The Wellesley Index to

VICTORIAN PERIODICALS

1824–1900

VOLUME II

Volume I

Volume II

The Wellesley Index
to Victorian Periodicals
1824-1900

VOLUME II

TABLES OF CONTENTS AND
IDENTIFICATION OF CONTRIBUTORS
WITH BIBLIOGRAPHIES
OF THEIR ARTICLES AND STORIES
AND AN INDEX OF
INITIALS AND PSEUDONYMS

WALTER E. HOUGHTON

EDITOR

Josef L. Altholz, Eileen Curran
Harold E. Dailey, Esther Rhoads Houghton
John A. Lester, Jr., Fr. Damian McElrath

ASSOCIATE EDITORS

UNIVERSITY OF TORONTO PRESS
ROUTLEDGE & KEGAN PAUL

© *University of Toronto Press 1972*

Toronto and Buffalo

Printed in Canada

Volume II
ISBN 0-8020-1910-2

Volumes I and II (the set)
ISBN 0-8022-1926-9
Microfiche ISBN 0-8020-0249-8
LC 66-5405

London: Routledge & Kegan Paul
ISBN 0-7100-7501-4

In memory of
Lady Nancy Houghton Cumming
whose able research on the *Dublin Review*
was a major contribution to this volume

Contents

Preface

Though many members of both the staff and the board of editors worked on the twelve periodicals in this volume, those who were primarily responsible for preparing the texts of each, including the introductions, were the following: for *Bentley's Quarterly Review*, the Editor; for the *Dublin Review*, John A. Lester, Jr. and Esther Rhoads Houghton, assisted by Lady Nancy Houghton Cumming; for the *Foreign Quarterly Review*, Eileen Curran; for the *Fortnightly Review*, Esther Rhoads Houghton; for *Fraser's Magazine*, the Editor, assisted by Patricia Crunden and Mary Ruth Hiller; for the *London Review* (1829), the Editor; for the *National Review*, Kazuko Dailey and Harold E. Dailey; for the *New Quarterly Magazine*, the Editor, assisted by Meredith Luyten; for the *Nineteenth Century*, Meredith Luyten; for the *Oxford and Cambridge Magazine*, Walter K. Gordon and the Editor; for the *Rambler*, Esther Rhoads Houghton with the collaboration of Josef L. Altholz and the assistance of Fr. Damian McElrath; and for the *Scottish Review*, Antoinette Petersen.

Among those who have aided in various ways with the preparation of the MS., including its proofreading and typing, were Mary Ann Bukovitch, Mary Cannon, Eleanor Clemence, Marianne Durgin, Gail Edmands, Barbara Erskine, Caroline Hatch, Mary Ruth Hiller, Anne Meixsell, Lindsay Miller, Sheila Morrison, Sydney O'Malley-Keyes, Elizabeth White.

In England we have been greatly indebted to Anne Byars, Elizabeth Falsey, and Ann Palmer, our research assistants in London. In various ways the *Index* is grateful to Margaret Skerl, recently retired Assistant Librarian, University College, London, and her colleague, Janet Percival; Jeanne Pingree, archivist of the Imperial College; Henry and Sheila Rosenberg, editors of the demanding section on nineteenth-century periodicals in the new *Cambridge Bibliography of English Literature*; Elisabeth Poyser, archivist of the Westminster Diocesan Archives; Rosemary Rendel of the Catholic Record Society; Miss S. J. A. Muir, Director's Assistant, Royal Geographical Society; Richard Story of the National Register of Archives; R. K. Brown, Librarian, Writers' Library; and T. S. Blakeney of the Mt. Everest Foundation, who gave us crucial information about some Victorian Alpinists.

Outside of London S. Wright, Esq. of Bures, Suffolk, has taken the trouble to send us lists of relevant articles in the learned journals. Ian Fletcher of Reading University and Professor A. W. Coats of the University of Nottingham have kindly responded to requests for information; and David Collard, University of Bristol, was good enough to publish a letter of inquiry in the *History of Economic Thought Newsletter*. J. S. G. Simmons, now a fellow of All Soul's and recently librarian of the Taylor Institute, has been an invaluable and friendly source of material on Russian authors; and Charles C. Nickerson, presently at Trinity College, Oxford, aided this volume in various ways. At Cambridge Brendel Whitman Lang has handled our research with skill. Others we wish to thank are Father C. S. Dessain of the Birmingham Oratory, who has put his knowledge of Cardinal Newman and other Victorian Catholics at our service; the Abbé Alphonse Chapeau of the Université Catholique d'Angers, now writing a biography of Cardinal Manning, who kindly sent us a list of authors marked in the file of the *Dublin Review* at St. Mary of the Angels, Bayswater; James Sambrook, the University, Southampton, for his helpful letters on the *Oxford and Cambridge Magazine*; Priscilla Metcalf for her careful reading of our introduction to the *Nineteenth Century*; Allan J. Rands of Farnham, Surrey, for permission to examine many cuttings of essays by his grandfather, William Brighty Rands; and Charles W. Crawford, for sending us annotations in copies of the *Rambler* at Oscott College.

In Scotland our chief indebtedness has been, as it was in *Index* I, to T. I. Rae, Assistant Keeper of Manuscripts at the National Library in Edinburgh; also to Julian Russell of the library staff for his highly professional help on Scottish biography. Special thanks are due to Dr. E. F. D. Roberts, the keeper of manuscripts, for his generous gift of research assistance in the summer of 1970. Margaret Rae has kindly examined letters for us in the library. Finally, we are most grateful to the present Lord Bute for allowing us to quote from the unpublished letters of the third Marquis of Bute, who was the proprietor and in some degree editor of the *Scottish Review*, 1886–1900; and to his librarian, Catherine Armet, for bringing them to the National Library for examination.

From Australia Susan Eade of Canberra sent us an analysis of an unsuspected collaboration in the *Fortnightly Review*.

In North America, to mention only a few on whom we have depended, Jack Robson of Victoria College, University of Toronto, and Robert Tener of the University of Alberta at Calgary are old and kind friends of the *Index*. Wilbur J. Smith, Librarian of Special Collections, University of California at Los Angeles, and J. R. Dunlop, Associate Librarian, City College of New York, made significant contributions to our work on the *Oxford and Cambridge Magazine*. Mrs. David Bonnell Green lent us the papers of her late husband on J. W. Parker, Jr., editor of *Fraser's Magazine*. Extensive research at the Morgan Library in New York was ably carried out by Nancy Houghton Brown. In his review of *Index* I Professor V. C. Knoepflmacher of the University of California at Berkeley suggested that the final item of any series be indicated by adding a "concl.," thus sparing the reader the annoyance of searching in vain for Part IV of a three-part article—a suggestion we have gratefully adopted. A general note of praise and thanks goes to Maurianne Adams of Smith College, Robert A. Colby of Queen's University, New York, Gordon Haight of Yale, William E. Fredeman, University of British Columbia, W. Eric Gustafson, University of California at Davis, Robert H. Woodward of San José State College, California, Edgar W. Morse, University of California at Davis, William S. Peterson, Andrews

University, Edward M. White, California State College at San Bernardino, H. B. de Groot of University College, University of Toronto, Marjory Douglas of Coconut Grove, Florida, James Belliveau of the Boston Athenaeum, Lawrence Evans of Northwestern University, B. M. Langstaff of New York City, and Frank Fetter of Hanover, New Hampshire. We owe various debts to the scholars, here and abroad, who made the survey of Victorian periodical writers, editors, proprietors, and publishers which are mentioned in the *DNB*, and their chairman, William H. Scheuerle, State University System of Florida, who made their findings available to the *Index*.

The chief contributor to Appendix A (Corrections and Additions to Volume I) is Joanne Shattock who has written the section on the *North British Review*. Other scholars who have enabled us to tighten our previous work are Nicholas Boyle of Magdalen College, Cambridge; Beatrice Corrigan and Robert A. Fenn of the University of Toronto; Joseph Hamburger of Yale; Anne Lohrli of the University of New Mexico, Las Vegas; Allan J. Rands of Farnham, Surrey, grandson of William Brighty Rands; and D. J. Walder of Edinburgh University.

In a category of immense importance we wish to express our gratitude to those institutions and foundations which have supported the preparation of this volume— indeed, without whose generosity there would have been no second volume: the National Endowment for the Humanities; the John Simon Guggenheim Memorial Foundation and its president, Gordon N. Ray; the Council on Library Resources, as Mr. Verner Clapp was retiring as president and Dr. Fred C. Cole taking over; the American Council of Learned Societies and its president, Frederick Burkhardt; the Braitmayer Foundation of Marion, Massachusetts; and the Sophie C. Hart Fund at Wellesley College. In connection with more than one of these grants we appreciate the guidance and recommendation of the administrative staff of Wellesley College, above all its president, Ruth M. Adams, its dean, Phyllis Fleming, its vice-presidents, Philip Phibbs, Albert E. Holland, Robert J. Schneider, Joseph Kiebala, and Harry B. Jones, controller. Other institutions which have made small but important grants for typing, travel, and in some cases resident expenses in London are Colby College, Haverford College, Rutgers University Research Council, and the University of Minnesota.

We have, of course, depended heavily on the staff of the Wellesley College Library under the leadership of Helen Brown. Hannah French, Research Librarian for Special Collections, has helped us more than once on Victorian publishing history. Other libraries in the area have continued to respond to our needs, and some have been good enough to loan us periodicals, or parts of periodicals, which were not at Wellesley. I refer in particular and with special gratitude to the Boston Athenaeum (James Belliveau and Jack Jackson), the Dinand Library of Holy Cross College (James M. Mahoney), and the Forbes Library at Northampton (Lawrence E. Wikander and Violet Durgin).

The Editor wishes to express his personal appreciation to all of our Associate Editors. They have contributed unstintingly both from their stores of knowledge and from their personal contacts with foreign scholars and archivists. To our Assistant Editors we are also indebted, particularly those who worked primarily on this volume, Kazuko Dailey, Walter K. Gordon, and H. B. de Groot. We have had great satisfaction in broadening the scope of our Advisory Editors, the full list of whom now consists of Robert A. Colby, Beatrice M. Corrigan, William E. Fredeman, Gordon S. Haight, Howard M. Jones, Oscar Maurer, John M. Robson, Henry and Sheila Rosenberg, Robert H. Tener, and Michael Wolff.

Finally, we thank the University of Toronto Press for the handsome volumes it is publishing. The print, the paper, and the spatial allowance have been praised in more than one review of *Index* I. For this volume we much appreciate the editorial assistance of Miss Joan Bulger.

W.E.H. and E.R.H.

Wellesley College
January 12, 1972

Introduction

The present volume contains 12 more periodicals, supplementing the 8 in Volume I, and bringing us to the half-way point of our project. The goal of indexing about 40 of the principal monthlies and quarterlies, 1824–1900, will be completed in Volumes III and IV.

At this mid-stage we have gained sufficient experience to state the grounds on which we are choosing our periodicals. From the beginning "principal" meant journals of relatively high calibre in the writing and editing, and of considerable reputation in educated circles. Moreover, they were to be general as distinct from professional: they were to admit, like the Catholic *Dublin Review*, a range of material, however slanted, that would include literature, politics, religion, economics, science, etc.[1] Hence the exclusion of such distinguished serials as *Nature*, *Mind*, and the *Atlantis*. These two requirements are fulfilled in the eight journals of Volume I, and here, I should suppose, in the *Dublin Review*, *Fraser's Magazine*, the *Fortnightly Review*, and the *Nineteenth Century*. The *National Review*, edited by Bagehot and Hutton, the *British Quarterly Review*, and the *Westminster*, including Mill's *London Review*, coming in the next volumes, will complete a list of fifteen principal and general periodicals which no one, I think, would question.

But beyond that opinions would differ and the criteria of selection become more varied. Given our special objective of identifying the authorship of articles and stories, the availability of source materials for this purpose, in an age of anonymity, becomes a crucial matter. Though the tables of contents have independent value, an author index, especially from 1824 to 1865 when only 3.6 per cent of the prose is signed, would hardly justify its title if the attributions fell much below 80 per cent. Shall we include borderline journals like the *Monthly Chronicle* or *Ainsworth's Magazine*? Not if we are unable to find keys to unlock most of the authorships. Conversely, if a good record of identifications has already been published (as is the case with the *Monthly Repository* and the *Germ*),[2] this is reason for an omission. Finally, we decided to provide a reasonable balance between articles and fiction (the latter about 30 per cent), and a sufficient geographical and sectarian spread to represent Irish

---

[1]This sentence and part of another just below have been adapted from my report, "The *Wellesley Index*, Volumes II and III: Plans and Problems," *Victorian Periodical Newsletter*, no. 4 (April 1969), p. 3.

[2]By Francis E. Mineka and Robert S. Hosmon, respectively.

and Scottish concerns, Catholic, Anglican, and Dissenting points of view, and the chief political positions. Clearly, with these subjective and partly incompatible criteria, the problem of choice becomes baffling: insoluble by logic, impossible even by Newman's illative sense. Moreover, whatever the decision, it is never final. As one makes his way deeper into the periodicals, gaining knowledge and judgment, he begins to reconsider journals he had once confidently accepted or rejected, which leads to a slightly new list of 40—to be superseded a few years later by another, slightly different, slightly better, one hopes. I am confident that the editors will be able to defend the final choice, but will never succeed in explaining, even to themselves, some of the omissions.[3]

The selection in this volume—or indeed in any volume—is not ideal. We plan a pattern of associated periodicals, but "circumstances beyond our control"—the illness of an editor, the resistance of a given journal, for the time being, to the probing of its anonymity, the unexpected discovery that this particular combination makes the volume too large or too small—force us to make substitutions; and in doing this, we have to take some account of what fits the available space rather than what would be most appropriate. But the make-up of a given volume is of little consequence so long as it contributes to a total body of periodicals that makes sense. Nevertheless, Volume II is not without a rationale. It brings together the two leading periodicals of the later century, the *Fortnighly Review* and the *Nineteenth Century*; and since both are liberal, in different ways, they are partly balanced by the conservative *National Review*, 1883–1900. The *Dublin Review* and the *Rambler* (the predecessor of the *Home and Foreign Review* in Volume I), nicely represent the orthodox and liberal wings of Roman Catholicism. The *London Review* of 1829 and *Bentley's Quarterly Review* of 1859–1860 were highly literate periodicals which refused to adopt any party line, religious or political—and so met speedy death. It was only in the period after 1865 that the public became more tolerant of non-sectarian journals, an attitude significantly encouraged by Matthew Arnold's "The Function of Criticism at the Present Time" (1864). *Fraser's Magazine* belongs with *Blackwood's*, on which at first it was modeled, as well as with *Macmillan's* (both in Volume I), in representing the best monthly magazines that focused on politics, religion, and society. By contrast, the *Oxford and Cambridge Magazine* of 1856, founded by William Morris, and the *New Quarterly Magazine*, 1873–1880, like the general run of the new magazines of the 1860s (the *Cornhill* is in our first volume), were essentially literary, emphasizing fiction, literary criticism, and verse. The *Foreign Quarterly Review* is the

---

[3]Anyone wishing to know what periodicals are planned for Volumes III and IV should consult the report mentioned in n. 1, p. xiii, or The *British Studies Monitor*, I (Spring 1970), 23–24. *Temple Bar* and the *Theological Review* were shifted to volume III when lack of space forced them out of Volume II. In place of the *Church Quarterly Review* we have substituted the Anglican *English Review*, 1884–1853, because of its interesting juxtaposition with the *Christian Remembrancer*. The *Monthly Chronicle*, 1839–1841, the *London Quarterly Review*, 1853–1900, and the Jesuit *Month*, 1864–1900, have been added. The division between Volumes III and IV has not yet been definitely decided upon. The report, but not the *Monitor* article, explains why other periodicals were ruled out and mentions some which might have been included.

first of a large number of journals (others of which will be indexed in Volume III) designed to open up foreign affairs and foreign writing to a public largely untravelled but eager to broaden its outlook. The *Scottish Review*, a conscious successor to the *North British* (also in Volume I), provides special insight into thought and opinion north of the border in the 80s and 90s.

The score for Volume II is less spectacular than that for Volume I. Publishers' lists, marked files, and editorial correspondence have proved harder to come by; and we have often had to turn to internal evidence, that is, autobiographical references and/or stylistic characteristics, where the results are frequently negative. Many writers for the *Foreign Quarterly Review* were obscure foreigners; only determined perseverance made the percentage of attributions as high as it is. The large number of political articles, which at best are too ephemeral to be reprinted, and of anonymous serials never published as books, made *Fraser's* especially baffling; while its size (6562 items) gave it excessive weight in the final average. On the other hand, the discovery of an old, cobwebbed tea chest in the basement of Archbishop's House Library containing more than 2000 letters to the executive editor of the *Dublin Review* from 1837 to 1863—a period in which only 4 articles were signed—made possible a final score there of over 90 per cent. In addition, the finding of Richard Simpson's notebook at Downside Abbey and a large collection of the correspondence of T. H. S. Escott in the London home of a descendant threw extensive light on the contributions to the *Rambler* and the pseudonyms in the *Fortnightly*.

The following table gives the record for Volume II.

Periodical	Total entries	Total articles & stories	Total articles & stories where entries are still blank	Percentage of blanks
Bentley's Quart. Rev.	38	38	0	0.00
Dublin Rev.	2,738	2,338	218	9.32
Foreign Quart. Rev.	901	788	217	27.53
Fortnightly Rev.	4,558	4,432	178	4.02
Fraser's Mag.	6,562	6,562	2,411	36.74
London Rev. (1829)	24	24	3	12.50
National Rev. (1883–)	2,538	2,421	193	7.97
New Quart. Mag.	219	208	29	13.94
Nineteenth Century	3,773	3,773	3	.08
Oxford & Cambridge Mag.	65	65	0	0.00
Rambler (1848–1862)	1,137	889	182	20.47
Scottish Rev. (1882–)	704	547	36	6.58
	23,257	22,085	3,470	15.71

Thus, Volume II supplies the name of the author, or of a probable or possible one, for 84.29 per cent of the articles and stories.[4]

But regardless of the level of attributions, there is the value, so often noticed in the reviews of Volume I, of the tables of contents. They give a scholar access to the titles of articles and stories in a journal he does not have at hand, or has only in incomplete form; indeed, even if his library has the full run of a periodical, the *Index* enables him to size up its contents, or its changing contents under changing editors, far more easily and quickly than examining it volume by volume. Also, in no other way can one readily gain a sense of what public opinion was focussing on in a given year or series of years, since here one can utilize so many journals at once. What was being discussed in 1860, say? Look at our contents for *Bentley's Quarterly Review*, *Blackwood's*, the *Cornhill*, the *Edinburgh*, *Fraser's*, *Macmillan's*, the *North British*, and the *Quarterly*; and when Volumes III and IV appear, there will also be *Bentley's Miscellany*, the *British Quarterly Review*, the *Dublin University Magazine*, Bagehot's *National Review*, *Temple Bar*, and the *Westminster*. Of course I chose a good year to make this point, but to a lesser extent any year will provide a range of opinion from various journals.

It may be noted that the number of contributors to Volume II is 4776, of which 1543 had also contributed to Volume I. For both volumes the total is 9556; or, more accurately if we add the new contributors now discovered for Volume I (see the index to Appendix A), 9597.

Two generalizations made in the Introduction to Volume I require comment. I there estimated (p. xvi) that before 1870 about 97 per cent of the articles and stories were anonymous or pseudonymous, while for the whole period, 1824–1900, the number was probably 90 per cent. On the basis of the 20 periodicals in both volumes, the first figure is proving fair enough: the number before 1865, when the *Fortnightly* initiated the signed article as a policy, is 96.4 per cent. But the second figure was too high. It now stands at 70.7 per cent. The extent to which the signed article gained ground after 1865 everywhere except in the *Edinburgh* and the *Quarterly* is striking and unexpected. Indeed, while 96.4 per cent of the articles and stories from 1824 to 1864 were anonymous or pseudonymous, the figure dropped to 57 per cent for the later period, 1865–1900. It should be noted, however, that two-thirds of the articles in Volumes I and II appeared in or after 1865. When we can include the figures for the 20 periodicals in the next two volumes, where the median will move backward, the final average of anonymous articles during the whole period will be higher, perhaps about 75 per cent.

The omission of poetry has disappointed some readers. The decision was readily defensible but it required explanation. To have included verse would have added an enormous number of worthless items to Part A and a large number of obscure authors to be identified and then described in Part B. No one who has tried to read "Ode to

---

[4]It should be noted that where the number of total entries given here for a periodical is larger than the last number in the text, this is probably because articles were accidentally omitted in the manuscript and had to be added with a lower case "a"—as for *Fraser's* no. 1286a.

the Coming Year," by M. J. Chapman, or "Pitt and Peel; or, 'Tis fifty years since . . .
By an old Parliamentary Rhyme Maker," starting

> Tis half a century ago,
>   And but one twelvemonth more,
> Since leagued the Whigs to overthrow
>   Will Pitt in '84 . . .

could think the *Index* the worse for their omission, or imagine that the hours
required to try and discover the contributors (full names, life dates, vocations) could
not have been better spent on prose and its authors. Some of the verse, of course, is
good (Tennyson himself published in *Macmillan's* and the *Nineteenth Century*), and
while we were doing the job, a complete listing of material, once and for all, had its
logic. But since the prose alone is requiring so many years of intensive work and so
much funding, we simply cannot afford to include the verse.

At least, not as a rule. When it illustrates a critical or historical introduction, notably in the case of translations from ancient and modern literature, we have made an
exception. Maginn's "Homeric Ballads" and his "Comedies of Lucian," with their
prefatory essays and footnotes, are a very different thing, in kind, from occasional
verse: they could hardly have been ignored. Wherever a significant headnote can
stand alone, we have retained it and omitted the verse (see *Blackwood's* no. 2999).
In both cases the critic or critic-translator, not the poet, is entered in Part B. Anyone
concerned with periodical material on Homer or Lucian, for example, should go to
Poole's *Index to Periodical Literature*, and use our *Index* for the authors of critical
articles or translations with prose introductions.

We are also now including what have been called satiric imitations—that is, satires
of life and politics in Victorian England which are modeled, for example, on the
epistles of Horace or the satires of Juvenal. The series of nine written by J. E. Thorold
Rogers, the economist, for *Temple Bar* (1873, 1874) are as relevant to the study of
the age as they would have been in prose.

Volume II contains one unique feature of great importance—Appendix: Corrections and Additions to Volume I. This appendix is deceptively long because it covers
every change, however minute, including the spelling of a middle name, and even new
biographical sources which change nothing in the Part B entry, though they provide
further information. Had we limited the appendix to new and wrong attributions of
articles and stories, only a few pages would have sufficed. At the present time, the
new attributions, including those now found definite in cases of conflict, number 172,
and there are 42 new contributors (each marked with an asterisk [*] in the index
to the Appendix). Incorrect attributions—whether outright, probable, or questioned
—number 84 out of 27,903 articles and stories, which is three-tenths of one per cent
(0.301 per cent). Considering the nature of the *Index* and the size of Volume I, this
seems an acceptable margin of error. It will increase as our research goes on and as
readers write, though not, I should suppose, very much. Certainly new attributions
will emerge. Both will be taken account of in Appendix A to Volume III.

The utility of compiling such corrections and additions depends heavily upon the reader. Unless he examines the brief Explanatory Note to Appendix A and follows the simple rules it lays down for determining possible errors or new discoveries— and not simply of authorships but of every kind—the labor and expense of this work is wasted, and much worse, wrong information is perpetuated.

Besides increasing the accuracy of Volume I, the appendix provides some valuable insight into the hazards of identification; for an examination of why the 83 misattributions occurred throws light, of course, on where the pitfalls lie. Under scrutiny, only two causal patterns are conspicuous: the assumption that a credible name like Constance Eaglestone is not a pseudonym (see *Blackwood's* no. 6629), and the tendency to falsify a correct surname by giving it someone else's first or middle name and life dates. "Poachers and poaching" (*Contemporary Review* no. 1976, September 1883) is signed James Purves but he is wrongly identified in Part B as James Liddell Purves.

I see no adequate way of guarding against the first pattern. When one has looked in vain into a dozen or more sources, he begins to suspect that the name may be a pseudonym and therefore checks it in Halkett & Laing's *Dictionary of Anonymous and Pseudonymous English Literature*, Cushing's *Initials and Pseudonyms*, and similar reference works; but not finding it, as is the case with Constance Eaglestone (and he will not find it unless the author wrote a book or a pamphlet, and one which the editors have discovered to be by Constance Sutcliffe), he can only accept it as genuine; and place it with the hundred or so "hard core" names, on our list of 12,000 contributors, who are equally without specific identification. The practice was extensive. To take an example at random, *Temple Bar* for 1898 contains articles and stories signed E. Greck, Adam Penne, Helen Cartwright, John Le Breton, Wirt Gerrare, Christian Carneige, Maarten Maartens, A. B. Romney, Cicely L'Estrange, Naranja Amarga, James Neirn, Reay Mackay, Powell Millington—all of which are pseudonyms.

Sometimes—as with most of the examples just cited—a publisher's list will happily do what the standard reference works cannot: provide the real name. A novel called *A Philosopher's Romance*, serialized in *Macmillan's*, 1896–1897, under the signature (in the Contents) of John Berwick, was published in 1898 as by the same man, and so appears in the *British Museum Catalogue of Printed Books*. The Macmillan list of contributors, however, assigns the novel to "Mrs. Haggard, British Consulate, Trieste," who would be Mrs. John George Haggard, according to the *Foreign Office List*, and Agnes Marion (Baber) Haggard, according to *Landed Gentry*. In this way the *Index* is discovering that names supposed to be genuine are in fact pseudonymous, and passing on the information to John Horden, Esq., of the School of English at Leeds University, who is editing a new edition of Halkett & Laing.

The misattributions that result from starting with a correct name, signed or attributed, and then jumping to the wrong person, can be reduced only by checking and double checking the first conclusion, however persuasive it seems. In the search for James Purves one comes on James Liddell Purves, 1843–1910, in Venn's *Alumni Cantabrigienses*, Foster's *Men at the Bar*, and *Who Was Who*; and though he spent much of his life in Melbourne, he was in England while at Cambridge and later at Lincoln's Inn, becoming a barrister in 1865 before returning to Australia. He might have contributed later to the *Contemporary*. However, there was a plain James

Purves, 1853–1922, a solicitor before the Supreme Court of Scotland, who wrote a number of Scottish essays in *Fraser's*, 1880–1882; and upon examination, we found that "Poachers and Poaching" in 1883 was definitely by a Scotsman (see the correction in Appendix A below). Though when Volume I was prepared *Fraser's* was not yet indexed and the only conspicuous Purves was James Liddell, the date of the article and the presence of James Purves in the *British Museum Catalogue* should have given us pause.

Or, to take a case where two people have precisely the same name: after assuming, rightly, that the contributor of three animal stories in *Macmillan's*, the first in April 1889, signed "W. H. Hudson" or, if not signed, so attributed in the Macmillan list, was the famous author of *Green Mansions*, whose life dates were 1841–1922, we did not hesitate to add to his bibliography "Jacques Tahureau," published a few months earlier in the same journal and signed "William Henry Hudson." But in *Who Was Who* and the *British Museum Catalogue* there is a William Henry Hudson, 1862–1918, a literary historian who later wrote several books on French literature and French writers, a field far from the naturalist's interests. The moral is plain: more skepticism and more biographical research.

Less common than these mistakes are others that occasionally occurred or might have occurred. Attributions based simply on Mr. X's offer to review such-and-such a book or an editor's letter requesting him to do so are, or should be, marked: "Unidentified. Perhaps Mr. X, who . . . ." If there is additional reason to show that the offer or the request was accepted, Mr. X is given the authorship with a "?". If he is to have a "prob.," there must be evidence that he did in fact write a review and that such a review appeared in the editor's periodical. For an outright attribution a note from the editor enclosing a cheque is needed, or a positive claim to the review by Mr. X. The entry for the *Quarterly Review* no. 1136 shows that the only evidence we had for Layard was a request from Whitwell Elwin, the editor, that he review Moltke's *The Russians in Bulgaria and Rumelia*. The correction below adds further evidence against any claim for Layard.

This type of error is not uncommon. Professor C. L. Cline, in his edition of George Meredith's letters, prints a note from J. W. Parker, Jr., editor of *Fraser's*, to Meredith, dated [Sept. 20, 1854], in which Parker writes: "What say you to an article on the *Songs of the Dramatists?* for next month, about 8 or 10 pages." The footnote cites *Fraser's*, 50 (Nov. 1854), 583–594, which bears this title, followed by Mr. Cline's comment: "It was unsigned, but internal evidence as well as the evidence of this letter clearly points to GM as the author." I do not know what internal evidence, whether autobiographical references or stylistic characteristics or both, were in his mind. All I know is that the article was reprinted by William Bodham Donne as his own in his *Essays on the Drama*, published in 1858 when both men were alive. No one who has ever examined an editor's correspondence (as we did for the *North British Review* under A. C. Fraser, where scores of suggestions came to nothing) will be tempted to take the proposal for the deed. It can only be an hypothesis to investigate in hope of finding solid evidence of its validity (as in the case of the *Quarterly Review* no. 847).

Another hazard is the tendency to assume that the name on a publisher's list is that of the author; and since it is, 99 times out of a 100, one is lulled into acting as though it always were. Publishers' lists, roughly speaking, are of two kinds, though the same list may be partly one, partly the other. The first is a memorial record drawn up some time later from memory, old notes, and letters: for instance the Murray "Register of Authors and Articles in the *Quarterly Review*, 1809–1879," and "Blackwood's Contributors' Book" down to 1870, after which the entries in both are contemporary; or H. R. Bagshawe's incomplete list for the *Dublin Review*, 1837–1863, compiled in 1863. The second type is a contemporary list, kept month by month or quarter by quarter, of people to whom payment was made, normally adding their addresses and the amount of the cheque: the Macmillan list, the Smith Accounts for the *Cornhill*, and the Longman account book for the *Edinburgh Review*, 1847–1900, are examples.

The liabilities of the first type are not only faulty memory, but the assumption that a person mentioned in notes and letters in connection with a particular article was the author, when in fact he may simply have procured the article and been paid for it, or he may have been only the editor or translator. The *Quarterly Review* no. 984 in March 1850, "*Diary of a Dutiful Son*" [by Thomas George Fonnereau], is attributed in the Murray "Register" to J. G. Lockhart. However, almost the entire article consists of passages called "March of Intellect," "Homer," "Modern Poetry," and the like, written by Fonnereau himself. Lockhart made the selection, and besides a short preface wrote one paragraph of comment on the author's introduction. He was only the editor. But since he had been invited to make any use of the book he chose (see the preface), it became *his* article for which *he* was paid. Hence the entry in the "Register." And because Lockhart was a regular contributor and the "Register" for March 1850 is full of genuine authors, it is all too easy to assume the piece was a review and assign it to him.

In the case of collaborations, names of contributors may be completely suppressed. *Blackwood's* no. 2388, "The Burn's festival," in September 1844, is assigned to W. E. Aytoun in the "Blackwood's Contributors' Book," but he wrote only 12 of its 29 pages. Theodore Martin in his *Memoir of Aytoun* assigns him simply the description of the event; and the article itself is found to be a series of speeches, one by Aytoun, but others by Professor John Wilson, Sir John McNeill, Henry Glassford Bell, etc., all of whom "collaborated" with Aytoun, who was, in effect, a reporter sent by Blackwood to cover the festival, which he did in this *his* article for which undoubtedly he was paid. The other speakers are simply omitted from the Contributors' Book. The correction in our Appendix A identifies Aytoun's work and lists his chief collaborators. The moral, which can also be drawn from many types of error, is simple enough: read or at least skim every article no matter what attribution is given by a publisher's list, a bibliography, or a letter.

The second type of publishers' list might seem to be more reliable because it is contemporary, but unhappily that is not the case. Since here the name is that of the person paid, it is normally that of the author, but not always. It may be that of an agent, like W. A. Watts; or, if the writer was abroad, some relative or friend; or, as before, simply an editor or translator; or perhaps a lifelike pseudonym which was used in the correspondence. Furthermore, here too a collaborator may be concealed if his partner contributes the article in his own name and is paid. The illustration of this which follows is chosen because it also exposes another difficulty—the ambiguity of the term "collaboration." *Macmillan's Magazine* no. 2886, June 1890, "On the character of Nero," signed Janus, is attributed in the publisher's list, and in our text, to **H. W. Orange.** However, Arthur W. Patrick in his *Lionel Johnson, Poète et Critique* (Paris, 1939), p. 238, attributes it to Johnson and Orange in collaboration, which we might well have adopted. But "collaboration" would have carried its inevitable suggestion of approximately an equal share in the work, and in this case that would have been wrong. For in January 1890 Johnson wrote a letter to Campbell Dodgson saying, "You remember that Nero essay, which I wrote, and which Orange slightly altered and read [presumably to some Oxford literary society]? He has got it accepted by Macmillan"[5]—and therefore he alone was on the list and received the cheque. The right attribution would have been: **"Lionel Johnson,** somewhat revised by **W. H. Orange."** We are now trying to make such distinctions, either by explaining them (see the correction of Macmillan no. 2886 in Appendix A) or at least by saying: "Mr. X, with the assistance of Mr. Y." But such information, which still leaves the exact role of each contributor uncertain, is hard to come by.[6] Most of the time one has to use "collaboration" loosely, to imply only that both authors apparently had some share in the work.

Any full account of the hazards of attribution would be endless. I conclude simply by mentioning a few others: the dangers of stylistic tests except where a given writer has a conspicuous manner of his own; the too ready use of parallel ideas, phrases, and quotations as evidence of common authorship (a later writer may have adopted them, consciously or unconsciously); the everlasting lure of interpreting "we wrote" such-and-such a paper to mean "I wrote"—which it sometimes does; the tendency to forget that a bishop's "surname" is that of his diocese (and therefore to think that Harvey Carlisle is a Carlisle and not a Goodwin, Bishop of Carlisle); the care required to determine which Churchill could sign himself Marlborough or which Fitz-Patrick was Lord Castletown at the particular date of publication; the baffling question of pseudonyms which are used by two men ("Bon Gaultier" first by Theodore Martin and "after they met" by Martin and W. E. Aytoun or by either alone; or still worse, the independent adoption of the same pen name by two contemporaries, like "A London Physician" by both James Howard and W. A. Guy, leading to endless confusion about the authorship of their books and in turn that of the articles printed therein); and the possibility that a volume of collected essays published posthumously may contain another man's essay because a "cut" or offprint of it was found among the dead man's papers. But once bitten, twice cautious. Though misattributions will never be eliminated and some can be corrected only by stumbling on the real author in unlikely places, they can be considerably reduced by being aware of their major sources.

A NOTE ON BIBLIOGRAPHY

Since 1966 there have been, I think, only three major works of a general kind relevant for our purposes. (Articles and monographs on particular journals will be found be-

[5]B.M. Add. MS. 46363. I owe my knowledge of this letter to the kindness of Ian Fletcher of the University of Reading.
[6]For a "brave" effort see my letter in the *Times Literary Supplement*, Sept. 3, 1971, p. 1057.

low, either at the end of the introductory essays or at the start of the corrections and additions for each periodical in Appendix A.) The new *CBEL*, III (1969) contains a long chapter called "Newspapers and Magazines," in which the original section in *CBEL*, III (1940) by H. G. Pollard and the supplement in *CBEL*, V (1957), by R. D. Altick, have been much expanded and revised by Henry and Sheila Rosenberg. They have put secondary scholarship into a separate section and arranged it under each periodical, added the names of proprietors wherever possible, dated the journal or its various series by month as well as year, and added many new editors and sub-editors. Furthermore, with scrupulous accuracy they have made liberal use of question marks to warn readers of information that is not firmly established. All in all, this is the best bibliography of its subject that exists. A second significant development has been the *Victorian Periodicals Newsletter*, conceived and edited by Michael Wolff. It first appeared in January 1968 and is still flourishing, having reached its twelfth number in June 1971. To the vast surprise of lonely periodical scholars, *VPN* suddenly revealed many others like themselves and a number of projects already under way or proposed, some of them large cooperative undertakings, such as the survey of all editors, contributors, and proprietors cited in the *DNB*, the alphabetical listing of all periodicals published in the U.K., 1824–1900, and a checklist of manuscript sources for Victorian editors and journalists. It is not too much to say that *VPN* was the creator of the Research Society for Victorian Periodicals (RSVP), and when that was established in the fall of 1968, it became, as it should have, the society's official organ. Finally, Christopher Kent's "Higher Journalism and the mid-Victorian Clerisy," *Victorian Studies*, XIII (Dec. 1969), 181–198, seems to me the best general article of recent years. It documents the changing attitude toward journalists and the increasing number of educated men who, about 1850–1870, began to write for the top periodicals, and relates these developments to the controversy of anonymity versus the signed article.

A NOTE TO THE READER

As in Volume I, references to books without mention of the number of volumes or date of publication are short titles: see section called Abbreviations and Short Titles for full bibliographical information. If the date is given and the number of volumes, where more than one, but the place of publication is omitted, the latter is to be understood as London. The footnotes to the several introductory essays may refer the reader to the Bibliographical Note or the Note on Attributions, both of which appear at the end of the essay and there indicate exactly what book or article is being cited.

W.E.H.

PART A

TABLES OF CONTENTS AND IDENTIFICATION OF CONTRIBUTORS

Editor's Note

THE BASIC FORMATS for Part A, described in the Editor's Note to Part A of Volume I of the *Index* (pp. 3–5), have remained the same, and most of the modifications which have been introduced in Volume II to provide clearer or fuller accounts of the items require no explanation.

Special mention, however, must be made of two changes. The first is of major significance. In Volume I the term "Signature" was distinguished from "Signed." Where "Signed" meant that the name of the author, without regard to any title or address, appeared in the text exactly as we gave it, "Signature" indicated that the editors had deduced the attribution from some name or other, the reader knew not what, which had been printed at the start or end of the paper. This practice has now been almost wholly discontinued. The entry in Volume I for *Macmillan's*, no. 2079— "**Elizabeth Mayhew Edmonds.** Signature; *BMCat.*"—concealed the precise name signed to the item. It would now appear as: "**Elizabeth Mayhew Edmonds.** Signed E. M. Edmonds; see *BMCat.* for her concern with modern Greek literature." Or, instead of "**Herbert W. Wilson.** Signature and *DNB*" (*Macmillan's* no. 3710), the entry would now be written: "**Herbert W. Wilson.** Signed H. W. Wilson; see *DNB*." Another mode of getting rid of the mysterious "Signature" involves a cross-reference in Part B. "Mrs. **Julia Ady.** Signature; see *WWW*" would now become: "**Julia Cartwright.** Signed." An entry in Part B would then read: "**Cartwright,** Julia: see Ady, Julia Mary (Cartwright)," under whom the item would be found. Only for those few cases where an abbreviated form of a name is used over and over again, have we retained the old "Signature" simply to avoid innumerable repetitions of the full facts. Instead of writing "**Eliza Lynn Linton.** Signed E. Lynn Linton; see *DNB*" 121 times, because our rule is always to give the feminine name if known, we continue to say, "**Eliza Lynn Linton.** Signature." But with this important difference in Volume II— that all ten such cases are herewith listed: Articles and stories entered as

"Alphonse Bellesheim. Signature" are signed A. Bellesheim.

"Matilda Betham-Edwards. Signature" are signed M. Betham-Edwards.

"Ellen M. Clerke. Signature" are signed E. M. Clerke.

"Emile Erckmann and Alexandre Chatrian. Signature" are signed MM. Erckmann-Chatrian.

"Andrew Lang. Signature" are signed A. Lang.

"Eliza Lynn Linton. Signature" are signed E. Lynn Linton.

"Friedrich Max Müller. Signature" are signed F. Max Müller.

"Margaret Oliphant. Signature" are signed Mrs. Oliphant.
"John Ruskin. Signature" are signed J. Ruskin.
Thus, in Volume II the reader is always informed of the precise name attached to the article or story, either at once in the entry for Part A, or here in the list of the ten "Signatures" retained.

This is by no means a pedantic piece of precision. In Volume I a scholar had to accept a thing like *Blackwood's* no. 7268, which read: "**Robert Anderson,** 1841–1918. Signature and Table of Contents," trusting our deductions from some signature or other and its illumination by whatever it was which the contents gave. He would now be told: "**Robert Anderson,** 1841–1918. Signed R. Anderson; Contents adds 'C.B., LL.D'; see *WWW*." Thus, by knowing the facts and seeing how our conclusion was reached, the reader is in a far better position to accept our attribution or to "consider it again." It should be added that any article or story that is not followed by a name and the word "Signed" or "Signature" is anonymous; for in the case of an unsolved pseudonym, one finds, "Signed: A Barbarian Eye"; or in that of a solved pseudonym or the title of a peer or bishop, the author's name is followed by "Signed Toby Allspy," or "Signed Northcote," or "Signed Harvey Carlisle," followed by elucidation.

The other change is less significant but requires explanation. In order to avoid repeating a pseudonym like "The Author of *Friends and Enemies at the Old Mill*" for fifteen entries of a novel, and yet not being able now to use the dubious "Signature" employed in Volume I to avoid such repetitions, we have devised "Evidence for no. 000," where the number is the beginning of the serial. Since such a statement must apply to the whole evidence block, it must cover the pseudonym, now placed at its beginning.

SPECIAL NOTE
The reader should remember that letters criticizing an article, and the author's reply, if any, as well as later notes or postscripts, are entered with the article itself and not at their chronological place. See, for example, *National Review* no. 796. Consequently, in the Correspondence sections, *National Review* nos. 830 and 841, these letters are omitted.

Bentley's Quarterly Review, 1859-1860

SOMETIME IN 1858 Richard Bentley decided to complement his monthly magazine, *Bentley's Miscellany*, with a quarterly review that would rival even the famous *Edinburgh* and *Quarterly*. Indeed, with a burst of initial enthusiasm he wrote to W. H. Prescott on September 3, 1858, "I am about to commence . . . a New Quarterly Review, which will be supported by most of the ablest writers of England, France, Germany, [and] Italy."[1] This was a dream, but Bentley succeeded in procuring as remarkable a group of editors and contributors as any Victorian periodical could have boasted, before or since—unless it was the *Saturday Review*. The general editor was Douglas Cook, director of the *Saturday Review*; the literary editor William Scott, editor of the *Christian Remembrancer* and leader-writer for the *Saturday*; and the political editor the brilliant young Lord Robert Cecil, later to be third Marquis of Salisbury and Prime Minister of England, who was on the staff of the same weekly.[2] Of the twenty contributors—among them Sarah Austin, Cecil, Dean Church, W. B. Donne, E. A. Freeman, Anne and J. B. Mozley, H. L. Mansel, and Goldwin Smith— nineteen are in the *Dictionary of National Biography*, and eight were already contributing to the *Saturday*. Bentley's high hopes, therefore, rested on a foundation of *Saturday* editors and reviewers who had made that weekly the outstanding periodical of its kind, to be supplemented by other writers of similar powers. Might they not create a new quarterly of high distinction?

Judging by its critical reception, they could and did. The *Spectator* praised the variety of subjects and the "judicious mixture of practical with literary and art topics. . . . The writing itself is often distinguished by smartness, power, almost eloquence, and always by careful or solid composition." The *Times*, finding the older quarterlies not "altogether equal to the intellectual wants of the present day," saw *Bentley's* as meeting a contemporary need, and praised its articles for their "natural thought and deep thought well expressed, and showing an original cast of mind in the writers." As such, it showed promise of a "distinguished career."[3]

[1]B.M. Add. MS. 46642, fol. 289.

[2]Bentley (cited in Note on Attributions.) Here and in the next sentence we are indebted to M. M. Bevington, *"The Saturday Review," 1855–1868* (New York, 1941), pp. 10–17 and the appendix, "Authorship of Articles."

[3]*Spectator*, Mar. 5, 1859, p. 267; *Times*, Aug. 20, 1859, p. 7. Also, in similar vein, see the *Examiner*, Mar. 26, 1859, p. 197, and the *Athenaeum*, Mar. 26, 1859, pp. 423–424. It should be noted, however, that the article in the *Times* was either written by William Scott or inspired by him, so that it is not a disinterested estimate: see Robert Cecil's remark in the *Life* (cited in Bibliographical Note), I, 87.

The first issue appeared on February 28, 1859. On May 31 Bentley wrote to his general editor, Douglas Cook:

My dear Sir,

It is with extreme regret and mortification I find that the sale of the First Number of the Quarterly Review remains very nearly what it was soon after its publication, leaving me the heavy loss of £ 600.

I must in consequence avail myself of the course pointed out by the Agreement, and give notice of my intention to terminate it on the publication of No. 2.[4]

But since the sale of No. 1 soon picked up—the issue was still selling in September[5]— Bentley carried on to a fourth number, which came out on January 2, 1860, before terminating publication. "All the Talents" had not saved his *Quarterly* from speedy collapse. How did such an incredible fate overtake it?

Not, I feel sure, because of left-handed work by the contributors. Dean Church's paper, "Mill, *On Liberty*" (no. 34) has recently been described by a modern specialist as "in many ways the most intelligent and considered" of all the contemporary reviews of that famous book, and a Victorian critic called another article (no. 14) "the most thoughtful and searching criticism of *Adam Bede* which has appeared."[6] The only adverse criticism I have discovered is the *Spectator's* caveats on three papers in the first issue.[7]

This specific evidence, in addition to the general estimates already cited, argues that the reasons for the failure of *Bentley's Quarterly* were extrinsic. Two of them are clear. The first was a matter of policy. When the three editors met with Mr. Bentley on July 24, 1858, it was agreed as follows: "*The Review to be Progressive in Politics. Moderate and unobtrusive in religion. The religious controversies which are in agitation between the Oxford and Exeter Hall Schools to be, as a rule, avoided.*"[8] Though the later prospectus spoke of "a defined aim" and a "definite policy" rather than the various opinions of individual writers, Cecil was to point out that this was not, in fact, the case; indeed, the prospectus itself had gone on to talk of the periodical as "temperate and independent," making "the country, and not party, its object."[9] Certainly the journal's neutrality was its striking feature, with implications pointed out by the *Saturday Review*: "Whatever it is, it is not launched as the mere organ of any political faction or literary fraternity. Herein are, of course, its dangers as well as its

---

[4]B.M. Add. ms. 46642, fol. 322. Bentley had decided (letter to Cook of June 30, 1858, cited in n. 8) that the Review would "require 3,300 copies to pay"; by June 8, 1859, the sale of No. 1 had been only 629 copies, with a loss to date of £639 18s. 5d.: see Gettman, *Bentley*, p. 146.

[5]According to Cecil, *Life*, I, 88.

[6]Professor Harold E. Dailey, author of a Columbia University dissertation (1970) on the reception of Mill's book, in a letter to the present writer; the *Saturday Review*, July 16, 1859, p. 82. The latter also praised nos. 11, 13, 15, and 16; the *Examiner* (cited in n. 3 above) chose nos. 1, 3, 7, and 9 for special mention; and the *Times* (ibid.) singled out nos. 3 and 10, 14 and 16.

[7]Namely, nos. 1, 6, and 8; the reference is in n. 3 above.

[8]Quoted from Bentley (see Note on Attributions) under 1859. For similar statements of policy, see Bentley's letter to Cook, June 30, 1858, B.M. Add. ms. 46642, fol. 280 (which is digested in Gettman, *Bentley*, p. 145) and a later letter of July 16, 1858, ibid., fol. 282.

[9]The prospectus was printed in the *Spectator*, Feb. 19, 1859, p. 220, and in the *Saturday Review*, Jan. 8, 1859, p. 53. Cecil's "correction" is in his letter to William Scott, Dec. 12, 1858, Sion Coll. London.

promises."[10] In the event, dangers that ended its promises. After its opening salute, the *Spectator* continued:

> But literary merit will not alone suffice to secure success in a leading periodical. There must be a definite purpose and some public want must be supplied. . . .
> A representative organ of some defined principle, if not of some party, has a great advantage, if not an essential, to permanent success. . . . Besides the more tangible benefit of party subscribers, a representative organ enlists in its cause the "choice spirits," the active, zealous, rising, and ambitious men of the party, and secures the best information of all kinds in possession of the party, while it is just as able as the most isolated work to obtain literary, scientific, or artistical aid. It has, moreover, a great advantage in its continuous power. Individuals die, remove, change their objects, or get exhausted; but a party continually furnishes new recruits. . . .
> These notions are supported by the actual fact. The two most enduring and successful Quarterlies are the organs of the two great parties into which the country is even yet divided."[11]

But, alas, *Bentley's Quarterly* is full of various and independent opinions. Its failure is assured.

One remembers that only five years later Arnold was to protest against "our organs of criticism" being "organs of men and parties having practical ends to serve," and the fact that "a free, disinterested play of mind meets with no favour." Witness the extinction in 1864 of the *Home and Foreign Review*. "Perhaps in no other organ of criticism in this country," he went on, "was there so much knowledge, so much play of mind; but these could not save it." Had he been speaking in 1860, Arnold might have written a similar epitaph for *Bentley's Quarterly*.[12] But the tide was turning. In the *Fortnightly* (1865) and still more in the *Nineteenth Century* (1877), individual play of mind came into its own, signatures and all. Had Bentley had the foresight to initiate the signed article, his great array of talent would have been immediately apparent, and this might have counteracted the waning insistence on party organs with practical purposes.

The second reason why the Review failed was its form, as distinct from its substance. It was a quarterly at the moment when the taste for quarterlies was declining; indeed, a *new* quarterly at the precise moment when the new periodicals were either monthly magazines like *Macmillan's* (1859) and the *Cornhill* (1860), or, still more challenging to *Bentley's*, monthly reviews like the *Fortnightly* (1865) and the *Contemporary* (1866). The fact was that the tempo of life had greatly increased since the early days of the great quarterlies. People no longer had the leisure—or the patience— to pore over long articles or to wait three months for the criticism of new books or the analysis of current politics. It is significant that few quarterlies of a general character

---

[10]Cited in n. 6, p. 81.

[11]Reference in n. 3. The reviewer goes on to lament that "English Politics and Parties" (no. 1) "is not a paper to form a party creed."

[12]From "The Function of Criticism at the Present Time," *Essays in Criticism, First Series*, 1865. R. B. [Richard Bentley II], *Some Leaves from the Past* (1896), p. 100, remarked, with simple assurance, that in 1859 his grandfather "started a *Quarterly Review*, which, holding a perfectly neutral political position, had but a brief career." Cf. the policy and fate of the *London Review* of 1829, discussed below in *Index*, II, 524–525.

were undertaken after 1850, and that only one of these, the *London Quarterly Review* (1853), which was supported by the Wesleyan Conference, survived to 1900. Even Bagehot's *National Review* lasted only ten years.[13] Clearly, Bentley's new journal, if not signed, should at least have been a monthly.

On his return to England in mid-September 1859, Cecil wrote his wife at Boulogne that as yet he had heard "nothing of B.Q.R.'s fate. But the printer seems strongly of opinion that it never could pay. Even the old Quarterly is falling off."[14] The new one was soon to do so completely.

EDITORS

John Douglas Cook, general editor.
William Scott, literary editor.
Lord Robert Cecil, political editor.

PROPRIETOR AND PUBLISHER

Richard Bentley & Son.

NOTE ON ATTRIBUTIONS

This periodical is unsigned. The attributions for Nos. 1, 3, and 4 are given in *A List of the Principal Publications Issued from New Burlington Street, 1829–1898*, ed. Richard Bentley II (8 vols., London, 1893–1920), Vol. III, under the years 1859 and 1860. This is referred to below as "Bentley." For No. 2 Bentley lists the contributors without mentioning the titles of their contributions. A little research has matched the writers to their articles.

BIBLIOGRAPHICAL NOTE

The only other account of this fine periodical is by Royal A. Gettman, *A Victorian Publisher: A Study of the Bentley Papers* (Cambridge, 1960), pp. 145–147. Besides the contemporary sources mentioned above in notes 3, 6, and 9, see Lady Gwendolen Cecil, *Life of Robert Marquis of Salisbury* (2 vols., London, 1921), I, 83–88, and eleven letters from Lord Cecil to William Scott at Sion College, London, discussing possible articles in future issues and mentioning some potential contributors whose work was not written or not used.

[13]See the list, edited by Henry and Sheila Rosenberg, in the new *CBEL*, III, 1857–1858.
[14]*Life*, I, 87.

BENTLEY'S QUARTERLY REVIEW, 1859-1860

The Dublin Review, 1836-1900

THE DECADES FOLLOWING WATERLOO brought immense changes in the social and political structure of Britain. They brought changes in the religious and spiritual climate as well. One trend, perhaps too seldom recognized, was the beginning of a Catholic revival in England. There were at least 67 Catholic newspapers, journals, and periodicals launched in the British Isles in the first half of the nineteenth century; the admission of Catholics to Parliament (1829) and their wider participation in the franchise (1832) gave added force to the revival.[1]

Of these trends Nicholas Wiseman, Rector of the English College at Rome (1828–1840), was well aware. With the intention of seizing a propitious moment to accelerate the Catholic revival, he returned to England in 1835–1836 to deliver a notable series of lectures. While the lectures were in progress, Wiseman was approached by Michael Quin, an Irish lawyer in London, with the suggestion of founding a new Catholic review. Wiseman at once saw in the proposal the possibility of reaching both Catholics and Tractarians more directly than the *Catholic Magazine* had done. The new review might stir the enthusiasm of the faithful for their own religion, and draw them from their years of isolation into renewed and vital contact with the Papacy; to the more general audience of non-Catholics, and especially to the Tractarians, it could speak with breadth of learning and a ready persuasiveness.[2] Quin enlisted as well the support of Daniel O'Connell, the great Irish nationalist, and together Wiseman and O'Connell became the first proprietors of the *Dublin Review*.

Precisely why the title *Dublin* was chosen for the review is uncertain. Wiseman, with his strong antipathy to controversy and his desire for conciliation, may have felt that the word "Catholic" in the title would have suggested militant partisanship; and he certainly would have wished to avoid any confusion with the *Catholic Magazine*.[3] It may have been partly in deference to O'Connell and his valuable influence among

---

[1]John R. Fletcher, "Early Catholic Periodicals in England," *DR*, 198 (April–June 1936), 284–310.

[2]That the review did speak directly to Newman is attested by his cry of distress, *Letters and Correspondence during his Life in the English Church*, ed. Anne Mozley (2 vols., 1897), II, 256, upon reading Wiseman's article of August 1839—"the first real hit from Romanism which has happened to me."

[3]Wiseman scorned the idea "of establishing the truth of our doctrines by overthrowing others." Quoted Ward, *Wiseman*, I, 236. Cf. [Nicholas Wiseman], "The High Church Theory of Dogmatical Authority," *DR*, 3 (July 1837), 79: "We covet their brotherhood in the faith, and their participation in our security of belief and their being bound to us in cords of love, through religious unity."

Irish liberals—and his financial backing—that the *Dublin* name was chosen; or partly to counter the "Edinburgh" of the *Edinburgh Review*.[4] The *Dublin Review* was always intended primarily for English readers, and it was always published in London. Yet it first appeared clad in green, and its first series bore the motto *Éire go bráth*.[5]

The *Dublin Review* began inauspiciously, with a succession of different editors for the first five numbers and an irregularity of publication date which was not fully overcome until the 1860s. It was plagued from the start by financial difficulties, chiefly that of attracting subscribers. The *Dublin* came late into the field. To some readers the O'Connell connection may have made it suspect—though O'Connell very early, if not from the very start, warmly approved the moderate line of the *Dublin*; to others, paradoxically, its very moderation detracted from its appeal. Wiseman himself was quite determined "that no extreme political views should be introduced into the Review." With his steady guidance, and with the acquisition (July 1836) of C. W. Russell of Maynooth as contributor and H. R. Bagshawe as editor (as of October 1837), the administration and policy of the first series of the *Dublin* became reasonably secure.[6]

The range, quality, and quantity of Russell's contributions in the *Dublin*'s first twenty years are astonishing. He supplied at least one article for almost every issue in this period, and in one instance (March 1850) four; a later contributor described him as "perhaps . . . the most gifted Catholic scholar of our times."[7] More than this, Russell gathered together, from among his friends and his colleagues at Maynooth, an active group of Irish contributors; he scrutinized their contributions, selected and forwarded the ones for publication, and distributed the remunerations. He was responsible for perhaps one third of every issue, and on one occasion at least he exercised a veto on an article accepted by Bagshawe and already set up in print.[8] In the fall of 1840 Wiseman returned from Rome and virtually took over direction of the *Review*. He claimed simply "to represent the theological and religious elements in the journal," but in fact he was its proprietor and censor; and from his pen flowed a series of impressive and influential articles on various subjects, many of which (though by no means all) are to be found in his collected *Essays*.[9]

---

[4]Matthew Russell, *Irish Monthly*, 21 (1893), 78, viewed the *Dublin* as setting itself up as a Catholic rival of the Whig *Edinburgh* and the Tory *Quarterly*.

[5]The attempt in 1961 to shed the implication of Irish origin by renaming the *Dublin* the *Wiseman Review* was short-lived, and as of 1965 it again became the *Dublin*.

[6]On O'Connell's approbation of the *Dublin* policy, see his letters of Feb. 18, 1838, quoted in L. C. Casartelli, "Our Diamond Jubilee," *DR*, 118 (Apr. 1896), 254, and of Jan. 19, 1844, quoted in W. J. Fitzpatrick, ed., *Correspondence of Daniel O'Connell, the Liberator* (2 vols., 1888), II, 315–316. Wiseman in retrospect gave deep praise "to the illustrious O'Connell, . . . that wrapped up as his whole external life was in politics, he consented that the new quarterly should not involve itself in their vortex . . ." [Nicholas Wiseman], "The Present Catholic Dangers," *DR*, 41 (Dec. 1856), 441. For Wiseman's stated resistance to extreme views, see Ward *Wiseman*, I, 249.

[7]Casartelli, "Our Diamond Jubilee," p. 260.

[8]Russell to Bagshawe, June 23, 24, 25, 1848, Bagshawe Papers, demands suppression of an article by Lord Shrewsbury, "whatever the delay and the cost." Cf. letter from Lord Shrewsbury to A. De Vere, Aug. 21, 1848, De Vere Papers, Natl. Lib. Ireland: "I send you a suppressed article I wrote for the last 'Dublin Review.' "

[9]Ward, *Wiseman*, I, 249.

From all of this it is clear that Bagshawe's designation as editor must be qualified. Bagshawe was titular editor, and he did yeoman service as *executive* editor, reading manuscripts, soliciting contributions, and dealing with publishers and printers; but he was never in full command. Russell in 1844 states that it will not do "for me *as yet* to be known as acting so much as editor."[10] L. C. Casartelli states roundly that "Wiseman was practically the literary editor of the REVIEW, Bagshawe being little more than a business editor."[11] Such was the ambiguity of the editorial position from 1837 to 1863 that Wiseman could proclaim late in 1844, "I hereby appoint and declare Henry R. Bagshawe Esq. Editor of the Dublin Review . . . ," and write in dismay to Russell early in 1846, "A report has reached me that you are thinking of retiring from the editorship of the 'Review'."[12]

Once organized and functioning with reasonable stability, the *Review* accomplished its dual purpose with great success. Between 1836 and 1850 it was not only the central voice of Catholicism in England, aiding and abetting its rise in many ways; it was also possibly a frequent means by which Anglo-Catholics became Roman Catholics. For Wiseman, indeed, "the main *religious* object" of the *Dublin Review* in the first decade of its life had been "to watch, to second, and to correct, where necessary," the Tractarian Movement.[13] Hundreds of converts turned to Rome, of whom J. H. Newman and W. G. Ward are the best known.

But even as Wiseman looked back on the successes of his policy of reconciliation in December 1845, and rejoiced that "the controversial period of our Review is . . . now over," a new conflict was developing.[14] The influx of distinguished converts to the Roman Church was gratifying, but it now represented a new element within the Church, one which roused both fear and suspicion among the old Catholics. For the most part the converts were men of superior education and broad outlook; this in itself was an assurance of tensions to be met and resolved. Wiseman himself was subjected to strong criticism for welcoming the converts, and for trying to smooth their difficult period of transition.[15] Reflecting on the accession of new writers hoped for among the converts, Wiseman wrote to Russell in 1846, "It is of great importance that the Catholic element of the 'Review' should be kept as much together as possible, and as strong an infusion of old Catholicism as possible be kept in it. This I mean for the sake of keeping up confidence from the Catholic body, which will be jealous of seeing the 'Review' pass too much into neophyte hands."[16]

In spite of Wiseman's pleas for mutual understanding, rancour smoldered. By December 1856 he felt called upon to write on "The Present Catholic Dangers."[17] Two articles in the *Rambler* were the immediate occasion for Wiseman's pronounce-

---

[10]Russell to Bagshawe, Nov. 22, 1844, Bagshawe Papers.

[11]"Our Diamond Jubilee," p. 254.

[12]Wiseman, Nov. 27, 1844, Bagshawe Papers; Ward, *Wiseman*, I, 445. Note that *DNB*, under C. W. Russell, refers to Russell as co-editor of the *Dublin Review* with Wiseman.

[13][Nicholas Wiseman], "The Religious Movement," *DR*, 19 (Dec. 1845), 538–539.

[14]Ibid., p. 545.

[15]Ward, *Wiseman*, I, 447–449, quotes a moving Wiseman memorandum on the lonely agonies he suffered for dealing mercifully with converts.

[16]Ward, *Wiseman*, I, 445.

[17]*DR*, 41 (1856), 441–470.

ment.[18] The *Rambler* articles had somewhat arrogantly and injudiciously poured scorn on the "Catholic remnant," and had aroused even the long-suffering Wiseman to bitter reproach. Wiseman begins with a poignant apologia for his conduct of the *Dublin*, and goes on to speak of the lack of Christian charity and understanding which could allow such a "wholesale and degrading charge, by a few persons, against the great bulk of their brethren in religious belief."[19] But Wiseman's chief concern was with the "intellectual separation of a knot of able persons" from the united body of the Church and "the creation of party, upon the very worst ground, that of a distinction of old, and new, catholics."[20] Such separation was a negation of all that Wiseman had striven for. It foreshadowed difficulties which were to beset not only the *Dublin* and the *Rambler*, but the whole of the Roman Catholic Church, for many years to come—the split between liberals and conservatives.

The *Rambler*, and its successor the *Home and Foreign Review*, were both eventually suppressed, while the *Dublin* staggered on from crisis to crisis. In part this unhappy situation was due to Wiseman's ill health, and in part to his increasing immersion in Church affairs, as first Cardinal Archbishop of the restored Hierarchy (1850). At a time when Wiseman himself knew the *Dublin* needed deeper and more varied and vital articles, his own contributions became fewer and fewer.[21] More and more problems of editorial policy devolved upon Bagshawe, who was by nature inclined to avoid difficult topics and controversial issues. In the summer of 1858 Bagshawe actually resigned as editor. Lord Acton, editor of the *Rambler*, formally offered to take over editorship of the *Dublin* as well. "It has not kept pace with the intellectual movement of the country," Acton announced in February 1859.[22] But Wiseman could not abide Acton's liberalism; Bagshawe was persuaded to stay on, and to resume editorship of what many regarded as a dying publication.[23]

Salvation from this crisis was found in the appointment of William George Ward as editor in 1863, and the commencement of the "New Series" with the July number of that year. Ward came to the editorship with two resolves which were not mutually compatible. On the one hand he was resolved on a moderate and conciliatory line: he would enlist many different kinds of people as contributors; he added a supplement recording continental thought and events; he was insistently diffident as to his ability to lead the *Dublin* with distinction.[24] Ward in fact left virtually all matters of politics, literature, and secular history to competent sub-editors—Edward Healy Thompson (1863–1865) and Cashel Hoey (1865–1878).

[18]This journal was founded in 1848, in some measure to give freer scope for the writings of converts, especially to that group of converts which had not felt unconditionally welcomed by the *Dublin*; see below, p. 732.

[19]"Present Catholic Dangers," pp. 441–442, 449.

[20]Ibid., p. 450.

[21]For Wiseman's awareness of the *Dublin's* need for revitalization in the early 1850's, see his letters, in Casartelli, "Our Diamond Jubilee," p. 256.

[22]"The Catholic Press," in Acton, *Essays on Church and State*, p. 266; reprinted from *Rambler*, no. 980.

[23]A good account of this crisis in the *Dublin's* history is given in Josef L. Altholz, *The Liberal Catholic Movement in England* (1962), pp. 34–39, 72–73, 182–184.

[24]See Newman's letter to Monsell, Nov. 19, [1862], Newmann MSS, and Ward's letter to Newman, Oct. 16, 1862, *Ward as Catholic*, p. 155.

On the other hand, in the matter of the absolute dogmatical authority of the Holy See, Ward was adamant. From the start he made it a primary aim of policy in his *Dublin* to attack liberalism in general within the Catholic faith of his day, and in particular to neutralize the poison of the *Home and Foreign Review*.[25] Lord Acton, editor of that journal, overtly welcomed the "principle of independent inquiry, within the bounds, and for the promotion, of the Catholic faith."[26] Little wonder that Ward lashed out at the *Home and Foreign* (1862–1864), and at its successor, the *North British Review*, in its final years (1869–1871). Both of these journals were short-lived. A papal brief struck counter to the position of the first; lack of a wide Catholic audience in Scotland, and illness of the editor, brought an end to the second. Ward was of course glad to see the end of them both, and of "their baneful influence over English Catholic thought."[27]

Two specific events impelled Ward still more aggressively to theological combat. On August 20 and 21, 1863, Count de Montalembert addressed the Congress of Catholics at Malines on "A Free Church in a Free Society" and "Liberty of Conscience"; his burden was a plea for separation of Church and State and a condemnation of the religious intolerance of the medieval Church. To W. G. Ward both theses were direct rebellion against Church teaching. Then in the following month, at the Munich Congress, Dr. Johann Döllinger struck another line which to Ward seemed highly dangerous. After paying tribute to the traditional Scholastic theology of the Church, he called for a newer, more flexible and free-ranging spirit of inquiry in theology, to give life and meaning to dogma in the modern age. For liberal Catholics the views of Montalembert and Döllinger were signs of new life in the Catholic revival; for Ward they were ominous questionings of the Church's infallibility, and heretical in their implication that modern liberties constitute *in principle* an advance over the truths of traditional theology.

Philosophically the issue between Ward and his liberal opponents was quite simple. To Ward's mind, indeed to his entire intellectual constitution, religious truth was the one thing needful to man's life; all other truths were peripheral, and gained whatever worth they possessed only from their proximity to and dependence on the Catholic faith. Hence Ward's lack of interest, editorially, in matters predominantly political, or historical, or literary. His field was that of theological belief, and his opponents, objects of his persistent *Dublin* onslaught, included all those who could not accept, in principle and in practice, his own position.

Ward thus made of the *Dublin* "a kind of theological battering-ram."[28] It was closely studied and exercised much influence in England and on the Continent; and, at the same time, as Newman was to observe, it gave the mournful impression that Ward was "never happy except when he [was] destroying the cohesive unity of Catholic brotherhood."[29]

It seems a paradox that Newman, whose faith in the *Via Media* was first shaken by

[25]W. G. Ward, "Preliminary Essay," in his *Doctrinal Authority*, pp. 2–5.
[26]"The Catholic Press," Acton, *Essays on Church and State*, p. 277.
[27]Ward, "Preliminary Essay," p. 34.
[28]Maisie Ward, "W. G. Ward and Wilfrid Ward," *DR*, 198 (April–June 1936), 237.
[29]Ibid., p. 240.

a Wiseman article in the *Dublin,* and who towered then as now in the estimation of many as one of the great masters of religious thought and expression, should have contributed but one article to the major Catholic review of his time.[30] Yet we must remember that, as a Catholic, Newman was more liberal than conservative—he even edited two issues of the *Rambler.* Furthermore, just as Ward was trying to persuade Newman to contribute, an article by H. E. Manning in Ward's very first number ("Work and Wants of the Catholic Church," July 1863) contained what Newman took to be a deliberate oversight of his work at Birmingham.[31] In any case Newman's deep longing for harmony and unity among the various elements within the faith was offended by Ward's disputatious and at times acrimonious vein, and he was led, as he had been led before, to take a line of neutrality, contributing neither to the *Dublin* nor to the *Home and Foreign* or *North British.*[32]

It followed, then, that Ward's theological contributions and editing were narrow and strong—"*very* narrow and *very* strong," as he told Cashel Hoey, who joined him as sub-editor in 1865.[33] Hoey took over those areas which were outside Ward's theological bailiwick, and became in fact, "rather . . . joint-Editor than sub-Editor. One-half of the REVIEW [was] in some sense under his supreme control."[34] Ward's own attention centred inevitably on the first premise of his position, the extent and power of the authority of the Church. "We cannot submit to the Church's authority by halves."[35]

Toward the end of his regime, after the Vatican Council had issued the dogma of Papal Infallibility (1870), Ward could conclude that his main position had been secured, and he moved to issues that were broader and less controversial. Bishop Hedley's editorship (1879–1884) confirmed this more temperate line, one which indeed was followed on into the twentieth century, of providing "for Catholic thought a focus, a centre and a medium of expression, that was at once wide-minded and loyal."[36] Hedley's training had not been in the wider sphere of Church affairs, as was

---

[30]Wiseman's article was the anonymous "Tracts for the Times," *DR,* 7 (Aug. 1839), 139–180; for its effects on Newman's Anglican beliefs, see his *Apologia pro Vita sua* (1864), chap. 3. Newman's single contribution to the *Dublin* was his anonymous review of Keble's *Lyra Innocentium,* 20 (June 1846), 434–461. His famous retraction of anti-Catholic statements, which appeared in 14 (April 1843), 271–275, was not strictly speaking a contribution; it was reprinted from the *Conservative Journal* of Feb. 1843 (see Newman, *Correspondence,* pp. 202–203), almost certainly without Newman's specific sanction.

[31]Henry Tristram, "Cardinal Newman and the *Dublin Review,*" *DR,* 198 (Apr.–June 1936), 228.

[32]See Newman's note to Ward's letter to him, Oct. 16, 1862, facsimile inserted before preface in *Ward as Catholic;* and Altholz, *Liberal Catholic Movement,* pp. 85, 213. A good account of Newman's continued alienation from the *Dublin after* the Ward period is given in Tristram, "Cardinal Newman and the *Dublin Review,*" pp. 231–234.

[33]*Ward as Catholic,* p. 223. It should be noted that throughout his editorship Ward had three ecclesiastical censors, approved by the Archbishop, to give security to the *Review's* theological doctrine.

[34]W. G. Ward, "Dr. Ward's Reply," in *DR,* 31 n.s., 83 o.s. (Oct. 1878), 277.

[35]Ward, "Preliminary Essay," p. 24. There was no room for tolerance, or for "minimizing tenets," in Ward's theology; see *Ward as Catholic,* p. 168, and W. G. Ward, "Preliminary Essay," p. 23. "If . . . Catholicism be true, . . . the one healthy, desirable, and legitimate state of civil society is, that the Church's doctrines, principles, and laws should be recognised without question as its one basis of legislation and administration" (*Ward as Catholic,* p. 177).

[36]Said by Maisie Ward of Wilfrid Ward's editorship, "W. G. Ward and Wilfrid Ward," p. 242.

Wiseman's, nor in the Union Debating Society at Oxford, where Ward's forensic weapons had been honed. Hedley's school was Ampleforth, where he was trained rigorously in Scholastic theology; for the eleven years preceding his editorship he had taught philosophy and theology in the monastery at St. Belmont's, Herefordshire.

A somewhat adventitious cause of the new and less controversial vein of the *Dublin* lay in the greater quantity and accelerated tempo of English books and periodicals in general. A quarterly could hardly enter now into the give-and-take of debate in a world where events, arguments, and counterarguments would not wait three months to get a hearing. "News, in these days," wrote Hedley, "accumulates so fast, and every topic is written on so quickly and so completely, that an organ which breaks silence only once in three months is forced to pass by many things."[37] In such circumstances, the role of a quarterly must be "to point out the tendencies of streams of thought, to sum up on large statements of fact and opinion, to draw lessons from the remote past and the recent past, and above all to keep in the sight of the intelligent public those deeper principles of speculative and practical truth which the dust and the noise of contemporary progress are apt to obscure."[38] In policy as well as in practice Bishop Hedley was resolved to make the *Dublin* more varied and less polemical. He sought to infuse the spirit of Catholicism "into literature, history, politics, and art. . . . Our readers need not fear that they will be importuned with religion."[39] No longer was the *Dublin* to be, as George Wenham put it, "the (unintentional) cause of offending and disuniting many."[40] The very confidence and coming-of-age of the restored English hierarchy must have had a direct effect on setting this course. The *Dublin* of the third series was committed not so much to wage campaigns which would defend or establish the faith, as to provide a medium for varied and vital expression by leading minds of that faith.

The full rationale of Hedley's policy was implied in his first lead article, "Catholicism and Culture" in January 1879. It was by no means a desertion of Ward's main position, and in no sense a capitulation to liberalism. Ward himself might have written the words, "There can be no Culture worthy the name which does not mean a widely extended acquaintance with Theology. . . . Catholic Culture is nearly the same thing as the cultivation of Theology."[41] The new accent in Hedley's article is his open recognition that "Culture . . . is as various as our faculties are various. There is intellectual, moral and spiritual culture. There is scientific, philosophical, linguistic, musical culture."[42] Hedley recognized the dangers to Catholic faith which lay in the multiplicity of new intellectual movements. "The stream of thought rushes on, disintegrating and undermining the banks which have been solid ground for so many centuries; sometimes laying bare seams of precious ore, oftener carrying away good land and wrecking houses and homes."[43] The weight of the *Dublin*, then, must be felt in the fray, cautioning against harmful "knowledge," insistently relating all modes of culture to

[37]"To Our Readers," *DR*, 1 3rd s., 84 o.s. (Jan. 1879), 1.
[38]Ibid., pp. 1–2.
[39]Ibid., p. 2.
[40]Dr. Wenham, quoted in Hedley, *Life*, p. 189. See also Dr. Ullathorne's comments, ibid.
[41]Hedley, "Catholicism and Culture," 1 3rd s., 84 o.s. (Jan. 1879), 9.
[42]Ibid., p. 5.
[43]Ibid., p. 10.

"the things in which lies man's substantial perfection," to the mysteries of the faith and the steadfast facts of revelation.[44]

The practical manifestations of this policy in the *Dublin*'s third series were many. Book notices were substantially expanded, and "Science Notes" and "Notes on Travel and Exploration" added. More foreign contributors were secured, and more writers of scholarly substance—this at a time when the *Dublin*'s payments to contributors (6s. 8d. per page) were lamentably low.[45]

A notable new element of the Hedley series was its practice of affixing signatures to contributed articles. Ward's series had on rare occasions relaxed the policy of strict anonymity; with Hedley the signed article became the general rule, though there were many exceptions to it. Signatures made it more readily possible to accept contributions without implying that the views expressed were entirely those of the *Review* itself.[46]

The editorships of Herbert Alfred Vaughan (1885–1891) and James Moyes (1892–1905) served to confirm and slightly to expand this new role. Vaughan widened the sphere of the *Review* to notice works of light literature and fiction—adding quickly that it was not his intention to *advocate* novel-reading, but to give caution and guidance to those who were tempted in that direction. Vaughan also established the proprietorship of the *Dublin Review* in perpetuity in his successors in the See of Westminster, which he himself assumed in 1892. The Very Reverend James Moyes, who became Canon Theologian of Westminster in 1895, initiated the fourth series of the *Dublin*, and, commencing his series with Volume 110, resumed the original sequence of volume numbering.

The *Dublin* of the nineteenth century had no wealthy patron; it addressed a rather limited public; as a quarterly publication there were many turns of events and controversy which it could not readily follow. But it was blessed in its associations with Church officialdom, and with editors who were nothing if not vigorous and valiant in the faith. In 1929 the *Edinburgh Review* ceased publication; the Catholic *Dublin* had outweathered the Protestant—and sometimes skeptical—*Edinburgh*. The centenary issue of 1936 was a cause for rejoicing and proud retrospect, and the *Dublin* continued well into the second quarter of its second century.[47]

EDITORS

Michael Joseph Quinn: May–July 1836, Vol. 1, nos. 1–2.
Mark Aloysius Tierney: Dec. 1836, Vol. 2, no. 3.

---

[44]Ibid., p. 9.

[45]See Hedley, *Life*, p. 190, where it is also observed that Bishop Hedley did not have, as Ward had had, financial resources to supplement payments to contributors out of his own pocket.

[46]In earlier years the same distinction had been made by the word "communicated": "We need hardly explain, that when we insert an article as 'communicated,' we by no means identify ourselves with the propositions contained in it: we only imply our humble opinion, that those propositions are such as any Catholic has full right to hold, and that their publication may lead to serviceable discussion" (*DR*, 23 n.s., 75 o.s., [July 1874], 172). See also *Index*, I, 549n.

[47]Unfortunately with the Winter issue of 1968–9, no. 518, the *Review* was forced to announce its retirement from the field: "It is regretted that owing to financial and production difficulties *The Dublin Review* can no longer continue an independent existence. It will in future be incorporated in *The Month*."

James Smith: Apr.–July 1837, Vol. 2, no. 4—Vol. 3, no. 5.

Henry Ridgard Bagshawe: Oct. 1837–Apr. 1863, Vol. 3, no. 6—Vol. 52, no. 104. Bagshawe was titular and executive editor, whereas Nicholas Wiseman and C. W. Russell were the persons who determined editorial policy: see above, p. 13.

CO-EDITOR

Frederick Lucas: Nov. 1839–Aug. 1842, Vol. 7, no. 14—Vol. 13, no. 25.[48]

William George Ward: July 1863–Oct. 1878, Vol. 1. n.s., no. 1—Vol. 31 n.s., no. 62.

SUB-EDITORS

Edward Healy Thompson: 1863–1865 prob.

John Cashel Hoey: 1865–1878.

John Cuthbert Hedley: Jan. 1879–Oct. 1884, Vol. 1 3rd s., no. 1—Vol. 12, no. 24.

SUB-EDITOR

W. E. Driffield: 1879–1884.

Herbert Alfred Vaughan: Jan. 1885–Oct. 1891, Vol. 13, 3rd s., no. 25—Vol. 26, no. 52.

SUB-EDITOR

W. E. Driffield: 1885–1891.[49]

James Moyes: Jan. 1892–Oct. 1900 (and later), Vol. 1 4th s., no. 1—Vol. 18, no. 36.

PROPRIETORS

Daniel O'Connell: May 1836–1847[?].[50]

Nicholas Wiseman: May 1836–1862.

Henry Edward Manning: 1862–1878.[51]

Herbert Alfred Vaughan: 1878–1900 (and later).

PUBLISHERS

William Spooner, London: 1836–1837, Vols. 1–3.

Booker and Dolman, London: 1838, Vols. 4–5.

C. Dolman, London: 1839–1844, Vols. 6–16.

Thomas Richardson and Son, London: 1844–1863, Vols. 17–52.

Burns and Lambert, London: 1863–1864, Vols. 1–2 n.s.

Burns, Lambert, and Oates, London: 1864–1867, Vols. 3–8 n.s.

Burns and Oates, London: 1867–1900, Vol. 9 n.s.—Vol. 127.

[48]See notation by Dolman, or one of his clerks, on a list of articles for the Nov. 1839 issue, Bagshawe Papers: "Mr. Lucas will in future be associated with Mr. Bagshawe as CoEditor." The connection was terminated some time in the summer or fall of 1842, since Russell to Bagshawe, Dec. 13, 1842, Bagshawe Papers, writes of Lucas' attack on the *Dublin* [in the *Tablet*].

[49]Driffield is referred to as virtually "the acting-editor" under Vaughan. See Casartelli, "Our Diamond Jubilee," p. 270.

[50]O'Connell continued his annual £25 contributions to the *DR* guarantee fund at least through 1843. It is not clear whether or not he continued as proprietor until his death on May 15, 1847.

[51]Manning's explicit statement that "in the year 1862 Cardinal Wiseman gave to me the legal proprietorship of the Dublin Review" (*DR*, 8 3rd s., 91 o.s. [Oct. 1882], 265) makes it difficult to credit Casartelli's attribution of proprietorship to W. G. Ward himself during this period. See Casartelli, "Our Diamond Jubilee," pp. 251, 263, 270.

NOTE ON ATTRIBUTIONS

Significant published studies of *Dublin Review* attributions are virtually all of the 1890s, and somewhat interdependent. They may be listed in chronological order as follows:

Matthew Russell, "Dr. [C. W.] Russell of Maynooth: Memorial Notes," *Irish Monthly*, 20 (1892), 1–3, 147–156, 264–276, 303–318, 383–388, 415–428, 485–496, 533–546, 594–598, 599–601, 652–658; 21 (1893), 44–50, 263–269, 317–330, 376–389, 410–422, 494–503; 22 (1894), 68–78, 162–168, 193–202, 270–280, 289–301. Referred to here as "Russell, 'Memorial Notes.' "

Matthew Russell, "The Early *Dublin* Reviewers," *Irish Monthly*, 21 (1893), 78–90, 137–146, 206–218. The first two installments rely heavily on the Bagshawe notebook described below; pp. 206–218 draw on notebooks (now lost) kept by W. G. Ward's sub-editor, J. Cashel Hoey. Russell attributions drawn directly from Hoey are referred to here as "Hoey notebooks"; other information and attributions in these articles are referred to as "Russell, Early Reviewers."

Matthew Russell, "Dr. [C. W.] Russell's Literary Work," *Irish Monthly*, 22 (1894), 632–642. Referred to here as "Russell, 'Literary Work.' "

Matthew Russell, "Dr. [C. W.] Russell and *The Dublin Review*," *Irish Monthly*, 23 (1895), 51–56. Referred to here as "Russell, *Dublin Review*."

[L. C. Casartelli], "The Dublin Review. General List of Articles. Vols. 1–108 (1836–1896)," *Dublin Review*, 118 (April 1896), 467–520. This list combines attributions given by Matthew Russell ("Early Reviewers," cited above) with evidence in the marked files of the *Dublin* at the library of Oscott College, Warwickshire; discrepancies between the two lists were submitted to Matthew Russell, and either resolved or else listed as conflicts. Referred to here as "*DR* list."

There are four manuscript sources of major importance:

(1) A collection of letters, most of them to or from Nicholas Wiseman, together with associated manuscripts which include a ledger sheet recording payments to Wiseman and others for articles contributed to the *Dublin Review*; in the Westminster Diocesan Archives, London. Referred to here as "Wiseman Papers."

(2) A notebook in the hand of H. R. Bagshawe, containing an incomplete list of contributors to Vols, 1–52, drawn up from notes, letters, and memory about 1863, now in the Westminster Diocesan Archives, London. Referred to here as "Bagshawe."

(3) Letters written to H. R. Bagshawe (editor, 1837–1863), in the Westminster Diocesan Archives, London, where they are called "*Dublin Review* Papers." Referred to here as "Bagshawe Papers."

(4) A collection of letters to Edward Healy Thompson, 1859–1890, the chief correspondents being J. H. Newman, W. G. Ward, J. H. Coleridge, H. E. Manning, and Herbert Vaughan. These letters shed light on the difficulties of the *Dublin*, 1858–1865, including an abortive plan to have Thompson as the new editor. The letters are the property of the Catholic Record Society and are on loan to the Westminster Diocesan Archives. Referred to here as "Healy Thompson Papers."

The *Index* is deeply indebted to Miss E. Poyser, Westminster Archivist, for many kindnesses, particularly for her persistence in discovering Bagshawe's notebook and

his voluminous editorial correspondence in the cellar and cupboards of Archbishop's House. Realizing the problem of examining such a mass of material in
time for this volume, she allowed Lady Cumming to work on them even before
they could be catalogued. She also procured access to the Healy Thompson Papers.

(5) In addition there are extensive markings in the set of the *Dublin* in Manning's
Library at Bayswater. They are not, according to Abbé Chapeau, in Manning's
hand but probably in that of Canon F. M. Wyndham, Superior at Bayswater, 1891–
1908. Many of the annotations could have been entered from "Russell, Early Reviewers," supplemented by Oscott II, but at least one attribution shows complete
independence of any sources we have been able to discover: the article "F. Augustine de Backer," April 1877, to Wilfrid C. Robinson. The file is referred to here as
"Bayswater."

(6) To these resources must be added the perplexing and often dubious markings in
the files of the *Dublin* now at Oscott College. It is clear to begin with that these are
not identical with those which Casartelli consulted. The main run of the *Dublin*
volumes seems to have been broken since 1896, and replacements made (with un-
marked volumes); some markings may have been made *after* Casartelli's "Dublin
list" appeared; independent speculations may have been made in the light of Matthew Russell's and Casartelli's work; and so forth. In any event, the marked files
now at Oscott lack several attributions which Casartelli found there, and provide
some evidence which he either did not find or did not use. Oscott markings are of
three kinds, which we have designated as follows:

"Oscott IA." Marked ascriptions in the Table of Contents of many volumes of the
Dublin Review.

"Oscott IB." Marked ascriptions in the short-title lists of articles for many *Dublin*
volumes; the lists are bound in a single volume at Oscott.

"Oscott II." Clearly the latest ascriptions made at Oscott, these are attributions written into the "Dublin list" in the Oscott copy of the April 1896 number.

BIBLIOGRAPHICAL NOTE

A journal of such pronounced ideological orientation as the *Dublin* is bound to be
self-conscious of its position, and to write a good deal of its history in its own pages.
The best general overview of the Review in the nineteenth century is still that given by
L. C. Casartelli in "Our Diamond Jubilee," April 1896, reprinted in the centennial
issue. Other essays in the centenary number (April–June 1936) give useful supplementary materials. Major sources for particular phases of the *Dublin*'s history are
the following, given chronologically by series, and in short-title when they have
already been cited in the foregoing essay.

FIRST SERIES. Wiseman, "Preface," *Essays on Various Subjects*, 1853, for a general
account of origins and policy; Wiseman, "Religious Movement," 1845, "Present
Catholic Dangers," 1856, "On Responsibility," 1862; the Bagshawe Papers and
the Healy Thompson Papers give vivid evidence of the parlous state of the *Dublin*
at the end of this series.

SECOND SERIES. Wilfrid Ward, *W. G. Ward and the Catholic Revival*, especially chap.
7, gives the fullest general account; W. G. Ward, "Two Criticisms on the Dublin

Review," *Dublin Review*, 8 n.s., 60 o.s. (January 1867), 164–172, and "Preliminary Essay," 1880; H. E. Manning, "Dr. Ward's Retirement," *Dublin Review*, 31 n.s., 83 o.s. (October 1878), 275–278 (which includes Ward, "Dr. Ward's Reply"); Manning, "William George Ward" (1882).

THIRD SERIES. Wilson, *Life of Hedley*, and J. E. Matthews, "Bishop Hedley as Editor," *Dublin Review*, 198 (April–June 1936), 253–266, for general view; Hedley, "To Our Readers" (1879), "Catholicism and Culture" (1879).

There are no significant special studies of the editorial regimes of Vaughan and Moyes, perhaps partly because they followed the policies of Hedley so closely. The best account of the *Dublin*, 1885–1900, though scanty, remains that of Casartelli in "Our Diamond Jubilee."

THE DUBLIN REVIEW, 1836–1900

VOLUME 1, MAY 1836

1 Economy of the earth, 1–27. **M. J. Quin.** Bagshawe.

2 Earl Mulgrave in Ireland, 28–46. Unidentified. This is the first of six articles defending the administration of Lord Mulgrave, nos. 2, 20, 25, 41, 83, and 93, which Bagshawe assigns to T. Drummond; but since Drummond was, in effect, the governor of Ireland and neither Catholic nor Irish, as were the writers of these arts., it is probable that he "arranged" for them as he did for *Edinburgh Review* nos. 1639 and 1647 (*Index*, I, 484) and as he must have done for no. 25.

3 Rienzi, 47–68. **M. J. Quin.** Bagshawe.

4 The Irish and English universities, 68–100. **A. M. Pollock** and **Michael Blount.** Bagshawe gives "Pollock and Blunt"; see *BMCat* and Allibone for Pollock, who presumably wrote pp. 68–88 on Irish universities, and *Landed Gentry*/1937 for a Michael H. M. Blount, who had Irish connections; see Part B below.

5 Ecclesiastical music [review of George Hogarth], 100–131. **George Hogarth** and **M. J. Quin.** Bagshawe; the art. is largely quotation from, and summary of, Hogarth's book, interlaced with admiring comment, prob. by Quin.

6 Raumer's *England in 1835*, 131–151. **M. J. Quin.** Bagshawe.

7 Maria Monk's "Black Nunnery," 151–174. **M. J. Quin.** Bagshawe.

8 The Edom of the prophecies, 174–200. **M. J. Quin.** Bagshawe.

9 Gerbet on the Eucharist, 200–221. **James Burton Robertson.** Bagshawe; claimed in his *Public Lectures on Ancient and Modern History* (1859), pp. 1–2.

10 The railway system in Ireland, 221–249. **C. B. Vignoles.** Bagshawe gives "Mr. Vignoles, C.E."—i.e., civil engineer; see *DNB*.

11 The Oxford controversy, 250–265. **Nicholas Wiseman.** Repr. as "The Hampden Controversy" in *Essays*, II.

12 *Declaration of the Catholic Bishops . . . In Great Britain* [short intro. and text signed by ten bishops], 265–278.

VOLUME 1, JULY 1836

13 State and prospects of Ireland, 281–313. **Michael Staunton.** Bagshawe gives "M. Stanton of Dublin"; on an offprint of this art., R. R. Madden, Madden Papers, Dublin Central Public Library, MS. 273, wrote: "This article was written by Michael Staunton, Esq."

14 *Six Months in a Convent*, 313–343. **Daniel O'Connell**, 1775–1847. On an offprint of this art. R. R. Madden, cited for no. 13, noted: "This article was written by O'Connell and was shown in MS. to M. J. Quin, Esq. of the *Morning Herald* and to Michael Staunton, Esq. of the *Morning Register* previous to publication"; this may explain Bagshawe's attr. to Quin.

15 Wraxall's *Memoirs*, 343–367. **M. J. Quin.** Bagshawe.

16 Versions of the Scripture, 367–399. **C. W. Russell.** Bagshawe gives "Dr. Russell of Maynooth"; Russell, "Literary Work," p. 637.

17 Recent poetry, 400–435. **M. J. Quin.** Bagshawe.

18 Philosophy of art, 435–460. **Nicholas Wiseman** and **John Steinmetz.** As transcribed by Matthew Russell, "Early Reviewers," p. 81, Bagshawe, gave "Mr. Skermetz" for Wiseman's collaborator; Wiseman was corresponding with John Steinmetz of Bruges in 1835 (Ward, *Wiseman*, I, 141) and Ward lists him among the foreign contributors to the early *DR* (ibid., p. 251).

19 Religion in Italy, 460–474. **Nicholas Wiseman.** Repr. *Essays*, III.

20 Pacata Hibernia [state of Ireland], 474–499. Unidentified. Assigned to T. Drummond by Bagshawe, but see no. 2.

21 The Protestant Association, 499–548. **M. J. Quin.** Bagshawe.

22   In miscellaneous intelligence, i–xiv. Conversion of the Rev. Pierce Connelly, v–xii, by **Pierce Connelly**—opening of 2nd paragraph.

VOLUME 2, DECEMBER 1836

23   Education in England, 1–35. **Thomas Wyse.** Bagshawe; confirmed in "List of papers received by Mr. Bagshawe for the *Dublin Review*" [dated 1840], Wiseman Papers.

24   The Fourth of October [1835: anti-Catholic, Protestant celebration], 35–51. **Nicholas Wiseman.** Repr. *Essays*, II.

25   A Poor Law for Ireland, 51–95. **Mark Perrin.** Thomas Drummond to Macvey Napier, July 25, 1837, Napier MS. 34,618, refers to Perrin's Poor Law art. in recent *DR*, and in letter to Napier, July 21, 1837, ibid. supplies first name; Bagshawe gives "T. Drummond," but cf. no. 2.

26   Medical statistics, 95–111. **James Frederick Palmer.** Bagshawe gives "J. F. Palmer"; see *DNB* and Gillow.

27   Literature of the aristocracy, and the literature of genius, 111–129. **William Howitt,** prob. Bagshawe gives "Mr. Howitt"; Oscott I supplies initial "W"; man cited wrote *The Aristocracy of England*, 1846 (H & L, I, 139), a subject, he says in the preface, he had thought about for ten years.

28   Maynooth College, 129–168. **E. C. Groves.** Bagshawe gives "Rev. Mr. Groves, Dublin"; see no. 56.

29   Persecution of Catholics in Prussia, 168–186. **Nicholas Wiseman.** Bagshawe; attr. in Ward, *Wiseman*, I, 270. (Note, pp. 613–620, by **Wiseman**—receipt by Bagshawe on account of Dr. Wiseman, Apr. 27, 1837, Bagshawe Papers.)

30   Chateaubriand's *Sketches of English Literature*, 187–198. **John Maguire.** Bagshawe gives "Rev. Dr. Maguire"; for man cited see Ward, *Wiseman*, index.

31   Irish absenteeism, 199–216. **Michael Staunton.** Bagshawe; four references back to no. 13 by Staunton.

32   Fishes and fishing, 216–226. **Robert Mudie?** Bagshawe gives "Mr. Mudie"; for man cited see *DNB*.

33   The [Royal] Dublin Society, 226–244. **C. W. Russell.** Bagshawe.

34   Life and writings of Mrs. Hemans, 245–275. **T. K. Hervey.** Bagshawe; for man cited see *DNB*.

VOLUME 2, APRIL 1837

35   Life and genius of John Hunter, 277–293. **J. F. Palmer.** Bagshawe; Palmer to Bagshawe, May [23, 1837], Bagshawe Papers, acknowledges payment for first art. in this issue.

36   Science and revealed religion, 293–329. **James Burton Robertson.** Bagshawe.

37   The "no-Popery" current, liberal and conservative, 329–338. **John O'Connell,** 1810–1858. Superscription by Bagshawe on letter from O'Connell May 3, 1837, Bagshawe Papers, notes payment to him for 3rd art. in this issue; Bagshawe gives "T. Drummond" but clearly in error.

38   Theory of probabilities (Part I), 338–354. **Augustus De Morgan.** Bagshawe; *Memoir*, list.

39   Recent opinions upon America, 354–367. **John O'Connell,** 1810–1858. Bagshawe; superscription by Bagshawe on letter cited for no. 37 notes payment to O'Connell for this art.

40   Modern English drama, 367–408. **Robert Bell,** 1800–1867. Bagshawe gives "Mr. Bell (Atlas)"; see *DNB.*; receipt in Bagshawe's hand for an art. in this issue written on Bell to Bagshawe [May 1837], Bagshawe Papers.

41   Ireland and her calumniators, 409–437. Unidentified. Probably by the author, or authors, of nos. 2, 20, 41, 83, and 93, all of which are attrib. to T. Drummond in Bagshawe; ref. p. 423n. relates it to no. 20.

42   Life and writings of Sir Humphry Davy, 437–474. **Edward Cox** and **J. F. Palmer.** Bagshawe gives "Rev. Dr. Cox and J. F. Palmer"; Palmer to Bagshawe, letter cited for no. 35, acknowledges payment for part of 8th art. in this issue.

43   Catholic versions of Scripture, 475–492. **Nicholas Wiseman.** Repr. *Essays*, I.

44   Present state and prospects of the Anglican Church, 493–508. **H. R. Bagshawe.** Bagshawe gives "B."; signed receipt for 10th art. in this issue, Apr. 27, 1837, Bagshawe Papers.

45   Turkey and its foreign diplomacy, 509–546. **Miles Stapleton.** Bagshawe gives "Mr. M. Stapleton (London)"; for man cited see Burke.

46   Anster's and Elliott's poems, 547–563. **H. R. Bagshawe.** Bagshawe gives "B."; receipt as in no. 44.

47   The Catholic Oath, 563–583. **H. R. Bagshawe.** Bagshawe gives "B."; receipt as in no. 44. With a letter to *The Times* which

was refused insertion there, signed **Henry Howard,** 583.

48 Declaration of the Irish Catholic Bishops [intro. and text signed by thirty bishops], 584–587.

49 Summary review of French Catholic literature, from September 1836 to March 1837, 588–603. **Nicholas Wiseman.** Receipt on account of Dr. Wiseman as in no. 44.

50 In miscellaneous intelligence, "Opening of the College of St. Paul's at Prior Park," 603–609, with an address by the Bishop of the Western District—**Peter Augustine Baines;** see *DNB*; "Important literary discovery" [Ebn Batoota's travels], 609–612, by **Daniel Rock**—Oscott I gives "Dr. Rock"; see *DNB*.

VOLUME 3, JULY 1837

51 De Jorio on Italian gesticulation, 1–15. **Nicholas Wiseman.** Repr. *Essays*, III.

52 Ireland, past and present, 15–43. **John O'Connell,** 1810–1858. Bagshawe; receipt for 2nd art. in this issue for O'Connell in hand of H. R. Bagshawe, dated Sept. 8, 1837, Bagshawe Papers.

53 The High Church theory of dogmatical authority, 43–79. **Nicholas Wiseman.** Repr. *Essays*, II.

54 The Canadian question, 79–113. **H. S. Chapman.** Bagshawe gives "Mr. Chapman (a Judge in the Colonies)"; Chapman to Bagshawe, Aug. 9, 1837, Bagshawe Papers, acknowledges payment for his art. on Canada in this issue. With a postscript, p. 276, prob. by **Chapman.**

55 Montémont's *London*, 113–133. **Miles T. Stapleton.** Stapleton to Bagshawe, Dec. 14, 1837, Bagshawe Papers, acknowledges payment for 5th art. in this issue.

56 The fisheries of Ireland, 133–150. **E. C. Groves.** Bagshawe; Groves to Bagshawe [Sept. 1837], Bagshawe Papers, acknowledges payment for this art. by name.

57 Early Italian scientific academies—attacks on the Holy See, 150–164. **Nicholas Wiseman.** Repr. *Essays*, III.

58 Christian political economy, 165–198. **Charles de Coux.** Bagshawe gives "M. de Coux (Université Catholique)"; for man cited see *Louvain Bibliography*, p. 138; de Coux to Bagshawe, Aug. 1, 1837, Bagshawe Papers, says he is glad his art. is liked.

59 The Danube and Black Sea, 198–236. **M. J. Quin.** Bagshawe; Quin to Bag-

shawe, Aug. 9, 1837, Bagshawe Papers, acknowledges payment for this art. by name.

60 Theory of probabilities (Part II, concl.), 237–248. **Augustus De Morgan.** Bagshawe; *Memoir*, list.

61 Summary review of Italian and German Catholic literature, from January to June, 1837, 249–253. Two separate receipts in the Bagshawe Papers, dated Sept. 8, 1837, indicate payments to Wiseman for arts. XI and XII; as this review and the following "miscellaneous intelligence" are merely cursory compilations, it is probable that Wiseman paid someone else to write them.

62 Notices of new books, 267–276. **James Smith.** Oscott IA; Smith to Bagshawe, Aug. 9, 1837, Bagshawe Papers, acknowledges payment for notices in this issue.

VOLUME 3, OCTOBER 1837

63 Life and writings of Novalis, 277–305. **James Burton Robertson.** Bagshawe; Edward Scott, Robertson's agent, to Bagshawe, Dec. 11, 1837, Bagshawe Papers, says Robertson complains of errors on pp. 298 and 301 of his art.

64 Ozanam's *English Chancellors*, 305–325. **T. Chisholm Anstey.** Bagshawe; Anstey to Bagshawe, Jan. 2, 1838, Bagshawe Papers, acknowledges payment for 2nd art. in this issue.

65 The Vaudois, 325–359. **T. C. Anstey** and **Nicholas Wiseman.** Bagshawe gives "T. C. Anstey"; but Wiseman to Bagshawe, Sept. 8, 1837, Bagshawe Papers, says Anstey is writing on the Vaudois "under my supervision"; that Wiseman's supervision was considerable is shown by refs. on p. 326 to no. 53 by Wiseman and on p. 334 to Newman's art. in *British Critic* of Oct. 1836 which was treated at length in no. 53, as well as by the scholarly knowledge of church history.

66 Pugin on modern and ancient ecclesiastical architecture, 360–384. **Nicholas Wiseman.** Bagshawe; receipt for 4th art. in this issue for Dr. Wiseman, signed by Bagshawe, Dec. 11, 1837, Bagshawe Papers.

67 Montalembert's *St. Elizabeth*, 384–401. **Nicholas Wiseman.** Repr. *Essays*, III.

68 English tourists in Ireland, 401–427. **Mr. Duff.** Bagshawe; [Nov. 1837] list by Bagshawe of arts. for this issue, plus a sec-

ond list including payments [Nov. 1837] gives 6th art. to "Duff."

69   The Bible and the Reformation, 428–452. **James Roche.** Claimed in Roche to Bagshawe, May 31, 1845, Bagshawe Papers; repr. *Essays*, I, when he was alive; attr. *DR* 31 (1851), 193.

70   The Irish in America, 452–468. **H. S. Chapman.** Bagshawe; Chapman to Bagshawe, Dec. 13, 1837, Bagshawe Papers, acknowledges payment for 8th art. in this issue.

71   Perceval's *Peace Offering* and *Roman Schism*, 468–525. **John Maguire.** Bagshawe; Edward Cox to Bagshawe, Dec. 19, 1837, Bagshawe Papers, sends receipt for Dr. Maguire for 9th art. in this issue.

72   Fallacious evidence of the senses, 525–549. **Daniel Rock.** Bagshawe; attr. in *DNB*.

73   Summary review of French Catholic literature, from March to September 1837, 550–557. **Nicholas Wiseman.** Receipt for 11th art. for Wiseman in this issue signed by Bagshawe, Dec. 11, 1837, Bagshawe Papers.

VOLUME 4, JANUARY 1838

74   Pozzo di Borgo [Russian diplomat], 1–32. **E. H. Michalowitz.** Bagshawe gives "Dr. Michelsen (Michelowicz, Russian)"; man cited claimed no. 92.

75   The religious system of the ancients—fate, 32–67. **R. H. Klausen.** Bagshawe gives "Dr. Klausen"; Edward Scott to Bagshawe, Dec. 11, 1837, Bagshawe Papers, inquires about a paper in English from Prof. Klausen on Roman mythology.

76   Principles of colonization: New Zealand, 67–96. **H. S. Chapman.** Bagshawe adds "(Judge in Colonies)"; Edward Wakefield to Bagshawe, Dec. 2, 1844, Bagshawe Papers, says Chapman told him *DR* had published arts. by him on New Zealand.

77   Christian antiquities, 96–104. **K. L. Urlichs.** Bagshawe; for man cited see *ADB*.

78   Breton, Norman, and Anglo-Norman poetry, 105–138. **S. A. Dunham.** Bagshawe; for man cited see *DNB*.

79   Saint-Simonism [Saint-Simonianism], 138–179. **Charles de Coux.** Bagshawe; de Coux to Bagshawe, Nov. 9, 1837, Bagshawe Papers, says he has collected his materials on Saint-Simonism. Translation by **Catherine E. Bagshawe**, prob.—de Coux to Bagshawe, Dec. 11, 1837, Bag-

shawe Papers, says he hopes Mrs. Bagshawe will take all needed liberties with the original.

80   The French in Africa, 179–201. **M. J. Quin.** Bagshawe; Quin to Bagshawe, Jan. 13, 1838, Bagshawe Papers, sends his "French in Africa."

81   Mesmerism, or animal magnetism, 202–232. **J. F. Palmer.** Bagshawe.

82   The Archbishop of Cologne, 232–245. **Jean Moeller.** *Louvain Bibliography*, p. 163; Bagshawe gives "M. C. de Coux," but Charles de Coux prob. sent in this MS. by his Louvain colleague.

83   Lord Mulgrave and the Protestants of Ireland, 246–264. Unidentified. Bagshawe gives "T. Drummond," but see no. 2.

84   In miscellaneous intelligence, a letter, 265–267, attr. to **Dr. [John] Lingard**—intro. note.

85   Review of new works, 277–278.

VOLUME 4, APRIL 1838

86   Trinity College, Dublin, 281–307. **Patrick McMahon.** Bagshawe gives "P. McMahon, M.P."; see Boase.

87   *Tracts for the Times* (Part I): Anglican claim of Apostolic Succession, 307–335. **Nicholas Wiseman.** Repr. *Essays*, II.

88   Records of olden outlaws, 335–368. **Dr. Johnson.** Bagshawe.

89   Catholic missions, 368–393. **Nicholas Wiseman.** Bagshawe.

90   *Pedro of Castile*, 393–407. **Mr. Vincent,** prob. Oscott I; Bagshawe interchanged this attribution with the next, which is known to be by O'Connell, q.v.

91   Miseries and beauties of Ireland, 407–440. **John O'Connell,** 1810–1858. Bagshawe; John O'Connell to Bagshawe [April, 1838], Bagshawe Papers, offers a review of Binns on Ireland, which this art. is; a note from Dolman, the publisher, [June 1843], ibid., shows that Daniel O'Connell paid for an art. by his son John in this issue.

92   Mehemet Ali, 440–461. **E. H. Michalowitz.** Bagshawe as in no. 74; Michalowitz claimed this in his application to R.L.F., July 24, 1838.

93   Dr. Meyler on Irish tranquillity, 461–485. Unidentified. Bagshawe gives "T. Drummond"; see no. 2.

94   The Bishop of Exeter and the Catholic Oath, 485–495. **E. C. Groves.** Bagshawe gives "Mr. Groves" and adds "Irish Parson"; cf. no. 56.

95   Irish novels and Irish novelists, 495–543.

Ellen O'Connell Fitzsimon. Bagshawe gives "Mrs. Fitzsimon (daughter of Dan O'Connell)"; John O'Connell to Bagshawe, letter cited for no. 91, refers to his sister's art.

96 Summary review of French and Italian Catholic literature, from September 1837 to March 1838, 543–558.

VOLUME 5, JULY 1838

97 The Roman Forum, 1–14. **Nicholas Wiseman.** Repr. *Essays*, III.

98 Ranke's *History of the Popes*, 14–51. **F. P. Papencordt.** Bagshawe's "Papenwordt" is corrected in Oscott I; for man cited see *ADB* and Ward, *Wiseman*, I, 251.

99 Prejudices of early education, 51–72. **C. W. Russell.** Bagshawe; Russell, "Literary Work," p. 638.

100 Galileo and the Roman Inquisition, 72–116. **Peter Cooper.** Attr. in R. R. Madden, *Galileo and the Inquisition* (1863), pp. 6, 92; *Cath. World*, 8 (Dec. 1868), 321; repr. Cincinnati, Ohio, 1844.

101 Irish election committees, 116–142. **Patrick McMahon.** Bagshawe.

102 Wallenstein, 142–187. **Jean Moeller.** *Louvain Bibliography*, p. 163; Bagshawe.

103 Peru, before and at the Spanish invasion, 187–224. **S. A. Dunham.** Bagshawe adds "(historian)"; cf. no. 78.

104 The plays of Talfourd and Knowles, 224–233. **H. R. Bagshawe?** Bagshawe gives "B." AND/OR, **Catherine E. Bagshawe?** Oscott I gives "Mrs. Bagshawe"; her granddaughter, Mother St. Edith, wrote the editors of this *Index*, June 5, 1961, that her grandmother contributed to the *DR* "and helped her husband," which suggests that many arts. which Bagshawe listed as his because he received payment were partly or wholly her work.

105 Authority of the Holy See in South America, 233–256. **Nicholas Wiseman.** Repr. *Essays*, I.

106 Notices of books, 273–279.

107 Catholic Institute of Great Britain, 280–284.

VOLUME 5, OCTOBER 1838

108 *Tracts for the Times* (Part II), 285–309. **Nicholas Wiseman.** Repr. *Essays*, II.

109 France: equality and centralization, 310–331. **Miles Stapleton.** Bagshawe; cf. no. 45.

110 Shakespeare's autobiographical poems, 331–348. **Mr. Sullivan.** Bagshawe.

111 Carlyle's works, 349–376. **T. C. Anstey.** Bagshawe; Charles Dolman, publisher, to Bagshawe, Bagshawe Papers, says £17 due Anstey for this issue.

112 *Memoirs of Scott* [by J. G. Lockhart], 377–407. **John O'Connell,** 1810–1858. Bagshawe; Dolman to Bagshawe, letter cited for no. 111, says £20 due O'Connell for this issue; note p. 388 explains why Daniel O'Connell's brother refused to hold a staghunt in honor of Sir Walter Scott.

113 The visible and the invisible, 407–436. **John Steinmetz.** Bagshawe; Dolman to Bagshaw, letter cited for no. 111, says £17 will be due Mr. Steinmetz. With a note, 411–414, by **J. F. Palmer**—Oscott I gives "Mr. Palmer"; opening sentence suggests this is by author of no. 81, q.v.

114 Orators in the reformed parliament (Part I), 437–462. Unidentified. Perhaps C. P. Cooper: although Bagshawe gives "Dr. Cooper, Dublin," (see no. 100), Oscott I gives "D. Cooper, Esq." and Dolman to Bagshawe, Feb. 21, 1839, Bagshawe Papers, says "Mr. Cooper" came to the office, in London, for his payment; the author is clearly familiar with the House of Commons, and is also an admirer of Lord Brougham, which suggests the possibility of C. P. Cooper, for whom see *DNB*.

115 Belgium and Holland, 463–496. **Charles de Coux.** Bagshawe. Translation by **Catherine E. Bagshawe,** prob.—Dolman to Bagshawe, letter cited for no. 111, includes £4.14.0 for his account for a translation; cf. no. 79.

116 Retribution due to Ireland, 496–533. **Michael Staunton.** Bagshawe.

117 Controversial novels: *Geraldine*, 533–555. **H. R. Bagshawe.** Bagshawe; Dolman to Bagshawe, letter cited for no. 111, says Bagshawe is owed £14.10.0 for art. X in this issue.

118 Summary review of French and Italian Catholic literature, from March to September, 1838, 574–584.

VOLUME 6, JANUARY 1839

119 Italian guides and tourists, 1–30. **Nicholas Wiseman.** Repr. *Essays*, III.

120 The life and writings of Görres, 31–74. **James Burton Robertson.** Bagshawe. Robertson to Bagshawe, Feb. 26, 1838,

Bagshawe Papers, refers to his paper on Görres.

121 Irish education: foundation schools in Ireland, 74–110. **R. J. Gainsford.** Bagshaw.

122 Charitable institutions of Rome, 111–132. **C. W. Russell.** Bagshawe; Russell, "Literary Work," p. 638; Russell to Bagshawe, Jan. 19, 1843, Bagshawe Papers, says no. 278 is a pendant to this art.

123 Orators in the Reformed Parliament (Part II), 133–162. Unidentified. Possibly C. P. Cooper; Bagshawe again gives "Dr. Cooper (Dublin)" but Dolman list for this issue refers to payment to Mr. Cooper; cf. no. 114.

124 Ecclesiastical seminaries, 162–207. **William Kyan.** Bagshawe gives "Rev. W. E. Kyan"; man cited accompanied Wiseman to Rome in 1836 (Ward, *Wiseman*, I, 253); was present at the retreat led by a Jesuit, which so much impressed Wiseman (ibid., p. 260); cf. the praise of the Jesuits here on pp. 187–194.

125 The railway system in Ireland, 207–269. **C. B. Vignoles.** Bagshawe; Vignoles to Bagshawe, Jan. 26, 1839, Bagshawe Papers, asks for his proof.

126 Comparative statistics of Irish and English crime, 269–276. **R. J. Gainsford.** Bagshawe; Gainsford to Bagshawe, Feb. 22, 1857, Bagshawe Papers, says he contributed this art. to issue of Jan. 1839.

127 Summary review of German Catholic literature, 277–288. **James Burton Robertson.** Bagshawe.

VOLUME 6, MAY 1839

128 Sylvester II and Gregory VII, 289–325. **F. P. Papencordt.** Bagshawe.

129 The Slavonians [on Poland], 325–357. **Stanislaus Koźmian,** prob. Dolman list of payments for this issue, June 1, 1839, Bagshawe Papers, which are not in the order of the printed arts., includes one to "Kormion," which could be a mistaken transcription; man cited was a Polish exile in London, a literary critic and an ardent Catholic; see *Cath. Ency.*

130 Trade with France, 357–395. **Charles de Coux,** prob. Dolman list, cited for no. 129, includes a payment to de Coux; he was a political economist, and is the one person on the list who was equipped to write this art.; cf. nos. 58, 79, and 115.

131 Dodd's *Church History of England*, 395–415. **John Lingard.** *Life*, list; Bagshawe.

132 Froude's *Remains*, 416–435. **Nicholas Wiseman.** Repr. *Essays*, II.

133 King John a Protestant reformer [on Bale's *King John*], 436–448. **Mr. Campbell.** Dolman list cited for no. 129 shows a payment to a Mr. Campbell for a relatively short art.

134 South Australia, 449–466. **H. S. Chapman?** Dolman list cited for no. 129 includes a payment to Chapman. cf. no. 76, to which reference is made here, p. 451; the subject reflects Chapman's interests; see *DNB*.

135 Lynch's *Measures for Ireland* [employment of laboring class], 466–480. **M. J. Quin,** prob. On p. 468, the author uses exactly same quotation from Spenser's *View of Ireland* as Quin uses in no. 209, pp. 218–219; on p. 476, as in no. 209, p. 242, the author acknowledges receipt of information from Mr. Mahony; here, p. 480, he makes same comment on early condition of Scotland as Quin makes in no. 209, p. 220; Quin also wrote nos. 176, 209, 219, and 248 on Ireland.

136 *Geraldine*: religious institutions, 480–490. **Nicholas Wiseman,** prob. Dolman list cited for no. 129 includes £31.17.6 for Wiseman, which would account for nos. 132 and this art.

137 Cooper's novels, 490–529. **H. R.** or **Catherine E. Bagshawe,** prob. Dolman list cited for no. 129 includes £39.11.0 to H. R. Bagshawe which would account for this art.; see no. 104.

138 Italian music, 529–545. **George Hogarth,** prob. Matthew Russell, "Memorial Notes," XX, 655, says by a brother of Mary Hogarth: see *DNB*; Oscott II gives "M. G. Hogarth"; cf. no. 5.

139 Summary review of French Catholic literature, from October 1838, to April 1839, 545–555.

VOLUME 7, AUGUST 1839

140 Library of the Fathers: St. Cyril, 1–36. **George Errington.** Bagshawe gives "Dr. Errington (Bishop of Plymouth)"; see *DNB*.

141 The judicature of the Commons on controverted elections, 36–69. **Patrick McMahon.** Bagshawe; Dolman list for this issue credits McMahon with a payment. (Note, p. 276.)

142 Roman history [by Arnold, Michelet, and Niebuhr], 69–98. **K. L. Urlichs.** Bagshawe; cf. no. 77; Urlichs to Wise-

man, Jan. 24, 1840, Ushawe Archives, acknowledges payment for an art.

143 Döllinger on the Mohammedan religion, 98–121. **James Burton Robertson.** Bagshawe; Dolman list for this issue credits Robertson with a payment.

144 The Normans in Sicily, 121–139. **F. P. Papencordt.** Bagshawe.

145 *Tracts for the Times* (Part III, concl.), 139–180. **Nicholas Wiseman.** Repr. *Essays*, II, and in *The High-Church Claims*, 1841.

146 Waterton and natural history, 180–197. **John Smith.** Bagshawe, who calls him "Rev. J. Smith, Formby"; see *CD/41*; Dolman list for this issue credits Smith with a payment.

147 Wiseman and Turton, 197–225. **John Maguire.** Bagshawe; Dolman list for this issue credits Maguire with a payment.

148 Modern English novels, 225–249. **H. R. Bagshawe.** Bagshawe.

149 Church architecture of the Middle Ages, 250–253. **Nicholas Wiseman.** Bagshawe; attr. in *DR* no. 2619, page 247n.

150 German Catholic literature, 253–263. **James Burton Robertson.** Bagshawe.

VOLUME 7, NOVEMBER 1839

151 Dr. Höninghaus' *Protestant Evidences of Catholicity*, 277–301. **C. W. Russell.** Claimed in *Correspondence of John Henry Newman with John Keble and Others, 1839–1845* (1917), p. 128. Bagshawe gives J. B. Robertson, but in error.

152 Medical notices, 301–333. **J. F. Palmer.** Bagshawe; Dolman list of payments for this issue, Bagshawe Papers.

153 Faith and literature of the Armenians, 333–356. **James Burton Robertson.** Dolman list of payments for this issue. With some translations in text by **Edward Cox** —Dolman list as above. Bagshawe gives Mr. Hattersley in error.

154 Henry of Monmouth, 356–398. **Frederick Lucas.** Bagshawe gives "Mr. F. Lucas (Tablet)"; see *DNB*; Dolman list of payments for this issue.

155 Transatlantic travelling, 399–429. **H. S. Chapman.** Dolman list of payments for this issue.

156 Library of the Fathers: *Confessions of St. Augustine*, 430–453. **C. W. Russell.** Bagshawe; Dolman list of payments for this issue.

157 Statistics of population, 454–483. **J. F. Palmer.** Bagshawe; Dolman list of pay-

ments for this issue. (Note, vol. 8, p. 288, by the Editor, **H. R. Bagshawe.**)

158 Poems by George Croker Fox, 484–499. **D. A. Durtnall.** Bagshawe; Dolman list of payments for this issue.

159 Modern English novels, 499–518. **H. R. Bagshawe.** Dolman list of payments for this issue.

160 The liberty of the press, 518–540. Unidentified. Possibly C. P. Cooper since Dolman list of payments for this issue includes one for Mr. Cooper (see no. 114).

161 Summary review of French Catholic literature from April to October 1839, 540–547. **Nicholas Wiseman.** Dolman list of payments for this issue.

VOLUME 8, FEBRUARY 1840

162 Arbitrary power: Popery, Protestantism (Part I), 1–55. **Patrick McMahon.** Bagshawe; Bagshawe list of payments for this issue, Bagshawe Papers.

163 Prejudices of our popular literature, 56–105. **C. W. Russell.** Bagshawe; Bagshawe list of payments for this issue.

164 *The Arabian Nights' Entertainments*, 105–133. **Mr. Hattersley.** Bagshawe and *DR* list; Bagshawe list of payments for this issue shows Frederick Lucas was paid for this art.; but Lucas was acting co-editor of the magazine, beginning with no. 14, and may have been transmitting a payment to Hattersley.

165 Halsted's *Life of Margaret Beaufort, Mother of Henry the Seventh*, 134–160. **Frederick Lucas.** Bagshawe list of payments for this issue.

166 German translation of the *Pickwick Papers*, 160–188. **C. W. Russell.** Bagshawe; Russell to Bagshawe, Jan. 8, 1840, Bagshawe Papers, offers a few pages on a German translation of *Pickwick*.

167 Gibbon; or, the infidel historian, and his Protestant editors, etc., 189–220. **John Miley.** Bagshawe gives "Rev. Dr. Miley (Dublin)"; see *DNB*; Charles Dolman to Bagshawe, Oct. 8 [1839], Bagshawe Papers, says Mr. Miley has sent part of an art. for next number.

168 Lamartine's poetry, 221–240. **P. A. Murray.** Bagshawe gives "Professor Murray (Maynooth)"; Murray to Bagshawe [Jan. 1840], Bagshawe Papers, encloses "Lamartine."

169 State and prospects of Catholicity in

England, 240–271. **Nicholas Wiseman.**
Bagshawe; Wiseman's account with *DR*
[May 1840], Bagshawe Papers, includes
a payment for this art.

170   Rise and fall of Chartism, 271–285.
John MacDonnell, 1795/96–1892? Bagshawe gives "J. MacDonnell"; man cited
was brother of Sir Alexander MacDonnell, chief clerk in office of T. Drummond during Lord Mulgrave's administration (Boase), who is mentioned in no.
2, p. 34n, as of great help to Drummond;
this art. is by an Irishman and an admirer of Lord Mulgrave and of Drummond (pp. 272, 273, 284).

VOLUME 8, MAY 1840

171   *Mores Catholici; or, Ages of Faith,*
289–316. **H. R. Bagshawe.** Bagshawe;
Bagshawe list of payments for this issue,
Bagshawe Papers.

172   Waterton's *Autobiography,* 317–334.
Charles Weld. Bagshawe list of payments
for this issue; Bagshawe gives "Mr.
Charles ———" but last name is il-
legible.

173   Did the Anglican Church reform herself? 334–373. **John Lingard.** Bagshawe;
Life, list; attr. in *DR* 32 (1852), 325.

174   Civil and religious education in Belgium, 373–414. **John Steinmetz.** Bagshawe; Bagshawe list of payments for this
issue.

175   Fraser's *Travels in Koordistan and
Mesopotamia,* 414–448. **Mr. Hattersley.**
Bagshawe; Bagshawe list of payments for
this issue.

176   Temperance movement in Ireland, 448–
484. **M. J. Quin.** Bagshawe; Bagshawe list
of payments for this issue.

177   Hon. and Rev. A. P. Perceval, and the
Dublin Review, 484–528. **John Maguire.**
Bagshawe; Bagshawe list of payments for
this issue.

178   Persecution in the East, 529–540.
Nicholas Wiseman. Bagshawe; Bagshawe
list of payments for this issue.

179   Allocution of the Pope, 540–548. **Pope
Gregory XVI.** Title. Edited and perhaps
translated by **H. R. Bagshawe**—in addition to payment for no. 171, Bagshawe
lists one in appendix for 4 pp. by himself.

180   Notices of books, 548–553. **George
Irvine,** prob. Bagshawe list of payments
for this issue includes, as appendix b,
one for Mr. Irvine for 5½ pp.; man cited

was to write on literary topics in nos.
188, 226, 292, and 343.

181   Summary review of South American
Spanish and Portuguese ecclesiastical
literature, 554–561. **Nicholas Wiseman.**
Bagshaw list of payments for this issue
includes as appendix c one to Wiseman
for 7½ pp.; on p. 555 there is a ref.
back to no. 104 by Wiseman; appendix c
of same list also includes one to Wiseman
for 4 pp., which would account for miscellaneous intelligence.

182   German literature, 561–568. **James Burton Robertson.** Bagshawe list of payments for this issue includes as appendix
d one to Robertson for 7 pp.

VOLUME 9, AUGUST 1840

183   Staudenmaier's *Spirit of Christianity,* 1–
25. **James Burton Robertson.** Bagshawe
list of payments for this issue, Bagshawe
Papers.

184   Recent no-Popery novels, 25–49. **C. W.
Russell.** Russell to Bagshawe, May 2,
1840, Bagshawe Papers, encloses part of
"No Popery novels"; on May 6 he says
he has worked hard to complete his
paper.

185   Necessity of legislation for life assurance, 49–88. **Augustus De Morgan.**
Memoir, list; Bagshawe list of payments
for this issue.

186   Hungary and Transylvania, 89–117.
M. J. Quin. Bagshawe list of payments
for this issue.

187   Affairs of Cologne: Hermesian doctrines, 117–156. **Joseph-Marie Axinger.**
Bagshawe list of payments for this issue.
Translated by **Catherine E. Bagshawe,**
prob.—Bagshawe list of payments for
this issue includes one to himself for
translation of this art.; Mrs. Bagshawe
had translated de Coux's arts.

188   Jean Paul F. Richter, 156–189. **George
Irvine.** Bagshawe list of payments for this
issue.

189   New Zealand, 189–214. **H. S. Chapman.**
Bagshawe list of payments for this issue;
Chapman to Bagshawe, [Aug. 1840], Bagshawe Papers, sends end of "New Zealand."

190   The [contemporary] stage, 215–250.
M. J. Quin. Bagshawe list of payments
for this issue.

191   Parties in church and state, 251–288.
M. J. Quin. Bagshawe list of payments
for this issue.

VOLUME 9, NOVEMBER 1840

192 Economy of the atmosphere, 289–316. **M. J. Quin?** His "Economy of the Earth" (no. 1) exhibits a similar knowledge and treatment of natural science; on Oct. 14, 1840, Bagshawe Papers, Quin tells Bagshawe he hopes all his other arts. [other than nos. 197 and 199] can be used in Nov. issue, and adds that Dolman has asked him to write on science, politics and current literature; on p. 310 is a brief discussion of Wrangel's expedition, the subject of no. 212 by Quin, a subject already proposed to Bagshawe in a letter from Quin, Sept. 23, ibid.

193 Shakespeare, 316–331.

194 The Brothers of the Christian Schools, 331–353. **P. A. Murray.** C. W. Russell to Bagshawe, July 2, 1840, Bagshawe Papers, says Murray is nearly ready with this art.; pages 332–333 were repr. by Murray, *Prose and Verse* (1867), pp. 77–78.

195 Modern French romance, 353–396. Unidentified. Possibly John Steinmetz who, in no. 218, makes the same attack on immorality in contemporary French novels, and there refers back on p. 452 to this art. OR, possibly Charles de Coux, whose letter to Bagshawe, March 7, 1838, Bagshawe Papers, offers to review "Balzac's *most immoral* novels," and who had spoken out against St. Simonianism in no. 79 (see p. 362 of this art.); the author's concern with Belgian booksellers would seem to identify him as of that nationality.

196 Arbitrary power: Popery, Protestantism (Part II), 396–454. **Patrick McMahon.** Cf. no. 162.

197 The Circassians, 454–477. **M. J. Quin.** Quin to Bagshawe, Sept. 3, 1840, Bagshawe Papers, says he will send about 25 pp. reviewing Longworth and Bell on Circassians.

198 Recent translations of the *Faust*: its sacred poetry, 477–506. **C. W. Russell.** Russell to Bagshawe, Sept. 22, 1840, Bagshawe Papers, says he will set about "Faust" instanter.

199 Foreign affairs, 506–527. **M. J. Quin.** Quin to Bagshawe, Sept. 30, 1840, Bagshawe Papers, refers to "my" art. on foreign policy.

200 Christian inscription found at Autun, 527–536. **Nicholas Wiseman.** Repr. *Essays*, III.

201 French Catholic literature, i–viii.

202 German Catholic literature, ix–xxix.

203 Miscellaneous literature, xxix–xxxi.

VOLUME 10, FEBRUARY 1841

204 Arbitrary power: Popery, Protestantism (Part III, concl.), 1–58. **Patrick McMahon.** Cf. no. 162.

205 Chevalier Artaud's *Life of Pius VII*, 59–97. **C. W. Russell.** Attr. Russell, "Memorial Notes," XXI, 411; confirmed Russell to Bagshawe, Jan. 16, 1841, Bagshawe Papers.

206 Hallam's *Literature of Europe* (Part I), 98–137. **John Steinmetz.** Frederick Lucas to Bagshawe, Dec. 17, 1840, Bagshawe Papers, says Steinmetz wants the two parts of his "Hallam" in two successive numbers.

207 The Horse Guards [court-martial of Capt. R. A. Reynolds], 138–184. Unidentified. Possibly by Maurice O'Connell, who wrote to Bagshawe, Mar. 27, 1841, Bagshawe Papers, that he was aware of the "rate of remuneration," which suggests an art. by him in Feb. issue; the art. is clearly written by a lawyer and prob. by a soldier; see Boase; the author praises proceedings in the Court of the Queen's Bench, whence Daniel O'Connell addressed a circular praising the *DR* in March 1844; see March 1844, Bagshawe Papers. (Note, p. 276.)

208 *The Quarterly Review* on "Romanism in Ireland" [see *QR* no. 663, this *Index*, vol. I] (Part I), 184–218. **David Leahy.** Leahy to Bagshawe, [July or Aug. 1841?], Bagshawe Papers, sends conclusion of subject already treated "in two preceding numbers" of *DR*; confirmed in Bagshawe list for Aug. 1841 issue, ibid.; Oscott II gives "Dr. Murray" in error.

209 The wants of Ireland, 218–248. **M. J. Quin.** Quin to Bagshawe, Mar. 5, 1841, Bagshawe Papers, asks for payment for this art.

210 *Scotland and the Scotch* [by Miss Catherine Sinclair], 248–254. **Charles Leslie.** Leslie to Bagshawe, July 2, 1840, Bagshawe Papers, sends criticisms of a recently published anti-Catholic (see p. 249) work by a woman; Phillip Howard to Bagshawe, Feb. 10, 1841, ibid., refers to Leslie's review of Miss Sinclair.

211 Recent poetry, 254–276. **M. J. Quin.** Quin to Bagshawe, Sept. 23, 1840, Bag-

shawe Papers, says he has left "Recent poetry" at Bagshawe's.

VOLUME 10, MAY 1841

212 Navigable Polar Sea, 277–300. **M. J. Quin.** Quin to Dolman [?], the publisher, Mar. 18, 1841, Bagshawe Papers, claims this.

213 On the present state of ecclesiastical architecture in England (Part I), 301–348. **A. W. N. Pugin.** Repr. under his name, 1843; see *BMCat.*

214 Mental epidemics, 348–382. **M. J. Quin.** Quin to Dolman, Mar. 18, 1841, Bagshawe Papers, says Bagshawe has this art. of his in MS.

215 Sporting in Ireland, 382–394. **Maurice O'Connell,** prob. Dolman to Bagshawe [May 1841], Bagshawe Papers, dealing with this issue, says, "Mr. Maurice O'Connell has sent for his money directly"; the art. includes, pp. 387–389, a description of hunting with Daniel O'Connell, Maurice's father.

216 Protestant evidence of Catholicity: Leibnitz, 394–429. **C. W. Russell.** *DR* list; Russell to Bagshawe, May [1841], Bagshawe Papers, sends "the close of Leibnitz."

217 Thomas Moore, 429–450. **P. A. Murray.** Claimed Murray to Bagshawe, Apr. 9, 1841, Bagshawe Papers.

218 Hallam's *Literature of Europe* (Part II, concl.), 450–489. **John Steinmetz.** Cf. no. 206.

219 Agricultural improvement in Ireland, 489–506. **M. J. Quin.** Quin to Bagshawe, Apr. 26, 1841, Bagshawe Papers, offers art. on Agricultural Assn. of Dublin; and on May 1, ibid., says he will try to send this art. by 10th.

220 *Lives of the Queens of England* [by Agnes Strickland], 506–518. Unidentified. Perhaps H. R. Bagshawe, who reviewed the 4th vol. of this work in no. 257.

221 The *Quarterly Review* on "Romanism in Ireland" (Part II), 518–543. **David Leahy.** Cf. no. 208.

222 Notices of books, 543–548.

VOLUME 11, AUGUST 1841

223 Southern Africa in 1840, 1–53. **T. C. Anstey.** Anstey to Bagshawe, Aug. [1841], Bagshawe Papers, sends the promised art. on Southern Africa; Bagshawe's list for this issue, ibid. (Note,

vol. 12, pp. 555–558, by **Bagshawe**—signed Ed. *Dub. Rev.*, with a quotation from *Cape Town Mail*.)

224 Moral and intellectual condition of Catholic Germany, 53–104. **James Burton Robertson.** Robertson to Bagshawe, Aug. 5, 1841, Bagshawe Papers, speaks of his art. with this title.

225 Jones on the value of annuities &c.: Society for the Diffusion of Knowledge, 104–133. **Augustus De Morgan.** *Memoir,* list.

226 German prose writers, 134–167. **George Irvine.** Irvine to Bagshawe, n.d. [Jan. or June 1841?], Bagshawe Papers, sends "the article on some of the German prose writers."

227 The ancient Church of England, and the liturgy of the Anglican Church [on William Palmer], 167–196. **John Lingard.** *Life,* list; Lingard to Bagshawe, July 1841, Bagshawe Papers, offers some remarks on Mr. Palmer's volumes.

228 The *Quarterly Review* on "Romanism in Ireland" (Part III, concl.), 196–228. **David Leahy.** Cf. no. 208.

229 Milnes' poems, 228–240. **W. D. Christie.** Frederick Lucas to Bagshawe, Aug. 31, 1841, Bagshawe Papers, says Christie's "Milnes" has been sent.

230 The Catholic and Anglican churches, 240–263. **Nicholas Wiseman.** Repr. *Essays,* II.

231 National English airs, 263–272. **J. W. Davison,** prob. Dolman, publisher, to Bagshawe, Nov. 10, 1841, Bagshawe Papers, says author of this art. requests payment; Nov. 25, ibid., says he has paid Mr. Davison; Davison was a music critic: see *DNB.* Bagshawe list for this issue gives "Mr. Bagshawe," apparently in error.

232 Notices of books, 273–276. **H. R. Bagshawe.** His own list for this issue.

VOLUME 11, NOVEMBER 1841

233 The successive discoveries of America, 277–310. **Francis Barham.** Claimed Barham to Bagshawe, Aug. 27, 1841, Bagshawe Papers.

234 The "Unity" and "Catholicity" of the English Protestant Established Church, 311–330. **David Leahy.** Leahy to Bagshawe, in [Aug. 1841], Bagshawe Papers, says he is writing an art. on Unity of the Church of England; in [Nov.], Richards, the printer, says he has an art. of Mr. Lahey's [sic] for this issue, ibid.

235 *The Elements of Euclid*, 330–355. **Augustus De Morgan.** *Memoir*, list.

236 Illegality of Crown grants of public fisheries in Ireland, 356–395. **Patrick McMahon.** McMahon to Bagshawe, Oct. 15 [1841], Bagshawe Papers, says his essay on Irish fisheries is ready. (Notes, vol. 12, pp. 278, 561–564, presumably by the author.)

237 Cardinal Mai's historical palimpsest, 395–426. **C. W. Russell.** Claimed by him in Russell, "Memorial Notes," XXI, 413.

238 Van Diemen's Land under the prison system, 426–477. **T. C. Anstey.** Anstey to Bagshawe, Nov. 1, 1841, Bagshawe Papers, asks for proofs of this art.

239 Schiller, 477–505. **Jane Sinnett.** Jane Sinnett to Bagshawe, Sept. 30, 1848, Bagshawe Papers, says she wrote an art. for *DR* some years ago on Schiller; this is only art. on Schiller in the 1840s; E. Percy Sinnett, her husband, to Bagshawe, Nov. 1841, ibid., writes of delay in receiving proofs.

240 Pope Boniface VIII, 505–549. **Nicholas Wiseman.** Repr. *Essays*, III.

241 *Annals of the Propagation of the Faith*, vols. I and II, 549–563. **M. J. Quin.** Quin to Bagshawe, June 19, 1841, Bagshawe Papers, is preparing a paper on the exertions of the Propaganda.

242 Notices of books, 564–568.

VOLUME 12, FEBRUARY 1842

243 Apostolics [Christian missions] and the eighteenth century, 1–38. **T. C. Anstey?** Marked "Mr. Anstey" in Minneapolis Public Library file; all other attributions in this issue appearing there have been confirmed; man cited wrote for *DR* at this time.

244 The literature of art (Part I) [ancient art], 38–80. **John Steinmetz.** Frederick Lucas to Bagshawe, Feb. 15, 1842, Bagshawe Papers, says Steinmetz wants to know if a second part of his "Literature of Art" will be acceptable.

245 The present state of ecclesiastical architecture in England (Part II, concl.), 80–183. **A. W. N. Pugin.** Cf. no. 213.

246 Stephens' *Ancient Cities of Central America*, 184–221. **C. W. Russell.** Russell to Bagshawe, Jan. 15, 1842, Bagshawe Papers, refers to "my" promised review of Stephens' *Antiquities*.

247 The Anglican system, 221–249. **Nicholas Wiseman.** Repr. *Essays*, II. (Letter signed **Charles Dodgson**, p. 558.)

248 Peel's government [and the state of Ireland], 250–278. **M. J. Quin.** Quin to Bagshawe, Feb. 13, 1842, Bagshawe Papers, says his paper is headed "The Peel Government." Postscript, pp. 277–278, by **H. R. Bagshawe**—Quin to Bagshawe, Mar. 6, 1842, ibid., says he is satisfied with Bagshawe's postscript.

VOLUME 12, MAY 1842

249 Miss Cox's *Hymns from the German*, 279–295. **C. W. Russell.** Bagshawe; Russell to Bagshawe, Jan. 15, 1842, Bagshawe Papers, promises a review of Miss Cox.

250 Lingard's *History of England*, 295–362. **Patrick McMahon.** Bagshawe; McMahon to Bagshawe, Oct. 15, [1841], Bagshawe Papers, promises review of Lingard. (Obituary notice of Henry Howard, 558–560.)

251 The Armenian convent of San Lazzaro, at Venice, 362–386. **C. W. Russell.** Bagshawe; Russell to Bagshawe, Mar. 10, 1842, Bagshawe Papers, says he will send art. on the monks of Lazzaro.

252 Affghanistan, 386–419. **Thomas Grimes.** Grimes to Bagshawe, May 25 and Nov. 24, [1842], Bagshawe Papers, discusses his "second" art. on Afghanistan, which does not seem to have appeared in *DR*.

253 St. Etienne-du-Mont, Paris, 419–446. **Matthew Kelly.** Repr. *Dissertations*.

254 Switzerland: convents of Argau, 446–466. **J. P. Leahy.** Bagshawe gives "Rev. Mr. Leahy, Dom[inican] Con[vent], Cork"; see Boase; Leahy to Bagshawe, April 14, 1842, Bagshawe Papers, says he will be happy with usual remuneration, and on May 19 speaks of the proof of an art. being delayed.

255 Weights, measures, and coinage, 466–493. **Augustus De Morgan.** Bagshawe; *Memoir*, list.

256 Frederic the Great and his times, 493–518. **T. C. Anstey.** Bagshawe; Anstey to Bagshawe, Dec. 1841, Bagshawe Papers, promises art. on [Frederick—illegible] the Great, edited by Campbell. (Note, vol. 13, p. 560.)

257 *Lives of the Queens of England* [by Agnes Strickland], Vol. IV, 518–525. **H. R. Bagshawe.** Bagshawe; T. C. Anstey to Bagshawe, Sept. 3, 1842, Bagshawe Papers, speaks of a "puff" of your art. on *Queens of England*.

258 Protestantism of the Anglican Church,

525–555. **Nicholas Wiseman.** Repr. *Essays*, II.

259   Notices of books, 564–565.

VOLUME 13, AUGUST 1842

260   Algeria, 1–33. **Thomas Grimes.** Grimes to Bagshawe, May 25, 1842, Bagshawe Papers, proposes art. on Algeria, based on Blanqui, Baude, and Scott; and on Nov. 24 [1842?] expresses thanks for *DR* insertion of two of his arts. in consecutive issues (see no. 252).

261   Literature of art (Part II, concl.) [Renaissance painting], 34–73. **John Steinmetz.** Cf. no. 244.

262   Progress of Australian discovery, 74–100. **H. S. Chapman,** prob. Chapman had contributed to the *DR* as early as 1837 when he was in Canada, and later on problems of colonization in Australia and New Zealand; see nos. 54, 76, 134, and 189.

263   Life of [Henry] Flood, 100–155. **E. V. H. Kenealy.** Kenealy to Bagshawe, [Sept. 1842], Bagshawe Papers, acknowledges payment for "Flood."

264   Why is Ireland exempted from the income tax? 155–206. **John O'Connell,** 1810–1858. O'Connell to Bagshawe, May 12, 1842, Bagshawe Papers, says he is completing an art. on Peel's taxation and Ireland.

265   The Spanish theatre, 207–239. **Dr. Lazeu.** Lazeu to Bagshawe, July 5 [1842], dated from 31 Keppel St., Bagshawe Papers, asks for payment for his "Spanish theatre," as he has to return to his country; on the 15th he acknowledges receipt of £20; *Boyle's Court Guide* for 1843 gives "Dr. Lazeu" at the above address. Translation of "passages" by **Angél de Villalobos**—Lazeu to Bagshawe, letter of July 15, speaks of giving passages of the art. "you wish to have translated" to a literary Spanish friend; Villalobos to Bagshawe, Aug. 24, [1842], ibid., returns Laz[eu's] art.

266   Ecclesiastical organization, 240–251. **Nicholas Wiseman.** Repr. *Essays*, I.

267   Notices of books, 251–276.

VOLUME 13, NOVEMBER 1842

268   Palmer's *Letters to Wiseman: on . . . Satisfaction*, 277–308. **P. A. Murray.** Murray to Bagshawe, Aug. 14, 1842, Bagshawe Papers; suggests this title for

his art.; claimed in *Irish Monthly*, 12 (1884), 154.

269   Spain and her resources [mainly on Prescott's *Ferdinand and Isabella*], 308–346. **M. J. Quin.** Quin to Bagshawe, Mar. 6, 1842, Bagshawe Papers, says he thinks he can promise an art. on Prescott's *Ferdinand and Isabell*a; Lord Shrewsbury to Bagshawe, Dec. 31, 1842, ibid., says Quin's account of Spanish clergy in his art. greatly exaggerated; see p. 343.

270   Chemistry, 346–376. **J. W. M'Gauley.** M'Gauley to Bagshawe, Apr. 5, 1843, Bagshawe Papers, says he is anxious to be paid for "Chemistry."

271   Faber's *Foreign Churches*, 377–413. **C. W. Russell.** Russell to Bagshawe, [Oct. 1842], Bagshawe Papers, says he will send a paper on Faber; Dolman to Bagshawe, Dec. 9, 1842, ibid., says Mr. Brodigan has called for payment for art. IV for Mr. Russell.

272   Science and rank, 413–448. **Augustus De Morgan.** *Memoir*, list.

273   Prayer and prayer-books, 448–485. **Nicholas Wiseman.** Repr. *Essays*, I.

274   The sepulchres of Etruria, 485–511. Unidentified. Possibly by Dominick Murphy, author of no. 294, whose opening sentence refers back to p. 507 of this art.

275   Depopulation: fixity of tenure, 512–560. **Patrick McMahon,** prob. Cf. no. 525, partly on same topic, where this art. is referred to or paraphrased on pp. 300, 308; pages 556–557 show this is by the author of "Ireland—Emigration, Employment," *Monthly Chronicle* 4 (1839), pp. 440–459, upon which McMahon's art., no. 525, leans heavily; Oscott II gives "Dr. Crolly," but we have found no confirmation.

VOLUME 14, FEBRUARY 1843

276   Recent charges, 1–66. **John Talbot.** Bagshawe gives "John, Earl of Shrewsbury"; confirmed Lord Shrewsbury to Bagshawe, Dec. 19 and 31, 1842, Bagshawe Papers; Russell, "Early Dublin Reviewers," p. 85, says that "if the Earl wrote this learned article, he must have been helped by his chaplain."

277   The Kirk of Scotland, 66–97. **W. B. D. D. Turnbull.** Nicholas Wiseman to Bagshawe, [June, 1842], Bagshawe Papers, says he has asked Turnbull to write for us on the Kirk; Turnbull to Bagshawe, Dec. 15, 1842, Bagshawe Papers, says

"from recent events in the Kirk" he will have to add a few pages. (Note, vol. 15, p. 558.)

278 Charitable institutions of Italy (Part I): Genoa, 97–120. **C. W. Russell.** Russell to Bagshawe, Jan. 19, 1843, Bagshawe Papers, sends rest of art. on charities of Genoa; Russell, "Literary Work," p. 638.

279 *Arundines Cami* [translations of modern poems into Latin and Greek], 121–141. **E. V. H. Kenealy,** prob. Kenealy to Bagshawe, Oct. 15, 1843, Bagshawe Papers, says "the paper to which I referred was that which appeared" in the Feb. no.; on Nov. 6, ibid., he says he had expected reply re *"Arundines Cami"* and that he is in need of money.

280 Education of the working classes, 141–177. **J. C. Symons.** Symons to Bagshawe, Feb. 3 [1843], Bagshawe Papers, refers to proofs of his art. to appear in next *DR*; and on Mar. 9 protests that last paragraph of his art. (on the Catholic Church) was not his; see p. 177.

281 The Irish Church [in Palmer's *Ecclesiastical History*], 178–223. **Matthew Kelly.** Repr. *Dissertations.*

282 The Catholic Church in Russia, 223–255. **Nicholas Wiseman.** Wiseman to Bagshawe, Feb. 21, 1843, Bagshawe Papers, says "you have the whole of my paper" and offers a short, light one to fill up if needed (see no. 283); attr. in P. A. Murray, *Irish Monthly*, 12 (1884), 152; P. A. Murray to Bagshawe, Mar. 2?, 1843, Bagshawe Papers, refers to W's promise at end of his art. in last no. (see p. 251), a promise fulfilled by no. 293.

283 Superficial travelling: Dickens, Mrs. Trollope, 255–268. **Nicholas Wiseman.** Repr. *Essays*, III.

284 Notices of books, 268–271.

285 Appendix, ["Retraction of anti-Catholic statements"], 271–273. **J. H. Newman.** Ascribed in prefatory note; repr. *Via Media* (3rd ed., 1877), II, 414–419, and there dated Feb. 1843; the retraction first appeared unsigned in the *Conservative Journal* of Feb. 1843 (Newman, *Correspondence*, pp. 202–203).

VOLUME 14, MAY 1843

286 Laing's *Travels*, 277–320. **Patrick McMahon.** Richards, the printer, to Bagshawe, [Mar. 1843], Bagshawe Papers, says he will put M'Mahon first in issue;

claimed in McMahon to Bagshawe's sec. [Nov. 1844], ibid.

287 Is Ranke an historian? 321–379. **John Ennis.** Ennis to Bagshawe, Feb. 19, 1843, Bagshawe Papers, sends art. with this title.

288 The Reformation and its consequences, 379–411. **John Talbot,** Earl of Shrewsbury. Claimed, Lord Shrewsbury to Bagshawe, Dec. 29 [1844], Bagshawe Papers.

289 Cardinal Mai's *Spicilegium Romanum* (Part I), 412–443. **C. W. Russell.** Russell to Bagshawe, Holy Saturday [April 15, 1843] Bagshawe Papers, sends first part of "Cardinal Mai"; Russell "Literary Work," p. 638.

290 The persecution of slander: *Edinburgh Review*; Borrow's *Bible in Spain*, 443–480. **P. A. Murray.** Claimed, Murray to Bagshawe, Oct. 15, 1843, Bagshawe Papers; *Irish Monthly*, 12 (1884), 155–156.

291 National holydays, 481–505. **Nicholas Wiseman.** Repr. *Essays*, I.

292 *Recollections of the Life of Johann Gottfried von Herder*, 505–534. **George Irvine.** Claimed in Irvine to Bagshawe, Nov. 26, 1844, Bagshawe Papers.

293 Russia in 1842, 534–560. **Nicholas Wiseman.** Wiseman to Bagshawe, May 9 [1843], Bagshawe Papers, sends "National Holidays" and one on Russia.

VOLUME 15, AUGUST 1843

294 Etruria-Celtica [review of William Betham], 1–28. **Dominick Murphy.** Murphy to Bagshawe, May 20, 1843, Bagshawe Papers, says he has written a review of Betham's *Etruscan Literature.*

295 Charitable institutions of Italy (Part II, concl.): Naples, 29–52. **C. W. Russell.** Russell to Bagshawe, June 6, 1843, Bagshawe Papers, says he is sending "Charitable Institutions of Naples"; Russell, "Literary Work," p. 638.

296 English agriculture: practice with science, 52–80. **Christopher Johnson.** John Lingard to Bagshawe, May 4, 1843, Bagshawe Papers, says his Lancaster friend will write on agricultural science; Johnson to Bagshawe, dated from Lancaster, July 15, 1843, ibid., sends art. on agriculture.

297 Anglo-Saxon literature, 80–103. **Thomas Flanagan.** Claimed Flanagan to Bagshawe, Dec. 26, 1844, Bagshawe Papers.

298 The religious movement [Oxford Movement with special reference to an art. by

W. G. Ward in *British Critic*, July 1843],
103–124. **A. L. M. Phillipps DeLisle.**
Attr. in Wiseman to Bagshawe, n.d.,
Wiseman Papers; DeLisle to Bagshawe,
Dec. 26, 1844, Bagshawe Papers, re-
nounces payment for "my art."

299 *Rome as It Was under Paganism, and
as It Became under the Popes* [by John
Miley], 125–147. **C. W. Russell.** Russell
to Bagshawe, Sept. 29, 1843, Bagshawe
Papers, says he has 3 arts. in this issue,
and especially wants authorship of
"Miley" kept secret.

300 Ireland and her grievances, 148–168.

301 Cardinal Pacca's *Memoirs* of his ministry under Pius VII, 168–181. **C. W. Russell.** Russell to Bagshawe, Sept. 8, 1843,
Bagshawe Papers, says he has got up a
paper on "Cardinal Pacca"; ref. on p.
181 to no. 205 by Russell also on Pius VII.

302 Carlyle's *Past and Present*, 182–200.
P. Le Page Renouf. Renouf to Bagshawe,
[Nov. 1844], Bagshawe Papers, claims
this as his first art. in *DR*; *Life-Work*,
IV, xxxii.

303 *Life of Grattan*, 200–252. **E. V. H.
Kenealy.** Claimed, Kenealy to Bagshawe,
Oct. 2, 1843, Bagshawe Papers.

304 Minor rites and offices (Part I), 253–
273. **Nicholas Wiseman.** Repr. *Essays*, I.

305 Notices of books, 273–276.

VOLUME 15, DECEMBER 1843

306 Archbishop Whately's *Petition to the
House of Lords*, 277–299. **C. W. Russell.**
Russell to Bagshawe, Oct. 26, 1843, Bag-
shawe Papers, promises a paper on Dr.
Whately.

307 The Scottish schism, 299–316. **W. B. D.
D. Turnbull.** Turnbull to Bagshawe, Mar.
17, 1843, Bagshawe Papers, is sending
"the Church in Scotland and its Schism."

308 The grievances of Ireland, 317–363.
John O'Connell, 1810–1858. O'Connell
to Bagshawe, Nov. 24, 1843, Bagshawe
Papers, says he has his review of a
speech by O'Brien, which this art. is,
nearly ready, and on Dec. 13, ibid., says
the art. goes off tonight.

309 The Ursuline and Presentation Orders
[of nuns]: Miss Nano Nagle, 363–386.
Dominick Murphy. Attr. in *DR* 18
(Mar. 1845), 270; repr. Cork, 1845.

310 *Life of Gerald Griffin*, 387–415. **C. W.
Russell.** Russell to Bagshawe, Dec. 10,
1843, Bagshawe Papers, sends end of
"Griffin." (Note, vol. 16, p. 573, by
Russell—Russell to Bagshawe [Feb. 22],

1844, Bagshawe Papers, sends note to
art. on Griffin in last no.)

311 *Life of Bishop Bedell*, 415–454.
Matthew Kelly. Repr. *Dissertations.*

312 History of St. Andrews, 454–469. **W. B.
D. D. Turnbull,** prob. Turnbull to Bagshawe, [Apr. 17], 1843, Bagshawe
Papers, says he will supply an art. on
schisms in Scotland [see no. 307] and
one on book clubs (this art. takes a slap
at Bannatyne Club on p. 455); Turnbull
wrote almost exclusively on Scotland.

313 O'Connell and Brougham: Irish agitation and French Revolution, 469–485.
P. A. Murray. Murray to Bagshawe, Dec.
19 [1843], Bagshawe Papers, sends art.
with this exact title.

314 Ancient and modern Catholicity, 485–
510. **Nicholas Wiseman.** Repr. *Essays*, I.

315 Dickens' *Christmas Carol*, 510–529.
C. W. Russell. Russell to Bagshawe, Dec.
29, 1843, Bagshawe Papers, promises
hasty art. on *Christmas Carol* by Jan. 1st
or 2nd.

316 New novels, 530–546. **H. R. Bagshawe?**
Richards to Bagshawe, Jan. 5, 1844, Bagshawe Papers, asks if Bagshawe intended
this to be an art. or a notice; the art. is
largely quotation and seems to have been
thrown together to fill out the issue.

317 Newman's *Sermons*, 547–557. **Nicholas
Wiseman.** Wiseman to Bagshawe, Jan. 1,
1844, Bagshawe Papers, proposes to send
art. on Newman's *Sermons*; in an undated letter, ibid., says he does not wish
to be known as the author of the paper
on Newman; reference in letter to announcement in *Tablet* that the *DR* was
about to collapse gives approx. date.

318 Notices [of books], 558.

VOLUME 16, MARCH 1844

319 Religious and social condition of
France, 1–36. **James Burton Robertson.**
Russell to Bagshawe, Mar. 17 [1844],
Bagshawe Papers, says Robertson's art.
touches on French universities, and suggests adding address of Paris Bishops.
With a memorial, pp. 37–44, by the
Archbishop of Paris and the bishops of
his province. (Appendix, pp. 261–272,
by **Robertson**—Russell to Bagshawe,
cited above.)

320 Prescott's *Conquest of Mexico*, 45–65.
John Sullivan. Russell to Bagshawe, Feb.
14, 1844, Bagshawe Papers, encloses
"Prescott" by a friend of Mr. Murphy of

Cork; on Apr. 16, ibid., he says he will have a paper "on China" from author of Prescott; and in [June], says he has marked Mr. J. Sullivan's address on his "China" (no. 335).

321   Dr. Mant's *Romish Corruptions*, 65–93. **C. W. Russell.** On p. 67, author speaks of "our" previous criticism of Dr. Mant in no. 249 (p. 295), by Russell; Russell to Bagshawe, Feb. 17, 1844, Bagshawe Papers, sends part of "Mant."

322   Moehler's *Symbolism*, 93–122. **C. W. Russell.** Russell, "Literary Work," p. 638; Russell to Bagshawe, [Mar. 1844], Bagshawe Papers, sends end of Möhler and says to use this title.

323   The Nestorian Christians of Kurdistan, 122–155. **Dominick Murphy.** Russell to Bagshawe, Apr. 16, 1844, Bagshawe Papers, says Mr. Murphy proposes an art. on Abyssinia like the Nestorians in this no.; Russell to Bagshawe, [Mar. 1844], sends this art. which "does credit . . . to a priest in an active city mission"; Russell here and hereafter refers to man cited as "Mr. Murphy"; Dominick Murphy was a personal friend and had been a classmate of Russell at Maynooth; he was a parish priest in Cork.

324   Irish Archaeological Society: Statute of Kilkenny, 156–185. **Matthew Kelly.** Repr. *Dissertations.*

325   State provision for the Irish clergy, 186–220. **Patrick Leahy.** Leahy to Bagshawe, Mar. 19, 1844, Bagshawe Papers, sends greater part of "Pension of Clergy of Ireland." (Note, p. 279.)

326   Recent publications on the Irish question, 220–237. **P. A. Murray,** prob. Dolman to Bagshawe, Feb. 27, 1844, Bagshawe Papers, says he has sent the pamphlet to Mr. Murray, i.e., prob. the pamphlet by Mr. Martin reviewed in this art.; Murray to Bagshawe, Mar. 22, 1844, ibid., says conclusion of his art. will be sent to-morrow; footnote on p. 234 shows this is almost certainly by author of no. 313, i.e., Murray.

327   Suppression of monasteries [by Henry VIII], 237–260. **Thomas Flanagan,** prob. Wiseman to Bagshawe, [Mar. 18, 1844], Bagshawe Papers, says he has put documents on suppression of monasteries into Mr. Flanagan's hands.

328   Notices of books, 272–278. Pages 272–276 by **Nicholas Wiseman**—claimed in Wiseman to Bagshawe [Apr. 15], 1844, Bagshawe Papers; pages 277–278 by **Nicholas Wiseman**—F. Searle to Bagshawe, Apr. 1, 1844, ibid., says Wiseman will send short art. on *Life of St. Stephen.*

VOLUME 16, JUNE 1844

329   *Works of Gerald Griffin*, 281–307. **C. W. Russell.** Russell to Bagshawe, [May 1844], Bagshawe Papers, says he has still to write "Griffin," and asks Bagshawe to copy out for him passages from vols. 3 and 8 of the *Works* (see pp. 299, 302); a second letter, [May 1844], ibid., refers to his work on Griffin being delayed by illness; Russell had earlier written no. 310 on the *Life of Griffin.*

330   Veneration of the saints in the early Church, 307–345. **P. Le Page Renouf.** Attr. *Life-Work*, IV, xxxii; claimed in Renouf to Bagshawe, Aug. 18, [1845], Bagshawe Papers.

331   Scriptural difficulties of geology, 345–373. **Dominick Murphy.** Russell to Bagshawe, Apr. 16, 1844, Bagshawe Papers, says he has a paper on geology by Mr. Murphy; on May 3, Russell sends Mr. Murphy's art.

332   The Irish State prosecution (Part I), 373–394. **P. M. Gartlan.** Russell, "Memorial Notes," XX, 3; Russell to Bagshawe, [May 1844], Bagshawe Papers, refers to Mr. Gartlan's "State Trials."

333   Neale's *Tour to the Ancient Churches of England*, 394–407. **C. W. Russell.** Russell to Bagshawe, Apr. 16, 1844, Bagshawe Papers, promises "Neale" for next issue.

334   French religious liberty—the Jesuits, 407–443. **Matthew Kelly.** Kelly to Bagshawe, day before Corpus Christi, [June 5, 1844], Bagshawe Papers, sends last sheets of art. with this exact title.

335   China, 444–463. **John Sullivan.** Russell to Bagshawe, [June 1844], Bagshawe Papers, says "I marked J. Sullivan's address on his paper (China)"; cf. no. 320.

336   Irish language and literature: Archbishop M'Hale, 463–482. **Dominick Murphy.** Russell to Bagshawe, [May 1844], Bagshawe Papers, says if Richards has not got Irish type, that part of Mr. Murphy's art. will have to be set in Dublin; reference back to no. 294, also by Dominick Murphy.

337   On minor rites and offices (Part II, concl.), 483–501. **Nicholas Wiseman.** Repr. *Essays,* I.

338   *Ordnance Memoir*: Ireland, 501–519. **C. W. Russell,** prob. Russell to Bag-

shawe, June 30, 1844, Bagshawe Papers, says he has bought "Kane's excellent book for review"; here on p. 502 the author promises to review "Kane's excellent work" (see no. 347 by Russell).

339 Rinuccini's *Memoirs of his Nunciature in Ireland*, 519–549. **C. W. Russell.** Russell to Bagshawe, Apr. 16, 1844, Bagshawe Papers, says he himself will send an art. on Rinuccini for next issue.

340 Appendix to article II: [*The Worship of the Blessed Virgin*], 550–571. **P. Le Page Renouf.** Renouf to Bagshawe, Aug. 18 [1845], Bagshawe Papers, asks for payment for nos. 330 and 340 by issue and number.

341 Notices of books, 572–573.

VOLUME 17, SEPTEMBER 1844

342 *Ireland and its Rulers*: O'Connell and the people, 1–34. **P. A. Murray.** Bagshawe's list, [Sept. 1844], Bagshawe Papers, for this issue, gives "Prof. Murray" (see *DNB*); P. A. Murray to Bagshaw, Apr. 17, 1844, ibid., hopes to have an art. on the above book for next issue, and on June 26, suggests holding his art. over (see note on p. 1).

343 Danish literature: Oehlenschläger's *Autobiography*, 34–69. **George Irvine.** Claimed, Irvine to Bagshawe, Nov. 26, 1844, Bagshawe Papers.

344 Classic scenes in Rome: Becker's *Gallus*, 69–92. **Dominick Murphy.** Bagshawe's list, [Sept. 1844] gives "Mr. Murphy, Cork"; Russell to Bagshawe, Aug. 27, 1844, Bagshawe Papers, hopes Bagshawe has received "life of the Romans" from Mr. Murphy.

345 Jesse's *Life of [George] Brummell*, 92–105. **P. M. Gartlan.** Bagshawe's list [Sept. 1844]; W. H. G. Bagshawe to Bagshawe, [Aug. 1844], Bagshawe Papers, says Gartlan is sending or has sent "Brummell."

346 The Christians of Abyssinia, 105–133. **Dominick Murphy.** Bagshawe's list, [Sept. 1844], gives "Mr. Murphy"; cf. no. 323.

347 Kane's *Industrial Resources of Ireland*, 133–158. **C. W. Russell.** Claimed in Russell to W. H. Bagshawe, [Sept. 1844], Bagshawe Papers.

348 Maitland's *Dark Ages*, 159–198. **George Crolly.** Bagshawe's list, [Sept. 1844], gives "Prof. Crolly"; Russell to Bagshawe, Sept. 12 [1844], Bagshawe Papers,

refers to Rev. Mr. Crolly of Maynooth's "Maitland."

349 The Irish State prosecution (Part II, concl.), 198–212. **P. M. Gartlan.** Cf. no. 332; Gartlan [to Bagshawe], Sept. 11, 1844, Bagshawe Papers, says he has finished continuation of "State Trials."

350 Edmund Burke's *Correspondence*, 212–236. **C. W. Russell.** Bagshawe's list, [Sept. 1844]; Russell to W. H. Bagshawe, [Sept. 1844], Bagshawe Papers, has sent closing sheets of "Burke."

351 Church and State [in England], 236–239; Catholic literary societies, 239–252. **Nicholas Wiseman.** Bagshawe's list, [Sept. 1844]; Wiseman to Bagshawe, [Sept. 1844], Bagshawe Papers, says to use above title and use letter signed by **Le Comte de Montalembert** as appendix (see pp. 241–252); Ledger sheet, Wiseman Papers.

352 Recent Italian apostates, 252–289. **Nicholas Wiseman.** Bagshawe's list, [Sept. 1844]; Wiseman to Bagshawe, [Sept. 1844], Bagshawe Papers, promises this art. by end of week; Ledger sheet, Wiseman Papers.

353 Notices of books, 289–293. **P. A. Murray** and **C. W. Russell.** Murray to Bagshawe, Aug. 9 [1844], Bagshawe Papers, hopes to send one or two short notices for the end of the issue; and Russell to W. H. Bagshawe, [Sept. 1844], ibid., promises a notice or two of books.

354 Note on Irish MSS., 293–296. **C. W. Russell.** Russell to W. H. Bagshawe, cited for no. 353, says he will send a report of the Archeological Society.

VOLUME 17, DECEMBER 1844

355 Chateaubriand's *Life of De Rancé*, 297–335. **Dominick Murphy.** Murphy to Bagshawe, Nov. 22 [1844], Bagshawe Papers, says Richardson has written for Mr. Murphy's "Chateaubriand."

356 Kendal's Texan expedition, 335–350. **John Sullivan?** Sullivan reviewed Prescott's *Conquest of Mexico* in no. 320, and here on p. 340 there is reference to p. 60 of that review; Russell to Bagshawe, Jan. 8, 1845, Bagshawe Papers, in discussing rates of payment for this issue, includes Sullivan.

357 Frederika Bremer's Swedish novels, 351–376. **C. W. Russell.** Russell to Bagshawe, Feb. 17, 1844, Bagshawe Papers, says he hopes to send a light paper on

Miss Bremer's Swedish novels, and in Dec. sends the end of this art.

358   Baron Cauchy's *Religious Orders*, 376–392. **Matthew Kelly.** He was the author of no. 334 on French religious associations to which reference is made here on p. 379; Russell to Bagshawe, June 30, 1844, Bagshawe Papers, says Mr. Kelly wants *Considérations sur les ordres religieux*, i.e., Cauchy's *Religious Orders*, ordered for him from Paris; Kelly had been at the Irish College in France, 1839–1841 (*DNB*), which would account for the knowledge of French academic and religious conditions exhibited here.

359   Canon Schmid's juvenile tales, 392–415. **C. W. Russell.** Russell to Bagshawe, Dec. 1844, Bagshawe Papers, says he has "Canon Schmid" ready.

360   *The Works of Edmund Spenser*, 415–447. **Matthew Kelly.** Kelly to Bagshawe, [Dec. 1844], Bagshawe Papers, refers to my "E[dmund] S[penser]."

361   The Papal supremacy anterior to the division of the East and the West, 447–487. **P. Le Page Renouf.** *Life-Work*, IV, xxxii; Renouf to Bagshawe, Dec. 9, [1844], Bagshawe Papers, sends bulk of what remained of his art.

362   The Church and the Empire in the thirteenth century, 487–516. **Thomas Flanagan,** prob. P. Renouf to Bagshawe, [Dec. 1844], Bagshawe Papers, says Flanagan was proposing an art. for this issue too; Flanagan to Bagshawe, Dec. 12, 1844, ibid., sends all but a few pages of an art.; cf. Russell to Bagshawe, Dec. 13, ibid., asks for subject of Flanagan's art.; Flanagan to Bagshawe, Jan. 8, 1845, Bagshawe Papers, does not find more than two or three mistakes in my paper; Flanagan was an ecclesiastical historian and this is only art. on that subject in this issue. The attr. to Renouf in the *DR* list is a confusion.

363   The life and writings of Miss [Frances] Brown, the blind poetess, 517–560. **George Crolly.** Russell to Bagshawe, Dec. 13, 1844, Bagshawe Papers, refers to "Miss Brown" by Crolly.

364   Dickens' *Chimes,* 560–568. **C. W. Russell.** Russell to Bagshawe, Dec. 4 [1844], Bagshawe Papers, promises a few pages on *Chimes.*

VOLUME 18, MARCH 1845

365   The Earl of Rosse's telescopes, 1–43. **C. W. Russell.** Russell to Bagshawe, Jan.

1, 1845, Bagshawe Papers, says he must keep "Lord Rosse" a while longer; on April 6, 1845, he describes himself as "the writer of arts. I and VII" in this issue.

366   The Maronites and Druses [in Syria], 43–74. **Dominick Murphy.** Russell to W. H. Bagshawe, Dec. 19, 1844, Bagshawe Papers, refers to Mr. Murphy's "Druses"; cf. no. 368.

367   Baily's repetition of the Cavendish experiment on the mean density of the earth, 75–112. **Augustus De Morgan.** *Memoir*, list; confirmed C. W. Russell to Bagshawe, Jan. 4, 1845, Bagshawe Papers.

368   *Memoirs of Father Ripa's Residence at the Court of Peking*, 112–128. **Dominick Murphy.** Russell to Bagshawe, May 14, 1845, Bagshawe Papers, has a notation saying he has transmitted payment to Rev. D. Murphy for arts. II, IV, and short notices.

369   The Anglo-Saxon and ancient British churches, 128–174. **Thomas Flanagan.** Russell to W. H. Bagshawe, Feb. 16, 1845, Bagshawe Papers, refers to Flanagan's "Lingard"; this art. is primarily a review of Lingard.

370   A Bill for the better Regulation of Medical Practice, throughout the United Kingdom, 174–205. **John Shaw Campbell.** Francis Searle, Wiseman's sec., to Bagshawe, Mar. 12, 1845, Bagshawe Papers, says Wiseman has told Richardson to insert Dr. Campbell's art. in the coming issue; see *DR*, 24 (March 1848), 227, which confirms that Campbell wrote on medical and sanitary reform in the *Dublin*—see no. 518.

371   Theiner's works: materials for Irish history, 205–230. **C. W. Russell.** Russell to W. H. Bagshawe, Jan. 13, 1845, Bagshawe Papers, says he will start at once on "Materials for Irish History"; cf. no. 365.

372   The Italian insurrections and Mr. Mazzini, 230–263. Unidentified. Possibly by Nicholas Wiseman, who, according to a letter from Francis Searle, his sec., Mar. 12, 1845, Bagshawe Papers, sent in a paper to fill in space; the author, originally unknown to Russell (see Russell to Bagshawe, [Mar. 1845], ibid.), ends this attack on Mazzini by speaking of his affection for the Italians, whose virtues few like us have had so many opportunities of admiring; and whose warmth and disinterestedness of friendship none more than ourselves has experienced and enjoyed (Wiseman had lived in Rome for over 20 years).

373   Notices of books, 264–282. Some by **Dominick Murphy**—Russell to Bagshawe, May 14, 1845, Bagshawe Papers, says he has paid Murphy for short notices in this issue; others by **C. W. Russell**—Russell to W. H. Bagshawe, Mar. 9, 1845, Bagshawe Papers, is sending "about a dozen short notices."

VOLUME 18, JUNE 1845

374   *German Reformation and its Times* [by Leopold Ranke], 283–320. **John Ennis.** Ennis to Bagshawe, Jan. 1, 1845, Bagshawe Papers, says he could have his "Ranke" ready by Feb. 1; Russell to W. H. Bagshawe, Feb. 16, 1845, refers to Ennis' "Reformation."

375   Tractarian poetry: Faber's *Sir Lancelot*, 320–331. **Dominick Murphy.** Russell to W. H. Bagshawe, Mar. 7, 1845, Bagshawe Papers, refers to Mr. Murphy's "Sir Lancelot."

376   Difficulties of the Ante-Nicene Fathers, 331–370. **P. Le Page Renouf.** *Life-Work*, IV, xxxii; Renouf to Bagshawe, Aug. 18, [1845], Bagshawe Papers, acknowledges payment for this art.

377   Spain, 370–485. **Nicholas Wiseman.** Repr. *Essays*, III.

378   Bokhara; its amir, and its people, 485–518. **Matthew Kelly.** Russell to Bagshawe, Mar. 2, 1845, Bagshawe Papers, refers to "Mr. Kelly on Bokhara"; Kelly to Bagshawe, Mar. 13, 1845, ibid., sends first part of "Bokhara."

379   *Lives of Men of Letters and Science, who flourished in the time of George III* [by Lord Brougham], 518–555. **James Roche.** Repr. *Essays*, I.

380   Cardinal Mai's *Spicilegium Romanum* (Part II, concl.), 555–576. **C. W. Russell.** Russell to Bagshawe, May 4, 1845, Bagshawe Papers, sends "a portion of my own 'Cardinal Mai'."

381   Notices of books, 576–586. Some by **C. W. Russell**—Russell to Bagshawe, [June 1845], Bagshawe Papers, says he has sent Richardson 6 pages of notices, including by name *Irish Watering Places* and Wills' poems, and on June 21, he says he wrote the short notice of Petrie.

VOLUME 19, SEPTEMBER 1845

382   The origin and uses of the round towers of Ireland, 1–67. **Matthew Kelly.** Repr. *Dissertations.*

383   Prichard's *Natural History of Man*, 67–98. **Dominick Murphy.** Russell to Bagshawe, May 4, 1845, Bagshawe Papers, encloses Mr. Murphy's "Prichard."

384   Speculators and speculations, 99–129. **Augustus De Morgan.** *Memoir*, list; confirmed by notation on De Morgan to Bagshawe, Nov. 18, 1845, Bagshawe Papers.

385   *Hawkstone, a Tale*, 129–145. **Emily Bowles.** Wiseman to Bagshawe, Aug. 14, [1845], Bagshawe Papers, says he has at hand for current issue Sewell's "*Hawkstone*" by Miss Bowles; Ledger sheet, Wiseman Papers, gives for 4th art. Miss Bowles; for woman cited see Newman, *L&D*, XI, index.

386   Ancient Irish Dominican schools, 145–174. **Bartholomew Russell.** Richardson, the printer, to Bagshawe, Aug. 25, 1845, Bagshawe Papers, says he has started to set up this art. by Rev. Mr. Russell, but has not yet received any art. from Dr. [C. W.] Russell; first name supplied from *Irish Monthly*, 18 (1890), 653.

387   Egypt and Mehemet Ali, 174–195. Unidentified. Ledger sheet, Wiseman Papers, assigns art. 6 in this issue to Wiseman, but Richardson to Bagshawe, letter cited for no. 386, says art. sent in by Dr. Wiseman but author unknown.

388   Mary, Queen of Scots, 195–229. **Thomas Flanagan.** Flanagan to W. H. G. Bagshawe, Nov. 17, 1845, Bagshawe Papers, acknowledges payment for "my article VII in No. 37"; endorsed on back by secretary, "Flanagan, Art. VII, No. 37, £10."; wrongly attributd to C. W. Russell by *DR* list and Russell, "Literary Work," p. 639.

389   The Reformation in Sweden: Gustavus Wasa [sic.], 229–265. **Dominick Murphy.** Russell to Bagshawe, May 4, 1845, Bagshawe Papers, encloses Mr. Murphy's "Gustavus Vasa."

390   *Palaeographia Sacra*, 265–271. **Nicholas Wiseman,** prob. Ledger sheet, Wiseman Papers, assigns him Art. IX.

391   Notices of books, 271–280. Pages 275–277 by **Dominick Murphy**—Russell to Bagshaw, Oct. 19, 1845, Bagshawe Papers, says this notice is by Murphy; pages 271–275, 277, 278 by **C. W. Russell**—Russell to Bagshawe, cited immediately above, lists these notices as his; the remainder by **Nicholas Wiseman** who was paid 17/1 for notices in this issue: Ledger sheet, Wiseman Papers.

VOLUME 19, DECEMBER 1845

392 O'Conor's *Military History of Ireland*, 281–311. **James Roche.** Repr. *Essays*, II.

393 Clarence Mangan's *German Anthology*, 312–331. **C. W. Russell.** Richardson, the printer, to Bagshawe, Dec. 17, 1845, Bagshawe Papers, has already printed off this art., assigned to man cited in Bagshawe's hand.

394 Religious and social condition of Belgium, 332–373. **James Burton Robertson.** Attr. in Richardson to Bagshawe, letter cited for no. 393.

395 The ballad poetry of Ireland, 373–390. **George Crolly.** Attr. in Richardson to Bagshawe, letter cited for no. 393.

396 Brownson's conversion, 390–400. **Nicholas Wiseman.** Ledger sheet, Wiseman Papers, assigns him Art. V; attr. Richardson to Bagshawe, letter cited for no. 393.

397 Dewar's *German Protestantism*, 401–433. **C. W. Russell.** Attr. Richardson to Bagshawe, letter cited for no. 393; Russell to Bagshawe, Oct. 24 [1845], Bagshawe Papers, sends end of "Dewar."

398 Book-keeping, 433–453. **Augustus De Morgan.** *Memoir*, list; claimed by De Morgan in R. P. Graves, *Life of W. R. Hamilton* (1882–1889), III, 631–632.

399 The plea of conscience for seceding from the Catholic Church to the Romish schism, in England, 453–458. **W. G. Ward.** Ledger sheet, Wiseman Papers, gives "VIII (Ward)"; letter cited for no. 393 gives "Mr. Ward."

400 *Le Prêtre, la Femme, et la Famille* [by T. Michelet]:—*Priests, Women, and Families*, 458–518. **George Crolly.** Russell to Bagshawe, Nov. 4 [1845], Bagshawe Papers, says Crolly is busy on Michelet's *Priests, Women, and Families.*

401 *A Short Series of Lectures, on the Parochial and Collegiate Antiquities of Edinburgh*, 519–521. **Nicholas Wiseman.** Ledger sheet, Wiseman Papers, assigns him Art. X; Richardson to Bagshawe, letter cited for no. 393, indicates an art. was expected from Wiseman.

402 The religious movement [the Oxford Movement], 522–538, with some reflections on the policy of the *Dublin Review*, 538–545. **Nicholas Wiseman.** Ledger sheet, Wiseman Papers, assigns him Art. XI; note also refs. to history of *DR*, and to Wiseman arts. nos. 11, 53, 87, 132, etc.

403 Notices of books, 545–555. Pages 549–551, 552 by **C. W. Russell**—Russell to Bagshawe, Dec . 6, 1845, Bagshawe

Papers, says he has written these notices and "some others."

VOLUME 20, MARCH 1846

404 The Scottish monks, 1–31. **Paul MacLachlan.** Bagshawe; Paul MacLachlan to W. H. G. Bagshawe, June 4, 1846, Bagshawe Papers, acknowledges payment for first art. in this issue.

405 D'Aubigné's *History of the Reformation*, 31–83. **James Roche.** Bagshawe; repr. *Essays*, I.

406 Prayers for England: the recent conversions, 83–106. **Frederick Oakeley,** prob. Bagshawe; Wiseman to W. H. Bagshawe, Mar. 5, 1846, Bagshawe Papers, lists this art. as by Oakeley; pp. 89–94 raise some question of Oakeley's authorship here, and suggests that Wiseman as editor (see Ledger sheet, Wiseman Papers, for this issue) may have revised these pages.

407 *The Lamp of the Sanctuary: a Catholic Story*, 107–120. **W. G. Ward.** Bagshawe; claimed in letter in *Rambler*, 3 (1848), 607n.

408 Rome, ancient and modern, 120–137. **Dominick Murphy.** Bagshawe gives "Rev. Dr. Murphy (Cork)"; Dominick Murphy to Bagshawe, Nov. 24, 1845, Bagshawe Papers, sends art. with this title.

409 Developments of Protestantism, 137–224. **T. W. M. Marshall.** Bagshawe; repr. under same title, 1849; see *BMCat* under T.W.M.

410 Dr. Pusey's sermon on absolution, 224–257. **Frederick Oakeley.** Bagshawe; Wiseman to W. H. Bagshawe, March 5, 1846, Bagshawe Papers, confirms.

411 Notices of books, 257–272. Pages 264–272, by **C. W. Russell**—Francis Searle to Bagshawe, May 21, 1846, Bagshawe Papers, says notices of books to no. VIII inclusive are by Dr. Wiseman, the remainder by Dr. Russell; pages 257–263 by **Nicholas Wiseman**—ibid.; Ledger sheet, Wiseman Papers.

VOLUME 20, JUNE 1846

412 Irish eloquence: Curran, 273–291. **Dominick Murphy.** Russell to Bagshawe, March 8, 1846, Bagshawe Papers, hopes Bagshawe has received Mr. Murphy's "Curran," and on April 22 [1846], says Mr. Murphy will write a short art. on O'Connell's speeches and combine it with his "Curran" if need be; on [June 1846], he sends in "a very well-written article on Curran by Mr. Murphy."

413   The deaf and dumb in Ireland: Dr. Kitto's *Lost Senses*, 291–319. **C. W. Russell.** Bagshawe; Russell to Bagshawe, Mar. 2, 1846, Bagshawe Papers, promises this by end of week.

414   Gosselin's *Power of the Pope in the Middle Ages*, 319–345. **John Gordon.** Bagshawe gives "Mr. J. Gordon (Inverness)"; Bishop John Murdoch to Bagshawe [?], Sept. 24, 1846, Bagshawe Papers, wants to know if this was by Rev. John Gordon, resident in France at the time; Wiseman to W. H. Bagshawe, March 5, 1846, Bagshawe Papers, gives "Gordon (Paris)."

415   *Autobiography of the Rev. Joseph Blanco White*, 345–386. **W. G. Ward.** Bagshawe gives "Mr. G. W. Ward" (see nos. 417, 473, 485); Ward to Bagshawe, [May–June 1846], Bagshawe Papers, wants proofs of his art. on "Mr. B. White."

416   Hood's poems, 386–408. **P. A. Murray.** Bagshawe; Murray to Bagshawe, Apr. 22 [1846], Bagshawe Papers, proposes to review Hood; on May 29, ibid., says he will add appendix on Davis.

417   Foreign lotteries, 408–427. Unidentified. Possibly John Ward, consul at Leipzig at this date and much interested in commerce and finance (see *DNB* and this *Index*, I, 1128). The Bagshawe attr. of "Mr. G. W. Ward" (to whom this topic would not be congenial) may stem from misinterpretation of an MS or oral attr. to "Ward"; Bayswater gives Mr. W. G. Ward.

418   Steinmetz's *Noviciate, or a Year among the English Jesuits*, 428–434. **Nicholas Wiseman.** Bagshawe; Ledger sheet, Wiseman Papers.

419   *Lyra Innocentium*, by the author of the *Christian Year*, 434–461. **J. H. Newman.** Bagshawe; repr. *Essays, Critical and Historical* (1871), II, as "John Keble."

420   Catholic Ireland, A.D. 600—the Church of St. Patrick, 461–500. **Matthew Kelly.** Bagshawe; repr. *Dissertations*.

421   Rite of ordination; moral training for the Church, 500–519. **Frederick Oakeley.** Bagshawe; Oakeley to Bagshawe, Sept. 23, 1846, Bagshawe Papers, acknowledges payment for an art., presumably in this issue.

422   Notices of books, 520–532. Pages 520–523 by **Dominick Murphy**, prob. Russell to Bagshawe, Apr. 22 [1846], Bagshawe Papers, says Mr. Murphy will write a

short art. on O'Connell's speeches; others by **C. W. Russell,** prob.; Russell to Bagshawe, [May 21], 1846, Bagshawe Papers, says he has some books sent him for notice, which he will forward shortly.

VOLUME 21, SEPTEMBER 1846

423   Mathematical bibliography, 1–37. **Augustus De Morgan.** Bagshawe; *Memoir*, list.

424   Devotion to the Most Holy Virgin—authority of the Church, 37–65. **W. G. Ward.** Bagshawe; Ward to Bagshawe, [May 1846], Bagshawe Papers, wants to write on a sermon on our Lady.

425   The great Irish insurrection [Carlyle's *Cromwell*], 65–131. **George Crolly.** Bagshawe; C. W. Russell to Bagshawe, Mar. 9, 1846, Bagshawe Papers, says Mr. Crolly wants to review *Cromwell* [by Thomas Carlyle].

426   Vincenzi's *Vindication of the Tridentine Canon of Scripture*, 131–163. **John Brande Morris.** Bagshawe; see *Ram* no. 516, p. 159n, where this is said to be by author of that art., i.e., J. B. Morris.

427   Flemish literature: Hendrik Conscience's tales, 163–184. **C. W. Russell.** Bagshawe; Russell to Bagshawe, Apr. 22 [1846], Bagshawe Papers, says he will write on Flemish tales.

428   Dickens's *Pictures from Italy*, 184–201. **P. A. Murray.** Bagshawe; repr. *Prose and Verse*, 1867.

429   Church music and choral regulations, 201–216. **Frederick Oakeley.** Bagshawe; Oakeley to Bagshawe, Jan. 22, 1847, Bagshawe Papers, acknowledges payment for an art. in Oct. issue.

430   The Benedictines of St. Maur: Mabillon, 217–246. **Dominick Murphy.** Bagshawe gives "Rev. D. Murphy, Maynooth"; Russell to Bagshawe, [Sept. 1846], Bagshawe Papers, lists this art. among those he has ready at Maynooth for the Sept. issue.

431   The fate of sacrilege, 246–258. **Nicholas Wiseman.** Bagshawe; repr. *Essays*, I.

432   Notices of books, 258–272. Pages 258–260, by **C. W. Russell**—Russell to Bagshawe, Jan. 20, 1847, Bagshawe Papers, says he has reviewed Burslem in next to last no.; Nicholas Wiseman did half the notices—Ledger sheet, Wiseman Papers.

VOLUME 21, JANUARY 1847

433   Devotional use of the breviary—Advent and Christmas, 273–305. **Frederick Oake-**

ley. Bagshawe; Richardson list [Jan. 1847] for this issue.

434   The reasonableness of forbearance towards some not yet converted, 305–336. **John Brande Morris.** Bagshawe; Richardson list [Jan. 1847] for this issue.

435   Vigilantius and his times, 337–372. **John Walker,** 1817–1878. John Walker to Bagshawe, Apr. 17, 1847, dated St. Mary's College, Oscott, acknowledges payment presumably for this art.; Richardson list [Jan. 1847] for this issue gives "Mr. Walker, St. Mary's Coll."; the attr. in Bagshawe to "Mr. Walker of Scarborough" is in error.

436   Paget: nature and religion, 372–401. **A. J. Christie.** Bagshawe, who adds "S.J."; Richardson list [Jan. 1847] for this issue.

437   The temples and tombs of Egypt and Palestine, 401–418. **Dominick Murphy.** Richardson list [Jan. 1847] for this issue; Bagshawe gives "Rev. Dr. Murray (Maynooth)."

438   Faith of Catholics: Waterworth, 419–427. **John Brande Morris.** Bagshawe; Richardson list [Jan. 1847] for this issue.

439   Maitland's *Church in the Catacombs,* 427–460. **C. W. Russell.** Bagshawe; claimed in Russell to Bagshawe, Nov. 12, 1846, Bagshawe Papers.

440   Unreality of Anglican belief, 461–493. **Nicholas Wiseman.** Bagshawe; repr. *Essays,* II.

441   Upper Canada, 494–509. **Nicholas Wiseman.** Bagshawe; Ledger sheet, Wiseman Papers; Richardson list [Jan. 1847] for this issue.

442   *Tales of the Century* [1746–1846], 509–514. **Nicholas Wiseman.** Bagshawe; Richardson list [Jan. 1847] for this issue.

443   Notices of books, 515–536. Pages 515–522 (exclusive of no. 1), and 527–534, by **C. W. Russell**—Russell to W. H. Bagshawe, Mar. 24, 1847, Bagshawe Papers, claims nos. 2–9 and 16–24.

VOLUME 22, MARCH 1847

444   The Order of Mercy and its foundress, 1–25. **Dominick Murphy.** Bagshawe; repr. *Sketches of Irish Nunneries,* 1865.

445   The physical cause of the death of Christ, 25–29. **A. J. Christie.** Bagshawe; Richardson list, 1847, for this issue.

446   Motherwell's poems, 59–74. **C. W. Russell.** Bagshawe; Richardson list, 1847, for this issue.

447   On helps to calculation, 74–92. **Augustus De Morgan.** Bagshawe; *Memoir,* list; Richardson list, 1847, for this issue.

448   McCabe's *Catholic History of England,* 92–124. **George Crolly.** Bagshawe; Richardson list, 1847, for this issue.

449   The aristocracies of Ireland, 124–135. **Matthew Kelly.** Bagshawe; Richardson list, 1847, for this issue.

450   Formby on Christian psalmody, 135–158. **Frederick Oakeley.** Bagshawe; Richardson list, 1847, for this issue.

451   Recent antiquarian researches in Lycia, 158–190. **C. W. Russell.** Bagshawe; Richardson list, 1847, for this issue.

452   Lord Brougham's *Men of Letters and Science*: D'Alembert, 190–229. **James Roche.** Bagshawe; repr. *Essays,* II.

453   Measures for Ireland, 230–260. **W. B. McCabe.** Bagshawe; Richardson list, 1847, for this issue.

454   Notices of books, 260–270. Pages 260–263, *From Oxford to Rome,* unidentified (letter, vol. 23, pp. 256–257, signed by The Author of *From Oxford to Rome*— **Furlong Elizabeth S. Harris:** see *Boase*); some notices by **Wiseman**—Ledger sheet, Wiseman Papers; Richardson list, 1847, for this issue gives notices to **Dr. Wiseman, Dr. Russell,** and **Mr. Bagshawe,** although Russell to Bagshawe, Apr. 23, 1847, Bagshawe Papers, says none of the notices are from his side [of the Irish Channel].

VOLUME 22, JUNE 1847

455   Answers to Mr. Allies—Mr. Thompson, Mr. Renouf, 271–317. **W. G. Ward.** Bagshawe; Richardson list, June 1847, for this issue.

456   Walsh's *Popular Irish Songs,* 317–325. **Dominick Murphy.** Bagshawe; Richardson list, June 1847, for this issue.

457   Doctrinal developments [on an art. by Brownson], 325–354. **W. G. Ward.** Bagshawe; Richardson list, June 1847, for this issue.

458   Auerbach's *Tales of the Black Forest,* 354–388. **C. W. Russell.** Bagshawe; Richardson list, June 1847, for this issue.

459   Colonial emigration [and population], 388–408. **J. S. Campbell.** Richardson list, June 1847, for this issue gives "Mr. J. S. Campbell"; Bagshawe gives "Mr. J. P. Campbell (S.J.)".

460   Irish Evangelicals—Dr. O'Brien, Lord Bishop of Ossory, etc., 408–427. **Matthew Kelly.** Richardson list, June 1847, for this issue gives "Rev. Mr. Kelly"; Bagshawe gives "Rev. P. Kelly (Maynooth)," but man cited was only Kelly on the

Maynooth staff and a frequent contributor to *DR*.

461	James II and Mary of Modena, 428–448. **Thomas Flanagan.** Bagshawe; Richardson list, June 1847, for this issue.

462	Dr. Wordsworth's *Letters to M. Gondon* [on the Church of Rome], 449–457. **David Lewis,** prob. Bagshawe and Richardson list, June 1847, for this issue, give only "Mr. Lewis," but D. Lewis to Bagshawe [July 1847], Bagshawe Papers, acknowledges payment for an art.; David Lewis later became a regular contributor to *DR*.

463	Catholic tradition and Scripture, 457–486. **F. H. Laing.** Bagshawe; Richardson list, June 1847, for this issue.

464	Christian art, 486–515. **Nicholas Wiseman.** Bagshawe; repr. *Essays*, III.

465	Notices of books, 515–535. Pages 524–525 (iv), 526–527 (vi, vii), 534–535 (xi–xiii), by **H. R. Bagshawe**—Richardson list, June 1847, for this issue; pages 525–526 (v), 527–529 (viii), 531–533 (x), by **C. W. Russell**—ibid.; pages 515–522 (i), by **Nicholas Wiseman**—ibid.

VOLUME 23, SEPTEMBER 1847

466	Lord Ellesmere's *Turkish Sieges of Vienna*, 1–26. **C. W. Russell.** Bagshawe, which, however, is almost illegible; confirmed by *DR* list; Russell to Bagshawe, Apr. 23, 1847, Bagshawe Papers, says this is being prepared in Ireland.

467	The Christian use of the Psalms of David, 27–58. **John Brande Morris.** Bagshawe.

468	Fortune's *Wanderings in China*, 59–77. **Dominick Murphy.** Bagshawe; Russell to Bagshawe, June 2, 1847, Bagshawe Papers, says he expects Mr. Murphy's "Fortune."

469	Dunlop's *Travels in Central America*, 78–89. **E. V. H. Kenealy.** Bagshawe; Kenealy to Bagshawe, Sept. 2, 1847, Bagshawe Papers, says he will keep "Dunlop" at half price.

470	The early Jesuit missions in North America, 89–104. **Dominick Murphy.** Bagshawe; Richardson list, [March] 1847, of arts. in hand gives "Rev. D. Murphy"; the art. was evidently held over.

471	The canon of sacred Scripture, 104–123. **Matthew Bridges.** Bagshawe; Bridges to Russell, May 24, 1847, Bagshawe Papers, offers art. with this title, and on Jan. 17, 1848, acknowledges payment.

472	The life of St. Philip Neri, 124–132. **H. R. Bagshawe.** Bagshawe.

473	Bunsen's *Church of the Future*, 132–145. **W. G. Ward.** Bagshawe, which, however, gives here and for nos. 415, 417, and 485 "Mr. G. W. Ward"; Richardson to Bagshawe, Sept. 2, 1847, Bagshawe Papers, sends proof of Mr. Ward's review of the *Church of the Future*.

474	Malou on the indiscriminate reading of the Bible, 145–178. **Henry Formby.** Richardson to Bagshawe, Aug. 20, 1847, Bagshawe Papers, speaks of Mr. Formby's art. of this title; Bagshawe gives "Rev. Dr. H. Formby (Mt. St.[?] Bernard)"; Formby to Bagshawe, [Aug.], 1847; dated from Mt. St. Bernard, Bagshawe Papers, says Wiseman gave him the task of reviewing Malou.

475	Our lady novelists—Lady Georgiana Fullerton, 178–203. **C. W. Russell.** Bagshawe; claimed Russell to Bagshawe, Sept. 3, 1847, Bagshawe Papers.

476	Johnson, his contemporaries and biographers, 203–228. **James Roche.** Bagshawe; repr. *Essays*, II.

477	Reform of the Dublin University—the scholarship question, 228–251. **John O'Hagan.** Bagshawe gives "Mr. J. O'Hagan (Dublin)": see *DNB*; Russell to Bagshawe, Aug. 15, 1847, Bagshawe Papers, says Mr. John O'Hagan has promised this art.

478	*The Rosary of the Blessed Virgin Mary: a Selection of Poetry*, 251–256. **Henry Formby.** Bagshawe; Formby to Bagshawe, Oct. 6, 1847, Bagshawe Papers, requests payment for his two contributions.

479	Notices of books, 257–272. Pages 261 (vi, vii, viii), 264 (xi), 265–267 (xiii), 268–269 (xv) by **C. W. Russell**—claimed in Russell to Bagshawe, Nov. 8, 1847, Bagshawe Papers; pages 257–259 by **W. G. Ward**—Russell to Bagshawe, Sept. 14, 1847, ibid., refers to Ward's notice of Cox's book.

VOLUME 23, DECEMBER 1847

480	Spanish novelists, 273–304. **W. B. McCabe.** Bagshawe.

481	Vestiges of the Catholic faith in Scandinavia, 305–322. **Edward Charlton.** Bagshawe gives "Dr. Charlton, Newcastle-on-Tyne"; see Boase; Richardson to Bagshawe [Nov.], 1847, Bagshawe Papers, says 2nd art. is by Dr. Charlton.

482	Prescott's *Conquest of Peru*, 322–340.

E. V. H. Kenealy. Bagshawe; Kenealy to Bagshawe, Mar. 1, 1848, Bagshawe Papers, asks for payment for "Prescott."

483   Adventures in the South Seas [on Melville's *Omoo*], 341–363. **John Bury Dasent.** Bagshawe gives "Mr. Dasent (Barr[ister]); see Boase; J. B. Dasent to Bagshawe, Mar. 27, 1848, Bagshawe Papers, speaks of payment due him.

484   Flanagan's *Manual of British and Irish History*, 364–373. **C. W. Russell.** Bagshawe; Russell to Bagshawe, Nov. 8, 1847, Bagshawe Papers, says he will send 8 or 10 pages on Mr. Flanagan's *History.*

485   Dr. Brownson on doctrinal developments, 373–405. **W. G. Ward.** Bagshawe (see no. 473); Ward to Bagshawe, Oct. 30 [1847], Bagshawe Papers, says he hopes to write one more art. on his controversy with Brownson.

486   The Russo-Greek and Oriental churches, 405–469. **T. W. M. Marshall.** Bagshawe; Richardson to Bagshawe, Sept. 2, 1847, Bagshawe Papers, says he has sent Mr. Marshall's art. to Bagshawe; it must have been held over.

487   The history and antiquities of Ireland, 469–496. **George Crolly.** Bagshawe; Richardson to Bagshawe, Dec. 6 and 17, 1847, Bagshawe Papers, shows there was an art. by Crolly in this issue of 28 pp.

488   Present position of the High-Church theory, 497–522. **Nicholas Wiseman.** Bagshawe; repr. *Essays,* II.

489   Notices of books, 522–536. Pages 522–524 by **W. B. McCabe**—McCabe to R. R. Madden, Dec. 18, 1847, Royal Irish Academy, speaks of his short review of Madden's book; see no. 492.

VOLUME 24, MARCH 1848

490   The Office of Holy Week, 1–31. **Frederick Oakeley.** Bagshawe; Richardson list, [March] 1848, for this issue, Bagshawe Papers.

491   Balmes's *Catholicism and Protestantism Considered in respect to Civilization* (Part I), 31–57. **James Burton Robertson.** Bagshawe; Richardson list, [March] 1848, for this issue. (Note, vol. 25, pp. 237–242, is by **Robertson**—see second sentence.)

492   Madden's *History of the Penal Laws,* 58–79. **W. B. McCabe.** Bagshawe; Richardson list, [March] 1848, for this issue; claimed in Madden's *Memoirs,* ed. his son, (1891), p. 219.

493   Vicary's *Residence at Rome in 1846,*

79–98. **C. W. Russell.** Bagshawe; Richardson list, [March] 1848, for this issue.

494   Irish fisheries, 98–109. **Patrick McMahon.** Bagshawe; Richardson list, [March] 1848, for this issue.

495   [Mrs.] Sinnett's *Byways of History,* 109–114. **Patrick McMahon.** Bagshawe; Richardson list, [March] 1848, for this issue.

496   Protestant learning: Dr. Hook and Mr. Eden, 115–143. **David Lewis.** Bagshawe gives "Mr. F. Lucas" and Richardson list, [March] 1848, for this issue gives "F. Lewis," but D. Lewis to Bagshawe, Aug. 19, 1847, Bagshawe Papers, says he has been asked to review Hook and Eden.

497   The apocryphal history of England, 143–163. **W. B. McCabe.** Bagshawe; Richardson list, [March] 1848, for this issue.

498   O'Donovan's *Annals of . . . Ireland, by the Four Masters,* 164–188. **C. W. Russell.** Bagshawe; Richardson list, [March] 1848, for this issue.

499   *Adventures in Mexico and the Rocky Mountains,* 188–217. **George Crolly.** Bagshawe; Richardson list, [March] 1848, for this issue.

500   *Loss and Gain* [by J. H. Newman], 218–226. **Nicholas Wiseman.** Bagshawe; Richardson list, [March] 1848, for this issue.

501   Death of Dr. [John Shaw] Campbell, 227–228. **Patrick McMahon.** Richardson to Bagshawe, Mar. 10, 1848, Bagshawe Papers, refers to Mr. McMahon's short notice of Dr. Campbell's death.

502   Notices of books, 228–268. Some by **C. W. Russell,** prob.—Richardson to Bagshawe, Mar. 11, 1848, Bagshawe Papers, refers to short notices written by Dr. Russell, who objected to inclusion of nos. vii, xviii, and xx as being out of date—which hence are presumably not his.

VOLUME 24, JUNE 1848

503   Protestant honesty: Dr. Christopher Wordsworth, 269–295. **David Lewis.** Bagshawe; Richardson list, [June] 1848, for this issue, Bagshawe Papers.

504   The Eastern Archipelago, and the Rajah of Sarawak, 295–316. **John Bury Dasent.** Bagshawe; Richardson list, [June] 1848, for this issue.

505   An Englishwoman [Sarah Maury] in America, 317–329. **W. B. McCabe.** Bagshawe; Richardson list, [June] 1848, for this issue.

506 On the monuments of Nineveh, and the cuneiform characters, 329–349. **Alexandre de Sainteville.** Bagshawe; Richardson list, [June] 1848, for this issue; claimed by de Sainteville in his application to R.L.F., July 1, 1848.

507 Tenure of land in Ireland, 349–380. **Jonathan Duncan.** Bagshawe; Richardson list, [June] 1848, for this issue.

508 Gibbon and his biographers, 381–408. **James Roche.** Bagshawe; repr. *Essays*, I.

509 The superstitions of unbelief, 408–427. **W. B. McCabe.** Bagshawe; Richardson list, [June] 1848, for this issue.

510 Audin's Henry VIII, 427–449. **D. C. Heron.** Bagshawe, which adds "(Dublin)": see Boase; Richardson list, [June] 1848, for this issue.

511 Pius the Ninth, 449–487. **Nicholas Wiseman.** Bagshawe; Richardson list, [June] 1848, for this issue.

512 Neale's *History of the Patriarchate of Alexandria*, 487–517. **C. W. Russell.** Bagshawe; Richardson list, [June] 1848, for this issue.

513 Notices of books, 517–531. Pages 517–527 (nos. i and ii) by **C. W. Russell**—Bagshawe to Russell [Sept.] 1848, Bagshawe Papers, encloses payment for these 2 notices.

VOLUME 25, SEPTEMBER 1848

514 The last eruption of Mount Hekla, 1–20. **Edward Charlton.** Bagshawe; Charlton to Bagshawe, Mar. 27, 1848, Bagshawe Papers, says he has an art. nearly ready on Mt. Hekla.

515 The University of Louvain, 20–40. **Henry Formby.** Bagshawe; Formby to Bagshawe, Oct. 6, 1847, Bagshawe Papers, proposes this art. and in [June 1848], complains that art. has not yet appeared; Richardson to Bagshawe, June 24, 1848, ibid., says Mr. Formby's art. can't be got into June issue.

516 The Austrian revolution and its results, 40–71. **W. B. McCabe.** Bagshawe; Russell to Bagshawe, July 23 and Aug. 3, 1848, Bagshawe Papers, says Mr. McCabe has sent a paper on Austrian Revolution.

517 The Church in Ceylon, 71–117. **J. G. Wenham.** Bagshawe, which adds "(Mortlake)": see Boase; Richardson to Bagshawe, Aug. 26, 1848, Bagshawe Papers, says Mr. Wenham's art. will stand no. 4.

518 Sanatory [sic] reform, 117–139. **J. S. Campbell** and **Patrick McMahon.** Bag-

shawe gives "Mr. P. McMahon, M.P.," but written above is "Dr. Campbell, London"; Campbell to Bagshawe, June 21, 1847, Bagshawe Papers, suggests this art. for Oct.; in [Oct.], ibid., he hopes it will appear in Jan. issue; since Campbell died in Dec., the art. was prob. finished by McMahon, who received some payment for this art., Bagshawe account, 1849, Bagshawe Papers.

519 Erman's *Travels in Siberia*, 139–164. **H. R. St. John.** Bagshawe; St. John to John Bagshawe, [Aug.] 1848, Bagshawe Papers, says he will forward "Siberia."

520 Milnes's *Life of Keats*, 164–179. **C. W. Russell.** Bagshawe; Russell to Bagshawe, [Aug. 1848], Bagshawe Papers, promises this art.

521 Liebig's philosophy, 179–204. **T. Lindley Kemp.** Bagshawe; Kemp to Bagshawe, Oct. 17, [1848], Bagshawe Papers, asks for payment for art. in last no.; on Feb. 8, [1848], Kemp had told Bagshawe he had finished "Liebig," ibid.

522 The Reformation as described by the reformers [on Döllinger's *Die Reformation*], 204–236. **C. W. Russell.** Bagshawe; Russell to Bagshawe, letter cited for no. 520, promises art. on Döllinger.

523 Notices of books, 242–266.

VOLUME 25, DECEMBER 1848

524 Tractarianism in the seventeenth century, 267–284. **C. W. Russell.** Bagshawe; Russell to Bagshawe, Sept. 14, [1848], Bagshawe Papers, says he will send an art. with this title; Bagshawe account book for this issue, ibid.

525 Measures for Ireland: tillage, waste lands, fixity of tenure, 284–345. **Patrick McMahon.** Bagshawe; Bagshawe account book for this issue.

526 The Stellinga [guilds]—Saxony in the ninth century, 345–370. **W. B. McCabe.** Bagshawe; Bagshawe account book for this issue.

527 Corrected editions of the Roman Gradual and Vesperal, 371–385. **Henry Formby.** Bagshawe; Bagshawe account book for this issue.

528 Artists of the Order of St. Dominic, 386–406. **J. M. Capes.** Bagshawe; Russell to Bagshawe, letter cited for no. 520, says Mr. Capes will have a paper with this title; Bagshawe account book for this issue.

529 Dr. Channing, 406–428. **Dominick Murphy.** Bagshawe; Russell to Bagshawe,

Dec. 3, 1848, Bagshawe Papers, says Mr. Murphy's "Channing" sent last week; Bagshawe account book for this issue.

530 Lord Castlereagh, 429–454. **George Crolly.** Bagshawe; Russell to Bagshawe, Dec. 3, 1848, Bagshawe Papers, says Mr. Crolly has "Castlereagh" ready; Bagshawe account book for this issue.

531 Oakeley's sermons, 454–463. **C. W. Russell.** Bagshawe; Russell to Bagshawe, [Dec.], 1848, Bagshawe Papers, asks for 6 or 8 pp. for an art. on "Oakeley's Sermons"; Bagshawe account book for this issue.

532 *Compitum* [by Kenelm Digby], 463–478. **H. R. Bagshawe.** Bagshawe; Bagshawe account book for this issue.

533 Spanish and English national art, 478–512. **Nicholas Wiseman.** Bagshawe; repr. *Essays*, III.

534 Notices of books, 512–529. Pages 512–515, 520–526, 527–528, 529 by **C. W. Russell**—claimed in Russell to Bagshawe, May 12, 1849, Bagshawe Papers.

VOLUME 26, MARCH 1849

535 Whiteside's *Italy in the Nineteenth Century*, 1–33. **Myles O'Reilly.** Bagshawe, who adds "M.P., Major"; Russell had planned to write on Whiteside (see his letters of Aug., Oct. 2, and Nov. 9, [1848], Bagshawe Papers), but on Dec. 3 offers to "give way" in favor of O'Reilly.

536 The siege of Monte Video, 33–59. **W. B. McCabe.** Bagshawe; claimed in McCabe to E. G. Bagshawe, June 1, 1849, Bagshawe Papers. (Note, vol. 28, p. 276, presumably by **H. R. Bagshawe**—editorial.)

537 The Duke of Marlborough: usages of war, 59–137. **Frederick Lucas.** Bagshawe; Lucas to Bagshawe, Sept. 4, 1849, Bagshawe Papers, acknowledges payment for his "Marlborough"; attr. in *DR* 99 o.s. (1886), 420.

538 Cervantes: *El Buscapie*, 138–152. **W. B. McCabe.** Bagshawe.

539 Emerson, 152–179. **Michael F. McCarthy.** Bagshawe gives "Mr. McCarthy"; Russell to Bagshawe, Nov. 9, 1848, Bagshawe Papers, says he has received "Emerson" from Mr. McCarthy of Cork; Richardson to Bagshawe, Mar. 15, 1850, ibid., speaks of a Mr. M. F. McCarthy of Cork as a contributor, and on April 29, gives his address as "Dunbar St., Cork"; *P. O.*

Directory for Cork, 1842–43, p. 56, lists a Michael F. McCarthy at 10 Dunbar St.

540 The Portuguese schism in India, 179–213. **J. G. Wenham.** Bagshawe; Russell to Bagshawe, letter cited for no. 539, says he has received this art. from Mr. Wenham.

541 Effects of Catholicism and Protestantism on civilization [on Balmes] (Part II, concl.), 214–241. **James Burton Robertson.** Bagshawe; Robertson to Bagshawe, Nov. 22, 1848, Bagshawe Papers, refers to second portion of his "Balmes."

542 Allies's *Journal in France*, 241–262. **Frederick Oakeley.** Bagshawe. Richardson to Bagshawe [March, 1849], Bagshawe Papers, says Oakeley's art. is 21 pages.

543 Notices of books, 263–272.

VOLUME 26, JUNE 1849

544 Ceylon: its ancient traditions and modern missionaries, 273–300. **W. B. McCabe.** Bagshawe; Richardson list [June 1849], Bagshawe Papers, of first six arts. for this issue.

545 Catholic hymnology, 300–315. **C. W. Russell.** Bagshawe; Richardson list as in no. 544.

546 Colonization and emigration [mainly on Maryland], 316–337. **Jane Sinnett.** Bagshawe gives "Mrs. Percy Sinnett"; see *BMCat.*; confirmed, Jane Sinnett to Bagshawe, Dec. 20, [1848], Bagshawe Papers; Richardson list as for no. 544.

547 The sacred congregations of Rome, 338–364. **Thomas Grant.** Bagshawe gives "Dr. Grant (Rome)"; see *DNB*; Richardson list as for no. 544.

548 Curzon's *Visits to Monasteries in the Levant*, 365–390. **Dominick Murphy.** Bagshawe; Richardson list as for no. 544; Richardson to E. G. Bagshawe, May 24, 1849, Bagshawe Papers, says he has received Mr. Murphy's "Curzon."

549 Macaulay's *History of England*, 390–441. **C. W. Russell.** Bagshawe; Russell to Bagshawe, [May 1849], Bagshawe Papers, says he has sent in most of "Macaulay."; Richardson list as for no. 544.

550 *Speculum Episcopi*, 441–480. **Nicholas Wiseman.** Bagshawe; Wiseman to Bagshawe, May 20, 1849, Bagshawe Papers, says he hopes to send part of his paper to-morrow.

551 Political state of Germany, 481–522. **James Burton Robertson.** Bagshawe;

Robertson to Bagshawe, Nov. 22, 1848, Bagshawe Papers, offers this, and on May 23, 1849, says it was sent off five days ago.

552　Notices of books, 522–533.

VOLUME 27, SEPTEMBER 1849

553　Maitland's *Essays on . . . the Reformation in England*, 1–34. **C. W. Russell.** Bagshawe; claimed in Russell to Bagshawe, Jan. 28, 1850, Bagshawe Papers.

554　*Historical Memorials of Greenland*, 35–74. **Edward Charlton.** Bagshawe.

555　Aytoun's *Lays of the Scottish Cavaliers*, 74–91. **C. W. Russell.** Bagshawe; claimed in letter cited for no. 553.

556　France since the revolution of February [1848], 91–122. **James Burton Robertson.** Bagshawe; Robertson to Bagshawe, Aug. 6, 1849, Bagshawe Papers, says he will forward "France."

557　*The Island of Cuba: its Resources, Progress and Prospects* [by R. R. Madden], 123–128. **W. B. McCabe.** Bagshawe; McCabe had earlier reviewed Madden in no. 492, to which ref. is made here on p. 127.

558　MacCabe's *Catholic History of England*, 128–146. **C. W. Russell.** Bagshawe; claimed in letter cited for no. 553.

559　The art of puffing, 146–162. **Nicholas Wiseman.** Bagshawe, supported by Wiseman himself in Casartelli, "Jubilee," p. 255.

560　Faber's *Hymns*, 163–181. **Frederick Oakeley.** Bagshawe.

561　The parables of the New Testament, 181–227. **Nicholas Wiseman.** Repr. *Essays*, I.

562　Notices of books, 227–266. Pages 227–244, 248–251, 258 by **C. W. Russell**— claimed in letter cited for no. 553.

VOLUME 27, DECEMBER 1849

563　Ways and means of the Church: the offertory, 267–291. **Frederick Oakeley.** Bagshawe; Oakeley to Bagshawe, Oct. 15, 1849, Bagshawe Papers, is endorsed "Oakeley . . . art. on offertory."

564　The miracles of the New Testament, 291–345. **Nicholas Wiseman.** Repr. *Essays*, I.

565　Ireland: spirit of recent legislation, 345–431. **Patrick McMahon.** Bagshawe; opening sentence refers to closing sentence of no. 494, note on p. 357 and first sentence

of p. 391, refer to no. 525 and note on p. 417 refers to no. 204, all by McMahon.

566　The Duke of Argyll on the ecclesiastical history of Scotland, 431–468. **C. W. Russell.** Bagshawe.

567　Irish factions, parsons, and landlords, 468–511. **George Crolly.** Bagshawe; Russell to Bagshawe, Apr. 17, 1849, Bagshawe Papers, says the Review has engaged a paper from Mr. Crolly on Irish land question.

568　The history of St. Cuthbert, 512–528. **W. B. McCabe.** Bagshawe; McCabe to Thos. Richardson, Nov. 14, 1849, Wiseman Papers, asks for his proof.

569　Sense v. science, 528–548. **Nicholas Wiseman.** Repr. *Essays*, III.

570　Notices of books, 548–549.

VOLUME 28, MARCH 1850

571　Merimée's *Life of Peter the Cruel*, 1–25. **C. W. Russell.** Bagshawe; Russell to Bagshawe, [Feb.] 17, 1850, Bagshawe Papers, says he has returned proofs of "Merimée."

572　The authorship of the *Imitation of Christ*, 26–50. **Dominick Murphy.** DR list has corrected Bagshawe's "Dr. Russell" to "Murphy"; Russell to Bagshawe, Sept. 2, 1848, Bagshawe Papers, says he has sent Mr. Murphy's art. on the Benedictine St. [sic] Thomas, but thinks it should be held over; this art. is on the controversial attr. of the *Imitation* to a Benedictine.

573　Hurter on the institutions, manners, and customs of the Middle Ages, 50–90. **James Burton Robertson.** Bagshawe; Bagshawe to Wiseman, Feb. 1 [?], 1850, Wiseman Papers, says Robertson has sent "Hurter."

574　The priest's hidden life, 90–122. **Nicholas Wiseman.** Bagshawe.

575　Miley's *History of the Papal States*, 123–141. **W. B. McCabe.** Bagshawe; Richardson to Bagshawe, Feb. 11, 1850, Bagshawe Papers, refers to a paper by McCabe for this issue; ref. back p. 129n. to no. 453 by McCabe.

576　Cambrensis and his adversaries: White and Lynch, 141–167. **C. W. Russell.** Bagshawe; Russell to Bagshawe, letter cited for no. 571, says he is busy with "Cambrensis."

577　M'Carthy's poems, 167–181. **John O'Hagan.** Russell to Bagshawe, Mar. 10, [1850], Bagshawe Papers, says he has sent "M'Carthy's poems" by O'Hagan; Bagshawe gives "C. W. Russell."

578 Newman's *Discourses Addressed to Mixed Congregations*, 181–209. **W. G. Ward**, prob. Oscott 1A, 1B, and *DR* list all give Ward; Bagshawe to Wiseman, Feb. 15, 1850, Wiseman Papers, says he has had no reply from Ward as to Newman's book; Richardson to Ward, Mar. 25, 1850, Bagshawe Papers, begs him to send corrected proof; Richardson to Bagshawe, Mar. 26, 1850, ibid., says Ward's failure to return proof of latter part of his art. is stopping the press, explaining that a portion of it had been set up on previous sheet (viz., pp. 181–194); Bagshawe gives "Dr. Russell," and Russell to Bagshawe, [Jan. 9, 1850], Bagshawe Papers, says he will write a paper on Newman's lectures [sic] immediately; but on [Feb. 17], he says if Ward will review Newman, that will do.

579 *Jane Eyre, Shirley*, 209–233. **H. R. Bagshawe.** Bagshawe.

580 The Gorham judgment, 233–273. **Nicholas Wiseman.** Bagshawe; Russell to Bagshawe, letter cited for no. 578, says Wiseman will barely have time to write "Gorham case" for next issue.

581 Notices of books, 274–276. Pages 274–275 by **C. W. Russell?**—Russell to Bagshawe, Jan. 28, 1850, Bagshawe Papers, says he will write a [good solid] notice of a title which is difficult to decipher but which could be *Annual Miscellany*.

VOLUME 28, JUNE 1850

582 Guizot's *English and French Revolutions*, 277–314. **James Burton Robertson.** Bagshawe; Bagshawe to Wiseman, Feb. 1, 1850, Wiseman Papers, says Robertson is writing this.

583 The Coptic Church, 314–330. **D. F. McLeod.** Bagshawe; Russell to Bagshawe, letter cited for no. 571, sends "Coptic church" by Rev. D. McLeod.

584 The government criminal returns, etc., 330–354. **James Morris.** Bagshawe gives "Mr. J. Morris (Brother Bishop Morris)"; James Morris to Bagshawe, Apr. 14, 1851, Bagshawe Papers, speaks of his previous art. on criminal statistics.

585 *Nineveh and its Remains* [by A. H. Layard], 354–398. **George Crolly.** Bagshawe; Russell to Bagshawe, letter cited for no. 571, says Crolly is at work on "Layard."

586 Hancock's *Impediments to the Pros-*

perity of Ireland, 399–420. **Patrick McMahon.** Bagshawe; Richardson list of arts. on hand for this issue, June 12, 1850, Bagshawe Papers.

587 The Inquisition, 421–469. **Thomas Grant** AND **C. W. Russell.** Bagshawe to Wiseman, Jan. 31, 1850, Wiseman Papers, sends Dr. Grant's paper, set in type, asking Wiseman to proofread the references; Bagshawe wishes Grant had stated "details of the actual prisoners" (cf. p. 464n); Russell to Bagshawe, [Feb.] 17, ibid., says he supposes the "Inquisition" will stand over, as it "would not do as it is"; on April 14, Russell says it has taken time to prepare the Inquisition paper, and on May 15 says he is "working at my Inquisition," which implies extensive rewriting; attr. to C. W. Russell only in Bagshawe, in Richardson list cited for no. 586, and *DR* list.

588 Dr. Achilli, 469–511. **Nicholas Wiseman.** *DR* list; Ward, *Wiseman*, II, 38–39. Bagshawe gives "Dr. Russell."

589 Notices of books, 511–537.

VOLUME 29, SEPTEMBER 1850

590 De Vere's *Sketches in Greece and Turkey*, 1–29. **C. W. Russell.** Bagshawe; Russell to Bagshawe, Aug. 6, 1850, Bagshawe Papers, speaks of his paper on De Vere.

591 Dyer's *Life of Calvin*, 30–70. **C. W. Russell.** Bagshawe; Russell to Bagshawe, letter cited for no. 590, promises to finish "Dyer" before Saturday.

592 De Rossi's *Ancient Christian Inscriptions*, 70–78. **Nicholas Wiseman?** Attr. in Russell, "Early Reviewers," p. 88; see Ward, *Wiseman*, I, 525, where Wiseman tells Bagshawe on Aug. 24 that he had sent a short art. from Paris; Bagshawe's attr. to Russell prob. due to fact that Russell frequently did review Rossi.

593 Early Norse poetry: translations of the Breton lays, 78–95. **Edward Charlton.** Bagshawe; Charlton to Bagshawe, June 13, 1851, Bagshawe Papers, acknowledges payment for art. 4 in this issue.

594 Ireland: review of the session, 96–120. **Patrick McMahon.** Bagshawe; McMahon to Bagshawe, May 29, 1851, Bagshawe Papers, acknowledges payment for art. 5 in this issue.

595 German prophecies on the state of the Church, 120–160. **James Burton Robertson.** Bagshawe; E. Scott to Bagshawe,

May 28, 1851, Bagshawe Papers, acknowledges payment for Robertson for art. 6 in this issue.

596 The life and death of Oliver Plunkett, 161–169. **Dominick Murphy.** Bagshawe; Richardson to Bagshawe, Sept. 18, 1850, Bagshawe Papers, says he is waiting for Mr. Murphy's corrections.

597 Carlyle's works, 169–206. **John O'Hagan.** Bagshawe; Casartelli, "Jubilee," p. 261.

598 Newman's [Lectures on] *Anglican Difficulties*, 207–225. **C. W. Russell.** Bagshawe; Richardson to Bagshawe, Sept. 9, 1850, Bagshawe Papers, says he has received "Newman's sermons[sic]" from Russell.

599 Ether and chloroform, 226–247. **Charles Hawkins.** Bagshawe; Hawkins to Bagshawe, May 28, 1851, Bagshawe Papers, acknowledges payment for an art. on chloroform.

600 Notices of books, 247–270. Pages 258–260 (x), 266–269 (xiv) by **William Maskell,** and prob. most of the others—Maskell to Bagshawe, [Sept. 1850], Bagshawe Papers, specifically claims x and xiv, and says he has sent 14 or more pp. of notices.

VOLUME 29, DECEMBER 1850

601 Ledru Rollin's *Decline of England*, 271–287. **Thomas Flanagan.** Bagshawe; Flanagan to Bagshawe, Aug. 6, 1851, Bagshawe Papers, acknowledges payment for an art. in this issue.

602 *Charles the Fifth's Correspondence*, 287–324. **C. W. Russell.** Bagshawe; Russell to Bagshawe, Nov. 3, 1850, Bagshawe Papers, says "Charles the Fifth" will soon be ready.

603 Poor [i.e., pauper] administration at home and abroad, 324–354. **Myles O'Reilly.** Bagshawe; O'Reilly to Bagshawe, May 26, 1851, Bagshawe Papers, asks for payment for "Poor Administration."

604 Northern literature, 354–370. **Edward Charlton.** Bagshawe; Richardson to Bagshawe, Dec. 3, 1850, Bagshawe Papers, says he has Charlton's art.

605 Allies on the Primacy, 370–415. **C. W. Russell.** Bagshawe; in letter cited for no. 602, Russell says he will set to on the Primacy at once.

606 Catholicism, a conservative principle, 416–432. **W. G. Ward.** Bagshawe.

607 Theological antiquarians; Merryweather's *Glimmerings in the Dark*, 432–456.

C. W. Russell. Bagshawe; Russell to Bagshawe, Dec. 15, 1850, Bagshawe Papers, says he will send off "Glimmerings."

608 Ireland: a peasant proprietary, 456–476. **Patrick McMahon.** Bagshawe; Richardson to Bagshawe, Sept. 6, 1850, Bagshawe Papers, says he has received art. with this title from McMahon.

609 Testimony of Grotius and Leibnitz to the truth of Catholic doctrines, 476–507. **T. W. Allies.** Bagshawe; repr. *Per crucem*, II.

610 The Hierarchy (No. I), 507–530. **Nicholas Wiseman.** Bagshawe. With an address to Cardinal Wiseman by the Catholics of England, 530–534, and the Cardinal's reply, 534–535; see no. 617.

VOLUME 30, MARCH 1851

611 Church offices and popular devotions, 1–23. **Frederick Oakeley.** Bagshawe; Richardson list for this issue [March 1851], Bagshawe Papers.

612 The Greek Church; a sketch: nationalism and Catholicism, 24–32. **T. W. Allies.** Bagshawe; Richardson list as for no. 611.

613 Cunningham's London, 33–68. **P. B. Maxwell.** Bagshawe reads "Mr. (MB) Maxwell" but Oscott IB and Richardson list as for no. 611 give "P. B. Maxwell"; cf. no. 646.

614 Modern historians of the Thirty Years' War:—Gfroerer's *Gustavus Adolphus*, 69–113. **C. F. Audley.** Bagshawe gives "Mr. Audley (Paris)"; but adds initials for no. 633; Richardson list as for no. 611.

615 "Mummeries of Superstition" in the early Church: the sign of the Cross, 113–152. **C. W. Russell.** Bagshawe; Richardson list as for no. 611.

616 Dr. Pusey's teaching and practice, 152–176. **Frederick Oakeley.** Bagshawe; Richardson list as for no. 611.

617 The Catholic Hierarchy (No. II), 176–207. **Nicholas Wiseman.** Bagshawe; Richardson list as for no. 611.

618 The Anglican universities as ecclesiastical training schools, 208–253. **T. W. Allies.** Bagshawe; repr. *Per crucem*, II.

619 Summary notice of . . . French Catholic publications, 253–273. **Laurence Gillie?** Russell to Bagshawe, Feb. 14, 1851, Bagshawe Papers, says he has asked Mr. Gillie in Paris for first summary of French literature.

620 Notices of books, 273–274. **H. R.**

Bagshawe? Richardson to Bagshawe, Mar. 26, 1851, Bagshawe Papers, begs Bagshawe to send a long notice of Ullathorne's pamphlet, which this is.

VOLUME 30, JUNE 1851

621 The monks and schoolmen of the Middle Ages, 275–331. **George Crolly.** Bagshawe; confirmed in Crolly to Bagshawe, July 22, 1850, Bagshawe Papers, and in Russell to Bagshawe, Mar. 12, 1851, ibid.

622 The witch mania of the four last centuries, 331–370. **Edward Charlton.** Bagshawe; confirmed in Richardson to Bagshawe, Apr. 7, 1851, Bagshawe Papers.

623 Dr. Jarcke's *Political Essays*, 371–409. **James Burton Robertson.** Bagshawe; confirmed in Robertson to Bagshawe, Mar. 21, 1851, Bagshawe Papers.

624 Sir Emerson Tennent's *Christianity in Ceylon*, 410–436. **J. G. Wenham.** Bagshawe; confirmed in Russell to Bagshawe, Mar. 12, 1851, Bagshawe Papers.

625 Merivale's *History of the Romans*, 436–453. **Thomas Flanagan.** Bagshawe; confirmed in Flanagan to Bagshawe, May 11, 1851, Bagshawe Papers.

626 Legends and legendary art: Mrs. Jameson, 453–484. **C. W. Russell.** Bagshawe; confirmed in letter cited for no. 624.

627 The industry of the poor, 484–532. **Nicholas Wiseman.** Bagshawe; confirmed in copy of letter to Richardson from H. R. Bagshawe, prob. [Aug. 1851], Bagshawe Papers.

628 Summary notice of . . . German Catholic publications, 532–557. **James Burton Robertson.** Bagshawe; Russell to Bagshawe, cited for no. 624, wants Robertson to do this summary; Robertson to Bagshawe, Apr. 26, 1851, Bagshawe Papers, agrees.

629 Notices of books, 557–563. **C. W. Russell,** prob. Russell to Bagshawe, Dec. 15, 1850, Bagshawe Papers, says he has sent some short notices, and on Xmas Day says he sent off a notice of Dr. Murray's *Miscellany*; there was no room for these in Dec. or Mar. issue.

VOLUME 31, SEPTEMBER 1851

630 Antagonist systems in the Anglican Church: Canterbury and Exeter, 1–39. **Edward Walford.** Bagshawe gives "Mr. E. Walford"; Richardson list of arts. on hand, Sept. 2, 1851, Bagshawe Papers.

631 The synod of Exeter, 39–52. **Edward Walford.** Bagshawe; Richardson list as cited for no. 630.

632 *Miscellany of the Celtic Society*, 53–88. **Matthew Kelly.** Bagshawe; attr. *Dissertations*, p. xv.

633 Public instruction in France under the new law, 89–121. **C. F. Audley.** Bagshawe gives "Mr. C. F. Audley (Paris)"; Richardson list as cited for no. 630.

634 Protestant ideas of the Confessional: "Pascal the Younger", 122–144. **Frederick Oakeley.** Bagshawe; Richardson list as cited for no. 630.

635 No Popery novels, 144–172. **C. W. Russell.** Bagshawe; Richardson list as cited for no. 630.

636 Essays of an octogenarian: James Roche, 172–196. **Dominick Murphy.** Russell to Bagshawe, July 20 [1851], Bagshawe Papers, says "Rev. D. Murphy is preparing an art. on Mr. Roche's *Essays*"; Richardson list as cited for no. 630; Bagshawe gives "Mr. Crolly," but clearly in error.

637 *The Catholic Florist* [on flowers for the altar], 196–201. **Edward Walford.** Bagshawe; Richardson list cited for no. 630.

638 The *Guardian* and "a theory on lying," 201–217. **W. G. Ward.** Bagshawe; Ward to Bagshawe, Sept. 17, 1851, Bagshawe Papers, says he will send art. on *Guardian* at once.

639 The moralities of legislation: the "Italian Church" [to be built in London], 218–258. **C. W. Russell,** 218–227. Bagshawe, who gives "Dr. Russell (summary of Irish letter)," referring to *Letter* being reviewed. AND **Nicholas Wiseman,** 227–258. Bagshawe; Wiseman to Russell, Aug. 12, 1851, Wiseman Papers, speaks of the art. on the Italian church he is writing in reply to the *Times*, which he begins by quoting.

640 Summary notices of French Catholic publications, 259–278. **Laurence Gillie.** Russell to Bagshawe, July 20, 1851, Bagshawe Papers, says he has asked Mr. Gillie in Paris for a further installment of French literature.

641 Notices of books, 279–312. Pages 296–297 by **T. W. Allies**—claimed in Allies to Bagshawe, July 19, 1852, Bagshawe Papers; page 295 by **H. R. Bagshawe?**—Richardson to Bagshawe, Apr. 7, [1851], ibid., requests notice of book on St. George's Cathedral; pages 284–286 by **William Maskell?**—Maskell to Bagshawe, Sept. 8, 1850, ibid., says he won't have time to review Benedict XIV, *On Heroic Virtue*, for Sept. 1850; pages

279–282, 282–283, 283–284, 292–293, 300–301, 306–309 by **C. W. Russell**—claimed Russell to Bagshawe [Apr. 8, 1852], ibid.; pages 288–291 by **Edward Walford**, prob.—he refers back to this notice in no. 721, p. 20n; page 299 by **Edward Walford?**—Walford to Bagshawe, June 21, 1851, Bagshawe Papers, wants to do brief review of Clifton Tracts.

VOLUME 31, DECEMBER 1851

642 Wordsworth's life and writings, 313–365. **George Crolly.** Bagshawe; confirmed in Russell to Wiseman, Oct. 31, 1851, Bagshawe Papers.

643 Father Gentili, 365–387. **Henry Formby.** Bagshawe; confirmed in series of letters between Formby, Bagshawe, and Richardson, Oct. 27–Nov. 9, 1852, Bagshawe Papers.

644 The actions of the New Testament, 387–437. **Nicholas Wiseman.** Repr. *Essays*, I.

645 Shepherd's *Early History of the Papacy*, 437–475. **C. W. Russell.** Bagshawe; confirmed Russell to Bagshawe, Nov. 2, 1851, Bagshawe Papers.

646 State bishops, 475–519. **P. B. Maxwell.** Bagshawe gives "Mr. Maxwell, MB"; claimed in P. Benson Maxwell to Bagshawe, July 14, 1852, Bagshawe Papers.

647 Papal aggression novels—*Cecile*, 519–529. **C. W. Russell.** Bagshawe; confirmed in Russell to Bagshawe, Nov. 20, 1851, Bagshawe Papers.

648 The Catholic University, 529–588. **T. W. Allies.** Bagshawe; repr. *Per crucem*, II.

649 The age of honesty [of dishonesty], 589–611. **Charles W. S. Brooks?** Bagshawe gives "Mr. Brooks, (CW)"; Richardson to Bagshawe, Dec. 16, 1851, Bagshawe Papers, confirms an art. by Brooks in this issue; the lively, non-sectarian tone makes attr. to man cited possible.

VOLUME 32, MARCH 1852

650 Philosophic researches on Christianity, 1–48. **James Burton Robertson.** Bagshawe; confirmed Robertson to Bagshawe, April 26, 1851, Bagshawe Papers.

651 Scipio de Ricci, 48–69. **Myles O'Reilly.** Bagshawe; confirmed Russell to Bagshawe, Sept. 13, 1851, Bagshawe Papers.

652 The Leeds experiment in Anglicanism,

69–97. **Edward Walford.** Bagshaw; confirmed Walford to Bagshawe, Jan. 21, 1852, Bagshawe Papers.

653 Scandinavian literature: *The Royal Mirror*, 97–125. **Edward Charlton.** Bagshawe; confirmed Richardson to Bagshawe, Jan. 26, 1852, Bagshawe Papers.

654 Are heroes always heroic? [a satire on leaders of Italian Revolution], 125–133. **Thomas Grant.** Bagshawe gives "Rt. Rev. Bishop Grant"; see *DNB*; Grant to Bagshawe, Feb. 24 [1852], Bagshawe Papers, says his paper is meant to be amusing; Richardson to Bagshawe, Feb. 25, 1852, ibid., has received an art. from Rt. Rev. Dr. Grant.

655 Mignet's *Mary Stuart*, 134–184. **C. W. Russell.** Bagshawe; Russell to Wiseman, Jan. 31, 1852, Wiseman Papers, says he is writing on Mignet's vile life of Mary Stuart.

656 Worsaae's *Account of the Danes and Norwegians in England, Scotland, and Ireland*, 184–220. **George Crolly.** Bagshawe; Russell to Wiseman, Jan. 31, 1852, Wiseman Papers, says Crolly is doing "Worsaae."

657 Dr. Newman's *Lectures on the Present Position of Catholics*, 220–257. **W. G. Ward.** Bagshawe; Ward to Bagshawe, Nov. 14, 1851, Bagshawe Papers, says he is glad to undertake Newman's Lectures for April No.

658 Lady theologians [Catherine Sinclair], 257–283. **Nicholas Wiseman.** Bagshawe; this issue was delayed waiting for a paper from the Cardinal.

659 Notices of books, 284–288.

VOLUME 32, JUNE 1852

660 Meyrick on the Church of Spain, 289–310. **Frederick Oakeley.** Bagshawe; confirmed in Richardson to Bagshawe, Mar. 12, 1852, Bagshawe Papers.

661 Scudamore on secession to Rome, 311–342. **Edward Walford.** Bagshawe; Richardson to Bagshawe, Jan. 26, 1852, Bagshawe Papers, says he has received "*Letters to a Seceder*" from Walford, i.e., the title of the book reviewed in this art.; confirmed in Walford to Bagshawe, Apr. 8, 1852, ibid.

662 Byle's *Sophisms of Free Trade and Popular Political Economy*, 343–385. **P. B. Maxwell.** Bagshawe gives "Mr. Maxwell (M.B.)."

663 The Jesuit in India, 386–406. **T. W. Allies.** Repr. *Per crucem*, II.

664 Patterson's *Tour in Egypt, Palestine, Syria, and Greece*, 407–435. **Edward Walford.** Bagshawe.

665 Miss Sellon and her sisterhood, 436–464. **Frederick Oakeley.** Bagshawe.

666 Jeffrey's *Life and Correspondence*, 464–511. **George Crolly.** Bagshawe; Russell to Bagshawe, Apr. 11, 1852, Bagshawe Papers, says Crolly is sending "Jeffrey."

667 Anglican views of church history: Foulkes's *Manual*, 512–529. **C. W. Russell.** Bagshawe; Russell to Bagshawe, May 24, 1852, Bagshawe Papers, says he will send a review of an ecclesiastical history, which describes Foulkes's *Manual*.

668 Summary of German Catholic literature, 530–539. **James Burton Robertson.** Bagshawe gives "Scott (Mr. J. B. Robertson)"; various letters from E. Scott to Bagshawe in Bagshawe Papers acknowledge receipt of payments for J. B. Robertson; Robertson to Bagshawe, Dec. 29, 1851, Bagshawe Papers, promises German summary for March No., but Russell to Bagshawe, Mar. 21, 1852, ibid., says it is too late.

669 Notices of books, 540–555. Pages 544–546 by **Edward Walford**—Walford to Bagshawe, June 7, 1852, Bagshawe Papers, sends notice of Mr. Lewin's book.

VOLUME 33, SEPTEMBER 1852

670 The lamas of Tibet, 1–45. **C. W. Russell.** Bagshawe; Richardson list, Aug. 23, 1852, Bagshawe Papers, for this issue.

671 The Countess Hahn Hahn's conversion, 46–77. **Edward Charlton.** Bagshawe; Richardson list for this issue.

672 The Mormons in America, 77–112. **Edward Walford.** Bagshawe; Richardson list for this issue.

673 The literature and romance of Northern Europe, 112–139. **Edward Charlton.** Bagshawe; Richardson list for this issue.

674 Cardinal Ximenes and his times, 140–183. **James Burton Robertson.** Bagshawe; claimed in his *Lectures on Modern History and Biography* (1864), p. 201n.

675 Historians of the Council of Trent, 184–219. **C. W. Russell.** Bagshawe; Richardson list for this issue.

676 The Bible in Maynooth, 220–264. **Nicholas Wiseman.** Bagshawe; opening sentence shows this to be by author of no. 561; i.e., Wiseman; repr. as *The Catholic Doctrine of the Use of the Bible*, 1853.

677 Notices of books, 264–268. **Edward Walford,** prob. Richardson to Bagshawe, Sept. 28, 1852, Bagshawe Papers, says 3 notices were written by Walford.

VOLUME 33, DECEMBER 1852

678 Japan, 269–292. **C. W. Russell.** Bagshawe; confirmed Russell to Bagshawe, Aug. 28 and Sept. 11, [1852], Bagshawe Papers.

679 The two dukes [Wellington and the Duke of Baylen], 293–303. **W. H. Anderdon.** Bagshawe gives "Rev. Mr. Anderdon"; see *DNB*. Richardson to Bagshawe, Oct. 28, 1852, Bagshawe Papers, says he has MS. from Rev. W. H. Anderdon.

680 Christian political economy, 303–321. **Myles O'Reilly.** Bagshawe; reference back to no. 603, also by O'Reilly, here on p. 315n.; O'Reilly to Bagshawe, Oct. 11, 1852, Bagshawe Papers, refers to his review of Perin, which this is.

681 The French controversy on the use of pagan literature in education, 321–336. **G. W. Abraham.** Bagshawe gives "Mr. Abraham"; man cited was a major contributor to *DR*.

682 Shetland and Iceland, by Plöyen and Madame Pfeiffer, 336–364. **Edward Charlton.** Bagshawe; confirmed in Richardson to Bagshawe, Nov. 11, 1852, Bagshawe Papers.

683 The newly-found treatise "Against all Heresies" [Originis Philosophumena], 365–408. **C. W. Russell.** Bagshaw; attr. by Wiseman in Casartelli, "Jubilee," p. 255. (See no. 717.)

684 Alison's *History of Europe*, 408–418. **H. R. Bagshawe.** Bagshawe.

685 Joseph de Maistre, 418–466. **James Burton Robertson.** Bagshawe; confirmed in Robertson to Bagshawe, Dec. 16, 1852, Bagshawe Papers.

686 Convents, 467–526. **Nicholas Wiseman.** Bagshawe; repr. under his name, 1853.

687 Notices of books, 526–532.

VOLUME 34, MARCH 1853

688 Ireland and Sir Francis Head, 1–32. **Edward Walford.** Bagshawe; Walford to Bagshawe, Dec. 6, [1852], Bagshawe Papers, refers to "my paper on Ireland."

689 The worship of the saints, 33–67. **Aubrey De Vere,** prob. Bagshawe;

claimed Aubrey De Vere to Bagshawe, Nov. 29, 1852, Bagshawe Papers. De Vere's list; *DR* list has a note: "Mr. A. de Vere disclaims these articles" (private note). See no. 697.

690 Edmund Burke, 68–104. **G. W. Abraham.** Bagshawe.

691 Lord John Russell's *Memoirs of Moore*, 104–139. **George Crolly.** Bagshawe.

692 Count de Montalembert's *Catholic Interests of the Nineteenth Century*, 139–174. **James Burton Robertson.** Bagshawe; confirmed Robertson to Bagshawe, Dec. 16, 1852, Bagshawe Papers.

693 Novel-morality: the novels of 1853, 174–203. **C. W. Russell.** Bagshawe.

694 The Madiai [Protestant activities in Italy], 203–244. **Nicholas Wiseman.** Bagshawe.

695 The case of Achilli, 244–314. **W. F. Finlason.** Bagshawe gives "Finlayson"; Finlason to Bagshawe, [Dec. 24, 1852], Bagshawe Papers, returns proofs of an art.; man cited a leading Catholic legal and historical writer, who wrote several arts. on the Achilli case in the *DR* and *Ram*, as well as a book on the subject.

VOLUME 34, JUNE 1853

696 Bishop Ken, 315–359. **W. H. Anderdon.** Bagshawe; confirmed Anderdon to Bagshawe, Jan. 12, 1854, Bagshawe Papers.

697 Longfellow's works, 359–407. **Aubrey De Vere.** Bagshawe; De Vere's list; claimed by him in letter in S. M. P. Reilly, *Aubrey De Vere* (Lincoln, Neb., 1953), pp. 141–142.

698 Charitable trusts, 407–441. **W. F. Finlason.** Bagshawe and *DNB*.

699 The life and writings of St. Paul, 441–482. **Edward Walford.** Bagshawe; Walford wrote a notice of one of the books here reviewed in June 1852; Walford to Bagshawe, letter cited for no. 669.

700 Catholic and Protestant hermeneutics: the Primacy, 482–510. **C. W. Russell.** Bagshawe.

701 What has the Church done for trade and manufactures? 510–540. **James Burton Robertson.** Bagshawe; E. Scott (Robertson's financial agent) to Bagshawe, Jan. 13, 1854, Bagshawe Papers, acknowledges payment for arts. presumably in nos. 67 and 68.

702 Cardinal Wiseman's *Essays*—periodical literature, 541–566. **Frederick Oakeley.** Bagshawe.

703 Notices of books, 566–579.

VOLUME 35, SEPTEMBER 1853

704 M. Libri and the public libraries of France, 1–69. **Edward Ryley.** Bagshawe gives "E. Ryley (Hampstead)"; see Boase, which notes he was a friend of Libri's; E. Ryley to Lord Brougham, July 14, 1853, Univ. Coll. London, shows he first submitted this art. to the *Edin. Rev.*

705 The Turco-Russian question: the holy places, 69–92. **G. W. Abraham.** Bagshawe.

706 Nineveh and Babylon, 93–138. **George Crolly.** Bagshawe.

707 De Saulcy's *Dead Sea and Bible Lands*, 139–172. **C. W. Russell.** Bagshawe.

708 The law of England with relation to moral theology, 172–199. **W. F. Finlason.** Bagshawe.

709 Our ministry of public instruction [anti-Catholicism in popular novels and the press], 199–229. **Nicholas Wiseman.** Bagshawe.

710 Archbishop Whately and the Board of Irish National Education, 229–266. **C. W. Russell.** Bagshawe.

711 Notices of books, 266–272.

VOLUME 35, DECEMBER 1853

712 The philosophy of the rule of faith, 273–336. **Aubrey De Vere.** Bagshawe; repr. *Essays*. Again, as for no. 689, *DR* list claims De Vere denied writing the art.

713 Modern deism, 336–362. **James Burton Robertson.** Bagshawe.

714 The ceremonies of the Church in their devotional and theological bearings, 362–382. **Frederick Oakeley.** Bagshawe; confirmed in Russell to Bagshawe, Jan. 6, 1854, Bagshawe Papers.

715 Wycliffe, 382–438. **W. F. Finlason.** Bagshawe; Finlason to Bagshawe, Jan. 6, 1855, Bagshawe Papers, says [his] "Wycliffe" was liked.

716 The *Emigrant Milesian*: *the Irish Abroad*, 438–447. **C. W. Russell.** Bagshawe.

717 Callistus and his accuser, 447–492. **C. W. Russell.** Bagshawe; claimed Russell to Bagshawe, Jan. 6, 1854, Bagshawe Papers; reference back to no. 683, of which this is really a continuation.

718 Merimée's *Demetrius the Imposter*, 492–516. **G. W. Abraham.** Repr. *Essays*.

719 Notices of books, 516–532. Pages 527–528 by **Edward Price**—Price to Wiseman, Oct. 25, Nov. 11, and Dec. 31,

1852, Wiseman Papers, says he is working on St. Teresa's *Interior Castle*.

VOLUME 36, MARCH 1854

720 Sermons and preachers, 1–19. **J. G. Wenham.** Bagshawe.
721 Domestic architecture in England, 20–45. **Edward Walford.** Bagshawe; C. W. Russell to Bagshawe, Jan. 18, 1854, Bagshawe Papers, says he is not happy about 2 arts. by Walford in this issue; cf. no. 722.
722 The doctrine of the Holy Eucharist [by R. I. Wilberforce], 45–79. **Edward Walford.** Bagshawe; Walford to Bagshawe, Jan. 12, 1854, Bagshawe Papers, proposes a review of Wilberforce; Russell to Bagshawe, letter cited for no. 721, reluctantly agrees that Walford should review Wilberforce.
723 Russia and Turkey, 79–165. **W. F. Finlason.** Bagshawe; Finlason to Bagshawe, Dec. 1, 1853, Bagshawe Papers, suggests an art. on Russia and Turkey.
724 Our resources: land, labour, and trade, 165–193. **Patrick McMahon.** Bagshawe.
725 Modern ascetic divinity: Father Faber, 194–212. **Frederick Oakeley.** Bagshawe.
726 Formularies of the Anglican Church: Maurice's *Essays*, 212–257. **C. W. Russell.** Bagshawe.
727 Notices of books, 257–268.

VOLUME 36, JUNE 1854

728 Church and state in Baden, 269–290. **James Burton Robertson.** Bagshawe; C. W. Russell to Bagshawe, Jan. 18, 1854, Bagshawe Papers, says he will propose this topic to Robertson; Scott to Bagshawe, Dec. 1, 1854, ibid., acknowledges payment for Robertson for an art. in June issue. Note that payments for this isue were made at end of Nov. and beginning of Dec.—C. W. Russell to Bagshawe, Dec. 2, 1854, Bagshawe Papers.
729 Editors and biographers of the Venerable Bede, 290–314. **John Walker,** 1800–1873. Bagshawe gives "Mr. Walker (Scarborough)"; Walker to Bagshawe, Dec. 3, 1854, dated from Scarbro', Bagshawe Papers, thanks him for a payment for an art. [in no. 72]; latter part of art. discusses Lingard, a close friend of Walker's—Newman, *L&D*, XI, index.
730 Oxford: its past and present (Part I),

314–351. **Edward Walford.** Bagshawe; Walford to Bagshawe, Nov. 30, 1854, Bagshawe Papers, acknowledges payment for this art.
731 The plague of controversy, 351–418. **Aubrey De Vere.** Bagshawe; De Vere's list; repr. *Religious Problems.*
732 Tendencies of modern logic, 419–451. **William Jennings.** Bagshawe gives "Rev. Mr. Jennings (Maynooth)"; see Boase.
733 Theory of Jesuit history, 451–494. **G. W. Abraham.** Repr. *Essays.*
734 Guizot's *Cromwell*, 494–520. **C. W. Russell.** Bagshawe.
735 Notices of books, 521–531.

VOLUME 37, SEPTEMBER 1854

736 Lord Holland's *Memoirs*, 1–37. **George Crolly.** Bagshawe.
737 Arctic discoveries, 37–67. **B. Cody.** Bagshawe; C. W. Russell to Bagshawe, June 10, 1855, Bagshawe Papers, asks for payment for Mr. Cody; *DR* list says Oscott gives "Rev. Mr. Jennings," but the subject most unlikely for him.
738 Oxford, its most past and present (Part II, concl.), 68–96. **Edward Walford.** Cf. no. 730.
739 Jansenism, Gallicanism and Jacobinism, 96–189. **W. F. Finlason.** Bagshawe.
740 Savonarola, 189–232. **Myles O'Reilly.** Bagshawe; a series of letters in 1854 and 1855 between C. W. Russell, W. F. Finlason and O'Reilly, Bagshawe Papers, all point to O'Reilly's authorship of this art.
741 Recent historians of the Papacy: Riddle and Robertson, 232–269. **C. W. Russell.** Bagshawe.
742 Notices of books, 270–272.

VOLUME 37, DECEMBER 1854

743 Monastic historians of England, 273–287. **G. W. Abraham.** Bagshawe; Richardson list for this issue, Dec. 4, 1854, Bagshawe Papers. *DR* list gives "Cody," but clearly in error.
744 The Irish sea-fisheries, 287–325. **Patrick McMahon.** Bagshawe; Richardson list for this issue.
745 St. Alphonsus and the *Christian Remembrancer*, 326–403. **William Walter Roberts?** Bagshawe gives "Mr. Roberts (neph.[?] of Dr. Manning)"; H. E. Manning to Bagshawe, Nov. 9, 1855, Bagshawe Papers, requests permission "to reprint the art. contributed by Mr.

Roberts in Dec. last on St. Alphonsus";
Richardson list for this issue; it is entirely possible that Roberts was inspired
by Manning and perhaps aided by him;
see Manning, *Life*, II, 37–44. *DR* list
gives "Dr. Manning."

746　Milman's *History of Latin Christianity*
(Vols. I–III), 404–449. **C. W. Russell.**
Bagshawe; Richardson list for this issue.

747　Wilberforce on the Church, 450–481.
George Crolly. Bagshawe; Richardson
list for this issue.

748　*The Church of the Catacombs* [by
Wiseman], 482–503. **C. W. Russell.** Bagshawe; Richardson list for this issue.

749　Cloister life of Charles V, 503–517.
Henry J. Lynch. Bagshawe gives "Mr. H.
Lynch"; confirmed in Henry J. Lynch to
Bagshawe, Dec. 31, 1854, Bagshawe
Papers.

750　Notices of books, 517–533.

VOLUME 38, MARCH 1855

751　"Bad Popes" [defense of Gregory VII,
Innocent VIII, Boniface VIII, Alexander
VI], 1–72. **W. F. Finlason.** Bagshawe;
Richardson list, Mar. 19, 1855, Bagshawe
Papers, for this issue.

752　Miss Strickland's *Mary Stuart*, 73–97.
G. W. Abraham. Richardson list for this
issue; repr. *Essays*; the Bagshawe attribution to C. W. Russell is prob. due to
paper being sent in by him.

753　Past and present state of chemical science, 98–112. **T. L. Kemp.** Bagshawe
gives "Dr. Kemp"; Richardson list for
this isue gives "T. L. Kemp, Esq."

754　Kemp's *Indications of Instinct*, 113–119.
William Seller. T. Lindley Kemp, subject
of this review, to Bagshawe, in letter
cited for no. 753, says he will send "Dr.
Seller's notice of two little works of mine
with my own paper"; Bagshawe's and
Richardson's attributions to Kemp prob.
due to this fact.

755　The Druses and their religion, 120–133.
G. W. Abraham. Bagshawe; Richardson
list for this issue.

756　Huc's *Chinese Empire*, 134–169. **C. W.
Russell.** Bagshawe; Richardson's list for
this issue. (See nos. 843 and 884.)

757　Legitimate influence of authority in
philosophy: Descartes, the Sensational-
ists, and Kant, 169–212. **William Jennings.** Bagshawe gives "Rev. Prof. Jenning (Maynooth)"; Richardson list for
this issue.

758　Lord J. Russell's Education Bill, 212–

232. **R. J. Gainsford.** Bagshawe, who
adds "(Sheffield)"; Richardson list for
this issue.

759　Marsden's *Puritans*, 232–253. **C. W.
Russell.** Bagshaw; Richardson list for this
issue.

760　Notices of books, 253–272. Page 253
by **H. R. Bagshawe,** prob.—Richardson
to Bagshawe, Mar. 26, 1855, Bagshawe
Papers, says "you sent on Sat. a short
notice of Faber"; pp. 261–262 also by
Bagshawe, prob.—Edward Walford to
Bagshawe, Mar. 15, 1855, ibid., asks him
to write a few lines on his "Peerage"; pp.
255–256 by **William Jennings,** prob.—
reference back to no. 732 on same topic;
pp. 259–260 by **C. W. Russell,** Richardson to Bagshawe, Mar. 24, ibid., says
"Desprez" is by Russell; p. 262 by **Edward Walford,** prob.—Walford to Bagshawe, cited immediately above, recommends Ince's *Outlines.* Richardson to
Bagshawe, Mar. 24, ibid., says "all the
short notices were sent by yourself, Dr.
Russell and Mr. Walford."

VOLUME 38, JUNE 1855

761　Who were the persecutors? [largely on
Bancroft's *History of the United States*],
273–299. **R. J. Gainsford.** Bagshawe;
Gainsford to Bagshawe, Dec. 29, 1855,
Bagshawe Papers, acknowledges pay-
ment for first art. in this issue.

762　De Vere's poems, 300–321. **C. W. Russell.** Bagshawe; Russell to Bagshawe, May
9, 1855, Bagshawe Papers, has sent this
art. to Richardson.

763　Richard Lalor Sheil, 321–354. **G. W.
Abraham.** Bagshawe; C. W. Russell to
Bagshawe, [May 1855], Bagshawe Papers,
says "Sheil is Abraham's."

764　St. Thomas of Canterbury, 355–413.
W. F. Finlason. Bagshawe; Finlason to
Bagshawe, May 10, [1855], Bagshawe
Papers, says "St. Thomas will be ready
on Monday."

765　Lord Cloncurry, 413–423. **Patrick
McMahon.** Bagshawe; McMahon to Bagshawe, Dec. 28, 1855, Bagshawe Papers,
acknowledges payment for art. 5 in this
issue.

766　The Turks in relation to prophecy, 424–
442. **G. W. Abraham.** Repr. *Essays.*

767　Mrs. Jameson's *Sisters of Charity*, 442–
460. **George Crolly.** Bagshawe; C. W.
Russell to Bagshawe, June 10, 1855,
Bagshawe Papers, speaks of an art. by
Crolly on Mrs. Jameson.

768 The Maynooth endowment, 461–506. **C. W. Russell.** Bagshawe; claimed in Russell to Bagshawe, June 16 [1855], Bagshawe Papers.

769 Dr. Faber on the Blessed Sacrament, 507–536. **William Jennings.** Bagshawe; C. W. Russell to Bagshawe, June 1 [1855], Bagshawe Papers, forwards a paper on Faber, and indicates an art. by Jennings for this issue, which would confirm Bagshawe.

770 Notices of books, 537–542. Pages 537–539 by **C. W. Russell**—Russell to Bagshawe, [Apr. 7, 1855], Bagshawe Papers, says he will notice Dr. Donovon's *Catechism*; pages 541–542 by **T. F. Wetherell?**—Wetherell to Bagshawe, Jan. 8, 1855, Bagshawe Papers, proposes a review of Hayward's [sic.] *Foreign Policy*.

VOLUME 39, SEPTEMBER 1855

771 Luther, 1–60. **W. F. Finlason.** Bagshawe; Finlason to Bagshawe, Sept. 17, 1855, Bagshawe Papers, complains he has not yet had revises of "Luther".

772 Food and its adulterations, 60–75. **T. L. Kemp.** Bagshawe; Kemp to Bagshawe, June 4, 1855, Bagshawe Papers, sends first part of paper on food.

773 Burton's *Pilgrimage to El Medinah*, 76–108. **C. W. Russell.** Bagshawe; claimed in Russell to Bagshawe, Sept. 22 [1855], Bagshawe Papers.

774 De Ravignan's *Times of Clement XIII and XIV*, 109–146. **G. W. Abraham.** Although Bagshawe gives "Dr. Russell," the art. is repr. in Abraham's *Essays*; again confusion is undoubtedly due to fact that Russell sent in most of the Irish arts.; see no. 778.

775 The action against the Cardinal [Boyle vs. Wiseman], 146–164. **W. F. Finlason.** Bagshawe; Finlason to Bagshawe, Sept. 17, 1855, Bagshawe Papers, acknowledges receipt of proofs of "the Cardinal's case."

776 Rome and Sardinia, 164–199. **George Bowyer.** Bagshawe; repr. from *Dublin Review* under his name, 1856.

777 Anglican rationalism, 199–244. **Nicholas Wiseman.** Bagshawe; Richardson to Bagshawe, Sept. 22, 1855, Bagshawe Papers, says "art. on Anglican rationalism *is* the Cardinal's."

778 Sidney Smith, 244–272. **George Crolly.** Bagshawe and *DR* list give "Dr. Russell," but Russell to Bagshawe, Sept. 22, [1855], Bagshawe Papers, says Sidney Smith is by Mr. Crolly.

779 Notices of books, 272.

VOLUME 39, DECEMBER 1855

780 *Sir Isaac Newton* [by David Brewster], 273–290. **G. W. Abraham.** Abraham to Bagshawe, Sept. 22, 1855, Bagshawe Papers, says he is hard at work on Brewster's *Newton*; Richardson to Bagshawe, Nov. 12, [1855], ibid., says "Life of Newton" was from Mr. Abraham; Bagshawe gives "Rev. Prof. Crolly (Maynooth)," clearly an error taken into account in the *DR* list.

781 Irish waste lands, 290–311. **Patrick McMahon.** Bagshawe; Richardson to Bagshawe, letter cited for no. 780, says "you will have proof of an art. by Mr. McMahon to-morrow."

782 Catholic reformatory schools, 312–328. **R. J. Gainsford.** Bagshawe; Gainsford to Bagshawe, Nov. 19, 1856, Bagshawe Papers, acknowledges payment for art. 3 in this issue.

783 The age of Edward III [review of John Lingard and Edward Foss], 328–384. **W. F. Finlason.** Bagshawe; Finlason to Bagshawe, Dec. 7, 1855, Bagshawe Papers, says he intended to put Foss at head of his art. as well as Lingard. (See no. 790.)

784 Pope Callistus on the Trinity, 384–412. **C. W. Russell.** Bagshawe; Russell to Bagshawe, Dec. 5, 1855, Bagshawe Papers, says he has sent most of "Callistus."

785 The Concordat with Austria, 413–432. **Thomas Grant.** Bagshawe; Grant to Bagshawe, Dec. 15, 1855, Bagshawe Papers, says he has added to his proof the note which appears on p. 413.

786 The study of eloquence in theological seminaries, 433–461. **Matthew Kelly.** Bagshawe; introduction to *Dissertations*, p. xv.

787 Lord John Russell on persecution [religious oppression], 462–482. **Nicholas Wiseman.** Bagshawe; Oscott IA and *DR* list assign to H. R. Bagshawe, but he simply edited Wiseman's lecture: see p. 480.

788 Christian theism, 482–489. **William Jennings.** Oscott IA; *DR* list; Russell to Bagshawe, Nov. 11, 1855, Bagshawe Papers, says Bagshawe may rely on this art. by Jennings.

789 Notices of books, 490–528. Pages 505–506 by **W. F. Finlason**—Finlason to Bagshawe, Aug. 21, 1855, Bagshawe Papers, encloses "Bonnechose."

VOLUME 40, MARCH 1856

790 The age of Morton, Wolsey, and More [sequel to no. 783], 1–66. **W. F. Finlason.** Bagshawe; Richardson to Bagshawe, Feb. 19, 1856, Bagshawe Papers, refers to Finlason's "Wolsey."

791 Mozley's *Augustinianism*, 67–134. **William Gowan Todd.** Bagshawe; Todd to H. E. Manning [Dec. 1855], Bagshawe Papers, says he cannot have "Mozley" ready before April.

792 The differences between the Holy See and the Spanish government, 134–155. **George Bowyer.** Bagshawe; repr. under his name, 1856.

793 Macaulay's *History of England*, 156–200. **C. W. Russell.** Bagshawe; claimed Russell to Wiseman, April 4, 1856, Wiseman Papers.

794 Bible-blasphemy, 200–252. **Nicholas Wiseman.** Bagshawe; Russell to Wiseman, April 4, 1856, Wiseman Papers, speaks of this as Wiseman's.

795 Mrs. Fitzherbert's marriage with H.R.H. the Prince of Wales, 252–271. **George Crolly.** Bagshawe; C. W. Russell to Bagshawe, Mar. 10, 1856, Bagshawe Papers, refers to Mr. Crolly's "Fitzherbert."

796 Notices of books, 271–280. Pages 278–280 (xiii) by **W. F. Finlason**—Richardson to Bagshawe, Jan. 25, 1856, Bagshawe Papers, says he has sent proof of *"Popes, Emperors"* to Finlason; pages 271–272 (i), 274–276 (v–viii) by **C. W. Russell**—claimed in Russell to Bagshawe, Mar. 18, 1856, ibid.

VOLUME 40, JUNE 1856

797 Milman's *Latin Christianity* (Vols. IV–VI), 281–299. **C. W. Russell.** Bagshawe; Russell to Bagshawe, Mar. 18, [1856], Bagshawe Papers, says he has finished "Milman."

798 *The Newcomes*, 299–309. **Frederick Oakeley.** Bagshawe; Oakeley to Bagshawe, Mar. 18, 1856, Bagshawe Papers, says he has forwarded a short art. on *The Newcomes*.

799 Londiniana, 309–338. **W. Sidney Gibson.** Repr. *Lectures and Essays on Various Subjects*, 1858.

800 Wordsworth's poems, 338–391. **W. F. Finlason.** Bagshawe; Finlason to Bag-

shawe, Jan. 21, 1856, Bagshawe Papers, says he has written on Wordsworth's poetry.

801 Hallam's works, 392–417. **G. W. Abraham.** Bagshawe; C. W. Russell to Bagshawe, Apr. 2 [1856], Bagshawe Papers, says Abraham's "Hallam" may be expected.

802 Digby's *Kathemerina*, 417–423. **H. R. Bagshawe.** Bagshawe.

803 *Fabiola* [by Nicholas Wiseman] and *Callista* [by J. H. Newman], 424–441. **C. W. Russell.** Bagshawe; Russell to Bagshawe, June 7, 1856, Bagshawe Papers, says he has sent off part of *"Fabiola and Callista."*

804 Montalembert's political future of England, 441–454. **W. H. Anderdon.** Bagshawe; Sutcliffe; Anderdon to Bagshawe, Mar. 5, 1856, Bagshawe Papers, hopes to have "Montalembert" ready for summer issue.

805 Prescott's *Philip II*, 454–481. **George Crolly.** Bagshawe; C. W. Russell to Bagshawe, Jan. 6, 1856, Bagshawe Papers, says Crolly's "Prescott" may be expected.

806 Peel's *Memoirs*: the Catholic question, 481–515. **C. W. Russell.** Bagshawe; Russell to Bagshawe, June 15, [1856], Bagshawe Papers, says he has sent off the rest of "Peel."

807 The religious war of words, 515–539. **Nicholas Wiseman** and **C. W. Russell.** Bagshawe gives "Wiseman" but Wiseman to Bagshawe, June 11, 1856, Wiseman Papers, shows that C. W. Russell was asked to write pp. 537–539 on Wiseman's own lecture, and Russell to Bagshawe, June 27, [1856], Bagshawe Papers, sends something to go at the end of the Cardinal's paper (pp. 537–539).

808 Notices of books, 540–552.

VOLUME 41, SEPTEMBER 1856

809 The Reformation the result of tyranny, 1–27. **W. F. Finlason.** Bagshawe; Finlason to Bagshawe, May 14, 1856, Bagshawe Papers, sends continuation of series on Eng. history; wants it in June No.

810 Burton's *Meccah* and *East Africa*, 27–66. **C. W. Russell.** Bagshawe; Russell to Bagshawe, cited for no. 801, says his "Burton" may be expected.

811 Curiosities of the anti-Jesuit crusade, 66–85. **Percy Fitzgerald.** Bagshawe gives "Mr. Fitzgerald"; Percy Fitzgerald to

Bagshawe [July 18, 1856], Bagshawe Papers, refers to his paper with this title.

812   Guizot's *Richard Cromwell*, 86–117. **G. W. Abraham.** Russell to Bagshawe, Aug. 16 and 24, 1856, Bagshawe Papers, refers to Abraham's "Cromwell"; repr. *Essays*; Bagshawe gives it to George Crolly, but clearly in error.

813   Passaglia on the prerogatives of Mary, 117–171. **William G. Todd.** Bagshawe; Todd to Bagshawe, July 14, [1856], Bagshawe Papers, wants to write on Passaglia; Acton to Döllinger, Mar. 20, [1858], refers to Todd's art. on Passaglia in *DR*, Conzemius, I, 135.

814   Italy and the Papal States, 171–226. **Nicholas Wiseman.** Bagshawe; repr. as: *A Vindication of Italy and the Papal States*, Cincinnati, 1856.

815   The Catholic University and legal education, 226–246. **Patrick McMahon.** Bagshawe; McMahon to Bagshawe, Sept. 6, 1856, Bagshawe Papers, acknowledges payment for 7th art. in this issue.

816   Notices of books, 247–277. Pages 260–261 (xii) and 261–262 (xiii) by **H. R. Bagshawe,** prob.—Richardson to Bagshawe, Sept. 11, 1856, Bagshawe Papers, presumes these notices were by Bagshawe; pages 266–267 (xix) by **H. R. Bagshawe,** prob.—Phillip Howard to Bagshawe, Mar. 26, 1856, ibid., refers to Bagshawe's notice of Mounsey; page 249 (ii) by **J. B. Robertson**—Robertson to Bagshawe, Sept. 19, 1856, ibid., sends notice of *Flemish Interiors*; pages 252 (vii), 253–259 (ix), 263 (xv) by **C. W. Russell,** prob.—Richardson to Bagshawe, Sept. 11, 1856, ibid., says these notices sent by Dr. Russell.

VOLUME 41, DECEMBER 1856

817   Cockburn's *Memorials of his Time*, 279–306. **G. W. Abraham,** prob. C. W. Russell to Bagshawe, Aug. 24 [1856], Bagshawe Papers, says he hopes to get Abraham to do "Cockburn"; repr. *Essays* during Abraham's lifetime. OR, **C. W. Russell?** Bagshawe and *DR* list; Russell to Bagshawe, Dec. 1, 1856, Bagshawe Papers, tells Bagshawe he has nothing for this issue.

818   An Anglican apology for tyranny [Froude's *History of England*], 307–344. **W. F. Finlason.** Bagshawe; cf. no. 809.

819   Recent writers on the temporal sovereignty of the Pope, 344–382. **W. B. McCabe.** Richardson to Bagshawe, Nov.

7, 1856, Bagshawe Papers, says Mr. McCabe's "Temporal Sovereignty" received, and continues, "Dr. Russell has approved of the art." Bagshawe assigns to C. W. Russell and *DR* list gives both with "?."

820   The Great Rebellion and the anti-Catholic faction, 383–411. **W. F. Finlason.** Bagshawe; Finlason to Bagshawe, Nov. 6, 1856, Bagshawe Papers, sends art. about Rebellion.

821   Madame D'Arbouville's poems and novels, 411–441. **W. E. Gloag.** Bagshawe; Gloag to Bagshawe, June 23, 1856, Bagshawe Papers, sends a review of Mme. D'Arbouville.

822   The present Catholic dangers [attack on the *Rambler*], 441–470. **Nicholas Wiseman.** Bagshawe; Richardson to Bagshawe, Dec. 16, 1856, Bagshawe Papers, says he has received a portion of the Cardinal's "Present Catholic Position." (Note, vol. 42, pp. 245–248, by **Wiseman**—Wiseman to Bagshawe, Apr. 1, 1857, Wiseman Papers, says he sent note on *Rambler* in the editor's name.)

823   The Irish in England, 470–521. **William G. Todd.** Repr. as a pamphlet under his name in 1857.

824   Notices of books, 521–535. Pages 527–528 by **H. R. Bagshawe**—A. Van Landau to Bagshawe, Dec. 23, 1856, Bagshawe Papers, thanks Bagshawe for himself writing notice of his pamphlet; pages 521–525 by **Thomas Grant**—Richardson to Bagshawe, Dec. 3, 1856, ibid., lists "Decline of Fun" by Dr. Grant for this issue, and on Dec. 16 allots 4 pp. to it.

VOLUME 42, MARCH 1857

825   Andersen's German stories, 1–25. **George Crolly.** Bagshawe; C. W. Russell to Bagshawe, Nov. 14, 1856, Bagshawe Papers, says Crolly promises a light paper on Andersen.

826   The Revolution [of 1688], the conspiracy of an oligarchy, 26–76. **W. F. Finlason.** Bagshawe; Finlason to Bagshawe, May 14, 1856, Bagshawe Papers, says the "Rebellion" and the "Revolution" will complete his series on the history.

827   Epidemic disease in Ireland, 76–95. **G. W. Abraham.** Bagshawe; C. W. Russell to Bagshawe, Mar. 1, [1857], Bagshawe Papers, says "Disease in Ireland" is by Abraham.

828   The latest phenomena of Anglicanism [on union with Rome], 95–123. **Frederick**

Oakeley. Bagshaw; confirmed by Wiseman to Bagshawe, Mar. 12, 1857, Wiseman Papers.

829   Works of charity, 123–142. **Frances M. Taylor.** Bagshawe gives "Miss Taylor"; Miss Taylor to Bagshawe, Feb. 12, 1857, Bagshawe Papers, says she wants to combine reviews of Mrs. Jameson and Miss Stanley's *Hospitals and Sisterhoods.*

830   English and Irish crime, 142–156. **R. J. Gainsford.** Bagshawe; Gainsford to Bagshawe, Feb. 22, 1857, Bagshawe Papers, says he is writing on this topic, and on Jan. 30, 1858, sends receipt for this art.

831   Recent antiquarian discoveries in Italy, 157–182. **C. W. Russell.** Bagshawe; Wiseman to Bagshawe, undated, Wiseman Papers, says the paper on Roman antiquities is Dr. Russell's.

832   *Legend of the Wandering Jew,* 183–195. **Nicholas Wiseman.** Bagshawe; Wiseman to Bagshawe, n.d., Wiseman Papers, says he has sent the *"Wandering Jew."*

833   The St. Barnabas judgment, 195–210. **C. W. Russell.** Bagshawe; Russell to Bagshawe, [Mar. 1857], Bagshawe Papers, says he will try to send 15 pp. on St. Barnabas judgment.

834   State of Catholic affairs, 211–230. **Nicholas Wiseman.** Bagshawe; confirmed by Wiseman to Bagshawe, n.d., Wiseman Papers, and Bagshawe to Wiseman, April 13, 1857, ibid.

835   *Flemish Interiors,* 230–244. **James Burton Robertson.** Bagshawe; Robertson to Bagshawe, Sept. 19, 1856, Bagshawe Papers, promises *"Flemish Interiors."*

836   Notices of books, 249–270. Pages 255–256 (vii), 266–268 (xv) by **C. W. Russell**—claimed in Russell to Bagshawe, Jan. 30, 1858, Bagshawe Papers; pages 257–258 (x) by **C. W. Russell,** prob.—Richardson to Bagshawe, Jan. 22, 1856/57, ibid., says Russell wants to review Northcote's *Catacombs*; Russell to Bagshawe [Mar. 1857], ibid., shows he contributed from 10 to 12 pages of notices in this issue.

VOLUME 42, JUNE 1857

837   Popular recreations and their moral influence, 271–293. **Frederick Oakeley.** Bagshawe; Oakeley to Bagshawe, May 29, [1857], Bagshawe Papers, says he has finished "Popular Recreations."

838   Helps' *Spanish Conquest in America,* 294–317. **G. W. Abraham.** Repr. *Essays.*

839   Christ, the Church, and the Bible, 317–

363. **William G. Todd.** Bagshawe; Todd to Bagshawe, Apr. 10, [1857], Bagshawe Papers, promises this art. by title for this issue.

840   "Souperism" [i.e., proselytism], tested by its own statistics, 363–382. **Frederick Oakeley.** Bagshawe; Oakeley to Bagshawe, May 29, [1857], Bagshawe Papers, says his "Irish Proselytism" will be sent to-morrow.

841   Bowring's *Siam,* 382–403. **G. W. Abraham.** Bagshawe.

842   Laforet's *Moral Philosophy,* 403–438. **D. B. Dunne.** Bagshawe; Dunne to Bagshawe, May 24, 1860, Bagshawe Papers, refers to "my" art. on Laforet in July 1857.

843   Huc's *Christianity in China,* (Part I), 438–480. **C. W. Russell.** Bagshawe; Russell to Bagshawe, Apr. 8, 1858, Bagshawe Papers, says he himself wrote all the arts. on Huc; see nos. 756 and 884.

844   Dodsworth on popular Protestant delusions, 481–490. **Frederick Oakeley.** Bagshawe; Oakeley to Bagshawe, June 9, 1857, Bagshawe Papers, has sent a short review of Dodsworth.

845   The Prince de Broglie's *Reign of Constantine,* 490–514. **C. W. Russell.** Bagshawe; Russell to Bagshawe, June 17, [1857], Bagshawe Papers, refers to "my De Broglie."

846   Notices of books, 514–536. Pages 528–529 (nos. xviii–xx), pages 530–532 (xxvi), by **C. W. Russell**—claimed in letter cited for no. 865; pages 515–516 by **W. G. Todd**—Todd to Bagshawe [1857], Bagshawe Papers, asks to send a notice of this Handbook.

VOLUME 43, SEPTEMBER 1857

847   The sequel of the Revolution [of 1688], 1–50. **W. F. Finlason.** Bagshawe; Finlason to Bagshawe, June 5, 1857, Bagshawe Papers, sends "Sequel of the Revolution."

848   Swedish poetry, 51–82. **F. D. Wackerbarth.** Bagshawe gives "Mr. Wackerbarth"; Richardson to Bagshawe, June 9, 1857, Bagshawe Papers, refers to receipt of an art. from Sweden; see Boase under Wackenbarth.

849   Goldsmith, 82–107. **A. L. Windsor.** Bagshawe gives "Mrs. Windsor, Richmond Terrace, Clifton"; A. L. Windsor to Bagshawe, from 6 Richmond Terrace, [Clifton], Feb. 24, 1858, Bagshawe Papers, sends receipt; some of the material

from this art. was used in his *Ethica* (1860), chap. vi.

850   Lord Campbell's *Chief Justices of England*, 108–128. **C. W. Russell.** Richardson to Bagshawe, Sept. 21, 1857, Bagshawe Papers, says Russell's "Campbell" will appear in this issue; Bagshawe gives "J. B. Robertson," but in error.

851   Madeleine Smith and Scottish jurisprudence, 128–171. **W. F. Finlason.** Bagshawe; Finlason to Bagshawe, Aug. 1, 1857, Bagshawe Papers, says "Madeleine Smith" will be finished this week.

852   Catholic unity and English parties, 172–206. **T. F. Wetherell.** Repr. under his name, 1858: *BMCat.*

853   Italy and India, 206–234. **Nicholas Wiseman.** Bagshawe; Wiseman to Bagshawe, Aug. 23, [1857?], Wiseman Papers, says he thinks he can write art. on this exact topic; Richardson to Bagshawe, Sept. 18, 1857, Bagshawe Papers, says Wiseman's paper will make at least 29 or 30 pp.

854   *The Creator and the Creature, or, The Wonders of Divine Love* [by F. W. Faber], 235–256. **Frederick Oakeley.** Bagshawe; Russell to Bagshawe, Sept. 25, [1857], Bagshawe Papers, says he did not want to change Oakeley's views about Faber; Oakeley to Bagshawe, Sept. 17, 1857, Bagshawe Papers, complains that Richardson has sent his art. on Faber to Faber.

855   Notices of books, 257–272. Pages 266–269 (nos. x–xiv) by **C. W. Russell**—claimed in Russell to Bagshawe, cited for no. 836.

VOLUME 43, DECEMBER 1857

856   Philip Howard, 273–287. **G. W. Abraham.** Repr. *Essays.*

857   Woodgate on secession, 287–322. **William Dodsworth.** Bagshawe gives "Mr. Dodsworth"; see *DNB*; Richardson to Bagshawe, Aug. 31, 1857, Bagshawe Papers, says Dodsworth has sent a review of [Woodgate's] *Anomalies.*

858   The Mayo Committee and Exeter Hall, 322–355. **W. F. Finlason.** Bagshawe; Finlason to Bagshawe, Aug. 1, 1857, Bagshawe Papers, says there should be an art. about Mayo and adds he is a master of the subject; Russell to Bagshawe, Oct. 31, 1857, says he has sent Finlason's art. to Richardson; Russell to Bagshawe, Nov. 25, [1857], ibid., says he hopes Wiseman's conclusion will make the art. all right.

859   The filibusters in Nicaragua, 355–391. **Thomas Arnold,** 1823–1900. Bagshawe gives "Mr. Arnold"; Russell to Bagshawe, July 1, [1857], Bagshawe Papers, says "Dr. Arnold of Rugby's son" has sent him "Filibusters."

860   Formalism, a charge against the Church, 391–427. **William G. Todd.** Bagshawe; W. G. Todd to Bagshawe, [Dec. 1857], Bagshawe Papers, says he is calling his art. "The Church and the Charge of Formalism."

861   Anglican propagandism, 427–449. **Frederick Oakeley.** Bagshawe; Oakeley to Bagshawe, Dec. 7 [1857], Bagshawe Papers, says he has sent this art. to Richardson.

862   Döllinger's *Relation of Heathenism and Judaism to Christianity*, 449–471. **C. W. Russell.** Bagshawe; Russell to Bagshawe, Nov. 25, [1857], Bagshawe Papers, says he expects to send about 20 pp. on Döllinger.

863   Trial by jury no boon to Catholics, 471–508. **W. F. Finlason.** Bagshawe.

864   Notices of books, 510–536. Pages 515–519 by **W. F. Finlason**—Finlason to Bagshawe, [Sept. 1857], Bagshawe Papers, complains that his notice of Blackstone was omitted from September issue; pages 510–511 (i), 514–515 (iii), 521–522 (viii), 524–526 (xi–xiv) by **C. W. Russell**—claimed in Russell to Bagshawe, letter cited for no. 836; pages 511–514 by **W. G. Todd**—Todd to Bagshawe, [Nov. 28, 1857], Bagshawe Papers, says he has written notice of Newman's *Sermons.*

VOLUME 44, MARCH 1858

865   Henry IV, 1–31. **J. D. Acton.** Bagshawe; Acton to Wiseman, Aug. 31, 1857, Wiseman Papers, says he is writing on "Henry IV"; Bagshawe, Jan. 30, 1858, Bagshawe Papers, inquires whether Acton will correct his proofs.

866   The German mystics of the fourteenth century, 31–99. **J. D. Dalgairns.** Repr. under his name, 1858.

867   Obstetric morality, 100–130. **George Crolly.** Bagshawe; C. W. Russell to Bagshawe, in letter cited for no. 865, refers to Mr. Crolly's "Obstetrics."

868   Evidences of the primacy of St. Peter from the catacombs, 130–157. **P. F. Moran.** C. W. Russell to Bagshawe, Jan. 30, 1858, Bagshawe Papers, refers to primacy in the catacombs by Rev. Dr.

Moran, Rome; man cited was in Rome at this time and contributed to *DR* in June and Dec. 1858, and Mar. 1859; the attr. to Russell in Bagshawe and *DR* list is due to the art. being sent in by Russell and the proofs corrected by him (letter cited above).

869 Recent African explorations (Part I), 158–180. **G. W. Abraham.** Bagshawe; C. W. Russell to Bagshawe, in letter cited for no. 865, says "African explorations—Abraham."

870 New versions of the Scriptures, 181–199. **William Dodsworth.** Bagshawe; W. Dodsworth to Bagshawe [Nov. 1857], from 7 York Terrace, Regents Park, Bagshawe Papers, inquiries about his review of translations of New Testament; man cited a convert who died at York Terrace in 1861: see *DNB*.

871 Crotchets and crotchettiness, 200–219. **Frederick Oakeley.** Bagshawe; Oakeley to Bagshawe, Jan. 5, 1858, Bagshawe Papers, offers "Crotchettiness"; Richardson to Bagshawe, Mar. 12, 1858, ibid., says he is saving 20 pp. for Mr. Oakeley.

872 *The Four Last Popes* [by Nicholas Wiseman], 219–243. **G. W. Abraham.** Russell to Bagshawe, Mar. 12 [1858], Bagshawe Papers, says Abraham has sent me the first of this art. and will send rest tomorrow; repr. *Essays*; both Bagshawe and *DR* list give "Dr. Russell," but in error.

873 Rome; its ruler and its institutions, 243–259. **H. R. Bagshawe.** Bagshawe; Richardson to Bagshawe, Mar. 17, 1858, Bagshawe Papers, refers to short paper you sent this a.m.; Mar. 20, ibid., says he will make "Rome" an art.

874 Notices of books, 260–268. Pages 262–264 (iii) by **S. B. A. Harper**—Harper to Bagshawe, Mar. 12, 1858, Bagshawe Papers, sends notice of book by a physician dealing with consumption; some notices by **Frances M. Taylor**—Richardson to Bagshawe, Mar. 17, 1858, Bagshawe Papers, shows that the latter had approved of notices by Miss Taylor for this issue.

VOLUME 44, JUNE 1858

875 *The Judges of England* [by Edward Foss], 269–290. **W. F. Finlason.** Bagshawe; Finlason to Bagshawe, Apr. 10, 1858, Bagshawe Papers, sends proof of "Foss."

876 Hillard's *Six Months in Italy*, 290–298. **R. J. Gainsford.** Bagshawe; Gainsford to Bagshawe, May 28, 1858, Bagshawe Papers, has returned proof of art. on Hillard.

877 The philosophy of religion and the religion of philosophy [review of William Smith's *Thorndale*], 299–335. **S. B. A. Harper.** Bagshawe gives "Mr. Harper"; S. B. A. Harper to Bagshawe, Mar. 12, 1858, Bagshawe Papers, says he has had no proof of "Thorndale."

878 English party struggles, 336–374. **W. F. Finlason.** Bagshawe; Finlason to Bagshawe, Apr. 17, 1858, Bagshawe Papers, asks for room for this art.

879 Geology and Protestantism, 375–395. **William Dodsworth.** Bagshawe; W. Dodsworth to Bagshawe, Mar. 24, 1858, Bagshawe Papers, suggests showing the Catholic Church is not hostile to science, which is theme of this art.

880 The Messiah [by Handel] at Exeter Hall, 395–412. **Frederick Oakeley.** Bagshawe; Oakeley to Bagshawe, Jan. 5, 1858, Bagshawe Papers, offers to write on Handel's music, and on June 2, [1858], ibid., says he is sending "Handel" to Derby.

881 The letters of St. Ignatius, 412–444. **P. F. Moran.** Bagshawe gives "Rev. Dr. Moran, Irish Col. Rome"; Russell to Bagshawe, May 29 [1858], Bagshawe Papers, has paper from Dr. Moran on St. Ignatius.

882 Froude's *History of England*, 445–485. **W. F. Finlason.** Bagshawe; Finlason to Bagshawe, Apr. 10, 1858, Bagshawe Papers, offers art. on new vol. of Froude just out.

883 Religious disabilities of Catholic prisoners, 485–501. **Frederick Oakeley.** Though Bagshawe assigns this art. to C. W. Russell and the next to Oakeley, he has reversed the names; Oakeley to Bagshawe June 5, [1858], Bagshawe Papers, promises an art. on Pentonville (see p. 485).

884 Huc's *Christianity in China* (Part II, concl.), 501–525. **C. W. Russell.** Cf. no. 883; Russell reviewed earlier vols. of this book in no. 843, q.v., and Russell to Bagshawe, May 25, [1858], Bagshawe Papers, says he will pursue "Huc" in June.

885 Notices of books, 526–533.

VOLUME 45, SEPTEMBER 1858

886 The Sunday on Protestant principles, 1–31. **R. J. Gainsford.** Bagshawe; Gainsford to Bagshawe, Nov. 21, 1858, Bag-

shawe Papers, acknowledges payment for first art. in this issue.

887 The latest Oxford view of the history of the Papacy, 32–53. **W. F. Finlason.** Bagshawe; Finlason to Bagshawe, July 28, 1858, Bagshawe Papers, wants to write on prophecy as applied to the Papacy, and in [Sept. 1855] says he has chosen the above title.

888 Child-murder: obstetric morality, 54–106. **William Burke Ryan.** Bagshawe; sections repr. at various places in his *Infanticide*, 1862.

889 Our judges, 107–130. **W. F. Finlason.** Bagshawe; Finlason to Bagshawe [Aug. 1858], Bagshawe Papers, wants to write art. on our judges for the last 20 years; Richardson to Bagshawe, Sept. 20, 1858, ibid., says Finlason has made a change on p. 112.

890 Jubilee of St. Cuthbert's College [Ushaw], 131–149. **Frederick Oakeley.** Bagshawe; confirmed by Bagshawe to Wiseman, Feb. 20, 1859, Wiseman Papers; Oakeley to Bagshawe, Sept. 9, [1858], Bagshawe Papers, says he has sent most of "Ushaw" to Richardson.

891 Father De Ravignan, 149–167. **E. S. Purcell.** Bagshawe; Purcell to Bagshawe, Mar. 7, 1859, Bagshawe Papers, refers to his former art. on Ravignan.

892 Recent African explorations (Part II, concl.), 168–187. **G. W. Abraham.** Bagshawe; Russell to Bagshawe, Sept. 1, 1858, Bagshawe Papers, says to send 4th and 5th vols. of book reviewed here to Abraham.

893 Appeal in criminal cases, 187–203. **Patrick McMahon.** Bagshawe; McMahon to Bagshawe, Aug. 8, 1858, Bagshawe Papers, says he is glad to print an art. on this subject. (Note, vol. 47, pp. 537–538, by **H. R. Bagshawe**—Richardson to Bagshawe, Jan. 27, 1860, Bagshawe Papers, speaks of his notice of Mr. McMahon's [Bill].)

894 The Confessional controversy, 203–221. **C. W. Russell.** Bagshawe; Richardson to Bagshawe, Sept. 20, 1858, Bagshawe Papers, says Russell promises his "Confessional" for Wednesday.

895 Chronicles of the Middle Ages, 221–250. **W. F. Finlason.** Bagshawe; Finlason to Bagshawe, Sept. 10, [1858], Bagshawe Papers, sends MS. of chronicles of middle ages.

896 Notices of books, 250–266. Pages 251 (ii) by **Catherine Bagshawe**, prob.— Richardson to Mrs. Bagshawe, Sept. 18, 1858, Bagshawe Papers, asks her to review book by St. J. Climacus; pages 255–

257 (v) by **H. R. Bagshawe**—Richardson to Mrs. Bagshawe cited for (ii) says *Merope* was by Mr. Bagshawe; page 263 (viii) by **H. R. Bagshawe**—Richardson to Bagshawe, Mar. 27, 1858, ibid., refers to his notice of *Pictures of the Heavens.*

VOLUME 45, DECEMBER 1858

897 Protestant "spiritual destitution," 267–290. **George Bowyer.** Bagshawe; Richardson to Bagshawe, Oct. 16, 1858, Bagshawe Papers, says Mr. Bowyer's paper has come; Bowyer to Bagshawe, Dec. 26, 1858, ibid., asks for extra copies of an art. in this issue.

898 The monuments of the catacombs: baptism, 290–313. **P. F. Moran.** *DR* list gives "Dr. Moran"; Russell to Bagshawe, Oct. 4, 1858, Bagshawe Papers, says he has "Catacombs" from Dr. Moran; Bagshawe gives "Mr. Abraham."

899 Miss Sewell and Miss Yonge, 313–328. **Frances M. Taylor.** Bagshawe gives "Miss Taylor"; F. M. Taylor to Bagshawe, [Nov. 8, 1858], Bagshawe Papers, says she has sent "Sewell and Yonge" to Richardson.

900 History in fiction, 328–364. **W. F. Finlason.** Bagshawe; Finlason to Bagshawe, [Sept. 1858], Bagshawe Papers, says he has written on historical novels; Russell to Bagshawe, Dec. 2, 1858, ibid., says Mr. F.'s title should be as above.

901 *La Belle Saison dans la Campagne, Conseils Spirituels,* 365–388. **G. W. Abraham.** Repr. *Essays.*

902 Justices' justice and the new Habeas Corpus Act, 388–403. **W. F. Finlason.** Bagshawe; Finlason to Bagshawe, letter cited for no. 900, proposes art. on decisions of magistrates re vagrancy and street obstruction (see p. 403).

903 German theories of Christianity and its origin, 404–413. **G. W. Abraham.** Repr. *Essays.*

904 Platform slanderers and newspaper libellers, 413–428. **W. F. Finlason.** Bagshawe; Finlason to Bagshawe, letter cited for no. 900, proposes an art. on libel.

905 The rise and fall of Jansenism, 428–484. **George Crolly.** Richardson to Bagshawe, Dec. 15, 1858, Bagshawe Papers, says they have received Mr. Crolly's "Jansenists"; Bagshawe gives "Prof. Jennings," but *DR* list is uncertain; see no. 917.

906 The Abbé Massé's *Life of St. Edmund of Canterbury,* 484–501. **Frederick Oakeley.** *DR* list; Oakeley to Bagshawe, Nov. 6, 1858, Bagshawe Papers, offers to review *Life of St. Edmund*; Bagshawe gives "Dr. Russell," but almost certainly in error.

907   Miss Kavanagh's *Summer and Winter in Two Sicilies*, 502–510. **Catherine E. Bagshawe.** Oscott IA and *DR* list assign to "Mrs. Bagshawe"; Bagshawe gives "B."

908   Abbé Domenech's *Missionary Life in Texas and Mexico*, 511–529. **C. W. Russell.** Bagshawe; Russell to Bagshawe, Aug. 24 [1858], Bagshawe Papers, says he has received Domenech, and on Dec. 18, says he hopes to finish "Domenech" to-morrow.

909   Notices of books, 530–547. Pages 534–535 by **C. W. Russell**—Russell to Bagshawe, Dec. 21, 1858, Bagshawe Papers, says he will write notice on Disraeli; pages 533–534 by **W. B. Ryan**—Ryan to Bagshawe, Nov. 20, 1858, Bagshawe Papers, says he will notice Wyse; pages 535–537 by **Frances M. Taylor**—letter cited for no. 899, says she has sent notice of Soeur Rosalie.

VOLUME 46, MARCH 1859

910   Norway, 1–18. **Edward Charlton.** Bagshawe; Charlton to Bagshawe, June 30, 1859, Bagshawe Papers, acknowledges payment for art. I in this issue.

911   The Mortara case and the Murphy case, 19–42. **W. F. Finlason.** Bagshawe; Finlason to Bagshawe, [1858], Bagshawe Papers, wants to write on the Jewish child, i.e., the Mortara case, and in [Nov.] says he has postponed it.

912   Syriac letters of St. Clement of Rome, 42–58. **P. F. Moran.** Bagshawe; Richardson to Bagshawe, Mar. 16, 1859, Bagshawe Papers, says proof of Dr. Moran's art. corrected by Dr. Russell, was sent; cf. no. 881.

913   The plea of insanity in trials for murder, 58–92. **W. F. Finlason.** Bagshawe; Finlason to Bagshawe, [Mar. 1859], Bagshawe Papers, sends proof of art. on madness.

914   *Anne Sherwood, or, The Social Institutions of England*, 93–109. **E. S. Purcell.** Bagshawe; J. B. Robertson to Bagshawe, Mar. 1859, Bagshawe Papers, refers to Purcell's review of *Anne Sherwood*.

915   The Cornwallis correspondence, 110–134. **C. W. Russell.** Bagshawe; Bagshawe to Wiseman, Feb. 10, 1859, Bagshawe Papers, says Russell will do "Cornwallis."

916   Lord Broughton's *Italy*, 135–151. **G. W. Abraham.** Repr. *Essays.*

917   Mgr. Parisis, Bishop of Arras, on philosophical tradition, 152–186. **William Jennings.** Russell to Bagshawe, Feb. 9, 1859, Bagshawe Papers, says that for next issue we shall have Jennings's "Philosophical Traditionalism"; Bagshawe's attr. to George Crolly is a confusion with no. 905, which he attribs. to Jennings.

918   The government of the Papal States (Part I), 187–251. **W. F. Finlason.** Bagshawe; Finlason to Bagshawe, [Mar. 1859], Bagshawe Papers, encloses art. on Papal government.

919   *Memoirs of the Court of George IV*, 252–258. **H. R. Bagshawe.** Bagshawe. Richardson to Bagshawe, Mar. 29, 1859, Bagshawe Papers, says he is sending proof of your art.

920   Notices of books, 259–268. Page 261 (no. ii) by **H. R. Bagshawe**, prob.—Richardson to Bagshawe, Mar. 30, 1859, Bagshawe Papers, pleads for a line or two on Faber's *Conferences*; page 264 by **C. W. Russell**—Richardson to Bagshawe, Mar. 7, 1859, ibid., says he has "Father Connell (Dr. Russell)" on hand; pages 259–260, 261 (no. iii), 262 (no. v) by **C. W. Russell?**—ibid., suggests these also may be by Russell.

VOLUME 46, JUNE 1859

921   Finland and Russian Lappmark, 269–283. **Edward Charlton.** Bagshawe; Charlton to Bagshawe, May 15, 1859, Bagshawe Papers, offers art. on Finland, and on Sept. 9, [1859], acknowledges payment for an art. in this issue.

922   The government of the Papal States (Part II, concl.), 283–409. **W. F. Finlason.** Bagshawe.

923   Harford's *Michael Angelo*, 410–423. **G. W. Abraham.** Repr. *Essays.*

924   Prison and workhouse grievances, 424–437. **Frederick Oakeley.** Bagshawe; Richardson to Bagshawe, June 10, 1859, Bagshawe Papers, lists this as by Oakeley.

925   Celebrated judges of England, 438–476. **W. S. Gibson.** Bagshawe; Gibson to Bagshawe, June 7, 1859, Bagshawe Papers, sends art. on judicial biography.

926   The Order of Malta, or of St. John of Jerusalem, 477–499. **George Bowyer.** Bagshawe; Bowyer to Bagshawe, June 6, [1859], Bagshawe Papers, says he is writing about Order of St. John, and on June 15 sends the art.

927   Cardinal Wiseman's *Tour in Ireland in 1858*, 499–510. **Frederick Oakeley.** Bagshawe; Oakeley to Bagshawe, Nov. 6,

1858, Bagshawe Papers, promises art. on Wiseman in Ireland.

928 Notices of books, 510–532. Pages 510–515, 526–527 by **H. R. Bagshawe?**—J. B. Robertson to Bagshawe, Sept. 1, 1859, Bagshawe Papers, thanks Bagshawe for review of his lectures; Richardson to Bagshawe, June 23, 1859, ibid., says Mr. Gillow and Dr. Newsham will appreciate Bagshawe's notice; pages 518–519, 524–526 by **C. W. Russell**—Richardson to Bagshawe, June 3, 1859, ibid., says these were sent by Dr. Russell.

VOLUME 47, SEPTEMBER 1859

929 Gilbert's *History of the City of Dublin*, 1–33. **C. W. Russell**. Bagshawe.

930 *Adam Bede* [by George Eliot]—foundling hospitals, 33–42. **Frances M. Taylor.** Bagshawe; F. M. Taylor to Bagshawe, Sept. 15, [1859], Bagshawe Papers, speaks of proofs of her art. and on Dec. 26, ibid., acknowledges payment for her last art. in *DR*.

931 The Church of Portugal since the times of Pombal, 43–77. **E. S. Purcell**. Bagshawe; Purcell to Bagshawe, Dec. 8, 1859, Bagshawe Papers, refers to his "Portugal."

932 [Nassau] Senior's *Turkey*, 77–97. **G. W. Abraham**. Repr. *Essays*.

933 Newland's *Life of Antonio De Dominis*, 97–110. **C. W. Russell**. Bagshawe; Russell to Bagshawe, Sunday [late Sept.], 1859, Bagshawe Papers, says he has finished "De Dominis" and sent it off.

934 Burke's *Vicissitudes of Families*, 111–131. **G. W. Abraham**. Bagshawe; Repr. *Essays*.

935 Carlyle's *Frederick the Great*, 132–168. **C. W. Russell**. Bagshawe; Richardson to Bagshawe, June 10, 1859, Bagshawe Papers, refers to Dr. Russell's "Carlyle."

936 The Massacre of Perugia, 168–264. **W. F. Finlason**. Bagshawe; Finlason to Bagshawe, [Nov. 1859], Bagshawe Papers, acknowledges acceptance of his "Perugia."

937 Notices of books, 264–272.

VOLUME 47, FEBRUARY 1860

938 Algeria under the French, 273–329. **Edmund Ffoulkes**. Bagshawe; claimed in Ffoulkes to Bagshawe, Mar. 15, 1860, Bagshawe Papers.

939 The north-eastern parts of European Russia, 330–345. **Edward Charlton.** Bagshawe; Charlton to Bagshawe, Nov. 21, 1859, Bagshawe Papers, promises paper on European Russia, and on May 17, 1860, ibid., acknowledges payment for an art. in last issue.

940 Irish national education, 345–445. **Aubrey De Vere.** Bagshawe; De Vere's list; Richardson list, Jan. 5, 1860, for this issue, Bagshawe Papers. Postscript, 442–445, by **C. W. Russell**—Richardson to Bagshawe, Feb. 2, 1860, ibid., says he has received Russell's note to De Vere art.

941 Ceylon, 445–468. **G. W. Abraham.** Repr. *Essays*.

942 Miracles—the natural and the supernatural, 468–500. **George Crolly.** Bagshawe; Richardson list for this issue.

943 Sources of ancient Egyptian history, 501–537. **C. W. Russell**. Bagshawe; Richardson list for this issue.

944 Notices of books, 538–542. Pages 538–541 by **E. S. Purcell**—Richardson to Bagshawe, Jan. 27, 1860, Bagshawe Papers, says notice of *Hebrew Lyrics* is by Purcell.

VOLUME 48, MAY 1860

945 On the origin and influences of Greek philosophy, 1–36. **Theobald F. Mathew.** Bagshawe gives "Rev. Mr. Mathews"; T. F. Mathew to Bagshawe, Mar. 23, 1860, Bagshawe Papers, refers to his art. on Greek philosophy.

946 The new glories of the Catholic Church [in the East], 37–50. **H. R. Bagshawe.** Bagshawe.

947 Darwin, *On the Origin of Species*, 50–81. **John Morris**, 1826–1893. Bagshawe; John Morris to Bagshawe, Apr. 9, 1860, Bagshawe Papers, says he corrected the proofs of "Darwin."

948 Modern principles of government—real progress, 81–106. **M. J. Rhodes.** Bagshawe; Rhodes to Bagshawe, Aug. 25, 1860, Bagshawe Papers, acknowledges payment for arts. IV and VII in this issue.

949 Modern humorists, 107–149. **Thomas Donnelly.** Bagshawe gives "T. Donnelly (Dublin)"; Thomas Donnelly to Bagshawe, Apr. 14, 1860, Bagshawe Papers, sends art., and on Aug. 27, ibid., acknowledges payment for art. V in this issue.

950 The Italian Revolution—its cause and character, 150–189. **E. S. Purcell.** Bagshawe; Purcell to Bagshawe, Apr. 21,

1860, Bagshawe Papers, says he has sent "Italian Revolution."

951   *The Minister's Wooing* [by Harriet Beecher Stowe], 190–228. **M. J. Rhodes.** Bagshawe; letter cited for no. 948.

952   The Roman Campagna, 228–252. **William Jennings.** Bagshawe; Russell to Bagshawe, Apr. 19, 1860, says Mr. Jennings has sent his paper on the Roman Campagna; Bagshawe gives "Russell," but Russell only sent in Jenning's art.

953   *St. Thomas Becket, Archbishop of Canterbury*, 253–266. **Thomas Grant.** Bagshawe gives "Rev. Canon Morris"; but this is a review of Morris; John Morris, 1826–1893, [May 2] and Aug. 22, 1860, to Bagshawe, Bagshawe Papers, speaks of Dr. Grant's paper on his *St. Thomas.*

954   Notices of books, 266–268. Pages 245–247 by **M. Georgina St. John**—Miss St. John to Bagshawe, Jan. 16, [1861], Bagshawe Papers, acknowledges payment for *Mary Templeton.*

VOLUME 48, AUGUST 1860

955   The English Poor Law and the Catholic poor, 269–316. **John Morris,** 1826–1893. Bagshawe; Morris to Bagshawe, June 17, 1860, Bagshawe Papers, sends art. with this exact title for next *DR*, and on Jan. 16, 1861, acknowledges payment for an art. in this issue.

956   Roger Bacon, 316–350. **C. W. Russell.** Bagshawe; Richardson to Bagshawe, July 11, 1860, Bagshawe Papers, says first part of Russell's "Bacon" has been received.

957   Ward's philosophical introduction to *Nature and Grace*, 351–400. **D. B. Dunne.** Bagshawe; Dunne to Bagshawe, May 24, 1860, Bagshawe Papers, proposes to review Ward, and on Nov. 15 says he has defended Mansel against Ward; see pp. 378–379.

958   Oliphant's *Japan*, 401–422. **C. W. Russell.** Bagshawe; this art. not only refers back to no. 678 in the opening line but also implies on p. 402 that this is a supplement to the earlier art.; Richardson to Bagshawe, Apr. 5, 1860, Bagshawe Papers, says he is trying to find Oliphant for Dr. Russell.

959   P[ère] Félix on real progress, 422–451. **M. J. Rhodes.** Bagshawe; notation by Bagshawe on letter, Rhodes to Bagshawe, Oct. 6, 1860, Bagshawe Papers, says fifth art. in Jan. issue by Rhodes.

960   The science of legislation, 451–497. **Thomas Donnelly.** Bagshawe; Donnelly to Bagshawe, Aug. 13, 1860, Bagshawe Papers, says he wrote this art. only to oblige author being reviewed.

961   Civil correspondence of the Duke of Wellington, 497–526. **Charles A. Russell,** 1832–1900. Bagshawe; Charles A. Russell to Bagshawe, [Nov. 1860], Bagshawe Papers, asks when to expect payment for "Wellington Correspondence."

962   *Evenings on the Thames*, 526–533. **H. R. Bagshawe.** Bagshawe.

963   *Tyborne*, 534–539. **M. Georgina St. John.** Bagshawe; Miss St. John to Bagshawe, Jan. 16, [1861], Bagshawe Papers, acknowledges payment for "*Tyborne*."

964   Notices of books, 539–552. Pages 542–548 by **John Morris,** 1826–1893—Morris to Bagshawe, June 17, 1860, Bagshawe Papers, says he would like to send notices of Dr. Husenbeth's two books; pages 549 (no. iv), 552 (no. vii) by **M. Georgina St. John,** prob.—Richardson to Bagshawe, July 13, 1860, ibid., says he has received two short notices from Miss St. John; Miss St. John to Bagshawe, May 18, [1860], ibid., had spoken of writing on Parisian religious views (both these notices are of French religious books).

VOLUME 49, NOVEMBER 1860

965   St. Thomas and Battle Abbey, 1–40. **John Morris,** 1826–1893. Bagshawe; Morris to Bagshawe, Dec. 4, 1860, Bagshawe Papers, returns proof of his art.; pp. 20–40 repr. *Life and Martyrdom of Saint Thomas Becket,* 2nd ed., 1885.

966   Glaciers, 40–104. **D. B. Dunne.** Bagshawe; Dunne to Bagshawe, Nov. 15, 1860, Bagshawe Papers, has had to recast his art. on getting Tyndall's "*Glaciers.*"

967   Bonapartism [in Italy], 104–146. **E. S. Purcell.** Bagshawe; Purcell to Bagshawe, Oct. 26, 1860, Bagshawe Papers, refers to his "Triumph of Bonapartism."

968   Book hawking, 146–155. **M. Georgina S. St. John.** Bagshawe; Miss St. John to Bagshawe, Jan. 16, [1861], Bagshawe Papers, requests payment for "Book-hawking."

969   Joseph Wolff, 156–189. **R. J. Gainsford.** Bagshawe; Gainsford to Bagshawe, Nov. 7, 1860, Bagshawe Papers, refers to his remarks on Wolff and says he will agree

to any additions or substitutions by Wiseman.

970   King James II's *Irish Army List*, 190–238. **W. Burke Ryan.** Bagshawe; Ryan to Bagshawe, [Dec. 1860], Bagshawe Papers, says he has forwarded pedigree [of Burke family] to Richardson, see pp. 212–213, and will send rest of art. tomorrow.

971   Notices of books, 238–262. Pages 249–255 edited by **John Morris,** 1826–1893—Morris to Bagshawe, Dec. 26, 1860, Bagshawe Papers, says he has pasted extracts together from report on reformatories; pages 256–262 also by **Morris**—in same letter Morris says he sent the book on prophecy with the notice and says the notice of school books is his; pages 238–245 by **E. S. Purcell**—Purcell to Bagshawe, Jan. 10, 1861, ibid., refers to "my notice of *Undercurrents*."

VOLUME 49, FEBRUARY 1861

972   Froude's [*History of England*]: Edward VI and Mary, 263–300. **C. W. Russell.** Bagshawe; Russell to Bagshawe, Dec. 19, 1860, Bagshawe Papers, says he will send end of "Froude."

973   Thomas Hood, 300–347. **Thomas Donnelly.** Bagshawe; claimed in Donnelly to Bagshawe, Oct. 10, 1861, Bagshawe Papers.

974   Rawlinson's *Herodotus*, 348–367. **Bernard Smith.** Bagshawe; Smith to Bagshawe, Jan. 16, 1861, Bagshawe Papers, says he will send "*Herodotus*" at once.

975   *The Courts and Cabinets of William IV and Victoria* [by Duke of Buckingham], 368–383. **Edward Walford.** Bagshawe; Walford to Bagshawe, Jan. 27, 1861, Bagshawe Papers, encloses his "Buckingham."

976   Recent discoveries at Carthage, 383–416. **C. W. Russell.** Bagshawe; Russell to Bagshawe, Feb. 18, [1861], Bagshawe Papers, says he has finished "Carthage."

977   Our foreign policy in 1860–61, 416–433. **H. W. Barron.** Bagshawe; Barron to Bagshawe, Nov. 17, [1860], Bagshawe Papers, sends a short art. on our foreign policy.

978   De Montalembert's *Western Monks*, 434–457. **G. W. Abraham.** Repr. *Essays.*

979   Anglican Neo-Christianity: the *Essays and Reviews* (Part I), 457–502. **C. W. Russell.** Bagshawe; Russell to Bagshawe, Jan. 17, 1861, Bagshawe Papers, says he

will write a careful art. on *Essays & Reviews.*

980   Living English poets, 503–542. **E. S. Purcell.** Bagshawe; J. B. Robertson to Bagshawe, Jan. 7, 1861, Bagshawe Papers, reminds Bagshawe that Purcell is to do this art.; Robertson is one of the poets reviewed.

981   Notices of books, 543–546. Pages 543–545 by **Bernard Smith**—Smith to Bagshawe, Jan. 25, [1861], Bagshawe Papers, says he will attempt a notice of Palmer; pages 545–546 by **H. R. Bagshawe,** prob.—Bagshawe account book for this issue shows he paid himself 10/ for notices.

VOLUME 50, MAY 1861

982   Iceland, 1–59. **D. B. Dunne.** Bagshawe; Dunne to Bagshawe, Mar. 4, 1861, Bagshawe Papers, says he is sending 1st part of "Iceland."

983   Popular education in England, 60–91. **John Morris,** 1826–1893. Bagshawe; Morris to Bagshawe, Jan. 10, 1862, Bagshawe Papers, acknowledges payment for 2nd art. in May issue.

984   Dr. Stanley's *Lectures on the History of the Eastern Church*, 92–121. **E. S. Ffoulkes.** Bagshawe; Ffoulkes to Bagshawe, Jan. 10, 1862, Bagshawe Papers, acknowledges payment for "Stanley."

985   *Antiquities of the Irish Academy* [by W. R. Wilde], 122–150. **C. W. Russell.** Bagshawe; Russell to Bagshawe, Mar. 18, 1861, Bagshawe Papers, says he hopes to get wood-cuts of Wilde's book for an illustrated art. for next issue.

986   Crime and its detection, 150–194. **Thomas Donnelly.** Bagshawe; claimed in Donnelly to Bagshawe, Oct. 10, 1861, Bagshawe Papers.

987   Döllinger and the temporal power of the Popes, 195–234. **E. S. Purcell.** Bagshawe; Purcell to Bagshawe, Jan. 13, 1862, Bagshawe Papers, acknowledges payment for his "contributions"; payments for this issue were made in Jan.; all other arts. except this and no. 988 are attributed; ref. back on p. 200 to no. 967 by Purcell.

988   The Law of Divorce: *a Tale*, 234–242. **E. S. Purcell.** Bagshawe; see evidence for no. 987.

989   The Convocation on *Essays and Reviews* (Part II, concl.), 242–259. **C. W. Russell.** Bagshawe; Russell to Bagshawe, Mar. 18, 1861, Bagshawe Papers, says he is sending a postscript on new Convocation and hopes it is not too late for Feb. issue, but it clearly was; ref. back on p. 243 to first pt. of this art. by Russell.

990   Notices of books, 259–265.

VOLUME 50, AUGUST 1861

991   "Saint Worship," and monotheistic religions, 267–301. **P. LePage Renouf.** Bagshawe; J. B. Robertson to Bagshawe, Jan. 7, 1862, Bagshawe Papers, complains of this issue coming out in Dec. and adds "Renouf's paper is excellent."

992   Cockerell's *Aegina*, etc., 302–312. **Edward Walford.** Bagshawe; Walford to Bagshawe, Apr. 10, 1862, Bagshawe Papers, acknowledges payment for 2nd art. in this issue.

993   Biblical hermeneutics, 312–329. **G. W. Abraham.** Bagshawe.

994   Calumnies against the "Society of Jesus," 329–340. **R. R. Madden.** Bagshawe; claimed and parts repr. in *Memoirs*, ed. his son (1891), p. 262.

995   Genealogy, 340–349. **Edward Walford.** Bagshawe; Walford to Bagshawe, letter cited for no. 992, acknowledges payment for 5th art. in this issue.

996   Austria and Hungary, 349–396. **R. J. Gainsford.** Bagshawe; Gainsford to Bagshawe, Apr. 10, 1862, Bagshawe Papers, acknowledges payment for 6th art. in this issue.

997   Rights of governments and of populations, 397–423. **Myles O'Reilly.** Bagshawe; O'Reilly to Bagshawe, Apr. 12, 1862, Bagshawe Papers, acknowledges payment for 7th art. in this issue.

998   Moran's *Life of Oliver Plunket*, 423–457. **C. W. Russell.** Bagshawe.

999   De Vere's *Inisfail*, 457–474. **C. W. Russell.** Bagshawe, who reversed nos. 999 and 1000, giving this to Gilbert and that to Russell.

1000 O'Curry's *Ancient Irish Historical Literature*, 475–498. **J. T. Gilbert.** *Life*, pp. 93–94, 446.

1001 Secret history of James, seventeenth Earl of Desmond (Part I), 499–529. **Denis F. McCarthy**, prob. Bagshawe gives "Mr. MacCarthy"; D. McCarthy to Bagshawe, Apr. 10, 1862, Bagshawe Papers, acknowledges payment for an art. (this is the date when payments were being made for this issue [cf. evidence for nos. 992, 995, and 996]); Aubrey De Vere to Bagshawe, Sept. 30,

1861, Bagshawe Papers, suggests Mr. MacCarthy, "a person of great literary acquirements and antiquarian as well as historical knowledge," write on the "Desmond War": see *DNB*.

1002 Notices of books, 529–533. Pages 529–533 by **E. S. Purcell**—[Purcell, identified by the handwriting] to Bagshawe, Oct. 12, 1861, Bagshawe Papers, asks for space for notice of Normanby's introduction on Modena.

VOLUME 51, FEBRUARY 1862

1003 Secret history of James, seventeenth Earl of Desmond (Part II, concl.), 1–25. **Denis F. McCarthy.** Cf. no. 1001.

1004 Palmer's *Egyptian Chronicles*, 25–51. **Edmund S. Ffoulkes.** *DR* list gives "E. J. Ffoulkes,"; E. S. Ffoulkes to Bagshawe, Dec. 26, 1861, Bagshawe Papers, says he has finished "Palmer."

1005 The Old Countess of Desmond, 51–91. **J. G. Nichols.** *DR* list gives "Nichol"; J. G. Nichols to Bagshawe, Sept. 2, 1862, from 25 Parliament St., Bagshawe Papers, acknowledges payment for 3rd art. in No. 10[?1–last digit torn off]; 25 Parliament St., London, was address of one of the offices of J. Nichols, Son, & Bentley: see *DNB* under John Bowyer Nichols.

1006 Dalgairns, *The Holy Communion*, 92–133. **D. B. Dunne.** Bagshawe; Dunne to Bagshawe, Mar. 4, 1862, Bagshawe Papers, says he has added a brief notice of Dalgairns' earlier career to his art.; see pp. 130–133.

1007 D'Abbadie's Ethiopic literature: *The Shepherd of Hermas*, 133–153. **C. W. Russell.** Bagshawe; Russell to Bagshawe, Feb. 15, 1862, Bagshawe Papers, says he will set about "D'Abbadie" tomorrow.

1008 Porson, 153–186. **C. W. Russell.** Bagshawe; Russell to Bagshawe, in letter cited for no. 1007, says he has finished "Porson."

1009 Papal allocutions and revolutionary principles, 186–219. **E. S. Purcell.** Bagshawe; Purcell to Bagshawe, Jan. 18, 1862, Bagshawe Papers, says he will send "Allocutions" as soon as possible.

1010 Marshall's *Christian Missions*, 219–257. **C. W. Russell.** Bagshawe; claimed in Russell to Bagshawe, Mar. 1, 1862, Bagshawe Papers.

1011 Pugin and Turner, 257–273. **E. S. Purcell.** Bagshawe; Purcell to Bagshawe, in letter cited for no. 1009, says he wishes to send "Pugin and Turner."

VOLUME 51, MAY 1862

1012 Modern periodical literature, 275–308. **Thomas Donnelly.** Bagshawe; Donnelly to Bagshawe, Apr. 28, 1863, Bagshawe Papers, acknowledges payment for first art. in this issue.

1013 The Established Church in Ireland, 308–359. **R. J. Gainsford.** Bagshawe; Gainsford to Bagshawe, May 12, 1862, Bagshawe Papers, hopes to be able to send "Irish Church" this week.

1014 Life and labours of John O'Donovan, LL.D., 359–378. **J. T. Gilbert.** Bagshawe; *Life*, pp. 96–97, 446.

1015 Irish Church history, 379–404. **G. W. Abraham.** Bagshawe; repr. *Essays*; C. W. Russell to Bagshawe, May 30, 1862, Bagshawe Papers, says this was written "under my direction."

1016 *Frederick the Great* [by Thomas Carlyle], 404–428. **G. W. Abraham.** Bagshawe; repr. *Essays*.

1017 Recent explorations in equatorial Africa, 428–481. **D. B. Dunne.** Bagshawe; Dunne to Bagshawe, Mar. 10, 1863, Bagshawe Papers, complains he has not been paid for "Equatorial Africa" in May issue.

1018 Sicily: the Italian revolution and the Papacy, 481–509. **E. S. Purcell.** Bagshawe; claimed in Purcell to Bagshawe, June 30, 1862, Bagshawe Papers.

1019 Notices of books, 510–529. Pages 510–516, 520–525, by **W. Charles Kent**—Bagshawe gives "Mr. Kent, Mr. Purcell," for these notices; Charles Kent to Bagshawe, Apr. 28, 1862, Bagshawe Papers, says he will do the short notices, and on Apr. 27, 1863, acknowledges a payment (Richardson to Bagshawe, Apr. 9, 1863, ibid., establishes date of payment for this issue); pages 516–520, 526–529, by **E. S. Purcell**—Purcell to Bagshawe, Mar. 12, 1862, Bagshawe Papers, says he is sending a notice of Jager's *Church of France*; and on June 30, says he wants to write notice of *Religious Orders*.

VOLUME 52, NOVEMBER 1862

1020 The employment of women, 1–44. **H. J. Wrixon.** Bagshawe gives "Mr. Wrixon, T.C.D.(Pr)"; there is no record in *Alum. Dub.* of any prof. of this name

at T.C.D.; man cited took his B.A. there in 1861 and was admitted to the Irish Bar in same year; claimed H. J. Wrixon to Bagshawe, Mar. 13, 1863, Bagshawe Papers.

1021 Rome on the Day of Pentecost, 1862 [canonization of the Japanese martyrs], 44–70. **F. R. Wegg Prosser.** Bagshawe; Richardson list of arts. on hand, Oct. 27, 1862, Bagshawe Papers; Prosser to Bagshawe, Oct. 15, 1862, ibid., agrees to toning down his reference to *Home and Foreign Review*, i.e., liberal Catholics.

1022 Earl Stanhope's *Life of Pitt*, 70–106. **C. W. Russell.** Bagshawe; Richardson list of arts. on hand, Oct. 27, 1862.

1023 The connection of the state with education in England and Ireland, 106–154. **Myles O'Reilly.** Repr. *Two Articles on Education*, 1863.

1024 On responsibility, 155–184. **Nicholas Wiseman.** Bagshawe gives "C.W."; Wiseman to Bagshawe, Oct. 11, 1862, Bagshawe Papers, says he is sending "On Responsibility" at once.

1025 Mendelssohn, 184–244. **D. B. Dunne.** Bagshawe; Dunne to Bagshawe, Mar. 10, 1863, Bagshawe Papers, asks for payment for "Mendelssohn."

1026 The duty of the state, its rules and limits, 245–271. **Myles O'Reilly,** prob. O'Reilly to Bagshawe, Nov. 12, 1862, Bagshawe Papers, encloses an art., which he indicates is not the 2nd art. planned on education (see no. 1031); Richardson to Bagshawe, Dec. 1, 1862, ibid., says they have Major O'Reilly's paper, which "will complete the present number." Bagshawe gives "Dr. Russell" but *DR* list shows the art. was marked "Major O'Reilly" in Oscott list.

1027 Notices of books, 271–278. Pages 271–275 by **E. S. Purcell**—Bagshawe gives "Mr. Purcell (Notice)," and Purcell to Bagshawe, Oct. 13, 1862, Bagshawe Papers, says he wishes to notice Robertson's *Free-Masonry*.

VOLUME 52, APRIL 1863

1028 The Liberal party in England and Ireland, 280–318. **G. W. Abraham.** Repr. *Essays*.

1029 The public records of Ireland, 318–390. **J. T. Gilbert.** Bagshawe; *Life,* pp. 122, 138. (Note, vol. 2 n.s., p. 278.)

1030 Modern intellectualism and the Catholic Church, 391–423. **E. S. Purcell.** Bagshawe; Purcell to Bagshawe, Nov. 13, 1862, Bagshawe Papers, regrets this is not to be in Nov. issue; Richardson list for this issue, Feb. 2, 1863, Bagshawe Papers.

1031 University education, 423–467. **Myles O'Reilly.** Repr. *Two Articles on Education*, 1863.

1032 Dr. Döllinger's *Protestantism and the Papacy*, 467–503. **C. W. Russell.** Bagshawe; Russell to Bagshawe, Dec. 1, 1862, Bagshawe Papers, says he has sent 1st part of "Dollinger"; Richardson list for this issue.

1033 The Roman state, 503–569. **R. J. Gainsford.** Bagshawe; Richardson list for this issue.

1034 Notices of books, 570–580. Pages 570–573, unidentified, possibly by H. R. Bagshawe—Richardson to Bagshawe, Mar. 24, 1863, Bagshawe Papers, asks for "a word or two more commending the beauty" of Birmingham's book.

VOLUME 1 N.S., 53 O.S., JULY 1863

1035 Popular devotion in Spain, 1–32. **Herbert Vaughan.** Claimed in Vaughan to Mgr. Talbot, June 20, [1863], Talbot Papers, no. 703, English College, Rome.

1036 The Abyssinian schism, 33–65.

1037 Intrinsic end of civil government, 66–111. **W. G. Ward.** Bayswater; in his *Doctrinal Decisions*, p. 72n, Ward claims an art. in the issue for July, 1863.

1038 Rosa Ferrucci, 111–138.

1039 The work and the wants of the Catholic Church in England, 139–166. **H. E. Manning.** Repr. *Miscellanies*, I. (Note, p. 612; letter vol. 3 n.s., pp. 251–252, signed by author.)

1040 Historical notes of the Tractarian Movement (Part I), 167–190. **Frederick Oakeley.** Signed; repr. under that title, 1865. Intro. note called "Essays and Miscellaneous Papers," 167–169, by the new editor, **W. G. Ward.**

1041 The French elections, 191–219. Signed: Δ. (Note, p. 274.)

1042 Notices of books, 220–262. Pages 220–224 by **W. G. Ward,** prob.—opening sentences link this to no. 1037 and it is cited in no. 1510, p. 40n. (Hereafter notices of this kind with typical references to earlier or later arts. by Ward, or presumably his, and supported by his known manner and interests, are cited as: cf. no. 1042.)

1043 Foreign periodical literature, 262–274.

E. H. Thompson and **Harriet Thompson.** W. G. Ward to E. H. Thompson, Jan. 3, 1865, Healy Thompson Papers, says he hopes Thompson and Mrs. Thompson will retain foreign periodical literature, which implies this department was in their hands until the final break with Thompson; it was omitted in the Apr. 1865 issue for lack of space, ibid., and ceased after Dec. of that year.

VOLUME 1 N.S., 53 O.S., OCTOBER 1863

1044 Dr. Hook's *Lives of the Archbishops of Canterbury*, 275–321.

1045 The curé of Ars, 322–355.

1046 Prison Ministers Act, 356–397. Unidentified. Possibly Edward Ryley, who according to Boase, aided Manning in obtaining equal rights for Roman Catholics in prison (see *Ram* no. 1054); since C. W. Russell was complaining in letter cited for no. 1050 that the regular "old" contributors were not being sufficiently represented in the new series, an art. by Ryley could be considered part of the complete changeover that Thompson, Ward and Manning desired: see Thompson to Ward, Oct. 3, 1862, Healy Thompson Papers, where he says "I positively refuse to have anything to do with the old hands."; the reference to John Morris's art. (no. 955) on workhouses on p. 358 may be viewed as a kind of introduction into the subject in hand; while Frederick Oakeley who had written nos. 883 and 924 on Catholic prisoners was suffering from bad eyesight (Oakeley to E. H. Thompson, Sept. 19, [1862], Healy Thompson Papers) and was working on his history of the Tractarians.

1047 The newly discovered Jewish catacomb at Rome, 397–418. **C. W. Russell.** Claimed in Russell to Wiseman, June 27 and 30, 1863, Wiseman Papers.

1048 The letters of S. Teresa, 419–457. **H. J. Coleridge.** Sutcliffe; attrib. in Russell, "Early Reviewers," p. 209.

1049 The dogmatic principle, 458–481. **W. G. Ward.** Manning's list; claimed by Ward, *Doctrinal Authority*, p. 101.

1050 The Catholic Congress of Malines, 482–493. **E. S. Purcell,** prob. C. W. Russell to Wiseman, June 30, 1863, Wiseman Papers, says Ward tells him he has an art. by Purcell as well as his own "Jewish catacomb," (no. 1047); Purcell was present at the Congress (Manning,

Life, I, 679); Purcell to E. H. Thompson, Dec. 12, 1864, Healy Thompson Papers, regrets trouble caused Thompson by his "papers," indicating earlier arts. in this series; on p. 491 the author speaks with pride of the Academia of the Catholic Religion, for whose costs Purcell lent money to Manning: see Boase.

1051 Historical notes of the Tractarian Movement (Part II), 494–508. **Frederick Oakeley.** Cf. no. 1040.

1052 Notices of books, 509–567. Pages 521–523 by **Patrick Murray**—claimed in his diary; pages 518–521 by **W. G. Ward**—cf. no. 1042.

1053 Foreign periodical literature, 568–582. **E. H. Thompson** and **Harriet Thompson.** Cf. no. 1043.

1053a Foreign events of Catholic interest, 583–612.

VOLUME 2 N.S., 54 O.S., JANUARY 1864

1054 Life and times of Dr. Blomfield, 1–23.

1055 Tourists and sight-seers in Rome, 23–57.

1056 Theological errors of the day: Brownson's *Review*, 58–95. **Patrick Murray.** Claimed in diary, Nov. 19, 1863.

1057 Gongora, 95–127.

1058 Music in its religious uses, 128–158. **James Burns,** prob. Both Gillow and Percy Fitzgerald, *Fifty Years of Catholic Life and Social Progress* (2 vols., 1901), I, 43, say James Burns, publisher of *DR* beginning with issue of July, 1863, wrote several arts. on music for it.

1059 Father Faber, 159–163. **H. E. Manning.** Repr. *Miscellanies*, I.

1060 Historical notes of the Tractarian Movement (Part III), 164–179. **Frederick Oakeley.** Signed.

1061 Theories of sensitive perception, 179–189. Signed: M.D.T.

1062 Notices of books, 190–237.

1063 Foreign periodical literature, 238–249. **E. H. Thompson** and **Harriet Thompson.** Cf. no. 1043.

1063a Foreign events of Catholic interest, 250–278. Unidentified. (Letter, p. 552, signed **Rowland Blennerhasset.**)

VOLUME 2 N.S., 54 O.S., APRIL 1864

1064 The "Union" movement, 279–312. **W. G. Ward,** prob. Pages 301–302 and ref. to editor's intro. note to no. 1040,

pp. 167–169, indicate authorship of Ward; the whole art. and its appendix reflect Ward's bitter hostility to "Unionism." (Appendix, p. 533 by **Ward**—by the author.)

1065 Father [Theobald] Mathew, 313–327.

1066 Slavery and the war in America, 328–362. **H. W. Wilberforce,** prob. This and no. 1110, both on slavery and the Civil War, are similar in their opposition to the South; both show close knowledge of American politics of the time; the author of no. 1110 quotes (p. 346n) a passage taken from p. 339 of this art.

1067 The Laureate [Tennyson] and his school, 363–385. **C. W. Russell?** The author has high praise for De Vere's introduction to the *Selections from the Poets* (cf. enthusiasm for De Vere in nos. 590, 762, and 999), including stress on religious office of poetry; reference to exaggerated praise of Tennyson, p. 364, parallels that in no. 1525, p. 462; on pp. 374–375 the author interjects an admiring notice of R. S. Hawker, a very minor poet, whom Russell praises again in no. 1579, p. 160; Matthew Russell, "Dr. Russell of Maynooth," *Irish Monthly*, 22(1894), 636, says Russell continued to contribute to almost every number, except towards the end.

1068 Renan's *Vie de Jesus*, 386–419. **H. J. Coleridge.** Sutcliffe; Russell, "Early Reviewers," p. 209.

1069 The Santiago catastrophe and its critics, 419–432.

1070 Spiritualism, 433–463. Signed: X.F.

1071 Science and the mystery of the blessed Eucharist, (Part I—no more published), 464–480. **T. F. Mathew.** Signed T.F.M.; attr. in Russell, "Early Reviewers," p. 209; Mathew to [?Bagshawe or Editor of *DR*], Apr. 11, 1863, Bagshawe Papers, offers art. with this precise title.

1072 Notices of books, 481–512. Pages 489–492 by **Matthew Russell**—Russell, "Early Reviewers," p. 210n.; pages 482–486, by **W. G. Ward,** prob.—cf. nos. 1042 and 1194.

1073 Our contemporaries [periodicals], 512–522. Edited and prob. largely written by **H. J. Coleridge.** E. H. Thompson to W. G. Ward, Nov. 25, 1864, Healy Thompson Papers, says "you entrusted 'Our Contemporaries' to him [Coleridge]."

1074 Foreign periodical literature, 523–532. **E. H. Thompson** and **Harriet Thompson.** Cf. no. 1043.

1074a Foreign events of Catholic interest, 534–554.

VOLUME 3 N.S., 55 O.S., JULY 1864

1075 The late judgment of the Privy Council, 1–26.

1076 Venn's *Life & Labours of S. Francis Xavier*, 27–64. **H. J. Coleridge.** Sutcliffe; Russell, "Early Reviewers," p. 210.

1077 Rome and the Munich Congress, 64–96. **W. G. Ward.** Largely repr. *Doctrinal Authority*; pp. 79–96 repr. *Doctrinal Decisions.* (Note, p. 217, by **W. G. Ward**—repr. *Doctrinal Decisions.*)

1078 Froude's *History of England*: Mary Stuart, 97–131. **C. W. Russell.** Russell, "Early Reviewers," p. 210; on p. 110 the author refers to having reviewed several years ago Mr. Mignet's *History of Mary Stuart*: see no. 655 by Russell, to which ref. is also made on pp. 113, 114, 118, 119.

1079 Garibaldi in England, 132–155.

1080 Newman's *Apologia Pro Vitâ Suâ*, 156–180. **H. J. Coleridge.** Sutcliffe.

1081 Historical notes of the Tractarian Movement (Part IV, concl.), 181–199. **Frederick Oakeley.** Signed.

1082 Foreign periodical literature: Dr. Döllinger and the Munich Congress (Part I), 200–217. **E. H. Thompson** and **Harriet Thompson.** Cf. no. 1043.

1083 Notices of books, 218–238. Pages 234–238 by **H. E. Manning?** or **William Roberts?**—this is a kind of supplement to no. 745 q.v.; pages 218–220 by **W. G. Ward**—repr. *Doctrinal Decisions.*

1084 Our contemporaries [periodicals], 239–251. **H. J. Coleridge**, prob. Cf. no. 1073.

VOLUME 3 N.S., 55 O.S., OCTOBER 1864

1085 The principles of '89 (Part I), 253–277. **Harriet Thompson.** W. G. Ward to E. H. Thompson, Jan. 3, 1865, Healy Thompson Papers, speaks of Mrs. Thompson's invaluable arts. on this subject; the attr. to E. H. Thompson in Oscott II no doubt reflects the fact that payment was made to him.

1086 The Christian schools of Alexandria (Part I), 278–310. **J. C. Hedley.** *Life*, pp. 64, 173–174, 220.

1087 Hedwige, Queen of Poland, 311–343.

1088 Surnames, in relation to the history of society, 344–371.

1089 University education for English Catholics, 372–401. **W. G. Ward.** Claimed in no. 1280, pp. 95–96; *Ward as Catholic*, p. 193n. (Appendix, pp. 520–

521, largely quotations from **Patrick Murray;** letter from the *Times*, pp. 521–522, by **John Francis Arundell**—signed Arundell of Wardour.)

1090 Christian art, 402–421. **E. I. Purbrick.** Attr. Russell, "Early Reviewers," p. 210; Oscott II.

1091 Outlines of the Gospel history, 421–454. **H. J. Coleridge.** Attr. *DR*, 12 n.s. (Apr. 1869), 496; Sutcliffe.

1092 Reformatory schools, 455–482. **R. J. Gainsford?** He had been a contributor in the first series, and had written a book with this title, 1857; he founded two reformatory schools, one of which, Market Weighton, is discussed in this art.; see Newman, *L&D*, XIV, 393n.

1093 Foreign periodical literature: Dr. Döllinger and the Munich Congress (Part II), 483–487. **E. H. Thompson** and **Harriet Thompson.** Cf. no. 1043.

1094 Notices of books, 488–508.

1095 Our contemporaries [periodicals], 508–519. **H. J. Coleridge,** prob. Cf. no. 1073.

VOLUME 4 N.S., 56 O.S., JANUARY 1865

1096 Holy Scripture in its Catholic aspects, 1–20.

1097 Rio's *Shakespeare*, 21–41. **J. C. Earle?** In a signed art., no. 1804, in 1882, Earle says on p. 34: "It has been shown by Mr. Rio, and in a former No. of this Review, that Shakespeare was a Catholic"; in no. 1804, signed by Earle, p. 34, and here on p. 22, Carlyle is cited as holding that Shakespeare was a Catholic.

1098 Extent of the Church's infallibility: the encyclical "Mirari Vos," 41–69. **W. G. Ward.** Pages 41–58, 68, 69 repr. *Doctrinal Decisions.*

1099 Madame de Maintenon, 70–107. **J. C. Earle,** prob. Oscott II; opening sentences of no. 1120, known to be by Earle, show he considered it as a companion-piece to this art.

1100 The Irish Church establishment, 107–125. Unidentified. Possibly by Edward Ryley since Ward wrote to Thompson on Dec. 11, [1864], Healy Thompson Papers, that they had better have Ryley's article which he thinks will make 18 sheets [sic], and Ryley wrote to Thompson on Dec. 14, ibid., saying he would do what was wanted "when the proofs come"; this is the only art. in this issue of 18 pp. (clearly the "sheets" was an inadvertence); in spite of refs. which seem to tie this art.

to no. 1013 by R. J. Gainsford, the style is much more polemic and rhetorical; Ryley, according to Boase, had worked with Wiseman on prison reform, wanted to bring Catholics back to Tory principles, and was a friend of Brougham's— see quotations from Brougham and Disraeli on pp. 122–124.

1101 The university question, 125–140. **W. G. Ward.** Attr. in *Ward as Catholic*, p. 193n; Frederick Oakeley to E. H. Thompson, Dec. 19, [1864], Healy Thompson Papers, says Ward tells him he will attack him in Jan. issue, as the author does here, pp. 125–133.

1102 Thiers, *Waterloo*, 141–170.

1103 The Belgian constitution and the Church, 171–192. **E. S. Purcell**, prob. Purcell to E. H. Thompson, Dec. 12, 1864, Healy Thompson Papers, refers to "my" Belgium art. (Note, pp. 581–582.)

1104 Cardinal Wiseman's sermons, 192–213. **H. E. Manning**, prob. Oscott II; no. 1107 begins with expression of joy at having closed last issue with account of Wiseman's mission in England (see here, p. 204).

1105 Foreign periodical literature: Dr. Döllinger and the Munich Congress (Part III), 214–226. **E. H. Thompson** and **Harriet Thompson.** Cf. no. 1043.

1106 Notices of books, 227–250. Pages 239–240, by **E. H. Thompson** or **Harriet Thompson**, prob.—W. G. Ward to Thompson, Dec. 11, 1864, Healy Thompson Papers, asks for notice of Mme. Mallac; pages 227–230, by **W. G. Ward,** prob.—cf. nos. 1042 and 1064; pages 230–234, also by **Ward**—H. J. Coleridge to E. H. Thompson, Dec. 15, 1864, Healy Thompson Papers, says he has asked Ward to insert in his notice of Manning the note which appears on p. 233.

1106a Foreign events of Catholic interest, 251–266.

VOLUME 4 N.S., 56 O.S., APRIL 1865

1107 Memorial of His Eminence Cardinal Wiseman, 267–278. **H. E. Manning.** Repr. *Miscellanies*, I.

1108 The principles of '89 (Part II, concl.), 279–302. **Harriet Thompson.** Cf. no. 1085.

1109 Recent Irish poetry, 302–328. **J. C. Hoey** and **Frances C. Hoey**, prob. Hoey notebook and Oscott II give "Hoey," but as in the case of the Bagshawes and the Healy Thompsons, the husband's name

was often the only one given, even for an art. actually written by the wife alone (see nos. 104 and 1085); the first part of this art. is a political discussion (cf. no. 1113), but the remainder is literary criticism, Mrs. Hoey's chief interest; C. A. Read, *Cabinet of Irish Literature,* 1880, IV, 253 refers to her as "a constant contributor to high class periodical literature, being at her best in such writings as a critic"; see also *BMCat., Temple Bar* (to be indexed in *Index* III), and *St. Paul's Magazine,* VIII [May 1871], 163–176; for a comparable collab., see no. 1301; during her husband's subeditorship, she prob. wrote most of the literary arts.—see nos. 1336, 1395, 1485, 1525 and others.

1110 Causes and objects of the war in America, 328–372. **H. W. Wilberforce.** Hoey notebook; Oscott II.

1111 Theiner's materials of Irish history, 372–395. **C. W. Russell.** Hoey notebook; cf. no. 371, to which detailed ref. is made here in opening paragraph.

1112 Consalvi's *Memoirs,* 396–423. **H. J. Coleridge?** Ward to E. H. Thompson, Jan. 3, 1865, Healy Thompson Papers, says April issue is full because of "Father Coleridge's unexpected return"; this is only unassigned art.; it reviews a pro-Jesuit author (Coleridge was a Jesuit).

1113 Wanted a policy for Ireland, 423–440. **J. C. Hoey.** Attr. by Russell, "Early Reviewers," p. 211; Hoey became associate editor in 1865, and treated contemporary politics with vigor (C. A. Read, *Cabinet of Irish Literature,* 1880, IV, 251–253); H. J. Coleridge to Healy Thompson, Dec. 17, 1864, Healy Thompson Papers, says "Ward writes as if Mr. Hoey were a great catch"; he was a barrister and journalist and wrote many of the political arts. in the Ward period on Italy, France, and Ireland as well as domestic affairs. (See *DR* no. 1650, p. 277, where Ward says Hoey had major responsibility for secular politics.)

1114 The Encyclical and Syllabus, 441–499. **W. G. Ward.** Claimed by Ward in *Ward as Catholic*, p. 281; pages 441–450, 498, 499 repr. *Doctrinal Decisions.*

1115 Text and translation of the Encyclical and Syllabus [embracing the principal errors of our time—censured by Pius IX], 500–529. **Pius IX.** Signed.

1116 Notices of books, 530–559. Pages 553–557, by **J. C. Earle**—Hoey notebook; pages 538–542, by **E. H. Thompson**—

Hoey notebook; pages 558–559, by **W. G. Ward?**—cf. no. 1121, which is an expanded review of the same book.

1116a Foreign events of Catholic interest, 560–581.

1117 Public school education, 1–43. Unidentified. (Appendix, 568–570, by **W. G. Ward** prob.—editor.)

1118 The Christian schools of Alexandria (Part II): Origen, 43–68. **J. C. Hedley.** *Life*, pp. 64, 220.

1119 The Celtic language and dialects, 69–87. Hoey notebook gives "B.D."; Oscott II.

1120 Madame Récamier and her friends, 88–121. **J. C. Earle.** Hoey notebook; Oscott II.

1121 Rome, unionism, and indifferentism, 121–173. **W. G. Ward.** Pages 121–132, 163–171 repr. *Doctrinal Decisions.*

1122 Proposed manual of English history, 173–189.

1123 Doctor Pusey's lectures on Daniel, 189–205. **W. G. Ward?** He constantly referred back to his own arts. as he does here on p. 192 to no. 1121; in the earlier art. he praises Pusey's lectures on Daniel, p. 160, as he does here (his seven-part attack on Pusey did not begin until Jan. 1866).

1124 The Mexican empire and the Canadian confederation, 206–226.

1124a Foreign events of Catholic interest, 227–245.

1125 Foreign periodical literature, 246–255. **E. H. Thompson** and **Harriet Thompson,** prob. Although this department did not appear in Apr. issue, prob. because it was crowded (see no. 1112), it was resumed in July and October, after which it no longer appeared during Ward's editorship.

1126 Notices of books, 256–280. Pages 257–258 by **William Clifford,** 1823–1893—intro. note; pages 258–259 by **W. G. Ward,** prob.—ref. to no. 1037 by Ward; pages 259–261 by **Ward**—headnote to no. 1163, and H. E. Manning to Ward, June 15, 1865, Ward letters, writes of "your review of the Bp. of Aquila"; pages 261–263 by **Ward**—pp. 262, 263 repr. *Doctrinal Decisions*; pages 268–270 by **Ward** —cf. no. 1128; page 279 by **Ward**— Manning to Ward, June 10, 1865, Ward letters, refers to Ward's notice of Dupanloup.

1127 The massacre of St. Bartholomew, 281–318. Unidentified. Possibly C. W. Russell, who was much interested in Catholic history; the author shows on p. 298n. that he was familiar with early *DR*, and on p. 311 accuses Froude, for whom Russell had little respect, of "whitewashing" historical figures.

1128 Mr. Oxenham and the *Dublin Review*, 319–351. **W. G. Ward.** Manning's list; Bayswater.

1129 Catholicism in Geneva (Part I), 352–375. Unidentified. (See no. 1147.)

1130 Doctrinal decrees of a pontifical congregation: The case of Galileo, 376–425. **W. G. Ward.** Repr. *Doctrinal Decisions.* (Appendix, vol. 6 n.s., pp. 260–267 by **W. G. Ward**—repr. *Doctrinal Decisions.*)

1131 *The Formation of Christendom* [by T. W. Allies], 425–453. **H. W. Wilberforce.** Repr. *The Church.*

1132 The Irish land question, 453–473. **J. C. Hoey,** prob. Cf. no. 1113; this is a more detailed treatment of a point raised by Hoey in that art. pp. 435–436.

1133 Calderwood and Mill upon Hamilton, 474–504. **R. E. Guy.** Signed R.E.G.; Oscott II gives "R. Guy, O.S.B."; see *BMCat* and *Benedictine Bibliog.* With a prefatory note by **W. G. Ward**—editor.

1133a Foreign events of Catholic interest, 505–516.

1134 Foreign periodical literature, 517–532. **E. H. Thompson** and **Harriet Thompson,** prob. Cf. no. 1125.

1135 Notices of books, 533–567. Pages 537–540 by **W. G. Ward**—cf. no. 1042; defense of *DR*; attack on Unionism.

1136 California and the Church, 1–35. **Herbert Vaughan.** J. G. Snead-Cox, *Life of Cardinal Vaughan* (1910), I, 153.

1137 The viceroys of Ireland [by J. T. Gilbert], 36–59. **C. W. Russell?** He had reviewed Gilbert's *History of Dublin* in no. 929 (Sept. 1859), which is here highly praised on pp. 36, 37; the art. is characterized by Russell's interest in and knowledge of Irish history.

1138 The foundress of the Faithful Companions of Jesus [Mme de Bonnault d'Houet], 59–78.

1139 Catholic instincts, 78–107.

1140 Cromwell's conquest and settlement of Ireland (Part I), 107–137.

1141 The papal allocution on freemasonry, 137–176. Unidentified. (Two letters, pp. 589–598, signed **William Lockhart**, with a reply by the author.)

1142 The new Parliament, 177–187. **J. C. Hoey**, prob. The art. deals with the treatment of Ireland by Parliament in 1866; on p. 183 the author refers back to his review of a pamphlet on Ireland in the April issue, no. 1113 by Hoey, and on p. 185 paraphrases a passage from p. 470 of no. 1132.

1143 Dr. Pusey's apology for Anglicanism, 188–239. **W. G. Ward.** Partly repr. *Doctrinal Authority* as "Historical Argument for the Church's Claims."

1144 Letter to Dr. Pusey by Mr. Allies, 239–259. **T. W. Allies.** Signed; repr. *Per crucem*, I.

1145 Notices of books, 268–296. Pages 268–271 by **Patrick Murray**—claimed in his diary, p. 112; pages 274–281, 281–288 by **W. G. Ward**, prob.—both notices are continuations of his controversy with Oxenham and with the *Union Review*.

VOLUME 6 N.S., 58 O.S., APRIL 1866

1146 Rome the civilizer of nations, 297–325. Unidentified. Possibly W. G. Ward, since the underlying theme is defence of Papal response to progress, particularly in science, and the author refers back on p. 320 to no. 1130 by Ward; Veuillot, one of the authors reviewed here, is referred to in no. 1263, p. 226, as "the leading opponent (in the press) of French 'liberal Catholicism,'" which would have made him doubly interesting to Ward.

1147 Catholicism restored in Geneva, 325–348.

1148 Christian political economy, 348–377.

1149 The Christian schools of Alexandria (Part III, concl.): Origen, 377–412. **J. C. Hedley.** *Life*, pp. 64, 220.

1150 Dr. Pusey's project of union, 412–449. **W. G. Ward.** Repr. *Doctrinal Authority*.

1151 Champagny on the Roman Empire, 449–485. **H. W. Wilberforce.** Repr. *The Church*.

1152 Signs of an Irish policy, 485–496. **J. C. Hoey**, prob. Oscott II with a ?; the author regrets lack of an Irish policy (cf. no. 1113), and pp. 485–486 imply that this is by same author.

1153 The Council of Florence, 496–541. **W. G. Ward.** Repr. *Doctrinal Authority*.

1154 Notices of books, 542–560. Pages 544–546 by **W. G. Ward**—claimed by him in *Devotional Essays*, p. 84n; pages 547–548 by **W. G. Ward**—repr. *Doctrinal Authority*, pp. 160–163; pages 548–555 (2 notices) by **W. G. Ward**, prob.—the first notice is part of his attack on E. B. Pusey, the second is a continuation of the controversy with the *Union Review*.

1154a Foreign events of Catholic interest, 561–588.

VOLUME 7 N.S., 59 O.S., JULY 1866

1155 *Julius Caesar*, by Napoleon III, 1–32. **H. W. Wilberforce?** Ref. back on p. 11 to our review of Champagny (no. 1151); same position taken about overriding importance of Christianity in Roman empire; Wilberforce was a major contributor to the *DR* under Ward.

1156 Canon Oakeley's *Lyra Liturgica*, 33–50. **C. W. Russell.** Russell, "Early Reviewers," pp. 211–212.

1157 Lecky's *History of Rationalism*, 51–79.

1158 F. Hyacinth Besson, 79–87.

1159 Irish writers on university education, 88–101. **W. G. Ward.** Manning's list; claimed by Ward, *Doctrinal Authority*, p. 2n.

1160 Interests of the Catholic poor, 101–115.

1161 The negro in Africa and the West Indies, 116–142. **H. W. Wilberforce**, prob. Start of no. 1169 links that art. closely with this.

1162 Dr. Pusey on Marian devotion, 142–199. **W. G. Ward.** Repr. *Devotional Essays* as "Catholic Devotion to our Blessed Lady."

1163 The Gaume controversy on classical studies, 200–228. **R. B. Vaughan.** Signed R.B.V.; Oscott II.

1164 Papal brief in favour of *La Civiltà Cattolica*, 229–233. **Pius IX.** Pope in 1866.

1165 Notices of books, 234–272. Pages 234–236, 240–246, 247–251 by **W. G. Ward**, prob.—cf. no. 1042; pages 236–237, 237–239 by **W. G. Ward**—partly repr. *Devotional Essays*.

VOLUME 7 N.S., 59 O.S., OCTOBER 1866

1166 S. Pius V., the father of Christendom, 273–304. Unidentified. Possibly C. W. Russell since art. reflects same interest in rehabilitation of Pius V as that shown in no. 1127, and quotes that art. here on p. 296; the author also uses de Falloux as a principal source here as in that art.

1167 Protestant proselytism in eastern lands, 305–331.

1168 Origen at Caesarea, 332–362. **J. C. Hedley.** Willson list; Oscott II; opens with definite link to nos. 1118, 1149.

1169 Jamaica, 362–414. **H. W. Wilberforce.** Attr. in *Ward as Catholic*, pp. 282–283.

1170 Pius IX and the *Civiltà Cattolica*, 414–432. **W. G. Ward.** Attr. in E. C. Butler, *Bishop Ullathorne* (1926), II, 41.

1171 Cromwell's conquest and settlement of Ireland (Part II), 433–454.

1172 Dr. Pusey on Marian doctrine: peace through the truth, 455–514. **W. G. Ward.** Largely repr. *Devotional Essays*. (Appendix, vol. 8 n.s., pp. 219–220, by **Ward**—Oscott II.)

1173 Notices of books, 515–551. Pages 519–523 by **W. G. Ward**—page 520 announces nos. 1177 and 1194 in some detail (both are Ward's); pages 523–526, 527–528, 533–538, 538–542 by **W. G. Ward,** prob.—cf. no. 1042; pages 528–533, by **W. G. Ward,** prob.—cf. no. 1042 (letter, vol. 8 n.s., pp. 253–254, by **William Lockhart**—signed; reply, p. 254, by **Ward**—as editor.)

VOLUME 8 N.S., 60 O.S., JANUARY 1867

1174 Dr. Whately, 1–25.

1175 The relations of St. Paul with St. Peter, 26–53. **W. G. Ward.** Repr. *Devotional Essays.*

1176 Mediaeval Manichaeism and the Inquisition, 53–82. **L. S. Ives.** Hoey notebook gives "Dr. Ives"; see *DAB*.

1177 Dr. Pusey on ecclesiastical unity, 83–118. **W. G. Ward.** Repr. *Doctrinal Authority.*

1178 Joan of Arc and her mission, 118–154.

1179 The *Directorium Anglicanum*, 155–164.

1180 Two criticisms on the *Dublin Review*, 164–172. **W. G. Ward.** Attr. in Casartelli, "Jubilee," pp. 264–265. (Note, pp. 493–495, presumably by **Ward.**)

1181 Dr. M'Cosh's *Intuitions of the Mind* and *Examination of Mill's Philosophy*, 172–191. **R. E. Guy.** Signed R.E.G.; editor's note, p. 172, assigns to author of no. 1133.

1182 The state of affairs [in Italy], 192–220. **J. C. Hoey,** prob. As sub-editor Hoey was almost entirely responsible not only for Irish but also for Continental political affairs; this is the first of a series of arts. dealing with the collapse of Napoleon

III and subsequent events—see nos. 1221 (the opening sentence of which suggests it is a continuation of this) and 1338, which is assigned to him in the Hoey notebook.

1183 Notices of books, 221–252. Pages 221–223, by **W. G. Ward,** prob.—cf. no. 1042.

VOLUME 8 N.S., 60 O.S., APRIL 1867

1184 Science, prayer, free will, and miracles, 255–298. **W. G. Ward.** Repr. *Essays on Theism*, II.

1185 English Catholic poor-schools, 299–315. **James Boone Rowe.** Hoey notebook gives "Father Rowe"; see *DR*, 28 n.s. (Jan. 1877), 250.

1186 New America [mainly on the Mormons], 316–348. **H. W. Wilberforce.** Hoey notebook.

1187 St. Cyril and the tumults of Alexandria, 349–381. **J. C. Hedley.** Hoey notebook; *Life*, pp. 64, 220.

1188 Catholic and party politics, 382–395. **W. H. Anderdon,** prob. Hoey notebook; Oscott II; assigned to W. G. Ward in Manning's list, but the list is not entirely reliable and the style very unlike Ward's.

1189 Mr. Ffoulkes on Christendom's divisions, 396–435. **David Lewis.** Hoey notebook gives "Lewis," Oscott II, "D. Lewis"; for man cited see Gorman; Manning's list assigns to Ward but Ward in effect denies authorship in the "Notice" preceding this issue, inserted before p. 254. (Letter, vol. 9 n.s., pp. 246–248, signed **Edmund S. Ffoulkes,** with reply, pp. 248–249 by **Lewis,** presumably.)

1190 Mary in the Gospels, 435–455. **W. G. Ward.** Repr. *Devotional Essays.* (Two letters, vol. 9 n.s., pp. 249–252, one quoted from *The Tablet*, signed "A Priest," the other to the Editor of the *DR* signed "J. B. M."—**John Brande Morris?**

1191 The Church and the Roman Empire, 456–481. **C. F. Audley.** Hoey notebook; Oscott II.

1192 The state of Ireland, 482–492. **J. C. Hoey.** Hoey notebook; Oscott II.

1193 Notices of books, 496–544. Pages 512–518 by **J. C. Hedley**—Hoey notebook; pages 541–543, 543 (DeBrett) by **J. C. Hoey**—Hoey notebook; pages 521–523 by **E. S. Keogh**—Hoey notebook; pages 538–541 by **Elizabeth Lockhart**—Hoey notebook; pages 496–500, 505–509, 527–529, 530–531 by **W. G. Ward,** prob.—cf. no. 1042.

VOLUME 9 N.S., 61 O.S., JULY 1867

1194 Dr. Pusey on papal prerogatives, 1–34. **W. G. Ward.** Repr. *Doctrinal Authority.*

1195 John Tetzel, 35–47.

1196 Lord Plunket's life and speeches, 48–79.

1197 The gods of the nations when Christ appeared (Part I), 80–109. **T. W. Allies.** Repr. *Formation of Christendom* (1865–1896), II.

1198 Archbishop Manning on England and Christendom, 110–125. **H. W. Wilberforce.** Hoey notebook; Oscott II.

1199 St. Jane Frances de Chantal, 125–154. **Elizabeth Lockhart.** Hoey notebook.

1200 F. Ryder and Dr. Ward, 154–162. **W. G. Ward.** Manning's list; Oscott II. (Letter inserted after p. 544 by **Ward**—title.)

1201 The Holy See and the Spanish Inquisition, 163–199. **L. S. Ives.** Hoey notebook; opening sentence links this closely with no. 1176.

1202 Irish questions, 200–207. **J. C. Hoey.** Oscott II; ref. back to this art. in no. 1212 by Hoey, p. 518; cf. evidence for no. 1113.

1203 Notices of books, 208–245. Pages 221–230 by **David Lewis**—cf. no. 1263; pages 210–213 by **W. G. Ward**, prob.—opening sentences are an editorial apologia; pages 213–214 by **W. G. Ward**, prob.—reference to Ryder controversy; pages 214–217 by **W. G. Ward**, prob.—cf. no. 1042.

VOLUME 9 N.S., 61 O.S., OCTOBER 1867

1204 Spiritism and modern devil-worship, 253–280. **P. A. Murray.** Diary for Aug. 11, 1867.

1205 Dr. Pusey on the Syllabus, 280–301. **W. G. Ward.** Claimed by Ward, *Doctrinal Authority*, p. 410n.

1206 Life of St. Aloysius Gonzaga, 301–333. **Aubrey De Vere.** Repr. *Essays on Poetry*, II as "A Saint."

1207 Minor doctrinal judgments, 333–381. **W. G. Ward.** Claimed by him in *Doctrinal Authority*, p. 438n.

1208 English Catholic university education, 381–440. **Herbert Vaughan.** Hoey notebook; Herbert Vaughan to Mgr. George Talbot, Oct. 10, 1867, Talbot Papers, English College, Rome, says he expects to be attacked for his art. on university education. The art. is attr. to R. W. R. Vaughan by *DNB* but in error.

1209 The first and second man [Adam and Christ] (Part I), 441–472. **T. W. Allies.** Repr. *Formation of Christendom* (1865–1896), II.

1210 The centenary [of Sts. Peter and Paul] of 1867, 473–482. **Sullivan.** Hoey notebook.

1211 Father Ryder's theological citations, 483–512. **W. G. Ward.** Ward to Baron von Hügel, July 16, [1876], at St. Andrews, claims this art.; Manning's list.

1212 An Irish session, 512–527. **J. C. Hoey.** Oscott II; attr. in Russell, "Early Reviewers," p. 213.

1213 Notices of books, 528–544. Pages 528–532, by **Patrick Murray** and **W. G. Ward** —Murray's diary, p. 112, gives "528–to bottom of page 529, ending France and Spain: the rest by Dr. Ward"; pages 539–543 by **C. W. Russell?**—De Rossi's excavations were a pet subject of his, cf. no. 1294; pages 535–536, by **W. G. Ward**, prob.—cf. no. 1042.

VOLUME 10 N.S., 62 O.S., JANUARY 1868

1214 Count de Montalembert's *Monks of the West*, 1–44. **H. W. Wilberforce.** Hoey notebook.

1215 Archbishop Manning on the Centenary [of St. Peter], 45–60. **W. G. Ward.** Claimed in *Doctrinal Authority*, p. 28.

1216 St. Thomas of Canterbury (Part I), 60–84. **Frances Mary Ward.** Repr. *Biographical Sketch of St. Thomas of Canterbury*, 1880, as by "Mrs. Ward"; attr. to Mrs. W. G. Ward in *Tablet*, Aug. 13, 1898, p. 265.

1217 Doctrinal Apostolic letters, 84–130. **W. G. Ward.** *Ward as Catholic*, p. 184n; Ward quotes pp. 129–130 as his own in *Doctrinal Authority*, p. 27n.

1218 Popular education in England, 131–165. **Herbert Vaughan.** Hoey notebook; repr. under his name, 1868.

1219 Tizzani on St. Cyprian, 165–176. **J. C. Hedley.** Hoey notebook; *Life*, pp. 64, 220.

1220 The second man [Christ] verified in history (Part II), 177–210. **T. W. Allies.** Note on p. 177 identifies this as a continuation of no. 1209 by Allies.

1221 Rome and the Revolution, 210–223. **J. C. Hoey.** Hoey notebook. Opening sentence strongly suggests this is a continuation of no. 1182.

1222 Notices of books, 224–278. Hoey notebook assigns these to "Mr. [David] Lewis, Dr. [Patrick] Murray, Fr. [E. S.] Keogh, and Mr. [Edward] Ryley." Pages 264–269 by **James Burns**, prob.—see evidence for no. 1058; this art. advocates, as does no. 1058, the use of both plain chant and ornamental music; see also no. 1249, where this notice and no. 1232 are referred to; pages 245–251, by **Murray**—Diary, pp. 55–56, 56, 112; pages 235–237 by **W. G. Ward**, prob.—referred to in no. 1289, p. 299; pages 269–274 by **W. G. Ward**—continuation of controversy in no. 1207.

1223 Roman documents on a philosophical controversy in Belgium [bearing on no. 1222, pp. 237–240], 279–290. (Letter, pp. 569–582, signed Vindex, with a brief introduction, apparently by **Ward**; answer to Vindex, vol. 11 n.s., pp. 295–306 signed The Writer of "Kleutgen versus Vindex"; letter, vol. 12 n.s., pp. 532–536, from four Louvain professors.)

VOLUME 10 N.S., 62 O.S., APRIL 1868

1224 The Duke of Wellington's *Despatches*, 291–319. **J. C. Hoey.** Hoey notebook.

1225 The witness of heretical bodies to Mariology, 320–361. **W. G. Ward.** Oscott II; Russell, "Early Reviewers," p. 214, assumes this is by Ward; sounds very like him.

1226 First age of the martyr Church, 362–395. **T. W. Allies.** Repr. *Formation of Christendom* (1865–1896), II.

1227 S. Jerome, 395–430. **J. C. Hedley.** Hoey notebook; Willson list; attr. by Barry, *Memories*, p. 135.

1228 The ritualists, 430–458. **H. W. Wilberforce.** Hoey notebook. (Note, p. 568.)

1229 S. Thomas of Canterbury (Part II, concl.), 458–489. **Frances Mary Ward.** Cf. no. 1216.

1230 S. Leo's dogmatic letter [in A.D. 449], 489–497. **W. G. Ward.** Manning's list; Bayswater.

1231 The case of Ireland before Parliament, 498–518. **J. C. Hoey.** Hoey notebook; ref. back, p. 508, to no. 1113.

1232 Notices of books, 519–568. Pages 540–541 by **James Burns**, prob.—see evidence for no. 1058; claimed in opening sentence by author of no. 1249; pages 523–527, 543–547 by **W. G. Ward**—cf. no. 1042, and nos. 1235 and 1251 respectively; pages 564–565, 566–567, 567–568 by **W. G. Ward**—part of his controversy with Ryder: see vol. 11 n.s., p. 200n.

VOLUME 11 N.S., 63 O.S., JULY 1868

1233 Dr. Smith on the Pentateuch, 1–39. **T. G. Law**, prob. Hoey notebook; included in "Bibliography" in Law's *Essays*.

1234 *Le Récit d'une Soeur; Souvenirs de Famille* [de la Ferronnays], 38–71. **H. W. Wilberforce.** Hoey notebook.

1235 The Irish disestablishment, 72–86. **W. G. Ward.** Hoey notebook; Bayswater.

1236 Glastonbury, 86–117. **W. H. Anderdon.** Hoey notebook.

1237 Female life in prison, 117–150. **Elizabeth Lockhart.** Hoey notebook.

1238 Rio's *Christian Art*, 150–173. **C. F. Audley.** Hoey notebook.

1239 National tendencies and the duties of Catholics, 173–199. **Herbert Vaughan.** Hoey; repr. under his name, 1868.

1240 Mr. Renouf on Pope Honorius, 200–233. **W. G. Ward.** Manning's list; see no. 1261 for reprint.

1241 Notices of books, 234–294. Pages 248–249, 249–250 by **Patrick Murray**—Diary, p. 112; pages 235–237, 246–247, 247–248 by **W. G. Ward**, prob.—cf. no. 1042; pages 243–244 by **W. G. Ward**—the controversy with Ryder, see above, p. 200n; pages 250–253, unidentified (letter, vol. 13 n.s., pp. 512–514, signed The Writer of the Notice on Dr. Melia.)

1242 In correspondence: On church music, 307–315, signed **Frederick Oakeley**; On Father Ryder, 315–316, by **T. F. Knox** —signed F. Knox, with title "Superior of the London Oratory"; see *DNB*.

VOLUME 11 N.S., 63 O.S., OCTOBER 1868

1243 Dr. O'Brien on justifying faith, its nature and effects, 317–363. **P. A. Murray.** Diary for Aug. 14, 1868, quoted in Russell, "Early Reviewers," p. 208.

1244 The Master of the Rolls' Irish publications, 364–373. **C. W. Russell?** Reference on p. 366n to no. 1111; a hostile ref. to J. A. Froude on p. 367, which reflects Russell's attitude.

1245 Cartwright, *On Papal Conclaves*, 374–391.

1246 The present and future of Oxford University, 391–425. Unidentified. In no. 1280, pp. 108–109, W. G. Ward claims "an extremely small portion" of this and adds that the facts on pp. 424–425 were furnished by a convert "whose Oxford career is quite recent." (See nos. 1273 and 1280.)

1247 Father Bottalla on papal supremacy, 426–440. **W. G. Ward.** Manning's list; Bayswater.

1248 The case of St. Liberius, 441–455. **J. C. Hedley.** *Life*, pp. 64, 179, 220. Oscott II seems to give to W. G. Ward but probably means 1247.

1249 Church music and church choirs (Part I), 455–486. **James Burns**, prob. See evidence for no. 1058.

1250 St. Paula, 486–500. Unidentified. Possibly J. C. Hedley, to whom it is attr. in Oscott II with a "?."

1251 The coming Council, 500–527. **W. G. Ward.** Manning's list.

1252 Apostolic letters related to the Council, 528–537. **Pius IX.** Signed.

1253 Notices of books, 538–568. Pages 546–549 by **W. G. Ward**, prob.—cf. nos. 1042 and 1261; pages 555–556 by **W. G. Ward** —see *Essays on Theism*, II, 200.

1254 Correspondence: The *Month* on church choirs, a letter to the editor, 568–574. **Frederick Oakeley.** Signed F. Oakeley, his usual signature.

VOLUME 12 N.S., 64 O.S., JANUARY 1869

1255 [N.W.] Senior's Irish voyages, 1–27.

1256 Theories on development of the faith, 28–70. **W. G. Ward**, prob. H. J. Coleridge to E. H. Thompson, Apr. 6 [1869], Healy Thompson Papers, refers to Ward's note on p. 47 of his Jan. number.

1257 *The Jesuits in Canada* [by Francis Parkman], 70–86.

1258 Principles of Catholic higher education, 86–106. **W. G. Ward.** Manning's list; Bayswater. (See nos. 1273 and 1280.)

1259 The Church and Napoleon I, 107–139. **H. W. Wilberforce.** Repr. *The Church.* (See nos. 1349 and 1372.)

1260 Church music and church choirs (Part II, concl.), 140–172. **James Burns**, prob. Cf. no. 1249.

1261 The orthodoxy of Pope Honorius, 173–202. **W. G. Ward.** Repr. under his name in *The Condemnation of Pope Honorius*, 1879.

1262 Ireland and the new ministry, 203–211. **Cashel Hoey.** Oscott II; cf. no. 1113, which is cited here, p. 203n.

1263 Notices of books, 212–268. Pages 217–218, 223–224. by **W. G. Ward**, prob.— cf. no. 1042, and for the second, also cf. nos. 1130, 1272; pages 218–220, 227–228,

by **W. G. Ward**, prob.—cf. nos. 1042, 1678, and 1293 respectively; p. 226, by **Ward**, prob.—H. J. Coleridge to E. H. Thompson, Apr. 6, [1869], Healy Thompson Papers, refers to Ward's blunder in this notice; pages 252–257 by **W. G. Ward** and **David Lewis**—repr. in Ward, *Strictures on Mr. Ffoulkes's Letter to Archbishop Manning*, 1869, where Ward, p. 4, assigns pp. 255, next to last paragraph, to 257 through paragraph ending "the Catholic Faith" to author of no. 1189 and the notice of Ffoulkes in no. 1203; pages 251–252, unidentified (letter from **A. P. Stanley** with reply signed **Alexius Mills**, pp. 512–517; second letter by **Mills**, vol. 13 n.s., pp. 527–530.)

VOLUME 12 N.S., 64 O.S., APRIL 1869

1264 Mr. Ffoulkes's *Letter to Archbishop Manning*, 269–308. **W. G. Ward.** Repr. under his name as *Strictures on Mr. Ffoulkes's Letter to Archbishop Manning*, 1869.

1265 Father Newman's Oxford *Parochial Sermons*, 309–330. **H. W. Wilberforce.** Newman to H. W. Wilberforce, Apr. 1869, Wilberforce Mss. at Georgetown University, thanks him for this review.

1266 S. John Damascene, 331–361. **J. C. Hedley.** *Life*, pp. 64, 220.

1267 Catholic controversies, 361–384. **W. G. Ward.** Manning's list; Ward claims it, *Doctrinal Authority*, p. 545.

1268 The convent case, 385–398.

1269 Father Perez and Mr. Longfellow's *Dante*, 399–425.

1270 Ritualistic divinity and law, 425–451. **P. A. Murray** and **H. William Wilberforce**, prob. Murray's diary for Mar. 28, 1869, which is quoted in Russell, "Early Reviewers," p. 208, shows he wrote pp. 425–439; note in diary, p. 111, assigns pp. 439–451 to "William Wilberforce"; since the philanthropist died in 1833, he almost certainly meant the man cited, who was writing for the *DR*; Bayswater gives only "Dr. Murray."

1271 Mr. Gladstone's Irish policy, 452–464. **J. C. Hoey**, prob. He wrote many of the arts. on Irish politics at this period (cf. nos. 1113, 1152, 1192, and 1262); Oscott II.

1272 Notices of books, 465–511. Pages 476–481, 497–500, 500–501 by **W. G. Ward**, prob.—cf. no. 1042.

1273 Correspondence: Catholic higher education [a letter bearing on *DR* nos. 1246 and 1258], 512–529 signed **John Gillow;** repr. with same title, 1869, with a comment, 529, by **W. G. Ward,** author of no. 1258 and some of no. 1246 (letters, vol. 13 n.s., pp. 246–260, signed **Frederick Oakeley,** see no. 1287; pp. 515–527, by **John Gillow**—signed **J. Gillow.**)

1274 Ecclesiastical documents, 530–536.

VOLUME 13 N.S., 65 O.S., JULY 1869

1275 The early Irish Church, 1–32. **R. J. Gainsford.** Hoey notebook; repr. under his name as *The Religion of St. Patrick and the Ancient Irish,* 1869.

1276 Authority of the Scholastic philosophy, 33–47. **W. G. Ward.** Repr. *Doctrinal Authority.* (Corrigendum, p. 531.)

1277 *The Ring and the Book,* 48–62. **John Doherty.** Hoey notebook and Russell, "Early Reviewers," pp. 214–215, give "Rev. J. Doherty"; see *BMCat* for prob. first name.

1278 Mill, On Liberty, 62–75. **Edward Lucas,** prob. Hoey notebook lists "E. Lucas" after "Doherty" and before "Cruikshank"; Russell, "Early Reviewers," p. 214, gives this to Ward, but surely not his style.

1279 The suppression of Italian monasteries, 76–87. **A. P. J. Cruikshank.** Hoey notebook lists "Rev. A. Cruikshank" after Lucas; cf. similar interest in no. 1439 known to be his; Russell, "Early Reviewers," p. 215, assigns to Lucas but see no. 1278; Cruikshank was himself a monk; see Gorman.

1280 Misunderstandings on Catholic higher education, 88–109. **W. G. Ward.** Manning's list; Bayswater; opens with close link to no. 1258.

1281 Life of Father Faber, 109–143. **H. W. Wilberforce.** Hoey notebook; Russell, "Early Reviewers," pp. 214–215. (Note, pp. 531–532, by **H. W. Wilberforce**—signed The Writer of the Article in the *Dublin* on F. Faber.)

1282 Philosophical axioms, 144–169. **W. G. Ward.** Manning's list; Russell, "Early Reviewers," p. 214; claimed in *NC* 3 (1878), 543n.

1283 The revolution in Spain, 169–180. **Herbert Vaughan.** Hoey notebook; Russell, "Early Reviewers," pp. 214–215.

1284 A glance at Catholic home politics, 180–184. **J. C. Hoey.** Hoey notebook; Oscott II.

1285 Roman documents, 185–197.

1286 Notices of books, 198–245. Pages 214–215, by **C. W. Russell,** prob.—he reviewed books noticed here in nos. 1303 and 1294; pages 231–235, by **W. G. Ward,** prob.—cf. nos. 1042 and 1297, pp. 496–499; pages 235–236, by **W. G. Ward**—continues the controversy of no. 1280 with the *Month;* page 237, by **W. G. Ward,** prob.—he starts off no. 1289, with ref. to this notice; pages 238–242, by **W. G. Ward**—cf. no. 1042; pages 216–222 by **H. W. Wilberforce,** prob.—he reviewed book noticed here in no. 1291.

1287 Correspondence: On a liberal education in its bearing on mental discipline and culture [a letter to the Editor], 246–260. **Frederick Oakeley.** Signed. (Letter to the *Tablet,* p. 531, signed **Frederick Oakeley.**)

VOLUME 13 N.S., 65 O.S., OCTOBER 1869

1288 The religious tendencies of India, 261–296. **H. L. Harrison.** Hoey notebook gives "Mr. Harrison"; Russell, "Early Reviewers," p. 207, gives initials; man cited spent most of his life in India; see Boase.

1289 Psychologism and ontologism, 297–318. **W. G. Ward,** prob. Hoey notebook; opening remarks and many refs. to Kleutgen throughout, link this to nos. 1276 and 1282, both by Ward; in no. 1360, Ward pretty clearly refers to this art. as his.

1290 *The Ladder of Perfection* [by Walter Hilton], 319–328. **R. W. Bede Vaughan.** Hoey.

1291 The Gallican Assembly of 1682, 328–361. **H. W. Wilberforce.** Repr. *The Church.*

1292 Mr. Trollope's last Irish novel [*Phineas Finn*], 361–377. **J. C. Hoey,** perhaps with collaboration of **Frances Hoey.** Hoey notebook gives only Hoey, but the combination of political and literary criticism suggests a joint authorship as in no. 1109.

1293 Catholic controversy, 377–392. **W. G. Ward.** Carries on his controversy with the *Month:* cf. no. 1267, discussed here, pp. 385 ff.; and no. 1280.

1294 Subterranean Rome, 393–421. **C. W. Russell.** Hoey notebook; this is a subject in which Russell had been much interested; see nos. 868, and 748, among others.

1295 Explicit and implicit thought, 421–442.

W. G. Ward. Manning's list; repr. *Essays on Theism* II.

1296 The landlord and tenant question in Ireland (Part I), 443–468. **J. C. Hoey,** prob. Cf. no. 1132; attr. by Russell, "Early Reviewers," p. 215, with a "probably"; Oscott II.

1297 Notices of books, 469–511. Page 482 by **Edward Redmond?**—see no. 1335 on the same subject by him, in which there is ref., p. 395n., to this notice; pages 469–474, 477–480 by **W. G. Ward,** prob.—cf. no. 1042, and nos. 1305 and 1346 respectively; pages 485–491, by **W. G. Ward,** prob.—cf. no. 1042; pages 496–499 by **W. G. Ward**—letter to William Maskell, Oct. 2, 1869, BM Add. MS. 37,824.

VOLUME 14 N.S., 66 O.S., JANUARY 1870

1298 The theory of denominational education, 1–13; Prospects of legislation on poor schools, 13–27. Pages 1–13 by **W. G. Ward,** prob. On page 2 the author refers to the points made in no. 1295, and adds the following note: "We incorporate here and there in this article a few sentences from its predecessor," showing that he regards this as a continuation; the art. reflects Ward's concern with education; the remainder of the art. may have been written by someone else.

1299 Rome, 28–56. **A. P. J. Cruikshank.** Hoey notebook.

1300 The English Protestant Marriage Law, 56–78.

1301 Mr. Aubrey de Vere's *Irish Odes*, 79–95. **J. C. Hoey** and **Frances Hoey,** prob. Cf. no. 1109 and 1292, where there was a similar combination of a brief political discussion followed by literary comments; two refs. back to no. 1109.

1302 Father Faber's work in the Church, 95–123.

1303 Mary Queen of Scots—the casket papers, 123–164. **C. W. Russell.** Attr. by Matthew Russell, "Early Reviewers," p. 215; opens with references to nos. 655 and 1078, both by Russell.

1304 The landlord and tenant question in Ireland (Part II, concl.), 165–184. **J. C. Hoey.** Cf. no. 1296.

1305 Infallibility and the Council, 184–224. **W. G. Ward.** Oscott II; Bayswater gives "? W. G. Ward"; opening link with no. 1251; references to other Ward arts. on p. 212n; referred to in text, no. 1512, p. 100; but p. 210n. shows that someone else contributed a few paragraphs.

1306 Notices of books, 225–298. Page 246 (Janus) by **Edward Redmond?**—he is author of no. 1335, in which he refers to his promise in this notice to deal with the Assumption; pages 225–227 by **W. G. Ward**—repr. *Devotional Essays*; pages 249–257, 257–259, 296–297 by **W. G. Ward,** prob.—cf. no. 1042, and other arts. by Ward.

VOLUME 14 N.S., 66 O.S., APRIL 1870

1307 Janus and false brethren, 299–312. **W. G. Ward.** Manning's list; Bayswater.

1308 Indian theism, 313–346. **H. L. Harrison,** prob. Opens with close link to no. 1288; same general topic.

1309 Fra Paolo Sarpi, 347–371. **J. C. Hedley.** Attr. in *Life*, p. 220; Willson list.

1310 Mr. Renouf's reply on Pope Honorius, 372–402. **W. G. Ward.** Repr. under his name; see no. 1261.

1311 Dr. Molloy on geology and revelation, 403–417. **P. A. Murray.** Claimed in his diary, Mar. 8, 1870, p. 80; also see p. 111.

1312 Mr. Tennyson's Arthurian poems, 418–429.

1313 The Ministerial Education Bill, 430–450.

1314 Is Ireland irreconcilable? 451–481. **J. C. Hoey.** Attr. and partially repr. "with permission of the author" in Charles A. Read, *Cabinet of Irish Literature* (4 vols., 1880), IV, 251–253.

1315 Controversies on the Council, 481–497. **W. G. Ward.** Oscott II; references to no. 1305.

1316 Roman documents, 497–522.

1317 Notices of books, 523–573. Pages 523–534 (4 notices) by **W. G. Ward**—cf. no. 1042; pages 537–542 by **H. W. Wilberforce?**—no. 1337 is a longer review of same book and refers to this notice.

VOLUME 15 N.S., 67 O.S., JULY 1870

1318 Protestant London, 1–26. **H. W. Wilberforce?** In no. 1331, p. 294, Wilberforce speaks of our having recently introduced to our readers the book reviewed here; and a note cites this art.; on p. 21 the author implies that he frequently attended services at the London Oratory and since Wilberforce had written with enthusiasm of Father Faber, he probably did attend services there (in his art. on convents, no. 1331, Wilberforce particularly defends the Oratorians, pp. 291–295).

1319 Chronicle of Evesham Abbey, 26–56. **David Lewis.** Attr. Russell, "Early Reviewers," p. 215.

1320 The authorship of the Epistle to the Hebrews, 57–85.

1321 Memoirs of Madame de Lafayette and Madame de Montagu, 85–109. **Elizabeth Lockhart.** Oscott II; Gillow, IV, 298.

1322 Dr. Lee on Anglican orders, 110–122.

1323 The Education Bill, 122–155.

1324 *Lothair* [by Disraeli], 156–178. **J. C. Hoey** and **Frances C. Hoey?** Cf. evidence for no. 1109.

1325 The Land Bill and the Lords, 178–185. **J. C. Hoey,** prob. Author speaks of no. 1314 as our previous art. on Gladstone, also cf. no. 1296.

1326 The Council, 186–207. **W. G. Ward.** Manning's list.

1327 Dogmatic constitution of the Catholic faith, 208–223. Promulgated by the Vatican Council.

1328 Brief addressed by the Holy Father to Dr. Ward, 224. **Pius IX.** Signed. [Translation, p. 509.]

1329 Roman documents, 225–235. Pages 225–231 letter signed by **Cardinal Giacomo Antonelli.**

1330 Notices of books, 236–269. Pages 244–246, 254 by **Patrick Murray**—Diary, p. 112; pages 236–237 by **W. G. Ward,** prob.—cf. no. 1042.

1330a Note concerning Mary Queen of Scots, 270, by **C. W. Russell,** prob. He was much interested in this subject; see nos. 655 and 1078.

VOLUME 15 N.S., 67 O.S., OCTOBER 1870

1331 The Convent Committee, 271–299. **H. W. Wilberforce.** Hoey notebook.

1332 Father Lopez on the Irish Trinitarians, 299–318. **M. W. O'Reilly.** Hoey notebook.

1333 The American Church, 319–355. **T. W. M. Marshall.** Hoey notebook.

1334 Lacordaire and the conferences of Notre Dame, 356–393. **J. C. Hedley.** Hoey notebook; *Life,* p. 220.

1335 The Assumption of the Blessed Virgin Mary, an Apostolical tradition, 393–430. **Edward Redmond.** Hoey notebook; Russell, "Early Reviewers," p. 215.

1336 Jane Austen and her novels, 430–457. **Frances Cashel Hoey.** Hoey notebook; Russell, "Early Reviewers," p. 215.

1337 The unity of the Church, 457–478.

W. H. Wilberforce. Hoey notebook; attr. Ward, *Doctrinal Authority,* p. 354.

1338 The fall of the French Empire, 479–495. **J. C. Hoey.** Hoey notebook; Oscott II; this art. exhibits attitudes which characterize the whole series on French politics, beginning with no. 1182, namely scorn of Napoleon and his generals, except Marshal MacMahon, for whom there is high praise, hostility to masonry, and the view that the present disaster is a visitation of God upon a licentious and atheist nation.

1338a First dogmatic constitution of the Church of God, 496–507. Promulgated by the Vatican Council. Translation by **J. E. Wallis,** 1821–1888, prob.—attr. in Russell, "Early Reviewers," p. 215.

1339 Notices of books, 510–539.

VOLUME 16 N.S., 68 O.S., JANUARY 1871

1340 Pius IX and the revolution, 1–36. **J. C. Hoey,** prob. This art. is linked with nos. 1182 and 1338 in that it traces the history of the attacks on the Papacy from 1848 until the current collapse of the French Empire.

1341 Grignon de Montfort and his devotion, 37–57. **W. G. Ward.** Partly repr. *Devotional Essays.* (Appendix, 448–458, by **Ward.**)

1342 Dean Stanley on Westminster Abbey, 58–84.

1343 Champagny's *Caesars of the Third Century,* 85–111. **H. W. Wilberforce.** Repr. *The Church.*

1344 *Life and Labours of St. Thomas of Aquin* [by R. B. Vaughan, Vol. I], 111–138. **J. C. Hedley.** *Life,* pp. 220–221. (See no. 1449.)

1345 The Erckmann-Chatrian novels, 138–170. **Frances C. Hoey,** prob. She was a trans. of many French works, and in 1871 trans. *The Outbreak of the Great French Revolution* by the above authors.

1346 The definition of Papal Infallibility, 171–201. **W. G. Ward.** Manning's list; Bayswater.

1347 Notices of books, 202–252. Pages 203–205 by **A. P. J. Cruikshank,** prob.—ref. on p. 204 to no. 1299 by him, great stress upon "devotions" would reflect Cruikshank's interest in saints (see no. 1391), religious symbolism and poetical prose style both to be found in no. 1299; pages 216–219, unidentified (letter, 514–515, signed **William Maskell,** with answer, presumably by the reviewer); page 202 by **Pius IX**—papal decree "Urbis et Orbis"; page 211 by **W. G. Ward**—cf. no. 1042; pages 245–250 unidentified; almost certainly by the author of no. 1393, who refers to it there, p. 360n., and refers to Blunt (author noticed here), pp. 356n., 357n., 358, 359, 361, 362.

VOLUME 16 N.S., 68 O.S., APRIL 1871

1348 Certitude in religious assent [on Newman's *Grammar of Assent*], 253–274. **W. G. Ward.** Repr. *Essays on Theism,* II. (Reply, vol. 18 n.s., pp. 223–226, presumably by **Ward,** to attack in *Fraser's Magazine* for Jan. 1872, pp. 23–42.)

1349 Pius VII and Napoleon I, 275–302. **H. W. Wilberforce.** Repr. *The Church.* (See nos. 1259 and 1372.)

1350 *The Priest on the Mission* [by Frederick Oakeley], 302–315.

1351 Two English novelists: Dickens and Thackeray, 315–350. **Frances Hoey,** prob. She was contributing arts. on literary figures at this time; she had come to London originally with an introduction to Thackeray (see *DNB*); she wrote on Dickens in *Temple Bar.*

1352 Copernicanism and Pope Paul V, 351–368. **W. G. Ward.** Claimed by him in *Essays on Theism,* II, 170n.

1353 *The See of Rome in the Middle Ages,* 368–385.

1354 The Brehon Law of Ireland, 385–411.

1355 Devotion to St. Joseph, 412–427. **A. P. J. Cruikshank,** prob. This art. is considered by its author as a development of a notice by Cruikshank, no. 1347, in the previous issue; like that notice it constantly reiterates the word "devotion" and repeatedly stresses the harmony and proportion in all to do with the Church; the style is characterized by religious symbolism and poetic prose.

1356 Paris and France, 428–447. **J. C. Hoey,** prob. This is another of the series on the fall of the Second Empire (cf. no. 1182); characterized by praise of Marshal MacMahon, pp. 431, 433, and statement that best policy for France is restoration of Comte de Chambord, p. 447, both of which attitudes are repeated in later arts. in the series: see nos. 1387 and 1450.

1357 Roman documents, 459–472.

1358 Notices of books, 473–513. Pages 473–

474, 476–478, 487–490, 490–492 by **W. G. Ward,** prob.—cf. no. 1042.

VOLUME 17 N.S., 69 O.S., JULY 1871

1359 Evolution and faith, 1–40. **J. C. Hedley.** Attr. in *Ward as Catholic,* pp. 405–406; repr. *Evolution.*

1360 The rule and motive of certitude, 40–66. **W. G. Ward.** Attr. in *Ward as Catholic,* p. 320; repr. *Essays on Theism,* I.

1361 Dr. Hampden and Anglicanism, 66–108. **H. W. Wilberforce.** Attr. in Newman to Wilberforce, Aug. 4, 7, and Sept. 12, 1871, Wilberforce MSS., Georgetown University.

1362 The fall of Paris, 109–122. **J. C. Hoey,** prob., perhaps with collab. of **Frances Hoey.** This carries on the series on fall of Second Empire begun in no. 1182, q.v., remaking many of the same points; that Mrs. Hoey may have collaborated is suggested by a more literary and somewhat more moralistic tone than that characterizing the earlier arts.; she had been in Paris on Easter Day, 1871, whence she returned next day with news of the Commune: see *DNB.*

1363 The opinions of Joseph de Maistre, 122–140.

1364 Galileo and the Pontifical congregations, 140–169. **W. G. Ward.** Claimed by him, *Doctrinal Authority,* p. 477n.

1365 The case of Louise Lateau, 170–179.

1366 Berkeley's life and works, 180–211.

1367 The jubilee of Pius IX, 212–218.

1368 Notices of books, 219–257. Pages 251–254 by **Frances C. Hoey,** prob.—she had reviewed the 1st ed. of *Jane Austen* in no. 1336; pages 223–224 by **W. G. Ward?** —his special topic and logistic form; page 237 by **W. G. Ward**—cf. no. 1042.

1369 Father Franzelin on the subject and object of infallibility [a translation], 258–268. **J. B. Franzelin.** Title and p. 223 of this issue.

VOLUME 17 N.S., 69 O.S., OCTOBER 1871

1370 Oxford, as it is and as it was, 269–285.

1371 Mr. Mill's denial of necessary truth, 285–318. **W. G. Ward.** Manning's list; repr. *Essays on Theism,* I.

1372 Pius VII at Savona and Fontainebleau, 318–360. **H. W. Wilberforce.** Repr. *The Church.* (See nos. 1259 and 1349.)

1373 Reply by Father Bottalla to Mr. Renouf (No. I), 361–377. **Paul Bottalla.** Title; Sutcliffe.

1374   Oppression of Catholics in Switzerland, 378–383.

1375   The Archbishop of Westminster [Manning] on the evils of the day, 384–402.

1376   The basilica of San Clemente, 402–420. Unidentified. Possibly C. W. Russell, who had always been interested in Roman ruins and in Rossi's researches, one of whose books is listed at head of this art.

1377   The Roman question, 421–446.

1378   The International Society [L'Internationale], 447–464. **J. C. Hoey,** prob. This series of arts. on the collapse of Second Empire frequently attacks secret societies and the Internationale, particularly singling out Mazzini and Cluseret, as here on pp. 453, 454 and 459 (cf. no. 1356, pp. 428–429 and no. 1362, p. 120).

1379   On the folly of the war waged by politicians against the dogma of Papal Infallibility: translated from the *Civiltà Cattolica*, 465–474.

1380   Notices of books, 475–523. Pages 495–496 by **A. P. J. Cruikshank,** prob.—referred to in no. 1391 by Cruikshank; pages 482–484 by **W. G. Ward,** prob.—his special topic of papal infallibility, and cf. no. 1042.

VOLUME 18 N.S., 70 O.S., JANUARY 1872

1381   Liberalism religious and ecclesiastical, 1–24. **W. G. Ward.** Pages 1–15 repr. *Doctrinal Authority,* where that is called first portion of his art.

1382   Nature and the poets, 25–44. **N. Sinnott?** Oscott II.

1383   Mr. Mill on the foundation of morality, 44–76. **W. G. Ward.** Manning's list; repr. *Essays on Theism* I.

1384   Fictions of the future [imaginative creations of future societies], 76–103.

1385   Imperial and republican diplomacy in France from 1866 to 1870, 103–135.

1386   The world turned atheist: how it has become so, 135–168. **P. A. Murray.** Diary, p. 111, quoted in Russell, "Early Reviewers," p. 209.

1387   The Pope and Europe in 1872, 168–184. **J. C. Hoey,** prob. The author is a partisan of the Comte de Chambord, but regrets his refusal to come to the throne except by hereditary right and under his own White Flag; specific ref. back to this art. in no. 1450, p. 483; praise of Marshal MacMahon as in no.

1356; hostility to masonic societies as in no. 1378, and allusion to Tarpeian Rock, p. 183 as in no. 1338, p. 494, all combine to place this in the series on French politics beginning with no. 1182.

1388   Notices of books, 185–248. Pages 218–223, 223–226 by **W. G. Ward**—cf. no. 1042 and for the first notice, cf. no. 1435.

VOLUME 18 N.S., 70 O.S., APRIL 1872

1389   The philosophy of subjective religion, 249–284. **Richard F. Clarke,** prob. Hoey notebook gives "Father Clarke"; Oscott II; see Boase, and Sutcliffe for his philosophical interests, which were also reflected at this time in the *Month.*

1390   Father Liberatore, Father Harper, and Lord Robert Montagu, 285–308. **W. G. Ward.** Manning's list; Hoey notebook. (Note vol. 19 n.s., p. 196 by **Ward.**)

1391   Saints' lives as spiritual reading, 309–333. **A. P. J. Cruikshank.** Hoey notebook.

1392   Protestant lectures on modern scepticism, 333–350. **Richard F. Clarke,** prob. Hoey notebook, as in no. 1389; Oscott II gives "Clarke," for no. 1393, but this art. represents his interests as no. 1393 does not.

1393   Revised English version of the Psalms, 351–362.

1394   Mr. Plummer's translation of Dr. Döllinger on the Popes, 363–379. **J. D. Dalgairns.** Hoey notebook.

1395   The works of Charles Lever, 379–408. **Frances Cashel Hoey.** Hoey notebook.

1396   Parliament and Catholic education, 409–440. **W. G. Ward.** Hoey notebook.

1397   The Gothic revival (communicated), 440–451. Signed: H.W.B. **H. W. Brewer.** Russell, "Early Reviewers," p. 216.

1398   Notices of books, 452–504.

VOLUME 19 N.S., 71 O.S., JULY 1872

1399   Unsectarianism and scientific secularism, 1–28.

1400   S. Mary Magdalene in the Gospels, 28–49. **W. G. Ward.** Repr. *Devotional Essays.*

1401   The Carte papers, 49–84. **C. W. Russell,** prob. Bayswater with a ? Matthew Russell, "Early Reviewers," p. 216, "suspects" Dr. Russell to be the reviewer, even though Russell was one of the editors of the Carte Papers; much of same history as related in no. 1468 is dealt with here; see also no. 339.

1402 Reply to Mr. Renouf by F[ather] Bottalla (No. II); orthodoxy of Pope Honorius I, 85–103. **Paul Bottalla.** Title; cf. no. 1373.

1403 The priesthood at Irish elections, 103–113. **W. G. Ward.** Manning's list; Oscott II. (See nos. 1408 and 1423.)

1404 Dr. Bain on the relativity of human knowledge (communicated), 114–154. **Richard F. Clarke?** Cf. nos. 1389 and 1392.

1405 The life and times of Sixtus the Fifth, 155–164.

1406 Catholic primary education in England, 164–195. **W. G. Ward.** Reply to attack on no. 1396; written in Ward's usual manner.

1407 Notices of books, 197–256. Pages 198–203 by **A. P. J. Cruikshank**—stress on hagiological method of writing saints' lives characteristic of him; pages 204–206, 208–214 by **W. G. Ward**, prob.—cf. nos. 1042 and 1416, pp. 477, 488; pages 215–218, by **W. G. Ward**—note on p. 528 (letter, p. 528, signed **T. S. Preston**).

VOLUME 19 N.S., 71 O.S., OCTOBER 1872

1408 The priesthood in Irish politics, 257–293. **W. G. Ward.** Manning's list; Oscott II. (See no. 1423.)

1409 The Middle Ages: their position in church history, 294–335. **A. P. J. Cruikshank**, prob. This is clearly by the author of no. 1355: he not only refers back to the previous art. on pp. 299, 318, 327, but on p. 301 he repeats almost verbatim the expression "the perfect harmony and beauty of proportion . . . of everything connected with the Church"; style is similar to that of no. 1355; reference back, p. 312n. to no. 1279 by Cruikshank.

1410 Catholicity in Germany, 335–351. Unidentified. (Note vol. 20 n.s., p. 208, by **T. W. Allies.**)

1411 *The Legends of St. Patrick* [by Aubrey De Vere], 351–384. **James Murphy.** Attr. Russell, "Early Reviewers," p. 216, from letters of C. W. Russell.

1412 A word on classical studies, 384–392. **W. G. Ward?** This was a subject on which Ward felt and wrote strongly; on p. 390 the author speaks of our own views on this subject which turn out closely to resemble those expressed by

Ward—see especially *Ram* no. 77 and *DR* no. 1258.

1413 The novels of Mr. Anthony Trollope, 393–430. **Frances Cashel Hoey?** Mrs. Hoey was writing most of the literary arts. in this period; see no. 1109.

1414 Lord Arundell on tradition, 431–447.

1415 Rio's *Memoirs on Christian Art*, 448–475. **C. F. Audley?** He had reviewed previous book by Rio in no. 1238, which is cited here at start.

1416 The present Anglican position, 476–505. **W. G. Ward.** *Doctrinal Authority*, pp. 413–420, reprints a few paragraphs.

1417 Notices of books, 506–527.

VOLUME 20 N.S., 72 O.S., JANUARY 1873

1418 Ireland in the reign of James I, 1–48.

1419 The labourers and political economy, 48–59. **W. G. Ward**, prob.—cf. no. 1042, as well as references to nos. 1371, 1383, and 1396, all by Ward.

1420 A study of relations (communicated), 59–76. **Richard F. Clarke?** Intro. note says by author cf. no. 1404; cf. nos. 1389 and 1392.

1421 The Queen's colleges in Ireland, 77–103. **J. C. Hoey**, prob. The author's view on the failure of the Queen's Colleges in Ireland is a restatement of Hoey's remarks on p. 434 of no. 1113, which appear again on p. 463 of no. 1433.

1422 Italian church architecture (communicated), 104–119. **A. P. J. Cruikshank?** Author says he is not an architect, but had lived many years in Rome—Cruikshank was in Rome 1850–1860 (Newman *L&D*, XIII, index); he lays great stress upon the word "unity," cf. nos. 1355, 1409 by Cruikshank; this art. may be an expansion of the idea touched upon in the note on pp. 318–319 in no. 1409; high praise of the Catholicism of the Middle Ages, p. 112, reflects the attitude in no. 1409.

1423 Irish priests and landlords, 120–137. **W. G. Ward.** Manning's list; Oscott II. (See nos. 1403 and 1408.)

1424 Reply to M. Renouf by Father Bottalla (No. III, concl.), 137–158. **Paul Bottalla.** Title; cf. no. 1373.

1425 The Vatican Council: its authority, its work, 159–207. **P. A. Murray.** Diary, p. 111, cited in Russell, "Early Reviewers," p. 209.

1426 Notices of books, 209–280. Pages 258–259, 264–270, 273–275 by **C. W. Russell**, prob.—on p. 258 the author refers to

Meline's *Life of Mary Queen of Scots,* which he reviews 264–270 (Russell's particular interest), on p. 259 he praises Lecky's dispraise of Froude whom Russell constantly attacked, on pp. 273–275 he reviews Hendrik Conscience whom he had reviewed more than once in first series; see no. 427; pages 213–220, 220–221 by **W. G. Ward,** prob.—cf. no. 1042.

VOLUME 20 N.S., 72 O.S., APRIL 1873

1427 The relation of scholastic to modern philosophy: Mr. Hutton and Mr. Martineau, 281–325. **J. B. D. Dalgairns.** Assigned to him in *DR,* 28 n.s. (Jan. 1877), 240.

1428 The true mission of the Teutonic race, 326–356.

1429 *Literature and Dogma* [by Matthew Arnold], 357–380.

1430 The Gordon Riots (Part I), 381–401. **Alexius Mills.** Repr. *The History of Riots in London in 1780,* 1883.

1431 The Church and modern men of science, 401– 420.

1432 Mr. Froude on the English in Ireland [in the eighteenth century], 421–448.

1433 The Irish University Bill, 448–469. **J. C. Hoey,** prob. He was the regular contributor on Irish political affairs; the author's hostility to Cardwell, p. 453, suspicion of Disraeli's rhetoric, pp. 455–458, and praise of Gladstone's moderation and sincerity, p. 459, are all to be found in other arts. attributed to Hoey: cf. respectively nos. 1113, 1378, and 1421.

1434 Notices of books, 470–532. Pages 503–505 by **Richard F. Clarke?**—author cites no. 1392 and the subject is in Clarke's field; pages 470–477 by **A. P. J. Cruikshank,** prob.—ref. back to no. 1391 in opening sentence and weighing of relative values of hagiological and biographical approach to saints' lives seem to indicate his authorship.

VOLUME 21 N.S., 73 O.S., JULY 1873

1435 Mr. Mill's reply to the *Dublin Review,* 1–49. **W. G. Ward.** Manning's list; repr. *Essays on Theism,* I.

1436 The progress of the Gordon Riots (Part II, concl.), 50–67. **Alexius Mills.** Cf. no. 1430.

1437 Authority and the Anglican Church—

Mr. Garbett and Canon Liddon, 67–102. **T. W. M. Marshall.** Hoey notebook.

1438 *The Bremen Lectures . . . on Religious Questions,* 102–115. **Richard F. Clarke?** Hoey notebook gives "Mr. Clark"; style and metaphysical material suggest man who wrote nos. 1389, 1392, etc.

1439 *Terra Incognita, or Convent Life in England,* 115–145. **A. P. J. Cruikshank.** Hoey notebook.

1440 The Irish brigade in the service of France, 145–191. **Mr. Fenton.** Hoey notebook.

1441 Canon Estcourt on Anglican ordination, 191–210. **David Lewis.** Hoey notebook gives "Mr. Lewis"; Oscott II gives "D. Lewis"; see Gorman.

1442 The case of Mr. O'Keeffe, 211–238. **John O'Hagan.** Hoey notebook; Casartelli; "Jubilee," p. 261.

1443 Notices of books, 239–272.

VOLUME 21 N.S., 73 O.S., OCTOBER 1873

1444 Pilgrimage and Paray-le-Monial, 273–295. **A. P. J. Cruikshank?** The author is almost obsessed with devotions and refers back to his previous discussion of them in the *DR,* cf. no. 1355, and repeats the point made in that art. and no. 1409, of the unity of the mystical life of the Church.

1445 *Rousseau* [by John Morley], 295–322.

1446 Usury (No. I), 323–348.

1447 The Ignatian Epistles: their genuineness and their doctrine, 349–402. **W. E. Addis,** prob. Assigned in Oscott IA to "Dr. Addis" (see *WWW*); ref. back to this art. in no. 1492 by Addis. (Note vol. 27 n.s., pp. 241–244 by the author.)

1448 Father Newman, *The Idea of a University,* 403–428. **W. G. Ward.** Manning's list. (Letter vol. 22 n.s., pp. 265–266 signed L.K., with brief reply by **Ward.**)

1449 *The Life and Labours of S. Thomas of Aquin* [by R. B. Vaughan, Vol. II], 429–462. **J. C. Hedley.** Attr. in *Life,* p. 220; Willson list.

1450 Marshal MacMahon's government of France, 462–484. **J. C. Hoey,** prob. A continuation of the analyses of French politics begun with no. 1182, q.v., not only is this a panegyric of MacMahon (particularly as Ireland's gift to France), but it also defends at length the position taken by the Comte de Chambord: for both cf. no. 1356.

1451 A few words on the authority of S.

Alphonsus (communicated), 485–490. **E. Rouse.** Signed E.R. Oscott II, which adds "Dr."

1452 Notices of books, 491–536. Pages 493–496, 499–501, 503–506, by **A. P. J. Cruikshank,** prob.—in the first two notices the superiority of the hagiological as against the biographical treatment of saints' lives is stressed; see no. 1391 by Cruikshank; pages 503–506 are on devotion to St. Joseph; see no. 1355.

VOLUME 22 N.S., 74 O.S., JANUARY 1874

1453 Mr. Mill's philosophical position, 1–38. **W. G. Ward.** Manning's list; repr. *Essays on Theism,* I.

1454 Taine's *History of English Literature,* 39–68. **A. P. J. Cruikshank?** Author exhibits same great admiration of Middle Ages as that displayed in no. 1409. See pp. 56, 61, 63, including a ref. back to that art. on p. 60.

1455 Usury and the canon law (No. II), 69–99.

1456 Mr. Jervis on the Church of France, 100–145. **Anne Hope.** *Memoir,* p. xxxvii. (See no. 1466.)

1457 The Archbishop of Westminster on the Sacred Heart, 146–161. **W. G. Ward.** Repr. *Devotional Essays.*

1458 The religious education of women, 162–187.

1459 Catholic higher studies in England, 187–204. **W. G. Ward,** prob. Ref. back on p. 189 to no. 1089 by Ward, coupled with claim that editorial policy had consistently opposed education of Catholic youth at Oxford or Cambridge; see also nos. 1101, 1159, 1258, 1280, and 1448.

1460 The situation in France, 204–210. **J. C. Hoey,** prob. This is clearly by the author of no. 1450, who here speaks of the efforts he had made therein to show that the Comte de Chambord could have negotiated with the National Assembly to establish a moderate monarchical constitution, and expresses deep regret that he did not do so; the same high praise of MacMahon appears as in no. 1450.

1461 Church architecture (communicated), 210–227. **St. George Mivart.** Signed M.J.F.; repr. in expanded form in *Contemporary Evolution* (1876), chap. vi.

1462 Notices of books, 228–264. Page 230 by **W. G. Ward**—defense of an attack on no. 1130.

VOLUME 22 N.S., 74 O.S., APRIL 1874

1463 Prussian and Italian diplomacy in 1866, 267–301.

1464 American poets (Part I), 302–325. **J. C. Earle.** Cf. no. 1474.

1465 Mr. Mill's denial of freewill, 326–361. **W. G. Ward.** Manning's list; repr. *Essays on Theism,* I. (See no. 1478.)

1466 Mr. Jervis on the Jansenistic and Gallican movement, 362–401. **Anne Hope.** *Memoir,* p. xxxvii. (See no. 1456.)

1467 Caesarism and Ultramontanism: Mr. Fitzjames Stephen, 402–423. **W. G. Ward.** Cf. no. 1042.

1468 Rinuccini's Irish nunciature, 424–449. **C. W. Russell,** prob. He had reviewed the Italian account of Rinuccini's nunciature in no. 339 (June 1844) and here on p. 429 he refers back to a point made there on p. 527; here he is somewhat mechanically retelling the same story with no signs of fresh interest or enthusiasm; see also no. 1401.

1469 The fall of Mr. Gladstone's government, 450–461. **J. C. Hoey,** prob. Hoey was the editor mainly responsible for political arts.; an Irishman, and a correspondent of Gladstone's (see no. 1481), the sentiments and tone of this art. would be characteristic of him; the last four pages deal with the unfortunate consequences to be expected by Ireland from the change of government (cf. no. 1262 and no. 1113, which is cited here, p. 203n.)

1470 Notices of books, 462–504. Pages 487–488 by **A. P. J. Cruikshank,** prob.—this reflects his view of the hagiological treatment of saints' lives, see no. 1391; pages 466–468 by **W. G. Ward**—ref. on p. 467 to no. 1448; the author speaks of being at Oxford, 1831–1845: see Foster.

VOLUME 23 N.S., 75 O.S., JULY 1874

1471 The Vatican definition on infallibility, 1–28. **W. G. Ward.** Cf. no. 1042; in *Doctrinal Authority,* p. 432, he quotes note on p. 2 as his; ref. back to this in no. 1506, p. 455. (Note pp. 522–523 by **Ward.**)

1472 London poor and London work, 29–53.

1473 A reply on necessary truth, 54–63. **W. G. Ward.** Headnote. (See no. 1510.)

1474 American poets (Part II, concl.), 64–86. **J. C. Earle.** Claimed in no. 1831, pp. 126–127.

1475 John Wesley and the rise of Methodism, 87–118.

1476 Castaniza's *Spiritual Conflict and Conquest*, 119–132.

1477 The fall of the Duc de Broglie and the crisis in France, 133–159. **J. C. Hoey,** prob. This continues the current accounts of French politics begun in no. 1182; both MacMahon and the Duc de Broglie are again highly praised, as in no. 1450, but the author now appears completely disillusioned with the Comte de Chambord and bitter about the extreme Legitimiste party in France (in letter to Gladstone cited for no. 1481, Hoey notebook refers to the "peculiar views" of that party).

1478 Appendix to article on freewill [no. 1465], 159–172. **W. G. Ward.** Manning's list; repr. *Essays on Theism*, I.

1479 Plain-Chant (communicated), 172–204. (Letters, pp. 537–538, signed Sacerdos Alter; p. 538 by **James Burns?**—signed Laicus, author commends position of author of no. 1058.)

1480 Notices of books, 205–258. Pages 207–209 by **C. W. Russell**—he had reviewed in no. 1303, the first vol. of the work noticed here; author proposes Oct. review, viz., no. 1483, which is by Russell.

VOLUME 23 N.S., 75 O.S., OCTOBER 1874

1481 The sovereignty in modern states: The Count de Chambord and the Pope's civil princedom, 259–312. **W. G. Ward.** Manning's list; J. C. Hoey to W. E. Gladstone, Nov. 6, 1874, BM Add. MS. 44,445, says Ward has written "in some degree at my instance" on sovereign powers in civil society; although the author regrets the action of the Comte de Chambord, he asserts that he has no right to the throne of France; ref. back to the author's having dealt with the same subject in nos. 1037 and 1390 both by Ward; the author stresses his belief in the obedience due to civil government, pp. 261, 293, 310; this art. is entirely different in intent and style (very characteristic of Ward) from the series probably written by J. C. Hoey. (Letters, vol. 24 n.s., pp. 530–535, signed W.P.; reply by **Ward** no. 1510; vol. 25 n.s., pp. 539–543, signed W.P.)

1482 Saint Caecilia and Roman society, 312–335. **C. W. Russell?** The author on

p. 318 refers to "our" earlier discussion in no. 1294; catacombs and DeRossi, pp. 318–319, were favorite topics of Russell's.

1483 The Babington Conspiracy: Mary Stuart, 338–378. **C. W. Russell.** Attr. Matthew Russell, "Early Reviewers," p. 217, opens with reference to no. 1303 as "our last art." on this topic.

1484 The pilgrimage to Pontigny, 378–412. **H. A. Vaughan?** Vaughan was an advocate of pilgrimages and had gone to Paray-le-Monial (see J. G. Snead-Cox, *Life of Cardinal Vaughan* [2 vols., 1910], I, 260, and Vaughan, *Letters*, p. xviii); this art. is prob. written by someone with ties to St. Edmund's, Ware, (p. 384), of which Vaughan had been vice-president in 1855 (*DNB*); and seems to be an official reply to attacks in the periodical press on the pilgrimage and on Manning's support of it, ibid.

1485 Mr. Aubrey de Vere's *Alexander the Great*, 412–440. **C. W. Russell,** prob. Opening sentence refers to author's previous admiring arts. on De Vere, see nos. 590, 762, 999; unlike nos. 1109, 1301, this art. makes almost no mention of De Vere's political thinking, but stresses with great praise his Catholicism, p. 440, and closes by saying only Catholics can truly appreciate De Vere.

1486 The infidelity of the day: the new scheme of Catholic higher education, 441–475. **W. G. Ward.** Manning's list; Ward to Baron von Hugel, Apr. 27, 1879, at St. Andrews, claims this.

1487 An examination of Mr. Herbert Spencer's *Psychology* (Part I) (communicated), 476–508. **St. George Mivart.** Signed M; evidence for no. 1515.

1488 Church music (communicated), 509–521. Signed: Monachus.

1489 Notices of books, 524–536. Pages 528–529 by **W. E. Addis?**—reference to this at start of no. 1503; pages 525–528, by **W. G. Ward,** prob.—ref. on p. 526 to Ward's art. on temporal sovereignty in this issue (no. 1481).

VOLUME 24 N.S., 76 O.S., JANUARY 1875

1490 Prussian law and the Catholic Church, 1–26.

1491 Bishop Pecock, his character and fortunes, 27–55.

1492 Gnosticism and the rule of faith in

St. Irenaeus, 56–113. **W. E. Addis.** Attr. in Ward, *Doctrinal Authority*, p. 397n.

1493 Music and plain chant, 113–127.

1494 Replies to Lord Acton, 127–153. **E. S. Keogh** and **Thomas Doyle.** Signed E.S.K.; Oscott II assigns to Keogh; however, pp. 130–143 on Pius V are by Doyle—see p. 129; Keogh to Ward, Apr. 25, 1877, Ward letters, refers to the Mr. Doyle who wrote on Pius V in reply to Acton; Thomas Doyle wrote a series of arts. on Pius V in the *Tablet*: see Boase.

1495 Bermuda, 153–169.

1496 Mr. Gladstone's *Expostulation*, 170–208. **W. G. Ward.** Manning's list; Bayswater.

1497 Notices of books, 209–254. Pages 209–211 by **Ward,** prob.—cf. nos. 1042 and 1496 and ref. to p. 210 of this art. in no. 1506, p. 457 (letter signed **W. B. Ullathorne,** p. 530); pages 211–215 by **W. G. Ward,** prob.—cf. nos. 1042, 1496, and 1520, p. 285n; pages 215–216 by **W. G. Ward**—cited as "ours" in the reprint of no. 1516 in *Devotional Essays*, p. 343.

VOLUME 24 N.S., 76 O.S., APRIL 1875

1498 Cardinal Manning, 255–271.

1499 Miracles: the objections against their possibility and antecedent probability [on *Supernatural Religion*], 271–304. **H. I. D. Ryder.** Hoey notebook. (Letter vol. 27 n.s., pp. 508–513 from *Tablet.*)

1500 Fair play in literature [toward Catholicism]: William and Robert Chambers, 305–323. **C. W. Russell.** Hoey notebook.

1501 Bishop Fessler on infallibility, 323–346. **W. G. Ward.** Claimed in his *Doctrinal Authority*, p. 499n. (Note, vol. 25 n.s.)

1502 The use and abuse of ritual, 346–356. **Frederick Oakeley.** Hoey notebook.

1503 *Supernatural Religion* [by W. R. Cassels], 357–411. **W. E. Addis.** Hoey notebook.

1504 The Protestation of 1789 and the Irish Catholic Oath, 412–438. **J. C. Hoey.** Hoey notebook.

1505 *Days near Rome* [by Augustus J. C. Hare], 438–454. **Emily Bowles,** prob. Hoey notebook gives "Miss Bowles"; see Newman, *L&D*, XI, 334.

1506 Mr. Gladstone and his Catholic critics, 454–509. **W. G. Ward.** Hoey notebook; Manning's list.

1507 Notices of books, 510–529. Pages 516–518, 519–522 by **W. G. Ward,** prob.—on the Gladstone controversy: cf. nos. 1496, 1506.

1508 Papal brief addressed to Charles Perin, 535–536. **Pius IX.** Signed.

VOLUME 25 N.S., 77 O.S., JULY 1875

1509 Modern society and the Sacred Heart, 1–38. **William Francis Barry.** *Memories,* pp. 112–113; claimed in no. 1932, p. 283n.

1510 A reply to two criticisms: "Civil Sovereignty" and "Necessary Truth," 39–62. **W. G. Ward.** Manning's list; Bayswater; cf. nos. 1473 and 1481; on p. 52n. he identifies himself with the editorial "we".

1511 Secularism in elementary education, 63–82.

1512 The purport of Bishop Fessler's treatise, 83–105. **W. G. Ward.** Claimed in his *Doctrinal Authority*, p. 499n. [Note by **Ward,** p. 219.]

1513 Prince Bismarck's speeches, 106–134.

1514 F[ather] Dumas on the Syllabus [translated], 134–143. **Henri Dumas.** Title and *EUI.* With an introduction and translation, 134–136, by **W. G. Ward,** prob. Cf. no. 1042 and refs. to other arts. by Ward.

1515 An examination of Mr. Herbert Spencer's *Psychology* (Part II) (communicated), 143–172. **St. George Mivart.** Signed M; pp. 158–164 repr. *Lessons from Nature* (1876), pp. 69–77.

1516 Father Coleridge on the gospels, 173–188. **W. G. Ward.** Repr. *Devotional Essays.*

1517 The European situation, 189–201. **J. C. Hoey,** prob. Like no. 1182 this art. takes an overall view of the situation on the Continent, but closes with a discussion of the current political outlook for France; reiterates regrets over action of Comte de Chambord and high praise of MacMahon and Duc de Broglie: cf. nos. 1460, 1477.

1518 Catholic liberalism (Part I), 202–218. **Henri Ramière.** Signed H. Ramière; see *Grand Larousse*. Trans. from *Etudes* by **W. G. Ward,** prob.—he was in correspondence with Ramière (*Ward as Catholic*, p. 187), and in agreement with his anti-liberalism.

1519 Notices of books, 219–272. Pages 223–227 by **William Francis Barry**—*Memories,* 113–114 (letter, pp. 543–544, signed

W[illiam] **Lockhart,** with reply by Barry as author of notice and of an art. to come, no. 1524); pages 219–223 by **W. G. Ward,** prob.—cf. no. 1042; pages 228–233 by **Ward,** prob.—cf. his controversy with Pusey beginning in no. 1143.

VOLUME 25 N.S., 77 O.S., OCTOBER 1875

1520 Father Newman on ecclesiastical prudence, 273–307. **W. G. Ward.** Manning's list; claimed in Ward to Baron von Hugel, July 5, [1876], at St. Andrews. (Note, vol. 26 n.s., p. 203, by **Ward,** as Editor.)

1521 Ranke's and Green's histories of England, 308–341. **Anne Hope.** *Memoir,* p. xxvii.

1522 Anglicans of the day, 342–375. **T. W. M. Marshall.** The reprint in 1875 is assigned to him by H&L, I, 82.

1523 The deification of the Roman emperors, 375–404.

1524 St. Thomas on the theory of human knowledge, 405–434. **William Francis Barry.** *Memories,* p. 114.

1525 Mary Tudor [two dramas by Sir Aubrey De Vere, 1788–1846, and Tennyson], 434–471. **C. W. Russell?** The author in the opening paragraphs shows great interest in and knowledge of the historical facts behind these dramas, referring frequently to scholarly evidence, admiring Maitland for his objectivity (cf. no. 553); his admiration of De Vere's conception and execution is extremely high and he also commends the son's preface (cf. no. 1485, p. 413); he feels Tennyson's poem is on a lower level, that it lacks organic wholeness; on p. 426 he refers to the exaggerated and indiscriminate praise of Tennyson; cf. no. 1067. In spite of Matthew Russell's "guess" that this might have been by Mrs. Hoey, the treatment and style both are characteristic of Russell's literary criticism; Bayswater gives "? Mrs. Cashel Hoey."

1526 Ireland and O'Connell, 472–499. **J. C. Hoey.** Attr. and partially repr. "by permission of the author" in Charles A. Read, *Cabinet of Irish Literature* (4 vols., 1880), IV, 251–253.

1527 Letter from M. Albert Dechamps to Rev. Father Gratry [translated from *Le-Monde*], 500–508. **Albert Dechamps.** Title.

1528 Notices of books, 509–538. Pages 512–516 by **William Francis Barry**—*Memories,* p. 113; pages 509–511 by **W. G. Ward**—repr. *Devotional Essays.*

VOLUME 26 N.S., 78 O.S., JANUARY 1876

1529 Catholic miracles, 1–36. **H. I. D. Ryder,** prob. Bayswater gives "? Fr. Ryder"; opening sentence links this closely to no. 1499. (Letter on this and no. 1499 from *Tablet,* vol. 27 n.s., pp. 508–513.)

1530 Dr. Brownson's philosophy, 36–55. **W. G. Ward,** prob. Oscott II with a ?, but see pp. 37–38, which imply this art. is by the editor, i.e., Ward.

1531 Paris, 55–73. **Frances C. Hoey?** She was very familiar with France and contemporary French literature, as is the author of this art.—see *BMCat.,* no. 1345, *Temple Bar,* and *St. Paul's Magazine* VIII (May 1871), 163–176; cf. no. 1109.

1532 Father O'Reilly on society and the Church, 73–96. **W. G. Ward.** Manning's list; Oscott II. (Note by **Ward,** 483–486, including a letter from **H. I. D. Ryder**—signed H.I.D.R.)

1533 Mr. Carlyle, 97–122.

1534 The Isle of Man, 122–148.

1535 The scholastic doctrine of science, 148–184. **William Francis Barry.** Claimed by him, *DR,* 19 3rd. s. (1888), 398n.

1536 The French Catholic universities, 185–202. **J. C. Hoey?** Art. begins by pointing out parallel position of the universities in France to those in Ireland (cf. no. 1421 and 1433); it expresses the hostility to revolutionists, p. 189, which was characteristic of Hoey; as the author of no. 1558, p. 209, the third in this series on education, says, "education is, then, for the moment the main battleground in France," which suggests that these three arts. are in essence political and therefore in the area of Hoey's usual contributions.

1537 Catholic liberalism [translated] (Part II, concl.), 204–226. **Henri Ramière.** Signed as in no. 1518. With introductory note, 204–205, by **W. G. Ward**—see his *Doctrinal Authority,* p. 28.

1538 On a letter of Montalembert's [from the *Month*], 226–228. **Prosper de Haulleville.** Signed P. de Haulleville; see Seyn.

1539 Notices of books, 229–270. Pages 229–231 by **W. G. Ward**—cf. no. 1042.

VOLUME 26 N.S., 78 O.S., APRIL 1876

1540 Tradition and Papal Infallibility, 271–300. **W. G. Ward.** Manning's list; Ward cites pp. 285–286 as his own in *Doctrinal*

Authority, p. 557n. (Letter, vol. 27 n.s., p. 214, signed **H. N. Oxenham.**)

1541 Professor Mivart's *Lessons from Nature*, 301–321. **W. G. Ward?** Oscott II; ref. on p. 315 to arts. on "necessary truth" by **Ward**; ref. p. 318n. to no. 1435 also by **Ward.**

1542 Catholic intermediate education: St. Mary's Orphanage, Blackheath, 322–331. **William Monsell.** J. C. Hoey to Monsell, Aug. 29, 1876, Monsell Papers, Nat. Lib. Ireland, refers to Monsell's art. in last issue about Middle Class Catholic Schools.

1543 Ranke's *History of England*, 332–350. **Anne Hope,** prob. Opening sentences link this closely with no. 1521.

1544 Church and state, 351–373. **W. G. Ward.** Manning's list; Oscott II; refs. back to nos. 1037, 1390 and 1501, all by Ward.

1545 Art in the provinces—*Keramic Art of Japan*, 374–400.

1546 The scholastics on intellect and abstraction, 400–441. **William Francis Barry.** Claimed by him, *DR*, 19 3rd. s. (1888), 398n., with title slightly changed.

1547 Secular education in England and the United States, 442–482. **T. W. Marshall.** Bayswater; art. repr. simultaneously in *American Catholic Quarterly Review* (see headnote on p. 442), where it is assigned in Contents, I, April 1876.

1548 On liberal Catholicism [seven Papal briefs], 487–493. **Pius IX.** Signed. (Note, vol. 28 n.s., p. 507.)

1549 The Church's social conflict, 494–500. **Henri Ramière.** Signed as in no. 1518. Translated from *Etudes*, by **W. G. Ward,** prob., see no. 1518.

1550 Notices of books, 501–533. Pages 524–526 by **W. G. Ward**—admitted in a letter, vol. 27 n.s., p. 214. (Letter, vol. 27 n.s., p. 214, signed **G. R. Kingdon.**)

VOLUME 27 N.S., 79 O.S., JULY 1876

1551 Professor Mivart on the rights of conscience, 1–37. **W. G. Ward.** Manning's list; Oscott II. (Quotation from **H. E. Manning,** pp. 508–509; reply by **Mivart,** pp. 555–567, with answer by **Ward,** pp. 567–568.)

1552 Cremation, 37–57.

1553 Mr. Mill on causation, 57–82. **W. G. Ward.** Manning's list; repr. *Essays on Theism,* I.

1554 The United States of America, 82–116.

1555 The witness of St. Irenaeus to Catholic doctrine, 117–155. **W. E. Addis.** Attr. in Ward, *Doctrinal Authority*, p. 397n.

1556 Mr. Alfred Austin's *Human Tragedy*, 155–182.

1557 A few more words on Fessler, 182–197. **W. G. Ward.** Claimed in his *Doctrinal Authority*, p. 499n.

1558 The republican victory in France, 198–213. **J. C. Hoey?** Not only is this the third in a series of arts. on education in its relation to the political situation of the time (cf. nos. 1536 and 1542), but also it expresses what was certainly the view of Ward, Manning, and Hoey: "that pest of our time, Liberal Catholicism," p. 202.

1559 Note to the April number, including a letter to the *Saturday Review*, 213–214. **W. G. Ward.** Signed Editor of the *Dublin Review.*

1560 On religious unity and toleration, 215–233. **Henri Ramière.** Signed as in no. 1518. Translated from *Etudes* by **W. G. Ward,** prob.

1561 Notices of books, 234–276. Pages 241–244 by **W. E. Addis?**—reply to an attack on no. 1447; pages 239–241 by **J. C. Hedley**—cf. opening of no. 1565; pages 237–238 by **W. G. Ward**—repr. *Devotional Essays*; pages 234–237 by **W. G. Ward,** prob.—cf. no. 1042.

1562 Pronouncement on Rosmini's works [in *Osservatore Romano*], 277–280. **Vincenzo Maria Gatti.** Signed.

VOLUME 27 N.S., 79 O.S., OCTOBER 1876

1563 Pomponio Leto on the Vatican Council, 281–299. **P. A. Murray.** Diary, pp. 111, 160–161; Russell, "Early Reviewers," p. 209.

1564 The Gospel narrative of the Resurrection, 299–336. **W. G. Ward.** Partly repr. *Devotional Essays.* ("Appendix" by **Ward,** vol. 28 n.s., pp. 220–228).

1565 Father Baker's *Sancta Sophia*, 337–367. **J. C. Hedley.** Repr. *Evolution* as "Prayer and Contemplation"; *Life*, pp. 220, 287, 306.

1566 Anglicanism in Australia, 368–399.

1567 Critical history of the sonnet (Part I), 400–430. **C. W. Russell.** Attr. *DNB.*

1568 Mr. Tyndall and contemporary thought, 431–469. **William Francis Barry.** *Memories*, p. 121, says he wrote a "series of articles" on Tyndall in *DR*; Oscott II.

1569 The Earl of Strafford, 469–499. **C. W. Russell?** The subject lies directly in the field of Russell's interest in and knowledge of Irish history; the treatment is factual and objective, even when dealing with Strafford's antipathy towards Irish Catholics, p. 487.

1570 The impending [Russo-Turkish] War, 499–508. **J. C. Hoey?** He was the main contributor on political topics under Ward (see no. 1113); this is the first of a series of arts. on Russo-Turkish war; the bitter disillusionment with Gladstone is expressed even more sharply than in no. 1542; see pp. 500, 504, 505, 508.

1571 Notices of books, 514–554. Pages 523–528, 530–531 by **W. G. Ward**—cf. no. 1042 and the reiteration on pp. 523–528 of his comment on W. S. Lilly in no. 1551, p. 18n.

1572 Liberty of conscience [reply to no. 1551], 555–567. **St. George Mivart.** Signed. With a comment by **W. G. Ward**, 567–568.

VOLUME 28 N.S., 80 O.S., JANUARY 1877

1573 Civil intolerance of religious error: Professor Mivart on liberty of conscience, 1–46. **W. G. Ward.** Claimed by Ward, *NC*, 1 (1877), 536n; Manning's list. (Appendix, pp. 503–506; letter signed **St. George Mivart**, pp. 557–558.)

1574 St. Josaphat, Martyr of Catholic unity, 46–74.

1575 Cardinal Antonelli, 74–84.

1576 Roman history a foremost bulwark of the Christian cause against the antichrist of our times, 85–111. **Henry Formby.** Signed. Intro. note denying editorial responsibility by **W. G. Ward.** (Also see no. 1604.)

1577 The past and present of France [review of de Tocqueville], 111–127.

1578 The character of Julius Caesar, 127–141.

1579 Critical history of the sonnet (Part II, concl.), 141–180. **C. W. Russell.** Cf. no. 1567.

1580 The cloud in the East [Russian-Turkish relations], 181–191. **J. C. Hoey?** This is a continuation of no. 1570, and the author as in the former art. is clearly bitter against Gladstone, p. 190; as in the series of French arts. beginning with no. 1182 the author expresses scorn of Napoleon III.

1581 An examination of Mr. Herbert Spencer's *Psychology* (Part III) (communicated), 192–219. **St. George Mivart.** Evidence for no. 1515.

1582 Notices of books, 229–274. Pages 229–

232 by **W. G. Ward**—cf. no. 1678, p. 317n.; pp. 232–233 by **W. G. Ward**—Bayswater; pp. 240–244 by **W. G. Ward**—cf. no. 1042.

1583 Papal brief [on assent to Papal infallibility], 275–276. **Pius IX.** Signed.

VOLUME 28 N.S., 80 O.S., APRIL 1877

1584 Russia [and Catholicism], 277–303. **H. E. Manning?** Attr. in *Athenaeum*, April 1877, p. 547; the art. expresses Manning's hostility to Russia and the Orthodox Russian Church and his disagreement with Gladstone's position (see W. E. Gladstone, *Letters on Church and Religion* (2 vols., 1910), I, 114); the singling out for special censure the universal drunkenness of the Russian peasants, p. 295, reflects Manning's concern with the alcohol problem: see *DNB*.

1585 Frederic Ozanam, 304–324. **H. E. Manning.** Repr. *Miscellanies*, II.

1586 Father Coleridge's *Life of Our Life*, 325–352. **W. G. Ward.** Repr. *Devotional Essays*.

1587 Primitive man in Somme Valley, 352–377.

1588 The study of medieval history, 377–425. **W. S. Lilly,** prob. This art. is very similar in subject and style to no. 1617, by Lilly; there is same wealth of footnotes, the same wide knowledge of contemporary English writers, and the same concern with historiography; in a notice in no. 1813, Lilly makes the same point about modern writers, p. 250, as that made here on p. 421, and in both cases uses the same quotation from R. C. Trench. W. G. Ward had commented (*DR* no. 1551, p. 18) upon an essay by Lilly in the *Month* for June 1876 that it "effectively set forth the true mediaeval spirit" and was impressive in its remarkable knowledge of modern literature, clearly implying that he hoped for Lilly's support in the *DR*.

1589 English martyrs, 426–451.

1590 Father Augustine de Backer, 452–472. **Wilfrid C. Robinson.** Bayswater; de Backer was a Belgian Jesuit; man cited was a Jesuit with strong interests in Belgium: *Catholic WW*/1919.

1591 The War [the Russo-Turkish War], 473–478. **J. C. Hoey?** Opening paragraph indicates this is a continuation of nos. 1570 and 1580; author repeats, p. 474, his distress that treaties are being ignored; cf. no. 1570, p. 500, and no. 1580,

p. 184; Gladstone is again sharply attacked as he was throughout no. 1570.

1592 An examination of Mr. Herbert Spencer's *Psychology* (Part IV) (communicated), 479–502. **St. George Mivart.** Evidence for no. 1515.

1593 Notices of books, 508–556. Pages 514–515 signed **H. J. Coleridge** [from the *Month*].

VOLUME 29 N.S., 81 O.S., JULY 1877

1594 Is the Roman question at an end? [the independence of the Holy See], 1–28. **William Francis Barry.** In *Memories*, p. 132, under date of 1879, he says he has written "articles and reviews" on the Roman question for the *DR*; cf. no. 1615.

1595 The age of Elizabeth, 28–68.

1596 General Ignatieff, 68–93. **J. C. Hoey?** Very anti-Russian as were the previous arts. on the Russo-Turkish wars, nos. 1570, 1580, and 1591; makes the same attack p. 69 on the gullibility of British statesmen, p. 69, as he had made in no. 1580, p. 190, this time particularly on Salisbury, concluding that the English Cabinet was the tool of Russia; again deplores the abrogation of treaties, p. 93, cf. no. 1591.

1597 Mr. Florence MacCarthy's [translations of] Calderon, 94–119.

1598 The true view of the Protestant Reformation, 120–146. **W. S. Lilly,** prob. In no. 1813, p. 254, Lilly, in speaking of the Reformation, refers to the point made here on pp. 140–142; in this art. as in that notice Brewer is quoted with admiration, see also no. 1617, p. 58; here as in no. 1588 there is repeated praise and expressions of respect for Newman; also a display of wide reading in contemporary literature; here on p. 120 is a remark which Lilly repeated in no. 1813, p. 251.

1599 The Elementary Education Act of last session, 146–171.

1600 Artificial memory, 172–190.

1601 Modern ideals and the liberty of the press, 191–222.

1602 Marshal MacMahon's appeal to France, 222–230. **J. C. Hoey, prob.** The art. is a further defence of Marshal MacMahon (cf. nos. 135, 1387, 1450, and 1477), this time on the occasion of his dissolving the ministry of Jules Simon; there is also a plea for the support of the

Duc de Broglie, who was also highly praised in nos. 1450, 1477, and 1517.

1603 Notices of books, 231–273. Pages 261–262. Unidentified. (Letter, p. 542, signed **Edward Healy Thompson.**)

1604 Correspondence: the primitive religion of the city of Rome, 274–282. **Henry Formby.** Signed.

VOLUME 29 N.S., 81 O.S., OCTOBER 1877

1605 The Channel Islands, 283–307.

1606 Hergenröther on church and state, 308–339. **W. G. Ward.** Oscott II; cf. no. 1042 and opening sentence refs. to no. 1544, p. 373, where Ward promises this art.

1607 The poetry of a pessimist [Louise Ackermann], 339–360.

1608 Christian charity and political economy (Part I), 360–386. **C. S. Devas.** Claimed in his *Groundwork of Economics* (1883), p. 655.

1609 Turkey and Russia [and the War], 387–417. **J. C. Hoey?** This is a continuation of the series of arts. on the Russo-Turkish war beginning with no. 1570, and like them expresses hostility to Russia and praise for the Turks, and again (p. 416) deplores the violation of treaties, especially under pretext of promoting Christianity.

1610 Catholicity and national prosperity, 418–441.

1611 Simon de Montfort, Earl of Leicester, 441–468. **Anne Hope.** *Memoir*, p. xxxvii.

1612 Recent German thought—its influence on Mr. Tyndall, 469–487. **William Francis Barry.** *Memories*, p. 121, where it is called "a study of Hartmann, Dühring, and Lange," which is the title of one of the books being reviewed here.

1613 The French President and the new Chamber of Deputies, 488–510. **J. C. Hoey?** This is a sequel to no. 1602 and opens with a ref. to prediction in that art. (p. 230) and argues anew that Marshal MacMahon must not resign (p 489); there is again a series of parallels drawn between the position and powers of MacMahon and the president of the United States of America, particularly Lincoln (see there p. 228 and here p. 490); in both cases the author exhibits a fairly detailed knowledge of Alexander Hamilton's *Federalist* (there p. 226; here p. 497, where he says he has previously quoted Hamilton in the July issue—indeed the same footnote appears, verbatim);

high praise not only of MacMahon throughout but also, on p. 510, of the Duc de Broglie (cf. no. 1602).

1614 Notices of books, 511–541. Pages 511–517 by **W. G. Ward**, prob.—E. S. Keogh to Ward, Oct. 19, 1877, Ward letters, says he looks forward to seeing the notice of Newman and telling Ward his opinion of it; this notice deals with vol. I of the *Via Media*, while vol. II is noticed in next issue; editorial refs. to case of Galileo (see especially no. 1130); p. 532 top, unidentified (letter, vol. 30 n.s., p. 258 signed **H. W. Lloyd**).

VOLUME 30 N.S., 82 O.S., JANUARY 1878

1615 Father Curci and the Roman question, 1–32, **William Francis Barry.** *Memories*, p. 121: speaks of defending Pope's temporal power against Padre Curci. (Note, vol. 31 n.s., pp. 208–212, by **Barry**.)

1616 De Rossi's *Roma Sotterranea*, 32–52.

1617 The Renaissance and liberty [on Symonds' *Renaissance*], 53–88. **W. S. Lilly.** Repr. *Chapters in European History* (1888), I.

1618 Christian charity and political economy (Part II), 89–110. **C. S. Devas.** Cf. no. 1608.

1619 Arundel Castle: The Fitzalans and Howards, 110–141. **Philip Henry Howard?** He was a member of the Howard family and an antiquary (Boase); this art., as well as nos. 1818, and 1846, is antiquarian in subject, and is especially concerned with Elizabethan persecutions; here the author deals with history of Howard family and in no. 1818 with "Belted Will" Howard in particular, direct ancestor of man cited (*Landed Gentry*); Gillow, III, 442, points out that Howard's pen was ever ready to defend the rights of Catholics; ref. to Walter Scott in this and no. 1846 as well as his interest in Durham may reflect Howard's connection with the north of England.

1620 The winter campaign [Russo-Turkish War], 141–156. **J. C. Hoey?** Art. opens with ref. to our review of the war in Oct., no. 1609, and second paragraph outlines in some detail what was said there; as in previous arts. in this series on Russo-Turkish war, beginning with no. 1570, the author attacks Russian barbarism, p. 156; he also makes a passing gibe at Gladstone's distress over the Bulgarian atrocities, ibid.

1621 An examination of Mr. Herbert

Spencer's *Psychology* (Part V), 157–194. **St. George Mivart.** Evidence for no. 1515.

1622 On some recent commentaries on the Syllabus, 195–202. **François Desjacques.** Signed Père Desjacques; he was frequent contributor to *Études* from which this art. is trans.: see *DBF*. Translation by **W. G. Ward**, prob.—he signed the note on p. 198 Ed. D.R.

1623 Two philosophical papers by Dr. Ward [repr. from the *Nineteenth Century*], 202–211. **W. G. Ward.** Title.

1624 Notices of books, 212–257. Pages 217–219 by **W. G. Ward**, prob.—cf. no. 1614.

VOLUME 30 N.S., 82 O.S., APRIL 1878

1625 Pius the Ninth, 259–291.

1626 Mr. Froude and St. Thomas of Canterbury, 292–327. **Anne Hope.** *Memoir*, p. xxxvii.

1627 Catholic college education in England, 327–359. **W. G.Ward.** Quoted as his by Ward, *Devotional Essays*, p. 234n.

1628 Mr. Motley's historical works (Part I), 359–397.

1629 Islam, 398–427.

1630 *The Douai Diaries*, 427–446. **J. C. Hedley.** *Life*, p. 86.

1631 Archbishop Trench on medieval church history, 446–464. **W. S. Lilly.** The subject is closely related to that of no. 1588 in general; in that art., p. 383, Lilly praised Trench's *Essays*, and, ibid., admired Bowden's *Gregory VII*, as here on p. 447; in no. 1617, p. 81, Lilly commended Trench's *Study of Words* as he does here on p. 448; on p. 456 the author refers back to what we said a year ago about the nature of history (see no. 1588, p. 395); the art., like no. 1588, contains frequent admiring references to Newman.

1632 England and Russia [re the Russo-Turkish War], 465–472. **J. C. Hoey?** This is one more discussion of the Russian aggression in Europe begun in no. 1570, attacking Russia for violation of treaties and barbarity and now urging the importance of English might in frustrating Russian ambitions on the Continent.

1633 Italy and Leo XIII, 473–498. **William Francis Barry,** prob. This continues the discussion of Father Curci and the Roman question: cf. no. 1615. (Note, vol. 31 n.s., pp. 208–212.)

1634 Address on school-work, 498–504. **J. C. Hedley.** Intro. note.

1635 Notices of books, 505–532. Pages 507–511 by **Anne Hope**, prob.—cf. no. 1626 on same topic.

VOLUME 31 N.S., 83 O.S., JULY 1878

1636 The centenary of Voltaire, 1–12.
1637 Christian charity and political economy (Part III, concl.), 12–42. **C. S. Devas.** Cf. no. 1608.
1638 The legend of Provence, 42–73.
1639 A bishop's liberty of conscience under the new German Empire, 74–86.
1640 Catholic college discipline, 86–97. **W. G. Ward.** Manning's list; Bayswater; opening sentence links this to no. 1627. (Letter, pp. 532–536, signed F.B.M., with reply by **Ward**.)
1641 Large or small schools, 98–105. **William J. P. Petre.** Signed William Petre; see Boase. Intro. note by **W. G. Ward**, prob.—clearly editorial and by the author of nos. 1640 and 1627.
1642 Canossa, 106–138.
1643 Dr. Bateman on Darwinism, 139–152.
1644 The assent due to certain Papal utterances (Part I), 152–173.
1645 The conflict between church and state, 173–207. **François Desjacques?** Oscott II gives "Desjacques."
1646 Note to the articles on Father Curci [nos. 1615 and 1633], 208–212. **William Francis Barry.** This is clearly by the writer of the arts.
1647 Encyclical [with translations, on the Apostolic See], 213–227. **Leo PP. XIII.** Signed.
1648 Notices of books, 228–260.
1649 Correspondence: A philosophy of history indispensable to Catholic education, 261–267. **Henry Formby.** Signed. With a comment, presumably by **W. G. Ward**, 267, and a translation of a German review of Formby's books by **H. Riess, S.J.**, 268–274.

VOLUME 31 N.S., 83 O.S., OCTOBER 1878

1650 Dr. Ward's retirement: letters by **H. E. Manning** and **W. G. Ward**, 275–278.
1651 Catholic colleges and Protestant schools, 279–315, with an appendix, 315–318. **W. G. Ward.** Manning's list; the author in opening sentence bows himself out of his editorial autonomy.
1652 The poetry of Michael Angelo, 319–338. **Ellen M. Clerke?** She had lived in Italy, 1867–1877, was much interested in

Italian literature (*DNB*), and wrote on Italian authors in *DR*, *FM*, and *NatR-II* (see below, Part B).
1653 Primer of English literature, 338–348.
1654 Mr. Motley's historical works (Part II), 349–380.
1655 The reasonable basis of certitude [repr. from *Nineteenth Century*], 381–399. **W G. Ward.** Signed.
1656 Mr. Senior's character of M. Thiers, 400–411.
1657 An examination of Mr. Herbert Spencer's *Psychology* (Part VI), 412–439. **St. George Mivart.** Evidence for no. 1515.
1658 Catholic fiction, 439–462.
1659 The assent due to certain Papal utterances (Part II), 463–478.
1660 The peace of Berlin, 479–486. **J. C. Hoey?** A further account of the European situation; on p. 479 author regrets that England signed Peace of Berlin instead of going to war with Russia in the summer; on p. 482 he refers to General Ignatieff's "extortionate diplomacy" (cf. no. 1596).
1661 Notices of books, 487–531. Pages 487–490 by **W. G. Ward**, prob.—cf. no. 1651, also nos. 1627 and 1640 on this topic.

VOLUME 1 3RD S., 84 O.S., JANUARY 1879

1662 To our readers, 1–2. **J. C. Hedley.** *DR* list.
1663 Catholicism and culture, 3–26. **J. C. Hedley.** *DR* list; repr. *Evolution*.
1664 The relief of the poor in the early Church, 26–49. **C. S. Devas.** Signed.
1665 The works and wants of the Church in England, 49–73. **Henry Edward Manning.** Signed; repr. *Miscellanies*, III.
1666 The Bristol pulpit in the days of Henry VIII, 73–95. **T. E. Bridgett.** Signed.
1667 Afghanistan, 95–119.
1668 The Paris Exhibition of 1878, 119–141. **W. H. Bower.** Signed.
1669 An examination of Mr. Herbert Spencer's *Psychology* (Part VII), 141–163. **St. George Mivart.** Evidence for no. 1515.
1670 Pre-Homeric legends of the voyage of the Argonauts, 164–182. **F. A. Paley.** Signed.
1671 The evangelisation of Africa, 182–208. **H. A. Vaughan.** Signed "Herbert, Bishop of Salford."
1672 Parental authority in matters of re-

ligion, 208–223. (Note by the author, pp. 504–505.)

1673 The winter session [of Parliament], 223–229.

1674 Science notices, 230–236. Signed: F.R.G.S. [i.e., Fellow Royal Geographical Society].

1675 Notices of Catholic continental periodicals, 236–250. Pages 246–250 by **Alfons Bellesheim**—signature, Bellesheim says "The present editor of the *Dublin Review* has desired me to contribute . . . a quarterly review of our prominent Catholic periodicals in Germany."

1676 Notices of books, 250–260.

VOLUME 1 3RD S., 84 O.S., APRIL 1879

1677 Catholicism and Mr. H. W. Mallock, 261–280. **J. C. Hedley.** Attr. in *Life*, p. 220.

1678 Free will, 281–322. **W. G. Ward.** Signed; repr. *Essays on Theism*, I.

1679 Thomas Moore, 323–368.

1680 An examination of Mr. Herbert Spencer's *Psychology* (Part VIII), 368–396. **St. George Mivart.** Signed.

1681 The Christians of the East: their present position and their hopes, 397–425. **T. J. Lamy.** Signed.

1682 Catholics and the school boards, 426–447. Unidentified. Perhaps J. G. Wenham, who probably wrote no. 1709, opening paragraph of which closely links that art. to this.

1683 Alcohol: its action and uses, 447–454. **J. R. Gasquet.** Signed.

1684 The map of British India, 454–476. Signed: E.

1685 The eighteenth century (Part I), 477–492. **W. S. Lilly.** Signed; repr. *Chapters in European History* (1886), II.

1686 Church and school in France, 493–503.

1687 Encyclical [on man's obedience to God], 506–512. **Leo PP. XIII.** Signed.

1688 Science notices, 513–520. Signed: F.R.G.S.

1689 Notices of Catholic continental periodicals, 520–533. Pages 523–527 by **Alfons Bellesheim**—signature.

1690 Notices of books, 534–552. Pages 542–546 by **Edmund Bishop**—*Life*, pp. 92, 493.

VOLUME 2 3RD S., 85 O.S., JULY 1879

1691 The liquor traffic; should it be pro-

hibited? 1–32. **Thomas P. Whittaker.** Signed.

1692 *One Generation of a Norfolk House* [by Augustus Jessopp], 32–57.

1693 Origen against Celsus, 58–90. **Robert Ornsby.** Signed.

1694 On the origin of the "Solar Myth," and its bearing on the history of ancient thought, 90–111. **F. A. Paley.** Signed.

1695 Brittany and the Bretons, 111–136.

1696 The demands of Ireland, 137–154. **Henry F. Neville.** Signed.

1697 The education question in Belgium, 154–183, with an appendix, 183–187. **T. J. Lamy.** Signed.

1698 Cardinal Newman, 187–203. **J. C. Hedley.** *Life*, pp. 199–202, 220.

1699 Science notices, 204–221. Pages 207–211 are signed O.

1700 Notices of Catholic continental periodicals, 221–236. Pages 221–225 by **Alfons Bellesheim**—signature.

1701 Notices of books, 236–256. Pages 236–240 by **W. G. Ward**—signed.

VOLUME 2 3RD S., 85 O.S. OCTOBER 1879

1702 The early Scottish Church, 257–279. **James Augustine Campbell.** Signed J. A. Campbell; *DR* list gives "Dr. Campbell, Scots' Col. Rome": for man cited see *CD/79*.

1703 The age of Dante in the Florentine chronicles, 279–303. **Ellen M. Clerke.** Signed E. M. Clerke; *DR* list gives "Miss E. M. Clerke"; she consistently used this signature for her many contributions.

1704 Supplementary remarks on free will, 304–329. **W. G. Ward.** Signed; repr. *Essays on Theism*, II.

1705 The eighteenth century (Part II), 330–350. **W. S. Lilly.** Signed.

1706 History of the Prussian "Kulturkampf" (Part I): up to the legislation of the year 1873, 350–363. *DR* list says "By a German Statesman."

1707 Gunpowder and modern warfare, 364–395. **F. R. Wegg-Prosser.** Signed F.R.W.P.; *DR* list.

1708 Lord Lawrence [Viceroy of India], 396–417. Signed: E.

1709 Our elementary schools and their work, 417–448. **J. G. Wenham?** Author "ventures," p. 440n., to refer the reader to a book by man cited and speaks of himself, p. 448, as one having had long experience with schools; Wenham was a school inspector (see Boase); on p. 435 he quotes from an art. by Wenham in *Ram* for Nov. 1856 (no. 790).

1710 Theology, past and present, at Maynooth, 449–464. **Henry F. Neville.** Signed. (Answered in no. 1721.)

1711 Encyclical [on Thomas Aquinas], 465–478. **Leo PP. XIII.** Signed.

1712 Notices of Catholic continental periodicals, 479–494. Pages 490–494 by **Alfons Bellesheim**—signature.

1713 Notices of books, 495–556. Pages 509–511 by **Edmund Bishop**—*Life*, pp. 100, 493.

VOLUME 3 3RD S., 86 O.S., JANUARY 1880

1714 Mauritius, 1–26.

1715 Mr. Herbert Spencer's system of philosophy (Part IX of his arts. on Spencer's *Psychology*, concl.), 26–73. **St. George Mivart.** Signed.

1716 The eighteenth century (Part III), 74–100. **W. S. Lilly.** Signed.

1717 Ethics in its bearing on theism, 101–133. **W. G. Ward.** Signed; repr. *Essays on Theism*, II.

1718 The land question and law reform, 134–165. **Aubrey St. John Clerke.** Signed.

1719 Legends of the Saxon saints, 165–189.

1720 Pope Leo XIII and modern studies, 190–210. **J. C. Hedley.** Oscott II; repr. *Evolution*.

1721 The alleged Gallicanism of Maynooth and of the Irish Clergy, 210–253. **William J. Walsh.** Signed.

1722 Letters on the study of St. Thomas of Aquin, on the works of St. Alfonso, and to the Société Scientifique of Brussels, 254–258. **Leo PP. XIII.** Signed.

1723 Notices of Catholic continental periodicals, 259–269. Pages 259–263 by **Alfons Bellesheim**—signature.

1724 Notices of books, 269–290. Pages 277–280, by **Alfons Bellesheim**—signed B., Bellesheim regularly reviewed continental, particularly German books and periodicals at this period and frequently used initial "B"; pages 280–283 by **Edmund Bishop**—*Life*, pp. 92, 493; pages 269–272 signed **W. G. Ward.**

VOLUME 3 3RD S., 86 O.S., APRIL 1880

1725 The birthplace of St. Patrick, apostle of Ireland, 291–327. **Patrick F. Moran.** Signed.

1726 History of the Prussian "Kulturkampf" (Part II): legislation of the years 1873 and 1874, 327–355. DR list says "By a German Statesman."

1727 A protestant life of St. Hugh, 355–372. **T. E. Bridgett.** Signed; repr. *Blunders and Forgeries*, 1890, as "A Saint Transformed."

1728 Recent research on the nerves and brain, 372–381. **J. R. Gasquet.** Signed.

1729 A new light on an old question [authorship of *The Imitation of Christ*], 382–409.

1730 The letters of Charles Dickens, 409–438.

1731 Text-books of philosophy, 439–464. **J. C. Hedley.** Oscott II; repr. *Evolution*.

1732 The distress in Ireland, 464–491.

1733 Encyclical on Christian marriage; and description of papal edition of St. Thomas Aquin, 492–506. **Leo PP. XIII.** Signed.

1734 Notices of Catholic continental periodicals, 507–517. Pages 507–511 by **Alfons Bellesheim**—signature.

1735 Science notices, 517–521.

1736 Notices of books, 521–574. Pages 553–558 by **J. S. Northcote**—signed J.S.N.; he was much interested in ecclesiastical archaeology, the subject of this notice.

VOLUME 4 3RD S., 87 O.S., JULY 1880

1737 The character of Cicero, 1–22. **Robert Ornsby.** Signed.

1738 The Greek Church: its history, dogma, discipline, rites, organization, and its future, 22–59. **T. J. Lamy.** Signed. (See no. 1776.)

1739 The apostle of Ireland and his modern critics, 59–87. **William Bullen Morris.** Repr. under his name, 1881.

1740 Church and school in Mauritius, 87–114.

1741 Dr. Ward's *Doctrinal Essays*, 115–127. **J. C. Hedley?** Attr. Matthews, "Hedley," p. 263.

1742 St. Catherine of Siena, 128–154.

1743 The suppression of the Congregations in France, 155–183.

1744 Notices of Catholic continental periodicals, 184–193. Pages 184–188 by **Alfons Bellesheim**—signature.

1745 Notices of books, 193–242. Pages 225–227 by **W. E. Addis**—signed; pages 227–231, by **Alfons Bellesheim**—signed B., cf. no. 1724; pages 200–207 by **Edmund Bishop**—*Life*, p. 493; pages 207–210 by **J. S. Northcote**—signed J.S.N.; his special topic.

VOLUME 4 3RD S., 87 O.S., OCTOBER 1880

1746 The writings of Mr. T. W. Allies [translated from two arts. in *Der Katholik*], 243–268. **Alfons Bellesheim.** The original arts. in *Der Katholik* are signed Dr. Bellesheim.

1747 Mr. Shadworth Hodgson on free will, 268–303. **W. G. Ward.** Signed; repr. *Essays on Theism*, II.

1748 Western Sussex: the borders of the Arun and the Adur (Part I), 303–321. **Alexander Wood.** *DR* list; Part II (no. 1768) is signed.

1749 Spenser as a textbook, 321–332. **Thomas Arnold,** 1823–1900. Signed T. Arnold; see *DNB.*

1750 The truth and the falsehood of M. Renan's lectures, 333–359. **W. E. Addis.** Signed.

1751 History of the Prussian "Kulturkampf" (Part III, concl.): the new legislative regulations, 360–386.

1752 Miracles and medical science, 386–398. **E. Mackey.** Signed, with addition of "M.D."

1753 Belgium and the Holy See, 399–438. **R. W. Petre.** Attr. in Gillow, V, 294.

1754 Papal brief on the affairs of Belgium, 439–442. **Pope Leo XIII.** Signed.

1755 Notices of Catholic continental periodicals, 443–456. Pages 443–446 by **Alfons Bellesheim**—signature.

1756 Notices of books, 457–520. Pages 479–481 signed **W. E. Addis;** page 485 by **Alfons Bellesheim,** prob.—signed B., cf. no. 1724; pages 463–467 by **T. E. Bridgett,** prob.—signed T.E.B., he was a regular contrib. at this period; pages 473–475 by **W. R. Brownlow,** prob.—signed W.R.B., he was much interested in archaeology; pages 476–478 by **Robert Ornsby,** prob.—signed R. O., he was a classicist.

VOLUME 5 3RD S., 88 O.S., JANUARY 1881

1757 Don Juan of Austria, 1–25.

1758 The brain and the mind, 25–56. **J. R. Gasquet.** Claimed at start of no. 1816.

1759 The Benedictines in western Australia, 56–76.

1760 Tractarianism and ritualism, 76–97.

1761 The position of Catholics in the United States, 97–116. **J. L. Spalding.** Signed J. W. Spalding, with title "Bishop of Peoria, Ill."; see *DAB.*

1762 Everlasting punishment, 117–145. **J. C. Hedley.** Oscott II; repr. *Evolution.*

1763 *Endymion* [by Disraeli], 145–165.

1764 Justice to Ireland, 165–195.

1765 Pope Leo XIII on St. Thomas of Aquin, 196–198. **Leo XIII.** Title.

1766 Notices of Catholic continental periodicals, 199–207. Pages 199–201 by **Alfons Bellesheim**—signature.

1767 Notices of books, 208–250. Pages 238–241 signed **W. E. Addis;** pages 234–238 by **Alfons Bellesheim**—signed B., cf. no. 1724; pages 246–250 signed **Gustave Masson.**

VOLUME 5 3RD S., 88 O.S., APRIL 1881

1768 Western Sussex (Part II, concl.), 251–268. **Alexander Wood.** Signed.

1769 Methods of historical inquiry (No. I), 269–288. **Henry Worsley.** Signed.

1770 A French study of Christian womanhood, 288–311.

1771 The days of the week, and the works of creation, 311–332. **William Clifford,** 1823–1893. Signed with title "Bishop of Clifton."

1772 The "Corpus Missal" and its probable date, 333–350. **Sylvester Malone.** Signed.

1773 Ritualism estimated from within and without, 350–371.

1774 The genius of George Eliot, 371–394. **William Francis Barry.** *Memories,* p. 143; repr. *Heralds of Revolt,* 1909.

1775 Catholic missions in Central Africa, 394–422. **Ellen M. Clerke,** prob. This is the first of a series of arts. on geographical and missionary topics by woman cited; some are signed and some are not, but they frequently refer back to previous ones (this art., for example, is cited in nos. 1914, p. 410, and 2404, p. 814, both signed E. M. Clerke); most of the earlier ones rely to a greater or less extent upon the weekly *Missions Catholiques,* even when the ostensible subject is not missions (see, for example, no. 1902, pp. 135, 145, 147); all are characterized by careful reading of contemporary sources, and by a factual approach combined with a lively narrative style.

It might be argued that since Herbert Vaughan wrote no. 1671 on missions in Africa, where *Les Missions Catholiques* is listed at head of art., he is the author of the series; but the schematic formalism of his work (see nos. 1208, 1218, 1239, 1871) is lacking in these arts., and in general his object is to instruct rather than to entertain; moreover, in no. 1671, the *Missions Catholiques* is not relied upon as it is throughout the series; but see last clause of evidence for no. 1964.

1776 The Russian Church; its history and present organization, 422–450. **T. J. Lamy.** Signed. (See no. 1738.)

1777 Encyclical on the Society for the Propagation of the Faith, 451–455, and letter to Cardinal Guibert, 455–458. **Leo PP. XIII.** Signed.

1778 Notices of Catholic continental periodicals, 459–472. Pages 459–462 by **Alfons Bellesheim**—signature.

1779 Notices of books, 472–510. Pages 488–489, 495–499 signed **W. E. Addis;** pages 489–495 by **Alfons Bellesheim**—signature; pages 472–478 by **Charles de Harlez**—signed C. de Harlez, first name given in Index; pages 478–483 by **W. S. Lilly**—signed W.S.L., he used these initials for an art. in *Month*, June 1876, which he subsequently repr. under his name, see *DR* no. 1571, p. 523; pages 500–504 signed **Gustave Masson.**

VOLUME 6 3RD S., 89 O.S., JULY 1881

1780 The [Protestant] religious press, 1–29.

1781 The extent of free will, 29–86. **W. G. Ward.** Signed; repr. *Essays on Theism*, II.

1782 The reorganization of our army, 86–105. **M. Laing Meason.** Signed.

1783 Recent works on the state of Germany in the fifteenth and beginning of the sixteenth century, by German authors (Part I), 106–127. **P. Alberdingk Thijm.** Signed, but with 2nd name ending with "x" instead of "k"; correctly printed on p. 111n. and at end of no. 1807.

1784 The revision of the New Testament, 127–144. **J. C. Hedley?** Attr. Matthews, "Hedley," p. 265; Oscott II, however gives "Dolman, O.S.B."; there was a Charles Vincent Dolman who was a canon of Newport at this time when Hedley was teaching at Belmont (*CD*/1900), but he does not appear in Snow, nor in *Benedictine Bibliog.*

1785 Catholic missions in Equatorial Africa, 144–175. **Ellen M. Clerke?** Belongs to the series on Catholic African missions listed in no. 1942, p. 28n; cf. no. 1775.

1786 A recent contribution to English history [T. E. Bridgett's *History of the Holy Eucharist*], 175–201. **Agnes Lambert.** Oscott II.

1787 On some reasons for not despairing of a national return to the faith, 201–219.

James Patterson. Signed James, Bishop of Emmaus; see *WWW*/1916 and *DR* list.

1788 Mr. Gladstone's second Land Bill, 220–249.

1789 Notices of Catholic continental periodicals, 250–259. Pages 250–253 by **Alfons Bellesheim**—signature.

1790 Notices of books, 259–306. Pages 287–292, 303–306 signed **W. E. Addis;** pages 297–299 by **Alfons Bellesheim**—signature; pages 294–296 signed S.M.; pages 280–286 signed **Gustave Masson.**

VOLUME 6 3RD S., 89 O.S., OCTOBER 1881

1791 The eighteenth century (Part IV, concl.), 307–336. **W. S. Lilly.** Signed.

1792 The Christian emperors and the pagan temples, 336–353. **W. R. Brownlow.** Signed.

1793 Literature for the young (Part I): periodical literature, 354–377.

1794 Minor poets of modern France (Part I), 377–406.

1795 Archbishop Lanfranc and his modern critics, 406–433. **Martin Rule.** Signed.

1796 The religion of George Eliot, 433–464. **William Francis Barry.** Signed William Barry.

1797 Prospects in Belgium, 464–498. **R. W. Petre.** Attr. in Gillow, V, 294.

1798 The days of creation: a reply [to criticisms of no. 1771], 498–507. **William Clifford,** 1823–1893. Signed.

1799 Constitution of Pope Leo XIII regarding the bishops and regular missionaries in England and Scotland, 508–522. **Leo XIII.** Title.

1800 Encyclical on political power, 522–530. **Leo PP. XIII.** Signed.

1801 Notices of Catholic continental periodicals, 531–541. Pages 539–541 by **Alfons Bellesheim**—signature.

1802 Notices of books, 541–566. Pages 551, 553–554 by **Alfons Bellesheim**—signed B., cf. no. 1724; pages 551–553, 554–555 by **Alfons Bellesheim**—signature.

VOLUME 7 3RD S., 90 O.S., JANUARY 1882

1803 The mission of the Zambesi, 1–31. **Ellen M. Clerke,** prob. Cf. no. 1775; referred to in nos. 2545, p. 267, and 2702, p. 59, both signed E. M. Clerke.

1804 English men of letters, 31–49. **John Charles Earle.** Signed.

1805 Philosophy of the theistic controversy,

49–85. **William George Ward.** Signed; repr. *Essays on Theism*, II.

1806   St. Francis de Sales: doctor of the Church (Part I), 86–115. **H. B. Mackey.** This and the succeeding parts repr. under his name as *Four Essays on . . . S. Francis de Sales*, 1883.

1807   Recent works on the state of Germany (Part II, concl.), 115–139. **P. Alberdingk Thijm.** Signed.

1808   The condition of the Catholics of Ireland one hundred years ago, 139–170. **Patrick Francis Moran.** Signed.

1809   Simoniacal casuistry in the established Church, 171–190.

1810   The canonization of the Eighth of December, 190–208. **J. C. Hedley.** Attr. in *Life*, p. 220.

1811   The Land League and the Land Act, 208–238.

1812   Notices of Catholic continental periodicals, 239–246. Pages 245–246 by **Alfons Bellesheim**—signature; pages 242–245 by **Martin Rule**—signed M.R., he had written no. 1795 on same subject.

1813   Notices of books, 247–290. Pages 267–271, 283–285 signed **W. E. Addis;** pages 273–275 by **Alfons Bellesheim**—signature; pages 258–260 signed E.; pages 250–258 by **W. S. Lilly**—signed W.S.L., cf. no. 1779.

VOLUME 7 3RD S., 90 O.S., APRIL 1882

1814   The voyage of the *Vega* and its results, 291–320. **Ellen M. Clerke.** Signature.

1815   County administration, 321–345. **N. J. Synnott?** This art. deals with same general subject as no. 1899 by Synnott: the role of the state in relation to local and individual self-determination; in no. 1899, p. 64, Synnott quotes from this art.; the style of both arts. is very direct and factual, and the author in both cases is well versed in current political thought.

1816   The physiological psychology of St. Thomas, 345–357. **J. R. Gasquet.** Oscott II; opening paragraph says this is by the author of no. 1728.

1817   Minor poets of modern France (Part II), 358–376.

1818   The household books of Lord William Howard, 376–394. **Philip Henry Howard?** See evidence for no. 1619.

1819   *John Inglesant*, 395–426. **William Francis Barry.** Signed as in no. 1796; repr. *Heralds of Revolt*, 1909.

1820   Recent evidence in support of 1 John v.7, 426–439.

1821   Literature for the young (Part II, concl.), 439–460.

1822   The Pope [and his political independence], 460–480. **J. C. Hedley.** Oscott II; attr. Matthews, "Hedley," p. 265; referred to in no. 2001, p. 148.

1823   Two letters to the bishops of Italy, 481–489. **Leo PP. XIII.** Signed.

1824   Science notices, 490–493.

1825   Notices of Catholic continental periodicals, 494–504. Pages 498–500 by **Alfons Bellesheim?**—he consistently did the section on German periodicals.

1826   Notices of books, 505–542. Pages 508–513 signed **W. E. Addis;** pages 507–508; 534–535 by **Ellen M. Clerke?**—she prob. wrote no. 1803 on same topic; pages 505–507 by **J. R. Gasquet?**—he wrote no. 1816 in this issue, on psychology and Thomas Aquinas, subject of these notices.

VOLUME 8 3RD S., 91 O.S., JULY 1882

1827   The sacred books of the East, 1–32. **W. S. Lilly.** Signed; repr. *Ancient Religion and Modern Thought* (1884), pp. 103–164.

1828   Electric lighting, 33–55. **Eric Stuart Bruce,** prob. This specialized account of specific details of production and use of electricity is very similar in matter and style to no. 1973 which is signed by Bruce; Bruce's conversion occurred in the following year, so he was prob. already in touch with Roman Catholics.

1829   The nomenclature of the days of the week, 56–73. **Sylvester Malone.** Signed.

1830   St. Francis de Sales: doctor of the Church (Part II), 74–104. **H. B. Mackey.** Cf. no. 1806.

1831   The vices of agnostic poetry, 104–127. **John Charles Earle.** Signed.

1832   Catholicism in North Africa, 127–158. **Ellen M. Clerke,** prob. This art. is included in the list of Catholic missions in Africa in no. 1942, p. 28n.; cf. no. 1775.

1833   Mr. Freeman's *William Rufus*, 158–182. **Martin Rule.** Oscott II; this art. expands and augments the passing objections taken by Rule in no. 1795 to Freeman's bias and inaccuracy.

1834   Ireland, 182–200.

1835   Letters to the bishops of Sicily, 201–208. **Leo PP. XIII.** Signed.

1836   Science notices, 209–213.

1837   Notices of Catholic continental periodicals, 213–225. Pages 213–217 by **Alfons Bellesheim**—signature.

1838 Notices of books, 225–264. Pages 232–235 by **Alfons Bellesheim**—signature.

VOLUME 8 3RD S., 91 O.S., OCTOBER 1882

1839 William George Ward, 265–272. **H. E. Manning.** Signed Henry Edward, Cardinal Archbishop; repr. *Miscellanies*, III.
1840 Alessandro Manzoni and his works, 273–302. **Ellen M. Clerke.** Signature; repr. *Fable and Song in Italy*, 1899.
1841 The resurrection of Ireland [Lecky's *History of England in the Eighteenth Century*], 302–330. **W. S. Lilly.** Signed.
1842 The childhood of religions, 331–354.
1843 Berthold Auerbach, 354–373. **William Francis Barry.** Signed as in no. 1796.
1844 The Corea, 373–397. **Ellen M. Clerke,** prob. This is another in the series on missions and the author again is relying on *Les Missions Catholiques*; cf. no. 1775; the book by Charles Dallet, used in writing this art., appears again at the head of no. 2478, signed E. M. Clerke.
1845 Taine's *French Revolution*, 397–416.
1846 Catholic memories of an old English city [Durham], 417–433. **Philip Henry Howard?** See evidence for no. 1619.
1847 Letter to the bishops of Ireland [on violence and secret societies], 434–437. **Leo PP. XIII.** Signed.
1848 Science notices, 438–441.
1849 Notices of Catholic continental periodicals, 441–453. Pages 441–444 by **Alfons Bellesheim**—signature.
1850 Notices of books, 454–524. Pages 466–467, 468–469 by **Alfons Bellesheim**—signature; pages 483–489 signed R.; pages 491–493 signed **W. S. Lilly.**

VOLUME 9 3RD S., 92 O.S., JANUARY 1883

1851 St. Martin and St. Patrick, 1–32. **W. B. Morris.** Signed.
1852 Bishop Clifford's theory of the days of creation, 32–47. **John S. Vaughan.** Signed.
1853 Fifty versions of "Dies Irae" (Part I), 48–77. **Orby Shipley.** Oscott II; Shipley was editor of various collections of hymns; see *BMCat*.
1854 Ireland under the legislative union, 78–100. **W. J. O'Neill Daunt.** Signed; repr. *Essays on Ireland*, 1886.
1855 The Third Order of St. Francis, 100–126.
1856 St. Francis de Sales, doctor of the Church (Part III), 127–153. **Henry Benedict Mackey.** Signed.

1857 Catholicism in Egypt, 153–181. **Ellen M. Clerke,** prob. This is another of the series on missions and the author is again using *Les Missions Catholiques*; cf. no. 1775.
1858 Ireland: her friends and foes, 181–200.
1859 Encyclical letter on St. Francis of Assisi and the spread of the Third Order, 201–207. **Leo PP. XIII.** Signed.
1860 Science notices, 208–213.
1861 Notices of Catholic continental periodicals, 213–222. Pages 213–215 by **Alfons Bellesheim**—signature.
1862 Notices of books, 222–259. Pages 225–228 by **Alfons Bellesheim**—signature; pages 241–244 by **Ellen M. Clerke?**—she was prob. author of no. 1803.

VOLUME 9 3RD S., 92 O.S., APRIL 1883

1863 Denis Florence MacCarthy, 261–293. **Ellen M. Clerke.** Signature.
1864 The Society of St. Vincent de Paul, 293–314. **Henry D. Harrod,** prob. This art. is concerned with serving the poor, a subject developed by Harrod in nos. 1915 and 1972; in no. 1915, p. 415, Harrod says he is repeating words from Ozanam which "we" quoted in the *DR* for April 1883, here on p. 294.
1865 The novels of Anthony Trollope, 314–334.
1866 Catholic political associations, 334–347. **Edmund Randolph** (Jun.). Signed.
1867 How the Union robs Ireland, 347–369. **W. J. O'N. Daunt.** Signed; repr. *Essays on Ireland*, 1886.
1868 Fifty versions of "Dies Irae" (Part II, concl.), 369–396. **Orby Shipley.** Oscott II. AND, **C. F. S. Warren,** who wrote 374–377 and signed the note on p. 377 C.F.S.W. (Note by **Shipley** and **C. F. S. Warren,** vol. 10 3rd s., pp. 243–244, where the latter's share in the art. is defined.)
1869 The days of creation: some further observations, 397–417. **William Clifford,** 1823–1893. Signed.
1870 The changed position of married women, 417–442. **John George Cox.** Signed.
1871 The sad experience of Catholics in non-Catholic universities, 442–462. **H. A. Vaughan.** Signed Herbert, Bishop of Salford; see *DNB*.
1872 Science notices, 463–467.
1873 Notices of Catholic continental periodicals, 467–477. Pages 471–474 by **Alfons Bellesheim**—signature.

1874 Notices of books, 478–512. Pages 493–494 by **J. S. Vaughan**, prob.—signed J.S.V.; man cited was a brother of H. A. Vaughan and was to be a frequent contributor.

VOLUME 10 3RD S., 93 O.S., JULY 1883

1875 On Catholic politics, 1–25. **St. George Mivart.** Signed.
1876 St. Francis de Sales, doctor of the Church (Part IV, concl.), 25–62. **Henry Benedict Mackey.** Signed.
1877 Freiligrath, 63–83. **William Francis Barry.** Signed as in no. 1796.
1878 Adrian IV. and Ireland, 83–103. **Francis Aidan Gasquet.** Signed. (See no. 1911.)
1879 Jane Austen, 103–129.
1880 The Tsar and his Holy Synod in 1840, 129–148.
1881 The Holy See, and the clergy of Ireland, 148–165. With the text of the "circular letter" discussed, 166. **J. C. Hedley.** Attr. in *Life*, p. 221; by Matthews, "Hedley," p. 265.
1882 Science notices, 167–172.
1883 Notices of Catholic continental periodicals, 172–182. Pages 172–175 by **Alfons Bellesheim**—signature.
1884 Notices of books, 182–243. Pages 211–213 by **Alfons Bellesheim**—signature; pages 199–201, 201–205 by **Edmund Bishop**—*Life*, pp. 96, 494.

VOLUME 10 3RD S., 93 O.S., OCTOBER 1883

1885 The three Fausts, 245–259. **L. C. Casartelli.** Signed.
1886 Modern Mexico, 260–291. **Ellen M. Clerke.** Signature.
1887 Some new English documents on Our Lady's Immaculate Conception, 291–305. **T. E. Bridgett.** Signed.
1888 Projects of the liberals in Belgium, 306–337. **R. W. Petre.** Attr. in Gillow, V, 294.
1889 Ireland in the time of Swift, 337–370. **W. J. O'N. Daunt.** Signed; repr. *Essays on Ireland*, 1886.
1890 Church discipline and Protestant historians, 370–389. **Sylvester Malone.** Signed.
1891 Elementary education; our position, prospects and policy, 389–401.
1892 Beginnings [of belief], 402–412. **J. C. Hedley.** Attr. in *Life*, p. 220.

1893 Letters on historical studies, 413–419, and on the Rosary, 420–424. **Leo PP. XIII.** Signed.
1894 Science notices, 425–429.
1895 Notices of Catholic continental periodicals, 429–438. Pages 431–434 by **Alfons Bellesheim**—signature.
1896 Notices of books, 439–490. Pages 441–447 signed **W. E. Addis;** pages 439–440 by **Alfons Bellesheim**—signature.

VOLUME 11 3RD S., 94 O.S., JANUARY 1884

1897 Secular education, 1–23. **David Lewis.** Signed D.L.; Oscott II; man cited wrote on public elementary education in 1871; see *BMCat.*
1898 Wycliffe and his teaching concerning the Primacy, 23–62. **Louis Delplace.** Signed L. Delplace, S.J.; see Seyn.
1899 Liberty, laisser-faire, and legislation, 62–80. **N. J. Synnott.** Signed.
1900 Alexander Farnese, 81–92.
1901 The Copts, 93–117. **Ellen M. Clerke,** prob. This is another in the series on missions, in which the author again uses *Les Missions Catholiques;* cf. no. 1775, and no. 1902.
1902 Madagascar past and present, 117–149. **Ellen M. Clerke.** Signature.
1903 The city of our martyrs [Douai], 149–186. **James Boniface Mackinlay.** Signed.
1904 New Testament Vaticanism, 186–201. **J. C. Hedley?** Attr. Matthews, "Hedley," p. 265.
1905 Science notices, 202–206.
1906 Notices of Catholic continental periodicals, 206–218. Pages 206–209 by **Alfons Bellesheim**—signature.
1907 Notices of books, 218–244. Pages 235–237 by **Alfons Bellesheim**—signature.

VOLUME 11 3RD S., 94 O.S., APRIL 1884

1908 *Dreizehnlinden* [by F. W. Weber], 245–272. **William Francis Barry.** Signed as in no. 1796.
1909 From logic to God, 273–307. **Thomas Harper.** Signed, with addition, "S.J."
1910 Life of St. Olaf, 307–316. **T. E. Bridgett.** Signed.
1911 Adrian IV. and Ireland [reply to no. 1878], 316–343. **Sylvester Malone.** Signed.
1912 The experiment of France, 344–366. **W. S. Lilly.** Signed.
1913 Christendom in ideal and in fact, 366–

392. **J. C. Hedley?** Attr. Matthews, "Hedley," p. 265; on Willson's list by internal evidence.

1914 The revolution in the Soudan, 392–414. **Ellen M. Clerke.** Signature.

1915 The dwellings of the poor, 414–437. **Henry D. Harrod.** Signed.

1916 Encyclical letter to the bishops of France, 438–443. **Leo PP. XIII.** Signed.

1917 Science notices, 444–448.

1918 Notices of Catholic continental periodicals, 449–458. Pages 449–452 by **Alfons Bellesheim**—signature.

1919 Notices of books, 458–495. Pages 466–467, 482–483 signed **W. E. Addis**; pages 470–471, 476 by **Alfons Bellesheim**—signature.

VOLUME 12 3RD S., 95 O.S., JULY 1884

1920 The first Sisters of Charity, 1–21.

1921 Recent editions of Aristophanes and Sophocles, 22–46. **Henry Hayman,** prob. Signed H.H.; Oscott II gives "H. Hayman"; see *DNB.*

1922 Ivan Tourguénief, 46–65. **G. V. Staratsky.** Signed.

1923 The conversion of England, 65–86. **St. George Mivart.** Signed.

1924 The primitive religion of the Chinese, 87–109. **Charles de Harlez.** Signed as in no. 1779.

1925 The *Encyclopoedia Britannica* on missions, 109–144. **A. Hilliard Atteridge.** Signed, with title "S.J."

1926 Pope Leo XIII and the freemasons, 144–165. **J. C. Hedley.** Attr. in *Life*, p. 220.

1927 Encyclical letter on freemasonry, 166–179. **Leo PP. XIII.** Signed.

1928 Science notices, 180–182.

1929 Notices of Catholic continental periodicals, 183–193. Pages 183–186 by **Alfons Bellesheim**—signature.

1930 Notices of books, 194–244. Pages 224–225 signed **W. E. Addis**; pages 219–220 by **Alfons Bellesheim**—signature; pages 241–242 signed **Henry D. Harrod;** pages 198–200 by **H. E. Manning**—signed as in no. 1839; repr. *Miscellanies,* III.

VOLUME 12 3RD S., 95 O.S., OCTOBER 1884

1931 Dryden as a hymnodist, 245–269. **Orby Shipley.** Signed.

1932 The battle of theism, 270–290. **Wil**liam Francis Barry. Signed as in no. 1796.

1933 Christianity in Lancashire in Roman and Celtic times, 290–316. **Robert Gradwell.** Signed; *DR* list adds title "Mgr."; see *Landed Gentry.*

1934 Abyssinia and its people, 316–345. **Ellen M. Clerke.** Signature.

1935 The vicissitudes of "vigil," 345–358. **Sylvester Malone.** Signed.

1936 The conversion of England: a reply [to no. 1923], 358–387. **Sydney H. Little.** Signed. (Reply, vol. 13 3rd s., p. 193. by **St. George Mivart**—title.)

1937 The Christian Brothers at the Health Exhibition, 387–411.

1938 Encyclical letter ordering the Rosary during October, 412–414. **Leo PP. XIII.** Signed.

1939 Science notices, 415–419.

1940 Notices of Catholic continental periodicals, 420–430. Pages 427–430 by **Alfons Bellesheim**—signature.

1941 Notices of books, 430–496. Pages 442–450 signed **W. E. Addis**; pages 455–457, 473–474 by **William Francis Barry**—signed as in no. 1796; pages 450–451, 461–463, 483–484 by **Alfons Bellesheim**—signature; pages 472–473 signed **Charles de Harlez**; pages 475–478 signed **Sylvester Malone.**

VOLUME 13 3RD S., 96 O.S., JANUARY 1885

1942 Commercial future of West Africa, 1–30. **Ellen M. Clerke,** prob. Oscott II; ref. back on p. 27 to no. 1775 and on p. 28n. to nos. 1785, 1803, 1832; woman cited contributed a number of signed arts. on commercial topics: see below Part B.

1943 The healing art in philosophy, 30–49. **Wilfrid Ward.** Signed.

1944 Mechanical devotions, 50–62. **R. F. Clarke.** Signed.

1945 Carlyle, 63–90. **William Francis Barry.** Signed as in no. 1796; repr. *Heralds of Revolt* (1909).

1946 Further remarks on the *Teaching of the Twelve Apostles* [see no. 1941, pp. 442–450], 91–106. **Henry Hayman.** Signed H. Hayman; man cited was a contributor at this time.

1947 Catholic boys' clubs, 107–123. **Henry D. Harrod.** Signed.

1948 English hagiology, 123–154. **Edmund Bishop.** Signed.

1949 The Catholic education question in England and Ireland (No. I): England—

elementary schools, 154–168. **John Kershaw.** Signed.

1950 The Catholic education question in England and Ireland (No. II): the Irish university question, 169–192. **Peter Huvetys.** Signed P. Huvetys, with title, "President, Blackrock College."

1951 Science notices, 194–205.

1952 Notices of Catholic continental periodicals, 206–216. Pages 212–216 by **Alfons Bellesheim**—signature.

1953 Notices of books, 217–242. Pages 220–222, 226–228 by **Alfons Bellesheim**—signature.

VOLUME 13 3RD S., 96 O.S., APRIL 1885

1954 The defender of the faith [Henry VIII], 243–268. **T. E. Bridgett.** Signed.

1955 Mrs. Inchbald, 269–293. **Peter Haythornthwaite.** Signed P. Haythornthwaite; for man cited see *Ward as Catholic,* p. 382.

1956 Protestant missions in Southern India: Tinnevelly and Ramnad, 294–316. **A. Hilliard Atteridge.** Signed.

1957 The educational crisis in Belgium, 316–331.

1958 The origin of terrestrial life, 332–339. **William Hamilton Bodley.** Signed.

1959 Recent explorations of ancient sites in Rome, 340–354. **Henry Hayman.** Signed as in no. 1946.

1960 The destiny of Khartoum, 355–381. **Ellen M. Clerke.** Oscott II; Casartelli, "Jubilee," p. 269; ref. back on p. 365 to no. 1914 signed E. M. Clerke.

1961 The brain and the mind, 381–392. **Andrew T. Sibbald.** Signed.

1962 Democracy: whither? 393–405. **Charles Weld Blundell.** Signed.

1963 Science notices, 406–410.

1964 Notes of travel and exploration, 411–420. **Ellen M. Clerke,** prob. The department here inaugurated reflects throughout the same basic concerns: missions, commercial potentials of newly discovered lands, particularly Africa, and improved modes of transportation (railroads and canals); many of these topics are dealt with at greater length in arts. signed E. M. Clerke (see below Part B); the easy journalistic style is the same as that characterizing her signed arts.; in the earlier issues the author makes use of *Les Missions Catholiques* and in at least two later ones of *Illustrated Catholic Missions* (see evidence for no. 1775); three installments are actually signed

E.M.C. (nos. 2345, 2356, and 2371), a fact which seems to be purely fortuitous, since all are so clearly by the same author; that here, as in the series of arts. on Catholic missions (no. 1775, etc.), the author may be writing under the guidance of Hedley or Vaughan is suggested by the frequent refs. to the Manchester Geographical Society which had been founded by the latter.

1964a Notes on novels, 420. Statement of policy with regard to reviewing novels; hereafter these will be included with regular notices.

1965 Notices of books, 420–430, 443–492. Pages 453–457 by **Alfons Bellesheim**—signature; pages 450–451 signed G.C.; pages 464–468 by **W. E. Driffield**—attr. in Bishop, *Life,* p. 495; pages 457–464 by **Joseph Van den Gheyn**—signed J. Van den Gheyn, S.J., M.R.A.S.

1966 Notices of Catholic continental periodicals, 431–443. Pages 431–435 by **Alfons Bellesheim**—signature.

VOLUME 14 3RD S., 97 O.S., JULY 1885

1967 Maritime canals, 1–19. **Ellen M. Clerke.** Signature.

1968 Studies in Oriental patrology: St. Ephrem, 20–44. **T. J. Lamy.** Signed.

1969 Catholics and modern literature, 45–64. **William Francis Barry.** Signed as in no. 1796.

1970 The present position of the arguments for the existence of God, 65–78. **J. R. Gasquet.** Signed.

1971 "The Holy Face," 78–102. **Ella B. Edes.** Signed.

1972 The Royal Commission on the homes of the poor, 102–119. **Henry D. Harrod.** Signed.

1973 Electric light and energy, 120–134. **Eric Stuart Bruce.** Signed.

1974 The Indian revenue and intoxicants, 135–148. **H. A. Phillips.** Signed.

1975 On the formation of knowledge, 148–171. **John G. Wenham.** Signed.

1976 Science notices, 172–177.

1977 Notes of travel and exploration, 177–186. **Ellen M. Clerke,** prob. Cf. no. 1964.

1978 Notices of books, 187–198, 210–242. Pages 222, 223, 237–238 by **Alfons Bellesheim**—signature; pages 234–235 signed H.W.; pages 226–227 unidentified, (letter from **Denis Gargan,** pp. 485–487, with reply from the reviewer, pp. 487–491.)

1979 Notices of Catholic continental periodicals, 199–210. Pages 199–203 by **Alfons Bellesheim**—signature.

VOLUME 14 3RD S., 97 O.S., OCTOBER 1885

1980 What has the Church to do with science? 243–253. **Joseph Rickaby.** Signed.

1981 The Irish question (No. I): a policy for Ireland, 254–265. **C. Raleigh Chichester.** Signed; *DR* list adds "Col."

1982 The Irish question (No. II): tithe rent-charge in Ireland, 265–275. **W. J. O'N. Daunt.** Signed; repr. *Essays on Ireland*, 1886.

1983 The gates of India, 276–301. **Ellen M. Clerke.** Signature.

1984 Souvenirs of a missionary college [Séminaire des Missions Étrangères in Paris], 301–324.

1985 Mr. Henry George and the land, 325–346. **J. C. Hedley.** Signed J.C.H.; *Life*, p. 221.

1986 The so-called "Sacred Books" of China, 346–369. **Charles de Harlez.** Signed as in no. 1779.

1987 The prophecies of St. Malachi, 369–386. **J. P. C. Stuart.** Signed Bute [Marquis of Bute]; repr. *Foreign Essays.*

1988 The outcome of Lutheranism in Prussia, 386–400. **Joseph Verres.** Signed.

1989 How shall Catholics vote at the coming Parliamentary election? 401–411. **H. E. Manning.** Signed as in no. 1839; repr. under this title, 1885.

1990 Science notices, 412–416.

1991 Notes of travel and exploration, 417–426. **Ellen M. Clerke,** prob. Cf. no. 1964.

1992 Notices of books, 426–433, 444–484. Pages 447–451 by **Alfons Bellesheim**—signature.

1993 Notices of Catholic continental periodicals, 433–444. Pages 433–436 by **Alfons Bellesheim**—signature.

VOLUME 15 3RD S., 98 O.S., JANUARY 1886

1994 Proportionate representation, 1–22. **Aubrey de Vere.** Signed; repr. *Essays.*

1995 Olier and Dupanloup, 22–40. **John S. Vaughan.** Signed.

1996 The nerves and over-pressure, 40–57. **Andrew T. Sibbald.** Signed.

1997 The Church and liberalism, 58–68. **F. R. Wegg-Prosser.** Signed.

1998 The story of Cowdray [House], 69–91. **William Francis Barry.** Signed as in no. 1796.

1999 Religion in the north [of England], 91–102.

2000 The Slav states of the Balkans, 102–133. **Ellen M. Clerke.** Signature.

2001 Catholic union and Catholic parties, 133–152. **J. C. Hedley.** *Life*, p. 221.

2002 Encyclical letter on the constitution of Christian states, 153–168. **Leo PP. XIII.** Signed.

2003 Letter to the bishops of England, 169–170. **Leo PP. XIII.** Signed.

2004 Science notices, 171–174.

2005 Notes of travel and exploration, 174–181. **Ellen M. Clerke,** prob. Cf. no. 1964.

2006 Notices of books, 181–190, 200–242. Pages 214–215, 225–226 signed T.A.B.; pages 205–207, 209, 210 by **Alfons Bellesheim**—signature; pages 211–214 signed J.W.D.; pages 200–205 by **J. R. Gasquet** —signed J.R.G.; he was writing notices for the *DR* at this time, some signed J.R.G. and others J. R. Gasquet, cf. particularly no. 2158.

2007 Notices of Catholic continental periodicals, 190–200. Pages 194–197 by **Alfons Bellesheim**—signature.

VOLUME 15 3RD S., 98 O.S., APRIL 1886

2008 The decay of the British Constitution, 243–260. **C. S. Devas.** Signed.

2009 The Archduchess Isabel [daughter of Philip II of Spain], 260–280. **Amy M. Grange.** Signed A. M. Grange; *DR* list adds "Mrs."; for woman cited see *BMCat.*

2010 Professor Jowett's *Politics of Aristotle,* 280–289. **Henry Hayman.** Oscott II; he was contributing at this time on classical subjects, cf. no. 2274.

2011 The patriarch of the "Active Orders" [Peter Fourier], 290–308.

2012 Burma and the farther East, 309–340. **Ellen M. Clerke.** Signature.

2013 The letters of the Popes, 340–358. **J. C. Hedley.** *DR* list; *Life*, p. 221.

2014 Methods of historical inquiry (No. II), 359–374. **Henry Worsley.** Signed. (Part I is no. 1769.)

2015 Symposium on Home Rule (No. I): the claim for Home Rule upon general principles, 374–394. **James Moyes.** Signed J. Moyes; man cited was canon of Salford under Vaughan and in 1892 succeeded him as editor of the *DR.*

2016 Symposium on Home Rule (No. II): the probable consequences of Home Rule, 394–403. Signed: An Irish Catholic Barrister.

2017 Science notices, 404–407.
2018 Notes of travel and exploration, 407–417. **Ellen M. Clerke,** prob. Cf. no. 1964.
2019 Notices of books, 417–426, 434–491. Pages 462–471 signed **W. E. Addis;** pages 449–450, 450–452 by **Alfons Bellesheim**—signature; pages 456–457 by **Edmund Bishop**—signed E.B., *Life,* p. 495; pages 472–478 signed **J. R. Gasquet;** pages 447–449 signed **T. B. Scannell;** pages 452–455 signed **Paul Alberdingk Thijm.**
2020 Notices of Catholic continental periodicals, 426–434. Pages 426–428 by **Alfons Bellesheim**—signature.

VOLUME 16 3RD S., 99 O.S., JULY 1886

2021 Novelists and novels, 1–9. **C. C. Longridge.** Signed.
2022 The progress of nihilism, 9–30. **William Francis Barry.** Signed as in no. 1796.
2023 The future of petroleum, 31–65. **Ellen M. Clerke.** Signature.
2024 *Pro vivis et defunctis:* some remarks upon Father Amherst's *History of Catholic Emancipation,* 65–91. **W. S. Lilly.** Signed.
2025 Plato's *Atlantis* and the *Periplus* of Hanno, 91–104. **Alexandre Motais.** Signed X; attr. in no. 2036, p. 351; *DR* list.
2026 The first Chinese philosopher, or, The system of Lao-tze, 105–127. **Charles de Harlez.** Signed as in no. 1779.
2027 Canadian opinion on the question of Home Rule, 128–144. **L. G. Power.** Signed, with address "Ottawa."
2028 Notes of travel and exploration, 145–153. **Ellen M. Clerke,** prob. Cf. no. 1964.
2029 Notices of books, 153–167, 176–241. Pages 194–195 signed **W. E. Addis;** pages 186–187, 207–208, 208 by **Alfons Bellesheim**—signature; pages 199–203 by **Edmund Bishop**—signed E.B., *Life,* p. 496; pages 210–211 by **J. R. Gasquet**—signed J.R.G.—cf. no. 2006; pages 213–215 signed **T. B. Scannell.**
2030 Notices of Catholic continental periodicals, 167–176. Pages 167–170 by **Alfons Bellesheim**—signature.

VOLUME 16 3RD S., 99 O.S., OCTOBER 1886

2031 What to do with the landowners, 243–260. **C. S. Devas.** Signed.
2032 Longfellow, 260–294. **Helen Atteridge.** Signed.

2033 Facilities of modern pilgrimage, 295–313. **F. R. Wegg-Prosser.** Signed.
2034 Where was St. Patrick born? (Part I), 314–334. **Sylvester Malone.** Signed. (See nos. 2063, 2088, and 2100.)
2035 Social disturbances: their cause and cure, 335–351. **John S. Vaughan.** Signed.
2036 The secret of Plato's *Atlantis*—a reply [to no. 2025], 351–363. **John Francis Arundell.** Signed Arundell of Wardour [Baron Arundell].
2037 Present position of China, 364–391. **Ellen M. Clerke.** Signature.
2038 Frederick Lucas, 392–428. **William J. Amherst.** Signed, with title "S.J."
2039 Brief in favour of the Society of Jesus, 429–430. **Leo PP. XIII.** Signed.
2040 Letters of Leo PP XIII: To the bishops of Hungary, 430–437. **Leo XIII.** Title. Constituting an episcopal hierarchy in India, 438–445. **Leo XIII.** Title.
2041 Notices of Catholic continental periodicals, 446–454. Pages 446–448 by **Alfons Bellesheim**—signature.
2042 Notes of travel and exploration, 454–463. **Ellen M. Clerke,** prob. Cf. no. 1964.
2043 Notices of books, 464–472, 476–492. Pages 484–488 signed **William Lockhart;** pages 480–481 signed **T. B. Scannell.**
2044 Science notices, 472–475.

VOLUME 17 3RD S., 100 O.S., JANUARY 1887

2045 Mr. John Morley, 1–29. **W. S. Lilly.** Signed.
2046 Protestant missions in Southern India: Tanjore, 30–44. **A. Hilliard Atteridge.** Signed.
2047 The English Constitution in theory and practice, 45–57. **T. B. Scannell.** Signed.
2048 Shakespeare as an economist, 57–80. **C. S. Devas.** Signed.
2049 Ancient Benedictine customs, 80–98. **Adam Hamilton.** Signed.
2050 The Portuguese in India, 98–124. **Ellen M. Clerke.** Signature.
2051 The influence of fatalism on public opinion, 125–139. **N. J. Synnott.** Signed.
2052 The story of the French exiles, 140–157. **T. E. Bridgett.** Signed.
2053 The lost, strayed and stolen of our Catholic poor children, 157–176. **Austin Oates.** Signed.
2054 Science notices, 177–188. Pages 180–181 signed **C. S. Devas;** pages 182–188 by **F. R. Wegg-Prosser**—signed F.R.W.-P.
2055 Notes of travel and exploration, 188–197. **Ellen M. Clerke,** prob. Cf. no. 1964.
2056 Notices of books, 197–202, 211–241.

Pages 221–223, 230, 231–232 by **Alfons Bellesheim**—signature; pages 233–234 signed **T. B. Scannell.**

2057 Notices of Catholic continental periodicals, 202–211. Pages 204–208 by **Alfons Bellesheim**—signature.

VOLUME 17 3RD S., 100 O.S., APRIL 1887

2058 Church extension and Anglican expansion, 243–265. **Thomas Arnold**, 1823–1900. Signed T. Arnold; see *DNB*.
2059 Barbour's *Legends of the Saints*, 265–277. **Mary M. Maxwell Scott.** Signed M. M. Maxwell Scott; repr. *Incidents.*
2060 War and ballooning, 278–287. **Eric Stuart Bruce.** Signed.
2061 Critics and class-lists, 287–306. **Edmund Gurney.** Signed.
2062 The Church after the Conquest, 306–333. **David Lewis.** Signed D.L.; Oscott II.
2063 Where St. Patrick was born (Part I), 334–359. **Colin C. Grant.** Signed. (See nos. 2034, 2088, and 2100.)
2064 Italy, present and future, 359–380. **A. Hilliard Atteridge.** Signed.
2065 Lightfoot's [conception of] St. Ignatius and the Roman Primacy, 380–399. **J. R. Gasquet**, prob. Signed J.R.G.; cf. no. 2006.
2066 The Catholic Truth Society, 400–413. **James Britten.** Signed.
2067 Notes of travel and exploration, 414–420. **Ellen M. Clerke**, prob. Cf. no. 1964.
2068 Notices of books, 420–424, 430–491. Pages 448, 449–450 by **Alfons Bellesheim**—signature; pages 430–437 by **H. E. Manning**—signed as in no. 1839; repr. *Miscellanies, III*; pages 481–482 signed **T. B. Scannell.**
2069 Notices of Catholic continental periodicals, 424–430. Pages 426–427 by **Alfons Bellesheim**—signature.

VOLUME 18 3RD S., 101 O.S., JULY 1887

2070 Bishop [Robert William] Willson, 1–26. **W. B. Ullathorne.** Signed.
2071 *The Throne of the Fisherman* [by T. W. Allies], 26–36.
2072 A glance at the history of Chinese philosophy, 36–54. **Charles de Harlez.** Signed as in no. 1779.
2073 The age of steel, 54–77. **Ellen M. Clerke.** Signature.
2074 The Venerable Richard Whiting, last

Abbot of Glastonbury, 78–110. **Francis Aidan Gasquet** and **Edmund Bishop.** Signed by Gasquet, but see Bishop, *Life*, p. 129, for proof of the collaboration.
2075 Pius VII. at Savona, 110–125. **T. B. Scannell.** Signed.
2076 The *Memoirs of Count Beust*, 126–151. **A. Hilliard Atteridge.** Signed.
2077 The work of the laity, 151–167. **James Britten.** Signed.
2078 Notes of travel and exploration, 168–180. **Ellen M. Clerke**, prob. Cf. no. 1964.
2079 Notices of books, 181–187, 197–242. Pages 205–206, 220–221 signed **W. E. Addis**; pages 238–240 signed **A. Hilliard Atteridge**; pages 210–211, 228–229, 233 by **Alfons Bellesheim**—signature; pages 208–210 signed G.C.; pages 240–241 signed **F. Landott**; pages 217–220 signed **W. S. Lilly**; pages 207–208, 213–215 by James Moyes, prob.—signed J.M., this and subsequent notices signed J.M. are prob. by man cited, who was already a contributor (see no. 2015) and in 1892 became editor; pages 224, 230 by **T. B. Scannell**, prob.—signed T.B.S., he wrote many notices in this period, some signed with his name and some with his initials; pages 224–225, 230–231 signed **T. B. Scannell.**
2080 Notices of Catholic continental periodicals, 187–197. Pages 187–190 by **Alfons Bellesheim**—signature; pages 195–197 signed **C. S. Devas.**

VOLUME 18 3RD S., 101 O.S., OCTOBER 1887

2081 M. Emery, Superior of St. Sulpice, 243–267. **H. I. D. Ryder.** Signed; repr. *Essays*, 1911.
2082 The native princes of India, 268–290. **Ellen M. Clerke.** Signature.
2083 Catholic women and night-work, 291–308. Signed: Catholica.
2084 The [Irish] Constitution of 1782, 308–323. **W. S. Lilly.** Signed.
2085 The Jews in France (Part I), 323–350. **F. Jeffrée.** Signed "Jeffrée"; *DR* list gives "F. Jeffrée," where the "F" may indicate Frère or Father.
2086 The Catholic University of Ireland, 350–360. **Thomas Arnold**, 1823–1900. Signed One of the Old Staff; *DR* list; man cited was a professor at Catholic University of Ireland under Newman.
2087 Dr. Stubbs on English ecclesiastical law, 360–386. **David Lewis.** Signed D.L.; Oscott II.
2088 Where was St. Patrick born? (Part II,

concl.), 387–401. **Sylvester Malone.** Signed. (See nos. 2034, 2063, and 2100.)

2089 Dr. Mivart on faith and science, 401–419. **John Cuthbert Hedley.** Signed. (Reply, vol. 19 3rd s., pp. 180–187 signed **St. George Mivart;** rejoinder pp. 188–189 by **Hedley**—signed J.C.H. and see no. 2115.)

2090 Science notices, 420–430. Pages 423–430 by **F. R. Wegg-Prosser**—signed F.R.W-P.

2091 Notes of travel and exploration, 430–439. **Ellen M. Clerke,** prob. Cf. no. 1964.

2092 Notices of books, 440–444, 451–492. Pages 466–467 by **Alfons Bellesheim**—signature; pages 462–463 by **L. C. Casartelli**—signed L.C.C., man cited a constant contributor to *DR*; pages 467–469 signed **C. S. Devas.**

2093 Notices of Catholic continental periodicals, 444–451. Pages 444–447 by **Alfons Bellesheim**—signature.

VOLUME 19 3RD S., 102 O.S., JANUARY 1888

2094 The rood of Boxley; or, How a lie grows, 1–33. **T. E. Bridgett.** Signed; repr. *Blunders and Forgeries,* 1890.

2095 The Jews in France (Part II, concl.), 34–61. **F. Jeffrée.** Signed "Jeffree"; *DR* list.

2096 The gospel and the Gospels [on the work of H. J. Coleridge], 62–89. Unidentified. (See no. 2113.)

2097 Church music and church choirs, 90–120. **Sydney H. Little.** Signed.

2098 Recent works on primitive Buddhism (Part I), 121–139. **Philémon Colinet.** Signed Ph. Colinet; see *DR* list and Seyn. (Part II is no. 2214.)

2099 *The Teaching of the Twelve Apostles,* 140–152. **J. R. Gasquet.** Signed.

2100 Where St. Patrick was born (Part II, concl.): a last reply, 153–166. **Colin C. Grant.** Signed. (See nos. 2034, 2063, and 2088.)

2101 The ethics of animal suffering, 166–179. **John S. Vaughan.** Signed.

2102 Science notices, 190–194.

2103 Notes of travel and exploration, 194–204. **Ellen M. Clerke,** prob. Cf. no. 1964.

2104 Notices of books, 204–212, 219–242. Pages 221–223, 230–233 by **Alfons Bellesheim**—signature; pages 241–242 signed **C. S. Devas.**

2105 Notices of Catholic continental periodicals, 213–219. Pages 216–219 by **Alfons Bellesheim**—signature.

VOLUME 19 3RD S., 102 O.S., APRIL 1888

2106 Henry VIII. and the English monasteries, 243–256. **H. E. Manning.** Signed as in no. 1839; repr. *Miscellanies,* III.

2107 A jubilee of science: a retrospect, 257–273. **Eric Stuart Bruce.** Signed.

2108 The Empire route to the East, 274–293. **Ellen M. Clerke.** Signature.

2109 An educational lesson from Berlin, 294–304. **L. C. Casartelli.** Signed.

2110 The nuns of Syon, 305–318. **Adam Hamilton.** Signed.

2111 An olive branch on state socialism, 319–335. **C. S. Devas.** Signed.

2112 Darwin's *Life and Letters,* 336–353.

2113 Two lives of our Lord: Father Coleridge's and Dr. Joseph Grimm's, 354–380. Unidentified. (See no. 2096.)

2114 Mr. Herbert Spencer's agnosticism, 381–399. **William Francis Barry.** Signed as in no. 1796.

2115 Dr. Mivart on faith and science, 400–411. **Jeremiah Murphy.** Signed J. Murphy; see p. 400. (Note, p. 411 by **H. A. Vaughan**—signed Editor.)

2116 Science notices, 412–419.

2117 Notes of travel and exploration, 419–427. **Ellen M. Clerke,** prob. Cf. no. 1964.

2118 Notices of books, 427–433, 447–492. Pages 484–485 by **Alfons Bellesheim**—signature; pages 461–465 signed **Orby Shipley.**

2119 Notices of Catholic continental periodicals, 433–446. Pages 433–436 by **Alfons Bellesheim**—signature; pages 438–441 by **L. C. Casartelli**—signed L.C.C. cf. no. 2092; pages 436–437 by **J. R. Gasquet**—signed J.R.G., cf. no. 2006.

VOLUME 20 3RD S., 103 O.S., JULY 1888

2120 Mr. R. H. Hutton as a religious thinker, 1–21. **Wilfrid Ward.** Signed.

2121 *Memoirs of a Royalist* [le Comte de Falloux], 22–42. **Ellen M. Clerke.** Signature.

2122 "Borough English" [descent of land to the youngest son], 43–54. **Edward Peacock.** Signed.

2123 *The Greville Memoirs,* 54–77.

2124 Catholics and county councils, 77–88. **W. S. Lilly.** Signed.

2125 Recent works on St. Augustine, 88–107. **P. A. Sheehan.** Signed.

2126 *The Quarterly Review* and the Church in England, 107–143. Signed: E.

2127 Can the Scriptures err? 144–165. **John Cuthbert Hedley.** Signed.

2128 Roman condemnation of Rosmini's *Propositions* [Latin text of the condemned propositions with Ital. trans.], 166–175.

2129 Science notices, 176–186.

2130 Notes of travel and exploration, 186–196. **Ellen M. Clerke,** prob. Cf. no. 1964.

2131 Notices of books, 196–201, 213–241. Pages 232–234, 234–236 by **Alfons Belleshem**—signature; pages 223–225 signed **C. S. Devas;** pages 225–229 **James Moyes,** prob.—signed J.M., cf. no. 2079; pages 239–240 signed **T. B. Scannell.**

2132 Notices of Catholic continental periodicals, 202–213. Pages 207–210 by **Alfons Bellesheim**—signature.

VOLUME 20 3RD S., 103 O.S., OCTOBER 1888

2133 Mr. Gladstone on the Elizabethan settlement of religion, 243–258. **John Morris,** 1826–1893. Signed, with title "S.J." (See no. 2207.)

2134 A missing page from the *Idylls of the King,* 259–274. **Jean Mary Stone.** Signed J. M. Stone; repr. *Studies.*

2135 The Apostles' Creed and the rule of faith (Part I), 275–290. **J. R. Gasquet.** Signed.

2136 The Lambeth Conference [of 1888], 291–311. **T. W. Allies.** Signed.

2137 Lady Georgiana Fullerton, 311–334. **Emily Bowles.** Signed.

2138 The National Gallery in 1888, 334–351.

2139 *The Quarterly Review* and the culture of our clergy, 352–377. **G. B. Lancaster Woodburne.** Signed.

2140 Irish industries, 378–399. **Ellen M. Clerke.** Signature.

2141 Letter to the bishops of Brazil, 400–410. **Leo PP. XIII.** Signed.

2142 Science notices, 411–419.

2143 Notes of travel and exploration, 419–428. **Ellen M. Clerke,** prob. Cf. no. 1964.

2144 Notices of books, 428–432, 443–487, 488–492. Pages 447, 468, 473–474 by **Alfons Bellesheim**—signature; page 474 signed G.C.; pages 462–463 signed **J. R. Gasquet;** pp. 480–481 signed **F. Landolt;** pages 463–467, 486–487 by **T. B. Scannell**—signed T.B.S., cf. no. 2079; page 467 signed **T. B. Scannell.**

2145 Notices of Catholic continental periodicals, 433–442. Pages 435–438 by **Alfons Bellesheim**—signature.

VOLUME 21 3RD S., 104 O.S., JANUARY 1889

2146 The new crusade [against the slave trade in Africa], 1–24. **Ellen M. Clerke.** Signature.

2147 The unity of theology, 25–42. **W. H. Kent.** Signed, with title "O.S.C."

2148 Were nuns ever immured? 43–51. **Edward Peacock.** Signed.

2149 The evolutionary hypothesis, 51–70. **Edwin de Lisle.** Signed.

2150 A Dominican story-teller [Augusta T. Drane], 70–86. **Florence M. Capes.** Signed F. M. Capes; *DR* list adds "Miss"; for woman cited see *BMCat.*

2151 Faith and folly [i.e., anti-religious science], 87–105. **John S. Vaughan.** Signed.

2152 The Cape in 1888, 106–113. **Agnes M. Clerke.** Signed A. M. Clerke; *DR* list adds "Miss"; see *DNB.*

2153 Louvain and Dublin [university education], 113–121. **Thomas Arnold,** 1823–1900. Signed T. Arnold; see *DNB.*

2154 A Protestant criticism of Protestant missions, 121–136. **A. Hilliard Atteridge.** Signed.

2155 Encyclical letter on liberty, 137–153. **Leo PP. XIII.** Signed.

2156 Science notices, 154–162.

2157 Notes of travel and exploration, 162–170. **Ellen M. Clerke,** prob. Cf. no. 1964.

2158 Notices of books, 170–178, 190–241. Pages 210–211 by **Alfons Bellesheim** — signature; pages 219–220 signed G.C.; pages 227–229 signed **C. S. Devas;** pages 225–227 by **J. R. Gasquet**—signed J.R.G.; identified in no. 2179, p. 82; pages 205–207 signed **J. R. Gasquet.**

2159 Notices of Catholic continental periodicals, 178–190. Pages 178–181 by **Alfons Bellesheim**—signature; pages 188–190 signed **C. S. Devas.**

VOLUME 21 3RD S., 104 O.S., APRIL 1889

2160 Henry VIII. and the suppression of the greater monasteries, 243–259. **H. E. Manning.** Signed as in no. 1839.

2161 Irish minstrelsy, 260–284. **Francis Thompson.** Signed.

2162 An apostle of Nirvana: H. F. Amiel, 285–298. **William Francis Barry.** Signed as in no. 1796; repr. *Heralds of Revolt,* 1909.

2163 Blue water, 299–307. **Andrew T. Sibbald.** Signed.

2164 The Apostles' Creed and the rule of faith (Part II, concl.), 307–321. **J. R. Gasquet.** Signed.

2165 Henrietta Maria, Queen Consort of England [queen of Charles I], 321–341. **Jean Mary Stone.** Signed as in no. 2134.

2166 The origins of the Church of Edessa, 342–352. **L. C. Casartelli.** Signed.

2167 Syndicates, trusts, and corners, 353–377. **Ellen M. Clerke.** Signature.

2168 Art and the people, 377–389. **James Britten.** Signed.

2169 The government and higher education in Ireland, 389–405. **Herbert Vaughan.** Signed Editorial; Editor of *DR*; a special interest of his.

2170 Letter on the conclusion of his jubilee year, 406–414. **Leo PP. XIII.** Signed.

2171 Science notices, 415–427.

2172 Notes of travel and exploration, 427–436. **Ellen M. Clerke,** prob. Cf. no. 1964.

2173 Notices of books, 436–441, 450–486, 487–492. Pages 465–467, 476–477, 483 by **Alfons Bellesheim**—signature; pages 470–471 by **L. C. Casartelli**—signed L.C.C., cf. no. 2092; pages 469–470 signed **T. B. Scannell.**

2174 Notices of Catholic continental periodicals, 441–449. Pages 441–444 by **Alfons Bellesheim**—signature; page 449 by **L. C. Casartelli**—signed L.C.C., cf. no. 2092.

VOLUME 22 3RD S., 105 O.S., JULY 1889

2175 The land and the works of St. Francis de Sales, 1–34. **Henry Benedict Mackey.** Signed.

2176 Rosminian ontologism, 35–47. **Thomas Esser.** Signed.

2177 The Buddhistic schools, 47–71. **Charles de Harlez.** Signed as in no. 1779.

2178 Faith and reason, 72–82. **John S. Vaughan.** Signed.

2179 Harnack on the "De Aleatoribus," 82–98. **H. I. D. Ryder.** Signed.

2180 Professor [T. H.] Green, 99–118. **W. S. Lilly.** Signed; repr. *Essays and Speeches*, 1897.

2181 The principles of '89, 118–139. **Ellen M. Clerke.** Signature.

2182 The *Macbeth* controversy, 140–156. **Francis Thompson.** Signed.

2183 Mental evolution in man, 157–173. **L. E. Baynard Klein.** Signed.

2184 Science notices, 174–184.

2185 Notes of travel and exploration, 184–193. **Ellen M. Clerke,** prob. Cf. no. 1964.

2186 Notices of books, 193–201, 213–242. Pages 235–237 by **Alfons Bellesheim**—

signature; pages 225–229 signed **C. S. Devas;** pages 222–223 by **Joseph Rickaby?**—signed J.R., man cited wrote no. 1980 on related topic; pages 237, 237–238 by **T. B. Scannell**—signed T.B.S., cf. no. 2079; pages 238–239 signed **T. B. Scannell.**

2187 Notices of Catholic continental periodicals, 201–213. Pages 201–203 by **Alfons Bellesheim**—signature; pages 211–213 signed **C. S. Devas;** pages 205–206 by **T. B. Scannell**—signed T.B.S., cf. no. 2079.

VOLUME 22 3RD S., 105 O.S., OCTOBER 1889

2188 W. G. Ward and the Oxford Movement, 243–268.

2189 Professor Weismann's hypotheses [about heredity], 269–296. **St. George Mivart.** Signed.

2190 An Indian Catholic mission, 297–318. **A. Hilliard Atteridge.** Signed.

2191 Vicars capitular, 318–340. **David Lewis.** Signed D.L.; cf. nos. 1897, 2062, 2087 where these initials are identified by Oscott II as Lewis's.

2192 "The Holy Helpers": Sts. Blaise and Erasmus, 340–350. **Ella B. Edes.** Signed.

2193 The early history of the Mass (Part I), 350–362. **J. R. Gasquet.** Signed.

2194 The youth of Mary Tudor, 363–385. **Jean Mary Stone.** Signed as in no. 2134.

2195 The dock labourers' strike (No. I): the labour market of East London, 386–406. **Ellen M. Clerke.** Signature.

2196 The dock labourers' strike (No. II): the great strike and the social question, 406–416. **C. S. Devas.** Signed.

2197 Science notices, 417–425.

2198 Notes of travel and exploration, 426–436. **Ellen M. Clerke,** prob. Cf. no. 1964.

2199 Notices of books, 436–442, 449–488, 488–490. Pages 476–477, 477–478, 478 by **Alfons Bellesheim**—signature; 481–482 [note misnumbering of pages here] signed **F. Landolt;** page 476 by **St. George Mivart,** prob.—cf. no. 2202 by Mivart, which fulfills promise made here; pages 479–480, 483–484 by **T. B. Scannell**—signed T.B.S., cf. no. 2079.

2200 Notices of Catholic continental periodicals, 442–449. Pages 447–449 by **Alfons Bellesheim**—signature.

VOLUME 23 3RD S., 106 O.S., JANUARY 1890

2201 University education in Ireland, 1–32.

John Healy. Signed; *DR* list adds "Bp.";
repr. *Papers and Addresses*, Dublin,
1909.

2202 Darwinism, 33–47. **St. George Mivart.**
Signed.

2203 Anglicanism and early British Christianity, 48–72. Signed: A Member of
the Cambrian Archaeol. Association.

2204 The potato, 73–84. **Donat Sampson.**
Signed as in no. 2587.

2205 "The Sacrifices of Masses [Art. 31 of
Thirty-nine Arts.]," 85–95. **Austin Richardson.** Signed.

2206 Aëropaedia, 95–110. **Andrew T. Sibbald.** Signed.

2207 Mr. Gladstone and Blessed John Fisher,
111–135. **John Morris,** 1826–1893. Signed.
(See no. 2133.)

2208 The Baltimore centenary [of the creation of a Catholic hierarchy in the U.S.],
135–153. **H. A. Vaughan.** Signed Editorial; Vaughan was editor of *DR*.

2209 Science notices, 154–164.

2210 Notes of travel and exploration, 165–
174. **Ellen M. Clerke,** prob. Cf. no. 1964.

2211 Notices of books, 175–182, 200–242.
Pages 215, 234–235 by **Alfons Belleshem**
—signature?—pages 230–231 by **James
Britten?**—signed J.B.; pages 228–229 by
J. R. Gasquet—signed J.R.G., cf. no.
2006; pages 200–202 by **James Moyes,**
prob.—signed J.M., cf. no. 2079; pages
216–219 signed J.S.; pages 202, 238, 240
by **T. B. Scannell**—signed T.B.S., cf. no.
2079; pages 239–240 signed **T. B. Scannell.**

2212 Notices of Catholic continental periodicals, 182–200. Pages 194–196 by **Alfons
Belleshem**—signature; pages 191–193 by
L. C. Casartelli—signed L.C.C., cf. no.
2092; pages 182–191 signed **Adam Hamilton.**

VOLUME 23 3RD S., 106 O.S., APRIL 1890

2213 Jesuits and seculars in the reign of
Elizabeth, 243–255. **John Morris,** 1826–
1893. Signed.

2214 Recent works on primitive Buddhism
(Part II, concl.), 256–285. **Philémon
Colinet.** Signed as in no. 2098.

2215 The early history of the Mass (Part
II), 286–299. **J. R. Gasquet.** Signed. (See
no. 2244.)

2216 Temperance legislation, 299–323.
James Halpin. Signed, with initials "C.C.";
see *Irish Catholic Directory*/1926.

2217 Mary, Queen of England, 324–341.
Jean Mary Stone. Signed as in no. 2134.

2218 The typical character of the Covenant
sacrifice, 342–350. **W. J. B. Richards.**
Signed.

2219 Were there four months before the
harvest?: an examination of John iv. 35,
351–367. **M. A. Power.** Signed, with
addition "S.J."

2220 Irishmen in the French Revolution,
368–383. **Pierce L. Nolan.** Signed.

2221 Cremation and Christianity, 384–402,
with English and Latin versions of the
decree of 1886 against cremation, 401–
402. **H. A. Vaughan.** Signed Editorial;
Vaughan was editor of *DR* at this time.

2222 Encyclical letter on the chief duties of
Christian citizens, 403–417. **Leo PP.
XIII.** Signed.

2223 Science notices, 418–426.

2224 Notes of travel and exploration, 426–
435. **Ellen M. Clerke,** prob. Cf. no. 1964.

2225 Notices of books, 435–443, 455–494.
Pages 463–465, 481 by **Alfons Belleshem**
—signature; pages 472–474 signed **C. S.
Devas;** page 475 by **T. B. Scannell**—
signed T.B.S., cf. no. 2079.

2226 Notices of Catholic continental periodicals, 443–454. Pages 448–450 by
Alfons Belleshem—signature; pages 447–
448 by **J. R. Gasquet?**—signed T.R.G.
but in possible error for J.R.G. since this
notice reflects interests of this frequent
contributor.

VOLUME 24 3RD S., 107 O.S., JULY 1890

2227 Charles Kingsley, 1–20. **Mary M. Mallock.** Signed M. M. Mallock; Index adds
"Miss."

2228 The final destiny of the earth, 21–36.
John S. Vaughan. Signed.

2229 The chansons de geste (Part I), 36–
53. **Mary Hayden.** Signed, with title
"M.A."; Index adds "Miss." (Part II is
no. 2431.)

2230 The Buddhist propaganda in Christian
countries, 54–73. **Charles de Harlez.**
Signed as in no. 1779.

2231 The early history of the Mass (Part
III, concl.), 74–88. **J. R. Gasquet.** Signed.

2232 Saint Augustine and his Anglican critics, 89–109. **Philip Burton.** Signed The
Author of *St. Augustine: an Historical
Study*; Oscott II gives "Dr. Burton,
C.M."; cf. no. 2381; see *Catholic World*
67 (April 1898), 113–116.

2233 Philip and Mary, 110–130. **Jean Mary
Stone.** Signed as in no. 2134.

2234 Deep-sea explorations and some of

their results, 131–144. **L. Baynard Klein.** Signed.

2235 Mediaeval guilds and modern competition, 145–164. **Ellen M. Clerke.** Signature.

2236 Science notices, 165–174.

2237 Notes of travel and exploration, 174–182. **Ellen M. Clerke,** prob. Cf. no. 1964.

2238 Notices of books, 182–191, 199–241. Pages 240–241 by **Alfons Bellesheim**—signature; pages 236–238, 238–240 by **T. B. Scannell**—signed T.B.S., cf. no. 2079.

2239 Notices of Catholic continental periodicals, 191–198. Pages 191–194 by **Alfons Bellesheim**—signature.

VOLUME 24 3RD S., 107 O.S., OCTOBER 1890

2240 Peter not Caesar; or, Mr. Allies' *Per Crucem ad Lucem*, 243–277. **Luke Rivington.** Signed.

2241 The Church and the social revolution, 278–301. **William Francis Barry.** Signed as in no. 1796.

2242 A royal elopement [Princess Clémentine and Prince Sobieski in 1719], 302–318. **Charlotte O'Conor Eccles.** Signed C. O'Conor Eccles; *DR* list gives "Miss C. O. Eccles"; *BMCat.* supplies first name.

2243 The labour problem: past and present, 319–336. **Thomas Canning.** Signed, with titles "M.A., Inst. C.E."

2244 Celebration of Mass in ante-Nicene times, 337–343. **J. R. Gasquet.** Signed. (See nos. 2193 and 2215.)

2245 Catholics and technical education, 344–365. **H. A. Vaughan.** Signed Editorial; Vaughan was editor at this period.

2246 Father [Theobald] Mathew's centenary, 366–390. **W. H. Cologan.** Signed.

2247 John Henry Cardinal Newman (No. I): in memoriam literature, 391–401.

2248 John Henry Cardinal Newman (No. II): some reminiscences of the early days of Cardinal Newman's Catholic life, 402–408. **Richard M. Stanton.** Signed, with title "priest of the Oratory."

2249 John Henry Cardinal Newman (No. III): Cardinal Newman; or, " 'Tis Fifty Years Since," 408–423. **William Lockhart.** Signed.

2250 John Henry Cardinal Newman (No. IV): our loss, and now our gain, 424–436. **Henry Hayman.** Signed.

2251 Science notices, 437–451.

2252 Notes of travel and exploration, 451–462. **Ellen M. Clerke,** prob. Cf. no. 1964.

2253 Notices of books, 462–469, 477–494. Pages 489–492 by **Alfons Bellesheim**—signature; page 487 by **Patrick Lynch**—signed P.L., man cited contributed in this period an art., no. 2516, and a signed notice, no. 2347, both on Irish history, the subject of this notice.

2254 Notices of Catholic continental periodicals, 469–477. Pages 469–472 by **Alfons Bellesheim**—signature.

VOLUME 25 3RD S., 108 O.S., JANUARY 1891

2255 Two Englishmen who served . . . abroad in the cause of Christendom: Sir Edward Wydville and Sir Thomas Arundell, 1–21. **J. F. Arundell.** Signed Arundell of Wardour [Lord Arundell].

2256 Richard Monckton Milnes, Lord Houghton, 22–35. **Edward Peacock.** Signed.

2257 The teaching of economic geography, 35–53. **Ellen M. Clerke.** Signature.

2258 The Maid of Orleans by the light of original documents, 54–72. **Francis M. Wyndham.** Signed.

2259 [Walter] Scott's *Journal*, 72–95.

2260 The Jacobin movement in Ireland, 95–109. **W. S. Lilly.** Signed.

2261 English Catholics and the social question, 110–121. **C. S. Devas.** Signed.

2262 The Lincoln Judgment [by the Privy Council]; or, Continuity [of the English Church], 121–146. **Luke Rivington.** Signed.

2263 Encyclical letter to the clergy and people of Italy, 147–156. **Leo PP. XIII.** Signed.

2264 Science notices, 157–169.

2265 Notes of travel and exploration, 169–177. **Ellen M. Clerke,** prob. Cf. no. 1964.

2266 Notices of books, 178–183, 193–237, 237–239. Pages 220–222 by **Alfons Belle-sheim**—signed B., cf. no. 1724; pages 219–220, 232–233, 236–237 by **Alfons Bellesheim**—signature.

2267 Notices of Catholic continental periodicals, 184–192. Pages 184–185 by **Alfons Bellesheim**—signature; pages 190–192 by **T. B. Scannell**—signed T.B.S., cf. no. 2079.

VOLUME 25 3RD S., 108 O.S., APRIL 1891

2268 Hypnotism, 241–254. **J. R. Gasquet.** Signed.

2269 The Scholastic movement and Catholic philosophy, 255–271. **Wilfrid Ward.** Signed.

2270 The Pope and Catholic philosophy in England, 272–289.

2271 Talleyrand's diplomatic letters, 1792–1799, 290–307. **T. B. Scannell.** Signed.

2272 The insurrection in Chile, 308–327. **Ellen M. Clerke.** Signature.

2273 The homage of Christ the King, 327–350. **Charles Coupe.** Signed, with addition "S.J."

2274 "The Constitution of the Athenians" ascribed to Aristotle, 351–370. **Henry Hayman.** Signed.

2275 The Anglican claim to historical Christianity, 371–401. **Luke Rivington.** Signed. (See no. 2289.)

2276 Apostolic letter of Pope Leo XIII on the government of the Anglo-Benedictine congregation, 402–409. **Leo PP. XIII.** Title.

2277 Encyclical letter to the bishops of the Catholic world on the abolition of slavery, 410–412. **Leo PP. XIII.** Signed.

2278 Science notices, 413–425.

2279 Notes on travel and exploration, 425–433. **Ellen M. Clerke,** prob. Cf. no. 1964.

2280 Notices of books, 433–438, 447–489. Pages 478, 483 by **Alfons Bellesheim**—signature; pages 451–456 by **James Moyes**—signed as in no. 2015; pages 488–489 by **T. B. Scannell**—signed T.B.S., cf. no. 2079.

2281 Notices of Catholic continental periodicals, 439–446. Pages 439–441 by **Alfons Bellesheim**—signature.

VOLUME 26 3RD S., 109 O.S., JULY 1891

2282 The Penal Laws: an historical retrospect, 1–26. **W. S. Lilly.** Signed.

2283 John MacHale, Archbishop of Tuam, 27–40. **Pius Devine.** Signed with initials "C.P."; Index adds "Rev."

2284 Trades unionism among women in Ireland, 41–48. **Henry Abraham.** Signed.

2285 The Augustinian System, 48–68. **Philip Burton.** Signed The Author of *St. Augustine; An Historical Study*; cf. no. 2232.

2286 A new system of Biblical history: the age of the Psalms, 69–91. **Charles de Harlez.** Signed.

2287 Catholic theology in England, 92–106. **W. H. Kent.** Signed.

2288 The internuncio at Paris during the Revolution, 107–123. **T. B. Scannell.** Signed.

2289 Independent national churches, 124–

152. **Luke Rivington.** Signed. (See no. 2275.)

2290 Leo XIII on "The Condition of Labour," 153–167. **H. E. Manning.** Signed as in no. 1839.

2291 Encyclical letter on the condition of labour, 168–189. **Leo PP. XIII.** Signed.

2292 Science notices, 190–198.

2293 Notes of travel and exploration, 198–208. **Ellen M. Clerke,** prob. Cf. no. 1964.

2294 Notices of books, 208–216, 222–239, 240–243.

2295 Notices of Catholic continental periodicals, 216–222. Pages 216–218 by **Alfons Bellesheim**—signature; pages 218–221 signed **T. B. Scannell.**

VOLUME 26 3RD S., 109 O.S., OCTOBER 1891

2296 Mr. Herbert Spencer on justice, 245–265. **St. George Mivart.** Signed.

2297 Sir John Franklin and the far North, 266–282. **Ellen M. Clerke.** Signed.

2298 Blessed Thomas More, 283–290.

2299 Benedictine government from the sixth to the eleventh century, 291–310. **Adam Hamilton.** Signed.

2300 Progress of the persecution under Elizabeth, 311–332. **Jean Mary Stone.** Signed as in no. 2134.

2301 Catholicism in the Waverley Novels, 333–352. **Thomas Canning.** Signed.

2302 Evolution and determinism, 353–373. **F. R. Wegg-Prosser.** Signed.

2303 The cultus of the Blessed Virgin as contained in the Sarum Breviary, 374–394. **F. E. Gilliat Smith.** Signed.

2304 How to save the voluntary schools, 395–411. **H. A. Vaughan.** Signed Editorial; *DR* list.

2305 Science notices, 412–426.

2306 Notes of travel and exploration, 426–436. **Ellen M. Clerke,** prob. Cf. no. 1964.

2307 Notices of books, 436–440, 440–496. Pages 483–486, 489–492 by **Alfons Bellesheim**—signature; pages 459–460 signed **J. R. Gasquet;** pages 471–475 by **T. B. Scannell**—signed T.B.S., cf. no. 2079.

VOLUME 1 4TH S., 110 O.S., JANUARY 1892

2308 England's devotion to St. Peter during a thousand years (Part I), 1–24. **H. A. Vaughan.** Index assigns to "Bishop of Salford."

2309 Pitt, 25–37. **Aubrey St. J. Clerke.** Signed in Index.

2310 A Bishop of Cork [Robert Barry] and

the Irish at Nantes (Part I), 38–51. **Patrick Hurley.** Signed, with title "P.P."

2311 Theism treated as a scientific hypothesis, 52–70. **John S. Vaughan.** Signed.

2312 Are agnostics in good faith?: a theological inquiry, 71–101. **Charles Coupe.** Signed.

2313 Spanish society in modern fiction, 102–122. **Ellen M. Clerke.** Signed.

2314 Early Russian fiction, 123–139. **H. Wilson.** Signed.

2315 Prevention of cruelty to children, 140–151. **Benjamin Waugh.** Signed.

2316 Old churchwardens' accounts, 152–159. **Edward Peacock.** Signed.

2317 Saving our schools and their catholic teaching, 160–171. **H. A. Vaughan.** Signed Editorial; Index assigns to "Bishop of Salford."

2318 Science notices, 172–177.

2319 Notes on social science, 177–183. Pages 177–180 signed **C. S. Devas.**

2320 Notes of travel and exploration, 184–194. **Ellen M. Clerke,** prob. Cf. no. 1964.

2321 Notices of books, 195–198, 205–240. Pages 228–229 by **Alfons Bellesheim**—signature; pages 210–213 by **T. B. Scannell**—signed T.B.S., cf. no. 2079.

2322 Notes on foreign periodicals, 198–205. Pages 202–205 by **Alfons Bellesheim**—title; pages 198–202 by **T. B. Scannell**—signed T.B.S., cf. no. 2079.

VOLUME 1 4TH S., 110 O.S., APRIL 1892

2323 England's devotion to St. Peter during a thousand years (Part II, concl.), 243–263. **H. A. Vaughan.** Cf. no. 2308.

2324 The Mosaic authorship of the Pentateuch, 264–281. **J. Aidan Howlett.** Signed.

2325 Six months at the Grand Chartreuse, 282–295. **Algar Thorold.** Signed.

2326 Anglican writers and the Council of Ephesus (Part I), 296–324. **Luke Rivington.** Signed.

2327 Protestantism in England, 325–336. **Edward Peacock.** Signed.

2328 Theosophy and its evidences, 337–350. **W. D. Strappini.** Signed.

2329 The Irish at Nantes (Part II, concl.): The Right Reverend Cornelius O'Keeffe, Bishop of Limerick, 1720–1737, 351–362. **Patrick Hurley.** Signed.

2330 An aspect of the temperance question, 363–371. **T. B. Griffith.** Signed.

2331 Some personal reminiscences of Cardinal Manning when Archdeacon of Chichester, 372–379. **William Lockhart.** Signed.

2332 Episodes in the life of Cardinal Manning in his Anglican days, 380–436. **Edmund Sheridan Purcell.** Signed.

2333 Science notices, 437–449.

2334 Notes of travel and exploration, 450–461. **Ellen M. Clerke,** prob. Cf. no. 1964.

2335 Notices of books, 461–468, 471–492. Page 478 by **Alfons Bellesheim**—signed B, cf. no. 1724; pages 474–475, 477, 490–491 by **Alfons Bellesheim**—signature; pages 479–482 signed **Henry Hayman;** pages 471–473 by **Patrick Lynch,** prob.—signed P.L., cf. no. 2253; pages 473–474 signed J.R.

2336 Notes on foreign periodicals, 468–471. Pages 468–471 by **Alfons Bellesheim**—signature.

VOLUME 2 4TH S., 111 O.S., JULY 1892

2337 Pastor's *History of the Popes* (Vols. I, II), 1–30. **T. B. Scannell.** Signed.

2338 Gardiner's *Civil War* [Vol. III], 31–62. **Henry Hayman.** Signed.

2339 Isaac Hecker, 63–95. **William Francis Barry.** Signed as in no. 1796.

2340 Recent discoveries in the cemetery of St. Priscilla, 96–116. **W. R. Brownlow.** Signed.

2341 Infanticide in China according to Chinese documents, 117–143. **Charles de Harlez.** Signed as in no. 1779.

2342 Anglican writers and the Council of Ephesus (Part II, concl.), 144–174. **Luke Rivington.** Signed.

2343 Science notices, 175–186.

2344 Notes on social science, 186–188. **C. S. Devas.** Signed.

2345 Notes of travel and exploration, 188–197. **Ellen Mary Clerke.** Signed E.M.C.; she was a regular contributor to *DR* and this was one major field of her interest; cf. no. 1964.

2346 Notes on foreign periodicals, 197–207. Pages 197–200 signed **Don Abbondio;** pages 205–207 by **Alfons Bellesheim**—signature; pages 204–205 signed **J. S. Vaughan.**

2347 Notices of books, 207–240. Pages 237–239 signed **Don Abbondio;** pages 215–216, 229–230, 236–237 by **Alfons Bellesheim**—signature; pages 239–240 signed **John Gerard;** page 226 signed H; page 239 signed **Gilbert Higgins;** pages 211–

212 signed **J. A. Howlett**; page 231 by **Patrick Lynch**—signed P. Lynch, cf. no. 2253; pages 233–236 by **James Moyes**, prob.—signed J.M., cf. no. 2079; pages 227–229, 231–232 signed **J. B. Milburn**; page 230 signed C.R.; pages 216–225 signed **G. Richardson**; pages 213–214, 214–215 signed **T. B. Scannell**; pages 207–210 signed **J. S. Vaughan**; pages 212–213 by **Thomas Whiteside?**—signed T. Whiteside.

VOLUME 2 4TH S., 111 O.S., OCTOBER 1892

2348 The authorship and composition of the Hexateuch (Part I), 245–267. **Christian van den Biesen.** Signed C. van den Biesen; see *BMCat*.

2349 Modern stellar astronomy, 268–296. **F. R. Wegg-Prosser.** Signed.

2350 The Spanish monarchy, 297–336. **Walter Fitzpatrick.** Signed; Index gives "W. F. Fitzpatrick."

2351 The great religious problem of the XIXth century, and *Lux Mundi* [by Charles Gore], 337–364. **Aubrey de Vere.** Signed; repr. *Religious Problems*.

2352 Probability and faith, 365–394. **John Morris**, 1826–1893. Signed.

2353 Charles Langdale (Part I), 395–425. **William J. Amherst.** Signed.

2354 *Shibboleths* [by W. S. Lilly], 426–437. **C. S. Devas.** Signed.

2355 Science notices, 438–442.

2356 Notes on travel and exploration, 443–452. **Ellen Mary Clerke.** Signed E.M.C.; cf. no. 1964.

2357 Notes on foreign periodicals, 453–457. Pages 453–455 signed **Don Abbondio**; pages 455–457 by **Alfons Bellesheim**—signature.

2358 Notices of books, 457–493. Pages 468–470 by **Alfons Bellesheim**—signed B., cf. no. 1724; pages 470–472, 484–485 by **Alfons Bellesheim**—signature; pages 475–477 by **J. R. Gasquet**—signed J.R.G., cf. no. 2158; pages 462–463 by **Daniel Iles**, prob.—signed D. Iles, man cited a prof. at Oscott; pages 491–492 signed **L. Baynard Klein**; pages 473–475 by **Patrick Lynch**, prob.—signed P.L., cf. no. 2253; pages 461–462 by **Patrick Lynch**—signed as in no. 2347; page 480 signed **J. B. Milburn**; page 493 signed C.R.; pages 477–479 by **T. B. Scannell**—signed T.B.S., cf. no. 2079; pages 465–466 signed **T. B. Scannell**; pages 486–489 by **Orby Shipley**—signed O. Shipley; pages

489–491 by **F. R. Wegg-Prosser**—signed F.R.W.P.

VOLUME 3 4TH S., 112 O.S., JANUARY 1893

2359 The Russian Church, 1–15. **Mary Elizabeth Herbert.** Signed.

2360 Vestiges of the Blessed Trinity in the material creation, 16–26. **John S. Vaughan.** Signed.

2361 The royal patronage in India, 27–39. **G. T. Mackenzie.** Signed.

2362 Authorship and composition of the Hexateuch (Part II, concl.), 40–65. **Christian van den Biesen.** Signed as in no. 2348.

2363 English scholars at Bologna during the middle ages, 66–83. **Antony Allaria.** Signed A. Allaria; see *CD*, 1889.

2364 The friars in Oxford, 84–106. **G. B. Lancaster Woodburne.** Signed.

2365 The minute book of the Cisalpine Club (Part I), 107–129. **W. J. Amherst.** Signed in Part II, p. 338, with title "S.J."

2366 Robert Surtees as a poet, 130–136. **Florence Peacock.** Signed.

2367 Evening continuation and recreative schools, 137–149. **W. M. Hunnybun.** Signed.

2368 Our educational outlook, 150–160. **W. Scott Coward.** Signed.

2369 Science notices, 161–168.

2370 Notes on social science, 169–175. **Charles S. Devas.** Signed.

2371 Notes of travel and exploration, 175–185. **Ellen Mary Clerke.** Signed E.M.C.; cf. no. 1964.

2372 Notes on foreign periodicals, 185–193. Pages 185–187 by **Alfons Bellesheim**—signature; pages 190–193 signed **Don Abbondio**.

2373 Notices of books, 194–241. Pages 196, 203, 223 by **Alfons Bellesheim**—signed B., cf. no. 1724; pages 195–196, 198–199, 221–222 by **Alfons Bellesheim**—signature; pages 196–198 by **Bruno De Splenter**—signed B. De Splenter, see *CD/89*; pages 212–214 by **J. A. Howlett**—signed J. C. Howlett, but cf. no. 2387 on same topic; pages 223–227 by **James Moyes**, prob.—signed J.M., cf. no. 2079; pages 228–229 signed **J. B. Milburn**; pages 204, 215–216 by **Austin Oates**, prob.—signed A.O., the notices signed with A. and A.G.O. are short and on a variety of subjects treated in a relatively superficial manner, Oates was also the author of no. 2053 and of a signed series in the *Month*, here no. 2485 reviews a history of Stony-hurst; pages 211–212 signed F.R.; page 240 by **George Richardson**, prob.—signed G. R., review of a textbook, cf. no. 2347; page 203 signed S.; pages 238–239 by **T. B. Scannell**—signed T.B.S., cf. no. 2079; pages 218–221 signed **T. B. Scannell**; pages 194–195 by **Victor Schobel**—signed V. Schobel, see *BMCat.*; pages 203–204, 236–237 by **J. S. Vaughan**, prob.—signed J.S.V., cf. no. 1874.

VOLUME 3 4TH S., 112 O.S., APRIL 1893

2374 The Papal jubilee (No. I): early English pilgrimages, 245–267. **James Moyes.** Signed as in no. 2015; *DR* list.
2375 The "Missa Catechumenorum" in the Greek liturgies, 268–292. **Herbert Lucas.** Signed.
2376 *Memoirs of Cardinal Massaja*, 293–320. **Ellen M. Clerke.** Signature.
2377 Minute book of the Cisalpine Club (Part II. concl.), 321–340. **W. J. Amherst.** Signed.
2378 Labour and capital, limited, 341–359. **William Francis Barry.** Signed as in no. 1796.
2379 A passage in the history of Charles I, 360–375. **Amy M. Grange.** Signed A. M. Grange.
2380 Tosti's *Life of St. Benedict*, 376–396. Signed: M.M.
2381 Saint Augustine and the Donatists, 397–419. **Philip Burton.** Signed The Author of *St. Augustine: An Historical Study*; Index gives "Rev. P. Burton"; cf. no. 2232.
2382 The canon of the New Testament, 420–434. **J. R. Gasquet.** Signed.
2383 Science notices, 435–441.
2384 Notes on social science, 442–447. **James Moyes**, prob. Signed J.M.; cf. no. 2079.
2385 Notes of travel and exploration, 447–459. **Ellen Mary Clerke**, prob. Cf. no. 1964.
2386 Notes on foreign periodicals, 460–467. Pages 460–463 by **Alfons Bellesheim**—signature; pages 463–465 signed **John S. Vaughan.**
2387 Notices of books, 467–493. Pages 482–483 by **Alfons Bellesheim**—signature; pages 486–487 signed J.J.C.; pages 476–479 by **Gilbert Higgins**, prob.—signed G.H., the notices with these initials are short and deal largely with books of

devotion or edification, no. 2497 deals with Lacordaire on whom Higgins wrote a signed notice, cf. no. 2347; pages 474–475 signed **J. A. Howlett;** pages 468–469 by **J. H. Matthews**—signed J.H.M., man cited was an antiquary and signed no. 2481 on a similar topic; pages 484–486, 492 by **T. B. Scannell**—signed T.B.S., cf. no. 2079.

VOLUME 4 4TH S., 113 O.S., JULY 1893

2388 Bishop Lightfoot and the early Roman See (Part I), 497–514. **E. Cuthbert Butler.** Signed, with title "O.S.B."
2389 The Hon. Charles Langdale (Part II), 515–531. **W. J. Amherst.** Signed.
2390 Some recent views on inspiration, 532–548. **J. A. Howlett.** Signed.
2391 Some English crosses, 549–563. **Florence Peacock.** Signed.
2392 The early Gallican liturgy (Part I), 564–588. **Herbert Lucas.** Signed.
2393 Evolution and ethics, 589–598. **L. M. Baynard Klein.** Signed.
2394 Queen Elizabeth and the revolution (Part I): her intrigues with the Huguenots, 1558–1563, 599–625. **Jean Mary Stone.** Signed as in no. 2134.
2395 The primitive saints and the See of Rome, 626–650. **Luke Rivington.** Signed.
2396 Science notices, 651–657.
2397 Notes on social science, 658–664. **Charles S. Devas.** Signed.
2398 Notes of travel and exploration, 665–674. **Ellen M. Clerke**, prob. Cf. no. 1964.
2399 Notes on foreign periodicals, 675–680. Pages 675–677 by **Alfons Bellesheim**—signature.
2400 Notices of books, 681–737. Pages 681, 682–683 by **Alfons Bellesheim**—signed B., cf. no. 1724; pages 681–682, 683–685, 728–729 by **Alfons Bellesheim**—signature; pages 734–735 signed G.A.G.; pages 696, 721–722 by **J. A. Howlett**—signed J.A.H., he was a frequent contributor under Moyes, primarily on Biblical scholarship, signing notices with his name or with these initials; pages 724–726 signed **J. A. Howlett;** pages 698–699 signed B.K.; pages 693–696, 730 signed **J. B. Milburn;** page 731 by **J. B. Milburn**—signed J.B.M., the notices signed with these initials are all written in the same easy literary manner, characterized by a special interest in format, maps, and illustrations, and they parallel

in form and style the notices signed J. B. Milburn; pages 699–702, 719–720, 721, 726–728 by **T. B. Scannell**—signed T.B.S., cf. no. 2079; pages 718–719 signed **T. B. Scannell;** pages 733–734 by **Algar Thorold**—signed A. Thorold, cf. no. 2325; pages 702–703 unidentified (correction, pages 940–942, by **James Moyes**—signed Editor).

VOLUME 4 4TH S., 113 O.S., OCTOBER 1893

2401 The propagation of Islam, 741–765. **Charles de Harlez.** Signed as in no. 1779.

2402 *Rome's Tribute to Anglican Orders,* 766–800. **J. D. Breen.** Assigned in Index.

2403 Temperance and the social question, 801–813. **James Halpin.** Signed.

2404 Father Ohrwalder's captivity, 814–835. **Ellen M. Clerke.** Signed.

2405 Bishop Lightfoot and the early Roman See (Part II, concl.), 836–857. **E. Cuthbert Butler.** Signed.

2406 The Hon. Charles Langdale (Part III, concl.), 858–873. **W. J. Amherst.** Signed.

2407 The Eucharistic Congress at Jerusalem, 874–885. **Mary Elizabeth Herbert.** Signed.

2408 Religious instruction in England during the fourteenth and fifteenth centuries, 886–914. **F. A. Gasquet.** Signed in Index; repr. *The Old English Bible, and Other Essays,* 1897.

2409 Science notices, 915–923.

2410 Notes of travel and exploration, 923–933. **Ellen M. Clerke,** prob. Cf. no. 1964.

2411 Notes on foreign periodicals, 933–939. Pages 933–936 by **Alfons Bellesheim**—signature.

2412 Notices of books, 940–984, 985–987. Pages 970–974 by **William Francis Barry** —signed as in no. 1796; pages 956–957 by **Alfons Bellesheim**—signature; pages 952–956 by **Christian van den Biesen,** prob.—signed C.V.B., this notice reflects Biesen's interest in Hebrew scholarship, cf. no. 2348; pages 946–947 by **James Moyes,** prob.—signed J.M., cf. no. 2079; page 976 by **George Richardson,** prob.— signed G.R., this notice of a manual would reflect his interest in textbooks, cf. no. 2347; pages 959–961 by **T. B. Scannell**—signed T.B.S., cf. no. 2079; pages 958–959 signed **T. B. Scannell;** page 950 by **J. S. Vaughan,** prob.—signed J.S.V., cf. no. 1874.

VOLUME 5 4TH S., 114 O.S., JANUARY 1894

2413 The art of burial, 1–21. **L. C. Casartelli.** Signed; repr. *Sketches.*

2414 England's ancient saints, 22–40. **F. E. Gilliat Smith.** Signed.

2415 The social difficulty, 41–60. **John S. Vaughan.** Signed.

2416 The gifts of a pontiff, 61–75. **A. E. P. Raymund Dowling.** Signed.

2417 A visitation of St. Mary Church in A.D. 1301, 76–94. **W. R. Brownlow.** Attr. to "Right Rev. Mgr. Brownlow" p. 76n.

2418 Alexander Pope, 95–111. **W. S. Lilly.** Signed; repr. *Essays and Speeches,* 1897.

2419 The early Gallican liturgy (Part II, concl.), 112–131. **Herbert Lucas.** Signed.

2420 Town fogs: their amelioration and prevention, 132–144. **Eric Stuart Bruce.** Signed.

2421 Mashunaland and its neighbours, 145–166. **Ellen M. Clerke.** Signature.

2422 Science notices, 167–175.

2423 Notes of travel and exploration, 176–186. **Ellen M. Clerke,** prob. Cf. no. 1964.

2424 Notes on foreign periodicals, 186–189. Pages 187–189 signed **John S. Vaughan.**

2425 Notices of books, 190–234, 235–241. Pages 216–217 by **Antony Allaria,** prob. —signed A.A., cf. no. 2363; pages 202–203 by **Alfons Bellesheim**—signed B., cf. no. 1724; pages 217–220 by **L. C. Casartelli**—signed L.C.C., cf. no. 2092; pages 226–228 by **J. A. Howlett**—signed J.A.H., cf. no. 2400; pages 206–208, 230–232 signed B.K.; pages 193–196 by **James Moyes,** prob.—signed J.M., cf. no. 2079; pages 214–216 by **J. B. Milburn**— signed J.B.M., cf. no. 2400; 208–209, 229–230, 232–233 by **T. B. Scannell**— Signed T.B.S., cf. no. 2079.

VOLUME 5 4TH S., 114 O.S., APRIL 1894

2426 Overlooked testimonies to the character of the English monasteries on the eve of their suppression, 245–277. **F. A. Gasquet.** Signed.

2427 The Popes as promoters of university education, 278–293. **John F. Hogan.** Signed J. F. Hogan; Index adds "Rev."; see *WWW*/1928.

2428 A missionary model farm in Borneo, 294–308. **Ellen M. Clerke.** Signature.

2429 Albi and the Albigensians, 309–332. **Robert W. Twigge.** Signed R. Twigge;

cf. no. 2466 where he is called "F.S.A.";
see *LCCat.*

2430 The Misericordia of Florence, 333–345. **Maria Zucchi.** Signed M. Zucchi; first name supplied by Index.

2431 The chansons de geste (Part II, concl.), 346–357. **Mary Hayden.** Signed. (Part I is no. 2229.)

2432 The Acacian troubles [having to do with Acacius, Bishop of Constantinople], 358–380. **Luke Rivington.** Signed.

2433 Penal times in Holland, 381–389. **Wilfrid C. Robinson.** Signed. With a note, p. 389, signed **W. S. Lilly.**

2434 Warham, an English primate on the eve of the Reformation, 390–414. With an appendix, 414–420. **James Moyes.** Signed as in no. 2015, p. 414.

2435 Science notices, 421–426.

2436 Notes of travel and exploration, 427–435. **Ellen M. Clerke,** prob. Cf. no. 1964.

2437 Notes on foreign periodicals, 436–440. Pages 438–440 by **Alfons Bellesheim,** prob.—he had consistently reviewed the German periodicals in this department, and he probably contributed pages 460–461 in no. 2438.

2438 Notices of books, 441–489, 490–493. Page 454 by **Antony Allaria,** prob.—signed A.A., cf. no. 2363; pages 460–461 by **Alfons Bellesheim**—signed B., cf. no. 1724; pages 441–448 signed C.B.; pages 479–482 signed J.I.C.; pages 449–452 by **J. B. Milburn**—signed J.B.M., cf. no. 2400; pages 464–466, 476–478 by **Henry Parkinson**—signed H. Parkinson, D.D.; pages 478–479 by **T. B. Scannell**—signed T.B.S., cf. no. 2079; pages 484–487 signed **Wilfrid Wilberforce.**

VOLUME 6 4TH S., 115 O.S., JULY 1894

2439 William George Ward, 1–29. **Wilfrid Wilberforce.** Signed.

2440 Textual criticism and the Acts of the Apostles, 30–53. **Herbert Lucas.** Signed, p. 52.

2441 Rings, 54–70. **Florence Peacock.** Signed.

2442 The higher criticism and archaeology, 71–95. **J. A. Howlett.** Signed.

2443 The vivisection controversy, 96–121. **Robert F. Clarke.** Signed.

2444 The pre-Reformation English Bible, 122–152. **F. A. Gasquet.** Signed; repr. *The Old English Bible*, 1897.

2445 Science notices, 153–161.

2446 Nova et vetera, 162–169. "Bidding the bedes," 162–167, by **James Moyes**—

signed as in no. 2015 (see no. 2460); Note on the translation "Full of Grace" in Luke I. 28, 168–169, by **J. R. Gasquet** —signed.

2447 Notes of travel and exploration, 170–178. **Ellen M. Clerke,** prob. Cf. no. 1964.

2448 Notices of books, 179–234, 235–239. Pages 197–202 signed **Don Abbondio;** pages 184–187, 189–191, 217–218 signed J.I.C.; pages 195–197, 202–205, 207–209 by **J. A. Howlett**—signed J.A.H., cf. no. 2400; pages 179–183 signed B.K., pages 187–189, 207, 214–216 by **James Moyes,** prob.—signed J.M., cf. no. 2079; pages 218–219, 222, 222–223 by **T. B. Scannell** —signed T.B.S., cf. no. 2079.

VOLUME 6 4TH S., 115 O.S., OCTOBER 1894

2449 The earliest Roman Mass-book, 245–278. **Edmund Bishop.** Signed; repr. with same title, 1894.

2450 The mediaeval service books of Aquitaine (Part I): Albi, 279–294. **Robert Twigge.** Signed as in no. 2429.

2451 The real Joan of Arc, 295–312. **Ellen M. Clerke.** Signed.

2452 The Church and the Bible: the two stages of their interrelation (Part I), 313–341. **Friedrich von Hügel.** Signed.

2453 The cures at Lourdes, 342–357. **J. R. Gasquet.** Signed.

2454 Queen Elizabeth and the revolution (Part II, concl.): the preparation for Saint Bartholomew, 358–381. **Jean Mary Stone.** Signed as in no. 2134.

2455 Lord Mar's Home Rule Bill, 382–386. **Stuart Erskine.** Signed, with title "Hon." in Index.

2456 The primitive church and the See of Peter, 387–401. **W. H. Kent.** Signed.

2457 Marlborough, 402–410. **G. T. Mackenzie.** Signed; reference to Bombay, p. 404, associates author with nos. 2361 and 2549, both with same signature.

2458 Some features of Papal jurisdiction in medieval England, 411–431. **James Moyes.** Signed as in no. 2015: *DR* list.

2459 Science notices, 432–443. Page 436 signed E.B.; pages 437–443 by **F. R. Wegg-Prosser**—signed F.R.W.P.

2460 Nova et vetera, 444–454. The rosary, 444–448, by **James Moyes**—signed as in no. 2015; The bidding of the bedes, 448–454, signed **Edmund Bishop.**

2461 Notes of travel and exploration, 455–462. **Ellen M. Clerke,** prob. Cf. no. 1964.

2462 Notices of books, 463–491, 492–493. Pages 468–471 by **Alfons Bellesheim**—

signature; pages 475–477 signed J.I.C.; pages 487–490 signed L.D.S.

VOLUME 7 4TH S., 116 O.S., JANUARY 1895

2463 Clerical and social life in Devon in 1287, 1–24. **W. R. Brownlow.** Signed Bishop of Clifton.

2464 Buddhist sects in Japan, 25–45. **Charles de Harlez.** Signed as in no. 1779; *DR* list.

2465 Two mediaeval Christmas offices, 46–62. **F. E. Gilliat Smith.** Signed.

2466 A Gascon city [Auch] and its church, 63–88. **Robert Twigge.** Signed R. Twigge, with title "F.S.A."

2467 Six weeks in Russia, 89–108. **Mary Elizabeth Herbert.** Signed.

2468 An electoral experiment in Belgium, 109–119. **Wilfrid C. Robinson.** Signed.

2469 Mrs. Augustus Craven, 120–135. **Ellen M. Clerke.** Signed.

2470 The early history of Baptism and Confirmation, 136–147. **J. R. Gasquet.** Signed.

2471 The dispensing power, 148–157. Signed: Z.

2472 Science in fetters (Part I), 158–178. **St. George Mivart.** Signed.

2473 Science notices, 179–187.

2474 Notes of travel and exploration, 188–195. **Ellen M. Clerke,** prob. Cf. no. 1964.

2475 Notices of books, 196–240. Page 201 by **Alfons Bellesheim**—signature; page 202 by **Alfons Bellesheim**—signed B., cf. no. 1724; pages 227–229 by **Christian van den Biesen**—signed C.v.d.B., cf. no. 2348; pages 217, 238–239 signed J.I.C.; pages 229–230 signed F.D.; page 220 by **Alfred Herbert?**—signed A.H., he wrote nos. 2633 and 2665; pages 220–222 by **J. A. Howlett**—signed J.A.H., cf. no. 2400; pages 218–219 signed R.H.; pages 199–200, 224–226 by **J. B. Milburn**—signed J.B.M., cf. no. 2400; pages 196–198, 223–224 by **T. B. Scannell**—signed T.B.S., cf. no. 2079; pages 202–205 signed T.M.S.; pages 212–214, 215–217, 219 signed J.T.; pages 214–215 by **R. W. Twigge,** prob.—signed R.T., topic reflects his antiquarian interests, cf. no. 2429; page 232 by **J. S. Vaughan,** prob.—signed J.S.V., cf. no. 1874.

VOLUME 7 4TH S., 116 O.S., APRIL 1895

2476 Eastern devotion to St. Joseph, 245–256. **W. H. Kent.** Signed.

2477 The Catholic Church in Japan, 257–289. **L. C. Casartelli.** Signed; repr. *Sketches.*

2478 The Church in Korea, 290–305. **Ellen M. Clerke.** Signature.

2479 The Church and the Bible (Part II, concl.), 306–337. **Friedrich von Hügel.** Signed.

2480 Mr. Swinburne's *Studies in Prose and Poetry*: a critique, 338–362. **Charles Coupe.** Signed.

2481 Welsh church history by non-Catholic writers, 363–374. **John Hobson Matthews.** Signed.

2482 Papal supremacy at the Council of Ephesus, 375–395. **Luke Rivington.** Signed.

2483 Science notices, 396–405.

2484 Notes of travel and exploration, 406–413. **Ellen M. Clerke,** prob. Cf. no. 1964.

2485 Notices of books, 414–490. Pages 428–432 by **William Francis Barry,** prob.—signed W.B., he wrote for *DR* on theology and philosophy; pages 435–437, 485 signed F.D.; pages 489–490 by **J. R. Gasquet**—signed J.R.G., cf. no. 2006; pages 443–444 signed W.G.; pages 457–460, 461–462 by **J. A. Howlett**—signed J.A.H., cf. no. 2400; pages 438–442, 444–446 by **W. H. Kent**—signed W.H.K., a constant contributor to *DR*; pages 414–416, 454–455 signed T.L.; page 448 by **Austin Oates?**—signed A.O., cf. no. 2373; pages 425–427 by **D. M. O'Connor**—signed D.M.O'C.; pages 472–484 signed R.C.S.

VOLUME 8 4TH S., 117 O.S., JULY 1895

2486 Science in fetters (Part II, concl.), 1–15. **St. George Mivart.** Signed.

2487 The bishops of Exeter in the thirteenth and fourteenth centuries, 16–26. **Adam Hamilton.** Signed.

2488 The Book of Daniel, 27–40. **J. A. Howlett.** Signed.

2489 Origin and history of the Septuagint, 41–56. **Christian van den Biesen.** Signed as in no. 2348; *DR* list.

2490 Mediaeval service-books of Aquitaine (Part II): Auch, 57–75. **Robert Twigge.** Signed as in no. 2429.

2491 Bells and bell customs, 76–86. **Florence Peacock.** Signed.

2492 The light of faith, 87–101. **David Fleming.** Signed Fr. David, O.S.F.; cf. no. 2544.

2493 Mary Tudor and the Reformers, 102–

127. **J. D. Breen.** Signed, with title "O.S.B."

2494 Mr. Balfour's philosophy, 128–152. **William Francis Barry.** Signed as in no. 1796.

2495 Science notices, 153–160.

2496 Notes of travel and exploration, 161– 169. **Ellen M. Clerke,** prob. Cf. no. 1964.

2497 Notices of books, 170–242. Pages 225– 226 by **Alfons Bellesheim**—signed A.B., review of a German work; pages 213– 217 by **William Francis Barry,** prob.— signed W.B., cf. no. 2485; pages 217– 220, 240–241 by **Gilbert Higgins,** prob.— signed G.H., cf. no. 2387; pages 204–208, 232–233 by **J. A. Howlett**—signed J.A.H., cf. no. 2400; pages 201–202, 203–204 signed R.L.K.; pages 185–188, 210–213, 221–224 by **J. B. Milburn**—signed J.B.M., cf. no. 2400; pages 176–180 signed H.P.; pages 182–184 by **Robert Twigge**—signed R.T., cf. no. 2475.

VOLUME 8 4TH S., 117 O.S., OCTOBER 1895

2498 Hallucinations, 245–264. **T. B. Snow.** Signed, with title "Abbot."

2499 The difficulties of the Catholic episcopate in Russian Poland, together with a short sketch of the life of Monsignor Charles Hryniewicki, Bishop of Vilna, 265–274. **Mary Elizabeth Herbert.** Signed.

2500 The Church and the Bible (Part III, concl.), 275–304. **Friederich von Hügel.** Signed.

2501 Pastor's *History of the Popes* (Vols. III, IV), 305–328. **T. B. Scannell.** Signed.

2502 The fall of the Knights of the Temple, 329–346. **Amy Grange.** Signed; Index adds "Mrs."

2503 The restoration of the Hierarchy and the Ecclesiastical Titles Bill, 347–372. **J. B. Milburn.** Signed.

2504 The church of Bordeaux during the last century of the English dominion (Part I), 373–395. **Ernest Allain.** Signed.

2505 Scientific evidence of the deluge, 396– 415. **F. R. Wegg-Prosser.** Signed.

2506 The English universities and the Reformation, 416–442. **L. C. Casartelli.** Signed; repr. *Sketches.*

2507 Science notices, 443–450.

2508 Notes of travel and exploration, 451– 458. **Ellen M. Clerke,** prob. Cf. no. 1964.

2509 Notices of books, 459–491. Pages 489–490 by **Gilbert Higgins,** prob.— signed G.H., cf. no. 2387; pages 467–474 by **D. M. O'Connor**—signed D.M.O'C.

VOLUME 9 4TH S., 118 O.S., JANUARY 1896

2510 Early Catholic witness upon Anglican orders, 1–39. **T. E. Bridgett.** Signed.

2511 The Lollards, 40–62. **T. B. Snow.** Assigned in Index to Right Rev. Abbot Snow; see no. 2498.

2512 The church of Bordeaux during the last century of the English dominion (Part II, concl.), 63–78. **Ernest Allain.** Signed.

2513 *Brother Luiz de Sousa* [by Garrett], 79–93. **Edgar Prestage.** Signed.

2514 Early Christian literature [by Harnack] (Part I), 94–116. **E. Cuthbert Butler.** Signed. (Part II is no. 2652.)

2515 *Catholic Socialism,* 117–128. **Charles S. Devas.** Signed.

2516 Maynooth College: its centenary history, 129–145. **Patrick Lynch.** Signed.

2517 Science notices, 146–153.

2518 Nova et vetera [on persecution of Catholics in 16th century], 154–172.

2519 Notes of travel and exploration, 173– 181. **Ellen M. Clerke,** prob. Cf. no. 1964.

2520 Notices of books, 182–242. Pages 201– 205 by **Edmund Bishop**—signed E.B., *Life,* p. 500; pages 232–234 by Dom **Bede Camm,** prob.—signed D.B.C., he signed no. 2574 also on an historical subject Dom Bede Camm; pages 234– 236 signed D.J.C.; pages 223–225 by **J. A. Howlett**—signed J.A.H., cf. no. 2400; pages 192–201 signed **Mary Elizabeth Herbert;** pages 216–220 by **Luke Rivington,** prob.—signed by L.R., cf. no. 2686; pages 225–228 by **J. S. Vaughan**— signed J.S.V., cf. no. 1874; pages 228– 230 signed F.W.

VOLUME 9 4TH S., 118 O.S., APRIL 1896

2521 Our diamond jubilee, 245–271. **L. C. Casartelli.** Signed; repr. *Sketches* as "The Makers of the *Dublin.*"

2522 Catholic antiquities of the Darenth Valley, Kent, 272–281. **A. M. Wilson.** Signed; *DR* list adds "Miss."

2523 Biblical science and the Bible, 282– 308. **J. A. Howlett.** Signed.

2524 Alexander VI, 309–333. **T. B. Scannell.** Signed.

2525 Wanderings of early Irish saints on the continent, 334–346. **Ellen M. Clerke.** Signed.

2526 One of Canon Gore's *Dissertations,* 347–369. **William Gildea.** Signed W. Gildea, D.D.; see *Tablet,* Nov. 14, 1914, p. 681.

2527 The place of the Holy Trinity in the *Divina Commedia*, 370–387. **D. Moncrieff O'Connor.** Signed.

2528 *The Life of Cardinal Manning* [by E. S. Purcell], 388–420. **W. H. Kent.** Signed.

2529 Science notices, 421–431.

2530 Notes on travel and exploration, 432–439. **Ellen M. Clerke,** prob. Cf. no. 1964.

2531 Notices of books, 440–466. Pages 449–450 by **Christian van den Biesen**—signed C.v.d.B., cf. no. 2348; pages 450–451 by **Gilbert Higgins,** prob.—signed G.H., cf. no. 2387; pages 445–448 by **J. A. Howlett**—signed J.A.H., cf. no. 2400; pages 460–461 signed R.K.; page 452 signed L.N.; pages 457–458 signed F.W.

2532 The *Dublin Review*: general list of articles, vols. 1–118 (1836–1896), 467–520.

VOLUME 10 4TH S., 119 O.S., JULY 1896

2533 A regius professor [William Bright] on the truthfulness of Catholics, 1–10. **John Chapman,** 1865–1933. Signed, with title "O.S.B."; see *Benedictine Bibliog.*

2534 A regius professor [William Bright] on the Roman See, 11–33. **Luke Rivington.** Signed.

2535 Sir Francis Englefield, 34–76. **Alfred Allen Harrison.** Signed.

2536 Papal elections and coronations, 77–96. **Egerton Beck.** Signed.

2537 The Cardinal of York [Prince Henry, brother of Prince Charles Stuart, the young pretender], 97–120. **Alice Shield.** Signed A. Shield; Index adds "Miss"; see Gorman.

2538 The Stratton churchwardens' accounts, 1512–1577, 121–131. **Florence Peacock.** Signed.

2539 Two English scholars and the beginnings of oriental studies in Louvain, 132–141. **L. C. Casartelli.** Signed; repr. *Sketches.*

2540 A handful of Irish books, 142–152. **Elsa D'Esterre-Keeling.** Signed.

2541 Science notices, 153–161.

2542 Notes of travel and exploration, 162–169. **Ellen M. Clerke,** prob. Cf. no. 1964.

2543 Notices of books, 170–240. Pages 208–214 by **Edmund Bishop**—signed E.B., *Life,* pp. 251, 501; pages 200–201 by Dom **Bede Camm,** prob.—signed D.B.C., cf. no. 2520; pages 196–198 signed M.C.; page 171 by **Gilbert Higgins,** prob.—signed G.H., cf. no. 2387; pages 205–207 by **John Hopwood,** prob.—signed J.H., he was an historian with special interest

in church history (see nos. 2595 and 2703), the topics treated in almost all notices signed with these initials, and all in the same genial manner; pages 177–178 signed J.M.I.; pages 202–205 signed A.A.M.W.

VOLUME 10 4TH S., 119 O.S., OCTOBER 1896

2544 Evolution and dogma, 245–255. **David Fleming.** Signed F. David, O.S.F.; attr. in Ralph Weber, *Notre Dame's John Zahm* (Notre Dame, Indiana, 1961), p. 92n.

2545 The crisis in Rhodesia, 256–270. **Ellen M. Clerke.** Signed.

2546 An idle hour amidst the art books of 1895, 271–282. **Francis Goldie.** Signed F. Goldie, S.J.; see Sutcliffe.

2547 Mediaeval service books of Aquitaine (Part III): Limoges, 283–301. **Robert Twigge.** Signed R. Twigge; cf. no. 2429.

2548 Theories of the beautiful and sublime, 302–318. **Joseph Louis Powell.** Signed, p. 317.

2549 An experiment in education [in Madras], 319–323. **G. T. Mackenzie.** Signed.

2550 Mr. Froude and the Council of Trent, 324–342. **W. H. Kent.** Signed.

2551 The Celtic sources of the *Divina Commedia*, 343–352. **Marion Mulhall.** Signed.

2552 The Orange conspiracy of 1688, 353–377. **Alice Shield.** Signed as in no. 2537.

2553 The extension of the Reformation, 378–391. **R. F. Conder.** Signed.

2554 Apostolic letter of Pope Leo XIII on Anglican ordinations, 392–401. **Leo PP. XIII.** Title.

2555 Science notices, 402–411.

2556 Nova et vetera, 412–427. A synodal sermon in the days of Queen Mary, 412–415, by **James Moyes**—signed as in no. 2015; Sermon delivered at the prorogation of the synod, 415–427, by **Thomas Watson,** 1513–1584—title.

2557 Notes of travel and exploration, 428–436. **Ellen M. Clerke,** prob. Cf. no. 1964.

2558 Notices of books, 437–494. Pages 474, 475–478 signed B.C.; page 469 signed J.C.; pages 487–488 signed J.I.C.; pages 463–465 by **John Hopwood,** prob.—signed J.H., cf. no. 2543; pages 448–451 signed J.M.J.; pages 442–443 signed F.T.L.; pages 488–490 by **G. T. Mackenzie,** prob.—signed G.T.M., on a book of Eastern travel, Mackenzie was a judge in India, and had contributed nos. 2361, 2457, and 2549; pages 438–439, 470–474 signed L.N.; pages 444–446, 455–459 signed H.P.; pages 474–475 signed F.W.; pages 459–460 signed **Wilfrid Wallace.**

VOLUME 11 4TH S., 120 O.S., JANUARY 1897

2559 The triangular battle for education, 1–16. **Herbert Vaughan.** Signed.

2560 The origin of the cope as a church vestment, 17–37. **Edmund Bishop.** Signed.

2561 Modern faith and the Bible, 38–55. **John McIntyre,** 1855–1934. Signed J. McIntyre, D.D.; see *WWW.*

2562 Can Christians consistently laugh or smile? 56–69. **T. E. Bridgett.** Signed.

2563 Notes on Catholic hymnology: a criticism of Dr. Julian's *Dictionary,* 70–87. **Charles T. Gatty.** Signed, with title "F.S.A."

2564 The Holy See and Pelagianism (Part I), 88–111. **John Chapman,** 1865–1933. Assigned to "Dom J. Chapman" in Index; repr. *Studies on the Early Papacy,* 1929.

2565 *Little Eyolf* [by Ibsen]: a plea for reticence, 112–125. **A. F. Spender.** Signed.

2566 Mr. Ottley's *Doctrine of the Incarnation,* 126–140. **W. L. Gildea.** Signed.

2567 The situation [between the Holy See and the Church of England], 1897, 141–182. **Luke Rivington.** Assigned in Index.

2568 Science notices, 183–192.

2569 Notes of travel and exploration, 193–199. **Ellen M. Clerke,** prob. Cf. no. 1964.

2570 Notices of books, 200–239. Pages 204–207, 208–210 by Dom **Bede Camm,** prob. —signed D.B.C., cf. no. 2520; pages 219–222 by F. A. Gasquet—signed F.A.G., man cited was contributing on religious history; pages 225–226 by **John Hopwood,** prob.—signed J.H., cf. no. 2543; pages 202–204 by **W. H. Kent**—signed W.H.K., cf. no. 2485; pages 212–216, 227-229 by **D. M. O'Connor**—signed D.M.O'C.; pages 231–234 signed H.P.

VOLUME 11 4TH S., 120 O.S., APRIL 1897

2571 How our fathers were taught in Catholic days, 245–265. **Francis A. Gasquet.** Signed.

2572 The Berkshire White Horse; and moraines in the Thames valley, 266-277. **Joseph Louis Powell.** Signed.

2573 The metaphysical basis of Protestantism, 278–298. **Mary M. Mallock.** Signed M. M. Mallock; cf. no. 2227.

2574 The Gunpowder Plot, 299–318. **Bede Camm.** Signed Dom Bede Camm.

2575 Charlotte Brontë and her circle, 319–333. **Elsa D'Esterre-Keeling.** Signed.

2576 What will be the creed of the future? 334–344. **J. G. Raupert,** prob. Signed Viator; man cited used this pseudonym for *Ten Years in Anglican Orders,* 1898, H&L, VI, 16.

2577 Alleluia's story, 345–350. **T. J. O'Mahony.** Signed, with title D.D.; see *BMCat.*

2578 Personal reminiscences touching Christian missionaries in China, Corea, Burma, etc., 351–372. **E. H. Parker.** Signed; repr. *China Past and Present,* N.Y. [1903].

2579 Devotion to the Sacred Heart in mediaeval England, 373–385. **Gilbert Dolan.** Signed, with title "O.S.B."

2580 The twenty-five years of Peter, 386–396. **Francis Bacchus.** Signed, p. 393.

2581 Science notices, 397–405.

2582 Notes of travel and exploration, 406–414. **Ellen M. Clerke,** prob. Cf. no. 1964.

2583 Notices of books, 415–489. Pages 422–423 signed C.; pages 415–416, 419 signed J.I.C.; pages 419–422 signed M.C.; pages 479–483 signed C.D.; pages 439–440 signed J.H.; page 461 by **James Halpin,** prob.—signed J.H., he was a great exponent of temperance, the subject of this notice; pages 468–470, 474–476, 477–479, by **J. A. Howlett**—signed J.A.H., cf. no. 2400; pages 437–439, 461–462 signed F.T.L.; pages 433–434, 450–451 by **John McIntyre**—signed J.M'I.; pages 423–429, 434–436 signed H.P.; pages 451–452, 453–458 by **A. F. Spender**—signed A.F.S., man cited contributed arts. on travel and literary figures, the notices signed with these initials deal with the same general topics.

VOLUME 12 4TH S., 121 O.S., JULY 1897

2584 Dr. Lea's *History of Indulgences,* 1–29. **W. H. Kent.** Signed.

2585 *Frithjof's Saga* [by Esaias Tegner], 30–40. **Margaret Watson.** Signed.

2586 The Apostolic age: Hort, Duchesne, Weizsäcker, 41–59. **E. Cuthbert Butler.** Signed.

2587 French expedition to Ireland in 1798, 60–79. **Donat Sampson.** Signed D. Sampson; first name in Contents on cover.

2588 The Communions [symbolic], with three blades of grass, of the knights-errant, 80–98. **Walter Sylvester.** Signed.

2589 The Holy See and Pelagianism (Part II, concl.), 99–124. **John Chapman,** 1865–1933. Signed; repr. *Studies on the Early Papacy,* 1929.

2590 Some troubles of the Elizabethan episcopate, 125–150. **Henry Norbert Birt.** Signed.

2591 St. Francis de Sales as a preacher (Part I), 151–174. **H. B. Mackey.** Signed; repr. under same title, 1898.

2592 Science notices, 175–184.

2593 Notes of travel and exploration, 185–192. **Ellen M. Clerke,** prob. Cf. no. 1964.

2594 Notices of books, 193–238. Pages 220–222 signed F.A.; pages 206–209, 230–231 by **Christian van den Biesen**—signed C.v.d.B., cf. no. 2348; pages 193–196 by Dom **Bede Camm,** prob.—signed D.B.C., cf. no. 2520; pages 209–213 signed J.C.; pages 196–199 by **C. S. Devas**—signed C.S.D., he had been a regular contributor since 1886, writing primarily on political economy, three of the notices signed with these initials are on socialism; pages 203–206 by **Gilbert Dolan,** prob.—signed G.D., Dolan was O.S.B. and the subject is St. Benedict; pages 199–200 by **J. A. Howlett**—signed J.A.H., cf. no. 2400; pages 213–218 signed J.M.I.; pages 227–230 signed F.T.L.; pages 225–227, 231–236 signed H.P.; pages 201, 202–203, 237–238 by **A. F. Spender**—signed A.F.S., cf. no. 2583.

VOLUME 12 4TH S., 121 O.S., OCTOBER 1897

2595 Sir Kenelm Digby, 245–268. **John Hopwood.** Signed, with title "D.D."

2596 Co-operative village banks, 269–283. **Virginia M. Crawford.** Signed.

2597 Richard Rolle, the hermit, 284–293. **T. E. Bridgett.** Signed.

2598 Life of General Gordon, 294–313. **Ellen M. Clerke.** Signed.

2599 St. Peter and the Roman Primacy, 314–322. **Francis Bacchus.** Signed.

2600 Education of women in France, 323–331. **Theresa Thorold.** Signed.

2601 The Gregorian melodies in the manuscripts and the editions, 332–354. **Wilfrid Corney.** Signed, with title "O.S.B."

2602 Mediaeval service books of Aquitaine (Part IV, concl.): Clermont-Ferrand, 355–377. **Robert Twigge.** Signed R. Twigge; cf. no. 2429.

2603 St. Francis de Sales as a preacher (Part II), 378–403. **H. B. Mackey.** Signed.

2604 Science notices, 404–414.

2605 Notes of travel and exploration, 415–422. **Ellen M. Clerke,** prob. Cf. no. 1964.

2606 Notices of books, 423–492. Pages 433–435 signed C.A.; pages 483–484 signed J.A.; pages 472–476 by **Edmund Bishop**—signed E.B., *Life,* pp. 269, 502; pages 450–453 by **E. Cuthbert Butler**—signed E.C.B., he used these initials in the *DNB*/ 1921, under list of contributors; pages 430–433, 435–436 by Dom **Bede Camm,** prob.—signed D.B.C., cf. no. 2520; pages 460–461 signed F.C.; pages 426–430, 436, 437, 461–464 signed J.C.; pages 446–449 by **C. S. Devas**—signed C.S.D., cf. no. 2594; pages 464–466 by **Gilbert Dolan,** prob.—signed G.D., man cited had already contributed one notice (cf. no. 2594) and was to contribute more; pages 440–444 by **John Hopwood,** prob.—signed J.H., cf. no. 2543; pages 424–426 by **W. H. Kent**—signed W.H.K., cf. no. 2485; pages 476–479 by **A. F. Spender**—signed A.F.S., cf. no. 2583.

VOLUME 13 4TH S., 122 O.S., JANUARY 1898

2607 English Biblical criticism in the thirteenth century, 1–21. **F. A. Gasquet.** Signed.

2608 The Hiberno-Danish predecessors of Columbus, 22–29. **Marion Mulhall.** Signed.

2609 Professor Jowett, 30–41. Signed: X.Y.Z.

2610 St. Jerome and Rome, 42–73. **John Chapman,** 1865–1933. Signed, with title "O.S.B."; repr. *Studies in the Early Papacy,* 1929.

2611 Impressions of the Holy Land, 74–92. **A. F. Spender.** Signed.

2612 St. Francis de Sales as a preacher (Part III, concl. [prob.]), 93–124. **H. B. Mackey.** Signed.

2613 Christian democracy, 125–144. **Charles Stanton Devas.** Signed.

2614 Two recent liturgical books, 145–156. **Edmund Bishop.** Signed.

2615 Science notices, 157–165.

2616 Notes of travel and exploration, 166–173. **Ellen M. Clerke,** prob. Cf. no. 1964.

2617 Nova et vetera: Eucharistic doctrine in the Eastern Church, 174–179. **Edmund Bishop.** *Life,* p. 502.

2618 Notices of books, 180–236. Pages 183–184 signed C.A.; pages 226–227, 229–230 by **E. C. Butler**—signed E.C.B., cf. no. 2606; pages 184–186 by Dom **Bede Camm,** prob.—signed D.B.C., cf. no. 2520; pages 182, 221–222 signed J.C.; pages 188, 222, 234, 235 signed J.I.C.; pages 223, 235–236 signed F.T.L.; pages 202–204, 207–209 signed E.N.; pages

181–182, 183, 206–207 signed L.N.; pages 214–216 signed J.O'L.; pages 180–181, 186–187, 218–220 by **A. F. Spender** —signed A.F.S., cf. no. 2583.

VOLUME 13 4TH S., 122 O.S., APRIL 1898

2619 Monuments to Cardinal Wiseman, 245–274. **T. E. Bridgett.** Signed.

2620 Craft guilds in the fifteenth century, 275–290. **T. B. Snow.** Signed.

2621 Queen Clementina [wife of the Old Pretender], 291–319. **Alice Shield.** Signed as in no. 2537.

2622 Textual criticism of the New Testament, 320–344. **J. A. Howlett.** Signed.

2623 Pictures of the Reformation period (Part I): Charitas Pirkheimer, 345–371. **Jean Mary Stone.** Signed as in no. 2134.

2624 Philosophy of the Renaissance, 372–390. **W. H. Kent.** Signed.

2625 Dr. Pusey's *Eirenicon*: why is it a failure? 391–417. **Luke Rivington.** Assigned in Index.

2626 Science notices, 418–425.

2627 Notes of travel and exploration, 426–434. **Ellen M. Clerke,** prob. Cf. no. 1964.

2628 Notices of books, 435–490. Pages 453–456 signed F.A.; pages 482–487 by **Edmund Bishop**—signed E.B., *Life*, p. 502; pages 480–482 signed J.C.; pages 445–448 by **C. S. Devas**—signed C.S.D., cf. no. 2594, on socialism; pages 439–444 by **Gilbert Dolan,** prob.—signed G.D., cf. no. 2594; pages 452–453, 456 signed E.G.; pages 448–449 by **John Hopwood,** prob.—signed J.H., cf. no. 2543; pages 450–452 by **J. A. Howlett** —signed J.A.H., cf. no. 2400; pages 435–438 signed F.T.L.; pages 460–462 by **John McIntyre**—signed J.McI.; page 472 signed D.M.; pages 457–460 signed H.P.; pages 462–464, 465–467 by **A. F. Spender** —signed A.F.S., cf. no. 2583.

VOLUME 14 4TH S., 123 O.S., JULY 1898

2629 William Ewart Gladstone, 1–40. **W. H. Kent.** Signed.

2630 The English mediaeval institute of cathedral canons, 41–64. **Edmund Bishop.** Signed.

2631 The Church and the universities (No. I): Bologna and Paris, 65–93. **J. B. Milburn.** Signed.

2632 The national establishments of England in mediaeval Rome (Part I), 94–

106. **William J. D. Croke.** Signed, Part II is signed with title "LL.D."

2633 Edmund of Abingdon and the universities, 107–120. **Alfred Herbert.** Signed.

2634 The modern critical and historical school, its methods and tendencies, 121–139. **E. Cuthbert Butler.** Signed.

2635 Some beliefs and customs relating to Holy Week, 140–158. **Florence Peacock.** Signed.

2636 Science notices, 159–167.

2637 Notes of travel and exploration, 168–175. **Ellen M. Clerke,** prob. Cf. no. 1964.

2638 Notices of books, 176–232. Pages 204–205 by **Christian van den Biesen**—signed C.v.d.B., cf. no. 2348; pages 179–180, 206–207 signed R.B.; page 231 signed J.J.C.; pages 222–223 by **C. S. Devas**— signed C.S.D., cf. no. 2594; pages 219–222 signed **Charles S. Devas;** pages 180–181 by **Gilbert Dolan?**—signed G.D., cf. no. 2594; pages 176–179 by **James Moyes,** prob.—signed J.M., cf. no. 2079; pages 196–203 signed R.C.S.

VOLUME 14 4TH S., 123 O.S., OCTOBER 1898

2639 Physical science and faith, 241–261. **John Cuthbert Hedley.** Signed.

2640 *Bards of the Gael and Gall* [translations by George Sigerson], 262–275. **Elsa D'Esterre-Keeling.** Signed.

2641 The succession of the first Roman bishops (Part I), 276–286. **Francis Bacchus.** Signed.

2642 The minnesinger Walther von der Vogelweide, 287–296. **Margaret Watson.** Signed.

2643 The principle of individualisation, 297–304. **A. J. Howard.** Signed, with titles "O.P., S.T.L., B.C.L."

2644 The national establishments of England in mediaeval Rome (Part II, concl.), 305–317. **William J. D. Croke.** Signed, with title "LL.D."

2645 Doctrine of the Eucharistic Presence and the Anglican divines, 318–336. **Edmund Bishop.** Signed.

2646 Father Dominic and the conversion of England, 337–355. **Bede Camm.** Signed, with title O.S.B.

2647 English scholarship in the thirteenth century, 356–373. **F. A. Gasquet.** Signed.

2648 Science notices, 374–382.

2649 Notes of travel and exploration, 383–390. **Ellen M. Clerke,** prob. Cf. no. 1964.

2650 Nova et vetera: how English Catholics prayed in the fourteenth century, 391–

401. Intro. note, pages 391–393, by **James Moyes**—signed as in no. 2015.

2651 Notices of books, 402–486. Pages 453–454 signed F.A.; pages 473–474 by **Christian van den Biesen**—signed C.v.d.B., cf. no. 2348; pages 402–406 by **Edmund Bishop**—signed E.B., *Life*, p. 503; pages 417–422, 426–428 by **E. C. Butler**—signed E.C.B., cf. no. 2606; pages 450–452 signed T.A.B.; page 423 signed M.E.D.; pages 460–463 by **W. L. Gildea** —signed W.L.G., cf. no. 2566; pages 415–417 by **John Hopwood, prob.**—signed J.H., cf. no. 2543; pages 439–443 by **J. A. Howlett**—signed J.A.H., cf. no. 2400; pages 412–415 signed J.M.I.; pages 464–469 by **W. H. Kent**—signed W.H.K., cf. no. 2485; pages 484–486 signed F.T.L.; pages 408–412 signed L.N.; pages 433–438 by **D. M. O'Connor**—signed D.M.O'C.; pages 407, 428–433 signed H.P.; pages 469–473 by **A. F. Spender**—signed A.F.S., cf. no. 2583.

VOLUME 15 4TH S., 124 O.S., JANUARY 1899

2652 Harnack's *Chronology of Early Christian Literature* (Part II, concl.), 1–24. **E. Cuthbert Butler.** Signed. (Part I is no. 2514.)

2653 Sir M. E. Grant Duff's *Notes from a Diary*, 25–35. **Wilfrid Ward.** Signed.

2654 Pictures of the Reformation period (Part II, concl.): the convent of St. Margaret and St. Agnes at Strassburg, 36–59. **Jean Mary Stone.** Signed as in no. 2134.

2655 Toscanelli and Vespucci, 60–77. **Ellen M. Clerke.** Signature.

2656 The liturgical books of the Russian Church, 78–106. **W. H. Kent.** Signed.

2657 Points of contact between Catholicism and spiritualism, 107–118. **Henry C. Corrance.** Signed.

2658 The foreshadowing of Christianity: the "Alcestis" of Euripides considered as a type of the Redemption, 119–140. **Moncrieff O'Connor.** Signed.

2659 The kingdom of the head master, 141–155. **R. B. S. Blakelock.** Signed.

2660 Science notices, 156–165.

2661 Notes of travel and exploration, 166–174. **Ellen M. Clerke, prob.** Cf. no. 1964.

2662 Nova et vetera, 175–193. Pages 175–178 by **James Moyes**—signed as in no. 2015; pages 178–193 copy of the letter

of foundation of the college or chantry of Halstede.

2663 Notices of books, 194–240. Pages 202–204 signed A.S.B.; pages 194–197 by **Christian van den Biesen**—signed C.v.d.B., cf. no. 2348; pages 197–200 signed E.H.B.; pages 215–216 by **Francis Bacchus?**—signed F.B., man cited was contributing on historical subjects at this time; pages 201–202, 228–229 by **J. A. Howlett**—signed J.A.H., cf. no. 2400; pages 231, 232 signed F.T.L.; pages 229–231 by **James Moyes, prob.**— signed J.M., cf. no. 2079; pages 206–207 signed E.N.; pages 208–211 by **D. M. O'Connor** —signed D.M.O'C., on Dante: see no. 2527; pages 227–228 by **T. B. Scannell** —signed T.B.S., cf. no. 2079.

VOLUME 15 4TH S., 124 O.S., APRIL 1899

2664 Lord Halifax and neo-Anglicanism, 241–264. **James Moyes.** Signed as in no. 2015, p. 261.

2665 Edward Thring of Uppingham, 265–290. **Alfred Herbert.** Signed, with title "M.A."

2666 Some historical notes from the margins of a manuscript [a Sarum breviary], 291–313. **Henry Norbert Birt.** Signed.

2667 The Church and the universities (No. II, concl.): Oxford, 314–341. **J. B. Milburn.** Signed.

2668 Divided hosts at treaty Communions: a query, 342–347. **Walter Sylvester.** Signed.

2669 Early Scottish saints, 348–372. **Michael Barrett.** Signed, with title "O.S.B."

2670 The succession of the early Roman bishops (Part II, concl.), 373–383. **Francis Bacchus.** Signed.

2671 Dr. Fairbairn on Catholicism, 384–407. **W. H. Kent.** Signed.

2672 Science notices, 408–415.

2673 Notes of travel and exploration, 416–423. **Ellen M. Clerke, prob.** Cf. no. 1964.

2674 Notices of books, 424–484. Pages 453–454 by **Edmund Bishop**—signed E.B., *Life*, p. 503; pages 469–472 by **C. S. Devas**—signed C.S.D., cf. no. 2594; pages 477–479 by **F. A. Gasquet**—signed F.A.G., cf. no. 2570; pages 424, 453, 472–474 by **John Hopwood, prob.**—signed J.H., cf. no. 2543; pages 450–452 by **J. A. Howlett**—signed J.A.H., cf. no. 2400; pages 437–439, 442, 483–484 signed F.T.L.; pages 425–428 by **John**

McIntyre—signed J.McI.; pages 433–436, 476–477 by **James Moyes**, prob.—signed J.M., cf. no. 2079; pages 425, 444–447 signed Jn.M.; pages 447–450 signed E.N.; pages 454–468 signed H.P.; pages 474–476 signed I.T.

VOLUME 16 4TH S., 125 O.S., JULY 1899

2675 Pastor's *Popes of the Renaissance*, 1–32. **W. H. Kent.** Signed.
2676 The triumph of St. Thomas, 33–42. **Merwin-Marie Snell.** Signed.
2677 Dramatic art and church liturgy, 43–55. **Edward King.** Signed, with title "S.J."
2678 The last Stuart princess [Louisa Mary, daughter of James II], 56–85. **Alice Shield.** Signed as in no. 2537.
2679 Will the gospel of materialism be the religion of the future? 86–96. **H. C. Corrance.** Signed.
2680 The reality of the external world, 97–120. **W. R. Carson.** Signed.
2681 Textual criticism of the Hebrew text, 121–143. **J. A. Howlett.** Signed.
2682 The Mazarinus manuscript and the primeval biography of St. Francis of Assisi, 144–152. **F. Andrew.** Signed, with title "O.F.M."; Index gives "Rev. Fr. Andrew."
2683 Mediaeval grammar schools, 153–178. **J. B. Milburn.** Signed.
2684 Science notices, 179–187.
2685 Notes of travel and exploration, 188–195. **Ellen M. Clerke,** prob. Cf. no. 1964.
2686 Notices of books, 196–240. Pages 206–207 signed R.B.; pages 208–210 by Dom **Bede Camm,** prob.—signed D.B.C., cf. no. 2520; pages 221–222 signed M.C.; pages 201–202 signed R.C.; page 208 by **John Hopwood,** prob.—signed H., cf. no. 2543; pages 218–220 by **Gilbert Higgins,** prob.—signed G.H., cf. no. 2387; page 203 signed J.H.; pages 203–204, 227–230 by **J. A. Howlett**—signed J.A.H., cf. no. 2400; pages 223–224 signed J.; pages 224–227 by **W. H. Kent**—signed W.H.K., cf. no. 2485; page 238 signed M.; pages 234–235 signed Jn.M.; pages 238–239 signed Jno.M.; pages 211–213, 233–234, 240 signed N.; pages 197–198 signed E.N.; pages 199–200 signed L.N.; pages 239–240 signed O.; page 239 by **Austin G. Oates,** prob.—signed A.G.O., cf. no. 2373; pages 216–218, 235–236 signed H.P.; page 197 signed M.P.; pages 214–216, 230–232 by **Luke Rivington**—signed L.R., identified on p. 232n.

VOLUME 16 4TH S., 125 O.S., OCTOBER 1899

2687 Robert Aiken, a sketch from memory, 245–268. **W. R. Brownlow.** Signed.
2688 A great French convent school before the Revolution: St. Cyr in the past (Part I), 269–283. **Barbara de Courson.** Signed, with title "Comtesse."
2689 The Oxford Movement: twelve years' converts, 284–295. **Edmund Jackson.** Signed.
2690 Renascence of Catholicism in France, 1796–1861, 296–314. **Moncrieff O'Connor.** Signed.
2691 Physical science versus matter and form, 315–341. **Cornelius Aherne.** Signed C. Aherne.
2692 Abbot Tosti, 342–359. **Bede Camm.** Signed.
2693 Scottish Benedictine houses of the past (Part I), 360–384. **Michael Barrett.** Signed.
2694 Iceland and the Faröe Islands, 385–401. **A. Clarke Little.** Signed.
2695 The making of French literature, 402–423. **W. H. Kent.** Signed.
2696 Science notices, 424–433.
2697 Notes of travel and exploration, 434–441. **Ellen M. Clerke,** prob. Cf. no. 1964.
2698 Nova et vetera: how our forefathers prepared for confession, 442–446. **H. N. Birt.** Signed.
2699 Notices of books, 447–492. Pages 462–463 signed P.A.; pages 478–479 by **E. C. Butler,** prob.—signed E.C.B., cf. no. 2606; pages 479–484 by **Francis Bacchus,** prob.—signed F.B., cf. no. 2663; pages 460–462 by Dom **Bede Camm,** prob.—signed D.B.C., cf. no. 2520; pages 468–469 signed D.; pages 491–492 signed G.; page 455 signed J.; pages 456–457 by **J. A. Howlett**—signed J.A.H., cf. no. 2400; pages 453–454 by **W. H. Kent**—signed W.H.K., cf. no. 2485; pages 472–473, 488–491 signed M.; pages 464–465, 471–472, 476–477, 484 signed Jn.M.; pages 484–488 signed N.; page 473 signed O.; pages 463–464, 474–475 by **A. G. Oates,** prob.—signed A.G.O., cf. no. 2373; pages 457–460 signed H.P.; page 477 signed M.P.; page 456 signed G.T.; pages 450–451, 454–455, 455–456 signed X.; pages 449–450 signed X.X.; page 451 signed Y.

VOLUME 17 4TH S., 126 O.S., JANUARY 1900

2700 The jubilee indulgence *a poena et a culpa*, 1–24. **Herbert Thurston.** Signed.

2701 The deprivation of clergy in Elizabeth's reign (Part I), 25–45. **Henry Norbert Birt.** Signed.

2702 The Catholic Church in South Africa, 46–66. **Ellen M. Clerke.** Signature.

2703 Professor Maitland's *Roman Canon Law in the Church of England*, 67–90. **John Hopwood.** Signed.

2704 St. Cyr in the present (Part II, concl.), 91–101. **Barbara de Courson.** Signed.

2705 Montalembert and French education, 102–120. **R. B. S. Blakelock.** Signed.

2706 The eve of the English Reformation, 121–150. **W. H. Kent.** Signed.

2707 Science notices, 151–160.

2708 Notes of travel and exploration, 161–168. **Ellen M. Clerke,** prob. Cf. no. 1964.

2709 Notices of books, 169–239. Pages 172–174, 187–189 signed A.S.B.; pages 179–182 by **E. C. Butler**—signed E.C.B., cf. no. 2606; page 175 by **Ellen M. Clerke** —signed E.M.C., cf. no. 2345; pages 204–206, 219–223 by **Henry C. Corrance** —signed H.C.C., he had contributed nos. 2657 and 2679 on similar topics; pages 201–202, 232–233 signed W.G.; pages 174–175 by **Alfred Herbert**, prob.— signed A.H., he was interested in education (see nos. 2633 and 2665); pages 213–218 by **Gilbert Higgins**—signed G.H., cf. no. 2387; pages 178–179 by **John Hopwood**, prob.—signed J.H., cf., no. 2543; pages 184–186, 223–225 by **J. A. Howlett**—signed J.A.H., cf. no. 2400; pages 196–201, 206–212 by **W. H. Kent**—signed W.H.K., cf. no. 2485; pages 233–236 signed F.T.L.; page 203 signed M.; pages 169–170 signed Jn.M.; pages 170–172 signed N.; pages 226–227, 227–228 signed E.N.; pages 189–193 by **D. M. O'Connor**—signed D.M.O'C.; pages 238–239 signed M.D.P.; page 237 signed W.; pages 176–178, 182–184, 194–195, 195–196, 212–213 signed X.

VOLUME 17 4TH S., 126 O.S., APRIL 1900

2710 The Syriac *Testament of Our Lord*, 245–274. **W. H. Kent.** Signed.

2711 Scottish Benedictine houses of the past (Part II), 275–296. **Michael Barrett.** Signed.

2712 The Nibelungenlied, 297–312. **Margaret Watson.** Signed.

2713 The deprivation of clergy in Elizabeth's reign (Part II, concl.), 313–342. **Henry Norbert Birt.** Signed.

2714 Physical science versus matter and form: a reply [to no. 2691], 343–355. **J. C. Bredin.** Signed. With note on p. 355 saying that to Edward Godwin "is due the metaphysical portion of the article."

2715 Noble Christian families in Rome under the pagan emperors, 356–378. **James Augustine Campbell.** Signed J. A. Campbell; *BMCat.*

2716 The catacombs of Syracuse (Part I), 379–390. **A. F. Spender.** Signed.

2717 Wellhausen and the chronicler [author of the Book of Chronicles], 391–411. **J. A. Howlett.** Signed.

2718 Science notices, 412–420.

2719 Notes of travel and exploration, 421–428. **Ellen M. Clerke,** prob. Cf. no. 1964.

2720 Notices of books, 429–490. Pages 468–471 by **Alfons Bellesheim**—signed B., cf. no. 1724; pages 483–484 signed C.B.; pages 430–434 by **Edmund Bishop**— signed E.B., *Life*, p. 504; pages 486–487 signed E.M.D.; pages 437–440 signed E.G.; pages 444–445, 450–451, 472–473, 479 signed W.G.; pages 462–463, 465 by **Gilbert Higgins**, prob.—signed G.H.; pages 465–468 by **J. A. Howlett**—signed J.A.H., cf. no. 2400; pages 440–444, 448–450 by **W. H. Kent**—signed W.H.K., cf. no. 2485; pages 454–456 by **Edmund Jackson**—signed E.J., see no. 2689; pages 429–430 signed F.T.L.; pages 437, 484–486 signed Jn.M.; pages 487–489 signed N.; pages 434–435, 446–447, 480–483, 489–490 by **A. G. Oates**, prob.—signed A.G.O., cf. no. 2373; pages 456–462 signed H.P.; pages 435–437 signed M.D.P.; pages 451–454 by **A. F. Spender** —signed A.F.S., cf. no. 2583; pages 430, 463–464 signed X.

VOLUME 18 4TH S., 127 O.S., JULY 1900

2721 The justice of the Transvaal War, 1–44.

2722 Scottish Benedictine houses of the past (Part III, concl.), 45–68. **Michael Barrett.** Signed.

2723 Edmund Burke and the Revolution, 69–94. **W. B. Morris,** Signed.

2724 A [nameless] Russian champion of the Church, 95–122. **W. H. Kent.** Signed.

2725 The catacombs of Syracuse (Part II, concl.), 123–144. **A. F. Spender.** Signed.

2726 Science notices, 145–153.

2727 Notes of travel and exploration, 154–163. **Ellen M. Clerke,** prob. Cf. no. 1964.

2728 Nova et vetera: extracts from the diary of an officer under William III (Part I), 164–192. **Thomas Bellingham.** Intro. note by **Sir Henry Bellingham**—signed H.B.; see p. 168 and Burke.

2729 Notices of books, 193–254. Pages 199–202 by **Francis Bacchus**, prob.—signed F.B., cf. no. 2663; pages 204–206 by **W. R. Brownlow?**—signed W.R.B., cf. no. 1756; pages 216–217 signed J.F.; pages 193–199, 250 signed W.G.; pages 236–238, 251–252 by **Gilbert Higgins**, prob.—signed G.H., cf. no. 2387; pages 226–227, 229–230, 234–235 by **John Hopwood**, prob.—signed J.H., cf. no. 2543; pages 202–204, 209–211, 223, 224–225, 233–234 by **J. A. Howlett**—signed J.A.H., cf. no. 2400; pages 211–215, 219–223, 244–245, 247–249 by **W. H. Kent**—signed W.H.K., cf. no. 2485; pages 218–219 signed M.; pages 231–232, 240–241 signed Jn.M.; pages 206, 215–216, 217–218 signed M.M.; pages 230–231, 232–233, 245–247, 250, 252–254 by **A. G. Oates**, prob.—signed A.G.O., cf. no. 2373; pages 227–229 signed M.D.P.; pages 207–208 by **A. F. Spender**—signed A.F.S., cf. no. 2583.

VOLUME 18 4TH S., 127 O.S., OCTOBER 1900

2730 Dr. Martineau on the notes of the church, 261–277. Signed: X.Y.Z.

2731 Physical science versus matter and form: a rejoinder [to no. 2714], 278–300. **Cornelius Aherne.** Signed C. Aherne.

2732 The Irish Church from the Danish to the Anglo-Norman invasion, 301–319. **E. A. D'Alton.** Signed.

2733 Theology and modern thought, 320–352. **W. H. Kent.** Signed.

2734 Scientific speculation and the unity of truth, 353–368. **Robert E. Froude.** Signed R. E. Froude with title "F.R.S."

2735 Science notices, 369–383.

2736 Notes of travel and exploration, 384–392. **Ellen M. Clerke,** prob. Cf. no. 1964.

2737 Nova et vetera: extracts from the diary of Colonel Thomas Bellingham (Part II, concl.), 393–416. **Thomas Bellingham.** Title.

2738 Notices of books, 417–500. Pages 489–491 signed E.C.; pages 417, 449–462 by **H. C. Corrance**, prob.—signed H.C.C., he used these initials for no. 2709; pages 419–420, 421–422, 466–467, 481, 483–484, 496 by **W. L. Gildea**—signed W.L.G., cf. no. 2566; pages 440–442, 443–445 by **Gilbert Higgins**, prob.—signed G.H., cf. no. 2387; pages 431–433 by **J. A. Howlett**—signed J.A.H., cf. no. 2400; pages 424–426 by **W. H. Kent**—signed W.H.K., cf. no. 2485; pages 417–418, 420–421, 447–448, 462–465, 481–483 signed F.T.L.; pages 484–488 by **John McIntyre**, prob.—signed J.McI.; pages 437–440, 442, 443 signed N.; pages 422–424, 427–430, 433–437, 469–475, 491–494 signed H.P.; pages 430–431 signed E.S.; pages 445–447, 448 signed X.

The Foreign Quarterly Review, 1827–1846

EVERY STUDY of the British reception of a foreign literature mentions the importance of the *Foreign Quarterly Review*. It ran for twenty years (1827–1846), longer than any other nineteenth-century review devoted exclusively or principally to the consideration of foreign thought and foreign literature. It included among its contributors many men who were prominent in their own day, and many whose reputations have survived the intervening century. The *Foreign Quarterly* sought to be the *Edinburgh* or *Quarterly* of its own special field, and any examination of the articles contained in its thirty-seven volumes will impress one with the extent of its success. It was established as a source of information on contemporary foreign literature, and its main importance lies in the articles which developed this purpose. At the same time it printed articles on a number of other subjects: on the Greek and Latin classics, on ancient and modern literatures of the Near and Far East, on medieval French and English poetry, on architecture, music, medicine, and the sciences. Many articles discuss England's position abroad, particularly in India; others plunge into religious controversy.

A "Foreign Quarterly Review" had been projected by the foreign bookselling firm of Treuttel and Co. in 1821; a prospectus was issued, but no review followed.[1] Others started short-lived reviews of foreign literature in 1822, 1823, and 1824; the public seemed unwilling to support such cosmopolitan ventures. Then in June 1826, in spite of these discouraging precedents, Sir Walter Scott suggested that Robert Pearse Gillies found and edit a quarterly periodical which would be part review, part miscellany of foreign literature; at the same time Scott warned that editing would involve "daily and constant drudgery." Gillies, who translated German drama for *Blackwood's*, was reckless, ineffectual, imprudent, improvident—a good translator, a poor critic, and an unpromising editor. He was, however, always happy projecting brilliant enterprises, and he was soon planning possible formats, soliciting contributions, seeking a publisher. After Blackwood and the leading London publishers turned him down, he turned to Treuttel and Würtz, who five years earlier had sought him as a contributor. They agreed, and in their determination to make the undertaking a success they allowed Gillies generous terms: his own stipend as contributing editor

---

[1] "The Foreign Quarterly Review . . . *versus* The Foreign Review . . ." (Nov. 17, 1827), p. 5; "Rejoinder of the Proprietors of the Foreign Quarterly Review to the 'Reply of the Foreign Review'" (Jan. 12, 1828), pp. 1–2. Both are bound with the copy of the *FQR*, Vol. I, in the British Museum.

would be £500 a year; contributors would be paid an average of 10 gns. per sheet, and such established reviewers as Robert Southey would receive as much as 100 gns. for two and a half sheets.[2] (The *Edinburgh*'s average pay was 20 gns. a sheet, the *Westminster*'s 10 gns. a sheet for those contributors who were paid.)[3]

During March 1827 Gillies planned the layout of the new Review, with the help of John George Cochrane, Treuttel's London manager: it was to contain reviews much like those in the *Edinburgh* and *Quarterly*, and in addition reports from correspondents in the chief continental cities. Gillies was responsible for collecting and editing the reviews, one of Treuttel's men for the "Miscellaneous Literary Notices." The first number was planned for June 15,[4] really too early a date; but surprisingly Gillies, or Treuttel, did not miss by too large a margin: the number actually appeared on July 28, selling for 7/6d.

All things considered, it was a good time for such a Review to appear. Though the end of the Napoleonic Wars in 1815 had once more made possible both travel on the Continent and importation of books from abroad, considerable interest in foreign works did not seem to develop until the late 1820s. The interest was stimulated by the presence of political refugees—in 1827 there were in London alone a thousand refugees from Spain and elsewhere. This group provided the tutors who taught foreign languages to the English; and they also provided some of the reviewers for such a periodical as the *Foreign Quarterly*. For whatever reason, 1826–1830 were the best years for the importation into England of French and Spanish books; imports then gradually declined until the nadir was reached in 1850.[5] Even up to 1835, two booksellers alone annually imported into England an average of 400,000 French books, the equivalent of one volume to every 53 inhabitants.[6] Another bookseller undertook to obtain German books within one month of the date of order, and also maintained a subscription service for twenty-two German periodicals.[7] Sometime before 1829 Treuttel and Würtz started the West London Foreign Circulating Library for those who could not afford the prices of foreign books, inflated by a duty of £5 per cwt. and the costs of carriage and insurance.[8] This availability of foreign books was important to the *Foreign Quarterly*, which remained remarkably true to its original policy of reviewing only books not yet available in English translation.

In its first years the *Foreign Quarterly*'s greatest problems were editorial. A self-appointed, unofficial sub-editor named William Fraser left after the first number to found the rival *Foreign Review*, taking with him actual and potential contributors, including Southey and Thomas Carlyle.[9] From the start Gillies looked down on the

---

[2]See Robert Pearse Gillies, *Memoirs of a Literary Veteran* (1851), III, 134–136, 143–146, 181; Sir Walter Scott, *Letters*, ed. H. J. C. Grierson (1932, 1937), X, 162; Gillies to Scott, Mar. 31, 1827, Nat. Lib. Scot.; "FQR *vs.* ForR" (n.1), p. 5.

[3][James Grant], *The Great Metropolis*, 2nd ed. (1837), II, 273, 281. Grant, II, 289, gives average *FQR* pay as 10–16 gns. a sheet (i.e., per 16 octavo pages).

[4]See Gillies to Scott, Mar. 31, 1827, Nat. Lib. Scot.

[5]Nigel Glendinning, "Spanish Books in England: 1800–1850," *Transactions of the Cambridge Bibliographical Society*, III (1959–1961), 77, 82.

[6]Marcel Moraud, *Le Romantisme française en Angleterre de 1814 à 1848* (Paris, 1933), p. 205 (figures from *New Monthly Magazine*, issue not identified).

[7]D. F. S. Scott, *Some English Correspondents of Goethe* (1949), pp. 73–74.

[8][John Ward], "Duties on Foreign Books," *FQR*, IX (Jan. 1832), 214.

[9]See Gillies, III, 169–170; "FQR *vs.* ForR" (n.1), pp. 1–8; "Rejoinder," pp. 1–11; *Selections from the Letters of Robert Southey*, ed. John Wood Warter (1856), IV, 57–58.

editorship and Cochrane had to assume the editorial duties. The latter seems justified in calling himself "the *real*, although not the *nominal* Editor . . . from the beginning." Finally, in March 1830, Gillies ceased to be even nominal editor. In the same month appeared the last issue of the *Foreign Review*. The two reviews then merged, retaining the name of the older and the price (6/) of its rival. Cochrane was now nominal, real, and sole editor, and remained such through 1834.[10]

Cochrane was a strong editor, and he was more responsible than any other for giving the *Foreign Quarterly* its character. He wrote later that he had wanted the Review to "exercise a salutary influence in the propagation of sound and liberal ideas, in the inculcation of charity and toleration in matters of politics and religion, and in making the nations of Europe better acquainted with each other."[11] To this end he gathered together an impressive, if seemingly disparate, group of contributors. They were well-informed and responsible; most were gentlemen, members of the gentlemen's universities, engaged in gentlemanly callings—lawyers and literary dilettantes like George Moir and Abraham Hayward, clergymen like Hugh James and Henry John Rose and Thomas Hartwell Horne, scholars like John Mitchell Kemble, professors like John Pringle Nichol and John Stevens Henslow. Several were active in Whig political and journalistic circles; many of these sat on parliamentary commissions and contributed to the *Edinburgh*, like George Cornewall Lewis, Charles Buller, and John Ward. Another important contributor who also wrote for the *Edinburgh* was the political economist, John Ramsey McCulloch, the originator of the wage-fund theory. A much smaller group of Benthamite reviewers contributed a great many articles, particularly John Bowring and Henry Southern, both editors of the *Westminster Review* and later, when they no longer contributed to the *Foreign Quarterly*, both holding diplomatic appointments. There were also important Tory contributors: Thomas Peregrine Courtenay, vice-president of the Board of Trade and a *Blackwood's* writer; Scott, who contributed for Gillies' sake; and others. A few literary hacks, who contributed prolifically, were Tories—Mrs. Busk, a *Blackwood's* contributor, and André Vieusseux, an Italian national; and they allowed their conservatism full freedom. All this produced a predominately liberal publication with occasional jarring notes of conservatism. The *Foreign Review* twitted it on its inconsistencies, political and critical, but the *Foreign Quarterly* took pride in them. Through the inconsistencies, too, in the opinion of John Stuart Mill, Cochrane achieved very much what he sought. As Mill observed, he "has a great love of fairness, and is above all an enemy of *extremes*—and . . . proves himself an impartial arbitrater between conflicting opinions by letting each in its turn speak through his pages, in as softened a voice as may be, whereby in truth his Review the better fulfils its mission, by representing the more correctly the attitude which English minds of all parties and sorts have taken up towards foreign nations . . . so that if [Carlyle] & the Right Hon. T. P. Courtenay appear side by side in it, we must not be shocked by the proximity."[12] Such bipartisanship was rare in early nineteenth-century journalism.

---

[10]See Gillies, II, 161, 203; Cochrane to Lord Brougham, Feb. 13, 1833, Univ. Col. Lond.; George Moir to Thomas Carlyle, Dec. 29, 1829, and Mar. 24, 1830, Nat. Lib. Scot.; Cochrane to Carlyle, July 3, 1830, Nat. Lib. Scot.

[11]Prospectus to *Cochrane's Foreign Quarterly Review* (1835), p. 2, in British Museum copy.
[12]To Carlyle, Dec. 27, 1832, in *Earlier Letters*, I, 132.

The *Athenaeum* considered the *Foreign Quarterly* "the best edited periodical in this country," partly because it reviewed only those books which were "best calculated to illustrate the spirit of the different nations from which they issued."[13] Abroad, articles from the *Foreign Quarterly* were translated into French (in the *Revue des deux Mondes*), German, and Dutch. Goethe praised the Review in *Ueber Kunst und Alterthum*, commending its writers for going about their work "höchst ernst, aufmerksam, mit Fleiss, umsichtig und allgemein wohlvollend"; it would moreover help create that "gehofften allgemeinen Weltliteratur" to which Goethe always looked.[14]

The Review circulated on the Continent as well as in Britain. From the start it was successful: a circulation of over 1,500 after the first two numbers remained fairly steady, never reaching 1,800.[15] These figures of course do not compare with the circulation of the giants, the *Edinburgh* and *Quarterly*, but they give a respectable showing in view of the special appeal of the *Foreign Quarterly*. Buyers were attracted not only by the Review's political fairness but also by its essentially romantic and nationalistic literary criteria, and by the variety of approaches taken in its articles.[16] Some were genuine reviews; some gave resumés of a whole body of national literature, going "over the ground rather as literary topographers than as literary critics" (Vol. III, p. 66); others provided careful summaries with lengthy quotation as substitutes for the originals; still others were the usual Victorian periodical essays parading as reviews. The first two types might well persuade readers to purchase foreign books—from Treuttel and Würtz, one hopes; the second two were not meant to win purchasers. Some books summarized were not readily obtainable; others were not fit for British eyes except in these carefully chosen extracts. Some of the essays, usually those which attracted most notice, were based on confidential official information, like two on Greece by James Murray, head of the Foreign Department of the *Times*.[17]

In 1833 the *Foreign Quarterly* encountered financial problems. After the twenty-fourth number (October 1833), Treuttel and Würtz was carried on by its junior member as Adolphus Richter and Co. In October 1834, Richter stopped payment, and in December Cochrane brought out the twenty-eighth number at his own risk, two months late. Also in December Richter declared bankruptcy; early in 1835 Cochrane, unable to work with Richter's trustees, left and set up *Cochrane's* (or *The New*) *Foreign Quarterly Review*. Richter tried, by legal injunction, to prevent any contributors from following Cochrane, but Cochrane succeeded in having the injunction modified.[18] At least six contributors did join Cochrane, but his new Review died after two numbers.

Cochrane's successor as conductor of the *Foreign Quarterly*, Frederic Shoberl, was experienced both as an editor and as a translator, and must have looked like an

---

[13]*Athenaeum*, Jan. 7, 1829, pp. 1–2. See also *Athenaeum*, Mar. 4, 1829, p. 136; May 27, 1829, p. 334.

[14]*Werke* (Weimar, 1903), XLI ,Teil 2, 348.

[15][Grant], II, 285–288; Moir to Carlyle, Dec. 29, 1829, Nat. Lib. Scot.

[16]For contemporary reactions see, for example, the *Athenaeum* reviews listed in n. 13.

[17]See *The Greville Memoirs, 1814–1860*, ed. Lytton Strachey and Roger Fulford (1938), I, 343, for contemporary comment on these articles.

[18]Cochrane's "Address to the Public," prefixed to the first number of *Cochrane's FQR* (1835), pp. 1–2, in copies at the British Museum and the Cambridge Univ. Lib.

excellent choice. He was known, however, both for his humbleness and his puffing.[19] He was a weaker editor than Cochrane, and the Review was no longer as well balanced as it had been. Undue emphasis was given to the pro-Turkish, anti-Russian school of David Urquhart (who himself became a contributor) and to antiquarian, philological, and Egyptological subjects. Much of the antiquarianism was in the hands of Thomas Wright, a new contributor and a young man just starting out to be one of the period's leading popularizers of Old English studies. Usually Egyptian studies were made to support religious orthodoxy; science was also put to a moral and orthodox use. Of national literatures, German was most adequately treated, thanks to the acquisition as a steady contributor of John Stuart Blackie, who adopted Carlyle's mannerisms but lacked Carlyle's intellectual clarity. Carlyle himself no longer contributed.

The *Foreign Quarterly* also encountered new competition. July 1835 saw the first issue of the *British and Foreign Review*, which pursued the same end Cochrane had pursued earlier: "We are desirous of seeing established, through the intervention of the press, a common standard of taste and public opinion among the enlightened and polished nations of Europe" (*British and Foreign Review*, Vol. I, p. 10). Whatever its impact, the fact is that the circulation of the now more parochial *Foreign Quarterly* fell considerably below 1,200.[20] Late in 1837 Black and Armstrong, already co-proprietors of the *Foreign Quarterly*, acquired Richter's remaining interest and became sole proprietor and publisher. Apparently Shoberl had been Richter's editor, for he was now replaced.

At this point the Review became ultra-Tory; the writing became turgid and italicized, hysterical and incoherent; and Benjamin Edward Pote, the new editor, was forever introducing his theories on the origins of languages and races. He was an inexpert and meddling editor: articles were substantially repeated, cut in two, or run together; proofreading, which had once been excellent, was forgotten. Worst of all, the Review forsook its purpose; never before would it have contended that, "The more widely we are separated from other and distant parts of the world the more natural is our indifference for its customs and manners; . . . we are bound to abstain from any thing beyond a casual notice of such uninteresting exotics" (Vol. XXII, p. 390). A few of the better reviewers stayed on from earlier years: Blackie, Courtenay, the American Henry Wheaton. H. L. Jones was probably the best of the new reviewers; occasionally someone of the stature of Basil Hall contributed a single review. Pote, however, was too intent on making the Review his own organ; he wrote most of his last number, that for January 1840, even though several other articles were on hand. He antagonized faithful authors and promising patrons and lost contributors

---

[19]Crabb Robinson spoke of someone being "as humble as Shoberl" (*On Books and their Writers*, ed. Edith J. Morley [1938], p. 355). Shoberl was co-founder of the *New Monthly Magazine* and co-edited it again in the 1840s, when he wrote many of its puffing reviews (see John Clubbe, *Victorian Forerunner. The Later Career of Thomas Hood* [Durham, N.C., 1968], pp. 132–133). He is identified as the new *FQR* editor in Antonio Panizzi, "To the Assignees of Messrs. A. Richter and Co. . . . Publishers and Proprietors of the Foreign Quarterly Review, now edited by Mr. Frederick Shoberl" (1835) and in a letter from Shoberl to an unidentified recipient, May 11, 1837 (MS., Staats- und Universitätsbibliothek Hamburg).

[20][Grant], II, 289.

like Wright. At the same time he invented a few interesting features, like "Music Abroad and at Home." Apparently it was not enough, though the immediate cause of his departure may have been an attack of brain-fever.[21]

He was succeeded by the Reverend Dr. James W. Worthington, a London rector and a Tory, whose numbers are more varied than Pote's. Many of his new contributors were Englishmen living abroad or foreigners living in England: George Stephens, professor first at Stockholm and later at Copenhagen; E. P. Sinnett, who had published an English-language newspaper in Hamburg; Antonio Gallenga, later a leader-writer for the *Times*; and a group of Slavic nationals who wrote on the life and literature of their homelands. Though one article, possibly by the editor, loudly hailed the Tories' return to power and called for "the cultivation of a close and intimate alliance" with the three Continental despotisms (Vol. XXVIII, p. 477), other articles precariously balanced with this a sympathy for the Liberals' pet causes, Poland and Italy. A strong Church of England bias was a natural concomitant of surpliced editorship. The *Foreign Quarterly* had been inimical to Roman Catholicism ever since Southey wrote the first review in the first number, but it had been generally no more attached to Anglicanism than to Dissent. Now the Review discovered not only that the one true church was that by law established (as proved by its establishment), but also that Puseyites were to be condemned as merely disguised, and therefore doubly pernicious, Papists.

If Worthington's issues were more interesting than Pote's, they were still not interesting enough to restore the Review's declining fortunes; it was moribund when, late in 1841, Chapman and Hall acquired the copyright and stock from Black and Armstrong. With John Forster "acting gratuitously as Prime Minister" and Jane Carlyle enlisted as his aide, the new publishers immediately began their effort to knock Worthington "on the head": he was, it was generally agreed, "sitting on [*FQR*] as an incubus." At least one candidate for the editorship put himself forward: William Makepeace Thackeray. However, there were objections (unspecified) to his taking over the office, and in the end Forster became temporary editor, to stay only as long as the patient needed his attention.[22]

The issue for April 1842 was a sort of interim issue. Some articles clearly came from Worthington's contributors; those by Thackeray and George Stovin Venables came through Chapman and Hall. Worthington claimed later that he left the *Foreign Quarterly* voluntarily, in protest against the failure of Chapman and Hall to maintain its conservative principles. Like other displaced editors, he founded a rival review, the *Foreign and Colonial Quarterly*, later rechristened the *New Quarterly*.[23] His

---

[21]In 1839 and later he suffered from "indisposition," sometimes lasting for months and sometimes described as "inflammation of the brain": see letters to J. S. Blackie, Macvey Napier, and Sir Robert Peel (Nat. Lib. Scot., MS. 2621, fols. 108–109; B.M. Add. MSS. 34,624, fols. 83–84, 472–474; 40,577, fols. 151–154). During the time he edited *FQR* Pote was frequently referred to as "the mad Editor," particularly by Baron Bunsen (uncatalogued MSS. in Deutsches Zentralarchiv, East Berlin).

[22]See letters from Jane Carlyle to John Sterling, Jan.–Feb. 1842 (*Letters and Memorials of Jane Welsh Carlyle*, ed. Thomas Carlyle and James Anthony Froude [N.Y., 1883], I, 100–103); Gordon N. Ray, *Thackeray: The Uses of Adversity, 1811–1846* (N.Y., 1955), p. 321.

[23]In addition to William Fraser and Cochrane, already mentioned, Frederic Shoberl started the *Foreign Monthly Review* a year after leaving *FQR*. The *Foreign and Colonial Quarterly*

claim that he took with him "nearly the whole staff of writers who have hitherto supported the Foreign Quarterly"[24] seems justified. They were not missed. Forster's first number, that of July 1842, carried articles by Bulwer Lytton, John Sterling, Walter Savage Landor, Thackeray, and Robert Browning. There was to have been an article by Giuseppi Mazzini, but because of problems of translation it appeared much later. Though subsequent numbers did not show this array of talent, they were still impressive. Landor and Thackeray continued to contribute, Forster wrote several articles, Blackie returned after an absence of almost two years, Carlyle interrupted his work on Cromwell to write something for Forster, and George Henry Lewes became a contributor. Though John Stuart Mill called him "the second worst critic of the age," Forster was a good editor. He was willing to take trouble; he was reliable; despite his pomposity and tyrannizing, his friends were loyal. Certainly he shaped the *Foreign Quarterly* in his own image. It was to treat foreign literature from a thoroughly English point of view.[25] This meant setting up earnestness, healthiness, sincerity, right-mindedness, manliness, and practicality as literary and philosophical standards. There was a shift back to liberal attitudes: Forster might allow Bulwer Lytton's conservatism to stand, but he warned George Stephens that he would print an article only if he were allowed to omit certain reactionary sentiments.[26]

The *Foreign Quarterly* prospered, but Forster wanted to give his ideas a wider circulation than that Review would ever provide; then he was bedridden through much of the summer and fall of 1843 with "a long and painful illness." The temporary editorship had become a burden, and Forster relinquished it after the October 1843 issue.[27]

Walter Keating Kelly claimed in his application to the Royal Literary Fund of July 5, 1864, to have been editor of the *Foreign Quarterly Review* from January 1844 to July 1846, and in a letter to the Committee of the Royal Literary Fund, March 8, 1852, the publishers Chapman and Hall said that Kelly had edited the *Foreign Quarterly Review* for three years. Indeed, in December 1844, we hear that "a Mr. Kelly is Editor of the *Foreign Quarterly*, and is soliciting articles from Englishmen in India"; while Thackeray spoke in a letter to Forster [c. 1846] of "Kelly of the *FQR*."[28] Kelly was active in the 1840s as a translator and journalist. He edited Chapman and Hall's Library of Travel from 1844 on, writing the first volume himself; he seems to have contributed to the *Foreign Quarterly Review* when Forster was editor, and he knew some of the active contributors like the St. Johns. He was to some uncertain but slight degree aided by the liberal Unitarian, Dr. John Relly Beard, who wrote to

---

Review, which changed its name to the *New Quarterly Review*, was the most successful of the rivals.

[24]"Prospectus," *Foreign and Colonial Quarterly Review*, Vol. I, of the New York Public Library copy.

[25]Statement of policy prefixed to the Cornell Univ. copy of Vol. XXIX (July 1842), i.

[26]Forster to Stephens, Feb. 9, 1843 (MS. in Kunglige Biblioteket, Stockholm). The article did not appear.

[27]Forster to Leigh Hunt, Nov. 11, 1843, BM Add. MS. 38,110, fol. 48; see also Forster to Macvey Napier, Feb. 12, 1844, BM Add. MS. 34,624, fols. 354–355.

[28]*The Letters of Philip Meadows Taylor to Henry Reeve*, ed. Sir Patrick Cadell (1947), p. 156, and letter signed W.M.T., dated "Thursday" from "13 Young St., Kensington," Huntington Lib. MS. 15277.

German friends about the *Foreign Quarterly* and even advertised in the *Augsburg Allgemeine Zeitung* for theological books to be reviewed in the English periodical.[29]

Certainly there are definite signs of a change of personnel in October 1844 or January 1845. Some contributors disappear; new ones appear. "Foreign Correspondence," which had disappeared after April 1843, reappears in October 1844. More and more the emphasis is on information drawn from personal observation rather than from published accounts.

The last eleven numbers of the *Foreign Quarterly* sustain the high level which Forster's numbers had attained. As never before in the Review's history, certain contributors are responsible number after number for the best articles. Many of them had contributed earlier, but few of them had written so much or so steadily. With Thackeray dropping out after a few numbers, some of the most important are George Henry Lewes, who reshaped British views of contemporary French literature through these pages; Thomas Adolphus Trollope, who sought through a vigorous and informal style to make the British reader feel the exuberance of Italian life and sympathize with the cause of Italian freedom; J. A. and Bayle St. John, father and son, writing particularly on Anglo-French relations in Africa and Asia; Andrew Valentine Kirwan, who divided his time between English law courts and French political circles and, like so many of these contributors, wrote from first-hand knowledge; J. S. Blackie, writing now of the Liberation War of 1813 rather than of German literature; Jane Sinnett, the translator of Fichte, who took over some of the German reviewing; Thomas Wright, returned after a five-years' absence and now often giving his antiquarian articles a contemporary point. Though the Review's colonial policy was imperialistic, it applauded and hoped for revolution and change in Europe. The political stir on the Continent took much of its attention, and it gave less space than it sometimes had to belles-lettres. German poetry received the most attention, for the Germans had cast off theory and become political, even in their poetry.

It seems a golden time when one reads the articles. However, 1846 and 1847 were difficult years for many periodicals; editors and publishers were overstocked with articles and understocked with money.[30] Chapman and Hall decided to combine two of their properties. The seventy-fourth number of the *Foreign Quarterly* was published in July 1846, followed in October by a periodical with two titles: on the title page, *The Westminster and Foreign Quarterly Review*, on page 1, *The Foreign Quarterly and Westminster Review*. The former title was used through Vol. 127 (1887), and at least through 1853 it was still sometimes spoken of as the *Foreign Quarterly*.[31] The first result of the merger was a reduction of the *Foreign Quarterly* to its "Critical Sketches" and "Foreign Correspondence," which followed the *Westminster*'s main articles. For our purposes the *Foreign Quarterly* can be thought of as ending with the merger. Inevitably it had never approached the ambitious design of

[29]Professor K. A. Credner to Beard, Apr. 8, 1844; Buchdruckerei Gebauer to Beard, Apr. 9, 1844, and rough draft of Beard's reply, all in Unitarian College, Manchester; *Augsburg Allgemeine Zeitung*, Oct. 29, 1844, p. 2422.

[30]See Gillies, III, 292.

[31]See George Cowell, *Life and Letters of Edward Byles Cowell* (1904), p. 92; Henry Sutherland Edwards, *Personal Recollections* (1900), p. 158.

its first editor, and as late as 1851–1852 Gillies was thinking of bringing out a "New Foreign Quarterly Review."[32] For twenty years, however, it had been the most successful and generally the most moderate, most perceptive, and best informed British interpreter of foreign literature and foreign attitudes.

EDITORS

Robert Pearse Gillies: July 1827–February 1830, Vol. 1—Vol. 5. Actual editor only of the first volume; nominal editor thereafter.
William Fraser: July 1827, Vol. 1, no. 1. Unofficial co-editor.
John George Cochrane: July 1827–December 1834, Vol. 1—Vol. 14. Actual editor almost from start; official editor from June 1830, Vol. 6.
Frederic Shoberl: March 1835–January 1838, Vol. 15—Vol. 20.
Benjamin Edward Pote: April 1838–January 1840,[33] Vol. 21—Vol. 24.
James William Worthington: April 1840–April 1842, Vol. 25—Vol. 29, no. 57.
John Forster: July 1842–October 1843, Vol. 29, no. 58—Vol. 32, no. 63.
Walter Keating Kelly: January 1844–July 1846, Vol. 32, no. 64—Vol. 37.

PUBLISHERS

Treuttel and Würtz, Treuttel, Jun. and Richter: Vols. 1–5.
Treuttel and Würtz, Treuttel, Jun. and Richter / Black, Young, and Young: Vols. 6–7.[34]
Treuttel and Würtz, and Richter / Black, Young, and Young: Vols. 8–12.
Adolphus Richter & Co. / Black, Young, and Young: Vols. 13–15.[35]
Adolphus Richter & Co. / Black and Armstrong: Vol. 16.
Black and Armstrong / Adolphus Richter & Co.: Vols. 17–19.
Black and Armstrong: Vols. 20–27.
Chapman and Hall: Vols. 28–37.

PROPRIETORS

Adolphus Richter, Charles G. Treuttel, and John Würtz (i.e., the publishers), July 1827–October 1833, Vols. 1—12.
Adolphus Richter, February 1834–August 1834, Vols. 13—14, no. 27.
The assignees of the bankrupt Adolphus Richter, December 1834 at least through March 1835, and probably through January 1836; Vol. 14, no. 28, at least through

---

[32]Gillies, III, 89; Gillies to Brougham, Mar. 18, 1852, Univ. Coll. London.

[33]Pote said he "became, for 1838-9, the Editor of the Foreign Quart Review" (letter to Macvey Napier, Sept. 9, 1842, BM Add. MS. 34,623). Usual procedure seems to have been for the Jan. no. to be prepared by the preceding year's editor. Worthington wrote George Stephens, Feb. 1, 1840, that "Mr Pote no longer remains the Editor" and that Worthington has assumed that position (MS. Kunglige Biblioteket, Stockholm).

[34]J. G. Cochrane contended that "the whole profit accruing from [*FQR*] had, ever since No. XI., been transferred from the pockets of the proprietors and editor into those of Messrs. BLACK, YOUNG, and YOUNG, of Tavistock Street, who had no interest in the work, and incurred not one farthing of the risk" ("Prospectus," *Cochrane's FQR*, p. 3).

[35]According to title pages. However, Vol. 14, no. 28, "was published by Mr. Cochrane, at his sole risk and responsibility" ("Address to the Public," *Cochrane's FQR*, p. 1).

Vol. 15, no. 29, and probably through Vol. 16.[36]
Alexander Black, April 1836–April 1838, Vols. 17—21, no. 41.[37]
Black and Armstrong, July 1838–July 1841, Vol. 21, no. 42—Vol. 27.
Chapman and Hall, October 1841–July 1846, Vols. 28—37.

NOTES ON ATTRIBUTIONS

All articles are unsigned; no initials or pseudonyms are used. Authors of articles in the first fourteen volumes are identified by John Macray, "List of Writers in 'Foreign Quarterly Review,' vols. I.–XIV., a Contribution to Literary History," *Notes and Queries*, 2nd ser., 8 (1859), 124–127. Macray was an employee of Treuttel and Würtz and then of Richter; his list seems to have been made from a marked file. It is virtually complete; only ten articles, mainly short critical sketches, are marked with a query.

Two copies of the *Foreign Quarterly* have been found with useful markings. In the copy of Volume XVI (October 1835) in the University of Minnesota library, four of nine articles are identified in the table of contents; two of these can be confirmed from other sources. The file of the *Foreign Quarterly* in the Wellesley College library contains a number of markings. Those in the first fourteen volumes are clearly copied from Macray's list, apparently by a German (he corrects Macray's misspelling of a German name but Germanizes other names); he does add one first initial that Macray did not know. After Volume 14 there are markings in fourteen numbers. A few of these are in a more recent hand, and sometimes wrong. The older markings, which seem reliable, were made in pencil and then copied or written over in pen; mainly they identify articles written by Germans or by Englishmen who had lived in Germany or Scandinavia.

One warning. The *Foreign Quarterly* itself once roundly stated that "we are bound to disbelieve all reports of articles in Reviews being written by *single* individuals" (Vol. VII, p. 229n.). The most meddlesome of all editors was B. E. Pote: "I had fancied Editors shortened, altered, or varied, & curtailed always: in truth I had . . . so acted myself, in every case."[38] Many articles in the issues edited by Pote more than bear out his admission: paragraphs, even pages, seem clearly the editor's insertions. We have noted some of his lengthier meddlings, but we could have added "and Pote" to many more attributions from April 1838 through January 1840.

BIBLIOGRAPHICAL NOTE

The only full study of the *Foreign Quarterly* is an unpublished doctoral dissertation by Eileen M. Curran, "The *Foreign Quarterly Review* (1827–1846): A British Interpretation of Modern European Literature" (Cornell, 1958). One chapter of this has been published as "The *Foreign Quarterly Review* on Russian and Polish Literature," *Slavonic and East European Review*, 40 (December 1961), 206–219.

---

[36]Complaints and Petitions, PRO C [Chancery Proceedings] 13/343/14, where the names are given.

[37]Black was the head of the firm of Black and Armstrong, which, with Vol. 17, became primary publisher. Sometime before May 22, 1838, Black was appointed Richter's assignee: Lewis and Lewis, solicitors for Black, to Lord Brougham, date given, Univ. Coll. London.

[38]To Macvey Napier, Sept. 10, 1843, BM Add. MS. 34,624.

THE FOREIGN QUARTERLY REVIEW, 1827–1846

"Monk (   ), of the Royal Marines," and *Army List*/27. (Note, p. 707.)

47 Lebrun, *The Voyage to Greece*, 591–595. **Leitch Ritchie**. Macray.

48 Modern Spanish comedy, 595–621. **S. D. Whitehead.** Macray.

49 Italian literature of the eighteenth century, 621–661. **André Vieusseux.** Macray.

50 Illyrian poetry, 662–671. **Thomas Keightley.** Macray.

51 Works of Henry Kleist, 671–696. **R. P. Gillies.** Macray.

52 Retzsch's *Outlines to Shakespeare: Hamlet*, 697–706. ——— **Staniforth.** Macray, who adds "Capt."

53 Critical sketches, 708–727. Page 727 by **J. G. Cochrane**; pages 718–719, 726–727 by **Robert Ferguson**, 1799–1865; pages 719–722 by **Thomas Hodgkin**, 1798–1866; pages 709–710, 724–726 by **Thomas Keightley**; pages 722–724 by **John Macray**; pages 715–718 by **Leitch Ritchie**; pages 710–715 by **André Vieusseux**—all attr. by Macray; page 708 by **Thomas Young**—attr. Macray, and in *FQR* no. 94, p. 468n., presumably by the editor; page 709, art. 14, by **Bartolomeo de Sanctis**—Macray as in no. 39.

54 Miscellaneous literary notices, 728–749. **John Macray.** Cf. no. 12.

standard catalogues and dictionaries; Whitehead was a frequent contributor to *FQR* at this time on similar subjects; cf. no. 31, pp. 83–89, with p. 184 here, and see no. 180.

61 French philosophers of the nineteenth century, 185–196. **Robert Ferguson**, 1799–1865. Macray as in no. 7.

62 Greece, 197–223. **H. J. T. Drury.** Macray gives "Rev. H. Drury, Harrow"; see *DNB*.

63 The Pyrenees, 223–254. **Henry Southern.** Macray.

64 Tegner's *Legend of Frithiof*, 254–282. **Mary Margaret Busk.** Macray.

65 Turkey and Russia, 282–301. ——— **Moore.** Macray; perhaps Niven Moore who was attached to the embassy at Constantinople in 1822: see Boase and p. 283 here.

66 Critical sketches, 302–321. Pages 307–309, 321 by **J. G. Cochrane**; pages 318–320 by **R. P. Gillies**; pages 302–307 by **T. H. Horne**; pages 309–310 by **T. J. Hussey**; pages 314–316 by **Henry Southern**; pages 316–318, 320–321 by **André Vieusseux**; pages 311–314 by **S. D. Whitehead**—all attr. Macray.

67 Miscellaneous literary notices, 322–344. **John Macray.** Cf. no. 12.

VOLUME 3, SEPTEMBER 1828

55 Arabic literature, 1–28. **W. D. Cooley.** Macray.

56 Language and literature of the Magyars, 28–76. **Károly György Rumy.** A signed MS. in German by Rumy, drawn up for Bowring Jan.–Mar. 1828, is now in the B.M. (German MS. 29,538); translated, with some abridgement and rearrangement, by **John Bowring**, to whom Macray assigned it, and who claims it in *Korrespondence*, p. 16.

57 French histories of the English revolution [Guizot], 76–92. **Herman Merivale.** Macray as in no. 13; Merivale, *Memoir*, p. 579.

58 French histories of the English revolution [F. A. J. Mazure], 93–111. **Henry Roscoe.** Macray.

59 Laplace's *Celestial Mechanics*, 111–148. **Thomas Galloway.** Macray; claimed in *Testimonials*.

60 Karamsin's *History of Russia*, 148–184. **S. D. Whitehead**, prob. Macray gives "J. D. Whitehurst," and for no. 83 "S. D. Whitehurst"; no such men found in

VOLUME 3, JANUARY 1829

68 Arts and manufactures in France, 359–400. **John Ward**, 1805–1890. Macray identifies him as "son of J. Ward, Esq., Inspector of Customs" (see *DNB*); *Experiences*, p. 3n.

69 Humboldt's *Political and Statistical Account of Cuba*, 400–433. **Charles Kenneth Mackenzie.** Macray gives "Charles McKenzie," adding "late Consul at Hayti": see Boase, *Gent. Mag.*, Oct. 1862, p. 504.

70 Meyer, *The Judicial Institutions of the Principal Countries of Europe*, 433–477. **J. H. Merivale.** Macray.

71 Oginski's *Memoirs on Poland*, 477–506. **André Vieusseux.** Macray.

72 Derode's *New Theory of Harmony*, 506–522. **Edward Holmes.** Macray, who adds "Prof. of Music, Islington"; see *DNB*.

73 *Memoirs of Vidocq*, 522–559. **Henry Southern.** Macray.

74 Raumer's *History of the Hohenstauffens*, 559–597. **Mary Margaret Busk.** Macray.

75 Louis Bonaparte's *Answer to Sir W. Scott's "History of Napoleon,"* 597–601. **Henry Southern.** Macray.

76 Language and literature of Friesland, 602–630. **John Bowring.** Macray.

77 Duke Bernard's *Travels in North America*, 630–635. **Charles Maclaren.** Macray.

78 Wine trade of France, 636–649. **J. R. McCulloch.** Macray.

79 Critical sketches, 650–673. Page 652 by "Mrs. (Anon)"; pages 655–660, 666–669 by **J. G. Cochrane**; pages 653–655 by **T. J. Hussey**; pages 665–666 by **H. E. Lloyd**; pages 660–662 by **John Macray**; pages 669–673 by **John Macray** and **J. G. Cochrane**; pages 662–665 by **André Vieusseux**—all attr. Macray; pages 650–651 by **John Ward**, 1805–1890—all attr. by Macray.

80 Miscellaneous literary notices, 674–692. **John Macray.** Cf. no. 12.

VOLUME 4, APRIL 1829

81 Sismondi's *History of France*, 1–35. **Henry Hallam.** Macray gives "H. Hallam"; see *DNB*.

82 Language and literature of Holland, 36–78. **John Bowring.** Macray; repr. as *Sketch of the Language and Literature of Holland*, Amsterdam, 1829.

83 Ancient national poetry of Spain, 78–102. **S. D. Whitehead.** See no. 60; sentence about Roman, Goth, and Moor sweeping over Spanish fields (pp. 78–79) repeats no. 48, p. 597, by Whitehead; low opinion of Spanish critics, p. 102, echoes no. 48, p. 596; review is partly of Depping, another of whose works Whitehead relies on heavily in no. 31.

84 Scandinavian mythology, 102–139. **Thomas Keightley.** Macray; letter cited in no. 35.

85 French criminal trials, 139–165. **Leitch Ritchie.** Macray.

86 Mexico, 165–204. **Charles Kenneth Mackenzie.** Macray; cf. no. 69.

87 Victor Hugo's poems and novels, 205–235. **Henry Southern; and C. A. Sainte-Beuve?** Macray gives Henry Southern; Jean Bonnerot, *Revue de Littérature Comparée*, 12 (Feb. 1932), 408–413, shows that St. Beuve wrote a ten-page MS. on Hugo's *Odes and Ballades* "destinée à la *Foreign Quarterly Review*," which contains various parallels with pp. 205–216 of the art., so that Southern may have translated and adapted St. Beuve's essay, and gone on himself to write the remainder of the art.

88 Von Hammer's *History of the Ottoman Empire*, 236–275. **W. D. Cooley.** Macray; claimed in application to R.L.F., Mar. 25, 1857.

89 Foreign views of the Catholic question, 275–306. **Hugh James Rose**, 1795–1838. Macray.

90 Critical sketches, 307–326. Pages 318–320 by **Mary Margaret Busk**; pages 312–313 by **T. H. Horne**; pages 313–318, 324–326 by **T. J. Hussey**; pages 307–312 by **Henry Southern**; pages 321–323 by **André Vieusseux**—all attr. by Macray.

91 Miscellaneous literary notices, 327–344. **John Macray.** Cf. in general no. 12; pages 335–336 on Dobrowsky by **John Bowring**—F. Chudoba, *Listy psané Johnu Bowringovive věcech české a slovanké literatury* (Prague, 1912), p. 31n.

VOLUME 4, AUGUST 1829

92 Revolutions of Naples in 1647 and 1648: Masaniello and the Duke of Guise, 355–403. **Walter Scott.** Macray; Scott's *Journal* (ed. 1950), pp. 632–633. Translated passages by **R. P. Gillies**—Gillies to Scott, May 9, 1829, Nat. Lib. Scot., agrees to translate "such passages as you wish to insert" in this art.

93 Mozart, 404–437. **Edward Holmes.** Macray.

94 Hieroglyphics, 438–469. **James Browne**, 1793–1841. Macray gives "Dr. James Brown," but changes spelling to "Browne" for no. 211; man cited wrote on hieroglyphics in *ER* (nos. 1162, 1179 in *Index*, I), to which this art. frequently refers; see *DNB*.

95 Lord Byron and M. Casimir Delavigne, 470–483. **Charles Barker.** Macray.

96 Letting of land—metayer system, 484–507. **J. R. McCulloch.** Macray; repr., with substantial additions, *Treatises and Essays* (Edin., 1859), pp. 165–222.

97 Spanish epic poetry: Ercilla's *Araucana*, 507–538. **Mary Margaret Busk.** Macray.

98 Wessenberg and the Roman Catholic Church in Germany, 539–573. **Hugh James Rose**, 1795–1838. Macray.

99 The Black Sea and the Caucasus, 574–601. **W. D. Cooley.** Macray.

100 Méry and Barthélemy, *The Son of the Man*, a poem, 602–607. **Leitch Ritchie.** Macray. (Postscript, p. 659n.)

101 History of the Knights Templars, 608–641. **Thomas Keightley.** Macray; claimed in letter cited in no. 20.

102 Rosini's *Nun of Monza*, 641–659. **For-**

tunato **Prandi.** Macray gives "F. Prandi, Esq. (ex-Military Officer of Ital. Army)": see Tosi.

103 Critical sketches, 660–678. Pages 661–664, 670–673 by **Mary Margaret Busk;** pages 673–677 by **J. G. Cochrane;** pages 667–669 by **W. D. Cooley;** pages 660–661 by **T. H. Horne;** pages 677–678 by **H. E. Lloyd;** pages 669–670 by **George Moir;** pages 664–667 by **Leitch Ritchie**—all attr. by Macray.

104 Miscellaneous literary notices, 679–694. **John Macray.** Cf. no. 12.

1835. Macray gives "Ἰακωπος δε Μορανια"; see Grant, *Metropolis*, II, 289.

117 Notice of M. Dumont, 317–324. **James Mackintosh.** Macray gives "Sir J. Mackintosh"; see *DNB*.

118 Critical sketches, 325–347. Pages 328–331, 337–342 by **Mary Margaret Busk;** pages 331–334 by **Leitch Ritchie;** pages 343–347 by **Henry Southern;** pages 325–328, 335–337 by **André Vieusseux**—all attr. by Macray.

119 Miscellaneous literary notices, 348–356. **John Macray.** Cf. no. 12.

VOLUME 5, NOVEMBER 1829

105 Bourrienne's *Memoirs of Napoleon*, 1–40. **Henry Southern.** Macray.

106 Wallenstein, 41–73. **George Moir.** Macray; attr. by William C. Taylor, ed., *The Cabinet of Friendship* (1834), p. 190n.

107 Present state of Spain, 73–108. **J. R. McCulloch** and **Mr. Buchanan.** Macray gives art. to McCulloch, but adds "principally from the communication of Mr. Buchanan, a commercial traveller," which explains indebtedness cited in art., p. 74; McCulloch calls his informant an "English gentleman" who met the "best-informed persons," p. 74; this and the fact that he was, like McCulloch, a political economist suggests David Buchanan (see *DNB*).

108 Greek romances, 108–141. **Leitch Ritchie.** Macray.

109 Heeren's *The Polity and Commerce of the Great Nations of Antiquity*, 141–157. **George Long.** Macray, who adds "Greek Prof., London University"; see *DNB*. (Notice to Correspondents, p. 718.)

110 Dialects and literature of Southern Italy, 158–190. **André Vieusseux.** Macray.

111 Pacho's *Travels in Marmarica and Cyrenaica*, 191–207. **Josiah Conder.** Macray; see *DNB*.

112 Early Roman history, 207–222. **Thomas Keightley.** Macray; claimed in letter cited in no. 20.

113 *Four Months in Belgium and Holland*, 222–231. **John Bowring.** Macray.

114 Pontécoulant: recent progress of physical astronomy, 231–256. **Thomas Galloway.** Macray; claimed in *Testimonials.*

115 The history of the fine arts, 256–271. **Thomas Jefferson Hogg.** Macray.

116 The Greek Revolution and European diplomacy, 271–317. **James Murray,** d.

VOLUME 5, FEBRUARY 1830

120 Present state of the Netherlands, 365–419. **John Ward,** 1805–1890. Macray; *Experiences*, p. 8n. (Postscript, p. 718.)

121 Rossetti's *Dante*, 419–449. **Charles Lyell,** 1767–1849, **Fortunato Prandi,** and **Charles Lyell,** 1797–1875. Macray gives "C. Lyell, Esq. of Kinnordy (revised by F. Prandi, Esq.)" see *DNB* for the Lyells and no. 102 for Prandi; Lyell senior to Dawson Turner, Apr. 12, 1830, Trin. Coll. Camb., referring to this art.: "Charles [i.e., Charles junior] licked the cub into shape, and put in some pepper and salt and gall."

122 Spix and Martius's *Travels in Brazil*, 449–475. **G. Cornewall Lewis.** Macray; attr. in *DNB*.

123 Bianca Cappello: The Medici family, 475–485. **Fortunato Prandi,** prob. Macray gives "T. Prandi," prob. a misprint for "F," who was a contributor at this time; cf. no. 102.

124 Christianity in China, 485–516. **J. A. St. John.** Macray.

125 French novels: Paul de Koch, 516–546. **Henry Southern.** Macray.

126 Life and works of Jovellanos, 547–568. **Antonio Alcalá Galiano.** Macray gives "Don Antonio Galiano (ex-Member of the Span. Cortes, Prof. of Span. in the London Univ.)" see *EUI*; in a signed article on Jovellanos in *Revista de Madrid*, II (1838), 301–324, Galiano says that he wrote one of the articles on Jovellanos that appeared in *FQR* and *Foreign Review* and that he will draw on that article in this (p. 302); although the Spanish article is not a simple translation of the *FQR* article, it makes many of the same points.

127 History of gnosticism, 569–598. **Thomas J. Hogg.** Macray.

128 Court of Chancery, 598–623. **James Bacon.** Macray, who adds "(Barrister, Author of 'Hist. of Francis I.')"; see H&L, III, 353.

129 Wilken and Michaud: history of the Crusades, 623–654. **Thomas Keightley.** Macray; claimed in letter cited in no. 20.

130 Jacotot's system of education, 655–668. **Henry Southern.** Macray; claimed in Southern to Thomas Coates, Mar. 15, 1830, Univ. Coll. London.

131 Sovereignty and final settlement of Greece, 668–698. **James Murray,** d. 1835. Macray as for no. 116, with further evidence cited there. (Note, vol. 6, p. 259.)

132 Critical sketches, 699–718. Pages 706–707 by **Antonio Alcalá Galiano;** pages 699–704 by **John Bowring;** pages 707–711 by **Mary Margaret Busk;** pages 704–706 by **T. H. Horne** pages 716–718 by **T. J. Hussey**—Macray gives "Rev. T. H. Hussey," but cf. nos. 26, 66, etc.; pages 712–716 by **André Vieusseux**—all attr. by Macray.

133 Miscellaneous literary notices, 719–725. **John Macray.** Cf. no. 12.

VOLUME 6, JUNE 1830

134 Daemonology and witchcraft, 1–47. **George Moir.** Macray; attr. in Cochrane to Carlyle, July 3, 1830, Nat. Lib. Scot.

135 Danish and Norwegian literature, 48–87. **John Bowring** and **George Borrow.** Macray assigns to John Bowring, but Bowring did only the prose part of the art. (see George Borrow, *Targum* [St. Petersburg, 1835], p. 51n.); For Borrow's translations, see C. K. Shorter, *George Borrow and His Circle* (Boston, 1913), pp. 146, 149.

136 Dutrochet's *New Researches on Vegetable Physiology*, 88–97. **J. S. Henslow.** Macray gives "Rev. J. J. Henslow"; prob. a misprint for J. S. Henslow, divine (see *DNB*), who wrote no. 269 on same subject.

137 Caillié's *Travels in Africa*, 97–121. **T. J. Hussey.** Macray.

138 Modern Swedish poetry, 122–141. **Mary Margaret Busk.** Macray.

139 History of the Amphictyonic confederacy, 141–147. **G. C. Lewis.** Macray; attr. in *DNB*.

140 The English in India, 148–180. **Thomas Campbell Robertson.** Macray.

141 State and prospects of the wool-growers, 181–194. ——— **Swann.** Macray.

142 Fétis—music made easy, 194–217. **Edward Holmes.** Macray.

143 Fontanier's *Travels in Asiatic Turkey*, 218–242. **Henry Southern.** Macray.

144 Critical sketches, 243–259. Pages 248–251 by **Mary Margaret Busk;** pages 256–259 by **T. H. Horne;** pages 252–253 by **T. J. Hussey;** pages 255–256 by **Fortunato Prandi;** pages 253–255 by **André Vieusseux**—all attr. by Macray; pages 243–247 by **G. C. Lewis,** attr. by Macray and *DNB*.

145 Miscellaneous literary notices, 260–273. **John Macray.** Cf. no. 12.

VOLUME 6, OCTOBER 1830

146 Norman conquest of England, 283–321. **Patrick Fraser Tytler.** Macray gives "P. Fraser Tytler, Esq., Author of the 'Hist. of Scotland' ": see *DNB*.

147 On codification, and its application to the laws of England, 321–349. **G. C. Lewis.** Macray; attr. in *DNB*. (Note, vol. 7, p. 263.)

148 Ferrario, *On Chivalry and Romance, and Italian Romantic Poetry*, 349–392. **André Vieusseux.** Macray.

149 French prohibitive system, 393–417. **George Austin.** Macray gives "G. Austin, Esq., brother of Prof. of Jurisp. in London Univer."; in Dec. 1828 Austin proposed writing a life of Colbert for the Soc. for the Diffusion of Useful Knowledge (Minutes of Sub-Committees, 1827–1829, p. 105, Univ. Coll. London); reference to Colbert in art., p. 394. (Letter, vol. 7, p. 263, signed **Charles Marryat.**)

150 Salverte, *The Occult Sciences of the Ancients*, 417–454. **T. J. Hussey.** Macray.

151 Modern French tragedy: Victor Hugo's *Hernani*, 455–473. **George Moir.** Macray.

152 French Revolution of 1830, 473–491. **G. C. Lewis.** Macray; attr. in *DNB*.

153 Commercial histories: financial reform, 491–497. **John Ward,** 1805–1890. Macray.

154 The Belgian Revolution, 497–515. **Henry Southern.** Macray; claimed in Southern to Macvey Napier, Dec. 16, 1830, Napier MS. 34, 614.

155 Critical sketches, 516–535. Pages 534–535 by **John Bowring;** pages 516–527 by **Mary Margaret Busk;** pages 528–529 by **Thomas Hodgkin,** 1798–1866; pages 527–528 by **T. J. Hussey;** pages 529–534 by **André Vieusseux**—all attr. by Macray.

156 Miscellaneous literary notices, 536–547. **John Macray.** Cf. no. 12.

157 Spirit of the twelfth and thirteenth centuries, 1–33. **Henry Southern.** Macray.

158 Mythology and religion of ancient Greece, 33–52. **G. C. Lewis.** Macray; attr. in *DNB*. (Note, vol. 8, p. 225–227, presumably by Lewis.)

159 Andral on consumption, 52–68. **John Conolly.** Macray gives "Dr. J. Conolly, Prof. of Med. in London University"; see *DNB*.

160 Carl Maria von Weber, 68–93. **William Dauney.** Macray, who adds "Advocate"; see Grove.

161 The fine arts of the middle ages, 93–129. **T. J. Hogg.** Macray gives "H. J. Hogg," undoubtedly in error: cf. no. 115.

162 History of the Hanseatic League, 130–145. **J. R. McCulloch.** Macray; repr. *Treatises* (see no. 96), pp. 373–386.

163 History of the ancient Germans, 145–180. **Mary Margaret Busk.** Macray.

164 *Correspondence between Schiller and Goethe*, 180–183. **George Moir.** Macray.

165 The Brunswick revolution, 184–193. **G. C. Lewis.** Macray; attr. in *DNB*.

166 The United States, 194–233. **Henry Tufnell.** Macray, who adds "co-translator of Müller's 'Dorians' "; see *DNB*.

167 German pocket books for 1831, 234–242. **George Moir.** Macray.

168 Critical sketches, 243–262. Pages 259–261 by **John Bowring;** pages 248–257 by **Mary Margaret Busk;** pages 257–259 by **Edward Holmes;** pages 243–245 by **John Ward,** 1805–1890—all attr. by Macray; pages 245–248 by **G. C. Lewis**—attr. by Macray and in *DNB*.

169 Miscellaneous literary notices, 264-274. **John Macray.** Cf. no. 12.

170 Herschel and Fresnel: theories of light, 283–306. **Thomas Galloway.** Macray; claimed in *Testimonials.*

171 Present state of Egypt, 307–336. **André Vieusseux.** Macray.

172 German manners in the sixteenth century, 337–354. **George Moir.** Macray.

173 Whale fishery, 355–370. **J. R. McCullough.** Macray.

174 Ancient Teutonic rhythmic gospel harmony, 371–387. **Joseph S. Stevenson.**

Macray; claimed in Stevenson to J. H. Newman, Sept. 10, 1840, Pusey House, Oxford.

175 French finance, 388–422. **George Taylor,** 1771/72–1851. Macray, who adds "Walton-le-Weir"; James Raine, in Taylor, *Surtees,* p. xiv, assigns such an art. to Taylor "in the Foreign Review," where no such art. appears.

176 Letters on Croatia and Italy, 423–432. **Edward Carleton Tufnell.** Macray gives "Edw. Tufnell, Esq."; man cited was brother of Henry Tufnell (see Foster) who wrote no. 166.

177 Modern architecture and architectural study, 432–461. **W. H. Leeds.** Macray; the style is typical of Leeds: use of foreign words and phrases, especially "*con amore*" and "*chefs d'œuvre*" (pp. 438, 457), his favorite terms, together with exaggerated and sometimes violent or raffish language (e.g. "puerile trifling, or anile superstition, is suffered . . . to exclude even a glimpse of common sense," p. 436); general concern with extension of knowledge and in particular architecture.

178 Greek texts of the Roman law, 461–478. **David Irving.** Macray; repr. in *Civil Law,* pp. 56–77, 163–164.

179 Paganini, 478–490. **William Dauney.** Macray; cf. no. 160.

180 Poland under Sobieski, 490–519. **S. D. Whitehead.** Macray.

181 Poland in 1830, 519–532. **André Vieusseux.** Macray.

182 Critical sketches, 533–547. Pages 539–541 by **H. G. Belinaye**—Macray gives "H. Belinaye, Esq., surgeon, Berners Street"; pages 533–539, 542–543 by **Mary Margaret Busk;** pages 544–547 by **André Vieusseux**—all attr. by Macray.

183 Miscellaneous literary notices, 548–555. **John Macray.** In general cf. no. 12; note on Kaufmann, p. 550 bottom, by **Thomas Carlyle**—Cochrane to Carlyle, Mar. 28, 1831, Nat. Lib. Scot: see Curran, *Vic. Periodicals Newsletter,* No. 2 (June 1968), 25–26.

184 Danish drama: Oehlenschläger, 1–32. **George Moir.** Macray.

185 Foreign policy of England: Lord Castlereagh, 33–60. **Thomas Peregrine Courtenay.** Macray; claimed in Courtenay to Blackwood, Feb. 11, 1832, Nat. Lib. Scot.

186 Lettish popular poetry, 61–78. **John Bowring.** Macray; claimed in Bowring, *Autobiographical Recollections* (1877), p. 127.

187 Second volume of Niebuhr's *Roman History*, 78–116. **Thomas Keightley.** Macray; claimed in letter cited in no. 20.

188 Russian novels and novelists: Bulgarin, 117–139. **W. H. Leeds.** Macray; Leeds to Macvey Napier, May 24, 1836, Napier MS. 34,617,. says he has contributed to *FQR* "several papers connected" with Russian literature—viz. *inter alia*, nos. 222 and 270.

189 Ancient municipal institutions of France, 140–149. **G. C. Lewis.** Macray; attr. in *DNB*.

190 Spain, 150–182. **James Browne,** 1793–1841. Macray; cf. nos. 94 and 211.

191 Toulotte's *History of the Roman Emperors*, 183–195. **Edward Carleton Tufnell.** Macray, as in no. 176.

192 Victor Hugo's *Notre Dame*, 196–215. **Henry Southern.** Macray.

193 The Low-German language and literature, 215–225. **Thomas Collins Banfield.** Macray gives "Dr. Thomas Banfield of Göttingen, translator of 'W. Tell' "; Banfield to Prof. F. W. Riemer, Feb. 15, 1832, Beinecke Lib., Yale Univ., signs his full name.

194 Critical sketches, 228–245. Pages 233–245 by **Mary Margaret Busk;** pages 228–233 by **George Moir**—all attr. by Macray.

195 Miscellaneous literary notices, 246–256. **John Macray.** Cf. no. 12.

VOLUME 8, OCTOBER 1831

196 German criminal trials, 265–302. **George Moir.** Macray.

197 Fourier, *Theory of Heat and Temperature of the Interior of the Earth*, 303–326. **Thomas Galloway.** Macray; claimed in *Testimonials*.

198 Châteaubriand's *Historical Discourses*: modern French schools of history, 326–346. **J. A. Roebuck.** Macray gives "R. A. Roebuck, Esq., Gray's Inn," whence man cited dates his letters at this time (see SDUK MSS., Univ. Coll. London); his brother Richard had been a naval officer, not known to have been a writer (Roebuck, (*Life*, p. 17); Cole, Diary, attrs. such an art. to "Roebuck," which is his usual term for J. A. Roebuck.

199 German literature of the fourteenth and fifteenth centuries, 347–391. **Thomas Carlyle.** Macray; repr. *Essays*, II.

200 Foreign policy of England: Mr. Canning, 391–431. **T. P. Courtenay.** Macray; claimed in letter cited for no. 185.

201 Diffusion of knowledge in France: necessity of public instruction, 431–438. **John Ward,** 1805–1890. Macray; cf. no. 68.

202 Beethoven, 439–461. **Edward Holmes.** Macray.

203 Pestilential cholera, 461–496. **James Copland.** Macray, who gives title "Dr." and adds "editor of 'Med. Repository' "; see *DNB*.

204 Critical sketches, 497–510. Pages 498–501, 503–508 by **Mary Margaret Busk;** pages 497–498 by **T. H. Horne;** pages 509–510 by **T. J. Hussey;** pages 501–502, 508–509 by **John Ward,** 1805–1890—all attr. by Macray.

205 Miscellaneous literary notices, 511–519. **John Macray.** Cf. no. 12.

VOLUME 9, JANUARY 1832

206 The Duke of Saint-Simon's *Memoirs*: The court of Louis the Fourteenth, 1–40. **Henry Southern.** Macray.

207 Literature and literary societies of Iceland, 41–77. **John Bowring.** Macray.

208 French drama [de Vigny, Hugo], 78–90. **George Moir.** Macray.

209 Mexican antiquities, 90–124. **Thomas Grimes.** Macray, who adds "Colchester (a Quaker)"; claimed in Grimes to Thomas Coates, June 4, 1832, Univ. Coll. London.

210 Grimm's *Teutonic Legal Antiquities*, 124–144. **Mary Margaret Busk.** Macray.

211 French expedition to Algiers: colonization of Africa, 145–175. **James Browne,** 1793–1841. Macray, who gives title "Dr."; cf. no. 94.

212 Poisson, *Capillary Action*, 175–181. **Thomas Galloway.** Macray; claimed in *Testimonials*.

213 Political state of Switzerland, 182–212. **André Vieusseux.** Macray.

214 Duties on foreign books, 212–217. **John Ward,** 1805–1890. Macray.

215 Critical sketches, 218–242. Pages 232–236 by **Mary Margaret Busk;** pages 218–222 by **W. H. Leeds;** pages 227–232, 241–242 by **George Moir;** pages 236–240 by **André Vieusseux**—all attr. by Macray; pages 223–227 by **C. C. de Pollon**—attr. by Macray, who adds "Copenhagen, editor of the 'Danske Bie.' "

216 Miscellaneous literary notices, 243–251. **John Macray.** Cf. no. 12.

VOLUME 9, MAY 1832

217 The reciprocity system (No. I), 261–289. **T. P. Courtenay.** Macray. (No. II is no. 233.)
218 Letters of a German Prince, 290–312. **Charles Buller.** Macray; see Mill, *Earlier Letters*, I, 107; identified in Cochrane to Carlyle, June 27, 1832, Nat. Lib. Scot., which refers to Mr. Buller's art. on "that princely personage."
219 Foscolo and his times, 312–344. **André Vieusseux.** Macray.
220 Recent French literature: *The Hundred and One*, 345–373. **George Moir.** Macray; Cochrane to Carlyle, June 27, 1832, Nat. Lib. Scot., assigns this art. to Moir.
221 Theodosian Code, 374–397. **David Irving.** Macray; repr. in *Civil Law*, pp. 23–25, 28–51, 116–119, with sections rearranged.
222 Russian poetry: Pushkin and Rilaeev, 398–418. **W. H. Leeds.** Macray; cf. letter cited in no. 188.
223 Quintana's *Spanish Biography*, 419–421. **Mary Margaret Busk.** Macray.
224 Penal colonies, 422–437. **Henry Southern.** Macray.
225 The Northern runes, 438–446. **Thomas Keightley.** Macray.
226 Minor French theatre: Scribe and his co-adjutors, 447–455. **George Moir.** Macray.
227 Prussian commercial policy (Part I), 455–470. **J. R. McCulloch.** Macray.
228 *Memoirs of Louis XVIII*, 470–482. **Henry Southern.** Macray.
229 Critical sketches, 483–500. Pages 493–495 by **Mary Margaret Busk;** pages 486–492 by **T. J. Hussey;** pages 499–500 by **George Moir;** pages 496–498 (Art. XVIII) by **André Vieusseux;** pages 483, 484–486 by **John Ward,** 1805–1890—all attr. by Macray.
230 Miscellaneous literary notices, 501–509. **John Macray.** Cf. no. 12.

VOLUME 10, AUGUST 1832

231 Goethe's *Works*, 1–44. **Thomas Carlyle.** Macray; repr. *Essays*, II.
232 Geology and climatology of Asia, 45–67. **Thomas Galloway.** Macray; claimed in *Testimonials*.

233 Free trade (No. II), 68–102. **T. P. Courtenay.** Macray. (No. III is no. 261.)
234 The Byzantine historians, 102–121. **William Cooke Taylor.** Macray gives "Dr. W. Cooke Taylor"; this and nos. 268, 274, 287 claimed in Taylor to Council of London Univ., Sept. 2, 1833.
235 American poetry [on Bryant], 121–138. **T. H. Lister.** Macray.
236 Thierry's *History of the Gauls*, 138–150. **G. C. Lewis.** Macray; attr. in *DNB*.
237 The German ultra-liberal press: Börne and Heine, 150–162. **George Moir.** Macray; claimed in Moir to Carlyle, n.d., Nat. Lib. Scot., MS. 1765, fols. 251–252.
238 Douville's *Travels in Central Africa*, 163–206. **W. D. Cooley.** Macray; claimed in a signed art., "The Geography of N'yassi," in *Journal of Royal Geographical Society of London*, 15 (1845), 235. (Note, p. 546.)
239 Thorvaldsen the sculptor, 207–213. **Mary Margaret Busk.** Macray.
240 American currency and banking, 214–249.
241 Critical sketches, 250–264. Pages 262–264 by **H. G. Belinaye;** pages 254–261 by **Mary Margaret Busk;** pages 250–254 by **George Moir;** pages 261–262 by **John Ward,** 1805–1890—all attr. by Macray.
242 Miscellaneous literary notices, 265–277. **John Macray.** Cf. no. 12.
243 Sir Walter Scott's "Farewell to his Readers," and M. Alphonse de Lamartine's "Reply" [in verse], 278–285. **Sir Walter Scott.** Title. Intro. note by **J. G. Cochrane?**—the tone is editorial.

VOLUME 10, OCTOBER 1832

244 Châteaubriand's *Works*, 297–334. **T. H. Lister.** Macray.
245 Italian pulpit eloquence: state of religion in Italy, 335–364.
246 German origin of the Latin language, 365–411. **J. M. Kemble.** Macray; Cochrane to Carlyle, Jan. 24, 1833, Nat. Lib. Scot., assigns to "Mr. John Kemble, the son of Mr. Charles Kemble." (Note, vol. 11, p. 215.)
247 Gouverneur Morris, 411–436. **Henry Southern.** Macray.
248 The poets of Portugal, 437–474. **Mary Margaret Busk.** Macray gives this to Henry Southern and then assigns no. 249 to Mrs. Busk, but that reverses the correct order; her characteristic style (see no. 345); cites her art. in *Blackwood's*, no.

567 (*Index*, I); her *Mediaeval Popes, Emperors, Kings, and Crusaders* (1854–1856), I, 411, refers to pp. 437–438 of this art.

249 French novels, 474–481. **Henry Southern.** Macray gives "Mrs. Busk," but cf. the start of evidence for the previous art.; pp. 475–476 cite no. 125, by Southern, as if by the same author.

250 On the present condition and future prospects of steam-carriages, 481–508. **John Scott Russell.** Macray gives "J. Scott Russell"; see *DNB*.

251 Sorelli's Italian translation of Milton, 508–513. **Arthur H. Hallam.** Macray; repr. *Writings of Arthur Hallam*, ed. Vail Motter, 1943.

252 The Revolution of 1830: government of Louis Philip, 514–540. **Henry Southern.** Macray.

253 Douville's *Reply* [to no. 238], 541–546. **W. D. Cooley.** Macray; in his *Inner Africa Laid Open* (1852), p. 48, Cooley implies that this as well as no. 238 is his.

254 Critical sketches, 547–558. Pages 553–558 by **Mary Margaret Busk;** pages 551–552 by **T. H. Horne**—all attr. by Macray; pages 547–551 by **George Moir**—attr. by Macray, and Cochrane to Carlyle, Oct. 29, 1832, Nat. Lib. Scot., assigns "the short article on Falk's Picture of Goethe" to Moir.

255 Miscellaneous literary notices, 559–566. **John Macray.** Cf. no. 12.

VOLUME 11, JANUARY 1833

256 Murat's *Sketch of the United States,* 1–29. ——— **Mark.** Macray. (Postscript, pp. 236–237.)

257 Modern Rome, and the Papal government, 29–72. **André Vieusseux.** Macray.

258 Albert Durer, 73–89. **Mary Margaret Busk.** Macray.

259 Restoration of the Bourbons: reign of Louis XVIII, 89–127. **Charles Buller.** Macray; attr. by Mill, *Earlier Letters*, I, 132.

260 Ancient history and constitution of Denmark, 128–140. **Henry Wheaton.** Macray; claimed by Wheaton in MS. list of his early articles, Pierpont Morgan Lib.

261 Results of free trade (No. III, concl.), 140–170. **T. P. Courtenay.** Macray.

262 Count Pecchio's works on England, 171–181. **André Vieusseux.** Macray.

263 Present state and prospects of French literature, 181–200. **George Moir.** Macray.

264 The young Napoleon, 201–215. **Henry Southern.** Macray.

265 [Critical sketches], 216–236: Victor Hugo, *Le Roi s'Amuse*, 216–217, by **Henry Southern**—Macray; Arrivabene, *The Charitable, &c., Institutions of England*, 218–222, by **André Vieusseux**—Macray; Letters on Italy, 222–227, by **Mary M. Busk**—Macray; Rask's *Anglo-Saxon Grammar*, 227–228, by **J. M. Kemble**—Macray; *The City of Refuge*, 228–229, by **John Ward,** 1805–1890—Macray; Roch, *Paris Malade*, 229–230, by **Mary M. Busk**—Macray; Italian novels, 230–236, by **Mary M. Busk**—Macray.

266 Miscellaneous literary notices, 238–253: pages 238–240, 247–253 by **John Macray** —cf. no. 12; pages 240–247 by **Théodore Lacordaire**—see p. 240; trans. with intro. and concluding notes by **W. D. Cooley**—on p. 240 translator plainly suggests he wrote nos. 238, 253, and claims the trans. of this notice.

VOLUME 11, APRIL 1833

267 Diderot, 261–315. **Thomas Carlyle.** Macray; repr. *Essays*, III.

268 Professor Schlegel and the Oriental Translation Fund, 315–333. **William Cooke Taylor.** Macray.

269 De Candolle's *Vegetable Physiology*, 334–382. **J. S. Henslow.** Macray; claimed in Henslow to W. J. Hooker, Jan. 23, 1833, Kew Gardens Lib.

270 Zagoskin's historical romances: the Russians in 1612, and in 1812, 382–403. **W. H. Leeds.** Macray; cf. letter cited in no. 188.

271 Prussian commercial policy (Part II, concl.), 403–406. **J. R. McCulloch.** Macray.

272 Niebuhr's *Roman History*, Vol. III: the Roman Reform Bill, 406–435. **Thomas Keightley.** Macray.

273 State of religious feeling in France, 435–441. **John Ward,** 1805–1890. Macray.

274 Jewish emancipation, 441–452. **William Cooke Taylor.** Macray.

275 Raumer's *Letters from Paris—History of the 16th and 17th Centuries*, 452–472. **Mary Margaret Busk.** Macray.

276 Pellico's memoirs of his ten years' captivity, 473–502. **George Moir.** Macray.

277 [Critical sketches], 503–527: Arago on lunar influences, 503–508, by **Thomas Galloway**—Macray; Armenian literature,

509–512, by **Mary M. Busk**—Macray; Count de Vigny's *Consultations of Dr. Black*, 513–517, by **Mary M. Busk**—Macray; *Meditations of Antonius, translated into Persian*, 518–519, by **William Cooke Taylor**—Macray; Douville's *Justification*, 519–527, by **W. D. Cooley**, perhaps with **J. G. Cochrane**—Macray gives Cochrane, but Cooley refers to this art., together with nos. 238, 253, and 266, in *Inner Africa Laid Open* (1852), pp. 48, 49; on p. 526 here, author implies that he is a member of the Royal Geographical Society, which Cooley was and Cochrane was not.

278   Miscellaneous literary notices, 528–537. **John Macray.** Cf. no. 12.

VOLUME 12, JULY 1833

279   French and English biographies of Newton, 1–27. **Thomas Galloway.** Macray.
280   Béranger, 28–49. **Herman Merivale.** Merivale, *Memoir*, p. 579.
281   The American systems of prison discipline, 49–80. **Henry Southern.** Macray.
282   Goethe's *Posthumous Works* (Part I): the second part of *Faust*, 81–109. **Abraham Hayward.** Macray.
283   *Philosophical History of Hypochondriasis and Hysteria*, 110–130. **John Conolly.** Macray; claimed in Conolly to Thomas Coates, May 15, 1834, Univ. Coll. London.
284   Geijer's *History of Sweden*, 131–141. **Thomas Keightley.** Macray.
285   The north of Italy and the Tyrol, 142–164. **H. Bellenden Ker.** Macray.
286   Poetry and the lives of the troubadours, 164–191. **W. J. Thoms.** Macray.
287   Mohammed and Mohammedanism, 192–208. **W. C. Taylor.** Macray.
288   Rush's *Residence in England*, 209–235. **T. H. Lister.** Macray gives "Thos. J. Lister"; undoubtedly an error for T. H. Lister, who had written no. 235 on a similar subject; Lister to Napier, July 12, 1833, Napier MS. 34,616, shows he read Rush's book at this time.
289   [Critical sketches], 236–256: Menzel's *Tour in Austria*, 236–241, by **George Moir**—Macray; *Russell de Albuquerque*, 241–245, by **Mary M. Busk**—Macray; Tromlitz's romances, 245–249, by **Mary M. Busk**—Macray; Retzsch's *Outlines to the Song of the Bell*, 250–251; Manno's *History of Sardinia*, 252–256, by **André Vieusseux**—Macray.

290   Miscellaneous literary notices, 257–266. **John Macray.** Cf. no. 12.

VOLUME 12, OCTOBER 1833

291   Cousin's *Report on the Prussian System of Education*: necessity and practicability of a national system of education, 273–301. **Sarah Austin.** Macray gives "Mrs. Austin"; see *DNB*. (Postscript, pp. 495–496.)
292   History of modern Italian freedom, 302–333. **André Vieusseux.** Macray.
293   D'Haussez, *Great Britain in 1833*, 334–352. **T. H. Lister.** Macray erroneously gives "P. H. Lister"; claimed in T. H. Lister to Napier, Sept. 1, 1833, Napier MS. 34,616.
294   Egyptian antiquities, 353–387. **Isaac Cullimore.** Macray gives "J. Cullimore"; claimed by Isaac Cullimore in *Fraser's*, no. 1148.
295   *Memoirs of the Duchess of Abrantes*, 387–398. **Mary Margaret Busk.** Macray.
296   Pellico's *Tragedies*, 398–412. **George Moir.** Macray.
297   Animal magnetism, 413–444. **Percival B. Lord.** Macray, who adds an Irishman "killed in India in an affray with the natives"; see *DNB*.
298   Retzsch's *Outlines: Macbeth*, 445–454.
299   Mirabeau, 455–495. **Charles Buller.** Macray; claimed in Buller to Carlyle, Aug. 5, 1833, Nat. Lib. Scot.
300   [Critical sketches], 497–513: Spindler's novels and romances: *The Nun of Gnadenzell*, 497–504, by **Mary M. Busk** —Macray; Dumas's *Gaul and France*, 504–507, by **William Cooke Taylor**— Macray; Ludvigh's *Tour in Hungary*, 507–510, by **Mary M. Busk**—Macray; Chambray's *Notes on Prussia*, 510–513, by **J. G. Cochrane**—Macray.
301   Miscellaneous literary notices, 514–527. **John Macray.** Cf. no. 12.

VOLUME 13, FEBRUARY 1834

302   Modern diplomacy, 1–35. **T. P. Courtenay.** Macray; claimed in Courtenay to Macvey Napier, Dec. 20, 1838, Napier MS. 34,619.
303   *Graphic History of the French National Convention*, 35–60. **Archibald Alison,** 1792–1867. Macray; repr. as "Reign of Terror" in *Miscellaneous Essays*, Boston, 1854.
304   Pronunciation of the Greek language,

60–73. **David Irving.** Macray.

305   The French in Algiers, 74–106. **André Vieusseux.** Macray.

306   Jacquemont's *Letters from India,* 107–132. **W. C. Taylor.** Macray.

307   Foreign poor: home colonies in Belgium and France, 132–152. **George Taylor,** 1771/72–1851. Macray, who adds "father of Henry T., Esq., author of 'Philip von Artevelde' "; see *DNB* under Henry Taylor, 1800–1886.

308   Lafontaine, the German novelist, 153–160. **Mary Margaret Busk.** Macray.

309   Turkey, Egypt, and Russia: the crisis in the East, 161-228. **Edward Villiers,** 1806–1843. Macray.

VOLUME 13, MAY 1834

310   Spanish painters, 237–271. **Edmund W. Head.** Macray; confirmed in Cochrane to Dawson Turner, Oct. 17, 1834, Trinity Coll. Lib., Cambridge.

311   Comparative mortality of different populations, 272–282. **J. P. Nichol.** Macray; confirmed in Mill, *Earlier Letters,* I, 222.

312   *Memoirs and Correspondence of Duplessis Mornay,* 282–313. **S. D. Whitehead.** Macray.

313   Swedish periodical literature, 314–340. **Mary Margaret Busk.** Macray.

314   The Austrian government and the Italian liberals, 340–354. **André Vieusseux.** Macray.

315   Ichthyology. 355–380.

316   Prince Pückler-Muskau's *Tutti Frutti,* 380–397. **Sarah Austin.** Macray gives "Mrs. Austin"; cf. no. 291.

317   Post office communication between England and foreign countries, 397–405. Unidentified. Possibly Hannibal Evans Lloyd, who had contributed previously to *FQR* and who was employed by the Foreign Post Office (see *Gent. Mag.* 182 [Sept. 1847], 325); art. shows intimate knowledge of the workings of F.P.O. and writer seems to have access to correspondence on F.P.O. matters.

318   Judicial system of British India, 406–441. **Humphrey B. Devereux.** Macray, who adds "son of Lord Hereford"; see Burke.

319   [Critical sketches], 442–460: *Ionian Anthology,* 442–444; Cousinéry's *Travels in Macedonia,* 445–451, by **W. C. Taylor** —Macray; Meidinger's *Gothico-Teutonic Dictionary,* 451–453, by **W. J. Thoms**— Macray; Rafn's *Faroe Islands,* 453–456,

by **Mary M. Busk**—Macray; *The Italian Insurrection of 1831,* 456–460, by **André Vieusseux** and **J. G. Cochrane**— Macray.

320   Miscellaneous literary notices, 461–473. **John Macray.** Cf. no. 12.

VOLUME 14, AUGUST 1834

321   Madame de Staël, 1–30. **T. H. Lister.** Macray.

322   German military history during the sixteenth century, 31–58. **Herman Merivale.** Macray; Merivale, *Memoir,* p. 579.

323   Central Asia, 58–92. **W. C. Taylor.** Macray.

324   The present school of architecture in Germany, 92–118. **W. H. Leeds.** Macray.

325   Alexander Dumas's *Travelling Impressions,* 119–130. **W. C. Taylor.** Macray.

326   Goethe's *Posthumous Works* (Part II, concl.), 131–162. **Abraham Hayward.** Macray; the first paragraph refers to this art. as a continuation of no. 282.

327   Dutch popular songs, 163–171. **W. J. Thoms.** Macray.

328   French commercial policy: new customs law, 172–197. **George Austin.** Macray gives "G. Austin"; cf. no. 149, cited here, p. 185n., as by same author.

329   History of the Phoenicians and Carthaginians, 197–228. **Thomas Keightley.** Macray.

330   [Critical sketch], 228–233. *Encyclopédie des Gens du Monde,* 228–233, by **J. G. Cochrane**—Macray.

331   Miscellaneous literary notices, 234–239. **John Macray.** Cf. no. 12.

VOLUME 14, DECEMBER 1834

322   Frederic the Great, 245–271. **Herman Merivale.** Macray; Merivale, *Memoir,* p. 579.

333   Madame Dudevant's novels: *Indiana, Valentine,* etc., 271–297. **Mary Margaret Busk.** Macray; claimed in Mrs. Busk to Blackwoods, Jan. 22, [1835], Nat. Lib. Scot.

334   Italy and Europe, 298–310. **André Vieusseux.** Macray.

335   Life and labours of Cuvier, 311–349. **John Conolly.** Macray.

336   New Arabian tales, 350–369. **W. C. Taylor.** Macray.

337   The countries, nations, and languages of the Oceanic region, 369–412. **John Crawfurd.** Macray; see *DNB.*

338 Van Artevelde, the brewer of Ghent, and his son Philip, 413–421. **Mary Margaret Busk.** Macray.

339 The Prussian government and administration, 422–456. **E. D. Friedländer.** Macray gives "Dr. Friedlander, of Dorpat"; see *BMCat*.

340 [Critical sketches], 457–469: Bronikowski's novels, 457–464, by **Mary M. Busk** —Macray; [Pompeo] Litta's *Celebrated Italian Families*, 464–465, by **André Vieusseux**—Macray; Pazos, *Historical and Political Memoirs*, 465–466, by **B. E. Pote**—Macray gives "Pote," see reference to Pazos in no. 429; Zieman's *Old German Rudiments*, 466–467, by **W. J. Thoms**—Macray; Depping's *State of the Jews in the Middle Ages*, 468–469, by **W. C. Taylor**—Macray.

341 Miscellaneous literary notices, 470–477. **John Macray.** Cf. no. 12.

VOLUME 15, MARCH 1835

342 Meyen's *Voyage Round the World*, 1–48. **W. D. Cooley?** Pages 12–13 of no. 387 refer in detail to this art. and to the reaction to it in terms which strongly suggest that the same author wrote both; there are many similarities of vocabulary and point of view between the two.

343 Bojardo's and Ariosto's *Orlando*: Italian romantic poetry [by Antonio Panizzi], 48–74. **Thomas Keightley.** Claimed in his *Reply to a Letter Addressed by Mr. A. Panizzi . . .* (1835), p. 1 and *passim*.

344 New theory of volcanoes, 74–83.

345 Sicily and Malta, 83–108. **Mary Margaret Busk.** The trademark of her writing in the conclusion, "we lay down our pen" (it is also found in nos. 346, 363, 373, 406, 414, 447); the general characteristics of style are the mixture of résumé and extensive quotation (which she sometimes calls "abstracts and extracts"), verse translations, and an occasional tone of shocked propriety; she reviews in most European languages, especially works of historical fiction and memoirs of titled women: here on p. 83 reference to no. 265, pp. 222–223, by Mrs. Busk.

346 Kosciuszko, 108–139. **Mary Margaret Busk.** Her trademark: cf. no. 345.

347 *Marco Visconti: a Story of the Fourteenth Century*, 139–145.

348 Principles of Grecian architecture, 145–158. **W. H. Leeds.** Leeds to Dawson Turner, Oct. 14, 1837, Trin. Coll. Camb., says he has received a note for £19 from Richter, the publisher, for arts. in *FQR* between Feb. 1834 and Jan. 1836 (nos. 324, 372, and this art. would represent payment at rate of 5 gns. per sheet); this opens with reference to no. 324 in words which imply a common authorship; it also makes many of the same points—modern buildings lack coherence, Romans and Italians debased Greek architecture, Palladian is "blundering," and the need for wider appreciation of architecture is great.

349 Pauperism in France, 159–182. **George Taylor,** 1771/72–1851. This is an elaboration of no. 307: same quotations are used in both arts. and many of the same points are made; this art. was drawn "in part, from our own investigation" (p. 159)—viz., in writing an elaborate report on the Poor Laws in 1832/33 (see Taylor, *Surtees*, p. xiii); the art. contains some observations of pauperism in Great Britain; for Taylor's interest in France, cf. nos. 175, 307.

350 Designs of Russia against Turkey, 183–194. **David Urquhart,** with a collab.? Various similarities of style and content between this art. and no. 381; anti-Russian point of view and discussion of Urquhart's anonymous publications throughout both essays; author has been in Near East, p. 191n., as Urquhart had. On possibility of a collab., see final statement in evidence for no. 364.

351 Progress and prospects of entomology, 194–209.

352 [Critical sketches], 209–226: *Leonardo da Vinci*, 209–216; *The Sweating Sickness*, 217–219; *Insurrection in Java*, 219–222; *Russia and Poland*, 222–224; *The revolution in Sweden*, 224–226.

353 Foreign criticisms on English works [translations from the *Götting[ische] Gelehrte Anzeigen*, for Aug. 14, 1834 (1833 in error), and Oct. 4, 1834, respectively], 227–228. Page 227 by **Arnold Hermann Ludwig Heeren**—signed Heeren, man cited was an editor of the *Göttingische Gelehrte Anziegen* (see *ADB*); p. 228 signed **Milford.**

354 Miscellaneous literary notices, 229–234.

VOLUME 15, JULY 1835

355 Rae's *New Principles of Political Economy, in Refutation of Adam Smith*, 241–266. **John Pringle Nichol?** At end of Aug. 1834, Nichol was writing a

"paper" for *FQR* (see Mill, *Earlier Letters*, I, 232); he and Mill discussed questions, particularly of definition, concerning political economy; this article reflects their current reading (e.g., Bacon's *Novum Organum*) and Nichol's emphasis on combination of utility and generosity (see *DNB*).

356   Present state of theatricals in France and England, 266–288.

357   Parrot's *Journey to Mount Ararat*, 288–303. **W. D. Cooley?** Cooley to Macvey Napier, May 9, 1835, Napier MS. 34,617, suggests a review of this book for the *Edin Rev.*, which will stress Parrot's admission of earlier errors and Humboldt's refusal to admit his own—a description which fits this art.; no such review in *ER*; Cooley was a frequent contrib. to *FQR*.

358   *Life of Keppler*, 304–325.

359   Discoveries and public works in the United States, 325–339.

360   Affairs of Spain, 339–347.

361   English literature, 347–360. **Mary Margaret Busk,** prob. Characteristic style and topic: see no. 345.

362   Marshal Soult, 360–387.

363   German history, 388–424. **Mary Margaret Busk.** Her trademark: cf. no. 345; pp. 388, 389 imply this is a continuation of no. 163.

364   Opinions and character of Turkish travellers (No. I), 424–464. **David Urquhart** with a collab.? Reviewer, p. 437n, appears to claim *FQR* no. 350; style, content and anti-Russian viewpoint are much the same as those of nos. 350 and 381; writer has been in Greece, p. 438, and in Turkey, "even in the ambassadorial circles" early in 1834 (see pp. 460–461 and *DNB*); reviewer, however, claims to have been converted to present view by Urquhart's book, which he praises, pp. 459–463, but Urquhart often used collabs. who admired his foreign policy and desired to promote it: he said himself, *Reminiscences*, p. 67, on Aug. 14, 1835, that he had "now to write" seven arts. for various periodicals "for which I have given the outline, found and converted the writers and editors."

365   [Critical sketches], 465–481: *Degeneracy of France*, 465–466; Peyronnet, *Thoughts of a Prisoner*, 466–468; *Reply of Lucien Buonaparte to Lamarque*, 468–470; *Democracy in America* [by de Tocqueville], 470–472; *Duchy of Savoy in 1833*, 473–476; Halley's comet, 477–481.

366   Miscellaneous literary notices, 482–490.

VOLUME 16, OCTOBER 1835

367   Menzel, *German Literature*, 1–26. **J. S. Blackie.** Stoddart, *Blackie*, I, 157.

368   Förster's *Life of Frederick-William I, King of Prussia*, 26–56. **Hannibal Evans Lloyd,** prob. Marked "Lloyd" in Univ. of Minnesota copy; man cited had reviewed German books previously in *FQR*—see nos. 79, 103.

369   Wilson's *Sanscrit Dictionary*, 56–77. **John Tytler.** Claimed in Tytler to Thomas Coates, Aug. 5, 1836, Univ. Coll. London; marked "Tytler" in Univ. of Minnesota copy.

370   Colletta's *History of Naples*, 78–113. **André Vieusseux,** prob. Author was in Naples in 1815, in company with officers of a Sicilian regiment (p. 92); Vieusseux was a lieutenant in such a regiment from 1811–1816 (see Boase), and wrote nos. 292, 314, 334 on Italy.

371   On the French and English "Chansons de Geste," 113–147. **Thomas Wright,** 1810–1877. Repr. *Literature*, I.

372   Landscape and ornamental gardening, 148–165. **W. H. Leeds,** prob. This and no. 324, known to be Leeds's, are claimed in no. 417, pp. 162, 171; see no. 177 for same general characteristics.

373   *Italy as It Is*, 165–177. **Mary Margaret Busk.** Her trademark: cf. no. 345.

374   On the political constitution of Spain, and the insurrection of Don Carlos, 177–205.

375   Objects and advantages of statistical science, 205–229. **William Cooke Taylor,** prob. Marked as his in Univ. of Minnesota copy; author makes frequent references to having attended recent meetings of the British Association (pp. 208, 209, 229); see Taylor in *DNB*, which also shows his interest in statistics.

376   Miscellaneous literary notices, 230–240.

VOLUME 16, JANUARY 1836

377   Italy and the Italians, 245–279. **André Vieusseux?** Page 267 cites no. 11; art. refers to many authors Vieusseux had reviewed in *FQR*; also echoes Vieusseux's earlier stated beliefs about the support of Austrian rule in Lombardy (see nos. 314, 334) and the need for statistical knowledge (see no. 215, p. 236).

378   Lichtenberg and Hogarth, 279–303. **W. H. Leeds.** In letter cited for no. 348, Leeds estimated that the new publisher

of *FQR*, Black and Armstrong, owed him about £30 for contributions since Jan. 1836; nos. 417, 435, 448, and this art. would represent payment at rate of £5 per sheet, a slight reduction after Richter's bankruptcy (see no. 348); Leeds had long been interested in Lichtenberg, writing on him for the *London Mag.* (see Leeds to Dawson Turner, Aug. 31, 1820, Trin. Coll. Camb.); Leeds to Dawson Turner, Dec. 30, 1821, ibid., claimed "Biographical Essay on the Genius and Productions of Hogarth," prefixed to 1822 folio ed. of Hogarth; many observations there are echoed in this art.

379   Antiquarian research in Egypt; its progress, disclosures, and prospects, 303–327. **Edward Clarkson.** Clarkson to C. P. Thomson, Sept. 29, 1836, BM Add. MS. 31,218, says he has written four arts. on Egyptian antiquity in the *Brit. & Foreign Rev.* and the *FQR* (those in the *FQR* are presumably nos. 379, 391); art. shows Clarkson's concern with historical validity of Scripture and, p. 326, with the existence once of a "causeway or railroad" across the desert from Karnac to Kosseir (cf. no. 425). (Note, vol. 17, p. 235.)

380   Goethe's correspondence with Zelter and Bettina Brentano, 328–360. **J. S. Blackie.** Stoddart, *Blackie*, I, 157.

381   Russian policy in Greece, 361–385. **David Urquhart,** prob. alone. Sir John Ponsonby in Urquhart's *Reminiscences*, p. 94, strongly criticizes Urquhart for his art., speaking as though he wrote it himself without a collab. (cf. evidence for no. 364).

382   On the Anglo-Latin poets of the twelfth century, 386–407. **Thomas Wright,** 1810–1877. Repr. *Literature,* I.

383   Guizot's *Course of Modern History,* 407–437. **Herman Merivale?** *DNB* credits only five articles to H. Merivale in *FQR* and this would be a sixth, but the reviewer speaks, p. 433, of no. 57 in words which imply a common authorship; both arts. stress "general sentiments" and the mass, in opposition to Guizot's stress on great men and the individual; both stress moderation and tolerance; both talk of classical and romantic historians.

384   Mythology of the north, 437–444. **Mary Margaret Busk,** prob. Characteristic style (see no. 345) and topic (see nos. 64, 138); the art. is closely related to her essay in *Blackwood's* no. 1400 (*Index,* I), published six months earlier, which was also on Grundtvig's *Northern Mythology* and utilized many of the same quotations.

385   [Critical sketches], 445–456; Russian annuals, 445–450, by **W. H. Leeds**—author implies in no. 470 that he wrote this, and p. 446n. cites no. 222, p. 417; Huber's *Sketches of Spain* [Vol. II], 450–452 by **Mary M. Busk?**—the reader is at once referred to her review of Hubert's *Cid* (no. 155, p. 524); *The Count of Candespina,* 452–456, also by **Mary M. Busk?**—she frequently noticed Spanish works, and in this case the art. begins with a point which she made in no. 182, p. 542; *The Life and Memoirs of Count Schulenburg,* 456.

386   Miscellaneous literary notices, 457–473.

VOLUME 17, APRIL 1836

387   Poeppig's *Travels in Chili, Peru, and on the River Amazons* [sic.], 1–48. **W. D. Cooley?** He originally wrote a review of this book for *ER* (see Cooley to Macvey Napier, May 9, Aug. 17, Sept. 9, Nov. 21, 1835 and Jan. 31, 1836, Napier MS. 34,617); it did not appear there; this review makes all the points that Cooley makes in his letters, and has an addition, pp. 46–48, described as such in the letter of Nov. 21, 1835.

388   Civil law: Barkow, Böcking, Blume, and Hänel, 48–59. **David Irving.** Repr. *Civil Law,* pp. 263–276.

389   General history of modern Italy, 60–96.

390   Michel: French metrical romances, 97–109. **Thomas Wright,** 1810–1877. Attr. by Sir Frederic Madden in MS. journal, April 29, 1836, Bodleian Lib.; usually Wright lent Sir Frederic his copy of *FQR* and identified his own contributions: see entry in journal for Jan. 30, 1836.

391   Monuments of Egypt and Nubia, 110–120. **Edward Clarkson.** First paragraph suggests that this is an extension of no. 379; first paragraph of no. 411 implies that author also wrote nos. 379 and 391; art. shows Clarkson's concern with corroboration of the Bible: cf. no. 379.

392   Niccolini's *Tragedies,* 121–139.

393   History of the Franks, 139–156.

394   On the study of natural history, 156–176.

395   Character and opinions of travellers in Turkey (No. II), 176–209. **David Urquhart,** with a collab.? Page 176 states that this art. resumes the task begun in no. 364; characteristics mentioned in no. 350 reappear here.

396 Raumer's *England in 1835*, 209–216. **Mary Margaret Busk?** Pp. 212–214 contain a long quotation from Niemeyer, whom Mrs. Busk had reviewed in no. 194; references to two other reviews of Raumer on pp. 209, 216 (viz., nos. 74 and 275) in words which imply a common authorship.

397 [Critical sketches], 217–235: Duden's *Europe and America*, 217–221; Von Mosel's *History of the Court Library at Vienna*, 221–224; Rhyming chronicle of the City of Cologne, 225–227; *The World as It Is*, 228–231, by **Mary Margaret Busk**—ends with her trademark, cf. no. 345; Dr. Wurm on *The Portfolio* [extracts of his critical remarks reprinted], 232–235, by **C. F. Wurm**—see opening paragraph; editor-translator may be Edmund S. Williams, who returned to London from Hamburg, where Wurm edited a journal early in 1836 and began to contribute to *FQR*: see opening paragraph here and nos. 420, 461.

398 Miscellaneous literary notices, 236–247. Unidentified. (Letter from Paris, p. 238, by **Francisque Michel**—claimed by Michel in *Galfridi de Monemuta Vita Merlini*, ed. Michel and Thomas Wright [Paris, 1837], p. xcii.)

VOLUME 17, JULY 1836

399 Prince Pückler-Muskau and his new tour, 253–271. **J. S. Blackie.** Claimed in Blackie to his father, Aug. 21, 1836, Nat. Lib. Scot.; Stoddart, *Blackie*, I, 158.

400 Martin, *On the Formation of the Minds of Women*, 272–286.

401 Meon, Chabaille, Mone, and Grimm: *Reynard the Fox*, 286–317. **W. J. Thoms.** Claimed in his *History of Reynard the Fox* (1844), p. xi, n.; repr., enlarged, as "Introduction" to book cited, pp. v–lxxxviii.

402 Thibaudeau's *Memoirs of Napoleon*, 317–361.

403 Guizot's Commission Historique and the English Record Commission, 362–390. **Thomas Wright**, 1810–1877. Reviewer, p. 377, is now editing the life of Hereward from Gale's transcript of the *Liber Swaffham*; in signed preface dated "20 juin 1838" in Francisque Michel, *Chroniques Anglo-Normandes*, II (Rouen, [1839]), Wright says he had been editing this work but was deflected from the task.

404 *Letters to John Henry Merck, from Göthe, Herder, Wieland, &c.*, 391–417.

Elizabeth Rigby Eastlake. Claimed in Elizabeth Rigby to Dawson Turner, her uncle, June 21, 1836, Trin. Coll. Camb.

405 Victor Hugo's *Marie Tudor*, 417–427.

406 Maffei's *History of Italian Literature*, 428–456. **Mary Margaret Busk.** Her trademark: see no. 345; the author's claim on p. 437 that *terza rima* is a difficult form to translate also appeared in no. 248, p. 450.

407 *Recollections of Russia, Turkey, and Greece*, 457–471.

408 [Critical sketches], 472–489: Italian novels, 472–482, by **Mary M. Busk**, prob.—characteristic style and topic (see no. 345), apparently by someone who has reviewed Italian novels previously (see nos. 215, 265), letter quoted in evidence for no. 497 repeats statements on p. 472 here; Jal's *Tour from Paris to Naples*, 482–489.

409 Miscellaneous literary notices, 490–498.

VOLUME 18, OCTOBER 1836

410 Eckermann's *Conversations with Göthe*, 1–30. **J. S. Blackie.** Stoddart, *Blackie*, I, 158; claimed in Blackie to Blackwoods, Oct. 20, 1836, Nat. Lib. Scot.

411 Mexican antiquities, 31–63. **Edward Clarkson.** Claims art. in *FQR*, Oct. 1836, called "Central American Antiquities," on title-page of his *Suez Canal*.

412 Retzsch's *Outlines* [illustrations for works by Goethe, Schiller, and Shakespeare], 63–88.

413 Poggio Bracciolini's *Letters*, 89–97.

414 *Otho the Great and His Times*, 97–109. **Mary Margaret Busk.** Her trademark: see no. 345.

415 Modern painting in Germany [Raczynski's *History of Modern Art in Germany*, Vol. I], 109–118. **Henry Wheaton.** *Wheaton*, p. 320.

416 Ancient Persian poetry, 119–158. **B. E. Pote,** prob. Cf. general evidence for no. 493 where on p. 322 there is a reference to page 142 of this art. in words that are surely personal rather than editorial; cf. comments on Eastern sensuousness and idleness with Pote's preface to his *The Assassins of the Paradise* (1831), pp. vi–vii.

417 Athenian architecture and polychrome embellishment, 159–179. **W. H. Leeds.** On p. 162 author claims no. 324.

418 Friar Rush and the frolicsome elves of popular mythology, 180–202. **Thomas Wright**, 1810–1877. Repr. *Literature*, II.

419   Ideler's *System of Psychology*, 203–218. **Edmund Sydney Williams?** See evidence for no. 461; Williams later published a psychological quarterly.

420   [Critical sketches], 219–243. *Chronicle of the Country of Dithmarsch*, 219–225, by **E. S. Williams**, prob.—see evidence for no. 461; book reviewed, which was published three years earlier in Hamburg, concerns an area in Denmark unheard of by "nineteen out of twenty English readers," and Williams had just returned to England after spending almost all his life in Hamburg; Davids' *Turkish Grammar*, 226–231, by **B. E. Pote**, prob.—cf. general evidence for no. 493, noting the ref. back to this in that art., p. 331; *New Greek Testament*, 231; Hennequin's *Voyage Philosophique*, 232–238; *La Campania Sotteranea*, 238–241; Endlicher's *Catalogue*, 241–242; D'Avezac's *Northern Africa*, 242–243.

421   Miscellaneous literary notices, 244–251.

VOLUME 18, JANUARY 1837

422   Foreign policy and internal administration of the Austrian Empire, 257–304.

423   French and English schools of medicine, 304–316. **John Conolly**, prob. Author "once" attended a lecture by Alibert at Hospital of St. Louis in Paris, p. 313; Conolly had gone to Paris twice before 1837 specifically to visit "the Medical Schools" (Conolly to Leonard Horner, Oct. 17, 1827, Univ. Coll. London), while Alibert was at St. Louis; Conolly had written on medical topics for *FQR*, notably no. 283 on hypochondriasis.

424   Tyrol and the Tyrolese, 317–341.

425   Steam navigation to India, 342–392. **Edward Clarkson.** Claimed on title-page of his *Suez Canal*.

426   Chateaubriand, *On English Literature*, 392–418. **George Croly.** Croly to F. Shoberl, Sept. 16, 1836, U. of Iowa Lib., promises art. on Chateaubriand for next no. after Oct. if too late for latter.

427   Occupation of Cracow by Austria, 418–433.

428   Sternberg's tales and novels, 433–454. **Mary Margaret Busk,** prob. Characteristic style and topic (see no. 345); reviewer, p. 434, has "made the British public acquainted with living German novelists of the historical school" (cf. nos. 289, 300, 340).

429   South America, 455–477. **B. E. Pote.** Pote to Sir Robert Peel, Oct. 29, 1845, BM Add. MS. 40,577, discusses as his an art. in *FQR* for "October 1837, or the next number either way," based on information from Don V. Pazos (see pp. 468–470) and on "a large M.S. by a German Botanist in Peru" (see pp. 457, 476, which draw on Tadeo Haenke, a "German naturalist"), describing "on the Eastern side of the Andes vast rich plains of all produce" (see pp. 475–477). (Note, vol. 21, pp. 188–190.)

430   [Critical sketches], 478–486: Raumer's *Historical Pocket-Book*, 478–483, by **Mary Margaret Busk?**—she reviewed Raumer in nos. 275 and 396, the first of which is immediately referred to, p. 478, as though hers; Reinaud, *Invasions of France by the Saracens*, 483–486.

431   Miscellaneous literary notices, 487–494.

VOLUME 19, APRIL 1837

432   Rozet's *Algiers*, and [Pückler-Muskau's] *Semilasso in Africa*, 1–35.

433   Chateaubriand's translation of *Paradise Lost*, 35–50. **H. J. T. Drury**, prob. See no. 62 by man cited, who there shows same concern for correct translation (see p. 208) as does this reviewer; on p. 50 author says he was at Cambridge about the time Byron was at Harrow (Drury left Cambridge and started teaching at Harrow in 1801, the year Byron entered); other details—that author had explored "hundreds of libraries" and devoted many hours to the *Iliad* and *Aeneid* (p. 38), that he had been in Brussels and Florence (p. 37)—all fit Drury (see *DNB* and James T. Hodgson, *Memoir of the Rev. Francis Hodgson* [1878], II, 112, 116).

434   Literary gossip on novels and dramas, 51–61.

435   Influence of construction on style in architecture, 62–91. **W. H. Leeds.** Marked as his in Wellesley Coll. copy; on p. 75n. author claims no. 417; cf. style described for no. 177.

436   *Memoirs of the Countess of Königsmark*, 92–106. **Mary Margaret Busk.** The review of a memoir of a titled lady, the shocked reticence, and the phrase "we *cannot extract or even abstract*" (last two, p. 95) all illustrate the evidence for no. 345; view of the middle ages, pp. 92, 100, is echoed in her *Mediaeval Popes* (full title in no. 248), I, iii–iv.

437   Miltitz's *The Duties of Consuls*, 106–117.

438   *The Invention of Printing* [by J. Wetter], 118–134. Unidentified. Wellesley Coll. copy assigns to "J.W."

439   British continental connexions, 135–184. **T. P. Courtenay**, prob. Writer repeatedly refers to nos. 185, 200, and 302 ("xv. 7, 13," p. 136n., is an error for "xiii. 7, 13"—which is no. 302); moreover, similar points are made, especially in opposition to foreign entanglements; the style of all four pieces is similar, as is the extensive footnoting.

440   Sanchoniatho's *Early History of the Phoenicians* (No. I), 184–197.

441   Tamil historical manuscripts, 198–230. **B. E. Pote**, prob. Cf. general evidence for no. 493; there are 5 refs. in this art. back to no. 416, and it is later referred to in nos. 449 and 552.

442   Miscellaneous literary notices, 231–239.

VOLUME 19, JULY 1837

443   Nettement's *Memoirs of the Duchess de Berri*, 245–266.

444   Burkart's *Residence and Travels in Mexico*, 266–293.

445   Ludwig Uhland and the Swabian poets, 293–337. **J. S. Blackie**. Claimed in *Testimonials*.

446   Moral and physical evils of large towns, 338–357.

447   Rellstab's tales and novels, 358–376. **Mary Margaret Busk**. Her trademark: see no. 345.

448   Grecian and Italian architecture contrasted, 377–397. **W. H. Leeds**. Pages 377–378 refer to criticisms of no. 324 and "the other architectural papers in this Review" [see nos. 177, 348, 417, and 435] to which the author feels it "a duty we owe both to ourselves individually," as well as to the *FQR*, to reply.

449   History of Ottoman poetry, 398–415. **B. E. Pote**, prob. Cf. general evidence for no. 493; idea on pp. 402–403 on creation of songs appears in no. 493, p. 345, with reference back (although wrong month and title are given).

450   *Zumalacarregui*, 416–432.

451   Circassia, 433–437.

452   [Critical sketches], 437–455: Diez and Raynouard on the neo-Latin languages, 437–445, by **Thomas Wright**, 1810–1877, repr. as *On the Neo-Latin Languages*, n.d.; Volpicella, *The Greek Tragedies*, 446–452; Adventures on land and at sea, 452–455.

453   Miscellaneous literary notices, 456–463.

VOLUME 20, OCTOBER 1837

454   *Memoirs of Madame Lebrun*, 1–21.

455   History and present state of Bohemia and of the Slavonian nations, 21–38.

456   Statistics of insanity in Europe, 39–54. **John Conolly?** Author shows wide knowledge of literature of insanity, and, pp. 52–54, advocates abolition of restraints, citing the example of the Retreat at York; see Conolly in *DNB*; Conolly wrote no. 283, also reviewing French medical books.

457   *History of Pope Pius VII*, 54–72.

458   Carl Ritter's researches in the Island of Hayti, 73–97.

459   Sanchoniatho's *History of Phoenicia* (No. II, concl.), 97–104.

460   Ancient music, 105–120.

461   German literature, 121–136. **Edmund Sydney Williams?** Williams worked for Black & Armstrong from 1836 and "frequently wrote reviews of German books" in *FQR* while they published it (until 1842); he was interested in German liberal theology, philosophical history, and oriental studies: see *Academy*, Sept. 5, 1891, pp. 196–197, and cf. pp. 122, 135–136 here.

462   Fresnel's *Letters on the History of the Arabs*, 137–157. **B. E. Pote?** In no. 493, p. 345, Pote refers to a passage of his which appeared in no. 449, but he wrongly cites "Arabian Antiquity" as the title of the art. and "last October" as the issue, plainly suggesting that he did this art. too.

463   Causes of the declaration of war between Buenos Ayres and Bolivia, 157–178. **B. E. Pote**, prob. Cf. no. 493; page 157 cites and summarizes no. 429.

464   [Critical sketches], 179–206. *Journal of an Hungarian Traveller in England*, 179–187; Dr. Lassen, *Ancient Persian Inscriptions*, 187–201, by **B. E. Pote**, prob.— see general evidence for no. 493, and no. 416 for concern with ancient Persia; Meyen, *Botanical Geography*, 201–206.

465   Miscellaneous literary notices, 207–213.

VOLUME 20, JANUARY 1838

466   Knebel's *Posthumous Works and Correspondence*, 221–253. **J. S. Blackie**. Reference on p. 240 is clearly to no. 445, pp. 334–335, and could hardly be editorial; similar views of Goethe here and in nos. 367, 380; lengthy quotations gathered under subject headings, pp.

238–240, had been used in no. 410. Carlylean style and references to Carlyle betray the disciple, as Carlyle himself called Blackie.

467 Popular elementary instruction, 254–287.

468 Early German comic romances, 287–309. **W. J. Thoms,** prob. Marked "W. Thoms" in Wellesley Coll. copy; p. 302n. refers to "our accomplished friend, Mr. Thomas Wright," which rules out a man who wrote on similar subjects for *FQR*.

469 Münch's *Studies* and *Recollections*, 310–327. **Mary Margaret Busk,** prob. Characteristic style and topic (see no. 345); foreign mistakes with English titles, p. 316, are a favorite target of hers (cf. no. 361, p. 360).

470 Present state of art in Russia, 328–339. **W. H. Leeds.** The reviewer had seen *Jurnal Izyashtshtnik Iskustv* "about ten or twelve years ago," p. 329: Leeds translated parts of this in *Foreign Rev.*, 1 (Jan. 1828), 335–339 (Leeds to Dawson Turner, Jan. 28, 1828, Trin. Coll. Camb.); p. 338n. refers the reader to no. 222, known to be by Leeds.

471 Heeren on the rise and progress of political theories, aristocracy and democracy, 340–369. **T. P. Courtenay.** Robinson, Transcripts, Jan. 29, 1838, reports "reading Courtenay's review of Heeren in the For: Quart: which he gave me."

472 Spanish poetry, 369–377.

473 The Hanoverian Constitution, and Royal Patent of November, 378–402. Pages 378–394 unidentified; pages 394–402 by **B. E. Pote,** prob. From the last paragraph on p. 394 to the end, there is a distinct change in point of view, the preceding being a specific treatment of the development of the Hanoverian Constitution, the later part a digressive discussion of change in governments; the style of the later section is typical of Pote (see no. 493), who was editing *FQR* at this time.

474 Mineralogical travels in the Ural and Altai mountains, 402–428.

475 View of Spanish affairs, 428–436.

476 [Critical sketch]: *Jonathan's Evenings* [by] X. B. Saintine, 437–441.

477 Miscellaneous literary notices, 442–450.

VOLUME 21, APRIL 1838

478 The Thugs, or Phansigars, 1–32.

479 Modern Italian narrative poetry, 33–45. **Mary Margaret Busk,** prob. Cf. no. 345

for her verse translations and note ending here similar to her trademark; ref. on p. 33 to her notice (no. 408) on Italian novels.

480 Courtet, *Political Science,* 46–56.

481 Russian novel writing, 56–78. **W. H. Leeds,** prob. Cf. general evidence for no. 177; opening sentence refers to "our" earlier notices of Russian literature (see no. 188 and arts. cited there) and to no. 470.

482 *Isabel de Solis,* by Martinez de la Rosa, 79–89.

483 Discovery of America by the Northmen before Columbus, 89–118. **Henry Wheaton.** *Wheaton,* p. 320.

484 The Abbé de La Mennais, 118–131.

485 Danish literature: Ingemann's novels, poems, and plays, 132–149.

486 *Peregrinations* [mainly in Peru] *of a Pariah* by Madame Flora Tristan, 150–188. Unidentified. With a concluding note, called Peru, Guiana and Navigation of the Amazons, 188–190, by **B. E. Pote,** prob.—cf. no. 429 which is here cited on pp. 188, 190, in words that strongly suggest a common authorship.

487 Canada, 191–220. **T. P. Courtenay.** Attr. in Robinson, Transcripts, May 5, 1838, which says "read . . . Courtenay's article in For. Quart: on Canada."

488 European and Asiatic poetry and tradition, 221–230. **B. E. Pote,** prob. Cf. no. 493 for Pote's interests and manner; specific references back to nos. 416, 462.

489 Critical notices, 230–234.

490 Miscellaneous literary notices, 235–241.

VOLUME 21, JULY 1838

491 Jung Stilling: religious literature of Germany, 247–283. **J. S. Blackie.** Claimed in *Testimonials.*

492 Queen Hortense, 284–315.

493 American literature [on] Chinese and Egyptian writing, 316–359. **B. E. Pote.** Attr. by P. W. Banks in *Fraser's Mag.,* 22 (July 1840), 67–68, where he quotes p. 359 of this art. "by Mr. Pote."; Pote's chief concerns were with Oriental and Mid-Eastern languages and races (see *BMCat.*) and with So. America; his style, while occasionally plain and expository (as in nos. 429 and 463), is more often florid, with extensive use of italics, capitalized words, and a manner that is highly "literary" and self-conscious; there is frequent ref. back to his own arts.

494 Grimm's *German Mythology,* 360–374.

Thomas Wright, 1810–1877. Repr. *Literature*, I.

495   Chateaubriand, *Spain,* 375–396. **T. P. Courtenay,** prob. Author states, p. 375, that "one of our earliest efforts" in dealing with foreign policy took up the same historical events (the Spanish War in no. 200); author frequently refers to nos. 185, 200 and 439.

496   Dutch literature, 397–413. Verse translation, pp. 398–400, by **B. E. Pote**— Mary Margaret Busk to the Blackwoods [endorsed "30 July/39" but references in letter indicate 1838], Nat. Lib. Scot., identifies translator of poetry of Van Lennep "in the last number" of *FQR* as the editor. OR, entire art. may be by **B. E. Pote:** cf. no. 507, where he did the verse and apparently the prose too.

497   Italian novels, 414–421. **Mary Margaret Busk,** prob. Characteristic style and topic (see no. 345); Mrs. Busk to the Blackwoods, Dec. 5, [1837], Nat. Lib. Scot., offers to do an art. on Italian historical novels; however, no such paper appears in *Blackwood's*; this essay fits her description of the art. in the letter cited; Mrs. Busk had written nos. 215, 265, and 408 on this subject.

498   Eugène Sue: French naval romances, 422–444.

499   Phoenician inscriptions, 445–462. **B. E. Pote,** prob. Cf. no. 493; page 460 refers to no. 416, p. 145 (though the footnote cites the wrong date).

500   [Critical sketches], 462–464.

501   Miscellaneous literary notices, 465–479.

VOLUME 22, OCTOBER 1838

502   Restoration of the fine arts of the middle ages in France (Part I), 1–34. **Harry Longueville Jones.** Attr. by W. H. Leeds in *Studies and Examples of the Modern School of English Architecture* (1839), p. 13, a book containing essays by Leeds and Charles Barry. (Part II is no. 519.)

503   *Malkolm* [by Henrich Steffens], 34–44. **Mary Margaret Busk,** prob. Characteristic style and topic (see no. 345).

504   Cuvier's life and labours, 45–71.

505   Sillig's *Dictionary of the Artists of Antiquity,* 72–100. **B. E. Pote?** Cf. no. 493; page 73 cites no. 493; no. 563, p. 385, cites this art.

506   Strauss: *Life of Christ,* 101–135.

507   Polish poetry, 135–153. **B. E. Pote,** prob. Pote to Macvey Napier, Sept. 9, 1842, Napier MS. 34,623, says he versified "almost literally" the "Castle of

Kaniov" in the *FQR* (pp. 140–145 here), and offers to do an art. for the *Edin. Rev.* on Polish poetry, partly dealing with a poem by one of the poets here reviewed; the long paragraph, p. 138, echoes Pote's preface to his *Assassins of Paradise,* 1831.

508   *Fermer the Genius,* 154–166.

509   Schlegel's *Essay on Egypt,* 167–182. **B. E. Pote,** prob. Cf. no. 493; pages 169 and 175 refer to nos. 441 and 416, respectively.

510   Russian position and policy towards Turkey, Circassia, Persia, and Hindostan, 183–213.

511   Critical sketches, 214.

512   Miscellaneous literary notices, 214–221.

VOLUME 22, JANUARY 1839

513   The Archbishop of Cologne: Prussia and Rome, 231–264. **John Hills.** Baron Bunsen to Hills, frequent letters from Oct. 1838 to Jan. 1839, Deutsches Zentralarchiv, Merseburg, discuss his arts. on "the Cologne business" and the publication date in *FQR.*

514   The ghost-seer of Prevorst, 265–275.

515   The dispatches of La Mothe-Fénélon, 276–298.

516   French colonial duties and German commercial league, 299–324. Unidentified. By a fugitive German Catholic revolutionary: see Bunsen, *Memoir,* I, 504, 509.

517   Italy, 325–347.

518   Schiller's flight [from Stuttgart], 348–355.

519   The fine arts in the middle ages in France (Part II), 356–358. **H. L. Jones,** prob. This is really the last part of no. 502: the writer speaks, p. 357, of "the other works in our title" but here there is only one work, which was apparently the seventh book Jones was reviewing on the same subject (there are six in no. 502); note similarity of title and that this review is too short to be an art. in its own right.

520   Chile, Peru, and American blockades, 359–373. **B. E. Pote,** prob. Cf. no. 493; pages 361 and 362 cite no. 463; see no. 429.

521   Arabs in Italy, Sicily, &c., 374–390. **B. E. Pote?** Cf. no. 493; review echoes many of Pote's usual ideas: "European and Asiatic families of mankind" spring from a common source, climate responsible for development, etc.

522 Chinese courtship, 390–406.
523 Müller: English and German scholarship, 407–441. **J. S. Blackie.** Claimed in *Testimonials.*
524 Music abroad and at home, 442–445.
525 Miscellaneous literary notices, 446–451.

VOLUME 23, APRIL 1839

526 On the law of storms, 1–23. **Basil Hall.** Marked as his in Wellesley Coll. copy; Hall to W. C. Redfield, Apr. 18, 1839, Beinecke Lib. Yale Univ., sends copy of recent art. in *FQR* in which he discussed Col. Reid's "Book on the Law of Storms": see p. 1n. and many later comments.
527 Progress of chemistry: ancient and traditional origin of chemistry, 23–61. **Henry Christmas,** 23–52, and **B. E. Pote,** prob. 53–61. Christmas's *Shores and Islands of the Mediterranean* (1851), I, 301–303, repeats pp. 32–33 here (both are basically translated from book by Dumas under review here, but both add one detail—Lully's visit to England—not in Dumas); p. 52 ends with line across bottom and p. 53 has new running title; moreover, p. 53 takes issue with pp. 25–26; pp. 54, 55n. cite nos. 416 and 464, both by Pote; for style cf. general evidence for no. 493; Pote, as editor, seems to be adding a commentary to someone else's article.
528 Creuzer and Knight: ancient figurative language, 62–82. **B. E. Pote,** prob. Cf. the general evidence for no. 493, which the author all but claims on p. 64; he also refers to nos. 416, 441, and 509, all prob. by Pote; cf. what is said of imagination, p. 71, with Pote's *The Assassins of the Paradise*, p. vii.
529 Labanoff: *Unpublished Letters of Mary Stuart*, 83–92.
530 Late proceedings in India: English usurpation of Oude, 93–116. **B. E. Pote** and a collab. Pages 102–116 seem to be Pote's: see general evidence for no. 493; in no. 543, p. 423, this part of the art. is referred to three times.
531 German literature and composition, 117–142.
532 The Austrian treaty, 143–160. Unidentified. By the author of no. 516, according to Bunsen to Baroness Bunsen, [Feb. 12, 1839], Deutsches Zentralarchiv, Merseburg; the art. continues the discussion of the German Commercial League: cf. p. 150 here with no. 516, p. 319.
533 Russian actual policy: Persia, Hindostan, and Central Asia, 161–212.

534 Photogenic drawings, 213–218.
535 Music abroad and at home, 219–223.
536 Miscellaneous literary notices, 224–229.

VOLUME 23, JULY 1839

537 Greek rhythm and metres: Boeckh, Apel, Hermann, Porson, Blomfield, &c., 241–294. **J. S. Blackie.** Claimed in *Testimonials.*
538 Versailles, 295–315. **Harry Longueville Jones.** Repr. *Essays and Papers*, 1870.
539 Lomonosov and his contemporaries: Russian literary biography, 316–339. **W. H. Leeds.** Page 319 refers to Naraezhny's *The Bursak*, which Leeds had described in no. 188, p. 122; for Leeds' knowledge of Russian literature see also nos. 188, 222, 270, 385, 481.
540 Albites, *Origin of the French Language and Literature*, 339–357.
541 Tieck's *Collected Tales*, 358–380.
542 Danilefsky, *Campaign of the Russians in France in 1814*, 380–410.
543 Russia, Persia, Turkey, and France, 411–443. **B. E. Pote** and a collab. Large parts of this art., especially the beginning and the end, seem to be Pote's (see general evidence for no. 493); detailed reference back to this in no. 564, pp. 386, 387.
544 Music abroad and at home, 444–453.
545 Miscellaneous literary notices, 454–458.

VOLUME 24, OCTOBER 1839

546 Views and objects of Mahomet in the composition of the Korann, 1–25.
547 Hungary: Mailáth's *History of the Magyars*, 26–55. **Mary Margaret Busk?** Characteristic style (cf. no. 345); Hungary denominated "Magyar-Orszag" on p. 33, as in no. 340, p. 459.
548 German influence upon the civilzation and progress of uncultivated nations, 56–75. **Edmund S. Williams?** See evidence for no. 461, and cf. pp. 65, 70, 72–75 here; emphasis again on individual liberty.
549 Industrial and moral state of Belgium, 75–89. **Thomas Colley Grattan,** prob. According to *Dublin Univ. Mag.,* 42 (1853), 662, Grattan contrib. "to the British and Foreign Reviews" between 1835 and 1839, chiefly on Belgium; also, ibid., he lived in Brussels and other Belgian cities, and author of this art. knew Belgium at first hand; there are many similarities of idea and phrasing between

this art. and two arts. on Belgium in *Brit. and For. Rev.*, 3 (July 1836), 1–23, and 7 (Oct. 1839), 521–569, to be assigned to Grattan in *Index*, III.

550   The philosophy of Kant, 90–106. **E. H. Michalowitz.** Claimed in his application to the R.L.F., Mar. 29, 1841.

551   The opium trade with China, 106–138.

552   *Arabian Nights*, 139–168. **B. E. Pote,** prob. Cf. general evidence for no. 493; p. 146 cites no. 441, and no. 561, p. 321, refers to this art.

553   De Kock's novels, 168–199.

554   [Critical sketch]: Raynouard, *Literature of Provence*, 200–202.

555   Music abroad and at home, 203–209.

556   Miscellaneous literary notices, 210–217.

VOLUME 24, JANUARY 1840

557   Merits of Euripides, 229–267. **J. S. Blackie.** Claimed in *Testimonials*.

558   Shubert, *Travels in the East*, 268–279. **Johann Lhotsky,** prob. Marked "Lhotsky" in Wellesley Coll. copy; Lhotsky to W. J. Hooker, Aug. 5, [1843], Kew Gardens Lib., describes his reviewing style as being "to translate & somewhat to arrange the most interesting portions of the work," which is the style of this art.; pp. 268–270 show anti-Catholic and anti-Austrian bias common throughout Lhotsky's letters and in his *Regeneration of Society*, 1844.

559   Indications of philosophic progress in America, 279–287.

560   Architecture at home and abroad, 288–312. **W. H. Leeds.** Marked as his in Wellesley Coll. copy; author refers on p. 292 to Schinkel with admiration; cf. no. 448, p. 377 and no. 177, p. 457; see general evidence for no. 177.

561   Identity of English, classical, and Oriental literature and interests, 313–335. **B. E. Pote.** Marked as his in Wellesley Coll. copy; cf. no. 493: pp. 321 and 334 cite nos. 552 and 441, respectively.

562   *Whist*, par Deschappelles, 335–350. **B. E. Pote.** Attr. by "Rudolf H. Rhein-hardt" [i.e., George Hempl], *Whist Scores and Card-Table Talk* (Chicago, 1887), p. 29; marked as his in Wellesley Coll. copy.

563   The Ethiopians: Apocryphal books of Isaiah and Enoch, 351–385. **B. E. Pote.** Marked as his in Wellesley Coll. copy; an offprint with special title page is signed B. E. Pote: see *BMCat.*

564   Turkey, Egypt, France, Russia, Asia, and the British Ministry, 386–421. **B. E.**

Pote. Cf. no. 493; marked as his in Wellesley Coll. copy; ref. on p. 409 back to no. 543, p. 440.

565   Critical sketches, 422.

566   Music abroad and at home, 423–439.

567   Miscellaneous literary notices, 440–445.

VOLUME 25, APRIL 1840

568   Egyptian hieroglyphics, 1–24. **Samuel Birch.** Marked as his in Wellesley Coll. copy; attr. in *BMCat.*

569   The old popular ballads and songs of Sweden (Part I), 25–48. **George Stephens.** J. W. Worthington to Stephens, Feb. 1, 1840, Kunglige Biblioteket, Stockholm, acknowledges receipt of this art.; marked as his in Wellesley Coll. copy.

570   State of British and continental historical literature, 49–56.

571   Russian survey of the north eastern coast of Siberia, 56–89. **E. W. P. Sinnett,** prob. Marked as his in Wellesley Coll. copy; Henry Wheaton to Catherine Wheaton, May 30 [1844], Pierpont Morgan Lib., describes Sinnett, an old friend, as "connected with the 'Foreign Quarterly.' "

572   The two parts of Goethe's *Faust*, 90–113.

573   *School for Journalists* [by Mᵐᵉ E. de Girardin], 113–130.

574   Tholuck's *Miscellaneous Writings in Defence of Religion*, 131–158.

575   Polish literature, 159–188.

576   War with China, 188–206.

577   Music abroad and at home, 207–215.

578   Miscellaneous literary notices, 216–223. Pages 221–223 by **George Stephens**—letter cited in no. 569 states: "*The Notices and Necrology* are also extremely useful," and mentions Bladh's book, which is reviewed here.

VOLUME 25, JULY 1840

579   Lessing's life and writings, 233–253. **J. S. Blackie.** Marked as his in Wellesley Coll. copy; p. 235 quotes from no. 410; the contrast of the English with the German temper, p. 244, is elaborated in no. 445, p. 300; what is said of Carlyle in evidence for no. 466 is also true here.

580   Church and State: Prussia, 254–281.

581   Bernadotte and Charles XIV. John, 282–317. **George Stephens.** Attr. in Erslew, *Supplement*; marked as his in Wellesley Coll. copy.

582   Fossil osteography, zoology and geo-

logy, 318–336. **Johann Lhotsky,** prob. See letter to Hooker cited in no. 558 and another, July 9, 1842, ibid., where he said, "I write occasionally for some of the Quarterlies" on natural history; writer speaks of the future of Australia (p. 330) and of discoveries in Brazil (p. 336) —Lhotsky had lived in Brazil, 1830–1832, and in Australia, 1832–1836 (see *Journal Proc. Royal Soc. New South Wales,* 42 [1908], 72–73).

583 *The French Described by Themselves,* 336–351.

584 Raumer, *Italy*; [and] *The Sulphur Monopoly,* 352–373.

585 South Australia, 374–393. **J. W. Worthington?** Reviewer mentions among his sources, p. 374, a letter from "a relative"; then on p. 391 "we subjoin extracts from a letter" written by "Mr. F. Worthington"; J. W. Worthington was now ed. of *FQR*.

586 Capital punishment [review of Victor Hugo's *The Last Days of a Condemned*], 394–406.

587 Raczynski: *History of Modern Art in Germany* [Vol. II], 406–419. **Henry Wheaton.** W. B. Lawrence, "Intro. Remarks" to Wheaton's *Elements of International Law* (6th ed., Boston, 1855), p. cliii, reported that Raczynski's book "was the subject of successive notices" by Wheaton in *FQR* as "each of the three volumes" appeared: cf. nos. 415, 655.

588 Michelet, *History of France,* 420–446.

589 The Gutenberg jubilee in Germany, 446–457. **G. C. F. Mohnike,** prob. Marked "Mohnicke" in Wellesley Coll. copy; man cited wrote *Die Geschichte der Buchdruckerkunst in Pommern* (Stettin, 1840) for the Gutenberg Jubilee; pp. 3–4 there on effects of printing press echo p. 447 here; see *ADB*.

590 Music abroad and at home, 457–464.

591 Miscellaneous literary notices, 465–469.

VOLUME 26, OCTOBER 1840

592 Ranke's *History of the Popes of Rome,* 1–28. **J. W. Worthington,** prob. Marked "Dr. Worthington" in Wellesley Coll. copy; anti-Romanist and particularly anti-Jesuit attitude throughout is found in many of Worthington's sermons and pamphlets (for example, his *Romish Usurpation,* 1850).

593 The old popular ballads and songs of Sweden (Part II, concl.), 29–56. **George Stephens.** Cf. no. 569; marked as his in

Wellesley Coll. copy; attr. in Erslew, *Supplement.*

594 Sclavonian antiquities, 57–80.

595 Herder, the protector of aboriginal people, 80–94. **Saxe Bannister,** prob. Marked "Bannister" in Wellesley Coll. copy; man cited was one of the founders of the Aborigines' Protective Society: see *DNB.*

596 Printing and publishing at home and abroad, 95–126. **Edward Kater,** prob. Marked "Kater" in Wellesley Coll. copy; no. 606 (also so marked), p. 317, implies he was familiar with Print Dept. of the British Museum; not only is Edward Kater of Downing Coll. Camb. the only Kater listed in the BM registers of admissions (on Feb. 6, 1840) but he was recommended by, and living with, Dr. J. W. Worthington, who became ed. of *FQR* in April 1840.

597 Chinese literature, 127–144. **Samuel Birch.** Marked "S. Birch" in Wellesley Coll. copy; Birch to Charles Atkinson, June 16, 1843, Univ. Coll. London, says he has "endeavored to diffuse a knowledge of [Chinese literature] by translations made in the Asiatic and other Journals."

598 Catherine de Medici, 145–165. **Antonio Gallenga.** *Episodes,* II, 90n.

599 Sparks's *Life of Washington,* 166–192.

600 Critical sketches of recent continental publications, 193–210. Pages 197–200 by **George Stephens**—Erslew, *Supplement*; pp. 200–203 by **G. C. F. Mohnike,** prob. —marked "Mohnicke" in Wellesley Coll. copy, cf. no. 589, and man cited had read a paper on the Minnesinger—subject of book under review—to the Litterarischgeselligen Verein zu Stralsund in 1836: see its *Bericht,* 1836.

601 Music abroad and at home, 211–222.

602 Miscellaneous literary notices, 223–228.

VOLUME 26, JANUARY 1841

603 *Memoirs of Varnhagen von Ense,* 241–265. **J. S. Blackie.** Stoddart, *Blackie,* I, 196; claimed in Blackie to Robert Blackwood, June 30, 1845, Nat. Lib. Scot.

604 Songs of the Ukraine, 266–289.

605 Copyright in Italy, 289–311. **Antonio Gallenga.** Partly repr. *Italy,* II, 375–379, 381–384.

606 Engraving, ancient and modern (Part I), 312–336. **Edward Kater,** prob. Marked "Kater" in Wellesley Coll. copy; see no. 596.

607 Fiedler's *Journey through Greece*, 337–369. **Henry Morley.** *Early Papers and Some Memories* (1891), p. 12.

608 Prince Pückler Muskau, *The South-Eastern Picture Gallery*, 369–387. **E. W. P. Sinnett,** prob. Marked as his in Wellesley Coll. copy; Sinnett was connected with the *FQR*: see no. 571.

609 Liberia in Africa: Governor Ashmun, 388–401.

610 Archives of the Athenian navy, 401–427. Unidentified. Marked "Dr. W. Christmas" in Wellesley Coll. copy, but no such person has been found; perhaps Dr. [James William] Worthington and [Henry] Christmas: the former, who was now editing *FQR*, was referred to by his contributors, including Christmas, as "Dr. W." (Julia Pardoe to Christmas [March? 1842?], Berg Collec., N.Y. Public Lib.); the latter was a close friend of his, a member of Society of Antiquaries, and a classicist (*Gent. Mag.,* 69 [May 1868], 681).

611 France and England: the Syrian question, 428–456. Pages 428–452, unidentified; pages 452–456, **Edward Clarkson,** prob. On p. 3 of his *Suez Canal,* he says he "advocated . . . elaborately" the Egyptian route to India in *FQR* when it was edited by Worthington (see pp. 454–456); concern with historical validity of Scripture (pp. 452–453) typical of Clarkson; wording on p. 452 suggests that two reviews by separate contributors may have been joined here.

612 Music abroad and at home, 456–470.

613 Miscellaneous literary notices, 471–476.

VOLUME 27, APRIL 1841

614 Italian drama, 1–37. **Antonio Gallenga.** Partly repr. *Italy,* II, 101–103, 167, 177, 197–207, 209–210. (The poem, p. 22, and possibly other selections here, trans. by **J. W. Worthington,** ibid., II, 171n.)

615 Inedited memoirs of Admiral Chicha-goff, a Russian minister of state, 38–56. **Henry Acton?** Admiral Chichagoff became a British citizen in 1834 (*Mémoires, 1767–1849* [Leipzig, 1862], pp. 6, 7) and was living in Brighton in 1841 (see this art., p. 39); author of this art. had access to the yet unpublished MSS. of the *Mémoires* (see p. 38); Acton, a native of Lewes with long-standing connections with the Brighton area (see *DNB*), was named joint executor of Chichagoff's will and was bequeathed a cameo ring (*Mé-*

moires, pp. 226, 228); he was "an occasional contributor" to several periodicals ("Memoir" prefixed to Acton's *Sermons* [1846], p. xcvii).

616 Rahel, 57–74. **J. S. Blackie.** Stoddart, *Blackie,* I, 191.

617 Engraving, ancient and modern (Part II), 74–101. **Edward Kater,** prob. Cf. no. 606.

618 Tezcuco, 102–118.

619 Rousseau's *Nouvelle Heloise* and the modern Littérature Extravagante, 118–141.

620 Britanny, 142–162.

621 French manufactures, 162–184.

622 Romanism and Catholicism, 184–199.

623 Critical sketches of recent continental publications, 200–210.

624 Music abroad and at home, 211–222.

625 Miscellaneous literary notices, 223–229.

VOLUME 27, JULY 1841

626 State of the Jews in Poland, 241–264.

627 Geography of the Arabs, 265–283.

628 Punishments and prisons in Sweden, 283–296. **George Stephens.** Erslew, *Supplement.*

629 Education in Italy, 297–327. **Antonio Gallenga.** Partly repr. *Italy,* II, 265–274, 277–278, 283–296.

630 Bancroft's *History of the United States,* 327–361.

631 Clot-Bey's *General Observations on Egypt,* 362–393.

632 *Christian Doctrines and Modern Science* [by D. F. Strauss], 394–418. **J. W. Worthington,** prob. Article is clearly written by someone with theological training, close ties with the university world, and scientific, especially astronomical, interests; see Boase, and J. H. C. Wright to J. O. Halliwell, Nov. 26, 1839, Edin. Univ. Lib., referring to Worthington as "that prodigy of scientific and classical lore," who has great "zeal for astronomical pursuits."

633 France and Europe, 419–443.

634 Critical sketches of recent continental publications, 444–454. Pages 450–454 by **Ottavio degli Albizzi,** prob., who wrote George Long, Feb. 7, 1842, Univ. Coll. London, that he had "furnished some articles to the foreign quarterly Review, the frazer Magazine, etc. etc."; writer is Italian (p. 451) and has poorer command of English than other writers on Italy in *FQR*; pages 448–450 may be by **Henry Christmas**—reviewer has someone call him "Don Enrico," p. 449, and Christmas, in *Shore & Islands of the Mediterranean* (1851), I, 227, has someone call him "Señor Don Enrique"; book and notice stress pleasures of travelling with little luggage and on foot or horseback (*Shores*, I, ix, and p. 448 here).

635 Music abroad and at home, 455–465.

636 Miscellaneous literary notices, 466–475.

VOLUME 28, OCTOBER 1841

637 Roman tablets and cursive hand, 1–21.

638 Sybel's *History of the First Crusade*, 22–45.

639 Hügel's *Travels in Cashmere*, 45–63.

640 Rüppell's *Travels in Abyssinia*, 64–90. **W. D. Cooley?** Cooley to Macvey Napier, Sept. 9, 1835, Napier MS. 34,617, suggests this book for review while it is still "in preparation," and adds that Rüppell's observations confirm his own conclusions on Bruce's barometrical observations (cf. p. 65 here); the *ER* review was not by Cooley (see *Index*, I, 490).

641 The women of Italy, 91–115. **Antonio Gallenga.** Partly repr. *Italy*, II, 302–310, 313–315, 319–328, 330–331.

642 Kohl's *Travels in Southern Russia*, 116–142.

643 Sweden as it is (Part I), 143–173. **George Stephens.** J. W. Worthington to Stephens, Feb. 1, 1840, Kunglige Biblioteket, Stockholm, says "The condition of Sweden will also form an interesting article"; attr. in Erslew, *Supplement*.

644 *History of Romance Languages*, 173–205.

645 *The Convention of July 13*, 206–232.

646 Music abroad and at home, 232–245.

647 Miscellaneous literary notices, 246–249.

VOLUME 28, JANUARY 1842

648 Egyptian hieroglyphics, 263–286. **Samuel Birch.** Attr. in *BMCat.*; cf. no. 568.

649 Barante's *History of the Dukes of Burgundy*, 287–305.

650 Roepell's *History of Poland*, 306–333.

651 *The Works of William von Humboldt*, 334–362.

652 The aristocracy of Italy, 362–397. **Antonio Gallenga.** Largely repr. *Italy*, II, 235–260.

653 Kohl's *Sketches of St. Petersburg*, 398–434.

654 Sweden as it is (Part II, concl.), 434–455. **George Stephens.** Cf. no. 643.

655 Raczynski's *History of Modern Art in Germany* [Vol. III], 455–468. **Henry Wheaton.** *Wheaton*, p. 320; cf. nos. 415, 587.

656 Considerations upon England, 469–493.

657 Critical sketches of recent continental publications, 494–498. Pages 496–498 (5 notices) by **Ottavio degli Albizzi,** prob., see no. 634.

658 Miscellaneous literary notices, 499–505.

VOLUME 29, APRIL 1842

659 The past and present state of Servia, 1–31.

660 The Baltic provinces of Russia, 32–68.

661 *Letters of Henri Quatre*, 69–105.

662 The French police, 106–138. **George Stovin Venables.** John Forster to ?, Mar. 15, 1842, Huntington Lib., said that Venables and Thackeray (see no. 663) would have arts. in "this number"; this art. is clearly written by an English lawyer with a knowledge of the classics— cf. *DNB* and Thackeray, *Letters*, II, 64, on Venables; the latter implies, ibid., that "Venables" contributed to *FQR*; man cited was the only Venables mentioned in Thackeray's *Letters*; this art. expresses various sentiments, notably those on liberty, found in other contributions of his to the Review.

663 *The Rhine* [by Victor Hugo], 139–167. **W. M. Thackeray.** Thackeray, *Letters*, II, 42, 44, 830; repr. *New Sketch Book*.

664 The Druzes, their creed and its sources, 168–203. **B. E. Pote.** Claimed in Pote to Macvey Napier, Sept. 9, 1842, Napier MS. 34,623.

665 On the rise and progress of Magyar literature, 204–227. **Julia Pardoe.** Claimed in "Letters," p. 373.

666 Monumental history of Spain, 228–238.

667 Critical sketches of recent continental publications, 239–253. Pages 239–241 by **Ottavio degli Albizzi?**—cf. nos. 634, 657, and note reference by reviewer, p. 239, to "the Medici, Albizzi, Strozzi."

668 Miscellaneous literary notices, 254–259.

669 Music in Italy, 260–266.

VOLUME 29, JULY 1842

670 The Reign of Terror: its causes and results, 274–308. **E. G. Bulwer-Lytton.** Repr. *Prose Works*, I.

671   Characteristics of German genius, 309–329. **John Sterling.** Repr. *Essays*, I.

672   Latin poetry, ancient and modern: *The Writings of Catullus*, 329–369. **Walter Savage Landor.** Repr. *Works*, XI.

673   The German in England, 370–383. **W. M. Thackeray.** Thackeray, *Letters*, II, 70; repr. *New Sketch Book*.

674   The last fifteen years of the Bourbons, 384–420. **W. M. Thackeray.** Thackeray, *Letters*, II, 42, 70.

675   Friedrich Baron de la Motte Fouqué, 421–450.

676   Eugene Sue's *Mathilde*, 451–464.

677   Tasso and Chatterton, 465–483. **Robert Browning.** Repr. as *Browning's Essay on Chatterton*, ed. Donald Smalley, Cambridge, Mass., 1948.

678   The American envoy and the King of the French, 484–490. Unidentified. Possibly Walter Keating Kelly; comments on Louis Philippe and his government, pp. 486–487, 489, in content and even in wording, are closely echoed by Kelly's *Narrative of the French Revolution of 1848*, pp. 7, 10–11; cf. no. 771.

679   [Critical sketches], 491–534: Demidoff's *Travels in Russia*, 491–501; *The Coins and Antiquities of Afghanistan*, 501–510, is perhaps by Henry Christmas, numismatist (see *DNB*); *History of Holland*, 510–512; *The Kingdom of Venetian Lombardy*, 512–513; *Roman Letters of the Latter Period of the Republic*, 513–514; *Sights and Thoughts in Foreign Churches* [by F. W. Faber], 514–516; *Excursions along the Shores of the Mediterranean*, 516–518; *Memoirs of Baron von Asseburg*, 518–519; *The Court and Times of Frederick the Great*, 519–520; *Ecclesiastical History of the Present Day*, 520–521; Erman's *Journey round the World*, 522; *The Education of Mothers of Families*, 522–523; German tales and novels, 524–527; Frédéric Soulié, *Prétendus*, 527–528; Alphonse Karr's *Am Rauchen*, 529; Mme de Cubieres' *M. de Goldon*, 529–530; Mme Dudevant's *Horace*, 530–532; *Lays of the Middle Age*, 532–534.

680   Foreign correspondence, 542–550. Pages 548–550 by **George Stephens**—attr. in Erslew, *Supplement*.

681   Miscellaneous literary notices, 551–562.

VOLUME 30, OCTOBER 1842

682   French criticism of English writers, 1–12.

683   Anselm of Canterbury, 13–35.

684   *Celebrated Crimes* [by Alexandre Dumas], 36–60. **T. A. Trollope,** prob. Cf. the procedure of dealing successively with specific individuals with that of Trollope's *Decade of Italian Women*; for the fascination with crime, the skepticism about "the good old days," and the superiority of the nineteenth century, see evidence for no. 800.

685   The first philosophers of Greece, 61–92. **John Forster.** Included in a vol. of his *FQR* arts., bound together by Forster himself, Forster Collection, Victoria and Albert Museum.

686   Russegger's *Travels in Egypt*, 93–104. **Bayle St. John,** perhaps with **James Augustus St. John.** The writer of no. 765, p. 403, cites this art. in terms that suggest a common authorship; attitude toward Mehemet Ali in both arts. is the same; Egyptian opthalmia is dwelt upon to a disproportionate degree in this short review, pp. 101–103, undoubtedly because J. A. St. John contracted it in 1832–1834 and suffered ever after from its effects (see his *There and Back Again in Search of Beauty* [1853], II, 289); the style seems to be Bayle St. John's (for example, the Shakespearean quotation, p. 104, the delicate ironies, p. 93); *DNB* shows that Bayle St. John, unlike his father, had not yet been in Egypt, so that he might well have needed some first-hand information.

687   Travelling romancers: Dumas on the Rhine, 105–124. **W. M. Thackeray.** Attr. in Ray, *Thackeray*, I, 484, on the basis of an unpublished Thackeray letter which says that this art. was forwarded to Forster; p. 106 refers to "our" notice of Hugo, no. 663; the ironic sneers at the French, the frequent references of the author to himself, the sarcasm directed at pretentious writing and living are all characteristic.

688   *Letters of the Queen of Navarre*, 125–149. **W. K. Kelly?** Pages 127–142 are almost completely duplicated in Kelly's "Preface" and "Memoir" prefixed to *The Heptameron of Margaret, Queen of Navarre* (1855), pp. v, xix–xxxvii, xl; the one additional detail here, p. 135, is that a "demoiselle de Keilly" became a mistress of Francis I.

689   *Naples and the Neapolitans*, 150–157.

690   Gervinus, *German Literature*, 158–160.

691   *The Idyls of Theocritus*, 161–190. **Walter Savage Landor.** Repr. Landor, *Works*, XII.

692   *Memoirs of Barère*, 191–196.
693   The newspaper literature of America, 197–222. **John Forster.** Evidence for no. 685. (See no. 727.)
694   Short reviews of recent publications, 223–241.
695   Foreign correspondence, 251–258. Pages 255–258 by **George Stephens**—attr. in Erslew, *Supplement.*
696   Sismonde de Sismondi, 258–261.
697   Miscellaneous literary notices, 262–265.

VOLUME 30, JANUARY 1843

698   Hoffmeister on Schiller, 281–315. Unidentified. Attr. to a German in Crabb Robinson, Transcripts, Feb. 19, 1843, which is supported by the trans. of the title of book being reviewed, p. 281, and the unidiomatic English of the extracts.
699   Charles Gutzkow's *Paris*, 316–330. **A. V. Kirwan.** Reviewer has lived extensively in France since 1822 or earlier (see Kirwan, *FM* no. 4023, pp. 389–399); is interested in French journalism and Irish questions (p. 320; see "Essays" and Boase); knows German and Germans (Kirwan lived in Munich and Vienna, 1830–1831); finds English parallels to Continental people and situations (pp. 320, 321), a hallmark of Kirwan's style (cf. nos. 762, 768, 787); was apparently born a few years before 1806 (p. 321; Kirwan was born in 1804); the brief sketches of prominent French men—even the same men—are found in Kirwan's essays in *Modern France.*
700   Socrates and the Sophists of Athens, 331–368. **John Forster.** Evidence for no. 685.
701   Balzac's *Provincial Bachelor's Household*, 369–380.
702   The Countess Hahn-Hahn's *Letters*, 381–396.
703   Forti's *Civil Institutes*, 397–413.
704   George Sand's *Consuelo*, 414–428.
705   *The King of Saxony's Travels in Montenegro*, 429–434.
706   Musset's *White Thrush*, 435–438.
707   Klopstock, 439–465. **J. S. Blackie.** Claimed in *Testimonials*, dated 1841; Stoddart, *Blackie*, I, 220.
708   The newspaper press of France, 466–498. **J. F. Corkran.** Claimed in application to R.L.F., Mar. 31, 1862.
709   Short reviews of recent publications, 499–524.
710   Foreign correspondence, 531–533.
711   Miscellaneous literary notices, 534–544.

VOLUME 31, APRIL 1843

712   Immermann's new *Münchhausen*, 1–23.
713   Schlosser's *History of the Eighteenth Century*, 24–57.
714   George Herwegh's *Poems*, 58–72. **W. M. Thackeray.** In *Letters*, II, 100–101, Thackeray speaks of having done two arts. in March for this issue of *FQR*: one is certainly no. 726; this is much the most likely to be the second: see Ray, *Thackeray*, I, 484, 485; repr. *New Sketch Book.*
715   Von Lang's *Autobiography*, 73–81.
716   French poetry and translation, 82–91. **John Frazer Corkran?** Corkran was a friend of L. de Wailly, whose translation of Burns is noticed here; p. 83 quotes in full one of Corkran's favorites among the translations (see Henriette Corkran's *Celebrities*, p. 76); Corkran, who was a minor poet, lived in Paris for many years (Boase); he contributed to *FQR* (*Athenaeum*, Feb. 9, 1884, p. 186).
717   Kohl's *Hundred Days in Austria*, 92–117.
718   The politics and the verses of Lamartine, 118–129.
719   Facts and feelings from the life of Steffens, 130–139. **J. S. Blackie.** See evidence for no. 799.
720   English history and character on the French stage, 140–168. **W. M. Thackeray?** Attr. by Ray, *Thackeray*, I, 485, on basis of unpublished letter of Forster to Thackeray, Mar. 14, 1842, "I'll send you the French Order in the course of the day," which may refer to the French books he needs for his review; repr. *New Sketch Book*, where editor, R. S. Garnett, pp. ix–x, cites parallels in ideas and style between this art. and a chapter of the *Paris Sketch Book*; however, the letter cited in no. 714 refers to his having written only two arts. in Mar. for this issue—viz., almost surely nos. 714 and 726; perhaps this had been done earlier.
721   *Reminiscences of Ernest Maurice Arndt*, 169–181. **J. S. Blackie.** Claimed in Blackie to Robert Blackwood, June 30, 1845, Nat. Lib. Scot.
722   Balzac on the newspapers of Paris, 182–187. Unidentified. Attr. to W. M. Thackeray by Ray, *Thackeray*, I, 484, 485, and repr. *New Sketch Book*; but evidence Ray cites ("Did you think of Janin?"), coming immediately after the remark in Forster's letter quoted in no. 720, would more likely refer to adding Janin to "the French Order"; and we already have

suggested three arts. by Thackeray for an issue for which he wrote only two in Mar.: see evidence for no. 714.

723 Moeser's *Collected Works*, 188–192.

724 Victor Hugo's *Burgraves of the Rhine*, 193–198. **J. F. Corkran?** In his widow's application to R.L.F., May 7, 1884, she mentions his article on Hugo.

725 *The Comedies of Plautus*, 199–230.

726 Thieves' literature of France, 231–249. **W. M. Thackeray.** *Letters*, II, 92.

727 The answer of the American press, 250–281. **John Forster.** See evidence for no. 685. (See no. 693.)

728 Short reviews of recent publications, 282–288.

729 Foreign correspondence, 289–292.

730 Miscellaneous literary notices, 293–304.

VOLUME 31, JULY 1843

731 The life and works of Rabelais, 313–346.

732 Habits and superstitions of the Bretons, 347–375.

733 Niebuhr's *Posthumous Works*, 376–395.

734 Francesco Petrarca, 396–426. **Walter Savage Landor.** Repr. *Works*, XII.

735 The Marquis de Custine's *Russia*, 427–437.

736 Arago's *Life of Herschel*, 438–453.

737 Napoleon and Maria Louisa, 454–464.

738 Gautier in Spain, 465–470.

739 The Dialogues of Plato, 471–501. **John Forster.** See evidence for no. 685.

740 The Spanish drama: Lope de Vega and Calderon, 502–539. **G. H. Lewes.** "Receipts"; repr. as a signed pamphlet, 1846.

741 Capefigue's *Europe during the Revolution*, 540–543.

742 Dr. Francia, 544–589. **Thomas Carlyle.** Repr. *Essays*, IV.

743 Short reviews of recent publications, 590–599.

744 Miscellaneous literary notices, 600–612.

VOLUME 32, OCTOBER 1843

745 Jean Jacques Rousseau, 1–33. **T. A. Trollope?** Since Trollope had written on George Sand a few months earlier (*For. and Colonial Quart. Rev.*, Apr. 1843), he would have been interested in a new edition of the *Confessions* to which she contributed a "Notice," extensively quoted here, pp. 4–6; the style is often imitative of Carlyle (see pp. 3, 4, 12, 33, for examples), and contains some French

and Latin phrases, with an Italian quotation on p. 32n.: cf. evidence for no. 800.

746 Arndt's *Sketches of Swedish History*, 34–60. **J. S. Blackie.** *Letters to His Wife*, pp. 109–110.

747 Louis Blanc's *History of Ten Years* [Vols. I–III], 61–75. **G. H. Lewes.** Scrapbooks, IV; pp. 65–75 are, as Lewes partially acknowledges on p. 65, a précis of Blanc's *Histoire de Dix Ans, 1830–1840*, II (Paris, 1842), 41–72.

748 Death and dying in France, 76–89.

749 The English on the continent, 90–106.

750 Venetian embassies to France in the 16th century, 107–134.

751 The Hôtel de Rambouillet, 135–159. **J. F. Corkran.** Claimed as in no. 708.

752 Augustus William Schlegel, 160–181. **G. H. Lewes.** "Receipts."

753 Carus, *Göthe*, 182–189.

754 Capefigue's *Diplomatists*, 190–196.

755 German plays and actors, 197–225.

756 French romancers on England, 226–246. **W. M. Thackeray**, prob. Attr. by Ray, *Thackeray*, I, 485, on stylistic grounds; p. 226 refers to no. 726, and pp. 232, 234, to no. 663; sentiments on pp. 227, 228, 231, 245 are typical of Thackeray; repr. *New Sketch Book*.

757 [General] Espartero, 247–262.

758 Short reviews of recent publications, 263–273.

759 Miscellaneous literary notices, 274–283.

VOLUME 32, JANUARY 1844

760 American poetry, 291–324.

761 Buchez and Daunou on the science of history, 325–346. **G. H. Lewes.** "Receipts."

762 The Congress of Vienna, 347–370. **A. V. Kirwan.** Title listed in "Essays," but periodical not named; author speaks of having been in Moscow and St. Petersburg, p. 361, and of having known Nowosiltzoff in Poland, p. 362—all of which is true of Kirwan: see evidence for *FM* no. 2059 below.

763 Calendars and almanacs, 371–386. Unidentified. Possibly W. K. Kelly, later ed. *FQR*, whose *Proverbs of All Nations* (1859), p. 212, quotes (as here, p. 376), Sir Thomas Browne and popular sayings. OR, Thomas Wright, 1800–1877, whose *Literature*, I, 131, uses some of proverbs given here, pp. 376–377.

764 Mignet's *Historical Essays*, 387–401. **G. H. Lewes.** "Receipts."

765 Pallme's *Travels in Kordofan*, 402–423.

Bayle St. John, perhaps with **J. A. St. John.** Page 413 gives a description of native hairdos which first appears in J. A. St. John's *Egypt, and Mohammed Ali* (1834), I, 378; language here, however, is more like Bayle's; Bayle was co-author with his father of a new revision of *Egypt, and Mohammed Ali*, announced by Ollier as "in the Press" in June 1846 but never published.

766 The Ethnological Societies of London and Paris, 424–435. **Bayle St. John.** On p. 426 author discusses the formation of the Ethnological Society in such detail as to suggest he was personally involved, and on p. 435 he refers to Society materials as "our" materials (see *DNB*); on p. 429 a paper given at the Society by J. A. St. John, Bayle's father, is discussed in detail; reviewer, like Bayle at this time, had not been in Egypt but knew men who had (see p. 427).

767 M. L. de Tegoborski, *The Finances and Public Credit of Austria*, 436–462. **Cyrus Redding,** prob. In application to R.L.F., May 15, 1862, he claims a review of Tegoborski in "Foreign Review . . . 1843."

768 Maret, Duke of Bassano, 463–470. **A. V. Kirwan,** prob. Listed in "Essays"; this is only art. under "Maret" in Poole; the style is characteristic: cf. description in *FM* no. 2307.

769 New accounts of Paris, 470–490. **W. M. Thackeray.** Thackeray, *Letters*, II, 126; repr. *New Sketch Book*.

770 Sinde, its amírs, and its people, 491–524.

771 Short reviews of recent publications, 525–541. Pages 527–530 by **Walter K. Kelly**—page 530 is expanded in his *Narrative of the French Revolution of 1848* (1848), pp. 11–13, which on pp. 8–9 quotes from book here under review.

772 Miscellaneous literary notices, 542–556.

VOLUME 33, APRIL 1844

773 Dante Allighieri, 1–30. **Giuseppe Mazzini.** Repr. *Scritti*, XXIX. Trans. by **Geraldine Jewsbury**—*New Letters and Memorials of Jane Welsh Carlyle*, ed. Alexander Carlyle (1903), I, 123.

774 Zschokke's *Autobiography*, 31–58. **Jane Sinnett.** Attr. in Henry Wheaton to Catherine Wheaton, letter cited in no. 571, on basis of letter from Mrs. Sinnett's sister.

775 St. Marc Girardin's *Lectures on the Drama*, 59–78. **G. H. Lewes.** "Receipts."

776 English and French rivalry in eastern Africa, 79–111. **Bayle St. John** and **J. A. St. John.** See evidence for no. 765; J. A. St. John's collab. is supported by the use of "we ourselves" (see p. 81), implying that the author had been in Africa, which Bayle was not until 1846 (see *DNB*); moreover, there is a shift of style about p. 84, the earlier part of the art. being generally in J. A. St. John's manner, the latter part in Bayle's.

777 Geijer's *History of the Swedes*, 112–135.

778 Commercial policy of Russia, 136–152.

779 Popular poetry of the Bretons, 153–180.

780 Rise and progress of culinary literature and cookery, 181–212. **A. V. Kirwan.** Repr. *Host and Guest*, 1864, as "Ancient and Medieval Cookery."

781 Problematic invasion of British India, 213–229. Unidentified. Possibly W. M. Thackeray, who offered, Feb. 23, 1844 (see *Letters*, II, 161), to review this book for the next issue; the style, however, does not seem to be his.

782 Short reviews of recent publications, 230–243. Pages 230–233 by **John Relly Beard,** prob.—Prof. K. A. Credner of Giessen to Beard, Apr. 8, 1844, Unitarian Coll. Manchester, writes of Beard's work for *FQR*, referring in this context to the need for a sound and impartial history of Rationalism (cf. p. 232 here); see also first evidence cited for no. 796, pp. 520–523.

783 Miscellaneous literary notices, 244–260.

VOLUME 33, JULY 1844

784 Balzac and George Sand, 265–298. **G. H. Lewes.** "Receipts."

785 Fontanier's Eastern mission, 299–320. **J. A. St. John,** prob. The sentiment, p. 306, "better a bad religion than no religion at all" is also developed in *FQR* nos. 124, pp. 489–497, and 901, p. 522; style is J. A. St. John's carefully straightforward, correct usage, rather than the more playful and colloquial idiom of Bayle St. John, who also deals with similar subjects; moreover, writer seems to have been in East (pp. 304, 306), as Bayle had not.

786 Dahlmann's *History of the English Revolution*, 321–330.

787 The French and English Bar, 331–371. **A. V. Kirwan.** Characteristic subject and style (see *FM* no. 2307); in *FM* no. 4068, p. 196, known to be by Kirwan, four sentences are repeated, almost verbatim, from pp. 357, 358, and 365 of this art.

788 The German newspaper press, 371–387.
789 The Anglo-Indian army, 388–432.
790 Michiel's *England*, 433–442. **W. M. Thackeray,** prob. Attr. by Ray, *Thackeray*, I, 485 on stylistic grounds; on p. 436 author refers to his previous arts. on "Victor Hugo and Alexander Dumas" (see nos. 663 and 687); repr. *New Sketch Book*.
791 Recent revolutions in Hayti, 443–458.
792 German and English translators from the Greek, 459–477. **G. H. Lewes.** "Receipts."
793 Schiller's *Minor Poems*: [translations by E. Bulwer-Lytton and John Herman Merivale], 478–497. **G. S. Venables.** G. H. Lewes to E. G. Bulwer-Lytton, Dec. 22, 1846, Hertfordshire Public Record Office, assigns to "Venables"; man cited wrote on Varnhagen Von Ense in *Blackwood's*, July 1839 (see *Index*, I); cf. no. 662 for further identification.
794 *The Chronicle of the Kings of Norway*, 498–503.
795 The navy of France, 503–519. **A. V. Kirwan,** prob. Art. discusses mainly *The Ports, Arsenals, and Dockyards of France, by a Traveller*, explaining how it came to be written: book was by Kirwan himself (see Boase); ends abruptly with discussion of Irish independence, another of Kirwan's interests (see *FM* no. 4329).
796 Short reviews of recent publications, 520–526. Pages 520–523 by **J. R. Beard,** prob.—Beard to Gebauer (bookseller in Halle), Apr. 1844, draft at Unitarian Coll. Manchester, says he is responsible for reviews of theological works in *FQR*; same point is made in advertisement in *Augsburg Allgemeine Zeitung*, Oct. 29, 1844, p. 2422.
797 Miscellaneous literary notices, 527–532.

VOLUME 34, OCTOBER 1844

798 Ireland from 1645 to 1649: *Mission of Rinuccini as Papal Nuncio*, 1–26.
799 *Memoirs of Henry Steffens*: the Liberation War in Germany, 26–41. **J. S. Blackie.** Stoddart, *Blackie*, I, 220, gives this title but gives date of no. 719, of which this is a continuation; both are certainly Blackie's.
800 The plague of Milan in the year 1630, 42–69. **Thomas Adolphus Trollope.** From the 30s through the 60s, Trollope wrote an enormous number of arts. in reviews and magazines (see *What I Re-*

member, II, 1–2, 18, 215; III, 63–64), many of them dealing, like those for *Household Words*, with "tid-bits from the byways of Italian history" (ibid., II, 119)—and of French history too—with emphasis on tales of corruption, crime, and torture. His style is sometimes imitative of Carlyle in *The French Revolution*, is marked in greater or less degree by the use of foreign phrases and Latin tags, and is always lively, however, antiquarian the material, largely because it combines, as he pertinently says on p. 42, "the startling strangeness and the minuteness of detail by which fiction arrests our sympathies, with the absorbing interest inseparable from the . . . consideration, that 'these things really were'." The main recurring notes are distaste for talk of "the good old times" (see *Filipo Strozzi* [1860], pp. 9–10), confidence in the moral superiority of the nineteenth century (see *Girlhood of Catherine de Medici* [1856], p. vi), and especially complaint about the distortion of history by Italian writers under pressure of political or clerical censorship. Much of all this applies to this art., where the Latin quotation, p. 51, is also found in *What I Remember*, I, 212.

801 The Punjâb, 70–104.
802 Domestic life in the [American] slave states, 104–129.
803 Beneke's *Theory and Practice of Education*, 130–148. **J. S. Blackie.** Attr. in E. Beneke to Blackie, Mar. 15, 1845, Nat. Lib. Scot.
804 English opinions on Germany, 148–164.
805 French aggressions in the Pacific, 165–194. **Bayle St. John.** Attr. in *DNB*.
806 The military power of Russia, 194–221.
807 Sacrifice of British ambassadors in Central Asia, 221–238.
808 Short reviews of recent publications, 239–250.
809 Foreign correspondence, 251–254.
810 Miscellaneous literary notices, 255–260.

VOLUME 34, JANUARY 1845

811 Hormayr's *Reminiscences of the Wars in Germany*, 265–289. **J. S. Blackie.** Blackie to Robert Blackwood, June 30, 1845, Nat. Lib. Scot., says he reviewed "the German work the *Lebensbilder*" (title of work under review) in Jan. *FQR*.
812 Vico and the Princess Belgiojoso, 289–303. **T. A. Trollope,** prob. See the gen-

eral evidence for no. 800; the beautiful Princess Belgiojoso's salons and her playing duets with Liszt, p. 290, are described by Trollope in *What I Remember*, I, 286–287.

813 Bettina Brentano, 304–324.

814 Records of early Italian art, 324–352. **James Dennistoun.** Claimed in Dennistoun to William Mure, June 9, 1845, Nat. Lib. Scot.

815 [Ferdinand] Freiligrath's *Poems*, 352–369. **W. K. Kelly.** Claimed as in no. 831.

816 *Rambles and Recollections of an Indian Official*, 369–389.

817 Projected ship canal across the great American isthmus, 389–400. **Bayle St. John,** prob., perhaps with **Percy St. John.** Bayle St. John wrote "a series of papers" which advocated a railway from Cairo to Suez (*Village Life*, II, 176–177; see pp. 390–391 here); author adopts attitudes often found in Bayle's arts.: attacks French politicians, Louis-Philippe, and the Tories, all p. 390; Percy St. John, according to his father, "bestowed much attention on parts of Central America" before 1853 (J. A. St. John, *There and Back*, I, vii).

818 Music in Germany and Belgium: its progress, present state, and prospects, 400–420.

819 Field sports of South Africa, 421–431.

820 British intercourse with China, 432–449. **Bayle St. John,** prob. The art. is strongly anti-French and anti-Jesuit, as is no. 805; both arts. make use of unpublished MSS. by missionaries belonging to the London Missionary Society; at this time St. John was in contact with the Society and was writing on "political questions of the day" for *FQR* (see *DNB*).

821 Niebuhr, Michelet, and Mérimée, 450–478, **G. H. Lewes.** Scrapbooks, V.

822 Lord Ellenborough's Indian policy, 479–514.

823 Short reviews of recent publications, 515–519. Pages 515–517 by **W. J. Thoms** (all except last paragraph)— Samuel Naylor to H. C. Robinson, Jan. 10, 1845, Robinson Transcripts, attrs., on Thom's authority, the short notice of recent Reynards in *FQR* to Thoms, and adds that Thoms disclaimed the last paragraph.

824 Foreign correspondence, 520–534. Pages 520–527 by **T. A. Trollope,** who seems to have been the *FQR* correspondent in Florence, where he was living, from Nov. 1844 to Apr. 1846—cf. the cumulative evidence for nos. 837, 862, 877, 890 (in most of which "Mr. Editor" or "dear Mr.

Editor" are inserted, as here, normally in the first sentence), and Trollope's customary use of foreign phrases; what is said of Niccolini's history of the Hohenstauffen, p. 526, is paraphrased in Theodosia Garrow [Trollope's] trans. of Niccolini's *Arnold of Brescia* (1846), p. vi (see letter, vol. 35, pp. 259–260, signed **Cesare Balbo,** with title "Count"); pages 528–534 by **T. A. Trollope,** prob. —he was at this Congress (*Diario della sesta riunione degli scienziate italiani convocati in Milano nel settembre 1844*, Milan [1845]), and when recalling it in *Impressions of a Wanderer* (1850), p. 3, uses same phraseology as on p. 529 here.

VOLUME 35, APRIL 1845

825 Pictures and picture-dealing, 1–34. **James Dennistoun.** Claimed in *Memoirs of the Dukes of Urbino* (1851), II, 466.

826 The history of British India, 34–55.

827 The *Antigone* and its critics, 56–73. **G. H. Lewes.** "Receipts."

828 The heroic ages of the North, 74–98. **Jane Sinnett.** Henry Wheaton, letter cited in no. 571, has accepted Mrs. Sinnett's offer to review Guillot's trans. of Wheaton's *Hist. of the Northmen*, here under review.

829 Heinzen's prohibited book, *The Bureaucracy of Prussia*, 98–108.

830 Thiers' *History of the Consulate and the Empire*, 109–153. **A. V. Kirwan.** There are marked similarities of opinion, sometimes expressed in the same wording, between this art. and one on the same subject in *Fraser's*, 31 (May 1845), 505–520, by Kirwan: cf. discussions of Mt. St. Bernard, Kléber, rights at sea, Fouché and Tallyrand, the battle of Copenhagen, and Thiers' style; three phrases, pp. 110, 111, reappear verbatim in *Brit. Quart. Rev.*, 7 (Feb. 1848), 137 [to be assigned to Kirwan in *Index*, IV].

831 Men and manners in Auvergne in 1665, 154–169. **W. K. Kelly.** Claimed in application to R.L.F., July 5, 1864.

832 On the teaching of languages, 170–187. **J. S. Blackie.** See his *Horae Hellenicae* (1874), p. x.

833 Michelet on auricular confession and direction, 188–198. **G. H. Lewes.** "Receipts."

834 Léon Faucher's *Manchester in 1844*, 198–211.

835 M. Guizot and the right of search, 211–252. **J. A. St. John,** prob. Writer implies

he has lived in France and seen a slave-caravan in Africa (pp. 230, 244; see *DNB*); repeats arguments used by St. John elsewhere (cf. pp. 214 and 230 with no. 873, pp. 440–441, 443, and no. 785, p. 299).

836   Short reviews of recent publications, 253–254.

837   Foreign correspondence, 255–260. Pages 255–259 by **T. A. Trollope**, prob.—cf. general evidence for no. 824; p. 259 reiterates points made in no. 824, p. 522, on *Arnaldo da Brescia* and censorship; the flood of 1844 and Florentine balls are described in *What I Remember*, II, 96–99, 101–103.

838   Miscellaneous intelligence, 261–264.

VOLUME 35, JULY 1845

839   *History of the Counts of Flanders*, 269–290.

840   The rise and fall of the European drama, 290–334. **G. H. Lewes.** "Receipts."

841   The war in the Cevennes, 335–382.

842   Railways in India, 382–409.

843   Medieval stories, 410–428. **Thomas Wright**, 1810–1877. Repr. *Literature*, II, as "The History and Transmission of Popular Stories."

844   German political squibs and crotchets, 429–453. **G. S. Venables?** In no. 870, p. 386, the reference to this art. implies a common authorship; the defence of private property against Socialism or Communism and the attack on mawkish philanthropy, partly on politico-economic grounds, serve to link the arts. and, to that extent, to support the attrib. (Venables was always a good 19th-century liberal: cf. no. 662).

845   The surveys of the Indian navy, 454–488. **J. A. St. John.** On p. 464 author says that Lieutenants Wellsted and Carless "passed some time" with him in Thebes, before 1834; see J. A. St. John, *Egypt, and Mohammed Ali* (1834), I, 318, and II, 38, 133–135.

846   The Oregon Territory, 489–517.

847   Short reviews of recent publications, 518–528. Pages 518–520 by **J. S. Blackie?** —he had studied at German universities, wrote extensively on the subject of Scottish, English, and German higher education, and had applied military terms to university life in no. 523, p. 429 (cf. p. 519 here); pages 520–524 by **J. S. Blackie?**—the writer says he had already

twice reviewed Steffens' *Memoirs* (see nos. 719, 799).

848   Foreign correspondence, 529–533. Pages 532–533 by **James Dennistoun**, prob.—no. 825, pp. 3–5, gives accounts of the sales at the Fesch Gallery which preceded those discussed here, and pp. 27–30 comment on the National Gallery, as does this correspondence; also Dennistoun to William Mure, June 9, 1845, Nat. Lib. Scot., shows former was at Bologna for three weeks in May 1845.

849   Miscellaneous intelligence, 534–536.

VOLUME 36, OCTOBER 1845

850   Napoleon in the year 1813, 1–31. **J. S. Blackie.** Claimed in *Testimonials*.

851   The new classic drama in France, 32–39. **G. H. Lewes.** "Receipts."

852   State and prospects of Mexico, 40–69. **Frederick Hardman?** No. 897, p. 433, cites this art.; comments on pp. 44–50 on oppressiveness of Spanish rule in Mexico echo Hardman's remarks in *Blackwood's*, 57 (Feb. 1845), 252–257.

853   French literary journals, 70–73. **G. H. Lewes.** Scrapbooks, V.

854   The Spanish people, 74–107.

855   Johann Gottlieb Fichte, 108–141. **Jane Sinnett.** Claimed in J. G. Fichte, *The Destination of Man*, trans. by Mrs. [E. W.] Percy Sinnett [i.e., Jane Sinnett], 1846, translator's preface.

856   Comic and satirical literature in the middle ages, 142–168. **Thomas Wright**, 1810–1877. Repr. *Archaeological Subjects*, II.

857   Political rights of the German people, 168–178.

858   Recent Italian political poems [by Giusti], 179–196. **T. A. Trollope.** The author not only knows Tuscan character and Florentine slang (p. 182), but also, like Trollope, was apparently a resident of Florence (pp. 183, 193–194); what is said on p. 187 about the Dukes of Tuscany and of Lucca is said again in *What I Remember*, II, 107, 136; in general cf. the evidence for no. 800. The poetic translations, pp. 189–193, are prob. by Theodosia Garrow, close friend of Trollope's and later his wife, who published translations of Giusti's poems in the *Athenaeum*: see *What I Remember*, II, 360–362.

859   *Travels in Kashmir and Panjab*, 196–231.

860   Personality in French and English

novels: Balzac's new novel, 232–235.
G. H. Lewes. Scrapbooks, V.

861 Short reviews of recent publications, 236–244. Pages 241–242 by **G. H. Lewes** —Scrapbooks, V.

862 Foreign correspondence, 245–248. **T. A. Trollope,** prob.—cf. general evidence for no. 824; p. 245 discusses advantages of remaining at Florence in the summer when the English colony was away (cf. *What I Remember*, II, 131); Trollope stayed in Florence during this particular summer (see F. E. Trollope, *Frances Trollope* [1895], II, 47).

863 Miscellaneous intelligence, 249–251.

VOLUME 36, JANUARY 1846

864 Abelard and Heloise, 257–292. **G. H. Lewes.** "Receipts"; pp. 262–266, 268–271, repr. revised, *Biographical History of Philosophy* (1857 ed.), pp. 295–299.

865 The Countess Hahn-Hahn's novels, 292–306. **Jane Sinnett,** prob. Marked "Mrs. Sinnett" in Wellesley Coll. copy; for her other reviews of German works, see Part B below.

866 Indian railways and the Indian press, 306–323.

867 On Monkish legends and miracles, 324–332. **Thomas Wright,** 1810–1877. Marked "T. Wright" in Wellesley Coll. copy; first paragraph links the art. to no. 856: see last paragraph of latter.

868 Leigh Hunt on the Italian poets, 333–354. **G. H. Lewes.** "Receipts."

869 The late King of Prussia, 354–370. **J. S. Blackie.** Blackie, *Letters to His Wife*, p. 113; Blackie, *Testimonials.*

870 Niebuhr and Dahlmann on the French Revolution, 371–388. **G. S. Venables,** prob. Marked "Venable" [margin cut off] in Wellesley Coll. copy; for his command of German see no. 793; his major field was European politics; frequent comments on French Revolution in no. 662.

871 Mozart, 389–411.

872 Adalbert von Chamisso, 412–437. **W. K. Kelly.** Claimed as in no. 831.

873 Capefigue's *Europe Since the Accession of Louis Philippe*, 437–474. **J. A. St. John.** Copy ascribed to "St. John" in G. H. Lewes' hand, Scrapbooks, VI; writer was in France, 1830 (see *DNB* on J. A. St. John; Bayle was only 8 at time); comments on need for a faith, p. 474, echo St. John, no. 124, pp. 489–493.

874 Pictures of the English by the French, 474–486. **G. H. Lewes.** "Receipts."

875 The political prospects of our empire in the East, 486–505.

876 Short reviews of recent publications, 506–518.

877 Foreign correspondence, 519–527. Pages 519–525 by **T. A. Trollope,** prob. cf. general evidence for no. 824; opens with immediate link to no. 837; on pp. 524–525 very high praise of Theodosia Garrow, whom Trollope had met about March of 1845 and found "very delightful" (*What I Remember*, II, 157); her poem on these pages is published from a MS.

VOLUME 37, APRIL 1846

878 The progresistas and moderados in Spain, 1–21. (Postscript, pp. 234–235.)

879 George Sand's recent novels, 21–36. **G. H. Lewes.** "Receipts."

880 M. Michelet's book, *Le Peuple*, 36–50.

881 Bunsen on the future condition of the church, 50–63.

882 The English in Borneo, 63–105. **J. A. St. John.** Spencer St. John, *The Life of Sir James Brooke* (1879), p. 124, says that his father had written about Borneo in the *FQR* at this time; wording on p. 88 (birds' nests sold for their weight in gold) and p. 65 (Borneo scenery like the Arabian Nights with Alps) repeated in J. A. St. John's *Views in the Eastern Archipelago, Borneo, Sarawak, Labuan, etc.,* 1847, unpaginated.

883 Ireland, its evils and their remedies, 105–128.

884 The satirical literature of the Reformation, 129–159. **Thomas Wright,** 1810–1877. Repr. *Archaeological Subjects*, II.

885 Algeria, past and present, 159–184.

886 Hommaire's *Travels in the Steppes of the Caspian, &c.,* 185–206.

887 The recently discovered fresco attributed to Raffael, 206–212. **James Dennistoun.** Claimed in *Memoirs of the Dukes of Urbino* (1851), II, 224.

888 The Governor General of India, and the war in the Punjâb, 212–234.

889 Short reviews of recent publication, 236–238. Page 238 by **G. H. Lewes,** prob. —in *Biographical History of Philosophy* (1846), IV, 157ff., Lewes quotes trans. reviewed here, with similar comment, and on p. 156 the remark on Fichte echoes that made here in second paragraph.

890 Foreign correspondence, 239–253. Pages 243–248 by **T. A. Trollope**—opening

remarks refer to no. 837; pp. 244 and 247 speak of what "I mentioned in my last letter" (viz., no. 877); p. 248 brings in Hiram Powers, an old friend of Trollope's (see *What I Remember*, I, 175–177); on the first Roman carnival at Florence, p. 246, cf. ibid., II, 198.

VOLUME 37, JULY 1846

891 Stokes's *Discoveries in Australia*, 257–280.

892 Johann Gottlieb v. Herder, 281–304. **Jane Sinnett,** prob. Same evidence as for no. 865.

893 An episode in the history of Lucca, 304–320. **T. A. Trollope,** prob. See the evidence for no. 800; the man praised in p. 307n was an old friend of Trollope's; opening paragraph refers to no. 862, p. 246, in words that imply a common authorship.

894 The French political preachers of the sixteenth century, 321–346.

895 Ancient Scottish life, 347–379. **Thomas Wright,** 1810–1877, prob. Wright to J. O. Halliwell, June 1, 3, and 6, 1846, Edin.

Univ., show he was working on an art. for *FQR*; references here to Sir Simonds D'Ewes, Thomas Rymer, elves, and antiquarianism reflect Wright's interests; pp. 348–354 concern witchcraft in Scotland, as does Wright's *Narratives of Sorcery and Magic* (1851), chaps. 9–10, 27–28.

896 Nature in art [on Ruskin's *Modern Painters*, vols. I and II], 380–416.

897 The writings of Charles Sealsfield, 416–448. **Frederick Hardman.** Hardman to John Blackwood, July 6, 1846, Nat. Lib. Scot., says "I have noticed Sealsfield's works in this number of the Foreign Quarterly."

898 Portugal and its late rulers, 448–460. **R. R. Madden.** MS. of art., identified as Madden's, is in "Literary Fragments of the late Dr. R. R. Madden," Royal Irish Academy, Dublin.

899 *The Cadet of Colobrières*, by Madame Charles Reybaud, 461–478.

900 McKenney and Hall's *Indian Tribes*, 479–493.

901 The diffusion of Christianity, 494–528. **J. A. St. John?** On p. 505 author claims to have directed public attention to Borneo previously (see no. 882); cf. subject of no. 124.

The Fortnightly Review, 1865–1900

IN DECEMBER 1864 George Eliot noted in her journal that Mr. Trollope and Mr. F. Chapman came to dinner and discussed a new periodical of which it was hoped that Lewes might become the editor.[1] It was planned as an attempt "to be for England what the *Revue des Deux Mondes* was for France," that is, a national forum for responsible expression of a wide variety of opinion.[2] Besides Trollope and Frederic Chapman, who in 1864 had become head of the firm of Chapman & Hall, other supporters included Huxley, E. A. Freeman, Frederic Harrison, R. T. Burton, and Alfred Austin, as well as the less known Charles Waring and Danby Seymour.[3]

The Review was to appear on the first and fifteenth of each month, after the manner of its French model—an interval which was neither too distant for influence on passing questions, nor too brief for deliberation. This in itself was a novelty, but far more startling was the announcement in the *Saturday Review* of March 25, 1865:

We propose to remove all those restrictions of party and of editorial 'consistency' which in other journals hamper the full and free expression of opinion, and we shall ask each writer to express his own views and sentiments with all the force of sincerity. He will never be required to express the views of an Editor or of a Party.

And it went on to add:

It must not be understood from this that the Review is without its purpose, or without a consistency of its own; but the consistency will be one of tendency, not of doctrine; and the purpose will be that of aiding Progress in all directions. The Review will be liberal, and its liberalism so thorough as to include great diversity of individual opinion within its catholic unity of purpose.[4]

By the time the new periodical was advertised in the *Athenaeum* of May 27, it seems clear that the founders were becoming wary about stressing the tendency towards liberalism and progress, and were concerned rather with emphasizing instead the neutral or open platform. They limited themselves to a more general statement:

[1]*Letters* (see Bibliographical Note), IV, 169.

[2]Escott, *Trollope* (see Bibliographical Note), p. 173; the features of the *Revue* which particularly impressed the projectors of the *Fortnightly* were its inclusion of fiction, interim of publication, independence of party, and above all its policy of the signed article.

[3]Escott, pp. 173–174; for fuller discussions of the founding of the Review, see Everett (see Bibliographical Note), p. 336, n. 27, and Trollope, *Autobiography* (see Bibliographical Note), pp. 172, 173, 176.

[4]Page 362.

The object of the *Fortnightly Review* is to become an organ for the unbiased expression of many and various minds on topics of general interest in Politics, Literature, Philosophy, Science and Art.[5]

This was precisely Trollope's position, perhaps because he was at heart less than enthusiastic about liberal tendencies: "We would be neither conservative nor liberal, neither religious nor free-thinking, neither popular nor exclusive;—but we would let any man who had a thing to say . . . speak freely. But he should always speak with the responsibility of his name attached."[6]

The principle of independence of party, it is true, had been quietly anticipated in England by the short-lived *Bentley's Quarterly Review*, 1859, and even as early as the *London Review* of 1829, but had never been so boldly asserted.[7] Almost immediately it led to a slight tension between those who conceived of the Review as an organ of liberalism and progress and those who wished to maintain in it a true balance between the established and the new, a truly open platform. This tension, barely discernible at first, was to affect much of the subsequent history of the *Fortnightly*.

But at least all were agreed not to indulge in anonymity, and again the clearest statement came from Trollope: "I think," he said, "that the name of the author does tend to honesty, and that the knowledge that it will be inserted adds much to the author's industry and care. It debars him also from illegitimate license and dishonest assertions."[8]

However shocking the abandonment of anonymity appeared to readers and publishers alike, it had an almost immediate effect upon the periodical press. Within a few years the *Contemporary* (1866), the *Nineteenth Century* (1877), and the *National Review* (1882) all adopted the policy of signature.

After some hesitation because of uncertain health, Lewes was persuaded to accept the editorship, and on Saturday, May 13, he noted in his journal "The *First Number of the Fortnightly* appeared."[9] It boasted articles by Bagehot, George Eliot, J. F. W. Herschel, Frederic Harrison, and, of course, by Lewes himself, as well as the first installment of Trollope's *Belton Estate*. The new Review was clearly off to an auspicious start. Indeed, even the cautious Lewes admitted a month later that the Review was at present a great success.[10] In December George Eliot echoed the same elation, while adding, "the principle of signature, never before thoroughly carried out in England, has given it an exceptional dignity, and drawn valuable writers. It is a thoroughly serious periodical, intended for the few who will pay a high price [2 shillings], and is supported by proprietors unconnected with the publishing trade." Mr. Lewes finds that "superior contributors present themselves and brave the supposed perils of signature."[11]

[5]Page 732.
[6]*Autobiography*, pp. 172–173.
[7]See the introductions on pp. 6–7 and 524–525 respectively.
[8]*Autobiography*, pp. 175–176.
[9]Eliot, *Letters*, IV, 169–178, 184–185, 211. On p. 185n. in the journal for Mar. 21, Lewes spelt out the conditions which he agreed to accept: "I am to have £600 a year for editing, with a sub-editor—one John Dennis—and a clerk found me; and absolute power over the conduct of the Review."
[10]Ibid., p. 195.
[11]Ibid., p. 211.

By late February or early March 1866, George Eliot's dread lest the worry and anxiety of editing the periodical prove too much for Lewes had begun to be justified, and it soon became evident that he could not continue; George Eliot wrote in her journal for November 6 that he would give up the editorship after the December issue.[12]

In spite of its *succès d'estime*, the Review had not been a business success. "Financially," said Trollope, "as a Company, we failed altogether."[13] In the first place the English trade had shown itself averse to a fortnightly issue, and so by November 1866 the *Fortnightly* became a monthly. And in the second place he asserted, "No Review can stand long which shall be colourless. It must be either with, or must be against some recognised set of opinions, either as to religion, politics, philosophy or other subject of commanding interest."[14] After all a public accustomed for at least fifty years to the spice of more or less violently partisan periodicals was probably at a loss to place and therefore to subscribe to one which proclaimed its neutrality. At the same time the *Fortnightly* was suspect merely from the known moral and political views of its first editor which, of course, tended to frighten away both conservative contributors and subscribers alike.[15] Both explanations are no doubt true, as Lewes recognized when in January 1866 he expressed his fear that many "superior contributors" were not after all prepared to brave the perils of signature. "There are many who withhold their services from a half suspicion that because their views are not for the government, or against it, not in harmony with those of the editor or of some well-known contributors, they would on that account be unacceptable."[16] And yet neither fully accounts for the financial difficulties of the Review. What apparently was needed was time for the novelty of the undertaking to be accepted and also a firmer control by a professional publisher of the actual mechanics of the periodical.[17]

At the time of Lewes's resignation the original Company had spent the few thousands it had collected, and the almost valueless copyright was made over to Messrs. Chapman & Hall.[18] But the founders still evidently took a share in selecting Lewes's successor; for we find Trollope writing to Lewes on November 9 that "We hardly know enough of Mr. Morley . . . . I shall be very glad if you will tell me your opinion."[19]

Fortunately the Company and the new publisher listened to the advice of Morley's friend from Oxford days, James Cotter Morison, who was largely responsible for Morley's appointment.[20] The choice almost immediately proved a wise one. From a

[12]Ibid., pp. 233, 249; in the interim the Leweses took a two-month holiday, leaving Trollope in charge (p. 266), p. 313n.

[13]"George Henry Lewes," *FortR*, 31 o.s. (Jan. 1879), 21.

[14]Ibid. See also the comment in the *Spectator* for Mar. 5, 1859, on *Bentley's Quarterly Review*, quoted above in the introduction to the latter.

[15]See remark by Henry Rogers in his preface to *Essays from "Good Words"* (1868), quoted in *The Contemporary Review*, 7 (Mar. 1868), 469: "Nobody could be more impartial than Mr. Lewes . . . but this did not prevent its [the *FortR*] being extensively stigmatized as 'an infidel publication,' 'a positivist magazine, you know,' and the like."

[16]Eliot, *Letters*, IV, 211, and *FortR*, 3 (Jan. 1, 1866), 512.

[17]Trollope, *Autobiography*, p. 173.

[18]Ibid.

[19]*Letters*, ed. Bradford Booth (1951), p. 191.

[20]Morley, *Recollections* (see Bibliographical Note), 1, 85.

circulation of 1,400 at the time of its financial collapse, its subscriptions had risen by 1872 to 2,500 and Morley could say it "is quietly rising every month."[21] More important, while retaining the services of many of the outstanding pens which had written for Lewes, Morley brought into the circle of contributors a growing band of distinguished and diversified thinkers, with the conscious aim of making the *Fortnightly* for his age what the *Encyclopédie* had been for eighteenth-century France—a center "for the best observation of fresh-flowing currents of thought, interest and debate."[22] And by January 1873 such was the prestige of the periodical that Frederic Harrison could write to him, "I am struck by the fact that with entire unanimity and regularity the whole Press of every shade prints the *F.R.* first among the Reviews, and this is entirely your doing."[23]

In spite of his best efforts to maintain the non-sectarian character of the Review, Morley soon found people labeling it Comtist, Positivist, or Naturalist; and if none of these labels fitted, still there was "a certain concurrence in the writers," even though it could not be defined. This unity was the very liberalism which the prospectus had promised and the advertisement in the *Athenaeum* had shied away from.[24] Trollope commented shrewdly on this result in 1876:

Liberalism, free-thinking, and open inquiry will never object to appear in company with their opposites, because they have the conceit to think that they can quell those opposites; but the opposites will not appear in conjunction with liberalism, free-thinking, and open inquiry. As a natural consequence, our new publication became an organ of liberalism, free-thinking, and open inquiry.[25]

This is an over-simplification. But however open in theory the pages of the review were to liberals and conservatives alike, the innate sympathies of its first two editors tended inevitably to stamp the *Fortnightly* as a great liberal periodical. Its liberalism, however, should not be equated with the political party of that name; it was far more pervasive than any such partisan allegiance. Morley himself partially analysed it in his "Valedictory": "So far as the Review has been more specially identified with one set of opinions than another, it has been due to the fact that a certain dissent from received theologies has been found in company with new ideas of social and political reform."[26] In his *Recollections* he describes it as "Rationalism," a term referring in the Victorian period mainly to the application of reason to all subjects of investigation whether religious, scientific, or social.[27] In the first it tended towards agnosticism, in the second towards scepticism, and in the third towards radicalism.

It was perhaps this acknowledged tendency toward progress and liberalism which chiefly distinguished the *Fortnightly* from the *Nineteenth Century*. James Knowles in the latter successfully dedicated his efforts towards securing prominent men to debate specific questions in the pages of the same issue from all, and often opposite, points of

---

[21]Hirst, *Early Life* (see Bibliographical Note), I, 84. From this figure Morley deduced that they could count on 30,000 readers (Everett [see Bibliographical Note], p. 321).

[22]*Recollections*, I, 85.

[23]Hirst, I, 87.

[24]*Recollections*, I, 86, 88.

[25]*Autobiography*, p. 174.

[26]*FortR*, 38 o.s. (Oct. 1882), 519.

[27]I, 88.

view; in this way he was perhaps able to provide a more truly "open" platform.[28] However, Knowles laid himself open to the charge made by Sir Frederick Pollock that he was not an editor at all, but a literary showman, a literary lion-hunter.[29]

Morley's own difficulties with his father, when he refused to take orders in 1859, had unmistakably signaled his alientation from the established order in religion and politics, an alienation which became more marked as he came to know J. S. Mill and Frederic Harrison. In July 1873 he met Joseph Chamberlain. This was the beginning of an extremely close friendship which exerted a decisive influence both upon Morley and the *Fortnightly*. Already on August 11, Morley suggested to Chamberlain that he take the *Fortnightly* for his platform,[30] and, indeed, the lead article in the issue for September, which was signed by Chamberlain, "The Liberal Party and Its Leaders," outlined the main objectives of the radical element of the Liberal Party: *Free Church, Free Land, Free Schools,* and *Free Labour*.[31] Later, when Morley decided in 1876 to resuscitate the the commentaries on current events, he wrote to Chamberlain that he would count on him for help and advice.[32] Finally it was in some measure due to Chamberlain that Morley in 1882 threw himself actively into politics and decided to withdraw from the *Fortnightly*.

It was not, however, only in the realms of politics, religion, and science that the *Fortnightly* showed its liberalism. Its attitude towards literature and criticism reflected the emergence of new trends and new writers. Meredith and Swinburne were not only welcomed but became frequent contributors, while Morris and Rossetti were praised, and Morley himself reviewed Pater's *Renaissance* in April 1873 with enthusiasm. Most surprising of all, even the poet laureate was attacked for his "Victorianism," and a poet whose greatness was still largely unrecognized hailed as his superior:

The truth is, we have this long while been so debilitated by pastorals, by graceful presentation of the Arthurian legend for drawing-rooms, by idylls, . . . by verse directly didactic, that a rude inburst of air from the outside welter of human realities is apt to spread a shock, which might show in what simpleton's paradise we have been living. The little ethics of the rectory parlour set to sweet music, the respectable aspirations of the sentimental curate married to exquisite verse, the everlasting glorification of domestic sentiment, . . . all this would seem to be turning us into flat valetudinarians.

[From Browning] there comes out a long procession of human figures, infinitely various in form and thought, in character and act; a group of men and women, eager, passionate, indifferent; tender and ravenous, mean and noble, humorous and profound.[33]

Small wonder that the reading public was stirred either to rage or delight by this championship of fresh points of view.

[28]See introduction to *Nineteenth Century*, pp. 622–624.

[29]*For My Grandson: Remembrances of an Ancient Victorian* (1933), p. 93.

[30]Letter quoted by Hamer, *Morley* (see Bibliographical Note), p. 99.

[31]By Free Church was meant disestablishment of the Church of England; by Free Land, the abolition of primogeniture and entail and facilities for transfer of small properties; by Free Schools, free public education; by Free Labour, liberty of association (trades unions, etc.), *FortR* no. 981, pp. 295–299.

[32]Hamer, p. 116, and below, no. 1227; for the unusual degree of intimacy between the two men all the time that Morley was editor, see Austen Chamberlain, *Down the Years* (1935), pp. 195–196, and F. W. Hirst, *In the Golden Days* (1947), pp. 168–169.

[33]John Morley, "On *The Ring and the Book*," *FortR.*, 11 o.s. (Mar. 1869), 331, 333.

Looking back in 1882, as he was writing his "Valedictory," Morley reverted to the question of the signed article. Either time or the exigencies of his growing political activism had mellowed his approach:

I have attached less stern importance to signature as an unvarying rule than did my pre-decessor. . . . Our practice has been signature as the standing order, occasionally suspended in favour of anonymity when there seemed to be sufficient reason. . . . On the whole, it may be said that the change from anonymous to signed articles . . . has not led to one-half either of the evils or of the advantages that its advocates and its opponents foretold.[34]

Even Lewes had found it expedient on three occasions to yield to the necessity for anonymity (nos. 128, 240, 330), and throughout his editorship the "Public Affairs" were never signed.[35] Again under Morley the current events were unsigned—except for a series by Frederic Harrison in 1873–74—but it may be surmised with a fair degree of probability that the editor wrote the major number of them.[36] In addition, Morley had evidently felt it wiser to relax the policy of signature some twenty or so times during his fifteen years in command, most notably in the case of an article by Gladstone, no. 1689, and a four-part attack on Disraeli by Frank Harrison Hill, nos. 1452, 1466, 1477, and 1498.

By 1882, partly under Chamberlain's influence, Morley had entered the political arena; and also two years before he had taken on the editorship of the daily *Pall Mall Gazette*. The strain was beginning to tell, as he wrote his sister in May 1882, and was increased by what he described as "a pretty lively quarrel with the proprietors of the Fortnightly."[37] The quarrel evidently came to a head during the summer, for in the issue for October Morley presented his final assessment, modest in the extreme, of what the Review had accomplished under his aegis. "A certain number of people have been persuaded to share opinions that fifteen years ago were more unpopular than they are now. A certain resistance has been offered to the stubborn influence of prejudice and use and wont. . . . Whatever gives freedom and variety to thought, and earnestness to men's interest in the world, must contribute to a good end. The Review has been an attempt to do something in this direction."[38]

Whatever the source of the quarrel between Morley and the publishers—perhaps the distractions of his political life, or perhaps his radicalism—when the former resigned, T. H. S. Escott was already there in a position to take over the editor's chair, as he did with the issue of November 1882.[39] He was a journalist of long standing,

---

[34]*FortR* no. 1956, pp. 513–514.

[35]Everett, pp. 44, 55, assumes that Lewes wrote these, although admitting, pp. 70–71, that he may have had help from his sub-editor, Dennis. But this is by no means certain. We know, for example, that Henry Danby Seymour wrote at least part of no. 351, q.v., while Trollope asked Lewes, May 30, 1865, "Who is to do your chronique?" (Trollope, *Letters*, p. 165), which implies that Lewes himself was not expected to write it. The use of the word "chronique" for "Public Affairs" is a reminder of how closely the *FortR* was following the *Revue des Deux Mondes*; and interestingly enough the word recurs in the Escott-Chamberlain correspondence.

[36]See below, evidence for nos. 405 and 1227. However, as Morley became more and more involved in active politics, it is probable that he may have called upon T. H. S. Escott for occasional help with this department; see evidence for no. 1547.

[37]Hirst, *Early Life*, II, 114, 125.

[38]Pages 520, 521.

[39]*Athenaeum*, Oct. 21, 1882, p. 532. There is some doubt about what precisely had been Escott's connection with Morley or the *Fortnightly* before this date. He was available in Jan. 1879 to help

having written for daily and weekly papers, as well as for *Fraser's* and other monthlies, which he continued to do even after taking on the *Fortnightly*.[40] He had as sub-editor Major Arthur Griffiths, and as reader and trusted assistant, William Leonard Courtney, still a fellow and tutor at Oxford, but later destined to become editor himself. Escott, according to Janet Courtney, told the publishers what indeed may have been a reflection of their own views, that the Review should be conducted along broader and less partisan lines, and she added that there was almost immediately an incursion of Conservative contributors.[41] Although remaining, like Morley, in close alliance with Joseph Chamberlain and writing to Gladstone on October 8, 1883 (BM Add. MS 44,483) that he considered it the function of the Review to "cultivate a strong body of liberal opinion," Escott nevertheless made a great effort to rally the opposition to his periodical. T. E. Kebbel recalled that when Escott took over, "he proposed to give a dinner to the leaders of the Tory party, though hitherto the *Fortnightly* had not been avowedly a party publication . . . and [he] entertained Lord Salisbury, Sir Stafford Northcote and some of their colleagues at a sumptuous banquet."[42] So marked were his efforts that Labouchere wrote to him, "Don't compromise yourself too much in your articles in the F.R. as a conservative, for we mean to have you one of these days as a Liberal journalist."[43] Certainly Escott's tie with Chamberlain, which dated back to the time when the former was writing for the *Standard*, exerted a strong counter influence, not only in specific articles, as for example the series of articles on the Radical Programme, nos. 2073, 2085, 2096, 2098, 2120, but also particularly in the "Home and Foreign Affairs"; and it is clear from his letters to Chamberlain that much the same arrangement as had obtained between Morley and Chamberlain continued under Escott.[44]

Although many of Escott's literary and political articles were worthy of the *Fortnightly*'s tradition, by and large the Review declined in quality and in circulation; Escott was overstraining himself, and on October 17, 1885, Edmund Yates wrote to Chamberlain that Escott was seriously ill.[45] He continued as nominal editor through June 1886, but there were increasing periods of ill health, during which Courtney and Griffiths carried on. This time there was no farewell causerie, no valedictory; there was the bare remark in the *Athenaeum* for July 17 that Mr. Escott had worked so hard for so long that it was not surprising "that he should have brought upon himself a serious illness."[46]

Once again there was a successor ready to hand. Frank Harris, who had been

out with the "Home and Foreign Affairs" (see no. 1547), but that he was actually a sub-editor seems unlikely since Janet Courtney, *Making of an Editor* (see Bibliographical Note), p. 134, says his appointment as editor was a surprise.

[40] *WWW*/1928.

[41] Courtney, p. 134. The hopes of the Conservatives were expressed in a letter from the Earl of Carnarvon to Escott on Aug. 24, 1882, Escott Papers: "Though I readily understand that the Fortnightly Review under your guidance cannot be a decided party publication yet I believe . . . that it will wear a more conservative complexion such as will connect it with the friends of the Constitution and distinguish it from its old Jacobin and revolutionary tendencies."

[42] *Lord Beaconsfield and Other Tory Memories* (1907), pp. 244–245.

[43] Letter in the Escott Papers, dated "Tuesday."

[44] Letters in the Chamberlain and Escott Papers.

[45] Letter in Chamberlain Papers.

[46] Page 78.

gradually making himself extremely useful to Chapman and Escott, obtained the editorship "almost by force" according to Frank Swinnerton in the *DNB*. He was a brash young man (30 years old) with unbounded confidence. But he brought a new burst of energy and brilliance to the periodical and was able to boast that in his first year he nearly doubled its circulation.[47] He was to edit the Review for eight years, during which it was particularly noteworthy for the high quality of its creative and critical literature: almost every distinguished English writer and critic of the day was among his contributors.

In view of Harris's strong interest in literature, it is perhaps not without significance that after the first three issues he discontinued the commentary on current events, which had been of such concern to his predecessors. This is not to imply that the Review ceased to be a vehicle for political articles from recognized authorities in their several fields; questions of the day were vigorously discussed from varying points of view, more and more often either anonymously or under a psuedonym. An achievement of which Harris was particularly proud was that he paid his contributors, particularly poets, more highly than his predecessors, largely, he said, out of his own pocket.[48]

If it was surprising that Harris ever became editor of the Review, it was well nigh miraculous that he remained ensconced at Chapman & Hall as long as he did; perhaps in part through his very brashness, but also in part through the efforts of his sub-editor John Verschoyle. According to Sir Harry Johnston, Verschoyle "did far more work in those days for the *Fortnightly* than Frank Harris, his Editor . . . he gave . . . large dinners or small and cozy ones to . . . contributors, to politicians, and leaders of movements."[49] He also did much if not all of the proofreading and took a share in soliciting articles.[50] However, it was all but inevitable that a man of Harris's temperament should sooner or later run into difficulties. "I found it very easy at first," he said, "to get on with Frederic Chapman, but his directors were for the most part stupid, brainless business men." According to his account it was the stupidity of the directors in listening to criticism of his "Modern Idyll" in the issue for June 1891 which brought matters to a head. When they asked him not to insert any more of his stories, he at once tore up his agreement and told them to find a new editor as soon as they could.[51] Matters were smoothed over by the intervention of George Meredith, a long-time and highly-valued reader for the firm. Peace reigned for a few years, but gradually, wrote Harris, "my position as editor of the Fortnightly became less pleasant to me. . . . Chapman was naturally a conservative businessman of the old-fashioned English type . . . he disliked art and literature; he hated the social movement of the time . . . he looked upon a socialist as a sort of low thief, and pictured a communist as one who had his hand always in his neighbor's pocket."[52] An article by Charles Malato sym-

[47]*My Life and Loves* (see Bibliographical Note), p. 635.
[48]Ibid.
[49]*Story of My Life* (Indianapolis, 1923), p. 218; see Esther Rhoads Houghton, "John Verschoyle and the *Fortnightly Review*," *Victorian Periodicals Newsletter*, No. 3, (Nov. 1968), pp. 17–21.
[50]Frank Harris, *Contemporary Portraits*, 2nd series (N.Y., 1919), pp. 46–50; Brome, *Frank Harris* (see Bibliographical Note), p. 81.
[51]*My Life and Loves*, p. 635.
[52]Ibid., p. 639.

pathetic to anarchism in September 1894 was the signal for a final rupture.[53] Already by September 22 it was reported in the *Athenaeum* that Mr. Harris would retire from the *Fortnightly* at the end of the year, and on November 24 it was announced that the December issue would be the first "under the new editor."[54]

From the time when Chapman and Hall took over the ownership of the *Fortnightly* (1867), and indeed from the very beginning, we have noted a certain latent tension between the conservative and liberal elements in the enterprise. Trollope himself, for example, was at heart a conservative, and so no doubt were Chapman and his directors; but circumstances, including their own proclaimed goals, had originally convinced them that success depended upon a reasonably liberal stance. Morley had almost certainly overstepped the bounds of reasonableness.[55] Escott, as we have seen, made some attempt to redress the balance, but with Harris there was an outright flaunting of accepted standards of literary taste and political discussion. Now the directors were happy to secure the services of one who was seasoned in the amenities of the academic world and also in that of journalism, a man who gave every sign of being a balanced observer of the world about him with a very real concern for the highest public interest. Most important of all, W. L. Courtney was emphatically a safe man, whose judgment was never likely to bring his proprietors into trouble, an encomium which was attested by his remaining as editor for 34 years.

But safety in the case of Courtney did not mean stogginess. Breadth and adaptability were the keynotes of his temperament. Widely read in philosophy and literature, passionately fond of the theatre, and a member of the staff of the *Daily Telegraph* in constant and immediate touch with both domestic and foreign affairs, he was an ideal editor for the Review. The *Fortnightly* continued its distinguished performance under his guidance until shortly before his death in 1928. He was ably supported by Janet Hogarth, formerly his student and later his wife, and the Review flourished financially and in reputation.

The last six years of the century saw no startling innovations. The general tenor was more urbane, of course, and there was an increase in the number of feminine contributors, and in the anonymous or pseudonymous articles. The former reflects, no doubt, the influence of the sub-editor and the more and more prominent position of women as the century progressed; the latter may be explained by Courtney's connection with the *Daily Telegraph* where he was in first-hand communication with some of the most outstanding foreign correspondents of the time, whom he was thus able to recruit for the *Fortnightly*. Since their effectiveness depended upon the preservation of their anonymity, Courtney, like Lewes, like Morley, like Escott, like Harris, had to bow to expediency and sometimes suspend the rigorous enforcment of the principle of signed articles.[56] In general, however, the *Fortnightly* remained true to the ideals

---

[53]The whole garbled tale of this parting of the ways is given by Harris in his *Contemporary Portraits*, 1st series (N.Y., 1920), pp. 199–201, as well as in *My Life and Loves*, pp. 635–642.

[54]Pages 390, 718.

[55]Trollope, *Autobiography*, p. 176, spoke regretfully of "Morley's set of contributors whose modes of thought are what we may call much advanced."

[56]This is not to imply that it was only political and military articles that were anonymous, though they were in preponderance; there was a sprinkling of literary ones whose authors refused to take personal responsibility for their views.

of its founders: it proved beyond a doubt, Trollope notwithstanding, that, in the longer run, a periodical open to all points of view could succeed, that highly regarded men of widely different views would argue them out under their own names on the neutral ground provided by an outstanding journal.

EDITORS

George Henry Lewes: May 15, 1865–Dec. 1866, Vol. 1—Vol. 6.

John Morley: Jan. 1867–Oct. 1882, Vol. 7 o.s., 1 n.s.—Vol. 38 o.s., 32 n.s.

T. H. S. Escott: Nov. 1882–June 1886, Vol. 38 o.s., 32 n.s.—Vol. 45 o.s., 39 n.s.

Frank Harris: July 1886–Oct. 1894, Vol. 46 o.s., 40 n.s.—Vol. 62 o.s., 56 n.s.

William Leonard Courtney: Dec. 1894–Oct. 1928, Vol. 62 o.s., 56 n.s.—Vol. 130 o.s., 124 n.s.

Under Lewes, John Dennis acted as sub-editor (Eliot, *Letters*, IV, 185n.). Trollope took over the editorial role while the Leweses were abroad in June and July 1866 (ibid., pp. 266, 296).

Under Morley, T. H. S. Escott seems to have been, at least in the *later* years, some kind of sub-editor (see above, n. 36, 39). On the occasion of Morley's trip to America in the fall of 1867, George Meredith took over briefly (*DNB*).

Under Escott, W. L. Courtney was reader and general assistant, while Arthur Griffiths was Escott's deputy, especially during his periods of ill health (Janet Courtney, *The Making of an Editor*, p. 35).

Under Frank Harris, John Stuart Verschoyle carried a large share of the editorial duties (see p. 180).

Under Courtney, Janet Hogarth was reader and sub-editor.

PUBLISHER

Chapman and Hall: May 15, 1865–Dec. 1900, Vol. 1—Vol. 74 o.s., 68 n.s.

PROPRIETORS

A committee whose composition is difficult to determine, but of which Anthony Trollope was certainly one of the leading members, was the proprietor from the founding of the Review in 1865 until its sale at the end of 1866 to Chapman and Hall, whose property it remained. Among those mentioned as members of the original committee are Alfred Austin, Walter Bagehot, E. S. Beesly, Edward Chapman, Frederic Chapman, George Eliot, E. A. Freeman, Frederic Harrison, T. H. Huxley, G. H. Lewes, R. M. Milnes, J. Cotter Morison, Danby Seymour, Charles Waring.[57]

NOTE ON ATTRIBUTIONS

Since the announced policy of the *Fortnightly* was personal responsibility, i.e., the signed article, a great deal of the work on attributions has been biographical. A baffling problem, however, has been the unexpectedly large number of anonymous or pseudonymous articles, roughly 520. In proportion as the signed article became more and more the accepted standard, the more important it became that, when

[57]See the opening paragraph above, and Escott and Everett in n. 3.

resorted to, anonymity should be carefully safeguarded—at least until the immediate need for secrecy had passed.

BIBLIOGRAPHICAL NOTE (arranged in editorial order)

Anthony Trollope, *An Autobiography*, ed. Michael Sadleir (1947).

T. H. S. Escott, *Anthony Trollope* (1913).

George Eliot, *Letters*, ed. G. H. Haight (7 vols., New Haven, 1954–1955), Vol. IV.

G. H. Lewes, "Farewell Causerie," *FortR*, 6 (December 1866), 890–891.

Anthony Trollope, "George Henry Lewes," *FortR*, 31 o.s. (January 1879), 15–24.

Edwin M. Everett, *The Party of Humanity: the "Fortnightly Review" and Its Contributors 1865–1874* (Chapel Hill, 1939).

John Morley, *Recollections* (2 vols., N.Y., 1917).

——, "Valedictory," *FortR*, 38 o.s. (October 1882), 511–521.

F. W. Hirst, *Early Life and Letters of John Morley* (2 vols., 1927).

D. A. Hamer, *John Morley, Liberal Intellectual in Politics* (Oxford, 1968).

Frank Harris, *My Life and Loves*, ed. John F. Gallagher (N.Y., 1925).

Vincent Brome, *Frank Harris* (1959).

Janet Courtney, *The Making of an Editor, W. L. Courtney, 1850–1928* (1930).

"M," "The Fortnightly—a Retrospect," *FortR*, 75 o.s. (January 1901), 104–117.

Among the MS sources used have been the Gladstone letters at the British Museum, the Chamberlain Papers at Birmingham University Library, and the large collection of Escott Papers (estimated at about 2000 items), the property of his granddaughter, currently (1971) being listed by the Historical Manuscripts Commission.

THE FORTNIGHTLY REVIEW, 1865–1900

history (Part I), 149–160. **Frederic Seebohm.** Signed F. Seebohm; see *DNB*.

76 Liberals, conservatives, and the Church, 161–168. **John Russell,** 1842–1876. Signed Amberley [Viscount Amberley].

77 Mr. Grote's *Plato*, 169–183. **G. H. Lewes.** Signed Editor.

78 Social amusements under the Restoration (Part I), 193–205. **Robert Bell,** 1800–1867. Signed; see *DNB*.

79 The Belton estate (chaps. xv–xvi), 206–226. **Anthony Trollope.** Signed.

80 The political economy of copyright, 227–239. **W. Bridges Adams.** Signed.

81 Public affairs, 240–247.

82 Notices of new books, 248–256. Pages 252–254 signed **John Dennis;** pages 248–251 signed **G. D. Haughton;** pages 254–255 signed **F. T. Palgrave;** pages 255–256 signed **Anthony Trollope.**

VOLUME 2, SEPTEMBER 15, 1865

83 The principles of success in literature (chap. v): the principle of beauty, 257–268. **G. H. Lewes.** Signed Editor.

84 The Black Death, and its place in English history (Part II, concl.), 268–279. **Frederic Seebohm.** Signed as in no. 75.

85 Ireland without a church establishment, 280–298. **James Godkin.** Signed.

86 Social amusements under the Restoration (Part II), 299–309. **Robert Bell,** 1800–1867. Signed; see *DNB*.

87 On some unexpected results of the Crimean War, 310–318. **George Hooper.** Signed.

88 Civilisation and crime, 319–328. **Sheldon Amos.** Signed.

89 De profundis [Atlantic cable], 329–336. **William Howard Russell.** Signed W. H. Russell; called "LL.D." in Table of Contents; see *DNB*.

90 Personal recollections of Siam, 337–349. **John Bowring.** Signed.

91 The Belton estate (chaps. xvii–xviii), 350–370. **Anthony Trollope.** Signed.

92 Public affairs, 371–378.

93 Notices of new books, 379–384. Pages 380–382 by **G. H. Lewes**—signed Editor; pages 379–380 signed **Anthony Trollope;** pages 382–384 signed **A. R. Vardy.**

VOLUME 2, OCTOBER 1, 1865

94 The bibliography of Tennyson, 385–403. **J. Leicester Warren.** Signed.

95 The Belton estate (chaps. xix–xx), 404–423. **Anthony Trollope.** Signed.

96 The Calcutta cyclone of 1864, 424–431. **L. J. Jennings.** Signed.

97 Agricultural statistics, 431–438. **R. Arthur Arnold.** Signed.

98 An electoral reform, 439–442. **Thomas Hare.** Signed.

99 Fishing in Norway, 443–451. **Charles Taylor.** Signed; Contents adds "Bart.";   see Boase.

100 The bishops and clerical subscription, 452–459. **G. D. Haughton.** Signed.

101 Social amusements under the Restoration (Part III, concl.), 460–475. **Robert Bell,** 1800–1867. Signed; see *DNB*.

102 Public schools, 476–487. **Anthony Trollope.** Signed.

103 Apollonius of Tyana, 488–503. **W. M. W. Call.** Signed.

104 Public affairs, 504–510.

105 Notices of new books, 511–512. Page 511 signed **John Dennis;** pages 511–512 by **G. H. Lewes**—signed Editor.

VOLUME 2, OCTOBER 15, 1865

106 The Belton estate (chaps. xxi–xxii), 513–532. **Anthony Trollope.** Signed.

107 The proposed revision of the Swiss Federal Constitution, 533–548. **Edward A. Freeman.** Signed.

108 Pagan and Muslim Arabs, 549–570. **Reginald Stuart Poole.** Signed.

109 The ideality of the rainbow, 571–578. **C. M. Ingleby.** Signed; repr. *Essays,* 1888.

110 Authenticity of the *Paston Letters,* 579–594. **James Gairdner.** Signed.

111 The English Constitution (Part IV): the monarchy (continued), 595–612. **Walter Bagehot.** Signed.

112 The civil service, 613–626. **Anthony Trollope.** Signed.

113 Public affairs, 627–634.

114 Notices of new books, 635–640. Pages 637–638 signed **W. M. W. Call;** pages 635–636, 638–640 by **G. H. Lewes**— signed Editor.

VOLUME 2, NOVEMBER 1, 1865

115 International law, 641–650. **J. E. Cairnes.** Signed; repr. *Political Essays,* 1873.

116 The Belton estate (chaps. xxiii–xxiv), 651–671. **Anthony Trollope.** Signed.

117 Neo-evangelism, 672–688. **Peter Bayne.** Signed.

118 The principles of success in literature (chap. vi, concl.): the laws of style, 689–710. **G. H. Lewes.** Signed Editor.

VOLUME 3, JANUARY 15, 1866

162   The fourth commandment, 529–538. **Anthony Trollope.** Signed.

163   Vittoria (chaps. i–iii), 539–558. **George Meredith.** Signed; novel published 1867.

164   The keystone of parliamentary reform, 559–565. **Thomas Hare.** Signed.

165   History of Hebrew philology, 566–574. **Francis Barham.** Signed.

166   The feelings and the will, viewed physiologically, 575–588. **Alexander Bain.** Signed.

167   Leslie, 589–606. **Philip Gilbert Hamerton.** Signed; repr. *Thoughts.*

168   Sanitary reform: water supply, 607–616. **R. Arthur Arnold.** Signed; repr. *Social Politics* (1878), as "Water Supply, London and Elsewhere."

169   Underground perils [of mining], 617–625. **George Phillips Bevan.** Signed Phillips Bevan; man cited concerned with industrial statistics; see Boase and *BMCat.*

170   On the advisableness of improving natural knowledge; a lay sermon, delivered at St. Martin's Hall, on Sunday, Jan. 7, 1866, 626–637. **T. H. Huxley.** Signed; repr. *Collected Essays*, I.

171   Public affairs, 638–645.

172   Causeries (No. I), 646–649. **G. H. Lewes.** Signed Editor.

173   Critical notices, 650–656. Pages 655–656 by **G. H. Lewes**—signed Editor; pages 652–654 by **Donald McLennan**, prob.—signed D. McLennan; pages 650–652 signed **Anthony Trollope;** pages 654–655 signed **A. R. Vardy.**

VOLUME 3, FEBRUARY 1, 1866

174   The English Constitution (Part V): the House of Lords, 657–678. **Walter Bagehot.** Signed.

175   Vittoria (chaps. iv–vii), 679–704. **George Meredith.** Signed.

176   The American "Radicals" and their English censors, 705–720. **Moncure D. Conway.** Signed.

177   Spirit rapping a hundred and fifty years ago, 721–734. **George Salmon.** Signed; called "Rev. Dr." in Contents: see *DNB.*

178   The intellect, viewed physiologically, 735–748. **Alexander Bain.** Signed.

179   The casual poor of London, 749–759. **Joseph Charles Parkinson,** b. 1832. Signed J. C. Parkinson; see *LCCat.*

180   Public affairs, 760–767.

181   Causeries (No. II), 768–772. **G. H. Lewes.** Signed Editor.

182   Critical notices, 773–784. Pages 781–783 by **Robert Buchanan,** 1841–1901—signed, cf. no. 54; pages 777–781 signed **H. S. Fagan;** pages 783–784 by **G. H. Lewes**—signed Editor; pages 773–775 signed **F. T. Palgrave;** pages 775–777 signed **Anthony Trollope.**

VOLUME 4, FEBRUARY 15, 1866

183   On the relations of radiant heat to chemical constitution, color, and texture, 1–15. **John Tyndall.** Signed; repr. *Fragments*, I.

184   The old Church of Ireland, 16–31. **James Godkin.** Signed.

185   Vittoria (chaps. viii–ix), 32–48. **George Meredith.** Signed.

186   Practical considerations of the representation of minorities, 49–64. **J. Boyd Kinnear.** Signed.

187   Trollope's *History of Florence*, 70–86. **Oscar Browning.** Signed.

188   The population of England before the Black Death, 87–89. **Frederic Seebohm.** Signed as in no. 75.

189   The Peasants' War of 1381, 90–95. **James E. Thorold Rogers.** Signed.

190   Dr. Livingstone's errors, 96–110. **W. D. Cooley.** Signed.

191   Public affairs, 111–118.

192   Critical notices, 119–128. Pages 119–121 signed **Peter Bayne;** pages 125–127, 128 signed **John Dennis;** pages 121–125 signed **H. S. Fagan;** pages 127–128 signed **J. S. Watson.**

VOLUME 4, MARCH 1, 1866

193   The Irish judicial establishment, 129–141. **Marmion Savage.** Signed.

194   Proudhon as a writer on art, 142–162. **Philip Gilbert Hamerton.** Signed; repr. *Thoughts.*

195   Vittoria (chaps. x–xi), 163–183. **George Meredith.** Signed.

196   On a uniform poor-rate for London, 184–192. **Joseph Charles Parkinson,** b. 1832. Evidence for no. 179.

197   Were the ancient Britons savages? (Part I), 193–209. **W. Walter Wilkins.** Signed.

198   Modern reforms in paper money, 210–221. **William Latham.** Signed.

199   On the study of music, 222–227. **Leonora Schmitz.** Signed.

200   Work for parliament, 228–237. **Peter Bayne.** Signed.

201   Public affairs, 238–245.

202 Causeries (No. III), 246–251. **G. H. Lewes.** Signed Editor.

203 Critical notices, 252–256. Pages 255–256 signed **J. S. Watson;** pages 252–255 signed **David Wedderburn.**

VOLUME 4, MARCH 15, 1866

204 The English Constitution (Part VI): the House of Commons, 257–283. **Walter Bagehot.** Signed.

205 The case of Ireland, 284–300. **James Godkin.** Signed.

206 Vittoria (chaps. xii–xiii), 301–316. **George Meredith.** Signed.

207 Strauss's *New Life of Christ*, 317–337. **Peter Bayne.** Signed.

208 In the Mont Cenis tunnel, 338–349. **Edward Gould Buffum.** Signed; repr. in *Sights and Sensations in France, Germany and Switzerland*, N.Y., 1869.

209 Individual responsibility in representative government, 350–358. **Thomas Hare.** Signed.

210 The metropolis and the railways, 359–368. **George Dodd,** 1808–1881. Signed; man cited wrote on London and on railways: see *DNB*.

211 Public affairs, 369–376.

212 Critical notices, 377–384. Pages 381–383, 383 signed **John Dennis;** pages 377–381 signed **H. S. Fagan;** pages 383–384 by **G. H. Lewes**—signed Editor.

VOLUME 4, APRIL 1, 1866

213 Spinoza, 385–406. **G. H. Lewes.** Signed Editor.

214 The architecture of London, in relation to climate, 407–420. **Herman Merivale.** Signed.

215 Principles of representation, 421–436. **Edward Wilson,** 1814–1878, and **Catherine Helen Spence.** The art. is signed by Wilson, but in her *Autobiography* (Adelaide, 1910), p. 25, Catherine Helen Spence describes in detail her collaboration, necessitated by Wilson's blindness.

216 Vittoria (chaps. xiv–xv), 437–458. **George Meredith.** Signed.

217 Metropolitan infirmaries for the pauper sick, 459–463. **Ernest Hart.** Signed.

218 Were the ancient Britons savages? (Part II, concl.), 464–476. **W. Walker Wilkins.** Signed.

219 President Johnson and the reconstruction of the Union, 477–490. **Charles Mackay.** Signed.

220 Public affairs, 491–502.

221 Causeries (No. IV), 503–509. **G. H. Lewes.** Signed Editor.

222 Critical notice, 510–512. **Anthony Trollope.** Signed.

VOLUME 4, APRIL 15, 1866

223 The clergy in relation to modern dogmatism and modern thought, 513–532. **G. R. Wynne.** Signed.

224 Mr. Swinburne's *Chastelard*, 533–543. **R. M. Milnes.** Signed Houghton [Lord Houghton].

225 On the origin of language, 544–559. **Edward B. Tylor.** Signed.

226 The just demand of the working man, 560–568. **J. M. Capes.** Signed.

227 Kinship in ancient Greece (Part I), 569–588. **J. F. M'Lennan.** Signed; repr. *Studies in Ancient History*, 1886.

228 Vittoria (chaps. xvi–xviii), 589–606. **George Meredith.** Signed.

229 The massacre of the innocents [infanticide in London], 607–612. **Andrew Wynter.** Signed; repr. *Fruit between the Leaves* (1875), II.

230 New views on light, 613–622. **C. K. Akin.** Signed; called "Dr." in Table of Contents.

231 Public affairs, 623–634.

232 Causeries (No. V), 635–638. **G. H. Lewes.** Signed Editor.

233 Critical notice, 639–640. **Edward B. Tylor.** Signed.

VOLUME 4, MAY 1, 1866

234 The mythical and romantic elements in early English history, 641–668. **Edward A. Freeman.** Signed; repr. *Essays*, I.

235 Gustave Doré's Bible, 669–681. **Philip Gilbert Hamerton.** Signed.

236 Kinship in ancient Greece (Part II, concl.), 682–691. **J. F. M'Lennan.** Signed.

237 The gentle Euphemia or, "Love Shall Still be Lord of All," 692–699. **Anthony Trollope.** Signed.

238 A feudal epic: *La Chanson d'Antioche*, 700–709. **John G. Sheppard.** Signed; called "Dr." in Contents; see Boase.

239 Vittoria, (chaps. xix–xx), 710–728. **George Meredith.** Signed.

240 Indedited letters of Louis Philippe, 729–744.

241 Facts and figures about the fisheries, 745–753. **James G. Bertram.** Signed.

242 Public affairs, 754–763.
243 Critical notices, 764–768. Pages 764–766 signed **John Dennis;** pages 767–768 by **G. H. Lewes**—signed Editor.

VOLUME 5, MAY 15, 1866

244 The electoral laws of Hungary, 1–14. **Arthur J. Patterson.** Signed.
245 The Oxford reformers of 1498 (chap. i), 15–30. **Frederic Seebohm.** Signed; series repr. in book of same title, 1867.
246 Victor Hugo's new novel [*Les Travailleurs de la Mer*], 30–46. **G. H. Lewes.** Signed Editor.
247 A historical view of the theories of the soul, 47–62. **Alexander Bain.** Signed.
248 The revised educational code: in practice, 63–75. **John Wisken?** Signed J. Wisker; man cited a schoolmaster; no J. Wisker found.
249 Vittoria (chaps. xxi–xxii), 76–90. **George Meredith.** Signed.
250 Religious life in Scotland, 91–97. **H. G. Reid.** Signed.
251 The President's defence [Abraham Lincoln], 98–106. **Moncure D. Conway.** Signed.
252 Public affairs, 107–118.
253 Critical notices, 119–128. Pages 119–120 signed **John Dennis;** pages 124–126 signed **H. S. Fagan;** pages 120–123 signed **G. D. Haughton;** pages 126–128 signed **Anthony Trollope.**

VOLUME 5, JUNE 1, 1866

254 *Ecce Homo* [by J. R. Seeley], 129–142. **Peter Bayne.** Signed.
255 A week in Prince Edward Island, 143–157. **Charles Mackay.** Signed.
256 The "Standing Orders" of parliament, and private bill legislation, 158–166. **Thomas Hennell.** Signed.
257 The Oxford reformers of 1498 (chap. ii), 166–183. **Frederic Seebohm.** Signed.
258 Vittoria (chaps. xxiii–xxiv), 184–199. **George Meredith.** Signed.
259 A word for the Stuarts, 200–211. **Robert Bell,** 1800–1867. Signed; see *DNB*.
260 Gluck's *Iphigenia in Tauris*, 212–219. **John Hullah.** Signed.
261 Political economy and the tenure of land, 220–228. **T. E. Cliffe Leslie.** Signed; repr. *Land Systems*.
262 Public affairs, 229–240.

263 Causeries (No. VI), 241–246. **G. H. Lewes.** Signed Editor.
264 Critical notices, 247–256. Pages 254–255 signed **John Dennis;** pages 255–256 signed **H. S. Fagan;** pages 251–254 signed **Anthony Trollope;** pages 247–251 signed **John L. Warren.**

VOLUME 5, JUNE 15, 1866

265 Grouping of boroughs, 257–266. **Edward A. Freeman.** Signed.
266 The Oxford reformers of 1498 (chap. iii), 267–278. **Frederic Seebohm.** Signed.
267 Romanism, Anglicanism, and Evangelicalism logically identical, 279–297. **William Kirkus.** Signed; repr. *Miscellaneous Essays*, 2nd series, 1868.
268 Descriptive poetry in England from Anne to Victoria, 298–320. **F. T. Palgrave.** Signed.
269 Vittoria (chaps. xxv–xxvi), 321–342. **George Meredith.** Signed.
270 Two art philosophers [H. Taine, C. Lévêque], 343–351. **Philip Gilbert Hamerton.** Signed; repr. *Thoughts*.
271 Monte Cassino (Part I), 352–367. **W. E. Hall.** Signed.
272 Public affairs, 368–379.
273 Critical notices, 380–384. Pages 380–381 signed **James Hinton;** pages 381–384 signed **Anthony Trollope.**

VOLUME 5, JULY 1, 1866

274 Count Bismarck (Part I), 385–405. **Max Schlesinger.** Signed; called "Dr." in Contents.
275 The recruiting difficulty; its causes and its remedy, 406–420. **C. H. Malan.** Signed; called "Captain" in Contents; see Boase.
276 Cicero and Clodius, 421–441. **E. S. Beesly.** Signed; repr. *Catiline*.
277 Atlantic telegraph and its lessons, 442–461. **John Stephen.** Signed J. Stephen; see *BMCat*.
278 Monte Cassino (Part II, concl.), 462–479. **W. E. Hall.** Signed.
279 Vittoria (chap. xxvii), 480–496. **George Meredith.** Signed.
280 Public affairs, 497–508.
281 Critical notices, 509–512. Pages 509–510 signed **E. S. Beesly;** pages 510–512 signed **John Dennis.**

VOLUME 5, JULY 15, 1866

282 *Les Apôtres* [by Renan], 513–536.
Henry Rogers. Signed; repr. *Essays from "Good Words,"* 1867.
283 The Oxford reformers of 1498 (chap. iv), 537–553. **Frederic Seebohm.** Signed.
284 What is an oath? 554–559. **J. M. Capes.** Signed.
285 Vittoria (chaps. xxviii–xxix), 560–586. **George Meredith.** Signed.
286 Home travel (No. II): Devonshire, 587–599. **John Dennis.** Signed.
287 Count Bismarck (Part II, concl.), 600–623. **Max Schlesinger.** Signed.
288 Public affairs, 624–635.
289 Critical notice, 636–640. **E. Lyulph Stanley.** Signed.

VOLUME 5, AUGUST 1, 1866

290 The policy of Italy, 641–653. **W. C. Cartwright.** Signed.
291 The discovery of the Albert N'Yanza, 654–669. **Henry Kingsley.** Signed.
292 On the use of metaphor and "pathetic fallacy" in poetry, 670–684. **Roden Noel.** Signed.
293 Vittoria (chaps. xxx–xxxi), 685–704. **George Meredith.** Signed.
294 Country life in Hungary before the elections, 705–717. **Arthur J. Patterson.** Signed.
295 The sovereignty of the sea, 718–733. **J. K. Laughton.** Signed.
296 Shakespeare's sonnets, 734–741. **Robert Bell,** 1800–1867. Signed; see *DNB.*
297 Public affairs, 742–753.
298 Critical notices, 754–768. Page 768 signed **John Dennis;** pages 758–763 signed **H. S. Fagan;** pages 754–758 signed **G. D. Haughton;** pages 763–768 signed **John Lubbock.**

VOLUME 6, AUGUST 15, 1866

299 The war of the banks, 1–27. **R. H. Patterson.** Signed.
300 New facts in the life of Geoffrey Chaucer, 28–35. **Edward A. Bond.** Signed.
301 The Oxford reformers of 1498 (chap. v), 36–56. **Frederic Seebohm.** Signed.
302 Vittoria (chap. xxxii), 57–70. **George Meredith.** Signed.
303 The religion of savages, 71–86. **Edward B. Tylor.** Signed.

304 The Danubian principalities, 87–103. **Adam Gielgud.** Signed.
305 Public affairs, 104–115.
306 Critical notices, 116–128. Pages 116–123 signed **Peter Bayne;** pages 126–127 signed **Moncure D. Conway;** pages 127–128 signed **John Dennis;** pages 123–126 signed **James Gairdner.**

VOLUME 6, SEPTEMBER 1, 1866

307 A Hungarian election, 129–150. **Arthur J. Patterson.** Signed.
308 Holbein at the National Portrait Exhibition (Part I: no more published), 151–169. **Alfred Woltmann.** Signed.
309 The Oxford reformers of 1498 (chap vi), 170–188. **Frederic Seebohm.** Signed.
310 The elements of muscular strength, 189–199. **Michael Foster,** 1836–1907. Signed M. Foster, Jun.; see *DNB.*
311 The inscription at Ancyra, 200–218. **W. M. W. Call.** Signed.
312 Was Sir William Hamilton a Berkeleian? 218–228. **James Hutchison Stirling.** Signed.
313 Vittoria (chaps. xxxiii–xxxiv), 229–242. **George Meredith.** Signed.
314 Public affairs, 243–254.
315 Critical notices, 255–256. Page 255 signed **John Dennis;** pages 255–256 by **G. H. Lewes**—signed Editor.

VOLUME 6, SEPTEMBER 15, 1866

316 England and the annexation of Mysore, 257–271. **John Morley.** Signed.
317 A Russian poet, 272–288. **W. R. S. Ralston.** Signed.
318 Immorality in authorship, 289–300. **Robert Buchanan,** 1841–1901. Signed.
319 The forest of Dartmoor, 300–310. **Richard J. King.** Signed.
320 Vittoria (chaps. xxxv–xxxvi), 311–326. **George Meredith.** Signed.
321 The reform of the statute book, 327–340. **Thomas Erskine Holland.** Signed; repr. *Essays on the Form of the Laws,* 1870.
322 The valle lands of Venetia, 341–352. **Henry Ecroyd.** Signed.
323 Miracles no proofs, 353–357. **John Fiske.** Signed.
324 Public affairs, 358–369.
325 Causeries (No. VII), 370–375. **G. H. Lewes.** Signed Editor.

326 Critical notices, 376–384. Pages 376–380 signed **Robert Bell**, 1800–1867—see *DNB*; pages 380–382 signed **H. S. Fagan;** pages 383–384 signed **G. D. Haughton.**

VOLUME 6, OCTOBER 1, 1866

327 Comte and Mill, 385–406. **G. H. Lewes.** Signed Editor.
328 The origin of the English, 407–419. **George W. Cox.** Signed.
329 A new theory of supply and demand, 420–434. **William T. Thornton.** Signed; repr. *On Labour*, 1869.
330 The army, 435–445. **James F. Fuller.** Signed A (Late) Common Soldier; claimed in his *Omniana: Reminiscences of an Irish Octogenarian* (1916), p. 92.
331 Home travel (No. III): Westmoreland and Cumberland, 445–454. **John Dennis.** Signed.
332 Vittoria (chaps. xxxvii–xxxviii), 455–473. **George Meredith.** Signed.
333 The Oxford reformers of 1498 (chap. vii, concl.), 474–492. **Frederic Seebohm.** Signed.
334 Public affairs, 493–504.
335 Critical notices, 505–512. Pages 510–512 signed **James Hutton;** pages 508–510 signed **David Wedderburn;** pages 505–507 signed **W. Whitaker.**

VOLUME 6, OCTOBER 15, 1866

336 The English Constitution (Part VII): on changes of ministry, 513–537. **Walter Bagehot.** Signed.
337 Walt Whitman, 538–548. **Moncure D. Conway.** Signed.
338 Russian society (Part I), 549–566. **A. W. Benni.** Signed.
339 The progress of medicine, 567–578. **W. B. Cheadle.** Signed; called "Dr." in Contents; see *DNB*.
340 Vittoria (chaps. xxxix–xl), 579–604. **George Meredith.** Signed.
341 European Turkey and its subject races, 605–619. **Adam Gielgud.** Signed.
342 Public affairs, 620–631.
343 Critical notices, 632–640. Pages 636–640 signed **Peter Bayne;** page 640 signed **John Dennis;** pages 632–636 signed **Anthony Trollope.**

VOLUME 6, NOVEMBER 1866

344 Elizabeth and her England, 641–658.

William Kirkus. Signed; repr. *Miscellaneous Essays*, 2nd series, 1868.
345 Russia and America, 659–665. **Moncure D. Conway.** Signed.
346 Notes curious and critical made at Perugia, 666–681. **Alfred Austin.** Signed.
347 Cottage property in London, 681–687. **Octavia Hill.** Signed; repr. *Homes of the London Poor*, 1875.
348 Vittoria (chaps. xli–xliv), 688–713. **George Meredith.** Signed.
349 The theory of missionary effort, 714–728. **G. R. Wynne.** Signed.
350 Russian society (Part II, concl.), 729–744. **A. W. Benni.** Signed.
351 Public affairs, 745–756. Pages 745–750, at least, by **Henry Dangby Seymour**—remarks on p. 749 retracted in signed note to no. 377, p. 241.
352 Causeries (No. VIII), 757–762. **G. H. Lewes.** Signed Editor.
353 Critical notices, 763–768. Pages 763–765 by **G. H. Lewes**—signed Editor; pages 765–768 signed **Edward B. Tylor.**

VOLUME 6, DECEMBER 1866

354 The Church of England as a religious body (Part I), 769–789. **John Russell,** 1842–1876. Signed Amberley [Viscount Amberley].
355 The lost tales of Miletus, 790–801. **Benjamin Hall Kennedy.** Signed.
356 Italy and the Pope (Part I), 802–806. **Aurelio Saffi.** Signed.
357 The English Constitution (Part VIII): its supposed checks and balances, 807–826. **Walter Bagehot.** Signed.
358 The currency and its reform, 837–856. **R. H. Patterson.** Signed.
359 Vittoria (chaps. xlv–epilogue), 857–877. **George Meredith.** Signed.
360 Public affairs, 878–889.
361 Farewell causerie, 890–896. **G. H. Lewes.** Signed Editor.

VOLUME 7 O.S., 1 N.S., JANUARY 1867

362 France in the seventeenth century, 1–18. **John Morley.** Signed Editor.
363 Tukárám: a study of Hinduism, 27–40. **Alexander Grant.** Signed; called "Bart." in Contents; see *DNB*.
364 The white rose (chaps. i–v), 41–67. **G. J. Whyte-Melville.** Signed; novel published 1868.
365 The significance of ritualism, 68–77. **J. C. Morison.** Signed.

366 The English Constitution (Part IX, concl.): its history, and the effects of that history, 78–99. **Walter Bagehot.** Signed.

367 Causeries (No. I), 100–103. **John Morley.** Signed Editor.

368 Public affairs, 104–115. **John Morley?** Morley's editorship commenced with this issue and he prob. assumed this department as part of his editorial responsibility; no. 405 has a note clearly by the author, signed J.M.

369 Critical notices, 116–128. Pages 118–120 signed **John Dennis;** pages 123–125 signed **Thomas Fowler;** pages 120–123 signed **Adam Gielgud;** pages 126–128 signed **George Meredith,** repr. *Works,* XXIII, 81–86; pages 116–118, 125–126 by **John Morley**—signed Editor.

VOLUME 7 O.S., 1 N.S., FEBRUARY 1867

370 Edmund Burke (Part I), 129–145. **John Morley.** Signed Editor; partially repr. "considerably modified," *Edmund Burke: a Historical Study,* 1867.

371 Our admiralty, 146–160. **Sherard Osborn.** Signed.

372 Lady Herbert's *Impressions of Spain,* 161–178. **Abraham Hayward.** Signed A. Hayward.

373 A canoe voyage, 179–196. **Philip Gilbert Hamerton.** Signed.

374 The Church of England as a religious body (Part II, concl.), 197–216. **John Russell,** 1842–1876. Signed Amberley [Viscount Amberley].

375 The white rose (chaps. vi–viii), 217–233. **G. J. Whyte-Melville.** Signed.

376 Prospects of the session, 234–240. **Henry D. Seymour.** Signed.

377 Public affairs, 241–245. **John Morley?** Cf. no. 368.

378 Causeries (No. II), 246–248. **John Morley.** Signed Editor.

379 Critical notices, 249–259. Pages 249–252 signed **J. M. Capes;** pages 258–259 signed **Frances Power Cobbe;** pages 255–257 signed **J. C. Morison;** pages 257–258 by **John Morley**—signed Editor; pages 252–255 signed **Anthony Trollope.**

VOLUME 7 O.S., 1 N.S., MARCH 1867

380 Our Venetian constitution, 261–283. **Frederic Harrison.** Signed.

381 Religious utopias in the United States, 290–302. **J. Cotter Morison.** Signed.

382 Edmund Burke (Part II), 303–318. **John Morley.** Signed Editor.

383 The Amalgamated Society of Carpenters, 319–334. **Edward Spencer Beesly.** Signed.

384 The white rose (chaps. ix–xii), 335–356. **G. J. Whyte-Melville.** Signed.

385 What is progress, and are we progressing? 357–370. **Frances Power Cobbe.** Signed.

386 Public affairs, 371–379. **John Morley?** Cf. no. 368.

387 Critical notices, 380–388. Pages 385–388 signed **William Black;** pages 382–385 by **Joseph Knight,** 1829–1907—signed J. Knight, see *DNB*; pages 380–382 signed **George Meredith,** repr. *Works,* XXIII, 87–91; page 388 by **John Morley**—signed Editor.

VOLUME 7 O.S., 1 N.S., APRIL 1867

388 History of the reform question from 1832 to 1848, 389–409. **W. N. Molesworth.** Signed. (See no. 412.)

389 Music the expression of character, 410–419. **J. M. Capes.** Signed.

390 Edmund Burke (Part III), 420–435. **John Morley.** Signed Editor.

391 Italy and the Pope (Part II, concl.), 436–455. **Aurelio Saffi.** Signed.

392 The white rose (chaps. xiii–xvi), 456–479. **G. J. Whyte-Melville.** Signed.

393 The Canadian confederation, 480–490. **Auberon Herbert.** Signed.

394 Young England and the political future, 491–496. **John Morley.** Signed Editor.

395 Public affairs, 497–506. **John Morley?** Cf. no. 368.

396 Critical notices, 507–516. Pages 514–516 signed **J. M. Capes;** pages 512–514 signed **Henry Stuart Fagan;** pages 507–510 signed **Henry Jackson,** 1839–1921; pages 510–512 by **John Morley**—signed Editor.

VOLUME 7 O.S., 1 N.S., MAY 1867

397 The picture-gatherings of Paris (Part I), 517–537. **Henry O'Neil.** Signed.

398 The slave trade and slave life in Central Asia, 538–550. **Arminius Vambéry.** Signed A. Vambéry; Contents gives first name.

399 What determines the price of labour or rate of wages? 551–566. **W. T. Thornton.** Signed; repr. *On Labour* (1870), pp. 90–108.

400 The historical credibility of the Homeric poems, 567–580. **George W. Cox.** Signed.

401 The white rose (chaps. xvii–xx), 581–601. **G. J. Whyte-Melville.** Signed.

402 The case against Sir Walter Raleigh, 602–614. **Samuel R. Gardiner.** Signed.

403 The budget and the national debt, 615–620. **Vere Henry Hobart.** Signed Hobart [Baron Hobart].

404 England and the European crisis, 621–629. **John Morley.** Signed Editor.

405 Public affairs, 630–637. **John Morley?** Footnote, p. 630, clearly by the author, signed J.M.; cf. no. 368.

406 Critical notices, 638–644. Pages 638–640 signed **J. M. Capes;** page 644 signed **H. Buxton Forman;** pages 641–642 signed **Robert Giffen;** page 643 by **John Morley**—signed Editor.

VOLUME 7 O.S., 1 N.S., JUNE 1867

407 Miracles and special providences, 645–660. **John Tyndall.** Signed; repr. *Fragments,* II.

408 The Roman Molière [Plautus], 661–677. **W. R. S. Ralston.** Signed.

409 The picture-gatherings of Paris (Part II, concl.), 678–696. **Henry O'Neil.** Signed.

410 The relations between the crowns of England and Scotland, 697–714. **Edward A. Freeman.** Signed; repr. *Essays,* I.

411 The white rose (chaps. xxi–xxiii), 715–732. **G. J. Whyte-Melville.** Signed.

412 History of the reform question from 1848 to 1866, 733–747. **W. N. Molesworth.** Signed.

413 American prospects, 748–753. **Moncure D. Conway.** Signed.

414 Public affairs, 754–763. **John Morley?** Cf. no. 368.

415 Critical notices, 764–772. Pages 769–770 signed **W. S. Austin;** pages 765–768 signed **Henry Jackson,** 1839–1921; pages 770–772 by **Joseph Knight,** 1829–1907 —signed as in no. 387; pages 768–769 signed **W. T. Marriott;** pages 764–765 by **John Morley**—signed editor.

VOLUME 8 O.S., 2 N.S., JULY 1867

416 The Trades' Union Commission, 1–18. **Edward Spencer Beesly.** Signed.

417 Morris's *Life and Death of Jason,* 19–28. **Algernon Charles Swinburne.** Signed, repr. *Essays.*

418 Roman, Anglican, and Protestant sacred music, 29–37. **J. M. Capes.** Signed.

419 Emigration from Ireland, 38–46. **T. E. Cliffe Leslie.** Signed.

420 Edmund Burke (Part IV, concl.), 47–61. **John Morley.** Signed Editor.

421 The white rose (chaps. xxiv–xxvi), 62–76. **G. J. Whyte-Melville.** Signed.

422 The state and the currency, 77–95. **R. H. Patterson.** Signed.

423 *The Reign of Law* [by the Duke of Argyl], 96–111. **George Henry Lewes.** Signed.

424 Public affairs, 112–122. **John Morley?** Cf. no. 368.

425 Critical notices, 123–128. Pages 127–128 signed **J. M. Capes;** pages 124–126 signed **Robert Giffen;** pages 123–124 by **John Morley**—signed Editor.

VOLUME 8 O.S., 2 N.S., AUGUST 1867

426 Charitable endowments, in their relation to the state and to public taxation, 129–142. **Thomas Hare.** Signed.

427 Theodore Parker, 143–152. **Moncure D. Conway.** Signed.

428 Macbeth and Lady Macbeth, 153–168. **P. W. Clayden.** Signed.

429 Legal etiquette, 169–179. **Albert V. Dicey.** Signed.

430 Sir Cecil Beadon's defence, 180–191. **J. M. Capes.** Signed.

431 The white rose (chaps. xxvii–xxix), 192–209. **G. J. Whyte-Melville.** Signed.

432 The law of trade combinations in France (Part I), 210–225. **Francis D. Longe.** Signed.

433 Mr. Froude on the science of history, 226–237. **John Morley.** Signed. Editor.

434 Public affairs, 238–244. **John Morley?** Cf. no. 368.

435 Critical notices, 245–256. Pages 245–247 signed **Henry Stuart Fagan;** pages 250–253 signed **Robert Giffen;** pages 247–250 by **Marie Meredith,** prob.— signed M. Meredith; the knowledge of French manners and dress suggests an acquaintance with that country; see *DNB* under George Meredith; pages 255–256 by **John Morley**—signed Editor; pages 253–255 signed **David Wedderburn.**

VOLUME 8 O.S., 2 N.S., SEPTEMBER 1867

436 M. Guizot's *Own Time* [*Memoirs pour servir à l'Histoire de Mon Temps*], 257–271. **John Wilson.** Signed; prob. the

author of *Studies of Modern Mind and Character* who wrote on French topics; see *Index*, I, 1141–1142.

437 The authenticity of the works of Plato, 272–286. **W. L. Blackley.** Signed.

438 Anonymous journalism, 287–292. **John Morley.** Signed Editor.

439 The law of trade combinations in France (Part II, concl.), 296–309. **Francis D. Longe.** Signed.

440 Richard Brinsley Sheridan, 310–332. **W. F. Rae.** Signed.

441 The white rose (chaps. xxx–xxxiv), 333–358. **G. J. Whyte-Melville.** Signed.

442 The Liberal programme, 359–369. **John Morley.** Signed Editor.

443 Critical notices, 370–376. Pages 370–373 signed **Robert Black;** page 376 signed **Robert Giffen;** page 370, 373–376 by **John Morley**—signed Editor.

VOLUME 8 O.S., 2 N.S., OCTOBER 1867

444 De Quincey and Coleridge upon Kant, 377–397. **James Hutchison Stirling.** Signed.

445 Harvard and Yale Universities, 398–413. **G. M. Towle.** Signed.

446 Mr. Arnold's *New Poems*, 414–445. **Algernon Charles Swinburne.** Signed; repr. *Essays*.

447 The white rose (chaps. xxxv–xxxvii), 446–463. **G. J. Whyte-Melville.** Signed.

448 English painters and painting in 1867, 464–476. **Sidney Colvin.** Signed.

449 Stray chapters from a forthcoming work on labour (chap. i): the claims of labour, and its rights, 477–500. **W. T. Thornton.** Signed; series repr. *On Labour*, 1869.

VOLUME 8 O.S., 2 N.S., NOVEMBER 1867

450 The future of London architecture, 501–517. **Henry Conybeare.** Signed.

451 Physics and politics (Part I): the pre-economic age, 518–538. **Walter Bagehot.** Signed; treatise published 1872.

452 The last two Abyssinian books [by Samuel Baker and Henry Dufton], 547–556. **Henry Kingsley.** Signed.

453 The white rose (chaps. xxxviii–xliv), 557–589. **G. J. Whyte-Melville.** Signed.

454 Stray chapters from a forthcoming work on labour (chap. ii): the rights of capital, 592–602. **W. T. Thornton.** Signed.

455 Culture: a dialogue [on Matthew Arnold], 603–614. **Frederic Harrison.** Signed; repr. *Choice of Books*.

456 Critical notices, 615–620. Pages 615–617 signed **J. M. Capes;** pages 617–618 signed **H. Buxton Forman;** pages 619–620 signed **Robert Giffen;** page 619 by **John Morley**—signed Editor.

VOLUME 8 O.S., 2 N.S., DECEMBER 1867

457 Proposed remedies for Irish wrongs, 621–634. **J. Herbert Stack.** Signed.

458 The Emperor Tiberius; a lecture delivered at Bradford, March 27, 1867 (Part I), 635–648. **Edward Spencer Beesly.** Signed; repr. *Catiline*.

459 The white rose (chaps. xlv–xlviii), 649–670. **G. J. Whyte-Melville.** Signed.

460 The marriage law of Scotland, 673–687. **J. Campbell Smith.** Signed.

461 Stray chapters from a forthcoming work on labour (chap. iii): the origin of trades' unions, 688–702. **W. T. Thornton.** Signed.

462 Music and architecture, 703–710. **J. M. Capes.** Signed.

463 Financial questions for the reformed parliament, 711–726. **Robert Giffen.** Signed.

464 Critical notices, 732–736. Pages 732–734 signed **Moncure D. Conway;** pages 734–736 signed **James Cotter Morison.**

VOLUME 9 O.S., 3 N.S., JANUARY 1868

465 The legal boundaries of liberty, 1–13. **A. V. Dicey.** Signed.

466 The Emperor Tiberius (Part II, concl.), 14–30. **Edward Spencer Beesly.** Signed.

467 Rawlinson on ancient architecture, 31–43. **James Fergusson,** 1808–1886. Signed; see *DNB*.

468 The white rose (chaps. xlix–liii), 44–70. **G. J. Whyte-Melville.** Signed.

469 Stray chapters from a forthcoming work on labour (chap. iv): the ends of trades' unionism, 77–88. **W. T. Thornton.** Signed.

470 Ireland for the British, 89–94. **James Cotter Morison.** Signed.

471 Shall we continue to teach Latin and Greek? 95–105. **Thomas Fowler.** Signed T. Fowler; see *DNB*.

472 Critical notices, 106–120. Pages 117–120 signed **P. W. Clayden;** pages 106–110 by **James Godkin**—signed as in no. 30; pages 115–117 signed **George Meredith,**

repr. *Works*, XXIII, 92–95; pages 110–115 signed **Henry Morley.**

349 signed **Americ Palfrey Marras;** pages 345–348 by **John Morley**—signed Editor.

VOLUME 9 O.S., 3 N.S., FEBRUARY 1868

473 Three old Yorkshire poems, 121–130. **Henry Morley.** Signed.
474 Ireland in 1868, 131–144. **T. E. Cliffe Leslie.** Signed; repr. *Land Systems.*
475 The white rose (chaps. liv–lx, concl.), 145–177. **G. J. Whyte-Melville.** Signed.
476 On the Christian hypothesis, and the method of its verification, 178–190. **Frederic Seebohm.** Signed.
477 Fenianism and the Irish Church, 191–205. **James Godkin.** Signed.
478 Russian railways, 206–215. **Robert Giffen.** Signed.
479 Critical notices, 216–232. Pages 216–220 signed **Moncure D. Conway;** pages 222–225 signed **J. W. Kaye;** pages 229–232 by **George Meredith**—signed, repr. *Works*, XXIII, 96–102; pages 220–222 by **John Morley**—signed Editor; pages 225–228 signed **E. B. Tylor.**

VOLUME 9 O.S., 3 N.S, MARCH 1868

480 Public school education; lecture delivered at the Royal Institution, 31st January, 1868, 233–249. **F. W. Farrar.** Signed.
481 Junius, Francis, and Lord Mansfield in December 1770, 250–256. **Herman Merivale.** Signed.
482 On the theory of clerical obligation, 257–269. **Rowland Williams.** Signed; see *Life and Letters*, ed. Ellen Williams (1874), II, 262–263.
483 Leonora Casaloni (book I, chaps. i–iv), 270–294. **T. A. Trollope.** Signed; novel published 1868.
484 Historical prediction, 295– 310. **Lionel A. Tollemache.** Signed; repr. *Safe Studies*, 1893.
485 The internal conflict of America, 311–318. **Moncure D. Conway.** Signed.
486 Ireland and Scotland, 319–329. **James Godkin.** Signed.
487 A fragment on the genesis of morals, 330–338. **John Morley.** Signed Editor.
488 Critical notices, 339–352. Pages 342–345 signed **J. M. Capes;** pages 350–352 signed **Sidney Colvin;** pages 339–342 signed **Edward A. Freeman;** pages 349–350 signed **Robert Giffen;** pages 348–

VOLUME 9 O.S., 3 N.S., APRIL 1868

489 Mr. Darwin's hypotheses (Part I), 353–373. **George Henry Lewes.** Signed.
490 The transit of power, 374–396. **Frederic Harrison.** Signed.
491 Mr. Pearson's *Early and Middle Ages of England*, 397–404. **Edward A. Freeman.** Signed.
492 Leonora Casaloni (book I, chaps. v–vii), 405–418. **T. A. Trollope.** Cf. no. 483.
493 The origin and character of the Homeric poems, 419–436. **George W. Cox.** Signed.
494 Stray chapters from a forthcoming work on labour (chap. v): ways and means of trades' unions, 437–451. **W. T. Thornton.** Signed.
495 Physics and politics (Part II): the age of conflict, 452–471. **Walter Bagehot.** Signed.
496 Critical notices, 472–480. Pages 476–478 by **John Morley**—signed Editor; pages 475–476 signed **W. F. Rae;** pages 479–480 signed **J. Herbert Stack;** pages 472–474 signed **W. T. Thornton.**

VOLUME 9 O.S., 3 N.S., MAY 1868

497 Joseph de Maistre (Part I), 481–496. **John Morley.** Signed Editor; repr. *Miscellanies*, II.
498 The ecclesiastical organisations of English Dissent, 497–507. **P. W. Clayden.** Signed.
499 Sir Thomas Moore and Henry VIII's book against Luther, 508–519. **Frederic Seebohm.** Signed.
500 Stray chapters from a forthcoming work on labour (chap. vi, concl.): ways and means of trades' unions, 520–536. **W. T. Thornton.** Signed.
501 Confucius, 537–546. **John Bowring.** Signed J. Bowring; Contents adds "Sir"; see *DNB.*
502 Leonora Casaloni (book II, chaps. i–iii), 547–569. **T. A. Trollope.** Cf. no. 483.
503 Compulsory primary education, 570–581. **Dudley Campbell.** Signed; repr. *Compulsory Education*, 1870.
504 Critical notices, 582–592. Pages 586–589 signed **Robert Black;** pages 582–584 signed **Edward Dowden;** pages 589–591

signed **James Cotter Morison;** pages 584–586 by **John Morley**—signed Editor; pages 591–592 signed **George Stott.**

VOLUME 9 O.S., 3 N.S., JUNE 1868

505 Joseph de Maistre (Part II), 593–610. **John Morley.** Signed Editor.
506 Mr. Darwin's hypotheses (Part II), 611–628. **George Henry Lewes.** Signed.
507 Massimo d'Azeglio, 629–638. **Antonio Gallenga.** Signed A. Gallenga: see *DNB.*
508 Matthew Arnold on the London University, 639–647. **Walter Bagehot.** Signed.
509 Mr. Holman Hunt's "Isabel", 648–657. **Bernard Cracroft.** Signed.
510 Mr. Robert Lytton's poems, 658–672. **George Meredith.** Signed; repr. *Works,* XXIII.
511 Leonora Casaloni (book II, chaps. iv–vii), 673–697. **T. A. Trollope.** Cf. no. 483.
512 The Digest of Law Commission, 698–708. **William O'Connor Morris.** Signed.
513 Critical notices, 709–720. Pages 709–711 signed **Frederic W. Farrar;** pages 711–713 signed **Robert Giffen;** pages 718–720 signed **William Kirkus;** pages 713–715 by **John Morley**—signed Editor; pages 715–718 signed **E. B. Tylor.**

VOLUME 10 O.S., 4 N.S., JULY 1868

514 The question of Central Asia, 1–15. **Robert Giffen.** Signed.
515 Notes on designs of the old masters at Florence, 16–40. **Algernon Charles Swinburne.** Signed; repr. *Essays.*
516 Leonora Casaloni (book II, chap. viii–book III, chap. i), 41–60. **T. A. Trollope.** Signed.
517 Mr. Darwin's hypotheses (Part III), 61–80. **George Henry Lewes.** Signed.
518 Nations and international law, 90–102. **T. E. Cliffe Leslie.** Signed.
519 The political prelude, 103–114. **John Morley.** Signed Editor.
520 Critical notice, 115–116. **Joseph Knight,** 1829–1907—signed as in no. 387.

VOLUME 10 O.S., 4 N.S., AUGUST 1868

521 Nihilism in Russia, 117–138. **Peter Boboruikin.** Signed.
522 Mr. Disraeli, the novelist, 146–159. **Bernard Cracroft.** Signed.

523 Common errors on the mind, 160–175. **Alexander Bain.** Signed; repr. *Practical Essays,* 1884.
524 Leonora Casaloni (book III, chaps. ii–iv), 176–196. **T. A. Trollope.** Signed.
525 Technical education, 197–228. **Fleeming Jenkin.** Signed.
526 Critical notices, 229–236. Pages 229–231 signed **Edward Dowden;** pages 232–234 signed **Robert Giffen;** pages 234–236 by **John Morley**—signed Editor.

VOLUME 10 O.S., 4 N.S., SEPTEMBER 1868

527 The retentive power of the mind in its bearing on education, 237–249. **Alexander Bain.** Signed.
528 The right of women to vote under the Reform Act, 1867, 250–254. **R. M. Pankhurst.** Signed.
529 John Wilkes, 260–276. **W. F. Rae.** Signed.
530 The laws of history (Part I: no more published), 277–299. **John Fiske.** Signed.
531 Leonora Casaloni (book III, chap. v–book IV, chap. i), 300–319. **T. A. Trollope.** Signed.
532 Old parties and new policy, 320–336. **John Morley.** Signed Editor.
533 Critical notices, 337–348. Pages 343–346 signed **John Bowring;** pages 346–348 signed **Frederic W. Farrar;** pages 337–343 signed **Rowland Williams.**

VOLUME 10 O.S., 4 N.S., OCTOBER 1868

534 Kirk's *History of Charles the Bold,* 349–368. **Edward A. Freeman.** Signed; repr. *Essays,* I.
535 Palingenesis, 369–378. **Henry Morley.** Signed.
536 Mystery, and other violations of relativity, 383–395. **Alexander Bain.** Signed; repr. *Practical Essays,* 1884, as "Errors of Suppressed Correlatives."
537 Leonora Casaloni (book IV, chaps. ii–v), 396–425. **T. A. Trollope.** Signed.
538 Social condition and political prospects of the Lancashire workmen, 426–441. **W. A. Abram.** Signed.
539 Joseph de Maistre (Part III, concl.), 442–460. **John Morley.** Signed Editor.
540 Critical notices, 461–468. Pages 467–468 signed **P. W. Clayden;** pages 461–465 signed **James Cotter Morison;** pages 465–467 signed **John Burnell Payne.**

VOLUME 10 O.S., 4 N.S., NOVEMBER 1868

541 On some features of American scenery, 469–491. **Herman Merivale.** Signed.

542 Mr. Darwin's hypotheses (Part IV, concl.), 492–509. **George Henry Lewes.** Signed.

543 The *Ethiopics* of Heliodorus, 510–525. **J. D. Lester.** Signed.

544 Leonora Casaloni (book IV, chap. vi–book V, chap. i), 526–553. **T. A. Trollope.** Signed.

545 The medical and general education of women, 554–571. **Millicent Garrett Fawcett.** Signed.

546 The Church and her younger members, 572–579. **F. W. Farrar.** Signed.

547 Critical notices, 580–588. Pages 585–586 signed **Robert Giffen;** pages 586–588 signed **Joseph Knight;** pages 580–583 by **T. E. Cliffe Leslie**—signed, repr. *Land Systems*; pages 583–585 by **John Morley** —signed Editor.

VOLUME 10 O.S., 4 N.S., DECEMBER 1868

548 Arthur Hugh Clough, 589–617. **John Addington Symonds.** Signed; repr. *The Last and the First*, N.Y., 1919.

549 Philosophy as a subject of study, 623–638. **G. Croom Robertson.** Signed; repr. *Philosophical Remains*, 1894.

550 Leonora Casaloni (book V, chaps. ii–concl.), 639–667. **T. A. Trollope.** Signed.

551 The constitutional question in the United States, 668–680. **D. C. Lathbury.** Signed.

552 The chamber of mediocrity [Commons], 681–694. **John Morley.** Signed Editor.

553 Critical notices, 695–704. Pages 701–702 signed **J. M. Capes;** pages 697–699 signed **Sidney Colvin;** pages 699–701 signed **W. T. Marriott;** pages 695–697 signed **Henry Morley;** pages 702–704 signed **W. F. Rae.**

VOLUME 11 O.S., 5 N.S., JANUARY 1869

554 Lamennais, 1–26. **Edward Dowden.** Signed; repr. *Studies*.

555 The saga of Gunnlaug the Worm-Tongue and Rafn the Skald, 27–56. **Eiríkr Magnusson** and **William Morris.** Signed; repr. *Three Northern Love Stories and Other Tales*, 1875.

556 On the physiology of thinking, 57–71. **H. Charlton Bastian.** Signed. (See no. 584.)

557 The Luther monument at Worms and the German Reformation struggle, 72–79. **Karl Blind.** Signed.

558 Suez Canal (Part I), 80–100. **J. Clerk.** Signed; called "Captain" in Contents.

559 Mr. Gladstone's work in finance, 101–116. **Robert Giffen.** Signed; repr. *Economic Inquiries and Studies* (1904), I.

560 Critical notices, 117–128. Pages 123–125 signed **Sidney Colvin;** pages 117–120 by **H. Buxton Forman**—signed, repr. with substantial revision in *Our Living Poets*; pages 121–123 signed **George Stott.**

VOLUME 11 O.S., 5 N.S., FEBRUARY 1869

561 On the physical basis of life, 129–145. **T. H. Huxley.** Signed; repr. *Collected Essays*, I.

562 The woman of business (chaps. i–iv), 156–177. **Marmion W. Savage.** Signed; novel published 1870.

563 Necker and Calonne: an old story, 178–187. **Edward Spencer Beesly.** Signed; repr. *Catiline*.

564 Mr. Anthony Trollope's novels, 188–198. **J. Herbert Stack.** Signed.

565 Schubert, 199–205. **J. M. Capes.** Signed.

566 Suez Canal (Part II, concl.), 206–225. **J. Clerk.** Signed.

567 On chemical rays, and the light of the sky, 226–248. **John Tyndall.** Signed.

568 Critical notices, 249–252. Pages 249–250 signed **Robert Giffen.**

VOLUME 11 O.S., 5 N.S., MARCH 1869

569 Westphalia and the Ruhr basin, 253–265. **T. E. Cliffe Leslie.** Signed; repr. *Land Systems*.

570 Spenser's "Hobbinol" [Gabriel Harvey], 274–283. **Henry Morley.** Signed.

571 Public and private property considered as to its legal conditions (Part I): public property, 284–297. **Thomas Hare.** Signed.

572 The woman of business (chaps. v–viii), 298–321. **Marmion Savage.** Signed.

573 Religious tests, and the nationalising of the universities, 322–330. **F. A. Paley.** Signed.

574 On *The Ring and the Book*, 331–343. **John Morley.** Signed Editor; repr. *Studies*.

575 The social future of the working class, 344–363. **Edward Spencer Beesly.** Signed.

576 An international money question, 364–370. **Nathaniel Taran.** Signed.

577 Critical notices, 371–376. Pages 375–376 signed **P. W. Clayden;** pages 371–

373 signed **William Kirkus;** pages 373–374 signed **Americ Marras.**

VOLUME 11 O.S., 5 N.S., APRIL 1869

578 Endowments, 377–390. **J. S. Mill.** Signed; repr. *Dissertations,* IV.
579 Russian popular legends, 395–406. **W. R. S. Ralston.** Signed.
580 Mr. Huxley on M. Comte, 407–418. **Richard Congreve.** Signed.
581 Ferdinand Lassalle, the German Social-Democrat, 419–453. **J. M. Ludlow.** Signed.
582 Sir G. C. Lewis and longevity, 454–472. **Lionel A. Tollemache.** Signed; repr. *Safe Studies,* 1893.
583 The woman of business (chaps. ix–xii), 473–492. **Marmion Savage.** Signed.
584 A note on Dr. Bastian's paper "On the Physiology of Thinking" [no. 556], 493–498. **Alexander Bain.** Signed.
585 Critical notices, 499–504. Pages 499–500 signed **J. M. Capes;** pages 500–502 signed **Sidney Colvin.**

VOLUME 11 O.S., 5 N.S., MAY 1869

586 Thornton on labour and its claims (Part I), 505–518. **J. S. Mill.** Signed; repr., with no. 598, *Dissertations,* IV.
587 Mr. Lecky's first chapter [of *History of European Morals*], 519–538. **John Morley.** Signed Editor.
588 Notes on the text of Shelley, 539–561. **A. C. Swinburne.** Signed; repr. *Essays.*
589 Pacific railroads, 562–578. **William A. Bell.** Signed.
590 The philosophy of etching, 579–585. **Philip Gilbert Hamerton.** Signed.
591 Mr. Longman's *Life and Times of Edward The Third,* 586–596. **Edward A. Freeman.** Signed; repr. *Essays,* I.
592 The woman of business (chaps. xiii–xvi), 597–621. **Marmion Savage.** Signed.
593 Arbitration and conciliation, 622–628. **Henry Crompton.** Signed.
594 Critical notices, 629–632. Pages 629–630 by **George Meredith**—signed, repr. *Works,* XXIII, 77–80.

VOLUME 11 O.S., 5 N.S., JUNE 1869

595 Literary egotism, 633–652. **Lionel A. Tollemache.** Signed; repr. *Safe Studies,* 1893.

596 The scientific aspects of positivism, 653–670. **T. H. Huxley.** Signed.
597 The portraits in the Academy of 1869 (Part I), 670–679. **Bernard Cracroft.** Signed.
598 Thornton on labour and its claims (Part II, concl.), 680–700. **J. S. Mill.** Signed.
599 American feeling towards England, 704–712. **Edward Dicey.** Signed.
600 The woman of business (chaps. xvii–xix), 713–731. **Marmion Savage.** Signed.
601 Public and private property considered as to its legal conditions (Part II, concl.): private property, 732–747. **Thomas Hare.** Signed.
602 Critical notices, 748–756. Pages 750–752 signed **T. E. Cliffe Leslie;** page 748 by **John Morley**—signed Editor; pages 752–755 signed **Charles Smith**—called "Captain" in Contents; pages 748–750 signed **Anthony Trollope.**

VOLUME 12 O.S., 6 N.S., JULY 1869

603 Relations of the Christian theory of duty to universal morality, 1–12. **J. Llewelyn Davies.** Signed; repr. *Theology and Morality,* 1873.
604 Claude Tillier: an unknown satirist, 13–29. **Philip Gilbert Hamerton.** Signed.
605 The Trades-union Bill, 30–45. **Frederic Harrison.** Signed.
606 The Academy of 1869 (Part II, concl.), 46–57. **Bernard Cracroft.** Signed.
607 Physics and politics (Part III): nation making, 58–72. **Walter Bagehot.** Signed. (Part IV is no. 826.)
608 Victor Hugo. *L'Homme qui Rit,* 73–81. **Algernon Charles Swinburne.** Signed; repr. *Essays.*
609 The woman of business (chaps. xx–xxii), 82–102. **Marmion Savage.** Signed.
610 On the nature of emotion, 103–115. **G. Fielding Blandford.** Signed.
611 Critical notices, 116–120. Pages 116–118 signed **William Kirkus.**

VOLUME 12 O.S., 6 N.S., AUGUST 1869

612 Walter Savage Landor, 121–139. **Edward Dowden.** Signed; repr. *Studies.*
613 Influence of civilisation on health, 140–161. **John Henry Bridges.** Signed.
614 On the scientific study of poetry, 163–178. **Francis T. Palgrave.** Signed.
615 Henry Crabb Robinson, 179–188. **Walter Bagehot.** Signed; repr. *Works,* IV and *Studies,* III.

616   On emigration, 189–199. **Charles Eliot Norton.** Signed.

617   On teaching English, 200–214. **Alexander Bain.** Signed.

618   The woman of business (chaps. xxiii–xxv), 215–235. **Marmion Savage.** Signed.

619   Critical notices, 236–240. Pages 236–237 signed **George Stott.**

VOLUME 12 o.s., 6 n.s., SEPTEMBER 1869

620   Mr. Gladstone on the historical credibility of the *Iliad* and *Odyssey*, 241–249. **George W. Cox.** Signed.

621   Ancient and modern Russia, 250–269. **Karl Blind.** Signed.

622   The question of the House of Lords, 270–286. **J. Boyd Kinnear.** Signed.

623   Heinrich Heine, 287–303. **J. D. Lester.** Signed.

624   The woman of business (chaps. xxvi–xxx), 304–337. **Marmion Savage.** Signed.

625   Public education in Holland, 338–347. **C. K. Altmann.** Signed.

626   Critical notices, 348–352. Pages 351–352 signed **Robert Giffen;** pages 348–351 signed **William A. Hunter.**

VOLUME 12 o.s., 6 n.s., OCTOBER 1869

627   The morality of field sports, 353–385. **Edward A. Freeman.** Signed. (See nos. 640, 738.)

628   Old guilds and new friendly and trade societies, 390–406. **J. M. Ludlow.** Signed.

629   The worship of animals and plants (Part I): totems and totemism, 407–427. **J. F. M'Lennan.** Signed; series repr. *Studies in Ancient History*, 2nd s., 1896. (See no. 678.)

630   Samuel Richardson, as artist and moralist, 428–443. **H. Buxton Forman.** Signed.

631   The woman of business (chaps. xxxi–xxxiii), 444–466. **Marmion Savage.** Signed.

632   Critical notice, 467–468. **George Stott.** Signed.

VOLUME 12 o.s., 6 n.s., NOVEMBER 1869

633   The positivist problem, 469–493. **Frederic Harrison.** Signed.

634   Notes on Leonardo Da Vinci, 494–508. **Walter H. Pater.** Signed; repr. *The Renaissance*, 1873.

635   The Latter-Day Saints (Part I), 511–535. **John Russell,** 1842–1876. Signed Amberley [Viscount Amberley].

636   The woman of business (chaps. xxxiv–

xxxvii), 536–561. **Marmion Savage.** Signed.

637   The worship of animals and plants (Part II): totem-gods among the ancients, 562–582. **J. F. M'Lennan.** Signed.

638   Critical notices, 583–584.

VOLUME 12 o.s., 6 n.s., DECEMBER 1869

639   Masterly inactivity, 585–615. **J. W. S. Wyllie.** Signed; repr. *Essays on the External Policy of India*, 1875.

640   Mr. Freeman on the morality of hunting, 616–625. **Anthony Trollope.** Signed. (See no. 738.)

641   The land question (Part I): English tenures in Ireland, 626–640. **Frederic Seebohm.** Signed as in no. 75.

642   Pope's *Essay on Man*, 641–650. **T. E. Kebbel.** Signed.

643   The condition of France, 651–664. **Karl Blind.** Signed.

644   The Latter-Day Saints (Part II, concl.), 665–691. **John Russell,** 1842–1876. Signed Amberley.

645   The woman of business (chaps. xxxviii–xl), 692–712. **Marmion Savage.** Signed.

VOLUME 13 o.s., 7 n.s., JANUARY 1870

646   Climbing in search of the sky, 1–15. **John Tyndall.** Signed.

647   Condorcet (Part I), 16–40. **John Morley.** Signed Editor; repr. *Miscellanies*, II.

648   Political economy and land, 41–63. **J. E. Cairnes.** Signed; repr. *Economy*.

649   A few words on Mr. Trollope's defence of fox-hunting, 63–68. **Helen Taylor.** Signed.

650   Christopher Marlowe, 69–81. **Edward Dowden.** Signed; repr. *Transcripts*.

651   The death-laments of savages, 82–88. **George Grey,** 1812–1898. Signed G. Grey; Contents gives "Sir George Grey"; see *DNB*.

652   The land question (Part II): feudal tenures in England, 89–107. **Frederic Seebohm.** Signed.

653   The woman of business (chaps. xli–xliii), 108–125. **Marmion Savage.** Signed.

654   Critical notice, 126–128. **J. Llewelyn Davies.** Signed.

VOLUME 13 o.s., 7 n.s., FEBRUARY 1870

655   Condorcet (Part II, concl.), 129–151. **John Morley.** Signed Editor.

695 The first Lord Malmesbury, 23–38. **T. E. Kebbel.** Signed.

696 Professor Cairnes on M. Comte and political economy, 39–58. **Frederic Harrison.** Signed. (See no. 710).

697 Wendell Phillips, 59–73. **Moncure D. Conway.** Signed.

698 Anne Furness (chaps. i–iv), 74–102. **Frances Eleanor Trollope.** H & L and *LCCat*; novel published 1871.

699 On national compulsory education, 101–113. **Frederic Seebohm.** Signed as in no. 75; repr. *How Can Compulsory Education Be Made to Work in England?* 1870.

700 The misrepresentation of majorities, 114–117. **Edward Maitland.** Signed.

701 The *Fortnightly Review* and positivism: a note, 118–120. **John Morley.** Signed Editor.

702 Critical notice, 121–124. **J. S. Mill.** Signed; repr. *Dissertations*, IV, as "Taine's *De l'Intelligence*."

VOLUME 14 o.s., 8 n.s., AUGUST 1870

703 Sir Thomas More on the politics of today, 125–137. **Helen Taylor.** Signed.

704 Tales of Old Japan (No. II, concl.): the loves of Gompachi and Komurasaki, 138–154. **A. B. Mitford.** Signed.

705 A fragment on Sandro Botticelli, 155–160. **Walter H. Pater.** Signed; repr. *The Renaissance*, 1873.

706 The life of Turgot, 161–179. **John Morley.** Signed Editor; repr. *Miscellanies*, II. (See. No. 805.)

707 The subjective synthesis, 184–197. **Frederic Harrison.** Signed; repr. *Common Sense.*

708 Our uncultivated lands, 198–215. **Frederick A. Maxse.** Signed.

709 Anne Furness (chaps. v–ix), 216–246. **Frances Eleanor Trollope.** Cf. no. 698.

710 A note [in reply to no. 696], 246–248. **J. E. Cairnes.** Signed.

VOLUME 14 o.s., 8 n.s., SEPTEMBER 1870

711 The mystery of life, 249–261. **Lionel S. Beale.** Signed.

712 Hegel as a politician: his views on English politics, 262–276. **James Scot Henderson.** Signed J. S. Henderson; see Boase.

713 Russia under Alexander II, 277–293. **Francis Marx.** Signed F. Marx; see *BMCat.*

714 The Civil Code of New York, 294–306. **W. O'Connor Morris.** Signed.

715 Political reputations, 307–313. **T. E. Kebbel.** Signed.

716 Anti-utilitarianism, 314–337. **W. T. Thornton.** Signed; repr. *Old-fashioned Ethics and Common-sense Metaphysics,* 1873.

717 Anne Furness (chaps. x–xiv), 338–366. **Frances Eleanor Trollope.** Cf. no. 698.

718 France and Germany, 367–376. **John Morley.** Signed Editor.

VOLUME 14 o.s., 8 n.s., OCTOBER 1870

719 Father Arndt, 377–394. **W. L. Blackley.** Signed in Contents.

720 Ornamental art in England, 395–410. **W. B. Scott.** Signed.

721 Bastiat, 411–428, **J. E. Cairnes.** Signed; repr. *Economy.*

722 Trinity College, Dublin, 429–441. **Max Cullinan.** Signed. (See no. 740.)

723 Jack Cade's Rebellion, 442–455. **James Gairdner.** Signed.

724 Anne Furness (chaps. xv–xviii), 456–478. **Frances Eleanor Trollope.** Cf. no. 698.

725 England and the [Franco-Prussian] War, 479–488. **John Morley.** Signed Editor. (See no. 732.)

726 Critical notice, 488–490. **C. M. Ingleby.** Signed.

VOLUME 14 o.s., 8 n.s., NOVEMBER 1870

727 Schelling's life and letters, 491–516. **J. Scot Henderson.** Signed.

728 The International Working Men's Association, 517–535. **Edward Spencer Beesly.** Signed.

729 Stray thoughts on comparative mythology, 536–548. **Edward A. Freeman.** Signed.

730 The political economy of Adam Smith, 549–563. **T. E. Cliffe Leslie.** Signed; repr. *Political Economy.*

731 Bolivia and Brazil in the Amazon Valley, 564–580. **George E. Church.** Signed.

732 England and the French Republic: [a letter] to the Editor of the *Fortnightly Review*, 581–588. **Charles C. Chesney.** Signed.

733 A note to Colonel Chesney's letter [no. 732], 588–591. **John Morley.** Signed Editor.

734   Anne Furness (chaps. xix–xxii), 592–614. **Frances Eleanor Trollope.** Cf. no. 698.

VOLUME 14 O.S., 8 N.S., DECEMBER 1870

735   The future of France, 615–630. **Emile de Laveleye.** Signed; repr. in French, *Essais et Etudes,* 1st series, Paris, 1894.
736   Bismarckism, 631–649. **Frederic Harrison.** Signed; repr. *National and Social Problems.*
737   Byron, 650–673. **John Morley.** Signed Editor; repr. *Miscellanies,* I.
738   The controversy on field sports, 674–691. **Edward A. Freeman.** Signed.
739   Hand and soul [on Chiaro], 692–702. **Dante Gabriel Rossetti.** Signed.
740   Trinity College, Dublin: a reply [to no. 722], 703–714. **J. P. Mahaffy.** Signed.
741   Treaty obligations, 715–720. **J. S. Mill.** Signed; repr. *Dissertations,* IV.
742   Anne Furness (chaps. xxiii–xxv), 721–738. **Frances Eleanor Trollope.** Cf. no. 698.

VOLUME 15 O.S., 9 N.S., JANUARY 1871

743   The German Empire, 1–16. **Heinrich von Sybel.** Signed.
744   Balzac's novels, 17–39. **Leslie Stephen.** Signed; repr. *Hours,* I.
745   To what extent is England prosperous? 40–52. **Henry Fawcett.** Signed.
746   The result of French designs upon Germany, 53–66. **Karl Blind.** Signed.
747   Shelley in 1812–13: an unpublished poem, and other particulars, 67–85. **W. M. Rossetti.** Signed.
748   The claims of women, 95–110. **Katharine L. Russell.** Signed K. Amberley [Viscountess Amberley].
749   Anne Furness (chaps. xxvi–xxviii), 111–129. **Frances Eleanor Trollope.** Cf. no. 698.
750   The *Westminster Review* on the land question in England, 130–136. **Frederic Seebohm.** Signed as in no. 75.
751   Some books of the month, 137–144. **Sheldon Amos.** Signed.

VOLUME 15 O.S., 9 N.S., FEBRUARY 1871

752   The effacement of England, 145–166. **Frederic Harrison.** Signed; repr. *Problems,* as "The Duty of England."
753   Our defences: a national or a standing army? 167–198. **J. E. Cairnes.** Signed; repr. *Political Essays,* 1873.
754   Edgar Quinet, 199–218. **Edward Dowden.** Signed; repr. *Studies.*
755   Old criticisms on old plays and old players: Garrick as Hamlet, described by a German spectator [G. C. Lichtenberg] (Part I), 221–239. **Robert Lytton.** Signed.
756   A heterodox view of the Eastern question, 240–254. **Humphry Sandwith.** Signed.
757   The boarding-out of pauper children, 255–261. **Henry Fawcett.** Signed.
758   Anne Furness (chaps. xxix–xxxi), 262–280. **Frances Eleanor Trollope.** Cf. no. 698.
759   Some books of the month, 281–288. **Sheldon Amos.** Signed.

VOLUME 15 O.S., 9 N.S., MARCH 1871

760   Italy and the republic, 289–309. **Joseph Mazzini.** Signed; repr. in Italian, *Scritti,* XCII.
761   De Quincey, 310–329. **Leslie Stephen.** Signed; repr. *Hours,* I.
762   From Portsmouth to Oran to see the eclipse, 330–351. **John Tyndall.** Signed; repr. *Fragments,* I.
763   Old criticisms on old plays and old players (Part II, concl.), 352–362. **Robert Lytton.** Signed.
764   On the nature and origin of the moral ideas, 363–373. **Alexander Grant.** Signed as in no. 363.
765   Do military inventions promote peace? 374–386. **Lionel A. Tollemache.** Signed.
766   Anne Furness (chaps. xxxii–xxxiv), 387–408. **Frances Eleanor Trollope.** Cf. no. 698.
767   Critical notice, 409–411. **James Sully.** Signed.
768   Some books of the month, 412–418. **Sheldon Amos.** Signed.

VOLUME 15 O.S., 9 N.S., APRIL 1871

769   Morals and moral sentiments, 419–432. **Herbert Spencer.** Signed; repr. *Recent Discussions in Science, Philosophy and Morals,* N.Y., 1871.
770   The New Forest: a sketch, 433–451. **G. E. Briscoe Eyre.** Signed.
771   Paris and France, 451–458. **Helen Taylor.** Signed.

772 The present state of the land question, 459–471. **C. Wren Hoskyns.** Signed; called "Wren-Hoskyns" in Contents.

773 On the Mausoleum of Halikarnassos, 472–484. **Sidney Colvin.** Signed; repr. *A Selection from Occasional Writings on Fine Arts*, 1873.

774 Paris after the peace, 485–494. **Edward Dicey.** Signed.

775 Lord Lytton's *King Arthur*, 495–504. **F. W. Farrar.** Signed.

776 The aesthetics of human character, 505–520. **James Sully.** Signed; repr. in revised form, *Sensation and Intuition*.

777 Anne Furness (chaps. xxxv–xxxviii), 521–542. **Frances Eleanor Trollope.** Cf. no. 698.

VOLUME 15 O.S., 9 N.S., MAY 1871

778 Mr. Maine, *Village Communities*, 543–556. **J. S. Mill.** Signed; repr. *Dissertations*, IV.

779 The Revolution of the Commune, 556–579. **Frederic Harrison.** Signed.

780 Agrarianism, 580–594. **Charles S. Roundell.** Signed.

781 Italy and Rome, 595–613. **J. W. Probyn.** Signed.

782 Can war be avoided? 614–633. **John Russell,** 1842–1876. Signed Amberley [Viscount Amberley].

783 Anne Furness (chaps. xxxix–xlv), 634–673. **Frances Eleanor Trollope.** Cf. no 698.

784 Critical notices, 674–676. Pages 674–675. **Sidney Colvin.** Signed.

VOLUME 15 O.S., 9 N.S., JUNE 1871

785 Germany: past, present, and future, 677–708. **Robert Lytton.** Assigned to him in *Letters*, I, 250.

786 Beauty and realism, in construction and decoration, 709–730. **Edward J. Poynter.** Signed.

787 Some recent English novels, 731–746. **J. Herbert Stack.** Signed.

788 The three theories of the wanderings of Ulysses, 747–770. **Herman Merivale.** Signed.

789 Taxes on land, 771–784. **Robert Giffen.** Signed; repr. *Economic Inquiries and Studies* (1904), I.

790 Anne Furness (chaps. xlvi–l), 785–814. **Frances Eleanor Trollope.** Cf. no. 698.

791 Critical notices, 815–816.

VOLUME 16 O.S., 10 N.S., JULY 1871

792 The Eustace diamonds (chaps. i–iv), 1–27. **Anthony Trollope.** Signed; novel published 1873.

793 The French Republic and the suffrage question, 28–34. **Karl Blind.** Signed.

794 Earl Russell, the Commune, and Christianity, 35–41. **Humphry Sandwith.** Signed.

795 John Ford, 42–63. **A. C. Swinburne.** Signed; repr. *Essays.*

796 Political economy and laissez-faire, 80–97. **J. E. Cairnes.** Signed.

797 Anne Furness (chaps. li–liv), 98–124. **Frances Eleanor Trollope.** Cf. no. 698.

798 Some recent books, 125–128.

VOLUME 16 O.S., 10 N.S., AUGUST 1871

799 The fall of the Commune, 129–155. **Frederic Harrison.** Signed.

800 Senior's *Journals*, 156–165. **Walter Bagehot.** Signed; repr. *Works,* II.

801 Prohibitory legislation in the United States, 166–179. **Justin McCarthy,** 1830–1912. Signed.

802 The devil, 180–191. **Frances Power Cobbe.** Signed; repr. *Darwinism.*

803 The Eustace diamonds (chaps. v–viii), 191–219. **Anthony Trollope.** Cf. no. 792.

804 Anne Furness (chaps. lv–lviii, concl.), 235–260. **Frances Eleanor Trollope.** Cf. no. 698.

VOLUME 16 O.S., 10 N.S., SEPTEMBER 1871

805 Turgot's two discourses at the Sorbonne, 261–278. **John Morley.** Signed Editor; repr. *Miscellanies,* II. (See no. 706.)

806 The Eustace diamonds (chaps. ix–xii), 279–307. **Anthony Trollope.** Signed.

807 The Paris workmen and the Commune, 308–320. **Auguste Desmoulins.** Signed.

808 The use of historical documents, 321–336. **Edward A. Freeman.** Signed.

809 The opium trade, 351–358. **F. W. Chesson.** Signed.

810 Natural rights and abstract justice, 359–376. **W. T. Thornton.** Signed.

VOLUME 16 O.S., 10 N.S., OCTOBER 1871

811 Pico Della Mirandola, 377–386. **Walter H. Pater.** Signed; repr. *The Renaissance*, 1873.

812 The prospects of liberalism in Germany, 387–420. **Karl Hillebrand.** Signed.

813 The Eustace diamonds (chaps. xiii–xvi), 421–449. **Anthony Trollope.** Signed.

814 Voltaire at Berlin; a chapter from a forthcoming monograph, 450–477. **John Morley.** Signed Editor; repr. *Voltaire,* 1872.

815 *Balaustion's Adventure* [by Browning], 478–490. **Sidney Colvin.** Signed.

816 The House of Lords, 491–504. **Henry Fawcett.** Signed; repr. *Essays.*

VOLUME 16 O.S., 10 N.S., NOVEMBER 1871

817 Berkeley's life and writings, 505–524. **J. S. Mill.** Signed; repr. *Dissertations,* IV.

818 Administrative nihilism: an address to the members of the Midland Institute, Oct. 9, 1871, 525–543. **T. H. Huxley.** Signed; repr. *Collected Essays,* I.

819 The present position of the government, 544–558. **Henry Fawcett.** Signed.

820 The poetry of Michelangelo, 559–570. **Walter H. Pater.** Signed; repr. *The Renaissance,* 1873.

821 The Paris Commune, a chapter towards its theory and history, 571–598. **Jules Andrieu.** Signed.

822 The Eustace diamonds (chaps. xvii–xx), 599–626. **Anthony Trollope.** Signed.

VOLUME 16 O.S., 10 N.S., DECEMBER 1871

823 Specialized administration, 627–654. **Herbert Spencer.** Signed; repr. *Essays,* III.

824 Church and state in Italy, 655–667. **J. W. Probyn.** Signed.

825 The Eustace diamonds (chaps. xxi–xxiv), 668–695. **Anthony Trollope.** Signed.

826 Physics and politics (No. IV): nation-making, 696–717. **Walter Bagehot.** Signed.

827 A new attack on toleration, 718–727. **Helen Taylor.** Signed.

828 The Irish University question, 748–762. **Henry Dix Hutton.** Signed on p. 760.

VOLUME 17 O.S., 11 N.S., JANUARY 1872

829 The position and practice of the House of Lords, 1–13. **R. M. Milnes.** Signed Houghton [Lord Houghton].

830 Home Rule, 16–29. **William O'Connor Morris.** Signed.

831 Chaumette and the first Commune of Paris of 1793, 30–45. **Albert Regnard.** Signed A. Regnard; see *Bib. Nat. Cat.*

832 Physics and politics (No. V, concl.): the age of discussion, 46–70. **Walter Bagehot.** Signed.

833 New theories in political economy, 71–76. **J. E. Cairnes.** Signed.

834 St. Bernard of Clairvaux, 77–89. **James Cotter Morison.** Signed.

835 The Eustace diamonds (chaps. xxv–xxviii), 90–116. **Anthony Trollope.** Signed.

836 *The Life of Charles Dickens* [by Forster], 117–120. **J. Herbert Stack.** Signed.

VOLUME 17 O.S., 11 N.S., FEBRUARY 1872

837 The religion of an Indian province, 121–140. **A. C. Lyall.** Signed; repr. *Asiatic Studies.*

838 Dickens in relation to criticism, 141–154. **George Henry Lewes.** Signed; repr. *The Dickens Critics,* ed. G. H. Ford and L. Lane, Jr., Ithaca, N.Y., 1961.

839 Warburton, 155–175. **Leslie Stephen.** Signed; repr. *Freethinking.*

840 The Church of England and the people, 176–190. **George Potter.** Signed.

841 The International and the Manchester School, 191–195. **Vere Henry Hobart.** Signed Hobart [Baron Hobart].

842 Irish policy in the eighteenth century, 196–203. **John Morley.** Signed editor.

843 The political enfranchisement of women, 204–214. **Arthur Arnold.** Signed; repr. *Social Politics,* 1878.

844 The Eustace diamonds (chaps. xxix–xxxii), 215–242. **Anthony Trollope.** Signed.

VOLUME 17 O.S., 11 N.S., MARCH 1872

845 The aim of reform, 243–264. **Goldwin Smith.** Signed.

846 Richard Wagner, 265–287. **Franz Hüffer.** Signed; repr. *Richard Wagner,* 1874.

847 The historical aspect of the land question, 288–302. **Charles Elton.** Signed.

848 Estanislao Figueras, 303–309. **Emilio Castelar.** Signed.

849 Custom and sex, 310–323. **Edith J. Simcox.** Signed H. Lawrenny; W. B. Scott, *Notes,* II, 244, identifies the pseudonym.

850 Pierre Leroux's doctrine of humanity, 324–331. **Louis Pierre Leroux.** Signed.

178–196. **W. W. Story.** Signed; repr. *Excursions in Art and Letters*, Boston, 1891.

924 Louis Napoleon: 1851 and 1873, 197–204. **Albert Venn Dicey.** Signed.

925 Class legislation, 205–217. **Henry Crompton.** Signed.

926 The new cure for incurables [euthanasia], 218–230. **Lionel A. Tollemache.** Signed; repr. *Stones of Stumbling*, 1893.

927 Forty years of the House of Lords (Part II, concl.), 231–250. **Francis Bowen-Graves.** Signed as in no. 918.

928 The Eustace diamonds (chaps. lxxvii–lxxx, concl.), 251–275. **Anthony Trollope.** Signed.

929 Critical notices, 276–280. **Sidney Colvin.** Signed.

VOLUME 19 o.s., 13 N.S., MARCH 1873

930 Are we Christians? 281–303. **Leslie Stephen.** Signed; repr. *Freethinking*.

931 Servia and its new prince, 304–315. **Humphry Sandwith.** Signed.

932 The organization of a legal department of government, 316–332. **James Bryce,** 1838–1922. Signed.

933 On the historical element in Shakespeare's Falstaff, 333–344. **James Gairdner.** Signed; repr. *Studies*.

934 On the causes which operate to create scientific men, 345–351. **Francis Galton.** Signed.

935 The game laws and the committee of 1872, 352–372. **A. H. Beesly.** Signed.

936 *Rameau's Nephew*: a translation from the French of Diderot (Part I: no more published), 373–395. **Denis Diderot.** Title. Translation by **John Morley**, prob. —he wrote on Diderot in 1878; see no. 1121.

937 Critical notices, 396–404. Pages 396–398 signed **J. S. Mill,** repr. *Dissertations*, IV; pages 398–404 signed **Edith Simcox.**

VOLUME 19 o.s., 13 N.S., APRIL 1873

938 Public and private morality, 405–428. **Edward A. Freeman.** Signed.

939 The relation of witchcraft to non-Christian religions, 429–446. **A. C. Lyall.** Signed; repr. *Asiatic Studies.*

940 Restrictions on trade, from a colonial point of view, 447–464. **David Syme.** Signed.

941 Sedition, 465–469. **Henry Crompton.** Signed.

942 Mr. Pater's essays [on the Renaissance], 469–477. **John Morley.** Signed Editor.

943 Liquor and licensing, 478–494. **Arthur Arnold.** Signed; repr. *Social Politics* (1878), as "Intoxicating Liquors Question."

944 Dr. Stirling, Hegel, and the mathematicians, 495–514. **James Hutchison Stirling.** Signed.

945 Lady Anna (chaps. i–iv), 515–536. **Anthony Trollope.** Signed; novel published 1874.

946 Critical notices, 537–548. Pages 537–542 signed **D. G. Rossetti;** pages 543–548 signed **Edith Simcox.**

VOLUME 19 o.s., 13 N.S., MAY 1873

947 The incidence of local taxation, 549–563. **Henry Fawcett.** Signed.

948 The scientific character of Spinoza's philosophy, 567–585. **Frederick Pollock,** 1845–1937. Signed.

949 Poetry of the Renaissance in Portugal: Miranda and Ferreira, 586–605. **Oswald Crawfurd.** Signed; repr. *Portugal.*

950 Recent progress in weather knowledge, 606–617. **R. H. Scott.** Signed.

951 Mythology and fairy tales, 618–631. **Andrew Lang.** Signature.

952 Lady Anna (chaps. v–ix), 632–660. **Anthony Trollope.** Signed.

953 Critical notices, 661–668. **Edith Simcox.** Signed.

VOLUME 19 o.s., 13 N.S., JUNE 1873

954 The death of Mr. Mill, 669–676. **John Morley.** Signed Editor; repr. *Miscellanies*, III.

955 The religion of inhumanity, 677–699. **Frederic Harrison.** Signed; repr. as "The Religion of Humanity" in *The Positive Evolution of Religion*, 1913.

956 Robert Schumann, 700–717. **Francis Hueffer.** Signed F. Hüffer; repr. *Richard Wagner*, 1874.

957 The assumptions of agnostics, 718–731. **St. George Mivart.** Signed.

958 Deer-forests and culpable luxury, 732–753. **A. H. Beesly.** Signed.

959 The anarchy of London, 754–768. **John S. Storr.** Signed.

960 The gold mines and prices in England, 769–774. **T. E. Cliffe Leslie.** Signed; repr. *Political Economy.*

961 Lady Anna (chaps. x–xii), 775–793. **Anthony Trollope.** Signed.

962   Critical notices, 794–800. **Edith Simcox.** Signed.

VOLUME 20 O.S., 14 N.S., JULY 1873

963   The military side of the Commune (Part I), 1–24. **Gustave Cluseret.** Signed G. Cluseret; see *Grand Larousse*. (See no. 881.)
964   The government and class legislation, 25–40. **Henry Crompton.** Signed.
965   The abortiveness of French revolutions, 41–53. **James Cotter Morison.** Signed.
966   De Maillet, 54–63. **Carveth Read.** Signed.
967   A lost art [photography], 64–78. **John Coryton.** Signed.
968   Farm labourers and cow plots, 79–86. **Henry Evershed.** Signed H. Evershed; Contents gives first name.
969   Girton College, 87–93. **Emily Shirreff.** Signed.
970   Panslavism: its rise and decline, 94–112. **Elodie L. Mijatovics.** Signed E. L. Mijatovics; repr. 1885.
971   Lady Anna (chaps. xiii–xvi), 113–136. **Anthony Trollope.** Signed.
972   Critical notices, 137–142. **Edith Simcox.** Signed.

VOLUME 20 O.S., 14 N.S., AUGUST 1873

973   The struggle for national education (Part I), 143–162. **John Morley.** Signed Editor; treatise published 1873.
974   Poliziano's Italian poetry, 163–188. **J. A. Symonds.** Signed; repr. *Renaissance in Italy* (1910), IV.
975   Thomas Love Peacock, 189–206. **George Barnett Smith.** Signed; repr. *Poets and Novelists*, 1876.
976   Reforms in Persia, 206–212. **Reginald Stuart Poole.** Signed.
977   The military side of the Commune (Part II), 213–233. **Gustave Cluseret.** Signed as in no. 963.
978   Mr. Mill's doctrine of liberty, 234–256. **John Morley.** Signed Editor.
979   Lady Anna (chaps. xvii–xx), 257–281. **Anthony Trollope.** Signed.
980   Critical notices, 282–286. **Edith Simcox.** Signed.

VOLUME 20 O.S., 14 N.S., SEPTEMBER 1873

981   The Liberal party and its leaders, 287–302. **Joseph Chamberlain.** Signed J.

Chamberlain; Contents gives first name.
982   The struggle for national education (Part II), 303–325. **John Morley.** Signed Editor.
983   Greek beauty and modern art, 326–336. **F. W. Cornish.** Signed.
984   The history and present state of political economy in Germany, 337–350. **Gustav Cohn.** Signed.
985   The military side of the Commune (Part III, concl.), 351–370. **Gustave Cluseret.** Signed as in no. 963.
986   The perception of musical form, 371–381. **James Sully.** Signed; repr., enlarged, in *Sensation and Intuition*.
987   Lady Anna (chaps. xxi–xxiv), 382–405. **Anthony Trollope.** Signed.
988   Critical notices, 406–410. **Edith Simcox.** Assigned in Contents.

VOLUME 20 O.S., 14 N.S., OCTOBER 1873

989   The struggle for national education (Part III, concl.), 411–433. **John Morley.** Signed Editor.
990   The growth of commonwealths, 434–456. **Edward A. Freeman.** Signed; repr. *Essays*, IV.
991   The philosophy of inductive inference, 457–476. **W. Stanley Jevons.** Signed.
992   Popular and artistic song in Germany, 477–487. **Franz Hüffer.** Signed.
993   The House of Commons and Indian finance, 488–504. **Lepel Griffin.** Signed.
994   The promotion of scientific research, 505–524. **George Gore.** Signed.
995   Lady Anna (chaps. xxv–xxviii), 525–547. **Anthony Trollope.** Signed.
996   Public affairs, 548–556. **Frederic Harrison.** Signed.

VOLUME 20 O.S., 14 N.S., NOVEMBER 1873

997   Purchase of the railways by the state, 557–580. **William Galt.** Signed.
998   Replies to criticisms (Part I), 581–595. **Herbert Spencer.** Signed; repr. *Essays*, III.
999   Popular songs of Tuscany, 596–613. **J. Addington Symonds.** Signed; repr. *Sketches*, II.
1000   Statistical fallacies respecting public instruction, 614–628. **J. G. Fitch.** Signed.
1001   Plutarch's essays, 629–644. **W. J. Brodribb.** Signed.
1002   Mr. Jebb's translations, 645–655. **Frederic W. H. Myers.** Signed.
1003   Lady Anna (chaps. xxix–xxxii), 656–678. **Anthony Trollope.** Signed.

1004 Public affairs, 679–692. **Frederic Harrison.** Signed.

VOLUME 20 O.S., 14 N.S., DECEMBER 1873

1005 Taine's *History of English Literature*, 693–714. **Leslie Stephen.** Signed; repr. *Men and Mountains*.

1006 Replies to criticisms (Part II, concl.), 715–739. **Herbert Spencer.** Signed.

1007 The new Christology, 740–757. **Francis W. Newman.** Signed.

1008 The *Orlando Innamorato* of Boiardo, 758–777. **J. Addington Symonds.** Signed; repr. *Renaissance in Italy* (1910), IV.

1009 The use of hypothesis, 778–788. **W. Stanley Jevons.** Signed.

1010 Free schools, 789–796. **Charles Wentworth Dilke.** Signed.

1011 Lady Anna (chaps. xxxiii–xxxv), 797–814. **Anthony Trollope.** Signed.

1012 Public affairs, 815–822. **Frederic Harrison.** Signed.

VOLUME 21 O.S., 15 N.S., JANUARY 1874

1013 Mr. Mill's *Autobiography*, 1–20. **John Morley.** Signed Editor; repr. *Miscellanies*, III.

1014 The present state of the Eastern question, 21–42. **Lepel Griffin.** Signed.

1015 Marat, 43–74. **Francis Bowen-Graves.** Signed as in no. 918.

1016 The effect of an increased production of wealth on wages, 75–81. **Henry Fawcett.** Signed.

1017 Experiences of spiritualism, 82–91. **John Russell,** 1842–1876. Signed Amberley [Viscount Amberley].

1018 Banking, 92–108. **R. H. Inglis Palgrave.** Signed.

1019 New books, 109–120. **Edith Simcox.** Signed.

1020 Lady Anna (chaps. xxxvi–xxxviii), 121–140. **Anthony Trollope.** Signed.

1021 Public affairs, 141–152. **Frederic Harrison.** Signed.

VOLUME 21 O.S., 15 N.S., FEBRUARY 1874

1022 M. Renan and France, 153–174. **Joseph Mazzini.** Signed.

1023 Organized priesthood, 175–189. **F. W. Newman.** Signed.

1024 The position and prospects of co-operation, 190–208. **Henry Fawcett.** Signed.

1025 Belli's *Sonnets in the Roman Dialect*, 209–224. **Hans Sotheby.** Signed; Contents gives "H. W. Sotheby."

1026 Mr. Tennyson's social philosophy, 225–247. **Lionel A. Tollemache.** Signed; repr. *Safe Studies*, 1893.

1027 The incidence of imperial and local taxation on the working classes, 248–265. **T. E. Cliffe Leslie.** Signed; repr. *Political Economy*.

1028 Lady Anna (chaps. xxxix–xli), 266–281. **Anthony Trollope.** Signed.

1029 Public affairs, 282–296. **Frederic Harrison.** Signed. With a note, 293–294, signed **John Morley.**

VOLUME 21 O.S., 15 N.S., MARCH 1874

1030 The Conservative reaction, 297–309. **Frederic Harrison.** Signed; repr. *Order and Progress*.

1031 Two chapters on the reign of Louis XIV (chap. i): 1661–1679, 310–327. **James Cotter Morison.** Signed.

1032 Parliamentary government, 328–341. **F. W. Newman.** Signed.

1033 Some phases of English art under George III (Part I), 342–358. **Sidney Colvin.** Signed.

1034 M. Victor Hugo's new romance [*Quatrevingt-treize*], 359–370. **John Morley.** Signed Editor; repr. *Studies.*

1035 The internal working of railways, 371–384. **Edwin Phillips.** Signed.

1036 The Game Law Committee report, 385–406. **A. H. Beesly.** Signed.

1037 Lady Anna (chaps. xlii–xliv), 407–424. **Anthony Trollope.** Signed.

VOLUME 21 O.S., 15 N.S., APRIL 1874

1038 On compromise (chaps. i–ii, introduction): on the possible utility of error, 425–454. **John Morley.** Signed Editor; treatise published 1874.

1039 On Wordsworth, 455–465. **Walter H. Pater.** Signed; repr. *Appreciations.*

1040 Sex in mind and in education, 466–483. **Henry Maudsley.** Signed.

1041 The Indian famine and the press, 484–495. **Auckland Colvin.** Signed.

1042 Two chapters on the reign of Louis XIV (chap. ii): A.D. 1679–1715, 496–516. **James Cotter Morison.** Signed.

1043 The threatened exodus of agricultural labourers, 517–533. **Edwin A. Curley.** Signed.

1044 Lady Anna (chaps. xlv–xlviii, concl.), 534–555. **Anthony Trollope.** Signed.
1045 Public affairs, 556–564. **Frederic Harrison.** Signed.

VOLUME 21 O.S., 15 N.S., MAY 1874

1046 Siberia, 565–581. **Ashton W. Dilke.** Signed.
1047 Sex in mind and education: a reply [to no. 1040], 582–594. **Elizabeth Garrett Anderson.** Signed.
1048 Mr. Maurice's theology, 595–617. **Leslie Stephen.** Signed in Contents.
1049 Field sports and vivisection, 618–629. **Edward A. Freeman.** Signed.
1050 A defence of modern spiritualism (Part I), 630–657. **Alfred R. Wallace.** Signed; repr. *On Miracles and Modern Spiritualism*, 1875.
1051 Some phases of English art under George III (Part II, misprinted III, concl.), 658–673. **Sidney Colvin.** Signed.
1052 What are the Falk Laws? 674–694. **John Brown Paton.** Signed.
1053 Public affairs, 695–704. **Frederic Harrison.** Signed.

VOLUME 21 O.S., 15 N.S., JUNE 1874

1054 The movements of agricultural wages in Europe, 705–719. **T. E. Cliffe Leslie.** Signed; repr. *Political Economy*.
1055 On compromise (chap. iii): of intellectual responsibility and the political spirit, 720–741. **John Morley.** Signed Editor.
1056 Alienation of public lands in colonies, 742–759. **Emile de Laveleye.** Signed.
1057 Winckelmann (Part I), 760–784. **Karl Hillebrand.** Signed.
1058 A defence of modern spiritualism (Part II, concl.), 785–807. **Alfred R. Wallace.** Signed.
1059 The power of the farmers, 808–816. **Richard Jefferies.** Signed.
1060 Lord Lytton's *Fables in Song*, 817–823. **Robert Louis Stevenson.** Signed.
1061 The Afghan succession, 824–840. **Evans Bell.** Signed.
1062 France, 841–856. **Frederic Harrison.** Signed; repr. *Problems*.

VOLUME 22 O.S., 16 N.S., JULY 1874

1063 Is a republic possible in France? 1–26. **James Cotter Morison.** Signed.

1064 Winckelmann (Part II, misprinted III, concl.), 27–51. **Karl Hillebrand.** Signed.
1065 Missionary religions, 52–67. **A. C. Lyall.** Signed; repr. *Asiatic Studies*.
1066 A note on "Missionary Religions" [no. 1065], 68–75. **Friedrich Max Müller.** Signature; repr. *Chips*, IV, as "On the vitality of Brahmanism."
1067 Mr. Swinburne's "Bothwell," 76–88. **R. M. Milnes.** Signed Houghton [Lord Houghton].
1068 Mr. Lewes's *Problems of Life and Mind*, 89–101. **Frederic Harrison.** Signed; repr. *Common Sense*.
1069 On compromise (chap. iv): of religious conformity, 102–119. **John Morley.** Signed Editor.
1070 The power of the labourers, 120–132. **J. Charles Cox.** Signed.
1071 Justice abroad, 133–145. **Frederick Marshall.** Signed.
1072 Critical notice, 146–148. **Alexander Bain.** Signed A. Bain; Contents gives first name.

VOLUME 22 O.S., 16 N.S., AUGUST 1874

1073 The first partition of Poland, 149–170. **Heinrich von Sybel.** Signed H. von Sybel; see *ADB*.
1074 Froude's *English in Ireland*, 171–191. **J. E. Cairnes.** Signed.
1075 Imaginary geometry and the truth of axioms, 192–200. **George Henry Lewes.** Signed.
1076 Federalism and Home Rule, 204–215. **Edward A. Freeman.** Signed.
1077 *The Revolution of September, 1870* [by Jules Simon] (art. in French), 216–225. **Henri Rochefort.** Signed.
1078 On compromise (chap. v): realisation of opinion, 226–248. **John Morley.** Signed Editor.
1079 Beauchamp's career (chaps. i–iii), 249–272. **George Meredith.** Signed; novel published 1876.

VOLUME 22 O.S., 16 N.S., SEPTEMBER 1874

1080 An American view of emigration, 273–292. **Alfred Bishop Mason.** Signed.
1081 A novelty in French fiction, 293–307. **E. Robert Lytton.** Signed Lytton [Earl Lytton].
1082 Moral aspects of the religious difficulty, 308–322. **J. Allanson Picton.** Signed.
1083 The northern range of the Basques, 323–337. **W. Boyd Dawkins.** Signed.

1084 Mr. Flint's *Philosophy of History*, 338–352. **John Morley.** Signed Editor.
1085 The professional training of teachers, 353–376. **William Jolly.** Signed.
1086 Beauchamp's career (chap. iv–viii), 377–404. **George Meredith.** Signed.

VOLUME 22 O.S., 16 N.S., OCTOBER 1874

1087 The next page of the Liberal programme, 405–429. **Joseph Chamberlain.** Signed.
1088 Mr. Disraeli's novels, 430–450. **Leslie Stephen.** Signed; repr. *Hours*, II.
1089 The Caucasus, 451–470. **Ashton W. Dilke.** Signed.
1090 The history of republicanism in France, 471–494. **Edward Spencer Beesly.** Signed.
1091 The study of archaeology in schools, 495–503. **Oscar Browning.** Signed.
1092 A recent work on supernatural religion [*Supernatural Religion* by W. R. Cassels], 504–518. **John Morley.** Signed Editor. (See no. 1113.)
1093 Economic aspect of the endowment of research, 519–536. **C. E. Appleton.** Signed; repr. *Essays on Research*.
1094 Beauchamp's career (chaps. ix–xi), 537–554. **George Meredith.** Signed.

VOLUME 22 O.S., 16 N.S., NOVEMBER 1874

1095 On the hypothesis that animals are automata and its history, 555–580. **T. H. Huxley.** Signed; repr. *Collected Essays*, I.
1096 Must we then believe Cassandra? 581–604. **M. E. Grant Duff.** Signed. (See no. 1110.)
1097 The Third French Republic, 605–622. **Edward Spencer Beesly.** Signed.
1098 Free land, 623–633. **Henry Robert Brand.** Signed H. R. Brand; cf. no. 1775.
1099 Mr. Mill's three essays on religion (Part I), 634–651. **John Morley.** Signed Editor.
1100 A fragment on *Measure for Measure*, 652–658. **Walter H. Pater.** Signed.
1101 A recent contribution to political economy [Cairnes' *Some Leading Principles of Political Economy*], 661–675. **Vincent Henry Stanton?** Signed V. H. Stanton; man cited used this signature for *CR* no. 862 in the same year, but we have found no evidence of his interest in, or knowledge of economics.
1102 Beauchamp's career (chaps. xii–xiv), 676–700. **George Meredith.** Signed.

VOLUME 22 O.S., 16 N.S., DECEMBER 1874

1103 The Kafir Revolt of 1873, 701–713. **John Westlake.** Signed.
1104 Body and mind, 714–736. **W. K. Clifford.** Signed; repr. *Lectures*, II.
1105 Auvergne, 737–753. **T. E. Cliffe Leslie.** Signed; repr. *Political Economy*.
1106 Unsolved problems in national education, 754–766. **J. G. Fitch.** Signed.
1107 The blank verse of Milton, 767–781. **John Addington Symonds.** Signed; repr. *Blank Verse*, 1905.
1108 Clergy and laity, 782–797. **John Delaware Lewis.** Signed.
1109 *The Greville Journals*, 798–816. **E. Lyulph Stanley.** Signed. (Note, vol. 17 n.s., p. 304.)
1110 A short reply to Mr. Grant Duff's lecture on *Rocks Ahead* [no. 1096], 817–823. **W. R. Greg.** Signed.
1111 The Republican defeat in the United States, 824–835. **Edward Dicey.** Signed.
1112 Beauchamp's career (chaps. xv–xvii), 836–856. **George Meredith.** Signed.

VOLUME 23 O.S., 17 N.S., JANUARY 1875

1113 A reply to Professor Lightfoot's article on *Supernatural Religion*, 1–26. **Walter R. Cassels.** Signed The Author of *Supernatural Religion*; see *DNB*; repr. *A Reply to Dr. Lightfoot's Essays*, 1889.
1114 The tenure of land [in Great Britain], 27–43. **George Campbell,** 1824–1892. Signed G. Campbell; Contents gives first name and adds "Sir"; see *DNB*.
1115 Lucretius, 44–62. **John Addington Symonds.** Signed; repr. *Sketches*, III.
1116 Mr. Spencer on social evolution, 63–82. **J. E. Cairnes.** Signed.
1117 *King Lear*, 83–102. **J. W. Hales.** Signed; repr. *Notes*.
1118 Mr. Mill's three essays on religion (Part II, concl.), 103–131. **John Morley.** Signed Editor.
1119 Beauchamp's career (chaps. xviii–xix), 132–149. **George Meredith.** Signed.
1120 Critical notice, 150.

VOLUME 23 O.S., 17 N.S., FEBRUARY 1875

1121 Diderot (Part I), 151–168. **John Morley.** Signed Editor; treatise published 1878.
1122 The new relations of Church and State in Germany, 169–199. **J. B. Paton.** Signed.

1123 Mr. Spencer on the study of sociology, 200–213. **J. E. Cairnes.** Signed. (See no. 1124.)

1124 A note on the preceding article [Cairnes on Spencer's sociology], 214–216. **Herbert Spencer.** Signed; repr. *Various Fragments*, N.Y., 1898.

1125 An unknown poet [Wells], 217–232. **A. C. Swinburne.** Signed; repr. in Charles J. Wells, *Joseph and His Brethren*, 1876.

1126 Our canal population, 233–242. **George Smith,** 1831–1895. Signed; see *DNB* for his interest in this topic.

1127 The theory of exchange value, 243–253. **George H. Darwin.** Signed; see *DNB* for early interest in Jevons and economics.

1128 Public health, 254–270. **Humphry Sandwith.** Signed.

1129 Beauchamp's career (chaps. xx–xxii), 271–294. **George Meredith.** Signed.

1130 The Liberal eclipse, 295–304. **John Morley.** Signed Editor.

VOLUME 23 O.S., 17 N.S., MARCH 1875

1131 Maine's *Early History of Institutions*, 305–320. **T. E. Cliffe Leslie.** Signed.

1132 Mr. Charles Austin, 321–338. **Lionel A. Tollemache.** Signed; repr. *Safe Studies*, 1893.

1133 William Law, 339–359. **Leslie Stephen.** Signed; repr. *Hours* (1st ed. only, 1875), II.

1134 The land question and landed tenures of possession, 360–370. **Frederick S. Corrance.** Signed.

1135 The debt of English to Italian literature, 371–381. **J. A. Symonds.** Signed; repr. *Sketches*, II.

1136 Karl Marx and German socialism, 382–391. **John Macdonell.** Signed.

1137 The practice of medicine by women, 392–407. **Sophia Jex-Blake.** Signed.

1138 The Irish judges, 408–421. **George Fottrell, Jr.** Signed G. Fottrell, Jr.; Contents gives first name.

1139 A year of the Birmingham school-board, 422–434. **William Harris.** Signed.

1140 Vivisection, 435–437. **Richard Congreve** and **J. H. Bridges.** Signed.

1141 Beauchamp's career (chaps. xxiii–xxv), 438–464. **George Meredith.** Signed.

VOLUME 23 O.S., 17 N.S., APRIL 1875

1142 The first and the last catastrophe [the beginning and end of the earth], 465–484. **W. K. Clifford.** Signed; repr. *Lec-*

tures, I. (Note, p. 793, by **Clifford**—signed W.K.C.)

1143 Diderot (Part II), 485–504. **John Morley.** Signed Editor.

1144 The poor law and the peasantry, 508–521. **William Hazlitt Roberts,** prob. Signed W. H. Roberts; man cited wrote no. 1830 and other works in this field listed in *BMCat.*

1145 The Indian civil service examinations, 522–536. **Lepel Griffin.** Signed.

1146 *Isaac Casaubon* [by Mark Pattison], 537–551. **James Cotter Morison.** Signed.

1147 Tenant right, 552–565. **F. S. Corrance.** Signed.

1148 The economic definition of wealth, 566–574. **W. T. Thornton.** Signed.

1149 Homer and his recent critics, 575–589. **Andrew Lang.** Signature.

1150 Beauchamp's career (chaps. xxvi–xxviii), 590–612. **George Meredith.** Signed.

VOLUME 23 O.S., 17 N.S., MAY 1875

1151 The three stages of Shakespeare (Part I), 613–632. **Algernon Charles Swinburne.** Signed; repr. *A Study of Shakespeare*, 1880.

1152 The Agricultural Holdings Bill, 633–647. **William Edwin Bear.** Signed.

1153 Hesiod, 648–663. **John Addington Symonds.** Signed; repr. *Greek Poets*, II.

1154 The employment of mothers in factories, 664–679. **Whately Cooke-Taylor.** Signed.

1155 Diderot (Part III), 680–701. **John Morley.** Signed Editor.

1156 The old and the new economists in Italy, 702–713. **Cesare Pozzoni.** Signed C. Pozzoni; see *BMCat.*

1157 Report of the Civil Service Commission, 714–724. **T. H. Farrer.** Signed.

1158 A recent work on cosmic philosophy [John Fiske's *Outlines of Cosmic Philosophy*], 725–738. **Frederick Pollock,** 1845–1937. Signed.

1159 Beauchamp's career (chaps. xxix–xxxi), 739–762. **George Meredith.** Signed.

VOLUME 23 O.S., 17 N.S., JUNE 1875

1160 What could we have done for France or Belgium? 763–775. Unidentified. Perhaps George Tomkyns Chesney: see *Athenaeum*, June 19, 1875, p. 821.

1161 *The Unseen Universe* [by P. G. Tait and Balfour Stewart], 776–793. **W. K. Clifford.** Signed; repr. *Lectures*, I.

1162 The treatment of Indian immigrants in Mauritius, 794–819. **E. Lyulph Stanley.** Signed.

1163 *Order and Progress* [by Frederic Harrison], 820–834. **Leslie Stephen.** Signed.

1164 Results of the examination-system at the universities, 835–846. **A. H. Sayce.** Signed; repr. *Essays on Research*.

1165 Some popular fallacies about vivisection, 847–854. **Charles Lutwidge Dodgson.** Signed Lewis Carroll; see *DNB*.

1166 Marcion's gospel, 855–875. **William Sanday.** Signed W. Sanday; see *DNB*.

1167 Beauchamp's career (chaps. xxxii–xxxiv), 876–898. **George Meredith.** Cf. no. 1159.

1168 A day at Sedan, 899–910. **John Morley.** Signed Editor.

VOLUME 24 O.S., 18 N.S., JULY 1875

1169 The European situation, 1–21. **Emile de Laveleye.** Signed.

1170 Marriages between first cousins in England and their effects, 22–41. **George H. Darwin.** Signed; see *DNB* for his interest in this topic.

1171 The history of a pavement, 42–63. **Sidney Colvin.** Signed.

1172 Positivists and workmen, 64–74. **Edward Spencer Beesly.** Signed.

1173 Railway rates and fares, 75–92. **Joseph Parsloe.** Signed; repr. *Our Railways*, 1878.

1174 The history of German political economy, 93–101. **T. E. Cliffe Leslie.** Signed; repr. *Political Economy*.

1175 A note on representative government, 102–107. **Thomas Hare.** Signed.

1176 The military position of England, 108–122. Unidentified. Possibly George Tomkyns Chesney, as the point of view is the same as that in no. 1160, and on pp. 108 and 113 the author refers back to points made in that art.

1177 Beauchamp's career (chaps. xxxv–xxxvii), 123–148. **George Meredith.** Signed.

VOLUME 24 O.S., 18 N.S., AUGUST 1875

1178 Professor Cairnes, 149–154. **Henry Fawcett.** Signed.

1179 The inheritance of the Great Mogul, 155–177. **Rutherford Alcock.** Signed.

1180 Parliament and popular government, 189–204. **E. J. Payne.** Signed.

1181 The Mediterranean of Japan, 205–216. **Cyprian A. G. Bridge.** Signed.

1182 Mr. Cross's labour bills, 217–227. **W. A. Hunter.** Signed; called "Professor" in Contents; see *DNB*.

1183 The Eleatic fragments, 228–240. **John Addington Symonds.** Signed; repr. *Greek Poets*, II, as "Parmenides."

1184 A Home-Rule experiment in Ceylon, 241–258. **William Digby.** Signed.

1185 On certain clerical obliquities of mind, 259–266. **Percival Frost.** Signed.

1186 Beauchamp's career (chaps. xxxviii–xl), 267–290. **George Meredith.** Signed.

VOLUME 24 O.S., 18 N.S. SEPTEMBER 1875

1187 An American's impressions of England, 291–305. **Horace White.** Signed.

1188 On the origin and growth of divine myths in India, 306–323. **A. C. Lyall.** Signed; repr. *Asiatic Studies*.

1189 Sophocles, 324–338. **John Addington Symonds.** Signed; repr. *Greek Poets*, II.

1190 Women at the Swiss universities, 339–352. **George F. B. Jenner,** prob. Signed G. Jenner; man cited had lived in Berne in 1866; see *WWW/1928*.

1191 Diderot (Part IV): the *Encyclopaedia*, 353–398. **John Morley.** Signed Editor.

1192 The workmen's victory, 399–406. **Henry Crompton.** Signed.

1193 Beauchamp's career (chaps. xli–xliii), 407–428. **George Meredith.** Signed.

1194 Critical notice, 429–436. **E. Robert Lytton**—signed Lytton [Earl Lytton].

VOLUME 24 O.S., 18 N.S., OCTOBER 1875

1195 The Church of England and the universities, 437–448. **Herbert Richards.** Signed.

1196 The prose works of Wordworth, 449–470. **Edward Dowden.** Signed; repr. *Studies.*

1197 A ramble in Syracuse, 471–483. **A. H. Sayce.** Signed.

1198 Poor relief in foreign countries, 484–499. **W. A. Hunter.** Signed.

1199 Charles Baudelaire, 500–518. **George Saintsbury.** Signed; repr. *Essays*, IV.

1200 Reasoned realism [G. H. Lewes and positivism], 519–535. **J. Scot Henderson.** Signed.

1201 The place of geography in physical science, 536–550. **Richard Strachey.**

Signed; called "Lieut.-Gen." in Contents; see *DNB*.

1202 Beauchamp's career (chaps. xliv–xlvi), 551–578. **George Meredith.** Signed.

VOLUME 24 O.S., 18 N.S., NOVEMBER 1875

1203 "Materialism" and its opponents, 579–599. **John Tyndall.** Signed; repr. *Fragments*, II, as "James Martineau and the Belfast Address."

1204 England and Russia in the East, 600–610. **M. E. Grant Duff.** Signed.

1205 Sherman and Johnston, and the Atlanta Campaign, 611–624. **Charles C. Chesney.** Signed.

1206 The Book of Job and Plato's dialogue on justice, 625–641. **Henry William Hamilton-Hoare.** Signed Henry William Hoare; see *WWW*/1940.

1207 Is our cause in China just? 642–663. **J. H. Bridges.** Signed.

1208 Diderot (Part V, concl.): dialogues, 664–687. **John Morley.** Signed Editor.

1209 The reform of the magistracy, 688–698. **Henry Crompton.** Signed.

1210 Beauchamp's career (chaps. xlvii–li), 699–730. **George Meredith.** Signed.

VOLUME 24 O.S., 18 N.S., DECEMBER 1875

1211 A word on Alexander Dyce, 731–746. **John Forster.** Signed.

1212 The true Eastern question, 747–769. **Edward A. Freeman.** Signed.

1213 Right and wrong: the scientific ground of their distinction, 770–800. **W. K. Clifford.** Signed; repr. *Lectures*, II.

1214 Dutch Guiana (chaps. i–ii), 801–825. **W. Gifford Palgrave.** Signed.

1215 The post-office telegraphs and their financial results, 826–835. **W. Stanley Jevons.** Signed; repr. *Methods*.

1216 The value of political machinery, 836–852. **Leslie Stephen.** Signed.

1217 *The Provincial Letters* [by Pascal], 853–868. **H. D. Traill.** Signed; repr. *New Fiction*.

1218 Beauchamp's career (chaps. lii–lvi, concl.), 869–902. **George Meredith.** Cf. no. 1210.

VOLUME 25 O.S., 19 N.S., JANUARY 1876

1219 The Channel Islands and land tenure, 1–23. **F. B. Zincke.** Signed.

1220 The three stages of Shakespeare (Part

II, concl.), 24–45. **A. C. Swinburne.** Signed.

1221 The relations of western powers with the East, 46–66. **Rutherford Alcock.** Signed.

1222 German railways: a comparison, 67–81. **John Macdonell.** Signed.

1223 The myth of Demeter and Persephone (Part I), 82–95. **Walter H. Pater.** Signed; repr. *Greek Studies*.

1224 A glimpse of the Korea, 96–102. **Cyprian A. G. Bridge.** Signed.

1225 Courage and death, 103–125. **Lionel A. Tollemache.** Signed; pp. 103–115 repr. *Safe Studies*, 1893, as "Physical and Moral Courage"; pp. 116–125 repr. in expanded form, *Stones of Stumbling*, 1893, as "The Fear of Death" and "Fearless Deaths."

1226 The copyright question, 126–140. **Edward Dicey.** Signed.

1227 Home and foreign affairs, 141–156. **John Morley.** Morley to Joseph Chamberlain, Dec. 9, 1875, quoted by D. A. Hamer, *John Morley*, Oxford, 1968, pp. 115–116, mentions his plan to write commentaries on current events for the *FortR* and says he counts upon Chamberlain's assistance because "two heads are better than one, and previous discussion with you always makes my own ideas clearer"; it is probable that where we do not have conflicting evidence Morley wrote this department; F. W. Hirst, Morley's research assistant, *Early Life*, II, 27, says that Morley did this section at this time; Morley, *Recollections* (N.Y., 1917), I, 96–97 recalls that he "followed sedulously the course of home and foreign affairs in the pages of the Review"; Hamer, p. 120, speaks of the "editorial portion" of the Review (Morley's own phrase) as separated from the signed arts. with their variety of opinion, which implies Morley's own authorship on a consistent line.

VOLUME 25 O.S., 19 N.S., FEBRUARY 1876

1228 Our dealings with Egypt, and the possible results, 157–173. **George Campbell,** 1824–1892. Signed; called "Sir" in Contents.

1229 What are liberal principles? 174–193. **George C. Brodrick.** Signed.

1230 Dutch Guiana (chaps. iii–iv), 194–214. **W. G. Palgrave.** Signed.

1231 The postulates of English political

economy (No. I), 215–242. **Walter Bagehot.** Signed.

1232 Modern English prose, 243–259. **George Saintsbury.** Signed; repr. *Essays,* III.

1233 The myth of Demeter and Persephone (Part II, concl.), 260–276. **Walter H. Pater.** Signed.

1234 The new judicature, 277–294. **Montague Cookson.** Signed.

1235 Home and foreign affairs, 295–310. **John Morley,** prob. Cf. no. 1227.

VOLUME 25 o.s., 19 n.s., MARCH 1876

1236 The disestablishment movement, 311–339. **R. W. Dale.** Signed.

1237 The Upper Engadine, 340–369. **Lionel A. Tollemache.** Signed; pp. 340–356, 363–369 repr. *Safe Studies,* 1893.

1238 M. Taine's new work [*L'Ancien Régime*], 370–384. **John Morley.** Signed Editor; repr. *Miscellanies,* III, as "France in the Eighteenth Century."

1239 The Catholic peril in America, 385–405. **Francis E. Abbot.** Signed Francis E. Abbott; but see *DAB.*

1240 The Weddas [a tribe in Ceylon], 406–417. **Bertram F. Hartshorne.** Signed.

1241 On examinations, 418–429. **Thomas Fowler.** Signed T. Fowler; called "Professor" in Contents; see *DNB.*

1242 A national training to arms, 430–464. **H. M. Havelock-Allan.** Signed H. M. Havelock; called "Sir" in Contents; see *DNB.*

1243 Home and foreign affairs, 465–478. **John Morley,** prob. Cf. no. 1227.

VOLUME 25 o.s., 19 n.s., APRIL 1876

1244 Spiritualism and materialism (Part I), 479–493. **George Henry Lewes.** Signed.

1245 Macaulay, 494–513. **John Morley.** Signed Editor; repr. *Miscellanies,* I.

1246 The finances of India, 514–535. **George Campbell,** 1824–1892. Signed as in no. 1114.

1247 Dutch Guiana (chaps. v–vi, concl.), 536–555. **W. G. Palgrave.** Signed.

1248 On spelling, 556–579. **Friedrich Max Müller.** Signature; repr. *Chips,* V.

1249 Some truths about Egypt, 580–590. **Greville J. Chester.** Signed.

1250 On Mr. Mill's theory of value, 591–602. **Alfred Marshall.** Signed.

1251 Madame de Maintenon (Part I), 603–616. **J. Cotter Morison.** Signed.

1252 Home and foreign affairs, 617–630. **John Morley,** prob. Cf. no. 1227.

VOLUME 25 o.s., 19 n.s., MAY 1876

1253 The right method with the publicans, 631–651. **Joseph Chamberlain.** Signed as in no. 981.

1254 The Chinese Empire and its foreign relations, 652–670. **Rutherford Alcock.** Signed.

1255 Cruelty to animals: a study in sociology, 671–684. **W. Stanley Jevons.** Signed; repr. *Methods.*

1256 Some of the results of the Education Act and Code of 1870, 685–705. **James Kay-Shuttleworth.** Signed.

1257 Spiritualism and materialism (Part II, concl.), 707–719. **George Henry Lewes.** Signed.

1258 The postulates of English political economy (Part II, concl.), 720–741. **Walter Bagehot.** Signed.

1259 Some recent travels, 742–757. **John Morley.** Signed Editor.

1260 Madame de Maintenon (Part II, concl.), 758–770. **J. Cotter Morison.** Signed.

1261 A few words on the Oxford University Bill, 771–776. **James Bryce,** 1838–1922. Signed.

1262 Home and foreign affairs, 777–790. **John Morley,** prob. Cf. no. 1227.

VOLUME 25 o.s., 19 n.s., JUNE 1876

1263 The new Domesday Book, 791–809. **E. Lyulph Stanley.** Signed.

1264 The financial crisis in America, 810–829. **Horace White.** Signed.

1265 Early autumn on the lower Yang-tze, 830–839. **Cyprian A. G. Bridge.** Signed.

1266 An agnostic's apology, 840–860. **Leslie Stephen.** Signed; repr. *Agnostic's Apology.*

1267 James Northcote, R. A., 861–876. **J. Thackray Bunce.** Signed.

1268 India and Lancashire, 877–896. **R. Raynsford Jackson.** Signed.

1269 The laws on compulsory education, 897–918. **John White.** Signed.

1270 Home and foreign affairs, 919–932. **John Morley,** prob. Cf. no. 1227.

VOLUME 26 o.s., 20 n.s., JULY 1876

1271 Harvey and vivisection, 1–17. **J. H. Bridges.** Signed.

1272 Adam Smith as a person, 18–42. **Walter Bagehot.** Signed; repr. *Works,* III.
1273 English liberalism and Australasian democracy, 43–59. **David Wedderburn.** Signed; called "Sir" in Contents; see Boase.
1274 Reflections at the Royal Academy, 60–73. **H. H. Statham.** Signed.
1275 Political machinery and political life, 74–92. **Leonard Courtney.** Signed.
1276 Past and present, 93–105. **Frederic Harrison.** Signed; repr. *Choice of Books.*
1277 On some disputed points in music, 106–130. **Edmund Gurney.** Signed.
1278 Home and foreign affairs, 131–144. **John Morley,** prob. Cf. no. 1227.

VOLUME 26 O.S., 20 N.S., AUGUST 1876

1279 The territorial expansion of Russia, 145–166. **D. Mackenzie Wallace.** Signed.
1280 Robespierre (Part I), 167–197. **John Morley.** Signed Editor; treatise repr. *Miscellanies,* I.
1281 Unsettled problems of American politics, 198–213. **L. J. Jennings.** Signed.
1282 An excursion in Formosa, 214–222. **Cyprian A. G. Bridge.** Signed.
1283 Mr. Cross [Home Secretary] and the magistracy, 223–231. **Henry Crompton.** Signed.
1284 Hartmann's philosophy of the unconscious, 242–262. **James Sully.** Signed; repr. with additions in *Pessimism, a History and a Criticism,* 1877.
1285 Home and foreign affairs, 263–274. **John Morley,** prob. Cf. no. 1227.

VOLUME 26 O.S., 20 N.S., SEPTEMBER 1876

1286 Turkey in Europe, 275–306. **Albert Rutson.** Signed.
1287 On cruelty to animals, 307–320. **Jonathan Hutchinson.** Signed.
1288 A word on good citizenship, 321–325. **Octavia Hill.** Signed.
1289 Robespierre (Part II, concl.), 326–363. **John Morley.** Signed Editor.
1290 The Irish Domesday Book, 364–373. **W. O'Connor Morris.** Signed.
1291 Lord Fairfax at Colchester, 374–382. **Clements R. Markham.** Signed.
1292 [Fitzjames] Stephen's *Digest of the Law of Evidence,* 383–394. **Frederick Pollock,** 1845–1937. Signed.
1293 Home and foreign affairs, 395–408. **John Morley,** prob. Cf. no. 1227.

VOLUME 26 O.S., 20 N.S., OCTOBER 1876

1294 Present aspects of the Eastern question, 409–423. **Edward A. Freeman.** Signed.
1295 English influence in Japan, 424–443. **Charles Wentworth Dilke.** Signed.
1296 William Godwin, 444–461. **Leslie Stephen.** Signed.
1297 Mormonism from a Mormon point of view, 462–478. **David Wedderburn.** Signed.
1298 Modern English architecture, 479–495. **H. H. Statham.** Signed.
1299 The American centenary, 496–516. **Horace White.** Signed.
1300 England and Turkey, 517–536. **Richard Congreve.** Signed.
1301 Home and foreign affairs, 537–546. **John Morley,** prob. Cf. no. 1227.

VOLUME 26 O.S., 20 N.S., NOVEMBER 1876

1302 Fermentation and its bearings on the phenomena of disease, 547–572. **John Tyndall.** Signed J. Tyndall; repr. *Fragments,* II.
1303 Lord Althorpe and the Reform Act of 1832, 573–600. **Walter Bagehot.** Signed; repr. *Works,* III.
1304 *Daniel Deronda* [by George Eliot], 601–616. **Sidney Colvin.** Signed.
1305 The future of political economy, 617–631. **W. Stanley Jevons.** Signed.
1306 On popular culture: an address, 632–650. **John Morley.** Assigned in footnote p. 632; repr. *Miscellanies,* III.
1307 The Eastern situation, 651–670. **Ralph A. Earle.** Signed.
1308 The Rodiyas [a tribe in Ceylon], 671–680. **Bertram F. Hartshorne.** Signed.
1309 Home and foreign affairs, 681–690. **John Morley,** prob. Cf. no. 1227.

VOLUME 26 O.S., 20 N.S., DECEMBER 1876

1310 A visit to Lapland, with notes on Swedish licensing, 691–708. **Joseph Chamberlain.** Signed as in no. 981.
1311 Cross and crescent, 709–730. **Frederic Harrison.** Signed.
1312 The law of honour, 731–751. **Edward A. Freeman.** Signed.
1313 A study of Dionysus [No. I, no more published], 752–772. **Walter H. Pater.** Signed.

1314   Arthur Schopenhauer, 773–792. **Francis Hueffer.** Signed F. Hueffer; repr. *Musical Studies*, 1880.

1315   Russia and Turkey, 793–808. **James Bryce,** 1838–1922. Signed.

1316   A mediaeval Spanish writer [Juan Ruiz], 809–832. **Mary A. Ward.** Signed.

1317   Home and foreign affairs, 833–844. **John Morley,** prob. Cf. no. 1227.

VOLUME 27 O.S., 21 N.S., JANUARY 1877

1318   The Birmingham plan of public-house reform, 1–9. **Robert Lowe.** Signed.

1319   Charles Kingsley, 10–31. **G. A. Simcox.** Signed.

1320   Economic law and English land-ownership, 32–53. **G. Shaw-Lefevre.** Signed.

1321   Free schools, 54–72. **Joseph Chamberlain.** Signed as in no. 981.

1322   The geographical aspect of the Eastern question, 73–87. **Edward A. Freeman.** Signed.

1323   Three new novels [by William Black, George Macdonald, Rhoda Broughton], 88–96. **Andrew Lang.** Signature.

1324   On the formation of some clans and castes in India, 97–118. **A. C. Lyall.** Signed; repr. *Asiatic Studies.*

1325   Constantinople and our road to India, 119–134. **H. M. Havelock-Allan.** Signed H. M. Havelock; see *DNB.*

1326   Home and foreign affairs, 135–146. **John Morley,** prob. Cf. no. 1227.

VOLUME 27 O.S., 21 N.S., FEBRUARY 1877

1327   Municipal public-houses, 147–159. **Joseph Chamberlain.** Signed as in no. 981.

1328   Shall we create a new university? 160–171. **Robert Lowe.** Signed. (See no. 1461.)

1329   Titian, 172–187. **Andrew Lang.** Signature.

1330   Paul Louis Courier, 188–206. **Henry D. Traill.** Signed.

1331   On the organisation of a teaching profession, 207–219. **Lyon Playfair.** Signed.

1332   The reform of the Ottoman Empire, 220–236. **Rowland Blennerhassett.** Signed.

1333   American efforts after international copyright, 237–256. **C. E. Appleton.** Signed.

1334   A new work on Russia [by D. Mackenzie Wallace] , 257–274. **John Morley.** Signed Editor.

1335   Home and foreign affairs, 275–284. **John Morley,** prob. Cf. no. 1227.

VOLUME 27 O.S., 21 N.S., MARCH 1877

1336   On the habits of ants, 287–306. **John Lubbock.** Signed.

1337   Have we abolished imprisonment for debt? 307–316. **Robert Lowe.** Signed.

1338   The course of modern thought, 317–327. **George Henry Lewes.** Signed; repr. *Current Discussions*, II.

1339   Balthasar Gracian, 328–342. **M. E. Grant Duff.** Signed; repr. *Miscellanies.*

1340   The age of reason, 343–361. **Mark Pattison.** Signed.

1341   A penal code, 362–376. **James Fitzjames Stephen.** Signed J. F. Stephen.

1342   The commercial treaty with France, 377–391. **John Slagg.** Signed.

1343   An address to some miners, 392–409. **John Morley.** Signed Editor in Contents.

1344   Army promotion and retirement, 410–417. **A. D. H. Haversham.** Signed Arthur D. Hayter; see *WWW/*1928.

1345   Home and foreign affairs, 418–427. **John Morley,** prob. Cf. no. 1227.

VOLUME 27 O.S., 21 N.S., APRIL 1877

1346   The political destiny of Canada, 431–459. **Goldwin Smith.** Signed; repr. with same title, 1877, and in *Current Discussions*, I.

1347   Decay of feudal property in France and England, 460–477. **H. S. Maine.** Signed; repr. *Early Law and Custom*, 1883.

1348   On certain relations between plants and insects. 478–494. **John Lubbock.** Signed.

1349   Cicero as a politician, 495–515. **Anthony Trollope.** Signed.

1350   Miss Martineau, 516–537. **G. A. Simcox.** Signed.

1351   On stimulants, 538–558. **Isaac Burney Yeo.** Signed J. Burney Yeo with title "M.D."; see *WWW/*1960.

1352   Mazzini on the Eastern question, 559–579. **Giuseppe Mazzini.** Intro. note. Intro. note by **James Stansfeld**—signed J. Stansfeld, Contents adds "Rt. Hon."; see *DNB*; trans. by **Emilie Ashurst Venturi**—signed E.A.V.; see H&L, III, 197.

1353   Belligerent claims and neutral rights, 580–590. **David William Stanley Ogilvy.** Signed Airlie [Earl of Airlie].

1354   Home and foreign affairs, 591–599. **John Morley,** prob. Cf. no. 1227.

1355   Our Eastern policy, 603–626. **Leonard Courtney.** Signed.

1356   Bentham and Benthamism in politics and ethics, 627–652. **Henry Sidgwick.** Signed H. Sidgwick; repr. *Essays.*

1357   Church and state, 653–675. **Frederic Harrison.** Signed; repr. *On Society*, 1918, as "A State Church."

1358   Parties and politics in Germany, 676–693. **Herbert Tuttle.** Signed.

1359   The levirate and polyandry, 694–707. **J. F. M'Lennan.** Signed; partially repr. *Studies in Ancient History*, 2nd s., 1896, as the Levirate in the chapter "Examples of Fabricated Genealogies."

1360   Barry Cornwall, 708–718. **G. A. Simcox.** Signed.

1361   Turgot in Limousin, 722–739. **John Morley.** Signed Editor; repr. *Miscellanies*, II.

1362   The church crisis: a parallel and contrast, 740–753. **Alexander Taylor Innes.** Signed.

1363   Home and foreign affairs, 754–763. **John Morley,** prob. Cf. no. 1227.

1364   George Sand, 767–781. **Matthew Arnold.** Signed; repr. *Mixed Essays*, 1879.

1365   Maoris and Kanakas [of New Zealand], 782–802. **David Wedderburn.** Signed.

1366   The farther outlook in the East, 803–819. **George Campbell,** 1824–1892. Signed as in no. 1114.

1367   The Grosvenor Gallery, 820–833. **Sidney Colvin.** Signed.

1368   Disestablishment and disendowment: a practical sketch, 834–852. **Henry W. Crosskey.** Signed.

1369   Evolution and positivism (Part I), 853–874. **J. H. Bridges.** Signed. (Note, vol. 28, pp. 285–286, signed **Mark Pattison.**)

1370   A leaf of Eastern history [extracts from Nassau Senior's Journal], 875–883. **Nassau W. Senior.** Page 876. With intro. note by **Mary C. M. Simpson,** prob.— cf. no. 1403.

1371   Exogamy and endogamy, 884–895. **J. F. McLennan.** Signed.

1372   A short rejoinder [to nos. 1359 and 1371], 895–902. **Herbert Spencer.** Signed; repr. *Various Fragments*, N.Y., 1898.

1373   Home and foreign affairs, 903–914. **John Morley,** prob. Cf. no. 1227.

1374   The defeat of the Liberal party, 1–24. **Goldwin Smith.** Signed.

1375   British interests in the present crisis, 25–34. **Emile de Laveleye.** Signed.

1376   The ethics of religion, 35–52. **W. K. Clifford.** Signed; repr. *Lectures*, II.

1377   The Duc de Broglie, 53–68. **Frank H. Hill.** Signed.

1378   At the Royal Academy, 69–85. **H. Heathcote Statham.** Signed.

1379   Evolution and Positivism (Part II, concl.), 89–114. **J. H. Bridges.** Signed.

1380   The new plan of selecting and training civil servants for India, 115–125. **Lyon Playfair.** Signed.

1381   A new political organization, 126–134. **Joseph Chamberlain.** Signed as in no. 981.

1382   Home and foreign affairs, 135–146. **John Morley,** prob. Cf. no. 1227.

1383   Secret societies in Russia, 149–169. **D. Mackenzie Wallace.** Signed.

1384   A plea for a rational education, 170–194. **M. E. Grant Duff.** Signed; repr. *Miscellanies*, 1878.

1385   Sea or mountain? 195–218. **Isaac Burney Yeo.** Signed as in no. 1351; repr. *Health Resorts*, 1882.

1386   Cavour, 219–243. **H. M. Hyndman.** Signed.

1387   The Indian Civil Service—a reply [to no. 1380], 244–258. **Arthur James Balfour.** Signed.

1388   Three books of the eighteenth century. (Part I): Holbach's *System of Nature*, 259–284. **John Morley.** Signed Editor.

1389   Home and foreign affairs, 287–300. **John Morley,** prob. Cf. no. 1227.

1390   The policy of aggrandizement, 303–324. **Goldwin Smith.** Signed.

1391   Heine in relation to religion and politics, 325–339. **Leonard A. Montefiore.** Signed; repr. *Essays.*

1392 Art in the community, 340–354. **J. Thackray Bunce.** Signed.
1393 The scepticism of believers, 355–376. **Leslie Stephen.** Signed; repr. *Agnostic's Apology.*
1394 Chopin, 377–394. **Francis Hueffer.** Signed; repr. *Musical Studies*, 1880.
1395 Antithetic fallacies, 395–400. **Frank H. Hill.** Signed.
1396 Cicero as a man of letters, 401–422. **Anthony Trollope.** Signed.
1397 Home and foreign affairs, 423–434. **John Morley,** prob. Cf. no. 1227.

VOLUME 28 O.S., 22 N.S., OCTOBER 1877

1398 The New Reform Bill, 437–452. **Robert Lowe.** Signed.
1399 Walter Bagehot, 453–484. **R. H. Hutton.** Signed.
1400 M. Renan's new volume, [*Origins of Christianity*], 485–509. **Walter Richard Cassels.** Signed The Author of "Supernatural Religion"; see *DNB.*
1401 The liquidations of 1873–76, 510–525. **Robert Giffen.** Signed; repr. *Economic Inquiries and Studies* (1904), I.
1402 The school of Giorgione, 526–538. **Walter H. Pater.** Signed; repr. *The Renaissance*, 1873.
1403 Conversations with M. Thiers (Part I), 539–561. **Nassau W. Senior.** Intro. note. Intro. note by **Mary Simpson—** signed M.C.M.S.; see *DNB* under Nassau Senior.
1404 The moral and social aspects of health, 562–580. **J. H. Bridges.** Signed.
1405 Home and foreign affairs, 581–592. **John Morley,** prob. Cf. no. 1227.

VOLUME 28 O.S., 22 N.S., NOVEMBER 1877

1406 Science and man, 593–617. **John Tyndall.** Signed; repr. *Fragments*, II.
1407 The value to the United Kingdom of the foreign dominions of the Crown, 618–630. **Robert Lowe.** Signed.
1408 The future of our commons, 631–641. **Octavia Hill.** Signed.
1409 Conversations with M. Thiers (Part II), 642–658. **Nassau W. Senior.** Cf. no. 1403.
1410 Books and critics, 659–679. **Mark Pattison.** Signed.
1411 Dr. Newman's theory of belief (Part I), 680–697. **Leslie Stephen.** Signed; repr. *Agnostic's Apology.*

1412 A speculation on evolution, 698–704. **Arthur James Balfour.** Signed; repr. *A Defence of Philosophical Doubt* (1879), chap. 13.
1413 Three books of the eighteenth century (Part II, no more published): Raynal's *History of the Indies*, 705–718. **John Morley.** Signed Editor.
1414 Home and foreign affairs, 719–728. **John Morley,** prob. Cf. no. 1227.

VOLUME 28 O.S., 22 N.S., DECEMBER 1877

1415 Mr. Gladstone on manhood suffrage, 733–746. **Robert Lowe.** Signed.
1416 The Republic and the Marshal [MacMahon], 747–772. **Frederic Harrison.** Signed.
1417 Humming-birds, 773–791. **Alfred R. Wallace.** Signed.
1418 Dr. Newman's theory of belief (Part II, concl.), 792–810. **Leslie Stephen.** Signed.
1419 Political dissent, 811–826. **J. Guinness Rogers.** Signed.
1420 Florence and the Medici (Part I), 827–842. **J. A. Symonds.** Signed; repr. *Sketches*, II.
1421 Hell and the divine veracity, 843–862. **Lionel A. Tollemache.** Signed; repr. *Stones of Stumbling*, 1893, as "Divine Economy of Truth."
1422 Has India food for its people? 863–877. **H. J. S. Cotton.** Signed.
1423 Home and foreign affairs, 878–888. **John Morley,** prob. Cf. no. 1227.

VOLUME 29 O.S., 23 N.S., JANUARY 1878

1424 Ceremonial government (Part I), 1–24. **Herbert Spencer.** Signed; series repr. *Principles of Sociology* (N.Y., 1890), II.
1425 An inside view of Egypt, 25–47. **George Campbell,** 1824–1892. Signed, with "M.P." added in Contents: see *DNB.*
1426 Technical education, 48–58. **T. H. Huxley.** Signed; repr. *Collected Essays*, III.
1427 Jules Sandeau, 59–74. **George Saintsbury.** Signed; repr. *French Novelists.*
1428 The Reform Bill of the future, 75–84. **Thomas Hare.** Signed.
1429 University extension [in size and usefulness], 85–95. **Goldwin Smith.** Signed.
1430 The Dutch in Java, 96–120. **David Wedderburn.** Signed.
1431 Monsieur Guizot at Val Richer, 121–

138. **N. W. Senior.** Signed; called "the late" in Contents; see *DNB* for topic.

1432 Home and foreign affairs, 139–149. **John Morley,** prob. Cf. no. 1227.

VOLUME 29 O.S., 23 N.S., FEBRUARY 1878

1433 England and the [Franco-Turkish] War, 153–166. **Emile de Laveleye.** Signed.

1434 William Harvey, 167–190. **T. H. Huxley.** Signed.

1435 Kafir Land, 191–206. **Anthony Trollope.** Signed.

1436 Lord Melbourne, 207–227. **R. M. Milnes.** Signed Houghton [Lord Houghton].

1437 The Christian "conditions" (Part I), 228–246. **W. R. Cassels.** Signed The Author of *Supernatural Religion*: see *DNB*.

1438 Victor Cherbuliez, 247–265. **George Saintsbury.** Signed; repr. *French Novelists.*

1439 Ceremonial government (Part II): trophies, 266–276. **Herbert Spencer.** Signed.

1440 Florence and the Medici (Part II, concl.), 277–296. **J. A. Symonds.** Signed.

1441 Home and foreign affairs, 297–308. **John Morley,** prob. Cf. no. 1227.

VOLUME 29 O.S., 23 N.S., MARCH 1878

1442 Equality, 313–334. **Mathew Arnold.** Signed; repr. *Mixed Essays*, 1879.

1443 A plain view of British interests, 335–348. **Samuel Laing,** 1812–1897. Signed S. Laing; Contents adds "M.P.": see *DNB*.

1444 Lessing, 349–364. **Reginald W. Macan.** Signed.

1445 The new revelation (Part II, concl.), 365–383. **W. R. Cassels.** Evidence for no. 1437.

1446 The strength of England, 384–403. **T. H. Farrer.** Signed.

1447 Whigs and Liberals, 404–416. **Goldwin Smith.** Signed.

1448 Modern Japan (Part I), 417–428. **David Wedderburn.** Signed.

1449 Théophile Gautier, 429–446. **George Saintsbury.** Signed; repr. *French Novelists.*

1450 Ceremonial government (Part III): mutilations, 447–468. **Herbert Spencer.** Signed.

1451 Home and foreign affairs, 469–476. **John Morley,** prob. Cf. no. 1227.

VOLUME 29 O.S., 23 N.S., APRIL 1878

1452 The political adventures of Lord Beaconsfield (Part I), 477–493. **Frank Harrison Hill.** Attr. in *DNB*.

1453 Politics in Australasia, 494–512. **Charles W. Purnell.** Signed.

1454 Giuseppe Mazzini (Part I), 513–528. **Frederic W. H. Myers.** Signed; repr. *Essays.*

1455 Modern Japan (Part II, concl.), 529–542. **David Wedderburn.** Signed.

1456 The resettlement of the Turkish dominions, 543–559. **George Campbell,** 1824–1892. Signed, with "M.P." added in Contents: see *DNB*.

1457 The influence upon religious beliefs of a rise in morality, 560–574. **A. C. Lyall.** Signed; repr. *Asiatic Studies.*

1458 Gustave Flaubert, 575–595. **George Saintsbury.** Signed; repr. *Essays*, IV, and *French Novelists.*

1459 Memorials of a man of letters [*Correspondence of Macvey Napier*], 596–610. **John Morley.** Signed Editor; repr. *Studies.*

1460 Ceremonial government (Part IV): presents, 611–630. **Herbert Spencer.** Signed.

1461 University extension and the proposed Manchester University [a reply to no. 1429], 631–638. **William Jack.** Signed.

1462 Home and foreign affairs, 639–646. **John Morley,** prob. Cf. no. 1227.

VOLUME 29 O.S., 23 N.S., MAY 1878

1463 The Eastern crisis, 647–661. **Goldwin Smith.** Signed.

1464 The French Workmen's Congress, 662–677. **Frederic Harrison.** Signed.

1465 An anniversary [Voltaire and Rousseau], 678–690. **George Saintsbury.** Signed.

1466 The political adventures of Lord Beaconsfield (Part II): from 1826 to 1837, 691–709. **Frank Harrison Hill.** Cf. no. 1452.

1467 Giuseppe Mazzini (Part II, concl.), 710–728. **Frederic W. H. Myers.** Signed.

1468 Liberals and Whigs, 729–740. **George C. Brodrick.** Signed.

1469 Catullus, 741–751. **Henry Nettleship.** Signed H. Nettleship; repr. *Lectures and Essays*, 1885.

1470 Diderot at Saint Petersburg, 752–771. **John Morley.** Signed Editor; for reprint see no. 1121.

1471 Ceremonial government (Part V): obeisances, 772–792. **Herbert Spencer.** Signed.

1472 Home and foreign affairs, 793–802. **John Morley,** prob. Cf. no. 1227.

VOLUME 29 O.S., 23 N.S., JUNE 1878

1473 On the dread and dislike of science, 805–815. **George Henry Lewes.** Signed.

1474 Emilio Castelar (Part I), 816–834. **M. E. Grant Duff.** Signed; repr. *Miscellanies*, 1878.

1475 Employment of our Asiatic forces in European wars, 835–849. **W. R. Greg.** Signed; repr. *Miscellaneous Essays*, II.

1476 Shelley's last days, 850–866. **Richard Garnett,** 1835–1906. Signed.

1477 The political adventures of Lord Beaconsfield (Part III): from 1837 to 1852, 867–888. **Frank Harrison Hill.** Cf. no. 1452.

1478 Liberalism and disestablishment, 889–908. **John Edward Jenkins.** Signed Edward Jenkins; called "M.P." in Contents; see *DNB*.

1479 Charles de Bernard, 909–924. **George Saintsbury.** Signed; repr. *French Novelists.*

1480 The future of Asiatic Turkey, 925–936. **James Bryce,** 1838–1922. Signed.

1481 The Transvaal and the Zulu countries, 937–954. **John Sanderson.** Signed.

1482 Home and foreign affairs, 955–964. **John Morley,** prob. Cf. no. 1227.

VOLUME 30 O.S., 24 N.S., JULY 1878

1483 Lancashire, 1–25. **John Morley.** Signed Editor.

1484 Irish Catholicism and British liberalism, 26–45. **Matthew Arnold.** Signed; repr. *Mixed Essays,* 1879.

1485 Emilio Castelar (Part II), 46–73. **M. E. Grant Duff.** Signed.

1486 Davos in winter, 74–87. **J. A. Symonds.** Signed; repr. *Swiss Highlands.*

1487 A word for indignation meetings, 88–101. **Goldwin Smith.** Signed.

1488 Octave Feuillet, 102–118. **George Saintsbury.** Signed; repr. *French Novelists.*

1489 The position of sociology among the sciences, 119–138. **J. H. Bridges.** Signed.

1490 Ceremonial government (Part VI, concl.): forms of address, 139–149. **Herbert Spencer.** Signed.

1491 Home and foreign affairs, 150–158. **John Morley,** prob. Cf. no. 1227.

VOLUME 30 O.S., 24 N.S., AUGUST 1878

1492 The Convention with Turkey, 159–174. **Samuel Laing,** 1812–1897. Signed as in no. 1443.

1493 Iceland, 175–190. **Anthony Trollope.** Signed.

1494 Belgian politics, 191–199. **Emile de Laveleye.** Signed.

1495 Rectifications, 200–213. **W. R. Greg.** Signed.

1496 A chapter of Buddhist folk-lore, 214–230. **Bertram Fulke Hartshorne.** Signed.

1497 Henry Murger, 231–249. **George Saintsbury.** Signed; repr. *French Novelists.*

1498 The political adventures of Lord Beaconsfield (Part IV, concl.): from 1852 to August 1878, 250–270. **Frank Harrison Hill.** Cf. no. 1452.

1499 Greece at the Congress of Berlin, 271–283. **G. J. Shaw-Lefevre.** Signed.

1500 The position of English joint-stock banks, 284–302. **A. J. Wilson.** Signed.

1501 Home and foreign affairs, 303–312. **John Morley,** prob. Cf. no. 1227.

VOLUME 30 O.S., 24 N.S., SEPTEMBER 1878

1502 A political epilogue, 313–333. **John Morley.** Signed Editor.

1503 Dreams and realities, 334–352. **Leslie Stephen.** Signed; repr. *Agnostic's Apology.*

1504 Mrs. Gaskell's novels, 353–369. **William Minto.** Signed W. Minto; see *DNB*.

1505 Hallucinations of the senses, 370–386. **Henry Maudsley.** Signed.

1506 The prospects of moral progress in India, 387–398. **H. J. S. Cotton.** Signed.

1507 Brockden Brown, 399–421. **George Barnett Smith.** Signed.

1508 The doctrine of metempsychosis, 422–442. **William Angus Knight.** Signed William Knight; repr. *Essays on Philosophy Old and New,* 1890.

1509 Home and foreign affairs, 443–452. **John Morley,** prob. Cf. no. 1227.

VOLUME 30 O.S., 24 N.S., OCTOBER 1878

1510 Imperialism, 453–465. **Robert Lowe.** Signed.

1511 The character of the humourist:

Charles Lamb, 466–474. **Walter H. Pater.** Signed; repr. *Appreciations.*

1512 The English school of jurisprudence (Part I): Austin and Maine on sovereignty, 475–492. **Frederic Harrison.** Signed; repr. *On Jurisprudence and the Conflict of Laws,* 1919.

1513 The two fair cousins, a Chinese romance, 493–508. **David Wedderburn.** Signed.

1514 The beginning of nerves in the animal kingdom, 509–526. **George J. Romanes.** Signed.

1515 Alexandre Dumas, 527–542. **George Saintsbury.** Signed; repr. *French Novelists.*

1516 An economic address: with some notes, 547–567. **John Morley.** Signed Editor.

1517 Mr. Gladstone's policy and the new equilibrium, 568–588. **Ralph A. Earle.** Signed.

VOLUME 30 O.S., 24 N.S., NOVEMBER 1878

1518 Porro unum est necessarium, 589–604. **Matthew Arnold.** Signed; repr. *Mixed Essays,* 1879.

1519 The recent development of socialism in Germany and the United States, 605–615. **Henry Fawcett.** Signed.

1520 Two foreign opinions on the Treaty of Berlin, 616–627. **Emile de Laveleye.** Signed.

1521 Epping Forest, 628–645. **Alfred R. Wallace.** Signed; repr. *Studies,* II.

1522 The peasants of the Limagne (Part I), 646–660. **F. Barham Zincke.** Signed.

1523 On the study of classical art, 661–681. **Sidney Colvin.** Signed.

1524 The English school of jurisprudence (Part II): Bentham's and Austin's analysis of law, 682–703. **Frederic Harrison.** Signed.

1525 Civilisation and noise, 704–720. **James Sully.** Signed.

1526 The caucus, 721–741. **Joseph Chamberlain.** Signed as in no. 981.

1527 Home and foreign affairs, 742–750. **John Morley,** prob. Cf. no. 1227.

VOLUME 30 O.S., 24 N.S., DECEMBER 1878

1528 Imperial administration, 751–764. **H. H. M. Herbert.** Signed Carnarvon [Earl of Carnarvon]; repr. *Essays,* III.

1529 Prince Bismarck, 765–786. **Emile de Laveleye.** Signed.

1530 The chances for a long Conservative régime in England, 787–800. **Walter Bagehot.** Note, p. 800. (Note, p. 800, by **John Morley**—signed Editor.)

1531 The migration of centres of industrial energy, 801–820. **Leonard Courtney.** Signed.

1532 The peasants of the Limagne (Part II, concl.), 821–835. **F. Barham Zincke.** Signed.

1533 The principle of copyright, 836–851. **T. H. Farrer.** Signed.

1534 The Russians in Armenia, 852–866. **Alfred A. Wheeler.** Signed.

1535 The impoverishment of India not proven, 867–881. **John Morley.** Signed Editor.

1536 The failure of the City of Glasgow Bank and its lessons, 882–901. **William Newmarch,** prob. Newmarch was a banker and economist; he contributed anonymously to the *FortR* (see *DNB*); this and no. 1565 are the only unsigned arts. on banking and money. (Correction, vol. 31 O.S., p. 162, presumably by the editor, **John Morley.**)

1537 Home and foreign affairs, 902–910. **John Morley,** prob. Cf. no. 1227.

VOLUME 31 O.S., 25 N.S., JANUARY 1879

1538 The scientific frontier [north-west border of India], 1–14. **H. W. Norman,** 1826–1904. Signed; Contents gives first name and adds "Sir"; see *DNB*.

1539 George Henry Lewes, 15–24. **Anthony Trollope.** Signed.

1540 Political economy and sociology, 25–46. **T. E. Cliffe Leslie.** Signed; repr. *Political Economy.*

1541 The London medical schools, 47–61. **William Gilbert.** Signed.

1542 On certain present phenomena of the imagination, 62–79. **R. M. Milnes.** Signed Houghton [Lord Houghton].

1543 Rural Roumania, 80–95. **T. Wemyss Reid.** Signed.

1544 Chamfort and Rivarol, 96–113. **George Saintsbury.** Signed; repr. *Essays,* IV.

1545 The English school of jurisprudence (Part III, concl.): the historical method, 114–130. **Frederic Harrison.** Signed.

1546 Sir Stafford Northcote—a rejoinder, 131–151. **M. E. Grant Duff.** Signed.

1547 Home and foreign affairs, 152–162. **T. H. S. Escott.** Escott to Gladstone, Dec. 24, 1878, BM. Add. MSS., 44458, says he has written this for Jan. issue.

VOLUME 31 O.S., 25 N.S., FEBRUARY 1879

1548 Virgil, 163–196. **Frederic W. H. Myers.** Signed; repr. *Essays.*

1549 The electric light, 197–216. **John Tyndall.** Signed; repr. *Fragments*, II.

1550 Chapters on socialism (Part I), 217–237. **John Stuart Mill.** Intro. note signed **Helen Taylor.**

1551 Ecce, convertimur ad gentes, 238–252. **Matthew Arnold.** Signed; repr. *Irish Essays*, 1882.

1552 Agricultural depression, 253–272. **William E. Bear.** Signed.

1553 The *Loyal League*: a Japanese romance, 273–289. **David Wedderburn.** Signed.

1554 Shall we give up Greek? 290–300. **Edward A. Freeman.** Signed.

1555 Economic method, 301–318. **Henry Sidgwick.** Signed.

1556 Home and foreign affairs, 319–328. **John Morley,** prob. Cf. no. 1227.

VOLUME 31 O.S., 25 N.S., MARCH 1879

1557 The plain story of the Zulu War, 329–352. **John Morley.** Signed Editor.

1558 First impressions of the new [French] Republic, 353–372. **Frederic Harrison.** Signed.

1559 Chapters on socialism (Part II), 373–382. **John Stuart Mill.** Cf. no. 1550.

1560 An American view of American competition, 383–396. **Edward Atkinson.** Signed.

1561 Thomas Paine, 397–416. **Moncure D. Conway.** Signed; repr. in Ingersoll, Robert G., *A Vindication of Thomas Paine*, Chicago and Toronto, 1879.

1562 A fair day's wages for a fair day's work, 417–434. **Leonard Courtney.** Signed.

1563 The Liberal Party and the farmers, 435–448. **William E. Bear.** Signed.

1564 Black and white in the Southern States (Part I), 449–468. **George Campbell,** 1824–1892. Signed; called "Sir" in Contents; repr. in *White and Black: The Outcome of a Visit to the United States*, N.Y., 1879.

1565 The urgent need for amending our bankruptcy legislation, 469–485. **William Newmarch,** prob. Cf. evidence for no. 1536.

1566 Home and foreign affairs, 486–490. **John Morley,** prob. Cf. no. 1227.

VOLUME 31 O.S., 25 N.S., APRIL 1879

1567 On the choice of books, 491–512. **Frederic Harrison.** Signed; repr. *Choice of Books.*

1568 Chapters on socialism (Part III, concl.), 513–530. **John Stuart Mill.** Cf. no. 1550.

1569 Italian politics, 531–545. **Emile de Laveleye.** Signed.

1570 Further remarks on Zulu affairs, 546–562. **John Morley.** Signed Editor.

1571 What is money? 563–575. **Henry Sidgwick.** Signed.

1572 Conventions at whist, 576–587. **William Pole.** Signed.

1573 Black and white in the Southern States (Part II, concl.): the political situation in the South, 588–607. **George Campbell,** 1824–1892. Signed as in no. 1564.

1574 The bright clauses of the Irish Land Act: a supplementary plea for peasant proprietors, 608–626. **W. T. Thornton.** Signed.

1575 Burma, 627–635. **Albert Fytche.** Signed.

1576 Home and foreign affairs, 636–646. **John Morley,** prob. Cf. no. 1227.

VOLUME 31 O.S., 25 N.S., MAY 1879

1577 The French Republic and the Catholic Church, 647–666. **John Morley.** Signed Editor.

1578 William Kingdon Clifford, 667–687. **Frederick Pollock,** 1845–1937. Signed.

1579 Democracy in Victoria, 688–717. **Charles H. Pearson.** Signed.

1580 The expedition of Philip II to England, 718–734. **H. J. Moreton.** Signed Ducie [3rd Earl Ducie].

1581 The history of games, 735–747. **Edward B. Tylor.** Signed.

1582 Canadian protection vindicated, 748–762. **David McCulloch.** Signed D. McCulloch; Contents gives first name.

1583 Ancient ideas respecting the arrangement of codes, 763–777. **H. S. Maine.** Signed; repr. *Early Law and Custom*, 1883, as "Classification of early rules."

1584 A problem in human evolution [the lack of hair in man], 778–786. **Grant Allen.** Signed.

1585 The situation in Egypt, 787–797. **George Campbell,** 1824–1892. Signed, with "Sir" added in Contents.

1586 Home and foreign affairs, 798–806.

John Morley, prob. Attr. in *Early Life*, II, 79.

1625   Home and foreign affairs, 440–448. **John Morley,** prob. Cf. no. 1227.

VOLUME 32 O.S., 26 N.S., OCTOBER 1879

1626   South Africa once more, 449–473. **J. A. Froude.** Signed.
1627   The Channel Islands, 474–491. **G. Shaw-Lefevre.** Signed; repr. *English and Irish Land Question,* 1881.
1628   A reply to "Fallacies of Evolution" [*ER* no. 3203], 492–504. **George J. Romanes.** Signed.
1629   Parliamentary government in America, 505–517. **Horace White.** Signed.
1630   Antonio Scialoja, 518–529. **Edward Dicey.** Signed.
1631   National education and the London School Board, 530–558. **E. Lyulph Stanley.** Signed.
1632   The historical side of the conflict of laws, 559–576. **Frederic Harrison.** Signed; repr. *On Jurisprudence and the Conflict of Laws,* 1919. (See no. 1642.)
1633   A word with some critics, 577–584. **John Morley.** Signed Editor.
1634   The British Museum Library, 585–600. **W. P. Courtney.** Signed.
1635   Home and foreign affairs, 601–610. **John Morley,** prob. Attr. in *Early Life,* II, 84–85.

VOLUME 32 O.S., 26 N.S., NOVEMBER 1879

1636   A German view of the British Army, 611–628. **Rudolph von Schwert.** Signed.
1637   Winter quarters, 629–649. **Isaac Burney Yeo.** Signed as in no. 1351; repr. *Health Resorts,* 1882.
1638   The Austrians in Bosnia, 650–671. **R. Hamilton Lang.** Signed.
1639   Men and women (Part I), 672–685. **Maria G. Grey.** Signed; called "Mrs. William Grey" in Contents. (Part II is no. 1814.)
1640   Matthew Arnold's *Selections from Wordsworth,* 686–701. **J. A. Symonds.** Signed; repr. *Essays.*
1641   An Indo-Mediterranean railway: fiction and fact, 702–715. **Wilfrid Scawen Blunt.** Signed.
1642   The conflict of laws analytically considered [sequel to no. 1632], 716–731. **Frederic Harrison.** Signed.
1643   Assurance investments, 732–754. **Arnold Page.** Signed on p. 753.

1644   Home and foreign affairs, 755–766. **John Morley,** prob. Attr. in *Early Life,* II, 85.

VOLUME 32 O.S., 26 N.S., DECEMBER 1879

1645   Martial law in Kabul (Part I), 767–784. **Frederic Harrison.** Signed; partly repr. *Problems* as "Afghanistan."
1646   The Austro-German alliance, 785–802. **Emile de Laveleye.** Signed.
1647   Land law reform, 803–816. **George Osborne Morgan.** Signed.
1648   Carlyle's political doctrines, 817–828. **William L. Courtney.** Signed; repr. *Studies.*
1649   Italy, 829–844. **W. J. Stillman.** Signed.
1650   *The Letters of Charles Dickens,* 845–862. **William Minto.** Signed.
1651   Loyalty, 863–878. **Edward A. Freeman.** Signed.
1652   From Belgrade to Samakov, 879–898. **Humphry Sandwith.** Signed.
1653   Buddah's first sermon, 899–912. **T. W. Rhys Davids.** Signed on p. 910.
1654   Home and foreign affairs, 913–922. **John Morley,** prob. Cf. no. 1227.

VOLUME 33 O.S., 27 N.S., JANUARY 1880

1655   Ireland, 1–25. **W. Neilson Hancock.** Signed.
1656   Mr. Gladstone, 26–52. **Henry Dunckley.** Signed.
1657   Handel, 53–75. **H. H. Statham.** Signed; repr. *Thoughts on Music.*
1658   Freedom of land, 76–86. **T. H. Farrer.** Signed.
1659   Conversations with Adolphe de Circourt, 87–118. **Nassau W. Senior.** Intro. note; repr. *Conversations with Distinguished Persons,* 1878, 1880. Intro. note by **Mary C. M. Simpson**—signed M.C.M.S.; *DNB* under Nassau Senior, and a second note, pp. 87–90, by **Edmond Scherer**—note by **M. C. M. Simpson.**
1660   Colorado, 119–129. **James W. Barclay,** prob. Signed J. W. Barclay; clearly by the author of *NC* no. 955 on similar topic, who there used his first name.
1661   The England of to-day, 130–146. **H. D. Traill.** Signed. Note, 146–149 by **John Morley**—signed Editor.
1662   Home and foreign affairs, 150–160. **John Morley,** prob. Cf. no. 1227.

Signed; repr. *Les Fleurs du Mal and Other Studies*, 1913.

1700 The backwoods of Ceylon, 769–784. **Albert Gray.** Signed.

1701 Austro-Hungary, 785–800. **W. J. Stillman.** Signed.

1702 The development of Buddhism in India, 801–821. **J. Ware Edgar.** Signed.

1703 A plea for the abolition of outdoor relief, 822–833. **T. W. Fowle.** Signed.

1704 The Liberal victory: from a Conservative point of view, 834–847. **Alfred Austin.** Signed.

1705 The cost of the Mediaeval church in England: a chapter of historical economics, 848–864.

1706 Home and foreign affairs, 865–876. **John Morley,** prob. Cf. no. 1227.

VOLUME 34 o.s., 28 n.s., JULY 1880

1707 Religious liberty and atheism, 1–7. **John W. Probyn.** Signed.

1708 M. Gimel on the division of land in France, 8–15. **F. Barham Zincke.** Signed.

1709 The Sultan's heirs in Asia, 16–30. **Wilfrid Scawen Blunt.** Signed.

1710 A new poet [James Thomson], 31–41. **G. A. Simcox.** Signed.

1711 State education: a help or hindrance? 42–57. **Auberon Herbert.** Signed.

1712 Parties and the distribution of seats, 58–68. **W. A. Hunter.** Signed.

1713 Edgar Allan Poe, 69–82. **William Minto.** Signed.

1714 The railroads of the United States: their effects on farming and production in that country and in Great Britain, 83–104. **Edward Atkinson.** Signed.

1715 Democracy in Victoria: dangers of the democratic form of government, 105–125. **Charles H. Pearson.** Signed.

1716 Home and foreign affairs, 126–136. **John Morley,** prob. Cf. no. 1227.

VOLUME 34 o.s., 28 n.s., AUGUST 1880

1717 Land tenure in Ireland, 137–146. **Mountifort Longfield.** Signed M. Longfield; Contents gives first name; see *DNB*.

1718 Why the American Colonies separated from Great Britain, 147–163. **John Fiske.** Signed.

1719 Health resorts in the Pyrenees, 164–175. **Isaac Burney Yeo.** Signed as in no. 1351; repr. *Health Resorts*, 1882.

1720 Mr. Bradlaugh and his opponents, 176–187. **Leslie Stephen.** Signed.

1721 Friendly Societies: their position and prospects, 188–199. **James S. Randell.** Signed.

1722 The European concert [the great powers and the Eastern question], 200–209. **D. C. Lathbury.** Signed.

1723 The Deccan, 210–229. **David Wedderburn.** Signed.

1724 Public opinion and its leaders, 230–244. **T. Wemyss Reid.** Signed.

1725 The policy of coercion [in regard to the Ottoman Empire], 245–262. **William T. Stead.** Signed.

1726 Home and foreign affairs, 263–272. **John Morley,** prob. Cf. no. 1227.

VOLUME 34 o.s., 28 n.s., SEPTEMBER 1880

1727 The ways of orthodox critics, 273–299. **Grant Allen.** Signed.

1728 The administration of justice in Madras, 300–311. **J. H. Nelson.** Signed.

1729 Mental imagery, 312–324. **Francis Galton.** Signed F.G.; name given in Contents.

1730 California, 325–346. **R. H. Patterson.** Signed.

1731 A visible church, 347–358. **John Delaware Lewis.** Signed.

1732 A contemporary narrative of the fall of the Bastille, 359–380. **Louis-Guillaume Pitra.** Intro. note. Trans. and edited by **Augustus Craven**—he signed intro. note.

1733 Some reflections on the Afghan imbroglio, 381–397. **Arthur Hobhouse.** Signed.

1734 Home and foreign affairs, 398–408. **John Morley,** prob. Cf. no. 1227.

VOLUME 34 o.s., 28 n.s., OCTOBER 1880

1735 Irish rents, improvements, and landlords, 409–421. **Murrough O'Brien.** Signed.

1736 A century of English poetry, 422–437. **Algernon Charles Swinburne.** Signed; repr. *Miscellanies*.

1737 Cattle ranches in the far West, 438–457. **W. Baillie Grohman.** Signed.

1738 County constituencies: a plan of reform, 458–471. **T. W. Fowle.** Signed.

1739 Are we Englishmen? 472–487. **Grant Allen.** Signed.

1740 Political economy in the United States, 488–509. **T. E. C. Leslie.** Signed; repr. *Political Economy*.

1741 The tragic comedians: a study in an

old story (chaps. i–iv), 510–532. **George Meredith.** Signed; novel published 1881.

1742 Home and foreign affairs, 533–544. **John Morley,** prob. Cf. no. 1227.

VOLUME 34 O.S., 28 N.S., NOVEMBER 1880

1743 Political institutions (Part I): preliminary, 545–555. **Herbert Spencer.** Signed; series repr. *Principles of Sociology* (N.Y., 1890), II. (The successive parts in the following 7 months have different titles.)

1744 Greece and the Greeks, 556–576; with a postscript, 576–579. **W. J. Stillman.** Signed.

1745 Experiments in peasant proprietorship, 579–591. **Murrough O'Brien.** Signed.

1746 The future of Switzerland, 592–600. **Fritz Cunliffe-Owen.** Signed.

1747 Authority in the Church of England, 601–616. **Orby Shipley.** Signed.

1748 A story of annexation in South Africa, 617–634. **F. Reginald Statham.** Signed.

1749 Jomini, Moreau, and Vandamme, 635–652. **C. F. Cromie.** Signed.

1750 The tragic comedians (chaps. v–vii), 653–670. **George Meredith.** Signed.

1751 Home and foreign affairs, 671–680. **John Morley,** prob. Attr. in *Early Life,* II, 99.

VOLUME 34 O.S., 28 N.S., DECEMBER 1880

1752 Political organization in general (Part II), 681–695. **Herbert Spencer.** Signed; cf. no. 1743.

1753 Young Ireland, 696–707. **P. J. Smyth.** Signed.

1754 Short notes on English poets: Chaucer, Spenser, the sonnets of Shakespeare, Milton, 708–721. **Algernon Charles Swinburne.** Signed; repr. *Miscellanies.*

1755 The relations of the Houses of Parliament, 722–736. **W. St. John Brodrick.** Signed.

1756 Industrial shortcomings: an address, 737–751. **Mark Pattison.** Signed.

1757 *Spinoza* [by Frederick Pollock], 752–772. **Leslie Stephen.** Signed.

1758 Mr. Wallace's *Island Life,* 773–784. **Grant Allen.** Signed.

1759 The tragic comedians (chaps. viii–ix), 785–803. **George Meredith.** Signed.

1760 Home and foreign affairs, 804–812. **John Morley,** prob. Attr. in *Early Life,* II, 99–100.

VOLUME 35 O.S., 29 N.S., JANUARY 1881

1761 Political integration (Part III), 4–17. **Herbert Spencer.** Signed; cf. no. 1743.

1762 The land legislation for Ireland, 18–34. **George Campbell,** 1824–1892. Signed; "Sir" and "M.P." added in Contents.

1763 Etienne Dolet, 35–43. **Mark Pattison.** Signed.

1764 Freedom of contract, 44–65. **T. H. Farrer.** Signed.

1765 Notes on [Disraeli's] *Endymion,* 66–76. **R. M. Milnes.** Signed Houghton [Lord Houghton].

1766 Aerial navigation, 77–92. **William Pole.** Signed.

1767 County boards, 93–102. **Charles T. D. Acland.** Signed.

1768 The tragic comedians (chaps. x–xi), 103–118. **George Meredith.** Signed.

1769 Home and foreign affairs, 119–128. **John Morley,** prob. Attr. in *Early Life,* II, 100.

VOLUME 35 O.S., 29 N.S., FEBRUARY 1881

1770 Tennyson and Musset, 129–153. **A. C. Swinburne.** Signed; repr. *Miscellanies.*

1771 Political differentiation (Part IV), 154–169. **Herbert Spencer.** Signed; cf. no. 1743.

1772 Reform in parliamentary business, 170–187. **William Rathbone.** Signed, and called "M.P." in Contents.

1773 Léonce de Lavergne, 188–205. **T. E. C. Leslie.** Signed; repr. *Political Economy.*

1774 Peasant proprietors and small farmers: in south-western France, 206–217. **Wentworth Webster.** Signed.

1775 The dwellings of the poor in London, 218–228. **Henry R. Brand.** Signed.

1776 Our foreign and Irish policy, 229–243. **E. S. Beesly.** Signed.

1777 The tragic comedians (chaps. xii–xv, concl.), 244–260. **George Meredith.** Assigned in Contents.

1778 Home and foreign affairs, 261–270. **John Morley,** prob. Attr. in *Early Life,* II, 102.

VOLUME 35 O.S., 29 N.S., MARCH 1881

1779 Political forms and forces (Part V), 271–284. **Herbert Spencer.** Signed; cf. no. 1743.

1780 How to get out of the South African difficulty, 285–301. **F. Reginald Statham.** Signed.

1781   Notes of travel in Thessaly and Epirus, 302–318. **W. Valentine Chirol.** Signed; the "W" prefixed to name is perhaps an inverted "M" for Monsieur; see no. 1837.
1782   On the study of history, 319–339. **Edward A. Freeman.** Signed.
1783   Lights and shades of American politics, 340–357. **H. M. Hyndman.** Signed.
1784   Folgore da San Gemignano, 358–370. **J. A. Symonds.** Signed; repr. *Byways.*
1785   The anti-Jewish agitation in Germany, 371–384. **Ernest Schuster.** Signed.
1786   The land laws, 385–396. **William Alfred Jevons,** prob. Signed William A. Jevons; see *BMCat.*
1787   Home and foreign affairs, 397–406. **John Morley,** prob. Attr. in *Early Life,* II, 102.

VOLUME 35 O.S., 29 N.S., APRIL 1881

1788   England and Ireland, 407–425. **John Morley.** Signed Editor.
1789   On fruits and seeds, 426–455. **John Lubbock.** Signed.
1790   Carlyle's *Reminiscences,* 456–466. **James Cotter Morison.** Signed.
1791   The cost of the General Election of 1880, 467–487. **W. P. Courtney.** Signed.
1792   Modern Italian poets, 488–503. **Francis Hueffer.** Signed; repr. *Italian and Other Studies,* 1883, as "Poets of Young Italy."
1793   Suicide, 504–512. **J. W. Horsley.** Signed; repr. *Jottings from Jail,* 1887.
1794   The morality of the profession of letters, 513–520. **Robert Louis Stevenson.** Signed.
1795   Political heads—chiefs, kings, etc. (Part VI), 521–533. **Herbert Spencer.** Signed; cf. no. 1743.
1796   Home and foreign affairs, 534–542. **John Morley,** prob. Cf. no. 1227.

VOLUME 35 O.S., 29 N.S., MAY 1881

1797   Impressions of the Irish Land Bill (No. I), 543–551. **Alex. G. Richey.** Signed.
1798   Impressions of the Irish Land Bill (No. II), 552–559. **George Campbell,** 1824–1892. Signed; Contents adds "M.P."
1799   Statius, 560–571. **Alfred Church.** Signed.
1800   English and Eastern horses (Part I): Eastern horses, 572–587. **Francis Hastings Doyle.** Signed.

1801   Has our vaccination degenerated? 592–605. **Charles Cameron.** Signed; Contents adds "M.D., M.P."; see *WWW*/1928.
1802   The fortunes of literature under the American Republic, 606–617. **George Edward Woodberry.** Signed.
1803   Commercial union from a Canadian point of view, 618–633. **Francis Hincks.** Signed F. Hincks; Contents adds "Sir"; see *DNB.*
1804   Cobden's first pamphlets, 634–649. **John Morley.** Signed Editor.
1805   Political heads—chiefs, kings, etc. (Part VII), 650–661. **Herbert Spencer.** Signed; cf. no. 1743.
1806   Home and foreign affairs, 662–674. **John Morley,** prob. Attr. in *Early Life,* II, 106.

VOLUME 35 O.S., 29 N.S., JUNE 1881

1807   Comte's definition of life, 675–688. **J. H. Bridges.** Signed.
1808   The Royal Academy in 1881, 689–703. **Edmund W. Gosse.** Signed.
1809   English and Eastern horses (Part II, concl.): English horses, 704–728. **Francis H. Doyle.** Signed.
1810   The visions of sane persons, 729–740. **Francis Galton.** Signed.
1811   A Conservative view of the Irish Land Bill, 741–756. **Anthony Traill.** Signed.
1812   The emigration and waste-land clauses, 757–766. **Charlotte G. O'Brien.** Signed.
1813   Hindu households, 767–775. **William Knighton,** 1834–1900. Signed W. Knighton; Contents gives first name; see *WWW*/1916.
1814   Men and women (Part II): a sequel [to no. 1639], 776–793. **Maria G. Grey.** Signed.
1815   On the policy of commercial treaties, 794–800. **John Morley.** Signed Editor.
1816   Home and foreign affairs, 801–810. **John Morley,** prob. Cf. no. 1227.

VOLUME 36 O.S., 30 N.S., JULY 1881

1817   Conciliation with Ireland, 1–25. **John Morley.** Signed Editor.
1818   Italy; her home and foreign policy, 27–39. **Antonio Gallenga.** Signed A. Gallenga.
1819   *The Four Winds of the Spirit* [by Victor Hugo], 40–53. **George Saintsbury.** Signed.
1820   The compound political heads (Part

VIII, concl.), 54–75. **Herbert Spencer.** Signed; cf. no. 1743.

1821 Denmark, 76–90. **David Wedderburn.** Signed.

1822 Technical education in Saxony, 91–97. **Bernhard Samuelson.** Signed B. Samuelson; Contents gives "M.P."; see *DNB*.

1823 The Land Laws, 98–107. **Robert R. Torrens.** Signed.

1824 Bimetallism and free trade, 108–125. **Emile de Laveleye.** Signed.

1825 Home and foreign affairs, 126–136. **John Morley,** prob. Cf. no. 1227.

VOLUME 36 O.S., 30 N.S., AUGUST 1881

1826 Irish grammar schools, 137–148. **Matthew Arnold.** Signed; repr. as "An Unregarded Irish Grievance," *Irish Essays*, 1882.

1827 A new life of Voltaire [by James Parton], 149–167. **George Saintsbury.** Signed.

1828 Two acts of Union: a contrast, 168–178. **A. V. Dicey.** Signed.

1829 The moral colour of rationalism, 179–194. **Louisa S. Bevington.** Signed L. S. Bevington; Contents gives first name.

1830 Co-operative farming, 195–203. **William Hazlitt Roberts.** Signed.

1831 The future of Islam (Part I): census of the Mohammedan world; the Haj, 204–223. **Wilfrid Scawen Blunt.** Signed; repr. *The Future of Islam*, 1882.

1832 Leigh Hunt as a poet, 224–237. **Armine T. Kent.** Signed; repr. *Otia: Poems, Essays, and Reviews*, 1905.

1833 The land question in Europe, 238–252. **Rowland Blennerhassett.** Signed.

1834 Treaties of commerce a surrender of principle, 253–259. **James Bird.** Signed. (See no. 1905.)

1835 Home and foreign affairs, 260–270. **John Morley,** prob. Cf. no. 1227.

VOLUME 36 O.S., 30 N.S., SEPTEMBER 1881

1836 Radicals and Irish ideas, 271–283. **D. C. Lathbury.** Signed.

1837 Bulgaria, 284–293. **M. Valentine Chirol.** Signed; the "M" prefixed to the name prob. stands for "Monsieur."

1838 South Africa: an unspoken speech, 299–314. **M. E. Grant Duff.** Signed.

1839 The future of Islam (Part II): the modern question of the Caliphate, 315–332. **Wilfrid Scawen Blunt.** Signed.

1840 The recent excavations in Pergamon, 333–345. **Walter C. Perry.** Signed.

1841 A volume of French souvenirs [of Madame C. Jaubert], 346–354. **H. Schütz Wilson.** Signed.

1842 The dry bones of popular education, 355–373. **Mary Elizabeth Christie.** Signed. (See no. 1852.)

1843 Over-production, 374–387. **George Tomkyns Chesney.** Signed as in no. 1589.

1844 Home and foreign affairs, 388–398. **John Morley,** prob. Cf. no. 1227.

VOLUME 36 O.S., 30 N.S., OCTOBER 1881

1845 Reform in parliamentary business: the House of Lords, 399–413. **William Rathbone.** Signed.

1846 The Latter Day Saints as they are [the Mormons], 414–431. **Edward A. Thomas.** Signed.

1847 Railways and waterways, 432–440. **William Fleming.** Signed W. Fleming; Contents gives first name.

1848 The future of Islam (Part III): the true metropolis—Mecca, 441–458. **Wilfrid Scawen Blunt.** Signed.

1849 Italian realistic fiction, 459–477. **Frances Eleanor Trollope.** Signed.

1850 The history of English law as a branch of politics, 478–498. **Frederick Pollock,** 1845–1937. Signed.

1851 Nicholas Alexeivitch Nekrasoff, 499–512. **Charles Edward Turner.** Signed; repr. *Studies*.

1852 "The Dry Bones of Popular Education," a reply [to no. 1842], 513–526. **W. Scott Dalgleish.** Signed.

1853 Home and foreign affairs, 527–536. **John Morley,** prob. Attr. in *Early Life*, II, 109, 110.

VOLUME 36 O.S., 30 N.S., NOVEMBER 1881

1854 How is the law to be enforced in Ireland? 537–552. **A. V. Dicey.** Signed.

1855 Antonio Rosmini, 553–584. **Thomas Davidson.** Signed.

1856 The future of Islam (Part IV): a Mohammedan reformation, 585–602. **Wilfrid Scawen Blunt.** Signed.

1857 The king, in his relation to early civil justice, 603–617. **H. S. Maine.** Signed; repr. *Early Law and Custom*, 1883.

1858 The salmon fisheries, 624–639. **Fred Eden.** Signed.

1859 The history and future of interest and

profit, 640–659. **T. E. Cliffe Leslie.**
Signed; repr. *Political Economy*.

1860   Home and foreign affairs, 660–670.
John Morley, prob. Attr. in *Early Life*,
II, 110.

VOLUME 36 o.s., 30 n.s., DECEMBER 1881

1861   Atheists in parliament, 671–679. **D. C.
Lathbury.** Signed.

1862   Kioto, 680–700. **W. Gifford Palgrave.**
Signed; repr. *Ulysses*.

1863   Thriftless thrift, 701–714. **Hugh Seymour Tremenheere.** Signed on p. 713.

1864   Has conservatism increased in England since the last Reform Bill? 718–729.
Alfred Frisby. Signed.

1865   The Bergsturz at Elm, 730–738. **William Pole.** Signed.

1866   The scientific evidence of organic evolution, 739–758. **George J. Romanes.**
Signed.

1867   A page of diplomatic history, 759–777.
Charlotte Blennerhassett. Signed C. Blennerhassett; called "Lady" in Contents;
see Burke.

1868   A chapter in the ethics of pain, 778–
796. **Edmund Gurney.** Signed; repr. *Tertium Quid* (1887), I. (See no. 1876.)

1869   Home and foreign affairs, 797–806.
John Morley, prob. Cf. no. 1227.

VOLUME 37 o.s., 31 n.s., JANUARY 1882

1870   Mr. Caird and land-owning cultivators,
1–12. **F. Barham Zincke.** Signed.

1871   Note on the character of Mary Queen
of Scots, 13–25. **Algernon Charles Swinburne.** Signed; repr. *Miscellanies*.

1872   Photographic chronicles from childhood to age, 26–31. **Francis Galton.**
Signed.

1873   The future of Islam (Part V, concl.):
England's interest in Islam, 32–48. **Wilfrid Scawen Blunt.** Signed.

1874   Pietro Cossa: dramatist, 49–68. **Alfred
Austin.** Signed.

1875   Sir Charles Lyell, 69–87. **Grant Allen.**
Signed.

1876   Vivisection: four replies [to no. 1868
and to 3 arts. in *NC*], 88–104. **Frances
Power Cobbe.** Signed. (See no. 1884.)

1877   *The Journals of Caroline Fox*, 105–
124. **John Morley.** Signed Editor.

1878   Home and foreign affairs, 125–136.
John Morley, prob. Cf. no. 1227.

VOLUME 37 o.s., 31 n.s., FEBRUARY 1882

1879   The relations of religion to Asiatic
states, 137–154. **A. C. Lyall.** Signed;
repr. *Asiatic Studies*; and *Asiatic Studies
Second Series*, 1899.

1880   As others see us, 156–165. **Andrew
Carnegie.** Signed.

1881   Mr. Swinburne's trilogy [*Chastelard,
Bothwell, Mary Stuart*], 166–179. **G. A.
Simcox.** Signed.

1882   The king and his successor, 180–194.
H. S. Maine. Signed; repr. *Early Law and
Custom*, 1883, as "Royal Succession and
the Salic Law."

1883   The health resorts of the Western
Riviera, 198–224. **Isaac Burney Yeo.**
Signed as in no. 1351; repr. *Health Re-
sorts*, 1882.

1884   The *Nineteenth Century* defenders of
vivisection, 225–236. **John Duke Coleridge.** Signed Coleridge [Baron Cole-
ridge].

1885   The ethics of vivisection, 237–246. **William B. Carpenter.** Signed.

1886   William Lloyd Garrison, 247–263.
Robert Niven. Signed.

1887   Home and foreign affairs, 264–272.
John Morley, prob. Cf. no. 1227.

VOLUME 37 o.s., 31 n.s., MARCH 1882

1888   Jowett's *Thucydides*, 273–292. **Edward A. Freeman.** Signed.

1889   Italy as it is, 293–313. **James Melvin.**
Signed.

1890   Miss Ferrier's novels, 314–331. **George
Saintsbury.** Signed; repr. *Essays*, I.

1891   The anthropometric laboratory, 332–
338. **Francis Galton.** Signed.

1892   The decay of criticism, 339–351. **Grant
Allen.** Signed.

1893   The practice of vivisection in England, 352–368. **Gerald F. Yeo.** Signed.

1894   The results of protection in young
communities, 369–379, with a postscript,
379. **George Baden-Powell.** Signed; repr.
without the postscript, *State Aid*.

1895   Some Irish realities: an historical chapter, 380–399.

1896   Home and foreign affairs, 400–410.
John Morley, prob. Attr. in *Early Life*,
II, 116.

VOLUME 37 o.s., 31 n.s., APRIL 1882

1897   A few words about the nineteenth century, 411–426. **Frederic Harrison.** Signed; repr. *Choice of Books.*

1898 French diplomacy in Syria, 427–438. **M. Valentine Chirol.** Signed as in no. 1837.

1899 Emile Zola, 439–452. **Andrew Lang.** Signature.

1900 The present condition of Russia, 453–467. **E. F. G. Law.** Signed.

1901 Sir Charles Bell and physiological experimentation, 468–475. **William B. Carpenter.** Signed.

1902 *The Life of James Mill* [by Alexander Bain], 476–504. **John Morley.** Signed Editor.

1903 Africa and the Empire, 505–517. **Alfred Aylward.** Signed.

1904 On the development of the colour-sense, 518–529. **Montagu Lubbock.** Signed.

1905 No more commercial treaties, 530–536. **James Bird.** Signed.

1906 Home and foreign affairs, 537–546. **John Morley**, prob. Attr. in *Early Life*, II, 116.

VOLUME 37 O.S., 31 N.S., MAY 1882

1907 Substitutes for trial by jury in Ireland, 547–563. **I. S. Leadam.** Signed.

1908 Marcus Aurelius Antoninus, 564–586. **Frederic W. H. Myers.** Signed; repr. *Essays.*

1909 Curiosities of the law of treason (Part I), 587–601. **Frederic Harrison.** Signed.

1910 Finland, 602–611. **Antonio Gallenga.** Signed A. Gallenga.

1911 Unnatural children [ill-health in slums], 612–619. **Elizabeth Rossiter.** Signed; called "Mrs. Rossiter" in Contents.

1912 The House of Lords, 620–635. **T. E. Kebbel.** Signed.

1913 Wintering in the snow: a study of the mountain air cure, 636–650. **Isaac Burney Yeo.** Signed as in no. 1351.

1914 The Russian Revolutionary Party, 654–671. **Peter Aleksyeevich Kropotkin.** Signed P. Kropotkin; Contents adds "Prince."

1915 Home and foreign affairs, 672–682. **John Morley**, prob. Cf. no. 1227.

VOLUME 37 O.S., 31 N.S., JUNE 1882

1916 An Eton boy, 683–697. **Matthew Arnold.** Signed.

1917 History of the law of treason (Part II), 698–709, with an addendum, 709–710. **Frederic Harrison.** Signed.

1918 Troubles in the Pacific, 711–734. **John Wisker.** Signed with address "Melbourne." (See no. 1942.)

1919 The Salon of 1882, 735–746. **Edmund W. Gosse.** Signed.

1920 Ralph Waldo Emerson, 747–770. **Moncure D. Conway.** Signed.

1921 Mr. Morris's *Hopes and Fears for Art*, 771–779. **Edith Simcox.** Signed.

1922 England and Ireland: an American view, 780–794. **Henry George.** Signed.

1923 Newgate: a retrospect, 795–807. **Arthur Griffiths.** Signed; called "Major" in Contents; see *DNB.*

1924 Home and foreign affairs, 808–818. **John Morley**, prob. Attr. in *Early Life*, II, 123.

VOLUME 38 O.S., 32 N.S., JULY 1882

1925 Foes in council, 1–15. **William Minto.** Signed.

1926 The philosophic movement in the Roman Church, 16–35. **Thomas Davidson.** Signed.

1927 Mr. Lecky and George III, 41–59. **T. E. Kebbel.** Signed.

1928 Why is Mr. Millais our popular painter? 60–77. **Emilie Isabel Barrington.** Signed; repr. *A Retrospect*, 1896.

1929 *Democracy: An American Novel* [by Henry Adams], 78–93. **Mary A. Ward.** Signed.

1930 Egyptian policy: a retrospect, 94–123. **John Morley.** Signed Editor and claimed by Morley in his *Life of W. E. Gladstone* (N.Y., 1903), III, 75–76.

1931 Home and foreign affairs, 124–132. **John Morley**, prob. Cf. no. 1227.

VOLUME 38 O.S., 32 N.S., AUGUST 1882

1932 Some impressions of the United States (Part I), 133–155. **Edward A. Freeman.** Signed.

1933 Kompert's Jewish tales, 156–173. **H. Sutherland Edwards.** Signed.

1934 Equalisation of railway rates, 174–190. **T. H. Farrer.** Signed.

1935 Another side of a popular story [on India], 191–208. **R. D. Osborn.** Signed; Contents adds "Colonel"; see *DNB.*

1936 The history of the science of politics (Part I), 209–225. **Frederick Pollock, 1845–1937.** Signed; series repr. as *An*

Introduction to the History of the Science of Politics, 1890.

1937　Passionless reformers, 226–233. **Henrietta O. Barnett.** Signed; repr. *Practicable Socialism*.

1938　Great Britain and the Suez Canal, 234–240. **William Rathbone.** Signed.

1939　The next reform bill, 241–254. **Alfred Frisby.** Signed.

1940　Home and foreign affairs, 255–268. **John Morley,** prob. Attr. in *Early Life*, II, 116–117.

VOLUME 38 O.S., 32 N.S., SEPTEMBER 1882

1941　A study of sensibility, 269–293. **George Saintsbury.** Signed; repr. *French Novelists*.

1942　Queensland planters: an exculpation [reply to no. 1918], 294–307. **R. J. Jeffray.** Signed.

1943　Who was primitive man? 308–322. **Grant Allen.** Signed.

1944　Some impressions of the United States (Part II, concl.), 323–346. **Edward A. Freeman.** Signed.

1945　The analysis of humour, 347–357. **H. D. Traill.** Signed.

1946　The House of Lords, 358–375. **Arthur F. Leach.** Signed.

1947　The history of the science of politics (Part II), 376–391. **Frederick Pollock,** 1845–1937. Signed F. Pollock.

1948　Home and foreign affairs, 392–404. **John Morley,** prob. Cf. no. 1227.

VOLUME 38 O.S., 32 N.S., OCTOBER 1882

1949　The Russian Bayard: personal reminiscences of General Scobeleff, 405–419. **W. Kinnaird Rose.** Signed.

1950　The homes of the poor, 420–431. **W. St. John Brodrick.** Signed.

1951　A musical crisis, 432–452. **Edmund Gurney.** Signed.

1952　The history of the science of politics (Part III), 453–467. **Frederick Pollock,** 1845–1937. Signed F. Pollock.

1953　Herder, 468–484. **James Sully.** Signed.

1954　Local government in America, 485–495. **Albert Shaw.** Signed.

1955　An English land bill, 496–510. **William E. Bear.** Signed.

1956　Valedictory, 511–521. **John Morley.** Signed Editor; repr. *Studies*.

1957　Home and foreign affairs, 522–534. **John Morley,** prob. Attr. in *Early Life*, II, 118.

VOLUME 38 O.S., 32 N.S., NOVEMBER 1882

1958　Reform of Egypt, 535–547. **Samuel W. Baker.** Signed.

1959　Lucius Carey, Lord Falkland, 548–559. **Henry Howard Molyneaux Herbert.** Signed Carnarvon [Earl of Carnarvon]; repr. *Essays*, I.

1960　The French Republic and M. Gambetta, 560–567. **Léon Gambetta.** Escott explains in his *Politics*, p. 38, that this art. was dictated by Gambetta to one of his secretaries and was "untouched by any further hand." (See no. 1976.)

1961　Francis Maitland Balfour, 568–580. **H. N. Moseley,** 1844–1891. Signed.

1962　On the future of Zululand and South Africa, 581–595. **H. B. E. Frere.** Signed.

1963　A new eirenicon [*Natural Religion*, by J. R. Seeley], 596–607. **Frederic W. H. Myers.** Signed; repr. *Essays*.

1964　State and prospects of British agriculture in 1882, 608–624. **George C. Brodrick.** Signed; repr. *Literary Fragments*, 1891.

1965　The Irish Parliamentary Party, 625–633. **T. M. Healy.** Signed.

1966　Some aspects of American public life, 634–655. **James Bryce,** 1838–1922. Signed.

1967　The eleventh plague of Egypt [foreign intrigue], 656–667. **A. J. Wilson.** Signed.

1968　The state of the opposition, 668–676. **John Eldon Gorst** and **Henry Drummond Wolff,** probably speaking for Randolph S. Churchill. Signed Two Conservatives: T. H. S. Escott, editor of *FortR* at this time, says (*Randolph Spencer-Churchill* [1895], pp. 157–8, 162, 167, 178–179) that the ideas were Churchill's, but spoken through his lieutenants; R. R. James, *Lord Randolph Churchill* (1959), p. 131, attrs. to Churchill, Gorst, and Wolff; Janet Courtney, *Making of an Editor*, p. 135, says "It appears it was really written by Randolph Churchill."

1969　Home and foreign affairs, 677–686. **T. H. S. Escott,** prob. He had been acting editor for a time under Morley (see above, p. 178); as early as Dec. 1878 he claimed to have written the home and foreign affairs for the Jan. issue (see no. 1547); that he was in many cases, prob. in most, doing the "chronique," as he called this department, is made clear from a series of letters from Escott to Chamberlain in the Birmingham University Library (see nos. 1992, 2119, and other home and foreign affairs attrib. to Escott on this basis); the same letters also show how heavily Escott relied upon Chamberlain for advice and memoranda in preparing this department.

VOLUME 38 O.S., 32 N.S., DECEMBER 1882

1970 The Conservative leadership [reply to no. 1968), 687–692. Signed: Two Other Conservatives.
1971 The Liberal party in Germany, 693–717. **George von Bunsen.** Signed.
1972 Working men and war, 718–727. **Thomas Burt.** Signed; called "M.P." in Contents; see *DNB*.
1973 A lesson on democracy, 728–747. **J. A. Froude.** Signed.
1974 Egypt for the Egyptians, 748–761. **Emile de Laveleye.** Signed.
1975 Charles Dickens, 762–779. **Mowbray Morris.** Signed.
1976 "The French Republic and M. Gambetta": a reply [to no. 1960], 780–791. **Jules Dietz.** Signed.
1977 Shooting, 792–807. **T. E. Kebbel.** Signed.
1978 How our public improvements are carried out, 808–816. **H. H. Statham.** Signed.
1979 Below the opposition gangway: a dialogue, 821–828. **H. D. Traill.** Signed.
1980 Home and foreign affairs, 829–838. **T. H. S. Escott,** prob. Cf. no. 1969.

VOLUME 39 O.S., 33 N.S., JANUARY 1883

1981 The coming session, 1–18. **George W. E. Russell.** Signed.
1982 Will the new rules work? 19–24. **George Byron Curtis.** Signed.
1983 Merton College in the sixteenth century, 25–37. **George C. Brodrick.** Signed; repr. *Memorials of Merton College*, Oxford, 1885.
1984 Reconstruction in Egypt, 38–50. **George Campbell,** 1824–1892. Signed; Contents adds "K.C.S.I." and "M.P."; see *DNB*.
1985 Secret societies in France, 51–63. **Hector Depasse.** Signed Jehan de Paris; Camille Barrère to Escott, Nov. 4, [1882], Escott Papers, encloses art. on secret societies by M. Depasse; repr. *Topics of the Time*, no. 1.
1986 Home Rule, socialism, and secession, 64–74. **J. Woulfe Flanagan.** Signed; repr. *Topics of the Time*, no. 1.
1987 The impressionists, 75–82. **Frederick Wedmore.** Signed; repr. *Topics of the Time*, no. 6.

1988 The history of the science of politics (Part IV, concl.), 83–99. **Frederick Pollock,** 1845–1937. Signed.
1989 A study of Longfellow, 100–115. **Henry Norman,** 1858–1939. Signed; for his interest in America, see *WWW*.
1990 The Reform Act of 1832 and its critics, 116–131. **A. V. Dicey.** Signed.
1991 Political effect of religious thought in India, 132–143. **Richard Temple.** Signed; repr. *Oriental Experience*, 1883.
1992 Home and foreign affairs, 144–152. **T. H. S. Escott.** Escott to Joseph Chamberlain, Dec. 9, 1882, Chamberlain Papers, asks for advice on subjects which are included in this department, and on Dec. 13, thanks him for the same.

VOLUME 39 O.S., 33 N.S., FEBRUARY 1883

1993 The new army and the old test, 153–170. **W. F. Butler.** Signed; Contents adds "Colonel" and "C.B."; see *DNB*.
1994 The third Reform Bill: why delay it? 171–180. **T. W. Fowle.** Signed.
1995 Samuel Wilberforce, 181–196. **G. W. Dasent.** Signed.
1996 Lord Westbury and Bishop Wilberforce: a Lucianic dialogue, 197–204. **H. D. Traill.** Signed; repr. *The New Lucian, being a series of Dialogues of the Dead,* 1884.
1997 A radical in Russia, 205–220. **Jesse Collings.** Signed.
1998 English actors: yesterday and today, 221–232. **J. Comyns Carr.** Signed.
1999 The House of Lords, 233–249. **Edward A. Freeman.** Signed.
2000 The beginning of art, 250–254. **Stanley Lane-Poole.** Signed; repr. *Topics of the Time,* no. 6.
2001 England and France in 1793, 255–271. **Oscar Browning.** Signed; repr. *The Flight to Varennes,* 1892.
2002 Mexico and her railways, 272–284. **John Young Sargent.** Signed J. Y. Sargent; Lady Blanche Rosslyn to Escott, Jan. 12, 1885, Escott Papers, speaks of an art. by John Sargent, not on scholarship as she expected but on a Mexican topic.
2003 Gambetta, 285–297. **Camille Barrère** and **Hector Depasse,** prob. Announced in *Athenaeum,* Jan. 20, 1883, p. 87; Barrère to Escott, 2 undated letters in Escott Papers, refers to his art. on Gambetta (neither mentions collaboration).

2004 Home and foreign affairs, 293–304. Unidentified. Escott to Joseph Chamberlain, Jan. 19, 1883, Chamberlain Papers, says "I have just arranged for the writing of the Chronique—taking up three subjects: county franchises, Ireland, Egypt"; he asks Chamberlain for half a dozen lines about Egypt; the word "arranged" suggests that Escott may have delegated the writing of the department for this issue; he may also have included a brief passage from Chamberlain.

VOLUME 39 O.S., 33 N.S., MARCH 1883

2005 The government of Paris, 305–314. **Albert Gigot.** Signed.
2006 A politician in trouble about his soul (Part I), 315–334. **Auberon Herbert.** Signed; series repr. with this title, 1884.
2007 Dr. Pusey and the High-Church movement, 335–348. **Edward S. Talbot.** Signed.
2008 Abolition of slavery in India and Egypt, 349–368. **H. B. E. Frere.** Signed.
2009 A democrat on the coming democracy, 369–381. **Henry Labouchere.** Signed H. Labouchere; Contents adds "M.P."; see *DNB*; repr. *Topics of the Time*, no. 1.
2010 The future of the English universities, 382–403. **James Bryce,** 1838–1922. Signed.
2011 Brazil and her railways, 404–416. **Charles Waring,** d. 1887. Signed.
2012 The county system, 417–436. **T. F. Kebbel.** Signed.
2013 Transferred impressions and telepathy, 437–452. **Edmund Gurney** and **Frederic W. H. Myers.** Signed.
2014 Home and foreign affairs, 453–460. **T. H. S. Escott,** prob. Cf. no. 1969.

VOLUME 39 O.S., 33 N.S., APRIL 1883

2015 The French army, 461–474. **Hippolyte Barthélemy.** Signed H. Barthélemy; for man cited see *DBF*.
2016 The Affirmation Bill, 475–484. **John Campbell Gordon.** Signed Aberdeen [Earl of Aberdeen].
2017 The production and life of books, 485–499. **C. Kegan Paul.** Signed; repr. *Faith and Unfaith*, 1891.
2018 Departments of agriculture, 500–513. **William E. Bear.** Signed.
2019 A tour in the Troad [Asia Minor], 514–529. **R. C. Jebb.** Signed.
2020 Lord Lawrence and the Mutiny, 530–

547. **H. W. Norman.** Signed; Contents adds "General"; see *DNB*.
2021 The European terror, 548–561. **Emile de Laveleye.** Signed; repr. *Topics of the Time*, no. 1.
2022 Phantasms of the living, 562–577. **Edmund Gurney** and **Frederic W. H. Myers.** Signed.
2023 Prince Gortchakoff on Russian diplomacy, 578–591. **H. Sutherland Edwards.** Signed.
2024 Workmen's trains and the passenger duty, 592–596. **Francis W. Buxton.** Signed.
2025 The budget: what Mr. Childers should do, 597–604. **A. J. Wilson.** Signed.
2026 Home and foreign affairs, 605–612. **T. H. S. Escott,** prob. Cf. no. 1969.

VOLUME 39 O.S., 33 N.S., MAY 1883

2027 Elijah's mantle; April 19th, 1883 [reflections on Disraeli's fall from power in 1880], 613–621. **Randolph S. Churchill.** Signed.
2028 Carlyle in society and at home, 622–642. **G. S. Venables.** Signed.
2029 Nitro-glycerine and dynamite, 643–652. **Vivian Dering Majendie.** Signed.
2030 Henry J. Stephen Smith, 653–666. **J. W. L. Glaisher.** Signed.
2031 A politician in trouble about his soul (Parts II and III), 667–690. **Auberon Herbert.** Signed.
2032 The reform of local government in counties, 691–704. **George C. Brodrick.** Signed.
2033 A plea for a British institute at Athens, 705–714. **R. C. Jebb.** Signed. (Letter, vol. 48, pp. 455–458, signed **George A. Macmillan,** with note, pp. 458–459, by **T. H. S. Escott**—signed "Ed. F.R.")
2034 The political condition of Italy, 715–733. **F. Nobile Vitelleschi.** Signed with titles, "Marquis, Member of the Italian Senate."
2035 John Richard Green, 734–747. **Philip Lyttelton Gell.** Signed.
2036 England's duty in Egypt, 748–757.
2037 Home and foreign affairs, 758–764. **T. H. S Escott,** prob. Cf. no. 1969.

VOLUME 39 O.S., 33 N.S., JUNE 1883

2038 The social discipline of the Liberal party, 767–775. Signed: A Liberal.
2039 Blasphemy and the common law, 776–789. **John Macdonell.** Signed.

2040 The poetry of Arthur Hugh Clough, 790–807. **Richard Holt Hutton.** Signed.

2041 China and foreign powers, 808–821. **Demetrius Charles Boulger.** Signed; repr. *Central Asian Questions.*

2042 The Church of England (No. I): the legal aspects of disestablishment, 822–840. **A. V. Dicey.** Signed.

2043 The Church of England (No. II): the clergy and the law, 841–855. **Malcolm MacColl.** Signed.

2044 The duration of penal sentences, 856–863. **E. F. Du Cane.** Signed.

2045 Genre in the summer exhibitions, 864–872. **Frederick Wedmore.** Signed.

2046 A new exodus, 873–887. **Sydney C. Buxton.** Signed.

2047 Robert Browning, writer of plays, 888–900. **W. L. Courtney.** Signed; repr. *Studies.*

2048 Some aspects of Lord Ripon's policy [on India], 901–910. **H. G. Keene.** Signed.

2049 Home and foreign affairs, 911–920. **T. H. S. Escott,** prob. Cf. no. 1969.

VOLUME 40 O.S., 34 N.S., JULY 1883

2050 The future of the Radical party, 1–11.

2051 The stage in relation to literature (Part I), 12–26. **E. Robert Bulwer Lytton.** Signed Lytton [Earl Lytton].

2052 Egypt (No. I): non-political control in Egypt, 27–38. **F. J. Goldsmid.** Signed; described on p. 27 as ex-controller of the Daira Saniya: see *DNB.*

2053 Egypt (No. II): the international position of the Suez Canal, 39–49. **T. E. Holland.** Signed; repr. *Studies in International Law,* 1898.

2054 A chapter of autobiography, being some account of my Oxford private pupils, 1831–1833; with notices of the first athletic contests between Oxford and Cambridge, 50–71. **Charles Wordsworth.** Signed; called "Bishop of St. Andrew's" in Contents; see *DNB.*

2055 The limits of English revolution [reply to no. 2009], 72–84. **George Charles Spencer-Churchill.** Signed Blandford [Marquess of Blandford].

2056 Remarks on some of my reviewers [of *Life of Samuel Wilberforce*], 85–96. **R. G. Wilberforce.** Signed.

2057 The fate of the London bill, 97–110. **J. F. B. Firth.** Signed; Contents adds "M.P."; see Boase.

2058 South Kensington Hellenism: a dialogue, 111–119. **H. D. Traill.** Signed.

2059 Army hospital services, 120–135. **Douglas Galton.** Signed; called "Captain" in Contents; *DNB.*

2060 Cave tombs in Galilee, 136–145. **Laurence Oliphant.** Signed.

2061 Home and foreign affairs, 146–152. **T. H. S. Escott,** prob. Cf. no. 1969.

VOLUME 40 O.S., 34 N.S., AUGUST 1883

2062 France and England in Egypt, 153–162. **Leon Say.** Signed.

2063 The negotiations with M. de Lesseps, 163–174. **O. C. Waterfield.** Signed.

2064 Importation of disease, 175–188. **Charles Creighton.** Signed C. Creighton; called "M.D." in Contents; see *WWW/* 1928.

2065 Byron and his biographers, 189–202. **G. S. Venables.** Signed.

2066 Criminal jurisdiction over Englishmen in India, 203–214. **Charles Colin Macrae.** Signed C.C. Macrae; see *WWW/*1928.

2067 The stage in relation to literature (Part II, concl.), 215–226. **E. Robert Bulwer Lytton.** Signed Lytton [Earl Lytton]. Postscript, p. 456, signed **John Hollingshead.**

2068 France and Syria, 227–243. **C. R. Conder.** Signed; Contents adds "Capt., R.E."; see *DNB.*

2069 Medical family registers, 244–250. **Francis Galton.** Signed.

2070 New Guinea and annexation, 251–262. **Julius Vogel.** Signed.

2071 Miracles and medium-craft, 263–277. **Horatio B. Donkin.** Signed H. Donkin; called "M.D." in Contents; see *WWW/* 1928.

2072 Our Boer policy, 278–289. **Gavin Brown Clark.** Signed G. B. Clark; Contents adds F.R.C.S.; see *WWW/*1940.

2073 The radical programme(No. I): machinery, 290–297. **T. H. S. Escott.** Attr. in Chamberlain, *Memoir,* p. 108; repr. in *The Radical Programme.* Chamberlain says that all these articles under that title and reprinted in the book were "arranged with me beforehand and submitted to me in proof before publication."

2074 Home and foreign affairs, 298–304. **T. H. S. Escott,** prob. Cf. no. 1969.

VOLUME 40 O.S., 34 N.S., SEPTEMBER 1883

2075 Politics in the Lebanon, 305–314. **Laurence Oliphant.** Assigned in Contents to An English Resident; claimed Oliphant to Percy Bunting, Nov. 25, [1833], Bunting Papers.

2076 Yachting (No. I): cruising, 315–322. **Thomas Brassey.** Signed; Contents adds "K.C.B."; see *DNB*.

2077 Yachting (No. II): racing, 322–326. **Dixon Kemp.** Signed.

2078 Egypt for the Egyptians, 327–343. **Carl Malortie.** Signed Malortie [Baron de Malortie].

2079 Modern dress, 344–353. **G. Armytage.** Signed; called "Mrs." in Contents.

2080 A politician in trouble about his soul (Part IV), 354–376. **Auberon Herbert.** Signed.

2081 Twelve months of travel, 377–393. **Robert Brown,** 1842–1895. Signed; Contents adds "Dr."; see *DNB*.

2082 Forty years in the desert [plea for reclamation of waste lands in Ireland], 394–406. **Ernest Hart.** Signed; author describes himself, p. 395, as a London doctor; see *DNB*.

2083 Anglo-Indian complications and their cause, 407–421. **A. P. Sinnett.** Signed.

2084 Ralph Waldo Emerson: an ethical study, 422–432. **Henry Norman,** 1858–1939. Signed; for his interest in America, see *WWW*.

2085 The Radical programme (No. II): measures, 433–447. **T. H. S. Escott.** Attr. in Chamberlain, *Memoir*, p. 108. Cf. no. 2073.

2086 Home and foreign affairs, 448–455. **T. H. S. Escott,** prob. Cf. no. 1969.

VOLUME 40 O.S., 34 N.S., OCTOBER 1883

2087 The foreign policy of France, 457–465. **Paul Leroy-Beaulieu.** Signed.

2088 Mr. Irving's interpretations of Shakspeare, 466–481. **Edward R. Russell.** Signed.

2089 Indian princes at home, 482–496. **Lepel Griffin.** Signed

2090 Victor Hugo: *La Légende des Siècles*, Vol. V, 497–520. **Algernon Charles Swinburne.** Signed; repr. *A Study of Victor Hugo*, 1886.

2091 Russia, Austria, and the Danubian States, 521–535. **Camille Barrère.** T. H. S. Escott to W. E. Gladstone, Sept. 29, and Oct. 8, 1883, BM Add. MSS., 44483, says author is Barrère, a foreign diplomat of great distinction, now "going as French Consul General to Egypt"; see *Documents diplomatiques français*, 1st s. V, 162.

2092 Some recent biographies, 536–553. **W. F. Pollock,** 1815–1888. Signed; Contents gives "Sir Frederick, Bart."; see *DNB*.

2093 The present state of the German army, 554–570. **Ernst Braune.** Signed; Contents adds "Capt."

2094 Through Portugal, 571–580. **Isabella Augusta Gregory.** Signed. "Augusta Gregory"; Contents gives "Lady Gregory"; see *DNB*.

2095 Why have a hangman? 581–586. **Arthur Griffiths.** Signed as in no. 1923.

2096 The Radical programme (No. III): the housing of the poor in towns, 587–600. **Frank Harris.** Attr. in Chamberlain, *Memoir*, p. 108.

2097 Home and foreign affairs, 601–608. **T. H. S. Escott,** prob. Cf. no. 1969.

VOLUME 40 O.S., 34 N.S., NOVEMBER 1883

2098 The Radical programme (No. IV): the agricultural labourer, 609–625. **Jesse Collings.** Attr. in Chamberlain, *Memoir*, p.108.

2099 The restoration in Egypt, 626–638. **Ardern G. H. Beaman,** prob. Signed "A. Beaman"; for his interest in Egypt, see *WWW*/1940.

2100 Scotch universities, their friends and foes, 639–658. **John Nichol,** 1833–1894. Signed; Contents adds "Prof."; see *DNB*.

2101 Bazaine's vindication, 659–673. **Archibald Forbes.** Signed.

2102 A month in Connemara, 674–689. **Samuel Laing,** 1812–1897. Signed as in no. 1443.

2103 Elections of the future, 690–699. **J. E. Gorst,** 1835–1916. Signed; Contents adds "Q.C."; see *DNB*.

2104 The political conditions of Spain, 700–712. **Laureano Figuerola.** Signed.

2105 Poets of to-day, 713–727. **W. L. Courtney.** Signed.

2106 Ireland and the Tory party, 728–736. **T. M. Healy.** Signed; Contents adds "M.P."; see *DNB*.

2107 The trusteeship of the Suez Canal, 737–749. **Charles Waring,** d.1887. Signed.

2108 Home and foreign affairs, 750–760. **T. H. S. Escott,** prob. Cf. no. 1969.

VOLUME 40 O.S., 34 N.S., DECEMBER 1883

2109 Labourers' and artisans' dwellings, 761–776. **Joseph Chamberlain.** Signed as in no. 981.

2110 The ideas of an exile, 777–782. **Ibrahim Hilmy.** Signed; Contents adds "H. H. Prince."

2111 The educational work of the Royal Academy, 783–790. **Frederick A. Eaton.** Signed.

2112 A year after Gambetta's death, 791–805. **Hector Depasse.** Signed; Depasse to Escott, Oct. 16, 17, 1883, Escott Papers, says Camille Barrère is helping him to revise his "Gambetta."

2113 A politician in trouble about his soul (Part V), 806–823. **Auberon Herbert.** Signed.

2114 *Pro patriâ*: the South African problem, 824–832. **D. P. Faure.** Signed.

2115 Fire-discipline [military conduct in battle], 833–844. **Archibald Forbes.** Signed.

2116 In the wrong paradise; an occidental apologue, 845–854. **Andrew Lang.** Signature; repr. *In the Wrong Paradise*, 1886.

2117 Turkish intrigues in Egypt, 855–869. **A. M. Broadley.** Signed.

2118 Theories and practice of modern fiction, 870–886. **Henry Norman,** 1858–1939. Signed; he was writing on literature for *FR* at this time.

2119 Home and foreign affairs, 887–896. **T. H. S. Escott.** Escott to Joseph Chamberlain, Nov. 27, 1883, Chamberlain Papers, says he has got a good bit of Chamberlain's speech into the "Chronique"; see pp. 891–893.

VOLUME 41 O.S., 35 N.S., JANUARY 1884

2120 The Radical programme (No. V): free schools, 1–20. **Francis Adams.** Attr. in Chamberlain, *Memoir*, p. 108.

2121 Social reforms for the London poor (No. I): the need of recreation, 21–30. **Violet Greville.** Signed; called "Lady" in Contents; see *WWW*/1916.

2122 Social reforms for the London poor (No. II): the wives and mothers of the working classes, 30–36. **T. W. Brockett,** prob. Signed A London Artisan; six months earlier an article dealing with the poor and signed in the same way (*Mac* 48 [June 1883], 127–130) is known to be his.

2123 The fallacy of Irish history, 37–49. **Goldwin Smith.** Signed.

2124 A visit to philistia [America], 50–64. **Lepel Griffin.** Signed; repr. in *The Great Republic*, 1884.

2125 Hablot Browne and book-illustration, 67–73. **Frederick Wedmore.** Signed.

2126 Rational radicalism, 74–88. **Samuel Laing,** 1812–1897. Signed as in no. 1443.

2127 Old comedy on a new stage [Aristophanes' *Birds*], 89–98. **R. C. Jebb.** Signed.

2128 Two biographies (No. I): *Edward Bulwer, Lord Lytton*, 99–107. **G. W. Dasent.** Signed.

2129 Two biographies (No. II): *Lord Lyndhurst*, 107–117. **T. E. Kebbel.** Signed.

2130 Life and death, 118–137. **W. S. Lilly.** Signed; repr. *Ancient Religion and Modern Thought*, 1884, as "Matter and Spirit."

2131 Home and foreign affairs, 138–144. **T. H. S. Escott.** Escott to Joseph Chamberlain, Dec. 20, 1883, Chamberlain Papers, says he plans in "Chronique" for Jan. to deal with the topics discussed here, and asks to consult Chamberlain.

VOLUME 41 O.S., 35 N.S., FEBRUARY 1884

2132 Liberal versus Conservative finance, 145–162. **John Lubbock.** Signed.

2133 The Anglo-French alliance, 163–174. **Timothée Colani.** Signed T. Colani; see *Bib. Nat. Cat.*

2134 Parliamentary reform, 175–189. **Arthur Arnold.** Signed.

2135 Turkish Arabia, 190–201. **Trevor Chichele Plowden.** Signed.

2136 Mr. Goldwin Smith; present and past, 202–207. **R. Barry O'Brien.** Signed; repr. *Irish Wrongs.*

2137 Radicals and Whigs, 208–225. **Henry Labouchere.** Signed as in no. 2009.

2138 Mozart, 226–240. **H. H. Statham.** Signed; repr. *Thoughts on Music.*

2139 Our colonial policy, 241–255. **St. Leger Herbert.** Signed.

2140 Occupying ownership, 256–266. **Jesse Collings.** Signed.

2141 The Guide of Islam [the Mahdi], 267–277. **C. R. Conder.** Signed.

2142 Home and foreign affairs, 278–288: (No. I) political, 278–285, by **T. H. S. Escott,** prob.—cf. no. 1969; (No. II) finance, 286–288.

VOLUME 41 O.S., 35 N.S., MARCH 1884

2143 Blasphemy and blasphemous libel, 289–318. **J. F. Stephen.** Signed.

2144 Job and his comforters: Elihu's

parable, 319–327. **Henry C. Raikes.** Signed An English Tory; attr. in *Life and Letters*, p. 208.

2145 Machiavelli, 328–343. **P. F. Willert.** Signed.

2146 The enfranchisement of urban lease-holders, 344–353. **Henry Broadhurst.** Signed.

2147 A politician in sight of haven (Part VI), 354–376. **Auberon Herbert.** Signed.

2148 Glimpses of the Soudan, 377–384. **Augusta Gregory.** Signed; Contents adds "Lady"; see *DNB*.

2149 The harvest of democracy, 387–401. **Lepel Griffin.** Signed; repr. *The Great Republic*, 1884.

2150 A world in pawn (Part I), 402–413. **A. J. Wilson.** Signed.

2151 Mr. [Abraham] Hayward, 414–425. **T. H. S. Escott.** Signed; repr. *Politics*. Postscript, p. 425, by **Mary Montgomerie Singleton**—signed Violet Fane; see *DNB* under Mary M. Currie, 1843–1905. (See no. 2163.)

2152 Home and foreign affairs, 426–432: (No. I) political, 426–430, by **T. H. S. Escott**, prob.—cf. no. 1969; (No. II) finance, 430–432.

VOLUME 41 O.S., 35 N.S., APRIL 1884

2153 Homeric Troy [on Schliemann], 433–452. **R. C. Jebb.** Signed.

2154 A plea for an Anglo-Roman alliance, 453–462. **W. Maziere Brady.** Signed.

2155 Frederick Denison Maurice, 463–471. **Frederic W. Farrar.** Signed.

2156 Realism behind the footlights, 472–481. **Lewis Wingfield.** Signed.

2157 Is insanity on the increase? 482–494. **W. J. Corbet.** Signed; Contents adds "M.P."; see *WWW*/1916.

2158 The Tory party under Wyndham and Bolingbroke, 495–509. **T. E. Kebbel.** Signed.

2159 Assassination and dynamite, 510–521. **William Dillon.** Signed.

2160 The Kingdom of the Nizam, 522–530. **J. E. Gorst**, 1835–1916. Signed.

2161 Equestrian sculpture for London, 531–536. **Edmund Gosse.** Signed.

2162 The juggernaut of poor men's providence, 537–548. **William Lewery Blackley.** Signed.

2163 Mr. Hayward: postscripta [six comments by different contributors], 549–556. A. W. Kinglake was evidently the moving spirit behind this collection (see his letters to Escott of Mar. 19, 23, 26, 1884, in the Escott Papers, as well as a letter from Mrs. Bryan Procter to Escott, Mar. 21, ibid., in which she encloses a small record to please Escott "and Mr. Kinglake") No. I by **William C. Cartwright?** —Kinglake to Escott, Feb. 1884, Escott Papers, agrees Cartwright will write a more extensive memoir of Hayward; but Cartwright to Escott, Mar. 21, ibid., says he has only a column or two, enough for a daily paper and offers to send some notes to [E. H.] Bunbury re Hayward and Napoleon (see No. V); these pages are a schematized comment on Escott's Mar. art. on Hayward. No. II by **Algernon Borthwick**, prob.—Kinglake to Escott, Mar. 23, ibid., speaks of Borthwick's comment being hostile, which this comment is. No. III by **A. W. Kinglake**, prob.—on Mar. 23, ibid., Kinglake told Escott he would like his comment to come after Borthwick's. No. IV by **Jane O. Brookfield**, prob.—Kinglake to Escott, Mar. 19, ibid., says Mrs. Brookfield will send anecdote about Hayward's thoughtfulness to her daughter; Kinglake was a close friend of the W. H. Brookfields (C. & Frances Brookfield, *Mrs. Brookfield and her Circle*, 2 vols., 1905). No. V by **E. H. Bunbury**—W. C. Cartwright to Escott, Mar. 23, ibid., says Bunbury told him he had sent notes illustrating Hayward's relations with Louis Napoleon. No. VI by **Anne B. Procter**—Kinglake to Escott, Mar. 23, ibid., says there was a funny misprint in proof of Mrs. Procter's comment: "honest pater" for "honest hater." In his *Rambling Recollections* (1908), I, 77–78, H. D. Wolff says, "Mr. Kinglake and I wrote a joint art. about him [Hayward] in the *FR* after his death"; but there is no mention of Wolff in the Kinglake-Escott letters.

2164 Home and foreign affairs, 557–568: (No. I) political, 557–567, by **T. H. S. Escott**, prob.—cf. no. 1969; (No. II) finance, 567–568.

VOLUME 41 O.S., 35 N.S., MAY 1884

2165 The Radical programme (No. VI): religious equality, 569–592. **John Morley.** Attr. in Chamberlain, *Memoir*, p. 108.

2166 Russia revisited, 593–610. **Malcolm MacColl.** Signed.

2167 Personal recollections of Leopold,

Duke of Albany, 611–624. **Frederic W. H. Myers.** Signed; repr. *Future Life.*

2168 Lord Ripon's Indian land legislation, 625–636. **George Campbell, 1824–1892.** Signed R. Campbell; but clearly in error, since George Campbell to Escott, Oct. 4, 1883, Escott Papers, says he is writing on Lord Ripon's scheme, of which he approves; man cited had served in India, 1842–1874, and was interested in land tenancy there and in Ireland (*DNB*, 1st suppl.); he had been a regular contributor to *FortR* (see below Part B); no R. Campbell with Indian experience and interests has been found.

2169 Some educational errors, 637–644. **Reginald W. Sackville-West.** Signed De La Warr [Earl De La Warr].

2170 Europe's stake in the Soudan, 645–654. **Halil Ganem.** Signed H. Ganem: see *Bib. Nat. Cat.*

2171 The speculative basis of modern unbelief, 655–667. **David Greig.** Signed.

2172 Possibilities of ballooning, 668–674. **Frederick G. Burnaby.** Signed.

2173 Recasting the Oxford schools, 675–682. **W. L. Courtney.** Signed.

2174 The Lords and the Reform Bill, 683–692. **Thomas Nash.** Signed A Manchester Conservative; W. St. John Brodrick to Escott, May 7, 1884, Escott Papers, promises not to reveal that Escott has told him Nash was the author; man cited was a barrister of Manchester, described in *Momus*, Feb. 9, 1882, as a Conservative.

2175 Home and foreign affairs, 693–704: (No. I) political, 693–701, by **T. H. S. Escott**, prob.—cf. no. 1969; (No. II) finance, 701–704.

VOLUME 41 O.S., 35 N.S., June 1884

2176 England's foreign policy, 705–711. **T. H. S. Escott?** Signed G.; Chamberlain to Escott, Nov. 2, 1883, Escott Papers, says Morley should have time to do the "Free Church" well, from a Radical perspective; "if you could get his consent it would leave you free to deal with the Foreign policy art., about which I spoke to Dilke when I saw him last and obtained his promise to give you full notes on the subject." Morley's art. is no. 2165 in May 1884; this art. in June would seem to be Escott's with the help of Sir Charles Dilke, a member of Gladstone's cabinet. When Gladstone protested the

use of "G." implying his authorship, Escott replied, June 17, 1884, BM. Add. MS. 44,486: "The paper came to me from a quarter which justified me in attaching to it high importance, and reached me a few hours before the magazine was going to press. Had I foreseen the misconception to which the initial attached might give rise I might have asked the writer to reconsider it"; in similar vein Algernon Bourke told W. S. Blunt (Blunt, *Gordon at Khartoum* [1911], pp. 248, 250) that Escott said the art. was "from the pen of one of our most prominent statesmen, and that it represented Mr. Gladstone's views." It looks as if Escott, having justified to himself the use of "G." on grounds that the ideas were Gladstone's via Dilke, then met the unexpected anger of Gladstone by the half truth, half prevarication that the art. came from the pen of a prominent statesman—viz. Dilke (cf. the same kind of "blind" in evidence for no. 2198). Other authors who have been suggested are Arthur Godley, Herbert Gladstone, and Sir Julian Goldsmid.

2177 Le style c'est l'homme: a causerie, 712–723. **E. Robert Bulwer Lytton.** Signed Lytton [Earl Lytton].

2178 A world in pawn (Part II, concl.), 724–735. **A. J. Wilson.** Signed.

2179 Charles Stuart Calverley, 736–753. **Walter J. Sendall.** Signed.

2180 The bursting of the bubble, 754–762. **W. St. John Brodrick.** Signed.

2181 Diana of the Crossways (chaps. i–iii), 763–780. **George Meredith.** Novel published 1885.

2182 The religious question in France, 781–793. **Paul Bert.** Signed.

2183 Sophocles, 794–811. **S. H. Butcher.** Signed; repr. *Some Aspects of Greek Genius.*

2184 Joseph and his brethren; an Eastern apologue with a Western moral, 812–818. **Henry C. Raikes.** Signed An English Tory; attr. in *Life and Letters*, p. 213.

2185 International rivalries in Central Africa, 819–828. **E. F. G. Law.** Signed.

2186 Home and foreign affairs, 829–840: (No. I) political, 829–837, by **T. H. S. Escott**, prob.—cf. no. 1969; (No. II) finance, 837–840.

VOLUME 42 O.S., 36 N.S., JULY 1884

2187 England and the Conference, 1–16. **Julian Goldsmid.** Signed; Contents adds

"Bart."; see Burke under D'Avigdor-Goldsmid.

2188 Newspapers, 17–29. **Thomas Gibson Bowles.** Signed.

2189 The English Church on the Continent, 30–44. **Charles W. Sandford.** Signed C. W. Gibraltar [Bishop of Gibraltar].

2190 On the cross benches, 45–56. **George Charles Spencer-Churchill.** Signed "Marlborough" [Duke of Marlborough].

2191 General Gordon's message [on religion], 57–74. **W. H. Mallock.** Signed.

2192 Games and gamesters, 75–87. **Bernard H. Becker.** Signed.

2193 The Congo Treaty, 88–107. **W. C. Cartwright.** Signed.

2194 Diana of the Crossways (chaps. iv–vii), 108–125. **George Meredith.** Signed.

2195 Princess Alice, 126–138. **Malcolm MacColl.** Signed.

2196 Home and foreign affairs (No. I) political, 139–147, by **T. H. S. Escott**—Escott to Gladstone, July 2, 1884, BM Add. MS. 44487, refers to his defence of government in *FortR* for July.

2197 Home and foreign affairs (No. II) finance, 147–148.

VOLUME 42 O.S., 36 N.S., AUGUST 1884

2198 The Marquis of Salisbury, K. G., 149–163. **T. H. S. Escott.** Edward W. Hamilton, diary for Aug. 5, 1884, BM Add. MS. 48637, says Escott told him he wrote the art.; Hamilton adds that in calling it to Gladstone's attention (see BM Add. MS. 44487, fol. 119) Escott called it "probably the best art. he had ever had in his review . . . he appears to think such a 'blind' justifiable in his trade."

2199 Ideas about India (Part I): the agricultural danger, 164–178. **Wilfrid Scawen Blunt.** Signed; repr. *Ideas about India*, 1885.

2200 Measurement of character, 179–185. **Francis Galton.** Signed.

2201 Morocco, 186–198. **Frederick P. Warren.** Signed; Contents adds "Capt., R.N."; see *Navy List/84*, p. 348.

2202 Our obligations in Egypt, 199–210. **R. T. Reid.** Signed.

2203 Compulsory temperance, 211–219. **J. T. Agg-Gardner.** Signed.

2204 Thomas Hobbes, 220–236. **H. W. Hamilton-Hoare.** Signed H. W. Hoare; see *WWW/*1940.

2205 What is Judaism?: a question of to-day, 237–256. **Lucien Wolf.** Signed.

2206 The House of Lords, 257–270. **James E. Thorold Rogers.** Signed.

2207 Nubar, 271–277. Signed: A British Resident of Cairo. Possibly A. G. H. Beaman, barrister and correspondent in Cairo for the *Standard*, who wrote to Escott on May 18, 1884, Escott Papers, that he wanted to write on the press in Egypt and late incidents, and stressed unreliability of Nubar; this art. deals at some length with the intrigues connected with the suppression of the French newspaper, *Le Bosphore*, and lays much of the blame for unsatisfactory Egyptian affairs on Nubar; the author speaks of having left Egypt in early July, p. 276, and A. M. Broadley to Escott, Oct. 1, 1883, ibid., shows Beaman was in London in October.

2208 Home and foreign affairs, 278–284: (No. I) political, 278–283, by **T. H. S. Escott,** prob.—cf. no. 1969; (No. II) finance, 283–284.

VOLUME 42 O.S., 36 N.S., SEPTEMBER 1884

2209 An antidote to agitation, 285–291. **Randolph S. Churchill.** Signed.

2210 Modern mysticism, 292–308. **W. S. Lilly.** Signed; repr. in *The Great Enigma*, N.Y., 1892, as "The Inner Light."

2211 Sport and travel in Norway, 309–320. **C. N. Jackson.** Signed.

2212 The question of the hour (No. I): people and peers, 321–331. **Henry Labouchere.** Signed as in no. 2009.

2213 The question of the hour (No. II): people, parliament and peers, 332–344. **Arthur Arnold.** Signed.

2214 Diana of the Crossways (chaps. viii–xi), 345–362. **George Meredith.** Signed.

2215 Concerning Chili, 363–374. **Douglas M. B. H. Cochrane.** Signed Cochrane [Lord Cochrane]; see *DNB* for title and his interest in South America.

2216 London water supply, 378–384. **C. Norman Bazalgette.** Signed.

2217 Two colonial questions (No. I): the Germans in South Africa, 385–390. **William H. P. Greswell.** Signed William Greswell; see *WWW/*1928.

2218 Two colonial questions (No. II): what England has done for the Zulus, 391–400. **Frederic Mackarness.** Signed.

2219 Mr. Irving's work [as an actor], 401–410. **Edward R. Russell.** Signed.

2220 Home and foreign affairs, 411–420. **T. H. S. Escott,** prob. Cf. no. 1969.

VOLUME 42 O.S., 36 N.S., OCTOBER 1884

2221 Is England a great European power? 421–432.

2222 The second Duke of Wellington, 433–444. **G. R. Gleig.** Signed. (Correction, p. 716, by **Gleig.**)

2223 Ideas about India (Part II): race hatred, 445–459. **Wilfrid Scawen Blunt.** Signed.

2224 Charles Reade's novels, 460–471. **W. L. Courtney.** Signed; repr. *Studies.*

2225 The Lords as a senate, 472–483. **Percy Greg.** Signed.

2226 Diana of the Crossways (chaps. xii–xiv), 484–501. **George Meredith.** Signed.

2227 European cavalry, 502–515. **James Keith Fraser.** Signed Keith Fraser; Contents adds "Colonel"; see Boase.

2228 The future of the Soudan, 516–527. **E. A. De Cosson.** Signed.

2229 Lord Salisbury as Foreign Minister, 528–534. Signed: M.P.; and in Contents A Member of Parliament.

2230 Bernal Osborne, 535–543. **T. H. S. Escott** and **A. W. Kinglake.** The art. is signed by Escott and repr. in *Politics*, but he explains there on p. 31, that it was actually written in collaboration with A. W. Kinglake.

2231 Home and foreign affairs, 544–556. **T. H. Escott,** prob. Escott to Joseph Chamberlain, Sept. 27, 1884, Chamberlain Papers, says he stopped the press to include a page on Salisbury's art. in *NatR-II.*

VOLUME 42 O.S., 36 N.S., NOVEMBER 1884

2232 Mr. Gladstone, 557–568. **T. H. S. Escott.** Repr. *Politics.*

2233 Ancient organs of public opinion, 569–588. **R. C. Jebb.** Signed.

2234 Is this the Bill [for redistribution of boroughs]? 589–593. **Arthur Arnold.** Signed.

2235 *Carlyle's Life in London* [by J. A. Froude], 594–608. **G. S. Venables.** Signed.

2236 The future of industry, 609–623. **Charles Waring,** d.1887. Signed.

2237 Ideas about India (Part III): the Mohammedan question, 624–637. **Wilfrid Scawen Blunt.** Signed.

2238 A last word on sugar bounties, 638–648. **George Baden-Powell.** Signed.

2239 The Irish and the government, 649–656. **T. M. Healy.** Signed.

2240 Diana of the Crossways (chaps. xv–xviii), 657–674. **George Meredith.** Signed.

2241 Moderation and total abstinence, 675–687. **Sutton Sharpe.** Signed.

2242 John Wilson Croker, 688–702. **T. E. Kebbel.** Signed.

2243 Home and foreign affairs, 703–716. **T. H. S. Escott,** prob. Chamberlain to Escott, July 13, 1884, Escott Papers, congratulates him on his attack on Salisbury in Aug. issue, and advises him to continue to harp on Salisbury's contempt for peaceable demonstration; see pp. 703–707.

VOLUME 42 O.S., 36 N.S., DECEMBER 1884

2244 Mr. Chamberlain, 717–727. **T. H. S. Escott.** Joseph Chamberlain to Escott, mid-Nov., 1884, Escott Papers, says "your article is a double-handed slap in the face for Tyndall and Grenfell" (see pp. 719–720); Morley to Escott, Nov. 29, 1884, ibid., says he has read and approves Escott's "Chamberlain."

2245 The future of the peerage, 728–737. **Percy Greg.** Signed.

2246 Diana of the Crossways (chaps. xix–xxvi, concl.), 738–767. **George Meredith.** Signed.

2247 German socialism, 768–779. **Moritz Kaufmann.** Signed M. Kaufmann; Contents adds "Rev."; see *WWW/1928.*

2248 Samuel Johnson, 780–786. **Edmund Gosse.** Signed.

2249 Forty years of parliament, 787–797. **A. D. R. W. Cochrane-Baillie,** prob. Signed A Young England Peer; Cochrane-Baillie to Escott, Aug. 14, [1884], Escott Papers, suggests a non-political art. on parliamentary anecdotes; Cochrane-Baillie was the only member of the original Young Englanders who, like this author, had gone to Eton and Cambridge, and who was a peer in 1884 (John Manners did not succeed to the dukedom until 1888); he had served in Parliament since 1841; in Mar. 1890 he wrote an art. in *Blackwood's* on the Young England Party (*Bk* no. 6507), in which there are a large number of similar passages, too many to have been borrowed unacknowledged from a living contemporary.

2250 Progress to poverty, 798–810. **Moreton Frewen.** Signed.

2251 Eastern notes, 811–823. **Charles Gordon.** Signed Huntly [Marquis of Huntly]; repr. *Travels, Sport, and Politics in the East of Europe,* 1887.

2252 The presidential election campaign, 824–833. **E. F. G. Law.** Signed.

2253 Men of letters on themselves, 834–846. **T. H. S. Escott.** Signed; repr. *Politics.*

2254 Home and foreign affairs, 847–860. **T. H. S. Escott,** prob. Cf. no. 1969.

VOLUME 43 O.S., 37 N.S., JANUARY 1885

2255 The Revolution of 1884, 1–10. **T. H. S. Escott.** Chamberlain, *Memoir,* p. 108; repr. in *The Radical Programme* as the "Introduction."

2256 Coleridge as a spiritual thinker, 11–25. **John Tulloch.** Signed. (See no. 2276.)

2257 Redistribution by different lights (No. I): the Seats Bill, 26–36. **Leonard Courtney.** Signed.

2258 Redistribution by different lights (No. II): seats and no seats, 37–43. **Arthur Arnold.** Signed.

2259 Redistribution by different lights (No. III): the political resultant, 44–54. **Henry C. Raikes.** Signed A Candid Conservative; Raikes to Escott, Dec. 22, 1884, Escott Papers, says he is glad Escott liked quotation which appears on p. 50 of the art.

2260 The expansion of art, 55–69. **Ferdinand Rothschild.** Signed; Contents adds "Baron"; see *DNB.*

2261 Agricultural and commercial depression, 70–83. **Stephen Williamson.** Signed S. Williamson; Contents gives first name.

2262 Behind the scenes, 84–94. **F. C. Burnand.** Signed.

2263 Education for the hungry, 95–104. **Eric S. Robertson.** Signed.

2264 The state of the turf, 105–115. **George Henry Cadogan.** Signed Cadogan [Earl Cadogan].

2265 Persia *in extremis,* 116–129. **M. Valentine Chirol.** Signed as in no. 1837.

2266 Caroline Bauer, 130–137. **E. B. de Fonblanque.** Signed.

2267 Home and foreign affairs, 138–148. **T. H. S. Escott.** Escott to Joseph Chamberlain, Dec. 17, 1884, Chamberlain Papers, asks for "tips" for his proposed "Chronique," and on Dec. 20, thanks him for "brief" for H&F Affairs.

VOLUME 43 O.S., 37 N.S., FEBRUARY 1885

2268 The ideas of the new voters (No. I), 149–155. **Henry Broadhurst.** Signed.

2269 The ideas of the new voters (No. II), 155–160. **William J. Davis,** prob. Signed A Trades Union Official; Escott to Chamberlain, Jan. 12, 1885, Chamberlain Papers, says he has solicited replies to his "Revolution of 1884," no. 2255, and received answers from Broadhurst, see no. 2268, and Davis; man cited was a member of Trades Union Congress Parliamentary Committee; see William A. Dalley, *Life Story of W. J. Davis,* Birmingham, 1914.

2270 The ideas of the new voters (No. III), 160–167. **Alfred Simmons.** Signed.

2271 The Upper Engadine in winter, 168–176. **J. F. Main.** Signed; called "Professor" in Contents; see Boase.

2272 Review of the year: Newton Hall, 1 January, 1885 [on Positivism], 177–196. **Frederic Harrison.** Signed.

2273 The American audience, 197–201. **Henry Irving,** 1838–1905. Signed; see *DNB.*

2274 Representation and misrepresentation (No. I): the crusade for proportional representation, 202–215. **G. Shaw-Lefevre.** Signed.

2275 Representation and misrepresentation (No. II): the coming steps in representation, 216–222. **Thomas Hare.** Signed.

2276 A pious legend examined [Coleridge's reputation as a spiritual thinker], 223–233. **H. D. Traill.** Signed.

2277 Ideas about India (Part IV): the native states, 234–248. **Wilfrid Scawen Blunt.** Signed.

2278 Scientific *versus* bucolic vivisection, 249–252. **James Cotter Morison.** Signed.

2279 The Navy paralysed by paper, 253–261. **Thomas Gibson Bowles.** Signed.

2280 Jane Austen at home, 262–270. **T. E. Kebbel.** Signed.

2281 Home and foreign affairs, 271–284. **T. H. S. Escott,** prob. Cf. no. 1969.

VOLUME 43 O.S., 37 N.S., MARCH 1885

2282 The coming land bill, 285–296. **C. A. Fyffe.** Signed. (See no. 2304.)

2283 Radical theorists on land [a reply to no. 2282], 297–308. **Henry Edward John Stanley.** Signed Stanley of Alderley [Baron Stanley of Alderley]. (See no. 2304.)

2284 *The Life of George Eliot* [by J. W. Cross], 309–322. **Frederic Harrison.** Signed; repr. *Choice of Books.*

2285 Organic nature's riddle (Part I), 323–337. **St. George Mivart.** Signed. (See no. 2341.)

2286 The problem of empire (No. I): imperial federation, 338–344. **J. A. Farrer.** Signed.

2287 The problem of empire (No. II): the Imperial Federation League, 345–351. **Arthur Mills.** Signed.

2288 Squires, spires, and mires, 352–370. **William Bury,** 1839–1927, prob. Signed W. Bury; Contents adds "Rev."; see Venn.

2289 England's place in India (No. I): an Indian Thersites [W. S. Blunt], 371–385. **Lepel Griffin.** Signed.

2290 England's place in India (No. II): ideas about India (Part V, concl.): the future of self-government, 386–398. **Wilfrid Scawen Blunt.** Signed.

2291 Tasso, 399–408. **H. Schütz Wilson.** Signed.

2292 The Bank of England, 409–423. **Henry May.** Signed.

2293 Home and foreign affairs, 424–436. **T. H. S. Escott,** prob. Cf. no. 1969.

VOLUME 43 O.S., 37 N.S., APRIL 1885

2294 England and Europe (No. I): the bulwarks of empire, 437–449. **H. M. Hozier.** Signed.

2295 England and Europe (No. II): the armed strength of England, 450–460. **Col. Wilkinson,** with **Arthur Griffiths?** Signed A Field Officer. Arthur Griffiths, sub-editor of *FortR*, to Escott the editor, June 9, 1885, Escott Papers, thanks him for the "enclosure from the Foreign Resident" [i.e., a cheque to Griffiths from Escott, who used this pseudonym for a book a year later (see H&L)?], which "I will at once pass on to my friend Colonel Wilkinson of the Brighton Fencibles (you know the Wilkinsons? a very literary family) who, as you may not be aware, was the true author of the contribution [this art. is the only unidentified item between Jan. and June 1885]. Wilkinson will be glad to be assured of the *F.R.*'s secrecy"; he will be "obliged for the cheque" but will say it was not necessary. Since Escott must have thought that Griffiths wrote the art. if he sent him the cheque (and Griffiths *was* a Field Officer) and was apparently not aware of Wilkinson's role nor even who he was, and since Wilkinson was not, it would seem, expecting a cheque, it is likely that Griffiths had some share in the business —probably putting together Wilkinson's ideas from his notes or/and conversation.

Spencer Wilkinson was never a Field Officer and lived in Manchester.

2296 Albania and the Albanians, 461–475. **V. H. P. Caillard.** Signed.

2297 A minister of education, 476–490. **Henry Craik.** Signed.

2298 Social science on the stage, 491–499. **H. Sutherland Edwards.** Signed.

2299 Royalty and viceroyalty in Ireland (No. I): the Irish viceroyalty, 500–511. **Henry L. Jephson.** Signed Henry Jephson; see *BMCat.*

2300 Royalty and viceroyalty in Ireland (No. II): a new era for Ireland, 512–518. **Robert O'Hara.** Signed R. O'Hara; see Boase.

2301 Organic nature's riddle (Part II, concl.), 519–531. **St. George Mivart.** Signed. (See no. 2341.)

2302 Shakespeare's fugues, 532–543. **John G. Dow.** Signed.

2303 The transfer of land, 544–556. **George Charles Spencer Churchill.** Signed Marlborough [Duke of Marlborough].

2304 The arguments of a peer [a reply to no. 2283], 557–565. **C. A. Fyffe.** Signed.

2305 English interests in North Africa, 566–574. **A. M. Broadley.** Signed.

2306 Home and foreign affairs, 575–588. **T. H. S. Escott,** prob. Cf. no. 1969.

VOLUME 43 O.S., 37 N.S., MAY 1885

2307 Peace or war, 589–596. **Lepel Griffin.** Signed.

2308 Mr. Swinburne's poetry, 597–610. **W. L. Courtney.** Signed; repr. *Studies.*

2309 Conservatives on themselves (Part I): Conservative organization, 611–619. **George C. T. Bartley.** Signed.

2310 Conservatives on themselves (Part II): the past and the future of Conservatism, 620–631. **George N. Curzon.** Signed.

2311 Conservatives on themselves (Part III): Jonah, 632–639. **Henry C. Raikes.** Signed An English Tory; Raikes to Escott, Apr. 20, 1885, Escott Papers, sends "Jonah."

2312 Marriage and divorce, 640–653. **George H. Lewis.** Signed.

2313 Recent progress in electricity, 654–663. **Julius Maier.** Signed.

2314 Bismarck: a retrospect, 664–678. **George Bunsen.** Signed Prince Outisky; Bunsen to Escott, n.d., Escott Papers, says he will send art. with this exact title in a few days—insists on using a pseudonym.

2315 Give and take with the colonies: union

of the Empire by tariff, 679–688. **Thomas Gibson Bowles.** Signed.

2316   Gordon (Part I): how we lost Gordon, 689–700. **Charles Williams.** Signed.

2317   Buddhism and mock Buddhism, 703–716. **Frederika Macdonald.** Signed; Contents adds "Mrs."

2318   Union of Presbyterian churches, 717–724. **John Campbell Gordon.** Signed Aberdeen [Earl of Aberdeen].

2319   Home and foreign affairs, 725–740. **T. H. S. Escott,** prob. Cf. no. 1969.

VOLUME 43 O.S., 37 N.S., JUNE 1885

2320   Ismail: a vindication, 741–752. **Julian Goldsmid.** Signed.

2321   Eton in eighty-five, 753–765. **G. E. Marindin.** Signed.

2322   The Queen and her family, 766–771. **Arthur Arnold.** Signed.

2323   Specialism in medicine, 772–787. **Morell Mackenzie.** Signed; repr. *Essays*, 1893. (See no. 2339.)

2324   Wyclif and the Bible, 788–798. **William Milligan.** Signed.

2325   The Saskatchewan scare, 799–807. **John Douglas Sutherland Campbell.** Signed Lorne [Marquess of Lorne].

2326   The Hellenic after-world, 808–818. **Percy Gardner.** Signed; repr. with revisions as "Spartan Tombs and the Cultus of the Dead," *Greek History.*

2327   Paris as an English residence, 819–830. **Frederic Marshall.** Signed.

2328   Scotch and other townships, 831–841. **Emile de Laveleye.** Signed.

2329   An operatic crisis, 842–851. **H. Sutherland Edwards.** Signed.

2330   The Parnellite programme, 852–861. **Richard Pigott.** Signed.

2331   Oxford and Cambridge through foreign spectacles, 862–868. **Paul Vinogradoff.** Signed; repr. *Collected Papers* (1928), I.

2332   Peace with Russia, 869–878. **Samuel Laing,** 1812–1897. Signed as in no. 1443.

2333   Home and foreign affairs, 879–892. **T. H. S. Escott,** prob. Cf. no. 1969.

VOLUME 44 O.S., 38 N.S., JULY 1885

2334   The Radical programme (No. VII): local government and Ireland, 1–16. **T. H. S. Escott** and **George Fottrell.** Attr. in Chamberlain, *Memoir*, pp. 108, 152, 154.

2335   Victor Hugo, 17–31. **Henry Céard.** Signed.

2336   The wine duties, 32–41. **F. G. Walpole.** Signed.

2337   Two days in the Brixworth Union, 42–55. **Henry Edward John Stanley.** Signed Stanley of Alderley [Baron Stanley of Alderley].

2338   Roman life and character, 56–66. **F. Marion Crawford.** Signed T. Marion Crawford, but Contents corrects first initial.

2339   The dangers of medical specialism [a reply to no. 2323], 67–78. **H. B. Donkin.** Signed. (See no. 2356.)

2340   Mr. J. R. Lowell, 79–89. **H. D. Traill.** Signed.

2341   Professor Mivart on instinct [reply to nos. 2285, 2301], 90–101. **George J. Romanes.** Signed. (See no. 2410.)

2342   A joke or a job? [the election of A. S. Napier to the Merton Chair of English Language and Literature at Oxford], 102–107. Signed: A Member of Convocation.

2343   The future of South Africa, 108–119. **Frederic Mackarness.** Signed.

2344   Fleeming Jenkin: in memoriam, 120–122. **Sidney Colvin.** Signed.

2345   The Radical programme (No. VIII): taxation and finance, 123–135. **Francis Adams.** Attr. in Chamberlain, *Memoir*, p. 108.

2346   Home and foreign affairs, 136–148. **T. H. S. Escott,** prob. Cf. no. 1969.

VOLUME 44 O.S., 38 N.S., AUGUST 1885

2347   The Paris newspaper press, 149–165. **Theodore Child.** Signed.

2348   The International tribunals of Egypt, 166–177. **Charles Sumner Maine.** Signed.

2349   Pasteur's life and labours, 178–192. **Eliza Lynn Linton.** Signature.

2350   Yacht racing, 193–202. **Thomas Dykes.** Signed T. Dykes; see *BMCat*, and Allibone.

2351   Lord Peterborough, 203–217. **Thomas Lister.** Signed Ribblesdale [Baron Ribblesdale].

2352   Death—and afterwards, 218–227. **Edwin Arnold,** 1832–1904. Signed; Contents adds "C.S.I."; see *DNB*.

2353   Private bill legislation, 228–239. **E. Leigh Pemberton.** Signed.

2354   The new naturalism, 240–256. **W. S. Lilly.** Signed.

2355   Midsummer in the Soudan, 257–266. **Henry Brackenbury.** Signed.

2356   Medical specialism: a rejoinder [to no. 2339], 267–276. **Morell Mackenzie.** Signed; repr. *Essays*, 1893.

2357 Church and state in Scotland, 277–285. **Alexander Hugh Bruce.** Signed Balfour of Burleigh [Baron Balfour of Burleigh].

2358 Home and foreign affairs, 286–300. **T. H. S. Escott,** prob. Escott to Joseph Chamberlain, July 28, 1885, Chamberlain Papers, says he wants to consult on one point in "Rad. Pro." (see p. 289–292) and on the Chronique.

VOLUME 44 O.S., 38 N.S., SEPTEMBER 1885

2359 Catholic Italy and the temporal power, 301–318. **William Henry Hurlbert.** Signed.

2360 Ralph Waldo Emerson, 319–331. **W. L. Courtney.** Signed; repr. *Studies.*

2361 The truth about Turkish finance, 332–344. **Vincent Caillard.** Signed.

2362 Saving the innocents, 345–356. **Susan Mary E. Jeune.** Signed Mary Jeune; Contents adds "Hon. Mrs. F."; see *WWW*/1940 under St. Helier; repr. *Lesser Questions,* 1894.

2363 Industrial and commercial Spain, 357–369. **George Higgin.** Signed; repr. *Commercial and Industrial Spain,* 1886.

2364 Councils and comedians, 370–381. **F. C. Burnand.** Signed.

2365 Health-resorts and their uses, 382–394. **Robson Roose.** Signed; repr. *Waste.*

2366 The youngest of the saints [General Gordon], 395–412. **Mary St. Leger Harrison.** Signed Lucas Malet; see *DNB* for her pseudonym; attr. Courtney, *Making of an Editor,* p. 137.

2367 Norway to-day, 413–425. **William Archer.** Signed.

2368 Lord Houghton, 426–435. **T. H. S. Escott.** Signed; repr. *Politics.*

2369 Home and foreign affairs, 436–452. **T. H. S. Escott?** Escott had broken down in Aug., see Intro. above, p. 179, but since he had contributed no. 2368, he may have written this also.

VOLUME 44 O.S., 38 N.S., OCTOBER 1885

2370 From three platforms (No. I): new policy and old failures, 453–462. **Reginald B. Brett.** Signed.

2371 From three platforms (No. II): the plea of a malcontent liberal, 463–477. **Edward Dicey.** Signed.

2372 From three platforms (No. III): the promised land, 478–490. **Henry Labouchere.** Signed.

2373 Men and manners in Constantinople, 491–505. **Arthur Nicolson,** prob. Signed Philo-Turk; Nicolson to Escott, Oct. 18, 1883, Escott Papers, writing from British Embassy, Constantinople, says he will need time to arrange materials for an art. and discusses a proposed book on social life in general, which he never wrote; on Aug. 21, 1884, he hopes to send an art. for Escott's consideration; the estimates of Sir Henry Layard, G. J. Goschen, and Lord and Lady Dufferin parallel those given as his in *Portrait of a Diplomat: Life of Sir Arthur Nicolson* by Harold Nicolson (Boston, 1930), pp. 19–20, 22–24.

2374 Cheap telegrams, 506–515. **Charles Cameron.** Signed; Contents adds "M.P."; see *WWW*/1928.

2375 Carlyle as a political teacher, 516–530. **Standish O'Grady.** Signed.

2376 The present state of the turf, 531–543. **Henry Hawley Smart.** Signed Hawley Smart; Contents adds "Capt."; see *DNB.*

2377 Our future masters, 544–556. **Mary A. Lewis.** Signed.

2378 Five years of foreign policy, 557–565. **Lucien Wolf.** Signed Diplomaticus; Courtney, *Making of an Editor,* p. 173, identifies this pseudonym in the *FortR.*

2379 The London stock exchange, 566–580. **Henry May.** Signed.

2380 Cant in politics, 581–590. **George Charles Spencer Churchill.** Signed Marlborough [Duke of Marlborough].

2381 Home and foreign affairs, 591–604. **T. H. S. Escott.** Escott to Joseph Chamberlain, Sept. 18, 1885, Chamberlain Papers, says he is anxious to make Chronique strong this time and asks for hints.

VOLUME 44 O.S., 38 N.S., NOVEMBER 1885

2382 Ireland and the general election, 605–613. **Samuel Laing,** 1812–1897. Signed as in no. 1443.

2383 A retrospect, 614–629. **Eliza Lynn Linton.** Signature.

2384 The national theatre, 630–636. **Augustus Harris.** Signed.

2385 Human personality, 637–655. **Frederic W. H. Myers.** Signed.

2386 The Scotch village community, 656–668. **John Rae.** Signed.

2387 Helping the fallen, 669–682. **Susan Mary E. Jeune.** Signed as in no. 2362; repr. *Lesser Questions,* 1894.

2388 A Faust of the first century, 683–690. **H. Sutherland Edwards.** Signed.

2389 Our sea fisherman, 691–698. **Edward Marjoribanks.** Signed.

2390 Dualism in Austria-Hungary, 699–710. **Arthur J. Patterson.** Signed.

2391 Health and taste in English homes, 711–721. **Robert W. Edis.** Signed; Contents adds "F. S. A.": see *WWW*/1928.

2392 The future of the fellah, 722–728. **H. H. Kitchener.** Signed.

2393 Home and foreign affairs, 729–740. **T. H. S. Escott,** prob. Escott to Joseph Chamberlain, Oct. 8, 1885, Chamberlain Papers, says he sees Chamberlain has been to Hawarden and asks for guidance as to what is going on for "my writing."

VOLUME 44 O.S., 38 N.S., DECEMBER 1885

2394 The coming contests of the world, 741–751.

2395 France under Richelieu, 752–767. **Emilia F. S. Dilke.** Signed; repr. *Art in the Modern State,* 1888.

2396 Moral and merry England, 768–779. **H. Anstruther White.** Signed.

2397 Is the caucus a necessity? 780–790. **John Macdonell.** Signed.

2398 Progress in India, 791–810. **A. C. Lyall.** Signed Vamadeva Shastin; attr. in *Life,* p. 477; repr. *Asiatic Studies,* 2nd series.

2399 The evidences of spiritualism, 811–826. **F. H. Bradley.** Signed.

2400 The American newspaper press, 827–839. **Theodore Child.** Signed.

2401 The Bulgarian imbroglio, 840–851. **Vincent Caillard.** Signed.

2402 The Irish problem (No. I): Home Rule and its solution, 852–864. **Bernard E. B. FitzPatrick.** Signed Castletown [Baron Castletown].

2403 The Irish problem (No. II): Irish disaffection, its causes and its cure, 865–876. **William Rathbone.** Signed.

2404 Home and foreign affairs, 877–884.

VOLUME 45 O.S., 39 N.S., JANUARY 1886

2405 The Liberal reverses and their cause (No. I): procrastination or policy? 1–9. **Reginald B. Brett.** Signed.

2406 The Liberal reverses and their cause (No. II): the elections—and after? 10–17. **Arthur Arnold.** Signed.

2407 Aesculapia victrix, 18–33. **Robert Wilson.** Signed; repr. under same title, 1886.

2408 Darwinism and democracy, 34–50. **W. S. Lilly.** Signed.

2409 British Columbia, 51–60. **William A. Baillie-Grohman.** Signed.

2410 The rights of reason [rejoinder to no. 2341], 61–68. **St. George Mivart.** Signed.

2411 Impressions of a modern Arcadian [in Virginia], 69–82. **Edith M. Nicholl.** Signed E. M. Nicholl; Contents gives "Mrs. Nicholl."

2412 Mr. Gladstone as a theologian, 83–92. **Samuel Laing,** 1812–1897. Signed as in no. 1443.

2413 My contested election, 93–101. Signed: A Defeated Candidate.

2414 Mr. Irving's [portrayal of] Faust, 102–105. **W. L. Courtney.** Signed.

2415 Political parties in Spain, 106–120. **Manuel Gonzalez Llana.** Signed M. G. Llana; see *EUI* under Gonzalez Llana.

2416 Small talk and statesmen [review of Greville's *Journals* and Lord Malmesbury's *Memoirs*], 121–140. **T. H. S. Escott.** Signed; repr. *Politics.*

2417 Home and foreign affairs, 141–152.

VOLUME 45 O.S., 39 N.S., FEBRUARY 1886

2418 Sir H. Maine, *Popular Government,* 153–173. **John Morley.** Signed; repr. *Studies.*

2419 Try the Bahamas [for health], 174–183. **Henry A. Blake.** Signed.

2420 The church and the world, 184–199. **William Francis Barry.** Signed William Barry; Contents adds "Rev."; see *WWW*/1940.

2421 Wear and tear of London life, 200–208. **Robson Roose.** Signed; repr. *Waste.*

2422 France under Colbert, 209–220. **Emilia F. S. Dilke.** Signed; repr. *Art in the Modern State,* 1888.

2423 Through the States, 221–236. **Theodore Child.** Signed.

2424 Local self-government in the central provinces of India, 238–247. **A. H. L. Fraser.** Signed.

2425 What boys read, 248–259. **Edward G. Salmon,** prob. Signed G. Salmon; cf. *NC* no. 1328, written in the same year.

2426 Parliamentary procedure, 260–269.

2427 Tennyson's last volume, 270–272. **T. H. S. Escott.** Signed.

2428 A radical view of the Irish crisis, 273–284. **Joseph Chamberlain.** Signed A Radical; claimed in *Memoir,* p. 184.

2429 Home and foreign affairs, 285–296.

2472 Benndorf's travels in Lycia and Caria, 802–815. **Walter Copland Perry.** Signed.

2473 A plea for the playwright, 816–828. **William Archer.** Signed.

2474 Female labour in the nail trade, 829–838. **Ada Heather-Bigg.** Signed.

2475 Eton worthies, 839–844. **Walter Herries Pollock.** Signed.

2476 Is medicine a progressive science? 845–854. **Morell Mackenzie.** Signed; repr. *Essays*, 1893.

2477 The prospects of the coming election, 855–860.

2478 Irish interests, 861–868. **J. Townsend Trench.** Signed.

2479 Home and foreign affairs, 869–880.

VOLUME 46 O.S., 40 N.S., JULY 1886

2480 The Liberal wreck, 1–8.

2481 Pasteur, 9–22. **George Morland Crawford,** prob. Signed G. M. Crawford; because man cited died in Nov. 1885, the art. may have been finished by his wife, Emily Crawford; they were both Paris correspondents of the *Daily News*: see Boase for him, *MWT*, 15th ed., for her.

2482 The novelists and their patrons, 23–35. **Alexander Innes Shand.** Signed.

2483 The political education of the country voter, 36–48.

2484 History in *Punch* (Part I): from 1841 to 1854, 49–67. **F. C. Burnand** and **Arthur à Beckett.** Signed.

2485 Home Rule in the eighteenth century, 68–78. **F. Bayford Harrison.** Signed.

2486 Pollution of the Thames, 79–90. **Alfred S. Jones.** Signed.

2487 Is the House of Lords worth preserving? 91–97. **Arthur Mills.** Signed.

2488 The Irish crisis (No. I): natural laws and the Home Rule problem, 98–104. **Frank Harris.** Signed.

2489 The Irish crisis (No. II): local government in Ireland, 105–113. **Robert Staples.** Signed.

2490 The Irish crisis (No. III): behind the scenes, 114–125. Signed: An Irishman.

2491 Home and foreign affairs, 126–136.

VOLUME 46 O.S., 40 N.S., AUGUST 1886

2492 Political cross-roads, 137–151. **George Charles Spencer Churchill.** Signed Marlborough [Duke of Marlborough].

2493 Homburg [German spa], 152–159. **F. Hæber.** Signed; Contents adds "Dr."

2494 Competitive examinations, 160–176. **Gordon Grey.** Signed.

2495 Deer-stalking in the past, 177–194. **Edward C. R. Ross,** prob. Signed Edward Ross; man cited a barrister and an expert marksman; see Boase.

2496 Is there hope for Ireland? 198–213. **R. J. Mahony.** Signed.

2497 Greek peasant life, 214–224. **J. Theodore Bent.** Signed.

2498 Switzerland as a holiday resort, 225–234. **H. Schütz Wilson.** Signed.

2499 Oliver Wendell Holmes, 235–243. **Edward Delille.** Signed.

2500 The answer to Mr. Gladstone, 244–255. **Arthur Arnold.** Signed.

2501 A new departure [in dealing with Ireland], 256–262. **Robert Anderson,** 1841–1918. Signed R. Anderson; Contents adds LL.D.; see *WWW/1928*.

2502 Home and foreign affairs, 263–272.

VOLUME 46 O.S., 40 N.S., SEPTEMBER 1886

2503 The ordnance department and Colonel Hope: a personal explanation, 273–275. **William Hope.** Signed W. Hope; Contents adds "Lieut.-Col., V.C." and *BMCat.* gives first name. Postscript on conflict of interest, 275, by **Frank Harris**—signed The Editor, F.R.

2504 The riots in Belfast, 276–299. Signed in Contents: Our Special Commissioner.

2505 Romanes versus Darwin: an episode in the history of the evolution theory, 300–316. **Alfred R. Wallace.** Signed.

2506 Prospects of Home Rule, 317–333. **Edward A. Freeman.** Signed.

2507 Some notes on Fletcher's *Valentinian*, 334–345. **John Addington Symonds.** Signed; repr. *Key of Blue*.

2508 Liszt's life and works; a study of character, 346–357. **Francis Hueffer.** Signed A Musical Critic; claimed in his *Half a Century of Music in England* (1889), p. ix, and repr. there.

2509 Mr. Francis Gwyn's journal, 358–364. **Francis Gwyn.** Title. Edited with intro. note by **Charles T. Gatty.** Signed.

2510 The Wagner festival at Baireuth, 365–371. **Helen Matilda Folkestone.** Signed; Contents adds "Viscountess"; see *Complete Peerage* under Radnor.

2511 Russia and England; Batoum and Cyprus (No. I), 372–382. **Samuel W. Baker.** Signed.

2512 Russia and England; Batoum and Cyprus (No. II), 382–387. **Armin Vambéry.** Signed as in no. 398.

2513 Our national vice [intemperance], 388–394. **H. E. Manning.** Signed Henry Edward Cardinal Archbishop [of Westminster]; repr. *Miscellanies,* III.

2514 Home and foreign affairs, 395–406.

VOLUME 46 O.S., 40 N.S., OCTOBER 1886

2515 Total solar eclipses, 407–422. **Richard A. Proctor.** Signed.

2516 The condition of Kerry, 423–447. **John Verschoyle.** Signed; Contents adds "Rev."; see Venn.

2517 Concession to the Celt, 448–451. **George Meredith.** Signed; repr. *Works,* XXIII.

2518 Falling in love, 452–462. **Grant Allen.** Signed; repr. *Falling in Love,* 1889.

2519 Manual instruction, 463–472. **John Lubbock.** Signed.

2520 Bi-metallism (No. I): theory of international bi-metallism, 473–480. **Henry Sidgwick.** Signed H. Sidgwick; Contents adds "Prof."; see *DNB.*

2521 Bi-metallism (No. II): the bi-metallic standard of value, 481–497. **Henry H. Gibbs.** Signed.

2522 The higher education of woman, 498–510. **Eliza Lynn Linton.** Signature.

2523 Hawthorne's romances, 511–522. **W. L. Courtney.** Signed; repr. *Studies.*

2524 The statistics of morality, 523–532. **Henry Hayman.** Signed with title D.D. (Letter, vol. 47 o.s., pp. 158–160, signed **Hermann Adler.**)

2525 Universal penny postage, 533–541. **John Henniker Heaton.** Signed J. Henniker-Heaton; see *DNB* and later arts. in *FortR;* Contents adds "M.P."

2526 A word for the Colonial Institute, 542. **John Douglas Campbell.** Signed Lorne [Marquess of Lorne].

VOLUME 46 O.S., 40 N.S., NOVEMBER 1886

2527 Shelley's "Philosophical View of Reform," [abridged with quotations], 543–562. **Edward Dowden.** Signed; repr. *Transcripts.*

2528 The coming crisis in Turkey, 563–574. **G. de Hennin.** Signed, with a capital D, but Contents and no. 2662 give "de."

2529 Materialism and morality, 575–594. **W. S. Lilly.** Signed.

2530 The moujiks and the Russian democracy, 595–604. **S. M. Kravchinsky.** Signed Stepniak—see *LCCat;* repr. *The Russian Peasantry.*

2531 The Royal Academy of Painting and Sculpture in France, 605–616. **Emilia F. S. Dilke.** Signed; repr. *Art in the Modern State,* 1888.

2532 Metaphor as a mode of abstraction, 617–632. **Friedrich Max Müller.** Signature.

2533 Lady book lovers, 633–640. **Andrew Lang.** Signed.

2534 The convent of Helfta, 641–658. **A. Mary F. Robinson.** Signed; repr. *Middle Ages.*

2535 An English classic, William Barnes, 659–670. **Coventry Patmore.** Signed.

VOLUME 46 O.S., 40 N.S., DECEMBER 1886

2536 State purchase of Irish railways, 671–686. **Charles Waring,** d.1887. Signed; repr. *State Purchase of Railways,* 1887.

2537 Outcast London, 687–695. **George Sale Reaney.** Signed; Contents adds "Rev."; see *BMCat.*

2538 Mobs and revolutions, 696–711. **W. W. Knollys.** Signed.

2539 Parliamentary procedure, 712–720. **Samuel Plimsoll.** Signed.

2540 American jottings, 721–736. **Grant Allen.** Signed.

2541 History in *Punch* (Part II), 737–752. **F. C. Burnand** and **Arthur à Beckett.** Signed.

2542 The chess masters of to-day, 753–765. **Leopold Hoffer.** Signed L. Hoffer; man cited was editor of *Chess Monthly;* *LCCat.* (Letter, vol. 47 o.s., pp. 471–472, signed **H. E. Bird.**)

2543 The character of Shelley, 766–775. **John Verschoyle.** Signed.

2544 Emin Bey: Gordon's lieutenant, 776–787. **J. T. Wills.** Signed; repr. *Emin Bey: Gordon's Lieutenant in Central Africa,* 1887.

2545 Science and morals, 788–802. **T. H. Huxley.** Signed; repr. *Collected Essays,* IX. (Letter, vol. 47 o.s., p. 160, signed **W. S. Lilly;** see no. 2564.)

VOLUME 47 O.S., 41 N.S., JANUARY 1887

2546 The present position of European politics (Part I): Germany, 1–31. **C. W. Dilke.** Series repr. in *European Politics* by Author of *Greater Britain,* i.e., C. W. Dilke: *BMCat.*

2547 Last words with General Gordon, 32–49. **Gerald Graham.** Signed.

2548   M. Renan's later works, 50–60. **Andrew Lang.** Signed.

2549   Ireland beyond the pale [the Western part], 61–72. **Arthur D. Hayter.** Signed.

2550   Benvenuto Cellini's character, 73–87. **John Addington Symonds.** Signed; repr. as part of intro. to his translation of *Life of Benvenuto Cellini*, 1896.

2551   The iron and steel trade, 88–104. **Isaac Lowthian Bell.** Signed Lowthian Bell; Contents adds "Bart."; see *DNB*.

2552   Womanhood in old Greece, 105–123. **Eliza Lynn Linton.** Signature.

2553   The new reformation (No. I), 124–138. **Charles Voysey**, 1828–1912. Signed; Contents adds "Rev."; see *DNB*.

2554   The new reformation (No. II), 138–149. **William Clifford**, 1823–1893. Signed; Contents adds "Hon. and Rev."

2555   A word on Lord Randolph Churchill's resignation, 150–155. **Frank Harris.** Signed The Editor.

2556   Correspondence: Theodore Aubanel and the Provençal Renaissance, 156–158, signed **Edward Barker.**

VOLUME 47 o.s., 41 n.s., FEBRUARY 1887

2557   The present position of European politics (Part II): France, 161–195. **C. W. Dilke.** Cf. no. 2546.

2558   The state of our trade, 196–210. **George Howell.** Signed; Contents adds "M.P."; see *DNB*.

2559   Our noble selves, 211–224. **Grant Allen.** Allen to his father, Jan. 26 [1887] in the possession of T. B. Higginson, Sharbot Lake, Ontario, says he wrote this unsigned article.

2560   Small farms, 225–236. **Robert James Lindsay.** Signed Wantage [Baron Wantage].

2561   The Mir and the police, 237–248. **S. M. Kravchinsky.** Signed Stepniak—*LCCat.*; repr. *The Russian Peasantry*, 1888, as "Paternal Government."

2562   Infection and disinfection, 249–261. **Robson Roose.** Signed; repr. *Waste*.

2563   Earthquakes, 262–275. **G. H. Darwin.** Signed.

2564   The province of physics: a rejoinder to Professor Huxley [no. 2545], 276–293. **W. S. Lilly.** Signed.

2565   The Transcaspian railway, 294–311. **Armin Vambéry.** Signed as in no. 398.

2566   In correspondence: Democracy in New South Wales, 312–315, signed **Augustus Nash**; The Nääs Slöjd: a Swedish system of handwork, 315–318, signed **Adeline Pullar**; Houseless at night, 318–320, signed **Charles C. Bethune** and **Harold E. Boulton.**

VOLUME 47 o.s., 41 n.s., MARCH 1887

2567   The present position of European politics (Part III): Russia, 321–354. **C. W. Dilke.** Cf. no. 2546. (Letter, pp. 615–616, signed **A. Vambéry** [see no. 2565] and reply, p. 616 from **C. W. Dilke;** vol. 52 o.s. (1889), p. 884, from **Dilke**—signed The Writer of "The Present Position of European Politics.")

2568   Wealth and the working classes (Part I), 355–375. **W. H. Mallock.** Signed.

2569   Our task in Burmah, 376–383. Signed: Conservative. Possibly Garnet Wolseley from whom A. G. F. Griffiths, as sub. ed. under Escott, requested an art. on Burmah (Griffiths to Wolseley, Nov. 1, 1885, Wolseley Papers, Hove Public Library).

2570   The Imperial Institute, 384–393. **Kenric B. Murray.** Signed.

2571   A fresh field for the sportsman [Alaska], 394–406. **H. W. Seton-Karr.** Signed.

2572   Valentine Visconti (Part I), 407–420. **A. Mary F. Robinson.** Signed; repr. *Middle Ages*.

2573   The case for free education, 421–431. **E. North Buxton.** Signed E. N. Buxton; Contents adds middle name.

2574   French aggression in Madagascar, 432–441. **Digby Willoughby.** Signed.

2575   The new reformation (No. III): theology under its changed conditions, 442–458. **W. H. Fremantle.** Signed. (See no. 2585.)

2576   The Canadian fisheries dispute, 459–468. **John Douglas Campbell.** Signed Lorne [Marquess of Lorne].

2577   In correspondence: The new *Otello*, 469–470, signed **H. Sutherland Edwards;** Thanks from the House of Shelter, 472, signed **Charles C. Bethune** and **Harold E. Boulton.**

VOLUME 47 o.s., 41 n.s., APRIL 1887

2578   The present position of European politics (Part IV): Austro-Hungary, 473–498. **C. W. Dilke.** Cf. no. 2546.

2579   The British army, past and present, 499–515. **John Miller Adye**, 1819–1900. Signed, with title "General": see *DNB*, 1st suppl.

2580 On a Western ranche, 516–533. **John Baumann.** Signed.

2581 Fluctuations in trade and wages, 534–545. **George Howell.** Signed.

2582 History in *Punch* (Part III, concl.), 546–557. **Arthur à Beckett** and **F. C. Burnand.** Signed.

2583 A model land law, 558–572. **Arthur J. Williams.** Signed; Contents adds "M.P."; (see no. 2596).

2584 Valentine Visconti (Part II, concl.), 573–586. **A. Mary F. Robinson.** Signed.

2585 The new reformation (No. IV): "Theology Under Its Changed Conditions"—a reply to Canon Fremantle [no. 2575], 587–612. **John W. Burgon.** Signed.

2586 In correspondence: Shelley's separation from his first wife, 613–615, signed **John Addington Symonds.**

VOLUME 47 O.S., 41 N.S., MAY 1887

2587 The present position of European politics (Part V): Italy, 617–645. **C. W. Dilke.** Cf. no. 2546.

2588 Nature and books, 646–656. **Richard Jefferies.** Signed; repr. *Field and Hedgerow*, 1889.

2589 Wealth and the working classes (Part II), 657–675. **W. H. Mallock.** Signed.

2590 A visit to Japan, 676–699. **Frank Brinkley.** Signed V. Brinkley; Contents adds "Capt., R. A."; but see *WWW*/1916.

2591 The simplicity of language, 700–714. **Friedrich Max Müller.** Signature; repr. *Three Introductory Lectures on Science of Thought*, Chicago, 1888.

2592 Womanhood in Greece: in history and art, 715–731. **Eliza Lynn Linton.** Signature.

2593 Sleep and its counterfeits, 732–742. **A. de Watteville.** Signed, with title "M.D."

2594 The new reformation (No. V): Dean Burgon and Mr. Fremantle, 743–752. **William Benham.** Signed W. Benham; Contents adds "Rev."; see *DNB*.

2595 Modern etching, 753–763. **Frederick Wedmore.** Signed.

2596 "A Model Land-Law": a reply to Mr. Williams [no. 2583], 764–784. **George Douglas Campbell.** Signed Argyll [Duke of Argyll].

VOLUME 47 O.S., 41 N.S., JUNE 1887

2597 The present position of European politics (Part VI, concl.): the United King-

dom, 785–834. **C. W. Dilke.** Cf. no. 2546.

2598 Victorian literature, 835–867. **Edward Dowden.** Signed; repr. *Transcripts*.

2599 The progress of science from 1836 to 1886, 868–884. **Grant Allen.** Signed.

2600 The progress of thought in our time, 885–898. **John Addington Symonds.** Signed; repr. *Essays*, as "The Philosophy of Evolution."

2601 English music during the Queen's reign, 899–912. **Francis Hueffer.** Signed.

2602 The material growth of the United Kingdom from 1836 to 1886, 913–927. **Leone Levi.** Signed.

2603 Fifty years of colonial development, 928–938. **George Baden-Powell.** Signed.

2604 In Parliament, 939–944. Signed: A Gladstonian M.P.

VOLUME 48 O.S., 42 N.S., JULY 1887

2605 Letters from Central Africa: a fragment, 5–20. **Eduard Schnitzer.** Signed Emin Pasha, his adopted name: see Hill. Intro. note, 4–5, signed **Mary Rosalie Felkin,** who was Mrs. Robert William Felkin: *BMCat.* where the latter's trans. of a book by Emin Pasha is entered.

2606 Good and bad temper in English families, 21–30. **Francis Galton.** Signed.

2607 General Langiewicz and the last Polish rising, 31–49. **Karl Blind.** Signed.

2608 Our working women and their earnings, 50–63. **F. Mabel Robinson.** Signed.

2609 Salvation by torture at Kairwan, 64–76. **George N. Curzon.** Signed.

2610 The vampire gold, 77–90. **George Charles Spencer Churchill.** Signed Marlborough [Duke of Marlborough].

2611 The higher theism, 91–112. **W. S. Lilly.** Signed.

2612 The Land Transfer Bill, 113–122. **Arthur Arnold.** Signed.

2613 Georgian and Victorian expansion, 123–139. **J. R. Seeley.** Signed.

2614 Home affairs: a national party, 140–151.

2615 In correspondence: Burma and the Burmese, 152–155, signed **Florence Layard.** The Women's Protective and Provident League, 155–156, Signed **Frederick Verney.**

VOLUME 48 O.S., 42 N.S., AUGUST 1887

2616 The growth of co-operation in England, 157–169. **George Jacob Holyoake.** Signed.

2617 Whitmania, 170–176. **Algernon Charles Swinburne.** Signed; repr. *Studies.* (Letter, pp. 459–460, signed **John Addington Symonds.**)

2618 Wealth and the working classes (Part III), 177–197. **W. H. Mallock.** Signed.

2619 Three dreams in a desert: under a mimosa-tree, 198–203. **Olive Schreiner.** Signed; repr. *Dreams, 1891.*

2620 The material progress of Ireland, 204–213. **Leone Levi.** Signed.

2621 Well rowed, Cambridge! 214–222. **Frederick I. Pitman.** Signed.

2622 French peasant proprietors, 223–236. **Matilda Betham-Edwards.** Signature.

2623 The Roman matron and the Roman lady, 237–258. **Eliza Lynn Linton.** Signature.

2624 Thoughts on knowledge, opinion, and inequality, 259–266. **Coventry Patmore.** Signed.

2625 Greater Greece and its education, 267–282. **J. Theodore Bent.** Signed.

2626 Marie Antoinette's milliners' bills, 283–296. **George Augustus Sala.** Signed.

2627 Fine passages in verse and prose selected by living men of letters (No. I), 297–316. Introduction presumably by Frank Harris—the editor. Letters from **Matthew Arnold, Grant Allen, F. C. Burnand, H. H. M. Herbert** (Earl of Carnarvon), **G. G. Leveson-Gower** (Earl Granville), **Thomas Hardy, Andrew Lang, W. S. Lilly, Eliza Lynn Linton, George Meredith, Agnata F. Ramsay, G. A. Sala, A. C. Swinburne.** (Letter, p. 460, on Arnold's letter, signed **Ernest Rhys;** ibid., by **Grant Allen** on his selection.)

VOLUME 48 O.S., 42 N.S., SEPTEMBER 1887

2628 Is a National party possible? 317–328. **R. B. Haldane.** Signed.

2629 An incident of real life in Bengal, 329–341. **W. Stobie.** Signed.

2630 Victor Hugo, *Choses Vues,* 342–346. **Algernon Charles Swinburne.** Signed; repr. *Studies.*

2631 American museums (Part I): The Museum of Comparative Zoology, Harvard University, 347–359. **Alfred R. Wallace.** Signed; repr. *Studies,* II. (Letter, p. 740, signed **Alfred R. Wallace.**)

2632 General Boulanger, 360–371. **W. H. Gleadell.** Signed.

2633 Free dinners at national schools, 372–378. **George Herbert Sargant.** Signed.

2634 Mr. Katkoff and the *Moscow Gazette,* 379–394. **H. Sutherland Edwards.** Signed.

2635 Trade unions, 395–409. Signed: Trade Unionist.

2636 The present state of the novel (Part I): [in England], 410–417. **George Saintsbury.** Signed.

2637 Realism and idealism, 418–429. **John Addington Symonds.** Signed; repr. *Essays.*

2638 Fine passages in verse and prose; selected by living men of letters (No. II), 430–454. Letters from **Augustine Birrell, John Duke Coleridge, Frances Power Cobbe, Oswald Crawfurd, Wilkie Collins, Edward Dowden, Edmund Gosse,** "Vernon Lee" [**Violet Paget**], **John Lubbock, W. H. Mallock,** "Ouida" [**Marie Louise de la Ramée**], **Ernest Rhys, Olive Schreiner, Edward Henry Stanley** [Lord Derby], **A. C. Swinburne, J. A. Symonds, R. Y. Tyrrell, Theodore Watts.**

VOLUME 48 O.S., 42 N.S., OCTOBER 1887

2639 Last words on Shelley, 461–481. **Edward Dowden.** Signed; repr. *Transcripts.*

2640 The physical condition of the masses, 482–490. **Charles Roberts,** 1836–1901. Signed; Contents adds "F.R.C.S."; see *LCCat.*

2641 Byways of Greek song, 491–502. **Andrew Lang.** Signed.

2642 The story of Tonga, 503–513. **Coutts Trotter.** Signed.

2643 Wealth and the working classes (Part IV, concl.), 514–534. **W. H. Mallock.** Signed.

2644 Pascal, the sceptic, 535–544. **W. L. Courtney.** Signed; repr. *Studies.*

2645 The flight of Piero De' Medici, October-November, 1494, 545–558. **A. Mary F. Robinson.** Signed; repr. *Middle Ages.*

2646 The women of chivalry, 559–579. **Eliza Lynn Linton.** Signature.

2647 Fine passages in verse and prose; selected by living men of letters (No. III), 580–604. Letters by **Edwin Arnold,** 1832–1904, **Thomas Bailey Aldrich, Austin Dobson, J. Llewellyn Davies, W. H. Fremantle, Frederic Harrison, J. J. Hornby, F. W. H. Myers, Benjamin Ward Richardson, H. D. Traill, Thomas Herbert Warren.**

VOLUME 48 O.S., 42 N.S., NOVEMBER 1887

2648 The British army (Part I): introduction, 605–635. **C. W. Dilke** and **C. B. Brackenbury.** Signed The Author of *Greater Britain*. Dilke wrote *Greater Britain*: see *BMCat.*; claimed by Dilke in no. 3154, p. 793; series repr. in his *The British Army* (1888); Stephen Gwynn and G. M. Tuckwell, *Life of Sir Charles W. Dilke* (N.Y., 1917), II, 391, explain the collaboration with Brackenbury.

2649 Wealth and ability, a rejoinder [to W. H. Mallock, nos. 2568, 2589, 2618, and 2643], 636–648. **H. M. Hyndman.** Signed. (Letter, p. 879, signed **W. H. Mallock.**)

2650 Secret societies in the Two Sicilies, 649–664. **E. Strachan Morgan.** Signed.

2651 American Museums (Part II, concl.): museums of American pre-historic archeology, 665–675. **Alfred R. Wallace.** Signed; repr. *Studies*, II.

2652 The Papacy and the temporal power, 676–695. **Emilio Castelar.** Signed.

2653 Hermann Lotze and the mechanical philosophy, 696–702. **St. George Mivart.** Signed; repr. *Essays*, II.

2654 A Midland university [at Birmingham], 703–716. **J. R. Seeley.** Signed.

2655 Fine passages in verse and prose; selected by living men of letters (No. IV), 717–739. Letters by **Alfred Austin, Rowland Blennerhassett, F. C. Burnand, Sidney Colvin, Lady Emilia Dilke, F. W. Farrar, Oliver Wendell Holmes,** Master of Marlborough [**George C. Bell**], **Louise Chandler Moulton,** Dean of St. Paul's [**R. W. Church**], **E. H. Plumptre, Agnes Mary Robinson, William Sharp, Frederick Tennyson, Edmund Yates.**

VOLUME 48 O.S., 42 N.S., DECEMBER 1887

2656 The British army (Part II): the present position, 741–782. **C. W. Dilke** and **C. B. Brackenbury.** Cf. no. 2648.

2657 Count Leo Tolstoi, 783–799. **Matthew Arnold.** Signed; repr. *Essays*, II.

2658 The Thames, 800–817. **Benjamin Ward Richardson.** Signed.

2659 Mademoiselle Aïssé, 818–834. **Edmund Gosse.** Signed; repr. *French Profiles*, 1904.

2660 The sweating system, 835–856. **David F. Schloss.** Signed.

2661 The model, 857–861. **J. A. Symonds.** Signed; repr. *Essays*.

2662 A partition of Turkey, 862–866. **G. de Hennin.** Signed.

2663 Our national expenditure, 867–878. **Leone Levi.** Signed.

2664 In correspondence: Labour organization [on unemployment registries], 883–884. Signed **J. W. Leigh.** Contents gives "Hon. and Rev. Canon Leigh."

VOLUME 49 O.S., 43 N.S., JANUARY 1888

2665 The British army (Part III): modern armies, 1–41. **C. W. Dilke** and **C. B. Brackenbury.** Cf. no. 2648; in the *Life*, cited there, III, 391, Dilke says he was heavily indebted here to a letter from Gen. Garnet Wolseley.

2666 The old school of classics and the new: a dialogue of the dead—Bentley, Madvig, Porson, Shakspeare, Euripides, 42–59. **Robert Yelverton Tyrrell.** Signed.

2667 Right and wrong, 62–80. **W. S. Lilly.** Signed.

2668 Elk-hunting, 81–98. **Henry Pottinger.** Signed. (Note, p. 300, by **Pottinger.**)

2669 Charles Darwin and agnosticism, 99–108. **Frederic W. H. Myers.** Signed; repr. *Future Life*.

2670 The prospect of Egypt in 1888, 109–111. **Francis Duncan.** Signed F. Duncan; Contents adds "Col." and "M.P."; see *DNB*.

2671 The present state of the novel (Part II, concl.): [in France], 112–123. **George Saintsbury.** Signed; repr. *French Novelists*.

2672 The higher life: how is it to be sustained? 124–142. **J. Llewellyn Davies.** Signed.

2673 Distress in London (No. I): remedies, 143–153. **William G. S. S. Compton.** Signed Compton [Earl Compton]; see *Complete Peerage* under Northampton.

2674 Distress in London (No. II): a note on outdoor relief, 153–156. **H. E. Manning.** Signed as in no. 2513; repr. *Miscellanies*, III, as "Outdoor Relief."

VOLUME 49 O.S., 43 N.S., FEBRUARY 1888

2675 The British army (Part IV): our "System," 157–186. **C. W. Dilke** and **C. B. Brackenbury.** Cf. no. 2648.

2676 English and American federalism, 189–195. **Francis Cabot Lowell, III** (1855–

1911)? Signed C. R. Lowell; after much research, especially in American sources, no such person found living in 1888; on the cover of the Boston Athenaeum copy and at the end of the art., the author's name has been emended, in faded ink, to Francis C. Lowell; Francis Cabot Lowell, Jr., had died in 1874; the man cited, an American judge and student of history, "published sundry articles in the *Atlantic Monthly* and elsewhere" (*Harvard College: The Class of 1876, 8th Report* [Cambridge, Mass.], p. 22).

2677 The abolition of school fees: a plea for further consideration, 196–210. **Joseph R. Diggle.** Signed.

2678 Beauty, composition, expression, characterization, 211–222. **John Addington Symonds.** Signed; repr. *Essays.*

2679 The education of the emotions, 223–236. **Frances Power Cobbe.** Signed; repr. *Scientific Spirit.*

2680 Turgueneff, 237–251. **George Moore.** Signed; repr. *Impressions.*

2681 Italian women in the middle ages, 252–272. **Eliza Lynn Linton.** Signature.

2682 "The Ways of Orthodox Critics" [reply to nos. 2667 and 2672], 273–278. **F. Howard Collins.** Signed.

2683 The housing of the poor, 279–286. **Harold E. Boulton.** Signed.

2684 A Jacobean courtier [Lord Herbert of Cherbury], 287–299. **Arthur Benson.** Signed.

VOLUME 49 O.S., 43 N.S., MARCH 1888

2685 The British army (Part V): the ideal of a British army, 301–330. **C. W. Dilke** and **C. B. Brackenbury.** Cf. no. 2648.

2686 The study of English literature, 331–349. **Edward Dowden.** Signed; repr. *New Studies* as "The Teaching of English Literature."

2687 Social problems and remedies, 350–363. **F. W. Farrar.** Signed.

2688 Guy de Maupassant, 364–386. **Henry James.** Signed; repr. *Partial Portraits,* 1888.

2689 State colonization, 387–398. **Robert Collier,** 1845–1909. Signed Monkswell [2nd Baron Monkswell].

2690 Home rule in the western Pyrenees, 399–407. **Wentworth Webster.** Signed.

2691 Domestic service and democracy, 408–417. **Edward Salmon.** Signed.

2692 Dairy schools, 418–426. **Walter S. B. M'Laren.** Signed.

2693 Mr. Herbert Spencer as a moralist [rejoinder to no. 2682], 427–444. **W. S. Lilly.** Signed.

VOLUME 49 O.S., 43 N.S., APRIL 1888

2694 The British army (Part VI): practical approximations to the ideal, 445–476. **C. W. Dilke** and **C. B. Brackenbury.** Cf. no. 2648.

2695 Spring-time in rural Portugal, 480–493. **Oswald Crawfurd.** Signed; repr. in "March" in *Round the Calendar in Portugal,* 1890.

2696 The destruction of self-government, 494–505. **Thomas Gibson Bowles.** Signed.

2697 A nun's love letters [*Lettres Portugaises*], 506–517. **Edmund Gosse.** Signed; repr. *French Profiles,* 1904.

2698 Caricature, the fantastic, the grotesque, 518–525. **John Addington Symonds.** Signed; repr. *Essays.*

2699 Healthy homes for the working classes, 526–537. **David F. Schloss.** Signed.

2700 The art of George Eliot, 538–553. **Oscar Browning.** Signed.

2701 The everlasting hills, 554–567. **Richard A. Proctor.** Signed.

2702 Science et Poésie, dialogue d'esthétique, 568–588. **Paul Bourget.** Signed.

VOLUME 49 O.S., 43 N.S., MAY 1888

2703 The House of Lords and the county councils, 589–604. **Edward A. Freeman.** Signed.

2704 The British army (Part VII, concl.): national defence, 605–626. **C. W. Dilke** and **C. B. Brackenbury.** Cf. no. 2648.

2705 Trout-fishing, 627–646. **Henry Pottinger.** Signed.

2706 Pierre Loti, 647–664. **Henry James.** Signed; repr. *Essays in London and Elsewhere,* N.Y., 1893.

2707 The revival of architecture, 665–674. **William Morris.** Signed.

2708 Sunday at Concord [Mass.], 675–690. **Grant Allen.** Signed.

2709 The East African slave-trade, 691–706. **W. M. Torrens.** Signed.

2710 Notes from a prosperous agricultural country [Denmark], 707–718. **Frances Mary de Borring.** Signed.

2711 Matthew Arnold, 719–728. **Frederic W. H. Myers.** Signed.

2712 Correspondence: Consular protection in Morocco, 729–732. **Ion Perdicaris.** Signed.

Volume 49 o.s., 43 n.s., June 1888

2713 Can we hold our own [against military attack]? 733–744. **J. F. Maurice.** Claimed, *National Defences* (1887), p. 5.

2714 Mr. Whistler's lecture on art ["Ten O'Clock"], 745–751. **Algernon Charles Swinburne.** Signed; repr. in *"Ten O'clock," a Lecture by James McNeill Whistler*, Portland, Me., 1916, also in *Pericles and Other Studies*, 1914.

2715 The cloister in Cathay, 752–767. **George N. Curzon.** Signed.

2716 Goethe (Part I): *Wilhelm Meister*, 768–789. **Edward Dowden.** Signed; repr. *New Studies.*

2717 The Local Government Bill (No. I): compensation to the drink trade, 790–794. **H. E. Manning.** Signed as in no. 2513; repr. *Miscellanies*, III, as "Compensation to the Drink Trade."

2718 The Local Government Bill (No. II): the licensing clauses, 795–802. **F. W. Farrar.** Signed.

2719 Summer-time in rural Portugal, 803–815. **Oswald Crawfurd.** Signed; repr. in "August" in *Round the Calendar in Portugal*, 1890.

2720 French political women, 816–842. **Eliza Lynn Linton.** Signature.

2721 Social problems in America, 843–861. **W. H. S. Aubrey.** Signed.

2722 The Cape in 1888, 862–884. **Henry H. M. Herbert.** Signed Carnarvon [Earl of Carnarvon]; repr. *Essays*, II.

Volume 50 o.s., 44 n.s., July 1888

2723 Our true foreign policy, 1–9. **Frank Harris,** prob. J. F. Maurice, *National Defences* (1897), p. 5, calls this an "editorial article."

2724 The Boulangist movement, 10–23. **Henri Rochefort.** Signed.

2725 The miscellaneous works of Ben Jonson, 24–38. **Algernon Charles Swinburne.** Signed; repr. *A Study of Ben Jonson*, 1889.

2726 Through Bulgaria with Prince Ferdinand, 39–56. **J. D. Bourchier.** Signed.

2727 Lucian, 57–68. **Andrew Lang.** Signed.

2728 Pawnbroking in England and abroad, 69–88. **F. Mabel Robinson.** Signed.

2729 Goethe (Part II, concl.): Goethe in Italy, 89–111. **Edward Dowden.** Signed; repr. *New Studies.*

2730 Critics and campaigns [reply to *ER* 3536], 112–135. **John Frederick Maurice.**

Signed F. Maurice; Contents adds "Col."; see *DNB.*

2731 Custom, 136–141. **Edward Carpenter.** Signed.

2732 The ethics of Kant, 142–156. **Herbert Spencer.** Signed.

Volume 50 o.s., 44 n.s., August 1888

2733 Jobbery in our public offices, 179–196. **L. J. Jennings.** Signed.

2734 A visit to President Brand [of the Orange River Free State], 197–210. **J. E. C. Bodley.** Signed.

2735 Reflections in India, 1880–1888, 211–228. **Samuel W. Baker.** Signed.

2736 Baron Hirsch's railway, 229–239. **J. Theodore Bent.** Signed Theodore Bent; cf. no. 2625; see *DNB.*

2737 Genius and talent, 240–255. **Grant Allen.** Signed.

2738 Rêve, 256–259. **Pierre Loti.** Signed.

2739 Capital and culture in America, 260–278. **Richard A. Proctor.** Signed.

2740 Courage, 279–292. **G. J. Wolseley.** Signed Wolseley [Viscount Wolseley].

2741 Correspondence: Trades-unions among women, 293–296. **Frederick W. Verney.** Signed.

Volume 50 o.s., 44 n.s., September 1888

2742 Military Genius, 297–312. **G. J. Wolseley.** Signed Wolseley [Viscount Wolseley].

2743 The conduct of business during the present session, 313–323. **Arthur A. Baumann.** Signed.

2744 The fall of fiction [on Rider Haggard], 324–336. **William Watson.** Watson to Edward Clodd, Mar. 5, 1892, typescript at Yale Univ. Lib. (original in the Bodleian) claims this. (Letter by **Watson,** signed "The Writer of 'The Fall of Fiction'," pp. 684–688.)

2745 Imprisonment for debt, 337–346. **M. D. Chalmers.** Signed.

2746 An eighteenth-century abbé [Ferdinando Galiani], 347–362. **Eliza Lynn Linton.** Signature.

2747 The social status of women in India, 363–372. **Lester Ramsay de Fonblanque.** Signed.

2748 A hundred years ago, 373–380. **W. W. Knollys.** Signed.

2749 The naval manoeuvres, 381–404. **J. F.**

Maurice. Claimed, *National Defences* (1897), pp. 5–6.

2750   Shakespeare's wisdom of life, 405–424. **Edward Dowden.** Signed.

VOLUME 50 O.S., 44 N.S., OCTOBER 1888

2751   Ben Jonson's *Discoveries*, 425–447. **Algernon Charles Swinburne.** Signed; repr. *A Study of Ben Jonson*, 1889.

2752   Homicidal mania, 448–463. **George H. Savage.** Signed.

2753   British East Africa, 464–480. **H. H. Johnston.** Signed.

2754   *The Memoirs of Count Carlo Gozzi*, 481–487. **John Addington Symonds.** Signed; repr. in book of same title, 1896.

2755   The great missionary failure, 488–500. **Isaac Taylor**, 1829–1901. Signed; Contents adds "Canon"; see *DNB*, 2nd suppl.

2756   The *Journal* of the Brothers de Goncourt, 501–520. **Henry James.** Signed; repr. *Essays in London and Elsewhere*, N.Y., 1893.

2757   The irresponsibilities of genius, 521–536. **Eliza Lynn Linton.** Signature.

2758   Mr. Hubert Parry's *Judith*, 537–545. **C. Villiers Stanford.** Signed.

2759   Mosquito defence: an ignored lesson of the naval manoeuvres, 546–556. **George Baden-Powell.** Signed.

VOLUME 50 O.S., 44 N.S., NOVEMBER 1888

2760   What our navy should be: introduction, 557–562. **Frank Harris.** Signed The Editor.

2761   What our navy should be (No. I), 562–570. **Thomas Symonds.** Signed.

2762   What our navy should be (No. II), 571–577. **G. Phipps Hornby.** Signed.

2763   What our navy should be (No. III), 577–580. **Frederick B. P. Seymour.** Signed Alcester [Baron Alcester].

2764   Missionary finance, 581–592. **Isaac Taylor**, 1829–1901. Signed as in no. 2755.

2765   Where is Stanley? 593–602. **H. H. Johnston.** Signed.

2766   The revival of handicraft, 603–610. **William Morris.** Signed.

2767   Palmyra: past and present, 611–628. **William George Spencer Scott Compton.** Signed Compton [Earl Compton]; see *Complete Peerage* under Northampton.

2768   Our task in Egypt, 629–664.

2769   Apologia pro fide nostra [Positivism], 665–683. **Frederic Harrison.** Signed.

VOLUME 50 O.S., 44 N.S., DECEMBER 1888

2770   The negro as a soldier, 689–703. **G. J. Wolseley.** Signed Wolseley [Viscount Wolseley].

2771   A few thoughts by a patriarch about French women, 704–720. **Jules Simon.** Signed.

2772   The political outlook in Queensland, 721–727. **A. W. Stirling.** Signed.

2773   Style, 728–743. **Walter Pater.** Signed; repr. *Appreciations*.

2774   The Black Mountain campaign, 744–754. **Stephen Wheeler.** Signed.

2775   Wild shooting, 755–773. **Henry Pottinger.** Signed.

2776   The Church Missionary Society: financial accounts: a reply [to no. 2764], 774–781. **Eugene Stock.** Signed. With a note, pp. 782–784, by **Isaac Taylor**, 1829–1901—signed as in no. 2755.

2777   The fate of Roumania, 785–804. **James D. Bourchier.** Signed.

2778   A story of the lighthouses (Part I), 805–828. **John Tyndall.** Signed.

VOLUME 51 O.S., 45 N.S., JANUARY 1889

2779   War, 1–17. **G. J. Wolseley.** Signed Wolseley [Viscount Wolseley].

2780   The ethics of cannibalism, 18–28. **H. H. Johnston.** Signed.

2781   Victor Hugo, *Toute la Lyre* (Part I), 29–40. **Algernon Charles Swinburne.** Signed; repr. *Studies*.

2782   Pen, pencil, and poison: a study, 41–54. **Oscar Wilde.** Signed.

2783   A comparison of Elizabethan with Victorian poetry, 55–79. **John Addington Symonds.** Signed; repr. *Essays*.

2784   The scientific bases of optimism, 80–106. **W. H. Mallock.** Signed; repr. *Studies*.

2785   Ibsen's social dramas, 107–121. **Edmund Gosse.** Signed; repr. *Northern Studies*, 1890.

2786   A visit to Bokhara the Noble, 122–143. **George N. Curzon.** Signed.

2787   The future of agnosticism, 144–156. **Frederic Harrison.** Signed; repr. *Common Sense*.

VOLUME 51 O.S., 45 N.S., FEBRUARY 1889

2788   England and Germany in East Africa, 157–165. **J. P. Farler.** Signed; Contents adds "Archdeacon of Magila, Usambara"; see Venn.

2827   The Education Commission and the school rate, 732–756. **H. E. Manning.** Signed as in no. 2513.

2828   What the Revolution of 1789 did, 757–779. **Frederic Harrison.** Signed; repr. *The Meaning of History.*

2829   The French Revolution and war, 780–791. **G. J. Wolseley.** Signed Wolseley [Viscount Wolseley].

2830   A conversation in a balcony, 792–808. **Frederick Greenwood.** Signed.

2831   Five years' advocacy of provincial parliaments, 809–818. **John Douglas Campbell.** Signed Lorne [Marquess of Lorne].

2832   Turf reform, 819–832. **William Day.** Signed.

2833   The foreigner in England, 833–838. **E. C. K. Gonner.** Signed.

2834   The House of Habsburg in South-Eastern Europe, 839–851. **Edward A. Freeman.** Signed.

2835   Benefit societies and trades unions for women, 852–856. **Emilia F. S. Dilke.** Signed.

2836   The art of prolonging life, 857–870. **Robson Roose.** Signed; repr. *Waste.*

2837   The spoliation of the Egyptian bond-holders, 871–878. Signed: J. R.

2838   The women of Spain, 879–904. **Emilia Pardo Bazan.** Signed.

2839   Philip Massinger, 1–23. **Algernon Charles Swinburne.** Signed; repr. *Contemporaries of Shakespeare*, 1919.

2840   Swiss neutrality, 24–29.

2841   Ibsen and English criticism, 30–37. **William Archer.** Signed.

2842   In the Balkans with Prince Ferdinand, 38–56. **J. D. Bourchier.** Signed.

2843   Edward FitzGerald, 57–70. **Edmund Gosse.** Signed; repr. *Critical Kit-Kats*, N.Y., 1896.

2844   How H. M. the Shah travels when at home, 71–76. **J. Theodore Bent.** Signed.

2845   Goethe and the French Revolution, 77–96. **Edward Dowden.** Signed; repr. *New Studies.*

2846   Nordanskär [a Swedish islet], 97–111. **Henry Pottinger.** Signed.

2847   The ethics of punishment, 112–122. **W. S. Lilly.** Signed.

2848   Women's suffrage: a reply [to *NC* no. 1712], 123–131, with a "Declaration in favour of women's suffrage," signed by many women, 131–139.

2849   Father Damien and leprosy in India, 140–150. **Edward Clifford.** Signed.

2850   Leprosy and its causes, 150–152. **Phineas S. Abraham.** Signed.

2851   Mr. Gladstone and the civilized world, 153–172. **Karl Blind.** Signed.

2852   Downing Street *versus* chartered companies in Africa, 173–185. **Joseph Thomson.** Signed.

2853   Gounod's views on art and artists, 186–206. **Marie Anne de Bovet.** Signed.

2854   The fortress of Paris, 207–213.

2855   The great Servian festival, 214–233. **J. D. Bourchier.** Signed.

2856   Giordano Bruno, 234–244. **Walter Pater.** Signed; repr. *Gaston de Latour* (1888), chap. vii.

2857   The present discontent in Cyprus, 245–253. **W. D. Hogarth.** Signed.

2858   Roger Bacon, a forgotten son of Oxford, 254–262. **W. L. Courtney.** Signed; repr. *Studies at Leisure*, 1892.

2859   Spanish and Portuguese bull-fighting, 263–270. **Oswald Crawfurd.** Signed; repr. as part of "May," *Round the Calendar in Portugal*, 1890.

2860   Mr. Browning in a passion, 271–273. **Robert Yelverton Tyrrell.** Signed.

2861   Some truths about Russia, 274–292. **E. J. Dillon?** Signed A Former Resident in Russia; this is almost certainly by the author of the series on Russian characteristics which begins in the next month —the description "a former resident" would be an added precaution against identification (Dillon was in Russia in 1889 and it was essential not to jeopardize his access to information.).

2862   Parallels to Irish Home Rule, 293–298. **Edward A. Freeman.** Signed.

2863   Belgian neutrality, 299–306.

2864   What English people read, 307–321. **Walter Montagu Gattie.** Signed.

2865   The case against capital punishment, 322–333. **B. Paul Neuman.** Signed.

2866   The coming elections in France, 334–341. **Emilia F. S. Dilke.** Signed.

2867   Coleridge as a poet, 342–366. **Edward Dowden.** Signed; repr. *New Studies.*

2868   Dry-nursing the Colonies, 367–379. **Flora L. Shaw.** Signed.

2869   Our national pastime, 380–394. **William Day.** Signed.

2870   Notes of a fortnight in Bosnia, 395–409. **A. Hulme-Beaman.** Signed.

2871   Russian characteristics (Part I): lying, 410–432. **E. J. Dillon.** Signed E. B. Lanin; although a note by the editor, **Frank Harris,** on p. 432 speaks of the "authors" of this series using the pseudonym, Dillon later admitted sole authorship; see *FR* 140 (1933), 23–24; repr. 1892, catalogued under E. J. Dillon in *BMCat.*

VOLUME 52 O.S., 46 N.S., OCTOBER 1889

2872   The labour problem, 437–447. **David F. Schloss.** Signed.

2873   Plain words on the woman question, 448–458. **Grant Allen.** Signed.

2874   The armed strength of France in 1889, 459–471.

2875   Progress in China, 472–490. **R. S. Gundry.** Signed; repr. in expanded form in *China.*

2876   Some of Balzac's minor pieces, 491–504. **George Moore.** Signed; repr. in a much expanded form in *Impressions.*

2877   Eastern women, 505–515. **Horace Victor.** Signed.

2878   In the forests of Navarre and Aragon, 516–537. **John Verschoyle.** Signed.

2879   Last days of the Ottoman Empire, 538–550. **John Welsh.** Signed.

2880   African development: the Soudan, 551–572. **Samuel W. Baker.** Signed.

2881   Russian characteristics (Part II), 573–588. **E. J. Dillon.** Evidence for no. 2871.

VOLUME 52 O.S., 46 N.S., NOVEMBER 1889

2882   Wilkie Collins, 589–599. **Algernon Charles Swinburne.** Signed; repr. *Studies.*

2883   Science and the revolution, 600–619. **W. H. Mallock.** Signed; repr. *Studies.*

2884   Our damatists and their literature, 620–632. **George Moore.** Signed; repr. *Impressions.*

2885   A republic *in extremis* [France], 633–649. **William Henry Hurlbert.** Signed.

2886   The armed strength of Germany in 1889, 650–661. **A. M. Murray.** Signed; Contents adds "Major" and "R.A."; see *WWW*/1928.

2887   The British South Africa Company, 662–668. **Flora L. Shaw.** Signed.

2888   The extension of trade in political principle, 669–682. **Frederick Greenwood.** Signed.

2889   Folk-lore of Northern Portugal, 683–694. **Oswald Crawfurd.** Signed; repr. in parts of "June," *Round the Calendar in Portugal,* 1890.

2890   The organization of working women, 695–704. **Clementina Black.** Signed.

2891   A modern correspondence, 705–721. **Lucy Clifford.** Repr. *Love-Letters of a Worldly Woman,* 1891.

2892   Russian characteristics (Part III), 722–736. **E. J. Dillon.** Evidence for no. 2871.

VOLUME 52 O.S., 46 N.S., DECEMBER 1889

2893   Literary criticism in France, 737–753. **Edward Dowden.** Signed; repr. *New Studies.*

2894   Betting, gambling, and my critics, 754–763. **W. C. Magee.** Signed W. C. Peterborough [Bishop of Peterborough].

2895   A page of my life, 764–775. **John Addington Symonds.** Signed; repr. *Swiss Highlands.*

2896   Practical religion, 776–788. **Grant Allen.** Signed; repr. *The Hand of God,* 1909.

2897   The unmaking of England, 789–805. **Karl Blind.** Signed.

2898   The sentinel of the Balkans, 806–822. **J. D. Bourchier.** Signed.

2899   The factory half-timer, 823–831. **Thomas Percy Sykes.** Signed T. P. Sykes, dated from Great Horton Board School, Bradford; man cited wrote elementary music text-books; see *BMCat.*

2900   A new French novelist [Henri Lavedan], 832–845. **Marie Blaze de Bury.** Signed Mme.

2901   Lepers and leprosy in Norway, 846–853. **Robson Roose.** Signed.

2902   Russian characteristics (Part IV): dishonesty, 854–868. **E. J. Dillon.** Evidence for no. 2871.

2903   The war scare of 1875, 869–883.

VOLUME 53 O.S., 47 N.S., JANUARY 1890

2904   Personal recollections of Thomas Carlyle, 5–32. **John Tyndall.** Signed; repr. *New Fragments.*

2905   The state and the Sermon on the Mount, 33–46. **W. C. Magee.** Signed

W. C. Peterborough [Bishop of Peterborough].

2906 An eighteenth-century mystic [Marquis de Marsay], 47–66. **Edward Dowden.** Signed, repr. *Essays.*

2907 The homes of the poor, 67–80. **Susan Mary E. Jeune.** Signed as in no. 2362. repr. *Lesser Questions*, 1894.

2908 Stanley's expedition: a retrospect, 81–96. Unidentified. Possibly Mary Rosalie Felkin, personal friend and translator of Emin Pasha's book, cited here, pp. 82, 84; she published some letters by him in *FortR* 2605.

2909 Sacred stones, 97–116. **Grant Allen.** Signed.

2910 The Cretan insurrection of 1889, 117–123.

2911 The Black Mountain [Montenegro], 124–135. **A. Hulme-Beaman.** Signed.

2912 Portugal's aggressions [in Africa] and England's duty, 136–148.

VOLUME 53 O.S., 47 N.S., FEBRUARY 1890

2913 The Portuguese in East Africa, 149–163. **Daniel J. Rankin.** Signed.

2914 One view of the question [an Indian looks at the English], 164–176. **Rudyard Kipling.** Signed in Contents; repr. *Many Inventions*, 1893.

2915 The land purchase question, 177–184. **T. W. Russell.** Signed.

2916 Mr. Labouchere: the democrat, 185–194. **W. H. Mallock.** Signed.

2917 Was it a crime? 195–219. **Amélie Rives Troubetzkoy.** Signed Amélie Rives: see Amer. *WWW/1950.*

2918 The city of the Creed [Nicaea], 220–230. **J. Theodore Bent.** Signed.

2919 Art-teaching and technical schools, 231–241. **Emilia F. S. Dilke.** Signed.

2920 English and Americans (Part I), 242–255. **William Morton Fullerton.** Signed.

2921 Russian characteristics (Part V, concl.), 256–275. **E. J. Dillon.** Evidence for no. 2871.

2922 Marie Bashkirtseff: a personal reminiscence, 276–282. **Marian Hepworth Dixon.** Signed, but with Marion as first name: see below, Part B.

2923 The Swaziland question, 283–291. **Hercules Robinson.** Signed.

2924 In correspondence: Mr. Gladstone on German literature; a protest, 292–294, signed **Karl Blind;** Oxford tutors and their professorial critic [Thorold Rogers], 294–296, signed **W. L. Courtney.**

VOLUME 53 O.S., 47 N.S., MARCH 1890

2925 Some South African questions, 297–309. **John Xavier Merriman.** Signed John Merriman; Contents adds "Hon."; see *DNB.*

2926 The morality of marriage, 310–330. **Mona Caird.** Signed; repr. *Morality of Marriage and Other Essays*, 1897.

2927 The lyrism of the English romantic drama, 331–342. **John Addington Symonds.** Signed; repr. *Key of Blue.*

2928 The evil of betting and how to eradicate it, 343–360. **William Day.** Signed.

2929 Mistaken identity and police anthropometry, 361–376. **Edmund R. Spearman.** Signed.

2930 The legend of Madame Krasinska, 377–396. **Violet Paget.** Signed Vernon Lee—see *DNB*; repr. *Vanitas*, 1892.

2931 Field-Marshal Lord Napier of Magdala, 397–403. **W. W. Knollys.** Signed.

2932 Judicial torture in China, 404–420. **R. S. Gundry.** Signed; repr. *China.*

2933 King Plagiarism and his court [attack on R. Haggard], 421–439. **James Runciman.** Signed.

2934 Regulation by statute of the hours of adult labour, 440–454. **Charles Bradlaugh.** Signed C. Bradlaugh; Contents adds "M.P."; see *DNB.* With letters by **Graham Berry, Arthur Blyth, Saul Samuel, George Livesey, A. G. Church** (Director of London Omnibus Co.), **Tom Mann, Mark Beaufoy, S. M. Burroughs** (of Messrs. Burroughs, Welcome, & Co.), 454–460.

VOLUME 53 O.S., 47 N.S., APRIL 1890

2935 James Shirley, 461–478. **Algernon Charles Swinburne.** Signed; repr. *Contemporaries of Shakespeare*, 1919.

2936 Leaves from a diary on the Karun River (Part I), 479–498. **George N. Curzon.** Signed.

2937 The London stage, 499–516. **Oswald Crawfurd.** Signed. (See nos. 2964, 2965, 2965a, and letter, vol. 54 o.s., pp. 315–316, by the author.)

2938 Literature: then and now, 517–531. **Eliza Lynn Linton.** Signature.

2939 The sweating system, 532–551. **David F. Schloss.** Signed.

2940 Idealism in recent French fiction, 552–565. **Marie Blaze de Bury.** Signed B. de Bury; Contents adds "Madame"; see *DBF.*

2941 The physique of European armies, 566–585. **Walter Montagu Gattie.** Signed.

2942 On marriage: a criticism, 586–594. **Clementina Black.** Signed.

2943 A national want: a practical proposal [a periodical devoted to "the Empire at large"], 595–600.

2944 The reform of the College of Surgeons, 601–620. **Morell Mackenzie.** Signed; repr. *Essays*, 1893.

VOLUME 53 O.S., 47 N.S., MAY 1890

2945 Tennyson: and after? 621–637.

2946 The Irish Land Bill, 638–655. **T. W. Russell.** Signed.

2947 The working of woman suffrage in Wyoming, 656–669. **Horace Plunkett.** Signed; Contents adds "Hon."; see *DNB*.

2948 The lamentable comedy of Willow Wood, 670–681. **Rudyard Kipling.** Signed.

2949 The Danish drama of to-day, 682–693. **William Archer.** Signed.

2950 Leaves from a diary on the Karun River (Part II, concl.), 694–715. **George N. Curzon.** Signed.

2951 The Médoc vintage of 1889, 716–730. **W. Beatty-Kingston.** Signed.

2952 English and Americans (Part II, concl.), 731–740. **Morton Fullerton.** Signed.

2953 North American fisheries disputes, 741–760. **F. Heinrich Geffcken.** Signed.

2954 England's outlook in East Africa, 761–776.

VOLUME 53 O.S., 47 N.S., JUNE 1890

2955 The great equatorial forest of Africa, 777–790. **P. B. Du Chaillu.** Signed.

2956 The poetry of John Donne, 791–808. **Edward Dowden.** Signed; repr. *New Studies.*

2957 A visit to a great estate [in Norway], 809–825. **Henry Pottinger.** Signed.

2958 "Distinction," 826–834. **Coventry Patmore.** Signed.

2959 On early licensing laws and customs, 835–840. **J. Charles Cox.** Signed J. C. Cox; Contents adds middle name and "LL.D., F.S.A."; see *WWW*/1928.

2960 Protection *versus* free trade in Australia, 841–863. **G. H. D. Gossip.** Signed.

2961 A glance at contemporary Greece, 864–880. **James D. Bourchier.** Signed.

2962 The landlord's preferential position, 881–895. **R. C. Richards.** Signed.

2963 The latest discoveries in hypnotism (Part I), 896–921. **Jules Luys.** Signed J. Luys; Contents adds "Dr."; see *Larousse du XXme siècle.*

2964 The London stage: a reply (to no. 2937), 922–931. **Herbert Beerbohm Tree.** Signed. With a rejoinder, pp. 931–936, by **Oswald Crawfurd.** Signed. (See no. 2965a.)

VOLUME 54 O.S., 48 N.S., JULY 1890

2965 The actor-manager, 1–16. **Henry Arthur Jones.** Signed.

2965a A stage reply [rejoinder to Crawfurd in no. 2964], 16–19. **Herbert Beerbohm Tree.** Signed.

2966 Russian prisons: the simple truth, 20–43. **E. J. Dillon.** Signed E. B. Lanin—no. 2871.

2967 Meissonier and the Salon Julian, 44–55. **George Moore.** Signed; repr. *Impressions.*

2968 The protection of American literature, 56–65. **Edmund Gosse.** Signed.

2969 Mr. Stanley's expedition: its conduct and results, 66–81. **J. Scott Keltie.** Signed.

2970 The workmen of Paris in 1390 and in 1890, 82–106. **A. Mary F. Robinson.** Signed with addition "Madame James Darmesteter."

2971 Among the Euganean Hills, 107–118. **John Addington Symonds.** Signed; repr. *Key of Blue.*

2972 England and Germany in Africa (No. I), 119–127. **H. H. Johnston.** Signed.

2973 England and Germany in Africa (No. II), 129–143. **V. Lovett Cameron.** Signed.

2974 England and Germany in Africa (No. III), 144–163, with a postscript, 163–164. **Ernest W. Beckett.** Signed; and see p. 144n for the ascription of the postscript.

VOLUME 54 O.S., 48 N.S., AUGUST 1890

2975 The latest discoveries in hypnotism (Part II, concl.), 168–183. **Jules Luys.** Signed as in no. 2963.

2976 The stronghold of the Sphakiotes, 184–201. **James D. Bourchier.** Signed.

2977 Mickiewicz, the national poet of Poland, 202–217. **E. J. Dillon.** Signed.

2978 Hogarth's tour [to the Island of Sheppey], 218–223. **Austin Dobson.** Signed; repr. *Vignettes*, III, as "The Adventures of Five Days."

2979 Ethics and politics, 224–237. **Rowland Blennerhassett.** Signed.

2980 Labour disputes in America, 238–246. **W. H. S. Aubrey.** Signed.

2981 The educational outlook, 247–257. **Joseph R. Diggle.** Signed.

2982 Armenia and the Armenian people, 258–273. **E. J. Dillon.** Signed E. B. Lanin—no. 2871; a repr., 1890, catalogued under E. J. Dillon by *BMCat.*

2983 War in the future, 274–281. **W. W. Knollys.** Signed.

2984 The change of government in Germany, 282–304. **F. Heinrich Geffcken.** Geffcken to Percy Bunting, July 1, 1890, Bunting Papers, says he sent this article to *FortR.*

2985 The chocolate-makers' strike, 305–314. **Clementina Black.** Signed.

VOLUME 54 o.s., 48 n.s., SEPTEMBER 1890

2986 The Newfoundland fisheries dispute, 317–324. **William V. Whiteway, Robert Bond, A. W. Harvey,** and **George H. Emerson.** Signed.

2987 Human selection, 325–337. **Alfred R. Wallace.** Signed; repr. *Studies*, I.

2988 Goethe's last days: with a document hitherto unpublished, 338–354. **Edward Dowden.** Signed; repr. *New Studies*. The document is a letter, pp. 339–343, signed **W. Weissenborn** and dated Weimar, March 28, 1832.

2989 A Catholic theologian [Father Sebastian Bowden] on natural religion, 355–371. **W. H. Mallock.** Signed; repr. *Studies.* (See no. 3002.)

2990 Sexual morality in Russia, 372–397. **E. J. Dillon.** Signed E. B. Lanin—no. 2871.

2991 Pro bonò publico, 398–407. **J. M. Barrie.** Signed.

2992 A century of women's rights, 408–417. **Elizabeth Robins Pennell.** Signed.

2993 John Henry Newman: in memoriam, 418–438. **W. S. Lilly.** Signed; repr. *Essays and Speeches*, 1897.

2994 The Argentine crisis (No. I): its development, 439–447. **Henry B. Callander.** Signed.

2995 The Argentine crisis (No. II): its financial significance, 448–468. **W. R. Lawson.** Signed.

VOLUME 54 o.s., 48 n.s., OCTOBER 1890

2996 Some remarks about South Africa, 469–480. Signed: A South African.

2997 The Jews in Russia, 481–509. **E. J. Dillon.** Signed E. B. Lanin—no. 2871.

2998 John Milton, 510–519. **Frederick Pollock,** 1845–1937. Signed; Contents adds "Bart"; see *DNB.*

2999 In Ruthenia, 520–530. **Menie Muriel Dowie.** Signed.

3000 Work while ye have the light: a tale of the early Christians (intro.; chaps. i–iv), 531–558. **Leo Tolstoi.** Signed; repr. as "Walk in the Light while ye Have Light," in *Complete Works of Count Tolstoy*, Boston, 1905, XIX.

3001 The American tariff war, 559–569. **A. Egmont Hake** and **O. E. Wesslau.** Signed.

3002 Reason and religion [reply to no. 2989], 570–580. **H. S. Bowden.** Signed; Contents gives "Father S. Bowden"; see Newman, *L&D*, XVI, index.

3003 The tenth international medical congress,, 581–588. **A. Symons Eccles.** Signed.

3004 The new pictures in the National Gallery, 589–596. **George Moore.** Signed; repr. *Impressions.*

3005 Anthony Hamilton, 597–613. **George Saintsbury.** Signed; repr. *French Novelists.*

3006 One of our conquerors (chaps. i–vi), 614–640. **George Meredith.** Signed; novel published 1891.

VOLUME 54 o.s., 48 n.s., NOVEMBER 1890

3007 The coming session: breakers ahead, 641–656. **Frederick Greenwood.** Signed.

3008 The Burman and his creed, 657–673. **Lepel Griffin.** Signed.

3009 The national policy of the United States, 674–683. **Moreton Frewen.** Signed.

3010 Development of tropical Africa under British auspices, 684–706. **H. H. Johnston.** Signed.

3111 Work while ye have the light (chaps. v–x, concl.), 707–737. **Leo Tolstoi.** Signed L. Tolstoi.

3012 Rural life in France in the fourteenth century (Part I), 738–752. **A. Mary F. Robinson.** Signed as in no. 2970.

3013 Reason alone [insufficient for belief in God]: a reply to Father Sebastian Bowden [no. 3002], 753–773. **W. H. Mallock.** Signed.

3014 Robert Davenport, 774–781. **Algernon Charles Swinburne.** Signed; repr. *Contemporaries of Shakespeare*, 1919.

3015 My life in Russian prisons, 782–794. **Felix Volkhovsky.** Signed.

3016 One of our conquerors (chaps. vii–x), 795–816. **George Meredith.** Signed.

VOLUME 54 O.S., 48 N.S., DECEMBER 1890

3017 Mr. Stanley's rear-guard, 817–829. **J. Rose Troup.** Signed.
3018 Child-life insurance: a reply to the Rev. Benjamin Waugh [*CR* no. 2900] (No. I), 830–851. **Pembroke Marshall.** Signed; Contents adds "Capt." (See no. 3095.)
3019 Prosper Mérimée, 852–864. **Walter Pater.** Signed; repr. *Studies.*
3020 Rural life in France in the fourteenth century (Part II), 865–877. **A. Mary F. Robinson.** Signed as in no. 2970.
3021 Burton as I knew him, 878–884. **V. Lovett Cameron.** Signed.
3022 The outlook in France (Part I): how republics are made and unmade, 885–905. **William Henry Hurlbert.** Signed.
3023 The mask of Descartes, 906–913. **W. L. Courtney.** Signed; repr. *Studies at Leisure,* 1892.
3024 Dr. Koch's consumption-cure, 914–924. **Edward Berdoe.** Signed.
3025 Mr. Tree's Monday nights, 925–931. Signed: X.
3026 An averted crash in the city, 932–945. **W. R. Lawson.** Signed.
3027 English bankers and the Bank of England reserve, 946–958. **A. J. Wilson.** Signed.
3028 One of our conquerors (chaps. xi–xiv), 959–992. **George Meredith.** Signed.

VOLUME 55 O.S., 49 N.S., JANUARY 1891

3029 Ibsen's new drama [The Lady from the Sea], 4–13. **Edmund Gosse.** Signed.
3030 The truth about Stanley and Emin Pasha, 14–20. **A. Mounteney Jephson.** Signed.
3031 Scientific sins, 21–37. **Ernest M. Bowden.** Signed.
3032 Finland, 38–68. **E. J. Dillon.** Signed E. B. Lanin—no. 2871.
3033 "Chez Pousset": a literary evening, 69–81. **Edward Delille.** Signed; repr. *French Writers.*
3034 On the Black Sea with Prince Ferdinand, 82–101. **James D. Bourchier.** Signed.
3035 Anima naturaliter pagana: a quest of the imagination, 102–112. **J. B. Bury.** Signed.

3036 A Canadian people, 113–121. **George Baden-Powell.** Signed.
3037 The Irish leadership, 122–125. **Frederic Harrison.** Signed.
3038 "The Rake's Progress' in Irish politics, 126–142. **Auberon Herbert.** Signed.
3039 One of our conquerors (chaps. xv–xix), 143–172. **George Meredith.** Signed.

VOLUME 55 O.S., 49 N.S., FEBRUARY 1891

3040 Russian finance: the racking of the peasantry, 173–212. **E. J. Dillon.** Signed E. B. Lanin—no. 2871. With a note, p. 212, by the editor, **Frank Harris.**
3041 Public life and private morals, 213–228. **W. H. Mallock.** Signed M.; cf. no. 3119, with same signature and similar subject; attr. *Athenaeum,* Feb. 14, 1891, p. 220.
3042 An island deer-forest, 229–244. **Henry Pottinger.** Signed.
3043 The road to social peace, 245–258. **David F. Schloss.** Signed.
3044 The farms and trotting-horses of Kentucky, 259–266. **George Charles Spencer Churchill.** Signed Marlborough [Duke of Marlborough].
3045 The Celt in English art, 267–277. **Grant Allen.** Signed.
3046 The development of decorative electricity, 278–284. **Alice M. Gordon.** Signed.
3047 Critics "Over the Coals," 285–291. **William Archer.** Signed.
3048 The soul of man under socialism, 292–319. **Oscar Wilde.** Signed.
3049 Correspondence. Noncomformists and Unionism, 320–323. **Christopher Newman Hall.** Signed Newman Hall; Contents adds "Rev."; see *DNB,* 2nd suppl.
3050 One of our conquerors (chaps. xx–xxii), 324–344. **George Meredith.** Signed.

VOLUME 55 O.S., 49 N.S., MARCH 1891

3051 The outlook in France (Part II, concl.), 347–369. **W. Henry Hurlbert.** Signed.
3052 For conscience sake, 370–382. **Thomas Hardy.** Signed; repr. in *Life's Little Ironies,* 1894.
3053 The position of affairs in the Eastern Soudan, 383–393. **Hugh E. M. Stutfield.** Signed.
3054 The poet Verlaine, 394–405. **Edward Delille.** Signed; repr. *French Writers.*
3055 Rossetti and the moralists, 406–412.

J. Coulson Kernahan. Signed The Author of "A Dead Man's Diary": *BMCat.*; repr. essentially in *Sorrow and Song*, 1894, as "A Note on Rossetti."

3056   The Papuan and his master, 413–426. **Hume Nisbet.** Signed. (Letter, vol. 56 o.s., pp. 431–435, signed **Henry O. Forbes,** with reply, pp. 435–436, by the author.)

3057   The Macedonian question, 427–438. **A. Hulme-Beaman.** Signed.

3058   Conduct and Greek religion: a protest, 439–443. **Norah Gribble.** Signed.

3059   The slow destruction of the New Forest, 444–465. **Auberon Herbert.** Signed on p. 464.

3060   Canada and imperial federation, 466–479. **J. W. Longley.** Signed.

3061   A preface to "Dorian Gray," 480–481. **Oscar Wilde.** Signed.

3062   Correspondence. Madeira as a health resort, 482–484. **V. F. Benett Stanford.** Signed.

3063   One of our conquerors (chaps. xxiii–xxvi), 485–512. **George Meredith.** Signed.

VOLUME 55 O.S., 49 N.S., APRIL 1891

3064   How we occupied Mashonaland, 513–532. **John Willoughby.** Signed.

3065   The relations of church and state, 533–544. **Leo Tolstoi.** Signed.

3066   The second idyl of Theocritus: "Incantations," 545–552. Intro. note and translation by **John Addington Symonds** —signed.

3067   A celebrated Frenchwoman [Madame de Maintenon], 553–569. **Yetta de Bury.** Signed.

3068   Virginia mines and American rails (Part I), 570–583. **George Charles Spencer Churchill.** Signed Marlborough [Duke of Marlborough].

3069   Our illusions, 584–597. **Eliza Lynn Linton.** Signature.

3070   In Rhodope with Prince Ferdinand, 598–614. **James D. Bourchier.** Signed; repr. *Life,* appendix.

3071   Anglo-Saxon unity, 615–622. **Reginald Brabazon.** Signed Meath [Earl of Meath].

3072   *Amours de Voyage* [by Fabre d'Eglantine], 623–633. **Edward Dowden.** Signed; repr. *New Studies.*

3073   The Moncrieff defence, 634–641. Signed: R.

3074   Editorial horseplay [about the Elgin Marbles], 642–655. **Frederic Harrison.** Signed. (Letter, pp. 833–835, signed **George N. Curzon.**)

3075   One of our conquerors (chaps. xxvii–xxix), 656–680. **George Meredith.** Signed.

VOLUME 55 O.S., 49 N.S., MAY 1891

3076   *The Journal of Sir Walter Scott, 1825–1832,* 681–694. **Algernon Charles Swinburne.** Signed; repr. *Studies.*

3077   The midnight baptism: a study in Christianity, 695–701. **Thomas Hardy.** Signed; repr. with modifications as chap. xiv of *Tess of the D'Urbervilles,* 3 vols., 1891.

3078   Personal recollections of Mazzini, 702–712. **Mathilde Blind.** Signed.

3079   The Transatlantic cattle trade, 713–724. **Moreton Frewen.** Signed.

3080   The Ibsen question, 725–740. **Oswald Crawfurd.** Signed.

3081   Trades Unionism among women, 741–750. **Florence Routledge** and **Emilia F. S. Dilke.** Article is signed by the first writer, but the Contents adds "Lady Dilke" as collaborator.

3082   Private life in France in the fourteenth century (Part III): the middle class, 751–761. **A. Mary F. Robinson.** Signed as in no. 2970.

3083   Elementary education a municipal charge, 762–770. **Francis R. J. Sandford.** Signed Sandford [Baron Sandford].

3084   A chemist in the suburbs, 771–779. **Frederick Wedmore.** Signed; repr. *Renunciations,* 1893.

3085   Virginia mines and American rails (Part II, concl.), 780–797. **George Charles Spencer Churchill.** Signed Marlborough [Duke of Marlborough].

3086   The Russian censure, 798–824. **E. J. Dillon.** Signed E. B. Lanin—no. 2871.

3087   South African problems, 825–832. **J. Scott Keltie.** Signed.

3088   One of our conquerors (chaps. xxx–xxxii, concl.), 836–856. **George Meredith.** Signed.

VOLUME 55 O.S., 49 N.S., JUNE 1891

3089   The British army in 1891, 857–876. **Charles W. Dilke.** Signed.

3090   Influenza, 877–886. **Morell Mackenzie.** Signed; repr. *Essays,* 1893.

3091   An election at the English Academy, 887–897. **Edmund Gosse.** Repr. *Questions at Issue,* 1893.

3092   Archbishop Magee, 898–909. **William Benham.** Signed W. Benham; Contents adds "Rev. Canon"; see *DNB.*

3093 The future of American literature, 910–926. **Theodore Watts.** Signed.

3094 The Paris salons of 1891, 927–938. **Mabel Robinson.** Signed.

3095 Child-life insurance: a reply to the Rev. Benjamin Waugh (No. II), 939–946. **Pembroke Marshall.** Signed.

3096 Letters in Philistia, 947–962. **Grant Allen.** Signed.

3097 Bulgars and Serbs, 963–976. **A. Hulme-Beaman.** Signed.

3098 Baudelaire; the man, 977–984. **Edward Delille.** Signed; repr. *French Writers*.

3099 A modern idyll, 985–1008. **Frank Harris.** Signed; repr. *Elder Conklin and Other Stories*, 1894.

VOLUME 56 O.S., 50 N.S., JULY 1891

3100 The credit of Australasia, 3–12. **George Baden-Powell.** Signed.

3101 Foreign pauper immigration, 13–24. **S. H. Jeyes.** Signed.

3102 Sir John Macdonald, 25–36. **J. G. Colmer.** Signed.

3103 Card-sharping in Paris, 37–52. **Edward Delille.** Signed; repr. *French Writers*.

3104 Stray thoughts on South Africa (Part I), 53–74. **Olive Schreiner.** Signed A Returned South African; see *FortR* no. 3784, for pseudonym; book published 1923. (See nos. 3784, 3824, 3840.)

3105 Cycling, 75–88. **R. J. Mecredy.** Signed.

3106 Punitive expeditions on the north-west frontier of India, 89–100. **Edward E. Oliver.** Signed.

3107 A note on affairs in Chili, 101–105. **Edward Manby.** Signed.

3108 The rediscovery of the unique, 106–111. **H. G. Wells.** Signed.

3109 With King Gungunhana in Gazaland, 112–117. **Dennis Doyle.** Signed.

3110 Montes, the matador, 118–148. **Frank Harris.** Signed; repr. in *Montes the Matador and Other Stories*, 1910.

VOLUME 56 O.S., 50 N.S., AUGUST 1891

3111 The future of Portugal, 149–162. **Oswald Crawfurd.** Signed.

3112 Goethe's friendship with Schiller, 163–180. **Edward Dowden.** Signed; repr. *New Studies*.

3113 The labour movement in Australia, 181–195. **Francis W. L. Adams.** Signed Francis Adams; see *DNB*.

3114 Note on a new poet [William Watson], 196–202. **Grant Allen.** Signed.

3115 The new yachting, 203–224. **Morell Mackenzie.** Signed; repr. *Essays*, 1893.

3116 Military education, 225–234. **Walter Wren.** Signed.

3117 On the relation of Painter's *Palace of Pleasure* to the English romantic drama, 235–243. **John Addington Symonds.** Signed.

3118 Private life in France in the fourteenth century (Part IV), 244–258. **A. Mary F. Robinson.** Signed as in no. 2970.

3119 Marriage and free thought, 259–278. **W. H. Mallock.** Signed M.; repr. *Studies*.

3120 The old economy and the new, 279–292. **William Smart.** Signed.

VOLUME 56 O.S., 50 N.S., SEPTEMBER 1891

3121 On the origin, propagation, and prevention of phthisis [tuberculosis], 293–309. **John Tyndall.** Signed. (Letter, pp. 595–596, signed **Godfrey W. Hambleton.**)

3122 Lowell in his poetry, 310–324. **Sidney Low.** Signed.

3123 A survey of the thirteenth century, 325–345. **Frederic Harrison.** Signed; repr. *The Meaning of History*.

3124 A pessimist playwright [Maurice Maeterlinck], 346–354. **William Archer.** Signed.

3125 An old Greek explorer of Britain and the Teutonic north [Pytheas], 355–364. **Karl Blind.** Signed.

3126 A Balkan confederation, 365–377. **James D. Bourchier.** Signed.

3127 M. Maurice Barrès, 378–391. **Edward Delille.** Signed; repr. *French Writers*.

3128 Social life in Australia (Part I), 392–407. **Francis W. L. Adams.** Signed as in no. 3113; repr. in *The Australians*, 1893.

3129 Swiss athletic sports, 408–415. **John Addington Symonds.** Signed; repr. *Swiss Highlands*.

3130 A triptych, 416–430. **Frank Harris.** Assigned in Contents; first 2 parts repr. *Elder Conklin and Other Stories*, 1894.

VOLUME 56 O.S., 50 N.S., OCTOBER 1891

3131 The emancipation of women, 437–452. **Frederic Harrison.** Signed; pp. 441–452 repr. *Realities & Ideals*, 1908, as "The Future of Women."

3132 *La Bête Humaine*: a study in Zola's idealism, 453–462. **John Addington Symonds.** Signed; repr. *Key of Blue*.

3133 The demoralisation of Russia, 463–

486. **E. J. Dillon.** Signed E. B. Lanin—no. 2871. (Letter, p. 906, signed **Frederick Roberts,** dated from Headquarters of the Army in India.)

3134   Under the yoke of the butterflies [the idle rich] (Part I), 487–505. **Auberon Herbert.** Signed.

3135   The Berlin Renaissance Museum, 506–515. **Wilhelm Bode.** Signed W. Bode; Contents gives first name.

3136   A national pension fund, 516–524. **Edward Cooper.** Signed.

3137   English and American flowers (Part I), 525–534. **Alfred R. Wallace.** Signed; repr. *Studies,* I.

3138   Women and the Royal Commission, 535–538. **Emilia F. S. Dilke.** Signed.

3139   Social life in Australia (Part II, concl.), 539–553. **Francis W. L. Adams.** Evidence for no. 3128.

3140   Impressions of England, 554–562. Signed: A Son of Adam.

3141   A human document (intro.; chaps. i–iii), 563–594. **W. H. Mallock.** Signed; novel published 1892.

VOLUME 56 o.s., 50 n.s., NOVEMBER 1891

3142   The French armies, 597–635. **Charles W. Dilke.** Signed. (See no. 3154.)

3143   Famine in Russia, 636–652. **E. J. Dillon.** Signed E. B. Lanin—no. 2871.

3144   Irish local government, 653–662. **T. W. Russell.** Signed.

3145   The free stage and the new drama, 663–672. **William Archer.** Signed.

3146   The emancipation of women [reply to no. 3131], 673–685. **Millicent Garrett Fawcett.** Signed.

3147   An Anglo-Indian story-teller [Rudyard Kipling], 686–700. **Francis W. L. Adams.** Signed as in no. 3113; repr. *Essays in Modernity,* 1899.

3148   *French and English* [by P. G. Hamerton], 701–707. **Matilda Betham-Edwards.** Signature.

3149   Slavery and fanampóana [forced labor] in Madagascar, 708–714. **Francis Cornwallis Maude.** Signed Vazaha; repr. *Madagascar.*

3150   The Bard of the Dimbovitza [Roumanian folk-songs], 715–718. **Frederic Harrison.** Signed.

3151   The "interviewer" abroad, 719–733. **Edward Dowden.** Signed.

3152   Correspondence. The modern Mark Antony [Boulanger], 734–737. **G. B. Malleson.** Signed.

3153   A human document (chaps. iv–viii), 738–772. **W. H. Mallock.** Signed.

VOLUME 56 o.s., 50 n.s., DECEMBER 1891

3154   The British army: the critics criticized —our army and its detractors, 773–792. Unidentified. Signed B. William St. John Brodrick to E. B. Iwan-Müller, Nov. 20, 1891, BM Add. MS. 51316, sends proof of "Our army and its detractors," which has been inspired by the War Office; asks for strict secrecy about "how you got it, as our man must lie perdu." With a rejoinder, pp. 792–795, signed **Charles W. Dilke.**

3155   English and American flowers (Part II, concl.): flowers and forests of the far West, 796–810. **Alfred R. Wallace.** Signed; repr. *Studies,* I.

3156   Compulsory Greek: reflections suggested by the Greek victory at Cambridge, 811–821. **J. B. Bury.** Signed.

3157   Winter cycling, 822–832. **R. J. Mecredy.** Signed.

3158   The Canadian census, 833–841. **J. G. Colmer.** Signed.

3159   An eighteenth-century singer: an imaginary portrait [of Antonio Vivarelli], 842–880. **Violet Paget.** Signed Vernon Lee—*DNB.*

3160   Phases of crime in Paris, 881–895. **Hugues le Roux.** Signed.

3161   British administration in West Africa, 896–905. **Thomas Fowell Buxton,** 1837–1915, prob. Signed F. Buxton; man cited was grandson of leader of anti-slavery movement and was concerned with African natives; see *DNB.*

3162   A human document (chaps. ix–xi), 907–932. **W. H. Mallock.** Signed.

VOLUME 57 o.s., 51 n.s., JANUARY 1892

3163   The Conservative foreign policy, 1–9. **Charles W. Dilke.** Signed.

3164   The new astronomy: its methods and results, 10–23. **Robert S. Ball.** Signed.

3165   A handful of lead [on hunting in Norway], 24–43. **Henry Pottinger.** Signed.

3166   Under the yoke of the butterflies (Part II, concl.), 44–64. **Auberon Herbert.** Signed.

3167   The blind guides of Italy [modern destroyers of artistic landmarks], 65–80. **Marie Louise de la Ramée.** Signed Ouida—*DNB;* repr. *Views.*

3168   Philip Marston, the blind poet, 81–90. **Coulson Kernahan.** Signed.

3169   The administration of justice in America, 91–108. **William Roberts.** Signed.

3170   Victor Hugo, "Dieu," 109–114. **Alger-**

VOLUME 58 O.S., 52 N.S., SEPTEMBER 1892

3258 How to drive Home Rule home, 273–287. **Frederic Harrison.** Signed.

3259 Mars, 288–303. **Robert S. Ball.** Signed. (Letter, p. 556, by the author—signed.)

3260 Cholera and cleanliness in Russia, 304–318. **E. J. Dillon.** Signed E. B. Lanin—no. 2871.

3261 The Strand improvements, 319–325. **Herbert P. Horne.** Signed.

3262 August Strindberg, 326–334. **Justin Huntly M'Carthy,** 1861–1936. Signed.

3263 New Japan, 335–345. **F. T. Piggott.** Signed.

3264 Mulready, 346–351. **Emilia F. S. Dilke.** Signed.

3265 Two Australian writers [A. L. Gordon and Marcus Clarke], 352–365. **Francis W. L. Adams.** Signed as in no. 3113; repr. *The Australians,* 1893.

3266 The late Prince Victor of Hohenlohe, 366–373. **Albert E. W. Gleichen.** Signed G., and in Contents, His Son; man cited was only surviving son of Prince Victor; see *DNB,* 1st suppl. under "Victor."

3267 Profit and loss, 374–416. **Frank Harris.** Signed; repr. *Montes the Matador and Other Stories,* 1910.

VOLUME 58 O.S., 52 N.S., OCTOBER 1892

3268 Mr. Huxley's controversies, 417–437. **Frederic Harrison.** Signed; repr. *Common Sense.*

3269 Progress in aerial navigation, 438–449. **Hiram S. Maxim.** Signed. (Letter, p. 700, signed **William Pole.**)

3270 The trend of trade unionism, 450–457. **H. W. Massingham.** Signed.

3271 Raphael, 458–469. **Walter Pater.** Signed; repr. *Studies.*

3272 The University of Fez to-day, 470–484. **Stephen Bonsal, Jr.** Signed.

3273 Victor Hugo: notes of travel [*Choses Vues*], 485–492. **Algernon Charles Swinburne.** Signed; repr. *Studies.*

3274 Russia and China, 493–507. **R. S. Gundry.** Signed; repr. *China and Her Neighbours,* 1893.

3275 Our weekly reviews, 508–516. **W. Earl Hodgson.** Signed.

3276 The settlement of Wales, 517–524. **W. Boyd Dawkins.** Signed.

3277 On the essential characteristic of French literature, 525–538. **Ferdinand Brunetière.** Signed.

3278 *The Barren Ground of Northern Canada,* 539–544. **W. Basil Worsfold.** Signed.

3279 Silver and Indian finance, 545–555. **Samuel Montagu.** Signed.

VOLUME 58 O.S., 52 N.S., NOVEMBER 1892

3280 An apologetic irenicon, 557–571. **T. H. Huxley.** Signed.

3281 Our molten globe, 572–584. **Alfred R. Wallace.** Signed; repr. *Studies,* I.

3282 Mr. Morley's task in Ireland, 585–594. **William O'Brien,** 1852–1928. Signed.

3283 A future school of English art, 595–606. **George Charles Spencer Churchill.** Signed Marlborough [Duke of Marlborough].

3284 Burmese traits, 607–620. **Henry Charles Moore.** Signed.

3285 Fruit-growing in California: a warning, 621–627. **William Roberts.** Signed.

3286 The Woman's Art Exhibition in Paris, 628–637. Signed: A Frenchwoman.

3287 Our oldest school [St. Peter's, York], 638–650. **Arthur F. Leach.** Signed.

3288 The insurrection of women: a criticism, 651–666. **J. B. Bury.** Signed.

3289 The life of M. Renan, 667–677. **Emily Crawford.** Signed; Contents adds "Mrs."; see *Index,* I, 859.

3290 A chat about Renan, 678–684. **Albert D. Vandam.** Signed.

3291 Table-talk of Renan, 685–688. **Hugues Le Roux.** Signed.

3292 British officials and French accusations, 689–696. **F. D. Lugard.** Signed.

3293 Correspondence. A Brazilian poet [Antonio Gonçalves Dias], 697–699. **William G. Abbott.** Signed.

VOLUME 58 O.S., 52 N.S., DECEMBER 1892

3294 An Australian view of India, 704–712. **Charles W. Dilke.** Signed.

3295 Mr. Huxley's ironicon [sic], 713–721. **Frederic Harrison.** Signed; repr. *Common Sense.*

3296 A plea for amnesty, 722–732. **J. E. Redmond.** Signed.

3297 Jupiter's new satellite, 733–745. **Robert S. Ball.** Signed.

3298 The American tariff: its past and its future, 746–760. **J. Stephen Jeans.** Signed.

3299 Mrs. Meynell, poet and essayist, 761–766. **Coventry Patmore.** Signed.

3300 The story of eleven days, May 7th–18th, 1832, 767–779. **Graham Wallas.** Signed.

emancipation of the intellect in the four-teenth, fifteenth and sixteenth centuries, 427–444. **John Addington Symonds.** Signed; repr. *The Last and the First*, N.Y., 1919.

VOLUME 59 O.S., 53 N.S., APRIL 1893

3346 Verdi's *Falstaff*, 445–453. **C. V. Stan-ford.** Signed.
3347 Politics and progress in Siam, 454–467. **George N. Curzon.** Signed.
3348 Some plays of the day, 468–476. **A. B. Walkley.** Signed.
3349 Superannuation of elementary teachers, 477–489. **Richard Temple.** Signed.
3350 Are individually acquired characters inherited? (Part I), 490–498. **Alfred R. Wallace.** Signed; repr. *Studies*, I.
3351 The poems of Louise Chandler Moul-ton, 499–504. **Coulson Kernahan.** Signed; repr. *Sorrow and Song*, 1894.
3352 The social remedies of the Labour party, 505–524. **W. H. Mallock.** Signed.
3353 The India Civil Service and the univer-sities, 525–534. **F. J. Lys.** Signed.
3354 Poor Abel! 535–542. **Marie Louise de la Ramée.** Signed Ouida—*DNB*.
3355 The new patronage bill, 543–546. **Robert C. Jenkins.** Signed.
3356 Scenery and the imagination, 547–573. **Archibald Geikie.** Signed.
3357 The financial clauses of the Home Rule Bill (No. I), 574–590. Signed: Liberal Unionist.

VOLUME 59 O.S., 53 N.S., MAY 1893

3358 Irish opinion on the Home Rule Bill, 593–609. **Edward Dowden.** Signed.
3359 The financial clauses of the Home Rule Bill (No. II), 610–619. **J. J. Clancy.** Signed.
3360 Is the universe infinite? 620–632. **Robert Ball.** Signed.
3361 The West Indies in 1892, 633–654. **Thomas Brassey.** Signed Brassey [Earl Brassey].
3362 Are individually acquired characters inherited? (Part II), 655–668. **Alfred R. Wallace.** Signed; repr. *Studies*, I.
3363 The Chatham Islands and their story, 669–690. **Henry O. Forbes.** Signed.
3364 On the rise and development of syn-thetical chemistry, 691–701. **T. E. Thorpe.** Signed.
3365 Rome revisited, 702–721. **Frederic**

Harrison. Signed; repr. *The Meaning of History*.
3366 An exchange for Gibraltar [the Canary Islands], 722–733. **J. W. Gambier.** Signed.
3367 The Veto Bill from the trade point of view, 734–744. **Charles Walker.** Signed. (See no. 3372.)
3368 A Jesuit doctrine of obedience, 745–752. **John Addington Symonds.** Signed.

VOLUME 59 O.S., 53 N.S., JUNE 1893

3369 The bank panic in Australia, 753–761. **Julius Vogel.** Signed.
3370 The currency crisis in the United States, 762–773. **Moreton Frewen.** Signed.
3371 The two salons [art exhibitions in Paris], 774–782. **Elizabeth Robins Pen-nell.** Signed.
3372 Drink and crime [reply to no. 3367], 783–796. **F. W. Farrar.** Signed.
3373 African legends, 797–828. **Henry M. Stanley.** Signed; repr. *My Dark Com-panions and their Strange Stories*, 1893.
3374 *Le Secret du Précepteur* [by Victor Cherbuliez], 829–835. **Marie Louise de la Ramée;** Signed Ouida—*DNB*; repr. *Critical Studies*, 1900.
3375 The City Unification Commission, 836–845. **Charles Harrison.** Signed.
3376 The poor children's holiday, 846–855. **Susan Mary E. Jeune.** Signed May Jeune.
3377 The interstellar ether, 856–862. **Oliver Lodge.** Signed.
3378 The Comédie-Française in London, 863–873. **Ange Galdemar.** Signed.
3379 In memory of John Addington Symonds, 874–880. **A. R. Cluer.** Signed.
3380 The Royal Academy (No. I), 881–889. **D. S. MacColl.** Signed.
3381 The Empire and its Institute, 890–895. **George Baden-Powell.** Signed.
3382 In correspondence: The deadlock in Madagascar: a remedy, 896–900, by **Francis Cornwallis Maude**—signed Vaza-ha, repr. *Madagascar*; The royal Irish constabulary and schedule VI of the Home Rule Bill, 901–904, signed: An Unionist.

VOLUME 60 O.S., 54 N.S., JULY 1893

3383 A visit to Prince Bismarck, 1–27. **George W. Smalley.** Signed; repr. *Studies of Men*, 1895.
3384 The evolution of our race [on C. H. Pearson, *National Life and Character*],

28–41. **Frederic Harrison.** Signed. (See no. 3393.)

3385 Beautiful London, 42–54. **Grant Allen.** Signed.

3386 The recent solar eclipse, 55–70. **T. E. Thorpe.** Signed.

3387 The dynasty of the Brohans, 71–76. **Ange Galdemar.** Signed.

3388 "The mausoleum of Ibsen" [on criticism of his plays], 77–91. **William Archer.** Signed.

3389 The progress of women's trade-unions, 92–104. **Evelyn March-Phillipps.** Signed.

3390 The Russian intrigues in South-Eastern Europe, 105–115. **C. B. Roylance-Kent.** Signed.

3391 Advance of the United States during one hundred years, 116–141. **S. G. Brock.** Signed Brock; see *Amer. WW*/1918–1919, where this title is cited.

3392 French movements in eastern Siam, 142–148. **Richard Temple.** Signed.

VOLUME 60 o.s., 54 n.s., AUGUST 1893

3393 An answer to some critics, 149–170. **Charles H. Pearson.** Signed. (See no. 3384.)

3394 The wanderings of the North Pole, 171–183. **Robert S. Ball.** Signed.

3395 The British farmer and the deluge of foreign produce, 184–197. **James Long.** Signed; Contents adds "Professor."

3396 The serpent's tongue, 198–206. **W. H. Hudson,** 1841–1922. Signed.

3397 The poor of the world: India, Japan, and the United States, 207–222. **Samuel A. Barnett.** Signed; repr. *Practicable Socialism.*

3398 The limits of animal intelligence, 223–239. **C. Lloyd Morgan.** Signed.

3399 Missionaries in China, 240–254. **R. S. Gundry.** Signed; repr. *China*, as chap. xi, "Causes of Antagonism."

3400 Plays and acting of the season, 255–266. **William Archer.** Signed.

3401 Thomas Paine, 267–281. **Leslie Stephen.** Signed.

3402 The needs of the Navy, 282–289. **Thomas Symonds.** Signed.

3403 The loss of the *Victoria*, 290–296. **G. Phipps Hornby.** Signed.

VOLUME 60 o.s., 54 n.s., SEPTEMBER 1893

3404 Mr. Gladstone and the currency, 297–316. **W. H. Grenfell.** Signed.

3405 Immortality and resurrection, 317–

328. **Grant Allen.** Signed; repr. *The Hand of God*, 1909.

3406 The origins of crime, 329–344. **W. Bevan Lewis.** Signed.

3407 The climbing of high mountains, 345–357. **W. M. Conway.** Signed.

3408 The military and the magistrates, 358–364. **George Irving.** Signed.

3409 Under British protection, 365–376. **J. Theodore Bent.** Signed.

3410 1793–1893, 377–389. **Albert D. Vandam.** Signed.

3411 A palace in the Strand, 390–404. **Martin A. S. Hume.** Signed; repr. *The Year after the Armada and other Historical Studies*, N.Y., 1896.

3412 England's right to the Suez shares, 405–411. **Cope Whitehouse.** Signed. (See no. 3449.)

3413 Development of athletics in the United States, 412–424. **Caspar W. Whitney.** Signed.

3414 Passages from an autobiography [of Humphry Thomson], 425–440. **Edward Dowden.** Signed.

VOLUME 60 o.s., 54 n.s., OCTOBER 1893

3415 The causes of pessimism, 441–453. **Charles H. Pearson.** Signed.

3416 The unemployed, 454–463. **Arnold White.** Signed.

3417 Atoms and sunbeams, 464–477. **Robert Ball.** Signed.

3418 The royal road to history: an Oxford dialogue, 478–491. **Frederic Harrison.** Signed; repr. as "The History Schools" in *The Meaning of History*.

3419 The balance of trade, 492–498. **George Tomkyns Chesney.** Signed G. Chesney; Contents gives first name and adds "General."

3420 The industrial position of women, 499–508. **Emilia F. S. Dilke.** Signed.

3421 The Pomaks of Rhodope, 509–523. **James D. Bourchier.** Signed; repr. *Life*, appendix.

3422 University systems, past and present, 524–538. **Patrick Geddes.** Signed.

3423 The electric fishes, 539–550. **John G. McKendrick.** Signed. (See no. 3209.)

3424 Notes of a journey in South Italy [pages from a diary], 551–557. **J. A. Symonds.** Intro. note.

3425 Current arguments for the outlawry of silver, 558–565. **Dana Horton.** Signed.

3426 Correspondence. The rehabilitation of silver, 566–568. **A. G. Schiff.** Signed.

VOLUME 60 O.S., 54 N.S., NOVEMBER 1893

3427 To your tents, oh Israel! 569–589. **G. B. Shaw** and **Sidney Webb.** Signed The Fabian Society; attr. in Shaw, *Collected Letters, 1874–1897.* (N.Y., 1965), p. 407.

3428 Mr. Rudyard Kipling's verse, 590–603. **Francis W. L. Adams.** Signed as in no. 3113; repr. *Essays in Modernity,* 1899.

3429 The lock-out in the coal trade, 604–615. **Vaughan Nash.** Signed.

3430 The ice age and its work (Part I): erratic blocks and ice-sheets, 616–633. **Alfred R. Wallace.** Signed; repr. *Studies,* I.

3431 Deli, in Sumatra: notes of a holiday visit by an idle official, 634–645. **R. W. Egerton Eastwick.** Signed.

3432 Is money a mere commodity? 646–654. **William Smart.** Signed; repr. in revised form, *Studies in Economics,* 1895.

3433 How to save Egypt, 655–664. **Cope Whitehouse.** Signed.

3434 Carl Wilhelm Scheele, 665–675. **T. E. Thorpe.** Signed.

3435 The psychology of labour and capital, 676–685. **Robert Wallace, 1831–1899.** Signed R. Wallace; Contents adds "M.P."; see *DNB.*

3436 The Ireland of to-day, 686–706. **Harold Frederic.** Signed X; claimed in Robert Sherard, "Harold Frederic," *The Idler,* XII (Nov. 1897), 539–540; see also Horace Plunkett, *Ireland in the New Century* (1904), p. 162. (Letter, vol. 61 o.s., pp. 138–140, by **Frederic**—signed "The Writer of the First 'X' Article" [no. 2819].) (See nos. 3438 and 3450.)

3437 Correspondence. The Imperial British East Africa Company, 707–712. **A. B. Kemball.** Signed.

VOLUME 60 O.S., 54 N.S., DECEMBER 1893

3438 The rhetoricians of Ireland, 713–727. **Harold Frederic.** Signed X;—evidence for no. 3436.

3439 Some unedited letters of John Keats, 728–740. **John Keats.** Title. Edited by **A. Forbes Sieveking.** Signed.

3440 The unemployed, 741–749. **Samuel A. Barnett.** Signed.

3441 The ice age and its work (Part II): erosion of lake basins, 750–774. **Alfred R. Wallace.** Signed; repr. *Studies,* I.

3442 A South Sea island and its people [the Maoris], 775–786. **Frederick J. Moss.** Signed.

3443 Self-government, 787–806. **W. S. Lilly.** Signed.

3444 The hunt for happiness, 807–823. **Francis W. L. Adams.** Signed as in no. 3113; repr. *Essays in Modernity,* 1899.

3445 Gounod (No. I), 824–837. **Marie Anne de Bovet.** Signed.

3446 Gounod (No. II), 837–841. **Charles M. Widor.** Signed.

3447 Clothing as a protection against cold, 842–848. **Robson Roose.** Signed; repr. *Waste.*

3448 Sea power: its past and its future, 849–868. **W. L. Clowes.** Signed Nauticus—*DNB.*

3449 Correspondence: England's right to the Suez shares, 869–872. **Cope Whitehouse.** Signed.

VOLUME 61 O.S., 55 N.S., JANUARY 1894

3450 The Ireland of to-morrow, 1–18. **Harold Frederic.** Signed X; evidence for no. 3436.

3451 Mr. F. Thompson, a new poet, 19–24. **Coventry Patmore.** Signed.

3452 Football [on professionalism], 25–38. Signed: Creston.

3453 The employment of women: the lady assistant commissioners' report, 39–48. **A. Amy Bulley.** Signed.

3454 The true discovery of America, 49–64. **J. W. Gambier.** Signed. (Letter, pp. 559–560, signed **Stoddard Dewey.**)

3455 The chemical action of marine organisms, 65–73. **John W. Judd.** Signed.

3456 The origin of mankind, 74–82. **Ludwig Büchner.** Signed.

3457 The French in India, 83–92. **L. B. Bowring.** Signed.

3458 The report of the Leprosy Commission in India, 93–102. **George Thin.** Signed; Contents add "Dr."

3459 Prince Alexander of Battenberg, 103–118. **James D. Bourchier.** Signed.

3460 The Triple Alliance in danger: a warning to England, 119–137. **E. J. Dillon.** Signed E. B. Lanin—no. 2871.

VOLUME 61 O.S., 55 N.S., FEBRUARY 1894

3461 The late Professor Tyndall, 141–148. **Herbert Spencer.** Signed.

3462 Oxford revisited, 149–158. **Goldwin Smith.** Signed.

3463 Fabian economics (Part I), 159–182. **W. H. Mallock.** Signed; repr. *Studies.*

3464 Science and Monte Carlo, 183–193.

Wallace, 1831–1899. Signed R. Wallace; attr. in *Life*, p. 487.

3506 The Royal Academy (No. II), 721–730. **D. S. MacColl.** Signed.

3507 The two salons [art exhibitions in Paris], 731–737. **Elizabeth Robins Pennell.** Signed.

3508 The new factory bill: as it affects women, 738–748. **Evelyn March-Phillipps.** Signed.

3509 Rype-shooting in Norway without dogs, 749–757. **G. A. Scott.** Signed.

3510 Local taxation: its amount and burden, 758–784. **W. M. J. Williams.** Signed.

3511 The mechanism of thought, 785–799. **Alfred Binet.** Signed.

3512 William Robertson Smith, 800–807. **J. G. Frazer.** Signed; repr. *Sir Roger de Coverley*, 1920.

3513 The disaffection in Behar, 808–816. **Donald N. Reid.** Signed.

3514 The worship of pottery, 817–825. **William Roberts**, 1862–1940. Signed as in no. 3477.

3515 Some aspects of musical criticism in England, 826–831. **C. V. Stanford.** Signed.

3516 The proposed Channel bridge, 832–836. **Albert, Prince de Monaco.** Signed.

3517 Silver and the tariff at Washington [an interview], 837–838. **Thomas B. Reed.** Opening paragraph. Intro. note, p. 837, possibly by **Moreton Frewen,** who in no. 3527, p. 119, vouches for Mr. Reed's sanction of this interview.

VOLUME 62 O.S., 56 N.S., JULY 1894

3518 Socialism and natural selection, 1–21. **Karl Pearson.** Signed; repr. *Chances of Death*, I.

3519 Poems in prose, 22–29. **Oscar Wilde.** Signed.

3520 A lesson from the [U.S.S.] *Chicago*, 30–43. **W. L. Clowes.** Signed Nauticus—*DNB*.

3521 The poetry of Robert Bridges, 44–60. **Edward Dowden.** Signed; repr. *New Studies*.

3522 A great experiment [of the Irish Congested Districts Board], 61–69. **T. W. Russell.** Signed.

3523 Notes on England: myself as a French master, 70–80. **Paul Verlaine.** Signed.

3524 The King, the Pope, and Crispi, 81–93. **H. R. Haweis.** Signed.

3525 Working-class setlements in Mulhouse and Milan, 94–103. **Charles Hancock.** Signed.

3526 Every-day cruelty, 104–115. **Louis Robinson.** Signed.

3527 Silver and the tariff at Washington [reply to no. 3517], 116–118. **T. H. Farrer.** Signed Farrer [Baron Farrer]. Rejoinders to Farrer's reply: 119–124 signed **Moreton Frewen;** 124–126 signed **J. Shield Nicholson;** 126–131 signed **F. J. Faraday.**

3528 Faust: a story in nine letters, 132–160. **Ivan Tourgénieff.** Assigned in Contents. Translated by Miss **L[ena] Milman**—Contents; and see no. 3532.

VOLUME 62 O.S., 56 N.S., AUGUST 1894

3529 The Boer question, 161–169. **H. H. Johnston.** Signed.

3530 Musical criticism and the critics, 170–183. **John F. Runciman.** Signed.

3531 A visit to Corea, 184–190. **A. Henry Savage-Landor.** Signed.

3532 Hamlet and Don Quixote, 191–205. **Ivan Tourgénieff.** Signed in Contents. Translated by **Lena Milman**—signed.

3533 A week on a labour settlement [in Australia], 206–213. **Margaret Elise Harkness.** Signed John Law—H&L.

3534 Bookbinding: its processes and ideal, 214–224. **T. J. Cobden-Sanderson.** Signed.

3535 Government life insurance: how not to do it, 225–241. **Julius Vogel.** Signed.

3536 The gold standard: an historical study, 242–262. **Brooks Adams.** Signed.

3537 The American sportswoman, 263–277. **Elizabeth Cynthia Barney.** Signed.

3538 Side-lights on the Second Empire (Part I), 278–292. **William Graham.** Signed. (Letter, p. 468, signed **G. H. Jennings.**)

3539 Where to spend a holiday (No. I), 293–299. **Susan Mary E. Jeune.** Signed as in no. 2362.

3540 Where to spend a holiday (No. II), 300–304. **Arthur Symons.** Signed.

3541 Where to spend a holiday (No. III), 305–314. **John Verschoyle.** Signed.

VOLUME 62 O.S., 56 N.S., SEPTEMBER 1894

3542 Some anarchist portraits, 315–333. **Charles Malato.** Signed.

3543 Politics and science, 334–351. **Karl Pearson.** Signed; repr. *Chances of Death*, I.

3544 The work of Mr. Pater, 352–367. **Lionel Johnson.** Signed.

3545 Oxford *v.* Yale, 368–382. **W. H. Grenfell.** Signed.

3546 The naval manoeuvres, 383–392. **W. L. Clowes.** Signed Nauticus—*DNB.*

3547 A journey to the sacred mountain of Siao-Outai-Shan in China, 393–409. **A. Henry Savage-Landor.** Signed.

3548 The Rajahs of Saràwak, 410–424. **Hugues Le Roux.** Signed.

3549 Imaginative currency statistics, 425–439. **J. Barr Robertson.** Signed.

3550 Shakespeare and Racine, 440–447. **Paul Verlaine.** Signed.

3551 Professor Henry Drummond's discovery [the law of altruism], 448–457. **Eliza Lynn Linton.** Signature.

3552 The municipal museums of Paris, 458–467. **Frederic Harrison.** Signed; repr. *Realities and Ideals.*

VOLUME 62 O.S., 56 N.S., OCTOBER 1894

3553 The Crimea in 1854, and 1894 (Part I), 469–497. **Evelyn Wood.** Signed; this and the four succeeding parts repr., revised and enlarged, with this title, 1895.

3554 Side-lights on the Second Empire (Part II, concl.), 498–512. **William Graham.** Signed.

3555 Our workmen's diet and wages, 513–526. **Thomas Oliver.** Signed.

3556 An antiquarian ramble in Paris, 527–537. **Frederic Harrison.** Signed.

3557 The extermination of great game in South Africa, 538–551. **H. A. Bryden.** Signed.

3558 The legislation of fear, 552–561. **Marie Louise de la Ramée.** Signed Ouida—*DNB*; repr. *Views.* (Letter, pp. 757–760, by the author.)

3559 In Syria, 562–573. **Frederic Carrel.** Signed.

3560 Madagascar, 574–581. **Francis Cornwallis Maude.** Signed Vazaha; repr. *Madagascar.*

3561 A pretender and his family [Duc d'Aumale of the Bourbons], 582–592. **Albert D. Vandam.** Signed; repr. *Third Republic.*

VOLUME 62 O.S., 56 N.S., NOVEMBER 1894

3562 The Crimea in 1854, and 1894 (Part II), 593–617. **Evelyn Wood.** Signed.

3563 Corea, China, and Japan, 618–635. **R. S. Gundry.** Signed.

3564 Burning questions of Japan, 636–650. **A. Henry Savage-Landor.** Signed.

3565 Hermann von Helmholtz, 651–660. **Arthur W. Rücker.** Signed.

3566 Women's newspapers, 661–670. **Evelyn March-Phillipps.** Signed.

3567 Rambles in Norsk Finmarken, 671–684. **George Lindesay.** Signed.

3568 Wordsworth's *"Castle of Indolence* Stanzas"* [written in his copy of Thomson's poem], 685–704. **Thomas Hutchinson.** Assigned in Contents.

3569 Symmetry and incident, 705–710. **Alice Meynell.** Signed; repr. *Essays*, 1930.

3570 Venetian missals, 711–717. **Herbert P. Horne.** Signed.

3571 The posibility of life in other worlds, 718–729. **Robert Ball.** Signed.

3572 The heart of life (chaps. i–iv), 730–756. **W. H. Mallock.** Signed in Contents; novel published 1895.

VOLUME 62 O.S., 56 N.S., DECEMBER 1894

3573 Foreign views of Lord Rosebery (No. I): from a French standpoint, 761–770. **Augustin Filon.** Signed with title "Author of *Profils Anglais.*" Translated by **Janet E. Hogarth**—Courtney, *Making of an Editor*, p. 155.

3574 Foreign views of Lord Rosebery (No. II): from a German point of view, 770–775. **Hans Delbrück.** Signed with title "Editor of the *Preussische Jahrbücher.*" Translated by **Janet E. Hogarth**—Courtney, *Making of an Editor*, p. 155.

3575 Mr. Robert Louis Stevenson: a critical study, 776–792. **Stephen Gwynn.** Signed.

3576 A threatened city [Pekin], 793–802. **M. Rees Davies.** Signed.

3577 Modern historians and their methods, 803–816. **Herbert A. L. Fisher.** Signed.

3578 Russia and the Balkan peninsula, 817–827. **Edward Dicey.** Signed.

3579 A true university for London, 828–844. **Montague Crackanthorpe.** Signed.

3580 The Crimea in 1854, and 1894 (Part III), 845–872. **Evelyn Wood.** Signed.

3581 The spread of diphtheria, 873–881. **Robson Roose.** Signed; repr. *Waste.*

3582 Uganda and the East African Protectorates, 882–894. **George S. Mackenzie.** Signed.

3583 The heart of life (chaps. v–vii), 895–914. **W. H. Mallock.** Signed.

3584 Correspondence: The lesson of the American elections, 915–920. **E. J. Cattell.** Signed Francis H. Hardy—Amer. *WWW/*1942.

VOLUME 63 O.S., 57 N.S., JANUARY 1895

3585 The question of a second chamber (No. I): a short way with the House of Lords, 1–14. **J. G. Swift McNeill.** Signed.

3586 The question of a second chamber (No. II): the House of Lords since the Reform Act, 14–26. **C. B. Roylance Kent.** Signed.

3587 Rubinstein, 27–36. **H. R. Haweis.** Signed.

3588 Alien immigration, 37–46. **Geoffrey Drage.** Signed. (Letter, pp. 501–507, signed **Arnold White.**)

3589 Count Moltke, field-marshal, 47–59. **Sidney Whitman.** Signed; repr. *Teuton Studies*, 1895.

3590 Lady Blennerhassett's *Talleyrand*, 60–76. **Frederick Clarke.** Signed.

3591 Madagascar, 77–86. **Francis Cornwallis Maude.** Signed Vazaha; repr. *Madagascar*.

3592 The collapse of China at sea, 87–100. **S. Eardley-Wilmot.** Signed.

3593 The Crimea in 1854, and 1894 (Part IV), 101–122. **Evelyn Wood.** Signed.

3594 The ethics of shopping, 123–132. **Susan Mary E. Jeune.** Signed M. Jeune; Contents adds "Lady"; see *BMCat*.

3595 The heart of life (chaps. viii–xi), 133–164. **W. H. Mallock.** Signed.

VOLUME 63 O.S., 57 N.S., FEBRUARY 1895

3596 England and the Gothenburg licensing system, 165–179. **Edwin Goadby.** Signed.

3597 The novels of Mr. Hall Caine, 180–196. **George Saintsbury.** Signed.

3598 Turkey and Armenia, 197–210. **Richard Davey.** Signed.

3599 The method of organic evolution (Part I), 211–224. **Alfred R. Wallace.** Signed; repr. *Studies*, I.

3600 Ancestor worship in China, 225–237. **R. S. Gundry.** Signed; repr. *China*.

3601 London pen and gown in the sixties and since, 238–249. **T. H. S. Escott.** Signed.

3602 Sidelights on socialism (No. I): Belgian socialism, 250–259. **H. G. Keene.** Signed.

3603 Sidelights on socialism (No. II): experiments by colonisation, 260–266. **Edward Salmon.** Signed.

3604 Sidelights on socialism (No. III): woman and socialism, 267–276. **Karl Knödel.** Signed; Contents adds "Dr."

3605 A note on Ibsen's *Little Eyolf*, 277–284. **W. L. Courtney.** Signed.

3606 The Crimea in 1854, and 1894 (Part V, concl.), 285–310. **Evelyn Wood.** Signed. (Letter, pp. 507–508, signed **Evelyn Wood.**)

3607 The heart of life (chaps. xii–xvi), 311–336. **W. H. Mallock.** Signed.

VOLUME 63 O.S., 57 N.S., MARCH 1895

3608 Presidents and politics in France, 337–346. **Augustin Filon.** Signed.

3609 Parliamentary questions of the day (No. I): the Irish Land Bill, 347–361. **T. W. Russell.** Signed.

3610 Parliamentary questions of the day (No. II): church disestablishment, 362–368. **H. M. Bompas.** Signed.

3611 Acting: an art, 369–379. **Henry Irving,** 1838–1905. Signed; see *DNB*.

3612 Lord Randolph Churchill, 380–392. **T. H. S. Escott.** Signed.

3613 Two modern poets [William Watson and John Davidson], 393–407. **H. D. Traill.** Signed.

3614 Politics and the Poor Law, 408–422. **Thomas Mackay.** Signed T. Mackay; for man cited see *BMCat*.

3615 Venetian art at the New Gallery, 423–434. **Claude Phillips.** Signed.

3616 The method of organic evolution (Part II, concl.), 435–445. **Alfred R. Wallace.** Signed; repr. *Studies*, I.

3617 Stéphane Mallarmé, 446–455. **Frederic Carrel.** Signed.

3618 An Algerian winter-resort: Biskra, 456–466. **Arthur Griffiths.** Signed.

3619 The crisis in Newfoundland, 467–474. **William Greswell.** Signed; Contents adds "Rev."

3620 The heart of life (chaps. xvii–xx), 475–500. **W. H. Mallock.** Signed.

VOLUME 63 O.S., 57 N.S., APRIL 1895

3621 Frederic Chapman, 509. **W. L. Courtney,** prob. Editor; Chapman was managing director of Chapman and Hall, proprietors of *FortR*.

3622 The situation in Egypt, 510–525. **W. T. Marriott.** Signed.

3623 The Liberal party and its candid friends, 526–539. **W. B. Duffield.** Signed.

3624 Mr. Balfour's *Foundations of Belief*, 540–550. **William Wallace,** 1844–1897. Signed W. Wallace with addition "Whyte's Professor of Moral Philosophy in the University of Oxford": see *DNB*.

3625 A system of coast defence, 551–564. **W. Laird Clowes.** Signed.

3704 Ferdinand Brunetière, 497–511. **Yetta Blaze de Bury**. Signed.

3705 Ireland: from the point of view of a disenchanted nationalist, 512–527. Signed: An Irish Nationalist.

3706 The expressiveness of speech: or, mouth-gesture as a factor in the origin of language, 528–543. **Alfred R. Wallace**. Signed; repr. *Studies*, II.

3707 The foreign policy of England, 544–556. **J. W. Gambier**. Signed.

3708 The asserted growth of Roman Catholicism in England, 557–565. **F. W. Farrar**. Signed.

3709 National defence (No. I): the naval manoeuvres, 566–581. **W. Laird Clowes**. Signed.

3710 National Defence (No. II): advancement in the army, 582–592. **Arthur Griffiths**. Signed.

3711 A Roman reverie, 593–608. **Alfred Austin**. Signed.

3712 English industry and Eastern competition, 609–620. **R. S. Gundry**. Signed.

3713 Islam and its critics: a rejoinder, 621–640. **Malcolm MacColl**. Signed The *Quarterly* Reviewer; opening paragraph identifies author as writer of *QR* no. 182 (July 1895), 220–253, which Murray's Register assigns to MacColl.

VOLUME 64 O.S., 58 N.S., NOVEMBER 1895

3714 Illiberal liberalism, 641–661. **W. S. Lilly**. Signed.

3715 The Burns and Dunlop correspondence, with extracts from some unpublished letters of the poet, 662–673. **L. M. Roberts**. Signed.

3716 Sectarian criticism [reply to no. 3698], 674–681. **Karl Pearson**. Signed. (Letter, pp. 959–960, signed **St. George Mivart**.)

3717 Brahmanism and *The Foundations of Belief*, 682–698. **A. C. Lyall**. Signed Vamadeo Shastri; attr. in *Life*, p. 477; repr. *Asiatic Studies*, 2nd series.

3718 Book collecting as a fine art, 699–706. **Julian Moore**. Signed.

3719 The Afghan alliance, 707–716. **E. Kay Robinson**. Signed.

3720 Prisoners on the move, 717–722. **Edmund R. Spearman**. Signed.

3721 The new study of children, 723–737. **James Sully**. Signed; repr. *Studies of Childhood* (N.Y., 1896) as "Introductory Chapters."

3722 The improvement of working-class homes, 738–746. **H. M. Bompas**. Signed.

3723 How Cuba might have belonged to France, 747–752. **Georgina Colmache**. Signed "G. Colmache"; Contents adds "Madame"; see *Blackwood Papers Cat.*

3724 Vegetarianism, 753–764. **T. P. Smith**. Signed, with addition of "M.B."

3725 How to counteract the "Penny Dreadful," 765–775. **Hugh Chisholm**. Signed.

3726 The beginnings of a republic [the Third French Republic] (Part I), 776–789. **Albert D. Vandam**. Signed.

3727 The sultan and his harem, 790–799. **Richard Davey**. Signed; repr. *The Sultan and his Subjects* (1897), I.

VOLUME 64 O.S., 58 N.S., DECEMBER 1895

3728 Lord Salisbury: from a French point of view, 803–812. **Augustin Filon**. Signed.

3729 Gustave Flaubert, 813–828. **Ernest Newman**. Signed.

3730 England in Nicaragua and Venezuela: from an American point of view, 829–842. **G. H. D. Gossip**. Signed. (Letter, vol. 65 o.s., p. 176, signed Lex.)

3731 Parties and policies (No. I): the failure of government by groups, 843–848. **William Rathbone**. Signed.

3732 Parties and policies (No. II): Unionist policy, 849–862. **J. S. Stuart-Glennie**. Signed.

3733 Hamlet—from an actor's prompt book, 863–878. **Herbert Beerbohm Tree**. Signed.

3734 Corea and the Siberian railway, 879–892. Signed: M.F.A.F.; perhaps A. F. Mockler-Ferryman, who was prof. of topography at Sandhurst, since this is a factual account of trip, during which the author noted with precision distances, altitudes, and temperatures, and especially visited a military installation, where he bought maps from the topographical section; man cited was contributing to periodicals at this time: see *Index*, I, 1015.

3735 The report of the Secondary Education Commission, 893–901. **T. J. Macnamara**. Signed.

3736 The beginnings of a republic (Part II, concl.), 902–918. **Albert D. Vandam**. Signed; *Athenaeum*, Dec. 21, 1895, pp. 870–871, shows that the passages purporting to be from Vandam's diary were plagiarized from Ludovic Halevy's *L'Invasion: Souvenirs et Récits*, 1872.

3737 Alaudarum legio [on the preservation of larks], 919–925. **F. A. Fulcher**. Signed.

3738 Mendelssohn: a critical estimate, 926–942. **H. Heathcote Statham**. Signed.

(Part I), 457–462. **Herman Cohen.** Signed.

3781 In the land of the northernmost Eskimo, 466–482. **Eivind Astrup.** Signed. Translated by **Carl Siewers**—p. 482n.

3782 Rhodes and Jameson, 483–494. **John Verschoyle.** Signed J. Verschoyle; Contents gives first name.

VOLUME 65 O.S., 59 N.S., APRIL 1896

3783 Egypt and its frontier, 499–509. **Arthur Griffiths.** Signed.

3784 Stray thoughts on South Africa (Part II): the Boer, 510–540. **Olive Schreiner.** Signed. Prefatory note by A Returned South African, signed **Olive Schreiner,** explains why she delayed so long in publishing this second part; see no. 3104.

3785 The Italian awakening, 541–546. **Marie Louise de la Ramée.** Signed Ouida—see *DNB.*

3786 Jules Lemaitre, 547–561. **Yetta Blaze de Bury.** Signed.

3787 The navy estimates and imperial defence, 562–575. **W. Laird Clowes.** Signed.

3788 Cardinal Manning: a reminiscence, 576–594. **Sydney Buxton.** Signed.

3789 Viewy folk, 595–604. **Eliza Lynn Linton.** Signature.

3790 The story of an amateur revolution, 605–612. Signed: A Johannesburg Resident.

3791 Some fallacies about Islâm, 613–623. **Malcolm MacColl.** Signed.

3792 The modern Jew and the new Judaism (Part II, concl.), 624–634. **Herman Cohen.** Signed.

3793 The agricultural programme, 635–650. **James Long.** Signed.

3794 Sudermann's novels, 651–662. **Janet E. Hogarth.** Signed.

3795 Russia and Bulgaria, 663–676. **Edward Dicey.** Signed.

VOLUME 65 O.S., 59 N.S., MAY 1896

3796 Tories or opportunists? 677–688.

3797 A forgotten Oxford Movement—1681, 689–703. **W. W. Hunter.** Signed; repr. *India of the Queen*, 1908.

3798 South Africa (No. I): Rhodesian affairs, 704–715. **H. L. W. Lawson.** Signed.

3799 South Africa (No. II): the high commissionership of South Africa, 716–723. **William Greswell.** Signed.

3800 The theory of the ludicrous, 724–737. **W. S. Lilly.** Signed; repr. *Studies.*

3801 The integration of the Empire, 738–750.

3802 The poet on the wolds [Frederick Wedmore himself: see intro. note and *BMCat.*], 751–758. **Frederick Wedmore.** Signed.

3803 The election petitions of 1895–6, 759–766. **Hugh Chisholm.** Signed.

3804 Czar and Emperor, 767–774. **Karl Blind.** Signed.

3805 The women of George Meredith, 775–790. **Garnet Smith.** Signed.

3806 To Akasheh [in the Soudan], and after, 791–800. **Arthur Griffiths.** Signed.

3807 Life from the lost Atlantis, 801–807. **St. George Mivart.** Signed.

3808 National education (No. I): Disraeli on national education, 808–817. **James W. Hoste.** Signed.

3809 National education (No. II): some reasons for the school board rate, 818–829. **Charles A. Sim.** Signed; Contents add "Major-General"; see *Army List*/96.

3810 National education (No. III): secondary education and the London School Board, 830–838. **Charles L. A. Skinner.** Signed.

VOLUME 65 O.S., 59 N.S., JUNE 1896

3811 The plain truth about Mr. Rhodes and the Transvaal, 839–856. Signed: Imperialist. This art. and nos. 3900 and 4122 were presumably written by the same "Imperialist" who wrote *Cecil Rhodes, a Biography and Appreciation,* 1897, either J. R. Maguire or J. S. Verschoyle; for a detailed discussion see E. R. Houghton, "John Verschoyle and the *Fortnightly Review,*" *Victorian Periodical Newsletter,* no. 3 (Nov. 1968), 17–21.

3812 *Jude the Obscure* [by Thomas Hardy], 857–864. **Robert Yelverton Tyrrell.** Signed.

3813 Russia and England in the Far East, 865–878. Signed: W.

3814 The Irish Land Bill of Lord Salisbury's Government, 879–892. **William O'Connor Morris.** Signed.

3815 On things Persian, 893–901. **C. J. Wills.** Signed.

3816 The modern Persian stage, 902–918. **James Mew.** Signed.

3817 Our neglected Tories, 919–927. **H. D. Traill.** Signed.

3818 Deterioration of soul, 928–943. **Violet Paget.** Signed Vernon Lee; repr. *Gospels of Anarchy*, 1908.

3819 The Olympic games, 944–957. **George Stuart Robertson.** Signed "G. S. Robertson, competitor and prizewinner"; see *WW/1966.*

3820 The Academy and New Gallery exhibitions, 958–974. **H. Heathcote Statham.** Signed.

3821 From Cobden to Chamberlain, 975–984. **Edward Salmon.** Signed.

3822 The work of the Chartered Company, 985–996. **Edward Dicey.** Signed.

3823 Wilhelm Liebknecht, the veteran leader of the German socialists, 997–1008. **Edith Sellers.** Signed.

VOLUME 66 O.S., 60 N.S., JULY 1896

3824 Stray thoughts on South Africa (Part III), 1–35. **Olive Schreiner.** Signed.

3825 Charilaos Trikoupes [Greek statesman], 36–47. **James D. Bourchier.** Signed.

3826 Coincidences (No. I), 48–69. **Friedrich Max Müller.** Signature.

3827 The muddle of Irish land tenure, 70–82. **William E. Bear.** Signed.

3828 A highway robber [the tramway], 83–90. **Marie Louise de la Ramée.** Signed Ouida—see *DNB.*

3829 The development of Lord Salisbury, 91–99. **T. H. S. Escott.** Signed.

3830 Public sentiment in America on the silver question, 100–109. **E. J. Cattell.** Signed Francis H. Hardy—see no. 3584.

3831 The doomed board schools, 110–122. **Robert F. Horton.** Signed.

3832 The salons, 123–136. **Claude Phillips.** Signed.

3833 The analytical humorist, 137–147. **H. D. Traill.** Signed; repr. *New Fiction* as "The Future of Humour."

3834 A chat about Jules Simon, 148–158. **Albert D. Vandam.** Signed; repr. *Third Republic* as "Jules Simon."

VOLUME 66 O.S., 60 N.S., AUGUST 1896

3835 The future of China, 159–174. Signed: L.

3836 The gorge of the Aar and its teachings, 175–182. **Alfred R. Wallace.** Signed; repr. *Studies,* I.

3837 Sir John Seeley, 183–198. **Herbert A. L. Fisher.** Signed.

3838 Luck or leadership? 199–206.

3839 Bi-metallism and the nature of money, 207–224. **W. H. Mallock.** Signed.

3840 Stray thoughts on South Africa (Part IV, concl.), 225–256. **Olive Schreiner.** Signed.

3841 Zola's philosophy of life, 257–271. **R. E. S. Hart.** Signed.

3842 The human animal in battle, 272–284. **H. W. Wilson.** Signed.

3843 Sunday closing in operation, 285–290. **Harry L. Stephen.** Signed.

3844 On an old American turnpike, 291–301. **A. G. Bradley.** Signed.

3845 The new French naval programme, 302–308. **C. B. Roylance Kent.** Signed.

3846 The making of a president, 309–318. **E. J. Cattell.** Signed Francis H. Hardy—see no. 3584.

VOLUME 66 O.S., 60 N.S., SEPTEMBER 1896

3847 Dr. Jameson's raid and the trial at bar, 319–332. **Edward Dicey.** Signed.

3848 Edmond de Goncourt, 333–349. **Yetta Blaze de Bury.** Signed.

3849 Italy (No. I): the Marquis di Rudini and Italian politics, 350–362. **Marie Louise de la Ramée.** Signed Ouida—see *DNB.*

3850 Italy (No. II): the Italians in Africa, 363–372. **J. Theodore Bent.** Signed.

3851 A modern view of Jesus Christ, 373–390. **John Beattie Crozier.** Signed.

3852 Some notes on poetry for children, 391–407. **E. V. Lucas.** Signed.

3853 *The Present Evolution of Man* [by G. A. Reid], 408–415. **E. Ray Lankester.** Signed. (Letter, vol. 67 O.S., p. 160, signed **Herbert Spencer,** with note by **W. L. Courtney**—signed Ed. *F.R.*)

3854 Ireland as a field for tourists, 416–425. **John A. Steuart.** Signed.

3855 The humanities of diet, 426–435. **Henry S. Salt.** Signed.

3856 The schoolmaster [A. J. Balfour] at St. Stephen's, 436–442.

3857 John Everett Millais, painter and illustrator, 443–450. **Joseph** and **Elizabeth R. Pennell.** Signed J. and E. R. Pennell.

3858 The Cretan question, 451–460. Signed: W.

VOLUME 66 O.S., 60 N.S., OCTOBER 1896

3859 The Russian ascendency in Europe, 461–471. **Lucien Wolf.** Signed Diplomaticus—see no. 2378.

3860 M. Paul Hervieu, 472–482. **Hannah Lynch.** Signed.

3861 Is insanity increasing? [reply to nos. 3308 and 3777], 483–493. **Thomas**

3904 A general voluntary training to arms versus conscription, 85–97. **H. M. Havelock Allan.** Signed. (Letter, pp. 972–974, by **Reginald Brabazon**—signed Meath [Earl of Meath].

3905 Marine garrisons for naval bases, 98–103. **F. C. Ormsby-Johnson.** Signed.

3906 A brilliant Irish novelist [William Carleton], 104–116. **G. Barnett Smith.** Signed.

3907 The efficiency of voluntary schools, 117–124. **William Boyd Carpenter.** Signed W. B. Ripon [Bishop of Ripon].

3908 Dr. Carl Peters, the leader of the recent anti-English agitation in Germany, 125–138. **Edith Sellers.** Signed.

3909 Old guns and their owners, 139–147. **Jean A. Visger** and **Denham Jordan.** Signed A Son of the Marshes—Eric Parker, *Surrey Naturalist* (1952), pp. 194–196.

3910 Mr. McKinley's opportunity, 148–159. **J. Lowry Whittle.** Signed.

VOLUME 67 O.S., 61 N.S., FEBRUARY 1897

3911 The hand-writing on the wall, 161–169.

3912 Ireland (No. I): the new Irish movement, 170–179. **Standish O'Grady.** Signed.

3913 Ireland (No. II): the financial relations of England and Ireland, 180–193. **Allan Innes.** Signed.

3914 How to work, 194–206. **Friedrich Max Müller.** Signature.

3915 Coventry Patmore: the praise of the odes, 207–217. **Louis Garvin.** Signed.

3916 The child in recent English literature, 218–228. **James Sully.** Signed J. Sully.

3917 Reformatory and industrial schools: report of the Departmental Committee, 229–238. **Robert Collier,** 1845–1909. Signed Monkswell [Baron Monkswell].

3918 The mission of Tennyson, 239–250. **W. S. Lilly.** Signed; repr. *Studies.*

3919 Spencer and Darwin, 251–262. **Grant Allen.** Signed; repr. *The Hand of God,* 1909.

3920 Morals and civilisation, 263–268. **H. G. Wells.** Signed.

3921 The girlhood of Maria Josepha Holroyd [Lady Stanley of Alderley], 269–283. **Margaret L. Woods.** Signed.

3922 The doom of cane-sugar: a colonial problem, 284–291. **George Baden-Powell.** Signed.

3923 Pitt and the Eastern question, 292–302. **W. B. Duffield.** Signed.

3924 Leighton and Watts: two ideals in art, 303–310. **H. Heathcote Statham.** Signed.

3925 An "entente" with France, 311–320. Signed: Veteran.

VOLUME 67 O.S., 61 N.S., MARCH 1897

3926 To the Right Hon. Arthur James Balfour: an open letter, 325–331. Signed: A Most Loyal Supporter.

3927 A study in Turkish finance (translation), 332–348. Signed on p. 347: A Turkish Patriot.

3928 The genius of D'Annunzio, 349–373. **Marie Louise de la Ramée.** Signed Ouida; repr. *Critical Studies,* 1900.

3929 Workers' insurance legislation in Germany, 374–386. **Henrietta Jastrow.** Signed.

3930 Our gentlemanly failures, 387–398. **S. H. Jeyes.** Signed; repr. in Sidney Low and W. P. Ker, *Samuel Henry Jeyes: A Sketch of His Personality and Work,* 1915.

3931 Justice for the taxpayer, 399–408. **Hugh Chisholm.** Signed.

3932 Joris Karl Huysmans, 409–423. **Gabriel Mourey.** Signed. Translated by **Janet E. Hogarth**—signed J.E.H. on p. 423n.

3933 China's present and future: the Reform party's plea for British benevolent neutrality, 424–440. **Sun Yat Sen.** Signed. AND **Edwin Collins.** Signed, p. 424n.

3934 The man [Edward] Gibbon, 441–455. **J. C. Bailey.** Signed.

3935 Lord Salisbury and the Eastern question, 456–466. **Lucien Wolf.** Signed Diplomaticus—see no. 2378.

3936 Mr. Rhodes's speeches, 467–478. **Edward Dicey.** Signed; with copious quotations from Cecil Rhodes.

VOLUME 67 O.S., 61 N.S., APRIL 1897

3937 Russia and the re-discovery [or re-union] of Europe, 479–491. **Olga Novikoff.** Signed.

3938 A German poet of revolt [Arno Holz], 492–503. **Laurie Magnus.** Signed.

3939 Our learned philhellenes, 504–512. **H. D. Traill.** Signed.

3940 After Khartoum, 513–523. **Arthur Griffiths.** Signed.

3941 Feminism in France, 524–534. **Virginia M. Crawford.** Signed.

3942 Crete, an object lesson, 535–545. **Malcolm MacColl.** Signed.

3943 Market wrecking, 546–555. **William E. Bear.** Signed.

3944 1497–1897: East and West, 556–567. **Edward Salmon.** Signed.

3945 Dangers to British sea-power under the present rules of naval warfare, 568–581. **Nicholas Synnott.** Signed.

3946 Financial relations between Great Britain and Ireland, 582–596. **William O'Connor Morris.** Signed.

3947 The Free Church in England, 597–607. **Robert F. Horton.** Signed.

3948 "Candia rediviva" [on Crete], 608–616. **George Baden-Powell.** Signed.

3949 South Africa (No. I): federalism in South Africa, 617–631. **William Greswell.** Signed.

3950 South Africa (No. II): Cecil Rhodes, 632–638. **C. D. Baynes.** Signed with title "Ed. of *The Johannesburg Standard and Diggers' News.*"

VOLUME 67 O.S., 61 N.S., MAY 1897

3951 A study in Turkish reform (translation), 639–659. Signed: A Turkish Patriot.

3952 Unpublished letters from John Stuart Mill to Professor Nichol, 660–678. **John Stuart Mill.** Title. Intro. note signed **William Knight.**

3953 The twentieth Italian parliament, 679–686. **Marie Louise de la Ramée.** Signed Ouida—see *DNB.*

3954 Professor William Wallace, 687–696. **J. H. Muirhead.** Signed.

3955 *Epic and Romance* [by W. P. Ker]: a review, 697–710. **Pearl Mary Craigie.** Signed with addition "(John Oliver Hobbes)."

3956 The Island of Sakhalin, 711–715. **Harry de Windt.** Signed.

3957 Degrees for women at Cambridge, 716–727. **J. R. Tanner.** Signed.

3958 The wrong way with the navy, 728–745. **William Laird Clowes.** Signed.

3959 The idea of comedy and Mr. Pinero's new play, 746–756. **W. L. Courtney.** Signed.

3960 Russia on the Bosphorus, 757–759. **J. W. Gambier.** Signed.

3961 Madame Bartet, Sociétaire of the Comédie de Française, 760–771. **Yetta Blaze de Bury.** Signed.

3962 The case against Greece, 772–781. **Lucien Wolf.** Signed Diplomaticus—see no. 2378.

3963 Crete and the Cretans, 782–810. **E. J. Dillon.** Signed.

VOLUME 67 O.S., 61 N.S., JUNE 1897

3964 A plot against British interests in the Levant, 811–824. **Malcolm MacColl.** Signed Vindex; claimed in *Memoirs and Correspondence* (1914), p. 205 and 206n.

3965 The Queen's Diamond Jubilee (No. I): the literature of the Victorian era, 825–838. **H. D. Traill.** Signed.

3966 The Queen's Diamond Jubilee (No. II): postal and telegraphic progress under Queen Victoria, 839–849. **J. Henniker Heaton.** Signed on p. 848.

3967 The Queen's Diamond Jubilee (No. III): agriculture during the Victorian era, 850–861. **William E. Bear.** Signed.

3968 The Queen's Diamond Jubilee (No. IV): the colonial empire of 1837, 862–870. **Edward Salmon.** Signed.

3969 The modern French drama (Part I), 871–886. **Augustin Filon.** Signed; this and the six succeeding parts repr. under this title, 1898. Translated by **Janet E. Hogarth**—see *BMCat.*

3970 Corsican bandits, and others, 887–894. **Hamilton Aïdé.** Signed.

3971 Captain Mahan's *Nelson*, 895–910. **William O'Connor Morris.** Signed.

3972 The new era at Hyderabad, 911–922. **Joseph Rock.** Signed.

3973 The naval and colonial policy of Germany, 923–934. **H. W. Wilson.** Signed.

3974 Imperial free trade, 935–945. **George Baden-Powell.** Signed.

3975 The Paris salons, 946–958. **H. Heathcote Statham.** Signed.

3976 The Thessalian war of 1897, 959–971. **Charles Williams.** Signed.

VOLUME 68 O.S., 62 N.S., JULY 1897

3977 Pascal, 1–18. **Leslie Stephen.** Signed; repr. *Studies*, II.

3978 England's military position: its present weakness; its vast undeveloped strength, 19–41. **H. M. Havelock-Allan.** Signed.

3979 The modern French drama (Part II), 42–56. **Augustin Filon.** Signed.

3980 England and the European concert, 57–65. **James W. Gambier.** Signed.

3981 A woman poet [Marceline Valmore], 66–85. **Blanche Warre Cornish.** Signed.

3982 The Burmo-Chinese frontier and the Kakhyen tribes, 86–104. **Edward Harper Parker.** Signed.

3983 Pacific blockade, 105–118. **T. E. Holland.** Signed; repr. *Studies in International Law,* 1898.

3984 The Princes of Orleans, 119–133. **Constance Sutcliffe.** Signed.
3985 The Greek War, as I saw it, 134–151. **Bennet Burleigh.** Signed.
3986 A lecture at Oxford: Gustave Flaubert, 152–164. **Paul Bourget.** Signed. Translated by **C. Heywood**—p. 164.

Volume 68 o.s., 62 n.s., August 1897

3987 Toryism and toil, 165–175. **Claude G. Hay** and **Harold Hodge.** Signed.
3988 Maurice Maeterlinck, 176–187. **Virginia M. Crawford.** Signed.
3989 Twenty years of cycling, 188–197. **Joseph** and **Elizabeth R. Pennell.** Signed J. and E. R. Pennell.
3990 Famines in India and their remedy, 198–214. **Romesh C. Dutt.** Signed.
3991 Dante as a religious teacher (Part I), 215–232. **Edward Moore.** Signed E. Moore; repr. enlarged in *Studies*, II.
3992 The shortcomings of our sporting literature, 233–243. **W. A. Baillie-Grohman.** Signed. (Letters, pp. 797–802, signed **Hedley Peek;** vol. 69 o.s., pp. 337–340, signed **Christoph Biedermann,** with title "Baron" and address "Raeknitz, near Dresden"; p. 680, signed **Hedley Peek.**)
3993 Handel and the Handel festivals, 244–258. **H. Heathcote Statham.** Signed.
3994 "The King of the Journalists" [Emile de Girardin], 259–276. **Albert D. Vandam.** Signed; repr. *Third Republic.*
3995 Mrs. Oliphant, 277–285. **Annie L. Coghill.** Signed.
3996 The defeat of the Armada, an anniversary object-lesson, 286–296. **Martin Hume.** Signed.
3997 Old friends with a new face [revised spelling of Indian names], 297–303. **St. John E. C. Hankin.** Signed.
3998 The present agitation in India and the vernacular press, 304–313. **M. M. Bhownaggree.** Signed.
3999 The Sultan and the concert, 314–320. **Lucien Wolf.** Signed Diplomaticus—see no. 2378.

Volume 68 o.s., 62 n.s., September 1897

4000 The unrecognised essence of democracy, 324–340. **W. H. Mallock.** Signed.
4001 Georges Darien, 341–357. **Marie Louise de la Ramée.** Signed Ouida; repr. *Critical Studies*, 1900.

4002 Dürer's visit to the Netherlands, 358–367. **W. Martin Conway.** Signed.
4003 The modern French drama (Part III): the Théâtre Libre, 368–385. **Augustin Filon.** Signed.
4004 Gibraltar as a winter resort, 386–394. **J. Lowry Whittle.** Signed.
4005 Cricket old and new, 395–406. **Frederick Gale.** Signed.
4006 Peasants of Romagna, 407–417. **Evelyn March Phillipps.** Signed.
4007 The science of meaning, 418–431. **J. P. Postgate.** Signed.
4008 A royal slave [man to language], 432–434. **Victoria Welby-Gregory.** Signed V. Welby; Contents adds "Lady"; see *Times,* Apr. 1, 1912, p. 11c.
4009 The speed of warships, 435–444. **Ralph George Hawtrey.** Signed.
4010 Socialism in France from 1876–1896, 445–458. **Paul Lafargue.** Signed. Translated by **Edward Aveling**—p. 458n.
4011 The Commission on Agriculture, 459–463. **Francis Allston Channing.** Signed.
4012 The Clondyke gold fields, 464–470. **Mark S. Wade.** Signed with title "M.D."
4013 The German Emperor's foreign politics, 471–480.

Volume 68 o.s., 62 n.s., October 1897

4014 Khartoum in sight, 481–489. **Arthur Griffiths.** Signed.
4015 At Arcachon, 490–503. **W. M. Fullerton.** Signed.
4016 The Irish lord-lieutenancy and a royal residence, 504–512. **J. G. Swift MacNeill.** Signed.
4017 Imagination in modern art: random notes on Whistler, Sargent, and Besnard, 513–521. **Violet Paget.** Signed Vernon Lee—see *DNB.*
4018 An object lesson in politics, 522–542. **W. S. Lilly.** Signed.
4019 Some recent French literature (No. I); Madame Geoffrin and her daughter, 543–558. **Janet E. Hogarth.** Signed.
4020 Some recent French literature (No. II): the hates of Napoleon, 559–570. **Charles Whibley.** Signed.
4021 Some recent French literature (No. III): the love-letters of Guy de Maupassant, 571–582. **Hannah Lynch.** Signed; for the fictitious nature of the letters see the *Academy,* 52 (Nov. 6, 1897), 375, and Nov. 13, p. 400.
4022 A statesman's autobiography [H. H. M. Herbert], 583–591. **T. H. S. Escott.** Signed.

4023 Scandinavia and her king, 592–605. **Constance Sutcliffe**. Signed. (See no. 4064.)

4024 The speed of warships: a reply [to no. 4009], 606–616. **William Henry White**. Signed W. H. White: see *DNB*/1921.

4025 An apology for unprincipled Toryism, 617–625. **Arthur A. Baumann**. Signed.

4026 The triumph of the Cossack, 626–636. **Lucien Wolf**. Signed Diplomaticus—see no. 2378.

VOLUME 68 O.S., 62 N.S., NOVEMBER 1897

4027 Our military requirements, 637–649. **G. S. Clarke**. Signed.

4028 Some notes on recent poetry in France, 650–665. **Gabriel Mourey**. Signed.

4029 The spirit of Toryism, 666–672. **Walter Sichel**. Signed.

4030 A note on George Meredith, 673–678. **Arthur Symons**. Signed; repr. *Studies*.

4031 The Bering Sea dispute, 679–691. **H. W. Wilson**. Signed.

4032 The modern French drama (Part IV): round about the theatres, 692–707. **Augustin Filon**. Signed.

4033 The case for "the Bechuana rebels," 708–717. **H. R. Fox Bourne**. Signed.

4034 A new study of natural religion [by J. B. Crozier], 718–731. **W. H. Mallock**. Signed.

4035 The future of British trade, 732–749. **John B. C. Kershaw**. Signed with addition "F.I.C." [Fellow of Institute of Chemistry]; see *BMCat*.

4036 Lord Roberts and Indian frontier policy, 750–765. **J. M'Leod Innes**. Signed.

4037 The choice for the sugar consumer, 766–777. **Hugh Chisholm**. Signed.

4038 Tennyson: a study in poetic workmanship, 778–783. **Harold Spender**. Signed.

4039 Lord Salisbury's dealings with France, 784–796. **Lucien Wolf**. Signed Diplomaticus—see no. 2378.

VOLUME 68 O.S., 62 N.S., DECEMBER 1897

4040 A French view of the British Empire, 803–816. **Pierre de Coubertin**. Signed; Contents adds "Baron"; see *WWW*/1940.

4041 Shakespeare's sonnets: the case against Southampton, 817–834. **William Archer**. Signed.

4042 The influence of Henry George in Eng-

land, 835–844. **John A. Hobson**. Signed J. A. Hobson; Contents gives first name.

4043 Lord Rosebery's apostasy, 845–852. **J. L. Garvin**. Attr. in Courtney, *Making of an Editor*, p. 166.

4044 *Annals of a Publishing House* [Blackwoods], 853–861. **John Cecil Russell**. Signed C. Stein—Blackwood.

4045 *La Révolte*, 862–874. **Villiers de l'Isle Adam**. Signed. Translation by **Mrs. Theresa Barclay**—p. 874, with intro. note also prob. by Mrs. Barclay; repr. 1901.

4046 The crisis in Spain (No. I): the Carlist cause, 875–883. **Melville Massue de Ruvigny** and **Cranstoun Metcalfe**. Signed Ruvigny [Marquis de] and Cranstoun Metcalfe.

4047 The crisis in Spain (No. II): can Sagasta save Spain? 884–887. **Leonard Williams**. Signed.

4048 Dante as a religious teacher (Part II, concl.), 888–904. **Edward Moore**. Signed as in no. 3991; repr. enlarged in *Studies*, II.

4049 Mounet Sully, 905–916. **Yetta Blaze de Bury**. Signed.

4050 England and France in West Africa, 917–925. **William Greswell**. Signed.

4051 The monstrous regiment of women, 926–936. **Janet E. Hogarth**. Signed. (Letter, vol. 69 o.s., pp. 334–337, signed **Edith Bradley**.)

4052 The poetry of William Morris, 937–947. **Nowell Smith**. Signed.

4053 Parliamentary difficulties in Austria, 948–960. **Emil Richter?** Signed Germanicus; see *BMCat* under Germanicus; cf. *Index*, I, 1063.

4054 Correspondence. Long speeches and bores, 961–962. **Frederic Carne Rasch**. Signed.

VOLUME 69 O.S., 63 N.S., JANUARY 1898

4055 The future of liberalism (No. I): the nemesis of party, 1–11. Signed: A.B.C.

4056 The future of liberalism (No. II): popular feeling and liberal opportunities, 12–21. Signed: Expertus. Possibly Malcolm MacColl, who had used this pseud. for a pamphlet in 1870, *Is Liberalism a Failure?*; much praise of Gladstone, of whom MacColl was a fervent admirer: *DNB*.

4057 *Cacoethes Literarum* [obsession with literature]: a French example, 22–30. **Charles Bastide**. Signed.

4058 [Introductory note to] Rose-leaves

from Philostratus, [translated into verse], 31. **Percy L. Osborn.** Signed, on p. 35.

4059 The growth of a thinker's mind: a study in Platonic chronology, 36–56. **Lewis Campbell.** Signed.

4060 Cycles and cycling: some notes of the shows, 57–67. **Joseph Pennell.** Signed J. Pennell.

4061 Ideal land tenure and the best makeshift, 68–80. **William E. Bear.** Signed.

4062 The problem of Gérard de Nerval, 81–91. **Arthur Symons.** Signed; repr. *Symbolist Movement.*

4063 My friend Robin, 92–95. **Gilbert Coleridge.** Signed.

4064 The Norwegian-Swedish conflict [a reply to no. 4023], 96–110. **H. L. Braekstad.** Signed.

4065 The adoption of street Arabs by the state, 111–118. **Emma Samuels.** Signed; Contents gives "Mrs. A. Samuels."

4066 The modern French drama (Part V): the new comedy, 119–134. **Augustin Filon.** Signed.

4067 Anti-Semitism and the Dreyfus case, 135–146. **Lucien Wolf.** Signed.

4068 The struggle of religions and races in Russia, 147–159. **E. J. Dillon.** Signed.

4069 Russia and her patients [Turkey, Austria, and France], 160–172. **Olga Novikoff.** Signed.

VOLUME 69 O.S., 63 N.S., FEBRUARY 1898

4070 M. Hanotaux, 173–188. Signed: °°°.

4071 The Millais and Rossetti exhibitions, 189–196. **Ford Madox Hüffer.** Signed.

4072 The county council election, 197–209. **H. L. W. Lawson.** Signed.

4073 Shakespeare and the Earl of Pembroke, 210–223. **Sidney Lee.** Signed.

4074 Corea, 224–238. **E. H. Parker.** Signed.

4075 Forty years in the lobby of the House of Commons, 239–254. **Frederick Gale.** Signed.

4076 Authors, publishers, and booksellers, 255–263. **John A. Steuart.** Signed.

4077 From Canton to Mandalay, 264–279. **William A. Johnstone.** Signed.

4078 A remedy for baby-farming, 280–286. **Frances H. Low.** Signed.

4079 Mr. Wilfrid Ward's *Cardinal Wiseman*, 287–307. **W. S. Lilly.** Signed; repr. *Studies.*

4080 Hope for the West Indies, 308–320. **George Baden-Powell.** Signed.

4081 A Monroe Doctrine for China, 321–333. **Lucien Wolf.** Signed Diplomaticus— see no. 2378.

VOLUME 69 O.S., 63 N.S., MARCH 1898

4082 Contradictions of modern France (No. I): the military paradox, 341–353. **Pierre de Coubertin.** Signed. (See no. 4135.)

4083 Reminiscences of Judah Philip Benjamin, 354–361. **Charles E. Pollock.** Signed. With intro. note by **John Morley?**—signed J.M., which initials he used in *Macmillan's*; see *Index*, I, 1161.

4084 The French on the Nile, 362–377. **Frederick Augustus Edwards.** Signed.

4085 "Marriage Questions in Fiction": standpoint of a typical modern woman, 378–389. **Frances E. McFall.** Signed Sarah Grand—see *CBEL.*

4086 The Tirah Campaign, 390–400. Signed: Eyewitness.

4087 An Elysian conversation, 401–407. **Charles Bastide.** Signed.

4088 The end of the new unionism, 408–422. **Louis Garvin.** Signed.

4089 Methods of voting: an electoral revolution, 423–431. **W. H. Howe.** Signed.

4090 Tragedy and Mr. Stephen Phillips, 432–435. **William Watson.** Signed.

4091 Side-lights of the revanche idea, 436–447. **Albert D. Vandam.** Signed.

4092 Hunting and its future, 448–460. **H. A. Bryden.** Signed.

4093 Recent attempts at copyright legislation, 461–467. **G. Herbert Thring.** Signed.

4094 Paul Kruger: an apology and a defence, 468–478. **F. Reginald Statham.** Signed.

4095 The Westminster "improvement" scheme, 479–485. **Edward Prioleau Warren.** Signed.

4096 The modern French drama (Part VI): the new comedy, 486–502. **Augustin Filon.** Signed.

4097 England and Japan, 503–512. **H. W. Wilson.** Signed.

VOLUME 69 O.S., 63 N.S., APRIL 1898

4098 Where Lord Salisbury has failed, 513–523. **Lucien Wolf.** Signed Diplomaticus— see no. 2378.

4099 The broken gates of death, 524–536. **W. B. Yeats.** Signed.

4100 Liquor traffic with West Africa, 537–560. **Mary H. Kingsley.** Signed.

4101 The posthumous works of Robert Louis Stevenson, 561–575. **Stephen Gwynn.** Signed.

4102 The French on the Niger: the "open door" in West Africa, 576–591. **Frederic A. Edwards.** Signed.

4103   The National Gallery and common sense, 592–600. **H. M. Paull.** Signed.

4104   Felice Cavallotti, 601–603. **Marie Louise de la Ramée.** Signed Ouida—see *DNB*.

4105   Books on big game, 604–611. **Theodore Roosevelt.** Signed.

4106   Can we rely on our war news? 612–625. **Michael MacDonagh.** Signed.

4107   Juvenile reformatories in France, 626–639. **Edmund R. Spearman.** Signed.

4108   The *Maine* disaster and after: the naval positions of Spain and the United States, 640–649. **Frederick T. Jane.** Signed.

4109   The story-teller at large: Mr. Henry Harland, 650–654. **Henry James.** Signed; repr. *American Essays*, ed. Leon Edel, N.Y., 1956.

4110   Friendly societies for women, 655–663. **J. Frome Wilkinson.** Signed.

4111   British trade and the integrity of China, 664–679. **Holt S. Hallett.** Signed.

VOLUME 69 O.S., 63 N.S., MAY 1898

4112   Egypt, 1881 to 1897, 681–699. **Edward Dicey.** Signed.

4113   Painting in enamels, 700–704. **Hubert Herkomer.** Signed.

4114   Havana and the Havanese, 705–722. **Richard Davey.** Signed.

4115   The influence of Balzac, 723–736. **Emile Faguet.** Signed.

4116   The Irish Local Government Bill, 737–751. **William O'Connor Morris.** Signed.

4117   Aubrey Beardsley, 752–761. **Arthur Symons.** Signed; repr. singly with this title, 1898, and in *Two Literatures*.

4118   A cure for indolence, 762–780. **Maurice de Fleury.** Signed. Trans. by **Isabel Wilson Hunter**—p. 762n.

4119   Prison reform (No. I): prisons and prisoners, 781–789. **William Douglas Morrison.** Signed.

4120   Prison reform (No. II): our female criminals, 790–796. **Eliza Orme.** Signed.

4121   The insolvent poor, 797–804. **Edward A. Parry.** Signed.

4122   The position and policy of Mr. Rhodes, 805–815. Signed Imperialist. Possibly J. S. Verschoyle or J. R. Maguire: see evidence for no. 3811.

4123   The Spanish-American War (No. I): the United States and Cuban independence, 816–832. **Frederick J. Matheson.** Signed.

4124   The mournful case of Cuba, 833–843. **G. H. D. Gossip.** Signed.

4125   The breakdown of our Chinese policy, 844–854. **Lucien Wolf.** Signed Diplomaticus—see no. 2378.

VOLUME 69 O.S., 63 N.S., JUNE 1898

4126   Cuba and her struggle for freedom, from personal observations and experiences, 855–866. **Fitzhugh Lee.** Signed with title "Major-General, late Consul-General of the U.S. to Havana."

4127   Wagner's *Ring* and its philosophy, 867–884. **Ernest Newman.** Signed.

4128   Friedrich Nietzsche and Richard Wagner, 885–897. **Beatrice Marshall.** Signed.

4129   Our navy against a coalition, 898–909. **H. W. Wilson.** Signed.

4130   Lord Rosebery and his followers (No. I): the present state of the Liberal party, 910–919.

4131   Lord Rosebery and his followers (No. II): the leaderless Liberals and Lord Rosebery, 920–926. **W. L. Stobart.** Signed.

4132   Lord Rosebery and his followers (No. III): politics in Scotland, 927–942. Signed: Academicus.

4133   Alphonse Daudet, 943–956. **Hannah Lynch.** Signed.

4134   The misgovernment of Italy, 957–976. **Marie Louise de la Ramée.** Signed Ouida —see *DNB*.

4135   Contradictions of modern France (No. II): the political paradox, 977–991. **Pierre de Coubertin.** Signed. (See no. 4082.)

4136   The Paris salons, 992–1007. **H. Heathcote Statham.** Signed.

4137   Mr. Gladstone (No. I), 1008–1019. **Malcolm MacColl.** Signed.

4138   Mr. Gladstone (No. II), 1020–1028. **Walter G. F. Phillimore.** Signed.

4139   Lord Salisbury and the Far East, 1029–1038.

VOLUME 70 O.S., 64 N.S., JULY 1898

4140   Mr. Gladstone, 1–10. **Arthur Hamilton Gordon.** Signed Stanmore [Baron Stanmore].

4141   Some stray letters of Mr. Gladstone [to Henry Raikes], 11–16. **W. E. Gladstone.** Title. Edited by **Henry St. John Raikes**—signed.

4142   Giacomo Leopardi: poet, philosopher, 17–35. **W. Knox Johnson.** Signed.

4143   Wei Hai Wei, our latest leasehold possession, being recollections of Wei

Hai Wei, with suggestions for a definite policy in the Far East, 36–43. **R. S. Yorke.** Signed.

4144 Free trade and cheap sugar, 44–55. **Charles S. Parker.** Signed.

4145 A dissolving empire [Austria], 56–71. **Francis W. Hirst.** Signed.

4146 The Philippine Islanders, 72–87. **Lucy M. J. Garnett.** Signed.

4147 The theatre in its relation to the state, 88–97. **Henry Irving**, 1838–1905. Signed; see *DNB*.

4148 The modern French drama (Part VII, concl.): Edmond Rostand and Jean Richepin, 98–114. **Augustin Filon.** Signed.

4149 Heredity as a social force, 115–126. **T. H. S. Escott.** Signed.

4150 French women in French industry, 127–140. **Yetta Blaze de Bury.** Signed.

4151 Can we hold our own at sea? 141–147. **T. A. Brassey.** Signed.

4152 The Women's Factory Department, 148–156. **May Tennant.** Signed.

4153 Coincidences (No. II), 157–162. **Friedrich Max Müller.** Signed T. Max Müller, but Contents gives "Rt. Hon. Professor F." (Letter, p. 346, signed **A. A. Bevan.**)

4154 Is there an Anglo-American understanding? 163–174. **Lucien Wolf.** Signed Diplomaticus—see no. 2378.

VOLUME 70 O.S., 64 N.S., AUGUST 1898

4155 The dynastic crisis in Spain, 175–204. Signed: A Spaniard.

4156 The real Cyrano de Bergerac, 205–215. **Joseph Knight.** Signed.

4157 Sierra Leone troubles, 216–230. **H. R. Fox Bourne.** Signed. (Letter, vol. 71 o.s., pp. 172–174, signed **W. E. B. Copland-Crawford,** with address "Vice-Consulate, Warri, West Africa.")

4158 The two Byrons, 231–248. **Walter Sichel.** Signed.

4159 Mr. John Morley, 249–262.

4160 A Shropshire poet [A. E. Housman], 263–271. **William Archer.** Signed.

4161 Protestantism and sacerdotalism, 272–288. **Malcolm MacColl.** Signed.

4162 Edward Burne-Jones, 289–306. **William Sharp.** Signed; repr. *Writings*, II.

4163 The prevention of consumption, 307–316. **Malcolm Morris.** Signed.

4164 Mr. Chamberlain as Foreign Minister, 317–325. Signed: Δ

4165 The individualist (chaps. i–iii), 326–345. **W. H. Mallock.** Signed Wentworth

Moore; repr. under Mallock's name, 1899.

VOLUME 70 O.S., 64 N.S., SEPTEMBER 1898

4166 The British record in China, 347–356. **Alexis Krausse.** Signed.

4167 The original intention of the "Monroe Doctrine," shown by the correspondence of Monroe with Jefferson and Madison, 357–368. **Theodore Andrea Cook.** Signed.

4168 The sonnets of M. De Heredia, 369–384. **J. C. Bailey.** Signed.

4169 Imperial penny postage at last: the revolt of the daughters [the colonies], 385–395. **J. Henniker Heaton.** Signed.

4170 The spy-mania and the revanche idea, 396–409. **Albert D. Vandam.** Signed; repr. *Third Republic.*

4171 Take care of the boys, 410–421. **B. Paul Neuman.** Signed.

4172 An all-British, or Anglo-American, Pacific cable, 422–428. **Charles Bright.** Signed.

4173 The Carlist policy in Spain, 429–439. **Melville Massue de Ruvigny,** and **Cranstoun Metcalfe.** Signed Ruvigny [Marquis de] and Cranstoun Metcalfe.

4174 A biography, 440–449. **Edward H. Cooper.** Signed.

4175 Kitchener and Khartoum, 450–459. **Arthur Griffiths.** Signed.

4176 Prince Bismarck (No. I): personal recollections, 460–470. **William Harbutt Dawson.** Signed.

4177 Prince Bismarck (No. II): the peace of Bismarck, 471–480. **Lucien Wolf.** Signed Diplomaticus—see no. 2378.

4178 The individualist (chaps. iv–vi), 481–506. **W. H. Mallock.** Evidence for no. 4165.

VOLUME 70 O.S., 64 N.S., OCTOBER 1898

4179 A diary at Santiago from May 18th, 1898, the day before the arrival of the Spanish fleet to July 18th, the day after the Americans took possession of the city (Part I), 507–526. **F. W. Ramsden.** Signed, with title "*Late British Consul for the Province of Santiago de Cuba.*"

4180 Bismarck and Richelieu, 527–547. **John F. Taylor.** Signed.

4181 The German Emperor and Palestine, 548–555.

4182 An Italian goldsmith [Salvatore Farina], 556–564. **F. Spear.** Signed; Contents gives "Mrs. Spear."

4183   Twelve years' work on the Congo, 565–574. **Demetrius C. Boulger.** Signed.

4184   The report of the Committee on Old Age Pensions, 575–580. **Thomas Scanlon.** Signed.

4185   Canicide, 581–586. **Marie Louise de la Ramée.** Signed Ouida—see *DNB*.

4186   A forgotten aspect of the drink question, 587–594. **E. D. Daly.** Signed.

4187   Indian currency policy, 595–604. **Edward Frere Marriott.** Signed.

4188   Rhodes redivivus, 605–619. **Edward Dicey.** Signed.

4189   A builder of the Empire: Sir George Grey, 620–626. **Louis Becke** and **Walter Jeffery.** Signed.

4190   The Anglo-German agreement, 627–634. **Lucien Wolf.** Signed Diplomaticus—see no. 2378.

4191   The individualist (chaps. vii–x), 635–664. **W. H. Mallock.** Evidence for no. 4165.

VOLUME 70 o.s., 64 n.s., NOVEMBER 1898

4192   The Fashoda question, 665–676. **Lionel Decle.** Signed.

4193   Stéphane Mallarmé, 677–685. **Arthur Symons.** Signed; repr. *Symbolist Movement.*

4194   The theological situation in India, 686–702. **A. C. Lyall.** Signed Vamadeo Shastri; attr. in *Life*, p. 477; repr. *Asiatic Studies*, 2nd series.

4195   Mr. Henry Reeve, 703–714. **T. H. S. Escott.** Signed.

4196   A diary at Santiago (Part II), 715–725. **Frederick W. Ramsden.** Signed.

4197   Mr. [Andrew] Lang on the origin of religion, 726–740. **John M. Robertson.** Signed. With a reply, pp. 740–744, signed **A. Lang.**

4198   Adventurers at the Klondike, 745–755. **T. C. Down.** Signed.

4199   Cape politics and Colonial policy, 756–764. **H. L. W. Lawson.** Signed.

4200   The return [report] on secondary education in the light of proposed legislation, 765–777. **Cloudesley Brereton.** Signed.

4201   The report of the Fry Commission [on Irish land acts], 778–792. **William O'Connor Morris.** Signed.

4202   Elizabethan adventure in Elizabethan literature, 793–809. **George Wyndham.** Signed; repr. *Essays in Romantic Literature*, ed. Charles Whibley, 1919.

4203   France of to-day, 810–820. Signed: An Anglo-Parisian Journalist.

4204   The individualist (chaps. xi–xv), 821–848. **W. H. Mallock.** Evidence for no. 4165.

VOLUME 70 o.s., 64 n.s., DECEMBER 1898

4205   New light on the Bahr-Gazal frontier, 849–863. **J. T. Wills.** Signed.

4206   The French colonial craze, 864–871. **Gaston Donnet.** Signed.

4207   Parnell and his power, 872–883. **Louis Garvin.** Signed.

4208   American expansion and the inheritance of the race, 884–892. **William Laird Clowes.** Signed.

4209   The telephone tangle, and the way to untie it, 893–900. **A. H. Hastie.** Signed.

4210   A vindication of Vedânta, 901–910. Signed: A Student in Vedânta. (Letter, vol. 71 o.s., pp. 358–362, signed **John Beattie Crozier.**)

4211   Montenegro and her prince, 911–927. **J. D. Bourchier.** Signed.

4212   The progress of Zionism, 928–943. **Herbert Bentwich.** Signed.

4213   Charles Dickens, 944–960. **Andrew Lang.** Signed.

4214   Some economic aspects of the imperial idea, 961–967. **Ethel Richmond Faraday.** Signed.

4215   The centenary of lithography, 968–983. **Joseph** and **Elizabeth R. Pennell.** Signed J. and E. R. Pennell.

4216   Diary of the Bishop of Killalla, 1798, 984–1001. **St. George Stock.** Signed.

4217   Fashoda and Lord Salisbury's vindication, 1002–1014. **Lucien Wolf.** Signed Diplomaticus—see no. 2378.

4218   The individualist (chaps. xvi–xix), 1015–1038. **W. H. Mallock.** Evidence for no. 4165.

VOLUME 71 o.s., 65 n.s., JANUARY 1899

4219   Recreant leaders, 1–9. **George F. Millin.** Signed The Author of *Life in Our Villages*—see H&L, VII, 332.

4220   Dean Liddell: as I knew him, 10–24. **Friedrich Max Müller.** Signature; repr. *Last Essays.*

4221   The Tanganika railway, 25–33. **Lionel Decle.** Signed.

4222   A group of Celtic writers [including W. B. Yeats], 34–53. **William Sharp.** Signed Fiona Macleod—see *DNB*.

4223   The powers and Samoa, 54–73. **John George Leigh.** Signed.

4224 Charlotte Brontë, 74–84. **W. Basil Worsfold.** Signed.

4225 Competitive examinations for Woolwich and Sandhurst, 85–99. **Hely Hutchinson Almond.** Signed.

4226 Language and style, 100–109. **Charles Whibley.** Signed.

4227 Cycles and cycling, 110–123. **Joseph Pennell.** Signed.

4228 After reading Horace Walpole, 124–128. **G. S. Street.** Signed; repr. *A Book of Essays*, 1902.

4229 The Disraeli of Liberalism [Lord Rosebery], 129–143. **J. L. Garvin.** Attr. in Courtney, *Making of an Editor*, p. 166.

4230 The individualist (chaps. xx–xxiii), 144–171. **W. H. Mallock.** Evidence for no. 4165.

4231 Educating the Liberals: Lord Rosebery and Home Rule, 175–185.

4232 France since 1814 (Parts I and II), 186–211. **Pierre de Coubertin.** Signed.

4233 New light on Marlowe and Kyd, 212–225. **Frederick S. Boas.** Signed.

4234 Newfoundland's opportunity, 226–231. **Beckles Willson.** Signed.

4235 A prime minister [Gaurîshankar] and a child-wife, 232–248. **Friedrich Max Müller.** Signature.

4236 The Liberal party and local veto, 249–258. **Frederick Dolman.** Signed.

4237 The war game in South Africa, 259–266. **Morley Roberts.** Signed.

4238 A new novelist: Albert du Bois, 267–273. **Richard Davey.** Signed.

4239 The commercial future (No. I): the new struggle for life among nations (from an American standpoint), 274–283. **Brooks Adams.** Signed.

4240 The commercial future (No. II): the commercial sovereignty of the seas: the coming competition, 284–299. **Benjamin Taylor.** Signed.

4241 The United Irish League in County Mayo, 300–305. Signed: An Irish Unionist.

4242 Butler's *Life of Colley*, 306–315. **Arthur Griffiths.** Signed.

4243 Dangerous trades: a case for legislation, 316–325. **H. J. Tennant.** Signed.

4244 The settling day [with France], 326–335. **Geoffrey C. Noel.** Signed.

4245 The individualist (chaps. xxiv–xxv), 336–357. **W. H. Mallock.** Evidence for no. 4165.

4246 Lord Carnarvon and Home Rule, 363–380.

4247 The *Tourmaline* expedition and the opening of the Sus, 381–389. **A. Gybbon Spilsbury.** Signed; Contents adds "Major"; repr. much expanded, *The "Tourmaline" Expedition*, 1906, under A. Gibbon Spilsbury in *BMCat*.

4248 Pessimism and tragedy, 390–400. **William Archer.** Signed.

4249 General Wood at Santiago: Americanizing a Cuban city, 401–412. **Henry Harrison Lewis.** Signed.

4250 Wagner and Schopenhauer, 413–432. **William Ashton Ellis.** Signed.

4251 The Congo State and its critics, 433–444. **Demetrius C. Boulger.** Signed.

4252 Old age pensions made easy, 445–459. **George F. Millin.** Signed The Author of *Life in Our Villages*—see no. 4219.

4253 Italy (No. I): Vatican and Quirinal, 460–474. **Wilfrid Ward.** Signed. (Letter, p. 722, signed by **W. S. Lilly.**)

4254 Italy (No. II): Vilfredo Pareto on Italy, 475–485. **Vilfredo Pareto.** Title and intro. note. Intro. note and conclusion by **Marie Louise de la Ramée**—signed Ouida —see *DNB*.

4255 Jean Ingelow, 486–499. **Mabel C. Birchenough.** Signed.

4256 Is it peace?—the progress of Anglo-French negotiations, 500–510. **Lucien Wolf.** Signed Diplomaticus—see no. 2378.

4257 The individualist (chaps. xxvi–xxvii), 511–538. **W. H. Mallock.** Evidence for no. 4165.

4258 Lord Salisbury's new Chinese policy, 539–550. **Lucien Wolf.** Signed Diplomaticus—see no. 2378.

4259 Sir Robert Peel, 551–563. **Francis Allston Channing.** Signed.

4260 The debt and the deficit, 564–571. **Hugh Chisholm.** Signed.

4261 France since 1814 (Part III): the great juggling of 1830, 572–585. **Pierre de Coubertin.** Signed.

4262 The Great Central Railway, 586–592. **Charles G. Harper.** Signed.

4263 The present peace demonstrations an obstacle to the true cause of peace amongst mankind, 593–603. **V. Tchertkoff.** Signed.

4264 Romanism in fiction, 604–622. **Walter Sichel.** Signed W. Sichel; Contents gives first name.

4265 Lawlessness in the Church, 623–633.

4266 The spoiling of St. Paul's, 634–646. **Samuel Howe.** Signed.

4267 The origin of totemism (Part I), 647–665. **J. G. Frazer.** Signed; repr. *Totemism and Exogamy* (1910), I.

4268 The unity of the religious idea, 666–679. **Oswald John Simon.** Signed.

4269 Bonapartism, 680–693. Signed: An Anglo-Parisian Journalist.

4270 The individualist (chaps. xxviii–xxxi), 694–721. **W. H. Mallock.** Evidence for no. 4165.

VOLUME 71 O.S., 65 N.S., MAY 1899

4271 The Samoan crisis and its causes, 723–734. **John George Leigh.** Signed.

4272 Finland and the Tsar, 735–744. **R. Nisbet Bain.** Signed.

4273 Balzac, 745–757. **Arthur Symons.** Signed; repr. *Studies*.

4274 Cardinals, consistories, and conclaves, 758–773. **Richard Davey.** Signed.

4275 The lessons of the Irish county councils elections, 774–782. Signed: Milesius.

4276 A seventeen hours' working day, 783–788. **Gertrude M. Tuckwell.** Signed, with title "Hon. Sec. Women's Trade Union League."

4277 A character of "The Trimmer," 789–816. **Helen C. Foxcroft.** Signed H. C. Foxcroft; for woman cited see *BMCat.*

4278 France since 1814 (Part IV)—1846: Louis Philippe almost a king, 817–834. **Pierre de Coubertin.** Signed.

4279 The origin of totemism (Part II, concl.), 835–852. **J. G. Frazer.** Signed.

4280 The teacher problem, 853–862. **Harold Hodge.** Signed.

4281 Dramatic convention, with special reference to the soliloquy, 863–870. **H. M. Paull.** Signed.

4282 The vanishing of universal peace, 871–880. **Lucien Wolf.** Signed Diplomaticus—see no. 2378.

4283 The judgment of Borso: a little novel of Ferrara (chaps. i–iv), 881–898. **Maurice Hewlett.** Signed; repr. *Little Novels of Italy*, 1899.

VOLUME 71 O.S., 65 N.S., JUNE 1899

4284 Russia's great naval enterprise: the establishment of intercourse between the Baltic and the Black Sea (Part I), 899–906. Signed: S. Perhaps George Strachey, who wrote *FM* nos. 3214 and 3227 in 1854 showing the same detailed knowledge of Russia, especially of its navy (in particular, cf. p. 208 here on the wooden frames called camels with p. 613 and note in *FM* no. 3227); the author quotes from Foreign Office, diplomatic, and consular reports, all of which would have been readily accessible to Strachey; the style has the same straightforward, factual, sometimes statistical character as that of *FM* nos. 3214 and 3227; the author also exhibits the same distrust of Russia as in the *FM* arts. and in *QR* no. 1979 in 1878.

4285 The tercentenary of Valasquez, 907–916. **Havelock Ellis.** Signed; repr. *The Soul of Spain*, 1908.

4286 Joints in our educational armour, 917–930. **T. J. Macnamara.** Signed.

4287 Egypt after Omdurman, 931–942. **J. Lowry Whittle.** Signed.

4288 Two cities: London and Peking, 943–954. **Archibald Little.** Signed.

4289 The Declaration of Paris, 955–968. **J. G. Butcher.** Signed.

4290 Twenty-five years' financial policy, 969–986. **Joseph Ackland.** Signed.

4291 Thomas Hood's first centenary, 987–1003. **H. C. Shelley.** Signed.

4292 "Made in Germany" and how to stop it: a practical proposal [commercial education], 1004–1011. **H. de B. Gibbins.** Signed.

4293 Mr. Frazer's theory of totemism, 1012–1025. **Andrew Lang.** Signed.

4294 France since 1814 (Part V)—1848: four months a republic, 1026–1037. **Pierre de Coubertin.** Signed.

4295 The Transvaal crisis: a voice from the rand, 1038–1047. Signed: Uitlander.

4296 The judgment of Borso (chaps. v–x, concl.), 1048–1070. **Maurice Hewlett.** Signed.

VOLUME 72 O.S., 66 N.S., JULY 1899

4297 A Palmerston—with nerves [Lord Rosebery], 1–16.

4298 Rallying-points for the Liberal party, 17–25. Signed: K.

4299 Souvenirs of some court favourites, 26–36. **Emily Charlotte Boyle.** Signed E. C. Cork and Orrery [Countess of Cork and Orrery].

4300 China: spheres of interest, and the open door, 37–52. **R. S. Gundry.** Signed.

4301 The mean [typical] Englishman, 53–62. **Joseph Jacobs.** Signed.

4302 In the twilight, 63–72. **Jean Owen Visger** and **Denham Jordan.** Signed A Son of the Marshes—see Eric Parker, *Surrey Naturalist* (1952), pp. 194–196.

4303 Lamennais, 73–84. **W. S. Lilly.** Signed; repr. *Studies.*

4304 The legal advantages of being a drunkard, 85–100. **E. D. Daly.** Signed.

4305 The Academy, the New Gallery, and the Guildhall, 101–112. **H. Heathcote Statham.** Signed.

4306 Sarah Bernhardt, 113–122. **Yetta Blaze de Bury.** Signed.

4307 The Shop Seats Bill movement, 123–131. **Margaret Hardinge Irwin.** Signed.

4308 Plays of the season, 132–139. **William Archer.** Signed.

4309 A regenerated France (?), 140–150. Signed: An Anglo-Parisian Journalist.

4310 The International Council of Women (No. I), 151–155. **Gilbert Parker.** Signed.

4311 The International Council of Women (No. II), 156–159. **May Wright Sewall.** Signed.

4312 The "New Situation" in South Africa, 160–171. **Lucien Wolf.** Signed Diplomaticus—see no. 2378.

4313 Anima semplicetta, or The Duchess of Nona (chaps. i–v), 172–186. **Maurice Hewlett.** Signed at end of chap. xi; repr. *Little Novels of Italy,* 1899.

VOLUME 72 O.S., 66 N.S., AUGUST 1899

4314 British and Dutch in South Africa, 187–196. **H. A. Bryden.** Signed. (Cf. no. 4331.)

4315 Villiers de L'Isle Adam, 197–204. **Arthur Symons.** Signed; repr. *Symbolist Movement.*

4316 Russia's great naval enterprise (Part II, concl.), 205–216. Signed: S. Perhaps George Strachey; cf. no. 4284.

4317 Bicycles as railway luggage, 217–226. **J. Allsebrook Simon.** Signed.

4318 New lights on Ibsen's *Brand*, 227–239. **Mabel A. St. Clair Stobart.** Signed M. A. Stobart; claimed in *Miracles and Adventures* (1935), p. 359.

4319 France since 1814 (Part VI)—1856: a bright situation and the way out, 240–255. **Pierre de Coubertin.** Signed.

4320 Hotels at home and abroad, 256–263. **Arthur Griffiths.** Signed.

4321 The dying of death, 264–269. **Joseph Jacobs.** Signed.

4322 Morocco up to date, 270–281. **H. R. Haweis.** Signed.

4323 Why is Unionism unpopular? 282–290. **J. Louis Garvin.** Signed.

4324 London buildings, 291–316. **Christine Sinclair Bremner,** prob. Signed C. S. Bremner; see Part B below.

4325 Shakespeare and Molière, 317–334. **Jules Claretie.** Signed. Trans. by **William Beatty-Kingston**—p. 334n.

4326 The struggle for South African supremacy, 335–347. **Lucien Wolf.** Signed Diplomaticus—see no. 2378.

4327 Anima semplicetta (chaps. vi–xi, concl.), 348–370. **Maurice Hewlett.** Signed.

VOLUME 72 O.S., 66 N.S., SEPTEMBER 1899

4328 The philosophy of the Dreyfus case, 371–384. **André Godfernaux.** Signed.

4329 Wanted: a redistribution bill, 385–394. **F. St. John Morrow.** Signed.

4330 A new Caroline commonplace book, 395–416. **Alice Law.** Signed. (Letter, p. 720, signed **Joseph Knight.**)

4331 Peace or war in South Africa [reply to no. 4314], 417–428. **Edward Dicey.** Signed. (Letter, pp. 717–719, signed **H. A. Bryden.**)

4332 English head masters and their schools, 429–447. **John Charles Tarver.** Signed.

4333 The Yangtze region, 448–463, **R. S. Gundry.** Signed.

4334 King Alfred's country, 464–474. **William Greswell.** Signed.

4335 Literary courtships, 475–489. **Eleanor A. Towle.** Signed.

4336 The Alaskan Boundary question, 490–499. **Horace Townsend.** Signed.

4337 M. Brunetière, 500–509. **Charles Bastide.** Signed.

4338 Criminal appeal and the prerogative of mercy, 510–518. Signed: X.Y.Z.

4339 The arrest of Thomas Kyd, 519–522. **Frederick S. Boas.** Signed.

4340 The Government and London architecture, 523–532. **Charles G. Harper.** Signed.

4341 The genesis of the German clerk, 533–536. **J. J. Findlay.** Signed.

4342 Bergen and the coalition nightmare, 537–546. **Lucien Wolf.** Signed Diplomaticus—see no. 2378.

VOLUME 72 O.S., 66 N.S., OCTOBER 1899

4343 The Rennes verdict and the Dreyfus

case: its military aspect, 547–562. Signed: An English Officer.

4344 The "Dreyfus scandal" of English history [the Popish plot], 563–575. **Helen C. Foxcroft.** Signed as in no. 4277.

4345 History in advertisements, 576–588. **Andrew Reid.** Signed.

4346 The problem of the aged poor, 589–596. **Geoffrey Drage.** Signed.

4347 Eugene Piot: a precursor: anecdotes and recollections, 597–611. **Charles Yriarte.** Signed.

4348 Australian federation: from the inside, 612–621. **Harold G. Parsons.** Signed.

4349 The sea story of Australia, 622–632. **Louis Becke** and **Walter Jeffery.** Signed.

4350 Mrs. Gaskell's short tales, 633–643. **Frances H. Low.** Signed.

4351 The Lambeth decision, 644–658. **Malcolm MacColl.** Signed. (Letter, p. 896, signed **Lewis T. Dibdin.**) (Cf. no. 4374.)

4352 The true meaning of the "crisis in the Church," 659–668. Signed: An Oxford Tutor.

4353 Municipal trading, 669–682. **Walter Bond.** Signed.

4354 The Paris market-women, 683–695. **Albert D. Vandam.** Signed.

4355 A romance in scholarship, 696–704. **Joseph Jacobs.** Signed.

4356 Mr. Chamberlain's mistakes, 705–716. **Lucien Wolf.** Signed Diplomaticus—see no. 2378.

VOLUME 72 O.S., 66 N.S., NOVEMBER 1899

4357 A South African settlement, 721–733.

4358 John Donne, 734–745. **Arthur Symons.** Signed; repr. *Two Literatures*.

4359 The art of flying, 746–758. **W. E. Garrett Fisher.** Signed.

4360 Direct railway communication between India and China, 759–768. **James Stuart.** Signed with title "Engineer Assam-Bengal Railway."

4361 The menacing comet, 769–779. **Edward Vincent Heward.** Signed.

4362 *The Letters of Mary Sibylla Holland,* 780–792. **Edith Sichel.** Signed.

4363 The Venezuelan award [re British colonies in So. America], 793–802. **Harry R. Whates.** Signed as in no. 3760.

4364 Unwritten literary laws, 803–814. **Marie Louise de la Ramée.** Signed Ouida; repr. *Critical Studies,* 1900.

4365 Maritime expeditions in relation to sea-power, 815–826. **F. C. Ormsby-Johnson.** Signed.

4366 The need to believe: an agnostic's notes on Professor Wm. James, 827–842. **Violet Paget.** Signed Vernon Lee; repr. *Gospels of Anarchy,* 1908.

4367 France since 1814 (Part VII): the other slope of the mountain—1860, 843–855. **Pierre de Coubertin.** Signed.

4368 Transvaal independence and England's future, 856–865. **Karl Blind.** Signed.

4369 The war in South Africa (Part I), 866–878.

4370 The divine adventure (Part I), 879–895. **William Sharp.** Signed Fiona Macleod—see *DNB*; repr. *The Writings of Fiona Macleod* (N.Y., 1909–1910), IV.

VOLUME 72 O.S., 66 N.S., DECEMBER 1899

4371 Professor [James] Ward's *Naturalism and Agnosticism,* 897–904. **Herbert Spencer.** Signed.

4372 A gleam in the darkness, 905–913. **Hamilton Aidé.** Signed.

4373 The Russian railway policy in Asia, 914–925. **R. E. C. Long.** Signed.

4374 Canon MacColl's new convocation [reply to no. 4351], 926–935. **F. W. Maitland.** Signed; repr. *Collected Papers,* (Cambridge, 1911), III.

4375 A lost principle of beauty in architecture, 936–943. **Julian Moore.** Signed.

4376 Some lessons of the Peace Conference, 944–957. **T. E. Holland.** Signed.

4377 The darkest hour for England [May 1797], 958–967. **Sidney Low.** Signed.

4378 The sportsman's library: a note on the books of 1899, 968–976. **F. G. Aflalo.** Signed.

4379 France since 1814 (Part VIII): the Third Republic, 977–990. **Pierre de Coubertin.** Signed.

4380 [Frederick W.] Robertson of Brighton, 991–1004. **T. H. S. Escott.** Signed.

4381 Grant Allen, 1005–1025. **Richard Le Gallienne.** Signed.

4382 Some notes on the Transvaal question, 1026–1031. **J. Percy Fitzpatrick.** Signed.

4383 Sir Harry Smith: a reminiscence of the Boer War in 1848, 1032–1035. **George F. H. Berkeley.** Signed.

4384 Count Muravieff's "indiscretion," 1036–1045. **Lucien Wolf.** Signed Diplomaticus—see no. 2378.

4385 The war in South Africa (Part II), 1046–1057.

4386 The divine adventure (Part II, concl.), 1058–1076. **William Sharp.** Signed Fiona Macleod—see *DNB*.

VOLUME 73 O.S., 67 N.S., JANUARY 1900

4387 The conduct of the war, 1–10. **Arthur Griffiths.** Signed.

4388 Issues at stake in South Africa, 11–23. **Alfred Hillier.** Signed; repr. *South African Studies*, 1900.

4389 Some recent Catholic apologists, 24–44. **St. George Mivart.** Signed. (Letters, p. 352, 716, signed **W. L. Lilly;** p. 526, signed **St. George Mivart.**)

4390 Gains and losses in the Pacific, 45–58. **John George Leigh.** Signed.

4391 The paths of glory [primarily on *Who's Who*], 59–68. **Joseph Jacobs.** Signed.

4392 *Fécondité* versus the *Kreutzner Sonata*, or Zola versus Tolstoi, 69–78. **Hannah Lynch.** Signed.

4393 A suggestion as to the origin of gender in language, 79–90. **J. G. Frazer.** Signed; repr. *Garnered Sheaves*, 1931.

4394 Stevenson's *Letters,* 91–103. **J. C. Bailey.** Signed.

4395 Agricultural education of natives [in So. Africa], 104–109. **Edith?** or **Emma? M. Green.** Signed E. M. Green; see *BMCat.* and *LCCat.*

4396 The "French Shore" [of Newfoundland] acute again, 110–120. **P. T. McGrath.** Signed with title "Editor, *Evening Herald*, St. John's N.F."

4397 Philosophy and modern culture, 121–134. **James Sully.** Signed.

4398 On the growth of tragedy in Shakespeare, 135–153. **Lewis Campbell.** Signed.

4399 Professionalism and sport, 154–161. **N. L. Jackson.** Signed.

4400 The war in South Africa (Part III), 162–172.

VOLUME 73 O.S., 67 N.S., FEBRUARY 1900

4401 A lance for the French, 173–177. **Thomas Barclay.** Signed.

4402 The Dutch Church and the Boers, 178–190. **William Greswell.** Signed.

4403 A scene from Ibsen's *Love's Comedy*, 191–199. **C. H. Herford.** Signed.

4404 *Wellington* [by Herbert Maxwell], 200–213. **William O'Connor Morris.** Signed.

4405 The War Office: a retrospect and a forecast, 214–223. **Arthur Griffiths.** Signed.

4406 The Lambeth decision and the law, 224–242. **Malcolm MacColl.** Signed. (Letters, pp. 524–526, signed **Lewis T. Dibdin;** pp. 717–718, signed **Malcolm MacColl.**

4407 The English Terence [Richard Cumberland], 243–257. **G. Barnett Smith.** Signed.

4408 Russia and Morocco, 258–264. Signed: Calpe.

4409 Procrastination and parsimony, 265–272. **George Arthur.** Signed.

4410 The logic of non-dogmatic Christianity, 273–289. **W. H. Mallock.** Signed.

4411 British and foreign rifle shooting, 290–299. **W. A. Baillie-Grohman.** Signed.

4412 The new Education Office and the interests of the Empire, 300–316. **R. P. Scott.** Signed.

4413 A preface to *The Bending of the Bough*, 317–324. **George Moore.** Signed.

4414 The Ruskin Hall movement, 325–335. **L. T. Dodd** and **J. A. Dale.** Signed.

4415 The war in South Africa (Part IV), 336–351.

VOLUME 73 O.S., 67 N.S., MARCH 1900

4416 The army and the administration, 353–361. Signed: Administrator.

4417 Some aspects of the Boer War, 362–372. **William Greswell.** Signed.

4418 One cause of our defeats: the service rifle, 373–381. **W. A. Baillie-Grohman.** Signed. (Note, p. 714, signed **W. A. Baillie-Grohman.**)

4419 The ethics of performing animals, 382–391. **F. G. Aflalo.** Signed.

4420 The administration of the Cruelty to Animals Act of 1876, 392–398. **Stephen Coleridge.** Signed. (Letter, pp. 714–716, signed **Stephen Paget.**)

4421 Our game books, 399–406. **John Cecil Russell.** Signed C. Stein—Blackwood.

4422 Wanted: statesmen! 407–417.

4423 The truth about Ruskin, 418–426. **H. Heathcote Statham.** Signed. (Letter, pp. 712–714, signed **E. T. Cook.**)

4424 On some liberal movements of the last half-century, 427–441. **Lewis Campbell.** Signed.

4425 How to pay for the war, 442–452. **Hugh Chisholm.** Signed.

4426 Lord Monkswell's Copyright Bill, 453–463. **G. Herbert Thring.** Signed.

4427 A reply to Mr. Herbert Spencer [no. 4371], 464–476. **James Ward.** Signed. (Letter, pp. 710–711, signed **Herbert Spencer.**)

4428 The military forces of our colonies, 477–493. **John F. Owen.** Signed.

4429 The last efforts for peace, 494–506. **Lucien Wolf.** Signed Diplomaticus—see no. 2378.

4430   Iona (Part I), 507–523. **William Sharp.** Signed Fiona Macleod—*DNB*; repr. *Writings of Fiona Macleod* (N.Y., 1909–1910), IV.

VOLUME 73 O.S., 67 N.S., APRIL 1900

4431   Our military needs, 527–536. **Arthur Griffiths.** Signed.

4432   Fifty-eight years, as child and woman, in South Africa, 537–550. Edited by **Maynard Butler**—signed.

4433   The future of South Africa, 551–556. **William Hosken.** Signed, with addition "Chairman, Uitlander Council."

4434   The House of Molière [Théâtre Français], 557–574. **W. E. Garrett Fisher.** Signed.

4435   Ibsen's new drama [*When We Dead Awaken*], 575–590. **James A. Joyce.** Signed.

4436   The next agricultural census, 591–601. **William E. Bear.** Signed.

4437   Germany as a naval power, 602–614. **Karl Blind.** Signed.

4438   "With but After" [on need for naval engineers], 615–627. **Rollo Appleyard.** Signed; repr. with this title, 1900.

4439   Unchanging dogma and changeful man, 628–648. **Wilfrid Ward.** Signed; repr. *Problems and Persons*, 1903.

4440   A royal visit to Ireland, 649–659. **Michael MacDonagh.** Signed.

4441   An American parallel to the present campaign, 660–667. **E. S. Valentine.** Signed; Contents adds "Major."

4442   The Confederation of South Africa, 668–679. **Edward Dicey.** Signed.

4443   The late campaign in Natal, 680–691.

4444   Iona (Part II, concl.), 692–709. **William Sharp.** Signed Fiona Macleod—see *DNB*.

VOLUME 73 O.S., 67 N.S., MAY 1900

4445   The possibility of a war between England and France, 719–729. **Pierre de Coubertin.** Signed.

4446   Mr. Bryce's manifesto to the Americans, 730–742. **Alfred Hillier.** Signed; repr. *South African Studies*, 1900.

4447   The art and status of the actor, 743–754. **H. B. Irving**, 1870–1919. Signed; repr. *Occasional Papers*, Boston, 1907.

4448   William Cowper, 755–779. **Alice Law.** Signed.

4449   Our antiquated drill and tactics, 780–791. **Edward N. Newdegate.** Signed.

4450   The future of the British army from a foreign standpoint, 792–806. **Theodor von Sosnosky.** Signed.

4451   A permanent Shakespearean theatre, 807–814. **H. Hamilton Fyfe.** Signed.

4452   Joint stock enterprise and our manufacturing industries, 815–829. **John B. C. Kershaw.** Signed.

4453   The promise of international exhibitions, 830–839. **F. G. Aflalo.** Signed.

4454   Annexation and after, 840–859. **Lucien Wolf.** Signed Diplomaticus—see no. 2378.

4455   South African reconstruction, 860–871. **Edward Dicey.** Signed.

4456   The invasion of the Orange Free State, 872–883.

4457   By the Ionian Sea (chaps. i–iv), 884–898. **George Gissing.** Signed; repr. under this title, 1901.

VOLUME 73 O.S., 67 N.S., JUNE 1900

4458   The evolution of mystery, 899–921. **Maurice Maeterlinck.** Signed. Translated by **Alfred Sutro**—signed, p. 921.

4459   The price of party government, 922–932. **W. S. Lilly.** Signed.

4460   Consult Sir George Grey! 933–946. **James Milne.** Signed.

4461   Ernest Dowson, 947–957. **Arthur Symons.** Signed; repr. *Studies*.

4462   The last palace intrigue at Peking, 958–971. **R. S. Gundry.** Signed.

4463   The Government Factory Bill of 1900, 972–979. **Gertrude M. Tuckwell.** Signed.

4464   Eleonora Duse, 980–993. **Helen Zimmern.** Signed.

4465   The coming Afghan crisis, 994–1003. **Demetrius C. Boulger.** Signed.

4466   Trawlers and undersized fish, 1004–1022. **G. Shaw Lefevre.** Signed.

4467   At the Royal Academy, 1023–1032. **H. Heathcote Statham.** Signed.

4468   A great Anglo-Indian: Sir William Wilson Hunter and his work, 1033–1044. **J. A. R. Marriott.** Signed.

4469   The new mysticism [on Fiona Macleod], 1045–1056. **Ernest Rhys.** Signed.

4470   Paul Kruger: some scenes and traits, 1057–1068. **F. Edmund Garrett.** Signed.

4471   Lord Rosebery and a national cabinet, 1069–1082.

VOLUME 74 O.S., 68 N.S., JULY 1900

4472   The policy of peace, 1–16. **Edward Dicey.** Signed.

4473   An overworked minister [Secretary of State for the Colonies] and—a remedy [additional secretaries for individual colonies], 17–27. **Beckles Willson.** Signed.

4474 France, Russia, and the peace of the world, 28–38. **Karl Blind.** Signed.

4475 Two mottoes of Cardinal Newman, 39–51. **Wilfrid Ward.** Signed; repr. *Problems and Persons*, 1903.

4476 The staging of Shakespeare: a defence of the public taste, 52–66. **H. Beerbohm Tree.** Signed. (Letter, pp. 355–356, signed **William Poel.**)

4477 The Workmen's Compensation Act; what it was to be, and what it is, 67–73. **Edward Abbott Parry.** Signed.

4478 Concerning hosts and hostesses, 74–82. **T. H. S. Escott.** Signed.

4479 On climax in tragedy, 83–91. **Lewis Campbell.** Signed.

4480 With lancet and rifle on the Beira railway, 92–99. **Lina Orman Cooper.** Signed L. Orman Cooper; see *BMCat.*

4481 The naval strength of the seven sea-powers, 100–117. **J. Holt Schooling.** Signed.

4482 Poets as legislators, 118–130. **Albert D. Vandam.** Signed; repr. *Third Republic.*

4483 The Paris Exhibition, 131–142. **H. Heathcote Statham.** Signed.

4484 The crisis in the Far East, 143–151. **Lucien Wolf.** Signed Diplomaticus—see no. 2378.

4485 The march to Pretoria, 152–160.

4486 By the Ionian Sea (chaps. v–viii), 161–176. **George Gissing.** Signed.

VOLUME 74 O.S., 68 N.S., AUGUST 1900

4487 What Imperialism means, 177–187. **J. H. Muirhead.** Signed.

4488 The art of Watts, 188–197. **Arthur Symons.** Signed; repr. *Studies in Seven Arts*, 1906.

4489 Peking—and after, 198–207. **Demetrius C. Boulger.** Signed.

4490 An international wheat corner, 208–216. **J. D. Whelpley.** Signed.

4491 Papers of the Scottish Reformation, 217–227. **Andrew Lang.** Signature.

4492 The armaments of seven navies, 228–246. **J. Holt Schooling.** Signed.

4493 Settlers and settlements in South Africa, 247–261. **H. A. Bryden.** Signed.

4494 Our naval arrangements in the other hemisphere, 262–267. **John C. R. Colomb.** Signed.

4495 A few French facts, 268–284. **Richard Davey.** Signed.

4496 The decrease of the salmon, 285–294. **Horace Hutchinson.** Signed.

4497 The crux of foreign policy [relations between England and Germany], 295–307.

4498 From Ladysmith to Standerton, 308–313.

4499 Contemporary Ireland, 314–326. **William O'Connor Morris.** Signed.

4500 Have we a policy in China? 327–336. **Lucien Wolf.** Signed Diplomaticus—see no. 2378.

4501 By the Ionian Sea (chaps. ix–xii), 337–354. **George Gissing.** Signed.

VOLUME 74 O.S., 68 N.S., SEPTEMBER 1900

4502 The out-going government: a rough balance sheet, 357–371. **H. R. Whates.** Signed as in no. 3760.

4503 Gordon's campaign in China (Part I), 372–390. **Charles George Gordon.** Signed [a posthumous art.]; repr. 1900. Introduction and account of the Tai-ping rebellion, pp. 372–382, by **Robert H. Vetch**—signed, repr. 1900.

4504 The dramas of Gabriele D'Annunzio, 391–409. **William Sharp.** Signed; repr. *Writings*, II.

4505 The Delagoa Bay arbitration, 410–429. **Malcolm McIlwraith.** Signed.

4506 "We always are ready" [on shortage of stokers in the navy], 430–439. **Rollo Appleyard.** Signed.

4507 Irish witch doctors, 440–456. **W. B. Yeats.** Signed.

4508 A lead for liberalism, 457–471.

4509 Some writers on war, 472–485. **Frederic Lees.** Signed.

4510 Sipodo and Bernard [two assassins]—1858 and 1900, 486–491. **John F. Taylor.** Signed.

4511 The care of the sick and wounded in war, 492–503. **Francis H. Welch.** Signed with addition "F.R.C.S., Surgeon-Colonel (retired) Medical Staff."

4512 The staging of Shakespeare: a reply to Mr. Beerhohm Tree, 504–512. **W. Hughes Hallett.** Signed; Contents gives "Colonel W. Hughes-Hallett."

4513 The coming settlement in China, 513–522. **Lucien Wolf.** Signed Diplomaticus—see no. 2378.

4514 By the Ionian Sea (chaps. xiii–xv), 523–532. **George Gissing.** Signed.

VOLUME 74 O.S., 68 N.S., OCTOBER 1900

4515 The burden of empire, 533–543. **W. S. Lilly.** Signed.

4516 Socialism and anarchism, 544–558. **Geoffrey Langtoft.** Signed.

4517 Our military prestige abroad, 559–566. **J. W. Gambier.** Signed.

4518 The kingdom of matter, 567–576. **Maurice Maeterlinck.** Signed. Translated by **Alfred Sutro**—signed.

4519 Lord Russell of Killowen, 577–588. **Edward Dicey.** Signed.

4520 The public schools and the public services, 589–600. **J. C. Tarver.** Signed.

4521 Gordon's campaign in China (Part II), 601–617. **Charles George Gordon.** Signed.

4522 Heroes of the war, and others, 618–628. **Arthur Griffiths.** Signed.

4523 The decay of the chaperon, 629–638. **Susan Mary E. Jeune.** Signed as in no. 2362.

4524 The struggle for industrial supremacy, 639–652. **Benjamin Taylor.** Signed.

4525 The Saturnalia and kindred festivals (Part I), 653–676. **J. G. Frazer.** Signed; repr. *The Golden Bough* (1900), III.

4526 The Far Eastern Crisis (No. I): why not a treaty with Russia? 677–686.

4527 The Far Eastern Crisis (No. II): is Russia to preponderate in China? 687–693. **Demetrius C. Boulger.** Signed.

4528 The Far Eastern Crisis (No. III): Count Lamsdorff's first failure [as head of Russian Foreign Office], 694–700. **Lucien Wolf.** Signed Diplomaticus—see no. 2378.

4529 By the Ionian Sea (chaps. xvi–xviii, concl.), 701–712. **George Gissing.** Signed.

VOLUME 74 o.s., 68 n.s., NOVEMBER 1900

4530 The Peking legations: a national uprising and international episode, 713–739. **Robert Hart.** Signed R.H.; name given in Contents.

4531 Mr. Chamberlain, 740–752. **H. R. Whates.** Signed as in no. 3760.

4532 England and Belgium, 753–764. Signed: Y.

4533 The Reverend Thomas Edward Brown: poet, 765–777. **S. H. W. Hughes-Games.** Signed; Contents adds "Rev."

4534 Bryan and McKinley: the parting of the ways, 778–789. **J. Lowry Whittle.** Signed.

4535 Three years of progressivism at the London School Board, 790–802. **T. J. Macnamara.** Signed. (Letter, pp. 1071–1072, signed **Joseph R. Diggle.**)

4536 The general election (No. I): the downfall of Liberalism, 803–814. **Edward Dicey.** Signed.

4537 The general election (No. II): the vindication of democracy, 815–824.

4538 The Saturnalia and kindred festivals (Part II, concl.), 825–849. **J. G. Frazer.** Signed.

4539 Disillusioned daughters, 850–857. Signed: Pleasaunce Unite. (Letter, pp. 1070–1071, signed **Dorothea Beale.**)

4540 Problems and playwrights, 858–866. Signed: Zyx.

VOLUME 74 o.s., 68 n.s., DECEMBER 1900

4541 A cabinet of commonplace, 897–913. **J. Louis Garvin.** Signed Calchas—see Courtney, *Making of an Editor*, p. 161.

4542 The cyclist soldier, 914–928. **H. G. Wells.** Signed.

4543 The future of the Liberal party, 929–934. Signed: A Liberal without Adjectives.

4544 Lord Rosebery's chance, 935–946. **J. A. R. Marriott.** Signed.

4545 The German Emperor, 947–952. **Ludwig Klausner-Dawoc.** Signed.

4546 Society's duty to the tramp, 953–966. **William Harbutt Dawson.** Signed.

4547 The housing question and the L.C.C. [London County Council], 967–981. **Charles Sheridan Jones.** Signed.

4548 The Scottish University crisis, 982–993. **William Wallace,** 1843–1921. Signed; see *WWW*.

4549 Maeterlinck's latest drama, 994–997. **S. C. de Soissons.** Signed.

4550 A plea for peace: an Anglo-Russian alliance, 998–1008. **J. W. Gambier.** Signed.

4551 Imperial federation: the condition of progress, 1009–1019. **Edward Salmon.** Signed.

4552 From an eighteenth-century escritoire, 1020–1027. **Ethel M. M. McKenna.** Signed.

4553 The autumn's books, 1028–1038. **Stephen Gwynn.** Signed.

4554 The sportsman's library: some books of 1900, 1039–1048. **F. G. Aflalo.** Signed.

4555 St. Gervase of Plessy: a mystery, 1049–1069. **Maurice Hewlett.** Signed.

4556 Literary supplement. The wedding guest, 1–42. **J. M. Barrie.** Signed in Contents; repr. *Works* (N.Y., 1929–1941), XVIII.

Fraser's Magazine for Town and Country, 1830–1882

Fraser's Magazine could scarcely have been published for fifty years under the control of a variety of editors and proprietors, in a period of radical change, and have remained the same periodical. Nevertheless, if one reads its principal statements of policy in 1830, 1849, and 1879, he discovers three things that its 96 volumes have in common.

It was always, as Maginn described it in his opening statement, a "magazine" in the sense of "a literary miscellany," which is to say, it was not a literary magazine. Its main emphasis was on politics, religion, and social conditions, in contrast to journals like the *Cornhill* or *Temple Bar*, so largely devoted to literature and literary criticism.[1] But style was always important. Whatever else "a magazine" may be, wrote the editor in 1879, "it is primarily an organ of literary expression."[2] That, indeed, was the basic reason for *Fraser's* initial success in the 1830s and its establishment as a major periodical. In the second place, from start to finish, it was an outstanding organ, if not of open revolt, as Thrall would have it (*Rebellious Fraser's*), at least of progressive thought. Even its conservatism, in the period when Maginn was the dominant influence, was closer to that of Coleridge and Carlyle than to the Toryism of Wellington and the status quo. Finally, *Fraser's* was distinguished among Victorian journals which made politics a major concern by its focus on principles and measures. In 1849 Parker explicitly adopted the policy Maginn had inaugurated in "Our Confession of Faith" (February 1830):

It will be seen from that document, that we undertook to bolster up no faction; to pin our faith on no man, nor any set of men; to support, to the best of our ability, the established institutions of the country; and to deal with every public measure as it came before us, strictly according to its merits. ... That our leanings have been Conservative throughout, we freely allow.

A generation later, after quoting part of this statement, the new editor, John Tulloch, continued:

It is especially necessary to look at measures rather than at men, and to watch carefully the springs that move political action. A true Liberalism, which looks to the future and all the

---

[1]See the two policy statements by Maginn—1 (Feb. 1830), 1–7, and 16 (Nov. 1837), 528–529. In both cases "literature" is of secondary importance and is limited to the criticism of books. But Maginn's lordly exclusion of novelettes, drolleries, and verse from "what is generally considered *the* magazine" (vol. 16, p. 528) was scarcely true in practice, either in *Blackwood's* or *Fraser's*.

[2]John Tulloch, 20 n.s. (July 1879), 8.

higher interests of our national life and society, cannot afford to repeat the commonplaces either of Government or of Opposition. It must examine questions in a comprehensive manner. . . . It must, above all, be servile to no mere party watchwords, nor personal names however distinguished or even deserving of distinction.[3]

One would not argue that such fine principles were never violated, but in a period when Arnold complained that "our organs of criticism are organs of men and parties," *Fraser's* as a whole may claim to have approached his ideal of a criticism free from subserving the special interests of any sect.[4]

The founding of *Fraser's Magazine for Town and Country* is a twice-told tale. By 1830 William Maginn, the Irish wit who had been one of *Blackwood's* liveliest contributors, had proved, apparently, a little too bold or intractable. His articles began to be refused; and he began to look for a journal of his own which would make *Blackwood's* regret its mistake.[5] With a roll of manuscript under his arm, Maginn and his friend Hugh Fraser, possessor of the required cash, were walking down Regent Street, so the story goes, when they came to the shop of James Fraser the publisher, and Maginn exclaimed "Fraser! Here's a namesake of yours. Let's try him." By great good luck the publisher was just then thinking of trying a monthly magazine that would be both popular and scholarly. Since Maginn could promise both requisites, a bargain was soon struck, and a periodical named after Hugh Fraser began publication in February 1830.[6]

Naturally enough, it was modeled on *Blackwood's*. It too was to be a literary miscellany published monthly, to have a protean editor called Oliver Yorke, as *Blackwood's* had its Christopher North, and to adopt a soubriquet, specially designed to assert its superiority—"Regina," the Queen of Magazines—which is to say, of "Magas." Its politics would also be Tory. But above all it was to outdo the older journal in its special field of scurrilous satire, witty invective, and the high jinks of "topical parodies and sham symposia."[7] In short, *Fraser's*, in the words of Maginn himself, was "a successful intruder into what was once thought a peculiar preserve [of] *Blackwood*."[8]

Though not, I think, with intention of rivalry, this is also true of the most striking feature of the early magazine, say from 1830 to 1847 when Maginn was the dominating influence—namely, the extraordinary and surprising variety of its materials. It is

[3] 39 (Jan. 1849), 2; cited in n.1 above, pp. 11–12.

[4] From "The Function of Criticism at the Present Time" (1864), *Essays in Criticism*, First Series (1865). The general point is made by Thrall, p. 7.

[5] The precise facts are not known. This account is based on Thrall, p. 4; cf. Mackenzie, "Memoir" (Bibliographical Note), pp. lxii–lxiii.

[6] Thrall, p. 4; Mackenzie, pp. lxiv–lxv.

[7] The quoted phrase is by Michael Sadleir, " 'Kind William Maginn'," *Things Past* (1944), p. 55.

[8] 7 (June 1833), 750. The circulation after a year was said to be 8700 (3 [Mar. 1831], 260), a very respectable figure, not much below the *Edinburgh* and *Quarterly*, and above *Blackwood's* 8000: see R. D. Altick, *The English Common Reader* (Chicago, 1957), pp. 392, 393. But given the source, it should be taken with a grain of salt. There is no reason, however, to doubt the general success of Regina. In the 1840s the circulation seems to have dropped, and the *Bookseller*, June 26, 1860, p. 359, claimed that when the Parkers bought it in 1847, it was suffering from "denuded purses."

not simply that scholarly articles on Homer or Egyptian antiquities, Scottish and Irish stories, ecclesiastical warfare, political tracts, foreign travels, translations from Persian and Hebrew, satiric sketches of contemporaries, essays on German transcendentalism, and literary spoofs jostle each other in startling juxtaposition. The variety of styles is even more striking; the tone is scholarly or polemical or conversational, and the brilliant wit can be light, ironic, ingenious, cruel—sometimes all in a single piece. The mixture is astonishing. Turn a page and you jump into another world. Indeed, the adjustment often requires an alert and knowledgable reader to be aware of the topical references and outrageous hoaxes. He has to read closely to determine whether a letter signed David Brewster was really by Brewster or not, or if a sonnet by Bowles was by Bowles—or could it be by Maginn?[9] If the issues and the wit have now faded, we can recognize how exciting *Fraser's* must have been in the 1830s, especially perhaps to young readers. *Sartor Resartus* was first published there in 1833–1834, and naturally enough: its fusion of philosophical, literary, and political observations, its alliance of levity and seriousness, its satire of Bulwer and the dandies, its anti-Benthamism, and the demands it made on the reader are the very stuff out of which *Fraser's* was made—transformed by the imagination of genius.

For this complex richness we have to thank Maginn. His own versatility was described by Kenealy with little exaggeration:

Theologian, Historian, Poet, Metaphysician, Mathematician, Philosopher, Phrenologist, Stenographist, Fencer, Boxer, Orator, Dramatist, Reviewer, Sonneteer, Joker, Punster, Doctor of Laws, Hoaxer, Political Economist, Newspaper Editor, Wit, Duellist, Pedestrian, Linguist, Arithmetician, O'Doherty, Pamphleteer, Translator, Epigrammatist, Antiquarian, Scholar, Conversationalist, Novelist and true Tory to the backbone. In fact a man so various that he seems to be not one but all mankind's epitome.[10]

Anyone half so gifted or half so facile would not only himself have written on many topics in many voices; he would also have created a periodical equally "various."

Perhaps Maginn's finest achievement was "The Gallery of Illustrious Literary Characters" in which he wrote the letterpress for Daniel Maclise's pen-and-ink drawings. For the first time in publishing history, a large number of contemporary figures (81) were sketched in portrait and prose, some of them enemies, some Fraserians, and none of them damned completely or entirely praised. Here at a glance one can see, in shifting tones and allusive writing, what is meant by the "brilliance" of Maginn, and find exemplified the scurrilous satire which gave *Fraser's* its early reputation. Here is Francis Place, London tailor, public citizen, and "Author of *The Principles of Population*":[11]

This hero was found, we believe, in a dust-pan, upon the steps of a house in St. James's Place, about sixty years back, by an honest Charlie, who forthwith conveyed him to the next workhouse, where (for these were unenlightened times) the little stranger was kindly taken care of. He was christened *Francis*, that being the *surname* of his wet-nurse; while, in lieu of patronymic, they gave him *Place*, as a memorial of the locality where he had been

---

[9]See below, nos. 498 and 963.

[10]E. V. H. Kenealy, *Fraser's*, 25 (Jan. 1842), 73, as reproduced in "ordinary" English with a small change of word order by Michael Sadleir, *Things Past*, p. 54.

[11]The quotation is placed under the portrait; the letterpress is 13 (Apr. 1836), 427.

discovered. Such were the bulrushes out of which Westminster drew the future Moses of
the Preventive Check,—a philosophical decalogue well worthy to supersede the first, which
it so boldly contradicts, particularly in the absurd article about *murder*.

To begin with, there is no truth whatever in this account of Place's birth. He was born
in a debtor's prison near Drury Lane kept by his father, Simon Place, then a bailiff
to the Marshalsea Court. Maginn's story is sheer libel, made credible by specific detail,
or, to those who recognized the fabrication, made tolerable by the amusing irony of
his being well cared for in those unenlightened times and by the fantastic sources of
his name. Moreover, the story is needed to support the metaphor of a new Moses
(which adds an anti-Semitic slur?) with his philosophical (non-religious) decalogue,
the Preventive Check. Malthus had recommended only moral restraint to curb population, but Place, the foremost of the neo-Malthusians, had denounced that doctrine
as out of harmony with human nature. "The remedy can alone be found in preven-
tives," namely, "such precautionary measures as would, without being injurious to
health or destructive of female delicacy, prevent conception." At the time this was a
shocking and repulsive idea, often considered tantamount to contradicting the sixth
commandment.[12]

The Mount Sinai of the new lawgiver is, we need hardly say, a certain tailor's shop at
Charing Cross. It was there that Johnson said he delighted to contemplate "the full tide of
human existence." It is there Place has erected his grand *Mill*-dam, for the salutary purpose of arresting this same tide, and causing it, utterly deserting the ancient and perilous
water-course, to wander innocuous amidst the sands and shallows of the Palus Pseudaphrodisiaca.

The mill-dam check has the salutary purpose of arresting the natural tide of human
life, and causing it, deserting what Place considers the old-fashioned and *perilous*
(because too reproductive) channel, to wander innocuous (*safe*) in the sands and
shallows of the Palus Pseudaphrodisiaca, the swamp of false love. But the printed
word is "*Mill*-dam," and Maginn was surely referring to both the Mills, especially to
John Stuart, whose distribution of the "diabolical handbills" of 1823, written by
Place, had landed him in jail, charged with the promotion of obscenity.[13]

The next paragraph begins:

This is the *magnum opus* of the sagest of the snips; but he has also contributed, in many
lesser matters, to the expansion of our intellects. Place soon learned to take a just measure
of the fundamental features of the old system; and declared war, to the scissors' point,
against those grievous humbugs, the Boroughs, the Peers, and the Church.

This "*magnum opus*"—the book as well as the whole work of erecting his grand mill-
dam by letters, conversation, etc.—is that of the sagest of the "snips," contemptuous
slang for tailors. And the war against "those grievous humbugs" which were the
foundation of the Constitution, as the Tories viewed them, was war "to the scissors'

[12]*Encyclopedia of Social Sciences* (N.Y., 1937), art. "Birth Control," quoting Place's book,
chap. VI, sec. 3; the attitude of the time is described by Graham Wallas, *The Life of Francis
Place* (1898), p. 169.

[13]See James Mill's article, "Colony," in the supplement to the *Encyclopaedia Britannica* (5th
ed., 1818); the handbills, called *To Married Working People*, were a reduction of Place's *Principles of Population* to its essential teaching; a good account of J. S. Mill's experience is in M. St.
J. Packe, *The Life of John Stuart Mill* (1954), pp. 56–59, 59n.

point," the tailor's tool and the feeblest of weapons. But not being able to leave his shop at Charing Cross, Place had to delegate the parliamentary warfare to various subservient journeymen, all much more distinguished than he, and all at one time or another elected Radical M.P.s from Westminster, with the strong support of a committee he had organized. "Such was Burdett—such was Hobhouse—and such is Evans: we say *is*, for we hope there is no chance of the gallant lieut.-general having been personnally dealt with after the tender mercies of Mina." Francis Burdett and John Cam Hobhouse, but Evans?[14] and is "gallant" ironic? and is Mina the bird or the Greek coin, or what? To discover that George de Lacy Evans was elected M.P. from Westminster in 1833, but took temporary leave in 1835 to establish a British legion to support the Spanish government of the regent Christina against the Carlists, and returned in 1837 after more than one gallant victory; and to identify Mina as Francisco Espoz Y Mina, 1781–1836, the tough guerrilla leader and general who was placed in command of the Spanish army opposing the Carlists in 1835–1836, so that nominally he and Evans were allies; but that since the Spanish government systematically starved and neglected the legion, Evans might well have been dealt with after the tender mercies of Mina—all this may take a good hour of research today. But in 1836 any reader of the newspapers would have followed the shorthand with the pleasure of knowing his politics. (The "lieut.-general" may have been an unconscious error; Evans was a captain.)[15]

Maginn continues: "We understand, however" [in contrast to depending on parliamentary journeymen, but also in contrast to Evans fighting for England], "that Place has now feathered his nest to a comfortable extent," and may soon see himself in "the House, not of Call, but of Commons," [a House of Call—see the *NED*—being one "where journeymen taylors . . . and all other artificers meet, and may be heard"]. There he will sit with Silk Buckingham, Thomas Wakley, John Bowring, and J. A. Roebuck, all Radicals and "all his equals in birth"—which quadruples the initial libel. All too, like Place, were *Westminster* reviewers, but Place, the practical uneducated man, never much respected by editors Bowring and T. P. Thompson, is called—the hyperbole is wonderfully ridiculous—"at once the Jeffrey, the Playfair, and the Sidney Smith, the critic-poetical, the critic-mathematical, and the critic-theological, of the grand organ of Benthamism."

The sketch ends with a surprising shift of focus and tone. After continuing his irony with a fervent wish to see Place himself in Downing Street, Maginn continues, "where he would certainly look the thing a good deal better than Spring Rice" [the Whig Chancellor of the Exchequer], "whom we are confident he would pronounce a disgrace to any reputable shopboard." And the next sentences show that Maginn is now in earnest, for he breaks out with a characteristic onslaught:

We are weary of seeing the loaves and fishes abandoned, by those who have the real power in this land, to such miserable mendicant imbeciles, the very dregs and sweepings of the doomed and fated aristocracy, as Johnny Russell, Morpeth, Mulgrave, and Duncannon, together with such a handful of time-serving scamps, traitors to the *Plebs* that spawned them, as Hobhouse, Rice, Ellice, Wood, and Tallow Tomson. Away with these paltry

---

[14]Wallas, pp. 44–57, 132–139, 327.
[15]For Evans, see the *DNB*; for Mina, the *Ency. Brit.*, 11th ed.

mimes!—the time is come when the real actors ought to be bounding on the stage; while such despicable tools should shrink behind the scenes, there to perform the obscure, as well as dirty work, for which alone nature and art have qualified them. Away with these dwarf monsters! despised, far below the mark of that rather respectable sentiment called hatred, by every Tory—loathed in his secret soul by every Liberal.

"Secret" because all the men mentioned were Liberals, from Lord John Russell, to speak of him with appropriate dignity, leader of the Whigs in the Commons, to Sir Charles Wood, Secretary to the Admiralty; while the last, Tallow Tomson, was William Thompson, corpulent of build, I suppose, who began as a Benthamite and became a Socialist.[16] On to the end:

> Away with all such, we say. Give us men to whose proceedings we can apply some rational standard of calculation—honest, out-spoken fractions of men even; any thing but this base convention of hypocrisy and cowardice, whose God is their belly.

This is the angry Maginn spewing out all the savage invective he can command, but recognizing the vast superiority even of fractions of men like Place, honest, outspoken, who could live in Downing Street without making their belly their God. And knowing Place's life-long service to society, one cannot but feel that Maginn had pointed to his finest quality—only faintly, leaving the satire in place.

This sketch of Place leads us into the only field of Fraserian comment we have space to consider: politics. Its conservatism has been called progressive, but it was to the right of Coleridge and Carlyle. "We are church-*and*-state men," insisted Maginn,[17] and if the magazine supported the Reform Bill, it soon came to feel that the supposed alliance of Whigs and Radicals endangered the monarchy and the Church. A score of articles shouted wildly against them both, and also, mainly on political grounds, against Catholics, Anglo-Catholics, and Dissenters; and though the Tories were not exempt from charges of weakness, there was little disinterested play of mind on political parties and religious sects under Maginn. On socio-economic questions, however, *Fraser's* adopted a stance which stems from Coleridge and harmonizes with Southey of the *Colloquies* (1829) and Carlyle of *Past and Present* (1843). Laissez faire and the political economists are attacked and the "condition of England" exposed. In a review of the Wellington administration, Maginn told of the unanswered petitions of the people, complaining of distress:

> They came from the agricultural labourer, reduced to rags and pauperism—from the fathers and brothers of those whom long suffering and despair had driven to crime and spoliation, to rioting, pillaging, and burning. They came from the starving artisan; from thousands of weavers, whose utmost exertions could not earn more than five shillings per week; from miners and spinners, whom the currency bill of Sir Robert Peel had reduced to live like slaves upon truck, and whose miserable pittance of wages, instead of being paid in the king's coin . . . were paid in the rancid bacon and stale cheese of their employers.

From this criticism, the positive position that made the Tories more liberal in our sense than the Liberals of the period inevitably followed:

---

[16]All the names can be found in the *DNB* except Mulgrave, who is in Burke's *Peerage*. Rice, I assume, is another reference to Spring Rice. "Tomson" is a typographical error for "Thompson," who would properly close the list, being at the farthest left.

[17]7 (June 1833), 751.

Toryism ought to be the *protective* system, as the system of the Radicals is the *destructive* one. It ought to protect the agricultural labourer from the farmer, the factory-child from the mill-tyrant, the Spitalfields weaver from the competition of the men of Lyons; it ought to enlarge the circulation; lessen in every way the surplus-labour which presses down the market; and never rest till general employment and fair wages were universal.

It is scarcely surprising that a moment before Maginn had been denouncing the measures advocated by "the Bowrings and Thompsons, and Roebucks and Humes"— and he might have added "the Places"—of the *Westminster Review*.[18]

I have focused on Maginn because no one else represents the early *Fraser's* so well. He is said to have written for almost every issue down to No. 133 (December 1840), "one or two papers at an average," which makes him by far the leading contributor; and in addition he often asked anyone who chanced to be present to write an article on such-and-such a subject, and then altered the manuscript as he pleased.[19] Furthermore, though he was "editor" only until 1836, the Magazine was his creation until the Parkers took it over in 1847, and the Fraserians for the most part men of his own kind, if less brilliant and less scurrilous. The well known portrait of the group by Maclise in Volume 11 (January 1835) is misleading, for Southey, Coleridge, Lockhart, and David Brewster printed little, and nothing of importance, in the Magazine.[20] Its famous contributors were Carlyle, who published essays on Goethe, Schiller, "Boswell's *Life of Johnson*," "Biography," "Thoughts on History," and in narrative "The Diamond Necklace" and "Count Cagliostro," as well as *Sartor*; and Thackeray who placed much of his early work in *Fraser's*, including the *Yellowplush Papers*, *Catherine*, and *Barry Lyndon*. Of lower rank but still read are *The Reliquies of Father Prout*, that is, of Francis Mahoney, the Irish wit and classical scholar. At the time, John Galt, James Hogg ("The Ettrick Shepherd"), and David Moir ("Delta"), all Scotsmen; the Irishmen Percival Banks, T. C. Croker, and E. V. Kenealy; the poet and philosopher Abraham Heraud; the antiquary Thomas Wright; and the critic Robert Willmott were well known men of letters. In the first decade *Fraser's* stood with *Blackwood's* at the forefront of monthly magazines.

A decline began, as one might expect, with the decline of Maginn himself. In 1836 came scandal and marital estrangement, and a brutal attack on James Fraser which resulted from Maginn's savage review of a novel by Grantley Berkeley. After these catastrophes, which ended Maginn's official career with *Fraser's*, the tendency to pile up debts and to drink too much increased, leading eventually to a debtor's prison and an early death in 1842. For a while the traditional character of the Magazine was kept up with the special assistance of Mahoney (1836–1837) and Kenealy (1838–1841), but after Fraser's death in 1841, G. W. Nickisson, the new publisher and editor (1841 or 1842–1847) was unequal to the task. Many of the Fraserians were

---

[18] 3 (May 1831), 515, and 9 (Mar. 1834), 370. The subject is well treated in chap. VII, "Progressive Toryism," of Thrall's book, to which I am indebted for these quotations.

[19] Kenealy's article, *Dublin University Magazine*, 23 (Jan. 1844), 89; Malcolm Elwin, *Victorian Wallflowers* (1934), p. 114. For the reference to "editor" in the next sentence, see below under Editors.

[20] The most authoritative list is Maginn's in 21 (Jan. 1840), 20–21. That in 13 (Jan. 1836), 4, is unreliable, containing some names of people who hated *Fraser's*, which made their inclusion among the Fraserians an amusing insult: note Dr. Bowring, E. L. Bulwer, and Alaric Watts, for example. See 1 (July 1830), 738, for a partial list of contributors during the first six months.

dead, and the others scattered or otherwise occupied, beyond reach of the old *esprit de corps*; and more important, the spirit of the times had become too earnest to enjoy or tolerate the improprieties of Maginn and Co.

Looking back on the life of *Fraser's Magazine* in 1879, Principal John Tulloch divided its history into two phases: that of the early Fraserians, 1830–1847, and that initiated by the Parkers, 1847–1879—or, as we should now say, 1847 to the end in 1882, since Tulloch introduced no change.[21] One might argue that a third phase had begun in 1860 when J. A. Froude took over from Parker, but although Froude's bent was more radical in religion and more Carlylean in politics, the basic character of Parker's magazine was unaltered. That character was Victorian, whereas Maginn's magazine was plainly marked—and now (in 1847) thought marred—by the dash and "riotous mirth" of the Regency.

When the William John Parkers took command in July 1847, the father as publisher and the son as editor, there was a major, though not immediate, shift of attitude. "I tell you fairly," wrote Kingsley to the new editor in June 1848, "that *the* want which people feel in Fraser's is a want of earnest purpose and deep faith of any kind."[22] Though Parker came to agree with this, his own statement, not made until January 1849, was narrower and more explicit. In describing "the *tone* in which the various subjects taken up in *Fraser's Magazine*" were to be discussed, he confessed:

We are not ignorant of the charge which has sometimes been brought against us, of having dealt more than was quite becoming in personalities. . . . It will accordingly be found, that within the last year and a half the Fraserians, as they have ceased to attend imaginary *symposia* and to drink gallons of imaginery punch, so they have learned to temper their wit, that it might tell on men's principles of action, without unnecessarily wounding their self-love or ruffling their tempers. . . . The practice of calling hard names and imputing unworthy motives the Magazine has abondoned, and is not likely, under its present management to return to it.[23]

Which is to say, it is not likely to publish another "Francis Place." But what it lost in brilliance and variety, it gained in distinction of thought and literary calibre. The best of Parker's men, to name only those with at least five prose contributions—Fitz-Gerald, Froude, Arthur Helps, Kingsley, Landor, G. H. Lewes, Peacock—were more than a match for the Fraserians.[24]

Furthermore, as that roll-call would suggest, the new *Fraser's* was liberal. It was the Parkers who published the first organ of Christian Socialism, *Politics for the People*, from May to July 1848, and during this period "the younger Mr. J. W. Parker" often joined Kingsley and the co-editors, Maurice and Ludlow, in making up the numbers.[25] In the meanwhile, in May 1848 the Magazine's reaction to Chartism was ambivalent: the moral-force Chartists, with their desire "to obtain the franchise by the legitimate influence of argument," won *Fraser's* praise, while their physical-force

---

[21] Cited in n. 1 above, pp. 3 and 6; the 1849 date on p. 3 is corrected to 1847 on p. 6.
[22] Quoted in Margaret Farrand Thorp, *Charles Kingsley, 1819–1875* (Princeton, 1937), p. 56.
[23] 39 (Jan. 1849), 3.
[24] Others who appeared less frequently were H. T. Buckle, Carlyle, Clough, George Eliot, Meredith, Mill, Patmore, and Spencer.
[25] Frederick Maurice, *The Life of Frederick Denison Maurice* (2 vols., N.Y., 1884), I, 481.

associates, said to stem from Whig principles, were repudiated. The six "points" were mildly criticized, but the £10 franchise needed revision; and modern England was charged with lacking the "love of justice": "Our unequal taxation, our class legislation, our unnatural distinctions of rank, all attest this."[26] The article was followed by another, "Whig Professions, and Whig Performances," written by an old enemy of Maginn's, J. A. Roebuck. However, after Europe was swept by the tempest of revolution, Parker hastened to inaugurate 1849 with an editorial congratulating "England and the readers of *Fraser*" on "having ridden out the gale" ("We might have had Communist workshops set up by command of a Provisional Government. . . . There might have been no crowned Queen to sanction the decisions of the legislature," etc., etc.), and insisting, with a reference back to Maginn's "Confession of Faith" in February 1830, "that our leanings have been Conservative throughout. . . . They are Conservative still." "Our *leanings*": and a moment later the support which Parker promises to ministers who protect the Constitution in Church and State is limited to those who neither strive "to stop the course of events" nor madly provoke "change for its own sake." Whoever precipitates revolution or denounces improvement, we shall oppose. The fact is that Parker's sympathy with radical experiment was checked by the events of 1848, leaving him a liberal Conservative, or rather, like Arnold, a Liberal "tempered by experience, reflection, and renouncement."[27]

This is especially true in a broad sense beyond the limits of politics. In the very next paragraph of his editorial (January 1849), he proudly speaks of having published "The Plague of Beggars" and other papers by A. W. Guy on sanitary reform, as well as "that strange wild tale" called *Yeast* (with its criticism of landlords, game laws, banking practices, and its praise of healthy animal passions in marriage). Presently, Kingsley and Froude became his close friends and major contributors; and he sympathized with the Broad Churchmen, whose books were published by Parker & Sons, including the startling *Essays and Reviews* of 1860. But Parker was not at heart a reformer, and his Magazine is conspicuously free from polemics. His liberalism is therefore much less activist and progressive than open-minded and tolerant. Hence the significance of Froude's tribute in his obituary:

With definite convictions of his own, he was satisfied that the cause of truth was best served when the points on which men differed were submitted to the most free discussion, when the representatives of two different schools of opinion had the fullest opportunity of expressing themselves. The writings of Mill and Buckle, Trench and Helps, Kingsley and Miss Yonge, were all published by the Parkers' house, and names connected with views so extreme in their divergence shew how broad was his appreciation.[28]

This was an ideal—he had refused *Alton Locke* and Fitzgerald's version of the *Rubaiyat*—but he had professed as much and aimed as high.[29] After the death of Parker on November 9, 1860, it was natural enough that his father should have asked Froude, who had nursed his son through his last illness and was an established

---

[26]"Chartism," 37 (May 1848), 579–592.
[27]End of Introduction, *Culture and Anarchy* (1869).
[28]*Gentleman's Magazine*, 55 (Feb. 1861), 224. This was, or became, Froude's own conviction: see *FM* 68 (Sept. 1863), 291, quoted below.
[29]For the refusals, see Maurer (Bibliographical Note), pp. 214–215. His own profession is in the editorial note, 59 (June 1859), 644–645.

man of letters, to assume the editorship. He had already published, among other books, the first volumes of his famous *History of England* and at least thirty articles, sixteen in *Fraser's*.

Moreover, he shared the liberal leanings of both the Parkers; indeed, in some respects to a degree which neither would have approved. In the early half of 1861 Francis Newman and Frances Power Cobbe, both theists, began their long careers as contributors to *Fraser's*, though not at first on religious topics. But in May 1863 Newman attacked the doctrinal rigidity of the Church; and in September appeared Froud's more radical "Plea for the Free Discussion of Theological Difficulties." In the latter the clergy were lashed for refusing to face the problems of belief which were spreading so widely, and could not be resolved, in Froude's opinion, except by "full and fair investigation." In all other fields of learning that "liberty of opinion which is the life of knowledge" was accepted, while in theology the least doubt of Biblical or ecclesiastical authority, if not answered with worn-out arguments, was branded as sin or drowned in ridicule. In the course of this broadside, Froude's own religious belief is introduced:

Christianity has abler advocates than its professed defenders, in those many quiet and humble men and women who in the light of it and the strength of it live holy, beautiful, and self-denying lives. . . . So long as the fruits of the Spirit continue to be visible in charity, in self-sacrifice, in those graces which raise human creatures above themselves . . . thoughtful persons will remain convinced that with them in some form or other is the secret of truth.

But a moment later he candidly admits: "What that belief is for which the fruits speak thus so positively, it is less easy to define." "It may be," he suggests, "that the faith which saves is the *something* held in common by all sincere Christians," and that "the true teaching of our Lord is overlaid with doctrines."[30] Dogma and the Church have disappeared, and Froude is talking the language of Unitarianism or Christian Theism. Two years later Louise Octavia Hope wrote to Brougham: "Fraser's Magazine is really becoming ultra Unitarian & free-thinking—a pity for there is less trash of other kinds in it than most magazines."[31] It would have been more than a "pity" to either of the Parkers, though clearly this is but the next step beyond the Broad Church.

Froude centered his "Plea for Free Discussion" simply on religion, but that was only because he saw no problem in other areas of knowledge. At the close he remarked without qualification: "Free discussion through a free press . . . is the best instrument for the discovery of truth, and the most effectual means for preserving it." Such a statement might well imply the open platform which was partly advocated for the *Fortnightly* in 1865 and fully achieved in 1877 by the *Nineteenth Century*, but not many men of strong convictions are capable of such open-mindedness. J. S. Mill, yes, but not J. T. Knowles, who had no convictions beyond the financial value

---

[30]The article is 68 (Sept. 1863), 277–291, and is reprinted in all editions, I think, of *Short Studies on Great Subjects*, Vol. I. The initial quotations and references are mainly to pp. 290, 278, 282, 279, 282. Froude's own belief is on p. 283 (the italics are mine); also see his contrast of what he and Newman call "Christianity" in 81 o.s., 1 n.s. (May 1870), 578.

[31]Letter dated Feb. 28, 1865, at University College, London; quoted by kind permission of Miss Margaret Skerl, assistant librarian.

of displaying famous men in public debate. Froude did publish a wide range of opinion on the American Civil War in spite of being pro-Confederate himself: "In civil war of any magnitude there has always been something to say on both sides," he wrote Frances Cobbe, a propos of accepting Mill's "The Contest in America,"[32] and he printed Moncure Conway's articles "By an American Abolitionist." But a sentence which followed a request to Conway to tone down his rhetoric is highly revealing:

I do not wish to make my own opinion the absolute rule of what is to appear in *Fraser* . . . but I do not like to affect a tone of thinking and feeling the precise reverse of the truth.[33]

That is scarcely the open mind; and yet Froude brought himself to print a good many papers which he disliked. There was "Politics in our Parish" in March 1867 "By a Country Tory" [John Skelton]; and in literary criticism the fine article of February 1863 on Browning, also by Skelton, beginning "It is about time we began to do justice to Robert Browning," which Froude postponed, month after month, with querulous objections. Again, for all his personal repugnance, he admitted a favourable review of Swinburne's *Poems and Ballads* because he was unwilling "to follow the crew of Philistines and bite his heels like the rest of them." Morris and Rossetti also received, reluctantly, their meed of praise; and Michael Rossetti with William Bell Scott wrote on Pre-Raphaelite art.[34]

In politics, however, *Fraser's* veered from liberal to conservative. In the sixties Abraham Hayward wrote a series of attacks on Disraeli, but after 1870, annoyed by Gladstone's colonial policy, Froude changed horses, urging one contributor to "praise Dizzy as much as you please." Moreover, the influence of Carlyle became steadily stronger until, in Froude's final utterance in July 1874, he was advocating the assumption of power by "men of wealth and rank."[35]

But it was in religion, for all his old plea for free discussion, that Froude became most one-sided and illiberal. In the later sixties and early seventies, his anti-clericalism, encouraged by Carlyle, was ignited by Fitzjames and Leslie Stephen, and the three let go with a series of blasts against Roman Catholicism, the High Church, the Evangelicals, and even the Broad Churchmen. When one contributor, probably A. K. H. Boyd, asked to defend Ritualism, he was promptly refused, and Froude explained, "I grow more and more intolerant of certain things; and conscious humbug in religious matters is one of them."[36]

Froude had never thought of himself as primarily an editor, and in any event he had to struggle, as Parker had not, with strong competition from the new monthlies,

---

[32]Letter dated Nov. 26, n.y., at the Huntington Library. Froude, *Life*, II, 331–346, gives a full digest of the articles on the war.

[33]Quoted by Conway, "Working with Froude" (see Bibliographical Note), p. 379.

[34]On Browning, see Froude, *Life*, II, 327–328; on Swinburne, ibid., pp. 328–329; on the Pre-Raphaelites, Maurer (in Bibliographical Note), pp. 222, 232. In this section on Froude, I am much indebted to Professors W. H. Dunn and Oscar Maurer, especially the latter.

[35]For this paragraph, see Maurer, p. 220, with notes 29–31, and pp. 241–242 on Carlyle's influence.

[36]*Blackwood's*, 156 (Dec. 1894), 769. For some of the articles referred to, see no. 5077 by Froude; nos. 4469, 4549, 4558, 4659, 4665, and 5022 by Fitzjames Stephen; and nos. 5060, 5280, 5299 by Leslie Stephen, which were reprinted in his *Essays on Free Thinking and Plain Speaking* (1873).

especially *Macmillan's*, to which the Broad Churchmen had turned, and the *Cornhill*, with its double attraction of higher payments and wider circulation.[37] Moreover, after remarking that "*Fraser*, in spite of its distinguished editor, was beginning to lose its position," Leslie Stephen added, "He was hardly the man to attract eager young liberal writers. Carlylism appeared to them to be simply reactionary and cynical."[38] For some or all of these reasons Froude tried to resign in 1871, but not being able to find a successor, carried on until the death of his wife in 1874. William Allingham, who had been sub-editor since 1870, took over. Though a minor poet of some distinction, he had neither Froude's force nor his literary connections. Francis Newman and A. K. H. Boyd continued to write, and Allingham's friend Carlyle sent him a few papers, as did Froude, but on the whole the contributors were undistinguished, and worst of all from a commercial point of view, there was not a single novel coming out serially at a time when that was essential for the success of a magazine. By 1879 a crisis was reached. Though Mrs. Oliphant thought it useless to try to revive "a magazine which had outlived its reputation," Longmans decided to hold on.[39] Its resurrection was entrusted to Principal John Tulloch of St. Andrew's University, the aging but well known writer on religious thought, who assumed control of *Fraser's* in July 1879.

At long last a novel by Blackmore made an immediate appearance, and the new editor, in an initial statement, "Our Past and Our Future," found both to be good, and both essentially continuous. "In higher speculation—whether philosophical, theological, or political—*Fraser* will continue to be, as it has long been, genuinely liberal. . . . Its pages will be open to free inquiry and the most thorough handling of modern questions"; while in belles lettres the Magazine will be an organ "of the best and brightest thought of the time."

But it was not to be. Though the first two numbers showed a rise in circulation, the September issue was almost still-born: the circulation had dropped to 500.[40] Late in 1880, no doubt partly from editorial worries and keen disappointment, Tulloch's old ennui returned, producing fits of depression too deep for work. With the help of Angus Knight he got out the issue for January 1881, but it was his last. Though he sent in some manuscript during that month, he wrote Allingham, January 21, 1881, of "Mr. Longman's kind offer to manage 'Fraser' for a month or two" while he was ill—an offer he had accepted; but recovery was nine months away.[41] Longman tried his own hand at editing for nearly two years, with no better success. For "an old thing

[37]A propos of his lecture on Heine, Arnold wrote his mother, June 16, 1863, *Letters of Matthew Arnold*, ed. G. W. E. Russell (2 vols., 1901), I, 226: "I shall print it, if I can, in the *Cornhill*, because it both pays best and has much the largest circle of readers." Its circulation in 1865 has been estimated by Alvar Ellegård (see *Index*, I, xxiii), p. 32, as 30,000, and *Fraser's* at 8,000. However, on Mar. 8, 1863, Froude wrote to Skelton, reprinted in *Blackwood's* 156 (Dec. 1894), 760: "The Magazine prospers. The circulation now exceeds 3,000, and more copies must be printed"—which implies that under Parker it was even lower, and that Ellegård's estimate of 8000 two years later was probably high. He gives 6000 for 1870.

[38]*Some Early Impressions* (1924), p. 137. The essays were first printed in 1903 in the *National Review*.

[39]Margaret Oliphant, *Life of Tulloch* (Bibliographical Note), p. 349; cf. pp. 348 and 352.

[40]Mrs. Oliphant, pp. 357, 358; and for the facts that follow, pp. 368–370, 386.

[41]Allingham Correspondence, cited in Bibliographical Note. On p. 385 Mrs. Oliphant says that "the magazine . . . fell from his hands at the beginning of his illness."

cannot be revived—never has been," as Knowles, the successful editor, had told Tulloch with crisp finality.[42] The end came with the issue of October 1882.

EDITORS

William Maginn: February 1800–September (?) 1836, Vols. 1—14, no. 3 (?).

In Maginn's obituary, September 1842, G. W. Nickisson not only denied that Maginn had ever been editor, but even claimed that he never took part in "the editorial management of the Magazine." This Kenealy labelled "Nickisson's filth" (see evidence for no. 1738); and Thrall has shown, pp. 5, 307, that both Percival Banks and Francis Mahoney called him the editor. But all Kenealy himself would say, in his article of January 1844 (see Bibliographical Note), p. 87, was that Maginn was "intimately connected" with the "foundation and chief management" of the periodical. Some years later Espinasse made that conclusion more specific (see Bibliographical Note). Maginn, he said, was never the editor because *Fraser's* never had an editor [not, he means, in the sense that Jeffrey was Editor of the *Edinburgh* or Morley of the *Fortnightly*], "being a republic or ochlocracy rather than a monarchy, limited or absolute." But if this is true, as I think it was (also see Banks' remark below, quoted under Mahoney), Maginn was certainly chairman of the board, impressing his own views and personality on every issue. He was, *de facto*, the editor, until about September 1836.[43]

In the first three years, 1830–1833, Abraham Heraud was sub-editor (see *DNB*), in charge, I suggest, of philosophy and literary criticism, though he often collaborated with Maginn in both fields.[44] His departure probably reflects a temperament too serious to remain a Fraserian. It would be hazardous to guess at the editorial committee, which in any event was changeable. James Fraser and John Churchill, Maginn's assistant, must have been regular members, joined at times by Lockhart and others.

Francis Sylvester Mahoney: October (?) 1836–December 1837 (?), Vols. 14, no. 4 (?)—16 (?).

After Maginn dropped out, his place was taken, apparently, by his fellow-Irishman and boon companion, "Father Prout." On October 1, 1836, Percival Banks remarked about Oliver Yorke, "Of late he might be generally described as Proutean; but," he added significantly, "look on him for any length of time, and you will find that he is Protean." Thrall, who quotes this on p. 198, says explicitly, p. 5, that Mahoney was Maginn's "successor in the position of editor." He left London at the close of 1837 and soon started on his European travels (see *DNB*).

The history of *Fraser's* from this point until Nickisson became proprietor and probably the real editor, in late 1841 or early 1842, is very cloudy. Mackenzie,

---

[42]Quoted by Mrs. Oliphant, p. 360.

[43]For the terminal date, see Thrall, pp. 198 and 199. I assume that Mackenzie's remark ("Memoir," p. lxxxii), that in 1836–1837 Maginn was "deprived of the best, because the most certain part, of his income," refers to his editorship of *FM*. It may be noted, however, that Thackeray's letter to Fraser, Mar. 5, 1838, written from Boulogne (*Letters*, I, 351), refers to having seen Maginn and received his "commands about the hundredth number," which suggests that Maginn may still have exerted some remote control, at least occasionally.

[44]Heraud himself, in applying to R.L.F., May 18, 1847, says he was editor for six years.

"Memoir," p. lxxii, said that E. V. Kenealy "succeeded Mahoney on the Magazine" —but as a writer, his footnote implies, rather than editor—and Thrall always refers to him simply as a member of the staff. Perhaps James Fraser, the proprietor, who had always taken part in his journal's editorial work, had a strong hand in these years.[45]

George William Nickisson: November or December 1841 or January 1842–June 1847, Vol. 24, nos. 5 or 6, or Vol. 25, no. 1—Vol. 35.

James Fraser died on October 2, 1841, but his name remained as publisher on the title pages until March 1842, when Nickisson's took its place for the April issue. But the latter had bought the business and become proprietor some time earlier, keeping Fraser's name on the Magazine for its commercial value.[46] Francis Mineka dates his first publication of the journal in January 1842,[47] and we know that on February 6, 1842, Thackeray sent Nickisson some instruction about the engraving of two cuts for a March article (*Letters*, II, 41). But was he the editor? Kenealy's letter to Nickisson, February 25, 1843, complains that his "editor, G. R. Gleig," has refused his contributions.[48] However, most of Thackeray's letters to Nickisson (see index, *Letters*, IV, 541) clearly imply that he is writing to the man in charge; and both Gordon Ray (ibid., II, 41, n.3) and the Henry Rosenbergs (new *CBEL*, III, col. 1845) assume his editorship. G. R. Gleig, I suggest, was a sub-editor or executive editor, at least for a time, and Nickisson became editor when he became proprietor. When? Ray and the Rosenbergs say 1841; Mineka (quoted above) sets January 1842 as his first issue.

John William Parker, Jr.: July 1847–October 1860, Vol. 36—Vol. 62, no. 4.

G. H. Lewes wrote to John William Parker, either the father as publisher or the son as editor [April or May 1847], Beinecke Lib., Yale Univ., saying that Nickisson had informed him "of the transference of 'Fraser's Magazine' to your care." The son's policy statement in January 1849 refers, p. 3, to our change of tone "within the last year and a half." Parker became seriously ill in the late summer of 1860 and died on November 9, 1860.

James Anthony Froude: November 1860–August 1874, Vol. 36, no. 5—Vol. 10 n.s., no. 2.

Dunn, in Froude, *Life*, II, 286, suggests that while Parker must have collected most of the material for the November and December 1860 issues, Froude saw them through the press. His name first appeared as editor on the title page of Volume 1 of the new series, January 1870, and remained there until August 1874; a head-note announcing a new editor initiated the September issue.[49]

[45]Thackeray's letters to Fraser of Jan. 14, 1840 and Dec. 3, 1840 (*Letters*, I, 407, 488) address him as though editor.

[46]The *Leamington Chronicle*, quoted in *Bentley's Advertiser*, Oct. 1842, p. 27, together with other tributes to Nickisson's *Fraser* dating back many months, said that although Mr. Nickisson had bought the business, he "continues" to keep Mr. Fraser's name "appended to the Magazine, which acquired such high reputation during his career as a publisher."

[47]In J. S. Mill, *Earlier Letters*, II, 723, n. 1.

[48]Kenealy Papers, Huntington Library, Pasadena, California.

[49]Dunn, in Froude, *Life*, II, 349, says that Allingham succeeded Froude in June 1874, but this is an error. Froude wrote Allingham on June 2 [1874], Allingham Correspondence, thanking him for "having taken Fraser off my hands during these months," i.e., since his wife's death, Feb. 12,

Allingham was sub-editor, 1870–1874 (ibid., p. 349). At various times when Froude was doing research in Spain or lecturing in America, *Fraser's* was run by his friends: for May and June 1861 by Arthur Helps, Theodore Martin, and William Frederick Pollock; from May to August 1867, mainly by Charles Kingsley and with some help from Leslie Stephen; and at the end of 1872 by Allingham.[50]

William Allingham: September 1874–June 1879, Vol. 10 n.s., no. 3—Vol. 19 n.s.

John Tulloch: July 1879–January 1881, Vol. 20 n.s.—Vol. 23 n.s., no. 1.

Charles James Longman: February 1881–October 1882, Vol. 23 n.s., no. 2—Vol. 26 n.s., no. 4.[51]

PUBLISHERS AND PROPRIETORS

James Fraser: February 1830–c. December 1841, Vol. 1—Vol. 24.

George William Nickisson: c. January 1842–June 1847, Vol. 25—Vol. 35.[52]

John William Parker and Son: July 1847–December 1860, Vol. 36—Vol. 62.

Parker, Son, and Bourn: January 1861–October 1863, Vol. 63—Vol. 68, no. 4.

Longman, Green, Longman, Roberts, & Green: November 1863–June 1865, Vol. 68—Vol. 71.

Longmans, Green, & Co.: July 1865–October 1882, Vol. 72—Vol. 80 and n.s. Vol. 1—Vol. 26.

NOTE ON ATTRIBUTIONS

The difficulty of identifying anonymous and pseudonymous writing in *Fraser's* is unusually severe. There are no marked files or publishers' lists, so far as we can discover, and the editorial correspondences of Froude and Allingham cited in the Bibliographical Note are disappointing. Nickisson sent Kenealy a complete list of Maginn's contributions, which he in turn, apparently, sent to Robert Shelton Mackenzie when Mackenzie was preparing his edition of Maginn's *Miscellaneous Writings*, and that is the last anyone has heard of it.[53] Moreover, since little is signed (only 243 papers before 1865 and 845 after, out of a total of about 6560), the lack of good sources is especially unfortunate.

The only sizeable body of information is in Miriam Thrall's *Rebellious Fraser's*, where pp. 276–306 are devoted to the identification of authorship during the first decade, 1830–1840. We have used this heavily but uneasily. Only rarely is any evidence given; most of the time the attributions are simply educated guesses founded on the combination of subject, style, and a general knowledge of the Fraserians. Some lists are headed "Work probably attributable to Thackeray and Maginn in collaboration," or "Work presumably by Heraud alone," leaving this editor in some-

1874; in his letter of June 7, he announces his intention to stay on as editor. Allingham to Thomas Longman, Jan. 29, 1877, Allingham Correspondence, says Froude resigned in July 1874.

[50]See, respectively, Maurer, p. 216, and Froude, *Life*, II, 289, 294; the evidence below for nos. 4761, 4793, 4800, and Maurer, p. 216, n. 12; and Froude to Allingham, Jan. 30 [1873], Allingham Correspondence, enclosing a cheque for £100 which Froude promised him "for managing Fraser's while I was away."

[51]For the last three editors, see the final paragraphs of the *Fraser* essay above; and on Allingham's initial date, the previous evidence on Froude's terminal date.

[52]For Fraser's terminal date and Nickisson's initial date, see above under Editors: Nickisson.

[53]Thrall, p. 323, n. 5.

thing of a quandary. Along with much that is undoubtedly right, there are inevitably a good many errors. Candidus is not E. V. Kenealy (p. 286), nor is Pierce Pungent Lockhart and Maginn (pp. 35, 287); and R. Alexander did not write the series called "The Schoolmaster's Experience in Newgate" (p. 294).[54] Many of Miss Thrall's attributions to Thackeray are questioned in Edward White's able article (see Bibliographical Note). But I begin to feel like the dog who bit the hand that fed him. We have used Miss Thrall extensively, if reluctantly, and owe her our gratitude.

The lists in the Magazine are cited in n. 20 above.

BIBLIOGRAPHICAL NOTE

There is no account of *Fraser's Magazine* from start to finish except the sketchy essay above. The only book, *Rebellious Fraser's* (N.Y., 1934), by Miriam M. H. Thrall, covers simply the first decade, 1830–1840, and deals almost wholly with the work of Maginn and his close associates.

For the early years Thrall's book may be supplemented by many essays, all centering on Maginn: E. V. H. Kenealy wrote obituaries in *Fraser's*, 26 (September 1842), 377–378 [but see below, no. 1738, for Nickisson's insertion], *Bentley's Miscellany*, 12 (September 1842), 329–330, and *Ainsworth's Magazine*, 2 (September 1842), 218–220, reprinted in his *Brallaghan* (1845); also an important article in the *Dublin University Magazine*, 23 (January 1844), 72–101; in 1857 R. S. Mackenzie's "Memoir," prefixed to Maginn's *Miscellaneous Writings* (N. Y., 1855–1857), V, ix–cx, greatly improved on Kenealy and still should be read, along with Thrall; *The Maclise Portrait-Gallery; or, Illustrious Literary Characters*, ed. William Bates [1873], is a scholarly edition of the most original feature of the early Magazine; Richard Garnett wrote the *DNB* article on Maginn in 1893. Lockhart's famous elegy can be read in Thrall, p. 190.

In the present century the principal work on Maginn besides Thrall's, has been done by Michael Sadleir: in his *Bulwer; a Panorama. Edward & Rosina, 1803–1836* (Boston, 1931), and especially the brilliant and more sympathetic essay, " 'Kind William Maginn,' " in his *Things Past* (1944), pp. 54–56; there is also a useful chapter by Malcolm Elwin in *Victorian Wallflowers* (1934). Edward M. White in "Thackeray's Contributions to *Fraser's Magazine*," *Studies in Bibliography*, 19 (1966), 67–84, brought a sharp, skeptical eye to bear on previous scholarship, and threw out many a Thackeray attribution, perhaps a few too many.

There are various policy statements, often including some history of the early periodical and its contributors, in the Magazine itself, usually written by Maginn: see especially 1 (February 1830), 1–8; 7 (June 1833), 750–752; 11 (January 1835), 1–27; 13 (January 1836), 1–80; 16 (November 1837), 528–529; and 21 (January 1840), 15–31.

In his survey of the periodical press, Francis Espinasse, calling himself "Herodotus Smith," took up *Fraser's* in the *Critic*, 11 (April 15, 1852), 200–201, bringing the story down through Nickisson's period into Parker's. For the latter's editorship, the only essay is unfortunately unpublished: "The Identity of John William Parker,

---

[54]See below, nos. 1392, 33, 393, respectively, for what seem to us the correct attributions.

Junior," by the late David Bonnell Greene, which was kindly loaned to the *Index* by Mrs. Greene. The obituary by J. A. Froude in the *Gentleman's Magazine*, 55 (February 1861), 221–224, should be read; also Parker's own statement in *Fraser's*, 39 (January 1849), 1–3.

For Froude's editorial years, there are valuable primary and secondary sources. Among the first, see Moncure Conway's "Working with Froude on *Fraser's Magazine*," *The Nation*, November 22, 1894, pp. 378–379, and November 29, pp. 401–402; John Skelton's "Reminiscences of James Anthony Froude," *Blackwood's*, 156 (December 1894), 756–776, reprinted in his *Table-Talk of Shirley* (Edinburgh, 1895), pp. 119–166. There is a collection of 80 editorial letters to and from Froude in the Huntington Library at Pasadena, California, and 33 letters in the Allingham Correspondence at the University of Illinois at Urbana. The best modern account is by Oscar Maurer, Jr., "Froude and *Fraser's Magazine*, 1860–1874," *University of Texas Studies in English*, 28 (1949), 213–243; it should be supplemented by Waldo H. Dunn's chapter "Editing *Fraser's Magazine*" in his *James Anthony Froude, a Biography* (2 vols., Oxford, 1961–1963), II, 326–350; also see pp. 285–288, and the index to both volumes.

For Allingham's editorship the major source is a collection of about 800 letters at the University of Illinois, which have been used by the kind permission of the library. There is some material in his *Diary*, ed. Helen Allingham (1908), and in his *Letters*, ed. Helen Allingham and Mrs. E. B. Williams (1911).

The period of Tulloch's valiant and futile struggle is well described by Mrs. [Margaret] Oliphant, *A Memoir of the Life of John Tulloch* (Edinburgh, 1888), pp. 348–362, 367–370. For his first issue, July 1879, Tulloch wrote a retrospect sketch of the Magazine called "Our Past and Our Future."

29 Canadian sketches (No. II): the bell of St. Regis, 268–270. **John Galt.** Signed The Author of *Sir Andrew Wylie*; cf. no. 10, which is apparently No. I.

30 Odes from the German of Klopstock, 271–275. **J. A. Heraud.** Since sub-title gives him as translator, presumably he also did the critical commentary.

31 The state of the fine arts in Russia, 276–286. **W. H. Leeds,** prob. In 1828 Leeds wrote an art. on this subject for the *Foreign Rev.* which never appeared there (see Leeds to Dawson Turner, Jan. 28, 1828, Trin. Coll. Camb.); *FQR* no. 470 in Jan. 1838 is the same kind of learned, serious account of fine arts in Russia by someone who knew Russian—and that was by Leeds; cf. nos. 8, 99.

32 The philosophy of pottery, 287–291.

33 Literary characters (No. I): James Hogg, 291–300. **Thomas Powell.** Signed Pierce Pungent; see Allibone for Powell's use of this pseudonym in *FM*; also *DAB* and *H&L,* I, 300; Thrall's identification of Pierce Pungent with Lockhart and Maginn, p. 35, is very shaky at best.

34 Whewell's notation of political economy; a fragment, 303–308.

35 Scene in Trinity College, Dublin: sketches of Dr. M———, A——— of D——— [Dr. Magee, Archbishop of Dublin] and Dr. E———, B——— of F——— [Dr. Elrington, Bishop of Ferns], 310–313.

36 Specimens of Irish minstrelsy (No. II): rockite songs, 314–318. **T. Crofton Croker.** Signed.

37 Fashionable novels: *The Dominie's Legacy* [by Andrew Picken; and Bulwer's *Pelham*], 318–335. **William Maginn,** perhaps with **J. A. Heraud.** Thrall, pp. 268–269, 284–285.

38 On the state of the country: a letter to Christopher North, Esq. from an old friend, 336–340. **A. Templeton.** Signed; perhaps Andrew Templeton, Scottish poet (see *BMCat*); more probably a pseudonym.

39 Sacred poetry: *The Descent into Hell* [by J. A. Heraud], 341–352. **William Maginn?** Maginn wrote on this general subject in no. 12, the reception of which is here discussed at length, pp. 341–342, as though by either the author or the editor of *FM*.

40 Mrs. M'Crie, Charles Mathews's old Scotch lady, 353–356. **Andrew Picken?** Thrall, p. 292.

41 Letter from Lady Byron (No. I), 356–359. **Anna I. Noel Byron,** collab. Title. AND a collaborator who wrote the commentary. (No. II is no. 53.)

42 Richard Taylor's [edition of] Horne Tooke, 360–366.

VOLUME 1, MAY 1830

43 Buckingham Palace, 379–388. **W. H. Leeds,** prob. Cf. nos. 8, 285, and 1052 for evidence that Leeds was *Fraser's* architectural critic; his interest in London architecture led to his *Supplement*, 1838, to Britton and Pugin, *Illustrations of the Public Buildings of London*; his raffish English appears on pp. 381, 387, 388 (he would like to "chop off Mr. Seguier's head, and place it on the trunk of some decapitated leaden god").

44 Canadian affairs, 389–398.

45 Jean Paul Friedrich Richter's review of Mme. de Staël's *Allemagne* (Part II, concl.), 407–413. **J. P. F. Richter.** Title; signed FRIP, anagram of his initials.

46 The wounded spirit (chaps. i–iv), 417–426. **D. M. Moir.** See no. 74.

47 An expostulation with the law of divorce, 427–431. **William Maginn?** Thrall, p. 303.

48 The Magyars versus Dr. Bowring, 433–442. **John Churchill,** with **William Maginn.** Thrall, p. 280; in the series of satires on John Bowring, Churchill apparently did the poetry (see Maginn's remark in no. 292, where he attrs. the poetry in no. 203 to Churchill), and Maginn presumably served as commentator, but no doubt both had a hand in both verse and prose.

49 Recollections and observations of a Scottish clergyman, 443–450. **Edward Irving.** Editorial note, no. 778, p. 99.

50 On medical quackery and Mr. St. John Long (No. I), 451–456. **John Aitken Carlyle.** Claimed in letter cited in no. 75. (See nos. 117, 166.)

51 East India Company (No. II): Messrs. Rickards and Crawfurd, 457–479. (No. III is no. 73.)

52 Sketch of English manners by a Frenchman [translated from a French *itineraire*], 479–482.

53 Lord and Lady Byron (No. II, concl.), 484–488. By the collaborator in No. I (no. 41).

54 *Liltiecockie* [fictitious book], 488–489.

55 Notes on the Russian army of 1828, 490–495. **Charles Routledge O'Donnell.** Signed C. R. O'Donnell, with title Lieutenant Colonel, late of the 15th Hussars; *Army List*/30.

56 The election of editor for *Fraser's Maga-*

zine: from Mr. Gurney's shorthand notes, corrected by Mr. Alexander Fraser of Thavies Inn (Part I), 496–508. **William Maginn.** Repr. *Writings*, V.

VOLUME 1, JUNE 1830

57 Mr. Edward Lytton Bulwer's novels; and remarks on novel-writing, 509–532. **William Maginn**, perhaps with **J. A. Heraud.** Signed Ned Culpepper, the Tomahawk; Thrall, pp. 268–269, 285.

58 A gossip about arts and artists, 533–540. **Charles Molloy Westmacott?** The author had been a painter twenty years ago and then, or later, a frequenter of exhibitions (p. 533); Westmacott was trained as an artist, had published descriptive catalogues of exhibitions at the R.A., and was a contributor to *FM* (see, respectively, no. 689, *BMCat.*, and no. 84, p. 738); the personal, chatty style is unlike the work of Leeds, the other *Fraser* writer on art at this time, and he was never an artist.

59 On the civil disabilities of British Jews, 541–548. **William Maginn?** Thrall, p. 303.

60 *Three Courses and a Dessert*, 549–554.

61 Newnham's *Illustrations of the Exodus*, 555–559.

62 Literary characters (No. II): the bard of hope [Thomas Campbell], 563–571. **Thomas Powell.** Signed Pierce Pungent; see no. 33. (No. III is no. 231.)

63 Sicilian poetry, 572–576.

64 Comparative anatomy of O'Connell and Cobbett, 577–579.

65 Specimens of Irish minstrelsy (No. III): songs of the Brazilian emigrants, 580–583. **T. Crofton Croker.** Signed.

66 The *Edinburgh Review*; Mr. Thomas Babington Macaulay and Mr. Southey ['s *Colloquies*], 584–600. **William Maginn.** Repr. *Writings*, V, as "Maginn on Macaulay."

67 Kisfaludy's "Meeting of the Similes" [satire on Bowring], 601–604. **John Churchill**, with **William Maginn.** Continuation of no. 48, announced on p. 442.

68 The gallery of illustrious literary characters (No. I): William Jerdan, Esq., editor of the *Literary Gazette*, 605–606. **William Maginn.** Thrall p. 20; repr. *Gallery*.

69 Minor Greek poets (No. I): Meleager, 608–609. **Robert A. Willmott.** Signed The Harrovian; Thrall, p. 293.

70 The Anti-Slavery Society, 610–622.

VOLUME 1, JULY 1830

71 The desperate system: poverty, crime, and emigration, 635–642. **William Maginn?** Thrall, p. 303.

72 The playhouses and the players, 644–650. Signed: Theatralis.

73 East India question (No. III): evidence laid before parliament, 655–662.

74 The wounded spirit (chaps. v–x), 663–672. **D. M. Moir.** Signed.

75 Animal magnetism, 673–684. **J. A. Carlyle.** Carlyle to Thomas Carlyle, May 17, 1830, Nat. Lib. Scot.: has finished an art. on this topic for *FM*.

76 Letter from Sir Morgan O'Doherty, Bart., 685–688. **William Maginn.** Signed Morgan O'Doherty—see no. 77.

77 Review of *The Reproof of Brutus*, 688–694. **William Maginn.** Signed Dixi; attr. on pp. 688, 694 to Ensign Morgan O'Doherty, pseud. of Maginn: see "Memoir," p. xxx.

78 Webster's *Travels through the Crimea and Egypt*, and Burckhardt's *Arabic Proverbs*, 695–710. **William Maginn?** Thrall, p. 303.

79 [Introduction to] Poems to distinguished individuals, 711–713. Signed: Peter Pepper and Co.

80 The gallery of illustrious literary characters (No. II): Thomas Campbell, Esq., editor of the *New Monthly*, 714. **William Maginn.** Repr. *Gallery*.

81 Colonial question [on slavery in West Indies]: parallel cases of Esther Hibner and the Mosses, 715–719.

82 Robert Montgomery and his critics, 721–726. **William Maginn?** He wrote earlier attack in no. 12, and prob. wrote the continuation of this art., no. 97.

83 Thoughts on the Wellington administration, 729–737. **Thomas Powell.** Signed Pierce Pungent; see no. 33.

84 The election of editor for *Fraser's Magazine* (Part II), 738–757. **William Maginn.** Repr. *Writings*, V.

85 Death of George the Fourth, 758–762.

VOLUME 2, AUGUST 1830

86 Dr. Kennedy and Lord Byron, 1–9. **William Maginn?** Thrall, p. 303.

87 Monos and Daimonos [satire on Bulwer-Lytton's story of that title in *New Monthly Mag.*, 28 (May, 1830), 387–392], 10–15.

88 Journey from Hermanstadt to Bucharest,

and passage of the Rother Thurm defile in the Carpathians—1828, 16–31. **C. R. O'Donnell.** Signed; cf. no. 55.

89 The philosophy of apparitions, 33–41. **Thomas Richards.** Claimed in Richards to Lord Brougham, Dec. 3, 1830, Univ. Coll. London. (See no. 173.)

90 Specimens of Irish minstrelsy (No. IV): Keating, 41–44. **T. Crofton Croker.** Signed. (Part V is no. 586.)

91 On the Italian opera (No. I), 45–52. Unidentified. (No. II is no. 233.)

92 The minor Greek poets (No. II, concl.): Simonides, 53–58. **R. A. Willmott.** Evidence for no. 69.

93 Lardner's Cabinet [Library]: vol. *Cities and Towns*, 58–61. **William Maginn?** Thrall, p. 303.

94 Mackenzie's *Haiti*, and Bayley's *Four Years in the West Indies*, 61–66.

95 Brougham on the slave question [continuation of no. 94], 67–76.

96 The gallery of illustrious literary characters (No. III): John Gibson Lockhart, Esq., editor of *The Quarterly*, 77. **William Maginn.** Repr. *Gallery*.

97 On religious poetry, being a letter to the editor of the *Literary Gazette*, Mr. Edward Clarkson, and others, 78–89. **William Maginn?** Signed Theophilus; this art. is really a continuation of no. 82, renewing the attack on Montgomery and Clarkson, and citing, p. 79n, the book there reviewed; on p. 84 author refers in detail to "our" earlier criticism of *The Descent into Hell*, repeating the points made in no. 39, p. 343; furthermore, the title and subject of no. 39 is "Sacred poetry."

98 Letter from a Tory from principle, not prejudice, to Oliver Yorke, Esq., 89–90. Unidentified. Reply, 90–92, signed Oliver Yorke.

99 Strictures on art and exhibitions, 93–110. **W. H. Leeds.** Leeds was writing on art at this time for *Fraser's* (cf. nos. 8, 31, 43); the violent English and the foreign phrases (cf. nos. 8, 43) and the use of "*con amore*" on p. 97 (cf. *FQR* nos. 372, p. 156, and 448, p. 381, etc.) are all characteristic of his style.

100 The dead parliament, 111–118.

101 Eugenius Roche, 118.

VOLUME 2, SEPTEMBER 1830

102 *Life of Bishop Heber*, 121–152. **R. A. Willmott** and a collab.? Pages 121–131,

almost wholly on Heber's poetry, seem like an early art. by Willmott: the succession of comments on Taylor, Latimer, and Warburton (p. 121), the ornate description of Spenser (p. 123), the quotation from Milton (p. 124), the sentimental notes ("the heart melting with affection," p. 122), and the exaggerated praise of Protestantism and condemnation of Catholicism (p. 121), all suggest the work of Willmott (see arts. in Part B and his *Summer Time*); pages 131–152 with their statistical tables are clearly by another hand, as the horizontal line drawn on page 131 would imply.

103 The man-hunter, 153–159. **B. W. Procter.** Signed [L. Bethel]; repr. *Essays and Tales in Prose* (Boston, 1853), I.

104 On the march of intellect, and universal education, 161–170.

105 The unearthly witness [a ghost story], 171–178. **James Hogg.** Signed The Ettrick Shepherd; see *DNB*.

106 Fables, 178–179. **Thomas Carlyle.** Signed Pilpay Junior; repr. *Essays*, I.

107 Hon. Mrs. Norton's *Undying One*, 180–189. **William Maginn.** Repr. in *Writings*, V, as "The Sheridan Family."

108 The prospects of the [new] ministry, 190–199. Unidentified. (See no. 128.)

109 Savage life in America, 199–214. Signed, in first paragraph: Oliver Yorke.

110 The disasters of Jan Nadeltreiber, 215–221. **William Howitt.** Signed.

111 East India Company (No. IV, concl.): Mr. Buckingham's last humbug, 222–226.

112 *The Fate of the Colonies* [in the West Indies], 226–232.

113 The French Revolution of 1830, 233–235.

114 The gallery of illustrious literary characters (No. IV): Samuel Rogers, Esq., author of *The Pleasures of Memory*, p. 237. **William Maginn.** Repr. *Gallery.*

115 The election of editor for *Fraser's Magazine* (Part III, concl.), 238–250. **William Maginn.** Repr. *Writings*, V.

VOLUME 2, OCTOBER 1830

116 The death of Mr. Huskisson, and the approaching parliament, 251–263.

117 Medical quackery and Mr. John St. John Long (No. II, concl.), 264–265. **J. A. Carlyle.** Cf. no. 50.

118 The gallery of illustrious literary characters (No. V): Thomas Moore, Esq.,

Napier, Dec. 16, 1830, Napier MSS., claims art. on Belgium in December *Fraser's*.

154 Parliamentary reform: proceedings before committees of privileges, and the case of the Cinque Ports, 612–632, 633*–637.*

155 Ruminations round the remains of a punch bowl, on the resignation of Billy Holmes and others, 638*–640.* **William Maginn.** Signed M. O'D. [Morgan O'Doherty]—see no. 77.

VOLUME 2, JANUARY 1831

156 [Introductory note to Schiller's] *Wallenstein's Camp*, 633–636. **John Churchill.** See no. 1397, p. 21.

157 On the punishment of death, 666–672. **William Hazlitt.** W. C. Hazlitt, *Memoirs*, I, xxx; repr. *Works*, ed. Waller & Glover, XII, 666–669; *Works*, ed. Howe, XIX, 324–329.

158 Narratives of the late French Revolution, 673–686.

159 Dr. Phillpott, the bishop, 687–690. **William Maginn?** Thrall, p. 303. With a postscript by Oliver Yorke—signed O.Y.

160 Cruthers and Jonson; or The outskirts of life, 691–705. **Thomas Carlyle.** Repr. *Essays*, V.

161 West Indian slavery by John Galt, Esq. (Letter III, concl.), 706–713. **John Galt.** Title. (Letter, vol. 3, Feb. Table of Contents verso, by Oliver Yorke—signed O.Y.)

162 Swing's letter to Oliver Yorke, 714–715. Signed: Swing!

163 The gallery of illustrious literary characters (No. VIII): The Doctor [William Maginn], 716. **J. G. Lockhart.** Attr. in Maginn, "Memoir," p. lxx; repr. Maginn, *Gallery*.

164 Parliamentary reform, and the vote by ballot (No. I), 717–735. (No. II is no. 179.)

165 Boaden's *Life of Mrs. Jordan*, 736–739. **William Maginn?** Thrall, p. 303.

166 Some passages from the diary of the late Mr. St. John Long (No. I; no more published), 739–740. **J. A. Carlyle.** Attr. by Thomas Carlyle, *Letters*, p. 182. (Letter, vol. 3, Feb. Table of Contents verso, with reply.)

167 The Polish insurrection, 741–742.

168 Luther's psalm ["Eine feste Burg"], 743–744. **Thomas Carlyle.** Repr. *Essays*, II, 160.

169 L'Envoy: ourselves, the Grey administration, and things in general, 745–748.

VOLUME 3, FEBRUARY 1831

170 The repeal of the Union, 1–11.

171 [Introduction to satiric poems by] Peter Nimmo, 12. **Thomas Carlyle.** Signed O.Y. [Oliver Yorke]; *Bibliography*, p. 208; Thrall, p. 299.

172 A day in Kent [adventures of the Fraserians], 17–33.

173 Fatal presentiments, 34–39. **Thomas Richards.** This art. is a sequel to no. 89.

174 The only daughter: a Scottish tale, 44–53. **Andrew Picken?** Thrall, p. 292.

175 Southey's *Life of Bunyan*, 54–66. **J. A. Heraud** and **William Maginn**, prob. Thrall, p. 285.

176 The gallery of illustrious literary characters (No. IX): Crofton Croker, 67. **William Maginn.** Repr. *Gallery*.

177 Unrepresented London, 69–72.

178 *France in 1829–1830* by Lady Morgan, reviewed by Her Ladyship's cortejo, Morgan Rattler, 73–84. **Percival W. Banks.** Signed Morgan Rattler; attr. in Grant, *Metropolis*, II, 322; Thrall, p. 278; Cushing, *Initials*.

179 On the vote by ballot (No. II), 85–94.

180 The novels of the season, 95–113. **William Maginn?** Thrall, p. 303.

181 The colonists *versus* the Anti-Slavery Society (No. II, concl.), 114–126. Signed: A Late Resident [of the West Indies].

VOLUME 3, MARCH 1831

182 Schiller, 127–152. **Thomas Carlyle.** Repr. *Essays*, II.

183 Ars ridendi; or, Hook and Hood—on laughter, 154–162. **William Maginn,** with **J. G. Lockhart?** Last two paragraphs, 161–162, repr. as "Philosophy of Laughter" in Maginn, *Writings*, V; Thrall, p. 287, suggests the collab.

184 Letters on the history, laws, and constitution of England to Oliver Yorke, Esq. (No. I; no more published), 163–171. Signed: Catholicus.

185 The barber of Duncow, a real ghost story, 174–180. **James Hogg.** Signed The Ettrick Shepherd—see *DNB*.

186 The ballot (No. III, concl.), 183–194.

187 *The Siamese Twins* [by Bulwer Lytton], 195–204. **William Maginn?** Thrall, p. 303.

188 Stray notes on the *Anti-Slavery Monthly*

Reporter, 205–208. Signed: A Looker-on.

189   Mr. Sadler and the *Edinburgh Review* [of July 1830], 209–221. **William Maginn?** Thrall, p. 303.

190   The gallery of illustrious literary characters (No. X): Mrs. Norton, 222. **William Maginn.** Repr. *Gallery*.

191   Moral and political state of the British Empire, 223–229.

192   "What is the value of a virtuous woman's tear?" 230–231.

193   The *Quarterly Review* [of Feb. 1831] on reform, 231–235.

194   "The Althorp budget," 236–237.

195   Moore's *Life of Byron*, 238–252. **William Maginn.** Signed O.Y. [Oliver Yorke]; "Memoir," p. lxv.

196   On our national prospects and political history, 252–254. **William Maginn.** Signed W. Holmes, Esq., M.P. for Haslemere; repr. *Writings*, V, as "The Politics of 1831."

197   Symposiac the second, 253–268. **William Maginn,** collab. at least. Thrall, p. 303, who adds, "presumably with others."

VOLUME 3, APRIL 1831

198   Parliamentary reform, 269–280.

199   Montgomery's *Oxford*, 280–283. **William Maginn?** Thrall, p. 303.

200   Grant's notes on Byron's *Cain*, 285–304. **J. A. Heraud.** Thrall, p. 270.

201   Some passages in the life of an idler (Part II), 305–320. **Henry Mildmay.** Signed.

202   On alchemy and the alchemists, 321–334. **J. A. Carlyle.** Claimed in letter cited in evidence for no. 245.

203   The poetry of the Sandwich Islands, 334–345. **John Churchill, with William Maginn.** In this continuation of the satire on John Bowring (cf. nos. 48, 67, and especially no. 119, where pp. 267, 280, announced the coming visit to the Sandwich Islands, and p. 281 quoted stanzas from Hawaiin [cf. pp. 334n., 335 here]), the poetry is at once attr. to "Our Man of Genius" (no. 895, p. 76, says "Our Man Of Genius" translated *Wallenstein's Camp* [see no. 156]; *FM* no. 1397, p. 21, identifies the translator as Churchill); for Maginn's prob. collab. see Thrall, p. 280, and no. 48.

204   Means of lessening the West Indian distress, 346–350. **John Galt.** Signed.

205   Punch and Judy, 350–354. **Robert Macnish.** Signed A Modern Pythagorean; attr. in *Tales*, I, 189; repr. *Tales*, II.

206   Castilian poetry, 355–363. **Pablo Mendíbil?** Attr. by Llorens, "*Emigrados*," p. 134n.

207   The gallery of literary characters (No. XI): John Wilson, Esq., 364. **William Maginn.** Repr. *Gallery*.

208   Visit from Mr. Saint John Long, 365–368. **William Maginn?** Thrall, p. 303.

209   On quackery, twaddle, and other offences, 368–375. **William Maginn?** Signed Piper; Thrall, p. 303.

210   Lives of the statesmen of France (No. I): the Duc de Sully (Part I), 376–390.

211   To Petrus Maximus on the ejectment of Jeffrey; a monologue, 391–394. **William Maginn?** Thrall, p. 303.

VOLUME 3, MAY 1831

212   Parliamentary eloquence (No. I): House of Commons, 395–407. **William Phillips.** Signed Oliver Yorke; Phillips to Blackwood, Aug. 27, 1831, Blackwood Corres., states that art. with this title formerly offered to *Bk* had been published in *FM*; Phillips was parliamentary reporter for the *Times*.

213   On the libraries of celebrated literary men, 408–409.

214   The gallery of literary characters (No. XII): Mary Russell Mitford, 410. **William Maginn.** Repr. *Gallery*.

215   Singular passage in my own life, 411–422. **Robert Macnish.** Signed A Modern Pythagorean; claimed in *Tales*, I, 191; repr. *Tales*, II.

216   The Rev. Edward Irving and his adversaries, 423–428.

217   *Scottish Melodies*, 429–435.

218   *A Year in Spain*, 436–449. **Pablo Mendíbil?** On pp. 446–447 "we" promise to write on the Spaniard Campomanes in the next number of *FM*, a subject which would be a "natural" for Mendíbil: see no. 237 and its evidence; then on p. 447 a line separates pp. 436–447 on the book being reviewed from pp. 447–449 on the Spanish clergy without reference to the book, so that these final pages may be by a different writer.

219   Presentation of the Magazine [*Fraser's*] to their Majesties; abbreviated from the court circular, 450–452.

220   Lives of the statesmen of France (No. I): the Duc de Sully (Part II), 453–472. (No. II is no. 343.)

221   Felix Binocular, a legal sketch, 472–477. **William Mudford.** Signed at start The Author of "First and Last," at end

W.; see *Blackwood's* no. 665, *Index*, I, 29; repr. in his *Tales and Trifles* (1849), I.

222 *Principles of Dissent*, 478–488.

223 Reflections on the Highland character, with reference to the novels *Destiny* and *The Scottish Gael*, 489–492.

224 *The Metropolitan*, a "prospect"-ive puff of a new periodical, 493–495. **William Maginn?** Thrall, p. 303.

225 Mr. Buxton and West Indians, 509–511.

226 Dissolution of parliament, 512–522.

227 Nicolas and Palgrave, 522–524. **William Maginn?** Thrall, p. 303.

228 The *Quarterly Review* [of Apr. 1831] on reform, 525–532. **William Maginn?** Thrall, p. 303.

VOLUME 3, JUNE 1831

229 New poem by Percy Bysshe Shelley: "The Wandering Jew"—introduction, 533–536. **J. A. Heraud** perhaps with **William Maginn.** Thrall, p. 285; letter cited in evidence for no. 262.

230 National song of Ireland, 537–556. **William Maginn?** Thrall, p. 303.

231 Literary characters (No. III, concl.): Mr. Wordsworth, 557–566. **Thomas Powell.** Signed Pierce Pungent; see no. 33.

232 Godwin's *Thoughts on Man*, 569–586. **J. A. Heraud** perhaps with **William Maginn.** Thrall, p. 285; letter quoted in evidence for no. 262.

233 On the Italian opera (No. II): Desdemona, 587–597. Signed R.P.E.

234 Romantic poetry of the Italians [on book by Panizzi], 598–603. **William Maginn?** Thrall, p. 303.

235 The honourable House and the reform debate, 604–612. **William Maginn, prob.** Author refers to himself as "Oliver the Great" and later "the Prime Mover of this Magazine"; the many references to periodicals and remarks on personalities which are at once subtle and insulting (see for clear examples the treatment of J. W. Croker and the poet Praed, p. 607) are characteristic: cf. no. 644.

236 The gallery of literary characters (XIII): Don Telesforo de Trueba y Cozio, 613. **William Maginn.** Repr. *Gallery*.

237 Life of Count Campomanes, 614–622. **Pablo Mendibil, prob.** Llorens "*Emigrados*," pp. 136–137n.; like Campomanes, Mendibil had been educated as a lawyer (see obit. *Athenaeum*, Jan. 7, 1832, p.

19); on p. 616n. there is a bibliography of Spanish books on ecclesiastical law.

238 The Colonial crisis, 625–630.

239 The result of the late elections, with the abstract of returns, 632–637.

240 The new parliament, 637–647. Unidentified. (Reply, Table of Contents, Aug. 1831, verso, to criticism in the *Times*.)

241 Rumbling murmurs of an old Tory over the fate of his quondam friends, 648–654. **William Maginn.** Signed at start The Baronet, at end M. O'D [Morgan O'Doherty]—see no. 77.

VOLUME 3, JULY 1831

242 The King's speech, 655–665.

243 The Suffolk Street exhibition, 678–685. **W. H. Leeds, prob.** Cf. no. 838 which Leeds wrote on the rival Somerset exhibition (mentioned here, p. 678) in the same form and something of the same style: the "wild" language conspicuous on pp. 678–680, including two puns, is characteristic of Leeds; also cf. no. 99.

244 The gallery of literary characters (No. XIV): The Earl of Munster, 686. **William Maginn.** Repr. *Gallery*.

245 *Natural Philosophy* [by J. F. W. Herschel], 698–702. **J. A. Carlyle.** J. A. Carlyle to his brother Thomas, May 11, 1831, Nat. Lib. Scot., is scribbling "a review of Herschel's introductory lectures for Fraser"; the full title of the book is *A Preliminary Discourse on the Study of Natural Philosophy*.

246 The Italian merchant, a tale; from the German of Goethe [from *Unterhaltungen Deutscher Ausgewanderten*], 704–712. **J. W. von Goethe.** Title.

247 Autobiography of Edward Lytton Bulwer, Esq. [in *New Monthly Mag.*, May 1831], 713–719. **William Maginn?** Thrall, p. 303.

248 Aunt Susan, 720–726. **James Hogg.** Signed The Ettrick Shepherd—see *DNB*.

249 Hewitt Davis on foreign corn importation, 727–735.

250 Landor's poems, 736–744. **J. A. Heraud** and **William Maginn, prob.** Thrall, pp. 285, 303; Malcolm Elwin, *Savage Landor* (N.Y., 1941), p. 247, attrs. last paragraph definitely to Maginn.

251 Parliamentary eloquence (No. II): House of Commons, 744–757. **William Phillips.** Evidence for no. 212.

252 The Oxford controversy, 758–767.

253 Burial of Mrs. Siddons, 768–770. Unidentified. (Reply, Table of Contents,

Aug. 1831, verso, presumably by the author of this art., to an art. in *New Monthly Mag.* on same subject.)

254 A word at parting, 771.

VOLUME 4, AUGUST 1831

255 An apology for a preface to our fourth volume, 1–7. **William Maginn.** Signed O.Y. [Oliver Yorke]; this is an editorial whose author boasts (p. 2) he has never written a book, and who makes the extensive use of italics for English words and foreign phrases common in Maginn's writing; also attr. by Thrall, p. 303. (See no. 271.)

256 Novels of the season; batch the second, 8–25. **William Maginn?** Thrall, p. 303.

257 Political state of Europe, 25–31.

258 Louis Philip's speech, 31–32.

259 *Bubble and Squeak* [fictitious book], 33–41. **William Maginn,** collab. at least. Thrall, p. 303, who adds "presumably with others." (See no. 294.)

260 On the *Metropolitan English Lexicon,* 41–44. **William Maginn?** Thrall, p. 303.

261 Poetical plagiaries: Thomas Moore (Part I), 45–52. **William Maginn.** Repr. *Writings,* V.

262 Rationalism, 53–63. **J. A. Heraud,** prob. Heraud to W. Blackwood, Mar. 10, 1834, Blackwood Corres: "Nearly all the poetical and metaphysical criticism in Fraser's Magazine is from my pen"; in this case, the quotations from Coleridge and the references to obscure Kantians make Heraud's authorship very likely.

263 The gallery of literary characters (No. XV): Lord John Russell, 65. **William Maginn.** Repr. *Gallery.*

264 The Bill, the whole Bill, and nothing but the Bill [the Reform Bill], 66–78.

265 Ensign O'Donoghue's "first love," 79–84. **Thomas Crofton Croker.** Signed Ensign O'Donoghue; pseudonym attr. by Thrall, pp. 35–36.

266 The march of humbug, 85–93.

267 On the innovations of Lord Brougham (No. I, no more printed), 93–95. Signed: A True Tory.

268 American traditions (No. II): The early missionaries; or, The discovery of the falls of Niagara, 96–100. **John Galt.** Signed. (No. III is no. 368.)

269 *Sketches of Irish Character* [by Anna M. Hall], 100–112. **William Maginn?** Thrall, p. 303.

270 Oliver Yorke at home (No. I): a col-

loquy with Robert Southey, 113–126. **J. A. Heraud,** prob. Signed (in first par.) Oliver Yorke; Thrall, p. 284; letter quoted in evidence for no. 262; many refs. to genius recall no. 7.

VOLUME 4, SEPTEMBER 1831

271 The *Literary Gazette,* the *Court Journal,* the *Spectator,* and Regina, Table of Contents verso. **William Maginn?** Reply to criticisms of *FM* provoked by no. 255.

272 Influence of the newspapers (Part I), 127–142.

273 Some passages in the life of an idler (Part III), 143–155. **Henry Mildmay.** Cf. no. 151. (Part IV is no. 489.)

274 Parliamentary eloquence (No. III): House of Lords, 155–166. **William Phillips.** Evidence for no. 212.

275 German poetry (No. I): Mr. Taylor's *Historic Survey of German Poetry,* 167–179. **J. A. Heraud.** Thrall, p. 271.

276 Peter Robertson versus the *Edinburgh Review,* 180–186. **William Maginn.** Thrall, p. 304; in no. 2090, p. 155, P. W. Banks attribs. "former mentions of Robertson" in *FM* to Maginn.

277 A pilgrimage to Loch Dherrig, 187–202.

278 Poland (No. I): the Piasts and Jagellos, 202–217.

279 The principle of the [Reform] Bill, 217–224.

280 On the Italian opera (No. III), 224–239. Signed: L.C.H. (No. IV is no. 416.)

281 Gallery of literary characters (No. XVI): Right Hon. John Wilson Croker, 240. **William Maginn.** Repr. *Gallery.*

282 Report of the select committee on the city of Dublin election, and also the minutes of evidence taken before them, 241–252.

283 *Barney Moore: A Vision of Covent Garden and St. Giles,* 253–260. **William Maginn.** Repr. *Writings,* V.

VOLUME 4, OCTOBER 1831

284 Religious missions, 261–274. Unidentified. Perhaps Andrew Picken, a Fraserian, who published *Travels . . . of Eminent English Missionaries* early in 1831, where he said, p. vi, he hoped to write on further "religious travellers, and other points of Missionary history," a statement which fits this art.

285 Pie-crust; or, Architectural madness [on

Peter Legh], 277–292. **W. H. Leeds.**
Leeds was "doing" architecture for
Fraser's in the 30s (cf. nos. 8, 17, 43,
1052); the use of foreign phrases
("*chefs-d'oeuvre*," p. 279, was a favorite
of his) and the extravagant, slangy English are hallmarks of Leeds' style: cf.
nos. 8, 43.

286 The white lady: a tale of the Highlands,
293–301. Signed: I.

287 Lord Brougham and the Court of Chancery, 301–307. Signed: W. Attr. by
Thrall, p. 293, to R. A. Willmott, but
neither subject nor style resemble Willmott's work.

288 Scenes in the law courts: the Court of
Chancery, 308–310. **Edward Marlborough
Fitzgerald?** Signed Θ; Thrall, pp. 282–
283.

289 Influence of the newspapers (Part II,
concl.), 310–321.

290 Parliamentary eloquence (No. IV):
House of Lords, 321–328. **William Phillips.** Evidence for no. 212.

291 Who murdered Begbie? a stage-coach
romance, 329–332. **Robert Macnish.**
Signed A Modern Pythagorean; repr.
Tales, II.

292 Gallery of literary characters (No.
XVII); Tydus-pooh-pooh [John Bow-
ring], 333. **William Maginn.** Repr. *Gallery*; the title is a pseudonym of John
Churchill (cf. no. 948) because in his
ironic satires of Bowring's poetry (notably
no. 203, here referred to), he pretended
to be Bowring; this explanation, suggested by Thrall, p. 20, is confirmed by
the incident in no. 310, p. 498.

293 Poland (No. II): the elective monarchy
to the reign of John Casimir, 334–346.

294 *Bubble and Squeak*: course the second,
347–355. **William Maginn,** collab. at
least. Cf. no. 259.

295 What ought the Lords to do with the
Reform Bill? 355–360.

296 Oliver Yorke at home (No. II): a
conversation with Walter Savage Landor,
361–373. **J. A. Heraud,** prob. Cf. no.
270.

297 Coronation coronal; or, Verses on the
coronation of their Majesties, King William IV and Queen Adelaide, by the
most eminent poets of the day [Words-
worth, Scott, Morgan O'Doherty, Heraud,
Hogg, Moir, Coleridge, Southey, James
Montgomery], 374–386. **William Maginn,**
collab. at least. On p. 378 author claims
the parody of O'Doherty, Maginn's
pseudonym; attr. by Thrall, p. 304, who
also adds "presumably with others."

VOLUME 4, NOVEMBER 1831

298 Life and times of Bishop Ken, 388–401.

299 The ancient commerce of England, prior
and to the reign of Edward III inclusive,
403–421. **John Galt.** Signed.

300 French, German, and English philosophy, 428–433. **J. A. Heraud,** prob.
Thrall, p. 284; letter quoted in evidence
for no. 262.

301 Gallery of literary characters (No.
XVIII): Washington Irving, 435. **William Maginn.** Repr. *Gallery*.

302 England and her colonies in the West,
436–446.

303 *Tales from Tieck* [trans. by Julius
Hare], 446–460. Unidentified. Author
claims, p. 447, he heard Tieck in Dresden
reading *Midsummer Night's Dream*; Edwin H. Zeydel, *Ludwig Tieck and England* (Princeton, 1931), pp. 154–156,
suggests Henry Crabb Robinson, who
heard Tieck in Dresden in 1829, or John
Strang, who had just returned from Dresden and hearing Tieck, and who wrote
very favorably of Tieck in his *Germany
in 1831*, 1836; a further possibility is
Sarah Austin who identified Hare as the
translator of these *Tales* and praises
Tieck's dramatic readings in her *Fragments from German Prose Writers*,
(1841), p. 343.

304 Parliamentary eloquence (No. V,
concl.): House of Lords, 461–469. **William Phillips.** Evidence for no. 212.

305 Temperance societies, 469–474.

306 "What must be done with the Lords?"
475–480.

307 [Lives of the statesmen of France] (No.
II): The life of Mazarin (Part I), 480–
484.

308 The re-election of Alderman Key, 485–
489.

309 The Briareus of the press, 490–495.
William Maginn? Thrall, p. 304. (Note,
p. 514, signed O.Y. [Oliver Yorke].)

310 Oliver Yorke's levee, 495–502. **William
Maginn,** collab. at least. Thrall, p. 304,
who adds, "presumably with others."

311 The reaction against reform 502–512.

VOLUME 4, DECEMBER 1831

312 National unions, 515–519.

313 Epistles to the literati (No. I): letter to
Edward Lytton Bulwer, 520–526. **William
Maginn,** prob. Signed Robin Roughhead;
opening paragraph, p. 525 col. ii, and
Thrall, p. 304. With a postscript, 526–

John Galt who used this pseud. in *Black-wood's* and wrote on colonial subjects there and in *FM*.

347 Resurrectional recreations, 85–95. **John Churchill** and **William Maginn?** Signed A Poor Devil; Thrall, pp. 280–281.

348 Gallery of literary characters (No. XXI): James Hogg, 97. **William Maginn.** Repr. *Gallery*.

349 The people of England—who are they? 98–106.

350 A good tale badly told by Mr. Edward Lytton Bulwer [*Eugene Aram*], 107–113. **William Maginn,** prob. Thrall, p. 304; Sadleir's *Bulwer*, p. 253.

351 The great and celebrated Hogg dinner, reported especially for *Fraser's Magazine*, 113–126. **William Maginn.** Attr. in "Memoir," p. lxxiii.

VOLUME 5, MARCH 1832

352 The spirit and practice of the Whig executive, 127–143. **Robert B. Seeley?** Signed An Independent Pittite; claims in first par. to have written no. 327, and to have adopted here a new pseudonym "which will serve for all topics."

353 The climax of cemeteries! 144–154.

354 The stock exchange (No. III, concl.), 155–165.

355 Schiller, Goethe, and Madame de Staël, 171–176. **Thomas Carlyle.** Repr. *Essays*, I, appendix.

356 Theological Library: *Life of Wiclif*, 177–197.

357 On recent manifestations of spiritual gifts (No. II), 198–205. **Edward Irving.** Signed.

358 Gallery of literary characters (No. XXII): Baron von Goethe, 206. **Thomas Carlyle.** Repr. *Essays*, II, and Maginn, *Gallery*.

359 Historical romance: Sir Walter Scott and his imitators (No. II), 207–217. **J. A. Heraud?** Thrall, p. 284.

360 Invasion of Portugal, 218–226.

361 Rencontres on the road (No. III): Mary Fenwick, 228–234. **Amelia Gillespie Smyth.** Cf. no. 342.

362 Letters to the learned professions (No. I; no more published): to the students of medicine, 238–243. **D. M. Moir.** Signed Gabriel Cowitch; attr. in Macnish, *Tales*, I, 219.

363 John Black's "Lord Plunkett and John Galt's Archibald Jobbry," [art. partly a reprint from *Morning Chronicle*], 244–246. Signed: Oliver Yorke.

364 Epistles to the literati (No. II): Place to Wilson; Wilson to Place, 247. **William Maginn,** prob. In title and style this continues no. 313 and initiates the trick of signing real names to fictitious letters: cf. nos. 378, etc., and no. 497.

365 Are we to have new peers or not? 248–252.

VOLUME 5, APRIL 1832

366 Biography [review of Boswell's *Johnson*] (Part I), 253–260. **Thomas Carlyle.** Repr. *Essays*, III. (Part II is no. 379.)

367 Twenty-second report on the revenue: packet establishments, home station, 261–275. Unidentified. (Letter, vol. 8, pp. 379–382.)

368 American traditions (No. III, concl.), 275–280. **John Galt.** Signed.

369 German poetry (No. III, concl.): Burger—Gotter—Voss—Holty, 280–294. **J. A. Heraud.** Thrall, p. 271.

370 The present balance of parties in the state, and the results of the Reform Bill, 294–316.

371 On recent manifestations of spiritual gifts (No. III, concl.), 316–320. **Edward Irving.** Signed.

372 Gallery of literary characters (No. XXIII): Israel D'Israeli, Esq., 321. **William Maginn.** Repr. *Gallery*.

373 Shipping interest, silk manufacture, and glove trade, 322–336. **R. B. Seeley?** Signed An Independent Pittite; cf. no. 352.

374 Trollope and Paulding on America, 336–350. **William Maginn?** Thrall, p. 304.

375 The Duke of Newcastle's *Address to All Classes and Conditions of Englishmen*, 351–360.

376 The perils of a political unionist, 360–368. Signed: A Member of the Jacobin Club.

377 *The Member: an Autobiography* [by John Galt], 369–375.

378 Epistles to the literati (No. III): letter of William Holmes, Esq., M.P., to Archibald Jobbry, Esq., Ex-M.P., viz., John Galt: see above, p. 245, 376–378. **William Maginn.** Signed William Holmes —see no. 196.

VOLUME 5, MAY 1832

379 Boswell's *Life of Johnson* (Part II,

concl.), 379–413. **Thomas Carlyle.** Repr. *Essays,* III.

380   The Great Plague in the fourteenth century, 415–419. Unidentified. Perhaps D. M. Moir who published a book on the history of medicine in 1831, and contributed to *FM.*

381   The reports of the commissioners on Common Law Reform, 420–431.

382   The sock and the buskin (No. III, concl.): Miss Fanny Kemble's *Francis the First,* and Mr. Sheridan Knowles's *Hunchback,* 432–447. (Author's reply to letter from W. C. Macready, vol. 6, p. 256, with comment by Oliver Yorke— signed O.Y.)

383   On [political] parties (No. I), 448–462. **R. B. Seeley?** Signed An Independent Pittite; cf. no. 352.

384   Voyages and Travels; Captain Basil Hall and the Landers, 462–474.

385   Gallery of literary characters (No. XXIV): the antiquaries, 475. **William Maginn.** Repr. *Gallery.* (See illustration, p. 490.)

386   Shiel versus the tithes, 476–482.

387   *The Altrive Tales* [by James Hogg], 482–489. **William Maginn?** No other Fraserian except Lockhart—and the references to him on pp. 487 and 488 seem to rule him out—had such knowledge of the Blackwood circle; the claim, p. 485, that Hogg was wrong to identify arts. signed Timothy Tickler with Mr. Sym could well be made by Maginn, who used the pseudonym himself; in no. 902, p. 200n., Maginn cites this review.

388   Dorf Juystein, 489–492.

389   A speech, by way of rider to a late debate, 493–501. Signed: W.I.H.

390   Epistles to the literati (No. IV): letter of Viscount Duncannon, M.P., to Archibald Jobbry, Esq., Ex-M.P., [viz., John Galt; see p. 245], 502–504. **William Maginn,** prob. This continues the series described in nos. 364 and 497, so that Duncannon is fictitious.

VOLUME 5, JUNE 1832

391   The present condition of public affairs, 505–514. Signed: A Country Gentleman.

392   *The American Chesterfield,* 515–519. **William Maginn?** Thrall, p. 304.

393   The schoolmaster's experience in Newgate (No. I), 521–533. **Charles Wall.** Francis Place, when sitting on a committee to supply spring water to London with man cited, heard that he was the

author of this series of arts. in *FM* and would therefore be a convicted felon; Place looked into the matter and Wall was dropped from the committee: see BM Add. MS. 35145, Sect. I, fol. 128; for his first name see no. 756 below; series repr. anon. as *Old Bailey Experience,* 1833. (Note, vol. 6, p. 256, by Oliver Yorke—signed O.Y.)

394   *Tour of a German Prince,* Vols. III and IV, 533–544.

395   The Archbishop of Canterbury's Bill on Pluralities, 545–551.

396   Discoveries of the modern geologists (No. I), 552–566.

397   Rencontres on the road (No. IV): Saturday, 567–577. **Amelia Gillespie Smyth.** Cf. no. 342.

398   On the doctrine of free trade, 577–582.

399   Gallery of literary characters (No. XXV): Louis Eustache Ude, 584. **William Maginn.** Repr. *Gallery.*

400   Some account of Coleridge's philosophy [*Aids to Reflection*], 585–597. **J. A. Heraud.** Thrall, p. 270.

401   On the domestic manners of the British [satire on Mrs. Trollope] (Part I), 598–602. Signed: Colonel Richard H. Hickory, of Cedar Swamp.

402   On political parties (No. II), 603–620. **R. B. Seeley?** Signed An Independent Pittite; cf. no. 352.

403   A cool dialogue on passing events, between Oliver and his chum, 621–629. **William Maginn?** Thrall, p. 304.

404   A growl at the Lords, 630–632. **William Maginn.** Signed Sir Morgan O'Doherty; see no. 434.

VOLUME 5, JULY 1832

405   Canada, by Tiger [William Dunlop], Galt, Picken, 633–642. **William Maginn.** Claimed in no. 543.

406   The book of JASHUR, from the Æthiopic, 643–648.

407   Thomson's *Life of Sir Walter Raleigh,* 649–658.

408   Allan Cunningham's *Maid of Elvar,* 659–666. **J. A. Heraud,** prob. Thrall, p. 264; on pp. 263–266 a case is made for the collab. of Carlyle because of (i) the sympathetic attitude toward Byron, but see Heraud's other arts. on Byron (listed in Part B); and (ii) a parallel with Carlyle's *Heroes,* eight years later, which can be attributed to conversation with Heraud.

409 Letter on the doctrine of St. Simon, 666–669. **J. A. Heraud?** Signed Fair-Play; Thrall, pp. 274, 285, who suggests that Carlyle may have had a hand in it.

410 Historical drama [histories of drama by Pennie and Collier], 670–682. **J. A. Heraud,** prob. Thrall, p. 284; p. 673 refers to Byron's *Cain* (cf. no. 200), and in footnote the author says he hopes to write on Byron's excellence as a dramatist (cf. no. 767); the discussion on pp. 670–671 with its reference to Regina has a tone of editorial pride.

411 The domestic manners of the British (Part II), 690–695. Signed: Colonel Richard H. Hickory, of Cedar Swamp.

412 Gallery of literary characters (No. XXVI): Reverend Doctor Lardner, 696. **William Maginn.** Repr. *Gallery.*

413 Lady Mary Shepherd's metaphysics, 697–708. **Mary Shepherd.** Signed; *DNB* under Sir Samuel Shepherd.

414 Our Royal-Academical lounge, 709–720. **W. H. Leeds.** Cf. the evidence for no. 285; here pp. 712–715 deal with architectural drawings; Latin tags and his extravagant English are again conspicuous.

415 What is an Irish orator? 721. **William Maginn?** Signed S. T. Coleridge; attr. Thrall, p. 281.

416 On the opera (No. IV, concl.): introduction, the management, the dancers, 722–735. Signed: J.J.M.

417 The schoolmaster's experience in Newgate (No. II); hurried trials, 736–749. **Charles Wall.** Cf. no. 393.

418 Meeting, at Oxford, of the British Association for the Advancement of Science, 750–753.

VOLUME 6, AUGUST 1832

419 Recollections of a gentlewoman (No. I): Madame du Barri, 1–9. **Miss Monckton.** On p. 3 author calls herself "Miss M***n"; biographical facts given in the art. show that she was a niece of Dowager Lady Galway, 1738–1792, and of Lady Cork, 1748–1840, and therefore prob. a daughter of John or Edward Monckton. See Burke and *Complete Peerage* under Cork and Galway.

420 Doctor O'Gorman, 9–11.

421 The schoolmaster's experience in Newgate (No. III): necessity of an appeal court, 12–23. **Charles Wall.** Cf. no. 393.

422 Geographical and statistical account of the All-in-myne-Eees, or Fancy Isles [with author's intro. letter signed Jacob Sly, mariner], 24–31. Signed: J.S. [Jacob Sly].

423 Epistles to the literati (No. V): Nathan Butt, Esq., the radical, to Dr. Bowring, editor of the *Westminster Review* [reply to *WR*, 17 (July 1832), 182–193], 32. **John Galt.** Signed Nathan Butt (he was the hero of Galt's *Radical,* reviewed in *WR* art.); see opening sentence.

424 Mary Hughes: a tale of the Welsh Highlands, 33–44.

425 Romantic poetry of Spain, 44–53.

426 Discoveries of modern geologists (No. II), 54–66.

427 Elizabeth Brownrigge, a tale; dedicated to the author of *Eugene Aram, a Novel* [by Edward Bulwer-Lytton], (Part I), 67–68. **William Maginn?** Sadleir, *Bulwer,* pp. 221–243, argues persuasively for Maginn's personal vendetta in the attack on Bulwer-Lytton; attr. by Thrall, pp. 62–64, adding "possibly with the help of Lockhart"; White, "Thackeray," pp. 72–74, reviews and rejects the case for Thackeray's authorship.

428 The Church of England and the Liberals, 88–104.

429 The domestic manners of the British (Part III), 105–109. Signed: Col. Richard H. Hickory, of Cedar Swamp.

430 Historical documents (No. I): secret instructions to General Wolfe for the conquest of Quebec, 109–111. **George II.** Signed G.R. [George Rex], and see text.

431 Gallery of literary characters (No. XXVII): Edward Lytton Bulwer, Esq., 112. **William Maginn.** Repr. *Gallery.*

432 On national economy (No. I): Chalmers on political economy (Part I), 113–118. **William Maginn?** Thrall, p. 304.

433 The contagious character of cholera, 119–121. **D. M. Moir?** His "gallery portrait" (no. 600) calls him "great upon contagion," referring to his battle against cholera [on which he wrote a book in 1832] and speaks of him as a contrib. to *FM.* With a letter, 121–123, by **William Dunlop**—signed Q.HY., attr. in postscript, signed O.Y., to "Tyger, whom we introduced . . . last month as the 'Backwoodsman' " (cf. no. 405, p. 633, which identifies the last two pseudonyms as Dunlop's).

434 Letter to the Primate of Ireland on the state of the Irish Church, and other matters, 124–126. **William Maginn.** Signed at start Sir Morgan O'Doherty:

see his "Memoir," p. xxx. (Note, p. 256, signed O.Y.—Oliver Yorke.)

467 Gallery of literary characters (No. XXX): Sir David Brewster, K.H. [in the form of a letter to Fraser], 416. **William Maginn**, prob. Signed James Hogg, which is accepted by Batho, *Shepherd*, p. 215, but attr. to Maginn both by Thrall, p. 288, and by Wm. Bates in Maginn's *Gallery*, where he remarks, p. 83, that the signature was just "one of the many rogueries perpetrated" by *Fraser's* (cf. no. 632, also in letter form); the reference to Hogg having written his own life three times had been made by Maginn in no. 348, and the tone of the sketch is very Maginnish; the poet Hogg would have been a curious choice to write on Brewster the scientist, and he had little interest in politics (contrast the last sentences). (See nos. 497, 498.)

468 My contemporaries, from the note-book of a retired barrister (Part III), 417–431.

469 Rencontres on the road (No. V): the hen and chickens, 431–436. **Amelia Gillespie Smyth.** Cf. no. 342.

470 The colonies, 437–446.

471 Portraits of eminent philosophers (No. II, concl.): Marquess de la Place, 446–449. **David Brewster**, prob. Claimed by author of no. 458, p. 351.

472 Ewan M'Gabhar, 450–459. **James Hogg.** Signed The Ettrick Shepherd—see *DNB*.

473 The schoolmaster's experience in Newgate (No. V, concl.): crimes, 460–498. **Charles Wall.** Cf. no. 393.

474 A dish of wholesome proverbs, 499–508.

VOLUME 6, NOVEMBER 1832, PART II

475 State of political feeling in the west of Scotland, 535–540.

476 Miss Edgeworth's tales and novels, 541–558.

477 The curse, 559–566.

478 Archbishop Whately's *Secondary Punishments* dissected, 566–575. **William Maginn**, prob. Maginn wrote no. 434 attacking Whately in similar style; Thrall, p. 304. (Note, p. 256, by **Maginn**, prob.—signed O.Y. [Oliver Yorke] in editorial tone, promises this art.)

479 *Zohrab the Hostage*, 576–592.

480 The free-trade question (No. I), 593–598. **John Galt.** Signed.

481 Landscape illustrations of the *Waver-*

ley Novels, 600–604. **J. A. Heraud**, prob. On p. 604 the author emphasizes the importance of knowledge in the activity of genius, which is exactly the point made at the beginning of nos. 340 and 359, also on Scott and prob. by Heraud; Heraud wrote no. 7 on genius.

482 New edition of Wordsworth's *Poetical Works*, 607–625. **J. A. Heraud.** Thrall, p. 284; in no. 740, p. 391, Heraud claims this as "our" art.

483 Our first double number and the reason why, 626–636. Signed: O.Y. [Oliver Yorke].

VOLUME 6, DECEMBER 1832

484 Whig foreign policy, 637–652. **R. B. Seeley?** Signed An Independent Pittite; cf. no. 352.

485 The *Friendship's Offering, Amulet, Book of Beauty*, and annual pocket books, 653–672. Unidentified. Listed in Thackeray, "Bibliography," but White, "Thackeray," p. 74, rejects the attr.

486 Physical evidences of the characteristics of ancient races among the moderns, 673–679.

487 Captain Forman, Lords Brougham, and John Russell, 680–684.

488 Gallery of literary characters (No. XXXI): William Roscoe, Esq., 685. **William Maginn.** Repr. *Gallery*.

489 Some passages in the life of an idler (Part IV, concl.), 689–700. **Henry Mildmay.** Cf. no. 151; notes are signed H.M.

490 Walter Vivian the smuggler, 704–711.

491 The books of aphorisms; with a running commentary, by Sir Morgan O'Doherty, Bart., 712–728. **Robert Macnish.** Signed An Oriental Author; claimed in *Tales*, I, 237–238. Commentary by **William Maginn**—see title and no. 434.

492 Dialogues of the dead on sepulchral rites and rights, 728–746. Signed in intro. letter: Pioneer Truepenny, M.D.

493 Historical documents (No. II): a memorial from Joseph Buonaparte to the Grand Duke of Tuscany begging hard for the honour of being knighted as one of the descendents from a Tuscan family, 747–748. **Joseph Buonaparte.** Title.

494 Appeal of the King of the Netherlands, to heaven, 749–750.

495 The departed of thirty-two, 751–754. **William Maginn**, prob. Thrall, p. 304;

quoted at length as "our" art. in no. 1397, pp. 17–18, 18.

VOLUME 7, JANUARY 1833

496 Address to contributors and readers by Oliver Yorke, 1–15, **William Maginn?** Signed Oliver Yorke; Thrall, p. 304.

497 Epistles to the literati (No. VI): James Hogg, Esq., to Oliver Yorke, Esq., 16. **William Maginn?** Signed James Hogg, who purports to take account of a criticism made by Brewster (see no. 498) of a remark in no. 467; and no. 467 is prob. by Maginn; the "Epistles to the literati" have been a series of fictitious spoofs (see nos. 313, 364, 378, 390, 423), and there is no reason to believe that this letter or the following, no. 498, represents a change to real signatures; "Hogg's" reference to his new poem "The Boread" in twelve books can hardly be genuine.

498 Epistles to the literati (No. VII): Sir David Brewster, the philosopher, to James Hogg, Esq., the shepherd, 16. **William Maginn?** Signed David Brewster; Brewster may well have complained to Maginn, as ed. of *FM* and an old acquaintance, about 3rd sentence of no. 467 because the question of his public speaking ability became of vital importance right after its publication, as he was being considered for the newly vacated professorship of Natural Philosophy at Edinburgh; but see the evidence for no. 497 on the pseudonymity of these "Epistles" and note both the exaggerated defence and the obvious spoof in the P.S. at a time when Brewster was in financial difficulties; since this letter is really an integral part of no. 497, it is natural to assume the same possible author.

499 My contemporaries, from the note-book of a retired barrister (Part IV), 44–53.

500 Errors of the Reformation, 57–64.

501 The contested election, 65–68. Unidentified. Thrall, p. 257, suggests Thackeray; White, "Thackeray," p. 74, rejects the attrib.

502 Magiana; or, The mysteries of natural and artificial magic, 73–78.

503 Gallery of literary characters (No. XXXII): Prince de Talleyrand, 80. **William Maginn. Repr.** *Gallery.* (Letter, pp. 246–247.)

504 The celebrated but hitherto unpublished poem of Lord Byron on Mr. Rogers, 81–

84. Intro. by **William Maginn**, who obviously did the notes too—Kenealy, "Maginn," p. 89. (Letters, pp. 240–243.)

505 The scarlet witch, 85–96. **Thomas Aird.** Attr. by Robert Macnish, *Tales*, I, 238; Macnish sent the MS. to Fraser.

506 Asinarii scenici, 96–106. **J. A. Heraud** and **William Maginn,** prob. Thrall, p. 285.

507 The free-trade question, (Letter II, concl.), 106–111. **John Galt.** Signed.

508 The last *Quarterly*, 112–115.

509 *Oeuvres de Platon, traduites par Victor Cousin*, 116–122. **J. A. Heraud,** prob. See letter quoted for no. 262; Heraud was an enthusiastic Platonist.

510 The elections, 122–124.

VOLUME 7, FEBRUARY 1833

511 An Englishman's remonstrance to the Whig aristocracy, 127–136. **R. B. Seeley?** Signed An Independent Pittite; cf. no. 352.

512 Discoveries of modern geologists (No. IV), 139–147.

513 A remarkable Egyptian story, written by Barek, a learned Jew of Egypt, about the latter end of the reign of Cambyses, the Persian, discovered and communicated by the Ettrick Shepherd [James Hogg], 147–158. **James Hogg.** Attr. in Batho, *Shepherd*, p. 216.

514 Gallery of literary characters (No. XXXIII): James Morier, Esq., 159. **William Maginn.** Repr. *Gallery.*

515 Masters and servants, 160–171. **Charles Wall.** Signed The Author of "The Schoolmaster's Experience in Newgate" —see no. 393.

516 [Introduction and notes to] The two round spaces on the tombstone, being an epitaph on the late James Mackintosh, by S. Taylor Coleridge, with an epitaph on himself, by the same, 175–177. **William Maginn,** prob. Kenealy, "Maginn," p. 89. (See p. 367, and p. 620 signed J.S.)

517 My contemporaries; from the note-book of a retired barrister (Part V), 178–190.

518 *The Greek Revolution*, 191–198.

519 English poetry: Barry Cornwall, Motherwell, and Leigh Hunt, 198–222.

520 On the chances of the reconstruction of the Tory Party (chap. i; no more published): sketch of the history of parties from the Revolution to Burke, 223–230. **William Maginn?** Thrall, p. 304.

521 Irish agitation (Part I), 232–239.

522 The Fraser papers for February, 240–250. **William Maginn**, with **John Churchill** as collab., and sometimes others. Maginn, "Memoir," p. lxxiv; Kenealy, "Maginn," p. 89; Thrall, p. 297; here and in later issues the "papers" are full of letters, some with pseudonymous signatures, so that Maginn was acting partly as commentator; Churchill prob. arranged the whole department and wrote some commentaries; in this issue, pp. 244–246, containing a letter signed Scotophilus, are prob. by **J. G. Lockhart**—see Sadleir, *Bulwer*, pp. 258–260; Thackeray's participation (see Thrall, pp. 281, 302) is ruled out by White, "Thackeray," p. 74.

VOLUME 7, MARCH 1833

523 Ireland and the priests, 251–266.
524 Gallery of literary characters (No. XXXIV): Countess of Blessington, 267. **William Maginn**. Repr. *Gallery*.
525 The student Morgenstern; a tale of Berne, 268–281.
526 National economy (No. IV): surplus labour and the remedies proposed: Poor Laws for Ireland, 282–291. **William Maginn?** Thrall, p. 304. (Letter, pp. 498–499, signed **Frank Freeman**, with reply, pp. 499–500, by the writer.)
527 Disasters of three days, 292–303.
528 Critical illustrations of Lord Byron's poetry, 303–317. **J. A. Heraud**, and **William Maginn**, prob. Thrall, p. 285; Carlyle, *Letters to Mill*, p. 48, guesses Heraud.
529 Notes on Italian scenery and manners, (No. I): a day at Loretto, 318–323.
530 Don Quixote's library (Part I), 324–331. Parts II and III are signed (b.).
531 Magiana; or, The mysteries of natural and artificial magic (No. II, concl.), 331–340.
532 [Intro. to] Lord Byron's verses on the Reverend Dr. Nott, 341. **William Maginn?** By analogy with no. 504; cf. no. 528.
533 Historical documents (No. III, concl.): a very curious and important document [letter from Lord Elgin to Sidney Smith about treaty between Spencer Smith and Bonaparte], 343. **James Bruce**. Intro. note.
534 Church reform: the Irish Althorpean (Part I), 346–349.
535 Rencontres on the road (No. VI): the loves of Aloyo and Teresa, 349–359. **Amelia Gillespie Smyth**. Cf. no. 342.
536 Naval evolutions, 359–364.

537 The birth, parentage, and education of Higgledy-piggledy, a serious history, 364–367.
538 The Fraser papers for March, 367–376. **William Maginn**, prob. with **John Churchill**. See evidence for no. 522.

VOLUME 7, APRIL 1833

539 National economy (No. V): the factory system—the Ten Hours Bill, 377–392. **William Maginn?** Thrall, p. 304.
540 Celebrated trials of the nineteenth century (No. I): Schinderhannes, the robber of the Rhine, and Pierre Coignard, otherwise Pontis, Comte de Sainte Hélène, 393–415. The series is almost a literal trans., with some omissions, of the chapters on the criminals named in the French collection cited here, p. 393n.
541 The reformed House of Commons, 415–425.
542 Rencontres on the road (No. VII, concl.): April fools, 425–435. **Amelia Gillespie Smyth**. Cf. no. 342.
543 Gallery of literary characters (No. XXXV): The Tiger [William Dunlop], 436. **William Maginn**. Repr. *Gallery*.
543a *The Seven before Thebes* [a trans. of Aeschylus], 447–458. **Thomas Medwin**. Signed.
544 Irish agitation (Part II, concl.), 458–470.
545 Piozziana [on *Recollections of the Late Mrs. Piozzi*], 471–475. **William Maginn?** Thrall, p. 304.
546 Church reform: the Irish Althorpean (Part II, concl.), 476–481.
547 Taylor's *Life of Cowper*, 482–497. **J. A. Heraud**, prob. Author of no. 657, p. 159, comes close to claiming this art.; attr. to Heraud by Carlyle, *Letters to Mill*, p. 48, in reply to Mill, *Earlier Letters*, I, 41.
548 The Fraser papers for April, 498–506. **William Maginn**, with **John Churchill**. See evidence for no. 522.

VOLUME 7, MAY 1833

549 Speeches delivered in banquo Reginae before Oliver [Yorke], Lord Protector of the world of letters, and a jury of Fraserians; with notes and comments by Morgan Rattler (No. I): Mirabeau v. Macaulay and others, 507–526. **P. W. Banks**, prob. Signed Sir Charles Botherall; Thrall, p. 278, assignes the series to Banks; certainly notes and commentary

are by **Banks**—his pseud. is in the title, cf. no. 178.

550 The Irish jury-bill, 527–531.

551 Hayward's translation of Goethe's *Faust*, 532–554. **J. A. Heraud**, prob. Heraud was a great admirer of Goethe and German philosophy; the discussions of genius, pp. 532, 538, especially the reference to lovers of "genius in the abstract," recall no. 7.

552 My contemporaries, from the note-book of a retired barrister (Part VI, concl.), 555–564.

553 Don Quixote's library, (Part II), 565–577. Signed: (b.).

554 Discoveries of modern geologists (No. V, concl.), 578–585.

555 *Quae cogitavit*, 585–589. **Thomas Carlyle.** Assigned in intro. note, which is signed O.Y. [Oliver Yorke], to D.T. [Diogenes Teufelsdröckh]; attr. *Memoirs*, I, 118; repr. *Essays*, III.

556 The female character, 591–601. Unidentified. (Letter, vol. 8, pp. 118–119.)

557 Gallery of literary characters (No. XXXVI): Benjamin D'Israeli, Esq., 602. **William Maginn.** Repr. *Gallery*.

558 On national economy (No. VI): Dr. Chalmers on a right moral state of the community, 603–614. **William Maginn?** Thrall, p. 304.

559 Meditations for May-Day, by Sir Morgan O'Doherty, Bart., 615–619. **William Maginn.** Signed M. O'D. [Morgan O'Doherty]—see "Memoir," p. xxx.

560 The Fraser papers for May, 620–632. **William Maginn**, with **John Churchill**. See evidence for no. 522.

VOLUME 7, JUNE 1833

561 Ancient country gentlemen of England, 633–657.

562 The poets of the day—batch the first, 658–667. **William Maginn?** Thrall, p. 297, who suggests collab. with Thackeray, but White, "Thackeray," p. 74, rejects this.

563 Mr. Thorburn's MS.—the original "Lawrie Todd" [hero of John Galt's book] (Part I), 668–681. **Grant Thorburn.** Attr. in *DNB*. With intro. and concluding notes by O.Y. [Oliver Yorke]. (See vol. 15, p. 531, with letter signed **Grant Thorburn.**)

564 Speeches delivered in banco Reginae (No. II): Mirabeau v. Dumont (Part I), 682–705. **P. W. Banks**, prob. Evidence for no. 549. (No. III is no. 815.)

565 Gallery of literary characters (No.

XXXVII): Thomas Carlyle, 706. **William Maginn.** Repr. *Gallery*.

566 The commission for perpetuating factory infanticide, 707–715.

567 *Six Weeks on the Loire*, 716–730.

568 *Miserrimus*; or, the Thelluson Job, 730–733.

569 The early days of Edmund Kean, 734–750. Unidentified. (Letters, vol. 8, pp. 125–126, by **P. W. Banks**—signed Morgan Rattler, see no. 178; author's reply, pp. 499–502; letters from Dr. **John Keate**, pp. 753–754.)

570 A wind-up for our seventh volume, literary, political, and anti-Peelish, 750–752. **William Maginn**, prob. Attr. by Sadleir, *Bulwer*, pp. 283–284; subject and phrasing are editorial.

VOLUME 8, JULY 1833

571 Sir Walter Raleigh and Sir Robert Cecil, 1–18.

572 Count Cagliostro: in two flights—flight first, 19–28. **Thomas Carlyle.** Repr. *Essays*, III.

573 Political unions: the Northern Political Union, 28–35.

574 New edition of *Rejected Addresses* [by James and Horace Smith], 36–44. **William Maginn?** Thrall, p. 297, who suggests Thackeray as collab., but White, "Thackeray," p. 74, rejects this claim. (Letter, p. 377.)

575 James Montgomery's *Lectures on Poetry*, 45–48.

576 The Shepherd's *Noctes* and the reason why they do not appear in *Fraser's Magazine*, 49–54. **William Maginn** and **James Hogg**. Signed Oliver Yorke; Batho, *Shepherd*, pp. 102–103, 216.

577 Mr. Thorburn's MS. (Part II, concl.), 55–63. **Grant Thorburn.** Attr. in *DNB*.

578 Gallery of literary characters (No. XXXVIII): Samuel Taylor Coleridge, Esq., 64. **William Maginn.** Repr. *Gallery*. (Letter, p. 503, signed A Friend to Free Inquiry [living in Newport, Isle of Wight].)

579 The Bridgewater treatises (No. I), 65–80. **J. A. Heraud** with **William Maginn**, prob. Thrall, p. 285.

580 The whole West Indian question, 81–90. **John Galt.** Signed.

581 The philosophical marriage, 90–99.

582 A letter to Earl Grey on the ministerial construction of the coronation oath, 100–103. Signed: One who has great respect for your order and office—one who pities

him who is weak enough to disgrace both, or either—and one who holds in sovereign contempt those who are slaves enough to betray their rights and duties.

583   On national economy (No. VII): free trade—Col. Thompson's and Mr. Booth's pamphlets, 103–112. **William Maginn?** Thrall, p. 304.

584   The triumph of humbug; a homily for July, 113–117. **William Maginn.** Signed M. O'D. [Morgan O'Doherty]—see "Memoir," p. xxx.

585   Fraser papers for July, 118–126. **William Maginn,** with **John Churchill.** See evidence for no. 522.

VOLUME 8, AUGUST 1833

586   Specimens of Irish minstrelsy (No. V): Keens, 127–132. **T. Crofton Croker.** Cf. no. 22.

587   Count Cagliostro: in two flights—flight last, 132–155. **Thomas Carlyle.** Repr. *Essays,* III.

588   The last duel I had a hand in, 156–167. **T. C. Croker.** Signed C. O'Donoghue, late Ensign 18th Royal Irish—see Thrall, p. 36.

589   Babbage on machinery and manufactures, 167–175. **William Maginn?** Thrall, p. 304.

590   [Introductory note to] Paraphrases of the twenty-third and forty-sixth psalms, by the late Rev. Thomas Saint Lawrence, Rector of Moviddy, in the diocese of Ross, Ireland, 175–176.

591   Notes on Italian scenery and manners, (No. II, concl.), 177–189.

592   Gallery of literary characters (No. XXXIX): George Cruikshank, Esq., 190. **William Maginn.** Repr. *Gallery.*

593   Hells in London, 191–206. **Charles Wall.** Signed The Author of "The Schoolmaster's Experience in Newgate" (no. 393, etc.).

594   Celebrated trials of the nineteenth century (No. II): Mingrat, ex-curé de Saint-Quentin—Francis Salis Reimbauer —Lelièvre, (otherwise Chevallier)—Anna Schonleben, 207–221. Cf. no. 540.

595   On national economy (No. VIII): on the Corn Laws—Colonel Thompson's and Mr. Booth's pamphlets, 222–231. **William Maginn?** Thrall, p. 304.

596   Hodges' *Narrative of the Expedition to Portugal,* 231–247.

597   The encounter of a squire of the Lord-Primate with Harry the Chancellor,

wherein the latter is signally defeated, 247–258.

VOLUME 8, SEPTEMBER 1833

598   The Bridgewater treatises (No. II): Dr. Chalmers and Sir Charles Bell, 259–278. **J. A. Heraud** and **William Maginn,** prob. Thrall, p. 285. (No. III is no. 869.)

599   The joke, 279–289. **John Galt.** Signed The Author of *The Annals of the Parish, The Member,* etc. etc.—see H&L; repr. *The Howdie.*

600   Gallery of literary characters (No. XL): Doctor Moir, 290. **William Maginn.** Repr. *Gallery.*

601   On intellectual endowments, 291–301. **Egerton Brydges.** Signed.

602   The philosophy of sneering, 302–310. **Robert Macnish.** Signed A Modern Pythagorean; attr. in *Tales,* I, 311.

603   On military promotion, 311–330. **John Mitchell.** Signed Bombardinio; pseud. attr. in Schmitz, *Mitchell,* p. xiv. With a letter and notes by **William Maginn**— signed Morgan O'Doherty, see no. 434.

604   The press and the Tories, 330–338. Unidentified. Repr. under same title, 1833, with preface signed H.D.

605   Touching things theatrical, 339–359. **P. W. Banks.** Signed Morgan Rattler— see no. 178.

606   The poets of the day—batch the second, 360–375. **William Maginn?** See evidence for no. 562.

607   Fraser papers for September, 376–384. **William Maginn,** with **John Churchill.** See evidence for no. 522.

VOLUME 8, OCTOBER 1833

608   Taylor's *History of the Civil Wars in Ireland,* 385–395.

609   Autobiography of a Scottish borderer, 396–412. **Agnes C. Hall.** Signed H; attr. in *Gent. Mag.,* 181 (Jan. 1847), 98, repr., Jedburgh, 1874.

610   On the French peerage, ancient and modern, 413–432.

611   Gallery of literary characters (No. XLI): Miss [Letitia Elizabeth] Landon, 433. **Francis Mahony.** Thrall, p. 290.

612   Persian women, 434–444.

613   Don Quixote's library (Part III, concl.): *The Austriada* of Juan Rufo Gutierrez, 445–455. Signed: (b.).

614   Celebrated trials of the nineteenth century (No. III, concl.): Marie Adelaide

Bodin (widow Boursier) and Nicolas Kostolo, 455–470. Cf. no. 540.

615 Specimens of the art of governing "by commission," 470–478. **William Maginn.** Thrall, p. 304; opening sentence attribs. to author of series starting with no. 432.

616 Bulwer, Westmacott, Cobbett, John Wood of Preston, and others, 479–488. **William Maginn?** He was engaged in a personal feud with Bulwer at the time (cf. Sadleir, *Bulwer*, pp. 221–243); on p. 480 the author seems to claim vol. 4, pp. 525–526 (see no. 313).

617 On yeomanry cavalry, and other military matters, 488–494. Signed: Ebenezer Shabrach.

618 My father's house: a tale, 495–498. **John Galt.** Signed; repr. *The Howdie.*

619 Fraser papers for October, 499–510. **William Maginn** with **John Churchill.** See evidence for no. 522.

VOLUME 8, NOVEMBER 1833

620 The Book of Enoch, 511–530. **J. A. Heraud** and **William Maginn,** prob. Thrall, p. 285.

621 The doctor bewitched, 530–535.

622 Boaden's *Memoirs of Mrs. Inchbald,* 536–556. **William Maginn?** See evidence for no. 562.

623 An account, by an eye-witness, of the wreck of the *Amphitrite,* August 31st and September 1st, 1833, on the coast of Boulogne, 557–560.

624 First session of the reformed parliament, 561–568.

625 The arcana of Freemasonry, 568–575.

626 Gallery of literary characters (No. XLII): Miss Harriet Martineau, 576. **William Maginn.** Repr. *Gallery.*

627 Reminiscences of an ill-used wretch, 577–580.

628 Sartor Resartus (book I, chaps. i–iv), 580–592. **Thomas Carlyle.** Repr. Boston, 1836, and in all editions of his writings.

629 India and England [on Capt. Basil Hall's *Voyages*], 593–603.

630 On national economy (No. IX): the *Westminster Review* on free-trade, absenteeism, [and] the greatest happiness principle, 604–613. **William Maginn?** Thrall, p. 304.

631 Lady Morgan's *Dramatic Scenes,* 613–621. **William Maginn?** See evidence for no. 562. (Letter, vol. 9, pp. 623–624, signed X.X.)

632 The Miller correspondence [fictitious letters from Coleridge, Hunt, Words-

worth *et al.*], 624–636. **William Maginn.** "Memoir," pp. lxxiii–lxxiv; editorial note, p. 754, presumably by **Maginn,** admits the "hoax."

VOLUME 8, DECEMBER 1833

633 On the periods of the erection of the Theban temple of Ammon, 637–649. **Isaac Cullimore.** Signed Hermes; attr. in *DNB.*

634 The Galt manuscripts [an introduction to no. 635 and other tales], 650–651. Signed: Oliver Yorke.

635 The gudewife, 651–657. **John Galt.** Signed The Author of the *Annals of the Parish*; repr. *The Howdie.*

636 Poets of the day—batch the third, 658–670. **William Maginn?** See evidence for no. 562. (Batch the fourth is no. 738.)

637 Sartor Resartus (book I, chaps. v–xi), 669 (sic)–684. **Thomas Carlyle.** Cf. no. 628.

638 Political unions (No. II): the members of the Northern Union (Part I), 685–699.

639 Gallery of literary characters (No. XLIII): Grant Thorburn, the original "Lawrie Todd," 700. **William Maginn.** Repr. *Gallery.*

640 Household servants, 701–716. **Charles Wall.** Signed The Author of *Old Bailey Experience*; cf. nos. 393, 756.

641 Old English political songs, 717–732. **Thomas Wright,** 1810–1877. Repr. *Literature,* II.

642 The last news, with three cheers for the Earl of Durham, as a tail-piece, 740–742. **William Maginn?** Thrall, p. 304.

643 Fraser papers for December, 742–754. **William Maginn** with **John Churchill.** See evidence for no. 522.

VOLUME 9, JANUARY 1834

644 The state and prospects of Toryism, January, 1834, 1–25. **William Maginn.** In no. 1397 (Jan. 1840), p. 19, Maginn listed those articles which had been reprinted as pamphlets: two called "The State and Prospects of Toryism" (viz., this one alone—see p. 240 below—and this one and the next, no. 675—see *BMCat.* under Toryism), and nos. 604, 654, 731, 781, 832, 924, and 987; and then went on to say that "who wrote the majority of these articles is a secret known only to ourselves," that he could "add no small testimony" about his character, that he would "violate no confidence" in saying his zeal for his country "is not confined to the pages of this Magazine" [i.e., he writes elsewhere too], that he knows no other Conservative writer who has written with greater talent and perseverance, "combined with so much statistical knowledge and perfect disinterestedness," and concludes: "Why should he be angry with us when we say, with every respect, that his name is ——— ?"—all of which sounds very much like Maginn on Maginn. The first two arts. (on Toryism) are, in fact, attr. to Maginn by Thrall, p. 304; all the others, with the notable exception of nos. 604 and 654, not only share the same view of Conservatism, but show markedly similar characteristics of method and style: the use of statistics, many quotations from contemporary journals, acid sarcasms, (the "*offal* of the Whig party," that "miserable, mischievous idiot" Lord John Russell), an extensive employment of italics, especially for single words, including their insertion into quotations —all are found in Maginn's known writing, and when most are found together become presumptive evidence of his hand; but since he was the editor of *FM*, one cannot be sure that he did not sometimes have what amounts to a collaborator whose MS. he retouched or partly rewrote so that the attribs. have usually been given a "prob." (Note, p. 240.)

645   Ensign O'Donoghue's last communication, 32–41. **T. C. Croker.** Signed Cornelius O'Donoghue—see Thrall, p. 36.

646   *Men and Manners in America*, 42–63.

647   Gallery of literary characters (No. XLIV): Captain [John] Ross, 64. **William Maginn.** Repr. *Gallery.*

648   Political unions (No. III, concl.): the members of the Northern Union (Part II), 65–71.

649   Present condition of the people, class I: labourers in cities and towns, 72–87. **Charles Wall.** Signed The Author of *Old Bailey Experience*; cf. nos. 393 and 756.

650   Thames fishing, 88–96. **Edward Jesse.** Signed Author of *Gleanings in Natural History*; repr. *An Angler's Rambles*, 1836.

651   Extraordinary history of a border beauty, 97–110. **James Hogg.** Signed The Ettrick Shepherd—see *DNB.*

652   Men and manners: a series of satires (No. I), 111–117. **Thomas Powell.**

Signed Pierce Pungent—see no. 33. The short "Arguments" that precede each satire in the series, signed Oliver Yorke, are presumably by **Powell.**

653   Notes written on the last day of the year thirty-three, 117–126. **William Maginn?** Signed O.Y. [Oliver Yorke]; Thrall, p. 304.

VOLUME 9, FEBRUARY 1834

654   The case of the Church of England [against Dissenters], 127–145.

655   Gallery of literary characters (No. XLV): Sir Egerton Brydges, 146. **William Maginn.** Repr. *Gallery.*

656   Dulce domum, 147–159. **T. C. Croker.** Signed Cornelius O'Donoghue—see Thrall, p. 36.

657   Fanaticism and the natural historian of enthusiasm [Isaac Taylor], 159–171. **J. A. Heraud,** prob. On p. 159n. author cites a passage in vol. 3, p. 294, from an art. known to be Heraud's; Thrall, p. 284; cf. no. 1000.

658   Men and manners (No. II), 171–176. **Thomas Powell.** Evidence for no. 652.

659   Sartor Resartus (book II, chaps. i–iv), 177–195. **Thomas Carlyle.** Cf. no. 628.

660   The singular trial of Francis Ormiston, 196–203.

661   The Lords' jurisdiction over peerage claims, 204–224.

662   Allan Cunningham's *Fifty Years*, 224–240. **William Maginn?** See evidence for no. 562.

663   Fraser papers for February, 240–252. **William Maginn,** prob. with **John Churchill.** Signed O.Y. [Oliver Yorke]—see evidence for no. 522.

VOLUME 9, MARCH 1834

664   Ireland, and the progress of the "repeal question," 253–267.

665   The Frasers in the Correi [in Scotland], 273–278. **James Hogg.** Signed The Ettrick Shepherd—see *DNB.*

666   Hints for a history of highwaymen, 279–287. Unidentified. Although often attr. to Thackeray, by Thrall and Gulliver, for example, the fact that the author was married before 1834 (p. 279) and that he first saw London in company with his father (p. 285) dispose of the case for Thackeray; prob. by the author of no. 1414.

667   Noah's journal of the ark, 288–299.

Isaac Cullimore. Signed Hermogenes—see no. 1005.

668   Gallery of literary characters (No. XLVI): Daniel O'Connell, Esq., and Richard Lalor Sheil, Esq., 300. **William Maginn.** Repr. *Gallery.*

669   Sartor Resartus (book II, chaps. v–vii), 301–313. **Thomas Carlyle.** Cf. no. 628.

670   Reforms and reformers, 314–325.

671   Original annals of the parish, extracted from *Private Letters, now first printed from the MSS. of the Rev. Professor* [Robert] *Wodrow, of Glasgow, 1694–1732,* 326–334.

672   *The Divine System of the Universe,* 335–347.

673   Men and manners (No. III), 348–355. **Thomas Powell.** Evidence for no. 652.

674   On national economy (No. X, concl.): the *Westminster Review* on "the economy of paying twice over," 356–364. **William Maginn?** Thrall, p. 304.

675   The state and prospects of Toryism in March 1834, 364–370. **William Maginn?** Thrall, p. 304; cf. no. 644. Postscript, 370–371, apparently added by **Maginn** —signed O.Y. [Oliver Yorke], see opening sentence.

676   The Fraser papers for March, 371–378. **William Maginn** with **John Churchill.** Signed O.Y. [Oliver Yorke]—see evidence for no. 522. Including a letter, 375–378, by **T. C. Croker**—signed Cornelius O'Donoghue, Thrall, p. 36.

VOLUME 9, APRIL 1834

677   Church matters: church-rates and tithes, and the alliance between Church and State; Dissenters' Marriage-Bill; [admission of Dissenters to] the Universities; Church and State in America, 379–398.

678   Cunningham's *Life of Burns,* 400–410. **Thomas Carlyle,** prob. Thrall, pp. 92, 274–275; *PMLA,* 39 (1924), 925.

679   The dead alive, 411–424. **Amelia Gillespie Smyth.** Repr. *Selwyn in Search of a Daughter,* 1835.

680   Mares'-nests, found by the materialists, the Owenites, and the craniologists, 424–434.

681   Gallery of literary characters (No. XLVII): Theodore E. Hook, Esq., 435. **William Maginn.** Repr. *Gallery.*

682   The lays of the unspoken, 436–442.

683   Sartor Resartus (book II, chaps. viii–x), 443–455. **Thomas Carlyle.** Cf. no. 628.

684   A dozen of novels, 456–487. **William**

Maginn, at least collab. Thrall, pp. 256, 297–298, who suggests partly by Thackeray but White, "Thackeray," p. 75, rejects this.

685   Father Prout's apology for Lent: his death, obsequies, and an elegy, 487–501. **Francis S. Mahony.** Repr. *Reliques.*

686   Bridlegoose Brougham, 501–506. **William Maginn?** Thrall, p. 304.

VOLUME 9, MAY 1834

687   The report on the Poor Laws, 507–522. Unidentified. Thrall, p. 304, attribs. to William Maginn, but the simple, expository style makes this very doubtful.

688   *The Judgement of the Flood* [by J. A. Heraud], 522–534.

689   Gallery of literary characters (No. XLVIII): Charles Molloy Westmacott, Esq., 536. **William Maginn.** Repr. *Gallery.*

690   Father Prout's plea for pilgrimages, and hospitable reception of Sir Walter Scott when he visited the Blarney Stone, 537–552. **F. S. Mahony.** Repr. *Reliques.* Intro. note by **Mahony**—signed Oliver Yorke, repr. *Reliques.*

691   Present condition of the people, class II (concl.): lower metropolitan tradesmen, 574–585. **Charles Wall.** Signed The Author of *Old Bailey Experience*; cf. nos. 393 and 756.

692   Ireland and the Irish, (No. I): stories of home; story the first, concerning knocking and Billy Foxleigh (chaps. i–iii), 586–600. **P. W. Banks.** Signed Morgan Rattler—see no. 178.

693   Sir Harris Nicolas and Joseph Ritson—his [Ritson's] life, letters, and labours, 601–615. **Thomas Wright,** 1810–1877. Pages 601 and 607 both refer to "our" previous art., no. 641, which is also on Ritson, and also quotes early lyrics.

694   The Fraser papers for May, 615–628. **William Maginn** with **John Churchill.** Signed O.Y. [Oliver Yorke]—see evidence for no. 522.

VOLUME 9, JUNE 1834

695   Dr. Young and Mrs. Belzoni [on Egyptian sculpture], 629–637. **Isaac Cullimore.** Signed Hermogenes—see no. 1004.

696   Men and manners (No. IV), 638–643. **Thomas Powell.** Evidence for no. 652. Intro. note signed Oliver Yorke.

697 Gallery of literary characters (No. XLIX): Leigh Hunt, 644. **William Maginn.** Repr. *Gallery.*

698 Imprisonment for debt and the insolvent debtors' court, 645–654. **Charles Wall.** Signed The Author of *Old Bailey Experience*; cf. nos. 393 and 756.

699 Ireland and the Irish (No. II, no more published): stories of home; story the first (chap. iv, concl.), 654–663. **P. W. Banks.** Evidence for no. 692.

700 Sartor Resartus (book III, chaps. i–v), 664–674. **Thomas Carlyle.** Cf. no. 628.

701 Horae Sinicae (No. I): Chinese anthology, translations from the Pih-Mei-She-Yung, or songs of a hundred women; to which is added a discourse in verse, dehorting the people from the practice of eating beef, 675–678. **D. M. Moir.** Cf. No. III (no. 816), which is signed Δ, Moir's famous signature; pages 675–677 are a selection, partly verbatim, partly rewritten (especially the verse) of Peter Perring Thoms' extractions "from the Pih-mei-she-yung, 'The Songs of a Hundred Beautiful Women,'" in his *Chinese Courtship*, (1824), pp. 249–280; the "Discourse," treated in similar fashion, was a trans. by Robert Morrison in his *Horae Sinicae* (1812), pp. 65–68.

702 Father Prout's carousal, 679–697. **F. S. Mahony.** Repr. *Reliques.*

703 Haydon's "*Reform Banquet,*" 702–710.

704 The first man I was near seeing hanged, 711–724. **T. C. Croker.** Signed C. O'Donoghue, Late Ensign (18th) Royal Irish—see Thrall, p. 36.

705 High-ways and low-ways; or Ainsworth's dictionary, with notes by Turpin [on Ainsworth's *Rookwood*], 724–738. **John Churchill,** prob. Attr. by Ainsworth in Ellis, *Ainsworth*, I, 259n., and by Thrall, p. 247; Thackeray has been suggested in Malcolm Elwin, *Thackeray, a Personality* (1932), p. 381, and Melville, *Thackeray*, I, 135, but White, "Thackeray," p. 75, rejects the attrib.

706 Defeat of the Whigs, or, The Perthshire elections—the turmoil in the cabinet, and the end of Grey, 739–743.

707 Postscript [a defense of Fraserian politics], 745–748.

VOLUME 10, JULY 1834

708 *Lay Sermons*: by the Ettrick Shepherd [James Hogg], 1–10. **Allan Cunningham.** Thrall, p. 282.

709 Men and manners (No. V), 11–18. **Thomas Powell.** Evidence for no. 652.

710 Dean Swift's madness; a tale of a churn—from the "Prout Papers," 18–32. **Francis Mahony.** Repr. *Reliques* and *Works.* Intro. note by Mahony—signed Oliver Yorke, repr. *Reliques.*

711 Poetry (No. I): the old poets, 33–47. **Egerton Brydges.** Signed.

712 Gallery of literary characters (No. L): W. H. Ainsworth, Esq., 48. **William Maginn.** Signed O.Y. [Oliver Yorke], with postscript signed M.O'D. [Morgan O'Doherty]. Repr. *Gallery.*

713 The national fairy mythology of England, 51–62. **Thomas Wright,** 1810–1877. Repr. *Literature*, I.

714 Some account of the late proceedings in our parish, 66–77. (See nos. 944, 1036.)

715 Sartor Resartus (book III, chaps. vi–viii), 77–87. **Thomas Carlyle.** Cf. no. 628.

716 Blackie's and Syme's translations of *Faust*, 88–96. **J. A. Heraud,** prob. Cf. no. 551, where Hayward's trans., here often praised, had been favorably reviewed; p. 94, indeed, quotes a passage from Hayward's second ed., in which he thanks "Mr. Heraud" for correcting an error in the first ed.; Heraud was planning a trans. of his own, as the Editor of *FM* knew (p. 94n.); moreover, this would have equipped him for the close analysis of the translations which is made here.

717 On manners, fashion, and things in general, a work in two chapters (chap. i), 97–104. **John Mitchell.** Signed Bombardinio—see no. 603. With notes by **William Maginn**—signed Sir Morgan O'Doherty, see no. 434.

718 Some passages in a visit to the Royal Academy, 106–119. **P. W. Banks.** Signed Morgan Rattler—see no. 178.

719 Oxford and Lord Brougham, 119–124.

VOLUME 10, AUGUST 1834

720 Domestic manners of Sir Walter Scott [on James Hogg's *Life of Scott*], 125–156. **William Maginn.** Attr. in J. G. Lockhart to Blackwood in *Blackwood and Sons*, II, 123; Grant's attr. to Lockhart (*Metropolis*, II, 321) is flatly denied by Maginn in no. 1024, p. 719. (Note, p. 378.)

721 The Mem, or schoolmistress; from the papers of the late Rev. Micah Balwhither

of Dalmailing, 157–162. **John Galt.** Signed; repr. *The Howdie.*

722 Men and manners (No. VI), 164–171. **Thomas Powell.** Evidence for no. 652.

723 Gallery of literary characters (No. LI): Thomas Hill, Esq., F.A.S., 172. **William Maginn.** Repr. *Gallery.*

724 La Guglielmina of Milan; a tale of Italy, from a manuscript in the monastery of St. Victor, 173–182. **William H. Ainsworth.** Signed W*; attr. by Ellis, *Ainsworth,* I, 229.

725 Sartor Resartus (book III, chaps. ix–xii, concl.), 182–193. **Thomas Carlyle.** Cf. no. 628.

726 The rogueries of Tom Moore, from the "Prout Papers," 194–210. **Francis Mahony.** Repr. *Reliques.* Intro. note by **Mahony**—signed Oliver Yorke, repr. *Reliques.*

727 Universal history: the earliest ages, 210–221.

728 Horae Sinicae (No. II): one hundred quatrains in honour of tea, by the celebrated Chinese juggler and poet, Broo-Hum-Fou, 222–226. **D. M. Moir?** Moir "collaborated" with P. P. Thoms and others on Nos. I, III, IV, V, of this series, but this No. is a spoof he wrote alone—if he wrote it.

729 On manners, fashion, and things in general (chap. ii, concl.), 226–237. **John Mitchell.** Signed Bombardinio—see no. 603. Notes by **William Maginn**—signed Sir Morgan O'Doherty, see no. 434. (No. 846 is really chap. iii.)

730 "The last chance" of the Whigs, 241–250.

VOLUME 10, SEPTEMBER 1834

731 Politics: The past session of parliament, 251–260, and The state and prospects of Toryism, September 1834, 260–265. **William Maginn,** prob. The man who wrote nos. 644 and 675 on Toryism continued the series here (and in no. 822), since we again find the method and style described in evidence for no. 644; pp. 251–260 are an art. listed in no. 1397, p. 19, and described in evidence for no. 644.

732 The maelstrom: a fragment, 267–281. **E. Wilson Landor.** Signed L*; the poem on p. 270 is reprinted in Landor's *Adventures in Northern Europe* (1836), I, 77–78, with a footnote saying it had been published in this paper in *FM*; since the book is full of stories of Norwegian life and this paper is about a Norwegian ship

in a hurricane, Landor prob. wrote the whole art.

733 Gallery of literary characters (No. LII): The Rev. George Robert Gleig, 282. **William Maginn.** Repr. *Gallery.*

734 Men and manners (No. VII), 283–294. **Thomas Powell.** Evidence for no. 652.

735 Concerning internal intercourse [by rail] in the British Islands, 294–309.

736 Literature and the Jesuits; from the "Prout Papers," 310–327. **Francis Mahony.** Repr. *Reliques* and *Works.* Intro. note by **Mahony**—signed Oliver Yorke, repr. *Reliques.*

737 Whig foreign policy, 327–337.

738 The poets of the day—batch the fourth, 338–364. **William Maginn?** Thrall, p. 297, who thinks Thackeray collaborated; White, "Thackeray," p. 75, rejects the collab.

739 Fraser papers for September, 365–378. **William Maginn,** prob. with **John Churchill.** Signed O.Y. [Oliver Yorke]; cf. no. 522.

VOLUME 10, OCTOBER 1834

740 Reminiscences of Coleridge, biographical, philosophical, poetical, and critical, 379–403. **J. A. Heraud.** Thrall, pp. 270–271, 284; author refers, pp. 379, 391, to nos. 369 and 400 as "our" arts.

741 Signor Paganini and Ensign O'Donoghue, larking at Boulogne, 409–416. **T. C. Croker.** Signed Cornelius O'Donoghue—see Thrall, p. 36.

742 Men and manners (No. VIII), 416–422. **Thomas Powell.** Evidence for no. 652.

743 Poetry (No. II, concl.): the modern poets, 423–436. **Egerton Brydges.** Signed.

744 Chrestomathy; or, analects and apologues from various sources, 437–447. **Jean Paul Richter,** 1763–1825, collab. Pages 437–442 attr. by translator, p. 439, to Richter.

745 Life and correspondence of Mrs. Hannah More, 448–462. **William Maginn?** Thrall, p. 298, who suggests collab. with Thackeray, but White, "Thackeray," p. 75, rejects it.

746 Gallery of literary characters (No. LIII): William Godwin, Esq., 463. **William Maginn.** Repr. *Gallery.*

747 The songs of France: on wine, war, woemen, wooden shoes, filosophy, frogs, and free trade, from the "Prout Papers," (chap. i): wine and war, 464–480. **Francis Mahony.** Repr. *Reliques.* Intro. note

by **Mahony**—signed Oliver Yorke, repr. *Reliques.*

748 Dinner to Earl Grey, 480–487. **William Maginn.** The "ballad," pp. 481–487, is signed Sir Morgan O'Doherty, Maginn's pseudonym; and the style of pp. 480–481 is characteristic.

749 An autumn in the north (chap. i), 488–493. **John Galt.** Attr. by Macnish, *Pythagorean*, I, 333.

750 Mr. Duncombe and Mr. Fraser, 494–504. **William Maginn?** Signed Oliver Yorke; Thrall, p. 304.

VOLUME 10, NOVEMBER 1834

751 The books on my table, 505–522. **P. W. Banks.** Signed Morgan Rattler—see no. 178.

752 Religious toleration in South America [in Venezuela], 523–529. Unidentified. The last five paragraphs are a postscript by another hand, signed: P.I.

753 Men and manners (No. IX), 530–537. **J. G. Lockhart,** and **William Maginn?** Signed Pierce Pungent; Thrall, pp. 35, 287.

754 Gallery of literary characters (No. LIV): James Smith, Esq., 538. **William Maginn.** Repr. *Gallery.*

755 Spanish legends, 539–556. Signed: A Berkeleian.

756 Metropolis water supply, 561–572. **Charles Wall.** Signed The Author of *Old Bailey Experience*; see evidence for no. 393; on fol. 120 of MS. cited there, this art. "by Charles Wall" is listed for inclusion with the documents Place planned to use in a projected "Narrative of the Proceedings of the Pure Spring Water Company."

757 An autumn in the north (chap. ii), 573–586. **John Galt.** Cf. no. 749.

758 The songs of France (chap. ii): woemen and wooden shoes, 587–601. **Francis Mahony.** Repr. *Reliques.* Intro. note by Mahony—signed Oliver Yorke, repr. *Reliques.*

759 Two articles on the annuals: judgment of the annuals (No. I), 604–609. **Bryan W. Procter.** Signed Barry Cornwall—see *DNB.* Intro. note, 602–604, which also applies to next item, by O.Y. [Oliver Yorke]—see p. 623, at end of no. 760.

760 Two articles on the annuals: judgment of the annuals (No. II), 610–623. **John Churchill.** Signed The Man of Genius—see no. 203.

VOLUME 10, DECEMBER 1834

761 The grievances of a country overseer, 629–639.

762 Gallery of literary characters (No. LV): Comte D'Orsay, 645. **William Maginn.** Repr. *Gallery.*

763 A Cambrian colloquy on the decline and fall of poetry, 646–665. **Joseph Downes.** Downes to Lockhart, n.d., Nat. Lib. Scot., MS. 934, fol. 135, says his "Colloquy on Poetry" was in last Dec. issue of *Fraser's.*

764 The songs of France (chap. iii): filosophy, 666–682. **Francis Mahony.** Repr. *Reliques.* Intro. note by **Mahony**—signed Oliver Yorke, repr. *Reliques.*

765 An autumn in the north (chap. iii), 682–691. **John Galt.** Cf. no. 749.

766 Men and manners (No. X, concl.), 692–698. **Thomas Powell.** Evidence for no. 652.

767 Lord Byron's dramas, 699–711. **J. A. Heraud** and **William Maginn,** prob. Thrall, p. 285, refs. back to "our" arts. on Byron, mentioning nos. 200, 439.

768 The Rev. Mr. Croly and the Irish Roman Catholics, 711–725.

769 Sir Egerton Brydges' reply to the *Edinburgh Review* [59 (July, 1834), 439], 725–735. **Egerton Brydges.** Title.

770 The wind-up of the year; being the last news of the ministry, a ballad on the woes of the Whigs, our closer, [and] the final song of XXXIV, 736–748. **William Maginn,** at least collab. The ballad, pp. 736–741, is signed M.O'D. [Morgan O'Doherty], Maginn's pseudonym; the political prose, pp. 736, 742–747, is very like Maginn in its view of Wellington (see Thrall's index) and its style (cf. evidence for no. 644); on p. 744 the principal journals Maginn wrote for are mentioned together in words very like those in no. 644, p. 10; and on p. 745 appears a strong editorial pronouncement on the future policy of *FM*; the poem on p. 748, signed O.Y., may not be Maginn's.

VOLUME 11, JANUARY 1835

771 The Fraserians; or, The commencement of the year thirty-five: a fragment, 1–27. **William Maginn.** Signed O.Y. [Oliver Yorke]; repr. *Gallery.* With a paper, "On the Universality of Goethe's Genius," pp. 11–12, ascribed to **David Brewster:** the sharp attack on Brougham, who was a friend and patron of Brewster, could suggest a Fraser spoof, but it was more likely an editorial insertion intended to be an impudent joke, for the material about Goethe's theory of colors reflects Brewster's known ideas (cf. *Edin. Rev.*, no. 1743 in *Index*, I); moreover, Brewster sits with the Fraserians in the frontispiece by Maclise which precedes this art., and most of the group give acknowledged speeches in prose or verse.

772 Europe during the middle ages, 28–32. **Thomas Wright,** 1810–1877. No. 840 opens with a close link to this art.; attr. by Francisque Michel, *Bibliothèque Anglo-Saxonne* (Paris, 1837), pp. 154–155.

773 Notes of a journey from Paris to Ostend, 33–49. **Robert Macnish.** Signed A Modern Pythagorean; repr. *Tales*, II.

774 Coleridgeiana, 50–58. **J. A. Heraud.** In opening sentence author all but claims no. 740, to which this is presented as a sequel.

775 *France, Social, Literary, Political* [by Henry Lytton Bulwer], 59–65. **William Maginn?** See evidence for no. 745.

776 An autumn in the north (chap. iv), 66–79. **John Galt.** Cf. no. 749.

777 The songs of France (chap. iv, concl.): frogs and free trade, 83–99. **Francis Mahony.** Repr. *Reliques.* Intro. note by Mahony—signed Oliver Yorke, repr. *Reliques.*

778 Death of the Rev. Edward Irving (No. I), 99–101. **B. W. Procter.** Attr. by A. L. Drummond, *Edward Irving and his Circle* (1937), p. 84.

779 Death of the Rev. Edward Irving (No. II), 101–103. **Thomas Carlyle.** Repr. *Essays*, III.

780 Anecdotes of ghosts and apparitions, 103–112. **James Hogg.** Signed The Ettrick Shepherd—see *DNB*.

781 A few words to the supporters of Earl Grey's administration, 113–120. **William Maginn,** prob. Cf. evidence for no. 644.

VOLUME 11, FEBRUARY 1835

782 The songs of Italy (chap. i), 121–135. **Francis Mahony.** Repr. *Reliques.* Intro. note by Mahony—signed Oliver Yorke, repr. *Reliques.*

783 Gallery of literary characters (No. LVII): Charles Lamb, Esq., 136. **William Maginn.** Repr. *Gallery.*

784 Country quarters, 137–147. **T. C. Croker.** Signed Ensign O'Donoghue, Late 18th, or Royal Irish—see Thrall, p. 36.

785 The Spanish question, 148–157.

786 Carrington's poems, 157–169.

787 An autumn in the north (chap. v, concl.), 170–178. **John Galt.** Cf. no. 749.

788 Of Ireland in 1834 (Part I), 193–217. **William Maginn,** prob. Signed An Officer in a Marching Regiment; pp. 197–199 are repr. *Writings*, V, as "Irish Genius," and the remainder of the art. is written in the same style—viz., that described in evidence for no. 644.

789 Popular superstition of modern Greece, 218–225. **Thomas Wright,** 1810–1877. Repr. *Literature*, I.

790 A very ridiculous sermon, 226–231. **James Hogg.** Signed The Ettrick Shepherd—see *DNB*.

791 The politics of the month, 234–246. **William Maginn,** prob. Thrall, p. 304; style here is described in evidence for no. 644.

VOLUME 11, MARCH 1835

792 Church reform, 247–258.

793 The songs of Italy (chap. ii, concl.), 259–274. **Francis Mahony.** Repr. *Reliques.* Intro. note by **Mahony**—signed Oliver Yorke, repr. *Reliques.*

794 The Cliffords of Craven; a tradition, 275–292. **Andrew Picken.** Signed; repr. *Waldie's Select Circulating Library* (Philadelphia, 1835), V.

795 Gallery of literary characters (No. LVIII): Pierre-Jean de Béranger, 300. **Francis Mahony.** Thrall, p. 290; repr. Maginn, *Gallery.*

796 A few observations on the crime of forgery, and its punishment, 301–309.

797 History of corporations, 309–325.

798 "Quarrels of" zoologists, 325–329. **Charles Waterton.** Signed. Intro. note by **J. J. Audubon**—Waterton to George Orde, July 3, 1835, in Waterton's *Essays on Natural History*, ed. Norman Moon, 1871.

799 Odd thoughts on strange subjects, 330–337. **J. A. Heraud,** prob. Signed Mordaunt Couplet, Esquire; Thrall, p. 284; pp. 335–336 in particular reflect Heraud's interests.

800 Of Ireland in 1834 (Part II, concl.), 342–350. **William Maginn,** prob. Evidence for no. 788.

801 The sea-sprite; or, A voice from the deep, 353–356.

802 Prospects of the ministry, 360–368. **William Maginn,** prob. The style is that

described in evidence for no. 644; the enemies are largely the same Whigs and Radicals named in no. 930, who are called "the *Destructives*" (pp. 361, 363), as they are in no. 675, p. 370, etc.

VOLUME 11, APRIL 1835

803 April fools; or One hundred matrimonial letters, 369–403. **William Maginn,** perhaps with **Theodore Hook.** Kenealy, "Maginn," p. 89, who explains that 18 persons wrote a hundred of these letters in answer to a fake advertisement, printed here p. 370, from a wealthy young Anglo-Indian lady seeking a husband; "her" replies are by Maginn and perhaps some by Hook.

804 Gallery of literary characters (No. LIX): Miss Jane Porter, 404. **William Maginn.** Repr. *Gallery.*

805 *The Book of the Season* [by William Howitt], 414–427. **William Maginn,** collab. at least. Thrall, p. 304, who adds, "presumably with others."

806 Corporation reform, 428–440. Signed: An Englishman.

807 Notte romane nel palazzo Vaticano; from the "Prout Papers," 441–456. **Francis Mahony.** Repr. *Works* as "Barry in the Vatican."

808 Church affairs—the Ecclesiastical Commission and church-rates, 457–464.

809 A quintette of novels, 465–490. **William Maginn?** See evidence for no. 745.

810 The Irish Church, 491–496.

VOLUME 11, MAY 1835

811 Mr. Sharon Turner's *Sacred History of the World* [Vol. II], 497–507. **J. A. Heraud?** Cf. no. 456, to which this is a sequel (see first paragraph), and which is referred to in detail on p. 499.

812 Northern Germany, 507–515.

813 Foreign literature (No. I): Spain and Portugal, 518–528.

814 Gallery of literary characters (No. LX): Lady [Sydney] Morgan, 529. **William Maginn.** Repr. *Gallery.*

815 Speeches delivered in banco Reginae (No. III, concl.): Mirabeau v. Dumont (Part II), 530–541. **P. W. Banks,** prob. Evidence for no. 549.

816 Horae Sinicae (No. III, concl.), 542–549. **D. M. Moir.** Signed Δ, Moir's famous signature (see *DNB*); Moir did only the editing, paraphrasing, and initial commentary, for most of the art., as he says himself on pp. 542 and 544, is taken from *The History of Sung-kin,* trans. by **P. P. Thoms,** 1820. (Nos. IV–V are no. 1173.)

817 Anonymous publications, 549–551. **John Galt.** Signed.

818 The mask; or, Part of a story, 552–558. **William Maginn.** Repr. *Magazine Miscellanies,* 1841.

819 The days of Erasmus, from the "Prout Papers," 559–575. **Francis Mahony.** Repr. *Works.* Intro. note signed Oliver Yorke.

820 A father's confession, 576–581. **William Maginn.** Repr. *Magazine Miscellanies,* 1841.

821 A decade of novels and nouvellettes, 586–609. **William Maginn?** See evidence for no. 745.

822 The state and prospects of Toryism in May, 1835, 610–616. **William Maginn,** prob. Cf. initial evidence for no. 731.

823 A letter to Francis Baring, Esq., joint secretary to the treasury, by an old whipper-in, [viz., Tory Whip], 617–620. **William Maginn?** Signed W.H. [William Holmes]; Thrall, p. 304.

VOLUME 11, JUNE 1835

824 The martial elegies of Tyrtaeus, 621–629. **William Maginn?** Thrall, p. 304.

825 Return from leave, 630–642. **T. C. Croker.** Signed C. O'Donoghue—see Thrall, p. 36.

826 A chapter of accidents, 642–650. **J. A. Heraud,** prob. Signed Mordaunt Couplet, Esquire—see no. 799; many of the topics reflect Heraud's interests.

827 Gallery of literary characters (No. LXI): Mr. Alaric Attila Watts, 652. **William Maginn.** Repr. *Gallery.*

828 Holman's *Voyage round the World,* 653–666.

829 Foreign literature (No. II, concl.): French system of universal instruction, 680–688.

830 Wordsworth's new volume of poetry [*Yarrow Revisited*], 689–707. **J. A. Heraud,** prob. Thrall, p. 284.

831 The poets of the day—batch the fifth [and last], 708–728. **William Maginn?** See evidence for no. 738.

832 The duty of a Conservative at the present juncture, 729–735. **William Maginn,** prob. Cf. evidence for no. 644.

833 The Whigs' last trick, 736–738.

VOLUME 12, JULY 1835

834 Whig friendship for institutions, 1–11.

835 The Jordans of Grange and the old maids of Balmogy; a tradition of the Dominie, 12–32. **Andrew Picken.** After he wrote *The Dominie's Legacy*, 1830, he was known as "The Dominie" (Thrall, p. 292); repr. in *Waldie's Select Circulating Library* (see no. 794), VI.

836 Of politicians, public opinion, and the press, 32–42. **P. W. Banks.** Signed Morgan Rattler—see no. 178.

837 Gallery of literary characters (No. LXII): Lord Francis Egerton, 43. **William Maginn.** Repr. *Gallery*. (See no. 845.)

838 The Somerset House annual [exhibition], 49–62. **W. H. Leeds.** Cf. no. 414, of which this is the exact analogue in subject, form, and style; it even includes the *"con amore"* p. 51, which is like a signature: see evidence for no. 99 (also on exhibitions) for a few references, and nos. 1052, 1291 for others.

839 M'Vicar's Balaam-box (No. I): tales of mystery, 63–75.

840 On Anglo-Saxon poetry, 76–88. **Thomas Wright,** 1810–1877. Repr. *Literature*, I.

841 Victor Hugo's *Hunchback of Notre Dame*, with specimens, from the "Prout Papers," of his lyrical poetry, 89–105. **Francis Mahony.** Repr. *Works*.

842 The stock exchange: panic the second, 105–111.

843 Duty of the Conservative lords and commoners: the Corporation Bill, 114–122.

VOLUME 12, AUGUST 1835

844 Coleridge's *Table-Talk*, 123–135. **J. A. Heraud.** Thrall, pp. 271, 284.

845 Epistles to the literati (No. VI): [John Stuart] Blackie to Yorke [with Yorke's reply], 136. **William Maginn?** Signed John S. Blackie, but the silly solemnity of the protest against a passing phrase in no. 837 and the fictitious character of these epistles (see no. 497) make his authorship very unlikely; the learned and witty reply on the etymology of "ragamuffin" points to Maginn, who prob. wrote the letter for the sake of the reply.

846 Bombardinio on manners, fashion, foreign travelling, and things in general,

137–153. John Mitchell. Pseudonym "Bombardinio" is identified in Schmitz, *Mitchell*, p. xiv.

847 Gallery of literary characters (No. LXIII): Henry O'Brien, A.B., 154. **Francis Mahony.** Repr. *Reliques* and Maginn, *Gallery*.

848 Of internal intercourse and communication in the British Islands [Thomas Grahame on canals], 155–163.

849 The barbarian eye [of the Fraserians], 164–173.

850 The dissenters and the universities, 174–191. **James Reid Brown,** prob. In letter of June 19, 1851, Chalmers Papers, New Coll. Edinburgh, addressed from the Manse of Greenock, the writer (last page of letter lost) says he wrote for the *Times* in favor of Dr. Chalmers' appointment to the Divinity Chair at Glasgow, vacant through the death of Mr. McGill in 1840; goes on to claim this art. and also nos. 874 and 883 below; man cited was minister of Greenock Middle Parish 1843–1860, and had earlier been a leader-writer for the *Times* (Scott, *Fasti*, III, 202), where an editorial, Oct. 1, 1840, p. 4, cols. d–e, strongly recommends the appointment of Chalmers; the only other pro-Chalmers statement in the *Times* was a letter, Oct. 20, p. 6, col. d, signed William Cunningham and Robert Candlish, both ministers in Edinburgh in 1851.

851 A series of modern Latin poets, from the "Prout Papers" (chap. i): "The Silkworm" by Jerome Vida [the poem is on 198–206], 192–197. **Francis Mahony.** Repr. *Reliques*. Intro. note by Mahony—signed Oliver Yorke; repr. *Reliques*.

852 Cobbett, 207–222. **William Maginn?** Thrall, p. 304.

853 The Greek pastoral poets—Theocritus, Bion, and Moschus (Part I): Theocritus, 222–241. **R. A. Willmott.** Attr. in *FM*, 21 (Jan. 1840), 21.

854 The national controversy [on politics], 242–248.

VOLUME 12, SEPTEMBER 1835

855 Recollections of Sir Walter Scott (No. I): his boyhood and youth, 249–266. **R. P. Gillies.** Repr. *Recollections*.

856 A few words of advice to clerks, shopmen, and apprentices, 267–279.

857 Gallery of literary characters (No. LXIV): Michael Thomas Sadler, Esq., 280. **William Maginn.** Repr. *Gallery*.

858 On Ker's *Nursery Rhymes and Proverbs*, 283–290. **Thomas Wright**, 1810–1877. Repr. *Literature*, I, as last half of "Proverbs and Popular Sayings."

859 The metropolitan emigrant, 291–299. **John Galt**. Signed; repr. *The Howdie*.

860 Preservation of the monarchy and empire, 301–312.

861 Modern Latin poets; from the "Prout Papers" (chap. ii): Casimir Sarbiewski, S. Sannazar, Jerome Fracastor, 313–326. **Francis Mahony.** Repr. *Reliques*. Intro. note by **Mahony**—signed Oliver Yorke; repr. *Reliques*.

862 Miss Fanny Kemble and her critics [largely from her *Journal*], 327–337.

863 Lochead's daughter, 338–356. **Agnes C. Hall.** Signed H.; attr. in *Gent. Mag.*, 181 (Jan. 1847), 98.

864 Bombardinio in Italy, 356–369. **John Mitchell.** Cf. no. 846.

865 A letter to Viscount Melbourne, 371–374. Signed: An English Elector.

VOLUME 12, OCTOBER 1835

866 Lord Brougham on natural theology, 375–393. **G. R. Gleig.** Repr. *Essays*, I.

867 The Greek pastoral poets (Part II): Theocritus concluded, 394–408. **R. A. Willmott.** Cf. no. 853.

868 Washington Irving's *Miscellanies*, 409–415. **William Maginn?** See evidence for no. 745.

869 The Bridgewater treatises (No. III): the Rev. Wm. Kirby and Doctor Roget, 415–429. **J. A. Heraud** and **William Maginn**, prob. Thrall, p. 285. (No. IV is no. 1147.)

870 Gallery of literary characters (No. LXV): William Cobbett, M.P. for Oldham, 430. **William Maginn.** Repr. *Gallery*.

871 A tale of truth, 431–437.

872 A fishing excursion into Galway, 437–447. **Samuel O'Sullivan.** Repr. *Remains* (Dublin, 1853), III.

873 Modern Latin poets, from the "Prout Papers" (chap. iii, concl.): Theodore Beza, Father Vanière, George Buchanan, 448–463. **Francis Mahony.** Repr. *Reliques*. Intro. note by **Mahony**—signed Oliver Yorke; repr. *Reliques*.

874 America and church establishments (Part I), 464–474. **James Reid Brown**, prob. Cf. no. 850.

875 Bombardinio at Rome, 477–492. **John Mitchell.** Cf. no. 846.

VOLUME 12, NOVEMBER 1835

876 Monologues by the late Samuel Taylor Coleridge (No. I): [on] life, 493–496. **S. T. Coleridge.** Title. Reported with intro. remarks by **J. A. Heraud**—closely linked to no. 844.

877 The confessions of a metempsychosis, 496–501. **Andrew Picken.** Signed The Dominie—see no. 835.

878 Recollections of Sir Walter Scott (No. II): his early manhood, 502–515. **R. P. Gillies.** Repr. *Recollections*.

879 Memorabilia Bacchanalia (No. I), 522–539. **C. J. Apperley.** Signed Nimrod—see *DNB*.

880 Gallery of literary characters (No. LXVI): Earl of Mulgrave, 540. **William Maginn.** Repr. *Gallery*.

881 The Greek pastoral poets (Part III): Bion, 541–550. **R. A. Willmott.** Cf. no. 853.

882 Horae Lutetianae: the cognate cities [Rome, Venice, Paris], 551–574. **P. W. Banks.** Signed Morgan Rattler—see no. 178.

883 America and church establishments (Part II), 575–600. **James Reid Brown**, prob. Cf. no. 850.

884 The state of parties, 605–618.

VOLUME 12, DECEMBER 1835

885 Monologues of the late Samuel Taylor Coleridge (No. II): science and system of logic, 619–629. **S. T. Coleridge.** Title. Reported with intro. remarks by **J. A. Heraud**—cf. no. 876.

886 The Baron of Courtstown, 629–641. **Andrew Picken.** Signed The Dominie—see no. 835.

887 Gallery of literary characters (No. LXVII): Robert Macnish, Esq., 650. **William Maginn.** Repr. *Gallery*.

888 Scottish ecclesiastical history, 651–664.

889 Authentic narrative of facts which occurred during a march in India; from an officer's sketch book, 664–672. **William Dunlop?** Thrall, p. 282.

890 The king and the people, 674–687.

891 Recollections of Sir Walter Scott (No. III): "honour, love, obedience, troops of friends," 687–703. **R. P. Gillies.** Repr. *Recollections*.

892 Shewing how the Tories and the Whigs extend their patronage to science and literature, 703–709.

893 Bombardinio on manners, war, and

Prince Puckler Muskau, 709–721. **John Mitchell.** Cf. no. 846.

894   The "disgraceful" coalition, 725–735.

VOLUME 13, JANUARY 1836

895   Parliamentary report of the proceedings of *Fraser's Magazine*, followed by an account of the grand Fraserian festival, 1–79. **William Maginn, with Francis Mahony.** Kenealy, "Maginn," p. 89, and Maginn, "Memoir," p. lxxiii, assign to Maginn; most of p. 79, from "The Ghost of Father Prout . . ." to the end, is repr. in Mahony's *Works* as "Father Prout's Dirge."

896   Regina's maids of honour: list the first, 80. **William Maginn.** Repr. *Gallery*.

897   A few words more to the Conservatives, 81–91. **William Maginn,** prob. The whole point of view as well as the style and method are those described in the evidence for no. 644; reference, p. 85, to "the Destructive party," a term used in no. 675, p. 370, no. 832, p. 729, and no. 1397, p. 15.

898   The Greek pastoral poets (No. IV, concl.): Moschus, 92–104. **R. A. Willmott.** Cf. no. 853.

899   Recollections of Sir Walter Scott (No. IV, concl.): "the sere and yellow leaf," 104–120. **R. P. Gillies.** Repr. *Recollections.*

900   Mr. Alaric *Alexander* Watts, 129–131. Unidentified. (See next item.)

901   The speech of William Erle, Esq., K.C., in the case of Watts *v.* Fraser and Moyes, on the 5th of December, 1835, in the King's Bench, Westminster, before Lord Denham and a special jury, 132–142. **William Erle.** Title.

VOLUME 13, FEBRUARY 1836

902   Lord Bacon, his character and philosophy, 143–153.

903   A glance at Russia in 1835, 160–169. **Henry Mildmay.** Signed.

904   Sketches of savage life (No. I): Kondiaronk, Chief of the Hurons, 169–176. **William Dunlop?** Thrall, p. 282.

905   Spain: illustrated, by Lewis, Roberts, and Roscoe, 177–181. **P. W. Banks.** Signed Morgan Rattler—see no. 178.

906   The present state of Ireland, 181–194. **Horatio Townshend.** Signed Senex; Thrall, pp. 293, 305, and *DNB.*

907   Willis's *Pencillings*, 195–202. **William**

Maginn. Repr. *Writings*, V. With a postscript, 202–203, by **Maginn**—signed O.Y. [Oliver Yorke].

908   Another glance at the "appropriation" clause [on the Irish Church], 203–209.

909   *Paris and the Parisians in 1835* [by Frances Trollope], 209–223. Unidentified. Thrall, p. 297, suggests Thackeray, but White, "Thackeray," p. 75, rejects this.

910   Gallery of literary characters (No. LXIX): Michael Faraday F.R.S., Hon. D.C.L. Oxon., etc., 224. **William Maginn.** Repr. *Gallery.*

911   Bacchanalia memorabilia (No. II), results of wine-bibbing, 225–235. **C. J. Apperley.** Signed Nimrod—see *DNB.*

912   *Dramas*, by Joanna Baillie, 236–249.

913   New churches, 249–254.

914   Stray reflections [largely a memoir of Sir John Sinclair], 254–259. **William Maginn,** at least collab. Thrall, p. 304, who adds, "presumably with others."

915   Political memoranda, 259–268. **William Maginn,** at least collab. The style and method here are those described in no. 644; on p. 262 author attacks the same Radicals and Whig lords who appear in no. 930, again with a reference to the *Westminster Rev.*; also Spring-Rice and Lord John Russell, here pp. 264 and 268, are criticized with similar acerbity in no. 930; however, pp. 259–262 top may be by another hand.

VOLUME 13, MARCH 1836

916   The conquest of Ireland by the Anglo-Normans [12th-cent. MS.], 269–288. **Thomas Wright,** 1810–1877. Repr. *Literature*, II.

917   M'Vicar's Balaam-box (No. II, concl.): tales of solitude and society, 289–299.

918   Gallery of literary characters (No. LXX): Rev. William Lisle Bowles, 300. **William Maginn.** Repr. *Gallery.* (See no. 937.)

919   The republics of the New World, 301–307.

920   Female education, and modern matchmaking, 308–316.

921   Sketches of savage life (No. II): Shaa-Naan-Dithit, or the last of the Boëothics, 316–323. **William Dunlop?** Thrall, p. 282.

922   *The Reliques of Father Prout, late parish priest of Watergrasshill, in the County Cork, Ireland*; collected and arranged by US; illustrated and lamplighted by Alfred Croquis, Esq., 333–343. **Fran-**

cis **Mahony.** Repr. *Works* as "Father Prout's Self-examination."

923 My acquaintance with the late Charles Mathews, 343–350. **George Wightwick.** Attr. in *DNB* under Charles Mathews to "Wightwick," though with slightly different title and the date 1833; for man cited see Thrall, p. 293.

924 Operative Conservative associations, 351–361. **William Maginn,** prob. Cf. evidence for no. 664.

925 Asinarii scenici, second series, [review of Browning's *Paracelsus* and Taylor's *Philip van Artevelde*], 362–377. **J. A. Heraud,** perhaps with **William Maginn?** Furnivall, p. 89, gives Heraud alone; Thrall, p. 285, suggests Maginn as a prob. collab.

926 Orangeism versus Romanism, 377–393.

VOLUME 13, APRIL 1836

927 The familiar letters of Cowley, with notices of his life, and sketches of some of his friends and contemporaries, now first printed (Part I), 395–409. **R. A. Willmott.** Pages 398–399 from Cowley's "Myself" are used in the opening selection of Willmott's *Parlour Book* (1841), pp. 1–3; Thrall, pp. 293–294; cf. Part II, which is no. 985. The actual letters, here and in Part II, are concoctions of Willmott's: see J. McL. McBryde, Jr., *Journ. of Germanic Philol.,* II, (1898–1899), 459–467, and *Athenaeum,* July 17, 1897, p. 99.

928 Père la Chaise, 409–415.

929 Morning musings with favourite old poets (No. I; no more published): the *Antigone* of Sophocles, 416–426. **R. A. Willmott.** Thrall, p. 294; he wrote series on Greek comedy, starting with no. 1050; the title and style are characteristic (for latter see evidence for no. 1549).

930 Gallery of literary characters (No. LXXI): Francis Place, 427. **William Maginn.** Repr. *Gallery.*

931 Memoirs of a homicide, 428–440.

932 J. Sheridan Knowles' plays, 451–468. **J. A. Heraud.** Author claims, p. 451, to have written *Quarterly Rev.,* 35 (Mar. 1827), 351–363, which is by Heraud (see *Index,* I); attr. in Macready, *Diaries,* I, 293.

933 [*Recollections*] *of the Private Life of Lafayette,* 468–474.

934 What is the use of a Lord-Lieutenant of Ireland? 475–487.

935 Another caw from the rookwood—Tur-

pin out again [on Ainsworth's *Rookwood*], 488–493. **William Maginn.** Thrall, pp. 247–248; repr. *Writings,* V.

936 On the sea-fed engine, for propelling vessels instead of steam, 494–496. **John Galt.** Signed.

937 Epistles to the literati (No. VII): Bowles to Yorke, 498–499. **William Maginn?** Signed W. L. Bowles; but this amusing and ridiculous protest against no. 918 can hardly be genuine; indeed, no "Epistle" so far has been (cf. nos. 497, 498, 845); since Maginn wrote no. 918, one might guess he would have written the spurious reply, as was the case apparently, with J. S. Blackie: see nos. 837 and 845. (See nos. 953, 963.)

938 Sketches of savage life (No. III, concl.): Tecumseh, chief warrior of the Shawanees, 499–511. **William Dunlop?** Thrall, p. 282.

939 The "no-popery" cry, 511–519.

VOLUME 13, MAY 1836

940 Union of Papists and Dissenters to achieve the disunion of Church and State, 521–525.

941 Goethe's *Tasso,* 526–539. **R. P. Gillies.** Attr. in Douglas F. S. Scott, *Some English Correspondents of Goethe* (1949), p. 42.

942 On courts-martial and the cat-o'-nine-tails, 539–552. **T. C. Croker.** Signed Cornelius O'Donoghue—see Thrall, p. 36.

943 Collier on Shakespeare, 553–559.

944 Some further particulars of the late proceedings in our parish [cf. no. 714], 559–567.

945 Gallery of literary characters (No. LXXII): Sir John C. Hobhouse, 568. **William Maginn.** Repr. *Gallery.*

946 My grandfather; a tale of Bath (Part I), 569–579.

947 Archaeographia—the Jewish theocracy, 579–593. **Isaac Cullimore.** Signed Hermogenes; claimed at start of no. 1005.

948 The poems of Quaffypunchovicz, the expatriated Pole; done into English by Tydus-pooh-pooh, our man of genius, 593–599. **John Churchill** with **William Maginn.** Cf. nos. 203, 292.

949 *The Greek Pastoral Poets,* 600–607. **R. A. Willmott.** Author claims, p. 601, to have written nos. 853, 867, 881. 898.

950 The Turners, 609–619. **James Hogg.** Signed The Ettrick Shepherd—see *DNB.*

951 The morning and evening papers, 620–631.

952 *England in 1835* [by Von Raumer], 631–638.

953 Epistles to the literati (No. VIII): Yorke to Bowles, 643–644. **William Maginn**, prob. Signed Oliver Yorke; a reply to Bowles' protest in no. 937—if it was his—against Maginn's portrait (no. 918) would probably come from the original author; on p. 644 the writer twice claims to be the conductor of the magazine (see especially the P.S.).

VOLUME 13, JUNE 1836

954 Corporal-punishment Commission: defects in military education, and promotion from the ranks, 645–656. **T. C. Croker.** Signed Ensign O'Donoghue—see Thrall, p. 36.

955 Cutting-out ashore; or, A bold stroke during the peace of Amiens, 657–665. **Augustus Collingridge.** H&L, I, 471.

956 On the charge that men of genius and high talents want judgment and practical sense, 673–682. **Egerton Brydges.** Signed.

957 My grandfather (Part II, concl.), 682–693.

958 Immortality and immateriality [on Lord Brougham, Thomas Wallace, and Thomas Turton], 694–707.

959 A letter from Cambridge to Oliver Yorke, about the art of plucking, etc., 707–715. **R. A. Willmott**, prob. Signed T.G.; pseudonym attr. by Thrall, pp. 251–252, on basis of similarity of style to that of no. 995, pp. 357–358; end of art., pp. 714–715, recommends a new book, *Conversations at Cambridge*, which Willmott had just published anonymously (see H&L, *BMCat.*) and includes two sentences that suggest the identity of author and reviewer (1st sentence of last par., p. 714, col. i, and last sentence, p. 715); though Willmott was at Trinity, the subscription "St. John's" allows for the ironic satire on Sir Launcelot Shadwell, p. 709, and Mr. [Thomas] Whytehead, p. 714, the latter of whom had just won the Chancellor's Medal (see Venn); both were at St. John's. White, "Thackeray," pp. 75–76, rejects the case for Thackeray's authorship, as does Thrall, pp. 251–252.

960 Gallery of literary characters (No. LXXIII): Mrs. S. C. Hall, 718. **William Maginn.** Repr. *Gallery.*

961 "Justice to Ireland" [speeches of Daniel O'Connell], 719–725. (See no. 969.)

962 Bacchanalia memorabilia (No. III): drinking experiences, 727–737. **C. J. Apperley.** Signed Nimrod—see *DNB.*

963 Sonnet that might have been written in May, by the Rev. Wm. Lisle Bowles, 737–738. **William Maginn?** This takes off from the request in the P.S. to no. 953 and continues the Yorke-Bowles exchange which seems entirely to be by Maginn (see nos. 937, 953, and cf. evidence for no. 497); the self-praise ("What sonnets are those of Bowles!") rules out Bowles at once; the verse parody as well as the knowledge of Byron also points to Maginn.

964 The odes of Horace, 739–746.

965 The book of blunders [books by James Grant on House of Commons and House of Lords], 747–754. **William Maginn?** Thrall, p. 304.

966 Our present position, 755–759.

VOLUME 14, JULY 1836

967 The books on my table: of *Hamlet,* 1–18. **P. W. Banks.** Signed Morgan Rattler—see no. 178; Thrall, pp. 248, 306; repr. in Maginn's *Writings,* V, and see p. lxxx, but Thrall, p. 306, rejects the attr.

968 Le Revenant, 30–42.

969 More "Justice to Ireland" [sequel to no. 961], 45–54.

970 On Anglo-Norman poetry, 55–67. **Thomas Wright,** 1810–1877. Repr. *Literature,* I.

971 Gallery of literary characters (No. LXXIV): Mr. Sergeant Talfourd, 68. **William Maginn.** Repr. *Gallery.*

972 Southey's *Life of Cowper,* 69–86. **J. A. Heraud**, prob. Cf. no. 547, called our "former paper" in p. 69 and paraphrased on pp. 69 and 70; the opening sentences immediately point to Heraud.

973 The songs of Horace (Part I): decade the first, from the "Prout Papers," 87–103. **Francis Mahony.** Series repr. *Reliques,* 2nd ed., and *Works.* Intro. notes by **Mahony**—signed Oliver Yorke introduce each part of the series; repr. *Reliques.*

974 A most talented family (Part I), 104–116.

975 A second letter from Cambridge to Oliver Yorke, Esq.: pluck examination questions; critical paper, 117–122. **R. A. Willmott**, prob. Signed T.G.; cf. no. 959, where, p. 713, author twice promises a second letter. (See no. 980.)

976   For the present instant: the ministers; the people, 123–130.

VOLUME 14, AUGUST 1836

977   On the principle of church establishments, 131–149.
978   A most talented family (Part II, concl.), 150–167.
979   Sandhurst College and Woolwich Academy, 168–179. **T. C. Croker.** Signed Ensign O'Donoghue—see Thrall, p. 36.
980   A postscript to the second letter from Cambridge [no. 975], 180–182. **R. A. Willmott.** Signed T.G.; cf. no. 959.
981   O'Hanlon and his wife, 184–201. **R. P. Gillies.** Signed W.F.; *Memoirs*, III, 219.
982   Gallery of literary characters (No. LXXV): Sir John Soane, 202. **William Maginn.** Repr. *Gallery*.
983   The songs of Horace (Part II), 203–217. **Francis Mahony.** Cf. no. 973.
984   *Ion* [by T. N. Talfourd] and *The Provost of Bruges*, 218–233. **J. A. Heraud.** Thrall, p. 284; on p. 218 the author affirms his "love" of Wordsworth and Coleridge, and whatever favors their influence: see Part B below.
985   The familiar letters of Cowley (Part II), 234–241. **R. A. Willmott.** Cf. no. 927; Thrall, pp. 293–294; the comparison of Cowley's Goliath with Milton's Satan, p. 239, appears in Willmott's *Summer Time*, pp. 57–58.
986   Mr. Grantley Berkeley and his novel [*Berkeley Castle*], 242–247. **William Maginn.** Attr. in *DNB*. (See nos. 1038, 1039.)
987   Notes of the month: the House of Peers; the ministry, 248–255. **William Maginn,** prob. Cf. evidence for no. 644.

VOLUME 14, SEPTEMBER 1836

988   Ireland and the conciliatory system [toward Roman Catholicism], 257–271.
989   Gallery of literary characters (No. LXXVI): Sheridan Knowles, Esq., 272. **William Maginn.** Repr. *Gallery*.
990   Bacchanalia memorabilia (No. IV, concl.): drinking experiences continued, 273–285. **C. J. Apperley.** Signed Nimrod —see *DNB*.
991   The *Possums* of Aristophanes, recently recovered and "translated" [with notes], 285–297.
992   The Jew of York, 298–314. **John Roby.** Attr. by his wife in his *Legendary and Poetical Remains* (1854), p. 32.

993   Scottish universities, 315–332.
994   Captain Gardiner's *Journey to the Zoolu Country*, 332–348.
995   A letter from Athens to Oliver Yorke, 349–359. **R. A. Willmott?** Signed T.G.; opening par. links this closely to no. 980; Thrall, p. 252.
996   The songs of Horace (Part III): decade the third, 360–372. **Francis Mahony.** Cf. no. 973.
997   General results of the past session, and prospects of the next, 373–392.

VOLUME 14, OCTOBER 1836

998   *The Statesman* [by Henry Taylor], 393–398. **William Maginn.** Repr. *Writings*, V.
999   The remembrances of a monthly nurse (No. I), 398–407. **Harriet Downing.** Series repr. 1852 under that title.
1000   Isaac Taylor's *Physical Theory of Another Life*, 407–424. **J. A. Heraud.** Starts with long extract from Coleridge (Heraud was his disciple); refers, p. 409, to our last paper on Taylor, citing no. 657; attr. Thrall, p. 88.
1001   The Ettrick Shepherd's last tale; Helen Crocket, 425–440. **James Hogg.** Attr. in text, p. 425. Intro. note signed Oliver Yorke.
1002   Bombardinio on manners, fashions, and things in general: affectation—male and female, 441–456. **John Mitchell.** Cf. no. 846.
1003   Gallery of literary characters (No. LXXVII): Lord Lyndhurst, 457. **William Maginn.** Repr. *Gallery*.
1004   Conservatism in the West Riding of Yorkshire, 458–460.
1005   Archaeographia: the exodi of the Jews and Greeks, 461–474. **Isaac Cullimore.** Signed Hermogenes; footnote, p. 461, assigns author nos. 633, 667, 695, etc.
1006   M'Namara Russel's lark in the Bight of Benin, 474–483. **T. C. Croker.** Signed Cornelius O'Donoghue—see Thrall, p. 36.
1007   The songs of Horace (Part IV), 484–499. **Francis Mahony.** Cf. no. 973.
1008   Palmerston policy, 506–513.

VOLUME 14, NOVEMBER 1836

1009   The state and prospects of Whiggism, 515–530. **William Maginn,** prob. Cf. title of no. 644, from which this art. takes off, quoting "our views in December 1833,"; the statistics, the quotations from periodicals, the use of italics, the strikes at leading Whigs and Radicals so often attacked before (Russell, Durham, Duncannon, Spring-Rice; "the Roebucks and Wakleys and Humes," pp. 517, 518, 525) are all paralleled in no. 644, no. 915, and elsewhere.

1010 The remembrances of a monthly nurse (No. II): General Harcourt, 531–544. **Harriet Downing.** Cf. no. 999.

1011 Secret history of the Irish Insurrection of 1803, **Samuel McSkimmin,** perhaps with the assistance of **T. Crofton Croker.** Claimed in McSkimmin to James Hope of Belfast, end of Nov. or early Dec. 1836, Madden Papers, Trin. Coll. Dublin; John A. Russell to R. R. Madden, Feb. 27, 1843, ibid., has reason to think the art. was put together by Crofton Croker from stories suggested by "a low fellow named McSkimming (sic.) of Carrickfergus."

1012 The last of the lairds; a tale of the highlands (Part I; no more published), 568–582. **W. H. Leeds.** Signed Candidus —cf. nos. 1392, 1479, 1542; though this is a story, Leeds' architectural interests appear in pp. 569 and 581–582. (Note, p. 694, from the Editor of *FM*.)

1013 The British Association: Bristol meeting, 582–594. **Joseph Henry Green?** S. T. Coleridge's marginalia on *Robinson Crusoe*, quoted at start, was in Green's possession at this time and still unpublished (see *DNB*); the religio-scientific outlook suggests that of the physician who edited the works of Coleridge. (Letter, pp. 593–594n., signed **Andrew Crosse.**)

1014 Gallery of literary characters (No. LXXVIII): Edmund Lodge, Esq., 595. **William Maginn.** Repr. *Gallery.*

1015 Wraxall's posthumous *Memoirs*, 596–617. **Egerton Brydges.** Signed.

1016 Unmerciful flagellation of a voluntary [Dissenting] doctor and his friends at Belfast, 625–630.

1017 Story's *Songs and Lyrical Poems*, 631–635.

1018 The spear-head [parody of J. M. Kemble's *Anglo-Saxon Poems of Beowulf*], 637–639. **William Maginn.** Signed J.M.K. [J. M. Kemble]; repr, in Maginn's *Magazine Miscellanies*, 1841.

VOLUME 14, DECEMBER 1836

1019 The songs of Horace (Part V, concl.), 641–656. **Francis Mahony.** Cf. no. 973.

1020 The statesman, 657–662. **John Galt.** Signed.

1021 Oliver Yorke at Paris (No. I): a conversation with Chateaubriand upon English literature, 662–680. **R. A. Willmott,** prob. This art. and Part II (no. 1091) have the distinctive qualities of Willmott's writing: the piling up of quotations, especially from Milton, Dryden, and the eighteenth-century poets and critics, Gray (cf. nos. 1688, 1987) and Johnson in particular, together with descriptions of nature, quoted or original, which are sensuous and often over lush (see his *Summer Journal* and many arts. listed in Part B); in addition, pilgrimages to the homes of the poets, p. 663, was an enthusiasm of Willmott's, the high opinion of Jeremy Taylor (p. 667 and Part II, p. 31) could point forward to Willmott's *Taylor*; Robert Hall and John Foster (Part II, p. 31) are dealt with together in Willmott's no. 2254, and both Parts focus on English rather than French literature. Attr. to J. A. Heraud by Thrall, p. 284, perhaps because Coleridge is quoted on p. 677, but Willmott was often quoting Coleridge and the style is very unlike Heraud's.

1022 The radicals, the dissenters, and the papists, 681–694.

1023 Sir Egerton Brydges to Oliver Yorke [on English poets of eighteenth century], 695–710. **Egerton Brydges.** Title.

1024 Mr. Grant's *Great Metropolis*, 710–719. **William Maginn.** Repr. *Writings*, V; the possibility of collab. with Thackeray is rejected by White, "Thackeray," p. 76. (Note, vol. 16, p. 24, by **Maginn**—signed O.Y. [Oliver Yorke], letter, pp. 24–25 signed **John Galt.**)

1025 Gallery of literary characters (No. LXXIX): John Baldwin Buckstone, 720. **William Maginn.** Repr. *Gallery.*

1026 The remembrances of a monthly nurse (No. III): Sergeant Chatterton, 722–732. **Harriet Downing.** Cf. no. 999.

1027 *Crichton* [by W. H. Ainsworth], 733–747. **Francis Mahony.** Ellis, *Ainsworth*, I, 323. (Criticism and reply, vol. 15, pp. 547–549.)

1028 Epistles to the literati (No. IX): Joanna Baillie on the character of Romiero, 748–749. **Joanna Baillie.** Though the "Epistles" to this point have been fictitious (see evidence for nos. 497, and nos. 845, 937, 963), they now become genuine—certainly in the case of No. X by Carlyle (no. 1342), and very probably here, given the highly favorable review of Miss Baillie's work in no. 912. (Letter, vol. 15, pp. 664–665, signed B.N.) (The remaining "Epistles" are nos. 1342, 1357, 1401, 1421, 1462 (two), 1522, 1596, and 1876.)

VOLUME 15, JANUARY 1837

1029 A septennial address, iii–vi. Signed: Oliver Yorke.

1030 The diamond necklace (chaps. i–vii), 1–19. **Thomas Carlyle.** Repr. *Essays*, III.

1031 Humours of the North (No. I): Baron Kalchenvogel at Edinburgh, 20–29. **R. P. Gillies.** Most of the reminiscences in this series were used in altered form in his *Memoirs*; also see no. 1041.

1032 A scourging soliloquy about the annuals, 33–48. **R. A. Willmott?** Signed T.G.; like all arts. signed T.G., this too is subscribed "St. John's": see no. 959.

1033 *Case of the Protestants of Ireland* [by Mortimer O'Sullivan], 49–61.

1034 The remembrances of a monthly nurse (No. IV): Mrs. Fortescue, 61–75. **Harriet Downing.** Cf. no. 999.

1035 *The Story of Eustace the Monk*, 75–85. **Thomas Wright**, 1810–1877. Repr. *Literature*, II.

1036 Something more about the late proceedings in our parish [cf. no. 944], 85–92.

1037 A point for the consideration of the Conservative leaders, 94–99.

1038 The trial of Fraser v. Berkeley and another, and Berkeley v. Fraser [transcript of trial arising from no. 986], 100–137.

1039 Defence of *Fraser's Magazine* in the Berkeley affair, 137–143. **William Maginn.** Signed.

VOLUME 15, FEBRUARY 1837

1040 Church rates: Lord Althorp's plan; the plan of the Dissenters and Radicals; the plan proposed by the archdeacons; further suggestions, 145–160. (See no. 1060.)

1041 Humours of the North (No. II): hints on parsimony, 161–169. **R. P. Gillies.** Signed W.F.—see no. 981; cf. no. 1031.

1042 [Introductory remarks to] Prince Henry to the Countess of Essex, six sonnets by Sir Egerton Brydges, 169–170. **Egerton Brydges.** Signed C. of S. [Chandos of Sudeley]; title and *DNB*.

1043 The diamond necklace (chaps. viii–xvi,

concl.), 172–189. **Thomas Carlyle.** Repr. *Essays*, III.

1044 Staithes: the smuggler's daughter, 190–215. **John Roby.** Attr. by his wife in his *Legendary and Poetical Remains* (1854), p. 35.

1045 Fox's *Book of Martyrs,* 215–223.

1046 Blue friar pleasantries (No. I): a scene in Ticklebrook Church, 223–228. **George Wightwick.** Signed in intro. note Locke, at end Roger; in no. 923, written by man cited, he claims, p. 345, to be "a Blue Friar"; cf. signatures for no. 1057; attr. Thrall, p. 293.

1047 Dress, dandies, fashions, &c., 232–243.

1048 The remembrances of a monthly nurse (No. V): Signora Bassano, 243–261. **Harriet Downing.** Cf. no. 999.

1049 Lord Brougham's Record Commission, 261–278. **Henry Cole.** *Fifty Years of Public Work* (1884), II, 64.

VOLUME 15, MARCH 1837

1050 Greek comedy (No. I): Aristophanes, 285–304. **R. A. Willmott.** No. 1397, 21, cites him as author of "Aristophanes" and "The Greek pastoral poets" [viz., no. 853, etc.]; see no. 1227.

1051 Whigs and Tories of old times (No. I), 304–315. (No. II is no. 1093.)

1052 A batch of architects, 324–339. **W. H. Leeds.** Leeds had been writing on architecture for *FM* (see Part B below); on p. 333 the attrib. of an art. in the *London and Westminster* signed W.E.H. to W. R. Hamilton had recently been argued by Leeds in the *FQR*, no. 417, p. 161n.; the combination of many foreign phrases, including Leeds' two favorites, *con amore* and *chefs d'oeuvre* (pp. 328, 331), and rather violent English strongly support the attrib.

1053 Embarking for the colonies, 339–354. **T. C. Croker.** Signed Ensign O'Donoghue —see Thrall, p. 36.

1054 Humours of the North (No. III): recollections of the Earl of B. [Buchan], 355–361. **R. P. Gillies.** Cf. no. 1031. (No. V is next in this series, no. 1074.)

1055 *Mammon* [on philanthropy], 362–370.

1056 Cibaria memorabilia (No. I), 371–381. **C. J. Apperley.** Signed Nimrod—see *DNB*.

1057 Blue friar pleasantries (No. II): playgoing days, 382–386. **George Wightwick.** Signed at start Brother Locke, at end Locke, B.F. [Blue Friar?]; cf. no. 1046.

1058 Prior's *Life of Goldsmith*, 387–400. **William Maginn?** Thrall, p. 304.

1059 Courtenay's *Life of Sir William Temple, Bart.*, 400–417.

1060 The topics of the moment [the Irish Corporation Bill; Church-rates and the ministerial plans for them], 418–422.

VOLUME 15, APRIL 1837

1061 Should clergymen take part in politics? 423–434.

1062 Cibaria memorabilia (No. II, concl.), 434–447. **C. J. Apperley.** Signed Nimrod —see *DNB*.

1063 Revolutionary parallels between 1685– 1689 and 1833–1837 (Part I), 448–460.

1064 The remembrances of a monthly nurse (No. VI): Ada Lascelles, 461–476. **Harriet Downing.** Cf. no. 999.

1065 *The River Sambatyon*, by Rabbi Moses Edrehi, 477–486.

1066 Three years of my life; or, Ellen Vere, 487–497. **Augustus Collingridge.** See evidence in Thrall, p. 281.

1067 One or two words on one or two books [by Landor and Bulwer-Lytton], 498–514. **J. A. Heraud,** with **William Maginn?** Thrall, p. 284, attrs. simply to Heraud, but he prob. combined on no. 250 on Landor; on p. 503 a passage from Landor is described as quoted in "our" previous art. (no. 250, p. 738): Bulwer-Lytton, here attacked, was an old enemy of Maginn's, though of *Fraser's* too.

1068 The weakness and the strength of the Conservative party (Part I), 515–523.

1069 The Fraser papers for April, 528–553. **William Maginn,** prob. with **John Churchill.** Cf. no. 522.

VOLUME 15, MAY 1837

1070 Hardiman's *Irish Minstrelsy; or, Bardic Remains of Ireland*, 555–570.

1071 Blue friar pleasantries (Nos. III–V), 571–577. **George Wightwick,** prob. Signed, respectively, Somno, B.F.; Tuck, B.F.; and Roger, B.F.; for the last see no. 1046.

1072 A Greek fragment lately discovered at Derrynane [satire on classical scholarship], 578–580.

1073 An essay on originality of mind, 581– 590. **Egerton Brydges.** Signed.

1074 Humours of the North (Nos. V and VI): John Philip Kemble; Sir Brooke

Boothby, 591–599. **R. P. Gillies.** Cf. no. 1031.

1075 An April voyage [review of poetry], 599–621. **R. A. Willmott,** prob. Intro. pages, 599–601, at once show Willmott's passion for nature and for quoting "the poets"; they also reveal, as does the title and the final paragraph, p. 621, his sentimental imagery; the spotting of hidden sources, p. 601, is characteristic; pp. 599, 603, 610 show that the author feels he is a "Fraserian": Willmott had published at least 18 arts., most of them, like this, on poetry.

1076 Revolutionary parallels between 1685– 1689 and 1833–1837 (Part II), 622–634.

1077 Mélange from the journal and notes of an employé (No. I), 635–646.

1078 The weakness and the strength of the Conservative party (Part II, concl.), 646–653.

1079 The Fraser papers for May, 654–679. **William Maginn,** prob. with **John Churchill.** Cf. no. 522.

VOLUME 15, JUNE 1837

1080 Roman Catholic College of Maynooth, 681–703.

1081 The Whiteboy, 704–714.

1082 German philosophy, 716–735. **R. P. Gillies.** In his application to R.L.F., April 9, 1838, Gillies claims "since mid- 1837" an art. in *FM* on "German Metaphysics."

1083 Revolutionary parallels between 1685– 1689 and 1833–1837 (Part III, concl.) 736–747.

1084 The mysterious bachelor, 747–764.

1085 *The Irish Tourist*, 765–773.

1086 Disraeli's *Venetia*, 773–789.

1087 Lord Carnarvon in Spain, 789–802.

VOLUME 16, JULY 1837

1088 Now or never, for our Queen and our native land! 3–8.

1089 The anatomy of gaming (No. I), 9– 24. **C. J. Apperley.** Signed Nimrod—see *DNB*.

1090 No entry.

1091 Oliver Yorke at Paris (No. II): conversation the second—Alphonso de Lamartine, 25–32. **R. A. Willmott,** prob. Cf. no. 1021.

1092 Rough sketches afloat (No. I): the lieutenant, part the first, 33–51. **Augustus**

Collingridge. H&L, V, 142; series repr. 1843 anon. under that title.

1093 Whigs and Tories (No. II), 51–66. (No. III is no. 1242.)

1094 The remembrances of a monthly nurse (No. VII): Sir George Knatchbull, 67–84. **Harriet Downing.** Cf. no. 999.

1095 T. Carlyle's *French Revolution*, 85–104. **J. A. Heraud.** J. S. Mill, *Earlier Letters*, I, 339–340: "evidently by Heraud"; the opening page reiterates Heraud's love of Wordsworth, Coleridge, and the German Romantics; the review is highly laudatory of Heraud's friend: see Thrall, pp. 89–91.

1096 What could Irish rebels effect against the power of Britain? 105–121.

1097 The philosophy of party politics, 122–129.

1098 Death of William the Fourth, 130–135.

VOLUME 16, AUGUST 1837

1099 The new features in the Spanish contest, 137–150.

1100 Blue friar pleasantries (Nos. VI–IX), 151–164. **George Wightwick.** Signed Locke; cf. no. 1046.

1101 Principles of police, and their application to the metropolis, 169–178.

1102 Three play-things: Bulwer's *Duchess de la Vallière*; [Mrs.] Butler's *Star of Seville*; Harper's *Bertrand*, 179–194.

1103 The May carnival at Exeter Hall, 194–199. Signed: Oliver Yorke.

1104 Mélange from the journal and notes of an employé (No. II): the minister and the marshal of France, 199–208.

1105 Cooper's *England*, 233–241. **William Maginn?** Thrall, p. 304.

1106 Rough sketches afloat (No. II): the lieutenant, part the second, 242–253. **Augustus Collingridge.** Cf. no. 1092. (No. III is no. 1282.)

1107 The Rev. W. J. Irons, *On Final Causes*, 254–265. **J. A. Heraud.** Thrall, p. 284; the author reviews the book as an attempt to apply the Coleridgean philosophy to the doctrine of final causes; cf. evidence for no. 262.

VOLUME 16, SEPTEMBER 1837

1108 The late election: character of "The Melbourne Parliament"; probable results of this election, 267–282.

1109 Tableaux of the taverns: the Wrekin, 283–288. Signed: Bibo.

1110 The poll or the ballot, 289–294.

1111 The highland sergeant, 294–307.

1112 A batch of voluntary Dissenters, 308–322.

1113 Humours of the North (No. VII): notanda respecting the Order of W.S.S., 323–330. **R. P. Gillies.** Cf. no. 1031.

1114 Recollections of our last parish minister (No. I), 330–345. Signed: The Precentor of the Parish. Intro. note signed Oliver Yorke.

1115 Bulwer's *Athens*, 347–356.

1116 Blue friar pleasantries (Nos. X–XIII), 357–367. **George Wightwick.** Signed Locke; cf. no. 1046.

1117 The anatomy of gaming (No. II), 368–378. **C. J. Apperley.** Signed Nimrod —see *DNB*.

1118 Works on Boulogne, 379–389.

1119 To T. P. Thompson, Esq., ex-M.P. for Hull, colonel in I know not what service, ci-devant editor of the *Westminster Review*, guitarist, Benthamite, fiddler, philosopher, and so forth, 390–399. Signed: Menenius.

VOLUME 16, OCTOBER 1837

1120 The pyramids (chap. i): interior mathematical characters, 401–410. **Isaac Cullimore.** Signed Hermogenes—see no. 1005. Intro. note signed O.Y. [Oliver Yorke].

1121 Mélange from the journal and notes of an employé (No. III), 410–416.

1122 Respectability: a sketch, 417–432. **R. P. Gillies.** Signed The Author of "O'Hanlon and His Wife" (no. 981).

1123 The life of Lord Clive, 433–450.

1124 Vagaries of an old traveller [with author's intro. note signed Diogenes Quis] (No. I): ancient Rome, 457–466.

1125 The Rockite, 466–476.

1126 *666 or* χξς, the Apocalyptic Number [an anti-Papal art.], 477–484.

1127 The Spanish contest; movements of the Carlists in Valencia and Lower Aragon; followed by Zaratiegui's expedition to Segovia, 485–497.

1128 The remembrances of a monthly nurse (No. VIII; concl.): Lord Walter Maxwell, 497–512. **Harriet Downing.** Cf. no. 999.

1129 The verdict of the nation; or, On which side are the educated classes? 513–525.

VOLUME 16, NOVEMBER 1837

1130 Shakespeare, Ben Jonson, Beaumont
and Fletcher, etc., 527–536. **William
Maginn**, prob. William Bates, in his
edition of Maginn's *Gallery*, p. 26,
attribs. an *FM* art. on Shakespeare in
1837 to Maginn: this is the only such
art.; the discussion, pp. 527–530, of the
purpose, aims and forms of magazine
writing, for *FM* in particular, is decidedly editorial in tone; the frequent
use of single italicized words is very
characteristic of Maginn's style. (Letter,
p. 775, signed **Alexander Dyce**.)
1131 Portraits of Spanish Carlist chiefs
(No. I), 536–548.
1132 The sacrifice; or, The country, the
town, and the continent (chaps. i–ii),
549–561. **Thomas Medwin.** Medwin list.
1133 Emigration and the United States,
562–577. **John B. Brown.** Signed A Sixteen Years' Resident; Brown to Henry
Brougham, Jan. 31, 1838, Brougham
Papers, Univ. Coll. London, claims he
wrote two papers in *FM* on emigration:
cf. no. 1144.
1134 Mélange from the journal and notes
of an employé (No. IV), 578–588. (No.
V is no. 1216.)
1135 The Whigs and "non-intervention,"
590–600.
1136 Vagaries by an old traveller (No. II,
concl.): modern Rome, 601–609. Signed,
p. 458: Diogenes Quis.
1137 Colonel Crockett, 610–627.
1138 The pyramids (chap. ii): exterior
mathematical characters, 627–636. **Isaac
Cullimore.** Evidence for no. 1120.
1139 Blue friar pleasantries (Nos. XIV–
XV), 637–644. **George Wightwick.**
Signed Locke, B.F. [Blue Friar?] ; cf. no.
1057.
1140 The Yellowplush correspondence:
fashionable fax and polite annygoats
(No. I), 644–649. **W. M. Thackeray.**
Signed Charles Yellowplush, Esq.; attr.
Letters, I, 348n; repr. *Works*, XXV.
Postscript signed O.Y. [Oliver Yorke].
1141 The Grenville Act, 650–655. Unidentified. (See nos. 1184, 1196.)

VOLUME 16, DECEMBER 1837

1142 *The Doctor, &c.* [by Robert Southey]
(Part I), 657–676. **William Maginn.**
Kenealy, "Maginn," p. 91.
1143 Travelling titles; or, Omnibus customers, 676–680.

1144 Emigration and the Canadas, 683–696.
John B. Brown. Signed A Sixteen Years'
Resident; see evidence for no. 1133.
1145 The sacrifice; or, The country, town,
and continent (chap. iii, concl.), 696–
710. **Thomas Medwin.** Cf. no. 1132.
1146 The use and abuse of friendship [on
speeches of Daniel O'Connell], 711–719.
1147 The Bridgewater Treatises (No. IV,
concl.): Dr. Buckland and Dr. Prout,
719–731. **J. A. Heraud** and **William
Maginn** prob. Thrall, p. 285.
1148 The pyramids (chap. iii, concl.): their
builders and historical epochs, 736–747.
Isaac Cullimore. Evidence for no. 1120;
this chap. iii was reprinted [1837] under
his name.
1149 Anatomy of gaming (No. III), 748–
757. **C. J. Apperley.** Signed Nimrod—
see *DNB*.
1150 A word on the annuals, 757–763. **W.
M. Thackeray.** Repr. *Works*, XXV; Ray,
Thackeray, I, 222, quotes a passage as
his.
1151 The new predicament of parties, 764–
775.

VOLUME 17, JANUARY 1838

1152 Homeric ballads (No. I), 1–12. **William Maginn.** Signed; series repr. *Writings*, IV.
1153 Portraits of Spanish Carlist chiefs
(No. II, concl.), 13–19.
1154 The new Frankenstein, 21–30.
1155 Lord Teignmouth's *Sketches of the
Coasts and Islands of Scotland*, 31–38.
1156 The Yellowplush correspondence (No.
II): Miss Shum's husband, 39–49. **W. M.
Thackeray.** Signed C.Y. [Charles Yellow-
plush]; cf. no. 1140.
1157 The newspaper press of Paris (No. I),
50–61.
1158 The prospects of the new year, 69–78.
1159 Our batch of novels for Christmas,
1837, 79–103. **W. M. Thackeray**, pp. 79–
92. *Letters*, I, 514; repr. *Works*, Furniss
ed., VIII. AND **William Maginn**, pp. 92–
103? Thrall, p. 295.
1160 *The Doctor, &c* [by Robert Southey]
(Part II), 106–122. **William Maginn.** Cf.
no. 1142.
1161 How long can it last [the political state
of affairs]? 123–132.

VOLUME 17, FEBRUARY 1838

1162 *Whitfield's Life and Times*, 133–147.

1163 Blue friar pleasantries (Nos. XXI–XXII) [nos. XVI–XX were verse], 147–155. **George Wightwick.** Signed Locke, B.F. [Blue Friar?]; cf. no. 1057.

1164 The state of the stage [largely on Shakespeare], 156–170.

1165 Imprisonment for debt: a bill prepared and brought into parliament by Mr. Attorney-General and Mr. Hawes, 171–188.

1166 The fabulists (No. I): Aesop, Phaedrus, Gay, and Fontaine, 188–207. **R. A. Willmott.** Pages 198–202, col. i were reprinted as his in Willmott's *Parlour Book* (1841), pp. 147–154.

1167 The newspaper press of Paris (No. II, concl.), 208–229.

1168 The three florists, 230–232. **Robert A. Armstrong.** Attr. in *DNB*.

1169 State of lower Canada, 233–242.

1170 The Yellowplush correspondence (No. III): dimond cut dimond, 243–250. **W. M. Thackeray.** Signed C. Yellowplush; cf. no. 1140.

1171 Homeric ballads (No. II): the song of the Trojan horse, sung to Ulysses by the minstrel Demodocus, 251–254. **William Maginn.** Signed.

1171 The rehearsal [Catholicism in Ireland and in Canada], 255–258.

VOLUME 17, MARCH 1838

1173 Horae Sinicae (Nos. IV–V, concl.), 259–268. **D. M. Moir** and **P. P. Thoms** for No. IV. See nos. 701, 816; here Moir is using Thoms' *Chinese Courtship in Verse*, 1824, as he admits, pp. 263–264. AND, **D. M. Moir** and **John Francis Davis** for No. V. Here Moir uses two translations by "Mr. Davis," as he says on p. 264; for man cited see *DNB*.

1174 Anatomy of gaming (No. IV), 269–279. **C. J. Apperley.** Signed Nimrod—see *DNB*.

1175 Half-a-crown's worth of cheap knowledge, 279–290. **W. M. Thackeray.** *Letters*, I, 407n, 515; repr. *Works*, ed. Furniss, VIII.

1176 Captain Orlando Sabertash to Oliver Yorke, Esq., on manners, fashion, and things in general (No. I), 291–309. **John Mitchell.** Pseudonym in title and the series attr. in Schmitz, *Mitchell*, p. xiv; see no. 2087, p. 114. (For an earlier series see nos. 717, 729, 846.)

1177 *The Doctor, &c.* (Part III, concl.), 310–326. **William Maginn.** Cf. no. 1142.

1178 "I can't think how it is!" 327–337.

1179 Gallery of literary characters (No. LXXX): Sir William Molesworth, 338. **William Maginn.** Repr. *Gallery*; M. G. Fawcett, *Life of Sir William Molesworth* (1901), pp. 16–17, suggests Thackeray as author or collab. but only on internal evidence; this is rejected by White, "Thackeray," p. 76.

1180 Recollections of our last parish minister (No. II): clerical sports—Robert Hall—Chalmers—Henry Melville's plagiarisms—Edward Irving, 339–352. Signed: The Precentor and Schoolmaster of the Parish.

1181 The Yellowplush correspondence (No. IV): skimmings from *The Diary of George IV*, 353–359. **W. M. Thackeray.** Signed Charles Yellowplush; cf. no. 1140. (See no. 1218.)

1182 Homeric ballads (No. III): [the return of the chiefs from Troy], 359–377. **William Maginn.** Signed.

1183 Murphy the meteorological quack, 378–384. **William Maginn?** Thrall, p. 304.

1184 The election petitions and the Grenville-Act, 384–392.

VOLUME 17, APRIL 1838

1185 A hundred months of Liberalism, 393–403.

1186 The Yellowplush correspondence (No. V): foring parts, 404–408. **W. M. Thackeray.** Signed C.Y. [Charles Yellowplush]; cf. no. 1140.

1187 Our club at Paris (No. I), 409–420. **John Wilks,** d. 1846. Claimed in Wilkes (sic) to John Blackwood, Mar. 14, 1838, Blackwood Corres.; see *DNB*.

1188 Railroads: their past history, present condition, and future prospects, in two chapters (chap. i): past history, 421–432.

1189 Ensign O'Donoghue's packet from Belgium (No. I), 432–446. **T. C. Croker.** Signed C. O'Donoghue—see Thrall, p. 36. Intro. note signed O.Y. [Oliver Yorke].

1190 The fabulists (No. II, concl.): Phaedrus, Fontaine, Fenelon, Vanbrugh, Boursault, etc., 447–466. **R. A. Wilmott.** Cf. no. 1166.

1191 Gallery of literary characters (No. LXXXI): The reverend Sydney Smith, 468–470. **William Maginn.** Thrall, p. 289.

1192 "Letters on the subject of the Catholics, to my brother Abraham, who lives in the country, by Peter Plymley" [extracts], 470–484. **Sydney Smith.** Intro. note presumably by **William Maginn**—continuation of no. 1191.

1193   Mitchell's *Life of Wallenstein*, 484–505. **William Maginn.** Repr. *Magazine Miscellanies*, 1841.

1194   Homeric ballads (No. IV): the cloak, 506–512. **William Maginn.** Signed.

1195   Artaphernes the Platonist, or The supper at Sallust's; a Roman fragment, 513–520. **Rosina Bulwer-Lytton.** Signed Mrs. Edward Lytton Bulwer; see *DNB* under Lytton, Rosina.

1196   More of the Grenville-Act, 521–526.

VOLUME 17, MAY 1838

1197   Lessons of illiberalism, 527–534.

1198   The anatomy of gaming (No. V, concl.), 538–545. **C. J. Apperley.** Signed Nimrod—see *DNB*.

1199   What would be the effect of abolishing all laws relating to debtor and creditor? 545–552.

1200   The newspaper press of Scotland (No. I): the Edinburgh papers, 559–571.

1201   Naval novelists, [mainly on Capt. Marryot], 571–577.

1202   Our club at Paris (No. II), 580–602. **John Wilks.** Cf. no. 1187.

1203   Mitchell's *Thoughts on Tactics*, 602–615. **William Maginn?** Thrall, p. 305.

1204   The Yellowplush correspondence (No. VI): Mr. Deuceace at Paris (chaps. i–iv), 616–627. **W. M. Thackeray.** Signed C.Y. [Charles Yellowplush]; cf. no. 1140.

1205   Channing's *Literary and Political Essays* (Part I): remarks on Milton, 627–635.

1206   The great fire of B ———, 644–646.

1207   Homeric ballads (No. V): the dog Argus, 648–652. **William Maginn.** Signed.

VOLUME 17, JUNE 1838

1208   The poetry of Shelley, 653–676. **J. A. Heraud,** prob. Thrall, p. 284; the religio-metaphysical emphasis supports the attrib.

1209   Blue friar pleasantries (Nos. XXIII–XXV), 677–690. **George Wightwick.** Signed Locke, B. F. [Blue Friar ?]; cf. no. 1057.

1210   Nothing [on Bulwer-Lytton's *England and the English*], 692–703. **P. W. Banks,** prob. Signed An Old Hand; cf. nos. 1726, 2108.

1211   Our club at Paris (No. III), 703–727. **John Wilks.** Cf. no. 1187.

1212   Homeric ballads (No. VI): funeral of Achilles, 728–733. **William Maginn.** Signed.

1213   The Yellowplush correspondence (No. VII): Mr. Deuceace at Paris (chaps. v–vii), 734–741. **W. M. Thackeray.** Signed C.Y. [Charles Yellowplush]; cf. no. 1140.

1214   Chalmers and the church establishment question (No. I), 742–758.

1215   Strictures on pictures, 758–764. **W. M. Thackeray.** Signed Michael Angelo Titmarsh; repr. *Works*, XXV.

1216   Mélange from the journal and notes of an employé (No. V, concl.), 766–771.

1217   Notes of the month: the election petitions; the appropriation-clause; general prospects, 773–778.

VOLUME 18, JULY 1838

1218   The *Edinburgh Review*, Lord Brougham, and the press, 1–28.

1219   Mary de Crousa, 28–42. Signed: An Old Physician.

1220   Railroads (chap. ii, concl.): their present condition and future prospects, 43–58.

1221   The Yellowplush correspondence (No. VIII): end of Mr. Deuceace's history (chap. viii), 59–71. **W. M. Thackeray.** Signed C.Y. [Charles Yellowplush]; cf. no. 1140.

1222   Homeric ballads (No. VII): the introduction of Penelope, 71–74. **William Maginn.** Signed.

1223   History of the Scottish press (No. II): the provincial papers (Part I), 75–85.

1224   Ensign O'Donoghue's packet from Belgium (Part II), 86–101. **T. C. Croker.** Signed Ensign O'Donoghue; cf. no. 1189.

1225   A rigmarole on taverns and things in general, with a glance at Panton Square, 102–117. Signed: Rory Rattlebrain.

1226   "Little men and little measures" (No. I): Lord John Russell, 118–125.

VOLUME 18, AUGUST 1838

1227   Greek comedy (No. II): the *Birds* of Aristophanes (Part I), 127–139. **R. A. Willmott.** Pages 130, col.i–131, col.ii, were reprinted as his in Willmott's *Parlour Book* (1841), pp. 296–299.

1228   Ensign O'Donoghue's packet from Belgium (Part III, concl.), 140–155. **T. C.**

Croker. Signed Ensign O'Donoghue; cf. no. 1189.

1229 Our club at Paris (No. IV), 155–178. **John Wilks.** Cf. no. 1187.

1230 A tale of the heptarchy, 179–186.

1231 Treason within the Church [on the Anglo-Catholics—R. H. Froude, William Palmer, J. H. Newman] (No. I), 187–195. Unidentified. (See no. 1279, 1308.)

1232 The Yellowplush correspondence (No. IX, concl.): Mr. Yellowplush's ajew [adieu], 195–200. **W. M. Thackeray.** Signed C.Y. [Charles Yellowplush]; cf. no. 1140.

1233 History of the Scottish press (No. III, concl.): the provincial papers (Part II, concl.), 201–209.

1234 Homeric ballads (No. VIII): the last appearance of Penelope, 209–212. **William Maginn.** Signed.

1235 "Little men and little measures" (No. II): Lord Palmerston, 213–219.

1236 English officers in the Carlist camp: Viscount Ranelagh, Lieut. Macmillan, Captain Hawkins, Ensign Devereux, 220–234.

1237 Coronation claims: O'Connell's plea for a peerage, 235–245. Signed fictitiously: D.O'C. [Daniel O'Connell]. Intro. note signed O.Y. [Oliver Yorke].

1238 Report of the Select Committee on Postage, 250–252. **Henry Cole.** Diary, July 25 and Aug. 4, 1838.

VOLUME 18, SEPTEMBER 1838

1239 *Life of [William] Wilberforce* [by R. I. and Samuel Wilberforce], 253–269.

1240 Jack among the lawyers; or, The cruise on shore of Bill George and Ned Blake of her majesty's ship *Magna Charta*, 270–285.

1241 Channing's *Literary and Political Essays* (Part II, concl.): remarks on Napoleon Bonaparate, 286–297.

1242 Whigs and Tories (No. III), 298–316.

1243 Greek comedy (No. III): the *Birds* of Aristophanes (Part II), 317–329. **R. A. Willmott.** Cf. no. 1050.

1244 The religious periodical press [newspapers], 330–338.

1245 Autobiography of the Hammersmith ghost, 338–347.

1246 Specimens of Persian poetry (No. I), 348–360. Unidentified. E. V. H. Kenealy is suggested by Thrall, p. 286, but in his *Poems and Translations* (1864), p. vi, Kenealy reported that he "knew but little of the Orient when the earlier versions

into foreign languages first appeared," which apparently was in the volume of prose cited, p. 1n.—viz. *Brallaghan*, 1845.

1247 "Little men and little measures" (No. III): the Earl of Durham, 361–367.

1248 Homeric ballads (No. IX): the prophecy of Theoclymenus the seer, 367–371. **William Maginn.** Signed.

1249 The Conservative policy for 1838–1839, 371–378.

VOLUME 18, OCTOBER 1838

1250 Genius and the public, 379–396.

1251 Chalmers and the Church establishment question (No. II, concl.), 396–404.

1252 A day among the mountains, 406–412. **R. A. Willmott,** prob. The subject and treatment, even in the first two paragraphs alone, are so characteristic of Willmott as to leave little doubt of his authorship: cf. the evidence for no. 1549.

1253 Foreign policy of the Whig cabinets of 1807 and of 1838, 413–424.

1254 The Constable of Bourbon, and the sacking of Rome, 424–444.

1255 Our club at Paris (No. V, concl.), 448–461. **John Wilks.** Cf. no. 1187.

1256 "Little men and little measures" (No. IV): Lord Brougham and Vaux, 461–470.

1257 Passages from the diary of the late Dolly Duster (No. I), 471–481. Signed: Knarf. Repr. in Thackeray *Works*, ed. Furniss, VIII; E. M. White, *Rev. of Eng. Studies*, 16(Feb. 1965), 35–43, rejects the attr.

1258 Sporting literature, 481–488.

1259 Homeric ballads (No. X): the story of the swineherd, 489–494. **William Maginn.** Signed.

1260 Loose thoughts, 495–504.

VOLUME 18, NOVEMBER 1838

1261 Recollections of our last parish minister (No. IV, concl.) [no No. III published], 540–550. Signed at start: His Own Precentor, at end: The Precentor of the Parish.

1262 Present state of mental philosophy in Italy, 550–557.

1263 State and prospects of Protestantism in France, 563–573.

1264 The Maidschenstein; a tradition of the Saxon Swiss, 574–591. **G. R. Gleig.** Repr. *Essays*, II.

discusses an art. Ogle is writing on Mr. Stevenson's *Letter* (see p. 205 here); she gives Ogle facts relating to her personal case which appear almost verbatim here, p. 214.

1295a Comedies of Lucian (No. II): *Timon* [Act II, concl.), 215–221. **William Maginn.** Cf. no. 1286a.

1296 Selections from the diary of a traveller in the Alps (No. I), 221–236. **William Brockedon.** Cf. no. 1305.

1297 The land of perjury and murder [Ireland], 236–242.

1298 The Luddite's sister, 243–253.

1299 A railway glance at the Corn Laws; or, A few words which passed, between Watford and Tring, on the 20th of January, 1839, 254–260.

VOLUME 19, MARCH 1839

1300 Statistics of Popery in Great Britain and the colonies (Part I): Roman Catholic statements, 261–277. **John Cumming?** The opening sentences of no. 1601 come close to claiming this two-part art.; the subject of that art., the Roman Catholic Institute, is discussed here, pp. 274–277; the rabid anti-Catholicism of all these arts. is characteristic of Cumming's *Lectures on Romanism*, Boston, 1854, and other works.

1301 Hazlitt in Switzerland: a conversation, 278–283. **Thomas Medwin.** Signed T. Medwin; attr. in Lovell, *Medwin*, p. 208.

1302 Talleyrand (Part II, concl.), 287–309. **John Wilks.** Cf. no. 1290.

1303 Deschapelles, the chess-king, 310–319. **George Walker.** Repr. *Chess and Chess-Players*, 1850.

1304 Blue friar pleasantries (No. XXX): Locke in London, 319–328. **George Wightwick.** Signed Locke, B. F.; cf. no. 1057.

1305 Selections from the diary of a traveller in the Alps (No. II, concl.), 329–348. **William Brockedon.** Author claims, p. 348, to have contributed sketches to William Beattie's *Waldenses*, 1838; the sketches named here are signed Brockedon in the book.

1306 The British navy, 348–358.

1307 Voyaging in Hindostan (Parts I–II), 359–366.

1308 Treason within the Church, 367–370. Unidentified. (Cf. nos. 1231, 1279.)

1309 Epaminondas Grubb, or Fenimore Cooper, versus the memory of Sir Walter Scott, 371–377. **William Maginn.** Repr. *Writings*, V.

1310 Notes of the month, 379–386.

VOLUME 19, APRIL 1839

1311 Statistics of Popery in Great Britain and the colonies (Part II, concl.): Protestant statements, 387–407. **John Cumming?** See evidence for no. 1300.

1312 Horae Catnachianae: a dissertation on ballads, with a few unnecessary remarks on Jonathan Wild, John Sheppard, Paul Clifford, and ——— Fagin, Esqrs., 407–424. **W. M. Thackeray,** prob. Closely linked in opening sentences to no. 1175; reference, p. 416, to Yellowplush; the strike at Dickens and *Oliver Twist* seems to be expanded in no. 1412, p. 211; White, "Thackeray," p. 80, lists as probable but still open to doubt.

1313 Rough sketches afloat (No. IV, concl.): the post-captain, part the second, 425–441. **Augustus Collingridge.** Cf. no. 1092.

1314 Alchemy, 446–455. Signed: An Alchemist.

1315 The autobiography and other philosophical researches of a poor scholar, 457–469. Signed: Peregrine South.

1315a Comedies of Lucian (No. III): *Timon* [Act III], 470–476. **William Maginn.** Cf. no. 1286a.

1316 The Pasha's vow, 478–485.

1317 Specimens of Persian poetry (No. III), 486–500. Unidentified. Cf. no. 1246.

1318 French parties and prospects, 502–512.

VOLUME 19, MAY 1839

1319 Oneiromancy [on dreams], 513–528.

1320 One or two guesses at one or two truths [on Augustus and Julius Hare], 529–542. **R. A. Willmott.** In his *Summer Time*, pp. 29–31 on Landor reproduce, often verbatim, the account given here on pp. 541–542.

1321 *The Sacred Poets* [review of R. A. Willmott], 543–555. Unidentified. (See no. 1370.)

1322 Practical reasoning versus impracticable theories [on Harriet Martineau's *Society in America*], 557–592.

1323 Catherine, a story (chap. i), 604–617. **W. M. Thackeray.** Signed Ikey Solomons, Esqr., Junior. *Letters*, I, 407, 408, 412; repr. *Works*, XXIV.

1324 *Cheveley; or, The Man of Honour* [by E. G. Bulwer-Lytton], 618–629.

1324a Comedies of Lucian (No. IV): *Charon; or, The Lookers-on* [scenes i–iii], 630–638. **William Maginn.** Cf. no. 1286a.

VOLUME 19, JUNE 1839

1325 Greek comedy (No. IV): the *Knights* of Aristophanes (Part I), 639–652. **R. A. Willmott.** Cf. no. 1050.

1326 The devil's diary; or, Temptations (Part I), 653–667.

1327 Domestic Jesuitism, 667–677.

1328 Croker's *Popular Songs of Ireland*, 678–684. **William Maginn?** Thrall, p. 305.

1329 *The Modern Pythagorean* [by Robert Macnish], 685–693.

1330 Catherine (chaps. ii–iv), 694–709. **W. M. Thackeray.** Evidence for no. 1323.

1331 Paris pastimes for the month of May, 710–716. Signed: You know Who. Attr. by Thrall, p. 295, to W. M. Thackeray, but White, "Thackeray," p. 77, rejects this.

1332 Anatomy of the chess automaton, 717–731. **George Walker.** Signed G. W.; repr. *Chess and Chess-Players*, 1850.

1332a Comedies of Lucian (No. V): *Charon* [scene iv], 732–737. **William Maginn.** Cf. no. 1286a.

1333 Familiar epistle to the hereditary Grand Duke of Russia, 738–742. **William Maginn.** Signed Morgan O'Doherty—see no. 434.

1334 A second lecture on the fine arts: the exhibitions, 743–750. **W. M. Thackeray.** Signed M.A.T. [Michael Angelo Titmarsh]; cf. no. 1215; repr. *Works*, XXV.

1335 The approaching dissolution, 751–757.

VOLUME 20, JULY 1839

1336 The trinity of the gentiles: Egyptian mythology (chap. i), 1–9. **Isaac Cullimore.** Signed Hermogenes—see no. 633.

1337 The ruling vice of modern politics, 11–15.

1338 A case of clairvoyance, 17–30.

1339 A chapter on sorcerers, loups-garoux, and other mauvais sujets, 30–38.

1340 Voyaging in Hindostan (Parts III–VI, concl.), 42–64.

1341 Whigs and Tories (No. IV, concl.), 64–76.

1342 Epistles to the literati (No. XI): Thomas Carlyle to Oliver Yorke, on the sinking of the *Vengeur*, 76–84. **Thomas Carlyle.** Title; repr. *Essays*, IV. (See no. 1421.)

1343 The Eastern question, 85–97.

1344 Catherine (chaps. v–vi), 98–112. **W. M. Thackeray.** Evidence for no. 1323.

1345 *Bunyan's Life and Times*, 115–125.

VOLUME 20, AUGUST 1839

1346 Specimens of Persian poetry (No. IV), 127–138. Unidentified. Cf. no. 1246.

1347 My private log (No. I): the *Glorioso*, a tale of the sea, 138–151. Unidentified. (No. II is no. 1527.)

1348 John Bull's castle, 152–166. **R. P. Gillies.** Signed The Author of "O'Hanlon and His Wife" (no. 981).

1349 Sketches of the University of Heidelberg, 171–181.

1350 A handful of [literary] trash, 181–188.

1351 Captain Orlando Sabertash, on manners, fashions, and things in general (No. III), 189–199. **John Mitchell.** Evidence for no. 1176. (No. IV is no. 1428.)

1352 The trinity of the gentiles: Egyptian mythology (chap. ii), 200–211. **Isaac Cullimore.** Evidence for no. 1336.

1353 The Paris rebels of the twelfth of May, 212–223. Signed: You know Who. See comment on no. 1331.

1354 Catherine (chap. vii), 224–232. **W. M. Thackeray.** Evidence for no. 1323.

1355 Sydney Smith, John Styles, and Grantley Berkeley, 233–247. **William Maginn?** Thrall, p. 305.

1356 The progress of disorganisation, 247–252.

VOLUME 20, SEPTEMBER 1839

1357 Epistles of the literati (No. XII): Dr. Maginn to Oliver Yorke, on Farmer's *Essay on Shakespeare*, 253–254. **William Maginn.** Title; repr. *Writings*, III.

1358 Dr. Farmer's *Essay on the Learning of Shakspeare* considered (Part I), 254–273. **William Maginn.** Signed; repr. *Writings*, III.

1359 A ramble in St. James's Bazar; or, Comments on the designs for the Nelson monument, 274–284. **W. H. Leeds.** The footnote in no. 1479, p. 370, seems to be the author's reference to what he, Leeds, said here, p. 279, and the note on p. 371 condemns Hosking, as author does here, p. 277; the extensive use of foreign phrases and extravagant language (both combined in the note, p. 275, where the author also uses the expression *chef d'oeuvre*, almost as common in Leeds as *con amore*) are very characteristic.

1360 The devil's diary (Part II, concl.), 284–299.

1360a Comedies of Lucian (No. VI): *Menippus; or, The Necyomantia*, 300–309. **William Maginn.** Cf. no. 1286a.

1361 New educational gems; or, A brace of scripture perversions, 310–321. **William Maginn?** Thrall, p. 305.

1362 The trinity of the gentiles: Egyptian mythology (chap. iii–iv, concl.), 326–332. **Isaac Cullimore.** Evidence for no. 1336.

1363 Blue friar pleasantries (Nos. XXXI–XXXIII), 333–347. **George Wightwick.** Signed Locke, B. F.; cf. no. 1057.

1364 The fêtes of July, 348–359. Unidentified. Signed: You know Who. See comment on no. 1331.

1365 "What is our real position?" 360–369.

1366 Canova; leaves from the autobiography of an amateur, 370–375. **Thomas Medwin.** Signed T. Medwin; attr. in Lovell, *Medwin*, p. 112n.

1367 A quatrain on the Queen; with a dozen octaves of translation of Her Majesty's last speech, 376–378. **William Maginn.** Signed M.O'D. [Morgan O'Doherty]—see no. 77.

1368 Greek comedy (No. V, concl.): the *Knights* of Aristophanes (Part II), 379–388. **R. A. Willmott.** Cf. no. 1050.

1369 The legend of Becket (Part I), 389–399.

1370 The elder sacred poets [sequel to no. 1321], 400–414.

1371 Recollections of James Hogg, 414–430. **R. P. Gillies.** Signed The Author of "Humours of the North" (no. 1031); much of this material used in his *Memoirs*.

1372 The Church [on *Essays on the Church*, by a Layman (Robert Benton Seeley)], 431–446.

1373 The French Plutarch: Cartouche, Poinsinet, 447–459. **W. M. Thackeray.** Repr. *Paris Sketch Book*, 1840, and *Works*, XXII.

1374 The youth of Julia Howard (Part I), 460–475.

1375 Dr. Farmer's *Essay on the Learning of Shakspeare* considered (Part II), 476–490. **William Maginn.** Signed; repr. *Writings*, III.

1376 Don Carlos, Christina, and the Spanish question, 491–504.

1377 A passage in the second year of the reign of Queen Victoria, 509–511.

1378 Of Rabelais (No. I), 513–529. **P. W. Banks.** Signed An Apprentice of the Law —see Thrall, p. 278.

1379 Catherine (chaps. viii–x), 531–548. **W. M. Thackeray.** Evidence for no. 1323.

1380 The Oxford nonjurors; or, The apostolical succession in the Anglican Church denied by the writers of the *Tracts for the Times*, 549–559.

1381 The legend of Becket (Part II, concl.), 560–571.

1382 The opium trade with China, 572–588.

1383 A newspaper editor's reminiscences (Part I), 588–603. **Gibbons Merle.** Thrall, pp. 28, 291. (Part II is no. 1477.)

1384 The youth of Julia Howard (Part II, concl.), 604–618.

1385 The Church and the Chartists, 619–629.

1386 A "sly drive" from the Post-Office to Parliament Street: penny plans and puzzling prognostics, 630–634. Signed: John Broad.

1387 The registration of 1839, 635–646.

1388 Dr. Farmer's *Essay on the Learning of Shakspeare* considered (Part III), 647–666. **William Maginn.** Signed; repr. *Writings*, III.

1389 My Irish tutorship (chaps. i–iii), 667–677. Signed: A Trinity Bachelor.

1390 On the French school of painting; with appropriate anecdotes, illustrations, and philosophical disquisitions, in a letter from Mr. Michael Angelo Titmarsh to Mr. Macgilp of London, 679–688. **W. M. Thackeray.** Signed M.A.T. [Michael Angelo Titmarsh]; repr. *Paris Sketch Book*, 1840, and *Works*, XXII.

1391 Some thoughts on the connexion of crime and punishment, 689–696.

1392 A chapter about boutiques and gin-palaces, 697–714. **W. H. Leeds.** Signed Candidus; the art. is by an architectural critic whose style is peppered with foreign words and phrases (including Leeds' favorite "*con amore*," p. 703) and punctuated with slangy English (the old Greek orders are here "minified," p. 704; "Soanean *moonificence*," p. 712): cf. no. 1052; Thrall guessed, p. 286, that Candidus, here and elsewhere, was E. V. Kenealy, but neither the knowledge of architecture nor the style are Kenealy's. (See no. 1542.)

1393 [Introductory note to] The great Cossack epic of Demetrius Rigmarolovicz, 715. **W. M. Thackeray.** Signed A Lady; Contents gives "Jemima Grundy"; see *Letters*, I, 408n., IV, 32; ballad repr. in *Miscellanies, Prose and Verse* (1855), I, as "The Legend of St. Sophia of Kioff."

1394 Cesar Otway's *Tour in Connaught*, 728–745.

1395 How to make a newspaper, without credit or cash, 746–752. Signed: An Old Journalist.

1396 A budget of bards, as a wind-up of the last of the thirties, 752–765.

VOLUME 21, JANUARY 1840

1397 Preface to our second decade, 1–31. **William Maginn.** Signed O.Y. [Oliver Yorke]; Maginn, "Memoir," pp. lxvi–lxvii.

1397a Comedies of Lucian (No. VII): "Menippus and Charon," 32. **William Maginn.** Cf. no. 1286a.

1398 My Irish tutorship (chaps. iv–vi), 33–45. Signed: A Trinity Bachelor.

1399 The Bocage and its poets: Basselin and Le Houx, 46–53. **Louisa S. Costello.** Repr. *A Summer amongst the Bocages* (1840), I, 134–172.

1400 Recollections of Germany, 53–70. **R. P. Gillies.** Partly repr. *Memoirs*, II, chap. xiii.

1401 Epistles to the literati (No. XIII): Ch-s Y-ll-wpl-sh, Esq. to Sir Edward Lytton Bulwer, Bart. [and] John Thomas Smith, Esq. to C--s Y--h, Esq.; notus, 71–80. **W. M. Thackeray.** Attr. in *Letters*, I, cvii; repr. *Works*, V.

1402 Discovery of a premeditated assassination, 81–90.

1403 Constantinople, 90–106. **Octavian Blewitt.** Signed Brother Peregrine; art. and pseudonym attr. to Blewitt in *Biograph*, V, 183; see *DNB*.

1404 Catherine (chaps. xi–xiii), 106–115. **W. M. Thackeray.** Evidence for no. 1323.

1405 The crisis; and, what is to follow? 116–124.

1406 Sonnets prophetical of civil dudgeon, 125–126. **William Maginn.** Signed Morgan O'Doherty—see no. 77.

VOLUME 21, FEBRUARY 1840

1407 Mrs. Hemans and the picturesque school, 127–146. **R. A. Willmott.** The style, especially of pp. 139–146, is unmistakably that described in the evidence for no. 1549; the passages from Warton and Akenside, p. 142, and from Dyer, p. 143, are again quoted as examples of the picturesque in Willmott's *Summer Time*, pp. 194–195, 196–197.

1408 Characteristics in the nineteenth century, 147–164.

1409 The star of the fountain, 165–176.

1410 Poland, England, and Russia, 177–190. **Richard Graves McDonnell.** Lord Dudley Coutts Stuart, to Prince Adam Czartoryski, Jan. 20, 1840, photostat in Harrowby MSS., original in Czartoryski Museum, Cracow, speaks of McDonnell's art. on Poland coming out in next number of *FM*; see *DNB*.

1411 On the present state of literary criticism in England, 190–200. Signed: One of the Reviewed.

1412 Catherine (chap. xiv, concl.), 200–212. **W. M. Thackeray.** Evidence for no. 1323.

1413 Of Rabelais (No. II): *The Chronicles*, 212–227. **P. W. Banks.** Evidence for no. 1378.

1414 William Ainsworth and *Jack Sheppard*, 227–245. Unidentified. Attr. to W. M. Thackeray by Thrall, pp. 73–74; but White, "Thackeray," p. 80, considers the attr. very "doubtful," and Thackeray himself in criticizing a review of *Jack Sheppard* (*Letters*, I, 437), cites only the end of "Catherine" (no. 1412) for a statement of his attitude and not his own review of the book, as he surely would have had he written this art. Possibly Percival Banks, in part if not entirely: see Ellis, *Ainsworth*, I, 375, where he offers to promote the book with a review in *FM*.

1415 Political memoranda, 245–253.

VOLUME 21, MARCH 1840

1416 Eloquence (Part I), 255–273. **R. A. Willmott.** The unmistakable style is described in the evidence for no. 1549; four phrases and a quotation on pp. 268–270 reappear in Willmott's *Jeremy Taylor* (1848), pp. 271–273.

1417 My Irish tutorship (chaps. vii–ix), 274–291. Signed: A Trinity Bachelor.

1418 Hints for biographers, 291–301. **R. A. Willmott,** prob. These anecdotes of poets and critics from Shakespeare to Byron, most of them packed with references and quotations (see especially pp. 294–295 on Macpherson, where there are two citations of Gray, a special favorite) strongly suggest the authorship of Willmott (see evidence for no. 1549); the devotional writings of Hooker and Taylor, mentioned on p. 301, were being discussed by Willmott at this very time in nos. 1416 and 1445.

1419 Chess without the chess-board, 302–318. **George Walker.** Signed at start A Chess-Player, at end G.W.; repr. *Chess and Chess-Players*, 1850.

1420 Modern Egypt, 319–331. **Octavian Blewitt.** Signed Brother Peregrine—see no. 1403.

1421 Epistles to the literati (No. XIV): On French criticism of the English, and notably in the affair of the *Vengeur* [cf. no. 1342], 332–345. **W. M. Thackeray.** Signed Nelson Tattersall Lee Scupper, Esq., Late Ensign in her Majesty's Horse-Marines; attr. in *Letters*, I, cvii.

1422 Scenes in the desert (Part I), 346–364. **A. Aylmer Staunton.** Attr. in intro. note.

1423 The opium question, and the suspended trade with China, 365–375.

1424 Privilege v. law, 376–379.

VOLUME 21, APRIL 1840

1425 Charles Dickens and his works, 381–400.

1426 Blue friar pleasantries (Nos. XXXIV–XXXV), 401–414. **George Wightwick.** Cf. no. 1057.

1427 Specimens of Persian poetry (No. V, concl.), 414–425. Unidentified. Cf. no. 1246.

1428 On manners, fashion, and things in general (No. IV): a summer tour, 425–441. **John Mitchell.** Evidence for no. 1176.

1429 What's what, 442–460.

1430 Another book of blunders [Grant's *Metropolitan Pulpit*], 461–472. Signed: A Pundit.

1431 Scenes in the desert (Part II), 473–486. **A. A. Staunton.** Cf. no. 1422.

1432 Who are you? or, The modern Salathiel, 487–493. **Theodore Martin.** Signed Bon Gaultier; Martin, *Memoir of W. E. Aytoun* (1867), pp. 61–62, says he used this pseudonym alone before he and Aytoun adopted it in 1842.

1433 On Shakspeare, 493–504. With an intro. note by **William Maginn,** prob.—

signed O.Y. [Oliver Yorke], and see Part B for his arts. on Shakespeare.

VOLUME 21, MAY 1840

1434 Primitive traditions of heathen nations, 507–517.

1435 A tale of the year 1685, 534–541.

1436 The history and mystery of secret societies and secret political clubs (Part I), 542–553.

1437 The Church in the Isle of Man, 557–572. Signed: A Member of the Manx Church.

1438 A trip across the Spanish frontier (Part I), 573–581. **John J. R. Manners.** Attr. by Charles Whibley, *Lord John Manners and His Friends* (1925), I, 82; confirmed by refs. to "my brother G ———" and "Lord R ———," p. 573, who are Lord Granby and Lord Ranelagh: see Whibley, I, 75.

1439 Guizot's *Progress of European Civilisation*, 582–589.

1440 A chapter on duelling, 594–605. Signed: One of the People Called Christians.

1441 Did Hannibal know the use of gunpowder? adversaria (No. I), 608–619. **William Maginn.** The "Adversaria" series was reprinted in his *Magazine Miscellanies*, 1841. (For other entries in this series see nos. 1451, 1466.)

1442 Brougham's *Demosthenes*, 620–632.

VOLUME 21, JUNE 1840

1443 Milman's *History of Christianity*, 633–647.

1444 Modern Greece (Part I), 649–658. **Octavian Blewitt.** Signed Brother Peregrine—see no. 1403.

1445 Eloquence (Part II, concl.), 659–676. **R. A. Willmott.** Cf. no. 1416.

1446 A shabby genteel story (chaps. i–ii), 677–689. **W. M. Thackeray.** *Letters*, I, 469, 488; repr. *Works*, XVIII.

1447 Woman and the social system [mainly on Socialism and free love], 689–702.

1448 Extracts from my journal between Chili and Jamaica (Part I), 703–719. Signed: An Absentee, Homeward-Bound.

1449 A pictorial rhapsody (Part I), 720–732. **W. M. Thackeray.** Signed M. A. Titmarsh; *Letters*, I, 450; repr. *Works*, XXV.

1450 The ashes of Buonaparte, 732–739.

1451 A few notes upon Shakspeare: adversaria (No. II), 740–742. **William Maginn.** Signed M.; cf. no. 1441.

1452 Lord Stanley's Bill [on registration of voters in Ireland], 743–754.

VOLUME 22, JULY 1840

1453 Occult science, 1–16. **D. M. Moir.** Author claims, p. 3, he wrote no. 816 which is signed Δ; medical history is a subject Moir was much interested in.

1454 Il Bondocani, from Weisser's *Mährchen der Scherezade*, 17–42. **Friedrich Christoph Weisser.** Title; *ADB*.

1455 Here or there, 43–60.

1456 Of Rabelais (No. III): "knowledge"— "education," 60–80. **P. W. Banks.** Evidence for no. 1378.

1457 Modern Greece (Part II, concl.), 81–89. **Octavian Blewitt.** Signed Brother Peregrine—see no. 1403.

1458 A shabby genteel story (chaps. iii–iv), 90–101. **W. M. Thackeray.** Cf. no. 1446.

1459 A trip across the Spanish frontier in July, 1839 (Part II, concl.), 102–112. Cf. no. 1438.

1460 A pictorial rhapsody (Part II): followed by a remarkable statement of facts by Mrs. Barbara, 112–126. **W. M. Thackeray.** Signed, p. 124, Michael Angelo Titmarsh; cf. no. 1449.

VOLUME 22, AUGUST 1840

1461 Ranke's *History of the Popes of the Sixteenth and Seventeenth Centuries*, 127–142.

1462 Epistles to the literati (Nos. XV–XVI): on old-fashioned oaths; on the London Library, 143–149. No. XV, signed Ernulphus Eyes-and-Limbs, is listed in Thackeray "Bibliography" but White, "Thackeray," p. 77, rejects the attr. No. XVI is by **G. H. Lewes**—signed Oliver Yorke, Lewes Scrapbooks, II.

1463 Going to see a man hanged, 150–158. **W. M. Thackeray.** Signed W.M.T.; Thackeray, *Letters*, I, 453; repr. *Works*, XXVI.

1464 Tableaux of the most eminent soldiers of the eighteenth century (No. I): field-marshal Schulenberg, Max Emmanuel, and Charles XII, 159–176. **John Mitchell.** Signed Captain Orlando Sabertash; series repr. *Biographies of Eminent Soldiers of the Last Four Centuries*, 1865.

1465 Blue friar pleasantries (No. XXXVI, concl.), 177–189. **George Wightwick.** Signed Locke, B.F.; cf. no. 1057.

1466 Darley's edition of Beaumont and Fletcher: adversaria (No. III): Peter-See-Mee, 189–192. **William Maginn.** Cf. no. 1441.

1467 Extracts from my journal between Chili and Jamaica (Part II, concl.), 193–212. Signed: An Absentee, Homeward-Bound.

1468 Sketches of national literature (Part I): [Greek literature], 213–225. **R. A. Willmott?** For Willmott's previous arts. in *FM* on Greek literature, see Part B below; like this, all are "literary" rather than learned; the praise of Euripides as "the most tragic" of ancient poets, p. 220, is found in no. 1227, p. 130; the desire, p. 220, to institute a series of parallels was carried out in no. 1665 and throughout *Summer Time*; the remark, p. 219, that "Sappho swims and sings in a sea of soft and luxurious emotion" is the very note of Willmott's sentimentalism.

1469 A shabby genteel story (chaps. v–vi), 226–237. **W. M. Thackeray.** Cf. no. 1446.

1470 A railway trip, 238–242. Signed: Miles Ryder, Esq.

1471 The history and mystery of secret societies (Part II, concl.), 243–252.

VOLUME 22, SEPTEMBER 1840

1472 Present state and prospects of the Jews, 253–276.

1473 Life on the Leinster, 277–287. Signed: A Member of the Circuit.

1474 The condemned cells; from the notebook of the ordinary of Newgate (chap. i), 288–306. **C. H. Wall.** Claimed in undated list of arts., R.L.F.

1475 The Revocation of the Edict of Nantes, 307–319.

1476 *The Confessions of Harry Lorrequer* [by Charles Lever] considered, 320–336. **P. W. Banks.** Signed Morgan Rattler—see no. 178.

1477 A newspaper editor's reminiscences (Part II), 336–345. **Gibbons Merle.** Cf. no. 1383.

1478 North American boundary, 346–358.

1479 Wightwickism [on Wightwick's *Palace of Architecture*], 359–372. **W. H. Leeds.** Signed Candidus—see no. 1392, 1542 on architecture, written in the same style; "*quantum suff*," p. 364, had been used by Leeds in no. 414, p. 710; claimed by the author of no. 1542, p. 328. (Reply, p. 751, by **George Wightwick**—signed Wightwick Himself.)

1480 Close of the session of 1840, 373–381.

perley. Signed Nimrod—see *DNB*; repr. *My Horses*, 1928.

1514 The condemned cells (chaps. iv–v): poisoning; the incendiary, 21–32. **C. H. Wall.** Cf. no. 1474.

1515 The Scottish liturgies, 33–52.

1516 On manners, fashion, and things in general (No. V): the philosophy of flirtation, 53–65. **John Mitchell.** Evidence for no. 1176.

1517 The greater and lesser stars of old Pall Mall (chaps. iii–vi), 66–80. **William Henry Pyne.** Cf. no. 1493.

1518 The three great epochs: Book I— 1830 (chaps. vi–vii), 81–90.

1519 Father [Theobald] Mathew, 90–101.

1520 A batch of almanacks for 1841, 101– 108.

1521 Rustic controversies (No. II): the uncannie woman, 109–117. **Allan Cunningham,** prob. Cf. no. 1498.

1522 Epistles to the literati (No. XVII): Galt, fils, to a friend of Galt, père, 118. **Alexander Tilloch Galt.** Signed A. S. Galt; see *DNB* under John Galt.

1523 *Life and Times of Montrose*, 119–123.

1524 Lamentations and perplexities of the Liberals, 123–128.

VOLUME 23, FEBRUARY 1841

1525 Religious authority the principle of social organisation, 129–148. James Fraser, *Correspondence of Emerson and Carlyle*, ed. J. Slater (N.Y., 1964), p. 298, described the author as "an entirely unknown man in the country."

1526 Winslow's *Physic and Physicians*, 149– 153.

1527 My private log (No. II, concl.): the pirate fight, a tale of the sea, 154–168.

1528 *The Tower of London* [by W. H. Ainsworth], 169–183. Unidentified. Listed in Thackeray "Bibliography," but White, "Thackeray," p. 77, rejects the attr.

1529 Tableaux of the most eminent soldiers of the eighteenth century (No. II): Prince Eugene, 187–194. **John Mitchell.** Evidence for no. 1464.

1530 The three great epochs: Book I—1830 (chaps. viii–x), 195–205.

1531 Rustic controversies (No. III): England and Scotland, 205–212. **Allan Cunningham,** prob. Cf. no. 1498.

1532 Bishop Sanderson's *Sermons*, 213–215.

1533 The modern Socrates; or, The life and history of John Jeremy Downingson, M.D., better known to the learned as Dr. Johannes Hierome Catabasides, written by himself, 216–223.

1534 The condemned cells (chap. vi): the criminal brothers, 224–234. **C. H. Wall.** Cf. no. 1474.

1535 Our foreign policy, and home prospects, 235–252. **R. G. McDonnell.** Opening paragraph shows this art. to be a continuation of no. 1512.

VOLUME 23, MARCH 1841

1536 Non-intrusion, vetoism, and other Scotch church matters, 251*–268. **John Cumming?** Attr. by Hugh Miller, *The Witness*, Mar. 10, 1841, 3rd page, on internal evidence; the positions adopted —the opening attack on Radicalism and Tractarianism, the support of Presbyterian polity against the Free Church claims, the dogmatic and abusive language (for example, on pp. 258, 268 col. ii), and the fact, p. 267, that the author has considerable acquaintance with Scottish ministers—would all support Miller's attrib.: see *DNB*.

1537 A chapter about Faustus and the devil, 269–283. Unidentified. See no. 1554.

1538 Tableaux of the most eminent soldiers of the eighteenth century (No. III): The Duke of Marlborough, 284–294. **John Mitchell.** Evidence for no. 1464.

1539 Of *Macbeth* (Part II), 295–305. **P. W. Banks.** Evidence for no. 1499.

1540 The greater and lesser stars of old Pall Mall (chap. vii), 306–313. **William Henry Pyne.** Cf. no. 1493.

1541 *The City of the Magyar*, 316–327.

1542 A codicil to "A chapter about boutiques &c.," [no. 1392], 328–338. **W. H. Leeds.** Signed Candidus; see evidence for no. 1392.

1543 The condemned cells (chap. vii): the man of colour, 339–350. **C. H. Wall.** Cf. no. 1474.

1544 Rustic controversies (No. IV): the spiritual folk, 351–359. **Allan Cunningham,** prob. Cf. no. 1498.

1545 Local courts, and the independence of the bar, 359–367.

1546 Ports of France and admiralty of England [reviews of *Ports, Arsenals, and Dockyards of France* by A. V. Kirwan], 368–376. **A. V. Kirwan** and a collaborator. Kirwan wrote what is obviously a preface, 368–370 (after urging every M.P. and every naval officer to read the book, p. 369, author adds: "We speak thus in no vain-glorious mood, nor under the influence of any ambitious spirit"); p. 370, col. ii, reads like the start of the review, repeating facts already stated in the "preface" and urging only a "general perusal"; later, p. 375, Kirwan's style is criticized.

VOLUME 23, APRIL 1841

1547 Delenda est Carthago: the Poor-Law Commission must be determined, 377–390.

1548 The greater and lesser stars of old Pall Mall (chap. viii), 393–401. **William Henry Pyne.** Cf. no. 1493.

1549 Some remarks on the latest biographer of our poets [on Robert Bell's *Lives of the British Poets*], 402–419. **R. A. Willmott.** In no. 1596 Willmott says he is willing to rest his case against the *Spectator* on the reply to its remarks on Collins in *FM*, which is a reference to pp. 405–406 of this art.; that Willmott wrote the reply—and therefore this art.—is further supported by the distinctive style that is found in all his work: the massive quotations from "the poets" (especially English poets from Milton to Cowper) with anecdotes of their lives, similar or contrasting passages arranged in parallel columns, the quick and superficial analogies between poets and painters, and the self-conscious search for epigrams, and the sentimental treatment of things, nature in particular.

1550 The condemned cells (chap. viii): the confessions of a swindler, 420–432. **C. H. Wall.** Cf. no. 1474.

1551 Specimen leaders of a would-be editor, 433–450. Signed: Ephraim Tackletoo.

1552 Rustic controversies (No. V): the penny wedding, 451–459. **Allan Cunningham,** prob. Cf. no. 1498.

1553 Lin the commissioner: an autobiogram, with lucubrations, transmitted from the island of Tchousang, by Brian O'Lynn the younger, volunteer attached to her Majesty's eighteenth, or Royal Irish, regiment of foot, 459–463. **Brian O'Lynn, Jun.** Title and Preface, but O'Lynn may be a pseudonym.

1554 A second chapter about Faustus and the devil [sequel to no. 1537], 464–477.

1555 *Norway and the Norwegians,* 478–484.

1556 War-office examination paper for 1841, 485.

1557 Tableaux of the most eminent soldiers of the eighteenth century (No. IV): Marshal Saxe, 486–493. **John Mitchell.** Cf. no. 1464.

1558 War with America a blessing to mankind, 494–502.

VOLUME 23, MAY 1841

1559 The Scotch non-intrusionists and their more eminent chiefs, 503–518. Signed: A Strathbogie Churchman [but see p. 503n.].

1560 Rural scenes of Pope and Milton, 519–528. **R. A. Willmott.** The style is that described in evidence for no. 1549; cf. remarks on Chalfont, p. 526, and quotation from Dunster, p. 527, with Willmott's *Lives of Sacred Poets,* 2nd Ser. (1838), II, 41, 47.

1561 The literary labours of Daniel O'Connell, Esq., M.P., 528–546.

1562 Murder and mystery; an incident, 547–559.

1563 Tableaux of the most eminent soldiers of the eighteenth century (No. V): Frederick II, 559–574. **John Mitchell.** Evidence for no. 1464.

1564 Specimens of the table-talk of the late John Boyle, Esq. (Part I), 574–583. **E. V. H. Kenealy.** Repr. *Brallaghan.*

1565 Gisquet's *Memoirs,* 584–593. **W. M. Thackeray.** Claimed in Thackeray to James Fraser, Mar. 25, 1841, printed in *Nineteenth-Century Fiction,* 22 (Dec. 1967), 281–282.

1566 The *Tracts for the Times* (No. I), 594–603.

1567 The three great epochs: Book I—1830 (chaps. xi–xii, concl.), 605–613.

1568 Rustic controversies (No. VI): Mysie's mermaid, 614–622. **Allan Cunningham,** prob. Cf. no. 1498.

1569 St. Jean d'Acre, 622–628.

VOLUME 23, JUNE 1841

1570 The *Tracts for the Times* (No. II, concl.): No. 90 [by J. H. Newman], 627–637.

1571 The row in the tea-shop, 638–644.

1572 Three months at a *maison de santé,* 645–658. Signed: Trim.

1573 Dissent in 1841, 658–670.

1574 My first literary adventure, 670–674. Signed: Palmoni.

1575 The greater and lesser stars of old Pall Mall (chaps. ix–xii): Carlton House, 677–691. **William Henry Pyne.** Cf. no. 1493.

1576 The scientific ass-sociates [on Glasgow meeting of British Association], 692–698.

1577 A newspaper editor's reminiscences (Part IV, concl.), 699–710. **Gibbons Merle.** Cf. no. 1383.

1578 Memorials of gormandising, in a letter

to Oliver Yorke, 710–725. **W. M. Thackeray.** Signed M. A. Titmarsh; claimed in *Letters*, II, 281; repr. *Works*, XXV.

1579 Howitt's *Visits to Remarkable Places*, 725–730.

1580 Specimens of the table-talk of the late John Boyle, Esq. (Part II), 731–748. **E. V. H. Kenealy.** Signed C.C.; cf. no. 1564; pp. 740–748, repr. in *Brallaghan* as "Moore's plagiarisms," pp. 289–307.

VOLUME 24, JULY 1841

1581 The age we live in, 1–15. **Antonio Gallenga.** Repr. in book by same title, 1845, under pseudonym L. Mariotti; claims pseudonym in *Episodes*, II, 238.

1582 Rustic controversies (No. VII): Will-o'-wisp Wednesday, 16–24. **Allan Cunningham,** prob. Cf. no. 1498.

1583 The condemned cells (chap. ix): the approver, 32–47. **C. H. Wall.** Cf. no. 1474.

1584 The last new life of Shakspeare [De Quincey's art. in *Ency. Brit.*], 48–57. **R. A. Willmott,** prob. The "literary" and sentimental style, together with many quotations from the poets, is the very sound of Willmott; also, like this author, he was fond of visiting the homes of famous poets.

1586 Rambling remarks with reference to the German opera, 69–75.

1587 The life and writings of Dean [Richard] Graves, 76–88.

1588 The greater and lesser stars of old Pall Mall (chap. xiii): the period of the Commonwealth, 88–97. **William Henry Pyne.** Cf. no. 1493.

1589 On men and pictures, à propos of a walk in the Louvre, 98–111. **W. M. Thackeray.** Author calls himself Titmarsh, p. 99; *Letters*, II, 19; repr. *Works*, XXV.

1590 A serio-comic review of the sayings and doings of the Scotch non-intrusionists in, and connected with, the last General Assembly, 112–126. Signed: A Strathbogie Churchman.

VOLUME 24, AUGUST 1841

1591 Sparta and Athens: Greece at the breaking out of the Peloponnesian War, 127–139.

1592 The Scotch chambermaid, 140–147.

1593 The three great epochs: Book I— 1830 (chaps. xv–xvi), 148–158.

1594 Sewell and Hewell; or, The rival shopkeepers! 159–166.

1595 Ruy Lopez, the chess-bishop, 168–177. **George Walker.** Repr. *Chess and Chess-Players*, 1850.

1596 Epistles to the literati (No. XVIII): R. A. Willmott to Oliver Yorke, Esq., 178. **R. A. Willmott.** Signed.

1597 Anecdotes of actors (No. I), 179– 189. **Anne Mathews.** Series publ. 1844.

1598 A summer holiday (Part I): morning, 190–197. **R. A. Willmott.** He wrote Part II (no. 1634).

1599 Confusion worse confounded [political satire], 198–207.

1600 Men and coats, 208–217. **W. M. Thackeray.** *Letters*, II, 33; repr. *Works*, XXV.

1601 The Roman Catholic Institute (No. I; no more published): Bonaventure's psalter, or Romish idolatry, 218–233. **John Cumming?** This art. seems to be the first sketch of a subject Cumming dealt with later (in *Lectures on Romanism* [Boston, 1854], pp. 303–310, and in *St. Bonaventura: the Psalter of the Blessed Virgin*, 1852); in all three cases the "substitution" of the Virgin for God or Christ—in the Te Deum and the litany as well as the psalms—is attacked, and Catholicism treated with fanatical hatred.

1602 To the messieurs of the diurnal press: an unpublished letter found in the desk of a deceased editor, 234–236.

1603 The "felo de se" of the Whigs, 237– 252.

VOLUME 24, SEPTEMBER 1841

1604 The end of the beginning [on the defeat of the Whigs], 253–268.

1605 The journal of an autumn in the country (Part I), 269–288. **R. A. Willmott.** His *Summer Time*, pp. 9, 20–21, 123–126, reproduces passages in art. on pp. 270, 275, 280, often verbatim; the diary structure, and the form of short essays peppered with quotations is characteristic of the book; the style is that described in evidence for no. 1549; also cf. Part III, no. 1625.

1606 A chapter on tailors, 288–296.

1607 Budget of a blue jacket of the *Belle Poule* frigate; or, Journal of the journey from Toulon to St. Helena, and thence to the Invalides at Paris [with fictitious intro. note signed Tom Jenkin ap Jones ap Barnacle] (chap. i), 297–309. **Hérou.**

Attr. in intro. note: chap. iii, p. 558, is signed Le Hérou, with addition, "Maintop man aboard the *Belle Poule*"; possibly P. N. M. Hérou who wrote *Opuscule à la mémoire de Napoléon*, Senlis, 1840: see *Bib. Nat. Cat.*

1608 The three great epochs: Book I— 1830 (chaps. xvii–xviii), 310–323.

1609 The history of Samuel Titmarsh and the great Hoggarty diamond, edited and illustrated by Sam's cousin, Michael Angelo (chaps. i–v), 324–343. **W. M. Thackeray.** *Letters*, II, 440; repr. *Works*, VI.

1610 Rustic controversies (No. VIII): the water kelpie, 344–351. **Allan Cunningham,** prob. Cf. no. 1498.

1611 Notes on the north what-d'ye-callem election (Letters I–II), 352–358. **W. M. Thackeray.** Signed Napoleon Putnam Wiggins of Passimaquoddy; *Letters*, II, 27n., 30. Intro. note signed O.Y. [Oliver Yorke].

1612 The dissenting convention at Manchester, 361–378.

VOLUME 24, OCTOBER 1841

1613 Sir Robert Peel's claim to the confidence of the clergy, 378–388.

1614 History of Samuel Titmarsh and the great Hoggarty diamond (chaps. vi–vii), 389–399. **W. M. Thackeray.** Cf. no. 1609.

1615 Of *Macbeth* (Part III): sources and characteristics of the play, 401–412. **P. W. Banks.** Evidence for no. 1615.

1616 Notes on the north what-d'ye-callem election (Letters III–IV), 413–427. **W. M. Thackeray.** Evidence for no. 1611.

1617 Budget of a blue jacket (chap. ii), 428–443. **Hérou.** Cf. no. 1607.

1618 Sir David Wilkie and his friends, 443–454. **William Henry Pyne,** prob. On p. 448 author relates an anecdote concerning "the author of the *Microcosm*" which includes such knowledgeable expressions as "the author was most agreeably surprised" and "the author felt at fault," and the author was Pyne; on pp. 452–453 he tells an anecdote about "Mr. Ackerman. . . . This worthy and most liberal trader"—a man for whom Pyne worked (see *DNB*); according to *Gent. Mag.,* 174 (July 1843), 100, Pyne contributed to *FM* and was intimately acquainted with all the principal artists of the time, as was the author of this art.; Pyne wrote several books in the style of *tête-à-tête* table gossip and anecdotes,

which is similar to that of this art. and in which appears a favorite word, *recherché*, (p. 451 here, pp. 95, 267 in *Wine and Walnuts* [1823], I); author is an older man (see pp. 448, 449, 453)— Pyne was born in 1769.

1619 The journal of an autumn in the country (Part II), 455–474. **R. A. Willmott.** Cf. no. 1605.

1620 Anecdotes of actors (No. II): George Frederick Cooke in London, America, and Scotland, 474–479. **Anne Mathews.** Cf. no. 1597.

1621 The great Reformation (Part I): its preparatives, 479–491. Unidentified. (Part II is no. 1705.)

1622 M'Leod's case, 492–504.

VOLUME 24, NOVEMBER 1841

1623 The Battle of Waterloo [on R. H. Horne's *History of Napoleon*], 505–518.

1624 Theodore Edward Hook, 518–524.

1625 The journal of an autumn in the country (Part III, concl.), 524–544. **R. A. Willmott.** Cf. no. 1605; entries on pp. 538–539 for Sept. 26 and 27 are largely reproduced in *Summer Time,* pp. 197–201.

1626 Budget of a blue jacket (chap. iii, concl.), 545–558. **Hérou.** Signed Le Hérou, but see evidence for no. 1607.

1627 The three great epochs: Book I—1830 (chaps. xix–xx, concl.), 559–570.

1628 Rustic controversies (No. IX, concl.): the Scotch Jacobite, 571–577. **Allan Cunningham,** prob. Cf. no. 1498.

1629 A chapter on the dogs of several of my acquaintances (chaps. i–ii), 578–583.

1630 Free and easy; or, A radical system of education, 584–594.

1631 The history of Samuel Titmarsh and the great Hoggarty diamond (chaps. viii–x), 594–611. **W. M. Thackeray.** Cf. no. 1609.

1632 The Chinese and our "great plenipotentiary" [Sir Charles Elliott], 612–627.

1633 The late Mr. [James] Fraser, 628–630.

VOLUME 24, DECEMBER 1841

1634 A summer holiday (Part II): noon, 631–647. **R. A. Willmott.** His *Summer Time,* pp. 61, 65, and 65–66, reproduces phrases and passages on pp. 636 and 638 of this art. almost verbatim.

1635 The greater and lesser stars of old Pall Mall (chaps. xiv–xviii, concl.), 648–662. **William Henry Pyne.** Cf. no. 1493.

1636 The condemned cells (chap. x, concl.): receivers of stolen goods, 663–674. **C. H. Wall.** Cf. no. 1474.

1637 Parties in the kirk; with a note to Sir Robert Peel from Oliver Yorke, Esq., 677–681, 681–683.

1638 Anecdotes of actors (No. III), 684–693. **Anne Mathews.** Cf. no. 1597.

1639 "A plea for the porkers," [on Baptist Noel's *Plea for the Poor*], 695–698. Signed: Timothy Knowall, Esq.

1640 Signs of the times, 698–701.

1641 A chapter on the dogs of several of my acquaintances (chaps. iii–iv), 702–716.

1642 The history of Samuel Titmarsh, and the great Hoggarty diamond (chaps. xi–xiii, concl.), 717–734. **W. M. Thackeray.** Cf. no. 1609.

1643 A Dublin "mayor's" nest [evaluation of Robert Peel's policies], 735–750.

VOLUME 25, JANUARY 1842

1644 Eighteen hundred and forty-one, our old year, 1–8.

1645 My life and times (Part I), 9–25. **C. J. Apperley.** Signed Nimrod—see *DNB*; series repr., ed. E. D. Cuming (N.Y., 1927), pp. 1–214.

1646 A chapter on the dogs of several of my acquaintances (chaps. v–vi), 25–32.

1647 A summer holiday (Part III, concl.): evening, 33–42. **R. A. Willmott.** Cf. no. 1634.

1648 A journey from Genoa to Rome, 43–50.

1649 Historical researches: the Camden Society's publications (No. II), 50–65. Unidentified. (No. III is no. 1701).

1650 A letther from Mr. Barney Brallaghan, piper at the Paddy's Goose public-house, Ratcliffe Highway, to Oliver Yorke, Exquire, containing a divarting account of the late Richard Alfred Millikin, author o' *The Groves of Blarney*, and some of his kintemporaries, 65–80. **E. V. H. Kenealy.** Signed Barney Brallaghan; repr. *Brallaghan.*

1651 Of *Macbeth* (Part IV, concl.): Witchcraft; the idea of the play; the man and woman, 81–100. **P. W. Banks.** Evidence for no. 1499.

1652 Recollections of the fairest hours to cheer the latest hours of life, from Jean Paul Richter, 101–104. **Jean Paul Rich-**ter, 1763–1825. Title.

1653 Saturday night and Sunday noon at sea, 105–114.

1654 The works of Flavius Josephus, 115–126.

VOLUME 25, FEBRUARY 1842

1655 My life and times (Part II), 127–143. **C. J. Apperley.** Evidence for no. 1645.

1656 On manners, fashion, and things in general (No. VI): courtship and love-making, 144–159. **John Mitchell.** Evidence for no. 1176. (No. VII is no. 1841.)

1657 A sickund letther from Mr. Barney Brallaghan, 160–181. **E. V. H. Kenealy.** Evidence for no. 1650.

1658 *The Spas of England, and Principal Sea-Bathing Places*, 182–191.

1659 A chapter on the dogs of several of my acquaintances (chap. vii), 192–201.

1660 The history of a wet afternoon; in a letter to Oliver Yorke, Esq., 202–208. **R. A. Willmott.** Signed M.A. with address "Valley of Rocks"; passages quoting Hill and Rogers, Steele, Hooker, Tickell, and Fuller on pp. 203–206 are repeated verbatim in Willmott's *Summer Time*, pp. 213–214, 216–217.

1661 A chapter on L.S.D. [pounds, shillings, and pence], 208–215.

1662 A day and night among the mountains, 216–227.

1663 Early Scottish poetry [on Chateaubriand's *Sketches of English Literature*], 228–237.

1664 Russian fabulists, with specimens (No. II, concl.), 237–250. **W. H. Leeds.** Cf. no. 1291 (No. I) and its evidence, some of which is drawn from this sequel. (No. I was no. 1291.)

VOLUME 25, MARCH 1842

1665 Hints for a new book of literary parallels: Dante, Virgil, Chaucer, Milton, and Petrarch, 251–264. **R. A. Willmott.** Pages 253 (Price on Claude), 256 (Virgil and the picturesque), 257 (quotation from Spenser), 261 (Nichols on Dante) are picked up again, with verbal echoes, in Willmott's *Summer Time*, pp. 111, 194, 172, 230 respectively; the very subject of the art., let alone the style, point to Willmott: cf. the evidence for no. 1549.

1666 The forsthaus in the Solling, 264–288.

1667 My life and times (Part III), 288–303. **C. J. Apperley.** Evidence for no. 1645.

1668 A chapter on the dogs of several of my acquaintances (chaps. viii–ix), 304–317.

1669 A sketch of Scotch diablerie in general, 317–331.

1670 The vagrants' lodging-house, 331–341.

1671 Dickens in France [lampoon of *Nicholas Nickleby*], 342–352. **W. M. Thackeray.** *Letters*, II, 41, 45; repr. *Works*, XXVI.

1672 New edition of Campbell's *Poets*, 353–362. **R. A. Willmott?** He wrote no. 1549 on a similar book in a similar style, which is described in the evidence for that art.

1673 The Conservatives in power, 363–376.

VOLUME 25, APRIL 1842

1674 Something upon an old subject; or, Ben Jonson and William Drummond, 377–389. **R. A. Willmott?** Though a little more factual and scholarly than Willmott's usual work, the mass of references, pp. 380–382, 385, to his favorite poets (notably Pope, Dryden, Crabbe, Gray, Goldsmith) and the many verse quotations immediately suggest his authorship; the quotation from Dryden, p. 385, col. i, reappears in Willmott's *Summer Time*, p. 79.

1675 A chapter on the dogs of several of my acquaintances (chaps. x–xi, concl.), 390–402.

1676 Detached thoughts, from Jean Paul Richter, 403–408. **Jean Paul Richter,** 1763–1825. Title.

1677 My life and times (Part IV), 409–427. **C. J. Apperley.** Evidence for no. 1645.

1678 Notes written in the margins of books, 428–431. **R. A. Willmott.** His *Summer Time*, pp. 116–118 reproduces most of pp. 428–429 of this art., often in identical phrases; cf. evidence for no. 1549.

1679 Anecdotes of actors (No. V, concl.), 436–440. **Anne Mathews.** Cf. no. 1597.

1680 Right of search, to Lord Ashburton (Letters I–III), 442–457. **A. V. Kirwan,** prob., and an older collaborator. Signed A Sailor and a Seldonite; letters I and II, 442–447, are by a naval officer, then on half pay, who had shed his blood for England about 1808 (p. 444); letter III, 447–457, is clearly by another hand, prob. Kirwan: in no. 2059, Kirwan says, p. 520, "we" have already treated a particular aspect of rights at sea, referring to this art.; also phrases here in no. 1680, pp. 452, 453, and two on p. 454, are identical with phrases in *FQR* no. 830, pp. 145–146, an art. by Kirwan; furthermore, letter III is clearly by a lawyer.

1681 *Les poissons d'Avril*; or, The French April-Fool Day, 457–465.

1682 "The city of the dead," a continuation of O'Donoghue's fountain: a new legend of the Lakes of Killarney, 466–469.

1683 Illustrations of Mirabeau, and of the first three years of the French Revolution (Part I), 470–487. **P. W. Banks.** Signed Morgan Rattler—see no. 178.

1684 The superfluities of life: a novel, translated from Ludwig Tieck (Part I), 488–500. **Ludwig Tieck.** Title; he wrote *Des Lebens "Überfluss."*

VOLUME 25, MAY 1842

1685 My life and times (Part V), 503–520. **C. J. Apperley.** Evidence for no. 1645.

1686 Homeric ballads (No. XIV): the arming of Achilles, 521–525. **William Maginn.** Signed.

1687 The superfluities of life (Part II, concl.), 526–540. **Ludwig Tieck.** Cf. no. 1684.

1688 Characters of celebrated authors, ancient and modern; biographical, critical, and anecdotical (No. I): Gray, 541–552. **R. A. Willmott.** In his *Summer Time*, pp. 128–129 repeat, in similar phrasing, the two anecdotes here on p. 547; cf. p. 111 of book on landscape in Gray and Claude Lorraine with art. p. 549; cf. p. 134, on his mother with art. p. 541; in general, cf. no. 1549.

1689 The philosophy of the insane [fiction], 553–571.

1690 May-day in the country and May-day in town, 572–583. **R. A. Willmott.** Content, method; and style clearly fulfil the description of Willmott's writing in no. 1549; the art. is divided into a number of short essays, each with its own title, exactly like no. 1695.

1691 De re vehiculari [history of coaches] (chap. i), 584–596. **Bayle St. John.** Attr. in *DNB*.

1692 Hoaxing histories (No. I): the enchanted postilion, 597–609.

1693 The premier [Robert Peel] at home and abroad, 610–619.

1694 The prisoner among the Circassians; translated from the German, 620–628.

1720 My life and times (Part VII), 159–175. **C. J. Apperley.** Evidence for no. 1645.

1721 The two Victorines; a tale of La Vendée (chaps. i–iv), 184–197.

1722 The way to set about it, 197–212.

1723 Rushings; or, British popular vagaries, 213–223.

1724 *The Art of Conversation* [by John Mitchell], 224–228.

1725 "Milor Trotter Chigswell," 228–235.

1726 The Italian theatre [i.e., opera], 236–244. **P. W. Banks,** prob. Signed An Old Hand; cf. pseudonym for no. 2108; this art., like that one, is on Italian opera, a subject Banks frequently wrote on (see Part B) and in a similar style.

1727 Alfred Waters, 245–252. Signed: Geoffrey Russell.

VOLUME 26, SEPTEMBER 1842

1728 The first session of Sir Robert Peel's Parliament, and its probable results, 253–264.

1729 Wilkie and his works, 265–271. **Peter Cunningham,** prob. On p. 265 author comments on the coming biography of Wilkie and says, "We expect much from Mr. Allan Cunningham's hands,—that he will allow the great subject of the life . . . to tell in his own unaffected language what he saw and felt . . ."—which is exactly the approach taken by Allan Cunningham in the biography for which Peter, his son, later wrote an "Introduction"; on p. 270 author quotes a comment of Wilkie's, which appears in the biography, II, p. 228, thus indicating that author had access to the letters being used by Allan Cunningham; on p. 269 author complains that everyone has forgotten Sir Francis Chantrey, who was a friend of his father's (see *DNB* under both); Peter Cunningham contributed to *FM* (see *DNB*).

1730 Hoaxing histories (No. IV): an affair of honour, 271–279; (No. V): James Smith and Count Boruwlaski, 279–281.

1731 Excursion to Port Arthur [in Van Diemen's Land], 281–298.

1732 The two Victorines; a tale of La Vendée (chaps. v–ix, concl.), 299–312.

1733 Neglected French poets: Du Bartas, 312–320.

1734 My life and times (Part VIII), 321–334. **C. J. Apperley.** Evidence for no. 1645.

1735 Some of the picture-galleries of England (No. I), 335–347. **R. A. Willmott.** Pages 159–160 of his *Summer Time* are a rewriting, often in the same phrases, of the passage on Dryden, Virgil, and Poussin on pp. 340–341; the style of book and art. is very similar.

1736 Reminiscences of men and things (No. I): my first love, 347–360. **John Wilks,** d.1846. Signed One Who Has a Good Memory; see evidence for no. 1852.

1737 Meeting of the British Association at Manchester, 361–376. Signed: Alfred Stubbs, C.B.M.I. [Chairman of the Bloomsbury Mechanics' Institute].

1738 The late William Maginn, LL.D., 377–378. **E. V. H. Kenealy.** R. Graves McDonnell to Kenealy, Aug. 31, [1842], Huntington Lib.: "I have seen the Fraser *with all Nickisson's filth* in the middle of the article"; with the letter is a copy of this obit. of Maginn with square brackets around the passage from "It was almost universally . . ." to ". . . impression when once formed"; marked by Kenealy: "The part between brackets is 'Nickisson's filth.' "

VOLUME 26, OCTOBER 1842

1739 The life of Sir Murray Maxwell (chaps. i–ii), 379–394. Unidentified. Intro. note signed O.Y. [Oliver Yorke].

1740 Fitz-Boodle's confessions (No. II): Miss Löwe, 395–405. **W. M. Thackeray.** Cf. no. 1702, but not signed and not repr. in *Works*, XXIV.

1741 *Pictures of Christian Life* [by R. A. Willmott], 406–419.

1742 My life and times (Part IX), 420–438. **C. J. Apperley.** Evidence for no. 1645.

1743 The last of the Homeric ballads (No. XVI): Nestor's first essay in arms, 439–446. **William Maginn.** Signed. Intro. and notes by **E. V. H. Kenealy**—signed The Templar—see no. 1711.

1744 *Charles O'Malley* and "Jack Hinton" [by Charles Lever]: Irish dragoons and English guardsmen, 447–465. **William Maginn?** Attr. by W. J. Fitzpatrick, *Life of Lever* (1879), I, 44, 274, where he quotes passages here, pp. 454, 453, as Maginn's; Maginn had died in Aug. 1842, but *O'Malley* had been published in 1841, and "Jack Hinton" appeared in the *Dub. Univ. Mag.*, Mar. to Dec. 1842, so that the art. could have been done by Maginn; the fact that it breaks off without reference to the last chapters of

"Hinton" supports this possibility, since otherwise a review of that novel would have been held over until its completion.

1745 Some of the picture-galleries of England (No. II, concl.), 466–476. **R. A. Willmott.** Cf. no. 1735, written in the same style; on p. 474 is the foundation for Willmott's *Summer Time*, p. 49.

1746 The fine and froggy art of swimming, 477–486. **R. H. Horne.** Signed Sir Julius Cutwater, Bart., K.C.B.; *Bibliography*, p. 3.

1747 Affghanistan (Part I), 493–504.

VOLUME 26, NOVEMBER 1842

1748 Affghanistan (Part II, concl.), 505–513.

1749 Midway [middle age], 514–526.

1750 The life of Sir Murray Maxwell (chaps. iii–iv), 527–542.

1751 Children, 543–552.

1752 Notes by a reader of history (No. I; no more published), 553–565.

1753 Hoaxing histories (No. VI, concl.): the fat old gentleman in the Kent Road, 566–578.

1754 The Ashburton Treaty, 579–594.

1755 La Venere di Scampadoglio, 594–609.

1756 Peep of day in Paris, 613–616.

1757 Dickens's *American Notes*, 617–629.

VOLUME 26, DECEMBER 1842

1758 [Thomas] Arnold and [William] Smyth on modern history, 631–645. **R. A. Willmott,** prob. This would seem to be a companion art. to no. 1717 on ancient history, where on pp. 128 and 132–133 Arnold's *Lectures on Modern History* are already being discussed (in particular, cf. p. 633 here with p. 128 there); the style is very similar; the reviewer here had been at Cambridge (pp. 632–633) as had Willmott; in no. 1994, p. 481, prob. by Willmott, this art. is referred to.

1759 My namesake, 649–660. **Theodore Martin** and **W. E. Aytoun.** Signed Bon Gaultier; evidence for no. 1712.

1760 My life and times (Part X, concl.), 668–677. **C. J. Apperley.** Evidence for no. 1645.

1761 Sir Ewen Cameron of Lochiel, 677–687.

1762 Proverbs displayed (No. I): "Half a loaf is better than no bread," 687–697.

1763 The life of Sir Murray Maxwell (chaps. v–vi), 698–709.

1764 The pound; or, Moral courage, 710–714.

1765 Movements in the Church, 715–729.

1766 Reminiscences of men and things (No. II): [Armand Carrel, Henri Heiné, Arago, Victor Hugo], 730–742. **John Wilks.** Evidence for no. 1852.

1767 Public affairs, 744–750.

VOLUME 27, JANUARY 1843

1768 Oliver Yorke at home, 1–35. **E. V. H. Kenealy.** Repr. *Brallaghan* as "A night with the Deipnosophist Club."

1769 Pleasures, objects, and advantages of literature indicated (No. I), 35–41. **R. A. Willmott.** Series repr., in revised form, as *Pleasures, Objects, and Advantages of Literature*, 1851.

1770 Jack Moriarty and his contemporaries T.C.D. [Trinity College Dublin] (No. I), 41–58.

1771 Macaulay's *Lays of Ancient Rome*, 59–75.

1772 Confessions of George Fitz-Boodle (No. III): Dorothea, 76–84. **W. M. Thackeray.** Signed G.F.B. [George Fitz-Boodle]; cf. no. 1702.

1773 Life of Sir Murray Maxwell (chaps. vii–viii), 85–98.

1774 Reminiscences of men and things (No. III): Berryer, 99–106. **John Wilks.** Evidence for no. 1852.

1775 Our Eastern policy [on China], 108–123.

VOLUME 27, FEBRUARY 1843

1776 Pleasures, objects, and advantages of literature indicated (No. II), 125–134. **R. A. Willmott.** Cf. no. 1769.

1777 A tale of Bramber Castle, 136–145.

1778 Reminiscences of men and things (No. IV): Guizot, David, 145–154. **John Wilks.** Evidence for no. 1852.

1779 Jack Moriarty and his contemporaries (No. II), 155–165.

1780 Notes of a tour in Flanders, 166–175.

1781 Wan Tang Jin Wŭh, 176–184. Signed: A Barbarian Eye.

1782 French romances [George Sand, Jules Janin, Balzac], 184–194.

1783 Graf de Tropp, 195–202.

1784 Life of Sir Murray Maxwell (chaps. ix–x), 203–213.

1785 Confessions of George Fitz-Boodle (No. IV): Ottilia, 214–224. **W. M.**

Thackeray. Signed G.S.F.B. [George Savage Fitz-Boodle]; cf. no. 1702.
1786 The dramatic works of Henry Taylor, 225–234. **P. W. Banks.** Signed An Apprentice of the Law—see no. 1378.
1787 What is to be done for Ireland? 235–250.

VOLUME 27, MARCH 1843

1788 Thoughts on *The Recreations of Christopher North*: "The Moors," 251–259.
1789 Pilgrimages in Paris (No. I): La Morgue, 260–271. **Julia Pardoe.** Claimed in Julia Pardoe to Sir John Phillipart, Oct. 10, 1843, Berg Coll., N.Y. Pub. Lib.; repr. *Pilgrimages in Paris*, 1862.
1790 The Ashburton Treaty again [cf. no. 1754], 272–289.
1791 Reminiscences of men and things (No. V): M. Thiers, 289–301. **John Wilks.** Evidence for no. 1852.
1792 The lost pearl, 302–311.
1793 Life of Sir Murray Maxwell (chaps. xi–xiii), 311–327.
1794 Jack Moriarty and his contemporaries (No. III), 327–343.
1795 Pleasures, objects, and advantages of literature indicated (No. III, concl.), 344–348. **R. A. Willmott.** Cf. no. 1769.
1796 Confessions of George Fitz-Boodle (No. V): men's wives (No. I), Mr. and Mrs. Frank Berry, 349–361. **W. M. Thackeray.** Signed G.S.F.B. [George Savage Fitz-Boodle]; repr. *Men's Wives*, 1853, and *Works*, V.
1797 The crisis of the Church of Scotland, 362–376.

VOLUME 27, APRIL 1843

1798 Mediterranean sketches, 377–392.
1799 The potter's daughter of Corinth, 393–398.
1800 Illustrations of discount, 398–409. **Deady Keane.** Attr. in Thackeray, *Letters*, II, 103–105.
1801 Victor Hugo's *Letters*: Champagne, Flanders, and the Rhine (Part I), 411–426. (Part II is no. 1815.)
1802 Jack Moriarty and his contemporaries (No. IV), 427–443.
1803 The trial of Daniel M'Naughten, and the bar of the Central Criminal Court, and the plea of insanity, 444–454.
1804 Reminiscences of men and things (No. VI, misnumbered V): De Lamartine,

454–464. **John Wilks.** Evidence for no. 1852.
1805 Confessions of George Fitz-Boodle (No. X, concl.): men's wives (No. II), the Ravenswing (chap. i), 465–475. **W. M. Thackeray.** Signed George Fitz-Boodle; cf. no. 1796. (Hereafter only the subtitle is used.)
1806 Life of Sir Murray Maxwell (chap. xiv), 476–483.
1807 The north-west (American) boundary question, 484–502.

VOLUME 27, MAY 1843

1808 The Anti-Corn-Law League and the country, 503–517.
1809 The dancing doctor—a highland tale founded on fact, 517–520.
1810 A batch of novels, 520–535.
1811 On the decoration of the new houses of Parliament, 535–542.
1812 Pilgrimages in Paris (No. II): the Temple, 543–556. **Julia Pardoe.** Cf. no. 1789.
1813 Life of Sir Murray Maxwell (chaps. xv–xvii, concl.), 557–571.
1814 The forsaken, 571–578.
1815 The Rhine and Rhenish affairs: the pretensions of France to the left bank of the Rhine (Part II), 584–596. (Part I is no. 1801.)
1816 Men's wives (No. II): the Ravenswing (chaps. ii–iii), 597–608. **W. M. Thackeray.** Evidence for no. 1805.
1817 Reminiscences of men and things (No. VII, misnumbered VI): the history and mystery of St. Simonianism, 609–614. **John Wilks.** Evidence for no. 1852.
1818 Boat ahoy! 615–619. **Richard John Smith.** Attr. in *Gent. Mag.*, 43 n.s. (Mar. 1855), 323.
1819 The government plan of education, 620–628.

VOLUME 27, JUNE 1843

1820 Walpole and his friends (Part I), 629–642. Signed: An Old Man.
1821 Northern Italy, 643–652.
1822 Proverbs displayed (No. II): "Never begin that of which you have not well considered the end," 652–663.
1823 Sir Francis Chantrey and Allan Cunningham, 664–677. **Peter Cunningham,** prob. Author is very familiar with the personal views, conversations, and experiences of Allan Cunningham, father

of man cited, and makes frequent complaints about the unfairness of Chantrey's will because Cunningham's legacy of £2000 was left with conditions which make it impossible for the family to collect (see p. 676 especially); cf. authorship of nos. 1729 and 2300.

1824   Titmarsh's travels in Ireland [Thackeray's *Irish Sketch Book*], 678–686. **E. V. H. Kenealy,** prob. Nickisson to Kenealy, May 6, 1843, Huntington Lib., sends him Thackeray's book and asks him to write "a kind but honest review" of it; if Kenealy had refused, there would hardly have been time to send someone else another copy, and get a review written, proofread, and published in the June issue (advertized in the *Athenaeum,* May 27, 1843, p. 498); Kenealy was an Irish contrib. to *FM.*

1825   Reminiscences of men and things (No. VIII, misnumbered VII): Chateaubriand and De Genoude, 687–704. **John Wilks.** Evidence for no. 1852.

1826   Jack Moriarty and his contemporaries (No. V): the college election, 705–717.

1827   *Conversations on the Parables,* 718–722.

1828   Men's wives (No. II): the Ravenswing (chap. iii), 723–733. **W. M. Thackeray.** Evidence for no. 1805.

1829   Colonisation—the only cure for national distress: Mr. Charles Buller's speech, 735–750.

VOLUME 28, JULY 1843

1830   The non-intrusion schism [in the Scottish Church], 1–14.

1831   Walpole and his friends (Part II, concl.), 15–30. Signed: An Old Man.

1832   Jack Moriarty and his contemporaries (No. VI): the scholar's death—the college breakfast, 30–43.

1833   Jeffrey and Gifford versus Shakspeare and Milton, 43–52.

1834   The last sitting [for a portrait], 52–59. **W. H. Leeds.** Signed Candidus—see nos. 1392, 1479, 1542; Leeds also wrote on painting (cf. nos. 99, 838); the style of this facetious Platonic dialogue has Leeds' combination of foreign phrases and raffish English, including puns.

1835   Reminiscences of men and things (No. IX, misnumbered VIII): Lafayette (Part I), 60–72. **John Wilks.** Evidence for no. 1852.

1836   On aesthetical criticism as applied to works of art, 72–79.

1837   Proverbs displayed (No. III, concl.): "Faint heart ne'er won fair lady," 79–85.

1838   Abælard and Heloisa, 86–99. (See no. 1876.)

1839   Pilgrimages in Paris (No. III): the passage Vendôme, 99–112. **Julia Pardoe.** Cf. no. 1789.

1840   Can the Queen's government be carried on? 117–126.

VOLUME 28, AUGUST 1843

1841   On manners, fashions, and things in general (No. VII): matrimony, 127–142. **John Mitchell.** Evidence for no. 1176. (No. VIII is no. 1940.)

1842   Addison (Part I), 143–159. **R. A. Willmott,** prob. The extensive knowledge of Dryden, Pope, Gay, and Johnson, combined with a style approaching that described in no. 1549, point to Willmott; this is especially true of Part II below.

1843   A night at Peleg Longfellow's, 160–168. **Theodore Martin** and **W. E. Aytoun.** Signed Bon Gaultier; see evidence for no. 1712.

1844   Reminiscences of men and things (No. IX, misnumbered VIII): Lafayette (Part II), 169–182. **John Wilks.** Evidence for no. 1852.

1845   Men's wives (No. II): the Ravenswing (chaps. v–vi), 188–205. **W. M. Thackeray.** Evidence for no. 1805.

1846   The late Lord Sydenham, 206–227.

1847   Jack Moriarty and his contemporaries (No. VII, concl.), 228–236.

1848   Owre true a tale, 237–241. Signed: An Object.

1849   The repeal question [Ireland and O'Connell], 242–252.

VOLUME 28, SEPTEMBER 1843

1850   *Letters of Mary Queen of Scots,* 253–268.

1851   The things we don't know, 269–277. **John Doran.** Claimed in *Athenaeum,* Dec. 1, 1860, p. 753; repr. *New Pictures and Old Panels,* 1859.

1852   Reminiscences of men and things (No. X, misnumbered IX): Louis Philippe, King of France (Part I), 278–295. **John Wilks,** d.1846. Signed One Who Has a Good Memory; *DNB,* drawing on *N&Q,* 5th s., 7 (Mar. 3, 1877), 180, says that after his return from Paris Wilks "was a constant contributor to *FM,* supplying reminiscences of Louis-Philippe and other notable Frenchmen"; *N&Q* adds that he had returned to London by 1840 and that he usually began his reminiscences "When I first saw . . ."; the series was attr. to Col. John Mitchell, without any concrete evidence, by Thrall, pp. 27–28, 291.

1853 The pearl of Bruges, 295–303.

1854 Addison (Part II, concl.), 304–320. **R. A. Willmott,** prob. Cf. no. 1842.

1855 Men's wives (No. II): the Ravenswing (chaps. vii–viii), 321–337. **W. M. Thackeray.** Evidence for no. 1805.

1856 Parliamentary pickings; or, The wonders and marvels of the session of 1843, contained in a letter addressed to Thomas Duncombe, Esq., M.P., by one of his Finsbury constituents, 337–345. Signed: A Finsbury Constituent.

1857 *Jerome Paturot*; with considerations on novels in general—in a letter from M. A. Titmarsh, 349–362. **W. M. Thackeray.** Signed M. A. Titmarsh; repr. Works, XXV.

1858 The Lady Francesca; a legend of Sorrento, 362–368.

1859 The late session of parliament, 369–378.

VOLUME 28, OCTOBER 1843

1860 Reminiscences of men and things (No. X, misnumbered IX), Louis Philippe (Part II), 379–403. **John Wilks.** Evidence for no. 1852.

1861 A treatise concerning the nature, origin, and destination of the soul; written at Margate in the latter end of December, 1793, by the Right Honourable Warren Hastings (chaps. i–iv), 403–412. **Warren Hastings.** Title. Intro. note signed O.Y. [Oliver Yorke].

1862 Bluebeard's ghost, 413–425. **W. M. Thackeray.** Signed M. A. Titmarsh; repr. *Works*, XXVI.

1863 New South Wales: colonial immigration—the bounty system and its frauds, 426–441.

1864 Pilgrimages in Paris (No. IV, concl.): the Pont-Neuf, 442–457. **Julia Pardoe.** Cf. no. 1789.

1865 Cloudy hours in summer days, 460–469. **R. A. Willmott.** Addressed, p. 462, from "Valley of Rocks" (cf. nos. 1660 and 1879); the style is unmistakable (cf. description in evidence for no. 1549).

1866 My journey to Scotland, and tremen-dous nocturnal adventure among the mountains of Braemar, 470–484.

1867 A heroine and a mock-hero in the days of the Fronde (chaps. i–iii), 485–493. **T. A. Trollope.** Repr. *Sketches from French History*, 1878.

1868 Men's wives (No. III): Dennis Haggarty's wife, 494–504. **W. M. Thackeray.** Evidence for no. 1805.

VOLUME 28, NOVEMBER 1843

1869 The Swedish romances [Frederika Bremer, trans. by Mary Howitt], 505–525.

1870 A heroine and a mock-hero in the days of the Fronde (chaps. iv–x, concl.), 526–538. **T. A. Trollope.** Cf. no. 1867.

1871 Reminiscences of men and things (No. X): Louis Philippe (Part III), 539–563. **John Wilks.** Evidence for no. 1852.

1872 Maid servants, 564–572.

1873 Treatise concerning the nature, origin and destination of the soul (chaps. v–vii, concl.), 573–581. **Warren Hastings.** Cf. no. 1861.

1874 Men's wives (No. IV): the ———'s wife, 581–592. **W. M. Thackeray.** Evidence for no. 1805.

1875 Architectural revivalism and Puginism, 593–605. **W. H. Leeds.** The art. is by an architectural critic who dislikes the exclusiveness of schools (pp. 593–595; cf. Leeds, start of no. 8 and elsewhere), and who combines the extensive use of foreign phrases (including Leeds' special hallmark, "*con amore*," p. 597), with raffish English; also, Leeds had written a *Supplement* to a work by Pugin (see no. 43).

1876 Epistles to the literati (No. XIX, concl.): Le Chevalier de Chatelain to Oliver Yorke, 608. **Jean-Baptiste-François-Ernest de Chatelain.** Signed Le Chevalier de Chatelain; see *DNB*.

1877 The two old houses, 609–614.

1878 O'Connell and the government, 615–630.

VOLUME 28, DECEMBER 1843

1879 The history of a week, 631–646. **R. A. Willmott.** Address "Valley of Rocks," p. 632 (cf. no. 1660); passages on Demosthenes, Xenophon, and Evelyn, 632–633, reappear, largely verbatim, in Willmott's *Summer Time*, pp. 148–149; attr. in E. V. H. Kenealy to T. J. Ouseley, Dec. 10, 1843, Huntington Lib., to "Parson Willmott."

1880 Reminiscences of men and things (No. XI, misnumbered X), Leopold I, king of the Belgians, 647–665. **John Wilks.** Evidence for no. 1852.

1881 Essay on the effects of moral causes on the prosperity of nations; written in 1814 by the Right Honourable Warren Hastings, 667–675. **Warren Hastings.** Title. Intro. note signed O.Y. [Oliver Yorke].

1882 Portrait of a tramp, 676–680.

1883 A continental tour (Part I), 681–694. **E. V. H. Kenealy.** Attr. in Arabella Kenealy, *Memoirs of E. V. H. Kenealy* (1898), p .104.

1884 Military tableaux; or, Scenes from the wars of Napoleon, sketched in the manner of Callot (No. I), 695–701. **John Mitchell.** Signed Captain Orlando Sabertash—see no. 1176.

1885 Grant in Paris [Grant's *Paris and Its People*], 702–712. **W. M. Thackeray.** Signed G.S.F.B. [George S. Fitz-Boodle]; *Letters*, II, 126, 139n.; repr. *Works*, ed. Furniss, VIII.

1886 Fanny Elssler (No. I): at the Havanah, 713–728. **Fanny Elssler** and **Henry Wikoff.** Intro. note; letter in no. 1912, p. 275n.

1887 What is to be done with Ireland now? 729–748.

VOLUME 29, JANUARY 1844

1888 Regina's Regina: or, Reminiscences of Her Most Gracious Majesty Queen Victoria, 1–24. **John Mitchell.** Evidence for no. 1852.

1889 Drummond's *Noble English Families*, 25–34.

1890 The luck of Barry Lyndon; a romance of the last century (chaps. i–ii), 35–51. **W. M. Thackeray.** Signed Fitz-Boodle; novel repr. *Miscellanies, Prose and Verse* (1854–1857), III, and *Works*, VII.

1891 An adventure in Bythinia, 52–67. **Julia Pardoe.** Claimed in Julia Pardoe to Sir John Phillipart, Oct. 10, 1843, Berg Coll., N.Y. Pub. Lib.

1892 A fine day in Fleet Street (No. I), 68–77. **Peter Cunningham,** prob. Cunningham explains that his *Handbook for London* (1849) had been "seven years in hand" (Preface, p. vii); the sources he used—manuscripts, old works on London, English poetry, etc. (see pp. viii–x) —are those used by the author of this series of arts.; Cunningham says, pp. vii–

viii, he had intended to write that work "as one continuous text," which is the form adopted here, and had "advanced to a great length" before shifting to a dictionary form; many histories narrated in the series reappear, abbreviated, in the *Handbook*, as do many of the quotations: see, for examples, pp. 68, 73 here, and *Handbook*, I, 179 and II, 563.

1893 Fanny Elssler (No. II): at Paris, 78–90. **Fanny Elssler** and **Henry Wikoff.** Cf. no. 1886.

1894 Great cities, their decline and fall (Part I), 91–96.

1895 The Gitano, 97–102.

1896 Military tableaux (No. II): Scenes from the wars of Napoleon (No. II): march to Moscow, 103–109. **John Mitchell.** Evidence for no. 1176.

1897 Kate Kearney [of Killarney], 110–111.

1898 English alliances and European prospects, 112–126.

VOLUME 29, FEBRUARY 1844

1899 French university writers, 127–143.

1900 Fanny Elssler (No. III): at Paris, 144–152. **Fanny Elssler** and **Henry Wikoff.** Cf. no. 1886.

1901 A box of novels, 153–169. **W. M. Thackeray.** Signed M. A. Titmarsh; *Letters*, II, 139; repr. *Works*, ed. Furniss, VIII.

1902 The speculative parricide: a Platonic study [popularization of "Euthyphron"], 170–180.

1903 The drama, 181–186.

1904 The luck of Barry Lyndon (chaps. iii–iv), 187–202. **W. M. Thackeray.** Evidence for no. 1890.

1905 Great cities, their decline and fall (Part II, concl.), 203–211.

1906 The artist's despair, 212–219.

1907 Reminiscences of men and things (No. XII): Prince de Metternich (Part I), 219–234. **John Wilks.** Evidence for no. 1852.

1908 Translations of Provençal and French songs, 235–238.

1909 The state and prospects of the government, 239–252.

VOLUME 29, MARCH 1844

1910 A summer hour in Pope's garden at Twickenham: Pope, Bolingbroke, Arbuthnot, and Swift, 253–260. **R. A. Willmott.** The style alone could settle the attrib.

(see the evidence for no. 1549); in addition, pp. 259–260 on the "natural" in Homer preceding the "picturesque" in later writers are drawn upon for Willmott's *Summer Time*, p. 192.

1911 Parallel between the collections of science and art in London and in Paris, 261–272.

1912 Fanny Elssler (No. IV, concl.): in London, at New York, and at the Havannah, 274–290. **Fanny Elssler** and **Henry Wikoff.** Cf. no. 1886.

1913 A walk across Bohemia, 290–301.

1914 Military tableaux (No. III): the burning of Moscow, 302–312. **John Mitchell.** Evidence for no. 1176.

1915 The monk Campanella and his works, 313–317.

1916 The luck of Barry Lyndon (chaps. v–vi), 318–330. **W. M. Thackeray.** Evidence for no. 1890.

1917 Reminiscences of men and things (No. XII, concl.): Prince de Metternich (Part II, concl.), 331–343. **John Wilks.** Evidence for no. 1852.

1918 The turret-clock, 344–353.

1919 Chemists of the eighteenth century (Part I), 354–361. Signed: An Old Man.

1920 The country versus the [Anti-Corn-Law] League, 364–378.

VOLUME 29, APRIL 1844

1921 A fine day in the Strand (No. II), 379–391. **Peter Cunningham,** prob. Cf. no. 1892.

1922 The luck of Barry Lyndon (chaps. vii–ix), 391–410. **W. M. Thackeray.** Evidence for no. 1890.

1923 Mrs. Grant, of Laggan, and her contemporaries, 411–418.

1924 Glimpses of the gifted: a legend of Venice, 418–424. **Julia Pardoe,** prob. This is the first of three "legend" arts. (see also nos. 1968, 2026) where the word always appears in the subtitle, precisely as it does in Julia Pardoe's *Trails and Traditions of Portugal*, 1833: "Donna Reta, a Legend of Lisbon," "The Fidalgo's Daughter, a Legend of Rio Mayor," "Father Eustacio, a Monastic Legend" (the last paralleling no. 2026); the form of these arts., as of the book, is fictional; these "legend" stories in *FM*, published in 1844, fall between the limits of Miss Pardoe's known contributions, Mar. 1843 and Dec. 1845.

1925 Chemists of the eighteenth century

(Part II, concl.), 425–438. Signed: An Old Man.

1926 The heroine of Ostend, 439–441.

1927 The Christian highlands of Æthiopia, 442–449.

1928 A continental tour (Part II, concl.), 449–464. **E. V. H. Kenealy.** Cf. no. 1883.

1929 Historical researches on the pretended burning of the library of Alexandria by the Saracens, 465–471.

1930 Lord Ellenborough, and the affairs of India, 472–484.

1931 Military tableaux (No. IV): Napoleon at the Battle of Wagram, 487–495. **John Mitchell.** Evidence for no. 1176.

1932 Some passages, private and professional, in the life of Herr [Joseph] Staudigl [opera singer], 496–502. **P. W. Banks.** Signed Morgan Rattler—see no. 178.

VOLUME 29, MAY 1844

1933 On railways, 503–516.

1934 Little travels and road-side sketches (No. I): from Richmond in Surrey to Brussels in Belguim, 517–528. **W. M. Thackeray.** Signed Titmarsh; series repr. *Works*, XXII.

1935 On emotional culture, 528–535. **David Masson.** *Memories of London in the 'Forties* (1908), p. 57n.

1936 An episode of the times of Philip V of Spain (Part I), 536–545.

1937 Memory, 546–547.

1938 The luck of Barry Lyndon (chaps. x–xi), 548–563. **W. M. Thackeray.** Evidence for no. 1890.

1939 Marshal Soult [sketch of Napoleon's campaigns], 564–579.

1940 On manners, fashions, and things in general (No. VIII, concl.): the sliding scale of manners, 580–597. **John Mitchell.** Evidence for no. 1176.

1941 Illustrations of national customs (No. I; no more published): Hebrew, translated from the modern Sanscrit, 597–603. **Hezekiah Moss.** Signed.

1942 The classics of the table (No. I): gastronomy, 604–615. **A. V. Kirwan.** Portions of the series repr. *Host and Guest*, 1864.

1943 The Factory Bill, 617–628.

VOLUME 29, JUNE 1844

1944 Oxford professors of poetry—Copleston and Keble, 629–639. **R. A. Willmott.** The style and critical method are exactly those of no. 1963, which is a sequel to this, as the author says, p. 639; p. 633 on Spenser repeats what "we" said on a former occasion—viz., no. 1910, pp. 257–258.

1945   An episode of the times of Philip V of Spain (Part II, concl.), 640–654.

1946   Of the red Indian, 655–676. **P. W. Banks.** Signed Morgan Rattler—see no. 178.

1947   Animal magnetism and neurhypnotism (Part I), 681–699. Signed in intro. note: R.S.S. (Part II is no. 2078.)

1948   May gambols; or, Titmarsh in the picture-galleries, 700–716. **W. M. Thackeray.** Signed M. A. Titmarsh; repr. *Works*, XXV. Intro. note signed O.Y. [Oliver Yorke].

1949   Napoleon and the poet de Lille, 717–721.

1950   The luck of Barry Lyndon (chaps. xii–xiii), 723–738. **W. M. Thackeray.** Evidence for no. 1890.

1951   Vagaries of Lentin-tide: Lord Ellenborough, and Lord Ashley, 740–750.

VOLUME 30, JULY 1844

1952   The Emperor Nicholas, 1–16.

1953   The Battle of Waterloo, 17–31.

1954   Secrets of the lecture-room: a surgeon's story, 31–36.

1955   On the state of the Peruvian empire previous to the arrival of the Spaniards, 37–47. **William Miller,** 1795–1861. Signed "General W. Miller, Her Majesty's Consul-General in the Pacific"; see *DNB*.

1956   The classics of the table (No. II): dinner, dessert, wines, coffee, and liqueurs, 48–61. **A. V. Kirwan.** Cf. no. 1942.

1957   Posting in the seventh year of Our Lady Queen Victoria, 62–71.

1958   *Coningsby; or, The New Generation* [by Disraeli], 71–84. Unidentified. (Cf. no. 2034.)

1959   Southey's sale and Southey's poems, 87–93. **R. A. Willmott.** The style is unmistakable: cf. the description in evidence for no. 1549.

1960   The luck of Barry Lyndon (chaps. xiv–xv), 93–108. **W. M. Thackeray.** Evidence for no. 1890.

1961   The modern troubadours, 108–118. **Hannah Lawrance?** Having dealt with the *trouvères* of northern France in *Blackwood's* (nos. 1509 and 1530, *Index*, I), the shift to the troubadours of the south and the langue d'Oc would be natural;

the same method of survey and digest is followed, and here runs to the 18th century, which is the limit of her range; in contrast to antiquaries like Thomas Wright, the approach is definitely literary: the long sentences with their studied rhythms and sensuous imagery (see especially pp. 108, 111, 118), the enthusiastic but restrained tone, and the note of nostalgia make one think immediately of Pater and the "Two Early French Stories" which begin *The Renaissance*.

1962   The state of parties, 119–126.

VOLUME 30, AUGUST 1844

1963   The lectures of Professor Keble, considered with a particular reference to some of the Latin poets, 127–138. **R. A. Willmott.** In his *Summer Time*, pp. 136 and 137–138 reproduce large parts of pp. 129 and 130 of this art. almost verbatim; on p. 129, the author claims nos. 853 and 867.

1964   The Marquise de Sévigné, Lady of Bourbilly, 139–153.

1965   [Raphael's] "The Transfiguration," and [del Piombo's] "The Raising of Lazarus," 154–170.

1966   Temperance societies, 170–175.

1967   Military tableaux (No. V): the Pomeranian Landwher at the Battle of Dennewitz, 176–189. **John Mitchell.** Evidence for no. 1176.

1968   Il Ghirlandajo, a legend of Florence, 190–197. **Julia Pardoe,** prob. Cf. no. 1924.

1969   A fine day in Piccadilly (No. III), 197–210. **Peter Cunningham,** prob. Cf. no. 1892.

1970   *Lord-Chancellor Eldon*, 211–226.

1971   The luck of Barry Lyndon (chaps. xvi–xvii), 227–242. **W. M. Thackeray.** Evidence for no. 1890.

1972   Incendiarism, its causes and cure, 243–252.

VOLUME 30, SEPTEMBER 1844

1973   A fortnight's novel-reading, 253–266.

1974   Classics of the table (No. III): dessert, fruits, sweetmeats, and liqueurs, 269–279. **A. V. Kirwan.** Cf. no. 1942.

1975   The Suniassie [Indian religious sect], 280–287. **R. Calder Campbell.** Repr. *Rough Recollections* (1847), III, 138–175.

1976   The pulpit in the nineteenth century,

287–294. **David Masson.** *Memories of London in the 'Forties* (1908), p. 57n.

1977 French fashionable life two hundred years ago: monarchs, ministers, and courtiers, 294–309.

1978 *Historic Fancies*, by the Hon. Sydney Smythe, 310–321.

1979 Concerning dog-stealing, 322–330. Signed: Larry Bow-wow-wow.

1980 An ethnological speculation on salt, 331–341.

1981 Campbelliana [on Thomas Campbell], 342–352. **Peter Cunningham,** prob. Attr. by S. C. Hall in *A Book of Memories* (1871), p. 349n.; autobiographical details in art., pp. 342, 347, support Hall's attrib.; Cunningham was writing for *FM* at this time (see *Index*, Part B).

1982 The luck of Barry Lyndon (Part II, chap. i), 353–364. **W. M. Thackeray.** Evidence for no. 1890.

1983 Some account of the official jesters, or court fools, 365–368. **John Doran?** Doran published *The History of Court Fools* in 1858, in which he says, p. 380, that he has "almost an encyclopedia of notes"; this art. discusses in shorter form many of the same people and cites many of the same reference works; it reads like a series of notes; Doran was writing for *FM* at this time (see no. 1851).

1984 The late session, 368–378.

VOLUME 30, OCTOBER 1844

1985 An election to the Long Parliament, 379–393. **Thomas Carlyle.** Repr. *Essays,* IV.

1986 The state murder; a tale [adaptation and abridgement of George Sand's *Le Secrétaire Intime*] (Part I), 394–412. **G. H. Lewes.** "Receipts."

1987 Some account of a poet's friend [Norton Nicholls, friend of Gray], 412–417. **R. A. Willmott.** Signed A. [Aris?], with address Trinity; in Willmott's *Summer Time,* pp. 230–231, two anecdotes reappear, verbatim, one after the other, as they are found here on p. 414; Willmott was a Trinity graduate and probably there on a visit; he wrote no. 1688 on Gray; the style fits most of the description in no. 1549.

1988 [John] Bull and Nongtongpaw, 418–426. **Antonio Gallenga.** Signed Anglomane; *Episodes,* II, 247; repr. *The Age We Live In,* 1845.

1989 Classics of the table (No. IV): sweet-meats, beer, cider, perry, liqueurs, and wines, 427–436. **A. V. Kirwan.** Cf. no. 1942.

1990 Of matters musical and of the Italian opera, 436–450. **P. W. Banks.** Signed Morgan Rattler—see no. 178.

1991 *Greece under the Romans* [by George Finlay], 450–465.

1992 Little travels and road-side sketches (No. II): Ghent, Bruges, 465–471. **W. M. Thackeray.** Evidence for no. 1934.

1993 Apology for art-unions, 471–478.

1994 Courses of English reading, 479–491. **R. A. Willmott,** prob. Characteristic style (described in evidence for no. 1549); the remark by Hallam on *MacFlecknoe* (p. 487, col. i) seems echoed in Willmott's *Summer Time,* p. 231; the grasp of Tayler (pp. 482, 484, 485–486) would be expected from a man who published a book on him in 1847.

1995 The general policy of the government, 491–502.

VOLUME 30, NOVEMBER 1844

1996 A fine day at Stratford-upon-Avon (No. IV), 505–517. **Peter Cunningham,** prob. The title, the antiquarian approach, the style and tone of this art. make it clearly one of the "Fine day" series which begins with no. 1892; Cunningham was treasurer of the Shakespeare Society and edited various works which it published: see *DNB.*

1997 The Smiths, 518–536.

1998 Prichard's *Natural History of Man,* 537–549. **P. W. Banks.** Signed An Apprentice of the Law—see no. 1378.

1999 Military tableaux (No. VI, concl.): the Brandenburgh Hussars in the campaigns of 1813 and 1814, 550–562. **John Mitchell.** Evidence for no. 1176.

2000 The state murder (Part II, concl.), 563–571. **G. H. Lewes.** "Receipts."

2001 Hints on the modern governess system, 571–583.

2002 The luck of Barry Lyndon (Part II, chap. ii), 584–597. **W. M. Thackeray.** Evidence for no. 1890.

2003 *Scotland and England*, by Kohl, 597–609.

2004 Classics of the table (No. V): ancient and modern wines, 610–621. **A. V. Kirwan.** Cf. no. 1942.

2005 A few words anent the labouring classes [and on Young England], 624–630.

2035 Classics of the table (No. VII): modern wines of France, 223–236. **A. V. Kirwan.** Cf. no. 1942.

2036 The widow, 236–243.

2037 The coming session, 244–252.

VOLUME 31, MARCH 1845

2038 Some rambling remarks on Horace and others (Part II), 253–271. **P. W. Banks.** Signed Morgan Rattler, Esq., M.A., An Apprentice of the Law—see nos. 178, 1378.

2039 The curate's volume of poems (chap. iii), 271–282.

2040 [Introduction and notes to] A winter carol, respectfully inscribed to a young lady whom the author met in *The Cambridge Star*, 283–292. Introduction signed: O.Y. [Oliver Yorke]; notes by "another hand."

2041 A passage in the lives of Rubens and Rembrandt, 293–307.

2042 Bunyan and Bunhill Fields, 308–319. Unidentified. Perhaps by R. A. Willmott: the opening pages are on Southey's prose (cf. nos. 1959, 2693); numerous literary references and quotations, especially from 17th- and 18th-century writers, are characteristic of Willmott's work.

2043 My log: Blue Squid, the sea ghost, 320–329.

2044 A walk from London to Fulham (Part III): from Little Chelsea to Walham Green, 330–342. **T. C. Croker.** Cf. no. 2017.

2045 The great Ward business [on W. G. Ward's *Ideal of a Christian Church*], 343–353. **R. A. Willmott?** In no. 2028, p. 136, Ward and Oakeley are mentioned as leading Tractarians; cf. this art., opening sentence, with no. 2056, pp. 477, 478, on Oakeley, for same central charge; Garbett and Moberly are frequently referred to in both arts.; the piled up allusions and quotations, notably on pp. 343, 349, 353, are characteristic of Willmott's writing; cf. no. 2166.

2046 Classics of the table (No. VIII, concl.): modern wines of France, 355–366. **A. V. Kirwan.** Cf. no. 1942.

2047 The policy of ministers, 368–378.

VOLUME 31, APRIL 1845

2048 Contemporary orators (No. I): Sir Robert Peel, 379–392. **G. H. Francis.**

Series revised and repr. in *Orators of the Age*, 1847.

2049 The wolves of Esthonia, 392–400. **Elizabeth Rigby Eastlake.** Attr. Marion Lockhead, *Elizabeth Rigby, Lady Eastlake* (1961), p. 32.

2050 Foscolo and English hospitality, 401–414. **Antonio Gallenga.** Signed Anglomane—see no. 1988; repr. *Italy*, II.

2051 Bon Gaultier's *Book of Ballads* [by Theodore Martin and W. E. Aytoun], 415–421.

2052 The curate's volume of poems (chap. iv), 422–432.

2053 Reminiscences of a ride in a *schnell wagen*, 433–444.

2054 A walk from London to Fulham (Part IV, concl.): Walham Green to Fulham, 445–457. **T. C. Croker.** Cf. no. 2017.

2055 *Modern Cookery in all its Branches*, 465–474.

2056 Mr. Oakeley's *Letter to the Bishop of London*, 475–481. **R. A. Willmott?** The parallel columns, pp. 479–480, are very characteristic; the literary references to Gray, Arbuthnot, and Pope, pp. 475, 477, are commonplaces of Willmott's work; see evidence for nos. 2028 and 2045; a common authorship of all three arts. seems probable.

2057 Two events in the life of an empiric, 482–492.

2058 The Treasury benches, 493–504.

VOLUME 31, MAY 1845

2059 *Histoire du Consulat et de L'Empire*, [by Thiers; Vols. I–III], 505–520. **A. V. Kirwan.** On p. 520 author speaks of knowing Nicholas Novositzoff "in Germany, Poland & Russia"; Kirwan was in Warsaw, Moscow, and St. Petersburg in 1828–1829, and in Munich 1830 (his *Letter to Lord Palmerston* was written from Munich, 1830); indeed, in the *FQR* no. 762, p. 362, Kirwan specifically says he knew "Nowosiltzoff" in Poland; cf. *FM* no. 2973.

2060 The mourner and the comforter, 521–534.

2061 A holiday trip to Gravesend and Rochester, 534–545.

2062 The curate's volume of poems (chap. v), 546–560.

2063 Some rambling remarks on Horace and others (Part III, concl.), 561–580. **P. W. Banks.** Evidence for no. 2038.

2064 The Royal Academy of Arts: its state and prospects, 583–597.

2065 The Non-Jurors and the Prayer-Book, 598–611.

2066 Anecdotes of highwaymen, 612–619.

2067 The Maynooth question, 620–630.

VOLUME 31, JUNE 1845

2068 Contemporary orators (No. II): Lord John Russell, 631–638. **G. H. Francis.** Repr. *Orators.*

2069 A night in the Champ de Mars, 639–646. **Julia Pardoe.** Repr. *Pilgrimages in Paris*, 1862.

2070 *Lives of Men of Letters and Science who Flourished in the Time of George III* [by Henry Brougham; Vol. I], 647–659. Unidentified. (See no. 2214.)

2071 The curate's volume of poems (chap. vi), 660–673.

2072 Early English actresses, 673–688. **Peter Cunningham.** Many passages and phrases reappear, sometimes verbatim, in Cunningham's *Nell Gwynn* (1852): for examples cf. pp. 681, 682, 686 with the book, pp. 35, 126, 124 respectively; the style is characteristic of this antiquarian writer for *FM* in the 1840s.

2073 The Duke of Marlborough (Part I), 689–702.

2074 An inquiry into the state of girls' fashionable schools, 703–712.

2075 Picture gossip: in a letter from Michael Angelo Titmarsh, 713–724. **W. M. Thackeray.** Signed Michael Angelo Titmarsh; *Letters*, II, 191; repr. *Works*, XXV.

2076 Mr. Benjamin Disraeli, M.P. [on *Sybil*], 727–737.

2077 On the Italian opera, 740–749. **P. W. Banks.** Signed Morgan Rattler, Esq., M.A., an Apprentice of the Law—see nos. 178, 1378.

VOLUME 32, JULY 1845

2078 Animal magnetism and neurhypnotism (Part II, concl.): throwing a few rays of light upon witchcraft, demonology, &c., 1–19. Signed: R.S.S.: see no. 1947 and opening paragraph here.

2079 The cross of Danzig, 20–26.

2080 Poets, painters, and other shadows, 27–48. **R. A. Willmott.** In his *Summer Time*, pp. 17 and 18 reproduce large parts of pp. 27 and 28 of this art. almost verbatim.

2081 Contemporary orators (No. III): Lord Lyndhurst, 49–54. **G. H. Francis.** Repr. *Orators.*

2082 The smuggler's daughter, 55–61.

2083 The spiritual perils of British travellers [in Rome], 62–71. **John Cumming?** The opening par. repeats the theme of nos. 1300 and 1311—indeed, the art. seems to be another expression of Cumming's fanatical distress at the spread of Roman Catholicism.

2084 The curate's volume of poems (chap. vii), 77–90.

2085 Three epochs of the [French] Revolution (No. I): destruction, 91–99.

2086 Monsieur Lecocq and his lodgers—a sketch of the "bourgeoise" life of Paris; from the French of Albéric Second (chaps. i–v), 99–111. **Albéric Second.** Title.

2087 *The Fall of Napoleon* by John Mitchell, 112–126. **A. V. Kirwan,** prob. The author had visited Dresden, p. 121 (Kirwan had travelled in Germany—see no. 2059); he speaks, p. 125, of having written "elsewhere" [i.e., not in *FM*?] of Napoleon "as a reformer of the laws" (see *FQR*, no. 830 [Apr. 1845], pp. 129–132, by Kirwan); and on p. 123 says he "knew Sir Hudson [Lowe] well," and that his manner was against him (cf. Kirwan in no. 3122, p. 151: "We had not ourselves the honour of Sir Hudson Lowe's personal acquaintance; but knowing his person well, we can aver that it was the reverse of prepossessing"); Kirwan had already written at least two arts. on Napoleon (no. 2059 and *FQR*, no. 830, both in this year); cf. the general evidence for no. 2307.

VOLUME 32, AUGUST 1845

2088 Something between the showers; in a letter to Oliver Yorke, 127–140. **R. A. Willmott.** Signed M.A.; cf. signature and style of no. 1660; passages quoting Johnson and Lord Collingwood, followed by a description of a blackbird and an anecdote about Watt, pp. 128–129, reappear, partly verbatim, in Willmott's *Summer Time*, pp. 13–14.

2089 A brace of worthies (No. I): the most honest man of France and Navarre—Gassion, 141–154.

2090 Some notices of Lord Robertson's *Leaves from a Journal*, 155–158. **P. W. Banks.** Signed An Apprentice of the Law —see no. 1378.

2091 Monsieur Lecocq and his lodgers (chaps. vi–vii, concl.), 159–164. **Albéric Second.** Cf. no. 2086.

2092 The late Sir William Follett, 165–174. **A. V. Kirwan.** Such an art. is listed for his "Essays"; pp. 170–171, 173, were clearly drawn upon for the sketch of Follett in *Brit.Quart.Rev.*, 11 (Feb. 1850), 186 [an art. to be assigned to Kirwan in *Index*, III]; Kirwan was closely connected with the trial mentioned on p. 173, col. i: see Boase.

2093 The curate's volume of poems (chap. viii), 179–193.

2094 The Scilly Islands, 194–205. **Frederick Holme,** prob. Holme to T. C. Croker, Jan. 15, [1845], from Corpus Christi Coll., Nat. Lib. Ireland, says he sent Nickisson a paper on the Scilly Islands on Jan. 1st.

2095 The Duke of Marlborough (Part II, concl.), 205–219.

2096 The fortunate painter [Velasquez], 220–223.

2097 Lady Hester Stanhope, 224–239.

2098 Tory policy, 240–252.

VOLUME 32, SEPTEMBER 1845

2099 Greek and Roman domestic interiors, 253–267. **R. A. Willmott.** In his *Summer Time*, pp. 171, 172, 168, 169 reproduce facts and anecdotes, often verbatim, found here on pp. 254, 256, 265, 265 respectively. (See no. 2116.)

2100 La fleuriste: an o'er true tale, 268–286. Signed: Selina.

2101 Ardmore [in Ireland], 286–300. Un-identified. (See no. 2111.)

2102 The curate's volume of poems (chap. ix), 301–313.

2103 Touching Antony the triumvir and Cicero the orator, 314–329. **P. W. Banks.** Signed Morgan Rattler—see no. 178.

2104 A brace of worthies (No. II, concl.): the most polite man of France and Navarre—Coîlin, 330–341.

2105]John] Bulwer's *Muscles of the Mind*, 341–349.

2106 On the character of the ghost in *Hamlet*, 350–356. **R. H. Horne.** Signed Professor Grabstein, Phil.D. of Göttingen; *Bibliography*, p. 4.

2107 Of Victor Hugo's lyrics, 358–372. Un-identified. (See no. 2191.)

2108 Of the Italian opera [in the 1845 season], 373–378. **P. W. Banks,** prob. Signed The Old Hand; author says, p.

373, that he intends to make a "few observations supplementary to my first article of the year" [i.e., of this opera season], which would refer to no. 2077 by Banks.

VOLUME 32, OCTOBER 1845

2109 Drops from the leaves: collected, after the showers, for Oliver Yorke, 379–388. **R. A. Willmott.** Signed M.A.; cf. no. 2088, which author claims in opening sentence, and on pp. 380, 386, and 387 recalls pp. 129, 137–138, 139 of no. 2088, dated from St. Edmund's Parsonage, not far from Launton where Willmott was curate in 1845: see *DNB*.

2110 Three adventures before midnight, 389–393.

2111 Ardo: the sequel to Ardmore [no. 2101], 393–403.

2112 Mark O'Shaugnessy's mistake: a piper's story, founded on fact, 403–410.

2113 The curate's volume of poems (chap. x), 416–428.

2114 Spain as it was, and Spain as it is; an historical sketch (Part I; no more published): Spain as it was—the cobbler of Seville, 428–440.

2115 Links of society, 441–452.

2116 Private life of the Romans, 453–469. **R. A. Willmott.** This is a sequel to no. 2099, in which another book of Becker's is reviewed in the same manner.

2117 A legend of Flodden Field, 469–478.

2118 Three epochs of the [French] Revolution (No. II), 478–484.

2119 England and Yankee-land, 485–496. **Antonio Gallenga.** Signed Anglomane—see no. 1988.

2120 Ourselves, our critics, and the general policy of the government, 496–504. Un-identified. Perhaps G. W. Nickisson, who was editor at this time.

VOLUME 32, NOVEMBER 1845

2121 Contemporary orators (No. IV): Lord Stanley, 505–512. **G. H. Francis.** Repr. *Orators*.

2122 Paulet la Lionne, 513–526.

2123 Out of town, 527–536.

2124 The curate's volume of poems (chap. xi, concl.), 537–559.

2125 Sea-side reading [recent books], 559–571.

2126 Old Homer, 572–577.

2127 White-chalk days of a wanderer (No. I; no more published): Rhodes, 577–583.

2128 Barmecide banquets, with Joseph Bregion and Anne Miller, 584–593. **W. M. Thackeray.** Signed G.S.F.B. [George Savage Fitz-Boodle]; repr. *Works*, ed. Furniss, X.

2129 Charles Bannister, 593–598.

2130 The defensible state of the country, 599–610. Unidentified. (See no. 2139.)

2131 The belle's choice, 610–622.

2132 *The Zoology of the English Poets Corrected by the Writings of Modern Naturalists*, 624–630. **R. A. Willmott.** In his *Summer Time*, pp. 22–23, he speaks of this book and uses phrases and illustrations that had appeared on pp. 624, 625–626 of this art.; *Summer Time* and art. are written in the same style, described in evidence for no. 1549.

VOLUME 32, DECEMBER 1845

2133 The Pryor's Bank, Fulham, 631–646. **T. C. Croker.** Repr. cited in no. 2017.

2134 Three scenes in the life of Count de Guiche, 647–662. **Julia Pardoe.** Repr., *Pilgrimages in Paris*, 1862.

2135 Cambridge studies, 663–675. **R. A. Willmott,** prob. In his *Conversations at Cambridge*, 1836, Willmott wrote an essay on this subject; the argument there on pp. 281–282 reappears here on pp. 664–665; the extensive piling up of quotations is characteristic as are the refs. to Gray (pp. 664, 667, 667n.); pp. 672–673 are a discussion of historical studies in which reference is made to Prof. Smyth (cf. no. 1758).

2136 Old London signs, 676–687. **Peter Cunningham,** prob. See evidence for no. 1892, all of which is applicable here; also cf. the reference to the waiter at the Cock (there, p. 75, here, p. 676).

2137 Contemporary orators (No. V): The Duke of Wellington, 688–691. **G. H. Francis.** Repr. *Orators*.

2138 Painted glass, 691–695.

2139 A few more words on the defensible state of the country [sequel to no. 2130], 696–707.

2140 The first bridal visit, 707–718.

2141 Of railways (Part I), 719–739. **P. W. Banks.** Signed Morgan Rattler, Esq. M.A., an Apprentice of the Law—see nos. 178, 1378.

2142 A day's excursion in Newfoundland, 740–742.

2143 About a Christmas book; in a letter from Michael Angelo Titmarsh to Oliver Yorke, 744–748. **W. M. Thackeray.** Signed Michael Angelo Titmarsh; repr. *Works*, ed. Furniss, VIII.

VOLUME 33, JANUARY 1846

2144 Our chimes for the New Year, 1–6. **R. A. Willmott.** Page 1 on Pope and Poussin, p. 2 on church bells, and the last sentence, p. 6, reappear, almost verbatim, in Willmott's *Summer Time*, pp. 99–102.

2145 The philosophy of crime, with illustrations from familiar history (No. I): William Horne, 7–21.

2146 Principal campaigns in the rise of Napoleon (No. I): the Italian campaigns (chaps. i–ii), 22–42. **John Mitchell.** Attr. Schmitz, *Mitchell*, p. xvii.

2147 On the history of pantomimes, in a letter to Oliver Yorke, Esq., 43–45. **G. H. Lewes.** Signed Vivian Latouche; Lewes, "Receipts."

2148 The pride of a spoiled beauty; adapted from the French of H. de Balzac (Part I), 46–57. **Honoré de Balzac.** Title. Translation of "Le Bal de Sceaux" by **Agnes Lewes**—Lewes, "Receipts."

2149 Public patronage of men of letters, 58–71.

2150 The first flower-painter, a legend of Sicyon, 72–77.

2151 Contemporary orators (No. VI): the Right Hon. T. B. Macaulay, 77–84. **G. H. Francis.** Repr. *Orators*.

2152 Titmarsh's tour through Turkeydom [Thackeray's *Tour from Cornhill to Cairo*], 85–96.

2153 Of railways (Part II, concl.), 97–113. **P. W. Banks.** Evidence for no. 2141; Thrall, p. 278.

2154 The lady of Elm-wood, 113–119.

2155 Mysteries of the cabinet, 121–126.

VOLUME 33, FEBRUARY 1846

2156 An illustrative chapter on straws [passing remarks of writers that reveal their characters]; being the first specimen of a new dictionary, 127–135. **R. A. Willmott.** Page 128 on Gray, on Bacon, and on the effect of sunlight on the eye and great literature on the mind, is the basis, often verbally, of Willmott's *Summer Time*, pp. 10–11.

2157 Contemporary orators (No. VII): the

Right Hon. Sir James Graham, 136–143. **G. H. Francis.** Repr. *Orators.*

2158 The legend of Gelnhausen; from the history of the twelfth century, 143–156. **Marian E. Martin?** Signed M.E.M.; in the Crone file of the *Dublin University Magazine,* Central Library, Belfast, all arts. signed M.E.M. are attrib. to Mrs. Martin of Ross (whose first name, but without the "E.," is given in *Landed Gentry of Ireland* under Robert Martin of Ross); her arts. there deal mainly with legends and medieval history; the fact that her last art. there appeared in Jan. 1856 and the last art. in *FM* by M.E.M. in Sept. 1855 supports the attrib., since Marian Martin died in 1855.

2159 Principal campaigns in the rise of Napoleon (No. II): the Italian campaigns (chaps. iii–iv), 157–180. **John Mitchell.** Cf. no. 2146.

2160 The pride of a spoiled beauty (Part II), 180–194. **Honoré de Balzac.** Cf. no. 2148.

2161 Latin pamphleteers: Sallust, 194–211. **R. A. Willmott,** prob. Cf. the content and the style of no. 1717, and the description of Willmott's style in no. 1549.

2162 A letter from Rippoldsau, 211–225. Signed: Selina.

2163 A dinner in ancient Egypt, 229–232.

2164 The philosophy of crime, with illustrations from familiar history (No. II, concl.): Francis David Stern, 235–246.

2165 The position of ministers, 246–252.

VOLUME 33, MARCH 1846

2166 Mr. Newman: his theories and character [as revealed in his *Essay on Development*], 253–268. **R. A. Willmott,** prob. The quotation of Davidson on Taylor, p. 257, appears, verbatim, in Willmott's, *Bishop Jeremy Taylor* (2nd ed., 1848), p. 284; other quotations from Taylor occur on pp. 255, 257, 259, the last from a rather obscure work which Willmott quotes in his book, p. 143; Newman's *Essay* is quoted by Willmott in no. 2144, p. 5; the references to numerous writers, together with many short quotations following rapidly upon one another, on pp. 256–257, and in general the literary character of the essay, support the attrib.

2167 Le Jeu de Noel; from the notes of an old traveller, 269–275.

2168 Principal campaigns in the rise of Napoleon (No. III): the Italian campaigns (chap. v), 276–287. **John Mitchell.** Cf. no. 2146.

2169 Counsel mal-à-propos, 288–292.

2170 Margaret Lucas, Duchess of Newcastle, 292–307.

2171 Milliners' apprentices, 308–316.

2172 Contemporary orators (No. VIII): Lord Palmerston, 317–322. **G. H. Francis.** Repr. *Orators.*

2173 The village of Lorette, and the new settlement of Vale Cartier [in Quebec province], 323–331.

2174 A brother of the press on the history of a literary man, Laman Blanchard, and the chances of the literary profession, in a letter to the Reverend Francis Sylvester at Rome, from Michael Angelo Titmarsh, Esq., 332–342. **W. M. Thackeray.** Title; *Letters,* II, 230; repr. *Works,* XXV.

2175 The common lodging-house, 342–357.

2176 *Modern Painters, &c.* [by Ruskin], 358–368.

2177 What is the position of Sir Robert Peel and his cabinet? 369–378.

VOLUME 33, APRIL 1846

2178 Of the Spains and the Spaniards, 379–394. **P. W. Banks.** Signed Morgan Rattler—see no. 178.

2179 Milly L———; a tale of fact in humble life, 395–412.

2180 Principal campaigns in the rise of Napoleon (No. IV): the Italian campaigns (chaps. vi–vii), 413–433. **John Mitchell.** Cf. no. 2146.

2181 An anecdote about an old house, 434–437.

2182 Musæus, 437–444.

2183 Dining out, 445–455. **Peter Cunningham,** prob. On p. 452 author refers to the discussion in no. 2136, p. 676, of William and James, waiters at the Cock in Fleet Street; the antiquarian approach is similar to that of Cunningham's other arts. on London (see nos. 1892, etc.).

2184 *Velasco; or, Memoirs of a Page* [by Cyrus Redding], 456–460.

2185 Female authorship, 460–466.

2186 Contemporary orators (No. IX): Earl Grey and Lord Morpeth, 466–477. **G. H. Francis.** Repr. *Orators.*

2187 The Sikhs—their rise and progress, 478–487.

2188 Murillo; or, The painter without ambition, 488–494.

2189 On some illustrated children's books [Gammer Gurton], 495–502. **W. M. Thackeray.** Signed Michael Angelo Titmarsh; *Letters*, II, 260n. and 261; repr. *Works*, XXV.

2222 Red Finlay of the deer, 166–171.

2223 Hampton Court: past and present, 172–181. **Katherine Thomson.** Repr. *Recollections.* (Letter, p. 479, signed William Ewart.)

2224 Principal campaigns in the rise of Napoleon (No. VIII): the campaign of Friedland, 182–197. **John Mitchell.** Cf. no. 2146.

2225 Holly cottage, 198–211.

2226 Contemporary orators (No. XII): some members of Lord John Russell's administration, 212–222. **G. H. Francis.** Repr. *Orators.*

2227 Memoranda and mementos of Madrid in 1845, 223–230. **A. V. Kirwan?** Kirwan to Blackwood, May 5, 1862, Nat. Lib. Scot.: "To Fraser . . . I have been a constant contributor for two and twenty years on French and Spanish literature, on Political and social subjects"; author says he had first been in Madrid at end of 1826, when he was just past the time of inexperienced boyhood (p. 223); Kirwan, who was born in 1804, later said, in 1860, that he was returning from Spain in the summer of 1825 (*FM* no. 4036, p. 575)—which may be a discrepancy, or may be a slip of memory; author had been in Moscow (p. 225), as had Kirwan (see evidence for *FM* no. 2059).

2228 Apparitions, 231–236.

2229 Proposals for a continuation of *Ivanhoe*, in a letter to Monsieur Alexandre Dumas (Part I), 237–245. **W. M. Thackeray.** Signed Monsieur Michael Angelo Titmarsh; claimed in preface to *Rebecca and Rowena*, and repr. in revised and expanded form, *Works*, XIV.

2230 Will the Whig government stand? 245–252.

VOLUME 34, SEPTEMBER 1846

2231 Life of a strolling player [John Cunningham], 253–261. **Peter Cunningham?** The antiquarian approach, the interest in a lesser known Cunningham, the use of poetry and occasional first-person, all suggest this Cunningham, who was writing for *FM* at this time and who later wrote a life of the actress Nell Gwynn (see *DNB*).

2232 Michel de Montaigne in the cradle, the nursery, and the college, 261–271. **Bayle St. John.** Attr. in *Men of the Time/59*; St. John wrote *Montaigne*, 1858, where I, 35, 51, 54, contain facts and phrasing similar to art. pp. 265–266, 268, 269.

2233 The story of the pretty old woman of Vevay, 272–282.

2234 Principal campaigns in the rise of Napoleon (No. IX): the campaign of Wagram (chap. i), 283–300. **John Mitchell.** Cf. no. 2146.

2235 The "ecrivain public"; a sketch from Parisian life, 301–322.

2236 Manners, traditions, and superstitions of the Shetlanders (Part III), 323–339.

2237 A glance at Prague during the Feast of St. Nepomuk, 339–346.

2238 Contemporary orators (No. XIII) [mainly on T. S. Duncombe], 347–352. **G. H. Francis.** Repr. *Orators.*

2239 A Portuguese bull-fight, 353–358.

2240 Proposals for a continuation of *Ivanhoe* (Part II, concl.), 359–367. **W. M. Thackeray.** Evidence for no. 2229.

2241 National education, 370–378.

VOLUME 34, OCTOBER 1846

2242 Commercial relations of the Indian archipelago, 379–391.

2243 Ham House in the days of the Cabal, 392–406. **Katherine Thomson.** Repr. *Recollections.*

2244 Morell's *History of Modern Philosophy*, 407–415. **G. H. Lewes.** "Receipts." (Note, p. 630, by **Lewes.**)

2245 A boar-hunt in Brittany, 416–427. **Charles J. Wells.** Signed a Resident [of Brittany]; attr. by Theodore Watts, *Athenaeum*, Mar. 8, 1879, p. 313.

2246 Principal campaigns in the rise of Napoleon (No. X): the campaign of Wagram (chap. ii), 428–435. **John Mitchell.** Cf. no. 2146.

2247 The rector's daughter (chap. i), 436–450.

2248 Contemporary orators (No. XIV): Mr. Wakley and Dr. Bowring, 450–466. **G. H. Francis.** Repr. *Orators.*

2249 Retrospective gleanings (No. II, concl.), 467–478. **Cyrus Redding.** Evidence for no. 2021.

2250 Manners, traditions, and superstitions of the Shetlanders (Part IV, concl.), 480–497.

2251 What is thought of our commercial policy on the continent? 499–504.

VOLUME 34, NOVEMBER 1846

2252 *The History of Etruria* (Part I), 505–521.

2253 Nightmare on the rails, 522–528.
2254 A postscript about John Foster [no. 2219], in a note to Oliver Yorke, 529–535. **R. A. Willmott.** Signed M.A., with address and date, as in nos. 1660, 2088, 2109, all of which are essays in the form of letters to Oliver Yorke; the sentimental description of nature and the piled-up quotations are hallmarks of Willmott's work.
2255 The new Werther, 536–550.
2256 Principal campaigns in the rise of Napoleon (No. XI, concl.): Battle of Wagram (chap. iii), and termination of the War, 551–566. **John Mitchell.** Cf. no. 2146.
2257 The rector's daughter (chap. ii), 567–581.
2258 Contemporary orators (No. XV): Mr. Roebuck, 582–598. **G. H. Francis.** Repr. *Orators.*
2259 The portrait, 599–602.
2260 Bohn's *De Grammont* [by Anthony Hamilton], 603–617.
2261 Politics and personality; being a few gleanings from the session and some traits of the debates, 618–630.

VOLUME 34, DECEMBER 1846

2262 English journalism, 630–640.
2263 Hair-love, 641–646.
2264 Contemporary orators (No. XVI, concl.): Sir Robert Inglis, Mr. W. E. Gladstone, Mr. Christie, 647–663. **G. H. Francis.** Repr. *Orators.*
2265 Passages from an unpublished French novel [satire on Jules Gabriel Janin and French Romantic school], 664–675.
2266 *The History of Etruria* (Part II, concl.), 676–685.
2267 The young country clergyman; a Scottish story, 686–697.
2268 Proposed commercial mission to Japan, 698–707.
2269 The Lord-Mayor and Lord-Mayor's day, 708–718. **Peter Cunningham?** The antiquarian approach, the use of poetry, the knowledge of old works on London are all typical of Cunningham's earlier and later arts. on London subjects (see nos. 1892 and 2300); see *DNB* [for his interest in antiquarian subjects and societies].
2270 Is she happy? 718–723.
2271 A few words about the cabinet and things in general, 725–731.
2272 *Wit and Humour* [by Leigh Hunt], 735–750. **R. A. Willmott.** Passage on Cowper, Prior, Butler, and Goldsmith,

p. 735, is echoed, with some verbal repetition, in *Summer Time*, pp. 204–205; an image from Cowper, p. 737, reappears in the latter, p. 164; cf. the youthful Milton gathering flowers from Sylvester, p. 737, with the book, pp. 34–35; the style is that described in the evidence for no. 1549.

VOLUME 35, JANUARY 1847

2273 The past, the present, and the coming, 1–14. **R. A. Willmott,** prob. The style seems unmistakably that described in the evidence for no. 1549; on p. 10 the comment on Correggio's Notte is found again in Willmott's *Summer Time*, p. 58.
2274 Scenes in the wilds of Mexico (No. I): Cayetano, the contrabandista, 25–28. **Gabriel Ferry.** Page 15n. The series was adapted and trans. by **Agnes Lewes**—p. 15n.; G. H. Lewes to J. W. Parker, [May 1847], Yale Univ. Lib., reported that the last two "adaptations from the French" in this series were ready; and see Lewes, "Receipts."
2275 *Favourite Haunts and Rural Studies*, 29–39. Unidentified. Perhaps R. A. Willmott who prob. wrote no. 2290 on a similar subject—indeed, p. 218 there on Milton seems to be a reference to p. 31 here; but there is more extensive quotation from the book reviewed than is normal in Willmott's work, though if he also wrote no. 2273 in this issue, as he seems to have done, this art. might have been put together rapidly and hence with many quotations.
2276 The sacrifices; a tale of ancient Rome, 40–53. Signed: MEM. Unidentified. Perhaps Marian E. Martin: cf. nos. 2158 and 3386, both of which are signed M.E.M.
2277 *Gatherings from Spain*, by the author of *The Hand-Book of Spain* [Richard Ford], 53–63. **A. V. Kirwan?** This art. draws heavily on *Brit. Quart. Rev.*, 4 (Aug. 1846), 143–179 [to be assigned to Kirwan, with a "prob.," in *Index*, III]: cf. ideas and sometimes same phrasing on pp. 52–54 with *BQR*, pp. 144–145, and remark on railroads, p. 59, with *BQR*, p. 178; 5 sentences on climate, p. 56, are taken almost verbatim from *BQR*, p. 177; both arts. are centered on Richard Ford's *Handbook*, here on an abridged edition; pp. 61–63 deal with two subjects Kirwan wrote on in *Host and Guest*, cookery and wines; also see initial evidence for *FM* no. 2227.

2278 A word or two about Mark Antony, 64–74.

2279 A legend of Forfarshire (Part I), 74–78.

2280 Literary legislators (No. I): Mr. B. Disraeli, 79–95. **G. H. Francis.** Partly repr. with additions in his *Critical Biographies: Benjamin Disraeli*, 1852.

2281 Touching Head's book and Canada [F. B. Head's *Emigrant*], 96–110. **P. W. Banks.** Signed Morgan Rattler, Esquire, M.A., an Apprentice of the Law—see nos. 178, 1378. (See no. 2311.)

2282 A grumble about Christmas-books, 111–126. **W. M. Thackeray.** Signed Michael Angelo Titmarsh; *Letters*, II, 263–264; repr. *Works*, ed. Furniss, VIII. AND **G. H. Lewes,** prob. Attr. White, "Thackeray," p. 83, and see Lewes, "Receipts," p. 368, where he speaks of writing "Titmarsh," prob. meaning the paragraph, p. 121, on Titmarsh's *Mrs. Perkin's Ball*.

VOLUME 35, FEBRUARY 1847

2283 On the abuse of language, in science and in common life, 127–140. **Alexander Bain.** *Autobiography*, ed. W. L. Davidson (1904), p. 426.

2284 The old judge (Part II): the tombstones, 141–147. **T. C. Haliburton.** Evidence for no. 2190.

2285 Holland House, and its inhabitants, 148–163. **Katherine Thomson.** Repr. *Recollections.*

2286 Some notices of a Shakspearian book [by J. P. Collier], 163–169. **P. W. Banks.** Signed Morgan Rattler—see no. 178.

2287 Scenes in the wilds of Mexico (No. II): the Mexican horse-tamer, 169–182. **Gabriel Ferry.** Evidence for no. 2274.

2288 Old London cries, 183–193. **Peter Cunningham?** Cf. title of no. 2136; art. is written in the same antiquarian style as his earlier and later arts. on London (see nos. 1892, etc. and no. 2300).

2289 Literary legislators (No. II): Mr. B. Disraeli; Mr. Mackinnon, 193–209. **G. H. Francis.** Cf. no. 2280.

2290 *Homes and Haunts of the British Poets* [by William Howitt], 210–227. **R. A. Willmott,** prob. The defence of Cowley (a favorite of Willmott's—cf. no. 927), the high praise of Addison on p. 219 (cf. nos. 1842, 1854), with a characteristic reference to painters; the emphasis on eighteenth-century poets, pp. 219–225, the strongly religious-moral

stance, pp. 210–218, and the subject of visiting literary shrines (cf. no. 1560, which is apparently referred to on p. 218—see pp. 524–525 of that art.), all suggest this regular contributor on poetry to *FM*.

2291 A legend of Forfarshire (Parts II–III), 228–243.

2292 What are we to expect (of the new parliament]? 244–252.

VOLUME 35, MARCH 1847

2293 Education of the people, 253–269. Unidentified. (See no. 2349.)

2294 Scenes in the wilds of Mexico (No. III): Matasiete, the hunter, 270–284. **Gabriel Ferry.** Evidence for no. 2274.

2295 The condition of authors in England, Germany, and France, 285–295. **G. H. Lewes.** "Receipts."

2296 A legend of Forfarshire (Part IV, concl.), 295–300.

2297 Mythological system of the Hellenes, 301–307.

2298 The old judge (Part III): How many fins has a cod? or, Forty years ago, 308–321. **T. C. Haliburton.** Signed The Author of *Sam Slick the Clockmaker*; cf. no. 2190.

2299 Literary legislators (No. III): Lord John Manners, 321–339. **G. H. Francis.** Cf. no. 2280.

2300 *Chronicles of Charter House*, 340–352. **Peter Cunningham.** Thackeray, *Letters*, II, 283–284.

2301 Minutiae literariae (No. I; no more published), 354–359. **R. A. Willmott.** Signed M.A.—signature used for nos. 1660, 2088, 2109, 2254, which are examples of the type of writing here described; on p. 354 the remark about Rubens reappears, almost verbatim, in Willmott's *Summer Time*, p. 222.

2302 Geraldine Fitsmaurice; from the recollections of a retired barrister, 360–369.

2303 "The great and comprehensive measure" [George Bentinck's solution to the Irish problem], 370–378.

VOLUME 35, APRIL 1847

2304 Aspect of contemporary literature, 379–385.

2305 The ancient palace of Greenwich (Placentia), and the days of the Tudors, 386–400. **Katherine Thomson.** Repr. *Recollections.*

2306 Scenes in the wilds of Mexico (No. IV): the bison-hunters, 401–411. **Gabriel Ferry.** Evidence for no. 2274.

2307 Chronique de Paris (No. I): or, The Restoration and the Revolution compared, 418–428. **A. V. Kirwan,** prob. Kirwan's letter (quoted in evidence to no. 2227) says he was a "constant" contributor to *FM*, 1840–1862, on French and Spanish politics, literature, and society; this range, with the inclusion of French journalism, is apparent in his *Modern France*, 1863; he was also interested in lawyers and physicians and in gastronomy (see Part B below); in *FM* no. 4023, p. 394, he reports that he visited Paris at least once every year from about 1818 (his first visit) to 1848 or 1849.

Though not highly distinctive, his work has several characteristics: it is normally a broad survey with factual emphasis, and in the case of memoirs—a primary subject—considerable use of anecdotes; he often refers to himself; some arts. are written in the first person; previous arts. referred to in the text turn out, as a rule, to be his, and he often borrows the substance and some of the phrasing from his previous work; English analogies to foreign men or events are commonly given; French and English translations of French are often mixed; parentheses are used; the attitude and language tend to be critical, sometimes sharply so, and few people or events are praised; the style is never sensuous or "poetic," nor often metaphorical; the political outlook is Whiggish—more specifically, somewhat anti-Republican, strongly anti-Socialist, and extremely hostile to Napoleon III.

In this particular case, one finds the knowledge of French journals, pp. 426–427, the mixture of French and English translation, pp. 427–428, and the rapid survey of many men and events; also Kirwan wrote Chroniques Nos. II and III, viz. nos. 2422, 2799.

2308 The old judge (Part IV): asking a governor to dine, 429–446. **T. C. Haliburton.** Evidence for no. 2190.

2309 Literary legislators (No. IV): Lord Mahon, 447–454. **G. H. Francis.** Cf. no. 2280.

2310 The teacher of music; a tale of epidemic, 455–466.

2311 Touching Canada [sequel to no. 2281], 467–482. **P. W. Banks.** Signed Morgan Rattler—see no. 2281.

2312 An adventure in the Apennines; translated from the German, 483–490.

2313 Famine in the south of Ireland, 491–504.

VOLUME 35, MAY 1847

2314 The Somerset family: the siege of Ragland Castle, 505–520. **Katherine Thomson.** Repr. *Recollections.*

2315 Mr. Cary, the translator of Dante, 521–537. **R. A. Willmott.** In his *Summer Time,* p. 187, he cites a line of Darwin's in conjunction with Cary's praise of *The Botanic Garden* (cf. art. p. 523); in ibid., pp. 108–109, he speaks of the flowers which Clare was able to find in Northamptonshire, though desolate and not picturesque (cf. art. p. 531); the style here is that described in no. 1549.

2316 Scenes in the wilds of Mexico (No. V): the robber and the Alcade, 538–547. **Gabriel Ferry.** Evidence for no. 2274.

2317 Spring novels, 548–552, 503–510 (sic.).

2318 The old judge (Part V): Horse-shoe Cove; or, Hufeisen Bucht, 511–528 (sic.). **T. C. Haliburton.** Evidence for no. 2190.

2319 Literary legislators (No. V): Mr. Smythe; Mr. Poulett Scrope, 529–544 (sic.). **G. H. Francis.** Cf. no. 2280.

2320 Anecdotical sketches on the life, manners, and eccentricities of the French authors of the present day, 545–552 (sic.).

2321 *The Life of Henry IV, King of France and Navarre* [by G. P. R. James], 553–565. **A. V. Kirwan,** prob. The author ends the art. with a specific promise to write no. 2328 for the June issue, and that art., which is prob. by Kirwan, begins with an immediate link back to this; to wish that Mr. James had given his work "a more distinct, individual, anecdotal, and biographical character," p. 564, is to ask it to be Kirwan's own form of writing history; the personal reference, p. 555, col. i, is characteristic of Kirwan and the facts are entirely compatible with his biography.

2322 A chapter on names, 566–570.

2323 Measures, not men, 571–580.

VOLUME 35, JUNE 1847

2324 Bunsen's *Egypt,* 631–638 [which follows p. 580]. **Edward Clarkson?** Clarkson wrote all of the Egyptian arts. for the *British and For. Rev.* (title-page of his *Suez Canal*, 2nd ed., 1843), including the one quoted here, p. 635n., written back in 1836; p. 636, mid-col. ii, contains echoes, nearly verbatim, of *FQR* no. 379, pp. 312, 326, by Clarkson, also written in 1836; author's remarks on p. 633 about writing on an Egyptian problem in "various magazines and reviews" since "our younger days" would fit Clarkson, who lectured on ancient Egypt as early as 1811 and edited numerous journals in the 1820's.

2325 A chronicle of Kenilworth Castle, its heroes and its heroines, 638–654. **Katherine Thomson.** Repr. *Recollections.*

2326 Love-passages in the life of Perron the Breton, being a sequel to the chasseurs' "Boar-hunt in Brittany" [no. 2245], 655–667. **Charles J. Wells.** Cf. no. 2245.

2327 Scenes in the wilds of Mexico (No. VI): Perico, the Mexican vagabond, 668–683. **Gabriel Ferry.** Evidence for no. 2274.

2328 *Louis XIV, and the Court of France in the Seventeenth Century* [by Julia Pardoe], 684–699. **A. V. Kirwan,** prob. Four remarks in similar phrasing, one sentence verbatim, and a quotation from Mme. de Motteville, here on p. 681, reappear in *Brit. Quart. Rev.*, 16 (Nov. 1852), 371–372, written by the author of *FM* nos. 3083 and 3142 (see *BQR*, 17 [May 1853], 480n.)—who was Kirwan; also cf. the evidence for no. 2321, a companion art.

2329 The old judge (Part VI): the keeping-room of an inn; or, Judge Beler's ghost, 700–713. **T. C. Haliburton.** Evidence for no. 2190.

2330 Literary legislators (No. VI, concl.): The Earl of Ellesmere; Mr. Monckton Milnes, 714–726. **G. H. Francis.** Cf. no. 2280.

2331 Of the two Italian operas [Her Majesty's Theatre and the Royal Italian Opera, Covent Garden], 728–738. **P. W. Banks.** Signed Morgan Rattler—see no. 178.

2332 Lord Grey, and his plans of colonisation, 738–749.

VOLUME 36, JULY 1847

2333 Three days of the famine at Schull, 1–13. **Richard Chenevix Trench.** Signed.

2334 A ramble at the foot of Mount Olympos, 13–19.

2335 *Ninfa*, 20–35.

2336 "I owe you nothing, sir," 36–42.

2337 Lathom House and the Stanley family, 44–53. **Katherine Thomson.** Repr. *Recollections.*

2338 Wilkie and Haydon, 53–61. **Cyrus Redding.** Passages and stories, notably pp. 54–57, reappear often verbatim in Redding's *Fifty Years Recollections* (1858), I, 120–251.

2339 Sensations of a summer night and morning on the Thames, 62–67. **Andrew Wynter.** Repr. *Social Bees.*

2340 Russian serfage: the relation between lord and serf, 68–75.

2341 The old judge (Part VII): the keeping-room of an inn; or, Seeing the devil, 76–87. **T. C. Haliburton.** Evidence for no. 2190.

2342 The deserted bazar, 88–93.

2343 Outlines in parliament (No. I): some members of the "Irish Party," 94–108. **G. H. Francis.** Signed The Author of "Literary Legislators" (no. 2280, etc.).

2344 Death-in-life, 108–112. **G. H. Lewes.** "Receipts."

2345 The Portuguese question, 115–126.

VOLUME 36, AUGUST 1847

2346 A day in Dalmatia, 127–139.

2347 Recollections of Dr. Chalmers, 140–155.

2348 Scenes in the wilds of Mexico (No. VII, concl.): José Juan, the pearl-fisher, 156–168. **Gabriel Ferry.** Evidence for no. 2274.

2349 Education of the people [sequel to no. 2293], 169–181. Unidentified. (Postscript, p. 252.)

2350 The memoirs of a lady; from the German, 182–188.

2351 Basing House, its besieged and its besiegers, 189–198. **Katherine Thomson.** Repr. *Recollections.*

2352 Book-love, 199–203. **R. A. Willmott,** prob. The style seems unmistakably that described in the evidence for no. 1549; the subject is another variation on nos. 1674, 1769, 1776, 1795, 2018, etc.

2353 The old judge (Part VIII): the keeping-room of an inn; or, A long night and a long story, 204–212. **T. C. Haliburton.** Evidence for no. 2190.

2354 Outlines in parliament (No. II): the railway potentates, 213–227. **G. H. Francis.** Evidence for no. 2343.

2355 Van Dyck and his works, 229–240.

2356 Sir Robert Peel's letter and the elections, 241–251.

VOLUME 36, SEPTEMBER 1847

2357 The Girondists, Jacobins, and M. de Lamartine, Deputy for Macon, 253–276. **A. V. Kirwan.** Cf. general evidence for no. 2307; the author calls himself, p. 257, an assiduous reader of French newspapers, naming three which Kirwan often mentions; on p. 264 discusses journalists; on p. 274 speaks of the *Moniteur* and "our excellent friend Plon," who has published 31 volumes of the journal; the survey of many figures is characteristic of Kirwan, as is the abrasive language about M. Roland, p. 273; p. 260, col. i, seems based on *FQR* no. 780, p. 208, by Kirwan.

2358 A defence of a classical education, 276–281.

2359 Juan Moreda, the slave-hunter, 282–289.

2360 Hands and gloves, 290–301.

2361 A visit to the wine country of Portugal, 302–309.

2362 A batch of parliamentary barristers (No. III—see no. 2376), 310–324. **G. H. Francis.** Evidence for no. 2343.

2363 The old judge (Part IX): the keeping-room of an inn; or, The cushion-dance, 324–334. **T. C. Haliburton.** Evidence for no. 2190.

2364 The orator of the shop, 336–344.

2365 Walter Scott—has history gained by his writings? 345–351.

2366 The merchant of Marseilles, 352–355.

2367 A day on the moors, 356–365.

2368 The sanitary question, 366–378. **W. A. Guy.** In no. 3716, p. 487, Guy speaks of "our" first taking up "The Sanitary Question" in Sept. 1847, and of recurring to the subject in Jan. 1848, citing no. 2408 in the note; there he speaks of "several other papers on Sanitary Reform" (cf. nos. 2380, 2427, etc.); "some on military matters, especially . . . a paper . . . in April 1855" (no. 3335); the *Biograph*, 6 (1881), 335, calls Guy a frequent contributor to *FM* of "essays on Sanitary Reform," some signed (nos. 3716, 3750), others anonymous; see *DNB*.

VOLUME 36, OCTOBER 1847

2369 Free Church sites [largely on Chalmers], 379–390.

2370 Mabel Earnley, 391–404.

2371 The Carlovingien romances of the middle ages, 404–415. **Hannah Lawrance?** Here, as in no. 1961, we have survey and digest written with the same literary quality; on p. 409 is a touch-and-go reference to a term used by the *trouvères*, on whom Hannah Lawrance had written three articles.

2372 Chartley Castle and the Ferrers family: Laurence, Earl Ferrers; Whitefield; and Lady Huntingdon, 415–425. **Katherine Thomson.** Repr. *Recollections.*

2373 The symbolism of the Greeks, 426–431.

2374 Some words about music and the modern opera, 432–446.

2375 The old judge (Part X): the keeping-room of an inn; or, A chase for a wife, 447–461. **T. C. Haliburton.** Evidence for no. 2190.

2376 A group of parliamentary oddities (No. IV, concl.), 461–471. **G. H. Francis.** The "No. IV" makes the art. a sequel to nos. 2343, 2354, and 2362, which are by Francis, and though the pseudonym used for them is absent here, the method of a series of profiles is continued in the same style.

2377 The Praslin tragedy: families of Choiseul, Praslin, and Sebastiani, 472–479.

2378 Goethe and his critics, 481–493.

2379 The first of October [current politics], 494–504.

VOLUME 36, NOVEMBER 1847

2380 The Sanitary Commission, and the health of the metropolis, 505–517. **W. A. Guy.** Cited in no. 2408, p. 42; Guy wrote *The Unhealthiness of Towns*, 1845, and arts. for *FM* on sanitary questions; see evidence for no. 2368; see *DNB*.

2381 Recent poetry: lyrical and dramatic [R. C. Trench, Aubrey De Vere], 518–537. **R. A. Willmott,** prob. The style seems very like that described in the evidence for no. 1549; as in Willmott's arts., Dryden and the neo-classical poets, esp. Gray, are often cited or quoted.

2382 *Lives of Simon, Lord Lovat, and Duncan Forbes of Culloden,* 537–545.

2383 The guerilla (Part I), 546–557.

2384 Hints upon history [mainly on Nelson's *Despatches and Papers*], 558–567. **Cyrus Redding.** Claimed as in no. 2709.

2385 Tieck's *Vittoria Accorombona,* 567–575.

2386 The old judge (Part XI): a pippin; or, Sheepskins and garters, 576–587. **T. C. Haliburton.** Evidence for no. 2190.

2387 The barrack-yard [character of British officers], 588–602.

2388 Aunt Laura's room, 606–609.

2389 A chapter on the art of eating, 610–617. **A. V. Kirwan,** prob. The essay in the form of fiction, the episode dealing with the highest level of French social life, the reference to "the illustrious Carême" and other French chefs, the mixture of French with English translation, and the use of parentheses all suggest Kirwan; also a common authorship with no. 2439, where the opening of the evidence is relevant.

2390 An adventure in Wicklow, 618–623.

2391 Thoughts on Jewish disabilities, 623–630. **F. D. Maurice.** Signed. (See no. 2403.)

VOLUME 36, DECEMBER 1847

2392 Thirty-five unpublished letters of Oliver Cromwell, communicated by Thomas Carlyle, 631–654. **Thomas Carlyle.** Signature, as editor and commentator. Title. The letters turned out to be fraudulent: see C. H. Firth's intro. to *Cromwell*, ed. S. C. Lomas, 1904.

2393 Coincidences: a tale of facts, 655–664.

2394 Dialogue on English hexameters: Marcus, Ernest (Part I), 665–670. **William Whewell.** Todhunter, *Whewell*, I, 289, 290. (Part II is no. 2568.)

2395 The fortifications of Paris strategically considered, 670–677.

2396 Count Henckel Von Donnersmarck's *Reminiscences*, 677–686.

2397 Recent novels: French and English [including *Jane Eyre*], 686–695. **G. H. Lewes.** "Receipts."

2398 The old judge (Part XII, concl.): a ball at a government house, 696–710. **T. C. Haliburton.** Evidence for no. 2190.

2399 The Manchester bishoprick, 710–718.

2400 The guerilla (Part II, concl.), 719–727.

2401 Currency and banking, 728–732.

2402 Felix Mendelssohn, 732–738. Unidentified. (See no. 2444.)

2403 Jewish disabilities: a letter from A. G. Stapleton, in reply to Professor Maurice [no. 2391], 738–742. **A. G. Stapleton.** Signed.

2404 What will the government do? 743–750.

VOLUME 37, JANUARY 1848

2405 The manufacturing poor, 1–16. **Robert Lamb.** Repr. *Free Thoughts*, I, as "A Manufacturing District." (See no. 2549.)

2406 Modern condottieri, 16–30.

2407 Faust in the German puppet-show, 32–40.

2408 1774 and 1844; or, The prisoner and the labourer, 40–54. **W. A. Guy.** Described by Guy in no. 3716, pp. 487–488, as though his (see evidence for no. 2368 specifically and in general); pages 42–43 are closely followed in text of Guy's *Public Health* (1874), p. 177.

2409 A Venetian story, 54–66.

2410 Ranke's *Servia*, 67–72.

2411 The literary circles of the last century: Mrs. Montagu and her friends, 72–81. **Katherine Thomson.** Repr. *Recollections.*

2412 Our national defences, 82–88.

2413 The King of Bavaria, Munich, and Lola Montez, 89–104. **John Palgrave Simpson?** Author knows Bavaria and has visited in the house of Lola Montez (see pp. 101–102); Simpson had spent some time "at German courts—notably at Munich" and is said to have been contributing to *FM* at this time: see *DNB* and *Biograph*, 1 n.s. (1882), 399.

2414 The Hampden controversy, 105–112. Unidentified. (See pp. 359–360 for further comment.)

2415 Current history: chronicle and commentary, 113–126. (Later entries for this department omit the subtitle.)

VOLUME 37, FEBRUARY 1848

2416 The Poughkeepsie Seer [Andrew Davis] and his revelations, 127–142.

2417 The witches' stone, 143–155. **John Palgrave Simpson?** Story begins with thanks to "the writer of the *Letters from the Baltic*," who was Elizabeth Eastlake, a cousin of Simpson's to whom he had dedicated his *Letters from the Danube*, 1847; in 1844 Simpson had written a similar story called "The Witchfinder" (*Blackwood's*, no. 2383, *Index*, I); see end of evidence for no. 2413.

2418 *L'Uscoque* [by George Sand], 156–166.

2419 Some new members of the new parliament: Mr. J. Walter, Mr. Feargus O'Connor, Mr. G. Cornewall Lewis, 167–176. **G. H. Francis,** prob. Cf. nos. 2343, 2354, 2362. (Reply, p. 357, to section on the late John Walter, may well be by **R. A. Willmott**—signed A Berkshire Clergy-

man, who says he knew Walter personally and here defends him vigorously;
Willmott was appointed rector of St.
Catherine's Church, Bearwood, Berks.,
by Walter himself in 1846: see *DNB*.)

2420 Sweden and Oscar I, 178–187.

2421 Life and remains of John Sterling [*Essays and Tales*, ed. J. C. Hare], 187–200.
R. A. Willmott. The style fulfils much of
the description in the evidence for no.
1549; the writer's disapproval of Sterling's non-Christian development would
be Willmott's; the quotation from Foster
on Coleridge commanding words like a
magician, p. 189, is also in no. 2219,
p. 145; the remark on Cambridge studies,
p. 188, is the central theme of no. 2135;
the references to seventeenth-century
divines, pp. 192, 195, reflect Willmott's
taste.

2422 Chronique de Paris (No. II): Madame
Adelaide—Louis Philippe, 201–208. **A.
V. Kirwan.** See evidence for no. 2799;
five comments on Louis Philippe, pp.
205–207, appear in *Brit. Quart. Rev.* of
the same month (vol. 7, p. 147, to be
assigned to Kirwan in *Index*, IV), the
first three almost verbatim.

2423 Alexander Von Humboldt's *Kosmos*,
208–222.

2424 The guerilla (Part III), 224–231.

2425 Current history, 234–244.

VOLUME 37, MARCH 1848

2426 The state of morals and education in
Wales, 245–256.

2427 Church Lane, St. Giles', 257–260.
W. A. Guy. Guy was on the committee
whose report is here reviewed (p. 257n.),
and author speaks as if from experience;
concern with amount of air in rooms, pp.
258–259, appears in nos. 2368, p. 375,
3335, p. 403, and 3716, p. 493; as in no.
2368, lament for defeat of Lord Morpeth's bill on sanitary reform in last
session; the statistics, p. 258, are characteristic (see *DNB*).

2428 Childhood and its reminiscences, 261–
272.

2429 Romance of Portuguese revolution,
272–285.

2430 A plea for physicians, 286–294.

2431 *Evangeline, A Tale of Acadie* [by
Longfellow], 295–298. **William Whewell.**
Attr. Todhunter, *Whewell*, I, 290–291.

2432 Mr. Sewell and the College of St.
Columba, 299–311.

2433 The armourer of Munster: a page from

the history of fanaticism (chaps. i–vi),
312–327. **Robert Bell,** 1800–1867. Novelette repr. in *Hearts and Altars* (1852),
II, 131—III, 100.

2434 Kingsley's *Saints' Tragedy*, 328–337.
John Conington, prob. After seeing a
letter of Conington's, containing praise
and criticism of his play, Kingsley wrote
him, Jan. 15, 1848, protesting against
the charge of condemning political economy in act. ii, scene 9, and defending
the anachronism of discussing the subject
in a medieval story by claiming he had
followed "the Shakespearian method of
bringing the past up to my readers, and
not the modern one of bringing my
readers down to the past" (*Letters*, I,
152–153); that this *FM* art. is Conington's review is strongly suggested on p.
331 by what is apparently an answer to
Kingsley's objections: criticizing the introduction of political economy in act
ii, scene 9—but omitting any claim that
Kingsley condemned the science—the
author writes: "It may be urged in reply,
that Shakespeare has frequently indulged
in . . . anachronisms, choosing rather to
raise the past to his own age than to
lower that to the past," and proceeds to
a counter argument; and the last part of
the review is full of praise; Conington
was a contributor to *FM*.

2435 Prospects of the opera, 337–342. **Edward Holmes,** prob. Cf. no. 2490.

2436 *The Bushman* [in Western Australia],
343–356.

2437 Current history, 358–370.

VOLUME 37, APRIL 1848

2438 The French Revolution of 1848—its
causes and consequences, 371–387.

2439 The reveries of a gastronome, 388–
395. **A. V. Kirwan.** Kirwan had written
"Classics of the Table" for *FM* (no. 1942,
etc.); on p. 388 is a personal reference
to entering the Café de Paris in 1833,
and Kirwan was an "habitué" of that café
for many years, starting in the 1820's
(see no. 4023, p. 399); on p. 389 author
discusses Spanish character as well as
food (cf. letter in evidence for no. 2307);
for the last pages on travel and eating
in Constantinople and the Near East, one
should recall that Kirwan (*FM* no. 4036,
pp. 575, 590) said he had "visited the
filthiest towns in Europe and Africa" and
been "in many lands, European and
Eastern," and that his major travelling

was done in the 1820's (ibid., pp. 575, 589, and no. 4068, p. 184); the use of untranslated sentences of French is frequent in Kirwan's work.

2440 The plague of beggars, 395–402. **W. A. Guy.** Attr. by J. W. Parker, Jr., the editor, in Jan. 1849 (no. 2535, p. 3), to the "same pen" that has been writing other papers for *FM* on "social questions," meaning since July 1847 when his editorship began; this must refer to nos. 2368, 2380, 2408, 2427, 2510, all of which are by Guy; also attr. in *Biograph*, 6 (1881), 335; the reprs. of the art., 1848 and 1868, were signed "By a London Physician," which the *BMCat.* decided was James Howard, but the same pseudonym was used by Guy (see H&L, IV, 430); besides, the notions about indiscriminate almsgiving, preventive rather than palliative charity, on fining donors and flogging beggars, as well as the anti-Irish prejudice are found in other papers by Guy; the reference, p. 401, is to an art. by Guy (no. 2427), a common practice of his.

2441 *Letters from the Danube* [art. is on Hungary], 403–411.

2442 On the social position of governesses, 411–414. **Sarah Lewis.** Signed The Author of *Woman's Mission*—see H&L, IX, 371.

2443 Railway prospects of India, 414–425.

2444 Recollections of Felix Mendelssohn [partly in reply to no. 2402], 426–428. **Sarah Austin.** Signed at start Mrs. Austin, at end S.A.

2445 Campbell's *Lives of the Lord Chancellors*, 429–440.

2446 The armourer of Munster (chaps. vii–xiii), 441–455. **Robert Bell,** 1800–1867. Cf. no. 2433.

2447 Signs of the times; by a rambler on the French coast, 457–466. **F. O. Ward.** Signed.

2448 Why should we fear the Romish priests? 467–474. **Charles Kingsley.** Thorp, *Kingsley*, pp. 50–51; attr. in Coleridge, *Life*, I, 216.

2449 Current history, 474–488.

VOLUME 37, MAY 1848

2450 Recent discoveries in astronomy, 489–509. Unidentified. Possibly Charles Richard Weld who wrote no. 2792, which also discusses the Herschels and the character of nebulae.

2451 A charming Frenchwoman [Mme. de Staël], 509–518. **G. H. Lewes.** "Receipts."

2452 Landor's *Hellenics* and Latin poems, 519–525.

2453 A campaign in Algiers, 525–539.

2454 Hospital nurses as they are and as they ought to be, 539–542.

2455 Heligoland, 543–549.

2456 The armourer of Munster (chaps. xiv–xx), 549–565. **Robert Bell,** 1800–1867. Cf. no. 2433.

2457 Australian colonies or republics? 566–578.

2458 Chartism, 579–592.

2459 Whig professions, and Whig performance (No. I), 593–608. **John A. Roebuck.** J. G. Lockhart to J. W. Croker, May 31 [1848], *N&Q*, 187 (Oct. 21, 1944), 187n.

2460 Current history, 608–614.

VOLUME 37, JUNE 1848

2461 France: her revolutions, her republics, her national assemblies, her parties, and present prospects, 615–629. **A. V. Kirwan.** The extensive similarities of thought and phrasing on pp. 616, 618–620, with the *Brit. Quart. Rev.*, 7 (May 1848), 497–498, 500–502, [an art. to be identified as Kirwan's in *Index*, IV], leave no doubt of a common authorship—the more so because the *BQR* art., appearing in May, was too late to be used in the June issue of *FM* by anyone except the author.

2462 Morven: a manuscript, 631–645. Signed: E.H.S.

2463 Quackery and the quacked [in medicine], 645–657.

2464 The last struggle of Abd el Kader; a glance at French policy in the Levant, 658–665.

2465 *Memoirs of the Reign of George the Second*, 665–683.

2466 The armourer of Munster (chaps. xxi–xxxii, concl.), 684–700. **Robert Bell,** 1800–1867. Cf. no. 2433.

2467 The Secret Committee on Military Expenditure, 701–711.

2468 Whig professions, and Whig performance (No. II, concl.), 711–723. **John A. Roebuck.** Cf. no. 2459.

2469 Current history, 724–734.

VOLUME 38, JULY 1848

2470 Spanish affairs, 1–14. **A. V. Kirwan?** Cf. letter quoted in no. 2227; on p. 10 author speaks of having travelled in the

north of Spain among gallant moun-
taineers (Kirwan spent the summer of
1825 or 1826 in the Pyrenees—see no.
4036, p. 575); the defence of Palmerston, p. 12, might be expected from
Kirwan.

2471 Hyas the Athenian, 16–31. **Dinah
Mulock.** Repr. *Romantic Tales*, 1859, as
"The Story of Hyas."

2472 Recent novels, 33–40.

2473 The state of the acted drama, 41–48.

2474 Denmark and the duchies of Holstein
and Schleswig, 49–58.

2475 The autobiography of a young French
widow (Part I), 59–71. Part II (no.
2484) is signed: Nina.

2476 The naturalist in Norway (Part I):
trout and their haunts, 71–79.

2477 Confessions of a nervous soldier; or,
The adventures of a night in County
Clare, 79–90. **R. H. Horne.** *Bibliography*,
p. 5.

2478 Sketches of the Mexican War, 91–102.

2479 Yeast; or, The thoughts, sayings, and
doings of Lancelot Smith, Gentleman
(chaps. i–ii), 102–115. **Charles Kingsley.**
Novel published 1851.

2480 Current history, 116–126.

VOLUME 38, AUGUST 1848

2481 Weld's *History of the Royal Society*,
127–135.

2482 Republican literature [in France], 136–
149. **A. V. Kirwan.** Cf. general evidence
for no. 2307; pp. 140–146 deal with
Spanish affairs, cf. no. 2470, and with
an art. in *Heraldo*; the defence, p. 136,
of "anecdotes, light sketches, casual observations" as sometimes having great
historical value would be Kirwan's view;
the language on pp. 144, 145, and 149,
is abrasive.

2483 Religious stories [including Newman's
Loss and Gain], 150–166.

2484 The autobiography of a young French
widow (Part II, concl.), 169–179. Signed:
Nina.

2485 The naturalist in Norway (Part II):
Char and their haunts, 180–187.

2486 Leaves from the life of a princess,
187–193.

2487 Yeast (chaps. iii–iv), 195–210. **Charles
Kingsley.** Cf. no. 2479.

2488 The army and the people (Part I),
211–219.

2489 Loch Vennachar: an idyllic reminiscence of the Highlands, 219–225.

2490 The lyric drama in 1848 [opera], 225–

232. Edward Holmes. In applying to
R.L.F., Oct. 30, 1848, he says he has
written on modern opera for *FM*.

2491 Current history, 233–244.

VOLUME 38, SEPTEMBER 1848

2492 Mill's *Political Economy*, 245–260.

2493 Arthur de Boisfleury; a chronicle of
1407, 261–274.

2494 An account of the first steam voyage
on the British seas; performed by the
Thames steam-packet, from Glasgow to
London, in the year 1815, 275–283.

2495 Yeast (chaps. v–vi), 284–300. **Charles
Kingsley.** Cf. no. 2479.

2496 *Annals of the Artists of Spain* [by
Stirling-Maxwell], 300–308.

2497 The naturalist in Norway (Part III,
concl.), 311–319.

2498 *Vanity Fair* [by Thackeray], 320–333.
Robert Bell, 1800–1867. Thackeray, *Letters*, II, 423.

2499 Modern Frankfort, 334–344. **Elizabeth
Rigby Eastlake.** Claimed in *Correspondence*, I, 216.

2500 The legends of Ulster: the unlucky
birthright, 344–351. **Frances Brown,**
prob. A series in *Tait's Edinburgh Mag.*,
signed by woman cited and called "The
Legends of Ulster," begins in June, 1849;
this story appearing in Sept. 1848 looks
like the first of the series.

2501 Current history, 352–362.

VOLUME 38, OCTOBER 1848

2502 *The Convent Witch* [by J. W. Mein-
hold], 363–378. **J. W. Meinhold.** A précis
of the story. Intro. and concluding notes
by an unknown translator-editor.

2503 Major-General Sir John Hunter Littler,
K.C.B., 379–391.

2504 Animal legends, 392–394. Compiler
unidentified. Footnote attribs. much of
the material to the German collectors
"Bechstein and Nork"—viz. Ludwig
Bechstein and either Friedrich or Selig
Korn [who are given as the real names
of "F. Nork" in *ADB*].

2505 The inundation of Pest (chaps. i–ii),
395–410.

2506 Publishers and authors, 411–420.
Katherine Thomson. Repr. *Recollections*.

2507 Hector Berlioz, 421–427. **Edward
Holmes,** prob. Attr. by A. W. Ganz,
Berlioz in London (1950), p. 74.

2508 *Harold*, and *Amymone* [by Bulwer-

Lytton, and by Eliza Lynn Linton], 429–433. **W. S. Landor.** E. Lynn Linton, "A Protest," *Athenaeum*, Aug. 31, 1881, p. 208; R. H. Super, *Walter Savage Landor*, (N.Y., 1954), pp. 373, 586, n.33.

2509 United States' aggrandisements and projects on the side of Mexico, 434–443.

2510 The Public Health Bill: its letter and its spirit, 444–446. **W. A. Guy.** Since Guy had lamented the defeat of Lord M's first Bill in the previous session (see no. 2368), it would be natural for him to review his second and successful Bill; like Guy in no. 2368, pp. 371–372 and 376–378, the reviewer praises the Bill for combining centralization and local boards and hails its clause blocking the opposition of local authorities; high praise of Edwin Chadwick with special regard to his role in the Sanitary Commission, p. 445, which author says he has stated before: see no. 2380, p. 505, which is by Guy.

2511 Yeast (chaps. viii–ix), 447–460. **Charles Kingsley.** Cf. no. 2479.

2512 Report of the Committee on the French Insurrection of June, 461–470. **J. M. Ludlow.** Ludlow's list.

2513 Current history, 471–480.

VOLUME 38, NOVEMBER 1848

2514 Views of Edinburgh, 481–494.

2515 Keats and his school [on *Life and Letters of Keats*, ed. Monckton Milnes], 495–502.

2516 The inundation of Pest (chaps. iii–iv), 503–515.

2517 *The Aristocracy of England*, 516–527.

2518 Yeast (chaps. x–xi), 530–547. **Charles Kingsley.** Cf. no. 2479.

2519 The present condition of the British navy, 548–563.

2520 General Cavaignac and his father [Jean Baptiste Cavaignac], 563–573.

2521 *The Fairfax Correspondence*, 573–582.

2522 The Universities [Oxford and Cambridge], 583–590.

2523 Current history, 592–602.

VOLUME 38, DECEMBER 1848

2524 The Arctic expeditions, 603–615. **C. R. Weld.** In his *Arctic Expeditions*, 1850, Weld drew heavily on this art.; one passage, pp. 25–26, repeats a passage here on p. 605, verbatim.

2525 *Memoirs and Correspondence of Vis-count Castlereagh, second Marquess of Londonderry*, 615–628.

2526 Fuss in a book-club; as related by a copy of Miss Martineau's *Eastern Life*, etc., etc., 628–634.

2527 The army and the people (No. II), 635–641.

2528 The inundation of Pest (chaps. v–vi, concl.), 642–653.

2529 Life and works of Leopardi, 659–669. **G. H. Lewes.** "Receipts."

2530 Christmas festivities in Russia, 670–677.

2531 The Austro-Italian question, 677–685. Unidentified. (See no. 2556.)

2532 The Thames: its uses and abuses [water pollution], 685–688.

2533 Yeast (chaps. xii–xiv, concl.), 689–711. **Charles Kingsley.** Cf. no. 2479.

2534 Current history, 713–722.

VOLUME 39, JANUARY 1849

2535 A happy New Year, 1–3. **John W. Parker,** 1820–1860. The art. is an editorial.

2536 Macaulay's *History of England*, 4–16.

2537 Memoir of a song, 17–28.

2538 Loose leaves from the note-book of a schemer (Part I), 28–35.

2539 *Die Royalisten*, 35–43. The art. is largely a digest of this novel by P. A. von Ungern-Sternberg.

2540 Snow pictures [travels in Canada], 45–58. **E. B. Hamley.** Signed Lieutenant Michael South; attr. in Shand, *Hamley*, I, 36.

2541 London from the crow's nest, 58–64. **Cyrus Redding.** Signed: Nerke; claimed as in no. 2709.

2542 The Swedenborgians, 64–78. **J. A. Froude.** *Life*, I, 128; Froude list.

2543 New Zealand and its recent progress under Governor Grey, 79–89.

2544 The national debt and colonization, 90–92. Signed (in intro. letter sent from Mauritius): R.A. and A Staff Officer.

2545 The self-seer (chaps. i–iii), 92–103. **Dinah Mulock.** Repr. *Romantic Tales*, 1859 and *Avillion*, 1855.

2546 *The Bothie of Toper-na-Fuosich* [by Clough], 103–110. **Charles Kingsley.** Attr. in John Conington to Kingsley, Jan. 13, 1849, Parrish Collect., Princeton Univ. Lib.; and in Clough, *Correspondence*, I, 240.

2547 The tale of an Arab story-teller, 112–117.

2548 Current history, 119–126.

VOLUME 39, FEBRUARY 1849

2549 The manufacturing poor [sequel to no. 2405]: the means of elevating their moral condition—education, 127–143. **Robert Lamb.** Repr. *Free Thoughts*, I, as "Our Manufacturing Populations."

2550 The Jesuits and their historian, Andrew Steinmetz, 143–155.

2551 The golden peninsula; a vision, 155–158.

2552 The self-seer (chaps. iv–vii), 159–170. **Dinah Mulock.** Cf. no. 2545.

2553 Loose leaves from the note-book of a schemer (Part II), 179–188.

2554 A modern Republican tragedy [*Catalina* by Alexandre Dumas], 188–196.

2555 Sacred and profane, 197–201. **John Conington.** Claimed in Conington to Kingsley, Jan. 13, 1849, Parrish Collect., Princeton.

2556 The Austro-Italian question [sequel to no. 2531], 201–212.

2557 Lamartine's *Raphael*, 212–220. **A. V. Kirwan.** In general cf. the evidence for no. 2307; on p. 212 the reference to no. 2357 suggests a common authorship, especially since both arts. are on Lamartine; on p. 218, in a personal allusion, the author speaks of mixing in Parisian society "in our youth" 20 or 22 years ago—viz. in 1827–1829, when Kirwan, aged 23–25, was in Paris three times a year (cf. no. 4023, p. 399).

2558 The late Mr. Charles Buller, 221–224. **Sarah Austin.** Signed S.A.; attrib. in *DNB* under Buller.

2559 The Conservative party, 224–236.

2560 Current history, 237–244.

VOLUME 39, MARCH 1849

2561 Wakefield's *View of the Art of Colonization*, 245–258.

2562 L'Enlumineuse; or, The three flower-markets of Paris, 259–277. Signed: Selina.

2563 The poetry of sacred and legendary art, 283–298. **Charles Kingsley.** Repr. *Works*, XX.

2564 The army and the people (Part III, concl.), 298–307.

2565 The self-seer (chaps. viii–x, with concl.), 308–319. **Dinah Mulock.** Cf. no. 2545.

2566 Catullus, 320–331.

2567 Madame de Maintenon, 331–341.

2568 Dialogues on English hexameters (Part II, concl.): [on Clough's *Bothie*], 342–

347. **William Whewell.** Attr. in Todhunter, *Whewell*, I, 292.

2569 Vienna during the siege and after it; rough sketches of rough scenes (chaps. i–ii), 347–354.

2570 Vestigia veri (Part I, no more published): evolution and revolution, 355–357. **F. O. Ward.** Signed.

2571 Current history, 358–362.

VOLUME 39, APRIL 1849

2572 The peace campaigns of Ensign Faunce (Part I), 363–377. **E. B. Hamley.** Signed Michael South; attr. in Shand, *Hamley*, I, 36.

2573 *The Poetry of Science*, 378–382.

2574 Joseph de Maistre, 383–396. **William Maccall.** Repr. *Foreign Biographies* (1873), I; see Carlyle, *Memoirs*, II, 25.

2575 Letter of advice from an experienced matron to a young married lady, 397–405.

2576 Recent novels [including Mrs. Gaskell's *Mary Barton*], 417–432. **Charles Kingsley.** Thorp, *Kingsley*, bibliography.

2577 An episode in the history of the Eddystone Lighthouse, 432–445. Signed, p. 445n.: W.S.W., who professes to be only the editor of the MS., which was written, he says, by a pauper named Richard Smith.

2578 Layard's *Nineveh*, 446–454.

2579 Vienna during the siege and after it (chaps. iii–v, concl.), 457–465.

2580 Six and four, 465–470.

2581 Insolvent members of parliament, 471–481.

2582 Current history, 482–488.

VOLUME 39, MAY 1849

2583 *Lays of the Scottish Cavaliers* [by W. E. Aytoun], 489–498.

2584 The peace campaigns of Ensign Faunce (Part II), 499–516. **E. B. Hamley.** Evidence for no. 2572.

2585 Loose leaves from the note-book of a schemer (Part III, concl.), 517–527.

2586 *Sacred Latin Poetry* [by R. C. Trench], 527–532. **William Whewell.** Todhunter, *Whewell*, I, 172.

2587 Matrimony (Part I), 533–544.

2588 Froude's *Nemesis of Faith*, 545–560. **J. M. Ludlow.** C. B. Mansfield to Ludlow, May 19, 1849, Univ. Lib. Camb., compliments him on his review of *Nemesis* in *Fraser*; confirmed in J. F. Maurice, *Life of F. D. Maurice* (1884), I, 539.

2589   Indian meal, 561–563. **Thomas Carlyle.** Signed C; claimed in Carlyle to Emerson, Apr. 19, 1849, *Correspondence of Emerson and Carlyle*, ed. Joseph Slater (1964), pp. 451–452.

2590   The two operas [Her Majesty's Theatre and the Royal Italian Opera], 563–569. **Edward Holmes,** prob. Cf. p. 569 on Lind with no. 2435, p. 339.

2591   Recent poetry, and recent verse [including *The Strayed Reveller* by Arnold], 570–586. **Charles Kingsley.** Attr. by Thorp, *Kingsley*, bibliog.; in letter to Arnold, Dec. 3, 1853 (quoted in R. B. Martin, *The Dust of Combat* [1959], p. 160), Kingsley admits he had criticized Arnold's poetry earlier in *FM*; this is the only review of Arnold before that date.

2592   Military policy—the late reductions, 586–598.

2593   Current history, 600–605.

VOLUME 39, JUNE 1849

2594   Railways (Part I), 607–618. **Edmund Beckett Denison?** Author has great knowledge of railway laws and uses legal terms such as *locus standi* and *pretium affectionis* (p. 616); Denison was a lawyer, who about this time had "acquired a large practice, chiefly in connection with railway bills"—see *DNB*; he wrote no. 2686 for *FM* a few months later and was asked by Parker to contribute to his *Bookselling Question*, 1852.

2595   The Macedonian and the English campaigns in the Punjaub, 618–624. Unidentified. Possibly by J. W. Kaye who briefly compared the two campaigns in the *North Brit. Rev.*, 12 (Nov. 1849), 194: cf. that page with this art., p. 621; the view of Lord Gough, pp. 623–624, is similar to that in another of Kaye's arts. on the wars against the Sikhs, ibid., 11 (Aug. 1849), 657–660. (For Kaye's authorship of the *NBR* papers, see "Additions . . . to Vol. I.")

2596   Roebuck on the colonies, 624–638.

2597   The unseen charities of London, 639–647.

2598   Matrimony (Part II), 648–660.

2599   The coincidence of form [in natural objects], 660–670.

2600   The peace campaigns of Ensign Faunce (Part III), 671–686. **E. B. Hamley.** Evidence for no. 2572.

2601   The Hungarian question, 687–701.

2602   Diplomacy in the last century [R. M. Keith's *Memoirs*], 701–712.

2603   The Anthesphoria at Athens, 713–721.

2604   Current history, 722–726.

VOLUME 40, JULY 1849

2605   North Devon (Part I), 1–14. **Charles Kingsley.** Repr. *Miscellanies*, II.

2606   The peace campaigns of Ensign Faunce (Part IV), 15–32. **E. B. Hamley.** Evidence for no. 2572.

2607   A chapter on balloons, 33–42.

2608   A fire in the backwoods, 42–52.

2609   The adventures of Prince Rupert, 52–62.

2610   Matrimony (Part III, concl.), 63–72.

2611   The Fine Arts' Exhibitions of 1849, 73–81.

2612   Tacitus the historian, 86–95.

2613   Queen's College, London, 96–106. Unidentified. (Note, p. 244.)

2614   Railways (Part II, concl.), 106–120. **Edmund Beckett Denison?** Cf. no. 2594.

2615   Current history, 121–126.

VOLUME 40, AUGUST 1849

2616   Wanderings through the conservatories at Kew, 127–135. **Philip H. Gosse.** Passages on pp. 126 and 128 reappear, either verbatim or slightly reworded, in Gosse's *Wanderings at Kew* (1857), pp. 19 and 40–44; the verse on p. 132 is printed in the book, p. 130; the art. is simply a brief, popular account of what was handled at greater length for semi-specialists in the volume which shortened the title.

2617   Our new curate, 136–147.

2618   [Holden's edition of] Aristophanes, 147–158.

2619   *Of Music in Italy* [by Berlioz], and other matters, 159–171. **P. W. Banks.** Signed Morgan Rattler—see no. 178.

2620   On Mr. Macaulay's praise of superficial knowledge, 171–175. **William Whewell.** Attr. in Todhunter, *Whewell*, I, 172.

2621   Outlines from Calderon, 175–187.

2622   Sketches in blue water: the funeral at sea; a sketch from memory, 188–191.

2623   The peace campaigns of Ensign Faunce (Part V), 194–206. **E. B. Hamley.** Evidence for no. 2572.

2624   Ulrich von Hutten and his times, 207–218.

2667 *Friends in Council* [by Arthur Helps], 636–644.

2668 Fanny Graham's dreams (Part III, concl.), 645–652.

2669 North Devon (Part II), 652–663. **Charles Kingsley.** Cf. no. 2605.

2670 M. Thiers and Trafalgar (Part II, concl.), 663–669.

2671 Occasional discourse on the Negro question, 670–679. **Thomas Carlyle.** Repr. *Essays*, IV. (See no. 2677.)

2672 The peace campaigns of Ensign Faunce (Part IX, chaps. xxxviii–xli), 679–691. **E. B. Hamley.** Evidence for no. 2572.

2673 New novels [including Charlotte Brontë's *Shirley*], 691–702. **W. G. Clark,** prob. In Hort, *Life and Letters*, I, 147, "Clark" is said to have reviewed *Shirley* in *FM*; presumably he wrote the whole art.; W. G. Clark was Hort's tutor; *DNB* reports he was frequent contributor to *FM.*

2674 Cholera gossip, 702–711. **W. A. Guy.** This art. is written by a medical statistician and a sanitary reformer (see pp. 702–704, 705, and cf. *DNB*); on p. 707 author tells reader to look at no. 2427 for picture of London slums; Guy often refers back to his own arts.; see evidence for no. 3716.

VOLUME 41, JANUARY 1850

2675 "Labour and the poor," 1–18. **J. M. Ludlow.** Signed J.T.; Ludlow's list; Kingsley, *Letters*, I, 221–222; initials attrib. in C. E. Raven, *Christian Socialism* (1920), pp. 110, 154.

2676 The Micmac's bride [a tale of New Brunswick; see nos. 2694, 2706] (Part I), 19–25.

2677 The Negro question, 25–31. **John Stuart Mill.** Signed D.; Mill, *Bibliography*, 72.

2678 Göthe's *Herman and Dorothea*, 33–40. **William Whewell.** Attr. in Todhunter, *Whewell*, I, 293.

2679 The bright room of Cranmore, 41–49.

2680 Leaves from a naturalist's note-book (Part I), 50–52. **William J. Broderip.** Series repr. *Leaves from the Notebook of a Naturalist*, 1852.

2681 The Dom of Dantzic; founded on fact (Part I), 53–68.

2682 The stage and its prospects, 69–75.

2683 The peace campaigns of Ensign Faunce (Part X), 76–89. **E. B. Hamley.** Evidence for no. 2572.

2684 Bülow-Cummerow on the German question, 90–97.

2685 Sir E. B. Lytton and Mrs. Grundy [review of *The Caxtons*], 98–111. **Charles Kingsley.** Thorp, *Kingsley*, bibliography; A. F. Hort, *Life and Letters*, I, 126.

2686 Marriage with a wife's sister [partly on books by Pusey and Keble], 112–134. **Edmund Beckett Denison.** Repr., enlarged as a pamphlet, 1851: see *BMCat.*

VOLUME 41, FEBRUARY 1850

2687 The state and prospects of the country, 135–151.

2688 *The Lamps of Architecture* [by Ruskin], 151–159. **William Whewell.** Attr. in Todhunter, *Whewell*, I, 173.

2689 Leaves from the note-book of a naturalist (Part II), 160–165. **W. J. Broderip.** Cf. no. 2680.

2690 North Devon (Part III, concl.): Clovelly, 167–177. **Charles Kingsley.** Cf. no. 2605.

2691 The Dom of Dantzic (Part II, concl.), 177–190.

2692 The drainage of the metropolis, 190–199.

2693 Southey's *Life and Correspondence*, 200–217. **R. A. Willmott.** The style seems unmistakable (see description in evidence for no. 1549); he wrote no. 1959 on Southey and prob. no. 2042, pp. 308–310, on Southey's prose; the men quoted are the familiar names in most of Willmott's essays: Dryden, Milton, Pope, Thomson, Young, Johnson, Crabbe, Cowper, and Coleridge.

2694 The Micmac's bride: a tale of New Brunswick (Part II), 217–223.

2695 The post-office, 224–232. **Andrew Wynter.** Repr. *Social Bees.*

2696 Linné, the woodland flower, 233–236.

2697 Touching opinion and evidence [on *An Essay on the Influence of Authority in Matters of Opinion* by G. C. Lewis], 237–249. **P. W. Banks.** Signed Morgan Rattler—see no. 178.

2698 Ireland, 250–260.

VOLUME 41, MARCH 1850

2699 Sketches of American society (No. I): the upper ten thousand, 261–271. **Charles Astor Bristed.** Signed A New Yorker; series repr. *Upper Ten Thousand: Sketches of American Society*, 1852, under pseud. Frank Manhattan; book attr. in *BMCat.*

2700 Letters from General Conway and the Countess of Ailesbury to Horace Walpole, Earl of Orford, from the originals formerly in the possession of the late Right Hon. Sir Alexander Johnston (Part I), 272–283. **Henry Seymour Conway** and **Caroline Campbell Conway.** Title and *DNB*.

2701 Leaves from the note-book of a naturalist (Part III), 283–291. **W. J. Broderip.** Cf. no. 2680.

2702 A ride in a hurricane through the sugar-canes; fragment from the unpublished memoirs of Reginald Hardy, Esq., late a West India planter, etc., etc., 292–294. **Reginald Hardy.** Title. Since no trace of Hardy has been found, this may be a pseudonym.

2703 Hints from Hygea, 295–306. **C. B. Mansfield.** Signed Ithi Kefalende; claimed in Mansfield to J. M. Ludlow, Jan. 1850, Univ. Lib. Camb.

2704 Gertrude Bohun, 307–321.

2705 The works of Beaumont and Fletcher, 321–332. **William B. Donne.** Repr. *Essays.*

2706 The Micmac's bride: a tale of New Brunswick (Part III, concl.), 333–339.

2707 Monsieur Guizot and the English revolution, 340–347.

2708 The peace campaigns of Ensign Faunce (Part XI), 347–359. **E. B. Hamley.** Evidence for no. 2572.

2709 Words about Oxford, 360–366. **Cyrus Redding.** Signed Zeta; claimed in his application to R.L.F., May 5, 1862; repr. erroneously in Everyman Library ed. of J.A. Froude's *Essays in Literature and History*, 1906.

2710 Colonial reform, 366–378.

VOLUME 41, APRIL 1850

2711 Spanish literature, 381–398.

2712 Operatic and other musical matters, 398–405. **Edward Holmes?** See ref. to "our last notice of music," no. 2770, p. 335; cf. praise of Berlioz, pp. 401–402, with no. 2507.

2713 Thomas Carlyle [in *Latter-Day Pamphlets*] and John Howard, 406–410. **W. A. Guy.** It would be as natural for Guy to sympathize with Carlyle's anti-philanthropy as to attack his disparagement of Howard; the main points he had already made on Howard in no. 2368, pp. 374–375, and no. 2408, pp. 42–43, reappear here on pp. 407, 408, 409; and Guy later wrote a book on Howard.

2714 Leaves from the note-book of a naturalist (Part IV), 411–423. **W. J. Broderip.** Cf. no. 2680.

2715 Letters from General Conway and the Countess of Ailesbury to Horace Walpole (Part II), 423–434. **H. S. Conway.** Despite the title, all letters are initialed H.S.C.; cf. no. 2700.

2716 Hilda D'Ehrenburg, 435–442. Signed: Eli Blackgown, D.D.

2717 A batch of biographies, 443–459.

2718 The peace campaigns of Ensign Faunce (Part XII, concl.), 460–477. **E. B. Hamley.** Evidence for no. 2572.

2719 Hungarian books, 477–485.

2720 Poor-laws in Ireland, 487–498.

VOLUME 41, MAY 1850

2721 A Study of Shakespeare in *The Merchant of Venice* (Part I), 499–512. **George Fletcher.** Signed.

2722 Queen's College and the *Quarterly*: a review reviewed [*Quart.Rev.*, 86 (Mar. 1850)], 513–522. **J. M. Ludlow.** Signed J.T.—see no. 2675; Ludlow's list.

2723 Sketches of American society (No. II): a wedding "above Bleecker," 523–528. **C. A. Bristed.** Evidence for no. 2699.

2724 *The Fables of Babrius* [ed. G. C. Lewis], 529–538.

2725 The story of The Requiem [by Mozart], 539–550.

2726 Leaves from the note-book of a naturalist (Part V), 551–564. **W. J. Broderip.** Cf. no. 2680.

2727 *The United States of America* [by Sir Charles Lyell], 564–578. **F. B. Zincke.** Claimed in *Days of my Years* (1891), p. 113.

2728 Of the English Bar, 578–588. **A. V. Kirwan.** This essay, by a lawyer, is an attack on the profession, claiming that the prize of battle is not to the strong or swift but to the cunning and political, and that those who "have struggled well and earnestly have yet failed," p. 579; it ends, p. 588, "We are tired . . . of the whole . . . legal tribe, and shall now take our leave of them" with a satiric poem by Baron Dawson; Kirwan retired from legal practice in 1850 when he was only 46, so that the art. looks like his apologia; moreover, both the author, p. 583, and Kirwan (no. 4270, p. 571) heard and admired the lectures of Dr. Macartney, Professor of Anatomy and Physiology at the University of Dublin, 1817–1831; Kirwan wrote on both lawyers and physicians.

2729 The legend of Pourpagne, 588–600.

2730 The good dame Bertha, 601–604.

2731 Diplomacy, diplomatists, and diplomatic servants of England: economical and organic reform of the system (Part I), 605–616.

VOLUME 41, JUNE 1850

2732 University reform (No. I): Cambridge, 617–629.

2733 Letters from General Conway to Horace Walpole (Part III), 631–640. **H. S. Conway.** Title; cf. no. 2700.

2734 Readables and unreadables [review of current poetry], 640–653. **Charles Kingsley.** Thorp, *Kingsley*, bibliography.

2735 Leaves from the note-book of a naturalist (Part VI), 654–666. **W. J. Broderip.** Cf. no. 2680.

2736 Diplomacy, diplomatists, and diplomatic servants of England (Part II, concl.), 666–676.

2737 *Lives of the Chief Justices* [by Lord Campbell], 677–689.

2738 Something about a murder; founded on fact, 690–696.

2739 A study of Shakespeare in *The Merchant of Venice* (Part II, concl.), 697–712. **George Fletcher.** Signed.

2740 Traits of an old soldier [Count Suwarrow], 713–720.

2741 Ireland's sins and Ireland's hopes: a letter to an Irish Member of Parliament, 721–736. **Aubrey De Vere.** Signed An Irishman; DeVere's list.

VOLUME 42, JULY 1850

2742 The English in the nineteenth century, 1–9.

2743 American poetry [R. W. Griswold, Bryant, Halleck, Longfellow, Whittier, Poe], 9–25. **C. A. Bristed.** Repr. in part, *Pieces*, III.

2744 Leaves from the note-book of a naturalist (Part VII), 25–38. **W. J. Broderip.** Cf. no. 2680.

2745 *"The Tempest"* as a Lyrical Drama [i.e., as an opera], 38–43.

2746 Recent travellers, 44–62.

2747 The woods and forests, 63–73.

2748 Ledru Rollin's *Decline of England*, 74–85. **A. V. Kirwan.** On p. 76 the description of *La Réforme*, the French radical newspaper, is simply a rewriting, in good part verbatim, of a page in Kirwan's art. *Brit. Quart. Rev.*, 3 (May 1846), 513—an art. repr. in his *Modern France*; the extensive knowledge of English law, pp. 80–83, would be expected of Kirwan, as would his hostility to Rollin's politics.

2749 University reform (No. II, concl.): Oxford, 86–95.

2750 The heirs of Gauntry; a tale (chap. i), 95–106.

2751 The island of Cuba, 107–118.

VOLUME 42, AUGUST 1850

2752 Wordsworth's posthumous poem [*The Prelude*], 119–132.

2753 A chapter on our political relations with St. Domingo, 133–136.

2754 Touching fly-fishing, 136–148. **P. W. Banks.** Signed Morgan Rattler—see no. 178.

2755 Madame de Pompadour, 149–164.

2756 Strictures on a pair of public structures [Houses of Parliament and British Museum], 165–175. **W. H. Leeds,** prob. See Part B for a long list of his architectural arts. in *FM*; the high respect for Greek style, p. 171, is characteristic; climate and architecture, p. 167, are discussed in nos. 8 and 17; the combination of foreign phrases, French and Latin, with raffish or violent language is typical of Leeds' style.

2757 The heirs of Gauntry (chaps. ii–iii), 175–187.

2758 Leaves from the note-book of a naturalist (Part VIII), 187–202. **W. J. Broderip.** Cf. no. 2680.

2759 Fruits of the season [recent novels], 203–214.

2760 A gossip about the Lakes, 214–221. **Andrew Wynter.** Repr. *Social Bees.*

2761 The late Sir Robert Peel, 223–236. **G. H. Francis.** Repr. under his name, 1852.

VOLUME 42, SEPTEMBER 1850

2762 The age of veneer: introduction, 237–245. (See no. 2780, etc.)

2763 Tennyson [*In Memoriam, The Princess,* and *Poems*, 1842], 245–255. **Charles Kingsley.** Repr. *Miscellanies*, I, and *Works*, XX.

2764 Sketches of American society (No. III): catching a lion, 255–266. **C. A. Bristed.** Evidence for no. 2699.

2765 The sounding statue of Memnon, 267–278.

2766 Leaves from the note-book of a naturalist (Part IX), 279–295. **W. J. Broderip.** Cf. no. 2680.

2767 *Eminent Etonians*, 296–302.

2768 The heirs of Gauntry (chap. iv—the last), 305–319.

2769 Familiar epistles from Ireland (No. IV, concl.), 319–328. Signed: T.F. [Terence Flynn].

2770 The late musical season, 329–336. **Edward Holmes?** Cf. praise of Berlioz, p. 332, with no. 2507, and praise of Bach, p. 336, with no. 2855; see *DNB* and Mackerness in *Music and Letters*, 45 (July 1964), 213–227.

2771 Letters from General Conway to Horace Walpole (Part IV, concl.), 337–344. **H. S. Conway.** Title; cf. no. 2700.

2772 Watering-places and summer haunts of England, 344–354.

VOLUME 42, OCTOBER 1850

2773 Geology versus development [mainly on *Vestiges of the Natural History of Creation*], 355–372.

2774 Sketches of American society (No. IV): life at a watering-place—accidents will happen, 373–379. **C. A. Bristed.** Evidence for no. 2699.

2775 Berlioz on *Der Freischütz*, 380–384. **Hector Berlioz.** Title. Trans. with an intro. note, 380–382, by **P. W. Banks**— note signed Morgan Rattler, see no. 178.

2776 A visit to the Mammoth Cave of Kentucky, 385–396. Signed: An Officer of the Royal Artillery.

2777 Public nurseries, 397–399.

2778 The foreign prince, 400–412.

2779 Leaves from the note-book of a naturalist (Part X), 413–429. **W. J. Broderip.** Cf. no. 2680.

2780 The age of veneer (chap. i), 437–445.

2781 The latest books on Germany and Italy, 446–462.

2782 Canterbury, New Zealand, 463–472.

VOLUME 42, NOVEMBER 1850

2783 The comfortable doctrine of compensations, 473–479.

2784 Captain Hervey's *Ten Years in India*, 479–495. **J. M. Ludlow.** Ludlow's list.

2785 Caesarism, 495–502.

2786 A legend of Oniaugara [North American Indians], 503–520.

2787 Talleyrand, 522–537.

2788 Leaves from the note-book of a naturalist (Part XI), 537–551. **W. J. Broderip.** Cf. no. 2680.

2789 The Wallachs in Transylvania, 552–560.

2790 Sketches of American society (No. V): life at a watering-place—Oldport Springs, 562–574. **C. A. Bristed.** Evidence for no. 2699.

2791 A triad of novels [including *Alton Locke*], 574–590.

VOLUME 42, DECEMBER 1850

2792 The Leviathan telescope and its revelations, 591–601. **Charles Richard Weld.** Repr. *Vacations in Ireland*, 1857, as chaps. xviii and xix.

2793 A tale of mystery, 601–614.

2794 Leaves from the note-book of a naturalist (Part XII), 614–632. **W. J. Broderip.** Cf. no. 2680.

2795 The records of the ancient Kings of Persia, 632–637.

2796 Touching things theatrical, 637–647.

2797 Walter Savage Landor, Esq., to the Rev. C. Cuthbert Southey, Curate of Plumbland [on Robert Southey], 647–650. **Walter Savage Landor.** Signed; repr. *Last Fruit* (1853), II.

2798 The ghetto of Rome, 651–662.

2799 Chronique de Paris (No. III): a letter from Dudley Digges Doolittle, Esq., secretary to H. B. M. Embassy at ———, to Charles Carleton Bulstrode, Esq., H. B. M. Envoy at ———, 663–672. **A. V. Kirwan.** A comparison of pp. 666–667 with Chronique no. II (no. 2422), p. 202, shows the same survey of restaurants, with various phrasal parallels, and both arts. contain attacks on Montalembert (here, pp. 664–665, there pp. 207–208); the fact that Kirwan's later autobiographical essay, no. 4023, pp. 398–400, again takes up four of these cafés, again making many of the same points in some of the same words, and that it too, written in the same personal, nostalgic tone, is focussing on Kirwan's youth in Paris, 1825–1830, supports the attrib. of both this art. and no. 2422; legal phrases here, pp. 663, 670, are common in Kirwan's work; cf. the similar title to no. 2202, which begins with a reference to Verdier Olive (cf. no. 2422, p. 202).

2800 New translations of Horace, 672–678.

2801 The Quaker, 680–685.

2802 Poland as it is, 686–689.

2803 Our musical autumn, 690–697. Unidentified. Perhaps Edward Holmes, who wrote on music for *FM*; cf. title of no. 2855.

2804 Charles Dickens and *David Copperfield*, 698–710.

VOLUME 43, JANUARY 1851

2805 The first half of the nineteenth century, 1–15. **John W. Parker,** 1820–1860, prob. The character of p. 15 shows that he certainly wrote that, and the remainder of the art. seems similar in style.

2806 Phantoms and realities; an autobiography (Part I), 16–29. **Robert Bell,** 1800–1867. Novelette, enlarged and revised, repr. in *Hearts and Altars* (1852), I—II, 129.

2807 Commerce with Africa, 30–36.

2808 A gossip about the Christmas books [including Mrs. Gaskell's *Moorland Cottage*], 37–46. **William Whewell?** Mrs. Gaskell, *Letters*, p. 142, believed "Dr. Whewell" wrote this review; she had received a complimentary note from him, evidently making similar points.

2809 The Abbé de Voisenon and his times, 48–58.

2810 W. M. Thackeray and Arthur Pendennis, Esquires; Robert Bell's *Ladder of Gold*, 75–90.

2811 Sketches of American society (No. VI): Life at a watering-place—the Lionne, 91–101. **C. A. Bristed.** Evidence for no. 2699.

2812 Louis de Saintaine, 102–113.

2813 Railway companies and railway law, 114–126. **Edmund Beckett Denison?** Art. begins with reference to nos. 2594, 2614 and a brief summary of their contents; author is clearly an expert and uses legal phrases such as *locus standi*; cf. evidence for no. 2594.

VOLUME 43, FEBRUARY 1851

2814 London in 1851, 127–137.

2815 German quarrels and unities, 137–146.

2816 The age of veneer (chap. ii), 147–152.

2817 [Note to] Thrieve Castle, Galloway: a tower of the Black Douglas, 153–155. **Richard John King,** prob. The ballad is signed R.I.K.; King had written a book on the early ballad poetry of England and Scotland in 1842; the note that follows describing the castle is characteristic of his work (see *BMCat.* for his

handbooks for travellers); he was a frequent contrib. to *FM* about this time (see nos. 3055, etc.), and signed four arts. with initials, but the initials were R.J.K.

2818 A scramble among the Pyrenees in the autumn of 1850 (Part I), 157–169. **Thomas Crofton Croker.** Signed Colonel Cornelius O'Donoghue, F.N.S.—see Thrall, p. 36. (Part II is no. 2872.)

2819 Mr. and Mrs. Browning, 170–182. **Charles Kingsley,** prob. Kingsley to Parker, n.d., Parrish Collection, Princeton Univ., promises "searching review of Browning for next month"; other arts. explicitly on R. Browning, *FM* nos. 3435 and 4810, are otherwise assigned; attr. by R. B. Martin, *The Dust of Combat* (1959), p. 161.

2820 Phantoms and realities (Part I concluded; Part II), 182–197. **Robert Bell,** 1800–1867. Cf. no. 2806.

2821 The search for Sir John Franklin, 198–202. **C. R. Weld.** Many paragraphs on pp. 200–202. reappear verbatim in Weld's *The Search for Sir John Franklin* (1851), pp. 48–50, 53–56.

2822 Leaves from the note-book of a naturalist (Part XIII), 202–219. **W. J. Broderip.** Cf. no. 2680.

2823 Lord Holland's *Foreign Reminiscences*, 220–236.

2824 Foreign competition and British agriculture, 236–248.

VOLUME 43, MARCH 1851

2825 Ancient fishing and fish, 249–272. **C. D. Badham.** Repr., expanded, *Prose.*

2826 *Lavengro* [by George Borrow]—"The Master of Words," 272–283. **W. Stirling-Maxwell.** Attr. in Borrow, *Life*, I, 92n, and C. K. Shorter, *George Borrow and his Circle* (Boston, 1913), p. 278.

2827 The force of fictions, 286–291.

2828 An inedited letter of Edward Gibbon, 291–293. **Edward Gibbon.** Signed.

2829 Gabrielle; or, The sisters, 295–307.

2830 Public vehicles of London: the cabs, 307–313.

2831 Sketches of American society (No. VII): life at a watering-place—the dog of Alcibiades, 313–325. **C. A. Bristed.** Evidence for no. 2699.

2832 Phantoms and realities (Part II, cont'd.), 326–338. **Robert Bell,** 1800–1867. Cf. no. 2806.

2833 Alfieri, 338–349. **Edgar A. Bowring.**

Claimed in preface, p. ix, to his trans. of *The Tragedies of Alfieri*, 1876.

2834 *History of French Journals, and Biography of French Journalists*, 350–366. **A. V. Kirwan.** Pages 350–351 take up the early journals in the same order and often with the same phrasing Kirwan had used in "Journalism in France" (cited in evidence for no. 2202), repr. *Modern France* (cf. pp. 2–13); in like manner cf. p. 354 at end with the book, p. 38.

VOLUME 43, APRIL 1851

2835 The cloister-life of the Emperor Charles V (Part I), 367–380. **William Stirling-Maxwell.** Series repr. 1852.

2836 *Episodes of Insect Life* (Part I), 381–396. **W. J. Broderip?** Although insects were not among Broderip's main concerns, his series of "Leaves . . . of a Naturalist" (no. 2680, etc.) was completed, or almost so (the last No. is in the next issue of *FM*), leaving him time to take on this 3-part review for Parker; the author at once explains, p. 381, why the subject should be of interest to all, and on p. 385 lists a series of entymologists whose works on insects are "in the hand and head of every naturalist"; the approach, popular but learned, with bits of poetry and historical references, is characteristic; the praise of Richard Owen, p. 392, is often found in Broderip (for example, in nos. 3177, 3779), and the admiration (in Part II of this art., no. 2862, p. 674n.) for Hunter and the Museum of the College of Surgeons appears in nos. 2735, p. 663, and 2852, p. 55; though C. D. Badham had written on insects and contributed to *FM*, his view of their possession of intellect is exactly opposite to that found here, in Part III.

2837 "The best of three"; or, The officer's charger, 397–409.

2838 Sketches of American society (No. VIII): life at a watering-place—the lion in the toils, 409–417. **C. A. Bristed.** Evidence for no. 2699.

2839 Materialism: Miss Martineau and Mr. Atkinson, 418–434. **J. A. Froude.** Claimed in *Life*, I, 182, 183.

2840 Phantoms and realities (Part II, cont'd.), 434–448. **Robert Bell,** 1800–1867. Cf. no. 2806.

2841 *The Philosophy of Living* [medicine], 448–452.

2842 Mozart's pianoforte, 453–462. **Edward Holmes,** prob. He wrote no. 2855 and other "occasional arts. on music for FM"; published an analytical index of Mozart's pianoforte works, 1852, and a life of Mozart, 1845; see *DNB.*

2843 The ministry and the papal bull, 463–469.

2844 An antediluvian romance, 470–472.

2845 The age of veneer (chap. iii), 472–476.

2846 Financial projects and calculations, 476–484.

VOLUME 43, MAY 1851

2847 *Travels in My Garden,* 485–492.

2848 The prevailing epidemic [on recent poetry], 492–509. **Charles Kingsley.** Thorp, *Kingsley*, bibliography; W. R. W. Stephens, *Life and Letters of E. A. Freeman* (1895), I, 83.

2849 Singular circumstance in the life of the late S. C ———, Esq., barrister-at-law, 510–513.

2850 Scenes at Malmaison, 515–528.

2851 The cloister-life of the Emperor Charles V (Part II, concl.), 528–545. **William Stirling-Maxwell.** Attr. in *Essays*, p. 463; claimed in his letter to J. W. Parker, Jan. 11, 1851, Fraser Papers.

2852 Leaves from the note-book of a naturalist (Part XIV, concl.), 545–563. **W. J. Broderip.** Cf. no. 2680.

2853 "Memoir" of Bishop Stanley [by A. P. Stanley], 564–574. **George Brimley.** Attr. in L. J. Phelan, "Life and Letters of George Brimley," unpublished dissertation, Harvard Univ., 1938, pp. 223, 440.

2854 Phantoms and realities (Part III), 574–585. **Robert Bell,** 1800–1867. Cf. no. 2806.

2855 Our musical spring, 586–595. **Edward Holmes.** Attr. by Mackerness, p. 222 (see work cited for no. 2770), though the correct date of the *Musical Times*, where part of this art. was repr., was not Oct. 1, 1851, as Mackerness says, but June 1, 1851.

2856 Legislating under difficulties, 595–602.

VOLUME 43, JUNE 1851

2857 Hartley Coleridge as man, poet, essayist, 603–615.

2858 A visit to the museum of practical geology, 618–630.

2859 A bit of our boyhood, 631–642.

2860 *Montrose and His Times* [ed. Mark Napier], 642–648.

2861 Sketches of American society (No. IX): a trot on the island, 648–663. **C. A. Bristed.** Evidence for no. 2699.

2862 *Episodes of Insect Life* (Part II), 663–675. **W. J. Broderip?** Cf. no. 2836.

2863 Are the English a musical people? 675–681.

2864 Chronique de Paris (No. IV), 682–689. **A. V. Kirwin.** He had written the previous Chroniques (nos. 2307, 2422, 2799); the French press, p. 684, was a main field of his writing: see no. 2834 and its evidence.

2865 Phantoms and realities (Part III, concl.), 690–707. **Robert Bell,** 1800–1867. Cf. no. 2806.

2866 The story of free trade, 716–722. **G. W. Dasent.** Signed Herodotus, Jun.; repr. *Jest and Earnest* (1873), II.

VOLUME 44, JULY 1851

2867 Palgrave's *History of Normandy and of England*, 1–18.

2868 A jungle recollection, 18–25. Signed: Captain Hardbargain.

2869 Little books with large aims, 26–40. **Charles Kingsley.** Attr. to Charles Kingsley in Thorp, *Kingsley*, bibliography.

2870 The deserted mansion, 40–43.

2872 The revelations of a common-place man, (Part I), 47–62.

2872 A scramble among the Pyrenees in the autumn of 1850 (Part II, concl.), 64–76. **T. C. Croker.** Evidence for no. 2818.

2873 The Homeric life, 76–92. **J. A. Froude.** Froude list; repr. *Studies*, I.

2874 Poulailler, the robber, 92–101.

2875 Wordsworth (Part I), 101–118. **George Brimley.** Repr. *Essays.*

VOLUME 44, AUGUST 1851

2876 Memorabilia of the Exhibition season [mainly on the Crystal Palace], 119–132.

2877 Chamois hunting, 133–148. **G. H. Kingsley.** Repr. *Sport and Travel.*

2878 The mineral waters of Germany, 149–155.

2879 The opera and concert season, 155–164. **Edward Holmes?** Cf. no. 2855, a

similar review art.; cf. no. 2842 on Mozart, who is discussed here, pp. 161–162.

2880 Translations of Schiller [by E. A. Bowring], 165–171.

2881 The revelations of a common-place man (Part II), 171–186.

2882 Wordsworth (Part II, concl.), 186–198. **George Brimley.** Cf. no. 2875.

2883 Soyers *Modern Housewife, or Ménagère*, 199–209. **Mary Meredith.** Attr. by Clement Shorter, *Sphere*, 64 (Mar. 1916), 328, though he confused *Blackwood's* with *FM*; about 1850 Parker, the publisher of *FM*, announced a cookbook by Mrs. Meredith, but it never appeared, ibid.; T. J. Hogg to Mrs. Meredith, Nov. 22, 1851, BM Add MS. Ashley 5730, said he looked forward to her "next article in *Fraser's*," which could well be an implied reference to this; the "next" could be no. 2915.

2884 The Bridgewater Gallery, 210–217. **William Stirling-Maxwell.** Attr. in *Essays*, p. 480.

2885 Travellers' books for 1851, 219–236.

VOLUME 44, SEPTEMBER 1851

2886 Rome and Italy, from 1815 to 1850, 237–256.

2887 English synonyms, 256–266. **William Davy Watson.** In no. 2921, p. 692, author speaks of not needing to repeat "opinions we have already expressed in a recent paper . . . on etymology" and goes on to point out its limitations as a key to the meaning of words; the reference must be to this art. (see pp. 256–257); cf. letter of 1851 quoted in evidence for no. 3327.

2888 Crebillon, the French Aeschylus, 267–277.

2889 Sketches of American society (No. X, concl.): a country gentleman at home, 277–290. **C. A. Bristed.** Signed at start A New Yorker, at end Frank Manhattan —see no. 2699.

2890 *Episodes of Insect Life* (Part III, concl.), 290–305. **W. J. Broderip?** Cf. no. 2836.

2891 Revelations of a common-place man (Part III), 305–320.

2892 Bishop Copleston, 320–332. Unidentified. (Letter, pp. 666–668, signed **R. Morey Weale.**)

2893 The age of veneer (chap. iv): the science of deception, 332–339.

2894   Notes on the newspaper stamp, 339–354.

57, is typical of Broderip (for example, in nos. 2689, pp. 164–165, and 3217, p. 534); the culinary interest expressed on pp. 49, 57, appears in nos. 3140, p. 391, and 3177, pp. 103–106.

2927 Autobiography of Captain Digby Grand (chaps. iv–v), 60–74. **G. J. Whyte-Melville.** Cf. no. 2904.

2928 King Alfred, 74–87. **J. A. Froude.** Claimed in *Life*, I, 185.

2929 The age of veneer (chap. v, concl.): the science of puffing, 87–93.

2930 History of the Hungarian War (chap. iii), 94–104. **Otto von Wenckstern.** Repr. *History*.

2931 An election row in New York, 104–110. **C. A. Bristed.** Signed Frank Manhattan—see no. 2889.

2932 The coup d'état in France: a letter to the people of England, 110–126. **A. V. Kirwan.** Signed.

VOLUME 45, FEBRUARY 1852

2933 Mr. Benjamin Disraeli as leader and legislator, 127–141. **G. H. Francis.** Repr. under his name, 1852.

2934 Suggestions about gift-books, 141–147.

2935 The licence of the streets, 147–150. Signed: A Grumbler.

2936 The late Joseph Mallord William Turner, 150–156. **Cyrus Redding.** Signed.

2937 Hypatia (chaps. iii–iv), 157–170. **Charles Kingsley.** Evidence for no. 2923.

2938 Modern history, and other matters, at Cambridge [mainly on Sir James Stephen], 170–182.

2939 Autobiography of Captain Digby Grand (chaps. vi–vii), 182–195. **G. J. Whyte-Melville.** Cf. no. 2904.

2940 Dialogue between John Dryden & Henry Purcell, in the year 1691, on the subject of their forthcoming *Dramatick Opera of King Arthur*, 196–200. Unidentified. Attr. by T. J. Wise and S. Wheeler, *Bibliography of . . . Walter Savage Landor* (1919), p. 333, on basis of style, but R. H. Super, *Walter Savage Landor* (N.Y., 1954), p. 593, n. 83, argues convincingly against this.

2941 History of the Hungarian War (chaps. iv–v), 200–214. **Otto von Wenckstern.** Repr. *History*.

2942 Romantic fables and popular superstitions [dragons], 215–224.

2943 The state and prospects of England, 225–244.

VOLUME 45, MARCH 1852

2944 *The History of the Whig Ministry of 1830 to the Passing of the Reform Bill* [by J. A. Roebuck], 245–260.

2945 Denis and Mountjoy—God and My Right [on Sir James Stephen's lectures], 261–272.

2946 Autobiography of Captain Digby Grand (chaps. viii–ix), 273–290. **G. J. Whyte-Melville.** Cf. no. 2904.

2947 Horæ dramaticæ (No. I): Querolus; or, The buried treasure, 291–302. **Thomas Love Peacock.** Signed M.S.O.; repr. *Works*, X.

2948 Hypatia (chaps. v–vi), 303–320. **Charles Kingsley.** Evidence for no. 2923.

2949 *Lord Palmerston, England, and the Continent*, 320–328.

2950 History of the Hungarian War (chap. vi), 328–340. **Otto von Wenckstern.** Repr. *History*.

2951 Clarendon and his contemporaries, 341–352.

2952 State and prospects of France and the continent of Europe, 352–362. **A. V. Kirwan.** This art. is a sequel to no. 2932, as p. 354 suggests; phrases on pp. 358 and 360 about the drums being removed on Dec. 1, 1851, and Napoleon III wearing the dress of a French general officer are found in Kirwan's *Modern France*, pp. 339–340; the quatrain from Byron on p. 362 was again quoted at end of *FM* no. 3884—signed by Kirwan.

VOLUME 45, APRIL 1852

2953 The colleges of Oxford, 363–379. **Goldwin Smith.** Attr. by T. Arnold Haultain, Smith's secretary, in a note in the Goldwin Smith Papers, Cornell Univ.

2954 The naturalist in Jamaica [P. H. Gosse], 379–398. **W. J. Broderip,** prob. The reviews of two other books by Gosse seem to be by Broderip, viz., nos. 3140 and 3253, both of which refer back to this; p. 394n. comments on a discovery by William Buckland, a close friend of Broderip's (see *FM* no. 3844, p. 489); p. 397 mentions a feat by Waterton which Broderip had discussed in the *Quart. Rev.* (no. 577, *Index*, I); except on p. 393, the art. lacks Broderip's usual footnotes, but otherwise the style seems to be his.

2955 Autobiography of Captain Digby Grand (chap. x), 398–410. **G. J. Whyte-Melville.** Cf. no. 2904.

2956 Preserved meats, 410–417. **Andrew Wynter.** Repr. *Social Bees.*

2957 Hypatia (chaps. vii–viii), 417–434. **Charles Kingsley.** Evidence for no. 2923.

2958 Lord Holland's *Memoirs of the Whig Party*, 434–448.

2959 Horæ dramaticæ (No. II): *The Phaëthon* of Euripides, 448–458. **T. L. Peacock.** Signed M.S.O.; repr. *Works*, X. (No. III is no. 3655.)

2960 History of the Hungarian War (chap. vii), 459–472. **Otto von Wenckstern.** Repr. *History.*

2961 The East and the West, 472–484.

VOLUME 45, MAY 1852

2962 Memoirs, letters, papers, and histories of the earlier years of the reign of George III, 485–501.

2963 Floreal [for May], 501–508.

2964 The shark and his cartilaginous cousins, 508–523. **C. D. Badham.** Repr. in expanded form, *Prose.*

2965 Opening of the musical season, 525–533. **Edward Holmes?** Pages 526–530 are on Berlioz, on whom Holmes wrote no. 2507; no. 2855 is a similar review art. and one also discussing Hullah's concerts.

2966 *Tauromachia; or, The Spanish Bull-Fights*, 533–541. **William Stirling-Maxwell.** Repr. *Essays.*

2967 Hypatia (chaps. ix-x), 541–556. **Charles Kingsley.** Evidence for no. 2923.

2968 *Lord Jeffrey's Life* [by Lord Cockburn], 557–563.

2969 Nursery literature, 563–574.

2970 History of the Hungarian War (chap. viii), 575–585. **Otto von Wenckstern.** Repr. *History.*

2971 Autobiography of Captain Digby Grand (chaps. xi–xii), 585–595. **G. J. Whyte-Melville.** Cf. no. 2904.

2972 Rosas, the dictator of Buenos Ayres, 596–602.

VOLUME 45, JUNE 1852

2973 Thiers' *History of the Consulate and Empire* [Vols. III–IV], and its applicability to coming events, 605–623. **A. V. Kirwan.** On p. 606, the author says he resumes the task of reviewing this work by Thiers (cf. no. 2059); on p. 614 he

refers to the Seine, the Neva, and the Liffey as though known at firsthand, and Kirwan was familiar with Paris, St. Petersburg (cf. evidence for no. 2059) and Dublin, where he grew up; attr. in Poole, I, 476; passage, p. 609, on France in 1802 and 1852 is taken almost verbatim from *Brit. Quart. Rev.*, 15 (May 1852), 561, an art. repr. by Kirwan in *Modern France*; and cf. the warning to England, pp. 618 and 623, with *BQR*, p. 573.

2974 A chair vacant in Edinburgh [University], 624–631.

2975 More marine stores: the narke, 631–648. **C. D. Badham.** Repr., expanded, *Prose.*

2976 Danish ballads, 649–659. **Whitley Stokes.** *Bibliography.* (See no. 3309.)

2977 The sketcher in Rhine-land, 659–673.

2978 Autobiography of Captain Digby Grand, (chaps. xiii–xiv), 673–687. **G. J. Whyte-Melville.** Cf. no. 2904.

2979 History of the Hungarian War (chap. ix, concl.), 687–698. **Otto von Wenckstern.** Repr. *History.*

2980 Hypatia (chaps. xi–xii), 700–710. **Charles Kingsley.** Evidence for no. 2923.

2981 The makers, sellers, and buyers of books, 711–724. **John W. Parker, Sr. and Jun.,** prob. The firm of John W. Parker and Son, who published *FM*, was deeply involved in the question here debated (see p. 715n. for two pamphlets they had published); the son was a writer (see no. 4053) but in this case the father must have had a share in the substance.

VOLUME 46, JULY 1852

2982 Chalmers, 1–18.

2983 Sketches of Rome under the Pope and the Republic (chaps. i–v), 19–29. Signed: An Eye Witness.

2984 Hypatia (chaps. xiii–xiv), 31–46. **Charles Kingsley.** Evidence for no. 2923.

2985 The Government School of Mines, 47–57.

2986 Niebuhr, 58–67.

2987 Autobiography of Captain Digby Grand (chaps. xv–xvi), 68–82. **G. J. Whyte-Melville.** Cf. no. 2904.

2988 Fish tattle: the conger, 83–98. **C. D. Badham.** Repr., expanded, *Prose.*

2989 The general assembly of the Kirk: an epistle to the Rev. Augustus Merivale, curate of P———, Hants, 98–106. Signed: E. FitzPleydell. Unidentified. The name is not Scotch and does not appear in any Scottish directories, clerical, university, or postal: it therefore seems to be a pseudonym; moreover, Augustus Merivale is not in *CCD* and is apparently fictitious.

2990 The training schools of Price's Patent Candle Company, 106–112. **Andrew Wynter.** Repr. *Pictures of Town and Country Life*, 1855.

2991 The government and the elections, 112–126.

VOLUME 46, AUGUST 1852

2992 Gold and emigration, 127–138.

2993 Hypatia (chaps. xv–xvi), 138–151. **Charles Kingsley.** Evidence for no. 2923.

2994 Familiar epistles from Ireland (No. V), 151–160. Signed: T.F. [Terence Flynn].

2995 A fortnight in North Wales, 161–172. **Andrew Wynter.** Repr. *Social Bees*.

2996 *Memoirs of Lord Langdale*, 173–188.

2997 Autobiography of Captain Digby Grand (chaps. xvii–xviii), 188–203. **G. J. Whyte-Melville.** Cf. no. 2904.

2998 Sketches of Rome under the Pope and the Republic (chaps. vi–viii), 203–213. Signed: An Eye-Witness.

2999 Austrian poets, 213–227. **George Meredith.** See D. B. Green, *Modern Language Review*, 54 (July 1959), 329–331.

3000 Art and the Royal Academy, 228–236.

3001 Uncle Tom's Cabin, 237–244. **Arthur Helps.** Signed A.H.; repr. *Correspondence*, pp. 117–133.

VOLUME 46, SEPTEMBER 1852

3002 Recent travels, 245–263.

3003 Mullets and mullomaniacs, 263–272. **C. D. Badham.** Repr. *Prose*.

3004 Hypatia (chaps. xvii–xviii), 272–284. **Charles Kingsley.** Evidence for no. 2923.

3005 The musical season, 284–290.

3006 Neglected French authors: Chamfort, 291–304.

3007 Autobiography of Captain Digby Grand (chaps. xix–xx), 305–320. **G. J. Whyte-Melville.** Cf. no. 2904.

3008 Ethical doubts concerning Reineke Fuchs, 321–330. **J. A. Froude.** Froude list; repr. *Studies*, I, as "Reynard the Fox."

3009 Sketches of Rome under the Pope and the Republic (chaps. ix–x), 331–341. Signed: An Eye-Witness.

3010 The new Orphan House at Ashley Down, Bristol, 341–346.

3011 The presidential election for America: to the editor of *Fraser's Magazine*, 347–351. **H. Arthur Bright.** Signed A Cambridge Man in the West; attr. by W. E. A. Axon, *Academy*, May 17, 1884, p. 349.

3012 The personnel of the new parliament, 351–364.

VOLUME 46, OCTOBER 1852

3013 The Duke of Wellington, 365–373.

3014 Bear hunting in India, 373–385.

3015 Hypatia (chaps. xix–xx), 386–403. **Charles Kingsley.** Evidence for no. 2923.

3016 On the character of Sir John Falstaff, 403–410.

3017 Autobiography of Captain Digby Grand (chaps. xxi–xxii), 411–426. **G. J. Whyte-Melville.** Cf. no. 2904.

3018 Sketches of Rome under the Pope and the Republic (chaps. xi–xiii), 427–438. Signed: An Eye-Witness.

3019 Edward Gibbon, 438–452.

3020 The gurnard group [of fish], 452–464. **C. D. Badham.** Repr. *Prose*.

3021 Tea table literature [Martin Farquhar Tupper's works], 466–475. **Henry Morley?** See *Life*, pp. 205, 211 for evidence that he published an anti-Tupper art. at this time; he was writing for *FM* in Jan. 1853.

3022 Slavery in the southern states, 476–490. **Edward J. Pringle.** Signed A Carolinian; the art. is a reprint of a pamphlet with same title and same pseudonym published at Cambridge, Mass., 1852; the 3rd ed., 1853, carries the author's name.

VOLUME 46, NOVEMBER 1852

3023 The Exhibition Jury reports, 491–502.

3024 Hypatia (chap. xxi), 503–518. **Charles Kingsley.** Evidence for no. 2923.

3025 Some account of Mrs. Beecher Stowe and her family, 518–525. Signed: An Alabama Man.

3026 The Northmen in Britain, 525–536.

3027 Autobiography of Captain Digby Grand (chaps. xxiii–xxiv), 537–552. **G. J. Whyte-Melville.** Cf. no. 2904.

3028 "The new Reformation": to the editor of *Fraser's Magazine*, 553–558. **Adolphus Bernays,** prob. Signed A.B.; art. reviews two German books and contains a quote in German, p. 555; Bernays was prof. of German at Kings Coll., London, and was asked to contribute to Parker's *Bookselling Question*, 1852; Parker was editor of *FM*.

3029   Sketches of Rome under the Pope and the Republic (chaps. xiv–xvi, concl.), 559–570. Signed: An Eye-Witness.

3030   Advocates and juries, 571–585. **A. V. Kirwan.** Author regrets that one writer he is reviewing had not read two arts. on the French bar in *For. Quart. Rev.* (July 1844) and *Brit. Quart. Rev.* (Feb. 1850), both of which were by Kirwan; Kirwan was a lawyer who wrote on legal history and biography in a style very like that used here; moreover, author, like Kirwan, has special knowledge of periodicals.

3031   A few words to Mr. Bull on his return from the continent, 585–593.

3032   The Ionian islands and their government, 593–608. **John Craufurd,** prob. Craufurd was secretary to the senate of the Ionian islands; and he had been asked to contribute to Parker's *Bookselling Question*, 1852; Parker edited *FM*.

VOLUME 46, DECEMBER 1852

3033   Lord John Russell, 609–621.
3034   New novels [one being Thackeray's *Esmond*], 622–636.
3035   Disraeli's *The New Curiosities of Literature*, 637–643. **William Stirling-Maxwell.** Attr. *Essays*, p. 480.
3036   Iceland in the year one thousand, 643–652.
3037   Architects and architecture, 653–659. **Coventry Patmore.** Attr. by Reid, *Patmore*, bibliography.
3038   Autobiography of Captain Digby Grand (chaps. xxv–xxvi, concl.), 660–672. **G. J. Whyte-Melville.** Cf. no. 2904.
3039   Niebuhr's *Ancient History*, 672–687.
3040   Hypatia (chap. xxii), 687–695. **Charles Kingsley.** Evidence for no. 2923.
3041   *Lands of the Messiah, Mahomet, and the Pope*, 696–703.
3042   The Empire in France: its probable consequences in Europe, 704–711. **A. V. Kirwan?** The style and point of view are very like those of nos. 2932 and 2952 earlier in the year; here, p. 705, as in no. 2932, p. 111, author blames the factionalism of a "half-dozen parties" for Napoleon's *coup d'état*; on p. 710 the humming French dockyards and the need for English preparedness was the

theme of Kirwan's *Ports, Arsenals, and Dockyards*, 1841; and cf. evidence for no. 3059.

3043   The magic chessmen, 711–713. **Mortimer Collins.** Attr. in *Dub. Univ. Mag.*, 90 (Oct. 1877), 495.

3044   How India is governed, 713–728.

VOLUME 47, JANUARY 1853

3045   Thomas Moore, 1–17.
3046   The fish of many names: the thunny, 17–30. **C. D. Badham.** Repr. *Prose*.
3047   American statesmen [Clay, Webster, Sumner], 31–39.
3048   Bison hunting in India, 39–48.
3049   Conrad Gesner, 48–61. **Henry Morley.** Repr. *Clement Marot and Other Studies* (1871), II.
3050   Hypatia (chaps. xxiii–xxiv), 62–74. **Charles Kingsley.** Evidence for no. 2923.
3051   Quarantine, 74–83.
3052   A visit to the Burgundian Library at Brussels, 83–87.
3053   Indian teas and Chinese travellers, 88–99.
3054   Mr. Thackeray in the United States: to the editor of *Fraser's Magazine*, 100–103. **W. M. Thackeray?** Signed John Small; repr. *Works*, XXV; White, "Thackeray," p. 84, accepts the attr. on basis of internal evidence but feels it must be "doubtful."
3055   Robert Herrick and his vicarage, 103–109. **R. J. King.** Signed Rev. M. Howlett of Devonshire; repr. *Sketches*.
3056   Wenham Lake ice, 110–113. **Andrew Wynter.** Repr. *Social Bees*.
3057   Concerning free British Negros: to the editor of *Fraser's Magazine*, 114–126. Signed: Utrinque.

VOLUME 47, FEBRUARY 1853

3058   *Wanderings through London* (Part I), 127–135.
3059   Napoleon III—invasion—French pamphlets and the English press, 135–148. **A. V. Kirwan.** On pp. 142–144 the subject of French plans to invade England continues what was said in no. 2973, pp. 618 ff.; indeed, on p. 143 the author speaks of no. 2973 in words that strongly imply a common authorship; the attitude toward Napoleon III is as hostile as Kirwan's in no. 2932; cf. the general evidence for no. 2307.
3060   Nanette, 148–155.
3061   Financial changes; with a word or two

about the income-tax, 157–160. Signed:
A Grumbler.

3062 The Wetherbys—father and son: sundry chapters of Indian experience (chap. i), 160–172. **John Lang.** Novel published 1853.

3063 *Classical School-Books*, 173–183. **John W. Donaldson.** Repr. *Classical School Books*, 1853.

3064 Canada, 183–190. **H. Arthur Bright.** Attr. by W. E. A. Axon, *Academy*, May 17, 1884, p. 349.

3065 A cruise on the Danube, 190–196.

3066 Hypatia (chaps. xxv–xxvi), 196–212. **Charles Kingsley.** Evidence for no. 2923.

3067 Military education, 212–220.

3068 Christopher Marlowe, 221–234.

3069 The government and the country [partly on *Quarterly Rev.*], 235–244.

VOLUME 47, MARCH 1853

3070 Shakespeare, and the new discovery [1632 folio], 245–256. **W. G. Clark?** Clark's concern with Shakespearean scholarship (see *DNB*) and the use of a large number of foreign, mainly classical, words and phrases (cf. no. 3359, for example) makes his authorship quite possible; the *DNB* calls him a frequent contributor to *FM*.

3071 The last of the scombers: the mackerel, etc., 257–272. **C. D. Badham.** Repr. *Prose.*

3072 The Wetherbys (chap. ii), 272–287. **John Lang.** Cf. no. 3062.

3073 *The Octavius of Minucius Felix*, 288–297. **W. B. Donne.** Attr. Johnson, *Donne*, list.

3074 Familiar epistles from Ireland (No. VI), 297–307. Signed: T.F. [Terence Flynn].

3075 Hypatia (chap. xxvii), 309–322. **Charles Kingsley.** Evidence for no. 2923.

3076 Life of the Rev. W[illiam] Kirby, 322–331.

3077 The personnel of the new ministry, 332–339.

3078 The proposed new national galleries and museums, 341–353.

3079 Law reform—its progress and prospects, 355–366. **A. V. Kirwan?** Kirwan, who was a barrister, wrote a number of arts, on lawyers and the history of law (see Part B below); the tendency to speak of *"the* Hullocks, *the* Bayleys," etc., here pp. 356, 358, is a stylistic trait of these arts., varied sometimes with *"a* Scarlett, *a* Copley," etc. (cf. no. 3030, p. 571; no. 4004, p. 127; no. 4068, p.

195); the author was apparently a young member of the profession in the late 20s, as was Kirwan: see p. 356, col. ii, l. 12, and p. 358, col. i, l. 42.

VOLUME 47, APRIL 1853

3080 Longfellow, 367–382. **Aubrey De Vere.** De Vere's list.

3081 The Wetherbys (chap. iii), 383–395. **John Lang.** Cf. no. 3062.

3082 New compositions for the harp, 396–401. **Edward Holmes.** Attr. in *BMCat.*

3083 Modern French memoirs—more particularly since the Revolution of 1789 (No. I), 401–416. **A. V. Kirwan.** Napoleon's usual menu, p. 414, reappears almost verbatim, in Kirwan's *Host & Guest*, p. 379; on p. 414 author says that with many superficial observers it has been a moot point "whether Napoleon ever seriously meant an invasion of England" (cf. no. 2973, p. 617) and then refers to abundant evidence to the contrary in "two or three articles which appeared in this magazine during the last sixteen months"; no. 2973, pp. 617–622, and no. 3059, pp. 142–144, in June 1852 and Feb. 1853, must be meant—and both are by Kirwan (there is some brief evidence in no. 2943, Feb. 1852, p. 234); the survey of French memoirs is the main line of Kirwan's writing, and the extensive use of French words and quotations in French is a characteristic of his arts.

3084 Hypatia (chaps. xix–xx, concl.), 417–434. **Charles Kingsley.** Evidence for no. 2923.

3085 Layard's second visit to Nineveh, 434–444.

3086 Our military schools, 444–452.

3087 *Wanderings through London* (Part II, concl.), 452–460.

3088 Little books with large aims [sequel to no. 2869], 460–473. **W. D. Watson,** prob. Here, in reviewing Trench's *Proverbs*, the author claims he had written no. 2921, also on a book by Trench; cf. no. 3394 too.

3089 Progress of the India question, 473–484. **W. D. Arnold.** Claimed in no. 3129, p. 237 and note.

VOLUME 47, MAY 1853

3090 Lord Grey's colonial administration, 485–499.

3091 *Policy of the Restoration in 1822–23,*

499–505. **A. V. Kirwan?** Kirwan prob. wrote no. 2895 on the Restoration; the defense of trivial incidents, p. 500, is a familiar position; in general, cf. evidence for no. 2307.

3092 Photography, 505–517.

3093 The Wetherbys (chap. iv), 517–532. **John Lang.** Cf. no. 3062.

3094 Kircaldy of Grange: a chapter out of Scottish history, 533–548. **J. A. Froude.** Froude list.

3095 Opsophagy: ancient fish-dealers, 548–562. **C. D. Badham.** Repr., expanded, *Prose*.

3096 Turkey and the east of Europe in relation to England and the west, 562–573.

3097 The music of the season—present and prospective, 574–580. **Edward Holmes?** He was writing on music for *FM* at the time (see no. 3082); cf. his praise of Berlioz in no. 2507 with pp. 574–577 here, and the enthusiastic comment, pp. 578–580, on Mozart, on whom Holmes wrote two books.

3098 The chosen of the people [political elections], 580–588.

3099 Manners and miseries of the French clergy, 590–602.

3100 A few words about the budget, 604–610. **Chichester Fortescue,** prob. O. W. Hewett, ed., . . . *And Mr. Fortescue* (1958), p. 46, shows that he proofread an art. for *FM* on Apr. 27, 1853; Fortescue was a liberal M.P. (Disraeli is here attacked) and was made a junior lord of the treasury in Mar. 1854: see *DNB*.

VOLUME 47, JUNE 1853

3101 Manchester, 611–626. **Robert Lamb.** Signed A Manchester Man; repr. *Free Thoughts*, I.

3102 Lieutenant Governor Gore and Upper Canada, 627–639.

3103 The Wetherbys (chap. v, concl.), 639–656. **John Lang.** Cf. no. 3062.

3104 *History of the Romans under the Empire* [by Charles Merivale], 657–669.

3105 "Flies" and feasts [among the ancients], 670–686. **C. D. Badham.** Repr., expanded, *Prose*.

3106 National galleries, museums, public parks, and gardens, 686–698.

3107 *The Factory of the Hanseatic Merchants in the City of London*, 699–706. **J. M. Kemble?** Attr. by Dickins, *Kemble*, p. 82.

3108 The Royal Academy exhibition, 707–713.

3109 Charles James Fox, 714–730.

VOLUME 48, JULY 1853

3110 The navy of France (No. I), 1–17.

3111 *Las Alforjas*, 18–23.

3112 The tables turned, 24–30. Unidentified. Attr. by Poole, I, 1279, to W. B. Carpenter (i.e., William Benjamin Carpenter), but Poole may have been confusing this art. with one by Carpenter on same subject in the *Quart. Rev.* for Sept. 1853, or with two arts. on mesmerism in *FM* in 1877 signed by Carpenter; in *FM* no. 5911, p. 399n., when Carpenter cites his previous work on such topics, he claims the *QR* art. but makes no mention of this.

3113 Wanted—an owner: some account of certain bones found in a vault beneath Rothwell Church, Northamptonshire, 31–42.

3114 Bertha's love (Part I), 43–59.

3115 *History of the Prussian Court and Aristocracy, and of the Prussian Diplomacy*, 59–70. **J. M. Kemble?** Attr. by Dickins, **Kemble,** p. 82.

3116 Carpiana, 71–86. **C. D. Badham.** Repr. *Prose*.

3117 *Lorenzo Benoni* [by Giovanni Ruffini], 87–94.

3118 Chimney pots, 95–97. Signed: A Grumbler.

3119 Emily Orford (chaps. i–viii), 98–114. Unidentified. (See headnote to no. 3135.)

3120 Belgium, Leopold, and the Duke of Brabant in relation to France and to Europe, 116–126.

VOLUME 48, AUGUST 1853

3121 *History of Scotland, from the Revolution to the Extinction of the Last Jacobite Insurrection* [by J. H. Burton], 127–142. **J. A. Froude.** Froude list; Froude to Parker, July [1853], Morgan Lib., sends this art.

3122 Napoleon Bonaparte, Sir Hudson Lowe, and Dr. O'Meara, 143–155. **A. V. Kirwan.** On p. 149 author speaks of being at Boulogne when Napoleon III arrived there in August 1840; on p. 112 of no. 2932, Kirwan says he was at Boulogne in August 1840 when Napoleon III landed on coast of France at Vimereux [Wimereux, five miles from Boulogne]; on p. 148 the author thinks "that a really Irish gentleman is the most perfect model of the character to be found," a remark only an Irish gentleman would make—and Kirwan was an Irish gentleman (see Boase); he wrote "Napoleonism" in *Modern France*; in general, see no. 2307.

3123 My first night in the jungle, 156–164. Signed: Captain Hardbargain.

3124 Memoir of James Bartleman, 164–170.

3125 Bertha's love (Part II, concl.), 173–186.

3126 Recollections of Ravenna, 186–197.

3127 The navy of France (No. II, concl.), 205–219.

3128 Emily Orford (chaps. ix–xviii), 220–233.

3129 What is the Indian question? 234–248. **W. D. Arnold.** Attr. by Matthew Arnold, *Letters to Arthur Hugh Clough*, ed. H. F. Lowry (Oxford, 1932), p. 142.

VOLUME 48, SEPTEMBER 1853

3130 By land and sea [exploration], 249–264.

3130a [Introduction to] Madonna Pia: a tragedy in one act, adapted from the French [of Auguste Belloy], 264–265. Intro. note (and trans. of play) by **Theodore Martin.** Two new acts were added to this text and published anonymously in 1855 as *Madonna Pia*, with an expanded headnote making the same points, sometimes in the same phrasing; this is attrib. to Martin in H&L and *BMCat*.

3131 A German first of September, 277–285. **G. H. Kingsley.** Repr. *Sport and Travel*.

3132 The toad's curse, 286–299.

3133 American diplomacy, 299–307.

3134 *Autobiography of B. R. Haydon*, 307–325. **George Brimley.** Attr. in source cited for no. 2853, pp. 242, 444.

3135 Emily Orford (chaps. xix–xxiii), 326–341.

3136 Plays and their providers, 342–349. **W. B. Donne.** Repr. *Essays*.

3137 Mademoiselle Clairon [French actress], 353–363.

3138 The session and the ministry, 364–370.

VOLUME 48, OCTOBER 1853

3139 Morals of Queen Elizabeth (Part I), 371–387. **J. A. Froude.** Claimed in *Life*, I, 197.

3140 *The Naturalist in Devonshire* [by P. H. Gosse], 388–400. **W. J. Broderip,** prob. Page 392n. mentions an obscure note by Broderip appended to an art. by someone else in the *Zoological Journal*; the style is very characteristic: see evidence for no. 3669.

3141 Emily Orford (chaps. xxiv–xxix), 401–416.

3142 Modern French memoirs (No. II, concl.), 418–433. **A. V. Kirwan.** Cf. no. 3083, written in same style and form; cited in text of no. 3169, p. 26.

3143 Uncle Peter (Part I), 434–445.

3144 *Sketches of the Courts of the House of Brunswick in Germany and England*, 445–451. **J. M. Kemble?** Attr. by Dickins, *Kemble*, p. 82.

3145 Alexander Smith and Alexander Pope, 452–466. **Charles Kingsley.** Repr. *Miscellanies*, I, and *Works*, XX.

3146 Pike, salmon, silurus, herring, and company, 467–482. **C. D. Badham.** Repr. *Prose*.

3147 A few words from Belgium: le mariage Autrichien, 482–488. Signed: C.

VOLUME 48, NOVEMBER 1853

3148 Morals of Queen Elizabeth (Part II, concl.), 489–505. **J. A. Froude.** Cf. no. 3139.

3149 Extracts from the journal of a visit to New South Wales in 1853 (Part I), 506–518.

3150 Propertius and his English editor [F. A. Paley], 518–525.

3151 Uncle Peter (Part II, concl.), 526–534.

3152 The North-West Passage [Captain M'Clure's voyage in search of Sir John Franklin], 535–538. **C. R. Weld?** The reference to previous arts. in *FM* on Franklin's last voyage, p. 536, suggests that this is another in the series Weld wrote on Franklin and the loss of his ship: see Part B below under Weld.

3153 Anatomy in long clothes, 539–550. **Henry Morley.** Repr. *Clement Marot and Other Studies* (1871), II, as "Andreas Vesalius."

3154 *The Story of Corfe Castle*, 551–567.

3155 Thoughts on Shelley and Byron, 568–576. **Charles Kingsley.** Repr. *Miscellanies*, I, and *Works*, XX.

3156 Dartmoor prison: as it was, and as it is, 577–587.

3157 The North American fisheries, 587–595.

3158 The insurrection in China, 596–606.

VOLUME 48, DECEMBER 1853

3159 The new Crystal Palace at Sydenham, 607–622. **Andrew Wynter.** Repr. *Pictures of Town and Country Life*, 1855.

3160 Greek and Roman philology, 623–632. **W. B. Donne.** Johnson, *Donne*, list.

3161 Extracts from the journal of a visit to New South Wales in 1853 (Part II, concl.), 634–647.

3162 *Profitable Poultry*, 647–659. **W. J. Broderip,** prob. Author comments, p. 659, on the current "poultry mania," a theme which Broderip takes up again in nos. 3296, 3307; the first part of evidence for no. 3177 is equally applicable here.

3163 Emily Orford (chaps. xxx–xxxvii, concl.), 659–670.

3164 The internal resources of Turkey, 670–677.

3165 *History of the War of the Sicilian Vespers*, 679–688.

3166 The last of the fins: cods, gadus, 689–710. **C. D. Badham.** Repr., expanded, *Prose.*

3167 The Russo-Turkish question, 711–726.

VOLUME 49, JANUARY 1854

3168 Decline and fall of the Corporation of London (Part I): the constitution, 3–18.

3169 Dr. Véron's *Memoirs*, 19–30. **A. V. Kirwan.** The author, p. 25, cites Kirwan's "Classics of the Table" (no. 1942, etc.); also, ibid., says he was well acquainted with Baron Capelle, as was Kirwan (see his autobiographical art., no. 4036, p. 587), and adds, contra Véron, that he was a comedian in early life, and later, when in exile, dined with Wellington—facts which Kirwan also affirms, with other parallels, in no. 4036, pp. 588–589.

3170 General Bounce; or, The lady and the locusts (chaps. i–ii), 31–47. **G. J. Whyte-Melville.** Signed The Author of *Digby Grand*; novel published 1855.

3171 Lord Palmerston and the presbytery of Edinburgh, 47–53. **Charles Kingsley.** Thorp, *Kingsley*, bibliog.

3172 The freight of the *Jacobina*, 54–61.

3173 A visit to the hospital for sick children, 62–67.

3174 The principle of the Grecian mythology; or, How the Greeks made their gods, 69–79.

3175 Young Germany, 81–88.

3176 Cambridge life according to C. A. Bristed [with some account of Yale and

Harvard], 89–100. Signed in text, p. 89: Philemon Jenkinson.

3177 Gallinaceana (No. I): [poultry], 101–112. **W. J. Broderip,** prob. The antiquarian erudition, the quotations from literature, especially poetry and the Classics, the anecdotal style, the use of occasional Latin and French phrases; the admiring references to Richard Owen, as here, p. 103, are all characteristic of Broderip's many arts. on natural history and birds in *FM*.

3178 A few words on Irish antiquities, 112–117.

3179 Derbyism [politics], 118–126.

VOLUME 49, FEBRUARY 1854

3180 Ruskin's *Stones of Venice* (Part I), 127–138.

3181 Poems by Matthew Arnold, 140–149. **Charles Kingsley.** Thorp, *Kingsley*, bibliog.; Kingsley's letter to Arnold, Dec. 3, 1853 (for source see no. 2591) not only says he hopes to review this book, but makes two points that appear here, p. 142, and calls "Sohrab and Rustum" the best poem in the volume (cf. here, pp. 143–146); moreover, no. 2591 is referred to in similar terms in both the letter and on p. 143, and is cited as "ours" on p. 143 where the earlier praise of the "Forsaken Merman" is repeated.

3182 Parliamentary reform from within, 149–156.

3183 The great ant-eater, 157–168. **W. J. Broderip,** prob. Signed *; this art. is cited in no. 3669 (p. 642) which contains various references to writers and subjects here discussed: d'Azara, Cuvier, Owen, Buffon, and ant-eaters; the author, p. 157, mentions Dickens' art. on "The Good Hippopotamus," as does Broderip in no. 2794, p. 626; Richard Owen, whom Broderip greatly admired, is highly praised, p. 168; cf. evidence for no. 3669.

3184 General Bounce (chaps. iii–iv), 169–184. **G. J. Whyte-Melville.** Evidence for no. 3170.

3185 Researches in Dutch literature (Part I), 185–194. **Mark Prager Lindo.** Attr. *Athenaeum*, Mar. 24, 1877, p. 386; cf. signature of no. 3294.

3186 Paris gossip, 195–198. **A. V. Kirwan?** This report on Paris is similar to that in *Brit. Quart. Rev.*, 22 (Oct. 1855), 428–455, partly repr. in Kirwan's *Modern France*; in both cases Napoleon III's improvements in Paris and his unpopularity are noted; this art. in *FM* is written in the first person; on p. 196 the author visits the courts of justice, and on p. 197 comments on the press: cf. no. 2307.

3187 The decline and fall of the Corporation of London (Part II): the Corporation as conservators of the Thames, 198–209.

3188 Russia, Finland, Norway, Denmark, and the Baltic, 214–224. **George Strachey,** prob. Author speaks, p. 218, of his personal inspection of the Baltic ports (for Strachey see no. 3214), and asserts, pp. 217, 218 that most of the Baltic ships are rotten because they are built of unseasoned wood (cf. no. 3227, pp. 615–616, which includes a ref. back to this art.); on p. 215 the author attacks the scare tactics of the "Protectionist Press" (the press is again taken to task in no. 3214, particularly "our own correspondent," pp. 496, 497, 505; no. 3227, p. 624; no. 3249, p. 132, and no. 3268, all prob. by Strachey).

3189 *Les Femmes,* 225–234.

3190 The Irish tenant-right question, 234–244.

VOLUME 49, MARCH 1854

3191 *The Plurality of Worlds* [by William Whewell], 245–256. **J. D. Forbes.** The MS. is at St. Andrews; included in MS. list of his arts. in Forbes Papers, St. Andrews.

3192 Villemain's *Memoirs* [Vol. I; but art. largely on Count Louis de Narbonne], 257–268. **A. V. Kirwan.** On p. 267 author discusses de Feletz in association with Dussaulx and Hoffman, as Kirwan did in *Modern France,* p. 32, and on p. 268 de Feletz is described in a sentence that reappears verbatim in that book, p. 32; in general cf. no. 2307.

3193 A day's curling, 269–274.

3194 Gallinaceana (No. II): peacocks, 275–287. **W. J. Broderip,** prob. Cf. no. 3177.

3195 A pageant which meant something [recent diplomatic meeting in the Punjab], 288–289.

3196 General Bounce (chaps. v–vi), 290–304. **G. J. Whyte-Melville.** Evidence for no. 3170.

3197 The British Jews: to the editor of *Fraser's Magazine,* 304–314. **Ernest Abraham Hart.** Signed E.A.H.; attr. in *DNB,* 1st suppl.

3198 Sinope after the battle [of Nov. 1853 between Turkish and Russian fleets], 314–317. Signed: Φ.

3199 Decline and fall of the Corporation of London (Part III): Corporation as suitors, justices, and judges, 318–329.

3200 Beaumarchais, 330–348.

3201 Researches in Dutch literature (Part II), 349–357. **M. P. Lindo.** Cf. no. 3185.

3202 *Oxford Reform and Oxford Professors,* 358–368.

3203 England at war, 369–370. **John W. Parker,** 1820–1860, prob. Editorial tone and brevity, with abandonment of the double-column format, strongly suggest a Parker editorial: cf. no. 2535.

VOLUME 49, APRIL 1854

3204 Frederick Denison Maurice, 371–387. **John Llewellyn Davies?** *Dub. Univ. Mag.,* 93 (1879), 585, ascribes to him "an article on Maurice's writings" in *FM* "about 1850"; this is the only possibility.

3205 A day at Marathon, 396–400.

3206 The electric telegraph, 401–411.

3207 General Bounce (chaps. vii–viii), 411–425. **G. J. Whyte-Melville.** Evidence for no. 3170.

3208 Glaciers [rev. of J. D. Forbes, *Norway and its Glaciers*], 426–438. **John Ball?** Ball's study of glaciers led to conclusions that coincided so closely with those of Forbes that he refrained from publishing them (*DNB*); on p. 437 the author outlines Forbes' opinions which 10 yrs.' experience has confirmed (Prof. Forbes sees no reason to change them and "neither do we"); cf. *ER* no. 2489 (*Index,* I, 510), where Ball concluded that Tyndall had merely completed, not overthrown, Forbes' theory.

3209 Old stores [books of the past year], 439–452.

3210 Decline and fall of the Corporation of London (Part IV): the Corporation in its works and ways, 453–462.

3211 Ruskin's *Stones of Venice* (Part II, concl.), 463–478.

3212 International law: Grotius, *On War and Peace,* 479–487.

3213 The Reform Bill and the War, 487–492.

VOLUME 49, MAY 1854

3214 Cronstat and the Russian fleet, 493–510. **George Strachey,** prob. F. J. A. Hort, *Life and Letters,* I, 278) sent the anon. repr. of this art. to his father, May 10, 1854, calling the author "one of our attachés at St. Petersburg driven home by the War . . . a very sharp-eyed and intelligent little creature"; man cited filled the post Feb. 21, 1852 to Feb. 1854 (*Foreign Office List*/59), and was a contemporary of Hort's at Trinity Coll. Camb.; he later combined journalism and diplomacy; there seems to be no reason to connect the other two attachés, S. Lumley and R. Kerr, with either Hort or Cambridge.

3215   The three Racans: an anecdote dramatized, 511–517. **Marmion W. Savage.** Signed The Author of *The Bachelor of the Albany*; see H&L, I, 170.

3216   Massaniello, 517–522.

3217   Gallinaceana (No. III, concl.): pheasants, 523–537. **W. J. Broderip,** prob. Cf. no. 3177.

3218   General Bounce (chaps. ix–x), 537–553. **G. J. Whyte-Melville.** Evidence for no. 3170.

3219   *Cautions for the Times* [ed. by Richard Whately], 553–558.

3220   Lord John's [John Russell's] sacrifice, 559–560.

3221   Decline and fall of the Corporation of London (Part V): the Corporation in relation to commerce, 561–571.

3222   The Danube: from Vienna to Constantinople, 571–577.

3223   Researches in Dutch literature (Part III), 578–587. **M. P. Lindo.** Cf. no. 3185.

3224   Wolf nurses in India, 587–590.

3225   Sirius; a fairy tale, 591–596.

3226   Party government, 602–610.

VOLUME 49, JUNE 1854

3227   Russian ships and Russian gunners, 611–631. **George Strachey,** prob. On pp. 611, 622 (3 references in text) author cites no. 3214 as though his; the subject is precisely the same.

3228   *Forlorn Hope* [ship that searched for Sir John Franklin], 633–645. **C. R. Weld,** prob. He wrote nos. 2524, 2821, and 3941 on this topic; all four arts. are similar in style.

3229   The personnel of the Russo-European question, 645–656.

3230   General Bounce (chaps. xi–xii), 657–673. **G. J. Whyte-Melville.** Evidence for no. 3170.

3231   Smyth's *Mediterranean*, 674–687.

3232   Decline and fall of the Corporation of London (Part VI, concl.): patronage and revenues of the Corporation—conclusion, 687–697.

3233   Music militant—our spring campaign, 697–702.

3234   Frederick Tennyson's poems, 703–717. **Charles Kingsley.** Thorp, *Kingsley*, bibliog.

3235   Germany, Greece, and the Scandinavian powers in reference to Russia and Turkey, 718–729. **George Strachey,** prob. The author refers, p. 727, to no. 3188, and the similarity of phrasing in the titles, indicating that both are studies in the relations between Russia and the European powers, points to a common authorship; on p. 728 he shows that he reads Russian readily; he also makes the point, ibid., that vigorous blows are necessary in the Baltic and the Euxine to prove the superior power of England and France (cf. no. 3188, p. 215); on p. 723 he claims that arts. in *Kreuz-Zeitung* are inspired by Russia (cf. no. 3268, p. 348); if it be objected that Strachey had also written no. 3227 in June, cf. nos. 3268 and 3269 in Sept. issue.

VOLUME 50, JULY 1854

3236   The Royal Institution and education, 1–15.

3237   Phases of music in Russia, 16–25.

3238   Prophecy of the Russians at Constantinople, 25–27.

3239   Etchings from the Euxine (No. I): flitting at Kostendje, 28–30. Signed: Φ.

3240   General Bounce (chaps. xiii–xiv), 31–46. **G. J. Whyte-Melville.** Evidence for no. 3170.

3241   The astronomy of comets, 47–59.

3242   *Balder* [by Sydney Dobell], 59–73.

3243   The latest aspect of the slavery question in the United States, 73–79.

3244   "Unpublished Journals of Travel," 80–94. Unidentified. (Editorial comment, p. 440.)

3245   Researches in Dutch literature (No. IV), 95–105. **M. P. Lindo.** Cf. no. 3185.

3246   My cousin William; a simple tale, 105–111.

3247   An excursion to Buitenzorg, in the interior of Java, 111–120.

3248   War and its obligations before peace, 121–126. **George Strachey?** The author speaks, p. 125, of his personal knowledge of the Euxine and the Baltic (for Strachey see no. 3214); pp. 125–126 are an expansion of the last pp. of no. 3227, where Strachey regretted that Odessa had not been destroyed, and maintained that misplaced leniency would prove costly to England (see also no. 3268); on pp. 125, 126, the author thinks that now is the time to capture Sebastopol, a statement referred back to in no. 3269, p. 363.

VOLUME 50, AUGUST 1854

3249 The Russian army (Part I), 127–153. **George Strachey,** prob. On p. 133 author refers to our former lists of the Russian fleets (no. 3214) and gives similar tables of the Russian army.

3250 Haydon's picture of Napoleon Musing, 154–156.

3251 "Glorious John" [Dryden], 157–172.

3252 General Bounce (chaps. xv–xvii), 173–190. **G. J. Whyte-Melville.** Evidence for no. 3170.

3253 *The Aquarium* [by P. H. Gosse], 190–203. **W. J. Broderip,** prob. Page 200n mentions arts. by Broderip in *Zoological Journal* and in the *Penny Cyclopedia*; the style is very characteristic: see evidence for no. 3669.

3254 A chapter on golf, 204–209.

3255 Photographs from Russian life [largely taken from a work by Turgenev], 209–222. Unidentified. Perhaps by John Duke Coleridge, who in a letter to Parker, Mar. 8, 1854, Haverford Coll., suggested a translation of a French story "giving a good deal of insight into Russian life"; that trans. never appeared, but this art., five months later, is based on a French edition of Turgenev, and the author, p. 210, proposes to give a "conception of the true character of Russian interior life." We owe this suggestion to David Greene: see Bibliographical Note at end of Introduction to *FM*.

3256 Sketches of campaigning life: the storming of Badajos, 223–237.

3257 Neglected health, 238–244. **W. A. Guy,** prob. Guy had reviewed the Public Health Act in no. 2510; this art. discusses what it had achieved (summary on p. 239, including its preventive war against cholera—cf. no. 2674), the unjust criticism of Chadwick (p. 239; cf. evidence for no. 2368), and the outrageous opposition of local interests to government action (pp. 241–242; cf. evidence for no. 2510); the author twice refers to supporting statistics (pp. 242, 243); see *DNB*.

3258 Politics and pronunciamentos of Spain, 246–252.

VOLUME 50, SEPTEMBER 1854

3259 The session and the ministry, 253–258.

3260 How to get on at the Bar, 261–271. Signed: An Experienced Junior.

3261 The Church among the tall chimneys, 272–288. **Robert Lamb.** Repr. *Free Thoughts*, I.

3262 Hafiz [the Persian poet] (Part I), 288–295. **E. B. Cowell.** List in *Life*; Fitz-Gerald, *Letters*, I, 232. (Part II is no. 4071.)

3263 Etchings from the Euxine (No. II, concl.): the Danube and the Crimea, 296–298. Signed: Φ.

3264 General Bounce (chaps. xviii–xix), 299–316. **G. J. Whyte-Melville.** Evidence for no. 3170.

3265 A handful of Italian patois books (No. I), 316–327. **J. M. Ludlow.** Signed Vicesimus Smatterling, B.L.; Ludlow's list.

3266 The great bustard, 328–340. **W. J. Broderip,** prob. The evidence in support of no. 3579 is equally applicable here.

3267 The mercantile marine, 340–348.

3268 Phases of war in St. Petersburg, 348–356. **George Strachey,** prob. On p. 348 author refers to his statement of May 1st on Russian gun-boats (this is in no. 3214, p. 507); first part of this art. is on Cronstat (cf. no. 3214); pp. 349n, 350, 351 refer to no. 3227; p. 348 refers to "Our own correspondent" (cf. no. 3214); author on pp. 355–356 objects to misguided leniency in sparing Odessa (cf. nos. 3227, 3248).

3269 The garrisons of the Crimea, 356–368. **George Strachey,** prob. The second paragraph refers to "our" description of the Russian Black Sea fleet, which gave the names of its ships, viz. no. 3214, pp. 508–510 (also see no. 3227, pp. 621–624); here the author continues to discuss Russian ships on pp. 357, 365, 367; referring to no. 3249, p. 358n., author adds further details to "our" August art.; in no. 3278, p. 483, author refers to "our last month's art. on the 'Garrisons of the Crimea' "; these facts seem strong enough to withstand the objection that this would be a second art. in succession in the same issue by the same author, which is very unusual in *FM* at this date.

VOLUME 50, OCTOBER 1854

3270 *Psychological Inquiries*, 371–387.

3271 The Turk and his future, 388–392.

3272 A week on the Tweed, 393–400.

3302 Field sports in foreign lands, 15–31.

3303 A soldier's view of the campaign of 1854, 32–39.

3304 Edward Forbes, 39–44. **W. W. Smyth.** Attr. in George Wilson and A. Geike, *Memoir of Edward Forbes* (1861), p. 140n.

3305 An inedited fragment [Boswell supposedly reports a conversation with Johnson on railways], 45–46. **James Craigie Robertson,** prob. Cf. no. 3578, p. 282, where author claims this fragment.

3306 Alwyn's first wife (chaps. i–ii), 47–58. **Dinah Mulock.** Repr. *Nothing New,* N.Y., 1857.

3307 Alectryomania [on poultry], 59–73. **W. J. Broderip.** Page 59 cites no. 3296 in words which clearly make this a continuation of that art.

3308 Paris demolished and Paris embellished: a walk about it and a talk about it, 73–86. **C. A. Bristed.** Signed The Author of *The Upper Ten Thousand*— see *BMCat.*

3309 A second batch of Danish ballads, 86–95. **Whitley Stokes.** Cf. no. 2976, to which this is a sequel.

3310 The hospital nurse: an episode of the War, founded on fact, 96–105.

3311 The old civilians [on Justinian's *Institutes*], 105–115. **W. B. Donne.** Attr. Johnson, *Donne,* p. 340.

3312 The ten days' session, 116–125.

VOLUME 51, FEBRUARY 1855

3313 Massey's *History of England* [*during the Reign of George III*], 127–144.

3314 Japan and its intercourse with foreign nations, 145–156. **M. P. Lindo.** Signed M.P.L.—see nos. 3185, 3294; author notes, p. 145, that he used Dutch version of book reviewed.

3315 Verse-books of 1854, 157–172. **George Brimley,** prob. Pages 157–163 repr. in his *Essays* as "Poetry and Criticism."

3316 A week in the wolds of Lincolnshire, 173–181.

3317 Alwyn's first wife (chaps. iii–iv, concl.), 181–191. **Dinah Mulock.** Cf. no. 3306.

3318 North and south [books on Europe], 192–207.

3319 St. Stephen's Chapel, 208–212.

3320 Barnum [on his *Autobiography*], 213–223.

3321 Hinchbrook (chaps. i–iii), 224–237. **J. C. Jeaffreson.** Cf. no. 3328.

3322 The War and the government, 238–244.

VOLUME 51, MARCH 1855

3323 Moral insanity—Dr. Mayo's *Croonian Lectures,* 245–259.

3324 An August at Felixstow, 259–272. **C. D. Badham.** Signed C.D.B.; attr. in no. 3630, p. 163.

3325 Cyrano de Bergerac, 273–288. **Henry Morley.** Signed H.M.; repr. *Clement Marot and Other Studies* (1871), II.

3326 The old world and the new, 291–306. **George Whyte-Melville.** Signed G.W.M.; claims use of these initials in *FM* in letter to Parker, Sept. 15 [1857], cited in *N&Q,* 208 o.s., 10 n.s. (Dec. 1963), 452.

3327 The rule of good nuns [trans. of *The Ancren Riwle*], 307–315. **W. D. Watson.** Signed W.D.W.; Arthur Helps to J. W. Parker, Jr., June 27, 1851, Historical Soc. of Penn., urges him strongly to give "literary employment" to the "old college friend" of his (both graduated at Trinity in 1835: see Venn); he is "a very thoughtful man, well read in literature," and a barrister who has rarely seen a brief; cf. earlier arts. that followed close upon this letter (nos. 2887, 2921, 3088); no other W.D.W. found in the *English Catalogue* or Boase seems the least likely.

3328 Hinchbrook (chaps. iv–vi), 316–330. **J. C. Jeaffreson.** Signed.

3329 Germany: past and future, 331–340. **Henry Ottley?** Signed H.O.; Ottley wrote on diplomacy in *FM*: see no. 4460, etc.

3330 Ye oyl of whelps: an incident in the life of the great French chirurgeon, Ambrose Paré, 341–345.

3331 Whitelocke's *Embassy to Sweden,* 345–354.

3332 The government, the aristocracy, and the country, 354–362.

VOLUME 51, APRIL 1855

3333 *Oxford Essays,* 363–383.

3334 A passage from the life of Ninian Holdfast, minister in Balmaclellan, A.D. 1624, 384–399. **John Skelton?** He wrote two stories about the Holdfasts: no. 4639 below on Martin, and one in his *Essays* called "Passage in the ministry of Stephen Holdfast."

3335 Military hospitals a century ago, 399–

407. **W. A. Guy**, prob. Cited in no. 3716, p. 487n.; p. 403 here and p. 493 there discuss precisely the same question in the same way; see *DNB*.

3336 Huc's *China*, 409–421. **George Whyte-Melville**. Signed G.W.M.—see no 3326.

3337 Hinchbrook (chaps vii–ix), 422–436. **J. C. Jeaffreson**. Signed.

3338 *Four Years at the Court of Henry VIII*, 441–454. **J. A. Froude**. Signed J.A.F.; Froude list.

3339 The naval school on board the *Illustrious*, 455–466. **Caroline Frances Cornwallis**. *Letters*, p. 443.

3340 Lady Blessington's *Life and Correspondence*, 467–475.

3341 The War Committee, the ministry, and the conference, 476–484.

VOLUME 51, MAY 1855

3342 The regimental system, 485–505. **Charles Edward Stuart Gleig**. Signed C.E.S.G.; at this time captain in 92nd (Highland) Regiment of Foot: *Army List/55*.

3343 *Westward Ho!* [by Kingsley], 506–517. **George Whyte-Melville**. Signed G.W.M.; cf. no. 3326.

3344 Servian proverbs, 517–526. **Whitley Stokes**. *Bibliography*.

3345 Periwinkles in pound, 531–548. **C. D. Badham**. Signed C.D.B.; Badham wrote on natural history for *FM*, using his initials: see no. 3324, etc.

3346 Hinchbrook (chaps. x–xiv), 549–562. **J. C. Jeaffreson**. Signed.

3347 Henry Lawes, 563–568. **John Hullah**. Signed J.H.; attr. in J. D. Coleridge to W. E. Gladstone, May 8, 1855, BM Add. MS. 44138, fol. 47b.

3348 Paris in little, and some of its vanities, 568–586. **C. A. Bristed**. Signed The Author of *The Upper Ten Thousand*; repr. *Pieces*, I.

3349 A visit to the Yezidis, or, Devil-worshippers of Armenia, 587–592.

3350 The Sebastopol Committee, 593–606.

VOLUME 51, JUNE 1855

3351 The administrative reform "movement"—an attempt to put it on wheels, 607–627. **David Masson**. Signed D.M.; cf. no. 3787 for his use of initials; see *North Brit. Rev.*, no. 410, in *Index*, I, for his interest in the topic at this time.

3352 Sir Robert Strange, 628–644. **William Stirling-Maxwell**. Signed W.S.; repr. *Essays*.

3353 *Wine, its Use and Taxation*, 645–650. **Cyrus Redding**. Signed C.R.; he published *Wine Duties Reduction*, 1852, and wrote for *FM*: see no. 2936.

3354 Hinchbrook (chaps. xv–xxi), 653–669. **J. C. Jeaffreson**. Signed.

3355 Possibilities of an Americo-Russian alliance, 670–675. **C. A. Bristed**. Signed C.A.B.; cf. no. 3364.

3356 Recent French literature, 676–693. **A. V. Kirwan**. This review of three French memoirs seems to supplement two of Kirwan's earlier pieces (on Véron and on Villemain, nos. 3169 and 3192), which the reader is referred to on pp. 683 and 689; a paragraph in *Modern France*, pp. 363–364, appears here, p. 677, in another form but using many of the same phrases.

3357 Sir Henry T. de la Beche, 694–699. **W. W. Smyth**. Signed W.W.S.; cf. no. 3304, also on a geologist.

3358 Three months in Weimar, 699–706. **George Eliot**. *Letters*, II, 201; repr. *Essays*.

3359 On some pictures in the Royal Academy Exhibition of 1855, 707–715. **William George Clark?** Signed W.G.C.; *DNB* calls him a contr. to *FM* "for some years"; on p. 708 author confesses he is neither artist nor connoisseur.

3360 The political crisis, 715–724.

VOLUME 52, JULY 1855

3361 An ascent of Mont Blanc [in 1851], 1–20. **Charles Greenwood Floyd**. Signed C.G.F.: pp. 3–4 show party led by Albert Smith; *FortR* no. 2460, p. 638 says three young Oxonians joined the expedition; Smith's own account, *Story of Mont Blanc* (1853), p. 184, names his three university companions as Floyd, Philips, and West; man cited only C. G. Floyd in Foster.

3362 *Velazquez and his Works*, 21–29. Signed: A.Y.

3363 An essay on humbug, 30–41. **Robert Lamb**. Signed at start A Manchester Man, at end R.L.; repr. *Free Thoughts*, I.

3364 The English press and the American public, 42–47. **C. A. Bristed**. Signed at start The Author of *The Upper Ten Thousand*, at end C.A.B.; repr. *Pieces*, III.

3365 Liszt, Wagner, and Weimar, 48–62.

George Eliot. *Letters*, II, 205; repr. *Essays.*

3366 Our cavalry horse, 62–66. Signed: C.

3367 Hinchbrook (chaps. xxii–xxvii), 67–82. **J. C. Jeaffreson.** Signed.

3368 *Sydney Smith* [by Lady Holland], 84–91. **Charles Kingsley.** Signed C.K.; Thorp, *Kingsley,* bibliog.

3369 Statistics, 91–95. Signed: A Grumbler.

3370 The drama, past and present, 96–104. **W. B. Donne.** Repr. *Essays.*

3371 Spurious antiques [some historical novels], 104–114.

3372 Parliament, the press, and the War, 115–122.

VOLUME 52, AUGUST 1855

3373 Lord Dalhousie, 123–135. **W. D. Arnold.** Signed W.D.A.; on p. 133 author seems to claim no. 3277; attr. by Frances J. Woodward, *The Doctor's Disciples* (1954), p. 234.

3374 *Queens of England of the House of Hanover,* 135–149. **J. M. Kemble,** prob. Signed T.M.K. (misprint for J.M.K.?); attr. "certainly" by Dickins, *Kemble,* p. 83; Kemble used his initials for nos. 3438, 3546.

3375 The law of marriage and divorce, 149–151. **William Stirling-Maxwell.** Attr. in *Essays,* p. 481.

3376 Cambridge in the last century, 153–162. Signed: H.L.

3377 Austrian nationalities and Austrian policy, 163–173. **John W. Wilkins?** Signed J.W.W.; Wilkins wrote on continental politics at this time: see *Index,* I, 1138–1139.

3378 Hinchbrook (chaps. xxviii–xxxiv), 173–190. **J. C. Jeaffreson.** Signed.

3379 The adulteration of food, 191–202.

3380 *Lands of the Slave and the Free,* 206–217.

3381 The opera in 1855, 217–222.

3382 Algeria—its past, present, and future, 223–231.

3383 Gilchrist's *Life of Etty,* 232–235. **F. T. Palgrave.** Signed F.; *Opuscula,* vol. I, item no. 13.

3384 Politics of the month, 235–240.

VOLUME 52, SEPTEMBER 1855

3385 Helps's *Spanish Conquest in America* [Vols. I and II], 241–256. **W. B. Donne.**

Johnson, *Donne,* list. (See nos. 3644, 4183.)

3386 The Kingdom of Sardinia, 257–263. **Marian E. Martin?** Signed M.E.M.; cf. no. 2158.

3387 Tennyson's *Maud,* 264–273. **Charles Kingsley.** Claimed in letter cited in Thorp, *Kingsley,* p. 95.

3388 American parties, past and present (Part I): national parties to the time of President Pierce, 274–285. **C. A. Bristed.** Signed at start The Author of *The Upper Ten Thousand,* at end C.A.B.; cf. no. 3364.

3389 *Italy,* and art in Italy (Part I): Rome, 286–296. **John Skelton.** Signed Shirley; repr. *Nugae Criticae,* as "Terra Santa."

3390 The bright side of war, 297–300. Signed: A Grumbler.

3391 Hinchbrook (chaps. xxxv–xlii), 300–317. **J. C. Jeaffreson.** Signed.

3392 Burton's *Pilgrimage to El Medinah and Meccah,* 318–329. **Henry A. Murray.** Signed H.A.M.—see no. 3946.

3393 The Continent in 1855, 330–339. Signed at start: A Resident, at end: C.

3394 *English, Past and Present* [by R. C. Trench], 340–349. **W. D. Watson.** Signed W.D.W.; cf. no. 3327.

3395 The story of a great discovery [circulation of blood], 352–356. **G. H. Lewes.** Signed G.H.L.; Lewes, "Receipts."

3396 The past session, 356–362.

VOLUME 52, OCTOBER 1855

3397 *Noctes Ambrosianae* [by John Wilson], 363–378. **James Craigie Robertson.** Signed J.C.R.; all that the author says of himself pp. 363–364, fits the man cited (see *DNB*); attr. by Bevington, *Saturday Review,* p. 368.

3398 Sketches and studies from Belgium (No. I): Mechlin, 378–390. **R. J. King.** Signed R.J.K.; repr. *Sketches.*

3399 An excursion to Point Manabique, in Central America, 391–397. Signed at start: A Naturalist, at end: J.M.D.

3400 Shakspeare's minor poems, 398–411.

3401 Hinchbrook (chaps. xliii–lii, concl.), 412–429. **J. C. Jeaffreson.** Signed.

3402 *Italy,* and art in Italy (Part II, concl.): the Northern Republics, 429–442. **John Skelton.** Evidence for no. 3389.

3403 The Hanoverian coup d'état, 443–454.

3404 Niebuhr and Lewis on the early Roman history, 455–469.

3405 Cantegrel, 469–475.

3406 The War and its opponents, 479–484.

3438 Macaulay's *History of England*, 147–166. **J. M. Kemble.** Signed J.M.K.—see no. 3374; attr. by Macaulay in G. O. Trevelyan, *Life and Letters of Lord Macaulay* (N.Y., 1876), II, 372.

3439 Ladak and Tibet, 166–172. **Francis Marx,** prob. The opening paragraph makes this almost a supplement to no. 3301.

3440 Kate Coventry (chaps. v–viii), 173–188. **G. J. Whyte-Melville.** Evidence for no. 3432.

3441 Scotch preaching and preachers, 189–198. **A. K. H. Boyd.** Repr. *Recreations,* 2nd series, as "Concerning the Pulpit in Scotland."

3442 Six months in India (Part II, concl.), 198–211. **Walter Scott Seton-Karr.** Signed W.S.S-K.; cf. no. 3434.

3443 Bain, *The Senses and the Intellect,* 212–230. **David Masson.** Signed D.M.; see no. 3787 for his use of initials; he wrote on British philosophy.

3444 Old rings (Part I), 230–241. **C. D. Badham.** Attr. in no. 3630, p. 163; note signature of Part II, which is no. 3465.

3445 On orthography: to the Rev. Augustus Jessopp, 243–244. **Walter Savage Landor.** Signed. (Note, p. 418, by the author of no. 3459.)

3446 Moldo-Wallachia, 245–252. **Mihail Kogălniceanŭ?** Attr. by Michael Sturdza in letter to the editors of the *Index,* Feb. 5, 1968; Kogălniceanŭ was in London at this time and met A. H. Layard, who may have put him in touch with *FM*; the *BMCat.* shows that Kogălniceanŭ was a Roumanian who might well have written this learned and first-hand account of the country.

VOLUME 53, MARCH 1856

3447 *Tristram Shandy* or *The Caxtons?* 253–267.

3448 A few mediæval painters, 267–274.

3449 The Dutch army, 275–281. **M. P. Lindo.** Signed M.P.L.—see nos. 3185, 3294.

3450 The rose garden of Sadi, 281–292. **E. B. Cowell.** List in *Life.*

3451 Kate Coventry (chaps. ix–xii), 293–311. **G. J Whyte-Melville.** Evidence for no. 3432.

3452 *The Dead Sea Route,* and *The Pilgrimage to Mecca* [by Richard Burton], 311–326. **Henry A. Murray.** Signed H.A.M.—see no. 3946.

3453 Protestantism: Zwingli and his times,

326–341. **W. D. Arnold,** prob. Signed W.D.A.—see no. 3373; he used these initials in *FM,* but usually on Indian subjects.

3454 Butler's *Poems,* 342–355.

3455 *The Organ,* 355–369. **John Hullah.** Signed J.H.; cf. no. 3347.

3456 The peace conferences, 369–378.

VOLUME 53, APRIL 1856

3457 A journey along the western frontier of north Finland in the summer of 1855, 379–394.

3458 *The Table-Talk of Samuel Rogers,* 395–403.

3459 On the treatment of love in novels, 405–418.

3460 Kate Coventry (chaps. xiii–xvi), 419–437. **G. J. Whyte-Melville.** Evidence for no. 3432.

3461 *Pinocchi,* 438–442.

3462 Imaginary conversations (No. II, concl.): Alfieri and Metastasio; Menander and Epicurus, 443–460. **Walter Savage Landor.** Signed; repr. *Works,* III and I.

3463 *Poetical Works of Geoffrey Chaucer,* 461–472.

3464 Sketches on the north coast (No. I): a naturalist at home, 472–479. **John Skelton.** Signed at start A Naturalist, at end Shirley; repr. *Nugae Criticae* as "At the Seaside."

3465 Old rings (Part II), 479–489. **C. D. Badham.** Signed C.D.B.; cf. no. 3444.

3466 *Poems,* by Edward Capern, 489–495. **J. A. Froude.** Signed J.A.F.; claimed in *Blackwood's,* 156 (Dec. 1894), 762.

3467 Foreign and domestic politics, 495–504.

VOLUME 53, MAY 1856

3468 College life at Glasgow, 505–522. **A. K. H. Boyd.** Repr. *Leisure Hours.*

3469 The United States, Cuba, and Canada, 522–533.

3470 Kate Coventry (chaps. xvii–xx), 535–554. **G. J. Whyte-Melville.** Evidence for no. 3432.

3471 Sketches on the north coast (No. II): the rocks in spring, 555–562. **John Skelton.** Evidence for no. 3464.

3472 M. Montalembert and John Wilson Croker; or, *traduttore traditore,* 563–583. **A. V. Kirwan.** Pages 565–567n. contain a half-dozen sentences which are found again, in good part verbatim, in Kirwan's *Modern France*, pp. 300–303. (Letter p. 749, signed **John Murray**, with reply, pp. 749–750 by the author, and note, p. 750, by **John W. Parker**, 1820–1860—signed Ed. of *Fraser's Magazine*.)

3473 Old rings (Part III): medical rings, 584–596. **C. D. Badham.** Cf. no. 3444.

3474 Alison's *History of Europe*, 597–611. **Fitzjames Stephen**, prob. Signed F.S.–I.T.; Stephen was "called to the bar of the Inner Temple" in 1854 (*Life* by Leslie Stephen [1905], p. 136); he attacked Alison on similar grounds in a similar style in the *Saturday Rev.*, Dec. 22, 1855, pp. 137–139 (Bevington, *Saturday Review*, p. 244); Leslie Stephen, *Life*, p. 485, says that before 1863, when his brother began to contribute regularly to *FM*, he had written "a few earlier articles" for the magazine.

3475 *The New Pitaval* [German collection of criminal trials], 612–626.

3476 The Treaty [of peace with Russia], 627–630.

VOLUME 53, JUNE 1856

3477 A Whit-week in Manchester, 631–647. **Robert Lamb.** Signed at start Edited by a Manchester Man; at end, R.L.; repr. *Free Thoughts*, I.

3478 Ruskin on the ancient and the modern poets: Homer and Tennyson, 648–659. **John Skelton.** Signed J.O.S.; partly repr. *Nugae Criticae*, as "A Critic on Criticism."

3479 *The Organ Question*, 660–668. **A. K. H. Boyd.** Repr. *Critical Essays* and *Leisure Hours*.

3480 Kate Coventry (chaps. xxi–xxiv, concl.), 669–685. **G. J. Whyte-Melville.** Evidence for no. 3432.

3481 Pre-Raphaelitism from different points of view, 686–693. Signed: A.Y.—R.S.

3482 Kars, and the parliamentary debate, 694–710.

3483 Decline of French romantic literature, 711–721. **A. V. Kirwan**, prob. On p. 711 the author refers to our previous sketches of Dr. Véron's, *Memoirs*, citing nos. 3169 and 3356, pp. 683–689; pp. 711, 713, 714, 718 show firsthand knowledge of French periodicals (cf. *Modern France*, chaps. i–ii); cf. general evidence for no. 2307.

3484 The art of story-telling, 722–732.

3485 Arago's *Popular Astronomy*, 733–742.

3486 Political ruminations, 743–748.

VOLUME 54, JULY 1856

3487 Edinburgh during the general assembly, 1–18.

3488 Old rings (Part IV, concl.), 18–30. **C. D. Badham.** Signed C.D.B.; cf. no. 3465.

3489 Froude's *History of England* [Vols. I–II], 31–46. **W. B. Donne.** Johnson, *Donne*, list.

3490 Sir Edwin Landseer as a naturalist and landscape painter, 47–53. **Charles Boner.** Signed.

3491 Lost at cards, 54–64.

3492 *The Campaigns of Paskiewitch and Omer Pacha in Asia*, 64–78. **Henry A. Murray.** Signed H.A.M.—see no. 3946.

3493 Lord Cockburn's *Memorials*, 79–89.

3494 Sketches on the north coast (No. III): the shores of the Scamander, 90–97. **John Skelton.** Evidence for no. 3464.

3495 De Bazancourt's *Crimean Expedition*, 97–110.

3496 An overland mail adventure [to the East], 111–121. **W. D. Arnold.** Signed W.D.A.—see no. 3373.

3497 The American questions, 121–126.

VOLUME 54, AUGUST 1856

3498 A peep into the principalities [Wallachia and Moldavia], 127–139. **George Whyte-Melville.** Signed G.W.M.—see no. 3326.

3499 Dwarfs and giants (Part I), 140–153. **G. H. Lewes.** Signed G.H.L.; Lewes, "Receipts."

3500 Sir Archibald Alison, 154–169. **Fitzjames Stephen**, prob. Signed F.S.—I.T.—see no. 3474.

3501 The double house, 170–186. **Dinah Mulock.** Signed The Author of *John Halifax, Gentleman;* repr. *Nothing New*, N.Y., 1857.

3502 The opera season of 1856, 186–196.

3503 Life at the water cure, 197–207. **A. K. H. Boyd.** Repr. *Critical Essays.*

3504 Curiosities of contemporary literature from the two Sicilies, 208–219. **J. M. Ludlow.** Signed Vicesimus Smatterling, B.L.; Ludlow's list.

3505 *Life and Manners in Persia*, 220–230.

3506 A midsummer day with the poets,

231–237. **John Skelton.** Signed Shirley
—see *DNB*.

3507 The last naval campaign in the Pacific, 238–244. **Francis Marx.** Signed F.M.; repr. *The Pacific and the Amoor*, 1861.

3508 The session of 1856, 247–252.

VOLUME 54, SEPTEMBER 1856

3509 Science by the seaside [in Devon], 253–260. **George Tugwell.** Signed T.; attr. by G. H. Lewes in Eliot, *Letters*, II, 274.

3510 Gilfillan's *History of a Man* [i.e., of himself], 260–269.

3511 Prospects of the Indian civil service: the "open" system, 270–285.

3512 Dwarfs and giants (Part II, concl.), 286–293. **G. H. Lewes.** Evidence for no. 3499.

3513 Maud Vivian, 294–314. Signed G.F.P. Perhaps George Frederick Pardon, who published several books under these initials in the 1850s and wrote some short stories.

3514 *Hours with the Mystics*, 315–328. **Charles Kingsley.** Signed C.K.; repr. *Miscellanies*, I and *Works*, XX.

3515 Sketches on the north coast (No. IV): the yellow sands, 329–335. **John Skelton.** Evidence for no. 3464.

3516 Stanley's *Sinai and Palestine*, 336–345. **Thomas C. Sandars.** Signed T.C.S.—see nos. 3583, 3650.

3517 *Pius IX. and Lord Palmerston* [by Montalembert], 345–347. **William Stirling-Maxwell.** Attr. in *Essays*, p. 481.

3518 Aytoun's *Bothwell*, 347–358.

3519 Jack Sepoy, 359–362. **W. D. Arnold.** Signed W.D.A.—see no. 3373.

3520 *France before and since the Revolution of 1789* [by de Tocqueville], 363–374.

VOLUME 54, OCTOBER 1856

3521 The Bashi-Bazouks [Turkish soldiers], 375–392.

3522 The last house in C—— Street, 392–398. **Dinah Mulock.** Repr. *Nothing New*, N.Y., 1857.

3523 Protestantism from a Roman-Catholic point of view, 398–406. Signed: A.R.B.

3524 Journal of a tour in the Crimea, 1856 (Part I), 407–420. Signed: H.F.V.

3525 Ancient gems (Part I): ornamental

stones, 421–432. **C. D. Badham.** Signed C.D.B.; attr. in no. 3630, p. 163.

3526 *Richard Cromwell and the Dawn of the Restoration* [by Guizot], 433–445. **John W. Wilkins?** Signed J.W.W.; Wilkins had reviewed other French historians: see this *Index*, I, 1139.

3527 Shakspeare and his native county, 446–456. Signed: J.W.

3528 James Montgomery, 457–473. **A. K. H. Boyd.** Repr. *Critical Essays.*

3529 *The Angel in the House* [by Coventry Patmore], 473–484. **George Brimley.** Repr. *Essays.*

3530 The two Tuppers, 484–486. **Charles John Evans.** Signed C.J.E.; this is an anecdote of Eton life under Dr. Keats, in fictional form, ending with the author's going to King's Coll. Camb. where he was the friend of a man who later became a Fellow; Evans is the only C.J.E. in Venn (1752–1900) who went to Eton, and he was a Fellow of King's, 1853–1866.

3531 The kingdom of the two Sicilies: its present state and future prospects, 486–500.

VOLUME 54, NOVEMBER 1856

3532 Glasgow down the water, 501–511. **A. K. H. Boyd.** Repr. *Recreations*, 2nd series.

3533 *Memoirs of Frederick Perthes*, 512–523. Signed: G.E.F.

3534 Journal of a tour in the Crimea, 1856 (Part II, concl.), 524–538. Signed: H.F.V.

3535 Meg of Elibank; recovered from a pigeon-hole in an ancient escritoir: the MSS. modernized in language, and with occasional interpolations, 539–559. **Henrietta Keddie.** Repr. in *Meg of Elibank and Other Tales*, by the Author of *The Nut-Brown Maids*, 1860: see H&L under both books, and *BMCat.* under Henrietta Keddie.

3536 Ancient gems (Part II, concl.), 560–573. **C. D. Badham.** Evidence for no. 3525.

3537 Communications with the Far East [plea for Suez Canal], 574–581.

3538 Sketches on the North coast (No. V): the Land's End, 582–591. **John Skelton.** Evidence for no. 3464.

3539 Mansfield's *Paraguay, Brazil, and the Plate*, 591–601. **Charles Kingsley.** Repr. *Miscellanies*, II.

3540 Jámi, the Persian poet, 603–610. **E. B. Cowell.** Signed E.B.C.—see list in *Life*.

3541 What are the United States coming to? 611–622. **W. H. Hurlbert,** prob. Charles Kingsley to A. C. Fraser, Feb. 6, 1856, Fraser Papers, reports that a South Carolinian called Hurlbert has an art. in the forthcoming *Edin. Rev.* on the American crisis (viz., no. 2324 in *Index*, I, Oct. 1856) and another in the forthcoming *Fraser* on the feeling of the South towards the North; both adopt the same historical approach and anti-Southern view; the quotation from Judge Story, *ER*, p. 593, is repeated here, p. 618; cf. the Kansas election in *ER*, p. 584, and p. 620 here; in both arts. the author pretends to be an Englishman; on Hurlbert see *DAB*.

VOLUME 54, DECEMBER 1856

3542 An essay on popularity, 623–636. **Robert Lamb.** Signed at start A Manchester Man, at end R.L.; repr. *Free Thoughts*, I.

3543 Professorial elections [Ferrier's *Scottish Philosophy, the Old and the New*], 637–643. **H. H. Lancaster.** Ferrier accused him of writing this attack and interpreted his refusal to answer as tacit admission of authorship: copy of corres. in Nat. Lib. Scot., MS. 4717, fols. 256 ff.

3544 The friends; an episode of Italian life, 644–653.

3545 Sketches on the north coast (No. VI, concl.): the fauna of the frost, 654–664. **John Skelton.** Evidence for no. 3464.

3546 Pauli's *History of England*, 665–680. **J. M. Kemble.** Signed J.M.K.—see no. 3374.

3547 The night mail train in India, 680–684. **W. D. Arnold.** Signed W.D.A.—see no. 3373.

3548 The muniment chamber at Losely Place [in Surrey], 685–701. Signed: Devonia.

3549 Some talk about Scotch peculiarities, 702–714. **A. K. H. Boyd.** Signed at Start Charles Oliver Ardersier-Macdonald, Esq., of Craig-Houlakim, near Whistle-Binkie, N.B., at end C.O.A.M.; repr. *Leisure Hours*. (See no. 3615.)

3550 *What Every Christian Must Know*, 716–728. **J. M. Ludlow.** Signed J.M.L.—see Ludlow's list.

3551 The Denison case, 732–735. **F. D. Maurice.** Signed.

3552 Politics, foreign and domestic, 736–742.

VOLUME 55, JANUARY 1857

3553 The interpreter; a tale of the War (chaps. i–v), 1–17. **G. J. Whyte-Melville.** Signed; novel published 1858.

3554 Tuscan proverbs, 18–28. **Whitley Stokes.** *Bibliography*.

3555 Ticket of leave, 29–38. Unidentified. (See no. 3572.)

3556 A trip to Scotland, 39–44. **V. H. Hobart.** Signed H.; repr. *Fragments*, 1875, and *Writings*, I.

3557 Cornelius Agrippa and the alchemists, 45–58. **John Ormsby.** Signed J.O.; attr. by Whitley Stokes, in *Letters to Allingham*, ed. Helen Allingham and Mrs. E. Braumer Williams (1911), p. 270.

3558 A visit to a model farm in Asia Minor, 59–63. Signed: θ.

3559 Archbishop Whately on Bacon, 64–79. **A. K. H. Boyd.** Repr. *Critical Essays* and *Autumn Holidays*.

3560 The last salmon before close time: extract from a letter from my brother, Percy Popjoy, Esq., in North Britain, 79–83. **G. H. Kingsley.** Signed G.H.K.; repr. *Sport and Travel*. (Note, p. 83, by **Charles Kingsley,** prob.—signed C.K.)

3561 Sermons and sermonizers, 84–94.

3562 Sketches and studies from Belgium (No. III, concl.): Bruges from the belfry tower, 94–101. **R. J. King.** Signed R.J.K.; repr. *Sketches*.

3563 Staff officer on the war in the Crimea, 103–112.

3564 The triumph of barbarism, 118–126. **Charles A. Bristed.** Signed at start A New Yorker, at end C.A.B.—see nos. 2699 and 3364.

VOLUME 55, FEBRUARY 1857

3565 Gleanings from the Record Office (Part I): the dissolution of the monasteries, 127–143. **J. A. Froude.** Signed; repr. *Studies*, I, as "The Dissolution of the Monasteries." (Part II is no. 3614.)

3566 The interpreter (chaps. vi–ix), 144–160. **G. J. Whyte-Melville.** Signed.

3567 A visit to Kars while in the hands of the Russians, 160–173.

3568 Emanuel Swedenborg, 174–182. **Coventry Patmore.** Signed C.P.—Reid, *Patmore*, bibliog.

3569 The three numbers, 183–194.

3570 Life in its simpler forms, 194–203. **G. H. Lewes.** Signed G.H.L.—Lewes, "Receipts."

3571 A Christmas week at Glasgow, 204–216. **A. K. H. Boyd.** On p. 204 he reminds his readers of no. 3532; no. 3532 ends, p. 511, with a promise to write this companion piece.

3572 Mr. Justice Willes on tickets of leave and transportation, 216–217. Unidentified, but half the art. is a quotation from James Shaw Willes.

3573 Little lessons for little poets, 218–235. **George Brimley?** On p. 233 author speaks of "our" previous criticism of *The Angel in the House* for its radical error in construction, which was in no. 3529, p. 483; in general cf. this review of poetry with that in no. 3315; attr. by L. J. Phelan, "Life and Letters of George Brimley," Harvard Univ. dissertation, 1938, pp. 328, 447.

3574 A glimpse of the temple caves of Ajunta, 236–238. Signed: J.W.B.

3575 The war with China, 239–248.

VOLUME 55, MARCH 1857

3576 Literary style (Part I), 249–264. **William Forsyth.** Repr. *Essays*, 1874.

3577 The interpreter (chaps. x–xiii), 265–281. **G. J. Whyte-Melville.** Signed.

3578 Boswell's *Letters*, 282–296. **James Craigie Robertson,** prob. Signed J.C.R.—see no. 3397, also on a Scottish subject.

3579 Rooks, 297–311. **W. J. Broderip,** prob. The use of an epigraph, the quotations from literature, especially from the Classics, the personal anecdotes, and the citation of standard authorities on ornithology like Yarrell and Macgillivray are all characteristic of the series of arts. on birds Broderip wrote for *FM* (see no. 3591, etc.).

3580 A few notes on Canadian matters (Part I), 312–328. **W. C. Keppel.** Signed Beta Mikron; cf. no. 3622.

3581 *The Gladiator of Ravenna* [by Friedrich Halm], 329–345. **Theodore Martin.** Repr. *Essays*, I.

3582 A chapter on flowerless plants, 345–353. Signed: Devonia.

3583 Kemble's *State Papers*, 354–363. **T. C. Sandars.** Signed T.C.S.; see no. 3650 and *DNB*; attr. in Bevington, *Saturday Review*, p. 370.

3584 Public affairs, 364–370.

VOLUME 55, APRIL 1857

3585 Siam and the Siamese, 371–386.

3586 The laird's seam, 387–396. **Henrietta Keddie.** Signed The Author of "Meg of Elibank"—see no. 3535.

3587 *German Love*, 396–399. **J. A. Froude.** Attr. confidently by Susanna Winkworth in Catherine Winkworth, *Letters and Memorials* (1883), II, 192.

3588 Six months at Kertch, 400–408. **Lascelles Wraxall.** Signed L.W.; many facts and phrases here, pp. 400–405, reappear in Wraxall's *Scraps and Sketches*, I, chap. ii, "A Winter at Kertch," pp. 28–34, 40, 43–45, 47; the chapter had been reprinted from *Bentley's Miscellany*, 39 (June 1856), 585–598.

3589 The interpreter (chaps. xiv–xvii), 409–423. **G. J. Whyte-Melville.** Signed.

3590 Literary style (Part II, concl.), 424–437. **William Forsyth.** Repr. *Essays*, 1874.

3591 The raven: where is Ralpho? 438–454. **W. J. Broderip.** Signed β—see no. 3844, p. 487.

3592 Calderon, 455–470. **W. B. Donne.** Signed W.B.D.; Johnson, *Donne*, list; FitzGerald, *Letters*, I, 253.

3593 Ancient history of Sunbury, 471–473. **Jesse Watts Russell.** Signed J.W.R.; this and four later arts. (see below, Part B) are all highly learned, antiquarian essays; man cited had been a F.S.A. since 1821: see list of Fellows, *Prods. of the Soc. of Antiquaries*, 4 (Apr. 1857).

3594 Some talk about food, 474–484. Signed: E.R.H. Perhaps Edward Rupert Humphreys, classicist and writer of miscellaneous essays (see *BMCat.*); the art. partly discusses special dishes of the Greeks and Romans.

3595 The elections, 486–492.

VOLUME 55, MAY 1857

3596 Imperialism, 493–506. **Goldwin Smith.** Signed G.S., as in no. 3947; attr. by Patricia H. Gaffney, *Goldwin Smith Bibliography* (Ithaca, N.Y., 1972), addenda to p. 6.

3597 Crows and choughs, 507–523. **W. J. Broderip.** Signed β—see no. 3844, p. 487.

3598 The mythology of Finnland, 523–537. **Whitley Stokes.** Signed Macc dá cherda [son of the craft]; *Bibliography*.

3599 The interpreter (chaps. xvii–xix), 538–553. **G. J. Whyte-Melville.** Signed.

3600 A few notes on Canadian matters (Part II), 554–568. **W. C. Keppel.** Signed Beta Mikron; cf. no. 3622.

3601 *Charlotte Brontë* [by Mrs. Gaskell], 569–582. **John Skelton.** Signed Shirley; repr. *Essays.*

3602 Taste in France, 583–589. **F. T. Palgrave.** Signed F.T.P.—see no. 4212.

3603 Mr. Warren's *Miscellanies*, 590–601.

3604 Excursions in Armenia, 602–611.

3605 John Mitchell Kemble, 612–618. **W. B. Donne.** Attr. Johnson, *Donne*, list.

VOLUME 55, JUNE 1857

3606 What are the functions of the artist? [on Ruskin's *Modern Painters*], 619–635. **John Skelton.** Signed Shirley—see *DNB.*

3607 A wooing and wedding of 17—, 636–649. **Henrietta Keddie.** Signed The Author of "Meg of Elibank"—see no. 3535.

3608 The press and the public service, 649–662.

3609 The interpreter (chaps. xxi–xxiv), 663–679. **G. J. Whyte-Melville.** Signed.

3610 Blackey at school [on natives of Hindostan], 679–684.

3611 Edgar Allan Poe, 684–700. **A. K. H. Boyd.** Signed K.P.I.; repr. *Critical Essays.*

3612 Deer (Part I), 701–717. **W. J. Broderip.** Signed β—see no. 3844, p. 487.

3613 Abdallah and Saida; a tale of Mesopotamia, 718–722.

3614 Gleanings from the Record Office (Part II): Henry the Eighth and Mary Boleyn, 724–738. **J. A. Froude.** Signed.

VOLUME 56, JULY 1857

3615 Some further talk about Scotch affairs, 1–15. **A. K. H. Boyd.** Signed C. A. Macdonald; repr. *Autumn Holidays* as if by C. A. Macdonald—see no. 3549.

3616 Palgrave's *History of Normandy and of England* [in 10th Century], 16–33. **John Mounteney Jephson,** prob. Signed J.M.J.; Jephson became F.S.A. in 1855 and later wrote book on a tour of Brittany.

3617 A day at Beaconsfield [where Burke lived], 33–38. Signed: H.T.

3618 The Philobiblon Society, 39–46.

3619 The interpreter (chaps. xxv–xxvii), 47–63. **G. J. Whyte-Melville.** Signed.

3620 A chapter on the sea, 64–71. **V. H.**

Hobart. Signed H.; repr. *Fragments,* 1875, and *Writings,* I.

3621 Deer (Part II), 72–89. **W. J. Broderip.** Evidence for no. 3612, p. 487.

3622 Notes on Canadian matters (Part III, concl.), 90–105. **W. C. Keppel.** Signed "Viscount Bury, M.P."; cf. no. 3580.

3623 Alfred de Musset, 106–113. **Eliza Lynn Linton.** Signed E.L., as is no. 3666, also on a modern French writer.

3624 Origin of the name of England, 114–118. **Jesse Watts Russell.** Signed J.W.R.; cf. no. 3593.

3625 The militia, 118–126.

VOLUME 56, AUGUST 1857

3626 Our past, present, and future policy in Persia, 127–140.

3627 High and low latitudes, 141–150. **William Stirling-Maxwell.** Signed W.S.; attr. in *Essays,* p. 481.

3628 The opera season of 1857, 151–157.

3629 A few words on France and French affairs, 157–161. **A. V. Kirwan?** The political position and the general style, with its tart criticism, are characteristic of *Fraser's* main writer on contemporary French politics; see Kirwan's letter quoted in evidence for no. 2307.

3630 Charles David Badham: in memoriam, 162–163. **John W. Parker,** 1820–1860. Signed P.; written in the name of *FM* and giving list of his contributions.

3631 The Indian army, 164–172. **Augustus Andrews?** Signed A.A.; the art. was written by an Indian army officer of considerable experience (pp. 164, 165), but written in England (pp. 164, 172); the subject is the dangerously large native element in the Indian army and how to render it benign; General Andrews went to India in 1793, officered 5 native regiments between 1829 and 1856, and was home on furlough in 1857: see Boase and *East-India Register and Army List.* Possibly by August Abbott, Indian army officer in *DNB,* 1st suppl., who was a writer—on the Afghan War.

3632 The interpreter (chaps. xxviii–xxxi), 173–191. **G. J. Whyte-Melville.** Signed.

3633 *George Stephenson and the Railway* [by Samuel Smiles], 191–203. **A. K. H. Boyd.** Signed K.P.I.; repr. *Critical Essays.*

3634 Deer (Part III, concl.), 204–221. **W. J. Broderip.** Evidence for no. 3612.

3635 English social life from the thirteenth to the sixteenth centuries, 222–237. Signed: Devonia.

3636 The Indian mutinies, 238–241. Unidentified. (See no. 3668.)

3637 The session of 1857, 244–252.

VOLUME 56, SEPTEMBER 1857

3638 *Handel,* 253–271. **John Hullah.** Signed J. H.—see no. 3347.

3639 Magpies, 272–287. **W. J. Broderip.** Signed β—see no. 3844, p. 487.

3640 The taste of the day (Part I), 288–296. **John Zephaniah Bell.** Signed at start A Professional Painter, at end J.Z.B.; man cited is the only J.Z.B. in Algernon Graves, *The Royal Academy of Art: a Complete Dictionary of Contributors* (8 vols., 1905–1906), I, 85–418; Bell, who was a painter, is on p. 175.

3641 A visit to Eton, 296–298.

3642 The interpreter (chaps. xxxiii–xxxv), 299–317. **G. J. Whyte-Melville.** Signed.

3643 Naval education, 318–330. **Caroline Frances Cornwallis.** *Letters,* p. 443.

3644 Helps's *Conquest of Spanish America* [Vol. III], 331–345. **W. B. Donne.** Johnson, *Donne,* List.

3645 Perfumery, 346–350.

3646 An essay on crotchets, 350–362. **Robert Lamb.** Signed at start A Manchester Man, at end R.L.; repr. *Free Thoughts,* I.

3647 Rise and progress of the subalpine kingdom [Piedmont], 363–378. Signed: S.

VOLUME 56, OCTOBER 1857

3648 Manchester, and its Exhibitions of 1857, 379–395. **Robert Lamb.** Signed at start A Manchester Man, at end R.L.; repr. *Free Thoughts,* II.

3649 The origin and function of music, 396–408. **Herbert Spencer.** Signed H.S.; repr. *Essays,* I.

3650 Buckle's *History of Civilization in England,* 409–424. **T. C. Sandars.** Signed T.C.S.; attr. in Buckle, *Life,* pp. 132n., 487.

3651 The interpreter (chaps. xxxvi–xxxviii), 425–443. **G. J. Whyte-Melville.** Signed.

3652 Shooting in Albania, 443–456. **Robert B. Mansfield.** Signed at start The Author of *The Log of the Water-Lily,* at end R.B.M.; repr. *New and Old Chips from an Old Block,* 1896, as chap. vi.

3653 Jays and nutcrackers, 457–472. **W. J. Broderip.** Signed β—see no. 3844, p. 487.

3654 The curate of Edenholm, 473–480.

W. D. Arnold. Signed W.D.A.—see no. 3373.

3655 Horæ dramaticæ (No. III, concl.): the "flask" of Cratinus, 482–488. **T. L. Peacock.** Signed The Author of *Headlong Hall;* repr. *Works,* X. (No. II was no. 2959.)

3656 Wanderings on Exmoor, 489–498. **George Tugwell.** Signed T.; attr. by G. H. Lewes in Eliot, *Letters,* II, 274.

3657 Art and history, 498–504. **Robert Alfred Vaughan.** Signed R.A.V.; repr. *Essays and Remains* (1858), II.

VOLUME 56, NOVEMBER 1857

3658 About Edinburgh, 505–520. **A. K. H. Boyd.** Signed K.P.I.—see no. 3633.

3659 Lord Macaulay of Rothley, 521–526. **T. E. Kebbel.** Signed T.E.K.; Kebbel wrote under these initials for *Cornhill;* a paper on Macaulay, dated Feb. 1860, is in his *Essays.*

3660 A precursor of the *Vestiges* [Robinet's *De la Nature*], 526–531. **G. H. Lewes.** Signed G.H.L.; Lewes, "Receipts."

3661 Metropolitan communications [in London], 532–547. Signed: A.W.

3662 The interpreter (chaps. xxxix–xlii), 551–570. **G. J. Whyte-Melville.** Signed.

3663 Rollers and kingfishers, 571–589. **W. J. Broderip.** Signed β—see no. 3844, p. 487.

3664 *Memoirs of St. Simon,* 590–604. **A. V. Kirwan.** Pages 590–591 contain at least 7 borrowings verbatim from the *Brit.Quart. Rev.,* 16 (Aug. 1852), 105, 109, 110, 111, 118, in an art. on French memoirs written by the author of *FM,* nos. 3083, 3142 (see *Brit.Quart.Rev.,* 17 [May 1853], 480n.)—who was Kirwan; pp. 591, 595–596 contain four borrowings nearly verbatim from *Brit.Quart.Rev.,* 16 (Nov. 1852), 388–390—also by Kirwan, on the same evidence.

3665 The taste of the day (Part II), 604–611. **John Zephaniah Bell.** Evidence for no. 3640.

3666 Daniele Manin, 612–619. **Eliza Lynn Linton.** Signed E.L.; Eliza Lynn did not become Mrs. Linton until 1858; author knew Manin in Paris and often noticed his "intense affection" for his daughter (p. 619): see G. S. Layard, *Mrs. Lynn Linton* (1901), p. 80.

3667 The Birmingham Congress, 619–626. **Mark Pattison.** Signed M.P.; Bodleian Lib., Pattison MS. 40, f. 24, records receipt from *FM* for art. in this issue; attr. in *DNB.*

3668 The Indian mutinies, 627–630. Unidentified. (See nos. 3721 and 3736,
which were also sent like this from Jes-
sore.)

VOLUME 56, DECEMBER 1857

3669 Waterton's *Essays on Natural History,
Third Series,* 631–649. **W. J. Broderip,**
prob. Broderip, a "most important and
frequent contributor" to *FM* (see no.
3844, p. 485) began writing his popular
but learned arts. on natural history in
Jan. 1850; they are marked by quotations and footnotes from many antiquarian sources, bits of poetry, scattered
Latin and French phrases; p. 649 repeats
an episode related by Broderip in no.
2758, p. 292; he had reviewed an earlier
series of Waterton's essays in the *Quart.
Rev.* (no. 577, *Index,* I).

3670 The story of an Edinburgh church,
650–656.

3671 Recent metaphysical works: Lewes,
Maurice, Fleming, 657–672. **A. K. H.
Boyd.** Signed A.K.H.B.; repr. *Critical
Essays.*

3672 Antiquities of the Jumnah, 672–674.
Jesse Watts Russell. Signed J.W.R.—see
no. 3593.

3673 The interpreter (chaps. xliii–xlvii),
675–698. **G. J. Whyte-Melville.** Signed.

3674 *Memorials and Correspondence of
Charles James Fox,* 698–709. Signed: W.

3675 On the use of proverbs in grave composition, 710–718. **W. D. Watson,** prob.
On p. 710 the extensive summary of no.
3088, pp. 470–473, which "we" wrote,
clearly implies a common authorship; on
p. 711, the same art. is quoted; Watson
regularly reviewed Trench for *FM*: besides no. 3088, see nos. 2921, 3394.

3676 The "Englishman's-house-his-castle"
theory; or, A glance at the police of the
streets, 719–724. Signed: A Grumbler.

3677 Lord Normanby and *A Year of
Revolution,* 724–735. **A. V. Kirwan,**
prob. This art. on French politics in the
1840s is typical of Kirwan's work in
general; in particular, cf. the view of
Cavaignac, p. 733, with no. 3629, p. 159;
of Guizot and Duchâtel, p. 728, with
Brit. Quart. Rev., 7 (Feb. 1848), 135–
136, 146 [to be assigned to Kirwan on
good evidence in *Index,* IV].

3678 India in mourning, 737–750. **W. D.
Arnold.** Attr. by F. J. Woodward, *The
Doctor's Disciples* (1954) pp. 215, 234.

VOLUME 57, JANUARY 1858

3679 On the life and writings of Henry
Fielding (Part I), 1–13. **Thomas Keight-
ley.** Signed; repr. *Life and Writings of
Henry Fielding, taken from the Pages of
"Fraser's Magazine,"* and edited by
Frederick Stover Dickson, Cleveland,
1907. (Postscript, pp. 762–763, by
Keightley—signed T.K.)

3680 Lady Strathmore's daughter (chaps.
i–v), 14–32. **Henrietta Keddie.** Signed
The Author of "Meg of Elibank" —no.
3535.

3681 A visit to the châteaux of Rubens and
Teniers, 32–40. **R. J. King.** Repr.
Sketches.

3682 Table-talk on Shakspeare: *Love's
Labour's Lost,* 41–45. **Edward Strachey,**
prob. Attr. by Sanders, *Strachey Family,*
p. 152.

3683 Woodpeckers, 46–62. **W. J. Broderip.**
Signed β—see no. 3844, p. 487.

3684 The physician's art: Dr. Watson, 94–
104. **G. H. Lewes.** Signed G.H.L.;
Lewes, "Receipts."

3685 Northern lights: city poems and city
sermons, 105–118. **John Skelton.** Signed
Shirley—see *DNB.*

3686 Livingstone's *Travels in South Africa,*
118–132. **T. C. Sandars.** Signed T.C.S.—
see nos. 3583, 3650.

3687 "A mad world, my masters," 133–142.
Charles Kingsley. Signed at start A
Sanitary Reformer, at end C.K.; repr.
Miscellanies, I, and *Works,* XVIII.

VOLUME 57, FEBRUARY 1858

3688 *Thorndale; or, The Conflict of
Opinions* [by William Smith], 143–159.
A. K. H. Boyd. Signed A.K.H.B.; repr.
Critical Essays and *Leisure Hours.*

3689 [Headnote to] The tapiser's tale;
attempted in the manner of Chaucer,
160–163. **Leigh Hunt.** Signed.

3690 Lady Strathmore's daughter (chaps.
vi–xii, concl.), 163–183. **Henrietta Keddie.** Evidence for no. 3680.

3691 How we escaped from Delhi, 184–189.
C. T. Le Bas. Signed.

3692 *The Physical Geography of the Sea,*
191–204.

3693 On the life and writings of Henry
Fielding (Part II, concl.), 205–217.
Thomas Keightley. Signed. (Postscript,
pp. 762–763, by **Keightley**—signed T.K.)

3694 False views of meanness, 218–221. Signed: A Grumbler.

3695 A ride in Mexico, 222–231. Signed: W.C.

3696 A word about our theatres, 231–241. **Theodore Martin.** Signed D.G.; repr. *Essays*, I.

3697 Cyrus Redding's *Personal Recollections*, 242–253.

3698 Charles James Napier; a study of character, 254–268. **John Skelton.** Signed Shirley; repr. *Essays*.

VOLUME 57, MARCH 1858

3699 An Anglo-Indian view of the Indian crisis (Part I), 269–282. **W. D. Arnold.** Signed The Author of "India in Mourning"—see no. 3678.

3700 The history of science; and some of its lessons [on William Whewell's *History of the Inductive Sciences*], 283–294. **J. D. Forbes.** Signed.

3701 Concerning country houses and country life, 295–311. **A. K. H. Boyd.** Signed A.K.H.B.; repr. *Recreations*, 1st series.

3702 Recruiting, 311–323. **William O'Malley.** Signed W.O.; pp. 315–316 show that author was at the siege of Sebastopol in Crimean War; see *Army List*/60, where O'Malley is the only "W.O." who is said to have been at Sebastopol.

3703 Lone-house Dale; a tale in six chapters, 323–341. **Eliza Lynn Linton.** Signed E.L.—see nos. 3622, 3666; Miss Lynn was not married until Mar. 24, 1858.

3704 Bee-eaters, wrynecks, creepers, and nuthatches, 342–357. **W. J. Broderip.** Signed β—see no. 3844, p. 487.

3705 Extent of the Indian mutinies, 358–362. Unidentified. (See no. 3721.)

3706 Aaron Burr, 363–370.

3707 The India Bill: a letter to the editor on the proposed Council of Eight, 371–376. **Arthur Helps.** Signed A.H.; repr. *Correspondence*, pp. 201–215.

3708 *Phantasmata*, 376–385.

3709 Decline and fall of Lord Palmerston's ministry, 386–394.

VOLUME 57, APRIL 1858

3710 Influence of women on the progress of knowledge, 395–407. **Henry Thomas Buckle.** Signed; repr. *Miscellaneous and Posthumous Works* (1872), I.

3711 My winter-garden, 408–425. **Charles**

Kingsley. Signed at start A Minute Philosopher, at end C.K.; repr. *Miscellanies*, I.

3712 *History of Italian Literature* [mainly on Dante], 426–439. Signed: A.R.B.

3713 *The Rambles of a Naturalist*, 441–458. **W. J. Broderip,** prob. Passage on p. 453 is cited in no. 3749, p. 69; on p. 453 high praise of Owen, whom Broderip greatly admired (see no. 3829, p. 487); the learned footnotes and popular style are characteristic of this man's many arts. on natural history in *FM*.

3714 Squire Bolton's transgression (chaps. i–iii), 459–473. **Henrietta Keddie.** Signed The Author of "Meg of Elibank"—see no. 3535.

3715 An Anglo-Indian view of the Indian crisis (Part II, concl.), 473–487. **W. D. Arnold.** Evidence for no. 3699.

3716 Mortality in the army: its causes and remedies, 487–502. **W. A. Guy.** Signed.

3717 Chapelle and Bachaumont, 502–511. **T. L. Peacock.** Signed The Author of *Headlong Hall*; repr. *Works*, X.

3718 The new ministry, 511–516.

VOLUME 57, MAY 1858

3719 A threnode to the east wind, 517–527. **Robert Lamb.** Signed at start A Manchester Man, at end R.L.; repr. *Free Thoughts*, II.

3720 *Oulita, the Serf*, 528–543. **A. K. H. Boyd.** Signed A.K.H.B.; repr. *Critical Essays* and *Leisure Hours*.

3721 The Indian mutinies: our past and future policy, in religion and colonization, 544–549. Unidentified. (See no. 3668.)

3722 Bürger and his translators, 549–554. **W. D. Watson.** Signed W.D.W.—see no. 3327.

3723 The taste of the day (Part III, concl.): our houses, 555–562. **John Zephaniah Bell.** Evidence for no. 3640.

3724 Squire Bolton's transgression (chaps. iv–vi), 563–578. **Henrietta Keddie.** Evidence for no. 3714.

3725 The unsocial evil: its nature, origin, and remedy; with a few well authenticated cases [a story], 579–585. **John Ormsby.** Signed O.; repr. *Stray Papers*, 1876.

3726 Gulls, 585–601. **W. J. Broderip.** Signed β—see no. 3844, p. 487.

3727 [Headnote to] The shewe of faire

seeming; attempted in the manner of Spenser, 602–610. **Leigh Hunt.** Signed.

3728 Robert Stephen Rintoul: in memoriam, 611–613. **John W. Parker,** 1820–1860. Signed P.—see no. 3630; Rintoul was a fellow editor.

3729 Passports and turnpikes, 614–616. Signed: A Grumbler.

3730 Ancient name of the Island of Mersey, 617–619. **Jesse Watts Russell.** Signed J.W.R.—see no. 3593.

3731 Barthomley, 620–635. **James Craigie Robertson.** Signed J.C.R.—see nos. 3397, 3578.

3732 An Anglo-Indian lament for John Company, 635–642. **W. D. Arnold.** Begins by quoting no. 3129 as his.

VOLUME 57, JUNE 1858

3733 Memoirs of Percy Bysshe Shelley (Part I), 643–659. **T. L. Peacock.** Signed; repr. *Works*, VIII. (Part II is no. 3932.)

3734 Political and social prospects of the Australian colonies, 659–670.

3735 Recent French memoirs [Guizot and Louis Blanc], 673–685. **A. V. Kirwan,** prob. Ideas and phrasing on pp. 674, 676, 678 are very similar to those in *Brit. Quart. Rev.*, 7 (Feb. 1848, 126, 127, 129 [to be assigned to Kirwan in *Index*, III]; in general cf. evidence for no. 2307.

3736 The men of the Indian mutinies, 686–690. Unidentified. (See no. 3668.)

3737 Matthew Arnold's *Merope*, 691–701. **John Conington?** Signed J.C.; he wrote for *FM* and was a classical scholar: see *DNB*.

3738 Squire Bolton's transgression (chaps. vii–xi, concl.), 702–713. **Henrietta Keddie.** Evidence for no. 3714.

3739 The albatross, 713–728. **W. J. Broderip.** Signed β—see no. 3844, p. 487.

3740 A mutiny of provincial troops; from Tacitus [applied to the Indian mutiny], 729–736. **Sarah Austin.** Signed S.A.; she used these initials for nos. 2558, 2629, 4618.

3741 Poems from Eversley, by the Rector [Charles Kingsley]; a spring-time study, 736–747. **John Skelton.** Signed Shirley—see *DNB*.

3742 Autumn travels, 747–761. **V. H. Hobart.** Signed H.; repr. *Fragments*, 1875, and *Writings*, I.

3743 Lord Derby's three months of power, 764–770.

VOLUME 58, JULY 1858

3744 Hanworth (chaps. i–iv), 1–15. Unidentified. This novel, published anon. 1858, is perhaps by Juliet Pollock: when W. F. Pollock dined with Parker, the editor of *FM*, on June 17, 1858, he "brought home proofs of 'Hanworth' coming out in *Fraser's Magazine*" (*Remembrances*, II, 71–72); since he says (II, 71) that no. 3927 in Jan. 1860 was his own first contribution to *FM*, it seems more than possible that he was bringing the proofs to his wife, who was also a writer.

3745 Froude's *History of England* [Vols. III–IV], 15–32. **W. B. Donne.** Signed W.B.D.; Johnson, *Donne*, list.

3746 *Teneriffe*—a summer above the clouds, 35–46. **Nevil Story-Maskelyne.** Signed N.S.M.—see no. 3419; man cited was now Professor of Mineralogy at Oxford (see *DNB*); last part of review is on volcanic geology.

3747 Concerning churchyards, 47–59. **A. K. H. Boyd.** Signed A.K.H.B.; repr. *Recreations*, 2nd series.

3748 Delhi as it is, 59–64.

3749 Man-of-war birds, boobies, and noddies, 65–80. **W. J. Broderip.** Signed β— see no. 3844, p. 487.

3750 Consumption in the guards [mortality in the foot guards], 80–86. **W. A. Guy.** Signed.

3751 Catarina in Venice: a study on the lagoon (Part I), 87–104. **John Skelton.** Repr. *Essays in Romance*.

3752 The zoologist about town, 104–110. **John Ormsby.** Signed O.; repr. *Stray Papers*, 1876.

3753 Petrie's *Ancient Music of Ireland*, 111–120. **Margaret McNair Stokes.** Signed Ingen dá cerda [daughter of the craft]; cf. no. 3598 for similar signature by her brother; see *DNB* for her interest in the subject, and *BMCat.* for her edition of Petrie's *Christian Inscriptions*.

3754 How we went up Snowdon, 121–126. Signed: B.G.J.

VOLUME 58, AUGUST 1858

3755 The commonplace book of Richard Hilles, 127–144. **J. A. Froude.** Signed.

3756 Telegraph-cable laying in the Mediterranean, with an excursion in Algeria, 145–157. **Thomas Fisher,** prob. Signed T.F.; man cited used these initials for nos. 3417, 3431, written in a similar style.

3757　Trafalgar Square, 157–160. Signed :A Grumbler.

3758　Hints for vagabonds (No. I): the Eifel, 160–167. **John Ormsby.** Signed at start One of themselves, at end O; Ormsby signed nos. 3725 and 3752 with an "O."; wrote travel arts. for *FM*: see *DNB*.

3759　The Thames and its difficulties, 167–172. **Arthur Helps,** prob. Signed A.H.— see nos. 3001 and 3707; the treatment of the topic is mainly political.

3760　Hanworth (chaps. v–vii), 173–189. Cf. no. 3744.

3761　*The Geology and Extinct Volcanoes of Central France* [by G. P. Scrope], **W. J. Broderip?** Broderip had once been Secretary of the Royal Geological Society and owned a large collection of fossil shells and stones (*DNB*); he was a close associate of William Buckland's, who is mentioned here pp. 194, 197, 200 (cf. evidence for no. 3825); on p. 206 the reader is told to " 'Go and see' " for himself exactly as he was at start of no. 3140, p. 388; Broderip had been a regular contributor to *FM* on natural history for years.

3762　Catarina in Venice (Part II), 207–222. **John Skelton.** Cf. no. 3751.

3763　Concerning a great Scotch preacher [John Caird], 222–238. **A. K. H. Boyd.** Repr. *Leisure Hours.*

3764　The opera season of 1858, 238–244.

3765　The Indian mutinies (No. I): native feeling and knowledge of natives by Englishmen, 245–249.

3766　The Indian mutinies (No. II, concl.): the Company *versus* the Crown, 249–252.

VOLUME 58, SEPTEMBER 1858

3767　Concerning work and play, 253–265. **A. K. H. Boyd.** Signed A.K.H.B.; repr. *Recreations,* 1st series.

3768　Sketches from Egypt (No. I; no more published): the dahabiah, 266–270. **Charles Augustus Murray,** prob. Signed C.A.M.; the author refers, p. 270, to "the whole time of my residence in Egypt"; man cited was consul-general in

Egypt, 1846–1853, and published *Hassan,* a novel of Egyptian life, in 1857.

3769　Hanworth (chaps. viii–x), 271–284. Cf. no. 3744.

3770　An English scholar in Greece [William G. Clark], 285–291. **George John Cayley,** prob. Signed G.J.C.; cf. no. 4171; Cayley signed nos. 4171, 4264, and prob. wrote no. 4149 signed G.J.C.; he matriculated at Trinity Coll. Camb. just after Clark became a fellow.

3771　Cormorants, 292–308. **W. J. Broderip.** Signed β—see no. 3844, p. 487.

3772　Catarina in Venice (Part III, concl.), 309–322. **John Skelton.** Cf. no. 3751.

3773　Chalk-stream studies, 323–343. **Charles Kingsley.** Signed at start A Minute Philosopher, at end C.K.; repr. *Miscellanies,* I.

3774　Shipwrecks, waifs, and strays, 343–347. Signed: R.M.

3775　"The Lawful Regiment of Women" [by Henry Howard, Earl of Northampton], 348–353. Signed: A.R.B.

3776　The Oude proclamation and the proprietors of the land, 354–358.

3777　The *Edinburgh Review* and Mr. Froude's *History* [on *ER*, no. 2389, *Index,* I, by Goldwin Smith], 359–378. **J. A. Froude.** Signed.

VOLUME 58, OCTOBER 1858

3778　The yellow gown; a ghost story, 379–391. **G. J. Whyte-Melville.** Signed.

3779　*The Cruise of the "Betsey"* [by Hugh Miller], 392–410. **W. J. Broderip?** Page 400 cites no. 3761 in words which strongly suggest a common authorship; both arts. are on geology and both begin with verse epigraphs, a form which Broderip often used at this time (see nos. 3771, 3791 for example); p. 406 praises Richard Owen, as Broderip frequently does (see evidence for nos. 3177, 3183).

3780　The murders at Deutz, 411–422. **G. H. Lewes.** Lewes, "Receipts."

3781　Richard Ford: in memoriam, 422–424. **Thomas Hughes.** Signed T.H.; Hughes was married to Ford's niece; Ford's last art. (*QR*, no. 1236, *Index,* I) was a review of *Tom Brown's School-days.*

3782　Recent travellers in Central America, 425–436. Signed: T.E.M.

3783　Hanworth (chaps. xi–xiv), 437–454. Cf. no. 3744.

3784　Hints for vagabonds (No. II): the Moselle, 455–462. **John Ormsby.** Evidence for no. 3758.

3785 The political pulpit of the [English] Civil War, 463–470. Signed: G.G.B.
3786 How I killed a cariboo, 470–478. **Thomas Godfrey Faussett.** Signed T.G.F.; cf. no. 4032 for subject and evidence.
3787 Sylvester's *Du Bartas*, 480–491. **David Masson.** Signed D.M.; Pratt list.
3788 British Columbia and Vancouver's Island, 493–504. **W. C. Keppel.** Signed Beta Mikron—see no. 3580.

VOLUME 58, NOVEMBER 1858

3789 Our failures, 505–523. **Robert Lamb.** Signed at start A Manchester Man, at end R.L.; repr. *Free Thoughts*, II.
3790 Concerning tidiness: being thoughts upon an overlooked source of human content, 523–536. **A. K. H. Boyd.** Signed at start A Very Particular Man, at end A.K.H.B.; repr. *Recreations*, 1st series.
3791 Pelicans, 537–553. **W. J. Broderip.** Signed β—see no. 3844, p. 487.
3792 Hanworth (chaps. xv–xviii), 554–569. Cf. no. 3744.
3793 The taming of horses, and Mr. Rarey, 570–582. **G. J. Whyte-Melville.** Signed G.J.W.M.; see *DNB* for his interest in this subject.
3794 Hector Garret of Otter (chaps i–iii), 583–596. **Henrietta Keddie.** Signed The Author of "Meg of Elibank"; repr. in *Days of Yore*, 1866.
3795 Demetrius Galanus; Greek translations from Sanscrit, 596–608. **T. L. Peacock.** Signed The Author of *Headlong Hall*; repr. *Works*, X.
3796 The Indian rebellion: the village system and the policy of annexation, 609–614.
3797 The expensive luxury of waste, 614–617. **John W. Parker,** 1820–1860, prob. Signed P.—see nos. 3630, 3728; it is very unlikely that having adopted "P." himself, editor Parker would have wanted anyone else to use the same signature; most of Parker's arts. are short.
3798 Studies of the Great Rebellion, 618–630. **W. B. Donne.** Johnson, *Donne*, list.

VOLUME 58, DECEMBER 1858

3799 Carlyle's *Frederick the Great* [Vols. I–II], 631–649. **G. H. Lewes.** Signed at start The Author of *The Life of Goethe*, at end G.H.L.; Lewes, "Receipts."

3800 Our new treaty with Japan, 650–658. **Mark Praeger Lindo.** Signed M.P.L.—see nos. 3185, 3294; cf. no. 3314.
3801 Snake-birds, 659–675. **W. J. Broderip.** Signed β—see no. 3844, p. 487.
3802 Hanworth (chaps. xix–xxii, concl.), 676–688. Cf. no. 3744.
3803 Concerning villas and cottages, 689–705. **A. K. H. Boyd.** Signed A.K.H.B.; repr. *Recreations*, 1st series.
3804 Hector Garret of Otter (chaps. iv–vi, concl.), 706–718. **Henrietta Keddie.** Evidence for no. 3794.
3805 People who are not respectable: a lay sermon, 719–729. **John Skelton.** Signed Shirley; repr. *Nugae Criticae*.
3806 India in a mess, 730–741. **W. D. Arnold.** Signed The Author of "India in Mourning"—see no. 3678.
3807 George Peacock, Dean of Ely: in memoriam, 741–746.
3808 M. de Montalembert and the Emperor of the French, 747–754. **A. V. Kirwan.** This reads like another of Kirwan's bitter attacks on Napoleon III, which began with no. 2932; moreover, phrases on pp. 751, 752, 753, and the postscript are found verbatim in Kirwan's *Modern France*, pp. 373, 373–374, 377.

VOLUME 59, JANUARY 1859

3809 Holmby House; a tale of old Northamptonshire (chaps. i–iv), 1–19. **G. J. Whyte-Melville.** Signed; novel published 1860.
3810 Concerning the art of putting things: being thoughts on representation and misrepresentation, 19–35. **A. K. H. Boyd.** Signed A.K.H.B.; repr. *Recreations*, 1st series.
3811 Schloss-eishausen; a mystery (Part I), 36–50. Signed [at end of Part III]: I.R.C.
3812 *Homer and the Homeric Age* [by W. E. Gladstone] (Part I), 50–65. **Barham Zincke.** Signed.
3813 Dramatic treasure-trove, 65–77. **Coventry Patmore.** Reid, *Patmore*, bibliog.
3814 Mushrooms, 78–93. **W. J. Broderip.** Signed β—see no. 3844, p. 487.
3815 Furniture books [illustrated books], 95–102.
3816 Hints for vagabonds (No. III): the Low Countries, 104–113. **John Ormsby.** Evidence for no. 3758.
3817 Antecedents of the Reformation, 114–

120. **Mark Pattison.** Signed M.P.; repr. *Essays*, I.

3818 How Queen Victoria was proclaimed at Peshawar, 120–126. **W. D. Arnold.** Signed W.D.A.—see no. 3373.

VOLUME 59, FEBRUARY 1959

3819 Hodson of Hodson's Horse, 127–145. **Thomas Hughes.** Signed.

3820 How I mused in the railway train; being thoughts on rising by candlelight, on nervous fears, and on vapouring, 146–158. **A. K. H. Boyd.** Signed A.K.H.B.; repr. *Recreations*, 1st series.

3821 Sketches at the Antipodes: New Zealand, 159–169.

3822 Holmby House (chaps. v–viii), 173–191. **G. J. Whyte-Melville.** Signed.

3823 *Homer and the Homeric Age* (Part II, concl.), 192–207. **Barham Zincke.** Signed.

3824 Schloss-eishausen (Part II), 207–226. Signed [at end of Part III]: I.R.C.

3825 Buckland's *Bridgewater Treatise*, 227–243. **W. J. Broderip.** On p. 230, author relates an incident concerning Buckland and Broderip (who is the "young undergraduate of Oriel" referred to: cf. first quotation on p. 231 with the same quotation on p. 486) which only Broderip would have known in such detail; since Broderip initiated Buckland's study of geology (see p. 486, col. i), he would have been an obvious person to review his *Treatise*.

3826 A fear for the future that women will cease to be womanly, 243–248.

3827 On playgoing, 249–252.

VOLUME 59, MARCH 1859

3828 War; an essay and conversation by friends in council, 253–279. **Arthur Helps.** Repr. *Friends in Council*, (1859), I.

3829 The shark, 280–298. **W. J. Broderip.** Signed β—see no. 3844, p. 487; art. attr. ibid., p. 485.

3830 Holmby House (chaps. ix–xi), 299–318. **G. J. Whyte-Melville.** Signed.

3831 *James Watt*, 318–329.

3832 Schloss-eishausen (Part III, concl.), 330–346. Signed: I.R.C.

3833 Hints for vagabonds (No. IV): Venice, 347–356. **John Ormsby.** Evidence for no. 3758.

3834 Müller and Donaldson's *History of Greek Literature*, 357–377. **T. L. Peacock.** Signed; repr. *Works*, X.

3835 William Hickling Prescott: in memoriam, 378–382. **William Stirling-Maxwell.** Signed W.S.; repr. *Essays*.

VOLUME 59, APRIL 1859

3836 Sword and gown (chaps. i–iv), 383–397. **George Alfred Lawrence.** Signed The Author of *Guy Livingstone*; novel published, 1859.

3837 Concerning two blisters of humanity: being thoughts on petty malignity and petty trickery, 398–414. **A. K. H. Boyd.** Signed A.K.H.B.; repr. *Recreations*, 1st series.

3838 The court of Russia a hundred years ago, 414–427. Signed: R.H.

3839 Holmby House (chaps. xii–xiii), 427–443. **G. J. Whyte-Melville.** Signed.

3840 Professional sectarianism: Dr. Brown's *Horae Subsecivae*, 443–451. **John Skelton.** Signed Shirley—see *DNB*.

3841 Hints for vagabonds (No. V): Connemara, 452–462. **John Ormsby.** Evidence for no. 3758.

3842 Russian dinners [but on dining in general], 462–472. **W. F. Pollock.** Frederic Pollock, his father, to man cited, May 2, 1859, in possession of Sir George F. Pollock, says he has read this paper with pleasure "and let me add *some pride.*"

3843 Excursions in the Eastern Pyrenees, 473–485. **C. R. Weld.** Repr. substantially, *The Pyrenees, West and East* (1859), pp. 338–381, 383.

3844 William John Broderip: in memoriam, 485–488. **John W. Parker,** 1820–1860. Parker liked to do short obituaries of his contributors (cf. nos. 3630, 3728), and this art. is clearly written from the inside: see remarks (p. 487, and last paragraph) which show an editor's knowledge and activity.

3845 Recent writers on reform [John Austin, James Lorimer, Thomas Hare], 489–508. **John Stuart Mill.** Signed J.S.M.; *Bibliography*, p. 92; repr. *Dissertations*, III.

VOLUME 59, MAY 1859

3846 Mill on liberty, 509–542. **Henry Thomas Buckle.** Signed; repr. *Miscel-*

laneous and Posthumous Works (1872), I. (See nos. 3855 and 3856.)

3847 Notes on the national drama of Spain (Part I), 543–557. **J. R. Chorley.** Signed.

3848 Holmby House (chaps. xiv–xv), 558–571. **G. J. Whyte-Melville.** Signed.

3849 Gower's *Confessio Amantis*, 571–586. **W. B. Donne.** Signed W.B.D.; Johnson, *Donne*, list.

3850 Wild sports of the Far South [Australia], 587–597. **Henry Kingsley**, prob. Signed H.K.; Kingsley was in Australia, 1853–1858; wrote on sport in *Macmillan's* under these initials; contributed to *FM* (see *MWT*, 9th ed.)

3851 Sword and gown (chaps. v–vii), 597–609. **G. A. Lawrence.** Evidence for no. 3836.

3852 Alexis de Tocqueville: in memoriam, 610–615. **A. V. Kirwan.** Signed.

3853 The domestic annals of Scotland—Chambers and Macaulay, 615–628. **John Skelton.** Signed Shirley—see *DNB*.

3854 Politics, home and foreign, 629–634.

VOLUME 59, JUNE 1859

3855 Mr. Buckle and Sir John Coleridge [reply to no. 3846], 634–644. **John Duke Coleridge.** Signed. (Note, 644–645, by **J. W. Parker**, 1820–1860—signed Ed. *F.M.*)

3856 Concerning *Man and his Dwelling-Place* [with a reply to no. 3846], 645–661. **A. K. H. Boyd.** Signed A.K.H.B.; repr. *Recreations*, 1st series.

3857 The exhibitions of 1859, 662–672.

3858 Early history of the Isle of Thanet, 673–678. **Jesse Watts Russell.** Signed J.W.R.—see no. 3593.

3859 Holmby House (chaps. xvi–xviii), 679–697. **G. J. Whyte-Melville.** Signed.

3860 Bacon's *History of King Henry the Seventh*, 697–709.

3861 *Poems and Ballads of Goethe* [trans. by Aytoun, D.C.L., and Theodore Martin], 710–717. **A. H. Clough.** Signed A.H.C.; claimed in *Correspondence*, II, 568.

3862 Sword and gown (chaps. viii–x), 717–730. **G. A. Lawrence.** Evidence for no. 3836.

3863 The future value of gold, 730–744. **Percy Greg.** Signed.

3864 The Roman question: the Pope—his church, court, and ministers, 744–753. **A. V. Kirwan?** A paragraph in no. 3884, p. 250, brings together the focal points of this art.—Pius IX, Napoleon

III, and the book by About here reviewed; Kirwan was writing on Italian politics for *FM* at this time (cf. list in evidence for no. 3904); the political standpoint, especially the notion that the Italians should act alone, p. 753, is found in all these arts.; the phrase, p. 750, "at the shady side of seventy," reminds one of "on the shady side of fifty" (no. 2422, p. 203, by Kirwan), and Kirwan's own use of "A man on the Shady Side of Fifty" as a pseudonym for nos, 4004, 4023, etc.; the extensive use of the book reviewed is not, however, Kirwan's unusual practice, but in this case he may have had little first-hand knowledge to go on.

3865 The elections and the War [between France and Austria], 757–762.

VOLUME 60, JULY 1859

3866 The irrationale of speech, 1–14. **Charles Kingsley.** Signed at start A Minute Philosopher, at end C.K.; repr. as *Hints to Stammerers*, 1864.

3867 Alexander von Humboldt: in memoriam, 15–23. Signed: B.P. Perhaps Baden Powell, whose interest in science and religion (see the end of the art.) makes him a likely "B.P."; moreover, author quotes, p. 22, from *Proceedings of the Royal Society*, and Powell was an F.R.S.

3868 Holmby House (chaps. xix–xxii), 24–41. **G. J. Whyte-Melville.** Signed.

3869 Egyptian and sacred chronology, 42–48. Signed: E.E.

3870 Notes on the national drama of Spain (Part II), 49–71. **J. R. Chorley.** Signed.

3871 On war in general, and modern French wars in particular, 71–81.

3872 Sword and gown (chaps. xi–xii), 81–95. **G. A. Lawrence.** Evidence for no. 3836.

3873 Thoughts on modern English literature, 97–110. **V. H. Hobart.** Signed H.; repr. *Fragments*, 1875 and *Writings*, I.

3874 A visit to Mount Ararat, 111–121.

3875 The new administration, 122–126.

VOLUME 60, AUGUST 1859

3876 The barons of Buchan: a contribution to local history, 127–145. **John Skelton.** Signed Shirley—see *DNB*.

3877 Concerning hurry and leisure, 145–

162. **A. K. H. Boyd.** Signed A.K.H.B.; repr. *Recreations*, 1st series.

3878 Holmby House (chaps. xxiii–xxv), 167–186. **G. J. Whyte-Melville.** Signed.

3879 A journey across the Fjeld [in northern Norway], 186–199. **John Young Sargent.** Signed J.Y.S.; man cited wrote books on Norwegian subjects: see *BMCat.*

3880 Sword and gown (chaps. xiii–xv), 199–211. **G. A. Lawrence.** Evidence for no. 3836.

3881 Alison's *History of Europe from 1815 to 1852* (Part I), 211–226. Signed [at end of Parts II and III]: Topaze.

3882 Thoughts on reserved people, 227–232. Signed: A Candid Man. Attr. by Poole, I, 1100, to A. K. H. Boyd, but the style lacks his personal note, and he never, we think, contributed two arts. to the same issue (he wrote no. 3877).

3883 Alpine literature, 232–242. **John Ball,** prob. Ball's "Alpine Travelers," *BentQR* no. 27, Oct. 1859, takes up the same themes as this art., two of which— English love of action and the founding of the Alpine Club—also appear in Ball's art. *ER* no. 2489 (*Index*, I), pp. 222, 224; a digression on the Forbes-Tyndall controversy, p. 237, reaches same conclusion adopted in *ER* art., p. 237; praise of Ball's own contributions to *Peaks, Passes, and Glaciers* both here, p. 239, and in *BentQR*, p. 232.

3884 The peace of Villafranca, 244–252. **A. V. Kirwan.** Signed A.V.K.; cf. general evidence for no. 2307.

VOLUME 60, SEPTEMBER 1859

3885 Machiavelli and his *Prince* explained and illustrated, 253–266. Signed: W.W.

3886 Essay towards an experimenal solution of the gold question (Part I), 267–278. **John E. Cairnes.** Signed; repr. *Economy.*

3887 Holmby House (chaps. xxvi–xxvii), 279–292. **G. J. Whyte-Melville.** Signed.

3888 Some remarks on Mr. Buckle's *History of Civilization*, 293–300. **Thomas Mayo.** Signed.

3889 *Idylls of the King* [by Tennyson], 301–314.

3890 Notes on the national drama of Spain (Part III), 314–330. **J. R. Chorley.** Signed.

3891 Sword and gown (chaps. xvi–xviii), 330–343. **G. A. Lawrence.** Evidence for no. 3836.

3892 Concerning *Friends in Council* [by

Arthur Helps], 344–360. **A. K. H. Boyd.** Signed A.K.H.B.; repr. *Critical Essays,* and *Recreations,* 2nd series.

3893 Much ado about nothing [on Charles Kean], 361–372.

3894 Naples, France, and Austria, 373–386. **A. V. Kirwan,** prob. Cf. no. 3904.

VOLUME 60, OCTOBER 1859

3895 Bacon's *Philosophical Works,* 387–409. Signed: G.D.H.

3896 On the life of Edmund Spenser, 410–422. **Thomas Keightley.** Signed.

3897 Notes on the national drama of Spain (Part IV, concl.), 423–434. **J. R. Chorley.** Signed.

3898 Holmby House (chaps. xxviii–xxix), 434–448. **G. J. Whyte-Melville.** Signed.

3899 About the West Riding, 449–465. Signed: Devonia.

3900 Last spring in Rome: a bird's-eye view, 467–470.

3901 Sword and gown (chaps. xix–xx), 471–480. **G. A. Lawrence.** Evidence for no. 3836.

3902 Bakers and builders, 480–482. Signed: A Grumbler.

3903 Port Royal and the Port Royalists, 482–497. **John Tulloch?** Signed J.T.; Tulloch was writing on such subjects by the mid-1850's (for the *North Brit. Rev.*) and was later ed. of *FM*; cf. no. 4056; though Ludlow used J.T. for nos. 2675, 2722, neither this nor no. 4056 are on his own list nor like his other work.

3904 Piedmont and Italy in 1849 and 1859, 498–512. **A. V. Kirwan,** prob. Nos. 3884 (signed A.V.K.), 3894, and this art. seem to form a series in which the evolving situation in Italy is discussed in the same style from the same viewpoint: the Peace of Villafranca is examined here, pp. 510–512, as in no. 3884, and found unworkable; the conclusion that Italy must depend on her own efforts to become a unified and important European power is stated or implied in all three (on pp. 252, 385, 511–512 respectively); that Napoleon's motive is not to free Italy but to check Austria is the common assumption.

VOLUME 60, NOVEMBER 1859

3905 Pitt and Canning: fifty years of political history, 513–533. **John Skelton.** Signed Shirley; repr. *Essays* as "From

Chatham to Canning," and *Nugae Criticae* as "The Statesmen of the Tories."

3906 Indian finance, 534–543. Signed: S.

3907 Holmby House (chaps. xxx–xxxii), 544–559. **G. J. Whyte-Melville.** Signed.

3908 Sir James Stephen, K.C.B., LL.D: in memoriam, 560–563. **Robert Vaughan.** Signed R.V., with address, "Uxbridge," where Vaughan was living at the time (see *DNB*); Parker, publisher of *FM*, had just published his *Revolutions in English History*, 1859.

3909 Religious and philosophical guides: Mansel and Maurice, 563–578. **Francis Garden?** Signed F.G. on p. 577; Garden was a theologian who, like the author of this art., greatly admired Maurice: see *DNB*.

3910 Sketches [of Nice] framed in olive wood, 579–591. Signed: E.H.M.

3911 Sword and gown (chaps. xxi–xxii), 591–603. **G. A. Lawrence.** Evidence for no. 3836.

3912 Alison's *History of Europe from 1815 to 1852* (Part II), 603–620. Signed: Topaze. (Part III is no. 4043.)

3913 Isambard Kingdom Brunel: in memoriam, 620–624. Signed: R.B. Perhaps Richard Beamish, who published a life of Brunel's father, 1862.

3914 Hallucinations, 625–631. Signed: G.

3915 Has political freedom receded? 631–642. Signed: W.W.

VOLUME 60, DECEMBER 1859

3916 The national defences, 643–660. **J. E. Addison.** Signed J.E.A.; this army officer had translated a French work on the defence of England in 1852 (see *BMCat.*); cf. no. 4103.

3917 Robert Stephenson: in memoriam, 661–667. **Samuel Smiles.** Signed.

3918 Long vacation readings, 672–683. **John Skelton.** Signed Shirley—see *DNB*.

3919 Holmby House (chaps. xxxiii–xxxv), 684–696. **G. J. Whyte-Melville.** Signed.

3920 England's literary debt to Italy, 697–708. **J. Montgomery Stuart.** Signed.

3921 Earthquakes, 708–720. **C. R. Weld.** Signed.

3922 Some account of Morocco, 720–738.

3923 The Victoria cross, 739–747.

3924 English poerty versus Cardinal Wiseman, 747–766. **Leigh Hunt.** Signed.

3925 A few words on non-intervention, 766–776. **John Stuart Mill.** Signed; repr. *Dissertations*, III.

VOLUME 61, JANUARY 1860

3926 Concerning disappointment and success, 1–20. **A. K. H. Boyd.** Signed A.K.H.B.; repr. *Recreations*, 2nd series.

3927 British novelists: Richardson, Miss Austen, Scott, 20–38. **W. F. Pollock.** Signed W.F.P.; *Remembrances*, II, 71; FitzGerald, *Letters*, I, 274–275.

3928 Essay towards a solution of the gold question (Part II, concl.), 38–53. **John E. Cairnes.** Signed; repr. *Economy*.

3929 The Shakespearian discovery [by Payne Collier], 53–64. **Thomas James Arnold.** Signed T.J.A.; attr. by H. B. Wheatley, *Notes of the Life of John Payne Collier* (1884), p. 54, where he speaks of Arnold's arts. in *FM*; see *DNB*. (See nos. 3938 and 3982.)

3930 Holmby House (chaps. xxxvi–xxxviii), 64–79. **G. J. Whyte-Melville.** Signed.

3931 Conversations with Prince Metternich, 79–91. **Robert R. Noel.** Signed R. R. Noel; opening discussion of phrenology identifies author with man cited: see *BMCat.*

3932 Memoirs of Percy Bysshe Shelley (Part II, concl.), 92–109. **T. L. Peacock.** Signed; repr. *Works*, VIII. (See no. 4198.)

3933 Wheat and tares (chaps. i–iv), 111–123. **Henry Stuart Cunningham.** Novel published anon. 1861; attr. to Cunningham in H&L and *BMCat.*

3934 The literary suburb of the eighteenth century [Twickenham] (chap. i), 124–133.

3935 Egypt and the Suez Canal, 134–150.

VOLUME 61, FEBRUARY 1860

3936 Concerning giving up and coming down, 151–167. **A. K. H. Boyd.** Signed A.K.H.B.—see no. 3671.

3937 The battle-fields of 1859, 168–175. **John Ormsby.** Signed O.—see no. 3752, etc.

3938 The "old corrector" [on Payne Collier], 176–187. **T. J. Arnold.** Signed T.J.A.—see no. 3929.

3939 Representation in practice and in theory, 188–204. **Thomas Hare.** Signed. (See no. 3964.)

3940 Holmby House (chaps. xxxix–xli), 204–221. **G. J. Whyte-Melville.** Signed.

3941 Franklin's fate, and the voyage of the *Fox*, 221–227. **C. R. Weld.** Signed C.R.W.; cf. nos. 2821, 2907 on this subject; see *DNB*.

3942 Points of view, 228–237. **V. H. Hobart.** Signed H.; repr. *Fragments*, 1875, and *Writings*, I.

3943 The idler in the Hague, 238–254. Signed: Topaze.

3944 Wheat and tares (chaps. v–vii), 255–267. **H. S. Cunningham.** Cf. no. 3933.

3945 The literary suburb of the eighteenth century (chap. ii): Alexander Pope, 267–276.

3946 The United States through English eyes, 276–288. **Henry A. Murray.** Signed H.A.M.; the author's first-hand remarks about Nicholas Longworth and Catawba Wine, p. 278, both of which he says he has praised "in another place," closely parallel those in Murray's *Lands of the Slave and the Free* (1855), I, 152–153; the book had been published by J. W. Parker, so that Parker might naturally have turned to Murray for a review of new books on the U.S.

3947 Why not the Lords too? 290–300. **Goldwin Smith.** Signed G.S.; a copy of this art. is among the Goldwin Smith Papers at Cornell Univ.; attr. by Elizabeth Wallace, *Goldwin Smith: Victorian Liberal* (Toronto, 1957), p. 155.

VOLUME 61, MARCH 1860

3948 Unpublished letters of Percy Bysshe Shelley, from Italy—1818 to 1822, 301–319. **P. B. Shelley.** Title. Edited with intro. and notes by **T. L. Peacock**—signed. (Postscript, p. 738, signed **T. L. Peacock.**)

3949 Concerning the worries of life, and how to meet them, 320–337. **A. K. H. Boyd.** Signed A.K.H.B.; repr. *Recreations*, 1st series.

3950 Holmby House (chaps. xlii–xlvi, concl.), 338–359. **G. J. Whyte-Melville.** Signed.

3951 Female labour, 359–371.

3952 Louis Napoleon's intentions tested by his conduct, 371–386. Signed: W.W.

3953 The literary suburb of the eighteenth century (chap. iii), 387–395.

3954 Madame Récamier, 396–416. **A. V. Kirwan,** prob. A characteristic review of a memoir (see Part B under Kirwan and cf. evidence for no. 2307); on pp. 396, 410, the same derogatory epithets are applied to Chateaubriand as in *Brit. Quart. Rev.*, 20 (July 1854), 238, repr. in Kirwan's *Modern France*; there are personal references on pp. 398, 413.

3955 The wine question reviewed, 416–424. Signed: F.G.

3956 Wheat and tares (chaps. viii–x), 425–433. **H. S. Cunningham.** Cf. no. 3933.

3957 The budget, 434–446. **Leone Levi.** Signed.

VOLUME 61, APRIL 1860

3958 Gryll Grange (chaps. i–v), 447–462. **Thomas Love Peacock.** Signed The Author of *Headlong Hall*; novel published 1861.

3959 William the Silent: a study of character, 463–474. **John Skelton.** Signed Shirley; repr. *Essays* and *Nugae Criticae*.

3960 Why virtue and merit are rarely rewarded, 474–485. Signed: W.W.

3961 *Revolutions in English History* [by Robert Vaughan, Vol. I], 485–500. Unidentified. (See no. 4411.)

3962 The metaphysician: a retrospect [from Hume to Hamilton], 503–517. **T. E. Webb.** Signed; repr. in substance in *The Veil of Isis; a Series of Essays on Idealism*, 1885.

3963 Hints for vagabonds (No. VI, concl.): Tyrol, 517–526. **John Ormsby.** Evidence for no. 3758.

3964 Representation of every locality and intelligence [sequel to no. 3939], 527–543. **Thomas Hare.** Signed.

3965 Literary suburb of the eighteenth century (chap. iv), 544–554.

3966 Military education, 554–560.

3967 The publication-of-letters nuisance, 561–563.

3968 Wheat and tares (chaps. xi–xii), 564–574. **H. S. Cunningham.** Cf. no. 3933.

3969 Philanthropic societies in the reign of Queen Anne, 576–582. **Mark Pattison.** Signed M.P.; repr. *Essays*, II.

3970 What are we coming to?—a conversation in a railway carriage, 583–592.

VOLUME 61, MAY 1860

3971 Compromise: the terms on which everybody surrenders, 593–610. **G. J. Whyte-Melville.** Signed.

3972 Gryll Grange (chaps. vi–xi), 611–627. **T. L. Peacock.** Evidence for no. 3958.

3973 *Ceylon*, 627–642. **T. Harlin.** Signed.

3974 The "Finding of Christ in the Temple," by Mr. Holman Hunt, 643–647. **F. T. Palgrave.** Signed F.T.P.—see no. 4212; attr. by W. M. Rossetti in Scott, *Notes*, II, 58.

3975 Concerning the dignity of dulness, 648–660. **A. K. H. Boyd.** Signed A.K.H.B.; repr. *Recreations*, 1st series.

3976 On certain aspects of toleration, 660–674. **John Skelton.** Signed Shirley—see *DNB*.

3977 The latest translator of Horace [Theodore Martin], 675–680.

3978 Wheat and tares (chaps. xiii–xv), 681–691. **H. S. Cunningham.** Cf. no. 3933.

3979 Phrenology and psychology, 692–708. **Alexander Bain.** Signed.

3980 The late prize-fight [Sayers vs. Heenan], 708–712.

3981 *The Life and Writings of Madame Swetchine*, 713–721.

3982 Mr. Collier's *Reply* [to Hamilton, on Shakespeare MS. controversy], 722–738. **T. J. Arnold.** Signed T.J.A.—see no. 3929.

VOLUME 61, JUNE 1860

3983 Physical theories of the phenomena of life [mainly on Darwin's *Origin of Species*] (Part I), 739–752. **William Hopkins.** Signed.

3984 A reverie after reading Miss Nightingale's *Notes on Nursing*, 753–757.

3985 Gryll Grange (chaps. xii–xiv), 757–772. **T. L. Peacock.** Evidence for no. 3958.

3986 Suggestions for the improvement of the reading department in the British Museum, 773–777. **James Spedding.** Signed.

3987 *Self-Help* [by Samuel Smiles], 778–786.

3988 Concerning growing old, 787–801. **A. K. H. Boyd.** Signed A.K.H.B.; repr. *Recreations*, 1st series.

3989 Wheat and tares (chaps. xvi–xviii), 802–813. **H. S. Cunningham.** Cf. no. 3933.

3990 A raid among the rhymers [J. S. Blackie, E. B. Browning, Morris], 814–828. **John Skelton.** Signed Shirley—see *DNB*.

3991 Difficulties of political prophecy, 829–834.

3992 Literary suburb of the eighteenth century (chaps. v–vi), 834–843.

3993 Life at Nice, 844–860. Signed: E.H.M.

3994 The Rochdale pioneers, 861–872. **Percy Greg.** Signed P.G.; attr. by Hill, *Memoir*, p. 386.

3995 The exhibitions of 1860, 874–882.

VOLUME 62, JULY 1860

3996 Froude's History of the Reigns of Edward VI. and Mary [*History of England*, Vols. V–VI], 1–17. **W. B. Donne.** Signed W.B.D.; Johnson, *Donne*, list.

3997 Wheat and tares (chaps. xix–xxi), 18–30. **H. S. Cunningham.** Cf. no. 3933.

3998 The volunteer course at Hythe School of Musketry, 31–46. **W. C. Keppel.** Signed Viscount Bury; see *DNB*.

3999 Gryll Grange (chaps. xv–xviii), 47–62. **T. L. Peacock.** Evidence for no. 3958.

4000 On the importance of energy in life, 63–74. Signed: W. W.

4001 Physical theories of the phenomena of life (Part II, concl.), 74–90. **William Hopkins.** Signed.

4002 The literary suburb of the eighteenth century (chaps. vii–ix, concl.), 94–107.

4003 A plea for truth in advertisement, 108–112. Signed: Verax.

4004 Social and political life five-and-thirty years ago, 113–132. **A. V. Kirwan.** Signed A Man on the Shady Side of Fifty; listed in "Essays"; claimed in Kirwan to Blackwood, May 5, 1862, Nat. Lib. Scot.

4005 Chronicle of current history, 135–146. **T. C. Sandars.** Thomas Hughes to Alexander Macmillan, Nov. 4, 1861, BM Add. MS. 54917, has arranged with [Charles S. C.] Bowen for monthly articles for *Macmillan's Mag.* (nos. 227, etc., called "Passing events": see *Index*, I, 818), "the sort of political digest and commentary which Sanders did till lately for Fraser"; this monthly series ran to no. 4133 at end of Aug. 1861; "Sanders" is surely an error for Sandars, the young barrister from Oxford who, from about 1855, was a frequent contributor to periodicals on history, politics, and contemporary affairs; he had already written 4 arts. for *FM* and about 80 for the *Saturday Review* (see Bevington, pp. 369–371), which accounts for Hughes' confidence he need mention only the surname.

VOLUME 62, AUGUST 1860

4006 Concerning summer days, 147–166. **A. K. H. Boyd.** Signed A.K.H.B.; repr. *Recreations*, 2nd series.

4007 The Ireland forgeries, 167–178. **T. J. Arnold.** Signed T.J.A.—see nos. 3929, etc., on forgeries.

4008 On the relations of the public to the

science and practice of medicine, 179–190. **Thomas Mayo.** Signed.

4009 Gryll Grange (chaps. xix–xxi), 191–205. **T. L. Peacock.** Evidence for no. 3958.

4010 Novels of the day: their writers and readers, 205–217. Signed: M-M.

4011 The proposed national defences, 218–227.

4012 *Essays and Reviews*, 228–242. **W. D. Watson.** Signed W.D.W.—see no. 3327.

4013 Wheat and tares (chaps. xxii–xxv, concl.), 242–259. **H. S. Cunningham.** Cf. no. 3933.

4014 Pope's MS. notes on Tickell's *Homer*, now first edited, with illustrations, by Professor Conington, 260–273. **John Conington.** Title; see *DNB*.

4015 Chronicle of current history, 273–284. **T. C. Sandars.** Cf. no. 4005.

VOLUME 62, SEPTEMBER 1860

4016 Ida Conway (chaps. i–ii), 285–298. **John Moore Capes?** Signed J.M.C.; Capes had already written at least one novel in the *Rambler* (no. 276 etc.; also perhaps two more, nos. 646, etc. and 714, etc.), and had recently ceased to contribute to that journal, which seems to have been his sole outlet (his last art. appeared in Feb. 1859); for his later novels in the 60s see *BMCat*.

4017 Hymns and hymn-tunes for congregational worship, 299–318. **Robert Lamb.** Signed at start A Manchester Man, at end R.L.; repr. *Free Thoughts*, II.

4018 A story of 1848–1849, 319–330. **Margaret Roberts.** Signed The Author of *Mademoiselle Mori*—see *BMCat*.

4019 The propensities, according to phrenology, examined (Part I), 331–347. **Alexander Bain.** Signed. (Part II is no. 4040.)

4020 Gryll Grange (chaps. xxii–xxvi), 348–364. **T. L. Peacock.** Evidence for no. 3958.

4021 Kingsley's *Miscellanies*, 364–372. Signed: S.M.P.

4022 Conversations at Athens on local topics, 375–389.

4023 France and Paris forty, thirty, and twenty years ago (No. I), 389–408. **A. V. Kirwan.** Signed A Man on the Shady Side of Fifty; listed in Contents of his "Essays"; claimed in letter cited for no. 4004.

4024 Chronicle of current history, 411–422. **T. C. Sandars.** Cf. no. 4005.

VOLUME 62, OCTOBER 1860

4025 Concerning Scylla and Charybdis; with some thoughts upon the swing of the pendulum, 423–437. **A. K. H. Boyd** and **Richard Whately.** Signed A.K.H.B.; repr. *Recreations*, 2nd series: for Whately see p. 423n.

4026 A "last word" on Lord Macaulay, 438–446. **John Skelton.** Signed Shirley; repr. *Nugae Criticae*.

4027 Ida Conway (chaps. iii–iv), 447–462. **J. M. Capes?** Evidence for no. 4016.

4028 A ride for the ring, 463–483. **G. J. Whyte-Melville.** Signed.

4029 The financial condition of Turkey, 483–488.

4030 Gryll Grange (chaps. xxvii–xxix), 489–503. **T. L. Peacock.** Evidence for no. 3958.

4031 *Palaeontology* [by Richard Owen], 505–525. Signed: F.T.C.

4032 A snow picnic [in Canada], 526–538. **T. G. Faussett.** Signed T.G.F.—see no. 4266; in Faussett's *Memorials*, (2nd ed., 1878), p. xv, W. J. Loftie says that before 1861 Faussett had been contributing to *FM*.

4033 The English Pompeii [Wroxeter], 539–542. **G. P. Bevan.** Signed.

4034 Chronicle of current history, 543–552. **T. C. Sandars.** Cf. no. 4005.

VOLUME 62, NOVEMBER 1860

4035 The philosophy of marriage, studied under Sir Cresswell Cresswell, 553–569. **Robert Lamb.** Signed at start A Manchester Man, at end R.L.; repr. *Free Thoughts*, II.

4036 France and Paris forty, thirty, and twenty years ago (No. II), 569–590. **A. V. Kirwan.** Evidence for no. 4023.

4037 Alexander von Humboldt at the Court of Berlin, 592–598. **R. Monckton Milnes.** Signed; repr. *Monographs, Personal and Social*, 1873.

4038 Gryll Grange (chaps. xxx–xxxii), 599–612. **T. L. Peacock.** Evidence for no. 3958.

4039 Hunting and hunters, 613–619. Signed: W.S.A.

4040 The sentiments, according to phrenology, examined (Part II), 620–636. **Alexander Bain.** Signed. Part I is no. 4019.

4041 Ida Conway (chap. v), 637–651. **J. M. Capes?** Evidence for no. 4016.

4042 Political economy in the clouds [on Ruskin], 651–659.

4043 Alison's *History of Europe from 1815 to 1852* (Part III, concl.), 660–678. Signed: Topaze.

4044 Chronicle of current history, 679–688. **T. C. Sandars.** Cf. no. 4005.

VOLUME 62, DECEMBER 1860

4045 Concerning screws: being thoughts on the practical service of imperfect means, 689–705. **A. K. H. Boyd.** Signed A.K.H. B.; repr. *Recreations*, 2nd series.

4046 Gryll Grange (chaps. xxxiii–xxxv, concl.), 705–718. **T. L. Peacock.** Evidence for no. 3958.

4047 Mr. Ruskin at the sea-side: a vacation medley, 719–734. **John Skelton.** Signed Shirley; repr. partly *Nugae Criticae* as "A Critic on Criticism."

4048 Ida Conway (chaps. vi–ix), 735–752. **J. M. Capes?** Evidence for no. 4016.

4049 Recollections of Ceylon: its forests and its pearl fishery, 753–767. Signed: S.W.

4050 On modern competition, 767–780. Signed: W.W.

4051 Life and Writings of Thomas de Quincey (Part I), 781–792. **H. W. Sotheby.** Signed H.W.S.; attr. by T. E. Kebbel, *Lord Beaconsfield and Other Tory Memories* (N.Y., 1907), p. 204.

4052 *The Glaciers of the Alps* [by John Tyndall], 793–809. **William Hopkins.** On p. 805 the author quotes a letter he wrote to the editor of the *Philosophical Magazine* of Mar. 1845; the letter appears there, vol. 26, p. 237, and is signed.

4053 In memoriam [John William Parker, 1820–1860], 810–813.

4054 Chronicle of current history, 814–822. **T. C. Sandars.** Cf. no. 4005.

VOLUME 63, JANUARY 1861

4055 Good for nothing; or, All down hill (chaps. i–iv), 1–22. **G. J. Whyte-Melville.** Signed The Author of *Digby Grand, The Interpreter*, etc.; novel published 1861.

4056 The life of Schleiermacher, 23–41. **John Tulloch,** prob. Signed J.T.; the author's knowledge of German theology and philosophy and his sympathy with Schleiermacher, together with the initials, point to Tulloch; cf. no. 3903.

4057 A January day, 41–50. **T. G. Faussett.** Signed T.G.F.; see no. 4266, and the antiquarian material on p. 50.

4058 Life and writings of Thomas de Quincey (Part II, concl.), 51–69. **H. W. Sotheby.** Unsigned but called "Second Paper": cf. no. 4051.

4059 Ida Conway (chaps. x–xi), 70–83. **J. M. Capes?** Evidence for no. 4016.

4060 On the propriety of abolishing the writing of books, 92–97. **John Skelton.** Signed Shirley—see *DNB*.

4061 A blue mutiny [of ryots against indigo planters in Bengal], 98–107. **T. H. Bullock,** prob. The strong defence of the ryots is made again in the next art. on indigo-planting, no. 4218, by Bullock, where many specific points are reiterated (cf. pp. 99–101, 103 here with pp. 616–617, 611, and 623 there); the same topic is pursued in no. 4320, also by Bullock.

4062 The modern Medusa; an o'er-true tale, 107–113. Signed: A.M.

4063 *The Horse and his Rider* [by Francis B. Head], 114–124.

4064 Chronicle of current history, 125–134. **T. C. Sandars.** Cf. no. 4005.

VOLUME 63, FEBRUARY 1861

4065 English policy in Europe, 135–150. **F. W. Newman.** Repr. *Miscellanies*, III, as "European Freedom."

4066 A strange story of Titahua, 151–162.

4067 Good for nothing (chaps. v–viii), 162–183. **G. J. Whyte-Melville.** Evidence for no. 4055.

4068 France and Paris forty, thirty, and twenty years ago (No. III, concl.), 184–197. **A. V. Kirwan.** Evidence for no. 4023.

4069 Ida Conway (chaps. xii–xiii), 198–213. **J. M. Capes?** Evidence for no. 4016.

4070 Concerning solitary days, 215–227. **A. K. H. Boyd.** Signed A.K.H.B.; repr. *Recreations*, 2nd series.

4071 Hafiz, the Persian poet (Part II, concl.), 228–234. **E. B. Cowell.** List in *Life*. (Part I is no. 3262.)

4072 My last governess, 235–245.

4073 The sentiments, according to phrenology, examined (Part III, sequel to no. 4040), 246–259. **Alexander Bain.** Signed. (Part IV is no. 4109.)

4074 Chronicle of current history, 260–268. **T. C. Sandars.** Cf. no. 4005.

VOLUME 63, MARCH 1861

4075 Good for nothing (chaps. ix–xii), 269–

289. **G. J. Whyte-Melville.** Evidence for no. 4055.

4076 The progress and prospects of astronomy (Part I), 289–298.

4077 Dante: his works and wanderings, 299–318.

4078 Another chapter on the Amoor [cf. no. 3301], 318–328. **Francis Marx.** Signed F.M.; repr. *The Pacific And the Amoor*, 1861.

4079 Ida Conway (chap. xiv), 329–338. **J. M. Capes?** Evidence for no. 4016.

4080 A few words on tours and tourists, 340–355.

4081 A mount on shanks's mare, 356–367. **T. G. Faussett.** Signed T.G.F.—see no. 4266, and note the antiquarian material here on pp. 366–367.

4082 Mrs. Piozzi, 368–384.

4083 The inquisition in England, 385–390. **John Skelton.** Signed Shirley—see *DNB*.

4084 Chronicle of current history, 393–402. **T. C. Sandars.** Cf. no. 4005.

VOLUME 63, APRIL 1861

4085 The American quarrel, 403–414. **F. W. Newman.** Newman to Messrs. Parker, Son, & Bourne, n.d., John Ryland's Lib., Manchester, acknowledges check for paper in *FM* with this exact title.

4086 Good for nothing (chaps. xiii–xvi), 415–434. **G. J. Whyte-Melville.** Evidence for no. 4055.

4087 Public schools, 434–440.

4088 Concerning future years, 441–458. **A. K. H. Boyd.** Signed A.K.H.B.; repr. *Recreations*, 2nd series.

4089 The progress and prospects of astronomy (Part II, concl.), 458–467.

4090 Ida Conway (chaps. xv–xvii), 468–482. **J. M. Capes?** Evidence for no. 4016.

4091 Toleration within the Church of England [on *Essays and Reviews*], 483–492.

4092 British sculpture; its condition and prospects, 493–505. **W. M. Rossetti.** Signed; repr. *Fine Art*.

4093 Java (Part I), 506–520. Signed: An Anglo-Batavian.

4094 Chronicle of current history, 521–528. **T. C. Sandars.** Cf. no. 4005.

VOLUME 63, MAY 1861

4095 Some thoughts on the conduct of business in parliament, 529–544.

4096 Good for nothing (chaps. xvii–xx),

545–563. **G. J. Whyte-Melville.** Evidence for no. 4055.

4097 The Turkish difficulty, 564–569.

4098 Concerning things slowly learnt, 570–585. **A. K. H. Boyd.** Signed A.K.H.B.; repr. *Leisure Hours*.

4099 The May east winds, 586–593. Signed: B.K.

4100 The individual and the crowd, 593–604. **T. E. C. Leslie.** Signed T.E.C.L.; repr. *Essays in Political and Moral Philosophy*, Dublin, 1879.

4101 Poland: its state and prospects, 605–624.

4102 Ida Conway (chaps. xvii–xviii), 626–638. **J. M. Capes?** Evidence for no. 4016.

4103 *Soldiers and Their Science*, 639–650. **J. E. Addison.** Signed.

4104 Chronicle of current history, 651–658. **T. C. Sandars.** Cf. no. 4005.

VOLUME 63, JUNE 1861

4105 Queen Elizabeth, Lord Robert Dudley, and Amy Robsart; a story from the archives of Simancas, 659–669. **J. A. Froude.** Signed.

4106 The city of the sun [Baalbec in Lebanon], 670–684. **Frances P. Cobbe.** Signed; repr. *Cities*.

4107 Good for nothing (chaps. xxi–xxv), 685–702. **G. J. Whyte-Melville.** Evidence for no. 4055.

4108 Arnold on translating Homer, 703–714. **James Spedding.** Signed J.S.; repr. *Reviews*, as "English Hexameters." (See note to no. 4228.)

4109 The intellectual faculties, according to phrenology, examined (Part IV, concl.), 715–730. **Alexander Bain.** Signed. (Previous parts are nos. 4019, 4040, 4073.)

4110 Ida Conway (chaps. xix–xx), 730–745. **J. M. Capes?** Evidence for no. 4016.

4111 The British salmon fisheries, 745–761.

4112 Where fancy is bred, 762–773. **John Ormsby.** Signed O.; repr. *Stray Papers*, 1876.

4113 Historical art in England [mainly on John Cross], 773–780. **F. T. Palgrave.** Signed.

4114 Chronicle of current history, 783–790. **T. C. Sandars.** Cf. no. 4005.

VOLUME 64, JULY 1861

4115 William Pitt [by Earl Stanhope, Vols. I–II], 1–17. Unidentified. (See no. 4246.)

4116 Good for nothing (chaps. xxvi–xxix),

18–35. **G. J. Whyte-Melville.** Evidence for no. 4055.

4117   *Ancient Law* [by H. S. Maine], 36–46.

4118   *Catullus* [trans. by Theodore Martin], 47–53.

4119   The sphynx; a discourse on the impotence of history, 54–70. **John Skelton.** Signed Shirley; repr. *Nugae Criticae.*

4120   Ida Conway (chaps. xxi–xxiii), 71–87. **J. M. Capes?** Evidence for no. 4016.

4121   Savings banks in connexion with the post office, 88–98.

4122   Petrarch and his times, 99–115.

4123   Saint Saturday, 116–123. Signed: J.E.C.

4124   Chronicle of current history, 125–134. **T. C. Sandars.** Cf. no. 4005.

VOLUME 64, AUGUST 1861

4125   A few more words from the archives of Simancas [sequel to no. 4105], 135–150. **J. A. Froude.** Signed.

4126   Good for nothing (chaps. xxx–xxxiii), 151–170. **G. J. Whyte-Melville.** Evidence for no. 4055.

4127   Italian states and rulers in the last half of the fifteenth century, 170–190.

4128   The Edda, 190–198. **Carl Lottner.** Signed.

4129   A discourse of immaturity; or, Concerning veal, 199–216. **A. K. H. Boyd.** Signed A.K.H.B.; repr. *Leisure Hours.*

4130   Ida Conway (chaps. xxiv–xxv, concl.), 219–233. **J. M. Capes?** Evidence for no. 4016.

4131   Causes of the disruption of the American Union, 234–245. Signed: X.Y.

4132   Reminiscences of New Zealand, 246–256. **Thomas Arnold,** 1823–1900. Claimed in *Life,* pp. 73, 74n.

4133   Chronicle of current history, 257–264. **T. C. Sandars.** Cf. no. 4005.

VOLUME 64, SEPTEMBER 1861

4134   Barren honour, a tale (chaps. i–iii), 265–282. **George Alfred Lawrence.** Signed The Author of *Guy Livingstone, Sword and Gown,* etc.; novel pub. 1862.

4135   Literature and philosophy of the early Christian ascetics, 283–295.

4136   Gone, 296–300. **A. K. H. Boyd.** Signed A.K.H.B.; repr. *Leisure Hours.*

4137   A few words on the census of Ireland, 300–307. **William O'Connor Morris.** Signed W.O'C.M.; claimed in Morris to

Blackwood, Aug. 19, 1861, Nat. Lib. Scot.

4138   Manners and morals, as affected by civilization, 307–316.

4139   Good for nothing (chaps. xxxiv–xxxvii), 317–336. **G. J. Whyte-Melville.** Evidence for no. 4055.

4140   Homœopathy: a letter to J.S.S., Esq., 337–340. **Benjamin Brodie.** Signed; repr. *Works of Sir Benjamin C. Brodie* (1865), I.

4141   Modern art in Berlin, 341–356. Signed: Topaze.

4142   Parish registers: their history and contents, 357–365.

4143   Said Bey Jumblatt [Lebanese Chief], 366–374. Signed: Libanus.

4144   Belligerents' rights at sea, 375–379.

4145   Java (Part II, concl.), 379–390. Signed: An Anglo-Batavian.

VOLUME 64, OCTOBER 1861

4146   Utilitarianism (chaps. i–ii), 391–406. **John Stuart Mill.** Signed. Treatise printed 1863.

4147   Barren honour (chaps. iv–v), 407–423. **G. A. Lawrence.** Evidence for no. 4134.

4148   Concerning people of whom more might have been made, 423–438. **A. K. H. Boyd.** Signed A.K.H.B.; repr. *Leisure Hours.*

4149   Working in gold, 439–451. **George John Cayley,** prob. Signed G.J.C.; cf. no. 4264.

4150   Some poets of the year, 452–466.

4151   Good for nothing (chaps. xxxviii–xli), 467–486. **G. J. Whyte-Melville.** Evidence for no. 4055.

4152   The Sunday question, 487–503.

4153   Something about modern Arabic, 504–516.

4154   Austria and Hungary, 517–524.

VOLUME 64, NOVEMBER 1861

4155   Utilitarianism (chaps. iii–iv), 525–534. **John Stuart Mill.** Signed.

4156   Barren honour (chaps. vi–vii), 535–549. **G. A. Lawrence.** Evidence for no. 4134.

4157   Clubs, 552–564.

4158   Concerning people who carried weight in life; with some thoughts on those who never had a chance, 565–579. **A. K. H. Boyd.** Signed A.K.H.B.; repr. *Leisure Hours.*

4159 The London exhibitions of 1861, 580–592. **W. M. Rossetti.** Signed; repr. *Fine Art.*

4160 Good for nothing (chaps. xlii–xlv), 593–611. **G. J. Whyte-Melville.** Evidence for no. 4055.

4161 The meeting in Manchester of the British Association for the Advancement of Science, 1861, 612–627. **Robert Lamb.** Signed at start A Manchester Man, at end R.L.; repr. *Free Thoughts*, II.

4162 *L'Italie est-elle la Terre des Morts?* 628–635.

4163 The proposed removal of the courts of law, 635–643. **Thomas Erskine Holland.** Signed T.E.H.; he was professor of International Law, Oxford.

4164 *Irish History and Irish Character* [Goldwin Smith], 644–658. **W. O'Connor Morris.** Signed W.O'C.M.—see no. 4137.

VOLUME 64, DECEMBER 1861

4165 Utilitarianism (chap. v, concl.), 659–673. **John Stuart Mill.** Signed.

4166 Duties of England to India, 674–689. **F. W. Newman.** Repr. *Miscellanies*, III.

4167 Good for nothing (chaps. xlvi–xlix, concl.), 690–699. **G. J. Whyte-Melville.** Evidence for no. 4055.

4168 Cowper's poems, 700–717. **W. B. Donne.** Signed W.B.D.; Johnson, *Donne*, list.

4169 Mexico, 717–731. Signed: L.

4170 Barren honour (chaps. viii–x), 732–752. **G. A. Lawrence.** Evidence for no. 4134.

4171 Between the cataracts [of the Nile] without a dragoman, 755–771. **G. J. Cayley.** Signed.

4172 Shakspeare, and his latest stage interpreters, 772–786. **Theodore Martin.** Repr. *Essays*, I.

VOLUME 65, JANUARY 1862

4173 Thalatta! Thalatta! a study at sea (Part I), 1–15. **John Skelton.** Signed The Author of "Catarina in Venice"—see no. 3751.

4174 Early Scottish poetry, 16–34. **John Skelton.** Signed Shirley—see *DNB*.

4175 Concerning the world's opinion: with some thoughts on cowed people, 35–50. **A. K. H. Boyd.** Signed A.K.H.B.; repr. *Leisure Hours.*

4176 A few words on the marriage law of the Empire, 51–58. **W. O'Connor Morris.** Signed W.O'C.M.—see no. 4137.

4177 Santa Teresa; a psychological study, 59–74. **J. A. Froude.** Signed I.A.F.; repr. *Armada*, in revised form.

4178 Barren honour (chaps. xi–xiii), 75–90. **G. A. Lawrence.** Evidence for no. 4134.

4179 A Greek ballad: Megas and Davéli, 91–94.

4180 Comets, 95–110.

4181 Max Müller on the science of language, 111–123.

4182 The close of 1861, 123–134.

VOLUME 65, FEBRUARY 1862

4183 *The Spanish Conquest in America* [by Arthur Helps, Vol. IV], 135–150. **W. B. Donne.** Johnson, *Donne*, list.

4184 Thalatta! Thalatta! (Part II), 151–168. **John Skelton.** Evidence for no. 4173.

4185 Editors and newspaper writers of the last generation (Part I), 169–183. **A. V. Kirwan.** Signed An Old Apprentice of the Law; listed in his "Essays"; he claimed Part II (no. 4217) in Kirwan to Blackwood, May 5, 1862, Nat. Lib. Scot.

4186 Westborough Fair, 183–197. **T. G. Faussett.** Signed T.G.F.; cf. no. 4266, and note the reference here, p. 185, to the antiquarian *History and Antiquities of Westborough.*

4187 Sidney Herbert, first Baron Herbert of Lea, 198–212.

4188 1831–32; a sketch, 213–228. **William Frederick Campbell.** Signed Lord Campbell; see p. 213n. and *Complete Peerage* under Stratheden.

4189 Celibacy v. marriage, 228–235. **F. P. Cobbe.** Signed F.P.C.; repr. *Pursuits of Women.*

4190 Barren honour (chaps. xiv–xvi), 236–252. **G. A. Lawrence.** Evidence for no. 4134.

4191 Muse of the drawing-room, 252–257.

4192 The contest in America, 258–268. **John Stuart Mill.** Signed; repr. Boston, 1862. (Comment, vol. 67, 192n. [on a remark here, p. 264], by **J. A. Froude**—signed Editor *FM*.)

VOLUME 65, MARCH 1862

4193 Thalatta! Thalatta! (Part III), 269–284. **John Skelton.** Evidence for no. 4173.

4194 The non-regulation provinces of India,

285–303. **T. H. Bullock?** Author speaks of his own experience in a non-regulation province, p. 298, which Berar was (see p. 296) and corrects Mr. Laing's misunderstanding of the Hyderabad accounts, p. 296 (Berar was a part of Hyderabad) —see no. 4286; the idea, p. 286, that famine, though caused directly by drought, is really caused by the price of food rising above what the poor can pay, is one of the main contentions of no. 4739; last part of evidence for no. 4237 is also applicable here.

4195   Concerning the sorrows of childhood, 304–317. **A. K. H. Boyd.** Signed A.K.H.B.; repr. *Leisure Hours.*

4196   The city of victory [Cairo], 317–331. **F. P. Cobbe.** Repr. *Cities.*

4197   *Popol Vuh* [sacred writings of Indians of Central America], 332–343. **Friedrich Max Müller.** Repr. *Chips,* I.

4198   Percy Bysshe Shelley: supplementary notice [to nos. 3733 and 3932], 343–346. **T. L. Peacock.** Signed; *Works,* VIII.

4199   The twice-revised code [of public education], 347–365. **Matthew Arnold.** *Letters of Matthew Arnold,* ed. G. W. E. Russell (2 vols., 1895), I, 183, 185, 187–188, 190–191, 193–194.

4200   Barren honour (chaps. xvii–xix), 366–382. **G. A. Lawrence.** Evidence for no. 4134.

4201   Austria and Hungary, 384–402. **Bonamy Price.** Signed. (See no. 4224, pp. 709–714.)

VOLUME 65, APRIL 1862

4202   The income-tax, and the plans for its reform, 403–414.

4203   Thalatta! Thalatta! (Part IV), 415–431. **John Skelton.** Evidence for no. 4173.

4204   The Roman book-trade under the Empire, 432–438. **George Cornewall Lewis.** Signed Sir George Lewis; author refers to his *Inquiry into the Credibility of Early Roman History.*

4205   Notes from Numidia (No. I), 438–447. **John Ormsby.** Series repr. *Autumn Rambles.*

4206   Mrs. Delany; or, A lady of quality in the last century, 448–457.

4207   Humming-birds, 457–468. **Charles Richard Weld.** Signed C.R.W.—see no. 3941.

4208   Barren honour (chaps. xx–xxi), 469–485. **G. A. Lawrence.** Evidence for no. 4134.

4209   Mental epidemics [in religion], 490–505.

4210   My Highland home, 506–518. **Arthur T. Malkin.** Attr. by Johnson, *Donne,* pp. 320–321.

4211   *The Engineers* [by Samuel Smiles], 519–527.

4212   Arthur Hugh Clough, 527–536. **Francis Turner Palgrave.** Signed F.T.P.; repr. Clough, *Poems,* 1862, as "Memoir."

VOLUME 65, MAY 1862

4213   Thalatta! Thalatta! (Part V), 537–550. **John Skelton.** Evidence for no. 4173.

4214   The colonies, 551–564.

4215   The Eternal City—in a temporary phase, 565–579. **Frances Power Cobbe.** Signed; repr. *Cities.*

4216   The *Vita Nuova* of Dante [translations by Theodore Martin and D. G. Rossetti], 580–594.

4217   Editors, and newspaper and periodical writers of the last generation [largely on James Mackintosh] (Part II), 595–609. **A. V. Kirwan.** Evidence for no. 4185. (See no. 4234.)

4218   Indigo-planting in Bengal, and the breach-of-contract bill, 610–626. **Thomas Henry Bullock.** Signed T.H.B.; in no. 4320, p. 531, Bullock speaks of this art. as "ours"; both arts., like all of his work, deal with India; see no. 4286.

4219   Barren honour (chaps. xxii–xxiv), 627–642. **G. A. Lawrence.** Evidence for no. 4134.

4220   Practical remarks on the law of the diffusion of gases in relation to social life, 643–651. Signed: G.K. Perhaps George Kemp who was a chemist and physiologist; see Venn.

4221   Science of history, 651–660.

4222   Notes from Numidia (No. II): across the Atlas, 661–670. **John Ormsby.** Cf. no. 4205.

VOLUME 65, JUNE 1862

4223   Thalatta! Thalatta! (Part VI, concl.), 671–697. **John Skelton.** Evidence for no. 4173.

4224   Hungary, 698–714. Signed: A.C.S.

4225   Going on, 715–732. **A. K. H. Boyd.** Signed A.K.H.B.; repr. *Everyday Philosopher.*

4226   The Reign of Terror [largely on Marie Antoinette] (Part I), 733–750.

4227 Barren honour (chaps. xxv–xxvii, concl.), 751–768. **G. A. Lawrence.** Evidence for no. 4134.

4228 Homeric translations, 769–780. Unidentified. Note [to no. 4108], 780–784, by **James Spedding**—signed J.S., repr. *Reviews.*

4229 Essays on political economy; being a sequel to papers which appeared in the *Cornhill Magazine* (No. I), 784–792. **John Ruskin.** Signed; repr., heavily revised, in *Munera Pulveris, Works,* XVII.

4230 The International Exhibition (No. I), 793–806.

VOLUME 66, JULY 1862

4231 A first friendship (chaps. i–iv), 1–21. **Henry Jackson,** 1831–1879. Novel published 1863 as by H.J.; assigned to Jackson in H&L and *BMCat.*

4232 Universal suffrage in the United States, and its consequences, 21–31. **Hiram Fuller.** Signed A White Republican; repr. *North and South,* 1863.

4233 Editors, and newspaper and periodical writers of the last generation (Part III, concl.), 32–49. **A. V. Kirwan.** Evidence for no. 4185.

4234 The late John Adolphus [on part of no. 4217], 49–53. **John Leycester Adolphus.** Signed.

4235 Notes from Numidia (No. III): the Sahara, 54–64. **John Ormsby.** Cf. no. 4205.

4236 The Royal Academy Exhibition, 65–76. **W. M. Rossetti.** Signed; repr. *Fine Art.*

4237 Public works in India: the navigation of the Godavery River, etc., 77–93. **T. H. Bullock,** prob. The author speaks from "very extended experience" of the geography of Behar, pp. 82–83, and of its politics since the annexation of 1853, p. 85 (cf. the evidence for no. 4286); the sympathy with native feelings and the candid criticism of the British government at home and in India are characteristic of Bullock's arts. for *FM.*

4238 A model and a wife, 95–113. **Isa Blagden.** Signed at start The Author of *Agnes Tremorne,* at end I.B.; see *BMCat.*

4239 The ordeal by oath: a plea for enfranchisement, 115–121. **John Skelton.** Signed Shirley—see *DNB.*

4240 Historical records and record commissions, 122–134.

VOLUME 66, AUGUST 1862

4241 A first friendship (chaps. v–viii), 135–152. **Henry Jackson,** 1831–1879. Cf. no. 4231.

4242 The Reign of Terror (Part II, concl.), 153–171.

4243 Concerning disagreeable people, 173–188. **A. K. H. Boyd.** Signed A.K.H.B.; repr. *Everyday Philosopher.*

4244 The fine art of the International Exhibition, 188–199. **W. M. Rossetti.** Signed.

4245 *Aids to Faith* and *Replies to "Essays and Reviews,"* 200–206. **A. P. Stanley.** Attr. by H. H. Milman, *Life,* p. 278; in no. 4608, p. 738, Stanley refers to this art. as if it were his.

4246 William Pitt—last ten years [Earl Stanhope's biography, Vols. III–IV], 207–220.

4247 Adrian (chaps. i–v), 221–239. Unidentified. Novel published anon. 1863 as *Adrian L'Estrange:* see *Eng.Cat.,* 1863–1872.

4248 The field and the forest, 240–255.

4249 *North America* [by Anthony Trollope], 256–264.

VOLUME 66, SEPTEMBER 1862

4250 Essays on political economy (No. II), 265–280. **John Ruskin.** Signed.

4251 A first friendship (chaps. ix–xi), 281–298. **Henry Jackson,** 1831–1879. Cf. no. 4231.

4252 North and South: the controversy in a colloquy, 299–318. **Hiram Fuller.** Signed A White Republican; repr. *North and South,* 1863.

4253 The post-office, 319–336. **M. D. Hill.** *Memoir,* p. 248.

4254 Henry Thomas Buckle, 337–345. **W. B. Donne.** Johnson, *Donne,* list.

4255 Adrian (chaps. vi–x), 346–362.

4256 Our manufacturing districts and operative classes, 363–382. **Robert Lamb.** Signed at start A Manchester Man, at end R.L.; repr. *Free Thoughts,* II, as "Our Cotton Trade and Factory Operatives."

4257 Corneille and Dryden: principles of the drama, 383–398.

VOLUME 66, OCTOBER 1862

4258 The opium revenue of India considered in connexion with Mr. Laing's last budget, 399–417. **T. H. Bullock,** prob. Author remarks, p. 412, that the ryots have "refused to grow indigo for the mere benefit of the European capitalist," as does Bullock in no. 4286, p. 7; the criticisms of Laing (cf. no. 4320), the knowledge of land rights in India, the sympathy for the ryots, and criticisms of the British government are characteristic of Bullock's arts. in *FM*; Bullock had published a pamphlet on opium in 1840 entitled "The Chinese Vindicated" which defended the Chinese attempts to halt the opium trade and criticized the contraband traders, as does the author here (see especially pp. 403–404).

4259 A first friendship (chaps. xii–xiii), 419–432. **Henry Jackson,** 1831–1879. Cf. no. 4231.

4260 North and South: the two constitutions, 433–448. **Hiram Fuller.** Signed A White Republican; repr. *North and South,* 1863.

4261 Notes from Numidia (No. IV, concl.): the "Grande Kabylie," 449–460. **John Ormsby.** Cf. no. 4205.

4262 What is truth? a page from the Covenant, 461–471. **John Skelton.** Signed Shirley—see *DNB*.

4263 Adrian (chaps. xi–xiv), 472–488.

4264 Art for artificers, 489–496. **G. J. Cayley.** Signed.

4265 Concerning Sundays long ago, 496–502. **A. K. H. Boyd.** Signed A.K.H.B.; repr. *Graver Thoughts of a Country Parson,* 1st series, 1863.

4266 The sixth quarter of the world [Romney Marsh in Kent], 502–515. **T. G. Faussett.** Signed T.G.F.; Faussett was an antiquary especially interested in Kent (see *DNB*) and a contributor to *FM*.

4267 Spiritualism, 516–528.

VOLUME 66, NOVEMBER 1862

4268 *Letters and Life of Bacon* [ed. James Spedding], 528–548. **W. B. Donne.** Johnson, *Donne,* list; FitzGerald-Donne, p. 65.

4269 A first friendship (chaps. xiv–xv), 549–565. **Henry Jackson,** 1831–1879. Cf. no. 4231.

4270 Physicians and surgeons of a bygone generation, 566–578. **A. V. Kirwan.** Signed A Man on the Shady Side of Fifty —see no. 4023; listed in his "Essays."

4271 Ernest Renan, 579–593.

4272 "What shall we do with our old maids?" 594–610. **Frances Power Cobbe.** Signed; repr. *Pursuits of Women.*

4273 Adrian (chaps. xv–xvii), 616–630.

4274 The International Exhibition (No. II, concl.), 631–646.

4275 North and South; or, Who is the traitor? 647–662. **Hiram Fuller.** Signed A White Republican; repr. *North and South,* 1863.

VOLUME 66, DECEMBER 1862

4276 The reaction in Naples, 662–678.

4277 A first friendship (chaps. xvi–xix), 679–694. **Henry Jackson,** 1831–1879. Cf. no. 4231.

4278 Present position of the Church of England, 695–709.

4279 Autumn days, 715–726. **John Skelton.** Signed Shirley—see *DNB*.

4280 Laurel and cypress: a chapter in the history of Australian exploration [the crossing of the continent by Burke and Wills], 726–741. Signed: R.R.

4281 Essays on political economy (No. III), 742–756. **John Ruskin.** Signed.

4282 To work again, 757–760. **A. K. H. Boyd.** Signed A.K.H.B.; repr. *Everyday Philosopher.*

4283 Adrian (chaps. xviii–xx), 761–773.

4284 Female charity: lay and monastic, 774–788. **Frances Power Cobbe.** Signed; repr. *Pursuits of Women.*

4285 "Sippurim" [on the Bohemian Jews], 789–798.

VOLUME 67, JANUARY 1863

4286 The sale of waste lands and redemption of land-tax in India, &c., considered, 1–16. **Thomas Henry Bullock.** Signed J.H.B., but in error for T.H.B., the signature of no. 4320, where p. 533, this art. is cited as "ours" and the same subject is under discussion; on p. 9 author calls himself "the responsible Government agent for the land settlement" in Berar from 1853 for seven years; p. 14 shows he is now living at Cheltenham; in *Walford's County Families of the U.K.* (1920), p. 192, the man cited is referred to as "Deputy Commissioner of Berar, India, who died in 1869"; the records of the India Office (Range 202, vol. 5) add the title "Captain"; the *Cheltenham P.O. Directories* for 1862 and 1863 list Captain Bullock; Meadows Taylor to A. H. Layard, Jan. 18, 1863, BM Add. MS. 44428, attribs.

this art. to "Capt. Bullock a brother Commissioner [in India]."

4287　A first friendship (chaps. xx–xxiii), 17–28. **Henry Jackson,** 1831–1879. Cf. no. 4231.

4288　On the treatment of female convicts, 31–46. **Mary Carpenter.** Signed.

4289　Maurice de Guérin, 47–61. **Matthew Arnold.** Signed; repr. *Essays,* 1st series.

4290　*Edward Irving* [by Margaret Oliphant], 62–73. **C. Kegan Paul.** *Memories* (1899), p. 179; repr. *Biographical Sketches,* 1883.

4291　Adrian (chaps. xxi–xxiv, concl.), 81–95.

4292　Naval architecture, 96–113.

4293　The late Sir Benjamin Brodie, 113–120. A. V. Kirwan. Signed An Old Apprentice of the Law—see no. 4185; listed in "Essays."

4294　The decypher of ancient inscriptions, 121–134. **F. W. Newman?** Cf. no. 4597 written in similar style from same skeptical point of view; Rawlinson and Hincks, referred to here, p. 133, reappear there on pp. 589, 590.

VOLUME 67, FEBRUARY 1863

4295　My wanderings in West Africa: a visit to the renowned cities of Wari and Benin (Part I), 135–157. **Richard F. Burton.** Signed F.R.G.S. [Fellow Royal Geographical Society]; attr. in N. M. Penzer, *Annotated Bibliography of Sir R. F. Burton,* 1923.

4296　A first friendship (chaps. xxiv–xxvi), 158–171. **Henry Jackson,** 1831–1879. Cf. no. 4231.

4297　The late Lady Morgan and her autobiography, 172–191.

4298　Negroes and slavery in the United States, 192–204. **Hiram Fuller.** Signed A White Republican; repr. *North and South,* 2nd ed., 1864.

4299　Concerning cutting and carving: with some thoughts on tampering with the coin of the realm, 205–219. **A. K. H. Boyd.** Signed A.K.H.B.; repr. *Everyday Philosopher.*

4300　A day at the Dead Sea, 226–238. **Frances Power Cobbe.** Signed; repr. *Cities.*

4301　Robert Browning, 240–256. **John Skelton.** Signed Shirley; repr. *A Campaigner at Home,* 1865.

4302　The moral philosophy of garotting, 258–264. Signed: A Retired Practitioner of the Science.

4303　Shams, 265–272. **Elizabeth Cleghorn**

Gaskell, prob. Signed E.C.G.; the art. deals with life in a country town in a manner reminiscent of *Cranford;* Froude to Mrs. Gaskell, Oct. 20, 1863, John Rylands Library, says he can now offer more than J. W. Parker because Longman is to be publisher, which implies an art. by Mrs. Gaskell under Parker's ownership and on March 20 [1864], ibid., asks her whether she wishes her "*name* to appear with 'French Life' or not," which suggests an earlier art., in which her name did not appear.

VOLUME 67, MARCH 1863

4304　My wanderings in West Africa (Part II), 273–289. **R. F. Burton.** Evidence for no. 4295.

4305　A first friendship (chaps. xxvii–xxxi, concl.), 290–303. **Henry Jackson,** 1831–1879. Cf. no. 4231.

4306　Law and lawyers in England and Scotland, 304–316.

4307　Mountaineering in 1861, 317–332. **A. T. Malkin.** Many facts given about himself by the author exactly parallel those in "Leaves from the Diary of the late Mr. A. T. Malkin," *Alpine Journal,* X, 40, 120, 205; on p. 325 the author says "my own notes of a tour in 1843" are included in Murray's *Handbook [for Travellers in Switzerland and the Alps of Savoy]* "down even to the latest editions"; notes in the 1854 ed., p. 181–183, are signed A.T.M.

4308　A chapter on innocents [on Scottish madhouses], 333–348. **Patrick C. Beaton.** Signed P.C.B.—see no. 4343.

4309　Theology in Holland, 358–370. **M. E. Grant Duff.** Partly repr. *Studies.*

4310　Victor Hugo, 372–382.

4311　Italian poetry and patriotism (Part I), 383–395. **Louisa A. Merivale.** Signed L.A.M.; woman cited published a book of selections from Italian poetry, 1865.

4312　The Japanese martyrs, 396–406.

VOLUME 67, APRIL 1863

4313　My wanderings in West Africa (Part III, concl.), 407–422. **R. F. Burton.** Evidence for no. 4295.

4314　Late laurels (chaps. i–iii), 423–440. **H. S. Cunningham.** Novel published 1864, ascribed to man cited in *BMCat.*

4315　Essays on political economy (No. IV, concl.), 441–462. **John Ruskin.** Signed.

W. Y. Sellar], 246–252. **F. T. Palgrave.** Signed.

4358 The popular novels of the year, 253–269.

4359 The last from Nineveh, 270–276.

VOLUME 68, SEPTEMBER 1863

4360 A plea for the free discussion of theological difficulties, 277–291. **J. A. Froude.** Repr. *Studies*, I.

4361 Late laurels (chaps. xiv–xvi), 292–306. **H. S. Cunningham.** Cf. no. 4314.

4362 Our manufacturing districts under a cloud, 309–325. **Robert Lamb.** Signed at start A Manchester Man, at end R.L.; repr. *Free Thoughts*, II, as "Lancashire under a Cloud."

4363 The periodical press of the United States of America, 325–334.

4364 A fortnight in Belgium in the June and July of 1863, 335–352. **A. V. Kirwan.** Listed in "Essays."

4365 Recreations of a London recluse (No. I), 353–363.

4366 A chapter on Madagascar, 375–391. **P. C. Beaton.** Signed P.C.B.—see no. 4343.

4367 On the credibility of old song-history and tradition, 394–401. **William Barnes.** Attr. by Dugdale, *Barnes*, p. 243.

4368 On the forest-hill: with some thoughts touching dream-life, 403–410. **A. K. H. Boyd.** Signed A.K.H.B.; repr. *Autumn Holidays*.

4369 The Prussian crisis, 410–418.

VOLUME 68, OCTOBER 1863

4370 England and America, 420–437. **J. F. Stephen.** Attr. in J. S. Mill to Henry Fawcett, Oct. 14, 1863, to appear in the forthcoming *Later Letters of J. S. Mill*, ed. Francis Mineka.

4371 Late laurels (chaps. xvii–xix), 438–453. **H. S. Cunningham.** Cf. no. 4314.

4372 England and her colonies [on Goldwin Smith], 454–470. **Bonamy Price.** Claimed in Price to A. C. Fraser, Oct. 13, 1863, Fraser Papers.

4373 A rough ride on classic ground, 470–483. **John Ormsby.** Repr. *Autumn Rambles*.

4374 On certain physical and natural-history phenomena of the Atlantic: especially with reference to the proposed telegraphic communication between Ireland and Newfoundland, 484–496. **William**

King, 1809–1886. Signed, with title "Professor": see *DNB*.

4375 The second part of Göthe's *Faust*, 497–512.

4376 The sketcher in the Ardennes and Moselle land, 513–525. **Charles R. Weld,** prob. Signed C.W.F.; initials prob. misprint for C.R.W., his signature for no. 4621, art. of similar title and subject.

4377 Recreations of a London recluse (No. II), 527–533.

4378 On the present state of Russia, and the advantages to Europe of a constitution for that empire, 534–548.

VOLUME 68, NOVEMBER 1863

4379 The new struggle for German federative reform, 549–569. **Henry Ottley?** Signed H.O.; cf. no. 3329, which is cited here on p. 562.

4380 Late laurels (chaps. xx–xxi), 570–584. **H. S. Cunningham.** Cf. no. 4314.

4381 The rights of man and the claims of brutes, 586–602. **Frances Power Cobbe.** Signed; repr. *Studies*.

4382 Italian poetry and patriotism (Part II, concl.), 603–618. **Louisa A. Merivale.** Evidence for no. 4311.

4383 How do fish live and grow? 619–627.

4384 Three days at Wilna [in Poland], 627–634. **Henry A. Tilley.** Claimed in no. 4395, p. 792.

4385 Concerning the close of holiday-time: with some thoughts on pulpits, 648–654. **A. K. H. Boyd.** Signed A.K.H.B.; his usual signature.

4386 Mendelssohn's *Letters*, 655–665. **John Hullah.** Signed I.H.; Frances Hullah, *Life of John Hullah* (1886), pp. 108–109.

4387 Strong-minded women, 667–678. **George Whyte-Melville.** Signed G.W.M. —see no. 3326.

VOLUME 68, DECEMBER 1863

4388 Women and scepticism, 679–698. **James Fitzjames Stephen.** Stephen list.

4389 Sketches in China, 699–712.

4390 The [political] reforms of the future, 713–729.

4391 A chapter on croakers, 730–745. **P. C. Beaton.** Signed P.C.B.—see no. 4343.

4392 An episode in the modern history of the English church [in 1772], 746–753.

4393 Plays, players, and critics, 767–776. **Theodore Martin.** Repr. *Essays*, I.

4394 Late laurels (chaps. xxii–xxiv), 777–790. **H. S. Cunningham.** Cf. no. 4314.

4395 The Polish women and the Insurrection, 792–800. **Henry A. Tilley.** Claimed in his *Eastern Europe and and Western Asia* (1864), p. 169n.

4396 *My Beautiful Lady* [by Thomas Woolner], 801–806. Unidentified. Possibly William Allingham, friend and admirer of Woolner's and of the poem (*Diary*, p. 91; *Letters*, pp. 283–293); he was asked to review the poem for *Mac* (no. 426 in *Index*, I, 570) but apparently refused [because he was committed to *FM*, which he had been writing for?]. (Additional note on the poem, vol. 69, p. 283n, by **John Skelton**—see no. 4416.)

4397 The English turf, 806–814.

VOLUME 69, JANUARY 1864

4398 The highway of nations [rights at sea], 1–17.

4399 Late laurels (chaps. xxv–xxvi), 18–36. **H. S. Cunningham.** Cf. no. 4314.

4400 [Fitzjames] Stephen on criminal law, 37–48.

4401 Criticism and the Gospel history, 49–63. **J. A. Froude.** Repr. *Studies*, I.

4402 The Royal Academy Commission, 64–77. **Henry Ottley,** prob. Signed H.O.; man cited wrote a *Dictionary of Painters and Engravers*, 1866; contributed no. 4460 to August issue.

4403 The poetry of the eighteenth century, 78–88.

4404 Japan, 101–117. **J. F. Stephen.** Stephen list.

4405 Concerning ugly ducks; being some thoughts on misplaced men, 119–127. **A. K. H. Boyd.** Signed A.K.H.B.; repr. *Autumn Holidays.*

4406 Recreations of a London recluse (No. III), 127–134. Unidentified. (No. IV is no. 4492.)

VOLUME 69, FEBRUARY 1864

4407 The political temper of the nation, 135–159. **Bonamy Price.** Signed.

4408 Late laurels (chaps. xxvii–xxviii, concl.), 160–170. **H. S. Cunningham.** Cf. no. 4314.

4409 Public works [in London], 173–186.

4410 Village life in Oudh (No. I): the village and its inhabitants, 187–198. **William Knighton.** Attr. in *MWT*, 14th ed.

4411 *Revolutions in English History* [by Robert Vaughan, Vol. III], 199–212. Signed: K.

4412 A campaigner at home (Nos. I and II): Laburnum Lodge; how we elected the beadle, 214–228. **John Skelton.** Series repr. 1865.

4413 Life and writings of Theodore Parker, 229–245. **J. F. Stephen.** Stephen list.

4414 Rambles with the lion-hunters of Algeria, 246–260. **John Ormsby.** Repr. *Autumn Rambles.*

VOLUME 69, MARCH 1864

4415 The Congress [of Vienna] correspondence [on a proposal made by Napoleon III], 261–278.

4416 A campaigner at home (No. III): memorial poetry—an essay by the doctor, 279–292. **John Skelton.** Cf. no. 4412.

4417 Hades, 293–311. **Frances Power Cobbe.** Signed; repr. *Studies.*

4418 Village life in Oudh (No. II, concl.): births, marriages, deaths, and 'wolf-boys,' 316–327. **William Knighton.** Cf. no. 4410.

4419 A week in bed, 327–335. **George Whyte-Melville.** Signed G.W.M.—see no. 3326.

4420 Jem Nash, the dull boy, 336–346. **Margaret Elliot.** Attr. by Mrs. Gaskell (*Letters*, p. 747) to "Miss (Maggie) Elliott . . . daughter of the Dean of Bristol"; the dean's name is given with one "t" (Rev. Gilbert Elliot) in Venn and Boase.

4421 *The Gladiators* [by G. T. Whyte-Melville], 347–356. Signed: M.

4422 Land tenure question, 357–377. **F. W. Newman.** Repr. *Miscellanies*, IV, as "Feudality versus Ownership."

4423 The parish priest (Part I), 377–386. **Harry Jones,** 1823–1900. Signed H.J.; series repr. *Priest and Parish*, 1866. (Parts II and III are nos. 4473 and 4539.)

VOLUME 69, APRIL 1864

4424 Russia and her dependencies: the Caucasus, 387–399. **Henry A. Tilley.** Signed H.A.T.; Tilley published *Eastern Europe and Western Asia* early in 1864; both Tilley in the book, pp. 244–245, and H.A.T. in art., p. 396, describe talking with Circassian boys and men about Schamyl; pp. 212–213, 243–246 in the book on emigration of Circassians into Turkey parallel, pp. 387, 388 in this art., sometimes in similar phrasing.

4425 Mr. Thackeray, 401–418. **J. F. Stephen.** Stephen list.

4426 Mr. Gardiner's *History of James I*, 419–434.

4427 French life (Part I), 435–449. **Elizabeth C. Gaskell.** Gaskell, "Bibliography," p. xvii; Froude to Mrs. Gaskell, Oct. 20, 1863, cited in *Bull. of John Rylands Lib.*, 19 (Jan. 1935), 160.

4428 Our private play, 461–480.

4429 The nineteenth century, 481–494. **Frances Power Cobbe.** Repr. *Studies* as "Decemnovenarianism."

4430 A campaigner at home (No. IV): about taking down the sun—a provincial letter, 496–506. **John Skelton.** Cf. no. 4412.

4431 How may a peace income-tax be supplanted? 507–520. Signed: E.S.

VOLUME 69, MAY 1864

4432 The Privy Council and the Church of England, 521–537. **J. F. Stephen.** Stephen list.

4433 Carlyle's *Frederick the Great* [Vol. IV], 539–550. Signed: V.

4434 Gilbert Rugge (chaps. i–ii), 551–565. **Henry Jackson,** 1831–1879. Signed The Author of *A First Friendship*; novel published 1866.

4435 Early days of George I: Lady Cowper's *Diary*, 566–574.

4436 French life (Part II), 575–585. **Elizabeth C. Gaskell.** Cf. no. 4427.

4437 Children of this world, 586–590. **F. T. Palgrave.** Opuscula, vol. II, inserted between items no. 1 and 2.

4438 A campaigner at home (No. V): politics: the old world and the new, 591–600. **John Skelton.** Claimed in his *Essays*, pp. xxii–xxiii.

4439 The *Infant Bridal, and other Poems* [by Aubrey De Vere], 601–617. **Henry Taylor,** prob. Froude to Taylor, March 3, n.y., Bodleian Lib., praises the part of his art. on De Vere which has arrived; Taylor added the year "1865," in error apparently for 1864.

4440 The pleasures of difficulty, 618–625. **L. Owen Pike.** Signed.

4441 A reminiscence of the old time: being some thoughts on going away, 627–638. **A. K. H. Boyd.** Signed A.K.H.B.; repr. *Autumn Holidays.*

4442 Mr. Whitworth and Sir Emerson Tennent [on artillery], 639–654. Unidentified. (See no. 4450.)

VOLUME 69, JUNE 1864

4443 Public schools: report of the Commission (No. I), 655–669.

4444 Gilbert Rugge (chaps. iii–v), 670–690. **Henry Jackson** 1831–1879. Evidence for no. 4434.

4445 Indian barracks and hospitals, 691–703.

4446 A campaigner at home (Nos. VI and VII): among the wild fowl; natural historians: St. John and Russel, 705–718. **John Skelton.** Cf. no. 4412.

4447 Three years of war in America, 719–738. **C. C. Chesney.** Signed C.C.C.—see no. 4938; Chesney published a book on the Civil War in 1863.

4448 French life (Part III, concl.), 739–752. **Elizabeth C. Gaskell.** Cf. no. 4427.

4449 Capital punishments, 753–772. **J. F. Stephen.** Signed J.F.S.; claimed at start of no. 4627.

4450 "Mr. Whitworth and Sir Emerson Tennent" [a reply to no. 4442], 773–786. **J. Emerson Tennent.** Signed. Notes, p. 786, by **J. A. Froude**—signed Ed. *F.M.*; and, pp. 786–790, signed The Reviewer, [that is, the author of no. 4442]. (Reply to Froude's note, vol. 70, pp. 133–134, signed **J. Emerson Tennent**; reply to that, p. 134n, by **Froude.**)

VOLUME 70, JULY 1864

4451 The Irish church, 1–19. **H. S. Cunningham.** Repr., signed, as *Is the "Good News from Ireland" True? Remarks on the Position and Prospects of the Irish Church Establishment*, 1864.

4452 Gilbert Rugge (chaps. vi–viii), 20–36. **Henry Jackson,** 1831–1879. Evidence for no. 4434.

4453 The land revenue of India: the perpetual settlement, 37–51. **T. H. Bullock.** Signed T.H.B.—see no. 4286; cf. no. 4320, cited here, p. 38.

4454 Two chapters [on gossip], 51–56. Signed: C.S.S.

4455 The Royal Academy Exhibition, 57–74. **W. M. Rossetti.** Signed; repr. *Fine Art,* in revised form.

4456 A campaigner at home (Nos. VIII–

IX): idealism: poetical and religious; a realist, 75–88. **John Skelton.** Cf. no. 4412; footnote on J. F. Ferrier, 76–78, repr. in *Essays*.

4457 The judges of England, 89–105.

4458 Tunis and Carthage, 109–122. **John Ormsby.** Repr. *Autumn Rambles*.

4459 The morals of literature, 124–133. **Frances Power Cobbe.** Signed; repr. *Studies*.

VOLUME 70, AUGUST 1864

4460 Notes on diplomacy and diplomatic history (Part I), 135–157. **Henry Ottley.** Signed.

4461 Gilbert Rugge (chaps. ix–xi), 159–178. **Henry Jackson,** 1831–1879. Evidence for no. 4434.

4462 Elizabethan gardening, 179–191.

4463 Concerning unpruned trees, 192–198. **A. K. H. Boyd.** Signed A.K.H.B.; repr. *Autumn Holidays*.

4464 A campaigner at home (Nos. X–XI): church logic and Dr. Robert Lee; our camp in the woodland; a day with the gentle poets, 199–213. **John Skelton.** Cf. no. 4412.

4465 *Natural History and Sport in Moray*, 214–221. Unidentified. Possibly by John Skelton who had noticed this book briefly, and also favorably, in vol. 69, pp. 715–716.

4466 Mendelssohn's *Letters*, second series, 226–233. **John Hullah.** Signed J.H.—see no. 4386.

4467 A pilgrimage to Compostella [in Spain], 234–244. **Henry Fanshawe Tozer?** Signed H.F.T.; Tozer wrote many travel books in which religious shrines were often described; he had written "The Monks of Mount Athos" in 1862 (see *BMCat.*).

4468 The transcendentalists of Concord, 245–264. **M. D. Conway.** Burtis list; *Autobiography*, I, 361.

VOLUME 70, SEPTEMBER 1864

4469 Dr. Newman's *Apologia*, 265–303. **J. F. Stephen.** Stephen list.

4470 Gilbert Rugge (chaps. xii–xiii), 305–318. **Henry Jackson,** 1831–1879. Evidence for no. 4434.

4471 Public schools: report of the Commission (No. II, concl.), 319–330.

4472 Notes on diplomacy and diplomatic history (Part II), 331–350. **Henry Ottley.** Signed.

4473 The parish priest (Part II), 351–359. **Harry Jones.** Evidence for no. 4423.

4474 A campaigner at home (Nos. XII–XIII): mater saeva cupidinum; an old commonplace book, 361–370. **John Skelton.** Cf. no. 4412.

4475 The philosophy of the poor-laws, 373–394. **Frances Power Cobbe.** Signed; repr. *Studies*.

VOLUME 70, OCTOBER 1864

4476 The decline and fall of Whiggery, 395–406.

4477 From Auckland to Awamutu, 407–424. **P. C. Beaton.** Signed P.C.B.—see no. 4343. (See no. 4490.)

4478 Gilbert Rugge (chaps. xiv–xvii), 425–442. **Henry Jackson,** 1831–1879. Evidence for no. 4434.

4479 The census of England and Wales, 1861, 443–457.

4480 A campaigner at home (Nos. XIV–XV): thunder in the air; among the heather, 457–465. **John Skelton.** Cf. no. 4412.

4481 Rae Gifford, 467–481. **Henrietta Keddie.** Repr. in *Garden of Women*, 1875, as "A Lent lily."

4482 Notes on diplomacy and diplomatic history (Part III), 482–505. **Henry Ottley.** Signed.

4483 Imogen in Shakspeare and in sculpture, 506–511.

4484 Glimpses into village life in the seventeenth century, 512–528.

VOLUME 70, NOVEMBER 1864

4485 The peasant proprietors of the Drôme, 529–538. Signed: X.

4486 Mr. Forster on the reign of Charles I, 539–555.

4487 The mysterious maid; a sensation tale, 557–581.

4488 Popular education, 582–592.

4489 Gilbert Rugge (chaps. xviii–xx), 593–605. **Henry Jackson,** 1831–1879. Evidence for no. 4434.

4490 A chapter showing how we live at Awamutu [in New Zealand], 606–626. **P. C. Beaton.** Signed P.C.B.—see no. 4343.

4491 A campaigner at home (No. XVI): Nancy's tryst—a reminiscence of the

Highlands, 627–636. **John Skelton.** Cf. no. 4412.

4492 Recreations of a London recluse (No. IV, concl.), 637–643.

4493 Dr. Pusey and the Court of Appeal, 644–662. **J. F. Stephen.** Stephen list.

VOLUME 70, DECEMBER 1864

4494 Ireland, 663–677.

4495 The drama in Paris, 678–694. **Abraham Hayward.** Claimed in *Correspondence*, II, 107.

4496 Gilbert Rugge (chaps. xxi–xxiii), 694–710. **Henry Jackson,** 1831–1879. Evidence for no. 4434.

4497 *Vie de Shakespeare* [by Victor Hugo], 711–725. **Juliet Pollock.** Macready to Lady Pollock, Jan. 9, 1864 (in error, surely, for 1865), *Diaries*, II, 460: "I shall send for the December number of *Fraser's* for the pleasure of reading your article"; Lady Pollock's interests in drama and in contemporary French literature (see *Index*, I, 1051) fit this art. perfectly, while they are not found in the issue for Dec. 1863 (except in no. 4393 written by Theodore Martin).

4498 A campaigner at home (Nos. XVII–XVIII, concl.): the Scottish Royalists; what they all made of it, 725–740. **John Skelton.** Cf. no. 4412.

4499 Concerning ten years: with some account of things learned in them, 741–756. **A. K. H. Boyd.** Signed A.K.H.B.; repr. *Lessons*.

4500 Kaye's *History of the Indian Mutiny*, 757–774. **J. F. Stephen.** Stephen list.

4501 Curiosities of the Patent Office, 775–780.

4502 Notes on diplomacy and diplomatic history (Part IV, concl.), 781–797. **Henry Ottley.** Signed.

4503 The Cambridge Apostles [defence of no. 4457], 797–798. **Charles Merivale.** *Autobiography*, p. 247.

VOLUME 71, JANUARY 1865

4504 President Lincoln, 1–21. **Moncure D. Conway.** Signed An American Abolitionist; claimed in *Autobiography*, II, 185.

4505 Spiritualism, as related to religion and science, 22–42. **Abraham Hayward.** *Correspondence*, II, 110.

4506 Gilbert Rugge (chaps. xxiv–xxvi), 43–

60. **Henry Jackson,** 1831–1879. Evidence for no. 4434.

4507 Condition and prospects of the navy, 61–82.

4508 Richardson [the novelist], 83–96.

4509 The hierarchy of art (Part I), 97–108. **Frances Power Cobbe.** Signed; repr. *Studies*.

4510 On mountain beauty [largely on Ruskin], 111–123.

4511 The drama in London, 124–134. **Theodore Martin.** Repr. *Essays*, I.

VOLUME 71, FEBRUARY 1865

4512 Rebellion, diplomacy, and progress in China, 135–153.

4513 Corporal punishments, and penal reformation, 154–166. **F. W. Newman.** Repr. *Miscellanies*, III.

4514 Gilbert Rugge (chaps. xxvii–xxix), 167–183. **Henry Jackson,** 1831–1879. Evidence for no. 4434.

4515 The story of Saneha: an Egyptian tale of four thousand years ago, 185–202. **Charles Wycliffe Goodwin.** Signed.

4516 Bristol churches, 203–209. **Thomas Arnold,** 1823–1900. Claimed in *Life*, p. 176.

4517 The amulet: a tale of Spanish California (chaps. i–v), 210–224. Unidentified. Novel published anon. 1865.

4518 What is the law of the Church of England? 225–241. **J. Fitzjames Stephen.** Signed.

4519 The rest of it [continuation of no. 4499], 243–250. **A. K. H. Boyd.** Signed A.K.H.B.; repr. *Lessons*.

4520 Theology of the nineteenth century, 252–268. **A. P. Stanley.** Repr. *Essays Chiefly on Questions of Church and State, from 1850–1870*, 1870.

VOLUME 71, MARCH 1865

4521 Clerical Subscription Commission: speech of the Dean of St. Paul's, Friday, April 22, 1864, 269–276. **H. H. Milman.** *DNB*.

4522 Virginia, first and last, 277–294. **M. D. Conway.** Burtis list.

4523 Gilbert Rugge (chaps. xxx–xxxiii), 295–312. **Henry Jackson,** 1831–1879. Evidence for no. 4434.

4524 How Ireland was governed in the sixteenth century, 312–315. **J. A. Froude.** Signed.

4525 The law of honour [and duelling], 316–333.

4526 The hierarchy of art (Part II, concl.), 334–346. **Frances Power Cobbe.** Signed; repr. *Studies.*

4527 The amulet (chaps. vi–ix), 347–362.

4528 Merivale's sermons on the conversion of the Roman Empire, 363–382. **J. F. Stephen.** Stephen list.

4529 Working men's clubs and institutes, 383–395. **Henry Solly.** Repr. as a pamphlet, preserved in a collection of tracts at the BM called *Social and Industrial Tracts, 1845–1874*; this one contains Solly's name as author with a note, "reprinted by permission from Fraser's Magazine, March 1865." Pamphlet and article are identical.

4530 Law reporting, 395–402.

VOLUME 71, APRIL 1865

4531 The [Papal] court of Rome: its parties and its men, 403–420.

4532 Regulars and volunteers, 421–433. **C. C. Chesney.** Signed C.C.C.—see no. 4938.

4533 A visit to General Butler and the Army of the James (Part I; no more published), 434–448.

4534 Gilbert Rugge (chaps. xxxiv–xxxvi), 449–466. **Henry Jackson,** 1831–1879. Evidence for no. 4434.

4535 The embankment of the Thames [on pollution], 466–477.

4536 Nooks and byways (Part I): what they are doing in Edinburgh, 478–489. **John Skelton.** Signed An Old Campaigner; cf. no. 4555.

4537 The amulet (chaps. x–xiii), 490–506.

4538 British sea-fish, fishermen, and fisheries, 507–525. Signed: A.B.

4539 The parish priest (Part III, concl.): on preaching, 526–536. **Harry Jones.** Evidence for no. 4423.

VOLUME 71, MAY 1865

4540 Mayflowerings [New England], 537–557. **M. D. Conway.** Burtis list.

4541 The Bishop of Oxford [Samuel Wilberforce] and the reverend cabmen of Paris, 558–570.

4542 Gilbert Rugge (chaps. xxxviii–xl), 571–588. **Henry Jackson,** 1831–1879. Evidence for no. 4434.

4543 Letters of Maria Theresa and Marie Antoinette, 588–597.

4544 Mr. Madox Brown's exhibition, and its place in our school of painting, 598–607. **W. M. Rossetti.** Signed; repr. *Fine Art.*

4545 French criticism on Spinoza, 608–626.

4546 The amulet (chaps. xiv–xvii), 627–642.

4547 Hinchliff's *South American Sketches,* 643–654.

4548 *Histoire de Jules César* [by Napoleon III], 655–670. **W. B. Donne,** prob. Among arts. bound up as Donne's, in three volumes, Johnson Papers.

VOLUME 71, JUNE 1865

4549 English ultramontanism (Part I): the relation of the Church of Rome to modern science, 671–687. **J. F. Stephen.** Stephen list.

4550 The Bank Charter Act of 1844, 688–701. **Bonamy Price.** Signed.

4551 Gilbert Rugge (chaps. xli–xliv), 702–718. **Henry Jackson,** 1831–1879. Evidence for no. 4434.

4552 England's future attitude towards Europe and towards the world, 719–735. **W. R. Greg.** Signed W.R.G.; repr. *Political Problems for our Age,* 1870.

4553 The Royal Academy Exhibition, 736–753. **W. M. Rossetti.** Signed; repr. *Fine Art.*

4554 The amulet (chaps. xviii–xx), 754–771.

4555 Nooks and byways (Part II): Mr. Swinburne's poems, 772–784. **John Skelton.** Signed An Old Campaigner; claimed in *Blackwood's,* 156 (Dec. 1894), 763.

4556 On subterranean ice, 784–790. **George Forrest Browne.** Attr. in *MWT,* 14th ed.

4557 The assassination of President Lincoln, 791–806. **M. D. Conway.** Signed An American Abolitionist; claimed in *Autobiography,* II, 78, 185.

VOLUME 72, JULY 1865

4558 English ultramontanism (Part II): 1–35. **J. F. Stephen.** Cf. no. 4549.

4559 Gilbert Rugge (chaps. xlv–xlvii), 36–55. **Henry Jackson,** 1831–1879. Evidence for no. 4434.

4560 The writings of M. Edmund About, 58–76. **Abraham Hayward,** prob. The method adopted here—a survey of the works of a contemporary French author, with his books listed at length on the first page—is found again in no. 4591, known to be Hayward's, but nowhere else in *FM*, perhaps in no other magazine as distinct from a review; furthermore, both essays outline certain novels, quoting a number of passages, always in English, and are written in the same sophisticated style; thus if Hayward did not write this piece, he copied it closely in no. 4591, which is highly unlikely.

4561 The right of occupancy in Oude and Bengal: the rent case—Hills *vs.* Issar Ghos, 77–91. **T. H. Bullock.** Signed T.H.B.—see no. 4286.

4562 The amulet (chaps. xxii–xxiv, concl.), 92–104.

4563 Fish culture, 105–115.

4564 Brodie's *Autobiography*, 116–124.

4565 Late operations on the [pollution of the] Serpentine, 125–134.

VOLUME 72, AUGUST 1865

4566 Parliamentary reform: true mode of proceeding, 135–159.

4567 John Dryden: a vindication, 160–179. **John Skelton.** Signed Shirley; repr. *Essays*.

4568 Gilbert Rugge (chaps. xlviii–xlix), 180–193. **Henry Jackson,** 1831–1879. Evidence for no. 4434.

4569 Her Majesty's Court of Probate, 193–204.

4570 Religious toleration, 205–221. **F. W. Newman.** Repr. *Miscellanies*, III.

4571 Reminiscences of the court and times of the Emperor, Paul I of Russia, up to the period of his death; from the papers of a deceased Russian General Officer (Part I), 222–241. **Nikolay Alexandrovich Sablukov.** Page 222n; Leo Loewenson, *Slavonic and East European Review,* 29 (1950/51), 215, n.12; *Bol'shaía Sovatskaía entsiklopediía,* vol. 37, p. 561.

4572 Spectrum analysis and the sun's physical constitution, 242–246. **Frederick Gard Fleay.** Signed F.G.F.; see *DNB*.

4573 Public virtue and Lord Westbury, 247–255.

4574 From an old gentleman's diary, 256–260. **Caroline Clive.** Signed The Author of *Paul Ferroll*—see *BMCat.*

4575 Miss Kate Terry in Viola, 261–268. **James Spedding.** Repr. *Reviews* as "*Twelfth Night* at the Olympic Theatre."

VOLUME 72, SEPTEMBER 1865

4576 Mannahatta [New York], 269–287. **M. D. Conway.** Burtis list.

4577 Gilbert Rugge (chaps. l–lii), 288–301. **Henry Jackson,** 1831–1879. Evidence for no. 4434.

4578 Reminiscences of the Emperor Paul I of Russia (Part II, concl.), 302–327. **N. A. Sablukov.** Cf. no. 4571.

4579 On lessening the irksomeness of elementary instruction, 328–334.

4580 On rifle-shooting, 335–340.

4581 Abigail, 341–370. **Henrietta Keddie.** Repr. in *Garden of Women*, 1875, as "Love lies bleeding."

4582 Free translation from the Icelandic of the *Edda*: "Helgakvida Hundingsbana," II, st. 28, 370–374. **Edmund Head.** Signed.

4583 The priest in the congregation, 375–386. **Harry Jones.** Signed H.J.; repr. *Priest and Parish*, 1866.

4584 Some passages from the history of the Chomley family, 387–402.

VOLUME 72, OCTOBER 1865

4585 Ireland and her exhibition in 1865, 403–422. **Frances Power Cobbe.** Signed.

4586 A chapter on Pai Marire, the new religion of the Maoris, 423–438. **P. C. Beaton.** Signed P.C.B.—see no. 4343.

4587 Gilbert Rugge (chaps. liii–lvii), 439–456. **Henry Jackson,** 1831–1879. Evidence for no. 4434.

4588 Austrian politics, 457–474.

4589 Writings of Bolingbroke, 475–491. **T. E. Kebbel,** prob. Cf. no. 4331, which ends with a promise to deal with Bolingbroke's writings later.

4590 From London to Rio de Janeiro: letters to a friend (Nos. I–II), 492–503. **Richard F. Burton.** Signed.

4591 Charles de Bernard, 504–520. **Abraham Hayward.** Claimed in *Correspondence,* II, 115.

4592 The organ in Scotland, 520–524. **A. K. H. Boyd.** Signed A.K.H.B.; repr. *Lessons.*

4593 William Henry Hunt, water-colour painter, 525–536. **F. G. Stephens.** Signed F.G.S.—see *DNB.*

VOLUME 72, NOVEMBER 1865

4594 Mr. Lecky on rationalism, 537–564. **J. F. Stephen.** Stephen list; attr. in *Memoir of W. E. H. Lecky* (by his wife, 1909), p. 44.

4595 The Beauclercs, father and son (chaps. i–iii), 565–579. **Charles Clarke.** Signed; novel published 1867.

4596 *Letters from Egypt, 1863–1865* [by Lady Duff-Gordon], 580–588.

4597 Cuneiform inscriptions: Gobineau versus Rawlinson, 589–613. **F. W. Newman.** Claimed in *Memoir*, p. 188.

4598 Gilbert Rugge (chaps. lviii–lx), 614–628. **Henry Jackson,** 1831–1879. Evidence for no. 4434.

4599 Nooks and byways (Part III, concl.): some song books, 629–636. **John Skelton.** Signed An Old Campaigner; cf. no. 4555.

4600 The wishes shop, 637–643.

4601 Town life in the south of France [mainly on Avignon], 644–664.

4602 Lord Palmerston, 665–670. **Abraham Hayward.** Claimed in *Corespondence*, II, 116.

VOLUME 72, DECEMBER 1865

4603 Politics and prospects of Spain, 671–691. **Abraham Hayward.** Claimed in *Correspondence*, II, 115, 123.

4604 The Beauclercs (chaps. iv–vi), 692–709. **Charles Clarke.** Signed.

4605 The military situation in India, 710–718.

4606 Concerning roadside stations; with some thoughts on the *terminus ad quem*, 719–725. **A. K. H. Boyd.** Signed A.K. H.B.; repr. *Lessons.*

4607 Days of Derry, 726–737.

4608 The gains of the Church of England in 1865, 738–746. **A. P. Stanley.** Attr. in *Life*, list of arts.

4609 Fiction and its uses, 746–760. **Edward Dowden.** Signed Decem; *Letters* (1914), pp. 24–25; J. A. Froude to Dowden, Sept. 4, n.y., at Pusey House, Oxford, is glad to accept his paper on fiction; "Decem" may stand for "Dowden Edward, *C.E.M.*": he signed *Temple Bar*, 8 (July 1863), 494–502, "C.E.M."

4610 Gilbert Rugge (chaps. lxi–lxiv), 760–777. **Henry Jackson,** 1831–1879. Evidence for no. 4434.

4611 Mr. Carlyle, 778–810. **J. F. Stephen.** Attr. by Hayward, *Correspondence*, II, 120.

VOLUME 73, JANUARY 1866

4612 Policy and prospects of the government, 1–15. **Abraham Hayward.** Claimed in *Correspondence*, II, 131.

4613 Church temporalities in Ireland, 16–26. **W. Maziere Brady.** Repr. *Essays.*

4614 Gilbert Rugge (chaps. lxv–lxviii, concl.), 27–41. **Henry Jackson,** 1831–1879. Evidence for no. 4434.

4615 The queen of the West [America], 42–68. **M. D. Conway.** Burtis list; attr. in J. A. Froude to Conway, n.d., Columbia Univ. Lib.

4616 The priest in the world, 69–78. **Harry Jones.** Signed H.J.; repr. *Priest and Parish*, 1866.

4617 From London to Rio de Janeiro (Nos. III–IV), 78–92. **Richard F. Burton.** Signed.

4618 The cholera in Malta, 93–103. **Sarah Austin.** Signed S.A.; she was in Malta in 1837 when the epidemic here described occurred; see *DNB.*

4619 The Beauclercs (chaps. vii–ix), 104–119. **Charles Clarke.** Signed.

4620 How we retook Dewangiri [in India], 120–129.

4621 The sketcher in the Eifel [country of Germany], 129–142. **Charles Richard Weld.** Signed C.R.W.—see no. 3941.

VOLUME 73, FEBRUARY 1866

4622 The indigent class: their schools and dwellings, 143–160. **Frances Power Cobbe.** Signed; repr. *Hours.*

4623 Jamaica, and the recent insurrection there [under Governor Eyre], 161–179. Signed: A Late Resident in the Island.

4624 Presbyterian sermons from archiepiscopal churches, 180–191. **A. K. H. Boyd.** Signed A.K.H.B.; repr. *Lessons.*

4625 Elements of the military balance of power in Europe, 192–214.

4626 The dawk bungalow; or, "Is his appointment pucka?" [satire on administration in India] (Part I), 215–231. **G. O. Trevelyan.** Signed; series repr. 1863.

4627 Report of the Capital Punishment Commission, 232–256. **J. Fitzjames Stephen.** Signed.

4628 An Alpine storm, 257–263. **Alfred Wills,** prob. The subject is the destructive effects of the storm upon "The Eagle's Nest," a house built in the Alps by an "English gentleman" (p. 258); though not present at the storm, the author arrived 10 days later to inspect the damage and collect information (pp. 258, 260), especially from the majordomo (p. 259); the author shows great knowledge of the area, knows the name of the blacksmith (p. 261), and realizes the owner's purpose in erecting a palisade around the "Nest" (p. 259); Alfred

Wills built the house in 1858–1859 and wrote *The Eagle's Nest*, 1860.

4629 Sundays, ancient and modern, 264–276. **James Gairdner.** Signed J.G.; repr. *Studies.*

VOLUME 73, MARCH 1866

4630 The Jamaica problem, 277–305. **W. R. Greg.** Repr. *Literary and Social Judgements* (4th ed., 1877), II, as "The Doom of the Negro Race."

4631 Concerning beards: being thoughts on progress, specially in Scotland, 306–321. **A. K. H. Boyd.** Signed A.K.H.B.; repr. *Lessons.*

4632 The minister's Sandy and Jess, 322–341. **Henrietta Keddie.** Repr. in *Garden of Women*, 1875, as "A sprig of heather."

4633 Clubs, 342–367. **Abraham Hayward,** prob. Cf. no. 4651, which is a complementary art. (see that art., pp. 610, 628); on p. 351 quotation from Hayward's own *Art of Dining* without citing author's name; the criticism of Derby and Disraeli, p. 364, is characteristic of Hayward at this time (cf. nos. 4612, 4819); Hayward belonged to the Atheneum and Carlton Clubs (see *Correspondence*, I, 52, 54), both of which are discussed here, the former spoken of by the author from "personal knowledge," p. 365.

4634 *The Domesday of Hampshire*, 368–381.

4635 The dawk bungalow (Part II, concl.), 382–391. **G. O. Trevelyan.** Signed.

4636 Admiral Smyth, 392–398. **Nevil Story-Maskalyne.** Signed N.S.M.—see nos. 3419, 3746; Smyth was engaged in a scientific survey of parts of the Mediterranean: hence his appeal to the author.

4636a Ballads from the Spanish, 399–401. Translated with intro. note by **Edmund Head**—signed.

4637 *British Conchology*, 402–410.

VOLUME 73, APRIL 1866

4638 Grote's *Plato*, 411–423. **William Whewell.** Attr. in intro. note, apparently by **H. R. Luard;** Todhunter, *Whewell*, I, 241, says art. "not quite finished by the author and was put into state for printing by the Rev. H. R. Luard."

4639 The passion of Martin Holdfast, 424–446. **John Skelton.** Repr. *Essays in Romance.*

4640 Thoreau, 447–465. **M. D. Conway.**

Attr. by Francis H. Allen, *Bibliography of Thoreau*, 1908, p. 122, and in Louisa Alcott to Ellen Conway, n.d., and in Sophia Thoreau to Ellen Conway, n.d., Columbia Univ. Lib.

4641 The native army in India, 466–476.

4642 The Reform Bill and the government, 477–495. **Abraham Hayward.** Cf. no. 4655; in *Correspondence*, II, 134–135, under Apr. 21, 1866, he is called "*Fraser*" for advocating these ideas.

4643 From London to Rio de Janeiro (Nos. V–VI), 496–510. **Richard F. Burton.** Signed.

4644 The Beauclercs (chaps. x–xiv), 511–530. **Charles Clerke.** Signed.

4645 Native tribes on the Zambési River; an East African sketch, 531–548. **L. J. Procter.** Signed L.J.P.; Procter and J. A. Blair published a grammar of the Manganja language in 1875, and the principal tribe described here is the Manganja; cf. no. 5367, which focuses on the Zambési.

VOLUME 73, MAY 1866

4646 On prayer in connection with certain public calamities, 549–557.

4647 The English troops in the East, 558–568.

4648 A chapter on clerical song-writers in the North [Scotland] (Part I), 569–583. **P. C. Beaton.** Signed P.C.B.—see no. 4343. (Part II is no. 4776.)

4649 The priest in the school, 584–591. **Harry Jones.** Signed H.J.; repr. *Priest and Parish*, 1866.

4650 How are European armies officered? 592–609.

4651 Salons, 610–629. **Abraham Hayward.** Repr. *Essays* (1873), I.

4651a The death of old King Gorm: a ballad, 630–631. Translated with an intro. note by **Edmund Head**—signed.

4652 Forest life, 632–651.

4653 Our commons and open spaces, 652–666. **Henry Warwick Cole.** Repr. as pamphlet, 1866.

4654 The Beauclercs (chaps. xv–xvii), 667–682. **Charles Clarke.** Signed.

VOLUME 73, JUNE 1866

4655 Parliamentary reform and the government, 683–704. **Abraham Hayward.** The *DNB* assigns him a series of arts. in *FM* on the reform question in 1866, attempting to avert a split in Lord John Russell's party: see nos. 4612, 4642, this one, and the post-mortem art. no. 4679.

4656   Superstition; a lecture delivered at the Royal Institution, April 24, 1866, 705–716. **Charles Kingsley.** Signed C. Kingsley; repr. *Works*, XIX.

4657   Anomalies of the American constitution, 717–734. **M. D. Conway.** Signed An American; Burtis list.

4658   *Les Travailleurs de la Mer* [by Victor Hugo], 735–745.

4659   *Ecce Homo* [by J. R. Seeley]: first notice, 746–765. **J. F. Stephen.** Stephen list.

4660   Church politics in Scotland, 767–780. **John Skelton.** Signed Shirley—see *DNB*.

4661   The Beauclercs (chaps. xviii–xx), 781–794. **Charles Clarke.** Signed.

4662   Belgium, 795–816. **M. E. Grant Duff.** Repr. *Studies*.

VOLUME 74, JULY 1866

4663   Ireland, 1–14. Unidentified. (Letter, p. 276, signed **Aubrey De Vere.**)

4664   Science; a lecture delivered at the Royal Institution, 15–28. **Charles Kingsley.** Signed as in no. 4656; repr. *Works*, XIX.

4665   *Ecce Homo*: second [and last] notice, 29–52. **J. F. Stephen.** Stephen list.

4666   The site of the National Gallery reconsidered, 53–71.

4667   Legends of Charlemagne, 72–83. **Philip Henry Stanhope.** Signed Earl Stanhope; repr. *Retreat from Moscow* and *Miscellanies*, 2nd series, 1872.

4668   A conversation: the portraits at South Kensington, 84–93. **W. F. Pollock.** *Remembrances*, II, 145, 149. (See no. 4781.)

4669   George Petrie, 1790–1866, 94–100. **William Allingham.** Signed W.A.; *Diary*, p. 138; repr. *Varieties*, III.

4670   *Operations against Charleston*, 101–111. **Henry Brackenbury.** Claimed in *Some Memories of My Spare Time* (1909), p. 37.

4671   The Beauclercs (chaps. xxi–xxiv), 112–128. **Charles Clarke.** Signed.

4672   Domestic servants, 129–134.

VOLUME 74, AUGUST 1866

4673   Stanley's *Jewish History*, 135–158. Unidentified. Perhaps Henry John Rose: author refers, p. 145n, to an anon. art. in the *Quart.Rev.* [no. 1417 in *Index*, I, by Rose], which gives more information on the topic under discussion—the discrepancy between different biblical scholars engaged in the "higher criticism" —and that art. was by Rose; the hostile attitude toward biblical criticism in general, seen in both arts., is also found in Rose's contribution to *Replies to "Essays and Reviews,"* 1862; the note, p. 144, cites Smith's *Dictionary of the Bible*, to which Rose contributed extensively.

4674   From London to Rio de Janeiro (No. VII, concl.), 159–178. **Richard F. Burton.** Signed.

4675   The German Knights, 179–198.

4676   The Brahmo Samaj [the Brahmin Church], 199–211. **Frances Power Cobbe.** Signed; repr. *Hours*.

4677   The Beauclercs (chaps. xxv–xxix), 212–228. **Charles Clarke.** Signed.

4678   The financial pressure and ten per cent, 229–242.

4679   The ministry: last and present, 243–258. **Abraham Hayward.** Claimed in *Correspondence*, II, 147.

4680   The War [Austro-Prussian] in its political and military bearings, 259–276.

VOLUME 74, SEPTEMBER 1866

4681   Recent movements in the Church of England, 277–296.

4682   The Exposition of Arcachon [in France] and its object [the relation of the fishing industry to a navy], 297–308.

4683   The poet of middle-aged men [Horace], 309–326.

4684   Washington, 327–346. **M. D. Conway.** Burtis list; art. based on Conway's "Life in Washington," MS. in Columbia Univ. Lib.

4685   Concerning the advantages of being a cantankerous fool; with some thoughts on the treatment of incapacity, 347–352. **A. K. H. Boyd.** Signed A.K.H.B.; repr. *Lessons*.

4686   Administration of medical relief to the destitute sick of the metropolis, 353–365. **Edwin Chadwick.** Signed.

4687   The reconstruction of Germany, 366–384. **W. C. Cartwright.** Signed.

4688   The Beauclercs (chaps. xxx–xxxiii, concl.), 385–403. **Charles Clarke.** Signed.

4689   The Reform League and the parks, 404–410. **Abraham Hayward.** Claimed in *Correspondence*, II, 147.

VOLUME 74, OCTOBER 1866

4690   Notes on Florence, 411–426. **C. R. Weld.** Most of the first paragraph is identical with paragraph in his *Florence, the New Capitol of Italy* (1867), p. 14; many other facts and phrases reappear in the book.

4691 The Indian civil service, 427–442.

4692 Munro's *Lucretius*, 443–455.

4693 Em's first and last lodger, 456–488. **Henrietta Keddie.** Repr. in *Garden of Women*, 1875, as "London pride."

4694 Mignet's *Charles V. and Francis I.*, 489–500. **Gustave Bergenroth.** Signed G.B.; claimed in W. C. Cartwright, *Gustave Bugenroth* (Edin., 1870), pp. 48, 49.

4695 On living in perspective, 501–508. **Dinah Maria Mulock.** Signed Author of *John Halifax, Gentleman*; repr. *The Unkind Word and Other Stories*, New York, 1870.

4696 On the education of girls, 509–524. **Dorothea Beale.** Signed A Utopian; attr. in Elizabeth Raikes, *Dorothea Beale of Cheltenham* (1909), p. 10; confirmed by comparison of art. with entry in *DNB*.

4697 Arthur Hugh Clough, 1819–1861, 525–535. **William Allingham.** Signed W.A.— see no. 4669; claimed by Allingham in Amy Woolner, *Thomas Woolner* (1917), p. 274.

4698 On the Welsh triads; with a confirmation of an ancient one from other sources, 536–544. **William Barnes.** Signed.

VOLUME 74, NOVEMBER 1866

4699 Why we want a reform bill, 545–563.

4700 Field-Marshal Viscount Combermere, 564–587. **Abraham Hayward.** Claimed in *Correspondence*, II, 148.

4701 Heinrich Heine, 588–609.

4702 A lost man, 610–632. **Henrietta Keddie.** Repr. in *Garden of Women*, 1875, as "A tiger lily; a goldenrod."

4703 Mr. Swinburne and his critics, 635–648. **John Skelton.** Claimed in *Blackwood's*, 156 (Dec. 1894), 763.

4704 Gregory VII [Hildebrand], 649–666.

4705 The conventional laws of society, 667–673. **Frances Power Cobbe.** Signed.

4706 The provision trade of Ireland [in pigs], 674–680.

VOLUME 74, DECEMBER 1866

4707 Military reform (Part I), 681–697. **Henry Brackenbury.** Claimed in *Some Memories of My Spare Time* (1909), p. 38.

4708 The Marstons (chaps. i–iv), 698–717.

C. H. Aïdé. Novel published 1868: see *BMCat.*

4709 Was Lord Bacon an impostor? [on Justus von Liebig's *Bacon*], 718–740. Unidentified. (See no. 4749.)

4710 Bribery and its remedies, 741–752. **J. E. Thorold Rogers.** Froude to Rogers, Sept. 23, [1866], Rogers Papers, asks for art. on "Bribery at Elections"; John Bright to Rogers, Dec. 12, 1866, ibid., is glad to see that Rogers is writing in *FM*.

4711 Down the Ohio to the underworld, 753–770. **M. D. Conway.** Burtis list.

4712 Mr. Dallas, *The Gay Science*: the laws and functions of criticism, 771–786. **John Skelton.** Signed Shirley—see *DNB*.

4713 Lunatics: being a letter to John Bull from Brother Jonathan, 787–793. **M. D. Conway.** Signed Jonathan; claimed in *Nation*, Nov. 22, 1894, p. 379.

4714 The theory of compensation [on Pierre Hyacinthe Azaïs], 794–815.

VOLUME 75, JANUARY 1867

4715 Parliamentary reform: labour and capital, 1–12.

4716 The Marstons (chaps. v–vii), 13–32. **C. H. Aïdé.** Cf. no. 4708.

4717 *The Cromwellian Settlement of Ireland*, 33–45.

4718 A day's fishing in the Bush [Irish river], 1848, 46–64.

4719 St. Katharine's Hospital, 65–82.

4720 Conington's *Aeneid*, 83–88.

4721 Theatrical licenses, 89–102.

4722 Athens and Pentelicus, 103–113. **T. W. Hinchliff.** Assigned in index to this vol.

4723 On the influence of Arabic philosophy in mediaeval Europe: a lecture delivered at the Royal Institution . . . February 2, 1866, 114–124. **Philip Henry Stanhope.** Signed Earl Stanhope; repr. *Miscellanies*, 2nd series, 1872.

4724 Among south-western cathedrals, 125–130. **A. K. H. Boyd.** Signed A.K.H.B.; repr. *Lessons.*

4725 Ministerial prospects, 131–142. **Abraham Hayward,** prob. Page 136 refers to no. 4689 as though his; the style and point of view (anti Disraeli, Lord Derby and Robert Lowe, pro Gladstone and Lord Russell) are those adopted by Hayward in his political arts. of 1866 for *FM*.

VOLUME 75, FEBRUARY 1867

4726 The land system of the country a

reason for a reform of Parliament, 143–162. **T. E. Cliffe Leslie.** Signed; repr. *Land Systems.*

4727   Fragment on the reign of Elizabeth; from the posthumous papers of Mr. Buckle (Part I), 163–186. **H. T. Buckle.** Title; all three parts repr. *Miscellaneous and Posthumous Works* (1872), I. Edited with an intro. note by **Helen Taylor**—signed H.T., cf. no. 4786.

4728   Banks and banking, 187–204. **Bonamy Price.** Signed.

4729   The Marstons (chaps. viii–xii), 205–226. **C. H. Aïdé.** Cf. no. 4708.

4730   Penance and absolution, 227–242.

4731   The [national] purpose and the President of the United States [Johnson], 243–261. **M. D. Conway.** Assigned in Contents.

4732   British merchant seamen (Part I), 262–276. **William Dawson.** Signed A Commander, R.N.; cf. no. 5226 where man cited is called a Commander, R.N., and where note, p. 181, refers to this art. (Part II is no. 4940.)

4733   Sunshine at the Land's End, 277–284. **Morgan George Watkins.** Repr. *In the Country.*

VOLUME 75, MARCH 1867

4734   Military reform (Part II), 285–300. **Henry Brackenbury.** Cf. no. 4707.

4735   Village sketches in Oudh (No. I): village joys and festivities, 301–315.

4736   Concerning the treatment of such as differ from us in opinion, 316–329. **A. K. H. Boyd.** Signed A.K.H.B.; repr. *Lessons.*

4737   The Marstons (chaps. xiii–xvi), 330–344. **C. H. Aïdé.** Cf. no. 4708.

4738   Politics in our parish, 345–357. **John Skelton.** Signed at start A Country Tory, at end Shirley—see *DNB.*

4739   Prevention of famine in India, 358–369. **T. H. Bullock.** Signed T.H.B.—see no. 4286, and Part B below.

4740   *The Foul Smells of Paris* [morals], 370–380.

4741   Costume in sculpture, 382–394. **F. G. Stephens.** Signed.

4742   Lord Russell's *Life of Fox*, 395–400. Signed: C.

4743   The American Sanitary Commission and its lesson, 401–414. **Frances Power Cobbe.** Signed.

4744   Ministerial prospects and reform, 415–422. **Abraham Hayward,** prob. Cf. the title of no. 4725; the point of view is that described in evidence for no. 4725; at

end author strikes at the Adullamites as Hayward had.

VOLUME 75, APRIL 1867

4745   Military reform (Part III), 423–434. **Henry Brackenbury.** Cf. no. 4707.

4746   Nisard's *History of French Literature*, 435–447.

4747   The Gracchi, 448–461.

4748   The Marstons (chaps. xvii–xx), 462–481. **C. H. Aïdé.** Cf. no. 4708.

4749   Was Lord Bacon an impostor? [reply to no. 4709], 482–495. **Justus von Liebig.** Signed Baron Liebig. Second paragraph of intro. and notes apparently by the author of no. 4709: see p. 493n.

4750   The new confessional, 501–511.

4751   American dairies, 512–522. **Stephen Buckland.** Signed.

4752   On poetry, 523–536. **William Allingham.** Signed W.A.; repr. *Varieties*, III.

4753   France under Richelieu and Colbert [on Positivism and history], 537–544.

4754   The life of Archbishop Whately, 545–556.

VOLUME 75, MAY 1867

4755   On the defence of India, 557–569. **Alexander Fraser.** Signed Lieut.-Col. A. Fraser, R.E., C.B.; see Boase.

4756   Journal of an officer of the Swiss Guards of Louis XVI, bearing upon the events of August 10, 1792 [trans. from a French MS.], 570–585. **Deville O'Keeffe?** Intro. note.

4757   Recent lectures and writings of Emerson, 586–600. **M. D. Conway.** Burtis list; Froude to Conway, mm. 9, [1867], Huntington Lib., returns art. on growth of Emerson's mind (which may have been no. 4879) and asks for an art. dealing with his opinions.

4758   The Marstons (chaps. xxi–xxiii), 601–617. **C. H. Aïdé.** Cf. no. 4708.

4759   Our deep sea fisheries, 618–625. Signed: W.B.

4760   The modern spirit, 626–639. **James Macdonell.** Attr. by Nicoll, *Macdonell*, p. 154.

4761   New America in its religious aspect [on W. H. Dixon's *New America*], 640–656. **G. O. Trevelyan?** Kingsley to unknown correspondent, Mar. 26, 1867, Parrish Collect., Princeton Univ., says Froude told Kingsley, as vice-editor during his absence, to expect an art. on "Dixon's America" and other papers on politics from said correspondent; Kingsley to Trevelyan, Apr. 2, 1867, has not yet received proofs of his art.; man cited more likely to be author referred to than Sir Charles Trevelyan: he was an M.P., had recently contributed nos. 4626 and 4635 to *FM*, and wrote art. on Amer. literature for *Macmillan's* in Apr. 1868 (see *Index*, I, 581).

4762 Charles Lamb, 657–672. **Gerald Massey**. Signed.

4763 On the chief methods of preparation for legislation, especially as applicable to the reform of Parliament, 673–690. **Edwin Chadwick**. Signed.

VOLUME 75, JUNE 1867

4764 Education, 691–703.

4765 The Marstons (chaps. xxiv–xxvii), 704–720. **C. H. Aïdé**. Cf. no. 4708.

4766 The teaching of Mr. Maurice, 721–734.

4767 Charlotte Corday, 735–742.

4768 Military reform (Part IV), 743–755. **Henry Brackenbury**. Cf. no. 4707.

4769 Over the Moro [Alpine pass], 758–768.

4770 The exclusion of the clergy from seats in the House of Commons, 769–778. **J. E. Thorold Rogers**. Signed.

4771 Concerning the heads of battering-rams, with some thoughts touching the revivification of mummies, 779–784. **A. K. H. Boyd**. Signed A.K.H.B.; repr. *Lessons*.

4772 The functions of an upper house of parliament, 785–801. **F. W. Newman**. Signed; repr. *Miscellanies*, III.

4773 "A charm of birds," 802–810. **Charles Kingsley**. Signed as in no. 4656; repr. *Prose Idylls*, 1873.

4774 The late Lord Plunket, 811–825.

VOLUME 76, JULY 1867

4775 Julius Caesar, 1–15.

4776 A chapter on clerical song-writers in the North (Part II, concl.), 16–29. **P. C. Beaton**. Signed P.C.B.—see no. 4648.

4777 Village sketches in Oudh (No. II), 30–41.

4778 Sylvester Judd, 45–60. **M. D. Conway**. Claimed in *Nation*, Nov. 29, 1894, p. 104.

4779 The Marstons (chaps. xxviii–xxxi), 60–78. **C. H. Aïdé**. Cf. no. 4708.

4780 Mr. Cobden and the land question, 79–91. **R. Arthur Arnold**. Signed.

4781 A conversation—the portraits at South Kensington: second exhibition, 93–102. **W. F. Pollock**. Cf. subject and text of no. 4668. (See no. 4880.)

4782 Two salutations, 103–109. **Henrietta Keddie**. Repr. *Garden of Women*, 1875, as "A Scotch rose."

4783 Some characteristics of South American vegetation, 110–116. **Charles J. F. Bunbury**. Signed.

4784 Irish difficulties: a review of recent events [on Fenianism], 117–130.

4785 Beckford's statue: a city episode, 131–134.

VOLUME 76, AUGUST 1867

4786 Fragment on the reign of Elizabeth; from the posthumous papers of Mr. Buckle (Part II), 135–150. **H. T. Buckle**. Title. Edited by **Helen Taylor**—J. S. Mill to J. A. Froude, Mar. 21, 1867, Bodleian Lib., says his daughter will send "the second installment of Buckle."

4787 The Marstons (chaps. xxxii–xxxiv), 151–168. **C. H. Aïdé**. Cf. no. 4708.

4788 Marriage laws, 169–189. **F. W. Newman**. Signed; repr. *Miscellanies*, III.

4789 A Spanish and a Danish novel [Caballero's *Gaviota*, and *The Parsonage of Noddēbo*], 190–203.

4790 Military reform (Part V, concl.), 204–215. **Henry Brackenbury**. Cf. no. 4707.

4791 Cox's *Mythology*, 216–220.

4792 The church and land question in Ireland, 221–236.

4793 Notes in South Germany in the autumn of 1866, 238–249. **George Meredith**. Signed G.M.; Charles Kingsley to Meredith, Apr. 11, 1867, Parrish Collect., Princeton Univ., encloses proof of your "Notes in South Germany."

4794 The plot of the Mexican drama [on politics], 250–268. **Abraham Hayward**. Claimed in *Correspondence*, II, 221.

VOLUME 76, SEPTEMBER 1867

4795 The late Prince Consort, 269–283. **J. A. Froude**. Attr. in Froude to Sir Arthur Helps, n.d., owned by E. A. P. Helps, his grandson.

4796 Fragment on the reign of Elizabeth; from the posthumous papers of Mr. Buckle (Part III, concl.), 284–300. **H. T. Buckle**. Title. Edited by **Helen Taylor**—cf. no. 4786.

4797 The Marstons (chaps. xxxv–xxxviii), 301–319. **C. H. Aïdé**. Cf. no. 4708.

Translated with a concluding note by **Edmund Head**—signed.

4834 Coloured suns, 95–101. **Richard A. Proctor.** Signed; repr. *Essays on Astronomy*, 1872.

4835 The controversy on free banking, between M. Wolowski and M. Michel Chevalier, members of the Institute of France (Part I), 102–120. **Bonamy Price.** Signed.

4836 Household service, 121–134. **Frances Power Cobbe.** Signed.

VOLUME 77, FEBRUARY 1868

4837 University organisation, 135–153. **Leslie Stephen.** Signed A Don; Ullmann list, p. 243; Stephen published *Sketches from Cambridge*, 1865, under this pseudonym.

4838 *Leaves from the Journal of our Life in the Highlands* [by Queen Victoria], 154–167. **Charles Kingsley.** Thorp, *Kingsley*, bibliog.

4839 The Marstons (chaps. liv–lvi), 170–186. **C. H. Aïdé.** Cf. no. 4708.

4840 Max Müller's *Chips*, 187–204. **Frances Power Cobbe.** Signed F.P.C.; repr. *Darwinism* as "Religions of the East."

4841 By the river side, 205–214.

4842 Rambles (No. IV): in the New Forest, 215–232. **William Allingham.** Evidence for no. 4807.

4843 The great nebula in Orion, 234–241. **Richard A. Proctor.** Signed.

4844 Village sketches in Oudh (No. III, concl.): echoes of the Mutiny, 242–258.

4845 How the Irish land system breeds disaffection, 259–268.

VOLUME 77, MARCH 1868

4846 England and America, 269–285. **M. D. Conway.** Burtis list.

4847 *Madame Tallien*, 286–300.

4848 Public school education, 301–319.

4849 The Marstons (chaps. lvii–lix, concl.), 320–332. **C. H. Aïdé.** Cf. no. 4708.

4850 The politics of young England (Part II, concl.), 333–352. **James Macdonell.** Evidence for no. 4833.

4851 *Westminster Abbey* [by A. P. Stanley], 353–364. Unidentified. Perhaps W. F. Pollock: the opening of no. 4943 by Pollock suggests he may have written this art. on an analogous subject.

4852 The religious crisis, 365–384. **Robert E. Bartlett,** prob. Signed B—see nos. 5438, 5822; the basic evidence for no.

6033 supports the attrib.: see especially pp. 374, 375–376, 380–381.

4853 Diary in Libby Prison [Richmond, Virginia], 385–406. **Imre Szabad.** Headnote.

VOLUME 77, APRIL 1868

4854 Vikram and the vampire; or, Tales of Indian devilry (Part I), 407–432. **Richard F. Burton.** Signed as "adapted" by him; series repr. 1870.

4855 How to save Ireland from an ultramontane university, 433–451. **James Lowry Whittle.** Signed.

4856 The controversy on free banking (Part II, concl.), 455–465. **Bonamy Price.** Signed.

4857 State papers of the reign of Henry VIII, 466–487. **James Gairdner,** prob. Cf. no. 4933 on similar subject, reviewing a supplementary volume to the one here noticed, where the author, p. 40, twice refers to this as our former art.

4858 Volcanos, 488–500. **C. R. Weld.** Signed.

4859 Oatnessiana (Part I, in 21 chaps.; Part II not published): Captain Ord's return (chaps. i–ii), 501–520.

4860 A school for young ladies in Genoa, 521–524. **Agrippina Catucci-Masi.** Signed.

4861 The Caucasian administration and the Irish difficulty [attack on Disraeli], 525–544. **Abraham Hayward.** Page 534 refers to a plagiarism of Disraeli's from Thiers which Hayward had discussed with Thiers and had written on previously (see *Correspondence*, I, 174); in no. 4819, p. 655, Hayward had spoken of Disraeli as our "Caucasian leader" (see pp. 525 and 542 here and title); see evidence for nos. 4870 and 4937.

VOLUME 77, MAY 1868

4862 The reorganisation of the army, 546–559.

4863 Vikram and the vampire (Part II), 560–576. **R. F. Burton.** Signed as in no. 4854.

4864 Women's votes: a dialogue, 577–590.

4865 Life of Sir Philip Sydney (Part I), 591–610. **Robert Southey.** Signed, and called "the late."

4866 Political economy and emigration, 611–624. **T. E. Cliffe Leslie.** Signed; repr. *Land Systems.*

4867 Oatnessiana (chaps. iii–iv), 625–640.

4868 Australia, 642–654.
4869 *Spiritual Wives* [by W. H. Dixon], 655–665.
4870 The Caucasian administration in trouble [over the Irish Church question], 666–678. **Abraham Hayward**, prob. The quotation from Macaulay, p. 666, which "we" had cited "not long since," is a reference to pp. 667–668 of no. 4819 by Hayward; cf. no. 4861, where Hayward's liking for italics is also evident; the point of view is described in evidence for no. 4725; cf. evidence for no. 4937.

VOLUME 77, JUNE 1868

4871 *Emanuel Swedenborg*, 679–699. **W. B. Donne.** Johnson, *Donne*, list.
4872 Vikram and the vampire (Part III), 700–716. **R. F. Burton.** Signed as in no. 4854.
4873 Life of Sir Philip Sydney (Part II), 717–733. **Robert Southey.** Signed.
4874 Rambles (No. V), 734–756. **William Allingham.** Evidence for no. 4807.
4875 Oatnessiana (chaps. v–vii), 757–775.
4876 The progress of civilisation in Northern and Western Europe in prehistoric times, 776–782. **W. Boyd Dawkins.** Signed.
4877 Bunsen's life and last book [*God in History*], 783–800. **Frances P. Cobbe.** Signed F.P.C.; repr. *Darwinism* as "Religions of the World."
4878 Spiritualism in the United States, 801–813. **Stephen Buckland**, prob. Signed S.B.; the author was living in N.Y. (p. 808); no. 4751 and *Macmillan's Mag.* no. 782 (*Index*, I) both by Buckland, are about life in N.Y. at this time.

VOLUME 78, JULY 1868

4879 The culture of Emerson, 1–19. **M. D. Conway.** In p. 1n. author claims no. 4757; Burtis list.
4880 A conversation: the portraits at South Kensington: third exhibition, 20–33. **W. F. Pollock.** *Remembrances*, II, 145, 187.
4881 Bolsover Forest (Part I), 34–52. **George Rooper.** Signed The Author of "The Autobiography of Salmo Salar" [*Macmillan's Mag.*, Aug. 1866]; series repr. *Flood, Field, and Forest*, 1871.
4882 Elements of Romanism [on J. H. Newman], 53–63.
4883 Oatnessiana (chaps. viii–ix), 64–80.
4884 Political economy and the rate of

wages, 81–95. **T. E. Cliffe Leslie.** Signed; repr. *Land Systems.*
4885 Life of Sir Philip Sydney (Part III, concl.), 96–118. **Robert Southey.** Signed.
4886 Kinglake's *Invasion of the Crimea* [Vols. III–IV], 119–142. **Abraham Hayward**, prob. On p. 121 the footnote reveals extensive knowledge of an art. on the Crimean campaign in the *North Brit. Rev.* which only the author would have been likely to have—and he was Hayward (see no. 458 in *Index*, I); besides describing the French translation of the art., with title and place of publication, the note states that the information, here on p. 121 and with similar phrasing in the *NBR*, p. 502, had been given the author by Lord Lyons to help counteract the anti-British statements of M. de Bazancourt, whose book was then under review; finally Hayward had reviewed Vols. I and II of Kinglake's book—and with equal approval—in *NBR* no. 715, and the phrasing there, pp. 364–365, is clearly echoed partly verbatim, here in *FM*, pp. 120–121.

VOLUME 78, AUGUST 1868

4887 The Irish policy of the Disraeli administration, and its results, 143–158. **William O'Connor Morris.** Signed W.O'C.M.; Morris wrote on Irish subjects in *FM*; see *Memories* (1895), p. 202.
4888 Trades unionism in the City and May Fair (Part I), 159–174. **James Macdonell.** Signed M.; Nicoll, *Macdonell*, p. 158.
4889 Oatnessiana (chaps. x–xii), 175–194.
4890 Rambles (No. VI), 195–213. **William Allingham.** Evidence for no. 4807.
4891 Sentimental religion, 218–229. **Frances P. Verney.** Repr. *Essays and Tales*, 1891.
4892 Vikram and the vampire (Part IV), 230–248. **R. F. Burton.** Signed as in no. 4854.
4893 Lands and seas of another world, 249–256. **R. A. Proctor.** Signed.
4894 The French army in 1734, 257–262.
4895 Metaphysicus and scientia; a parable for the present day, 265–276.

VOLUME 78, SEPTEMBER 1868

4896 The alcoholic controversy, 277–299.
4897 Recent developments of Protestantism [related to Biblical criticism], 300–312.
4898 Oatnessiana (chaps. xiii–xiv), 313–332.

4899 School and university system in Scotland, 333–352. **Alexander Craig Sellar**, prob. Signed A.C.S.; Sellar was assistant education commissioner for Scotland at this time (Boase), and later published essays on Scottish education (*BMCat.*)

4900 On the failure of "natural selection" in the case of man, 353–362. **W. R. Greg.** Attr. by Charles Darwin, *Descent of Man* (1871), Part I, chap. v.

4901 The religious creed and opinions of the Caucasian champion of the Church [Disraeli], 363–374. **Abraham Hayward.** Cf. nos. 4861, 4870, 4937; the chap. on the Jews in Disraeli's *Life of Lord George Bentinck* is quoted both here, p. 364, and in no. 4870, p. 671; p. 373 refers to "our Caucasian Premiér" as does no. 4861, pp. 525 and 542.

4902 The moon, 375–390. Signed: בֶּן יֶרַח אָנֹכִי ['Anoki ben Ierah = I am the son of the moon].

4903 Gustavus III of Sweden and the counter revolution, 391–410.

VOLUME 78, OCTOBER 1868

4904 Church policy, 411–424.

4905 Oatnessiana (chaps. xv–xvi), 425–442.

4906 Trades unionism in the City and May Fair (Part II, concl.), 443–460. **James Macdonell.** Evidence for no. 4888. (See no. 4977, pp. 689–694.)

4907 News from Sirius, 461–467. **R. A. Proctor.** Signed; repr. *Essays on Astronomy*, 1872.

4908 Poetry and George Eliot; a letter from a hermitage, 468–479. **John Skelton.** Signed Shirley—see *DNB*.

4909 Vikram and the vampire (Part V), 480–497. **R. F. Burton.** Signed as in no. 4854.

4910 Bolsover Forest (Part II), 498–517. **George Rooper.** Evidence for no. 4881.

4911 Translations of the *Iliad* [by P. S. Worsley and John Conington], 518–531.

4912 The *Kalewipoeg* [Esthonian epic], 534–544. **Sabine Baring-Gould.** Signed S. Baring-Gould—see *DNB*/1930.

VOLUME 78, NOVEMBER 1868

4913 Oxford, 545–566. **Bonamy Price.** Signed.

4914 Facts and phantasms on the ecclesiastical question, 567–583. **Robert E. Bartlett**, prob. Signed B—see nos. 4852, 5438, 5822; the man described in the evidence for no. 6033 seems clearly to be the author here: see especially pp. 572, 575, 576, 577, 583.

4915 Vikram and the vampire (Part VI), 584–602. **R. F. Burton.** Signed as in no. 4854.

4916 The Mancinis: an Italian episode in French history, 603–622. **T. A. Trollope?** Between Dec. 1868 and Jan. 1874, Trollope wrote a series of articles on seventeenth-century French history, focussed mainly, as here, on the period of the Fronde, which were reprinted in his *Sketches of French History*, 1878; the sources used for them are also used here (St. Simon, Mme. de Motteville, and the writers listed on p. 606); moreover, Trollope's major interest in Italians would have made Mazarin and his family especially attractive; extensive use of foreign words and phrases is a commonplace of his writing.

4917 Poetical theology and theological poetry, 623–641.

4918 Oatnessiana (chaps. xvii–xviii), 642–656.

4919 Prussia and Mr. Carlyle; a letter from a hermitage, 657–659. **John Skelton.** Signed Shirley—see *DNB*.

4920 Spain, 660–674. **Abraham Hayward.** Harriet Grote to Hayward, Dec. 15, 1868, Beinecke Lib., Yale Univ., thanks him for this art.; *Correspondence*, II, 194; opening sentences place the art. as a sequel to no. 4603.

VOLUME 78, DECEMBER 1868

4921 The Irish Church in the sixteenth century, 675–689.

4922 Oatnessiana (chaps. xix–xxi, concl.), 690–710.

4923 American torpedo warfare, 711–727. **William Dawson.** Page 723, first and third paragraphs, reappear somewhat rearranged but largely verbatim, and without quotation marks or reference to source, in Dawson's lecture, "Offensive Torpedo Warfare," given on Jan. 30, 1871, before the Royal United Service Institution: see its *Journal*, vol. 15, pp. 93, 93–94; this art. is cited in no. 5226, p. 176, where several phrases here, p. 725, reappear.

4924 "Landowners, land, and those who till it," 728–747. **Edward Girdlestone.** Signed.

4925 Vikram and the vampire (Part VII,

concl.), 748–761. **R. F. Burton.** Signed as in no. 4854.

4926 The great nebula in Argo, 762–768. **R. A. Proctor.** Signed; repr. *The Universe of Suns*, 1884.

4927 Prison labour, 769–776. **R. Arthur Arnold.** Signed.

4928 "Criminals, idiots, women, and minors," 777–794. **Frances Power Cobbe.** Signed.

4929 Dean Milman, 795–801. **Frances P. Verney.** Repr. *Peasant Properties*, II. (Note, vol. 79, p. 134, by **Frances Verney.**)

VOLUME 79, JANUARY 1869

4930 Educational endowments, 1–15. **J. G. Fitch.** Signed.

4931 The materials of the universe [on spectroscopy], 16–26.

4932 Bolsover Forest (Part III, concl.), 27–38. **George Rooper.** Evidence for no. 4881.

4933 Facts and fictions about Katharine of Arragon, 40–59. **James Gairdner.** Repr. *Studies*.

4934 Wanderings westward [to Ireland], 60–79. **Francis Francis.** Signed.

4935 Trench's *Realities of Irish Life*, 80–98.

4936 Log of a cruise at the mouth of the Thames, 99–112.

4937 The ministry and the Irish Church, 113–134. **Abraham Hayward.** Claimed this art. in *FM*, giving exact title, *Correspondence*, II, 189, in a letter dated Feb. 25, 1868, an error of forgetfulness or mistranscription for 1869; clearly by the author of nos. 4861, 4870, 4901 (the political attitudes are similar in tone and substance); the *Life of Lord George Bentinck* is again quoted, p. 122, as in nos. 4870 and 4901; and cf. no. 5004.

VOLUME 79, FEBRUARY 1869

4938 Chinese Gordon, 135–157. **C. C. Chesney.** Signed C.C.C.; repr. *Essays on Military Biography*, 1874.

4939 The two comets of the year 1868 (Part I), 158–164. **Richard A. Proctor.** Signed.

4940 British merchant seamen (Part II), 169–187. **William Dawson.** Signed A Commander, R.N.; cf. no. 4732. (Part III is no. 5013.)

4941 Jabez Oliphant; or, The modern prince (book I, chaps. i–iii), 188–201. **J. H. Burrow.** Bentley; novel published anon. 1870.

4942 A voice from the colonies on the colonial question, 202–216. **John Robinson,** 1839–1903. Signed J.R.; claimed in his *Life Time in South Africa* (1900), p. xxi.

4943 Milman's *Annals of St. Paul's Cathedral*, 217–229. **W. F. Pollock.** Remembrances, II, 196.

4944 William Morris and Matthew Arnold; a letter from a hermitage, 230–244. **John Skelton.** Signed Shirley—see *DNB*.

4945 A visit to La Creuse, 245–252. **T. E. Cliffe Leslie.** Signed; repr. *Land Systems*.

4946 Modern preaching, 254–268.

VOLUME 79, MARCH 1869

4947 What is a bishop? 269–280.

4948 A note on pauperism, 281–290. **Florence Nightingale.** Signed.

4949 The Cretan insurrection of 1866–1868, 291–311. **W. J. Stillman.** Signed A Resident in Crete; claimed in *Autobiography of a Journalist* (Boston, 1901), II, p. 486.

4950 *The Pilgrim and the Shrine*; or, scepticism, 312–321.

4951 Jabez Oliphant (book I, chaps. iv–v), 322–335. **J. H. Burrow.** Cf. no. 4941.

4952 A deaf and dumb service, 336–340.

4953 Life in India (chaps. i–ii): prefatory; general view of northern and southern India, 341–359. **Edward Braddon.** Book published 1872.

4954 The devil in Leipzig, 360–379. **M. D. Conway.** Signed.

4955 The grand force! [advertising], 380–383. **William Jerdan.** Signed W.J.; obit. in *N&Q*, 4th series, 4 (July 17, 1869), 67 says that in recent numbers of *FM* are contributions from his pen.

4956 Mr. Henry Taylor's *Plays and Poems*, 384–397. **Horace M. Moule?** Signed H.M.M.; Moule signed no. 5254 on two other Victorian poets; the primary interest in the medieval history embodied in Taylor's plays is analogous to Moule's viewpoint in discussing the Arthurian writers in *Macmillan's Mag.*, no. 1152 (see *Index*, I, where the "Noule" is a typographical error for "Moule").

4957 The ethics of disendowment [of the Irish Church], 398–402.

VOLUME 79, APRIL 1869

4958 On the relative demand for labour in the agricultural and manufacturing districts: its causes and effects, 403–416.

4959 Fergusson's *Tree and Serpent Worship*, 417–430. **Frances P. Cobbe.** Signed F.P.C.; repr. *Darwinism*, as "Prehistoric Religion."

4960 Jabez Oliphant (book I, chaps. vi–ix), 431–450. **J. H. Burrow.** Cf. no. 4941.

4961 Scottish characteristics: a prelection, 451–465. Signed: A Scoto-Celt.

4962 The greatest wonder [lack of common sense in legislation], 466–474. **William Jerdan.** Signed W.J.; author says, p. 466, he wrote no. 4955.

4963 Concerning depreciation: with some thoughts on dislike, 475–486. **A. K. H. Boyd.** Signed A.K.H.B.; repr. *Landscapes*.

4964 Whist and whist-players, 487–510. **Abraham Hayward.** Repr. *Essays* (1873), I.

4965 Mr. Longman's *Edward the Third*, 511–524.

4966 Mendelssohn as an influence, 525–536. Signed: F.R.

VOLUME 79, MAY 1869

4967 Women's education, 537–552.

4968 A visit to my discontented cousin (chaps. i–vii), 553–568. **James Moncreiff.** Attr. in *DNB* and *BMCat.*; novel published anon. 1871.

4969 Erie campaigns in 1868; or, How they manage things on the New York Stock Exchange, 569–584.

4970 Life in India (chap. iii): India eighty years ago—a retrospect, 585–601. **Edward Braddon.** Cf. no. 4953.

4971 President Grant, 602–621.

4972 Jabez Oliphant (book II, chaps. i–iii), 622–642. **J. H. Burrow.** Cf. no. 4941.

4973 A route from the Atlantic to the Pacific through British territory, 643–650. **Harry Verney.** Signed.

4974 Lord Vernon's *Inferno di Dante*, 651–660. **W. F. Pollock.** Signed W.F.P.—see no. 3927; Pollock translated the *Divine Comedy*, 1854.

4975 The Habitual Criminals Bill, 661–677. **Henry Taylor,** 1800–1886. Signed; identified, p. 666n.: see *BMCat.*

4976 Milton and Galileo, 678–684. **Richard Owen.** Signed R. Owen; *Life*, II, 370.

(Note, p. 819, by **J. A. Froude**—signed The Editor of *Fraser.*)

VOLUME 79, JUNE 1869

4977 The working man and his friends, 685–701. Signed: J.H.F.

4978 A visit to my discontented cousin (chaps. viii–x), 702–720. **James Moncrieff.** Cf. no. 4968.

4979 Life in India (chap. iv): domestic interiors, 721–738. **Edward Braddon.** Cf. no. 4953.

4980 The two comets of the year 1868 (Part II, concl.), 739–746. **Richard A. Proctor.** Signed.

4981 Spedding's *Life and Letters of Bacon*, 747–762. **W. B. Donne.** Johnson, *Donne*, list.

4982 Spanish poetry before A.D. 1500, 763–779. **Charles Welsh Mason,** b.1830/31. Signed C. Welsh-Mason, B.A.; see Venn, *BMCat.* under Mason, who published some translations of Spanish poetry, 1863.

4983 On the names of places in Ireland, 780–793. **William Allingham.** Signed.

4984 Jabez Oliphant (book II, chaps. iv–vi), 794–807. **J. H. Burrow.** Cf. no. 4941.

4985 Saddling and bitting, 808–819.

VOLUME 80, JULY 1869

4986 The Comtist Utopia, 1–21. **Leslie Stephen.** Ullmann list, p. 243.

4987 A visit to my discontented cousin (chaps. xi–xv), 22–39. **James Moncreiff.** Cf. no. 4968.

4988 *Currency* [by Bonamy Price], 40–57. **F. W. Newman.** Repr. *Miscellanies*, IV, as "Peel's Act of 1844." (See no. 5018.)

4989 A midnight ride with Henry the Second, 58–66.

4990 Life in India (chap. v): in the Moffussil, 67–86. **Edward Braddon.** Cf. no. 4953.

4991 The ever-widening world of stars, 90–96. **Richard A. Proctor.** Signed.

4992 Poaching on Mont Blanc a dozen years ago, 97–111. **T. W. Hinchliff.** Attr. in *Alpine Journal*, VIII, appendix, p. 13, and XI, 39–40.

4993 Why skilled workmen don't go to church, 112–118.

4994 The autobiography of consciousness; or, The experiences of an indoor servant [on philosophy from Descartes to J. S. Mill], 119–128.

4995   Jabez Oliphant (book II, chap. vii), 129–134. **J. H. Burrow.** Cf. no. 4941.

VOLUME 80, AUGUST 1869

4996   Primary education, 135–154. Signed: B.

4997   A visit to my discontented cousin (chaps. xvi–xix), 155–177. **James Moncreiff.** Cf. no. 4968.

4998   Two [classes of] Irish tourists, 178–199.

4999   A May ramble, 200–206. **A. K. H. Boyd.** Signed A.K.H.B.; repr. *Landscapes.*

5000   Credit and crises, 207–222. **Bonamy Price.** Signed.

5001   Jabez Oliphant (book III, chaps. i–iii), 223–236. **J. H. Burrow.** Cf. no. 4941.

5002   Shakespeare's vocabulary and style, 237–247.

5003   A few words on Utilitarianism, 248–256. **Robert Williams,** 1843–1886. Signed R.W.; Contents gives full name; man cited was at this time a fellow of Merton Coll. Oxford (see Boase) who translated Aristotle's *Nicomachean Ethics,* 1869 (see *BMCat.*); the art. is a professional essay on the utilitarian ethic.

5004   The Irish Church Bill, 257–272. **Abraham Hayward,** prob. On p. 267 author mentions a point "we" had proved earlier in no. 4937; Hayward had long supported both Gladstone and the Disestablishment of the Irish Church.

VOLUME 80, SEPTEMBER 1869

5005   Mr. Lecky's *History of European Morals,* 273–284. **Leslie Stephen?** Attr. in Ullmann list, p. 243, but (see p. 235) only on basis of close resemblance to a review of the same book in the *Nation* attrib. to Stephen by Maitland.

5006   A visit to my discontented cousin (chaps. xx–xxiii, concl.), 285–299. **James Moncreiff.** Cf. no. 4968.

5007   The earldom of Wiltes, 300–317.

5008   The sun's journey through space, 318–325. **Richard A. Proctor.** Signed; repr. *Essays on Astronomy,* 1872.

5009   Life in India (chap. vi): the natives of the country, 326–347. **Edward Braddon.** Cf. no. 4953.

5010   Jabez Oliphant (book III, chaps. iv–viii), 350–365. **J. H. Burrow.** Cf. no. 4941.

5011   Female education in France, 366–379. **F. P. Verney.** Repr. *Essays and Tales,* 1891.

5012   Of unconsciousness and annihilation, 380–385. **A. K. H. Boyd.** Signed A.K.H.B.; repr. *Landscapes.*

5013   British merchant seamen (Part III, concl.), 386–406. **William Dawson.** Evidence for no. 4732.

VOLUME 80, OCTOBER 1869

5014   *Suggestions on Academical Organisation* [by Mark Pattison], 407–430. Unidentified. Possibly A. V. Dicey. Froude to Dicey, Aug. 1, 1869, Bodleian Lib., asks him to review this book; the author was clearly, as he suggests, p. 407, one who knew "the internal condition of the University" [viz., of Oxford], and though residing in London, Dicey had been a Fellow of Trinity since 1860. W. H. Dunn reported to the said *Index* that the art. is bound up in a volume, owned by him, in which the other arts. are known to be by J. A. Froude, but Froude was not in close touch with Oxford.

5015   A new phase of the Irish question: convent life in Ireland, 431–444. Signed: C. (See no. 5065.)

5016   Pindar, 445–462.

5017   Little Miss Deane, 463–476.

5018   Reply to the article on currency, July 1869 [no. 4988], 477–493. **Bonamy Price.** Signed.

5019   Professor Tyndall's theory of comets, 504–512. **Richard A. Proctor.** Signed; repr. *The Orbs around Us,* 1872.

5020   Jabez Oliphant (book III, chap. ix), 513–521. **J. H. Burrow.** Cf. no. 4941.

5021   Henry Crabb Robinson, 522–536. **W. B. Donne.** Johnson, *Donne,* list.

VOLUME 80, NOVEMBER 1869

5022   The present state of religious controversy, 537–574. **J. F. Stephen.** Stephen list.

5023   A third Irish tourist [cf. no. 4998], 575–596. Signed: F. (Note, vol. 81 o.s., p. 142.)

5024   Lord Byron vindicated, 598–617.

5025   Jabez Oliphant (book IV, chaps i–iii), 618–634. **J. H. Burrow.** Cf. no. 4941.

5026   The baths of Santa Catarina, 635–648. **Leslie Stephen.** Repr. *Playground.*

5027   Ghosts, present and past, 649–661. **F. J. S. Edgcombe.** Signed.

5028 The poetry of the year: an autumnal review, 622–678. **John Skelton.** Signed Shirley—see *DNB*.

VOLUME 80, DECEMBER 1869

5029 Charity, 679–703. **J. G. Fitch.** Signed.

5030 Life in India (chap. vii): the rulers, the public, and the press, 704–721. **Edward Braddon.** Cf. no. 4953.

5031 Dr. Pusey and Dr. Temple, 722–737. **Leslie Stephen.** Ullmann list, p. 243.

5032 Jabez Oliphant (book IV, chaps. iv–v), 738–753. **J. H. Burrow.** Cf. no. 4941.

5033 The Rosse telescope set to new work, 754–760. **Richard A. Proctor.** Signed; repr. *The Orbs around Us*, 1872.

5034 A poet of the Lower French Empire [Baudelaire], 769–775. **William Allingham.** Repr. *Varieties*, III.

5035 To know, or not to know? 776–787. **Frances Power Cobbe.** Signed; repr. *Scientific Spirit*.

5036 Orthodoxus tyrannus: a parable, 788–797.

5037 Victor Hugo's *L'Homme qui rit*, 798–805. Unidentified. Perhaps W. F. Pollock: Froude to Pollock, May 30, n.d., Bodleian Lib., welcomes an art. for September and mentions Hugo's book; letter of Oct. 5 asks when he may expect an art.; but perhaps by his wife, Juliet Pollock, who was more likely to write on contemporary French literature.

VOLUME 81 O.S., 1 N.S., JANUARY 1870

5038 England and her colonies, 1–16. **J. A. Froude.** Signed at start The Editor, at end J.A.F.; repr. *Studies*, II.

5039 Westward: a grandfather's dream (Part I), 17–35. **Herman Merivale.** Claimed in Merivale to Henry Taylor, Feb. 4, 1870, Bodleian Lib.

5040 Lunar warmth and stellar heat, 36–43.

5041 Irish elections and the influence of the priests, 44–58. **J. Lowry Whittle.** Signed J.L.W.; name given in Contents.

5042 Rambles (No. VII): Devon, 59–71. **William Allingham.** Evidence for no. 4807.

5043 Laissez-faire, 72–83. **Robert Williams,** 1843–1886. Signed R.W.; full name in Contents; cf. no. 5003.

5044 Dr. Robert Lee of Edinburgh, 86–106. **John Skelton.** Signed Shirley; partly repr. *Essays*.

5045 The last "field-day" in the New York "gold-room" [on the New York Stock Exchange], 107–120.

5046 Ireland and the Irish land question, 121–142. **Abraham Hayward,** prob., Hayward spoke on Dec. 23, 1869, *Correspondence*, II, 211, of having been exclusively occupied for many days with Irish Tenant Right; on Dec. 24, ibid., p. 213, Lord Lytton was looking forward to his art. on the Irish Land Question; on p. 124 author speaks of the amnesty meetings as "formidable" as does Hayward in *Correspondence*, II, 209; Hayward had written on Irish questions for *FM*.

VOLUME 81 O.S., 1 N.S., FEBRUARY 1870

5047 Mr. Mill on the subjection of women, 143–165. **Henry Taylor.** Signed; repr. *Works* (1877–1878), V.

5048 The fate of Paraguay, 166–184. **Thomas W. Hinchliff.** Signed T.W.H.; name given in Contents.

5049 The enclosure of commons, 185–196. **Henry Fawcett.** Signed, with addition of "M.P."

5050 Rambles (No. VIII): still in Devon, 197–210. **William Allingham.** Evidence for no. 4807.

5051 Westward: a grandfather's dream (Part II, concl.), 211–219. **Herman Merivale.** Cf. no. 5039.

5052 A bishop of the twelfth century [St. Hugo of Avalon], 220–236. **J. A. Froude.** Signed J.A.F.; repr. *Studies*, II.

5053 Strange discoveries respecting the aurora, 237–245. **Richard A. Proctor.** Signed; repr. *Light Science*.

5054 The merchant and his wife; an apologue for the Colonial Office, 246–247. **J. A. Froude.** Repr. *Studies*, II.

5055 Our rule in India (Part I), 248–254. **Campbell Walker.** Claimed at start of no. 5131.

5056 Jabez Oliphant (book IV, chap. vi–book V, chap. i), 255–277. **J. T. Burrow.** Cf. no. 4941.

5057 Literary and musical copyrights, 278–284. **Roberton Blaine.** Signed.

VOLUME 81 O.S., 1 N.S., MARCH 1870

5058 Reciprocal duties of state and subject, 285–301. **J. A. Froude.** Signed at start The Editor, at end J.A.F.; repr. *Studies*, II.

5059 On dust and disease, 302–310. **John Tyndall.** Signed.

5060 The Broad Church, 311–325. **Leslie Stephen.** Signed; repr. *Free Thinking.*

5061 *Faraday*, 326–342. **W. F. Pollock.** *Remembrances*, II, 167, 199.

5062 *Ancient and Mediaeval India*, 343–361. **Frances Power Cobbe.** Signed; repr. *Darwinism* as "The Religion and Literature of India."

5063 Rabelais and the Renaissance, 363–372. **Andrew Lang.** Signed A.L.; attr. by Falconer, *Writings of Lang*, p. 18, and R. L. Green, *Andrew Lang, a Critical Biography* (Leicester, 1946), p. 251.

5064 Practical working of the ballot in the United States, 373–380. **John Torrey Morse,** Jr. Signed J. T. Morse; see *Amer. WWW*/1942 and *LCCat.*

5065 Another paper on convent life [reply to no. 5015], 381–387. Signed: An Irish Catholic.

5066 Jabez Oliphant (book V, chaps. ii–v, concl.), 388–407. **J. H. Burrow.** Cf. no. 4941.

5067 Secularisation of university education in Ireland, 408–426. Signed: R.O.B.L.

5068 The agricultural labourer, 427–443.

5069 Lectures on the science of religion (No. I), 444–455. **Friedrich Max Müller.** Signature.

5070 Life in India (chap. viii, concl.): the overland route, 456–473. **Edward Braddon.** Cf. no. 4953.

5071 The cost of a Napoleon [Napoleon III], 474–488. **W. R. Greg.** Signed W.R.G.—see no. 4552.

5072 Irish politics and Irish priests, 491–499. **James Macdonell,** prob. Signed M.—see nos. 4833, 5675, etc.

5073 Capital—labour—profit,   500–512. **James E. Thorold Rogers.** Signed.

5074 A fortnight in Kerry (Part I), 513–530. **J. A. Froude.** Signed. J.A.F.; repr. *Studies*, II.

5075 The future of Turkey, 531–539. **John Vickers.** Signed; prob. the John Vickers, author of *The New Koran . . . or, Textbook on Turkish Reformers*, 1861: see *BMCat.*

5076 National armies and modern warfare, 543–560. **Francis D. Dwyer.** In no. 5135, pp. 518–519, and again in no. 5146, p. 657, Dwyer refers to this art. as "ours"; the subject is characteristic.

5077 Father Newman, *The Grammar of Assent*, 561–580. **J. A. Froude.** Assigned in Contents to "The Editor"; repr. *Studies*, II.

5078 Lectures on the science of religion (No. II), 581–593. **Friedrich Max Müller.** Signature.

5079 Arundines Nili [on Egypt], 594–607. **William Howard Russell.** Signed W.H.R.; assigned to W. H. Russell in Contents; see *DNB.*

5080 The poems of Dante Gabriel Rossetti, 609–622. **John Skelton.** Signed Shirley—see *DNB.*

5081 The religious difficulty, 623–634. **Leslie Stephen.** Assigned in Contents.

5082 The opposition of Mars, 636–641.

5083 Alexander Pope, 642–656. **John Dennis.** Claimed in *Studies*, preface.

5084 The Shannon improvements, 658–666.

5085 The objects of art, 667–676. **Frances P. Verney.** Repr. *Peasant Properties*, II.

5086 Mr. Gardiner's *Prince Charles and the Spanish Marriage*, 677–694. **James Spedding.** Signed. (See no. 5197.)

5087 Lectures on the science of religion (No. III), 695–717. **Friedrich Max Müller.** Signature.

5088 The adulteration of food and drugs, 718–730.

5089 Fresh evidence about Anne Boleyn (Part I), 731–748. **J. A. Froude.** Signed J.A.F.; Contents gives "The Editor."

5090 Adam and Mally; a story of Scottish farm-life, 749–765. **Henrietta Keddie.** Repr. in *Garden of Women*, 1875, as "A Scotch thistle."

5091 Ultramontane text-books, 766–776.

5092 Omar Khayyám, the astronomer-poet of Persia, 777–784. **T. W. Hinchcliff.** Claimed in *Letters of Edward FitzGerald to Bernard Quaritch* (1926), p. 43.

5093 Some remarks on the London Art Exhibitions of 1870, 785–789. **J. Jackson Jarves?** Signed An American; Jarves (see *DAB*) wrote no. 5143 on modern Italian art in a similar style of quiet self-assurance; no. 5143 was repr. in a book "by An American Amateur in Europe."

5094 Mr. Disraeli's *Lothair*, 790–805. **John Skelton.** Signed Shirley; see *Blackwood's*, 156 (Dec. 1894), 765.

5095 The House of Condé, 806–829.

VOLUME 82 O.S., 2 N.S., JULY 1870

5096 Emerson's *Society and Solitude*, 1–18. **M. D. Conway.** Assigned in Contents.

5097 Telegraph time, 19–30. **James Carpenter.** Assigned to "J. Carpenter" in Contents; see Boase.

5098 Indian finance, 31–43. Signed: S.

5099 Fresh evidence about Anne Boleyn (Part II, concl.), 44–65. **J. A. Froude.** Evidence for no. 5089.

5100 The water we should not drink, 66–72. **W. M. Higgins.** Signed.

5101 The story of the dog-worshipper, 73–92. **Amir Dihlávi Khusrau.** Page 73n and *BMCat.* Translated by **Henry Copinger**—Froude to Allingham, June 20 [1871], Allingham Corres. speaks of "Col. Copinger the 'dog-worshipper'"; *Army List*/69.

5102 The greatest sea wave ever known, 93–99. **Richard A. Proctor.** Signed; repr. *Light Science.*

5103 Lectures on the science of religion (No. IV, concl.), 100–112. **Friedrich Max Müller.** Signature.

5104 Reminiscences of Walter Savage Landor, 113–120. **Eliza Lynn Linton.** Signature.

5105 Government from above and from below, 121–129. **F. W. Newman.** Signed; repr. in *Miscellanies*, III, as "Guidance or Anarchy."

5106 Charles Dickens, 130–134.

VOLUME 82 O.S., 2 N.S., AUGUST 1870

5107 Seven hundred years ago; an historic sketch [of Ireland], 135–158. **William Allingham.** Signed; repr. *Varieties*, III.

5108 In memory of George Villiers, Earl of Clarendon, 159–166. **Henry Reeve.** Signed H.R.; Contents gives full name.

5109 The Alps in the last century, 167–180. **Leslie Stephen.** Signed; repr. *Playground* as "The Old School."

5110 Daniel Webster, 181–197.

5111 Mahometanism in the Levant (Part I), 198–217. **William Gifford Palgrave.** Signed G.; repr. *Eastern Questions.*

5112 Gunpowder and modern artillery, 218–223. **Francis Montagu Smith.** Signed F.M.S.; in the next year Captain Smith, assistant superintendent of Royal Gunpowder Factory, published *A Handbook of the Manufacture and Proof of Gunpowder*: see *BMCat.*, *Army List*/70.

5113 Prince Paul's betrothal, 224–242.

Henrietta Keddie. Repr. in *Garden of Women*, 1875, as "A Balsam."

5114 An early stroll to Zermatt, 243–250. **George Carless Swayne.** Signed.

5115 *Hereditary Genius* [by Francis Galton], 251–265. **F. W. Farrar.** Assigned in Contents.

5116 Causes of the War [Franco-Prussian], 266–268.

VOLUME 82 O.S., 2 N.S., SEPTEMBER 1870

5117 The colonies once more, 269–287. **J. A. Froude.** Signed at start The Editor, at end J.A.F.; repr. *Studies*, II.

5118 *Letters of Sir George Cornewall Lewis*, 288–293. **Harriet Grote.** Claimed in *The Lewin Letters*, ed. T. H. Lewin (1909), II, 288.

5119 The planet Saturn, 294–302. **Richard A. Proctor.** Signed; repr. *Essays on Astronomy*, 1872.

5120 Mahometanism in the Levant (Part II), 303–321. **W. G. Palgrave.** Evidence for no. 5111.

5121 Fashions in hair and head-dresses, 322–331.

5122 The dominie's sons; a story, 332–347. **Henrietta Keddie.** Repr. in *Garden of Women*, 1875, as "A Lammas Lily."

5123 East and West [Ends of London] (Part I), 348–360. Unidentified. By a woman who had worked extensively in the Parochial Mission Women Association (see p. 348), and who was a friend of Charlotte F. F. Spencer. **Charlotte Spencer** wrote the intro. and sent the art. to *FM*—signed "Contributed by Countess Spencer": see *Complete Peerage.*

5124 The plot and dramatis personnae of *Titus Andronicus,* 361–372. **R. G. Latham.** Signed.

5125 The future of labour, 373–384. **J. Lowry Whittle.** Signed.

5126 The War [Franco-Prussian] (No. I), 385–402. **Francis Doyne Dwyer.** Froude to Allingham, Aug. 2, [1870], Allingham Corres., discussing the next issue: "Major Dwyer (he has been in Germany 30 years and is a shrewd and good officer) will have a paper on the war" (for man cited see refs. below in Part B); the all-important date—1870—is settled by ibid. to ibid., July 21, [1870], where Froude's reference to Reeve adding a few words to his paper on Clarendon (no. 5108) is followed by plans for the

"Sept." issue, including "a third of Miss Keddie's stories" (no. 5122) and "another paper" of his own "on the Colonies" (no. 5117).

VOLUME 82 O.S., 2 N.S., OCTOBER 1870

5127 *Home Politics*, 403–413. Signed: F.P. Possibly Frederick Pollock, 1845–1937: cf. no. 5448.

5128 Mr. Matthew Arnold and the Church of England, 414–431. **Leslie Stephen.** Signed.

5129 East and West (Part II, concl.), 432–442. Cf. no. 5123.

5130 The internal relations of Europe, 443–457. **Francis W. Newman.** Signed; repr. *Miscellanies*, III, as "Conditions of permanent peace."

5131 Our rule in India (Part II, concl.), 458–467. **Campbell Walker.** Signed.

5132 Mahometanism in the Levant (Part III, concl.), 468–482. **W. G. Palgrave.** Signed; cf. no. 5111.

5133 A month with the belligerents [the French and Germans]: notes from a diary, 483–502. **Moncure D. Conway.** Attr. by Friedrich Max Müller, *Life and Letters* (1902), I, 407; cf. *DAB*.

5134 A novel way of studying the stars, 503–513. **Richard A. Proctor.** Signed; repr. *Essays on Astronomy*, 1872.

5135 The War (No. II), 518–536. **Francis D. Dwyer.** See opening reference to no. 5126.

VOLUME 82 O.S., 2 N.S., NOVEMBER 1870

5136 Mr. Cardwell's military policy, 537–553.

5137 The present condition of China, 554–568. Signed: A Resident.

5138 Rambles (No. IX): in London, 569–583. **William Allingham.** Evidence for no. 4807.

5139 The new Dominion [Canada], 584–589. **Charles Marshall.** Signed at start A Recent Visitor, at end C.M.; p. 586, last part of col. i, is repeated almost verbatim in Marshall's *The Canadian Dominion* (1871), pp. 256, 258.

5140 Mystic trees and flowers (Part I), 590–608. **M. D. Conway.** Claimed in *Autobiography*, II, 322.

5141 In the Highlands: holiday thoughts, 609–617. **A. K. H. Boyd.** Signed A.K.H.B.; repr. *Landscapes*.

5142 On the drowning of Shelley, 618–625. **R. H. Horne.** Signed.

5143 Some notes on modern Italian art, 626–630. **J. Jackson Jarves.** Signed J. Jackson Tarves, but corrected in Index; repr. *Art Thoughts*, 1870.

5144 The Fiji Islands in 1868, 1869, and 1870, 631–636.

5145 The personal history of imperialism in 1870, 637–651. **Abraham Hayward.** Claimed in *Correspondence*, II, 218.

5146 The War (No. III, concl.), 652–670. **Francis D. Dwyer.** See opening reference to no. 5135.

VOLUME 82 O.S., 2 N.S., DECEMBER 1870

5147 On progress, 671–690. **J. A. Froude.** Signed at start The Editor, at end J.A.F.; repr. *Studies*, II.

5148 Athletic sports and university studies, 691–704. **Leslie Stephen.** Signed.

5149 Mystic trees and flowers (No. II, concl.), 705–723. **M. D. Conway.** Signed.

5150 The eclipse of the present month, 724–734. **R. A. Proctor.** Signed.

5151 Rambles (No. X): at Liverpool, 735–753. **William Allingham.** Evidence for no. 4807.

5152 The federal movement in Ireland, 754–764. Signed: An Irishman who is not a Federalist.

5153 The temptation of the Reverend Stephen Holdfast (Part I), 767–782. **John Skelton.** Signed Dionysius Diamond, M.D.; repr. *Essays in Romance* as "A Passage in the Ministry of Stephen Holdfast."

5154 Primogeniture, 783–792. **Arthur Joseph Munby?** Signed A.J.M.; Munby was a barrister and a conveyancer in the Ecclesiastical Commissioners' office (see Venn); he had contributed verse to *FM* in Sept. 1862 and July 1864.

5155 Two great wars: an historical parallel [between the Civil War and the Franco-Prussian War], 793–805. **Adam Badeau.** Signed, with the title "Brevet Brigadier-General, United States Army."

VOLUME 83 O.S., 3 N.S., JANUARY 1871

5156 On the causes of the Crimean War, 1–13. **F. W. Newman.** Signed.

5157 The Indian deficit, 14–27. **Henry Fawcett.** Stephen, *Fawcett*, appendix.

5158 A fortnight in Kerry (Part II, concl.),

28–45. **J. A. Froude.** Signed at start The Editor, at end J.A.F.; repr. *Studies*, II.

5159 The free-grant lands of Canada, 46–54. **Charles Marshall.** Signed; repr. *The Canadian Dominion* (1871), chap. v.

5160 The schoolmaster abroad, 55–67. **M. P. Lindo.** Signed, with address, "The Hague."

5161 The loss of H.M.S. *Captain*, 68–83. **Edmund Robert Freemantle.** Signed E.R.F.; claimed in *The Navy as I Have Known It* [1919], p. 177.

5162 Annals of a border county [Hereford-shire], 84–98. **Charles John Robinson.** Signed C.J.R.; attr. in *Biograph*, 6 (1881), 145; pp. 87, 98, refer to his *Castles of Herefordshire*, 1870.

5163 The temptation of the Reverend Stephen Holdfast (Part II, concl.), 99–116. **John Skelton.** Evidence for no. 5153.

5164 Scotland in the sixteenth century: pre-reformation period, 117–134. **Alexander Falconer.** Signed A.F.; attr. to "Mr. A. Falconer" in *Athenaeum*, Jan. 7, 1871, p. 19; cf. no. 5275.

VOLUME 83 O.S., 3 N.S., FEBRUARY 1871

5165 England's war [on the home front], 135–150. **J. A. Froude.** Repr. *Studies, II.*

5166 Meteors and meteor systems, 151–161. **Richard A. Proctor.** Signed; repr. *The Orbs around Us,* 1872.

5167 Virgil as translated by Dryden and Conington, 162–173. Signed: A.M.L.

5168 The Eastern question, 174–183.

5169 Adamnán's vision [trans. of a MS. in Royal Irish Academy], 184–194. **Whitley Stokes.** Signed in introduction Mac dá cherda; see *DNB*, 2nd suppl., for his interest in medieval Irish literature and no. 3598 for the pseudonym.

5170 The monastery of Sumelas, 195–206. **W. Gifford Palgrave.** Signed; repr. *Eastern Questions* and *Ulysses*.

5171 Prussia and Germany, 207–229. **Reinhold Pauli.** Signed Professor Pauli of Göttingen; see *ADB*, which also shows he had visited Edinburgh, where this lecture had been delivered.

5172 Kaye's Indian Mutiny [i.e., his *Sepoy War*], 232–245. Signed: S.

5173 The Orange Society, 246–256. Signed: An Ulster Protestant.

5174 The crisis in France, 257–272. **Francis D. Dwyer.** This is a sequel to no. 5146, as the writer points out, p. 257.

VOLUME 83 O.S., 3 N.S., MARCH 1871

5175 The last instalment of Irish policy, 273–283. **J. Lowry Whittle.** Signed.

5176 Mr. Elwin's edition of Pope, 284–301. **Leslie Stephen.** Signed L.S.; repr. *Hours* (1st ed. only, 1875), I.

5177 Thomas Ingoldsby (Barham), 302–316.

5178 The sun's corona, 317–327. **Richard A. Proctor.** Signed; repr. *The Orbs around Us,* 1872.

5179 Chinese statesmen and state papers (No. I), 328–342.

5180 Rambles (No. XI): a bird's-eye view from Crow Castle, 343–363. **William Allingham.** Evidence for no. 4807.

5181 Giordano Bruno, 364–377.

5182 Isambard Kingdom Brunel, 383–394.

5183 What the Chinese really think of Europeans [a trans. from Chinese], 395–406. Signed: at start A Native Literate, at end A Wanderer on a Raft.

VOLUME 83 O.S., 3 N.S., APRIL 1871

5184 Life peerages, 407–418.

5185 A pilgrimage to St. David's, 419–431. **R. J. King.** Repr. *Sketches.*

5186 The Emperor Julian, 432–450. **C. G. Prowett.** Signed.

5187 Two solutions [to the Malthusian problem of population], 451–456. **John Edward Jenkins.** Signed The Author of *Ginx's Baby*; see *BMCat*.

5188 Mr. Voysey and Mr. Purchas, 457–468. **Leslie Stephen.** Ullmann list, p. 243.

5189 The government scheme of army reform, 469–486.

5190 Arabiana: the poet 'Omar, 487–502. **W. Gifford Palgrave.** Signed; repr. *Eastern Questions.*

5191 Chinese statesmen and state papers (No. II), 503–514.

5192 What, then, *is* the corona? 515–528. **Richard A. Proctor.** Signed; repr. *The Orbs around Us,* 1872.

5193 The French government of national defence, 529–540. Signed: E.B.M.

VOLUME 83 O.S., 3 N.S., MAY 1871

5194 The condition of French politics, 541–554. **W. R. Greg.** Signed W.R.G.—see no. 4552; cf. no. 5071.

5195 "Ours" in Japan, 555–562. Unidentified. Burtis list, suggests M. D. Conway on internal evidence, but is doubtful.

5196 The working man's political question, 563–570.

5197 James I. and Lord Digby: a reply to Mr. Spedding [no. 5086], 571–583. **Samuel R. Gardiner.** Signed.

5198 Malthusianism, true and false, 584–598. **Francis W. Newman.** Signed.

5199 Australian tendencies, 599–605. Signed: An Old Colonist.

5200 Education in the navy, 606–612. **James G. Goodenough.** Signed. (Note, vol. 4 n.s., p. 134, by **Goodenough**—signed J.G.G.)

5201 Chinese statesmen and state papers (No. III, concl.), 613–628.

5202 The original Merry Andrew [Andrew Boorde], 629–640.

5203 The agricultural labourer of Scotland, 641–653.

5204 Paris, 1588–1594: Commune versus King; an historical study, 654–669.

5205 The poetry of the Siege [of Paris], 670–674. Signed: J.H.F.

VOLUME 83 o.s., 3 n.s., JUNE 1871

5206 The tenure of land in Europe, 675–691. **Daniel Grant.** Assigned to "D. Grant" in Contents; man cited had been asked to write for *FM* (Froude to Allingham, Aug. 2, [1870], Allingham Corres.) and published a book on land tenure in Ireland in 1881.

5207 Characteristics of Mormonism; by a recent visitor to Utah, 692–702. **Charles Marshall.** Signed.

5208 The travels and adventures of a philosopher in the famous empire of Hulee [i.e., matter]; from an old MS., A.D. 2070 [on materialist philosophy], 703–717.

5209 Deflective education [training for domestic service], 718–723.

5210 Volundur, a Scandinavian legend [based upon the Danish version of A. G. Öhlenschläger], 729–750. **Peter Toft.** Signed in intro. note.

5211 English republicanism, 751–761. **Thomas Wright.** Signed A Working Man; repr. *Masters*, pp. 159–185.

5212 On architecture and its relation to modern life, 762–777. Signed: An Architect.

5213 Rambles (No. XII): in the land of the Kymry, 778–797. **William Allingham.** Evidence for no. 4807.

5214 The Commune of 1871, 798–809. Signed: E.B.M.

VOLUME 84 o.s., 4 n.s., JULY 1871

5215 Home government for Ireland, 1–12. Signed: An Irish Liberal.

5216 Traces of animal worship among the old Scandinavians, 13–25. **Jón A. Hjaltalín.** Signed.

5217 Don Carlos [of Spain, son of Philip II], 26–42.

5218 Touraine in April 1871, 43–61.

5219 The English working classes and the Paris Commune, 62–68. **Thomas Wright.** Signed "The Journeyman Engineer"; repr. *Masters.*

5220 Erasmus Montanus: an old Danish comedy, translated with a short sketch of Holberg's life, 69–96. **Ludwig Holberg.** Intro. note. The sketch, 69–71, and trans. by **Peter Toft**—signed.

5221 Salt Lake City and the valley settlements, 97–108. **Charles Marshall.** Signed.

5222 Great Britain confederated; new chapter to be added to the old school books for the rising generation of the twentieth century, 109–114. (See no. 5231.)

5223 *Suum cuique*: the moral of the Paris catastrophe, 115–134. **W. R. Greg.** Signed W.R.G.—see no. 4552; cf. no. 5194, which is cited here, p. 119n.

VOLUME 84 o.s., 4 n.s., AUGUST 1871

5224 The defence of Canada, 135–149.

5225 John Asgill; and the cowardliness of dying, 150–166. **Keningale Cook.** Signed.

5226 Future naval battles, 167–181. **William Dawson.** Signed Commander W. Dawson, R.N.; see *WWW*/1916.

5227 The art season of 1871, 182–192. **William Bell Scott.** Signed W.B.S.; *Notes*, pp. 133, 137, 139, 142; Scott to Allingham, July 7, [1871], Allingham Corres., returns proof of this art.

5228 Rambles (No. XIII): on the Wye, 193–213. **William Allingham.** Evidence for no. 4807.

5229 Concerning John's Indian affairs (Part I), 214–225. **Robert H. Elliot.** Part II is signed R.H.E.; series repr. under this title, 1872.

5230 At Paris, just before the end [of the Commune], 230–248. **H. S. Fagan.** Signed at start A Vicar of the Church of England, at end H.S.F.; see Boase; he used his initials for no. 5610. With an intro. note by **J. A. Froude**—signed Ed. *F.M.*

5231   More on Great Britain confederated [sequel to no. 5222], 249–250. Unidentified. With intro. note by **J. A. Froude**—signed Ed.

5232   The campaigns of 1859, 1866, and 1870–71, 251–268.

VOLUME 84 O.S., 4 N.S., SEPTEMBER 1871

5233   The future of university reform, 269–281. **Leslie Stephen.** Signed.

5234   The study of astronomy, 282–292. **Richard A. Proctor.** Signed; repr. *Essays on Astronomy*, 1872.

5235   The preservation of commons, 293–306.

5236   *Village Communities in the East and West* [by H. S. Maine], 308–322.

5237   The sheik and his daughter; or, Wisdom and folly, an Eastern tale, 323–333. Unidentified. Perhaps by Amir Dihlávi Khusrau since Froude to Allingham, June 20, [1871], Allingham Corres., says "Col. Copinger 'the dog-worshipper' has sent four more of his *Eastern Tales*"; cf. no. 5101. Trans. by **Henry Copinger,** prob.—cf. no. 5101.

5238   Jottings from an examiner's note-book, 337–345.

5239   Joaquin Miller's *Songs of the Sierras*, 346–355.

5240   A sketch from Portugal and Aragon, 356–368.

5241   *The Service of the Poor* [on religious sisterhoods], 369–383. (See no. 5258.)

5242   The imperial connection, from an Australian colonist's point of view, 384–402. **W. Jardine Smith.** Signed.

VOLUME 84 O.S., 4 N.S., OCTOBER 1871

5243   The English statesman's imperial question, 403–416.

5244   As to the decoration of St. Paul's Cathedral, 417–425. Signed: An Architect.

5245   On the condition of the working classes, 426–440. **Thomas Wright,** the "Journeyman Engineer." Signed; repr. *Masters.*

5246   Two German schools [Gymnasium and Real Schule], 446–457. Signed: E.E.M.

5247   Rambles (No. XIV): at Edinburgh, 458–480. **William Allingham.** Evidence for no. 4807.

5248   The proposed Roman Catholic university for Ireland, 481–491. **James Macdonell.** Signed M.; cf. no. 5072 with same initial on very similar subject.

5249   Concerning John's Indian affairs (Part II), 492–511. **Robert H. Elliot.** Evidence for no. 5229.

5250   Evidence: historical, religious, and scientific, 512–524. **Frances P. Verney.** Repr. *Peasant Properties*, II.

5251   French politics, 525–536. **Léon Veer.** Signed.

VOLUME 84 O.S., 4 N.S., NOVEMBER 1871

5252   Reports on the military forces of Prussia and the North German Confederation, 1868–1870 (Part I), 537–562. **Eugène G. H. C. Stoffel.** Assigned in Contents to Baron Stoffel; see *LCCat.* Trans. with an intro. note by **C. E. H. Vincent**—signed.

5253   The Lofoden Islands, 563–574. **Edmund W. Gosse.** Signed; repr. *Studies.*

5254   The story of Alcestis [on William Morris's and Robert Browning's adaptations], 575–585. **Horace M. Moule.** Signed.

5255   The trial of Mary Stuart, sometime Queen of Scots (Part I), 586–605. **John Skelton.** Signed as edited by Shirley; attr. in intro. note to Dionysius Diamond, another pseudonym; repr. *Essays.*

5256   Epicureanism, ancient and modern, 606–617. **Francis W. Newman.** Signed; repr. *Miscellanies*, V.

5257   A pilgrimage on the Ammer, 618–637. **Moncure D. Conway.** Signed M.D.C.; see *Autobiography*, II, 227.

5258   Sisters and sisterhoods [partly a reply to no. 5241], 638–649. Signed: An English Roman Catholic.

5259   Mr. D. Wilder, of Boston, U.S., on gold and currency, 653–670. **Bonamy Price.** Signed.

VOLUME 84 O.S., 4 N.S., DECEMBER 1871

5260   Reports on the military forces of Prussia (Part II, concl.), 671–694. **E. G. H. C. Stoffel.** Evidence for no. 5252.

5261   The Anglicani and their XXXIX medical formulae [satire on Church of England], 695–708.

5262   Wanted: a religion for the Hindoos,

709–726. **Robert H. Elliot.** Signed R.H.E.—see no. 5229.

5263 Trial of Mary Stuart (Part II, concl.), 727–745. **John Skelton.** Evidence for no. 5255.

5264 Rambles (No. XV): in Scotland, 746–764. **William Allingham.** Evidence for no. 4807.

5265 The constitution of Sweden, 765–775. Signed: T., but complete initials prob. W.D.T.: see no. 6074.

5266 Papal Ireland, 776–792.

5267 Modern seamanship, 793–801. **William Dawson.** Signed as in no. 5226.

VOLUME 85 O.S., 5 N.S., JANUARY 1872

5268 Political prospects [largely on Gladstone], 1–16.

5269 The fate of the "Jardin d'Acclimatation" during the late sieges of Paris, 17–22. **Richard Owen.** Signed Zoologus; *Life,* II, 372.

5270 On certitude in religious assent: a letter to the author of an article in the *Dublin Review* for Apr. 1871 [by W. G. Ward: see *DR* no. 1348], 23–42. **J. F. Stephen.** Signed F.; Stephen list.

5271 A few October days, 43–54. **A. K. H. Boyd.** Signed A.K.H.B.; repr. *Landscapes.*

5272 The Irish university question, 55–64. **Keningale Cook?** Signed An Irish Graduate; Cook was unable to go to Oxford for financial reasons, and therefore took a B.A. at Trin. Coll. Dublin, "crossing St. George's Channel for each examination" [*Biograph,* 2 (1879), 39]; he contributed to *FM* in 1871 (see no. 5225) and also, according to *Biograph,* p. 44, in 1872; in the art., p. 56, the author stops to describe the role of non-resident students at T.C.D., quoting the specific requirement of "paying eight visits to Dublin, and passing eight term-examinations"—a point that has no bearing on the central theme; the latter is the financial difficulty preventing many Irish students from attending their own universities.

5273 Perfidious woman, 65–77.

5274 A new survey of the northern heavens, 78–91. **Richard A. Proctor.** Signed; repr. *Mysteries of Time and Space,* 1883.

5275 Laing's *Sir David Lyndsay,* 92–104. **Alexander Falconer.** Signed.

5276 The early life of Charles Dickens [on Forster's biography], 105–113. Unidentified. Langstaff's "Bibliography" credits

Andrew Lang with a contribution to this issue; the other unassigned arts. seem unlikely; Lang wrote on Dickens in *Good Words,* 1888, and the *Fortnightly,* 1898.

5277 Von Moltke's *Letters from Turkey, 1835–1839,* 114–130.

VOLUME 85 O.S., 5 N.S., FEBRUARY 1872

5278 The drink traffic and the Permissive Bill, 131–147. **Francis William Newman.** Signed.

5279 Notes on East Greenland, 148–155. **Adolf Pansch,** prob. Signed A. Pansch, M.D., of the German Arctic Expedition of 1869–70; see *BMCat.*

5280 Religion as a fine art, 156–168. **Leslie Stephen.** Signed L.S.; repr. *Free Thinking.*

5281 The burgomaster's family; or, Weal and woe in a little world (chaps. i–iv), 169–192. **E. C. W. van Gobie.** Signed Christine Müller; see *BMCat.*; novel published under pseudonym, 1873. Translated by **John Shaw Lefevre**—signed.

5282 Concerning John's Indian affairs (Part III, concl.), 193–205. **Robert H. Elliot.** Evidence for no. 5229.

5283 Ireland's experiences of Home Rule, 206–217.

5284 On longevity, 218–233. **Richard Owen.** Signed; *Life,* II, 372. (See no. 5338.)

5285 An American on representation [Simon Sterne], 234–241. **Millicent G. Fawcett.** Signed M.G.F.; repr. Fawcett, *Essays.*

5286 The Kriegsspiel, 242–245.

5287 The Mahometan revival, 246–260. **W. Gifford Palgrave.** Signed; repr. *Eastern Questions.*

VOLUME 85 O.S., 5 N.S., MARCH 1872

5288 The new royal warrants [army reform], 261–276.

5289 A French anarchist [P. J. Proudhon], 277–288.

5290 Tea-planting in India, and the Lewshai tribes, 289–295.

5291 The new Irish Land Law, 296–309. Signed: L.

5292 The burgomaster's family (chaps. v–vii), 310–330. **E. C. W. van Gobie.** Evidence for no. 5281.

5293 Recent publications bearing on the War [Franco-Prussian] (Part I), 331–340. **C. E. H. Vincent?** Page 333 refers to no. 5252 which was trans. by Vincent; this art. which contains many trans. from other French publications, opens with a comment that the "Special Correspondent" phase of the War is finished: Vincent had been a special correspondent for the Daily Telegraph in 1871, but rejoined his regiment in 1872 (see *Life of Sir Howard Vincent* by S. H. Jeyes [1912], pp. 22–23, 33).

5294 The city of the monk [Munich], 341–359. **M. D. Conway.** Burtis list; cited in no. 5366, p. 609.

5295 The new Hindoo theism, 360–369. **Robert H. Elliot.** Signed R.H.E.—see no. 5229.

5296 Taine's *English Literature*, 370–380.

5297 The American case under the *Alabama* claims, 381–394. **Henry Ottley.** Signed H.O.; pp. 382–383 and 385 were largely reprinted, partly verbatim, in Ottley's *On the Errors and Mischiefs of Modern Diplomacy* (1872), pp. 81–83, 84, 87, 108–109.

VOLUME 85 O.S., 5 N.S., APRIL 1872

5298 The assassination of Lord Mayo, 395–408. **Robert H. Elliot.** Signed.

5299 Darwinism and divinity, 409–421. **Leslie Stephen.** Signed L.S.; repr. *Free Thinking.*

5300 The interview at Aubervilliers [on the Commune], 422–429. **G. P. Cluseret.** Signed General Cluseret; letters of Froude, *Journal of the Rutgers University Library*, 11 (Dec. 1947), 6–8.

5301 The burgomaster's family (chap. viii), 430–447. **E. C. W. van Gobie.** Evidence for no. 5281.

5302 Monks of La Trappe [in Belgium], 448–460. **John Macdonald.** Signed, with title "M.A."

5303 Torpedoes, 461–476. **E. R. Freemantle.** Signed E.R.F.—see no. 5161; he later wrote on this subject in *Nineteenth Century*, Oct. 1885, and *Blackwood's*, Apr. 1887.

5304 Parisiana, 477–490.

5305 John Hookham Frere, 491–510.

5306 The story of the pretended de Caille, 511–524.

VOLUME 85 O.S., 5 N.S., MAY 1872

5307 Irish nationality, 525–540. Signed: A.C.

5308 Antoine Wiertz, 541–552. **Frederika Richardson,** prob. Signed F. Richardson; Richard Garnett to Allingham, May 9, 1872, Allingham Corres., is glad to see

"Miss Richardson's paper at last"; see *BMCat.*

5309 Recent publications bearing on the War (Part II, concl.), 553–569. **C. E. Howard Vincent?** Cf. no. 5293.

5310 The burgomaster's family (chaps. ix–x), 570–587. **E. C. W. van Gobie.** Evidence for no. 5281.

5311 Novelties in [Pre-Raphaelite] poetry and criticism, 588–596.

5312 Reorganisation of the army, 597–611. **G. R. Gleig.** Signed.

5313 Recollections of a winter in Brazil, 612–622. **F. W. Longman.** Signed.

5314 American traits, 632–638. Signed: W.C.M.

5315 Mazzini, 639–650. **John Sale Barker.** Signed.

VOLUME 85 O.S., 5 N.S., JUNE 1872

5316 The agricultural strike, 651–666.

5317 *Kalevala*; or, The Finnish national epic, 667–677. **Andrew Lang.** Signature; repr. *Custom and Myth*, 1884.

5318 *Voltaire* [by John Morley], 678–691. **Leslie Stephen.** Signed L.S.; Ullmann, list, p. 244.

5319 The Historical Manuscripts Commission (No. I), 696–713. **John Piggot, Junior.** Signed. (No. II is no. 5494.)

5320 The burgomaster's family (chaps. xi–xiii), 714–736. **E. C. W. van Gobie.** Evidence for no. 5281.

5321 The duties of the State, 737–750. **J. Herbert Stack.** Signed in Contents.

5322 The misadventures of Mr. Catlyne, Q.C., an autobiography (chaps. i–iv), 751–767. **Martin Francis Mahony.** Signed Matthew Stradling, Author of *Cheap John's Auction*, etc.—H&L, I, 323; novel published 1873.

5323 The unsettlement of the *Alabama* claims, 768–781. **Thomas G. Bowles.** Signed in Contents.

VOLUME 86 O.S., 6 N.S., JULY 1872

5324 Commercial bribery and corruption, 1–10.

5325 Clever fishes, 11–20. **Francis Francis.** Signed.

5326 The Royal Academy Exhibition, 21–30. **W. F. Pollock.** FitzGerald, *Letters*, I, 341–342.

5327 My connection with Fenianism, 31–46. **G. P. Cluseret.** Signed G. Cluseret; claimed in Cluseret to Froude, May 8,

1872, Froude Collection, Beinecke Lib., Yale Univ.

5328 The burgomaster's family (chaps. xiv–xv), 47–66. **E. C. W. van Gobie.** Evidence for no. 5281.

5329 Of competitive examination and selection thereby, 67–73. **A. K. H. Boyd.** Signed A.K.H.B.; repr. *Landscapes.*

5330 From Cairo to Athens, 74–87. **Matilda Betham-Edwards.** Signature.

5331. Rahel and Varnhagen von Ense, 88–101. **Kate Vaughan Jennings.** Signed.

5332 The misadventures of Mr. Catlyne (chaps. v–vii), 102–116. **Martin F. Mahony.** Evidence for no. 5322.

5333 Rambles (No. XVI): at Canterbury, 117–134. **William Allingham.** Evidence for no. 4807.

VOLUME 86 O.S., 6 N.S., AUGUST 1872

5334 The disestablished Church in Ireland, 135–149.

5335 Social macadamisation, 150–168. **Leslie Stephen.** Signed L.S.; Ullmann list, p. 244.

5336 Donna Olimpia Maldachini: "Olim pia; nunc o l'impia," 169–184.

5337 The misadventures of Mr. Catlyne (chaps. viii–xi), 185–200. **Martin F. Mahony.** Evidence for no. 5322.

5338 The longevity of the patriarchs [with comments on no. 5284], 201–206.

5339 The burgomaster's family (chaps. xvi–xviii), 209–232. **E. C. G. van Gobie.** Evidence for no. 5281.

5340 The pronunciation of Latin, 233–243. **Danby Fry?** Signed D.F.; a learned linguistic art.; man cited was a member of the Philological Society: see *DNB.*

5341 Hananda, the miracle worker, 244–250. **Richard Garnett,** 1835–1906. Signed R.G.; full name in Contents; repr. *Twilight of Gods.*

5342 *Sir Henry Lawrence,* 251–264.

VOLUME 86 O.S., 6 N.S., SEPTEMBER 1872

5343 Strikes, short hours, poor-law, and *laissez-faire,* 265–281. **W. R. Greg.** Signed W.R.G.—see no. 4552.

5344 A pilgrimage to Port-Royal, 282–295.

5345 The legend of the monkey; from the Chinese, 296–309. **Miss H. E. Wodehouse.** Intro. note, signed H. E. Wodehouse, shows author adapted and translated the legend; another Chinese legend three years later (see *CM* no. 1463 in

Index, I) was by woman cited. (See no. 5475.)

5346 Domestic life and economy in France, 310–317. Signed: G.E.

5347 The burgomaster's family (chaps. xix–xxi), 318–340. **E. C. W. van Gobie.** Evidence for no. 5281.

5348 *Servia,* 341–356. **Francis Dwyer.** Signed D.; Contents gives "Major F. Dwyer"; see no. 5126 and Allibone.

5349 Our great-grandmothers; or, Sketches from Montagu House (Parts I–II), 357–374. **Julia C. Busk Byrne.** Signed The Author of *Flemish Interiors*—see H&L, II, 302.

5350 The misadventures of Mr. Catlyne (chaps. xii–xv), 375–390. **Martin F. Mahony.** Evidence for no. 5322.

5351 Premier and president, 391–398. **Nathan Sheppard,** prob. Signed An American; attr. in *Athenaeum,* Sept. 7, 1872, p. 305.

VOLUME 86 O.S., 6 N.S., OCTOBER 1872

5352 Peasant proprietors, 399–414.

5353 Luxury, 415–434. Signed: A. W.

5354 Norwegian poetry since 1814, 435–449. **Edmund W. Gosse.** Signed; repr. *Studies.*

5355 The burgomaster's family (chaps. xxii–xxiv, concl.), 450–473. **E. C. W. van Gobie.** Evidence for no. 5281.

5356 Horace Greeley, 474–490. **M. D. Conway.** Signed M.D.C.; Burtis list; Froude to Conway, Sept. 19, n.y., Huntington Lib., will correct parts of art. on Greeley.

5357 The Irish Roman Catholic laity, 491–496. **Thomas Croskery.** Signed T.C.; see no. 5845; that is also on Ireland, as are his arts. in *Edin. Rev.* (see *Index,* I, Part B); this essay is clearly by a Protestant: see *DNB.*

5358 The public lands of the United States, 497–504. Signed: W.C.M.

5359 The misadventures of Mr. Catlyne (chaps. xvi–xvii, concl.), 505–523. **Martin F. Mahony.** Evidence for no. 5322.

5360 With a trout rod, 524–532. **M. G. Watkins.** Signed.

VOLUME 86 O.S., 6 N.S., NOVEMBER 1872

5361 Autumn manoeuvres, 533–544. **G. R. Gleig.** Signed.

5362 A bad five minutes in the Alps, 545–561. **Leslie Stephen.** Repr. *Free Thinking.*

5363 The Panthays of Yün-nan, 562–571.

William Frederick Mayers. Signed W.F.M.; attr. in *DNB*.

5364 Our great-grandmothers (Parts III–IV, concl.), 572–585. **Julia C. B. Byrne.** Evidence for no. 5349.

5365 Movements in the star-depths, 586–595. **Richard A. Proctor.** Signed.

5366 Demonology (Parts I–II), 596–613. **M. D. Conway.** Signed in Contents; Burtis list.

5367 Dr. Livingstone, 614–627. **L. J. Procter.** Signed.

5368 *New Tales from the Norse*, 629–640. **W. R. S. Ralston.** Signed.

5369 Mis-education, 641–650. **Thomas Wright,** the "Journeyman Engineer." Signed; repr. *Masters*.

5370 Six months of prefecture under Gambetta, 651–666. **Camille Barrère.** Signed at start An Ex-Secretary, at end C.B.; attr. in *Athenaeum*, Nov. 16, 1872, p. 637.

VOLUME 86 O.S., 6 N.S., DECEMBER 1872

5371 Empire or no empire? 667–685. **W. Jardine Smith.** Signed at start A Colonist, at end W.J.S.; on p. 669 author says he wrote no. 5242.

5372 Without a guide [at Oxford], 686–696. Signed: E.P.

5373 Demonology (Parts III–IV, concl.), 697–719. **M. D. Conway.** Evidence for no. 5366.

5374 Six weeks in North and South Tyrol, 720–731. **William Longman.** Signed, with title "F.G.S."

5375 The Irish Brigade in the service of France, 1698–1791, 732–740.

5376 The true school for architects, 743–750. Signed: C.

5377 Possibilities of free religious thought in Scotland, 751–769.

5378 Concerning the disadvantages of living in a small community, 770–774. **A. K. H. Boyd.** Signed A.K.H.B.; repr. *Landscapes*.

5379 Domestic sanitary arrangements, 775–781. **Robert Rawlinson.** Signed.

5380 Behind the scenes at the Commune, 782–801. **G. P. Cluseret.** Signed General Cluseret at start, G. C. at end; cf. no. 5300.

VOLUME 87 O.S., 7 N.S., JANUARY 1873

5381 Address by J. A. Froude delivered November 30, in the Association Hall, New York [in answer to Father Thomas N. Burke], 1–21. **J. A. Froude.** Title.

5382 New edition of *The Paston Letters*, 22–26. **Lucy Toulmin Smith.** Signed L. Toulmin Smith; see *DNB*, 2nd suppl.

5383 A visit to Shamyl's country [the Caucasus] in the autumn of 1870, 27–42. **Edwin Ransom.** Signed, with titles F.R.A.S. and F.R.G.S.

5384 Some curiosities of criticism, 43–51. **William Allingham.** Repr. *Varieties*, III.

5385 Thorwaldsen in Copenhagen and in Rome, 52–66. **J. Beavington Atkinson.** Signed; repr. *Art Tour to Northern Capitals of Europe*, 1873.

5386 Of alienation, 67–73. **A. K. H. Boyd.** Signed A.K.H.B.; repr. *Landscapes*.

5387 Shaftesbury's *Characteristics*, 76–93. **Leslie Stephen.** Signed L.S.; full name in Contents; repr. *Free Thinking*.

5388 A sketch of M. Thiers, 94–100. Signed: S.

5389 On prisons; some observations on the International Prison Congress held in London from July 3 to 13, 1872, 101–108. **Walter Crofton.** Signed, with titles "The Right Hon. Sir" and "C.B."

5390 Dulwich College, 109–115. **J. G. Fitch.** Signed F.; attr. in A. L. Lilly, *Sir Joshua Fitch* (1906), p. 256.

5391 Hereditary improvement, 116–130. **Francis Galton.** Signed.

VOLUME 87 O.S., 7 N.S., FEBRUARY 1873

5392 The Dominion of Canada, 131–155. **Cyril Graham.** Signed in Contents.

5393 Wittenberg and Cologne, 156–159. **Alexander Schwartz.** Signed A.S.; Contents gives "Dr. Schwartz"; for Schwartz's interest in Germany, see *Index*, I, 1077.

5394 Justices of the Peace, 160–170. **John Roland Phillips?** Signed J.R.P.; man cited was a barrister and magistrate (see Boase) and later a known contributor to *FM*.

5395 Jagannath and his worship, 171–179. **Alexander Allardyce,** prob. Signed A.A.; Allardyce was a journalist in India, 1868–1875 or 1876 (see *DNB*, 1st suppl.), also writing on India for English journals (see *Index*, I, 791); his piece in the *Cornhill Mag.*, no. 1544 (see *Index*, I), was, like this one, a story of human sacrifice in India.

5396 *Charles de Montalembert* [by Mrs. Oliphant], 180–189.

5397 A sketch of Charles Lever, 190–196.

William John Fitzpatrick. Signed W.J.F.; man cited published a life of Lever, 1879.

5398 Daily work in a north-west district, 197–208. Signed in Contents: An Indian Official.

5399 Plymouth: the story of a town, 209–221. **Richard John King.** Signed.

5400 The original prophet [Joseph Smith], 225–235. **Charles Marshall.** Signed at start A Visitor to Salt Lake City, at end C.M.; cf. no. 5207.

5401 Suggestions towards making better of it, 236–244. **A. K. H. Boyd.** Signed A.K.H.B.; repr. *Landscapes.*

5402 The *Peking Gazette* (Part I), 245–256. **Rutherford Alcock.** Signed, with titles "Sir" and "K.C.B."

5403 Guns and armour, 257–264. **William Dawson.** Signed.

VOLUME 87 O.S., 7 N.S., MARCH 1873

5404 The transfer of land [in Ireland], 265–278. **Arthur Arnold.** Signed; repr. *Social Politics*, 1878.

5405 A plea for Black Bartholomew, 279–292. **James Macdonell.** Signed.

5406 Causes of the friction between the United States and England, 293–303. **Nathan Sheppard,** prob. Signed The Author of "Premier and President"—see no. 5351.

5407 A few words on philology, 304–321. Signed: M.T.

5408 The coming transit of Venus, and British preparations for observing it, 322–331. **Richard A. Proctor.** Signed.

5409 Our seamen [and the ships they sail], 332–340.

5410 *The Peking Gazette* (Part II, concl.), 341–357. **Rutherford Alcock.** Signed.

5411 The Paris Commune of 1871: its origin, legitimacy, tendency, and aim, 360–384. **G. P. Cluseret.** Signed at start as in no. 5300, and at end as in no. 5327.

5412 The Irish schoolmaster and the Irish priest, 385–390. Signed: J.J.S.

VOLUME 87 O.S., 7 N.S., APRIL 1873

5413 The story of the death of Thomas, Earl of Strafford, A.D. 1641, 391–408. **Reginald F. D. Palgrave.** Signed.

5414 Ought government to buy the railways? 409–421. Signed: B.

5415 Episodes in the life of a musician, 422–441. **Matilda Betham-Edwards.** Signature.

5416 Stanley's *Lectures on the Church of Scotland*, 442–457. **Alexander Falconer.** Signed.

5417 On some gradations in the forms of animal life, 458–476.

5418 The late Lady Becher, 477–481. **William John Fitzpatrick.** Signed W.J.F.; cf. no. 5397, so signed and another biographical sketch of an Irish figure; see *MWT*, 10th ed.

5419 Mr. Buckle's contribution to the new philosophy of history, 482–499. **J. S. Stuart-Glennie.** Signed.

5420 A peep at ancient Etruria, 500–513.

5421 The Irish University question—attempts at legislation, 514–524.

VOLUME 87 O.S., 7 N.S., MAY 1873

5422 Lectures on Mr. Darwin's philosophy of language (No. I), 525–541. **Friedrich Max Müller.** Signature.

5423 Peasantry of the south of England (Part I), 542–558. **George Jennings Davies.** Signed A Wykehamist; the Rev. George J. Davies to J. E. Thorold Rogers, Apr. 10, 1873, Rogers Papers: "I am writing on the present agricultural position—of which you will see somewhat in the next number of Fraser"; Davies used "A Wykehamist" as his pseudonym for a book in 1861 (see *BMCat.*) and in 1873 was vicar of Timsbury near Winchester (*CCD/76*).

5424 Gerard de Nerval, 1810–1855, 559–566. **Andrew Lang.** Signed.

5425 A "note" of interrogation, 567–577. **Florence Nightingale.** Signed.

5426 Over the marches of civilised Europe [the Balkans], 578–596. Signed: A.E.

5427 Present aspects of the labour question, 597–604. Signed at start: An Artisan, at end: W.S.

5428 Vienna, 605–619. **M. D. Conway.** Signed in Contents.

5429 On the regeneration of Sunday, 620–630. **F. W. Newman.** Signed.

5430 The Jesuits, and their expulsion from Germany, 631–646.

5431 Bodley and the Bodleian, 647–658. **Richard John King.** Signed.

VOLUME 87 O.S., 7 N.S., JUNE 1873

5432 Lectures on Mr. Darwin's philosophy of language (No. II), 659–678. **Friedrich Max Müller.** Signature.

5433 Peasantry of the south of England

(Part II), 679–692. **George Jennings Davies.** Evidence for no. 5423.

5434 A week of camp life in India, 693–701. Signed: An English Lady.

5435 On the extension of railways in America, 702–712. **John W. Cross.** Repr. *Impressions.*

5436 *The Fable of the Bees* [by Mandeville], 713–727. **Leslie Stephen.** Signed L.S.; full name in Contents; repr. *Free Thinking.*

5437 The workmen of Paris during the siege (Part I), 728–737. **Jean de Bouteiller,** prob. Signed J. de Bouteiller; see *Bib. Nat.Cat.* for man cited, a translator of English books.

5438 Principal Tulloch, *Rational Theology and Christian Philosophy*, 738–749. **Robert E. Bartlett,** prob. Signed B—see no. 5822; much of the evidence for no. 6033 applies to this art.: see especially pp. 740, 741, 744 cols. i–ii.

5439 The coming transit of Venus, and foreign preparations for observing it, 750–759. **Richard A. Proctor.** Signed.

5440 The ethics of St. Paul, 760–777. **Alexander Schwartz.** Signed A.S.—see nos. 5393, 5488.

5441 Our Irish policy, 778–789.

VOLUME 88 O.S., 8 N.S., JULY 1873

5442 Lectures on Mr. Darwin's philosophy of language (No. III, concl.), 1–24. **Friedrich Max Müller.** Signature.

5443 A sub-"note of interrogation" [sequel to no. 5425] (Part I; no more published): what will be our religion in 1999? 25–36. **Florence Nightingale.** Signed.

5444 Froissart's *Chronicles*, 37–49. **J. F. Stephen.** Stephen list.

5445 A turn through Gaelic Ireland in 1872, 50–56. **John Francis Campbell.** Signed J. F. Campbell, Author of *Popular Tales of the West Highlands*: see *DNB.*

5446 Peasantry of the south of England (Part III, concl.), 57–73. **George Jennings Davies.** Evidence for no. 5423.

5447 Royal Academy Exhibition [1873], 74–85. **W. F. Pollock.** Signed P.; FitzGerald, *Letters*, I, 358.

5448 *Liberty, Equality, Fraternity* [by J. F. Stephen], 86–97. Signed: F.P. This may well be Frederick Pollock, 1845–1937, who began writing about this time on philosophy, politics, and jurisprudence; his father was an old contributor to *FM.*

5449 A visit to Cashmere, 98–113. Signed: A Captain in Her Majesty's Service.

5450 *Literature and Dogma* [by Matthew Arnold], 114–134. **F. W. Newman.** Signed.

VOLUME 88 O.S., 8 N.S., AUGUST 1873

5451 Our food supply and the Game Laws, 135–147.

5452 *The Life and Teachings of Mohammed*, 148–157. **F. W. Newman.** Signed.

5453 A visit to Ireland at election time, 158–171.

5454 The workmen of Paris between the two sieges (Part II, concl.), 175–190. **Jean de Bouteiller,** prob. Cf. no. 5437.

5455 The relation of metaphysics to literature and science, 191–200. **John Stuart Blackie.** Signed.

5456 A singer from Killarney [Alfred Perceval Graves], 201–206. **George Barnett Smith.** Signed.

5457 The functions of government in India, 207–211. Signed: S.

5458 Mr. Dixon's *History of Two Queens*, 212–225. **Joseph Knight.** Signed.

5459 The fourrière [Paris bureau of lost and found], 226–232. **Julia C. B. Byrne.** Signed The Author of *Flemish Interiors* —see no. 5349.

5460 Lucian, 233–249. **C. G. Prowett.** Signed.

5461 British merchant seamen, 250–261. **William Dawson.** Signed.

5462 Of growing old, 262–272. **A. K. H. Boyd.** Signed A.K.H.B.; repr. *Landscapes.*

VOLUME 88 O.S., 8 N.S., SEPTEMBER 1873

5463 A policy for Ireland, 273–283.

5464 St. Paul's Cathedral, 284–297. **Charles Locke Eastlake,** 1836–1906. Signed C. L. Eastlake; first name added in Contents.

5465 MacConglinny's vision; a humorous satire, translated from the original Irish in the "Leabhar Brec," a manuscript transcribed about the year 1400 [with translator's intro. note], 298–323. **W. M. Hennessy,** trans. Signed, p. 299.

5466 Birds of the Humber, 324–337. **M. G. Watkins.** Signed.

5467 Prayer, miracle, and natural law; from a theological point of view, 338–347. **Leonard Woolsey Bacon.** Signed.

5468 Mrs. Archer Clive, 348–352. Signed: H.A. After Mrs. Clive's sudden death,

Froude wrote Allingham, July 23, 1873, Allingham Corres.: "Will you write a few pages about her, taking *Paul Ferroll* and the *Poems* by V. as a text," reminding him that she had once contributed to *FM*; on Aug. 14 he had received a MS. of "the notice of Mrs. Clive," and asked for more extracts to be included; "H.A." might be a printer's error for "W.A.," or it might stand for Hugh Allingham, William's half-brother, who wrote *Ballyshannon* in 1879; Allingham did not marry Helen Paterson until 1874.

5469   The Central Asian question, 335–365.

5470   The story of the Woodhouselee ghost; an incident in Scottish history, 366–382. **William Williamson,** and **David Ker?** The postscript, 381–382, signed D.K., shows that D.K. wrote the art. from materials "collected by the late Mr. W. Williamson," who is described as a partner "in a large mercantile house in the City"; a William Williamson was a partner ·in Wyllie, James & Co., 13 Leadenhall Street (*London Directory*, 1872); the "D.K." who published *The Broken Image and Other Tales*, Edin., 1870, is identified with a ? in the *BMCat.* as the second man cited.

5471   The Protestant restoration in France in the last century, 383–398. **James Macdonell.** Signed M.—see nos. 4833, 5675.

VOLUME 88 o.s., 8 n.s., OCTOBER 1873

5472   Irish Orangeism: its past and its future, 399–417. **George Whyte-Melville,** prob. Signed M. or N.; Whyte-Melville published a novel entitled *M., or N.* in 1869; a note, p. 417, by **J. A. Froude**—signed Ed. *F.M.*, shows that "M. or N." was a single contributor.

5473   Gravelotte revisited, 418–432. **M. D. Conway.** Assigned in Contents.

5474   The Indian civil service (Part I): what it is, 433–446. Unidentified. Parts II and III are signed: Y.

5475   The dragon's head: being the conclusion of "The legend of the monkey [no. 5345]", 447–463. **Miss H. E. Wodehouse.** Evidence for no. 5345.

5476   Apuleius, 464–482. **C. G. Prowett.** Signed.

5477   The naval war game, 483–493. **William Dawson.** Signed.

5478   Some elements of the land question, 494–507.

5479   *Lombard Street* [by Walter Bagehot], 508–528. **Bonamy Price.** Signed.

VOLUME 88 o.s., 8 n.s., NOVEMBER 1873

5480   Jonathan Edwards, 529–551. **Leslie Stephen.** Signed; repr. *Hours,* I.

5481   The Indian civil service (Part II): what it does, 552–566. Signed: Y.

5482   St. Symeon Salos, 567–574. **Sabine Baring-Gould.** Signed as in no. 4912, with titles "Rev. . . . M.A."

5483   The authorship of the *Odyssey,* 575–592. **Francis W. Newman.** Signed; repr. *Miscellanies,* V.

5484   Sissipara; an Indian mountain sketch, 593–599. **M. J. Walhouse.** Signed M.J.W.; man cited was civil servant in India (see Part B, below); cf. signature of no. 6006.

5485   A proposed reform of the English constitution, 600–607. Signed in Contents: A Colonist [in Australia: see p. 600].

5486   Pilgrimages and Catholicism in France, 608–614. **Camille Barrère.** Signed.

5487   British policy in Persia and Central Asia, 615–630. **Henry Ottley.** Signed.

5488   The new birth, according to St. Paul, 631–647. **Alexander Schwartz.** Signed A. S.; Contents gives "Dr. A. Schwartz"; cf. no. 5393.

5489   Into ballad-land [Scotland], 648–662. **M. G. Watkins.** Signed; repr. *In the Country.*

VOLUME 88 o.s., 8 n.s., DECEMBER 1873

5490   John Stuart Mill [on his *Autobiography*], 663–681. **Abraham Hayward.** Attr. in Kate Russell to Helen Taylor, Dec. 7, 1873, Mill-Taylor Collection, British Lib. of Pol. and Econ. Science, London School of Econ., Box XIX, item 61.

5491   St. Nicolas of Trani, 682–686. **Sabine Baring-Gould.** Signed as in no. 4912.

5492   The future of farming, 687–697. **Richard Jefferies.** Signed.

5493   A trip into Bosnia, 698–713. **Humphry Sandwith.** Signed.

5494   The Historical Manuscripts Commission (No. II): third report, 714–727. **John Piggot.** Signed. (No. I is no. 5319; No. III is no. 5656.)

5495   Of quarrelsome folk, 728–738. **A. K. H. Boyd.** Signed A.K.H.B.; repr. *Landscapes.*

5496   A review of Spanish struggles for liberty, 739–756. **Alexander Johnstone Wilson,** prob. Signed A.J.W.—see no. 5849; his special field was trade and finance, but he also wrote on politics.

5497   A Cutcherry intrigue [in India], 757–763. Signed: Y.

5498 The child of miracle [the Count de Chambord], 764–772.

5499 The folk-lore of Devonshire, 773–785. **Richard John King.** Signed.

VOLUME 89 O.S., 9 N.S., JANUARY 1874

5500 The Home Rule Conference, 1–13.

5501 *The Convents of the United Kingdom*, 14–24.

5502 Archbishop Laud, 25–41. **Peter Bayne.** Repr. *Chief Actors in the Puritan Revolution*, 1878.

5503 Original letters of Bernardo Tasso; a chapter of Italian history, 42–54. **George F. Goddard,** prob. Signed G.; Froude to Allingham, Nov. 20, [1873], Allingham Corres. says Goddard writes that he has heard from him [Allingham] about his Tasso; man cited wrote on Italian subjects: see *BMCat.*

5504 An artist's dream, 55–60. **W. F. Pollock,** prob. Signed P.—see no. 5447, on same subject.

5505 Rambles (No. XVII): London Bridge to Cabourg, 61–77. **William Allingham.** Evidence for no. 4807.

5506 The Patarines of Milan, 78–99. **Sabine Baring-Gould.** Signed as in no. 4912.

5507 The future of the agricultural labourers' emigration, 100–111. **John W. Cross.** Signed; repr. *Impressions.*

5508 The restoration of the Moghul buildings at Agra, 112–115. **G. R. Aberigh-Mackay.** Signed G.R.A.-M.; man cited professor of Eng. lit. at the Delhi Coll. at this time: see Buckland.

5509 Three days in Sark, 116–123. **William Forsyth.** Signed; repr. *Essays*, 1874.

5510 The Ashantee war unnecessary and unjust, 124–134. **Thomas Gibson Bowles.** Signed. (Note, p. 268, signed **Thomas Gibson Bowles.**)

VOLUME 89 O.S., 9 N.S., FEBRUARY 1874

5511 John Smith's shanty, 135–149. **Richard Jefferies.** Signed; repr. *The Toilers of the Field*, 1892.

5512 A Christmas in India, 150–156. **M. J. Walhouse.** Signed M.J.W.—see no. 5484.

5513 Petronius Arbiter, 157–173.

5514 The present condition of Norway, 174–185. **Edmund W. Gosse.** Signed.

5515 The Christian Brothers [Jesuits] and their lesson-books, 186–199.

5516 Woman's place in the economy of creation, 200–209. **Mary Francis Cusack.** Signed M. F. Cusack; attr. to "Miss

Cusack, 'the Nun of Kenmare,' " p. 779; see *BMCat.*

5517 Rambles (No. XVIII): from Cabourg to St. Malo, 210–226. **William Allingham.** Evidence for no. 4807.

5518 The *Gripis-Spa*: from the *Elder Edda*, 227–234. **Andrew Lang.** Signed A.L.; attr. by Falconer, *Writings of Lang*, p. 18.

5519 Modern comedy, 235–244. Signed: F. Possibly Percy Fitzgerald who, in *Principles of Comedy and Dramatic Effect* (1870), chap. ii, had adopted a similar critical position.

5520 Idle days in the High Alps, 245–248. **J. F. Hardy.** Signed.

5521 The religious question in Switzerland, 249–267. **G. P. Cluseret.** Signed G. Cluseret; Contents gives "General Cluseret": cf. no. 5411. (See no. 5529.)

VOLUME 89 O.S., 9 N.S., MARCH 1874

5522 The turn of the [political] tide: what does it mean? 269–280.

5523 Salmon fishing, 281–292. **M. G. Watkins.** Signed.

5524 The Indian civil service (Part III, concl.): what it does, 293–311. Signed: Y.

5525 Stone monuments of Sardinia: their mysterious origin and destination, 312–322. **S. P. Oliver.** Signed; repr. *Nuragghi Sardi, and Other Non-historic Stone Structures of the Mediterranean Basin*, Dublin, 1875.

5526 University endowments, 323–335. **Leslie Stephen.** Ullmann list.

5527 The Teutonic and the Celtic epic: *The Nibelungen Lied* and the *Tain bo Cuailgne*, 336–354. **Alexander G. Richey.** Signed A. G. Richey; Contents gives first name.

5528 German minne-singers on the struggle between Kaiser and Pope, 355–363.

5529 The Old Catholic movement in Western or "Romande" Switzerland [sequel to no. 5521] (Part I), 364–376. **G. P. Cluseret.** Signed as in no. 5327.

5530 Idols of society, 377–388. **Maria G. Grey.** Signed M. G. Grey; called "Mrs. Grey" in Contents; see *DNB*, 2nd suppl.

5531 The Irish elections, 389–402.

VOLUME 89 O.S., 9 N.S., APRIL 1874

5532 Germany and the Papacy, 403–418.

5533 Shakespeare's son-in-law: a study of

old Stratford, 419–425. **C. Elliot Browne.** Signed.

5534   Modern missions [to the working class], 426–436. Signed at start: A Church of England Clergyman, and at end: F.

5535   The postal telegraph service, 437–449. **Archibald Granger Bowie.** Signed.

5536   Romance of an old Yorkshire village, 450–465. **M. D. Conway.** Signed.

5537   The strivings of ancient Greece for union, 466–476. **Francis W. Newman.** Signed; repr. *Miscellanies*, V.

5538   The Old Catholic movement in Western or "Romande" Switzerland (Part II, concl.), 477–494. **G. P. Cluseret.** Cf. no. 5529.

5539   Some old-fashioned parsons, 495–507. **R. J. King.** Signed R.J.K.; attr. Boase and Courtney, II, 860, under "Welsh."

5540   Green London, 508–519. **William Allingham.** Signed P.W. [Patricius Walker]—see nos. 4807, 5714.

5541   Political novels [mainly Disraeli's], 520–536. **T. H. S. Escott.** Signed.

VOLUME 89 O.S., 9 N.S., MAY 1874

5542   The working of the Irish Land Act, 537–549. Signed: F.N.

5543   Val Maggia, 550–558. **Douglas W. Freshfield.** Signed; repr. *Italian Alps*, 1875.

5544   Scott and his publishers [largely on Archibald Constable], 559–568.

5545   English and German sailors, 569–573. Signed: An English Sea-Captain.

5546   The story of a Yorkshire blacksmith, 574–587. **M. D. Conway.** Signed.

5547   The moral character of Roman conquest, 588–601. **Francis W. Newman.** Signed; repr. *Miscellanies*, V.

5548   Intellectual wild oats, 602–609. **Bertha Thomas.** Signed B.T.—see no. 5759; the Editor of *FM*, in Table of Contents for Nov. 1874 verso, calls author of this art. and no. 5575 "an English lady who has a perfect right to those initials."

5549   The father of universal suffrage in France [Ledru-Rollin], 610–619.

5550   John Webster, 620–634. **Edmund W. Gosse.** Signed; repr., with revisions, *Seventeenth-Century Studies*, 1883.

5551   The place of Albany Fonblanque in English journalism, 635–644. **T. H. S. Escott.** Signed.

5552   A few London exteriors, 645–657. **William Allingham.** Signed P.W. [Patricius Walker]—see nos. 4807, 5714.

5553   A railway-accidents bill, 658–670. **Richard Jefferies.** Signed.

VOLUME 89 O.S., 9 N.S., JUNE 1874

5554   Russia and Turkey, 671–687.

5555   Mr. Ruskin's recent writings [mainly *Fors Clavigera*], 688–701. **Leslie Stephen.** Signed.

5556   Assyrian discoveries: a lecture delivered at the London Institution, January 28, 1874, 702–711. **A. H. Sayce.** Signed.

5557   Ornithological reminiscences, 712–730. **John Skelton.** Signed Shirley—see *DNB*.

5558   Religion at the bar of ethics, 731–739. **F. W. Newman.** Signed; repr. *Miscellanies*, V.

5559   My vestry windows, 740–751. **A. K. H. Boyd.** Signed A.K.H.B.; repr. *Landscapes*.

5560   Sussex cottages, 752–764.

5561   Bulwer's last three books, 765–777. **T. H. S. Escott.** Signed.

5562   Convent boarding-schools for young ladies, 778–786. **May (Laffan) Hartley,** prob. An art. on "Convent Schools" in *FM* for 1876 (sic.) is attr. to woman cited (in *Women of the Day*, p. 111); no such art. in 1876; the Irish background supports the attrib., since Mrs. Hartley lived in Dublin. (See no. 5604.)

5563   Things we have eaten: rambling thoughts of a rambling feeder, 787–794. **J. F. Hardy.** Signed.

5564   Political consequences of army reform, 795–801. Signed: C.G.

VOLUME 90 O.S., 10 N.S., JULY 1874

5565   Party politics, 1–18. **J. A. Froude.** Assigned in Contents to "The Editor"; repr. *Studies*, III.

5566   Paris vehicles, 19–31.

5567   Fiji, 32–39. Signed at start: A Recent Resident, at end: W.C.M.

5568   Atheism, poetry, and music [on D. F. Strauss's *Old Faith and the New*], 40–54. **G. D. Haughton.** Signed.

5569   Puddlers and iron-smelters, 55–61.

5570   Sketches from southern India (No. I): coffee planting in South Travancore, 64–68. Signed G.C.

5571   Sketches from southern India (No. II): forest service in India, 69–74. Signed G.C.

5572   Sketches from southern India (No. III, concl.): the great elephant forest, 74–85. **M. J. Walhouse.** Signed M.J.W. —see nos. 5484, 6006.

5573 The masons of La Creuse, 86–93. **Camille Barrère.** Signed.

5574 Liberal Protestantism, 94–108. **Robert Bell.** Signed; perhaps the divine listed in *CCD*/76 and Foster, b.1797/98.

5575 A professor extraordinary, 109–121. **Bertha Thomas.** Signed B.T.—See nos. 5548, 5759.

5576 Redistribution of seats in Ireland, 122–134.

VOLUME 90 O.S., 10 N.S., AUGUST 1874

5577 The farmer at home, 135–152 **Richard Jefferies.** Signed; repr. *The Toilers of the Field*, 1892.

5578 The Southern States since the War (Part I): their present condition and future prospects, 153–163. **Edwin De Leon.** Signed Edwin de Leon; see *Amer. WWW*/96.

5579 Who wrote "Shakspere"? 164–178. Signed: J.V.P. J. V. Prichard is suggested by Cushing, *Initials*, I, with a ?, and called a Shakespearean scholar; Prichard has been found only in *BMCat.*, writing on Bishop Percy and Montesquieu, but at this time.

5580 Our great London hospitals (No. I), 179–185. **Horatio Nelson Hardy.** Signed H.N.H.; in *Medical Directory*/1920, Hardy says he wrote on London hospitals and wrote for *FM*.

5581 Philo the Jew, 186–200. **Charles Gipps Prowett.** Signed, with addition "the late."

5582 On Ottery East Hill, 201–213. **M. G. Watkins.** Signed; repr. *In the Country.*

5583 The decoration of St. Paul's Cathedral, 214–222. **Edward W. Godwin.** Signed.

5584 Motley's *John of Barneveld*, 223–245. **Alexander Falconer.** Signed.

5585 Greenwich School forty years ago, 246–253. Signed: An Old Boy.

5586 Mr. Disraeli's *Letters of Runnymede*, 254–268.

VOLUME 90 O.S., 10 N.S., SEPTEMBER 1874

5587 The principles of Friendly Society legislation, 269–283. **A. J. Wilson.** Signed A.J.W.—see no. 5849.

5588 A day at Fotheringhay, 284–292. **Richard John King.** Signed.

5589 The Indian famine, 293–303.

5590 Between June and May, 304–315. **A. K. H. Boyd.** Signed A.K.H.B.; repr. *Landscapes.*

5591 Colonial distinctions, 316–324.

5592 "Junius" and his time, 325–344. **J. M. Hawkins.** Signed.

5593 The Southern States since the War (No. II): industrial and financial condition, 346–366. **Edwin De Leon.** Signed as in no. 5578.

5594 Supernatural religion, 367–377. **Malcolm MacColl.** Signed.

5595 The poet-king of Scotland [James I], 378–387. Signed: W.G.

5596 Contrasts of ancient and modern history (No. I), 388–398. **Francis W. Newman.** Signed; repr. *Miscellanies*, V.

5597 Frau Rath, 399–406. **J. W. Sherer.** Signed.

VOLUME 90 O.S., 10 N.S., OCTOBER 1874

5598 Dr. Priestley, 407–419. **F. S. Turner.** Signed F.S.T.; assigned in Contents.

5599 The Empress Eugénie sketched by Napoleon III, 420–423. **Louis Napoleon.** Title. Trans., with intro. note, signed J.C.

5600 From India by the Euphrates route, 424–436. **William Brown Keer.** Signed, with title "Rev.," of Bombay.

5601 The National Workshops of 1848, and M. Louis Blanc, 437–447. **Camille Barrère.** Signed.

5602 The dangerous glory of India, 448–464. **Francis William Newman.** Signed; repr. *Miscellanies*, III.

5603 "My Lydia" [daughter of Laurence Sterne], 465–472. **Percy Fitzgerald.** Signed.

5604 A word for the convent boarding-schools [in answer to no. 5562], 473–483. Signed: An Old Convent-Girl.

5605 A Chinese love story [translation with intro. note] (Part I), 484–503.

5606 The House of Commons: its personnel and its oratory, 504–517. **T. H. S. Escott.** Signed.

5607 At a Highland hut, 518–529. **J. S. Stuart-Glennie.** Signed.

5608 Church reform, 530–540. **Robert Arthur Arnold,** prob. Signed R.A.A.—see no. 5626; the art. is on ecclesiastical politics, which would be an appropriate topic for Arnold.

VOLUME 90 O.S., 10 N.S., NOVEMBER 1874

5609 Trading benefit and burial societies, and post-office insurance, 541–555. **A. J. Wilson.** Signed A.J.W.—see no 5849, and 5587, to which this is really a sequel.

5610 The Scilly Islands, 556–569. **H. S. Fagan.** Signed H.S.F.; Boase and Courtney, III, 1178.

5611 Contrasts of ancient and modern history (No. II), 570–584. **Francis William Newman.** Signed; repr. *Miscellanies*, V.

5612 A Chinese love story (Part II, concl.), 585–610.

5613 Legislation on betting [on horse racing], practically considered, 611–619. **James Glass Bertram.** Signed J.G.B.; Bertram wrote arts. on gambling on horses in the *Contemp. Rev.* at this time (nos. 732 and 1164, *Index*, I) and later published two books on horse-racing under pseudonym Louis Henry Curzon.

5614 The Southern States since the War (Part III, concl.): "the conflict of races," 620–637. **Edwin De Leon.** Signed as in no. 5578.

5615 Du Quesne and the French navy of the seventeenth century, 638–653. **J. K. Laughton.** Signed; repr. *Studies*.

5616 The labourer's daily life, 654–669. **Richard Jefferies.** Signed; repr. *The Toilers of the Field*, 1892.

5617 Our great London hospitals (No. II, concl.), 670–678. **H. N. Hardy.** Evidence for no. 5580.

VOLUME 90 o.s., 10 n.s., DECEMBER 1874

5618 General representation, 679–692.

5619 On the Vatna Jökull [in Iceland], 693–705. **W. L. Watts.** Signed; repr. *Snioland; or, Iceland, Its Jökulls and Fjalls* (1875), pp. 106–139.

5620 Training-schools for nurses, 706–713.

5621 The literary partnership of Canning and Frere [in the *Anti-Jacobin*], 714–727. Signed: J.C.

5622 Primary education in Ireland, 728–740. (See no. 5684.)

5623 The ethics of Jesus Christ, 741–748. **F. R. Conder.** Signed F.R.C.; his later arts., starting with no. 5942, are signed; Conder wrote on theology as well as engineering: see *BMCat.*

5624 Contrasts of ancient and modern history (No. III), 749–762. **Francis W. Newman.** Signed; repr. *Miscellanies*, V.

5625 Latest intelligence from the planet Venus [on woman's suffrage], 763–766. **Bertha Thomas.** Signed B.T.—see no. 5759.

5626 The agricultural strikes, 767–776. **R. A. Arnold.** Signed R.A.A.; Arnold published a book on land laws and wrote

for *FM*; later in life he dropped his first name and became Arthur Arnold.

5627 The Greville memoirs, 777–788. **Geraldine Jewsbury,** prob. Signed G.J.; cf. no. 5645, where, on p. 210, author comments on the contrast between Prince Albert's time and that of George IV "as displayed in the Greville Memoirs"; the feminine, sentimental style, the emphasis on duty (cf. p. 788 here, p. 210 there), the interest in gossipy trivia rather than political history, all indicate a common authorship.

5628 Bulwer as politician and speaker, 789–801. **T. H. S. Escott.** Signed.

5629 Scottish churches and the Patronage Act, 802–813.

VOLUME 91 o.s., 11 n.s., JANUARY 1875

5630 Early kings of Norway (chaps. i–vii), 1–26. **Thomas Carlyle.** Book published 1875.

5631 The Bayou Tèche [in Louisiana], 27–39. **Edwin De Leon.** Assigned in Contents.

5632 German home life (No. I): servants, 40–49. **Marie von Bothmer.** Signed A Lady; series reprinted 1876: see *BMCat.* (Letter, p. 540, signed A German; reply, p. 787, by **Marie von Bothmer**—signed The Author of "German Home Life.")

5633 Langalibalele [an African chief], 50–61. **H. S. Fagan.** Signed H.S.F.—see no. 5610. (Letter, p. 272, by **David Erskine** —signed D. Erskine, Colonial Secretary.)

5634 Quaint corners of mediaeval biography: Meinwerk, Bishop of Paderborn, 62–71. **Sabine Baring-Gould.** Signed as in no. 4912.

5635 The financial policy of New Zealand, 74–87. **Charles Fellows.** Signed. (See no. 5649.)

5636 Sir Charles Bell, 88–99. **Frederick Arnold.** Signed F.A.; *Reminiscences of a Literary and Clerical Life* (1889), I, 266. (Letter, vol. 12 n.s., pp. 129–130, by **Charles Bell**—signed with titles "M.D., F.R.C.P.")

5637 Opinions of the contemporaries of the Evangelists [on the invisible world], 100–109. **F. R. Conder.** Signed F.R.C.; cf. no. 5623.

5638 Contrasts of ancient and modern history (No. IV, concl.): on the stability of civilisation, 110–120. **Francis W. Newman.** Signed; repr. *Miscellanies*, V.

5639 The settlement of Vineland in New

Jersey, 121–134. **Charles K. Landis.**
Signed.

VOLUME 91, O.S., 11 N.S., FEBRUARY 1875

5640 Early kings of Norway (chaps. viii–x),
135–155. **Thomas Carlyle.** Cf. no. 5630.
5641 Vegetarianism, 156–172. **Francis William Newman.** Signed.
5642 German home life (No. II): furniture,
173–183. **Marie von Bothmer.** Evidence
for no. 5632.
5643 The Brussels Conference, 184–198.
Henry Ottley. Signed.
5644 On the limits of science, 199–207.
William Forsyth. Signed.
5645 *Prince Albert* [by Theodore Martin],
209–222. **Geraldine Endsor Jewsbury,**
prob. Signed G.E.J.; Miss Jewsbury, who
was writing reviews in the 70's, was an
old friend of the Martins and was aware
of the difficulties the author had in
writing the book (see *Life,* pp. 186, 192,
and index under the Martins); the review is highly laudatory and a little sentimental.
5646 The literary history of the word Messiah, 223–233. **F. R. Conder.** Signed
F.R.C.; cf. no. 5623.
5647 The Shipton accident, 234–242. **Richard Jefferies.** Signed.
5648 Personal recollections about Ledru-
Rollin, 243–253. **Karl Blind.** Signed.
5649 The finances of New Zealand [a reply
to no. 5635], 254–272. **Julius Vogel.**
Signed. (See no. 5659.)

VOLUME 91 O.S., 11 N.S., MARCH 1875

5650 Early kings of Norway (chaps. xi–xvi,
concl.), 273–288. **Thomas Carlyle.** Cf.
no. 5630.
5651 German home life (No. III): food,
289–298. **Marie von Bothmer.** Evidence
for no. 5632.
5652 The place of Sterndale Bennett in
music, 299–305. **H. H. Statham.** Signed
H.H.S; repr. *Thoughts on Music.*
5653 Sidgwick's *Methods of Ethics,* 306–
325. **Leslie Stephen.** Signed.
5654 Recollections of the stage, 326–337.
Robert R. Noel. Signed R. R. Noel;
Contents gives "Major Noel"; author's
knowledge of German literature, p. 336
and note, identifies him with man cited:
see *BMCat.*
5655 Some political aspects of Sir Samuel

Baker's expedition, 338–347. **A. J. Wilson.** Signed A.J.W.—see no. 5849.
5656 The Historical Manuscripts Commission (No. III): fourth report, 348–367.
John Piggot. Signed. (Nos. I and II are
nos. 5319 and 5494; No. IV is no.
6028.)
5657 The dangers of the sea, 368–372.
Signed: The Captain of an Ocean
Steamer.
5658 The literary character of the fourth
gospel, 373–383. **F. R. Conder.** Signed
F.R.C.; cf. no. 5623. (See no. 5690;
letter, p. 666, signed **T. L. Hill** and
reply, p. 802, by **Conder**—signed F.R.C.)
5659 A rejoinder on the debts of New Zealand [a reply to no. 5649], 384–392.
Charles Fellows. Signed.
5660 Charles Kingsley, 393–406. **Richard
John King.** Signed.

VOLUME 91, O.S., 11 N.S., APRIL 1875

5661 The portraits of John Knox, 407–439.
Thomas Carlyle. Repr. in *Early Kings of
Norway,* 1875.
5662 Tetuan [a city in Morocco], 440–449.
Signed: R.
5663 Recruiting and the militia, by two
officers of Her Majesty's army (No. I):
recruiting, 450–459. Signed: C.G.
5664 Recruiting and the militia (No. II):
the militia, 459–466. Signed: S.
5665 Some remarks on unions of nations,
467–477. Signed: W.B.
5666 Cleveland [part of northeast York-
shire], 478–492. **Richard John King.**
Signed.
5667 The proposed Indian Institute, 493–
501.
5668 Secret papers of the Empire, 502–510.
Signed: F.
5669 Socialism in America, 511–520.
5670 Vivisection, 521–528. **George Hoggan.**
Signed, with titles "M.B. and C.M."
5671 Three experiments in co-operative
agriculture, 529–539. **Matilda Betham-
Edwards.** Signed M.B.E.; attr. by Hill,
Memoir, p. 397.

VOLUME 91, O.S., 11 N.S., MAY 1875

5672 Sea studies, 541–560. **J. A. Froude.**
Signed J.A.F.; full name in Contents;
repr. *Studies,* III.
5673 Girton College, 561–567. **Matilda
Betham-Edwards.** Signed M.B.-E.—see
no. 6063.

5674 The story of Swindon, 568–580. **Richard Jefferies.** Signed; repr. *The Hills and the Vale*, 1909.

5675 The new army of France, 581–591. **James Macdonell.** Signed M.—see no. 4833, etc.; he was special correspondent for the *Times* in France, 1870–1871; published *France since the First Empire*, 1880.

5676 A note on Cervantes and Beaumont and Fletcher, 592–597. Signed: J.C.

5677 The first London dispensaries, 598–607. **H. N. Hardy.** Signed at end H.N.H.; Contents adds "A Surgeon"; cf. no. 5580.

5678 The Royal Navy of England, 608–615. Signed at start: A Commander, at end: B.

5679 Along the western coast of India, 616–628. **M. J. Walhouse.** Signed M.J.W.; cf. no. 6006.

5680 The King Messiah of history, 629–641. **F. R. Conder.** Signed F.R.C.; cf. no. 5623.

5681 An old story of a feast and a battle, 642–654. **William Allingham.** Signed P.W. [Patricius Walker]—see nos. 4807, 5714.

5682 German home life (No. IV): manners and customs, 655–665. **Marie von Bothmer.** Evidence for no. 5632.

VOLUME 91 O.S., 11 N.S., JUNE 1875

5683 Moral estimate of Alexander the Great, 667–685. **F. W. Newman.** Signed; repr. *Miscellanies*, V.

5684 Primary education in Ireland [reply to no. 5622], 686–695. **John Ormsby,** prob. Signed J.O.—see no. 3557; Ormsby was educated in Ireland (see *DNB*) and was a frequent contributor to *FM*.

5685 Letter of Hemsterhuys on atheism, 696–703. **Francis Hemsterhuys.** Title and p. 696. Intro. note, 696–698, unsigned.

5686 Peasant life in north Italy, 704–719.

5687 The civil service, 720–729. **Aucher Cornwall Taylor.** Signed A.C.T.; *Foreign Office List*, 1884.

5688 Fire-burial among our Germanic forefathers, 730–749. **Karl Blind.** Signed.

5689 Angling worthies, 750–763. **M. G. Watkins.** Signed.

5690 A reply to an article on the literary character of the fourth gospel [no. 5658], 764–773. **Alfred Edersheim.** Signed. (See no. 5698.)

5691 German home life (No. V): language, 774–787. **Marie von Bothmer.** Evidence for no. 5632.

5692 Arctic expeditions, 789–801. **John Piggot.** Signed.

VOLUME 92 O.S., 12 N.S., JULY 1875

5693 Our future army, 1–19. **James Macdonell.** Signed M.—see no. 4833.

5694 Some recollections of Sir Sterndale Bennett, 20–24.

5695 The dalesfolk of Cumberland and Westmoreland, 25–35. Signed: One of Themselves.

5696 On a logical trick of the modern experiential philosophy, 36–40. **C. F. Keary.** Signed.

5697 Politics and the press, 41–50. **T. H. S. Escott,** prob. Signed E.; Escott wrote on both subjects and their interconnections; the art. shows the same characteristics of style as those described in evidence for no. 5894; Escott was contributing to *FM* at this time.

5698 The debate as to the fourth gospel [reply to no. 5690], 51–64. **F. R. Conder.** Signed F.R.C.; cf. no. 5658. (Letter, pp. 270–272, signed **Alfred Edersheim.**)

5699 The *Merchant of Venice* at the Prince of Wales's Theatre, 65–71. **James Spedding.** Signed J.S.; repr. *Reviews.*

5700 The International Working Men's Association (Part I), 72–87. **Matilda Betham-Edwards.** *Reminiscences* (1898), p. 223n.; *Academy*, Oct. 16, 1875, p. 404.

5701 Essay on poetical translation, 88–96. **Francis W. Newman.** Signed.

5702 *The Ancient Irish* [by Eugene O'Curry], 97–110. **David Fitzgerald.** Signed.

5703 Jersey affairs, 111–122.

5704 The condition of Palestine, 123–128. **Adolphus Rosenberg.** Signed.

VOLUME 92 O.S., 12 N.S., AUGUST 1875

5705 The bluejackets and marines of the Royal Navy, 131–155. Signed: A Naval Officer.

5706 Old rings and seals: a gossip about engraved gems, 156–165. **R. H. Cave.** Signed, with title "Rev."

5707 Impressions of Madeira, 166–180. **William Longman.** Signed.

5708 The International Working Men's Association (Part II), 181–194. **Matilda Betham-Edwards.** Cf. no. 5700.

5709 German home life (No. VI): dress

and amusements, 195–209. **Marie von Bothmer.** Evidence for no. 5632.

5710 What was primitive Christianity? 210–223. **Francis William Newman.** Signed.

5711 The kingdom of Burmah in 1875, 224–232. **Edmond Browne.** Signed, with title "Captain . . . 21st Royal North British Fusiliers."

5712 Remarks on a recent Irish election, 233–242. **John Ormsby,** prob. Signed at start One of the Electors, at end J.O.—see nos. 3557, 5684.

5713 Armin, the liberator of Germany, 243–254. **Karl Blind.** Signed.

5714 Artist and critic, 255–269. **William Allingham.** Signed P.W. [Patricius Walker]; repr. *Varieties*, III.

VOLUME 92 O.S., 12 N.S., SEPTEMBER 1875

5715 On national universities, 273–284. **F. W. Newman.** Signed.

5716 Old English metrical romances, 285–299. **J. W. Hales.** Signed; repr. *Folia*.

5717 The International Working Men's Association (Part III, concl.), 300–311. **Matilda Betham-Edwards.** Cf. no. 5700.

5718 Two years in Natal, 312–334. Signed: An English Lady.

5719 Ladies as clerks, 335–340. Signed: A Government Official.

5720 The gulf between the old law and the new, 341–352. **F. R. Conder.** Signed F.R.C.—see no. 5623; attr. in Poole, I, 730.

5721 Some account of a German boarding school [for girls], 353–363. Signed: E.M. Perhaps by E.E.M., who wrote no. 5246.

5722 Our military system and the national debt, 364–381. **Francis Dwyer?** Signed D.—see no. 5348; author called "an experienced military officer," p. 364n., and art. largely on subject of the foreign soldier serving as a volunteer, a role played by Dwyer for most of his life.

5723 Field-faring women, 382–394. **Richard Jefferies.** Signed; repr. *Toilers of the Fields*, 1892.

5724 Mr. Green's *Short History of the English People* (No. I): is it trustworthy? 395–410. **James Rowley.** Signed.

VOLUME 92 O.S., 12 N.S., OCTOBER 1875

5725 Is monarchy an anachronism? 411–436. Signed: J.V.

5726 On petroleum and oil-wells, 437–449.

Richard Owen. Signed Professor Owen; *Life*, II, 374; claimed in Richard Owen to Allingham, Aug. 26, 1875, Allingham Corres.

5727 Some remarks on our relations with Russia, 450–456. Signed: H.S.

5728 The character of Mary Tudor, 457–474. **John Piggot.** Signed.

5729 Proper uses of wealth, 475–482. Signed: W.M.

5730 The Venetian navy in the sixteenth century, 483–500. **J. K. Laughton.** Signed.

5731 Old china, 501–507. **R. H. Cave.** Signed.

5732 Recollections of a cruise in the Baltic, 508–518. **John Skelton.** Signed An Old Campaigner—see no. 4555.

5733 How history is sometimes written, 519–527. **A. H. Wratislaw.** Signed.

5734 The Science Congress at Nantes, 528–538. **Matilda Betham-Edwards.** Signed M.B.-E.—see no. 6063.

5735 On a university curriculum, 539–548. **F. W. Newman.** Signed.

VOLUME 92 O.S., 12 N.S., NOVEMBER 1875

5736 A ride through Bosnia, 349–365. **Henry Vignoles** and **O. J. Vignoles.** Signed V.; art. was founded on notes of former (*Athenaeum*, Nov. 6, 1875, p. 611) and was written by the latter (*CCD/76*).

5737 The history of twins, as a criterion of the relative powers of nature and nurture, 566–576. **Francis Galton.** Signed.

5738 The ventilation of hospitals, 577–591. Signed: S.E.

5739 De la Grange's diary, 592–597. **Julia C. B. Byrne.** Signed The Author of *Flemish Interiors*—see no. 5349.

5740 Mohammedanism and the Negro race; by a negro, 598–615. **Edward W. Blyden.** Signed.

5741 German home life (No. VII): women, 616–626. **Marie von Bothmer.** Evidence for no. 5632.

5742 Alfonso the Wise [of Spain], 627–639. Signed: J.C.

5743 The survival of paganism, 640–651.

5744 An autumn in western France (Part I): Angers, 652–660. **Matilda Betham-Edwards.** Signed M.B.-E.—see no. 6063.

5745 *The Papal Drama*, 661–673. **F. W. Newman.** Signed.

5746 Notes on the navy, 674–686. Signed: An Old Sailor.

VOLUME 92 O.S., 12 N.S., DECEMBER 1875

5747 The capitalist in society [on G. J. Holyoake's *History of Co-operation*], 687–700. **Francis William Newman.** Signed; repr. *Miscellanies*, IV.

5748 The Wagner Festival of 1876, 701–709. **Franz Hueffer.** Signed.

5749 Mr. Green's *Short History of the English People* (No. II, concl.), 710–724. **James Rowley.** Signed.

5750 Land and labour in Russia, 725–735. Signed at start: An English Resident in Russia, at end: O., with address, St. Petersburgh.

5751 British merchant seamen, 736–744. **William Dawson.** Signed.

5752 A monk's daily life, 745–756. **Walter Thornbury.** Signed W.T.; claimed in letter to Allingham, Apr. 27, 1875, Allingham Corres.

5753 The Bukowina [province of Austria]: an historical study, 757–773. **E. H. Kilian.** Signed E. Kilian, with address, Vienna; cf. no. 5867.

5754 German home life (No. VIII): men, 774–784. **Marie von Bothmer.** Evidence for no. 5632.

5755 Scenery of an Indian stream, 785–798. **M. J. Walhouse.** Signed M.J.W.; cf. no. 5484.

5756 Letter from New South Wales, 799–807. **Robert Dudley Adams.** Signed, with address, Sydney, N.S.W.

5757 The Malay outbreak, 808–814.

VOLUME 93 O.S., 13 N.S., JANUARY 1876

5758 Turkey, Egypt, and the Eastern question, 1–12.

5759 Critics in Wonderland: a study, 13–21. **Bertha Thomas.** Signed B.T.; Bertha Thomas to Allingham, Feb. 12, 1876, Allingham Corres., speaks of Alfred Austin having assumed that "B. T. was a man!"

5760 The French fishery claims on the coast of Newfoundland, 22–31. **James Whitman.** Signed.

5761 Erasmus (Part I), 32–50. **St. George Stock.** Part II is signed S.; claimed in Stock to Blackwood, Mar. 20, [1876], Nat. Lib. Scot.

5762 An autumn in western France (No. II): Morbihan, 51–59. **Matilda Betham-Edwards.** Evidence for no. 5744.

5763 *The Unseen Universe*, 60–68. **Edward

Caird?** Signed E.C.; art., written by a Scotsman, is on metaphysics (see *DNB* on Caird), and reviews a book by two Scotsmen.

5764 The Flemings and the Walloons of Belgium, 69–80. **Karl Blind.** Signed.

5765 A few words on interment, 81–85. **George Sherston Baker.** Signed.

5766 Employment in India, 86–99. Signed: G.C. Unidentified. (Letter, p. 536, signed A North-West Civilian.)

5767 German home life (No. IX, concl.): marriage and children, 100–113. **Marie von Bothmer.** Evidence for no. 5632.

5768 On the weakness of Roman Empire, 114–129. **Francis William Newman.** Signed; repr. *Miscellanies*, V.

5769 The place of the Judicature Acts in English law, 130–134. **E. S. Roscoe.** Signed.

VOLUME 93 O.S., 13 N.S., FEBRUARY 1876

5770 English capital and foreign loans, 135–144. **Francis William Newman.** Signed; repr. *Miscellanies*, IV.

5771 The royal Bengal tiger, 145–161. **M. G. Watkins.** Signed.

5772 The truth about the Bastille, 162–169. **H. S. Fagan.** Signed H.S.F.—see nos. 5230, 5610.

5773 The Illyrians, past and present [now Albanians and Wallachians], an ethnological and philological essay, 170–177. Signed: W.

5774 Erasmus (Part II, concl.), 178–191. **St. George Stock.** Evidence for no. 5761.

5775 Natal fruits and vegetables, 192–196. Signed: P.

5776 The story of a limestone cave: an account of the Victoria Cave near Settle, 197–220. **John Edward Field.** Signed J.E.F.; Field was curate of Settle, 1872–1874 (see *CCD*/76) and wrote geological and archeological arts. for *Blackwood's*: see *Index*, I, 894.

5777 An autumn in western France (No. III): Finisterre, 221–228. **Matilda Betham-Edwards.** Evidence for no. 5744.

5778 Our public schools and public schoolmasters, 229–245. **E. H. Knatchbull-Hugessen.** Signed.

5779 The proposed Byron Memorial, 246–260. **William Allingham.** Repr. *Varieties*, III, as "Disraeli's Monument to Byron."

5780 The mobilisation of the army, 261–268. Signed: A Military Officer.

VOLUME 93 O.S., 13 N.S., MARCH 1876

5781 Great Britain and her colonies, 269–282. Signed: A Victorian.

5782 Armenian folk songs, 283–297. **Evelyn Carrington Martinengo-Caesaresco.** Signed E.C.; repr. *Folk Songs.*

5783 Sainte Perine, or the City of the Gentle: "Villa de la Reunion," 298–300. **Julia C. B. Byrne.** Signed The Author of *Gheel, the City of the Simple*: see *BMCat.*

5784 A tour in Lapland, 1875 (Part I), 301–319. Signed: W.D.T.

5785 The education of barristers, 320–324. **E. S. Roscoe,** prob. Signed E.S.R.; man cited a barrister who wrote legal arts. for *FM.*

5786 English prisons, 325–337. Signed: J.H.

5787 Maxims and reflections; from the German of Goethe, 338–348. **Johann Wolfgang von Goethe.** Title. Trans. by **Matilde Blind**—*MWT*, 14th ed.

5788 An autumn in western France (No. IV): more of Finisterre, 349–359. **Matilda Betham-Edwards.** Evidence for no. 5744.

5789 Local taxation, local debt, and local government, 360–366. **F. R. Conder.** Signed F.R.C.; cf. no. 5623.

5790 Life and labours of Francis Deak, 1803–1876 [Hungarian patriot], 374–385. **Karl Blind.** Signed.

5791 Army recruiting, 386–402. Signed: A General.

VOLUME 93 O.S., 13 N.S., APRIL 1876

5792 Secondary education in Scotland (Part I), 403–422. **G. G. Ramsay.** Signed, with title "Professor . . . University of Glasgow."

5793 Sicilian fairy tales, 423–433. **W. R. S. Ralston.** Signed.

5794 A beam of light [on the physical nature of light], 434–441. Signed: B.

5795 India's expectations, 442–457. **W. Harris.** Signed.

5796 The Irish census of 1871, 458–467.

5797 In Arden, 468–478. **C. Elliot Browne.** Signed.

5798 A tour in Lapland (Part II, concl.), 479–495. Signed: W.D.T.

5799 *Norman Macleod,* 497–505. **A. K. H. Boyd.** Signed A.K.H.B.; repr. *Recreations*, 3rd s.

5800 Waste of power in sanitary improve-ment, 506–513. **F. R. Conder.** Signed F.R.C.; cf. nos. 5623, 5823.

5801 An autumn in western France (No. V, concl.): Côtes du Nord, 514–522. **Matilda Betham-Edwards.** Evidence for no. 5744.

5802 On cruelty, 523–536. **Francis W. Newman.** Signed; repr. *Miscellanies*, III.

VOLUME 93 O.S., 13 N.S., MAY 1876

5803 English foreign policy and the Eastern question, 537–545.

5804 Shakespeare and history, 546–553. **Edward Rose.** Signed.

5805 Christianity and the Negro race; by a negro, 554–568. **Edward W. Blyden.** Signed.

5806 Some remarks respecting the purchase of books in Germany, 569–572. **Albert Stutzer.** Signed.

5807 The Agricultural Children's Act, 573–581. **Whately Cooke Taylor.** Signed.

5808 Bonivard, "the prisoner of Chillon," 582–587. **Robert Edward Bartlett.** Signed R.E.B.—see no. 6033; Bonivard was a religious liberal.

5809 Secondary education in Scotland (Part II, concl.), 588–612. **G. G. Ramsay.** Signed.

5810 Our Indian army, 614–631. **M. Laing Meason.** Signed.

5811 Izaak Walton, 632–644. **M. G. Watkins.** Signed.

5812 The present aspect of some legal customs, 645–651. **E. S. Roscoe.** Signed E.S.R.; cf. no. 5785.

5813 *The Indian Alps,* 652–658. Signed: C.

5814 The life and lays of Ferdinand Freiligrath, 659–674. **Karl Blind.** Signed.

VOLUME 93 O.S., 13 N.S., JUNE 1876

5815 Lord Macaulay, 675–694. **J. A. Froude.** Signed J.A.F.; *Life*, I, 213.

5816 Remarks on modern warfare, 695–699. **Percy Scudamore Cunningham,** prob. Signed at start A Military Officer, at end P.S.C.; in *Army List/*76, man cited only officer with those initials. (See no. 5835.)

5817 Modern newspaper enterprise, 700–714. **T. Wemyss Reid.** Signed X.; Reid began his journalistic career in Newcastle, was London correspondent of the *Leeds Mercury*, 1867–1870, and editor, 1870–1887, establishing a London office of the newspaper in 1873, which was shared with the *Glasgow Herald* (see *DNB*, 2nd suppl.); in the article the achievements of the provincial press are extolled, pp. 709–712, with references to the daily press of Newcastle, the *Leeds Mercury*, and the *Glasgow Herald* on pp. 711, 709 and 713, 709 and 712–713, respectively; p. 710 describes the London correspondent of a provincial paper, making some of the same points made by Reid in his "'Our London Correspondent',", *Macmillan's* (no. 1965 in *Index*, I)—cf. pp. 709–710 here with pp. 21, 25, 26 there, and the use of "X" as signature here with the same letter applied to a London correspondent in *Mac.*, p. 18; the *Biograph*, 1 (1879), 118, reported that Reid was a contributor to *FM*.

5818 The poor and the hospitals, 715–727. Signed: S.E.

5819 The Russian imperial title: a forgotten page of history, 728–732. **Karl Blind.** Signed.

5820 Quarter sessions (No. I): under Queen Elizabeth; from original records, 733–746. **A. H. A. Hamilton.** Signed; repr. *Quarter Sessions from Queen Elizabeth to Queen Anne*, 1878.

5821 Runes and rune-stones, 747–757. **R. J. King.** Signed.

5822 Calvin at Geneva, 758–768. **Robert Edward Bartlett.** Signed B.; the author not only refers, p. 762, to the source of an incident in no. 5808, but also draws heavily in both arts. from the Registers of the Council of the City of Geneva, which he here says, p. 758n., he recently examined; moreover, he shows the same sympathy with religious liberalism (here, p. 761 in particular) as does Bartlett in nos. 5808 and 6033.

5823 On the government of London (No. I): by a civil engineer, 769–776. **F. R. Conder.** Signed F.R.C.; cf. no. 5623; Conder was a civil engineer.

5824 On the government of London (No. II): by a lawyer, 776–785. Signed: P.

5825 The financial position of Egypt, 786–806. **A. J. Wilson.** Signed.

VOLUME 94 O.S., 14 N.S., JULY 1876

5826 Austria and Turkey, 1–24. **E. H. Kilian,** prob. This is subscribed "Vienna" with month and year, exactly like no. 5753; no. 5867 is also subscribed "Vienna."

5827 The fable of Wagner's Niebelungen trilogy, 25–38. **Bertha Thomas.** Signed B.T.—see no. 5759.

5828 The new education bill [the Agricultural Children's Act], 39–44. **A. H. A. Hamilton.** Signed.

5829 The future sources of the illumination and water supply of London, 45–52. **F. R. Conder.** Signed F.R.C.; attr. by Poole, I, 766; cf. no. 5623.

5830 At the General Assembly, 53–62. **A. K. H. Boyd.** Repr. *Recreations*, 3rd s.

5831 A Scottish Kirk sessions-book, 1691, 63–71. **William B. Scott.** Signed.

5832 The Koran *versus* Turkish reform, 72–83. **Henry Sneyd.** Signed.

5833 Stockbroking and the Stock Exchange, 84–103. Signed: W. (See nos. 5864, 5875.)

5834 Etruscan translation, 104–120. **Francis William Newman.** Signed.

5835 Modern warfare [reply to no. 5816], 121–123. **John Ruskin.** Signature; repr. *Works*, XXXIV, 522–525.

5836 Autobiography of a vegetarian: a true narrative of a successful career, 124–134. **C. O. Groom Napier.** Signed.

VOLUME 94 O.S., 14 N.S., AUGUST 1876

5837 Russia in Europe, 135–149. **Arthur Arnold.** Signed.

5838 Society in Italy in the last days of the Roman Republic, 150–162. **J. A. Froude.** Signed J.A.F.; repr. *Studies*, III.

5839 The extradition of criminals, 163–175. **E. S. Roscoe.** Signed.

5840 A Burmese "ilpon," [i.e. a] tale, 176–180. **Janet Ross.** Signed.

5841 The French in Cochin-China, 181–192. **Horace A. Browne.** Signed, with title "Colonel."

5842 High-pressure agriculture, 193–199. **Richard Jefferies.** Signed.

5843 Quarter sessions (No. II): under James I; from original records, 200–212. **A. H. A. Hamilton.** Signed.

5844 The University of London and its influence on education in Scotland, 213–218. **Walter Marlow Ramsay.** Signed.

5845 Ulster and its people, 219–229. **Thomas Croskery.** Signed T.C.; Croskery spent much of his life in Ulster and was a contrib. to *FM*: see *DNB*.

5846 From Belgrade to Constantinople overland, 230–249. **Humphry Sandwith.** Signed.

5847 The Irish Land question; by a landlord, 250–256. **W. Bence Jones.** Signed.

5848   Barbados, 257–268. Assigned, p. 536n., to L.-A.

VOLUME 94 O.S., 14 N.S., SEPTEMBER 1876

5849   British trade (No. I), 269–284. **A. J. Wilson.** Signed A.J.W.; repr. *Resources of Modern Countries*, 1878.
5850   Fairy plays, 285–293. **Edward Rose.** Signed.
5851   The Bloody Parliament of Wilemow, 294–301. **A. H. Wratislaw.** Signed.
5852   Taxation in India, 302–324. **Shoshee Chunder Dutt.** Signed; repr. *India, Past and Present*, 1880. (Letter, pp. 669–670, signed **F. E. Gibson,** with addition "Madras Civil Service.")
5853   Last century magazines, 325–333. Signed: T.H. Perhaps Thomas Hughes who used these initials for no. 3781, and in *Macmillan's Mag.* a few months earlier (no. 1456, *Index*, I); one of his interests was magazines.
5854   The future of the Roman Church, 334–340. **Francis William Newman.** Signed.
5855   The Cistercian abbeys of Yorkshire, 341–362. **John Piggot.** Signed.
5856   The *Golden Ass* of Apuleius, 363–374. **W. H. Mallock.** Signed.
5857   Arabian horses, studied in their native country in 1874–1875, 375–402. **Roger Upton.** Signed, and called "Captain . . . Author of *Newmarket and Arabia*": see *BMCat.*

VOLUME 94 O.S., 14 N.S., OCTOBER 1876

5858   On the present condition of our navy, 403–418.
5859   Lucian, 419–437. **J. A. Froude.** Signed J.A.F.; repr. *Studies*, III.
5860   The Chinese in the Straits of Malacca, 438–445. **W. A. Pickering.** Signed, with title, "Chinese Interpreter to the Government of the Straits Settlements."
5861   Amongst the sea-birds, 446–456. **M. G. Watkins.** Signed; repr. *In the Country.* (Note, p. 670, by **William Allingham**—signed Ed.)
5862   British trade (No. II): the economic position of India, 457–476. **A. J. Wilson.** Evidence for no. 5849.
5863   Quarter sessions (No. III): under James I; from original records of the County of Devon, 477–492. **A. H. A. Hamilton.** Signed.
5864   A defence of the Stock Exchange

[reply to no. 5833], 493–503. **Charles Branch.** Signed. (See no. 5875.)
5865   Christian missions in West Africa; by a negro, 504–521. **Edward W. Blyden.** Signed.
5866   Cause and objects of the Crimean War, 522–536. **Francis William Newman.** Signed.

VOLUME 94 O.S., 14 N.S., NOVEMBER 1876

5867   The Bulgarians, 537–560. **E. H. Kilian.** Signed, with title "Dr." and address "Vienna."
5868   The rings of Saturn: recent discoveries, 561–571. **Richard A. Proctor.** Signed; repr. *Myths and March of Astronomy*, 1889.
5869   British trade (No. III): the United States, 572–592. **A. J. Wilson.** Evidence for no. 5849.
5870   The astronomy of the future; a speculation, 593–599. **Newton Crosland.** Signed; repr. revised *Pith: Essays and Sketches*, 1881, and *The New Principia*, 1884. (Letters, vol. 15 n.s., p. 134 signed **F. W. Newman** and **N. Levitt;** reply, p. 406, signed **Newton Crosland.**)
5871   Heinrich Heine's life and work, 600–623. **Henry G. Hewlett.** Signed.
5872   Islam and race distinctions; by a negro, 624–637. **Edward W. Blyden.** Signed. (Letter, pp. 809–810, signed **Robert Osborn.**)
5873   The Australian colonies and confederation, 641–652. **H. M. Hyndman.** Signed.
5874   An English homestead, 653–660. **Richard Jefferies.** Signed; repr. *The Toilers of the Field*, 1892.
5875   The Stock Exchange again [reply to no. 5864], 661–668. Signed: The Writer of the Article in *Fraser* on the Stock Exchange [no. 5833]; that was signed W.

VOLUME 94 O.S., 14 N.S., DECEMBER 1876

5876   On the uses of a landed gentry, 671–685. **J. A. Froude.** Signed.
5877   Notes on the Turk, 686–697. **Edwin De Leon.** Signed.
5878   Eyes and eye-glasses; a friendly treatise, 698–722. **Richard Hengist Horne.** Signed.
5879   Melanchthon: a chapter in the history of education, 723–735. **John Hutchison.** Signed J. Hutchison with address, "Glasgow High School"; see entry in Part B below.

5880   British trade (No. IV): Russian progress, 736–755. **A. J. Wilson.** Evidence for no. 5849.

5881   Biology in schools, 756–770. **Andrew Wilson,** 1852–1912. Signed; repr. *Leisure-Time Studies,* 1879.

5882   Our arctic voyage: an unscientific account, 771–808. **Charles E. Hodgson.** Signed The Chaplain of the *Discovery*; *Navy List*/76.

VOLUME 95 O.S., 15 N.S., JANUARY 1877

5883   Jòn Jònsonn's saga: the genuine autobiography of a modern Icelander, 1–33. **Jòn Jònsonn.** Title; edited with intro. note by **George Ralph Fitz-Roy Cole**—signed, with title "C.E."

5884   Considerations on municipal government, 34–42. **F. R. Conder.** Signed F.R.C.—see no. 5623.

5885   Fields and field sports in Madras, 43–55. **M. J. Walhouse.** Signed M.J.W.; cf. no. 6006.

5886   Quarter sessions (No. IV): under Charles I; from original records of the County of Devon, 56–67. **A. H. A. Hamilton.** Signed.

5887   The *Roman de Renart* and La Fontaine, 68–81. **Jules Andrieu.** Signed.

5888   British trade (No. V): Austro-Hungary and Germany, 82–100. **A. J. Wilson.** Evidence for no. 5849.

5889   The Teutonic tree of existence, 101–117. **Karl Blind.** Signed.

5890   Mariuccia, 118–133.

VOLUME 95 O.S., 15 N.S., FEBRUARY 1877

5891   Mesmerism, odylism, table-turning, and spiritualism: considered historically and scientifically (Lecture I), 135–157. **William Benjamin Carpenter.** Signed William B. Carpenter; lectures repr. *Mesmerism, Spiritualism, &c.,* 1877.

5892   Our new frigates, 158–165. Signed: A Naval Officer.

5893   English local etymology, 166–172. **Henry Bradley.** Signed.

5894   The House of Lords, 173–186. **T. H. S. Escott,** prob. Art. begins with a reference to no. 5606 in words which suggest a common authorship; both arts. emphasize Parliamentary oratory; comments on Lord Rosebery, p. 179, are repeated in Escott's *Personal Forces of the Period* (1898), p. 55; the anecdotal style, excep-

tionally long paragraphs, occasional Gallicisms, and exaggerated phraseologies (such as "fossil traditions" and "lavish profusion," pp. 174, 175; cf. "flaming passage" [of a bill] and "unparalleled confusion" in no. 5606, p. 504) are typical of Escott's *FM* arts. and later books.

5895   Public instruction in Egypt, 187–200. **J. C. McCoan.** Signed; repr. *Egypt As It is,* N.Y., 1877.

5896   Carnot's plan for invading England, 201–205.

5897   The technical trade schools of north Germany, 206–218. **Henry Solly.** Signed, and called "Principal of 'The Artisans' Institute.' "

5898   The Cornish pilchard fisheries, 219–223. **James Quick.** Signed.

5899   Tuscan peasant plays, 224–234. **Violet Paget.** Signed V. Paget: see *DNB*/1940.

5900   British trade (No. VI): France, 235–253. **A. J. Wilson.** Evidence for no. 5849.

5901   Charles Kingsley [on his *Letters and Memoirs*], 254–268. **A. K. H. Boyd.** Signed A.K.H.B.; repr. *Recreations,* 3rd s.

VOLUME 95 O.S., 15 N.S., MARCH 1877

5902   Discipline and seamanship in the navy, past and present, 269–284. **E. R. Freemantle.** Signed E.R.F.—see no. 5161; cf. his book cited there.

5903   Imperial Delhi and the English Raj, 285–297. **William Simpson,** 1823–1899. Signed; see *DNB*/1st suppl.

5904   On certain government annuities in France, 298–301. **F. R. Conder.** Signed F.R.C.—see no. 5623.

5905   Etruscan interpretation, 302–321. **Francis William Newman.** Signed. (See no. 5922.)

5906   A long look-out, 322–330. **A. K. H. Boyd.** Signed A.K.H.B.; repr. *Recreations,* 3rd s.

5907   The religion of the great pyramid, 331–343. **Richard A. Proctor.** Signed; repr. *Myths and March of Astronomy,* 1889, and *The Great Pyramid,* 1883.

5908   British trade (No. VII): Italy, 344–358. **A. J. Wilson.** Evidence for no. 5849.

5909   Foreign relations of China, 359–373. Signed: A Chinese [who had lived in London two years and wrote in English, p. 359n.].

5910   The Norfolk Broads, 374–381.

5911 Mesmerism, odylism, table-turning and spiritualism (Lecture II, concl.), 382–405. **William Benjamin Carpenter.** Signed as in no. 5891. (See no. 5984.)

VOLUME 95 O.S., 15 N.S., APRIL 1877

5912 Popular songs of Tuscany, 407–421. **Janet Ross.** Signed; repr. *Old Florence.*
5913 Our inland navigation, 422–431. **F. R. Conder.** Signed F.R.C.—See no. 5623.
5914 On the Bedaween of the Arabian desert: notes of a recent visit, 432–443. **Roger D. Upton.** Signed.
5915 The moral treatment of insanity: a sketch of its rise and progress, 444–459. **Ellice Hopkins.** Signed.
5916 Quarter sessions (No. V): during the Civil War; from original records, 460–469. **A. H. A. Hamilton.** Signed.
5917 An apology for the competitive system [in the civil service], 470–487. **James Macdonell.** Signed M.—see no. 4833.
5918 Master Robert Shallow; a study of the Shakespeare country, 488–498. **C. Elliot Browne.** Signed.
5919 Local control of the drink traffic: two alternatives, 499–506. **Francis William Newman.** Signed; repr. *Miscellanies,* III. (Note, p. 674, signed **F. W. Newman.**)
5920 Old and young—cities and men, 507–518. **G. A. Simcox.** Signed.
5921 British trade (No. VIII): Spain, Portugal, and the Netherlands, 519–537. **A. J. Wilson.** Evidence for no. 5849.
5922 Notes on certain Etruscan interpretations [reply to no. 5905], 537–540. **Isaac Taylor,** 1829–1901. Signed; see *DNB,* 2nd suppl. (Note, p. 540, signed **F. W. Newman.**)

VOLUME 95 O.S., 15 N.S., MAY 1877

5923 The causes of pre-eminence in war, 541–562. Signed: A General.
5924 Slavery in Egypt, 563–570. **J. C. McCoan.** Signed; repr. *Egypt As It Is,* N.Y., 1877.
5925 Titian, 571–588. **Josiah Gilbert.** Signed Joseph Gilbert, but corrected, p. 806.
5926 Contemporary French poetry, 589–598. **Matilda Betham-Edwards.** Signed M.B.-E.—see no. 6063.
5927 Quarter sessions (No. VI): under the Commonwealth; from original records, 599–608. **A. H. A. Hamilton.** Signed.

5928 A northern *Hamlet* [on the Danish *Amleth* by Öhlenschläger], 609–621. **Edward Rose.** Signed.
5929 Unequal agriculture, 622–628. **Richard Jefferies.** Signed; repr. *The Hills and the Vale,* 1909.
5930 British trade (No. IX): Canada and South Africa, 629–650. **A. J. Wilson.** Evidence for no. 5849.
5931 Studies in Russian literature (Nos. I and II) [Lomonosoff and Kantemier], 651–664. **C. E. Turner.** Signed; series repr. *Studies.*
5932 On modern automatism, 665–674. **Francis William Newman.** Signed.

VOLUME 95 O.S., 15 N.S., JUNE 1877

5933 The war in Asia: recollections of the last campaign [1854–1856], 675–688. **J. C. McCoan.** Signed.
5934 Studies in Russian literature (Nos. III and IV) [Catherine the Second and Sumarokoff], 689–700. **C. E. Turner.** Signed.
5935 British trade (No. X): Australia and New Zealand, 701–722. **A. J. Wilson.** Evidence for no. 5849.
5936 An old German poem and a Vedic hymn [the "Wessobrunn Prayer" and the 129th song of the *Rig-Veda*], 723–730. **Karl Blind.** Signed.
5937 Quarter sessions (No. VII): in Devonshire under Charles II (Part I); from original records, 731–742. **A. H. A. Hamilton.** Signed.
5938 Molière, 743–757. **Henry M. Trollope.** Signed.
5939 The probable results of disestablishment, 758–767. **R. E. Bartlett.** Signed R.E.B.—see no. 6033.
5940 Experience of ambulances (Part I), 768–785. **Jessie White Mario.** Signed.
5941 Italian masks, 786–796. **Edward Rose.** Signed.
5942 The battles of peace, 797–806. **F. R. Conder.** Signed, with title "C.E."

VOLUME 96 O.S., 16 N.S., JULY 1877

5943 The Schliemannic Ilium, 1–16. **William Simpson,** 1823–1899. Signed; cf. no. 5903.
5944 Bassano, 17–28. **Bertha Thomas.** Signed B.T.—see no. 5759.
5945 Quarter sessions (No. VIII): in Devonshire under Charles II (Part II, concl.);

from original records, 29–39. **A. H. A. Hamilton.** Signed.

5946 Studies in Russian literature (Nos. V and VI) [von Viezin and Derzhavin], 40–53. **C. E. Turner.** Signed.

5947 Experience of ambulances (Part II), 54–74. **Jessie White Mario.** Signed.

5948 An exposition of betting and book-making, 75–84. **James Glass Bertram.** Signed B.—see no. 5613, cited in opening sentence; pp. 77, 79, 81 reappear, sometimes verbatim, in Bertram's *The Blue Ribbon of the Turf* (1890), pp. 174, 176–179.

5949 The money cost of the mineral traffic on railways, 85–112. **F. R. Conder.** Signed. Intro. note by **William Allingham** —signed Ed.

5950 British trade (No. XI): Mexico and Brazil, 113–122. **A. J. Wilson.** Evidence for no. 5849.

5951 A peculiar holiday [in London], 123–133. **A. K. H. Boyd.** Repr. *Recreations*, 3rd s.

5952 Some remarks on the resources of New Zealand, 134–138. **Julius Vogel.** Signed.

VOLUME 96 O.S., 16 N.S., AUGUST 1877

5953 *The City* [book on financial district of London], 139–151. **Arthur Arnold.** Signed; repr. *Social Politics*, 1878.

5954 Sexagenarian mountaineering, 152–178. **F. Barham Zincke.** Signed.

5955 The annexation of the Transvaal, 179–185. Signed: An Eye-Witness.

5956 Studies in Russian literature (Nos. VII and VIII) [Karamsin and Jukovsky], 186–203. **C. E. Turner.** Signed.

5957 British trade (No. XII): the River Plate, Chili, and Peru, 204–221. **A. J. Wilson.** Evidence for no. 5849.

5958 The purple head, 222–227. **Richard Garnett**, 1835–1906. Signed; repr. *Twilight of Gods.*

5959 Quarter sessions (No. IX): under James II; from original records, chiefly of the County of Devon, 228–240. **A. H. A. Hamilton.** Signed.

5960 What is disestablishment and disendowment? 241–246. **Francis William Newman.** Signed; repr. *Miscellanies*, III.

5961 Experience of ambulances (Part III, concl.), 247–266. **Jessie White Mario.** Signed.

5962 Concerning the longest day, 267–272.

A. K. H. Boyd. Signed A.K.H.B.; repr. *Recreations*, 3rd s.

VOLUME 96 O.S., 16 N.S., SEPTEMBER 1877

5963 Modern prophets [mainly scientists], 273–292. **William Allingham.** Signed Unus de Multis; repr. *Varieties*, III.

5964 Third-class passengers, 293–305. **F. R. Conder.** Signed.

5965 Christianity in India, 306–319. **Meredith Townsend?** Signed at start One Long Resident in India, at end M.T.; Townsend was in India, 1848–1860, returned to edit the *Spectator* and write thousands of arts.; his pessimistic view of the future of Christianity in India (see *DNB*/2nd suppl.) is precisely that adopted here and more especially in no. 5999.

5966 The transfer of "real" property; from a client's point of view, 320–332. Signed: R.T.

5967 Veii [one of the states in the Etruscan League], 333–347. Signed: R.C.

5968 Studies in Russian literature (Nos. IX and X) [Kriloff and Gogol], 348–367. **C. E. Turner.** Signed.

5969 Notes on the Slavonian races, 368–374. **Edward F. Willoughby.** Signed.

5970 Of vulgarity in opinion, 375–381. **A. K. H. Boyd.** Signed A.K.H.B.; repr. *Recreations*, 3rd s.

5971 British trade (No. XIII, concl.): the West Indies, &c., 382–398. **A. J. Wilson.** Evidence for no. 5849. (Letter, p. 540, signed **J. L. Ohlson.**)

5972 The Caliphate, 399–405. **J. C. McCoan.** Signed.

VOLUME 96 O.S., 16 N.S., OCTOBER 1877

5973 Austria, Germany, and the Eastern question, 407–416.

5974 William Longman; in memoriam, 417–421. **Henry Reeve.** Signed H.R.; attr. in *DNB* under Longman.

5975 Progress of colonisation in Algeria, 422–441. **Matilda Betham-Edwards.** Signed M.B.-E.—see no. 6063.

5976 Clericality, 442–451. **R. E. Bartlett.** Signed R.E.B.; cf. no. 6033.

5977 Garibaldi in France (Part I), 452–477. **Jessie White Mario.** Signed.

5978 Quarter sessions (No. X): under William and Mary; from original records, 478–485. **A. H. A. Hamilton.** Signed.

5979 On the comparative stupidity of politicians, 486–490. Signed: H.

5980 Studies in Russian literature (No. XI): a further account of the writings of Nicholas Gogol, 491–504. **C. E. Turner.** Signed.

5981 Some of the moral aspects of political economy, 505–515. **William Morton.** Signed.

5982 Dean Stanley at St. Andrews, 516–525. **A. K. H. Boyd.** Signed A.K.H.B.; repr. *Recreations*, 3rd s.

5983 Australian federation and imperial union, 526–539. **W. Jardine Smith.** Signed at start A Colonist, at end S.; cf. nos. 5242, 5371.

VOLUME 96 O.S., 16 N.S., NOVEMBER 1877

5984 Psychological curiosities of spiritualism, 541–564. **William Benjamin Carpenter.** Signed as in no. 5891. (Note, p. 806; see no. 5994.)

5985 English orthography, 565–574. **F. W. Newman.** Signed.

5986 Rambles (No. XIX): in Devon and Cornwall, 575–591. **William Allingham.** Evidence for no. 4807.

5987 Studies in Russian literature (No. XII): Poushkin, 592–601. **C. E. Turner.** Signed.

5988 Garibaldi in France (Part II), 602–618. **Jessie White Mario.** Signed.

5989 An old story now [on memory], 619–625. **A. K. H. Boyd.** Signed A.K.H.B.; repr. *Recreations*, 3rd s.

5990 Budhist schools in Burmah; by the director of public instruction in British Burmah, 626–634. **Peter Hordern.** Signed P. Hordern; see *Index*, I, 945.

5991 Three weeks with the hop-pickers, 635–648.

5992 The West India question, 649–674. **H. E. Watts.** Signed.

VOLUME 96 O.S., 16 N.S., DECEMBER 1877

5993 Mycenae; from personal investigation, 675–693. **William Simpson,** 1833–1899. Signed; cf. no. 5903.

5994 Psychological curiosities of scepticism: a reply to Dr. Carpenter [no. 5984], 694–706. **Alfred R. Wallace.** Signed. (Note, vol. 17 n.s., p. 134, signed **William B. Carpenter.**)

5995 The progress of marine insurance in England, 707–719. **E. S. Roscoe.** Signed.

5996 Garibaldi in France (Part III, concl.), 720–735. **Jessie White Mario.** Signed.

5997 Free trade in land, 736–747. **Francis W. Newman.** Signed; repr. *Miscellanies*, IV, as "Small Freeholds."

5998 Quarter sessions (No. XI, concl.): under Queen Anne; from original records, 749–761. **A. H. A. Hamilton.** Signed.

5999 Can India be Christianised? [sequel to no. 5965], 762–771. **Meredith Townsend?** Signed M.T.; cf. no. 5965, which is claimed, p. 762.

6000 Studies in Russian literature (No. XIII, concl.): the works of Poushkin, 772–782. **C. E. Turner.** Signed.

6001 Transcaucasia, 783–791. **G. R. Fitz-Roy Cole.** Signed. (Note, vol. 17 n.s., p. 268, from **Cole.**)

6002 Rambles (No. XX, concl.): in Thanet, 792–806. **William Allingham.** Evidence for no. 4807.

VOLUME 97 O.S., 17 N.S., JANUARY 1878

6003 England and her colonies, 1–17. **George Baden-Powell.** Signed.

6004 On teaching English, 18–21. **Francis W. Newman.** Signed.

6005 On the position of the Evangelical party in the Church of England, 22–31. **R. E. Bartlett.** Signed R.E.B.—see no. 6033.

6006 The great fourfold waterfall [of Garsoppa in India], 32–45. **M. J. Walhouse.** Signed.

6007 Spinozism: the religion of gladness, 46–57. **Arthur Bolles Lee.** Signed.

6008 The city of Kiyôto, 58–70. **Cyprian A. G. Bridge.** Signed.

6009 Thurot: a biographical sketch, 71–88. **J. K. Laughton.** Signed; repr. *Studies*.

6010 Free trade or reciprocity? 89–92. **C. Halford Thompson.** Signed.

6011 The kingdom of Fife, 93–113. **T. Hutchison.** Signed.

6012 How to invest money with safety [in railways], 114–126. **Francis Roubiliac Conder.** Signed.

6013 Ivy-leaves; from the Hermitage, Epping Forest (No. I), 127–134. **William Allingham.** Signed Eastern Hermit; attr. in his *Diary*, p. 307.

VOLUME 97 O.S., 17 N.S., FEBRUARY 1878

6014 The policy of Lord Beaconsfield's government, 135–141.

6015   Origen and Celsus, 142–167. **J. A. Froude.** Signed; repr. *Studies*, IV. (See no. 6049.)

6016   Professor [Robert] Buchanan of Glasgow, 168–175. **A. K. H. Boyd.** Signed A.K.H.B.; repr. *Recreations*, 3rd s.

6017   The capture and shooting of wild-fowl, 176–184. **M. G. Watkins.** Signed.

6018   Count Cavour, 185–199. Signed: S. S.

6019   May's *Democracy in Europe*, 200–206. Signed: D.

6020   Educational missions in India, 207–219. **Peter Hordern.** Signed as in no. 5990.

6021   The Hospital of S. Maria della Scala at Siena, 220–227. **Agnes D. Atkinson.** Signed.

6022   A visit to Dr. Schliemann's Troy, 228–239. **William C. Borlase.** Signed.

6023   The past and future of the High Church party, 240–249. **R. E. Bartlett.** Signed R.E.B.—see no. 6033.

6024   The Kaffir War, 250–258. Signed at start: An English Officer in South Africa, at end: H.S.

6025   Ivy-leaves (No. II), 259–268. **William Allingham.** Evidence for no. 6013.

VOLUME 97 O.S., 17 N.S., MARCH 1878

6026   The science of naval architecture, 269–276.

6027   Working men's conventions, 277–287. **Francis R. Conder.** Signed.

6028   The Historical Manuscripts Commission (No. IV, concl.): fifth report, 288–308. **John Piggot.** Signed P.; cf. no. 5319.

6029   The functions of government regarding public works, 309–314. **Horace Bell.** Signed.

6030   Spenser's Irish rivers, 315–333. **P. W. Joyce.** Signed.

6031   Barga, 334–345. **Linda Villari.** Signed; repr. *On Tuscan Hills and Venetian Waters*, 1885.

6032   Coroners, 346–352. **J. Roland Phillips.** Signed.

6033   The Broad Church movement, 353–364. **Robert Edward Bartlett.** Signed R.E.B.; C. R. Sanders, *Coleridge and the Broad Church Movement*, 1942, p. 10n., says "probably" by Bartlett; very probably because the position adopted here is found in the articles in the *Contemp. Rev.* which Bartlett signed (see *Index*, I, 806): the concern with the Christian Church but the refusal to identify it with any party in the Anglican Church or even with that Church to the exclusion

of other Christian churches; the playing down of doctrinal and ceremonial criteria and the emphasizing of "the devotional and saintly side of the religious life"; the readiness to accept freedom of inquiry (what Tulloch called rationalism) and therefore the confirmed results of contemporary science; and everywhere the plea for wide sympathy, mutual understanding, tolerance, etc.

6034   A great agricultural problem, 365–373. **Richard Jefferies.** Signed.

6035   Intermediate education in Ireland, 374–384. **W. G. Huband.** Signed.

6036   Of country work, 385–392. **A. K. H. Boyd.** Signed A.K.H.B.; repr. *Recreations*, 3rd s.

6037   Ivy-leaves (No. III), 393–402. **William Allingham.** Evidence for no. 6013.

VOLUME 97 O.S., 17 N.S., APRIL 1878

6038   Recent illustrations of naval warfare, 403–412. **John C. Paget.** Signed.

6039   At Stratford-on-Avon; an historical association, 413–427. **John W. Hales.** Signed; repr. *Notes*.

6040   Martin's *Western Islands* [*of Scotland*], 428–448. Signed: E.F.I.T.

6041   Church restoration, 449–457. **George Crabbe.** Signed, with title "Rev."

6042   The laws and customs of the ancient Irish, 458–481. **David Fitzgerald.** Signed.

6043   The limit of the habitability of London, 482–492. **F. R. Conder.** Signed.

6044   The Hon. Mrs. Norton and married women, 493–500. **Arthur Arnold.** Signed; repr. *Social Politics* (1878), as "The legal position of married women."

6045   Paul Jones, "the pirate," 501–522. **J. K. Laughton.** Signed; repr. *Studies*.

6046   A romance of the east coast, 523–528. **Emily L. Cornish.** Signed.

6047   Ivy-leaves (No. IV), 529–536. **William Allingham.** Evidence for no. 6013.

VOLUME 97 O.S., 17 N.S., MAY 1878

6048   Can England easily bear the cost of a great war? 537–547. Signed: W.

6049   Three letters on "Origen and Celsus" [no. 6015], 548–555. **F. W. Newman, J. A. Froude,** and **F. W. Newman.** Signed.

6050   The Azores, 556–568. Signed: R.M.D.

6051   Ximenes Doudan [French letter-writer], 569–577.

6052   British quadrupeds, 578–595. **M. G. Watkins.** Signed.

6053 On keeping silence from good [religious] words, 596–603. **Robert Edward Bartlett.** Signed R.E.B.—see no. 6033; on p. 599 author cites no. 6005.

6054 English and German party government, 604–616. Signed: A German.

6055 Louis Börne, 617–631. **Kate Vaughan Jennings.** Signed J.; long passage, pp. 620–621, is largely a paraphrase from her *Rahel, Her Life and Letters* (1876), pp. 39–40; she wrote no. 5331 on a closely related subject.

6056 Colonial and Indian custom-houses, and Manchester, 632–637. **Archibald Michie.** Signed. (See no. 6105.)

6057 Basque customs, 638–653. Signed: E.S.

6058 The legal position of the Dardanelles and the Suez Canal, 654–662. **John Macdonell.** Signed.

6059 Ivy-leaves (No. V), 663–670. **William Allingham.** Evidence for no. 6013.

VOLUME 97 O.S., 17 N.S., JUNE 1878

6060 Vice-Admiral Baron von Tegetthoff, 671–692. **J. K. Laughton.** Signed; repr. *Studies.*

6061 On Jewish proselytism before the War of Titus, 693–700. **Francis W. Newman.** Signed.

6062 The nemesis of the Renaissance, 701–717. **Henry G. Hewlett.** Signed.

6063 Jean Reynaud, French mystic and philosopher, 718–728. **Matilda Betham-Edwards.** Signed M.B.-E.; repr. *French Men, Women and Books*, 1910.

6064 Ups and downs in philology, 729–740. Signed: M.T.

6065 Of the Lengten-tide, 741–747. **A. K. H. Boyd.** Signed A.K.H.B.; repr. *Recreations*, 3rd s.

6066 Mary Wollstonecraft; a vindication, 748–762. **C. Kegan Paul.** Signed.

6067 The railway commissioners and the companies, 763–773. **James Howard, 1821–1889.** Signed; for the attr. to this agriculturalist, see his address on p. 773, the *DNB*, and the footnote, p. 773, in which he thanks Joseph Parsloe "for much of the information required in the preparation of this paper."

6068 Garden allotments, 774–778. **Alfred Hopkinson.** Signed.

6069 The Academy of the Árcadi: a study of Italian literary life in the eighteenth century (Part I), 779–798. **Violet Paget.** Signed Vernon Lee; repr. *Studies.*

6070 Ivy-leaves (No. VI), 799–806. **William Allingham.** Evidence for no. 6013.

VOLUME 98 O.S., 18 N.S., JULY 1878

6071 The defence of our Empire, 1–19. **George Baden-Powell.** Signed.

6072 Hydrological survey of England, 20–32. **F. R. Conder.** Signed.

6073 The Academy of the Árcadi (Part II, concl.), 33–59. **Violet Paget.** Evidence for no. 6069.

6074 The constitution of Norway, 60–72. Signed at start: The Author of "The Constitution of Sweden" (no. 5265), at end: W.D.T.

6075 Letters of Coleridge, Southey, and Lamb to Matilda Betham, hitherto unpublished, 73–84. **Matilda Betham-Edwards.** Signed M.B.-E.; repr. *Six Life Studies of Famous Women*, 1880.

6076 Among the Burmese (Part I), 85–102. **Peter Hordern.** Signed as in no. 5990.

6077 "L'École Française" at Athens and at Rome, 103–112. **M. Wolfe Capes.** Signed.

6078 The religions of Asiatic Turkey, 113–129. **J. C. McCoan.** Signed; repr. *Our New Protectorate.*

6079 Ivy-leaves (No. VII), 130–134. **William Allingham.** Evidence for no. 6013.

VOLUME 98 O.S., 18 N.S., AUGUST 1878

6080 The races of Asiatic Turkey, 135–147. **J. C. McCoan.** Signed; repr. *Our New Protectorate.*

6081 On the controversy of life, 148–166. **Edmund Gurney.** Signed; repr. *Tertium Quid* (1887), I.

6082 A June day's fancies, 167–177. **A. K. H. Boyd.** Signed A.K.H.B.; repr. *Recreations*, 3rd s.

6083 Africa and the Africans; by a negro, 178–196. **Edward W. Blyden.** Signed.

6084 Facts and fallacies of pauper education, 197–207. **Walter R. Browne.** Signed; repr. under same title, 1878.

6085 Social aspects of the Paris Exhibition, 208–225. **Matilda Betham-Edwards.** Signed M.B.-E.—see no. 6063.

6086 Trial of two Quakers in the time of Oliver Cromwell; from original records, 226–235. **A. H. A. Hamilton.** Signed.

6087 Peasants and proprietors in Tuscany, 236–244. Signed: C.

6088 Among the Burmese (Part II), 245–261. **Peter Hordern.** Signed as in no. 5990.

6089 Ivy-leaves (No. VIII), 262–268. **William Allingham.** Evidence for no. 6013.

VOLUME 98 O.S., 18 N.S., SEPTEMBER 1878

6090 The resources and products of Asiatic Turkey, 269–278. **J. C. McCoan.** Signed; repr. *Our New Protectorate.*

6091 The multiplication of universities, 279–295. **J. Bass Mullinger.** Signed.

6092 Among the Burmese (Part III), 296–307. **Peter Hordern.** Signed as in no. 5990.

6093 The public career and personal character of Francis Bacon, 308–325. **James Rowley.** Signed; repr. *Wordsworth.*

6094 Some remarks on the employment of English capital, 326–338. **Francis R. Conder.** Signed.

6095 Studies of Italian musical life in the eighteenth century (Part I), 339–361. **Violet Paget.** Signed Vernon Lee; repr. *Studies.*

6096 Holidays in eastern France (No. I): Seine et Marne, 362–380. **Matilda Betham-Edwards.** Signed M.B.-E.; series repr., 1879.

6097 "Peace with honour" [in Turko-Russian War], 385–395.

6098 Ivy-leaves (No. IX), 396–402. **William Allingham.** Evidence for no. 6013.

VOLUME 98 O.S., 18 N.S., OCTOBER 1878

6099 Slavery and polygamy in Turkey, 403–413. **J. C. McCoan.** Signed; repr. *Our New Protectorate.*

6100 Is schoolmastering a learned profession? 414–422. Signed: A. (See no. 6136.)

6101 Studies of Italian musical life in the eighteenth century (Part II), 423–446. **Violet Paget.** Evidence for no. 6095.

6102 John Chinaman abroad, 447–457. **G. R. Fitz-Roy Cole.** Signed.

6103 Sub-aqueous warfare, ancient and modern, 458–470. **Cyprian Bridge.** Signed.

6104 Among the Burmese (Part IV), 471–481. **Peter Hordern.** Signed as in no. 5990.

6105 Colonial custom-houses [reply to no. 6056], 482–489. **Edward Langton.** Signed, with addition "Member of the Executive Council of Victoria, Honorary Member of the Cobden Club."

6106 The progress of some of our railways towards bankruptcy, 490–502. **F. R. Conder.** Signed.

6107 Some aspects of modern nonconformity, 503–515. **Robert Edward Bartlett.** Signed R.E.B.; cf. no. 6033.

6108 Holidays in eastern France (No. II): Le Doubs, 516–529. **Matilda Betham-Edwards.** Evidence for no. 6096.

6109 Ivy-leaves (No. X), 530–536. **William Allingham.** Evidence for no. 6013.

VOLUME 98 O.S., 18 N.S., NOVEMBER 1878

6110 How Turkey in Asia is governed, 545–558. **J. C. McCoan.** Signed; repr. *Our New Protectorate.*

6111 Engineers in India, 559–565. Signed: U. Perhaps Frederick Robert Upcott, engineer and member Public Works Dept., India, since 1868: see *WWW/1928.*

6112 Studies of Italian musical life in the eighteenth century (Part III, concl.), 566–579. **Violet Paget.** Evidence for no. 6095.

6113 Strafford, 580–594. **A. H. A. Hamilton.** Signed.

6114 Among the Burmese (Part V), 599–608. **Peter Hordern.** Signed as in no. 5990.

6115 The organisation of unremunerative industry, 609–621. **Edith Simcox.** Signed.

6116 Colorado: the home of the farmer, 622–630. Signed at start: An English Farmer Now Settled Three Years in the State, at end: O.O.O.

6117 Holidays in eastern France (No. III): still in Le Doubs, 631–646. **Matilda Betham-Edwards.** Evidence for no. 6096.

6118 On the economy of speed in transport, 647–661. **F. R. Conder.** Signed.

6119 Ivy-leaves (No. XI), 662–666. **William Allingham.** Evidence for no 6013.

VOLUME 98 O.S., 18 N.S., DECEMBER 1878

6120 Tory finance, 667–678. Signed: W.

6121 "Frisco," 679–696.

6122 Public works in Asiatic Turkey: existing and projected, 697–712. **J. C. McCoan.** Signed; repr. *Our New Protectorate.*

6123 Mr. [Spencer] Walpole on England in the nineteenth century, 713–725. **G. Barnett Smith.** Signed.

6124 The question of the Thames, 726–736. **F. R. Conder.** Signed.

6125 Holidays in eastern France (No. IV,

concl.): the Jura, 737–757. **Matilda Betham-Edwards.** Evidence for no. 6096.

6126 Among the Burmese (Part VI, concl.), 758–766. **Peter Hordern.** Signed as in no. 5990.

6127 Hoffmann's *Kreisler*: the first of musical romanticists, 767–777. **Violet Paget.** Signed Vernon Lee; repr. *Belcaro*, 1881, as "Chapelmaster Kreisler."

6128 Solvency and resources of India [by H. M. Hyndman]: a reply to an article [by H. M. Hyndman] in *The Nineteenth Century*, 778–794. Signed: D.

6129 Ivy-leaves (No. XII, concl.), 796–798. **William Allingham.** Evidence for no. 6013.

VOLUME 99 O.S., 19 N.S., JANUARY 1879

6130 The Bhutan frontier: geographical and ethnical notes, 1–21. **T. Durant Beighton.** Signed.

6131 Trade-unions: their nature, character, and work, 22–31. **George Howell.** Signed.

6132 Starvation wages and political economy, 32–41. Signed: G.S. (See no. 6184.)

6133 The writing of history, and the first twenty-five years of Stuart rule in England, 42–54. **James Rowley.** Signed.

6134 The new Factory Act, 55–62. **Whately Cooke-Taylor.** Signed.

6135 Public instruction in Turkey, 63–78. **J. C. McCoan.** Signed; repr. *Our New Protectorate.*

6136 "Is schoolmastering a learned profession?" [reply to no. 6100], 79–87. **C. A. Vansittart Conybeare.** Signed.

6137 Negro slavery under English rule, 88–106. **Francis William Newman.** Signed.

6138 How to treat India, 107–114. Signed: X.

6139 Corsica, 115–133. **Roden Noel.** Signed.

VOLUME 99 O.S., 19 N.S., FEBRUARY 1879

6140 Bourbon [island near Mauritius], 135–158. **W. E. Montague.** Signed; cf. no. 6151.

6141 English parties and Irish faction; with suggestions for rearrangement, 159–169. Signed at start: A Conservative, at end: J.C.P.

6142 Negro slavery in the American union, 170–182. **Francis W. Newman.** Signed.

6143 *The Wonder-Working Magician* [by Calderon], 183–196. **Richard Hengist Horne.** Signed.

6144 Reciprocity, 197–210. **C. Halford Thompson.** Signed.

6145 On song, 211–224. **Edmund Gurney.** Signed.

6146 The best friend of the working man [the machine], 225–237. **F. R. Conder.** Signed.

6147 Mesmerism, planchette, and spiritualism in China, 238–245. **Herbert A. Giles.** Signed.

6148 The industrial employment of women, 246–255. **Edith Simcox.** Signed.

6149 A portfolio of ancient engravings, 256–263. **William B. Scott.** Signed. (See no. 6152.)

6150 A query on *Hamlet*, 263–264. **William Allingham.** Signed P.W. [Patricius Walker]—see no. 4807. (See no. 6160.)

VOLUME 99 O.S., 19 N.S., MARCH 1879

6151 Mauritius (Part I), 265–288. **William Edward Montague.** Signed W. E. Montague; man cited stationed at Mauritius in that year: see *Army List*/77, p. 340.

6152 A second portfolio of ancient engravings [sequel to no. 6149], 289–297. **William B. Scott.** Signed.

6153 Walter Bagehot, 298–313. **G. Barnett Smith.** Signed.

6154 Land titles and transfer, 314–324. **Arthur Arnold.** Signed; repr. *Free Land* (1880), chap. ix.

6155 White of Selborne, 325–340. **M. G. Watkins.** Signed.

6156 Technical training for girls, 343–351. **Bertha Thomas.** Signed B.T.—see no. 5759.

6157 A west-end poet [Thomas Haynes Bayly], 352–357. Signed: P.

6158 Realities of Bengali life, 358–370. Signed: A.S.B.

6159 Metastasio and the opera of the eighteenth century (Part I), 371–393. **Violet Paget.** Signed Vernon Lee; repr. *Studies.*

6160 The *Hamlet* difficulty [a reply to 6150], 394. Signed: W.P.

VOLUME 99 O.S., 19 N.S., APRIL 1879

6161 The trade guilds of the city of London, 395–405.

6162 On the escape of Prince Louis Napoleon from the fortress of Ham: my interview with H.R.H. the Duke of Brunswick, December 3, 1845, 406–420. **Joseph Orsi.** Signed; repr. *Recollections,* pp. 171–220.

6163 Residual phenomena, 421–427. **M. M. Pattison Muir.** Signed.

6164 The bankruptcy laws and mercantile corruption, 428–437. Signed: W.

6165 Mauritius (Part II, concl.), 438–467. **W. E. Montague.** Signed; cf. no. 6151.

6166 On nursing as a career for ladies, 468–479. **George Barraclough.** Signed, with title "M.R.C.S., Eng."; attr. in *Med. Directory*/90.

6167 The crisis in trade: its cause and cure, 482–494. **E. A. Ryder.** Signed.

6168 Metastasio and the opera of the eighteenth century (Part II), 495–510. **Violet Paget.** Evidence for no. 6159.

6169 Squatters and peasant proprietors in Victoria, 511–518. **Robert Niven.** Signed.

6170 Wagner as a dramatist, 519–532. **Edward Rose.** Signed.

VOLUME 99 O.S., 19 N.S., MAY 1879

6171 The game of Egyptian finance, 533–547. **A. J. Wilson.** Signed.

6172 On Chinese fans, 548–556. **Herbert A. Giles.** Signed.

6173 Are explosions in coal mines preventible? 557–568. **Francis R. Conder.** Signed.

6174 Metastasio and the opera of the eighteenth century (Part III, concl.), 583–614. **Violet Paget.** Evidence for no. 6159.

6175 John Aikin, M.D., 615–625. **Mary Emma Martin.** Signed Mrs. Herbert Martin: see *BMCat.*

6176 The Church of the future, 626–634. **Robert Edward Bartlett.** Signed R.E.B.—see no. 6033.

6177 Reforms in Asiatic Turkey, 635–649. Signed at start: One Who has Lived There, at end: S.

6178 The true Omar Khayam, 650–659. **Jessie E. Cadell.** Signed J.E.C.; attr. in obit. notice, *Athenaeum*, June 28, 1884, p. 824.

6179 The dark side of a bright picture, 660–664. Signed at start: A Colorado Settler, at end: C.S.

6180 The Byron monument, 665–666. **William Allingham.** Signed One Who Loves and Honours English Poetry; repr. *Varieties*, III.

VOLUME 99 O.S., 19 N.S., JUNE 1879

6181 Indian budgets and Indian deficits, 667–679.

6182 A pedestrian's route from the Italian Lakes to the Rhone Valley, 680–689. **Arthur Cust.** Signed A. Cust, with title "M.A."; see Venn.

6183 Wandering thoughts about Germany, 690–696. **R. E. Bartlett.** Signed R.E.B.; cf. no. 6033, etc.; last paragraphs of this art. deal with Christianity from a liberal position.

6184 Starvation wages and political economy: a reply [to no. 6132], 697–702. Signed: C.E.

6185 Experiences of a coffee planter in southern India, 703–708. Signed: G.C.

6186 Mr. Caird, *The Landed Interest and the Supply of Food*, 709–730. Signed: G.S.

6187 The command of the sea, 731–740. Signed: C.

6188 Ausonius, 741–760. **James Mew.** Signed.

6189 A visit to the New Zealand geysers, 761–768. **Robert Clement Bunbury,** prob. Signed Clement Bunbury; see Venn.

6190 Schopenhauer on men, books, and music, 769–777. **Matilda Betham-Edwards.** Signed M.B.-E.—see no. 6063.

6191 The revival of the warlike power of China, 778–789. **Cyprian A. G. Bridge.** Signed.

6192 Some fifty years ago [on *FM* in 1830's], 790–800. **William Allingham.** Carlyle *Bibliography*, p. 506.

VOLUME 100 O.S., 20 N.S., JULY 1879

6193 Our past and our future, 1–12. **John Tulloch.** Signed the Editor in index.

6194 Mary Anerley: a Yorkshire tale [the subtitle was added in 2nd installment, no. 6201, etc.] (chaps. i–vi), 13–37. **Richard D. Blackmore.** Novel published 1880.

6195 Shelley as a lyric poet, 38–53. **J. C. Shairp.** Signed; repr. *Aspects of Poetry*, 1881

6196 A Royal Commission upon the Scotch Universities, 54–70.

6197 Bibliomania in 1879: a chat about rare books, 71–88. **John Skelton.** Signed Shirley—see *DNB.*

6198 Gossip and gossip [largely on the "Society journals"], 90–102. **T. Wemyss Reid?** In Reid's " 'Our London Correspondent' " published 10 months later in *Macmillan's* (no. 1965 in *Index*, I), pages 18–19, and 22–23, also describe good and bad gossip in a similar style, though with a shift in emphasis from "bad" gossip here to "good" gossip there; there too the "society journals" are cited on pp. 20, 26; and see evidence for *FM* no. 5817.

6199 Three small books: by great writers [Browning, Eliot, Tennyson], 103–124.

6200 A government on its defence, 125–142.

VOLUME 100 O.S., 20 N.S., AUGUST 1879

6201 Mary Anerley (chaps. vii–x), 143–170. **R. D. Blackmore.** Cf. no. 6194.

6202 Egypt and the pre-Homeric Greeks, 171–185. **Andrew Lang.** Signature.

6203 Of parting company, 186–194. **A. K. H. Boyd.** Signed A.K.H.B.; repr. *Our Little Life*, 1882.

6204 A Gallician novelist [Leopold Ritter von Sacher-Masoch], 195–209. **Helen Zimmern.** Signed.

6205 Prince Louis Napoleon's expedition to Boulogne, August 1840; an original narrative, 210–229. **Joseph Orsi.** Signed; repr. *Recollections*, pp. 116–162.

6206 *Familiar Photographs in Verse*, 230–241. **Arthur Hill.** Signed.

6207 Weather forecasting, 242–254. **J. K. Laughton.** Signed.

6208 Studies in biography, 255–275.

6209 The state of public business, 276–290.

VOLUME 100 O.S., 20 N.S., SEPTEMBER 1879

6210 Mary Anerley (chaps. xi–xiii), 291–314. **R. D. Blackmore.** Cf. no. 6194.

6211 Mr. Froude's *Caesar*, 315–337. **W. Y. Sellar.** Signed.

6212 My journal in the Holy Land (Part I), 338–350. **Annie Brassey.** Signed.

6213 Tenant right in Ireland, 351–359.

6214 Cheneys [in Buckinghamshire] and the House of Russell, 360–385. **J. A. Froude.** Signed; repr. *Studies*, IV.

6215 A Hungarian episode: Zigeuner music, 390–396. **Julia C. B. Byrne.** Signed The Author of *Flemish Interiors*—see no. 5349.

6216 Holiday travel-books, 397–418.

6217 The close of the session, 419–432.

VOLUME 100 O.S., 20 N.S., OCTOBER 1879

6218 Mary Anerley (chaps. xiv–xvi), 433–455. **R. D. Blackmore.** Cf. no. 6194.

6219 French tragedy before Corneille, 456–474. **George Saintsbury.** Signed.

6220 Partridges and politics, 478–493. **T. E. Kebbel.** Signed.

6221 The failure of altruism, 494–503.

6222 Prince Napoleon and European democracy; reminiscences, 504–521. **Karl Blind.** Signed.

6223 My journal in the Holy Land (Part II), 522–533. **Annie Brassey.** Signed.

6224 Afghanistan: its races and rulers, 534–541. Signed: G.T.P.

6225 Recent novels, 542–563.

6226 The cost of a foreign policy [the Afghan War], 564–578.

VOLUME 100 O.S., 20 N.S., NOVEMBER 1879

6227 Mary Anerley (chaps. xvii–xix), 579–603. **R. D. Blackmore.** Cf. no. 6194.

6228 What Shakespeare learnt at school (Part I), 604–621. **Thomas S. Baynes.** Signed; repr. *Shakespeare Studies*, 1894.

6229 A siding at a railway station (Part I, no more published), 622–633. **J. A. Froude.** Signed J.A.F.; repr. *Studies*, IV.

6230 The land question, and report on land titles and transfer, 634–646. **Arthur Arnold.** Signed; repr. *Free Land* (1880), chap. x.

6231 Little to shew, 647–656. **A. K. H. Boyd.** Signed A.K.H.B.; repr. *Our Little Life*, 1882.

6232 Mr. Gladstone as a man of letters, 657–672. **John Tulloch.** Attr. in *Biograph* 3 (1880), 428.

6233 How we got away from Naples; a story of the time of King Bomba, 673–684. Signed: H.

6234 Professor Clifford, 685–701.

6235 Lord Salisbury and Mr. Cross in Lancashire, 702–722.

VOLUME 100 O.S., 20 N.S., DECEMBER 1879

6236 Mary Anerley (chaps. xx–xxii), 723–747. **R. D. Blackmore.** Cf. no. 6194.

6237 First impressions of the New World (Part I), 748–766. **George Douglas Campbell.** Signed Argyll [Duke of Argyll].

6238 Strikes: their cost and results, 767–783. **George Howell.** Signed.

6239 My life in Paris during and following the Commune, 784–797. **Joseph Orsi.** Signed Count Orsi; repr. *Recollections*.

6240 Homeric mythology and religion: a reply to Mr. Gladstone [in *Nineteenth Century*, 6 (Oct. 1879), 746–768], 798–807. **George W. Cox.** Signed.

6241 My journal in the Holy Land (Part

III, concl.), 808–821. **Annie Brassey.** Signed.

6242 *Edward and Catherine Stanley* [*Memoirs*, ed. A. P. Stanley], 822–830.

6243 Our sons at Eton and Oxford; with elucidations [intermittently, in smaller print] by one of the sons, 831–850. Signed: A "Parent."

6244 England and the Councils of Europe, 851–866.

VOLUME 101 O.S., 21 N.S., JANUARY 1880

6245 Mary Anerley (chaps. xxiii–xxv), 1–23. **R. D. Blackmore.** Cf. no. 6194.

6246 Some aspects of Indian finance, 24–39. **W. W. Hunter.** Signed.

6247 First impressions of the New World (Part II, concl.), 40–57. **George Douglas Campbell.** Signed Argyll; cf. no. 6237.

6248 A type of the Renaissance [Andrea del Sarto], 58–71. **Ellen M. Clerke.** Signature; Index adds "Miss"; see *DNB*.

6249 Ireland and England, 73–82. Signed at end: M.P., in Index An M.P.

6250 What Shakespeare learnt at school (Part II), 83–102. **Thomas S. Baynes.** Signed.

6251 Mr. Gladstone in Scotland, 103–117.

6252 Earthbound; a story of the seen and the unseen, 118–144. **Margaret Oliphant.** Signature.

VOLUME 101 O.S., 21 N.S., FEBRUARY 1880

6253 Mary Anerley (chaps. xxvi–xxx), 145–173. **R. D. Blackmore.** Cf. no. 6194.

6254 The late Canon [J. B.] Mozley, 174–188. **J. C. Shairp.** Signed.

6255 Ancient Buddhist remains in Afghanistan, 189–204. **William Simpson,** 1823–1899. Signed; cf. no. 5903.

6256 Wordsworth, 205–221. **Edward Caird.** Signed; repr. *Essays on Literature and Philosophy* (1892), I.

6257 English Liberals and continental liberals, 222–234.

6258 An imprisoned princess—Leonora Christina of Denmark, 235–247. Signed: K.D.M.

6259 What is money? 248–260. **Bonamy Price.** Signed.

6260 The English nation and the Zulu War, 261–271. **George W. Cox.** Signed.

6261 The *Crookit Meg*; a story of the year one (chaps. i–v), 272–288. **John Skelton.** Author's intro. note signed Shirley; novel

published 1880 and repr. *Table Talk*, 2nd series (1896), I.

VOLUME 101 O.S., 21 N.S., MARCH 1880

6262 Mary Anerley (chaps. xxxi–xxxiv), 289–313. **R. D. Blackmore.** Cf. no. 6194.

6263 Free trade principles and taxation, 314–323. **Frederick Romilly.** Signed.

6264 On the origin of a written Greek literature, 324–336. **F. A. Paley.** Signed.

6265 Burton's *Reign of Queen Anne*, 337–352. **John Tulloch.** Signed J.T.; assigned to "The Editor" in Index.

6266 *Russia Before and After the War*, 353–360. **Olga (Kiréeff) de Novikoff.** Signed O.K.; she published *Russia and England*, 1880, under these initials.

6267 Thomas Henry Buckle, 361–377.

6268 Irish land reform; from an Irish point of view, 378–391. **J. C. McCoan.** Signed.

6269 Among French friends in Burgundy: Dijon, 392–402. **Matilda Betham-Edwards.** Signature.

6270 The *Crookit Meg* (chaps. vi–xii), 403–420. **John Skelton.** Cf. no. 6261.

6271 The coming election, 421–432.

VOLUME 101 O.S., 21 N.S., APRIL 1880

6272 Mary Anerley (chaps. xxxv–xxxviii), 433–458. **R. D. Blackmore.** Cf. no. 6194.

6273 A Swiss novelist [Gottfried Keller], 459–476. **Helen Zimmern.** Signed.

6274 The Zulu campaign; from a military point of view, 477–488. **Arthur Harness.** Signed.

6275 The *Crookit Meg* (chaps. xiii–xvii), 489–503. **John Skelton.** Cf. no. 6261.

6276 Contesting the counties, 504–515. **William Minto.** Signed.

6277 MacPherson, Burns, and Scott in their relation to the modern revolution, 516–531. **J. S. Stuart-Glennie.** Signed.

6278 National thrift and its practical promotion, 532–547. **William Lewery Blackley.** Signed.

6279 Blues and buffs [Tories and Whigs]; a sketch of a contested election (chaps. i–ix), 548–570. **Arthur Mills.** Series published 1880: see *BMCat*.

6280 The electoral crisis, 571–576.

VOLUME 101 O.S., 21 N.S., MAY 1880

6281 Mary Anerley (chaps xxxix–xli), 577–599. **R. D. Blackmore.** Cf. no. 6194.

6282 The variations of the Roman Church, 600–611. **A. P. Stanley.** Signed.

6283 A Russian lady's book [by Olga de Novikoff], 612–618. **Adelina P. Irby.** Signed A. P. Irby; Index adds "Miss"; see *BMCat.*

6284 What Shakespeare learnt at school (Part III, concl.), 619–641. **Thomas S. Baynes.** Signed; cf. no. 6228.

6285 The *Crookit Meg* (chaps. xviii–xxii), 642–651. **John Skelton.** Cf. no. 6261.

6286 The atheistic view of life, 652–667. **Richard H. Hutton.** Signed.

6287 What is a bank? and what does it deal in? 668–682. **Bonamy Price.** Signed.

6288 Blues and buffs (chaps. x–xiii), 683–697. **Arthur Mills.** Cf. no. 6279.

6289 The grievances of women, 698–710. **Margaret Oliphant.** Signed M.O.W.O.; assigned to "Mrs. Oliphant" in Index.

6290 The past election, 711–720.

VOLUME 101 O.S., 21 N.S., JUNE 1880

6291 The *Crookit Meg* (chaps. xxiii–xxxi, concl.), 721–746. **John Skelton.** Signed Shirley; cf. no. 6261.

6292 Effects of western competition on the eastern states of America, 747–754. **Lyon Playfair.** Signed.

6293 Last years of the Prince Consort [Theodore Martin's biography], 755–768. **John Tulloch.** Signed J.T.; assigned to "The Editor" in the Index.

6294 Geology and history, 769–780. **Grant Allen.** Signed.

6295 Mary Anerley (chaps. xlii–xlv), 781–804. **R. D. Blackmore.** Cf. no. 6194.

6296 Mr. Gladstone's ancestors—the Gledstanes of Gledstanes and Coklaw; a chapter in old Scottish history, 805–816. **John Veitch.** Signed J. Veitch; repr. *Border Essays*, 1896.

6297 Diamonds, natural and artificial, 817–830. **Agnes M. Clerke.** Signed.

6298 Blues and buffs (chaps. xiv–xxii), 831–848. **Arthur Mills.** Cf. no. 6279.

6299 Painting and popular culture, 849–856. **T. C. Horsfall.** Signed.

6300 The new departure [in parliament], 857–864.

VOLUME 102 O.S., 22 N.S., JULY 1880

6301 Blues and buffs (chaps. xxiii–xxxii, concl.), 1–28. **Arthur Mills.** Cf. no. 6279.

6302 The Austrian power, 29–47. **Edward A. Freeman.** Signed.

6303 The poetry of Lewis Morris, 48–59. **Thomas Bayne.** Signed.

6304 Montaigne as an educationalist, 60–72. **S. S. Laurie.** Signed.

6305 Mary Anerley (chaps. xlvi–xlviii), 73–95. **R. D. Blackmore.** Cf. no. 6194.

6306 The migration of popular stories, 96–111. **George W. Cox.** Signed.

6307 Hospital nursing, 112–125. **Henry C. Burdett.** Signed.

6308 The Book of Job; a literary and biographical study, 126–134. **T. K. Cheyne.** Signed.

6309 The ministry and its work, 135–144.

VOLUME 102 O.S., 22 N.S., AUGUST 1880

6310 Theeda: an allegory, 145–163. **Julian Hawthorne.** Signed.

6311 Russia and China, 164–174. **Demetrius Charles Boulger.** Signed; repr. *Central Asian Questions.*

6312 Béranger: his songs and politics, 175–184. **Eliza Clarke.** Signed; Index adds "Mrs."

6313 The water supply of London, 185–198. **F. R. Conder.** Signed.

6314 An artist on art [E. J. Poynter], 199–211. **Harry Quilter.** Signed.

6315 The up-bringing of pauper children in Scotland, 212–222. **John Skelton.** Signed.

6316 A forgotten empire in Asia Minor [the Hittite empire], 223–233. **A. H. Sayce.** Signed.

6317 Mary Anerley (chaps. xlix–liii), 234–260. **R. D. Blackmore.** Cf. no. 6194.

6318 The House of Lords and popular education, 261–275. **S. S. Laurie.** Signed An Old Educationalist; see his *The Training of Teachers*, 1882, Preface.

6319 A bather's ideal, 276–278. **Ernest James Myers.** Signed Ernest Myers; for man cited see *DNB*/1921; in *FM* and elsewhere he apparently did not use his middle name.

6320 Parliamentary difficulties and political parties, 279–288.

VOLUME 102 O.S., 22 N.S., SEPTEMBER 1880

6321 The romance of the first radical; a prehistoric apologue, 289–300. **Andrew Lang.** Signature; repr. *In the Wrong Paradise*, 1886.

6322 Russel of *The Scotsman*, 301–317. **H. G. Graham.** Signed.

6364 The prophetic power of poetry, 53–66. **J. C. Shairp.** Signed; repr. *Aspects of Poetry*, 1881.

6365 Prehistoric science en fête [congress of anthropologists], 67–72.

6366 Henry John Codrington, Admiral of the Fleet, 73–86. **J. K. Laughton.** Signed.

6367 Folk lullabies, 87–99. **Evelyn Martinengo-Cesaresco.** Signed Evelyn Carrington, her maiden name; repr. *Folk-Songs.*

6368 The last chapter of Irish history, 100–116. **George C. Brodrick.** Signed; repr. *Literary Fragments*, 1891.

6369 Our ideals, 117–122. **Violet Greville.** Signed.

6370 A plea for our dull boys, 123–134. Signed: An Oxford Tutor.

6371 Rumours [in current politics], 136–144.

VOLUME 103 O.S., 23 N.S., FEBRUARY 1881

6372 In trust; the story of a lady and her lover (chaps. i–iii), 145–165. **Margaret Oliphant.** Novel published 1882.

6373 Wanted: a new constitution for India, 166–186. **Robert H. Elliot.** Signed.

6374 Macaulay, 187–196. **Ernest Myers.** Signed; cf. no. 6319.

6375 Greek dinners, 197–206. **F. A. Paley.** Signed.

6376 Alone in college, and what came of it, 211–226.

6377 Flight natural and artificial, 227–246. **J. Bell Pettigrew.** Signed.

6378 Concerning the cheerfulness of the old, 247–262. **A. K. H. Boyd.** Signed A.K.H.B.; repr. *Our Little Life*, 1882.

6379 Village life of George Eliot, 263–276. **T. E. Kebbel.** Signed.

6380 The parliamentary situation, 277–286.

VOLUME 103 O.S., 23 N.S., MARCH 1881

6381 In trust (chaps. iv–vi), 287–309. **Margaret Oliphant.** Cf. no. 6372.

6382 The truth about American competition, 310–324. **George Baden-Powell.** Signed.

6383 A new house for the Commons, 325–333. **H. W. Lucy.** Signed.

6384 *Lord Campbell*, 334–352. **A. K. H. Boyd.** Signed A.K.H.B.; repr. *Our Little Life*, 1882.

6385 John Gilpin as a solar hero, 353–371.

6386 A publisher's view of international copyright, 372–378. **Charles James Longman.** Signed.

6387 A landscape painter's tale, 379–389. **Mary C. McCallum.** Signed M. C. Sterling, under which name she wrote fiction (see *BMCat.*); see Part B below.

6388 Tyningtown, 390–399. **James Purves.** Signed.

6389 A stormy passage in politics, 411–422.

VOLUME 103 O.S., 23 N.S., APRIL 1881

6390 In trust (chaps vii–ix), 423–446. **Margaret Oliphant.** Cf. no. 6372.

6391 The Lancashire witches, 447–460. **Alexander Charles Ewald.** Signed; repr. *Stories from the State Papers* (1882), II.

6392 The Indian uncovenanted service, 461–473. Signed: An Official [in the Indian Civil Service].

6393 The City companies and technical education, 474–481. **John Roland Phillips.** Signed J. R. Phillips; see *Index*, I, 1048.

6394 Jewish home life, 482–500. **Helen Zimmern.** Signed.

6395 Hospital reform, 501–514. **Henry C. Burdett.** Signed.

6396 Mr. Carlyle's *Reminiscences,* 515–528. **Andrew Lang.** Signature.

6397 The Royal Commission on Church Courts, 530–552. **John Oakley.** Signed.

6398 March gusts [in politics], 553–566.

VOLUME 103 O.S., 23 N.S., MAY 1881

6399 In trust (chaps. x–xii), 567–589. **Margaret Oliphant.** Cf. no. 6372.

6400 The colleges as landlords, 590–600. Signed: Oxoniensis.

6401 A Lancashire poets' corner, 601–610. **J. A. Noble.** Signed.

6402 The *Sunbeam* in a storm: an extract from Mrs. Brassey's diary, 611–617. **Annie Brassey.** Title; the diary shows she was the wife of Thomas Brassey, 1836–1918, in *DNB.*

6403 Young Oxford, 618–636. Signed: An Oxford Tutor.

6404 On the origin of the Prince of Wales' feathers, 637–649. **William Simpson,** 1833–1899. Signed W. Simpson, full name in Index, with title "F.R.G.S."; see *DNB*/1st suppl.

6405 Autobiography of an agnostic, 650–669. **Bertha Thomas,** prob. Signed B. Thomas; woman cited wrote frequently for *FM.*

6406 Mr. Thrale, 670–679. **T. E. Kebbel.** Signed.

6407 Employers' liability for accidents to workpeople, 680–692. **Edwin Chadwick.** Signed.

6408 The first act [of parliament], 693–702.

VOLUME 103 O.S., 23 N.S., JUNE 1881

6409 In trust (chaps. xiii–xv), 703–726. **Margaret Oliphant.** Cf. no. 6372.

6410 The revised version of the English New Testament, 727–740. **Alexander Roberts.** Signed.

6411 A Japanese bride, 741–757. **Matilda Betham-Edwards.** Signature.

6412 Our winter storms, 758–770. **J. K. Laughton.** Signed.

6413 Consolations, 771–782. **Edith Simcox.** Repr. *Episodes.*

6414 Malpractices at elections, 783–799. **W. M. Torrens.** Signed.

6415 In Umbria; a study of artistic personality, 800–816. **Violet Paget.** Signed Vernon Lee; repr. *Belcaro*, 1881.

6416 A pilgrimage to Cyprus in 1395–1396, 818–821. **J. Theodore Bent.** Signed.

6417 Conservative tactics, 822–832.

VOLUME 104 O.S., 24 N.S., JULY 1881

6418 In trust (chaps. xvi–xviii), 1–27. **Margaret Oliphant.** Cf. no. 6372.

6419 Léon Michel Gambetta, 28–41.

6420 A diptych, 42–56. **Edith Simcox.** Signed The Author of "Consolations" (no. 6413); repr. *Episodes.*

6421 The honorary element in hospital administration, 57–67. **B. Burford Rawlings.** Signed.

6422 Parliament and the higher education, 68–83. **J. E. Thorold Rogers.** Signed.

6423 Beauchamp and Co., 84–98. **Mary E. Martin.** Signed Mrs. Herbert Martin, Author of *Bonnie Lesley*, etc.; see *BMCat.*

6424 The failure of protection in the United States, 99–112. **George Baden-Powell.** Signed; repr. *State Aid.*

6425 The late Governor of Madras [William Adam], 113–122. **Alexander Craig Sellar.** Signed.

6426 Party politics, 132–140.

VOLUME 104 O.S., 24 N.S., AUGUST 1881

6427 In trust (chaps. xix–xxi), 141–165. **Margaret Oliphant.** Cf. no. 6372.

6428 Mr. Max Müller's philosophy of mythology, 166–187. **Andrew Lang.** Signature.

6429 Tractarianism and ritualism, 188–203. **Malcolm MacColl.** Signed.

6430 Midsummer noon, 204–211. **Edith Simcox.** Signed The Author of "Consolations" (no. 6413); repr. *Episodes.*

6431 The finance of unendowed hospitals, 212–223. **B. Burford Rawlings.** Signed.

6432 The great southern comet of 1880, 224–234. **Agnes M. Clerke.** Signed A. M. Clerke; see *DNB*/2nd suppl.

6433 A film of gossamer; a story of the chestnut harvest, 235–249. **Ellen M. Clerke.** Signature.

6434 Historic memorials of the Norfolk Coast (Part I), 253–267. **C. Rachel Jones.** Signed Mrs. Herbert Jones; repr. *Sandringham Past and Present*, 1883.

6435 Closing scenes [in parliament], 268–276.

VOLUME 104 O.S., 24 N.S., SEPTEMBER 1881

6436 In trust (chaps. xxii–xxiv), 277–300. **Margaret Oliphant.** Cf. no. 6372.

6437 Nassau Senior's journals and conversations, 301–319. Signed: E.E.

6438 The capercaillie [Scottish game bird], 320–326. **M. G. Watkins.** Signed.

6439 Historic memorials of the Norfolk coast (Part II, concl.), 327–344. **C. Rachel Jones.** Signed as in no. 6434.

6440 Registry of title, 345–357. **W. M. Torrens.** Signed.

6441 Mary Schönewald; a study in prophecy, 358–384. **A. Mary F. Robinson.** Signed.

6442 Swift and Ireland, 385–400. **Stanley Lane-Poole.** Signed.

6443 The House of Lords, 401–414.

VOLUME 104 O.S., 24 N.S., OCTOBER 1881

6444 In trust (chaps. xxv–xxvii), 415–436. **Margaret Oliphant.** Cf. no. 6372.

6445 Life in mediaeval Venice, 437–447. **J. Theodore Bent.** Signed.

6446 Love and friendship, 448–461. **Edith Simcox.** Signed The Author of "Consolations" (no. 6413); repr. *Episodes.*

6447 Privateers and privateering in the eighteenth century (No. I): Fortunatus Wright, 462–478. **J. K. Laughton.** Signed; repr. *Studies.*

6448 The electric telegraphs, 479–491. **A. H. Japp.** Signed in Index.

6449 Under false colours; or, "A Roland

for an Oliver," 492–514. **Mary Gleed Tuttiett.** Signed The Author of *The Broken Tryst*: see *BMCat*.

6450　The letters of Goethe's mother, 515–525. **Eliza Clarke.** Signed; Index gives "Mrs. Clarke."

6451　An Athenian archbishop of the Dark Ages [Michael Acominatus], 526–532. **John Edward Kempe.** Signed J. Kempe in Index; see Venn and *WWW*/1916.

6452　The House of Commons, 533–546.

VOLUME 104 O.S., 24 N.S., NOVEMBER 1881

6453　In trust (chaps. xxviii–xxx), 547–570. **Margaret Oliphant.** Cf. no. 6372.

6454　Leopardi and his father: a study, 571–588. **Linda Villari.** Signed.

6455　Privateers and privateering in the eighteenth century (No. II, concl.): George Walker, 589–603. **J. K. Laughton.** Signed; repr. *Studies*.

6456　England under protectionism and under free trade, 604–623. **A. J. Wilson.** Signed.

6457　At anchor, 624–629. **Edith Simcox.** Signed The Author of "Consolations" (no. 6413); repr. *Episodes*.

6458　German student life, 630–645. **A. H. Baynes.** Signed.

6459　Of the opposition, 646–657. **A. K. H. Boyd.** Signed A.K.H.B.; repr. *Our Little Life*, 1882.

6460　The physical revolution of the nineteenth century, 658–667. **F. R. Conder.** Signed.

6461　The Rev. Jeremiah's thorn, 668–672. **Helen K. Wilson.** Signed.

6462　The recess [of parliament], 673–682.

VOLUME 104 O.S., 24 N.S., DECEMBER 1881

6463　In trust (chaps. xxxi–xxxiii), 683–708. **Margaret Oliphant.** Cf. no. 6372.

6464　The new departure in Russia, 709–729. **Olga (Kiréeff) de Novikoff.** Signed O.K.—see no. 6266.

6465　Stefano; a reminiscence of Sorrento, 730–741. **Ellen M. Clerke.** Signature.

6466　Of mistakes; a consolatory essay, 742–752. **A. K. H. Boyd.** Signed A.K.H.B.; repr. *Our Little Life*, 1882.

6467　English satire in the nineteenth century, 753–761. **Ernest Myers.** Signed; cf. no. 6319.

6468　A chat about good cheer, 762–776. **Mrs. Elizabeth Stone.** Signed Sutherland Menzies; see *BMCat*.

6469　The *chansons de geste*: the "Song of Roland," 777–789. **C. F. Keary.** Signed.

6470　Charles Tennyson Turner, 790–799. **Thomas Bayne.** Signed.

6471　The House of Commons, 800–812.

VOLUME 105 O.S., 25 N.S., JANUARY 1882

6472　In trust (chaps. xxxiv–xxxvi, concl.), 1–27. **Margaret Oliphant.** Cf. no. 6372.

6473　The seed-time of health, 28–45. **Benjamin Ward Richardson.** Signed.

6474　Mr. Darwin on earth-worms, 46–53. **F. A. Paley.** Signed.

6475　The tercentenary of Siberia, 54–71. **Olga (Kiréeff) de Novikoff.** Signed O.K. —see no. 6266.

6476　Labédoyère's doom, 72–90. **Malcolm MacColl.** Signed.

6477　The Irish Land Act of 1881: its origin and its consequences, 91–106. **George C. Brodrick.** Signed; repr. *Literary Fragments*, 1891.

6478　Cervo, 107–117. **J. Theodore Bent.** Signed.

6479　The political outlook, 118–128.

VOLUME 105 O.S., 25 N.S., FEBRUARY 1882

6480　Exchange no robbery; or, Fated by a jest (Part I), 129–144. **Matilda Betham-Edwards.** Signature; novel published 1883.

6481　The claim of tenant-right for British farmers, 145–155. **George C. Brodrick.** Signed; repr. *Literary Fragments*, 1891.

6482　Dr. Sheridan [friend of Swift's], 156–172. **Stanley Lane-Poole.** Signed.

6483　John Dryden, 179–191. **John Dennis.** Signed.

6484　"Lord of all"; a love story, 192–205. **Mary E. Martin.** Signed as in no. 6175.

6485　[*Correspondence of*] *Robert Southey and Caroline Bowles*, 206–213.

6486　The human ideal, 214–232. **Edmund Gurney.** Signed; repr. *Tertium Quid* (1887), I.

6487　William Ellis and his work as an educationist, 233–252. **Florence Fenwick Miller.** Signed.

6488　Clôture, 253–260.

VOLUME 105 O.S., 25 N.S., MARCH 1882

6489　The Lady Maud (chaps. i–iii), 261–291. **William Clark Russell,** Assigned in Index to "The Author of *The Wreck of the 'Grosvenor'* "; novel published 1882.

6490 Montepulciano, 292–306. **J. A. Symonds.** Signed; repr. *Byways.*

6491 How Gilbert Sherard fared in the flood, 307–328. **Frances P. Verney.** Signed F. P. Verney; Index gives "Lady Verney"; see *DNB.*

6492 Basuto, 329–342. **Alfred Aylward.** Signed. Translation of speeches in the art. by **Martin Hopkins**—p. 342n.

6493 The French privateers (No. I): Jean Bart, 343–360. **J. K. Laughton.** Signed; repr. *Studies.*

6494 Exchange no robbery (Part II), 361–375. **Matilda Betham-Edwards.** Signature.

6495 The poetry of Dante Gabriel Rossetti, 376–384. **Thomas Bayne.** Signed.

6496 Tenant-right; or, Security v. confidence, 385–394. **I. S. Leadam.** Signed.

VOLUME 105 O.S., 25 N.S., APRIL 1882

6497 The Lady Maud (chaps. iv–vi), 395–425. **William Clark Russell.** Evidence for no. 6489.

6498 M. Léon Say on the prosperity of France, and the state purchase of railways, 426–437. **Francis R. Conder.** Signed.

6499 How far is the present House of Commons represented in the roll of the Long Parliament? 438–445. **C. W. Kennedy.** Signed.

6500 Exchange no robbery (Part III), 446–463. **Matilda Betham-Edwards.** Signature.

6501 Correspondence of Niccolò Paganini, 464–476. **J. Theodore Bent.** Signed.

6502 Perry's *Greek and Roman Sculpture*, 477–485. **George W. Cox.** Signed.

6503 Among the tors [on Dartmoor], 486–497. **B. Burford Rawlings.** Signed.

6504 The French privateers (No. II, concl.): Du Guay-Trouin, 498–518. **J. K. Laughton.** Signed; repr. *Studies.*

6505 The new coalition, 519–530.

VOLUME 105 O.S., 25 N.S., MAY 1882

6506 The Lady Maud (chaps. vii–viii), 531–567. **William Clark Russell.** Evidence for no. 6489.

6507 A pre-Raphaelite magazine [*The Germ*], 568–580. **J. Ashcroft Noble.** Signed; repr. *Sonnet in England.*

6508 The Public Worship Regulation Act, 581–585. **George W. Cox.** Signed.

6509 Exchange no robbery (Part IV, concl.),

586–598. **Matilda Betham-Edwards.** Signature.

6510 *John Inglesant* [by J. H. Shorthouse], 599–605. **Samuel R. Gardiner.** Signed.

6511 Charles Lamb and his friends, 606–617. **John Dennis.** Signed.

6512 Irregular warfare, 618–631. **Alfred Aylward.** Signed.

6513 A visit to the Queen of Burmah, 632–642. **Ellen Rowett.** Signed.

6514 Life in Old Florence, 643–655. **J. Theodore Bent.** Signed.

6515 The new departure in Ireland, 656–666.

VOLUME 105 O.S., 25 N.S., JUNE 1882

6516 The Lady Maud (chaps. ix–x), 667–703. **William Clark Russell.** Evidence for no. 6489.

6517 The earliest Scottish university [St. Andrews] (Part I), 704–719. **J. C. Shairp.** Signed; repr. *Sketches in History and Poetry*, Edin., 1887.

6518 The case of the special hospitals, 720–733. **B. Burford Rawlings.** Signed.

6519 Primitive belief and savage metaphysics, 734–744. **Andrew Lang.** Signature.

6520 National necessities as the bases of national education, 745–767. **Benjamin Ward Richardson.** Signed.

6521 The hangman's rope: a story of North Devon superstition, 768–778.

6522 Whigs and Liberals, 779–788. **Ernest Myers.** Signed; cf. no. 6319.

VOLUME 106 O.S., 26 N.S., JULY 1882

6523 The Lady Maud (chaps. xi–xiii), 1–34. **William Clark Russell.** Evidence for no. 6489.

6524 The earliest Scottish university (Part II, concl.), 35–51. **J. C. Shairp.** Signed.

6525 Apollo the fiddler: a chapter on artistic anachronism, 52–67. **Violet Paget.** Signed Vernon Lee; repr. *Juvenalia* (1887), I.

6526 "The Lord of the World" [Jagannatha, Hindu deity], 68–84. **William Simpson,** 1823–1899. Signed; cf. no. 5903.

6527 Goneril; a story, 85–98. **A. Mary F. Robinson.** Signed.

6528 Æthelston: a northern sketch, 99–112. **James Purves.** Signed.

6529 The Irish difficulty, 120–140. Signed: A Foreign [i.e. Continental] Liberal.

VOLUME 106 O.S., 26 N.S., AUGUST 1882

6530 The Lady Maud (chap. xiv), 141–171. **William Clark Russell.** Evidence for no. 6489.
6531 Three trips to Tartarus, 172–183. **Helen Zimmern.** Signed.
6532 The contention between the carriers and the manufacturers of Great Britain, 184–201. **F. R. Conder.** Signed.
6533 Lost love: a Lothian tale, 202–221. **James Purves.** Signed.
6534 A turning point in the history of co-operation, 222–235. **Edith Simcox.** Signed.
6535 Personal recollections about Garibaldi (Part I), 236–254. **Karl Blind.** Signed.
6536 An Indian romance—and the reality [finance and public works in India], 255–276. **A. J. Wilson.** Signed.

VOLUME 106 O.S., 26 N.S., SEPTEMBER 1882

6537 The Lady Maud (chaps. xv–xvii), 277–312. **William Clark Russell.** Evidence for no. 6489.
6538 Race and life on English soil, 313–334. **Benjamin Ward Richardson.** Signed.
6539 The "Cock," [tavern in Fleet Street], 335–344. Signed: An Old Templar.
6540 Better away, 345–356. **A. K. H. Boyd.** Signed A.K.H.B.; repr. *Our Little Life*, 2nd series, 1884.

6541 Historical cookery, 357–362. **Christina G. J. Reeve.** Signed Mrs. Henry Reeve: see *DNB* under her husband.
6542 A Venetian medley, 363–380. **J. A. Symonds.** Signed; repr. *Byways.*
6543 Personal recollections about Garibaldi (Part II, concl.), 381–404. **Karl Blind.** Signed.

VOLUME 106 O.S., 26 N.S., OCTOBER 1882

6544 The Lady Maud (chaps. xviii–xx, concl.), 405–428. **William Clark Russell.** Evidence for no. 6489.
6545 English: its ancestors, its progeny, 429–457. **Jennett Humphreys.** Signed.
6546 On the antiquity of some of our familiar agricultural terms, 458–468. **F. A. Paley.** Signed.
6547 Mr. Swinburne's trilogy [on Mary Queen of Scots], 469–479. **Thomas Bayne.** Signed.
6548 What makes people to live, 480–496. **Léon Tolstoy.** Signed. Trans. by **Olga (Kiréeff) de Novikoff**—signed O.K., see no. 6266.
6549 Old Scotch judges, 497–508. **James Purves.** Signed.
6550 Literary criticism and biography, 509–520. **John Dennis.** Signed.
6551 How I introduced the telephone into Egypt, 521–534. **Edwin De Leon.** Signed, but incorrectly, Edwin de Leon.

The London Review, 1829

THE AMBITIOUS PROJECT of a new quarterly review in the field already occupied by the *Edinburgh*, the *Quarterly*, and the *Westminster* first occurred to Nassau Senior, Professor of Political Economy at Oxford, sometime in the spring of 1828.[1] After engaging the support of his friend Richard Whately, then Principal of St. Alban Hall and soon to be Archbishop of Dublin, he used the good offices of Dr. Thomas Mayo to persuade Blanco White, on July 27, to become the editor.[2] White was an Englishman brought up as a Catholic in Spain, now a convert to the Church of England and a tutor at Oxford, where he enjoyed the privileges of the Oriel common room. During the next months the three associates were busy approaching potential contributors, attempting to draw up a prospectus—which was never written (the policy is in the first article, "Journals and Reviews")—and choosing a title. Because they themselves and two-thirds of the contributors were connected with Oxford, the *Oxford Review* must have been considered; but no doubt the desire to avoid a parochial and university appearance dictated the choice of something more metropolitan. The first issue appeared on February 20, 1829, the second on, or just before, June 10.[3] There was no third. The periodical, as White was to say, "totally failed of success."[4]

He meant—or he should have meant—failed to survive. For even a glance at the roll of contributors is sufficient to suggest that intrinsically it could hardly have been a failure. Fourteen of the fifteen contributors uncovered are in the *Dictionary of National Biography* by virtue of outstanding contributions to theology, medicine, economics, and criticism. Besides White, Senior, and Whately, the names include Edwin Chadwick, J. H. Newman, and Baden Powell. This promise of high quality is confirmed by examination. Though some of the articles are slight, most of them show a grasp of the subject matter that is informed and intelligent. Two in particular are of major importance: Chadwick's "Preventive Police," which helped to transform the antiquated system of nightwatchmen into the modern police system established under Peel, and Newman's famous essay on poetry, one of the principal statements of critical theory in the Victorian period.

But above all, what distinguishes the *London Review* of 1829 is what Arnold was to call the critical spirit. With the rival quarterlies and their party lines (Whig, Tory,

[1]Blanco White, *Life* (Bibliographical Note), I, 448.

[2]Ibid., I, 448. David Masson, referring to 1829, *North British Review*, 13 (Feb. 1850), 45–46, spoke of Senior having been "engaged, together with Dr. Whately, now Archbishop of Dublin, in bringing out the *London Review*, the nominal editor of which was Mr. Blanco White."

[3]*Athenaeum*, Feb. 18, 1829, p. 112; June 10, p. 360.

[4]*Life*, III, 130.

and Utilitarian) in mind, Blanco White—if it was he—laid down an astonishing policy in the opening article, "Journals and Reviews." Likening the able reviewer to a judge rather than an advocate, he continued:

Unless he can resolve to consider the case in question strictly on the basis of its own merits, . . . to afford a clear and ungarbled detail of the arguments on both sides, and especially to maintain the dignity of his court . . . by severely checking personal rancour or wilful misconstruction of motives, the sooner the common consent of the public deposes him from his self-constituted office, the better. . . .

We conceive that the portion of society who choose to be . . . free in the exercise of their political judgment, is increasing both in number and consideration: and that in compliment to their decency and good sense, party virulence is gradually retreating to the shelter of parish vestries. It is on our belief in the existence of this class that we found our hopes of that which has been considered as doubtful, that a Review can exist without espousing any ready-made political creed; and it is from such that we look for a fair trial.

Moreover, a program like this promised a new function of criticism: "to stimulate . . . curiosity," and "instead of manufacturing thoughts for the reader, to induce him to think for himself."[5] Were ideas like these anywhere expressed before Arnold wrote his own "Function of Criticism" in 1864? His protest there against the sectarian temper of the great reviews and his call for a free play of the mind were anticipated by thirty-five years. Doubtless the calibre of the *London Review* was not so high as that of the *Home and Foreign*, which Arnold singled out for its dispassionate intelligence, but the spirit of impartiality and the aim of stimulating "curiosity" (a term also used by Arnold) were striking innovations in 1829. They reflect the highest ideals of academic life, however rarely achieved.

Though its neutral position was recognized at the time,[6] the new Review was often thought of as a potential rival of the Tory *Quarterly*. Lockhart wrote to Scott on October 23, 1828, that Blanco White was setting up "an opposition Review" and threatening to steal the services of Robert Southey—news which so alarmed John Murray he attempted to persuade the new editor to drop the whole project. Southey himself thought that the two reviews would "promote the same cause" and might even "assist each other."[7] Since Senior and Whately were liberals, and the position stated in the initial article was "a sincere desire for social improvement," and in religion no more than "a sincere attachment" to Christianity in general, this now seems curious. But such a broad policy was capable of broad interpretation. Though in its third article the Review advocated the reform of the Church, the reforms proposed were very minor and the point of view not far from Newman's.

[5]The quotations are on pp. 8, 9, and 6 respectively.

[6]The *Athenaeum*, Feb. 25, 1829, p. 117, reviewing the first number, thought readers would like its "tone of anxious impartiality and moderation."

[7]Andrew Lang, *Life and Letters of John Gibson Lockhart* (2 vols., 1897), II, 32; White, *Life*, I, 451. In a vituperative article on Whately in *Fraser's Magazine*, 6 (Nov. 1832, Part II), 568, the writer, probably William Maginn (see no. 478 above), claimed that the *London Review* was "planned in Oxford, by some dull people whose articles had been rejected by *The Quarterly*. Fired with indignation against Lockhart, they determined to run down Murray; and the papers rejected in Albemarle-street appeared under the patronage of Saunders and Otley." Since Senior's earlier articles on Scott had been published in the *Quarterly* under Gifford, it is possible that he had offered no. 2 below to Lockhart and had had it rejected. But the writer's tone hardly commands much credence.

Moreover, the association with Oxford seemed to guarantee an essential conservatism. And yet it was possible, from the same broad stance, for White to tell Perronet Thompson, the new proprietor and joint editor of the *Westminster Review*, that "the *London Review* is to advocate all manner of improvement, and be as liberal as the *Westminster*, bating its anti-religious tendency."[8] And possible too for him to ask Thompson as well as Southey for contributions.[9]

Though it may or may not have been true that in 1829 "the temper of the general mass of society" was becoming "more moderate on political subjects, and more skeptical as to the motives of contending parties"[10]—and therefore ready to welcome an impartial periodical—there were two particular circumstances that made the time favorable for the new venture. As Newman pointed out, the *Quarterly* "was not at the moment altogether satisfactory to the great political and religious party, which it has ever represented." He meant that its Toryism was too "high-and-dry," too unresponsive to the winds of reform, especially in the Church. Furthermore, it seemed to lack a firm hand at the helm, for after Gifford's retirement in 1824, a succession of editors had followed; and as yet no one could foresee the long reign of Lockhart, who had taken over in 1826.[11] This second weakness, resulting from a failure of editorial continuity, was equally true of the *Westminster*, where the Mills and their allies had walked out when Bowring and Perronet Thompson took over in 1828. Here the resulting gain for the new *London* is demonstrated by an unpublished letter from J. S. Mill to Nassau Senior, Jan. 5 [1829], introducing Edwin Chadwick. Mill explained: "He has been a writer in the Westminster Review but has seceded like the rest of us, in consequence of the recent changes in that work." He had collected materials for an article on the metropolitan police which he now wanted to publish in the new periodical.[12] In this way the latter procured one of its best essays and best contributors.

But for all its virtues and all these encouraging factors, the *London Review* failed to survive. Why? Newman offered two explanations. "The new publication," he suggested, "required an editor of more vigorous health and enterprising mind, of more cheerful spirits, and greater power of working, and with larger knowledge of the English public, than Mr. White possessed; and writers, less bookish and academical than those, able as they were, on whom its fate depended." As a result, "the Review was dull."[13] Newman was probably right about the editor. At any rate, as early as September 1828, within six weeks of his happy acceptance of the post, Blanco White was lamenting that in an unguarded moment he had been swept "into the broad and tempestuous sea of the Reviews" and that now it was too late to draw back. Small wonder that before the second issue appeared, he had resigned his "compact with the evil spirit, the demon of the book market" and was hoping soon "to be entirely free from the nightmare of the London Review."[14] Newman's second

---

[8]As reported by Thompson in a letter to John Bowring, Feb. 23, 1829, quoted in L. G. Johnson, *General T. Perronet Thompson* (1957), p. 151.

[9]Ibid.; White, *Life*, I, 451.

[10]"Journals and Reviews," *London Review*, pp. 6–7.

[11]J. H. Newman, *Essays* (Bibliographical Note), I, 27, makes both points.

[12]Blanco White Papers, R.P. XVIII.10.1 (2), Liverpool Univ. Lib.

[13]*Essays*, I, 27–28.

[14]Newman, *Letters* (Bibliographical Note), I, 193; White, *Life*, I, 467.

charge is a half-truth. The Review was not dull, but it lacked what Macaulay once called the essential requirement for periodical success: that the writing have "spirit and vivacity."[15] White had been warned of this at the time, when Southey told him that if it were to sell widely the Review must be "entertaining."[16] Still, to the modern reader at least, this quality is often lacking in the *Edinburgh* and the *Quarterly*. All one can say is that relatively speaking the *London Review* was a little heavier than its rivals.

Moreover, and more important, its two major competitors were long established fixtures, with solid subscription lists. At best the odds were against a new quarterly of equal calibre, based like them on university graduates for writers and readers. But the circumstances were closer to worst than best. For though in 1828 the time may have seemed ripe to a group of Oxford intellectuals for a broad impartial examination of the great issues of the age, the fact was that a fresh and violent wave of controversy—political, religious, and social—was on the point of erupting. Catholic Emancipation in 1829, the Reform Bill of 1832, and the initiation of Newman's Oxford Movement in 1833 are only the main signs of a new period of sharp conflict. This development, in which a nonpartisan journal was almost certain to be wrecked, struck the *London Review* directly in February 1829, shortly after the first issue appeared. In the clash over the re-election of Peel as M.P. for Oxford, Senior, Whately, and the Editor voted for him, while Newman and other contributors voted against him.[17] Later in the year Blanco White wrote the inevitable obituary: "It will not die away unregretted," he said, "but die it must,—leaving those two numbers behind, to show the melancholy truth, that no really impartial work of that kind is as yet generally liked in England."[18] Even a generation later the zeitgeist seemed to Arnold no more favorable; but by the 1860s the skepticism of sectarian authority that White had mistakenly counted upon for support had become widespread. The new reviews—the *Home and Foreign* in 1862, the *Fortnightly* in 1865, the *Contemporary* in 1866—finally achieved the high goal which the *London Review* of 1829 had been the first to attempt.

PROPRIETOR

Nassau W. Senior.[19]

EDITOR

Joseph Blanco White.[20]

---

[15]G. O. Trevelyan, *Life and Letters of Lord Macaulay* (2 vols., N.Y., 1876), II, 102.

[16]White, *Life*, I, 451.

[17]White, *Life*, I, 455, realized the consequences of his vote: "I know that I shall be abused by those who have hitherto praised me. Let it be so, though it is most painful in my peculiar circumstances." Newman, *Essays*, I, 28, saw White's action as a causal factor in the failure of the Review.

[18]*Life*, I, 469.

[19]White, *Life*, I, 449, shows that Senior went to London to make arrangements with a publisher; Leon Levy, *Senior* (Bibliographical Note), p. 133, calls the *LR* Senior's "own periodical." Whately, however, may have shared the role of proprietor: see Masson in n. 2 above.

[20]But to some degree, certainly, Senior and Whately had something to say about the choice of articles: see Masson in n. 2 above, and Whately's letter which is quoted as evidence for article no. 14.

PUBLISHER
Saunders and Otley, London.

NOTE ON ATTRIBUTIONS
The Review is completely anonymous. There is no marked file, publisher's list, or editorial correspondence known to us. A few attributions were made from the Blanco White Papers in the Liverpool University Library.

BIBLIOGRAPHICAL NOTE
There is no history of the Review. The above essay has been founded on *The Life of the Rev. Joseph Blanco White, Written by Himself*, ed. J. H. Thom (3 vols., 1845), I, 448–457, 467–469, and III, 130–132; J. H. Newman, *Letters and Correspondence*, ed. Anne Mozley, (2 vols., 1891), I, 192–195; Newman's note in his *Essays, Critical and Historical*, 2nd ed. (2 vols., 1872), I, 27–28; and S. Leon Levy, *Nassau W. Senior, the Prophet of Modern Capitalism* (Boston, 1943), pp. 130–136, 388–389, 389–390, 395. The two issues were reviewed in the *Athenaeum*, Feb. 25, 1829, pp. 117–118, and June 10, 1829, p. 360, but each review centers on a single article. There is a wild attack, probably by William Maginn, in *Fraser's*, 6 (Nov. 1832, Part II), 568.

THE LONDON REVIEW, 1829

VOLUME 1, No. I, 1829

1 Journals and reviews, 1–9. **Joseph Blanco White.** Marked as his in the Bodleian copy; the style supports the attrib.

2 Sir Walter Scott's novels, 10–43. **Nassau W. Senior.** Repr., revised and expanded, *Essays on Fiction* (1864), pp. 1–8, 138–188; claimed in letter in Levy, *Senior*, p. 395.

3 Writers on Church reform, 44–85.

4 Anecdotes of Napoleon, 86–112. **Henry Nelson Coleridge.** Coleridge to Blanco White, Oct. 13, 1828, White MSS., Liverpool Univ., discusses art. on book here being reviewed.

5 Transportation, 112–139. **Richard Whately.** Repr. *Miscellaneous Lectures and Reviews*, 1861.

6 Diet, 139–153. **A. B. Granville.** Granville to Blanco White, Nov. 5, 1828, White MSS., Liverpool Univ., suggests a humorous art. on diet for first number.

7 Greek tragedy, 153–171. **J. H. Newman.** Repr. *Essays*, I, as "Poetry, with reference to Aristotle's *Poetics*."

8 Social life of England and France, 171–198.

9 Insanity and its moral preventive, 198–222. **Thomas Mayo,** prob. Author clearly a doctor who knew the scholarship on insanity; Dr. Mayo wrote books on mental diseases in 1817, 1834, 1838, 1854 (see *BMCat.*), was a fellow of Oriel Coll., a friend of Senior's, and the man who invited White to become editor (see White, *Life*, I, 448).

10 Internal corn trade, 222–233. **N. W. Senior.** Claimed in letter in Levy, *Senior*, p. 395.

11 *The Course of Time* [poem by Robert Pollock], 233–251. **J. B. White.** List in *Life*.

12 Preventive police, 252–308. **Edwin Chadwick.** *Life*, bibliography; claimed in Chadwick to Charles Buller, Apr. 17, 1839, Univ. Coll. London.

VOLUME 1, No. II, 1829

13 Mineral waters, 313–333. **C. G. B. Daubeny.** Repr. *Miscellanies* (1867), I.

14 Records of history [on Isaac Taylor's *History of the Transmission of Ancient Books*], 334–365. **Samuel Hinds?** Whately to Blanco White, Apr. 5, 1829, White MSS., Liverpool Univ., says he will bring "Hinds' and my own article finished, and perhaps Coplestone's"; Whately's is no. 17; this is likely to be Hinds's, since he had written *The Rise and Early Progress of Christianity*, 1828, and was also concerned, like Taylor, with the validity of early Christian documents.

15 Brand's *Peru*, 366–387. **Edward Stanley,** 1779–1849. Stanley to Blanco White, Mar. 1 [1829], White MSS., Liverpool Univ., sends this art. as promised.

16 Spanish poetry and language, 388–403. **J. B. White.** List in *Life*.

17 Juvenile library, 404–419. **Richard Whately.** Repr. *Miscellaneous Lectures and Reviews*, 1861.

18 Fashionable novels [including Disraeli's *Vivian Gray* and Bulwer-Lytton's *Pelham*], 419–446. Unidentified. Since Senior reviewed novels (cf. no. 2), he would seem a likely author, but he claimed that he wrote only nos. 2 and 10 for the *LR* (see Levy, *Senior*, p. 395); Whately had written on modern novels in the *Quart. Rev.*, 1822, but the remarks quoted for no. 14 sound as though he did only one art. for this issue, viz., no. 17; this might be Coplestone's art. in the evidence for no. 14.

19 Progress of mathematics, 467–486. **Baden Powell.** Attr. in *Notices*, p. 30.

20 Human physiology, 486–502.

21 War [of Russia] with Turkey, 502–521. **Joseph Dornford,** prob. Newman, *Letters*, I, 194, shows that White asked Dornford to do a military art. for the *LR*; *DNB* says "his talk ran much on wars"; the art. is mainly geographical and historical.

22 Game Laws, 521–536. Unidentified. Possibly Charles Neate who suggested two subjects for arts., both approved by White (Newman, *Letters*, I, 194); Neate published *Game Laws*, anon., 1830 (see *DNB*), which is not a reprint of this art., but resembles it at various points; he was fond of riding and steeplechasing, and was already studying at Lincoln's Inn.

23 Centralization: public charities in France, 536–565. **Edwin Chadwick.** Same evidence as for no. 12.

24 Bishop Heber, 566–589. **John Philips Potter.** Repr. *Essays on the Lives of Cowper, Newton, and Heber*, 1830.

The National Review, 1883–1900

IN THE FIRST NUMBER of the *National Review* its editor, Alfred Austin, described a conversation he had had with Disraeli in April 1881, scarcely a fortnight before the Conservative chieftain's death. Picking up a copy of "a celebrated and able Review" [undoubtedly the *Nineteenth Century* with its famous symposia] " 'Curious, is it not?' he said. 'Reading an article in this publication, I find it demonstrated that there is no God. Going a little further, and perusing another paper in the same number, I discover that the Pope is God's vicegerent. Well, this is a little perplexing.' " That observation and what followed led Austin to remark on the singular fact that "the Conservative Party had no monthly Review, dedicated, like the one to which [Disraeli] had referred, to the discussion of subjects, not only political, but philosophical, literary, and social," and addressed to "the more intellectual portion of the public." Such a Review "might present to the nation the various aspects of Conservative sentiment and opinion . . . which fair and reasonable minds would find to be substantially consentaneous, and practically one." Thus, the *National Review* had its origin—though not necessarily on this day—in the need for a new force at a time when the quarterlies were losing influence and the leading monthlies were the liberal *Fortnightly* and the many-opinioned, "perplexing" *Nineteenth Century*.

As the discussion ended, Disraeli "suddenly added, with much emphasis, 'But, above all, no Programme.' " Austin demurred. Disraeli explained that any program would be misrepresented by opponents. "Besides, we are all of us short-sighted; and, therefore, the fewer promises men make the better." Having found this qualification approved by Disraeli's supporters, Austin adopted it. In the same article, significantly called " 'Above all, no programme'," he insisted: "The *National Review* is not a Party organ. To no Party is it under the faintest obligation, and by no Party will it be enslaved. The views that may be advanced in it will be the views of the individual writer by whom they are propounded," and any attempt to identify them with the leaders of the Conservative party would be irresponsible. "Its pages will be open to all Conservatives who have anything to say, and who know how to say it."[1]

But in point of fact Austin made no real effort to dissociate the Review from the Conservative party beyond this profession of "no programme." Indeed, only a few pages later the note of political warfare is plainly heard. Since right reason, Austin claims, is now "rather on the side of Conservatism than on the side of its opponents

---

[1] "Above all, no programme," 1 (Mar. 1883), 24–26.

... it must be put into the field [that is, into the country by a national review] and brought face to face with the enemy. It will win no victories, and retrieve no defeats [the reference is to the general election of 1880 when Gladstone's Midlothian campaign swept the Conservatives out of office] so long as it remains rigidly passive in winter quarters."[2] Plainly, right reason is going to arm the *National* with the best of all possible programs. It is hardly surprising that, with this article especially in mind, the liberal *Daily Telegraph* pointedly asked, "When is a Party organ not a Party organ?"[3] To which Austin could have replied only by saying, "When it is dealing with literature and philosophy."

For Austin was a party man,[4] and his professions of independence were exaggerated. The first public announcement of the *National* came during a meeting at the Junior Carleton Club in which plans for a new Conservative Club were also launched. Lord Carnarvon, Colonial Secretary in the Disraeli cabinet, was in the chair at this meeting, and his biographer says he had obtained Lord Salisbury's approval for the "new literary venture." The circular, seeking subscribers for the *National*, was issued under the names of such ranking Conservatives as Lord Carnarvon, Lord Lytton, Lord Stanhope and his son, Edward Stanhope, Arthur James Balfour, and Henry Cecil Raikes, in addition to those of Austin and his joint editor, William John Courthope.[5] Lord Salisbury and Sir Stafford Northcote, who divided the party's leadership in the post-Disraeli years, did not sign the circular, but along with the most prominent Conservatives of the time they contributed articles to the *National*. Indeed, T. E. Kebbel later recalled that the favoritism shown Austin by Conservative writers "occasioned some little soreness in quarters where similar recognition and assistance had not been experienced, though the services rendered were at least equally meritorious."[6]

In its first months the *National* was badly received by much of the competitive press. The *Academy* suggested that its "most distinct feature" seemed to be "back to Queen Anne." The *Spectator* found it "somewhat thin." And other writers, commonly Liberals, spoke openly of its "mediocrity" and "dullness." *Punch* accompanied a cartoon of Austin seated on Pegasus wearing a cocked hat and holding the *National Review*, with some verses ending, "He has no programme, and he'll have no readers." Austin seems to have been somewhat untypically abashed by the criticisms, even in the satiric dialogue intended as a reply to them.[7]

Yet the *National* made its way to its share of the public, and in the long run probably outlived most of the journals which had belittled it. The difficulties of the Gladstone government in meeting the demands of its awkwardly diverse supporters

---

[2]Ibid., p. 28.

[3]Quoted in the *NatR-II*, 1 (Apr. 1883), 168–169.

[4]After two unsuccessful bids for a seat in the House of Commons, the more recent in 1880, Austin had ceased to think of himself as a politician; but between 1876 and 1898 he was very active as a writer of leading articles for the *Standard*, a Conservative London daily. See his *Autobiography* (1911), I, 214–215; II, 129–132, 178–179.

[5]Arthur H. Hardinge, *The Life of Henry Howard Molyneux Herbert* (1925), III, 86–88. Two months before the *National* first appeared, Carnarvon described himself as "more engaged in it than anyone else except the two editors."

[6]T. E. Kebbel, *Lord Beaconsfield and Other Tory Memories* (1907), p. 243.

[7]*NatR*, 1 (Apr. and May 1883), 161–174, 376–386, where the *Spectator* and *Punch* are quoted, p. 165; for the *Academy*, see Mar. 3, 1883, p. 152.

provided abundant subject matter for Austin's slashing style of political journalism.[8] And the many big names among the contributors kept the Review in the public eye: an article by Lord Salisbury on "Labourers' and Artisans' Dwellings" made a genuine sensation in November 1883.

Nor was the appeal of the *National* limited to the purely political. The appointment of W. J. Courthope as joint editor with Austin gave some sort of literary pretension to the journal. As a winner at Oxford of the Newdigate Prize (1864) and the Chancellor's Prize (1868), and as an editor and biographer of Pope, Courthope brought responsible literary credentials with him. An article on "Conservatism and Art" in the first number established a kind of keynote for Courthope's contribution to the venture. He continued to publish articles in the same vein over the first few years, including a series on "The Liberal Movement in English Literature" which became a well known book.[9] And it may have been Courthope rather than Austin who attracted to the Review articles by T. E. Kebbel, W. H. Mallock, H. D. Traill, William Archer, and others, which were fully in keeping with the character and quality of the *Fortnightly* or the *Nineteenth Century*.[10] The *National* published little fiction under Austin and Courthope, although Mallock's novel, *The Old Order Changes*, first came out in its pages. Austin's poetry appeared rather frequently there, but so did William Watson's political sonnets in the Miltonic tradition, "Ver Tenebrosum," as well as the well known "Wordsworth's Grave."

After Courthope resigned as editor in August 1887 to become a Civil Service Commissioner, the *National* tended to coast through the remaining six years of Austin's editorship. Under the pressure of full editorial responsibility, he seems to have found time to contribute fewer signed articles himself. Or perhaps his relative reticence was a product of Conservative party dominance in the politics of those years: it is always easier to attack than to praise, and livelier reading too. In some degree William Watson tended to take Courthope's place as a writer of articles on the conservative element in literature, and at one point he was offered, though he may not have accepted, the post of editor *pro tempore* for the period of Austin's annual holiday on the Continent.[11] Between 1891 and 1893 Austin secured the ser-

[8]See, for example, *NatR-II*, 1 (May 1883), 321–335, where Austin draws upon rumor and personality to gloat over a "Prime Minister's dilemma" which seems certain to have existed only in his own mind.

[9]If the title seems curious in the Conservative *National*, cf. Courthope's remarks in the preface to the book (1885), pp. ix–x: "I have not used the words 'Liberalism' and 'Conservatism' in any invidious or party sense. By 'Liberalism' I mean the disposition which leads men to seek above all things the enlargement of individual liberty: by 'Conservatism' that which makes them desire primarily to preserve the continuity of national development. Between these two principles I can see no essential contradiction, nor do I think that they can be safely separated." On p. viii he says, as we can now understand, that his book might have been called " 'The Romantic Movement in English Literature'."

[10]Walter Graham, *English Literary Periodicals* (N.Y., 1930), p. 264, attributes the literary elements in the *NatR-II* wholly to Courthope's labors, but only a generally impressionistic estimate of Courthope's editorial contribution can be made on the basis of available evidence. Courthope's letter of resignation, published in Austin's *Autobiography*, II, 176, says the joint editors "worked together . . . in practically unbroken harmony," with "a congruity of feeling, instinct, sympathy, and taste." For the best memoir of Courthope, see that by J. W. Mackail in *Proceedings of the British Academy*, IX (1917–1918), 581–590.

[11]In a letter dated Feb. 5, [1890], in the Dowden Papers, Trinity College, Dublin, Watson says, "I am too doubtful of my own equipment for the task to jump at it precipitantly."

vices of William Earl Hodgson as sub-editor. Hodgson had been a contributor since 1883, and Austin came to value him highly for his knowledge of the literary market and his talent for buying articles at a reasonable rate. However, a symptom of the journal's decline was the admiration that Austin privately expressed for Hodgson's ability to obtain "interesting correspondence which is not paid."[12] As a twentieth-century editor later remarked, the *National Review* "led a blameless, if rather dull existence" in the years before July 1893, at which time it was sold to and began to be edited by Leopold James Maxse.[13]

Leo Maxse, then not quite thirty, had recently been forced by ill health to give up his parliamentary ambitions and his hopes for a career in law. His father, Admiral Frederick Augustus Maxse, was casting about for a suitable occupation for his son. Though the elder Maxse apparently provided the money to buy the Review, the actual negotiations for its purchase were conducted by the younger Maxse during June and July 1893. Austin sold the Review for £1500, out of which he returned £350 as reimbursement for unexhausted subscriptions. Beyond the purchase price, Austin's overriding concern at the time of sale was to maintain the Conservatism of the *National*. Admiral Maxse had been a close political ally of the Radical chieftain Joseph Chamberlain since 1872 and, like Chamberlain, had recently become a Liberal Unionist. Leo Maxse had himself been a Liberal Unionist and an admirer of Chamberlain, but by mid-1893 he seems to have looked upon himself as too confirmed an Imperialist for such liberal labels. Austin asked Maxse to assure him that "in the improbable event of the Conservative Party and the Liberal Unionist Party growing apart, [the *National Review*] shall not be carried over to the cause of the latter as against the former." Maxse pledged, "No attempt shall be made either now or hereafter to carry it into the Liberal Unionist camp," and he remained faithful to this promise, though he never became the dutiful party man that Austin was.[14]

Under Maxse the *National* remained nominally a Conservative journal, but its character, first and last, was unmistakably Maxse's—Conservative yet capable of mounting a successful campaign (in 1911) to oust a Conservative government under the slogan "B.M.G." ("Balfour Must Go"). Not surprisingly, Maxse's capacity for independent judgment tended to change the Review from a rather staid Conservative journal to a lively journal of Conservative tendencies. Years later he explained that he obtained the *National* in order to be able to express his views with complete freedom, and he modified its format somewhat for this purpose. For the more than thirty-eight years of his editorship he led off each number with an unsigned but easily attributable article of news and opinion entitled "Episodes of the month"; and as his interest in colonial affairs began to crowd the confines of this monthly column, he devised a second column, in May 1897, devoted to the concerns of Greater Britain. When he was able to employ a reporter with a temperament akin to his own, he added yet a third column, "The month in America." Maxse was a man "with views of his own on most subjects of thought, and with liberty to express them," and he did not

---

[12]Austin to L. J. Maxse, June 28, 1893, Maxse Papers, no. 445.

[13]Edward Grigg, "Leopold Maxse is dead," *NatR-II*, 98 (Feb. 1932), 139. Grigg edited the *NatR* from 1948 to its suspension of publication in June 1960.

[14]Austin-Maxse Letters of June–July 1893, Maxse Papers, no. 445; Grigg, pp. 137–139.

hesitate to use the *National Review* to forward his favorite causes with the public, to castigate the errors of public officials, and to "bait" those in power "for excellent ends." As a journalist he was colorful, single-minded, and pugnacious. He also knew himself to be something of a "crank"; he was, as G. K. Chesterton described him, "very right-minded about some things; rather wrong-headed about others." Yet for all his intransigence he exerted a strong public influence because his motives were regarded as unfailingly patriotic and his facts were known to be highly accurate.[15]

Not all the energy behind the success of the *National* in these years was Maxse's own, however. Leo's sister Violet recalled that no sooner was the Review purchased than the entire Maxse family "flung themselves into the new venture," although they were all amateurs. Admiral Maxse, who was the model for the hero in George Meredith's novel *Beauchamp's Career*, contributed thirteen articles between 1893 and 1900, while Leo's brother, Frederick Ivor Maxse, contributed six. Perhaps even more important were the copious letters the father and brother sent back from wherever they happened to be—South Africa, Egypt, the Sudan—containing first-hand facts and observations which might be useful to Leo in his monthly columns.[16]

Even the family friend, George Meredith, seems to have been partly enlisted in the cause, contributing at least one review—a rare thing for Meredith at that date—and helping to steer talented writers in Leo's direction. It was almost certainly Meredith who arranged the publication of three short series by Gissing in the *National* during 1893 to 1895. Perhaps it was also he who procured the numerous contributions by Leslie Stephen on literary and ethical topics, for as an editor Leo Maxse probably took a less than average interest in literary topics. Though he tended to publish more fiction than Austin had, he generally relied on what was easily obtainable from the usual agents.[17]

Probably the most striking causes behind which Maxse threw his considerable energies were the vindication of Captain Dreyfus and the mobilization of British public opinion against Germany. With the help of Sir Godfrey Lushington and F. C. Conybeare, and after prolonged investigations of his own in France and Germany, Maxse scored a journalistic coup of sorts in August 1898, when in a signed article he convincingly demonstrated that one of the key documents used to convict Dreyfus had been forged by Colonel Henry, then head of the Intelligence Department of the French War Office. This exposé was shortly followed by the Colonel's arrest, confession, and suicide. Many persons at the time assumed that Maxse had been provided with information by Clemenceau, another family friend, although the French statesman denied the charge.[18] Maxse's near obsession with "the German danger"

---

[15]H. W. Massingham, "The Ethics of Editing," *Nat-R*, 35 (Apr. 1900), 256; Grigg, p. 150; L. J. Maxse, "*Germany on the Brain*" (1915), p. 9; and *NatR*, 98 (Feb. and Mar. 1932), 157, 159–160, 309.

[16]Violet Milner, *My Picture Gallery* (1951), pp. 32–33. The unrestricted portion of the Maxse Papers contains numerous examples of informational letters to Leo from other members of the Maxse family.

[17]Milner, *loc.cit.*; the Maxse Papers contain several letters which reveal the extent to which contributors to the *NatR-II* were provided by professional literary agents.

[18]See the numerous articles on the Dreyfus case in the *NatR-II* between June 1898 and Oct. 1899, especially L. J. Maxse, "M. Cazaignac's *Vindication of Captain Dreyfus*," 31 (Aug. 1898), 814–834. See also Grigg, p. 141.

began before the turn of the century and reached a fever pitch well before the outbreak of World War I. Not only did he hammer away on the topic in his monthly columns, but he also enlisted the aid of like-minded, able analysts such as Sir Rowland Blennerhassett and H. W. Wilson to write under their own names and under pseudonyms.[19]

The success Maxse found with the public on these two topics probably contributed more than anything else to the widening circulation and influence of the *National*. As might be expected, the journal came to be one which was sometimes hated and not seldom feared, but under Maxse, at least, no one ever called it either dull or mediocre.

EDITORS

Alfred Austin and William John Courthope, joint editors: March 1883–August 1887, Vol. 1—Vol. 9.
Alfred Austin: September 1887–July 1893, Vol. 10—Vol. 21, 5th issue.
SUB-EDITOR
William Earl Hodgson: 1891–1893.
Leopold James Maxse: August 1893–December 1900, and later, Vol. 21, 6th issue—Vol. 36, 4th issue, and later.

PROPRIETORS

Alfred Austin: March 1883–July 1893.
Leopold James Maxse: August 1893–December 1900, and later.

PUBLISHERS

W. H. Allen & Co.: March 1883–May 1891, Vol. 1—Vol. 17, no. 3.
Edward Arnold: June 1891–December 1891, Vol. 17, no. 4—Vol. 18, no. 4.
W. H. Allen & Co.: January 1892–June 1894, Vol. 18, no. 5—Vol. 23, no. 4.
Edward Arnold: July 1894–December 1900, Vol. 23, no. 5—Vol. 36, no. 4.

NOTE ON ATTRIBUTIONS

About 78 per cent of the articles in the *National Review* are signed. There is no publisher's list or other comprehensive source to aid in the identification of anonymous and pseudonymous contributions. The Maxse Papers, in the archives of the West Sussex County Record Office, are now partly open to the public, and letters to and from L. J. Maxse have been invaluable in establishing the authorship of a number of pseudonymous articles.

BIBLIOGRAPHICAL NOTE

There is no comprehensive history of the *National Review*. Robert Murray Christian's unpublished doctoral dissertation, "Leo Maxse and the *National Review*: A Study in the Periodical Press and British Foreign Policy, 1893–1914" (University of Virginia, 1940), is a history of the Review in its relation to British foreign policy, 1893–1914. Arthur H. Hardinge, *Life of Henry Howard Molyneux Herbert, Fourth*

---

[19]Robert Murray Christian, "Leo Maxse and the *National Review*" (see Bibliographical Note). See also the preface to Maxse's "*Germany on the Brain*," p. 9.

Earl of Carnarvon (3 vols., 1925), Alfred Austin's *Autobiography* (2 vols., 1911), and T. E. Kebbel's *Lord Beaconsfield and Other Tory Memories* (1907) contain fragmentary accounts of the Review's founding and early history. A series of articles in the February 1932 issue, on the occasion of L. J. Maxse's death, and another series in March 1933 commemorating the fiftieth anniversary of the *National*, contain personal recollections of varying usefulness. The last number of the Review, in June 1960, contains a brief historical sketch by its last editor, J. E. P. Grigg. At the present time (1971) John A. Hutcheson, Jr., is working on a dissertation called "Leo Maxse and the *National Review*," in the Department of History at the University of North Carolina, Chapel Hill.

THE NATIONAL REVIEW, 1883–1900

VOLUME 1, MARCH 1883

1 A dialogue and a moral, 1–23. **Alfred Austin.** Signed Thomas Tantivy; that Austin, proprietor and co-editor, should lead off—and with a pseudonym meaning Thomas Tory (see *N.E.D.*)—seems highly appropriate; the 7 arts. Signed Thomas Tantivy frequently deal with matters of editorial concern (e.g., replies to critics of the Review in nos. 12 and 26), display editorial foreknowledge (cf. no. 12, p. 170), and amplify ideas presented in arts. signed by Austin, especially on party government and Gladstone's political character. No doubt Courthope, his co-editor, read these arts. in manuscript and made suggestions, but his main interests were literary rather than political, and when he wrote alone on politics, his work was more abstract, rarely satirical.

2 "Above all, no programme," 24–39. **Alfred Austin.** Signed.

3 The first of March, 1711 [on *Spectator* and *National Rev.*], 40–50. **H. H. M. Herbert.** Signed Carnarvon [Earl of Carnarvon]; repr. *Essays*, I.

4 The work of the Church [of England] during the present century (Part I), 51–67. **Robert Gregory.** Signed.

5 Conservatism in art, 72–84. **W. J. Courthope.** Assigned in Contents.

6 Bishop Berkeley's *Life and Letters* (Part I), 85–100. **Arthur James Balfour.** Signed; repr. *Essays and Addresses*, 1893.

7 Radicalism and the people, 101–111. **W. H. Mallock.** Signed.

8 France and judicial reform in Egypt, 113–125. **Harold A. Perry.** Signed.

9 The paintings of Mr. Rossetti, 126–134. **David Hannay.** Signed.

10 Irish legislation and its results, 135–151. **William Brodrick,** 1830–1907. Signed Midleton; Contents adds "Viscount."

11 Current politics, 152–158. **Alfred Austin** and **W. J. Courthope.** Assigned in Contents to "The Editors."

VOLUME 1, APRIL 1883

12 Our critics [i.e. of the Review], 161–174.

Alfred Austin. Signed Thomas Tantivy, cf. no. 1.

13 An essayist of three hundred years ago [Montaigne], 175–192. **Robert B. Lytton.** Signed Lytton [Earl of Lytton].

14 Imperial emigration, 193–207. **George Potter.** Signed. Intro. note by **Alfred Austin** and **W. J. Courthope**—signed The Editors.

15 Lord Ripon's new Indian policy, 208–223. **W. S. Seton-Karr.** Signed.

16 Homes of the criminal classes (Part I), 224–239. **Hugh E. Hoare.** Signed.

17 The redistribution of political power, 240–256. **Henry Cecil Raikes.** Signed.

18 The new school of fiction [Henry James and W. D. Howells], 257–268. **Arthur Tilley.** Signed.

19 Coalitions—a centenary anniversary, 269–285. **T. E. Kebbel.** Signed T. H. Kebbel, in error; man cited was a frequent contributor to the Review; cf. no. 220, which is partly a sequel to this art.

20 Lord Lawrence and masterly inactivity, 286–298. **Demetrius Charles Boulger.** Signed; repr. *Central Asian Questions.*

21 Berkeley's *Life and Letters* (Part II, concl.), 299–313. **Arthur James Balfour.** Signed.

22 Current politics, 314–320. **Alfred Austin** and **W. J. Courthope.** Assigned in Contents to "The Editors."

VOLUME 1, MAY 1883

23 The prime minister's dilemma [on Gladstone's retirement], 321–335. **Alfred Austin.** Signed.

24 Liberty and socialism, 336–361. **G. R. C. Herbert.** Signed Pembroke [Earl of Pembroke].

25 Life and work of the Church of Scotland, 364–375. **James H. Rankin.** Signed James Rankin; Contents provides middle initial and adds "D.D."

26 On the literary advantages of Grub Street, 376–386. **Alfred Austin.** Signed Thomas Tantivy—see no. 1.

27 Names and characters in the *Vicar of Wakefield*, 387–394. **Edward Ford.** Signed

E. Ford; Contents provides first name.

28 The municipality of London (Part I), 395–407. **Margaret E. Harkness.** Signed M. E. Harkness; see *BMCat.*; cf. *NC* nos. 625, 782.

29 Sir Francis Drake: some points in his character and career, 408–423. **Walter Herries Pollock.** Signed.

30 Suggestions for the development of our yeomanry cavalry, 424–438. **W. A. Baillie-Hamilton.** Signed.

31 The incidence and administration of local taxes, 442–451. **Albert Pell.** Signed; Contents adds "M.P."

32 On the study of classical archaeology (Part I), 452–467. **C. T. Newton.** Signed; Contents adds title "C.B."

33 Current politics, 468–475. **Alfred Austin** and **W. J. Courthope.** Signed The Editors.

VOLUME 1, JUNE 1883

34 "Veiled obstruction" [in parliament], 478–489. **Arthur James Balfour.** Signed.

35 England and France in Indo-China, 490–506. **Archibald R. Colquhoun.** Signed.

36 The radicalism of the market-place, 507–530. **W. H. Mallock.** Signed.

37 What is a Whig? 540–547. **H. G. Percy.** Signed Percy [Earl Percy].

38 [Browning's] *Jocoseria* and the critics: a plea for the reader, 548–561. **William John Courthope.** Signed.

39 On national unity, 562–574. **Robert Scott Moffat.** Signed.

40 A paradox on Quinet, 575–587. **George Saintsbury.** Signed; repr. *Essays*, IV.

41 The story of the escape of Prince Metternick, 588–605. **Carl von Hügel.** Signed. Intro. note, 588–589, by **Friedrich von Hügel**—signed F.v.H., initials of son of author of art., see *DNB*.

42 The work of the Church of England during the present century (Part II): elementary education, 606–623. **Robert Gregory.** Signed.

43 English tenant right, 624–632. **Clare Sewell Read.** Signed.

44 Current politics, 633–640. **Alfred Austin** and **W. J. Courthope.** Signed The Editors.

VOLUME 1, JULY 1883

45 Figures, facts and fallacies, 641–645. **Stafford Henry Northcote.** Signed N.; Alfred Austin to Northcote, June 28, 1883, BM Add. MS. 50041, thanks him for this art.

46 A stroll with Corkhouse, 646–657. **Alfred**

Austin. Signed Sangfroid, and Contents gives to "Lord Sangfroid," who does not exist; cf. Sangfroid's sarcastic reference, p. 656, to "the laws of political ecoonmy, at that moment descending from Saturn," with Austin's remark, no. 75, p. 95, "Have we not already relegated Political Economy to Saturn? from which planet, however, it will probably return, whenever it suits the convenience of a great statesman [Gladstone?], or the exigencies of an embarrassed Party [the Liberals], to bring it back again"; the art. is a sequel, in characterization, content, and style, to the satirical dialogue of no. 1, in which Sangfroid had already appeared.

47 The gold question and the fall of prices, 658–676. **Henry H. Gibbs.** Signed; repr. *Bimetallic Controversy*, 1886.

48 Mr. Irving as a tragedian: a criticism, 677–686. **B. Brooksbank.** Signed.

49 Conservative instincts in the English people (No. I): the middle classes, 687–701. **T. E. Kebbel.** Signed T. C. Kebbel in error; attr. to man cited, vol. 2, p. 243n., below.

50 Conservative instincts in the English people (No. II): the working classes, 701–711. **Percy Greg.** Signed.

51 The future of Whiggism, 718–725. **George Byron Curtis.** Signed.

52 Roma nuova—Roma vecchia, 726–736. **A. D. R. W. Cochrane-Baillie.** Signed Lamington [Baron Lamington].

53 The Suez Canal, 737–743. **Arthur Mills.** Signed.

54 The art of essay writing, 744–757. **John Dennis.** Signed.

55 The Lords and the Deceased Wife's Sister Bill, 758–766. **A. J. B. Beresford-Hope.** Signed.

56 An introduction to the *Pensées* of Pascal, 767–782. **Henry William Hamilton-Hoare.** Signed H. W. Hoare: see *WWW/1940*.

57 Current politics, 783–790. **Alfred Austin** and **W. J. Courthope.** Signed The Editors.

VOLUME 1, AUGUST 1883

58 England and France in the East, 791–809. **Harold A. Perry.** Signed.

59 Thoughts on family politics, 810–823. **Alfred Austin.** Signed Thomas Tantivy —see no. 1; opens with a personal claim to no. 26.

60 Homes of the criminal classes (Part II, concl.), 824–840. **Hugh E. Hoare.** Signed.

61 The Engadine, 841–855. **G. F. Browne.** Signed; Contents adds "Rev."

61a The ride of the dead: a Greek ballad

of the tenth century, 856–863. Translation and note by **W. H. Mallock**—signed.

62 National education, 864–873. **St. George Mivart.** Signed.

63 The Mahmal and the British troops in Egypt, 874–884. **Philip Vernon Smith.** Signed.

64 The cattle-ranche country of Canada, 885–893. **Alexander Staveley Hill.** Signed.

65 The scientific novel and Gustave Flaubert, 894–907. **Hugh E. Egerton.** Signed.

66 The volunteers as a military force, 908–918. **Francis Radcliffe.** Signed.

67 The defence of sport, 919–932. **Richard Jefferies.** Signed; repr. *Life of the Fields*, 1884.

68 Current politics, 933–940. **Alfred Austin and W. J. Courthope.** Signed The Editors.

VOLUME 2, SEPTEMBER 1883

69 Have we a colonial policy? 1–22. **H. B. E. Frere.** Signed.

70 The art of preaching, 23–34. **H. H. M. Herbert.** Signed Carnarvon [Earl of Carnarvon]; repr. *Essays*, III.

71 Are we despoiling India? a rejoinder [to *Nineteenth Century*, vol. 14, pp. 1–22], 35–48. Signed: John Indigo.

72 English art in 1883, 49–60. **Henry Blackburn.** Signed.

73 The New Guinea question; from a colonial point of view, 61–69. **W. Delisle Hay.** Signed.

74 The development of cricket, 70–80. **G. R. C. Harris.** Signed Harris [Baron Harris].

75 On the relation of literature to politics, 81–95. **Alfred Austin.** Signed; repr. *The Bridling of Pegasus*, 1910.

76 The municipality of London (Part II, concl.), 96–105. **Margaret E. Harkness.** Signed as in no. 28.

77 Lord Monboddo and Mrs. Garrick: a love episode, 106–112. **Edward Ford.** Signed.

78 An American on America, 113–128. **Harriet Waters Preston.** Signed M. Preston; Contents adds "Miss"; on p. 114 author quotes from an art. of hers in *Atlantic Monthly*, 44 (Nov. 1879), 677, which is assigned to "H. W. Preston" in the *Atlantic Index* for 1857–1888, p. 178; see *DAB*.

79 Radicalism and the working classes, 129–145. **W. H. Mallock.** Signed.

80 Current politics, 146–152. **Alfred Austin and W. J. Courthope.** Signed The Editors.

VOLUME 2, OCTOBER 1883

81 Are parliamentary institutions in danger? 153–167. Signed: A Retired Politician. (Letter, pp. 754–755, signed An Active Politician.)

82 Gottfried Keller: the modern novel in Germany, 168–188. **Charles Grant**, 1841–1889. Signed; see Boase.

83 The new law of elections, 189–204. **Henry Cecil Raikes.** Signed.

84 The era of the torpedo, 205–211. **E. Kay Robinson.** Signed.

85 Sismondi's political ideas, 212–224. **R. C. E. Abbot.** Signed Colchester [Baron Colchester].

86 Points for Conservative consideration (No. I): the representation of Ireland, 225–235. **Robert Staples, Jr.** Signed R. Staples, Jr.: see *BMCat*.

87 Points for Conservative consideration (No. II): why Conservatism fails in Scotland, 235–243. **William Earl Hodgson.** Signed.

88 Evolution and a priori ethics, 244–258. **G. A. Simcox.** Signed.

89 Miss Austen and George Eliot, 259–273. **T. E. Kebbel.** Signed.

90 The work of the Church of England during the present century (Part III, concl.): organisation, 277–293. **Robert Gregory.** Signed.

91 Current politics, 294–300. **Alfred Austin and W. J. Courthope.** Signed The Editors.

VOLUME 2, DECEMBER 1883

92 Labourers' and artisans' dwellings, 301–316. **Robert Cecil.** Signed Salisbury [Marquess of Salisbury] (Letters, pp. 753–754, signed **Manley Hopkins;** pp. 755–756, signed Vox Clamantis.)

93 Johnson and Carlyle: common sense versus transcendentalism, 317–332. **William John Courthope.** Signed.

94 Subsidising the Ameer [of Afghanistan], 333–340. **Demetrius Charles Boulger.** Signed; repr. *Central Asian Questions*.

95 The transformations of chivalric poetry, 341–353. **Violet Paget.** Signed V. Paget; see *DNB*.

96 The statesmanship of the streets, 354–368. Signed: An Old Diplomatist.

97 Italians and English, 369–375. **Linda Villari.** Signed L. Villari; cf. no. 188.

98 Will Norway become a republic? 376–392. **Carl Siewers.** Signed.

99 On the study of classical archaeology

by **H. H. M. Herbert**—signed Carnarvon [Earl of Carnarvon].

130   Forty years of income tax, 771–785. **John G. Hubbard.** Signed. (Letter, vol. 3, pp. 291–292, signed **W. Barrow Simonds.**)

131   The two Lucians: a dialogue on popular religion, 786–798. **William John Courthope.** Signed.

132   The representation of the people (No. I): can any class be trusted? 799–806. Signed: A Moderate Liberal.

133   The representation of the people (No. II): redistribution—right and wrong directions, 807–823. **Percy Greg.** Signed.

134   The tale of Tristram and Iseult, 826–837. **Mathilde Blind.** Signed.

135   Our game laws, 838–850. **W. S. Seton-Karr.** Signed.

136   The Boers, 851–858. **R. N. Fowler.** Signed. (Letter, vol. 4, pp. 138–143, signed **R. Paver**, with address "Bloemfontein, O.F.S., South Africa.")

137   Ethical theism, 859–869. Signed: Fidens.

138   Primary education in India, 870–879. **Frederic Pincott.** Signed.

139   Social deterioration and its remedy, 880–888. **Eustace G. Cecil.** Signed.

140   The landlords and the national income: illustrated by a chart, showing the exact proportion obtaining between the rental of the country, and the gross income of the country, 889–891. **W. H. Mallock.** Signed.

VOLUME 3, MARCH 1884

141   The opposition and the country, 1–8.

142   A sequel to "Rich man's dwellings" [no. 105], 9–19. **Janetta Manners.** Signed; repr. *Writings*, I. (Letter, pp. 284–285, signed One of the Upper Ten.)

143   Our geographical position and future trade, 20–33. **Edward B. Hamley.** Signed E. C. Hamley, apparently in error: see *DNB*.

144   Manet and the French Impressionist School, 34–44. **Arthur Baignères.** Signed.

145   A short survey of the Ecclesiastical Courts Commission Report, 45–60. **George Henry Sumner.** Signed. (See no. 184; letters, pp. 285–287, signed **G. R. Portal**; pp. 428–432, signed **W. F. Hobson.**)

146   The aristocracy of letters, 61–77. **Alfred Austin.** Signed.

147   The Northern Territory of South Australia, 78–88. **J. Langdon Parsons.**

Signed, with address "Adelaide, South Australia." (Letter, pp. 427–428, by **William Feilding**—signed W. Feilding, with title "Major-Gen," *Army List*/84.)

148   Reminiscences of John Reynolds, goldsmith, 89–98. Signed: John Reynolds; given an anonymous entry in Contents.

149   Mr. Irving and Diderot's *Paradox*, 99–108. **J. Ramsay.** Signed.

149a The dual policy: a cabinet council reported, 109–112. Signed: One Who Overheard.

150   Hospital problems: the children of the poor, 113–124. **Nestor Tirard.** Signed, with title, "M.D., London." (Letter, pp. 289–291, signed **Coldstream Tuckett**, with address "The Croft, Bristol.")

151   A fortnight in French Cochin China and Cambodgia [sic], 125–137. **G. R. C. Harris.** Signed Harris [Baron Harris].

152   In Correspondence: The operation of the Irish Land Act, 142–144, signed **W. R. Ancketill.**

VOLUME 3, APRIL 1884

153   Dissolution or anarchy? 145–150. Unidentified. (Letters, p. 425, signed A Reader Both of the *National* and the *Quarterly*; p. 426, signed A County Voter.)

154   Christopher North, 151–160. **Gathorne Gathorne-Hardy.** Signed Cranbrook [Viscount Cranbrook], p. 151. (Letter, pp. 426–427, signed An Old Fogey.)

155   The Merchant Shipping Bill, 161–171. **Roper Lethbridge.** Signed.

156   A Hampshire trout, 172–185. Signed: Sirion.

157   Cattle disease and the food supply, 186–198. **William E. Bear.** Signed.

158   [Tommaso] Salvini, 199–210. **W. E. Henley.** Signed.

159   The friendship of France, 211–226. **Harold A. Perry.** Signed.

160   Letters from Ruricola (No. II), 227–237. **H. H. M. Herbert.** Evidence for no. 129.

161   [Russia's annexation of] Merv!—What next? 238–252. **Demetrius Charles Boulger.** Signed; repr. *Central Asian Questions.*

162   American poetry, 256–269. **Percy Greg.** Signed.

163   The Bengal Tenancy Bill: Sir J. Caird and Bishop Heber, 270–283. **C. T. Buckland.** Signed. (See no. 297.)

164   In Correspondence: The dead-lock in

Irish land, 287–288, signed **W. R. Ancketill.**

774. **Richard Temple.** Signed; repr. *Cosmopolitan Essays,* 1886, as "Social Science in England."

200 The attitude of Carlyle and Emerson towards Christianity, 775–778. **R. C. Seaton.** Signed.

201 Hodson of Hodson's horse, 789–817. **T. R. E. Holmes.** Signed; repr. in *Four Famous Soldiers,* 1889. (Letters, vol. 4, pp. 423–428 by **George Hewitt Hodson** —signed George M. Hodson in error, since writer claims, p. 424, to be brother who prefixed a "vindication" to new ed. of W. S. R. Hodson, *Hodson of Hodson's Horse,* 1883: see *BMCat., Landed Gentry;* reply, pp. 862–866, by **Holmes**— signed.)

202 The clergy and Church defence, 818–835. **William Lewery Blackley.** Signed. (Letter, vol. 4, pp. 143–144, signed Vicar.)

203 Radicalism and reality, 836–845. **Norman Pearson.** Signed.

204 The French *versus* the London Missionary Society in Madagascar, 846–859. **Alfred Smith.** Signed.

205 In Correspondence: Elementary education—over-pressure and the "Mundella Code," 860–863, signed An Educator, Not a Teaching Machine.

VOLUME 4, SEPTEMBER 1884

206 Democracy and the House of Lords, 1–16. **W. T. Quin.** Signed Dunraven [Earl of Dunraven]. (See no. 226.)

207 The liberal movement in English literature (Part II), 17–29. **William John Courthope.** Signed.

208 Sir Bartle Frere in Sind, 30–44. **F. J. Goldsmid.** Signed.

209 The burning of Bristol: a reminiscence of the first Reform Bill, 45–62. **G. Lathom Browne.** Signed.

210 "Personal sacrifices," and the Conservative cause, 63–70. **A. M. Brookfield.** Signed.

211 Protection from the workman's point of view, 71–85. **William J. Harris.** Signed; Contents adds "M.P."

212 A woman's work, 86–90. **Reginald Brabazon.** Signed Brabazon [Lord Brabazon]; repr. *Social Arrows.* (Letter, p. 288, signed **F. B. Money Coutts.**)

213 The younger Pitt as an orator, 91–108. **C. F. Keary.** Signed. (Letter, pp. 282–283, signed **Edward Herries.**)

214 The rights of laymen in the Church, 109–125. **Henry Hayman.** Signed.

215 In the forest of Arden [a performance of *As You Like It*], 126–136. **Alfred Austin.** Signed.

VOLUME 4, OCTOBER 1884.

216 The value of redistribution: a note on electoral statistics, 145–162. **Robert Cecil.** Signed Salisbury [Marquess of Salisbury].

217 The development of classical learning, 163–176. **Arthur Tilley.** Signed.

218 The industrial crisis in France, 178–189. **W. H. Hume.** Signed.

219 Corkhouse at home, 190–194. **Alfred Austin.** Signed Sangfroid; and in Contents assigned to "Lord Sangfroid"— see no. 46.

220 Tory prime ministers (No. I): Mr. Pitt, 195–214. **T. E. Kebbel.** Signed; series repr. with extensive revisions as *A History of Toryism,* 1886.

221 Letters from Ruricola (No. IV), 215–221. **H. H. M. Herbert.** Evidence for no. 129.

222 A Pickwickian positivist [Frederic Harrison], 222–237. **Wilfrid Ward.** Signed.

223 Settlements of land in England, 238–251. **Hugh M. Humphry.** Signed.

224 Italian social life, 252–265. **Antonio Gallenga.** Signed A. Gallenga; see *DNB.*

225 India, 1880–4: an unofficial retrospect, 266–281. **James Durie.** Signed.

226 In Correspondence: "Possumus"; or, The constitutional aspect of the House of Lords, 283–288, signed **Walter S. Sichel.**

VOLUME 4, NOVEMBER 1884

227 The navy; its duties and capacity, 289–299. **William Henry Smith,** 1825–1891. Signed W. H. Smith; Contents adds "Right Hon." and "M.P.": see *DNB.*

228 *The Memoirs of Madame de Tourzel,* 300–316. **Catherine Mary Phillimore.** Signed.

229 The Russo-Afghan Boundary Commission, 317–329. **Arminius Vambéry.** Signed.

230 Some lessons from Carlyle's life, 330–341. **Alfred Austin.** Signed.

231 Four years of Egyptian finance, 342–355. **C. F. Moberly Bell.** Signed.

232 Past and present: Lord Malmesbury's *Memoirs,* 356–364. **Henry Mervyn.** Signed.

233 Imperial federation (No. I), 365–380. **Montagu Burrows.** Signed. Intro. note,

p. 365, by **Alfred Austin** and **W. J. Courthope**—signed Editors *N.R.* (Letter, pp. 710–711, signed **T. B. Collinson.**)

234 Imperial federation (No. II), 380–386. **Samuel Wilson.** Signed; Contents adds "Sir."

235 Alexandre Dumas and his plagiarisms, 387–402. **Francis Hitchman.** Signed.

236 Medical relief of the rural poor, 403–409. **C. M. Campbell.** Signed, with title "M.D." (Letter, p. 572, signed J.O.)

237 A review of fashionable thought, 410–422. **William Earl Hodgson.** Signed.

238 In Correspondence: What ails trade? 428–432, by **Arthur Phelps**—signed A. Phelps, with titles "Colonel, Commissary-General of the Bombay Army": see *WWW/1928.*

VOLUME 4, DECEMBER 1884

239 The adjustment of the quarrel [on electoral reform], 433–440.

240 The myths of Romeo and Juliet, 441–450. **William Archer.** Signed.

241 Tory prime ministers (No. II): the "mediocrities"—Lord Liverpool, the Duke of Portland, Mr. Percival, 451–465. **T. E. Kebbel.** Signed.

242 The nature of evidence in matters extraordinary [psychical research], 472–491. **Edmund Gurney.** Signed.

243 Notes in the Morbihan [Brittany], 492–503. **Emily Lawless.** Signed.

244 The unity of the Empire: federation, intercolonial and imperial, 504–511. **William Westgarth.** Signed W. Westgarth; man cited wrote frequently on colonial affairs; see *DNB.*

245 The liberal movement in English literature (Part III), 512–527. **William John Courthope.** Signed.

246 The Church of England abroad, 528–545. **Frederick Arnold.** Signed.

247 A French critic: M. Edmond Scherer, 546–559. **Frank T. Marzials.** Signed.

248 Improvement of the plants of the farm, 560–567. **Henry Evershed.** Signed.

249 In Correspondence: The coming reform and the representation of minorities, 569–572, by **Philip Vernon Smith**—signed P. V. Smith, cf. no. 279; Evolution v. socialism, 573–576, signed A Country Doctor.

VOLUME 4, JANUARY 1885

250 Buddhism and Christianity, 577–591.

Margaret Elizabeth Child-Villiers. Signed M. E. Jersey [Countess of Jersey].

251 The poetry and the prose of the crofter question, 592–606. **W. R. Lawson.** Signed.

252 Della Crusca and Anna Matilda [Hannah Cowley]: an episode in English literature, 607–619. **Armine T. Kent.** Signed; repr. *Otia: Poems, Essays and Reviews,* 1905. (Letter, pp. 867–868, signed Nemo.)

253 Railways in Asiatic Turkey, 620–630. **Demetrius C. Boulger.** Signed.

254 Women's suffrage, 631–641. **Henry Cecil Raikes.** Signed. (Letters, vol. 5, pp. 575–576, signed **F. A. Cameron,** with address "Waverley House, Lockharton, Edinburgh"; pp. 864–865, signed **E. A. Sarel.**) (See no. 279.)

255 The lowlands of Moray in the fourteenth and nineteenth centuries, 642–657. **Constance F. Gordon Cumming.** Signed as in no. 100.

256 Letters from Ruricola (No. V), 660–668. **H. H. M. Herbert.** Evidence for no. 129.

257 Chivalry, marriage, and religion: a woman's protest, 669–682. Signed: A Woman. (See no. 272.)

258 Ivan Turgénieff (Part I), 683–697. **Arthur Tilley.** Signed. (Part II is no. 341.)

259 A key to social difficulties [satirical argument for marriage by competitive examination], 698–701. Signed: Democratic Tory.

260 The judgement in the "Mignonette" case, 702–709. **George Sherston Baker.** Signed Sherston Baker; Contents adds "Sir": see *WWW/1928.*

261 In Correspondence: Recent Irish land legislation, 712–714, signed **J. Pulling Heath,** with description "Tenant Farmer" and address "47, Southernhay, Exeter"; Stray thoughts of a Liberal on the House of Lords, 714–718, signed **J. Thornton Hoskins;** Board schools and compulsory education, 718–720, signed J.J.

VOLUME 4, FEBRUARY 1885

262 An appeal to the Conservative Party, 721–740. **C. Gavan Duffy.** Signed. (Letter, vol. 5, pp. 142–144, signed An Irish Conservative.)

263 The two roads [Tory v. Liberal]: an after-dinner argument, 741–754. **Alfred Austin.** Signed Thomas Tantivy—see no. 1.

264 Gainsborough, 755–765. **Walter Armstrong**. Signed.

265 Our national future, 766–775. **George Baden-Powell**. Signed.

266 Stimulants and narcotics, 776–795. **Percy Greg**. Signed.

267 Hadrian's "Address to His Soul" [as translated by Byron, Prior, Pope and Charles Merivale], 796–800. **H. H. M. Herbert**. Signed Carnarvon [Earl of Carnarvon]; repr. *Essays*, II. (Letters, vol. 5, pp. 134–135, 280, signed **W. F. Hobson**; p. 280, signed **R. W. Wintle**; p. 281, signed **Edwin Arnold**, 1832–1904; p. 580 signed **John F. Rolph;** p. 580, signed Qualiscumque.)

268 Tory prime ministers (No. III): Mr. Canning, 801–818. **T. E. Kebbel**. Signed.

269 Two dramatic criticisms (No. I): voice and emotion, with reference to the "Juliet" of Miss Mary Anderson, 819–832. **G. E. Humphreys**. Signed.

270 Two dramatic criticisms (No. II): Ophelia's madness, 833–841. **Gilbert Venables**. Signed.

271 Caucus and *camorra* [Italian form of political caucus], 842–849. **T. A. Trollope**. Signed.

272 A reply to "A Woman's Protest" [no. 257], 850–856. Signed: A Man. (Letter, vol. 5, pp. 289–292, signed A Woman [author of no. 257].)

273 In Correspondence: Australasia or Australia? 857–861, signed **Francis Joseph Stevenson**.

VOLUME 5, MARCH 1885

274 The root of our misfortunes, 1–7. **Alfred Austin**. Signed.

275 The stage (No. I): the stage as a profession for women, 8–19. **Eliza Lynn Linton**. Signature.

276 The stage (No. II): the social status of the actor, 20–28. **John Coleman**. Signed.

277 Is an imperial fiscal policy possible? 29–42. **Roper Lethbridge**. Signed.

278 A French drama upon Abelard [by Charles de Rémusat], 43–59. Signed: A Conceptualist.

279 Women's suffrage: a reply [to no. 254], 60–70. **Philip Vernon Smith**. Signed.

280 Some aspects of the Salvation Army, 71–93. **Leopold Katscher**. Signed.

281 Ireland and the Redistribution Bill, 94–103. **F. H. Blackburne Daniell**. Signed.

282 Recruits and recruiting; or, Recruiting past and present, 104–119. **Frederick Robinson**. Signed.

283 Nature in folk-songs, 120–133. **Evelyn Martinengo Cesaresco**. Signed; repr. *Folk-Songs*.

284 In Correspondence: Land owners and land law, 136–139, signed **Lewis Marks Biden;** The City Guilds Commission, 139–141.

VOLUME 5, APRIL 1885

285 Eighteen hundred and fifty-three and eighteen hundred and eighty-five [policy toward Russia], 145–148.

286 Letters from Ruricola (No. VI, concl.), 149–157. **H. H. M. Herbert**. Evidence for 129.

287 The party system (No. I): the new Radicals, 158–172. **Percy Greg**. Signed.

288 The party system (No. II): the future of the Conservative party, 172–185. Signed: An Imperialist.

289 An appeal to men of leisure, 186–189. **Reginald Brabazon**. Signed Brabazon [Lord Brabazon], repr. *Social Arrows*. (Letter, pp. 570–572, on difficulties of a retired army man in adjusting to civilian life, by **Oswald Mosley Bradshaw**—signed O. Bradshaw; man cited a career officer who retired in 1885 [*Army List/* 85] and was called "O. Bradshaw" in source for *Cornhill*, no. 795 in *Index*, I; *not* Octavius Bradshaw in *WWW*/1928.)

290 Archaeological frauds in Palestine, 190–206. **G. F. Browne**. Signed; Contents adds "Rev."

291 Lord Bury and imperial federation, 207–219. **Harold Finch-Hatton**. Signed. (Letter, pp. 572–575, by **Charles Hodges Nugent**—Signed C. H. Nugent, who says he had joined the Imperial Federation League, "Colonel, Sir Charles Nugent, K.C.B." appears in list of members published with Imperial Federation League, 1886; see *WWW*/1916.)

292 The liberal movement in English literature (No. IV), 220–237. **William John Courthope**. Signed.

293 The Irish loyalists and Home Rule (No. I): a Conservative view, 238–244. **James H. Stronge**. Signed.

294 The Irish loyalists and Home Rule (No. II): a Liberal view, 244–257. Signed: Broughshane [a pseudonym: see Contents and p. 245n.].

295 The German abroad, 259–267. **C. E. Dawkins**. Signed.

296 The London livery companies, 268–279. **Lewis T. Dibdin**. Assigned in Contents to "L. F. Dibdin"; man cited wrote on

same subject in *Quart. Rev.* in Jan. 1885: see no. 2210, *Index*, I.

297   In Correspondence: The Bengal Tenancy Bill, 281–286, signed **Walter Scott Seton-Karr** (letter, pp. 432–436, signed **Roper Lethbridge**); Representation of minorities, 286–289, signed **Frederick Calvert.**

VOLUME 5, MAY 1885

298   The advance of Russia towards India, 293–307. **G. B. Malleson.** Signed.

299   How the blind dream, 309–319. **B. G. Johns.** Signed.

300   Tory prime ministers (No. IV): The Duke of Wellington, 320–336. **T. E. Kebbel.** Signed.

301   Poetry and theological polemics, 337–347. **Alfred Austin.** Signed.

302   The border ballads, 348–360. **Mary A. Baillie Hamilton.** Signed.

303   Politics and political economy, 361–367. **A. J. Balfour.** Signed: repr. *Essays and Addresses*, 1893.

304   The bells of Carlisle Cathedral, 368–381. **Henry Whitehead.** Signed H. Whitehead; see Boase.

305   Body and music [epistemology], 382–390. **E. Carey.** Signed.

306   An apology for jingoism, 391–402. **Walter Copland Perry.** Signed.

307   Mr. Ruskin's museum at Sheffield, 403–412. **Edward Schroder Prior,** prob. Signed E.S.P.; in 1883, Prior was a member of the St. George's Art Society, and later Slade Professor of Fine Art at Cambridge: see *WWW*/1940.

308   A scarce book [Cobbett's *Rural Rides*], 413–428. **Hugh E. Egerton.** Signed.

309   In Correspondence: The two million [newly enfranchised electors], 429–432. **George R. Portal.** Signed G. R. Portal, with address "Burghclere, Newbury"; see Part B, below.

VOLUME 5, JUNE 1885

310   A word to country gentlemen by one of themselves, 437–443. **H. H. M. Herbert.** Signed A Country Gentleman; attr. in *Life*, I, 71; repr. *Essays*, II.

311   The fate of Marocco, 444–457. **Harold Arthur Perry.** Signed.

312   The [Royal] Academy and the Salon, 458–473. **Walter Armstrong.** Signed.

313   A seat in the House, 474–483. **Alfred Austin.** Signed.

314   Mr. Goschen on national insurance, 490–503. **William Lewery Blackley.** Signed.

315   The liberal movement in English literature (No. V), 504–518. **William John Courthope.** Signed. (Letter, p. 723, signed F. H. Doyle.)

316   Notes on native questions, South Africa, 519–539. **Cecil Ashley.** Signed.

317   A vigil in Stonehenge, 540–546. **H. H. M. Herbert.** Signed Carnarvon [Earl of Carnarvon]; repr. *Essays*, I.

318   On the remuneration of labour in England, 547–558. **F. R. Conder.** Signed.

319   M. Lessar's triumph: and after? [Afghanistan border question], 559–569. **Edward Stanhope.** Signed.

320   In Correspondence: An elected peerage, 576–580, signed **Frederick William Heygate.**

VOLUME 5, JULY 1885

321   The late crisis and the new cabinet, 581–588.

322   The nineteenth century Ishmael [industrial schools for juvenile prisoners], 589–605. **Hugh Egerton.** Signed.

323   Imperial federation and home rule: a Conservative solution, 606–615. **G. B. Lancaster Woodburne.** Signed. (Letter, pp. 857–859, by **F. R. Wegg-Prosser**—signed F.R.W.P., signature used by Wegg-Prosser for *DR* nos. 1707, 2358, 2459; he was an M.P. and wrote on politics.

324   Sir William Napier, 616–633. **T. R. E. Holmes.** Signed; repr. *Four Famous Soldiers*, 1889.

325   The Conservative provincial press, 634–645. **Algernon Borthwick?** Signed B; author is believed to be a person in "the inner circle of Conservative journalism" (p. 866); Borthwick was proprietor of the ultra-Tory *Morning Post* and member of the Primrose League, on which he wrote *NC* no. 1294 a year later. (Letter, pp. 866–868, signed **H. Byron Reed.**) (See no. 340.)

326   A glance at the stage, 646–651. **W. H. Pollock.** Signed.

327   What is public opinion? 652–664. **H. D. Traill.** Signed.

328   An appeal to men of wealth, 665–667. **Reginald Brabazon.** Signed Brabazon [Lord Brabazon]; repr. *Social Arrows.*

329   Our work in Egypt, 668–680. **Carl de Malortie.** Signed Baron de Malortie.

330   Some higher aspects of mesmerism,

681–703. **Edmund Gurney** and **Frederic W. H. Myers.** Signed.

331   The strength and weakness of Conservatism, 704–715. Signed: A Looker-On.

332   In Correspondence: Free trade, 716–717, signed Fretensis (letters, pp. 865–866, signed It; vol. 6, pp. 294–295, 435–436, signed Fretensis; pp. 432–435, signed **Robert Scott Moffat**); Schoolboys and their ways, 718–720, signed **Henry M. Trollope;** Women and women's suffrage, 721–722, signed **Sarah Steward** with address "Beck Hall, Billingfard, Dereham, Norfolk" (letter, pp. 863–864, signed "Vera"); General Gordon, 723–724, signed **R. Crawley,** who may be the Richard Crawley, 1840–1893, who wrote *Election Rhymes* in 1880 (see *DNB*), since the letter ends with a political quatrain.

VOLUME 5, AUGUST 1885

333   Gordon or Gladstone? 725–733. **Stanley Leighton.** Signed.

334   Wanted, a new constitution, 734–749. **Alfred Austin.** Signed. (Letter, vol. 6, pp. 141–144, signed **W. F. Hobson.**)

335   Elements in the Irish question (No. I): Irish industrial schools, 751–763. **A. G. C. Liddell.** Signed, with the third initial misprinted "G". (Letter, vol. 8, pp. 137–140, signed **Alfred Harris.**)

336   Elements in the Irish question (No. II): The cultivation of tobacco in Ireland, 764–769. **Robert Staples, Jr.** Signed as in no. 86.

337   The liberal movement in English literature (No. VI, concl.), 770–786. **William John Courthope.** Signed.

338   An address to the Liberty and Property Defence League; with a word to the Conservative party, 787–800. **G. R. C. Herbert.** Signed Pembroke [Earl of Pembroke].

339   Tory prime ministers (No. V): Sir Robert Peel and the "Great Conservative Party," 1835 and 1885 (Part I), 801–817. **T. E. Kebbel.** Signed.

340   The establishment of newspapers, 818–828. Signed: A Conservative Journalist.

341   Ivan Turgénieff (Part II, concl.), 829–841. **Arthur Tilley.** Signed.

342   Competition and industrial organization, 842–856. **Robert Scott Moffat.** Signed.

343   In Correspondence: A proposed address of the British army to the Queen and nation, 859–862, signed **Charles A. Spaeth,** with address "Mannheim, Baden."

VOLUME 6, SEPTEMBER 1885

344   Conservative prospects at the general election, 1–10.

345   My lecturing tour in England, 11–25. **Arminius Vambéry.** Signed A. Vambéry; Contents gives first name.

346   The value of the ideal: a conversation, 26–42. **Violet Paget.** Signed Vernon Lee; repr. *Baldwin*, 1886. (Letter, pp. 295–296, signed Inquirer.)

347   The Scottish Church question, 43–52. **A. N. Cumming.** Signed.

348   Road repair: its wastefulness and inefficiency, 53–67. **H. Revell Reynolds, Jr.** Signed. (Letter, pp. 724–727, signed **Joseph Hall,** with title "Assoc. M. Inst. C.E. [Civil Engineers]"; reply, vol. 7, pp. 430–432, by **Reynolds**—signed.)

349   Tory prime ministers (No. VI): Sir Robert Peel (Part II), 68–83. **T. E. Kebbel.** Signed.

350   A dark page in Italian history, [Barbara Sanseverino-Sanvitale, 1551–1612], 84–104. **Antonio Gallenga.** Signed as in no. 224.

351   The Catholic vote, 105–111. **Edward Styche Hart.** Signed.

352   Some uses of a parliamentary seat, 112–122. **Percy Greg.** Signed.

353   A political colloquy, 123–133. Signed: Audax.

354   The future of the Soudan, 134–140. **V. Lovett Cameron.** Signed.

355   In Correspondence: Our junior conservatives, 145–146, signed **Kendall Robinson,** with address "Blyth"; An Indian officer's view of the Afghan question, 146–152, signed **Cecil B. Brownlow.**

VOLUME 6, OCTOBER 1885

356   The electoral campaign, 153–161.

357   An Anglo-Chinese commercial alliance, 162–173. **Archibald R. Colquhoun.** Signed.

358   Friendly societies: their best form, 184–191. **J. B. Sweet.** Signed; Contents adds "Rev."

359   [Charles] Churchill, 192–199. **Joseph Devey.** Signed J. Devey: see Boase.

360   The national party (No. I): are parties and principles breaking up? 200–206. **Eustace G. Cecil.** Signed; Contents adds "Lord" and "M.P."

361   The national party (No. II): a word from the Reform Club, 207–210. Unidentified. Intro. note, p. 207, by **Alfred**

Austin and **W. J. Courthope**—signed Editors *N.R.*

362 The stage *Faust*, 211–222. **Walter S. Sichel.** Signed. (Letter, p. 862, signed **Walter Sichel.**)

363 How to popularize unpopular political truths, 223–241. **W. H. Mallock.** Signed.

364 Tory prime ministers (No. VII): Lord Derby, 242–253. **T. E. Kebbel.** Signed in Contents.

365 The situation in Burmah, 254–265. **A. R. McMahon.** Signed.

366 The clergy and politics, 266–270. **H. George Morgan.** Signed; Contents adds "Rev."

367 Voluntary schools, 271–288. **Henry Hayman.** Signed.

368 In Correspondence: What are moderate Liberals to do? 289–292, signed **E. C. Clark,** with title "Regius Professor of Civil Law, Cambridge"; Shakespear and Epictetus, 292–294, signed C.J.I.

VOLUME 6, NOVEMBER 1885

369 "Skeletons at the Feast" [Liberal opponents of Joseph Chamberlain], 297–315. **Alfred Austin.** Signed.

370 The history of an Indian district [Sirsa, Punjab]: an example of the benefits of British rule in India, 316–328. **James Wilson,** 1853–1926. Signed J. Wilson; man cited was Indian Civil Servant in Punjab in 1875 and after: see *WWW*.

371 The Church question and the coming election, 333–342. **Philip Vernon Smith.** Signed.

372 The peasant proprietor of the south [of France], 345–357. **Frances Mary de Borring.** Signed.

373 The local working of the Birmingham caucus, 358–369. Signed: A Birmingham Tory.

374 Low prices and hostile tariffs, 370–383. **A. W. Roberts.** Signed on p. 380.

375 The theatre (No. I): Shakespeare as a dramatic model, 384–400. **William Spink.** Signed.

376 The theatre (No. II): the stage of Greater Britain, 401–413. **William Archer.** Signed; repr. *About the Theatre*, 1886.

377 Tory prime ministers (No. VIII, concl.): Lord Beaconsfield, 414–431. **T. E. Kebbel.** Signed.

378 In Correspondence: Great artists and portraiture in England—a protest, 436–440, signed **Marian L. Hatchard** and **Ada Heather-Bigg** (letter, pp. 727–728, signed

W. D. Gainsford; reply, vol. 7, pp. 287–288, signed **Marian L. Hatchard**).

VOLUME 6, DECEMBER 1885

379 The old order changes (Book I, chaps. i–iv), 441–463. **W. H. Mallock.** Assigned in Contents; novel published 1886.

380 The selection for regimental commands, 464–473. Assigned in Contents to "Centurion."

381 The opium-poppy cultivation of Bengal, 474–488. **C. T. Buckland.** Signed.

382 The Radical programme, 489–501. **Henry Cecil Raikes.** Signed.

383 Poetry, politics and conservatism, 502–518. **George N. Curzon.** Signed.

384 Aspects of the national Church (No. I): the tribune of the people, 519–529. **Walter L. Bicknell.** Signed Austen Pember; see below, App. A, *Mac.* no. 2459.

385 Aspects of the national Church (No. II): the Church and the age, 530–536. Signed: John Reynolds, Citizen and Goldsmith [pseudonym: see no. 148]. (Letter, pp. 862–868, signed One in Earnest.)

386 Reform in the tenure of land: a panacea for agricultural distress, 537–552. **E. Leigh Pemberton.** Signed.

387 A plea for orthodox political economy, 553–563. **J. Shield Nicholson.** Signed.

388 The London School Board: its past and future, 566–571. **Arthur Mills.** Signed.

389 The electoral triumph, 572–576.

390 In Correspondence: Some Liberal lights, 577–580, by **James Frazer Cornish**—signed J.F.C., cf. no. 1209, pp. 284–288, for close similarity of subject and style; Of the general depression, 580–584, signed **W. F. Hobson.**

VOLUME 6, JANUARY 1886

391 The old order changes (Book I, chaps. v–viii), 585–615. **W. H. Mallock.** Assigned in Contents.

392 The plague of tongues [campaign oratory], 616–630. **H. D. Traill.** Signed.

393 Persia as an ally, 631–639. **A. C. Yate.** Signed.

394 Poetry and politics: form and subject, 640–650. **William John Courthope.** Signed.

395 Parochialism or imperialism, 651–658. Signed: An Ex-Liberal M.P.

396 Frederic Mistral, 659–670. **Arthur Symons.** Signed.

397 Colonial governors, 671–678. **William Greswell.** Signed.
398 The original institution of the Turkish army, 679–692. **Andrew T. Sibbald.** Signed.
399 An American view of the English land problem, 693–706. **John Swann.** Signed.
400 My recollections of what I saw and heard during the East Leicestershire election, 707–715. **Janetta Manners.** Signed.
401 Mr. Gladstone's latest manoeuvre [separate parliament for Ireland], 716–719.
402 In Correspondence: The older system of political economy, 720–724, signed **Archer Gurney** (letter, pp. 870–872, signed **W. F. Hobson**).

VOLUME 6, FEBRUARY 1886

403 The laws relating to land, 729–744. **J. F. Stephen.** Signed. (Letter, vol. 7, pp. 132–135, signed **Edmund Lawrence,** with address "Armagh.")
404 The old order changes (Book II, chaps. i–iv), 745–771. **W. H. Mallock.** Assigned in Contents.
405 Is crime increasing or diminishing with the spread of education? 772–783. **Robert Gregory.** Signed. (Letter, vol. 7, pp. 135–138, signed **J. Satchell Hopkins,** with address "Edgbaston, Birmingham.")
406 Millais, 784–795. **Walter Armstrong.** Signed.
407 North Queensland separation, 796–809. **Harold Finch-Hatton.** Signed.
408 The reform of the laws relating to Church patronage, 810–832. **W. C. Magee.** Signed W. C. Peterborough [Bishop of Peterborough]. (Letter, vol. 7, pp. 143–144, by **James Ferguson,** 1857–1917—signed A Scottish Conservative, cf. no. 831.)
409 *Faust* at the Lyceum, 833–837. **W. H. Pollock.** Signed.
410 The land question in the Highlands, 838–847. **C. C. Grant.** Signed; Contents adds "Rev."
411 *Glenaveril* [by Robert Lytton], 849–861. **William John Courthope.** Signed.
412 In Correspondence: International trade, 868–870, signed **W. D. Gainsford.**

VOLUME 7, MARCH 1886

413 The Liberal party and Home Rule, 1–6. **R. Bosworth Smith.** Signed.
414 The old order changes (Book II, chaps.

v–ix), 7–39. **W. H. Mallock.** Assigned in Contents.
415 The depression of trade and state-directed colonization, 40–53. **J. F. Boyd.** Signed.
416 French interests in Egypt, 57–66. **Harold A. Perry.** Signed.
417 A Venetian playwright [Carlo Gozzi], 67–82. **Linda Villari.** Signed.
418 Ireland under her own parliament, 83–102. **John Leith Veitch.** Signed J. L. Derwent—see *BMCat.* (Letter, pp. 422–428, signed **Henry McClintock Alexander,** with title "Captain R.N.")
419 The newer North-West [Canada] as a field for Englishmen, 103–119. **George Alexander.** Signed.
420 Party and patriotism, 120–131. **Alfred Austin.** Signed. (Letters, pp. 283–284, signed **Edmund Lawrence;** pp. 284–285, signed **J. Laister.**)
421 In Correspondence: A glance at voluntaryism, 139–143, signed **Frank Banfield.**

VOLUME 7, APRIL 1886

422 The falsehoods of the political situation, 145–149.
423 The old order changes (Book III, chaps. i–iv), 150–175. **W. H. Mallock.** Assigned in Contents.
424 Canvassing experiences in an agricultural constituency, 176–189. **Clara E. L. Strutt.** Signed Clara E. L. Rayleigh [2nd Baroness Rayleigh].
425 The spirit of the age, 190–198. **Perceval C. Gaussen.** Signed.
426 An Irish Churchman's view of the rights of the laity, 199–213. **Henry Jellett.** Signed; Contents gives "Archdeacon of Cloyne." (See nos. 488, 508.)
427 The fame of Turner, 230–238. **Walter Armstrong.** Signed.
428 The cuckoo, 239–249. **William Hodgson.** Signed.
429 Hendrik Conscience and the Flemish revival, 250–260. **George Edmundson.** Signed.
430 The English gentleman, 261–271. **W. R. Browne.** Signed W.R.B.; Cover gives "the late W. R. Browne."
431 Butter *versus* Home Rule; or, The economic condition of Ireland, 272–279. **William J. Harris.** Signed.
432 In Correspondence: The needs of the Welsh Church, 280–282, signed **R. S. Mylne,** with title "M.A." and address, "Oxford"; Conservative organization, 285–287, signed Προαίρεσις (letter, pp. 429–430, signed Προαίρεσις).

VOLUME 7, MAY 1886

433 Dismemberment disguised, 289–295. **Gathorne Gathorne-Hardy.** Signed Cranbrook [Viscount Cranbrook].

434 The old order changes (Book III, chaps. v–x), 296–324. **W. H. Mallock.** Assigned in Contents.

435 France: its finances and its freedom, 325–342. **C. B. Norman.** Assigned in Contents, with title "Captain."

436 The establishment and endowment of nonconformity, 343–352. **Stanley Leighton.** Signed.

437 A reverie on the Riviera, 353–363. **Alfred Austin.** Signed Rambler; claimed, although misdated 1885, in *Autobiography* (1911), II, 268–269.

438 The Crofters Bill in Orkney, 364–375. **A. M. Sutherland Graeme.** Signed. (Letter, 568–571, signed **Alfred W. Johnston.**)

439 Hobbes and the modern radical, 376–391. **H. D. Traill.** Signed.

440 Social aspects of the revolution of 1789, 392–412. **Francis Hitchman.** Signed.

441 The Primrose League, 413–418. **Susan Harris.** Signed S. H. Malmesbury [Countess of Malmesbury].

442 In Correspondence: The British House of Peers, 419–422, signed **Archer Gurney.**

VOLUME 7, JUNE 1886

443 The old order changes (Book IV, chaps. i–v), 433–464. **W. H. Mallock.** Assigned in Contents.

444 The political prospect (No. I): a Liberal view—the new questions and the new constituencies, 465–474. **J. A. Doyle.** Signed.

445 The political prospect (No. II): a Conservative view—prophecy and politics, 475–486. **William John Courthope.** Signed.

446 Théodore Agrippa d'Aubigné, 487–501. **P. F. Willert.** Signed.

447 State-and-rate-paid education, 502–518. **Hugh Fortescue, 1818–1905.** Signed Fortescue [Earl Fortescue]. (Letter, pp. 719–720, by **Hugh Fortescue**—signed as above.)

448 The [Royal] Academy and the Salon, 519–538. **Walter Williams.** Signed.

449 The development of North-west Canada by the Hudson's Bay trade-route, 541–551. **William Shelford.** Signed W. Shelford, with title "M. Inst. C.E. [Civil Engineers]: see *DNB*.

450 The revival of common sense, 552–565. **Alfred Austin.** Signed.

451 In Correspondence: Political equality and uniformity, 566–568, signed A Sociologist; Free libraries under the "Act" and their promotion, 571–576, signed **Alfred Cotgreave;** repr. with same title, [1886].

VOLUME 7, JULY 1886

452 Mr. Gladstone's coming defeat, 577–582. **Alfred Austin** and **W. J. Courthope.** Signed The Editors.

453 The old order changes (Book V, chaps. i–iii), 583–606. **W. H. Mallock.** Assigned in Contents.

454 Glimpses of Bürger and Bauer life in Homburg and the Taunus region, 607–617. **Janetta Manners.** Signed.

455 Ritual litigation, 618–633. **George Trevor.** Signed, with title "D.D."

456 Poetry compared with the other fine arts, 634–648. **F. T. Palgrave.** Signed.

457 National enemies and national defences, 652–667. **Henrietta O. Barnett.** Signed H. A. Barnett, but repr. by woman cited in *Practicable Socialism* as "The Poverty of the Poor."

458 Mallet du Pan, 668–677. **R. C. E. Abbot.** Signed Colchester [Baron Colchester].

459 Why is the provincial press radical? 678–682. Signed: A Conservative Journalist.

460 The novelists of Naples, 683–697. **A. Mary F. Robinson.** Signed.

461 Imperial federation (No. I): Colonial home rule, 698–703. **George Baden-Powell.** Signed; repr. *The Saving of Ireland,* Edin., 1898, as "The Colonial Analogy."

462 Imperial federation (No. II): Impossible constitutions, 704–711. **Charles Bowyer Adderley.** Signed Norton [Baron Norton].

463 In Correspondence: Australia and annexation, 712–714, signed **C. S. W. Pfoundes;** Future Irish policy, 714–719, signed **E. J. Gibbs.**

VOLUME 7, AUGUST 1886

464 Party or Empire? 721–729.

465 The old order changes (Book V, chaps. iv–vii, concl.), 730–753. **W. H. Mallock.** Assigned in Contents.

466 Agricultural depression and its remedies, 754–769. **Wilbraham Egerton.** Signed Egerton of Tatton [2nd Baron Egerton of Tatton]. (See no. 494.)

Signed. (Letters, pp. 861–862, and vol. 9, p. 144, signed **R. W. Wintle.**)

498 Burma and the Burmese, 332–350. **A. R. McMahon.** Signed.

499 Democracy and taste, 351–360. Signed: A Lover of the Classics.

500 Social reforms in India, 361–368. **Nanda Lal Ghosh.** Signed; see *BMCat.* under Nandalāla.

501 Sir Francis Doyle's *Reminiscences*, 369–378.

502 Chaucer and Boccaccio, 379–391. **Ellen Mary Clerke.** Signature.

503 The relation of women to the state in past times, 392–399. **Helen Blackburn.** Signed.

504 Sullivan's *Golden Legend*, 400–407. **C. V. Stanford.** Signed.

505 Our grandmothers, 408–419. **Margaret Elizabeth Child-Villiers.** Signed M. E. Jersey [Countess of Jersey].

506 In Correspondence: The Eastern question, 431–432, signed Προαίρεσις.

VOLUME 8, DECEMBER 1886

507 An Empire institute, 433–442. **George Baden-Powell.** Signed.

508 Lay representation in Church synods in Australia, 443–454. **Alfred Barry.** Signed Alfred Sydney [Bishop of Sydney].

509 France as it is and was: government and society, 455–476. Signed: A Parisian.

510 The British merchant service, 477–482. **W. B. Whall.** Signed.

511 Open spaces and physical education, 483–490. **Reginald Brabazon.** Signed Brabazon [Lord Brabazon]; repr. *Some National and Board School Reforms*, 1887. (Letter, vol. 10, pp. 144–148, signed **Ernest E. James.**)

512 Modern philosophy: Realism *v.* Idealism, 491–511. **Robert Scott Moffat.** Signed.

513 A practicable experiment in Home Rule, 512–520. **Almeric FitzRoy.** Signed.

514 Why should we break up the marriage code? A reply to Lord Bramwell [*Nineteenth Century*, vol. 20, pp. 403–415], 522–532. **Percy Greg.** Signed. (See no. 528.)

515 Life at the Scottish universities, 533–541. **John Kirkwood Leys?** Signed J. Leys; man cited was educated at Glasgow Univ.: see *WWW*/1916 and note that *Temple Bar*, 72 (Oct. 1884), 187–208, is assigned in Bentley to John Leys, while 113 (Mar. 1898), 389–403, is signed John K. Leys.

516 The present state of peasant proprietors in Germany, 542–548. **Walburga Paget.** Signed W. Paget; Contents adds "Lady"; see *WWW*/1940.

517 Canon Kingsley as a naturalist and country clergyman, 549–558. **Henry Evershed.** Signed. (Letter, pp. 862–863, signed **H. D. S. Powell.**)

518 Corporation reform, 559–564. Signed: John Reynolds [pseudonym: see no. 148].

519 In Correspondence: Ireland's only chance, 565–568, signed **C. Hamilton.**

VOLUME 8, JANUARY 1887

520 Conservatism and young conservatives, 577–587. **George N. Curzon.** Signed.

521 Carlyle, the "pious editor" of Cromwell's speeches, 588–604. **Reginald F. D. Palgrave.** Signed.

522 Jubilee reigns in England, 605–617. **Arthur Burney.** Signed.

523 Thoughts on Dowden's *Life of Shelley*, 618–633. **William John Courthope.** Signed.

524 Some miscalled cases of thought transference, 634–640. **Ada Heather-Bigg** and **Marian L. Hatchard.** Signed. (Letter, vol. 9, pp. 437–439, signed **Edmund Gurney.**)

525 "Locksley Hall" and liberalism, 641–647. **Mortimer Dyneley.** Signed. (Letter, vol. 9, pp. 147–149, signed **H. P. Tregarthen.**)

526 The Colonial Conference and imperial defence, 648–658. **William Greswell.** Signed.

527 The Rachel-Cremieux correspondence, 659–672. **Nina Kennard.** Signed.

528 The marriage code of Henry VIII. and Mr. Greg, 673–679. **Edmund Beckett.** Signed Grimthorpe [Baron Grimthorpe]. Intro. note by **Alfred Austin** and **W. J. Courthope**—signed Editors. (Letter, pp. 858–860, signed **W. F. Hobson.**)

529 "Owen Meredith," Earl of Lytton, 680–701. **Alfred Austin.** Signed.

530 Politics at home and abroad, 702–710. Unidentified. Intro. note by **Alfred Austin** and **W. J. Courthope**—signed Editors *N.R.*

531 In Correspondence: A policy for Ireland, 711–716, signed An Irishman Belonging to No Party (letter, vol. 9, pp. 139–141, signed **Charles Crosthwaite**); Technical education: a workman's view, 716–720, signed **H. J. Pettifer**, with title "Secretary, Workmen's Association for Defence of British Industry."

Charles L. Graves. Signed. (Letter, pp. 577–581, signed **Charles Catty.**)

569 The Russian frontiers of the Austro-Hungarian Empire, 330–340. **A. Hilliard Atteridge.** Signed.

570 A spring holiday [in France and Italy], 341–351. **Alfred Austin.** Signed Rambler —see no. 437.

571 On the direct influence over style in poetry, exercised by the other fine arts, sculpture and painting especially; with illustrations ancient and modern (Part I), 352–369. **F. T. Palgrave.** Signed. (Part II is no. 632.)

572 The law of theft, 370–381. **Hugh Hall.** Signed.

573 *Lothair* and *Endymion* [by Disraeli], 382–394. **Francis Hitchman.** Signed.

574 The re-organization of the Indian army, 395–406. **C. B. Norman.** Signed.

575 A French critic [Ferdinand Brunetière] on Victor Hugo, 407–417. **Francis Paul.** Signed.

576 The municipalities on their trial, 418–426. **Stanley Leighton.** Signed.

577 Politics at home and abroad, 427–434.

578 In Correspondence: The lion's share of the world's trading, 435–436, signed **J. Pulling Heath,** with address "47, Southernhay, Exeter."

VOLUME 9, JUNE 1887

579 Our Indo-Chinese frontier, 441–450. **Richard Temple.** Signed.

580 Old and new Oxford, 451–464. **T. E. Kebbel.** Signed.

581 Queen's plates [prize money]: horse supply, 465–478. **Thomas Lister.** Signed Ribblesdale [Baron Ribblesdale]. (Letter, p. 861, by **Thomas Lister**—signed Ribblesdale.)

582 The Byron ladies, 484–498. **Henry Hayman.** Signed.

583 Notes on New Zealand, 499–512. **E. Brodie Hoare.** Signed.

584 The Royal Academy and the Salon, 513–524. **William Sharp.** Signed.

585 State-directed colonization, 525–537. **Reginald Brabazon.** Signed Brabazon [Lord Brabazon].

586 The foreign missions of the Church of England, 538–553. **Frederick Arnold.** Signed.

587 England in the Mediterranean, 554–568. **Harold Arthur Perry.** Signed.

588 Politics at home and abroad, 569–576.

589 In Correspondence: The working man and the crisis, 583–584, signed Προαίρεσις.

VOLUME 9, JULY 1887

590 The true lessons of the Jubilee, 585–590.

591 Alsace-Lorraine and the European situation, 591–601. Signed: An Old German Resident.

592 Art at the public schools, 602–617.

593 Leasehold enfranchisement, 618–629. **J. W. Flanagan.** Signed.

594 Irish dairy-farming, 630–637. **Henry Evershed.** Signed.

595 Burke and the French Revolution, 638–658. **James Rowley.** Signed J. Rowley; repr. *Wordsworth.*

596 Fifty years of women's work, 659–667. **Louisa Twining.** Signed.

597 Character and ability in politics, 668–679. **Alfred Austin.** Signed.

598 Some minor worries [charity fund drives, etc.], 680–685. Signed: A Member of Parliament.

599 The strength and weakness of Russia, 686–689. **Hubert Foster.** Signed; Contents adds "Capt., R.E."

600 Postal communication, past and present (Part I), 690–704. **H. W. Linford.** Part II (no. 714) is signed.

601 The separatist attack on fundamental principles, 705–710. **Leonard H. West.** Signed.

602 Politics at home and abroad, 711–716.

603 In Correspondence: The Crimes Bill for Ireland—its justification, 717–721, signed **George W. Ruxton** (letters, vol. 10 pp. 139–144, pp. 582–585, signed **George W. Ruxton**); Tithes, 721–723, signed **W. Barrow Simonds;** Tory democracy, 724–728, signed **Frank Banfield** (letter, vol. 10, pp. 289–293, signed **Thomas M. Watt,** with description "Ulster Presbyterian" and address "Hovingham").

VOLUME 9, AUGUST 1887

604 The position of the Liberal Unionists, 729–734. **Alfred Austin** and **W. J. Courthope.** Signed The Editors.

605 The opinion of "the civilized world [on British policy]," 735–745. **Roundell Palmer.** Signed Selborne [Earl of Selborne].

606 The country clergy, 746–756. **E. W. Bowling.** Signed.

607 Wagner's letters to Frau Eliza Wille, 757–776. **Francis Paul.** Signed.

608 Are we worthy of our Empire? 781–792. **C. C. Penrose Fitzgerald.** Signed.

609 Ancient and modern painted glass, 793–810. **E. G. Howard.** Signed.

610 The other side of the medal, 811–823. **H. D. Traill.** Signed.

611 The agricultural crisis in north Italy, 824–832. **Evelyn Martinengo-Cesaresco.** Signed E. Martinengo Cesaresco; Contents adds "Countess"; cf. no. 283.

612 The mystical side of Wordsworth, 833–843. **John Hogben.** Signed.

613 Objections of an Oxford Liberal to Home Rule, 844–853. **W. R. Anson.** Signed.

614 Politics at home and abroad, 854–860.

615 In Correspondence: the Spalding and Paddington elections, 861–862, signed Προαίρεσις; The Church house, 862–865, signed Clericus; The invasion of America, 865–868, signed **Selwyn Blackett.**

VOLUME 10, SEPTEMBER 1887

616 Mr. Gladstone's concessions, 1–10. **E. R. Wodehouse.** Signed.

617 Keats' place in English poetry, 11–24. **William John Courthope.** Signed. (Letter, p. 590, signed **Joseph John Murphy.**)

618 Allotments [of land for cottage gardens], 25–39. **Henry Evershed.** Signed.

619 *The Service of Man* [by Cotter Morison], 46–58. **P. F. Willert.** Signed.

620 Donatello, and the unveiling of the façade of the Duomo at Florence, 59–69. **Catherine Mary Phillimore.** Signed.

621 Cobden's dream, 70–79. **H. R. Farquharson.** Signed.

622 Gustav Freytag, 80–105. **Konrad Sittenfeld.** Signed Conrad Alberti; See *Grosse Brockhaus.*

623 The last day of Windsor Forest, 106–111. **T. L. Peacock.** Signed; repr. *Works,* VIII. Intro. note by **Richard Garnett,** 1836–1906—signed R.G., repr. *Calidore & Miscellanea,* 1891.

624 Recent literature in China, 112–124. **H. N. Shore.** Signed.

625 Parliamentary procedure, 125–132. **Hugh Fortescue,** 1854–1932. Signed Ebrington [Viscount Ebrington].

626 Politics at home and abroad, 133–138.

627 In Correspondence: The poverty of India, 148–152, signed **H. G. Keene.**

VOLUME 10, OCTOBER 1887

628 Has the session been unfruitful? 153–165. **C. A. Whitmore.** Signed.

629 The effects of town life upon the human body, 166–172. **J. Milner Fothergill.** Signed.

630 The protection of national industry, 173–190. **James Plaisted Wilde.** Signed Penzance [Baron Penzance].

631 Shall women graduate at Cambridge? 191–201. **J. P. Postgate.** Signed.

632 On the direct influence over style in poetry, exercised by the other fine arts (Part II), 202–218. **F. T. Palgrave.** Assigned in Contents.

633 The new electorate in France and the men of the Third Republic, 219–241. **Marie Blaze de Bury.** Signed Madame Blaze de Bury; see *DBF.*

634 Richard Jefferies, and the open air, 242–250. **Newton Wallop.** Signed Lymington [Viscount Lymington].

635 Our first amphictyonic council, 251–266. **William Greswell.** Signed.

636 The eruptive force of modern fanaticism, 268–280. **Frank Banfield.** Signed.

637 Politics at home and abroad, 281–288.

638 In Correspondence: Home Rule, an exploded myth, 293–295, signed **S. H. Boult;** Would the extension of the franchise to women be advantageous? 295–296, signed Sackville Dorset [apparently a pseudonym].

VOLUME 10, NOVEMBER 1887

639 The decay of British agriculture: pictures from life drawn by a landowner, 297–312. **William J. Harris.** Signed W. J. Harris; Contents provides first name.

640 Comfort and safety in London theatres, 313–325. **Charles L. Floris.** Signed.

641 Tory foreign policy sixty years ago: Canning, Castlereagh, and Wellington, 326–334. **T. E. Kebbel.** Signed.

642 Dogs in disgrace [rabies control], 335–340. **William Hillier Onslow.** Signed Onslow [Earl of Onslow].

643 Competition and free trade, 341–354. **C. A. Cripps.** Signed. (Letter, pp. 730–734, signed **Charles Catty.**)

644 French socialism, 355–375. **Moritz Kaufmann.** Signed M. Kaufmann; Contents adds "Rev."; man cited was a prolific writer on socialism: see *WWW*/1928.

645 What women write and read, 376–381. **Florence Layard.** Signed. (Letter, pp. 727–729, by **Florence Mary Ramsay**—signed Florence M. Ramsey, cover gives "Lady Ramsey," but see Burke.

646 Pauperism, distress, and the coming winter, 382–394. **Hugh P. Tregarthen.** Signed.

647 On the killing of the chimaera [on poetry], 395–414. **Alfred Austin.** Signed.

648 Fresh work for parliament, 415–421. **Edward S. Norris.** Signed.

649 Politics at home and abroad, 422–428.

650 In Correspondence: State emigration, 429–434, signed **W. Allen Smith**, with address "Jersey" (letter, pp. 871–876, signed **David Evans**, with title "Chairman, Fore Street Warehouse Company"); The road for stenography, 435–436, signed G.C.H.W.; Mr. Gladstone's five parliaments, 436–440, signed **T. J. Scott.**

VOLUME 10, DECEMBER 1887

651 A reply to Lord Randolph Churchill [on free trade], 441–460. **William J. Harris.** Signed.

652 Lord Macaulay and Madame D'Arblay, 461–477. **Coker Adams.** Signed; Contents adds "Rev."

653 "Go ye and teach!": a hint to political organizations, 478–[514]. **W. H. Mallock.** Signed.

654 An easy solution of the Irish land question, 515–520. **George Holloway.** Signed. (Letter, pp. 725–727, signed **Arthur Smith.**)

655 Slipshod English, 521–528. **Isaac Gregory Smith?** Signed I.G.S.; Smith used these initials for *Temple Bar* 109 (Oct. 1896), 214–217, and for works listed in *BMCat.* and H&L. (Letter, pp. 879–880, signed **Hamilton P. Lyne**, with address "Medical College, London Hospital.")

656 English farms and the price of food, 529–541. **Albert J. Mott.** Signed.

657 Heine's visit to London, 542–548. **Thomas Pryde.** Signed.

658 Peasant properties in France, 1787–1887, 549–564. **Frances P. Verney.** Signed F. P. Verney; repr. *Peasant Owners.*

659 Practical Tory administration, 565–574. **George Baden-Powell.** Signed.

660 Politics at home and abroad, 575–581.

661 In Correspondence: The Irish question, 585–588, signed A Lover of Ireland; The dissemination of Conservative papers among the poor, 588–590, signed **F. A. Millington,** with address "National Conservative Club, Pall Mall."

VOLUME 10, JANUARY 1888

662 Lord Salisbury's foreign policy, 591–606. Signed: Q.

663 Two views of the novelist, 607–616. **Hugh E. Egerton.** Signed.

664 Mercantile Ireland versus Home Rule, 617–625. **Richard Patterson.** Signed A Belfast Merchant; attr. on p. 871.

665 Personal experiences of Bulgaria, 626–636. **T. W. Legh.** Signed.

666 The "malaise" and its causes: an examination of Mr. Giffen's address to the Economic Science Section of the British Association, 637–655. **James Mavor.** Signed.

667 Some abuses in public speaking, 656–661. **Edward S. Norris.** Signed.

668 A Magyar musician [Lizst], 662–675. **Pauline Schletter.** Signed Paul Sylvester— see *BMCat.*

669 Rome and malaria, 676–684. **E. Strachan Morgan.** Signed.

670 The rise and progress of the poor-law system in relation to the Church, 685–700. **Morris Fuller.** Signed.

671 Charity in Talmudic times: Or, Ancient solvings of a modern problem, 701–709. **Katie Magnus.** Signed; Contents gives "Lady Magnus"; see *WWW/*1928.

672 The protectionist fallacy, 710–715. Signed: A Liberal Unionist. (Letter, vol. 11, pp. 295–296, signed **H. R. Ware,** with address "19, Farnham Road, Guildford": see Venn.)

673 Politics at home and abroad, 716–721.

674 In Correspondence: Mr. Arnold Forster's scheme for Ireland, 722–725, signed **F. A. Millington.**

VOLUME 10, FEBRUARY 1888

675 Conservatism and female suffrage, 735–752. **Goldwin Smith.** Signed. (See no. 692.)

676 [Correspondence of] the Marquess of Wellesley and the Earl of Iddesleigh, 753–756. **Richard Colley Wellesley** and **Stafford Henry Northcote.** Title. Intro. note signed **H. Stafford Northcote.**

677 The landowners' convention in Dublin, 757–767. **Anthony Traill.** Signed.

678 Mr. Matthew Arnold on the loves of the poets, 768–778. **Alfred Austin.** Signed.

679 How to revive British industries without taxing food, 779–789. **George Holloway.** Signed. (Letters, vol. 11, pp. 428–430, signed **James John Barrett**, with title "Late District Hon. Sec., Finsbury Conservative Association"; pp. 430–434, by **Henry Harrison,** prob.—signed H. Harrison, with address "Newcastle-on-Tyne," see *P.O. Directory/*87.)

680 Notes taken during a visit to a Kerry nationalist, 790–798. **Amos Reade.** Signed.

681 Extension of the episcopate, 799–810. **Robert Gregory.** Signed.

682 The evolution of humour, 811–830. **H. D. Traill.** Signed.

683 The prospects of fair trade, 831–835. **Hugh Fortescue,** 1854–1932. Signed Ebrington [Viscount Ebrington].

684 Are rich landowners idle? 836–840. **Janetta Manners.** Signed.

685 Two centenaries (No. I): the centenary of the *Times*, 841–856. **Alexander Innes Shand.** Signed.

686 Two centenaries (No. II): the centenary of Australia, 857–865. **John Henniker-Heaton.** Signed J. Henniker-Heaton; Contents adds "M.P.": see *DNB*.

687 Politics at home and abroad, 866–870.

688 In Correspondence: Union versus separation, pp. 876–879, signed **George W. Ruxton.**

VOLUME 11, MARCH 1888

689 Disestablishment in Wales, 1–13. **Matthew Arnold.** Signed. (See no. 712.)

690 Medical science in relation to homoeopathy, 14–30. **Robert B. Carter.** Signed R.B.C.; Carter was an opthalmic surgeon who wrote for non-technical journals (see *Index*, I, 840); diseases of the eye are discussed on pp. 24–27. (Letters, pp. 283–289, 427, 723–726, and vol. 12, pp. 279–282, signed **R. E. Dudgeon;** pp. 578–581, and vol. 12, pp. 136–138, signed E.P.T., p. 581 adds "M.D. Cantab"; vol. 12, pp. 282–284, signed **Rowland Allan,** with titles "M.B., Fr.," and address "Bridgman Place, Bolton.")

691 Coryat's *Crudities*, 1611, 31–43. **M. S. Dimsdale.** Signed.

692 Women's suffrage: a reply [to no. 675], 44–61. **Millicent Garrett Fawcett.** Signed.

693 Who are "the English people"? 62–71. Signed: An Englishman.

694 Free trade and the economists, 72–86. **C. A. Cripps.** Signed. (See no. 708; letter, pp. 425–427, by **Richard Walter Chetwynd**—signed Chetwynd [Viscount Chetwynd].)

695 Plain facts about Ireland, 87–102. **George C. Brodrick.** Signed; repr. *Literary Fragments*, 1891.

696 What we have done for Cyprus, 103–114. **Ulick Ralph Burke.** Signed.

697 A purified British senate: the "status quo," 115–134. **George N. Curzon.** Signed. (See no. 700.)

698 Politics at home and abroad, 135–141.

699 In Correspondence: Compulsory emigration of English paupers to Western Australia, 142–144, signed **Richard Varley** with address, "Eversley, South Park Road, Harrogate" (letter, pp. 439–440, signed **Frederic Pincott**); Retiring pensions for the clergy, 145–150, signed **H. George Morgan** (Cover adds "Rev."); Currency and prices, 150–152, signed **Charles Wilson,** with address "Cheltenham" (letter, pp. 434–438, signed **Charles Wilson**).

VOLUME 11, APRIL 1888

700 The reconstruction of the House of Lords: the "modus operandi," 153–175. **George N. Curzon.** Signed.

701 The character of the devil in the middle ages, 176–191. **A. C. Champneys.** Signed.

702 Education in agriculture, 192–199. **Robert Wallace,** 1853–1939. Signed; Contents adds "Professor."

703 The Liberal Unionists and the government, 202–209. **Newton Wallop.** Signed Lymington [Viscount Lymington]. (Letters, vol. 12, pp. 135–136, 862, signed Προαίρεσις.)

704 Lavater, 210–223. **Arthur Benson.** Signed.

705 Intemperance in India, 224–234. **C. T. Buckland.** Signed.

706 Pindar and athletics, ancient and modern, 235–258. **Charles Wordsworth.** Signed; Cover adds "Bishop of St. Andrews."

707 The certainties of chance, 259–267. **R. A. Proctor.** Signed. (Letter, pp. 438–439, signed J.C.M.)

708 Cripps versus free trade, 268–275. **G. R. C. Herbert.** Signed Pembroke [Earl of Pembroke]. (See no. 718.)

709 Politics at home and abroad, 276–282.

710 In Correspondence: "Local option" in the new Local Government Bill, 289–295, signed **Joseph Alan Scofield** (letter, pp. 576–577, signed **Joseph Alan Scofield**).

VOLUME 11, MAY 1888

711 Peers' eldest sons on the reform of the House of Lords, 297–299.

712 Disestablishment in Wales, 300–308. **Roundell Palmer.** Signed Selborne [Earl of Selborne].

713 Italy in England, 309–316. **Antonio Gallenga.** Signed as in no. 224.

714 Postal communication, past and present

Churchill [translated from *Revue des Deux Mondes*], 326–340. **Pierre Marie Augustin Filon.** Attr. in intro. note to "M. Filon"; in *Revue des Deux Mondes*, 89 (Sept. 15, 1888), 176, to "Augustin Filon"; see *Grande Encyclopédie*. Intro. note by the editor—**Alfred Austin.**

784 The physiological bearing of waist-belts and stays, 341–349. **C. S. Roy** and **J. G. Adami.** Signed. (Letter, pp. 857–861, signed **W. Wilberforce Smith,** with titles, "M.D., M.R.C.P.")

785 The French clergy exiles in England, A.D. 1792–1797, 350–360. **Frederick George Lee.** Signed.

786 Ecclesiastical grants in India, 361–372. **W. S. Seton-Karr.** Signed. (Letter, p. 566, signed **H. G. Keene.**)

787 The oratory of the House of Commons, 373–388. **C. W. Radcliffe Cooke.** Signed.

788 The democracy and the drama, 389–400. **Edward Salmon.** Signed.

789 The income of a university, and how it is spent, 401–413. **G. F. Browne.** Signed; Contents adds "Rev. Prof."

790 Politics at home and abroad, 414–419.

791 In Correspondence: The unity of Christians, 420–422, signed **T. G. Headley,** Cover adds "Rev."; A fool's paradise [free trade], 423–427, signed **Digby W. Cayley.**

VOLUME 12, DECEMBER 1888

792 The social problem (No. I): East London and crime, 433–443. **Henrietta O. Barnett.** Signed.

793 The social problem (No. II): The sinking and the sunken; the state lever, 444–449. **Charles Henry Bromby.** Signed C. H. Bromby, with the title "Bishop": see *DNB*.

794 The social problem (No. III): The Elberfeld poor-law system, 450–466. **Hugh P. Tregarthen.** Signed.

795 "The black art," or English manner of engraving, 467–485. **W. Lewery Blackley.** Signed.

796 Conservatism in Scotland, 486–491. **W. Earl Hodgson.** Signed. (Letters, pp. 849–850, signed A Perthshire Landlord; pp. 850–851, signed **Frederick Wicks;** vol. 13, p. 144, signed **William Earl Hodgson.**)

797 Notes on *King Lear*: an essay in Shakespearian interpretation, 492–503. **Lewis Campbell.** Signed.

798 Authorized and systematic lay agency, 504–517. **George Huntington.** Signed.

799 The marriage question, 518–523. **H. G. Keene.** Signed.

800 The great hospitals of London, 524–532. **A. O'D. Bartholeyns.** Signed.

801 *Monti di Pieta*, 533–543. **E. Strachan Morgan.** Signed.

802 English farms and the cost of increased production, 545–553. **Albert J. Mott.** Signed; Contents adds "F.G.S."

803 Politics at home and abroad, 554–559.

804 In Correspondence: Denominational education for Ireland, pp. 560–564, signed **Charles Crosthwaite;** Competitive examination, 566–570, by **Hugh P. Tregarthen,** prob.—signed H.P.T., man cited wrote for *NatR-II* on legislative subjects; The Royal Commission on gold and silver, 571–575, signed **Charles Wilson** (letters, pp. 715–720, and vol. 13, pp. 136–141, 425–429, signed **Charles Wilson;** vol. 13, pp. 141–142, by **William Walker**—signed An Old Banker, with address "Edinburgh," claimed in his first letter, no. 853).

VOLUME 12, JANUARY 1889

805 The European outlook for 1889, 577–582.

806 Machine guns and coast defence, 583–597. **Willoughby Verner.** Signed.

807 Irish novelists on Irish peasants, 598–611. **R. E. Prothero.** Signed.

808 Islam as a political system, 612–626. **Andrew T. Sibbald.** Signed. (Letter, p. 856, signed **Herbert Haines.**)

809 *The Wise and Foolish Virgins* [medieval trope], 627–637. **Ivan S. Andrew Herford.** Signed J. S. A. Herford, man cited wrote on mystery plays in 1889: see *BMCat*.

810 The value of the Chinese alliance, 638–650. **Demetrius C. Boulger.** Signed.

811 Politics, A.D. 1705–1707, 651–662. **G. B. Lancaster Woodburne.** Signed.

812 The higher education of women, 663–668. **Katie Magnus.** Signed. (Letters, pp. 851–853, signed A Mother of a Girton Student; vol. 13, pp. 279–280, signed **Julia M. Cohen.**)

813 The satires of Ariosto, 669–680. **Ellen Mary Clerke.** Signature; repr. *Fable and Song in Italy*, 1899.

814 Forest science: its aim and scope, 681–691. **John Nisbet.** Signed J. Nisbet; see *WWW/1916*.

815 A reception at the French Academy, 692–703. **Gabriel Paul Othenin de Clé-**

ron. Attr. in intro. note to "Comte d'Haussonville": see *Bib. Nat. Cat.* and *Grand Larousse* under Haussonville. Intro. note apparently by the editor, **Alfred Austin.** Trans. by **Pauline Schletter**—attr. p. 692n. to Paul Sylvester—see *BMCat.* (See no. 816.)

816   A reception at the French Academy: reply [to no. 815], 703–709. **J. L. F. Bertrand.** Attr. in intro. note to "M. Bertrand"; see *DBF.* Trans. as in no. 815.

817   In Correspondence: The volunteer movement, 713–714, signed **C. Willis.**

VOLUME 12, FEBRUARY 1889

818   The value of voluntary schools, 721–729. **J. E. H. Gascoyne Cecil.** Signed Cranborne [Viscount Cranborne].

819   "Feares" or "Teares"; *Macbeth*, Act V, Scene 5, 730–735. **Wyke Bayliss.** Signed.

820   Technical education for women in England and abroad, 736–750. **Mary Jeune.** Signed; repr. *Lesser Questions*, 1894.

821   The fruit-growing folly, 751–759. **Albert J. Mott.** Signed.

822   The Westminster slough of despond, 760–771. Signed: M.P. [Member of Parliament].

823   American and English girls, 772–780. **J. Acton Lomax.** Signed.

824   The elections for the London County Council, 781–786. **C. A. Whitmore.** Signed.

825   Some curiosities of diet, 787–806. **Alfred J. H. Crespi.** Signed.

826   A poet's corner, 807–817. **W. H. Gresswell.** Signed.

827   The sick poor of the metropolis, 818–829. **A. O'Donnel Bartholeyns.** Signed. (Letter, vol. 13, p. 288, signed **A. O'D. Bartholeyns.**)

828   The housing of the poor, 830–841. **Newton Wallop.** Signed Lymington [Viscount Lymington].

829   Politics at home and abroad, 842–848.

830   In Correspondence: Midnight drinking in London, 863–864, signed **F. A. Millington.**

VOLUME 13, MARCH 1889

831   Scottish conservatism, 1–21. **James Ferguson,** 1857–1917. Signed A Scottish Conservative; claimed by Ferguson in an

art. with the same signature, *Scottish Rev.*, 26 (Oct. 1895), 379 (see *ScotR* no. 502 for the evidence of his authorship).

832   A reminiscence of the late Crown Prince Rudolf of Austria, 22–32. **Willoughby Verner.** Signed.

833   The higher education of women, 33–44. **Eva Knatchbull-Hugessen.** Signed. (Letters, pp. 276–279, signed **Katie Magnus;** pp. 419–420, by **Mary Bramston,** prob.—signed M. Bramston, signature used for *Macmillan's Mag.* no. 3238, *Index,* I.)

834   The Negro tenants of the Southern States, 45–60. **Arthur Granville Bradley.** Signed A. G. Bradley: see *WWW/* 1950.

835   Bimetallism: a dialogue, 61–66. **E. Brodie Hoare.** Signed.

836   Radicals and the unearned increment, 69–91. **W. H. Mallock.** Signed. (Letter, p. 416, signed J.B., with address "Liverpool.")

837   Divination in the seventeenth century, 92–104. **George Francis Legge.** Signed F. Legge; see *BMCat.* (Letters, pp. 712–713, by **Alice L. Cleather**—signed A. L. Cleather, cf. no. 924; vol. 14, pp. 142–143, by **Legge**—signed as above.)

838   The pastor's duty in reference to benefit and burial clubs, 105–117. **C. T. Cruttwell.** Signed.

839   Our true policy in India: a rejoinder [to *FortR*, nos. 2796 and 2797], 118–124. **George N. Curzon.** Signed.

840   Politics at home and abroad, 125–130.

841   In Correspondence: Irish and other difficulties, 131–136, signed **Charles Wilson.**

VOLUME 13, ARIL 1889

842   Some sound French novels, 151–168. **Marie Blaze de Bury.** Signed as in no. 633. (Letter, pp. 414–416, by **Denis F. Hannigan**—signed D. F. Flannigan, with address "27, Lower Mount Street, Dublin"; man cited was living at that address [see *Royal National Directory for Ireland/*94], and was a translator of French novels: see *BMCat.*)

843   The brain-power of plants, 169–172. **Arthur Smith.** Signed.

844   Open coast towns and international law, 173–180. **Herbert Haines.** Signed.

845   Macbeth, considered as a Celt, 181–190. **Jessie Douglas Montegomery.** Signed.

846 The sonnet in America, 191–201. **William Sharp.** Signed.

847 The [National] Congress and modern India, 202–219. **Gilbert Leslie Smith.** Signed G. Leslie Smith; see Part B below. (See no. 870.)

848 Women as social reformers, 220–225. **Mrs. F. M. Foster.** Signed F. M. Foster; cf. no. 1052, where Contents adds "Mrs." to this signature.

849 The first special correspondent [Melchior Grimm], 226–245. **Pauline Schletter.** Signed Paul Sylvester—see *BMCat.*

850 Selfishness in competition, 246–258. **C. A. Cripps.** Signed.

851 The finest deer in the world, 259–270. **Henry Seton-Karr.** Signed H. Seton-Karr; Contents adds "M.P."; see *WWW*/1916.

852 Politics at home and abroad, 271–275.

853 In Correspondence: A suggestion: what to do about land, 281–284, signed **Amos Reade;** The history and geography of our colonies, 285, by **Charles Wilson,** prob.—signed C.W., cf. no. 862; Bimetallism and currency, 285–288, signed **W. D. Gainsford** (letters, pp. 417–419, and vol. 14, pp. 286–290, signed **R. T. Redmayne,** with addresses "32, Jutland Street, Preston" and "95, Barton Terrace, Preston"; pp. 432, 864, by **W. D. Montagu**—signed Manchester [Duke of Manchester]; pp. 567–568, and vol. 14, pp. 146–148, signed **Charles Wilson;** pp. 569–570, and vol. 14, pp. 148–149, 284–286, by **William Walker**—signed The Old Banker, with address "Edinburgh," Walker claimed in a signed letter from Edinburgh, vol. 14, p. 721 (see no. 943), to have written before on this subject under pseudonym; p. 570 signed **Henry H. Gibbs**).

VOLUME 13, MAY 1889

854 Silver and the fall of prices, 289–310. **Moreton Frewen.** Signed.

855 The Madame de Maintenon of Wurtemberg [Francesca von Hohenheim], 311–324. **C. A. Montrésor.** Signed.

856 The music of the British army, 325–342. **Frederick J. Crowest.** Signed. (Letter, pp. 570–571, by **Charles Wilson,** prob.—signed C.W., cf. no. 862.)

857 Scientific education in relation to industrial prosperity, 343–353. **Percy Faraday Frankland.** Signed.

858 Doctoring in China, 354–368. **H. N. Shore.** Signed; Contents adds "R.N."

859 The lessons of emigration, 369–376. **Stephen Thompson.** Signed.

860 Balzac's view of the artistic temperament, 377–385. **Darcy Lever,** perhaps with **H. C. A. Keith.** Signed Philip Kent; ledger for *Temple Bar* (BM Add. MS. 46,564 vol. 5) for *Temple Bar*, 75 (Nov. 1885), 325–342, lists Philip Kent as pseudonym for H. C. A. Keith, but for vol. 109 (Oct. 1896), 261–266, gives both Keith and Darcy Lever; *NatR-II* no. 1341 is signed Darcy Lever but attr. in Contents to Philip Kent.

861 The progress of modern Birmingham, 386–411. **Alfred J. H. Crespi.** Signed.

862 In Correspondence: The Salisbury-Balfour success [in reducing crime in Ireland], 420–425, signed **George W. Ruxton** (letters, pp. 575–576, by **Charles Wilson** —signed C.W. and dated from Cheltenham, as are most of Wilson's letters; pp. 714–716, signed **George W. Ruxton;** pp. 719–720, by **John Kingston**—signed J. Kingston, cf. content and tone of his letters in no. 956); The leadership in the House and in the country, 429–432, signed **R. St. J. Corbet.**

VOLUME 13, JUNE 1889

863 Vaccination and the *Encyclopedia Britannica*, 433–455. **Herbert Preston-Thomas.** Signed H. Preston-Thomas; see *WWW*/1916.

864 An Italian nun of the seventeenth century [Galileo's daughter, Pollissema], 456–469. **Alfred J. Sanders.** Signed.

865 International law and food supplies (No. I): food supplies and international law, 470–478. **Herbert Haines.** Signed. (Letters, p. 708, by **Vincent Kennett-Barrington**—signed V. Kennett-Barrington, see p. 857; pp. 709–712, signed **John Cropley;** pp. 857–858, signed **Herbert Haines.**)

866 International law and food supplies (No. II): our food supply, 479–483. **Robert Scott Moffat.** Signed.

867 Mr. Gladstone and Italy, 484–502. **Antonio Gallenga.** Signed as in no. 224.

868 The pacification of Burmah, 503–516. **Demetrius C. Boulger.** Signed.

869 England's climatic phenomena, 517–525. **Newton Wallop.** Signed Lymington [Viscount Lymington].

870 The Indian National Congress; the other side [reply to no. 847], 526–538. **Frederic Pincott.** Signed.

871   The Roman family, 539–551. **E. Strachan Morgan.** Signed. (Letter, p. 717, signed **J. W. Slater,** with address "36 Wray Crescent, N."; see *Kelly's Suburban Directory* (1892), p. 298.)

872   The Sugar Convention, 552–560. **Robert Grant Webster.** Signed.

873   Politics at home and abroad, 561–566.

874   In Correspondence: Let Mr. Gladstone speak out [on Irish Home Rule], 571–574, signed **George W. Ruxton;** A tax on Christian names, 574–575, signed **F. A. Millington** (letter, pp. 717–719, signed One Who Has Paid Taxes for over Half a Century).

VOLUME 13, JULY 1889

875   The threatened abdication of man [women's suffrage], 577–592. **Eliza Lynn Linton.** Signature. (Letter, vol. 15, pp. 716–720, signed **F. Neville.**

876   Dr. Johnson on modern poetry, an interview in the Elysian Fields, A.D. 1900, 593–604. **William Watson.** Signed; repr. *Excursions.*

877   "Vaccination" in the *Encyclopaedia Britannica*—a reply [to no. 863], 605–616. **Charles Creighton.** Signed C. Creighton, with title "M.D."; see *WWW/ 1928.*

878   The Church's gymnasium, 617–629. **Walter L. Bicknell.** Signed Austen Pember; see no. 384.

879   Poor Law infirmaries and their needs, 630–642. **Louisa Twining.** Signed.

880   George Sand at an English school, 643–653. **J. G. Alger.** Signed.

881   The present feeling of the working classes, 654–676. **G. Rome Hall.** Signed.

882   William Gifford, 677–687. **Cyril A. Waters.** Signed.

883   Some parliamentary incidents, 688–701. **C. W. Radcliffe Cooke.** Signed.

884   Politics at home and abroad, 702–707.

885   In Correspondence: The Australian aborigines, 713–714, signed **Charles Wilson.**

VOLUME 13, AUGUST 1889

886   Grouse shooting, 721–737. **George Campion.** Signed.

887   The religion of our boys, 738–749. **Walter L. Bicknell.** Signed Austen Pember: see no. 384. (Letters, vol. 14, pp. 149–150, signed **L. J. Pope,** with address "Edgbaston"; pp. 293–294, signed One

who has Taught Boys; pp. 431–433, signed **Charles Crosthwaite** [misspelled Crothwaite, but corrected on Cover; and cf. no. 897].)

888   The South African problem, 750–761. **Henry Elsdale.** Signed H. Elsdale; Contents adds "Maj., R.E."; see *LCCat.*

889   Land League ballads, 762–770. **C. J. Hamilton.** Signed.

890   On Professor [T. H.] Green's political philosophy, 771–787. **F. C. Conybeare.** Signed.

891   Some East-End workwomen, 788–793. **Clementina Black.** Signed.

892   Some few Thackerayana, 794–803. Signed: D.D.

893   The French Revolutionary calendar, 804–818. **Francis Hitchman.** Signed. (Letter, vol. 14, p. 145 by **Philip Vernon Smith**—signed P. V. Smith.)

894   An empire of crofters, 819–830. **John Rae.** Signed.

895   A Frenchman's impressions of London in the seventeenth century, 831–844. **Arthur Irwin Dasent.** Signed.

896   Politics at home and abroad, 845–850.

897   In Correspondence: Fiscal federations: reflections on the annual report of the Imperial Federation League, 1888–89, 851–857, signed **Digby W. Cayley;** Rome's demands as to university education, 858–861, signed **Charles Crosthwaite;** Currency, 861–863, signed **R. T. Redmayne.**

VOLUME 14, SEPTEMBER 1889

898   The work of the session, 1–9. **C. A. Whitmore.** Signed.

899   The origin of modern occultism, 10–22. **G. Francis Legge.** Signed F. Legge; see *BMCat.* (See no. 913.)

900   On Tuscan rhymes, 23–35. **Pauline Schletter.** Signed Paul Sylvester—See *BMCat.*

901   Secular and honorary deacons, 36–55. **A. J. H. Crespi.** Signed.

902   Orchids and hybridizing, 56–66. **Frederick Boyle.** Signed.

903   Wordsworth and the Quantock hills, 67–83. **William Greswell.** Signed.

904   A Conservative plea for the rights of man, 84–91. **W. Earl Hodgson.** Signed.

905   Cow-keeping by farm labourers, 92–108. **Henry Evershed.** Signed.

906   The Age of Reason: some literary aspects of the French Revolution of 1789, 109–124. **H. G. Keene.** Signed.

907   Politics at home and abroad, 125–130.

908   In Correspondence: On the revival of famous fruit trees, 131–135, signed **H. Y. J. Taylor,** with address "Conservative Club, Gloucester"; Indian pensions—the covenant, 135–137, signed Indicus; The Gladstonians should fight fairly, 138–140, signed **George W. Ruxton;** The West Australian constitution, 140–141, signed **Charles Wilson** (letters, vol. 15, pp. 141–142, 423–425, signed **Charles Wilson**); Proposed aggression on the Soudan, 143–145, signed **Charles Wilson.**

VOLUME 14, OCTOBER 1889

909   On the proposed endowment of a Roman Catholic university in Ireland, 151–166. **F. C. Conybeare.** Signed. (Letters, pp. 290–293, 857–863, signed **Charles Crosthwaite;** pp. 579–580, signed **Edward Stanley Robertson;** p. 581, signed Irish Landlord.)

910   Fiction: plethoric and anaemic, 167–183. **William Watson.** Signed.

911   The Empire (No. I): the Imperial Federation League, 184–199. **William Greswell.** Signed. (Letter, pp. 429–431, signed **H. G. Keene,** with address "Fontenay, Jersey.")

912   The Empire (No. II): the crown and the colonies, 200–207. **Edward Salmon.** Signed.

913   The genesis of theosophy, 208–217. **H. S. Olcott.** Signed. (Letter, 435–436, signed **Sydney G. P. Coryn,** with title "Fellow of the Theosophical Society.") (See no. 924.)

914   Women and tobacco, 218–228. **J. D. Hunting.** Signed. (Letter, pp. 573–574, signed A Woman of Holland.)

915   The British workman, 229–242. **G. Rome Hall.** Signed.

916   Wild ducks and duck decoying, 243–255. **John Watson,** d.1928. Signed; for man cited see *WWW.*

917   The education of the blind and of the deaf in the United Kingdom, 256–269. **Charles E. D. Black.** Signed. (Letter, pp. 436–438, signed **W. H. Addison,** with title "Head Master, West of England Institution for the Deaf and Dumb, Exeter.")

918   Politics at home and abroad, 270–274.

919   In Correspondence: Women's rights, 275–278, signed **Esther Delaforce;** Village ethics, 279–282, by **Margaret Anne Curtois**—signed M. A. Curtois, novelist of village life, see *BMCat.;* The preservation, protection, and cultivation of fluvial fishes, 282–284, signed **W. August Carter,** with title "Secretary of the Midland Counties Fish Culture Establishment."

VOLUME 14, NOVEMBER 1889

920   Armenia and the armenians, 295–315. **F. C. Conybeare.** Signed.

921   The lepers of Crete, 316–320. **Charles Edwardes.** Signed.

922   Morals and manners in Richardson, 321–340. **Leonora B. Lang.** Signed L. B. Lang; Contents gives "Mrs. Andrew Lang."

923   The oil wells of Burma, 341–348. **Charles Marvin.** Signed.

924   Colonel Olcott's theosophy; a reply [to no. 913], 349–357. **George Francis Legge.** Signed F. Legge; see *BMCat.* (Letter, pp. 721–722, by **Alice Leighton Cleather**—signed A. L. Cleather, see *LCCat.*)

925   Fisher life in Scotland, 358–370. **J. G. Bertram.** Signed.

926   Ekenames and nicknames, 371–382. **Arthur Gaye.** Signed.

927   Compulsory games at public schools, 383–391. **Ernest Gambier-Parry.** Signed E. Gambier-Parry; Contents adds "Major": see *WWW/1940.*

928   Teplitz [spa in Bohemia], 392–400. **E. C. Papillon.** Signed.

929   The woman's part in politics, 401–418. **Annie M. Payne.** Signed.

930   Politics at home and abroad, 419–423.

931   In Correspondence: The Primrose League v. the National League in Ireland, 424–429, signed **Amos Reade;** Criminal members of Parliament, 434–435, signed **Robert S. Moffat.**

VOLUME 14, DECEMBER 1889

932   The L. S. D. [£. s. d.] of Home Rule, 439–445. **George Baden-Powell.** Signed; repr. *The Saving of Ireland,* Edin., 1898.

933   The early pheasants, 446–457. **T. E. Kebbel.** Signed; repr. *Sport and Nature,* 1893.

934   Socialism and the Papacy, 458–478. **Moritz Kaufmann.** Signed M. Kaufmann; Contents adds "Rev.": cf. no. 644.

935   Patrician pugilism, 479–490. **Walter L. Bicknell.** Signed Austen Pember; see no. 384.

936   Pope, 491–503. **H. D. Traill.** Signed.

937   The Archbishop's jurisdiction [Canterbury], 504–519. **Morris Fuller.** Signed.

938   Poetry by men of the world [Alfred

Lyall and W. S. Blunt], 520–529. **William Watson.** Signed.

939 A Lothian fair, 530–537. **George Eyre-Todd.** Signed.

940 Hydrophobia: its treatment by Pasteur, 538–546. **George Herring.** Signed; Contents adds "Dr." and "L.F.P.S." (Letter, p. 863, signed **George Herring.**)

941 Women of today, yesterday, and tomorrow, 547–561. **Mary Jeune.** Signed; repr. *Lesser Questions*, 1894.

942 Politics at home and abroad, 562–567.

943 In Correspondence: A plea for scholarships, 568–572, signed **Herbert Haines;** A deficient currency and the natural result, 575–578, signed **Charles Wilson** (letters, pp. 720–721, signed **William Walker,** with address "Edinburgh"; pp. 863–865, signed **Charles Wilson**); Proposed bishopric for Birmingham, 582, signed A Churchman.

VOLUME 14, JANUARY 1890

944 Portuguese claims in Africa, 583–591. **V. Lovett Cameron.** Signed.

945 Robert Browning, 592–597. **H. D. Traill.** Signed.

946 Public health and politics, 598–615. **G. Rome Hall.** Signed.

947 Theosophy, the "divine wisdom," 616–622. **H. S. Olcott.** Signed.

948 An economic cure for socialism, 623–636. **W. Earl Hodgson.** Signed. (Letter, pp. 868–870, signed **A. Egmont Hake.**)

949 The proposed miners' federation, 637–645. **Sydney Wyatt.** Signed.

950 Mr. Stevenson's methods in fiction, 646–657. **A. Conan Doyle.** Signed.

951 Bird life in Romney Marsh, 658–672. **Willoughby Verner.** Signed; Contents adds "Captain."

952 The persian poetry of Avicenna, 673–679. **Charles J. Pickering.** Signed.

953 Tithe rent-charges and peasant tenancies, 680–693. **R. E. Prothero.** Signed. (Letter, vol. 15, pp. 143–144 by **Wilbraham Egerton**—signed Egerton of Tatton [2nd Baron Egerton of Tatton].)

954 Lord Tennyson's new volume [*Demeter and Other Poems*], 694–702. **Alfred Austin.** Signed.

955 Politics at home and abroad, 703–709.

956 In Correspondence: The tithe question and Church reform, 710–715, signed **Arthur Smith,** with address "Smallford, St. Albans"; The selection of public servants—a suggestion, 715–719, signed **W. J. Curran Sharp;** Church defence,

719, by **John Kingston**—signed J. Kingston, with title "Chaplain R.N., Retired, sometime Rector of Cattistock," with address "Bembridge, Isle of Wight," see *CCD*/1908, (letters, vol. 15, pp. 142–143, signed **W. S. Lach-Szyrma;** vol. 16, p. 280, signed **John Kingston**); Methods of charitable relief, 722–726, signed **Vincent G. Borradaile.**

VOLUME 14, FEBRUARY 1890

957 Political economy in its relation to strikes, 727–739. **Guilford L. Molesworth.** Signed. (Letter, vol. 15, pp. 139–140, signed **Herbert Haines.**)

958 The fairy mythology of Ireland, 740–764. **C. S. Boswell.** Signed.

959 The second-class clergy, 765–775. **A. Marwood Wilcox.** Signed. (See no. 1050; letter, vol. 15, pp. 417–420, signed **F. T. Marsh,** with address "Liverpool.")

960 A dialogue with a mummy, 776–780. **Giacomo Leopardi.** Signed. Trans. by **Patrick Maxwell**—signed; p. 776n. adds "Major-General."

961 Local government for Ireland, 781–787. **Hugh Fortescue,** 1818–1905. Signed Fortescue [3rd Earl Fortescue].

962 Temperance and the public-houses, 788–797. **R. E. Macnaghten.** Signed. (Letter, vol. 15, pp. 431–432, signed **Cordy Manby.**)

963 Firdausî's lyrical poetry, 798–810. **Charles J. Pickering.** Signed.

964 Random recollections of Corsica, 811–825. **Cecil F. Parr.** Signed.

965 The seige of Helicon, 826–834. **William Watson.** Signed.

966 Out of the depths, 835–850. **A. E. Gathorne-Hardy.** Signed; repr. *Autumns in Argyleshire,* 1901.

967 Politics at home and abroad, 851–856.

968 In Correspondence: Irish mountebanks and mendicants, 865–868, signed **George W. Ruxton.**

VOLUME 15, MARCH 1890

969 Africa south of the equator, 1–17. Signed: Anglo-African.

970 Servants and domestic service, 18–28. **Ernest Gambier-Parry.** Signed E. Gambier-Parry; Contents adds "Major"; see *WWW*/1940. (Letter, pp. 421–422, signed **R. Arthur Kinglake.**)

971 Can there be a science of character? 29–38. **W. L. Courtney.** Signed.

972 Wat Tyler and his cause, 39–58. **Henry Evershed.** Signed.

973 Some Irish traits of thought and speech, 59–64. **Hugh Hall.** Signed.

974 [Wallace's] *Darwinism*, 65–76. **Albert J. Mott.** Signed.

975 Talleyrand [in England], 77–85. **R. C. E. Abbot.** Signed Colchester [Baron Colchester].

976 The mother of the Strozzi, a family history of the fifteenth century, 86–100. **Lily Wolffsohn.** Signed Edith Marget; woman cited used this pseudonym in *ScotR* 206.

977 The centenary of White's *Selborne*, 101–113. **Arthur Gaye.** Signed.

978 Tithes, considered by a tithe-payer, 114–128. **E. L. Pemberton.** Signed. (Letter, pp. 430–431, signed A Tithe-owner.)

979 Politics at home and abroad, 129–134.

980 In Correspondence: The Toryism of tomorrow, 135–139, signed **R. St. J. Corbet.**

VOLUME 15, APRIL 1890

981 Needed amendments of the Factory Act, 145–152. **Arthur A. Baumann.** Signed.

982 Winter and spring exhibitions, 1890, 153–166. **Julia M. Ady.** Signed.

983 Colliery explosions and their prevention, 167–173. **Cyril Parkinson.** Signed C. Parkinson; Contents adds "F.G.S."; *Mac* no. 3819, *Index*, I, provides first name.

984 The Yorkshire dalesman, 174–189. **J. Dickinson.** Signed.

985 Problems of living (No. I): the cost of a shorter working day, 190–202. **John A. Hobson.** Signed J. A. Hobson; Contents provides first name.

986 Problems of living (No. II): our farmers in chains, 203–211. **Harry Jones.** Signed; Contents adds "Rev." (Letter, pp. 429–430, signed **W. M. Acworth.**) (See no. 1022.)

987 A Surrey home, 212–218. **Evelyn Pyne.** Signed.

988 Rabies and muzzling, 219–231. **Arthur Shadwell.** Signed. (Letter, p. 709, signed **Charles Bell Taylor.**)

989 In Calabria, 232–246. **Charles Edwardes.** Signed.

990 *A Dictionary of Christian Biography*, 247–260. **Alfred Church.** Signed.

991 Home rule for India, 261–276. **H. G. Keene.** Signed. (See no. 996.)

992 Politics at home and abroad, 277–282.

993 In Correspondence: Railway communication between India and upper Burma, 283–285, signed **H. P. Babbage** (letter, vol. 16, pp. 131–134, signed **F. N. Burn,** with address "Rangoon"); Africa south of the equator, 285–288, signed Anglo-African.

VOLUME 15, MAY 1890

994 The real cause of Prince Bismarck's retirement, 289–294.

995 Was I also hypnotized? 300–311. **T. Adolphus Trollope.** Signed.

996 Home Rule not wanted for India, 312–326. **Frederic Pincott.** Signed; Contents adds "M.R.A.S." (Letters, pp. 564–565, 853–854, signed **Herbert Haines;** pp. 710–712, 854–856, signed **Frederic Pincott.**)

997 A Persian Chaucer [Rûdagî], 327–340. **Charles J. Pickering.** Signed.

998 A year under county councils, 341–347. **Leonard H. West.** Signed.

999 A visit to Count Mattei, 348–355. **Walburga Paget.** Signed Wally Paget; Contents adds "Lady"; see *WWW*/1940. (See no. 1024.)

1000 Dancing as a fine art, 356–367. **J. F. Rowbotham.** Signed.

1001 The mining federations: their first fight, 368–378. **Sydney Wyatt.** Signed.

1002 Music hall land, 379–391. **Percy Fitzgerald.** Signed. (Letter, pp. 565–566, signed **Frederic Pincott.**)

1003 Insect communists, 392–403. **Florence Fenwick Miller.** Signed.

1004 Newfoundland and the French fishery question, 404–411. **H. C. Goldsmith.** Signed; Contents adds "R.N."

1005 Politics at home and abroad, 412–416.

1006 In Correspondence: Increase of revenue without extra taxation, 422–423, signed **W. J. Hodges;** Sight test for volunteers, 425–429, signed **E. F. Cash,** with title "Major" and address "Ding Wall, N.B."; postscript by the editor—**Alfred Austin.**

VOLUME 15, JUNE 1890

1007 *Problems of Greater Britain* [by C. W. Dilke], 433–445. **W. J. Courthope.** Signed. (Letter, pp. 708–709, by **H. G. Keene**—signed H.G.K., with address "Jersey," cf. no. 911; reply, pp. 848–851, signed **W. J. Courthope.**)

1008 Great and big: a dialogue [on greatness

vs. bigness], 446–451. **T. O. Brown.** Signed.

1009 Mr. Gladstone's disestablishment of the Greek pantheon, 452–463. **Karl Blind.** Signed.

1010 Chartered companies in Africa, 464–473. **V. Lovett Cameron.** Signed.

1011 Vermin in England, 474–482. **Walter Peace.** Signed Discipulus; Contents gives "W. Peace"; cf. no. 2459.

1012 The bishop-elect's oath of canonical obedience, 483–499. **Morris Fuller.** Signed.

1013 The evil May-Day [1517], 500–505. **Herbert Haines.** Signed.

1014 A plea for Sunday observance, 506–517. **Charles Hill.** Signed.

1015 The Lancashire laureate [Edwin Waugh], 518–528. **William Watson.** Signed; repr. *Excursions.*

1016 Laws and government of "brutes," 529–535. **J. W. Slater.** Signed.

1017 A Kentish pilgrim road, 536–544. **H. F. Abell.** Signed.

1018 The case for the tithe-payer, 545–554. **Henry R. Farquharson.** Signed. (See no. 1044; letter, p. 720, signed A Tithe-owner.)

1019 Politics at home and abroad, 555–561.

1020 In Correspondence: Why is Scotland radical? 562–564, signed **James Ballantyne,** with address "Adelphi, Aberdeen"; Notes about Ireland, 567–571, signed, **George W. Ruxton;** Currency and the case of Ireland, 561–573, signed **R. T. Redmayne;** Rabbit pest in Australia, 574–576, signed **John Henry Metcalfe,** with address "Leyburn Wensleydale, Yorkshire" (letter, pp. 862–864, signed **H. Speight,** with address "West Bowling, Bradford").

VOLUME 15, JULY 1890

1021 A scandalous session, 577–582. Signed: Q.

1022 Our farmers in chains—a sequel [to no. 986], 583–591. **Harry Jones.** Signed. (Letter, vol. 19, pp. 135–141, signed **Harry Jones.**)

1023 Dacoity in upper Burma, 592–605. **H. D. Keary.** Signed.

1024 Count Mattei and his treatment of cancer: a reply to Lady Paget [no. 999], 606–613. **Herbert Snow.** Signed. (See nos. 1035, 1047.) (Letters, pp. 857–859, and vol. 16, pp. 431–432, signed **Arthur J. Danyell,** with address "6, Via Serragli, Florence"; pp. 859–860, by **Walburga**

Paget—signed L. Paget, where the initial seems to stand for "Lady," cf. no. 999.)

1025 His Excellency the Governor [on colonial governors], 614–624. Signed: Ex-Governor. Perhaps George Ferguson Bowen who had been governor of various colonies, including Victoria and New Zealand (see *DNB*); he sent a letter to *NatR-II* in 1891 (no. 1231).

1026 The social records of a Scotch family [the *Caldwell Papers*], 625–640. **Leonora B. Lang.** Signed Mrs. Lang; assigned in Contents to Mrs. Andrew Lang.

1027 Charitable endowments, 641–653. **Bernard H. Holland.** Signed.

1028 Pasteur's prophylactic, 654–666. **Charles Bell Taylor.** Signed. (Letter, pp. 860–861, by **George Herring**—signed G. Herring, cf. no. 940.)

1029 Compensation for [public-house] licences, 667–672. Signed: A Radical Teetotaler. (Letters, pp. 861–862, signed **Charles Wilson;** vol. 16, pp. 134–135, signed **R. E. Macnaghten.**)

1030 The beginnings of Persian literature, 673–687. **Charles J. Pickering.** Signed.

1031 Angelic immorality [in Goldsmith's *Vicar of Wakefield*], 688–696. **Frederic H. Balfour.** Signed.

1032 Some curiosities of Irish farming, 697–707. **Miss C. L. Cooper.** Signed C. L. Cooper; Contents adds "Miss."

1033 In Correspondence: Sunday in Ireland under the Parnellites, 712–713, signed **George W. Ruxton;** Remedial legislation for Ireland and India, 713–716, by **Charles Wilson,** prob.—signed C.W., cf. no. 862.

VOLUME 15, AUGUST 1890

1034 Our rights and prospects in Africa, 721–740. **V. Lovett Cameron.** Signed.

1035 Count Mattei's system, 741–747. **Walburga Paget.** Signed as in no. 999. (See no. 1047; note, vol. 16, p. 10, signed **T. R. Allinson;** letters, vol. 16, pp. 279–280, signed An Old Matteist; p. 432, signed **Heneage Legge;** pp. 718–720, signed **M. de Bunsen.**)

1036 Political and social life in Holland, 748–763. Signed: S.T.

1037 The punishment of genius [on Keats], 764–769. **William Watson.** Signed; repr. *Excursions.*

1038 Triumphant democracy in the seventeenth century, 770–781. **George Francis Legge.** Signed F. Legge; see *BMCat.*

1039 The stage in Shakspeare's day, 782–

791. **William Poel.** Signed.

1040   "Snake Jim Hollunder?" [on Heligoland], 792–801. **Arthur Gaye.** Signed.

1041   What is education? 802–814. **Frederic Pincott.** Signed.

1042   The last singers of Bukhârâ, 815–823. **Charles J. Pickering.** Signed.

1043   A western trout-stream [the Monnow in Wales], 824–831. **Cyril Parkinson.** Signed as in no. 983.

1044   The case for the tithe-owner, 832–841. **William Gildea.** Signed W. Gildea; attr. to man cited, *WWW*/1928.

1045   Politics at home and abroad, 842–847.

1046   In Correspondence: Liberal Unionism [on Home Rule], 851–853, signed An Average Liberal Unionist; France and Heligoland, 856–857, signed **Herbert Haines.**

VOLUME 16, SEPTEMBER 1890

1047   Mattei v. the knife: the rational treatment of cancer, 1–9. **Samuel Kennedy.** Signed; Contents adds "F.R.C.S.E." (See no. 1069.)

1048   The leather industry in Ireland, 11–25. **George G. Chisholm.** Signed.

1049   The progress of weather study, 26–39. **Henry Harries.** Signed; Contents adds "F.R. Met. Soc."

1050   "Second-class" clergy—a reply [to no. 959], 40–49. **Henry Sutton.** Signed; Contents adds "Rev."; attr. *WWW*/1928.

1051   Electoral blackmailing, 50–54. **Joseph J. Davies.** Signed.

1052   A Princess of Condé, 55–76. **Mrs. F. M. Foster.** Signed F. M. Foster; Contents adds "Mrs."

1053   Carlyle and old women, 77–83. **Pauline W. Roose.** Signed P. W. Roose; Contents provides first name.

1054   Feathered and furred marauders, 84–92. **Walter Peace.** Signed Discipulus: cf. no. 1011.

1055   Russian sects, 93–104. **C. T. Hagberg Wright.** Signed.

1056   A cobbler-artist, 105–112. **George Eyre-Todd.** Signed.

1057   The immigration of destitute foreigners, 113–124. **W. H. Wilkins.** Signed.

1058   Politics at home and abroad, 125–130.

1059   In Correspondence: The scramble for African territory, 135–136, signed **Charles Wilson;** State-owned railways, 137–142, signed **W. J. Hodges** (letter, pp. 280–282, by **Charles Wilson,** prob.—signed C.W., cf. no. 862); The currency and banking, 142–144, by **Charles Wilson,** prob.—signed C. W., cf. no. 862.

VOLUME 16, OCTOBER 1890

1060   The Colonial Office and the colonies, 145–160. **Stanley Leighton.** Signed. (Letter, pp. 424–425, signed **Richard Norton Lowe,** with address "Lincoln's Inn.")

1061   The girl graduate: a few statistics, 161–165. **William Gallatly.** Signed M.A. London; Contents gives "W. Gallatly"; man cited wrote on education and received M.A. Univ. of London, 1884: see Venn. (See no. 1099.)

1062   The age of disfigurement [billboard advertising], 166–182. **Richardson Evans.** Signed.

1063   Homicide, as a misadventure [on patent medicines], 183–189. **Henry W. Hubbard.** Signed. (Letter, pp. 571–574, signed **John Morgan Richards;** reply, pp. 853–856, by **Hubbard.**)

1064   The reform of public dinners, 190–199. **Harry Jones.** Signed.

1065   Lewis Devrient, 200–208. **Janet Ross.** Signed.

1066   The cases for the tithe-payer and tithe-owner, 209–225. **Charles E. Shea.** Signed.

1067   Stendhal's autobiography, 226–239. **Marie Blaze de Bury.** Signed as in no. 633.

1068   The new ordeal by battle [labor strikes], 240–251.

1069   The knife v. Mattei, 252–258. **Herbert Snow.** Signed. (Letters, pp. 426–430, 716–718, signed **Samuel Kennedy;** pp. 430–431, signed **Alfred W. Stokes,** with titles "F.C.S., F.I.C."; pp. 575–576, signed **Arthur J. Danyell;** p. 720, signed **Herbert Snow.**)

1070   The potato blight in Ireland, 259–266. **W. H. Wilkins.** Signed.

1071   Politics at home and abroad, 267–272.

1072   In Correspondence: Baiting a bishop, 273–279, signed **George W. Ruxton;** The degeneracy of the modern sonnet, 282–286, signed **J. G. F. Nicholson;** State granaries: national insurance against war, 286–288, signed **W. J. Hodges.**

VOLUME 16, NOVEMBER 1890

1073   Mr. Gladstone and Malta, 289–302. **George Baden-Powell.** Signed.

1074   The obliteration of Florence, 303–309.

Marie Louise de la Ramée. Signed Ouida; see *DNB*.

1075	The history of socialism (Part I): the early period, 1817–1852, 310–334. **Alice Oldham.** Signed.

1076	Newman from Newman's points of view, 335–346. **Charles S. Jerram.** Signed.

1077	Card-playing and free whist, 347–359. **Lowis d'Aguilar Jackson.** Signed Aquarius: see H&L, *BMCat*. (See no. 1100; letter, vol. 17, pp. 142–145, from **Jackson**—signed Aquarius.)

1078	Reform of the marriage laws of India, 360–369. **Lionel Ashburner.** Signed. (Letters, pp. 567–568, signed **Frederic Pincott;** vol. 17, pp. 295–296, signed **Nana Moroji** with address "Bombay."

1079	America and protection, 370–382. **A. N. Cumming.** Signed. (Letter, pp. 712–714, signed **R. T. Redmayne.**)

1080	Fruit-culture in Worcestershire orchards, 383–396. **Cyril Parkinson.** Signed as in no. 983.

1081	The great Australian strike, 397–406. **A. Patchett Martin.** Signed.

1082	Lord Iddesleigh, 407–416. **T. E. Kebbel.** Signed.

1083	Politics at home and abroad, 417–423.

1084	In Correspondence: Church reform, 425, signed A Churchman.

VOLUME 16, DECEMBER 1890

1085	Mr. Gladstone and the Church of Scotland, 433–445. **James Ferguson,** 1857–1917, prob. The anti-disestablishment position adopted here and in no. 547 is precisely that which Ferguson expressed in *ScotR* no. 350, two years later: Presbyterian reunion and a national church; moreover, there are many instances of similarities in thought among the three arts., including attacks on Gladstone, and in two cases almost verbatim passages on Gladstonian speeches: cf. pp. 439, 440 here and *ScotR* no. 350, p. 180.

1086	The talent of motherhood, 446–459. **Arabella Kenealy.** Signed; Contents adds "Dr."; see *WWW*/1940. (Letter, pp. 850–853, signed **Beatrice J. Hay.**)

1087	The history of socialism (Part II): anarchism—nihilism—the beginning of German socialism—Ferdinand Lassalle, 460–485. **Alice Oldham.** Signed.

1088	Gambling at Monte Carlo, 486–495. **Norwood Young.** Signed.

1089	The eight-hours movement, 496–505. **Frederic Pincott.** Signed.

1090	'Umar of Nîshâpûr, 506–521. **Charles J. Pickering.** Signed.

1091	Christian colonies and brotherhoods. 522–532. **Harry Jones.** Signed.

1092	Château Malbrouk, 533–544. **Henry W. Wolff.** Signed.

1093	Technical agricultural education, 545–557. **R. Henry Rew.** Signed.

1094	Who shall inherit Constantinople? 558–563. Signed: Quis?

1095	In Correspondence: Will the miners strike? 564–567, signed **S. Turner,** with address "Barnsley," see Robinson's *Barnsley Directory*/1902; New aspects of rabbit farming, 569–571, signed **H. Paget,** with address "Bowden House, College Road, Harrow"; Mr. Pitt on home rule, 575, signed **T. N. Beasley.**

VOLUME 16, JANUARY 1891

1096	"A happy new year," 577–581. Signed: Unionist.

1097	Our boys (No. I): School-boys' parents, 582–593. **Walter L. Bicknell.** Signed Austen Pember; see no. 384.

1098	Our boys (No. II): Modern schoolbills, 594–608. **Arthur Gaye.** Signed.

1099	The girl graduate: a reply [to no. 1061], 609–613. **Frances E. Ashwell.** Signed; Cover adds "Girton College."

1100	Free whist: a reply [to no. 1077], 614–620. **Henry A. Cohen.** Signed.

1101	The history of socialism (Part III, concl.): German socialism—Karl Marx—Christian socialists—future of socialism, 621–649. **Alice Oldham.** Signed.

1102	A winter cruise on the Severn Sea, 650–658. **Cyril Parkinson.** Signed as in no. 983.

1103	Matthew Arnold: criticism of life, 659–666. **W. A. Appleyard.** Signed.

1104	Are animals automata? 667–687. **F. C. Conybeare.** Signed.

1105	Winter in the country of the passion play, 688–696. **H. C. Ward.** Signed; Contents adds "Captain"; see *WWW*/1916.

1106	"General" Booth's scheme, 697–711. **Susan Mary E. Jeune.** Signed as in no. 732.

1107	In Correspondence: "As sheep led to the slaughter" [on a Dockers' Union strike], 714–716, signed **Hamilton P. Lyne.**

VOLUME 16, FEBRUARY 1891

1108	The Mashonaland trek [in South Africa], 721–733. Signed: Anglo-African.

1109	Life and labours of Schliemann, with

personal recollections, 734–748. **Karl Blind.** Signed.

1110 Morals and politics, 749–758. **Julia Wedgwood.** Signed.

1111 The history and nature of hypnotism, 759–780. **A. Campbell Clark.** Signed, with title "M.D."

1112 "In darkest England": suggestions, 781–788. Signed: An Ex-(Colonial) Attorney-General.

1113 Critics and their craft, 789–793. **William Watson.** Signed; repr. *Excursions.*

1114 The Royal Dublin Society, 794–803. **Thomas E. Galt-Gamble.** Signed.

1115 Wit and pathos in Suetonius, 804–809. **M. S. Dimsdale.** Signed.

1116 Hagenau and Trifels, 810–822. **Henry W. Wolff.** Signed.

1117 The socialist reaction, 823–843. **C. A. Cripps.** Signed.

1118 Sport under National Hunt Rules, 844–849. **Hwfa Williams.** Signed.

1119 In Correspondence: Preserving the vital balance in inland fisheries, 857–858, signed **W. August Carter;** An appeal for single women, 859–864, signed L.M.S.

VOLUME 17, MARCH 1891

1120 Can England keep her trade? 1–11. **John A. Hobson.** Signed.

1121 The abdication of Mrs. Grundy, 12–24. **H. D. Traill.** Signed.

1122 The Behring's Sea question, 25–36. **J. Bell.** Signed.

1123 Salmon leistering [spearing], 37–49. **James Purves.** Signed.

1124 The radical at home [entitled "Rylands & Co., Unlimited" in Contents], 50–55. **H. C. Raikes,** prob. Signed H.C.R.; man cited ridiculed the radicals in earlier numbers: see especially no. 382.

1125 American literature, 56–71. **William Sharp.** Signed.

1126 The fair Ophelia of a highland glen, 72–79. **William Earl Hodgson,** prob. Signed W. Hodgson; man cited wrote frequently on Scottish subjects for the Review.

1127 Hindu marriage customs and British law, 80–90. **T. Vijaya-Raghavan.** Signed.

1128 Workers in woodcraft, 91–104. **John Watson,** d.1928. Signed Rusticus; Contents gives name.

1129 The Rubâ'iyât of Abû Sa'îd, 105–117. **Charles J. Pickering.** Signed.

1130 The London hospital and its nurses, 118–129. **W. H. Wilkins.** Signed.

1131 In Correspondence: Mr. Parnell—his naughtinesses and the storm they raised, 130–133, signed **George W. Ruxton** (letters, pp. 294–295, signed **George W. Ruxton;** p. 583, signed **Harry Vane Milbank,** with address "Thorpe Perrow, Bedale"); To allay Irish discontent, 133–135, signed **W. J. Hodges;** The immorality of hypnotism, 136–139, signed **James F. MacNamara,** with title "R.I.C." [Royal Irish Constabulary]; Quack medicines and the duty of the medical profession, 139–142, signed **James Mason,** with titles "M.D., L.R.C.P.."; Cyprus under British rule, 145–146, signed **Charles Wilson;** Are we to retain capital punishment? 147–149, signed **Anthony C. Deane;** Army clerks and reserves, 150–152, signed Reform.

VOLUME 17, APRIL 1891

1132 The censuses of the century, 153–169. **F. Bayford Harrison.** Signed.

1133 The garden of death, 170–178. **Evelyn Pyne.** Signed.

1134 The Hindû marriage agitation, 179–194. **Frederic Pincott.** Signed. (Letter, pp. 861–863, signed **Frederic Pincott,** with address "12 Wilson Road, Camberwell.")

1135 The sun's radiation of heat: a new theory, 195–205. **William Goff,** prob. Signed W. Goff; man cited lived in Dublin (see Foster); Kingstown, address given in letter below, is a suburb of Dublin. (Letters, pp. 578–579, signed **E. S. Ridsdale,** but perhaps "S" is an error for "A" and the author Sir Edward Aurelian Ridsdale, who wrote a study of cosmic evolution in 1889, and the writer speaks with authority about science; pp. 858–860, and vol. 21, pp. 143–144, signed **W. Goff,** with address "Kingstown.")

1136 The fine art of fragrance, 206–213. **Llewellyn Bullock.** Signed.

1137 The problem of domestic service, 214–227. **Frances McLaughlin.** Signed. (Letter, pp. 721–723, by **Mrs. L. M. Battine** —signed L.M.B., with address "105, Gloucester Terrace, Hyde Park, W."; Kelly/84 lists "Mrs. Battine" at that address.

1138 The Church and dissent in Wales, 228–237. **T. Lloyd Williams.** Signed; Cover adds "Rev."; calls himself S.P.G. Sec. for Wales, p. 228 (cf. *CCD*/1902). (See no. 1160.)

1139 English and German music, 238–244. **J. F. Rowbotham.** Signed. (Letters, p. 433, signed **Cecil B. Hilliard;** pp. 574–576, signed **Louis Zissler,** with address

"145, Wardour Street, W."; p. 577, signed **G. Byng Gattie,** with title "late H.M.C.S."; see no. 1162.)

1140   The Gibeonites of the stage: work and wages behind the scenes, 245–261. **C. H. d'E. Leppington.** Signed.

1141   Lord Beaconsfield—after ten years, 262–274. **Edward Salmon.** Signed.

1142   In Correspondence: Luxury and Greek, 275–279, signed **Gilbert Faber;** Hints for single women of the United Kingdom, 279–285, signed **Jessie Weston** (letter, pp. 580–582, signed **R. R. Hunt,** with address "Aukland, N.Z.") Literature for the blind, 285–287, by **F. Neville**—signed F. Nevill but see no. 875 and Part B below; Spoilers of Churches who read the lessons [on disestablishment in Wales], 287–289, signed **Charles Crosthwaite** (letter, pp. 571–574, signed **Charles Crosthwaite**); The aggressive teetotaller, 290–292, signed **James F. Macnamara;** Egyptian canals, 292–294, signed **Charles Wilson.**

VOLUME 17, MAY 1891

1143   On the present state of the law relating to the married, 297–311. **J. Edmondson Joel.** Signed.

1144   The story of swordmanship, 312–330. **Egerton Castle.** Signed.

1145   The hill-men around Manipur, 331–336. **C. N. Barham.** Signed.

1146   Luck, merit, and success, 337–348. **George R. Gallaher.** Signed. (Letter, pp. 583–584, signed **Herbert Haines.**)

1147   How I became a Conservative: a tragedy in five acts, 349–369. **Bertha Thomas.** Signed.

1148   A modern high-school girl, 370–378. **Emily Constance Cook.** Signed.

1149   The agricultural problem as a whole, 379–389. **Compton Reade.** Signed.

1150   The revolt of Strephon, 390–401. **George Morley.** Signed.

1151   Some jail experiences in India, 402–412. **C. T. Buckland.** Signed.

1152   The Mazeppa legend, 413–423. **Henry Spalding.** Signed H. Spalding; Contents adds "Lieut.-Col.": see *Army List*/88.

1153   Preservation of the colonies and the price of bread, 424–432. **H. E. J. Stanley.** Signed Stanley of Alderley [3rd Baron Stanley of Alderly].

1154   In Correspondence: Wanted, sick nurses for India, 434–437, signed **Edith E. Cuthell;** Obelisks, round towers and sun-worship, 437–440, signed **Charles Wilson.**

VOLUME 17, JUNE 1891

1155   Shall we dissolve this year? 441–451.

1156   A neglected factor of the Irish question, 452–465. **Fanny W. Currey.** Signed.

1157   The pictures of the year, 466–476. **Julia Cartwright.** Signed.

1158   The physical conscience, 477–493. **Arabella Kenealy.** Signed.

1159   A diligence journey in Spain, 494–502. **Willoughby Verner.** Signed.

1160   The Church in Wales: a reply [to no. 1138], 503–513. **W. Jenkyn Thomas.** Signed. (Letter, pp. 849–853, signed J.D.J.)

1161   Italy as a field for emigration, 514–522. **E. Strachan Morgan.** Signed.

1162   German and English music, 523–527. **Walter Austin.** Signed. (Letter, pp. 863–867, signed **J. F. Rowbotham.**)

1163   German or Greek? 528–543. **Arthur Gaye.** Signed.

1164   Nasir of Balkh, 544–564. **Charles J. Pickering.** Signed.

1165   Training in patriotism, 565–570. **L. K. Trotter.** Signed.

VOLUME 17, JULY 1891

1166   Five years of resolute government, 585–592.

1167   Eton, 593–607. **Arthur C. Benson.** Signed.

1168   After the galleries: a studio talk, 608–619. **D. S. MacColl,** prob. Signed D.S.M. —cf. nos. 2027 and 2172 on very similar subjects; man cited was an art critic; see *DNB.*

1169   Police work in Ceylon, 620–638. **Constance F. Gordon-Cumming.** Signed as in no. 100.

1170   The first Handel festival, 639–648. **Richard Edgcumbe.** Signed.

1171   To-day in Morocco, 649–664. **Charles Rolleston.** Signed; Contents adds "Captain."

1172   The farmer-monk, 665–680. **A. E. P. Raymund Dowling.** Signed.

1173   Mr. Harris and Mr. Oliphant, 681–691. **Janet Phillips.** Signed Janet Phillips (Beryl); Cover gives "Mrs. A. Phillips ('Beryl')."

1174   The diet of great men, 692–706. **Alfred J. H. Crespi.** Signed.

1175   Two biographies [of Robert Browning

and Laurence Oliphant], a novel [Meredith's *One of Our Conquerors*], and a study [of Meredith], 707–711. **Frances Colvin.** Attr. by E. V. Lucas, *The Colvins and Their Friends* (1928), p. 206.

1176 In Correspondence: Wanted: a style, 712–718, signed **Gilbert Coleridge**, with address "11, Roland Gardens, S.W."; The outcome of the Manipur Disaster, 718–721, signed **Henry P. Babbage;** Lord Beaconsfield and Imperial unity, 723–727, signed **W. Basil Worsfold;** Where were women's rights in the last century? 727–728, by **H. Y. J. Taylor**—signed H. J. J. Taylor, with address "Gloucester Conservative Club," second initial clearly a misprint, cf. nos. 908, 1292.

VOLUME 17, AUGUST 1891

1177 The session: its domestic questions, 729–742.
1178 The historical drama and the teaching of history, 743–753. **Hugh E. Egerton.** Signed.
1179 Rousseau's ideal household, 754–766. **Leonora B. Lang.** Signed L. B. Lang; Contents gives "Mrs. Andrew Lang."
1180 A plea for the Triple Alliance, 767–783. **Karl Blind.** Signed.
1181 The degradation of British sports, 784–798. **W. Earl Hodgson.** Signed.
1182 Some famous pirates, 799–807. **Tighe Hopkins.** Signed.
1183 The Anglo-Indians, 808–817. **E. L. Robertson.** Signed; Cover gives "Mrs. James C. Robertson."
1184 A materialist's paradise, 818–827. **Maurice Hewlett.** Signed.
1185 The persecuted Russian Jews, 828–837. **C. B. Roylance Kent.** Signed.
1186 Contemporary literature, 838–848.
1187 In Correspondence: The geology of the Channel, 854–856, by **Charles Wilson,** prob.—signed C.W., cf. no. 862; Postal reform, 856–858, signed **Erdmann** and **Schanz** [a corporation], with address "4, Salcott Road, Clapham Junction, London"; A ride to Tokar, 868–872, signed **Richard Fortescue Phillimore,** with title "Lieut. R.N."

VOLUME 18, SEPTEMBER 1891

1188 Democracy and Irish local government, 1–11. Signed: Unionist.
1189 An unscientific view of vivisection, 12–18. **Walburga Paget.** Signed Walb. Paget;

Contents adds "Lady"; see *WWW*/1940. (Letters, pp. 858–861, signed **Allan Grant** with address "Madras"; vol. 19, pp. 144–145, signed **Frances Power Cobbe.**)
1190 The new emperor [Wilhelm II] and his new chancellor [Bismarck], 19–42. **Charles Lowe.** Signed.
1191 September, 43–57. **T. E. Kebbel.** Signed.
1192 The fittest and the luckiest; which survives? 58–70. **G. W. Bulman.** Signed.
1193 Ernest Daudet on Coblentz and the emigration, 71–84. **R. C. E. Abbot.** Signed Colchester [Baron Colchester].
1194 The county councillor: a study, 85–92. **H. D. Traill.** Signed.
1195 Woman's life in old Italy, 93–114. **Richard Davey.** Signed.
1196 Free law? a scheme, 115–124. **J. Acton Lomax.** Signed.
1197 Contemporary literature, 125–134.
1198 In Correspondence: Club life in East London, 135–139, signed **W. Pett Ridge,** with address "Birkbeck Literary and Scientific Institution"; Voluntary socialism, 139–144, signed **Gilbert Faber.**

VOLUME 18, OCTOBER 1891

1199 Scotland and her home rulers, 145–159. **A. N. Cumming.** Signed.
1200 "Drink": ethical considerations and physiological, 160–176. **J. Mortimer Granville.** Signed; Contents adds "M.D." (Letters, pp. 426–427, signed F.P.; pp. 427–429, signed **J. James Ridge,** with title "M.D."; pp. 429–432, signed **R. E. Dudgeon,** with title "M.D."
1201 Austria: its society, politics and religion, 177–188. **Suzette van Zuylen van Nyevelt.** Signed S. I. de Zuylen de Nyevelt; Contents adds "Baroness"; see *Titled Nobility* under Zuylen.
1202 The Mahatma period, 189–200. **W. Earl Hodgson.** Signed.
1203 French school-girls, 201–209. **A. Strobel.** Signed; Contents adds "Madame."
1204 A Cape farmer in Kent, 210–226. **Hendrik B. Knoblauch.** Signed.
1205 From a simian point of view, 227–235. **H. Knight Horsfield.** Signed; repr. *In the Gun Room,* 1892.
1206 The pessimists and womankind, 236–251. **Charles Edwardes.** Signed.
1207 Parish councils, 252–258. **P. H. Ditchfield.** Signed.

1278 In defence of phantasms, 234–251. **Frank Podmore.** Signed. (Letter, pp. 427–431, signed **Lionel A. Weatherly,** with title "M.D.")

1279 The "Progressive" victory [in London County Council elections], 252–257. **C. A. Whitmore.** Signed.

1280 Among the books, 258–269.

1281 In Correspondence: Clapham-by-the-Sea [fiction, in a series of letters to "Reginald Klaussen"], 270–278, signed **Robert Brett,** which may be a pseudonym; Recurring ideas, 284–285, signed **J. Cuming Walters;** the revival of Jacobinism, 290–293, signed **George H. Powell;** Fair trade and authority, 293–296, signed **M. S. Constable.**

VOLUME 19, MAY 1892

1282 Fallacies of modern socialism, 300–311. **George C. Brodrick.** Signed.

1283 The female Quixote [Charlotte Lennox], 312–317. **Austin Dobson.** Signed; repr. *Vignettes,* I.

1284 Mr. Chaplin and the cattle trade, 318–327. **William E. Bear.** Signed.

1285 The new wedlock, 328–337. **Violet Greville.** Signed.

1286 The consolations of M. Renan, 338–348. **Sidney J. Low.** Signed.

1287 Society in Corsica, 349–360. **Basil Thomson.** Signed.

1288 The Guanches of Tenerife, 361–380. **Charles Edwardes.** Signed.

1289 Voltaire and King Stanislas, 381–400. **Henry W. Wolff.** Signed.

1290 In the wake of the red van, 401–408. **Gertrude Blake.** Signed; Contents adds "Lady."

1291 Among the books, 409–418.

1292 In Correspondence: The misadventures of Calvinism in Scotland, 419–423, signed W.H., with address "Fife, N.B." (letter, pp. 576–580, signed Jonathan Oldbuck [prob. a pseudonym: Cover puts name in quotation marks], with address "Edinburgh"); Outside the chamber of mirrors, 431–437, signed **H. Knight Horsfield,** repr. *In the Gun Room,* 1892; How poison was detected a hundred years ago, 438–440, signed **H. Y. J. Taylor,** with address "Conservative Club, Gloucester."

VOLUME 19, JUNE 1892

1293 Ulster, 449–456.

1294 Stage-struck, 457–466. **H. D. Traill.** Signed.

1295 The Dutch peasantry, 467–475. **Suzette van Zuylen van Nyevelt.** Signed as in 1201.

1296 Authors, individual and corporate, 476–487. Signed: A London Editor. (See no. 1308.)

1297 A poseuse of the eighteenth century [Madame de Genlis], 488–500. **Leonora B. Lang.** Signed as in no. 1179.

1298 Paul Verlaine, 501–515. **Arthur Symons.** Signed.

1299 Ancient Rome and modern London, 516–525. **Edward J. Gibbs.** Signed, with title "M.A." (Letter, p. 867, signed **Herbert Haines.**)

1300 The Earl of Albemarle, 526–547. **Roden Noel.** Signed.

1301 Yeomen and sportsmen, 548–562. **T. E. Kebbel.** Signed.

1302 Among the books, 563–575.

1303 In Correspondence: Mutterings from India, 582–584, signed Loyalist, with address "61, Brodies Road, Mylapore, Madras, India."

VOLUME 19, JULY 1892

1304 The appeal to the country, 585–590.

1305 Suggested by Cobbett's ghost, 591–602. **Frederick Greenwood.** Signed.

1306 A critical taboo, 603–611. **Andrew Lang.** Signature.

1307 Historical Rimini, 612–625. **Evelyn Martinengo-Cesaresco.** Signed as in no. 611.

1308 Authors, individual and corporate: a reply [to no. 1296], 626–635. **Walter Besant.** Signed. (Rejoinder, pp. 635–638, signed A London Editor.)

1309 Polynesian labour traffic, 639–647. **Richard Temple.** Signed.

1310 Newspaper copyright, 648–666. **Sidney J. Low.** Signed. (Letters, pp. 855–859, signed **Harold Hardy** with address "1, South Square, Gray's Inn"; pp. 859–864, signed **Spencer Brodhurst,** with address "The Temple."

1311 Common sense at last [on tariffs], 667–674. **C. E. Howard Vincent.** Signed.

1312 The candidate for West Drum, 675–695. **W. Earl Hodgson.** Signed.

1313 Among the books, 696–703.

1314 In Correspondence: Jacobinism and other follies [first publication of a manuscript letter], 704–706, signed **Robert Southey,** with an intro. note by **D. S. MacColl,** prob.—signed D.S.M.—see no. 1168; What the Labour Party may achieve, 706–715, signed **Norwood Young;** An intolerable priesthood, 715–719, signed An Irish Justice of the Peace; "With all hands!" [on assistance to fishermen's widows], 719–723, by **Gertrude Blake**—signed G. Blake, cf. no. 1261; Modern life and sedatives, 723–728, signed **Thomas Robinson,** with title "M.D.", and address "London" (letter, vol. 20, pp. 280–288, signed A Nervous Man).

VOLUME 19, AUGUST 1892

1315 The general election (No. I): a bird's-eye view, 730–740. **Arthur A. Baumann.** Signed.
1316 The general election (No. II): the real Radical programme, 740–746. **C. A. Whitmore.** Signed.
1317 Rivarol, 747–761. **Gertrude E. Campbell.** Signed; Contents gives "Lady Colin Campbell."
1318 The unpopularity of the Poor Law, 762–771. **Thomas Mackay.** Signed as in no. 1255.
1319 The first ascent of Mont Blanc, 772–782. **Richard Edgcumbe.** Signed.
1320 Voltaire and England, 783–801. **Nina H. Kennard.** Signed N. H. Kennard; Contents gives "Mrs. Arthur Kinnard": see *BMCat.*
1321 Beginnings of the drama in America, 802–811. **Richard Davey.** Signed.
1322 Along Hadrian's British wall, 812–823. **H. F. Abell.** Signed.
1323 The Row'tilly girl, 824–835. **David S. Meldrum.** Signed.
1324 Among the books, 836–846.
1325 In Correspondence: Railway servants' eye-sight, 847–851, signed **W. M. Beaumont;** Gunners and gunsmiths: a true story, 851–855, by **H. E. J. Stanley** —signed Stanley of Alderley [3rd Baron Stanley of Alderley]; The immorality of Chinamen [immigrants in America], 865–866, signed **Locksley Lucas;** Antiquarianism in modern art, 867–872, signed **Charles John Shebbeare.**

VOLUME 20, SEPTEMBER 1892

1326 The old and the new ministry, 1–9. Signed: Regulus.
1327 Country gentlemen, 10–24. **Herbert Maxwell.** Signed.
1328 Wanted: a new Corrupt Practices Act, 25–40. **W. H. Mallock.** Signed.

1329 The revival of ethics, and of laughter, 41–53. **W. Earl Hodgson.** Signed.
1330 Notre-Dame de Boulogne, 54–66. **R. S. Gundry.** Signed.
1331 The children of fiction, 67–82. **Henry Sutton.** Signed H. Sutton; attr. in *WWW/* 1928.
1332 Should clergymen take to trade? 83–92. **C. N. Barham.** Signed.
1333 The decay of Scotch Radicalism, 93–107. **James Ferguson,** 1857–1917. Signed A Scottish Conservative—see no. 831.
1334 The tall master, 108–119. **Gilbert Parker.** Signed.
1335 Among the books, 120–128.
1336 In Correspondence: A striking electoral anomaly, 129–131, signed **C. H. d'E. Leppington;** An Auld Licht causerie, 132–135, signed W.R.N.; From a suburban window, 136–140, signed **J. Ashton Ainscough;** A theory of brain waves, 140–144, signed **E. Wynter Wagstaff,** with title "M.S.E." and address "Katha, Upper Burma."

VOLUME 20, OCTOBER 1892

1337 The future of the Tory Party (No. I): a plea for progress, 145–151. **Francis R. Y. Radcliffe.** Signed.
1338 The future of the Tory Party (No. II): a plea against "progression," 151–159. Signed: An Old-School Tory.
1339 Society in ancient Venice, 160–176. **Charles Edwardes.** Signed.
1340 The ruin of English agriculture, 177–187. **P. Anderson Graham.** Signed.
1341 The rise and fall of words, 188–194. **Darcy Lever.** Signed; Contents attr. to "Philip Kent": cf. no. 860. (Letter, pp. 430–432, signed **W. H. Johnstone,** with address "Worthing.")
1342 The Song of Roland and the Iliad, 195–205. **Andrew Lang.** Signature.
1343 Coming and going, 206–214. **George T. Shettle.** Signed; repr. *John Wiclif, of Wycliffe,* Leeds, 1922.
1344 The boyhood and youth of Columbus, 215–228. **Richard Davey.** Signed.
1345 Gamekeepers, 229–240. **T. E. Kebbel.** Signed.
1346 The organization of real credit, 241–256. **H. de F. Montgomery.** Signed.
1347 Among the books, 257–269.
1348 In Correspondence: Barbados as a winter resort, 270–274, signed **T. Herbert Bindley;** The Institute of Journalists, 274–278, signed An Old Journalist; The new danger in Ireland, 278–280, signed An Irish J.P.

VOLUME 20, NOVEMBER 1892

1349 Constitutional revision, 289–300. **Robert Cecil.** Signed Salisbury [Marquess of Salisbury]. (Letter, pp. 573–574, signed **Edward Stanley Robertson.**)

1350 M. Renan and Christianity, 301–309. **Richard H. Hutton.** Signed.

1351 Free trade a variable expedient, 310–326. **Frederick Greenwood.** Signed. (See nos. 1362 to 1366.)

1352 "The controverted question" [what is an agnostic?] 327–344. **W. Earl Hodgson.** Signed.

1353 A remonstrance with Mr. Jesse Collings [on agricultural land allotments], 345–350. **H. E. J. Stanley.** Signed Stanley of Alderley [3rd Baron Stanley of Alderley]. (Reply, pp. 565–567, signed **Jesse Collings.**

1354 The general chapter of the Jesuits, 351–359. **Robert Beauclerk.** Signed; Contents adds middle initial "S."

1355 London fog: a scheme to abolish it, 360–367. **B. H. Thwaite.** Signed; Contents adds "C.E." (Letters, pp. 576–577, signed **J. Horton Ryley;** pp. 577–578, signed **J. Cecil Bull.**)

1356 A French abbé of the seventeenth century, 368–376. **Lewis Latimer.** Signed.

1357 Madagascar and Mauritius, 377–381. **Frederic Condé Williams.** Signed. (Letter, vol. 21, p. 422, by **Virgile Naz**—signed V. Naz, see *WWW*/1916, with an excerpt from the Debates of the Council of Mauritius, pp. 422–424.)

1358 The comedy of courtship, 382–400. **David S. Meldrum.** Signed.

1359 Among the books, 401–413. Unidentified. (Letter, pp. 575–576, signed **Frederick Wicks.**)

1360 A poet's funeral [Tennyson], 414.

1361 In Correspondence: In the club smoking room, 415–421, signed **H. Knight-Horsfield;** Criminal contagion, 422–427, signed **Arthur MacDonald,** with address "Washington, D.C."; An honest and sufficient currency, 427–430, signed **Charles Wilson.**

VOLUME 20, DECEMBER 1892

1362 Fair trade and bad trade (Part I): who profits by free trade? (No. I), 433–436. **Leonard Courtney.** Signed; Contents adds middle initial, "H." (See no. 1380.)

1363 Fair trade and bad trade (Part I): who profits by free trade? (No. II), 436–

440. Samuel Cunliffe Lister. Signed Masham [1st Baron Masham].

1364 Fair trade and bad trade (Part II): the effect of an import duty, 441–445. **James Edgcome.** Signed.

1365 Fair trade and bad trade (Part III): the views of labour (No. I), 446–450. **J. Keir Hardie.** Signed.

1366 Fair trade and bad trade (Part III): the views of labour (No. II), 450–453. **Frederick J. Whetstone.** Signed, with title "Past Chairman of the Amalgamated Society of Engineers."

1367 Tennyson's literary sensitiveness, 454–460. **Alfred Austin.** Signed.

1368 Physical education, 461–468. **Reginald Brabazon.** Signed Meath [Earl of Meath].

1369 Merchandise marks legislation, 469–476. **Charles Stuart-Wortley.** Signed C. Stuart-Wortley; Contents adds "M.P.": see Burke under Wharncliff.

1369a Episode tiré des mémoires inédits du Marquis de ——— (1780) [in French] (Part I), 477. **Walter Herries Pollock.** Signed. (Part II is no. 1412a.)

1370 Glanders and farcy [animal diseases], 478–481. **Charles Colville.** Signed, with titles "Lt.-Col., Director, London Road Car Company."

1371 The devastation of the Soudan, 482–494. **W. T. Marriott.** Signed.

1372 Early treatises on Ireland, 495–508. **George C. Brodrick.** Signed.

1373 The private life of an eminent politician [fiction] (Part I), 509–552. **Eduoard Rod.** Signed.

1374 Among the books, 553–564.

1375 In Correspondence: Parliamentary registration: a plea for reform, 567–571, signed **F. W. Palliser,** with address "Poole Park, Fulham, S.W."; A climate for the consumptive [Gran Canaria], 571–572, signed **John W. Hayward,** with title "M.D."; Free trade and our shipping supremacy, 574–575, signed **Andrew W. Arnold;** The mental and moral character of mobs, 578–580, signed **C. H. d'E. Leppington.**

VOLUME 20, JANUARY 1893

1376 Agricultural union, 587–593. **M. E. G. Finch-Hatton.** Signed Winchilsea [Earl of Winchilsea].

1377 Lord Winchilsea's proposal [in no. 1376], 594–599. **George Byron Curtis.** Signed.

1378 The correlation of the moral forces, 600–606. **William A. Knight.** Signed

William Knight; Contents adds title "Professor"; see *WWW*/1928.

1379 Disabilities of democracy, 607–623. **W. Earl Hodgson.** Signed.

1380 The Farreresqueries of free trade, 624–634. **Frederick Greenwood.** Signed.

1381 State regulation of the price of bread, 635–639. **H. E. J. Stanley.** Signed Stanley of Alderley [Baron Stanley of Alderley].

1382 Authors, publishers, and reviewers, 640–650. **Frederick Wicks.** Signed.

1383 Toryism and progression, 651–660. **Francis R. Y. Radcliffe.** Signed.

1384 Byeways in Sicily, 661–667. **Susan Keppel.** Signed; Contents adds "Lady."

1385 The Church in Wales, 668–678. **Arthur Griffith-Boscawen.** Signed.

1386 The private life of an eminent politician (Part II), 679–716. **Edouard Rod.** Signed.

1387 Among the books, 717–724.

VOLUME 20, FEBRUARY 1893

1388 French lessons for English politicians, 732–742. **Frank H. Hill.** Signed.

1389 Tyranny of the paragraph, 743–748. **Arthur Waugh.** Signed. (See no. 1401.)

1390 Current sophisms about labour, 749–763. **Henry Gourlay.** Signed.

1391 Electricity in country houses, 764–766. **B. H. Thwaite** and **J. F. S. Russell.** Signed B. H. Thwaite and Russell [Earl Russell].

1392 The epistles of the Mahdi, 767–781. **Alfred E. Turner.** Signed; Contents adds "Colonel, R.A."

1393 Agriculture and economics, 782–793. **C. A. Cripps.** Signed.

1394 Extravagance in dress, 794–804. **Mary Jeune.** Signed; repr. *Lesser Questions*, 1894.

1395 The private life of an eminent politician (Part III), 805–838. **Edouard Rod.** Signed.

1396 Among the books, 839–848.

1397 In Correspondence: In defence of outdoor poor relief, 849–855, signed **William E. Welby-Gregory** (letter, vol. 21, pp. 283–285, signed **Archer M. White**); The reference library of the British Museum, 856–859, signed **Robert Scott Moffat**; Political parties and the drink trade, 859–868, signed W.G.

VOLUME 21, MARCH 1893

1398 The Bill of Wrongs [Home Rule Bill for Ireland], 1–13.

1399 Mr. Irving's Becket [performance in Tennyson's play], 14–21. **H. D. Traill.** Signed.

1400 A common ground of agreement for all parties (Parts I–III), 22–37. **W. H. Mallock.** Signed. (Parts IV–V are no. 1411.)

1401 In defence of the paragraph, 38–43. **Oliver A. Fry.** Signed.

1402 Russian propaganda, 44–50. **Arminius Vambéry.** Signed as in no. 345.

1403 The French Canadian *habitant*, 51–57. **Harriet J. Jephson.** Signed; Contents adds "Lady."

1404 Lieutenant Mackenzie's ride, 58–61. **T. Rice Holmes.** Signed.

1405 Restaurants for the labouring classes, 62–70. **Mary Margaret Mallock.** Signed M. M. Mallock; Contents adds "Miss."

1406 Victims of vanity, 71–79. **Violet Greville.** Signed.

1407 The private life of an eminent politician (Part IV, concl.), 80–117. **Edouard Rod.** Signed.

1408 Among the books, 118–129.

1409 In Correspondence: The Liberals and the Labour party, 130–134, signed **J. L. Mahon,** with address "Leeds"; Experiences of Irish official life, 134–139, signed **Alfred E. Turner;** How agriculture is affected by the currency, 139–143, signed **Charles Wilson.**

VOLUME 21, APRIL 1893

1410 The Home Rule Bill and the army, 145–150. **Edward Gibson.** Signed Ashbourne [Baron Ashbourne].

1411 The causes of the national income [continuation of no. 1400, and therefore marked Parts IV–V], 151–161. **W. H. Mallock.** Assigned in Contents.

1412 The Radical rush, 162–173. **T. E. Kebbel.** Signed.

1412a Episode tiré des mémoires inédits du Marquis de ——— (Part II, concl.), 174. **Walter Herries Pollock.** Signed. (See no. 1369a.)

1413 Conservatives and the London County Council, 175–186. **C. A. Whitmore.** Signed.

1414 England in relation to Mohamedan states, 187–195. **Rafiüddin Ahmad.** Signed.

1415 Seven and three [as numbers], 196–209. **Arthur Gaye.** Signed.

1416 Reorganization of the army: a scheme, 210–217. **Cecil W. Battine.** Signed C. W.

Battine, with title "Lieut. 7th Dragoon Guards"; Contents gives first name.

1417   At the edge of Italy [Bosco Chiesanuova], 218–229. **Linda Villari.** Signed.

1418   The attack on the Church, 230–239.

1419   The watchmaker's wife, 240–265. **Frank R. Stockton.** Signed.

1420   Among the books, 266–278.

1421   In Correspondence: The cuckoo in the west of England, 279–280, by **H. Y. J. Taylor**—signed H.Y.J.T., with address "Gloucester"—see no. 1292; The ancient Scottish parliament, 281–282, signed **J. A. Lovat-Fraser;** Abattoirs, 285–288, by **W. A. Hollis**—signed Pyx Hawes, with address "Brighton"; Cover gives man cited.

VOLUME 21, MAY 1893

1422   Ireland's "decay" and Ulster's defiance, 292–302. **Sidney J. Low.** Signed.

1423   Amusements of the poor, 303–314. **Susan Mary E. Jeune.** Signed M. Jeune; Contents gives "Lady Jeune"; see *WWW*/ 1940. (Letter, p. 556, signed A Country Woman.)

1424   The destinies of the Far East, 315–331. **George N. Curzon.** Signed. (Letter, vol. 22, pp. 574–576, signed A British Merchant.)

1425   Romance of the National Gallery, 332–345. **Emily Constance Cook.** Signed; Contents gives "Mrs. E. T. Cook."

1426   The causes of the national income (Parts VI–VII), 346–356. **W. H. Mallock.** Signed. (Letters, pp. 552–553, signed **Henry Arthur Jones;** pp. 719–720, signed **Frederick Wicks.**)

1427   The Tory press and the Tory party (Part I): a complaint, 357–362. **FitzRoy Gardner.** Signed.

1428   The Tory press and the Tory party (Part II): an answer (No. I), 363–367. **Henry Cust.** Signed.

1429   The Tory press and the Tory party (Part II): an answer (No. II), 367–368. **Walter Herries Pollock.** Signed.

1430   The Tory press and the Tory party (Part II): an answer (No. III), 368–371. **W. E. Henley.** Signed.

1431   The Tory press and the Tory party (Part II): an answer (No. IV), 371–374. **Sidney J. Low.** Signed.

1432   The London programme, 375–385. **C. A. Whitmore.** Signed.

1433   Two proper prides, 386–406. **H. D. Traill.** Signed.

1434   Among the books, 407–421.

1435   In Correspondence: The revival of the spiritual ideal in France, 424–430, signed **Laura M. Lane,** with description "Author of *The Life and Writings of Alexandre Vinet*"; The bitter cry of the superannuated, 430–432, by **William Routh**— signed W. Routh, with address "Bedale, Yorks.", see Venn.

VOLUME 21, JUNE 1893

1436   The collapse in Australia, 436–448. **Harold Finch-Hatton.** Signed.

1437   The new humour and the non-humourists, 449–458. **J. L. Toole.** Signed; Contents gives full name.

1438   The art of the year, 459–473. **William Sharp.** Signed.

1439   The causes of the national income (Parts VIII–IX), 474–485. **W. H. Mallock.** Signed.

1440   The study of English language and literature as part of a liberal education, 486–499. **W. J. Courthope.** Signed.

1441   The exile of the Marquise de Falaiseau, 500–509. **Suzette van Zuylen van Nyevelt.** Signed as in no. 1201.

1442   The new era in letters, 510–517. **Arthur Waugh.** Signed.

1443   At the sign of the eagle, 518–540. **Gilbert Parker.** Signed.

1444   Among the books, 541–551.

1445   In Correspondence: The police clauses of the Home Rule Bill, 553–556, signed A British Citizen; Absurdities of the Registration Bill, 557–562, signed **F. E. Eddis,** with address "St. Stephen's Club, Westminster"; The witness of the monuments, 562–567, signed **J. H. S. Moxly;** Thoughts for defenders of the Church, 567–571, signed **H. George Morgan;** The abuse of tobacco, 571–576, signed **G. J. Cowley-Brown.**

VOLUME 21, JULY 1893

1446   France, England, and Siam, 577–593. **R. S. Gundry.** Signed; repr. *China and Her Neighbours*, 1893, as "France and Siam."

1447   A modern conversation, 594–605. **W. Earl Hodgson.** Signed.

1448   Sir Richard Owen and old-world memories, 606–619. **Lionel A. Tollemache.** Signed.

1449   The causes of the national income

(Parts X–XI), 620–631. **W. H. Mallock.**
Signed.

1450   The argument for belief, 632–646. **H. M. Bompas.** Signed.

1451   In defence of the Post Office, 647–658. Signed: One Who Knows.

1452   The *Persiles* of Cervantes, 659–681. **James Mew.** Signed.

1453   A grey romance, 682–703. **Lucy Clifford.** Signed; Contents gives "Mrs. W. K. Clifford."

1454   Among the books, 704–712.

1455   In Correspondence: A word with Mr. Huxley, 713–715, signed A Layman; Boom cities [in western United States], 716–717, signed **Locksley Lucas;** Modern criticism, 717–719, signed **Arthur Rickett.**

VOLUME 21, AUGUST 1893

1456   Episodes of the month, 724–738. **L. J. Maxse.** Maxse became editor with this number; with rare exceptions, the monthly arts. with this title "were known to be Maxse's unpartnered composition": see J. S. Sandars, H. W. Wilson, and Lord Newton, *NatR-II*, vol. 98, p. 156, and vol. 100, pp. 176, 185–186; cf. nos. 2082, 2365.

1457   The personal gratification bill, 739–750. **Frederick Greenwood.** Signed.

1458   Herman Sudermann, 751–770. **Mary Elizabeth Braddon.** Signed M. E. Braddon; Contents adds "Miss."

1459   Alexis de Tocqueville, 771–784. **A. V. Dicey.** Signed.

1460   *Fin de siècle* medicine, 785–791. **A. Symons Eccles.** Signed; Contents adds "M.B."

1461   The causes of the national income (Parts XII–XIII, concl.), 792–804. **W. H. Mallock.** Signed.

1462   Closing of the Indian mints, 805–816. **William H. Houldsworth.** Signed.

1463   Guy de Maupassant, 817–826. **George Saintsbury.** Signed.

1464   The Royal Welsh Land Commission, 827–840. **H. E. J. Stanley.** Signed Stanley of Alderley [Baron Stanley of Alderley].

1465   A fresh puzzle of Home Rule, 841–844. **Frederick Pollock.** Signed.

1466   The white seal, 845–859. **Rudyard Kipling.** Signed; repr. *Writings*, VIII, from the *Second Jungle Book*.

1467   Among the books, 860–869.

1468   In Correspondence: Courts martial, 870–872, signed **Vernon Lushington** (letter, vol. 22, pp. 141–144, signed **Vernon Lushington**).

VOLUME 22, SEPTEMBER 1893

1469   Episodes of the month, 1–18. **L. J. Maxse.** Cf. no. 1456.

1470   The Behring Sea arbitration award, 19–24. **A. W. Staveley Hill.** Signed, but no "W." in *DNB* or Hansard; Contents adds "M.P."

1471   An Englishwoman in Thibet, 25–35. **Annie R. Taylor.** Signed; Contents adds "Miss."

1472   For weary citizens [on Home Rule Bill], 36–45. **H. D. Traill.** Signed.

1473   The immorality of evolutionary ethics [Spencer's *Ethics*], 46–58. **W. Earl Hodgson.** Signed.

1474   Hops and hop-pickers, 59–67. **Charles Edwardes.** Signed.

1475   The rupee difficulty, 68–82. **Evelyn Hubbard.** Signed.

1476   The Tuscan nationality, 83–96. **Grant Allen.** Signed.

1477   A warning from Wales, 97–103. **Arthur Griffith-Boscawen.** Signed A. Griffith-Boscawen: cf. no. 1385.

1478   "Judas" [defense of Joseph Chamberlain], 104–114. **Frederick A. Maxse.** Signed.

1479   Young genius, 115–130. **Frederick Greenwood.** Signed.

1480   Among the books, 131–140.

VOLUME 22, OCTOBER 1893

1481   Episodes of the month, 145–160. **L. J. Maxse.** Cf. no. 1456.

1482   The crowning mercy [defeat of Home Rule Bill], 161–170. **Edward Gibson.** Signed Ashbourne [Baron Ashbourne].

1483   Biography, 171–183. **Leslie Stephen.** Signed; repr. Stephen, *Men and Mountains.*

1484   Is golf a first-class game? 184–188. **Alfred Lyttelton.** Signed. (Letters, pp. 427–428, signed **Arthur James Balfour;** pp. 568–572, signed **Horace G. Hutchinson.**)

1485   The new Chamber of Deputies, 189–202. **Emily Crawford.** Signed.

1486   *Via media*, 203–214. **G. J. Cowley-Brown.** Signed.

1487   A fortnight in Finland, 215–229. **J. D. Rees.** Signed.

1488   The session (No. I): its personal aspects, 230–241. Signed: M.P. [Member of Parliament].

1489   The session (No. II): its barren labour, 242–248. **George Baden-Powell.** Signed.

1490 A missing page in Alpine history, 249–257. **Richard Edgcumbe.** Signed.

1491 The garden that I love (Part I), 258–278. **Alfred Austin.** Signed; series published as book, 1894.

1492 "For God's judgment," 279–288. **Millicent Sutherland.** Signed Erskine Gower [names of her father and husband]; Duchess of Sutherland to L. J. Maxse, n.d., Maxse Papers, MS. 443, insists on this pseudonym for her "story"; this is only use of the name in *NatR-II.*

VOLUME 22, NOVEMBER 1893

1493 Episodes of the month, 289–303. **L. J. Maxse.** Cf. no. 1456.

1494 The European outlook, 304–315. **Frederick A. Maxse.** Signed.

1495 The garden that I love (Part II), 316–334. **Alfred Austin.** Signed.

1496 Reflections on the way home [from India], 335–351. **H. E. M. James.** Signed. (See no. 1536.)

1497 Robert Lowe as a journalist, 352–364. **A. Patchett Martin.** Signed.

1498 Parish councils (No. I), 365–375. **T. W. Fowle.** Signed. (Letter, pp. 572–574, by **Thomas Mackay**—signed as in no. 1255.)

1499 Parish councils (No. II), 375–381. **John W. E. Douglas-Scott-Montagu.** Signed John Scott Montagu; Contents adds "M.P.": see *WWW/1940.*

1500 Golf—the monstrous regiment of the Englishry, 382–386. **Thomas Mackay.** Signed as in no. 1255.

1501 Church and press, 387–393. **J. Thackray Bunce.** Signed.

1502 South African policy, 394–399. **William Greswell.** Signed.

1503 In Cabinet council, 400–408. **H. D. Traill.** Signed.

1504 The Brudenels, 409–417. **Hamilton Aïde.** Signed.

1505 Among the books, 418–426.

1506 In Correspondence: The silver lining [on Irish Home Rule], 429–432, signed An Irish Girl.

VOLUME 22, DECEMBER 1893

1507 Episodes of the month, 433–448. **L. J. Maxse.** Cf. no. 1456.

1508 Is our sea-power to be maintained? 449–457. **George Hamilton.** Signed; Contents adds "Lord" and "M.P."

1509 Matthew Arnold, 458–477. **Leslie Stephen.** Signed; repr. *Studies,* II.

1510 The voluntary schools crisis, 478–490. **Henry Hayman.** Signed.

1511 Our Lady of Pootoo [Buddhist goddess], 491–503. **R. S. Gundry.** Signed; repr. *China* as "The Goddess of Mercy."

1512 The Kirk, and Presbyterian union, 504–514. **Robert Herbert Story.** Signed R.H.S.; Contents gives "Rev. H. Story, D.D."; see *DNB.*

1513 The garden that I love (Part III), 515–530. **Alfred Austin.** Signed.

1514 The unsolved Irish problem, 531–541. **Charles Owen O'Conor.** Signed O'Conor Don: see *DNB.*

1515 Silver in the fifty-third congress [of the United States], 542–557. **Moreton Frewen.** Signed.

1516 The day of silence, 558–567. **George Gissing.** Signed; repr. *Human Odds and Ends,* 1898.

VOLUME 22, JANUARY 1894

1517 Episodes of the month, 577–591. **L. J. Maxse.** Cf. no. 1456.

1518 W. H. Smith as a colleague, 592–600. **Edward Gibson.** Signed Ashbourne [Baron Ashbourne].

1519 Imperial insurance, 601–611. **F. N. Maude.** Signed, with title "Captain, late R. E."

1520 Notes of a tour in north Italy, 612–623. **Emily Crawford.** Signed.

1521 The decline of urban immigration, 624–635. **Edwin Cannan.** Signed.

1522 People's banks, 636–647. **Thomas Mackay.** Signed T. Mackay; repr. *Methods of Social Reform,* 1896.

1523 The garden that I love (Part IV, concl.), 648–663. **Alfred Austin.** Signed.

1524 Incidents of the autumn session, 664–672. Signed: M.P. [Member of Parliament].

1525 Featherstone and other riots, 673–680. **Harry L. Stephen.** Signed.

1526 How we lost the United States of Africa, 681–698. **F. Edmund Garrett.** Signed.

1527 Some recent fiction (No. I), 699–703. **Frances Balfour.** Signed; Contents adds "Lady."

1528 Some recent fiction (No. II), 703–707. **Edith Lyttelton.** Signed; Contents gives "Mrs. Alfred Lyttelton."

1529 Some recent fiction (No. III), 707–713. **Margot Tennant.** Signed; Contents adds "Miss."

1530   Some recent fiction (No. IV), 713–
717. **Constance Lytton.** Signed; Contents
adds "Lady."
1531   Correspondence: A Spanish experience,
718–720, signed **A. H. Studd.**

VOLUME 22, FEBRUARY 1894

1532   Episodes of the month, 721–737. **L. J.
Maxse.** Cf. no. 1456.
1533   An appeal to the Lords, 738–741. **St.
Loe Strachey.** Signed. (See nos. 1549
through 1553.)
1534   *The Life of Arthur Stanley* [by R. E.
Prothero and G. G. Bradley], 742–761.
Mountstuart E. Grant Duff. Signed; repr.
Out of the Past (1903), II.
1535   An English master [Hubert Parry, the
composer], 762–771. **Violet (Maxse) Milner,** prob. Signed V.; she was a sister of
the editor; she knew Parry well and chose
his Wedding March for her first wedding
in June 1894: see Violet Milner, *My
Picture Gallery* (1951), p. 61.
1536   Some further reflections on India, 772–
782. **H. E. M. James.** Signed.
1537   The living wage, 783–795. **Hugh Bell.**
Signed.
1538   Roman society a century ago, 796–813.
Charles Edwardes. Signed.
1539   Why the Imperial Federation League
was dissolved, 814–822. **Robert Beadon.**
Signed.
1540   Mr. Ruskin in relation to modern
problems, 823–834. **E. T. Cook.** Signed.
1541   The university for Wales, 835–841.
J. Ellis McTaggart. Signed.
1542   Edward Stanhope, 842–849. **W. St.
John Brodrick.** Signed St. John Brodrick;
Cover gives first initial and title "M.P."
1543   The service of a village knight, 850–
864. **Marian Bower.** Signed; Contents
adds "Miss."

VOLUME 23, MARCH 1894

1544   Episodes of the month, 1–15. **L. J.
Maxse.** Cf. no. 1456.
1545   Reasons for a coalition, 17–28. Signed:
A Conservative M.P.
1546   Luxury, 29–48. **Leslie Stephen.** Signed;
repr. *Social Rights and Duties* (1896), II.
1547   French feeling towards England, 49–
56. **André Lebon.** Signed, with title
"Deputy of the French Chamber."
1548   Heresies in salmon-fishing, 57–64. **W.
Earl Hodgson.** Signed. (See no. 1578.)
1549   The referendum (No. I), 65–72. **A. V.
Dicey.** Signed.

1550   The referendum (No. II), 72–76.
George N. Curzon. Signed.
1551   The referendum (No. III), 76–77.
Frederick A. Maxse. Signed.
1552   The referendum (No. IV), 78–79.
H. G. Grey. Signed Grey [Earl Grey].
1553   The referendum (No. V), 79–80. **T. H.
Farrer.** Signed Farrer [Baron Farrer].
(See no. 1564.)
1554   Some notes on Tibet, 81–88. **Annie R.
Taylor.** Signed.
1555   The Royal Welsh Land Commission,
89–97. **H. E. J. Stanley.** Signed Stanley of
Alderley [Baron Stanley of Alderley].
1556   A family budget, 98–109. Signed: A
Family Man. Unidentified. (See no. 1583;
letter, pp. 285–288, by **Henrietta M. A.
Strachey**—signed Amy Strachey, cf. no.
1687.)
1557   *The Influence of Sea Power* [by A. T.
Mahan], 110–117. **F. N. Maude.** Signed.
1558   Our Cleopatra [Egypt], 118–127. **H. D.
Traill.** Signed.
1559   Some side aspects of disestablishment,
128–138. Signed: Z.
1560   A fragmentary correspondence, 139–
144. **Beatrix Duff.** Signed; Contents adds
"Miss."

VOLUME 23, APRIL 1894

1561   Episodes of the month, 145–163. **L. J.
Maxse.** Cf. no. 1456.
1562   Mr. Gladstone's retirement, 175–180.
Signed: M.P. [Member of Parliament].
1563   The destruction of British birds, 181–
195. **T. L. Powys.** Signed Lilford [Baron
Lilford].
1564   The referendum, 196–200. **St. Loe
Strachey.** Signed.
1565   The Labour Commission, 201–212.
Signed: Observer.
1566   The art of reading books, 213–218.
J. E. C. Welldon. Signed.
1567   The position of Liberal Unionists (No.
I), 219–221. **T. W. Russell.** Signed.
1568   The position of Liberal Unionists (No.
II), 222–225. **H. O. Arnold-Forster.**
Signed.
1569   The position of Liberal Unionists (No.
III), 226–227. **J. Parker Smith.** Signed.
1570   The position of Liberal Unionists (No.
IV), 227–231. **Frederick A. Maxse.**
Signed.
1571   When life stirs, 232–235. **Denham Jordan** and **Jean A. Visger.** Signed A Son of
the Marshes: see evidence for *Blackwood's Mag.*, no. 6516, *Index*, I, 177.
1572   The discontent in the Civil Service,
236–249. Signed: X.Y.

1573 The cause and effect of the Matabele War, 250–272. **F. C. Selous.** Signed.

1574 A capitalist, 273–284. **George Gissing.** Signed; repr. *The House of Cobwebs*, 1906.

VOLUME 23, MAY 1894

1575 Episodes of the month, 289–304. **L. J. Maxse.** Cf. no. 1456.

1576 The Home Rule campaign, 305–318. **Joseph Chamberlain.** Signed as in no. 1243.

1577 The duties of authors, 319–339. **Leslie Stephen.** Signed; repr. *Social Rights and Duties* (1896), II.

1578 Heresies in salmon fishing, 340–349. **Herbert Maxwell.** Signed.

1579 Kossuth and the Hungarian war of liberation, 350–363. **Sidney J. Low.** Signed.

1580 A stroll in Boccaccio's country, 364–371. **Janet Ross.** Signed; repr. *Old Florence*.

1581 The House of Commons and the Indian Civil Service, 372–389. **Theodore Beck.** Signed.

1582 Lord Wolseley's *Marlborough*, 391–402. Signed: A.J.

1583 Another family budget, 403–408. Signed: Felicitas. Unidentified. (See no. 1500.)

1584 Questions in the House on naval matters, 409–423. **H. O. Arnold-Forster.** Signed.

1585 Eton cricket, 424–432. **R. H. Lyttelton.** Signed.

VOLUME 23, JUNE 1894

1586 Episodes of the month, 433–448. **L. J. Maxse.** Cf. no. 1456.

1587 The attack on the Church, 449–459. **Richard E. Webster.** Signed. AND **Arthur Griffith-Boscawen.** Signed as in no. 1477.

1588 A substitute for the Alps, 460–467. **Leslie Stephen.** Signed; repr. Stephen, *Men and Mountains*.

1589 Enthusiasm or hysteria? [on politics], 468–481. **Thomas Mackay.** Signed as in no. 1255.

1590 Ocean highways: their bearing on the food and wages of Great Britain, 482–499. **George Hamilton.** Signed; Contents adds "Lord" and "M.P."

1591 Some developments of tennis, 500–513. **J. M. Heathcote.** Signed.

1592 The great conspiracy [concerning religion in education], 514–526. **Athelstan Riley.** Signed.

1593 New evidence on agricultural depression, 527–543. **William E. Bear.** Signed.

1594 "The actualists: some impressions of Shilito Jessop, artist," 544–565. **Mortimer Menpes.** Signed.

1595 The Niger territories, 566–576. **Leonard Darwin.** Signed; Contents adds "Major" and "M.P."

VOLUME 23, JULY 1894

1596 Episodes of the month, 577–592. **L. J. Maxse.** Cf. no. 1456.

1597 The colonies and maritime defence, contributed on behalf, and by authority of, The Imperial Federation (Defence) Committee, 593–610. (See nos. 1622, 1651.)

1598 "Fair women" at the Grafton Gallery, 611–625. **Claude Phillips.** Signed.

1599 An Irish landlord's budget, 626–636. Unidentified. (See no. 1613.)

1600 The Labour party and the general election, 637–649. **J. L. Mahon.** Signed.

1601 Gogol, the father of Russian realism, 650–661. **Arthur Tilley.** Signed.

1602 Campaigning in Matabeleland, 662–669. Signed: A Member of the Bechuanaland Border Police.

1603 Harrow cricket, 670–681. **Spencer W. Gore.** Signed.

1604 Lord Sherbrooke and Sir Alfred Stephen, 682–686. **A. Patchett Martin.** Signed. (Letter, p. 861, by **S. R. Lowry-Corry**—signed Belmore [Earl Belmore].

1605 Socialism and the rentier, 687–691. Signed H.L.

1606 The currency question, 692–707. **David Barbour.** Signed.

1607 Mrs. Martin's company, 708–718. **Jane Barlow.** Signed.

1608 In Correspondence: An unpublished episode of the Peninsular War, 719–720, by **John Edward Cornwallis Rous**—signed Stradbroke [2nd Earl of Stradbroke], with intro. note signed **Arthur Lyon Fremantle.**

VOLUME 23, AUGUST 1894

1609 Episodes of the month, 721–741. **L. J. Maxse.** Cf. no. 1456.

1610 Lords and Commons: a dialogue, 742–754. **H. D. Traill.** Signed.

1611 The part of religion in human evolution, 755–763. **Francis Galton.** Signed. (Note, 763–765, signed **Benjamin Kidd.**)

1612 The outskirts of Europe, 766–780. **J. D. Rees.** Signed.

1613 An Irish landlord's budget, 781–785. **T. W. Russell.** Signed. (See no. 1630.)

1614 Debased silver and British trade, 788–796. **E. E. Isemonger.** Signed, with title "Colonial Treasurer, Straits Settlements."

1615 Sleeplessness, 797–805. **A. Symons Eccles.** Signed.

1616 The position of women in industry, 806–814. **Helen D. Bosanquet.** Signed H. Dendy; repr. *Aspects of the Social Problem*, ed. Bernard Bosanquet, 1895.

1617 The heroic couplet, 815–835. **St. Loe Strachey.** Signed.

1618 Colliery explosions and coal-dust, 836–846. **W. N. Atkinson.** Signed.

1619 Margaret: a sketch in black and white, 847–860. **Augusta Zelia Fraser.** Signed The Author of *A Study in Colour*—see *BMCat.*

1620 In Correspondence: A protest from the south [of England], 861–864, by **Frederic Case**—signed F. Case, with address "Tudeley Vicarage, Tonbridge"; see Venn.

VOLUME 24, SETEMBER 1894

1621 Episodes of the month, 1–22. **L. J. Maxse.** Cf. no. 1456.

1622 The colonies and the Empire, contributed on behalf of the United Empire Trade League, 23–28. **C. E. Howard Vincent.** Signed.

1623 Hobbes, 29–41. **Frederick Pollock.** Signed.

1624 The prospects of flying, 42–47. **Hiram S. Maxim.** Signed.

1625 The bar as a profession, 49–57. Signed: The Ordinary Man.

1626 To the brink of Pirene, 58–68. **Morton Fullerton.** Signed.

1627 How to save the rupee, 69–85. **Harold Cox.** Signed.

1628 Some features of the session in the House of Commons, 86–96. Signed: Conservative M.P.

1629 Autumn thoughts, 97–111. **T. E. Kebbel.** Signed.

1630 An Irish landlord's budget and its critics, 112–122. Signed: The Annotator of "An Irish Landlord's Budget" [no. 1599].

1631 Rosemary, 123–144. **Frederick Greenwood.** Signed.

VOLUME 24, OCTOBER 1894

1632 Episodes of the month, 145–164. **L. J. Maxse.** Cf. no. 1456.

1633 Shall we degrade our standard of value? 165–189. **T. H. Farrer.** Signed Farrer [Baron Farrer]; repr. *Studies in Currency*, 1898. (See no. 1670.)

1634 The drift of psychical research, 190–209. **Frederic W. H. Myers.** Signed.

1635 A country-house question [gratuities for servants], 210–215. Signed: X.

1636 The invisible government; or, Ireland a nation, *temp.* 19—, 216–231. **St. Loe Strachey.** Signed.

1637 Some Oxford memories of the praeaesthetic age, 232–244. **T. H. S. Escott.** Signed.

1638 An American utopia [reform of municipal governments], 245–252. **Edward Porritt.** Signed. (See no. 1785.)

1639 The poor man's cow: a suggestion to the coming parish councils, 253–262. **Henry W. Wolff.** Signed.

1640 *Problems of the Far East* [by George Curzon], 263–277. **F. Ivor Maxse.** Signed.

1641 A very light railway, 278–288. **Jane Barlow.** Signed.

VOLUME 24, NOVEMBER 1894

1642 Episodes of the month, 289–306. **L. J. Maxse.** Cf. no. 1456.

1643 London Progressives v. London education, 307–315. **Joseph R. Diggle.** Signed.

1644 The attack on Lord Stratford de Redcliffe, 316–333. **Stanley Lane-Poole.** Signed.

1645 The situation in Belgium, 334–346. **Luis de Lorac.** Signed.

1646 Etoniana, 347–354. **Walter Durnford.** Signed.

1647 A sham crusade [by Liberals against House of Lords], 355–365. **Robert Wallace**, 1831–1899. Signed A Radical M.P.; cf. no. 2270 bearing same signature; Wallace supplements this argument in a signed art., *NC* no. 2696.

1648 Leafless woods and grey moorlands, 366–374. **Denham Jordan** and **Jean A. Visger.** Signed A Son of the Marshes; see evidence for *Blackwood's Mag.*, no. 6516, *Index*, I, 177.

1649 Native India and England, 375–391. **Theodore Beck.** Signed.

1650 The Hans Sachs celebration in Germany, 392–403. **Karl Blind.** Signed.

1651 What is imperial defence? 404–414. **P. H. Colomb.** Signed.

1689 Colonial problems (No. II): the commercial collapse of Newfoundland, 822–827. **A. R. Whiteway.** Signed.

1690 The work and policy of the London County Council, 828–846. **R. M. Beachcroft** and **H. Percy Harris.** Signed, with Beachcroft's middle name added in Contents as "Melville," but see *WWW*/1928 and *BMCat.*

1691 A lodger in Maze Pond, 847–862. **George Gissing.** Signed; repr. *The House of Cobwebs*, 1906.

VOLUME 25, MARCH 1895

1692 Episodes of the month, 1–20. **L. J. Maxse.** Cf. no. 1456.

1693 Tunis and Egypt, 21–34. **J. St. Loe Strachey.** Signed. (See no. 1716.)

1694 Mr. Balfour's *Foundations of Belief*, 35–47. **Benjamin Kidd.** Signed.

1695 The present condition of wood-engraving in England and America, 48–58. **Marion H. Spielmann.** Signed M. H. Spielman; see *WWW*/1950. (See no. 1720.)

1696 Friendly Societies and old-age pensions: a reply to Mr. Chamberlain [no. 1667], 59–71. **J. Lister Stead.** Signed.

1697 Drink as a trade, 72–80. **J. Satchell Hopkins.** Signed.

1698 Bishop Thirlwall and the Irish Church Bill of 1869, 81–96. **William Alexander.** Signed William Derry and Raphoe [Bishop of Derry and Raphoe].

1699 The future of poetry, 97–104. **Arthur Christopher Benson.** Signed.

1700 The present depression: its causes, consequences, and continuance, 105–118. **R. H. Inglis Palgrave.** Signed.

1701 Lord Randolph Churchill, 119–131. **Herbert Maxwell.** Signed.

1702 The scrap-book of Canon Alberic, 132–141. **M. R. James.** Signed.

VOLUME 25, APRIL 1895

1703 Episodes of the month, 145–157. **L. J. Maxse.** Cf. no. 1456; apology for emphasis on the currency problem, p. 149, is editorial.

1704 Cheques [Government support of Irish M.P.'s], 158–164. **William Waldegrave Palmer.** Signed Wolmer [Viscount Wolmer].

1705 The choice of books, 165–182. **Leslie Stephen.** Signed.

1706 Twelve hundred miles in a waggon: a short account of a journey through the British South Africa Company's territory in 1894 (Parts I–V), 183–206. **Alice Balfour.** Signed; series repr. same title, 1896.

1707 The currency question: for laymen [bimetallism] (No. I): introductory, 207–213. **Herbert C. Gibbs.** Signed.

1708 The currency question: for laymen (No. II): trade and industry, 213–219. **W. H. Houldsworth.** Signed.

1709 The currency question: for laymen (No. III): India, 219–225. **David Miller Barbour.** Signed D. Barbour; Cover adds "Sir David" and "K.C.S.I."; see *DNB*/1930. (See nos. 1733, 1734, 1802.)

1710 Sir Geoffrey Hornby, 226–238. **W. Laird Clowes.** Signed.

1711 The Progressive [party] check [in recent election], 239–246. **C. A. Whitmore.** Signed.

1712 Twenty-five years of a German court theatre, 247–258. **John G. Robertson.** Signed.

1713 Resolutions of the House of Commons, 259–276. **G. W. Prothero.** Signed.

1714 Recent finance, 277–288. Signed: Observer.

VOLUME 25, MAY 1895

1715 Episodes of the month, 289–305. **L. J. Maxse.** Cf. no. 1456.

1716 Some Anglo-French problems, 306–317. **James W. Lowther.** Signed.

1717 Coleridge's *Letters*, 318–327. **Leslie Stephen.** Signed.

1718 Headaches, 328–336. **A. Symons Eccles.** Signed.

1719 A dialogue on bimetallism, 337–342. **Leonard Courtney.** Signed. (See nos. 1733, 1734.)

1720 The true condition of wood-engraving in England and America, 343–350. **Joseph Pennell.** Signed.

1721 Twelve hundred miles in a waggon (Parts VI–IX, concl.), 351–373. **Alice Balfour.** Signed.

1722 The English public-house, 374–387. **Arthur Shadwell.** Signed; repr. with additions, *Drink*. (Note, p. 640, by **Shadwell.**)

1723 Pontresina, 388–398. **G. F. Browne.** Signed; Contents gives "Bishop of Stepney."

George Edwards. Signed A. G. St. Asaph [Bishop of St. Asaph].

1805   Christian reunion, 415–421. **Charles Lindley Wood.** Signed Halifax [Viscount Halifax].

1806   Correspondence: The American "sound money" problem and its solution, 422–424, signed **Anthony Higgins;** reply, 425–428, signed **Moreton Frewen.**

VOLUME 26, DECEMBER 1895

1807   Episodes of the month, 429–447. **L. J. Maxse.** Cf. no. 1456.

1808   The crisis in religious education, 448–470. **John Bilsborrow.** Signed John, Bishop of Salford; see *WWW*/1916.

1809   Matthew Arnold in his *Letters*, 471–483. **Alfred Austin.** Signed.

1810   The greater Eastern question, 484–493. **Robert K. Douglas.** Signed.

1811   The air-car, or man-lifting kite, 494–500. **Baden F. S. Baden-Powell.** Signed B. Baden Powell; Cover gives title "Lieutenant"; see *WWW*/1940.

1812   Investors and their money, 501–511. **Hugh E. M. Stutfield.** Signed.

1813   A great singer's last home [Elizabeth Billington], 512–518. **William Barclay Squire.** Signed.

1814   Child distress and state socialism, 519–528. **Joseph R. Diggle.** Signed.

1815   A new theory of gout: what it is not, what it is, and how to avoid it, 529–544. **Mortimer Granville.** Signed.

1816   Our military problem: for civilian readers (Part I), 545–557. **F. Ivor Maxse.** Signed; series repr. with slight revisions, 1896.

1817   The decline of drunkenness, 558–568. **Arthur Shadwell.** Signed.

1818   A Turkish note on the Turkish question [in French], 569–572. By "a Turkish gentleman of high position, . . . one of the leaders of the Young Turkish Party." See intro. note by **L. J. Maxse**—signed Ed. *N.R.*

VOLUME 26, JANUARY 1896

1819   Episodes of the month, 573–594. **L. J. Maxse.** Cf. no. 1456.

1820   American politics, 595–608. **Moreton Frewen.** Signed.

1821   The armed peace: new style, 609–618. **Sidney Low.** Signed.

1822   Is British housekeeping a success? 619–627. **Ellen W. Darwin.** Signed; in Contents "Mrs. Francis Darwin," with first name misspelled "Frances."

1823   The claims of voluntary schools, 628–640. **E. R. Wodehouse.** Signed.

1824   A plea for variety in taxation, 641–649. **Hartley Withers.** Signed.

1825   Advertisement as a gentle art [on literary agents], 650–656. Signed: An Editor.

1826   Our military problem: for civilian readers (Part II), 657–669. **F. Ivor Maxse.** Signed.

1827   George Borrow, 670–684. **James Hooper.** Signed.

1828   National Church Sustentation Fund, 685–702. **William Lefroy,** 1836–1909. Signed, with title "Dean of Norwich"; see *DNB*.

1829   The squeeze, 703–716. **Frederick Greenwood.** Signed.

VOLUME 26, FEBRUARY 1896

1830   Episodes of the month, 717–740. **L. J. Maxse.** Cf. no. 1456.

1831   The key-note of our foreign policy, 741–757. **J. St. Loe Strachey.** Signed. (See no. 1841.)

1832   The command of the sea and British policy, 758–769. **Spenser Wilkinson.** Signed; repr. *War and Policy*, 1900.

1833   The evolution of editors, 770–785. **Leslie Stephen.** Signed; repr. *Studies*, I.

1834   The Chartered Company and Matabililand, 786–797. **Frederick G. Shaw.** Signed, with titles "A.M.I.C.E., F.G.S." (See no. 1842.)

1835   The German colony in London, 798–810. **Arthur Shadwell.** Signed.

1836   Our military problem: for civilian readers (Part III, concl.), 811–826. **F. Ivor Maxse.** Signed.

1837   Tiflis, 827–835. **Walter B. Harris.** Signed.

1838   The company-monger's elysium, 836–848. **Hugh E. M. Stutfield.** Signed.

1839   The problem of poverty in old age, 849–876. **Lionel Holland.** Signed.

VOLUME 27, MARCH 1896

1840   Episodes of the month, 1–20. **L. J. Maxse.** Cf. no. 1456.

1841   Should we seek an alliance? 21–32. Signed: Balance of Power.

1842   The Chartered Company [in Africa]: the other side [of no. 1834], 33–50. **F. Reginald Statham.** Signed.

1843 National biography, 51–65. **Leslie Stephen.** Signed; repr. *Studies*, I.

1844 The development of Dodos [West African Negroes], 66–79. **Mary H. Kingsley.** Signed.

1845 Volunteers, 80–91. **J. H. A. Macdonald.** Signed; Cover gives "Lord Kingsburgh"; see *DNB*/1921.

1846 Beautifying London, 92–102. **C. A. Whitmore.** Signed.

1847 Workmen directors, 103–110. **George Livesey.** Signed.

1848 The conversion of Manning, 111–123. **Bernard Holland.** Signed.

1849 The worship of the ugly, 124–132. **Cosmo Monkhouse.** Signed.

1850 Our food supply in the event of war, 133–144. **William E. Bear.** Signed. (See no. 1854; letter, pp. 302–304, signed **R. B. Marston.**)

VOLUME 27, APRIL 1896

1851 Episodes of the month, 145–165. **L. J. Maxse.** Cf. no. 1456.

1852 Egypt and England, 166–177. **T. H. Farrer.** Signed Farrer [Baron Farrer]. (Note, p. 488.)

1853 Slatin Pasha and the Sudan, 178–196. **F. D. Lugard.** Signed.

1854 National granaries, 197–207. **R. A. Yerburgh.** Signed.

1855 John Byrom, 208–221. **Leslie Stephen.** Signed; repr. *Studies*, I.

1856 The humorous aspect of childhood, 222–236. **James Sully.** Signed J. Sully; author refers, p. 236n., to his *Studies in Childhood*; see *WWW*/1928.

1857 The militia, 237–256. **G. F. H. Somerset.** Signed Raglan [Baron Raglan].

1858 *Infirma vincula caritatis* [England's reputation abroad], 257–261. **Charles Darling.** Signed; Contents adds "Q.C., M.P."

1859 The forces of temperance, 262–276. **Arthur Shadwell.** Signed; repr., with revisions, *Drink*.

1860 The British case against Venezuela, 277–301. **L. J. Maxse.** Signed.

VOLUME 27, MAY 1896

1861 Episodes of the month, 305–324. **L. J. Maxse.** Cf. no. 1456.

1862 France and Egypt [in French], 325–337. **François Deloncle.** Signed.

1863 Can England be invaded? 338–356.

G. S. Clarke. Signed; repr. Thursfield, *Navy and the Nation.*

1864 The throne of thunder, 357–374. **Mary H. Kingsley.** Signed.

1865 The Manitoba school question, 375–383. **Charles Hibbert Tupper.** Signed.

1866 Mr. Hardy as a decadent, 384–390. **A. J. Butler.** Signed.

1867 The imperial note in British statesmanship, 391–400. **G. R. Parkin.** Signed.

1868 The Unionist leaders: Lord Salisbury (No. I; no more published), 401–411. **H. D. Traill.** Signed.

1869 Kaffir finance, 412–423. **W. R. Lawson.** Signed.

1870 A recent visit to Japan, 424–434. **Arthur Griffith-Boscawen.** Signed A. G. Boscawen; Contents adds "M.P."; see *WWW*/1950.

1871 The Education Bill, 1896, 435–448. **Joseph R. Diggle.** Signed.

VOLUME 27, JUNE 1896

1872 Episodes of the month, 449–469. **L. J. Maxse.** Cf. no. 1456.

1873 The relations between the United States and Great Britain, 470–482. **J. B. Moore.** Signed; p. 470n. states that the author was "Assistant-Secretary of State in the United States . . ."

1874 Justice to Egypt, 483–488. **Thomas Henry Farrer.** Signed Farrer [Baron Farrer].

1875 Arthur Young, 489–504. **Leslie Stephen.** Signed; repr. *Studies*, I.

1876 Editors, 505–515. Signed: A Contributor. (See no. 1898.)

1877 South Africa, 516–530. **H. O. Arnold Forster.** Signed.

1878 Two years in Rhodesia: a French view of the Chartered Company, 531–545. **Lionel Decle.** Signed.

1879 The money of the Far East, 546–554. **Arthur George V. Peel.** Signed George Peel; Contents adds "Hon."; see *WWW*/1960.

1880 Some gossiping reflections [on foreign affairs], 555–568. **Frederick Greenwood.** Signed.

1881 Union, spiritual or ecclesiastical? 569–575. **William Boyd Carpenter.** Signed W. B. Ripon [Bishop of Ripon].

1882 Emancipation from the Jews, 576–592. **William Francis Barry.** Signed A Quarterly Reviewer; writer claims, p. 576, an art. on the modern Jew in *Quarterly Rev.* "at the beginning of the year": see evidence for *QR* no. 2653, *Index*, I, 777, 805.

VOLUME 27, JULY 1896

1883   Episodes of the month, 593–613. **L. J. Maxse.** Cf. no. 1456.

1884   The historic protest of the Church of England, and the question of reunion with Rome, 614–625. **William Sinclair.** Signed; Contents assigns to "Archdeacon of London"; see *WWW*/1928.

1885   Oliver Wendell Holmes, 626–641. **Leslie Stephen.** Signed; repr. *Studies*, II.

1886   A plea for amateur artists, 642–652. **Maria Theresa Earle.** Signed.

1887   The commercial federation of the Empire, 653–662. **J. G. Colmer.** Signed; Contents adds "C.M.G."; see *WWW*/1940.

1888   The science of change of air, 663–672. **Louis Robinson.** Signed; Contents adds "M.D."

1889   Canada and the Empire, 673–685. **G. M. Grant.** Signed; Cover adds "Principal" and "D.D. (Queen's University, Canada)"; *DNB*, 2nd suppl.

1890   The American silver rebellion, 686–700. **T. E. Powell.** Signed.

1891   Cycling in the desert, 701–709. **D. G. Hogarth.** Signed.

1892   The injustice of rural rating, 710–718. **J. St. Loe Strachey.** Signed.

1893   Mr. Rhodes' raid, 719–736. **L. J. Maxse.** Signed.

VOLUME 27, AUGUST 1896

1894   Episodes of the month, 737–761. **L. J. Maxse.** Cf. no. 1456.

1895   Mrs. Meynell's two books of essays [*Rhythm of Life* and *Colour of Life*], 762–770. **George Meredith.** Signed.

1896   Mr. Chamberlain, 771–782. **B. C. Skottowe.** Signed.

1897   The monetary situation and the United States, 783–792. **Francis A. Walker.** Signed. (See nos. 1909, 1910.)

1898   Contributors, 793–801. Signed: An Editor.

1899   The unpopularity of the House of Commons, 802–815. **Thomas Mackay.** Signed as in no. 1255.

1900   The secret of Catholicism [Zola's *Rome*], 816–833. **William Francis Barry.** Signed William Barry; Contents adds "Rev." and "D.D."; see *WWW*/1940.

1901   Five years' political and social reform

in New Zealand, 834–850. **W. P. Reeves.** Signed.

1902   A midsummer night's marriage, 851–871. **John Meade Falkner.** Signed Meade Falkner; Contents adds initial "J.": see *DNB*/1940.

1903   Our naval weakness, 872–880. **Ben Tillett.** Signed; Contents adds "Alderman."

VOLUME 28, SEPTEMBER 1896

1904   Episodes of the month, 1–25. **L. J. Maxse.** Cf. no. 1456.

1905   Mr. Gladstone's return, 27–35. **H. D. Traill.** Signed.

1906   The Christian motive, 36–46. **Bernard Holland.** Signed.

1907   The Family Council in France, 47–58. **Matilda Betham-Edwards.** Signature.

1908   The American crisis (No. I), 59–64. **Thomas Lloyd.** Signed T. Lloyd; said in no. 1929, p. 269, to be associated with *The Statist*: see *BMCat.*

1909   The American crisis (No. II), 64–70. **Arthur George V. Peel.** Signed as in no. 1879.

1910   The American crisis (No. III), 70–74. **J. H. Tritton.** Signed.

1911   Sir Henry Irving's claims, 75–86. **William Wallace,** 1843–1921. Signed; man cited was a correspondent of L. J. Maxse: see Maxse Papers.

1912   Crocodile tears and fur seals, 87–92. **Charles Hibbert Tupper.** Signed.

1913   The origin of Oxford, 93–102. **Arthur F. Leach.** Signed.

1914   A bird's eye view of the north-west frontier [of India], 103–118. **John Dickson-Poynder.** Signed; Contents adds "Sir" and "M.P."

1915   The study of man, 119–125. **W. M. Flinders Petrie.** Signed.

1916   The coming crisis in consols, 126–138. **Hugh Chisholm.** Signed.

1917   Correspondence: Tithe redemption: a solution, 139–140, signed **Compton Reade.**

VOLUME 28, OCTOBER 1896

1918   Episodes of the month, 141–164. **L. J. Maxse.** Cf. no. 1456.

1919   The Empire and the gold standard, 165–179. **Henry Hucks Gibbs.** Signed Aldenham [Baron Aldenham].

1920   Anglophobia, 180–188. **Frederick A. Maxse.** Signed.

1921 The political outlook in the United States, 189–198. **B. R. Tillman.** Signed; Contents adds title "Senator"; see *DAB*.

1922 A visitor's glimpse of the contest [U.S. political campaign], 199–204. **A. Symons Eccles.** Signed.

1923 The aesthetics of the dinner table, 205–219. **Arthur Kenney-Herbert.** Signed as in no. 1672.

1924 Russia's strength, 220–227. **Spenser Wilkinson.** Signed; repr. *War and Policy*, 1900.

1925 The apology of Dives, 228–241. **William Francis Barry.** Signed as in no. 1900, with same titles in Contents.

1926 Canada as a field for mining investment, 242–251. **George M. Dawson.** Signed.

1927 The real Robert Elsmere, 252–261. **F. Reginald Statham.** Signed.

1928 The state of the bar, 262–268. **S. A. T. Rowlatt.** Signed.

1929 The bimetallic side of the American crisis (No. I), 269–276. **T. E. Powell.** Signed, with title "Vice-President of the Bimetallic League."

1930 The bimetallic side of the American crisis (No. II), 276–280. **Arnold Hepburn.** Signed, with title "Assistant Secretary of the Bimetallic League."

1931 The bimetallic side of the American crisis (No. III), 280–284. **Hermann Schmidt.** Signed, with title "Vice-President . . . of the Executive Council of the Bimetallic League."

VOLUME 28, NOVEMBER 1896

1932 Episodes of the month, 14 unnumbered pages and 285–296. **L. J. Maxse** and unidentified collaborator. Maxse usually wrote arts. with this title (cf. no. 1456, etc.); unnumbered pages are written from N.Y., and vol. 29, p. 135, says that when Maxse was in the U.S. studying the presidential campaign, he was most impressed by moderation of the followers of Bryan, which receives the emphasis in these pages; pp. 285–296 show evidence of another author, perhaps Frederick A. Maxse, father of the editor and a contributor, who would have been old enough to remember the Orsini bomb attack of 1858, which is recalled on p. 295.

1933 The Church and the Unionist Party, 297–308. Signed: A Layman.

1934 Lord Rosebery's resignation, 309–314. Signed: Conservative M.P.

1935 The value of Constantinople, 315–324. **Spenser Wilkinson.** Signed; repr. *War and Policy*, 1900.

1936 The government's opportunity, 325–333. **Joseph R. Diggle.** Signed.

1937 Homeric warfare, 334–344. **J. B. Bury.** Signed.

1938 The economic aspects of the bicycle, 345–353. **Arthur Shadwell.** Signed as in no. 1744. (See no. 1975.)

1939 Trafalgar and to-day, 354–369. **H. W. Wilson.** Signed; Contents adds "Author of *Ironclads in Action*"; see *BMCat*.

1940 Principles of local taxation, 370–377. **Edwin Cannan.** Signed.

1941 Untaxed imports and home industries, 378–383. **W. Farrer Ecroyd.** Signed.

1942 The functions of a governor-general, 384–389. **Charles Hibbert Tupper.** Signed. (See no. 1955.)

1943 The working of the Old-Age Relief Law in Copenhagen, 390–399. **Edith Sellers.** Signed.

1944 The American elections of 1896, 400–405. **Moreton Frewen.** Signed.

1945 The metropolitan water question, 406–428. **Lionel Holland.** Signed.

VOLUME 28, DECEMBER 1896

1946 Episodes of the month, 429–451. **A. Maurice Low** and, prob., **L. J. Maxse.** In pp. 429–442, written from Denver, use of first person singular pronoun suggests Low (cf. no. 1971); remark on p. 430 about distance between N.Y. and the West is claimed by Low in no. 2062, p. 82; pp. 443–451 state usual editorial opinions, strongly indicating Maxse (cf. no. 1456).

1947 The presidential contest (No. I): Altgeld of Illinois, 452–473. **Francis F. Browne.** Signed; Contents adds "Editor of *The Dial*, Chicago"; see *DAB*.

1948 The presidential contest (No. II): notes on the currency question, 473–476. **W. E. Chandler.** Signed.

1949 Church reform, 477–488. **Arthur Griffith-Boscawen.** Signed A. Griffith-Boscawen; cf. no. 1385.

1950 Denominational schools and the Government, 489–504. **J. Frome Wilkinson.** Signed J. Frome-Wilkinson; Contents adds Rev.; see Foster.

1951 Lord Leighton's sketches, 505–518. **Emilie Isabel Barrington.** Signed.

1952 Llanthony Abbey and two of its priors, 519–531. **Arthur C. Benson.** Signed.

1953 A guess at the origin of *Hamlet*, 532–542. **Arthur T. Lyttelton.** Signed.

1954 The native problem in South Africa, 543–553. **William F. Bailey.** Signed.

1955 The functions of a governor-general, 554–558. **W. P. Reeves.** Signed; Contents adds "Agent-General for New Zealand"; see *WWW*/1940.

1956 Registered Friendly Societies for women, 559–566. **Elizabeth S. Haldane.** Signed.

1957 Some remarks on modern nurses, 567–572. **Emma L. Watson.** Signed. (See no. 1970.)

VOLUME 28, JANUARY 1897

1958 Episodes of the month, 573–597. **L. J. Maxse.** Cf. no. 1456; opinions on pp. 588–593 are similar to those described as Maxse's in vol. 29, p. 135.

1959 The United States and Cuba: a new Armenia, 598–604. **W. Hallett Phillips.** Signed [misspelled Philips]: see *LCCat*.

1960 Trifling with national defence, 605–615. **Spenser Wilkinson.** Signed; repr. *War and Policy*, 1900.

1961 Lord Pembroke, 616–629. **A. V. Dicey.** Signed.

1962 Some Irish history and a moral, 630–640. **Bernard Holland.** Signed.

1963 Ibsenism (No. I): the craze, 641–647. **H. D. Traill.** Signed.

1964 Ibsenism (No. II): *Little Eyolf*, 648–653. **Ronald McNeill.** Signed.

1965 A manufactured land question, 654–667. **C. Morgan Richardson.** Signed with a hyphen; Contents and *BMCat.* give name as cited.

1966 Hampton Court in by-gone years, 668–680. **Eleanor Vere Boyle.** Signed.

1967 Two British battles (No. I): "It was a glorious victory"—Sluys, 1340, 681–687. **Alfred T. Story.** Signed.

1968 Two British battles (No. II): The Battle of Hastings, 687–695. **J. H. Round.** Signed.

1969 National education: a proposal, 696–700. **John E. Dorington.** Signed.

1970 Modern nurses: a reply [to no. 1957], 701–706. **Nancy Paul.** Signed.

1971 The month in America, 707–716. **Alfred Maurice Low.** First installment of a regular monthly series of which Low is known to have written nos. 1983, 2021, and 2062 onward; use of first person singular pronoun with frequent cross references throughout the series indicates a single author; sections of this art. are claimed in no. 2125, p. 898, and in no. 2161, pp. 405–406.

VOLUME 28, FEBRUARY 1897

1972 Episodes of the month, 717–738. **L. J. Maxse.** Cf. no. 1456.

1973 The over-taxation of Ireland, 739–751. **Charles Owen O'Conor.** Signed, p. 751, O'Conor Don: see *DNB*. With The Report of the Financial Relations Commission, 751–768.

1974 Wordsworth's youth, 769–786. **Leslie Stephen.** Signed; repr. *Studies*, I.

1975 The hidden dangers of cycling, 787–796. **Arthur Shadwell.** Signed as in no. 1744.

1976 Bimetallism in Europe (No. I): France, 797–803. **Edmond d'Artois.** Signed, with title "Assistant General Secretary, French Bimetallic League."

1977 Bimetallism in Europe (No. II): Germany, 803–808. **Otto Arendt.** Signed, with title "Member of Prussian Diet"; see *NDB*.

1978 Bimetallism in Europe (No. III): Great Britain, 808–815. **Henry Hucks Gibbs.** Signed Aldenham [Baron Aldenham.]

1979 The rebellion in the Philippine Islands, 816–825. **John Foreman.** Signed.

1980 Curates, 826–832. **Anthony C. Deane.** Signed.

1981 Food crops and famine in India, 833–843. **William E. Bear.** Signed.

1982 Lord Roberts in Afghanistan, 844–853. **Spenser Wilkinson.** Signed.

1983 The month in America, 854–866. **A. Maurice Low.** Attr. by editor, p. 724n.

VOLUME 29, MARCH 1897

1984 Episodes of the month, 1–29. **L. J. Maxse.** Cf. no. 1456.

1985 Some home truths about Rhodesia, 30–41. **W. E. Fairbridge.** Signed; Cover gives "Editor of *The Rhodesian Herald*."

1986 The defence of London, 42–50. **Spenser Wilkinson.** Signed; repr. with revisions, *War and Policy*, 1900.

1987 Gibbon's autobiography, 51–67. **Leslie Stephen.** Signed L. Stephen; repr. *Studies*, I.

1988 Reminiscences of the Oxford Union: an address to the Sydney University Union, 68–83. **B. R. Wise.** Signed.

1989 Mr. [Grover] Cleveland, 84–98. **Edward P. Clark.** Signed, with description "An Editorial Writer for the New York *Evening Post*."

1990 The Irish claim and some replies, 99–112. **Bernard Holland.** Signed.

1991 "Hidden dangers": a reply [to no.

1975], 113–117. **Frederick Pollock.** Signed.

1992 John Bull and silver, 118–129. **F. J. Faraday.** Signed.

1993 "The other grace" [on fictional heroines], 130–134. **Jane H. Findlater.** Signed; repr. *Stones from a Glass House,* 1904.

1994 The month in America, 135–146. **A. Maurice Low.** Pages 138–139 are claimed in no. 2004, p. 270; cf. no. 1971.

VOLUME 29, APRIL 1897

1995 Episodes of the month, 149–168. **L. J. Maxse.** Cf. no. 1456. (See no. 2005.)

1996 Trade and training in Germany, 169–188. **Philip Magnus.** Signed.

1997 Helpless Europe, 189–199. **Spenser Wilkinson.** Signed; repr. *War and Policy,* 1900.

1998 Arthur Hugh Clough, 200–212. **F. Reginald Statham.** Signed.

1999 Fishing in West Africa, 213–227. **Mary H. Kingsley.** Signed; repr. *West African Studies,* 1899.

2000 President McKinley, 228–237. **A. Maurice Low.** Signed.

2001 A recent glance at Spain, 238–242. **John Foreman.** Signed.

2002 The story of a philanthropic pawnshop, 243–252. **Edith Sellers.** Signed.

2003 The patriotic editor in war, 253–263. **P. H. Colomb.** Signed.

2004 The month in America, 264–275. **A. Maurice Low.** Pages 272–273 are claimed in no. 2021, pp. 439–440; cf. no. 1971. (Letter, pp. 478–481, signed **Moreton Frewen.**)

2005 Episodes of the month [supplement to no. 1995], 278–292. **L. J. Maxse.** Cf. no. 1456.

2006 Appendix: reply of the Bimetallic League to the memorial of the Gold Standard Defence Association, 293–295. **Henry Hucks Gibbs.** Signed. With signatures of the League members, 295–300.

VOLUME 29, MAY 1897

2007 Episodes of the month, 301–324. **L. J. Maxse.** Cf. no. 1456.

2008 The case for the Transvaal, 325–351. **F. Reginald Statham.** Signed.

2009 Europe and Greece, 352–363. **Frederick A. Maxse.** Signed.

2010 Canadian poetry, 364–381. **John A. Cooper.** Signed; described, p. 302, as editor of *Canadian Mag.*

2011 In defence of worldly mothers, 382–391. **Ellen Desart.** Signed; Contents adds "Countess."

2012 The spoliation of Irish landlords: introductory, 392–393. **James Hamilton.** Signed Abercorn [Duke of Abercorn].

2013 The spoliation of Irish landlords (No. I), 393–402. **James C. Lowry.** Signed, with address "County Tyrone"; Contents adds "Colonel."

2014 The spoliation of Irish landlords (No. II), 402–404. **Anthony Traill.** Signed.

2015 The spoliation of Irish landlords (No. III), 405–406. **Richard Bagwell.** Signed.

2016 The spoliation of Irish landlords (No. IV), 406–407. **George O'Callaghan-Westropp.** Signed G. O'Callaghan Westropp; Contents adds "Capt.": see *WWW*/1950.

2017 The spoliation of Irish landlords (No. V), 407–409. **James Wilson,** 1832–1907. Signed, with title "D.L." and address "County Longford"; see Burke's *Ireland.*

2018 The spoliation of Irish landlords (No. VI), 409–414. **H. de F. Montgomery.** Signed.

2019 Shipping charges and the fall of prices, 415–420. **A. W. Flux.** Signed.

2020 English weather, 421–432. **C. A. Whitmore.** Signed.

2021 The month in America, 433–442. **A. Maurice Low.** Attr. by editor, p. 319n.

2022 *Jowett's Life,* 443–458. **Leslie Stephen.** Signed; repr. *Studies,* II.

2023 A colonial chronicle, 459–477. **L. J. Maxse.** This monthly series (later called "Greater Britain"), an offshoot of the "Episodes of the month" (see no. 1995, p. 168n.), is discussed as Maxse's by knowledgable correspondents (F. I. Maxse, Nov. 23, 1897; W. H. Hutchinson to L. J. Maxse, Apr. 6, 1898; and W. P. Schreiner to L. J. Maxse, Aug. 9, 1898, Maxse Papers, MS. 446); author indicates intimate editorial knowledge by frequent references to matters published in the same numbers (vol. 30, pp. 307, 947; vol. 32, p. 147; vol. 33, p. 341, and vol. 34, p. 958).

VOLUME 29, JUNE 1897

2024 Episodes of the month, 485–513. **L. J. Maxse.** Cf. no. 1456.

2025 War through peace spectacles, 514–524. **G. S. Clarke.** Signed.

2026 The downfall of Greece, 525–535. **H. W. Wilson.** Signed.

2027 The [Royal] Academy, 536–541. **D. S. MacColl.** Signed.

2028 The retrospect of the reign, 542–556. **T. E. Kebbel.** Signed.

2029 Newman and Renan, 557–576. **William Francis Barry.** Signed as in no. 1900.

2030 Ireland and bimetallism, 577–582. **E. F. V. Knox.** Signed.

2031 The month in America, 583–593. **A. Maurice Low.** Pages 590–591 are claimed in no. 2044, p. 748; cf. no. 1971.

2032 London as a Jubilee city, 594–603. **H. Heathcote Statham.** Signed.

2033 Archbishop Benson, 604–614. **E. C. Wickham.** Signed.

2034 A colonial chronicle, 615–632. **L. J. Maxse.** Cf. no. 2023.

VOLUME 29, JULY 1897

2035 Episodes of the month, 635–659. **L. J. Maxse.** Cf. no. 1456.

2036 British interests and the Wolcott Commission (No. I): the monometallist view, 660–665. **Thomas Lloyd.** Signed as in no. 1908.

2037 British interests and the Wolcott Commission (No. II): the bimetallist view, 666–676. **Elijah Helm.** Signed; Cover adds "Secretary of the Manchester Chamber of Commerce."

2038 British interests and the Wolcott Commission (No. III): the monetary relations of Great Britain and the colonies, 676–687. **F. J. Faraday.** Signed.

2039 The present position of the Anglican Church, 688–702. **Bernard Holland.** Signed.

2040 The new *Nelson* [biography by A. T. Mahan], 703–710. **Spenser Wilkinson.** Signed; repr. *War and Policy*, 1900, as "Nelson."

2041 Women, 711–720. **Ellen Desart.** Signed.

2042 Europe's new invalid [Spain], 721–734. **John Foreman.** Signed.

2043 The multiplication of musicians, 735–743. **J. Cuthbert Hadden.** Signed.

2044 The month in America, 744–755. **A. Maurice Low.** Page 747 is claimed in no. 2092, p. 438; cf. no. 1971.

2045 War, trade, and food supply, 756–769. **G. S. Clarke.** Signed.

2046 A colonial chronicle, 770–792. **L. J. Maxse.** Cf. no. 2023.

VOLUME 29, AUGUST 1897

2047 Episodes of the month, 793–819. **L. J. Maxse.** Cf. no. 1456; in no. 2067, p. 178, reference to "editorial vanity" in this art.

2048 An understanding between Russia and Great Britain, 820–838. Signed in Contents: An Official.

2049 Golden Rhodesia: a revelation, 839–851. **J. Y. F. Blake.** Signed.

2050 The uses of humour, 852–866. **James Sully.** Signed.

2051 Concerning pugilism, 867–876. **William Broadfoot.** Signed W. Broadfoot; Contents adds "Major, R.E.": see *WWW/* 1928.

2052 Oxford Liberalism, 877–891. **R. A. Johnson** and **O. W. Richards.** Signed; Cover adds that Johnson was "lately President of the Oxford Union" (see *WWW/*1940); Owen William Richards was his contemporary at Oxford (see *Landed Gentry*).

2053 The month in America, 892–903. **A. Maurice Low.** On page 899 author claims no. 2044; cf. no. 1971.

2054 The sequel to Gibbon's love-story, 904–915. **Edith Lyttelton.** Signed.

2055 Naval warfare of the future, 916–926. **P. H. Colomb.** Signed. (See no. 2080.)

2056 A colonial chronicle, 927–944. **L. J. Maxse.** Cf. no. 2023.

VOLUME 30, SEPTEMBER 1897

2057 Episodes of the month, 1–30. **L. J. Maxse.** Cf. no. 1456.

2058 Shall agriculture perish? 31–45. **William E. Bear.** Signed.

2059 The British civilian in India, 46–60. **Herbert Birdwood.** Signed.

2060 Johnsoniana, 61–76. **Leslie Stephen.** Signed; repr. *Studies*, I.

2061 The worship of athletics, 77–81. **A. H. Gilkes.** Signed.

2062 The month in America, 82–94. **A. Maurice Low.** Assigned in Contents. Postscript, 94–95, by **L. J. Maxse**— signed Editor *N.R.*

2063 The treatment of ancient buildings, 96–110. **H. Heathcote Statham.** Signed.

2064 A French naval hero [Jean Bart], 111–121. **Alfred T. Story.** Signed.

2065 African religion and law, 122–139. **Mary H. Kingsley.** Signed; repr. *West African Studies*, 1964.

2066 A colonial chronicle, 140–162. **L. J. Maxse.** Cf. no. 2023.

VOLUME 30, OCTOBER 1897

2067 Episodes of the month, 163–191. **L. J. Maxse.** Cf. no. 1456; reference, p. 178, to "editorial vanity."

2068 The risings on the Indian frontier, 192–206. **Robert C. Low.** Signed R. C. Low; Contents gives "Lt.-General Sir Robert Low."

2069 The Canadian enigma, 207–216. **Arthur Shadwell.** Signed as in no. 1744.

2070 Native Rhodesia, 217–225. **J. Y. F. Blake.** Signed. (See nos. 2083, 2140.)

2071 Run-getting [in cricket], 226–232. **Gilbert L. Jessop.** Signed.

2072 Great Britain's opportunity (No. I): an appeal to the government, 233–238. **Edward Sassoon.** Signed.

2073 Great Britain's opportunity (No. II): our contributions, 238–241. **Charles Hoare.** Signed.

2074 Great Britain's opportunity (No. III): silver v. cotton, 241–246. **Albert Simpson.** Signed; described, p. 191, as "a prominent Lancashire employer"; Cover adds "J. P."

2075 Great Britain's opportunity (No. IV): the operatives' view, 246–250. **James Mawdsley.** Signed; Contents adds "J.P."

2076 Great Britain's opportunity (No. V): can France and the United States maintain the ratio of 15½ to 1? 250–257. **H. R. Beeton.** Signed.

2077 George Gissing's novels, 258–266. **Frederick Dolman.** Signed.

2078 The month in America, 267–279. **A. Maurice Low.** Assigned in Contents.

2079 The religious issue at the London School Board election, 280–283. **Evelyn Cecil.** Signed.

2080 Naval warfare of the present and future: a reply to Admiral Colomb [no. 2055], 284–296. **H. J. May.** Signed.

2081 A colonial chronicle, 297–322. **L. J. Maxse.** Cf. no. 2023.

VOLUME 30, NOVEMBER 1897

2082 Episodes of the month, 323–353. **L. J. Maxse.** Cf. no. 1456; authorship of pp. 344–346 is acknowledged in no. 2103.

2083 Native Rhodesia: a rejoinder [to no. 2070], 354–359. **Hugh Marshall Hole.** Signed.

2084 The working of compulsory arbitration in labour disputes, 360–370. **W. Pember Reeves.** Signed.

2085 Life of Tennyson, 371–390. **Leslie Stephen.** Signed; repr. *Studies*, II.

2086 The Harrow and Eton match, 391–395. Signed: An Old Harrow Captain.

2087 Great Britain's duty [in bimetallism crisis] (No. I): a Radical's appeal to the government, 396–403. **R. L. Everett.** Signed.

2088 Great Britain's duty (No. II): a panic, 403–405. **J. P. Heseltine.** Signed.

2089 Great Britain's duty (No. III): India, 405–411. **A. S. Ghosh.** Signed; Cover adds "Prof. of Economics, Calcutta University."

2090 Great Britain's duty (No. IV): Greater Britain, 411–414. **Donald Reid, Jr.** Signed, with address "Dunedin, [New Zealand]."

2091 Great Britain's duty (No. V): "the bimetallic intrigue": an elementary exposition, 414–430. **L. J. Maxse.** Signed on p. 427.

2092 The month in America, 431–444. **A. Maurice Low.** Signed in Contents.

2093 A school journey in Germany, 445–452. **Catherine I. Dodd.** Signed.

2094 The true place of the volunteer force in imperial defence, 453–470. **Eustace Balfour.** Signed; Contents adds "Lieut.-Colonel."

2095 A colonial chronicle, 471–490. **L. J. Maxse.** Cf. no. 2023.

VOLUME 30, DECEMBER 1897

2096 Episodes of the month, 491–518. **L. J. Maxse.** Cf. no. 1456.

2097 The ruin of the West Indies, 519–534. **Henry De Worms.** Signed Pirbright [Baron Pirbright].

2098 Rural administration in Ireland, 535–541. **Richard Bagwell.** Signed.

2099 Prisoners in the witness-box, 542–546. **Alfred Lyttelton.** Signed. (See no. 2113.)

2100 The state of Spain, 547–560. **John Foreman.** Signed.

2101 The economic problem (No. I): an Australian appeal, 561–566. **F. A. Keating.** Signed.

2102 The economic problem (No. II): the world's interest in the reopening of the Indian mints, 566–573. **F. J. Faraday.** Signed.

2103 The economic problem (No. III): an apology to Lord Farrer [concerning no. 2082], 573–577. **L. J. Maxse.** Signed Editor *National Review*. (Letter, p. 744, by **Thomas Henry Farrer**—signed Farrer [Baron Farrer]; reply, pp. 744–750, by Maxse—signed Editor *National Review*.)

2104 The Queen as a Mahomedan sovereign, 578–590. **Herbert Birdwood.** Signed.

2105 The month in America, 591–604. **A. Maurice Low.** Signed.

2106 A cross-bench view of foreign missions, 605–618. **H. Hensley Henson.** Signed.

2107 The importation of German, 619–635. **Leslie Stephen.** Signed; repr. *Studies*, II.

2108 A colonial chronicle, 636–658. **L. J. Maxse.** Cf. no. 2023.

VOLUME 30, JANUARY 1898

2109 Episodes of the month, 659–686. **L. J. Maxse.** Cf. no. 1456.

2110 The test of loyalty: an object lesson from the West Indies, 687–693. **Nevile Lubbock.** Signed.

2111 The trade-union triumph: Allen v. Flood, 694–714. **Godfrey Lushington.** Signed.

2112 Suicide by typhoid fever, 715–727. **Arthur Shadwell.** Signed as in no. 1744.

2113 Prisoners in the witness-box, 728–730. **Evelyn Ashley.** Signed.

2114 The month in America, 731–743. **A. Maurice Low.** Signed.

2115 A defence of the muzzle, 751–761. **Gerald Arbuthnot.** Signed.

2116 Edmund Burke, statesman and prophet, 762–778. **William Francis Barry.** Signed as in no. 1900.

2117 Education and the Conservative party, 779–786. **Athelstan Riley.** Signed.

2118 A colonial chronicle, 787–810. **L. J. Maxse.** Cf. no. 2023.

VOLUME 30, FEBRUARY 1898

2119 Episodes of the month, 811–836. **L. J. Maxse.** Cf. no. 1456.

2120 Sir Wilfrid Laurier at Washington, 837–843. **J. W. Longley.** Signed; identified, p. 947, as Attorney-General of Nova Scotia.

2121 The Russian advance on India, 844–858. **E. C. Ringler Thomson.** Signed, with titles "Late Assistant Agent to the Governor-General of India and H. M. Vice-Consul for Khorasan and Sistan."

2122 Mining and politics in the Transvaal, 859–866. Signed: M.

2123 An Eton master [William Johnson], 867–877. **Bernard Holland.** Signed.

2124 Raiding the clergy, 878–885. **Arthur Griffith-Boscawen.** Signed as in no. 1477.

2125 The month in America, 886–899. **A. Maurice Low.** Signed.

2126 The tragedy of Arthur Crawford [public trial in Bombay], 900–917. Signed: Circumspecte Agatis.

2127 Mind as disease-producer, 918–928.

Herbert Coryn. Signed; Contents adds "Dr."

2128 The British bounty to Asia, 929–935. **H. Kopsch.** Signed. Postscript, 935–936, by **L. J. Maxse**—signed Editor, *N.R.*

2129 The engineering struggle, 937–946. **Benjamin C. Browne.** Signed.

2130 A colonial chronicle, 947–970. **L. J. Maxse.** Cf. no. 2023.

VOLUME 31, MARCH 1898

2131 Episodes of the month, 1–28. **L. J. Maxse.** Cf. no. 1456.

2132 Face to face in West Africa, 29–38. **Frederick A. Maxse.** Signed.

2133 The British army, 39–52. **E. G. Bulwer.** Signed.

2134 The Indian crisis and a remedy, 53–62. **Herbert C. Gibbs.** Signed.

2135 The sorrows of scribblers—being the confessions of a magazine contributor, 63–74.

2136 The higher rascality [finance], 75–86. **Hugh E. M. Stutfield.** Signed.

2137 The coming partition of China, 87–95. **John Foreman.** Signed.

2138 An artist of many methods [Mortimer Menpes], 96–104. **A. L. Baldry.** Signed.

2139 The month in America, 105–117. **A. Maurice Low.** Signed. Postscript, 117, by **L. J. Maxse**—signed Editor *N.R.*

2140 Second thoughts on Rhodesia, 118–129. **J. Y. F. Blake.** Signed.

2141 The Irish Land Acts at work: Report of the Royal Commissioners upon the procedure and practice and methods of valuation followed under the Irish Land Acts and Land Purchase Acts, 130–144. **Anthony Traill.** Signed A. Traill; Contents gives first name. Postscript, 144, by **L. J. Maxse**—signed Editor *N.R.* (Letter, pp. 776–780, signed **Anthony Traill.**)

2142 A colonial chronicle, 145–161. **L. J. Maxse.** Cf. no. 2023.

2143 Correspondence: The sugar crash and after? 162–164, by **Charles G. Walpole** —signed C. G. Walpole; Contents gives first name and adds "Sir."

VOLUME 31, APRIL 1898

2144 Episodes of the month, 165–190. **L. J. Maxse.** Cf. no. 1456.

2145 Great Britain and her rivals in Asia, 191–205. **Arminius Vambéry.** Signed H. Vambéry: see *BMCat.* under "Vambéry,

Hermann"; Cover gives "Prof. A. Vambéry."

2146 The policy of Russia, 206–217. **A. V. Markoff.** Signed; Cover adds "Dr." and "F.R.G.S."

2147 Russia's sinews of war, 218–232. **W. R. Lawson.** Signed.

2148 The army as a career; a voice from the ranks, 233–243. Signed: T. Atkins [Tommy Atkins].

2149 The "religious" novel, 244–252. **Anthony C. Deane.** Signed.

2150 The month in America, 253–262. **A. Maurice Low.** Signed.

2151 Our defeat and some morals [London politics], 263–268. **C. A. Whitmore.** Signed.

2152 Constitution making in Australia, 269–279. **W. Harrison Moore.** Signed.

2153 Should inebriates be imprisoned? 280–291. **Arthur Shadwell.** Signed as in no. 1744.

2154 Front bench invertebrates, 292–301. **H. W. Wilson.** Signed.

2155 A colonial chronicle, 302–324. **L. J. Maxse.** Cf. no. 2023. (Letter, pp. 626–628, by **Melius de Villiers**—signed An Afrikander; de Villiers to Maxse, June 27, 1898, from Bloemfontein, Maxse Papers, MS. 446, sends thanks for publishing his letter on the Transvaal in the "current number.")

VOLUME 31, MAY 1898

2156 Episodes of the month, 325–350. **L. J. Maxse.** Cf. no. 1456.

2157 The advance in the Soudan, 351–360. **Charles Williams.** Signed.

2158 Surprise in war, from a military and a national point of view, 361–373. **T. Miller Maguire.** Signed.

2159 The Chartered Company [South Africa], 374–385. **L. March-Phillipps.** Signed.

2160 Handicaps [in horse racing], 386–402. **G. Herbert Stutfield.** Signed.

2161 The month in America, 403–416. **A. Maurice Low.** Signed. Postscript, 416–417, by **L. J. Maxse**—signed Editor, *N.R.*

2162 The autocrat of the sick-room, 418–421. **Margaret Vane.** Signed.

2163 A publicist's view of France, 422–431. **Matilda Betham-Edwards.** Signature.

2164 Plunder by death duties, 432–448. **C. Morgan Richardson.** Signed as in no. 1965.

2165 A colonial chronicle, 449–471. **L. J. Maxse.** Cf. no. 2023.

2166 Correspondence: Indian currency, 472–476, signed **William Fowler.**

VOLUME 31, JUNE 1898

2167 Episodes of the month, 477–501. **L. J. Maxse.** Cf. no. 1456.

2168 Great Britain v. France and Russia, 502–522. **J. N. Hampson.** Signed.

2169 First impressions of the [Spanish-American] War, 523–535. **P. H. Colomb.** Signed. (See no. 2191.)

2170 Mr. Gladstone—fragments of personal reminiscences, 536–540. **Evelyn Ashley.** Signed.

2171 The truth about the Dreyfus case, 541–558. **Frederick C. Conybeare.** Signed Huguenot; claimed by man cited in no. 2186, pp. 755–756; cf. no. 2218.

2172 The international exhibition of art at Knightsbridge, 559–564. **D. S. MacColl.** Signed.

2173 The month in America, 565–577. **A. Maurice Low.** Signed.

2174 A descendant of the prophet: in memoriam, Sir Syed Ahmad Khan Bahadur, 578–586. **Theodore Morison.** Signed.

2175 Two foreign criticisms of Australasian democracy, 587–601. **W. P. Reeves.** Signed.

2176 A colonial chronicle, 602–625. **L. J. Maxse.** Cf. no. 2023.

VOLUME 31, JULY 1898

2177 Episodes of the month, 629–653. **L. J. Maxse.** Cf. no. 1456.

2178 Our future policy in China, 654–670. **Alexander Michie.** Signed A. Mitchie; see *DNB.*

2179 The truth about the *Maine* disaster, 671–682. **H. W. Wilson.** Signed.

2180 The unreadiness of the volunteers, 683–693. **Lonsdale Hale.** Signed.

2181 Mr. Kensit [zealous Protestant and anti-Ritualist]—and after, 694–699. **H. Hensley Henson.** Signed.

2182 Is cricket degenerating? 700–709. **H. F. Abell.** Signed.

2183 The month in America, 710–720. **A. Maurice Low.** Signed.

2184 India in deep waters, 721–733. **Robert H. Elliot.** Signed.

2185 The street music question, 734–744. **H. Heathcote Statham.** Signed.

2186 The military terror in France, 745–756. **L. J. Maxse.** Signed.

2187 A colonial chronicle, 757–775. **L. J. Maxse.** Cf. no. 2023.

VOLUME 31, AUGUST 1898

2188 Episodes of the month, 781–801. **L. J. Maxse.** Cf. no. 1456.

2189 The Russian bogey, 802–813. **Arnold White.** Signed.

2190 M. Cavaignac's vindication of Captain Dreyfus, 814–834. **L. J. Maxse.** Signed.

2191 Second impressions of the [Spanish-American] War, 835–844. **P. H. Colomb.** Signed.

2192 Journalism as a profession, 845–855. **Arthur Shadwell.** Signed. (See no. 2214.)

2193 A reminiscence of Manila, 856–867. **Frank T. Bullen.** Signed.

2194 The report on old-age pensions, 868–885. **Lionel Holland.** Signed.

2195 The German elections, 886–895. **W. H. Dawson.** Signed.

2196 Married women in American society, 896–901. Signed: Maryland.

2197 The recent insurrections in Italy, 902–913. **Antonio de Viti de Marco.** Signed De Viti de Marco; Contents adds "Marquis"; see *LCCat*.

2198 A colonial chronicle, 914–932. **L. J. Maxse.** Cf. no. 2023.

VOLUME 32, SEPTEMBER 1898

2199 Episodes of the month, 1–28. **L. J. Maxse.** Cf. no. 1456.

2200 The Morocco question and the [Spanish-American] War, 29–35. **Walter B. Harris.** Signed.

2201 An Anglo-Russian understanding? 36–45. **H. W. Wilson.** Signed.

2202 The letters of an innocent [in English translation], 48–65. **Alfred Dreyfus.** Signed. Intro. note, 46–48, by **F. C. Conybeare**—signed Huguenot: see nos. 2171, 2218.

2203 A study in school children, 66–74. **Catherine I. Dodd.** Signed, with middle initial given as "J."; see *WWW/1940*.

2204 The month in America, 75–88. **A. Maurice Low.** Signed.

2205 The scientific work of Lord Rayleigh, 89–102. **Oliver Lodge.** Signed.

2206 Company promoting *à la mode*, 103–115. **W. R. Lawson.** Signed.

2207 A lady's impressions of the House of Commons (No. I), 116–122. Signed: Grille. (No. II is no. 2346.)

2208 French rights in Newfoundland, 123–

128. **Patrick Thomas McGrath.** Signed P. McGrath; Cover adds "St. Johns, Newfoundland": see Wallace.

2209 A colonial chronicle, 129–148. **L. J. Maxse.** Cf. no. 2023. (For continuation under new title, see no. 2220.)

VOLUME 32, OCTOBER 1898

2210 Episodes of the month, 149–173. **L. J. Maxse.** Cf. no. 1456.

2211 "A Daniel come to judgment," or, The War Office on its trial, 174–191. **H. O. Arnold-Forster.** Signed.

2212 India's currency problem, 192–200. **Nathan Meyer Rothschild.** Signed Rothschild [Baron Rothschild].

2213 The Tsar's manifesto, 201–210. **Arnold White.** Signed.

2214 Journalism as a career: a reply to "Journalism as a profession" [no. 2192], 211–219. **Sidney J. Low.** Signed A Veteran Journalist; attr. by D. Chapman-Huston, *The Lost Historian: A Memoir of Sir Sidney Low* (1936), p. 361, where it is dated Aug. 1898 in confusion with the art. to which Low is replying.

2215 The month in America, 220–229. **A. Maurice Low.** Signed.

2216 On some fresh facts indicating man's survival of death, 230–242. **Frederic W. H. Myers.** Signed.

2217 A Muhamadan university, 243–249. **Theodore Morison.** Signed.

2218 Side-lights on the Dreyfus case, 250–267. **Frederick C. Conybeare.** Signed, together with the pseudonym "Huguenot."

2219 The key to the mystery [of the Dreyfus case], 268–283. **L. J. Maxse.** Signed.

2220 Greater Britain [continuation of "A colonial chronicle," no. 2023, etc.], 284–300. **L. J. Maxse.** Cf. no. 2023.

VOLUME 32, NOVEMBER 1898

2221 Episodes of the month, 301–325. **L. J. Maxse.** Cf. no. 1456.

2222 Shall the Indian Government ruin India? 326–336. **Thomas Lloyd.** Signed as in no. 1908.

2223 French military justice, 337–356. **Frederick C. Conybeare.** Signed.

2224 Russia and Captain Dreyfus, 357–373. **L. J. Maxse.** Signed.

2225 The confessional in the national

Church, 374–380. **H. Hensley Henson.** Signed.

2226 The month in America, 381–391. **A. Maurice Low.** Signed.

2227 The Empire of the Philippines, 392–400. **John Foreman.** Signed.

2228 Concerning sharks, 401–410. **Frank T. Bullen.** Signed.

2229 The financial strain on France, 411–423. **W. R. Lawson.** Signed.

2230 Persons and politics in Peking, 424–433. **Alexander Michie.** Signed as in no. 2178.

2231 Greater Britain, 434–452. **L. J. Maxse.** Cf. no. 2023.

VOLUME 32, DECEMBER 1898

2232 Episodes of the month, 453–480. **L. J. Maxse.** Cf. no. 1456.

2233 The alternatives before the Indian government, 481–490. **Thomas George Baring.** Signed Northbrook [Earl of Northbrook].

2234 Shall the Open Door [to China] be closed? 491–495. **Gilbert Reid.** Signed; Contents adds "Rev."

2235 Treason in the French War Office, 496–513. **F. C. Conybeare.** Signed.

2236 Lord Lister's anodyne to public conscience [on vivisection], 514–519. **Stephen Coleridge.** Signed. (See no. 2291; letter, pp. 755–756, signed **E. A. Shäfer;** reply, pp. 882–884, signed **Stephen Coleridge.**)

2237 Tact, 520–523. Signed: Barbara.

2238 The month in America, 524–536. **A. Maurice Low.** Signed.

2239 A study of town and country children, 537–551. **Catherine I. Dodd.** Signed.

2240 A secret mission, 552–566. **Philip H. Bagenal.** Signed.

2241 A recent glimpse of South Africa, 567–573. **Evelyn Ashley.** Signed.

2242 The company scandal: a City view, 574–584. **Hugh E. M. Stutfield.** Signed.

2243 Greater Britain, 585–604. **L. J. Maxse.** Cf. no. 2023.

VOLUME 32, JANUARY 1899

2244 Episodes of the month, 605–630. **L. J. Maxse.** Cf. no. 1456.

2245 The policy of jingoism, 631–641. **H. W. Wilson.** Signed.

2246 The leaderless opposition, 642–654. **Robert Wallace,** 1831–1899. Signed A Radical M.P.—see no. 2270.

2247 Admiral Lord Lyons, 655–669. **Frederick A. Maxse.** Signed.

2248 The future of Morocco, 670–679. **Henry M. Grey.** Signed.

2249 The month in America, 680–692. **A. Maurice Low.** Signed.

2250 Boarding-out under ladies' committees, 693–699. **Margaret Vane.** Signed; Contents adds "Lady."

2251 The navy as a profession, 700–714. Signed: Captain, R.N.

2252 The point of view [in fiction], 715–718. **Jane H. Findlater.** Signed.

2253 The new Irish revolutionary movement, 719–730. **F. St. John Morrow.** Signed.

2254 Some international aspects of the Dreyfus scandal, 731–741. **L. J. Maxse.** Signed.

2255 Greater Britain, 742–754. **L. J. Maxse.** Cf. no. 2023.

VOLUME 32, FEBRUARY 1899

2256 Episodes of the month, 757–771. **L. J. Maxse.** Cf. no. 1456.

2257 The Dreyfus case (No. I): the scope of the enquiry, 772–786. **Godfrey Lushington.** Signed.

2258 The Dreyfus case (No. II): a clerical crusade, 787–806. **Frederick C. Conybeare.** Signed; repr. *Roman Catholicism.*

2259 The Dreyfus case (No. III): the only mystery, 807–817. **L. J. Maxse.** Signed.

2260 The New Zealand Old-Age Pensions Act, 818–825. **W. P. Reeves.** Signed.

2261 The Grub Street of the arts, 826–834. **Austin Dobson.** Signed; repr. *A Paladin of Philanthropy,* 1899.

2262 My two chiefs in the Crimea [Admirals Dundas and Lyons], 835–849. **Frederick A. Maxse.** Signed.

2263 The month in America, 850–861. **A. Maurice Low.** Signed.

2264 A threatened railway monopoly: South-Eastern and Chatham Railways "working union," 862–881. Signed: Shareholder.

2265 The provincial obligations of South Kensington Museum; or, A note on the Circulation Department of South Kensington Museum, 885–894. **David A. E. Lindsay.** Signed Balcarres [Earl Balcarres].

2266 The rule of the Chartered Company, 895–908. **H. C. Thomson.** Signed.

2267 Greater Britain, 909–924. **L. J. Maxse.** Cf. no. 2023.

VOLUME 33, MARCH 1899

2268 Episodes of the month, 1–24. **L. J. Maxse.** Cf. no. 1456.
2269 The misgovernment of the Transvaal, 25–38. **H. C. Thomson.** Signed.
2270 The future of the House of Commons, 39–51. **Robert Wallace,** 1831–1899. Signed A Radical M.P.; Wallace to Maxse, March 5, 1899, Maxse Papers, MS. 446, thanks him for cheque; author says, p. 39, he has been "more than twelve years in the House of Commons": see *DNB.*
2271 Secret societies in the Church of England, 52–61. **Walter Walsh,** 1847–1912. Signed, and called "Author of *The Secret History of the Oxford Movement*"—see *WWW.*
2272 Lord Raglan's traducers, 62–73. **Frederick A. Maxse.** Signed.
2273 The comedy of Christian Science, 74–86. **W. H. Mallock.** Signed.
2274 The month in America, 87–98. **A. Maurice Low.** Signed.
2275 The aged poor, 99–106. **John Hutton.** Signed; Contents adds "M.P."
2276 Cyclones and hurricanes, 107–114. **John Madden.** Signed.
2277 An American religious crusade, 115–128. **William Francis Barry.** Signed as in no. 1900.
2278 The Dreyfus affair (No. I): M. de Beaurepaire and M. Dupuy, 129–140. **Godfrey Lushington.** Signed.
2279 The Dreyfus affair (No. II): *il caso Dreyfus*; or, The Jesuit view, 140–158. **Frederick C. Conybeare.** Signed; repr. *Roman Catholicism.*
2280 The Dreyfus affair (No. III): the sins of the syndicate, 158–168. **L. J. Maxse.** Signed.
2281 Greater Britain, 169–184. **L. J. Maxse.** Cf. no. 2023.

VOLUME 33, APRIL 1899

2282 Episodes of the month, 185–212. **L. J. Maxse.** Cf. no. 1456.
2283 The Established Church, 213–227. **Hugh Cecil.** Signed; Contents adds title "Lord" and "M.P."
2284 A disease in imperial finance, 228–231. **Arthur George V. Peel.** Signed as in no. 1879.
2285 The Balfour legend, 232–238. Signed: A Conservative M.P.
2286 Some hints to young bowlers [in cricket], 239–245. **Gilbert L. Jessop.** Signed.

2287 The war correspondent at bay, 246–253. **Frederick A. Maxse.** Signed.
2288 The month in America, 254–265. **A. Maurice Low.** Signed.
2289 King Alfred, 266–284. **Frederick Pollock.** Signed.
2290 Anarchy in Uganda, 285–295. **Edmund Heathcote Thruston.** Signed.
2291 Mr. [Stephen] Coleridge's attack [in no. 2236], 296–301. **E. A. Schäfer.** Signed.
2292 Dropmore, 302–316. **Eleanor Vere Gordon Boyle.** Signed E.V.B.; Contents gives "Mrs. R. Cavendish Boyle": see *BMCat.*
2293 General de Boisdeffre? 317–340. **Frederick C. Conybeare.** Signed.
2294 Greater Britain, 341–354. **L. J. Maxse.** Cf. no. 2023.

VOLUME 33, MAY 1899

2295 Episodes of the month, 355–379. **L. J. Maxse.** Cf. no. 1456.
2296 The coming crisis in the Transvaal, 380–388. **Arnold White.** Signed.
2297 The belligerent Papacy, 389–400. **W. J. Stillman.** Signed.
2298 The Browning letters, 401–415. **Leslie Stephen.** Signed; repr. *Studies,* III.
2299 Scenes and scandals on the London vestries, 416–429. Signed in Contents: Ratepayer.
2300 St. Paul's, 430–436. **John Stirling Maxwell.** Signed.
2301 The month in America, 437–448. **A. Maurice Low.** Signed.
2302 A few fallacies in the ritual controversy, 449–461. **H. C. Beeching.** Signed.
2303 An Irish poet ["A.E.," G. W. Russell], 462–471. **Victor A. G. R. Bulwer Lytton.** Signed Lytton [Earl Lytton].
2304 Fresh evidence on the Dreyfus case, 472–491. **Frederick C. Conybeare.** Signed.
2305 A Garibaldi reminiscence, 492–500. **Evelyn Ashley.** Signed.
2306 The moral of the Indian countervailing duties, 501–512. **Mayson M. Beeton.** Signed.
2307 Greater Britain, 513–530. **L. J. Maxse.** Cf. no. 2023.

VOLUME 33, JUNE 1899

2308 Episodes of the month, 531–555. **L. J. Maxse.** Cf. no. 1456.
2309 The case for dissolution, 556–567.

Sidney J. Low, prob. Signed Carltonensis; cf. no. 2389.

2310 Our American competitors, 568–580. **Benjamin C. Browne.** Signed.

2311 The coming Russian loan, 581–594. **W. R. Lawson.** Signed.

2312 Ethics of horse-racing, 595–609. **R. F. Meysey Thompson.** Signed; Contents adds "Lieut.-Col."

2313 The month in America, 610–621. **A. Maurice Low.** Signed.

2314 A study of the early instruction of twin boys, 622–636. **Catherine I. Dodd.** Signed.

2315 The threatened railway monopoly in Ireland, 637–642. **Thomas Spring-Rice,** 1849–1926. Signed Monteagle [2nd Baron Monteagle].

2316 The present popularity of Omar Khayyam, 643–652. **Bernard Holland.** Signed.

2317 The invasion of England, 653–663. **H. W. Wilson.** Signed.

2318 Greater Britain, 664–682. **L. J. Maxse.** Cf. no. 2023.

2319 The conspiracy against Dreyfus [supplement to the June number, with separate pagination], 1–64. **Godfrey Lushington.** Signed on p. 60.

VOLUME 33, JULY 1899

2320 Episodes of the month, 683–708. **L. J. Maxse.** Cf. no. 1456.

2321 Is the Unionist party committed to old-age pensions? (No. I), 709–718. **C. A. Whitmore.** Signed.

2322 Is the Unionist party committed to old-age pensions? (No. II), 719–726. **John E. Dorington.** Signed.

2323 Is the Unionist party committed to old-age pensions? (No. III), 727–733. **Edward Bond.** Signed; Cover adds "M.P."; see *WWW/1928.*

2324 The civil war in France, 734–739. **Frederick A. Maxse.** Signed.

2325 Studies of a biographer: Southey's letters, 740–757. **Leslie Stephen.** Signed; repr. *Studies,* IV.

2326 The British Sunday, 758–769. **H. Hensley Henson.** Signed.

2327 The month in America, 770–782. **A. Maurice Low.** Signed.

2328 A study in Jew-baiting [French policy in Algeria], 783–801. **Frederick C. Conybeare.** Signed.

2329 The genesis of Germany, 802–812. **Henry Cust.** Signed.

2330 The Commonwealth of Australia, 823–844. **B. R. Wise.** Signed.

2331 Greater Britain: South Africa, 845–866. **L. J. Maxse.** Cf. no. 2023.

VOLUME 33, AUGUST 1899

2332 Episodes of the month, 867–891. **L. J. Maxse.** Cf. no. 1456.

2333 The rapprochement between France and Germany, 892–901. **H. W. Wilson.** Signed Ignotus—see no. 2377.

2334 Our duty towards China, 902–916. **R. A. Yerburgh.** Signed.

2335 Jean Calas, 917–933. **Frederick C. Conybeare.** Signed; repr. *Roman Catholicism.*

2336 Klondike: a study in booms, 934–944. **Ernest E. Williams.** Signed.

2337 The Church as a profession, 945–955. **Douglas Macleane.** Signed.

2338 The month in America, 956–967. **A. Maurice Low.** Signed.

2339 British expansion in West Africa, 968–979. **Leonard Darwin.** Signed.

2340 An open-air reformatory, 980–991. **Edith Sellers.** Signed.

2341 The Australian view of the South African crisis, 992–999. **W. H. Fitchett.** Signed.

2342 Greater Britain, 1000–1018. **L. J. Maxse.** Cf. no. 2023.

VOLUME 34, SEPTEMBER 1899

2343 Episodes of the month, 1–25. **L. J. Maxse.** Cf. no. 1456.

2344 Anglophobia: a French warning to England, 26–46. **Urbain Gohier.** Signed; Cover adds "Author of *L'Armée contre la Nation*"; see *Bib. Nat. Cat.*

2345 The court-martial at Rennes [Dreyfus case], 47–64. **Godfrey Lushington.** Signed.

2346 Impressions of the House of Commons from the ladies' gallery (No. II), 65–72. Signed: Grille. (No. III is no. 2501.)

2347 Can gardening be made to pay? 73–83. **S. Whyndham Fitzherbert.** Signed S. W. Fitzherbert; Contents provides middle name.

2348 The month in America, 84–96. **A. Maurice Low.** Signed.

2349 The keepers of literature, 97–109. **William Francis Barry.** Signed as in no. 1900.

2350 Don Miraglia, 110–118. **Adelina Paulina Irby.** Signed A. P. Irby; Contents adds "Miss": see *BMCat.*

2351 The reform policy of the Chinese Emperor, 119–131. **George S. Owen.** Signed.

2352 Greater Britain, 132–148. **L. J. Maxse.** Cf. no. 2023.

VOLUME 34, OCTOBER 1899

2353 Episodes of the month, 149–178. **L. J. Maxse.** Cf. no. 2365.
2354 The verdict at Rennes [Dreyfus case], 179–202. **Godfrey Lushingon.** Signed.
2355 Sword and cassock, 203–219. **F. C. Conybeare.** Signed; repr. *Roman Catholicism.*
2356 Mr. Chaplin's [political] kite, 220–229. **Ernest E. Williams.** Signed.
2357 Cricket reform, 230–235. **Alfred Lyttelton.** Signed.
2358 The cult of infirmity, 236–245. **Arnold White.** Signed.
2359 The month in America, 246–257. **A. Maurice Low.** Signed.
2360 Tarpon-fishing, 258–267. **W. H. Grenfell.** Signed.
2361 William Morris and the arts and crafts, 268–271. **W. A. S. Benson.** Signed.
2362 Compulsory arbitration at work; a New Zealand experiment, 272–288. **John MacGregor,** 1850–1936. Signed J. Mac-Gregor; Cover adds "Member of Legislative Council, New Zealand"; man cited was a critic of compulsory arbitration and member of the Council: see *New Zealand Biog.*
2363 The Archbishops' judgment, 289–300. **H. Hensley Henson.** Signed.
2364 Greater Britain: South African crisis, 301–316. **L. J. Maxse.** Cf. no. 2023.

VOLUME 34, NOVEMBER 1899

2365 Episodes of the month, 317–347. **L. J. Maxse.** Cf. no. 1456; pp. 317–320 are repr. in *"Germany on the Brain,"* ed. Maxse, 1915; among the reprints there of arts. with this title, Maxse specifies those which are not his (cf. no. 2464).
2366 "After" in South Africa, 348–352. **Evelyn Ashley.** Signed. (Letters, pp. 632–635, signed **H. M. Meysey-Thompson;** reply, pp. 801–803, signed **Evelyn Ashley.**)
2367 Moral factors in the [Boer] War, 353–357. **Spenser Wilkinson.** Signed; repr. *War and Policy,* 1900.
2368 The role of the Roman Catholic Church in France, 358–377. **Urbain Gohier.** Signed. (Letters, pp. 635–636, signed **Henry Gibbs,** who calls himself

"an English Catholic"; reply, pp. 803–804, signed **Urbain Gohier.**)
2369 The cosmopolitan spirit in literature, 378–391. **Leslie Stephen.** Signed; repr. *Studies,* IV.
2370 A playgoer's protest, 392–398. **Eveline C. Godley.** Signed.
2371 The month in America, 399–411. **A. Maurice Low.** Signed.
2372 German finance, 412–428. **W. R. Lawson.** Signed.
2373 A summer trip in Alaska, 429–438. **William F. Bailey.** Signed, with the title "Assistant Irish Land Commissioner."
2374 Redistribution, 439–446. **C. A. Whitmore.** Signed.
2375 Greater Britain: South Africa, 447–468. **L. J. Maxse.** Cf. no. 2023.

VOLUME 34, DECEMBER 1899

2376 Episodes of the month, 469–493. **L. J. Maxse.** Cf. no. 1456.
2377 The coming storm in the Far East, 494–505. **H. W. Wilson.** Signed Ignotus; Wilson to Maxse, Dec. 15, 1899, Maxse Papers, MS. 446, says he has mentioned his *"nom de plume"* to no one and encloses receipt for payment "for two articles in the December number"; no. 2378 is one, this art. the only other possibility.
2378 Democracy and the [Boer] War, 506–514. **H. W. Wilson.** Signed.
2379 The Vatican at work, 515–531. **Richard Bagot.** Signed. (See no. 2439.)
2380 Walter Bagehot, 532–544. **M. E. Grant Duff.** Signed; repr. *Out of the Past* (1903), II.
2381 On the evolution of a tendency of adopting symbols as the universal written language of the world, 545–549. **Chihchen Lofengluh.** Signed; Cover adds "Chinese Minister in London."
2382 The month in America, 550–562. **A. Maurice Low.** Signed.
2383 The pupil teacher in rural schools, 563–575. **Evelyn Strutt.** Signed Evelyn Rayleigh [3rd Baroness Rayleigh].
2384 A winter's camp in Gippsland [Australia], 576–583. **C. Bogue Luffmann.** Signed.
2385 The transports and the troops, 584–594. **Arthur Shadwell.** Signed as in no. 1744.
2386 John Donne, 595–613. **Leslie Stephen.** Signed; repr. *Studies,* III.
2387 Greater Britain, 614–631. **L. J. Maxse.** Cf. no. 2023.

VOLUME 34, JANUARY 1900

2388 Episodes of the month, 637–661. **L. J. Maxse.** Cf. no. 1456; selections from pp. 653–658 repr. as in no. 2365.

2389 Ought we to have a coalition? 662–669. **Sidney J. Low,** prob. Signed Carltonensis; Low to Maxse, Jan. 9, 1900, Maxse Papers, MS. 447, thanks him for cheque and approves Maxse's toning down of the art., which suggests partisan politics.

2390 The cankers of a long peace, 670–682. **Arnold White.** Signed.

2391 The last of the Dervishes, 683–695. **F. Ivor Maxse.** Signed F. I. Maxse; Contents adds "Major"; see *WWW*/1960.

2392 Some recent impressions of South Africa, 696–707. **George C. T. Bartley.** Signed.

2393 The art of narration, 708–713. **Jane H. Findlater.** Signed; repr. *Stones from a Glass House,* 1904.

2394 The month in America, 714–726. **A. Maurice Low.** Signed.

2395 The war of winds: a commentary on weather forecasts, 727–733. **John M. Bacon.** Signed.

2396 Hospital chaos, 734–748. **Honnor Morten.** Signed. (Letter, pp. 970–972, signed **Timothy Holmes,** with title "Consulting Surgeon and Treasurer to St. George's Hospital.")

2397 An episode of the Bakrid, 749–766. **Charles Randal Marindin.** Signed An Indian Magistrate; claimed in Marindin to Maxse, Aug. 2, 1899, Maxse Papers, MS. 446.

2398 Popular Catholicism in France, 767–780. **Frederick C. Conybeare.** Signed; repr. *Roman Catholicism.*

2399 Greater Britain: the South African War, 781–800. **L. J. Maxse.** Cf. no. 2023.

VOLUME 34, FEBRUARY 1900

2400 Episodes of the month, 805–829. **L. J. Maxse.** Cf. no. 1456; pp. 811–817 repr. as in no. 2365.

2401 The causes of reverse [in South Africa], 830–842. **H. W. Wilson,** prob. Signed An Englishman; cf. no. 2479.

2402 War and government, 843–851. **Spenser Wilkinson.** Signed; repr. *War and Policy,* 1900.

2403 The war chest of the Boers, 852–866. **W. R. Lawson.** Signed. (Letter, vol. 35, pp. 178–180, signed **Alfred Marks.**)

2404 The present feeling in Germany towards England, 867–874. **Mary Annette Russell.** Signed A German Lady; "Elizabeth" to Maxse, Jan. 11, 1900, and Gräfin von Arnim (she was then married to Count von Arnim) to Maxse, same month, Maxse Papers, MS. 447, agrees to write this art. but insists on pseudonym of "A German Woman"; see *DNB.*

2405 School children's ideals, 875–889. **Catherine I. Dodd.** Signed.

2406 The month in America, 890–900. **A. Maurice Low.** Signed Moreton C. Bradley; Low to Maxse, Jan. 11, 1900, Maxse Papers, MS. 447, explains his use of a pseudonym "this month"; he regularly wrote the arts. under this title.

2407 Goethe and Victor Hugo: a comparison, 901–913. **Maurice Baring.** Assigned in Contents.

2408 Mars as a world, 914–922. **Richard Arman Gregory.** Signed R. A. Gregory; Contents adds "Professor": see *WWW*/1960.

2409 The London housing problem, 923–931. **H. Percy Harris.** Signed.

2410 The Roman danger [Catholicism], 932–943. **Robert F. Horton.** Signed.

2411 Greater Britain: South African war —a retrospect, 944–969. **L. J. Maxse.** Cf. no. 2023.

VOLUME 35, MARCH 1900

2412 Episodes of the month, 1–27. **L. J. Maxse.** Cf. no. 1456.

2413 Great Britain and the European powers, 28–39. **Rowland Blennerhassett.** Signed.

2414 The War Office and the [Boer] War, 40–60. **H. O. Arnold Forster.** Signed.

2415 The man in the cabinet, 61–74. **H. W. Wilson.** Signed The Man in the Street; Wilson to L. J. Maxse, Mar. 4, 1900, Maxse Papers, MS. 447, thanks him for cheque; the only other art. unaccounted for in the March issue is no. 2419, but since Wilson was not "a diplomate" (signature of no. 2419) and since the subject of this art. is war and Wilson was military editor of *Daily Mail* (*Times,* July 13, 1940), this seems to be his.

2416 *Red Pottage,* 75–80. **Edith Lyttelton.** Signed.

2417 A chance for the public schools, 81–87. **C. J. Cornish.** Signed.

2418 The month in America, 88–100. **A. Maurice Low.** Signed Moreton C. Bradley; cf. no. 2406.

Reeves, with title "Agent-General for New Zealand"; 644–645, signed **Andrew Clark,** with titles "Sir" and "Agent General for Victoria and Tasmanis"; 645, signed **Walter Peace,** with title "Sir"; 645, signed **Philip Oakley Fysh.**

2460   The Mivart episode, 646–660. **H. Hensley Henson.** Signed.

2461   Lord Herbert of Cherbury, 661–673. **Leslie Stephen.** Signed.

2462   Count Mouravieff's triumph ["Open Door" policy in China], 674–678. **Robert Yerburgh.** Signed.

2463   Greater Britain, 679–696. **L. J. Maxse.** Cf. no. 2023.

VOLUME 35, JULY 1900

2464   Episodes of the month, 697–720. Unidentified. L. J. Maxse, *"Germany on the Brain"* (1915), p. 31, says this art. was "written by another hand," because of the death of his father.

2465   A Khaki dissolution, 721–726. Signed: A Conservative M.P.

2466   The conspiracy against the French Republic, 727–745. **Frederick C. Conybeare.** Signed; repr. *Roman Catholicism.*

2467   Dante's realistic treatment of the ideal, 746–757. **Alfred Austin.** Signed; repr. *The Bridling of Pegasus,* 1910.

2468   The rights of the weak, 758–772. **W. H. Mallock.** Signed.

2469   The house of Usna: a drama in a wood, as produced at the Globe Theatre by the Stage Society, 773–788. **William Sharp.** Signed Fiona Macleod: see *DNB/* 2nd suppl.

2470   The parlous condition of cricket, 789–799. **Horace G. Hutchinson.** Signed.

2471   The month in America, 800–811. **A. Maurice Low.** Signed.

2472   A plea for military history, 812–822. **Charles W. C. Oman.** Signed C. Oman; Cover adds "Fellow of All Souls' College, Oxford": see *DNB/*1950.

2473   A trip from Uganda to Khartoum, 823–838. **Moreton F. Gage.** Signed.

2474   The Swiss army: its lessons for England, 839–849. **G. G. Coulton.** Signed.

2475   Some final impressions of the Roman Catholic Church, 850–865. **Arthur Galton.** Signed.

2476   Greater Britain, 866–876. Unidentified. Prob. not by L. J. Maxse; perhaps the explanation for not writing no. 2464 was true for this art. too.

2477   The story of the Boer War [supplement to the July number with separate pagination], 1–36. **H. W. Wilson.** Signed; Cover adds "Author of *Ironclads in Action.*"

VOLUME 35, AUGUST 1900

2478   Episodes of the month, 877–901. **L. J. Maxse.** Cf. no. 1456.

2479   "Having eyes they see not" [on military preparedness], 902–912. **H. W. Wilson,** prob. Signed An Englishman; author claims "inside acquaintance" with at least three newspapers, p. 905; Wilson, a naval expert and military editor for the *Daily Mail,* had been on the staff of three major papers (cf. *Times,* July 13, 1940); L. J. Maxse, *"Germany on the Brain"* (1915), p. 8, says Wilson wrote for the *National Review* under various pseudonyms; detailed knowledge of naval matters and concern about the German military menace in this art., pp. 906–907, and two other arts. with same signature (no. 2401, pp. 834, 840, and no. 2516, pp. 332–333, 337–339) are consistent with Wilson's known views.

2480   The sick and wounded in South Africa, 913–921. **Arthur Stanley.** Signed; Contents adds "M.P."; see *DNB/*1950.

2481   The economic revolution in Germany, 922–935. **Ernest E. Williams.** Signed.

2482   Walter Bagehot, 936–950. **Leslie Stephen.** Signed; repr. *Studies,* III.

2483   The pious pilgrimage, 951–971. **Mary Annette Russell.** Assigned in Contents to "Author of *Elizabeth and her German Garden*": see *DNB/*1950.

2484   The month in America, 972–981. **A. Maurice Low.** Signed.

2485   A case of paternal desertion [on need for conscription], 982–988. **Thomas Wodehouse Legh.** Signed Newton [Baron Newton].

2486   The Judicature Acts at work, 989–1002. **Rollo F. Graham-Campbell.** Signed on p. 998.

2487   Compulsion v. volunteering; or, Facts and fancies about the press-gang, 1003–1016. **Cyprian A. G. Bridge.** Signed.

2488   Is the Broad Church party extinct? 1017–1024. **William Page Roberts.** Assigned in Contents to "Page Roberts," with title "Rev. Canon"; see Venn.

2489   Some lessons of the Boer War, 1025–1038. Assigned in Contents to "The Military Critic of *Westminster Gazette.*"

2490   Greater Britain, 1039–1048. **L. J. Maxse.** Cf. no. 2023.

VOLUME 36, SEPTEMBER 1900

2491 Episodes of the month, 1–24. **L. J. Maxse.** Cf. no. 1456; pp. 1–6 repr. as in no. 2365.

2492 Japan and the new Far East, 25–36. **H. W. Wilson.** Signed Ignotus—see no. 2377.

2493 The foreign policy of the German Empire, 37–51. **Rowland Blennerhassett.** Signed.

2494 Will the United States withdraw from the Philippines? 52–62. **John Foreman.** Signed.

2495 Church parade in the army, 63–66. Signed: R.A., with address "Natal Field Force"; assigned in Contents to "Royal Artillery." (See no. 2531.)

2496 The schoolboy's view of schoolmasters, 67–72. **Ralph George Hawtrey.** Signed.

2497 The month in America, 73–83. **A. Maurice Low.** Signed.

2498 The coal problem, 84–99. **A. D. Provand.** Signed.

2499 Drawn matches at cricket, 100–109. **W. J. Ford.** Signed.

2500 Expression in poetry, 110–119. **H. C. Beeching.** Signed; repr. *Two Lectures*, Cambridge, 1901.

2501 Impressions of the House of Commons from the ladies' gallery (No. III, concl.), 120–127. Signed: Grille. (No. I is no. 2207.)

2502 An Africander's reflections on the future of South Africa, 128–138. **Adrian Hofmeyr.** Signed.

2503 Greater Britain, 139–152. **L. J. Maxse.** Cf. no. 2023.

VOLUME 36, OCTOBER 1900

2504 Episodes of the month, 153–177. **L. J. Maxse.** Cf. no. 1456.

2505 The German danger in the Far East, 178–195. **James Louis Garvin.** Signed X; Garvin to Maxse, Oct. 4, 1900, Maxse Papers, MS. 447, thanks him for cheque and prominent position given his art., and continues the argument of the art.; Garvin used "X" as pseudonym in *FortR*; see Courtney, *Making of an Editor*, p. 161.

2506 Electors and the navy, 196–209. **C. McL. McHardy.** Signed.

2507 A plea for the control of China, 210–220. **Francis Edward Younghusband.** Signed.

2508 Vatican and Quirinal, 221–230. **Richard Bagot.** Signed.

2509 General Wolfe's letters, 231–240. **Eveline C. Godley.** Signed.

2510 The Oxford undergraduate, 241–250. **H. Brodrick.** Signed.

2511 The month in America, 251–260. **A. Maurice Low.** Signed.

2512 The investor's opportunity, 261–272. **W. R. Lawson.** Signed.

2513 The Roman Catholic hierarchy in Australia, 286–290. Signed: An English Catholic.

2514 Greater Britain, 291–304. **L. J. Maxse.** Cf. no. 2023.

VOLUME 36, NOVEMBER 1900

2515 Episodes of the month, 305–329. **L. J. Maxse.** Cf. no. 1456.

2516 Reconstruction or catastrophe? 330–340. **H. W. Wilson,** prob. Signed An Englishman—see no. 2479.

2517 The problem of invasion, 341–360. **W. E. Cairnes.** Signed.

2518 The universities and national defence, 361–365. **T. F. C. Huddleston.** Signed.

2519 The Japanese navy, 366–376. **C. C. P. Fitzgerald.** Signed.

2520 The history of a small estate in Wales, 377–385. **Stanley Leighton.** Signed.

2521 The month in America, 386–398. **A. Maurice Low.** Signed.

2522 The moderates and the [London] School Board, 399–406. **William C. Bridgeman.** Signed.

2523 Civil engineering as a profession, 407–419. **L. F. Vernon-Harcourt.** Signed.

2524 The war correspondent: a suggestion for the future, 420–429. **H. F. Prevost Battersby.** Signed.

2525 The sacrifice of Canada, 430–439. **Ernest E. Williams.** Signed.

2526 Greater Britain, 440–456. **L. J. Maxse.** Cf. no. 2023.

VOLUME 36, DECEMBER 1900

2527 Episodes of the month, 457–482. **L. J. Maxse.** Cf. no. 1456; pp. 480–481 repr. as in no. 2365.

2528 A new fourth party, 483–494. Signed: Young England.

2529 Some personal impressions of the army, 495–506. **Arthur Griffith-Boscawen.** Signed as in no. 1870; Contents adds "Captain" and "M.P."

2530 The military education of officers, 507–516. **T. Miller Maguire.** Signed.

2531 Church parade in the army, 517–522. **C. B. Mayne.** Signed, with title "Major R.E."

2532 Is Emerson a poet? 523–536. **Coulson Kernahan.** Signed.

2533 Government House [on colonial governors], 537–544. **Arthur Galton.** Signed.

2534 American affairs, 545–556. **A. Maurice Low.** Signed.

2535 A comparison of German and English school-children, 557–567. **Catherine I. Dodd.** Signed.

2536 Her Majesty's judges, 568–578. **Ernest Bowen-Rowlands?** Signed E.; wrote arts. on law and lawyers in *Strand Mag.* in 1899 signed E. (Bowen-Rowlands, *In Court and out of Court* [1925], pp. 184–185), and a life of Judge Henry Hawkins also signed E.; p. 571 of art. and *In Court*, p. 60, deal with same case in which R. W. Wright was the judge; art., p. 577, praises chief justice Alverstone, while *In Court*, pp. 52–54, criticizes him, but the book is 25 years later; in the five chapters of the book on judges and lawyers, no mention is made of this art.

2537 Colonial governments as moneylenders, 579–591. **W. P. Reeves.** Signed.

2538 Greater Britain, 592–608. **L. J. Maxse.** Cf. no. 2023.

The New Quarterly Magazine, 1873–1880

THE *New Quarterly Magazine* was a bold experiment. It was the first general periodical written for educated readers which was both a magazine and a quarterly; or, to speak more exactly, a magazine which appeared at quarterly intervals, since all other magazines of this kind were weeklies or monthlies. This meant that it could not publish a novel, as Oswald Crawfurd, the founder and editor, not only realized but, curiously enough, emphasized in his prospectus: "The Magazine will contain . . . Two or more Tales of considerable length by Eminent Writers. *The Tales will invariably be completed in the Numbers in which they appear.*"[1] Obviously, this was a reassurance to the reader that he would not have to wait three months to continue a story, but the italics suggest that the single-issue tale was a virtue, a selling-point. One wonders if some readers of the ubiquitous serialized fiction were not finding a month's delay between chapters I–IV and V–VIII, etc. sufficiently annoying to welcome Crawfurd's innovation.[2]

To some degree, however, the quarterly spacing had a personal source, as did the other special features brought forward in the prospectus. The Magazine was to be "a High-Class Literary and Social Periodical" which, in addition to the important tales, would contain "Papers on Topics of Social and General Interest," including "TRAVEL and BIOGRAPHY." As this would imply—and the fact confirms—serious comment on the major issues of the time was to be avoided. Some years later a specific policy was defined which dated from the beginning: "The 'New Quarterly Magazine' avoids disputed religious questions, and theology is wholly apart from the regions of thought with which it is concerned."[3] No doubt this was welcome after the successive blows of Darwin, *Essays and Reviews*, Colenso, and Huxley in the sixties, but the policy of exclusion went much further to cover politics, science, and philosophy, with the tension of controversy which they too, as much within the individual as in the public, were bound to provoke. In Crawfurd's period, October 1873–January 1878, there are only three articles on controversial subjects: one on vivisection (no. 50), one on railway reform (no. 125), and the third on a spiritualistic seance (no. 5). When the last brought a batch of letters, the frightened editor refused to print them on the ground that the skeptical author had proved his point so well that any further

[1] *Athenaeum*, Sept. 6, 1873, p. 319. The italics are Crawfurd's.

[2] Crawfurd himself may well have had in mind the deleterious effect of serial publication on the quality of novels: see, for example, the discussion in *Fraser's Magazine*, 23 (Feb. 1841), 169–171.

[3] *NQM*, 2 n.s. (Oct. 1879), 445. The new editor was Kegan Paul.

discussion could provide "neither instruction nor entertainment" to the "educated and intelligent persons" for whom the *New Quarterly* was written.[4]

Crawfurd meant persons like himself, for the Magazine was shaped in his own image. Though he early joined the foreign service and was consul in Oporto, Portugal, from 1866 to 1890, literary pursuits and country sport were his primary interests. The obituary in the *Athenaeum* is revealing:

> Mr. Crawfurd's attitude to the literary life was always that of the cultured amateur rather than that of the professional worker. Books and "the play" were to him the most amenable diversions of a busy career, and he was never obliged, like many of his contemporaries, to adopt them as his principal means of support. It was not unnatural, therefore, that such work as he did should have possessed the shortcomings, no less than the qualities, of work undertaken mainly as a means of recreation. He dabbled in editorship and in publishing, but his hold upon these rather arduous undertakings was essentially tentative. He was guided by the taste of the dilettante rather than by the business instinct of the man of commerce. . . . He was a man of lively ideas, incapable of discussing any subject without assuming his own definite relation to the problems it suggested, and it was one of his pet beliefs that such problems could be effectively discussed in the form of a story.[5]

Though this betrays the bias of the professional journalist with his living to make, it explains a good deal: the fact that having to edit four issues a year was quite enough work, and that controversial questions had best be discussed, if at all, indirectly, their edges blunted, in the form of tales. Crawfurd would publish a quarterly magazine, and if it lost money, no harm done; and what it lacked in depth, it would make up for in entertaining articles on Portugal, fishing, riding, wine, and "The spirit of modern agriculture" (one suspects that his main audience was the landed gentry), or biographical sketches of Rabelais, Macaulay, Goethe, and Sir Philip Sidney, told with the accent on anecdote.

At the start Crawfurd wrote most of the periodical himself—four out of the seven pieces in each of the first three numbers; and during his editorship contributed at least 36 of the 134 papers. He used four pseudonyms, left many of his papers anonymous, and with seemingly modest infrequency contributed an article signed "The Editor." Though his promise of attracting "Eminent Writers" of fiction scarcely came true (he did publish two stories by Meredith and a few by Henry Kingsley and Eliza Lynn Linton), he was more successful with essays, by Frances Power Cobbe, Richard Jeffries, Francis Hueffer, Robert Buchanan, and—the big plum—Meredith's "On the idea of comedy, and of the uses of the comic spirit." There are no figures available on the circulation. All we know is that within a few days the first issue had to be reprinted.[6]

Then, after a good but not specially notable record, the *New Quarterly* came out in January 1876 with an original feature that captured immediate attention and made the three-month interval genuinely functional. Indeed, one suspects that the interval may have inspired the idea. At any rate, Crawfurd started a department called "Current literature and current criticism" in which each review made a point of quoting

---

[4] 1 (Jan. 1874), 442. For Crawfurd's self-assurance, see the end of the extract just below.
[5] Feb. 6, 1909, p. 164, signed A.W.
[6] *Athenaeum*, Oct. 11, 1873, p. 451.

several earlier reviews which had appeared during the quarter, thus exposing the variety of critical opinion and warning readers against the dogmas of their favourite journal. Crawfurd explained:

The many-sidedness of modern criticism . . . is familiar enough to those whose business is general literature, but the great mass of the reading public can have few opportunities of learning how much a hasty and narrow literary judgment may be prevented by a comparison of the many intelligent and honest opinions continually being formed from various and independent standpoints.

However reasonable, even obvious, this was, it met with considerable displeasure from editors, reviewers, and publishers.[7] Hence the apologia, which continues:

It is distinctly not in our idea, as it has been hastily implied that it was, to set the various divergences of current critical judgment in curious and impertinent apposition, but while we take careful note of these occasional divergences, we shall always endeavour to arrive at sound and safe conclusions of our own. Where there is any conflict of opinions we shall quote these opinions, and give the reader the opportunity of assisting his own judgment by their help.[8]

When Francis Hueffer, the second editor, continued the section, he too was at pains to deny any subversive or arrogant attitude, and to argue a further advantage gained by the quarterly delay:

The 'New Quarterly Magazine' does not claim the privileges or pretend to the superior wisdom of a Court of Appeal. The only advantage over its more ephemeral brethren it lays claim to is that of time. Even the lapse of a few months is frequently of infinite avail in calming down the heat of passion and clearing away the prejudices of a first impression; and traces of this greater clearness and tranquillity of critical atmosphere will, it is hoped, be found in this summary.[9]

But the innovation came to an end when Kegan Paul took command in 1879 for the simple reason that the third editor was also a publisher, who had no intention of alienating the reviewers of books by invidious comparisons.

The two issues of Volume 9 (October 1877 and January 1878) were the only ones not to contain at least one paper by Crawfurd, and all the issues of 1877 were without his long review section. It seems likely that the amateur was tiring of the labor demanded even by a quarterly magazine. Moreover, he may well have had to spend more than he wished to sustain a journal whose audience was limited. In any event, about November 1, 1877, Crawfurd sold his periodical to Francis Hueffer, who had been an assistant editor of the *Academy* for six years and a contributor to the *New Quarterly*.

---

[7]See the *Academy*, Jan. 8, 1876, p. 32, partly quoted below in n. 9; but our main source is the fact that both Crawfurd and Hueffer felt obliged to deny charges and defend the policy: see the next two extracts.

[8]*NQM*, 6 (Apr. 1876), 231. How seriously Crawfurd took his new review section is revealed by the next paragraph: "In order that we may perform the duty we have set ourselves with the fullest impartiality to all the parties most immediately concerned, we have thought it well to exclude from the pages of THE NEW QUARTERLY the advertisements of publishing firms."

[9]*NQM*, 10 (Apr. 1878), 213. This reads like an answer to the criticism in the *Academy*, Jan. 8, 1876, p. 32: "If there is a class of readers who wish to be not more than a quarter behind the world, and do not mind being that, the editor of the *New Quarterly* seems in a position to cater for them."

Hueffer then assigned the copyright to Chatto and Windus, arranging to have them publish the Magazine at their own expense and risk, and to divide the profits. Hueffer was to be editor at £10 per issue, with "a further sum of £5 for every 500 copies sold beyond 2000 of each number." The agreement was for four years, though Chatto and Windus was given permission to transfer its interest at any time to another publisher, subject to the same arrangements.[10] But despite this escape hatch, editor and publisher were optimistic, as the expected sale would suggest. In a letter of April 29, 1878, they spoke of their first number as promising "to inaugurate a new era," and on June 5 told Sir Charles Dilke that the *New Quarterly* "takes a much higher literary position than formerly." What they had in mind is revealed by their request to Dilke for an "article on 'Royal Partisanship in Politics' in opposition to the views advocated in the article on 'The Crown and Constitution' in the last no. of the 'Quarterly Review.' "

So enter politics and controversy (the April issue contained "Parliamentary forms and reforms," " 'What can we do for Greece?' " and a long analysis of Panslavonianism); the review of reviews department is revived; the fiction is reduced to one tale; and the level of contributors is clearly raised by the arrival of Sidney Colvin, Edmund Gosse, Thomas Hardy, Andrew Lang, R. L. Stevenson, and T. A. Trollope. Nevertheless, among the Chatto and Windus papers one suddenly comes upon a letter to Hueffer of December 13, 1878, beginning: "We have seen Messr. Kegan Paul & Co. and settled with them for the transfer of all rights in the 'New Quarterly Magazine' commencing with the January number." This could hardly have caused Hueffer much distress. He received £300 from the publishers as penalty for terminating their four-year agreement; and since he quickly secured the post of music critic on the *Times*,[11] he was exchanging the task of editing a periodical—and one which, despite its improvement in quality, must have been selling well under the 2000 copies expected—for an activity far more congenial. Whether or not he sold his Magazine, we do not know. Certainly by January 1879 Kegan Paul was editor and publisher, if not proprietor as well.[12]

Paul's periodical differed little from Hueffer's. It carried on the extended range of subject matter and the restriction of fiction to one tale. Moreover, some new contributors of ability were procured: Richard Garnett, J. J. Jusserand, Justin McCarthy, Mark Pattison, among others; but with no better effect on sales than Hueffer's similar improvement. With the issue for April 1880 the *New Quarterly* "died for want of capital."[13]

The experiment had failed, primarily I think because of the quarterly appearance. This prevented the publication of serialized fiction, still much in demand, and when Hueffer and Paul extended their coverage to political and controversial questions, they brought their periodical into impossible competition with the *Edinburgh*, the *Quar-*

---

[10]The documents are at Chatto and Windus, and are here used by the kind permission of the firm. See the Bibliographical Note for precise references in the letterbooks.

[11]*Academy*, Dec. 21, 1878, p. 582.

[12]Because of the bad fire in 1883, documents about the transfer do not now exist at Routledge and Kegan Paul.

[13]According to W. F. Haydon in H. St. J. Raikes, *Life and Letters of Henry Cecil Raikes* (1898), p. 203, writing in late Oct. 1883.

terly, and the *Westminster*. But the Magazine did not fail; it succeeded, especially under its last editors. A writer in the *Academy* for 1899, announcing the commencement of a *New Quarterly* dealing with the Church, predicted it would have "little in common with the *New Quarterly* which many of us read with so much interest a few decades ago."[14]

EDITORS

Oswald John Frederick Crawfurd: October 1873–January 1878, Vol. 1—Vol. 9.
Francis Hueffer: April 1878—October 1878, Vol. 10.[15]
C. Kegan Paul: January 1879–April 1880, Vol. 1—Vol. 3 n.s.[16]

PROPRIETORS

O. F. J. Crawfurd: October 1873–January 1878, Vol. 1—Vol. 9.
Francis Hueffer: April–October, 1878, Vol. 10.
C. Kegan Paul and Co., probably, but possibly Francis Hueffer: January 1879–April 1880, Vol. 1—Vol. 3. n.s.[17]

PUBLISHERS

Ward, Lock and Tyler: October 1873–January 1877, Vol. 1—Vol. 7.
Ward, Lock & Co.: April 1877–January 1878, Vol. 8—9.
Chatto and Windus: April 1878–October 1878, Volume 10.
C. Kegan Paul and Co.: January 1879–April 1880, Vol. 1—Vol. 3 n.s.

NOTE ON ATTRIBUTIONS

About 60 per cent of the articles are signed with the author's name. There is no known publisher's list or comprehensive source from which unsigned articles can be identified and pseudonyms resolved.

BIBLIOGRAPHICAL NOTE

No account of the *New Quarterly Magazine* exists, nor are there any lives of its editors or histories of its publishing houses which give information about it.

On Crawfurd, two obituaries, in the *Times*, Feb. 1, 1909, p. 13d, and the *Athenaeum*, Feb. 6, 1909, p. 164, signed A.W., supplement the article in the *DNB*, 2nd suppl. The letterbooks at Chatto and Windus in London deal almost entirely with the business arrangements connected with Vol. 10 and Francis Hueffer: Vol. 8, fols. 213, 220, 430, 434, 490, 491; Vol. 9, fols. 414, 438, 448, 483, 538, 582, 599, 773,

[14]Feb. 4, 1899, p. 148.

[15]See the *Athenaeum*, Nov. 17, 1877, p. 631, and Dec. 21, 1878, p. 806.

[16]It should be noted, however, that when Kegan Paul & Co. bought "the entire copyright and the right of continuation" from Chatto and Windus, they also agreed to pay for all articles which Hueffer had accepted for publication (mainly, no doubt, for the Jan. 1879 number), as well as to pay him £10 "for services already rendered," which was his full salary for an issue: letter of Chatto and Windus to C. Kegan Paul and Co., Dec. 12, 1878, Chatto and Windus documents. Under these circumstances it is highly unlikely that Paul did not use some of Hueffer's articles for his first issue. Thus, in some degree, Hueffer and Paul were joint editors of the Jan. 1879 number.

[17]See the introduction above, at end of the account of Hueffer's editorship, p. 611.

786, 801, 804, 819, 820, 821, 828. In the article on Paul, *DNB*, 2nd suppl., the date at which he assumed the editorship should have been 1879, not 1873.

The prospectus is printed in the *Athenaeum* for Sept. 6, 1873, p. 319, and Sept. 20, p. 383. For a comment on the first issue, see the *Academy*, Nov. 1, 1873, pp. 403–404. Editorial remarks are found in *NQM*, 6 (April 1876), 230–232; 10 (April 1878), 213–214; and 2 n.s. (October 1879), 445.

THE NEW QUARTERLY MAGAZINE, 1873–1880

29 The mistakes of a day, 865–886. **Henry Coe Coape.** Signed Mervyn Merriton, Author of *The Ringwoods of Ringwood*, etc.: see H&L, V, 126.

VOLUME 3, OCTOBER 1874

30 Notes of travel in Portugal (chap. xii), 1–25. **O. J. F. Crawfurd.** Evidence for no. 8.
31 The fauna of fancy, 26–49. **Frances Power Cobbe.** Signed; repr. *False Beasts and True*, 1875.
32 A sea changeling, 50–134. **Frances E. M. Notley.** Signed F. M. Notley, Author of *Olive Varcoe*: see H&L, IV, 251.
33 Spiritualism in England, 135–155. **Nathaniel A. Harness.** Signed.
34 The character of Goethe, 156–186. **Robert Buchanan,** 1841–1901. Signed; repr. *A Look round Literature*, 1887.
35 The size of farms, 187–202. **Richard Jefferies.** Signed.
36 In the Rue Froide, 203–239. **Katharine S. Macquoid.** Signed The Author of *Patty* (see *BMCat.*).

VOLUME 3, JANUARY 1875

37 Canada: an emigrant's journal, 241–273. **Lewis Parker.** Signed.
38 Nathaniel Hawthorne, 274–303. **George Barnett Smith.** Signed; repr. *Poets and Novelists*, 1876.
39 The mad Willoughbys, 304–372. **Eliza Lynn Linton.** Signature; repr. *The Mad Willoughbys and Other Tales*, [1876].
40 English flower gardens, 373–398. **O. J. F. Crawfurd.** Signed Archibald Banks; repr. *Country House Essays*, 1876, and *Horses and Riders*, [1885].
41 Notes of travel in Portugal (supplementary chapter), 399–415. **O. J. F. Crawfurd.** Evidence for no. 8.
42 Sir Philip Sidney, 416–442. **Henry Kingsley.** Signed; repr. *Fireside Studies*, (1876), II.
43 A tragedy queen, 443–474. **O. J. F. Crawfurd.** Signed John Dangerfield—see no. 10; repr. *The Fool*, II.

VOLUME 4, APRIL 1875

44 On allotment gardens, 1–32. **Richard Jefferies.** Signed.
45 The religious element in Chaucer, 33–48. **T. H. L. Leary.** Signed, with titles "Rev." and "D.C.L."

46 The fool of the family, 49–126. **O. J. F. Crawfurd.** Signed John Dangerfield—see no. 10; repr. *The Fool*, I.
47 Trout fishing, 127–158. **O. J. F. Crawfurd.** Signed Archibald Banks; repr. *Country House Essays*, 1876, and *Horses and Riders*, [1885].
48 Richard Wagner and his *Ring of the Niblung*, 159–186. **Francis Hueffer.** Signed F. Hueffer; repr. *Musical Studies*, 1880.
49 Only an episode, 187–221. **Frances Hoey.** Signed F.C.H.; Contents gives "Mrs. Cashel Hoey"; repr. *No Sign*, 1876.
50 The moral aspects of vivisection, 222–237. **Frances Power Cobbe.** Signed; repr. under that title, 1876.
51 Thomas Love Peacock: a personal reminiscence, 238–255. **Robert Buchanan,** 1841–1901. Signed; repr. *A Look round Literature*, 1887.

VOLUME 4, JULY 1875

52 De Quincey, 257–287. **O. J. F. Crawfurd.** Signed The Editor.
53 Affonso Henriquez, and the rise of Portugal, 288–324. **Oswald Crawfurd.** Signed; repr. *Portugal* as "The Rise of Portugal" and "The First King of Portugal."
54 The modern stage, 325–362. **Robert Buchanan,** 1841–1901. Signed; repr. *A Look round Literature*, 1887.
55 Dark cybel, 363–443. **Frances Hoey.** Contents gives "Mrs. Cashel Hoey"; repr. *No Sign*, 1876.
56 Lord Bute, the premier, 444–474. **Frederick Arnold.** Signed.
57 The town mouse and the country mouse, 475–510. **Frances Power Cobbe.** Signed; repr. *Scientific Spirit*.
58 By the law, 511–549. **Eliza Lynn Linton.** Signature; repr. *The Mad Willoughbys and Other Tales*, [1876].

VOLUME 5, OCTOBER 1875

59 Village organization, 1–35. **Richard Jefferies.** Signed; repr. *The Hills and the Vale*, 1909.
60 Philip Massinger, 36–64. **George Barnett Smith.** Signed.
61 Nino Bixio, 65–84. **Evelyn Carrington.** Signed; repr. *Italian Characters of the Epoch of Unification*, 1890.
62 No sign, 85–145. **Frances Hoey.** Signed Mrs. Cashel Hoey; repr. *No Sign*, 1876.
63 The artistic spirit in modern poetry, 146–165. **J. W. Comyns Carr.** Signed; repr. *Essays on Art*, 1879.

repr. *The Troubadours* (1878), pp. 228–271.

101 The house on the beach: a realistic tale, 329–410. **George Meredith.** Signed; repr. *Works*, XXII.

102 Revolutions and Russian conquests in Central Asia, 411–434. **J. H. Tremenheere.** Signed.

103 Goethe in his old age [and Johann Eckerman], 435–459. **Edward Barrington De Fonblanque.** Signed.

104 The Pompeii of the Tannenwald, 460–471. **H. Schütz Wilson.** Signed.

105 Kate Cronin's dowry, 472–501. **Frances Hoey.** Signed Mrs. Cashel Hoey; repr. under same title, N.Y., 1877.

VOLUME 8, APRIL [PRINTED JANUARY] 1877

106 On the idea of comedy, and of the uses of the comic spirit, 1–40. **George Meredith.** Signed; repr. *Works*, XXIII.

107 The tourist in Portugal (No. II): farms and farming, 41–80. **O. J. F. Crawfurd.** Evidence for no. 86.

108 Mrs. Jack, 81–155. **Frances Eleanor Trollope.** Signed.

109 The art of lying [tall stories in literature], 156–185. **C. Elliot Browne.** Signed.

110 Musical expression and the composers of the eighteenth century, 186–202. **Violet Paget.** Signed H. Vernon Lee; see Peter Gunn, *Vernon Lee* (1964), p. 66.

111 A glance at the comets, 203–223. **Edward V. Heward.** Signed.

112 The mystic; or, A journey to Edinburgh, 224–254. **O. J. F. Crawfurd.** Signed John Dangerfield—see no. 10.

VOLUME 8, JULY 1877

113 The tourist in Portugal (No. III, concl.): a Portuguese Troy, 255–282. **O. J. F. Crawfurd.** Evidence for no. 86.

114 The peak in Darien: the riddle of death, 283–293. **Frances Power Cobbe.** Signed; repr. *Peak in Darien*, 1882.

115 The Countess von Labanoff; or, The three lovers: a novelette, 294–351. **Richard Hengist Horne.** Signed; repr. under same title, 1877.

116 The literary aspects of Schopenhauer's work, 352–378. **Francis Hueffer.** Signed; repr. *Italian and Other Studies*, 1883.

117 The future of country society, 379–409. **Richard Jefferies.** Signed R. Jefferies.

118 Edgar Allan Poe, 410–427. **James Ashcroft Noble.** Signed.

119 The case of General Ople and Lady Camper, 428–478. **George Meredith.** Signed in Contents; repr. *Works*, XXI.

VOLUME 9, OCTOBER 1877

120 Count Giacomo Leopardi, 1–33. **Helen Zimmern.** Signed.

121 Lord Chancellors and Chief Justices since Lord Campbell, 34–67. **Frederick Arnold.** Signed as in no. 23, with title "Rev."; see Boase.

122 Misericordia, 68–142. **Eliza Lynn Linton.** Signature; repr. under that title, N.Y., 1878.

123 Sir John Sinclair, and some other Scotch improvers, 143–168. **Henry Evershed.** Signed.

124 Giotto, 169–202. **Julia Cartwright.** Signed J. Cartwright; Contents gives first name.

125 Railway reform, 203–217. **Joseph Parsloe.** Signed.

126 The curé's housekeeper, 218–259. **Frances Eleanor Trollope.** Signed.

VOLUME 9, JANUARY 1878

127 The story of Dr. Faustus, 261–284. **Francis Hueffer.** Signed.

128 An idyl of Euboea, 285–298. **Chrysostom Dion.** See pp. 285–286. Trans. with intro. and concluding notes by **Helen Zimmern**—signed.

129 Esau's choice, 299–323. **Frances Hoey.** Contents gives "Mrs. Cashel Hoey."

130 Early literary journals, 324–341. **C. Elliot Browne.** Signed.

131 The popular preaching of the past, 342–362. **T. H. L. Leary.** Signed.

132 Cool haunts in the Italian highlands, 363–389. **Evelyn Carrington.** Signed.

133 The devil in English poetry, 390–416. **Henry G. Hewlett.** Signed.

134 The fortunes of the Sundew family: a social nightmare in seven chapters, 417–442. **Bertha Thomas,** prob. Signed B. Thomas; see *BMCat.*

VOLUME 10, APRIL 1878

135 Unknown correspondence by Edgar Poe [including several letters by friends], 1–30. **Edgar A. Poe.** Title. Edited with intro. note, signed **John H. Ingram.**

136 The Apollo Belvedere, 31–46. **Sidney Colvin.** Signed.
137 Mrs. Gainsborough's diamonds, 47–109. **Julian Hawthorne.** Signed; repr. *The Laughing Mill and Other Stories,* 1879.
138 Panslavonianism, 110–132. **H. Sutherland Edwards.** Signed; repr. *Russians At Home,* II.
139 Parliamentary forms and reforms, 133–157. **Henry W. Lucy.** Signed.
140 Alfred de Musset and physiognomic poetry, 158–179. **Theodore Watts.** Signed.
141 "What can we do for Greece?" 180–200.
142 The tapping of Thirlmere [for a reservoir], 201–212.
143 Current literature and current criticism, 213–240. **Francis Hueffer** and others. See p. 213, first sentence.

154 Martin Luther, 502–524. **Henry Hayman.** Signed.
155 Our professor, 525–558. **Eliza Lynn Linton.** Signature; repr. under same title, N.Y., 1879.
156 Théodore de Banville, 559–578. **Andrew Lang.** Signature; repr. *Essays in Little,* 1891.
157 The caucus system and the Liberal party, 579–590. **George Howell.** Signed.
158 Dictionaries of music, 591–613. **H. Sutherland Edwards.** Signed; repr. *Lyrical Drama* (1881), II.
159 The vernacular press of India and the Afghan crisis, 614–633. Contents gives "an Indian Editor."
160 A history of Italian folk-song, 634–654. **T. Adolphus Trollope.** Signed.
161 Current literature and current criticism, 655–684. **Francis Hueffer** and others. Cf. no. 143.

VOLUME 10, JULY 1878

144 A Dutch poetess of the seventeenth century [Tesselschade Visscher], 241–269. **Edmund W. Gosse.** Signed; repr. *Studies.*
145 General Cesnola's *Cyprus,* 270–291. **W. Watkiss Lloyd.** Signed.
146 Country life in Portugal, 292–314. **O. J. F. Crawfurd.** Signed John Latouche; repr. *Portugal* as "Modern Portugal: Country Life and Sport."
147 An indiscretion in the life of an heiress, 315–378. **Thomas Hardy.** Signed; repr., ed. C. J. Weber, Baltimore, 1935.
148 Reminiscences of Gustave Courbet at La Tour, 379–389. **Elizabeth E. Evans.** Signed.
149 Mary Wollstonecraft, 390–412. **Mathilde Blind.** Signed.
150 Socialism, 413–431. **Arthur Arnold.** Signed.
151 Current literature and current criticism, 432–460. **Francis Hueffer** and others. Cf. no. 143.

VOLUME 10, OCTOBER 1878

152 The gospel according to Walt Whitman, 461–481. **Robert Louis Stevenson.** Signed; repr. *Familiar Studies of Men and Books,* 1882.
153 The new Bulgaria, 482–501. **F. D. Millet.** Signed; Contents adds "late war correspondent of *The Daily News.*"

VOLUME 11 o.s., 1 n.s., JANUARY 1879

162 Prince Bismarck, 1–23. Unidentified. **C. Kegan Paul** wrote the footnote, p. 22: see *Memories,* p. 285.
163 Our public schools (No. I): Eton, 24–46. **C. Kegan Paul?** Paul graduated from Eton and later, 1853–1862, served as a chaplain and college master, which would account for the author's close knowledge of the school's organization; since this was Paul's first issue as editor and he must have planned these arts. on the public schools, we should expect him to take Eton himself (he also wrote *NC* no. 2296 on the same subject) and to initiate the series; some parallels exist between pp. 38–39 and 34 and Paul's *Memories,* pp. 89 and 227–228. The series, written by different contributors, was repr. anon. as *Our Public Schools,* 1881.
164 Max Müller on the origin of religion, 63–72.
165 A beleaguered city, 73–149. **Margaret Oliphant.** Signature in Contents.
166 *The Thousand and One Nights* (Part I), 150–174. **John Payne,** 1842–1916. Attr. by W. F. Kirby in Richard Burton, *The Book of the Thousand Nights and a Night* (1886), X, 496.
167 England's policy towards Afghanistan, 175–195. **Demetrius C. Boulger.** Repr. *Central Asian Questions.*
168 The custodians of learning in the middle ages, [the monks], 196–212.
169 Selected books of the quarter, 213–240.

Volume 11 o.s., 1 n.s., April 1879

170 South Africa, 241–272. **Frederic Rogers.** Attr. in *Athenaeum*, Apr. 26, 1879, p. 539, and in *Academy*, same date, p. 367, to Lord Blachford.

171 Our public schools (No. II): Harrow, 273–296. Unidentified. For reprint see no. 163.

172 Public libraries and their catalogues, 303–323. **Richard Garnett, 1835–1906.** Repr. *Essays*.

173 The distracted young preacher, 324–376. **Thomas Hardy.** Signed; repr. *Wessex Tales*, 1888.

174 *The Thousand and One Nights* (Part II, concl.), 377–401. **John Payne, 1842–1916.** Cf. no. 166.

175 Maladministration of charities by the City Companies, 402–417.

176 The early days of the French Academy, 418–436.

177 The poets of the Oxford Catholic Movement: 1827–1845, 437–450. **C. Kegan Paul.** Passages on pp. 439–440 and 441 are identical in phrasing and quotations with Paul's sketch of Keble in *Biographical Sketches* (1883), pp. 47, 48, respectively.

178 Selected books, 451–480.

Volume 12 o.s., 2 n.s., July 1879

179 The Greek frontier, 1829–1879: how it was won in 1829, 1–20. **Charles M. Church.** Pages 16–17 are an earlier draft of Church's "Reminiscences" in E. M. Church, *Chapters in an Adventurous Life: Sir Richard Church in Italy and Greece* (1895), pp. 320–321; attr. in *WWW*/1916.

180 Our public schools (No. III): Winchester, 21–34. Unidentified. For reprint see no. 163.

181 Disestablishment and its complications in Scotland, 46–56. **William Wallace, 1843–1921,** prob. Two years earlier in a signed art. in the *Contemp. Rev.* (no. 1157, *Index*, I), "The Religious Upheaval in Scotland," Wallace had taken much the same ground and discussed, in similar terms, some of the same people: the liberal nature of established churches (there p. 246, here p. 50); church music and church aesthetics, with a reference to Dr. Lee (p. 243 and p. 50); the "dogmatism of Strauss" (p. 245 and p. 49);

the Robertson Smith controversy (pp. 247–251 and pp. 52–53), etc.; *The Bookman* [London], Oct. 1893, reported that Wallace wrote "for the *Contemporary* and *New Quarterly*."

182 The tale of Chloe: an episode in the history of Beau Beamish, 57–113. **George Meredith.** Repr. under this title, 1895, and in *Works*, XXI.

183 A new dialect; or, Yokohama pidgin, 114–124. **Charles Godfrey Leland.** On p. 121 author says he "published, some years ago, a work on Chinese Pidgin"; Leland wrote *Pidgin-English Sing-Song; or Songs and Stories in the China-English Dialect*, 1876; on p. 121 author speaks of Rabelais Society, which Leland founded.

184 The Corporation of London and metropolitan government, 125–149.

185 The poetic phase in modern English art, 150–165.

186 The human face divine [on its evolution], 166–182. **Grant Allen?** On p. 168 the author refers to a signed art. in the *FortR* for May 1879 (no. 1584), but without mentioning the writer's name, which was Grant Allen; moreover, he points out that both that art. and this explain facts about the human body and the human face, respectively, on the same grounds—increased or decreased use of inherited mammalian features; Allen wrote many popular papers on evolution.

187 Cardinal Newman and his work, 183–202. **C. Kegan Paul.** See no. 177; cf. that art., p. 438, where Paul traces the origins of the Oxford Movement to Keble's Assize Sermon and his *Christian Year*, and quotes Newman's *Apologia*, to this art., p. 186; Paul wrote on Newman in *Biographical Sketches*, 1883, and had been closely associated with the Oxford Movement (see *Memories*, pp. 143, 219).

188 Selected books, 203–236.

Volume 12 o.s., 2 n.s., October 1879

189 India's need and England's duty, 237–254. **H. J. S. Cotton.** Claimed in *Indian and Home Memories* (1911), p. 163.

190 Our public schools (No. IV): Rugby, 255–279. **Arthur Sidgwick.** Attr. by E. G. Sandford in *Memoirs of Archbishop [Frederick] Temple*, ed. Sandford (1906), I, 205; for reprint see no. 163.

191 Workhouse visiting and management during twenty-five years, 283–306. **Louisa Twining.** Repr. *Recollections of Workhouse Visiting and Management during Twenty-five Years*, 1880.

192 The story of a lie, 307–355. **Robert Louis Stevenson.** Signed; repr. *Novels and Tales* (N.Y., 1895), III.

193 George Henry Lewes, 356–376. **James Sully.** George Eliot, *Letters*, VII, 198, 230, 231.

194 Realism in dramatic art [and Zola's work], 377–400. **John Westland Marston.** Attr. in *Athenaeum*, Nov. 1, 1879, p. 564; *CBEL*, III, 604.

195 What does Home Rule mean? 401–411. **Justin McCarthy,** 1830–1912. Signed A Home-Rule M.P.; attr. in *Athenaeum*, Oct. 18, 1879, p. 498, and *Academy*, same date, p. 281.

196 Mr. Hardy's novels, 412–431. **C. Kegan Paul.** Attr. George Douglas, *Hibbert Journal*, 26 (Apr. 1928), 392.

197 Can army short service be made to work? 432–444.

198 Selected books, 445–476. Pages 469–473 by **Thomas Hardy**—attr. with evidence in Carroll A. Wilson, *Thirteen Author Collections of the 19th Century*, (N.Y., 1950), I, 52; pages 445–448 by **C. Kegan Paul,** prob.—second sentence is plainly editorial and the topic, "St. Paul," would have attracted this writer.

VOLUME 13 O.S., 3 N.S., JANUARY 1880

199 The roads of England, and wayfaring life in the middle ages (Part I), 1–23. **J. J. Jusserand.** Signed Dr. Jusserand in Contents; cf. no. 211.

200 Our public schools (No. V): Westminster, 24–51. Unidentified. For reprint see no. 163.

201 The revival of the drama, 55–66.

202 Italian affairs, 67–91.

203 Michael and I, 92–135. **Julian Sturgis.** Signed; repr. *My Friends and I*, N.Y., 1884.

204 Shelta, the tinkers' talk, 136–141. **Charles G. Leland.** Signed.

205 The treatment of vagrancy, 142–149.

206 Middle-class education, 150–157. **Mark Pattison.** Signed.

207 The origin of poetry, 158–177.

208 Fucinus [in the Apennines]: a lost lake and a new found land, 178–188.

209 The anti-rent agitation in Ireland, 189–211.

210 Selected books, 212–232.

VOLUME 13 O.S., 3 N.S., APRIL 1880

211 The roads of England, and wayfaring life in the middle ages (Part II, concl.), 233–257. **J. J. Jusserand.** Signed.

212 Our public schools (No. VI): Marlborough, 258–283. **Everard F. Im Thurn.** In *Athenaeum*, Jan. 6, 1894, p. 19, man cited complains that an art. in *Ludgate Monthly Mag.*, Sept. 1893, is "cribbed" from one of his own in the *NQM*; cf. this art. with *Ludgate Monthly*, 5, (Sept. 1893), 451–460; for reprint see no. 163.

213 Miracle plays, 287–309.

214 Illusions of perception, 310–334. **James Sully.** Repr., expanded and revised, in *Illusions*, 1881.

215 Fellow-townsmen, 335–383. **Thomas Hardy.** Signed; repr. *Wessex Tales*, 1888.

216 Russia, 384–410.

217 Jacobins and levellers, 411–431.

218 The general election, 432–443.

219 Selected books, 444–460.

The Nineteenth Century, 1877–1900

A GENTLEMAN DINING at Willis' Rooms in London on the evening of April 21, 1869, might have been startled by the arrival of a curiously assorted party. For on this evening men of such fame and diverse interests as Tennyson, Huxley, James Martineau, and W. G. Ward were here brought together by James Knowles for the first meeting of the Metaphysical Society. This extraordinary Society, which met each month for twelve years, quickly expanded its membership to include fifty-nine distinguished names.[1] Unlike the members of most societies, they were chosen for their diversity of opinion, strong convictions, and an earnest desire to grapple with the religious and philosophic questions of their day. Knowles points out how far the diversity went:

At first it was intended that no distinct and avowed opponents of Christianity should be invited, though Anglicans of all shades, Roman Catholics, Unitarians and Nonconformists should be eligible. But it was soon felt that if any real discussion of Christian evidences was to take place, the opposition ought be fully and fairly represented.[2]

In the 1870s it took courage, a fine sense of courtesy, and a firm belief in the value of the "open platform" for the members of the Society to exchange opinions candidly, even in a private meeting, on religious questions. Few of them had not felt doubt or met challenge to their deepest beliefs; some had recently been converted to Catholicism, others had lost a traditional faith. All recognized that not only religious creeds, but the very principles and structure of faith itself, were being reconsidered by their more thoughtful contemporaries. The new emphasis on scientific method and Biblical criticism which was arising in the nineteenth century demanded such reconsideration. Hence the admission of "the opposition."

James Thomas Knowles, Jr. was not trained as a philosopher but as an architect. However, when he became editor of the *Contemporary Review* in 1870, he realized that by drawing the interests of the Society and its members into a review, he would be fulfilling a need among educated people. It was not only that the subjects of the papers—primarily religious and speculative—had an interest for the large audience of a periodical. Knowles also felt that its methods of debate and its concern with presentation of evidence could enrich discussions of politics or social questions—if

---

[1]Alan Brown (Bibliographical Note), pp. 25–27, describes this preliminary meeting and quotes the resolutions passed. The list of members is given by Knowles, *NC*, 18 (Aug. 1885), 178.
[2]Quoted in Hallam Tennyson, *Alfred Lord Tennyson: A Memoir* (N.Y., 1897), II, 166.

only full and frank exchange could be assured by an editor.[3] For some years he gained experience through directing the *Contemporary*; and the journal gained benefit from his acquaintance with the members of the Society, whose contributions he solicited. It welcomed the prestigious names of Gladstone and Manning, and the polished papers of Huxley and Ruskin. However, by 1877 the new proprietors of the *Contemporary* were a little perturbed by Knowles' editorial principles.[4] The sharp repartee and unfettered spirit of debate common to the Society's meetings were giving the Review an increasingly controversial tone. "The change made, after Mr. Knowles joined it, in the conduct of *The Contemporary*, by enlarging the comparatively limited 'platform' of the Dean [Dean Alford, first editor], and converting it into an entirely free and open field, where all forms of honest opinion and belief (represented by men of sufficient weight) should be not only tolerated, but equally welcomed," inevitably met with mixed response.[5] But Knowles was convinced, when he broke with the Review, that his experience in the Society had inspired new ideas about journalism which he alone must implement. For in that year, with the genius of a born entrepreneur and the same insight and enthusiasm which he had used in founding the Metaphysical Society, he embarked on the publication of the *Nineteenth Century*.

While editing the *Contemporary*, Knowles continued to work as an architect; but as sole editor and proprietor of a review as broad in scope as the *Nineteenth Century*, he found that his varied interests were absorbed in that one career. Gradually he took on fewer commissions, although he continued his interest in architecture and contributed articles on the subject to his periodical.

The first lively publications of the new Review were clearly indebted to the Metaphysical Society. Indeed, in many ways the young *Nineteenth Century* was an organ of the Society. A glance at the first two issues reveals that fifteen of the twenty-two contributors were members. Moreover, since Knowles had decided that all viewpoints ought to be fully represented, articles often stimulated enough controversy and interest to carry the original subject forward, through several issues, on waves of criticism, defence, and retort.

In the second issue (April 1877) the editor's "passion for organized controversy" took an interesting form.[6] He asked seven men to write on one subject, "The influence upon morality of a decline in religious belief," and called the resulting series of articles "A Modern 'Symposium'." The seven contributors, as we should expect, were all members of the Society. In a prefatory note the editor described the symposium:

A certain number of gentlemen have consented to discuss from time to time, under this title, questions of interest and importance. Each writer will have seen all that has been written before his own remarks, but (except the first writer) nothing that follows them.

---

[3]He recalled (*NC*, 18 [Aug. 1885], 177) that one of the distinguishing features of the Society had been its willingness to discuss theological subjects "after the manner and with the freedom of an ordinary scientific society."

[4]See introduction to the *Contemporary* in the *Index*, I, 211.

[5]The quotation is from the prospectus to the *NC*, written by Knowles himself: *Athenaeum*, Feb. 10, 1877, p. 205.

[6]The phrase quoted is by Michael Goodwin, *Nineteenth-Century Opinion* (1951), p. 9.

The first writer, as proposer of the subject, will have the right of reply or summing-up at the end.[7]

This method provided the framework for an exhaustive coverage of a particular subject, and the successive symposia presented the reader with a series of related papers, conveniently drawn together in one or two issues, which had the suspense found in actual debates. The term "Symposium" was hardly accidental: in setting up a framework within which eminent men could argue their views on serious subjects, Knowles was adapting the Socratic dialogue to the conditions of journalism, and affirming the Platonic faith in discourse, which has been called "the dominating feature of the intellectual life of the nineteenth century."[8]

But, however closely related, Knowles' Review differed from the Society in various respects. The reach of the *Nineteenth Century* extended to realms with which the group had not been concerned—notably those of practical science, social justice, and politics. This reflected a shift in national focus from the impact of science on religion in the 60s and 70s (the Society's life-dates were 1869–1880) to social and political problems in the 80s and 90s. The change is traceable partly to the crisis of Home Rule and the mounting colonial problem, especially in South Africa, partly to a weary skepticism of finding anything but dusty answers in the endless discourse on metaphysics.[9] Furthermore, as soon as the periodical centred attention on politics, it tended to adopt a Liberal position, and to that extent modified its open platform. The essays which appeared in July 1892 in the familiar form of a symposium were called "Why I shall vote for the Unionist candidate." It was only after the victory of the Home Rulers that Knowles followed this with another symposium in August, "Why I voted for Mr. Gladstone." And no political series, I believe, ever presented the Conservative position; Knowles left that to the *National Review*, founded in 1883. Again, to take an issue of a different kind—the proposed Channel Tunnel of 1882— Knowles was said by Gladstone to have single-handedly crushed the idea by soliciting a sufficient number of articles opposed to the plan from admirals and statesmen.[10]

Knowles' policy that all articles be signed, which was a hallmark of the *Nineteenth Century*, also had its roots in the Metaphysical Society. The members had taken individual responsibility for their views; contributors were similarly expected to acknowledge their opinions with signatures. This policy, however, had other and more important sources. Some reviews, notably the *Fortnightly* and the *Contemporary*, had begun to publish signed articles in the 1860s.[11] Furthermore, as the editor of a new review which did not have the patronage of a specific political or religious establishment, Knowles must have felt that a policy of anonymity would have had little *raison d'être*. In addition, being a man of business, he saw the advan-

[7] *NC*, 1 (Apr. 1877), 331. In *NC*, 18 (Aug. 1855), 179, Knowles acknowledged that the inspiration for the symposium came from the meetings of the Metaphysical Society.

[8] Brown (Bibliographical Note), p. xiv.

[9] See Walter E. Houghton, *The Victorian Frame of Mind* (New Haven, 1957), pp. 14–18, 179–180.

[10] John Marriott, "Our Fathers that Begat Us," *Nineteenth Century and After*, 122 (Aug. 1937), 184. See below, nos. 682–685, 697, 710–714.

[11] The principal reasons for the breakdown of anonymity are mentioned in the *Index*, I, xviii–xix, and n. 8.

tage of displaying names like Gladstone, Tennyson, Huxley, or Cardinal Manning on the cover of a periodical. What educated reader would not buy a journal in which most of the articles were by the leading men of the day discussing the great issues of the day? The authoritative ring of the title itself, from this point of view, was a stroke of genius. It was not the name of a town, or a place, or a publisher, or, still less, of a party. It was the name of the age it so brilliantly embodied.[12] Small wonder that, when Knowles died in 1908, the obituary in the *Times* found that he "combined in a remarkable way a sense of what interested the educated public with the keen eye of the man of business."[13] The fact that in the early years the *Nineteenth Century* sold over 10,000 copies per issue, far more than any other periodical of its kind,[14] and that this in turn, promising perhaps 50,000 readers, was bound to "steal" well known writers from other journals,[15] supports this estimate.

But to put it this way is misleading. It reduces the achievement to a lower level by ignoring the quality of the writing and the *editorial* skill of the editor. We need to balance our perspective by recalling Frederic Harrison's tribute in 1908:

It grew to be a literary power in the New World as well as in the Old; and has exercised a very striking influence not only on periodical literature but on liberal thought. In a few pages it is impossible to relate the story of a career of editorship of more than thirty years, with its multiplicity of interests, causes, and topics, and its singular list of eminent contributors. None know so well as his earliest colleagues in this task how entirely the result was the work of the energy, the boldness, the versatile tact, and the genial sympathy of the English Brunetière, Sir James Knowles.[16]

To my mind, the *Fortnightly* under Morley was the only review of the later Victorian period more distinguished than the *Nineteenth Century*.

In 1901 the Review became the *Nineteenth Century and After*, and in 1951 the *Twentieth Century*.[17] In 1908, upon the death of Knowles, his son-in-law, William Wray Skilbeck, became editor. Although the Review continued successfully with some of Knowles' old contributors, it inevitably lost the galaxy of famous men which once revealed its elite origin. This was the result of changing times. The symposia with their exhaustive dialogues, carried on by men who could combine active careers as statesmen or scholars with writing at length for the public, were no longer possible: careers became too demanding as competition increased; nor did the public have time

---

[12]Miss Priscilla Metcalf has kindly informed us that in a letter to Tennyson, Jan. 6, 1877, at the Tennyson Research Centre, Lincoln, Knowles credited Tennyson with having suggested the title. How explicit the suggestion was, or how much was due to Knowles' quick uptake of a vague remark, is uncertain.

[13]Feb. 14, 1908, p. 12e.

[14]Editor, "Our Thousandth Number," *Twentieth Century*, 167 (June 1960), 504. The statement on other periodicals (the *Edinburgh*, the *Quarterly*, the *Fortnightly*, and the *Contemporary*) is based on the figures for 1870 in Alvar Ellegård (see *Index*, I, xxiii), p. 27.

[15]Charles Wordsworth in a letter to W. A. Knight, Mar. 14, 1878, at the Morgan Library, N.Y., indicates the rewards of writing for Knowles: "I see the Number has reached its 20th thousand, owing no doubt to its attractive articles at the prow and stern, and so I shall have succeeded at all events in obtaining currency in many thoughtful minds for the views which I wished to express."

[16]*NC*, 63 (Apr. 1908), 695-696.

[17]In 1900 Knowles found that the title, *Twentieth Century*, had been appropriated by an enterprising rival. It was not until 1951 that the legal problems were settled and this title was available: see Goodwin, cited in n. 7, p. 15.

to study such great prose marathons. But Knowles, who was so sensitive to the pulse of his time, would have been the first to acknowledge that he should have to remold his Review to meet the temper of twentieth-century readers—a challenge its later editors have met, for it is still in publication.

EDITOR AND PROPRIETOR

James T. Knowles: March 1877–December 1900 (and after). Vol. 1—Vol. 48.
    Henry Hyde Champion was assistant editor for two years, 1890/91–1892/93.[18]
    William Wray Skilbeck assisted his father-in-law, starting about 1891, perhaps after Champion resigned.[19]

PUBLISHERS

Henry S. King and Co.: March 1877–December 1877, Vol. 1—Vol. 2.
C. Kegan Paul and Co.: January 1878–June 1881, Vol. 3—Vol. 9.
Kegan Paul, Trench and Co.: July 1881–June 1891, Vol. 10—Vol. 29.
Sampson Low, Marston and Co.: July 1891–December 1900, Vol. 30—Vol. 48.

NOTE ON ATTRIBUTIONS

The *Nineteenth Century* is a signed periodical, but a few signatures turn out to be pseudonyms: C. de Warmont (no. 269), Adalet (nos. 1907, 1973, 2245), Fiona Macleod (no. 3755), and Esmé Stuart (no. 2424). A *Catalogue of Contributors and Contributions* to the first fifty volumes was compiled by Knowles in 1902. Here the names of the authors, though not in strict alphabetical order, are to be found under the first letter of their surnames, all the As, then the Bs, etc., being brought together, so that the *Catalogue* provides a complete list of contributors, except for the four who used pseudonyms. In other respects, the information in this *Index* is more extensive and useful.

BIBLIOGRAPHICAL NOTE

Alan W. Brown, *The Metaphysical Society: Victorian Minds in Crisis, 1869–1880* (N.Y., 1947) is an essential source for the background of the Review: see especially chap. X, "Knowles and the Triumph of the *Nineteenth Century*." R. H. Hutton gave a reconstruction of a Society debate in "The Metaphysical Society," *NC*, 18 (August 1885), 179–196, where the introductory note by Knowles reveals the significance which the meetings had for the editor. In the memoir of Tennyson (see n. 2 above), pp. 166–169, Hallam Tennyson quotes descriptions of the Society contributed by Knowles and others.

   A prospectus published in the *Spectator*, Feb. 10, 1877, p. 191 (also in the *Athenaeum*, same date, p. 205) and Knowles' introduction to his *Catalogue of Contributors* are the only direct statements of policy which were made by the editor. However, good first-hand descriptions of the early years of the Review—its principles, contributors, and the quality of the articles—are given by Frederic Harrison,

---

[18]The obituary in the *Times*, May 2, 1928, p. 11c, says he worked for two years as sub-editor of the *NC* just before going to Australia, where he arrived in 1893.
[19]We wish to thank Miss Eirene Skilbeck, his granddaughter, for this information.

"The *Nineteenth Century*, No. D: A Retrospect," *NC*, 84 (October 1918), 785–796; Yves Guyot, "Ma Connexion avec la *Nineteenth Century*," *The Nineteenth Century and After*, 101 (March 1927), 305–312; and J. A. R. Marriott, "Our Fathers That Begat Us," *The Nineteenth Century and After*, 122 (August 1937), 179–188.

Several anniversary issues have contributed the following more historical articles on the Review, all in the *Nineteenth Century and After*: Sir Francis Younghusband, "The First Fifty Years," 101 (March 1927), 294–304; and as editorials, "Sixty Years Ago," 121 (March 1937), 424–432, and "Our Thousandth Number," 167 (June 1960), 498–507. In March 1952 the seventy-fifth anniversary number (Vol. 151) was entirely devoted to studies of the contributions to the Review between 1877 and 1901. These studies were based on Michael Goodwin's anthology of extracts, *Nineteenth-Century Opinion* (1951), which itself includes a preface, pp. 9–16.

In the issue of April 1908 (Vol. 63, pp. 683–696) six brief articles appeared which bear more specifically on Knowles' editorship and his personal qualities. Written by J. E. C. Welldon, Henry Birchenough, J. W. Cross, Frederick Wedmore, Herbert Maxwell, and Frederic Harrison, they were entitled, "James Knowles: a Tribute from Some Friends." Sydney K. Phelps also gave a personal account of Knowles in "Personal Reminiscences of Two Editors," 101 (March 1918), 313–319. The vivid impressions which these reminiscences give is supplemented by the more chronological treatment of Knowles' career by Sir Sidney Lee in the *DNB*, 2nd suppl., 1912, and the obituary notice in the *Times*, Feb. 14, 1908, p. 12e. Priscilla Metcalf writes us that she is preparing a manuscript for publication which is called "The Two Lives of James Knowles."

THE NINETEENTH CENTURY, 1877–1900

30 The present crisis in the Church of England, 417–435. **T. T. Carter.** Signed.
31 Social aspects of disestablishment, 436–457. **J. G. Rogers.** Signed.
32 The abuses of a landed gentry, 458–478. **Arthur Arnold.** Signed; repr. *Social Politics,* 1878. (Note, p. 926, by the editor, **James Knowles,** quoting letter from Sir James Caird.)
33 The true story of the Vatican Council (Part III), 479–503. **H. E. Manning.** Signed as in no. 8.
34 Recent science, 504–523. **James Knowles.** Evidence for no. 10.
35 An actor's notes on Shakspeare (No. II): Hamlet and Ophelia, act. III, scene 1, 524–530. **Henry Irving,** 1838–1905. Signed; see *DNB.* (No. III is no. 271.)
36 A modern "symposium": the influence upon morality of a decline in religious belief (No. VIII), 531–536. **W. G. Ward.** Signed Dr. Ward; see p. 536n and *DNB.*
37 A modern "symposium" (No. IX), 536–539. **T. H. Huxley.** Title gives "Professor Huxley."
38 A modern "symposium" (No. X), 539–545. **R. H. Hutton.** Signed.
39 A modern "symposium" (No. XI, concl.), 545–546. **James Fitzjames Stephen.** Evidence for no. 20.

VOLUME 1, JUNE 1877

40 Life and times of Thomas Becket (Part I), 548–562. **J. A. Froude.** Signed; repr. *Studies, IV.*
41 South Kensington (Part I), 563–582. **Edgar A. Bowring.** Signed.
42 The punishment of infanticide, 583–595. **C. A. Fyffe.** Signed.
43 The true story of the Vatican Council (Part IV), 596–610. **H. E. Manning.** Signed as in no. 8.
44 For and against the play: a dialogue, 611–622. **Juliet Pollock.** Signed.
45 The soul and future life (Part I), 623–636. **Frederic Harrison.** Signed; repr. in *Current Discussion,* II.
46 Teaching to read, 637–645. **James Spedding.** Signed; repr. *Reviews.*
47 Railway accidents, 646–664. **John Fowler.** Signed.
48 Our route to India, 665–685. **Edward Dicey.** Signed; repr. *England and Egypt,* 1881. (See no. 62.)
49 Disestablishment and disendowment, 686–706. **A. H. Mackonochie.** Signed. (See no. 162.)
50 Turkey (Part I), 707–728. **Stratford**

Canning. Signed Stratford de Redcliffe [Viscount Stratford de Redcliffe]; repr. in *Current Discussion,* I, and in *The Eastern Question,* 1881.

VOLUME 1, JULY 1877

51 Turkey (Part II, concl.), 729–752. **Stratford Canning.** Cf. no. 50.
52 The Ridsdale judgment and its results, 753–773. **C. J. Ellicott.** Signed as in no. 4.
53 Round the world in the *Sunbeam* (Part I), 774–789. **Thomas Brassey.** Signed; repr. *Voyages,* I.
54 The true story of the Vatican Council (Part V, concl.): infallibility, 790–808. **H. E. Manning.** Signed as in no. 8.
55 Greater or lesser Britain, 809–831. **Julius Vogel.** Signed. (See nos. 86 and 156.)
56 The soul and future life (Part II, concl.), 832–842. **Frederic Harrison.** Signed. (See no. 82 and following arts.)
57 Life and times of Thomas Becket (Part II), 843–856. **J. A. Froude.** Signed.
58 The five nights' debate [in parliament on the Eastern question], 857–878. **M. E. Grant Duff.** Signed.
59 Another lesson from the radiometer, 879–887. **William Crookes.** Signed.
60 Medical women, 888–901. **James Stansfeld.** Signed.
61 Rejoinder [to no. 16] on authority in matters of opinion, 902–926. **W. E. Gladstone.** Signed; repr. *Gleanings,* III.

VOLUME 2, AUGUST 1877

62 The future of Egypt, 3–14. **Edward Dicey.** Signed; repr. *England and Egypt,* 1881, and *Current Discussion,* I. (See nos. 71, 80.)
63 Life and times of Thomas Becket (Part III), 15–27. **J. A. Froude.** Signed.
64 Impatience in politics, 28–43. **George Jacob Holyoake.** Signed.
65 George Dawson: politician, lecturer, and preacher, 44–61. **R. W. Dale.** Signed.
66 South Kensington (Part II, concl.), 62–81. **Edgar A. Bowring.** Signed.
67 Round the world in the *Sunbeam* (Part II), 82–96. **Thomas Brassey.** Signed.
68 Harriet Martineau [her *Autobiography*], 97–112. **W. R. Greg.** Signed; repr. *Misc. Essays,* I.
69 Shall Manchester have a university? 113–123. **Thomas Bazley.** Signed.
70 Recent literature, 124–143. **Henry Morley.** Signed.

71 Aggression on Egypt and freedom in the East, 149–166. **W. E. Gladstone.** Signed; repr. *Gleanings*, IV. (See no. 80.)

VOLUME 2, SEPTEMBER 1877

72 Germany and Egypt, 167–176. **George von Bunsen.** Signed.
73 Famine and debt in India, 177–197. **W. G. Pedder.** Signed.
74 Improvement of the law by private enterprise, 198–216. **James Fitzjames Stephen.** Signed.
75 Life and times of Thomas Becket (Part IV), 217–229. **J. A. Froude.** Signed. (Part V is no. 88.)
76 England and South Africa, 230–250. **Edward D. J. Wilson.** Signed.
77 Is life worth living? (Part I), 251–273. **W. H. Mallock.** Signed; repr. in *Current Discussion*, II.
78 The precedents and usages regulating the Muslim Khalîfate, 274–282. **George Percy Badger.** Signed.
79 The practical side of cooperative housekeeping, 283–291. **Roswell Fisher.** Signed.
80 Mr. Gladstone and our Empire, 292–308. **Edward Dicey.** Signed.
81 Recent science, 309–328. **James Knowles.** Evidence for no. 10.
82 A modern "symposium": the soul and future life (No. I), 329–334. **R. H. Hutton.** Signed; series repr. in *Current Discussion*, II.
83 A modern "symposium" (No. II), 334–341. **T. H. Huxley.** Signed Professor Huxley.
84 A modern "symposium" (No. III), 341–348. **Frederic Rogers.** Signed Lord Blachford.
85 A modern "symposium" (No. IV), 349–354. **Roden Noel.** Signed. ("Symposium" continued with no. 94.)

VOLUME 2, OCTOBER 1877

86 The integrity of the British Empire, 355–365. **Frederic Rogers.** Signed Blachford [Lord Blachford].
87 The colour-sense, 366–388. **W. E. Gladstone.** Signed.
88 The murder of Thomas Becket (Part V of no. 40), 389–410. **J. A. Froude.** Signed.
89 Cosmic emotion, 411–429. **W. K. Clifford.** Signed; repr. *Lectures*, II.
90 Round the world in the *Sunbeam* (Part III), 430–445. **Thomas Brassey.** Signed.

91 Restoration and anti-restoration, 446–470. **Sidney Colvin.** Signed.
92 International relations; and how they may be maintained for the best interests of mankind, 471–487. **Stratford Canning.** Signed as in no. 50; repr. *The Eastern Question*, 1881.
93 Archbishop Trench's poems, 488–496. **Frederic W. H. Myers.** Signed; repr. *Essays.*
94 A modern "symposium": the soul and future life (No. V), 497–499. **Roundell Palmer.** Signed Lord Selborne.
95 A modern "symposium" (No. VI), 499–506. **Alfred Barry.** Signed Canon Barry: see *DNB.*
96 A modern "symposium" (No. VII), 506–511. **W. R. Greg.** Signed; repr. *Misc. Essays*, I.
97 A modern "symposium" (No. VIII), 511–517. **Baldwin Brown.** Signed, with title "Rev."
98 A modern "symposium" (No. IX), 517–521. **W. G. Ward.** Signed.
99 A modern "symposium" (No. X, concl.) [comment on Nos. I–IX], 521–536. **Frederic Harrison.** Signed.

VOLUME 2, NOVEMBER 1877

100 The county franchise and Mr. Lowe thereon, 537–560. **W. E. Gladstone.** Signed; repr. *Gleanings*, I. (See no. 132.)
101 The Russians, the Turks, and the Bulgarians: at the theatre of war, 561–582. **Archibald Forbes.** Signed; repr. in *Current Discussion*, I.
102 Sun-spots and famines, 583–602. **J. Norman Lockyer** and **W. W. Hunter.** Signed.
103 Indian famines, 603–620. **George Tomkyns Chesney.** Signed George Chesney; Contents adds "Colonel"; see *DNB*, 1st suppl.
104 A morning with Auguste Comte, 621–631. **Thomas Erskine Perry.** Signed E. Perry; Contents gives "Sir Erskine Perry"; see *DNB.*
105 The Church Congress on Nonconformity, 632–646. **J. Guinness Rogers.** Signed. (See no. 111.)
106 The Marshalate: a chapter of French history, May 1873–October 1877, 647–668. **E. D. J. Wilson.** Signed.
107 Life and times of Thomas Becket (Part VI, concl.), 669–691. **J. A. Froude.** Signed.
108 Recent literature, 692–712. **Henry Morley.** Signed.

184 The political destiny of Canada, 1074–1086. **Francis Hincks.** Signed F. Hincks; Contents gives "Sir Francis Hincks."

185 Mr. Froude and the landlords of Ireland, 1087–1097. **Peter Fitzgerald.** Signed, with title "Knight of Kerry."

186 Readjustment of Church and State, 1098–1119. **C. J. Ellicott.** Signed as in no. 4.

187 The social origin of nihilism and pessimism in Germany, 1120–1132. **Charles Waldstein.** Signed; Contents adds "Dr."

188 Recent science, 1133–1153. **James Knowles.** Evidence for no. 10.

189 Liberty in the East and West, 1154–1174. **W. E. Gladstone.** Signed.

VOLUME 4, JULY 1878

190 The place of conscience in evolution, 1–18. **T. W. Fowle.** Signed.

191 The history of the International Association, 19–39. **George Howell.** Signed.

192 Ironclad field artillery, 40–50. **C. B. Brackenbury.** Signed.

193 On music and musical criticism (Part I), 51–74. **Edmund Gurney.** Signed. (Part II is no. 320.)

194 What the sun is made of, 75–87. **J. Norman Lockyer.** Signed.

195 The will of Peter the Great, 88–97. **William J. Thoms.** Signed.

196 Impressions of America (Part IV): popular education, 98–115. **R. W. Dale.** Signed.

197 The Second Advent and the church question, 116–132. **George Vance Smith.** Signed G. Vance Smith; Contents adds "Rev."; see *DNB*, 2nd suppl.

198 Jews and Judaism: a rejoinder [to no. 172], 133–150. **Hermann Adler.** Signed.

199 Protected princes in India, 151–173. **David Wedderburn.** Signed.

200 A modern "symposium" (No. V): is the popular judgment in politics more just than that of the higher orders? 174–181. **W. R. Greg.** Signed; repr. *Misc. Essays*, I. (No. IV is no. 168.)

201 A modern "symposium" (No. VI), 181–184. **Robert Lowe,** 1811–1892. Signed Mr. Lowe; index gives "Rt. Hon. R. Lowe"; see *DNB*.

202 A modern "symposium" (No. VII), 184–189. **W. E. Gladstone.** Signed Mr. Gladstone.

203 A modern "symposium" (No. VIII, concl.) [comment on Nos. I–VII], 189–192. **Arthur Russell.** Signed; cf. no. 165.

VOLUME 4, AUGUST 1878

204 The people of India (Part I; no more published), 193–221. **Florence Nightingale.** Signed.

205 Liberty in Germany (Part I), 222–239. **Leonard A. Montefiore.** Signed; repr. *Essays.*

206 Senior's *Conversations,* 240–260. **M. E. Grant Duff.** Signed; repr. *Out of the Past* (1903), I.

207 Malta, 261–288. **Francis W. Rowsell.** Signed F.W.R.; Contents gives "F. W. Rowsell": see Boase.

208 A familiar colloquy [on fine arts], 289–302. **W. H. Mallock.** Signed. (See no. 351.)

209 The religion of the Greeks as illustrated by Greek inscriptions (Part II, concl.), 303–326. **C. T. Newton.** Signed; repr. *Essays.*

210 The "friends of the foreigner" seventy years ago, 327–346. **Edward D. J. Wilson.** Signed.

211 The future of Englishwomen: a reply [to no. 181], 347–357. **Millicent Garrett Fawcett.** Signed.

212 Some phases of early religious development, 358–376. **C. F. Keary.** Signed.

213 Recollections of the revival of Greek independence (Part I), 377–392. **Stratford Canning.** Signed as in no. 50; repr. *The Eastern Question,* 1881.

VOLUME 4, SEPTEMBER 1878

214 Foreign policy of Great Britain—imperial or economic? 393–407. **W. R. Greg.** Signed; repr. *Misc. Essays,* I.

215 Henri Gréville's sketches of Russian life, 408–422. **W. R. S. Ralston.** Signed.

216 The crown and the cabinet in Canada, 423–431. **Francis Hincks.** Signed as in no. 184.

217 Ethical philosophy and evolution, 432–456. **William A. Knight.** Signed William Knight; repr. *Essays in Philosophy Old and New,* 1890.

218 The ceremonial use of flowers, 457–477. **Agnes Lambert.** Signed A. Lambert; Contents gives first name. (See no. 441.)

219 Echoes of the late debate [on the Eastern question], 478–493. **M. E. Grant Duff.** Signed.

220 The new principle of industry, 494–511. **George Jacob Holyoake.** Signed.

221 Limits of modern art-criticism, 512–516. **R. S. Tyrwhitt.** Signed.

222 The Chinese as colonists, 517–527. **W. H. Medhurst.** Signed.
223 Recent literature, 528–542. **Henry Morley.** Signed.
224 Nubar Pasha and our Asian protectorate, 548–559. **Edward Dicey.** Signed.
225 England's mission [on the Eastern question], 560–584. **W. E. Gladstone.** Signed. (See no. 338.)

VOLUME 4, OCTOBER 1878

226 The bankruptcy of India (Part I), 585–608. **H. M. Hyndman.** Signed; repr. under the same title, 1886.
227 The "fiasco" of Cyprus, 609–626. **Archibald Forbes.** Signed.
228 A suggested act for the separation of Church and State [with draft of bill], 627–642. **A. H. Mackonochie.** Signed, p. 637.
229 Barry Cornwall [based on an autobiographical fragment], 643–652. **Henry G. Hewlett.** Signed.
230 Animal intelligence, 653–672. **G. J. Romanes.** Signed G.J.R.; Contents gives name cited.
231 Faith and verification, 673–694. **W. H. Mallock.** Signed.
232 The caucus and its consequences, 695–712. **Edward D. J. Wilson.** Signed.
233 Impressions of America (Part V, concl.): religion, 713–734. **R. W. Dale.** Signed.
234 Liberty in Germany (Part II), 735–751. **Leonard A. Montefiore.** Signed.
235 The slicing of Hector, 752–764. **W. E. Gladstone.** Signed.
236 Recent science, 765–784. **James Knowles.** Evidence for no. 10.

VOLUME 4, NOVEMBER 1878

237 The progress of personal rule [in government], 785–808. **Henry Dunckley.** Signed. (See nos. 256 and 276.)
238 Virchow and evolution, 809–833. **John Tyndall.** Signed J. Tyndall; repr. *Fragments*, II.
239 National insurance: a cheap, practical, and popular means of abolishing poor rates, 834–857. **William Lewery Blackley.** Signed; repr. *Collected Essays on the Prevention of Pauperism*, 1880. (See no. 375.)
240 Recent attacks on political economy, 858–868. **Robert Lowe.** Signed.

241 Chrysanthema gathered from the Greek anthology, 869–888. **William M. Hardinge.** Signed.
242 University work in great towns, 889–909. **J. G. Fitch.** Signed.
243 The democracy and foreign policy, 910–924. **H. D. Traill.** Signed.
244 The three colours of Pre-Raphaelitism (Part I), 925–931. **John Ruskin.** Signed; repr. *Works*, XXXIV.
245 Recollections of the revival of Greek independence (Part II, concl.), 932–954. **Stratford Canning.** Cf. no. 213.
246 Electoral facts (No. I), 955–968. **W. E. Gladstone.** Signed. (No. II is no. 1811.)

VOLUME 4, DECEMBER 1878

247 The Afghan crisis, 969–989. **Henry C. Rawlinson.** Signed H.C.R.; Contents gives name cited.
248 *Beauty and the Beast*, 990–1012. **W. R. S. Ralston.** Signed.
249 Dogma, reason, and morality, 1013–1036. **W. H. Mallock.** Signed.
250 Some difficulties in zoological distribution, 1037–1052. **P. L. Sclater.** Signed.
251 What is a colonial governor? 1053–1071. **Edward D. J. Wilson.** Signed.
252 The three colours of Pre-Raphaelitism (Part II, concl.), 1072–1082. **John Ruskin.** Signed.
253 The future of India, 1083–1104. **Thomas Erskine Perry.** Signed as in no. 104, with same evidence.
254 Religion of the ancient Egyptians, 1105–1120. **John Newenham Hoare.** Signed.
255 The Cape: a descriptive sketch, 1121–1138. **Henry W. Tyler.** Signed.
256 Personal rule: a reply [to no. 237], 1139–1150. **T. E. Kebbel.** Signed.

VOLUME 5, JANUARY 1879

257 Passing events in Turkey: remarks and suggestions, 2–12. **Stratford Canning.** Signed as in no. 50; repr. *Current Discussion*, I.
258 Receiving strangers, 13–23. **Caroline Emilia Stephen.** Signed.
259 Novel-reading: the works of Charles Dickens; the works of W. Makepeace Thackeray, 24–43. **Anthony Trollope.** Signed.
260 Shorter parliaments, 44–63. **John Holms.** Signed.

261 The logic of toleration, 64–88. **W. H. Mallock.** Signed.
262 Verify your compass [on moral conscientiousness], 89–96. **W. R. Greg.** Signed; repr. *Misc. Essays*, I.
263 The depreciation of silver and the Indian finances, 97–111. **George Tomkyns Chesney.** Signed as in no. 103.
264 Cyprus and Mycaenae, 112–131. **A. S. Murray.** Signed.
265 "Saddling the right horse": a dialogue [on the Eastern question], 132–148. **William Minto.** Signed.
266 Recent science, 149–167. **James Knowles.** Evidence for no. 10.
267 The friends and foes of Russia, 168–192. **W. E. Gladstone.** Signed.

VOLUME 5, FEBRUARY 1879

268 The financial condition of India, 193–218. **Henry Fawcett.** Signed; repr. *Indian Finance*, 1880.
269 Félix Antoine Dupanloup, Bishop of Orleans, 219–246. **Charlotte Blennerhassett.** Signed C. de Warmont; Acton, *Correspondence*, pp. 50–57, especially p. 52n.; Lady Blennerhassett to Sir Wilfrid Ward, March 4, 1912, Camb. Univ. Lib., Add. MS. 7486.52, says she used a "nom de guerre" for this article; the counts of Leyden lived near a town called Warmont. Prefatory letter by **Ignaz von Döllinger**—signed J. Doellinger.
270 Animals and their native countries, 247–259. **Alfred R. Wallace.** Signed; repr. *Studies*, I, as "Evolution and the distribution of animals."
271 An actor's notes on Shakespeare (No. III): "Look here, upon this picture, and on this," 260–263. **Henry Irving,** 1838–1905. Signed; see *DNB*. (No. IV is no 1415.)
272 Liberty in Germany (Part III, concl.), 264–284. **Leonard A. Montefiore.** Signed.
273 The chemical elements, 285–299. **J. Norman Lockyer.** Signed.
274 Old masters at the winter exhibitions, 300–318. **Sidney Colvin.** Signed.
275 The poor in France, 320–339. **W. Walter Edwards.** Signed.
276 Personal rule: a rejoinder [to no. 256], 340–361. **Henry Dunckley.** Signed.
277 Co-operative stores: a reply to the shopkeepers, 362–367. **J. H. Lawson.** Signed. (See no. 301.)
278 The government and its critics, 368–384. **Edward D. J. Wilson.** Signed.

VOLUME 5, MARCH 1879

279 The place of will in evolution, 385–404. **T. W. Fowle.** Signed.
280 The drink difficulty, 405–417. **Wilfrid Lawson.** Signed.
281 Artistic copyright, 418–424. **W. Holman Hunt.** Signed.
282 Psychometric facts, 425–433. **Francis Galton.** Signed.
283 The grave perplexity before us [on the labor problem], 434–442. **W. R. Greg.** Signed; repr. *Misc. Essays*, I.
284 The bankruptcy of India (Part II, concl.), 443–462. **H. M. Hyndman.** Signed.
285 On epithets of movement in Homer, 463–487. **W. E. Gladstone.** Signed.
286 The meaning of life, 488–512. **St. George Mivart.** Signed; repr. *Essays*.
287 Philosophy of the pure sciences: universal statements of arithmetic, 513–522. **W. K. Clifford.** Signed.
288 Is insanity increasing? 523–533. **J. Mortimer Granville.** Signed J. Mortimer-Granville; see Boase.
289 Banking and commercial legislation, 534–546. **Henry R. Grenfell.** Signed.
290 The evils of "piece work," 547–563. **William Lattimer,** prob. Signed W. Lattimer; man cited wrote on trade depressions: see *BMCat*.
291 The causes of the Zulu War, 564–574. **Frederic Rogers.** Signed Blachford [Lord Blachford].

VOLUME 5, APRIL 1879

292 Past and future policy in South Africa, 583–596. **Henry George Grey.** Signed Grey; Contents gives "Rt. Hon. Earl Grey."
293 On sensation and the unity of structure of sensiferous organs, 597–611. **T. H. Huxley.** Signed; repr. *Collected Essays*, VI.
294 The business of the House of Lords, 612–617. **Robert N. C. G. Curzon.** Signed Zouche [15th Baron Zouche].
295 A few words on Mr. Freeman, 618–637. **J. A. Froude.** Signed.
296 Reciprocity the true free trade, 638–649. **Alfred R. Wallace.** Signed; repr. *Studies*, II.
297 Count Leo Tolstoy's novels, 650–669. **W. R. S. Ralston.** Signed.
298 The Egyptian crisis, 670–689. **Edward Dicey.** Signed; repr. *England and Egypt*, 1881, as "The Nubar-Wilson Ministry."

380 Government and the artists, 968–984. **Henry T. Wells.** Signed. Intro. letter signed **Frederick Leighton.**

381 The literary calling and its future, 985–998. **James Payn.** Signed; repr. *Private Views.*

382 Modern atheism and Mr. Mallock (Part II, concl.), 999–1020. **Louisa S. Bevington.** Signed as in no. 359.

383 The functions of the brain, 1021–1032. **Julius Althaus.** Signed.

384 *The Domesday Book of Bengal*, 1033–1050. **Francis W. Rowsell.** Signed.

385 Mistress and servants, 1051–1063. **Caroline E. Stephen.** Signed.

386 Reasons for doubt in the Church of Rome, 1064–1067. **John Thomas Freeman Mitford.** Signed Redesdale [Earl of Redesdale]. (See nos. 411, 422.)

387 Irish politics and English parties, 1068–1081. **Edward D. J. Wilson.** Signed.

388 A plea for the eighteenth century, 1082–1092. **William Stebbing.** Signed; repr. *Verdicts* as "Notes on Lecky's *Eighteenth Century.*"

389 On the present state of the French church, 1093–1118. **J. P. P. Martin.** Signed as in no. 135; repr. in volume cited there.

390 Escape from pain: the history of a discovery [ether], 1119–1132. **James Paget.** Signed.

VOLUME 7, JANUARY 1880

391 Russian nihilism, 1–26. **Fritz Cunliffe-Owen.** Signed.

392 George Canning: his character and motives, 27–42. **Stratford Canning.** Signed as in no. 50.

393 Athletics in public schools, 43–57. **Edward Lyttelton.** Signed.

394 Phaedra and Phèdre, 58–77. **Lionel Tennyson.** Signed.

395 Purchase in the Church, 78–92. **John Martineau.** Signed.

396 The origin of species and genera, 93–106. **Alfred R. Wallace.** Signed; repr. *Studies*, I.

397 Dr. Abbott and Queen Elizabeth, 107–127. **James Spedding.** Signed.

398 Old fashioned gardening, 128–135. **Margaret A. Paul.** Signed.

399 The criminal code (1879), 136–160. **James Fitzjames Stephen.** Signed.

400 Atheistic Methodism, 161–184. **W. H. Mallock.** Signed.

401 War correspondents and the authorities, 185–196. **Archibald Forbes.** Signed. (See no. 416.)

VOLUME 7, FEBRUARY 1880

402 The situation in Afghanistan, 197–215. **H. C. Rawlinson.** Signed.

403 Lord Chelmsford and the Zulu War, 216–234. **Archibald Forbes.** Signed.

404 The present conditions of art, 235–255. **G. F. Watts.** Signed.

405 Paganism in Paris, 256–275. **Charles Loyson.** Signed Hyacinthe Loyson; Contents gives "Père Hyacinthe" [Carmelite Monk].

406 An eye-witness of John Kemble, 276–296. **Theodore Martin.** Signed; repr. *Essays*, II, as "Ludwig Tieck on the English Stage."

407 Free land and peasant proprietorship, 297–317. **Arthur Arnold.** Signed.

408 Ritualists and Anglicans, 318–332. **A. F. Northcote.** Signed.

409 Our Egyptian protectorate, 333–352. **Edward Dicey.** Signed; repr. *England and Egypt*, 1881, as "The Anglo-French Protectorate."

410 On historical psychology, 353–360. **Henry Sidgwick.** Signed.

411 Reasons for doubt in the Church of Rome: a reply [to no. 386], 361–366. **T. J. Capel.** Signed.

412 Free trade, railways, and the growth of commerce; or, An attempt to estimate the comparative effects of (1) liberation of intercourse and (2) improvement of locomotion upon the trade and wealth of the United Kingdom during the last half-century, 367–388. **W. E. Gladstone.** Signed.

VOLUME 7, MARCH 1880

413 England as a naval power, 389–405. **Robert Spencer Robinson.** Signed.

414 The common-sense of Home Rule, 406–421. **Justin McCarthy,** 1830–1912. Signed. (See nos. 426, 427.)

415 Sham admiration in literature, 422–433. **James Payn.** Signed; repr. *Private Views.*

416 Newspaper correspondents in the field, 434–442. **G. J. M. K. Elliot.** Signed Melgund [Viscount Melgund].

417 The next reform bill, 443–463. **Henry Fawcett.** Signed.

418 Burns and Béranger, 464–485. **Charles Mackay.** Signed.

419 The proper use of the City churches, 486–492. **C. Kegan Paul.** Signed.

420 Irish land agitation, 493–502. **Peter G. Fitzgerald.** Signed Peter Fitzgerald, Knight of Kerry.

421   God and nature, 503–515. **Harvey Goodwin.** Signed Harvey Carlisle [Bishop of Carlisle]; repr. *Science and Faith.*

422   Reasons for doubt in the Church of Rome: a rejoinder [to no. 411], 516–520. **John T. F. Mitford.** Signed Redesdale [Earl of Redesdale].

423   Recent science, 521–537. **James Knowles.** Evidence for no. 10.

424   *Russia and England* [by Mme Novikoff], 538–556. **W. E. Gladstone.** Signed.

VOLUME 7, APRIL 1880

425   The docility of an "imperial" parliament, 557–566. **Robert Lowe.** Signed. (See no. 450.)

426   The common-sense of Home Rule: a reply [to no. 414], 567–582. **Edward D. J. Wilson.** Signed.

427   The common-sense of Home Rule: a rejoinder [to no. 426], 583–592. **Justin McCarthy,** 1830–1912. Signed.

428   The deep sea and its contents, 593–618. **William Benjamin Carpenter.** Signed William B. Carpenter; repr. *Nature and Man,* 1888.

429   Agnosticism and women, 619–627. **Bertha Lathbury.** Signed; Contents adds "Mrs." (See no. 443.)

430   A Nonconformist's view of the election, 628–637. **J. Guinness Rogers.** Signed. (See no. 450.)

431   Days in the woods, 638–657. **Windham Thomas W. Quin.** Signed Dunraven [4th Earl of Dunraven]; repr. *Canadian Nights.*

432   British interests in the East, 658–676. **M. E. Grant Duff.** Signed.

433   The present crisis at Guy's Hospital, 677–684. **Margaret Lonsdale.** Signed. (See no. 447.)

434   Native armies of India, 685–709. **John Miller Adye,** 1819–1900. Signed as in no. 347.

435   Religion, Achaian and Semitic, 710–725. **W. E. Gladstone.** Signed.

436   Imperialism and Socialism, 726–736. **Frederic Seebohm.** Signed F. Seebohm; Contents gives first name.

VOLUME 7, MAY 1880

437   Marc-Aurèle, 742–755. **Ernest Renan.** Signed.

438   Atheism and the rights of man, 756–777. **W. H. Mallock.** Signed.

439   Modern English landscape-painting, 778–794. **A. W. Hunt.** Signed.

440   Penal servitude, 795–807. **Charles Bowyer Adderley.** Signed Norton [Lord Norton].

441   The ceremonial use of flowers: a sequel [to no. 218], 808–827. **Agnes Lambert.** Signed.

442   The pound of flesh [on Shylock], 828–839. **Moncure D. Conway.** Signed.

443   Agnosticism and women: a reply [to no. 429], 840–844. **Jane Hume Clapperton.** Signed J. H. Clapperton; Contents adds "Miss"; *Westminster Rev.,* 130 (Dec. 1888), 717, gives full name.

444   John Donne, 845–863. **William Minto.** Signed.

445   The pinch of poverty, 864–870. **James Payn.** Signed; repr. *Private Views.*

446   Irish absenteeism, 871–883. **Henry L. Jephson.** Signed.

447   On the nursing crisis at Guy's Hospital (No. I), 884–891. **William W. Gull.** Signed.

448   On the nursing crisis at Guy's Hospital (No. II), 892–901. **S. O. Habershon.** Signed.

449   On the nursing crisis at Guy's Hospital (No. III, concl.), 902–904. **Alfred G. Henriques.** Signed.

450   A Conservative view of the elections, 905–916. **T. E. Kebbel.** Signed.

VOLUME 7, JUNE 1880

451   England and Russia in Asia, 917–928. **Arminius Vambéry.** Signed A. Vambéry; see *WWW*/1916.

452   On the method of Zadig: retrospective prophecy as a function of science, 929–940. **Thomas H. Huxley.** Signed; repr. *Collected Essays,* IV.

453   Fiction: fair and foul (Part I), 941–962. **John Ruskin.** Signed; repr. *Works,* XXXIV, 265–394. (Letter, vol. 8, p. 760, signed **Thea Berg.**)

454   Some Indian suggestions for India, 963–978. **Syed Ameer Ali.** Signed Ameer Ali; see *DNB*/1930, under Ameer.

455   Our national art collections and provincial art museums (Part I), 979–994. **John Charles Robinson.** Signed J. C. Robinson; see *DNB*/1921.

456   Familiar conversations on modern England (No. II), 995–1019. **Karl Hillebrand.** Signed. (No. I is no. 361.)

457   A programme of reforms for Turkey, 1020–1039. **Edwin Pears.** Signed.

458 Landscape painting, 1040–1056. **R. P. Collier.** Signed.

459 The Conservative party and the late election: a sequel [to no. 450] 1057–1064. **T. E. Kebbel.** Signed.

460 The crisis in Indian finance, 1065–1077. **Samuel Laing,** 1812–1897. Signed S. Laing; see *DNB*.

461 The Indian budget estimates, 1078–1088. **Richard Strachey.** Signed.

462 Doctors and nurses (No. I), 1089–1096. **Octavius Sturges.** Signed.

463 Doctors and nurses (No. II), 1097–1104. **Seymour J. Sharkey.** Signed.

464 Doctors and nurses (No. III, concl.), 1105–1108. **Margaret Lonsdale.** Signed.

VOLUME 8, JULY 1880

465 The future of Liberalism, 1–18. **Matthew Arnold.** Signed; repr. *Irish Essays,* 1882.

466 Atheism and repentance: a familiar colloquy, 19–41. **W. H. Mallock.** Signed.

467 The clôture in parliament, 42–55. **Edward D. J. Wilson.** Signed.

468 Modern French art, 56–66. **Gerard Baldwin Brown.** Signed.

469 A stranger in America, 67–87. **George Jacob Holyoake.** Signed; repr. in book of same title (1881), pp. 209–246.

470 Story-telling, 88–98. **James Payn.** Signed; repr. *Private Views.*

471 The commercial treaty between France and England, 99–106. **E. Raoul Duval.** Signed.

472 The House of Lords and national insurance, 107–118. **William Lewery Blackley.** Signed.

473 The French clergy and the present republic, 119–139. **J. P. P. Martin.** Signed as in 135.

474 The Palais-Royal Theatre, 140–156. **Francisque Sarcey.** Signed.

475 Bleeding to death [on the Indian empire], 157–176. **H. M. Hyndman.** Signed; repr. *The Bankruptcy of India,* 1886.

VOLUME 8, AUGUST 1880

476 An Englishman's protest [on Church and State], 177–181. **H. E. Manning.** Signed as in no. 8; repr. *Miscellanies,* III.

477 Peasant proprietors at home, 182–194. **J. H. Tuke.** Signed J.H.T.; Contents gives name cited.

478 Fiction: fair and foul (Part II), 195–206. **John Ruskin.** Signed.

479 The creed of the early Christians, 207–217. **A. P. Stanley.** Signed.

480 Iceland, 218–236. **David Wedderburn.** Signed.

481 Representative government in the colonies, 237–248. **Arthur Mills.** Signed.

482 Our national art collections and provincial art museums (Part II), 249–265. **John Charles Robinson.** Signed as in no. 455.

483 The future of China, 266–274. **Demetrius Charles Boulger.** Signed; repr. *Central Asian Questions.*

484 State aid and control in industrial insurance, 275–293. **Hugh Seymour Tremenheere.** Signed.

485 Political optimism: a dialogue, 294–304. **H. D. Traill.** Signed.

486 The landowners' panic, 305–312. **Justin McCarthy,** 1830–1912. Signed.

487 Recent literature, 313–340. Compiled by **W. Mark W. Call, Alfred Church, H. G. Hewlett, Clements R. Markham, William Minto, James Payn, G. J. Romanes, F. W. Rudler, Lionel Tennyson, E. D. J. Wilson.**

VOLUME 8, SEPTEMBER 1880

488 Ireland (No. I; no more published), 341–369. **J. A. Froude.** Signed.

489 A real "saviour of society" [profit-sharing], 370–383. **Sedley Taylor.** Signed; repr. *Profit-sharing.*

490 A few more words on national insurance, 384–393. **H. H. M. Herbert.** Signed Carnarvon [Earl of Carnarvon]; repr. *Essays,* II.

491 Fiction: fair and foul (Part III), 394–410. **John Ruskin.** Signed. (Letter, vol. 8, p. 760, signed **Ralph Thicknesse.**)

492 The thoroughbred horse: English and Arabian, 411–423. **Wilfrid Scawen Blunt.** Signed.

493 English rational and irrational, 424–444. **Fitzedward Hall.** Signed.

494 A Colorado sketch, 445–457. **W. T. W. Quin.** Signed Dunraven [4th Earl of Dunraven]; repr. *Canadian Nights.*

495 The Egyptian liquidation, 458–473. **Edward Dicey.** Signed; repr. *England and Egypt,* 1881, as "The Commission of Liquidation."

496 Hypnotism, 474–480. **G. J. Romanes.** Signed.

497 François Villon, 481–500. **John Payne.** Signed.

498 The Burials Bill and disestablishment,

501–512. **Alfred Barry.** Signed. (See no. 532, p. 1022.)

VOLUME 8, OCTOBER 1880

499 Obstruction or "clôture", 513–525. **Robert Lowe.** Signed Sherbrooke [Viscount Sherbrooke].

500 The creeds: old and new [impact of science and philosophy on religion] (Part I), 526–549. **Frederic Harrison.** Signed.

501 The chase: its history and laws (Part I), 550–563. **A. E. Cockburn.** Signed.

502 The unstable equilibrium of parties, 564–577. **Edward D. J. Wilson.** Signed.

503 Petty Romany [clans of gipsies], 578–592. **Joseph Lucas.** Signed.

504 Wapiti-running on the plains [of America], 593–611. **W. T. W. Quin.** Signed Dunraven [4th Earl Dunraven]; repr. *Canadian Nights.*

505 Diary of Liu Ta-Jên's mission to England, 612–621. **Liu Ta-Jên.** Title. Trans. signed **F. S. A. Bourne.**

506 The philosophy of crayfishes [on T. H. Huxley's *The Crayfish*], 622–637. **Harvey Goodwin.** Signed Harvey Carlisle [Bishop of Carlisle]; repr. *Science and Faith.*

507 Political fatalism, 638–645. **H. D. Traill.** Signed.

508 Demoniacal possession in India, 646–652. **William Knighton.** Signed W. Knighton; see *WWW*/1916.

509 Alexandre Dumas, 653–671. **Walter Herries Pollock.** Signed.

510 The "Portsmouth custom" [tenant rights], 672–676. **Newton Wallop.** Signed Lymington [Viscount Lymington].

VOLUME 8, NOVEMBER 1880

511 Legislation for Ireland, 677–689. **Robert Lowe.** Signed Sherbrooke [Viscount Sherbrooke]. (See no. 524.)

512 The Sabbath, 690–714. **John Tyndall.** Signed; repr. *New Fragments.*

513 Evils of competitive examinations, 715–723. **A. R. Grant.** Signed.

514 The philosophy of Conservatism, 724–747. **W. H. Mallock.** Signed.

515 Fiction: fair and foul (Part IV), 748–760. **John Ruskin.** Signed J. Ruskin. (Part V is no. 634.)

516 Our new wheat-fields at home, 761–765. **Frederic F. Hallett.** Signed.

517 The government of London, 766–786.

W. M. Torrens. Signed; repr. under same title, 1884.

518 The creeds: old and new (Part II, concl.): the human synthesis, 787–809. **Frederic Harrison.** Signed; repr. *Common Sense.*

519 The works of Sir Henry Taylor, 810–823. **Henry G. Hewlett.** Signed.

520 Bribery and corruption, 824–843. **Sydney C. Buxton.** Signed.

521 Recent science, 844–860. **James Knowles.** Evidence for no. 10.

VOLUME 8, DECEMBER 1880

522 Ireland in '48 and Ireland now, 861–875. **Justin McCarthy,** 1830–1912. Signed.

523 The Irish "poor man," 876–887. **Charlotte G. O'Brien.** Signed.

524 The Irish land question, 888–894. **James Hewitt.** Signed Lifford [4th Viscount Lifford].

525 Explosions in collieries and their cure, 895–920. **Samuel Plimsoll.** Signed. (See nos. 548, 549.)

526 Music and the people, 921–932. **Florence A. Marshall.** Signed.

527 South Africa, 933–954. **H. G. Grey.** Signed Grey; Contents as in no. 292.

528 The chase: its history and laws (Part II, concl.), 955–970. **A. E. Cockburn.** Signed.

529 The obligations of the New Testament to Buddhism, 971–994. **J. Estlin Carpenter.** Signed.

530 Earl Russell during the Eastern question, 1853–1855, 995–1007. **Hallam Tennyson.** Signed.

531 The sculptures of Olympia, 1008–1017. **A. S. Murray.** Signed.

532 The probable results of the Burials Bill, 1018–1030. **J. Guinness Rogers.** Signed.

533 Parliamentary obstruction and its remedies, 1031–1046. **Henry Cecil Raikes.** Signed.

VOLUME 9, JANUARY 1881

534 The dawn of a revolutionary epoch, 1–18. **H. M. Hyndman.** Signed.

535 The historical claims of tenant right, 19–36. **Frederic Seebohm.** Signed as in no. 436.

536 The present anarchy, 37–52. **Edward D. J. Wilson.** Signed.

537 The three "F's" [on the land question],

53–61. **John R. W. de Vesci.** Signed de Vesci [4th Viscount de Vesci].

538 The High Court of Justice, 62–85. **James Fitzjames Stephen.** Signed.

539 A glimpse at Newfoundland, 86–107. **W. T. W. Quin.** Signed Dunraven [4th Earl Dunraven]; repr. *Canadian Nights* as "Newfoundland in the 'Seventies."

540 A day with a war balloon, 108–122. **Henry Elsdale.** Signed.

541 The exhibiting of pictures, 123–130. **T. Villiers Lister.** Signed.

542 A census of religions, 131–144. **J. G. Hubbard.** Signed.

543 Penny fiction, 145–154. **James Payn.** Signed; repr. *Private Views*.

544 The religion of Zoroaster, 155–176. **Monier Monier-Williams.** Signed Monier Williams; Contents adds "Professor . . . C.I.E."; see *DNB*, 1st suppl.

545 The Basutos and the constitution of the Cape of Good Hope, 177–200. **H. B. E. Frere.** Signed. (See no. 569.)

VOLUME 9, FEBRUARY 1881

546 Ritualism, 201–210. **R. W. Church.** Signed.

547 The Transvaal, 211–236. **H. B. E. Frere.** Signed.

548 Explosions in collieries and their cure, 237–244. **John Herman Merivale.** Signed J. H. Merivale; Contents gives "J. Herman Merivale"; man cited was a collier manager; see *BMCat*.

549 Fire-damp, 245–248. **J. D. Shakespear.** Signed.

550 The breaking up of the land monopoly, 249–268. **G. C. Spencer Churchill.** Signed Blandford [Marquess of Blandford].

551 La Rochefoucauld, 269–291. **E. S. Dallas.** Signed.

552 The United States as a field for agricultural settlers, 292–301. **D. W. S. Ogilvy.** Signed Airlie [Earl of Airlie].

553 The philosophy of Liberalism, 302–323. **Robert Wallace,** 1831–1899. Signed; *Life*, p. 292.

554 The city parochial charities, 324–337. **R. H. Hadden.** Signed.

555 A Jewish view of the anti-Jewish agitation, 338–357. **Lucien Wolf.** Signed.

556 Irish emigration, 358–371. **J. H. Tuke.** Signed.

557 Abolition of landlords, 372–384. **Thomas Spring-Rice,** 1849–1926. Signed Monteagle [2nd Baron Monteagle].

558 The Irish police, 385–396. **Henry A. Blake.** Signed.

VOLUME 9, MARCH 1881

559 Eighty years [1800–1880 in Ireland], 397–414. **Charlotte G. O'Brien.** Signed.

560 Radicalism: a familiar colloquy, 415–438. **W. H. Mallock.** Signed.

561 Art needlework (No. I), 439–449. **Marian Alford.** Signed.

562 Art needlework (No. II), 450–454. **G. F. Watts.** Signed.

563 The creed of a layman, 455–477. **Frederic Harrison.** Signed; repr. *Creed of a Layman*, 1907.

564 Smoke prevention, 478–490. **W. F. Pollock.** Signed.

565 The state of parties, 491–499. **T. E. Kebbel.** Signed.

566 The Pārsīs, 500–516. **Monier Monier-Williams.** Signed as in no. 544.

567 Our next leap in the dark [on reform acts], 517–535. **Hugh Fortescue,** 1818–1905. Signed Fortescue [3rd Earl Fortescue]; repr. under same title, 1884.

568 Transplanting to the colonies, 536–546. **W. M. Torrens.** Signed.

569 The Basutos and Sir Bartle Frere, 547–557. **William Fowler,** 1828–1905. Signed; See *WWW*.

570 Long and short service, 558–572. **Garnet Wolseley.** Signed G. J. Wolseley with title "Lieutenant-General." (See no. 591.)

571 Holland and the Transvaal, 573–576. **W. H. de Beaufort.** Signed; Contents as in no. 144.

VOLUME 9, APRIL 1881

572 Military impotence of Great Britain, 577–610. **Alexander Kirchhammer.** Signed, with addition "Captain in the General Staff Imperial Royal Austrian Army."

573 Working men and the political situation, 611–622. **Thomas Burt.** Signed.

574 Persia and its passion-drama, 623–648. **Lionel Tennyson.** Signed.

575 The child-criminal, 649–663. **Elizabeth Surr.** Signed; Contents adds "Mrs."

576 Reform of feudal laws, 664–680. **G. C. Spencer Churchill.** Signed Blandford [Marquess of Blandford].

577 Jules Jacquemart, 681–690. **Frederick Wedmore.** Signed; repr. *Four Masters of Etching*, 1883.

578 Rebeccaism [protest against fishing regulations], 691–694. **R. D. Green Price.** Signed.

579 La philosophie de Diderot; or, Le dernier mot d'un matérialiste, 695–708. **Paul Janet.** Signed.

580 The incompatibles [the Irish Land Bill] (Part I), 709–726. **Matthew Arnold.** Signed; repr. *Irish Essays*, 1882.

581 Business in the House of Commons, 727–736. **Robert Lowe.** Signed Sherbrooke [Viscount Sherbrooke].

VOLUME 9, MAY 1881

582 The "silver streak" [the Channel], 737–755. **Edward Plunkett.** Signed Dunsany [16th Baron Dunsany]. (Letter, p. 1066, signed **Robert Spencer Robinson**; see no. 681, in particular the note there on p. 304.)

583 Peace in the Church, 756–777. **A. J. B. Beresford Hope.** Signed; repr. *Worship and Order*, 1883.

584 George Eliot, 778–801. **Edith Simcox.** Signed.

585 Profit-sharing, 802–811. **Sedley Taylor.** Signed; repr. *Profit-sharing.*

586 French verse in English, 812–837. **William M. Hardinge.** Signed.

587 Religious fairs in India, 838–848. **William Knighton.** Signed as in no. 508.

588 West-End improvements, 849–855. **Maude Stanley.** Signed.

589 Carlyle's lectures on the periods of European culture: from Homer to Goethe, 856–879. **Thomas Carlyle** and **Edward Dowden.** Signed Edward Dowden; he put together large extracts from the lectures, together with a critical commentary.

590 The new Irish Land Bill, 880–904. **George D. Campbell.** Signed Argyll [8th Duke of Argyll]. (See no. 599.)

VOLUME 9, JUNE 1881

591 A civilian's answer to Sir Garnet Wolseley, 905–916. **H. O. Arnold-Forster.** Signed.

592 A reviser on the new revision [of the New Testament], 917–936. **G. Vance Smith.** Signed.

593 What is a pound? 937–948. **H. R. Grenfell.** Signed; repr. in Gibbs, *Bimetallic Controversy.*

594 Ernest Renan, 949–968. **Frederic W. H. Myers.** Signed; repr. *Essays.*

595 Pawnbroking abroad and at home, 969–991. **W. Walter Edwards.** Signed.

596 Intelligence of ants (Part I), 992–1008. **George J. Romanes.** Signed.

597 Carlyle's *Reminiscences*, 1009–1025. **Henry Taylor**, 1800–1886. Signed; attr. by Una Taylor, *Guests and Memories* (Oxford, 1924), p. 389.

598 The incompatibles (Part II, concl.), 1026–1043. **Matthew Arnold.** Signed; repr. *Irish Essays*, 1882.

599 The Duke of Argyll and the Irish Land Bill, 1044–1065. **G. Shaw Lefevre.** Signed.

VOLUME 10, JULY 1881

600 The early life of Thomas Carlyle, 1–42. **J. A. Froude.** Signed; repr. *Thomas Carlyle: The First Forty Years of His Life* (1882), I, 1–61.

601 New markets for British produce, 43–55. **George Baden-Powell.** Signed; repr. *State Aid* as "Low Tariffs for the British Empire."

602 Second chambers [on House of Lords], 56–62. **David Wedderburn.** Signed.

603 Gossip of an old bookworm, 63–79. **William J. Thoms.** Signed.

604 Health and physique of our city populations, 80–89. **Reginald Brabazon.** Signed Brabazon [Lord Brabazon]; repr. *Social Arrows*, 1886.

605 M. Renan and miracles, 90–106. **F. W. H. Myers.** Signed; repr. *Essays* as "Ernest Renan."

606 Confiscation and compensation, 107–119. **Edward D. J. Wilson.** Signed.

607 Unity in the Church of Christ, 120–130. **Horatio Nelson.** Signed Nelson [3rd Earl Nelson].

608 A dredging ground, 131–141. **Emily Lawless.** Signed.

609 Man's place in nature, 142–160. **Harvey Goodwin.** Signed Harvey Carlisle [Bishop of Carlisle]; repr. *Science and Faith.*

VOLUME 10, AUGUST 1881

610 Isolated free trade (No. I), 161–180. **Edward Sullivan.** Signed.

611 Isolated free trade (No. II), 181–183. **W. D. Montagu.** Signed Manchester [7th Duke of Manchester].

612 "The Revolutionary Party" [in English politics], 184–205. **W. T. W. Quin.** Signed Dunraven [4th Earl Dunraven].

613 The coming age of the volunteers, 206–

216. **R. J. Lindsay.** Signed R. Loyd-Lindsay; see *DNB*, 2nd suppl.

614   Hereditary rulers, 217–235. **G. C. Spencer Churchill.** Signed Blandford [Marquess of Blandford].

615   President Garfield, 236–244. **Robert Shindler.** Signed.

616   Intelligence of ants (Part II, concl.), 245–258. **George J. Romanes.** Signed.

617   My return to Arcady: and how I find things looking, 259–275. **Augustus Jessopp.** Signed; repr. *Arcady*.

618   The Arab monuments of Egypt, 276–283. **Frank Dillon.** Signed.

619   Pantheism, and cosmic emotion, 284–295. **Frederic Harrison.** Signed; repr. *Creed of a Layman*, 1907.

620   County characteristics: Kent, 296–307. **Henry G. Hewlett.** Signed. (See nos. 1031, 1173.)

621   What shall we do with our bankrupts? 308–316. **Robert Lowe.** Signed Sherbrooke [Viscount Sherbrooke].

VOLUME 10, SEPTEMBER 1881

622   The deadlock in the House of Commons, 317–340. **Frederic Harrison.** Signed.

623   How to eat bread, 341–356. **Louisa S. Bevington.** Signed as in no. 359.

624   Scrutin de liste and scrutin d'arrondissement [on universal suffrage], 357–368. **Joseph Reinach.** Signed.

625   Women as civil servants, 369–381. **Margaret E. Harkness.** Signed; Index adds "Miss."

626   The place of revelation in evolution, 382–404. **T. W. Fowle.** Signed.

627   *Four Centuries of English Letters*, 405–422. **Henry Taylor.** Signed.

628   Worry, 423–429. **J. Mortimer Granville.** Signed.

629   The workman's view of "fair trade," 430–447. **George Potter.** Signed.

630   France and North Africa, 448–454. **Reginald W. Sackville-West.** Signed De la Warr [7th Earl De la Warr].

631   The future of gold, 455–472. **Emile de Laveleye.** Signed.

VOLUME 10, OCTOBER 1881

632   Ireland and the Land Act, 473–493. **E. H. Stanley.** Signed Derby [15th Earl of Derby].

633   The Jewish question, 494–515. **Goldwin Smith.** Signed. (See no. 652.)

634   Fiction: fair and foul (Part V, concl.): the two servants, 516–531. **John Ruskin.** Signed.

635   On commercial "corners," 532–537. **William B. Halhed.** Signed.

636   Disease-germs, 538–554. **William Benjamin Carpenter.** Signed W. B. Carpenter; see *DNB*.

637   Our highways, 555–566. **William Brodrick,** 1830–1907. Signed Midleton [8th Viscount Midleton].

638   Child life for children, 567–572. **Elizabeth Rossiter.** Signed.

639   Scientific optimism, 573–587. **James Sully.** Signed.

640   Fair trade, 588–605. **W. Farrer Ecroyd.** Signed.

641   The proposals of the Fair Trade League, 606–628. **Thomas P. Whittaker.** Signed.

VOLUME 10, NOVEMBER 1881

642   Administrative machinery of Egypt, 641–659. **Francis W. Rowsell.** Signed.

643   Sir Walter Ralegh in Ireland, 660–682. **John Pope Hennessy.** Signed.

644   Sheep-hunting in the mountains, 683–700. **W. T. W. Quin.** Signed Dunraven [4th Earl Dunraven]; repr. *Canadian Nights*.

645   The last great dream of the crusade [on Columbus], 701–722. **J. Baldwin Brown.** Signed.

646   International copyright, 723–734. **W. Fraser Rae.** Signed.

647   The future cathedral of Liverpool, 735–743. **Edmund Venables.** Signed.

648   The Order of Corporate Reunion, 744–760. **Frederick George Lee.** Signed. With a postscript, 761–762, by **John T. Seccombe**—signed Lawrence, Bishop of Caerleon; see Henry R. T. Brandreth, *Dr. Lee of Lambeth* (1951), pp. 120, 129 and *DNB*, 2nd suppl. under Lee.

649   A new love poet [William Scawen Blunt], 763–784. **Robert Lytton.** Signed Lytton [1st Earl Lytton].

VOLUME 10, DECEMBER 1881

650   The Irish Jacobins, 785–793. **J. Woulfe Flanagan.** Signed.

651   The Scotch land question: Aberdeenshire agitation, 794–812. **H. B. E. Frere.** Signed. (See no. 680.)

652   Recent phases of Judaeophobia, 813–829. **Hermann Adler.** Signed. (Note, vol. 12, p. 7, by **Goldwin Smith**—signed G.S.,

695 Vivisection and the use of remedies, 479–487. **T. Lauder Brunton.** Signed.

696 An Englishman's protest [against the parliamentary oath], 488–492. **H. E. Manning.** Signed as in no. 8; repr. *Miscellanies*, III. (See no. 766.)

VOLUME 11, APRIL 1882

697 The proposed Channel tunnel: a protest, 493–500. **James Knowles.** Signed. With an intro. list of protesters against the Channel tunnel. (See nos. 710–714.)

698 What is money? 501–509. **Robert Lowe.** Signed Sherbrooke [Viscount Sherbrooke]; repr. in Gibbs, *Bimetallic Controversy.*

699 New theory of the sun: the conservation of solar energy, 510–525. **C. William Siemens.** Signed.

700 Small-pox and vaccination in 1871–1881, 526–546. **William Benjamin Carpenter.** Signed William B. Carpenter; see *DNB.*

701 A heathen apocalypse [sources of apocalyptic literature], 547–554. **Eduard Zeller.** Signed C. Zeller, but attr. to man cited in his *Kleine Schriften* (3 vols., Berlin, 1911), III, 551.

702 Landowning as a business: a reply [to no. 686], 555–566. **James Howard,** 1821–1889. Signed.

703 A school of dramatic art: a dialogue between Millbrook and his friend Haughton, 567–571. **Hamilton Aïdé.** Signed. (See no. 719.)

704 Oiling the waves: a safeguard in tempest, 572–585. **Constance F. Gordon Cumming.** Signed C. F. Gordon Cumming; see *BMCat.*

705 The superstitions of modern Greece, 586–605. **Paul B. d'Estournelles.** Signed P. d'Estournelles; Contents adds "M. le Baron"; see *Grand Larousse.*

706 A notable secession from the Vatican [Henry Count di Campello], 606–625. **R. J. Nevin.** Signed.

707 A sketch of the criminal law, 626–649. **James Fitzjames Stephen.** Signed.

708 The agnostic at church (No. I), 650–652. **J. Henry Shorthouse.** Signed.

709 The agnostic at church (No. II), 653–656. **Jane Hume Clapperton.** Signed as in no. 443.

VOLUME 11, MAY 1882

710 The proposed Channel tunnel: a pro-

test; [being a further list of names, compiled by the Editor], 657–662. Cf. no. 697.

711 The Channel tunnel (No. I): a national question, 663–667. **J. L. A. Simmons.** Signed.

712 The Channel tunnel (No. II), 668–671. **W. C. Keppel.** Signed Bury [Viscount Bury].

713 The Channel tunnel (No. III), 672–674. **E. B. Hamley.** Signed.

714 The Channel tunnel (No. IV): a French reply, 675–679. **Joseph Reinach.** Signed.

715 A word about America, 680–696. **Matthew Arnold.** Signed; repr. *Civilization in the United States*, Boston, 1888.

716 The goal of modern thought, 697–718. **W. S. Lilly.** Signed; repr. *Ancient Religion and Modern Thought*, 1884.

717 The Arcady of our grandfathers, 719–739. **Augustus Jessopp.** Signed; repr. *Arcady.*

718 What is a standard [on bimetallism]? 740–752. **H. R. Grenfell.** Signed; repr. in Gibbs, *Bimetallic Controversy.*

719 A school for dramatic art, 753–757. **F. C. Burnand.** Signed.

720 Notes on Turner's *Liber Studiorum*, 758–781. **Stopford A. Brooke.** Signed.

721 Anti-vaccination, 782–802. **P. A. Taylor.** Signed.

722 The duty of moderate Liberals, 803–825. **E. H. Knatchbull-Hugessen.** Signed Brabourne [1st Baron Brabourne].

723 Town and country politics, 826–840. **J. Guinness Rogers.** Signed.

VOLUME 11, JUNE 1882

724 Home Rule (No. I), 841–857. **G. C. Spencer Churchill.** Signed Blandford [Marquess of Blandford].

725 Home Rule (No. II), 858–868. **Justin McCarthy,** 1830–1912. Signed.

726 Peel and Cobden, 869–889. **Goldwin Smith.** Signed.

727 Thought-reading, 890–900. **W. F. Barrett, Edmund Gurney,** and **Frederic W. H. Myers.** Signed. With extracts, 900–901, from a paper by **James Knowles**—signed The Editor of this Review. (See no. 744.)

728 The Tower of London, 902–914. **A. B. Mitford.** Signed.

729 Shakespearian criticism, 915–933. **Walter Herries Pollock.** Signed.

730 The friends of the farmer, 934–948. **J. Woulfe Flanagan.** Signed.

[Lord Brabazon]; repr. *Social Arrows*, 1886.

770 The French educational system, 533–555. **J. P. P. Martin.** Signed as in no. 135.

771 The site of paradise: an ancient problem solved by modern scholarship, 556–571. **Charles H. H. Wright.** Signed.

772 Roumanian peasants and their songs, 572–582. **C. F. Keary.** Signed.

773 Profit-sharing in agriculture, 583–590. **Sedley Taylor.** Signed; repr. *Profit-sharing.*

774 A glimpse of Mexico, 591–601. **Francis Francis.** Signed as in no. 687.

775 Handwork for children, 602–612. **Eglantyne L. Jebb.** Signed E. L. Jebb; Contents adds "Mrs."; see *WWW*/1960 under Richard Jebb, and *BMCat.*

776 About Voltaire, 613–632. **Alexander A. Knox.** Signed.

VOLUME 12, NOVEMBER 1882

777 The present state of the army: sequel to a Mansion House speech, 633–646. **Frederick S. Roberts.** Signed Frederick Roberts; Contents adds "Sir" and initial "S."

778 Irish revolution and English liberalism, 647–666. **John Morley.** Signed.

779 Public works in London, 667–686. **G. Shaw Lefevre.** Signed.

780 The Jews: a deferred rejoinder [to no. 652], 687–709. **Goldwin Smith.** Signed.

781 A Liverpool address, 710–720. **Matthew Arnold.** Signed.

782 Railway labour, 721–732. **Margaret E. Harkness.** Signed.

783 Superstition in Arcady [on antiquarian research], 733–755. **Augustus Jessopp.** Signed; repr. *Arcady* as "Arcady in Some Phases of Her Faith."

784 The Irish land commissioners, 756–765. **Hugh Fortescue,** 1854–1932. Signed Ebrington [Viscount Ebrington].

785 Modern miracles, 766–780. **Richard F. Clarke.** Signed with title "S.J.": see Boase.

786 Notes on school board questions, 781–796. **Sydney C. Buxton.** Signed.

787 The ministry and the clôture, 797–803. **J. Guinness Rogers.** Signed.

788 England in Egypt, 804–820. **Edward Dicey.** Signed.

VOLUME 12, DECEMBER 1882

789 The Egyptian question and the French alliance, 821–838. **Joseph Reinach.** Signed.

790 England and the Suez Canal, 839–860. **Edward Plunkett.** Signed Dunsany [16th Baron Dunsany].

791 The second division at Tel-El-Kebir, 861–870. **E. B. Hamley.** Signed.

792 The fallacy of materialism (No. I): mind and body, 871–888. **George J. Romanes.** Signed.

793 The fallacy of materialism (No. II): matter and mind, 889–902. **Harvey Goodwin.** Signed Harvey Carlisle [Bishop of Carlisle].

794 Walt Whitman, 903–918. **G. C. Macaulay.** Signed.

795 Must it be "all or nothing" [in matters of faith]? 919–924. **Frederick R. Wynne.** Signed.

796 *Uncle Pat's Cabin,* 925–938. **Philip H. Bagenal.** Signed.

797 Farming and taxation, 939–946. **E. L. Stanley.** Signed Stanley of Alderley [Baron Stanley].

798 The Hamlet saga: from Saxo-Grammaticus, 947–957. Signed Falbe [Count de Falbe].

799 Is the Education Act of 1870 a just law? 958–968. **H. E. Manning.** Signed as in no. 8; repr. *Miscellanies,* III. (See nos. 805, 822.)

800 Instructions to my counsel, 969–996. **Ahmed Arábi.** Signed with addition "the Egyptian"; see Hill under Ahmad 'Urābi Pasha.

VOLUME 13, JANUARY 1883

801 Our position as a naval power, 1–13. **H. O. Arnold-Forster.** Signed.

802 Scotland's version of Home Rule, 14–26. **W. Scott Dalgleish.** Signed.

803 Russian prisons, 27–44. **Peter A. Kropotkin.** Signed P. Krapotkine; Contents adds "Prince"; repr. *In Prisons.*

804 On taste in dress, 45–57. **G. F. Watts.** Signed.

805 Cardinal Manning's demand on the rates [for all schools], 58–75. **R. W. Dale.** Signed. (See no. 823.)

806 Girl-children of the state, 76–87. **Maria Trench.** Signed.

807 "Puss in Boots," 88–104. **W. R. S. Ralston.** Signed.

808 The procedure of the High Court of Justice, 105–116. **Alfred Hill.** Signed.

809 Origin of the National Party in Egypt, 117–134. **John Ninet.** Signed.

810 Modern miracles: a rejoinder [to no.

785], 135–139. **E. S. Shuckburgh.** Signed; repr. in *Topics of the Time*, no. 5.

811   The functions of an opposition, 140–154. **Henry Cecil Raikes.** Signed.

812   The functions of Conservative opposition, 155–165. **W. St. John Brodrick.** Signed.

813   A sweet-water ship-canal through Egypt, 166–172. **John Fowler** and **Benjamin Baker.** Signed.

VOLUME 13, FEBRUARY 1883

814   On the economic condition of the Highlands of Scotland, 173–198. **G. D. Campbell.** Signed Argyll [Duke of Argyll].

815   *The Creed of Christendom* [by W. R. Greg], 199–216. **James Martineau.** Signed.

816   The theatrical revival, 217–228. **Frederick Wedmore.** Signed.

817   Middle-class education, 229–248. **C. B. Adderley.** Signed Norton [Baron Norton].

818   Village life in Norfolk six hundred years ago: a village lecture, 249–272. **Augustus Jessopp.** Signed; repr. *Coming of the Friars.*

819   Election prospects of the Conservatives, 273–278. **Charles E. Lewis.** Signed.

820   Concerning the unknown public, 279–296. **Thomas Wright.** Signed; Contents adds "the 'Journeyman Engineer' "; repr. in *Topics of the Time*, no. 3.

821   Local government in England and Wales (Part I), 297–313. **William Rathbone.** Signed.

822   Religion and the rates (No. I), 314–326. **H. E. Manning.** Signed as in no. 8; repr. *Miscellanies*, III, as "The Working of the Education Act of 1870 Unequal." (See nos. 833, 842.)

823   Religion and the rates (No. II), 327–337. **Robert Gregory.** Signed.

824   The unmounted Bucephalus [France], 338–356. **Joseph Reinach.** Signed.

VOLUME 13, MARCH 1883

825   Our hospitals, 359–384. **Henry C. Burdett.** Signed.

826   A few words about the eighteenth century, 385–403. **Frederic Harrison;** repr. *Choice of Books.*

827   The truth about Rossetti, 404–423. **Theodore Watts.** Signed.

828   Party obligations to-day, 424–433. **T. E. Kebbel.** Signed.

829   Wagner and wagnerism, 434–452. **Ed-**

mund Gurney. Signed; repr. in *Topics of the Time*, no. 6.

830   The "canker-worm": outdoor relief, 453–457. **James Hewitt.** Signed Lifford [4th Viscount Lifford].

831   Common sense in dress and fashion, 458–464. **Walburga E. Paget.** Signed W. Paget; see *WWW/1940.*

832   French elementary education, 465–472. **E. Lyulph Stanley.** Signed.

833   The Cardinal [Manning] and the schools: a rejoinder [to no. 822], 473–492. **R. W. Dale.** Signed. (See no. 842.)

834   The suppression of poisonous opinions (Part I), 493–508. **Leslie Stephen.** Signed; repr. *Agnostic's Apology.*

835   Local government in England and Wales (Part II, concl.), 509–528. **William Rathbone.** Signed.

836   The weakness of the army, 529–544. **J. L. A. Simmons.** Signed.

VOLUME 13, APRIL 1883

837   Practicable socialism, 554–560. **Samuel A. Barnett.** Signed; repr. *Practicable Socialism.*

838   Our national balance-sheet, 561–577. **John Lubbock.** Signed.

839   "What shall I do with my son?" 578–586. **William Feilding.** Signed W. Feilding; Contents adds "Major-Gen."; see Part B below. (See nos. 878, 925.)

840   Isaiah of Jerusalem (Part I), 587–603. **Matthew Arnold.** Signed; repr. as intro. to his *Isaiah of Jerusalem*, 1883.

841   The Highland crofters, 604–616. **John Stuart Blackie.** Signed.

842   Is the Christianity of England worth preserving? 617–634. **H. E. Manning.** Signed as in no. 8; repr. *Miscellanies*, III.

843   An unsolved historical riddle [Antonio Perez] (Part I), 635–652. **J. A. Froude.** Signed; repr. *Armada.*

844   The suppression of poisonous opinions (Part II, concl.), 653–666. **Leslie Stephen.** Signed.

845   Servants of the sick poor, 667–678. **Florence Craven.** Signed.

846   The future "Constitutional Party," 679–699. **W. T. W. Quin.** Signed Dunraven [4th Earl Dunraven].

847   England and South Africa, 700–728. **John McKenzie.** Signed.

VOLUME 13, MAY 1883

848   Desultory reflections of a Whig, 729–

739. **F. T. de Grey Cowper.** Signed Cowper [7th Earl Cowper]. (See no. 862.)

849 Questions of the day in India, 740–758. **Julian Goldsmid.** Signed.

850 The man of the future, 759–764. **E. Kay Robinson.** Signed.

851 Detective police, 765–778. **M. Laing Meason.** Signed.

852 Isaiah of Jerusalem (Part II, concl.), 779–794. **Matthew Arnold.** Signed.

853 Shall we retain the marines? 795–800. **G. A. Schomberg.** Signed.

854 An unsolved historical riddle (Part II, concl.), 801–823. **J. A. Froude.** Signed.

855 The past and future of Cambridge University, 824–840. **G. W. Hemming.** Signed.

856 Subjective difficulties in religion; or, Does unbelief come chiefly from something in religion or in ourselves? 841–861. **Aubrey De Vere.** Signed; repr. *Essays on Poetry*, II.

857 A glimpse into the art of singing, 862–871. **Margaret Watts Hughes.** Signed; Contents gives "Mrs. Watts Hughes."

858 The law a respecter of persons, 872–885. **Charles Cameron.** Signed.

859 France and China, 886–895. **Demetrius Charles Boulger.** Signed; repr. *Central Asian Questions*.

860 Social reform, 896–912. **Samuel Smith.** Signed.

VOLUME 13, JUNE 1883

861 Why send more Irish to America? 913–919. **Goldwin Smith.** Signed. (See no. 882.)

862 A protest against Whiggery, 920–927. **George W. E. Russell.** Signed. (See no. 875.)

863 The fortress prison of St. Petersburg, 928–949. **Peter A. Kropotkin.** Signed P. Krapotkine; repr. revised *In Prisons*, chaps. iii and vii.

864 The painted poetry of Watts and Rossetti, 950–970. **Emilie Isabel Barrington.** Signed; repr. in *A Retrospect*, 1896.

865 Falling trade and factory legislation, 971–977. **Archibald W. Finlayson.** Signed.

866 Fox-hunting, 978–991. **William Bromley-Davenport.** Signed W. Bromley Davenport; see *Landed Gentry*.

867 The dwellings of the poor, 992–1007. **George Howell.** Signed.

868 The improvement of the "Campagna Romana," 1008–1015. Count Conestabile. Signed.

869 The farmers and the Tory party, 1016–1035. **James Howard,** 1821–1889. Signed.

870 The new Agricultural Holdings Bill, 1036–1044. **William E. Bear.** Signed.

871 Wallenstein, 1045–1063. **H. Schütz Wilson.** Signed.

872 The English in Egypt, 1064–1079. **Francis W. Rowsell.** Signed.

873 The manufacture of public opinion, 1080–1092. **Blanchard Jerrold.** Signed.

VOLUME 14, JULY 1883

874 The spoliation of India (Part I), 1–22. **J. Seymour Keay.** Signed. (Note, p. 356, signed **J. Seymour Keay;** Part II is no. 980.)

875 The Whigs: a rejoinder [to no. 862], 23–30. **F. T. de Grey Cowper.** Signed Cowper [Earl Cowper].

876 House-lighting by electricity, 31–52. **W. C. Keppel.** Signed Bury [Viscount Bury].

877 Supernaturalism: mediaeval and classical, 53–64. **W. S. Lilly.** Signed; partially repr. *Chapters in European History* (1888), I.

878 Whither shall I send my son [to which colony]? 65–77. **William Feilding.** Signed.

879 The coming of the friars, 78–100. **Augustus Jessopp.** Signed; repr. *Coming of the Friars.*

880 New Guinea, 101–108. **Coutts Trotter.** Signed.

881 The sirens in ancient literature and art, 109–130. **Walter Copland Perry.** Signed.

882 Why send more Irish out of Ireland? 131–144. **A. M. Sullivan.** Signed.

883 Cheap fish for London, 145–164. **Samuel Plimsoll.** Signed.

884 The critical condition of the army, 165–188. **J. L. A. Simmons.** Signed.

VOLUME 14, AUGUST 1883

885 Why not purchase the Suez Canal? 189–205. **Edward Dicey.** Signed.

886 The German and British armies: a comparison, 206–227. **H. M. Hozier.** Signed.

887 A leaf from the real life of Byron, 228–242. **J. A. Froude.** Signed.

888 Painters and their patrons, 243–256. **W. Archer Shee.** Signed.

889 France and the slave trade in Madagascar, 257–261. **Lawrence C. Goodrich.** Signed.

890	After death, 262–284. **Norman Pearson.** Signed; repr. *Some Problems of Existence*, 1907.

891	Women and representative government, 285–291. **Millicent Garrett Fawcett.** Signed.

892	American and Canadian notes, 292–299. **George Jacob Holyoake.** Signed.

893	The locust war in Cyprus, 300–316. **Constance F. Gordon-Cumming.** Signed as in no. 704.

894	Aix-Les-Bains and Annecy, 317–328. **A. D. R. W. Cochrane-Baillie.** Signed Lamington [Baron Lamington].

895	Our Indian stewardship, 329–338. **Florence Nightingale.** Signed.

896	Italian policy in the East, 339–345. **Francesco Nobili-Vitelleschi.** Signed F. Nobili Vitelleschi; Contents adds "Marchese"; see *BMCat.*

897	The cholera and our water-supply, 346–355. **Percy Faraday Frankland.** Signed.

VOLUME 14, SEPTEMBER 1883

898	Ireland and the Empire (Part I), 361–384. **H. G. Grey.** Signed Grey [3rd Earl Grey].

899	The Liberal idea and the colonies, 385–401. **H. O. Arnold-Forster.** Signed.

900	Salmon-fishing, 402–413. **William Bromley-Davenport.** Signed as in no. 866.

901	Clergymen as head-masters, 414–420. **C. Kegan Paul.** Signed.

902	The life-problem of Bengal, 421–440. **Syed Ameer Ali.** Signed as in no. 454.

903	The theatre and the mob, 441–456. **Henry Arthur Jones.** Signed; repr. *Renascence.*

904	The wish to believe: a dialogue in a Catholic college [sequel to no. 675], 457–479. **Wilfrid Ward.** Signed; repr. *Witnesses.*

905	Memories of Ischia, 480–500. **William Howard Russell.** Signed.

906	Have we an army? 501–516. **P. L. MacDougall.** Signed.

907	Inequality in punishment, 517–530. **Edward Fry.** Signed; repr. *Studies by the Way*, 1900, as "The Theory of Punishment."

908	Republican prospects in France, 531–540. **Joseph Reinach.** Signed.

VOLUME 14, OCTOBER 1883

909	Foundations of the government of India, 541–568. **J. F. Stephen.** Signed.

910	Recent events in India, 569–589. **Evelyn Baring.** Signed.

911	Clouds over Arcady [on agricultural labor], 590–609. **Augustus Jessopp.** Signed; repr. *Arcady.*

912	The politics of literature: a dialogue, 610–621. **H. D. Traill.** Signed; repr. *New Fiction.*

913	After-images, 622–638. **Sydney Hodges.**

914	Short service: one cause of its failure, 639–653. **G. R. Gleig.** Signed.

915	The poetry of the early mysteries, 654–673. **Florence M. Capes.** Signed F. M. Capes; see *BMCat.*

916	The Agricultural Holdings Act, 1883, 674–694. **G. Shaw Lefevre.** Signed.

917	Mesmerism (Part I, no more published), 695–719. **Edmund Gurney** and **Frederic W. H. Myers.** Signed.

918	The present and future of the Australasian colonies, 720–732. **Archibald Forbes.** Signed.

VOLUME 14, NOVEMBER 1883

919	Ireland and the Empire (Part II, concl.), 733–752. **H. G. Grey.** Signed Grey [3rd Earl Grey].

920	The Jews and the malicious charge of human sacrifice, 753–778. **Charles H. H. Wright.** Signed.

921	An academy of literature for Great Britain, 779–793. **Henry Taylor.** Signed, p. 780. With letter from Henry Brougham to Robert Southey, 793–794, and reply by Robert Southey, 794–797.

922	Great cities and social reform (No. I), 798–809. **Reginald Brabazon.** Signed Brabazon [Lord Brabazon], p. 803; repr. *Social Arrows*, 1886.

923	Great cities and social reform (No. II), 810–818. **Samuel A. Barnett.** Signed; repr. *Practicable Socialism* as "Town Councils and Social Reform."

924	The French army of to-day, 819–839. **C. B. Norman.** Signed C. Norman; Contents adds "Captain"; cf. no. 1000.

925	Blue-blooded boys: an Australian criticism [of no. 839], 840–853. **W. Jardine Smith.** Signed.

926	Land as property, 854–862. **Newton Wallop.** Signed Lymington [Viscount Lymington].

927	Our orchards and paraffin oil, 863–873. **Henry P. Dunster.** Signed.

928	The sun's corona, 874–883. **Richard A. Proctor.** Signed; repr. *The Universe of Suns*, 1884.

929	The new departure in legal reform, 884–906. **Montague Cookson.** Signed.

930 The progress of democracy in England, 907–924. **George C. Brodrick.** Signed; repr. *Literary Fragments*, 1891.

VOLUME 14, DECEMBER 1883

931 Common sense and the dwellings of the poor (No. I): improvements now practicable, 925–933. **Octavia Hill.** Signed.

932 The dwellings of the poor (No. II): the mischief of state aid, 934–939. **A. A. Cooper.** Signed Shaftsbury [Earl of Shaftsbury].

933 The dwellings of the poor (No. III): the existing law, 940–951. **H. O. Arnold-Forster.** Signed.

934 The dwellings of the poor (No. IV): a workman's reflections, 952–963. **William Glazier.** Signed.

935 Outcast Russia: the journey to Siberia, 964–976. **Peter A. Kropotkin.** Signed as in no. 803; repr. *In Prisons.*

936 Recreation, 977–988. **James Paget.** Signed.

937 Extracts from the diary of the Marquis Tsêng, 989–1002. **Tsêng Chitsê.** Title; called Chinese minister to England and France, p. 989; see H. A. Giles, *A Chinese Biographical Dictionary*, 1898. Intro. note and trans. by **J. N. Jordan** —signed.

938 Ungrateful Ireland (Part I), 1003–1029. **C. Gavan Duffy.** Signed.

939 Rachel, 1030–1044. **Nina H. Kennard.** Signed.

940 A recent visit to the Boers, 1045–1061. **Robert Lindsay.** Signed R. Loyd-Lindsay; see *DNB*.

941 The revival of the West Indies, 1062–1074. **Nevile Lubbock.** Signed.

942 Manhood suffrage on the principle of shareholding, 1075–1089. **Norman Pearson.** Signed.

943 Covert-shooting, 1090–1106. **William Bromley-Davenport.** Signed as in no. 900.

VOLUME 15, JANUARY 1884

944 Religion: a retrospect and prospect, 1–12. **Herbert Spencer.** Signed. (See nos. 977, 1002.)

945 The pretensions of M. de Lesseps, 13–27. **Charles Magniac.** Signed C. Magniac; see Venn.

946 Statues and monuments of London, 28–48. **G. Shaw Lefevre.** Signed.

947 Lord Melbourne: a sketch, 49–56. **F. T. de Grey Cowper.** Signed Cowper [Earl Cowper].

948 A treatise on love, 57–67. **Algernon Sidney.** With note on the family of Sidney, 67–70, by **James P. Ley**—signed, with addition "M.A. Cantab."

949 Ungrateful Ireland (Part II, concl.), 71–93. **C. Gavan Duffy.** Signed.

950 Floods, 94–99. **R. A. Haldane-Duncan.** Signed Camperdown [3rd Earl Camperdown].

951 Daily life in a mediaeval monastery, 100–122. **Augustus Jessopp.** Signed; repr. *Coming of the Friars.* (See no. 1043.)

952 The new Bribery Act and the York election, 123–137. **E. T. Wilkinson.** Signed, with title "Liberal Agent at York."

953 Our growing Australian empire, 138–149. **Henry Parkes.** Signed.

954 Homes of the poor, 150–166. **Richard Assheton Cross.** Signed.

955 A new view of Mormonism, 167–184. **James W. Barclay.** Signed.

VOLUME 15, FEBRUARY 1884

956 On the inspiration of scripture, 185–199. **John H. Newman.** Signed, with title "Cardinal."

957 The House of Lords (No. I): its reform, 200–216. **W. T. W. Quin.** Signed Dunraven [4th Earl Dunraven].

958 The House of Lords (No. II): on its abolition, 217–227. **T. E. Kebbel.** Signed.

959 The state and the medical profession, 228–238. **T. H. Huxley.** Signed; repr. *Collected Essays*, III.

960 A walk to Coomassie, 239–254. **Godfrey Y. Lagden.** Signed.

961 The universities and the poor, 255–261. **Samuel A. Barnett.** Signed; repr. *Practicable Socialism* as "University Settlements."

962 "Cramming" in elementary schools, 262–273. **C. B. Adderley.** Signed Norton [Baron Norton].

963 India, her wheat and her railways, 274–292. **William Fowler,** 1828–1905, prob. Signed. Fowler wrote *Indian Currency*, 1899: see *WWW*.

964 Proportional representation, 293–304. **Robert B. Hayward.** Signed.

965 An ecclesiastical olive branch, 305–316. **A. J. B. Beresford-Hope.** Signed.

966 The germ-theory of zymotic diseases; considered from the natural history point of view, 317–336. **William Benjamin Carpenter.** Signed as in no. 636; see *DNB*.

967 Christian agnosticism, 337–344. **G. H. Curteis.** Signed, but with initials reversed; see Boase.

968   On rainbows, 345–360. **John Tyndall.** Signed; repr. *New Fragments.*

VOLUME 15, MARCH 1884

968a   A society for the enforcement of sanitary laws and the improvement of dwellings, 361–362. **James Knowles.** Signed.

969   Our protectorate in Egypt, 363–388. **Edward Dicey.** Signed.

970   Peasants' homes in Arcady, 389–408. **Augustus Jessopp.** Signed; repr. *Arcady.*

971   Platform women, 409–415. **Margaret Lonsdale.** Signed.

972   Opening national institutions on Sunday, 416–434. **W. T. W. Quin.** Signed Dunraven [4th Earl Dunraven]. (See no. 987.)

973   The brutes on their master [animals discussing man], 435–444. **H. D. Traill.** Signed.

974   Ship insurances and the loss of life at sea, 445–454. **Thomas Brassey.** Signed.

975   My schooldays from 1830 to 1840, 455–474. **George Granville Bradley.** Signed.

976   The exile in Siberia, 475–493. **Peter A. Kropotkin.** Signed as in no. 803; repr. *In Prisons.*

977   The ghost of religion, 494–506. **Frederic Harrison.** Signed; repr. *Common Sense.* (See nos. 1012, 1033 and 1063.)

978   The House of Commons, 507–536. **H. G. Grey.** Signed Grey [3rd Earl Grey].

VOLUME 15, APRIL 1884

979   The prophet of San Francisco [Henry George], 537–558. **G. D. Campbell.** Signed Argyll [8th Duke of Argyll]; repr. in George's *Property in Land*, N.Y., 1884. (See no. 1018.)

980   The spoliation of India (Part II), 559–582. **J. Seymour Keay.** Signed.

981   Wordsworth and Byron (Part I), 583–609. **Algernon Charles Swinburne.** Signed; repr. *Miscellanies.*

982   The Arundel Society, 610–625. **W. H. Gregory.** Signed.

983   Democracy and socialism, 626–644. **George C. Brodrick.** Signed; repr. *Literary Fragments*, 1891.

984   King John of Abyssinia, 645–651. **E. A. De Cosson.** Signed.

985   Luther and recent criticism, 652–668. **John Tulloch.** Signed.

986   Numbers; or, The majority and the remnant, 669–685. **Matthew Arnold.** Signed; repr. *Discourses in America,* 1885.

987   The day of rest, 686–702. **Charles Hill.** Signed, with addition "Secretary to the Working Men's Lord's Day Rest Association."

988   Proportional representation (No. I), 703–713. **John Lubbock.** Signed. With a list of members of parliament who belong to the Proportional Representation Society, 713–715.

989   Proportional representation (No. II): a test election, 716–720. **H. O. Arnold-Forster.** Signed.

VOLUME 15, MAY 1884

990   The spoliation of India (Part III, concl.): rackrenting the land and the water, 721–740. **J. Seymour Keay.** Signed. (See no. 1049.)

991   Colour, space, and music for the people, 741–752. **Octavia Hill.** Signed.

992   The forthcoming Arab race at Newmarket, 753–763. **Wilfrid Scawen Blunt.** Signed.

993   Wordsworth and Byron (Part II, concl.), 764–790. **Algernon Charles Swinburne.** Signed.

994   Apparitions (Part I), 791–815. **Edmund Gurney** and **Frederic W. H. Myers.** Signed. (Part II is no. 1015.)

995   The Mahdi and Mohammedan predictions concerning the last days, 816–822. **Charlotte E. Stern,** prob. Signed C. E. Stern; woman cited wrote historical books on the Bible at this time: see *BMCat.*

996   A voyage in the *Sunbeam* in 1883, 823–839. **Thomas Brassey.** Signed T. Brassey; repr. *11,506 Knots in the "Sunbeam,"* 1884.

997   "Sanitary Aid" [Committee], 840–848. **Rosalind Marryat.** Signed.

998   Frederick Denison Maurice, 849–866. **J. Henry Shorthouse.** Signed.

999   Australia and the imperial connection, 867–872. **Henry Parkes.** Signed.

1000   The colonies of France, 873–896. **C. B. Norman.** Signed.

VOLUME 15, JUNE 1884

1001   "How long halt ye between two opinions [about Egypt]?" 897–904. **C. F. Moberly Bell.** Signed, but with an "S." as second initial; man cited was in Egypt at the time and signed *NatR-II* no. 231, in Nov. 1884, on same topic.

1002　The unknowable and the unknown, 905–919. **James Fitzjames Stephen.** Signed.

1003　What do the Irish read? 920–932. **J. Pope-Hennessy.** Signed.

1004　The continental Sunday, 933–944. **William Rossiter.** Signed.

1005　False coin [on natural religion], 945–968. **Agnes Lambert.** Signed.

1006　The art of public speaking, 969–978. **Hamilton Aïdé.** Signed.

1007　With Baker and Graham in the Eastern Soudan, 979–1003. **John Macdonald.** Signed; on p. 993 author refers to "a fellow-correspondent" at the battle he was describing: cf. no. 3357.

1008　Forgotten bibles, 1004–1022. **Friedrich Max Müller.** Signature; repr. *Last Essays.*

1009　The Yorkshire Association, 1023–1036. **Charles Milnes Gaskell.** Signed. (Letter, vol. 16, p. 168, from **Gaskell.**)

1010　Eight years of co-operative shirtmaking, 1037–1054. **Edith Simcox.** Signed.

1011　Free trade in the army, 1055–1074. **Frederick Roberts.** Signed; Contents gives "Lieut. Gen. Sir Frederick S. Roberts."

VOLUME 16, JULY 1884

1012　Retrogressive religion, 3–26. **Herbert Spencer.** Signed.

1013　Egypt's proper frontier, 27–46. **Samuel White Baker.** Signed.

1014　City of London livery companies, 47–67. **Richard Assheton Cross.** Signed.

1015　Visible apparitions (Part II, concl.), 68–95. **Edmund Gurney** and **Frederic W. H. Myers.** Signed. (Letter, p. 851, signed **Frederick H. Balfour,** with reply, pp. 851–852, signed **Edmund Hornby.**)

1016　The federal states of the world, 96–117. **J. N. Dalton,** 1839–1931. Signed, with title "Rev." in Contents; see Venn.

1017　The letters of Heinrich Heine, 118–133. **Walter S. Sichel.** Signed.

1018　The "reduction to iniquity" [reply to no. 979], 134–155. **Henry George.** Signed; repr. *Property in Land,* N. Y., 1884.

1019　The surrender of Egypt, 156–167. **Edward Dicey.** Signed.

VOLUME 16, AUGUST 1884

1020　The House of Lords and the country (No. I), 169–173. **William A. A. De Vere.** Signed St. Albans [10th Duke of St. Albans].

1021　The House of Lords (No. II), 174–181. **Arthur James Balfour.** Signed.

1022　The House of Lords (No. III), 182–188. **E. Lyulph Stanley.** Signed.

1023　The House of Lords (No. IV), 189–195. **George Howell.** Signed.

1024　The House of Lords (No. V), 196–209. **Newton Wallop.** Signed Lymington [Viscount Lymington].

1025　Leprosy, present and past (Part I): present, 210–227. **Agnes Lambert.** Signed.

1026　An American criticism of the Egyptian campaign, 228–237. **Archibald Forbes.** Signed.

1027　A tangled skein unravelled; or, The mystery of Shakespeare's sonnets, 238–262. **Charles Mackay.** Signed.

1028　A limit to evolution, 263–280. **St. George Mivart.** Signed; repr. *Essays.*

1029　The prophet of walnut-tree yard [Lodowick Muggleton], 281–300. **Augustus Jessopp.** Signed; repr. *Coming of the Friars.*

1030　Technical education: report of the Royal Commissioners, 301–319. **Henry Solly.** Signed.

1031　County characteristics: Sussex, 320–338. **Henry G. Hewlett.** Signed.

1032　English sisterhoods, 339–352. **Maria Trench.** Signed.

VOLUME 16, SEPTEMBER 1884

1033　Agnostic metaphysics, 353–378. **Frederic Harrison.** Signed; repr. *Common Sense.*

1034　Storm-clouds [of anarchy] in the Highlands, 379–395. **J. A. Cameron.** Signed.

1035　Chatter versus work in parliament, 396–411. **J. Guinness Rogers.** Signed.

1036　The dawn of the new Italy, 412–433. **Francesco Nobili-Vitelleschi.** Signed F. Nobili-Vitelleschi; cf. no. 896.

1037　The Darwinian theory of instinct, 434–450. **G. J. Romanes.** Signed.

1038　The opportunity of the peers, 451–459. **Newton Wallop.** Signed Lymington [Viscount Lymington].

1039　A democrat's defence of the House of Lords, 460–466. **Maltman Barry.** Signed.

1040　Leprosy, present and past (Part II, concl.): past, 467–489. **Agnes Lambert.** Signed.

1041　English supremacy in the East, 490–504. **Francis Bulkeley Johnson.** Signed F. Bulkeley Johnson; see Venn under Johnson.

1042　Imperial federation: its impossibility,

505–516. **C. S. Adderley.** Signed Norton [Baron Norton].

VOLUME 16, OCTOBER 1884

1043 Daily life in a modern monastery, 517–529. **Elphege G. Cody.** Signed, with title "O.S.B." and address "Fort Augustus, N.B."

1044 The emigrant in New York, 530–549. **Charlotte G. O'Brien.** Signed.

1045 Charles Reade, 550–567. **A. C. Swinburne.** Signed; repr. *Miscellanies.*

1046 A farm that pays, 568–575. **Catherine Milnes Gaskell.** Signed. (See no. 1135.)

1047 Our deaf and dumb, 576–597. **Elisabeth J. M. Blackburn.** Signed.

1048 England as a market garden, 598–610. **Henry P. Dunster.** Signed.

1049 The spoliation of India: a reply [to no. 990], 611–618. **Lionel Ashburner.** Signed.

1050 An experiment [in class understanding], 619–623. **C. Kegan Paul.** Signed.

1051 The classification of literature, 624–629. **J. Taylor Kay.** Signed.

1052 Progress and wages: a workman's view, 630–638. **James G. Hutchinson.** Signed.

1053 The art treasures of Prussia, 639–662. **J. Beavington Atkinson.** Signed.

1054 Lord Beaconsfield's Irish policy, 663–680. **J. Pope Hennessy.** Signed.

VOLUME 16, NOVEMBER 1884

1055 A corrected picture of the Highlands, 681–701. **G. D. Campbell.** Signed Argyll [8th Duke of Argyll]. (See no. 1104.)

1056 The people of England versus their naval officials, 702–714. **H. O. Arnold-Forster.** Signed.

1057 The Sisters of Thibet, 715–730. **Laurence Oliphant.** Signed; repr. *Fashionable Philosophy and Other Sketches,* 1887.

1058 What will the peers do? 731–745. **E. H. Knatchbull-Hugessen.** Signed Brabourne [1st Baron Brabourne].

1059 *Faust, "ein Fragment"* [by Goethe], 746–763. **Nina Kennard.** Signed.

1060 State-directed emigration: its necessity, 764–787. **Reginald Brabazon.** Signed Brabazon [Earl Brabazon]; repr. *Social Arrows,* 1886.

1061 Karlsbad: the queen of Bohemian watering places, 788–805. **W. Fraser Rae.** Signed.

1062 "Over-pressure" [in schools], 806–825. **Sydney C. Buxton.** Signed.

1063 Last words about agnosticism and the religion of humanity, 826–839. **Herbert Spencer.** Signed.

1064 Lord Northbrook's mission, 840–850. **Edward Dicey.** Signed.

VOLUME 16, DECEMBER 1884

1065 Imperial federation from an Australian point of view, 853–868. **John Douglas.** Signed.

1066 The expansion of Germany, 869–878. **George Baden-Powell.** Signed.

1067 Miss Anderson's Juliet, 879–900. **Robert Lytton.** Signed Lytton [Earl Lytton].

1068 The proposed new cathedral for Liverpool, 901–914. **James Fergusson,** 1808–1886. Signed; see *DNB.*

1069 The black death in East Anglia (Part I), 915–934. **Augustus Jessopp.** Signed; repr. *Coming of the Friars.*

1070 Proportional versus majority representation, 935–964. **Albert Grey.** Signed. (See no. 1094.)

1071 English songs, ancient and modern, 965–983. **Charles Mackay.** Signed.

1072 Mission women, 984–990. **Maud C. Hamilton.** Signed.

1073 Something better than emigration: a reply [to no. 1060], 991–998. **H. M. Hyndman.** Signed.

1074 The Democratic victory in America, 999–1026. **William Henry Hurlbert.** Signed.

1075 Conservative and Liberal finance, 1027–1036. **Edward G. Clarke.** Signed Edward Clarke; see *DNB.* With a letter, 1036–1038, signed **W. E. Gladstone.**

VOLUME 17, JANUARY 1885

1076 Caesarism, 1–14. **Francis T. de Grey Cowper.** Signed Cowper [Earl Cowper].

1077 The new reform [Redistribution Bill], 15–24. **J. O'Connor Power.** Signed.

1078 Will Russia conquer India? (Part I), 25–42. **Arminius Vambéry.** Signed as in no. 451.

1079 The centenary of *The Times,* 43–65. **W. Fraser Rae.** Signed.

1080 Charles Lamb and George Wither, 66–91. **Algernon Charles Swinburne.** Signed; repr. *Miscellanies.*

1081 Cycling and cyclists, 92–108. **W. C. Keppel.** Signed Bury [Viscount Bury].

1082 The savage, 109–132. **Friedrich Max Müller.** Signature; repr. *Last Essays.*

1083 Locusts and farmers of America, 133–153. **Constance F. Gordon Cumming.** Signed as in no. 704.

1084 Religion and the stage, 154–169. **Henry A. Jones.** Signed; repr. *Renascence.*

1085 Confessions of an Eton master. 170–184. **H. S. Salt.** Signed.

1086 The navy and the admiralty, 185–200. **Robert Spencer Robinson.** Signed.

VOLUME 17, FEBRUARY 1885

1087 Imperial federation, 201–217. **W. E. Forster.** Signed. With a postscript, 217–218, signed **James Service.**

1088 A word more about America, 219–236. **Matthew Arnold.** Signed; repr. *Civilization in the United States*, Boston, 1888.

1089 Reform of the House of Lords, 237–248. **G. R. C. Herbert.** Signed Pembroke [Earl of Pembroke].

1090 The duties of dramatic critics, 249–262. **William Archer.** Signed; repr. *About the Theatre*, 1886, as "The Ethics of Theatrical Criticism."

1091 Abolition of proprietary madhouses, 263–279. **John Charles Bucknill.** Signed.

1092 State aid to emigrants: a reply to Lord Brabazon [no. 1060], 280–296. **J. H. Tuke.** Signed.

1093 Will Russia conquer India (Part II, concl.), 297–311. **Arminius Vambéry.** Signed as in no. 451.

1094 Proportional representation: objections and answers, 312–320. **John Lubbock, Leonard Courtney, Albert Grey,** and **John Westlake.** Signed; Contents gives "John" as Westlake's first name, which signature gives as "J."

1095 Light from the East on the colour question, 321–330. **James W. Furrell.** Signed.

1096 Democracy and England, 331–341. **C. B. Adderley.** Signed Norton [Baron Norton].

1097 Irrigation in Egypt, 342–351. **C. C. Scott-Moncrieff.** Signed.

1098 Private bill legislation, 352–368. **Alexander Craig Sellar.** Signed.

1099 Socialism and rent-appropriation: a dialogue, 369–380. **Henry George** and **H. M. Hyndman.** Signed.

VOLUME 17, MARCH 1885

1100 The unity of the Empire (No. I),

381–396. **W. C. Keppel.** Signed Bury [Viscount Bury].

1101 The unity of the Empire (No. II), 397–404. **J. D. S. Campbell.** Signed Lorne [Marquis of Lorne].

1102 The volunteers in time of need, 405–423. **Edward Hamley.** Signed; repr. *National Defence*, 1889.

1103 Egypt and the Soudan: on the other side of the hill, 424–436. **William H. Gregory.** Signed.

1104 The Highland crofters: a vindication of the report of the Crofters' Commission, 437–463. **Francis Napier.** Signed Napier and Ettrick [Baron Napier and Ettrick].

1105 George Eliot's *Life*, 464–485. **J. D. Acton.** Signed Acton [Lord Acton]; repr. *Historical Essays.*

1106 The Eton tutorial system, 486–495. **John S. Bligh.** Signed Darnley [6th Earl of Darnley].

1107 Whispering machines [to record books on discs], 496–499. **R. Balmer.** Signed, with address "Bibliothèque Nationale, Paris."

1108 The political situation of Europe, 500–520. **Francesco Nobili-Vitelleschi.** Signed as in no. 1036.

1109 The actor's calling: a reply [to several writers on acting], 521–526. **Hamilton Aïdé.** Signed.

1110 Finland: a rising nationality, 527–546. **Peter A. Kropotkin.** Signed P. Kropotkin; Contents adds "Prince."

1111 Turkey and England, 547–551. **A. C. Hobart-Hampden.** Signed Hobart Pasha; see *DNB.*

1112 A few more words on imperial federation, 552–556. **W. E. Forster.** Signed.

VOLUME 17, APRIL 1885

1113 The Russian advance in Central Asia, 557–574. **H. C. Rawlinson.** Signed.

1114 An Anglo-Turkish alliance (No. I), 575–582. **A. C. Hobart-Hampden.** Signed as in no. 1111.

1115 An Anglo-Turkish alliance (No. II), 583–589. **J. Picton Warlow.** Signed, with addition, "late Military Vice-Consul in Anatolia."

1116 A scheme for imperial federation, 590–598. **Samuel Wilson.** Signed; Contents adds "Sir"; see Boase.

1117 The black death in East Anglia (Part II, concl.), 599–622. **Augustus Jessopp.** Signed.

1118 The comparative study of ghost stories, 623–632. **Andrew Lang.** Signed.

1119 In case of invasion, 633–643. **Archibald Forbes.** Signed.

1120 The proper sympathy between France and England, 644–657. **Joseph Reinach.** Signed.

1121 The eastern pediment of the Parthenon, 658–675. **Charles Waldstein.** Signed.

1122 The sun's corona, 676–689. **William Huggins.** Signed.

1123 A short tract upon oaths, 690–700. **Stephen E. De Vere.** Signed.

1124 Marivaux, 701–712. **Yetta Blaze de Bury.** Signed J. Blaze de Bury; called "Mlle." in Contents; see Part B below for other arts. in *NC* on French subjects by woman cited.

1125 Gordon at Gravesend: a personal reminiscence, 713–722. **Arthur Stannard.** Signed.

1126 Since 1880, 723–732. **George J. Goschen.** Signed.

VOLUME 17, MAY, 1885

1127 Egypt and the Soudan, 733–744. **Muhammad 'Abd al-Halīm Pasha.** Signed Halim; called "Prince Halim Pasha" in Contents; see *Hill* under Muhammad. (See nos. 1153, 1188.)

1128 The coming war [on Afghan frontier], 745–754. **Peter A. Kropotkin.** Signed as in no. 1110.

1129 Variations in the punishment of crime, 755–776. **James Fitzjames Stephen.** Signed.

1130 Diet in relation to age and activity, 777–799. **Henry Thompson.** Signed.

1131 Shakespeare and stage costume, 800–818. **Oscar Wilde.** Signed.

1132 The Red Man, 819–826. **J. H. McNaughton.** Signed.

1133 Death, 827–832. **Arthur E. Shipley.** Signed.

1134 Our system of infantry tactics: what is it? 833–846. **P. L. MacDougall.** Signed.

1135 A farm that really pays, 847–856. **John Bowen-Jones.** Signed J. B. Bowen-Jones; see *WWW/1928* under Jones.

1136 Lunacy law reform, 857–868. **J. R. Gasquet.** Signed.

1137 Lord Bramwell on drink: a reply [to no. 1138], 869–878. **Frederic W. Farrar.** Signed.

1138 Drink, 878–882. **George W. W. Bramwell.** Signed Lord Bramwell; see *DNB*, 1st suppl. (See nos. 1147, 1159.)

1139 Why I left Russia, 883–904. **Isidor Goldsmith.** Signed.

1140 The "great wall" of India, 905–908. **William Henry R. Green.** Signed Henry Green; Contents gives "Sir Henry Rhodes Green"; see *BMCat*.

VOLUME 17, JUNE 1885

1141 Mr. Gladstone as a foreign minister, 909–925. **J. Guinness Rogers.** Signed.

1142 Housing the poor, 926–947. **Richard Assheton Cross.** Signed.

1143 Genius and insanity, 948–969. **James Sully.** Signed.

1144 The Irish Parliament of 1782, 970–987. **Henry L. Jephson.** Signed Henry Jephson; see *BMCat*.

1145 James Russell Lowell, 988–1008. **G. Barnett Smith.** Signed.

1146 Our armies in India, 1009–1020. **Frederick W. Verney.** Signed.

1147 Drink: a rejoinder [to no. 1137], 1021–1030. **G. W. W. Bramwell.** Signed Bramwell [Baron Bramwell].

1148 *The Faithfull Shepherdesse*, 1031–1042. **Janey Sevilla Campbell.** Signed.

1149 Letters from a private soldier in Egypt, 1043–1054. **William H. Saunders.** Signed.

1150 Mining inspection a sham: by a miner, 1055–1063. **J. M. Foster.** Signed. (See no. 1163.)

1151 Leasehold enfranchisement, 1064–1071. **Henry Broadhurst.** Signed.

1152 The Crimes Act, 1072–1076. **Thomas Spring-Rice**, 1849–1926. Signed Monteagle [2nd Baron Monteagle].

VOLUME 18, JULY 1885

1153 The Khedivate of Egypt, 1–13. **Edward Dicey.** Signed.

1154 The work of Victor Hugo (Part I), 14–29. **Algernon Charles Swinburne.** Signed; repr. *A Study of Victor Hugo*, 1886.

1155 Modern Catholics and scientific freedom, 30–47. **St. George Mivart.** Signed.

1156 A swain of Arcady, 48–57. **Augustus Jessopp.** Signed; repr. *Arcady.*

1157 Parliamentary manners, 58–68. **Henry W. Lucy.** Signed.

1158 Public business in the House of Commons, 69–77. **Henry H. Fowler.** Signed.

1159 Drink: a last word to Lord Bramwell, 78–87. **Frederic W. Farrar.** Signed.

1160 To within a mile of Khartoum, 88–100. **Frederick Richard T. T. Gascoigne.**

Signed R. F. T. Gascoigne; Contents adds "Capt."; man cited fought in Egyptian war in 1884; see *WWW*/1940.

1161 Recent progress in biology, 101–110. **E. Ray Lankester.** Signed.

1162 The armed strength of Turkey, 111–123. **Henry Felix Woods.** Signed Woods Pasha; see *WWW*/1940.

1163 Mine inspection: a reply [to no. 1150], 124–129. **George Blake Walker.** Signed.

1164 Transylvanian superstitions, 130–150. **Jane Emily Gerard.** Signed E. Gerard; Contents gives "Mme. Emily de Laszowska Gerard": see *DNB*, 2nd suppl.

1165 The true "scientific frontier" of India, 151–159. **John Slagg.** Signed.

1166 England or the admiralty? 160–176. **H. O. Arnold-Forster.** Signed.

VOLUME 18, AUGUST 1885

1167 The Metaphysical Society: a reminiscence, 177–196. **R. H. Hutton.** Signed.

1168 A defence of deer forests, 197–208. **Donald Cameron.** Signed, with addition "of Lochiel."

1169 Aristocracy in America, 209–217. **Matthew M. Trumbull.** Signed.

1170 Violins, 218–233. **William Huggins.** Signed.

1171 The burden of Ireland, 238–248. **J. Leslie Field.** Signed.

1172 A Jesuit reformer and poet [Frederick Spee], 249–273. **H. I. D. Ryder.** Signed; repr. *Essays*, 1911.

1173 County characteristics: Surrey, 274–293. **Henry G. Hewlett.** Signed.

1174 The work of Victor Hugo (Part II, concl.), 294–311. **Algernon Charles Swinburne.** Signed.

1175 The recent rebellion in North-West Canada, 312–327. **G. J. M. K. Elliot.** Signed Melgund [Viscount Melgund].

1176 The London flower trade, 328–337. **Edward A. Arnold.** Signed.

1177 Anti-cholera inoculation, 338–352. **Charles Cameron.** Signed. (See no. 1182.)

VOLUME 18, SEPTEMBER 1885

1178 What is a moderate Liberal to do? 353–361. **Francis T. de Grey Cowper.** Signed Cowper [Earl Cowper].

1179 The radical programme for Ireland, 362–373. **Edward William O'Brien.** Signed.

1180 An episode of the Armada, 374–387.

H. J. Moreton. Signed Ducie [3rd Earl of Ducie].

1181 War horses, 388–397. **Frank S. Russell.** Signed.

1182 The cholera-inoculation fallacy, 398–407. **Edward F. Willoughby.** Signed.

1183 Thibet, 408–431. **Charles H. Lepper.** Signed.

1184 Why men will not be clergymen, 432–438. **Hubert Handley.** Signed.

1185 The enclosure of commons, 439–452. **H. R. Grenfell.** Signed.

1186 Vittoria Colonna, 453–473. **H. Schütz Wilson.** Signed.

1187 Reservation of the Sacrament, 474–484. **T. W. Belcher.** Signed.

1188 A reply to my critics, 485–492. **Muhammad 'Abd al-Halim Pasha.** Signed Halim; cf. no. 1127.

1189 The recent progress of democracy in Switzerland, 493–512. **Emile de Laveleye.** Signed.

VOLUME 18, OCTOBER 1885

1190 The question of the land, 513–531. **G. Shaw Lefevre.** Signed.

1191 The uniformity of nature, 532–544. **Harvey Goodwin.** Signed H. Carlisle [Bishop of Carlisle].

1192 Parliament and the Church, 545–560. **William C. Borlase.** Signed. (See no. 1331.)

1193 The novel of manners, 561–576. **H. D. Traill.** Signed; repr. *New Fiction*.

1194 Eton reform, 577–592. **F. W. Warre-Cornish.** Signed F. W. Cornish; see *DNB*/1921.

1195 Gold scarcity and the depression of trade, 593–613. **Moreton Frewen.** Signed.

1196 Natural heirship; or, All the world akin, 614–625. **Henry Kendall.** Signed; repr., enlarged, *The Kinship of Man*, Boston, 1888.

1197 The lesson of "Jupiter," 626–650. **Friedrich Max Müller.** Signature.

1198 Female labour in Australia: an appeal for help, 651–656. **Jeannie Lockett.** Signed.

1199 Ironclads and torpedo flotillas, 657–673. **E. R. Fremantle.** Signed.

1200 The new star in the Andromeda nebula, 674–684. **Richard A. Proctor.** Signed; repr. *Other Suns than Ours*, 1887.

VOLUME 18, NOVEMBER 1885

1201 Dawn of creation and of worship:

reply to Dr. Réville, 685–706. **W. E Gladstone.** Signed. (See nos. 1218, 1237.)

1202   Irish wrongs and English remedies: a statement of facts, 707–721. **R. Barry O'Brien.** Signed; repr. *Irish Wrongs.*

1203   Sir Herbert Stewart's desert march, 722–744. **Douglas Dawson.** Signed.

1204   State Christianity and the French elections, 745–762. **William Henry Hurlbert.** Signed.

1205   Disestablishment in Wales, 763–770. **George Osborne Morgan.** Signed.

1206   The restoration of Westminster Hall, 771–782. **James Fergusson,** 1808–1886. Signed; see *DNB.*

1207   Some experiences of work in an East-End district, 783–793. **Katrine C. Cowper.** Signed Katie Cowper; Contents adds "Countess."

1208   Foreign opinions on peasant properties, 794–803. **Frances P. Verney.** Signed F. P. Verney; repr. *Peasant Owners.*

1209   Free schools, 804–818. **C. B. Adderley.** Signed Norton [Baron Norton].

1210   The coup d'état in Eastern Roumelia: a narrative, 819–832. **Edgar Whitaker.** Signed.

1211   The Radicals and socialism, 833–839. **H. M. Hyndman.** Signed.

1212   The vote of a moderate Liberal, 840–848. **Edward Dicey.** Signed.

VOLUME 18, DECEMBER 1885

1213   The interpreters of Genesis and the interpreters of nature, 849–860. **T. H. Huxley.** Signed; repr. *Collected Essays,* IV, and *Controverted Questions.* (See no. 1226.)

1214   Our insular ignorance, 861–872. **John Robert Seeley.** Signed.

1215   Small holdings, 873–878. **Horatio Nelson.** Signed Nelson [3rd Earl Nelson].

1216   The Red Cross, 879–892. **John Furley.** Signed.

1217   Insanity and crime, 893–899. **G. W. W. Bramwell.** Signed Bramwell [Baron Bramwell].

1218   Solar myths, 900–919; with a postscript, 919–922. **Friedrich Max Müller.** Signature. (See nos. 1226 and 1230.)

1219   Stimulants and narcotics: their use and abuse, 923–939. **Fortescue Fox.** Signed.

1220   What geography ought to be, 940–956. **Peter A. Kropotkin.** Signed as in no. 1110.

1221   Prevention [of vice by "The Girls' Friendly Society"], 957–964. **Theresa Shrewsbury.** Signed; Contents gives "Dowager Countess of Shrewsbury."

1222   The new French chamber, 965–977. **Yves Guyot.** Signed.

1223   Leopardi, 978–992. **Constance Fletcher.** Signed.

1224   A strategical view of Turkey, 993–1002. **A. C. Hobart-Hampden.** Signed as in no. 1111.

1225   Capital and the improvement of land, 1003–1010. **G. D. Campbell.** Signed Argyll [8th Duke of Argyll].

VOLUME 19, JANUARY 1886

1226   Proem to Genesis: a plea for a fair trial, 1–21. **W. E. Gladstone.** Signed. (Postscript, p. 176, by **Gladstone**—signed W.E.G.)

1227   The fallacy of "imperial federation," 22–34. **Henry Thring.** Signed.

1228   Federal union with Ireland, 35–40. **R. Barry O'Brien.** Signed; repr. *Irish Wrongs.*

1229   Home Rule in Austria-Hungary, 41–49. **David Kay.** Signed.

1230   Myths and mythologists, 50–65. **Andrew Lang.** Signed.

1231   The little ones and the land [of Arcady], 66–86. **Augustus Jessopp.** Signed; repr. *Arcady.*

1232   A pedantic nuisance [use of original spelling of ancient names], 87–105. **Frederic Harrison.** Signed; repr. *The Meaning of History,* as "Paleographic Purism." (See no. 1271.)

1233   The administration of the navy, 1880–85, 106–126. **Thomas Brassey.** Signed.

1234   Irish education, 127–137. **Mervyn Wingfield.** Signed Powerscourt [7th Viscount Powerscourt].

1235   Thomas Middleton, 138–153. **Algernon Charles Swinburne.** Signed; repr. *The Age of Shakespeare,* 1908.

1236   The battle of Abu-Klea, 154–159. **Reginald A. J. Talbot.** Signed R. Talbot, with addition "Lieut-Colonel"; Contents adds "Hon."; see *WWW/1940.*

1237   "Dawn of creation": an answer to Mr. Gladstone [no. 1201], 160–175. **Albert Réville.** Signed.

VOLUME 19, FEBRUARY 1886

1238   An American view of popular government, 177–190. **E. L. Godkin.** Signed; repr. *Problems of Modern Democracy,*

N.Y., 1896, as "Popular Government." (See no. 1252.)

1239　Mr. Gladstone and Genesis (No. I), 191–205. **T. H. Huxley.** Signed; repr. *Collected Essays*, IV, and *Controverted Questions*. (Letter, vol. 20, p. 304, from **W. E. Gladstone.**)

1240　Mr. Gladstone and Genesis (No. II), 206–214. **Henry Drummond.** Signed.

1241　Shall we desert the Loyalists? 215–225. **H. O. Arnold-Forster.** Signed.

1242　Rural Italy and peasant properties, 226–237. **Frances P. Verney.** Signed as in no. 1208; repr. *Peasant Owners.*

1243　William Cobbett, 238–256. **Charles Milnes Gaskell.** Signed.

1244　A court of lunacy, 257–263. **C. F. A. C. Ponsonby.** Signed De Mauley [2nd Baron De Mauley].

1245　Have we an army reserve? 264–270. **Arthur D. Hayter.** Signed.

1246　Food accessories: their influence on digestion, 271–279. **J. Burney Yeo.** Signed.

1247　Sensationalism in social reform, 280–290. **Samuel A. Barnett.** Signed; repr. *Practicable Socialism.*

1248　Samoa, 291–311. **Clement Kinloch-Cooke.** Signed C. Kinloch Cooke; see *WWW/1950.*

1249　Alternative policies in Ireland, 312–328. **James Bryce,** 1838–1922. Signed.

VOLUME 19, MARCH 1886

1250　The economic value of Ireland to Great Britain, 329–345. **Robert Giffen.** Signed; repr. *Economic Inquiries and Studies* (1904), I.

1251　The evolution of theology: an anthropological study (Part I), 346–365. **T. H. Huxley.** Signed; repr. *Collected Essays*, IV, and *Controverted Questions.*

1252　Mr. Godkin on popular government, 366–379. **H. S. Maine.** Signed; Contents gives "Sir Henry Sumner Maine."

1253　The free-trade idolatry (Part I), 380–395. **J. P. Wilde.** Signed Penzance [1st Baron Penzance]. (See no. 1282.)

1254　Turner's drawings at the Royal Academy, 396–406. **W. G. Rawlinson.** Signed.

1255　In French prisons, 407–423. **Peter A. Kropotkin.** Signed as in no. 1110; repr. *In Prisons.*

1256　Home Rule (No. I): precedents, 424–442. **G. Shaw Lefevre.** Signed.

1257　Home Rule (No. II): in Austria, 443–

465. **E. G. Petty-Fitzmaurice.** Signed Edmond Fitzmaurice; see *DNB/1940.*

1258　Home Rule (No. III): for Scotland, 466–475. **Arthur D. Elliot.** Signed.

1259　Home Rule (No. IV): the impending English answer, 476–484. **Frank H. Hill.** Signed.

VOLUME 19, APRIL 1886

1260　The evolution of theology (Part II, concl.), 485–506. **T. H. Huxley.** Signed.

1261　The Church and the villages: what hope? 507–527. **Augustus Jessopp.** Signed; repr. *Country Parson.*

1262　The second part of *Faust*, 528–538. **John Stuart Blackie.** Signed.

1263　Thrift among the children, 539–560. **Agnes Lambert.** Signed. (See no. 1438.)

1264　Women's suffrage, 561–569. **Theodosia Chapman.** Signed; Contents adds "Mrs."; see *WWW/1928* under Edward W. Chapman.

1265　The factors of organic evolution (Part I), 570–589. **Herbert Spencer.** Signed.

1266　The free-trade idolatry (Part II, concl.), 590–605. **J. P. Wilde.** Signed as in no. 1253.

1267　Liberal election addresses, 606–619. **Hugh Fortescue,** 1854–1932. Signed Ebrington [Viscount Ebrington].

1268　Three attempts to rule Ireland justly, 620–635. **R. Barry O'Brien.** Signed; repr. *Irish Wrongs.*

1269　A "nationalist" parliament, 636–644. **W. E. H. Lecky.** Signed.

VOLUME 19, MAY 1886

1270　The nadir of Liberalism, 645–663. **Matthew Arnold.** Signed; repr. *Essays*, ed. Fraser Neiman.

1271　A few more words about names, 664–672. **Frederic Harrison.** Signed.

1272　The jubilee of the Reform Club, 673–688. **W. Fraser Rae.** Signed.

1273　Whence came the comets? 689–696. **Richard A. Proctor.** Signed; repr. *Other Suns than Ours*, 1887.

1274　Mr. Donnelly's Shakespeare cipher, 697–709. **Percy M. Wallace.** Signed.

1275　The National Indian Congress, 710–721. **John Slagg.** Signed.

1276　The case of Galileo, 722–739. **Jeremiah Murphy.** Signed J. Murphy, with addition "C.C." [Catholic curate]; see no. 1155, pp. 32–36.

1277　Women's suffrage: a reply [to no.

1317 The Hindu widow, 364–373. **Devendra N. Dás.** Signed; repr. *Sketches of Hindoo Life,* 1887.

1318 A visit to some Austrian monasteries, 374–390. **St. George Mivart.** Signed; repr. *Essays.*

1319 How a provincial paper is managed, 391–402. **Arnot Reid.** Signed.

1320 Marriage with a deceased wife's sister, 403–415. **G. W. W. Bramwell.** Signed Bramwell [Baron Bramwell]. (See nos. 1338, 1361.)

1321 Merely players [the theatre and morality], 416–422. **Dinah Maria Mulock.** Signed D. M. Craik; see *DNB.*

1322 Egyptian divine myths, 423–440. **Andrew Lang.** Signed.

1323 Our superstition about Constantinople, 441–452. **H. O. Arnold-Forster.** Signed.

VOLUME 20, OCTOBER 1886

1324 Prisoners as witnesses, 453–472. **J. F. Stephen.** Signed.

1325 Comte's famous fallacy, 473–490. **Harvey Goodwin.** Signed H. Carlisle [Bishop of Carlisle]. (See no. 1342.)

1326 The civil service as a profession, 491–502. **Benjamin Kidd.** Signed.

1327 The chase of the wild fallow deer, 503–514. **Gerald Lascelles.** Signed.

1328 What girls read, 515–529. **Edward G. Salmon.** Signed.

1329 Our craftsmen, 530–552. **Thomas Wright.** Signed, with addition "Journeyman Engineer."

1330 Not at home [emigration and immigration], 553–564. **John O'Neill.** Signed.

1331 The Church and parliament, 565–578. **J. G. Hubbard.** Signed.

1332 Disease in fiction, 579–591. **Nestor Tirard.** Signed.

1333 The Liberal split, 592–608. **G. Shaw Lefevre.** Signed.

VOLUME 20, NOVEMBER 1886

1334 The coming winter in Ireland, 609–616. **John Dillon.** Signed.

1335 France, China, and the Vatican, 617–632. **Rutherford Alcock.** Signed.

1336 Exhibitions, 633–647. **H. Trueman Wood.** Signed.

1337 Multiplex personality, 648–666. **Frederic W. H. Myers.** Signed.

1338 Sisters-in-law, 667–677. **J. F. Mackarness.** Signed J. F. Oxon [Bishop of Oxford].

1339 Distress in East London, 678–692. **Samuel A. Barnett.** Signed; repr. *Practicable Socialism* as "Relief Funds and the Poor."

1340 Gustave Flaubert and George Sand, 693–708. **Nina H. Kennard.** Signed N. H. Kennard; Contents gives "Mrs. Arthur Kennard."

1341 Workhouse cruelties, 709–714. **Louisa Twining.** Signed.

1342 The Bishop of Carlisle on Comte, 715–723. **Frederic Harrison.** Signed.

1343 The building up of a university, 724–741. **Augustus Jessopp.** Signed.

1344 Europe in the Pacific, 742–764. **Clement Kinlock Cooke.** Signed as in no. 1248.

VOLUME 20, DECEMBER 1886

1345 On the suppression of boycotting, 765–784. **James Fitzjames Stephen.** Signed.

1346 Nova Scotia's cry for home rule, 785–794. **Mrs. E. C. Fellows.** Signed E. C. Fellows; Contents adds "Mrs."

1347 The classes, the masses, and the glasses, 795–804. **Wilfrid Lawson.** Signed.

1348 The *Hamlet* of the Seine, 805–814. **Juliet Pollock.** Signed.

1349 Buying Niagara, 815–823. **J. Hampden Robb.** Signed.

1350 Massage, 824–828. **Janetta Manners.** Signed; Contents gives "Lady John Manners"; see *Complete Peerage.*

1351 A suspended conflict [the Church and State], 829–843. **J. Guinness Rogers.** Signed.

1352 Rural enclosures and allotments, 844–866. **E. G. Petty-Fitzmaurice** and **H. Herbert Smith.** Signed Edmond Fitzmaurice and H. Herbert Smith; for the former see *DNB*/1940.

1353 A thought-reader's experiences, 867–885. **Charles Garner.** Signed Stuart C. Cumberland: see *BMCat.,* H & L.

1354 Loyalty of the Indian Mohammedans, 886–900. **W. H. Gregory.** Signed.

1355 A flying visit to the United States, 901–912. **Thomas Brassey.** Signed Brassey [Lord Brassey].

VOLUME 21, JANUARY 1887

1356 "Locksley Hall" and the Jubilee, 1–18. **W. E. Gladstone.** Signed.

1357 The government of Ireland (Part I): a

reply [to Edward Dicey's book on Home Rule], 19–39. **John Morley.** Signed.

1358 Hill-digging and magic, 40–58. **Augustus Jessopp.** Signed; repr. *Random Roaming.* (See no. 1398.)

1359 Physiological selection, 59–80. **George J. Romanes.** Signed.

1360 Thomas Dekker, 81–103. **Algernon Charles Swinburne.** Signed; repr. *The Age of Shakespeare,* 1908.

1361 Bishops and sisters-in-law, 104–109. **G. W. W. Bramwell.** Signed Bramwell [Baron Bramwell].

1362 Schools as prisons and prisons as schools, 110–118. **C. B. Adderley.** Signed Norton [1st Baron Norton].

1363 The true reform of the House of Lords, 119–123. **Reginald Brabazon.** Signed Brabazon [Lord Brabazon].

1364 Pure beer, 124–132. **W. Cuthbert Quilter.** Signed.

1365 Rural life in Russia, 133–147. **Frances P. Verney.** Signed as in no. 1208; repr. *Peasant Owners.*

1366 The zenith of conservatism, 148–164. **Matthew Arnold.** Signed; repr. *Essays,* ed. Fraser Neiman.

VOLUME 21, FEBRUARY 1887

1367 Notes and queries on the Irish demand, 165–190. **W. E. Gladstone.** Signed; repr. *Irish Question.* (See no. 1382.)

1368 Scientific and pseudo-scientific realism, 191–205. **T. H. Huxley.** Signed; repr. *Collected Essays,* IV, and *Controverted Questions.* (See nos. 1377, 1387.)

1369 Notes on New York, 206–226. **G. W. Smalley.** Signed.

1370 Astronomical photography, 227–237. **A. A. Common.** Signed.

1371 The scientific bases of anarchy, 238–252. **Peter A. Kropotkin.** Signed as in no. 1110; repr. in *Revolutionary Pamphlets,* N.Y., 1927, as "Anarchist Communism."

1372 Local government in the rural districts, 253–261. **George Sclater-Booth.** Signed G. Sclater-Booth; Contents gives first name.

1373 Artisan atheism, 262–272. **William Rossiter.** Signed.

1374 Fair-trade fog and fallacy, 273–285. **George W. Medley.** Signed.

1375 Revelations of the after-world, 286–300. **H. I. D. Ryder.** Signed; repr. *Essays,* 1911.

1376 The government of Ireland (Part II, concl.), 301–320. **John Morley.** Signed.

VOLUME 21, MARCH 1887

1377 Professor Huxley on Canon Liddon, 321–339. **G. D. Campbell.** Signed Argyll [8th Duke of Argyll].

1378 The true position of French politics, 340–350. **Joseph Reinach.** Signed. (See no. 1408.)

1379 A colonial view of imperial federation, 351–361. **Robert Stout.** Signed.

1380 The trials of a country parson (Part I), 362–383. **Augustus Jessopp.** Signed; repr. *Country Parson.* (Part II is no. 1443.)

1381 The dulness of museums, 384–396. **J. G. Wood.** Signed.

1382 Mr. Gladstone on "the Irish demand," 397–414. **E. H. Knatchbull-Hugessen.** Signed Brabourne [1st Baron Brabourne].

1383 Cyril Tourneur, 415–427. **Algernon Charles Swinburne.** Signed; repr. *The Age of Shakespeare,* 1908.

1384 The prospect in South Africa, 428–451. **H. G. Grey.** Signed Grey [3rd Earl Grey].

1385 Twenty-four hours in a newspaper office, 452–459. **Arnot Reid.** Signed.

1386 The greater gods of Olympos (Part I): Poseidon, 460–480. **W. E. Gladstone.** Signed.

VOLUME 21, APRIL 1887

1387 Science and pseudo-science, 481–498. **T. H. Huxley.** Signed; repr. *Collected Essays,* IV, and *Controverted Questions.* (See no. 1412.)

1388 A "Friend of God" [perhaps John Tauler], 499–506. **Matthew Arnold.** Signed; repr. *Essays,* ed. Fraser Neiman.

1389 The closer union of the Empire, 507–516. **John Merriman.** Signed with title "Member of the Cape Legislative Assembly."

1390 Athletes of the present and past, 517–529. **H. Ellington.** Signed, with address "London Rowing Club."

1391 An act for the suspension of parliament, 530–541. **H. D. Traill.** Signed.

1392 England and Europe, 542–558. **Edward Dicey.** Signed.

1393 Demeter and the pig, 559–565. **Andrew Lang.** Signed.

1394 A militia regiment, 566–575. **W. W. Palmer.** Signed Wolmer [Viscount Wolmer].

1395 A glimpse of Russia, 576–584. **Mary A. A. Stewart.** Signed M. A. A. Galloway [Countess of Galloway].

1396 The "nineteenth century school" in art, 585–595. **Walter Armstrong**. Signed.

1397 On well-meant nonsense about emigration, 596–611. **G. Osborne Morgan**. Signed.

1398 A warning to the S. P. R. [Society for Psychical Research], 612–614. **Augustus Jessopp**. Signed.

1399 Liberal Unionists and coercion (No. I), 615–622. **Reginald B. Brett**. Signed.

1400 Liberal Unionists and coercion (No. II), 623–628. **F. T. de Grey Cowper**. Signed Cowper [7th Earl Cowper].

VOLUME 21, MAY 1887

1401 Up to Easter [the question of Home Rule], 629–643. **Matthew Arnold**. Signed; repr. *Essays*, ed. Fraser Neiman. (See no. 1447.)

1402 Playing at "coercion" [with Ireland], 644–653. **R. Barry O'Brien**. Signed.

1403 Mental differences between men and women, 654–672. **George J. Romanes**. Signed.

1404 Decay of bodily strength in towns, 673–676. **Reginald Brabazon**. Signed Brabazon [Lord Brabazon].

1405 How to ensure breathing spaces, 677–682. **C. L. Lewes**. Signed.

1406 Deer forests: past, present, and future, 683–701. **George Malcolm**. Signed.

1407 The ruin of Aurangzeb; or, The history of a reaction, 702–718. **W. W. Hunter**. Signed; repr. *India of the Queen*, 1908.

1408 Fallacies of the French press, 719–725. **Arthur Otway**. Signed; Contents adds "Sir."

1409 German life in London, 726–741. **Leopold Katscher**. Signed.

1410 A volunteer battalion, 742–747. **Robert W. Routledge**. Signed.

1411 The greater gods (Part II): Apollo, 748–770. **W. E. Gladstone**. Signed.

1412 Science falsely so called: a reply [to no. 1387], 771–774. **G. D. Campbell**. Signed Argyll [8th Duke of Argyll].

1413 A new title for the Crown, 775–780. **George Baden-Powell**. Signed.

VOLUME 21, JUNE 1887

1414 Our great competitor [the United States], 792–799. **James Keith**. Signed.

1415 An actor's notes (No. IV): M. Coquelin on actors and acting, 800–803.

Henry Irving, 1838–1905. Signed; see *DNB*. (No. III was no. 271.)

1416 Are animals mentally happy? (Part II) 804–824. **Briggs Carlill**. Signed B. Carlill; cf. no. 1310.

1417 French penal colonies, 825–842. **Arthur Griffiths**. Signed.

1418 Newnham College from within, 843–856. **Eva Knatchbull-Hugessen**. Signed.

1419 A beggar-poet [James Chambers], 857–872. **Thomas Woolner**. Signed.

1420 Comte's atheism, 873–882. **Harvey Goodwin**. Signed H. Carlisle [Bishop of Carlisle].

1421 South Africa as it is: from a colonist's point of view, 883–900. **John Robinson**, 1839–1903. Signed; see *DNB*.

1422 Strange medicines, 901–918. **Constance F. Gordon Cumming**. Signed as in no. 704.

1423 Lecky's *History of England in the Eighteenth Century*, 919–936. **W. E. Gladstone**. Signed.

VOLUME 22, JULY 1887

1424 After six years [away from England], 1–30. **Mountstuart E. Grant Duff**. Signed.

1425 The Catholic Church and biblical criticism, 31–51. **St. George Mivart**. Signed. (See no. 1467.)

1426 Mr. Gladstone and the income tax, 52–54. **W. E. H. Lecky**. Signed.

1427 A kitchen college, 55–59. **Harriette Brooke Davies**. Signed H. Brooke Davies; Contents gives first name.

1428 Art sales and Christie's, 60–78. **George Redford**, 1817–1895. Signed.

1429 The greater gods of Olympos (Part III, concl.): Athenê, 79–102. **W. E. Gladstone**. Signed.

1430 A regiment of infantry, 103–110. **Henry John T. Hildyard**. Signed H. T. Hildyard; Contents gives "Colonel"; see *WWW*/1928.

1431 Artisan atheism, 111–126. **William Rossiter**. Signed.

1432 "The House was still sitting when we went to press," 127–132. **G. Osborne Morgan**. Signed.

1433 A first visit to India, 133–148. **Herbert J. Gladstone**. Signed.

VOLUME 22, AUGUST 1887

1434 The coming anarchy, 149–164. **Peter A. Kropotkin**. Signed as in no. 1110;

repr. in *Revolutionary Pamphlets*, N.Y., 1927, as "Anarchist Communism."

1435   Europe revisited (Part I), 165–173. **Salar Jung**, 1863–1889, and **Moreton Frewen.** Signed Salar Jung; but see no. 1461.

1436   Where are the letters?: a cross-examination of certain phantasms, 174–194. **A. Taylor Innes.** Signed. (See no. 1463.)

1437   Dogs in Germany, 195–205. **Louisa Sarah Bevington.** Signed L. S. Guggenberger; see *BMCat.* under both names.

1438   Progress of "thrift among the children," 206–218. **Agnes Lambert.** Signed.

1439   The English and the American press, 219–233. **Arnot Reid.** Signed.

1440   The memorials of the dead, 234–241. **Charles Milnes Gaskell.** Signed.

1441   The creatures we breathe, 242–247. **Percy Faraday Frankland.** Signed.

1442   North Borneo, 248–256. **Thomas Brassey.** Signed Brassey [Lord Brassey].

1443   The trials of a country parson (Part II, concl.), 257–278. **Augustus Jessopp.** Signed.

1444   Mr. Lecky and political morality, 279–284. **W. E. Gladstone.** Signed.

1445   American opinion on the Irish question, 285–292. **E. L. Godkin.** Signed.

VOLUME 22, SEPTEMBER 1887

1446   A great lesson [attack on Darwin and Huxley], 293–309. **G. D. Campbell.** Signed Argyll [8th Duke of Argyll]. (See postscript to no. 2055.)

1447   From Easter to August [the Irish question], 310–324. **Matthew Arnold.** Signed; repr. *Essays*, ed. Fraser Neiman.

1448   Professional ignorance in the army, 325–334. **Lonsdale Hale.** Signed.

1449   Morphinomania, 335–342. **Seymour J. Sharkey.** Signed.

1450   Recent criticism on Raphael, 343–360. **Jean Paul Richter**, 1847–1937. Signed.

1451   The East End as represented by Mr. Besant, 361–375. **Jane Stuart-Wortley.** Signed; Contents adds "Mrs." With a table of wages paid to female operatives, 376–377, signed **J. B. Lakeman.**

1452   Church-going: a dialogue on hymns, 378–390. **Theodosia Chapman.** Signed as in no. 1264.

1453   The capacity of women, 391–402. **Edith Simcox.** Signed.

1454   Positivism in Christianity, 403–414. **Wilfrid Ward.** Signed.

1455   The working of school banks, 415–417. **Henry Whitehead.** Signed H. Whitehead; Contents gives first name.

1456   A German view of Mr. Gladstone, 418–434. **Theodor von Bunsen.** Signed.

1457   Electoral facts of 1887, 435–444. **W. E. Gladstone.** Signed.

VOLUME 22, OCTOBER 1887

1458   Ingram's *History of the Irish Union*, 445–469. **W. E. Gladstone.** Signed; repr. *Irish Question.* (See no. 1490.)

1459   The new Afghan frontier, 470–482. **West Ridgeway.** Signed.

1460   The dock life of East London, 483–499. **Beatrice Potter.** Signed.

1461   Europe revisited (Part II, concl.), 500–510. **Salar Jung**, 1863–1889, and **Moreton Frewen.** Signed Salar Jung; John R. S. Leslie, *Studies in Sublime Failure* (1932), p. 263, says "Moreton [Frewen] wrote an article which Salar Jung signed (*Nineteenth Century*, October 1887)," but the use of the first person throughout the article suggests that Frewen was writing from full notes taken down as Jung talked.

1462   *The Winter's Tale*, 511–521. **William Archer.** Signed.

1463   Letters on phantasms: a reply [to no. 1436], 522–533. **Edmund Gurney.** Signed.

1464   The position of the Unionists, 534–551. **Edward Dicey.** Signed.

1465   The parliamentary breakdown, 552–562. **Frank H. Hill.** Signed.

1466   Literature for the little ones, 563–580. **Edward Salmon.** Signed. (Note, p. 744, signed **Lewis Carroll.**)

1467   Mr. Mivart's modern Catholicism, 581–600. **J. F. Stephen.** Signed. (See nos. 1496, 1497, 1507.)

VOLUME 22, NOVEMBER 1887

1468   An olive branch from America (No. I): an Anglo-American copyright, 602–610. **R. Pearsall Smith.** Signed; repr. as *Anglo-American Copyright*, Phila., 1887. Intro. note to the series, 601–602, signed **James Knowles.**

1469   An olive branch from America (No. II), 611–612. **W. E. Gladstone.** Signed.

1470   An olive branch from America (No. III), 612. **Hallam Tennyson.** Signed.

1471   An olive branch from America (No. IV), 612–613. **G. D. Campbell.** Signed Argyll [8th Duke of Argyll].

1472 An olive branch from America (No. V), 613. **F. W. Farrar.** Signed.

1473 An olive branch from America (No. VI), 613. **H. Rider Haggard.** Signed.

1474 An olive branch from America (No. VII), 614–615. **Lewis Morris.** Signed.

1475 An olive branch from America (No. VIII), 615–616. **Justin McCarthy,** 1830–1912. Signed.

1476 An olive branch from America (No. IX), 616–617. **T. H. Farrer.** Signed.

1477 An olive branch from America (No. X), 617–619. **Walter Besant.** Signed.

1478 An olive branch from America (No. XI), 619. **Matthew Arnold.** Signed.

1479 An olive branch from America (No. XII), 620–624. **T. H. Huxley.** Signed.

1480 An olive branch from America (No. XIII), 624. **Kegan Paul,** and **Trench, &** Co. Signed.

1481 Science and the bishops, 625–640. **T. H. Huxley.** Signed. Letter 640–641, signed **John W. Judd.**

1482 Can English literature be taught? 642–658. **J. Churton Collins.** Signed.

1483 The nerve-rest cure: a plea for the nervous, 659–666. **James Muir Howie.** Signed.

1484 The antiquity of man in North America, 667–679. **Alfred R. Wallace.** Signed.

1485 County characteristics: Cornwall, 680–691. **Walter H. Tregellas.** Signed.

1486 Medical women, 692–707. **Sophia Jex-Blake.** Signed, with addition "M.D."

1487 British missions and missionaries in Africa, 708–724. **H. H. Johnston.** Signed.

1488 How to solve the Irish land question, 725–744. **H. O. Arnold-Forster.** Signed.

VOLUME 22, DECEMBER 1887

1489 "The power of loose analogies," 745–765. **G. D. Campbell.** Signed Argyll [8th Duke of Argyll].

1490 Mr. Gladstone and the Irish union: a reply [to no. 1458], 766–790. **T. Dunbar Ingram.** Signed.

1491 Mohammedanism in Africa, 791–816. **R. Bosworth Smith.** Signed.

1492 Picture-hanging at the National Gallery, 817–826. **Charles L. Eastlake,** 1836–1906. Signed; see *DNB.*

1493 The time it takes to think, 827–830. **J. McK. Cattell.** Signed.

1494 Doris, 831–843. **Augustus Jessopp.** Signed.

1495 The French Society of Authors, 844–849. **Edmund Gosse.** Signed.

1496 Catholicity and reason, 850–870. **St. George Mivart.** Signed. (See no. 1507.)

1497 Belief and doubt, 871–885. **Harvey Goodwin.** Signed H. Carlisle [Bishop of Carlisle].

1498 Flamingoes at home, 886–890. **Henry A. Blake.** Signed.

1499 Irish land purchase: a reply to my critics, 891–896. **H. O. Arnold-Forster.** Signed.

VOLUME 23, JANUARY 1888

1500 The progress of cremation, 1–17. **Henry Thompson,** 1820–1904. Signed; see *DNB.*

1501 The two paths: a dialogue [on contemporary culture], 18–22. **Frederic Harrison.** Signed.

1502 Shelley, 23–39. **Matthew Arnold.** Signed; repr. *Essays,* II.

1503 A river of ruined capitals [the Hugli], 40–53. **W. W. Hunter.** Signed; repr. *India of the Queen,* 1908.

1504 Home Rule in Norway, 54–70. **Theodor von Bunsen.** Signed.

1505 The decline of art, 71–92. **F. T. Palgrave.** Signed.

1506 American statesmen (Part I), 93–114. **Goldwin Smith.** Signed.

1507 A rejoinder to Mr. Mivart [to no. 1496], 115–126. **James Fitzjames Stephen.** Signed.

1508 Dethroning Tennyson: a contribution to the Tennyson-Darwin controversy, 127–129. **A. C. Swinburne.** Signed; repr. *Studies* as "Tennyson or Darwin?"

1509 Leo the Thirteenth and the civil power: an appeal to common sense, 130–141. **Herbert A. Vaughan.** Signed Herbert, Bishop of Salford.

1510 A great confession [Herbert Spencer's writings on Darwin], 142–160. **G. D. Campbell.** Signed Argyll [8th Duke of Argyll]; repr. *Organic Evolution Cross-Examined,* 1898. (See no. 1514.)

VOLUME 23, FEBRUARY 1888

1511 The struggle for existence: a programme, 161–180. **T. H. Huxley.** Signed.

1512 More air for London, 181–188. **Octavia Hill.** Signed.

1513 The Panama Canal and its prospects, 189–206. **J. Stephen Jeans.** Signed.

1514 A counter criticism [of no. 1510], 207–215. **Herbert Spencer.** Signed.

1515 The reign of pedantry in girls' schools,

216–238. **Elizabeth M. Sewell.** Signed; Contents adds "Miss." (See no. 1537.)

1516   How to live on £700 a year, 239–244. **George Somes Layard.** Signed.

1517   Chatter or business? [parliamentary procedure], 245–257. **Frank H. Hill.** Signed.

1518   The present position of the medical schism, 258–275. **Kenneth Millican.** Signed.

1519   The death of Abdul Aziz and of Turkish reform, 276–296. **Henry Elliot.** Signed; Contents adds "Sir."

1520   The Constitution of the United States (Part I), 297–316. **E. J. Phelps.** Signed.

VOLUME 23, MARCH 1888

1521   A pleading for the worthless, 321–330. **H. E. Manning.** Signed as in no. 8; repr. *Miscellanies*, III.

1522   The swarming of men, 331–353. **Leonard Courtney.** Signed.

1523   Is Japanese art extinct? 354–369. **Marcus B. Huish.** Signed.

1524   Long life and how to attain it, 370–393. **J. Burney Yeo.** Signed.

1525   Poor men's gardens, 394–402. **Hugh Fortescue**, 1818–1905. Signed Fortescue [Earl Fortescue].

1526   A lady's American notes, 403–413. **Emily A. Acland.** Signed; Contents gives "Mrs. W. A. D. Acland."

1527   The invasion of pauper foreigners, 414–422. **Arnold White.** Signed.

1528   Local government, 423–440. **Henry Thring.** Signed Thring [1st Baron Thring].

1529   The Constitution of the United States (Part II, concl.), 441–457. **E. J. Phelps.** Signed.

1530   Life on thirty shillings a week, 458–463. **Miranda Hill.** Signed.

1531   Life on a guinea a week, 464–467. **W. Roberts.** Signed.

1532   A few words on French revolutionary models, 468–480. **John Morley.** Signed; repr. *Studies.*

VOLUME 23, APRIL 1888

1533   Civilisation in the United States, 481–496. **Matthew Arnold.** Signed; repr. under same title, Boston, 1888.

1534   The breakdown of our industrial system, 497–516. **Peter A. Kropotkin.** Signed as in no. 1110.

1535   Snowed up in Arcady, 517–535. **Augustus Jessopp.** Signed; repr. *Country Parson.*

1536   A model factory, 536–540. **Reginald Brabazon.** Signed Meath [Earl of Meath].

1537   Girls' schools, past and present, 541–554. **Dorothea Beale.** Signed.

1538   Our auxiliary cavalry, 555–568. **G. J. M. K. Elliot.** Signed Melgund [Viscount Melgund].

1539   Mr. Max Müller's *Science of Thought* (Part I), 569–582. **J. F. Stephen.** Signed.

1540   Our day's sport in India, 583–588. **J. D. Rees.** Signed.

1541   Century for century [the papers of Augustin Tilon on England], 589–602. **Ferdinand Rothschild.** Signed; Contents adds "Baron."

1542   Ben Jonson (Part I), 603–616. **Algernon Charles Swinburne.** Signed; repr. *A Study of Ben Jonson*, 1889.

1543   The Chinese in Australia, 617–619. **John Pope Hennessy.** Signed.

1544   The House of Lords, 620–632. **Frank H. Hill.** Signed.

VOLUME 23, MAY 1888

1545   The defencelessness of London, 633–640. **Edward Hamley.** Signed; repr. *National Defence*, 1889.

1546   The Local Government Bill, 641–660. **Henry Thring.** Signed Thring [1st Baron Thring].

1547   The disenchantment of France, 661–681. **Frederic W. H. Myers.** Signed; repr. *Future Life.*

1548   In the Bahamas, 682–692. **Edith Blake.** Signed; Contents adds "Mrs."; see *WWW*/1928 under Sir Henry Arthur Blake.

1549   Ben Jonson (Part II, concl.), 693–715. **Algernon Charles Swinburne.** Signed.

1550   The clergy and the land, 716–723. **R. E. Prothero.** Signed.

1551   Niederbronn [in Alsace], 724–733. **Hugh C. E. Childers.** Signed.

1552   Tinkering the House of Lords, 734–742. **Newton Wallop.** Signed Lymington [Viscount Lymington].

1553   Mr. Max Müller's *Science of Thought* (Part II, concl.), 743–759. **J. F. Stephen.** Signed.

1554   The admiralty confusion and its cure, 760–765. **Charles Beresford.** Signed; Contents adds "Captain Lord"; see *DNB*.

1555   Robert Elsmere and the battle of belief, 766–788. **W. E. Gladstone.** Signed.

VOLUME 23, JUNE 1888

1556 The question of imperial safety (No. I): the minimum force requisite for security, 789–798. **Edward Hamley.** Signed; repr. *National Defence*, 1889.
1557 Imperial safety (No. II): our actual military strength, 799–808. **H. M. Hozier.** Signed.
1558 Imperial safety (No. III): a workable admiralty, 809–816. **Charles Beresford.** Signed.
1559 The coming reign of plenty, 817–837. **Peter A. Kropotkin.** Signed as in no. 1110.
1560 Pasteur, 838–857. **Eliza Priestley.** Signed; Contents adds "Mrs."
1561 Archbishop Trench's poems, 858–880. **Aubrey De Vere.** Signed; repr. *Essays.*
1562 American statesmen (Part II), 881–892. **Goldwin Smith.** Signed.
1563 Free Greece, 893–900. **Mary A. A. Stewart.** Signed M. A. A. Galloway [Countess of Galloway].
1564 The "scientific frontier" as accomplished fact, 901–917. **George N. Curzon.** Signed.
1565 A women's college in the United States [Bryn Mawr], 918–926. **Alys W. Pearsall Smith.**
1566 Local government and county councils in France (Part I), 927–936. **W. H. Waddington.** Signed Waddington; Contents adds "French Ambassador"; see Venn.

VOLUME 24, JULY 1888

1567 The Elizabethan settlement of religion, 1–13. **W. E. Gladstone.** Signed.
1568 Our missionaries, 14–29. **W. W. Hunter.** Signed; repr. *India of the Queen,* 1908.
1569 A few words about picture exhibitions, 30–44. **Frederic Harrison.** Signed.
1570 The vague cry for technical education, 45–52. **W. G. Armstrong.** Signed Armstrong [Baron Armstrong]. (See no. 1591.)
1571 The Engadine—summer and winter, 53–60. **Joseph Kidd.** Signed.
1572 A story of our lighthouses, 61–80. **John Tyndall.** Signed.
1573 The new Labour Party, 81–93. **H. H. Champion.** Signed.
1574 Liberating the slaves in Brazil, 94–105. **Walter J. Hammond.** Signed on p. 103.

1575 The curse of the War Office, 106–118. **Eustace G. Cecil.** Signed; Contents adds "Lord."
1576 Buddhism, 119–135. **R. S. Copleston.** Signed Reginald Stephen Colombo [Bishop of Colombo].
1577 Local government and county councils in France (Part II, concl.), 136–144. **W. H. Waddington.** Signed Waddington; cf. no. 1566.

VOLUME 24, AUGUST 1888

1578 Who owns the churches? 145–160. **Augustus Jessopp.** Signed.
1579 East London labour, 161–183. **Beatrice Potter.** Signed.
1580 On the geographical distribution of British intellect, 184–195. **A. Conan Doyle.** Signed.
1581 The new cure for "growing too fat," 196–206. **J. Burney Yeo.** Signed.
1582 The real Madame de Pompadour, 207–226. **Yetta Blaze de Bury.** Signed Y. Blaze de Bury; Contents adds "Mlle."; cf. no. 1714.
1583 Democracy and party, 227–237. **T. E. Kebbel.** Signed.
1584 Workers' songs, 238–250. **Laura Alexandrine Smith.** Signed; Contents adds "Miss."
1585 A mountain vineyard in California, 251–261. **William Maitland.** Signed, with address, "Santa Cruz, California."
1586 American statesmen (Part III, concl.), 262–275. **Goldwin Smith.** Signed.
1587 The public offices—from within, 276–281. **S. Arthur Blackwood.** Signed.
1588 What is left of Christianity? 282–300. **W. S. Lilly.** Signed; repr. revised in *The Great Enigma*, N.Y., 1892, as "Twilight of the Gods."

VOLUME 24, SEPTEMBER 1888

1589 Pages from a work-girl's diary, 301–314. **Beatrice Potter.** Signed.
1590 Socialism through American spectacles, 315–324. **Lloyd S. Bryce.** Signed.
1591 Lord Armstrong and technical education, 325–333. **Lyon Playfair.** Signed.
1592 An Armada relic, 334–339. **J. D. S. Campbell.** Signed Lorne [Marquess of Lorne].
1593 Chaucer and the Italian Renaissance, 340–359. **F. T. Palgrave.** Signed.

918. **Edith Blake.** Signed; Contents gives "Lady Blake."

1637 The protest against over-examination (No. I): a reply [to no. 1614], 919–924. **William A. Knight.** Signed William Knight; Contents adds "Professor."

1638 The protest against over-examination (No. II), 925–930. **Harold Arthur Perry.** Signed.

1639 The protest against over-examination (No. III), 931–932. **H. Temple Humphreys.** Signed H. Temple Humphrey, with addition "Mem. Inst. C. E."; I.C.E. *Minutes*, 108 (1892), 403, gives "Humphreys."

VOLUME 25, JANUARY 1889

1640 The British fleet and the state of Europe, 1–11. **Charles Beresford.** Signed.

1641 Isolation; or Survival of the unfittest, 12–34. **G. D. Campbell.** Signed Argyll [8th Duke of Argyll].

1642 The decay of lying: a dialogue [on art], 35–56. **Oscar Wilde.** Signed.

1643 "A thousand more mouths every day," 57–72. **Reginald Brabazon.** Signed Meath [12th Earl of Meath].

1644 Clubs for working girls, 73–83. **Maude Stanley.** Signed.

1645 Cathedral-room for neglected records, 84–103. **Augustus Jessopp.** Signed; repr. *Country Parson*.

1646 The posthumous vicissitudes of James the Second, 104–109. **J. G. Alger.** Signed.

1647 Australian side lights on English politics, 110–132. **Ernest W. Beckett.** Signed.

1648 A Brahmin school-girl, 133–139. **Georgiana Kingscote.** Signed.

1649 Mr. Bryce's *American Commonwealth*, 140–148. **Frederic Harrison.** Signed.

1650 Daniel O'Connell, 149–168. **W. E. Gladstone.** Signed; repr. *Irish Question*.

VOLUME 25, FEBRUARY 1889

1651 Agnosticism, 169–194. **T. H. Huxley.** Signed; repr. *Collected Essays*, V, and *Controverted Questions*. (See nos. 1673, 1674, 1684, 1706, 1707.)

1652 The future of Toryism: a sketch, 195–212. **W. T. W. Quin.** Signed Dunraven [4th Earl Dunraven].

1653 Noticeable books (No. I): *Divorce—a novel*, 213–215. **W. E. Gladstone.** Signed. Intro. note to the series, 213, by **James Knowles.**

1654 Noticeable books (No. II): *Lyrics*,

215–218. **Frederic Harrison.** Signed on p. 221; assigned in Contents.

1655 Noticeable books (No. III): *A Village Tragedy*, 218–221. **Frederic Harrison.** Signed.

1656 Noticeable books (No. IV): *Lives of Twelve Good Men*, 221–222. **R. E. Prothero.** Signed.

1657 Noticeable books (No. V): *Sophocles in English*, 222–224. **W. S. Lilly.** Signed.

1658 Noticeable books (No. VI): *Notes of Conversation with the Duke of Wellington*, 224–227. **Augustine Birrell.** Signed.

1659 Noticeable books (No. VII): *The Quick or the Dead* and *Virginia of Virginia*, 228–230. **Hamilton Aïdé.** Signed.

1660 Noticeable books (No. VIII): *English Wayfaring Life* [by J. J. Jusserand], 230–232. **Augustus Jessopp.** Signed.

1661 Noticeable books (No. IX): *In Castle and Cabin*, 232–235. **John Morley.** Signed.

1662 Is examination a failure? 236–255. **W. Baptiste Scoones.** Signed.

1663 The distractions of German statesmanship, 256–266. **Frederick Greenwood.** Signed.

1664 The fluctuating frontier of Russia in Asia, 267–283. **George N. Curzon.** Signed.

1665 The sacrifice of education to examination (No. V), 286–290. **Auberon Herbert.** Signed. With intro. note, 284–285, by **James Knowles,** and list of names, 285–286, compiled by him.

1666 The sacrifice of education (No. VI), 291–300. **Frederick Pollock,** 1845–1937. Signed; repr. *Oxford Lectures*, 1890, as "Examination and Education."

1667 The sacrifice of education (No. VII), 300–303. **Joseph Fayrer.** Signed.

1668 The sacrifice of education (No. VIII), 303–308. **Francis Galton.** Signed.

1669 The sacrifice of education (No. IX), 308–311. **W. O. Priestley.** Signed Dr. Priestley; see *DNB*.

1670 The sacrifice of education (No. X), 312–322. **Harvey Goodwin.** Signed The Bishop of Carlisle.

1671 To a friend, 323–324. **Oscar Fredrik.** Signed; Contents gives "King of Sweden and Norway."

VOLUME 25, MARCH 1889

1672 Twelve millions per annum wasted in the sea, 325–350. **Samuel Plimsoll.** Signed. (See nos. 1688, 1720.)

1673 Agnosticism: a reply to Professor Huxley [no. 1651] (No. I), 351–368. **Henry Wace.** Signed.

1674   Agnosticism: a reply to Professor Huxley (No. II), 369–371. **W. C. Magee.** Signed W. C. Peterborough [Bishop of Peterborough].

1675   The new rules and the old complaint [in parliament], 372–380. **Henry W. Lucy.** Signed.

1676   Tennyson as prophet, 381–396. **Frederic W. H. Myers.** Signed; repr. *Future Life.*

1677   Can we think without words? an answer to the Duke of Argyll, 397–408. **Friedrich Max Müller.** Signature; repr. *Last Essays.*

1678   Westminster Abbey and its monuments (No. I), 409–414. **William Morris.** Signed.

1679   Westminster Abbey (No. II): the cloisters, 415–417. **James Knowles.** Signed. (See no. 1896.)

1680   The London County Council, 418–430. **W. M. Acworth.** Signed.

1681   News from some Irish emigrants, 431–437. **J. H. Tuke** and **Martin Mahony.** Signed J. H. Tuke, but long letter quoted here, pp. 432–435, from Father Martin Mahony of Minnesota, whose name is on p. 431.

1682   The value of witness to the miraculous, 438–453. **T. H. Huxley.** Signed; repr. *Collected Essays,* V, and *Controverted Questions.*

1683   The new Reformation: a dialogue, 454–480. **Mary A. Ward.** Signed. (See no. 3551.)

VOLUME 25, APRIL 1889

1684   Agnosticism: a rejoinder [to no. 1673], 481–504. **T. H. Huxley.** Signed; repr. *Collected Essays,* IV, and *Controverted Questions.*

1685   Work for the London Council, 505–512. **Reginald Brabazon.** Signed Meath [12th Earl of Meath].

1686   On seals and savages, 513–526. **Edith Blake.** Signed.

1687   Casual notes about Ireland, 527–538. **Mervyn Wingfield.** Signed Powerscourt [7th Viscount Powerscourt].

1688   Are twelve millions per annum wasted in the sea? 539–551. **Thomas Scrutton.** Signed.

1689   Monte Carlo, 552–557. **Henry Sidebotham.** Signed, with address "Mentone, France"; Contents gives "Rev."

1690   Our reign in the Ionian Islands, 558–

571. **Walter Frewen Lord.** Signed; repr. *The Lost Possessions of England,* 1896, as "The Ionian Islands."

1691   Is an "Agricultural Department" desirable? 572–581. **R. E. Prothero.** Signed.

1692   A few more words on Daniel O'Connell, 582–594. **W. H. Gregory.** Signed; Contents gives "Sir William Gregory."

1693   Lunatics as patients, not prisoners, 595–607. **John Batty Tuke.** Signed.

1694   A suggestion for emigrants, 608–614. **J. D. S. Campbell.** Signed Lorne [Marquis of Lorne].

1695   Noticeable books (No. I): *For the Right,* 615–617. **W. E. Gladstone.** Signed.

1696   Noticeable books (No. II): *English Economic History* [by W. J. Ashley], 617–621. **Augustus Jessopp.** Signed.

1697   Noticeable books (No. III): *Toussaint Galabru,* 621–623. **Walter Pater.** Signed.

1698   Noticeable books (No. IV): *Madame de Montagu,* 623–625. **Hamilton Aïdé.** Signed.

1699   Noticeable books (No. V): *Letters of Thomas Carlyle from 1826 to 1836,* 625–628. **Frederic Harrison.** Signed.

VOLUME 25, MAY 1889

1700   The new naval programme, 629–640. **W. G. Armstrong.** Signed Armstrong [Baron Armstrong].

1701   The lesson of Birmingham, 641–652. **Edward Dicey.** Signed.

1702   The Hindu at home, 653–666. **Margaret E. Child-Villiers.** Signed M. E. Jersey [Countess of Jersey].

1703   A working woman's speech, 667–671. **Mrs. Briant.** See p. 667, where she is called "the secretary to the Nottingham and Leicester Cigar Makers' Union." Reported and edited by **Clementina Black**—signed.

1704   Church and state in Germany, 672–688. **F. H. Geffcken.** Signed H. Geffcken; Contents adds "Professor"; see *ADB.*

1705   With Father Damien and the lepers, 689–699. **Edward Clifford.** Signed; repr. in expanded form *Father Damien: a Journey from Cashmere to his Home in Hawaii,* 1889. (See no. 1719.)

1706   Christianity and agnosticism, 700–721. **Henry Wace.** Signed.

1707   An explanation to Professor Huxley [of no. 1674], 722–723. **W. C. Magee.** Signed W. C. Peterborough [Bishop of Peterborough].

1708   Society and democracy in France, 724–736. **Frederick Marshall.** Signed.

1709 Misery in great cities, 737–752. **Frederick Greenwood.** Signed.

1710 Are we making way [with the party system]? 753–762. **Frederic Harrison.** Signed.

1711 Italy in 1888–89, 763–780. **W. E. Gladstone.** Signed.

VOLUME 25, JUNE 1889

1712 An appeal against female suffrage, 781–785. A large number of women signatories listed, 785–787. With a further appeal for more signatories, 788, by **James Knowles.**

1713 The ethics of political lying, 789–794. **Edward Dicey.** Signed.

1714 The Théâtre Français, and its sociétaires (Part I), 795–811. **Yetta Blaze de Bury.** Signed.

1715 A bird's-eye view of India, 812–826. **M. E. Grant Duff.** Signed.

1716 Six generations of czars, 827–837. **Frances P. Verney.** Signed as in no. 1208; repr. *Essays and Tales*, 1891.

1717 The great French Revolution and its lesson, 838–851. **Peter A. Kropotkin.** Signed as in no. 1110.

1718 The mysteries of malaria, 852–867. **Eliza Priestley.** Signed; Contents adds "Mrs."

1719 A few more words on the Hawaiians and Father Damien [sequel to no. 1705], 868–880. **Edward Clifford.** Signed; for repr. see no. 1705.

1720 Twelve millions per annum wasted in the sea: a rejoinder [to no. 1688], 881–893. **Samuel Plimsoll.** Signed.

1721 An agricultural parcels post, 894–901. **Henry Peter Dunster.** Signed.

1722 Sardinia and its wild sheep, 902–920. **E. N. Buxton.** Signed.

1723 A bye-election in 1747, 921–936. **Hugh Fortescue,** 1854–1932. Signed Ebrington [Viscount Ebrington].

1724 Agnosticism and Christianity, 937–964. **T. H. Huxley.** Signed; repr. *Collected Essays,*V, and *Controverted Questions.*

VOLUME 26, JULY 1889

1725 Plain speaking on the Irish union, 1–20. **W. E. Gladstone.** Signed; repr. *Irish Question.* (See no. 1745.)

1726 The eight hours question, 21–34. **Harold Cox.** Signed.

1727 The Forth Bridge, 35–42. **John Fowler,** 1817–1898, and **Benjamin Baker.** Signed John Fowler and B. Baker; Contents gives "Sir John Fowler" and "Benjamin Baker"; for both see *DNB*, 1st suppl. under Fowler.

1728 The first-night judgment of plays, 43–59. **Henry Arthur Jones.** Signed; repr. *Renascence.*

1729 Sport in Nepal, 60–64. **Eva Wyndham Quin.** Signed: Contents adds "Lady."

1730 The last illness of Lord Beaconsfield, 65–71. **Joseph Kidd.** Signed, with addition "M.D."

1731 The Théâtre Français and its sociétaires (Part II, concl.), 72–85. **Yetta Blaze de Bury.** Signed.

1732 The appeal against female suffrage (No. I): a reply [to no. 1712], 86–96. **Millicent Garrett Fawcett.** Signed. (See no. 1757.)

1733 The appeal against female suffrage (No. II), 97–103. **Margaret M. Dilke.** Signed M. M. Dilke; Contents gives "Mrs. Ashton Dilke"; see Burke.

1734 The appeal against female suffrage (No. III) [a list of names to be added to the protest of no. 1712], 104–105. A large number of women signatories.

1735 Giordano Bruno and new Italy, 106–119. **Karl Blind.** Signed.

1736 Health-seeking in Tenerife and Madeira, 120–135. **Morell Mackenzie.** Signed; repr. *Essays*, 1893.

1737 Mr. Dandelow: a story half told, 136–159. **Augustus Jessopp.** Signed.

1738 The Persia of the Shah, 160–172. **J. D. Rees.** Signed.

VOLUME 26, AUGUST 1889

1739 A breakfast-party in Paris, 173–185. **Frederic Harrison.** Signed.

1740 The new Liberalism, 186–193. **L. A. Atherley-Jones.** Signed. (See no. 1766.)

1741 On change of air, 194–207. **J. Burney Yeo.** Signed.

1742 Wanted: a gospel for the century, 208–217. **William Francis Barry.** Signed William Barry; Contents gives "Father Barry"; see *WWW/*1940.

1743 The deadly wild beasts of India, 218–240. **Joseph Fayrer.** Signed J. Fayrer; Contents gives first name and "Sir."

1744 The works of Henrik Ibsen, 241–256. **Walter Frewen Lord.** Signed.

1745 Mr. Gladstone's "plain speaking," 257–272. **E. H. Knatchbull-Hugessen.** Signed Brabourne [1st Baron Brabourne].

1746 The art of conversation, 273–279. **Thomas Lister.** Signed Ribblesdale [4th Baron Ribblesdale].

1747 Phoenician affinities of Ithaca, 280–293. **W. E. Gladstone.** Signed.

1748 The French in Germany, 294–311. **F. Heinrich Geffcken.** Signed.

1749 Wool-gatherings [observations on love and kindness], (Part I; no more published), 312–323. **Frederick Greenwood.** Signed.

1750 Noticeable books (No. I): *The Critical Period of American History* [by John Fiske], 324–327. **John Morley.** Signed.

1751 Noticeable books (No. II): Lady Blennerhassett's *Frau von Staël*, 327–330. **W. S. Lilly.** Signed.

1752 Noticeable books (No. III): *Micah Clarke* [by A. Conan Doyle], 330–332. **R. E. Prothero.** Signed.

1753 Noticeable books (No. IV): *The Scientific Works of Sir William Siemens*, 333–337. **Frederick Bramwell.** Signed.

1754 Noticeable books (No. V): *A Tale of the House of the Wolfings*, 337–341. **Henry G. Hewlett.** Signed.

1755 Noticeable books (No. VI): Janet's *Psychical Automatism*, 341–343. **Frederic W. H. Myers.** Signed.

1756 Noticeable books (No. VII, concl.): *William George Ward* [*and the Oxford Movement*], 343–346. **Hallam Tennyson** and **Lady Emily Tennyson**—signed Hallam Tennyson, but see *Athenaeum*, Aug. 3, 1889, p. 164, for his mother's collab.

1757 The appeal against female suffrage: a rejoinder [to nos. 1732, 1733], 347–354. **Louise Creighton.** Signed. With a long list, called "Appendix," of women signatories, 355–384.

VOLUME 26, SEPTEMBER 1889

1758 Italy drifting, 385–408. **Carlo Alberto Alfieri.** Signed Alfieri; Contents gives "Marchese Alfieri di Sostegno"; see *Enci. Ital.* Trans., "ou plutôt récomposé," by **Marie Blaze de Bury**—Alfieri to Mme. Blaze de Bury, quoted in *Revue de litterature comparée*, 31 (1957), 251.

1759 Diseases caught from butcher's meat, 409–422. **Henry Behrend.** Signed, with addition "M.R.C.P."; Contents adds "Dr."

1760 Criticism as a trade, 423–430. **William A. Knight.** Signed as in no. 1637. (See no. 1791.)

1761 Das I. Garde-Dragoner-Regiment: an historical sketch, 431–434. **Lonsdale Hale.** Signed.

1762 Wordsworth's great failure, 435–451. **William Minto.** Signed.

1763 A few words to fresh workers, 452–461. **Octavia Hill.** Signed.

1764 What next in Egypt? 462–475. **Edward Dicey.** Signed.

1765 In search of a religion, 476–491. **W. S. Lilly.** Signed.

1766 The new Liberalism: a response [to no. 1740], 492–499. **George W. E. Russell.** Signed.

1767 The grievances of High Churchmen, 500–508. **George G. Perry.** Signed. (See no. 1790.)

1768 An eight-hour law, 509–522. **H. H. Champion.** Signed.

1769 Parliamentary misrule of our war services, 523–544. **H. O. Arnold-Forster.** Signed.

VOLUME 26, OCTOBER 1889

1770 The attack on the Native States of India, 545–560. **Mohsin-ul-Mulk** [Mehdi Ali]. Signed.

1771 The universities in contact with the people, 561–583. **J. Churton Collins.** Signed.

1772 Rome in 1889, 584–601. **Julia M. Ady.** Signed.

1773 *Journal de Marie Bashkirtseff*, 602–607. **W. E. Gladstone.** Signed.

1774 A résumé of the Irish land problem, 608–621. **T. W. Russell.** Signed.

1775 The comparative insensibility of animals to pain, 622–627. **William Collier.** Signed W. Collier; Contents adds "Dr."; see *WWW/1940*.

1776 On some war-songs of Europe, 628–650. **Laura Alexandrine Smith.** Signed; Contents adds "Miss."

1777 Old country houses, 651–658. **Edward Strachey.** Signed.

1778 Mental and physical training of children, 659–667. **Jessie Oriana Waller.** Signed; Contents gives "Mrs."

1779 Lady Toad, 668–680. **Friedrich Max Müller.** Signature.

1780 The city of Lhása, 681–694. **Graham Sandberg.** Signed.

1781 Water poachers, 695–709. **John Watson**, d.1928. Signed; see *WWW*.

1782 The middle class and new Liberalism, 710–720. **J. Guinness Rogers.** Signed.

VOLUME 26, NOVEMBER 1889

1783 The new trades-unionism, 721–732. **Frederic Harrison.** Signed; repr. *National and Social Problems.*

1784 The new Tories, 733–745. **George Charles Spencer Churchill.** Signed Marlborough [8th Duke of Marlborough].

1785 The new national party, 746–753. **Montague Crackanthorpe.** Signed.

1786 Australia fifty years ago, 754–775. **Henry Elliot.** Signed; Contents adds "Sir."

1787 Women of to-day, 776–784. **Catherine Milnes Gaskell.** Signed.

1788 The history of a star, 785–800. **J. Norman Lockyer.** Signed.

1789 Roman Catholicism in America, 801–824. **J. E. C. Bodley.** Signed.

1790 Are they grievances? [splits within the Church], 825–832. **Augustus Jessopp.** Signed.

1791 Criticism as a trade: a reply [to no. 1760], 833–839. **Alfred J. Church.** Signed.

1792 Modern gambling and gambling laws, 840–860. **G. Herbert Stutfield.** Signed.

1793 "Memo" on classes in the Soudan, 861–862. **C. G. Gordon.** Signed; Contents gives "the late General." Intro. note signed **Clifford Lloyd.**

1794 A problem in money, 863–881. **Robert Giffen.** Signed; repr. *The Case against Bimetallism*, 1892. (See no. 1807.)

1795 The English Church under Henry the Eighth, 882–896. **W. E. Gladstone.** Signed.

VOLUME 26, DECEMBER 1889

1796 Is it open to the colonies to secede? 897–911. **Julius Vogel.** Signed.

1797 Stamping out Protestantism in Russia, 912–924. **Charles H. H. Wright.** Signed.

1798 The dreadful revival of leprosy, 925–941. **Morell Mackenzie.** Signed; repr. *Essays*, 1893.

1799 Parliamentary franchises, past and present, 942–962. **John Lambert.** Signed.

1800 The venomous snakes of India, 963–983. **Joseph Fayrer.** Signed J. Fayrer; Contents as in no. 1743.

1801 Noticeable books (No. I): *Memorials of a Southern Planter*, 984–986. **W. E. Gladstone.** Signed.

1802 Noticeable books (No. II): Mr. Courthope's *Life of Pope*, 987–991. **Augustine Birrell.** Signed.

1803 Noticeable books (No. III): *A Cen-*

tury of Revolution [by W. S. Lilly], 992–994. **Walter Pater.** Signed.

1804 Noticeable books (No. IV): *The Despot of Broomsedge Cove*, 994–997. **Hamilton Aïdé.** Signed.

1805 Noticeable books (No. V.): *Correspondance Inédite du Prince de Talleyrand et du Roi Louis XVIII*, 998–1000. **Walter Frewen Lord.** Signed.

1806 The awakening of Persia, 1001–1013. **Edward Fitzgerald Law.** Signed. E. F. G. Law; see *DNB*, 2nd suppl.

1807 Mr. Giffen's attack on bimetallists, 1014–1023. **J. Shield Nicholson.** Signed; repr. *Treatise on Money*, 2nd ed., 1893.

1808 The Irish malady, and its physicians, 1024–1042. **Frank H. Hill.** Signed.

1809 Notes on the latest land programme, 1043–1046. **Henry de la Poer.** Signed Waterford [5th Marquess of Waterford].

1810 In praise of London fog, 1047–1055. **M. H. Dziewicki.** Signed.

1811 Electoral facts of to-day (No. II), 1056–1066. **W. E. Gladstone.** Signed. (No. I is no. 246; No. III is no. 2092.)

VOLUME 27, JANUARY 1890

1812 On the natural inequality of men, 1–23. **T. H. Huxley.** Signed; repr. *Collected Essays*, I. (See no. 1857.)

1813 The German daily press, 24–37. **Ludwig Bamberger.** Signed L. Bamberger; Contents gives "Dr."; see Hyamson.

1814 The Melbourne government: its acts and persons, 38–55. **W. E. Gladstone.** Signed.

1815 Ourselves and our foremothers, 56–64. **Margaret E. Child-Villiers.** Signed M. E. Jersey [Countess of Jersey].

1816 The decline of reserve among women, 65–71. **Katie Cowper.** Signed; Contents gives "Countess Cowper."

1817 The future of the city charities, 72–88. **Robert Hunter.** Signed.

1818 The actual and the political Ireland, 89–101. **T. W. Russell.** Signed.

1819 Ten years of British art, 102–118. **Marcus B. Huish.** Signed.

1820 Absolute political ethics, 119–130. **Herbert Spencer.** Signed; repr. *Essays* (1914 ed.), III.

1821 The ascertainment of English, 131–144. **Charles Mackay.** Signed.

1822 The dangers of electric lighting, 145–149. **Charles W. Vincent.** Signed.

1823 The government and the tithes, 150–

172. **H. G. Grey.** Signed Grey [Earl Grey].

VOLUME 27, FEBRUARY 1890

1824 Natural rights and political rights, 173–195. **T. H. Huxley.** Signed; repr. *Collected Essays*, I. (See no. 1844.)
1825 The future of Russia in Asia, 196–212. **Arminius Vambéry.** Signed.
1826 The illustration of books and newspapers, 213–224. **Henry Blackburn.** Signed.
1827 A Chinese view of railways in China, 225–239. **Fung Yee.** Signed, with addition, "Late Secretary of the Chinese Legation in London."
1828 Play and players on the Riviera, 240–257. **W. Fraser Rae.** Signed.
1829 The glut of junior officers in the army, 258–267. **John Miller Adye,** 1819–1900. Signed as in no. 347.
1830 The naturalist on the Pampas, 268–283. **W. H. Hudson,** 1841–1922. Signed.
1831 The land and its owners in past times, 284–302. **Augustus Jessopp.** Signed; repr. *Studies.*
1832 Crete and the Sphakiots, 303–311. **Charles Edwardes.** Signed.
1833 Party prospects [for the Unionists], 312–326. **T. E. Kebbel.** Signed.
1834 Dante and the "new Reformation," 327–343. **J. W. Cross.** Signed; repr. *Impressions.*
1835 The working of "The People's Palace" [clubs for low-income groups], 344–356. **Edmund Hay Currie.** Signed.

VOLUME 27, MARCH 1890

1836 The report of the Parnell Commission, 357–383. **Michael Davitt.** Signed.
1837 On books and the housing of them, 384–396. **W. E. Gladstone.** Signed. AND **Mary Gladstone Drew,** collab? Attr. to her in her *A Forty Years' Friendship*, ed. S. L. Ollard (N.Y., 1919), p. 131n., in a letter which Ollard dates 1889.
1838 A battle described from the ranks, 397–407. **Arthur V. Palmer.** Signed, with addition, "Late Sergeant, 79th Highlanders." (Letter, p. 708, by **Edward Everett**—signed E. Everett, with addition "Colonel Commanding Cameron Highlanders", with note on it by **James Knowles**—signed Editor; see nos. 1882, 1903.)
1839 Wallace on "Darwinism," 408–423.

Harvey Goodwin. Signed H. Carlisle [Bishop of Carlisle]. (See no. 1875.)
1840 A seventeenth-century prelate [Bishop Ken], 424–434. **J. Jessop Teague.** Signed.
1841 On justice (Part I), 435–448. **Herbert Spencer.** Signed; repr. *The Principles of Ethics* (1893), II, 3–35.
1842 Property, 449–455. **G. W. W. Bramwell.** Signed Bramwell [Baron Bramwell].
1843 Brain work and manual work, 456–475. **Peter A. Kropotkin.** Signed as in no. 1110.
1844 A working man's reply to Professor Huxley, 476–483. **J. D. Christie.** Signed, with addition, "Pastrycook." (See no. 1824.)
1845 Our merchant service: its condition, and suggestions for its improvement, 484–496. **Thomas Brassey.** Signed Brassey [1st Earl Brassey].
1846 The suppression of rabies in the United Kingdom, 497–512. **George Fleming.** Signed.
1847 Capital: the mother of labour, 513–532. **T. H. Huxley.** Signed.

VOLUME 27, APRIL 1890

1848 The labour movement (No. I): a multitude of counsellors, 533–552. **H. H. Champion.** Signed.
1849 The labour movement (No. II): the case for an eight-hours day, 553–565. **J. A. Murray Macdonald.** Signed. (See nos. 1935–1937.)
1850 The French fishery claims in Newfoundland, 566–575. **Robert J. Pinsent.** Signed.
1851 Was I hypnotised? 576–581. **Hamilton Aïdé.** Signed.
1852 Continental and English painting, 582–591. **J. A. Crowe.** Signed.
1853 Horseflesh, 592–607. **Lees Knowles.** Signed.
1854 On justice (Part II, concl.), 608–620. **Herbert Spencer.** Signed.
1855 The English conquest of Java, 621–632. **Walter Frewen Lord.** Signed; repr. *The Lost Possessions of England*, 1896, as "Java."
1856 Hunting at Gibraltar, 633–638. **Thomas Lister.** Signed Ribblesdale [4th Baron Ribblesdale].
1857 Professor Huxley's attacks, 639–650. **Michael Flürscheim.** Signed.
1858 Noticeable books (No. I): a new book on the gospels [*The First Three Gospels* by J. E. Carpenter], 651–658. **Mary A. Ward.** Signed.

1859 Noticeable books (No. II): *Appreciations* [by Walter Pater], 658–662. **W. J. Courthope.** Signed.

1860 Noticeable books (No. III): *An Epitome of Mr. Herbert Spencer's Philosophy,* 662–667. **W. S. Lilly.** Signed.

1861 Noticeable books (No. IV): *Walpole* [by John Morley], 667–671. **Henry G. Hewlett.** Signed.

1862 Ireland then and now, 672–687. **T. W. Russell.** Signed.

1863 Prince Bismarck, 688–707. **Rowland Blennerhassett.** Signed.

VOLUME 27, MAY 1890

1864 The development of the labour movement, 709–720. **Tom Mann.** Signed.

1865 England and Germany in East Africa, 721–726. **Francis De Winton.** Signed, but with "de" instead of "De": see *DNB,* 1st suppl.

1866 The good time coming [Home Rule], 727–732. **W. W. Palmer.** Signed Wolmer [Viscount Wolmer].

1867 The story of a conspirator [Wolfe Tone] (Part I), 733–755. **G. D. Campbell.** Signed Argyll [8th Duke of Argyll].

1868 The art of the painter-etcher, 756–765. **Francis Seymour Haden.** Signed. (See no. 2045.)

1869 The tithes bill, 766–772. **G. W. W. Bramwell.** Signed Bramwell [Baron Bramwell].

1870 Left-leggedness, 773–778. **Walter K. Sibley.** Signed.

1871 Ireland (No. I): retiring the landlord garrison, 779–794. **Michael Davitt.** Signed.

1872 Ireland (No. II): the government plan for the congested districts, 795–798. **J. O'Connor Power.** Signed.

1873 Ireland (No. III, concl.): the ultimate guarantee, 799–802. **Hugh Fortescue,** 1854–1932. Signed Ebrington [Viscount Ebrington].

1874 The Comte de Clermont, 803–822. **Ferdinand Rothschild.** Signed.

1875 Darwin's latest critics, 823–832. **George J. Romanes.** Signed.

1876 The newspaper press, 833–842. **Frederick Greenwood.** Signed.

1877 Government: anarchy or regimentation, 843–866. **T. H. Huxley.** Signed; repr. *Collected Essays,* I.

1878 Charles the Twelfth: a memoir (Part I), 867–884. **Oscar Fredrik.** Signed as in no. 1671.

VOLUME 27, JUNE 1890

1879 The Lords and the sweating system [in labor], 885–905. **Beatrice Potter.** Signed.

1880 A penny post for the Empire, 906–920. **J. Henniker Heaton.** Signed.

1881 Racing in 1890, 921–936. **G. Herbert Stutfield.** Signed.

1882 "A battle described from the ranks" [no. 1838], 937–941. **Joseph Alexander Campbell.** Signed J. A. Campbell, with addition, "Staff Adjutant, Volunteer Forces, Western Australia (formerly Sergeant-Major 'The Queen's Own Cameron Highlanders')": see *Irish Who's Who*/1908. (See no. 1903.)

1883 New wine in old bottles, 942–956. **Wilfrid Ward.** Signed; repr. *Witnesses.*

1884 Something about village almshouses, 957–976. **Augustus Jessopp.** Signed; repr. *Random Roaming.*

1885 An atheist's pupil [Paul Bourget], 977–986. **W. S. Lilly.** Signed; repr. *The New France,* 1913, as "L'Ame Moderne."

1886 Labour disputes and the Chamber of Commerce, 987–997. **S. B. Boulton.** Signed. With a report, 998–1000, "Adjustment of Labour Disputes," adopted by the London Chamber of Commerce.

1887 The story of a conspirator (Part II, concl.), 1001–1025. **G. D. Campbell.** Signed Argyll [8th Duke of Argyll].

1888 Lord Rosebery and the London County Council, 1026–1039. **Frederic Harrison.** Signed.

1889 Actor-managers (No. I), 1040–1051. **Bram Stoker.** Signed.

1890 Actor-managers (No. II), 1052–1053. **Henry Irving,** 1838–1905. Signed; see *DNB.*

1891 Actor-managers (No. III), 1054–1058. **Charles Wyndham.** Signed.

VOLUME 28, JULY 1890

1892 The African bubble, 1–4. **J. Pope Hennessy.** Signed. (See no. 1905.)

1893 The lights of the Church and the light of science, 5–22. **T. H. Huxley.** Signed; repr. *Collected Essays,* IV, and *Controverted Questions.*

1894 Compensation or confiscation [on temperance], 23–38. **T. W. Russell.** Signed.

1895 The French opera, 39–53. **Yetta Blaze de Bury.** Signed.

1896 The threatened disfigurement of Westminster Abbey, 54–58. **James Knowles.** Signed.

1897 Charles the Twelfth: a memoir (Part

II, concl.), 59–79. **Oscar Fredrik.** Signed as in no. 1671.

1898 Increase of cancer: its probable cause, 80–88. **Herbert Snow.** Signed.

1899 Official polytheism in China, 89–107. **A. C. Lyall.** Signed; repr. *Asiatic Studies, 2nd Series,* as "On the Relations between the State and Religion in China" (Part II).

1900 The press and government, 108–118. **Frederick Greenwood.** Signed.

1901 The crisis in the post office, 119–122. **J. L. Mahon.** Signed.

1902 The true function and value of criticism, with some remarks on the importance of doing nothing: a dialogue (Part I), 123–147. **Oscar Wilde.** Signed.

1903 What I saw at Tel-El-Kebir: a rejoinder [to no. 1882], 148–156. **Arthur V. Palmer.** Signed.

1904 The Irish Land Purchase Bill, 157–168. **H. G. Grey.** Signed Grey [3rd Earl Grey].

VOLUME 28, AUGUST 1890

1905 The value of Africa: a reply to Sir John Pope Hennessy [in no. 1892], 169–175. **H. H. Johnston.** Signed.

1906 Mr. Cecil Rhodes as premier, 176–185. **Edward Dicey.** Signed.

1907 A voice from a harem: some words about the Turkish woman of our day, 186–190. Signed: Adalet. Publisher's note in *Hadjira*, by Adalet, 1896, calls the author "a young Turkish lady" who wrote the novel "in English."

1908 The loyalty of the colonies: a dialogue between a globe-trotter and a colonist, 191–200. **R. H. Bakewell.** Signed. (See no. 1958.)

1909 Charles the First as a picture collector, 201–211. **Henry G. Hewlett.** Signed. With extracts, 211–217, from an inventory made in 1649.

1910 On the rim of the desert, 218–235. **E. N. Buxton.** Signed.

1911 Noticeable books (No. I): *With Essex in Ireland,* 236–238. **W. E. H. Lecky.** Signed.

1912 Noticeable books (No. II): *Life and Letters of the Rev. Adam Sedgewick,* 238–241. **Augustus Jessopp.** Signed.

1913 Noticeable books (No. III): *The English Novel in the Time of Shakespeare,* 242–244. **R. E. Prothero.** Signed.

1914 Noticeable books (No. IV): Mr. Symonds's *Essays Speculative and Suggestive,* 244–248. **W. S. Lilly.** Signed.

1915 Noticeable books (No. V): *Trente Ans de Paris* [by Alphonse Daudet], 248–251. **Millicent Lord.** Signed; Contents gives "Mrs. Frewen Lord."

1916 The power of "suggestion," 252–259. **C. Theodore Ewart.** Signed.

1917 The soldier's barrack-room, 260–268. **A. B. McHardy.** Signed.

1918 The Hebrew hell, 269–285. **James Mew.** Signed.

1919 Domestic service, 286–296. **Ellen W. Darwin.** Signed. (See no. 1944.)

1920 Primitive natural history, 297–308. **George John Romanes.** Signed.

1921 The American silver bubble, 309–324. **Robert Giffen.** Signed; repr. *The Case against Bimetallism,* 1892.

VOLUME 28, SEPTEMBER 1890

1922 The private soldier on the private soldier's wrongs, 325–336. **Arthur V. Palmer.** Signed. (See nos. 1960–1962.)

1923 Mutual aid among animals (Part I), 337–354. **Peter A. Kropotkin.** Signed P. Kropotkin; repr. *Mutual Aid.*

1924 How Art Kavanagh fought Richard the King: a fourteenth century chronicle, 355–368. **Emily Lawless.** Signed; repr. *Traits and Confidences,* 1898.

1925 Behind the scenes in English politics [the Crimean crisis in 1855], 369–380. **Nassau W. Senior.** Signed; Contents adds "the late."

1926 A Pompeii for the twenty-ninth century, 381–391. **Frederic Harrison.** Signed; repr. *Realities and Ideals,* as "A Pompeii for the Thirtieth Century."

1927 American railways and British farmers, 392–409. **J. Stephen Jeans.** Signed.

1928 Bion of Smyrna, 410–424. **William Morton Fullerton.** Signed.

1929 Water in Australian Saharas, 425–434. **Thomas Allnutt Brassey.** Signed T. A. Brassey; see *WWW*/1928.

1930 The true function and value of criticism (Part II, concl.), 435–459. **Oscar Wilde.** Signed.

1931 Ruin of the civil service, 460–470. **R. G. C. Hamilton.** Signed.

1932 A mediaeval popular preacher [Brother Nicholas Bozon], 471–477. **Maurice Hewlett.** Signed.

1933 Is Central Africa worth having? (No. I), 478–487. **J. Pope Hennessy.** Signed.

1934 Is Central Africa worth having? (No. II), 488–500. **Edward Dicey.** Signed.

VOLUME 28, OCTOBER 1890

1935 The labour revolution (No. I): a multitude of counsellors, 501–516. **H. H. Champion.** Signed.

1936 The labour revolution (No. II): the new departure in trades unionism, 517–525. **T. R. Threlfall.** Signed.

1937 The labour revolution (No. III): what are the ideals of the masses? 526–533. **Reginald B. Brett.** Signed.

1938 The awakening of Jamaica, 534–544. **Henry A. Blake.** Signed.

1939 Tuberculous meat and its consequences, 545–562. **Henry Behrend.** Signed.

1940 Some aspects of Newman's influence, 563–574. **Wilfrid Ward.** Signed; repr. *Witnesses*.

1941 Manners and customs of Sicily in 1890, 575–587. **Hamilton Aïdé.** Signed.

1942 Bees and Darwinism, 588–600. **Harvey Goodwin.** Signed H. Carlisle [Bishop of Carlisle].

1943 Dahomey and the French, 601–615. **Archer P. Crouch.** Signed.

1944 In defence of domestic service: a reply [to no. 1919], 616–626. **Mary E. Benson.** Signed M. E. Benson; Contents gives "Miss"; see Boase.

1945 The weaknesses of Congregationalism (No. I): seen from the pews, 627–635. **B. Paul Neuman.** Signed.

1946 The weaknesses of Congregationalism (No. II): seen from the pulpit, 635–639. **T. Herbert Darlow.** Signed.

1947 An Armenian's cry for Armenia, 640–647. **James Aratoon Malcolm.** Signed James A. Malcolm; Contents gives middle name.

1948 A model government office, 648–659. **L. J. Jennings.** Signed.

1949 Meddling with Hindu marriages, 660–676. **J. D. Rees.** Signed.

VOLUME 28, NOVEMBER 1890

1950 Mr. Carnegie's "gospel of wealth": a review and a recommendation, 677–693. **W. E. Gladstone.** Signed. (See no. 2007.)

1951 In peril from parliament (Part I), 694–698. **H. G. Grey.** Signed Grey [3rd Earl Grey].

1952 Mutual aid among animals (Part II, concl.), 699–719. **Peter A. Kropotkin.** Signed as in no. 1923.

1953 The destruction of Egyptian monuments, 720–732. **Henry Wallis.** Signed.

1954 Irish chronicles: Gerald the Great (Part I), 733–749. **Emily Lawless.** Signed. (Part II is no. 2013.)

1955 The Aryan question and pre-historic man, 750–777. **T. H. Huxley.** Signed; repr. *Collected Essays*, VII.

1956 French boycotting and its cure, 778–785. **R. E. Prothero.** Signed.

1957 The guilds of the early Italian painters, 786–800. **J. Paul Richter,** 1847–1937. Signed.

1958 The loyalty of the colonies, 801–811. **Alfred Barry.** Signed.

1959 The Oxford movement of the fifteenth century, 812–830. **F. T. Palgrave.** Signed.

1960 The private soldier's wrongs (No. I): an officer's reply, 831–834. **T. S. Baldock.** Signed.

1961 The private soldier's wrongs (No. II): boy-sergeants, 835–839. **Joseph Byrne.** Signed.

1962 The private soldier's wrongs (No III): life in a cavalry regiment, 840–853. **Wilfrid Gore-Browne.** Signed.

1963 The latest Midlothian campaign, 854–860. **Michael Davitt.** Signed.

VOLUME 28, DECEMBER 1890

1964 Shall we Americanise our institutions? 861–875. **Joseph Chamberlain.** Signed J. Chamberlain; Contents gives first name.

1965 Irresponsible wealth (No. I), 876–885. **H. E. Manning.** Signed as in no. 8.

1966 Irresponsible wealth (No. II), 886–889. **Hermann Adler.** Signed.

1967 Irresponsible wealth (No. III), 890–900. **Hugh Price Hughes.** Signed.

1968 The trade league against England, 901–913. **L. J. Jennings.** Signed.

1969 Birds, 914–926. **Herbert Maxwell.** Signed; repr. *Meridiana: Noontime Essays*, 1892.

1970 Constantinople revisited, 927–944. **G. Shaw Lefevre.** Signed.

1971 Idealism and the masses, 945–949. **R. B. Cunninghame Graham.** Signed.

1972 Women as public servants, 950–958. **Louisa Twining.** Signed.

1973 Life in the harem, 959–966. Signed: Adalet. See no. 1907.

1974 The keepers of the herd of swine [on Mr. Gladstone's biblical criticism], 967–979. **T. H. Huxley.** Signed; repr. *Collected Essays*, V, and *Controverted Questions*.

1975 Give back the Elgin Marbles, 980–

troversial method, 455–467. **T. H. Huxley.** Signed; repr. *Collected Essays*, V, and *Controverted Questions*. (Letter, p. 690, signed **W. E. Gladstone**; acknowledgment by **Huxley**. pp. 924–925.)

2016 The New World [of America and the Colonies], 468–476. **J. W. Cross.** Signed; repr. *Impressions*.

2017 John Wesley, 477–494. **Hugh Price Hughes.** Signed.

2018 The joke about the Elgin Marbles, 495–506. **James Knowles.** Signed.

2019 Commercial union within the Empire, 507–522. **Windham T. W. Quin.** Signed Dunraven [4th Earl Dunraven].

VOLUME 29, APRIL 1891

2020 The seamy side of Australia, 523–537. **J. W. Fortescue.** Signed. (See nos. 2089 and 2100.)

2021 Mutual aid among savages, 538–559. **Peter A. Kropotkin.** Signed as in no. 1110.

2022 Slum-mothers and death-clubs: a vindication, 560–563. **Edward Berdoe.** Signed.

2023 The story of Bianca Cappello, 564–582. **H. Schütz Wilson.** Signed; repr. *History and Criticism*, 1896.

2024 State-made farmers, 583–587. **William E. Bear.** Signed.

2025 A stone book [the sculpture of Westminster Abbey], 588–600. **Emily T. Bradley.** Signed; Contents adds "Miss"; later Mrs. Emily Tennyson Smith.

2026 The progress of Welsh disestablishment, 601–607. **G. Osborne Morgan.** Signed.

2027 Is it to be civil war? [the Scottish rail strike], 608–614. **A. P. Laurie.** Signed.

2028 A department of health, 615–623. **F. A. Rollo Russell.** Signed Rollo Russell; see *WWW*/1916.

2029 A model dairy, 624–627. **Reginald Brabazon.** Signed Meath [12th Earl of Meath].

2030 Science and a future life, 628–647. **Frederic W. H. Myers.** Signed; repr. *Future Life*.

2031 Five thousand miles with range-cattle, 648–669. **Nele Loring.** Signed.

2032 Talleyrand's *Memoirs*, 670–684. **J. D. Acton.** Signed Acton [1st Baron Acton]; repr. *Historical Essays*.

2033 Professor Huxley and the Duke of Argyll, 685–689. **G. D. Campbell.** Signed Argyll [8th Duke of Argyll]. (See postscript to no. 2055.)

VOLUME 29, MAY 1891

2034 The judicial shock to marriage, 691–700. **Eliza Lynn Linton.** Signature.

2035 Italy and the United States, 701–718. **Jessie White Mario.** Signed, with addition, "(Vedova)" after "White."

2036 Resuscitation by oxygen, 719–726. **Henry Elsdale.** Signed.

2037 Town and country parsons, 727–746. **Harry Jones,** 1823–1900. Signed; see Venn; repr. *Fifty Years*, 1895.

2038 Kaiser-I-Hind and Hindoostani, 747–753. **Rafiüddin Ahmad.** Signed.

2039 Noticeable books (No. I): *Esther Pentreath*, 754–756. **Leonard Courtney.** Signed.

2040 Noticeable books (No. II): Mr. Lecky's new volumes [*A History of England in the Eighteenth Century*], 756–759. **W. S. Lilly.** Signed.

2041 Noticeable books (No. III): *Untrodden Ground in Astronomy and Geology*, 760–763. **J. C. Cowell.** Signed, with addition, "Major-General."

2042 Noticeable books (No. IV): *The Religious Renascence in Italy*, 763–766. **Maurice Hewlett.** Signed.

2043 Noticeable books (No. V): *Animal Life and Intelligence*, 766–768. **George John Romanes.** Signed.

2044 Noticeable books (No. VI): *Philomythus*, 768–774. **Mary A. Ward.** Signed.

2045 The Royal Society of Painter Etchers, 775–781. **Francis Seymour Haden.** Signed.

2046 The warfare of the future, 782–795. **Archibald Forbes.** Signed; repr. *Camps*.

2047 The "enormous antiquity" of the East, 796–810. **Friedrich Max Müller.** Signature.

2048 The realm of the microbe, 811–831. **Eliza Priestley.** Signed.

2049 "Trusts": an alarm, 832–844. **Samuel Plimsoll.** Signed.

2050 Is it Aristotle's tomb? 845–850. **Charles Waldstein.** Signed.

VOLUME 29, JUNE 1891

2051 The opium "resolution," 851–856. **James Fitzjames Stephen.** Signed.

2052 On the analysis of voluntary movement, 857–870. **Victor Horsley.** Signed.

2053 A description of Manipur, 871–887. **James Johnstone.** Signed J. Johnstone; Contents gives "Sir James Johnstone."

2054 Social aspects of American life, 888–903. **Hamilton Aïdé.** Signed.

2055　Hasisadra's adventure, 904–924. **T. H. Huxley.** Signed; repr. *Collected Essays*, IV, and *Controverted Questions*. With a postscript, 924–926, on Gladstone's letter (see no. 2015) and on nos. 1446, 2033.

2056　The duel between public schools and private "coaches," 927–940. **Walter Wren.** Signed.

2057　Mohammedan women, 941–952. **Annie Reichardt.** Signed. (See no. 2097.)

2058　From the Albert Nyanza to the Indian Ocean, 953–968. **W. G. Stairs.** Signed.

2059　Tsar v. Jew, 969–978. **Ellen Desart.** Signed; Contents adds "Countess"; see *WWW*/1940.

2060　Witnesses to the unseen, 979–997. **Wilfrid Ward.** Signed; repr. *Witnesses*.

2061　The bombardment of Iquique, 998–1015. **Archer P. Crouch.** Signed.

2062　Morocco: the world's last market, 1016–1021. **Charles F. Goss.** Signed.

2063　Is free education a bribe? 1022–1026. **T. E. Kebbel.** Signed.

2064　The McKinley Bill, 1027–1036. **Andrew Carnegie.** Signed.

VOLUME 30, JULY 1891

2065　Gambling and the law, 1–6. **James Fitzjames Stephen.** Signed.

2066　The army as a public department, 7–25. **George Tomkyns Chesney.** Signed as in no. 103.

2067　Woodlands, 26–39. **Herbert Maxwell.** Signed; repr. *Post Meridiana.*

2068　A fair taxation of ground-rents, 40–55. **Robert Hunter.** Signed.

2069　Pasquale de Paoli: a study, 56–70. **Walter Frewen Lord.** Signed; repr. *The Lost Possessions of England*, 1896, as "Corsica."

2070　The industries of ancient India, 71–78. **Murli Manohar.** Signed; Contents adds "Rajah"; prob. repr. *Indian Industries and Other Essays*, Madras, 1897.

2071　The wild women (Part I): as politicians, 79–88. **Eliza Lynn Linton.** Signature. (See nos. 2182, 2321.)

2072　A labour inquiry, 89–99. **H. H. Champion.** Signed.

2073　1799: a rustic retrospect, 100–111. **Augustus Jessopp.** Signed; repr. *Random Roaming.*

2074　How to utilise the naval volunteers, 112–117. **H. O. Arnold-Forster.** Signed.

2075　The Congregationalist Council, 118–129. **J. Guinness Rogers.** Signed.

2076　The poet of the Klephts: Aristoteles Valaoritis, 130–144. **Rennell Rodd.** Signed.

2077　The "Commonwealth of Australia," 145–153. **G. H. Reid.** Signed.

2078　Sir John Macdonald on imperial federation: a personal reminiscence, 154–160. **S. B. Boulton.** Signed.

VOLUME 30, AUGUST 1891

2079　Our dealings with the poor, 161–170. **Octavia Hill.** Signed.

2080　The next parliament, 171–184. **Edward Dicey.** Signed.

2081　A war correspondent's reminiscences (Part I), 185–196. **Archibald Forbes.** Signed; repr. *Memories* as "Ten Years of War Correspondence."

2082　The future of landscape art, 197–209. **James Stanley Little.** Signed.

2083　Demography, 210–216. **Douglas Galton.** Signed.

2084　On certain ecclesiastical miracles, 217–236. **H. I. D. Ryder.** Signed; repr. *Essays*, 1911.

2085　The "confusion worse confounded" at the War Office, 237–257. **George Tomkyns Chesney.** Signed as in no. 2066, which is claimed here, p. 237. (See no. 3599.)

2086　The drama of the moment, 258–274. **H. A. Kennedy.** Signed.

2087　Théodore de Banville, 275–284. **R. E. Prothero.** Signed.

2088　The French in Tonquin, 285–291. **C. W. A. N. R. Cochrane-Baillie.** Signed Lamington [2nd Baron Lamington].

2089　"The seamy side of Australia": a reply from the colonies [to no. 2020], 292–302. **Howard Willoughby.** Signed.

2090　Identification by finger-tips, 303–311. **Francis Galton.** Signed.

2091　Frontiers and protectorates, 312–328. **Alfred Lyall.** Signed.

VOLUME 30, SEPTEMBER 1891

2092　Electoral facts (No. III, concl.), 329–340. **W. E. Gladstone.** Signed. (No. II is no. 1811.) (Note, p. 676, by **Gladstone** —signed W.E.G.)

2093　The British in East Africa, 341–345. **John D. S. Campbell.** Signed Lorne [Marquis of Lorne].

2094　The last bit of natural woodland, 346–360. **Auberon Herbert.** Signed.

2095　Ferdinand Lassalle, 361–379. **Nina Kennard.** Signed.

2096 Compulsory insurance in Germany, 380–386. **F. Heinrich Geffcken.** Signed.

2097 The real status of women in Islâm. 387–399. **Syed Ameer Ali.** Signed as in no. 454.

2098 Can railway-passenger fares be lowered? 400–413. **W. M. Acworth.** Signed.

2099 A war correspondent's reminiscences (Part II, concl.), 414–429. **Archibald Forbes.** Signed.

2100 Guileless Australia: a rejoinder [to no. 2089], 430–443. **J. W. Fortescue.** Signed.

2101 Our worn-out parsons, 444–455. **Augustus Jessopp.** Signed; repr. *Peasantry.*

2102 A French ambassador at the court of Charles II, 456–479. **J. J. Jusserand.** Signed.

2103 Imperial federation (No. I): an English view, 480–489. **Thomas Brassey.** Signed Brassey [1st Earl Brassey].

2104 Imperial federation (No. II): an American view, 490–508. **Andrew Carnegie.** Signed.

VOLUME 30, OCTOBER 1891

2105 Federating the Empire: a colonial plan, 509–520. **Charles Tupper.** Signed; Contents adds "High Commissioner for Canada."

2106 The question of disestablishment, 521–539. **Goldwin Smith.** Signed; repr. *Essays on Questions of the Day,* N.Y., 1893.

2107 The private life of Sir Thomas More, 540–563. **Agnes Lambert.** Signed.

2108 Welsh fairies, 564–574. **John Rhys.** Signed.

2109 The wisdom of Gombo [Franco-negro proverbs], 575–582. **Edward Wakefield.** Signed.

2110 Immigration troubles of the United States, 583–595. **W. H. Wilkins.** Signed.

2111 The wild women (Part II, concl.): as social insurgents, 596–605. **Eliza Lynn Linton.** Signature.

2112 The naval policy of France, past and future, 606–627. **G. Shaw Lefevre.** Signed.

2113 The military forces of the Crown, 628–637. **John Miller Adye,** 1819–1900. Signed as in no. 347.

2114 Stray thoughts of an Indian girl, 638–642. **Cornelia Sorabji.** Signed.

2115 A bardic chronicle, 643–657. **Emily Lawless.** Signed.

2116 On the ancient beliefs in a future state, 658–676. **W. E. Gladstone.** Signed. (See no. 2137.)

VOLUME 30, NOVEMBER 1891

2117 On spurious works of art, 677–698. **John Charles Robinson.** Signed as in no. 455.

2118 Unpublished pages of Pepys's diary, 699–711. **Henry B. Wheatley.** Signed.

2119 The Christian hell, 712–734. **James Mew.** Signed.

2120 Is man the only reasoner? 735–745. **James Sully.** Signed.

2121 The *Mimes* of Herodas, 746–752. **Charles Whibley.** Signed; repr. *Studies in Frankness,* 1898.

2122 Byron at Pisa, 753–763. **Janet Ross.** Signed.

2123 The Psychical Society's ghosts: a challenge renewed, 764–776. **A. Taylor Innes.** Signed.

2124 The House of Commons and the Church, 777–782. **Edward L. Stanley.** Signed Stanley of Alderley [4th Baron Stanley of Alderley].

2125 French authors on each other, 783–798. **Edward Delille.** Signed.

2126 Is our yeomanry worth preserving? 799–812. **David W. S. Ogilvy.** Signed Airlie [Earl of Airlie].

2127 Life in a Jesuit college [at Pau], 813–830. **Michael S. Dziewicki.** Signed H. Dziewicki; man cited adopted name of Michael Henry Dziewicki when he was at a Jesuit seminary in Pau: see *Index,* I, 881.

2128 Darwinism in the nursery, 831–842. **Louis Robinson.** Signed.

2129 My critics, 843–852. **Edward Dicey.** Signed.

VOLUME 30, DECEMBER 1891

2130 The German newspaper press, 853–871. **Charles Lowe.** Signed.

2131 "Hibernia Pacata" [on union with Ireland], 872–884. **John R. W. de Vesci.** Signed De Vesci [4th Viscount de Vesci].

2132 How to re-organise the War Department, 885–902. **George Tomkyns Chesney.** Signed as in no. 103.

2133 Gardens, 903–918. **Herbert Maxwell.** Signed; repr. *Post Meridiana.*

2134 Milton's Macbeth, 919–932. **John W. Hales.** Signed; repr. *Folia.*

2135 The diminution of drunkenness in Norway, 933–938. **Reginald Brabazon.** Signed Meath [12th Earl of Meath].

2136 Women and the glove trade, 939–950. **Ada Heather-Bigg.** Signed.

2137 Ancient beliefs in immortality: a reply

to Mr. Gladstone, 951–968. **T. K. Cheyne.** Signed.

2138 A railway journey with Mr. Parnell, 969–974. **Thomas Lister.** Signed Ribblesdale [4th Baron Ribblesdale]; repr. *Impressions and Memoirs*, 1927.

2139 The new science: preventive medicine, 975–993. **M. Armand Ruffer.** Signed.

2140 A suggestion for my betters [the need for studying history], 994–1001. **Augustus Jessopp.** Signed; repr. *Studies*.

2141 Trade in the Malay Peninsula, 1002–1005. **Martin Lister.** Signed; Index adds "Hon."

2142 Shakespeare and modern Greek, 1006–1017. **John Stuart Blackie.** Signed.

2143 Moltke and Moltkeism, 1018–1035. **Archibald Forbes.** Signed; repr. *Memories* as "Moltke before Metz."

2144 The Labour "platform" at the next election, 1036–1042. **H. H. Champion.** Signed.

VOLUME 31, JANUARY 1892

2145 The horrors of hunger, 1–6. **Nicholas Shishkoff.** Signed N. Shishkoff; Contents gives first name. (Notes, pp. 340, 712 by **James Knowles**—signed Editor; see no. 2220.)

2146 Lord Rosebery and Mr. Pitt, 7–23. **Reginald B. Brett.** Signed.

2147 Hypnotism and humbug, 24–37. **Ernest Hart.** Signed.

2148 Protection: free trade, fair trade, colonial trade, 38–60. **Henry G. Grey.** Signed Grey [3rd Earl Grey].

2149 Our minor poets, 61–72. **H. D. Traill.** Signed.

2150 Electrical transmission of power, 73–89. **William C. Keppel.** Signed Albemarle [7th Earl of Albemarle].

2151 Imperial federation for naval defence, 90–100. **Thomas Brassey.** Signed Brassey [1st Earl Brassey].

2152 Mutual aid among the barbarians, 101–122. **Peter A. Kropotkin.** Signed as in no. 1110; repr. *Mutual Aid*.

2153 Man, East and West, 123–133. **Samuel A. Barnett.** Signed.

2154 Taxes on transport, 134–149. **W. M. Acworth.** Signed.

2155 The rural voter (No. I): the law, the land, and the labourer, 150–159. **Henry Thring.** Signed Thring [1st Baron Thring].

2156 The rural voter (No. II): farm labourers and their friends, 160–173. **William E. Bear.** Signed.

2157 The rural voter (No. III): Hodge at home, 174–180. **Henrietta M. Batson.** Signed; Contents gives "Mrs. Stephen Batson." (See no. 2173.)

VOLUME 31, FEBRUARY 1892

2158 Cross-examination, 183–187. **George W. W. Bramwell.** Signed Bramwell [Baron Bramwell].

2159 The accused as a witness, 188–196. **Frederick Mead.** Signed.

2160 The traffic in sermons, 197–207. **B. G. Johns.** Signed.

2161 Two moods of a man: by a woman, 208–223. **Mary Montgomerie Singleton.** Signed with addition "(Violet Fane)"; repr. *Two Moods of a Man* by Violet Fane, 1901.

2162 The London water supply, 224–232. **John Lubbock.** Signed.

2163 Recollections of Tewfik Pacha, 233–242. **Edward Dicey.** Signed.

2164 The "ideal" university, 243–254. **J. Churton Collins.** Signed.

2165 A trip to Travancore, 255–262. **Eva Wyndham Quin.** Signed.

2166 Castle Acre, 263–279. **Augustus Jessopp.** Signed; repr. *Random Roaming*.

2167 Cardinal Manning in the Church of England, 280–292. **R. G. Wilberforce.** Signed.

2168 The present state of the Panama Canal, 293–311. **E. H. Seymour.** Signed.

2169 *A New Calendar of Great Men* [by Auguste Comte], 312–328. **John Morley.** Signed; repr. *Miscellanies*, IV.

2170 Influenza and salicin, 329–339. **T. J. Maclagan.** Signed.

VOLUME 31, MARCH 1892

2171 New stars, 341–351. **J. Norman Lockyer.** Signed.

2172 The settlement of landed property, 352–358. **George W. H. Venables-Vernon.** Signed Vernon [7th Baron Vernon].

2173 Hodge and his parson [the rural laborer], 359–362. **Arnold D. Taylor.** Signed.

2174 Italia non farà da se [why Italy cannot get on without foreign assistance], 363–374. **Walter Frewen Lord.** Signed.

2175 French eighteenth-century art in England, 375–390. **Ferdinand Rothschild.** Signed.

2176 Household clubs: an experiment, 391–398. **Ishbel M. Gordon.** Signed Ishbel Aberdeen [Countess of Aberdeen].

2177 The latest electrical discovery, 399–402. **J. E. H. Gordon.** Signed.

2178 Repayment of the metropolitan debt, 403–409. **Alfred Hoare.** Signed.

2179 Minor poets—and others, 410–418. **H. D. Traill.** Signed.

2180 Napoleon the Third at Sedan, 419–432. **Archibald Forbes.** Signed; repr. *Memories* as "Dark Days of Sedan."

2181 The Muslim hell, 433–454. **James Mew.** Signed.

2182 The partisans of the wild women, 455–464. **Eliza Lynn Linton.** Signature.

2183 Some social changes in fifty years, 465–473. **Emily C. Boyle.** Signed E. C. Cork [Countess of Cork].

2184 The French newspaper press, 474–486. **Edward Delille.** Signed.

2185 Famine relief in Samara, 487–495. **Nicholas Shishkoff.** Signed as in no. 2145. Intro. note by **James Knowles**—signed Editor.

2186 The London County Council (No. I): towards a commune, 496–514. **John Burns.** Signed.

2187 The London County Council (No. II): towards common sense, 515–524. **R. E. Prothero.** Signed. (See no. 2199.)

VOLUME 31, APRIL 1892

2188 How to federate the Empire: a reply to critics, 525–536. **Charles Tupper.** Signed.

2189 Prospects of marriage for women, 537–552. **Clara E. Collet.** Signed.

2190 Chicago and its Exhibition, 553–565. **Henry Trueman Wood.** Signed.

2191 Lord Lytton's rank in literature, 566–576. **Wilfrid Scawen Blunt.** Signed.

2192 Vegetable diet, 577–585. **Walburga Paget.** Signed; Contents gives "Lady Paget."

2193 The story of Gifford and Keats, 586–605. **David Masson.** Signed.

2194 The attack on the credit of Australasia, 606–622. **R. M. Johnston.** Signed.

2195 Camp life and pigsticking in Morocco, 623–630. **Henrietta Grey Egerton.** Signed.

2196 Impressions of the Canadian North-West, 631–647. **Michael Davitt.** Signed.

2197 Colour-blindness, its pathology and its possible practical remedy, 648–660. **A. E. Wright.** Signed.

2198 Austrian stud farms, 661–672. **Frederick Wrench.** Signed.

2199 Let London live! 673–685. **John Burns.** Signed.

2200 Noticeable books (No. I): *The Platform, Its Rise and Progress*, 686–689. **W. E. Gladstone.** Signed.

2201 Noticeable books (No. II): *The Recollections of a Happy Life*, 689–692. **Augustus Jessopp.** Signed.

2202 Noticeable books (No. III): *Grania* [by Emily Lawless], 693–695. **R. E. Prothero.** Signed.

2203 Noticeable books (No. IV): Mr. Burd's *Machiavelli*, 696–700. **J. D. Acton.** Signed Acton [1st Baron Acton].

2204 Noticeable books (No. V): Dr. Westcott on religious thought, 700–703. **W. S. Lilly.** Signed.

2205 Noticeable books (No. VI): *Poems* by Emily Dickinson, 703–706. **Hamilton Aïdé.** Signed.

2206 Noticeable books (No. VII): *The Spirit of Islam*, 707–711. **Stanley Lane-Poole.** Signed.

VOLUME 31, MAY 1892

2207 Memorable dissolutions, 713–734. **G. Barnett Smith.** Signed.

2208 The Liberal outlook, 735–742. **T. Wemyss Reid.** Signed.

2209 Recent science, 743–761. **Peter A. Kropotkin.** Signed as in no. 1110.

2210 Studies of New York society, 762–777. **Mayo Williamson Hazeltine.** Signed.

2211 A Maori meeting, 778–786. **Reginald Brabazon.** Signed Meath [12th Earl of Meath].

2212 How General Gordon was really lost, 787–794. **Thomas Heazle Parke.** Signed.

2213 The meaning of a baby's footprint, 795–806. **Louis Robinson.** Signed.

2214 Household clubs: how will they affect small households? 807–810. **Margaret Hamilton.** Signed; Contents adds "Lady."

2215 A defence of the so-called "wild women," 811–829. **Mona Caird.** Signed; repr. *Morality of Marriage and Other Essays*, 1897.

2216 The decay of the landed aristocracy in India, 830–838. **Odai Partab Singh.** Signed.

2217 Lost in the Rockies, 839–849. **W. H. Grenfell.** Signed.

2218 One of the "six hundred" on the Balaclava charge, 850–863. **J. W. Wightman.** Signed with addition "late 17th Lancers."

2219 Stevens and the Wellington memorial, 864–870. **Walter Armstrong.** Signed.

2220 The Shishkoff Russian famine fund, 871–873. **E. W. Brooks.** Signed. With list of subscribers, 873–876, compiled by **James Knowles**—signed Editor.

VOLUME 31, JUNE 1892

2221 Ulster and Home Rule, 877–884. **St. Loe Strachey.** Signed.
2222 The inefficiency of the army, 885–898. **J. L. A. Simmons.** Signed.
2223 Ireland blocks the way, 899–904. **Herbert J. Gladstone.** Signed.
2224 Some great Jewish rabbis, 905–924. **Charles H. H. Wright.** Signed.
2225 A butler's view of men-service, 925–933. **John Robinson.** Signed.
2226 Ovid metamorphosed, 934–937. **Janet Ross.** Signed.
2227 The Tuscan sculpture of the Renaissance, 938–949. **Violet Paget.** Signed V. Paget; repr. *Renaissance Fancies and Studies,* 1895.
2228 The increase of crime, 950–957. **William Douglas Morrison.** Signed.
2229 An Indian funeral sacrifice, 958–963. **J. D. Rees.** Signed.
2230 A fourteenth-century parson [John de Gurnay], 964–984. **Augustus Jessopp.** Signed; repr. *Random Roaming.*
2231 The invasion of destitute aliens, 985–1000. **Windham T. W. Quin.** Signed Dunraven [4th Earl of Dunraven].
2232 Women and worship in Burmah, 1001–1007. **Violet Greville.** Signed; Contents adds "Lady."
2233 The story of an unhappy queen [Sophia Dorothea], 1008–1026. **Millicent Erskine Wemyss.** Signed.
2234 Protection as labour wants it, 1027–1031. **H. H. Champion.** Signed.
2235 Did Dante study in Oxford? 1032–1042. **W. E. Gladstone.** Signed.

VOLUME 32, JULY 1892

2236 The choice of England [in the elections], 1–12. **Edward Dicey.** Signed.
2237 The American newspaper press, 13–28. **Edward Delille.** Signed.
2238 The astronomy and mythology of the ancient Egyptians, 29–51. **J. Norman Lockyer.** Signed.
2239 A journey to England in the year 1663, 52–66. **J. J. Jusserand.** Signed; repr. *English Essays from a French Pen,* 1895.
2240 Music for the masses, 67–76. **Florence A. Marshall.** Signed.
2241 The tercentenary of Trinity College, Dublin, 77–96. **J. P. Mahaffy.** Signed.

2242 Jamaica resurgens, 97–103. **William A. A. De Vere.** Signed St. Albans [10th Duke of St. Albans].
2243 The situation in central Asia, 104–117. **Arminius Vambéry.** Signed as in no. 451.
2244 Sir John Franklin, 118–129. **Henry Elliot.** Signed.
2245 Turkish marriages viewed from a harem, 130–140. Signed: Adalet. See no. 1907.
2246 The impending elections in England and America, 141–150. **Andrew Carnegie.** Signed.
2247 Why I shall vote for the Unionist candidate (No. I), 151–154. **Robert Gregory.** Signed. Intro. note by **James Knowles** —signed The Editor.
2248 Why I shall vote for the Unionist candidate (No. II), 155–157. **S. H. Butcher.** Signed.
2249 Why I shall vote for the Unionist candidate (No. III), 157–159. **E. H. Carbutt.** Signed.
2250 Why I shall vote for the Unionist candidate (No. IV), 159–161. **H. N. Hamilton Hoare.** Signed.
2251 Why I shall vote for the Unionist candidate (No. V), 161–163. **John Glover.** Signed.
2252 Why I shall vote for the Unionist candidate (No. VI), 163–165. **Arthur Mursell.** Signed; Contents adds "Rev."
2253 Why I shall vote for the Unionist candidate (No. VII), 165–168. **W. H. Dallinger.** Signed.
2254 Why I shall vote for the Unionist candidate (No. VIII), 169–171. **G. J. Romanes.** Signed.
2255 Why I shall vote for the Unionist candidate (No. IX), 172–173. **Thomas W. Allies.** Signed.
2256 Why I shall vote for the Unionist candidate (No. X), 173–176. **Aubrey De Vere.** Signed.

VOLUME 32, AUGUST 1892

2257 Why I voted for Mr. Gladstone (No. I), 177–178. **T. H. Farrer.** Signed.
2258 Why I voted for Mr. Gladstone (No. II), 178–180. **J. Franck Bright.** Signed.
2259 Why I voted for Mr. Gladstone (No. III), 181–182. **William Markby.** Signed W. Markby; Contents gives "Sir William Markby."
2260 Why I voted for Mr. Gladstone (No. IV), 182–185. **Alfred R. Wallace.** Signed.
2261 Why I voted for Mr. Gladstone (No. V), 185–187. **Henry G. Hewlett.** Signed.

Contents gives "Mrs. Josceline Bagot"; see *WWW*/1940.

2308 Railways in native Indian states, 752–762. **Edward Dicey.** Signed.

2309 The art of cooking, 763–772. **Arthur Kenney-Herbert.** Signed as in no. 2266.

2310 The Inns of Court as schools of law, 773–790. **Montague Crackanthorpe.** Signed.

2311 A picture of the past, 791–803. **Eliza Lynn Linton.** Signature. (See no. 2321.)

2312 The morality of "vivisection" (No. I), 804–811. **Victor Horsley.** Signed.

2313 The morality of "vivisection" (No. II), 812–817. **M. Armand Ruffer.** Signed. (See no. 2327.)

2314 Michelangelo, 818–830. **Janet Ross.** Signed.

VOLUME 32, DECEMBER 1892

2315 Labour leaders on the labour question (No. I): the unemployed, 845–863. **John Burns.** Signed.

2316 Labour leaders (No. II): Mr. Chamberlain's programme, 864–874. **Thomas Burt.** Signed.

2317 Labour leaders (No. III): Mr. Chamberlain's programme, 875–882. **H. H. Champion.** Signed.

2318 Labour leaders (No. IV): Mr. Chamberlain's programme, 883–890. **J. Keir Hardie.** Signed.

2319 Labour leaders (No. V): Mr. Chamberlain's programme, 891–898. **Sam Woods.** Signed.

2320 Happiness in hell, 899–919. **St. George Mivart.** Signed. (See nos. 2338, 2355, 2459, 2496.)

2321 Walling the cuckoo [Mrs. Linton and women's rights], 920–929. **Herbert Maxwell.** Signed.

2322 Squandered girlhood, 930–937. **Edith Lyttelton Gell.** Signed.

2323 Railway mismanagement, 938–951. **W. M. Acworth.** Signed.

2324 Aspects of Tennyson (No. I), 952–966. **H. D. Traill.** Signed.

2325 £38,000,000 per annum! [agricultural imports for 1891], 967–974. **Jesse Collings.** Signed.

2326 A "candidates' protection society," 975–979. **J. A. Farrer.** Signed.

2327 The morality of vivisection: a reply [to nos. 2312, 2313], 980–983. **James Moorhouse.** Signed J. Manchester [Bishop of Manchester].

2328 "Spheres of influence" [occupation of Uganda], 984–990. **George Taubman-Goldie.** Signed.

2329 Alaska and its glaciers, 991–1001. **Henrietta Grey Egerton.** Signed.

2330 Recent science, 1002–1020. **Peter A. Kropotkin.** Signed as in no. 1110.

2331 Our national art museums and galleries, 1021–1034. **John Charles Robinson.** Signed as in no. 455.

VOLUME 33, JANUARY 1893

2332 Signs of the times (No. I): false democracy, 4–18. **W. S. Lilly.** Signed.

2333 Signs of the times (No. II): sham education, 19–35. **J. P. Mahaffy.** Signed.

2334 Signs of the times (No. III): trained workers for the poor, 36–43. **Octavia Hill.** Signed.

2335 Irving's *King Lear*: a new tradition, 44–51. **Edward R. Russell.** Signed.

2336 Three weeks in Samoa (Part I): the rival monarchs—a night in the rebel camp, 52–64. **Margaret E. Child-Villiers.** Signed M. E. Jersey [Countess of Jersey].

2337 *Architecture: A Profession or an Art?* 65–82. **Edmund Beckett.** Signed Grimthorpe [1st Baron Grimthorpe]. (See nos. 2361 and 2380.)

2338 Happiness in hell: a reply [to no. 2320], 83–92. **Richard F. Clarke.** Signed R. F. Clarke; Contents adds "Rev. Father"; see Boase.

2339 Modern poets and the meaning of life, 93–111. **Frederic W. H. Myers.** Signed; repr. *Future Life*.

2340 Urmi—a poisoned queen: a true story, 112–115. **Cornelia Sorabji.** Signed.

2341 The silver question and India, 116–126. **George Tomkyns Chesney.** Signed G. Chesney; Contents gives "General Sir George Chesney."

2342 A reformation of domestic service, 127–138. **Elizabeth Alicia M. Lewis.** Signed. (See nos. 2354, 2365.)

2343 The priest in politics, 139–155. **Michael Davitt.** Signed.

2344 Où allons-nous? 156–163. **Yves Guyot.** Signed.

2345 Aspects of Tennyson (No. II): a personal reminiscence, 164–188. **James Knowles.** Signed.

VOLUME 33, FEBRUARY 1893

2346 "Passing the wit of man" [Gladstone on Irish affairs], 189–202. **Henry L. Jephson.** Signed as in no. 1144.

2347 An experiment in federation and its lessons, 203–218. **Robert Stout.** Signed.

2348 Shall Uganda be retained? 219–234. **J. Guinness Rogers.** Signed.

2349 What is "fashion"? 235–248. **Ada Heather-Bigg.** Signed, but without the hyphen; cf. no. 2136.

2350 Three weeks in Samoa (Part II, concl.): natives and missionaries, 249–260. **Margaret E. Child-Villiers.** Signed M. E. Jersey [Countess of Jersey].

2351 Medical women in fiction, 261–272. **Sophia Jex-Blake.** Signed.

2352 Aspects of Tennyson (No. III): the real Thomas Becket, 273–292. **Agnes Lambert.** Signed.

2353 The taxation of ground-rents, 293–308. **J. Powell Williams.** Signed.

2354 The doom of the domestic cook, 309–319. **George Somes Layard.** Signed.

2355 Happiness in hell (Part I): a rejoinder [to no. 2338], 320–338. **St. George Mivart.** Signed. (Part II is no. 2382.)

2356 Commercial unity with the colonies, 339–346. **Augustus Loftus.** Signed.

2357 The revival of witchcraft, 347–368. **Ernest Hart.** Signed.

VOLUME 33, MARCH 1893

2358 The Home Rule Bill, 369–374. **Justin McCarthy,** 1830–1912. Signed.

2359 The financial causes of the French Revolution (Part I), 375–390. **Ferdinand Rothschild.** Signed.

2360 Inaccessible valleys: a study in physical geography, 391–404. **Alfred R. Wallace.** Signed; repr. *Studies,* I.

2361 Architecture: a profession or an art, 405–415. **T. G. Jackson.** Signed.

2362 The inner history of the Waterloo campaign, 416–429. **Archibald Forbes.** Signed; repr. *Camps.*

2363 A contemporary letter on the battle of Waterloo, 430–435. **Felton Hervey.** Intro. note by **Fanny G. Osborne**—signed Fanny G. Leeds [Duchess of Leeds].

2364 Aspects of Tennyson (No. IV): the classical poems, 436–453. **Herbert Paul.** Signed.

2365 The dislike to domestic service, 454–456. **Clementina Black.** Signed.

2366 Jewish wit and humour, 457–469. **Hermann Adler.** Signed.

2367 Hansoms and their drivers, 470–479. **W. H. Wilkins.** Signed.

2368 The decrease of crime, 480–492. **E. F. Du Cane.** Signed. Contents gives "Sir Edmund F. Du Cane."

2369 A Britisher's impressions of America and Australasia, 493–514. **Reginald Brabazon.** Signed Meath [12th Earl of Meath]. (See no. 2443.)

2370 The rupee and the ruin of India, 515–524. **Syed Ameer Ali.** Signed as in no. 454.

2371 Alfred de Musset, 525–540. **Leopold Katscher.** Signed.

2372 Enlargement of the House of Commons, 541–544. **Charles Barry.** Signed.

VOLUME 33, APRIL 1893

2373 A bill for the weakening of Great Britain [Home Rule Bill], 545–558. **Joseph Chamberlain.** Signed as in no. 1964.

2374 Second thoughts on the Home Rule Bill, 559–570. **J. E. Redmond.** Signed.

2375 Lord Cromer and the Khedive [Abbās], 571–585. **Wilfrid Scawen Blunt.** Signed; *Academy,* Apr. 1, 1893, p. 284, claims that this is an authoritative statement, made through Mr. Blunt, of the Khedive's own view of the quarrel which he wanted to put before the British public; cf. opening paragraph.

2376 The lives and loves of North American birds, 586–605. **John Worth.** Signed.

2377 The Behring Sea question, 606–610. **Michael Culme-Seymour.** Signed M. Culme-Seymour; Contents gives first name and adds "Vice-Admiral Sir."

2378 The art of breathing, 611–618. **A. W. Drayson.** Signed.

2379 Bimetallism once more, 619–630. **Leonard Courtney.** Signed.

2380 "Architecture: an art or nothing," 631–634. **Edmund Beckett.** Signed Grimthorpe [1st Baron Grimthorpe].

2381 Cardinal Newman on the eternity of punishment, 635–636. **Henry W. Probyn-Nevins** and **John H. Newman.** Signed W. Probyn-Nevins (see Boase); Probyn-Nevins wrote the commentary on a letter signed John H. Newman.

2382 Last words on the happiness in hell (Part II, concl.), 637–651. **St. George Mivart.** Signed. (See no. 2459.)

2383 The financial causes of the French Revolution (Part II, concl.), 652–670. **Ferdinand Rothschild.** Signed.

2384 Recent science, 671–689. **Peter A. Kropotkin.** Signed as in no. 1110.

2385 The reading of the working classes, 690–701. **George R. Humphery.** Signed.

2386 The Lion King of Sweden, 1710–13 [Charles VII], 702–724. **Oscar Fredrik.** Signed; Contents as in no. 1671.

VOLUME 33, MAY 1893

2387 The invasion of India by Russia, 727–748. **G. J. Younghusband.** Signed.
2388 St. William of Norwich, 749–766. **Augustus Jessopp.** Signed; repr. *Peasantry.*
2389 Esoteric Buddhism, 767–788. **Friedrich Max Müller.** Signature; repr. *Last Essays.* (See nos. 2414, 2444.)
2390 My maverick [a story of western United States], 789–795. **R. B. Townshend.** Signed.
2391 The Agram mummy, 796–802. **M. L. McClure.** Signed; Contents gives "Mrs."
2392 *Falstaff* and the new Italian opera, 803–812. **J. A. Fuller Maitland.** Signed.
2393 A walk in Alexandria, 813–829. **Alfred E. P. Raymund Dowling.** Signed.
2394 The Hawaiian revolution, 830–835. **Theophilus H. Davies.** Signed Theo. H. Davies; see *LCCat.*
2395 Aspects of Tennyson (No. V): Tennyson as a nature-poet, 836–856. **Theodore Watts.** Signed.
2396 An imperial university for women, 857–861. **G. F. Browne.** Signed.
2397 The influence of climate on race, 862–873. **J. W. Fortescue.** Signed.
2398 Cavour on the repeal of the union [of England and Ireland], 874–882. **Mary Wood.** Signed; Contents adds "Lady."
2399 Noticeable books (No. I): Tocqueville's *Souvenirs*, 883–886. **J. D. Acton.** Signed Acton [1st Baron Acton].
2400 Noticeable books (No. II): *The Naturalist in La Plata* [by W. H. Hudson], 886–889. **George John Romanes.** Signed.
2401 Noticeable books (No. III): *Lena's Picture*, 889–892. **M. E. Grant Duff.** Signed.
2402 Noticeable books (No. IV): *National Life and Character*, 892–896. **A. C. Lyall.** Signed.
2403 Noticeable books (No. V): *Journal des Prisons de Mon Père, de Ma Mère et des Miennes*, 896–899. **R. E. Prothero.** Signed.
2404 Noticeable books (No. VI): the poetry of Lord de Tabley, 899–904. **Richard Le Gallienne.** Signed.

VOLUME 33, JUNE 1893

2405 The Gospel of Peter (Part I), 905–926. **James Martineau.** Signed.
2406 Ulster and the Confederate states, 927–931. **Camille de Polignac.** Signed C. de Polignac; Contents adds first name and title "Prince."
2407 Six hundred years of English poverty: a study in the fluctuations of the purchasing power of wages, 932–951. **Gustav F. Steffen.** Signed.
2408 Rare books and their prices, 952–965. **William Roberts**, 1862–1940. Signed W. Roberts, with addition "Editor of *The Bookworm*": see *WWW.*
2409 An impossible correspondence—1892 [satire of an editor's rejections of poems], 966–969. **R. F. Murray.** Signed.
2410 The Rothamsted experiments [in fertilizing crops], 970–980. **Caroline Creyke.** Signed; Contents adds "Mrs."
2411 The Poldi-Pezzoli collection at Milan, 981–993. **Charles L. Eastlake,** 1836–1906. Signed.
2412 Post office "plundering and blundering," 994–1008. **J. Henniker Heaton.** Signed.
2413 Habitual drunkards, 1009–1014. **John Batty Tuke.** Signed.
2414 Esoteric Buddhism: a reply to Professor Max Müller, 1015–1027. **A. P. Sinnett.** Signed.
2415 How to attract capital to the land, 1028–1037. **G. W. H. Venables-Vernon.** Signed Vernon [7th Baron Vernon].
2416 A naturalist's view of the fur-seal question, 1038–1045. **P. L. Sclater.** Signed.
2417 The craving for fiction, 1046–1061. **Herbert Maxwell.** Signed; repr. *Post Meridiana.*
2418 Protection and the Empire, 1062–1074. **Walter Frewen Lord.** Signed.

VOLUME 34, JULY 1893

2419 The "arts and crafts" exhibition at Westminster [the Home Rule question], 1–9. **Edward Dicey.** Signed.
2420 The ninth clause [of the Home Rule Bill], 10–21. **Robert Wallace,** 1831–1899. Signed R. Wallace; Contents adds "Dr."; see *DNB*, 1st suppl.
2421 The new South Sea bubble, 22–33. **J. W. Fortescue.** Signed.
2422 The Siamese boundary question, 34–55. **George N. Curzon.** Signed.
2423 "Robbing God," 56–64. **Augustus Jessopp.** Signed; repr. *Great Pillage.*
2424 Charles Baudelaire and Edgar Poe: a literary affinity, 65–80. **Amélie Claire Leroy.** Signed Esmè Stuart; see *LCCat.*
2425 The Pan-Britannic gathering, 81–93. **J. Astley Cooper.** Signed.

2426 Some day dreams and realities [unity among Christian churches], 94–100. **Harry Jones,** 1823–1900. Signed; see Venn.

2427 How to catalogue books, 101–109. **J. Taylor Kay.** Signed.

2428 Cookery as a business, 110–120. **Mary Harrison.** Signed.

2429 Great Britain as a sea-power, 121–130. **T. A. Brassey.** Signed.

2430 The situation at Washington, 131–144. **Goldwin Smith.** Signed.

2431 Mediaeval medicine, 145–151. **E. Augusta King.** Signed E. A. King; see *LCCat.*

2432 The Apostles' Creed (No. I): a translation and introduction, 152–158. **Mary A. Ward.** Signed.

2433 The Apostles' Creed (No. II): historically examined, 158–176. **Adolf Harnack.** Signed.

VOLUME 34, AUGUST 1893

2434 India between two fires, 177–186. **George N. Curzon.** Signed.

2435 The crisis in Indo-China, 187–197. **Demetrius C. Boulger.** Signed.

2436 Evolution in Professor Huxley, 198–211. **St. George Mivart.** Signed.

2437 The future of education, 212–229. **J. P. Mahaffy.** Signed.

2438 "My stay in the highlands," 230–247. **Catherine Milnes Gaskell.** Signed.

2439 Recent science, 248–266. **Peter A. Kropotkin.** Signed as in no. 1110.

2440 Public playgrounds for children, 267–271. **Reginald Brabazon.** Signed Meath [12th Earl of Meath]; repr. *Thoughts.*

2441 The Abbé Grégoire and the French Revolution, 272–283. **William Gibson.** Signed; see *WWW/1950* under Baron Ashbourne.

2442 The poetry of D. G. Rossetti, 284–290. **W. Basil Worsfold.** Signed.

2443 An open letter to Lord Meath, 291–295. **O. P. Fitzgerald.** Signed.

2444 Esoteric Buddhism: a rejoinder [to no. 2414], 296–303. **Friedrich Max Müller.** Signature; repr. *Last Essays.*

2445 The art of household management, 304–313. **Arthur Kenney-Herbert.** Signed as in no. 2226.

2446 An incident in the career of the Rev. Luke Tremain, 314–328. **Augustus Jessopp.** Signed; repr. *Peasantry.*

2447 "How long, O Lord, how long?" [women's working conditions], 329–336. **W. H. Wilkins.** Signed.

VOLUME 34, SEPTEMBER 1893

2448 Weariness, 337–352. **Michael Foster.** Signed.

2449 "Protestant science" and Christian belief, 353–368. **W. J. Knox Little.** Signed.

2450 The transformation of Japan (Part I): feudal times, 369–383. **Margaret E. Child-Villiers.** Signed M. E. Jersey [Countess of Jersey].

2451 Father Archangel of Scotland, 384–398. **R. B. Cunninghame Graham.** Signed. (See no. 2481.)

2452 The conduct of friendship, 399–415. **Herbert Maxwell.** Signed; repr. *Post Meridiana.*

2453 "La jeune Belgique" [young Belgian writers], 416–436. **William Sharp.** Signed; repr. *Writings,* II.

2454 The Malay Peninsula, 437–451. **Alfred Keyser.** Signed.

2455 A new stage doctrine, 452–457. **Hamilton Aïdé.** Signed.

2456 A question of taste [aesthetic theories], 458–469. **E. F. Benson.** Signed.

2457 Poaching, 470–475. **L'Aigle Cole.** Signed.

2458 American life through English spectacles, 476–488. **A. S. Northcote.** Signed.

2459 The verdict of Rome on "the happiness in hell," 489–500. **Richard F. Clarke.** Signed as in no. 2338. (See nos. 2320, 2382.)

VOLUME 34, OCTOBER 1893

2460 A cabinet minister's vade-mecum [politicians' tactics], 504–522. **Auberon Herbert.** Signed.

2461 "Setting the poor on work," 523–532. **James Mavor.** Signed.

2462 Through the Khyber Pass, 533–542. **Spenser Wilkinson.** Signed; repr. *War and Policy,* 1900.

2463 Dr. Pearson on the modern drama, 543–550. **Henry Arthur Jones.** Signed; repr. *Renascence.*

2464 The position of geology, 551–559. **Joseph Prestwich.** Signed; repr. *Collected Papers on Controversial Questions of Geology,* 1895.

2465 The archaic statues of the Acropolis museum, 560–569. **Reginald Lister.** Signed.

2466 The transformation of Japan (Part II, concl.): the era of Meiji "enlightened government," 570–583. **Margaret E. Child-Villiers.** Signed M. E. Jersey [Countess of Jersey].

2510 The new winter-land [French North Africa], 99–114. **William Sharp.** Signed.

2511 Chinese poetry in English verse, 115–125. **Herbert A. Giles.** Signed.

2512 Chartered government in Africa, 126–131. **Arthur Silva White.** Signed.

2513 Protection for surnames, 132–140. **Douglas M. B. H. Cochrane.** Signed Dundonald [12th Earl of Dundonald].

2514 Recent science, 141–157. **Peter A. Kropotkin.** Signed as in no. 1110. (See no. 2535.)

2515 Charles the Twelfth and the campaign of 1712–13, 158–176. **Oscar Frederik.** Signed; Contents as in no. 1671.

VOLUME 35, FEBRUARY 1894

2516 The Khedive [Abbās] and Lord Cromer, 177–188. **Wilfrid Scawen Blunt.** Signed; on p. 177 Blunt claims "the same high sources" he had used in writing no. 2375, which would include Abbās himself.

2517 The position of the Liberal party, 189–202. **J. Guinness Rogers.** Signed.

2518 The political future of "Labour," 203–216. **T. R. Threlfall.** Signed, with addition "Secretary to Labour Electoral Association of Great Britain and Ireland."

2519 Noticeable books (No. I): *Arthur Stanley*, 220–226. **Goldwin Smith.** Signed.

2520 Noticeable books (No. II): *William George Ward and the Catholic Revival*, 226–229. **R. H. Hutton.** Signed.

2521 Noticeable books (No. III): Mr. [Francis] Thompson's poems, 229–233. **H. D. Traill.** Signed.

2522 Noticeable books (No. IV): Griffiths' *Secrets of the Prison House*, 234–236. **W. S. Lilly.** Signed.

2523 Noticeable books (No. V): "Edition de luxe" of *Alexander Dumas*, 237–240. **Theodore Watts.** Signed.

2524 Noticeable books (No. VI): Launcelot and Guenevere, 240–244. **Hamilton Aïdé.** Signed.

2525 Noticeable books (No. VII): Mr. Weyman's *Gentleman of France*, 244–247. **Rowland E. Prothero.** Signed.

2526 The Queen and her second prime minister [Sir Robert Peel], 248–258. **Reginald B. Brett.** Signed.

2527 Old Wenlock and its folklore, 259–267. **Catherine Milnes Gaskell.** Signed.

2528 New Zealand under female franchise, 268–275. **R. H. Bakewell.** Signed.

2529 Feeble-minded children, 276–283. **Douglas Galton.** Signed.

2530 Bores, 284–301. **Herbert Maxwell.** Signed; repr. *Post Meridiana*.

2531 Mohammedanism and Christianity, 302–312. **Friedrich Max Müller.** Signature; repr. *Last Essays*.

2532 Mothers and daughters, 313–322. **Ethel B. Harrison.** Signed E. B. Harrison; Contents gives "Mrs. Frederic Harrison."

2533 A letter to the Opium Commission, 323–329. **G. W. Des Voeux.** Signed; Contents gives "Sir William Des Voeux."

2534 Italian art at the new gallery, 330–336. **Charles Whibley.** Signed.

2535 The glacial theory, 337–342. **G. D. Campbell.** Signed Argyll [8th Duke of Argyll].

2536 Prospects of free trade in the United States, 343–352. **Chauncey M. Depew.** Signed.

VOLUME 35, MARCH 1894

2537 The impeding revolution: political England revisited, 353–366. **Goldwin Smith.** Signed.

2538 The Chamberlain coalition programme, 367–378. **Edward Dicey.** Signed.

2539 Western nations and Eastern markets, 379–396. **Holt S. Hallett.** Signed.

2540 Devil-hunting in Elizabethan England, 397–411. **T. G. Law.** Signed; repr. *Essays.*

2541 Elementary education and the decay of literature, 412–423. **Joseph Ackland.** Signed.

2542 The revolt of the daughters (No. I): a last word on "the revolt," 424–429. **Blanche A. Crackanthorpe.** Signed as in no. 2503.

2543 The revolt of the daughters (No. II): daughters and mothers, 430–436. **Mary E. Haweis.** Signed M. E. Haweis; Contents adds "Mrs."; see *DNB*, 2nd suppl. under Hugh R. Haweis.

2544 A reply from the daughters (No. I), 437–442. **Kathleen Cuffe.** Signed; Contents adds "Lady."

2545 A reply from the daughters (No. II), 443–450. **Alys W. Pearsall Smith Russell.** Signed.

2546 The Shah of Persia in England, 451–458. **Arminius Vambéry.** Signed as in no. 451.

2547 The mystery of Monsieur Regnier, 459–469. **Archibald Forbes.** Signed; repr. *Camps.*

2548 Improvement of Irish hunters, 470–480. **Frederick Wrench.** Signed.

2549 Some great churches of France (Part

I): Notre Dame d'Amiens, 481–488. **Walter Pater.** Signed; repr. *Studies.*

2550   Women as official inspectors, 489–494. **Louisa Twining.** Signed.

2551   In the mountains of Egypt, 495–512. **E. N. Buxton.** Signed.

2552   The lotos eaters [the opium trade], 513–522. **Lepel Griffin.** Signed.

VOLUME 35, APRIL 1894

2553   The House of Lords (No. I): an unfair penalty on peers, 525–537. **William St. John Brodrick, George N. Curzon,** and **William W. Palmer.** Signed St. John Brodrick, George N. Curzon, and Wolmer [Lord Wolmer]. With a bill allowing peers to sit in the House of Commons, 538.

2554   The House of Lords (No. II): reform by "resolution," 539–546. **Goldwin Smith.** Signed.

2555   The House of Lords (No. III): a dangerous anachronism, 547–552. **Thomas Burt.** Signed.

2556   The House of Lords (No. IV): abolish its veto, 553–559. **T. Wemyss Reid.** Signed.

2557   The evicted tenants problem, 560–573. **Michael Davitt.** Signed. (See no. 2600.)

2558   A neglected sense [smell], 574–587. **Edward Dillon.** Signed.

2559   Simon Ryan the Peterite (Part I), 588–601. **Augustus Jessopp.** Signed; repr. under same title, N.Y., 1896.

2560   The insignificance of the trades union vote, 602–617. **Frederick Wicks.** Signed.

2561   Realism of to-day, 618–627. **Katie Cowper.** Signed; Contents gives "Countess Cowper."

2562   Early social self-government, 628–638. **John Simon,** 1816–1904. Signed, with addition "K.C.B."; see *DNB*, 2nd suppl.

2563   The Queen and her "permanent minister" [Lord Palmerston], 639–648. **Reginald B. Brett.** Signed.

2564   Frau Aja [Goethe's mother], 649–659. **H. Schütz Wilson.** Signed.

2565   Professor Sayce on "The Higher Criticism," 660–666. **T. K. Cheyne.** Signed.

2566   The cow agitation; or, the mutiny-plasm in India, 667–672. **Oday Pertap Singh.** Signed; Contents adds "C.S.I. (Rajah of Bhinga)."

2567   Recent science, 673–691. **Peter A. Kropotkin.** Signed as in no. 1110.

2568   The utter corruption in American politics, 692–700. **Amyas Stafford Northcote.** Signed.

VOLUME 35, MAY 1894

2569   Shall Indian Princes sit in the House of Lords? 710–716. **Reginald Brabazon.** Signed Meath [12th Earl of Meath]; repr. *Thoughts.*

2570   Democratic ideals, 717–728. **William Francis Barry.** Signed as in no. 1742.

2571   Intellectual progress in the United States, 729–745. **George F. Parker.** Signed.

2572   Simon Ryan the Peterite (Part II, concl.), 746–760. **Augustus Jessopp.** Signed.

2573   Aspects of Tennyson (No. VII): as a humorist, 761–774. **H. D. Traill.** Signed.

2574   Modern surgery, 775–795. **Hugh Percy Dunn.** Signed.

2575   The English libro d'oro [of real nobility], 796–806. **J. H. Round.** Signed.

2576   The profits of coal-pits, 807–812. **G. P. Bidder,** 1836–1896. Signed; attr. in I.C.E. *Minutes*, 125 (1896), 427.

2577   Life in a Russian village, 813–827. **J. D. Rees.** Signed.

2578   The new and the old art criticism, 828–837. **Mary Whitall Costelloe.** Signed; Contents adds "Mrs."

2579   Sunshine and microbes, 838–844. **Percy Frankland.** Signed.

2580   Recent archaeology, 845–862. **J. P. Mahaffy.** Signed.

2581   Nile reservoirs and Philae, 863–872. **Benjamin Baker.** Signed.

VOLUME 35, JUNE 1894

2582   Checks on democracy in America, 873–889. **George Washburn Smalley.** Signed.

2583   India—the political outlook, 890–904. **George Tomkyns Chesney.** Signed as in no. 2341.

2584   Art at the salons, 905–911. **Charles Whibley.** Signed.

2585   The Queen and Lord Palmerston, 912–921. **Reginald B. Brett.** Signed.

2586   Pedigrees of British and American horses, 922–937. **James Irvine Lupton.** Signed.

2587   Noticeable books (No. I): *Life of Bishop Wilberforce*, 938–942. **Francis T.**

de Grey Cowper. Signed Cowper [7th Earl Cowper].

2588 Noticeable books (No. II): African Spir, 1837–1890, 942–945. **Friedrich Max Müller.** Signature.

2589 Noticeable books (No. III): *Ten Years of Armed Peace Between France and England* (1783–1793), 946–948. **A. C. Lyall.** Signed.

2590 Noticeable books (No. IV): *Witnesses to the Unseen* [by Wilfrid Ward], 948–951. **W. S. Lilly.** Signed.

2591 Noticeable books (No. V): Mr. John Davidson's poetry, 952–955. **Richard Le Gallienne.** Signed.

2592 Noticeable books (No. VI): *The History of Trade Unionism* [by Sidney and Beatrice Webb], 956–958. **Frederic Harrison.** Signed.

2593 Noticeable books (No. VII): *A Study in Colour*, 959–962. **James Knowles.** Signed.

2594 Some great churches of France (No. II, concl.): Vézelay, 963–970. **Walter Pater.** Signed; repr. *Studies*.

2595 A recent run to the East, 971–986. **Thomas Brassey.** Signed Brassey [1st Earl Brassey]; repr. *Voyages*, II.

2596 Modern explosives, 987–998. **Wentworth Lascelles-Scott.** Signed.

2597 Love, 999–1012. **Herbert Maxwell.** Signed.

2598 The proposed Nile reservoir (No. I): the devastation of Nubia, 1013–1018. **J. P. Mahaffy.** Signed.

2599 The proposed Nile reservoir (No. II): the submergence of Philae, 1019–1025. **Frank Dillon.** Signed.

2600 The Evicted Tenants Bill, 1026–1032. **Thomas Spring-Rice,** 1849–1926. Signed Monteagle [2nd Baron Monteagle].

2601 The crying need for reforms in our Company Law, 1033–1050. **Alfred Emden.** Signed.

VOLUME 36, JULY 1894

2602 The failure of the Labour Commission, 2–22. **Beatrice Webb.** Signed. (See no. 2638.)

2603 The partition of Africa, 23–37. **A. Silva White.** Signed.

2604 Delusions about tropical cultivation, 38–54. **G. William Des Voeux.** Signed.

2605 Religion in primary schools, 55–70. **J. G. Fitch.** Signed. (See no. 2665.)

2606 A night in India, 71–78. **Mary S. C.**

Logan. Signed S. C. Logan; Contents adds "Mrs."; see *LCCat.*

2607 The "Virgin of the Rocks" [by Leonardo da Vinci], 79–86. **Frederic W. Burton.** Signed.

2608 Competitive examinations in China, 87–99. **Thomas Lowndes Bullock.** Signed T. L. Bullock; see *WWW/1916.*

2609 Proposed overthrow of the Church in Wales, 100–110. **Lewis T. Dibdin.** Signed.

2610 The art of dying, 111–125. **Ida A. Taylor.** Signed I. A. Taylor; Contents adds "Miss"; see *LCCat.*

2611 College discipline, 126–136. **L. A. Selby-Bigge.** Signed.

2612 A land of incredible barbarity [Morocco], 137–145. **Reginald Brabazon.** Signed Meath [12th Earl of Meath].

2613 The centenary of Edward Gibbon, 146–156. **Frederic Harrison.** Signed.

VOLUME 36, AUGUST 1894

2614 The place of heresy and schism in the modern Christian church, 157–174. **W. E. Gladstone.** Signed. (Letter, p. 664, signed W. E. Gladstone; see no. 2629.)

2615 The Italian case against France, 175–182. **W. L. Alden.** Signed.

2616 Mutual aid in the mediaeval city (Part I), 183–202. **Peter A. Kropotkin.** Signed as in no. 1110; repr. *Mutual Aid.*

2617 The farce of "university extension" (No. I), 203–210. **Charles Whibley.** Signed. (See nos. 2632, 2633, 2648.)

2618 Behind the scenes of nature, 211–221. **A. P. Sinnett.** Signed.

2619 A part of a ghost: a mystery, 222–229. **William Howard Russell.** Signed W. H. Russell; Contents adds "Dr."; see *DNB*, 2nd suppl.

2620 The war-chests of Europe, 230–243. **Heinrich Geffcken.** Signed.

2621 In the Tarumensian woods, 244–252. **R. B. Cunninghame Graham.** Signed.

2622 Death and two friends: a dialogue, 253–258. **Richard Le Gallienne.** Signed.

2623 The labour war in the United States, 259–267. **J. S. Jeans.** Signed.

2624 The present position of Egyptology, 268–278. **J. P. Mahaffy.** Signed.

2625 Facts from Bihar about the mud-daubing, 279–285. **William Egerton.** Signed W. Egerton, Bengal Civil Service; see *Army List/93*, p. 900.

2626 Some pictures and their prices, 286–300. **William Roberts,** 1862–1940. Signed W. Roberts; see *WWW.*

2627　Is our race degenerating? 301–314. **Hugh Percy Dunn.** Signed.

VOLUME 36, SEPTEMBER 1894

2628　True and false conceptions of the Atonement [as understood by Annie Besant], 317–331. **W. E. Gladstone.** Signed. (See no. 2769.)

2629　Heresy and schism from another point of view [contra. no. 2614], 332–340. **G. Vance Smith.** Signed.

2630　Our warning from the naval manoeuvres, 341–355. **William Laird Clowes.** Signed.

2631　"Known to the police," 356–370. **Edmund R. Spearman.** Signed.

2632　The facts about university extension (No. I), 371–382. **M. E. Sadler.** Signed.

2633　The facts about university extension (No. II), 383–388. **Laura E. Stuart.** Signed.

2634　Smoke [smoking by women], 389–396. **Ethel B. Harrison.** Signed in text; Contents as in no. 2532.

2635　Mutual aid in the mediaeval city (Part II, concl.), 397–418. **Peter A. Kropotkin.** Signed as in no. 1110.

2636　The Hadramut: a journey in southern Arabia, 419–437. **J. Theodore Bent.** Signed.

2637　The gold question: an appeal to mono-metallists, 438–451. **J. P. Heseltine.** Signed. (See no. 2661.)

2638　Mrs. Sidney Webb's attack on the Labour Commission, 452–467. **Geoffrey Drage.** Signed.

2639　The parish priest in England before the Reformation, 468–488. **Augustus Jessopp.** Signed; repr. *Great Pillage*.

VOLUME 36, OCTOBER 1894

2640　The seven Lord Roseberies, 489–506. **St. Loe Strachey.** Signed.

2641　Wagner at Bayreuth, 507–514. **Mary A. A. Stewart.** Signed M. A. A. Galloway [Countess of Galloway].

2462　The alleged sojourn of Christ in India, 515–521. **Friedrich Max Müller.** Signature; repr. *Last Essays*. With a letter on Buddist monasteries, 521–522, from an English lady in India. (See no. 2919.)

2643　English art connoisseurship and collecting, 523–537. **John Charles Robinson.** Signed as in no. 455.

2644　Cholera and the Sultan, 538–554. **Ernest Hart.** Signed.

2645　Did Omar destroy the Alexandrian library? 555–571. **R. Vasudeva Rau.** Signed.

2646　A dialogue on dress, 572–582. **Theodosia Chapman.** Signed as in no. 1264.

2647　A Scottish vendetta, 583–597. **Herbert Maxwell.** Signed.

2648　The farce of university extension (No. II), 598–603. **Charles Whibley.** Signed.

2649　A suggestion to Sabbath-keepers, 604–611. **Alfred R. Wallace.** Signed; repr. *Studies*, II, as "A Counsel of Perfection for Sabbatarians."

2650　The Chinaman abroad, 612–620. **Edmund Mitchell.** Signed.

2651　A trip to Bosnia-Herzegovina, 621–644. **H. G. A. Opper de Blowitz.** Signed Blowitz; Contents gives "Mons. de Blowitz"; see *WWW/*1916.

2652　The perilous growth of Indian state expenditure, 645–663. **Auckland Colvin.** Signed.

VOLUME 36, NOVEMBER 1894

2653　What has become of Home Rule? 665–677. **J. E. Redmond.** Signed.

2654　England and the coming thunderstorm: a German view [of English foreign policy], 678–689. **Felix Boh.** Signed.

2655　Christian Socialism, 690–707. **G. D. Campbell.** Signed Argyll [8th Duke of Argyll].

2656　The parliaments of the world, 708–715. **J. Taylor Kay.** Signed.

2657　The press in Turkey, 716–726. **H. Anthony Salmoné.** Signed.

2658　Babies and monkies, 727–743. **S. S. Buckman.** Signed.

2659　The people's kitchens in Vienna, 744–753. **Edith Sellers.** Signed.

2660　More light on Antonio Perez, 754–769. **Martin A. S. Hume.** Signed.

2661　The Monometallist creed: a reply to a challenge [in no. 2637], 770–780. **Henry Dunning MacLeod.** Signed.

2662　The Corean crux: a word for China, 781–789. **Demetrius C. Boulger.** Signed.

2663　Nonconformist forebodings [about government policy], 790–806. **J. Guinness Rogers.** Signed.

2664　Fruit ranching, 807–816. **A. C. Twist.** Signed, with address "El Toro, California."

2665　The Bible in elementary schools, 817–823. **J. G. Fitch.** Signed.

2666　"Justice to England": a rallying cry, 824–836. **Edward Dicey.** Signed.

VOLUME 36, DECEMBER 1894

2667 Lord Rosebery's enterprise against the House of Lords, 837–845. **L. A. Atherley-Jones.** Signed L. A. Atherley Jones.

2668 If the House of Commons were abolished? 846–863. **Sidney Low.** Signed.

2669 About that skeleton [modern drama], 864–874. **H. D. Traill.** Signed.

2670 Criminal and prison reform, 875–889. **Michael Davitt.** Signed.

2671 Why I am not an agnostic, 890–895. **Friedrich Max Müller.** Signature; repr. *Last Essays.*

2672 The estate duty and the road round it, 896–899. **Andrew H. Hastie.** Signed A. H. Hastie; see *BMCat.*

2673 The music of Japan, 900–918. **Laura Alexandrine Smith.** Signed.

2674 New sources of electric power (No. I): electric energy direct from the coalfields, 919–926. **B. H. Thwaite.** Signed.

2675 New sources of electric power (No. II): electricity from peat, 927–931. **John Munro.** Signed J. Munro; see *WWW/1940.*

2676 The decay of bookselling, 932–938. **David Stott.** Signed.

2677 Wanted, an imperial conference, 939–946. **John C. R. Colomb.** Signed.

2678 How to multiply small holdings, 947–958. **Harold E. Moore.** Signed. Intro. note, 947–948, by **C. R. Wynn-Carrington**—signed Carrington [3rd Baron Carrington].

2679 Lord Bacon versus Professor Huxley, 959–969. **G. D. Campbell.** Signed Argyll [8th Duke of Argyll].

2680 The cry against home work, 970–986. **Ada Heather-Bigg.** Signed.

2681 Recent science, 987–1007. **Peter A. Kropotkin.** Signed as in no. 1110.

VOLUME 37, JANUARY 1895

2682 The Independent Labour party, 1–14. **J. Keir Hardie.** Signed.

2683 The collectivist prospect in England, 15–31. **William Graham.** Signed.

2684 The Queen and Lord Beaconsfield, 32–44. **Reginald B. Brett.** Signed.

2685 Birds and their persecutors, 45–56. **Marie L. de la Ramée.** Signed Ouida; see *DNB,* 2nd suppl.

2686 Women under Islam: their social status and legal rights, 57–70. **Lucy M. J. Garnett.** Signed.

2687 Auricular confession and the English

Church, 71–85. **T. Teignmouth Shore.** Signed. (See no. 2704.)

2688 The paintings at Pompeii, 86–94. **H. A. Kennedy.** Signed.

2689 Defoe's *Apparition of Mrs. Veal,* 95–100. **George A. Aitken.** Signed. (Letters, pp. 271–273, by R. S. Cleaver and Walter Scott.)

2690 Night travelling in India, 101–111. **Mary S. C. Logan.** Signed as in no. 2606.

2691 St. Martin of Tours, 112–130. **Augustus Jessopp.** Signed; repr. *Peasantry.*

2692 The political situation, 131–137. **Wemyss Reid.** Signed.

2693 Stony Sinai, 138–155. **E. N. Buxton.** Signed.

2694 The triumph of Japan, 156–164. **Robert K. Douglas.** Signed.

2695 Francesco Crispi: an appreciation, 165–176. **W. L. Alden.** Signed.

VOLUME 37, FEBRUARY 1895

2696 Single chamber "Democrats," 177–194. **Robert Wallace,** 1831–1899. Signed R. Wallace; attr. in *Life,* p. 487.

2697 How to "mend" the House of Lords, 195–205. **Reginald Brabazon.** Signed Meath [12th Earl of Meath]; repr. *Thoughts.*

2698 Infringing a political patent, 206–214. **St. Loe Strachey.** Signed.

2699 Should we hold onto the Mediterranean in war? 215–225. **Henry Elsdale.** Signed H. Elsdale; Contents gives "Lieut.-Col."; see *LCCat.*

2700 *Social Evolution* [reply to criticisms], 226–240. **Benjamin Kidd.** Signed.

2701 Delphi, 241–257. **Reginald Lister.** Signed.

2702 Ghost-stories and beast-stories, 258–270. **Andrew Lang.** Signed.

2703 Is bimetallism a delusion? 274–280. **Edward Tuck.** Signed.

2704 Auricular confession and the Church of England, 281–289. **T. T. Carter.** Signed. (See no. 2720.)

2705 Language versus literature at Oxford, 290–303. **J. Churton Collins.** Signed.

2706 The Crown's "right of reply," 304–312. **Alfred Cock.** Signed.

2707 The making of a shrine [Madonna di Pompei], 313–324. **Lily Wolffsohn.** Signed; Contents adds "Mrs."

2708 Marriage of innocent divorcées, 325–336. **Edmund Beckett.** Signed Grimthorpe [1st Baron Grimthorpe].

2709 Noticeable books (No. I): *The Libera-*

tion of Italy, 337–340. **Frederic Harrison.** Signed.

2710 Noticeable books (No. II): *Europe from 1815 to 1871*, 341. **Frederic Harrison.** Signed.

2711 Noticeable books (No. III): *The Life of Mr. J. A. Symonds*, 342–346. **H. D. Traill.** Signed.

2712 Noticeable books (No. IV): *Mrs. Augustus Craven*, 346–349. **W. S. Lilly.** Signed.

2713 Noticeable books (No. V): *The Life of Mr. Bradlaugh*, 349–354. **Augustine Birrell.** Signed.

2714 Reminiscences of Christina Rossetti, 355–366. **Theodore Watts.** Signed.

VOLUME 37, MARCH 1895

2715 The millstone round the neck of England [her policy on the Mediterranean], 369–381. **William Laird Clowes.** Signed. (See nos. 2729, 2756.)

2716 The good sense of the English people, 382–392. **T. E. Kebbel.** Signed.

2717 On some legal disabilities of trade unions, 393–408. **Bernard Holland.** Signed. Intro. note, 393–394, by **S. C. Cavendish**—signed Devonshire [8th Duke of Devonshire].

2718 How to organise a people's kitchen in London, 409–420. **Edith Sellers.** Signed.

2719 The builder of the round towers: a chronicle of the eighth century, 421–434. **Emily Lawless.** Signed.

2720 What is church authority? 435–439. **T. Teignmouth Shore.** Signed. (See no. 2742.)

2721 The wanton mutilation of animals, 440–461. **George Fleming.** Signed; Contents adds "Dr."

2722 Rembrandt and Sir Joshua Reynolds: a notice of two landscape pictures, 462–466. **John Charles Robinson.** Signed as in no. 455.

2723 Officers' expenses in the cavalry and other arms of the service, 467–476. **David W. S. Ogilvy.** Signed Airlie [Earl of Airlie].

2724 Written gesture [character in handwriting], 477–490. **John Holt Schooling.** Signed.

2725 Maurice Maeterlinck, 491–496. **Richard Hovey.** Signed.

2726 The Chinese drama, 497–515. **George Adams.** Signed.

2727 A night in the reporters' gallery, 516–526. **Michael MacDonagh.** Signed.

2728 Mr. Balfour's attack on agnosticism

(Part I; no more published), 527–540. **T. H. Huxley.** Signed.

VOLUME 37, APRIL 1895

2729 England and the Mediterranean: a reply to Mr. Laird Clowes [in no. 2715], 541–551. **G. S. Clarke.** Signed; repr. in Thursfield, *The Navy and the Nation*, 1897.

2730 *The Foundations of Belief* [by A. J. Balfour], 552–566. **James Martineau.** Signed.

2731 The decline of the House of Commons, 567–578. **Sidney Low.** Signed.

2732 Penalties of ignorance, 579–592. **Eliza Priestley.** Signed.

2733 Domestic architecture in Paris, 593–606. **Alphonse de Calonne.** Signed.

2734 Sex in modern literature, 607–616. **Blanche A. Crackanthorpe.** Signed as in no. 2503.

2735 The greater antiquity of man, 617–628. **Joseph Prestwich.** Signed.

2736 The latest Irish land bill: a suggestion, 629–633. **Thomas Spring-Rice**, 1849–1926. Signed Monteagle [2nd Baron Monteagle].

2737 Some American "impressions" and "comparisons," 634–645. **Elizabeth L. Banks.** Signed.

2738 The historical and classical plays of Thomas Heywood, 646–656. **A. C. Swinburne.** Signed; repr. *The Age of Shakespeare*, 1908.

2739 London and the water companies, 657–664. **John Lubbock.** Signed.

2740 The *Diatessaron* of Tatian, 665–681. **Walter R. Cassels.** Signed.

2741 The art of Skopas and of Praxiteles in the British Museum, 682–691. **Eugénie Sellers Strong.** Signed Eugénie Sellers; see *WWW*/1950.

2742 What is church authority? 692–696. **T. T. Carter.** Signed.

2743 Manufacturing a new pauperism, 697–708. **C. S. Loch.** Signed.

VOLUME 37, MAY 1895

2744 An object-lesson in "prohibition," 709–718. **T. C. Down.** Signed.

2745 The real rulers of Turkey, 719–733. **H. Anthony Salmoné.** Signed.

2746 A May Queen festival: with letters from Mr. Ruskin, 734–747. **John P. Faunthorpe.** Signed.

2747 The ancient English office of the

Easter Sepulchre, 748–764. **Henry J. Feasey.** Signed.

2748 A love episode in Mazzini's life, 765–785. **Dora Melegari.** Signed D. Melegari; Contents adds "Mademoiselle"; see *LCCat.*

2749 Mr. Irving on the art of acting, 786–797. **Marie L. de la Ramée.** Evidence for for no. 2685.

2750 Women in French prisons, 798–812. **Edmund R. Spearman.** Signed.

2751 True and false notions of prayer, 813–818. **Norman Pearson.** Signed; repr., much revised, *Some Problems of Existence*, 1907, as "Possibilities of Prayer." (See no. 2801.)

2752 Colour-shadows, 819–831. **A. E. Wright.** Signed.

2753 Georgian treaties with Russia, 832–847. **V. N. Cherkezov.** Signed, but with initials "V.E."; attr. by Boris Nikolaevsky in "Varlaam Nikolaevich Cherkezov (1846–1925)," *Katorga i ssylka* No. 25 (Moscow, 1926), p. 231.

2754 Joan of Arc, 848–858. **Caroline Southwood Hill.** Signed C. Southwood Hill; Contents adds "Mrs."; see *DNB*/1921 under Octavia Hill.

2755 The false Pucelle, 859–874. **Andrew Lang.** Signed.

2756 Braggadocio about the Mediterranean: a rejoinder [to no. 2729], 875–888. **W. Laird Clowes.** Signed.

VOLUME 37, JUNE 1895

2757 England and France on the Niger: "the race for Borgu," 889–903. **F. D. Lugard.** Signed.

2758 Alliance or fusion? (No. I): the case for alliance, 904–917. **J. St. Loe Strachey.** Signed.

2759 Alliance or fusion? (No. II): the case for fusion, 918–925. **Edward Dicey.** Signed.

2760 The Mussalmans of India and the Armenian question, 926–939. **Ghulam-us-Saqlain.** Signed; Index adds "(Khwaji)."

2761 "In the days of her youth" [women's education], 940–954. **Harry Quilter.** Signed.

2762 The after-careers of university-educated women, 955–960. **Alice M. Gordon.** Signed.

2763 The celestial empire of the West [Rome and the Anglican Church], 961–967. **Augustus Jessopp.** Signed.

2764 Advertising as a trespass on the public, 968–980. **Richardson Evans.** Signed.

2765 Chitral and frontier policy, 981–990. **Lepel Griffin.** Signed.

2766 Bimetallism (No. I): as a bubble, 991–1000. **Henry Dunning MacLeod.** Signed.

2767 Bimetallism (No. II): as a new way to pay old debts—an appeal to Mr. Balfour, 1001–1007. **J. W. Cross.** Signed.

2768 The two salons, 1008–1020. **Alphonse de Calonne.** Signed.

2769 "True and false conceptions of the Atonement" [reply to no. 2628], 1021–1026. **Annie Besant.** Signed.

2770 Provincial patriotism [Home Rule], 1027–1035. **J. P. Mahaffy.** Signed.

2771 A journey to Scotland in the year 1435, 1036–1052. **J. J. Jusserand.** Signed; repr. *English Essays from a French Pen*, 1895.

2772 The recent "witch-burning" at Clonmel, 1053–1058. **E. F. Benson.** Signed.

2773 The gentle art of book lending: a suggestion, 1060–1070. **George Somes Layard.** Signed.

VOLUME 38, JULY 1895

2774 The Conservative programme of social reform, 3–16. **John E. Gorst,** 1835–1916. Signed; see *DNB*.

2775 The Irish fiasco, 17–26. **Henry L. Jephson.** Signed as in no. 1144.

2776 An object-lesson in "payment of members," 27–40. **Alexander B. Tulloch.** Signed.

2777 Intellectual detachment, 41–56. **Herbert Maxwell.** Signed.

2778 Dr. Pusey and Bishop Wilberforce, 57–67. **R. G. Wilberforce.** Signed.

2779 My native salmon river [the Spey], 68–81. **Archibald Forbes.** Signed; repr. *Camps.*

2780 Recent science, 82–102. **Peter A. Kropotkin.** Signed as in no. 1110.

2781 How to obtain a school of English opera, 103–110. **J. F. Rowbotham.** Signed.

2782 The Church in Wales, 111–124. **Alfred G. Edwards.** Signed A. G. Asaph [Bishop of Asaph].

2783 Colour-music: a suggestion of a new art, 125–134. **William Schooling.** Signed.

2784 Religion in elementary schools: proposals for peace, 135–141. **George A. Spottiswoode.** Signed.

2785 The Society of Comparative Legislation, 142–155. **C. P. Ilbert.** Signed.

2786 A Moslem view of Abdul Hamid and

the powers, 156–164. **Rafiüddin Ahmad.** Signed.

2787 Some lessons from Kiel, 165–176. **W. Laird Clowes.** Signed.

VOLUME 38, AUGUST 1895

2788 The general election (No. I): what does it all mean? 177–187. **J. Guinness Rogers.** Signed.

2789 The general election: (No. II): the rout of the faddists, 188–198. **Edward Dicey.** Signed.

2790 The House of Lords, 199–213. **Thomas Lister.** Signed Ribblesdale [4th Baron Ribblesdale]; repr. *Impressions and Memoirs*, 1927.

2791 Theological pessimism, 214–226. **Frederic Harrison.** Signed. (See no. 2824.)

2792 Orgeas and Miradou: a dream of Provence, 227–235. **Frederick Wedmore.** Signed; repr. *Dream of Provence*, 1907.

2793 New British markets (No. I): western China, 236–246. **Holt S. Hallett.** Signed.

2794 New British markets (No. II): Tibet, 247–260. **C. E. D. Black.** Signed.

2795 Spencer versus Balfour, 261–277. **St. George Mivart.** Signed. (Letter, p. 536, signed **Herbert Spencer.**)

2796 The Prison Committee report, 278–294. **E. F. Du Cane.** Signed.

2797 Stars and molecules, 295–307. **Edmund Ledger.** Signed E. Ledger; Contents gives first name and adds "Rev."

2798 University extension in America; with a prize essay ["The influence of Puritanism on national character"], 308–321. **Anne M. Earle.** Signed.

2799 A dialogue on the drama, 322–337. **H. A. Kennedy.** Signed.

2800 The old-age homes in Austria, 338–347. **Edith Sellers.** Signed.

2801 A defence of prayer, in reply to Mr. Norman Pearson [in no. 2751], 348–360. **William Francis Barry.** Signed as in no. 1742.

VOLUME 38, SEPTEMBER 1895

2802 Islam and its critics, 361–380. **Syed Ameer Ali.** Signed as in no. 454.

2803 Permanent dominion in Asia, 381–396. **A. C. Lyall.** Signed; repr. *Asiatic Studies, 2nd Series.*

2804 The romantic and contemporary plays of Thomas Heywood, 397–410. **Algernon Charles Swinburne.** Signed; repr. *The Age of Shakespeare*, 1908.

2805 The romance of Leonardo da Vinci, 411–425. **Alphonse de Calonne.** Signed.

2806 Americans and the Pan-Britannic movement, 426–441. **J. Astley Cooper.** Signed.

2807 New British markets (No. III): tropical Africa, 442–454. **F. D. Lugard.** Signed.

2808 Africanists in council, 455–465. **A. Silva White.** Signed.

2809 The picture sales of 1895, 466–473. **William Roberts,** 1862–1940. Signed W. Roberts; see *WWW*.

2810 Lion hunting beyond the Haud, 474–493. **H. C. Lowther.** Signed.

2811 The Kutho-Daw, 494–505. **Friedrich Max Müller.** Signature; repr. *Last Essays.*

2812 A foreign affairs committee, 506–518. **Sidney Low.** Signed.

2813 The present condition of Russia, 519–535. **Peter A. Kropotkin.** Signed as in no. 1110.

VOLUME 38, OCTOBER 1895

2814 The gold-mining madness in the city, 537–547. **S. F. van Oss.** Signed.

2815 The political situation in Italy, 548–560. **Antonio De Viti de Marco.** Signed De Viti de Marco; Contents gives "Marchese"; see *Enci. Ital.*

2816 Ruskin as master of prose, 561–575. **Frederic Harrison.** Signed; repr. *Tennyson, Ruskin, Mill.*

2817 The Trafalgar captains, 576–594. **W. Laird Clowes.** Signed.

2818 The land of frankincense and myrrh [Dhofar, Arabia], 595–613. **J. Theodore Bent.** Signed.

2819 A medical view of the miracles at Lourdes, 614–618. **Edward Berdoe.** Signed.

2820 The new spirit in history, 619–633. **W. S. Lilly.** Signed.

2821 Frederick Locker-Lampson, 634–643. **Coulson Kernahan.** Signed.

2822 In Germany: a sketch, 644–648. **Millicent Sutherland.** Signed.

2823 The closing of the Indian mints, 649–660. **Thomas Brassey.** Signed Brassey [1st Earl Brassey].

2824 The religion of humanity: a reply to Mr. Frederic Harrison [in no. 2791], 661–672. **W. H. Mallock.** Signed.

2825 The religion of the undergraduate, 673–680. **Anthony C. Deane.** Signed. (See nos. 2840, 2841, 2851.)

2826 The proper pronunciation of Greek, 681–698. **Joannes Gennadius.** Signed J.

Gennadius; see *WWW*/1940. (See no. 2868.)

2827 A great university for London, 699–705. **Lyon Playfair.** Signed Playfair [Baron Playfair].

2828 The need for an Antarctic expedition, 706–712. **Clements R. Markham.** Signed.

VOLUME 38, NOVEMBER 1895

2829 Bishop Butler and his censors (Part I): [Bagehot, Miss Hennell, Leslie Stephen], 715–739. **W. E. Gladstone.** Signed; repr. *Studies Subsidiary to the Works of Bishop Butler*, 1896.

2830 Lord Salisbury on evolution, 740–757. **Herbert Spencer.** Signed.

2831 Great Britain, Venezuela, and the United States, 758–768. **H. Somers Somerset.** Signed.

2832 The Chinese view of missionaries, 769–777. **T. C. Hayllar.** Signed.

2833 Islâm and Canon MacColl, 778–785. **Syed Ameer Ali.** Signed as in no. 454.

2834 The rigidity of Rome, 786–804. **Wilfrid Ward.** Signed; repr. *Problems and Persons*, 1903.

2835 Hulderico Schmidel, 805–813. **R. B. Cunninghame Graham.** Signed.

2836 The past and the future of Gibraltar, 814–827. **John Adye,** 1857–1930. Signed, with title "Major R.A. and Brevet Lt. Colonel."

2837 The change of our musical pitch, 828–837. **J. Cuthbert Hadden.** Signed.

2838 Art connoisseurship in England: mutation or decline? 838–849. **John Charles Robinson.** Signed as in no. 455.

2839 Author, agent, and publisher: by one of "the trade," 850–855. **T. Werner Laurie.** Signed. (See nos. 2849, 2850.)

2840 The religion of the undergraduate (No. I): reply from Cambridge [to no. 2825], 856–860. **Reginald B. Fellows.** Signed.

2841 The religion of the undergraduate (No. II): reply from Oxford [to no. 2825], 861–869. **Heneage Legge.** Signed H. Legge; see *WWW*/1916.

2842 Indian frontiers and Indian finance, 870–888. **Auckland Colvin.** Signed.

VOLUME 38, DECEMBER 1895

2843 The transformation of the army under the Duke of Cambridge, 889–904. **J. L. A. Simmons.** Signed.

2844 The policy of "killing Home Rule by kindness," 905–914. **J. E. Redmond.** Signed.

2845 Reopening the education settlement of 1870, 915–930. **E. Lyulph Stanley.** Signed. (See nos. 2864, 2865, 2889.)

2846 Kashmir, 931–946. **Lepel Griffin.** Signed.

2847 Le journal d'Eugène Delacroix et les peintres de l'école Anglaise, 947–957. **Charles Yriarte.** Signed.

2848 *Unto This Last* [by John Ruskin], 958–974. **Frederic Harrison.** Signed; repr. *Tennyson, Ruskin, Mill.*

2849 The society of authors: a reply [to no. 2839], 975–978. **W. Martin Conway.** Signed.

2850 The literary agent, 979–986. **Walter Besant.** Signed.

2851 The religion of the undergraduate: a reply to some criticisms, 987–990. **Anthony C. Deane.** Signed.

2852 The Eastern question (No. I): Turkish reforms and Armenia, 991–1000. **F. Heinrich Geffcken.** Signed.

2853 The Eastern question (No. II): the religious basis of Russian policy, 1001–1007. **Olga Novikoff.** Signed.

2854 The Eastern question (No. III): how the Sultan can save his empire, 1008–1014. **Rafiüddin Ahmad.** Signed.

2855 University settlements, 1015–1024. **Samuel A. Barnett.** Signed; repr. *Practicable Socialism.*

2856 Medicine and society, 1025–1040. **J. Burney Yeo.** Signed.

2857 Matthew Arnold, 1041–1055. **John Morley.** Signed.

2858 Bishop Butler and his censors (Part II, concl.) [Matthew Arnold, Maurice, Goldwin Smith, Mark Pattison], 1056–1074. **W. E. Gladstone.** Signed. (See no. 2870.)

2859 Canon MacColl on Islam: a correspondence, 1075–1082. **Malcolm MacColl** and **James Knowles.** Signed.

VOLUME 39, JANUARY 1896

2860 The issue between Great Britain and America, 1–6. **Henry M. Stanley.** Signed.

2861 Common sense and Venezuela, 7–15. **Edward Dicey.** Signed.

2862 Can the Empire feed its people? 16–27. **James Long.** Signed; see *BMCat.* for this James Long, writer on agriculture and farming.

2863 The ugliness of modern life, 28–43.

Marie L. de la Ramée. Evidence for no. 2685; repr. *Critical Studies*, 1900.

2864 Reopening the education settlement of 1870 (No. I): a reply to Mr. Lyulph Stanley [no. 2845], 44–50. **Joseph R. Diggle.** Signed.

2865 Reopening the education settlement of 1870 (No. II): a reply [to no. 2845], 51–57. **Athelstan Riley.** Signed. (See no. 2889.)

2866 In the wild west of China, 58–64. **Alicia Bewicke Little.** Signed.

2867 Mutual aid amongst modern men, 65–86. **Peter A. Kropotkin.** Signed as in no. 1110; repr. *Mutual Aid*, as "Mutual Aid Among Ourselves."

2868 Erasmus and the pronunciation of Greek, 87–97. **Joannes Gennadius.** Signed as in no. 2826.

2869 The rule of the laywoman, 98–105. **Henrietta M. Batson.** Signed.

2870 Bishop Butler's apologist [W. E. Gladstone], 106–122. **Leslie Stephen.** Signed.

2871 The advantage of fiction, 123–131. **Mary G. Tuttiet.** Signed M. G. Tuttiet, with addition "Maxwell Gray"; see *LCCat.*

2872 Church defence or Church reform? 132–149. **Augustus Jessopp.** Signed; repr. *Peasantry.* (Note, p. 356, signed **Augustus Jessopp.**)

2873 English prisons, 150–157. **Algernon West.** Signed.

2874 A septuagenarian's retrospect, 158–172. **J. Guinness Rogers.** Signed.

2875 Is the Sultan of Turkey the true Khaliph of Islam? 173–180. **H. Anthony Salmoné.** Signed.

VOLUME 39, FEBRUARY 1896

2876 The facts about the Venezuela boundary, 185–188. **John Bolton.** Signed.

2877 The relations of France and England, 189–203. **Francis de Pressensé.** Signed.

2878 Our true foreign policy, 204–217. **H. O. Arnold-Forster.** Signed.

2879 The protection of our commerce in war, 218–235. **H. W. Wilson.** Signed.

2880 Corn stores for war-time, 236–239. **R. B. Marston.** Signed.

2881 The proposed German barrier across Africa, 240–248. **J. W. Gregory.** Signed.

2882 The life of Cardinal Manning [by E. S. Purcell] (No. I), 249–253. **Herbert A. Vaughan.** Signed Herbert Cardinal Vaughan, Archbishop of Westminster. (See no. 2906.)

2883 The life of Cardinal Manning (No. II), 254–256. **Wilfrid Meynell.** Signed.

2884 Criticism as theft, 257–266. **William A. Knight.** Signed as in no. 1637; Contents gives "Professor."

2885 Dairy farming, 267–285. **G. W. H. Venables-Vernon.** Signed Vernon [7th Baron Vernon].

2886 Irish education, 286–294. **Mervyn Wingfield.** Signed Powerscourt [7th Viscount Powerscourt].

2887 Reasonable patriotism, 295–315. **Reginald Brabazon.** Signed Meath [12th Earl of Meath]; repr. *Thoughts.*

2888 Shakespeare, Falstaff, and Queen Elizabeth, 316–327. **H. A. Kennedy.** Signed.

2889 Mr. Diggle and Mr. Riley: a rejoinder [to nos. 2864, 2865], 328–331. **E. Lyulph Stanley.** Signed.

2890 Note on the Anglo-French convention in Siam, 332–334. **Frederick Verney.** Signed, with title "English Sec. of Siamese Legation."

2891 Slavery under the British flag, 335–355. **F. D. Lugard.** Signed.

VOLUME 39, MARCH 1896

2892 An army without leaders, 357–374. **Lonsdale Hale.** Signed.

2893 Chartered companies, 375–380. **J. D. S. Campbell.** Signed Lorne [Marquis of Lorne].

2894 In praise of the Boers, 381–389. **H. A. Bryden.** Signed.

2895 The seamy side of British Guiana, 390–398. **Francis Comyn.** Signed.

2896 Our invasion scares and panics, 399–415. **R. Vesey Hamilton.** Signed.

2897 Recent science, 416–432. **Peter A. Kropotkin.** Signed as in no. 1110.

2898 Matthew Arnold, 433–447. **Frederic Harrison.** Signed.

2899 The naval teachings of the crisis [mobilization of the fleet], 448–456. **W. Laird Clowes.** Signed.

2900 Australia as a strategic base, 457–464. **Arthur Silva White.** Signed.

2901 Lord Leighton and his art: a tribute, 465–476. **W. B. Richmond.** Signed.

2902 The agricultural position, 477–480. **F. W. Wilson.** Signed.

2903 Scenes in a barrack school, 481–494. **Henry W. Nevinson.** Signed. (Note, pp. 871–872, signed **Catherine Scott,** with addition "Hon. Sec. of the Metropolitan Association for Befriending Young Servants.")

2904 The encroachment of women, 495–501. **Charles Whibley.** Signed.

2905 Self-help among American college girls, 502–513. **Elizabeth L. Banks.** Signed.

2906 Poisoning the wells of Catholic criticism, 514–526. **Edmund S. Purcell.** Signed. With a letter, 526–528, from **W. E. Gladstone.** (See no. 2922, 2996.)

VOLUME 39, APRIL 1896

2907 International jealousy, 529–543. **J. P. Mahaffy.** Signed.

2908 "The burden of Egypt" (No. I): the difficulties of withdrawal, 544–556. **H. D. Traill.** Signed.

2909 "The burden of Egypt" (No. II): our promise to withdraw, 557–565. **Wemyss Reid.** Signed.

2910 A bill to promote the conviction of innocent prisoners, 566–575. **Herbert Stephen.** Signed. (See no. 2933.)

2911 Consols at 110 [Consolidated Stock], 576–582. **S. F. van Oss.** Signed.

2912 *Memoirs of the Duc de Persigny*, 583–595. **F. T. de Grey Cowper.** Signed Cowper [7th Earl Cowper].

2913 Sir Robert Peel, 596–607. **George Peel.** Signed.

2914 Picture conservation, 608–623. **John Charles Robinson.** Signed as in no. 455.

2915 A dialogue on vulgarity, 624–635. **Theodosia Chapman.** Signed as in no. 1264.

2916 The decay of classical quotation, 636–646. **Herbert Paul.** Signed.

2917 The fetich of publicity, 647–654. **John Macdonell,** 1845–1921. Signed; see *DNB.*

2918 What, then, did happen at the Reformation? 655–666. **Augustine Birrell.** Signed. (See nos. 2955, 3082, 3118.)

2919 The chief Lama of Himis on the alleged *Unknown Life of Christ,* 667–677. **J. Archibald Douglas.** Signed. With a postscript, 677–678, by **Friedrich Max Müller**—signature.

2920 Niccola Pisano and the renascence of sculpture, 679–688. **J. A. Crowe.** Signed.

2921 King and Pretender in Rome [Leo XIII], 689–693. **W. L. Alden.** Signed.

2922 Mr. Gladstone and Cardinal Manning, 694–696. **Sydney F. Smith.** Signed, with title "S.J."

VOLUME 39, MAY 1896

2923 Mr. Lecky on democracy, 697–720.

John Morley. Signed; repr. *Miscellanies,* IV.

2924 Why South Africa cannot wait, 721–738. **Edward Dicey.** Signed. (See no. 2980.)

2925 The truth of the Dongola adventure, 739–745. **Wilfrid Scawen Blunt.** Signed.

2926 If Ireland sent her M.P.'s to Washington? 746–755. **William O'Brien,** 1852–1928. Signed; see *DNB.*

2927 The Irish land question to-day, 756–761. **Thomas Spring-Rice,** 1849–1926. Signed Monteagle [2nd Baron Monteagle].

2928 Portrait-painting in its historical aspects, 762–778. **John Collier.** Signed.

2929 The new Education Bill (No. I): a radical commentary, 779–784. **T. J. Macnamara.** Signed.

2930 The new Education Bill (No. II): the Nonconformist case, 785–795. **J. Guinness Rogers.** Signed.

2931 A medical view of cycling for ladies, 796–801. **W. H. Fenton.** Signed.

2932 European coalitions against England, 802–811. **T. E. Kebbel.** Signed.

2933 A bill for the protection of innocent prisoners: in reply to Sir Herbert Stephen [in no. 2910], 812–825. **George Pitt-Lewis.** Signed G. Pitt-Lewis; see *WWW/1916.*

2934 Co-operation in agriculture, 826–836. **Wilbraham Egerton.** Signed Egerton of Tatton [2nd Baron Egerton of Tatton].

2935 Hungary at the close of her first millennium, 837–849. **Emil Reich.** Signed.

2936 The reunion of Christendom, 850–870. **Charles L. Wood.** Signed Halifax [2nd Viscount Halifax].

VOLUME 39, JUNE 1896

2937 The true motive and reason of Dr. Jameson's raid, 873–880. **G. Seymour Fort.** Signed.

2938 Some flaws in the Education Bill, 881–895. **J. G. Fitch.** Signed.

2939 Cardinal Manning's memory: fresh lights, 896–905. **Reginald G. Wilberforce.** Signed.

2940 America as a power, 906–913. **Alexander Maclure.** Signed.

2941 Mutual aid amongst ourselves, 914–936. **Peter A. Kropotkin.** Signed as in no. 1110; repr. *Mutual Aid.*

2942 Natural requital, 937–949. **Norman Pearson.** Signed; repr., much revised, *Some Problems of Existence,* 1907, as "Sanctity of Morality."

2982 The influence of Bayreuth, 360–366. **J. A. Fuller Maitland.** Signed.

2983 The baptism of Clovis, 367–382. **Augustus Jessopp.** Signed; repr. *Great Pillage.*

2984 Sketches made in Germany (No. I), 383–394. **Katherine Blyth.** Signed; Contents gives "Mrs."

2985 Some recollections of Cardinal Newman, 395–411. **Aubrey De Vere.** Signed; repr. *Recollections,* N.Y., 1897.

2986 At sea, 412–421. **Martin Morris.** Signed.

2987 The Jew-baiting on the Continent, 422–438. **Emil Reich.** Signed.

2988 On inductive morality, 439–453. **Francesco Nobili-Vitelleschi.** Signed as in no. 1036.

2989 Boiling milk, 454–460. **Grace C. Frankland.** Signed G. C. Frankland; Contents gives "Mrs. Percy Frankland"; see *WWW*/1950 under Percy E. Frankland.

2990 A northern pilgrimage, 461–473. **Wemyss Reid.** Signed.

2991 An attempt at optimism, 474–477. **Mary E. Ponsonby.** Signed.

2992 Sailing for ladies in Highland lochs, 478–486. **Caroline Creyke.** Signed.

2993 John Stuart Mill, 487–508. **Frederic Harrison.** Signed; repr. *Tennyson, Ruskin, Mill.*

VOLUME 40, OCTOBER 1896

2994 Why Russia distrusts England, 509–515. **Wemyss Reid.** Signed.

2995 The cry for fraudulent money in America, 516–532. **George F. Parker.** Signed.

2996 On the ethics of suppression in biography, 533–540. **Edmund S. Purcell.** Signed. With a postscript, 541–542, by **Purcell**—signed E.S.P., including a letter from **W. E. Gladstone.**

2997 Bhowáni, the cholera-goddess: some experiences in Hindoo sanitation, 543–558. **E. H. Hankin.** Signed.

2998 Of women in assemblies, 559–566. **Charles Selby Oakley.** Signed. (See no. 3023.)

2999 Lord Randolph Churchill as an official, 567–579. **Algernon West.** Signed; repr. *One City.*

3000 On the Dervish frontier, 580–595. **J. Theodore Bent.** Signed.

3001 County councils and rural education, 596–608. **Charles Thomas Dyke Acland.** Signed.

3002 Horse ambulances, 609–618. **Francis Dudley Leigh.** Signed Dudley Leigh; Contents adds "Hon."; see *WWW*/1940.

3003 A visit to Queen Elizabeth, 619–631. **J. H. Round.** Signed.

3004 The unavoidable uselessness of prison labour, 632–642. **E. F. Du Cane.** Signed.

3005 Fra Filippo Lippi, 643–653. **J. A. Crowe.** Signed.

3006 The massacres in Turkey (No. I), 654–659. **J. Guinness Rogers.** Signed.

3007 The massacres in Turkey (No. II), 660–664. **Reginald Brabazon.** Signed Meath [12th Earl of Meath].

3008 The massacres in Turkey (No. III), 665–670. **John Burns.** Signed.

3009 The massacres in Turkey (No. IV), 671–675. **H. Anthony Salmoné.** Signed.

3010 The massacres in Turkey (No. V), 676–680. **W. E. Gladstone.** Signed.

VOLUME 40, NOVEMBER 1896

3011 England and the continental alliances, 681–688. **Francis de Pressensé.** Signed.

3012 La Turquie et son souverain: la crise actuelle, ses origines, sa solution, 689–698. **Diran Kélékian.** Signed.

3013 The voluntary schools, 699–710. **John E. Gorst,** 1835–1916. Signed; see *DNB.*

3014 The Westralian mining "boom," 711–720. **S. F. van Oss.** Signed.

3015 Commercial morality in Japan, 721–728. **Robert Young.** Signed, with title "Editor, *Knobe Chronicle,* Japan."

3016 Sketches made in Germany (No. II, concl.), 729–742. **Katherine Blyth.** Signed.

3017 Arbitration in labour disputes, 743–758. **Sidney and Beatrice Webb.** Signed.

3018 Noticeable books (No. I): *The Well at the World's End* [by William Morris], 759–760. **Algernon Charles Swinburne.** Signed.

3019 Noticeable books (No. II): *Windfall and Waterdrift,* 760–765. **Marie L. de la Ramée.** Evidence for no. 2685; repr. *Critical Studies,* 1900, as "Auberon Herbert."

3020 Noticeable books (No. III): *Primogeniture,* 765–768. **W. S. Lilly.** Signed.

3021 Noticeable books (No. IV): *Illumination; The Scripture Reader of St. Mark's, A Lady of Quality,* 768–772. **Mabel C. Birchenough.** Signed.

3022 Noticeable books (No. V): *Charlotte Brontë and Her Circle,* 772–776. **Wemyss Reid.** Signed.

3023 "Of women in assemblies": a reply [to

VOLUME 41, MAY 1897

3105 The powers and the East in the light of the War [between Greece and Turkey], 681–686. **Francis de Pressensé.** Signed.

3106 Side-lights on the Cretan insurrection, 687–698. **Ernest N. Bennett.** Signed.

3107 Among the liars [in Crete], 699–706. **H. C. Lowther.** Signed.

3108 The Schleswig-Holstein question and its place in history, 707–716. **Friedrich Max Müller.** Signature; repr. under same title, 1916, and in *Last Essays*. (See no. 3210.)

3109 On bank holidays and a plea for one more, 717–721. **John Lubbock.** Signed; repr. *Essays and Addresses*, 1903.

3110 May carols, 722–733. **A. M. Wakefield.** Signed.

3111 The home of the Cabots, 734–738. **H. Cabot Lodge.** Signed.

3112 The progress of medicine during the Queen's reign, 739–758. **Malcolm Morris.** Signed.

3113 Goree: a lost possession of England, 759–768. **Walter Frewen Lord.** Signed.

3114 The apotheosis of the novel under Queen Victoria, 769–792. **Herbert Paul.** Signed.

3115 The speech of children, 793–807. **S. S. Buckman.** Signed.

3116 Tobacco in relation to health and character, 808–823. **Edward Vincent Heward.** Signed.

3117 Gongora, 824–836. **James Mew.** Signed.

3118 The sacrifice of the Mass, 837–849. **J. H. Round.** Signed.

3119 The Duke of Argyll's criticisms, 850–852. **Herbert Spencer.** Signed.

VOLUME 41, JUNE 1897

3120 British monarchy and modern democracy, 853–864. **W. S. Lilly.** Signed.

3121 India under Queen Victoria, 865–882. **A. C. Lyall.** Signed.

3122 The forthcoming naval review and its predecessors, 883–892. **H. W. Wilson.** Signed.

3123 Nelson, 893–906. **G. S. Clarke.** Signed.

3124 The new astronomy: a personal retrospect, 907–929. **William Huggins.** Signed.

3125 Roses of Jericho: a day in provincial France, 930–941. **Rowland E. Prothero.** Signed; repr. *The Pleasant Land of France*, 1908.

3126 The limits of French armament, 942–

956. **John Adye,** 1857–1930. Signed as in no. 2836.

3127 The significance of the Siamese visit, 957–963. **Percy Cross Standing.** Signed.

3128 Woman's place in the world of letters, 964–974. **Alice Stopford Green.** Signed.

3129 The island of Socotra, 975–992. **J. Theodore Bent.** Signed.

3130 Do foreign annexations injure British trade? 993–1004. **Henry Birchenough.** Signed.

3131 Chantilly and the Duc D'Aumale, 1005–1015. **Alphonse de Calonne.** Signed.

3132 The new Irish policy, 1016–1022. **Thomas Spring-Rice,** 1849–1926. Signed Monteagle [2nd Baron Monteagle].

VOLUME 42, JULY 1897

3133 England's opportunity: Germany or Canada? 1–8. **Henry Birchenough.** Signed.

3134 The Jameson expedition: a narrative of facts, 9–21. **John C. Willoughby.** Signed. (See no. 3150.)

3135 Recent science: Brain structure—the approach of the "Black Death"—snakebite, 22–43. **Peter A. Kropotkin.** Signed as in no. 1110.

3136 The growth of caste in the United States, 44–54. **Joseph Edgar Chamberlin.** Signed.

3137 Some reminiscences of English journalism, 55–66. **Wemyss Reid.** Signed.

3138 On conversation, 67–73. **James Payn.** Signed.

3139 Thomas Day, 74–86. **Amelius R. Mark Lockwood.** Signed M. Lockwood; see *DNB*/1930.

3140 Genius and stature, 87–95. **Havelock Ellis.** Signed; repr. *A Study of British Genius*, 1926. (Letters, p. 336, signed **Henry Troutbeck** and **R. G. Wilberforce.**)

3141 The Pope and the Anglican archbishops, 96–112. **H. I. D. Ryder.** Signed; repr. *Essays*, 1911.

3142 The French and the English treatment of research, 113–123. **Eliza Priestley.** Signed.

3143 Life in poetry (Part III, concl.): poetical decadence, 124–141. **W. J. Courthope.** Signed.

3144 The teaching of music in schools, 142–150. **J. Cuthbert Hadden.** Signed.

3145 The wrecking of the West Indies, 151–160. **Mayson M. Beeton.** Signed.

3146 How poor ladies live: a rejoinder [to no. 3098] and a "Jubilee" suggestion, 161–168. **Frances H. Low.** Signed.

3147 Women's suffrage again! 169–172.

Theodosia Chapman. Signed as in no. 1264.

White. Signed; *not* the author of no. 3160: see Contents and Index for both.

3186 The protection of wild birds, 614–622. **Harold Russell.** Signed.

3187 Philo-Zionists and anti-Semites, 623–635. **Herbert Bentwich.** Signed.

3188 Our custom house regulations, 636–639. **Algernon West.** Signed.

3189 The promised Irish Local Government Bill, 640–652. **J. E. Redmond.** Signed.

3190 Art and the daily paper, 653–662. **Joseph Pennell.** Signed.

3191 British suzerainty in the Transvaal, 663–672. **Edward Dicey.** Signed.

VOLUME 42, NOVEMBER 1897

3192 The Dual and the Triple Alliance, 673–677. **Francesco Crispi.** Signed F. Crispi; see *DEI*. (See no. 3206.)

3193 The monetary chaos, 678–689. **Robert Giffen.** Signed.

3194 Creeds in the primary schools, 690–702. **J. G. Fitch.** Signed.

3195 Modern education: an address delivered at the Mason College, Birmingham, 703–718. **J. P. Mahaffy.** Signed.

3196 The Italian novels of Marion Crawford, 719–733. **Marie L. de la Ramée.** Evidence for no. 2685; repr. *Critical Studies*, 1900.

3197 The fur-pullers of south London, 734–743. **Edith F. Hogg.** Signed.

3198 Some first impressions [of Eastern Europe and Russia], 744–754. **Wemyss Reid.** Signed.

3199 The genealogy of Nelson, 755–765. **W. Laird Clowes.** Signed.

3200 Liquor traffic in Africa, 766–784. **F. W. Lugard.** Signed.

3201 Sketches made in Germany (No. IV), 785–790. **Katharine Blyth.** Signed.

3202 On the financial relations of Great Britain and Ireland, 791–798. **John Lubbock.** Signed. (See no. 3244.)

3203 Recent science, 799–820. **Peter A. Kropotkin.** Signed as in no. 1110.

3204 Guicciardini, 821–844. **John Morley.** Signed; repr. *Miscellanies*, IV.

VOLUME 42, DECEMBER 1897

3205 The problem beyond the Indian frontier, 845–868. **Auckland Colvin.** Signed.

3206 The Dual and the Triple Alliance and Great Britain, 869–885. **Francis de Pressensé.** Signed.

3207 Our reserves for manning the fleet (No. I), 886–898. **Thomas Brassey.** Signed Brassey [1st Earl Brassey].

3208 Our reserves for manning the fleet (No. II): a critique of Lord Brassey, 899–906. **Charles Beresford.** Signed.

3209 Tammany, 907–917. **Frederick A. McKenzie.** Signed.

3210 The Danish view of the Schleswig-Holstein question, 918–927. **A. D. Jorgensen.** Signed; repr. in Max Müller, *The Schleswig-Holstein Question*, 1916.

3211 The new learning, 928–939. **Herbert Paul.** Signed. (Letters, vol. 43, pp. 165–168, signed **Gilbert Murray** and **Herbert Paul.**)

3212 Our public art museums: a retrospect, 940–964. **John Charles Robinson.** Signed as in no. 455.

3213 Billiards: some suggestions for the future, 965–974. **Dudley D. Pontifex.** Signed.

3214 The ways of "settlements" and of "missions," 975–984. **Samuel A. Barnett.** Signed.

3215 Some reminiscences of Thomas Henry Huxley, 985–998. **St. George Mivart.** Signed.

3216 In the sub-editor's room [of a newspaper], 999–1008. **Michael MacDonagh.** Signed.

3217 The present situation of England: a Canadian impression, 1009–1018. **George T. Denison.** Signed.

VOLUME 43, JANUARY 1898

3218 The War Office and its sham army (No. I), 1–7. **A. M. Brookfield.** Signed.

3219 The War Office (No. II), 7–10. **Frederick Carne Rasch.** Signed.

3220 The War Office (No. III), 10–16. **Frank S. Russell.** Signed.

3221 The War Office (No. IV), 16–22. **Alwyne Compton.** Signed.

3222 Do we need an army for home defence? 23–29. **E. F. Du Cane.** Signed.

3223 A recruiting sergeant's suggestions, 30–34. **Arthur V. Palmer.** Signed.

3224 A walk through deserted London, 35–46. **Algernon West.** Signed; repr. *One City*.

3225 Parish life in England before the great pillage (Part I), 47–60. **Augustus Jessopp.** Signed; repr. *Great Pillage*.

3226 The childhood and school days of Byron, 61–81. **R. E. Prothero.** Signed.

3227 At a technical institute, 82–90. **Michael Foster.** Signed M. Foster; Contents gives first name.

3228 The prisoners of the [ancient] gods [i.e., many of the dead, according to Irish peasants' beliefs], 91–104. **W. B. Yeats.** Signed.

3229 Arthur Hugh Clough: a sketch, 105–116. **Thomas Arnold**, 1823–1900. Signed T. Arnold; Contents gives first name; see *DNB*, 1st suppl.

3230 The higher education of women in Russia, 117–134. **Sophie Kropotkin.** Signed; Contents adds "Princess."

3231 Is the Liberal party in collapse? 135–153. **J. Guinness Rogers.** Signed.

3232 The partition of China, 154–164. **Holt S. Hallett.** Signed.

VOLUME 43, FEBRUARY 1898

3233 England at war, 171–181. **Frederick Greenwood.** Signed. (See nos. 3249, 3312.)

3234 The expansion of Germany, 182–191. **Henry Birchenough.** Signed.

3235 German versus British trade in the East, 192–196. **Clavell Tripp.** Signed.

3236 The quaint side of Parliament, 197–213. **Michael MacDonagh.** Signed; repr. *Parliament*, 1902.

3237 Lord Edward Fitzgerald, 214–229. **Ida A. Taylor.** Signed as in no. 2610, with same evidence.

3238 French officialism, 230–240. **Alphonse de Calonne.** Signed.

3239 The future of the Anglo-Afghan alliance, 241–249. **Rafiüddin Ahmad.** Signed.

3240 The permanent pacification of the Indian frontier, 250–255. **G. J. Younghusband.** Signed.

3241 More about Sheridan, 256–265. **W. Fraser Rae.** Signed.

3242 The native press in India, 266–276. **George MacLagan Chesney.** Signed G. M. Chesney; see Venn.

3243 The Manchester School and to-day, 277–283. **Andrew Carnegie.** Signed.

3244 Sir John Lubbock on the "financial relations commission": a reply [to no. 3202], 284–291. **D. R. W. Bourke.** Signed Mayo [7th Earl of Mayo].

3245 Captain Mahan's counsels to the United States, 292–300. **G. S. Clarke.** Signed.

3246 Dante and paganism, 301–311. **D. R. Fearon.** Signed.

3247 The real grievances of the Uitlanders, 312–327. **H. M. Meysey-Thompson.** Signed.

3248 Great Britain's opportunity in China, 328–335. **C. A. Moreing.** Signed.

VOLUME 43, MARCH 1898

3249 "England at War": a supplement by an old Tory [to no. 3233], 337–344. **T. E. Kebbel.** Signed.

3250 The army and the government's opportunity, 345–365. **H. O. Arnold-Forster.** Signed.

3251 The navy and the engineering dispute, 366–370. **Archibald S. Hurd.** Signed.

3252 A brief note on the North-West frontier policy, 371–375. **R. W. Napier.** Signed Napier of Magdala [2nd Baron Napier of Magdala].

3253 Millais's works at Burlington House, 376–388. **Claude Phillips.** Signed.

3254 The methods of the Inquisition, 389–405. **W. S. Lilly.** Signed; repr., expanded, *Christianity and Modern Civilization*, 1903.

3255 The short story, 406–416. **Frederick Wedmore.** Signed; repr. *On Books and Arts*, 1899.

3256 White slaves: a true tale, 417–430. **Margaret E. Child-Villiers.** Signed M. E. Jersey [Countess of Jersey].

3257 Parish life in England before the great pillage (Part II, concl.), 431–447. **Augustus Jessopp.** Signed.

3258 Specimen of a translation of the *Georgics* in blank verse, 448–456. **Herbert C. Gardner.** Signed, p. 456, Burghclere [Lord Burghclere]; see Venn.

3259 The reconstruction of the Diocese of Rochester, 457–465. **H. W. Yeatman-Biggs.** Signed Huyshe Southwark [Bishop Suffragan of Southwark in Diocese of Rochester]: see *WWW*/1928.

3260 Austria-Hungary and the Ausgleich, 466–480. **Emil Reich.** Signed.

3261 The future of Manchuria, 481–493. **F. E. Younghusband.** Signed.

3262 Some of the resources of Canada, 494–514. **Peter A. Kropotkin.** Signed as in no. 1110.

3263 Deaths under chloroform, 515–520. **E. Augusta King.** Signed E. A. King; Contents gives "Mrs. R. M. King"; see *LCCat.* under author cited. (See nos. 3277, 3278, 3304.)

VOLUME 43, APRIL 1898

3264 France and England, 521–533. **Francis de Pressensé.** Signed.

3265 The latest reconstruction of the navy, 534–548. **William Henry White.** Signed W. H. White; see *DNB*/1921.

3266 British ships in foreign navies, 549–

555. **Archibald S. Hurd.** Signed. (Note, pp. 866–868, signed W. H. White.)

3267 Why "vegetarian"? 556–569. **Henry Thompson, 1820–1904.** Signed; see *DNB*. (See nos. 3302, 3331.)

3268 Places and things of interest and beauty, 570–589. **Robert Hunter.** Signed.

3269 French ignorance of English literature in Tudor times, 590–603. **J. J. Jusserand.** Signed.

3270 The Conservative party and municipal elections, 604–611. **Joseph R. Diggle.** Signed.

3271 The Centenary of '98 [the Irish Insurrection], 612–624. **J. E. Redmond.** Signed.

3272 Eléonore d'Olbreuse and Queen Victoria, 625–632. **Adrienne van Amstel.** Signed.

3273 Cottage homes for the aged poor, 633–636. **John Hutton.** Signed.

3274 *Pot-Pourri from a Surrey Garden*, 637–647. **S. Reynolds Hole.** Signed.

3275 The Philosophical Radicals, 648–660. **Herbert Paul.** Signed.

3276 When Europe was on the brink of the Seven Years' War, 1754–56, 661–667. **A. C. Lyall.** Signed.

3277 Deaths under chloroform (No. I): a reply [to no. 3263], 668–675. **Dudley W. Buxton.** Signed.

3278 Deaths under chloroform (No. II): impure chloroform, 676–678. **William Ramsay, 1852–1916.** Signed; see *DNB*.

3279 A study in trade unionism, 679–692. **Benjamin Taylor.** Signed.

VOLUME 43, MAY 1898

3280 England's duties as a neutral, 693–705. **John Macdonell, 1845–1921.** Signed; see *DNB*.

3281 The growth of the world's armaments, 706–716. **H. W. Wilson.** Signed.

3282 The Caucasus and Tirah: a retrospect, 717–723. **R. W. Napier.** Signed Napier of Magdala [2nd Baron Napier of Magdala].

3283 The working girl of to-day, 724–730. **Albinia Hobart-Hampden.** Signed; Contents adds "Lady."

3284 The "limited-company" craze, 731–744. **S. F. van Oss.** Signed.

3285 Fox-hunting and agriculture, 745–754. **George F. Underhill.** Signed.

3286 Nicholas Culpeper: soldier, physician, astrologer, and politician, 755–763. **Sidney Peel.** Signed.

3287 A postal Utopia, 764–779. **J. Henniker Heaton.** Signed.

3288 The English Bible: Wyclif to Coverdale, 780–794. **H. W. Hamilton-Hoare.** Signed H. W. Hoare; see *WWW*/1940.

3289 A young lady's journey from Dublin to London in 1791, 795–808. **Jane Hester.** See p. 795.

3290 The Prisons Bill and progress in criminal treatment, 809–821. **E. F. Du Cane.** Signed.

3291 E. Meissonier: personal recollections and anecdotes, 822–840. **Charles Yriarte.** Signed.

3292 The romance of an ancient City church [Barking Church, London], 841–854. **A. J. Mason.** Signed; Contents adds "Professor."

3293 Representation of the colonies in the home parliament, 855–865. **Joseph Millerd Orpen.** Signed.

VOLUME 43, JUNE 1898

3294 "Splendid isolation" or what? 869–878. **Henry M. Stanley.** Signed.

3295 Our urgent need of a reserve of wheat, 879–889. **R. B. Marston.** Signed.

3296 Lord Salisbury's score in China, 890–898. **Holt S. Hallett.** Signed.

3297 The Workmen's Compensation Act, 1897, 899–914. **R. T. Thomson.** Signed.

3298 The difficulties and the limits of co-operation, 915–931. **Thomas Brassey.** Signed Brassey [1st Earl Brassey].

3299 On style in English prose, 932–942. **Frederic Harrison.** Signed.

3300 Breach of Church law: its danger and its remedy, 943–956. **Alfred Barry.** Signed.

3301 The Catholicism of the British army, 957–965. **Philip C. W. Trevor.** Signed.

3302 "Why vegetarian"?: a reply to critics [of no. 3267], 966–976. **Henry Thompson.** Signed.

3303 Wanted: an opera, 977–984. **J. A. Fuller Maitland.** Signed.

3304 Death and torture under chloroform: a rejoinder [to nos. 3277 and 3278], 985–993. **E. Augusta King.** Signed E. A. King; cf. no. 3263.

3305 The microbe in agriculture, 994–1001. **C. M. Aikman.** Signed.

3306 The first woman's hospital in Morocco, 1002–1007. **Mary Jane Brabazon.** Signed M. J. Meath; Contents adds Countess of Meath; repr. *Thoughts*.

3307 Fighting the bubonic plague in India, 1008–1016. **Kate Marion Hunter.** Signed

K. Marion Hunter; Contents adds "Miss"; see *Surgeon Index*.

3308 Among the elephants, 1017–1029. **J. D. Rees.** Signed.

3309 The fine-art of living, 1030–1042. **William Martin Conway.** Signed Martin Conway; see *DNB*/1940.

3310 Mr. Gladstone as a contributor to the *Nineteenth Century* [with a list of his articles], 1043–1046. **James Knowles.** Signed.

VOLUME 44, JULY 1898

3311 The Anglo-American future, 1–11. **Frederick Greenwood.** Signed. (See no. 3326.)

3312 A Russian comment on "England at war," 12–20. **Nicholas Shishkoff.** Signed as in no. 2145.

3313 Mr. Gladstone and the Roman Catholic Church, 21–29. **Wilfrid Meynell.** Signed Wilfred Meynell, evidently an error in transcription.

3314 Mr. Gladstone and the Nonconformists, 30–45. **J. Guinness Rogers.** Signed.

3315 The just punishments of heretics, 46–52. **William Wood.** Signed.

3316 The salons, 53–66. **Claude Phillips.** Signed.

3317 Sketches made in Germany (No. V), 67–78. **Katharine Blyth.** Signed.

3318 Civilisation in the western Soudan, 79–91. **Charles Henry Robinson.** Signed C. H. Robinson; see *WWW*/1928.

3319 Rural education, 92–101. **Edmund Verney.** Signed.

3320 Cyrano de Bergerac, 102–115. **Stanley Young.** Signed.

3321 The capture of Havana by England, 1762, 116–124. **John Adye,** 1857–1930. Signed as in no. 2836.

3322 The Wagner mania, 125–131. **J. Cuthbert Hadden.** Signed.

3323 The art of letter-writing, 132–150. **Herbert Paul.** Signed.

3324 The coal supplies of the world, 151–168. **Benjamin Taylor.** Signed.

VOLUME 44, AUGUST 1898

3325 Mr. Gladstone and his party, 169–185. **Wemyss Reid.** Signed.

3326 England and America, 186–195. **G. S. Clarke.** Signed.

3327 The Spaniards in Cuba, 196–207. **Antonio Gonzalo Perez.** Signed.

3328 The University of Oxford in 1898, 208–223. **George C. Brodrick.** Signed.

3329 The theatrical position, 224–233. **Frederick Wedmore.** Signed.

3330 The money-lending inquiry, 234–245. **T. W. Russell.** Signed.

3331 Vegetarian still: a reply to Sir Henry Thompson, 246–252. **Josiah Oldfield.** Signed; Contents adds "Dr."

3332 Commercial manslaughter [lead-poisoning], 253–258. **Gertrude Tuckwell.** Signed.

3333 Recent science, 259–280. **Peter A. Kropotkin.** Signed as in no. 1110.

3334 A plea for the better teaching of manners, 281–295. **Florence Bell.** Signed.

3335 A Gordon myth [about Chinese soldiers], 296–302. **Robert K. Douglas.** Signed.

3336 The taxation of ground values, 303–313. **Edward Sassoon.** Signed.

3337 Mr. Herbert Spencer: in self-defence, 314–327. **W. H. Mallock.** Signed. (See no. 3339.)

3338 American "yellow journalism," 328–340. **Elizabeth L. Banks.** Signed.

VOLUME 44, SEPTEMBER 1898

3339 What is social evolution? 348–358. **Herbert Spencer.** Signed.

3340 The art treasures of America (Part I), 359–372. **William Sharp.** Signed.

3341 The historical method of J. A. Froude, 373–385. **Frederic Harrison.** Signed; repr. *Tennyson, Ruskin, Mill.*

3342 A recent business tour in China, 386–399. **C. A. Moreing.** Signed.

3343 Vitalism, 400–413. **John Scott Haldane.** Signed John Haldane; see *WWW*/1940.

3344 Paris prisons during the Terror, 414–426. **H. Schütz Wilson.** Signed.

3345 Emigrant education, 427–436. **George Jacob Holyoake.** Signed.

3346 The return of the Jews to Palestine, 437–447. **Oswald John Simon.** Signed.

3347 An African adventure, 448–454. **Arthur Baring Koe.** Signed.

3348 A Catholic's view of *Helbeck of Bannisdale* [by Mrs. Humphry Ward], 455–467. **Richard F. Clarke.** Signed as in no. 2338. (See no. 3362.)

3349 Unparliamentary expressions, 468–486. **Michael Macdonagh.** Signed; repr. *Parliament*, 1902.

3350 The new American imperialism, 487–501. **Edward Dicey.** Signed.

3351 What was primitive Christianity? 502–

520. **W. S. Lilly.** Signed; repr., expanded, in *Christianity and Modern Civilization*, 1903, as "The Nascent Church."

VOLUME 44, OCTOBER 1898

3352 Should Europe disarm? 521–530. **Sidney Low.** Signed.

3353 The ritualist conspiracy, 531–544. **Cornelia H. M. Guest.** Signed Cornelia Wimborne [Lady Wimborne].

3354 The Benefices Act, 545–553. **Hugh Fortescue,** 1818–1905. Signed Fortescue [3rd Earl Fortescue].

3355 The French people, 554–566. **Hubert E. H. Jerningham.** Signed.

3356 The inventor of dynamite [Alfred Nobel], 567–581. **Henry de Mosenthal.** Signed.

3357 Fellah soldiers, old and new: a reminiscence and a moral, 582–590. **John Macdonald.** Signed; apparently by author of no. 1007: references to Graham and Baker, and on p. 585 to the author's personal knowledge of the "old army" in Egypt, 1881–1884; on p. 587 author says he was "Correspondent of the *Daily News*."

3358 The new great reform in the criminal law, 591–600. **George Pitt-Lewis.** Signed as in no. 2933.

3359 The art treasures of America (Part II, concl.), 601–617. **William Sharp.** Signed.

3360 Rough notes on the birds of the Bass Rock and neighbouring shores, 618–625. **Lionel Walter Rothschild.** Signed Walter Rothschild; see *DNB*/1940.

3361 The story of Murat and Bentinck, 626–640. **Walter Frewen Lord.** Signed.

3362 Another Catholic's view of *Helbeck of Bannisdale*, 641–655. **St. George Mivart.** Signed.

3363 The coming struggle in the Pacific, 656–672. **Benjamin Taylor.** Signed.

3364 Tuberculosis in man and beast, 673–687. **Herbert Maxwell.** Signed.

3365 The battle of Omdurman and the Mussulman world, 688–696. **Rafiüddin Ahmad.** Signed.

VOLUME 44, NOVEMBER 1898

3366 The Tsar's proposed conference and our foreign affairs (No. I), 697–706. **G. S. Clarke.** Signed.

3367 The Tsar's proposed conference and our foreign affairs, (No. II), 707–717. **J. Guinness Rogers.** Signed.

3368 Coal, trade, and the Empire, 718–723. **Archibald S. Hurd.** Signed.

3369 Confession, 724–730. **Theodosia Chapman.** Signed as in no. 1264.

3370 The O.C.R. [Order of Corporate Reunion] and its work, 731–747. **Frederick George Lee.** Signed.

3371 The clergy and the laity: an apologia, 749–753. **Augustus Jessopp.** Signed A. Jessopp; Contents gives "Rev. Dr. Jessopp."

3372 Sir George Grey: a South African tribute, 754–759. **John Robinson,** 1839–1903. Signed; see *DNB*, 2nd suppl.

3373 A lesson in acting: by two visible and one invisible actors, 760–768. **Hamilton Aïdé.** Signed.

3374 Ireland, real and ideal, 769–782. **Isabella Augusta Gregory.** Signed Augusta Gregory [Lady Gregory].

3375 Judging in the Gambia, 783–790. **Harry L. Stephen.** Signed.

3376 The historical method of Professor Freeman, 791–806. **Frederic Harrison.** Signed; repr. *Tennyson, Ruskin, Mill*.

3377 Fallacies about old age pensions, 807–818. **C. S. Loch.** Signed.

3378 Recent progress in German universities, 819–834. **Laurie Magnus.** Signed.

3379 Nursing the poor in their homes, 835–839. **Mabel Howard.** Signed; Contents adds "Lady."

3380 The Roman roads of Britain, 840–853. **W. B. Paley.** Signed.

3381 The legal status of women in India, 854–866. **Cornelia Sorabji.** Signed.

3382 How to circumvent "cramming" in Irish secondary education, 867–880. **J. P. Mahaffy.** Signed.

VOLUME 44, DECEMBER 1898

3383 The future of Egypt (No. I): our hampered trusteeship, 881–896. **Edward Dicey.** Signed.

3384 The future of Egypt (No. II): the Niger and the Nile: a warning, 897–904. **Henry Birchenough.** Signed.

3385 The future of Egypt (No. III): Egypt and Tunis: a study in international law, 905–914. **John Macdonell,** 1845–1921. Signed; see *DNB*.

3386 The proposed Muslim University in India, 915–921. **Rafiüddin Ahmad.** Signed.

3387 Does the Church of England teach anything? 922–939. **W. H. Mallock.** Signed.

3388 Neglecting our customers [on British

trade], 940–956. **Agnes Lambert.** Signed. (See no. 3428.)

3389   The Bohemian question, 957–970. **Francis Lützow.** Signed Lützow; Contents gives "Francis Count Lützow"; see *WWW*/1928 and *Titled Nobility*.

3390   The reorganisation of our national art museums, 971–979. **John Charles Robinson.** Signed as in no. 455.

3391   The London water supply, 980–990. **G. Shaw Lefevre.** Signed. (See no. 3423.)

3392   French views of an English university, 991–1003. **Margaret L. Woods.** Signed.

3393   Historical research, 1004–1014. **J. H. Round.** Signed.

3394   A girls' lodging-house, 1015–1023. **Désirée M. Leake.** Signed D. M. Leake; Contents gives "Mrs. Percy Leake"; see *WWW*/1950 under her husband.

3395   Is the lavish expenditure of wealth justifiable? 1024–1030. **Bradley Martin, Jun.** Signed.

3396   Cathedral reform, 1031–1040. **Samuel A. Barnett.** Signed; repr. *Practicable Socialism, New Series*, 1915.

3397   The Tirah and Khartoum expeditions, 1041–1047. **Lawrie Oppenheim.** Signed L. Oppenheim; see *WWW*/1928.

3398   Omdurman, 1048–1054. **John Frederick Maurice.** Signed F. Maurice; Contents gives "Major-General Frederick Maurice"; see *DNB*/1921.

VOLUME 45, JANUARY 1899

3399   The Liberal collapse (No. I): the party and its leaders, 1–9. **J. Guinness Rogers.** Signed.

3400   The Liberal collapse (No. II): a case for coalition, 10–19. **Sidney Low.** Signed.

3401   The Liberal collapse (No. III): the Independent Labour Party's programme, 20–38. **J. Keir Hardie** and **J. R. MacDonald.** Signed.

3402   British seamen for British ships, 39–45. **W. L. Ainslie** and **J. H. Yoxall.** Signed.

3403   France in Newfoundland, 46–55. **P. T. McGrath.** Signed.

3404   The colonial weakness of France, 56–66. **John Adye,** 1857–1930. Signed as in no. 2836.

3405   University education for Irish Catholics, 67–80. **Edward T. O'Dwyer.** Signed Edward Thomas, with addition, "Bishop of Limerick"; see *WWW*/1928.

3406   Vittoria Accoramboni, 81–89. **Margaret Maitland.** Signed.

3407   The open-air cure of consumption: a

personal experience, 92–101. **James Arthur Gibson.** Signed; repr. *Nordrach Treatment for Consumptives*, 1902. (See nos. 3425, 3433.)

3408   Impressions of American universities, 102–112. **Percy Gardner.** Signed.

3409   Fly fishing, 113–125. **Sydney Buxton.** Signed.

3410   Some recollections of Sir Edward Burne-Jones, 126–131. **Joseph Jacobs.** Signed.

3411   Are savage gods borrowed from missionaries? 132–144. **Andrew Lang.** Signed; repr. with revisions *Magic and Religion*, 1901, as "Theory of Loan Gods."

3412   The Alps in 1898, 145–148. **Reginald Hughes.** Signed.

3413   The Dreyfus drama and its significance, 149–172. **Yves Guyot.** Signed.

VOLUME 45, FEBRUARY 1899

3414   The present crisis in the Church of England, 173–187. **C. L. Wood.** Signed Halifax [2nd Viscount Halifax].

3415   Ritualism and disestablishment, 188–201. **George W. E. Russell.** Signed; repr. *The Household of Faith*, 1902.

3416   Some plain words about the Tsar's new gospel of peace, 202–215. **Henry H. Howorth.** Signed.

3417   War as the supreme test of national value, 216–225. **H. F. Wyatt.** Signed.

3418   An all-British cable system: cables as auxiliary weapons of imperial defence, 226–234. **Archibald S. Hurd.** Signed. With letter, 234, signed **C. J. Rhodes.**

3419   Sketches made in Germany (Part V), 235–244. **Katharine Blyth.** Signed.

3420   Lord Beaconsfield's novels, 245–260. **Walter Frewen Lord.** Signed.

3421   The new psychology, 261–272. **St. George Mivart.** Signed.

3422   On the *Maiolicia of Faenza*, 273–281. **C. D. E. Fortnum.** Signed.

3423   The London water supply: an answer [to no. 3391], 282–294. **Arthur Shadwell.** Signed.

3424   International fishery legislation, 295–303. **Otto Pettersson.** Signed O. Pettersson; Contents gives first name and title "Prof."

3425   The prevention of consumption, 304–314. **J. G. Sinclair Coghill.** Signed, with title "M.D." (See no. 3433.)

3426   Liberty of the press in France, 315–326. **John E. Power Wallis.** Signed J. P. Wallis; see *WWW*/1950.

3427 Florentine gardens in March, 327–335. **Emily Lawless.** Signed.

3428 Neglecting our customers: a postscript [to no. 3388], 336–340. **Agnes Lambert.** Signed.

VOLUME 45, MARCH 1899

3429 The nation and the ritualists, 341–357. **J. Guinness Rogers.** Signed.

3430 The crisis in the Church, 358–367. **R. Bosworth Smith.** Signed.

3431 The land and the labourers, 368–377. **C. R. Wynn-Carrington.** Signed Carrington [1st Earl Carrington].

3432 The French judicial system, 378–388. **Alphonse de Calonne.** Signed.

3433 The Nordrach cure [for consumption] practicable in this country, 389–403. **James Arthur Gibson.** Signed; repr. *Nordrach Treatment for Consumptives*, 1902.

3434 Recent science, 404–423. **Peter A. Kropotkin.** Signed as in no. 1110.

3435 The Menelik myth, 424–433. **Edmond de Poncins.** Signed; Contents adds "Vicomte."

3436 Sketches made in Germany (Part VI, concl.), 434–446. **Katharine Blyth.** Signed.

3437 The great tractarian [George Savile, Marquess of Halifax], 447–464. **Herbert Paul.** Signed.

3438 A university for the people, 465–476. **J. Churton Collins.** Signed.

3439 The retardation of the navy by the engineers' strike, 477–485. **Archibald S. Hurd.** Signed.

3440 The sack of Yangchow in 1644: a Chinese narrative, 486–501. **Wang Hsiu-ch'u.** Page 487. Trans. with an intro. note by **Robert K. Douglas**—signed.

3441 Is the party system breaking up? 502–511. **T. E. Kebbel.** Signed. (See no. 3461.)

3442 "Hands off Trinity" [Trinity Coll. Dublin], 512–524. **Anthony Traill.** Signed.

VOLUME 45, APRIL 1899

3443 Germany as an object-lesson, 525–537. **Charles Copland Perry.** Signed.

3444 The cry for new markets, 538–547. **Frederick Greenwood.** Signed.

3445 Australian federation, 548–557. **Thomas Brassey.** Signed Brassey [1st Earl Brassey].

3446 The "lawless" clergy of "this Church

and realm," 558–569. **George Arthur.** Signed.

3447 The natural decline of warfare, 570–578. **Alexander Sutherland.** Signed.

3448 The Thames as a salmon river, 579–589. **R. B. Marston.** Signed.

3449 A sample of Chinese administration, 590–597. **R. P. Cobbold.** Signed.

3450 Ladies' clubs, 598–611. **Eva Anstruther.** Signed.

3451 The new planet, "Eros," 612–619. **Edmund Ledger.** Signed as in no. 2797.

3452 The naval situation, 620–635. **H. W. Wilson.** Signed.

3453 Woman as an athlete, 636–645. **Arabella Kenealy.** Signed, with addition "L.R.C.P." [Licentiate of Royal Coll. of Physicians]. (See nos. 3463, 3479.)

3454 The English Bible from Henry the Eighth to James the First, 646–662. **H. W. Hamilton-Hoare.** Signed as in no. 3288.

3455 Higher education and the state, 663–670. **T. J. Macnamara.** Signed.

3456 Winged carriers of disease, 671–680. **Eliza Priestley.** Signed.

3457 Old age pensions: a suggestion, 681–688. **Spencer Walpole,** 1839–1907. Signed S. Walpole; Contents gives "Sir Spencer Walpole"; see *DNB*, 2nd suppl.

VOLUME 45, MAY 1899

3458 The hypocrisies of the Peace Conference, 689–698. **Sidney Low.** Signed.

3459 Russia in Finland, 699–715. **J. N. Reuter.** Signed.

3460 The ethics of war, 716–728. **H. I. D. Ryder.** Signed; repr. *Essays*, 1911.

3461 The failure of party government: a reply [to no. 3441], 729–732. **Goldwin Smith.** Signed.

3462 The Church of England as by law established, 733–744. **Edmund Robertson.** Signed.

3463 Woman as an athlete: a reply to Dr. Arabella Kenealy, 745–754. **Laura Ormiston Chant.** Signed L. Ormiston Chant; see *WWW*/1928.

3464 The influence of women in Islâm, 755–774. **Syed Ameer Ali.** Signed as in no. 454.

3465 Booksellers and bookselling, 775–784. **Joseph Shaylor.** Signed.

3466 An outburst of activity in the Roman congregations, 785–794. **William Gibson,** 1868–1942. Signed; see *WWW*/1950 under Ashbourne. (See no. 3483.)

3467 The House in the Wood [used for the

1899 peace conference], 795–801. **Elisabeth Lecky.** Signed.

3468 Germany as a naval power, 802–814. **G. S. Clarke.** Signed.

3469 Homing pigeons in war-time, 815–820. **George J. Larner.** Signed.

3470 Reminiscences of Lady Byron, 821–832. **Adelaide Ross.** Signed.

3471 The jackeroo [immigrant to Australia], 833–840. **A. C. Yorke.** Signed.

3472 The law as to "constructive murder," 841–849. **George Pitt-Lewis.** Signed as in no. 2933.

3473 British trade in 1898: a warning note, 850–856. **J. W. Cross.** Signed.

3474 Wireless telegraphy and "brain-waves" [letter to *Spectator* with intro. note], 857–864. **James Knowles.** Signed, p. 858.

VOLUME 45, JUNE 1899

3475 The cry of the villages, 865–879. **Augustus Jessopp.** Signed; repr. *Great Pillage.*

3476 Parnell and Ireland, 880–890. **Leonard Courtney.** Signed.

3477 The present position of the Friendly Societies, 891–905. **H. V. Toynbee.** Signed.

3478 An Imperial telegraph system, 906–914. **J. Henniker Heaton.** Signed.

3479 Woman as an athlete: a rejoinder [to no. 3463], 915–929. **Arabella Kenealy.** Signed.

3480 Shakespeare in France, 930–937. **Sidney Lee.** Signed.

3481 Beneficent germs, 938–943. **Henry S. Gabbett.** Signed, with title "M.D."

3482 The decline of the art of singing, 944–954. **Richard Davey.** Signed.

3483 Catholic apologetics: a reply [to no. 3466], 955–961. **Wilfrid Ward.** Signed.

3484 The gold diggings at Bathurst in 1851, 962–972. **Henrietta Huxley.** Signed; Contents gives "Mrs. Huxley"; see Huxley, *Life*, I, 39.

3485 The decay in our salmon fisheries and its remedy, 973–980. **Hely Hutchinson Almond.** Signed.

3486 Jainism: a chat with Raja Sivaprasad, 981–990. **Ernest M. Bowden.** Signed.

3487 Sea-power and sea-carriage, 991–1006. **Benjamin Taylor.** Signed.

3488 Some notes from Washington, 1007–1013. **Richard Weightman.** Signed.

3489 Erastianism, 1014–1022. **J. Llewelyn Davies.** Signed.

3490 The falling-off in the quantity and

quality of the clergy, 1023–1030. **Anthony C. Deane.** Signed.

VOLUME 46, JULY 1899

3491 Are we to lose South Africa? 1–7. **Sidney Shippard.** Signed. (See nos. 3522, 3523.)

3492 School children as wage-earners, 8–17. **John E. Gorst,** 1835–1916. Signed: *DNB.*

3493 The International Council of Women in congress, 18–25. **Ishbel M. Gordon.** Signed Ishbel Aberdeen [Countess of Aberdeen].

3494 The open spaces of the future, 26–35. **Octavia Hill.** Signed.

3495 The mediaeval Sunday, 36–50. **Herbert Thurston.** Signed, with title "S.J."

3496 The native Australian family, 51–64. **Edith Simcox.** Signed.

3497 Dante's ghosts, 65–76. **D. R. Fearon.** Signed.

3498 While waiting in a friend's room, 77–83. **Algernon West.** Signed; repr. *One City.*

3499 The teeth of the schoolboy, 84–93. **Edwin Collins.** Signed E. Collins, with addition "Editor of *The Dentist*"; Contents gives first name.

3500 The outlook at Ottawa, 94–101. **J. G. Snead Cox.** Signed.

3501 The English masque, 102–111. **Edward Dowden.** Signed; repr. *Essays.*

3502 Is there really a "crisis" in the Church? 112–122. **Charles A. Roe.** Signed.

3503 Lord Ellenborough, 123–130. **Spencer Walpole,** 1839–1907. Signed as in no. 3457. (See no. 3513.)

3504 Old-age pensions in France, 131–141. **Arthur F. Wood.** Signed.

3505 Parliamentary government in Japan, 142–152. **H. N. G. Bushby.** Signed.

3506 A Supreme Moment: a play in one act, 153–172. **Lucy Clifford.** Signed; Contents gives "Mrs. W. K. Clifford."

VOLUME 46, AUGUST 1899

3507 The excessive armies of Russia, 173–179. **J. L. A. Simmons.** Signed.

3508 The limitations of naval force, 180–191. **G. S. Clarke.** Signed.

3509 A woman's criticism of the Women's Congress, 192–202. **Frances H. Low.** Signed. (See no. 3531.)

3510 What church has "continuity"? 203–212. **St. George Mivart.** Signed.

3511 The recent fuss about the Irish

language, 213–222. **J. P. Mahaffy.** Signed.

3512 The connection of England with Newfoundland, 223–237. **George William Des Voeux.** Signed William Des Voeux; cf. nos. 2533, 2604.

3513 Lord Ellenborough: a reply [to no. 3503], 238–242. **Reginald C. E. Abbot.** Signed Colchester [3rd Baron of Colchester].

3514 Did Byron write "Werner"? 243–250. **Edward Frederick Leveson-Gower.** Signed F. Leveson Gower; Contents gives Frederick and adds "Hon."; see *DNB*, 2nd suppl.

3515 The Marlborough gems, 251–261. **Charles Newton-Robinson.** Signed.

3516 Why are our brains deteriorating? 262–272. **Henry Elsdale.** Signed as in no. 2699.

3517 Life on the Nile south of Fashoda, 273–281. **Arthur D. Milne.** Signed.

3518 "The humours of Ter-na-nog" [of Ireland], 282–288. **Lina Orman Cooper.** Signed L. Orman Cooper; Contents adds "Mrs."; see *BMCat.*

3519 The *Decameron* and its villas, 289–301. **W. J. Stillman.** Signed.

3520 Madame Necker, 302–316. **Marcia C. Maxwell.** Signed; Contents adds "Hon."

3521 The evolution of the parliamentary oath, 317–333. **Michael MacDonagh.** Signed; repr. *Parliament*, 1902.

3522 The casus belli in South Africa, 334–344. **Edmund Robertson.** Signed.

VOLUME 46, SEPTEMBER 1899

3523 Are we to lose South Africa?: a rejoinder [to no. 3522], 345–351. **Sidney Shippard.** Signed.

3524 The imperial function of trade, 352–366. **Henry Birchenough.** Signed.

3525 Rifle-shooting as a national sport, 367–382. **W. A. Baillie-Grohman.** Signed.

3526 The future of the great armies, 383–395. **Sidney Low.** Signed.

3527 A visit to the Craig Brook salmon hatchery, 396–409. **Moreton Frewen.** Signed.

3528 An Indian plague story, 410–431. **Cornelia Sorabji.** Signed.

3529 The father of letters [Cicero], 432–444. **Herbert Paul.** Signed.

3530 Rowton houses: from a resident, 445–454. **W. A. Sommerville.** Signed.

3531 A woman's criticism of the Women's Congress, a reply [to no. 3509], 455–458. **Fannie Humphreys Gaffney.** Signed;

with addition "President National Council of Women of the United States."

3532 The American negro and his place, 459–474. **Elizabeth L. Banks.** Signed.

3533 The Sierra Leone disturbances, 475–483. **Harry L. Stephen.** Signed.

3534 An all-British railway to China, 484–492. **C. A. Moreing.** Signed.

3535 Carlyle as an historian, 493–503. **G. M. Trevelyan.** Signed.

3536 The philosophy of poetry, 504–513. **Martin Morris.** Signed.

3537 The future of the Christian religion, 514–520. **Henry R. Percival.** Signed, with addition "Presbyter of the Diocese of Pennsylvania, U.S.A."

VOLUME 46, OCTOBER 1899

3538 The situation in South Africa: a voice from Cape Colony, 522–526. **C. Usher Wilson.** Signed, with address "The Rectory, Codesberg, Cape Colony."

3539 Liberalism and its cross-currents, 527–540. **J. Guinness Rogers.** Signed.

3540 The great unpaid [unpaid public servants], 541–549. **Algernon West.** Signed; repr. *One City.*

3541 The fear of over-education, 550–555. **Alexander Sutherland.** Signed.

3542 Electricity in India, 556–559. **C. C. Townsend.** Signed.

3543 Thirteenth-century Persian lustre pottery, 560–569. **Henry Wallis.** Signed.

3544 Town and country labourers (No. I), 570–582. **Henrietta M. Batson.** Signed as in no. 2157.

3545 Town and country labourers (No. II), 583–590. **Percy Wyndham.** Signed.

3546 The hospital where the plague broke out, 591–602. **Charlotte O'Conor-Eccles.** Signed C. O'Conor-Eccles; Contents adds "Miss"; see *WWW/1916.*

3547 North Clare: leaves from a diary, 603–612. **Emily Lawless.** Signed.

3548 A Tibetan poet and mystic [Milaraspa], 613–632. **Graham Sandberg.** Signed; Contents adds "Rev."

3549 Powder and paint, 633–640. **Ida A. Taylor.** Signed as in no. 2610.

3550 The cry of the consumptives, 641–653. **James Arthur Gibson.** Signed; repr. *Nordrach Treatment for Consumptives,* 1902.

3551 The new Reformation [sequel to no. 1683]: a conscience clause for the laity, 654–672. **Mary A. Ward.** Signed; Contents gives "Mrs. Humphry Ward."

3552 The Church crisis and disestablishment, 673–684. **W. F. Geikie-Cobb.**

Signed **W. F. Cobb**, with addition "D.D."; see *WWW*/1950.

3553 Lambeth and "liberation," 685–692. **George W. E. Russell.** Signed; repr. The *Household of Faith*, 1902, as "A Mockery, a Delusion, and a Snare."

VOLUME 46, NOVEMBER 1899

3554 After the present war [in South Africa], 693–707. **Edward Dicey.** Signed.
3555 Native unrest in South Africa, 708–716. **Emma M. Green.** Signed E. M. Green; see *RG*, *LCCat.*, and *Yearbook*/1922.
3556 The battle of Trafalgar: an unpublished narrative, 717–728. **William Pryce Cumby.** Signed. Intro. note, 717–718, signed **Erasmus Ommanney**, with title "Admiral." Footnotes by **Robert Patton** —intro. note.
3557 The future of Lord Rosebery, 729–733. **H. W. Massingham.** Signed.
3558 The Van Dyck exhibition at Antwerp, 734–752. **Claude Phillips.** Signed.
3559 The intellectual future of Catholicism, 753–768. **W. H. Mallock.** Signed.
3560 Horticulture as a profession for the educated, 769–781. **Ada Goodrich-Freer.** Signed A. Goodrich Freer; Contents adds "Miss"; see *WWW*/1940.
3561 The Dalmeny experiments: manuring with brains, 782–791. **D. Young.** Signed; see *BMCat.*
3562 Cricket in 1899: the valuation of drawn matches, 792–797. **A. C. Wootton.** Signed.
3563 Literature before letters, 798–813. **Friedrich Max Müller.** Signature; repr. *Last Essays.*
3564 A devil-dance in Ceylon, 814–817. **Caroline Corner-Ohlmüs.** Signed; Contents gives "Mrs."
3565 Charity versus outdoor relief, 818–826. **Samuel A. Barnett.** Signed.
3566 "The remittance man" [in the colonies], 827–832. **D. Wallace Duthie.** Signed, with addition "David Garth," his pseudonym.
3567 The plague in Oporto, 833–847. **Arthur Shadwell.** Signed A. Shadwell; see *WWW*/1940.
3568 The newspapers (No. I), 848–864. **Wemyss Reid.** Signed.

VOLUME 46, DECEMBER 1899

3569 South African problems and lessons (No. I), 865–880. **Sidney Low.** Signed.

3570 South African problems and lessons (No. II), 881–890. **Sidney Shippard.** Signed.
3571 English and Dutch in the past, 891–904. **Alice S. Green.** Signed A. S. Green; Contents gives "Mrs. John Richard Green"; see *WWW*/1940.
3572 Terms used in modern gunnery, 905–914. **John Frederick Maurice.** Signed as in no. 3398.
3573 Mr. Stephen Phillips's tragedy of *Paolo and Francesca*, 915–933. **Sidney Colvin.** Signed.
3574 Recent science: meteorites and comets, 934–946. **Peter A. Kropotkin.** Signed as in no. 1110.
3575 Cromwell and the electorate, 947–956. **J. Horace Round.** Signed.
3576 A negro on the position of the negro in America, 957–973. **D. E. Tobias.** Signed.
3577 Plagiarism, 974–981. **E. F. Benson.** Signed.
3578 The Churchman's politics: a dialogue, 982–987. **Anthony C. Deane.** Signed.
3579 The war-cloud in the farthest East, 988–995. **Holt S. Hallett.** Signed.
3580 A Hindu home, 996–1007. **J. D. Rees.** Signed.
3581 Austria at the end of the century, 1008–1019. **Francis Lützow.** Signed as in no. 3389.
3582 The newspapers (No. II), 1020–1034. **Wemyss Reid.** Signed.

VOLUME 47, JANUARY 1900

3583 The defence of the Empire and the militia ballot, 1–13. **G. S. Clarke.** Signed. Intro. note signed **James Knowles.**
3584 The military weakness of England and the militia ballot, 14–28. **Sidney Low.** Signed.
3585 The volunteers, 29–35. **J. G. B. Stopford.** Signed.
3586 Our Indian troops, 36–40. **Henry H. Howorth.** Signed.
3587 The South African conspiracy against British rule, 41–50. **A. Theodore Wirgman.** Signed, with addition "Canon of Grahamstown Cathedral."
3588 The continuity of Catholicism, 51–72. **St. George Mivart.** Signed. (See no. 3603.)
3589 The prince of journalists [Jonathan Swift], 73–87. **Herbert Paul.** Signed.
3590 The ghost of Doctor Harris (from an original MS. of Nathaniel Hawthorne, dedicated to Mrs. J. P. Heywood), 88–

93. **Nathaniel Hawthorne.** Signed. Intro. note signed **A. M. Wilberforce.**

3591   Climate and the atmosphere, 94–102. **John M. Bacon.** Signed.

3592   Can sentences be standardised? 103–115. **Montague Crackanthorpe.** Signed.

3593   The Jews in France, 116–120. **Paul Bettelheim.** Signed.

3594   The War relief funds, 121–129. **C. G. Lang.** Signed. (See no. 3616.)

3595   The common mule, 130–138. **R. B. Townshend.** Signed.

3596   The tinkering of hymns, 139–145. **J. Cuthbert Hadden.** Signed.

3597   Shakespeare and the modern stage, 146–156. **Sidney Lee.** Signed.

3598   The newspapers (No. III), 157–172. **Wemyss Reid.** Signed.

VOLUME 47, FEBRUARY 1900

3599   The "confusion worse confounded" at the War Office, 173–207. The article, 187–207, is by **George Tomkyns Chesney.** Reprint of no. 2085. Introduction, entitled "The general management of the army," 174–186, by **Spenser Wilkinson.** Signed. Intro. note for both arts. signed **James Knowles.**

3600   The militia, 208–222. **Herbert Maxwell.** Signed.

3601   The militia ballot, 223–226. **John R. W. de Vesci.** Signed De Vesci; Contents gives "Viscomte de Vesci"; see Burke and *RG.*

3602   Our peace training for war: guilty or not guilty? 227–243. **Lonsdale Hale.** Signed.

3603   Dr. Mivart on the continuity of Catholicism, 244–259. **Richard F. Clarke.** Signed as in no. 2338.

3604   The two reports of the Licensing Commission, 260–274. **Algernon West.** Signed. (See no. 3626.)

3605   The new mysticism in Scandinavia, 279–296. **Hermione Ramsden.** Signed.

3606   Electrical engineering and the municipalities, 297–303. **A. A. Campbell Swinton.** Signed.

3607   Harmonic literature, 304–307. **Joseph H. Choate, Jun.** Signed.

3608   Ancient Egyptian ceramic art, 308–320. **Henry Wallis.** Signed.

3609   Some stray shots and a moral [a story of the West in America], 321–329. **R. B. Townshend.** Signed.

3610   In the Alps of Dauphiné, 330–338. **Gertrude Lowthian Bell.** Signed.

3611   Neutrals and the [Boer] War [as seen

from the Hague conference], 339–349. **John Macdonell,** 1845–1921. Signed; see *DNB.*

3612   The newspapers (No. IV), 350–364. **Wemyss Reid.** Signed.

VOLUME 47, MARCH 1900

3613   The breakdown of voluntary enlistment, 365–377. **Sidney Low.** Signed.

3614   The actual strength of our forces at home, 378–381. **Thomas G. Baring.** Signed Northbrook [Earl Northbrook].

3615   The future of mounted infantry, 382–391. **Thomas Denman.** Signed Denman [3rd Baron Denman].

3616   The relief funds, 392–395. **Horatio Nelson.** Signed Nelson [3rd Earl Nelson].

3617   The civil and moral benefits of drill, 396–399. **G. Sale Reaney.** Signed.

3618   Senussi and his threatened holy war: a warning, 400–412. **T. R. Threlfall.** Signed.

3619   The problem of the Middle East, 413–424. **Thomas E. Gordon.** Signed T. E. Gordon; see *DNB/1921.*

3620   Scripture and Roman Catholicism, 425–442. **St. George Mivart.** Signed.

3621   Cromwell's constitutional experiments, 443–458. **John E. Power Wallis.** Signed as in no. 3426.

3622   On some difficulties incidental to middle age, 459–470. **Florence Bell.** Signed; repr. *The Minor Moralist,* 1903.

3623   Women workers: how they live, how they wish to live, 471–484. **Emily Hobhouse.** Signed.

3624   In defence of Sir David Chalmers, 485–497. **Janet A. Chalmers.** Signed J. A. Chalmers; Contents gives "Lady Chalmers"; see *WWW/1916* under Sir David Chalmers.

3625   The story of the Bulwer-Clayton Treaty, 498–509. **Benjamin Taylor.** Signed.

3626   The "temperance" reply to Sir Algernon West [in no. 3604], 510–525. **Thomas P. Whittaker.** Signed.

3627   The newspapers (No. V), 526–540. **Wemyss Reid.** Signed.

VOLUME 47, APRIL 1900

3628   The proper precautions for imperial safety, 541–553. **G. S. Clarke.** Signed.

3629   The insufficient proposals of the War Office, 554–567. **H. O. Arnold-Forster.** Signed.

3630 Are we misled about the fleet? 568–579. **H. W. Wilson.** Signed.

3631 The "parlous position" of England, 580–592. **W. S. Lilly.** Signed.

3632 The Boers and the native question, 593–602. **A. Theodore Wirgman.** Signed.

3633 Who is to pay for the [Boer] War? 603–608. **Robert A. Haldane-Duncan.** Signed Camperdown [3rd Earl of Camperdown].

3634 Planting out state children in South Africa, 609–611. **J. D. S. Campbell.** Signed Lorne [Marquis of Lorne].

3635 Mr. Ruskin at Farnley, 617–623. **Edith Mary Fawkes.** Signed.

3636 The autocrat of the dinner table [John Selden], 624–636. **Herbert Paul.** Signed.

3637 Excavations in the Roman Forum: "Hastae martiae et ops consiva," 637–651. **Giacomo Boni.** Signed.

3638 A Dutch fairy tale, 652–662. **Margaret Robinson.** Signed.

3639 The scarcity of coal, 663–668. **Bennett H. Brough.** Signed.

3640 A liberal Catholic view of the case of Dr. Mivart, 669–684. **Robert Edward Dell.** Signed.

3641 The French army, 685–697. **Paul Bettelheim.** Signed.

3642 The newspapers (No. VI), 698–712. **Wemyss Reid.** Signed.

VOLUME 47, MAY 1900

3643 The question of submarine boats, 713–722. **Edmund Robertson.** Signed.

3644 The dearth of naval engineers, 723–727. **Charles E. Lart.** Signed.

3645 Local beginnings of imperial defence: an example, 728–733. **Henry Birchenough.** Signed.

3646 The volunteers and the insecurity of England, 734–743. **J. G. B. Stopford.** Signed.

3647 American public opinion of the [Boer] War, 744–752. **H. H. Bowen.** Signed. (See no. 3706.)

3648 Marksmanship old and new, 753–766. **W. A. Baillie-Grohman.** Signed.

3649 The British sphere in Asia, 767–775. **Charles E. D. Black.** Signed.

3650 The elders of Arcady, 776–792. **Augustus Jessopp.** Signed; repr. *Peasantry*.

3651 The "Perseus and Andromeda" of Titian, 793–801. **Claude Phillips.** Signed.

3652 Woman's brain, 802–810. **Alexander Sutherland.** Signed.

3653 A chat about Jane Austen's novels, 811–820. **W. S. Northcote.** Signed Iddesleigh [2nd Earl of Iddesleigh].

3654 The true story of the prisoner of Chillon, 821–829. **Adrienne van Amstel.** Signed A. van Amstel; Contents adds "Baronne"; cf. no. 3272.

3655 On the merits and demerits of thrift, 830–838. **Florence Bell.** Signed; repr. *The Minor Moralist*, 1903.

3656 Growing bureaucracy and parliamentary decline, 839–846. **Alice Stopford Green.** Signed.

3657 Women's clubs in America, 847–854. **Margaret Polson Murray.** Signed, with address "Montreal" and title "Hon. Mem. General Federation of Women's Clubs."

3658 Imperial federation and some neglected colonial ties, 855–865. **John Macdonell,** 1845–1921. Signed; see *DNB*.

3659 The newspapers (No. VII), 866–880 **Wemyss Reid.** Signed.

VOLUME 47, JUNE 1900

3660 The future of South Africa (No. I): voice from Natal, 881–889. **F. S. Tatham.** Signed, with addition "Member of the Legislative Assembly of Natal."

3661 The future of South Africa (No. II): the native races, 890–898. **J. S. Moffat.** Signed.

3662 The cavalry rush to Kimberley, and in pursuit of Cronje, 899–915. **Cecil Boyle.** Signed. Intro. note, 899–902, signed **Sydney Buxton.**

3663 The cruel case of the wounded warhorses, 916–922. **Laurence W. Pike.** Signed.

3664 Enigmas of Empire, 923–935. **Sidney Low.** Signed.

3665 Swiss rifle clubs, 936–949. **J. H. Rivett-Carnac.** Signed.

3666 The prospects of Anglicanism, 950–959. **W. F. Geikie-Cobb.** Signed as in no. 3552.

3667 Liberalism and intransigeance, 960–973. **Wilfrid Ward.** Signed. (See no. 3686.)

3668 The vogue of the garden book, 974–987. **Henrietta M. Batson.** Signed as in no. 3544.

3669 The intellectual awakening of China, 988–992. **Robert K. Douglas.** Signed.

3670 Tycho Brahe, 993–1004. **Arthur Ponsonby.** Signed.

3671 The copyright bills, 1900, 1005–1019. **Henry Thring.** Signed Thring [1st Baron Thring].

3672 The genius of Handel, 1020–1029. **H. Heathcote Statham.** Signed.

3673 The Irish guards, 1030–1035. **Fitzalan Manners.** Signed, with addition "Captain, Scots Guards."

3674 The newspapers (No. VIII), 1036–1050. **Wemyss Reid.** Signed.

VOLUME 48, JULY 1900

3675 The lessons of the [Boer] War: a proposed association (No. I), 1–3. Signed by a large number of prospective members. (See nos. 3690 and 3757.)

3676 Our vacillation in China and its consequences, 4–16. **Henry Norman,** 1858–1939. Signed; see *WWW*.

3677 Soldier settlers in South Africa, 17–26. **J. G. B. Stopford.** Signed.

3678 The home generals and their work in the coming autumn, 27–41. **Lonsdale Hale.** Signed.

3679 Administrative reform in the Public Service, 42–53. **P. Lyttelton Gell.** Signed. (See no. 3734.)

3680 The National Gallery in 1900, and its present arrangements, 54–74. **Marion H. Spielmann.** Signed as in no. 3061.

3681 In the bye-ways of rural Ireland (Part I), 75–88. **Michael MacDonagh.** Signed.

3682 Hooliganism and juvenile crime: the only cure, 89–99. **Andrew A. W. Drew.** Signed.

3683 Town children in the country, 100–107. **Henrietta O. Barnett.** Signed.

3684 Sixpenny telegrams, 108–117. **J. Henniker Heaton.** Signed.

3685 Identification offices in India and Egypt, 118–126. **Francis Galton.** Signed.

3686 Mr. Wilfrid Ward's apologetics, 127–136. **Robert Edward Dell.** Signed.

3687 The prerogative of dissolution, 137–148. **Edmund Robertson.** Signed.

3688 Wanted a leader, 149–158. **J. Guinness Rogers.** Signed.

3689 The newspapers (No. IX), 159–172. **Wemyss Reid.** Signed.

VOLUME 48, AUGUST 1900

3690 The lessons of the War: a proposed association (No. II), 173–183. Signed by a large number of prospective members. (Note, p. 345, by **James Knowles** —signed Editor *NC*; see no. 3757.)

3691 "Ordinary business principles" (No. I), 184–188. **James Blyth.** Signed. Intro. note by **James Knowles**—claimed, p. 184.

3692 "Ordinary business principles" (No. II), 189–191. **Wemyss Reid.** Signed.

3693 "Ordinary business principles" (No. III), 191. **Andrew Fairbairn.** Signed.

3694 "Ordinary business principles" (No. IV), 192. **John Wolfe Barry.** Signed.

3695 "Ordinary business principles" (No. V), 192–193. **Alfred Harmsworth.** Signed.

3696 "Ordinary business principles" (No. VI), 193. **Frederick Bradford McCrea?** Signed Major McCrea; man cited was a major in the army and founded Army and Navy Cooperative Society Ltd.: see *WWW*/1916.

3697 "Ordinary business principles" (No. VII), 193–195. **Henry Birchenough.** Signed. (See no. 3712 on the series.)

3698 Our infantry, 196–197. **T. G. Baring.** Signed Northbrook [1st Earl Northbrook].

3699 How to breed horses for war, 198–206. **Wilfrid Scawen Blunt.** Signed.

3700 Missionaries in Egypt, 207–218. **Arnold Ward.** Signed.

3701 The new Commonwealth, 219–225. **Albert Graham Berry.** Signed.

3702 The slow growth of moral influence in politics, 226–235. **John Percival.** Signed J. Hereford [Bishop of Hereford].

3703 The imperial note in Victorian poetry, 236–248. **J. A. R. Marriott.** Signed.

3704 Notes on players and old plays, 249–255. **Frederick Wedmore.** Signed.

3705 The small industries of Britain, 256–271. **Peter A. Kropotkin.** Signed as in no. 1110.

3706 An American view of the Boer War, 272–284. **Edward J. Hodgson.** Signed.

3707 Some unseen stars, 285–297. **Edmund Ledger.** Signed as in no. 2797.

3708 In the bye-ways of rural Ireland (Part II, concl.), 298–314. **Michael MacDonagh.** Signed.

3709 The newspapers (No. X), 315–329. **Wemyss Reid.** Signed.

3710 The Chinese revolt, 330–338. **Frederick Greenwood.** Signed.

3711 Vengeance and afterwards [the Chinese revolt], 339–344. **Edward Dicey.** Signed.

VOLUME 48, SEPTEMBER 1900

3712 "Business principles" in the public service, 345–356. **Edmund Robertson.** Signed.

3713 The staff work in the [Boer] War, 357–372. **Lonsdale Hale.** Signed.

3714 The religions of China (Part I): Confucianism, 373–384. **Friedrich Max Müller.** Signature; entire series repr. *Last Essays.*

3715 The situation in Italy, 385–392. **Giovanni Dalla Vecchia.** Signed.

3716 American imperialism, 393–406. **Bradley Martin, Jun.** Signed.

3717 Our allies at Waterloo, 407–422. **Herbert Maxwell.** Signed. (See no. 3735.)

3718 The traditional "British sailor," 423–435. **W. J. Fletcher.** Signed.

3719 The Maiolica [pottery] of Siena, 436–450. **Langton Douglas.** Signed.

3720 The oldest picture-book of all [the sky], 451–464. **E. Walter Maunder.** Signed.

3721 Statistics of suicide, 465–482. **Reginald A. Skelton.** Signed.

3722 The burden of coal, 483–495. **Benjamin Taylor.** Signed.

3723 The newspapers (No. XI), 496–509. **Wemyss Reid.** Signed.

3724 The South African war hospitals, 510–520. **Murray Guthrie.** Signed.

VOLUME 48, OCTOBER 1900

3725 A nation of amateurs, 521–535. **George C. Brodrick.** Signed. (See no. 3772.)

3726 Ritualism and the general election, 536–550. **Cornelia H. M. Guest.** Signed Cornelia Wimborne [Lady Wimborne].

3727 Concerning petitions and electioneering pledges, 551–556. **Sophia M. Palmer.** Signed.

3728 Notes and impressions from a tour in China, 557–568. **Henry A. Blake.** Signed.

3729 The religions of China (Part II): Taoism, 569–581. **Friedrich Max Müller.** Signature.

3730 The working man and the war charges, 582–591. **Frederick Greenwood.** Signed.

3731 Nietzsche: an appreciation, 592–606. **Oswald Crawfurd.** Signed.

3732 Extravagance and economy in the London School Board, 607–617. **C. A. Elliott.** Signed.

3733 An American presidential campaign, 618–624. **James Boyle.** Signed.

3734 Administrative reform in the Public Service: a reply [to no. 3679], 625–628. **Algernon West.** Signed.

3735 The Dutch-Belgians at Waterloo, 629–638. **Charles W. C. Oman.** Signed C. Oman; see *DNB*/1950.

3736 Wanted—a new war poet: a handful of Crimean war poems, 639–647. **Mabel C. Birchenough.** Signed.

3737 Five new pictures in the National Gallery, 648–655. **M. H. Witt.** Signed.

3738 The breed of man, 656–669. **Hely Hutchinson Almond.** Signed.

3739 The newspapers (No. XII), 670–684. **Wemyss Reid.** Signed.

VOLUME 48, NOVEMBER 1900

3740 Cabinet government or departmentalism? 685–694. **J. A. R. Marriott.** Signed.

3741 Lessons of the [Boer] War (No. I): "place the War Office in commission," 695–701. **Henry Thring.** Signed Thring [1st Baron Thring].

3742 Lessons of the War (No. II): suggestions from the front, 702–716. **Charles à Court Repington.** Signed Charles à Court; see *DNB*/1930.

3743 Lessons of the War (No. III): our belated battleships, 717–729. **Archibald S. Hurd.** Signed.

3744 The religions of China (Part III, concl.): Buddhism and Christianity, 730–742. **Friedrich Max Müller.** Signature.

3745 The lake-dwellers, 743–754. **Augustus Jessopp.** Signed; repr. *Peasantry.*

3746 Extravagance in dress, 755–763. **Helen Guendolen Ramsden.** Signed Guendolen Ramsden; see *WWW*/1916.

3747 Voice culture, 764–776. **Caroline Creyke.** Signed.

3748 French Canada and the Empire, 777–784. **J. G. Snead Cox.** Signed.

3749 The Van Eycks, 785–790. **W. H. James Weale.** Signed.

3750 Electioneering women: an American appreciation, 791–800. **Elizabeth L. Banks.** Signed.

3751 The cradle of the human race, 801–806. **Samuel Waddington.** Signed.

3752 Army manoeuvres in France, 807–814. **H. Somers Somerset.** Signed.

3753 The casualties of war and of industry, 815–819. **F. Harcourt Kitchin.** Signed.

3754 The vulgarising of Oberammergau [Passion plays], 820–824. **L. C. Morant.** Signed. (Note, p. 1070 by **James Knowles.**)

3755 The Gael and his heritage, 825–841. **William Sharp.** Signed Fiona Macleod: see *DNB*, 2nd suppl.

3756 The newspapers (No. XIII), 842–856. **Wemyss Reid.** Signed.

3757 The administrative reform association, [including a draft of the constitution], 859–880. Signed by a large number of members. Intro. note by **James Knowles** —signed Editor *NC.*

VOLUME 48, DECEMBER 1900

3758 The strategical value of the Channel Islands, 881–890. **William Laird Clowes.** Signed.

3759 "Balfourian amelioration" in Ireland, 891–904. **Horace Plunkett.** Signed.

3760 Thomas Henry Huxley, 905–918. **Leslie Stephens.** Signed; repr. *Studies,* III.

3761 Recent science: unsuspected radiations, and insects and malaria, 919–940. **Peter A. Kropotkin.** Signed as in no. 1110.

3762 The role of women in society (Part I; cont. after 1900): in eighteenth-century France, 941–954. **Mary E. Ponsonby.** Signed.

3763 The defective addition to our Company Law, 955–971. **Alfred Emden.** Signed.

3764 A visit to the Boer prisoners at St. Helena, 972–983. **Alice Stopford Green.** Signed.

3765 The poet's end, 984–992. **Frederick Wedmore.** Signed.

3766 Present day progress in India, 993–1000. **Protap Chunder Mozoomdar.** Signed.

3767 *The Sources of Islam,* 1001–1004. **William Muir.** Signed W. Muir; Contents gives first name and "Sir."

3768 Negligence in recruiting, 1005–1012. **P. G. Elgood.** Signed.

3769 The return of the exile [from India]: a retrospect, 1013–1023. **Charles A. Roe.** Signed.

3770 The newspapers (No. XIV, concl.), 1024–1039. **Wemyss Reid.** Signed.

3771 The usages of war in South Africa, 1040–1050. **John Macdonell,** 1845–1921. Signed; see *DNB.*

3772 Are we really a nation of amateurs? 1051–1063. **Herbert Maxwell.** Signed.

3773 Lord Rosebery on the dangers to British trade, 1064–1070. **Henry Birchenough.** Signed.

The Oxford and Cambridge Magazine, 1856

The *Oxford and Cambridge Magazine* was founded by William Morris and Edward Burne-Jones while both were students at Oxford University. They were joined in the venture by William Fulford, who was to edit eleven of the periodical's twelve issues; Richard Watson Dixon, destined to become a poet in his own right and an associate of Patmore, Hopkins, and Bridges; Wilfred Heeley, later a civil servant in India; Vernon Lushington, who became Deputy Judge Advocate General in 1869; and Cormell Price, later headmaster in several public schools. About two-thirds of the periodical was written by these men, and the remainder by a variety of friends and fellow students at both universities.

These seven young writers formed a "Brotherhood," which suggests their enthusiasm, especially Morris's and Burne-Jones's, for Pre-Raphaelite painting;[1] and since both young men knew the Pre-Raphaelite periodical, the *Germ*, published briefly in 1850, the *Oxford and Cambridge Magazine* has come to be thought of as a second, more elaborate organ of the P.R.B.[2] But this is a half truth. The "Brotherhood" was not an imitation of the Pre-Raphaelite order, nor was its object the reform of art. Its aim, as Burne-Jones put it, was a "Crusade and Holy Warfare against the age," meaning specifically the appalling conditions of life in the great industrial areas and the indifference toward them of the upper classes, and more broadly the lack of idealism in contemporary society.[3] In his account of the founding of the Magazine, J. W. Mackail never mentions Pre-Raphaelitism, though no doubt it was in the back of his mind. Speaking of the Brotherhood in the summer of 1855, he says in his *Life of Morris*:

To find some united and organized method of bringing their beliefs and enthusiasms before the world, to join actively in the crusade of which Carlyle, Ruskin, and Tennyson were the accepted leaders, became the first object of their ambition; and their plans now took definite shape in the resolution to found and conduct a magazine of a really high order.[4]

[1]See J. W. Mackail, *The Life of William Morris* (2 vols., 1899), I, 71, 72. The following remark about the *Germ* is on p. 71.
[2]Walter Graham, *English Literary Periodicals* (New York, 1930), p. 300, remarks, for example: "After the failure of *The Germ*, much of the effort of the Pre-Raphaelites was turned into the *Oxford and Cambridge Magazine* (London) of 1856."
[3]Mackail, I, 63–65.
[4]Ibid., I, 67.

Canon Dixon's recollection of the periodical's origin confirms this account, but broadens it significantly:

Of this undertaking the central notion was, I think, to advocate moral earnestness and purpose in literature, art, and society. It was founded much on Mr. Ruskin's teaching: it sprang out of youthful impatience, and exhibited many signs of immaturity and ignorance: but perhaps it was not without value as a protest against some things. The Pre-Raphaelite movement was then in vigour: and this Magazine came to be considered as the organ of those who accepted the ideas which were brought into art at that time; and, as in a manner, the successor of the *Germ*, a small periodical which had been published previously by the first beginners of the movement.[5]

"To advocate moral earnestness and purpose in literature, art, and society" comes first, it will be noted. This is a central Victorian idea, heard among the Cambridge Apostles about 1830 (of whom Tennyson was one), in the sermons of Thomas Arnold, in Carlyle from the early essays to *Past and Present* (1843), and later, especially in Kingsley and Ruskin. This ethical strain and social concern, which had not been heard in the *Germ*, were then blended, as Dixon suggests, with the more specialized and aesthetic ideas associated with Pre-Raphaelitism. In Burne-Jones's review of Thackeray's *The Newcomes* (no. 7), which has been called "a manifesto of the magazine,"[6] the former is at first emphasized. Speaking with youthful enthusiasm of the dawn of a new age, he pays special tribute to "such great names as Tennyson and Holman Hunt, Ruskin and Carlyle, and Kingsley, and many others who have led on this most godly crusade against falsehood, doubt, and wretched fashion, against hypocrisy and mammon, and lack of earnestness, and among them—according to his rare and excellent gift—Thackeray." It is scarcely surprising that within the year the Magazine carried a five-part essay on Carlyle and a note on Kingsley's sermons. On the other hand, Burne-Jones's praise of Thackeray centers on his ability to describe human nature as it is because he has studied directly from life; he therefore belongs "with the great naturalists." And, Burne-Jones could have added, among the new Pre-Raphaelites, for Naturalism was the main principle of the movement.[7] Other elements found in the Magazine are the use of sharp and exact detail, the conscious search for beauty of form and word, and the concern with medieval architecture and chivalry, especially in Morris. Its Pre-Raphaelitism is also revealed by the essays on Ruskin's aesthetics (no. 24), Tennyson's poetry (nos. 2, 10, 16), and two pictures by Rossetti and Madox Brown (no. 45).

With Morris acting as editor, the first issue appeared on January 1, 1856, and sold for a shilling. The publisher initially printed 750 copies, but had to bring out 250 more later in the month. Attention to the minutiae of editing was not, how-

---

[5]Quoted by T. Hall Caine, *Recollections of Dante Gabriel Rossetti* (Boston, 1883), p. 36.
[6]*Academy*, July 2, 1898, p. 19.
[7]Cf. the opening paragraphs of Morris's Birmingham "Address on the Collection of Paintings of the English Pre-Raphaelite School," in *William Morris: Artist, Writer, Socialist*, ed. May Morris (Oxford, 1936), I, 296–302. There the "special and particular" doctrine of the School is called, "in one word, Naturalism. That is to say, the Pre-Raphaelites started by saying, 'You have Nature before you, what you have to do is to copy Nature and you will produce something . . . worth people's attention.' "

ever, to Morris' liking, and before the appearance of the February issue, he formally assigned editorial duties to William Fulford, to whom he paid a salary of £100 during the year the Magazine continued to appear. A survey of the contents shows that of the 70 contributions to its pages, there are 18 short stories (8 by Morris), 17 poems (5 by Morris), and 35 essays. About three-quarters of the essays are on literary topics, with papers on society, politics, religion, and philosophy filling out the remainder. The most frequently discussed authors are Shakespeare, Ruskin, Tennyson, Thackeray, and Browning; and in the case of two issues (January and May), medallions of Tennyson and Carlyle cast by the Pre-Raphaelite sculptor Thomas Woolner were offered for sale with the Magazine. Although the *Oxford and Cambridge* was politically neutral, the non-literary papers contain definite and sometimes outspoken attitudes on such topics as overpopulation, women's rights, the Crimean War, the mammonism of the age, and the effects of the factory system on English life.

A favorable reference to Dante Rossetti in the January issue caught his eye and prepared the way for his association with the periodical and its founders. Writing to a friend, he commented, "That notice in *The Oxford and Cambridge Magazine* was the most gratifying thing by far that ever happened to me—being unmistakeably [*sic*] genuine."[8] Ironically, Rossetti's association with the journal was responsible for the high point of its success as well as the beginning of its failure. Urged by Morris and Burne-Jones, Rossetti contributed three poems: "The Burden of Nineveh" (August), "The Blessed Damozel" (November), and "The Staff and the Scrip" (December). These represent the finest literary achievement of the Magazine. On the other hand, Rossetti used all his powers to exhort Morris and Burne-Jones to turn their attention to the field of art rather than literature, and to assist him in painting the ceiling of the Oxford Union with murals. His efforts were successful, and Burne-Jones recorded the shift in interest: "The Mag. is going to smash—let it go! the world is not converted and never will be. It has had stupid things in it lately. I shall not write again for it, no more will Topsay [Morris]—we cannot do more than one thing at a time, and our hours are too valuable to spend so."[9]

But in any event the end was in sight. The sales had been steadily declining, and when the final issue appeared in December, there was a large stock of unsold copies on the publisher's shelves.[10] The Magazine was too youthful and too Pre-Raphaelite to capture a sustaining audience.

EDITORS

William Morris: January 1856.
William Fulford: February 1856 – December 1856.

PROPRIETOR

William Morris.

[8]*Letters of Dante Gabriel Rossetti to William Allingham, 1854–1870*, ed. G. B. Hill (New York, [1897]), pp. 173–184.
[9]Quoted by Mackail, I, 108.
[10]Ibid., I, 89.

PUBLISHER
Bell and Daldy, London.

NOTE ON ATTRIBUTIONS

An authoritative list of attributions is a prize possession to the editor of an anonymous periodical and all too rarely found. For this Magazine there are no less than four such lists, together with several others of inferior quality—riches so welcome one is reluctant to complain that they involve discrepancies. But such is the case. We have therefore cited several sources, though not necessarily all (see no. 9), unless the evidence of one is so strong as to be unquestionable (no. 7); and where a single source is given in a debatable item, like that for Fulford in no. 52, one can assume that the attribution is not found elsewhere. If there is any doubt whatever, we have mentioned dissenting ascriptions (nos. 55 and 61), but not where the case seems proved (no. 29).

A full account of these lists has still to be written, describing them, dating them, assessing their relationships, and judging their reliability. Here we can only mention briefly those we have used, in what we think is their chronological order:

(1) "List of articles [with their authors] in *Oxford and Cambridge Magazine*, 1856, from a List supplied by Mr. Vernon Lushington and Mr. W. Bell Scott." This incomplete list is pasted onto the front flyleaf of the Wellesley College copy. Another list with the same title, varying slightly from this one, is attached to the copy of the Magazine in the Nottingham University library. Our abbreviation, "OxCam list," applies to both; where there is any significant difference, the variance is noted. The original has not been found.

(2) In 1897 Buxton Forman, in *The Books of William Morris*, pp. 28–33, included a complete catalogue of attributions, partly derived from Morris himself in the early 1870s, and partly from a Vernon Lushington list of contributors to the journal. We call this "Forman."

(3) The "Mackail 'MS. Notes'" were prepared by J. W. Mackail when he was writing *The Life of William Morris*, published in 1899, and their attributions would have been included in that book had not some of the contributors who were still living objected (see I, 90). In compiling this complete list Mackail had access not only to the Morris papers but also, through his wife, to those of Edward Burne-Jones. Among the latter he found at least a partial list of attributions drawn up in 1859 by Georgiana Macdonald, a contributor who later became Lady Burne-Jones, his mother-in-law. The "MS. Notes" have the added value of Mackail's marginalia, where he more than once challenges other attributions or documents his own source. He claims that his information is the best yet attained; in fact, all other published lists "are inaccurate in important particulars" (I, 90). But unfortunately so is his. The "MS. Notes" are located in the William Morris Gallery at Walthamstow. We are grateful to the Gallery for permission to use them.

(4) The "Price list" was drawn up by Cormell Price, a contributor, and enclosed in a letter to Falconer Madan, November 19, 1909. He there guarantees "its accuracy in the first 6 numbers," but admits that in the last six, he is uncertain about a few articles: some he attributes with question marks, and three he leaves without

authors (nos. 52, 58, 61). It should be recognized that Price was then an elderly man (he was born in 1835 or 1836), and though no doubt he consulted some old letters and perhaps a marked file, he was partly relying on memory. A second letter of December 22, 1909, in reply to some comments and queries of Madan, is of considerable importance. The "Price list" and the two letters are owned by Mr. J. R. Dunlop, Associate Librarian, The City College of New York, who generously put them at our service.

In addition to these major sources which aim at identifying all contributions to the Magazine, there are some which are more limited in scope: R. W. Dixon's contributions are discussed in James Sambrook, *A Poet Hidden: The Life of Richard Watson Dixon, 1833–1900* (1962), pp. 22–24; and Burne-Jones in the *Memorials*, I, 122, identifies the authorship of articles in the January and February issues.

Finally, four other partial, incomplete, and rather unreliable lists have been consulted and have been occasionally helpful in corroborating an attribution cited by one or another of the foregoing sources. These are Temple Scott, *A Bibliography of the Works of William Morris* (1897), p. 38; the *Athenaeum*, October 17, 1896, pp. 527–528; an anonymous manuscript in the British Museum (Ashley B.3679 PS8/11221), and, most important, a marked copy in the Powell Library, University of California at Los Angeles, called to our attention by Mr. Wilbur J. Smith, Head of the Department of Special Collections. The front flyleaf of this copy bears the name of Charles Fairfax Murray (1849–1919), the famous collector, and is therefore cited below as "Murray copy." Under the signature appears the following note:

On the covers at the end I have noted the names of most of the contributors. Some were written in pencil by an unknown hand before I purchased the book / others were supplied ~ confirmed by Mr. Swinburne who marked in W. Bell Scott's copy which is in my possession / a list was supplied to W. B. Scott also by Mr. Vernon Lushington.

The covers are those of each issue, and the names were partly derived, we take it, from those in a copy (which Murray also owned) originally belonging to W. B. Scott and afterwards to Swinburne, who added further attributions. Scott had had the benefit of a list supplied by Vernon Lushington.[11] The attributions, unfortunately, are uneven, a few being demonstrably wrong. Finally, much more recently, there is H. S. Hosmon's list in the *Victorian Periodicals Newsletter*, No. 4, April 1969, pp. 40–47, but since it suffers from ignorance of sources (1), (3), and (4) above, it has not been used.

BIBLIOGRAPHICAL NOTE

There is no definitive, full-length study of the *Oxford and Cambridge Magazine*. Brief accounts of the journal are contained in the books cited above by Forman, pp. 22–33; Mackail, I, 87–108; Burne-Jones, I, 115–130; and Sambrook, pp. 22–26.

[11]This reading of Murray's note is indebted to a clipping from a book catalogue pasted onto the back cover of the Wellesley College copy. After the full title, it continues: "A. C. Swinburne's copy (from the library of W. Bell Scott), with the author's names appended to the Index, *partly in the handwriting of Swinburne, who has also made additions, in pencil, on nine pages*; also an Autograph letter from Vernon Lushington (one of the contributors) to W. Bell Scott enclosing him a list of some of the authors with their articles." This is the second copy mentioned in Murray's note as being in his possession.

There is a perceptive criticism in the *Saturday Review*, February 28, 1857, pp. 196–197, called "Undergraduate Literature," written by T. C. Sandars (see Bevington, p. 370), and an article, "Burne-Jones and Thackeray," in the *Academy*, July 2, 1898, pp. 19–20, in which the writer calls our no. 7 "practically a *credo* of the school of young artists to which Edward Burne-Jones belonged, and a manifesto of the magazine." *In a Nook with a Book* (Cincinnati, n.d.) by Frederick William Macdonald, brother of Georgiana Burne-Jones, contains a useful chapter. More recent studies include Walter K. Gordon, A Critical Selected Edition of William Morris's "Oxford and Cambridge Magazine" (1856), unpublished dissertation, University of Pennsylvania, 1960, which gives a brief history of the journal, discusses its critical reception, and assesses the Magazine against the background of the nineteenth-century periodical. See also Walter K. Gordon, "Pre-Raphaelitism and the *Oxford and Cambridge Magazine*," *Journal of the Rutgers University Library*, 29 (June 1966), 42–51, which describes the journal's indebtedness to the *Germ* and its espousal of Pre-Raphaelite social and aesthetic causes.

THE OXFORD AND CAMBRIDGE MAGAZINE, 1856

26 Oxford, 234–257. **Godfrey Lushington.**
    OxCam list; Mackail "MS. Notes"; For-
    man, p. 29.

VOLUME 1, MAY 1856

27 Prometheus [in Aeschylus and Shelley],
    259–264. **Lewis Campbell.** *OxCam* list;
    Mackail "MS. Notes"; Forman, p. 30;
    Price list.
28 Unhealthy employments, 265–271. **C. J.
    Faulkner** and **Cormell Price.** Mackail
    "MS. Notes"; Forman, p. 30; Price list.
29 The sacrifice; a tale, 271–280. **Georgiana
    Macdonald.** Mackail "MS. Notes"; For-
    man, p. 30; Cormell Price to Falconer
    Madan, Dec. 22, 1909, owned by J. R.
    Dunlop of New York. "It was *not* their
    brother Henry [brother of Alice and
    Louisa Macdonald], a chum of mine at
    school & college, who wrote Tale p. 271,
    but the sister Georgiana, then about 17
    (or less). She is now widow of Sir E.
    B-Jones."
30 Shakespeare's *Troilus and Cressida*, 280–
    292. **William Fulford.** *OxCam* list; Mack-
    ail "MS. Notes"; Forman, p. 30.
31 Carlyle (Part II): "His Lamp for the
    Old Years," 292–310. **Vernon Lushing-
    ton.** Cf. no. 23.
32 A night in a cathedral, 310–316. **William
    Fulford.** Mackail "MS. Notes"; Forman,
    p. 30.
33 On popular lectures, considered as an
    irregular channel of national education
    (Part I), 316–319. **Bernard Cracroft?**
    OxCam list, Price list, and Forman, p.
    30. OR, **William Fulford?** Mackail "MS.
    Notes" reports, "B. Cracroft according to
    Cormell Price, but assigned to Fulford by
    Lady Burne-Jones in 1859"; the style
    favors Fulford whose writing, in con-
    trast to Cracroft's (see no. 34 for his),
    is more academic, pedestrian and moralis-
    tic, his arts. often starting with an out-
    line of the subject and an explanation of
    what he will cover.

VOLUME 1, JUNE 1856

34 Thackeray and Currer Bell, 323–335.
    Bernard Cracroft. *OxCam* list; Price list;
    Forman, p. 30; in Price to Madan (cited
    in evidence for no. 29), assigned con-
    fidently to Cracroft, with account of
    chief qualities of his style, which might
    have included the habit of using italics,
    even for remarks within quotations which

Cracroft wishes to stress (here, pp. 330,
333; cf., for one example, *National Rev.*,
19 (Nov. 1864), 181–230, repr. in his
Essays); in contrast to Fulford's, Cracroft's style has much more vitality,
subtlety, and metaphorical texture. Mackail "MS Notes" felt "almost certainly
Fulford."
35 Carlyle (Part III): another look at "The
    Lamp for the Old Years," 336–352.
    Vernon Lushington. Cf. no. 23.
36 Ruskin and the *Quarterly*, 353–361. **Wil-
    liam Morris** and **Edward Burne-Jones,**
    prob. *OxCam* list and Forman, p. 30,
    attr. to Morris; Price list to Burne-Jones;
    Mackail "MS. Notes" to both, adding
    "mainly Burne-Jones"; cf. no. 24; both
    authors are given by *CBEL*, III, 706, and
    in Ruskin, *Works*, V, lx n., and XXXVIII,
    136.
37 Froude's *History of England* [Vols. I–II],
    362–388. **Wilfred L. Heeley.** Mackail
    "MS. notes"; Forman, p. 30.

VOLUME 1, JULY 1856

38 On the life and character of Marshal St.
    Arnaud [of France in Crimean War],
    389–402. **Robert Campbell,** 1832–1912,
    prob. Forman, p. 31, gives "Robert
    Campbell"; see Venn for man cited;
    Mackail "MS. Notes" says "probably L.
    Campbell," apparently recalling no. 27,
    but that Campbell was a classical scholar
    and philosophical thinker; Price list attrs.
    to T. W. Jex-Blake; Murray copy to
    "Robert Campbell or Jex Blake."
39 Gertha's lovers (chaps. i–iii), 403–417.
    William Morris. *OxCam* list; Forman, p.
    31; repr. *Works*, I.
40 A study in Shakespeare: *Timon of
    Athens*, 417–441. **William Fulford** and
    Mrs. Hill (prob. Annie Scott Hill), prob.
    Attr. to Fulford in *OxCam* list and by
    Forman, p. 31; Mackail "MS. Notes"
    reads, "Mrs. Hill, but probably retouched
    by Fulford"; in letter cited in evidence for
    no. 29, Price says that this art. and no.
    54 "are evidently by the same hand," and
    that in his copy one of them is attr. to
    "Mrs. Hill," who was perhaps a relative
    of Birkbeck Hill; woman suggested was
    the wife of George Birkbeck Hill who
    was an Oxford friend of Fulford, Burne-
    Jones, and Morris (see *DNB*, 2nd suppl.)
41 Lancashire and *Mary Barton* [by Mrs
    Gaskell], 441–451. **Cormell Price.** *Ox-
    Cam* list; Mackail "MS. Notes"; Forman,
    p. 31; Price list.

VOLUME 1, AUGUST 1856

42 On popular lectures (Part II, concl.), 453–462. **Bernard Cracroft?** or **William Fulford?** Cf. no. 33.

43 Woman, her duties, education and position, 462–477. **William Fulford.** *OxCam* list; Mackail, "MS. Notes"; Forman, p. 31.

44 "Death the avenger" and "Death the friend," 477–479. **William Morris.** *OxCam* list; Forman, p. 31; repr. *Works*, I.

45 Two pictures [by Rossetti and Madox Brown], 479–488. **Vernon Lushington,** prob. Murray copy; *OxCam* list; Forman, p. 31; W. B. Scott, *Notes*, II, 37; Rossetti, *Letters*, I, 321 and note; Price list and Mackail's "MS. Notes" give "G. [Godfrey] Lushington," Mackail adding "Not V. Lushington"; but the subject, like the weight of evidence, points strongly to man cited—indeed, Price's letter, in evidence for no. 29, describes Vernon's style as "marked by the frequent use of the dash," which is certainly true here, and in other arts. in other journals.

46 Svend and his brethren, 488–499. **William Morris.** Mackail "MS. Notes"; Forman, p. 31; repr. *Works*, I.

47 Gertha's lovers (chaps. iv–v, concl.), 499–512. **William Morris.** Cf. no. 39.

VOLUME 1, SEPTEMBER 1856

48 Robert Herrick, 517–530. **William Aldis Wright.** Attr. in *DNB*, *OxCam* list, and Forman, p. 32; but Mackail's "MS. Notes" reads "a professional writer named Wright, got in by Fulford, not Aldis Wright," which may be correct, but cf. his almost certain error in no. 45.

49 Lindenborg pool, 530–534. **William Morris.** *OxCam* list; Forman, p. 32; repr. *Works*, I.

50 Cavalay: a chapter of a life (Part I), 535–548. **William Fulford.** *OxCam* list; Mackail "MS. Notes"; Forman, p. 32.

51 Alexander Smith, 548–558. **William Fulford.** *OxCam* list; Mackail "MS. Notes"; Forman, p. 32.

52 The work of young men in the present age, 558–564. **William Fulford?** Mackail "MS. Notes." OR, **Cormel Price?** Though marked with a "?" in Price's own list, attr. to him by Forman, p. 32, and in Murray copy; strong influence of *Past and Present* here and in no. 42, p. 448; after fifty years perhaps Price's memory failed him here.

53 The hollow land; a tale (chaps. i–ii), 565–577. **William Morris.** *OxCam* list; Forman, p. 32; *Works*, I.

VOLUME 1, OCTOBER 1856

54 *Twelfth night; or, What You Will*: a study in Shakespeare, 581–605. **William Fulford,** and **Mrs. Hill** (prob. Annie Scott Hill), prob. See all the evidence for no. 40.

55 The sceptic and the infidel (Part I), 605–620. **Bernard Cracroft.** *OxCam* list at Wellesley Coll.; Murray copy; Forman, p. 32; Price, in letter cited for no. 29, says "almost certainly Cracrofts"; the massive use of italics is alone nearly sufficient to make the attrib. (cf. evidence for no. 34). Attr. to William Fulford in Mackail "MS. Notes" on basis of Lady Burne-Jones' opinion, and in *OxCam* list at Nottingham, which adds, "not Cracroft."

56 Cavalay (Part II), 620–632. **William Fulford.** Cf. no. 50.

57 The hollow land (chap. iii, concl.), 632–641. **William Morris.** Cf. no. 53.

58 Rogers' *Table Talk*, 641–644. **William Fulford.** *OxCam* list; Forman, p. 32; Mackail "MS. Notes."

VOLUME 1, NOVEMBER 1856

59 The sceptic and the infidel (Part II), 645–663. **Bernard Cracroft.**

60 Cavalay (Part III, concl.), 664–676. **William Fulford.** Cf. no. 50.

61 The druid and the maiden, 676–697. **Edward Burne-Jones?** *OxCam* list, Murray copy, and also Forman, p. 32, but with some doubt; Mackail "MS. Notes" says by "a professional writer got in by Fulford."

62 Carlyle (Part IV): Carlyle as a writer, 697–712. **Vernon Lushington.** Cf. no. 23.

VOLUME 1, DECEMBER 1856

63 Recent poems and plays, 717–732. **John Nichol.** Repr. *Fragments of Criticism*, Edin., 1860; William Knight, *Memoir of John Nichol* (1896), p. 134.

64 Golden wings, 733–742. **William Morris.** *OxCam* list; Forman, p. 33; repr. *Works*, I.

65 Carlyle (Part V, concl.): "His Lamp for the New Years," 743–771. **Vernon Lushington.** Cf. no. 23.

The Rambler, 1848–1862

THE ROMAN CATHOLIC converts of the 1840s faced immediate problems both practical and psychological. Some had to give up their Anglican livings and find alternate means of livelihood. Some enrolled in Catholic seminaries, but for many the priesthood was barred because they were married. These practical difficulties, added to the sense of being adrift in a new world, tended to strengthen the ties of mutual understanding and, in spite of Wiseman's best efforts, to set them apart from their new co-religionists. There was, however, an additional source of distress: most of them were graduates of one or the other of the great universities and found themselves thrown among men of inferior education, and, indeed, often under their tutelage. The founding of the *Rambler* may be viewed as an attempt to bolster their spirits in a time of disillusionment.

J. M. Capes wrote to Newman in July 1846 of plans for establishing a magazine: "We should write for the present condition of the English mind, entering into all subjects of literary, philosophic and moral interest, treating them as a person would do who believes Catholicism to be the only true religion."[1] This sounded innocent enough, and indeed was so intended, but Newman with remarkable prescience foresaw danger in a periodical "being written by *converts* only or principally," and immediately warned of "collisions with old Catholics."[2]

The first number of the *Rambler* appeared on January 1, 1848.[3] It announced on its title page that it was a journal of home and foreign literature, politics, science, music, and the fine arts.[4] While commencing as a weekly of only sixteen quarto pages, in September 1848, the date at which this *Index* begins to deal with it, it became a monthly of eighty octavo pages. Although the articles were almost entirely anonymous, with only an occasional initial or signed letter, it was well known that at least until 1850 the *Rambler* was the work of "a single individual and a few friends."[5] The individual was John Moore Capes, and the two main friends, his brother Frederick

[1]Newman MSS at Birmingham Oratory.

[2]Newman, *L&D*, XI, 207.

[3]As for the title, the editor said, p. 2, "We take it, as Johnson assumed it, now nearly one hundred years ago, simply for want of a better."

[4]The omission of theology is striking and deliberate. In the first volume, p. 216, is the editorial phrase, "If our readers knew how cordially we detest theological and controversial tales . . ."; and for the second volume a contribution is refused because "too theological in subject for our pages" (Vol. 2, p. 119). But such a limitation, as its later history reveals, was impossible to maintain: see Newman, *L&D*, XVIII, 560.

[5]See editorial for 5 (Jan. 1850), 10.

and his colleague at Prior Park, J. Spencer Northcote. Discussions of music, literature, architecture, and archaeology took up a large portion of its pages, but Capes had
another interest, and a major one, the social question in its many ramifications—
housing, poverty, emigration, and education.[6] The result was a broad spectrum of
subjects treated with both intelligence and tolerance, and in a tone that was incisive,
occasionally witty, or even sarcastic.

Both because of its breadth and its tone, the *Rambler* found itself involved almost
from the beginning in controversy. In their over-eager and no doubt slightly arrogant
wish to ameliorate conditions in the Church which they had lately entered, the converts began to criticize church architecture and music as well as Catholic education,
lay and ecclesiastical. This, of course, aroused resentment, and when Capes in his
editorial for December 1848 declared in the closing sentence, "We are convinced
that the scanty ranks of our clergy continue as they are, chiefly because we are still,
to so great an extent, without a sound and complete system of ecclesiastical education," the storm broke. Bishop Ullathorne, who had originally favored the idea of the
Rambler, fulminated in the *Tablet* for December 9, "Those who are but as children
amongst us, forgetting their pupilage, have undertaken to rebuke, censure, and
condemn the acts" of those in authority in the Church.[7]

Far from being cowed by Ullathorne's invective, Capes returned to the charge with
what amounted to a declaration of editorial independence. After admitting that the
editors of a journal like the *Rambler* are not infallible, he went on to ask:

What is the Church Catholic? *She* is herself infallible; but her individual children in this
country, what are they? Are they not erring men, with many duties, many privileges, many
powers, but not one of them with the gift of omniscience or infallibility?[8]

But many, in fact, seemed to be acting on that authoritarian assumption. Under these
circumstances Capes became convinced that the role of the *Rambler* was to champion
the cause of progress within the Catholic Church. His manifesto appeared in April
1849, as he was "bringing the Third Volume . . . to a conclusion."[9]

Our education, clerical and secular, is universally *felt*, and generally admitted, to be still in
its infancy. . . . We are notoriously the most disputatious community in the kingdom,
quarreling with one another on every possible opportunity. . . . Add to this the mournful
truth, that we have as yet no Catholic literature. . . . In such a state of things can we dream
of continuing the same quiet, steady, easy-going ways? . . . In truth, quiescence is *impossible* to us. . . . The existence of such a Journal as the *Rambler*, and its boldness in pressing
upon its readers a variety of topics which the cautious, conservative spirit of other days
would have kept sacred from all public discussion . . . is a necessity of our day.

[6]Capes's interest in the poor, as well as his generally liberal point of view, inevitably led to
concern for Ireland and Irish emigrants in London.

[7]*Tablet*, IX, 787. Newman, in the meanwhile, had written to Capes on Dec. 6 that his article
was "very clever and very true. . . . Its truth is what gives it so much point"; but by Jan. 3 he
warned Capes that he would be in difficulties because the "article had the tone of a hostile attack,
instead of having a double dose of butter to introduce an unpleasant subject." *L&D*, XII, 365,
XIII, 6.

[8]From "The Duties of Journalists," 3 (Jan. 1849), 329.

[9]In the file of the *Rambler* generously loaned to this *Index* by the Forbes Library of Northampton, Mass., this is entitled "Preface" and is prefixed to Vol. 3, but the opening words show that it
should have been bound either at the beginning of the April issue or as an appendix to the whole
volume.

Thus to throw down the gauntlet was to invite further opposition, but the *Rambler* held firmly on its forthright course. Its circulation, though not overwhelming, was, considering the social and financial status of Catholic readers, respectable. In its editorial for January 1850 the magazine took occasion to do a little harmless boasting: "The commencement of our fifth volume finds us with a rapidly increasing circulation, with additional contributors, and with expressions from all quarters of the esteem in which our humble efforts are held."[10]

It would, however, be a mistake to think that the excitement of controversy alone was responsible for the *Rambler*'s success. True to its title-page, it covered, and covered very ably, a wide range of subjects, including fiction, much of it from the hand of Capes himself. His versatility of interests and fluency of pen were truly remarkable. Aside from his concern with social questions, he was a competent musician—performer, composer, and critic.[11] He was likewise a well-read and intelligent critic of literature, and a practical student of church architecture. In addition to his own contributions, he had a series of articles on the recent explorations of the catacombs from his colleague J. S. Northcote, who was in Rome in 1848–50, as well as first-hand reports on the all-absorbing events there in those years. He was also ably seconded by his younger brother Frederick, who combined with his legal experience many of the editor's tastes, particularly in the fine arts. No wonder that the *Rambler* was successful.

Nevertheless, Capes had begun to feel the strain of carrying so much of the burden on his own shoulders; and was also worried about finances. On Newman's advice, he decided to try to make the *Rambler* more readable by changing the format, "to throw it into a Review *shape*."[12] Accordingly, with the issue of January 1850 the magazine appeared as an octavo and no longer with the double-columned pages. Capes was disappointed, too, that Newman and the Oratorians hesitated to become contributors. Though willing at first to serve as theological censor, Newman did not wish to risk offending Wiseman as proprietor of the *Dublin*, either by writing for the *Rambler* or seeming to connect it with the Oratory.[13] Capes's editorial worries were complemented by anxieties over the encroaching blindness of his wife and problems with his own health. In these circumstances he decided, in the spring of 1852, to entrust his editorial responsibilities to his friend J. S. Northcote. But Northcote's editorship was not, at least in Capes's eyes, a success; he lacked Capes's breadth of interest and his witty approach. He was "cautious to an extreme."[14] The circulation suffered and the proprietor was much relieved when, after two years, Northcote proposed to resign.

In April 1854 Capes was hoping to enlist Richard Simpson as assistant editor,

---

[10] 5 (Jan. 1850), 10.

[11] In Newman, *L&D*, XIII, 28, Newman thanks Capes for composing some hymns for the Oratory, and on p. 167 refers to a mass composed by him.

[12] Newman, *L&D*, XIII, 312–315.

[13] The connection was so widely assumed that in 7 (June 1851), 542, it was considered necessary to publish a disclaimer of any connection between the *Rambler* and the Oratory, as well as, be it noted, its independence of either Wiseman or the Jesuits. The editor firmly shouldered personal responsibility for opinions expressed in the periodical. Newman, however, remained as theological censor through Vol. 9 (May 1852) (Newman, *L&D*, XV, 36), and, as will be seen, he stayed connected with the *Rambler* in people's minds, long after he had actually retired.

[14] Letter to Richard Simpson of July 6, 1854, in Simpson notebook at Downside.

explaining that he would count on him for critical and entertaining papers since the *Rambler* was "decidedly too theological." After all, he remarked, the Review is addressed to "3 classes," not only Catholics and Puseyites, but also to "Protestant men of the world."[15] The choice of Simpson was hardly surprising, for the two men were fundamentally alike—both liberally oriented, widely read, with a variety of interests, and both with an irresistible urge to poke fun at pomposity or hypocrisy.[16] But Simpson in his first known contribution startled even Capes with his account of religion and modern philosophy (*Ram* no. 249). Then in January 1852 he carried on the discussion with an article on the delicate subject of Galileo. Finally, with his papers on magic in October and December 1854, and the letter on original sin in July 1855, the *Rambler*, for the first time, became seriously embroiled with members of the Catholic hierarchy. Simpson was admittedly the author of the offending articles, but Capes loyally backed him up by defending them in the periodical.

Parallel to the developing independence of the *Rambler* was a gradual divergence between the more conservative and the more liberal members of the Catholic body. It soon became clear that the *Rambler* and its outspoken conductors were to be considered liberals or even radicals: they were claiming the right to "speculate a little on questions of moral, intellectual, social, or physical philosophy" (*Ram* no. 789, p. 316), and accordingly were judged dangerous to the faith. Then, before the furor over the article on original sin had abated, appeared the notice of *Brownson's Quarterly Review* in October 1856, which included the unfortunate remark that "the little remnant of Catholic England lives very much on tradition—lives by the past" (*Ram* no. 789, p. 316). This was understandably interpreted as a sneer at the so-called Old Catholics as well as at Wiseman, who was further incensed in the following month by an article on poor-schools. In December he took occasion to remonstrate in the *Dublin* in no uncertain terms (*Dublin* no. 822). Capes and Simpson rose stoutly to their own defence (*Ram* no. 819). Well might Wiseman, who had considered his greatest triumph the conversions of the 1840s, feel that the fruit of the blossom was bitter indeed. Bitter but attractive. In the very midst of his condemnation (*Dublin* no. 822) Wiseman was honest enough to remark:

We find the *Rambler* on the table of every respectable catholic house, in the hands of the clergy, in the library of colleges, in the reading room of every catholic Institute or club, under direction of laymen or clerks. We have never heard it spoken of save with respect, and even admiration: except in the theological views alluded to, and the paragraph on which we are commenting. Surely it has received its full share of public applause, as well as its fair share of so limited a patronage as catholic literature can well expect. While number after number of the Dublin Review is not favoured even with a passing notice by any catholic newspaper, scarcely a week is allowed to elapse by any of them, after the monthly appearance of the *Rambler*, without a glowing eulogium, and copious extracts in each.

But this very popularity made its liberalism all the more dangerous.

While this warfare invigorated Simpson, it was finally too much for Capes's failing

---

[15]Letters of Apr. 20 and July 1, 1854, ibid.

[16]Cf. Capes to Simpson, Sept. 23, 1857, Simpson notebook, with regard to Capes's article on La Salette (*Ram* no. 869): "I understand that Dr. Ullathorne was *confident* that *you* wrote the art. on La Salette. . . . I dare say many would have thought so too, for somehow whenever anything appears which people think bumptious . . . you get the credit of it."

energies, and in October 1857 he resigned the editorship and sold his interest in the undertaking, although continuing to write for almost another year.[17] The new proprietors were Simpson, Sir John Acton, and Frederick Capes. The accession of Acton brought respectability to the *Rambler*: he was not a convert, he had a position in society and politics, and he was a brilliant and highly trained scholar. But he was heartily in sympathy with the liberal views of Capes and Simpson, and while he spoke out with less verve, he did so with more weight and assurance. Any relief felt by anyone was clearly premature.

The *Rambler* had already shown its genius for stirring up opposition, and now as the new conductors moved forward to continue the original policies, they found themselves in an even more contentious atmosphere. Added to the periodical's sins of general independence was the resistance of Acton and Simpson to the suppression of intellectual liberty by Church authorities, and in particular the distortion of history by ecclesiastical censorship.[18] In his first issue Simpson castigated the Very Reverend Canon Flanagan, with characteristic disrespect, for being "afraid of following the truth too close at the heels, lest it kick his teeth out. His narrative is therefore, as it were, boneless and nerveless, boiled down to a jelly." And Acton, in August 1858, spoke out more judiciously but no less forcefully: "Partiality in judging great historical characters . . . implies a very imperfect idea of history, and among Catholics, a very imperfect trust in religion." And he added, "Because St. Augustine was the greatest doctor of the West, we need not conceal the fact that he was also the father of Jansenism," a remark which was to spark fresh controversy.[19] Nor was the hierarchy any happier about Acton's outspoken political views. Much of his education had taken place on the Continent and there in predominantly liberal circles; he was in close touch with such leaders as Döllinger and Montalembert; and he did not hesitate to criticize the conservative movements both at home and abroad.

The *Rambler*'s position became ever more precarious, aggravated by the popular suspicion, according to Acton, "that a crowd of converts have conspired together, half to become apostates, the rest to remain [in the Church] in the hope that, as ostensible Catholics, they might do more harm through the *Rambler*."[20] In addition, there was now a new party opposing any liberal tendencies—a party stressing unquestioning reliance upon the authority of Rome. This group included such leading converts as W. G. Ward, Frederick Faber, and H. E. Manning, and it was to them that Wiseman turned in his hope of sinking the *Rambler*.[21] The confrontation was not long in coming. Two articles by S. N. Stokes in January and February 1859 were the

---

[17]As early as July 1, 1856, Capes had begun to try and rid himself of his editorship. In this connection he wrote to Simpson (Simpson notebook) that he thought "the circulation was about 1,000; it was more before the [Crimean] war." Cf. Alvar Ellegård, *The Readership of the Periodical Press in Mid-Victorian Britain* (Göteborg, 1957), p. 30.

[18]Already in Vol. 12 (Nov. 1853) Capes had warned against playing tricks with Church history (no. 537, p. 343).

[19]*Ram* no. 882, p. 353, and no. 945, p. 135. On p. 136 of the latter, Acton spoke of the "shame" caused by the "disgraceful" treatment of Joan of Arc by the revered Catholic historian Lingard.

[20]Conzemius (see Bibliographical Note), I, 156–157; trans. in Altholz, p. 83.

[21]See Wiseman to Bagshawe, Aug. 1, 1858, Bagshawe Papers, and Newman, *L&D*, XX, 263n.; for Ward's "detestation" of the *Rambler* see his letters to Newman (*L&D*, XIX, 74n.).

given cause; but the underlying factor was the bishops' determination to suppress the periodical if possible, but at the least to get rid of Simpson. With this intention a meeting was held on February 12, 1859, at which Wiseman, Errington, and Ullathorne decided to force Simpson's withdrawal.[22] To encompass their design they turned to Newman, who was known to be friendly to Acton and Simpson. The subsequent negotiations were long and complicated, and the outcome was certainly unexpected. By March 21 Newman had agreed that he himself would undertake the editorship "for the present," but in almost the same mail he wrote to Ullathorne that the arrangement was "a most bitter penance to me."[23] And a bitter penance indeed it was to be.

Newman immediately advertised a new series of the *Rambler* to be "published at intervals of two months." The aim of the conductors, he said, will be "as it has ever been . . . to reconcile freedom of thought with implicit faith . . . and to encourage a manly investigation of subjects of public interest under a deep sense of the prerogatives of ecclesiastical authority."[24] But with the very first issue a veritable hornet's nest was stirred up by two letters of Newman's in the Correspondence: "Temporal Prosperity a Note of the Church" and "Questions and Answers"; and furthermore, Dr. Gillow of Ushaw objected strenuously, and in print, to a sentence on consultation of the faithful, also by Newman. The *Tablet* was only too happy to join the hue and cry, and in an article rumored to be by Frederick Oakeley, warned against the *Rambler*'s "discussing delicate and critical questions *coram populo*" and went on to hope that the magazine would not become a "mere dashing adventurer."[25] This was an inauspicious beginning, not very likely to persuade the bishops that the old spirit of the *Rambler* was dead.[26] At an interview with Ullathorne on May 22, it was "suggested" to Newman that he give up the editorship after the July issue, and this he promised to do.[27] "All through my life I have been plucked," he wrote to Henry Wilberforce on July 20, 1859. "The Bishop put his extinguisher on the Rambler. I never meant to have kept it for long—but it is one thing to set a thing off, another to be made to throw it away."[28]

Unfortunate as his attempt to save the *Rambler* had been to him personally, Newman's departure was equally so to the conductors. They were faced with the immediate need to make new editorial arrangements, for they were determined not to be driven from the field. On June 1 Simpson remarked with characteristic aggressiveness, "It must now come to an open fight, and the sooner and the more acid the better."[29] The chief difficulty was to find a sub-editor, since Acton was now engaging actively in politics and was also frequently forced to be abroad. The irrepressible

[22]Described by Simpson to Acton, Feb. 20 [1859], Woodruff MSS; quoted by Damian McElrath, "Richard Simpson and John Henry Newman," *The Catholic Historical Review*, 52 (Jan. 1967), 515.

[23]See Newman, *L&D*, VIII and XIX for the year 1859, particularly XIX, 86, 87, 96–97.

[24]Reproduced in Newman, *L&D*, XIX, 88.

[25]Quoted in Newman, *L&D*, XIX, 140.

[26]They still felt it "unsettled people," ibid., p. 142.

[27]He wrote a full account of the proceedings to Edward Healy Thompson on May 29, ibid., pp. 148–151.

[28]Ibid., p. 181.

[29]Ibid., p. 148n.

Simpson had to be replaced, for, as Acton recognized, he really did not understand his own imprudence.[30] Newman, although he had a high opinion of Simpson's powers and great respect for his character, spoke out forcefully on July 5, 1859, against allowing him to be sub-editor: "He will always be flicking his whip at Bishops, cutting them in tender places, throwing stones at sacred Congregations, and, as he rides along the high road, discharging pea shooters at Cardinals who happen by bad luck to look out of window."[31]

Presently it was arranged that T. F. Wetherell should serve as sub-editor. He had some qualms about joining the *Rambler*, but Newman was able to persuade him: "I am sure he [Acton] wishes to keep clear of what is likely to give offence to Catholics, and has no wish to make the *Rambler* the organ of a party."[32] Actually so desirous was Acton of reconciliation that he told Northcote his aim was "peace among Catholics; for Protestants of good will a golden bridge; polemics to be directed chiefly against freethinkers."[33] But he selected as the motto for the periodical *Seu vetus est verum diligo, sive novum* [I choose truth, whether old or new], which was not exactly what the authorities would have viewed as a gesture of peace. The issue for September 1859 did occupy itself almost exclusively with non-theological matter —even the article on Rosmini confining itself primarily to speculative philosophy, and in November Simpson made an attempt to pacify the suspicions that had been aroused by the question of Lingard's cardinalate (*Ram* no. 1011).

But things were not so smooth as they seemed on the surface. Acton was abroad, and Wetherell was overburdened at the War Office, so that Simpson was actually in charge of preparing the November and January issues.[34] Here then was the very situation that Newman had striven to correct. Simpson was just where he was before; "he *was* Editor"; and when a letter in the *Tablet* of October 29, 1859, referred to Newman as if he were still "the distinguished conductor of the *Rambler*," he believed that he owed it to the bishops to deny such a connection. This he did in a letter to the *Tablet* of November 12, thereby causing the circulation to decline drastically.[35] Acton was upset by this public statement, and in June he wrote to Newman about the whole problem of the *Rambler*, bemoaning the fact that Wetherell had deserted him— "so that I am without, any regular editorial help except what I can get from Simpson. . . . I greatly fear that without your countenance and aid there is very little chance of my going on with success."[36] But Newman's fingers had been burned and his heart was sore. After September 1860 he held himself more and more aloof.

Meanwhile the split among the Catholics was growing wider and more vituperative, fracturing primarily and ostensibly upon the question of temporal power, but there was an underlying friction with regard to the relative position of the ecclesiastical authorities and the laity, which ironically enough had been stirred up by Newman's original discussion "On Consulting the Faithful." Criticism rained upon the *Rambler* from every quarter, and Acton and Simpson and their few faithful contributors found

---

[30] Ibid., p. 155.
[32] Newman, *L&D*, XIX, 195, 198, 201.
[34] J. L. Altholz, pp. 120, 124.
[36] Ibid., pp. 371–372.

[31] Newman to Acton, July 6, 1861, *L&D*, XX, 4.
[33] Gasquet, p. 85n.
[35] Newman, *L&D*, XIX, 237, 371, 373.

themselves more and more isolated and embattled. They were suspect in Rome and threatened with censure unless they would come out in favor of temporal power. Moreover, they were openly sympathetic with Döllinger and the Catholic liberals on the Continent, and at war with Wiseman and Manning. The latter indeed urged Acton in no uncertain terms to give up the periodical as a means of avoiding censure.[37] But Acton preferred to face the condemnation from Rome, feeling that it would put the authorities in the wrong if they based a censure on what was primarily a political rather than a religious matter. Pressure was clearly applied to James Burns, the publisher, who was likewise the publisher for the hierarchy, and in September he in turn issued an ultimatum to Simpson, who was again acting as editor: either the *Rambler* must be surrendered to a committee named by Manning, Ward, and North-cote or find another publisher. This gambit backfired, at least for the moment, in much the same way as the removal of Newman had done. In the first case the bishops had removed the one and only possible moderating influence from the *Rambler*; now they had succeeded in putting the *Rambler* into the hands of a Protestant publisher.[38] Acton and Wetherell were only just able to restrain Simpson from blasting the authorities in a proposed article on Catholic liberty of the press as a lead-off to the first number issued by the new publishers, Williams and Norgate.[39] Instead they prefixed a statement to the May 1862 *Rambler*, "To Readers and Correspondents," announcing the change from a bi-monthly to a quarterly, and giving a revealing summary of the history and present position of the periodical.

The *Rambler* was commenced on the 1st of January 1848. . . . Its aim was to unite an intelligent and hearty acceptance of the Catholic dogma with free inquiry and discussion on questions which the Church has left open to debate. . . . It soon became evident that our design responded to a very serious need in the Catholic body. . . . During this period of ten years and a half [1848–1859], we at first endeavoured to restrict it to topics of social and literary interest. . . . But the events of the time, and the circumstances of English Catholicism, gradually modified our position, compelling us more and more to open our pages to investigations of a deeper and more complex nature.

As to the new *Rambler*, they continued, "It will abstain from direct theological discussion . . . and in dealing with those mixed questions into which theology indirectly enters, its aim will still be to combine devotion to the Church with discriminaton and candour in the treatment of her opponents; to reconcile freedom of inquiry with implicit faith." The program bears a striking resemblance not only to various statements by Capes but also to the notice prefixed by Newman to the issue for May 1859 —this leopard clearly was not changing its spots. There is, however, a more emphatic tone of independence, engendered no doubt by the immediate situation.

In the opening article of the May issue Simpson ventured to slip in the remark that "Perhaps, as in the ideal state, *so in the Church also*, the best temporal condition of Christendom is to be found in the due balance and harmony of the freedom of individual, of corporation, and of monarchy."[40] This could only horrify such advocates of total submission to ecclesiastical authority in all areas as Wiseman, Manning,

---

[37]Ibid., pp. 230, 517–518, 523–524.
[39]Ibid., p. 52, n. 2.

[38]Newman, *L&D*, XX, 47–52.
[40]Page 451, our italics.

and Ward. Even more direct and offensive was a full-scale attack on Ward's *Relation of Intellectual Power to Man's True Perfection* (no. 1133), holding the author up to ridicule and scorn.

Such a blatantly aggressive stance might well have led to the suppression of the *Rambler*, so long desired by Wiseman, had not Acton and Simpson already decided to make the change to a quarterly review under a new name. The resulting *Home and Foreign Review* was an even more distinguished periodical than its predecessor—but no more amenable to the dignitaries of the Church.[41]

EDITORS

John Moore Capes: January 1, 1848–1852.
James Spencer Northcote: 1852–September 1854.
John Moore Capes: October 1854–October 1857.
Richard Simpson: February 1858–February 1859.
John Henry Newman: May–July 1859.
Sir John Acton: September 1859–May 1862.

   SUB-EDITORS
   Richard Simpson, September 1856–January 1858; acting editor, October 1856–January 1857, November 1857–January 1858.
   Thomas F. Wetherell, August 1859–January 1860, September 1860–May 1862.[42]

PROPRIETORS

John Moore Capes, 1848–1858.
Sir John Acton, Richard Simpson, and Frederick Capes, 1858–1862.[43]

PUBLISHERS

Burns and Lambert, London: 1848–September 1861.
Williams and Norgate, London: November 1861–May 1862.

NOTE ON ATTRIBUTIONS

Few articles in the *Rambler* are signed and the initials which are used are rarely genuine. There are no publisher's lists. The most important primary source is a notebook that belonged to Richard Simpson, including (1) lists of articles (1848–1852 and 1859–1862) with generally accurate attributions of authorship (incomplete for the earlier years), but not apparently in Simpson's own hand; (2) *Rambler* accounts from September 1856 to February 1859, with indication of authorship usually merely by initials. This is supplemented by two lists prepared by James Spencer Northcote, of contributors known to him, and by an illuminating and extensive series of letters from Capes to Simpson, as well as a few letters from Charles Weld and T. F. Wetherell. These sources are now at Downside Abbey and were

[41] See *Index*, I, 547–553.
[42] Capes was acting editor for the July 1858 issue. Simpson was acting sub-editor Mar.–July 1860 and during Wetherell's illness, Mar.–Sept. 1861.
[43] Acton had two shares, Simpson and Frederick Capes each had one. A share was valued at £50. The new management took over in Feb. 1858, although the arrangements were not definitive until July.

examined by the kind permission of the Abbot. Especially for the period from 1858, the history of the *Rambler* is best traced through the correspondence of its editors. Acton's letters to Simpson (very imperfectly edited by Gasquet) are also at Downside. Simpson's letters to Acton and Acton's other correspondence (including that with Döllinger, edited by Conzemius) are in the possession of Mr. Douglas Woodruff, Marcham Abbey, Abingdon, Berkshire.[44] Newman's correspondence (being edited under the direction of Father Dessain) is at the Birmingham Oratory.

BIBLIOGRAPHICAL NOTE

Acton, John Emerich Edward Dalberg. *Essays on Church and State.* Ed. D. Woodruff. 1952. Introduction, and in particular essay IX, "The Catholic Press," taken from the *Rambler* for February 1859.

――――. *Essays on Freedom and Power.* Ed. Gertrude Himmelfarb, with a bibliography by Bert F. Hoselitz. Boston, 1948.

Altholz, Josef Lewis. *The Liberal Catholic Movement in England.* 1962. Chapters I–IX provide the most detailed history of the *Rambler.*

――――. "Bibliographical Note on the *Rambler,*" *Papers of the Bibliographical Society of America,* 56 (1962), 113–114.

――――. "On the Use of 'Communicated' in the *Rambler,*" *Victorian Periodical Newsletter,* January 1968, 28–29. For the use and meaning of the term "communicated" following a title, see also *Index,* I, 549.

――――, and Damian McElrath, eds. *The Correspondence of Lord Acton and Richard Simpson.* Vols. I and II. Cambridge, 1971–1972.

Capes, John Moore. *Four Years' Experience of the Catholic Religion.* Philadelphia, 1849.

――――. *To Rome and Back.* 1873. (See an interesting review of this book, as well as a sympathetic estimate of Capes by C. Kegan Paul in the *Theological Review,* 11 [1874], 256–262.)

Conzemius, Victor, ed. *Ignaz von Döllinger / Lord Acton: Briefwechsel 1850–1890.* Band I, *1850–1869.* München, 1963.

Gasquet, Francis Aidan, ed. *Lord Acton and his Circle.* 1906.

Houghton, Esther Rhoads. "Reviewer of Browning's *Men and Women* in the *Rambler* Identified," *Victorian Newsletter,* no. 33 (Spring 1968), p. 46.

McElrath, Damian. "Richard Simpson and Count de Montalembert, the *Rambler* and the *Correspondant,*" *Downside Review,* 84 (April 1966), 150–170.

――――. "Richard Simpson and John Henry Newman: the *Rambler,* Laymen, and Theology," *Catholic Historical Review,* 52 (January 1967), 509–533.

Newman, John Henry. *The Letters and Diaries of John Henry Newman.* Vols. XI–XX. Ed. by C. Stephen Dessain. 1961.

Ward, Wilfrid. *The Life of John Henry Cardinal Newman.* 2 vols. 1912.

Watkin, Aelred, and Herbert Butterfield. "Gasquet and the Acton-Simpson Correspondence," *Cambridge Historical Journal,* 10 (1950), 75–105.

――――――――――――

[44]The Acton-Simpson correspondence from Feb. 1858 to Aug. 1859 has now been published (see Bibliographical Note), too late unfortunately to allow for page references to be supplied by the *Index*: the dates of the letters, however, are sufficient guide to the printed text.

VOLUME 3, SEPTEMBER 1848

1 The first remedy for Ireland's sorrows, 1–5. **J. M. Capes,** prob. Capes projected the *Rambler* and almost single-handed carried it on from its inception until 1857 (see Newman, *L&D*, XIII, 312, and *Ram* no. 194, p. 10); he was almost certainly responsible for the editorials as well as for many arts. which reflect his known interests; see introduction above.

2 Aristocracy and democracy, 6–9. **J. M. Capes,** prob. This art. reflects views expressed in earlier editorials; see in particular that for June 24, 1848, "Monarchy and Republicanism."

3 St. Philip Neri and his times (Part I), 9–14. **J. D. B. Dalgairns.** Attr. by Newman, *L&D*, XII, 256, XV, 250.

4 Cardinal Consalvi, 14–18.

5 The new crook in the lot (chaps. i–ii), 18–30. **Gertrude Parsons,** prob. Northcote file gives "G.P." for nos. 113, 126, 135, 146; she was a prolific writer of religious novels, whose husband wrote for the *Rambler*.

6 Emigration; how possible for the poor, 30–33. **F. W. Jerningham.** Signed F.W.J.; man cited wrote a letter on New Zealand signed Frederick Jerningham in *Ram* 2 (May 1848), 56–57, and a pamphlet on emigration in the same year: *BMCat.*

7 The music of the fifteenth century; its character and its corruptions, 33–37. **J. M. Capes,** prob. Cf. no. 1 and introduction above.

8 St. John's Church, Salford, Manchester, 38. **J. M. Capes,** prob. Cf. no. 1 and introduction above.

9 Roman intelligence: agitation in the city —attempted assassination of Father Hearne, of Manchester, 39–41. **J. S. Northcote?** Signed Our Own Correspondent, Rome, August 14, 1848; Northcote, a close friend of Capes and later editor of the *Rambler*, was in Italy 1847–1850: *DNB.*

10 The Jesuits: their friends and their foes [review of Andrew Steinmetz and W. P. Ward], 41–53. Unidentified. Possibly W. A. Grant of Derby, who offered a review of Steinmetz on the Jesuits to H. R. Bagshawe for the *DR* (Grant to Bagshawe, May 12, 1848, Bagshawe Papers); it was apparently rejected and may then have been sent to the *Ram.*

11 Modern almsgiving in connexion with the education of the Catholic poor, 53–61. **J. M. Capes,** prob. Cf. no. 1 and introduction above. This art. introduces the topic Capes was to discuss later, the offertory; cf. no. 123.

12 Milnes' *Life of Keats,* 61–65.

13 Mr. Bell's new novel [*The Tenant of Wildfell Hall*], 65–66.

14 Short notices, 66–67.

15 In Ecclesiastical register: The Bishop of Langres on Christian education, 69–70, by **Pierre Louis Parisis**—title; Corea (Part I), 74–77, by **M. N. A. Daveluy** —opening paragraph.

16 Historic chronicle [current events], 79–80.

VOLUME 3, OCTOBER 1848

17 Will England ever be a Catholic country? 81–89. **J. M. Capes,** prob. Cf. no. 1.

18 St. Philip Neri and his times (Part II), 89–94. **J. D. B. Dalgairns.** Cf. no. 3.

19 The ideas of the deaf and dumb, 94–103.

20 The new crook in the lot (chaps. iii–v), 103–116. **Gertrude Parsons,** prob. Cf. no. 5.

21 Roman news: prorogation of the Parliament, 116–118. **J. S. Northcote?** Signed Our Own Correspondent, Rome, Sept. 14, 1848; evidence for no. 9.

22 Early Christian art, 118–124.

23 *Italy in the Nineteenth Century,* 124–133.

24 Ross's *Yacht Voyage,* 134–135.

25 The Middle-Age drama, 135–137.

26 Short notices, 137–140.

27 In Correspondence: Sedilia and stools, 140–141, signed A Lover of Christian Art; Screens and the Quarant' Ore, 141, signed S.; Rood-screens, 142–143, by

T. W. Marshall—signed T.W.M., identified, p. 446, this a continuation of a discussion from vol. 2; Rood-screens, 143, signed Y. (letters, pp. 212–222, by **W. G. Ward**—signed H., claimed p. 446; pp. 285–289, by **T. W. Marshall**—signed T.W.M.; pp. 374–376, by **W. G. Ward**—claimed p. 446).

28   In Ecclesiastical register: Letters on Lebanon (Part I), 147–150, by **Eugène Boré**—opening paragraph; Corea (Part II, concl.), 150–152, by **M. N. A. Daveluy**—cf. no. 15.

29   Historic chronicle [current events], 156–158.

VOLUME 3, NOVEMBER 1848

30   Pantheism, communism, and christianity, 159–165. **J. M. Capes**, prob. Cf. no. 1; while calling pantheism and communism "portentous monsters," the author nevertheless recognizes them as attempts to establish the principle of brotherhood; such liberal toleration would be characteristic of Capes.

31   St. Philip Neri and his times (Part III), 166–170. **J. D. B. Dalgairns.** Cf. no. 3.

32   The Roman catacombs (No. XI cont'd from vol. 2): their school rooms, baptisteries, and confessionals, 171–174. **J. S. Northcote.** Signed N.; claimed in preface, *Roman Catacombs* (1857), p. ix.

33   Discovery of a complete and authentic copy of the original Antiphonary of St. Gregory [translated from the *Revue de la Musique Religieuse*], 174–180. **Jean Louis Félix Danjou.** Footnote, p. 174. Translated by **Ambrose Lisle Phillipps**—signed "A.L.P."; Simpson notebook gives A. L. P[hillipps].

34   The new crook in the lot (chaps. vi–vii), 180–188. **Gertrude Parsons**, prob. Cf. no. 5.

35   Roman affairs: the new ministry, 188–190. **J. S. Northcote?** Signed Our Own Correspondent, Rome, October 14, 1848; evidence for no. 9.

36   The Chevalier Bunsen on biblical history, 191–194.

37   Spanish art, 194–201.

38   New novels; bad, good, and indifferent, 201–209.

39   *The Fairfax Correspondence*, 209–210.

40   Short notices, 210–211.

41   In Correspondence: The Architectural Association, 222, signed: A Catholic Architect.

42   Ecclesiastical register, 222–231.

43   Historic chronicle [current events], 231–234.

VOLUME 3, DECEMBER 1848

44   Catholic and Protestant collegiate education, 235–241. **J. M. Capes.** Simpson notebook; Gasquet, p. xv. (Letters, pp. 372–374, signed **Frederick Oakeley**, with a note by the editor, **J. M. Capes**; pp. 446–457, signed **W. G. Ward**, see no. 77; pp. 533–536, by **J. M. Capes?**—signed C.; pp. 604–614, signed **W. G. Ward**, see no. 107.)

45   Sketches ecclesiastical and secular (No. I): the poor priest, 241–247. **T. W. Marshall?** Simpson notebook gives for succeeding parts "?Marshall"; Marshall was involved in the controversy over rood-screens; see no. 27.

46   The Roman catacombs (No. XII): their churches and chapels, architecture and painting, 248–255. **J. S. Northcote.** Evidence for no. 32.

47   The new crook in the lot (chaps. viii–ix), 255–268. **Gertrude Parsons**, prob. Cf. no. 5.

48   *The Castlereagh Correspondence*, 268–276.

49   Memoirs of the reign of Charles I, 276–282.

50   Rev. F. Oakeley's *Sermons*, 282–284.

51   In Correspondence: Roman News: progress of the ministry and murder of Count Rossi, 284–285, by **J. S. Northcote?**—signed Our Own Correspondent, Rome, November 13, 1848; evidence for no. 9.

52   In Ecclesiastical register: Letters on Lebanon (Part II), 290–294, by **Eugène Boré**—cf. no. 28; The modern saints: including signed letters of **J. H. Newman, F. W. Faber, W. B. Ullathorne** and remarks from the *Tablet*, 298–300. Proposals for a corrected edition of the Bible, 300–301, signed A Lover of Consistency.

53   Historic chronicle [current events], 307–310.

VOLUME 3, JANUARY 1849

54   Music as a part of education, 311–317. **J. M. Capes**, prob. Cf. no. 1. Capes was much interested in musical education; cf. introduction above.

55   The Roman catacombs (No. XIII): their paintings, 318–325. **J. S. Northcote.** Evidence for no. 32.

91 Anglo-Saxonica: Soames, Paley, and Chambers, 527–529.
92 Short notices, 529–530.
93 In Correspondence: The revolution in Rome, 531–533, by **J. S. Northcote?**— signed Our Own Correspondent, Rome, Feb. 14, 1849; evidence for no. 9.
94 In Ecclesiastical register: Letters on Lebanon (Part V, concl.), 536–538, with a note on the author, signed **Eugène Boré.**
95 Historic chronicle [current events], 549–550.

VOLUME 3, APRIL 1849

96 Preface ["bringing the third volume of the *Rambler* to a conclusion"], iii–vi. **J. M. Capes**, prob. He was the editor.
97 Holy week, 551–557. **J. M. Capes**, prob. Cf. no. 1; the author regrets in passing the musical deficiencies in certain celebrations of the rites of Holy Week; see introduction above.
98 The Pope and the people of Rome, 557–564. **J. M. Capes**, prob. Cf. no. 1; the author praises Pius IX for his liberal reforms; the Pope's "independent and energetic movement in the cause of reform" (p. 563) would naturally appeal to Capes.
99 Sketches: ecclesiastical and secular (No. II cont'd.): Ignatius Dunstan Dominick Smith, 564–570. **T. W. Marshall?** Cf. no. 45.
100 The Roman catacombs (No. XVI, concl.): relics, 570–578. **J. S. Northcote.** Evidence for no. 32.
101 Cardinal Capaccini (Part II, concl.), 578–579.
102 Protestant views of the doctrine of the Incarnation, 579–593. **J. M. Capes.** See Newman, *L&D*, XIII, 68.
103 Revolutionised Italy, 593–597.
104 Catholicism in Scotland: the Association of St. Margaret, 597–599.
105 Quetelet, *On Probabilities*, 599–600. **J. M. Capes**, prob. Cf. no. 1; Capes was a professor of mathematics at Prior Park College, to whom the subject of this article would be of special interest.
106 Short notices, 600–601.
107 In Correspondence: The Roman republicans, 602–604, by **J. S. Northcote?**— signed Our Own Correspondent, Rome, Mar. 14, 1849, evidence for no. 9; The study of classical Greek and Latin: Mr.

Ward in reply to C., see no. 44, 604–614, signed **W. G. Ward.**
108 In Ecclesiastical register: Encyclical on the Immaculate Conception, 614–615, by **Pius IX**—title.
109 Historic chronicle [current events], 619–620.

VOLUME 4, MAY 1849

110 Where does our strength lie? 1–7. **J. M. Capes**, prob. Cf. no. 1; statement of contemporary condition of Catholics in England; p. 2, echoes that in the preface, above, no. 96.
111 Count Stolberg, 7–17. **James Burton Robertson.** Note at end of art. says an abridgement of this memoir has been prefixed to John Dalton's translation of Stolberg's *Little Book of the Love of God*; the author of the memoir is identified in a notice of the book in *Rambler*, 3, 441.
112 Sketches: ecclesiastical and secular (No. II cont'd., concl.): Ignatius Dunstan Dominick Smith, 17–24. **T. W. Marshall?** Cf. no. 45.
113 The new crook in the lot (chaps. xvi–xvii), 24–32. **Gertrude Parsons**, prob. Northcote file gives "G.P."; see no. 5.
114 Modern deism; Morell and Froude, 32–45.
115 Dr. Rock's *Church of our Fathers*, 45–48.
116 Thackeray's *Pendennis*, 48–51.
117 Allies' *Journal in France* (Part I), 51–63. **E. H. Thompson.** Claimed, Thompson to Allies, Mar. 13, 1849, Westminster Diocesan Archives.
118 Anglican misconceptions: *The Christian Remembrancer* [on Allies' *Journal in France*], 63–64.
119 Short notices, 65–67.
120 In Correspondence: The state of Rome; progress of plunder and tyranny, 67–69, by **J. S. Northcote?**—signed Our Own Correspondent, Rome, Apr. 11, 1849; evidence for no. 9.
121 Ecclesiastical register, 71–79.
122 Historic chronicle [current events], 79–80.

VOLUME 4, JUNE 1849

123 The offertory, 81–89. **J. M. Capes.** Simpson notebook. (Letters, pp. 208–210, 269–270, and 396–398, signed

Frederick Oakeley; pp. 398–399, signed **F. Betham.**)

124 English art; its weakness and its strength, 89–97. **J. M. Capes?** Cf. no. 1 and introduction above. (See nos. 144 and 185.)

125 The *Quarterly Review* and Mr. Macaulay, 97–106. **J. M. Capes?** Cf. no. 1; this defense of Macaulay from Croker's attack would be characteristic of Capes' liberal attitude; cf. the praise and blame of Macaulay in nos. 72 and 88.

126 The new crook in the lot (chaps. xviii–xix), 107–117. **Gertrude Parsons**, prob. Northcote file gives "G.P."; cf. no. 5.

127 Maitland on the Reformation; the lawfulness of persecution, 117–129. **J. M. Capes?** Cf. no. 1; the praise of Maitland for exposing cant would be characteristic.

128 Allies' *Journal in France* (Part II), 129–144. **E. H. Thompson.** Cf. no. 117.

129 Seymour's wedding-pilgrimage to Rome, 144–149.

130 Short notices, 149–150.

131 In Ecclesiastical register: Consecration of the Bishop of Bruges, 152–155, by **Frederick Oakeley**, prob.—signed F.O.

132 Historic chronicle [current events], 158–160.

VOLUME 4, JULY 1849

133 Four years' experience of the Catholic religion: with observations on its effects upon the character, intellectual, moral, and spiritual (Part I), 161–171. **J. M. Capes.** Signed A Late Member of the University of Oxford; claimed by Capes in letter to Wiseman, Oct. 29, 1854, Westminster Diocesan Archives; repr. *Four Years' Experience of the Catholic Religion*, Phila., 1849.

134 Protestant prophecies of the fall of the Papacy, 171–174.

135 The new crook in the lot (chaps. xx–xxi), 174–181. **Gertrude Parsons**, prob. Northcote file gives "G.P."; cf. no. 5.

136 *Loyola and Jesuitism* [by Isaac Taylor], (Part I), 181–192.

137 Ruskin's *Seven Lamps of Architecture*, 193–201. **J. M. Capes,** prob. Capes to Richard Simpson, July 6, 1854, Simpson notebook, warns Simpson not to clash with what Capes had said earlier about Ruskin.

138 Clough's poems [*Ambarvalia*], 201–205.

139 The water-cure at home, 205–207.

140 Short notices, 207–208.

141 In Ecclesiastical register: Allocution of

Pope Pius IX, pronounced in secret consistory at Gaeta on April 20, 1849, 210–217 by **Pius IX**—title.

142 Historic chronicle [current events], 219–220.

VOLUME 4, AUGUST 1849

143 Four years' experience of the Catholic religion (Part II), 221–233. **J. M. Capes.** Evidence for no. 133.

144 Modern church architecture, 233–236. **J. M. Capes,** prob. Cf. no. 1 and introduction above; also nos. 195 and 221. (See nos. 124 and 185.)

145 Catholic college difficulties, 236–239. **J. M. Capes?** The author expands the point made by Capes in no. 44, p. 236; the apathy of Catholic laity in paying as they ought for their children's instruction, and in general makes the same point about inferior education of Catholics.

146 The new crook in the lot (chap. xxii, concl.), 239–246. **Gertrude Parsons,** prob. Northcote file gives "G.P."; cf. no. 5.

147 [Francis] Newman on the soul, 246–252.

148 *Loyola and Jesuitism* [by Isaac Taylor], (Part II, concl.), 252–263.

149 The use of hymns: Catholic and non-Catholic poetry, 263–267. **J. M. Capes?** This article combines an appreciation of religious poetry and concern for the poor, both characteristic of Capes.

150 Short notices, 267–268.

151 In Ecclesiastical register: Allocution of Pope Pius IX: Latin text of no. 141, 270–277 by **Pius IX**—title; The English government and the French intervention in Rome [a series of letters from **Viscount Palmerston,** the **Marquis of Normanby, Prince Castelcicala,** and **Raffaele Fornari,** the Apostolic Nuncio in Paris], 278–280.

152 Historic chronicle [current events], 281–282.

VOLUME 4, SEPTEMBER 1849

153 Four years' experience of the Catholic religion (Part III, concl.), 283–295. **J. M. Capes.** Evidence for no. 133.

154 The life and writings of Augustus William von Schlegel (Part I), 295–304. **James Burton Robertson,** prob. The author of this 2-pt. art. says, p. 295n, that he has

drawn his materials partly from his own recollections of Schlegel; Robertson in his "advertisement" to the 2nd ed. of his translation of Frederick von Schlegel's *Philosophy of History*, 1845, speaks of having known W. A. Schlegel at Bonn; Robertson had already contributed to the *Ram* in 1848 (no. 111).

155 Non-religious education, 305–308. **J. M. Capes?** Cf. no. 1 and introduction above.

156 The Clapham Sect; Evangelicalism, 308–320.

157 Catholicism and civilisation, 320–331. **J. M. Capes,** prob. On p. 321, the author pleads for education of the poor and at the close for amelioration of their plight; also on p. 321 he bemoans lack of a Catholic literature; cf. no. 96 and introduction above.

158 *England in the Days of Wiclif*, 331–333.

159 *David Copperfield* and *Con Gregan*, 333–337.

160 Ecclesiastical register, 337–345.

161 Historic chronicle [current events], 345–346.

Volume 4, October 1849

162 Money prospects, 347–354. **J. M. Capes,** prob. Cf. no. 1; this editorial stresses the discrimination against the poor within the Catholic Church; see especially closing sentence; cf. no. 174, p. 423. (Letters, pp. 466–467, signed **Matthew Bridges**; pp. 467–469, signed **Y.**)

163 Catholic parochial ministrations: the visitation of the sick (Part I), 354–357.

164 Classical studies as pursued in the English universities, 357–371. **T. A. Paley,** prob. The author implies by his comments, pp. 359–360, that he is a Cambridge man, and says on p. 367 he can personally attest the proficiency of Ushaw students in Greek; Paley was a graduate of Cambridge and a Classical scholar; in July 1849 he spent a week at Ushaw and took part in public examinations and was favorably impressed by the attainments in the classics. (*Ushaw Magazine*, 1906, p. 27.)

165 The life and writings of Augustus William von Schlegel (Part II), 372–378. **James Burton Robertson.** Cf. no. 154.

166 Church festivals (Part I): The festivals of the angels, 378–381. Signed M.

167 Bible controversy and Bible reading, 381–388. **J. M. Capes?** Simpson notebook with a ?; see Newman, *L&D*, XIII, 397n.

(Note, p. 469, by **J. M. Capes**—signed Ed. *Rambler*; letter, pp. 469–470, signed P.)

168 Christian Rome (Part I), 389–396. **E. H. Thompson,** prob. Northcote file gives "E.H.T."

169 In Correspondence: Letter to the Editor of the *Christian Remembrancer*, 396–398, signed **Frederick Oakeley.**

170 Ecclesiastical register, 400–407.

171 Historic chronicle [current events], 407–408.

Volume 4, November 1849

172 Cheap books, 409–416. **J. M. Capes,** prob. Simpson notebook gives J. M. Capes?"; detailed refs. to problems of editing the *Rambler*, strongly suggest the editor.

173 Literature for the Catholic poor, 417–419. **J. M. Capes,** prob. This is a pendant to preceding no. (Letter, p. 526, signed **T. E. Bradley.**)

174 A Sunday in London (chaps. i–ii), 419–432. **J. M. Capes.** Repr. under this title, 1850.

175 Catholic parochial ministrations: the visitation of the sick (Part II), 432–435.

176 Church festivals (Part II): All Saints, All Souls, 435–441. Signed: M.

177 Socinianism, 442–451.

178 Christian Rome (Part II, concl.), 451–460. **E. H. Thompson,** prob. Cf. no. 168.

179 *Rome and the Abbey*, 460–465.

180 Short notices, 465–466.

181 Ecclesiastical register, 470–471.

182 Historic chronicle [current events], 472.

Volume 4, December 1849

183 The conversion of England, 473–482. **J. M. Capes,** prob. Cf. no. 1; reflects his concern over the discrimination against the poor; cf. no. 162. (Letters, vol. 5, pp. 185–188, 292–296, 388–390, all by **George Spencer**—signed Ignatius of S. Paul, Passionist [his name in religion].)

184 A Sunday in London (chaps. iii–iv), 483–498. **J. M. Capes.** Cf. no. 174.

185 Church decoration, 498–503. **J. M. Capes,** prob. A defence of the *Rambler's* previous article on modern church architecture (no. 144). (See nos. 124 and 144.)

186 Church festivals (Part III, concl.): Advent, Christmas, 503–509. Signed: M.

187 Protestant churches, 509–514. **J. M.**

Capes, prob. The author, like Capes, is concerned that churches should primarily reflect religious, rather than aesthetic, feelings; like Capes, he claims that when means are adequate, Catholics delight to build handsome churches, but where they are lacking, a simple, even an ugly building is a fit place for devotion; cf. no. 144.

188 Tithes, 514–518. **Frederick Betham**, prob. In an earlier letter (see no. 123), Betham offers to pursue this topic further. (Letter, vol. 5, pp. 100–103, prob. by **Betham**—signed The Writer of the Paper on Tithes.)

189 John Howard, 518–522.

190 Lord Cloncurry's *Autobiography*, 522–525.

191 Short notices, 525.

192 In Ecclesiastical register: Lord Minto in Rome [some of his letters], 526–528, by **Gilbert Elliot**—signed Minto [Earl Minto]; The Catholic bishops and the Prussian charter, 528–530.

193 Historic chronicle [current events], 530.

VOLUME 5, JANUARY 1850

194 Hopes and fears for 1850, 1–11. **J. M. Capes**, prob. Editorial; cf. no. 1.

195 Town churches (No. I), 11–18. **J. M. Capes** and **M. E. Hadfield**. See Newman, *L&D*, XIII, 398n.; for Hadfield's share see p. 16 of the art.

196 Catholic parochial ministrations: visitation of the sick (Part III, concl.), 19–25.

197 A Sunday in London (chaps. v–vi), 26–55. **J. M. Capes**. Cf. no. 174.

198 A few remarks on Gothic ecclesiastical building, and its cost, 57–61. **W. W. Wardell**. Signed.

199 Newman's *Discourses*, 62–83. Unidentified. Newman thought the review might have been by W. G. Ward: see *L&D*, XIII, 355–356.

200 Tate's *Algebra*, 83–88. **J. M. Capes**? He was prof. of mathematics at Prior Park; cf. no. 105.

201 Short notices, 88–91.

202 In Correspondence: Madeira, 92–100, possibly by F. A. Paley, classical scholar, and convert in 1846, who was in Madeira at about this time: see *DNB*.

203 Ecclesiastical register, 104–108.

VOLUME 5, FEBRUARY 1850

204 Communism, 109–124. **J. M. Capes**,

prob. The exposition of Christian communism, the attack on mammon-minded industrialists and praise of co-operative combinations for labour would all reflect Capes' attitudes; see for example no. 30.

205 Town churches (Part II, concl.), 124–126. **W. W. Wardell**. Attr. p. 124.

206 A Sunday in London (chap. vii), 127–139. **J. M. Capes**. Cf. no. 174.

207 The two kingdoms, 140–181. **J. M. Capes**, prob. Attr. in Newman, *L&D*, XIII, 397n.

208 Short notices, 181–185. Pages 181–182, by **J. M. Capes**—Newman, *L&D*, XIII, 397.

209 In Ecclesiastical register: Encyclical on present posture of affairs in Italy, 189–198, by **Pius IX**—signed; Correspondence between the Bishop of La Rochelle and the Rev. Father Newman on *The Essay on Development* (extracted and translated from the *Univers*), 198–202, by **Clément Villecourt** and **J. H. Newman**—title.

VOLUME 5, MARCH 1850

210 The progress of Catholic poverty, 203–216. **J. M. Capes**, prob. Editorial in tone; the plea for financial support of the Church parallels that in no. 622 in particular.

211 The canon of Holy Scripture, 216–226.

212 A Sunday in London (chaps. viii–ix, concl.), 226–250. **J. M. Capes**. Signed Herder; cf. no. 174.

213 Layard's *Nineveh*, 252–280.

214 The Irish church establishment, 280–286. **J. M. Capes**, prob. The article reiterates the views expressed in no. 1 with regard to the disestablishment of the Protestant Church in Ireland, and reflects Capes' interest in the Irish.

215 Urquhart's *Pillars of Hercules*, 287–289.

216 Short notices, 289–292.

VOLUME 5, APRIL 1850

217 Church reform, 297–318. **J. M. Capes**, prob. Cf. no. 1; and no. 96, quoted above, p. 733, where the need to move (to reform) is stressed; on p. 310 the author refers to previous discussions of our poverty, see among others no. 210; pp. 314–315 deal with the Catholic periodical press, including the *Rambler*.

218 Life of Frederic Hurter (chaps. i–iii),

318–335. **Alexandre de St. Cheron.** Title says "From the French of A. St. Cheron"; see *Bib. Nat. Cat.* Translated by **James Burton Robertson?**—he wrote on Hurter in *DR* in March, 1850, no. 573, in which, pp. 50, 58, it is implied that he translated Hurter's *Innocent III* (vols. III and IV).

219 Southey's *Life and Correspondence*, 338–354.

220 Carlylism, 354–366.

221 Mr. Pugin and the *Rambler*, 367–375. **J. M. Capes,** prob. Editorial reply to a pamphlet by Pugin attacking *Rambler* arts. on town churches: nos. 195, 205.

222 Migne's *Bibliothèque Universelle du Clergé*, 375–377.

223 Short notices, 378–388.

VOLUME 5, MAY 1850

224 Prospects of the Anglo-Catholic party in the Established Church [on Gorham judgment], 391–407. **J. M. Capes,** prob. Cf. no. 1 and also Capes' arts. on his experience of the Catholic religion, nos. 133, 143, and 153.

225 Life of Frederic Hurter (chaps. iv–vi, concl.), 407–424. **Alexandre de St. Cheron.** Cf. no. 218.

226 Images and image-worship (Part I), 427–450.

227 The church and the king before and after the Reformation, 450–476.

228 Short notices, 476–484.

VOLUME 5, JUNE 1850

229 Wants of the time, 485–504. **J. M. Capes,** prob. Cf. no. 1; the author is concerned with means of reaching the Catholic poor, such as lectures, periodical press, and recreation; he shows exact knowledge of Protestant periodicals and endeavors and urges the use of similar methods by Catholics; cf. the lectures organized by Capes in the following year (Newman, *L&D*, XIV, XV).

230 The Neapolitan catacombs, 504–525. **J. S. Northcote.** Signed N; Simpson notebook; opening sentence: "It is now more than a year ago since I despatched to you my last paper on the Roman Catacombs."

231 Town churches (No. III, concl.), 525–526. **Charles Parker.** Signed C.P.; two accompanying drawings signed C. Parker.

232 Cardinal Pacca's *Memoirs* (Part I), 529–548. **J. S. Northcote.** Simpson notebook.

233 Images and image-worship (Part II, concl.), 548–573.

234 Short notices, 573–578.

VOLUME 6, JULY 1850

235 Catholic funerals, 1–11. **Charles Eyre.** Simpson notebook; Northcote list; Northcote file.

236 Brief notices of some writers of the English Franciscan province since the era of the Reformation (No. I), 11–21. **George Oliver.** Dedication signed G.O.; repr. *Collections.*

237 The miraculous life of the saints, 22–57. **J. M. Capes.** Repr. as "Essay on the Miraculous Life of the Saints," prefixed to Georgiana Fullerton, *Life of St. Frances of Rome*, 1855.

238 Cardinal Pacca's *Memoirs* (Part II, concl.), 57–73. **J. S. Northcote.** Northcote list; Simpson notebook; Northcote file.

239 Rossi on the Christian inscriptions of Rome, 73–76. **J. S. Northcote.** Northcote list; Simpson notebook; Northcote file.

240 Hanmer on submission to the Catholic church, 76–80.

241 Short notices, 81–84. Pages 83–84, by **J. S. Northcote**—Northcote list; Simpson notebook; Northcote file.

242 In Ecclesiastical register: Allocution of Pius IX at the secret consistory of May 20, 1850, 85–88 by **Pius IX**—title.

VOLUME 6, AUGUST 1850

243 Popular education: Catholic poor schools and middle schools, 91–109. **J. M. Capes,** prob. Cf. no. 1 and introduction above.

244 Brief notices of some writers of the English Franciscan province (No. II), 110–119. **George Oliver.** Evidence for no. 236.

245 Balmez, 122–164.

246 Sir Robert Peel, 165–169.

247 Short notices, 170–171. Page 170 (Achilli) by **W. F. Finlason**—Northcote file.

248 In Ecclesiastical register: Decision of the Pope on national education in France, 171–173, by **Raffaele Fornari**—signed R. Archbishop of Nicaea, Nuncio Apostolic: see *NBG*; Prayers in Belgium for

the conversion of England, 174–177, signed P.

VOLUME 6, SEPTEMBER 1850

249 Religion and modern philosophy (Part I), 185–204. **Richard Simpson.** Capes to J. H. Newman, July 18, 1850, Newman MSS., says Simpson's art. startled him; see Newman, *L&D*, XIV, 43n. (Letter, vol. 7, pp. 177–179, by **Simpson**— signed S.)

250 Celebrated sanctuaries of the Madonna (Part I): States of the Church, 204–221. **J. S. Northcote.** Signed N.; repr. with this title, 1868.

251 Brief notices of some writers of the English Franciscan province (No. III, concl.), 222–236. **George Oliver.** Evidence for no. 236.

252 Theological science: Protestant preaching, 238–251. **J. M. Capes,** prob. He wrote no. 264 replying to criticisms of this art.; on pp. 239–240 the author defends the use of journalism in discussing theology.

253 The Papal States: Miley and Gaume [on this topic], 251–263.

254 Short notices, 264–265.

255 Ecclesiastical register, 266–278.

VOLUME 6, OCTOBER 1850

256 Religion and modern philosophy (Part II), 279–298. **Richard Simpson.** Cf. no. 249.

257 Celebrated sanctuaries of the Madonna (Part II): Naples, Tuscany, 298–314. **J. S. Northcote.** Evidence for no. 250.

258 Popular services, 315–351. **J. M. Capes.** Simpson notebook; see Newman, *L&D*, XIV, 259n. (Letters, pp. 454–457, by **J. S. Northcote**—signed M.N.H., Simpson notebook; p. 560, presumably by **Capes.**)

259 A Socinian view of Catholicism [in the *Prospective Review*], 351–359. **J. M. Capes,** prob. As a journalist himself, Capes was interested in other periodicals; the conclusion repeats the statements made in no. 224 and nos. 133, 143 and 153, about the reactions of the converts.

260 Short notices, 360–365. Page 362 (Achilli) by **W. F. Finlason**—Northcote file.

261 Ecclesiastical register, 365–372.

VOLUME 6, NOVEMBER 1850

262 Religion and modern philosophy (Part III), 373–390. **Richard Simpson.** Cf. no. 249.

263 Celebrated sanctuaries of the Madonna (Part III): Tuscany, 391–406. **J. S. Northcote.** Evidence for no. 250.

264 Extempore preaching, 406–408. **J. M. Capes.** Northcote list; see no. 252.

265 The Pope, 409–440. **J. M. Capes.** Simpson notebook; Newman, *L&D*, XIV, 104n.

266 *Mount St. Lawrence,* 440–448.

267 Short notices, 449–454. Perret, 453–454, by **J. S. Northcote**—Northcote file.

268 Ecclesiastical register, 458–466.

VOLUME 6, DECEMBER 1850

269 The hierarchy, 467–479. **J. M. Capes.** Simpson notebook; Newman, *L&D*, XIV, 127, 131.

270 Religion and modern philosophy (Part IV, concl.), 480–490. **Richard Simpson.** Cf. no. 249.

271 Collections illustrating the history of the English Benedictine congregation (No. I), 491–506. **George Oliver.** Dedication signed O.; repr. *Collections.*

272 Rise, progress, and results of Puseyism (Part I), 506–544. **J. M. Capes.** Simpson notebook; Northcote list; Newman, *L&D*, XIV, 131.

273 Ecclesiastical register, 544–559.

VOLUME 7, JANUARY 1851

274 Catholic prospects, 1–7. **J. M. Capes.** Simpson notebook; Northcote list; Northcote file; see Newman, *L&D*, XIV, 165.

275 Celebrated sanctuaries of the Madonna (No. IV): Milan, 7–33. **J. S. Northcote.** Evidence for no. 250.

276 Passion, love, and rest; or, the autobiography of Basil Morley (chaps. i–ii), 34–54. **J. M. Capes.** Simpson notebook; Northcote list; Northcote file.

277 Collections illustrating the history of the English Benedictine congregation (No. II), 54–60. **George Oliver.** Evidence for no. 271.

278 Rise, progress, and results of Puseyism (Part II), 60–89. **J. M. Capes.** Cf. no. 272.

279 Short notices, 89–90.

VOLUME 7, FEBRUARY 1851

280 The miracle of St. Januarius, 91–116. **J. S. Northcote.** Signed N.; Simpson notebook; Northcote file.

281 Passion, love, and rest; or, the autobiography of Basil Morley (chaps. iii–iv), 117–134. **J. M. Capes.** Cf. no. 276.

282 Collections illustrating the history of the English Benedictine congregation (No. III), 134–144. **George Oliver.** Evidence for no. 271.

283 Rise, progress, and results of Puseyism (Part III), 144–161. **J. M. Capes.** Cf. no. 272.

284 Miss Strickland's *Queens of Scotland*, 161–166.

285 Dr. Murray on miracles and on education, 166–171. **J. M. Capes,** prob. He had reviewed Vol. 1 of Murray's *Irish Annual Miscellany*, in no. 214; for his stand against secular education see, for example, no. 155.

286 Short notices, 171–177.

287 Ecclesiastical register: Reported attack on Father Ignatius, reprint of a letter from the *Tablet*, 180–182, by **George Spencer**—signed Ignatius of S. Paul, Passionist, his name in religion.

VOLUME 7, MARCH 1851

288 Celebrated sanctuaries of the Madonna (No. V): Reggio, 183–192. **J. S. Northcote.** Evidence for no. 250.

289 Passion, love, and rest; or, the autobiography of Basil Morley (chaps. v–vi), 192–214. **J. M. Capes.** Cf. no. 276.

290 Collections illustrating the history of the English Benedictine congregation (No. IV), 214–222. **George Oliver.** Evidence for no. 271.

291 Shilling churches and penny churches, 222–227. **J. M. Capes,** prob. This is a return to his favorite theme of the discrimination against the poor in churches.

292 Rise, progress, and results of Puseyism (Part IV, concl.), 228–248. **J. M. Capes.** Cf. no. 272.

293 How shall we meet the Protestant aggression? 249–258. **J. M. Capes,** prob. He was in correspondence with Newman on this subject and was organizing a series of lectures on it; see Newman, *L&D*, XIV, 216–218.

294 Townsend's *Journal in Italy*, 259–268.

295 Short notices, 268–273.

296 In Ecclesiastical register: The Bishop of

Birmingham and Lord J. Russell, 274–276, signed **W. B. Ullathorne.**

VOLUME 7, APRIL 1851

297 The Irish in London, 277–296. **J. M. Capes.** This editorial exhibits Capes's concern with both the poor and with the Irish, and on p. 292 speaks of the discrimination against the poor within the Church, cf. nos. 174, 210, and 291.

298 Passion, love, and rest; or, the autobiography of Basil Morley (chap. vii), 297–309. **J. M. Capes.** Cf. no. 276.

299 Anglo-Catholics in theory and in fact, 310–313. **J. M. Capes,** prob. This is a kind of supplement to or summary of the arts. on Puseyism, nos. 272, 278, 283, and 292.

300 Collections illustrating the history of the English Benedictine congregation (No. V), 313–322. **George Oliver.** Evidence for no. 271.

301 The church and the antiquarians, 323–337. **J. M. Capes,** prob. A further attack on Puseyism, particularly in the matter of architecture, including rood screens; see evidence for no. 299, and the controversy in the early issue (no. 27).

302 B[lessed] Ippolito Galantini, the apostolic silk-weaver, 337–349. **J. M. Capes.** Simpson notebook; Northcote file; Newman, *L&D*, XIV, 246. (Notice, p. 464, by **Capes**—Newman, ibid., p. 251.

303 Lord Holland's *Foreign Reminiscences*, 349–356.

304 Short notices, 356–358.

305 Ecclesiastical register, 359–370.

VOLUME 7, MAY 1851

306 Our position and policy, 371–382. **J. M. Capes,** prob. Newman, *L&D*, XIV, 260.

307 Celebrated sanctuaries of the Madonna (Part VI): Loreto, 383–408. **J. S. Northcote.** Cf. no. 250.

308 Passion, love, and rest; or, the autobiography of Basil Morley (chap. viii), 409–424. **J. M. Capes.** Cf. no. 276.

309 Collections illustrating the history of the English Benedictine congregation (No. VI), 424–435. **George Oliver.** Evidence for no. 271.

310 The Protestant feeling towards convents, 440–450. **J. M. Capes?** The author speaks of the near impossibility of Catholics by birth understanding Protestant prejudices against Catholic institutions; Capes repeatedly stressed Protestant inability to understand Catholic faith and practices.

311   The great debate on the penal bill, 450–463. **W. F. Finlason.** Signed W.F.F.; man cited a chief legal writer for the Catholic cause.

312   Short notices, 463–464.

VOLUME 7, JUNE 1851

313   Catholic epitaphs, 465–479. **Charles Eyre.** Simpson notebook; Northcote list; Northcote file.

314   A "loyal" bishop in the Middle Ages: Gilbert Folliot, Bishop of London, 480–494. **David Lewis.** Simpson notebook; Northcote list; Northcote file.

315   Passion, love, and rest; or, the autobiography of Basil Morley (chap. ix), 495–509. **J. M. Capes.** Cf. no. 276.

316   Collections illustrating the history of the English Benedictine congregation (No. VII, concl.), 509–516. **George Oliver.** Evidence for no. 271.

317   The mystery of the passion at Ober Ammergau [sic] in Bavaria, 517–525. **Richard Raby.** Signed. (Letter, vol. 8, pp. 162–164, with an intro. note by **J. S. Northcote,** prob.—signed N., an initial used by him for many of his contributions.) (See no. 736.)

318   *Yeast* [by Charles Kingsley], 525–533. **J. M. Capes?** The art. exhibits an interest in contemporary periodicals that was characteristic of Capes, as well as making a passing reflection on a "Puseyite young lady" (p. 527).

319   Ireland's duty to England, 534–541. **J. M. Capes?** This is an attack on the new penal laws mooted in Parliament as a result of restoration of the hierarchy; see no. 269.

320   Short notices, 541–542. Page 542, notice about the *Rambler*, by **J. M. Capes,** speaking as the editor.

321   Ecclesiastical register, 543–546.

VOLUME 8, JULY 1851

322   The Catholic university for Ireland, 1–12. **J. M. Capes.** The art. opens with what may be considered his credo: "the prosperity of the Catholic Church . . . is bound up with the education of her young ecclesiastics, and the progress of her schools for the poor."

323   State encroachments on the Church before the Reformation (Part I), 12–27. **W. F. Finlason?** This art. is referred to in *DR* 34 (1853), 413, as is also no. 461, in an art. known to be by Finlason; subject reflects his interests, but see Newman, *L&D*, XIV, 396n.

324   Passion, love, and rest; or, the autobiography of Basil Morley (chap. x), 27–41. **J. M. Capes.** See no. 276.

325   "Churches" versus "rooms," 41–45, with a supplementary statement, 45–46. **J. M. Capes,** prob. This is another statement of his position on church architecture; the supplement notices the personal attacks made on Capes by Pugin. For an account of this phase of the controversy see Newman, *L&D*, XIV, 258–259, 271.

326   Leigh Hunt's *Autobiography*, 46–57.

327   Queen Mary, 57–67.

328   Wright's *Narratives of Sorcery and Magic*, 67–78.

329   Short notices, 79.

330   In Correspondence: Proposal for a priest's portfolio, 80–81, by **John Morris, 1826–1893,** prob.—signed John Morris (John Brande Morris almost always used his middle initial), with a reply by **J. M. Capes**—signed Edit. *Rambler*; St Joseph and Mr. Pugin, 82, signed **J. J. Mulligan.**

331   Ecclesiastical register, 83–86.

VOLUME 8, AUGUST 1851

332   Historical sketches of devotions to the Blessed Sacrament (Part I): Holy Communion, 87–110. **J. S. Northcote.** Simpson notebook; Northcote list. (Letter, p. 339, signed Y.)

333   A lecture at ———— college, Ireland, 110–118. **J. M. Capes.** Simpson notebook; Northcote list; Northcote file.

334   State encroachments on the Church before the Reformation (Part II), 118–145. **W. F. Finlason?** Cf. no. 323.

335   Thoughts on the festival of the Assumption of the Blessed Virgin Mary, 145–155.

336   Domestic Gothic architecture, 156–159. **J. M. Capes,** prob. This art. reflects his stand that architecture of any building should conform to financial exigences or to common sense; there is no one style to be used under all circumstances.

337   Short notices, 160–162. Page 160 (Father Marchi), by **J. S. Northcote**—Northcote list; Northcote file.

338 In Correspondence: Representations of the Passion of our Blessed Lord in France, 162–164, with an intro. note by **J. S. Northcote**, prob.—signed N., he used this initial for many of his contributions.

339 Ecclesiastical register, 166–172.

VOLUME 8, SEPTEMBER 1851

340 Civil and religious liberty, 173–180. **J. M. Capes**, prob. Cf. no. 1; the author makes the same points as in no. 110, and on p. 180 echoes the title of that editorial: "when shall we see the day when we all of us know wherein our true strength lies."

341 Historical sketches of devotions to the Blessed Sacrament (Part II): communion of infants and of the sick—other uses of the most Holy Sacrament, 180–198. **J. S. Northcote.** Cf. no. 332.

342 Passion, love, and rest; or, the autobiography of Basil Morley (chap. xi), 198–207. **J. M. Capes.** Cf. no. 276.

343 St. Pudentiana and her Roman Church, 208–214. Unidentified. Possibly J. S. Northcote who had recently returned from a three-year residence in Rome, where he had made an intensive study of Roman churches and catacombs.

344 Archdeacon Wilberforce on Erastianism, 216–234. **T. W. Allies.** Repr. *Per crucem ad lucem* (1879), II.

345 Dr. Achilli and the Inquisition, 235–252. **J. M. Capes?** See Newman, *L&D*, XIV, 341n.

346 Short notices, 253–254. **J. S. Northcote.** Northcote list; Northcote file.

347 Correspondence, 254–257.

348 Ecclesiastical register, 257–258.

VOLUME 8, OCTOBER 1851

349 State encroachments on the Church before the Reformation (Part III), 259–285. **W. F. Finlason?** Cf. no. 323.

350 Passion, love, and rest; or, the autobiography of Basil Morley (chap. xii, concl.), 285–296. **J. M. Capes.** Cf. no. 276.

351 Animal magnetism, 296–326. **J. M. Capes**, prob. Newman, *L&D*, XIV, 368. (Letter, pp. 412–413, signed Romanus.)

352 Short notices, 326–327.

353 Correspondence: Catholic popular education, 328–339. Signed: Sacerdos.

354 Ecclesiastical register, 340–344.

VOLUME 8, NOVEMBER 1851

355 The old priest's parlour (Part I), 345–357. **J. M. Capes**, prob. This first part is taken up with the education of the poor (see introduction above), including drawing and music as means of recreation (see nos. 54, 229, 258); stress of common sense approach characteristic of Capes.

356 State encroachments on the Church before the Reformation (Part IV, concl.), 357–372. **W. F. Finlason?** Cf. no. 323.

357 Newman's *Lectures on the Position of Catholics in England*, 372–395. **J. M. Capes**, prob. In this review the author reverts to the themes of nos. 293 and 310, that Protestants are really possessed by suspicion and hatred of Catholics and the Catholic Church, and warns against making concessions in order to reach their reason.

358 English conservatives and French rationalists (Part I), 396–404.

359 The parson fly-fishing, 405–410.

360 Short notices, 410–412.

361 Ecclesiastical register, 413–422.

VOLUME 8, DECEMBER 1851

362 Historical sketches of devotions to the Blessed Sacrament (Part III): the altar and its furniture: the oblations, 423–443. **J. S. Northcote.** Cf. no. 332.

363 Miracles—Father Newman and the Bishop of Norwich [correspondence and comment], 443–461. Pages 444–452 reprint letters between **J. H. Newman** and **Samuel Hinds**; Newman's letters repr. *L&D*, XIV, 375, 382, 384, 397, and whole correspondence repr. as a note, *Lectures on the Present Position of Catholics in England*, 1851. (Introductory note clearly by **J. M. Capes**, the editor.)

364 English conservatives and French rationalists (Part II, concl.), 461–471.

365 The Protestant criticising, 471–486. **J. M. Capes**, prob. This is a further statement of the fact that Protestants are unable to think or reason objectively about Catholicism; cf. no. 357.

366 Quakerism, 486–498.

367 Short notices, 498–500.

368 Ecclesiastical register, 501–508.

VOLUME 9, JANUARY 1852

369 Galileo and his condemnation, 1–25.

Richard Simpson. Simpson notebook; Northcote file; Newman, *L&D*, XIV, 471n. (Comment, vol. 10, 2nd s., pp. 285–288, by **Richard Simpson**—*Rambler* accounts.)

370 The old priest's parlour (Part II, concl.), 25–32. **J. M. Capes**, prob. This second part is on the theme of meeting Protestant opposition head-on without attempting reconciliation by concessions.

371 The fugitive, an historical sketch (Part I), 33–55. **Simon Platzer.** Intro. note. Translation and intro. note by **Miss Buckle**—Simpson notebook; Northcote list; Northcote file.

372 The Roman revolution, 55–68. **J. S. Northcote.** Simpson notebook; Northcote list; Northcote file.

373 Lamartine's *History of the Restoration in France*, 68–79.

374 Protestant justice and royal clemency, 79–84. **J. M. Capes**, prob. Attr. in Newman, *L&D*, XIV, 477n and 443n where Capes makes the same point which is made in the opening paragraph here.

375 Short notices, 85–86.

VOLUME 9, FEBRUARY 1852

376 Monsignor Parisis on Catholic journalism [from the *Annales de Philosophie Chrétienne*, Sept. 1850], 87–100. **Pierre-Louis Parisis.** Title.

377 Kate Gearey; or, Irish life in London (chaps. i–ii), 100–115. **Miss Mason.** Northcote file; repr. same title, 1853.

378 The fugitive, an historical sketch (Part II, concl.), 116–139. **Simon Platzer.** Translation by **Miss Buckle.** Cf. no. 371.

379 [John Brande] Morris on the Incarnation: Catholic and Protestant preaching, 140–154. **J. M. Capes.** Attr. Newman, *L&D*, XIV, 456.

380 Ireland sixty years ago, 154–166.

381 Short notices, 166–168.

382 Correspondence, 168, signed Vox.

VOLUME 9, MARCH 1852

383 The French in London, 169–179. **J. M. Capes**, prob. This satirical account of how an attack by France might force the English to disestablish the Irish Establishment, repeats in humorous vein the theme of no. 1.

384 Murder in England and in Ireland [on landlord-killing], 179–185. **J. M. Capes**, prob. This attack on the hypocrisy of

English Protestants in thinking that England is less plagued with violence and crime than Ireland is characteristic of Capes; see no. 1 and introduction above.

385 Kate Gearey; or, Irish life in London (chaps. iii–iv), 185–206. **Miss Mason.** Cf. no. 377.

386 The gold-fields of the ancients (Part I), 206–210.

387 St. Teresa's *Life* of herself, 211–220. **J. M. Capes**, prob. The author on p. 211 pokes scorn at those who would "correct" saints' lives so as to make them acceptable to Protestants and Catholics; see no. 357. (Letter, vol. 12, p. 426, signed **John Dalton.**)

388 [Introductory note to] Yriarte's *Literary Fables*, 220–221. **J. M. Capes**, prob. This introductory note is almost certainly by the editor.

389 Mr. Mayhew among the thieves [on London poor], 228–235. **J. M. Capes**, prob. Author speaks of having previously written of Mayhew's experience among the Irish poor in London (see no. 297, pp. 282–283); the poor were a constant subject of concern to Capes.

390 Father Gavazzi, 236–244. **J. M. Capes**, prob. The article undertakes to expose the apostate Gavazzi and the bigotry of our fellow Protestant countrymen and the blind infatuation of their hatred against Catholicism.

391 In Ecclesiastical register: Obituary notice of the Rev. John Kirk, 244–249 (letter, pp. 425–426, signed **Frederick Oakeley**); The Ecclesiastical Titles Bill and the Catholic schools, 250–252, signed **Scott Nasmyth Stokes.**

VOLUME 9, APRIL 1852

392 The struggles of Catholic literature, 255–264. **J. M. Capes**, prob. Art. deals with problems of Catholic publication in general and of *Rambler* in particular; see no. 172.

393 Masters and workmen in the Middle Ages, 264–283.

394 Kate Gearey; or, Irish life in London (chaps. v–vi), 283–306. **Miss Mason.** Cf. no. 377.

395 Historical sketches of devotions to the Blessed Sacrament (Part IV): The festival of Corpus Christi, 307–324. **J. S. Northcote.** Cf. no. 332.

396 Dr. Murray and Dr. Whately, 327–333.

397 Sham biographies—*The Household of Sir Thomas More*, 333–338. **J. M. Capes?**

The word "sham" is almost a trademark of Capes; the concern on p. 337 with literature for Catholics would also be characteristic.

398 Short notices, 338–340.

VOLUME 9, MAY 1852

399 Historical sketches of devotions to the Blessed Sacrament (Part V): Benediction, 341–349. **J. S. Northcote.** Cf. no. 332.

400 Kate Gearey; or, Irish life in London (chaps. vii–viii), 349–376. **Miss Mason.** Cf. no. 377.

401 The gold-fields of the ancients (Part II, concl.), 376–382.

402 Catholic biography under the penal laws [*Life of Mrs. Dorothy Lawson*], 383–392. Unidentified. Possibly Richard Simpson, who was much interested in this period of English Catholic history.

403 Dr. Philpotts and the *Edinburgh Review*, 392–403.

404 The Life of Washington [by himself], 403–410.

405 *The Cape and the Kafirs*, 410–420.

406 Short notices, 421–425.

VOLUME 9, JUNE 1852

407 Historical sketches of devotions to the Blessed Sacrament (Part VI): Quarant' Ore—perpetual adoration, 427–437. **J. S. Northcote.** Cf. no. 332.

408 Kate Gearey; or, Irish life in London (chap. ix), 437–450. **Miss Mason.** Cf. no. 377.

409 The doctrine of the Immaculate Conception [taken from the *Civiltà Cattolica*, translated from the *Univers*], 451–468. Translation by **J. S. Northcote?**—he was editor at this time; see introduction above.

410 Pilgrimages to Jerusalem, 469–476. **J. S. Northcote.** Simpson notebook; Northcote list; Northcote file.

411 Duties and responsibilities of writers of fiction, 477–483. **J. A. Stothert?** Reference back to this art. in no. 479, known to be by Stothert, and on the same subject.

412 Anglican synods, 483–488.

413 Papal aggression in Thibet and Tartary, 488–508.

414 Short notices, 509–512.

VOLUME 10, JULY 1852

415 Popular education (Part I), 1–14. **J. M. Capes,** prob. This was one of his major preoccupations; see introduction above; the author reverts to the point made in no. 355 about the cramming of children's heads with facts they will never need to use (p. 7); bemoans lack of moral or religious instruction in state schools. (See nos. 423 and 430.)

416 Kate Gearey; or, Irish life in London (chap. x), 14–29. **Miss Mason.** Cf. no. 377.

417 Cathedral chapters, 29–36.

418 Translations and editors, 36–46. **J. S. Northcote.** Simpson notebook; Northcote list; Northcote file.

419 Protestant controversialists, 46–57. **J. S. Northcote.** Simpson notebook; Northcote list; Northcote file.

420 Gutzlaff's *Life of the Late Emperor of China*, 57–63.

421 The Roman catacombs, 63–69. **J. S. Northcote.** Simpson notebook; Northcote list; Northcote file.

422 Short notices, 69–71.

423 Correspondence: Popular education—the English statesman's idea and plan of popular education examined as to its aim, its details, and results, and contrasted with that of the Catholic Church (Part I), 72–82, signed: A Catholic Priest.

VOLUME 10, AUGUST 1852

424 Catholic lending-libraries, 83–88. **J. M. Capes,** prob. He had been constantly concerned, as he says on p. 83, with this topic. Cf. no. 172, 173 and the reference in opening paragraph to no. 415. (Letter, pp. 245–247, signed Y. *Miss. Ap.*)

425 Kate Gearey; or, Irish life in London (chaps. xi–xii), 88–119. **Miss Mason.** Cf. no. 377.

426 Christian pilgrimages, 119–135. **J. S. Northcote.** Simpson notebook; Northcote list; Northcote file.

427 Dr. Rock's *Church of Our Fathers*, 135–148.

428 Dr. Mackay's *Popular Delusions*, 149–153. **J. S. Northcote.** Simpson notebook; Northcote list; Northcote file.

429 Short notices, 154–155. Page 155 on *The Choir*, unidentified (letters, pp. 338–340, signed M.S.M., and pp. 510–512, signed A Chorister).

429a Ecclesiastical register, 156–160. Pastoral letter [on education of the poor].

Nicholas Wiseman. Signed N. Card. Archbishop.

430 Correspondence: Popular education (Part II), 160–167. Signed: A Catholic Priest.

VOLUME 10, SEPTEMBER 1852

431 Popular education (Part II, concl.), 169–179. **J. M. Capes,** prob. The author chides the Catholic laity for not supporting their own schools; cf. no. 11.

432 Historical sketches of devotions to the Blessed Sacrament (Part VII): Miracles wrought by the Holy Eucharist, 179–195. **J. S. Northcote.** Cf. no. 332.

433 Kate Gearey; or, Irish life in London (chaps. xiii–xiv), 195–219. **Miss Mason.** Cf. no. 377.

434 The hymns of the Catholic Church, 219–226. **Charles Eyre.** Simpson notebook; Northcote list; Northcote file.

435 Achilli *v.* Newman; or, the enchanted mirror, 226–239. **W. F. Finlason.** Northcote file.

436 Short notices, 239–241.

437 In Correspondence: The cultivation of singing in poor-schools, 242–244, signed Parochus; Devotion to St. Winefride, 244–245, signed Sacerdos.

438 Ecclesiastical register, 248–254.

VOLUME 10, OCTOBER 1852

439 Historical sketches of devotions to the Blessed Sacrament (Part VIII, concl.): Miracles wrought in the Holy Eucharist, 255–268. **J. S. Northcote.** Cf. no. 332.

440 Kate Gearey; or, Irish life in London (chaps. xv–xvii, concl.), 268–290. **Miss Mason.** Cf. no. 377.

441 The penal laws under Queen Elizabeth, 290–306. Unidentified. Possibly Richard Simpson who later wrote frequently and learnedly upon this subject; see nos. 798, 802, 808, 815, etc.

442 Manners and customs of the Sardinians, 306–322. **J. S. Northcote.** Northcote list; Northcote file.

443 A blue-stocking in the bush, 322–336.

444 Short notices, 336–338.

VOLUME 10, NOVEMBER 1852

445 Popular music a part of popular education, 341–353. **J. M. Capes,** prob. Cf. no. 1, and in particular nos. 54 and 355; on

p. 344 the author refers to Mr. Mayhew, whom he reviewed in nos. 297 and 389, and makes a plea for good teaching of music in Catholic poor-schools.

446 A pilgrimage to La Salette (Part I), 353–381. **J. S. Northcote.** Repr. with same title, 1852.

447 Robberies of religion, ancient and modern: Report of the Select Committee on the Law of Mortmain and of Testamentary Dispositions (Part I), 381–399. **W. F. Finlason.** Signed W.F.F.; subject reflects his interest; this art. referred to in *DR* 34 (1853), 416, known to be by Finlason and in Finlason, *An Essay on the History and Effects of the Law of Mortmain,* (1853), p. 12.

448 The wedding: a tale of the Tyrol [from the German], 399–413. Translated by **Miss Buckle.** Simpson notebook; Northcote list; Northcote file.

449 *Uncle Tom's Cabin; or, Life Among the Lowly* [by Harriet Beecher Stowe], 413–424. **J. S. Northcote,** prob. See nos. 481, and 499.

450 Short notices, 424–426.

VOLUME 10, DECEMBER 1852

451 A pilgrimage to La Salette (Part II, concl.), 427–441. **J. S. Northcote.** Cf. no. 446.

452 Robberies of religion, ancient and modern (Part II, concl.), 441–463. **W. F. Finlason.** Evidence for no. 447.

453 Convocation at last, 463–470.

454 The flight of the Pope: account by the Countess de Spaur, 470–485. **Thérèse de Spaur.** Title. Translated and abridged from *Revue des Revues,* June 1852, with an intro. note by **J. S. Northcote**—Northcote list; Northcote file.

455 Dialogue between John Bull and an Oxford divine, 485–489.

456 *Cloister Life of Charles V* [by William Stirling], 489–506. **J. S. Northcote.** Northcote file.

457 Short notices, 506–510, by **J. S. Northcote**—Northcote list; Northcote file gives p. 507 as the beginning of Northcote's contribution.

VOLUME 11, JANUARY 1853

458 Our position and prospects, 1–15. **J. E. Wallis,** 1821–1888. Northcote list and Northcote file give "Wallis"; for man cited see Boase.

459 Death-bed bequests; or, Catholic testators and Protestant conspirators: a true story, 16–29. **W. F. Finlason.** Northcote list; Northcote file.

460 A chapter in the history of the Reformation in Ireland (Part I), 29–41. **Matthew Kelly.** Repr. *Dissertations.*

461 The chancellors of England, 42–61. **W. F. Finlason.** Northcote list; Northcote file; art. is referred to in *DR* 34 (1853), 415, by Finlason.

462 *The Pilgrim: or, Scenes on the Road from England to Rome,* 61–79. **Aubrey De Vere.** Northcote list; Northcote file.

463 Miss Strickland's *Life of Mary Queen of Scots,* 79–87. **J. S. Northcote.** Northcote list; Northcote file.

464 The last struggles of Disraeli [from the *Tablet and Telegraph,* Dec. 25, 1852], 87–91.

465 Short notices, 91–93. Page 92 by **J. S. Northcote**—Northcote list.

VOLUME 11, FEBRUARY 1853

466 The Protestant Inquisition; or, Catholic interests before select committees of the House of Commons, 95–109. **W. F. Finlason.** Northcote list; Northcote file.

467 A chapter in the history of the Reformation in Ireland (Part II, concl.), 109–122. **Matthew Kelly.** Cf. no. 460.

468 The modern pilgrim's progress; or, the history of Puseyism in a dream, 122–135. **Maria S. R. Poole.** Northcote list gives "Mother I [melda] Poole," her name in religion; Northcote file gives "M.S.R.P."; attr. in Newman, *L&D,* XI, 353.

469 Circumstantial evidence: case of Mr. Kirwan, 135–146. **W. F. Finlason.** Northcote list; Northcote file.

470 Mrs. Chisholm and emigration, 148–166.

471 Money and morals, 166–173. **J. S. Northcote.** Northcote file; Northcote list.

472 Tennyson's *Ode on the Death of the Duke of Wellington,* 173–175.

473 Short notices, 176, by **J. A. Stothert.** Northcote file.

VOLUME 11, MARCH 1853

474 Dr. Newman's trial; Protestant morality and Protestant justice, 177–197. **W. F. Finlason,** prob. Finlason was the author of a report of Newman's trial and of no. 435; in no. 469, p. 146, he explained his

interest in the case of Kirwan as due to its being a parallel instance of prejudice subverting justice; the treatment of the subject and the legal refs. cited here indicate the author was, like Finlason, a lawyer.

475 The priest and the parson; a contrast, 197–213. **J. S. Northcote.** Northcote file; Northcote list.

476 Medieval games and festivals, 214–228. **J. S. Northcote.** Northcote file; Northcote list.

477 Madeleine, the Rosière (chaps. i–ii), 228–238. **Annette Marie Maillard,** prob. Northcote file gives "Madame Maillard"; see *BMCat.*

478 The temporal sovereignty of the Pope, 238–251. **J. S. Northcote.** Northcote file.

479 Catholic novelists, 251–262. **J. A. Stothert.** Northcote file.

VOLUME 11, APRIL 1853

480 Charitable trusts, ancient and modern (Part I), 263–278. **W. F. Finlason.** Northcote list; Northcote file; Finlason wrote on same subject in *DR* 34 (June, 1853), 407–441, and wrote *A Brief . . . Exposition of the Law of Charitable Trusts,* 1860.

481 American slavery and American Protestantism, 278–299. **J. S. Northcote,** prob. Although Northcote list gives both "Wallis" and "Northcote," it seems highly prob. from pages 495–496 that nos. 449, 481, and 499 were all by same author; Northcote file gives "J.S.N."

482 Important discovery of Father Secchi relative to the inscription on the chair of St. Mark at Venice, 300–304. **J. S. Northcote.** Northcote file; Northcote list.

483 Madeleine, the Rosière (chaps. iii–v), 304–319. **Annette Marie Maillard,** prob. Cf. no. 477.

484 M. Guizot's appeal to our common Christianity (Part I), 319–331. **Harriet D. Thompson.** Northcote list gives "Mrs. Healy Thompson"; Northcote file. (Part II is no. 491.)

485 *Legends of the Madonna* [by Mrs. Jameson], 331–336. **J. S. Northcote?** Northcote file gives both pp. 334 and 336 to "J.S.N."

486 A few more words on La Salette, 336–343. **J. S. Northcote.** Northcote file; cf. no. 446.

487 Short notices, 344–348. Page 347 by **J. S. Northcote**—Northcote list; Northcote file.

VOLUME 12, SEPTEMBER 1853

519 Catholic literature for the poor (Part II, concl.), 169–174. **Henry Formby.** Northcote list; cf. no. 511.

520 Historical notices of patron saints (No. III): patron saints of Scotland, 174–186. **J. S. Northcote?** Northcote file; he was the author of parts I and II. OR, **J. A. Stothert?** Oscott file; he was a priest in Scotland, and author in 1850 of book on St. Margaret of Scotland. OR, a collaboration.

521 A visit to Loyola, 186–191. **G. F. Wood?** Signed R; Northcote file gives "Cap[?] Wood, S.J."; man cited had been a naval officer and became a Jesuit. (Letter, p. 340, signed M.W.)

522 Leaves from the journal of a confessor of the faith during the French Revolution, 1793–1795, translated and abridged from *Les Serviteurs de Dieu*, ed. Léon Aubineau, 1852 (Part I), 191–201. **Louis-Pierre Leproust.** Introductory note. Translation by **J. S. Northcote?** Northcote file; Oscott file gives "trans. by Fr. de Lys."

523 A glance at the morality and religion of England, 201–217. **J. S. Northcote.** Northcote list; Northcote file; Oscott file.

524 Cardinal Wiseman and the Tractarians [on Wiseman's *Essays*], 217–237. **Robert Ornsby?** Northcote file; Northcote list; Oscott file; Ornsby had been a Tractarian. OR, **Richard Simpson?** J. M. Capes to Simpson, Dec. 17, 1854, Simpson notebook, refers to "your review of the Cardinal's *Essays*."

525 Tombs of heretics in the Roman catacombs, 238–245. **J. S. Northcote.** Northcote list; Northcote file; Oscott file.

526 On the cultivation of the musical faculty, 245–252. **Frederick Capes?** Northcote file and Oscott file give "F. Capes." OR, **J. M. Capes?** Northcote list gives "Capes," and J. M. Capes also was interested in music.

527 Short notices, 252–254. **J. M. Capes.** Northcote file.

VOLUME 12, OCTOBER 1853

528 Historical notices of patron saints (No. IV, concl.): patron saints of Ireland, 255–265. **Matthew Kelly.** Northcote file; Oscott file.

529 Testimonies of saints regarding religion in England (Part III, concl.), 265–268.

E. E. Estcourt. Northcote list; Northcote file; Oscott file.

530 Journal of a confessor of the faith during the French Revolution (Part II, concl.), 268–282. **Louis-Pierre Leproust.** Cf. no. 522.

531 Secret societies: worship of the devil [review of *L'Ebreo di Verona*] (No. I), 283–301. **J. S. Northcote.** Northcote list; Northcote file; Oscott file. (See nos. 540 and 564.)

532 Catholic singing, 302–312. **J. M. Capes,** prob. Northcote file gives "Capes"; Oscott file gives "Mr. Capes"; Northcote list gives "Formby," but he is the author under review.

533 The counter theory; or, the latest development of Puseyism, 312–325. **Aubrey De Vere.** Northcote list; Northcote file; Oscott file.

534 *Memorandums on Ireland*, 326–336. **J. S. Northcote.** Northcote list; Northcote file; Oscott file.

535 Importance of religious ceremonial, 336–338. **Frederick Oakeley.** Northcote list; Northcote file; Oscott file.

536 Short notices, 338–340.

VOLUME 12, NOVEMBER 1853

537 Savonarola: Catholicism in the fifteenth and in the nineteenth century (Part I), 341–356. **J. M. Capes.** Northcote list; Northcote file; Oscott file.

538 Catholic hymnology: a lost sequence found, 356–360. **Charles Eyre.** Northcote list; Northcote file; Oscott file.

539 St. Gregory and St. Anselm (Part I), 360–374. **J. S. Northcote.** Northcote list; Northcote file; Oscott file.

540 Anecdotes of the Roman Revolution [Review of *L'Ebreo di Verona*] (No. II), 374–384. **J. S. Northcote.** Northcote list; Northcote file; Oscott file; see nos. 531 and 564.

541 Table-turning and table-talking, 384–406. **J. S. Northcote?** Northcote file; Oscott file; Northcote list gives both Northcote and Morris for p. 384, almost certainly a confusion, although J. B. Morris was noted for his credulity (*DNB*), and would have found the topic congenial.

542 Haydon's *Autobiography*, 406–422. **J. M. Capes.** Northcote list; Northcote file; Oscott file.

543 Short notices, 422–426. Page 423, by **J. S. Northcote**—Northcote's list; Northcote file.

544 Correspondence: The orthography of St. Teresa's name, 426, signed **John Dalton.**

VOLUME 12, DECEMBER 1853

545 The editor to the readers of the *Rambler*, 427–430. **J. S. Northcote.** Title.

546 A visit to St. Mary's, Cabra; or, the education of the deaf and dumb, 431–442. **John Burke.** Northcote file gives "Rev. Burke of Phisborough"; Oscott file gives "Rev. Burke of Phisboro"; man cited was at the presbytery, St. Peter's, Phibsborough in 1852: see Thom/52, p. 980.

547 Celebrated visions of the Blessed Virgin, 442–449. **Adam B. Laing-Meason.** Sutcliffe; Northcote file; Oscott file.

548 Savonarola: Catholicism in the fifteenth and in the nineteenth century (Part II, concl.), 449–473. **J. M. Capes.** Cf. no. 537.

549 Interesting discoveries in the Holy Land, 473–480. **Richard Simpson.** Northcote list; Northcote file; Oscott file.

550 St. Gregory and St. Anselm (Part II, concl.), 480–499. **J. S. Northcote.** Cf. no. 539.

551 Science and religion, 499–503. **Richard Simpson.** Oscott file; J. M. Capes to Simpson, July 1, 1854, Simpson notebook, excuses his "operation" on Simpson's "Religion and Science."

552 Translations: a good specimen and a bad, 504–507. **J. S. Northcote.** Northcote file; Oscott file.

553 Short notice, 516.

VOLUME 13 o.s., 1 2ND s., JANUARY 1854

554 How to convert Protestants, 1–19. **J. M. Capes.** Northcote list; Northcote file; Oscott file.

555 *The Female Jesuit Abroad*, 19–40. **Elizabeth Anstice.** Northcote list; Northcote file; Oscott file.

556 Living novelists: Dickens, Thackeray, Bulwer, Lady G. Fullerton, Currer Bell, 41–51. **J. A. Stothert.** Northcote file.

557 Archdeacon Wilberforce on the Holy Eucharist, 51–69. **Aubrey De Vere.** Northcote list; Northcote file; Oscott file.

558 Dr. Madden's *Shrines and Sepulchres*, 70–80. **Myles O'Reilly.** Northcote file; Oscott file. (Letter, p. 306, by **O'Reilly**—signed Your Contributor; opening sen-

tence shows this to be by author of no. 558.)

559 *The Wandering Jew*, 80–87. **J. M. Capes.** Northcote list; Northcote file; Oscott file.

560 Short notices, 87–102. Pages 87–89, unidentified (letter, pp. 302–305, signed **M. A. Tierney**). Pages 97–98, by **J. S. Northcote**—Northcote list; pages 98–99, by **Richard Simpson**—Capes to Simpson, Apr. 24, 1854, Simpson notebook, says Simpson did Volpe charmingly; Oscott file, for the notices, lists **Capes, Northcote, [E. H.] Thompson, R. Simpson, J. B. Morris,** and **N[athaniel] Goldsmid,** etc.

VOLUME 13 o.s., 1 2ND s., FEBRUARY 1854

561 Religious toleration a question of first principles, 103–121. **E. H. Thompson.** Oscott file; Northcote file.

562 Our choirs: what they are and what they might become, 121–133. **Henry Bedford.** Northcote file; Oscott file, which gives "Mr. Bedford, All Hallows, Drumcondra": see no. 502. (Letters, 396–399, signed **F[rederick] Canon Oakeley;** 583–584, signed **J. G. Wenham.**)

563 Rites and ceremonies (No. I, no more published): Holy Water, 133–139. **Adam B. Laing-Meason.** Sutcliffe; Oscott file; Northcote file gives "Lang, S.J., R. I. P." (Letter, p. 302, signed **J. Dalton.**)

564 Anecdotes of the Roman Republic [review of *L'Ebreo di Verona*] (No. III), 140–150. **J. S. Northcote.** Northcote list; Northcote file; Oscott file. (See nos. 531 and 540.)

565 English and foreign historians: the massacre of St. Bartholomew, 150–169. **E. H. Thompson.** Northcote file; Oscott file.

566 Dr. Cahill's letter on transubstantiation, 169–177. **J. M. Capes.** Northcote list; Northcote file; Oscott file.

567 Napoleon and Sir Hudson Lowe, 178–183. **J. M. Capes.** Northcote list; Northcote file; Oscott file.

568 The religious census of England, 183–190. **Daniel Parsons?** Northcote list; Northcote file; see nos. 574 and 580. OR, **J. E. Wallis,** 1821–1888. Oscott file; see no. 458.

569 Short notices, 190–204. Pages 192, 197, by **J. S. Northcote**—Northcote list; pages 203–204, by **[Nathaniel] Goldsmid** and **J. S. Northcote**—Oscott file; Oscott file,

for notices, lists **J. M. Capes, J. S. North-cote, Richard Simpson, J. A. Stothert,** etc.

VOLUME 13 O.S., 1 2ND S., MARCH 1854

570 Shams and realities, 205–227. **J. M. Capes.** Northcote file; Oscott file.
571 The Turks and the Christians in Albania, 228–239. **William Wingfield.** Oscott file gives "Wingfield, Esq."; Northcote file adds "Ward's brother-in-law." (Letter, pp. 399–400.)
572 Miss Strickland's *Life of Mary Queen of Scots*, 239–248. **J. S. Northcote.** Northcote file; Northcote list; Oscott file.
573 *On the Study of Words* [by R. C. Trench], 249–257. **George Ryder.** Oscott file gives "G. Ryder, Esq.": Northcote file; man cited a convert.
574 Our picture in the census [of 1851] (Part I), 257–280. **Daniel Parsons.** Northcote list; Northcote file; Oscott file.
575 Music for amateur performance, 280–286. **J. M. Capes.** Northcote list; Northcote file; Oscott file.
576 Short notices, 286–301. Pages 291, 292, 297, 301 by **J. S. Northcote**—Northcote list; page 300 by **Daniel Parsons**—Northcote list; pages 295–296 unidentified (note, vol. 2, n.s., 92).

VOLUME 13 O.S., 1 2ND S., APRIL 1854

577 Equivocation, as taught by St. Alphonsus Liguori, 307–336. **J. M. Capes.** J. H. Newman, *L&D*, XVI, 9, 13, 161; Northcote list; Capes to Richard Simpson, Feb. 6, 1854, Simpson notebook, says he is writing on *Christian Remembrancer's* attack on St. Alphonsus. (Note, pp. 493–494, signed **James A. Stothert**; a second note, p. 494.)
578 Catholic hymnology: life of blessed Jacopone di Todi, 336–343. **J. S. Northcote.** Northcote list; Northcote file. (Note, vol. 2, n.s., 92, by **Northcote,** prob.)
579 *The Right Honourable Benjamin Disraeli*, 344–356.
580 Our picture in the census (Part II, concl.), 356–375. **Daniel Parsons.** Northcote list; Northcote file.
581 Dr. Newman's *Lectures on the Turks*: Catholic institutes, 375–385.
582 Short notices, 385–395. Page 388 by **J. S. Northcote**—Northcote list.

VOLUME 13 O.S., 1 2ND S., MAY 1854

583 Nuns, monks, and Jesuits, 401–410. **J. M. Capes.** Northcote list; Northcote file; Oscott file.
584 On the persecution of nuns and religious women during the French Revolution, 410–428. **John Simeon.** Northcote list; Northcote file; Oscott file.
585 The life of a conspirator [*Lorenzo Benoni* by Ruffini], 428–438. **J. M. Capes.** Northcote list; Northcote file; Oscott file.
586 The Hebraisms and Catholicisms of Disraeli's novels, 439–453. **W. F. Finlason.** Northcote file; Oscott file.
587 Recent Protestant tourists in Italy, 453–462. **J. S. Northcote?** Northcote list. OR, **J. S. Northcote** and **Richard Simpson?** Oscott file; Northcote file gives both single authorship and collab.
588 Illustrated books, 462–472. **J. M. Capes.** Northcote list; Northcote file; Oscott file.
589 Christian and pagan Rome, 472–486. **Aubrey De Vere.** Northcote list; Northcote file; Oscott file.
590 Short notices, 486–493. Page 492 by **J. S. Northcote**—Northcote list.

VOLUME 13 O.S., 1 2ND S., JUNE 1854

591 The state's best policy, 495–510. **J. M. Capes.** Oscott file.
592 The life of an editor, 510–519. **J. S. Northcote.** Northcote list; Northcote file; Oscott file.
593 Sufferings of English nuns during the French Revolution (Part I), 520–536. **J. S. Northcote.** Northcote list; Northcote file; Oscott file.
594 The Czar and his subjects, 536–552. **J. M. Capes.** Oscott file.
595 Chinese civilisation and Christian charity, 552–557. **Aubrey De Vere.** Northcote file; Oscott file.
596 The modern Protestant hypothesis relative to the gradual absorption of early Anglicanism by the popedom, 557–576. **William B. Waterworth.** Sutcliffe; Oscott file; Northcote file.
597 Short notices, 577–583. Page 582 by **J. S. Northcote**—Northcote list.

VOLUME 14 O.S., 2 2ND S., JULY 1854

598 Constantinople: its past and its future fall, 1–19. **J. M. Capes.** Northcote list; Northcote file; Oscott file.

599 Was Shakespeare a Catholic? 19–36. **W. F. Finlason.** Northcote file; Oscott file; claimed in Finlason to H. R. Bagshawe, May 31, 1855, Bagshawe Papers.

600 Sufferings of the English nuns during the French Revolution (Part II, concl.), 36–44. **J. S. Northcote.** Northcote list; Northcote file; Oscott file.

601 England and the English three hundred years ago, 45–55. **J. S. Northcote.** Northcote list; Northcote file; Oscott file.

602 A poet from the labouring class [Gerald Massey], 55–62. **Henry Bedford,** prob. Northcote file gives "Bedford"; Oscott file gives "G. Bedford, Drumcondra"; for Henry Bedford see no. 502, and *Cath. Ency.*

603 Travels in Transcaucasia, 62–68. **Richard Simpson.** Northcote list; Northcote file; Oscott file.

604 Waterworth's *England and Rome*, 69–74. **Richard Simpson.** Northcote list; Northcote file; Oscott file.

605 Musical criticism: Beethoven's Missa Solemnis, 75–85. **Richard Simpson.** Though attributed to Capes in Northcote list, Northcote file, and Oscott file, Capes himself wrote Simpson, July 1, 1854, Simpson notebook, praising Simpson's "Beethoven Mass," and adding that he himself was not acquainted with this particular Mass.

606 Short notices, 85–92. Page 86 by **Richard Simpson**—Northcote list; Northcote file; J. M. Capes to Simpson, July 24, 1854, Simpson notebook, suggests Simpson noticed Bowyer.

VOLUME 14 O.S., 2 2ND S., AUGUST 1854

607 Protestant authors and publishers, and Catholic readers, 93–105. **J. M. Capes?** Capes wrote many of the editorials while Northcote was officially editor; it deals with Protestant hostility to and fear of Catholics, a subject treated frequently by him and discusses the history of the *Rambler* itself, including its independence from any publisher. OR, **J. S. Northcote?** He was nominally the editor, and he had written nos. 545 and 592 dealing with the periodical and its problems.

608 Suppression of the English secular college at Douay during the French Revolution, 106–113. **John Gillow.** Gillow, II, 481, n. 4.

609 The evil effects of religious persecution, 113–129. **J. M. Capes.** Capes to Richard Simpson, July 1, 1854, Simpson note-

book, speaks of his own art. on the Edict of Nantes.

610 Modern philosophy: the plurality of worlds [Brewster's reply to Whewell], 129–137. **Richard Simpson,** prob. He certainly wrote nos. 369, 628, and 702, the last of which refers specifically to this art.

611 Talbot Gwynne's novels, 137–154.

612 Mr. Ruskin's art-philosophy (Part I), 155–162. **Frederick Capes,** prob. J. M. Capes to Richard Simpson, July 8, 1854, Simpson notebook, says he hopes his brother will do justice to Ruskin, and on July 24, says he has not seen his brother's "Ruskin."

613 Mrs. Austin's *Sketches of German Life*, 163–177.

614 Short notices, 178–188. Page 181 by **J. S. Northcote**—Northcote list; Northcote file; pages 178–179 by **Richard Simpson**—J. M. Capes to Simpson, May 8, 1855, Simpson notebook, deplores Simpson's puff of Buckley.

VOLUME 14 O.S., 2 2ND S., SEPTEMBER 1854

615 The Queen's government and the University [of Dublin], 189–209. **J. M. Capes.** Newman, *L&D*, XVI, 162, 200–201. Pages 203–209 repr. an art. by **J. H. Newman** from the *Catholic University Gazette*, page 202.

616 Hospitals and Sisterhoods, 209–229. **J. M. Capes,** prob. This art. reflects his interest in the poor; cf. nos. 570 and 659, as well as nos. 729 and 745.

617 De Castro's *Religious Intolerance in Spain*, 229–241.

618 Hannay's *Satire and Satirists*: the picturesque and the popular, 241–247.

619 Mr. Ruskin's art-philosophy (Part II), 247–258. **Frederick Capes,** prob. Cf. no. 612.

620 Finlay's *Byzantine Empire*, 258–271. **J. M. Capes.** Capes to Simpson, July 24, 1854, Simpson notebook, is writing a review of Finlay's *Byzantine History*; Aug. 20, 1854, ibid., is willing to have Simpson shorten his "Finlay."

621 Short notices, 271–276.

VOLUME 14 O.S., 2 2ND S., OCTOBER 1854

622 An appeal to the Catholic laity on the present condition of the poor, 277–290. **J. M. Capes.** Signed.

623 Oliver Cromwell, 291–317. **Matthew**

Bridges, prob. Capes to Simpson, Aug. 20, 1854, Simpson notebook, says "Cromwell" will be by Bridges and will prob. be second art. in issue; man cited had contributed to the *Ram* in Feb. 1848 (Matthew Bridges to H. R. Bagshawe, Jan. 25, 1848, Bagshawe Papers, says his sketch of *Sterling's Life* is to appear shortly in the *Ram*) and later contributed no. 779.

624 Magic (Part I), 317–330. **Richard Simpson.** J. M. Capes to Simpson, July 1, 1854, suggests this review to Simpson; on Aug. 24 praises it and discusses note on p. 321. (Letters, pp. 451–452, and vol. 15, pp. 248–250, by **T. W. Wilkinson**—signed W., J. M. Capes to Simpson, Sept. 27, 1854, Simpson notebook, identifies "W" as "Wilkinson of Ushaw"; pp. 538–540 and vol. 15, pp. 250–252, by **Richard Simpson**—signed The Author of the Articles on Magic.)

625 Huc's *Chinese Empire* (Part I), 331–344. **Richard Simpson,** prob. Capes to Simpson, Aug. 29, 1854, Simpson notebook, says "by all means do Huc's new book."

626 *The Christian Remembrancer* on medieval and Protestant preaching, 344–353. **J. M. Capes.** Capes to Simpson, Aug. 20, 1854, Simpson notebook, says Oct. No. will contain an art. of his (Capes) on *Christian Remembrancer*.

627 Dublin palace "fiction," 353–360. **T. N. Harper,** prob., and **J. M. Capes.** Capes to Richard Simpson, Aug. 20, 1854, Simpson notebook, says this is "by Harper (with head and tail by me)"; *Rambler* accounts give "T.H."

628 Short notices, 360–364. Pages 360–361 by **Richard Simpson?**—prob. by author of nos. 610 and 624; of the first Simpson was probably the author, of the second he definitely was; J. M. Capes to Simpson, Aug. 24, 1854, Simpson notebook, assures Simpson Oct. *Ram* will be sent to Whewell; pages 361–362 by **Simpson,** prob.—Capes to Simpson, Aug. 26, 1854, ibid., acknowledges receipt of *"Hard Times"*; page 363 by **Simpson**—Capes to Simpson, Aug. 24, 1854, ibid., says he has altered an expression in Simpson's notice of Miss Sewell.

VOLUME 14 O.S., 2 2ND S., NOVEMBER 1854

629 The "Civilisation" argument, 365–380. **J. M. Capes.** Capes to Simpson, Aug. 20, 1854, Simpson Notebook, says Oct.

No. will contain a paper by him on the civilisation argument, and that it will prob. be the first art.

630 Huc's *Chinese Empire* (Part II, concl.), 380–393. **Richard Simpson,** prob. Cf. no. 625.

631 Sporting and morals in Norway and Sweden, 394–401. **Richard Simpson,** prob. Capes to Simpson, Aug. 24, 1854, Simpson notebook, says he has altered nothing in this review except two words, which appear on pp. 394, 398.

632 The worship of Mary as practised by Catholics of the present day, 402–422. **J. M. Capes?** The author satirizes extreme hostility of Protestants to Catholics, a topic often treated by Capes; this is a review of the *Glories of Mary* by Liguori, whom Capes reviewed in no. 577.

633 Suggestions to "contented" Anglicans, 423–432.

634 Stuart's *Residence in Persia*, 433–442.

635 Short notices, 442–447. Pages 443–444 by **Richard Simpson**—J. M. Capes to Simpson, Sept. 27, 1854, Simpson notebook, regrets he will not get *"Siluria"* into Nov. No., but he did.

636 The printing-presses of the Abbé Migne, 447–450.

VOLUME 14 O.S., 2 2ND S., DECEMBER 1854

637 An estimate of the changes now taking place in the Church of England, 453–462. **J. M. Capes,** prob. This editorial, incidentally on the Oxford Reform Bill, regrets the latitudinarianism creeping into Established Church, since High Church Anglicans were more readily converted to Catholicism; the author cites the large number of converts from Oxford, "chief seat of Tory church-and-king exclusiveness"—(p. 459).

638 On common sense in Christian art, 463–479. **J. M. Capes,** prob. J. M. Capes to Simpson, Dec. 8, 1854, Simpson notebook, says this has been applauded; this art. stresses the importance of common sense as a guide in church architecture and the need to make the building conform to purposes of worship of whole congregation; cf. no. 137.

639 Hofer and the Tyrolese war of independence, 479–504.

640 Magic (Part II, concl.), 504–516. **Richard Simpson.** J. M. Capes to Simpson, Aug. 20, 1854, Simpson notebook, says he has looked through the 2nd art. on

magic. (Letter, pp. 538–540, by **Simpson** prob.)

641   Stories for the poor, 517–525.

642   Nolte's *Reminiscences of a Merchant's Life*, 525–534. **J. M. Capes.** Capes to Simpson, Aug. 24, 1854, Simpson notebook, says he will review Nolte himself.

643   Short notices, 534–535. Page 534 by **J. S. Northcote**—Northcote list; Northcote file.

VOLUME 15 O.S., 3 2ND S., JANUARY 1855

644   The editor to the reader, 1–2. **J. M. Capes.** Editor.

645   Jesuitism and anti-Jesuitism, 2–26. **J. M. Capes.** Capes to Richard Simpson, Aug. 29, 1854, Simpson notebook, says he would like to say his say on Jesuitism; on Sept. 1, 1854, ibid., says he will try his hand at it, and on Nov. 25, 1854, ibid., says it will be in Jan. No.

646   Compton Hall; or the recollections of Mr. Benjamin Walker (chaps. i–iii), 26–44. **J. M. Capes?** The framework of this story consists of experiences of a young journalist; Protestant hostility to Catholicism and Dissenting fanaticism play a part; Capes, who had complained of the dullness of *Ram* under Northcote, was probably trying to enliven the periodical with this tale of adventure.

647   A conversion under the old penal laws (Part I), 44–59. **Mary Anne (Grenville) Arundell.** Intro. note assigns this art. about her mother to "Lady A———"; many facts given in the account show that the mother was born Mary Elizabeth Nugent and her father was George Grenville, 3rd Earl Temple and Marquis of Buckingham; cf. pp. 45–46, 50–52, 57, 119, 124, 125, 365–366 with *DNB*/1900 under Grenville and Robert Nugent; confirmed by marginal notes in file of the *Rambler* at Oscott College. Introductory note, 44–45, signed **Thomas Brindle.**

648   De Vere's *Poems*, 59–66.

649   Lord Carlisle's *Turkish and Greek Waters*, 66–73.

650   Short notices, 73–84. Pages 75–77 by **J. M. Capes,** prob.—Capes to Richard Simpson, Nov. 25, 1854, Simpson notebook, proposes to write on mysticism à propos of B. Suso; pages 78–79 by **Capes**—Capes to Simpson, Dec. 8, 1854, ibid., says he will do *Heartsease*; pages 79–80 by **Capes,** prob.—Capes to Simpson, May 9, 1855, ibid., says *Rose and Ring* not worth my buying for reviewing;

pages 77–78 by **Richard Simpson**—Capes to Simpson, Nov. 25, 1854, ibid., Capes congratulates him on "Mrs. Jameson."; page 79 by **Simpson**—Capes to Simpson, Dec. 12, 1854, ibid., says "your estimate of DeQuincey is just mine"; page 80 by **Simpson**—Capes to Simpson, Nov. 25, 1854, ibid., says he is anxious to see your French Gothic theory.

VOLUME 15 O.S., 3 2ND S., FEBRUARY 1855

651   Catholic politics and Catholic M.P.s, 85–96. **J. M. Capes.** Capes to Richard Simpson, Dec. 17, 1854, Simpson notebook, says this art. of his will prob. appear in Feb. No.

652   Compton Hall (chaps. iv–v), 96–117. **J. M. Capes?** Cf. no. 646.

653   A conversion under the old penal laws (Part II), 117–126. **Mary Anne (Grenville) Arundell.** Cf. no. 647, and see no. 674.

654   Our camp disasters and their cause, 127–135. **J. M. Capes.** Capes to Simpson, Jan. 7, 1855, Simpson notebook, says he will write a short paper on *Our Camp in Turkey.*

655   Gleanings from the "Broad Church," 136–145. **Richard Simpson.** J. M. Capes to Simpson, Dec. 8, 1854, Simpson notebook, says he will make an art. out of four notices by Simpson with this title.

656   How did Scotland become Presbyterian? (Part I), 145–157.

657   The blind leading the blind, 158–162.

658   Short notices, 163–172. Page 165 by **Richard Simpson**, prob.—J. M. Capes to Simpson, Dec. 12, 1854, ibid., says "*Halieutics*" will do for Feb.; page 170 by **Richard Simpson**—Capes to Simpson, Jan. 9, 1855, ibid., says he will substitute Simpson's "Foreign Policy" for his own; page 163 by **William Simpson**—J. M. Capes to Richard Simpson, Jan. 7[?], 1855, Simpson notebook, says to send Simpson's brother's notice of the Aberdeen ritual.

VOLUME 15 O.S., 3 2ND S., MARCH 1855

659   The Patriotic Fund and proselytism, 173–181. **J. M. Capes,** prob. Cf. no. 1; while regretting Protestant bigotry, the author urges restraint in castigating it, and pleads for Catholic efforts to care for Catholic wounded, widows and orphans of Crimean War.

660 Compton Hall (chaps. vi–vii), 181–202. **J. M. Capes?** Cf. no. 646.

661 Protestantism at sea [in the navy], 202–207. Signed: W.

662 *The Englishwoman in Russia*, 208–221. **Richard Simpson.** J. M. Capes to Simpson, Nov. 25, 1854, Simpson notebook, suggests this review; on Jan. 7[?], 1855 says he is depending upon it for March, and on Jan. 28, ibid., has received the MS.

663 How did Scotland become Presbyterian? (Part II), 221–236.

664 Short notices, 237–247. Page 243 by **Richard Simpson**—J. M. Capes to Simpson, Nov. 25, 1854, Simpson notebook, says to give *Grace Greenwood* a "dressing"; p. 245 by **Simpson**—Capes to Simpson, ibid., suggests a notice of Doran; page 246 by **Simpson**—Capes to Simpson, Jan. 16, 1855, ibid., says he has added to the swipe at Poujoulat.

VOLUME 15 O.S., 3 2ND S., APRIL 1855

665 The true principle of religious controversy, 253–265. **J. M. Capes.** Capes to Richard Simpson, Dec. 12, 1854, Simpson notebook, is writing art. for Feb. or March on controversialists.

666 Compton Hall (chaps. viii–ix), 265–285. **J. M. Capes?** Cf. no. 646.

667 *Cardinal Wolsey*, 285–310.

668 Brownson's *Spirit-Rapper*, 310–317. **Richard Simpson**, prob. J. M. Capes to Simpson, Jan. 7?, 1855, Simpson notebook, suggests this review.

669 *The Microscope*, 318–320.

670 *Annals of the Holy Childhood*, No. 4, 321–324.

671 Short notices, 324–332.

VOLUME 15 O.S., 3 2ND S., MAY 1855

672 The Immaculate Conception, 333–344. **J. M. Capes.** Capes to Richard Simpson, Apr. 25, 1855, Simpson notebook, refers to his own paper on the Immaculate Conception.

673 Compton Hall (chaps. x–xi), 344–365. **J. M. Capes?** Cf. no. 646.

674 A conversion under the old penal laws (Part III, concl.), 365–366. Unidentified. Opening sentence says by a relative of Lady Arundell, see no. 647; Henry Benedict, eleventh Baron Arundell, her brother-in-law, John Francis, twelfth Baron Arundell, her nephew, or Richard Plantagenet Grenville, second Duke of Buckingham and Chandos, her grandson, are possibilities.

675 Education: the Maynooth report, 366–385. **J. M. Capes** and **Richard Simpson.** J. M. Capes to Simpson, Jan. 9, 1855, Simpson notebook, says "Weise" will do very well; on Mar. 30, ibid., Capes says he is adding something about Maynooth report to "Weise."

676 How did Scotland become Presbyterian? (Part III), 385–405.

677 Recent German Catholic poetry, 406–410.

678 Short notices, 410–420.

VOLUME 15 O.S., 3 2ND S., JUNE 1855

679 Catholic politics thirty years ago, 421–432. **J. M. Capes**, prob. This editorial, although it is in reality a review of Richard Lalor Sheil, commences with a reminder of Protestant hostility to Catholics in spite of improved political status, and a call to attend to the needs of the poor.

680 Compton Hall (chaps. xii–xiii, concl.), 433–449. **J. M. Capes?** Cf. no. 646.

681 Pombal and the expulsion of the Jesuits from Portugal, 449–470. (Note, vol. 16, p. 81.)

682 How did Scotland become Presbyterian? (Part IV), 470–484.

683 *Corsica* [by Gregorovius], 484–493. **J. M. Capes?** Capes to Richard Simpson, Apr. 19, 1855, Simpson notebook, says he will get Gregorovius "at your advice." OR, **Richard Simpson?** Capes may have entrusted the review to him.

684 Balmez' *Miscellanies*, 493–504. **Richard Simpson?** Capes to Simpson, Aug. 29, 1854, Simpson notebook, agrees Simpson should do Balmez by and by.

685 Short notices, 504–508. Pages 504–505 by **J. M. Capes**, prob.—Capes to Richard Simpson, May 8, 1855, Simpson notebook, says Donovan asked him to write this puff of his book.

VOLUME 16 O.S., 4 2ND S., JULY 1855

686 Priestcraft, 1–10. **J. M Capes**, prob. This editorial deals with the Protestant prepossession that a Catholic priest is "a compound of the conspirator, the conjuror, and the fanatic."

687 *The Conversion of Hermann the Pianist*, 10–25. **Jean-Baptiste Gergerès.** *Bib.Nat.*

Cat. Translation and précis of the book by **J. M. Capes?**—he was the editor and much interested in music.

688   The Immaculate Conception viewed in connection with the doctrine of Original Sin, [a letter to the editor], 25–37. **Richard Simpson**. Signed R.P.S.; attr. Gasquet, p. xxxi; J. M. Capes to Simpson, Mar. 30, 1855, Simpson notebook, asks him to do this in form of a letter. (Letters, vol. 17, pp. 476–479, by **Richard Simpson**—signed R.P.S., and pp. 479–480 by **John Stanislas Flanagan**—signed J.S.F.)

689   Protestant accounts of French convents, 37–50. **J. M. Capes**, prob. The author attacks the biased fear entertained by Protestants of convents; cf. no. 583.

690   How did Scotland become Presbyterian? (Part V, concl.), 50–67.

691   Sir Archibald Alison on Catholic emancipation, 67–72.

692   Short notices, 72–82. Pages 72–73 by **J. M. Capes**, prob.—he was the author of the *Rambler's* original defence of Liguori; see no. 577.

VOLUME 16 O.S., 4 2ND S., AUGUST 1855

693   The poor-school question, 83–93. **J. M. Capes**, prob. Editorial, cf. no. 1; poor-schools were of constant concern to Capes.

694   Mr. Montgomery's poetry: religious sentimentalism, 94–107.

695   Insanity in its relations to Catholicism, 108–119.

696   Beste's travels in America, 120–133.

697   Sydney Smith's *Life*, 133–144.

698   Maurice on Catholicism and civilisation, 144–150.

699   Short notices, 150–159.

VOLUME 16 O.S., 4 2ND S., SEPTEMBER 1855

700   Vain repetitions, 163–175. **J. M. Capes**, prob. This editorial returns to the subject of Protestant inability to understand Catholicism, in this case particularly prayers.

701   Burton's *Pilgrimage to El Medinah and Meccah*, 189–199. **Richard Simpson**. J. M. Capes to Simpson, Aug. 20, 1855, Simpson notebook, says Burton is in printer's hands as you sent it.

702   Brewster's *Life of Newton*: Galileo and the Inquisition, 199–207. **Richard Simpson**. J. M. Capes to Simpson, letter cited

for no. 701, says Brewster is in the printer's hands as you sent it.

703   Difficulties in the Protestant proof of the canon of Scripture (Part I), 208–223. (Part II is no. 716.)

704   The King of Oude's private life, 223–235.

705   Short notices, 236–242. Page 237 by **Richard Simpson**—J. M. Capes to Simpson, Aug. 20, 1855, Simpson notebook, particularly praises this notice of Macvicar.

VOLUME 16 O.S., 4 2ND S., OCTOBER 1855

706   *Quare fremuerunt gentes?* 243–252. **J. M. Capes**, prob. An editorial defence of the Pope upon his excommunication of Piedmontese who have participated in seizure of ecclesiastical property; the author satirizes the inconsistency or rather hypocrisy of the Protestant reaction.

707   Anthony, Earl of Shaftesbury: a Protestant champion of the seventeenth century, 252–277.

708   *The Newcomes* [by Thackeray], 277–284. Unidentified. Possibly John C. Whyte, whose review of the *Newcomes* for the *Dublin Review* was rejected in Sept.; he had asked to have it returned so that he could try elsewhere (Whyte to H. R. Bagshawe, Sept. 11, 1855, Bagshawe Papers).

709   *Hyppolytus and Callistus*: Döllinger, Bunsen and [Christopher] Wordsworth, 284–299.

710   The Duke of Buckingham's *Memoirs of the Court of George the Third*, 299–305.

711   Trenery's *City of the Crescent*, 305–316.

712   Short notices, 316–322. Pages 317–318. Unidentified (letters, p. 402, by **Frederick Meyrick** and **H. E. Manning**—both signed.)

VOLUME 16 O.S., 4 2ND S., NOVEMBER 1855

713   The miracle-plays of the middle ages (Part I), 323–336.

714   St. Oswald's; or, life in the cloister (chaps. i–iii), 336–357. **J. M. Capes?** This novelette is similar to "Compton Hall" (beginning with no. 646), simple in style, lively in matter, and with the same mystification in plot; in spite of the sub-title, the scene is really mainly in a county neighborhood; in both cases, as in "Passion, Love and Rest" (beginning with no. 276), the theme of Protestant hostility to Catholicism appears, offset by a slightly sentimental portrayal of Catholic virtue.

715   St. Charles Borromeo on church-building, 363–370. **J. M. Capes,** prob. Opens with a renewed attack on the exclusive use of Gothic Church architecture; cf. nos. 144 and 221.

716   The Anglican canon—Wordsworth and Lee (Part II, concl.), 370–389.

717   Laforet on scientific theology, 389–393.

718   Short notices, 393–402. Pages 393–394 by **Richard Simpson?**—this attack on Dr. Cumming reflects Simpson's scorn of him; see *BMCat.* for his discussion with Cumming in 1849.

Volume 16 o.s., 4 2nd s., December 1855

719   The miracle-plays of the middle ages (Part II, concl.), 403–414.

720   St. Oswald's; or, life in the cloister (chaps. iv–vi), 415–436. **J. M. Capes?** Cf. no. 714.

721   Catholicism and Protestantism in Liverpool, 436–442. **J. M. Capes?** He had acquaintances in Liverpool, and had lectured there (Newman, *L&D*, XIV, 216–218); the art. closes with a plea for increased financial support of the priesthood, as well as for increased vocations among young Catholics.

722   Cousin on the true, the beautiful and the good, 442–450.

723   Frederick Lucas, 450–460. **J. M. Capes,** prob. The author commences by saying that readers of the *Rambler* will naturally expect from us a notice of Lucas; Lucas as editor of the *Tablet* was a fellow journalist and Capes shared his view (p. 451) that reform of Catholicism itself should precede proselytizing.

724   Bailey's *Mystic*, 460–466. Unidentified. Possibly Richard Simpson, who in no. 732 begins his review of Browning with an extended reference back to this art.

725   Short notices, 466–474.

726   Correspondence: Bible-burning, 475–476, by **Richard Simpson**—signed Richard ap William (Simpson was Richard, son of William, see no. 737).

Volume 17 o.s., 5 2nd s., January 1856

727   Bible-burning and Bible reading, 1–11. **J. M. Capes,** prob. This editorial is essentially a renewed attack on Protestant

hostility to Catholics, prompted prob. by a letter from Simpson, no. 726.

728   St. Oswald's; or, life in the cloister (chaps. vii–ix), 12–33. **J. M. Capes?** Cf. no. 714.

729   Protestantism in the presence of the Church: the Austrian Concordat, 34–46. **J. M. Capes,** prob. This art. like the editorial is bitter about Protestant hypocrisy vis-à-vis Catholicism; stresses illogical fanaticism of Protestant thinking; and resents silence of Protestants in regard to services of Catholic nuns in Crimea; cf. the editorial for February, no. 734; p. 95.

730   Who are the real Bible-burners? 47–50. **Richard Simpson.** Signed R. ap W.; cf. no. 726.

731   Crown Court and the Austrian Concordat, 50–54. Signed: D. Unidentified. Possibly Richard Simpson, whose first name ended in "d," and who was an old opponent of Dr. Cumming, the subject of attack in this art.; cf. no. 718.

732   Browning's *Men and Women*, 54–71. **Richard Simpson.** Northcote list; Northcote file.

733   Short notices, 71–80.

Volume 17 o.s., 5 2nd s., February 1856

734   The war and its influence on Catholicism, 81–97. **J. M. Capes,** prob. This editorial opens with a point made by Capes in his preface (no. 96), about disputatiousness of Catholics among themselves, which vitiated all attempts at organization; it returns again to the charge of hypocritical Protestantism, p. 88.

735   St. Oswald's; or, life in the cloister (chaps. x–xi), 98–118. **J. M. Capes?** Cf. no. 714.

736   The mystery of the passion at Ober-Ammergau (Part II, concl.), 119–133. **Richard Raby.** Intro. note. (See no. 317.)

737   Misprision of flunkeyism, 137–140. **Richard Simpson.** Signed Richard ap William; Northcote list; Northcote file; see no. 726.

738   Macaulay's *History of England* [Vols. III–IV] (Part I), 140–157. **J. M. Capes,** prob. This and no. 743 review vols. III and IV of Macaulay's *History* and are clearly by the same author, who is increasingly bitter about Macaulay's anti-Catholic point of view; cf. no. 88, and see no. 758. (Letter, pp. 239–240, by **John Dalton**—signed J. Dalton with address, "Northampton," man cited was a

member of clergy of Northampton in 1856, see *DNB*.)

739   Short notices, 157–160.

VOLUME 17 O.S., 5 2ND S., MARCH 1856

740   Catholicity and English society, 161–178. **J. M. Capes,** prob. The author's general theme that "Protestantism is one great organized system of social persecution" is merely a further development of his preoccupation with the Protestant reaction to Catholicism.

741   St. Oswald's; or, life in the cloister (chaps. xii–xiv), 178–199. **J. M. Capes?** Cf. no. 714.

742   Paterfamilias on "Popery," 199–208. **Richard Simpson.** Northcote list; Northcote file.

743   Macaulay's *History of England* [Vols. III–IV] (Part II), 208–228. **J. M. Capes,** prob. Cf. nos. 738 and 758.

744   Short notices, 228–239.

VOLUME 17 O.S., 5 2ND S., APRIL 1856

745   Social tyranny of Protestantism, 241–258. **J. M. Capes,** prob. This editorial is clearly by the author of no. 740; it also deals largely with sabbatarianism, a subject treated by Capes in his leader for March 18, 1848.

746   St. Oswald's; or, life in the cloister (chaps. xv–xviii, concl.), 258–280. **J. M. Capes?** Cf. no. 714.

747   Medieval hymns, 280–294. Unidentified. Possibly Richard Simpson, author of no. 752 and of no. 812. (Letter, pp. 397–400, by the author.)

748   The prospects of America, 294–315. **J. M. Capes?** The author proposes, along with Catholicism, as a cure for the over-tension of American life, the due observance of the sabbath as a means of rest and recreation; cf. no. 745.

749   Short notices, 315–320.

VOLUME 17 O.S., 5 2ND S., MAY 1856

750   The body and the members, 321–326. **J. M. Capes,** prob. The author warns that the war now being settled, Catholics may expect renewed hostility from Protestants, and regrets that Catholics lack organisation to meet such opposition; cf. nos. 734, 740.

751   On original sin as affecting the destiny

of unregenerate man, 327–345. **Richard Simpson.** Signed R.P.S.; Northcote list; Northcote file.

752   Medieval Latin, 348–352. **Richard Simpson.** Signed Richard ap William; see no. 726.

753   Mrs. Fitzherbert and George IV, 352–370. (Letter, p. 480, by **John Dalton**—signed J. Dalton, cf. no. 738.)

754   The fish as a symbol in early Christian art: recent discoveries in the catacombs, 370–382. **J. S. Northcote?** The subject was of particular interest to him; see his book, *Roman Catacombs*, 1857, and no. 32.

755   Doran's *Knights and Their Days*, 382–391.

756   Short notices, 391–397.

VOLUME 17 O.S., 5 2ND S., JUNE 1856

757   On the exaggerations of modern art, 401–413. **J. M. Capes,** prob. This editorial complains that the present is an age of puffs or shams (Capes' favorite words), and of hasty restlessness (cf. editorials of Jan. 15 and 29, 1848); on pp. 408–409 there is a ref. to no. 714 ff., which may be Capes.

758   King William III, 413–433. **J. M. Capes,** prob. Although Macaulay's name does not appear in the title, this is a continuation of nos. 738 and 743, as well as a sequel to nos. 72 and 88; where the author of no. 72 praised Macaulay for his impartiality, his reaction gradually shifted as he went from volume to volume, until he begins no. 743 by saying he knows no writer who excels him [Macaulay] in ingenuity in distorting facts, in blackening characters . . . in whitewashing; already in no. 88, the author on p. 520 objects that Macaulay's enthusiasm for William was "utterly misplaced"; the themes of anti-Catholic bigotry and hypocrisy, characteristic of Capes run throughout the series, here particularly on pp. 413, 428, 433; on p. 414 is a ref. to large sums realized by Macaulay on his *History* (cf. nos. 72, 738 and 743).

759   Preston Hall and our new dignitaries (chaps. i–iii), 434–448. **Daniel Parsons.** Signed The Author of *Stumpingford*; nos. 777, 784, 792 of this novel attr. to him in *Rambler* accounts; novel published anonymously in 1854.

760   A few words about the moon, 448–455. **Richard Simpson.** Signed Richard ap

William; Northcote list; Northcote file; see no. 726.

761 Nuns and nurses in the East, 455–462. **J. M. Capes,** prob. The author recurs to the idea that English soldiers and sailors fighting together with "our Catholic allies" would gain a juster idea of Catholics, and particularly of Catholic sisters and nuns; cf. nos. 734 and 745.

762 Cuzco and Lima, 463–474.

763 Short notices, 474–476.

VOLUME 18 O.S., 6 2ND S., JULY 1856

764 A pilgrimage to the proto-monastery of Subiaco, and the Holy Grotto of St. Benedict (chaps. i–ii), 1–11. **W. B. Ullathorne.** Signed.

765 Preston Hall and our new dignitaries (chaps. iv–vi), 11–28. **Daniel Parsons.** Evidence for no. 759.

766 R. P. S. on the destiny of the unregenerate, in reply to J[ohn] S[tanislaus] F[lanagan], 28–47. **Richard Simpson.** Signed R.P.S.; Northcote list; Northcote file; see no. 688. (Postscript, p. 80, by **Simpson**—signed R.P.S.; Northcote file; Northcote list.)

767 Haxthausen's *Russian Empire*, 47–61.

768 *On the Origin of the Pallium*, 61–70.

769 Short notices, 71–80.

VOLUME 18 O.S., 6 2ND S., AUGUST 1856

770 The Chevalier Bunsen on *The Signs of the Times*, 81–96. **Richard Simpson.** Northcote list; J. M. Capes to Simpson, June 24, 1856, Simpson notebook, suggests Simpson review Bunsen as a leader for August.

771 A pilgrimage to the proto-monastery of Subiaco, and the Holy Grotto of St. Benedict (chaps. iii–v), 97–113. **W. B. Ullathorne.** Signed.

772 Preston Hall and our new dignitaries (chaps. vii–ix), 114–130. **Daniel Parsons.** Evidence for no. 759.

773 Secret history of the Catholic relief bill, 133–151. Unidentified. Possibly William Simpson, as J. M. Capes to Richard Simpson, July 1, 1856, Simpson notebook, asked him to touch up his brother's MS. and have it printed; this is the kind of subject on which William Simpson wrote, usually with his brother.

774 Short notices, 152–160. Pages 152–153 by **Richard Simpson**—J. M. Capes to Simpson, June 24, 1856, Simpson note-

book, asks him to extend his notice of Hecker.

VOLUME 18 O.S., 6 2ND S., SEPTEMBER 1856

775 The session of 1856, 161–168. **Richard Simpson.** *Rambler* accounts.

776 A pilgrimage to the proto-monastery of Subiaco and the Holy Grotto of St. Benedict (chaps. vi–vii), 169–186. **W. B. Ullathorne.** Signed; *Rambler* accounts.

777 Preston Hall and our new dignitaries (chap. x), 186–201. **Daniel Parsons.** *Rambler* accounts.

778 Catholicity and nationality, 203–216. **Richard** and **William Simpson.** *Rambler* accounts; Northcote file and Northcote list give just "Simpson."

779 Who wrote the *Waverley Novels*? 217–226. **Matthew Bridges.** *Rambler* accounts.

780 Scientific evidence: the trials of Palmer, Dove, etc. (Part I), 226–231. **Frederick Capes.** *Rambler* accounts.

781 Short notices, 231–240. Pages 234 (*Garden of the Soul*), 238 (*Beleaguered Heart*), 240 (Rio, *Four Martyrs*) by **J. M. Capes**—*Rambler* accounts; remainder by **Richard Simpson**—*Rambler* accounts.

VOLUME 18 O.S., 6 2ND S., OCTOBER 1856

782 A preacher of reform: the Dorsetshire Luther [Thomas Hancock], 241–250. **Richard Simpson.** *Rambler* accounts.

783 A pilgrimage to the proto-monastery of Subiaco and the Holy Grotto of St. Benedict (chap. viii), 251–265. **W. B. Ullathorne.** Signed; *Rambler* accounts.

784 Preston Hall and our new dignitaries (chaps. xii–xiii), 265–281. **Daniel Parsons.** *Rambler* accounts.

785 Dr. John Bird Sumner at Bath, 281–288. **Daniel Parsons.** *Rambler* accounts bracket this with no. 784.

786 The antecedents of the French Revolution (Part I), 288–299. **William** and **Richard Simpson.** *Rambler* accounts; Northcote file, which says "R. S. and his brother W. S."

787 Protestantism in the East, 299–308. **William** and **Richard Simpson.** *Rambler* accounts.

788 Scientific evidence: the trials of Palmer, Dove, etc. (Part II), 308–314. **Frederick Capes.** *Rambler* accounts.

789 Short notices, 314–320. **Richard Simpson.** *Rambler* accounts.

VOLUME 18 O.S., 6 2ND S., NOVEMBER 1856

790   The rising generation: our poor-schools, 321–334. **J. G. Wenham.** Gasquet, p. xxvi, n.; *Rambler* accounts.

791   A pilgrimage to the proto-monastery of Subiaco and the Holy Grotto of St. Benedict (chaps. ix–x, concl.), 334–345. **W. B. Ullathorne.** Signed; *Rambler* accounts.

792   Preston Hall and our new dignitaries (chaps. xiv–xvi, concl.), 345–362. **Daniel Parsons.** *Rambler* accounts.

793   A canonised controversialist [John Donne], 362–371. **Richard Simpson.** *Rambler* accounts.

794   The causes of the French Revolution (Part II), 372–382. **William and Richard Simpson.** Cf. no. 786.

795   *The Communion of Labour* [by Mrs. Jameson], 383–392. **Richard Simpson.** *Rambler* accounts.

796   What of the Denison decision? 392–396. **Richard Simpson.** *Rambler* accounts.

797   Short notices, 396–400. **Richard Simpson.** *Rambler* accounts.

VOLUME 18 O.S., 6 2ND S., DECEMBER 1856

798   A glimpse into the working of the penal laws under James I: from unpublished manuscripts, 401–418. **Richard Simpson.** *Rambler* accounts.

799   Catholicity and despotism, 418–434. **J. M. Capes.** *Rambler* accounts.

800   Instruction *v.* education, 434–444. **J. G. Wenham.** *Rambler* accounts give "J.G.W."; he contributed arts. on education.

801   The morals and politics of materialism, 445–454. **Richard Simpson.** *Rambler* accounts.

802   Ben Jonson, recusant and renegade, 455–465. **Richard Simpson.** *Rambler* accounts; Capes to Simpson, Nov. 26, 1856, Simpson notebook, asks Simpson to send Jonson at once.

803   Turner's pictures at Marlborough House, 466–468. **Frederick Capes.** *Rambler* accounts.

804   Conscience and faith, 468–472. **Richard Simpson.** *Rambler* accounts.

805   Short notices, 472–478. Pages 472–474 by **J. M. Capes**—*Rambler* accounts; remainder by **Richard Simpson**—*Rambler* accounts.

806   Correspondence: Theologia male ferrata, 479–480, by **J. B. Morris**—signed J.B.M. *Rambler* accounts (letter, vol. 19, pp. 154–159, by **W. H. Eyre**—signed

Sacerdos, Sutcliffe; notes, pp. 159–161, by **J. M. Capes,** the editor; letter pp. 239–242, by **J. B. Morris**—signed J.B.M. *Rambler* accounts).

VOLUME 19 O.S., 7 2ND S., JANUARY 1857

807   The Irish church establishment: can we upset it? 1–15. **J. M. Capes.** *Rambler* accounts; Capes to Simpson, Nov. 26, 1856, Simpson notebook, tells him to use this title for his [Capes'] art.

808   A morning at the Star-Chamber [on Edmund Campion], 15–37. **Richard Simpson.** *Rambler* accounts. (See nos. 880 and 900.)

809   Principles of education, 37–52. **J. G. Wenham.** *Rambler* accounts give "J.G.W."; see no. 800.

810   *Arctic Explorations,* 52–62. **Frederick Capes.** *Rambler* accounts.

811   *The Girlhood of Catherine de Medici* [by T. A. Trollope], 62–71. **J. M. Capes.** *Rambler* accounts; Capes to Simpson, Nov. 17, 1856, Simpson notebook, says he will review Trollope for Jan.

812   Southwell's *Poems,* 71–79. **Richard Simpson.** *Rambler* accounts; Capes to Simpson, n.d., Simpson notebook, tells him to do Southwell.

813   Short notices, 79–82. **Richard Simpson**—*Rambler* accounts; Capes to Simpson, Jan. 4, 1857, Simpson notebook, refers to "your remarks on the *Lamp*" (letter, pp. 161–162, signed **James Burke.**)

VOLUME 19 O.S., 7 2ND S., FEBRUARY 1857

814   The Catholic university: its difficulties and prospects, 83–98. **J. M. Capes.** *Rambler* accounts; Capes to Simpson, Jan. 4, 1857, refers to "my" university art.

815   Father Southwell and his capture, 98–118. **Richard and William Simpson.** *Rambler* accounts.

816   Notes of a visit to the coast of Albania, 119–126. **T. N. Harper?** *Rambler* accounts give "T.H."; Capes to Simpson, Jan. 11, 1857, Simpson notebook, says to tell Harper there is no room for his art. in the current issue, but perhaps more material was needed at last moment.

817   Critics and the fine arts, 126–132. **Frederick Capes.** *Rambler* accounts.

818   Memorials of the penal laws, 132–140. **Richard Simpson.** *Rambler* accounts.

819   The *Rambler* and the *Dublin Review,*

140–144. **Richard Simpson** AND **J. M. Capes.** *Rambler* accounts give "R.S.", but see Capes to Simpson, Jan. 8, 11, 13, and 16, 1857, Simpson notebook, which establish Capes's very large share in this art. (See nos. 789, notice of *Brownson's Quarterly Review*, and 790, and *DR* 822).

820 Modern Anglicanism: *The Union*, 144–150. **J. M. Capes.** *Rambler* accounts; Capes to Simpson, letter cited for no. 814, promises an art. on *The Union*.

821 Short notices, 151–154. **Richard Simpson.** *Rambler* accounts.

822 In Correspondence: The editorship of the *Rambler*, 162, by **J. M. Capes**— Capes to Simpson, Jan. 11, 1857, Simpson notebook, says he will insert a notice in the Feb. issue, stating that he is again the editor.

VOLUME 19 O.S., 7 2ND S., MARCH 1857

823 Literary cookery, 163–183. **J. M. Capes** and **Richard Simpson.** *Rambler* accounts give "J.M.C." but add "about 2pp. of this R. S." (Letter, p. 402, signed **George Bowyer**, with intro. note by **J. M. Capes** —*Rambler* accounts.)

824 The capture and death of Dr. John Storey, 183–201. **Richard Simpson.** Repr. *Under the Penal Laws*, 1930; *Rambler* accounts add "W. S. old documents."

825 Christianity in the Pacific, 202–212. **Frederick Weld.** *Rambler* accounts.

826 Chaldea and Persia, 213–226. **Frederick Capes.** *Rambler* accounts.

827 Whately on Bacon, 227–234. **Richard Simpson.** *Rambler* accounts.

828 Short notices, 234–239. Pages 236–237 by **J. M. Capes**—*Rambler* accounts, Capes to Newman, Apr. 7, 1857, Newman MSS., says he has Ullathorne's permission to say that the reviewer in the *DR* misunderstood *Ram* no. 790; other notices by **Richard Simpson**—*Rambler* accounts.

VOLUME 19 O.S., 7 2ND S., APRIL 1857

829 The civil rights of religious orders, 243–259. **Richard Simpson.** *Rambler* accounts; based on Rosmini's *Filosofia della Politica*: see p. 259n.

830 The scandal of goodness, 259–268. **J. M. Capes.** *Rambler* accounts.

831 The martyrs of Chichester, 269–284. **Richard Simpson.** *Rambler* accounts.

832 Guizot's *Memoirs of Sir Robert Peel*, 285–300. **J. M. Capes.** *Rambler* accounts; Capes to Simpson, Mar. 26, 1857, Simpson notebook, says he is glad Simpson likes his "Peel."

833 Prospects of Catholic philosophy, 300–310. **Charles Meynell.** *Rambler* accounts.

834 Short notices, 310–318. Pages 312–316 by **Frederick Capes**—*Rambler* accounts (letter, pp. 400–401, by **Frederick Capes** —signed F.C.); pages 316–318 by **Richard Simpson**—*Rambler* accounts; pages 310–312 by **H. M. Walker**—*Rambler* accounts.

835 Correspondence: The *Dublin Review* and the work of the converts, 318–322, signed **George Montgomery.**

VOLUME 19 O.S., 7 2ND S., MAY 1857

836 The political future, 323–337. **J. M. Capes.** *Rambler* accounts; see Newman, *Life*, I, 437, and *L&D*, XVIII, 29–30.

837 The controversy on the poor-school grant, 338–348. **S. N. Stokes.** Signed S.N.S.; *Rambler* accounts; he was an inspector of schools.

838 The rescue, 348–364. **Richard Simpson.** *Rambler* accounts.

839 Seymour's curse; or, the last Mass of Owslebury (Part I), 364–381. **Cecilia Caddell.** Signed; *Rambler* accounts. (Note, pp. 364–365, by **J. M. Capes**— signed Ed. *Rambler*.)

840 *The Kingdom and People of Siam*, 382–399. **Frederick Capes.** *Rambler* accounts.

841 Short notice, 399–400, by **Richard Simpson**—*Rambler* accounts.

VOLUME 19 O.S., 7 2ND S., JUNE 1857

842 Protestant criticisms on Catholic morals, 403–420. **J. M. Capes.** *Rambler* accounts.

843 Life and martyrdom of Thomas Alfield, 420–431. **Richard Simpson** and **William Simpson.** *Rambler* accounts; Northcote file; it is, however, repr. *Under the Penal Laws*, 1930, without reference to William Simpson.

844 Seymour's curse; or, the last Mass of Owslebury (Part II), 431–450. **Cecilia Caddell.** Signed; *Rambler* accounts.

845 A letter of Father Campion, 451–456. **Edmund Campion.** Title. Edited by **William** and **Richard Simpson.** *Rambler* accounts.

846 *Christianity in China, Tartary, and*

Thibet (Part I), 456–470. **Frederick Capes.** *Rambler* accounts.

847   A doctor's opinions on physic, 470–475. **J. M. Capes.** *Rambler* accounts.

848   Dr. Oliver's *Collections*, 476–480. **Charles Weld.** *Rambler* accounts give "C.W."; Weld to Simpson, Apr. 29, n.y., Simpson notebook, says he will send a short notice of Dr. Oliver's book for June.

849   Short notices, 480–482, by **J. M. Capes** and **Richard Simpson**—*Rambler* accounts give "J. M. C. one page and R.S. nearly two."

VOLUME 20 O.S., 8 2ND S., JULY 1857

850   Ultramontanism for England, 1–12. **J. M. Capes.** *Rambler* accounts; Capes to Simpson, June 4, 1857, Simpson notebook, says "I send you a leader for July."

851   Industrial education, 12–24. **S. N. Stokes.** *Rambler* accounts.

852   Biographical sketch of Thomas Poundes (Part I), 24–38. **Richard Simpson.** *Rambler* accounts.

853   The divorce bill, 38–47. **Richard Simpson.** *Rambler* accounts; Charles Weld to Simpson, [1859], Simpson notebook, says he sees himself writing on divorce—"not half so good as what you have already written."

854   Seymour's curse; or, the last Mass of Owslebury (Part III), 47–60. **Cecilia Caddell.** Signed.

855   A letter of Father Campion, 60–65. **Edmund Campion.** Title. Edited by **Richard Simpson.** *Rambler* accounts.

856   *Civilisation in the Fifth Century*, 65–76. **E. S. Ffoulkes.** *Rambler* accounts.

857   Short notices, 77–80. Pages 79–80 by **Frederick Capes** and **J. M. Capes**— *Rambler* accounts (letter, p. 160, by C.J.M.—signed The Editor of the Volume [*Alice Sherwin*], see *BMCat.*); pages 77–78 by **Richard Simpson**—*Rambler* accounts.

VOLUME 20 O.S., 8 2ND S., AUGUST 1857

858   The French Emperor, 81–94. **J. M. Capes.** *Rambler* accounts.

859   Biographical sketch of Thomas Poundes (Part II, concl.), 94–106. **Richard Simpson.** *Rambler* accounts.

860   Seymour's curse; or, the last Mass of Owslebury (Part IV, concl.), 106–114. **Cecilia Caddell.** Signed.

861   The Duke of Gueldres on the English martyrs, 114–122. **Richard Simpson.** *Rambler* accounts.

862   Faber's *The Creator and the Creature*, 122–135. **J. M. Capes.** *Rambler* accounts. With an additional criticism, 135–140, by **Louis de Buggenoms.** *Rambler* accounts give "L. B."; Capes to Simpson, Jan. 13, 1857, Simpson notebook, shows Buggenoms was in corres. with Simpson; Capes to Simpson, Feb. 17, 1859, ibid., explains Faber's anger at *Rambler* by saying it was due to Buggenoms' letter.

863   Phillipps on the unity of Christendom, 140–145. **Richard Simpson.** *Rambler* accounts; Capes to Simpson, Sept. 21, 1857, Simpson notebook, refers to "yours about A. Phillipps"; Northcote file.

864   *The History of Normandy and England* [by Francis Palgrave], 146–152. **Richard Simpson.** *Rambler* accounts.

865   *The Life of Handel*, 153–157. **Frederick Capes.** *Rambler* accounts.

866   Short notices, 157–160, by **J. M. Capes** and **Richard Simpson**—*Rambler* accounts give "page + ¼ R.S.; 3/4 page J. M. C."

VOLUME 20 O.S., 8 2ND S., SEPTEMBER 1857

867   Ireland's opportunity, 161–172. **J. M. Capes.** *Rambler* accounts.

868   A conversion in the reign of Charles I (Part I), 173–189. **Richard Simpson.** *Rambler* accounts.

869   *The Edinburgh Review* on La Salette, 189–200. **J. M. Capes.** *Rambler* accounts.

870   *Christianity in China, Tartary, and Thibet* (Part II, concl.), 201–215. **Frederick Capes.** *Rambler* accounts.

871   Converts and old Catholics, 216–230. **J. M. Capes.** *Rambler* accounts.

872   Short notices, 230–232, partly by **Richard Simpson.** *Rambler* accounts give "R. S. 1 [page]."

VOLUME 20 O.S., 8 2ND S., OCTOBER 1857

873   Amusements for the people, 233–245. **J. M. Capes.** *Rambler* accounts.

874   What books shall we use in our schools? 245–258. **J. G. Wenham.** *Rambler* accounts.

875   A conversion in the reign of Charles I (Part II, concl.), 258–272. **Richard Simpson.** Cf. no. 868.

876   Ultramontanism and despotism, 272–290. **J. M. Capes.** *Rambler* accounts.

877   On belief in reputed miracles, 290–301. **J. M. Capes.** *Rambler* accounts.

878   Ornsby's *Life of St. Francis de Sales*, 301–304. **J. M. Capes.** *Rambler* accounts.

VOLUME 20 O.S., 8 2ND S., NOVEMBER 1857

879   The Russian church, 305–322. **Richard Simpson.** *Rambler* accounts; Conzemius, I, 132. (See nos. 888, 892, and 899.)

880   Was Campion a traitor to his brethren? 322–331. **Richard Simpson.** *Rambler* accounts. (Letter, vol. 21, pp. 142–143, signed **Thomas Flanagan**, pp. 143–144, by **Simpson**—signed Ed.) (See nos. 808 and 900.)

881   Rough notes on Ruskin, 331–338. **Charles Weld.** *Rambler* accounts; Weld to Simpson, Oct. 7, [1857], Simpson notebook, promises to see what he can say about Ruskin.

882   Church-history of England [by T. Flanagan], 338–354. **Richard Simpson.** *Rambler* accounts. (Letter, vol. 21, pp. 142–143, signed **Thomas Flanagan**.)

883   Chinese life and manners, 354–368. **Frederick Capes.** *Rambler* accounts.

884   Döllinger's *Heathenism and Judaism*, 368–381. **Richard Raby.** J. M. Capes to Richard Simpson, Oct. 2, 1857, Simpson notebook, says Raby has sent a review of this book.

885   Short notices, 381–384, by **J. M. Capes** and **Richard Simpson**—*Rambler* accounts.

VOLUME 20 O.S., 8 2ND S., DECEMBER 1857

886   Catholicity in India, 385–399. **Richard Simpson** and **Thomas Grant.** *Rambler* accounts; Northcote file. (Letters, vol. 21, p. 72, by **Frederick Weld**, prob.—signed W., he was the author of no. 825; p. 288, by **Grant**—*Rambler* accounts.)

887   Laurence Vaux, 399–418. **Richard Simpson.** *Rambler* accounts; claimed Simpson to Acton, July 1, [1858], Acton-Simpson Corres.

888   The Greek rite, 418–429. **Richard Simpson.** *Rambler* accounts. (See nos. 879, 892, and 899.)

889   Translations of the Scriptures, 429–442. **John Maguire.** *Rambler* accounts.

890   Waterton's *Essays*, 442–455. **Frederick Capes.** *Rambler* accounts.

891   Short notices, 456, by **Richard Simpson** —*Rambler* accounts.

VOLUME 21 O.S., 9 2ND S., JANUARY 1858

892   The Russian and Anglican hierarchies, 1–21. **Richard Simpson.** *Rambler* accounts. (See nos. 879, 888, and 899.)

893   Musical humours, 22–35. **Richard Simpson.** *Rambler* accounts.

894   The Church and young America, 35–49. **Richard Simpson.** *Rambler* accounts.

895   Ideology of St. Thomas, 49–62. **Charles Meynell.** *Rambler* accounts.

896   Mozart's *Correspondence*, 62–70. **J. M. Capes.** *Rambler* accounts.

897   Short notices, 70–72, by **Richard Simpson**—*Rambler* accounts.

VOLUME 21 O.S., 9 2ND S., FEBRUARY 1858

898   A retrospect, 73–84. **J. M. Capes.** *Rambler* accounts.

899   The Anglican priesthood, 84–100. **Richard Simpson.** *Rambler* accounts. (See nos. 879, 888, and 892.)

900   Campion's alleged confessions, 100–113. **Richard Simpson.** *Rambler* accounts. (See nos. 808 and 880.)

901   Madame Elizabeth Galitzin, 113–121. Unidentified. Translated by **Elizabeth Mary Simpson**, prob.—*Rambler* accounts give E.M.S., initials of Mrs. Richard Simpson.

902   *Captivity of Two Russian Princesses in the Caucasus*, 121–129. **J. M. Capes.** *Rambler* accounts.

903   Caswall's *Poems*, 129–135. **J. M. Capes.** *Rambler* accounts.

904   A Bible distributor [George Borrow] painted by himself, 135–141. **J. A. Douglas** and **Richard Simpson.** *Rambler* accounts give "Douglas and R.S."; Northcote file; Charles Weld to Simpson, Oct. 7, [1857], and n.d., Simpson notebook, identifies Douglas as brother-in-law of Lord Petre; see Burke.

905   Short notices, 141–142, by **Richard Simpson**—*Rambler* accounts.

906   In Correspondence: Translation of the Scriptures, 144, signed Lector.

VOLUME 21 O.S., 9 2ND S., MARCH 1858

907   English Catholics and the English government, 145–157. **Richard Simpson.** *Rambler* accounts.

908   Liberty in France, 157–168. **J. M. Capes.** *Rambler* accounts.

909   What was the religion of Shakespeare? (Part I), 168–187. **Richard Simpson.**

Rambler accounts; H. S. Bowden, editor of Simpson's *The Religion of Shakespeare* (1899), asserts (Preface, p. vii) that Simpson contributed *three* articles on this subject to the *Rambler* in 1858: see nos. 914 and 922. (Letter, vol. 24, pp. 100–102, by **Richard Raby**, prob.—signed R.Y., Simpson to Acton, Apr. 6, 1859, Acton-Simpson Corres., mentions a letter from Raby, who lived in Munich and contributed to the *Rambler*; this letter reports a criticism by a professor at Prague of the *Rambler* series on Shakespeare.)

910   Modern poets, 188–207. **Charles Meynell**. *Rambler* accounts.

911   The English of the seventeenth century, 208–214. Unidentified. Possibly Abbot Walter Montagu; see p. 208n. and *DNB*. Edited with intro. note by **Richard Simpson**—*Rambler* accounts.

912   Short notices, 214–216, by **Richard Simpson**—*Rambler* accounts.

VOLUME 21 O.S., 9 2ND S., APRIL 1858

913   Are the interests of science opposed to the interests of religion? 217–232. **J. M. Capes**. *Rambler* accounts.

914   What was the religion of Shakespeare? (Part II), 232–249. **Richard Simpson**. Cf. no. 909.

915   India in 1848, 249–267. **J. M. Capes**. *Rambler* accounts.

916   The life and times of Edmund Burke, 268–273. **J. D. Acton**. *Rambler* accounts; Gasquet, p. 4; extract repr. in *Essays on Church and State*, pp. 455–457.

917   Sunny memories of Rome, 273–280. **Richard Simpson**. *Rambler* accounts. (Letter, pp. 425–432, signed **M. A. Tierney**.)

918   Cuddesdon casuistry, 280–285. **Richard Simpson**. *Rambler* accounts.

919   Short notices, 285–287, by **Richard Simpson**—*Rambler* accounts.

920   Correspondence, 288, by **Richard Simpson**—*Rambler* accounts.

VOLUME 21 O.S., 9 2ND S., MAY 1858

921   The mission of the laity, 289–302. **W. G. Todd**. *Rambler* accounts and Gasquet, p. 18, give "Dr. Todd"; for man cited see Newman, *L&D*, XIV, index.

922   What was the religion of Shakespeare? (Part III, concl.), 302–319. **Richard**

Simpson. Cf. no. 909.

923   Bossuet (Part I), 320–337. **J. M. Capes**. *Rambler* accounts; Capes to Simpson, Mar. 13, 1858, Simpson notebook, disclaims any idea of attacking Bossuet; Mar. 20, ibid., says he thinks Bossuet would make two arts.; May 6, ibid., sends 2nd part of Bossuet; May 9, ibid., refers to my 1st art. on Bossuet; the art. is repr. in error in Acton's *Essays on Church and State*. (Notice, vol. 22, p. 72, by **John Maguire**—*Rambler* accounts give "Dr. Maguire"; for man cited see Newman, *L&D*, XIII, 189, and index.)

924   Dr. Brownson's experiences, 337–346. **Richard Simpson**. *Rambler* accounts; Gasquet, p. 18.

925   Positivism, 346–352. **Richard Simpson**. *Rambler* accounts.

926   Noble on the mind and the brain, 353–356. **J. M. Capes**. *Rambler* accounts.

927   Short notices, 356–360. Pages 356–357, by **Charles Meynell**—*Rambler* accounts; remainder by **Richard Simpson**, ibid.

VOLUME 21 O.S., 9 2ND S., JUNE 1858

928   India for Exeter Hall, 361–373. **J. M. Capes**. *Rambler* accounts.

929   Bossuet (Part II, concl.), 373–390. **J. M. Capes**. *Rambler* accounts.

930   Modern individualism, 390–399. **Richard Simpson**. *Rambler* accounts.

931   Laforet's exposition of Catholic dogma, 399–412. **John Bonus**. *Rambler* accounts give "Bonus"; Gasquet, p. 25, gives "Rev. Mr. Bonus"; man cited noticed in no. 828, pp. 234–235, and in *DR* no. 845, p. 530, in both cases described as "B.D. Louvain"; Laforet was president of the Pope's College in the Catholic University of Louvain.

932   Louis Blanc's *Historical Revelations*, 412–416. **Frederick Capes**. *Rambler* accounts.

933   Lord Montague's troubles, 416–421. **William Simpson**. *Rambler* accounts give "W.S."; Richard Simpson to Acton, July 1, 1858, Acton-Simpson Corres., refers to his brother's paper on Lord Montague.

934   Short notices, 421–424, by **Richard Simpson**—*Rambler* accounts; however, the notice of Gladstone on Homer may be by J. D. Acton—Simpson to Acton, May 31, 1858, Acton-Simpson Corres., says "You may find in Gladstone enough to hang a review upon."

VOLUME 22 O.S., 10 2ND S., JULY 1858

935 The dead-lock in politics, 1–11. **J. M. Capes.** *Rambler* accounts; Gasquet, pp. 20, 23.

936 The influence of Catholics in England, 11–27. **Richard Simpson.** *Rambler* accounts; Gasquet, pp. 16, 19n, 25n.

937 Mr. Buckle's thesis and method, 27–42. **Richard Simpson.** *Rambler* accounts; Gasquet, pp. 17n., 19, 20, 23n.; Conzemius, I, 143. AND **J. D. Acton.** Gasquet, p. 23, quotes Acton as saying in ref. to this art., "The matter of Quetelet, and the termination introductory to Buckle No. 2, I did subjoin" (see pp. 36–37 and last paragraph).

938 Hogg's *Life of Shelley*, 42–53. **J. M. Capes.** *Rambler* accounts; Gasquet, p. 20n.

939 Queen Elizabeth in love, 54–61. **Richard Simpson.** *Rambler* accounts; Gasquet, p. 20.

940 Literary notices, 61–72. Pages 61–68, 70–72, by **J. D. Acton**—*Rambler* accounts give "Acton," but see Gasquet, pp. 17, 19n.; pp. 68–70 by **Charles Meynell**—Acton to Simpson, June 11, 1858, Acton-Simpson Corres., says "Meynell has done Poe."

VOLUME 22 O.S., 10 2ND S., AUGUST 1858

941 France, 73–88. **Richard Simpson.** *Rambler* accounts; Gasquet, p. 30.

942 Mr. Buckle's philosophy of history, 88–104. **J. D. Acton.** *Rambler* accounts; repr. *Historical Essays*.

943 German Jews and French reviewers, 104–120. **John Maguire.** *Rambler* accounts; Gasquet, p. 26.

944 Italian statistics, 120–134. **Richard Simpson.** *Rambler* accounts; Gasquet, p. 28.

945 Literary notices, 134–144, by **J. D. Acton, J. M. Capes,** and **Richard Simpson**—*Rambler* accounts, which give to each 7½, 1, and 1 pages respectively; pages 134–142 by **Acton**—see Gasquet, pp. 17, 34, where the reference is to last 2 lines of 1st paragraph on p. 135, not to "Bossuet" in June issue, Conzemius, I, 144 (letter, p. 216, by **Richard Simpson**—*Rambler* accounts); pages 142–143, 144, by **Capes**—Capes to Simpson, June 30, 1858, Simpson notebook, says he is noticing Trollope and George Eliot, and preparing Brialmont; pages 143 (White),

144 (von Humboldt), by **Simpson**—must be his 1 page.

VOLUME 22 O.S., 10 2ND S., SEPTEMBER 1858

946 The Pope and the patriarchs, 145–164, with a note, p. 164, acknowledging debt to late Anthony Tinnebroeck, S. J., "for the matter of our arguments." **Richard Simpson.** *Rambler* accounts.

947 The one true religion [on Comte's *Catechism of Positive Religion*], 164–173. **J. M. Capes.** *Rambler* accounts; Gasquet, p. 25.

948 The philosophy of the absolute, 173–190. **Charles Meynell.** *Rambler* accounts; see Gasquet, p. 25.

949 How doth the little busy bee! 190–199. **Richard Simpson.** *Rambler* accounts.

950 *Novels and Novelists*, 200–207. **Frederick Capes.** *Rambler* accounts.

951 Thomas Woodhouse, 207–212. **Richard Simpson.** *Rambler* accounts.

952 Literary notices, 212–216, by **Richard Simpson**—*Rambler* accounts.

VOLUME 22 O.S., 10 2ND S., OCTOBER 1858

953 M. Guizot and his contemporaries (Part I), 217–229. **Ferdinand d'Eckstein.** *Rambler* accounts; no. 988, p. 41. Translated by **Charles A. Spink**—Simpson to Acton, Aug. 25, 1858, Acton-Simpson Corres., refers to Mr. Spink's translation.

954 Jeremy Bentham's greatest-happiness principle, 229–250. **Richard Simpson.** *Rambler* accounts; Gasquet, p. 47n.

955 M. de Marsys on our martyrs, 250–265. **Richard Simpson.** *Rambler* accounts.

956 Father Theiner's publications, 265–267. **J. D. Acton.** *Rambler* accounts.

957 Catholic and Protestant missionary, book, and education societies, 268–279. **T. W. Allies** and **Richard Simpson,** who did last 2 pages. *Rambler* accounts.

958 Literary notices, 279–288, by **Richard Simpson**—*Rambler* accounts, Simpson to Acton, Monday [Sept. 1858], Acton-Simpson Corres., says "I send you the short notice of the *Dublin*."

VOLUME 22 O.S., 10 2ND S., NOVEMBER 1858

959 M. Guizot (Part II), 289–301. **Ferdinand d'Eckstein.** Cf. no. 953. Translated by **J. D. Acton**—Gasquet, p. 36.

960 The confessional, 302–314. **Richard Simpson.** *Rambler* accounts.

961 Longfellow's new poem ["Miles Standish's Courtship"], 314–325. **Richard Simpson.** *Rambler* accounts.

962 John Hambley, alias Tregwethan, martyr, 325–335. **Richard Simpson.** *Rambler* accounts; repr. *Under the Penal Laws*, 1930.

963 The late Archbishop of Cologne and Prussian diplomacy, 335–344. **Richard Raby.** *Rambler* accounts.

964 China, 345–356. **Frederick Capes.** *Rambler* accounts.

965 Literary notices, 356–360, by **Richard Simpson**—*Rambler* accounts.

VOLUME 22 O.S., 10 2ND S., DECEMBER 1858

966 The paternity of Jansenism, 361–373. **J. J. I. von Döllinger.** *Rambler* accounts. Intro. note, p. 361, by **Richard Simpson** —signed Ed. Translated by **J. D. Acton** —Acton to Simpson [Nov. 15, 1858], Acton-Simpson Corres., encloses half of Döllinger's letter and speaks of his difficulty in translating a certain phrase therein. (Letters, vol. 24, pp. 113– 114, by **J. H. Newman**—signed J.J., see Conzemius, I, 182–183, repr. Newman, *L&D*, XIX, 538–539; pp. 242–244 by **Richard Simpson**—signed R.S., Simpson notebook.)

967 Mr. George Combe and his phrenology, 373–388. **Richard Simpson.** *Rambler* accounts; Gasquet, pp. 36, 39n.

968 Belgium, 388–399. **Richard Simpson.** *Rambler* accounts; Gasquet, p. 39n.

969 William Harrington, 399–407. **Richard Simpson.** *Rambler* accounts; Gasquet, pp. 36, 39n.

970 Mansel's Bampton lectures, 407–415. **Richard Simpson.** *Rambler* accounts; Gasquet, p. 39n.; Capes to Simpson, Jan. 22, 1862, Simpson notebook, says he looked back at Simpson's art. on Mansel.

971 St. Ursula and the eleven thousand virgins, 415–421. **Richard Simpson.** *Rambler* accounts; Gasquet, p. 39n.; Conzemius, I, 144.

972 The Count de Montalembert, 421–428. **J. D. Acton.** *Rambler* accounts; Gasquet, pp. 40–41, show that Acton consulted Simpson about this art., and Acton to Simpson, Dec. 12, 1858, Acton-Simpson Corres., refers to "our" art., but this may be no more than the editorial "our"; extracts repr. *Essays on Church*

and State, p. 472. (Note, p. 432, by **Acton**—*Rambler* accounts, Gasquet, p. 42, shows that Acton asked Simpson to put in the note and in large measure dictated its wording.)

973 Literary notices, 429–432. Pages 429– 431, by **J. D. Acton**—*Rambler* accounts, Gasquet, p. 41, extract repr. *Essays on Church and State*, p. 467; pages 431– 432, by **Richard Simpson**—*Rambler* accounts.

VOLUME 23 O.S., 11 2ND S., JANUARY 1859

974 The Christmas of Christian art, 1–17. **Tommaso Minardi.** Intro. note. Translated by **Richard Simpson**—*Rambler* accounts; Simpson to Acton, Dec. 3, 1858, Acton-Simpson Corres., says he has translated one of Minardi's lectures. Intro. note by **Charles Weld**—*Rambler* accounts, Weld to Simpson, Mar. 7, [1859], Simpson notebook, refers to my preface to Minardi. (Letters, pp. 146– 148, by **Frederick Capes**—signed ***, *Rambler* accounts; p. 148, by **J. D. Acton**—signed Ed. R.)

975 The royal commission on education, 17–30. **S. N. Stokes.** *Rambler* accounts; Gasquet, p. 54n. (See no. 982.)

976 Political thoughts of the Church, 30– 49. **J. D. Acton.** *Rambler* accounts; repr. *History of Freedom.*

977 John Jones, martyr, 49–55. **Richard Simpson.** *Rambler* accounts.

978 Toasting the Pope, 55–63. **Richard Simpson.** *Rambler* accounts.

979 Literary notices, 64–72, by **Richard Simpson** and **Frederick Capes**—*Rambler* accounts reports "R.S. 6 pp., F.C. 2 pp."; given Capes' interest, he prob. did pp. 68–69.

VOLUME 23 O.S., 11 2ND S., FEBRUARY 1859

980 The Catholic press, 73–90. **J. D. Acton.** *Rambler* accounts; repr. *Essays on Church and State.*

981 Martineau's *Studies of Christianity*, 90– 103. **Richard Simpson.** *Rambler* accounts; Gasquet, pp. 43, 49, 51.

982 The royal commission and the *Tablet*, 104–113. **S. N. Stokes.** *Rambler* accounts.

983 Bureaucracy, 113–125. **Richard Simpson.** *Rambler* accounts; Gasquet, pp. 45, 53n., 54n., 61n.

984 Caesarism, Diabolism, and Christianity,

126–137. **J. M. Capes.** Signed C; *Rambler* accounts; Gasquet, pp. 46n., 49. (See nos. 975, 976, and 978.)

985 Foreign Protestant view of England in 1596, 137–146. **Richard Simpson.** *Rambler* accounts.

VOLUME 24 O.S., 1 3RD S., MAY 1859

986 The Mission of the Isles of the North (Part I), 1–22. **J. H. Newman.** Simpson notebook; repr. *Historical Sketches*, III, as "Northmen and Normans in England and Ireland."

987 Religious associations in the sixteenth century, 23–41. **Richard Simpson.** See Newman, *L&D*, XIX, 77.

988 The Abbé de Lamennais (communicated), 41–70. **Ferdinand d'Eckstein.** Intro. note. Intro. note, presumably by the editor, **J. H. Newman,** and historical annotations, 70–77, by **J. D. Acton**—signed A.D.J., Gasquet, p. 65, Conzemius, I, 154–155. Trans. by **Richard Simpson**—Newman, *L&D*, XIX, 86, 91.

989 The development of Gothic architecture (communicated), 77–89. **Richard Simpson.** Signed D.N.; Simpson wrote on Gothic architecture in no. 650, p. 80; Newman, now editor, refers to this art. as Simpson's (*L&D*, XIX, 102); Simpson used these initials for *NBR* no. 944, and for a letter on *Ram* no. 1098, q.v.; the attr. in a very partial list in the Simpson notebook for this issue gives "? Darnel," but apparently in error.

990 The ancient saints (Part I) (communicated), 90–98. **J. H. Newman.** Signed O; repr. *Historical Sketches*, II, as "Last Years of St. Chrysostom."

991 In Correspondence: Our martyrs of the sixteenth century, 99–100, by **Robert Monteith**—signed R.M., Richard Simpson to J. D. Acton, Apr. 6, 1859, Acton-Simpson Corres., refers to a letter from Monteith, Monteith built a church at Lanarck, (cf. Newman, *L&D*, XI, index, and first sentence of this letter) (letters, p. 242, by **Charles Meynell**, prob.—signed C.M., he used these initials in *Ram*; pp. 379–386, by **Victor de Buck**—signed Y.Z., Simpson notebook, Newman, *L&D*, XIX, 185; pp. 386–390, by **Charles Weld** and **Richard Simpson**—signed C.W., and letter of Acton to Newman, Aug. 15, 1859, cited for no. 1001, says he has letter from Weld on martyrs with extracts from MSS., but

Simpson notebook, in Simpson's hand, gives "CW & RS"; vol. 25, pp. 90–93, by **Richard Simpson**—signed R.S.).

Temporal prosperity a note of the Church, 102–105, by **J. H. Newman,** prob.—signed O.H.; see Newman, *L&D*, XIX, 166, repr. ibid., pp. 527–529 (letter, pp. 231–234, by **M. J. Rhodes**—signed M.S., Rhodes to Newman, May 24 [Feast of Our Lady], Newman MSS., sends reply to "Temporal Prosperity"; pp. 234–236, by **Frederick Oakeley,** prob.—signed F., he used this initial to sign a letter in no. 1050 and an art., no. 1074; pp. 236–238, by **J. H. Newman,** prob.—signed O.H.; vol. 25, pp. 93–97, by **Richard Simpson**—signed X, confirmed in Simpson to Acton, Oct. 4, 1859, Acton-Simpson Corres.).

Questions and answers, 105–109, by **J. H. Newman**—signed H.I.; see Simpson to Newman, May 1, 1859, Newman MSS., where he refers to your question about laymen studying theology (see no. 998).

The prospect of war, 109–113, by **J. H. Newman,** prob.—signed J.O., see no. 996 and Newman, *L&D*, XIX, 527n., repr. ibid., pp. 534–538 (letter, vol. 25, pp. 83–86, by **T. F. Wetherell**—signed Sigma, Gasquet, p. 83).

992 Literary notices, 114–116.

993 Contemporary events, 117–144. **J. H. Newman.** *Life*, I, 635.

VOLUME 24 O.S., 1 3RD S., JULY 1859

994 The Text of the Rheims and Douay version of Holy Scripture, 145–169. **J. H. Newman.** Repr. *Tracts Theological and Ecclesiastical*, 1874.

995 The Mission of the Isles of the North (Part II), 170–185. **J. H. Newman.** Cf. no. 986.

996 Thoughts on the causes of the present war (communicated), 186–198. **T. F. Wetherell.** Signed Sigma; Newman *L&D*, XIX, 153. (Letters, pp. 378–379, by **J. H. Newman**—signed J.O., Simpson notebook, Gasquet, p. 79; vol. 25, pp. 83–86, by **Wetherell**—signed Sigma, Gasquet, p. 83.)

997 On consulting the faithful in matters of doctrine (communicated), 198–230. **J. H. Newman.** Signed O.; Newman, *L&D*, XIX, 152; partly repr. in 3rd ed. of *Arians of the 4th Century* (1871). (Letter, pp. 390–391, by **Richard Simp-**

son—signed P.S., Newman, *L&D*, XIX, 185.)

998   In Correspondence: Lay students in theology, 238–241, by **J. H. Newman**—signed H.; in the *Rambler* he used one or another of his initials and O. [for Oratory], either singly or in various combinations; this letter, which answers his own question in no. 991, p. 109, is largely a quotation from his *Idea of a University*, Part II, chap. iv; Richard Simpson to Newman, May 19, 1859, Newman MSS., sends him a quotation from Victor de Buck, which is incorporated in the last paragraph, p. 241.

Designs and prospects of Russia, 244–247, by **J. H. Newman**—signed H.H.; see comment immediately above on Newman's use of his initials.

999   Literary notices, 247–250, by **J. D. Acton**, prob.—Gasquet, p. 70.

1000   Contemporary events, 251–288. Pages 251–258 by **J. H. Newman**, prob.—cf. no. 993; see Newman, *L&D*, XIX, 152, n.3, 153, n.2, 168; pages 258–277 by **J. D. Acton**—Gasquet, p. 70.

VOLUME 24 O.S., 1 3RD S., SEPTEMBER 1859

1001   The political system of the Bonapartes, 289–332. **Ferdinand d'Eckstein.** Simpson notebook; Acton to Newman, Aug. 15, 1859, Newman MSS., lists this art. for Sept.; Gasquet, p. 74n. Translated by **Richard Simpson**—Gasquet, p. 74.

1002   The theory of party, 332–352. **Richard Simpson.** Simpson notebook; Newman, *L&D*, XIX, 163; Acton to Newman, cited for no. 1001 says Simpson is rewriting this art.

1003   Rosmini and Gioberti (communicated), 353–370. **Charles Meynell.** Signed M.; Simpson notebook; Acton to Newman, cited for no. 1001, lists Meynell on Rosmini; Newman, *L&D*, XIX, 163. (Letters, vol. 25, pp. 97–98, by **Antonius Giunchi**—signed G., original of this letter in Italian, signed D. A. Giunchi, is in Westminster Diocesan Archives; pp. 232–236, by **Meynell**—signed M.; pp. 386–388, by **Giunchi**—signed A.G.)

1004   The captive's keepsake (communicated), 371–377. **Richard Simpson.** Signed R.S.; Simpson notebook; Acton to Newman, cited for no. 1001, is expecting a 2nd art. from Simpson, a short one; Gasquet, p. 77n.

1005   Notices, 391–396. Page 395 (Lamy), by **John Brande Morris**—Acton to Newman, cited for no. 1001, says he has accepted Morris's short notice, Simpson notebook gives "J.B.M. 1 page"; pages 391–395, 396, by **J. H. Newman**—Simpson notebook gives "Newman 4½ pp.," Newman, *L&D*, XIX, 198.

1006   Contemporary events, 397–432. **J. D. Acton.** Simpson notebook; Conzemius, I, 160; heavily revised by **Richard Simpson**—Gasquet, pp. 76n., 78n., 80.

VOLUME 25 O.S., 2 3RD S., NOVEMBER 1859

1007   The symbolism of the catacombs, 1–17. **J. S. Northcote.** Simpson notebook gives "?Northcote"; Gasquet, p. 83n., 92n.

1008   The forms of intuition (Part I), 18–41. **Richard Simpson.** Simpson notebook; Gasquet, pp. 88n., 116n.

1009   The ancient saints (Part II): St. John Chrysostom: the separation (communicated), 41–62. **J. H. Newman.** Evidence for no. 990.

1010   Mill, *On Liberty* (Part I) (communicated), 62–75. **Thomas Arnold**, 1823–1900. Signed A.; Simpson notebook; Gasquet, pp. 81, 83.

1011   Dr. Lingard's alleged cardinalate (communicated), 75–83. **Richard Simpson.** Signed Z; Simpson notebook; Gasquet, pp. 77, 112; claimed Simpson to Acton, Oct. 11, 1859, Acton-Simpson Corres.

1012   In correspondence: Palmerston on architecture, 86–90, by **Frederick Capes**, prob.—signed F.C.; though Simpson notebook gives "?Simpson," the attribution to Capes is confirmed in Simpson to Acton, Oct. 4, 1859, Acton-Simpson Corres.

Episcopal See of St. Martin, Canterbury, 98–104, by **Victor de Buck**—signed Y.Z., see Gasquet, p. 105, where Acton is shown to provide the "note to F. de Buck's letter," which appears here on p. 100.

1013   Literary notices, 104–110. Pages 104–107, by **J. D. Acton**—Gasquet, p. 81n., largely repr. *Essays on Church and State* (pp. 420–422); pp. 107–110, by **Richard Simpson**—Simpson to Acton, Oct. 11, 1859, Acton-Simpson Corres., says he can do Miller's geology.

1014   Contemporary events, 111–136. **Richard Simpson**, prob. Gasquet, pp. 89, 96, 108; Simpson to Acton Oct. 4, 1859,

Acton-Simpson Corres., describes his plans for this section.

VOLUME 25 O.S., 2 3RD S., JANUARY 1860

1015   The Roman question, 137–154. **J. D. Acton** and **Richard Simpson.** Simpson notebook gives "Simpson—substantially Acton."

1016   The political system of the Popes (Part I), 154–165. **Konstantin von Höfler.** Simpson notebook; cf. nos. 1035, 1072; repr. Acton, *Essays on Church and State.* Edited by **J. D. Acton** —cf. no. 1035.

1017   The forms of intuition (Part II), 166–186. **Richard Simpson.** Cf. no. 1008.

1018   A few words on philology (communicated), 186–199. **Richard Simpson.** Signed W.; Simpson to Acton, Dec. 7, 1859, Acton-Simpson Corres., says his collections in philology to be used if necessary; Simpson notebook gives "Wetherell," but this is crossed out, and "no" written in, and in another hand, "I think by Simpson," added.

1019   On the signs of martyrdom in the catacombs (communicated), 199–214. **George M. Conroy,** prob. Signed C. as are nos. 1027 and 1039; no. 1027 attr. simply to "Conroy" by Gasquet, pp. 115 and 120; for this art. Simpson notebook gives "C.," but for nos. 1027 and 1039, closely linked in subject, gives "Conroy"; man cited was prof. of theology, All Hallow's Coll., Dublin (Boase); Gasquet, p. 134n., attrs. the art. to Northcote, but Northcote attacked it in the letter on p. 386 and in no. 1047. (Letters, p. 386, by **J. S. Northcote**—signed J.S.N.; vol. 26, p. 114, by **Victor de Buck,** prob.— signed J.P., Conzemius, I, 175n., although Acton's actual wording, to which Conzemius's note refers, is ambiguous, see Gasquet, pp. 120, 128; pp. 222–223, by **J. D. Acton?** or **Richard Simpson?**—signed Ed., Gasquet, p. 128; pp. 253–260, by **John Morris,** 1826–1893, prob.—signed J.M., see Gasquet, p. 134, man cited was secretary to Cardinal Wiseman, and the present writer would seem to be speaking for the establishment.)

1020   A plea for bores (communicated), 214–226. **Richard Simpson.** Signed Rude Boreas; Simpson notebook; Gasquet, pp. 106–107.

1021   In Correspondence: Volunteers and recruits, 226–229, by **T. F. Wetherell,**

prob.—signed X, see Gasquet, pp. 109–110; The temporal power, 230–232, by **J. D. Acton**—signed C.C., attr. in Gasquet, p. 113n.; The theory of party, 237–243, by **August Reichensperger**—signed A. Reichensperger, with a note identifying him by **J. D. Acton**—signed Ed.

1022   Literary notice, 244–246. **Richard Simpson.** Capes to Simpson, Jan. 16, 1860 [mistakenly dated 1859], Simpson notebook, refers to "your" notice of Rawlinson.

1023   Contemporary events, 247–280. **J. D. Acton, Richard Simpson,** prob., and **T. F. Wetherell?** Minnesota file gives "Acton," but see Gasquet, pp. 91, 96, 109–110; see Newman, *L&D,* XIX, 209.

VOLUME 25 O.S., 2 3RD S., MARCH 1860

1024   The hopes of Ireland, 281–291. **John O'Hagan.** Simpson notebook; O'Hagan to Acton, Oct. 15, 1859, and Feb. 2, 1860, Woodruff Collection, show he wrote this art.; Gasquet, p. 85, 120.

1025   The states of the Church, 291–323. **J. D. Acton.** Simpson notebook; repr. *Essays on Church and State.*

1026   Forms of intuition (Part III), 324–343. **Richard Simpson.** Cf. no. 1008.

1027   The Church in the ancient symbols (Part I) (communicated), 343–361. **George Conroy,** prob. Signed C; Simpson notebook and Gasquet, pp. 115, 120, give only "Conroy." (See no. 1019.)

1028   Darwin, *On the Origin of Species* (communicated), 361–376. **Richard Simpson.** Signed R.S.; Simpson notebook; Northcote list; attr. by Lady Blennerhasset, *Edinburgh Review,* 197 (Apr. 1903), 504–505.

1029   Mill, *On Liberty* (Part II) (communicated), 376–385. **Thomas Arnold,** 1823–1900. Evidence for no. 1010.

1030   Correspondence: Belgian politics, 388–393, by **Victor de Buck**—signed Y.Z., the author is a Belgian (see p. 388), Minnesota file, and Gasquet, p. 120.

1031   Literary notices, 393–398. Pages 396–398 by **J. D. Acton**—Gasquet, p. 131; pages 393–396 by **Richard Simpson**—Northcote list, Simpson to Acton, Tuesday night [c. Dec. 20, 1859], Acton-Simpson Corres., says he has set to work on "Bacon"; p. 398 by **Simpson?**—Minnesota file.

1032   Contemporary events, 399–422. **Rich-**

ard Simpson, with assistance from **J. D. Acton.** Minnesota file; Gasquet, p. 119. (Letter, vol. 26, pp. 115–119, by **Simpson**—signed R.S., Simpson notebook, Gasquet, p. 126n.)

VOLUME 26 O.S., 3 3RD S., MAY 1860

1033   The Catholic University of Ireland, 1–10. **Thomas Arnold,** 1823–1900. Simpson notebook; Gasquet, pp. 122, 124; Conzemius, I, 175.
1034   Reform, 10–26. **Richard Simpson.** Simpson notebook; Gasquet, p. 122.
1035   The political system of the Popes (Part II), 27–38. **Konstantin von Höfler.** Acton to Simpson, Feb. 24, 1860, Acton-Simpson Corres., says he has not been able yet to go through more than one sheet of Höfler; and on Mar. 6 he refers to "Höfler on the Roman states-system"; Simpson notebook gives "Hoefler" with a faint "Acton" below [Höfler's art. which was sent through Acton?]. Edited by **J. D. Acton**—see first letter cited above, and cf. Simpson's role in no. 1072.
1036   Sir Walter Scott, 39–67. **Thomas Arnold,** 1823–1900. Simpson notebook; Gasquet, pp. 122, 124.
1037   The Church and science (Part I; no more published): the exact sciences (communicated), 68–83. **Ferdinand d'Eckstein.** Signed Le Baron d'Eckstein; Gasquet, p. 122; Simpson notebook gives "Simpson?," so it was prob. revised by Simpson in his editorial capacity.
1038   The limits of our thought (communicated), 83–106. **Charles Meynell.** Signed M.; Simpson notebook; Newman, *L&D,* XIX, 334.
1039   The Church in the ancient symbols (Part II) (communicated), 106–113. **George Conroy.** Evidence for no. 1027.
1040   In Correspondence: Russia, 119–123, signed W.—unidentified, possibly by J. Wassilieff, as the author is Russian and Wassilieff was the chaplain of Russian embassy at Paris, who is praised in no. 1059, p. 389, and may have sent this in by means of Victor de Buck, Conzemius, I, 175n., suggests this may have been by Ivan Gagarin, also a Russian, and also in France at this time; Belgium, 123–126, by **Victor de Buck**—signed Y.Z.; Conzemius, I, 175.
1041   Literary notice, 127–128. **Richard Simpson.** Minnesota file; Gasquet, pp. 123–124.
1042   Current events, 128–144. **Richard**

Simpson, with assistance from **J. D. Acton.** Gasquet, p. 123.

VOLUME 26 O.S., 3 3RD S., JULY 1860

1043   The House of Lords, 145–157. **Richard Simpson.** Simpson notebook; Gasquet, pp. 134, 135.
1044   Hefele's *Life of Ximenes,* 158–170. **J. D. Acton.** Simpson notebook; repr. *Essays on Church and State.*
1045   The negro race and its destiny (Part I), 170–189. **Thomas Arnold,** 1823–1900. Simpson notebook; Minnesota file; Gasquet, p. 137n.
1046   The ancient saints (Part III): St. Chrysostom—the exile (communicated), 189–203. **J. H. Newman.** Evidence for no. 990.
1047   On the signs of martyrdom in the catacombs (communicated), 203–222. **J. S. Northcote.** Signed J.S.N.; Simpson notebook; Gasquet, p. 134n.
1048   The philosopher's stone (communicated), 223–233. **Richard Simpson.** Simpson notebook; Gasquet, pp. 132n., 137n.
1049   A true report of the life and martyrdom of Mr. Richard White, schoolmaster (Part I) (communicated), 233–248. A sixteenth-century MS. edited by **Richard Simpson.** Repr. *Under the Penal Laws,* 1930.
1050   In Correspondence: Catholic education, 248–253, by **H. N. Oxenham**—signed X.Y.Z., Gasquet, p. 128n., Newman, *Life,* I, 512 (letters, pp. 398–401, by **J. H. Newman**—signed H.O., *Life,* I, 513, Gasquet, p. 148n.; pp. 401–408, by **Frederick Oakeley**—signed F., Simpson notebook, Gasquet, p. 148n.; vol. 27, pp. 100–117, by **H. N. Oxenham**—signed X.Y.Z., Newman, *Life,* I, 514, Gasquet, p. 150n.; pp. 237–273, by **W. G. Ward**—signed W.G.W., see no. 1076; p. 392, by **H. N. Oxenham**—signed X.Y.Z., Gasquet, p. 170n.; pp. 392–396, by **J. D. Acton** and **Richard Simpson,** prob.—signed S.A.B.S., see Gasquet, pp. 161–162, 165–170; pp. 396–410, by **Frederick Oakeley**—signed F., see Gasquet, p. 170; pp. 410–421, by **Richard Simpson**—signed Derlax, Gasquet, p. 171n.; vol. 28, pp. 100–117, by **W. G. Ward**—signed W.G.W.; pp. 118–122, by **Richard Simpson**—signed Derlax; pp. 122–124 correspondence between **Frederick Oakeley** and **H. N. Oxenham**—signed F. and X.Y.Z.

respectively; pp. 124–125, by **John Maguire**—signed P.Q.R., Simpson to Acton, Tuesday night [Mar. 15, 1861], Acton-Simpson Corres., says Maguire has had 17 years' experience as a professor: cf. art. p. 125).

1051 Literary notices, 260–264. Pages 262–264 by **J. D. Acton**—Hoselitz, p. 383.

1052 Current events, 265–288. **J. D. Acton,** prob. See Gasquet, p. 139.

VOLUME 26 O.S., 3 3RD S., SEPTEMBER 1860

1053 National defence, 289–300. **J. D. Acton.** Simpson notebook; Gasquet, pp. 128, 149; extracts repr. *Essays on Church and State.*

1054 The Prison Discipline Act, 300–317. **Edward Ryley.** Simpson notebook, and Gasquet, pp. 130, 143, 144, give "Ryley"; for man cited see Boase.

1055 The negro race and its destiny (Part II, concl.), 317–337. **Thomas Arnold,** 1823–1900. Cf. no. 1045.

1056 The ancient saints (Part IV, concl.): St. Chrysostom—the death (communicated), 338–357. **J. H. Newman.** Evidence for no. 990.

1057 The spirit-rappers (communicated), 357–365. **Richard Simpson.** Simpson notebook; Gasquet, p. 148n.

1058 A true report of the life and martyrdom of Richard White, schoolmaster (Part II, concl.) (communicated), 366–388. Edited by **Richard Simpson.** Cf. no. 1049.

1059 In Correspondence: The Russian Church, 388–398 by **Victor de Buck**—signed Y.Z., Newman, *L&D*, XIX, 396, Simpson notebook gives "a correspondent from Vienna"; Translated by **Richard Simpson**—Newman, *L&D*, ibid.

1060 Literary notices, 409–410.

1061 Current events, 411–432. Pages 418–419 by **J. D. Acton**—Gasquet, p. 149, attr. *Essays on Church and State,* p. 454; pages 419–432 by **Richard Simpson** and **J. D. Acton**—Gasquet, pp. 146, 148, 149.

VOLUME 27 O.S., 4 3RD S., NOVEMBER 1860

1062 The Roman question, 1–27. **Richard Simpson.** Simpson notebook; Gasquet, pp. 140, 144, 147, 150.

1063 The Poor-Law Amendment Act, 28–54. **Edward Ryley.** Simpson notebook; Gasquet, pp. 137n.

1064 Elementary school books, 54–66. **S. N. Stokes.** Minnesota file gives Stokes; for man cited see Boase.

1065 Mr. Kingsley (communicated), 66–80. **Florence M. Bastard.** Signed F.; Simpson notebook; attr. in Newman, *L&D*, XIX, 396; for woman cited see Newman, *L&D*, XVI, 335.

1066 George Eliot's novels (communicated), 80–100. **H. N. Oxenham.** Signed O.M.; Simpson notebook; Gasquet, p. 151n.

1067 In Correspondence: Our most noble selves, 117–120, by **Frederick Oakeley**—signed One Who Has Suffered, Simpson to Acton, Dec. 3, 1860, Acton-Simpson Corres., says Oakeley wrote this; The Austrian Empire, 121–124, by **Ludwig von Meyer**—signed M.v.L., Simpson notebook, Gasquet, p. 150.

1068 Literary notices, 125–128. Pages 126–128 by **Richard Simpson**, with revisions by **J. D. Acton**—Minnesota file gives "Simpson"; Hoselitz, p. 383, gives "Acton"; see Gasquet, p. 149.

1069 Current events, 129–144. Pages 129–133 by **T. F. Wetherell**, prob.—Gasquet, p. 151.

VOLUME 27 O.S., 4 3RD S., JANUARY 1861

1070 Döllinger's *History of Christianity,* 145–175. **J. D. Acton.** Simpson notebook; Gasquet, pp. 151, 152; partly repr. *Essays on Church and State.*

1071 The Grand Remonstrance, 176–183. **Richard Simpson.** Simpson notebook; Gasquet, pp. 153n., 162n.

1072 The political system of the Popes (Part III, concl.), 183–193. **Konstantin von Höfler.** Acton to Simpson, Aug. 27, 1860, Acton-Simpson Corres., says there will be another art. from Höfler, finishing the mediaeval popes; Simpson to Acton, Dec. 3, 1860, ibid., says he is engaged in rewriting Höfler. Edited by **Richard Simpson**—letter just cited.

1073 Notes on the present state of Austria (communicated), 193–205. **J. D. Acton, Ludwig von Meyer,** and **Richard Simpson.** Signed A.; repr. Acton, *Essays on Church and State*; Conzemius, I, 188; Simpson notebook gives "L. V. Meyer? chiefly Acton; final arrangement by Simpson."

1074 Preaching and public speaking (communicated), 205–216. **Frederick Oakeley.** Signed F.; Simpson to Acton, Dec. 3,

1860, Acton-Simpson Corres., says Oakeley has sent art. on preaching.

1075 Edmund Campion (Part I) (communicated), 216–237. **Richard Simpson.** Signed R.S.; repr. *Edward Campion, A Biography*, 1867.

1076 Correspondence: Catholic education, 237–273. **W. G. Ward.** Signed W.G.W.; Gasquet, pp. 152–153, 165n., 168, 169; see no. 1050.

1077 Current events, 274–286. Pages 275–276 by **T. F. Wetherell**—J. D. Acton to Richard Simpson, 1861, Acton-Simpson Corres., says Wetherell has sent one page on home affairs and promises New Zealand.

VOLUME 27 O.S., 4 3RD S., MARCH 1861

1078 The Neo-Protestantism of Oxford, 287–314. **H. N. Oxenham.** Simpson notebook; attr. in Newman, *L&D*, XIX, 472.

1079 The administration of charitable trusts, 314–332. **S. N. Stokes.** Attr. in Newman, *L&D*, XIX, 472.

1080 The Irish Church, 332–348. **Thomas Arnold**, 1823–1900. Attr. Newman, *L&D*, XIX, 472, where Acton adds "much revised" by himself; Conzemius, I, 195.

1081 Women, politics and patriotism (communicated), 349–362. **Florence M. Bastard.** Signed F.H.; attr. Newman, *L&D*, XIX, 472, where Acton adds that her initials are misprinted.

1082 Edmund Campion (Part II) (communicated), 362–391. **Richard Simpson.** Evidence for no. 1075.

1083 Current events, 422–432. **J. D. Acton.** Conzemius, I, 195.

VOLUME 28 O.S., 5 3RD S., MAY 1861

1084 Catholic policy, 1–17. **William Monsell.** Conzemius, I, 206; see Gasquet, p. 146.

1085 Political causes of the American Revolution, 17–61. **J. D. Acton.** Gasquet, pp. 171, 181; repr. *Essays on Church and State*.

1086 Dr. Ward's philosophy, 61–80. **Richard Simpson.** Simpson notebook; Gasquet, pp. 171, 176–177, 181. (Letter, pp. 269–272, by **Simpson**—signed The Reviewer of Dr. Ward's Philosophy.)

1087 Edmund Campion (Part III) (communicated), 80–100. **Richard Simpson.** Evidence for no. 1075. (Letter, vol. 29, pp. 124–129, by **Richard Simpson**—

signed The Writer of the "Life of Edmund Campion.")

1088 Current events, 126–140. Pages 126–132 by **J. D. Acton** and **Richard Simpson**, prob.—Gasquet, p. 182; pages 132–140 by **J. D. Acton**—Gasquet, pp. 182, 187.

VOLUME 28 O.S., 5 3RD S., JULY 1861

1089 Cavour, 141–165. **J. D. Acton.** Claimed in Newman, *L&D*, XIX, 522; repr. *Historical Essays and Studies*.

1090 Reason and faith (Part I), 166–190. **Richard Simpson.** Acknowledged by Simpson, *Bishop Ullathorne and The Rambler*, 1862: see *BMCat*.

1091 Expectation of the French Revolution, 190–213. **J. D. Acton.** Claimed in Conzemius, I, 216.

1092 Religion and civilisation [on Buckle's *History of Civilisation in England*, Vol. II], 213–227. **Richard Simpson?** Minnesota file; see Newman, *L&D*, XIX, 522, which may imply that the art. was by Simpson, "tamed" by J. D. Acton.

1093 Religious novels (communicated), 227–235. **H. N. Oxenham.** Signed H. A.; Minnesota file; Oxenham to Acton, May 26, 1861, Woodruff Collection, sends his "religious novels."

1094 Edmund Campion (Part IV) (communicated), 235–259. **Richard Simpson.** Evidence for no. 1075.

1095 In Correspondence: The Roman question, 259–268, two letters, the first by Father **Caccia**—signed ***, Gasquet, p. 190, Conzemius, I, 216, where Acton is quoted as saying that Caccia was a Rosminian (see here, p. 262); the second signed P.—identified by Acton as a Bolognese priest, Conzemius, ibid.; intro. letter signed J.R., and editorial note, 259–260, by **J. D. Acton**—signed Ed.; Ecclesiastical decisions, 268–269, signed B.

1096 Literary notices, 272–277.

1097 Current events, 277–290. Pages 277–286, by **J. D. Acton**—Conzemius, I, 216n.; pages 286–290, by **Richard Simpson**, prob.—Gasquet, p. 191.

VOLUME 28 O.S., 5 3RD S., SEPTEMBER 1861

1098 The Catholic Academy, 291–302. **J. D. Acton.** Simpson notebook; repr. *Essays on Church and State*. (Letters, vol. 28, pp. 387–391, by **Richard Simpson**—signed D.N., Simpson to Acton, Feb.[?],

1862, Acton-Simpson Corres., in listing contents for Mar., refers to "my old letter" in print 4 pages; pp. 526–534, by **J. D. Acton**—signed N.N., Simpson notebook, Gasquet, p. 269; the use of D.N. here by Simpson, as well as N.N. by Acton, is confirmed in Simpson to Acton, Apr. 29, 1862, Acton-Simpson Corres., where he says, "By the bye, talking of d--ning ---- D.N. to N.N. greetings.")

1099   *The Life of Dr. Doyle* (Part I), 302–326. **Aubrey de Vere.** De Vere's list; Simpson notebook; Gasquet, p. 191; for Acton's editing of this art. see Gasquet, p. 195 and Conzemius, I, 220n.

1100   Reason and faith (Part III, concl.), 326–346. **Richard Simpson.** Cf. no. 1090.

1101   English public schools and colleges in Catholic times (communicated), 346–360. **Frederick Oakeley.** Signed A.M.D.G. [prob. Ad Majorum Dei Gloriam]; attr. in Newman, *L&D*, XX, 35. (Letter, vol. 29, pp. 119–124, by **J. D. Acton?**—signed A., Hoselitz, Gasquet, p. 235, refers to a letter from H. N. Oxenham for this issue, but Oxenham to Acton, Dec. 31, 1861, Woodruff Collection, complains that his letter on public schools was omitted.)

1102   Aubrey de Vere's *Poems* (communicated), 360–372. Signed: T.C.; see Gasquet, pp. 191 and 220; in the second reference Acton speaks of "our Irish historical contributor" and this art. is primarily on Irish history.

1103   Edmund Campion (Part V) (communicated), 372–393. **Richard Simpson.** Evidence for no. 1075.

1104   In Correspondence: The Pugin testimonial, 393–394, by **H. N. Oxenham**—signed Justitia, Oxenham to Acton, Aug. 5, 1861, Woodruff Collection, sends a letter on Pugin testimonial, Newman, *L&D*, XX, 35; Recollections of Pugin, 394–402, by **Richard Simpson**—signed S., author speaks of being in Rome in 1847 as was Simpson, Simpson journal for May 3, 1847, Simpson notebook, says he visited many churches with Pugin at end of April.

1105   Literary notices, 402–406. Pages 403–406 by **J. D. Acton**—largely repr. *Essays on Church and State*, pp. 459–463.

1106   Current events, 407–432. **J. D. Acton.** Conzemius, I, 217, 221.

VOLUME 29 O.S., 6 3RD S., NOVEMBER 1861

1107   Döllinger on the temporal power, 1–62. **J. D. Acton.** Simpson notebook; repr. *History of Freedom.*

1108   The Education Commission, 62–85. **S. N. Stokes.** Simpson notebook gives "Stokes?"; T. F. Wetherell to Richard Simpson, Oct. 26, 1861, Simpson notebook, refers to an art. by Stokes for this issue; see Gasquet, p. 220. (Note, p. 146, by **J. D. Acton,** the editor, explaining that the art. should have been marked "Communicated"; see nos. 1115 and 1122.)

1109   *The Life of Dr. Doyle* (Part II, concl.), 85–106. **Aubrey de Vere.** Cf. no. 1099.

1110   Dr. Manning on the papal sovereignty (communicated), 106–119. **Richard Simpson.** Signed P.; Simpson notebook; Gasquet, p. 211–214, 221.

1111   Literary notice, 129–130. **Richard Simpson.** Minnesota file.

1112   Current events, 131–146. **Richard Simpson.** Minnesota file; Simpson to Acton, Oct. 20, 1861, Acton-Simpson Corres., says he will analyse Passaglia; see Gasquet, p. 206.

1113   Notice to readers and correspondents [explanation of change of *Rambler's* publishers], 147–148. **J. D. Acton, Richard Simpson,** and **T. F. Wetherell.** Gasquet, pp. 203n., 207–209, 216–217.

VOLUME 29 O.S., 6 3RD S., JANUARY 1862

1114   Tocqueville's *Remains,* 149–172. **Richard Simpson.** Simpson notebook; Gasquet, pp. 219, 226–229, 235; Conzemius, I, 249.

1115   The Commission on Education and the revised code, 172–190. **S. N. Stokes.** Simpson notebook gives "Stokes?"; Gasquet, pp. 220, 237, 242.

1116   Mr. Goldwin Smith's *Irish History,* 190–220. **J. D. Acton.** Claimed in Conzemius, I, 248; repr. *History of Freedom.* In the Simpson notebook, "Acton" appears to be written over "Oxenham" (see Gasquet, p. 181), which prob. refers to a notice of Smith by Oxenham that was not used.

1117   Rio on Christian art (communicated), 220–234. **Florence M. Bastard.** Signed F.H.; Simpson notebook; Gasquet, pp. 198, 224.

1118   Edmund Campion (Part VI) (communicated), 234–250. **Richard Simpson.** Evidence for no. 1075.

1119   Correspondence: The Oaths [required to hold office], 250–265. **T. L. Green.** Signed T.L.G.; Simpson notebook; Gasquet, pp. 198n., 247.

1120 Literary notices, 265–276. Pages 268–271 by **J. M. Capes**—Capes to Simpson, Nov. 28, 1861, and Jan. 22, 1862, Simpson notebook, refer to his notices of Brown and Forbes; pages 271–276 by **J. M. Capes, Richard Simpson,** and **J. D. Acton**—Capes to Simpson of Jan. 22, 1862, Simpson notebook, refers to his "Wolff" and "Dickens," but complains that Simpson really rewrote both notices, Acton to Simpson [Dec. 8, 1861], in Gasquet, pp. 241–242, shows that the former supplied the ideas on Dickens which Simpson used in his revision of Capes's notice; pages 265–267 by **D. C. Lathbury,** prob., heavily revised by **Simpson,** following detailed suggestions by **Acton** (see Gasquet, pp. 248–251).

1121 Current events, 277–292. **J. D. Acton.** Gasquet, p. 247; Minnesota file.

VOLUME 29 o.s., 6 3RD s., MARCH 1862

1122 The revised educational code, 293–300. **S. N. Stokes.** Simpson notebook. (See nos. 1108 and 1115.)

1123 Moral law and political legislation, 301–318. **Richard Simpson.** Simpson notebook; Gasquet, pp. 253–256, 258.

1124 The Protestant theory of persecution, 318–351. **J. D. Acton.** H. N. Oxenham to Acton, Feb. 16 or 19, 1862, Woodruff Collection, says "I hear you have written . . . in defense of persecution"; Conzemius, I, 240; repr. *History of Freedom.*

1125 Marshall on Christian missions (communicated), 352–366. **Richard Simpson,** prob. Although the art. is signed W., letters from Acton to Simpson [Jan. 13, 1862] and Thursday [Jan. 23, 1862], Acton-Simpson Corres., strongly indicate Simpson's authorship; attr. to Simpson in Northcote list; the signature W. suggests that Simpson got material from either Charles or Frederick Weld, the latter of whom had travelled much in the East: see *DNB.*

1126 Edmund Campion (Part VII) (communicated), 366–386. **Richard Simpson.** Evidence for no. 1075.

1127 In Correspondence: Colonies, 391–400, by **J. D. Acton**—signed C.C., initials used by Acton for no. 1021, see Gasquet, pp. 278–280, where Acton

outlines some of the ideas expressed here, Simpson to Acton, Thursday night [1862], Acton-Simpson Corres., says "your" letter will be 10 pages; Delation, 401–404, by **Victor de Buck,** prob.—signed V.P.; he was himself a victim of delation.

1128 Literary notices, 404–413. Pages 404–408 by **J. D. Acton,** prob.—extract repr. *Essays on Church and State,* pp. 456–457; pages 410–412 by **Richard Simpson** —Gasquet, pp. 237, 239.

1129 Current events, 414–428. Pages 417–418 by **Richard Simpson,** prob.—see Gasquet, p. 246.

VOLUME 29 o.s., 6 3RD s., MAY 1862

1130 Enlargement of the *Rambler,* 429–431. **J. D. Acton, Richard Simpson,** and **T. F. Wetherell.** Editorial; Gasquet, p. lix; Simpson notebook gives "Wetherell" only.

1131 The individual, the corporation and the state, 432–451. **Richard Simpson.** Simpson notebook; Wetherell to Simpson, Thursday, n.y., Simpson notebook, says to avoid a given expression in any other art. than the corporation one to prevent sameness.

1132 Dante's philosophy of love, 451–464. **Richard Simpson.** Simpson notebook; see Gasquet, p. 280; Acton to Simpson, Feb. 6, 1862, Acton-Simpson Corres., says he will send materials on Dante.

1133 Dr. Ward on intellect (communicated), 465–494. **J. W. Roberts.** Signed O.S.F.; *DR* no. 1222, p. 231 and *BMCat.*

1134 Galileo and Mendelssohn (communicated), 494–504. **Richard Simpson.** Signed G.P.; Simpson notebook; T. F. Wetherell to Simpson, Thursday, n.y., Simpson notebook, sends back Simpson's "Mendelssohn" with suggestions.

1135 Edmund Campion (Part VIII, concl.) (communicated), 504–526. **Richard Simpson.** Evidence for no. 1075.

1136 Literary notices, 534–538. Pages 536–538 by **Florence M. Bastard,** prob.—Wetherell to Simpson, ibid., says he is sending Mrs. B's notices; pages 534–536 by **Richard Simpson**—T. F. Wetherell to Simpson, Thurs., n.y., Simpson notebook, refers to your Dalhousie art.

1137 Current events, 538–572. Pages 546–572 by **J. D. Acton**—Gasquet, p. 269.

The Scottish Review, 1882–1900

WITH THE DEMISE of the *North British Review* in 1871 there was no periodical whose main concern was Scottish affairs, if indeed the late review could have been so described. And although Scotland possessed two influential newspapers, the *Glasgow Herald* and the *Scotsman*, no monthly or quarterly was engaged in the fight for Scottish Home Rule and other liberal-national measures.[1] To correct this situation, two men living in Paisley, both intensely Scottish, determined in 1882 to found a new quarterly in order to "protest against the idea that London is the center of Scottish life, as also against the idea that Scotland is not strong enough to have a literary organ of its own." The Reverend W. M. Metcalfe, a minister of the Established Church of Scotland, was "the originator and editor" of the *Scottish Review*.[2] His collaborator was the Paisley publisher whose name was associated with so many Scottish literary revivals, Alexander Gardner.[3] Gardner described the venture as one in which he was to take the pecuniary risk and Metcalfe was to do the editing, though in point of fact this division of labor was never precisely adhered to.[4]

The journal's first appearance in November 1882 was decently noticed by the important periodicals. Noting the liberal intention "to be the medium for the unfettered expression of opinions on all subjects," the *Spectator* went on to say, "The *Scottish Review* has made a modest and solid rather than a bold and brilliant beginning, a fact which shows the wisdom of the editor."[5] Its critics especially hailed the section of summaries of foreign reviews as an innovation.[6] These summaries, along

---

[1]As G. S. Pryde, *Scotland from 1603 to the Present Day* (1962), p. 216, pointed out, even these newspapers went over to the Liberal Unionist party after the Gladstone Home Rule defeat of 1886.

[2]The *Scots Magazine*, n.s. 4 (1888/89), 158. The previous quotation is from a letter of Metcalfe's to Lord Bute, Oct. 2, 1887, Bute papers.

[3]*Academy*, Nov. 25, 1882, p. 381.

[4]Gardner to Bute, July 5, 1886, Bute papers, makes this point. However, it is clear from Gardner's earlier letters to Lord Bute that he himself did much of the editorial work involving correspondence with authors and selection of articles. This was probably especially true with those authors whose books he published, and from whom he might naturally solicit articles.

[5]*Spectator*, Nov. 25, 1882, p. 1516. Locally, the *Glasgow Herald*, Nov. 27, 1882, glowingly reported, "The first number of the *Scottish Review* is so decidedly a success that it at once places the publication on a level of equality with the high-class quarterly reviews already in the field," whereas the *Scotsman* for Dec. 12, 1882, in placing the Review next to the "heavy dragoons of critical literature," wondered (with good cause) whether the public was disposed to buy more in this already crowded field, and wished for a lighter and cheaper production.

[6]*Academy*, cited in n. 3.

with the lengthy sections of book notices, assumed a position of importance through-out the life of the Review, and Metcalfe complained that "on this matter of summaries we have been subject almost from the beginning to something like wholesale theft. The first to steal the idea from us was that eminently religious quarterly, the *London R*. . . . A secular paper has this week stolen a whole column from us."[7] The journals chosen for inclusion in the summaries were from every major country on the contin-ent including Greece and Spain, and went as far afield as America and Iceland.

The collaboration of Gardner and Metcalfe lasted four years; financial necessity then forced a change of ownership. The pecuniary loss to Gardner had amounted to some £1000 by 1886, a sum too great for a small and struggling Scottish publisher to absorb.[8] In the fall of 1886 the journal was purchased by J. P. Crichton-Stuart, the third Marquess of Bute, who had been a contributor since the first issue and whose critical advice had always been sought by Gardner.[9] It was to provide him for the rest of his life with an outlet for his literary excursions as well as a voice for those programs which he supported. Lord Bute was a giant of the Scottish peerage, and munificent in the type of philanthropy practiced in the nineteenth century, for he was the possessor of a purse vast enough to erect great university and ecclesiastical buildings. He was also a Protestant who had been converted to Catholicism in the face of tremendous adverse pressure and with notorious publicity.[10] Although edu-cated at Oxford, his interest in Scottish education was extremely strong, and his own scholarly researches went deep into Scottish church history and antiquities in general.

In commending the Review to Lord Bute, Gardner hoped that the new proprietor would continue the policy of allowing two sides of a question to be heard, and he strongly recommended the retention of Mr. Metcalfe, "who has done the general work all this time without any recompense beyond the hope that he was helping to establish a national quarterly which might ultimately yield a reward."[11] He also recommended that the work be divided as it had been between Metcalfe and himself, with Metcalfe continuing to solicit and examine the articles and set up the notices and summaries of foreign reviews in print, and then sending all this material with his recommendations to Lord Bute, who would make the final selection and read all the proof.[12]

With the choice of articles in Lord Bute's hands commencing with the October issue of 1886, one senses a distinct heightening of quality. Gardner had always managed to have one or two good articles each issue, written by Lord Bute himself or by Metcalfe or by a fairly important scholar like Professor Henry Calderwood, but

---

[7]Metcalfe to Bute, Jan. 26, 1890, Bute papers. The "*London R*." must be the Methodist *London Quarterly Review*. On a smaller scale, this had been done earlier by the *Dublin Review*.

[8]Gardner to Bute, July 5, 1886, Bute papers.

[9]See the correspondence between Gardner and Lord Bute, 1884–1886, Bute papers. Unfor-tunately, few of Gardner's letters are preserved and none prior to 1884.

[10]Bute, *Memoir* (see Bibliographical Note), chaps. III and IV.

[11]Gardner to Bute, July 5, 1886, Bute papers.

[12]Ibid. Whatever financial reward Metcalfe received while Gardner owned the Review evi-dently came from the fees he accumulated as one of its steadiest contributors. A memorandum, probably in Lord Bute's hand, states that Metcalfe is willing to remain at the fee of 7/6 per page for articles written, but suggests that the more affluent new owner might offer him £20 per quarter for his editorial services.

there were also too many inferior ones, like those from the somewhat purple pen of Sophie Veitch, a frequent reviewer of fiction. These now virtually disappeared from its pages, along with the political writings of William Wallace, editor of the *Glasgow Herald*, who was too anti-Home Rule for Lord Bute's taste. Many more antiquarian and historical articles appeared, reflecting the interests of Metcalfe as well as of Lord Bute.

In spite of the improvements, the Review never attained the popularity to which it aspired. The charge of being "ponderous" was one levelled against it time and again, much to Lord Bute's disgust.[13] Though the scholarship was able, neither proprietor nor editor could give it lively form. The expression remained too often dry and academic. "The way in which a number of the newspaper people do their work is very peculiar and to those who try to be accurate, vexatious and contemptible," wrote Metcalfe in 1889. "Their writers might be squelched in a single sentence but for the honour it would do them to pay them the least attention."[14] And if by the 1890s, in reporting to Lord Bute on the reception of the current issue as he did each time, the editor could say, "They speak respectfully of the the S.R. as usual. We seem to be getting into a still better position in public opinion,"[15] that was more hope than fact.

Doubtless this goes far to explain its meagre circulation, this and its antiquarian flavor. In 1886, 600 copies were being printed, of which 300 were sold, the rest going out for review or being kept on hand.[16] Each new subscriber was triumphantly reported, and during the late 80s there was even an attempt to merge with the *Celtic Magazine*, or at least to acquire its elusive list of subscribers from its equally elusive editor. This was evidently given up as a lost cause by Metcalfe, who finally got the names of two subscribers, one of whom was already taking the *Scottish*. Another remedy suggested more than once was to take the Review to London, both as a means of widening its circulation and because "anything 'literary' must originate there." But, as Metcalfe notes, "*Scottish* is an important part of the S.R. 'The Edinburgh' and *NBR* went to London with the result that they lost whatever of the Scottish flavor they had."[17]

Scottish, therefore, the Review would remain, even though, as an unknown reviewer (probably Metcalfe) says in 1891, "*The Scottish Review* . . . has had from the first a much more cosmopolitan aim than its mere title might seem to indicate. While Scottish history, literature and life were to find in it a record and a reflex, or, at least, in their important features and phases a critical survey, the *Review* aimed at bringing within the notice of its readers the intellectual movements and products of other lands and races,—of, in fact, so far as possible within its limits, the wide Empire of Letters."[18] Both elements remained constant throughout. On the one hand

[13]Bute, *Memoir*, pp. 137, 138.
[14]Metcalfe to Bute, Oct. 21, 1889, Bute papers.
[15]Metcalfe to Bute, April 29, 1892, Bute papers.
[16]Memorandum cited in n. 12. Contrast the circulation of the *North British Review*, (*Index*, I, 663). Even the *Rambler*, which appealed to a limited audience, had a circulation of 1000: see Ellegård (*Index*, I, xxiii), p. 30.
[17]Metcalfe to Lord Bute, Oct. 2, 1887, Bute papers.
[18]*ScotR*, 17 (Jan. 1891), 253–254.

the Review presented its readers with at least one "Scottish" article in each issue—occasionally a discussion of Gaelic language and literature, but most often one dealing with a Scottish literary, historical, or antiquarian subject. In addition, the "political" article almost always took up a north-of-the-Tweed question. In 1886 the Conservative sweep and the defeat of Gladstone's Irish Home Rule Bill caused the proponents of Scottish Home Rule to dig in. The Scottish Home Rule Association was formed,[19] with Lord Bute as a member, and Metcalfe even went so far, in 1889, as to propose that a new Scottish national political party be formed with Lords Bute and Lothian at its head; and he added, "Conservatives and liberals have their organs in the *Quarterly* and the *Edinburgh*, why not the Scottish Party? The S.R. has always been national & without any inconsistency or break in its continuity might always of course, assuming that Your Lordship has a chief place in its [i.e. the party's] councils, become the organ of the National Party."[20]

On the other hand, the Review consistently sought to provide a wider scope. Besides the summaries of foreign reviews, there were frequent articles on Canada by Sir J. G. Bourinot and William Leggo, on Greece by Lord Bute's friend Demetrios Bikelas, on the continent by Karl Blind, on Italy by Lily Wolffsohn and H. R. F. Brown, on Ireland by William O'Connor Morris. F. R. Conder was a steady contributor on scientific and engineering topics. Robert Mark Wenley covered philosophy. By far the most frequent contributor was Metcalfe himself, who wrote more than fifty articles ranging over many areas, mainly language and literature. Lord Bute himself was the author or translator of a score of papers. James Ferguson of Kinmundy was another Scottish contributor, mostly on family and local history and on politics from a conservative point of view. William Wallace, mentioned before as the editor of the *Glasgow Herald*, had an interesting career with the Review. The "political" writer before the events of 1886 swung him into the Unionist camp, he later became a frequent contributor on literature.

With such a staff—though not men of the highest rank and certainly less well known than those who wrote for the major journals—the Review had nothing to be ashamed of. But financially it had always run at a loss, and was helpless without the support of its patron, Lord Bute. The seventy-second and final number appeared in October 1900, the month in which he died.[21]

EDITOR
William Musham Metcalfe[22]

PROPRIETORS
Alexander Gardner: November 1882–July 1886, Vol. 1—Vol. 8.
J. P. Crichton-Stuart, third Marquess of Bute: Oct. 1886–Oct. 1900, Vol. 9—Vol. 36.

---

[19]Pryde, p. 216.
[20]Metcalfe to Lord Bute, July 4, 1889, Bute papers.
[21]Bute *Memoir*, p. 146.
[22]But Gardner had his hand in the editorial work, 1882–1886 (see n. 4 above), as did Lord Bute, too, after he bought the periodical: see p. 786 at n. 12.

PUBLISHER
Alexander Gardner, Paisley.

NOTE ON ATTRIBUTIONS
The major sources for the authorship of articles, which are totally anonymous for the first three years and then become increasingly signed until the last three or four years, when about half are unsigned, are two manuscript collections. The present Marquess of Bute, of the Isle of Rothesay in Scotland, kindly allowed us to microfilm the extensive correspondence of the editor and the proprietor, Lord Bute. Most of the letters cover the years 1886–1900; a very few are from the first owner, Alexander Gardner, to Lord Bute in 1884 and 1886. The National Library of Scotland contains the other manuscript sources, comprising several collections of *Scottish Review* materials presented by the editor's son, William Metcalfe. In the editor's own hand is a list of contributors' addresses, dated 1891, which has proved invaluable, especially in establishing specific authors through the use of first names and addresses. We call this "Metcalfe Addresses." Accompanying this is a manuscript index to the authors of articles in the *Scottish Review*, probably in the hand of the younger Metcalfe. It is not complete, and there are some inaccuracies, but it does provide the authors of many unsigned articles. This is the "*ScotR* list." The same hand has added names or initials of authors in pencil at the ends of articles in the set of the Review he presented to the National Library, known to us as the "Metcalfe copy." Additional attributions are given in the index, many with question marks, indicating the uncertainty of the writer. Lastly, there is a volume of associated letters in the National Library addressed by various authors to William M. Metcalfe. Only one is prior to 1886, and the majority are of the late 1880s and the 1890s. The published *Catalogue of the Blackwood Papers* has provided biographical information about some rather obscure authors, and the Blackwood correspondence to which it has led has yielded attributions in several cases where rejected *Blackwood* articles later turned up in the *Scottish Review*. For all these materials we are indebted, directly or indirectly, to our kind friend T. I. Rae, Assistant Curator of Manuscripts, National Library, Scotland.

BIBLIOGRAPHY
The only account of the Review is a chapter in D. H. Blair, *John Patrick, Third Marquis of Bute: a Memoir*, 1921.

THE SCOTTISH REVIEW, 1882–1900

Loch and thus brought to light the hidden crannogs—see *Obit. Notices of the Fellows of the Royal Society*, II, pp. 388–389), both point to Maxwell as the probable author.

23 Agnosticism, 87–101. **George Matheson.** Metcalfe copy gives "G. Matheson"; see Donald Macmillan, *Life of George Matheson* (1908), pp. 204–206.

24 The future of the Highlands, 101–117. **William Anderson Smith.** *ScotR* list and *BMCat.*

25 Some results of Scotch theology, 117–126.

26 Mrs. Carlyle's *Letters* [ed. J. A. Froude], 127–146. **W. M. Metcalfe.** *ScotR* list.

27 Contemporary literature, 147–189.

28 Summaries of foreign reviews, 189–207.

VOLUME 2, SEPTEMBER 1883

29 The educational wrongs of the middle classes, 209–221.

30 Emerson's social philosophy, 222–234.

31 Scotland in the eighteenth century—1707 (Part I), 234–260.

32 "The mean" in politics, 261–281.

33 Walt Whitman, 281–300. **W. M. Metcalfe.** *ScotR* list.

34 Zola's Parisian middle classes [from his *Natural and Social History of a Family*], 301–334. **Émile Zola.** Title. Introd. note and trans. by **J. P. Crichton-Stuart**— *ScotR* list.

35 Three representative poets: Mr. Tennyson, Mr. Swinburne, and Mr. Browning, 334–358.

36 Scottish patriotism and Scottish politics, 358–382.

37 Contemporary literature, 383–400.

38 Summaries of foreign reviews, 401–416.

VOLUME 3, DECEMBER 1883

39 The relation of Scottish universities to those of England and Germany, 1–34. **James Donaldson,** 1831–1915. Attr. in *Athenaeum*, Nov. 10, 1883, p. 603, where running title of this art. is used.

40 The Irish language, 34–51.

41 M. Renan's *Souvenirs*, 51–75. **J. P. Crichton-Stuart.** *ScotR* list; repr. *Foreign Essays.*

42 A study from Turgénieff [his "Live Relics"], 75–91. **Ivan Turgénieff.** Title. Trans. by **J. P. Crichton-Stuart**—see *DNB*, 1st suppl.

43 Martin Luther, 91–105.

44 The theology of St. Paul, 105–125. **W. M. Metcalfe.** *ScotR* list.

45 Charles Dickens, 125–147.

46 What is the Conservative policy? 147–162. **James Ferguson,** 1857–1917? Ferguson to Blackwood, April 12, 1883, Blackwood Corres., says he is sending "a political article"; the only unidentified political art. in *Blackwood's* at this time, no. 5858, is very unlike Ferguson's known writings for *Bk* and *ScotR*, all of which deal with Scottish politics; see *Bk* 7002, *ScotR* 118, 441 and 502; Ferguson's articles for *ScotR* represented the Scottish Conservative point of view; *ScotR* nos. 63 and 88 had previously been rejected by *Blackwood's.*

47 Contemporary literature, 163–193.

48 Summaries of foreign reviews, 193–208.

VOLUME 3, APRIL 1884

49 Scotland in the eighteenth century (Part II, concl.), 209–248.

50 The Scots brigade, 248–266. **Mary M. Maxwell-Scott.** Attr. in Alexander Gardner to Bute, June 6, 1884, Bute Papers.

51 Mr. Swinburne's debt to the Bible, 266–285.

52 Flaws in philanthropy, 285–298.

53 The Eddic poems, 299–320. **W. M. Metcalfe.** *ScotR* list.

54 The life of St. Margaret [Queen of Scotland], 320–336. **Mary M. Maxwell-Scott.** Repr. *Incidents.*

55 Frederick Denison Maurice, 336–356. **W. M. Metcalfe.** *ScotR* list.

56 A minister for Scotland, 356–377.

57 Contemporary literature, 378–402.

58 Summaries of foreign reviews, 402–420.

VOLUME 4, JULY 1884

59 Unpublished notices of James Sharp, Archbishop of St. Andrews, 1–30. **Osmund Airy.** Attr. in *Academy*, July 19, 1884, pp. 43–44. (See no. 81.)

60 The Scottish language, 30–61. **W. M. Metcalfe.** *ScotR* list.

61 The new light upon St. Patrick, 62–85. **J. P. Crichton-Stuart.** *ScotR* list; repr. *Home Essays.*

62 The Scottish and English clergy, 85–96.

63 The Scottish loyalists [in the Great Civil War], 96–115. **James Ferguson,** 1857–1917. Ferguson to Blackwood, Sept. 6, 1882, Blackwood Corres., says he has a paper on the Aberdeenshire phase of the

Civil War; never published in *Bk*; see no. 88, another case of a rejected *Bk* article in *ScotR*.

64   A legend of vanished waters [Loch Spynie], 115–137. **Constance Gordon-Cumming.** Assigned to "Miss C. F. Gordon Cumming" in *ScotR* no. 257, p. 307n.

65   Highland land law reform, 137–163.

66   Contemporary literature, 164–186.

67   Summaries of foreign reviews, 186–200.

VOLUME 4, OCTOBER 1884

68   New South Wales, 201–223.

69   The teaching of Archdeacon Farrar, 224–245.

70   The battle of Otterburn, 245–259. **Charles Rampini.** Repr. *Tales of Old Scotland*, Edin., 1890.

71   The *De Imitatione Christi*: who wrote it? 259–287. **Alexander H. Fairly.** *ScotR* list, which adds "Rev." (See no. 100.)

72   The true reasonableness of Christianity, 287–301. Unidentified. *ScotR* list gives "R. M. Wenley?"; but this is not at all like Wenley's careful philosophical work and analysis, nor is the sentimental note characteristic.

73   Mystic novels, 302–323. **Annie M. Harris.** Claimed in A. M. Harris to W. M. Metcalfe, Feb. 29, 1892, Bute Papers.

74   The crisis [of the third Reform Bill]—beneath and after, 323–350. **William Wallace,** 1843–1921, prob. Wallace wrote many of the political articles prior to 1889; his liberal point of view is expressed here, and two of his heroes are written of in similar ways: cf. p. 324 here and p. 376, no. 16 on Gladstone, and p. 328 here and p. 161, no. 104 (on Morley).

75   Contemporary literature, 351–389.

76   Summaries of foreign reviews, 390–408.

VOLUME 5, JANUARY 1885

77   Froude's *Carlyle's Life in London*, 1–21. **W. M. Metcalfe.** *ScotR* list.

78   Correspondence of Sir Robert Moray with Alexander Bruce, second Earl of Kincardin, 1657–1660, 22–43. **Osmund Airy.** Attr. by Alexander Robertson, *Life of Sir Robert Moray* (1922), p. 204.

79   Behind the scenes in clerical life, 43–59.

80   Echoes of the eighteenth century, 59–75.

Sophie F. F. Veitch? Alexander Gardner (letter cited in no. 121) says she has "done some good things" for *ScotR*: nos. 15, 89, and this art., consisting largely of letters from Veitch family papers, could be in his mind.

81   A letter from James Sharp to the Earl of Middleton, proving his treachery in 1661, 75–82. **James Sharp** and **Osmund Airy.** Sharp's letter, pp. 77–79; surrounding commentary by Airy, see p. 76, which refers back to no. 59 in a paragraph plainly indicating the same author, and see the *Athenaeum*, Feb. 14, 1885, p. 217.

82   Archbishop Hamilton's *Catechism*, 83–103. **W. M. Metcalfe.** *ScotR* list.

83   Patmos, 103–137. **J. P. Crichton-Stuart.** *ScotR* list; repr. *Foreign Essays*.

84   The Lennox [family], 138–161. **Mary M. Maxwell-Scott.** Repr. *Incidents*.

85   Contemporary literature, 162–188.

86   Summaries of foreign reviews, 189–204.

VOLUME 5, APRIL 1885

87   Scottish art and artists, 205–226.

88   The American loyalists [in the Revolutionary War], 227–249. **James Ferguson,** 1857–1917. Ferguson to Blackwood, Nov. 13, 1884, Blackwood Corres., asks for return of his "American loyalists"; letter endorsed "Ms. retd. 17 Nov/84."

89   George Eliot, 250–264. **Sophie F. F. Veitch,** prob. Woman cited wrote no. 15 and other reviews of fiction (nos. 123 and 132) which contain many similarities of style and content (see especially pp. 251 and 254 here and no. 15, p. 333); she also wrote an art. on Victoria, no. 121, which, on p. 98, contains a phrase on the near-fatal illness of the Prince of Wales identical in wording to that on p. 259 here.

90   Hampole's *Psalter*, 264–284. **W. M. Metcalfe.** *ScotR* list.

91   Canada: its political development, 285–311. **J. G. Bourinot.** *ScotR* list.

92   Stuart pretenders, 311–332. **W. Maziere Brady.** Claimed in Brady to Alexander Gardner, May 13, 1885, Nat. Lib. Scot.; repr. *Anglo-Roman Papers*, Paisley, 1890, as "The Eldest Natural Son of Charles II."

93   Our foreign policy, 332–357.

94   Contemporary literature, 358–386.

95   Summaries of foreign reviews, 387–406.

VOLUME 6, JULY 1885

96   Disestablishment, 1–10. **John Douglas Campbell.** Signed Lorne [Marquess of Lorne].

97   *Natural Law in the Spiritual World* [by Henry Drummond], 10–37. **W. M. Metcalfe.** *ScotR* list.

98   Laing's *Popular and Romance Poetry of Scotland*, 37–48. **W. M. Metcalfe.** Attr. in Alexander Gardner to Lord Bute, July 5, 1886, Bute Papers.

99   Imperial federation from a Canadian point of view (Part I), 48–59. **William Leggo.** Signed.

100   Thomas à Kempis and *The Imitation of Christ*, 59–69. **Leonard Wheatley.** Attr. in *ScotR* no. 341, p. 468.

101   Winifred, Countess of Nithsdaill, 69–85. **Mary M. Maxwell-Scott.** Repr. *Incidents*.

102   Some Christian monuments of Athens, 85–123. **J. P. Crichton-Stuart.** *ScotR* list; repr. *Foreign Essays*.

103   Founding of the Congo Free State, 124–141. **W. M. Metcalfe.** *ScotR* list.

104   The political portrait gallery, 141–165. **William Wallace**, 1843–1921, prob. The author identifies himself, p. 143, as the writer of no. 16.

105   Contemporary literature, 166–188.

106   Summaries of foreign reviews, 189–204.

VOLUME 6, OCTOBER 1885

107   The Church of Scotland and the coming election, 205–220. **John Tulloch.** Signed.

108   York mystery plays, 220–248. **W. M. Metcalfe.** *ScotR* list.

109   Scotland's new departure in philosophy, 248–262. **R. M. Wenley**, prob. Man cited wrote nos. 269 and 286 which are reviews of other works by the philosophers reviewed here, as well as many other articles on philosophy and religion for *ScotR*; opening lines of no. 269 refer back to this art. and continue the discussion of Scottish philosophy.

110   Scottish Catholics under Mary and James, 263–275. **Mary M. Maxwell-Scott.** Repr. *Incidents*.

111   Records of Argyll, 275–294. **W. M. Metcalfe,** prob. Metcalfe copy; and *ScotR* list, which adds "?"; there are several references to favorite Metcalfe topics, such as the Eddic poems (cf. no. 53), Norsemen (cf. no. 335), and the Gaelic language (cf. no. 60).

112   The Scottish Parliament, 295–323.

113   The philosophy of stupidity, 323–333.

114   The Scotch disestablishment vote, 333–348. **George C. Hutton.** Signed.

115   Contemporary literature, 349–388.

116   Summaries of foreign reviews, 389–404.

VOLUME 7, JANUARY 1886

117   The Scottish peerage, 1–27. **J. P. Crichton-Stuart.** *ScotR* list; repr. *Home Essays*; Bute, *Memoir*.

118   The Conservative cause in Scotland in the light of the general election, 27–47. **James Ferguson**, 1857–1917. Signed A Conservative; claimed in opening sentence of nos. 441 and 502.

119   *The Greville Memoirs*, 47–72. **W. M. Metcalfe.** *ScotR* list.

120   What is astrology? 72–92. **Francis R. Conder.** *ScotR* list; editor's note, vol. 15, p. 252.

121   Victoria: a monograph, 93–100. **Sophie F. F. Veitch.** Alexander Gardner to Bute, Feb. 4, 1886, Bute Papers, acknowledges the latter's dislike of the "articles of the author of *Victoria* and *Fiction*," but adds that "she" has done some good things (see no. 15 for example); cf. no. 123, which ends, p. 128, with a purple passage eulogizing the virtues of Victoria similar to that here, p. 96.

122   *The Natural Truth of Christianity: Selections from the Writings of John Smith and Others*, 100–114. Unidentified. *ScotR* list gives "R. M. Wenley?" but the objection to no. 72 applies here also.

123   Current fiction, 115–128. **Sophie F. F. Veitch**, prob. Metcalfe copy, which adds a "?"; woman cited not only wrote religious novels, the subject of this art., but had already reviewed them in no. 15; certain characteristics of thought and style are similar to those of no. 15; cf. especially p. 126 here and pp. 336–337 there.

124   Political sidelights and prospects, 128–156. **William Wallace**, 1843–1921, prob. The author identifies himself, p. 151, as the writer of no. 104.

125   Contemporary literature, 157–189.

126   Summaries of foreign reviews, 190–200.

VOLUME 7, APRIL 1886

127   The Greek question, 201–231. **Demetrios Bikelas.** Signed ΔΗΜΗΤΡΙΟΣ

ΒΙΚΕΛΑΣ; repr. *Seven Essays*. Trans. by **J. P. Crichton-Stuart**—*BMCat.*

128   Barbour's *Legends of the Saints*, 232–263. **W. M. Metcalfe.** *ScotR* list.

129   On the water circulation of great cities, 264–286. **Francis R. Conder.** Editorial note cited for no. 120.

130   The Caldwell papers, 286–303. **W. M. Metcalfe.** *ScotR* list gives "Herbert Maxwell?"; however, this art. appears in a list of articles attr. to Metcalfe in Gardner to Bute, July 5, 1886, Bute Papers.

131   Fallacies of reading lists, 303–315. **Sophie F. F. Veitch.** Alexander Gardner to Bute, April 29, 1886, Bute Papers, says, "As to Miss V. I was not sure of in ms. and when in type was dissatisfied but thought as the subject of Books was a popular one, it might do no harm"; Sophie Veitch had been a contributor on literary topics to the *ScotR*.

132   Ethics and art in recent novels, 315–330. **Sophie F. F. Veitch?** Woman cited wrote nos. 15 and 123, which also were reviews of novels approached from a religious, ethical point of view; all three insist on the necessity of a moral tone: see p. 316 here; no. 15, p. 331; and no. 123, p. 116.

133   The prospects of Canadian confederation, 330–340. **Robert Ker.** Signed, with addition, "Trinity Church, Quebec."

134   Imperial federation from a Canadian point of view (Part II, concl.), 340–363. **William Leggo.** Signed.

135   Contemporary literature, 364–395.

136   Summaries of foreign reviews, 396–408.

VOLUME 8, JULY 1886

137   Home rule for Scotland, 1–20.

138   Sir William Hamilton, 20–40. **J. Clark Murray.** Signed.

139   The flowers of the forest [three versions of an old ballad], 41–45. Edited with an intro. note by **John Tod**—signed John Strathesk, see *BMCat.* and Cushing, *Initials*, I, 275.

140   Burton's *Anatomy of Melancholy*, 45–60. **W. M. Metcalfe.** *ScotR* list.

141   The Mesmerist; from the late Ivan Turgénieff, 61–87. **Ivan Turgénieff.** Title. Trans. by **J. P. Crichton-Stuart**—see headnote and *DNB*, 1st suppl.

142   Recent novels, 87–101.

143   Life and times of Longfellow, 101–126. **George Stewart, Jun.** Signed; repr. *Essays from Reviews*, Quebec, 1892.

144   The general election, and after, 126–139. **William Wallace**, 1843–1921. Signed.

145   Contemporary literature, 140–187.

146   Summaries of foreign reviews, 188–200.

VOLUME 8, OCTOBER 1886

147   Landed estate and farming in the southwest of Scotland, 201–226. **Charles G. Shaw.** Signed.

148   On inland transport, 227–258. **Francis R. Conder.** Editorial note cited for no. 120.

149   The Byzantine empire (Part I), 258–286. **Demetrios Bikelas.** Signed ΔΗΜΗΤΡΙΟΣ ΒΙΚΕΛΑΣ; repr. *Seven Essays*. Trans. by **J. P. Crichton-Stuart**—*BMCat.*

150   The Bayreuth festival, 287–309. **J. P. Crichton-Stuart.** *ScotR* list; repr. *Foreign Essays*.

151   The fishery question: a Canadian view (Part I), 309–334. **William Leggo.** Signed.

152   Ossianic ballad poetry—Ossian's prayer [from "The Book of the Dean of Lismore"], 334–367. Edited with an intro. note by **Alexander Cameron**—signed.

153   Saved [the Constitution], 368–380. **Herbert Maxwell.** *ScotR* list.

154   Contemporary literature, 381–403.

155   Summaries of foreign reviews, 403–416.

VOLUME 9, JANUARY 1887

156   On the jurisdiction of the English courts over Scotsmen, 1–31. **Andrew Jameson,** prob. J. B. Balfour to Pitman (Bute's commissioner), Aug. 19, 1886, Bute Papers, says Jameson has agreed to write this art.; Francis Anderson (Bute's secretary?) to Metcalfe, n.d., Bute Papers, speaks of "Andrew Jamieson (sic) an Advocate at the Scottish Bar" as the proposed author of this art.; see *DNB*, 2nd suppl.

157   Mr. Spencer's "Unknowable," 31–52. **W. M. Metcalfe.** *ScotR* list.

158   Byzantinism and Hellenism (Part II), 52–78. **Demetrios Bikelas.** Signed ΔΗΜΗΤΡΙΟΣ ΒΙΚΕΛΑΣ; repr. *Seven Essays*. Trans. by **J. P. Crichton-Stuart**—*BMCat.* (Part III is no. 166.)

159   St. Magnus of the Orkneys, 79–108. **Mary M. Maxwell-Scott** and **J. P. Crichton-Stuart.** *ScotR* list gives "Hon. Mrs. Maxwell-Scott"; Bute, *Memoir*, pp. 149–150; repr. *Incidents*.

160   The fisheries question: a Canadian view

(Part II, concl.), 108–137. **William Leggo.** Signed.

161 Egypt on the eve of the English invasion, 137–169. **Ahmed Nassif.** *ScotR* list; Bute, *Memoir*, p. 133, gives Amin as man's title instead of Ahmed. Trans. by **James Robertson**, 1840–1920—intro. note gives "Dr. Robertson, Professor of Oriental Languages in the University of Glasgow": see *WWW*. Intro. note by **J. P. Crichton-Stuart?**—see Butte, *Memoir*, p. 133.

162 Contemporary literature, 170–204.

163 Summaries of foreign reviews, 204–214.

VOLUME 9, APRIL 1887

164 The apocryphal character of the Moabite stone, 215–245. **Albert Löwy.** Signed.

165 French Canada, 245–272. **John George Bourinot.** Signed.

166 The subjects of the Byzantine empire (Part III, concl.), 272–297. **Demetrios Bikelas.** Signed ΔΗΜΗΤΡΙΟΣ ΒΙΚΕΛΑΣ; Metcalfe; repr. *Seven Essays*. Trans. by **J. P. Crichton-Stuart**—*BMCat*.

167 The gas industry of the United Kingdom, 297–316. **Thomas Newbigging.** Signed, with title "C.E."; Metcalfe to Bute, Sept. 10, 1886, Bute Papers, adds address, "Manchester."

168 Thomas of Erceldoune, 316–347. **W. M. Metcalfe.** Claimed in Metcalfe to Bute, March 30, 1887, Bute Papers.

169 Recent archaeology in Euboia, 347–356. **George Lampakes.** Intro. note. With an extract from an Athenian newspaper on Lampakes, pp. 347–349. Trans. by **J. P. Crichton-Stuart**—intro. note signed Bute [Marquess of Bute].

170 Professor Noiré on the origin of reason, 356–377. **T. B. Saunders.** Signed.

171 Egypt under the English invasion, 378–398. **Ahmed Nassif.** *ScotR* list. Trans. by **James Robertson**, 1840–1920—intro. note says by author and trans. of no. 161.

172 Contemporary literature, 398–439. Pages 426–431 by **J. P. Crichton-Stuart**—assigned in Metcalfe to Bute, March 30, 1887, Bute Papers.

173 Summaries of foreign reviews, 440–450.

VOLUME 10, JULY 1887

174 The modern cremation movement, 1–38. **Charles Cameron.** Signed.

175 The coronation of Charles II at Scone,

38–93. **J. P. Crichton-Stuart.** *ScotR* list; repr. *Scottish Coronations*, 1902.

176 The Hudson's Bay route, 94–124. **William Leggo.** Signed.

177 The redemption of astrology, 124–143. **Francis R. Conder.** Cf. no. 120.

178 The burning of Frendraught, 143–163. **Charles Rampini.** Signed.

179 Contemporary literature, 164–201. Pages 180–182 by **C. C. Grant**—claimed in Grant to Metcalfe, June 1, 1887, Nat. Lib. Scot.

180 Summaries of foreign reviews, 201–212.

VOLUME 10, OCTOBER 1887

181 The union of 1707 viewed financially, 213–234. **James Carmont.** Attr. in Bute to W. M. Metcalfe, Feb. 11, 1887, Bute Papers.

182 Salvatore Farina, 235–266. **Lily Wolffsohn.** *ScotR* list.

183 The coronation of Charles I at Holyrood, 266–322. **J. P. Crichton-Stuart.** *ScotR* list; repr. *Scottish Coronations*, 1902.

184 Alcohol and alcoholism, 322–337. **E. Fournier de Flaix.** Signed. Translated from the *Revue Scientifique* by **E. H. Lawrence Oliphant**—note on p. 322.

185 The two chancellors: James Betoun and Thomas Wolsey, 337–368. **G. Gregory Smith.** Signed.

186 The three evils of destiny, 369–387. **J. Theodore Bent.** Signed.

187 Adam Smith and his foreign critics, 387–411. **Moritz Kaufmann.** Signed M. Kaufmann; see *WWW*/1928.

188 Contemporary literature, 412–434. Pages 413–414 by **T. B. Saunders**—attr. in Metcalfe to Bute, Sept. 6, 1887, Bute Papers; pages 430–431 by **W. M. Metcalfe**—Metcalfe to Bute, October 2, 1887, Bute Papers, refers to his notice of Veitch's book.

189 Summaries of foreign reviews, 434–446.

VOLUME 11, JANUARY 1888

190 Scotland in times past, 1–34. **George Burnett.** Signed.

191 The Panama Canal, 35–59. **Francis R. Conder.** Cf. no. 120.

192 The earliest Scottish coronations, 60–102. **J. P. Crichton-Stuart.** *ScotR* list; repr. *Scottish Coronations*, 1902.

193 The peasant in North Italy, 103–117.

Title. Trans. by **J. P. Crichton-Stuart**— Bute to W. M. Metcalfe, Jan. 8, 1888, Bute Papers, says he is taking Turgénieff to Italy and will try to work on it; see *DNB*, 1st suppl.

233 The religious education difficulty in England, 105–122. **J. Edward Graham.** Signed. (Note, p. 188, by **Graham**— signed J.E.G.)

234 The last resting place of St. Andrew, 122–161. **J. P. Crichton-Stuart.** *ScotR* list; repr. *Foreign Essays.*

235 East Africa and the slave trade, 161–188. **A. M. Symington.** Signed A.M.S.; *ScotR* list.

236 Summaries of foreign reviews, 189–212.

237 Contemporary literature, 213–228. Pages 213–214 by **J. P. Crichton-Stuart**— claimed in Crichton-Stuart to Metcalfe, Jan. 16, 1889, Bute Papers.

VOLUME 13, APRIL 1889

238 Corporate re-union in the reign of Charles I, 229–248. **Jean M. Stone.** Signed J. M. Stone; repr. *Studies.*

239 The national music of Scotland, 249–273. **J. Cuthbert Hadden.** Signed.

240 The Panama scandal, 274–287. **Francis R. Conder.** Evidence for no. 120.

241 The tennis court [described in the *Moniteur* of June, 1789], 287–312. Trans. by **L. A. Barbé**—Metcalfe to Bute, March 18, 1889, Bute Papers: "I have seen Barbé and got him to work"; cf. no. 247.

242 A Scottish governing house, 312–338. **James Ferguson,** 1857–1917. *ScotR* list.

243 Greece before 1821, 339–370. **Demetrios Bikelas.** Signed ΔΗΜΗΤΡΙΟΣ ΒΙΚΕΛΑΣ; repr. *Seven Essays.* Trans. by **J. P. Crichton-Stuart**—ibid.

244 Julius Wolff, 370–409. **Lily Wolffsohn.** Signed Edith Marget; *ScotR* list.

245 Summaries of foreign reviews, 409–433.

246 Contemporary literature, 433–452.

VOLUME 14, JULY 1889

247 The taking of the Bastille; translated from the *Moniteur* newspaper of July 20–23, 23 and 24, 1789, 1–34. Trans. by **L. A. Barbé**—attr. in Metcalfe to Bute, Nov. 21, 1889, Bute Papers; see *WWW/ 1928.*

248 The railway race to Edinburgh, 34–68. **Francis R. Conder.** Evidence for no. 120.

249 The great palace of Byzantium, 68–93. **F. G. Kenyon.** *ScotR* list.

250 The salmon in Scotland, 93–111. **J. G. Bertram.** *ScotR* list.

251 The formation of the modern Greek state, 112–137. **Demetrios Bikelas.** Signed ΔΗΜΗΤΡΙΟΣ ΒΙΚΕΛΑΣ; repr. *Seven Essays.* Trans. by **J. P. Crichton-Stuart**— ibid.

252 The romance of Sir Tristrem, 138–172. **W. M. Metcalfe.** Metcalfe to Bute, May 27, 1889, Bute Papers, says "Sir Tristrem is drawing to a conclusion" and that he has only "to correct and add the notes."

253 Summaries of foreign reviews, 172–198.

254 Contemporary literature, 199–219.

VOLUME 14, OCTOBER 1889

255 The Scotch farm-labourer, 219–238. **Alexander Gordon.** Signed; repr., with changes, *The Folks o'Carglen; or, Life in the North,* 1891.

256 Byzantine ecclesiastical music, 239–280. **S. G. Hatherly.** *ScotR* list.

257 Florence Wilson, 281–310. **Charles Rampini.** Signed.

258 The fourth of August; translated from the *Moniteur* newspaper of August 4 and 5, 1789, 311–337. Trans. by **L. A. Barbé** —cf. no. 247.

259 Darwinism and the origin of reason, 337–361. **T. B. Saunders.** Signed.

260 The territory of the Hellenic Kingdom, 361–380. **Demetrios Bikelas.** Signed ΔΗΜΗΤΡΙΟΣ ΒΙΚΕΛΑΣ; repr. *Seven Essays.* Trans. by **J. P. Crichton-Stuart** —ibid.

261 The blind deaf-mute, Helen Keller, 380–398. **J. Clark Murray.** Signed.

262 Parliament in Scotland, 399–416. **J. P. Crichton-Stuart.** Signed Bute [Marquess of Bute]; repr. *Home Essays.*

263 Summaries of foreign reviews, 416–438.

264 Contemporary literature, 438–450.

VOLUME 15, JANUARY 1890

265 Ecclesiastical music in Presbyterian Scotland, 1–24. **J. Cuthbert Hadden.** Signed.

266 The prehistoric Levant, 25–54. **C. R. Conder.** *ScotR* list.

267 The Vikings, 55–82. **W. M. Metcalfe.** *ScotR* list.

268 The capture of Versailles; translated

305 The poetry of Rudolf Baumbach, 82–114. **Lily Wolffsohn.** Signed Edith Marget; *ScotR* list.

306 The correspondence of an old Scotch factor [William Tod, 1745–1821], 114–139. **Charles Rampini.** Signed.

307 Three Finnish scholars [H. G. Porthan, M. A. Castrem, Elias Lönnrot], 140–170. **William Nicolson.** *ScotR* list.

308 Mr. Lecky on Ireland, 171–208. **W. M. Metcalfe.** Metcalfe to Bute, Dec. 8, 1890, Bute Papers, says "I am trying to bring Lecky to an end and I hope to succeed in a day or two."

309 Summaries of foreign reviews, 209–247.

310 Contemporary literature, 248–258.

VOLUME 17, APRIL 1891

311 Modern socialism, 259–280. **James Ramsay MacDonald.** Signed J. Grant; Edith Ellis (in Havelock Ellis, *My Life*, pp. 284–285) was shocked when she learned that her friend Ramsay MacDonald "had written for the *Scottish Review* a pseudonymous article on Socialism which, though not exactly an attack, was a . . . warning . . . against the risks and dangers of Socialism."

312 A French envoy in 1745, 280–292. **J. G. Alger.** Signed.

313 The Tell Amarna tablets, 292–318. **C. R. Conder.** Signed.

314 Economic principles and university reform, 319–332. **J. S. Nicholson.** Signed.

315 The spread of Gaelic in Scotland: being the fifth Rhind Lecture, 332–349. **John Rhŷs.** Signed.

316 The Spanish Inquisition, 349–383. **George Francis Legge.** Signed F. Legge; obit. *Antiquaries Journal*, 3 (1923), 306.

317 *Lux Mundi* [by Charles Gore], 384–412. **W. M. Metcalfe.** *ScotR* list.

318 Is there an alternative for shorter parliaments? 412–425. **James Douglas Holms.** Signed.

319 Summaries of foreign reviews, 425–460.

320 Contemporary literature, 461–476. Pages 467–468 by **W. M. Metcalfe**—claimed in Metcalfe to Bute, April 7, 1891, Bute Papers.

VOLUME 18, JULY 1891

321 The oriental Jews, 1–23. **C. R. Conder.** Signed.

322 *A Publisher and his Friends* [John Murray], 24–53. **W. M. Metcalfe.** *ScotR* list, which adds a "?"; Metcalfe to Bute, May 7, 1891, Bute Papers, says he is "reading away at the life of Murray the Publisher," which "looks as though it would make an interesting article"; May 19, *ibid.*, reports he is getting along slowly with "Murray."

323 Philosophy of religion, 53–77. **R. M. Wenley.** Signed.

324 The legend of the Archangel Leslie, 77–110. **T. G. Law.** Signed; repr. *Essays*.

325 Mineral leases and royalties, 110–120. **Benjamin Taylor.** Signed.

326 Certain national names of the aborigines of the British Isles: being the sixth Rhind Lecture, 120–143. **John Rhŷs.** Signed.

327 Goethe's Faust and modern thought, 143–174. **Moritz Kaufmann.** Signed as in no. 187.

328 Laurence Oliphant, 175–197. **W. M. Metcalfe.** Claimed in Metcalfe to Bute, July 2, 1891, Bute Papers.

329 The Scotch Ploughmen's Union and its reforms, 197–211. **J. G. Dow.** Signed.

330 Summaries of foreign reviews, 211–245.

331 Contemporary literature, 246–256.

VOLUME 18, OCTOBER 1891

332 Witchcraft in Scotland, 257–288. **George Francis Legge.** Signed as in no. 316.

333 A retrospect on the Euxine and the Caspian, 288–301. **Andrew T. Sibbald.** Signed.

334 Gaelic historical songs, 301–341. **William A. Craigie.** *ScotR* list.

335 The Norse discovery of America, 341–366. **W. M. Metcalfe.** Claimed in Metcalfe to Bute, August 7, 1891, Bute Papers.

336 Beginnings of the Scottish newspaper press (Part I), 366–377. **J. D. Cockburn.** Signed. (Part II is no. 401.)

337 Scotch divines and English bishops, 1606, 377–393. **Florence MacCunn.** Signed.

338 The former proprietor of Abbotsford [Rev. Robert Douglas, 1747–1820], 393–405. **Paton J. Gloag.** Signed.

339 Local government and administration in Ireland, 405–435. **William O'Connor Morris.** Signed.

340 Summaries of foreign reviews, 435–461.

341 Contemporary literature, 462–479.

VOLUME 21, JANUARY 1893

384 Biblical studies in the middle ages, 1–33. **T. G. Law.** Signed; repr. *Essays.*

385 Fifeshire, 33–59. **J. H. Crawford.** Signed.

386 The low death-rate, 59–81. **Alfred J. H. Crespi.** Signed.

387 Simon Fraser: Lord Lovat, Ob. 1747, 81–115. **William Donaldson,** 1838–1924. Signed; Donaldson to Blackwood, Nov. 24, 1891, from Edinburgh, Nat. Lib. Scot., sends art. on "Lord Lovat"; returned to him on Jan. 7, 1892 [wrongly dated 1891]; see *WWW*/1928.

388 The origin of the mediaeval belief in witchcraft, 115–142. **George Francis Legge.** Signed as in no. 316.

389 The wedding-tour of James VI in Norway, 142–161. **A. H. Millar.** Signed.

390 The anthropological history of Europe (No. IV), 162–182. **John Beddoe.** Signed as in no. 360.

391 The Scotch education department, 183–207. **James Donaldson,** 1831–1915. Signed J. Donaldson; see *DNB*/1921.

392 Summaries of foreign reviews, 208–237.

393 Contemporary literature, 238–256.

VOLUME 21, APRIL 1893

394 The Scottish fisheries under the fishery board, 257–279. **William Anderson Smith.** Signed W. Anderson Smith: cf. nos. 5, 24.

395 The early languages of Syria, 279–296. **C. R. Conder.** Signed R. C. Conder; *ScotR* list.

396 George Buchanan and the Inquisition; from newly-discovered documents, 296–315. **P. Hume Brown.** Signed.

397 Book-plates, 315–329. **Henry Gough.** Signed H. Gough; *ScotR* list.

398 The wandering of the [German] nations, 329–349. **J. B. Bury.** Signed.

399 The anthropological history of Europe (No. V), 350–371. **John Beddoe.** Signed as in no. 360.

400 Brendan's fabulous voyage: a lecture delivered on January 19, 1893, before the Scottish Society of Literature and Art, 371–398. **J. P. Crichton-Stuart.** *ScotR* list; repr. *Home Essays.*

401 Beginnings of the Scottish newspaper press (Part II, concl.), 399–419. **James D. Cockburn.** Signed.

402 Regulation of the drink traffic, 419–445. **John Mann, Jr.** Signed; Metcalfe

Addresses and issues of *Glasgow Direct.* show he was the Sir John Mann in *WWW*/1960.

403 Summaries of foreign reviews, 446–473.

404 Contemporary literature, 474–491. Pages 478–479 by **W. M. Metcalfe**—claimed in Metcalfe to Bute, Nov. 2, 1892, Bute Papers.

VOLUME 22, JULY 1893

405 The Spanish Blanks and Catholic Earls, 1592–4, 1–32. **T. G. Law.** Metcalfe; repr. *Essays.*

406 The romance of *King Rother*, 33–61. **Allan Menzies.** Signed.

407 Andrew Fletcher, the Scottish patriot, 61–84. **James Ramsay MacDonald?** Signed J. R. MacDonald; man cited wrote no. 311.

408 The anthropological history of Europe (No. VI, concl.), 84–103. **John Beddoe.** Signed as in no. 360.

409 Galloway and her feudal sheriffs, 104–132. **James Ferguson,** 1857–1917. Signed J. Fergusson; cf. no. 350 where man cited is spelled with a double "s"; the several references to Mar and Buchan suggest his arts. on these subjects in *Quarterly Review* (see *Index*, I, 893); the many "Scottisms" and the introduction of verse quotations are characteristic of Ferguson's writing, both here and in the *Quarterly* arts.

410 Some heretic gospels, 133–162. **George Francis Legge.** Signed as in no. 316.

411 Shellfish culture, 162–173. **J. H. Fullarton.** Signed.

412 Barbour and Blind Harry as literature, 173–201. **W. A. Craigie.** Signed.

413 Summaries of foreign reviews, 202–233.

414 Contemporary literature, 234–256.

VOLUME 22, OCTOBER 1893

415 Sir John Clerk of Penicuik, 257–274. **W. G. Scott-Moncrieff.** Signed.

416 The earliest ages of Hebrew history, 274–292. **C. R. Conder.** Signed.

417 The Scottish paraphrases, 292–325. **J. Cuthbert Hadden.** Signed.

418 The meaning of the Russian name, 325–341. **Karl Blind.** Signed.

419 A Scottish merchant of the sixteenth century [David Wedderburn], 341–363. **A. H. Millar.** Signed.

420 An idyll during the French Revolution, 363–381. **J. G. Alger.** Signed.

508 Legendary lore of the inner Hebrides, 54–71. **Frank Rinder.** Signed.

509 Gustav Freytag, 71–82. **John G. Robertson.** Signed.

510 St. Andrews, 1645–46, 82–95. **Robert Williamson.** Signed R. Williamson; a list of names in Bute's handwriting, December, 1893, Bute Papers, contains a "Robert Williamson"; Bute to Metcalfe, June 16, 1887, Bute Papers, calls him his "Free Church friend"; see *Fasti-Free Church*.

511 The "Song to Aegir," 95–104. **Karl Blind.** Signed.

512 Bagpipe music, 105–117. **W. L. Calderwood.** Signed.

513 The seizure of a Turkish flagship, 117–125. **Demetrios Bikelas.** Signed. Trans. by **William Metcalfe**—intro. note gives "W. Metcalfe," with titles "Rev." and "B.D.": see *Fasti*, VIII, 650.

514 The political theories of St. Thomas Aquinas, 126–150. **R. W. Carlyle.** Signed A. J. Carlyle in error: see *DNB*/1940 under R. W. Carlyle.

515 Summaries of foreign reviews, 151–177.

516 Contemporary literature, 178–194.

VOLUME 27, APRIL 1896

517 The Orkney Isles, 195–225. **T. Pilkington White.** Signed.

518 The princes of the House of Condé, 226–253. **William O'Connor Morris.** Signed.

519 Spain and the Jacobites: the story of 1719, 253–275. **Benjamin Taylor.** Signed.

520 Pulvis Olympicus, 276–292. **John Letcher Patterson.** Signed John Patterson; Metcalfe addresses gives Prof. John Patterson of Louisville, Ky.; see *Amer WWW*/1942 for man cited.

521 The Runic Crosses of Northumbria, 292–304. **Jean M. Stone.** Signed as in no. 238; repr. *Studies*.

522 Mr. Purcell and Cardinal Manning, 304–324. **W. M. Metcalfe?** Metcalfe copy.

523 The Gledstanes of olden time, 324–336. **Florence M. Gladstone.** Signed.

524 Plagiarism and coincidence, 336–350. **J. Cuthbert Hadden.** Signed.

525 Summaries of foreign reviews, 351–381.

526 Contemporary literature, 382–400.

VOLUME 28, JULY 1896

527 Hjaltland, 1–33. **T. Pilkington White.** Signed.

528 Serapis: a study in religions, 33–55. **George Francis Legge.** Signed as in no. 316.

529 The universities of Europe in the middle ages, 56–78. **Joseph Wells.** Signed J. Wells; see *WWW*/1940.

530 The Asiatics in America, 78–103. **C. R. Conder.** Signed.

531 Scotland under the Roundheads, 103–122. **James Colville.** Signed.

532 Christina, Queen of Sweden, 122–152. **R. S. Mylne.** Signed.

533 Summaries of foreign reviews, 153–176.

534 Contemporary literature, 177–201.

VOLUME 28, OCTOBER 1896

535 *The Annandale Family Book*, 203–223. **A. H. Millar.** Signed.

536 Victor Hugo, the poet, 223–246. **Amélie C. Leroy.** Signed Esmé Stuart: see H&L.

537 Sutherland folk-lore, 246–264. **Frank Rinder.** Signed.

538 Music in Old England, 264–293. **J. Cuthbert Hadden.** Signed.

539 The coronation of James I of England, 293–310. **Guy le Strange.** Signed.

540 St. Mark's indebtedness to St. Matthew, 310–330. **F. P. Badham.** Signed.

541 The poetry of the Skalds, 331–346. **W. A. Craigie.** Signed.

542 A liberal education: the function of a university, 346–354. **G. W. Prothero.** Signed.

543 Journalism from the interior, 354–372. **William Wallace**, 1843–1921. *ScotR* list.

544 Summaries of foreign reviews, 373–406.

545 Contemporary literature, 407–425.

VOLUME 29, JANUARY 1897

546 The land system of Ireland, 1–30. **William O'Connor Morris.** Signed.

547 The history of the Roumanians, 30–55. **J. B. Bury.** Signed.

548 The cycling epidemic, 56–74. **T. Pilkington White.** Signed T.P.W.; *ScotR list.*

549 Alberoni and the Quadruple Alliance, 74–100. **Edward Armstrong.** Signed as in no. 471.

550 Scottish bibliography, 101–115. **Harry G. Aldis.** Signed.

551 Egyptian chronology, 116–127. **C. R. Conder.** Signed.

552 *An Editor's Retrospect* [by Charles A.

Cooper], 128–151. **William Wallace** (1843–1921)? Wallace wrote no. 543, also an account of journalism from the inside; on p. 145 the author points out that Cooper neglects to mention R. Wallace (brother of man cited) as one of the editors of the *Scotsman*.

553 Summaries of foreign reviews, 152–176.

554 Contemporary literature, 177–200.

VOLUME 29, APRIL 1897

555 *Pickle the Spy* [by Andrew Lang], 201–226. **A. H. Millar.** Signed.

556 Primitive religion and primitive magic, 226–246. **George Francis Legge.** Signed as in no. 316.

557 Lord Roberts in India, 247–275. **W. M. Metcalfe.** *ScotR* list.

558 Modern Greek folk-lore, 276–295. **William Metcalfe.** Signed W. Metcalfe; cf. no. 513. (See no. 571.)

559 New light on Burns, 295–311. **James Davidson.** Signed; prob. the James Davidson, b. 1862, assistant ed. of the *Glasgow Herald* (see *Aberdeen Graduates*); the book here reviewed, and very favorably, was edited by William Wallace, the ed. of the *Glasgow Herald*.

560 *Farthest North* [on arctic exploration], 311–321. **W. M. Metcalfe,** prob. *ScotR* list, which adds a "?"; man cited wrote other reviews of travel books (nos. 103, 557, 593, 626); the large blocks of quotations are characteristic.

561 The diary of Jane Porter, 321–337. **Ina Mary White.** Signed.

562 The financial relations of Great Britain and Ireland, 337–363. **William O'Connor Morris.** Signed.

563 Summaries of foreign reviews, 364–399.

564 Contemporary literature, 400–418.

VOLUME 30, JULY 1897

565 Victorian art, 1–33. **James L. Caw.** Signed.

566 Wyntoun's *Original Chronicle*, 33–54. **W. A. Craigie.** Signed.

567 *The Life of Nelson* [by A. T. Mahan], 55–92. **William O'Connor Morris.** Signed.

568 Early Christian miniatures, 93–117. **Jane Bury.** Signed.

569 George Thomson, the friend of Burns, 117–142. **J. Cuthbert Hadden.** Signed.

570 Literary culture in Canada, 143–163. **John George Bourinot.** Signed.

571 Modern Greek [in reply to no. 558], 164–166. **J. S. Stuart-Glennie.** Signed. With a rejoinder, 166–167, signed **William Metcalfe.**

572 Summaries of foreign reviews, 168–201.

573 Contemporary literature, 202–216.

VOLUME 30, OCTOBER 1897

574 Processions, 217–235. **J. Balfour Paul.** Signed.

575 Sheriffs and coroners, 235–251. **Hugh Cowan.** Signed.

576 Paolo Sarpi, 251–282. **Horatio F. Brown.** Signed; repr. *Studies in the History of Venice*, II, 1907.

577 Mrs. Oliphant and her rivals [especially George Eliot and Mrs. Humphry Ward], 282–300. **William Wallace,** 1843–1921. Signed An Old Personal Friend; *ScotR* list; supported by Wallace to Blackwood, Oct. 4, 1897, Blackwood Corres.

578 The new woman on the Bible, 300–322. **T. Pilkington White.** Signed T.P.W.; *ScotR* list.

579 Scandinavian literature, 322–340. **David Anderson.** Signed.

580 Greek art in Asia, 340–361. **C. R. Conder.** Signed.

581 Some anonymous Scottish songs, 361–374. **J. A. Duncan.** Signed; repr. *Some Family Leaves*, Edin., 1911.

582 Summaries of foreign reviews, 375–405.

583 Contemporary literature, 406–421.

VOLUME 31, JANUARY 1898

584 Scottish municipal heraldry, 1–23. **J. Balfour Paul.** *ScotR* list.

585 Lord Tennyson, 23–51. **J. Edward Graham.** Signed.

586 *Annals of a Publishing House* [by Mrs. Oliphant on Blackwood & Sons], 51–81.

587 A corner of Bretonland, 81–106. **T. Pilkington White.** Signed.

588 R. W. Cochran-Patrick, 106–126. **Neil K. Cochran-Patrick.** Metcalfe copy; Metcalfe addresses.

589 David, Earl of Huntingdon, 127–148. **Robert Aitken.** Signed.

590 Hanoverian letters of 1746—before Culloden, 148–165. **A. H. Millar.** Signed.

591 Summaries of foreign reviews, 166–199.

592 Contemporary literature, 200–216.

635 *The American Revolution*, 328–353.
636 The origins of political economy, 353–371. **St. George Stock.** *ScotR* list.
637 Odin and the royal family of England, 371–379. **Karl Blind.** Signed.
638 Summaries of foreign reviews, 380–414.
639 Contemporary literature, 415–426.

VOLUME 34, JULY 1899

640 Early struggles for the Indian trade, 1–22. **W. M. Metcalfe.** *ScotR* list.
641 Golf and its literature, 22–39. **William Wallace,** 1843–1921. Signed.
642 Roundell Earl of Selborne, 39–69. **William O'Connor Morris.** Signed.
643 Miss Ferrier's novels, 70–90.
644 Anent the Whitefoords, 90–101. **Florence M. Parsons.** Signed F. M. Parsons; Cover gives "Mrs. Clement Parsons": see *WWW*/1940.
645 The evolution of the procurator fiscal, 101–110. **Henry H. Brown.** Signed.
646 Famous sultanas, 110–124. **Lucy M. J. Garnett.** Signed.
647 Mrs. Oliphant's *Autobiography*, 124–138. **W. M. Metcalfe?** *ScotR* list, which adds the "?."
648 The story of Tusculum, 138–153. **Florence Gautier,** prob. Signed F. Gautier; *ScotR* list gives "Countess Gautier"; woman cited was author of a pamphlet on Roman monuments, now in Boston Public Library.
649 Some remarkable coincidences in customs and beliefs, 153–167. **F. R. Coles.** Signed.
650 Summaries of foreign reviews, 168–195.
651 Contemporary literature, 196–212.

VOLUME 34, OCTOBER 1899

652 The Royal Library, 213–235. **Jean M. Stone.** Signed; repr. *Studies*.
653 Discoveries in Western Asia, 236–259. **C. R. Conder.** Signed.
654 The Ossianic ballads, 260–290. **W. A. Craigie.** Signed.
655 Mr. Rudyard Kipling's prose writings, 291–309. **W. M. Metcalfe.** *ScotR* list.
656 *The Wedderburn Book* [by Alexander Wedderburn], 310–330. **A. H. Millar.** Signed.
657 A notable failure [Charles the Bold], 330–342. **H. J. Allen.** Signed; Cover adds "Professor."
658 Fermartine, 342–363. **James Ferguson,**

1857–1917. Though *ScotR* list assigns this to "J. A. Fergusson," all of the evidence given for no. 409 applies to this art.; Fermartine was a section of Buchan.
659 Summaries of foreign reviews,, 364–393.
660 Contemporary literature, 394–412.

VOLUME 35, JANUARY 1900

661 The alleged haunting of B--- House, 1–13. **J. P. Crichton-Stuart** and **Ada Goodrich-Freer.** Signed A. Goodrich-Freer; attr. to both as authors in *DNB*, 1st Suppl. under Stuart; repr. in book with same title, 1899, where both are presented as editors: see *BMCat*.
662 The life and limitations of [R. L.] Stevenson, 13–35. **William Wallace,** 1843–1921. Signed.
663 *Social Life in Scotland in the Eighteenth Century*, 36–59.
664 The South African crisis, 59–69. **William Metcalfe.** Signed A Resident in Contents; *ScotR* list; see *Fasti*, VII, 451, for Metcalfe's South African residency.
665 The coercion of custom, 69–89. **T. Pilkington White.** Signed T.P.W.; *ScotR* list.
666 The mythology of the nineteenth century [on Emile Zola], 89–105. **Fernande Blaze de Bury.** Signed.
667 The taxation of land values, 105–128. **J. Edward Graham.** Signed.
668 The first chapter of the War [in South Africa], 129–161. **Arthur M. White.** Assigned in Contents "Colonel U.U."; White to W. M. Metcalfe, Sept. 25, 1900, Nat. Lib. Scot., refers to his "three chapters" in *ScotR* on the War: cf. nos. 680, 692.
669 Summaries of foreign reviews, 162–186.
670 Contemporary literature, 187–215.

VOLUME 35, APRIL 1900

671 A Scot abroad [James Keith, b. 1696], 217–225. **Robert S. Rait.** Signed.
672 The Hudson Bay Company, 226–249. **W. M. Metcalfe.** *ScotR* list.
673 Wayland the Smith, 250–261. **Karl Blind.** Signed.
674 The literary inspiration of imperialism, 262–278. **William Wallace,** 1843–1921. *ScotR* list.
675 Sir William Henry Flower, K.C.B., etc., 279–291. **William C. M'Intosh.** Signed.
676 Julian and Jerusalem, A.D. 363, 291–

306. **J. M. Campbell.** Signed; Cover and Contents add "Sir."

677 The negotiations which preceded the war in South Africa, 306–325. **J. Edward Graham.** Signed.

678 Colours in Dante, 325–336. **J. L. Bevir.** Signed J. L. Bevis incorrectly; typescript of this art. in Harvard College Library with Joseph Louis Bevir as author; Bevir was a master at Wellington College: see *Wellington College Register, 1859–1923*.

679 The sons of Dom John, 337–353. **C. J. Willdey.** Signed.

680 The second chapter of the War, 353–378. **Arthur M. White.** Evidence for no. 668.

681 Summaries of foreign reviews, 379–402.

682 Contemporary literature, 403–424.

VOLUME 36, JULY 1900

683 Recent Scottish historians, 1–18. **A. H. Millar.** Signed.

684 The Kelmscott Press; a review and some statistics, 19–35. **Frank Rinder.** *ScotR* list.

685 Sir Walter Scott and the Blair Adam Antiquarian Club (1817–31), 35–44. **William Stephen** (1834–1901)? OR, **William Stephen** (1840–1912)? Signed W. Stephen; attr. to "Rev. William Stephen" by J. C. Corson, *A Bibliography of Sir Walter Scott* (1943), p. 358; both men cited were Scottish divines: see *Aberdeen Graduates*, I, and *Fasti-Free Church*, pp. 350–351, respectively.

686 Yiddish literature, 44–62. **W. M. Metcalfe.** *ScotR* list.

687 Recent Hittite discoveries, 62–80. **C. R. Conder.** Signed.

688 Admiral Baillie, 81–88. **F. P. Badham.** Signed.

689 The reaundancy of spinster gentlewomen, 88–112. **T. Pilkington White.** Signed T.P.W.; *ScotR* list.

690 The future in South Africa, 113–125. **William Metcalfe.** *ScotR* list.

691 A father of history [Ari Thorgilsson, 1067–1148], 126–142. **W. A. Craigie.** Signed.

692 The third chapter of the War, 142–159. **Arthur M. White.** Evidence for no. 668.

693 Summaries of foreign reviews, 160–180.

694 Contemporary literature, 181–200.

VOLUME 36, OCTOBER 1900

695 The love story of Drummond of Hawthornden, 203–229. **Louise Lorimer.** Signed.

696 *Quentin Metsys*; translated from the French of Monsieur Edward Van Even, 230–250. **Edward Van Even.** Title. Trans. by **Ina Mary White**—signed.

697 Daniel Defoe in Scotland, 250–269. **James D. Cockburn.** Signed.

698 The coming war of American dreams, 269–292. **William Wallace,** 1843–1921. Signed.

699 A lost art ["table-talk"], 292–302. **Oliphant Smeaton.** Signed.

700 The strath of Achéron, and its Homeric ghosts, 302–311. **J. S. Stuart-Glennie.** Signed.

701 The folk-lore of Icelandic fishes, 312–332. **Ólaf Davidsson.** Signed. Trans. by **W. A. Craigie**—Craigie to W. M. Metcalfe, Sept. 4, 1900, Nat. Lib. Scot.

702 Concerning birds, 332–359. **S. E. Saville.** Signed.

703 Summaries of foreign reviews, 360–384.

704 Contemporary literature, 385–403.

PART B

BIBLIOGRAPHIES OF CONTRIBUTORS

Bibliographies of Contributors

EXPLANATORY NOTE
The note in *Index*, I, 785–786, should be reread, with special attention to the definitions of the term "See" in the third paragraph. The changes of format in Volume II are mainly one omission and two additions.

Where the biographical source is simply the article or story that follows, we now omit it. In *Index*, I, 969, occurs the following entry, reprinted in its entirety:

> **Knight,** Dr. W. T., schoolmaster, Towcester
> School. See *Mac* no. 2746.
>
> A practical philanthropist [Jean Godin],
> **Mac** 2746

In this volume the "See *Mac* no. 2746" would be dispensed with on the theory that if no biographical source is given, the information must be contained in the text of Part A or in the article itself. However, had Knight written two or more articles, the particular one which explained his vocation would have had to be cited in the old way.

An extension of this new method occurs where part of the description is provided by the text of Part A or the article and part by a printed source. In this case we again omit the former but cite the latter. For example, the entry below for Richardson, Frederick Austin, adds: "R.C. abbé, prof. at the Institute St. Louis. *BMCat*." Since all one can discover in the *BMCat*. is the "R.C. abbé" he turns to the entry for the *Dublin Review* no. 2205 (which is listed below the name), where he finds nothing but a signature. Consequently, the remainder of the identification must be in the article itself, as it is.

In short, either the absence of any source for what description is given or the inadequacy of such a source warns the reader to turn back to the item in Part A, and if that fails, to the article itself.

One addition was forced upon us by the frequent and uncertain habits of collaboration adopted by the staff and/or the editors of certain journals, notably early *Fraser's* and the *Foreign Quarterly*. Though half a dozen possibilities exist, we have placed all ambiguous attributions in one of three main categories, each with its own format. The evidence may indicate (1) that the author may have written the whole paper but if not, he certainly collaborated—which appears below as "collab. at least" (see under Maginn, *Fraser's* no. 183); or (2) that the author seems to have collaborated, though we cannot be sure—where we simply use "collab.?" (see under Heraud, *Fraser's* no. 620); or (3) that the author may have collaborated, but we are by no means sure that he had anything to do with the paper—in which case we put a "?" before the title and add a "collab." after the code number (see under Urquhart, *Foreign Quarterly* no. 364). These formats are peculiar to Part B; the corresponding entries in Part A normally take other forms: compare the Part A entries for the examples just cited.

The second addition is the reference to Volume I, Part B in order to avoid repeating biographical facts and to call attention both to earlier articles or stories and, if need be, to corrected or additional information. The standard entry is, "Doe, John: see *Index*, I, 000." But if we have now discovered a change in his bibliography or in the facts of his life, the entry becomes, "Doe, John: see *Index*, I, 000, and II, App. A." For the specific reference in the latter, the reader should consult the Index to Appendix A under John Doe.

The abbreviations of the twelve periodicals indexed here are as follows:

BentQR:	*Bentley's Quarterly Review*	**NatR-II:***	*The National Review*, 1883+
DR:	*The Dublin Review*	**NQM:**	*The New Quarterly Magazine*
FQR:	*The Foreign Quarterly Review*	**NC:**	*The Nineteenth Century*
		OxCam:	*The Oxford and Cambridge Magazine*, 1856
FortR:	*The Fortnightly Review*		
FM:	*Fraser's Magazine*	**Ram:**	*The Rambler*, 1848–1862
LR(1829):	*The London Review*, 1829	**ScotR:**	*The Scottish Review*, 1882+

A

Abbās Hilmī Pasha, 1874–1944, Khedive of Egypt, 1892–1914. Hill.

See: **NC** 2375, 2516

Abbondio, Don, O.S.B.

Notes on foreign periodicals, **DR** 2346, 2357, 2372
Notices: 2347, 2448

Abbot, or Abbott, Francis Ellingwood, 1836–1903, divine. *DAB.*

The Catholic peril in America, **FortR** 1239

Abbot, Reginald Charles Edward, 3rd Baron Colchester, 1842–1919, barrister. *WWW.*

Sismondi's political ideas, **NatR-II** 85
Mallet du Pan, 458
The endowed schools inquiry, 560
Talleyrand [in England], 975
Ernest Daudet on Coblentz, 1193

Lord Ellenborough, **NC** 3513

Abbott, Augustus, 1804–1867, army officer. *DNB*, 1st suppl.

See: **FM** 3631

Abbott, William G.

A Brazilian poet [Antonio Gonçalves Dias], **FortR** 3293

'Abd al-Halim Pasha: see Muhammad 'Abd al-Halim Pasha.

À Beckett, Arthur William, 1844–1909, humorist. *DNB.*

History in *Punch*, **FortR** 2484, 2541, 2582, all collab.

Abell, Henry Francis, traveller, sketcher. *BMCat.*; *Kelly's Directory of Kent, Surrey, and Sussex* (1899), p. 653, gives full name at address of H. F. Abell.

A Kentish pilgrim road, **NatR-II** 1017
Along Hadrian's British wall, 1322
Is cricket degenerating? 2182

Aberigh-Mackay, George Robert, 1848–1881, educator in India. Buckland.

The restoration of Moghul buildings at Agra, **FM** 5508

*NatR-II** is adopted because **NatR-I** will be used in Volume III for *The National Review*, 1855–1864.

About, Edmond-François-Valentin, 1828–1885, journalist. *DBF.*

Clerical education in France, **NC** 352

Abraham, George Whitley, 1830–1885, Irish barrister and historian. Boase.

French controversy on use of pagan literature in education, **DR** 681
Edmund Burke, 690
The Turco-Russian question, 705
Merimée's *Demetrius the Imposter,* 718
Theory of Jesuit history, 733
Monastic historians of England, 743
Miss Strickland's *Mary Stuart,* 752
The Druses and their religion, 755
Richard Lalor Sheil, 763
The Turks in relation to prophecy, 766
De Ravignan's *Times of Clement XIII and XIV,* 774
Sir Isaac Newton [by Brewster], 780
Hallam's works, 801
Guizot's *Cromwell,* 812
Cockburn's *Memorials of his Time,* 817
Epidemic disease in Ireland, 827
Helps' *Spanish Conquest in America,* 838
Bowring's *Siam,* 841
Philip Howard, 856
Recent African explorations, 869, 892
The Four Last Popes [by Wiseman], 872
La Belle Saison dans La Campagne, 901
German theories of Christianity, 903
Lord Broughton's *Italy,* 916
Harford's *Michael Angelo,* 923
[Nassau] Senior's *Turkey,* 932
Burke's *Vicissitudes of Families,* 934
Ceylon, 941
De Montalembert's *Western Monks,* 978
Biblical hermeneutics, 993
Irish church history, 1015
Frederick the Great [by Carlyle], 1016
Liberal party in England and Ireland, 1028
See: 898

Abraham, Henry

Trades unionism among women in Ireland, **DR** 2284

Abraham, Phineas Simon, 1847–1921, dermatologist. *WWW, Surgeon Index.*

Leprosy and its causes, **FortR** 2850

Abram, William Alexander: see *Index,* I, 786.

The Lancashire workmen, **FortR** 538

Ackland, Joseph, misc. writer in Glasgow. *Blackwood Papers Cat.*

Twenty-five years of financial policy, **FortR** 4290

Elementary education and decay of literature, **NC** 2541
The growth of our seaports, 3169

Acland, Sir Charles Thomas Dyke: see *Index,* I, 786.

County boards, **FortR** 1767

County councils and rural education, **NC** 3001

Acland, Hon. Emily Anna (Smith), 1860–1942, novelist; wife of William Alison Dyke Acland. *Times,* Jan. 30, 1942, p. 1a.

A lady's American notes, **NC** 1526

À Court, Charles: see Repington, Charles à Court.

Acton, Henry, 1797–1843, Unitarian divine. *DNB.*

?Memoirs of Admiral Chicagoff, **FQR** 615

Acton, Sir John Emerich Edward Dalberg: see *Index,* I, 786.

Henry IV, **DR** 865

George Eliot's *Life,* **NC** 1105
Talleyrand's *Memoirs,* 2032
Notices: 1977, 2203, 2399

The life and times of Edmund Burke, **Ram** 916
Mr. Buckle's thesis and method, 937 collab.
Mr. Buckle's philosophy of history, 942
Father Theiner's publications, 956
The Count de Montalembert, 972
Political thoughts of the Church, 976
The Catholic press, 980
The Roman question, 1015 collab.
The temporal power, 1021
The states of the Church, 1025
Hefele's *Life of Ximenes,* 1044
National defence, 1053
Döllinger's *History of Christianity,* 1070
Notes on the present state of Austria, 1073 collab.
Political causes of the American Revolution, 1085
Cavour, 1089
Expectation of the French Revolution, 1091
The Catholic Academy, 1098
Döllinger on the temporal power, 1107
Mr. Goldwin Smith's *Irish History,* 1116
The Protestant theory of persecution, 1124
Colonies, 1127
Enlargement of the *Rambler,* 1130 collab.
Contemporary and current events, 1000, 1006 collab., 1023 collab., 1032 collab., 1042 collab., 1052, 1061 collab., 1083, 1088 collab., 1097, 1106, 1121, 1137

Acton, Sir John E. E. D. (*continued*)
Edited: 1016, 1035, 1099
Letters: 974, 1050, 1101, 1127
Notes: 988, 1002, 1019?, 1021, 1095, 1108
Notices: 940, 945, 973, 999, 1013, 1031, 1051, 1068 collab., 1105, 1113 collab., 1120 collab., 1128
Trans: 959, 966
See: 923, 934

Acworth, Sir William Mitchell: see *Index*, I, 787.

Letter: **NatR-II** 986

The London County Council, **NC** 1680
Can railway-passenger fares be lowered? 2098
Taxes on transport, 2154
Railway mismanagement, 2323

Adam, Juliette (Lamber): see *Index*, I, 787.

Woman's place in modern life, **FortR** 3201

Adam, William

Consanguinity in marriage, **FortR** 119, 129

Adami, John George, 1862–1926, pathologist. *DNB*.

Waist-belts and stays, **NatR-II** 784 collab.

Adams, Brooks, 1848–1927, economist. *DAB*.

The gold standard, **FortR** 3536
New struggle for life among nations, 4239

Adams, Coker, 1827–1891, divine. Foster, *Landed Gentry*.

Macaulay and Madame D'Arblay, **NatR-II** 652

Adams, Francis, sec. National Education League. Chamberlain, *Memoir*, p. 108; *BMCat*.

The Radical programme: free schools, **FortR** 2120
The Radical programme: taxation and finance, 2345

Adams, Francis William Lauderdale: see *Index*, I, 787.

The labour movement in Australia, **FortR** 3113
Social life in Australia, 3128, 3139
An Anglo-Indian story-teller [Kipling], 3147
Some Australian men of mark, 3176
Some recent novels, 3230
Shelley, 3249
Two Australian writers, 3265

Mr. Rudyard Kipling's verse, 3428
The hunt for happiness, 3444

Adams, George, Indian civil servant. *Army List*/87, p. 893.

The Chinese drama, **NC** 2726
India, 3176

Adams, Robert Dudley, b.1829, still alive in 1908, Australian journalist. Johns' *Notable Australians*, 1908.

Letter from New South Wales, **FM** 5756

Adams, William Bridges, 1797–1872, inventor. *DNB*.

Political economy of copyright, **FortR** 80

Adderley, Charles Bowyer: see *Index*, I, 787.

Impossible constitutions, **NatR-II** 462

How not to retain the colonies, **NC** 335
Penal servitude, 440
Middle-class education, 817
"Cramming" in elementary schools, 962
Imperial federation: its impossibility, 1042
Democracy and England, 1096
Free schools, 1209
Schools as prisons, 1362
Two conflicting "reports" on education, 1633

Adderley, Hon. James, 1861–1942, prebendary of St. Paul's. *WWW*.

A sermon for the season, **NatR-II** 1731

Addis, William Edward, 1844–1917, R.C. priest. *WWW*.

The Ignatian Epistles, **DR** 1447
Gnosticism and faith in St. Irenaeus, 1492
Supernatural Religion [by W. R. Cassels], 1503
Witness of St. Irenaeus to Catholic doctrine, 1555
Truth and falsehood of M. Renan's lectures, 1750
Notices: 1489?, 1561?, 1745, 1756, 1767, 1779, 1790, 1813, 1826, 1896, 1919, 1930, 1941, 2019, 2029, 2079

Addison, Joseph Edward, 1821–1890, army officer. Boase.

The national defences, **FM** 3916
Soldiers and Their Science, 4103

Addison, William Hall, headmaster, West of England Institution for the Deaf and Dumb, Exeter. *BMCat*.

Letter: **NatR-II** 917

Addleshaw, William Percy, 1866–1916, critic. *LCCat.*, Foster.

Wilfrid Blunt's poetry, **NatR-II** 1782

Adler, Hermann, 1839–1911, chief rabbi of British Empire. *U.J.E.*

Letter: **FortR** 2524

Can Jews be patriots? **NC** 157
Jews and Judaism, 198
Recent phases of Judaeophobia, 652
Irresponsible wealth, 1966
Jewish wit and humour, 2366

Adolphus, John Leycester: see *Index*, I, 787.

The late John Adolphus, **FM** 4234

Ady, Julia Mary (Cartwright): see *Index*, I, 787.

Winter and spring exhibitions, **NatR-II** 982
The pictures of the year, 1157
A corner of Essex, 1236

Giotto, **NQM** 124

Jean-François Millet, **NC** 1599
Rome in 1889, 1772

Adye, Sir John, 1857–1930, army officer, *WWW.*

The past and the future of Gibraltar, **NC** 2836
Has our army grown with our empire? 2949
The limits of French armament, 3126
The capture of Havana by England, 3321
The colonial weakness of France, 3404

Adye, Sir John Miller: see *Index*, I, 788.

The British army, past and present, **FortR** 2579

The British army, **NC** 347
Native armies of India, 434
Glut of junior officers in the army, 1829
Military forces of the Crown, 2113
In defence of "short service," 2278

Aflalo, Frederick George: see *Index*, I, 788.

The sportsman's library, **FortR** 4378
Ethics of performing animals, 4419
Promise of international exhibitions, 4453
The sportman's library, 4554

Agar-Ellis, Leopold George Frederick Agar, 5th Viscount Clifden of Gowran, 1829–1899, M.P. Venn.

Irish local government, **NatR-II** 1242

Agg-Gardner, J. T.: see Gardner, J. T. Agg.

Aherne, Cornelius, 1861–1929, prof. at St. Joseph's Coll., Mill Hill. *Tablet,* June 1, 1929.

Physical science v. matter and form, **DR** 2691
Physical science v. matter and form, 2731

Ahmad, Maulvi Sir Rafiüddin, 1865–1954, Indian educationist. *WWW.*

In defence of Islâm, **FortR** 3754

England in relation to Mohamedan states, **NatR-II** 1414

Kaiser-I-Hind and Hindoostani, **NC** 2038
A Moslem view of Abdul Hamid, 2786
The Eastern question, 2854
India: is the British "Raj" in danger? 3177
A Moslem's view of the Pan-Islamic revival, 3179
Future of the Anglo-Afghan alliance, 3239
The battle of Omdurman and the Mussulman world, 3365
The proposed Muslim University in India, 3386

Aïdé, Charles Hamilton: see *Index*, I, 788.

Colour in domesticity and dress, **FortR** 2823
Corsican bandits, and others, 3970
A gleam in the darkness, 4372

The Marstons, in 16 installments from **FM** 4708 to 4849

The Brudenels, **NatR-II** 1504

A school of dramatic art, **NC** 703
The art of public speaking, 1006
The actor's calling, 1109
Was I hypnotised? 1851
Manners and customs of Sicily in 1890, 1941
Social aspects of American life, 2054
A new stage doctrine, 2455
A lesson in acting, 3373
Notices: 1659, 1698, 1804, 2205, 2524

Aikman, Charles Morton: see *Index*, I, 788.

The microbe in agriculture, **NC** 3305

Argon and atmosphere, **ScotR** 496

Ailesbury, Countess of: see Conway, Caroline (Campbell)

Ainscough, J. Ashton. *BMCat.*

From a suburban window, **NatR-II** 1336

Ainslie, William Langstaff, b.1858/59. Foster.

British seamen for British ships, **NC** 3402 collab.

Ainsworth, William Harrison, 1805–1882, editor, novelist. *DNB.*

La Guglielmina of Milan, **FM** 724

Aird, Thomas: see *Index*, I, 788.

The scarlet witch, **FM** 505

Airy, Osmund: see *Index*, I, 789.

Unpublished notices of James Sharp, Archbishop of St. Andrew's, **ScotR** 59
Correspondence of Sir Robert Moray with Alexander Bruce, 78
Letter from James Sharp to Earl of Middleton, 81 collab.

Aitken, David, 1796–1875, divine. *Fasti,* II, 133.

Germany in 1826, **ScotR** 449

Aitken, George Atherton: see *Index*, I, 788.

Defoe's *Apparition of Mrs. Veal*, **NC** 2689

Aitken, Robert

David, Earl of Huntingdon, **ScotR** 589
The Knights Templars in Scotland, 602

Akin, C. K., Dr.

New views on light, **FortR** 230

Alberdingk Thijm: see Thijm, Petrus Paul Maria Alberdingk.

Albert I, Prince of Monaco, 1848–1922. *LCCat.*

The proposed Channel bridge, **FortR** 3516

Albizzi, Count Rinaldo Ottavio degli, 1804–1851, a Florentine. Count Pompeo Litta, *Famiglie Celebri Italiane,* XI (Turin, 1876), disp. 178, table 9.

Notices: **FQR** 634, 657, 667?

Alcalá Galiano, Antonio, 1789–1865, Spanish statesman. *EUI.*

Life and works of Jovellanos, **FQR** 126
Notice: 132

Alcock, Sir Rutherford: see *Index*, I, 788.

Inheritance of the Great Mogul, **FortR** 1179
Relations of western powers with the East, 1221
Chinese Empire and foreign relations, 1254

The *Peking Gazette*, **FM** 5402, 5410

Opium and common sense, **NC** 654
France, China, and the Vatican, 1335

Alden, William Livingston: see *Index*, I, 789.

The Italian case against France, **NC** 2615
Francesco Crispi, 2695
King and Pretender in Rome [Leo XIII], 2921
Battle of the standards in America, 2970

Aldis, Harry Gidney, 1863–1919, bibliographer. *LCCat.*

Scottish bibliography, **ScotR** 550

Aldrich, Thomas Bailey, 1836–1907, American poet. *DAB.*

Letter: **FortR** 2647

Alexander, George

The newer North-West [Canada], **NatR-II** 419
Two coercion bills compared, 761

Alexander, Henry McClintock, 1834–1896, naval officer. *LCCat.*

Letter: **NatR-II** 418

Alexander, William, 1824–1911, Archbishop of Armagh. *DNB.*

Thirlwall and the Irish Church Bill of 1869, **NatR-II** 1698

Alfièri di Sostegno, Marchese Carlo Alberto, 1827–1897, politician. *Enci. Ital.*

Italy drifting, **NC** 1758

Alford, Viscountess Marianne Margaret (Compton), known as Lady Marian Alford, 1817–1888, artist. *DNB.*

Art needlework, **NC** 561

Alger, John Goldworth: see *Index*, I, 789.

George Sand at an English school, **NatR-II** 880
Women in the Reign of Terror, 1237
Vicissitudes of James the Second, **NC** 1646

A French envoy in 1745, **ScotR** 312
An idyll during the French Revolution, 420
Sir Andrew Melville, 485
Fall of Robespierre, 596

Alison, Sir Archibald, 1792–1867: see *Index*, I, 789.

History of the French National Convention, **FQR** 303

Allain, Ernest, 1847–1902, French archivist. *DBF.*

Church of Bordeaux during English dominion, **DR** 2504, 2512

Allan, H. M. Havelock: see Havelock-Allan, Henry Marshman.

Allan, Rowland, M.B.. Fr., of Bridgman Place, Bolton.

Letter: **NatR-II** 690

Allardyce, Alexander: see *Index*, I, 791.

Jagannath and his worship, **FM** 5395
Mr. Sempill's settlement, 6344

Allaria, Antony or Anthony, 1853–1921, Abbot of the Canons in England. *Tablet,* June 11, 1921, p. 769.

English scholars at Bologna, **DR** 2363
Notices: 2425, 2438

The Culdees, **ScotR** 464

Allen, Charles Grant Blairfindie: see *Index*, I, 792.

A problem in human evolution, **FortR** 1584
Some new books, 1606
The ways of orthodox critics, 1727
Are we Englishmen? 1739
Wallace's *Island Life,* 1758
Sir Charles Lyell, 1875
The decay of criticism, 1892
Who was primitive man? 1943
Falling in love, 2518
American jottings, 2540
Our noble selves, 2559
Progress of science from 1836 to 1886, 2599
Sunday at Concord [Mass.], 2708
Genius and talent, 2737
Plain words on the woman question, 2873
Practical religion, 2896
Sacred stones, 2909
The Celt in English art, 3045
Letters in Philistia, 3096
Note on a new poet [William Watson], 3114
Bates of the Amazons, 3302
Beautiful London, 3385
Immortality and resurrection, 3405
The new hedonism, 3480
The origin of cultivation, 3494
The mystery of birth, 3670
Spencer and Darwin, 3919
Letter: 2627

Geology and history, **FM** 6294
Landowning and copyright, 6324

The Tuscan nationality, **NatR-II** 1476

?The human face divine [on its evolution], **NQM** 186

Allen, H. J., professor.

A notable failure [Charles the Bold], **ScotR** 657

Allhusen, Beatrice May (Butt): see *Index*, I, 794.

Hester, **NQM** 93

Allies, Thomas William, 1813–1903, Catholic theologian. *DNB.*

Grotius and Leibnitz [on] truth of Catholic doctrines, **DR** 609
The Greek Church, 612
Anglican universities as ecclesiastical schools, 618
The Catholic University, 648
The Jesuit in India, 663
Letter to Dr. Pusey by Mr. Allies, 1144
Gods of the nations when Christ appeared, 1197
First and second man [Adam and Christ], 1209, 1220
First age of the martyr Church, 1226
The Lambeth Conference [of 1888], 2136
Note: 1410
Notice: 641

Why I shall vote for the Unionist candidate, **NC** 2255

Archdeacon Wilberforce on Erastianism, **Ram** 344
Catholic and Protestant missionary societies, 957 collab.

Allingham, Hugh, Irish writer, half-brother of William Allingham, q.v. *BMCat.*

See: **FM** 5468

Allingham, William: see *Index*, I, 794.

George Petrie, **FM** 4669
Arthur Hugh Clough, 4697
On poetry, 4752
Rambles, in 20 installments from 4807 to 6002
On the names of places in Ireland, 4983
A poet of the Lower French Empire [Baudelaire], 5034
Seven hundred years ago [Ireland], 5107
Some curiosities of criticism, 5384
Green London, 5540
A few London exteriors, 5552
A feast and a battle, 5681
Artist and critic, 5714

Allingham, William (*continued*)
The proposed Byron memorial, 5779
Modern prophets, 5963
Ivy leaves, in 12 installments from 6013 to 6129
A query on *Hamlet*, 6150
The Byron monument, 6180
Fifty years ago [on *FM* in 1830s], 6192
Notes: 5861, 5949
See: 4396, 5468

Allinson, Thomas Richard, M.D. *Med. Direc./* 1900.

Note: **NatR-II** 1035

Almond, Hely Hutchinson: see *Index*, I, 794.

Examinations for Woolwich and Sandhurst, **FortR** 4225

Football as a moral agent, **NC** 2489
The decay in our salmon fisheries, 3485
The breed of man, 3738

Althaus, Julius: see *Index*, I, 794.

The functions of the brain, **NC** 383

Altmann, C. K.

Public education in Holland, **FortR** 625

Ameer Ali, Syed, 1849–1928, Indian jurist. *DNB.*

Some Indian suggestions for India, **NC** 454
A cry from the Indian Mahommedans, 748
The life-problem of Bengal, 902
The real status of women in Islâm, 2097
The rupee and the ruin of India, 2370
Islâm and its critics, 2802
Islâm and Canon Mac Coll, 2833
The influence of women in Islâm, 3464

Amherst, William Joseph, S.J., 1820–1904. Sutcliffe.

Frederick Lucas, **DR** 2038
Charles Langdale, 2353, 2389, 2406
The minute book of the Cisalpine Club, 2365, 2377

Amos, Sheldon: see *Index*, I, 794.

Democracy in England, **FortR** 18
Civilisation and crime, 88
Some books of the month, 751, 759, 768

Amstel, Baronne Adrienne van

Eléonore d'Olbreuse and Queen Victoria, **NC** 3272
True story of the prisoner of Chillon, 3654

Ancketill, William Robert, 1820–1889, writer on Ireland. Boase (where the surname is misspelt Anketell), *BMCat., LCCat.*

Operation of Irish Land Act, **NatR–II** 152
Dead-lock in Irish land, 164
Letter: 120

Anderdon, William Henry, S.J., 1816–1890. *DNB.*

The two dukes [Wellington and Duke of Baylen], **DR** 679
Bishop Ken, 696
Montalembert's political future of England, 804
Catholic and party politics, 1188
Glastonbury, 1236
See: 1235

Anderson, David, later Lord St. Vigeons, 1862–1948, Scottish advocate. *WWW.*

Scandinavian literature, **ScotR** 579

Anderson, Elizabeth (Garrett): see *Index*, I, 794.

Sex in mind and education, **FortR** 1047
The history of [women in medicine], 3343

Anderson, James Maitland, 1852–1927, librarian, Univ. of St. Andrews. *WWW.*

The "Princely Chandos" and the University of St. Andrews, **ScotR** 466

Anderson, Joseph, 1832–1916, Scottish antiquary. *LCCat.*

The wicked clan Gregor, **ScotR** 297

Anderson, Sir Robert: see *Index,* I, 794.

Irish crisis: the general problem, **FortR** 2466
New departure [in dealing with Ireland], 2501

Andrew, F., O.F.M., b.1858. *Catholic Who's Who/*1924.

The Mazarinus manuscript and the biography of St. Francis of Assisi, **DR** 2682

Andrews, Augustus, 1779/1780–1858, general in Indian army. Boase.

?The Indian army, **FM** 3631

Andrieu, Jules, 1839–1895, historian. *DBF.*

The Paris Commune, **FortR** 821

The *Roman de Renart* and La Fontaine, **FM** 5887

Anson, Sir William Reynell, 1843–1914, warden of All Souls Coll., Oxon. *DNB.*

Objections of a Liberal to Home Rule, **NatR-II** 613

Anstey, Thomas Chisholm, 1816–1873, prof. Prior Park Coll. *DNB.*

Ozanam's *English Chancellors,* **DR** 64
The Vaudois, 65 collab.
Carlyle's works, 111
Southern Africa in 1840, 223
Van Diemen's Land under prison system, 238
?Apostolics and the eighteenth century, 243
Frederic the Great and his times, 256

Anstice, Elizabeth (Poole), 1807–1889, R.C. convert. Newman, *L&D,* XI, index.

The Female Jesuit Abroad, **Ram** 555

Anstruther, Hon. Eva Isabella Henrietta (Hanbury-Tracey), 1869–1935. *WWW,* Burke.

Ladies' clubs, **NC** 3450

Anton, Peter, 1850–1911, Scottish divine. *Fasti,* III, 481.

Frances Ridley Havergal, **FM** 6335

Antonelli, Giacomo, 1806–1876, Cardinal, Sec. of State to Pius IX. *Cath. Ency.*

Roman documents, **DR** 1329

Apperley, Charles James: see *Index,* I, 795.

Memorabilia Bacchanalia, **FM** 879, 911, 962, 990
Cibaria memorabilia, 1056, 1062
Anatomy of gaming, 1089, 1117, 1149, 1174, 1198
Go—going—gone!, 1513
My life and times, in 10 installments from 1645 to 1760

Appleton, Charles Edward Cutts Birch: see *Index,* I, 795.

Economic aspect of the endowment of research, **FortR** 1093
American efforts after international copyright, 1333

Appleyard, Rollo, 1867–1943, consulting engineer. *WWW.*

"With but After" [on need for naval engineers], **FortR** 4438
"We always are ready" [on shortage of stokers in the navy], 4506

Appleyard, W. A.

Matthew Arnold: criticism of life, **NatR-II** 1103

Arábi, Ahmed, 1840–1911, Egyptian revolutionary leader. Hill under Amad 'Urābi Pasha.

Instructions to my counsel, **NC** 800

Arbuthnot, Sir Alexander John: see *Index,* I, 795.

The opium controversy, **NC** 690

Arbuthnot, Gerald Archibald, 1872–1916, politician. *WWW.*

A defence of the muzzle, **NatR-II** 2115

Arch, Joseph, 1826–1919, politician. *DNB.*

The labourers and the vote, **NC** 123

Archer, Thomas Andrew: see *Index,* I, 796.

The Council of Clermont and the First Crusade, **ScotR** 498

Archer, William: see *Index,* I, 796.

Norway to-day, **FortR** 2367
A plea for the playwright, 2473
A plea for an endowed theatre, 2817
Ibsen and English criticism, 2841
The Danish drama of to-day, 2949
Critics "Over the Coals," 3047
Pessimist playwright [Maeterlinck], 3124
The free stage and the new drama, 3145
The stage and literature, 3178
The drama in the doldrums, 3243
"The mausoleum of Ibsen," 3388
Plays and acting of the season, 3400
Some recent plays, 3496
Eleanora Duse, 3685
George Henry Lewes and the stage, 3758
The blight on the drama, 3899
Shakespeare's sonnets, 4041
A Shropshire poet [A. E. Housman], 4160
Pessimism and tragedy, 4248
Plays of the season, 4308

The myths of Romeo and Juliet, **NatR-II** 240
The stage of Greater Britain, 376
A well-graced actress, 467

The duties of dramatic critics, **NC** 1090
The Winter's Tale, 1462

Arendt, Otto, 1854–1936, German politician. *NDB.*

Bimetallism in Europe: Germany, **NatR-II** 1977

Argyll, Duke of: see Campbell, George Douglas.

Armstrong, Edward: see *Index*, I, 796.

The Franco-Italian question, **ScotR** 471
Alberoni and the Quadruple Alliance, 549

Armstrong, Robert Archibald, 1788–1867, Gaelic lexicographer. *DNB.*

The three florists, **FM** 1168

Armstrong, Sir Walter, 1850–1918, art critic. *WWW.*

The Life and Works of Rembrandt, **FortR** 3468

The art harvest of the year, **NatR-II** 192
Gainsborough, 264
The [Royal] Academy and the Salon, 312
Millais, 406
The fame of Turner, 427
Pictures at Edinburgh, 487
"Nineteenth century school" in art, **NC** 1396
Stevens and the Wellington memorial, 2219

Armstrong, William George, Baron Armstrong of Cragside, 1810–1900, inventor, engineer. *DNB.*

The vague cry for technical education, **NC** 1570
The cry for useless knowledge, 1618
The new naval programme, 1700

Armytage, Mrs. G.; possibly Eliza Matilda Mary (Radcliffe), d.1898, wife of Sir George Armytage. Burke.

Modern dress, **FortR** 2079

Arnold, Andrew W.: see *Index*, I, 796.

Free trade and shipping supremacy, **NatR-II** 1375

Arnold, Sir Arthur: see *Index*, I, 796.

Agricultural statistics, **FortR** 97
Sanitary reform: water supply, 168
Political enfranchisement of women, 843
Liquor and licensing, 943
Parliamentary reform, 2134
People, parliament and peers, 2213
Is this the Bill [for redistribution of boroughs]? 2234
Redistribution by different lights, 2258
The Queen and her family, 2322
The elections: and after? 2406
Irish crisis: Gladstone's policy, 2464

The answer to Mr. Gladstone, 2500
The Land Transfer Bill, 2612

Cobden and the land question, **FM** 4780
Prison labour, 4927
The transfer of land, 5404
Church reform, 5608
The agricultural strikes, 5626
Russia in Europe, 5837
The City, 5953
The Hon. Mrs. Norton, 6044
Land titles and transfer, 6154
The land question: titles and transfer, 6230
Socialism, **NQM** 150
The abuses of a landed gentry, **NC** 32
Business aspect of disestablishment, 162
Free land and peasant proprietorship, 407

Arnold, Edward Augustus: see *Index*, I, 796.

The London flower trade, **NC** 1176

Arnold, Sir Edwin, 1832–1904, poet and essayist. *DNB.*

Death: and afterwards, **FortR** 2352
Letter: 2647
Letter: **NatR-II** 267

Arnold, Edwin Lester Linden, 1856/57–1935, cattle breeder, journalist. *WWW, Times,* Mar. 4, 1935, p. 19c.

The future of English tobacco, **NC** 1609

Arnold, Frederick, 1832–1891, divine. Boase.

Sir Charles Bell, **FM** 5636
The Church of England abroad, **NatR-II** 246
Foreign missions of the Church, 586
Personal history of Lord Macaulay, **NQM** 23
Lord Bute, the premier, 56
Lord Chancellors since Lord Campbell, 121

Arnold, Matthew: see *Index*, I, 796.

George Sand, **FortR** 1364
Equality, 1442
Irish Catholicism and British Liberalism, 1484
Porro unum est necessarium, 1518
Ecce, convertimur ad gentes, 1551
Copyright, 1673
Irish grammar schools, 1826
An Eton boy, 1916
Count Leo Tolstoi, 2657
Letter: 2627
The twice-revised code, **FM** 4199
Maurice de Guérin, 4289

Dante and Beatrice, 4328

Disestablishment in Wales, **NatR-II** 689

Falkland, **NC** 9
A guide to English literature, 117
The French play in London, 339
The future of Liberalism, 465
The incompatibles [Irish Land Bill], 580,
    598
A word about America, 715
Literature and science, 749
A Liverpool address, 781
Isaiah of Jerusalem, 840, 852
The majority and the remnant, 986
A word more about America, 1088
The nadir of Liberalism, 1270
The zenith of conservatism, 1366
A "Friend of God" [perhaps John Tauler],
    1388
Up to Easter [on Home Rule], 1401
From Easter to August [Irish question],
    1447
An olive branch from America, 1478
Shelley, 1502
Civilisation in the United States, 1533

Arnold, Robert Arthur: see Arnold, Sir
    Arthur.

Arnold, Thomas, 1823–1900: see *Index*, I,
    797.

The filibusters in Nicaragua, **DR** 859
Spenser as a textbook, 1749
Church extension and Anglican expansion,
    2058
The Catholic University of Ireland, 2086
Louvain and Dublin, 2153

Reminiscences of New Zealand, **FM** 4132
Bristol churches, 4516

Arthur Hugh Clough, **NC** 3229

Mill, *On Liberty,* **Ram** 1010, 1029
The Catholic University of Ireland, 1033
Sir Walter Scott, 1036
The negro race and its destiny, 1045, 1055
The Irish Church, 1080

Arnold, Thomas James, 1804?–1877, barris-
    ter, police magistrate. *DNB.*

The Shakespearian discovery, **FM** 3929
The "old corrector," 3938
Collier's *Reply,* [Shakespeare controversy],
    3982
The Ireland forgeries, 4007

Arnold, William Delafield, 1828–1859, Anglo-
    Indian official, novelist. *DNB.*

The India question, **FM** 3089
What is the Indian question? 3129
What is the Indian question now? 3277
Lord Dalhousie, 3373
Protestantism: Zwingli and his times, 3453
An overland mail adventure, 3496
Jack Sepoy, 3519
The night mail train in India, 3547
The curate of Edenholm, 3654
India in mourning, 3678
An Anglo-Indian view of the Indian crisis,
    3699, 3715
Anglo-Indian lament for John Company,
    3732
India in a mess, 3806
Queen Victoria proclaimed at Peshawar,
    3818

Arnold-Forster, Hugh Oakeley: see *Index*, I,
    797.

The political outlook, **FortR** 3254

The position of Liberal Unionists, **NatR-II**
    1568
Questions in the House on naval matters,
    1584
Emperor's new clothes [Irish Land Acts],
    1725
The new Council of Defence, 1768
South Africa, 1877
"A Daniel come to judgment"; or The War
    Office on its trial, 2211
The War Office and the [Boer] War, 2414

Civilian's answer to Sir Garnet Wolseley,
    NC 591
Our position as a naval power, 801
The Liberal idea and the colonies, 899
The dwellings of the poor, 933
Proportional representation, 989
The people of England v. their naval
    officials, 1056
England or the admiralty? 1166
Shall we desert the Loyalists? 1241
Our superstition about Constantinople,
    1323
How to solve the Irish land question, 1488
Irish land purchase, 1499
Misrule of our war services, 1769
How to utilise the naval volunteers, 2074
Our true foreign policy, 2878
Sisyphus in Ireland, 2981
Army and the government's opportunity,
    3250
Insufficient proposals of the War Office,
    3629

Arthur, Sir George Compton Archibald,
    1860–1946, army officer, biographer.
    WWW.

Arthur, Sir George C. A. (*continued*)
Procrastination and parsimony, **FortR** 4409

The "lawless" clergy, **NC** 3446

d'Artois, Edmond, sec. of French Bimetallic League. *Bib.Nat.Cat.*

Bimetallism in Europe: France, **NatR-II** 1976

Arundell, Henry Benedict, 11th Baron Arundell of Wardour, 1804–1862, *Complete Peerage.*

See: **Ram** 674

Arundell, John Francis, 12th Baron Arundell of Wardour, 1831–1906. *Complete Peerage.*

The secret of Plato's Atlantis, **DR** 2036
Sir Edward Wydville and Sir Thomas Arundel, 2255
Letter: 1089

See: **Ram** 674

Arundell, Lady Mary Anne (Grenville), 1787–1845, Catholic convert, wife of James Everard, 10th Baron Arundell of Wardour. *Complete Peerage.*

A conversion under the old penal laws, **Ram** 647, 653

Ashburner, Lionel Robert, 1827–1907, Bombay civil service. *WWW.*

Reform of marriage laws of India, **NatR-II** 1078

The spoliation of India, **NC** 1049

Ashley, Hon. Cecil, 1849–1932, statesman. *WWW.*

Native questions, South Africa, **NatR-II** 316

Ashley, Hon. Evelyn, 1836–1907, barrister. *DNB.*

Prisoners in the witness-box, **NatR-II** 2113
Mr. Gladstone, 2170
A recent glimpse of South Africa, 2241
A Garibaldi reminiscence, 2305
"After" in South Africa, 2366

Ashwell, Frances E., of Girton College.

The girl graduate, **NatR-II** 1099

Asquith, Emma Alice Margaret, or Margot, (Tennant), 1864–1945, Countess of Oxford and Asquith. *DNB.*

Some recent fiction, **NatR-II** 1529

Astrup, Eivind, 1871–1895, first officer in the Peary Expeditions. *LCCat.*

Land of the northernmost Eskimo, **FortR** 3781

Atherley-Jones, Llewellyn Archer, 1851–1929, judge. *WWW.*

An Irish compromise? **NatR-II** 1679

The new Liberalism, **NC** 1740
Lord Rosebery's enterprise, 2667

Atkinson, Agnes D., wife of Joseph Beavington Atkinson, q.v. *Blackwood Papers Cat.*

Hospital of S. Maria della Scala, **FM** 6021

Atkinson, Edward, 1827–1905, economist. *DAB.*

American view of American competition, **FortR** 1560
The railroads of the United States, 1714

Atkinson, Joseph Beavington: see *Index*, I, 797.

Thorwaldsen in Copenhagen and Rome, **FM** 5385

The art treasures of Prussia, **NC** 1053

Atkinson, Sir William Nicholas, 1850–1930, inspector of mines. *WWW.*

Colliery explosions and coal-dust, **NatR-II** 1618

Atteridge, Andrew Hilliard, 1851/52–1941, war correspondent, historian. *Times,* June 17, 1941, p. 9.

Encyclopaedia Britannica on missions, **DR** 1925
Protestant missions in Southern India, 1956, 2046
Italy, present and future, 2064
The *Memoirs of Count Beust,* 2076
Protestant criticism of Protestant missions, 2154
An Indian Catholic mission, 2190
Notice: 2079

The military frontier of France, **NatR-II** 541
Russian frontiers of Austro-Hungarian Empire, 569

Atteridge, Helen, novelist. *BMCat.*

Longfellow, **DR** 2032

Aubrey, William Hickman Smith: see *Index*, I, 798.

Social problems in America, **FortR** 2721
Labour disputes in America, 2980

Audley, Charles-Felix, 1807–c.1886, journalist. *Bib.Nat.Cat., DBF.*

Historians of the Thirty Years' War, **DR** 614
Public instruction in France, 633
The Church and the Roman Empire, 1191
Rio's *Christian Art*, 1238
?Rio's *Memoirs on Christian Art*, 1415

Audubon, John James, 1785–1851, ornithologist, *DAB.*

Note: **FM** 798

Austin, Alfred: see *Index*, I, 798.

Notes made at Perugia, **FortR** 346
The Liberal victory, 1704
Pietro Cossa: dramatist, 1874
A Roman reverie, 3711
Letter: 2655

A dialogue and a moral, **NatR-II** 1
"Above all, no programme," 2
Our critics [of the Review], 12
The prime minister's dilemma [Gladstone's retirement], 23
Literary advantages of Grub Street, 26
A stroll with Corkhouse, 46
Thoughts on family politics, 59
Relation of literature to politics, 75
Rich men's dwellings, 105
Will party government work? 109
Another talk with Corkhouse, 115
Divorce between literature and the stage, 122
Edward Bulwer, Lord Lytton, 127
The aristocracy of letters, 146
To-morrow [on politics], 169
Italia redenta, 175
In the forest of Arden [*As You Like It*], 215
Corkhouse at home, 219
Lessons from Carlyle's life, 230
The two roads [Tory v. Liberal], 263
The root of our misfortunes, 274
Poetry and theological polemics, 301
The seat in the House, 313
Wanted, a new constitution, 334
"Skeletons at the Feast" [Liberal opponents of Chamberlain], 369
Party and patriotism, 420
A reverie on the Riviera, 437
The revival of common sense, 450
Gladstone's coming defeat, 452 collab.
"Owen Meredith," Earl of Lytton, 529
A spring holiday [in France and Italy], 570
Character and ability in politics, 597

The position of the Liberal Unionists, 604 collab.
On the killing of the chimaera, 647
Matthew Arnold on loves of poets, 678
Matthew Arnold, 721
Tennyson's *Demeter and Other Poems*, 954
Tennyson's literary sensitiveness, 1367
The garden that I love, 1491, 1495, 1513, 1523
Matthew Arnold in his *Letters*, 1809
Dante's treatment of the ideal, 2467
Current politics, 11, 22, 33, 44, 57, 68, 80, 91, 103, all collab.
Notes: 14, 233, 361, 474, 528, 530, all collab.; 783, 815, 1006

Austin, George, b. post 1800, philologist, Anglo-Saxon scholar; younger brother of John and Charles Austin. Janet Ross, *Three Generations* (1892 ed.), p. 89.

French prohibitive system, **FQR** 149
French commercial policy: customs law, 328

Austin, Sarah (Taylor): see *Index*, I, 798, and II, App. A.

France, **BentQR** 16

Cousin's *Report, Prussian System of Education*, **FQR** 291
Prince Pückler-Muskau's *Tutti Frutti*, 316

Felix Mendelssohn, **FM** 2444
The late Mr. Charles Buller, 2558
Madame Récamier, 2629
A mutiny of provincial troops, 3740
The cholera in Malta, 4618
See: 303

Austin, Walter, amateur composer. *Brit. Mus. Biog.*

German and English music, **NatR-II** 1162

Austin, Wiltshire Stanton, 1826–1875, barrister and critic. Boase.

Notice: **FortR** 415

Aveling, Edward Bibbins, 1851–1898, socialist. Boase.

Trans: **FortR** 4010

Axinger, Joseph-Marie, 1806–1888, French controversialist. *DBF.*

Affairs of Cologne, **DR** 187

Aylward, Alfred S. (born Murphy, but apparently changed name), 1841–1889, Irish Fenian and So. African adventurer.

Aylward, Alfred S. (*continued*)
Rosenthal. (See *Index*, I, 798.)

Africa and the Empire, **FortR** 1903

Basuto, **FM** 6492
Irregular warfare, 6512

Aytoun, William Edmonstoune: see *Index*, I, 798.

The dead alive: an inn story, **FM** 1712 collab.
My namesake, 1759 collab.
A night at Peleg Longfellow's, 1843 collab.

B

Babbage, Henry Prevost, 1824–1918, army officer. *WWW*.

Railway between India and Burma, **NatR-II** 993
Outcome of the Manipur Disaster, 1176

Bacchus, Francis Joseph, 1860–1937, priest at Oratory of Edgbaston. Henry Tristram, *Francis Joseph Bacchus*, Birmingham, 1937.

The twenty-five years of Peter, **DR** 2580
St. Peter and the Roman Primacy, 2599
Succession of the first Roman bishops, 2641, 2670
Notices: 2663, 2699, 2729

Bacon, Sir James, 1798–1895, judge. *DNB*.

Court of Chancery, **FQR** 128

Bacon, John MacKenzie: see *Index*, I, 800, and II, App. A.

Weather forecasts, **NatR-II** 2395

Climate and the atmosphere, **NC** 3591

Bacon, Leonard Woolsey: see *Index*, I, 800.

Prayer, miracle, and natural law, **FM** 5467

Badeau, Adam: see *Index*, I, 800.

Two great wars [U.S. Civil War and Franco-Prussian War], **FM** 5155

Baden-Powell, Baden Fletcher Smyth: see *Index*, I, 800.

The air-car or man-lifting kite, **NatR-II** 1811

Baden-Powell, Sir George Smyth: see *Index*, I, 800.

Reform in Victoria, **FortR** 1596
Results of protection in young communities, 1894
A last word on sugar bounties, 2238
Fifty years of colonial development, 2603
Mosquito defence, 2759
Obstruction and its cure, 2805

A Canadian people, 3036
The credit of Australasia, 3100
The Empire and its Institute, 3381
The doom of cane-sugar, 3922
"Candia rediviva" [on Crete], 3948
Imperial free trade, 3974
Hope for the West Indies, 4080

England and her colonies, **FM** 6003
The defence of our Empire, 6071
The sugar question, 6326
The truth about American competition, 6382
Failure of protection in the U.S., 6424

Our national future, **Nat-II** 265
Colonial home rule, 461
An Empire Institute, 507
Practical Tory administration, 659
The L. S. D. [£. s. d.] of Home Rule, 932
Mr. Gladstone and Malta, 1073
The session: its barren labour, 1489

New markets for British produce, **NC** 601
The expansion of Germany, 1066
A new title for the Crown, 1413
Selecting colonial governors, 1635

Badger, George Percy: see *Index*, I, 800.

The Muslim Khalîfate, **NC** 78

Badham, Charles David: see *Index*, I, 800.

Ancient fishing and fish, **FM** 2825
Naples Bay and fish-market, 2901
The shark and his cousins, 2964
More marine stores: the narke, 2975
Fish tattle: the conger, 2988
Mullets and mullomaniacs, 3003
More fish tattle: the gurnard group, 3020
The fish of many names: the thunny, 3046
Last of the scombers: the mackerel, 3071
Opsophagy: ancient fish-dealers, 3095
"Flies" and feasts, 3105
Carpiana, 3116
Pike, salmon, silurus, herring, 3146
Last of the fins: cods, gadus, 3166
August at Felixstow, 3324
Periwinkles in pound, 3345
Old rings, 3444, 3465, 3473, 3488
Ancient gems, 3525, 3536

Badham, Francis Pritchett, b.1863/64. Foster.

St. Mark's indebtedness to St. Matthew, **ScotR** 540

Admiral Baillie, 688

Bagehot, Walter: see *Index*, I, 801.

The English Constitution, in 9 parts, **FortR** 1–366

Physics and politics, 451, 495, 607, 826, 832

Matthew Arnold on London University, 508

Henry Crabb Robinson, 615

Bad lawyers or good? 689

Senior's *Journals*, 800

Postulates of English political economy, 1231, 1258

Adam Smith as a person, 1272

Lord Althorpe and Reform Act of 1832, 1303

Chances for a long Conservative régime in England, 1530

Bagenal, Philip Henry Dudley: see *Index*, I, 801.

International [Exhibition] and its influence on English politics, **NatR-II** 101

Home Rule rehearsed: local government in Ireland, 720

A secret mission, 2240

Count Cavour on Ireland, **NC** 759 collab.

Uncle Pat's Cabin, 796

Bagot, Arthur Greville, 1849–1915, army officer. Burke.

Our naval reserves, **FortR** 3776

Bagot, Richard, 1860–1921, novelist. *WWW*.

The Vatican at work, **NatR-II** 2379

Anglophobia at the Vatican, 2439

Vatican and Quirinal, 2508

Bagot, Lady Theodosia (Leslie), 1865–1940, organised army hospitals, *WWW*, Burke under Leslie of Glaslough.

A north-country election, **NC** 2307

Bagshawe, Catherine Elizabeth (Gunning), wife of H. R. Bagshawe, q.v. Venn under her husband.

?The plays of Talfourd and Knowles, **DR** 104 collab.

?Cooper's novels, 137

Miss Kavanagh's *Summer and Winter in Two Sicilies*, 907

Notice: 896

Trans: 79, 115, 187

Bagshawe, Henry Ridgard, 1799–1870, barrister, executive ed. *Dublin Rev*. Newman, *L&D*, XII, index.

State and prospects of Anglican Church, **DR** 44

Anster's and Elliott's poems, 46

The Catholic Oath, 47

?Plays of Talfourd and Knowles, 104 collab.

Controversial novels: *Geraldine*, 117

?Cooper's novels, 137

Modern English novels, 148

Modern English novels, 159

Ages of Faith, 171

Lives of the Queens of England, 257

?New novels, 316

The Life of St. Philip Neri, 472

Compitum [by Kenelm Digby], 532

Jane Eyre – Shirley, 579

Alison's *History of Europe*, 684

Digby's *Kathemerina*, 802

Rome; its ruler and its institutions, 873

Memoirs of the Court of George IV, 919

New glories of the Catholic Church, 946

Evenings on the Thames, 962

Notes: 157, 223, 248, 536, 893

Notices: 232, 454, 465, ?620, ?641, 760, 816, 824, 896, 920, ?928, 981

Trans: 179

See: 220, 1034

Bagwell, Richard, 1840–1918, barrister, writer on Ireland, *WWW*.

Spoliation of Irish landlords, **NatR-II** 2015

Rural administration in Ireland, 2098

Baignères, Arthur, historical writer. *BMCat*.

Manet and the Impressionist School, **NatR-II** 144

Bailey, James Blake. *LCCat*.

Letter: **NatR-II** 750

Bailey, John Cann: see *Index*, I, 801

Matthew Arnold, **FortR** 3753

The man [Edward] Gibbon, 3934

The sonnets of M. De Heredia, 4168

Stevenson's *Letters*, 4394

Bailey, William Frederick, 1857–1917, Irish barrister. *WWW*.

Native problem in South Africa, **NatR-II** 1954

A summer trip in Alaska, 2373

Baillie, Joanna, 1762–1851, Scottish dramatist, poet. *DNB*.

The character of Romiero, **FM** 1028

Baillie-Grohman, William Adolph, 1851–1921, sportsman. *WW/1920, WW/1923* obit.

Cattle ranches in the far West, **FortR** 1737
British Columbia, 2409
Shortcomings of sporting literature, 3992
British and foreign rifle shooting, 4411
One cause of our defeats: the service rifle, 4418

Rifle-shooting as a national sport, **NC** 3525
Marksmanship old and new, 3648

Baillie-Hamilton, Lady Mary Aynscombe (Mossop): see *Index*, I, 801.

Border ballads, **NatR-II** 302

Baillie-Hamilton, Sir William Alexander, 1844–1920, barrister. *WWW.*

Development of our yeomanry cavalry, **NatR-II** 30

Bain, Alexander: see *Index*, I, 801.

The feelings and the will, **FortR** 166
Intellect, viewed physiologically, 178
Theories of the soul, 247
Common errors on the mind, 523
The retentive power of the mind, 527
Violations of relativity, 536
Dr. Bastian's paper on "Physiology of Thinking," 584
On teaching English, 617
Notice: 1072

On the abuse of language, **FM** 2283
Phrenology and psychology, 3979
Propensities, according to phrenology, 4019, 4040, 4073, 4109

Bain, Robert Nisbet, 1854–1909, historical writer. *DNB.*

Finland and the Tsar, **FortR** 4272

Baines, Peter Augustine, 1786–1843, R.C. prelate. *DNB.*

Opening of the college at Prior Park, **DR** 50

Baines, Talbot: see *Index*, I, 801.

Consequences of Imperial rally, **NatR-II** 2445

Baker, Sir Augustine FitzGerald, 1851–1922, lawyer. *LCCat.*

An unrealised national asset, **FortR** 2792

Baker, Sir Benjamin, 1840–1907, civil engineer. *DNB.*

A ship-canal through Egypt, **NC** 813 collab.
The Forth Bridge, 1727 collab.
Ship railways, 2008
Nile reservoirs and Philae, 2581

Baker, Sir George Sherston, 1846–1923, barrister. *WWW.*

A few words on interment, **FM** 5765

The judgment in the "Mignonette" case, **NatR-II** 260

Baker, Sir Samuel White: see *Index*, I, 801.

Reform of Egypt, **FortR** 1958
Russia and England; Batoum and Cyprus, 2511
Reflections in India, 2735
African development: the Soudan, 2880

Maritime dangers and defence, **NatR-II** 735

Egypt's proper frontier, **NC** 1013

Bakewell, Robert Hall, 1831–1908, physician, *New Zealand Biog.*

The loyalty of the colonies, **NC** 1908
New Zealand under female franchise, 2528

Balbo, Count Cesare, 1789–1853, Italian statesman. Tosi.

Letter: **FQR** 824

Baldock, Thomas Stanford, 1854–1937, army officer. *WWW.*

The private soldier's wrongs, **NC** 1960

Baldry, Alfred Lys, 1858–1939, painter. *WWW.*

An artist [Mortimer Menpes], **NatR-II** 2138

Balfour, Alice Blanche, 1850–1936, sister of Arthur James Balfour, q.v. *Times,* Jan. 13, 1936, p. 9d.

Twelve hundred miles in a waggon [in So. Africa], **NatR-II** 1706, 1721

Balfour, Arthur James: see *Index*, I, 802.

The Indian civil service, **FortR** 1387
A speculation on evolution, 1412

Berkeley's *Life and Letters,* **NatR-II** 6, 21
"Veiled obstruction" [in parliament], 34
Politics and political economy, 303
Letter: 1484

Morley's *Life of Cobden,* **NC** 664
The House of Lords, 1021

Balfour, Eustace James Anthony: see *Index*, I, 802.

Volunteer force in defence, **NatR-II** 2094

Balfour, Lady Frances (Campbell), 1858–1931, suffragist. *DNB.*

Some recent fiction, **NatR-II** 1527
The election of 1895, 1772

Balfour, Frederic Henry, journalist. *BMCat.,* *Yearbook*/1904.

Angelic immorality [in Goldsmith's *Vicar of Wakefield*], **NatR-II** 1031

Letter: **NC** 1015

Ball, John: see *Index,* I, 802.

Austrian Italy, **BentQR** 10
The campaign in Italy, 19
Alpine travellers, 27

?Glaciers [and J. D. Forbes], **FM** 3208
Alpine literature, 3883

Ball, Sir Robert Stawell: see *Index,* I, 802.

The new astronomy, **FortR** 3164
How long can the earth sustain life? 3197
Mars, 3259
Jupiter's new satellite, 3297
Is the universe infinite? 3360
The wanderings of the North Pole, 3394
Atoms and sunbeams, 3417
Significance of carbon in the universe, 3473
Possibility of life in other worlds, 3571

Ballantyne, James, of Aberdeen.

Why is Scotland radical? **NatR-II** 1020

Balmer, R., of the Bibliothèque Nationale, Paris.

Whispering machines [to record books on discs], **NC** 1107

Balzac, Honoré de: see *Index,* I, 803.

The pride of a spoiled beauty, **FM** 2148, 2160

Bamberger, Ludwig, 1823–1899, politician, writer, man of letters. Hyamson.

The German daily press, **NC** 1813

Banfield, Francis or Frank, b.1852/53, journalist. Foster, *BMCat.* (See *Index,* I, 803.)

A glance at voluntaryism, **NatR-II** 421
Tory democracy, 603
Eruptive force of modern fanaticism, 636
Interviewing in practice, 1800

Banfield, Thomas Collins, lektor of English, Univ. of Göttingen, 1828–1833. J. S. Pütter, *Versuch einer academischen Gelehrten-Geschichte von der . . . Universitat zu Göttingen* (4 vols., Göttingen, 1765–1838), IV, 502.

The Low-German language and literature, **FQR** 193

Banks, Elizabeth L., d. 1938, American-born journalist. *WWW, Amer. WWW.*

Some American "impressions," **NC** 2737
Self-help among American college girls, 2905
American "yellow journalism," 3338
The American negro and his place, 3532
Electioneering women, 3750

Banks, Percival Weldon, 1805–1850, Irish journalist. Dickens, *Letters,* I, 160n.

France in 1829–1830 by Lady Morgan, **FM** 178
Speeches delivered in banquo Reginae, 549, 564, 815
Touching things theatrical, 605
Ireland and the Irish, 692, 699
A visit to the Royal Academy, 718
The books on my table, 751
Of politicians, public opinion, and the press, 836
Horae Lutentianae: the cognate cities, 882
Spain: illustrated, by Lewis, Roberts, and Roscoe, 905
The books on my table: of *Hamlet,* 967
Nothing [on Bulwer-Lytton's *England and the English*], 1210
Of Rabelais, 1378, 1413, 1456
Confessions of Harry Lorrequer [by Charles Lever], 1476
Of *Macbeth,* 1499, 1539, 1615, 1651
Ilustrations of Mirabeau, 1683, 1719
Notices of the Shakspearian drama, 1697, 1707
The German opera, 1716
Italian theatre, 1726
Dramatic works of Henry Taylor, 1786
The life of Staudigl, 1932
Of the red Indian, 1946
Matters musical and Italian opera, 1990
Prichard's *Natural History of Man,* 1998
Remarks on Horace and others, 2020, 2038, 2063
On the Italian opera, 2077
Robertson's *Leaves from a Journal,* 2090
Antony and Cicero, 2103
The Italian opera, 2108
Of railways, 2141, 2153
Of the Spains and the Spaniards, 2178
Of the Italian opera, 2215

Banks, Percival Weldon (*continued*)
Head's book [*The Emigrant*], and Canada, 2281, 2311
Notices of a Shakspearian book [by J. P. Collier], 2286
Of the two Italian operas [houses], 2331
Of Music in Italy [by Berlioz], 2619
Horace's ode, 2634
Philosopher, patriot, and poet [Béranger], 2657
Opinion and evidence [on G. C. Lewis' *Essay*], 2697
Fly-fishing, 2754
Letter: 569
Trans: 2775
See: 1414

Bannister, Saxe, 1790–1877, misc. writer. *DNB.*

Herder, protector of aboriginal people, FQR 595

Barbé, Louis A., 1845–1926, Scottish professor. *WWW.*

Trans: ScotR 241, 247, 258, 268

Barbour, Sir David Miller, 1841–1928, Indian civil servant, economist. *DNB.*

The currency question, NatR-II 1606
The currency question—for laymen, 1709

Barclay, James W., grain merchant of Aberdeen, visited America, 1876–1883. *Blackwood Papers Cat.*, R. G. Athearn, *Westward the Briton* (N.Y., 1953), p. 188.

Colorado, FortR 1660

Grievances of the farmers, NC 680
A new view of Mormonism, 955

Barclay, Robert, 1829–1906, of the Manchester Chamber of Commerce. *BMCat.*; letter to this *Index* from Central Library, Manchester.

The appreciation of gold, FortR 3499

Barclay, Lady Thérèse Marie Camille (Pouget), wife of 13th baronet. Burke.

Trans: FortR 4045

Barclay, Sir Thomas: see *Index*, I, 803.

A lance for the French, FortR 4401

Barham, C. N., divine.

The hill-men around Manipur, NatR-II 1145
Should clergymen take to trade? 1332

Barham, Francis Foster, 1808–1871, editor. *DNB.*

Successive discoveries of America, DR 233

History of Hebrew philology, FortR 165

Baring, Evelyn, 1st Earl of Cromer, 1841–1917, diplomatist. *DNB.*

Recent events in India, NC 910

Baring, Maurice, 1874–1945, man of letters. *DNB.*

Goethe and Victor Hugo: a comparison, NatR-II 2407

Baring, Thomas George, 1st Earl of Northbrook, 1826–1904, statesman. *DNB.*

The natives of India, FM 6353

The Indian government, NatR-II 2233

Actual strength of our forces at home, NC 3614
Our infantry, 3698

Baring-Gould, Sabine: see *Index*, I, 803.

The *Kalewipoeg* [Esthonian epic], FM 4912
St. Symeon Salos, 5482
St. Nicolas of Trani, 5491
The Patarines of Milan, 5506
Meinwerk, Bishop of Paderborn, 5634

Barker, Charles, b.1797, d. before 1853, critic and journalist. Venn, editor's preface to Barker's *Characters . . . of Charles II*, 1853; in *Testimonials* (see *BMCat.*) he gives his birthdate.

Lord Byron and M. Casimir Delavigne, FQR 95

Barker, Edward Harrison: see *Index*, I, 803.

Theodore Aubanel and the Provençal Renaissance, FortR 2556

Barker, John Sale: see *Index*, I, 804.

Mazzini, FM 5315

Barlow, Jane, 1860–1917, Irish novelist. *LCCat.*

Mrs. Martin's company, NatR-II 1607
A very light railway, 1641

Barnes, William: see *Index*, I, 804.

Patmore's poems, FM 4349
Old song-history and tradition, 4367
On the Welsh triads, 4698

Barnett, Dame Henrietta Octavia Weston: see *Index*, I, 804.

Passionless reformers, **FortR** 1937

National enemies and defences, **NatR-II** 457
East London and crime, 792

The verdict on the barrack schools, **NC** 3051
Town children in the country, 3683

Barnett, Samuel Augustus: see *Index*, I, 804.

The poor of the world: India, Japan and U.S., **FortR** 3397
The unemployed, 3440

Practicable socialism, **NC** 837
Great cities and social reform, 923
The universities and the poor, 961
Sensationalism in social reform, 1247
Distress in East London, 1339
A scheme for the unemployed, 1625
Man, East and West, 2153
University settlements, 2855
"Settlements" and "missions," 3214
Cathedral reform, 3396
Charity versus outdoor relief, 3565

Barney, Elizabeth Cynthia

The American sportswoman, **FortR** 3537

Barraclough, George, b.1837, surgeon. Venn.

Nursing as a career for ladies, **FM** 6166

Barrère, Camille Eugène Pierre: see *Index*, I, 804.

Gambetta, **FortR** 2003 collab.
Russia, Austria, and the Danubian States, 2091
See: 2112

Six months of prefecture under Gambetta, **FM** 5370
Pilgrimages and Catholicism in France, 5486
The masons of La Creuse, 5573
Workshops of 1848, and M. Blanc, 5601

Barrett, James John; probably of the Finsbury Conservative Assoc.

Letter: **NatR-II** 679

Barrett, Michael, O.S.B., b.1848. *Benedictine Bibliog.*

Early Scottish saints, **DR** 2669
Scottish Benedictine houses of the past, 2693, 2711, 2722

Barrett, Sir William Fletcher, 1844–1925, prof. of physics. *WWW.*

Thought-reading, **NC** 727 collab.

Barrett-Lennard, J.; perhaps lt. col. John Barrett-Lennard, 1863–1935, army officer. *WWW/1940.*

Letter: **FortR** 3321

Barrie, Sir James Matthew: see *Index*, I, 804.

Pro bono publico, **FortR** 2991
The wedding guest, 4556

Barrington, Emilie Isabel (Wilson), 1841/42–1933, wife of Russell Henry Barrington. *WWW, Times,* Mar. 11, 1933, p. 12b.

Why is Mr. Millais our popular painter? **FortR** 1928

Lord Leighton's sketches, **NatR-II** 1951

Is a great school of art possible? **NC** 300
Painted poetry of Watts and Rossetti, 864

Barron, Sir Henry Winston, 1795–1872, Irish M.P. Boase.

Our foreign policy in 1860–61, **DR** 977

Barry, Alfred: see *Index*, I, 805.

Lay representation, Church synods in Australia, **NatR-II** 508

The soul and future life, **NC** 95
The good and evil of examination, 158
The Burials Bill and disestablishment, 498
The loyalty of the colonies, 1958
Breach of Church law, 3300

Barry, Charles, 1823–1900, architect. Chambers.

Enlargement of the House of Commons, **NC** 2372

Barry, Sir John Wolfe Wolfe; see Wolfe-Barry, Sir John Wolfe.

Barry, M. Maltman, labour leader, *LCCat., Blackwood Papers Cat.*

A democrat's defence of the House of Lords, **NC** 1039

Barry, William Francis: see *Index*, I, 805.

Modern society and the Sacred Heart, **DR** 1509
St. Thomas on the theory of knowledge, 1524
The scholastic doctrine of science, 1535

Barry, William Francis (*continued*)
Scholastics on intellect and abstraction, 1546
Mr. Tyndall and contemporary thought, 1568
Is the Roman question at an end? 1594
German thought: its influence on Mr. Tyndall, 1612
Father Curci and the Roman question, 1615
Italy and Leo XIII, 1633
The articles on F. Curci, 1646
The genius of George Eliot, 1774
The religion of George Eliot, 1796
John Inglesant, 1819
Berthold Auerbach, 1843
Freiligrath, 1877
Dreizehnlinden, 1908
The battle of theism, 1932
Carlyle, 1945
Catholics and modern literature, 1969
The story of Cowdray [House], 1998
The progress of nihilism, 2022
Herbert Spencer's agnosticism, 2114
An apostle of Nirvana: H. F. Amiel, 2162
The church and the social revolution, 2241
Isaac Hecker, 2339
Labour and capital, limited, 2378
Mr. Balfour's philosophy, 2494
Notices: 1519, 1528, 1941, 2412, 2485, 2497

The church and the world, **FortR** 2420

Emancipation from the Jews, **NatR-II** 1882
Catholicism [Zola's *Rome*], 1900
The apology of Dives, 1925
Newman and Renan, 2029
Edmund Burke, statesman and prophet, 2116
An American religious crusade, 2277
The keepers of literature, 2349

Wanted: a gospel for the century, **NC** 1742
Democratic ideals, 2570
A defence of prayer, 2801

Barthélemy, Hippolyte, 1840–1900, officer in French army. *DBF.*

The French army, **FortR** 2015

Bartholeyns, A. O'Donnel, misc. writer. *BMCat.*

The great hospitals of London, **NatR-II** 800
The sick poor of the metropolis, 827

Bartlett, Robert Edward: see *Index,* I, 806.

The religious crisis, **FM** 4852
Facts and phantasms on the ecclesiastical question, 4914

Tulloch, *Rational Theology and Christian Philosophy,* 5438
Bonivard, "the prisoner of Chillon," 5808
Calvin at Geneva, 5822
Probable results of disestablishment, 5939
Clericality, 5976
Evangelical party in Church of England, 6005
The High Church party, 6023
The Broad Church movement, 6033
On keeping silence from good [religious] words, 6053
Modern nonconformity, 6107
The church of the future, 6176
Wandering thoughts about Germany, 6183

Bartley, Sir George Christopher Trout, 1842–1910, banker. *DNB.*

Conservatives on themselves: organization, **FortR** 2309

Impressions of South Africa, **NatR-II** 2392

Barton, Sir Edmund, 1849–1920, Australian statesman. *DNB.*

Letter: **NatR-II** 2459

Bastard, Florence Mary (Scrope), d.1871, wife of Edmund Rodney Pollexfen Bastard. *Landed Gentry.*

Mr. Kingsley, **Ram** 1065
Women, politics and patriotism, 1081
Rio on Christian art, 1117
Notice: 1136

Bastian, Henry Charlton: see *Index,* I, 806.

On the physiology of thinking, **FortR** 556

Spontaneous generation, **NC** 136

Bastide, Charles, b.1875, French historian. *LCCat.*

Cacoethes literarum [obsession with literature], **FortR** 4057
An Elysian conversation, 4087
M. Brunetière, 4337

Bates, Edgar

Civil service pensions, **NatR-II** 741

Batson, Henrietta M.: see *Index,* I, 806.

The rural voter, **NC** 2157
The rule of the laywoman, 2869
Town and country labourers, 3544
The vogue of the garden book, 3668

Battersby, Henry Francis Prevost, 1862–1949, misc. writer. *LCCat., WWW.*

The war correspondent, **NatR-II** 2524

Battine, Cecil William, b.1867, army officer. *LCCat.*

Reorganization of the army, **NatR-II** 1416

Battine, Mrs. L. M., of London.

Letter: **NatR-II** 1137

Baumann, Arthur Anthony, 1856–1936, barrister, ed. *Saturday Rev. WWW.*

Conduct of business during present session, **FortR** 2743
An apology for unprincipled Toryism, 4025
The truth about Tory democracy, **NatR-II** 544
London clauses of Local Government Bill, 731
The Lords' committee on the sweating system, 768
Remedies for the sweating system, 780
Needed amendments of the Factory Act, 981
The general election, 1315

Baumann, John: see *Index*, I, 806.

On a Western ranche, **FortR** 2580

Bayliss, Sir Wyke: see *Index*, I, 806.

Art, contra world, flesh, devil, **NatR-II** 730
"Feares" or "Teares"; *Macbeth*, act. V, scene 5, 819

Bayne, Peter: see *Index*, I, 807.

Neo-evangelism, **FortR** 117
Work for parliament, 200
Strauss's *New Life of Christ*, 207
Ecce Homo [by J. R. Seeley], 254
Notices: 50, 192, 306, 343

Archbishop Laud, **FM** 5502

Bayne, Thomas Wilson, 1845–1931, Scottish man of letters. *WWW.*

The poetry of Lewis Morris, **FM** 6303
Lyric poetry, [Gosse, Lang, and Hake], 6345
Charles Tennyson Turner, 6470
Poetry of Dante Gabriel Rossetti, 6495
Mr. Swinburne's trilogy, 6547

Baynes, Arthur Hamilton, 1854–1942, divine. *WWW.*

German student life, **FM** 6458

Baynes, C. D., ed. *Johannesburg Standard and Diggers News.*

Cecil Rhodes, **FortR** 3950

Baynes, Thomas Spencer: see *Index*, I, 807.

What Shakespeare learnt at school, **FM** 6228, 6250, 6284

Bazalgette, Charles Norman, b.1847, barrister; father was a civil engineer. Allibone, *M at B.*

London water supply, **FortR** 2216

Bazan, Emilia Pardo: see Pardo Bazan.

Bazley, Sir Thomas, 1797–1885, manufacturer, politician. *DNB.*

Shall Manchester have a university? **NC** 69

Beachcroft, Sir Richard Melvill, 1846–1926, businessman. *WWW.*

London County Council, **NatR-II** 1690 collab.

Beadon, Robert John, b.1844, barrister. *M at B.*

Imperial Federation League, **NatR-II** 1539

Beale, Dorothea, 1831–1906, educator. *DNB.*

On the education of girls, **FM** 4696

Letter: **FortR** 4539

Girls' schools, past and present, **NC** 1537

Beale, Lionel Smith: see *Index*, I, 807.

The mystery of life, **FortR** 711

Beaman, Ardern George Hulme, 1857–1929, diplomatist in Near East. *WWW.*

The restoration in Egypt, **FortR** 2099
Notes of a fortnight in Bosnia, 2870
The Black Mountain [Montenegro], 2911
The Macedonian question, 3057
Bulgars and Serbs, 3097
See: 2207

Beamish, Richard, 1798–1873, civil engineer. Boase.

See: **FM** 3913

Bear, William Edwin, 1840/41–1918, agriculturalist. Death certificate at Somerset House; obit. in *Mark Lane Express Agricultural Journal*, June 17, 1918, p. 562. (See *Index*, I, 807.)

The strike of the farm labourers, **FortR** 877
Difficulties of tenant-farmers and legislative remedies, 890

Bear, William Edwin (*continued*)
The Agricultural Holdings Bill, 1152
Agricultural depression, 1552
The Liberal Party and the farmers, 1563
Revolt of the counties, 1696
An English land bill, 1955
Departments of agriculture, 2018
Irish crisis: peasant-proprietorship, 2465
The climax of agricultural disaster, 3696
The muddle of Irish land tenure, 3827
Market wrecking, 3943
Agriculture during the Victorian era, 3967
Ideal land tenure, 4061
The next agricultural census, 4436

Cattle disease and the food supply, **NatR-II** 157
Mr. Chaplin and the cattle trade, 1284
Evidence on agricultural depression, 1593
Our food supply in the event of war, 1850
Food crops and famine in India, 1981
Shall agriculture perish? 2058

The public interest in agricultural reform, **NC** 321, 358
The new Agricultural Holdings Bill, 870
State-made farmers, 2024
The rural voter, 2156

Beard, John Relly, 1800–1876, Unitarian minister. *DNB.*
Notices: **FQR** 782, 796

Beasley, T. N. *BMCat.*
Mr. Pitt on home rule, **NatR-II** 1095

Beaton, Patrick C., 1825–1904, Scottish divine. *Fasti,* VII, 535, and *FM* no. 4308, etc.
A chapter on innocents, **FM** 4308
A chapter on notables, 4317
A chapter on superstition, 4327
How Lord P——— [Patrick Robertson] became our rector, 4343
A chapter on Chalons and Aldershot, 4353
A chapter on Madagascar, 4366
A chapter on croakers, 4391
From Auckland to Awamutu [New Zealand], 4477
How we live at Awamutu, 4490
Pai Marire, new religion of Maoris, 4586
Clerical song-writers in the North, 4648, 4776

Beatty-Kingston, William: see *Index,* I, 807.
Foreign correspondents, **FortR** 2436
The Médoc vintage of 1889, 2951
Trans: 4325

Beauchamp, Henry King, 1866–1907, ed. *Madras Mail.* Burke.

The North-West Frontier of India, **FortR** 3636

Beauclerk, Robert S.
General chapter of the Jesuits, **NatR-II** 1354

Beaufort, Willem Hendrik de, 1845–1918, member of Dutch States General. *LCCat.*
Germany and Holland, **NC** 144
Holland and the Transvaal, 571

Beaufoy, Mark; probably Mark Hanbury Beaufoy, 1854–1922, M.P., business executive. Venn.
Letter: **FortR** 2934

Beaumont, Frederick Edward Blackett, 1833–1899, army officer. Boase.
The Channel tunnel, **NC** 682

Beaumont, William Mardon, 1851–1928, physician. *Surgeon Index/4* s.
Railway servants' eye-sight, **NatR-II** 1325

Bechstein, Ludwig, 1801–1860, German scholar. *ADB.*
See: **FM** 2504

Beck, Egerton William Townsend, 1858–1941, barrister, *WWW,* Venn.
Papal elections and coronations, **DR** 2536

Beck, Theodore, 1859–1899, principal of Anglo-Oriental College, Meerut, India. Venn.
The House of Commons and the Indian Civil Service, **NatR-II** 1581
Native India and England, 1649

Becke, Louis, 1855–1913, misc. writer. *LCCat.*
Builder of Empire: George Grey, **FortR** 4189 collab.
The sea story of Australia, 4349 collab.

Becker, Bernard Henry, 1833–1900, misc. writer. Boase.
Games and gamesters, **FortR** 2192

Beckett, Arthur à: see À Beckett, Arthur.

Beckett, Sir Edmund: see *Index,* I, 807, and II, App. A.
Marriage code of Henry VIII. and Mr. Greg, **NatR-II** 528
Architecture, a Profession or an Art? **NC** 2337

Architecture: an art or nothing, 2380
Marriage of innocent divorcées, 2708

?Railways, **FM** 2594, 2614
Marriage with a wife's sister [on books by
Pusey and Keble], 2686
?Railway companies and law, 2813

Beckett, Ernest William, 2nd Baron Grimthorpe, 1856–1917, M.P. Burke.

England and Germany in Africa, **FortR**
2974

Randolph Churchill, **NatR-II** 545

Australian side lights on English politics,
NC 1647

Beddoe, John, 1826–1911, physician. *DNB.*

Anthropological history of Europe, **ScotR**
360, 369, 379, 390, 399, 408

Bedford, Henry, 1816–1903, educator. *Cath.
Ency.*

All Hallow's College, Drumcondra, Dublin,
Ram 502
Our choirs, 562
A poet from the labouring class [Gerald
Massey], 602

Beeching, Henry Charles: see *Index,* I, 808.

Fallacies in ritual controversy, **NatR-II**
2302
Passion and imagination in poetry, 2457
Expression in poetry, 2500

Beesly, Augustus Henry: see *Index,* I, 808.

Game laws and the committee of 1872,
FortR 935
Deer-forests and culpable luxury, 958
Game Law Committee report, 1036

Beesly, Edward Spencer: see *Index,* I, 808.

Catiline as a party leader, **FortR** 14
Cicero and Clodius, 276
Amalgamated Society of Carpenters, 383
The Trades' Union Commission, 416
The Emperor Tiberius, 458, 466
Necker and Calonne, 563
Social future of the working class, 575
International Working Men's Association,
728
The Galway judgment, 875
History of republicanism in France, 1090
The Third French Republic, 1097
Positivists and workmen, 1172
Our foreign and Irish policy, 1776
A strong second chamber, 3673
Notice: 281

Beeton, Henry Ramié, advocate of bimetallism. *LCCat.*

The currency question—for laymen, **NatR-
II** 1802
Great Britain's opportunity, 2076

Beeton, Sir Mayson Moss, 1865–1947, West
Indies specialist. *LCCat., WWW.*

The Indian countervailing duties, **NatR-II**
2306
The wrecking of the West Indies, **NC** 3145

Behrend, Henry, 1828–1893, physician. *Jewish
Ency.*

Diseases caught from butcher's meat, **NC**
1759
Tuberculous meat and its consequences,
1939

Beighton, Thomas Durant, 1846–1906, Bengal
civil servant. "Bengal Civil Fund Family
Register" at India Office, II, 703.

The Bhutan frontier, **FM** 6130

Belcher, Thomas Waugh, 1831–1910, divine.
WWW.

Reservation of the sacrament, **NC** 1187

Belinaye, Henry George de la, 1799–1873,
French émigré, surgeon. BM Add. MS.
47,494.

Notices: **FQR** 182, 241

Bell, Charles, 1804/05–1891, M.D., F.R.C.P.;
nephew of Sir Charles Bell in *Index,* I.
Medical Direct./92.

Letter: **FM** 5636

Bell, Charles Frederick Moberly, 1847–1911,
news correspondent. *WWW.*

Four years of Egyptian finance, **NatR-II**
231
"How long halt ye between two opinions?"
[about Egypt], **NC** 1001

Bell, Evans: see Bell, Thomas Evans.

Bell, Lady Florence Eveleen Eleanore (Ol-
liffe), 1851–1930, misc. writer, wife of
Sir Hugh Bell, q.v. *LCCat., Yearbook/
1922.*

Better teaching of manners, **NC** 3334
Difficulties incidental to middle age, 3622
On the merits and demerits of thrift, 3655

Bell, George Charles, 1831/32–1913, divine,
Master of Marlborough. *WWW,* Foster.

Letter: **FortR** 2655

Bell, George Joseph, 1770–1843, prof. of Scottish law. *DNB.*

Mrs. Siddons as Lady Macbeth, **NC** 138 collab.

Bell, Gertrude Margaret Lowthian, 1868–1926, traveller, archaeologist. *DNB.*

In the Alps of Dauphiné, **NC** 3610

Bell, Henry Thomas Mackenzie, 1856–1930, critic, poet. *WWW.*

William Morris: a eulogy, **FortR** 3879

Bell, Horace, 1839–1903, civil engineer. *DNB.*

Regarding public works, **FM** 6029

Bell, Sir Hugh, 1844–1931, industrialist. *WWW.*

The living wage, **NatR-II** 1537

Bell, Sir Isaac Lowthian, 1816–1904, entrepreneur. *DNB.*

The iron and steel trade, **FortR** 2551

Bell, J.

The Behring's Sea question, **NatR-II** 1122

Bell, John, 1811–1895, sculptor. *DNB.*

Letter: **FM** 2030

Bell, John Zephaniah, 1794–1883, painter. Benezit, *Dictionnaire des Peintres*, 1924.

The taste of the day, **FM** 3640, 3665, 3723

Bell, Lowthian: see Bell, Isaac Lowthian.

Bell, Mackenzie: see Bell, Henry Thomas Mackenzie.

Bell, Robert, divine; perhaps the Robert Bell listed in *CCD*/76 and Foster, b.1797/98.

Liberal protestantism, **FM** 5574

Bell, Robert, 1800–1867: see *Index*, I, 808.

Modern English drama, **DR** 40

Social amusements under the Restoration, **FortR** 78, 86, 101
The comedies of Etherege, 145
A word for the Stuarts, 259
Shakespeare's sonnets, 296
Notices: 50, 132, 326

The armourer of Munster, **FM** 2433, 2446, 2456, 2466
Vanity Fair [by Thackeray], 2498

Phantoms and realities, 2806, 2820, 2840, 2854, 2865

Bell, Thomas Evans, 1825–1887, writer on India. Boase.

The Afghan succession, **FortR** 1061

Bell, William Abraham, 1841–1920, country gentleman. *LCCat.*, Venn.

Pacific railroads, **FortR** 589

Bellesheim, Alfons, 1839–1912, German historian. *LCCat.*

The writings of T. W. Allies, **DR** 1746
Notes on foreign periodicals: German periodicals, in 9 installments from 2322 to 2437
Notices: 1724, 1745, 1756, 1767, 1779, 1790, 1802, 1813, 1838, 1850, 1862, 1884, 1896, 1907, 1919, 1930, 1941, 1953, 1965, 1978, 1992, 2006, 2029, 2056, 2068, 2079, 2092, 2104, 2118, 2131, 2144, 2158, 2173, 2186, 2199, 2211, 2225, 2238, 2253, 2266, 2280, 2307, 2321, 2335, 2347, 2358, 2373, 2387, 2400, 2412, 2425, 2438, 2462, 2475, 2497, 2720
Notices of Catholic continental periodicals: German periodicals, in 51 installments from 1675 to 2295

Bellingham, Sir Alan Henry, 1846–1921, barrister. Burke.

Note: **DR** 2728

Bellingham, Thomas, 1645–1721, army officer. *LCCat.*

Diary of an officer under William III, **DR** 2728, 2737

Belloc-Lowndes, Marie Adelaide: see Lowndes, M. A. B.

Belloy, Auguste, Marquis de, 1815–1871, man of letters. *DBF.*

See: **FM** 3130a

Belmore, Somerset Richard, Earl Belmore, 1835–1913. Burke.

Fair play to landlords, **NC** 743

Benedict, Sir Julius, 1804–1885, musician. *DNB.*

The proposed university of music, **NC** 736

Benham, William: see *Index*, I, 809.

Dean Burgon and Mr. Fremantle, **FortR** 2594

Archbishop Magee, 3092

Archbishop Tait, **ScotR** 9

Bennett, Sir Ernest Nathaniel: see *Index*, I, 809.

Side-lights on the Cretan insurrection, **NC** 3106

Benni, A. W.

Russian society, **FortR** 338, 350

Benson, Arthur Christopher: see *Index*, I, 809.

Jacobean courtier [Herbert of Cherbury], **FortR** 2684

Lavater, **NatR-II** 704
Eton, 1167
Christina Rossetti, 1682
The future of poetry, 1699
Llanthony Abbey and two of its priors, 1952

Benson, Edward Frederic: see *Index*, I, 809.

From the diary of a lotus eater, **FortR** 3891

A question of taste, **NC** 2456
The recent "witch-burning" at Clonmel, 2772
Plagiarism, 3577

Benson, Mary Eleanor, 1863–1890, social worker. Boase.

In defence of domestic service, **NC** 1944

Benson, William Arthur Smith, 1854–1924, architect. *WWW.*

William Morris, **NatR-II** 2361

Bent, James Theodore: see *Index*, I, 809.

Greek peasant life, **FortR** 2497
Greater Greece and its education, 2625
Baron Hirsch's railway, 2736
How the Shah travels when at home, 2844
The city of the Creed [Nicaea], 2918
Road from Mashonaland [to the sea], 3175
Among the chiefs of Bechuanaland, 3210
Under British protection, 3409
The Italians in Africa, 3850

A visit to the oldest state in Europe [San Marino], **FM** 6359
Pilgrimage to Cyprus in 1395–1396, 6416
Life in mediaeval Venice, 6445
Cervo, 6478

Correspondence of Niccolò Paganini, 6501
Life in Old Florence, 6514

Mysterious amongst modern Greeks, **NatR-II** 561
Parallels to Homeric life in Greece to-day, 751

What St. John saw on Patmos, **NC** 1629
On the origin of the Mashonaland ruins, 2497
The Hadramut: in southern Arabia, 2636
The land of frankincense and myrrh [Dhofar, Arabia], 2818
On the Dervish frontier, 3000
The island of Socotra, 3129

Three evils of destiny, **ScotR** 186

Bentwich, Herbert, 1856–1932, barrister. *WWW.*

The progress of Zionism, **FortR** 4212

Philo-Zionists and anti-Semites, **NC** 3187

Berdoe, Edward, 1836–1916, physician, Browning scholar. *LCCat., Times,* Mar. 9, 1916, p. 12c.

Dr. Koch's consumption-cure, **FortR** 3024

Slum-mothers and death-clubs, **NC** 2022
A medical view of Lourdes, 2819

Beresford, Lord Charles William de la Poer, Baron Beresford, 1846–1919, admiral. *DNB.*

The admiralty confusion and its cure, **NC** 1554
Imperial safety: a workable admiralty, 1558
British fleet and the state of Europe, 1640
Questions for the Council of Defense, 3062
Our reserves for manning the fleet, 3208

Beresford-Hope, Alexander James: see *Index,* I, 810.

Deceased Wife's Sister Bill, **NatR-II** 55

Peace in the Church, **NC** 583
An ecclesiastical olive branch, 965

Berg, Thea, a Norwegian.

Letter: **NC** 453

Bergenroth, Gustav Adolph, 1813–1869, historian. *DNB.*

Mignet's *Charles V. and Francis I.*, **FM** 4694

Berkeley, George Fitz-Hardinge, 1870–1955,

Berkeley, George Fitz-Hardinge (*continued*)
army officer, historian. *LCCat., Times,*
Nov. 15, 1955, p. 1.

Sir Harry Smith and the Boer War, 1848,
FortR 4383

Berlioz, Louis-Hector, 1803–1869, French
composer. *DBF.*

Berlioz on *Der Freischütz,* **FM** 2775

Bernays, Adolphus, d.1864, prof. of German,
Kings Coll. London. Boase.

"The new Reformation," **FM** 3028

Berry, Albert Graham, nephew of Sir Graham
Berry, q.v.; of the London office of the
Colony of Victoria. See *NC,* 3701, pp.
219–220.

The new Commonwealth, **NC** 3701

Berry, Sir Graham, 1822–1904, Australian
statesman. *DNB.*

Letter: **FortR** 2934

Bert, Paul, 1833–1886, French Minister of
Public Instruction and Worship. *DBF.*

The religious question in France, **FortR**
2182

Bertram, James Glass: see *Index,* I, 810.

Fisheries, **FortR** 241

Legislation on betting, **FM** 5613
Betting and book-making, 5948

Oyster-growing, **NatR-II** 764
Fisher life in Scotland, 925

The salmon in Scotland, **ScotR** 250

Bertrand, Joseph Louis François, 1822–1903,
mathematician. *DBF.*

Reception at the French Academy: reply,
NatR-II 816

Besant, Annie (Wood), 1847–1933, theoso-
phist. *DNB.*

"Conceptions of the atonement," **NC** 2769
The conditions of life after death, 3027

Besant, Sir Walter: see *Index,* I, 810.

Authors, individual and corporate, **NatR-II**
1308

An olive branch from America, **NC** 1477
The literary agent, 2850

Betham, Frederick, of St. Andrews, Newcastle-on-Tyne. See *Ram* no. 123; Bat-
tersby/49.

Tithes, **Ram** 188
Letter: 123

Betham-Edwards, Matilda Barbara: see *Index,*
I, 810.

French peasant proprietors, **FortR** 2622
French and English [by P. G. Hamerton],
3148
Madame Bodichon, 3177

From Cairo to Athens, **FM** 5330
Episodes in the life of a musician, 5415
Co-operative agriculture, 5671
Girton College, 5673
International Working Men's Association,
5700, 5708, 5717
Science Congress at Nantes, 5734
An autumn in western France, 5744, 5762,
5777, 5788, 5801
Contemporary French poetry, 5926
Progress of colonisation in Algeria, 5975
Jean Reynaud, 6063
Letters of Coleridge, Southey, and Lamb
to Matilda Betham, 6075
Social aspects of the Paris Exhibition, 6085
Holidays in eastern France, 6096, 6108,
6117, 6125
Schopenhauer on men, books, and music,
6190
Among French friends in Burgundy, 6269
An autumn on the Côte-d'Or, 6325
A Japanese bride, 6411
Exchange no robbery, 6480, 6494, 6500,
6509

Conseil de Famille in France, **NatR-II**
1798
The Family Council in France, 1907
A publicist's view of France, 2163

Bethune, Charles Congleton, b.1849, alive in
1908, J.P. Venn.

Houseless at night, **FortR** 2566 collab.
Thanks from the House of Shelter, 2577
collab.

Bettelheim, Paul. *BMCat.*

The Jews in France, **NC** 3593
The French army, 3641

Bevan, Anthony Ashley: see *Index,* I, 811.

Letter: **FortR** 4153

Bevan, George Penry, b.1824/25. Foster.

The English Pompeii [Wroxeter], **FM** 4033

Bevan, George Phillips, 1830–1889, statistician. Boase. *BMCat.*

Underground perils [of mining], **FortR** 169

Bevan-Lewis, William, 1847–1929, pathologist. *WWW.*

The origins of crime, **FortR** 3406

Bevington, Louisa Sarah, b.1845, afterwards, Mrs. Ignatz Guggenberger, misc. writer. Miles, *Poets,* IX, 227–230.

The moral colour of rationalism, **FortR** 1829

Modern atheism and Mr. Mallock, **NC** 359, 382

How to eat bread, 623

Dogs in Germany, 1437

Bevir, Joseph Louis, b.1855/56, educator. Foster, *BMCat.*

Colours in Dante, **ScotR** 678

Bhownaggree, Sir Mancherjee Merwanjee, 1851–1933, Indian politician. *DNB.*

The present agitation in India, **FortR** 3998

Bicknell, Walter Lionel, b.1852/3, prob. a schoolmaster. Foster, *BMCat.* (Also see *Index,* I, 811; and I, 1045, under his pseudonym of Pember, Austen or Austin.)

Aspects of the national Church (No. I): the tribune of the people, **NatR-II** 384

The Church's gymnasium, 878

The religion of our boys, 887

Patrician pugilism, 935

Our boys (No. I): School-boys' parents, 1097

Bidder, George Parker, 1836–1896, barrister, civil engineer. I.C.E. *Minutes,* 125 (1896), 422–428. (See App. A below.)

The profits of coal-pits, **NC** 2576

Biden, Lewis Marks

Land owners and law, **NatR-II** 284

Biedermann, Baron Christoph, of Raeknitz near Dresden.

Letter: **FortR** 3992

Biesen, Christian van den, divine. *BMCat.*

Authorship and composition of Hexateuch, **DR** 2348, 2362

Origin and history of the Septuagint, 2489

Notices: 2412, 2475, 2531, 2594, 2638, 2651, 2663

Bigg, Ada Heather: see Heather-Bigg, Ada.

Bigge, Lewis Amherst Selby: see Selby-Bigge, Lewis Amherst.

Bikelas, Demetrios, 1835–1908, Greek historian. *EUI.*

The Greek question, **ScotR** 127

The Byzantine empire, 149, 158, 166

Greece before 1821, 243

Formation of the modern Greek state, 251

The territory of the Hellenic Kingdom, 260

The seizure of a Turkish flagship, 513

Bill, Charles, 1843–1915, M.P. *Landed Gentry.*

Colonial problems: Gibraltar, **NatR-II** 1688

Billing, Robert Claudius, 1834–1898, Bishop of Bedford. *WWW, MWT/99.*

Urban populations, **FortR** 3341

Bilsborrow, John, 1837–1903, R.C. Bishop of Salford. *WWW.*

Crisis in religious education, **NatR-II** 1808

Bindle Thomas Herbert: see *Index,* I, 811.

Barbados as a winter resort, **NatR-II** 1348

Binet, Alfred, 1857–1911, French psychologist. *Larousse xxme Siècle.*

Mental imagery, **FortR** 3237

The mechanism of thought, 3511

Birch, Samuel, 1813–1885, Egyptologist. *DNB.*

Egyptian hieroglyphics, **FQR** 568, 648

Chinese literature, 597

Birchenough, Sir Henry, 1853–1937, Pres. British S. African Co. *WWW.*

Do foreign annexations injure British trade? **NC** 3130

England's opportunity: Germany or Canada? 3133

The expansion of Germany, 3234

The future of Egypt: the Niger and the Nile, 3384

The imperial function of trade, 3524

Local beginnings of imperial defence, 3645

"Ordinary business principles," 3697

Lord Rosebery on British trade, 3773

Birchenough, Lady Mabel C. (Bradley), 1860–1936, novelist and critic. *WWW, Yearbook/1904.*

Jean Ingelow, **FortR** 4255

Birchenough, Lady Mabel C. (*continued*)
A new war poet: Crimean war poems, **NC** 3736
Notice: 3021

Bird, Henry Edward, b.1830, writer on chess. *LCCat.*

Letter:˙ **FortR** 2542

Bird, James; possibly Sir James Bird, 1863–1925, in *WWW*, although he would have been only 17 at date of first art.

Treaties of commerce a surrender of principle, **FortR** 1834
No more commercial treaties, 1905

Birdwood, Herbert Mills, 1837–1907, Indian civil servant. *WWW.*

The British civilian in India, **NatR-II** 2059
The Queen as Mahomedan sovereign, 2104

Birrell, Augustine: see *Index*, I, 812.

Letter: **FortR** 2638

What did happen at the Reformation? **NC** 2918
Notices: 1658, 1802, 2713

Birt, Henry Norbert, O.S.B., 1861–1919. *Benedictine Bibliog.*

Troubles of the Elizabethan episcopate, **DR** 2590
Notes from a manuscript [a Sarum breviary], 2666
How our forefathers prepared for confession, 2698
Deprivation of clergy in Elizabeth's reign, 2701, 2713

Bishop, Edmund, 1846–1917, liturgiologist. *DNB.*

English hagiology, **DR** 1948
The Venerable Richard Whiting, 2074 collab.
The earliest Roman Mass-book, 2449
The bidding of the bedes, 2460
Origin of cope as a church vestment, 2560
Two recent liturgical books, 2614
Eucharistic doctrine in the Eastern Church, 2617
Mediaeval institute of cathedral canons, 2630
Eucharistic Presence and Anglican divines, 2645
Notices: 1690, 1713, 1724, 1745, 1884, 2019, 2029, 2520, 2543, 2606, 2628, 2651, 2674, 2720

Bishop, Maria Catherine: see *Index*, I, 812.
Mrs. Craven and her work, **NC** 309

Black, Charles Edward Drummond: see *Index*, I, 812.
Education of the blind and deaf, **NatR-II** 917
New British markets: Tibet, **NC** 2794
The British sphere in Asia, 3649

Black, Clementina: see *Index*, I, 812
The organization of working women, **FortR** 2890
On marriage: a criticism, 2942
The chocolate-makers' strike, 2985
Some East-End workwomen, **NatR-II** 891
Letter: 725
The troubles of an automaton, **NQM** 89
The dislike to domestic service, **NC** 2365
Edited: 1703

Black, John, 1783–1855, journalist, ed. *Morning Chronicle*, 1817–1843. *DNB.*
See: **FM** 363

Black, Robert: see *Index*, I, 812.
Notices: **FortR** 443, 504

Black, William: see *Index*, I, 812.
Notice: **FortR** 387

Blackburn, Elisabeth J. M., prob. a teacher of the deaf and dumb.
Our deaf and dumb, **NC** 1047

Blackburn, Helen, 1842–1903, suffragette. *DNB.*
Relation of women to the state, **NatR-II** 503

Blackburn, Henry, 1830–1897, art critic. *WWW.*
English art in 1883, **NatR-II** 72
The art of illustration, 112
Illustration of books and newspapers, **NC** 1826

Blackett, Selwyn, 1854–1935, divine. *WWW.*
The invasion of America, **NatR-II** 615
Letter: 165

Blackie, John Stuart: see *Index*, I, 812.
Menzel, *German Literature*, **FQR** 367
Goethe's correspondence with Zelter and Bettina Brentano, 380

Prince Pückler-Muskau and his new tour, 399

Eckermann's *Conversations with Göthe*, 410

Ludwig Uhland and the Swabian poets, 445

Knebel's *Works and Correspondence*, 466

Jung Stilling: religious literature of Germany, 491

Müller: English and German scholarship, 523

Greek rhythm and metres: Boeckh, Apel, Hermann, Porson, Blomfield, &c., 537

Merits of Euripides, 557

Lessing's life and writings, 579

Memoirs of Varnhagen von Ense, 603

Rahel, 616

Klopstock, 707

Facts and feelings, life of Steffens, 719

Reminiscences of Ernest Maurice Arndt, 721

Arndt's *Sketches of Swedish History*, 746

Memoirs of Henry Steffens: the Liberation War in Germany, 799

Beneke's *Theory and Practice of Education*, 803

Hormayr's *Reminiscences of the Wars in Germany*, 811

On the teaching of languages, 832

Napoleon in the year 1813, 850

The late King of Prussia, 869

Notice: 847?

Metaphysics, literature, and science, **FM** 5455

See: 845

The Highland crofters, **NC** 841

The second part of *Faust*, 1262

Shakespeare and modern Greek, 2142

Bikelas on Scotland, **ScotR** 285

Blackley, William Lewery: see *Index*, I, 813.

Authenticity of the works of Plato, **FortR** 437

Father Arndt, 719

Juggernaut of poor men's providence, 2162

National thrift, **FM** 6278

English pauperism, 6339

The clergy and Church defence, **NatR-II** 202

Mr. Goschen on national insurance, 314

"The black art," English manner of engraving, 795

National insurance, **NC** 239

House of Lords and national insurance, 472

Blackmore, Richard Doddridge: see *Index*, I, 813.

Mary Anerley, in 15 installments, from **FM** 6194 to 6323

Blackwood, Harriot, or Harriet, Georgina (Rowan-Hamilton), Marchionesse of Dufferin and Ava, 1843–1936, wife of Frederick T. H. T. Blackwood. *Complete Peerage, DNB* 2nd suppl. under her husband.

The women of India, **NC** 2006

Blackwood, Sir Stevenson Arthur, 1832–1893. Principal sec. to the Post Office. Boase.

The public offices—from within, **NC** 1587

Blagden, Isa Jane: see *Index*, I, 813.

A model and a wife, **FM** 4238

Blaine, Delabere Roberton, 1806/07–1871, barrister; writer on copyright. Boase.

Literary and musical copyrights, **FM** 5057

Blake, Edith (Osborne), wife of Sir Henry Arthur Blake. *WWW*/1928 under her husband.

In the Bahamas, **NC** 1548

The Beothuks of Newfoundland, 1636

On seals and savages, 1686

Blake, Lady Emma Gertrude (Dawson), d.1924, wife of Sir Patrick James Graham Blake, 5th Baron. Burke.

Patchword in black and white, **NatR-II** 1261

In the wake of the red van, 1290

"With all hands!" [fishermen's widows], 1314

Blake, Sir Henry Arthur: see *Index*, I, 814.

Try the Bahamas [for health], **FortR** 2419

The Pan-Britannic olympiad, 3334

The Irish police, **NC** 558

Flamingoes at home, 1498

The awakening of Jamaica, 1938

Where did Columbus first land in 1492? 2292

Impressions from a tour in China, 3728

Blake, John Y. Fillimore, 1856–1907, army officer. *LCCat.*

Golden Rhodesia: a revelation, **NatR-II** 2049

Native Rhodesia, 2070

Second thoughts on Rhodesia, 2140

Blakelock, Ralph Blakelock Salt, 1867–1904, priest at Brompton Oratory. Gorman.

Blakelock, Ralph Blakelock Salt (*continued*)
The kingdom of the head master, **DR** 2659
Montalembert and French education, 2705

Blanc, Louis, 1811–1882, French politician, journalist. *DBF.*

See: **FQR** 747

Blanchamp, Henry, perhaps the translator in *BMCat.*, or perhaps Henry Frederick Ernest Blanchamp, b.1866, journalist, in Venn; or the two may be the same.

Thoughts of a human automaton, **FortR** 3190

Blandford, George Fielding: see *Index*, I, 814.

On the nature of emotion, **FortR** 610

Blaze de Bury, Fernande

The Abbé Prévost in England, **ScotR** 620
Mythology of the nineteenth century [on Zola], 666

Blaze de Bury, Baronne Marie Pauline Rose (Stuart): see *Index*, I, 814, and II, App. A.

The decadence of thought in France, **FortR** 2804
A new French novelist [Henri Lavedan], 2900
Idealism in recent French fiction, 2940

New electorate in France, **NatR-II** 633
Some sound French novels, 842
Stendhal's autobiography, 1067

Trans: **NC** 1758

Blaze de Bury, Yetta, d.1902, French critic. *DBF* under Ange Henri Blaze de Bury.

Celebrated Frenchwoman [Madame de Maintenon], **FortR** 3067
The Duc de Lauzun and court of Louis XV, 3655
Ferdinand Brunetière, 3704
Jules Lemaitre, 3786
Edmond de Goncourt, 3848
Anatole France, 3887
Mme. Bartet of the Comédie Française, 3961
Mounet Sully, 4049
French women in French industry, 4150
Sarah Bernhardt, 4306

Marivaux, **NC** 1124
The real Madame de Pompadour, 1582
Théâtre Français, and its sociétaires, 1714, 1731
The French opera, 1895

Blennerhassett, Lady Charlotte Julia (Gräffin von Leyden): see *Index*, I, 814.

A page of diplomatic history, **FortR** 1867
Félix Antoine Dupanloup, **NC** 269

Blennerhassett, Sir Rowland: see *Index*, I. 814.

Letter: **DR** 1063a
The reform of the Ottoman Empire, **FortR** 1332
The land question in Europe, 1833
Ethics and politics, 2979
Letter: 2655

Great Britain and European powers, **NatR-II** 2413
Great Britain and the dual monarchy, 2451
Foreign policy of the German Empire, 2493

Prince Bismarck, **NC** 1863

Blewitt, Octavian: see *Index*, I, 814.

Constantinople, **FM** 1403
Modern Egypt, 1420
Modern Greece, 1444, 1457
The Danube, 1494, 1506

Bligh, Edward Vesey: see *Index*, I, 814.

The magistracy, **NatR-II** 489

Bligh, John Stuart, 6th Earl of Darnley, 1827–1896, army officer. Burke.

The Eton tutorial system, **NC** 1106

Blind, Karl: see *Index*, I, 814.

The Luther monument and the German Reformation, **FortR** 557
Ancient and modern Russia, 621
The condition of France, 643
Result of French designs upon Germany, 746
French Republic and the suffrage question, 793
General Langiewicz, 2607
John Bright, personal recollections, 2820
Mr. Gladstone and the civilized world, 2851
The unmaking of England, 2897
Gladstone on German literature, 2924
An old Greek explorer of Britain [Pytheas], 3125
Czar and Emperor, 3804
Young Turkey, 3890
Transvaal independence, 4368
Germany as a naval power, 4437
France, Russia, and peace of the world, 4474

Recollections about Ledru-Rollin, **FM** 5648
Fire-burial among our forefathers, 5688

Armin, the liberator of Germany, 5713

The Flemings and Walloons of Belgium, 5764

Life and labours of Francis Deak 1803–1876 [Hungarian patriot], 5790

Ferdinand Freiligrath, 5814

The Russian imperial title, 5819

The Teutonic tree of existence, 5889

An old German poem and a Vedic hymn, 5936

Prince Napoleon and European democracy, 6222

Recollections about Garibaldi, 6535, 6543

Gladstone's disestablishment of Greek pantheon, **NatR-II** 1009

Life and labours of Schliemann, 1109

A plea for the Triple Alliance, 1180

The Hans Sachs celebration in Germany, 1650

Discovery of Odinic songs in Shetland, **NC** 322

The conflict in Germany, 679

Giordano Bruno and new Italy, 1735

A mistaken imperial celebration [of Barbarossa], 3046

Luther monuments and the German revolution of 1525, **ScotR** 288

Kossuth and Klapka, 380

The meaning of the Russian name, 418

Ale-drinking old Egypt and the Thrako-Germanic race, 465

The "Song to Aegir," 511

Strife of tongues in Belgium, 599

Odin and the royal family of England, 637

Wayland the Smith, 673

Blind, Mathilde, 1841–1896, poetess. Boase.

Recollections of Mazzini, **FortR** 3078

Trans: **FM** 5787

The tale of Tristram and Iseult, **NatR-II** 134

Mary Wollstonecraft, **NQM** 149

Bloomfield, Lady Georgiana (Liddell), 1822–1905, wife of John Arthur Douglas Bloomfield, 2nd Baron Bloomfield. *DNB.*

An episode in history [life of Empress Marie Louise], **NatR-II** 480

Irish wit and humour, 1220

Blount or Blunt; possibly Michael Henry Mary Blount, 1789–1874, J.P., who had Catholic connections through his wife, Elizabeth A. M. Petre, in *Landed Gentry/*1937, under Riddell-Blount.

The Irish and English universities, **DR** 4 collab.

Blowitz, Henri George Adolphe Opper de: see *Index,* I, 815, and II, App. A.

A trip to Bosnia-Herzegovina, **NC** 2651

Blundell, Charles Joseph Weld, 1844–1927. *Landed Gentry.*

Democracy: whither? **DR** 1962

Blundell, Mary E. (Sweetman): see *Index,* I, 815, and II, App. A.

Old folks' tales, **NatR-II** 1775

Blunt: see Blount.

Blunt, Wilfrid Scawen, 1840–1922, traveller, poet. *DNB.*

An Indo-Mediterranean railway, **FortR** 1641

Recent events in Arabia, 1695

The Sultan's heirs in Asia, 1709

The future of Islam, 1831, 1839, 1848, 1856, 1873

Ideas about India, 2199, 2223, 2237, 2277

England's place in India, 2290

The thoroughbred horse, **NC** 492

The Egyptian Revolution, 757

The forthcoming Arab race at Newmarket, 992

Lord Lytton's rank in literature, 2191

The release of Arabi, 2279

Lord Cromer and the Khedive [Abbās], 2375, 2516

The truth of the Dongola adventure, 2925

Turkish misgovernment, 3029

How to breed horses for war, 3699

Blyden, Edward Wilmot, 1832–1912, African educator. *LCCat.*

Mohammedanism and the Negro race, **FM** 5740

Christianity and the Negro race, 5805

Christian missions in West Africa, 5865

Islam and race distinctions, 5872

Africa and the Africans, 6083

Blyth, Sir Arthur, 1823–1891, agent-general for So. Australia. Boase.

Letter: **FortR** 2934

Blyth, Sir James, 1st Baron Blyth, 1841–1925. *WWW.*

"Ordinary business principles," **NC** 3691

Blyth, Mrs. Katharine, *BMCat., NC* no. 2984. Possibly the wife of Edmund Kell Blyth who published a book on Germany in 1897: see *BMCat.*

Blyth, Mrs. Katharine (*continued*)
Sketches made in Germany, **NC** 2984, 3016, 3072, 3201, 3317, 3419, 3436

Boas, Frederick Samuel, 1862–1957, English scholar. *WWW, LCCat.*
New light on Marlowe and Kyd, **FortR** 4233
The arrest of Thomas Kyd, 4339

Boboruikin, Petr, or Peter, Dmitrievich: see *Index,* I, 815.
Nihilism in Russia, **FortR** 521

Boborykine, Peter: see preceding entry.

Bockett, F. W.: see *Index,* I, 815.
The people and their friends, **FortR** 2431

Bode, Wilhelm Arnold von, 1845–1929, German art historian. *Grosse Brockhaus.*
The Berlin Renaissance Museum, **FortR** 3135
Old-age pensions: failure in Germany, **NatR-II** 1256

Bodley, John Edward Courtenay: see *Index,* I, 816.
A visit to President Brand [of the Orange River Free State], **FortR** 2734
Roman Catholicism in America, **NC** 1789

Bodley, William Hamilton, 1820–1900, R.C. priest. *Venn.*
The origin of terrestrial life, **DR** 1958

Boh, Felix, 1844–1929, German political writer. *EUI.*
German view [of English foreign policy], **NC** 2654

Bolton, John; possibly John Bolton of Lancashire, writer on geology. *Allibone.*
The facts about the Venezuela boundary, **NC** 2876

Bompas, Henry Mason: see *Index,* I, 816.
Nonconformists and Home Rule, **FortR** 3229
Church disestablishment, 3610
Improvement of working-class homes, 3722
The Education Bill, 3888
The argument for belief, **NatR-II** 1450

Bond, Edward, 1844–1920, M.P. *WWW.*

Unionist Party and old-age pensions, **NatR-II** 2323

Bond, Sir Edward Augustus, 1815–1898, librarian of British museum. *DNB.*
Facts in life of Geoffrey Chaucer, **FortR** 300

Bond, Richard Warwick: see *Index,* I, 816.
King Arthur on the stage, **FortR** 3635
Cymbeline at the Lyceum, 3874

Bond, Sir Robert, 1857–1927, Canadian statesman. *DNB.*
Newfoundland fisheries dispute, **FortR** 2986 collab.

Bond, Walter; possibly W. G. Bond, author of *The Rating of Electric Lighting,* 1902, in *BMCat.*
Municipal trading, **FortR** 4353

Boner, Charles, 1815–1870, misc. writer. *DNB.*
Sir Edwin Landseer, **FM** 3490

Boni, Giacomo, 1859–1925, Italian archaeologist. *Tosi.*
Excavations in the Roman Forum, **NC** 3637

Bonsal, Stephen: see *Index,* I, 816.
The University of Fez to-day, **FortR** 3272

Bonus, John 1828/29–1909, R.C. priest. *Foster;* Bonus, *Thoughts in Verse for my Friends* (1914), p. viii.
Laforet's exposition of Catholic dogma, **Ram** 931.

Booth, Arthur John, writer on socialism. *BMCat.*
Fourier, **FortR** 902, 909

Boré, Eugène, 1809–1878, French priest, orientalist. *DBF.*
Letters on Lebanon, **Ram** 28, 52, 65, 78, 94

Borlase, William Copeland: see *Index,* I, 816.
A visit to Dr. Schliemann's Troy, **FM** 6022
Parliament and the Church, **NC** 1192

Borradaile, Vincent Gawain, divine. *CCD/76.*
Methods of charitable relief, **NatR-II** 956

Borring, Frances Mary de: see *Index*, I, 816, and II, App. A.

A prosperous agricultural country [Denmark], **FortR** 2710

The peasant proprietor of the south [of France], **NatR-II** 372

Borromeo, St. Charles, 1538–1584, archbishop of Milan. *Cath.Ency.*

Letter: **Ram** 65

Borrow, George Henry: see *Index*, I, 816.

Danish and Norwegian literature, **FQR** 135 collab.

Borthwick, Sir Algernon, 1st Baron Glenesk, 1830–1908, newspaper proprietor, M.P. *DNB.*

Mr. Hayward, **FortR** 2163

?Conservative provincial press, **NatR-II** 325

The Primrose League, **NC** 1294

Borthwick, Lady Alice Beatrice (Lister), 1841–1898, misc. writer, wife of Sir Algernon Borthwick, q.v. *DNB* under her husband and her father, Thomas Henry Lister, 1800–1842.

The increasing duration of human life, **NC** 3167

Bosanquet, Helen (Dendy): see *Index*, I, 817.

Women in industry, **NatR-II** 1616
The socialist propaganda, 1774

Law and the laundry, **NC** 3067 collab.

Boscawen, A. Griffith: see Griffith-Boscawen, Arthur.

Boswell, Charles Stuart. *BMCat.*

The fairy mythology of Ireland, **NatR-II** 958
From Swedenborg to the modern philosopher, 1264

Bothmer, Countess Marie Maximillian von (von Fehleisen): see *Index*, I, 817.

German home life, in 9 installments from **FM** 5632 to 5767

Bottalla, Paul, S.J., 1823–1896. Sutcliffe.

Father Bottalla to Mr. Renouf, **DR** 1373, 1402, 1424.

Boulger, Demetrius Charles: see *Index*, I, 817.

China and foreign powers, **FortR** 2041
Twelve years' work on the Congo, 4183
The Congo State and its critics, 4251
The coming Afghan crisis, 4465
Peking—and after, 4489
Is Russia to preponderate in China? 4527

Russia and China, **FM** 6311

Lord Lawrence and masterly inactivity, **NatR-II** 20
Subsidising the Ameer [of Afghanistan], 94
[Russia's annexation of] Merv! 161
Railways in Asiatic Turkey, 253
The value of the Chinese alliance, 810
The pacification of Burmah, 868

England's policy towards Afghanistan, **NQM** 167

The future of China, **NC** 483
France and China, 859
The crisis in Indo-China, 2435
The Corean crux: a word for China, 2662

Boult, Swinton Henry, b.1835, barrister. *M at B.* (In *Index*, I, 817, an art. of his is wrongly listed under his father: see App. A below.)

Home Rule, an exploded myth, **NatR-II** 638
Letter: 483

Boulton, Sir Harold Edwin, 1859–1935, philanthropist. Burke.

Houseless at night, **FortR** 2566 collab.
Thanks from the House of Shelter, 2577 collab.
The housing of the poor, 2683
A London house of shelter, 3466

Boulton, Sir Samuel Bagster, 1830–1918, businessman. *WWW.*

Labour disputes and the Chamber of Commerce, **NC** 1886
Sir John Macdonald on imperial federation, 2078

Bourchier, James David: see *Index*, I, 817.

Through Bulgaria with Prince Ferdinand, **FortR** 2726
The fate of Roumania, 2777
The heritage of the Hapsburgs, 2803
In the Balkans with Prince Ferdinand, 2842
The great Servian festival, 2855
The sentinel of the Balkans, 2898
A glance at contemporary Greece, 2961
The stronghold of the Sphakiotes, 2976
On the Black Sea with Prince Ferdinand, 3034

Bourchier, James David (*continued*)
In Rhodope with Prince Ferdinand, 3070
A Balkan confederation, 3126
The Pomaks of Rhodope, 3421
Prince Alexander of Battenberg, 3459
Charilaos Trikoupes [Greek statesman], 3825
Montenegro and her prince, 4211

Beaconsfield [the town], **NatR-II** 738

Bourget, Charles-Joseph-Paul, 1852–1935, French novelist. *DBF.*

Science et poésie, **FortR** 2702
Gustave Flaubert, 3986

Bourinot, Sir John George: see *Index*, I, 817.

Canada: its political development, **ScotR** 91
French Canada, 165
Canada and the United States, 283
Canadian Dominion and Australian "Commonwealth," 486
Literary culture in Canada, 570

Bourke, Sir Dermot Robert Wyndham, 7th Earl of Mayo, 1851–1927. Burke.

The tourist in Ireland, **NC** 3149
Sir John Lubbock on the "financial relations commission," 3244

Bourne, Sir Frederick Samuel Augustus, 1854–1940, civil servant. *WWW.*

Trans: **NC** 505

Bourne, Henry Richard Fox: see *Index*, I, 817.

Malta, **FortR** 1591
The case for "the Bechuana rebels," 4033
Sierra Leone troubles, 4157

Bousfield, Sir William, 1842–1910, educationist. *WWW.*

Note: **NC** 3081

Bouteiller, Jean or Jehan-Charles de, 1840–1885, journalist. *DBF.*

Workmen of Paris during the siege, **FM** 5437, 5454

Bovet, Maria Anne de, b.1855, later Mme. de Bois-Hébert, French novelist. *DBF.*

Gounod's views on art and artists, **FortR** 2853
Gounod, 3445

Bowden, Ernest Monnington, 1859–1904, inventor. Venn.

Scientific sins, **FortR** 3031

Jainism: a chat with Raja Sivaprasad, **NC** 3486

Bowden, Henry George Sebastian, 1836–1920, R.C. priest. Newman, *L&D*, XVI, index.

Reason and religion, **FortR** 3002

Bowen, Sir George Ferguson: see *Index*, I, 818.

Corsica, **NatR-II** 1231
See: 1025

Bowen, H. Herldon, an American. *LCCat.*

American opinion of the [Boer] war, **NC** 3647

Bowen-Graves, Francis Robert Steele, b.1845/46, barrister. Foster, under Graves.

Forty years of the House of Lords, **FortR** 918, 927
Marat, 1015

Bowen-Jones, Sir John Bowen, 1840–1925, merchant. *WWW* under Jones.

A farm that really pays, **NC** 1135

Bowen-Rowlands, Ernest Brown, 1866–1951, barrister. *WWW.*

?Her Majesty's judges, **NatR-II** 2536

Bower, Marian, fiction writer. *BMCat.*

The service of a village knight, **NatR-II** 1543

Bower, William H., 1814/15–1905, of St. Edmund's Coll. *Tablet,* Jan. 21, 1905, p. 105.

The Paris Exhibition of 1878, **DR** 1668

Bowie, Archibald Granger. *BMCat.*

Postal telegraph service, **FM** 5535

Bowles, Emily, 1818–1904? R.C. critic. Newman, *L&D*, XI, index.

Hawkstone, a Tale, **DR** 385
Days near Rome [by Augustus J. C. Hare], 1505
Lady Georgiana Fullerton, 2137

Bowles, Thomas Gibson: see *Index*, I, 818, and *DNB.*

Newspapers, **FortR** 2188
The Navy paralysed by paper, 2279
Union of the Empire by tariff, 2315

Boyd, Andrew K. H. (*continued*)
Concerning cutting and carving, 4299
Concerning the estimate of human beings, 4321
On the forest-hill: thoughts touching dream-life, 4368
The close of holiday-time, 4385
Concerning ugly ducks, 4405
A reminiscence of the old time, 4441
Concerning unpruned trees, 4463
Concerning ten years, 4499
The rest of it, 4519
The organ in Scotland, 4592
Roadside stations, 4606
Presbyterian sermons, 4624
Concerning beards, 4631
Advantages of a cantankerous fool, 4685
Among south-western cathedrals, 4724
Treatment of such as differ from us in opinion, 4736
The heads of battering-rams, 4771
Depreciation: with some thoughts on dislike, 4963
A May ramble, 4999
Of unconsciousness and annihilation, 5012
In the Highlands, 5141
A few October days, 5271
Competitive examination and selection, 5329
Disadvantages of a small community, 5378
Of alienation, 5386
Making better of it, 5401
Of growing old, 5462
Of quarrelsome folk, 5495
My vestry windows, 5559
Between June and May, 5590
Norman Macleod, 5799
At the General Assembly, 5830
Charles Kingsley, 5901
A long look-out, 5906
A peculiar holiday [in London], 5951
Concerning the longest day, 5962
Of vulgarity in opinion, 5970
Dean Stanley at St. Andrews, 5982
An old story now, 5989
Professor [Robert] Buchanan of Glasgow, 6016
Of country work, 6036
Of the Lengten-tide, 6065
A June day's fancies, 6082
Of parting company, 6203
Little to shew, 6231
The cheerfulness of the old, 6378
Lord Campbell, 6384
Of the opposition, 6459
Of mistakes, 6466
Better away, 6540
See: 3882

Boyd, J. F. *BMCat.*

Depression of trade, colonization, **NatR-II** 415

Boyd, W.; possibly Sir Walter Boyd, 1833–1918, Irish barrister in *WWW*.

North-American fisheries question, **FortR** 2470

Boyle, Cecil William, 1853–1900, army officer. Burke under Cork.

The cavalry rush to Kimberley, **NC** 3662

Boyle, Eleanor Vere (Gordon): see *Index*, I, 818.

Autumn in a Buchan garden, **NatR-II** 1780
Hampton Court in by-gone years, 1966
Dropmore, 2292

Boyle, Emily Charlotte (de Burgh), Countess of Cork and Orrery, 1828–1912, wife of 9th Earl of Cork and Orrery. *Complete Peerage* under Cork.

Souvenirs of court favourites, **FortR** 4299

Some social changes in fifty years, **NC** 2183

Boyle, Frederick: see *Index*, I, 818.

Orchids and hybridizing, **NatR-II** 902

A thanksgiving for orchids, **NC** 2294

Boyle, James, 1853–1939, political correspondent. *Amer. WWW.*

An American presidential campaign, **NC** 3733

Brabazon, Lady Mary Jane (Maitland), 1847–1918, Countess of Meath, wife of Reginald Brabazon, q.v. *Complete Peerage.*

The first woman's hospital in Morocco, **NC** 3306

Brabazon, Reginald, 12th Earl of Meath, 1841-1929, diplomat. *DNB.*

Anglo-Saxon unity, **FortR** 3071
Depreciators of the nation, 3903
Letter: 3904

A woman's work, **NatR-II** 212
An appeal to men of leisure, 289
Appeal to men of wealth, 328
Open spaces and physical education, 511
State-directed colonization, 585
Physical education, 1368

Health and physique of our city populations, **NC** 604
The early closing movement, 769

Great cities and social reform, 922
State-directed emigration, 1060
The true reform of the House of Lords,
1363
Decay of bodily strength in towns, 1404
A model factory, 1536
"A thousand more mouths every day,"
1643
Work for the London Council, 1685
Labour colonies in Germany, 1986
A model dairy, 2029
Diminution of drunkenness in Norway,
2135
A Maori meeting, 2211
A Britisher's impressions of America and
Australasia, 2369
Public playgrounds for children, 2440
Shall Indian Princes sit in the House of
Lords? 2569
Land of incredible barbarity [Morocco],
2612
How to "mend" the House of Lords, 2697
Reasonable patriotism, 2887
Are manners disappearing from Great
Britain? 2964
The massacres in Turkey, 3007

Brackenbury, Charles Booth: see *Index*, I,
819.

The British Army, in 7 installments from
FortR 2648 to 2704, collab.

Ironclad field artillery, **NC** 192

Brackenbury, Sir Henry: see *Index*, I, 819.

Midsummer in the Soudan, **FortR** 2355

Operations against Charleston, **FM** 4670
Military reform, 4707, 4734, 4745, 4768,
4790

Braddon, Sir Edward Nicholas Coventry: see
Index, I, 819.

Life in India, in 7 installments from **FM**
4953 to 5070

The federation movement in Australasia,
NC 2966

Braddon, Mary Elizabeth, 1837–1915,
novelist, wife of John Maxwell. *DNB.*

Herman Sudermann, **NatR-II** 1458

Bradlaugh, Charles: see *Index*, I, 819.

The hours of adult labour, **FortR** 2934

Bradley, Arthur Granville: see *Index*, I, 819.

On an old American turnpike, **FortR** 3844

Alexander Hamilton, **NatR-II** 469
Negro tenants of the Southern states, 834

Bradley, Edith, household economist, of
Bredons Norton. *BMCat.*

Letter: **FortR** 4051

Bradley, Emily T.: see Smith, Emily Tennyson.

Bradley, Francis Herbert, 1846–1924, philosopher. *DNB.*

The evidences of spiritualism, **FortR** 2399

Bradley, George Granville: see *Index*, I, 820.

My schooldays from 1830 to 1840, **NC** 975

Bradley, Henry, 1845–1923, philologist, *DNB.*

English local etymology, **FM** 5893

Bradley, Thomas Earnshaw, ed. *The Lamp.*
BMCat.

Letter: **Ram** 173

Bradshaw, Oswald Mosley: see *Index*, I, 820.

Letter: **NatR-II** 289

Brady, William Maziere: see *Index*, I, 820,
and *Cath.Ency.*

A plea for an Anglo-Roman alliance,
FortR 2154

Church temporalities in Ireland, **FM** 4613
Irish Church in time of Queen Elizabeth,
4805

Stuart pretenders, **ScotR** 92

Braekstad, Hans Lien, 1845–1915, Anglo-
Norwegian journalist. *WWW, LCCat.*

The Norwegian-Swedish conflict, **FortR**
4064

Bramston, Mary: see *Index*, I, 820.

Letter: **NatR-II** 833

Bramwell, Sir Frederick Joseph, 1818–1903,
engineer. *DNB.*
Notice: **NC** 1753

Bramwell, George William Wilshere, Baron
Bramwell, 1808–1892, judge. *DNB.*

Drink, **NC** 1138
Drink: a rejoinder, 1147
Insanity and crime, 1217
Marriage with a deceased wife's sister,
1320

?On the universality of Goethe's genius, 771
See: 498

Briant, Mrs., sec. to the Nottingham and
Leicester Cigar Makers' Union in 1889.

A working woman's speech, **NC** 1703

Brickdale, Matthew Inglett Fortesque: see
Index, I, 822.

Phonetics, **FM** 2645
Poets and players, 2908

Bridge, Sir Cyprian Arthur George: see
Index, I, 822.

The Mediterranean of Japan, **FortR** 1181
A glimpse of the Korea, 1224
Early autumn on the lower Yang-tze, 1265
An excursion in Formosa, 1282

The city of Kiyôto, **FM** 6008
Sub-aqueous warfare, 6103
The revival of the warlike power of China,
6191

Compulsion v. volunteering, **NatR-II** 2487

Bridgeman, William Clive, 1864–1935, statesman. Venn.

The moderates and the London School
Board, **NatR-II** 2522

Bridges, John Henry, 1832–1906, philosopher.
DNB.

Influence of civilisation on health, **FortR**
613
Vivisection, 1140 collab.
Is our cause in China just? 1207
Harvey and vivisection, 1271
Evolution and positivism, 1369, 1379
Moral and social aspects of health, 1404
Position of sociology among sciences, 1489
Comte's definition of life, 1807

Bridges, Matthew, 1800–1894, R.C. priest.
Newman, *L&D,* XI, 164n.

The canon of sacred Scripture, **DR** 471

Oliver Cromwell, **Ram** 623
Who wrote the *Waverley Novels?* 779
Letter: 162

Bridgett, Thomas Edward: see *Index,* I, 823.

Bristol pulpit in the days of Henry VIII,
DR 1666
A Protestant life of St. Hugh, 1727
New English documents on Immaculate
Conception, 1887
Life of St. Olaf, 1910

The defender of the faith [Henry VIII],
1954
The story of the French exiles, 2052
The rood of Boxley; or, How a lie grows,
2094
Catholic witness upon Anglican orders,
2510
Can Christians consistently laugh or smile?
2562
Richard Rolle, the hermit, 2597
Monuments to Cardinal Wiseman, 2619
Notice: 1756

Bright, Sir Charles: see *Index,* I, 823.

Pacific cable, **FortR** 4172

Bright, Henry Arthur: see *Index,* I, 823.

Presidential election for America, **FM** 3011
Canada, 3064

Bright, James Franck, 1832–1920, Master of
Univ. Coll., Oxford. *DNB.*

Why I voted for Mr. Gladstone, **NC** 2258

Brimley, George, 1819–1857, essayist, librarian
of Trinity Coll., Cambridge. *DNB.*

"Memoir" of Bishop Stanley [by A. P.
Stanley], **FM** 2853
Wordsworth, 2875, 2882
Autobiography of B. R. Haydon, 3134
Verse-books of 1854, 3315
Men and Women [by Browning], 3435
The Angel in the House [by Coventry
Patmore], 3529
Little lessons for little poets, 3573

Brindle, Thomas, 1791–1871, regent of Prior
Park. Boase.

Note: **Ram** 647

Brinkley, Frank, 1841–1912, Tokyo correspondent of *Times. WWW.*

A visit to Japan, **FortR** 2590

Bristed, Charles Astor: see *Index,* I, 823

Sketches of American society, in 10 install-
ments, from **FM** 2699 to 2889
American poetry, 2743
An election row in New York, 2931
Paris, demolished and embellished, 3308
Paris, its vanities, 3348
An Americo-Russian alliance, 3355
English press and American public, 3364
American parties, past and present, 3388,
3409
Political press of America, 3422
The triumph of barbarism, 3564

Britten, James, botanist, sec. Catholic Truth Society. Gorman, *Cath.Ency.*

The Catholic Truth Society, **DR** 2066
The work of the laity, 2077
Art and the people, 2168
Notice: ?2211

Broadfoot, William: see *Index*, I, 823.

Concerning pugilism, **NatR-II** 2051

Broadhurst, Henry, 1840–1911, labour leader. *DNB.*

Enfranchisement of urban leaseholders, **FortR** 2146
The ideas of the new voters, 2268

Leasehold enfranchisement, **NC** 1151

Broadley, Alexander Meyrick: see *Index*, I, 823, and *WWW*/1928.

Turkish intrigues in Egypt, **FortR** 2117
English interests in North Africa, 2305

Brock, Sidney Gorham, b.1836, American lawyer, journalist. *Amer. WW*/1919.

Advance of the United States, **FortR** 3391

Brockedon, William: see *Index*, I, 823, under Brockendon (in error).

Diary of a traveller in the Alps, **FM** 1296, 1305

Brockett, T. W.: see *Index*, I, 823.

Social reforms for the London poor, **FortR** 2122

Brockway, Zebulon Reed, 1827–1920, penologist: *Amer. WWW.*

The Elmira reformatory, **FortR** 3217

Broderip, William John: see *Index*, I, 823 and II, App. A.

Leaves from the note-book of a naturalist, in 14 installments, from **FM** 2680 to 2852
?*Episodes of Insect Life*, 2836, 2862, 2890
?*Game Birds and Wild Fowl*, 2926
The naturalist in Jamaica [P. H. Gosse], 2954
The Naturalist in Devonshire [by P. H. Gosse], 3140
Profitable Poultry, 3162
Gallinaceana [poultry], 3177
The great ant-eater, 3183
Gallinaceana: peacocks, 3194
Gallinaceana: pheasants, 3217

The Aquarium [by P. H. Gosse], 3253
The great bustard, 3266
The Poultry Pentalogue, 3296
Alectryomania [on poultry], 3307
Rooks, 3579
The raven: where is Ralpho? 3591
Crows and choughs, 3597
Deer, 3612, 3621, 3634
Magpies, 3639
Jays and nutcrackers, 3653
Rollers and kingfishers, 3663
Waterton's *Essays on Natural History*, 3669
Woodpeckers, 3683
Bee-eaters, wrynecks, creepers, and nut-hatches, 3704
The Rambles of a Naturalist, 3713
Gulls, 3726
The albatross, 3739
Man-of-war birds, boobies, and noddies, 3749
?*Geology of Central France* [by Scrope], 3761
Cormorants, 3771
?*Cruise of the "Betsey"* [by Hugh Miller], 3779
Pelicans, 3791
Snake-birds, 3801
Mushrooms, 3814
Buckland's *Bridgewater Treatise*, 3825
The shark, 3829

Brodhurst, Bernard Edward Spencer: see *Index*, I, 823.

Letter: **NatR-II** 1310

Brodie, Sir Benjamin Collins: see *Index*, I, 823.

Homoeopathy, **FM** 4140

Brodribb, William Jackson, 1829–1905, translator. *DNB.*

Pliny the Younger, **FortR** 690
Plutarch's essays, 1001

Brodrick, George Charles: see *Index*, I, 823.

What are liberal principles? **FortR** 1229
Liberals and Whigs, 1468
British agriculture in 1882, 1964
Merton College in the sixteenth century, 1983
Reform of local government in counties, 2032
Huxley: personal reminiscences, 3686

The last chapter of Irish history, **FM** 6368
The Irish Land Act of 1881, 6477
Tenant-right for British farmers, 6481

Plain facts about Ireland, **NatR-II** 695

Fallacies of modern socialism, 1282
Early treatises on Ireland, 1372

Merton College before the Reformation, **NC** 763
The progress of democracy in England, 930
Democracy and socialism, 983
The University of Oxford in 1898, 3328
A nation of amateurs, 3725

Brodrick, H.

The Oxford undergraduate, **NatR-II** 2510

Brodrick, William, 8th Viscount Midleton, 1830–1907. Burke.

Surrey, **BentQR** 23

Irish legislation and its results, **NatR-II** 10

The Noxious Gases Bill, **NC** 373
Our highways, 637

Brodrick, William St. John Freemantle, 1st Earl Midleton, 1856–1942, M.P. *DNB.*

Relations of Houses of Parliament, **FortR** 1755
The homes of the poor, 1950
The bursting of the bubble, 2180

A reform of the House of Lords, **NatR-II** 173
Edward Stanhope, 1542

Functions of Conservative opposition, **NC** 812
The House of Lords, 2553 collab.

Bromby, Charles Henry: see *Index*, I, 824.

Disendowment: a compromise, **FortR** 3659

The sinking and the sunken [on poverty and crime], **NatR-II** 793

Bromley-Davenport, William, 1821–1884, M.P. *Landed Gentry.*

Fox-hunting, **NC** 866
Salmon-fishing, 900
Covert-shooting, 943

Brooke, Stopford Augustus: see *Index*, I, 824.

Notes on Turner's *Liber Studiorum*, **NC** 720

Brookfield, Arthur Montagu, 1853–1940, army officer. *WWW.*

"Personal sacrifices," and the Conservative cause, **NatR-II** 210

The War Office and its sham army, **NC** 3218

Brooks, Charles William Shirley: see *Index*, I, 824.

?The age of honesty [of dishonesty], **DR** 649

Brooks, E. W.; perhaps Ernest Walter Brooks, 1863–1955, Byzantine historian in *WWW* /1960.

The Shishkoff Russian famine fund, **NC** 2220

Brooksbank, B.

Mr. Irving as a tragedian, **NatR-II** 48
Poetic emotion and affinities, 181
Letter: 189

Brough, Bennett Hooper, 1860–1908, mining expert. *DNB.*

The scarcity of coal, **NC** 3639

Brougham, Henry Peter: see *Index*, I, 824 and II, App. A.

Letter: **NC** 921

Brown, Baldwin: see Brown, James Baldwin.

Brown, Frances, 1816–1879; called "The Blind Poetess of Ulster." Allibone; *LCCat.*

Legends of Ulster: the unlucky birthnight, **FM** 2500

Brown, Gerard Baldwin, 1849–1932, prof. of Fine Art, Edinburgh. *WWW.*

Modern French art, **NC** 468

Brown, Henry Hilton, 1856/57–1927, procurator-fiscal of Midlothian. *Scotsman*, Jan. 13, 1927.

Evolution of the procurator fiscal, **ScotR** 645

Brown, Horatio Robert Forbes: see *Index*, I, 828.

Paolo Sarpi, **ScotR** 576

Brown, J. J.

Madame de Douhault, **NatR-II** 1761

Brown, James, 1835–1890, Scottish divine. *LCCat.*

Thomas Carlyle's apprenticeship, **ScotR** 4

Brown, James Baldwin: see *Index*, I, 828.

Is the pulpit losing its power? **NC** 6
The soul and future life, 97

Brown, James Baldwin (*continued*)
The last great dream of the crusade [on Columbus], 645

Brown, James Reid, 1796–1860, journalist, later Scottish minister. Scott, *Fasti,* III, 202.

The dissenters and the universities, **FM** 850
America and church establishments, 874, 883

Brown, John B., a sixteen-years resident of U.S. and Canada. See *FM* no. 1133.

Emigration and the United States, **FM** 1133
Emigration and the Canadas, 1144

Brown, Peter Hume, 1849–1918, Scottish historian. *DNB.*

George Buchanan and the Inquisition, **ScotR** 396

Brown, Robert: see *Index,* I, 828.

Twelve months of travel, **FortR** 2081

Brown, T. O.

Great and big: a dialogue, **NatR-II** 1008

Browne, Sir Benjamin Chapman, 1839–1917, civil engineer. *WWW.*

The engineering struggle, **NatR-II** 2129
Our American competitors, 2310

Browne, C. Elliot, antiquary.

Shakespeare's son-in-law, **FM** 5533
In Arden, 5797
Master Robert Shallow, 5918

Wit of last generation [Joseph Jekyll], **NQM** 88
The art of lying [tall stories in literature], 109
Early literary journals, 130

Browne, Edmond Charles, b.1843, army officer. *Army List/75, LCCat.*

The kingdom of Burmah in 1875, **FM** 5711

Browne, Francis Fisher, 1843–1913, editor. *DAB.*

The presidential contest, **NatR-II** 1947

Browne, George Forrest: see *Index,* I, 829.

On subterranean ice, **FM** 4556

The Engadine, **NatR-II** 61
Archaeological frauds in Palestine, 290

Income of a university, and how it is spent, 789
Pontresina, 1723

An imperial university for women, **NC** 2396

Browne, George Lathom, 1815–1892, barrister, author. Allibone, *LCCat.*

The burning of Bristol, **Nat-R** 209

Browne, Horace Albert, 1832–1914, general. *WWW.*

The French in Cochin-China, **FM** 5841

Browne, James, 1793–1841: see *Index,* I, 829.

Hieroglyphics, **FQR** 94
Spain, 190
French expedition to Algiers, 211

Browne, Walter Raleigh, 1842–1884, civil engineer. Boase.

Pauper education, **FM** 6084

The English gentleman, **NatR-II** 430

Browning, Oscar: see *Index,* I, 829.

Trollope's *History of Florence,* **FortR** 187
The study of archaeology in schools, 1091
England and France in 1793, 2001
The art of George Eliot, 2700

Browning, Robert, 1812–1889, poet. *DNB.*

Tasso and Chatterton, **FQR** 677

Brownlow, Cecil Barry, 1854–1935, army officer. Venn.

Indian officer's view of the Afghan question, **NatR-II** 355

Brownlow, William Robert Bernard, 1830–1901, Bishop of Clifton. *WWW,* Gorman.

Christian emperors and pagan temples, **DR** 1792
The cemetery of St. Priscilla, 2340
A visitation of St. Mary Church in 1301, 2417
Clerical and social life in Devon in 1287, 2463
Robert Aiken, a sketch from memory, 2687
Notices: 1756, ?2729

Bruce, Alexander Hugh: see *Index,* I, 829.
Church and State in Scotland, **FortR** 2357

Bruce, Eric Henry Stuart, 1855–1935, aeronautical engineer. *WWW.*

Electric lighting, **DR** 1828

Electric light and energy, 1973
War and ballooning, 2060
A jubilee of science, 2107
Town fogs, 2420

Bruce, Thomas: see *Index*, I, 830.

Letter to Sidney [sic] Smith, **FM** 533

Brunetière, Ferdinand: see *Index*, I, 830.

Essential characteristic of French literature, **FortR** 3277

Brunton, Sir Thomas Lauder: see *Index*, I, 830.

Vivisection and the use of remedies, **NC** 695

Bryce, George, 1844–1931, divine, founder of Univ. of Manitoba. *WWW.*

Unique University of Manitoba, **NatR-II** 1223

Bryce, James, Viscount Bryce: see *Index*, I, 830.

A legal department of government, **FortR** 932
The Oxford University Bill, 1261
Russia and Turkey, 1315
The future of Asiatic Turkey, 1480
Some aspects of American public life, 1966
Future of the English universities, 2010

Alternative policies in Ireland, **NC** 1249

Bryce, Lloyd Stephens, 1851–1917, American general, editor. *DAB.*

Socialism through American spectacles, **NC** 1590

Bryden, Henry Anderson: see *Index*, I, 830.

Extermination of game in South Africa, **FortR** 3557
Hunting and its future, 4092
British and Dutch in South Africa, 4314
Settlers and settlements in South Africa, 4493
Letter: 4331

In praise of the Boers, **NC** 2894

Brydges, Sir Samuel Egerton: see *Index*, I, 830.

On intellectual endowments, **FM** 601
Poetry: the old poets, 711
Poetry: the modern poets, 743
Reply to the *Edinburgh Review*, 769
Men of genius want practical sense, 956
Wraxall's posthumous *Memoirs*, 1015

To Oliver Yorke, 1023
[Introductory remarks to] six sonnets, 1042
An essay on originality of mind, 1073

Buchanan, David: see *Index*, I, 830, and II, App. A.

Present state of Spain, **FQR** 107 collab.

Buchanan, Robert Williams: see *Index*, I, 831.

Thorvaldsen and his English critics, **FortR** 17
Old ballads of Denmark, 54
Immorality in authorship, 318
Notices: 142, 182

The character of Goethe, **NQM** 34
Thomas Love Peacock: a reminiscence, 51
The modern stage, 54
Aeschylus and Victor Hugo, 68
Lucretius and modern materialism, 75

Büchner, Friedrich Carl Christian Ludwig, 1824–1899, German biologist. *ADB, LCCat.*

The origin of mankind, **FortR** 3456

Buck, Victor de, 1817–1876, Belgian Bollandist. *Cath. Ency.*

Episcopal See of St. Martin, Canterbury, **Ram** 1012
Belgian politics, 1030
Belgium, 1040
The Russian Church, 1059
Letters: 991, 1019
See: 1127

Buckland, Charles Thomas: see *Index*, I, 831.

Ganjah [Indian drug], **NatR-II** 117
The Bengal Tenancy Bill, 163
The opium-poppy cultivation of Bengal, 381
Intemperance in India, 705
Some jail experiences in India, 1151
Men-servants in India, 1239

Buckland, Stephen: see *Index*, I, 831.

American dairies, **FM** 4751
Spiritualism in the United States, 4878

Buckle, Miss; probably Margaret Buckle, d.1891, daughter of William Hill Buckle of Chaceley. *Landed Gentry.*

Note: **Ram** 371
Trans: 378, 448

Buckle, Henry Thomas, 1821–1862, historian. *DNB.*

Influence of women on knowledge, **FM** 3710

Buckle, Henry Thomas (*continued*)
Mill on liberty, 3846
Fragment on the reign of Elizabeth, 4727,
4786, 4796

Buckman, Sydney Savory, 1860–1929, geologist. *Times*, Mar. 2, 1929, p. 14c, *LCCat.*
Babies and monkeys, **NC** 2658
The speech of children, 3115

Bucknill, Sir John Charles: see *Index*, I, 831.
Abolition of proprietary madhouses, **NC** 1091

Budrioli, Andrea, S.J., Italian scholar.
See: **Ram** 991

Buffum, Edward Gould, 1820–1867, American journalist. *Appleton's Cyclopedia of American Biography*, 6 vols., N.Y., 1888–1889.
In the Mont Cenis tunnel, **FortR** 208

Buggenoms, Louis de, 1816–1882, a Belgian Redemptorist working in London. Newman, *L&D*, XIII, 171n.
Faber's *Creator and the Creature,* **Ram** 862

Bulkeley-Johnson, Francis Head, 1862/63–1933, diplomat who served in Australia. Venn under Johnson.
English supremacy in the East, **NC** 1041

Bull, J. Cecil
Letter: **NatR-II** 1355

Bullen, Frank Thomas: see *Index*, I, 831.
A reminiscence of Manila, **NatR-II** 2193
Concerning sharks, 2228

Buller, Charles: see *Index*, I, 831.
Letters of a German Prince, **FQR** 218
Restoration, Bourbons: reign of Louis XVIII, 259
Mirabeau, 299

Bulley, Agnes Amy, misc. writer. *BMCat.*
The employment of women, **FortR** 3453

Bullock, Llewellyn Christopher Watson Bullock, 1866–1936, divine. *Landed Gentry.*
The fine art of fragrance, **NatR-II** 1136

Bullock, Thomas Henry, 1807–1868/69, army officer, civil servant in India. *Walford's*

County Families of U.K. (1920), p. 192: information from his grandson, Col. D. A. Bullock.
A blue mutiny [against indigo planters in Bengal], **FM** 4061
?Non-regulation provinces of India, 4194
Indigo-planting in Bengal, 4218
Public works in India, 4237
Opium revenue of India, 4258
Sale of waste lands in India, 4286
Laing's *England's Mission in the East,* 4320
The land revenue of India, 4453
Right of occupancy in Oude and Bengal, 4561
Prevention of famine in India, 4739

Bullock, Thomas Lowndes, 1845–1915, prof. of Chinese, Oxford. *WWW.*
Competitive examinations in China, **NC** 2608

Bulman, G. W., writer on science; "M.A., B.Sc." added to signature in *Westminster Review*, art. iv, May, 1893.
The fittest and the luckiest, **NatR-II** 1192

Bulwer, Sir Edward Earle Gascoyne, 1829–1910, general. *DNB.*
The British army, **NatR-II** 2133

Bulwer-Lytton, Edward George Earle Lytton: see *Index*, I, 832.
Reign of Terror: causes and results, **FQR** 670
Letter: **FM** 313

Bulwer-Lytton, Rosina Doyle (Wheeler), Lady Lytton, 1802–1882, novelist, wife of E. G. Bulwer-Lytton, Lord Lytton. *Concise DNB* under Lytton, Rosina.
Artaphernes the Platonist, **FM** 1195

Bulwer-Lytton, Victor Alexander George Robert, 2nd Earl of Lytton, 1876–1947, statesman. *DNB.*
Irish poet ["A.E.," G. W. Russell], **NatR-II** 2303

Bunbury, Sir Charles James Fox, 1809–1886, Sheriff of Suffolk. Boase.
South American vegetation, **FM** 4783

Bunbury, Sir Edward Herbert: see *Index*, I, 832.
Mr. Hayward, **FortR** 2163

Bunbury, Robert Clement Sconce, 1847–1930, barrister. *Venn.*

The New Zealand geysers, **FM** 6189

Bunce, John Thackray, 1828–1899, journalist. *WWW.* (See App. A below.)

James Northcote, **FortR** 1267
Art in the community, 1392

Church and press, **NatR-II** 1501

Bunsen, George von, 1824–1896, German politician. *DNB* 2nd suppl., under Ernest de Bunsen.

The Liberal party in Germany, **FortR** 1971
Prince Bismarck, 2314

Germany and Egypt, **NC** 72

Bunsen, M. de

Letter: **NatR-II** 1035

Bunsen, Theodor von, 1832–1892, diplomat. *DNB* 2nd suppl., under Ernest de Bunsen.

A German view of Mr. Gladstone, **NC** 1456
Home rule in Norway, 1504

Buonaparte, Joseph, 1768–1844, King of Naples. *DBF.*

To the Grand Duke of Tuscany, **FM** 493

Burdett, Sir Henry Charles, 1847–1920, ed. of *The Hospital. BMCat., WWW.*

Hospital nursing, **FM** 6307
Hospital reform 6395

Our hospitals, **NC** 825

Burgess, James John Haldane, 1862–1927, private teacher. *WWW.*

Shetland folk-lore, **ScotR** 468

Burgess, William, d.1899, animal breeder. *Boase.*

Letter: **NatR-II** 747

Burgon, John William: see *Index*, I, 833.
"Theology Under Its Changed Conditions," **FortR** 2585

Burke, James, 1819–1886, barrister, ed. of *The Lamp. Boase.*

Letter: **Ram** 813

Burke, John, R.C. priest; in 1852 at "Presby-

tery, St. Peter's, Phibsborough" (Thom, 1852, p. 980), disappears from *Battersby's Catholic Directory,* 1861.

Education of deaf and dumb, **Ram** 546

Burke, Ulick Ralph: see *Index*, I, 833.

What we have done for Cyprus, **NatR-II** 696

Burleigh, Bennet: see *Index*, I, 833, and *Times*, June 18, 1914, p. 6c.

The Greek War, as I saw it, **FortR** 3985

Burn, F. N., of Rangoon.

Letter: **NatR-II** 993

Burnaby, Frederick Gustavus, 1842–1885, army officer. *DNB.*

Possibilities of ballooning, **FortR** 2172

Burnand, Sir Francis Cowley: see *Index*, I, 833.

Behind the scenes, **FortR** 2262
Councils and comedians, 2364
History in *Punch*, 2484, 2541, 2582, all collab.
Letters: 2627, 2655

A school for dramatic art, **NC** 719

Burne-Jones, Sir Edward Coley, 1833–1898, painter. *DNB.*

The cousins, **OxCam** 3
Essay on *The Newcomes* [by Thackeray], 7
A story of the north, 11
Ruskin's *Modern Painters*, 24
Ruskin and the *Quarterly*, 36 collab.
?The druid and the maiden, 61

Burne-Jones, Lady Georgiana (Macdonald), 1839/40–1920, wife of Sir Edward Burne-Jones. *Annual Register/1920.*

The Sacrifice: a tale, **OxCam** 29
See: 63

Burnett, George: see *Index*, I, 833.

Scotland in times past, **ScotR** 190

Burney, Arthur; possibly Arthur George Burney, b.1849/50, in *M at B.*

Jubilee reigns in England, **NatR-II** 522
Patriotism of a hereditary peerage, 724

Burns, James, 1808–1871, publisher; published *Dublin Rev.* and *Rambler. Boase.*

Music in its religious uses, **DR** 1058

Burns, James (*continued*)

Church music and church choirs, 1249, 1260

Letter: ?1479

Notices: 1222, 1232

Burns, John Elliot, 1858–1943, labor leader, politician. *DNB*.

The London County Council, **NC** 2186

Let London live! 2199

Labour leaders on the labour question, 2315

The massacres in Turkey, 3008

Burroughs, afterwards Traill-Burroughs, Sir Frederick William, 1831–1905, army officer. *DNB*.

Land legislation, **NatR-II** 1217

Burroughs, Silas Mainville, 1846–1895, of Messrs. Burroughs, Welcome, & Co., London. Letter to this *Index* from the Welcome Foundation.

Letter: **FortR** 2934

Burrow, John Holme, B.A. Cambridge, 1855. Venn, *BMCat*.

Jabez Oliphant, in 13 installments from **FM** 4941 to 5066

Burrows, Montagu: see *Index*, I, 833.

Imperial federation, **NatR-II** 233

Burt, Thomas: see *Index*, I, 833.

Working men and war, **FortR** 1972

Working men and the political situation, **NC** 573

Labour leaders, 2316

The House of Lords: a dangerous anachronism, 2555

Burton, Sir Frederic William, 1816–1900, director National Gallery. *DNB*.

Glimpses of the Levant, **FortR** 24

The "Virgin of the Rocks" [by Leonardo da Vinci], **NC** 2607

Burton, Philip, C.M. [Congregation of the Mission], Catholic priest. See *DR* no. 2232.

Saint Augustine and his Anglican critics, **DR** 2232

The Augustinian System, 2285

Saint Augustine and the Donatists, 2381

Burton, Sir Richard Francis: see *Index*, I, 834.

Wanderings in West Africa, **FM** 4295, 4304, 4313

From London to Rio de Janeiro, 4590, 4617, 4643, 4674

Vikram and the Vampire, in 7 installments from 4854 to 4925

Bury, Blaze de: see Blaze de Bury.

Bury, Jane (Bury), wife of John Bagnell Bury, q.v. *DNB*/1930 under her husband.

Early Christian miniatures, **ScotR** 568

Bury, John Bagnell: see *Index*, I, 834.

Anima naturaliter pagana, **FortR** 3035

Compulsory Greek, 3156

The insurrection of women, 3288

Homeric warfare, **NatR-II** 1937

Freeman's *History of Sicily*, **ScotR** 343, 376

Hungarians: their origin and early homes, 364

Wandering of the [German] nations, 398

The Works and Days [by Hesiod], 426

The great palace of Constantinople, 436

Italy under the Lombards, 507

History of the Roumanians, 547

Bury, William, 1839–1927, divine. Venn.

Squires, spires, and mires, **FortR** 2288

Bushby, Henry North Grant, 1863–1926, barrister. Venn.

Parliamentary government in Japan, **NC** 3505

Busk, Mary Margaret (Blair): see *Index*, I, 834, and *Blackwood Papers Cat*.

Italian comedy, **FQR** 30

Tegner's *Legend of Frithiof*, 64

Raumer's *History of the Hohenstauffens*, 74

Spanish epic poetry, 97

Modern Swedish poetry, 138

History of the ancient Germans, 163

Grimm's *Teutonic Legal Antiquities*, 210

Quintana's *Spanish Biography*, 223

Thorvaldsen the sculptor, 239

The poets of Portugal, 248

Albert Durer, 258

Letters on Italy, 265

Roch, *Paris Malade*, 265

Italian novels, 265

Raumer's *Letters from Paris—History of the 16th and 17th Centuries*, 275

Armenian literature, 277

de Vigny's *Consultations of Dr. Black*, 277

Russell de Albuquerque, 289

Tromlitz's romances, 289
Memoirs of the Duchess of Abrantes, 295
Spindler's *Nun of Gnadenzell*, 300
Ludvigh's *Tour in Hungary*, 300
Lafontaine, the German novelist, 308
Swedish periodical literature, 313
Rafn's *Faroe Islands*, 319
Madame Dudevant's *Indiana*, *Valentine*, etc., 333
Van Artevelde and his son Philip, 338
Bronikowski's novels, 340
Sicily and Malta, 345
Kosciuszko, 346
English literature, 361
German history, 363
Italy As It Is, 373
Mythology of the north, 384
?Huber's *Sketches of Spain*, 385
?*The Count of Candespina*, 385
?Raumer's *England in 1835*, 396
The World as It Is, 397
Maffei's *History of Italian Literature*, 406
Italian novels, 408
Otho the Great and His Times, 414
Sternberg's tales and novels, 428
?Raumer's *Historical Pocket-Book*, 430
Memoirs of the Countess of Königsmark, 436
Rellstab's tales and novels, 447
Münch's *Studies* and *Recollections*, 469
Modern Italian narrative poetry, 479
Italian novels, 497
Malkolm [by Henrich Steffens], 503
?Hungary, 547
Notices: 90, 103, 118, 132, 144, 155, 168, 182, 194, 204, 215, 229, 241, 254

Butcher, Sir John George, Baron Danesfort, 1852–1935, Q.C., M.P. *WWW* under Danesfort.

The Declaration of Paris, **FortR** 4289

Butcher, Samuel Henry: see *Index*, I, 835.

Sophocles, **FortR** 2183

Why I shall vote for the Unionist candidate, **NC** 2248

Bute, Marquis of: see Crichton-Stuart, J. P.

Butler, Agnata Frances (Ramsay), 1867–1931, wife of Henry Montagu Butler. Burke under Ramsay; *Times*, May 29, 1931, p. 19d.

Letter: **FortR** 2627

Butler, Arthur John: see *Index*, I, 835.

Mr. Hardy as a decadent, **NatR-II** 1866

Butler, Edward Cuthbert, born Edward Joseph Aloysius, O.S.B., 1858–1934, abbot. *DNB.*

Bishop Lightfoot and the early Roman See, **DR** 2388, 2405
Early Christian literature, 2514, 2652
Hort, Duchesne, Weizsäcker, 2586
Modern critical and historical school, 2634
Notices: 2606, 2618, 2651, 2699, 2709

Butler, Maynard. *BMCat.*

Edited: **FortR** 4432

Butler, Sir William Francis: see *Index*, I, 835.

The new army and the old test, **FortR** 1993

Butt, Beatrice May: see Allhusen, Beatrice May (Butt).

Buxton, Dudley Wilmot, 1855–1931, anaesthetist. *WWW*, Surgeon Index.

Deaths under chloroform, **NC** 3277

Buxton, Edward North: see *Index*, I, 835.

The case for free education, **FortR** 2573
Sardinia and its wild sheep, **NC** 1722
On the rim of the desert, 1910
The father of all the goats, 1999
In the mountains of Egypt, 2551
Stony Sinai, 2693
Timber creeping in the Carpathians, 3069

Buxton, Francis William, 1847–1911, J.P., M.P. *WWW.*

Workmen's trains and passenger duty, **FortR** 2024

Buxton, Sydney Charles, Earl Buxton: see *Index*, I, 835.

Can the cost of elections be reduced? **FortR** 1668
A new exodus, 2046
Cardinal Manning, 3788
Bribery and corruption, **NC** 520
Notes on school board questions, 786
"Over-Pressure" [in schools], 1062
Fly fishing, 3409
Note: 3662

Buxton, Sir Thomas Fowell, 1837–1915, statesman. *DNB.*

British administration in West Africa, **FortR** 3161

Byrne, Joseph Magee, army officer. *Army List/87.*

The private soldier's wrongs, **NC** 1961

Byrne, Julia Clara (Busk): see *Index*, I, 835.

Our great-grandmothers, **FM** 5349, 5364
The fourrière, 5459
De la Grange's diary, 5739
Sainte Perine, or City of the Gentle, 5783

A Hungarian episode: Zigeuner music, 6215

Byron, Lady Anna Isabella (Milbanke) Noel, 1792–1860, wife of Lord Byron. Boase.

Letter: **FM** 41 collab.

C

Caccia,   , 1807–1882, Rosminian priest. Conzemius, I, 210n., *Cath. Ency.*

Letter: **Ram** 1095

Caddell, Cecilia Mary, 1813/14–1877, novelist. Boase.

Seymour's curse, **Ram** 839, 844, 854, 860

Cadell, Jessie Ellen, 1844–1884, novelist, Persian scholar. *DNB.*

The true Omar Khayam, **FM** 6178

Cadogan, George Henry, 5th Earl Cadogan, 1840–1915, statesman. *DNB.*

The state of the turf, **FortR** 2264

Caillard, Sir Vincent Henry Penalver, 1856–1930, administrator in Near East. *DNB.*

Albania and the Albanians, **FortR** 2296
The truth about Turkish finance, 2361
The Bulgarian imbroglio, 2401

Caird, Alice Mona (Alison), d.1932, writer, wife of J. A. Henryson-Caird. *BMCat.*, *WWW.*

The morality of marriage, **FortR** 2926

Defence of the so-called "wild women," **NC** 2215

Caird, Edward: see *Index*, I, 836.

?*The Unseen Universe*, **FM** 5763
Wordsworth, 6256

Caird, Sir James, 1816–1892, agriculturist. *DNB.*

India: the land and people, **NC** 332, 340, 356, 365
See: 32

Cairnes, John Elliot: see *Index*, I, 836.

International law, **FortR** 115
Political economy and land, 648
M. Comte and political economy, 680
Bastiat, 721
Our defences, 753

Political economy and laissez-faire, 796
New theories in political economy, 833
Froude's *English in Ireland*, 1074
Mr. Spencer on social evolution, 1116
Mr. Spencer on the study of sociology, 1123
Note: 710

Solution of the gold question, **FM** 3886, 3928

Cairnes, William Elliot: see *Index*, I, 836.

The problem of invasion, **NatR-II** 2517

Calderwood, Henry: see *Index*, I, 836.

Theology in Scotland, **ScotR** 10

Calderwood, William Leadbetter: see *Index*, I, 837.

Bagpipe music, **ScotR** 512

Call, Wathen Mark Wilks, 1817–1890, misc. author. Venn.

Apollonius of Tyana, **FortR** 103
The inscription at Ancyra, 311
Notices: 20, 114, 124

Notice: **NC** 487

Callander, Henry Barrington, Queen's foreign service messenger. *F.O. List/79.*

The Argentine crisis, **FortR** 2994

Calonne, Alfonse Bernard, Vicomte de: see *Index*, I, 837.

Domestic architecture in Paris, **NC** 2733
The two salons, 2768
The romance of Leonardo da Vinci, 2805
The Dame de Châteaubriant, 3054
Chantilly and the Duc D'Aumale, 3131
The French aristocracy, 3171
French officialism, 3238
The French judicial system, 3432

Calvert, Frederick, 1806–1891, barrister. Boase.

Representation of minorities, **NatR-II** 297

Cameron, Alexander, 1827–1888, divine. *LCCat.*

Edited: **ScotR** 152

Cameron, Sir Charles, 1841–1924, physician. *WWW.*

Has our vaccination degenerated? **FortR** 1801
Cheap telegrams, 2374

The law a respecter of persons, **NC** 858
Anti-cholera inoculation, 1177

?Medical reform, **ScotR** 14
The modern cremation movement, 174

Cameron of Lochiel, Donald, 1835–1905, statesman. *WWW.*

A defence of deer forests, **NC** 1168

Cameron, F. A., of Edinburgh.

Letter: **NatR-II** 254

Cameron, J. A.

Storm-clouds [of anarchy] in the Highlands, **NC** 1034

Cameron, Verney Lovett: see *Index*, I, 837.

England and Germany in Africa, **FortR** 2973
Burton as I knew him, 3021

The future of the Soudan, **NatR-II** 354
Slavery in Africa, 777
Portuguese claims in Africa, 944
Chartered companies in Africa, 1010
Our rights and prospects in Africa, 1034

Camm, Reginald Percy John, Dom Bede Camm, O.S.B., 1864–1942. Foster, *WWW.*

The Gunpowder Plot, **DR** 2574
Father Dominic and the conversion of England, 2646
Abbot Tosti, 2692
Notices: 2520, 2543, 2570, 2594, 2606, 2618, 2686, 2699

Campbell, Mr.; possibly James Augustine Campbell, q.v.

?King John a Protestant reformer, **DR** 133

Campbell, Charles Moss, M.D. *Medical Directory/90, BMCat.*

Medical relief of the rural poor, **NatR-II** 236

Campbell, Lord Colin, 1853–1895, barrister. Boase.

Annexation and South Africa, **NC** 692

Campbell, Dudley: see *Index*, I, 837.

Compulsory primary education, **FortR** 503

Campbell, Sir George: see *Index*, I, 837.

The tenure of land, **FortR** 1114
Our dealings with Egypt, 1228
The finances of India, 1246
The farther outlook in the East, 1366
An inside view of Egypt, 1425
Resettlement of the Turkish dominions, 1456
Black and white in the Southern States, 1564, 1573
The situation in Egypt, 1585
Home Rule in several countries, 1691
The land legislation for Ireland, 1762
Impressions of the Irish Land Bill, 1798
Reconstruction in Egypt, 1984
Lord Ripon's Indian land legislation, 2168

Campbell, George Douglas: see *Index*, I, 837.

"A Model Land-Law," **FortR** 2596
First impressions of the New World, **FM** 6237, 6247

Influence upon morality of a decline in religious belief, **NC** 25
The new Irish Land Bill, 590
Condition of the Highlands of Scotland, 814
The prophet of San Francisco [Henry George], 979
A corrected picture of the Highlands, 1055
Capital and the improvement of land, 1225
Huxley on Canon Liddon, 1377
Science falsely so called, 1412
A great lesson [Darwin and Huxley], 1446
An olive branch from America, 1471
"The power of loose analogies," 1489
A great confession [Spencer on Darwin], 1510
Isolation; or, Survival of the unfittest, 1641
Story of a conspirator [Wolfe Tone], 1867, 1887
Huxley on the warpath, 1982
Huxley and the Duke of Argyll, 2033
The glacial theory, 2535
Christian Socialism, 2655
Lord Bacon versus Huxley, 2679
Herbert Spencer and Lord Salisbury on evolution, 3080, 3096

Campbell, Lady Gertrude Elizabeth (Blood), 1861–1911, wife of Lord Colin Campbell, q.v. *MWT*/15th ed., *WWW*, and Crone, all under Lady Colin Campbell.

Domestic decorations, **NatR-II** 1233

Campbell, Lady Gertrude E. (*continued*)
Drawing-room entertainments, 1265
Rivarol, 1317

Campbell, Sir J. M.; perhaps Sir James Macnabb Campbell, 1846–1903, Indian civil servant, in Buckland.

Julian and Jerusalem, A.D. 363, **ScotR** 676

Campbell, James Augustine, d.1902, rector of Scots' Coll., Rome. *Times*, Feb. 21, 1902, p. 8e.

The early Scottish Church, **DR** 1702
Christian families under pagan emperors, 2715
See: 133

Campbell, Lady Janey Sevilla (Callander), 1846–1923, actress, wife of Lord Archibald Campbell. *WWW* under Lady Archibald Campbell, *LCCat.*

The Faithfull Shepherdesse, **NC** 1148
From Tyree to Glencoe, 3173

Campbell, John Douglas Sutherland: see *Index*, I, 838.

The Saskatchewan scare, **FortR** 2325
A word for the Colonial Institute, 2526
The Canadian fisheries dispute, 2576
Advocacy of provincial parliaments, 2831

The unity of the Empire, **NC** 1101
An Armada relic, 1592
A suggestion for emigrants, 1694
The British in East Africa, 2093
Chartered companies, 2893
Planting out state children in South Africa, 3634

Disestablishment, **ScotR** 96

Campbell, John Francis: see *Index*, I, 838.

Gaelic Ireland in 1872, **FM** 5445

Campbell, John Shaw, 1798–1847, London physician. *Dublin Rev.*, 24 (1848), 227–228, *BMCat.*

Regulation of medical practice, **DR** 370
Colonial emigration [and population], 459
Sanatory [sic] reform, 518 collab.

Campbell, Joseph Alexander, b.1844, army officer, served in Australia. *Irish WW/* 1908.

"A battle described from the ranks," **NC** 1882

Campbell, Lewis: see *Index*, I, 838.

A thinker's mind: Platonic chronology, **FortR** 4059
Growth of tragedy in Shakespeare, 4398
Liberal movements of the last half-century, 4424
On climax in tragedy, 4479
Notes on *King Lear*, **NatR-II** 797
Prometheus [on Aeschylus and Shelley], **OxCam** 27
See: 38

Campbell, Robert, 1832–1912, barrister. Venn.

Life of Marshal St. Arnaud [on Crimean War], **OxCam** 38

Campbell, Robert Calder, 1798–1857, army officer. *DNB.*

The Suniassie, **FM** 1975

Campbell, William Frederick, Baron Stratheden of Cupar and Baron Campbell, 1824–1893. *Complete Peerage.*

1831–32: a sketch, **FM** 4188

Campion, Edmund, 1540–1581, Jesuit martyr. *DNB.*

Letters: **Ram** 845, 855

Campion, George, 1846–1926, sheriff-substitute. *WWW.*

A chat about woodcock, **NatR-II** 770
Grouse shooting, 886

Cannan, Edwin, 1861–1935, economist. *DNB.*

The decline of urban immigration, **NatR-II** 1521
Principles of local taxation, 1940

Canning, Stratford, 1st Viscount Stratford de Redcliffe: see *Index*, I, 838.

Turkey, **NC** 50, 51
International relations, 92
The revival of Greek independence, 213, 245
Passing events in Turkey, 257
George Canning, 392

Canning, Thomas, 1849–1915, civil engineer. *Tablet*, Mar. 15, 1919, p. 325.

The labour problem, **DR** 2243
Catholicism in the Waverley Novels, 2301

Canton, William, 1845–1926, poet, sub-ed. of *Contemp. Rev. DNB.*

Contributors

?Poems of Dr. Walter C. Smith, **ScotR** 3

Capel, Thomas John, 1836–1911, R.C. prelate. *DNB.*

Doubt in the Church of Rome, **NC** 411

Capes, Florence M., social worker. *BMCat., Cath.WW*/1930.

Dominican story-teller [Augusta T. Drane], **DR** 2150

The poetry of the early mysteries, **NC** 915

Capes, Frederick: see *Index*, I, 838.

?Cultivation of the musical faculty, **Ram** 526

Ruskin's art-philosophy, 612, 619

Trials of Palmer, Dove, etc., 780, 788

Turner's pictures at Marlborough House, 803

Arctic Explorations, 810

Critics and the fine arts, 817

Chaldea and Persia, 826

The Kingdom and People of Siam, 840

Christianity in China, Tartary, and Thibet, 846, 870

The Life of Handel, 865

Chinese life and manners, 883

Waterton's *Essays,* 890

Louis Blanc's *Historical Revelations,* 932

Novels and Novelists, 950

China, 964

Palmerston on architecture, 1012

Letter: 974

Notices: 834, 857 collab., 979

Capes, John Moore: see *Index*, I, 838, and Newman, *L&D*, XI, index.

Artists of the Order of St. Dominic, **DR** 528

Just demand of working man, **FortR** 226

What is an oath? 284

Music the expression of character, 389

Sacred music, 418

Sir Cecil Beadon's defence, 430

Music and architecture, 462

Schubert, 565

Notices: 379, 396, 406, 425, 456, 488, 553, 585

?Ida Conway, in 12 installments from **FM** 4016 to 4130

First remedy for Ireland's sorrows, **Ram** 1

Aristocracy and democracy, 2

Music of the fifteenth century, 7

St. John's Church, Salford, Manchester, 8

Almsgiving: education of the Catholic poor, 11

Will England ever be a Catholic country? 17

Pantheism, communism and christianity, 30

Catholic and Protestant collegiate education, 44

Music as a part of education, 54

The duties of journalists, 56

Protestant hagiology, 58

The Church and the people, 67

?Macaulay's *History of England,* 72, 88

Kelly's *Plain-chant Manual,* 75

The fourth estate, 80

On exclusive use of plain-chant, 84

Caswall's *Breviary Hymns,* 89

Preface, 96

Holy Week, 97

The Pope and the people of Rome, 98

Protestant views of the doctrine of the Incarnation, 102

Quetelet, *On Probabilities,* 105

Where does our strength lie? 110

The offertory, 123

English art; its weakness and strength, 124

?The *Quarterly Review* and Macaulay, 125

?Maitland on the Reformation, 127

Four years' experience of the Catholic religion, 133, 143, 153

Ruskin's *Seven Lamps of Architecture,* 137

Modern church architecture, 144

Catholic college difficulties, 145

?Hymns: Catholic and non-Catholic poetry, 149

?Non-religious education, 155

Catholicism and civilisation, 157

Money prospects, 162

?Bible controversy and Bible reading, 167

Cheap books, 172

Literature for the Catholic poor, 173

A Sunday in London, 174, 184, 197, 206, 212

The conversion of England, 183

Church decoration, 185

Protestant churches, 187

Hopes and fears for 1850, 194

Town churches, 195 collab.

?Tate's *Algebra,* 200

Communism, 204

The two kingdoms, 207

The progress of Catholic poverty, 210

Irish church establishment, 214

Church reform, 217

Mr. Pugin and the *Rambler,* 221

Prospects of Anglo-Catholic party in Established Church, 224

Wants of the time, 229

The miraculous life of the saints, 237

Catholic poor schools and middle schools, 243

Theological science: Protestant preaching, 252

Capes, John Moore (*continued*)
Popular services, 258
A Socinian view of Catholicism [in *Prospective Review*], 259
Extempore preaching, 264
The Pope, 265
The hierarchy, 269
Rise, progress, and results of Puseyism, 272, 278, 283, 292
Catholic prospects, 274
Passion, love, and rest, in 9 installments from 276 to 350
Murray on miracles and education, 285
Shilling churches and penny churches, 291
How shall we meet the Protestant aggression? 293
The Irish in London, 297
Anglo-Catholics in theory and in fact, 299
The church and the antiquarians, 301
B[lessed] Ippolito Galantini, 302
Our position and policy, 306
?Protestant feeling towards convents, 310
?*Yeast* [by Charles Kingsley], 318
?Ireland's duty to England, 319
Catholic university for Ireland, 322
"Churches" versus "rooms," 325
A lecture at ——— college, Ireland, 333
Domestic Gothic architecture, 336
Civil and religious liberty, 340
?Dr. Achilli and the Inquisition, 345
Animal magnetism, 351
The old priest's parlour, 355, 370
Newman, *On the Position of Catholics in England*, 357
The Protestant criticising, 365
?Protestant justice and royal clemency, 374
Morris on the Incarnation, 379
The French in London, 383
Murder in England and in Ireland, 384
St. Teresa's *Life* of herself, 387
Mayhew among the thieves [on London poor], 389
Father Gavazzi, 390
?The struggles of Catholic literature, 392
?*The Household of Sir Thomas More*, 397
Popular education, 415, 431
Catholic lending-libraries, 424
Popular music a part of popular education, 445
?The cultivation of the musical faculty, 526
Catholic singing, 532
Savonarola, 537, 548
Haydon's *Autobiography*, 542
How to convert Protestants, 554
The Wandering Jew, 559
Cahill's letter on transubstantiation, 566
Napoleon and Sir Hudson Lowe, 567
Shams and realities, 570
Music for amateur performance, 575

Equivocation by St. Alphonsus Liguori, 577
Nuns, monks, and Jesuits, 583
The life of a conspirator [*Benoni* by Ruffini], 585
Illustrated books, 588
The state's best policy, 591
The Czar and his subjects, 594
Constantinople, 598
?Protestant publishers, Catholic readers, 607
Evil effects of religious persecution, 609
Queen's government and University [of Dublin], 615
Hospitals and sisterhoods, 616
Finlay's *Byzantine Empire*, 620
Appeal to Catholic laity on the poor, 622
The Christian Remembrancer on medieval and Protestant preaching, 626
Dublin palace "fiction," 627 collab.
The "Civilisation" argument, 629
?The worship of Mary, 632
Changes now taking place in the Church of England, 637
On common sense in Christian art, 638
Reminiscences of a Merchant's Life, 642
The editor to the reader, 644
Jesuitism and anti-Jesuitism, 645
?Compton Hall, 646, 652, 660, 666, 673, 680
Catholic politics and Catholic M.P.s, 651
Our camp disasters and their cause, 654
The patriotic fund and proselytism, 659
The true principle of religious controversy, 665
The Immaculate Conception, 672
Education: the Maynooth report, 675 collab.
Catholic politics thirty years ago, 679
?*Corsica* [by Gregorovius], 683
Priestcraft, 686
Protestant accounts of French convents, 689
The poor-school question, 693
Vain repetitions, 700
Quare fremuerunt gentes?, 706
?St. Oswald's, 714, 720, 728, 735, 741, 746
St. Charles Borromeo on church-building, 715
?Catholicism and Protestantism in Liverpool, 721
Frederick Lucas, 723
?Bible-burning and Bible reading, 727
?Protestantism, in the presence of the church: the Austrian Concordat, 729
The [Crimean] war and Catholicism, 734
?Macaulay's *History of England*, 738, 743
Catholicity and English society, 740
Social tyranny of Protestantism, 745
?The prospects of America, 748
The body and the members, 750
Exaggerations of modern art, 757
King William III, 758

Capes, William Wolfe, 1834–1914, divine.
   DNB.

Carbutt, Sir Edward Hamer, 1838–1905, engineer. *WW*/1906.

Carey, E.

Carl, or **Charles,** Prince of Sweden and Norway; probably Oscar Charles William,
   Duke of Västergotland, 1861–1951, in
   Burke/1953, p. xcvii, under Royal Family, James I.

Carlill, James Briggs, writer on psychology,
   father of Harold F. Carlill in Venn. (See
   Index, I, 839, under both B. Carlill and
   James B. Carlill, and II, App. A.)

Carlyle, John Aitken, 1801–1879, physician.
   DNB.

Carlyle, Robert Warrand, 1859–1934, Indian
   civil servant. *DNB.*

Carlyle, Thomas: see *Index*, I, 839.

Carlyle, Thomas (*continued*)
An election to the Long Parliament, 1985
Indian meal, 2589
The Negro question, 2671
Early kings of Norway, 5630, 5640, 5650
The portraits of John Knox, 5661
Edited: 2392
Trans: 4, 45, 448, 464
See: 25, 408, 409

Lectures [periods of European culture],
NC 589 collab.

Carmont, James, 1838/39–1922, of the Crichton Royal Institution; hon. sheriff-substitute for Dumphries. *Cath. Direct. for
Scotland*/1925; *Glasgow Herald*, Apr. 10,
1927, p. 7vi.

The union of 1707 viewed financially,
ScotR 181

Carnegie, Andrew: see *Index*, I, 839.

As others see us, **FortR** 1880

The advantages of poverty, **NC** 2007
The McKinley Bill, 2064
Imperial federation, 2104
Elections in England and America, 2246
The Manchester School and to-day, 3243

Carpenter, Edward: see *Index*, I, 839.

Custom, **FortR** 2731

Carpenter, James, 1840–1899, astronomer at
the Royal Observatory, Greenwich.
Boase.

Telegraph time, **FM** 5097

Carpenter, Joseph Estlin, 1844–1928, prof.
ecclesiastical history, Manchester New
Coll., London. *DNB*.

The obligations of the New Testament to
Buddhism, **NC** 529

Carpenter, Mary, 1807–1877, philanthropist.
DNB.

Treatment of female convicts, **FM** 4288

Carpenter, William Benjamin: see *Index*, I,
839.

The ethics of vivisection, **FortR** 1885
Sir Charles Bell and physiological experimentation, 1901

Mesmerism and spiritualism, **FM** 5891,
5911.
Curiosities of spiritualism, 5984
Note: 5994

See: 3112

The radiometer and its lessons, **NC** 14
The deep sea and its contents, 428
Disease-germs, 636
Small-Pox and vaccination in 1871–1881,
700
Germ-theory of zymotic diseases, 966

Carpenter, William Boyd: see *Index*, I, 840.

The efficiency of voluntary schools, **FortR**
3907

Union, spiritual or ecclesiastical? **NatR-II**
1881

Carr, Joseph William Comyns: see *Index*, I,
840, and II, App. A.

English actors: yesterday and today, **FortR**
1998

The artistic spirit in modern poetry, **NQM**
63
[Royal] Academy, and the Salon [in Paris],
87

Carrel, Frederic. *BMCat., Yearbook*/1916.

The College of France, **FortR** 3340
English and French manners, 3503
In Syria, 3559
Stéphane Mallarmé, 3617

Carrington, Charles Robert Wynn: see Wynn-
Carrington, Charles Robert.

Carrington, Evelyn: see Martinengo-Cesaresco, Evelyn.

"**Carroll,** Lewis": see Dodgson, Charles Lutwidge.

Carson, William Robert, 1874–1903, R.C.
priest. Gorman.

The reality of the external world, **DR** 2680

Carter, Ellis Warren

Sophie Kovalevsky, **FortR** 3640

Carter, Robert Brudenell: see *Index*, I, 840.

Medical science, homoeopathy, **NatR-II** 690

Carter, Thomas Thellusson: see *Index*, I, 840.

Present crisis in the Church of England,
NC 30
Auricular confession, 2704
What is church authority? 2742

Carter, W. August, sec. of the Midland Counties Fish Culture Assoc. See *NatR-II*, no.
919.

Preservation of fluvial fishes, **NatR-II** 919
Preserving inland fisheries, 1119

Cartwright, Julia: see Ady, Julia Mary (Cartwright).

Cartwright, William Cornwallis: see *Index*, I, 840.

The policy of Italy, **FortR** 290
?Mr. Hayward, 2163
The Congo Treaty, 2193

The reconstruction of Germany, **FM** 4687

Casartelli, Louis Charles, 1852–1925, Bishop of Salford. *WWW*.

The three Fausts, **DR** 1885
An educational lesson from Berlin, 2109
Origins of the Church of Edessa, 2166
The art of burial, 2413
The Catholic Church in Japan, 2477
English universities, and the Reformation, 2506
Our diamond jubilee, 2521
Beginnings oriental studies in Louvain, 2539
Notices: 2092, 2173, 2425
Notices of Catholic continental periodicals: 2119, 2174, 2212

Case, Frederic, 1849–1904, divine. Venn.

Protest from the south, **NatR-II** 1620

Case, Thomas, 1844–1925, prof. of philosophy, Oxford. *DNB*.

Against Oxford degrees for women, **FortR** 3668

Cash, E. F., instructor of musketry with volunteer movement.

Sight test for volunteers, **NatR-II** 1006

Cash, Frederick G. of Gloucester.

Letter: **NatR-II** 165

Cassels, Walter Richard: see *Index*, I, 840.

A reply to Professor Lightfoot's article on *Supernatural Religion*, **FortR** 1113
Renan's new volume [*Origins of Christianity*], 1400
The Christian "conditions," 1437, 1445

The *Diatessaron* of Tatian, **NC** 2740

Castelar y Ripoll, Emilio: see *Index*, I, 840.

Estanislao Figueras, **FortR** 848
The republican movement in Europe, 869, 873, 883, 891
The Papacy and the temporal power, 2652

Castelcicala, Prince Fabrico Rufo de, Neapolitan diplomat. *EUI*.

Letter: **Ram** 151

Castle, Egerton: see *Index*, I, 840.

The story of swordsmanship, **NatR-II** 1144

Cattell, Edward James: see *Index*, I, 840.

Lesson of the American elections, **FortR** 3584
America on the silver question, 3830
The making of a president, 3846
Battle of the ballots in America, 3867
Lessons from the American election, 3896

Cattell, James McKeen, 1860–1944, psychologist. *Amer. WWW*.

The time it takes to think, **NC** 1493

Catty, Charles

Letters: **NatR-II** 568, 643

Catucci-Masi, Agrippina

A school for young ladies in Genoa, **FM** 4860

Cave, Robert Haynes: see *Index*, I, 841, and *CCD*/76.

Old rings and seals, **FM** 5706
Old china, 5731

Cave, Thomas Sturmy, 1846–1936, army officer. *WWW*.

Volunteers and capitation grant, **NatR-II** 555

Cavendish, Lady Lucy Caroline (Lyttelton), 1841–1925, wife of Lord Frederick Charles Cavendish. *LCCat.*, Burke under Devonshire.

Law and the laundry, **NC** 3068

Cavendish, Spencer Compton, 8th Duke of Devonshire: see *Index*, I, 841.

Note: **NC** 2717

Cavour, Camillo Benso, Conte di, 1810–1861, statesman. *Enci.Ital.*

Count Cavour on Ireland, **NC** 759 collab.

Caw, Sir James Lewis: see *Index*, I, 841.

Victorian art, **ScotR** 565
Recent French painting, 594

Cayley, Digby William, 1862–1928. Venn.

Cayley, Digby William (*continued*)
Fool's paradise [free trade], **NatR-II** 791
Fiscal federations, 897

Cayley, George John: see *Index*, I, 841.

An English scholar in Greece [William G. Clark], **FM** 3770
?Working in gold, 4149
Between the cataracts [of the Nile] without a dragoman, 4171
Art for artificers, 4264

Céard, Henry, 1851–1924, French man of letters. *DBF.*

Victor Hugo, **FortR** 2335

Cecil, Edgar Algernon Robert, Viscount Cecil of Chelwood, 1864–1958, statesman. *WWW.*

Official assurances [loss of trees in Manchester Square], **NatR-II** 2434

Cecil, Lord Eustace Brownlow Henry Gascoyne, 1834–1921, army officer. *WWW,* Burke under Salisbury.

Social deterioration and its remedy, **NatR-II** 139
The national party, 360

The curse of the War Office, **NC** 1575
An autumn visit to Japan, 1632

Cecil, Evelyn, 1st Baron Rockley, 1865–1941, politician. Burke under Rockley.

Religious issue at London School Board election, **NatR-II** 2079

Cecil, Hugh Richard Heathcote Gascoyne, 1st Baron Quickswood, 1869–1956, M.P. *WWW* under Quickswood.

The Established Church, **NatR-II** 2283

Cecil, James Edward Hubert Gascoyne, 4th Marquess of Salisbury, 1861–1947, statesman. *DNB.*

The value of voluntary schools, **NatR-II** 818

Cecil, Robert Arthur Talbot Gascoyne: see *Index*, I, 841.

English politics and parties, **BentQR** 1
The faction-fights, 11
France and Europe, 20
The coming political campaign, 30

Labourers' and artisans' dwellings, **NatR-II** 92

Redistribution: electoral statistics, 216
Constitutional revision, 1349
Rosebery's plan [for a new House of Lords], 1654

Cesaresco, Evelyn M.: see Martinengo-Cesaresco, Evelyn.

Chadwick, Edwin: see Index, I, 842, and II, App. A.

Medical relief to the destitute sick, **FM** 4686
Methods of preparation for legislation, 4763
Police force and prevention of crime, 4829
Employers' liability for accidents, 6407

Preventive police, **LR (1829)** 12
Centralization: public charities in France, 23

Gladstone on local administration, **NatR-II** 566

Chaillu, Paul Bellom du: see Du Chaillu, Paul Bellom.

Chalmers, Lady Janet (Lorimer), wife of Sir David Patrick Chalmers. *WWW/1916* under her husband.

In defence of Sir David Chalmers, **NC** 3624

Chalmers, Sir Mackenzie Dalzell, 1847–1927, judge. *DNB.*

Imprisonment for debt, **FortR** 2745

Chamberlain, Joseph, 1836–1914, statesman. *DNB.*

The Liberal party and its leaders, **FortR** 981
Next page of the Liberal programme, 1087
The right method with the publicans, 1253
A visit to Lapland, 1310
Free schools, 1321
Municipal public-houses, 1327
A new political organization, 1381
The caucus, 1526
Labourers' and artisans' dwellings, 2109
A radical view of the Irish crisis, 2428
See: 1227, 1992, 2004, 2131

Old-age pensions, **NatR-II** 1243
The Home Rule campaign, 1576
Old-age pensions and Friendly Societies, 1667

Shall we Americanise our institutions? **NC** 1964
The labour question, 2303

A bill for the weakening of Great Britain [Home Rule Bill], 2373

Chamberlin, Joseph Edgar, 1851–1935, American editor. *Amer. WWW.*

Growth of caste in United States, **NC** 3136

Chambers, William, 1800–1883, of Edinburgh, Scottish legal authority. *LCCat.*

How crime is investigated in Scotland, **FortR** 68

Champion, Henry Hyde, 1859–1928, sec., Social Democrat Federation; ass't. ed. *Nineteenth Century. WWW.*

The new Labour Party, **NC** 1573
An eight-hour law, 1768
The labour movement, 1848
The labour revolution, 1935
Defeat of trade unionism in Australia, 1997
A labour inquiry, 2072
The Labour "platform," 2144
Protection as labour wants it, 2234
Labour leaders, 2317

Champneys, Arthur Charles, 1854–1924, master at Marlborough Coll. *Marlborough Coll. Register, 1843–1904,* Oxford, 1905; *Times,* Aug. 25, 1924, p. 1.

Devil in the middle ages, **NatR-II** 701

Chance, Sir William, 1853–1935, barrister. *WWW.*

Indoor v. outdoor relief, **NatR-II** 1748

Chandler, William Eaton, 1835–1917, Sec. of U.S. Navy. *DAB.*

The presidential contest: on the currency question, **NatR-II** 1948

Channing, Francis Allston, 1st Baron Channing of Wellingborough, 1841–1926, American-born agriculturalist. *WWW.*

The Commission on Agriculture, **FortR** 4011
Sir Robert Peel, 4259

Chant, Laura Ormiston (Dibbin), 1848–1923, suffragette. *WWW.*

Woman as an athlete, **NC** 3463

Chapman, Henry Samuel: see *Index,* I, 842.

The Canadian question, **DR** 54
The Irish in America, 70
Principles of colonization: New Zealand, 76
?South Australia, 134

Transatlantic travelling, 155
New Zealand, 189
Progress of Australian discovery, 262

Chapman, John, born Henry Palmer Chapman, 1865–1933, Abbot of Downside. *Benedictine Bibliog.*

On the truthfulness of Catholics, **DR** 2533
The Holy See and Pelagianism, 2564, 2589
St. Jerome and Rome, 2610

Chapman, Hon. Mrs. Theodosia (Spring-Rice), d.1926, wife of Edward W. Chapman. Burke under her father, 1st Baron Monteagle.

Women's suffrage, **NC** 1264
Church-going: on hymns, 1452
A dialogue on dress, 2646
A dialogue on vulgarity, 2915
Women's suffrage again! 3147
Confession, 3369

Charlton, Edward, 1814–1874, doctor, of Newcastle-on-Tyne. Boase.

Vestiges of Catholic faith in Scandinavia, **DR** 481
The last eruption of Mount Hekla, 514
Historical Memorials of Greenland, 554
Early Norse poetry, 593
Northern literature, 604
Witch mania of the four last centuries, 622
Scandinavian literature, 653
The Countess Hahn Hahn's conversion, 671
Literature and romance of Northern Europe, 673
Shetland and Iceland, 682
Norway, 910
Finland and Russian Lappmark, 921
Parts of European Russia, 939

Chatelain, le Chevalier Jean Baptiste-François-Ernest de, 1801–1881, journalist. *DNB.*

Epistle to Oliver Yorke, **FM** 1876

Cheadle, Walter Butler: see *Index,* I, 842.

The progress of medicine, **FortR** 339

Chenevix, Richard: see *Index,* I, 843.

Gall and Spurzheim—phrenology, **FQR** 29

Cherkezov, Varlaam Nickolaevich, 1846–1925, anarchist and Georgian nationalist. See essay cited in evidence for *NC* no. 2753.

Georgian treaties with Russia, **NC** 2753

Cherrill, Alfred King, 1839–1927, divine. Venn.

Nonconformists and the Church Congress, **NC** 111

Chertkóv, Vladimir Grigorevich, 1854–1936, Russian exile in England, disciple of Tolstoy. *Times,* Nov. 11, 1936, p. 21b.

The present peace demonstrations, **FortR** 4263

Chesney, Charles Cornwallis: see *Index,* I, 843.

England and the French Republic, **FortR** 732
Sherman and Johnston, and the Atlanta Campaign, 1205

Three years of war in America, **FM** 4447
Regulars and volunteers, 4532
Chinese Gordon, 4938

Chesney, George MacLagan: see *Index,* I, 843.

The native press in India, **NC** 3242

Chesney, Sir George Tomkyns: see *Index,* I, 843.

The Indian finances, **FortR** 1589
Over-production, 1843
The balance of trade, 3419
See: 1160, 1176

Indian famines, **NC** 103
The value of India to England, 134
Russia and India, 155
Depreciation of silver and Indian finances, 263
The Indian services, 319
The army as a public department, 2066
"Confusion worse confounded" at the War Office, 2085, 3599
How to reorganise the War Department, 2132
The silver question and India, 2341
India: the political outlook, 2583

Chesson, Frederick William, 1833/34–1888, journalist. Boase.

The opium trade, **FortR** 809

Chester, Greville John, 1830–1892, Egyptologist. Boase.

Some truths about Egypt, **FortR** 1249

Chetwynd, Richard Walter, 7th Viscount Chetwynd, 1823–1911. Burke.

Letter: **NatR-II** 694

Cheyne, Thomas Kelly: see *Index,* I, 844.

The Book of Job, **FM** 6308

Ancient beliefs in immortality, **NC** 2137
Professor Sayce on "The Higher Criticism," 2565

Chichester, Charles Raleigh: see *Index,* I, 844.

A policy for Ireland, **DR** 1981

Chi'en Lung, 1711–1799, Emperor of China. *Annals and Memoirs of the Court of Peking* by Backhouse and Bland, 1914.

From the Emperor of China to King George the Third, **NC** 2956

Chihchen Lofengluh: see Lo Feng-Luh, Sir Chich Chen.

Child, Theodore E.: see *Index,* I, 844, and II, App. A.

The Paris newspaper press, **FortR** 2347
The American newspaper press, 2400
Through the States, 2423
Society in Paris, 2447
Pictures in London and Paris, 2471

Child-Villiers, Margaret Elizabeth: see *Index,* I, 844.

Buddhism and Christianity, **NatR-II** 250
Our grandmothers, 505
The romance of a mine, 743

The Hindu at home, **NC** 1702
Ourselves and our foremothers, 1815
A French colony [New Caledonia], 2291
Three weeks in Samoa, 2336, 2350
The transformation of Japan, 2450, 2466
White slaves, 3256

Childers, Hugh Culling Eardley, 1827–1896, statesman. *DNB.*

Niederbronn [in Alsace], **NC** 1551

Chirol, Sir Ignatius Valentine: see *Index,* I, 844.

Notes of travel in Thessaly and Epirus, **FortR** 1781
Bulgaria, 1837
French diplomacy in Syria, 1898
Persia *in extremis,* 2265

Chisholm, George Goudie, 1850–1930, lecturer, Univ. of Edin. *WWW.*

The leather industry in Ireland, **NatR-II** 1048

Chisholm, Hugh, 1866–1924, journalist and ed. *Ency.Brit. DNB.*

University degrees for women, **FortR** 3650
How to counteract the "Penny Dreadful," 3725
The election petitions of 1895–6, 3803
Justice for the taxpayer, 3931
The choice for the sugar consumer, 4037
The debt and the deficit, 4260
How to pay for the war, 4425

The coming crisis in consols, **NatR-II** 1916

Choate, Joseph Hodges, Jun., 1876–1968, N.Y. lawyer. *Amer. WWW.*

Harmonic literature, **NC** 3607

Chorley, John Rutter, 1807?–1867, ed. of Spanish plays. *DNB.*

The national drama of Spain, **FM** 3847, 3870, 3890, 3897

Christie, Albany James, S.J., 1817–1891. Newman, *L&D*, XI, index.

Paget: nature and religion, **DR** 436
Physical cause of death of Christ, 445

Christie, J. D., pastrycook.

Working man's reply to Huxley, **NC** 1844

Christie, Mary Elizabeth: see *Index*, I, 845.

The dry bones of popular education, **FortR** 1842

Christie, William Dougal: see *Index*, I, 845.

Milnes' poems, **DR** 229
Lord Grey on the Reform Act of 1832, **FM** 4800

Christmas, afterwards Noel-Fearn, Henry, 1811–1868, misc. writer and numismatist. *DNB.*

Progress of chemistry, **FQR** 527 collab.
?*Coins and Antiquities of Afghanistan*, 679
See: 610 collab., 634

Church, A. G., Director of the London Omnibus Co.

Letter: **FortR** 2934

Church, Alfred John: see *Index*, I, 845.

Statius, **FortR** 1799

Dictionary of Christian Biography, **NatR-II** 990

Criticism as a trade, **NC** 1791
Notice: 487

Church, Charles Marcus, 1823–1915, Canon of Wells. *Times*, Feb. 10, 1915, p. 10b.

The Greek frontier, 1829–1879, **NQM** 179

Church, George Earl, 1835–1910, engineer. *WWW.*

Bolivia and Brazil in the Amazon Valley, **FortR** 731

Church, Richard William: see *Index*, I, 845.

Mill, *On Liberty*, **BentQR** 34

Letter: **FortR** 2655

Ritualism, **NC** 546

Churchill, George Charles Spencer, 8th Duke of Marlborough, 1844–1892. Burke.

The limits of English revolution, **FortR** 2055
On the cross benches, 2190
The transfer of land, 2303
Cant in politics, 2380
Political cross-roads, 2492
The vampire gold, 2610
Farms and trotting-horses of Kentucky, 3044
Virginia mines and American rails, 3068, 3085
A future school of English art, 3283

The breaking up of the land monopoly, **NC** 550
Reform of feudal laws, 576
Hereditary rulers, 614
Political opportunism, 676
Home Rule, 724
The new Tories, 1784

Churchill, John. Thrall, pp. 35, 280.

The Magyars, versus Dr. Bowring, **FM** 48 collab.
Kisfaludy's "Meeting of the Similes" [satire on Bowring], 67 collab.
Unpublished poems of a man of genius, 119
Schiller's *Wallenstein's Camp*, 156
Poetry of the Sandwich Islands, 203 collab.
?Resurrectional recreations, 347 collab.
The Fraser papers, in 14 installments from 522 to 1079, all collab.
Ainsworth's dictionary, 705
Judgment of the annuals, 760
The poems of Quaffypunchovicz, 948 collab.

Churchill, Randolph Henry Spencer, known as Lord Randolph Churchill, 1849–1894, statesman. *DNB.*

Churchill, Randolph H. S. (*continued*)
?State of the opposition, **FortR** 1968
collab?
Elijah's mantle [on Disraeli's fall in 1880],
2027
An antidote to agitation, 2209

Clancy, John Joseph: see *Index,* I, 845.

Financial clauses of Home Rule Bill, **FortR**
3359

The financial grievance of Ireland, **NC**
3044

Clapperton, Jane Hume. *BMCat.*

Agnosticism and women, **NC** 443
The agnostic at church, 709

Claretie, Arsène-Armand, known as Jules,
1840–1913, French author. *DBF.*

Shakespeare and Molière, **FortR** 4325

Clark, Archibald Campbell, 1851–1901, M.D.
*Surgeon Index/*3rd s.

Hypnotism, **NatR-II** 1111

Clark, Edward P., 1847–1903, American
journalist, *Amer. WWW.*

[Grover] Cleveland, **NatR-II** 1989

Clark, Edwin Charles, 1835–1917, regius
prof. of civil law, Cambridge. *WWW.*

What are Liberals to do? **NatR-II** 368

Clark, Gavin Brown, 1846–1930, consul-
general for Republic of So. Africa.
WWW.

Our Boer policy, **FortR** 2072

Clark, William George: see *Index,* I, 846.

New novels [including C. Brontë's *Shirley*],
FM 2673
?Shakespeare and the new discovery [of
1632 folio], 3070
Royal Academy Exhibition of 1855, 3359

Clarke, Andrew, 1824–1902, colonial official.
DNB.

Letter: **NatR-II** 2459

Clarke, Charles, 1814/15–1870, sportsman,
novelist. Boase, *BMCat.,* Foster.

The Derby of 1865, **FortR** 22

The Beauclercs, in 9 installments from **FM**
4595 to 4688

Clarke, Sir Edward George, 1841–1931, politician. *DNB.*

London government, **NatR-II** 1661 collab.
at least

Conservative and Liberal finance, **NC** 1075

Clarke, Mrs. Eliza; perhaps the Eliza Clarke
in *BMCat.* writing biography in the 80s.

Béranger: his songs and politics, **FM** 6312
The letters of Goethe's mother, 6450

Voltaire and Madame du Châtelet, **NC** 183

Clarke, Frederick; prob. the Frederick Seymour Clarke, 1855–1932, diplomat, in
WWW.

Lady Blennerhassett's *Talleyrand,* **FortR**
3590

Clarke, Sir George Sydenham: see *Index,* I,
846.

Our military requirements, **FortR** 4027

Can England be invaded? **NatR-II** 1863
War through peace spectacles, 2025
War, trade, and food supply, 2045

England and the Mediterranean, **NC** 2729
Nelson, 3123
Captain Mahan's counsels to United States,
3245
England and America, 3326
The Tsar's proposed conference, 3366
Germany as a naval power, 3468
The limitations of naval force, 3508
The Empire and the militia ballot, 3583
Proper precautions for imperial safety,
3628

Clarke, Richard Frederick, 1839–1900, Jesuit
priest. Boase.

The philosophy of subjective religion, **DR**
1389
Protestant lectures on modern scepticism,
1392
?Dr. Bain on relativity of human knowl-
edge, 1404
?A study of relations, 1420
?*Bremen Lectures . . . on Religious Ques-
tions,* 1438
Mechanical devotions, 1944
Notice: ?1434

Modern miracles, **NC** 785
Happiness in hell, 2338
Verdict of Rome on "the happiness in hell,"
2459
The training of a Jesuit, 2972

Catholic's view of *Helbeck of Bannisdale*
[by Mrs. Humphrey Ward], 3348
Mivart on continuity of Catholicism, 3603

Clarke, Robert Francis: see *Index*, I, 846.

The vivisection controversy, **DR** 2443

Clarkson, Edward, 1787/88–1871, writer on
Near East. *BMCat.*, death certificate at
Somerset House.

Antiquarian research in Egypt, **FQR** 379
Monuments of Egypt and Nubia, 391
Mexican antiquities, 411
Steam navigation to India, 425
France and England [the Syrian Question],
611

?Bunsen's *Egypt*, **FM** 2324

Clayden, Peter William: see *Index*, I, 846.

Peel and Palmerston, **FortR** 146
Macbeth and Lady Macbeth, 428
The ecclesiastical organisations of English
Dissent, 498
Notices: 472, 540, 577

Cleather, Mrs. Alice Leighton, misc. writer.
BMCat., *LCCat.*

Letters: **NatR-II** 837, 924

Cleaver, Richard Stuart. *WWW*/1950 under
his son Frederick Holden Cleaver.

Letter: **NC** 2689

Clerk, J., Capt.

Suez Canal, **FortR** 558, 566

Clerke, Agnes Mary: see *Index*, I, 847.

The Cape in 1888, **DR** 2152

Diamonds, natural and artificial, **FM** 6297
The great southern comet of 1880, 6432

Clerke, Aubrey St. John: see *Index*, I, 847.

The land question and law reform, **DR**
1718
Pitt, 2309

Clerke, Ellen Mary: see *Index*, I, 847.

?Poetry of Michael Angelo, **DR** 1652
Age of Dante in the Florentine chronicles,
1703
Catholic missions in Central Africa, 1775
?Catholic missions in Equatorial Africa,
1785
The mission of the Zambesi, 1803

Voyage of the *Vega* and its results, 1814
Catholicism in North Africa, 1832
Alessandro Manzoni and his works, 1840
The Corea, 1844
Catholicism in Egypt, 1857
Denis Florence MacCarthy, 1863
Modern Mexico, 1886
The Copts, 1901
Madagascar past and present, 1902
The revolution in the Soudan, 1914
Abyssinia and its people, 1934
Commercial future of West Africa, 1942
The destiny of Khartoum, 1960
Notes of travel and exploration, in 63 in-
stallments from 1964 to 2736
Maritime canals, 1967
The gates of India, 1983
The Slav States of the Balkans, 2000
Burma and the farther East, 2012
The future of petroleum, 2023
Present position of China, 2037
The Portuguese in India, 2050
The age of steel, 2073
The native princes of India, 2082
The Empire route to the East, 2108
Memoirs of a Royalist [le Comte de Fal-
loux], 2121
Irish industries, 2140
New crusade [against slave trade in Africa],
2146
Syndicates, trusts, and corners, 2167
The principles of '89, 2181
The dock labourers' strike, 2195
Mediaeval guilds and modern competition,
2235
The teaching of economic geography, 2257
The insurrection in Chile, 2272
Sir John Franklin and the far North, 2297
Spanish society in modern fiction, 2313
Memoirs of Cardinal Massaja, 2376
Father Ohrwalder's captivity, 2404
Mashunaland and its neighbours, 2421
A missionary model farm in Borneo, 2428
The real Joan of Arc, 2451
Mrs. Augustus Craven, 2469
The Church in Korea, 2478
Wanderings of early Irish saints, 2525
The crisis in Rhodesia, 2545
Life of General Gordon, 2598
Toscanelli and Vespucci, 2655
The Catholic Church in South Africa, 2702
Notices: ?1826, ?1862, 2709

A type of the Renaissance [Andrea del
Sarto], **FM** 6248
A story of the chestnut harvest, 6433
Stefano; a reminiscence of Sorrento, 6465

Circe in mediaeval song, **NatR-II** 172
Chaucer and Boccaccio, 502
The satires of Ariosto, 813

Cléron, Gabriel Paul Othenin de, comte d'Haussonville, 1843–1924. *Bib. Nat. Cat., Grand Larousse.*

Reception at French Academy, **NatR-II** 815

Clifford, Edward 1844–1907, Evangelistic Sec., the Church Army. *Memoir* of him by Mrs. R. Cholmeley (1907), pp. 160, 167–168.

Father Damien and leprosy in India, **FortR** 2849

"The first-born son of death," **NC** 1610
With Father Damien and the lepers, 1705
The Hawaiians and Father Damien, 1719

Clifford, Lucy (Lane): see *Index*, I, 848, and II, App. A.

A modern correspondence, **FortR** 2891
In case of discovery, 3702

A grey romance, **NatR-II** 1453

A Supreme Moment: a play in one act, **NC** 3506

Clifford, William Joseph Hugh, 1823–1893, Bishop of Clifton. Boase.

Days of the week, and works of creation, **DR** 1771
The days of creation, 1798, 1869
Notice: 1126

The new reformation, **FortR** 2554

Clifford, William Kingdon: see *Index*, I, 848.

Body and mind, **FortR** 1104
The first and the last catastrophe [beginning and end of earth], 1142
The Unseen Universe, 1161
Right and wrong, 1213
The ethics of religion, 1376

Influence upon morality of a decline in religious belief, **NC** 26
Cosmic emotion, 89
Virchow on the teaching of science, 161
Childhood and ignorance, 178
Philosophy of the pure sciences, 287

Clive, Caroline (Meysey-Wigley): see *Index*, I, 848.

From an old gentleman's diary, **FM** 4574

Clough, Arthur Hugh, 1819–1861, poet. *DNB.*
Poems and Ballads of Goethe, **FM** 3861

Clouston, Sir Thomas Smith, 1840–1915, physician. *WWW.*
The medical schools of Scotland, **ScotR** 425

Clowes, Sir William Laird: see *Index*, I, 848.

The uselessness of Gibraltar, **FortR** 3327
Sea power, its past and its future, 3448
A lesson from the [U.S.S.] *Chicago*, 3520
The naval manoeuvres, 3546, 3709
A system of coast defence, 3625
Navy estimates and imperial defence, 3787
The wrong way with the navy, 3958
American expansion, 4208

The next siege of Paris, **NatR-II** 1658
The Royal Navy in 1894, 1671
Sir Geoffrey Hornby, 1710

Toulon and the French navy, **NC** 2500
Our warning from the naval manoeuvres, 2630
Millstone round the neck of England [Mediterranean policy], 2715
Braggadocio about the Mediterranean, 2756
Some lessons from Kiel, 2787
The Trafalgar captains, 2817
The naval teachings of the crisis, 2899
The genealogy of Nelson, 3199
Value of the Channel Islands, 3758

Cluer, Albert Rowland, 1852–1942, judge. *WWW.*

John Addington Symonds, **FortR** 3379

Cluseret, Gustave Paul, 1823–1900, army officer, politician. *DBF.*

The military side of the Commune, **FortR** 963, 977, 985

The interview at Aubervilliers [on the Commune], **FM** 5300
My connection with Fenianism, 5327
Behind the scenes at the Commune, 5380
The Paris Commune of 1871, 5411
Religious question in Switzerland, 5521
Catholic movement in Switzerland, 5529, 5538

Coape, Henry Coe, b.1808/09, barrister. Foster, *BMCat.*

The mistakes of a day, **NQM** 29

Cobb, William Frederick: see Geikie-Cobb, William Frederick.

Cobbe, Frances Power: see *Index*, I, 848.

What is progress, are we progressing? **FortR** 385
The devil, 802
Vivisection, 1876
The education of the emotions, 2679
Letter: 2638
Notice: 379

City of the sun [Baalbec in Lebanon], **FM** 4106
Celibacy v. marriage, 4189
The city of victory [Cairo], 4196
The Eternal City, 4215
"What shall we do with our old maids?" 4272
Female charity: lay and monastic, 4284
A day at the Dead Sea, 4300
A day at Athens, 4325
The City of Peace [Jerusalem], 4333
Rights of man and claims of brutes, 4381
Hades, 4417
The nineteenth century, 4429
The morals of literature, 4459
The philosophy of the poor-laws, 4475
The hierarchy of art, 4509, 4526
Ireland and her exhibition in 1865, 4585
The indigent class, 4622
The Brahmo Samaj [the Brahmin Church], 4676
The conventional laws of society, 4705
The American Sanitary Commission, 4743
Household service, 4836
Max Müller's *Chips*, 4840
Bunsen's life and last book [*God in History*], 4877
Criminals, idiots, women, and minors, 4928
Fergusson's *Tree and Serpent Worship*, 4959
To know, or not to know? 5035
Ancient and Mediaeval India, 5062

Letter: **NatR-II** 1189

Animals in fable and art, **NQM** 18
The fauna of fancy, 31
The moral aspects of vivisection, 50
The town mouse and the country mouse, 57
Backward Ho! 67
Pessimism [Schopenhauer], 99
The peak in Darien: the riddle of death, 144

Cobbold, Ralph Patteson: see *Index*, I, 848.

A sample of Chinese administration, **NC** 3449

Cobden-Sanderson, Thomas James, 1840–1922, bookbinder, printer. *DNB*.

Bookbinding: its processes and ideal, **FortR** 3534

Cochran-Patrick, Sir Neil James Kennedy, 1866–1958, Scottish advocate. *WWW*.

R. W. Cochran-Patrick, **ScotR** 588

Cochran-Patrick, Robert William, 1842–1897,

statesman, archaeologist. *DNB, ScotR* no. 576.

See: **ScotR** 22

Cochrane, Douglas Mackinon Baillie Hamilton, 12th Earl of Dundonald, 1852–1935, army officer. *DNB*.

Concerning Chili, **FortR** 2215

Protection for surnames, **NC** 2513

Cochrane, John George, 1781–1852, ed. *FQR* 1827–1835. *DNB*.

Rizo, *Modern Greek Literature*, **FQR** 10 collab.
Russian literature, 25 collab.
Chambray's *Notes on Prussia*, 300
Italian Insurrection of 1831, 319 collab.
Encyclopédie des Gens du Monde, 330
Note: ?243
Notices: 39, 53, 66, 79 collab., 103
Trans: 39
See: 277

Cochrane-Baillie, Alexander Dundas Ross Wishart: see *Index*, I, 848.

Forty years of parliament, **FortR** 2249

Roma nuova—Roma vecchia, **NatR-II** 52
Political pessimism, 124

Aix-Les-Bains and Annecy, **NC** 894

Cochrane-Baillie, Charles Wallace Alexander Napier Ross, 2nd Baron Lamington, 1860–1940, statesman. *DNB*.

The French in Tonquin, **NC** 2088

Cock, Alfred, 1849–1898, barrister. Boase.

The Crown's "right of reply," **NC** 2706

Cockburn, Sir Alexander James Edmund, 1802–1880, Lord Chief Justice of England. *DNB*.

The chase: its history and laws, **NC** 501, 528

Cockburn, James D., of Glasgow. William Wallace, *Robert Wallace* (1903), p. ix.

Beginnings of Scottish newspaper press, **ScotR** 336, 401
Daniel Defoe in Scotland, 697

Cockerell, Samuel Pepys, b.1844, sculptor. Mallet.

Lord Leighton's drawings, **NC** 3026

Cody, B.

Arctic discoveries, **DR** 737
See: 743

Cody, George Elphege, 1847–1891, O.S.B., Bishop of Ross. Snow.

Daily life in a modern monastery, **NC** 1043

Coghill, Annie Louisa (Walker), d.1907, wife of Harry Coghill. *Blackwood Papers Cat.* under both her names, *BMCat.* under Mrs. Harry Coghill, and *LCCat.* under maiden name. (See *Index,* I, 1126, under Miss Walker and Annie Louisa Walker, and App. A below under Walker.)

Mrs. Oliphant, **FortR** 3995

A forgotten hero [Jacques Cartier], **FM** 6356

Coghill, John George Sinclair, 1834–1899, physician. *Surgeon Index*/3rd s.

The prevention of consumption, **NC** 3425

Cohen, Henry A.

Free whist, **NatR-II** 1100

Cohen, Hermann, 1842–1918, German philosopher. *NDB.*

The modern Jew and new Judaism, **FortR** 3780, 3792

Cohen, Julia Matilda (Waley), d.1917, social worker. *LCCat., WWW* under Mrs. Nathaniel Cohen.

Letter: **NatR-II** 812

Cohen, Nathaniel Louis, 1847–1913, member of London County Council. *Jewish Ency.*

Registries and marketing of labour, **NatR-II** 548

Cohn, Gustav, 1840–1919, German economist. *NDB.*

Political economy in Germany, **FortR** 984

Colajanni, Napoleone, 1847–1921, Italian statesman. *DEI.*

The Italian bank scandals, **FortR** 3488

Colani, Timothée, 1824–1888, French theologian. *DBF.*

The Anglo-French alliance, **FortR** 2133

Cole, George Ralph Fitz-Roy, d.1910, civil

engineer. *Landed Gentry*/1937; see *FM* no. 5883.

Transcaucasia, **FM** 6001
John Chinaman abroad, 6102
Edited: 5883

Cole, Sir Henry: see *Index,* I, 849.

Lord Brougham's Record Commission, **FM** 1049
Report of Committee on Postage, 1238

Cole, Henry Warwick: see *Index,* I, 849.

Our commons and open spaces, **FM** 4653

Cole, L'Aigle: see *Index,* I, 849.

Poaching, **NC** 2457

Coleman, John, 1831–1904, comedian. *Dramatic Portraits.*

Status of actor, **NatR-II** 276

Coleridge, Gilbert James Duke, 1859–1953, misc. writer, sculptor. *WWW.*

My friend Robin, **FortR** 4063

Wanted: a style, **NatR-II** 1176

Coleridge, Henry James, S.J., 1822–1893, ed. of *The Month. DNB.*

The letters of St. Teresa, **DR** 1048
Renan's *Vie de Jésus,* 1068
Our contemporaries [periodicals], 1073, 1084, 1095
Venn's *Life of St. Francis Xavier,* 1076
Newman's *Apologia Pro Vitâ Suâ,* 1080
Outlines of the Gospel history, 1091
?Consalvi's *Memoirs,* 1112
Notice: 1593

Coleridge, Henry Nelson: see *Index,* I, 849, and II, App. A.

Anecdotes of Napoleon, **LR (1829)** 4

Coleridge, Sir John Duke: see *Index,* I, 850.

Sir William Boxall, **FortR** 1664
The *Nineteenth Century* defenders of vivisection, 1884
Letter: 2638

Mr. Buckle and Sir John Coleridge, **FM** 3855
See: 3255

Coleridge, Samuel Taylor: see *Index,* I, 850.

Monologues, **FM** 876, 885
See: 415, 6075

Coleridge, Stephen William Buchanan: see
Index, I, 850.

Cruelty to Animals Act of 1876, **FortR**
4420

Lord Lister's anodyne [on vivisection],
NatR-II 2236

Coles, Frederick R., asst. keeper of the Na-
tional Museum of Antiquities, Edinburgh.
J. A. Duncan, *Some Family Leaves*
(Edin., 1911), p. 145; *BMCat.*

Coincidences in customs and beliefs, **ScotR**
649

Colinet, Philémon, 1853–1917, prof. at Louvain, orientalist. *Seyn.*

Recent works on primitive Buddhism, **DR**
2098, 2214

Collet, Clara E.: see *Index*, I, 850.

Prospects of marriage for women, **NC** 2189

Collier, John, 1850–1934, painter, *DNB.*

Portrait-painting, **NC** 2928

Collier, Robert, 2nd Baron Monkswell, 1845–
1909, statesman. *WWW* under Monkswell.

State colonization, **FortR** 2689
Reformatory and industrial schools, 3917

Collier, Robert Porrett, 1st Baron Monkswell,
1817–1886, judge, landscape painter.
DNB.

Landscape painting, **NC** 458

Collier, William, 1856–1935, pres. of British
Medical Assoc. *WWW.*

Insensibility of animals to pain, **NC** 1775

Collingridge, Augustus, naval officer. *BMCat.*,
H&L.

Bold stroke during the peace of Amiens,
FM 955
Three years of my life; or Ellen Vere, 1066
Rough sketches afloat, 1092, 1106, 1282,
1313

Collings, Jesse, 1831–1920, politician. *DNB.*

A radical in Russia, **FortR** 1997
The Radical programme: the agricultural
labourer, 2098
Occupying ownership, 2140

Letter: **NatR-II** 1353

£38,000,000 per annum! [for agricultural
imports], **NC** 2325

Collins, Edward James Mortimer, 1827–1876,
man of letters. *DNB*, Boase.

The magic chessmen, **FM** 3043

The Summerfield imbroglio, **NQM** 65
Almanacs, 72
Aristophanes, 92

Collins, Edwin, ed. *The Dentist.*

The teeth of the schoolboy, **NC** 3499

Collins, Edwin

China's present and future [plea for British
neutrality], **FortR** 3933 collab.

Collins, Frederick Howard, 1857–1910,
printer. *LCCat.*, *Yearbook/1916*

"The Ways of Orthodox Critics," **FortR**
2682

Collins, John Churton: see *Index*, I, 850.

Can English literature be taught? **NC** 1482
Universities in contact with the people, 1771
The "ideal" university, 2164
Language versus literature at Oxford, 2705
A university for the people, 3438

Collins, Mortimer: see Collins, Edward James
Mortimer

Collins, Wilkie: see Collins, William Wilkie

Collins, William Wilkie: see *Index*, I, 852.

Letter: **FortR** 2638

The Monktons of Wincot Abbey, **FM** 3407,
3421

Collinson, Thomas Bernard: see *Index*, I, 852.

Letter: **NatR-II** 233

Collyer, Adelaide Martha (Shuckburgh), wife
of D'Arcy Bedingfeld Collyer. *Landed
Gentry.* (See *Index*, I, 852.)

The salons of the ancien régime, **NC** 2293

Colmache, Georgina A.: see *Index*, I, 852.

How Cuba might have belonged to France,
FortR 3723

Colmer, Joseph Grose, 1856–1937, Canadian
statesman. *WWW.*

Sir John Macdonald, **FortR** 3102
The Canadian census, 3158

Colmer, Joseph Grose (*continued*)
Commercial federation of the Empire, **NatR-II** 1887

Cologan, William Henry, R.C. priest. *BMCat.*

Father [Theobald] Mathew's centenary, **DR** 2246

Colomb, Sir John Charles Ready: see *Index*, I, 852.

Naval arrangements in other hemisphere, **FortR** 4494

Waste and confusion in the navy, **NatR-II** 2422

The naval manoeuvres, **NC** 1612
Wanted, an imperial conference, 2677

Colomb, Philip Howard: see *Index*, I, 852.

What is imperial defence? **NatR-II** 1651
The patriotic editor in war, 2003
Naval warfare of the future, 2055
Impressions of [the Spanish-American] War, 2169, 2191

Colquhoun, Archibald Ross: see *Index*, I, 852.

England and France in Indo-China, **NatR-II** 35
Anglo-Chinese commercial alliance, 357

Colvile, Charles Frederick, lieut.-col., army officer. *Army List*/92

Glanders and farcy [animal diseases], **NatR-II** 1370

Colville, James: see *Index*, I, 852, and II, App. A.

The Complaynt of Scotlande, **ScotR** 429
Scotland under the Roundheads, 531

Colvin, Sir Auckland: see *Index*, I, 852.

The Indian famine and the press, **FortR** 1041

Growth of Indian state expenditure, **NC** 2652
Indian frontiers and Indian finance, 2842
Agra in 1857: a reply to Lord Roberts, 3095
The problem beyond the Indian frontier, 3205

Colvin, Lady Frances (Fetherstonhaugh), 1839–1924, married first to Albert Hurt Sitwell, second to Sidney Colvin. E. V. Lucas, *The Colvins and Their Friends* (1928), pp. 54, 63, 337.

Two biographies [Robert Browning, Laurence Oliphant], George Meredith's *One of our Conquerors*, **NatR-II** 1175

Colvin, Sir Sidney: see *Index*, I, 852.

English painters and painting in 1867, **FortR** 448
Notes on Albert Durer, 667
On the Mausoleum of Halikarnassos, 773
Balaustion's Adventure [by Browning], 815
The Bethnal Green Museum, 898
Phases of English art under George III, 1033, 1051
The history of a pavement, 1171
Daniel Deronda [by George Eliot], 1304
The Grosvenor Gallery, 1367
On the study of classical art, 1523
Art and criticism, 1611
Literature and the manual arts, 1687
Fleeming Jenkin: in memoriam, 2344
Letter: 2655
Notices: 488, 553, 560, 585, 784, 865, 872, 879, 886, 893, 913, 921, 929

The Apollo Belvedere, **NQM** 136

Restoration and anti-restoration, **NC** 91
Old masters at the winter exhibitions, 274
Tragedy of *Paolo and Francesca* [by Stephen Phillips], 3573

Common, Andrew Ainslie, 1841–1903, astronomer. *DNB.*

Astronomical photography, **NC** 1370

Compton, Lord Alwyne Frederick, 1855–1911, army officer. *WWW.*

The War Office, **NC** 3221

Compton, William George Spencer Scott, 13th Earl Compton, 1851–1913. *Complete Peerage* under Northampton.

Distress in London; remedies, **FortR** 2673
Palmyra: past and present, 2767

Compton-Rickett, Arthur: see *Index*, I, 852.

Modern criticism, **NatR-II** 1455

Comyn, Francis
The seamy side of British Guiana, **NC** 2895

Conder, Claude Reignier: see *Index*, I, 853.

France and Syria, **FortR** 2068
The Guide of Islam [the Mahdi], 2141

The prehistoric Levant, **ScotR** 266
Early Christians in Syria, 294

Rude stone monuments in Syria, 303
The Tell Amarna tablets, 313
The oriental Jews, 321
Ancient trade, 345
The Canary Islanders, 354
The natural basis of speech, 378
Early languages of Syria, 395
Earliest ages of Hebrew history, 416
Antiquities of Cyprus, 431
Modern Moslems, 440
Jerusalem, 459
Archaeology of the Pentateuch, 488
State of Turkey, 505
The Asiatics in America, 530
Egyptian chronology, 551
Greek art in Asia, 580
Discoveries in Western Asia, 653
Recent Hittite discoveries, 687

Conder, Francis Roubiliac: see *Index*, I, 853.

The ethics of Jesus Christ, **FM** 5623
Contemporaries of the Evangelists [on invisible world], 5637
Literary history of the word Messiah, 5646
Literary character of Fourth Gospel, 5658
The King Messiah of history, 5680
Debate as to the Fourth Gospel, 5698
The old law and the new, 5720
Local taxation, debt, local government, 5789
Sanitary improvement, 5800
On the government of London, 5823
Future sources of illumination and water supply, London, 5829
On municipal government, 5884
Government annuities in France, 5904
Our inland navigation, 5913
The battles of peace, 5942
The mineral traffic on railways, 5949
Third-class passengers, 5964
Invest money with safety [railways], 6012
Working men's conventions, 6027
The habitability of London, 6043
Hydrological survey of England, 6072
The employment of English capital, 6094
Progress of railways towards bankruptcy, 6106
Economy of speed in transport, 6118
The question of the Thames, 6124
The best friend of the working man [the machine], 6146
Explosions in coal mines, 6173
The water supply of London, 6313
The problem of railway safety, 6358
Physical revolution of the 19th century, 6460
Léon Say on the prosperity of France, 6498
Contention between the carriers and manufacturers, 6532

Remuneration of labour in England, **NatR-II** 318

What is astrology? **ScotR** 120
Water circulation of great cities, 129
On inland transport, 148
Redemption of astrology, 177
The Panama Canal, 191
The Panama scandal, 240
The railway race to Edinburgh, 248
The Nile and its work, 275

Conder, Josiah, 1789–1855, bookseller. *DNB.*

Pacho's *Travels in Marmarica and Cyrenaica,* **FQR** 111

Conder, René François Reignier, b.1857/58, librarian to Marquis of Bute. Gorman, Foster.

The extension of the Reformation, **DR** 2553

Condorcet, Jean Antoine Nicolas de Caritat, Marquis de, 1743–1794, metaphysician. *DBF.*

Condorcet's plea for women, **FortR** 691

Conestabile, Count; possibly Count Francesco Conestabile writing on agricultural improvements in 1884: see *Catalogo Generale della Libreria Italiana,* 1847–1899, and *BMCat.*

Improvement of the "Campagna Romana," **NC** 868

Congreve, Richard, 1818–1899, positivist. *DNB.*

Mr. Huxley on M. Comte, **FortR** 580
Vivisection, 1140 collab.
England and Turkey, 1300

Conington, John: see *Index,* I, 853.

Kingsley's *Saints' Tragedy,* **FM** 2434
Sacred and profane, 2555
?Matthew Arnold's *Merope,* 3737
Pope's MS. notes on Tickell's *Homer,* 4014

Connelly, Pierce, 1804–1883, R.C. priest, later reentered Episcopal ministry. Newman, *L&D,* XI, index.

Conversion of Rev. Pierce Connelly, **DR** 22

Conolly, John: see *Index,* I, 854.

Andral on consumption, **FQR** 159
History of Hypochondriasis and Hysteria, 283

Conolly, John (*continued*)
Life and labours of Cuvier, 335
French and English schools of medicine,
423
?Statistics of insanity in Europe, 456

Conroy, George, 1831–1878, bishop of Ar-
dagh. Boase.

The signs of martyrdom in the catacombs,
Ram 1019
The Church in the ancient symbols, 1027,
1039

Constable, Marmaduke Strickland, 1862–1898,
sec. of legation at Stockholm. *Landed
Gentry.*

Political crisis, Sweden and Norway, **FortR**
3644

Fair trade and authority, **NatR-II** 1281

Conway, Caroline (Campbell), Countess of
Ailesbury (by her first marriage), 1721–
1803. *Complete Peerage* under Ailesbury.

Letters to Horace Walpole, **FM** 2700 collab.

Conway, Henry Seymour, 1721–1795, army
officer. *DNB.*

Letters to Horace Walpole, **FM** 2700 collab., 2715, 2733, 2771

Conway, Moncure Daniel, 1832–1907, American divine, essayist. *DAB.*

Recollections of President Lincoln, **FortR** 4
Modern Times [a village in] New York, 32
America, France, and England, 155
American "Radicals," and their English
censors, 176
The President's defence [Lincoln], 251
Walt Whitman, 337
Russia and America, 345
American prospects, 413
Theodore Parker, 427
The internal conflict of America, 485
Wendell Phillips, 697
Thomas Paine, 1561
Ralph Waldo Emerson, 1920
Notices: 306, 464, 479

The transcendentalists of Concord, **FM**
4468
President Lincoln, 4504
Virginia, first and last, 4522
Mayflowerings [New England], 4540
Assassination of President Lincoln, 4557
Mannahatta [New York], 4576
The queen of the West [America], 4615
Thoreau, 4640

Anomalies of American constitution, 4657
Washington, 4684
Down the Ohio to the underworld, 4711
Lunatics, 4713
National purpose and the President of the
U.S. [Johnson], 4731
Recent lectures and writings of Emerson,
4757
Sylvester Judd, 4778
The new rebellion in America, 4817
England and America, 4846
The culture of Emerson, 4879
The devil in Leipzig, 4954
Emerson's *Society and Solitude*, 5096
A month with the belligerents [French and
Germans], 5133
Mystic trees and flowers, 5140, 5149
A pilgrimage on the Ammer, 5257
The city of the monk [Munich], 5294
Horace Greeley, 5356
Demonology, 5366, 5373
Vienna, 5428
Gravelotte revisited, 5473
Romance of an old Yorkshire village, 5536
Story of a Yorkshire blacksmith, 5546
See: 5195

The pound of flesh [on Shylock], **NC** 442

Conway, William Martin: see *Index*, I, 854.

The climbing of high mountains, **FortR**
3407
Dürer's visit to the Netherlands, 4002

The society of authors, **NC** 2849
The fine-art of living, 3309

Conybeare, Charles Augustus Vansittart,
1853–1919, barrister. *WWW.*

"Is schoolmastering a learned profession?"
FM 6136

Conybeare, Frederick Cornwallis, 1856–1924,
scholar. *WWW.*

[T. H.] Green's political philosophy, **NatR-
II** 890
Proposed endowment of a Catholic univer-
sity in Ireland, 909
Armenia and the Armenians, 920
Are animals automata? 1104
The Dreyfus case, 2171
Side-lights on the Dreyfus case, 2218
French military justice, 2223
Treason in the French War Office, 2235
The Dreyfus case, 2258
The Dreyfus affair: the Jesuit view, 2279
General de Boisdeffre? 2293
Fresh evidence on the Dreyfus case, 2304
Jew-baiting [French policy in Algeria], 2328

Jean Calas, 2335
Sword and cassock, 2355
Popular Catholicism in France, 2398
Conspiracy against French Republic, 2466
Note: 2202

Conybeare, Henry, engineer. See *WWW*/1928 under his son, Charles F. P. Conybeare, and I. C. E., *List of Members*, 1883.

The future of London architecture, **FortR** 450

Cook, Sir Charles Archer, 1849–1934, barrister. *WWW.*

A lawyer's love-letters, 1615, **NatR-II** 534

Cook, Sir Edward Tyas: see *Index*, I, 854.

Letter: **FortR** 4423

Ruskin in relation to modern problems, **NatR-II** 1540

Cook, Lady Emily Constance (Baird): see *Index*, I, 854.

A modern high-school girl, **NatR-II** 1148
Romance of the National Gallery, 1425

Cook, Keningale Robert, 1845–1886, journalist, ed. *Dub.Univ.Mag.* Boase, *Times*, June 28, 1886, p. 1a.

John Asgill; cowardliness of dying, **FM** 5225
?The Irish university question, 5272

Cook, Sir Theodore Andrea, 1867–1928, journalist. *WWW.*

The Monroe Doctrine, **FortR** 4167

Cooke, Charles Wallwyn Radcliffe, 1841–1911, barrister, agriculturist. Venn.

The Parnellites in Parliament, **NatR-II** 495
Oratory of the House of Commons, 787
Some parliamentary incidents, 883

Cooke, Clement Kinloch: see Kinloch-Cooke

Cooke-Taylor, Richard Whately: see *Index*, I, 854.

The employment of mothers in factories, **FortR** 1154

The Agricultural Children's Act, **FM** 5807
The new Factory Act, 6134

Cookson, Montague Hughes: see Crackanthorpe, M. H.

Cooley, William Desborough: see *Index*, I, 855, and II, App. A.

Turkey, **FQR** 36
Arabic literature, 55
Von Hammer's *History, Ottoman Empire*, 88
The Black Sea and the Caucasus, 99
Douville's *Travels in Central Africa*, 238
Douville's *Reply*, 253
Douville's *Justification*, 277
?Meyen's *Voyage Round the World*, 342
?Parrot's *Journey to Mount Ararat*, 357
?Poeppig's *Travels in Chili, Peru, and on the River Amazons*, 387
?Rüppell's *Travels in Abyssinia*, 640
Notices: 103
Trans: 266

Dr. Livingstone's errors, **FortR** 190

Cooper, Antony Ashley: see *Index*, I, 855.

The dwellings of the poor, **NC** 932

Cooper, Miss C. L.

Curiosities of Irish farming, **NatR-II** 1032

Cooper, Charles Purton: see *Index*, I, 855.

See: **DR** 114, 123, 160

Cooper, Edward; possibly Edward S. Cooper in *BMCat.*, who wrote on money and the poor.

A national pension fund, **FortR** 3136

Cooper, Edward Herbert, 1867–1910, novelist. *WWW, LCCat.*

A biography, **FortR** 4174

Cooper, John Alexander, 1868–1956, Canadian editor. Wallace.

Canadian poetry, **NatR-II** 2010

Cooper, John Astley, 1866–1898, writer on sports. Venn.

An Anglo-Saxon olympiad, **NC** 2280
The Pan-Britannic gathering, 2425
Americans and the Pan-Britannic movement, 2806

Cooper, Mrs. Lina Orman: see *Index*, I, 855; see *NC* no. 3518.

With lancet and rifle on Beira railway, **FortR** 4480

"The humours of Ter-na-nog" [of Ireland], **NC** 3518

Cooper, Peter, 1798?–1852, Catholic priest. Newman, *L&D*, XV, index.

Galileo and the Roman Inquisition, **DR** 100

Copinger, Henry, army officer. *Army List/69.*

Trans: **FM** 5101, 5237

Copland, James, 1791–1870, physician. *DNB.*

Pestilential cholera, **FQR** 203

Copland-Crawford, W. E. B., West African consular service.

Letter: **FortR** 4157

Copleston, Edward: see *Index*, I, 855.

See: **LR (1829)** 18

Copleston, Reginald Stephen: see *Index*, I, 855.

Buddhism, **NC** 1576

Corbet, Robert St. John, 1839–1907, political writer. Burke.

Resignation [of Randolph Churchill] and reconstruction, **NatR-II** 543
Leadership in the House and in the country, 862
Toryism of tomorrow, 980

Corbet, William Joseph, 1824–1909, of Irish Lunacy Office, M.P. *WWW.*

Is insanity on the increase? **FortR** 2157
The increase of insanity, 3308, 3777
Letter: 3861

Corkran, John Frazer, 1811–1884, journalist. Boase, *Athenaeum*, Feb. 9, 1884, 186, death certificate at Somerset House, R.L.F.

Newspaper press of France, **FQR** 708
?French poetry and translation, 716
?Victor Hugo's *Burgraves of the Rhine*, 724
Hôtel de Rambouillet, 751

Corner-Ohlmüs, later Corner-Ohlmütz, Caroline (Corner), lived in Ceylon. *BMCat., RG; RG* (1905–1909) and *NC* 58 (1905), 132, give later form of surname.

A devil-dance in Ceylon, **NC** 3564

Corney, Charles Wilfrid, O.S.B., 1851–1926, procurator in Curia Romanâ. Snow, *Benedicti Familiae.*

Gregorian melodies in the manuscripts, **DR** 2601

Cornish, Blanche Warre: see Warre-Cornish, Blanche.

Cornish, Charles John: see *Index*, I, 855.

A chance for the public schools, **NatR-II** 2417

Cornish, Emily L.

A romance of the east coast. **FM** 6046

Cornish, Francis Warre: see Warre-Cornish, F. W.

Cornish, James Frazer: see *Index*, I, 855.

Some Liberal lights, **NatR-II** 390
A Gladstonian meeting, 1209

"Cornwall, Barry": see Procter, Bryan Waller.

Cornwallis, Caroline Frances, 1786–1858, authoress. *DNB.*

Naval school on the *Illustrious*, **FM** 3339
Naval education, 3643

Corrance, Frederick Snowden, 1822–1906, M.P. Venn.

Land question and tenures of possession, **FortR** 1134
Tenant right, 1147

Corrance, Henry Clemence: see *Index*, I, 856, and II, App. A.

Catholicism and spiritualism, **DR** 2657
Will materialism be the religion of the future? 2679
Notices: 2709, 2738

Coryn, Herbert Alfred William, physician. *BMCat., Med. Reg./99.*

Mind as disease-producer, **NatR-II** 2127

Coryn, Sidney G. P., Fellow of the Theosophical Soc.

Letter: **NatR-II** 913

Coryton, John: see *Index*, I, 856.

A lost art [photography], **FortR** 967

Cosson, Emilius Albert De: see De Cosson.

Costello, Louisa Stuart, 1799–1870, artist, novelist. *DNB.*

The Bocage: Basselin and Le Houx, **FM** 1399

Costelloe, Mary Whitall (Smith), wife of Benjamin Francis Conn Costelloe. *WW/* 1900, under her husband.

The new and the old art criticism, **NC** 2578

Cotgreave, Alfred, 1849–1911, librarian. *LCCat.*

Free libraries under the "Act," **NatR-II** 451

Cotton, Sir Henry John Stedman, 1845–1915, Indian civil servant. Buckland, *LCCat.*

Has India food for its people? **FortR** 1422
Prospects of moral progress in India, 1506

India's need and England's duty, **NQM** 189

Coubertin, Baron Pierre de Fredi de, 1863–1937, French educator. *WWW.*

A French view of the British Empire, **FortR** 4040
Modern France: the military paradox, 4082
Modern France: the political paradox, 4135
France since 1814, in 8 installments from 4232 to 4379
Possibility of war between England and France, 4445

Coulton, George Gordon, 1858–1947, historian. *WWW.*

The Swiss army: its lessons for England, **NatR-II** 2474

Coupe, Charles, S.J., 1853–1910. Sutcliffe.

The homage of Christ the King, **DR** 2273
Are agnostics in good faith? 2312
Mr. Swinburne's *Studies,* 2480

Courson, Countess Barbara Frances Mary (Neave) de, wife of Count Roger de Courson. *LCCat.*

St. Cyr in the past and present, **DR** 2688, 2704

Courtenay, Thomas Peregrine: see *Index,* I, 856.

Foreign policy of England: Lord Castlereagh, **FQR** 185
Foreign policy of England: Mr. Canning, 200
The reciprocity system, 217
Free trade, 233
Results of free trade, 261
Modern diplomacy, 302
British continental connexions, 439
Heeren on political theories, aristocracy,

democracy, 471
Canada, 487
Chateaubriand, *Spain,* 495

Courthope, William John: see *Index,* I, 856.

Conservatism in art, **NatR-II** 5
Current politics, 11, 22, 33, 44, 57, 68, 80, 91, 103, all collab.
[Browning's] *Jocoseria* and the critics, 38
Johnson and Carlyle, 93
The two Lucians: on popular religion, 131
The liberal movement in English literature, 189, 207, 245, 292, 315, 337
Poetry and politics, 394
Glenaveril [by Robert Lytton], 411
The political prospect: a Conservative view, 445
Mr. Gladstone's coming defeat, 452 collab.
Dowden's *Life of Shelley,* 523
Position of the Liberal Unionists, 604 collab.
Keats' place in English poetry, 617
Problems of Greater Britain [by C. W. Dilke], 1007
Claudian's "Old Man of Verona," 1249
The study of English language and literature, 1440
Notes: 14, 233, 361, 474, 528, 530, all collab.

Life in poetry, **NC** 2975, 3071, 3143
Notice: 1859

Courtney, Janet Elizabeth (Hogarth): see Hogarth, Janet Elizabeth.

Courtney, Leonard Henry: see *Index,* I, 857.

Political machinery and political life, **FortR** 1275
Our Eastern policy, 1355
Migration of centres of industrial energy, 1531
A fair day's wages for a fair day's work, 1562
Turkish fallacies and British facts, 1675
Redistribution by different lights, 2257

Who profits by free trade? **NatR-II** 1362
A dialogue on bimetallism, 1719
At Saratoga Springs [convention on proportional representation], 1765

The representation of minorities, **NC** 333
Proportional representation, 1094 collab.
The swarming of men, 1522
Bimetallism once more, 2379
Presidential election [of McKinley], 3047
Canning and the Eastern question, 3165
Parnell and Ireland, 3476
Notice: 2039

Courtney, William Leonard: see *Index*, I, 857.

The new psychology, **FortR** 1618
Carlyle's political doctrines, 1648
Robert Browning, writer of plays, 2047
Poets of to-day, 2105
Recasting the Oxford Schools, 2173
Charles Reade's novels, 2224
Mr. Swinburne's poetry, 2308
Ralph Waldo Emerson, 2360
Mr. Irving's [portrayal of] Faust, 2414
George Meredith's novels, 2469
Hawthorne's romances, 2523
Pascal, the sceptic, 2644
Roger Bacon of Oxford, 2858
Oxford tutors and their professorial critic [Thorold Rogers], 2924
The mask of Descartes, 3023
Ibsen's *Little Eyolf*, 3605
Huxley as philosopher, 3689
Idea of comedy, Pinero's new play, 3959
Frederic Chapman, 3621
Note: 3853

Can there be a science of character? **NatR-II** 971
Momus: a Socratic dialogue, 1275

Courtney, William Prideaux, 1845–1913, journalist, *WWW*.

The British Museum Library, **FortR** 1634
Cost of the General Election of 1880, 1791

Coutts, Francis Burdett Thomas Money: see Money-Coutts, Francis Burdett Thomas

Coux, Charles, comte de, 1787–1865, prof. at Université Catholique de Louvain. *Louvain Bibliography*.

Christian political economy, **DR** 58
Saint-Simonism, 79
Belgium and Holland, 115
Trade with France, 130
See: 82, 195

Cowan, Hugh, 1833–1898, advocate, sheriff-substitute. Grant.

Sheriffs and coroners, **ScotR** 575

Coward, Walter Scott Vidal, b.1836/37 inspector of schools, convert to Rome. Venn, *BMCat*.

Our educational outlook, **DR** 2368

Cowell, Edward Byles: see *Index*, I, 857.

Hafiz, the Persian poet, **FM** 3262, 4071
The rose garden of Sadi, 3450
Jámi, the Persian poet, 3540

Cowell, Sir John Clayton, 1832–1894, army officer. Boase.

Notice: **NC** 2041

Cowley, Abraham, 1618–1667, poet. *DNB*.

See: **FM** 927, 985

Cowley-Brown, George James: see *Index*, I, 858.

The abuse of tobacco, **NatR-II** 1445
Via media, 1486

Cowper, Francis Thomas de Grey, 7th Earl Cowper, 1834–1905, Lord-Lieut. of Ireland. *DNB*.

Desultory reflections of a Whig, **NC** 848
The Whigs, 875
Lord Melbourne, 947
Caesarism, 1076
What is a moderate Liberal to do? 1178
Liberal Unionists and coercion, 1400
Memoirs of the Duc de Persigny, 2912
Notice: 2587

Cowper, Countess Katrine Cecilia (Compton), 1845–1913, wife of Francis Thomas de Grey Cowper, q.v. *Complete Peerage*.

Experiences of work in East-End district, **NC** 1207
The decline of reserve among women, 1816
Realism of to-day, 2561

Cox, Ambrose Francis, b.1844/45. Foster.

Evolution and equality, **NatR-II** 1216

Cox, Edward, 1802–1856, pres. of St. Edmund's Coll., Ware. Newman, *L&D*, XI, index.

Sir Humphry Davy, **DR** 42 collab.
Trans: 153

Cox, Sir George William: see *Index*, I, 858.

The origin of the English, **FortR** 328
Historical credibility of Homeric poems, 400
Origin and character of Homeric poems, 493
Gladstone on historical credibility of *Iliad* and *Odyssey*, 620
Norman Conquest of England [by E. A. Freeman], 666

Homeric mythology and religion, **FM** 6240
English nation and the Zulu War, 6260
The migration of popular stories, 6306
Cabul, Candahar, and India, 6330
Horses and their feet, 6357
Perry's *Greek and Roman Sculpture,* 6502
The Public Worship Regulation Act, 6508

Cox, Harold, 1859–1936, economist, journalist. *DNB.*

How to save the rupee, **NatR-II** 1627

The eight hours question, **NC** 1726

Cox, John Charles, 1843–1919, divine, antiquary. *WWW.*

The power of the labourers, **FortR** 1070
On early licensing laws and customs, 2959

Cox, John George Snead, 1855–1939, ed. *Tablet,* barrister. *BMCat., WWW* under Snead-Cox.

The changed position of married women, **DR** 1870

Mr. Laurier and Manitoba, **NC** 3102
The outlook at Ottawa, 3500
French Canada and the Empire, 3748

Crabbe, George: see *Index,* I, 859.

Church restoration, **FM** 6041

Crackanthorpe, Blanche Alethea (Holt): see *Index,* I, 859.

The revolt of the daughters, **NC** 2503, 2542
Sex in modern literature, 2734

Crackanthorpe, Montague Hughes: see *Index,* I, 859.

The morality of married life, **FortR** 895
The new judicature, 1234
A true university for London, 3579

The nation before party, **NC** 303
The new departure in legal reform, 929
The future of the Unionists, 1622
The new national party, 1785
The Inns of Court as schools of law, 2310
New ways with old offenders, 2470
Can sentences be standardised? 3592

Cracroft, Bernard: see *Index,* I, 859.

Holman Hunt's "Isabel," **FortR** 509
Disraeli, the novelist, 522
Portraits in the Academy of 1869, 597, 606

?On popular lectures, **OxCam** 33, 42
Thackeray and Currer Bell, 34
The sceptic and the infidel, 55, 59

Craigie, Pearl Mary Teresa (Richards), 1867–1906, novelist. *WWW* under her pseud. "John Oliver Hobbes."

Epic and Romance [by W. P. Ker], **FortR** 3955

Craigie, Sir William Alexander, 1867–1957, philologist. *WWW, BMCat.*

Gaelic historical songs, **ScotR** 334

Barbour and Blind Harry as literature, 412
Three tales of the Fiann, 456
The Vision of Tundale, 489
Poetry of the Skalds, 541
Wyntoun's *Original Chronicle,* 566
The Ossianic ballads, 654
A father of history [Ari Thorgilsson, 1067–1148], 691
Trans: 701

Craik, Mrs.: see Mulock, Dinah Maria.

Craik, Sir Henry: see Index, I, 859.

A minister of education, **FortR** 2297

Crane, Walter, 1845–1915, artist. *DNB.*

English revival of decorative art, **FortR** 3303

Craufurd, John, 1780–1867, sec. to senate of Ionian islands. Boase under his son, Edward H. J. Craufurd.

The Ionian islands and their government, **FM** 3032

Craven, Augustus, 1806–1884, sec. of legation, Stuttgart. F.O. Lists/84 and 1901, M. C. Bishop, *Memoir of Mrs. Augustus Craven* (1894), I, 33.

Trans: **FortR** 1732

Craven, Florence; prob. Florence Champagné (Cotton) Craven, d.1899. Burke under her husband, Augustus William Craven.

Servants of the sick poor, **NC** 845

Crawford, Emily (Johnstone): see *Index,* I, 859, and II, App. A.

The life of Renan, **FortR** 3289
See: 2338

The new Chamber of Deputies, **NatR-II** 1485
Notes of a tour in north Italy, 1520

Crawford, Francis Marion: see *Index,* I, 859.

Roman life and character, **FortR** 2338

Crawford, George Morland Crawford, 1816–1885, Paris correspondent of *Daily News.* Boase.

Pasteur, **FortR** 2481

Crawford, James Hunter, divine, writer on Scottish flora and fauna. *LCCat.*

Forfarshire, **ScotR** 375
Fifeshire, 385
Perthshire, 439

Crawford, Virginia Mary (Smith) 1862/63–1948, social reformer. *LCCat., Tablet,* Oct. 30, 1948, p. 284. (See *Index,* I, 860.)

Co-operative village banks, **DR** 2596

Object lesson in Christian democracy, **FortR** 3744

Emile Verhaeren: the Belgian poet, 3881

Feminism in France, 3941

Maurice Maeterlinck, 3988

Crawfurd, John: see *Index,* I, 860.

Countries and languages, Oceanic region, **FQR** 337

Crawfurd, Oswald John Frederick: see *Index,* I, 860.

Poetry of the Renaissance in Portugal, **FortR** 949

Spring-time in rural Portugal, 2695

Summer-time in rural Portugal, 2719

Spanish and Portuguese bull-fighting, 2859

Folk-lore of Northern Portugal, 2889

The London stage, 2937

The London stage, 2964

The Ibsen question, 3080

The future of Portugal, 3111

Letter: 2638

Travel in Portugal, **NQM** 1, 8, 15, 22, 30, 41

Miss Olivia Tempest, 3

Horses and riders, 6

Giulio Vescona: a tale, 7

Splendide mendax: a tale, 10

Winter in Madeira, 13

On the stage: a story, 14

William Blake: artist, poet, mystic, 16

Wine and wine-merchants, 19

Beechwood revel: a story, 21

Birds and beasts in captivity, 25

English flower gardens, 40

A tragedy queen, 43

The fool of the family, 46

Trout fishing, 47

De Quincey, 52

Affonso Henriquez, rise of Portugal, 53

Lawn tennis, 70

Current literature and criticism, 74, 82, 90, 98

The story of Alix Fairford, 77

Ancient and medieval music, 79

Artemus Ward and humourists of America, 80

The tourist in Portugal, 86, 107, 113

Professor Hoffman's "folly," 97

The mystic; or, A journey to Edinburgh, 112

Country life in Portugal, 146

Note: 5

Slavery in East Central Africa, **NC** 1600

Nietzsche, 3731

Crawley, R.; possibly Richard Crawley, 1840–1893, scholar. *DNB.*

General Gordon, **NatR-II** 332

Creighton, Charles: see *Index,* I, 860.

Importation of disease, **FortR** 2064

"Vaccination" in the *Britannica,* **NatR-II** 877

Creighton, Louise (von Glehn), 1850–1936, historian. *WWW.*

The appeal against female suffrage, **NC** 1757

Law and the laundries, 3067 collab.

Crespi, Alfred John Henry: see *Index,* I, 860, and *Med. WW/1915.*

Some curiosities of diet, **NatR-II** 825

Modern Birmingham, 861

Secular and honorary deacons, 901

The diet of great men, 1174

Odd foods, **ScotR** 289

The low death-rate, 386

Crewe-Milnes, Robert Offley Ashburton, 2nd Baron Houghton, 1858–1945. *DNB.*

Ireland unvisited, **NatR-II** 1741

Creyke, Caroline (Lawes-Wittewronge), d.1946, wife of Walter Pennington Creyke. Burke under Lawes.

The Rothamsted experiments, **NC** 2410

Sailing for ladies in Highland lochs, 2992

Skating on artificial ice, 3088

Fancy cycling for ladies, 3172

Voice culture, 3747

Crichton-Browne, Sir James, 1840–1938, physician, psychologist. *DNB* under Browne.

Handcraft, **NatR-II** 752

Crichton-Stuart, John Patrick, 3rd Marquis of Bute, 1847–1900, educator, proprietor of *ScotR. DNB.*

The prophecies of St. Malachi, **DR** 1987

Ancient Celtic Latin hymns, **ScotR** 11

M. Renan's *Souvenirs,* 41

The new light upon St. Patrick, 61

Patmos, 83

Christian monuments of Athens, 102

The Scottish peerage, 117

The Bayreuth festival, 150
St. Magnus of the Orkneys, 159 collab.
Coronation of Charles II, 175
Coronation of Charles I, 183
Earliest Scottish coronations, 192
Giordano Bruno before the Venetian In-
quisition, 213, 221
Last resting place of St. Andrew, 234
Parliament in Scotland, 262
David, Duke of Rothesay, 355
Brendan's fabulous voyage, 400
Alleged haunting of B——— House, 661
collab.
Note: ?161
Notices: 172, 237, 273
Trans: 34, 42, 127, 141, 149, 158, 166, 169,
232, 243, 251, 260, 613, 631.

Cripps, Charles Alfred, 1852–1941, 1st Baron
Parmoor, lawyer, politician. *DNB.*

Competition and free trade, **NatR-II** 643
Free trade and the economists, 694
To Lord Pembroke [on free trade], 718
Selfishness in competition, 850
The socialist reaction, 1117
Agriculture and economics, 1393

Crispi, Francesco: see *Index*, I, 860, and *DEI.*

The Dual and the Triple Alliance, **NC** 3192

Crofton, Sir Walter Frederic: see *Index*, I,
861.

On prisons, **FM** 5389

Croke, William J. D., b.1869, Canadian-born
scholar who lived at Rome. *Catholic
World*, 66 (Jan. 1898), 571–573.

National establishments of England in
mediaeval Rome, **DR** 2632, 2644

Croker, Thomas Crofton, 1798–1854, Irish
antiquary. *DNB.*

Specimens of Irish minstrelsy, **FM** 22, 36,
65, 90, 586
Ensign O'Donoghue's "first love," 265
Ensign O'Donoghue's first battle, 457
The last duel I had a hand in, 588
Ensign O'Donoghue's last communication,
645
Dulce domum, 656
First man I was near seeing hanged, 704
Signor Paganini and Ensign O'Donoghue,
741
Country quarters, 784
Return from leave, 825
Courts-martial and cat-o'-nine-tails, 942
Defects in military education, 954

Sandhurst College, Woolwich Academy,
979
Russel's lark in the Bight of Benin, 1006
?The Irish Insurrection of 1803, 1011
collab.?
Embarking for the colonies, 1053
Ensign O'Donoghue's packet from Belgium,
1189, 1224, 1228
A walk from London to Fulham, 2017,
2032, 2044, 2054
The Pryor's Bank, Fulham, 2133
Pyrenees in the autumn of 1850, 2818,
2872
Letter: 676

Crolly, George, 1813–1878, prof. at Maynooth. Healy, *Maynooth.*

Maitland's *Dark Ages*, **DR** 348
Life and writings of Miss [Frances] Brown,
363
The ballad poetry of Ireland, 395
Le Prêtre, la Femme, et la Famille [by T.
Michelet], 400
The great Irish insurrection, 425
McCabe's *Catholic History of England*, 448
History and antiquities of Ireland, 487
Adventures in Mexico, 499
Lord Castlereagh, 530
Irish factions, parsons, and landlords, 567
Nineveh and its Remains [by Layard], 585
Monks and schoolmen of the middle ages,
621
Wordsworth's life and writings, 642
Worsaae's *Account of Danes, Norwegians
in England, Scotland, Ireland*, 656
Jeffrey's *Life and Correspondence*, 666
Lord John Russell's *Memoirs of Moore*,
691
Nineveh and Babylon, 706
Lord Holland's *Memoirs*, 736
Wilberforce on the Church, 747
Mrs. Jameson's *Sisters of Charity*, 767
Sidney Smith, 778
Mrs. Fitzherbert's marriage, 795
Prescott's *Philip II*, 805
Andersen's German stories, 825
Obstetric morality, 867
The rise and fall of Jansenism, 905
Miracles, 942
See: 275, 636, 780, 812, 917

Croly, George: see *Index*, I, 862.

Chateaubriand, *On English Literature*,
FQR 426

Cromie, Charles Francis, 1858–1907, army
officer. *WWW.*

Jomini, Moreau, and Vandamme, **FortR**
1749

Crompton, Henry: see *Index*, I, 864.

Arbitration and conciliation, **FortR** 593
Class legislation, 925
Sedition, 941
The government and class legislation, 964
The workmen's victory, 1192
The reform of the magistracy, 1209
Mr. Cross and the magistracy, 1283

Cromwell, Oliver, 1599–1658, the Protector. *DNB*.

See: **FM** 2392

Crookes, Sir William, 1832–1919, scientist. *DNB*.

Possibilities of electricity, **FortR** 3174

Another lesson from the radiometer, **NC** 59

Crooklands, Joseph

Italian disunion, **FortR** 3654

Cropley, John, of Walthamstow.

Letters: **NatR-II** 734, 865

Croskery, Thomas: see *Index*, I, 864, under Croskerry (which is a misspelling) and *DNB*.

The Irish Roman Catholic laity, **FM** 5357
Ulster and its people, 5845

Crosland, Newton, 1819–1899, misc. writer. Boase.

The astronomy of the future, **FM** 5870

Cross, John Walter: see *Index*, I, 864, and *Times*, Nov. 4, 1924, p. 19a.

Railways in America, **FM** 5435
Agricultural labourers' emigration, 5507

Dante and the "new Reformation," **NC** 1834
The New World [America], 2016
Bimetallism, 2767
British trade in 1898, 3473

Cross, Richard Assheton: see *Index*, I, 864.

Homes of the poor in London, **NC** 750, 954
City of London livery companies, 1014
Housing the poor, 1142

Crosse, Andrew, 1784–1855, electrician. *DNB*.

Letter: **FM** 1013

Crosskey, Henry William: see *Index*, I, 864.

Disestablishment and disendowment, **FortR** 1368

Crosthwaite, Charles, 1806–1892, vicar general of Kildare. Boase.

Bishop of Liverpool's call for union, **NatR-II** 779
Denominational education for Ireland, 804
Rome's demands as to university education, 897
Spoilers of churches in Wales, 1142
Letters: 472, 482, 531, 550, 887, 909

Crouch, Archer Philip: see *Index*, I, 865.

Dahomey and the French, **NC** 1943
The bombardment of Iquique, 2061
The world beneath the ocean, 3034

Crow, Francis Edward, 1863–1939, foreign service. *WWW*.

English enterprise in Persia, **NC** 3057

Crowe, Sir Joseph Archer: see *Index*, I, 865.

Continental and English painting, **NC** 1852
Niccola Pisano, 2920
Fra Filippo Lippi, 3005

Crowest, Frederick James: see *Index*, I, 865.

Wanted: an English musical style, **NatR-II** 559
English opera *in nubibus*, 771
The music of the British army, 856

Crozier, John Beattie, 1849–1921, Canadian misc. writer. *WWW*.

A modern view of Jesus Christ, **FortR** 3851
Letter: 4210

Cruikshank, Alexander Patrick John, 1830–1900, R.C. priest. Gorman.

Suppression of Italian monasteries, **DR** 1279
Rome, 1299
Devotion to St. Joseph, 1355
Saints' lives as spiritual reading, 1391
Middle Ages in Church history, 1409
?Italian church architecture, 1422
Convent Life in England, 1439
?Pilgrimage and Paray-le-Monial, 1444
?Taine's *History of English Literature,* 1454
Notices: 1347, 1380, 1407, 1434, 1452, 1470

Cruttwell, Charles Thomas, 1847–1911, divine historian. *DNB*.

The pastor's duty, burial clubs, **NatR-II** 838

Cuffe, Lady Kathleen Mary Alexina, d.1938, wife of Sir Thomas Edward Milborne-Swinnerton-Pilkington. Burke under her husband.

A reply from the daughters, **NC** 2544

Cullimore, Isaac: see *Index*, I, 865.

Egyptian antiquities, **FQR** 294

Erection of the Theban temple of Ammon, **FM** 633
Noah's journal of the ark, 667
Dr. Young and Mrs. Belzoni [on Egyptian sculpture], 695
Archaeographia: the Jewish theocracy, 947
Exodi of the Jews and Greeks, 1005
The pyramids, 1120, 1138, 1148
The trinity of the gentiles, 1336, 1352, 1362

Cullinan, Maxwell Cormac, 1843–1884, prof. of Latin, Univ. Coll. London. Venn, Boase.

Trinity College, Dublin, **FortR** 722
Virgilius the enchanter, 867

Culme-Seymour, Sir Michael, 1836–1920, naval officer. *WWW* under Seymour.

The Behring Sea question, **NC** 2377

Cumby, William Pryce, naval officer at Battle of Trafalgar. *Navy List*/17.

The battle of Trafalgar, **NC** 3556

Cumming, Alexander Neilson: see *Index*, I, 865.

The Scottish Church question, **NatR-II** 347
America and protection, 1079
Scotland and her home rulers, 1199

Cumming, Constance F. Gordon: see Gordon-Cumming.

Cumming, John, 1807–1881, Scotch divine, controversialist. *DNB*.

?Statistics of Popery, **FM** 1300, 1311
?Scotch church matters, 1536
?Bonaventure's psalter, or Romish idolatry, 1601
?Spiritual perils of British travellers [in Rome], 2083

Cunliffe-Owen, Philip Frederick, apparently known as Fritz, 1855–1926, diplomat, journalist. *DAB* and *AmerWW*/1919, where he is said to have written for *NC* and *FortR*.

The future of Switzerland, **FortR** 1746
Russian nihilism, **NC** 391

Cunningham, Allan: see *Index*, I, 865.

Lay Sermons: by the Ettrick Shepherd [James Hogg], **FM** 708
Rustic controversies, in 9 installments from 1498 to 1628
?Doings in fresco, 1699 collab.?

Cunningham, Sir Henry Stewart: see *Index*, I, 866.

Wheat and tares, in 8 installments from **FM** 3933 to 4013
Late laurels, in 11 installments from 4314 to 4408
The Irish church, 4451

Cunningham, Percy Scudamore, army officer; served in Madras. *Army List*/76, pp. 42, 481, 510.

Remarks on modern warfare, **FM** 5816

Cunningham, Peter, 1816–1869, critic. *DNB*.

?Doings in fresco, **FM** 1699 collab.?
Wilkie and his works, 1729
Francis Chantrey and Allan Cunningham, 1823
A fine day in Fleet Street, 1892
A fine day in the Strand, 1921
A fine day in Piccadilly, 1969
Campbelliana, 1981
A fine day at Stratford-upon-Avon, 1996, 2012
A fine day in the Temple, 2022
British sculpture, 2030
Early English actresses, 2072
Old London signs, 2136
Dining out, 2183
Old London cries, 2288
Chronicles of Charter House, 2300

Curley, Edwin A. *BMCat*.

Exodus of agricultural labourers, **FortR** 1043

Currey, Fanny W. Allibone.

The Irish question, **NatR-II** 1156

Currie, Bertram Wodehouse, 1827–1896, banker. Boase.

The currency question, **NatR-II** 1734

Currie, Sir Edmund Hay, 1834–1913, chairman of London Hosp. *WWW*.

The working of "The People's Palace" [low-income club], **NC** 1835

Currie, Lady Mary Montgomerie (Lamb), 1843–1905, writer of fiction; used pseud. "Violet Fane"; wife of Henry Sydenham Singleton and in 1894 of Philip Henry Wodehouse, 1st Baron Currie. *DNB, WWW.*

Note: **FortR** 2151

Two moods of a man: by a woman, **NC** 2161

A Turkish "young pretender" [Prince Jemshid], 3094

Curteis, George Herbert: see *Index,* I, 866.

Christian agnosticism, **NC** 967

Curtis, George Byron, 1843–1907, journalist. *WWW.*

Will the new rules work? **FortR** 1982

The future of Whiggism, **NatR-II** 51
Some facts about redistribution, 118
Lord Winchilsea's proposal, 1377

Curtois, Margaret Anne, writer of fiction. *BMCat.*

Village ethics, **NatR-II** 919

Curzon, George Nathaniel: see *Index,* I, 866.

Conservatives on themselves, **FortR** 2310
Salvation by torture at Kairwan, 2609
The cloister in Cathay, 2715
A visit to Bokhara the Noble, 2786
From a diary on the Karun River, 2936, 2950
Politics and progress in Siam, 3347
Letter: 3074
The conservatism of Young Oxford, **NatR-II** 180
Poetry, politics and conservatism, 383

Conservatism and young conservatives, 520
A purified British senate: the "status quo," 697
Reconstruction of the House of Lords, 700
Our true policy in India, 839
The destinies of the Far East, 1424
The referendum, 1550
The "scientific frontier" as accomplished fact, **NC** 1564
Fluctuating frontier of Russia in Asia, 1664
The Siamese boundary question, 2422
India between two fires 2434
The House of Lords: unfair penalty on peers, 2553 collab.

Curzon, Robert Nathaniel Cecil George, 15th Baron Zouche, 1851–1914, army officer. Burke.

The business of the House of Lords, **NC** 294

Cusack, Mary Francis, 1830–1899, Irish R.C. nun. Allibone, *LCCat.*

Woman's place in creation, **FM** 5516

Cust, Arthur, 1842–1911, schoolmaster, mountaineer. Venn.

The Italian Lakes to the Rhone Valley, **FM** 6182

Cust, Henry John Cockayne, 1861–1917, politician, journalist. *DNB.*

Tory press and Tory party, **NatR-II** 1428
The genesis of Germany, 2329

Cuthell, Mrs. Edith E., misc. writer. *Yearbook*/1922.

Wanted, nurses for India, **NatR-II** 1154

D

Dale, J. A.

The Ruskin Hall movement, **FortR** 4414 collab.

Dale, Robert William: see *Index,* I, 867.

The disestablishment movement, **FortR** 1236
Liberal candidates at the next election, 1593
George Dawson: politician, lecturer, preacher, **NC** 65
Impressions of America, 146, 163, 176, 196, 233

Cardinal Manning's demand [on school rates], 805
The Cardinal [Manning] and the schools, 833

Dalgairns, John Dobrée: see *Index,* I, 867.

German mystics of the fourteenth century, **DR** 866
Plummer's translation of Döllinger on the Popes, 1394
Scholastic to modern philosophy: Hutton and Martineau, 1427

St. Philip Neri and his times, **Ram** 3, 18, 31, 70, 83

Dalgleish, Walter Scott, 1834–1897, editor. *Boase.*

"The Dry Bones of Popular Education," **FortR** 1852

Scotland's version of Home Rule, **NC** 802

Dallas, Eneas Sweetland: see *Index*, I, 867.

La Rochefoucauld, **NC** 551

Dallinger, William Henry: see *Index*, I, 867.

Why I shall vote for the Unionist candidate, **NC** 2253

D'Alton, Edward Alfred, 1860–1941, R.C. priest. *WWW, BMCat.*

Irish Church from Danish to Anglo-Norman invasion, **DR** 2732

Dalton, John, 1814–1874, R.C. priest, scholar. *DNB.*

Orthography of St. Teresa's name, **Ram** 544
Letters: 387, 563, 738, 753

Dalton, John Neale, 1839–1931, divine. *Venn.*

The federal states of the world, **NC** 1016

Daly, Edward D., writer on temperance. *BMCat.*

The drink question, **FortR** 4186
Legal advantages of being a drunkard, 4304

Daniell, Clarmont John: see *Index*, I, 868, and II, App. A.

Bimetallism: fixed ratio, **NatR-II** 475

Daniell, Francis Henry Blackburne, 1845–1921, barrister. *Venn.*

Ireland: Redistribution Bill, **NatR-II** 281

Danjou, Jean Louis Félix, 1812–1866, French musicologist. *LCCat., Grand Larousse.*

Original Antiphonary of St. Gregory, **Ram** 33

Danyell, Arthur Johnson, writer on Italy. *BMCat.*

Letters: **NatR-II** 1024, 1069

Darling, Charles John, 1st Baron Darling, 1849–1936, judge. *DNB.*

Infirma vincula caritatis [England's reputation abroad], **NatR-II** 1858

Darlow, Thomas Herbert, 1858–1927, divine. *WWW.*

Weakness of Congregationalism: seen from the pulpit, **NC** 1946

Darmesteter, Agnes Mary Frances (Robinson): see *Index*, I, 868, and II, App. A.

The convent of Helfta, **FortR** 2534
Valentine Visconti, 2572, 2584
The flight of Piero De' Medici, 2645
Workmen of Paris in 1390 and 1890, 2970
Life in France in the fourteenth century, 3012, 3020, 3082, 3118, 3189
Letter: 2655

Mary Schönewald; a study in prophecy, **FM** 6441
Goneril; a story, 6527

The novelists of Naples, **NatR-II** 460

Darwin, Ellen Wordsworth (Crofts), d.1903, lecturer at Newnham Coll. Camb.; second wife of Sir Francis Darwin. *DNB*/1930 under her husband.

British housekeeping, **NatR-II** 1822

Domestic service, **NC** 1919

Darwin, Sir George Howard: see *Index*, I, 868.

The theory of exchange value, **FortR** 1127
Marriages between first cousins, 1170
Earthquakes, 2563

Darwin, Leonard, 1850–1943, army officer. *WWW.*

The Niger territories, **NatR-II** 1595
Is our military administration hopeless? 1736
British expansion in West Africa, 2339

Dás, Devendra Nath, B.A. Cambridge, 1882. *Venn, BMCat.* under Devendranatha Raya.

The Hindu widow, **NC** 1317

Dasent, Arthur Irwin, 1859–1939, civil servant. *WWW, Landed Gentry.*

Frenchman's impressions of London, **NatR-II** 895

Dasent, Sir George Webbe: see *Index*, I, 868.

Samuel Wilberforce, **FortR** 1995

Dasent, Sir George Webbe (*continued*)
Edward Bulwer, Lord Lytton, 2128

The story of free trade, **FM** 2866

Dasent, John Bury, 1806–1888, barrister.
Boase.

Adventures in the South Seas [Melville's *Omoo*], **DR** 483
The Eastern Archipelago and the Rajah of Sarawak, 504

Daubeny, Charles Giles Bridle, 1795–1867, scientist. *DNB.*

Mineral waters, **LR (1829)** 13

Dauney, William: see *Index*, I, 869.

Carl Maria von Weber, **FQR** 160
Paganini, 179

Daunt, William Joseph O'Neill: see *Index*, I, 869, and Boase.

Ireland under legislative union, **DR** 1854
How the Union robs Ireland, 1867
Ireland in the time of Swift, 1889
Tithe rent-charge in Ireland, 1982

Daveluy, Mario Nicolas Antonio, 1818–1866, French missionary in Corea. *EUI.*

Corea, **Ram** 15, 28

Davenport, W. Bromley: see Bromley-Davenport, William.

Davey, Richard Patrick Boyle, b.1848, journalist. *WW/1913.*

Turkey and Armenia, **FortR** 3598
Muhammedan women in Turkey, 3665
The sultan and his harem, 3727
The sultan and his priests, 3740
Havana and the Havanese, 4114
A new novelist: Albert du Bois, 4238
Cardinals, consistories, and conclaves, 4274
A few French facts, 4495

Woman's life in old Italy, **NatR-II** 1195
Beginnings of the drama in America, 1321
The boyhood and youth of Columbus, 1344

The decline of the art of singing, **NC** 3482

Davids, Thomas William Rhys: see *Index*, I, 869.

Buddah's first sermon, **FortR** 1653

Davidson, James, 1862–1937, newspaper editor in Glasgow. Metcalfe addresses; *Aberdeen Graduates,* I and III.

New light on Burns, **ScotR** 559

Davidson, Thomas, 1840–1900, educator. Boase.

Antonio Rosmini, **FortR** 1855
Philosophic movement in Roman Church, 1926

Davidsson, Ólafur, 1862–1903, native of Iceland. *BMCat.,* Harvard Coll. Lib. Cat.

Folk-lore of Icelandic fishes, **ScotR** 701

Davies, George Jennings, 1826–1884, divine. Foster, *LCCat.*

Peasantry of the south of England, **FM** 5423, 5433, 5446

Davies, Harriette Brooke

A kitchen college, **NC** 1427

Davies, John Llewelyn: see *Index*, I, 869.

Christian theory of duty, universal morality, **FortR** 603
The higher life, 2672
Letter: 2647
Notice: 654

?Frederick Denison Maurice, **FM** 3204

Erastianism, **NC** 3489

Davies, Joseph J. *BMCat.*

Electoral blackmailing, **NatR-II** 1051
May Statute Fairs in East Anglia, doomed? 1242

Davies, M. Rees: see *Index*, I, 870.

A threatened city [Pekin], **FortR** 3576
The awakening of China, 3700

Davies, Theophilus Harris, d.1898, English merchant in Hawaii. *LCCat.,* R. S. Kuykendall, *The Hawaiian Kingdom, 1778–1854,* Honolulu, 1938, p. 302.

The Hawaiian revolution, **NC** 2394

Davies, William: see *Index*, I, 870.

Artist life in Rome, **FortR** 2454

Davis, Sir John Francis: see *Index*, I, 870.

Horae Senicae, **FM** 1173 collab.

Davis, William John, b.1848, alive in 1914, inspector of factories. William A. Dalley, *Life Story of W. J. Davis,* Birmingham, 1914.

The ideas of the new voters, **FortR** 2269

Davison, James William, 1813–1885, music critic. *DNB.*

National English airs, **DR** 231

Davitt, Michael: see *Index,* I, 870, 1194.

The Parnell Commission, **NC** 1836
Ireland: retiring the landlord garrison, 1871
The latest Midlothian campaign, 1963
The Canadian North-West, 2196
The priest in politics, 2343
Fabian fustian [and Home Rule], 2486
The evicted tenants problem, 2557
Criminal and prison reform, 2670

Dawkins, Sir Clinton Edward: see *Index,* I, 870.

The German abroad, **NatR-II** 295

Dawkins, Sir William Boyd: see *Index,* I, 870.

Northern range of Basques, **FortR** 1083
The settlement of Wales, 3276

Civilisation in Europe in prehistoric times, **FM** 4876

Dawson, Charles, Lord Mayor of Dublin. *BMCat.*

The Irish franchise, **FortR** 1670

Dawson, Douglas Frederick Rawdon, 1854–1933, army officer. *WWW.*

Sir Herbert Stewart's desert march, **NC** 1203

Dawson, George Mercer, 1849–1901, geologist. *DNB.*

Canada, mining investment, **NatR-II** 1926

Dawson, William: see *Index,* I, 871.

British merchant seamen, **FM** 4732, 4940, 5013
American torpedo warfare, 4923
Future naval battles, 5226
Modern seamanship, 5267
Guns and armour, 5403
British merchant seamen, 5461
The naval war game, 5477
British merchant seamen, 5751

Dawson, William Harbutt, 1860–1948, editor, critic. *WWW.*

Bismarck and Prussian monarchy, **FortR** 3638
Bismarck, 4176
Society's duty to the tramp, 4546

The German elections, **NatR-II** 2195
Letter: 1256

Day, William Henry, 1823–1908, trainer and breeder of race horses. *DNB.*

Turf reform, **FortR** 2832
Our national pastime, 2869
Evil of betting and how to eradicate it, 2928

Deane, Anthony Charles, 1870–1946, divine, journalist. *WWW.*

Retain capital punishment? **NatR-II** 1131
Greek at the universities and schools, 1220
Curates, 1980
The "religious" novel, 2149

Religion of undergraduate, **NC** 2825, 2851
The quantity and quality of the clergy, 3490
The churchman's politics, 3578

Dechamps, Albert

Letter from M. Albert Dechamps to Rev. F. Gratry, **DR** 1527

Decle, Lionel, 1859–1907, explorer, journalist. *WW/1907, LCCat.*

The Fashoda question, **FortR** 4192
The Tanganika railway, 4221

Two years in Rhodesia, **NatR-II** 1878

De Cosson, Emilius Albert, 1850–1889, army officer. *Hill.*

The future of the Soudan, **FortR** 2228

King John of Abyssinia, **NC** 984

de Fonblanque: see under Fonblanque.

Delaforce, Esther. *BMCat.*

Women's rights, **NatR-II** 919

de la Ramée, Marie Louise: see *Index,* I, 871.

Blind guides of Italy [destroyers of landmarks], **FortR** 3167
Death and pity, 3204
Conscription, 3248
The sins of society, 3301
Poor Abel! 3354
Le Secret du Précepteur, 3374
The Italy of to-day, 3467
L'uomo fatale [Francesco Crispi], 3478
L'Impérieuse Bonté, 3500
The legislation of fear, 3558
The Italian awakening, 3785
A highway robber [the tramway], 3828

de la Ramée, Marie Louise (*continued*)
Marquis di Rudini and Italian politics, 3849
The genius of D'Annunzio, 3928
The twentieth Italian parliament, 3953
Georges Darien, 4001
Felice Cavallotti, 4104
The misgovernment of Italy, 4134
Canicide, 4185
Unwritten literary laws, 4364
Letter: 2638
Note: 4254

Obliteration of Florence, **NatR-II** 1074

Birds and their persecutors, **NC** 2685
Mr. Irving on the art of acting, 2749
The ugliness of modern life, 2863
The quality of mercy, 2977
Italian novels of Marion Crawford, 3196
Notice: 3019

Delbrück, Hans, 1848–1929, German writer on politics. *Grosse Brockhaus.*

Rosebery: from a German point of view, **FortR** 3574

De Leon, Edwin: see *Index,* I, 871, and II, App. A.

The Southern States since the War, **FM** 5578, 5593, 5614
The Bayou Tèche [Louisiana], 5631
Notes on the Turk, 5877
How I introduced telephone into Egypt, 6551

Delille, Edward: see *Index,* I, 871.

Parisian hells [gambling halls], **FortR** 2432
Oliver Wendell Holmes, 2499
"Chez Pousset": a literary evening, 3033
The poet Verlaine, 3054
Baudelaire the man, 3098
Card-sharping in Paris, 3103
M. Maurice Barrès, 3127
Pierre Loti, 3179
M. Paul Bourget, 3211
Guy de Maupassant, 3233

French authors on each other, **NC** 2125
The French newspaper press, 2184
The American newspaper press, 2237

De Lisle, Ambrose Lisle March Phillipps, 1809–1878, Catholic writer. *DNB.*

Religious movement [Oxford Movement], **DR** 298

Trans: **Ram** 33

De Lisle, Edwin Joseph Lisle March Phillipps, 1852–1920, civil servant. *WWW.*

The evolutionary hypothesis, **DR** 2149

Dell, Robert Edward, 1865–1940, Catholic writer on politics. *LCCat.; Times,* July 22, 1940, p. 6f.

The case of Dr. Mivart, **NC** 3640
Mr. Wilfrid Ward's apologetics, 3686

Del Mar, Alexander, 1836–1926, American monetary expert. *Amer. WWW.*

Historical aspect of monetary question, **FortR** 3626

Deloncle, Antoine Benoît François, 1856–1922, politician. *DBF.*

France and Egypt, **NatR-II** 1862

Delplace, Louis, 1843–1928, Jesuit historian. Seyn.

Wycliffe and teaching concerning the Primacy, **DR** 1898

De Morgan, Augustus: see *Index,* I, 871.

Theory of probabilities, **DR** 38, 60
Legislation for life assurance, 185
Jones on value of annuities, 225
The Elements of Euclid, 235
Weights, measures, and coinage, 255
Science and rank, 272
Baily's repetition of Cavendish experiment on mean density of earth, 367
Speculators and speculations, 384
Book-keeping, 398
Mathematical bibliography, 423
On helps to calculation, 447

Dempster, Charlotte Louisa Hawkins: see *Index,* I, 871.

Pasteur and hydrophobia, **NatR-II** 468

Dendy, H.: see Bosanquet, Helen (Dendy).

Denison, Edmund Beckett: see Beckett, Sir Edmund.

Denison, George Taylor, 1839–1925, Canadian army officer. *WWW.*

Present situation of England, **NC** 3217

Denman, Thomas, 3rd Baron Denman, 1874–1954, army officer. *WWW.*

The future of mounted infantry, **NC** 3615

Dennis, John: see *Index,* I, 872.

Our rural poor, **FortR** 27
Surrey, 66
New Aldine edition of Cowper, 147
Robertson of Brighton, 156
Devonshire, 286

Westmoreland and Cumberland, 331
Notices: 11, 20, 39, 50, 82, 105, 124, 161,
192, 212, 243, 253, 264, 281, 298, 306,
315, 343, 369

Alexander Pope, **FM** 5083
John Dryden, 6483
Charles Lamb and his friends, 6511
Literary criticism and biography, 6550

The art of essay writing, **NatR-II** 54
Robert Southey, 536

Dennistoun, James: see *Index*, I, 872.

Records of early Italian art, **FQR** 814
Pictures and picture-dealing, 825
Foreign correspondence, 848
Recently discovered fresco attributed to
Raffael, 887

Dent, Clinton Thomas: see *Index*, I, 872.

Can Mount Everest be ascended? **NC** 2297

Depasse, Hector, 1842–1911, publicist, statesman. *DBF.*

Secret societies of France, **FortR** 1985
Gambetta, 2003 collab.
A year after Gambetta's death, 2112

Depew, Chauncey Mitchell, 1834–1928,
American railroad executive. *WWW.*

Free trade in the United States, **NC** 2536

De Saintville, Alexandre Dumenil, Frenchman
living in London. R.L.F.

Monuments of Nineveh, **DR** 506

Desart, Countess Ellen Odette (Bischoffsheim),
1857–1933, opponent of women's suff-
rage. *WWW.*

In defence of worldly mothers, **NatR-II**
2011
Women, 2041
Tsar v. Jew, **NC** 2059

Desjacques, François, 1831–1890, prof., journalist. *DBF.*

Recent commentaries on the Syllabus, **DR**
1622
?Conflict between Church and State, 1645

Desmoulins, Auguste, 1823–1892, French socialist. *DBF.*

Paris workmen and the Commune, **FortR**
807

De Splenter, Bruno, 1835–1899, teacher, R.C.
priest. Boase.

Notice: **DR** 2373

D'Esterre-Keeling,   Elsa,   1857/58–1935,
teacher, lecturer. *WW*/1900; *Times,* Jan.
15, 1935, p. 14e.

A handful of Irish books, **DR** 2540
Charlotte Brontë and her circle, 2575
Bards of the Gael and Gall [translations by
George Sigerson], 2640

Des Voeux, Sir George William: see *Index*, I,
873.

A letter to the Opium Commission, **NC**
2533
Delusions about tropical cultivation, 2604
The connection of England with Newfoundland, 3512

Devas, Charles Stanton, 1848–1906, political
economist. *WWW.*

Christian charity and political economy,
DR 1608, 1618, 1637
Relief of poor in early Church, 1664
Decay of British Constitution, 2008
What to do with the landowners, 2031
Shakespeare as an economist, 2048
An olive branch on state socialism, 2111
The dock labourers' strike, 2196
English Catholics and the social question,
2261
Notes on social science, 2319, 2344, 2370,
2397
Shibboleths [by W. S. Lilly], 2354
Catholic Socialism, 2515
Christian democracy, 2613
Notices of Catholic continental periodicals:
2080, 2159, 2187
Notices: 2054, 2092, 2104, 2131, 2158,
2186, 2225, 2594, 2606, 2628, 2638, 2674

De Vere, Aubrey Thomas: see *Index*, I, 873.

The worship of the saints, **DR** 689
Longfellow's works, 697
The philosophy of the rule of faith, 712
The plague of controversy, 731
Irish national education, 940
Life of St. Aloysius Gonzaga, 1206
Proportionate representation, 1994
Religious problem of the XIXth century,
and *Lux Mundi* [by Charles Gore], 2351

Ireland's sins and hopes, **FM** 2741
Longfellow, 3080
Letter: 4663

Subjective difficulties in religion, **NC** 856
Archbishop Trench's poems, 1561
Why I shall vote for the Unionist candidate,
2256
Some recollections of Cardinal Newman,
2985

De Vere, Aubrey Thomas (*continued*)
The Pilgrim, **Ram** 462
The counter theory, latest development of Puseyism, 533
Archdeacon Wilberforce on Holy Eucharist, 557
Christian and pagan Rome, 589
Chinese civilisation and Christian charity, 595
The Life of Dr. Doyle, 1099, 1109

De Vere, Sir Stephen Edward: see *Index*, I, 873.

A short tract upon oaths, **NC** 1123

Jesuit discoverers of the Mississippi, **Ram** 515

De Vere, William Amelius Aubrey, 10th Duke of St. Albans, 1840–1898, army officer. Burke.

The House of Lords and the country, **NC** 1020
Jamaica resurgens, 2242

Devereux, Humphrey Bohun: see *Index*, I, 873, and II, App. A.

Judicial system of British India, **FQR** 318

de Vesci, John Robert William, 4th Viscount de Vesci, 1844–1903, army officer. Burke.

The three "F's." [on the land question], **NC** 537
"Hibernia Pacata" [on union with Ireland], 2131
The militia ballot, 3601

Devey, Joseph, 1815–1897, barrister. Boase.

[Charles] Churchill, **NatR-II** 359

De Villiers, Melius, 1849–1938, Chief Justice, Orange Free State. Rosenthal.

Letter: **NatR-II** 2155

Why South Africa can wait, **NC** 2980
England's advance north of Orange River, 3079

Devine, Pius, R.C. priest.

John MacHale, Archbishop of Tuam, **DR** 2283

De Viti de Marco, Antonio, 1858–1943, economist, politician. *DEI, LCCat.*

The insurrections in Italy, **NatR-II** 2197

The political situation in Italy, **NC** 2815

Dewey, Stoddard, 1853–1933, newspaper correspondent. *Amer. WWW.*

Letter: **FortR** 3454

De Windt, Harry, 1856–1933, traveller. *N.Y. Times*, Dec. 2, 1933, p. 13iv, *BMCat.* (See *Index*, I, 1144, under Windt, Harry de.)

The Island of Sakhalin, **FortR** 3956

De Winton, Sir Francis Walter, 1835–1901, S. African administrator. *DNB.*

England and Germany in East Africa, **NC** 1865

De Worms, Henry, Baron Pirbright, 1840–1903, politician. *DNB.*

The ruin of the West Indies, **NatR-II** 2097

Dibdin, Sir Lewis Tonna: see *Index*, I, 874.

Letters: **FortR** 4351, 4406

The London livery companies, **NatR-II** 296

Overthrow of the Church in Wales, **NC** 2609

Dicey, Albert Venn: see *Index*, I, 874.

Legal etiquette, **FortR** 429
The legal boundaries of liberty, 465
Louis Napoleon: 1851 and 1873, 924
Two acts of Union, 1828
How is the law to be enforced in Ireland? 1854
The Reform Act of 1832, 1990
The Church of England, 2042

See: **FM** 5014

Alexis de Tocqueville, **NatR-II** 1459
The referendum, 1549
The constitutional question: Unionists and the House of Lords, 1674
Lord Pembroke, 1961

Dicey, Edward James Stephen: see *Index*, I, 874.

American feeling towards England, **FortR** 599
Paris after the peace, 774
Republican defeat in the United States, 1111
The copyright question, 1226
Antonio Scialoja, 1630
The plea of a malcontent liberal, 2371
Russia and the Balkan peninsula, 3578
The story of Stambouloff's fall, 3695
The isolation of England, 3769
Russia and Bulgaria, 3795

Dilke, Sir Charles Wentworth (*continued*)
Present position of European politics, 2546, 2557, 2567, 2578, 2587, 2597
The British Army, in 7 installments from 2648 to 2704, all collab.
Baluch and Afghan frontiers of India, 2798, 2807
The British army in 1891, 3089
The French armies, 3142
The Conservative foreign policy, 3163
An Australian view of India, 3294
The Uganda problem, 3319
Letter: 3154
See: 2176

Dilke, Lady Emilia Frances (Strong), 1840–1904: see *Index*, I, 1044, under Pattison, Emilia Frances.

Nicolas Poussin, **FortR** 857
France under Richelieu, 2395
France under Colbert, 2422
Royal Academy of Painting and Sculpture in France, 2531
The great missionary success, 2822
Benefit societies and trades unions for women, 2835
The coming elections in France, 2866
Art-teaching and technical schools, 2919
Trades unionism among women, 3081 collab.
Women and the Royal Commission, 3138
Mulready, 3264
The industrial position of women, 3420
Letter: 2655

Dilke, Margaret Mary (Smith), d.1914, wife of Ashton Wentworth Dilke. Burke.

The appeal against female suffrage, **NC** 1733

Dillon, Edward, c.1850–1914, art expert. *Times*, June 2, 1914, p. 10e.

A neglected sense [smell], **NC** 2558

Dillon, Emile Joseph: see *Index*, I, 875.

?Some truths about Russia, **FortR** 2861
Russian characteristics, 2871, 2881, 2892, 2902, 2921
Russian prisons, 2966
Mickiewicz, national poet of Poland, 2977
Armenia and the Armenian people, 2982
Sexual morality in Russia, 2990
The Jews in Russia, 2997
Finland, 3032
Russian finance, 3040
The Russian censure, 3086
The demoralisation of Russia, 3133
Famine in Russia, 3143
Cholera and cleanliness in Russia, 3260
The Triple Alliance in danger, 3460

The fiasco in Armenia, 3770
Germany's foreign policy, 3885
Crete and the Cretans, 3963
Religions and races in Russia, 4068

Dillon, Frank, 1823–1909, landscape painter. *DNB*.

The Arab monuments of Egypt, **NC** 618
Light and water-colors, 1311
The proposed Nile reservoir, 2599

Dillon, John, 1851–1927, Irish nationalist. *DNB*.

The coming winter in Ireland, **NC** 1334

Dillon, Valentine Blake, 1846/47–1904, Irish politician. *Irish Times*, May 1, 1904.

A Unionist policy for Ireland, **NatR-II** 1793

Dillon, William, b.1850, political writer. *LCCat*.

Assassination and dynamite, **FortR** 2159

Battle of the standards in America, **NC** 2971

Dimsdale, Marcus Southwell, 1860–1919, Latin scholar. Venn.

Coryat's *Crudities*, **NatR-II** 691
Wit and pathos in Suetonius, 1115

Dion, or **Dio,** Chrysostom, c.40–115, Greek sophist and rhetorician. *Ency.Brit.*/11th ed.

An idyl of Euboea, **NQM** 128

Ditchfield, Peter Hampton, 1854–1930, divine, prolific author. *WWW*.

Parish councils, **NatR-II** 1207

Dixie, Lady Florence Caroline (Douglas), 1857–1905, traveller. *DNB*.

Cetshwayo and Zululand, **NC** 755

Dixon, Charles, 1858–1926, naturalist. *WWW*.

A new law of geographical dispersal, **FortR** 3632

Dixon, Marian Hepworth (MacMahon), alive in 1904, wife of William Hepworth Dixon in *DNB. Yearbook*/1904, p. 335, and her daughter, Ella Hepworth Dixon (in *As I Knew Them*, [1930], p. 13) both call her "Marian", not "Marion."

Marie Bashkirtseff, **FortR** 2922

Dixon, Richard Watson, 1833–1900, historian, poet, divine. *DNB.*

The rivals, **OxCam** 5
The barrier kingdoms [in Crimean War], 9
The prospects of peace [in Crimean War], 21

Dobson, Henry Austin: see *Index*, I, 876.

Hogarth's tour [to Sheppey], **FortR** 2978
Letter: 2647

The female Quixote [Charlotte Lennox], **NatR-II** 1283
Polly Honeycombe, 1743
The Grub Street of the arts, 2261

Dodd, Catherine Isabel, 1860–1932, educator, writer. *WWW, LCCat.*

A school journey in Germany, **NatR-II** 2093
A study in school children, 2203
Town and country children, 2239
The early instruction of twin boys, 2314
School children's ideals, 2405
German and English school-children, 2535

Dodd, George: see *Index*, I, 876.

The metropolis and railways, **FortR** 210

Dodd, L. T.; perhaps the Rev. Llewellyn Theodore Dodd in *BMCat.*

The Ruskin Hall movement, **FortR** 4414 collab.

Dodgson, Charles, 1800–1868, divine. Boase; birthdate under son (next entry) in Boase.

Letter: **DR** 247

Dodgson, Charles Lutwidge, 1832–1898, mathematician, used pseud. "Lewis Carroll." *DNB.*

Fallacies about vivisection, **FortR** 1165

Note: **NC** 1466

Dodsworth, William, 1798–1861, R.C. theologian. *DNB.*

Woodgate on secession, **DR** 857
New versions of the Scriptures, 870
Geology and Protestantism, 879

Doherty; probably John Doherty, who contributed to *Essays on Religion*, ed. H. E. Manning, 1865; Russell, "Early Reviewers," p. 215, calls Doherty a "priest of Turnham Green."

The Ring and the Book, **DR** 1277

Dolan, Gilbert, 1853–1914, hagiologist. *Benedictine Bibliog.*

The Sacred Heart in mediaeval England, **DR** 2579
Notices: 2594, 2606, 2628, ?2638

Döllinger, Johann Joseph Ignaz von: see *Index*, I, 876.

Letter: **NC** 269
The paternity of Jansenism, **Ram** 966

Dolman, O.S.B.; perhaps Charles Vincent Dolman, Canon of Newport, in *CD/* 1900.

See: **DR** 1784

Dolman, Frederick, 1867–1923, journalist. *Times*, June 12, 1923; *WWW.*

Chamberlain's municipal career, **FortR** 3651
The Liberal party and local veto, 4236

George Gissing's novels, **NatR-II** 2077

Donaldson, Lady Albinia Frederica (Hobart-Hampden), d.1932. Burke under Buckinghamshire.

The working girl of to-day, **NC** 3283

Donaldson, Sir James, 1831–1915: see *Index*, I, 876.

Relation of Scottish universities to those of England and Germany, **ScotR** 39
The Scotch education department, 391

Donaldson, John William: see *Index*, I, 876.

Classical School-Books, **FM** 3063

Donaldson, William, 1838–1924, sec. of the Prison Commission for Scotland. *WWW.*

Simon Fraser—Lord Lovat, **ScotR** 387

Donisthorpe, Wordsworth, b.1847, barrister. Venn, *M at B.*

The future of marriage, **FortR** 3181

Donkin, Sir Horatio Bryan, 1845–1927, physician. *WWW.*

Miracles and medium-craft, **FortR** 2071
The dangers of medical specialism, 2339

A note on "thought-reading," **NC** 744

Donne, William Bodham: see *Index*, I, 876.

Horace Walpole, **BentQR** 7
The drama of the day, 17
Shakespearian literature, 21

Donne, William Bodham (*continued*)
Ben Jonson: life and works, 33

Works of Beaumont and Fletcher, **FM** 2705
The Octavius of Minucius Felix, 3073
Plays and their providers, 3136
Greek and Roman philology, 3160
Songs from the Dramatists, 3287
Charles Kemble, 3289
The old civilians [on Justinian's *Institutes*],
3311
Drama, past and present, 3370
Helps's *Spanish Conquest in America,* 3385,
3644, 4183
Froude's *History of England,* 3489, 3745,
3996
Calderon, 3592
John Mitchell Kemble, 3605
Studies of the Great Rebellion, 3798
Gower's *Confessio Amantis,* 3849
Cowper's poems, 4168
Henry Thomas Buckle, 4254
Letters and Life of Bacon, 4268, 4981
Tacitus and his Times, 4347
Histoire de Jules Cesar, 4548
Emanuel Swedenborg, 4871
Henry Crabb Robinson, 5021

Donnelly, Thomas, solicitor in Dublin. Thom/
52, p. 1009.

Modern humorists. **DR** 949
The science of legislation, 960
Thomas Hood, 973
Crime and its detection, 986
Modern periodical literature, 1012

Donnet, Gaston-Henri-Pierre, 1867–1908,
French journalist. *DBF.*

The French colonial craze, **FortR** 4206

Doran, John: see *Index,* I, 877.

The things we don't know, **FM** 1851
Account of jesters or court fools, 1983

Shakespeare in France, **NC** 127

Dorington, Sir John Edward, 1832–1911,
M.P. *WWW.*

National education, **NatR-II** 1969
Unionist Party committed to old-age pensions? 2322

Dornford, Joseph, 1794–1868, divine. *DNB.*

War [of Russia] with Turkey, **LR (1829)** 21

Dougall, James Dalziel, 1818–1891, rifle
maker. Boase.

Letter: **NatR-II** 116

Douglas, James Alexander, d.1862, of Grey's
Inn. Burke under 11th Baron Petre.

A Bible distributor [George Borrow], **Ram**
904 collab.

Douglas, James Archibald, prof. in Agra, India. *BMCat., NC* no. 2919, p. 672. Perhaps man of this name, b.1865/66, in
Foster.

The chief Lama of Himis, **NC** 2919

Douglas, John, 1828–1904, premier of Queensland. Serle.

Imperial federation, **NC** 1065

Douglas, Sir Robert Kennaway: see *Index,* I,
877.

The greater Eastern question, **NatR-II** 1810

The triumph of Japan, **NC** 2694
Some Peking politicians, 3035
A Gordon myth [about Chinese soldiers],
3335
The intellectual awakening of China, 3669
Trans: 3440

Douglas, Robert Langton, 1864–1951, art expert. *WWW.*

The maiolica [pottery] of Siena, **NC** 3719

Douglas, William Scott, 1867–1915, historian.
LCCat.

Cromwell before Edinburgh, 1650: "Gogar
Feight," **ScotR** 497

Douglas-Scott-Montagu, John Walter Edward,
2nd Baron Montagu of Beaulieu, 1866–
1929, civil engineer. *WWW.*

Parish councils, **NatR-II** 1499

Nature v. the chartered company, **NC**
2969

Dow, John George, 1858–1897, Scotsman who
became an American educator. Metcalfe
Addresses, *Glasgow Graduates.* (See
Index, I, 878.)

Shakespeare's fugues, **FortR** 2302

Scotch Ploughmen's Union, **ScotR** 329

Dowden, Edward: see *Index,* I, 878.

Lamennais, **FortR** 554
Walter Savage Landor, 612
Christopher Marlowe, 650
Edgar Quinet, 754
Victor de Laprade, 868
The prose works of Wordsworth, 1196

Shelley's "Philosophical View of Reform,"
2527
Victorian literature, 2598
Last words on Shelley, 2639
The study of English literature, 2686
Goethe, 2716, 2729
Shakespeare's wisdom of life, 2750
Hopes and fears for literature, 2789
Edmond Scherer, 2815
Goethe and the French Revolution, 2845
Coleridge as a poet, 2867
Literary criticism in France, 2893
An eighteenth-century mystic [Marquis de
Marsay], 2906
The poetry of John Donne, 2956
Goethe's last days, 2988
Amours de voyage [by Fabre d'Eglantine],
3072
Goethe's friendship with Schiller, 3112
The "interviewer" abroad, 3151
Meredith in his poems, 3186
Irish opinion on the Home Rule Bill, 3358
Autobiography [of Humphry Thomson],
3414
The poetry of Robert Bridges, 3521
Letter: 2638
Notices: 504, 526

Fiction and its uses, **FM** 4609
Mr. Browning's *Sordello*, 4810

Carlyle's lectures on European culture, **NC**
589 collab.
The English masque, 3501

Dowie, Ménie Muriel: see Norman, Ménie
Muriel.

Dowling, Alfred Edward Patrick Raymund:
see *Index*, I, 878.

The gifts of a pontiff, **DR** 2416

The farmer-monk, **NatR-II** 1172

A walk in Alexandria, **NC** 2393

Down, Thomas Christopher: see *Index*, I,
878.

Adventurers at the Klondike, **FortR** 4198

An object-lesson in "prohibition," **NC** 2744
The Manitoba schools question, 2962

Downes, Joseph: see *Index*, I, 878.

A Cambrian colloquy on poetry, **FM** 763

Downie, John

How the Scottish Union was effected,
ScotR 370
How the Scottish Union has worked, 381

Downing, Harriet, poet, novelist. *BMCat.*;
Dickens, *Letters*, I, 476n.

Remembrances of a monthly nurse, in 8
installments from **FM** 999 to 1128

Doyle, Sir Arthur Conan: see *Index*, I, 878.

Stevenson's methods in fiction, **NatR-II**
950

Distribution of British intellect, **NC** 1580

Doyle, Dennis, M.D., sanitary inspector at
Kimberley. Ian Colvin, *Life of* [Sir L. S.]
Jameson (1923), I, 32, 115.

With King Gungunhana in Gazaland, **FortR**
3109

Doyle, Sir Francis Hastings Charles: see *Index*, I, 878.

English and Eastern horses, **FortR** 1800,
1809

Letter: **NatR-II** 315

Doyle, John Andrew: see *Index*, I, 879.

Political prospect: a Liberal view, **NatR-II**
444

Doyle, Thomas, 1793–1879, provost of Southwark. Boase.

Replies to Lord Acton, **DR** 1494 collab.

Drage, Geoffrey: see *Index*, I, 879.

Alien immigration, **FortR** 3588
The problem of the aged poor, 4346

Mrs. Sidney Webb's attack on the Labour
Commission, **NC** 2638

Drage, Mildred

Monticelli [French painter], **FortR** 3775

Drapes, Thomas, 1874–1919, physician. *Surgeon Index*/3rd s.

Is insanity increasing? **FortR** 3861

Drayson, Alfred Wilks: see *Index*, I, 879,
and II, App. A.

The art of breathing, **NC** 2378

Drew, Andrew Augustus Wild: see *Index*, I,
879.

Hooliganism and juvenile crime, **NC** 3682

Drew, Mary (Gladstone): see *Index*, I, 879.

?On books and the housing of them, **NC**
1837 collab.

Dreyfus, Alfred, 1859–1935, French army officer. *DBF.*

The letters of an innocent, **NatR-II** 2202

Driffield, William Edward, 1843/44–1896, sub-editor *DR* under Hedley and H. A. Vaughan. *Tablet,* July 18, 1896, p. 105.

Notice: **DR** 1965

Drummond, Henry, 1851–1897, Scottish divine. *DNB.*

Gladstone and Genesis, **NC** 1240

Drummond, Thomas, 1797–1840, chief administrator in Ireland under Lord Mulgrave. *DNB.*

See: **DR** 2, 20, 25, 37, 41, 83, 93

Drummond, Hon. William Henry, 1845–1879, writer on Africa. Allibone.

Incidents of African travel, **NQM** 78

Drury, Henry Joseph Thomas, 1778–1841, scholar, master at Harrow. *DNB.*

Greece, **FQR** 62
Chateaubriand's translation of *Paradise Lost,* 433

Dubor, Georges de, 1848–1931, French popular writer. *DBF.*

The plays of Hroswitha, **FortR** 3778

Du Cane, Sir Edmund Frederick: see *Index,* I, 880.

The duration of penal sentences, **FortR** 2044
National defences, 2449

Experiments in punishment, **NC** 374
The decrease of crime, 2368
The Prison Committee report, 2796
The uselessness of prison labor, 3004
Turkish misgovernment, 3030
Do we need an army for home defence? 3222
The Prisons Bill and criminal treatment, 3290

Du Chaillu, Paul Bellom, 1837–1903, American traveler of French extraction. *EUI.*

The great equatorial forest of Africa, **FortR** 2955

Duclaux, Mary: see Darmesteter, Agnes Mary Frances.

Dudgeon, Robert Ellis, 1820–1904, M.D., homeopath. *DNB.*

Letters: **NatR-II** 690, 1200

Duff, Mr.; possibly Nicholas Duff, of Meath, Dunshaughlin, in Battersby/66.

English tourists in Ireland, **DR** 68

Duff, Beatrix; possibly Beatrice Duff in *BMCat.*

A fragmentary correspondence, **NatR-II** 1560

Duff, Sir Mountstuart E. Grant: see Grant Duff, M. E.

Duffield, William Bartleet: see *Index,* I, 880.

Liberal party and its candid friends, **FortR** 3623
Pitt and the Eastern question, 3923

Duffy, Sir Charles Gavan: see *Index,* I, 880.

An appeal to the Conservative Party, **NatR-II** 262

Ungrateful Ireland, **NC** 938, 949

Dumas, Henri, 1819–1902, French Jesuit. *EUI.*

Father Dumas on the Syllabus, **DR** 1514

Duncan, Francis: see *Index,* I, 880.

The prospect of Egypt in 1888, **FortR** 2670

Duncan, James Alexander, b.1849, Scottish poet. J. A. Duncan, *Some Family Leaves,* Edin., 1911, p. 22.

Anonymous Scottish songs, **ScotR** 581

Duncan, Jonathan, 1799–1865, currency reformer. *DNB.*

Tenure of land in Ireland, **DR** 507

Dunckley, Henry: see *Index,* I, 880.

Mr. Dillwyn's motion, **FortR** 1590
Mr. Gladstone, 1656

Personal rule [in government], **NC** 237, 276

Dunham, Samuel Astley, 1795/96–1858, historian. *DNB,* Boase.

Breton, Norman, Anglo-Norman poetry, **DR** 78
Peru and the Spanish invasion, 103

Dunlop, William: see *Index,* I, 881, and II, App. A.

Letter on cholera, **FM** 433

?A march in India, 889
?Sketches of savage life, 904, 921, 938

Dunn, Hugh Percy, 1854–1931, surgeon. *WWW.*

What London people die of, **NC** 2488
Modern surgery, 2574
Is our race degenerating? 2627

Dunne, David Basil, 1828?–1892, prof. at Cath. Univ. Dublin. Newman, *L&D,* XVI, index.

Laforet's *Moral Philosophy,* **DR** 842
Ward's *Nature and Grace,* 957
Glaciers, 966
Iceland, 982
Dalgairns, *The Holy Communion,* 1006
Explorations in equatorial Africa, 1017
Mendelssohn, 1025

Dunster, Henry Peter, 1814–1904, divine, botanist. *Times,* June 13, 1904, p. 8e, but correct birthdate is in *LCCat.* and Foster.

Our orchards and paraffin oil, **NC** 927
England as a market garden, 1048
An agricultural parcels post, 1721

Durie, James.

India, 1880–4, **NatR-II** 225

Durnford, Walter, 1847–1926, provost of King's College, Cambridge. *DNB.*

Etoniana, **NatR-II** 1646

Durtnall, Daniel Alban, classicist. *BMCat.*

Poems by George Croker Fox, **DR** 158

Duthie, David Wallace, divine in So. Africa and Australia. *CCD/1902.*

"The remittance man," **NC** 3566

Dutt, Romesh Chunder, 1848–1909, Indian civil servant. *WWW.*

Famines in India and their remedy, **FortR** 3990

Dutt, or Datt, Shoshee Chunder, or Sasi Chandra, 1824/25–1886, Bengal civil servant. Buckland, *LCCat.*

Taxation in India, **FM** 5852

Duval, Edgard Raoul, 1832–1887, politician. *Grand Larousse.*

Commercial treaty between France and England, **NC** 471

Dwyer, Francis Doyne: see *Index,* I, 881, and II, App. A.

National armies and modern warfare, **FM** 5076
The War [Franco-Prussian], 5126, 5135, 5146
The crisis in France, 5174
Servia, 5348
?Military system and the national debt, 5722

Dyce, Alexander, 1798–1869, editor of Elizabethan plays. *DNB.*

Letter: **FM** 1130

Dyer, Henry, 1848–1918, prof. of engineering in Japan. *WWW.*

Race across the Atlantic, **ScotR** 342

Dykes, Thomas: see *Index,* I, 881.

Yacht racing, **FortR** 2350
Ocean steamers, 2463

Dyneley, Mortimer.

"Locksley Hall" and liberalism, **NatR-II** 525

Dziewicki, Michael Henry: see *Index,* I, 881.

"Exorcizo Te" [exorcist literature], **NC** 1611
In praise of London fog, 1810
Life in a Jesuit college, 2127

E

Eardley-Wilmot, Sir Sydney Marow, 1847–1929, naval officer, *WWW.*

The collapse of China at sea, **FortR** 3592

Earle, Anne M., teacher in Philadelphia.

University extension in America, **NC** 2798

Earle, John Charles, 1814–1885, poet, R.C. priest. Gorman.

?Rio's *Shakespeare,* **DR** 1097
Madame de Maintenon, 1099
Madame Récamier and her friends, 1120
American poets, 1464, 1474

Earle, John Charles (*continued*)
English men of letters, 1804
The vices of agnostic poetry, 1831
Notice: 1116

Earle, Maria Theresa (Villiers), 1836–1925.
WWW.

A plea for amateur artists, **NatR-II** 1886

Earle, Ralph Anstruther E., 1835–1879, M.P.
Venn.

The Eastern situation, **FortR** 1307
Mr. Gladstone's policy, 1517

Eastlake, Charles Locke, 1836–1906: see
Index, I, 883.

St. Paul's Cathedral, **FM** 5464

Picture-hanging at the National Gallery,
NC 1492
The Poldi-Pezzoli collection at Milan, 2411

Eastlake, Lady Elizabeth (Rigby): see *Index*,
I, 883, and II, App. A.

Letters to John Henry Merck, from Göthe,
&c., **FQR** 404

The wolves of Esthonia, **FM** 2049
Modern Frankfort, 2499

Eastwick, Robert William Egerton, b.1847/48.
Foster.

Deli, in Sumatra, **FortR** 3431

Eaton, Sir Frederick Alexis: see *Index*, I, 883.

Educational work of the Royal Academy,
FortR 2111

Eccles, Arthur Symons, 1855–1900, physician.
Index-Catalogue.

Tenth International Medical Congress,
FortR 3003

Fin de siècle medicine, **NatR-II** 1460
Sleeplessness, 1615
Headaches, 1718
Visitor's glimpse [of U.S. political cam-
paign], 1922

Eccles, Charlotte O'Conor: see O'Conor-
Eccles, Charlotte.

d'Eckstein, Baron Ferdinand, 1790–1869,
Danish philosopher. *EUI.*

M. Guizot and his contemporaries, **Ram**
953, 959
The Abbé de Lamennais, 988
The political system of the Bonaparts, 1001
The Church and science, 1037

Ecroyd, Henry

The valle lands of Venetia, **FortR** 322

Ecroyd, William Farrer, 1827–1915, J.P.,
M.P. *Landed Gentry.*

Untaxed imports, home industries, **NatR-II**
1941
Fair trade, **NC** 640

Eddis, F. E.; possibly the F. E. Eddis in
BMCat.

The Registration Bill, **NatR-II** 1445

Eden, Frederick, b.1829, commissioner of
fisheries. *M at B*, Foster.

The salmon fisheries, **FortR** 1858

Edersheim, Alfred: see *Index*, I, 884.

Literary character of the Fourth Gospel,
FM 5690
Letter: 5698

Edes, Ella B., niece of Bishop J. M. Wain-
wright of New York. Gorman.

"The Holy Face," **DR** 1971
"The Holy Helpers"—Sts. Blaise and
Erasmus, 2192

Edgar, Sir John Ware, 1839–1902, Bengal
civil servant. *WWW.*

Development of Buddhism in India, **FortR**
1702

Edgcombe, Frederick Joseph Sydney: see
Index, I, 884, and II, App. A.

Ghosts, present and past, **FM** 5027

Edgcome, James. *BMCat.*

The effect of an import duty, **NatR-II** 1364

Edgcumbe, Richard John Frederick: see *Index*, I, 884, under Edgcumbe, Richard,
and II, App. A.

The first Handel festival, **NatR-II** 1170
The first ascent of Mont Blanc, 1319
A missing page in Alpine history, 1490

Edis, Sir Robert William, 1839–1927, architect. *WWW.*

Health and taste in English homes, **FortR**
2391

Edmundson, George: see *Index*, I, 884.

Hendrik Conscience and the Flemish revival, **NatR-II** 429

Edwardes, Charles: see *Index*, I, 884, and *Yearbook*/1920.

The lepers of Crete, **NatR-II** 921
In Calabria, 989
The pessimists and womankind, 1206
Society in Naples, 1246
The Guanches of Tenerife, 1288
Society in ancient Venice, 1339
Hops and hop-pickers, 1474
Roman society a century ago, 1538

Crete and the Sphakiots, **NC** 1832
The new football mania, 2299

Edwards, Alfred George, 1848–1937, bishop. *DNB*.

Some disestablishment fictions, **NatR-II** 1750
Church reform, 1804

The Church in Wales, **NC** 2782

Edwards, Frederick Augustus, 1854/55–1931. F.R.G.S. Death certificate, Somerset House; *BMCat*.

The French on the Nile, **FortR** 4084
The French on the Niger, 4102

Edwards, Henry Sutherland: see *Index*, I, 885, and II, App. A.

Kompert's Jewish tales, **FortR** 1933
Prince Gortchakoff on Russian diplomacy, 2023
Social science on the stage, 2298
An operatic crisis, 2329
A Faust of the first century, 2388
The new *Othello*, 2577
Katkoff and the *Moscow Gazette*, 2634

Panslavonianism, **NQM** 138
Dictionaries of music, 158

Edwards, Matilda Betham: see Betham-Edwards, Matilda.

Edwards, William Walter: see *Index*, I, 885.

The poor in France, **NC** 275
Compulsory providence, 375
Pawnbroking abroad and at home, 595

Egerton, Henrietta Grey: see Grey-Egerton, Henrietta.

Egerton, Hugh Edward, 1855–1927, historian. *DNB*.

Scientific novel and Gustave Flaubert, **NatR-II** 65
A scarce book [Cobbett's *Rural Rides*], 308
The nineteenth century Ishmael [industrial schools for juvenile prisoners], 322

Two views of the novelist, 663
Historical drama and the teaching of history, 1178

Egerton, Wilbraham Egerton, 1st Earl Egerton of Tatton, 1832–1909. *WWW*.

Agricultural depression, remedies, **NatR-II** 466
Letter: 953

The Manchester ship canal, **NC** 2502
Co-operation in agriculture, 2934

Egerton, William, Bengal civil servant. *Army List*/93, p. 900.

Facts from Bihar about the mud-daubing, **NC** 2625

Elam, Charles, 1824–1889, physician. *Surgeon Index*/2nd s. (See *Index*, I, 885.)

Man and science, **NC** 160

Elgood, Percival George, 1863–1941, army officer. *WWW*.

Negligence in recruiting, **NC** 3768

Eliot, George: see *Index*, I, 886.

The influence of rationalism [Lecky's *History*], **FortR** 3
Notice: 11

Three months in Weimar, **FM** 3358
Liszt, Wagner, and Weimar, 3365

Eliot-James, A. G. F.: see James, Mrs. A. G. F. Eliot.

Ellerton, Richard

A new franchise, **FortR** 46

Ellicott, Charles John: see *Index*, I, 886.

Church of England, present and future, **NC** 4
The Ridsdale judgment and its results, 52
Readjustment of Church and State, 186

Ellington, H., of the London Rowing Club.

Athletes of the present and past, **NC** 1390

Elliot, Arthur Ralph Douglas: see *Index*, I, 886.

Home Rule: for Scotland, **NC** 1258

Elliot, Gilbert, 2nd Earl of Minto, 1782–1859, diplomat. *DNB*.

Letter: **Ram** 192

Elliot, Gilbert John Murray Kynynmond: see *Index*, I, 887.

Newspaper correspondents in the field, **NC** 416

Recent rebellion in North-West Canada, 1175

Our auxiliary cavalry, 1538

Elliot, Sir Henry George, 1817–1907, diplomat. *DNB.*

The death of Abdul Aziz, **NC** 1519
Australia fifty years ago, 1786
Sir John Franklin, 2244

Elliot, Margaret; daughter of Rev. Gilbert Elliot, dean of Bristol, in Boase.

Jem Nash, the dull boy, **FM** 4420

Elliot, Robert Henry, 1837–1914, Irish landed proprietor. *WWW.*

John's Indian affairs, **FM** 5229, 5249, 5282
Wanted—a religion for the Hindoos, 5262
The new Hindoo theism, 5295
The assassination of Lord Mayo, 5298
Wanted: a new constitution for India, 6373

India in deep waters, **NatR-II** 2184

Elliot, William Gerald, 1858–1930, barrister. Venn.

The amateur acting of today, **NatR-II** 1669

Elliott, Sir Charles Alfred, 1835–1911, lieut.-gov. of Bengal. *DNB.*

The London School Board, **NC** 3732

Ellis, Henry Havelock: see *Index*, I, 887.

The tercentenary of Velasquez, **FortR** 4285
Letter: 3678

Genius and stature, **NC** 3140

Ellis, Sir John Whittaker, 1829–1912, Lord Mayor of London. *WWW.*

The Government of London Bill, **NatR-II** 178

Ellis, Leopold George Frederick Agar: see Agar-Ellis, L. G. F. A.

Ellis, William Ashton, 1853–1919, M.D., musicologist. *Surgeon Index/*3rd s.; *Times*, Jan. 4, 1919, p. 3c.

Wagner and Schopenhauer, **FortR** 4250

Elsdale, Henry: see *Index*, I, 888.

The South African problem, **NatR-II** 888

A day with a war balloon, **NC** 540
Resuscitation by oxygen, 2036
Should we hold on to the Mediterranean in war? 2699
Why are our brains deteriorating? 3516

Elssler, Fanny, 1810–1884, Austrian dancer. *Ency.Brit.*, 11th ed.

Fanny Elssler [her impressions], at the Havanah, **FM** 1886, 1893, 1900, 1912, all collab.

Elton, Charles Isaac: see *Index*, I, 888.

Historical aspect of the land question, **FortR** 847

Emden, Alfred, 1849–1911, judge of county courts. *WWW.*

Need for reforms in Company Law, **NC** 2601
Defective addition to our Company Law, 3763

Emerson, Hon. George Henry, 1853–1919, Newfoundland supreme court justice. *WWW.*

The Newfoundland Fisheries dispute, **FortR** 2986 collab.

Emerson, James: see Tennent, James Emerson.

Emin Pasha: see Schnitzer, Eduard C. O. T.

Ennis, John, d.1862, D.D., parish priest of Booterstown. Newman, *L&D*, XVI, 328; *Battersby/*63.

Is Ranke an historian? **DR** 287
German Reformation and its Times, 374

Erdmann and Shanz [a corporation].

Postal reform, **NatR-II** 1187

Erle, Sir William, 1793–1880, judge. *DNB.*

The case of Watts v. Fraser and Moyes, **FM** 901

Errington, George, 1804–1886, R.C. archbishop. *DNB.*

Library of the Fathers: St. Cyril, **DR** 140

Erskine, David, 1816–1903, colonial secretary of Natal. Burke.

Letter: **FM** 5633

Erskine of Marr, Hon. Stuart Ruaraidh

Contributors

EVERSHED 905

Joseph, 1869–1960, Gaelic scholar.
BMCat., *WWW*.

Lord Mar's Home Rule Bill, **DR** 2455

Escott, Thomas Hay Sweet: see *Index*, I, 889.

Home and foreign affairs, in 37 installments
from **FortR** 1547 to 2393 (nos. 2142 to
2208 collab.; no. 2369?)
The Radical programme, 2073, 2085
Mr. [Abraham] Hayward, 2151
?England's foreign policy, 2176
The Marquis of Salisbury, 2198
Bernal Osborne, 2230 collab.
Mr. Gladstone, 2232
Mr. Chamberlain, 2244
Men of letters on themselves, 2253
The Revolution of 1884, 2255
The Radical programme: local government
and Ireland, 2334 collab.
Lord Houghton, 2368
Small talk and statesmen [Greville's *Journal* and Malmesbury's *Memoirs*], 2416
Tennyson's last volume, 2427
The army and the democracy, 2434
London pen and gown in the sixties, 3601
Lord Randolph Churchill, 3612
The development of Lord Salisbury, 3829
England, Russia, and France, 3875
Statesman's autobiography [H. H. M. Herbert], 4022
Heredity as a social force, 4149
Mr. Henry Reeve, 4195
[Frederick W.] Robertson of Brighton, 4380
Concerning hosts and hostesses, 4478
Edited: 2163
Note: 2033
See: 2004

Political novels, **FM** 5541
Fonblanque in English journalism, 5551
Bulwer's last three books, 5561
The House of Commons, 5606
Bulwer as politician and speaker, 5628
Politics and the press, 5697
The House of Lords, 5894

Oxford memories, **NatR-II** 1637

Esser, Thomas, 1850–1926, German Dominican, theologian. *Grosse Brockhaus.*

Rosminian ontologism, **DR** 2176

Estcourt, Edgar Edmund, 1816–1884, R.C.
canon of St. Chad's Cathedral. *DNB.*

Testimonies of saints, **Ram** 505, 513, 529

d'Estournelles, Paul Balluat, Baron de Constant de Rebecques, 1852–1924, diplomat.
Grand Larousse.

The superstitions of modern Greece, **NC**
705

Evans, Sir Arthur John: see *Index*, I, 890.

The Austrian counter-revolution in the Balkans, **FortR** 1682

Evans, Charles John, 1830/31–1882, divine.
Venn, *Eton School Register, 1841–1850*,
pp. 38, 53.

The two Guppers, **FM** 3530

Evans, David, London businessman.

Letter: **NatR-II** 650

Evans, Elizabeth Edson (Gibson), 1832–1911,
misc. writer. *Amer. WWW*.

Gustave Courbet at La Tour, **NQM** 148

Evans, Joseph, Methodist minister of Denbigh. *BMCat.*

Letter: **NatR-II** 739

Evans, Richardson, 1846–1928, barrister.
WWW.

Age of disfigurement [billboard advertising], **NatR-II** 1062

Advertising as a trespass on the public, **NC**
2764

Everett, Edward, 1837–1920, army officer.
WWW.

Letter: **NC** 1838

Everett, Robert Lacey, 1833–1916, M.P.
WWW.

Great Britain's duty, **NatR-II** 2087

Evershed, Henry: see *Index*, I, 890, and II,
App. A.

Farm labourers and cow plots, **FortR** 968

Improvement of the plants of the farm,
NatR-II 248
Canon Kingsley as naturalist and clergyman, 517
Irish dairy-farming, 594
Allotments [of land for cottage gardens],
618
Cow-keeping by farm labourers, 905
Wat Tyler and his cause, 972

Habit in plants, **NQM** 27
Sir John Sinclair and other Scotch improvers, 123

Ewald, Alexander Charles: see *Index*, I, 890.

An historical love match [Duke of Suffolk and Queen Mary (Tudor) of France], **FM** 6334
The Lancashire witches, 6391

Ewart, Charles Theodore, 1856–1917, physician. *Surgeon Index*/3rd s.

The power of "suggestion," **NC** 1916

Ewart, William, 1798–1869, politician, *DNB*.

Letter: **FM** 2223

Eyre, Charles, 1817–1902, Catholic Archbishop of Glasgow. *WWW*.

Catholic funerals, **Ram** 235

Catholic epitaphs, 313
The hymns of the Catholic Church, 434
Catholic hymnology, 538

Eyre, George Edward Briscoe, 1840–1922, Verderer for the New Forest. *Landed Gentry*.

The New Forest, **FortR** 770

Eyre, William Henry, S.J., 1823–1898, rector of Stonyhurst. Boase.

Letter: **Ram** 806

Eyre-Todd, George: see *Index*, I, 890.

A Lothian fair, **NatR-II** 939
A cobbler-artist, 1056

F

Faber, Frederick William, 1814–1863, Superior of London Oratory. *DNB*.

Letter: **Ram** 52

Faber, Gilbert

Luxury and Greek, **NatR-II** 1142
Voluntary socialism, 1198

Fabian Society: see Shaw, George Bernard, and Webb, Sidney.

Fagan, Henry Stuart: see *Index*, I, 891.

Notices: **FortR** 182, 192, 212, 253, 264, 298, 326, 396, 435
At Paris, before the end [of the Commune], **FM** 5230
The Scilly Islands, 5610
Langalibalele [an African chief], 5633
The truth about the Bastille, 5772

Irish woollens, **NatR-II** 190

Faquet, Emile, 1847–1916, French critic. *Grand Larousse*.

The influence of Balzac, **FortR** 4115

Fairbairn, Sir Andrew, 1828–1901, Mayor of Leeds. *WWW*.

"Ordinary business principles," **NC** 3693

Fairbridge, William Ernest, 1863–1943, Rhodesian journalist. Information from Mr. Eric Rosenthal of Cape Town.

Some home truths about Rhodesia, **NatR-II** 1985

Fairly, Alexander H., Scottish divine; possibly Henry Alexander Fairlie, 1893–1903, in *Fasti*, III, 45.

De Imitatione Christi—who wrote it? **Scot R** 71

Falbe, Count de

The Hamlet saga: from Saxo-Grammaticus, **NC** 798

Falconer, Alexander; perhaps the Alexander Falconer, 1825–1892, Scottish divine, in *Fasti*, IV 305.

Scotland in the sixteenth century, **FM** 5164
Laing's *Sir David Lyndsay*, 5275
Stanley's *Lectures on the Church of Scotland*, 5416
Motley's *John of Barneveld*, 5584

Falkner, John Meade, 1858–1932, antiquary. *DNB*.

A midsummer night's marriage, **NatR-II** 1902

Falle, Bertram Godfray, 1st Baron Portsea, 1860–1948, judge. Burke, *WWW*.

Les Ecréhous (Channel islets), **NatR-II** 491 collab.

Fane, Violet: see Currie, Lady Mary Montgomerie (Lamb).

Faraday, Ethel Richmond, economist; possibly daughter of Frederick J. and Lucy Richmond Faraday: see under her brother, Wilfred B. Faraday, *WWW/* 1960.

Economic aspects of the imperial idea, **FortR** 4214

Faraday, Frederick J., economist on the *Manchester Guardian*; prob. father of Wilfred B. and Ethel Richmond Faraday, q.v. *Blackwood Papers Cat.*

Letter: **FortR** 3527

John Bull and silver, **NatR-II** 1992
The Wolcott Commission: monetary relations of Great Britain and colonies, 2038
Reopening of Indian mints, 2102

Farler, John Prediger, b.1845, missionary in Central Africa. Venn.

England and Germany in East Africa, **FortR** 2788

Farquharson, Henry Richard, 1857–1895, politician. Venn.

Cobden's dream, **NatR-II** 621
More tillage: a plea for the farm labourers, 747
The case for the tithe-payer, 1018
The Church and the tithe acts, 1801
Letter: 494

Farrar, Frederic William: see *Index,* I, 892.

Public school education, **FortR** 480
The Church and her younger members, 546
Lord Lytton's *King Arthur,* 775
Frederick Denison Maurice, 2155
Social problems and remedies, 2687
Local Government Bill, licensing clauses, 2718
Drink and crime, 3372
Growth of Roman Catholicism in England, 3708
Letter: 2655
Notices: 513, 533

Hereditary Genius [by Francis Galton], **FM** 5115

Lord Bramwell on drink, **NC** 1137, 1159
An olive branch from America, 1472

Farrer, James Anson: see *Index,* I, 892, and II, App. A.

The problem of empire, **FortR** 2286

A "candidates' protection society," **NC** 2326

Farrer, Sir Thomas Henry: see *Index,* I, 892.

Report of the Civil Service Commission, **FortR** 1157
The strength of England, 1446
The principle of copyright, 1533
Freedom of land, 1658
Freedom of contract, 1764
Equalisation of railway rates, 1934
Silver and the tariff at Washington, 3527

The referendum, **NatR-II** 1553
Shall we degrade our standard of value? 1633
The currency question [monometallism], 1733
Taking stock of employers' liability, 1799
Egypt and England, 1852
Justice to Egypt, 1874

An olive branch from America, **NC** 1476
Why I voted for Mr. Gladstone, 2257

Faulkner, Charles Joseph, 1834–1892, dean at Univ. Coll. Oxford. Boase.

Unhealthy employments, **OxCam** 28 collab.

Faunthorpe, John Pincher, 1839–1924, educator, pres. London Ruskin Society. *WWW.*

A May Queen festival with letters from Mr. Ruskin, **NC** 2746

Faure, David Pieter, 1842–1918, founder of Unitarian Church in So. Africa. Rosenthal.

Pro patriâ: the South African problem, **FortR** 2114

Faussett, Thomas Godfrey, later T. G. Godfrey-Faussett, 1829–1877, barrister, antiquary. *DNB.*

How I killed a cariboo, **FM** 3786
Snow picnic [in Canada], 4032
A January day, 4057
A mount on shanks's mare, 4081
Westborough Fair, 4186
The sixth quarter of the world [Romney Marsh in Kent], 4266

Fawcett, Henry: see *Index,* I, 892.

To what extent is England prosperous? **FortR** 745
The boarding-out of pauper children, 757
The House of Lords, 816
Present position of the government, 819
The nationalisation of the land, 907
The incidence of local taxation, 947
Effect of increased production of wealth on wages, 1016

Fawcett, Henry (*continued*)
Position and prospects of co-operation, 1024
Professor Cairnes, 1178
Recent development of socialism in Germany and United States, 1519
The enclosure of commons, **FM** 5049
The Indian deficit, 5157
Financial condition of India, **NC** 268
The proposed loans to India, 310
The new departure in Indian finances, 362
The next reform bill, 417

Fawcett, Dame Millicent (Garrett): see *Index*, I, 892.
Medical and general education of women, **FortR** 545
The electoral disabilities of women, 683
The Women's Suffrage Bill, 2813
The emancipation of women, 3146
An American on representation, **FM** 5285
Women's suffrage, **NatR-II** 692
The future of Englishwomen, **NC** 211
Women and representative government, 891
Women's suffrage, 1277
The appeal against female suffrage, 1732

Fawkes, Edith Mary (Cleasby), wife of Ayscough Fawkes. *Landed Gentry*.
Mr. Ruskin at Farnley, **NC** 3635

Fayrer, Sir Joseph, 1824–1907, surgeon-general. *DNB*.
The sacrifice of education, **NC** 1667
The deadly wild beasts of India, 1743
The venomous snakes of India, 1800

Fearon, Daniel Robert: see *Index*, I, 893.
Dante and paganism, **NC** 3246
Dante's ghosts, 3497

Feasey, Henry John, 1863–1908, Benedictine monk. Gorman, *BMCat*.
English office of the Easter Sepulchre, **NC** 2747

Feilding, Hon. William-Henry-Adelbert, 1836–1895, army officer. Lodge /74 under Denbigh, *Army List* /84, Whitaker /1915.
Imperial migration and settlement, **NatR-II** 537
Letter: 147
"What shall I do with my son?" **NC** 839
Whither shall I send my son [to which colony]? 878

Felkin, Mary Rosalie, wife of Robert William

Felkin in *Index*, I, 893. *BMCat.*; see *FortR* no. 2605.
Note: **FortR** 2605
See: 2908

Fellows, Charles; prob. a businessman with special interest in New Zealand. See *FM* no. 5659, p. 386.
Financial policy of New Zealand, **FM** 5635
The debts of New Zealand, 5659

Fellows, Mrs. E. C. *BMCat*.
Nova Scotia's cry for home rule, **NC** 1346

Fellows, Reginald Bruce, b.1871, barrister, later priest. Venn.
The religion of the undergraduate, **NC** 2840

Fenn, William Wilthew, b. about 1827, a landscape painter who turned to writing after becoming blind. Allibone.
The welfare of the blind, **FortR** 2446

Fenton, Mr.; possibly Edward Dyne Fenton, d.1880, retired army officer in Boase.
Irish brigade in the service of France, **DR** 1440

Fenton, William Hugh, 1854–1928, senior surgeon, Chelsea Hospital for Women, *WWW*.
A medical view of cycling for ladies, **NC** 2931

Fenwick, Ethel Gordon (Manson), 1857–1947, nurse, ed. of *Journal of Nursing*. *WWW*.
Nurses à la mode, **NC** 3075

Ferguson, James, 1857–1917: see *Index*, I, 893 and II, App. A.
The church question in Scotland, **NatR-II** 547
Scottish conservatism, 831
Gladstone and Church of Scotland, 1085
The growth of Conservatism in Scotland, 1251
The decay of Scotch radicalism, 1333
Letter: 408
?What is the Conservative policy? **ScotR** 46
Scottish loyalists [in the Great Civil War], 63
The American loyalists [in the Revolutionary War], 88
The Conservative cause in Scotland, 118
A Scottish governing house, 242

Presbyterian reunion and a national church, 350
Galloway and her feudal sheriffs, 409
Scotland and the Unionist cause, 441
The gay Gordons, 476
Scottish elections of 1895, 502
Letters of last earl-marischal [George Keith, 1693–1788], 615
Fermartine, 658

Ferguson, Robert, 1799–1865: see *Index*, I, 893.

Berard, *Influence of Civilization on Public Health*, **FQR** 7
Progress of metaphysics in Germany: Cousin's *Philosophical Fragments*, 15
French philosophers, nineteenth century, 61
Notices: 39, 53

Fergusson, James, 1808–1886: see *Index* I, 893, and II, App. A.

Rawlinson on ancient architecture, **FortR** 467

Proposed new cathedral for Liverpool, **NC** 1068
The restoration of Westminster Hall, 1206

Ferry, Gabriel [well-established pseudonym of Louis de Bellemarr], 1809–1852, French novelist. *Grand Larousse.*

Scenes in the wilds of Mexico, in 7 installments from **FM** 2274 to 2348

Ffoulkes, Edmund Salisbury or Salusbury: see *Index*, I, 894.

Algeria under the French, **DR** 938
Stanley's *Lectures on the Eastern Church*, 984
Palmer's *Egyptian Chronicles*, 1004
Letter: 1189

Civilisation in the Fifth Century, **Ram** 856

Field, Basil; possibly Basil Field, 1868/69–1938, divine, in Venn.

Fly-fishing, **FortR** 3487

Field, John Edward: see *Index*, I, 894, and II, App. A.
The story of Victoria Cave, **FM** 5776

Field, Joshua Leslie, b.1857, barrister. *M at B.*

The burden of Ireland, **NC** 1171

Figuerola y Ballester, Don Laureano, 1816–1903, statesman, economist. *EUI.*

The political condition of Spain, **FortR** 2104

Filon, Pierre Marie Augustin, 1841–1916, French man of letters. *Larousse XXme.*

Rosebery from a French standpoint, **FortR** 3573
Presidents and politics in France, 3608
Salisbury from a French point of view, 3728
The modern French drama, in 7 installments from 3969 to 4148

Foreign estimate of R. Churchill, **NatR-II** 783

Finch-Hatton, Harold Heneage, 1856–1904, M.P. Burke.

Lord Bury, imperial federation, **NatR-II** 291
North Queensland separation, 407
The collapse in Australia, 1436

Finch-Hatton, Murray Edward Gordon, 1851–1898, 12th Earl of Winchilsea. Burke.

Agricultural union, **NatR-II,** 1376

Findlater, Jane Helen: see *Index*, I, 894, and II, App. A.

"The other grace" [fictional heroines], **NatR-II** 1993
The point of view [in fiction], 2252
The art of narration, 2393
The slum movement in fiction, 2443

Findlay, Joseph John, 1860–1940, educator. *WWW.*

The genesis of the German clerk, **FortR** 4341

Finlason, William Francis, 1818–1895, legal writer. *DNB.*

The case of Achilli, **DR** 695
Charitable trusts, 698
The law of England with relation to moral theology, 708
Wycliffe, 715
Russia and Turkey, 723
Jansenism, Gallicanism and Jacobinism, 739
"Bad Popes" [defense of maligned Popes], 751
St. Thomas of Canterbury, 764
Luther, 771
The action against the Cardinal [Boyle v. Wiseman], 775
The age of Edward III, 783
The age of Morton, Wolsey, and More, 790
Wordsworth's poems, 800
The Reformation the result of tyranny, 809
An Anglican apology for tyranny [Froude on Henry VIII], 818

Finlason, William Francis (*continued*)
The Great Rebellion, 820
The Revolution [of 1688], 826
Sequel of the Revolution, 847
Madeleine Smith and Scottish jurisprudence, 851
The Mayo Committee and Exeter Hall, 858
Trial by jury no boon to Catholics, 863
The Judges of England [by Foss], 875
English party struggles, 878
Froude's *History of England*, 882
Oxford view of the Papacy, 887
Our judges, 889
Chronicles of the Middle Ages, 895
History in fiction, 900
Justices' justice and the Habeas Corpus Act, 902
Platform slanderers, 904
The Mortara case, 911
The plea of insanity in trials, 913
The government of the Papal States, 918, 922
The massacre of Perugia, 936
Notices: 789, 796, 864

The great debate on the Penal Bill, **Ram** 311
?State encroachments on the Church, 323, 334, 349, 356
Achilli v. Newman, 435
Robberies of religion, 447, 452
Death-bed bequests, 459
The chancellors of England, 461
The Protestant Inquisition, 466
Circumstantial evidence: case of Kirwan, 469
Dr. Newman's trial, 474
Charitable trusts, 480, 488, 495
Hebraisms and Catholicisms of Disraeli's novels, 586
Was Shakespeare a Catholic? 599
Notices: 247, 260

Finlayson, Archibald W., of Finlayson, Bousfield and Co., linen thread manufacturers of Glasgow. *Glasgow Directory*/1880–1900, *LCCat.*

Falling trade and factory legislation, **NC** 865

Firth, Joseph Firth Bottomley, 1842–1889, barrister. Boase.

The fate of the London bill, **FortR** 2057

Fisher, Herbert Albert Laurens: see *Index*, I, 895.

Modern historians and their methods, **FortR** 3577
Sir John Seeley, 3837

Fisher, Roswell Corse: see *Index*, I, 895, and II, App. A.

Cooperative housekeeping, **NC** 79

Fisher, Thomas, 1810–1891, naval officer. Boase.

Last August in the Baltic, **FM** 3417, 3431

Fisher, William Edward Garrett: see *Index*, I, 895.

Glasgow—a model municipality, **FortR** 3630
The art of flying, 4359
House of Molière [Théâtre Français], 4434

Fiske, John, 1842–1901, American historian. *DAB.*

Miracles no proofs, **FortR** 323
The laws of history, 530
Why the American Colonies separated from Great Britain, 1718

Fitch, Sir Joshua Girling: see *Index*, I, 895.

Statistical fallacies respecting public instruction, **FortR** 1000
Unsolved problems in national education, 1106

Educational endowments, **FM** 4930
Charity, 5029
Dulwich College, 5390

University work in great towns, **NC** 242
The Chautauqua reading circle, 1604
Religion in primary schools, 2605
The Bible in elementary schools, 2665
Some flaws in the Education Bill, 2938
The London University problem, 3065
Creeds in the primary schools, 3194

Fitchett, William Henry: see *Index*, I, 895.

Australian view of So. African crisis, **NatR-II** 2341

Fitzgerald, Charles Cooper Penrose: see *Index*, I, 895, and *WWW*/1928.

Are we worthy of our empire? **NatR-II** 608
Sir Samuel Baker on maritime defence, 765
"Fraternal France," 1787
Training of seamen in Royal Navy, 2458
The Japanese navy, 2519
Letter: 770

Fitzgerald, David, 1847–1920, judge. *WWW.*

The Ancient Irish [by Eugene O'Curry], **FM** 5702
The ancient Irish, 6042

Fitzgerald, Edward Marlborough, b.1802, Irish journalist. Dickens, *Letters,* I, 233n.; Venn.

?The Court of Chancery, **FM** 288

Fitzgerald, John D., member Labour Council of Australia.

Mr. H. H. Champion on the Australian strike, **NC** 2014

Fitzgerald, Oscar Penn, 1829–1911, bishop. *Amer. WWW.*

An open letter to Lord Meath, **NC** 2443

Fitzgerald, Percy Hetherington: see *Index,* I, 896, and II, App. A.

The anti-Jesuit crusade, **DR** 811

"My Lydia," **FM** 5603
See: 5519

What is "the scene"? **NatR-II** 110
Music hall land, 1002

The world behind the scenes, **NQM** 95

Fitzgerald, Sir Peter George: see *Index,* I, 896.

Mr. Froude and landlords of Ireland, **NC** 185
Irish land agitation, 420

Fitzherbert, Samuel Wyndham, b.1854, writer on gardening. Venn.

Can gardening be made to pay? **NatR-II** 2347

Fitzmaurice, Edmond: see Petty-Fitzmaurice, Edmond.

Fitz-Patrick, Bernard Edward Barnaby, 2nd Baron Castletown of Upper Ossory, 1849–1937. *WWW* under Castletown. (See *Index,* II, App. A.)

Home Rule and its solution, **FortR** 2402

A Unionist policy for Ireland, **NatR-II** 1794

FitzPatrick, Sir James Percy, 1862–1931, So. African statesman. *DNB.*

Notes on the Transvaal question, **FortR** 4382

Fitzpatrick, Walter; prob. the man in the *BMCat.*

The Spanish monarchy, **DR** 2350

Fitzpatrick, William John, 1830–1895, Irish biographer. *DNB.*

A sketch of Charles Lever, **FM** 5397
The late Lady Becher, 5418

FitzRoy, Sir Almeric William, 1851–1935, sec. to the Privy Council. *WWW.*

Experiment in Home Rule, **NatR-II** 513

Fitzsimon, or Fitz-Simon, Ellen (O'Connell), c.1805–1883, wife of Christopher Fitz-simon, daughter of Daniel O'Connell. *DNB* under her father, *Landed Gentry of Ireland.*

Irish novels and novelists, **DR** 95

Flaix, Ernest Fournier de: see Fournier de Flaix, Ernest.

Flanagan, John Stanislas, 1821–1905, theologian. Newman, *L&D,* XII, index.

Letter: **Ram** 688

Flanagan, John Woulfe, 1852–1929, Irish journalist. Crone.

Home Rule, socialism, and secession, **FortR** 1986

Leasehold enfranchisement, **NatR-II** 593

The Irish Jacobins, **NC** 650
The friends of the farmer, 730

Flanagan, Thomas, 1814–1865, historian. *DNB.*

Anglo-Saxon literature, **DR** 297
Suppression of monasteries, 327
Church and Empire, thirteenth century, 362
Anglo-Saxon and British churches, 369
Mary, Queen of Scots, 388
James II and Mary of Modena, 461
Ledru Rollin's *Decline of England,* 601
Merivale's *History of the Romans,* 625

Letters: **Ram** 880, 882

Fleay, Frederick Gard: see *Index,* I, 896.

Spectrum analysis and the sun, **FM** 4572

Fleming, David, 1851–1915, Franciscan, *EUI* appendix.

The light of faith, **DR** 2492
Evolution and dogma, 2544

Fleming, George, 1833–1901, veterinary surgeon. *DNB.*

Vivisection and diseases of animals, **NC** 694

Fleming, George (*continued*)
The suppression of rabies, 1846
The wanton mutilation of animals, 2721

Fleming, William; possibly the William
Fleming in *BMCat.* who was a railway
timetable constructor.

Railways and waterways, **FortR** 1847

Fletcher, George, critic, *BMCat.*

The Merchant of Venice, **FM** 2721, 2739

Fletcher, Julia Constance: see *Index*, I, 896.

Leopardi, **NC** 1223

Fletcher, Walter John: see *Index*, I, 896, and
II, App. A.

The traditional "British sailor", **NC** 3718

Fleury, Maurice de, 1860–1931, physician.
Grand Larousse.

A cure for indolence, **FortR** 4118

Floris, Charles L.

Comfort and safety in London theatres,
NatR-II 640

Floyd, Charles Greenwood, 1830–1903, divine. Burke.

An ascent of Mont Blanc, **FM** 3361

Flürscheim, Michael, 1844–1912, writer on
social reform. *NDB.*

Professor Huxley's attacks, **NC** 1857

Flux, Sir Alfred William, 1867–1942, economist, statistician. *DNB.*

Shipping charges and fall of prices, **NatR-
II** 2019

Folkestone, Viscountess Helen Matilda
(Chaplin), 1846–1929, musician. *Complete Peerage* under Radnor.

The Wagner festival at Baireuth, **FortR**
2510

Fonblanque, Edward Barrington de, 1821–
1895, in foreign service. Boase.

Caroline Bauer, **FortR** 2266

Caspar Hauser, **NQM** 94
Goethe in his old age [and Johann Ecker-
mann], 103

Fonblanque, Lester Ramsay de, father of

Maj. Gen. Philip De Fonblanque in
WWW/1940.

Social status of women in India, **FortR**
2747

Forbes, Archibald: see *Index*, I, 897.

Bazaine's vindication, **FortR** 2101
Fire-discipline [military conduct], 2115
Russians, Turks, and Bulgarians, **NC** 101
The "fiasco" of Cyprus, 227
The political situation in Burmah, 302
Flogging in the army, 360
War correspondents and the authorities,
401
Lord Chelmsford and the Zulu War, 403
The Australasian colonies, 918
Criticism of the Egyptian campaign, 1026
In case of invasion, 1119
Soldiers' rations, 1630
The recruiting problem, 2009
The warfare of the future, 2046
A war correspondent's reminiscences, 2081,
2099
Moltke and Moltkeism, 2143
Napoleon the Third at Sedan, 2180
The French Empress and the German War,
2272
Inner history of the Waterloo campaign,
2362
The mystery of Monsieur Regnier, 2547
My native salmon river [the Spey], 2779

Forbes, Henry Ogg: see *Index*, I, 897, and
WWW/40.

The Chatham Islands, **FortR** 3363
Antarctica: a vanished Austral land, 3465
Letter: 3056

Forbes, James David: see *Index*, I, 897.

The Plurality of Worlds [by William
Whewell], **FM** 3191
The history of science, 3700

Ford, Edward; perhaps Edward Ford, 1825–
1902, divine, schoolmaster in Venn.

Characters in the *Vicar of Wakefield*,
NatR-II 27
Lord Monboddo and Mrs. Garrick, 77

Ford, Ford Maddox: see *Index*, I, 897.

Millais and Rossetti exhibitions, **FortR**
4071

Ford, William Justice, 1853–1904, cricketer.
DNB.

Drawn matches at cricket, **NatR-II** 2499

Foreman, John, 1853/54–1937, F.R.G.S. Death certificate, Somerset House. (See *Index*, I, 898.)

Rebellion in Philippine Islands, **NatR-II** 1979
A recent glance at Spain, 2001
Europe's new invalid [Spain], 2042
The state of Spain, 2100
The coming partition of China, 2137
The Empire of the Philippines, 2227
Will United States withdraw from Philippines? 2494

Forman, Henry Buxton: see *Index*, I, 898.

Samuel Richardson, artist and moralist, **FortR** 630
Notices: 406, 456, 560

Formby, Henry, 1816–1884, priest, musicologist. *Dict. of Cath. Biog.*

Malou on indiscriminate reading of Bible, **DR** 474
The Rosary of the Blessed Virgin Mary, 478
The University of Louvain, 515
Editions of the Roman Gradual and Vesperal, 527
Father Gentili, 643
Roman history a bulwark of the Christian cause, 1576
Primitive religion of Rome, 1604
A philosophy of history indispensable to Catholic education, 1649

Catholic literature for the poor, **Ram** 511, 519

Fornari, Raffaele [or Nicolo?], 1788–1854, Cardinal, Nuncio-Apostolic to the French Republic. Newman, *L&D*, XVI, 614, *NBG* under Nicolo Fornari.

The Pope on national education in France, **Ram** 248
Letter: 151

Forster, H. O. Arnold: see Arnold-Forster, H. O.

Forster, Henry William, first Baron of Lepe, 1866–1936, government administrator, M.P. *WWW*.

Letter: **FortR** 3307

Forster, John: see *Index*, I, 898.

The first philosophers of Greece, **FQR** 685
The newspaper literature of America, 693
Socrates and the Sophists of Athens, 700
The answer of the American press, 727
The Dialogues of Plato, 739

A word on Alexander Dyce, **FortR** 1211

Forster, William Edward: see *Index*, I, 898.

Imperial federation, **NC** 1087, 1112

Forsyth, William: see *Index*, I, 898.

Literary style, **FM** 3576, 3590
Three days in Sark, 5509
On the limits of science, 5644

Fort, George Seymour, 1858–1951, sec. to governor of Cape Colony. *WWW*.

Dr. Jameson's raid, **NC** 2937

Fortescue, Chichester Samuel, later Parkinson-Fortesque, Baron Carlingford, 1823–1898, statesman. *DNB*.

A few words about the budget, **FM** 3100

Fortescue, Hugh, 3rd Earl Fortescue, 1818–1905. *DNB*.

State-rate-paid education, **NatR-II** 447
Gladstone's claims to confidence, 558
Local government for Ireland, 961

Our next leap in the dark [on reform], **NC** 567
Poor men's gardens, 1525
"Imperium in imperio" [the Local Government Act], 1603
The Benefices Act, 3354

Fortescue, Hugh, Viscount Ebrington and later (1905) 4th Earl Fortescue, 1854–1932. Burke.

Parliamentary procedure, **NatR-II** 625
The prospects of fair trade, 683

The Irish land commissioners, **NC** 784
Liberal election addresses, 1267
A bye-election in 1747, 1723
Ireland: the ultimate guarantee, 1873

Fortescue, Sir John William: see *Index*, I, 898.

Jamaica and Mauritius, **NatR-II** 1230

The seamy side of Australia, **NC** 2020
Guileless Australia, 2100
The influence of climate on race, 2397
The new South Sea bubble, 2421

Fortnum, Charles Drury Edward, 1820–1899, art collector. *DNB*.

On the *Maiolicia of Faenza*, **NC** 3422

Foster, Mrs. F. M.

Women as social reformers, **NatR-II** 848

A Princess of Condé, 1052

Foster, Hubert John, b.1855, army officer. *LCCat., BMCat.*

Strength and weakness of Russia, **NatR-II** 599

Foster, J. M., a miner.

Mining inspection a sham, **NC** 1150

Foster, Sir Michael: see *Index*, I, 899.

The elements of muscular strength, **FortR** 310

Weariness, **NC** 2448
At a technical institute, 3227

Fothergill, John Milnea: see *Index*, I, 899.

Effects of town life upon body, **NatR-II** 629

Fottrell, Sir George, 1849–1925, Irish solicitor. *WWW.*

The Irish judges, **FortR** 1138
Local government and Ireland, 2334 collab.

Land purchase in Ireland, **NC** 3028

Fournier de Flaix, Ernest, 1824–1904, economist. *Larousse XXᵉ Siècle.*

Alcohol and alcoholism, **ScotR** 184

Fowle, Thomas Welbank: see *Index*, I, 899.

Decay of self-government in villages, **FortR** 1610
Plea for the abolition of outdoor relief, 1703
County constituencies: a plan of reform, 1738
The third Reform Bill: why delay it? 1994

Parish Councils, **NatR-II** 1498

The place of conscience in evolution, **NC** 190
The place of will in evolution, 279
The place of revelation in evolution, 626

Fowler, Sir Henry Hartley: see *Index*, I, 899.

Public business in the Commons, **NC** 1158

Fowler, Sir John, 1817–1898, civil engineer. *DNB.*

Railway accidents, **NC** 47
The Channel passage: an alternative, 685
A ship-canal through Egypt, 813 collab.
The Forth Bridge, 1727 collab.

Fowler, Sir Robert Nicholas, 1828–1891, Lord Mayor of London. *DNB.*

The Boers, **NatR-II** 136

Fowler, Thomas: see *Index*, I, 899.

Shall we continue to teach Latin and Greek? **FortR** 471
On examinations, 1241
Notice: 369

Fowler, William: see *Index*, I, 900.

Indian currency, **NatR-II** 2166

The Basutos and Sir Bartle Frere, **NC** 569
India, her wheat and railways, 963

Fox, Robert Fortescue, 1858–1940, physician. *Times*, June 17, 1940, p. 2.

Stimulants and narcotics, **NC** 1219

Fox, Stephen N.: see *Index*, I, 900.

Truck legislation, **FortR** 3629

Fox-Bourne, Henry Richard: see Bourne, Henry Richard Fox.

Foxcroft, Helen Charlotte, 1865–1950, biographer, journalist. *WWW, LCCat.*

A character of "The Trimmer," **FortR** 4277
"Dreyfus scandal" of English history [the Popish Plot], 4344

Foxwell, Herbert Somerton: see *Index*, I, 900.

Farrer on the monetary standard, **NatR-II** 1670

Francis, Francis, 1822–1886, writer on angling and travel. *DNB.*

Salmon fisheries and their prospects, **FM** 4825
Wanderings westward [to Ireland], 4934
Clever fishes, 5325

The Yellowstone geysers, **NC** 687
A glimpse of Mexico, 774

Francis, George Henry, 1817?–1866, journalist, editor. Boase.

Contemporary orators, in 16 installments from **FM** 2048 to 2264
Sir Robert Peel, 2048
Lord John Russell, 2068
Lord Lyndhurst, 2081
Lord Stanley, 2121
The Duke of Wellington, 2137
T. B. Macaulay, 2151
Sir James Graham, 2157

Frankland, Sir Edward, 1825–1899, chemist.
DNB.

Frankland, Grace C. (Toynbee), 1858–1946,
bacteriologist. *WWW*, under Mrs. Percy
Frankland.

Frankland, Percy Faraday, 1858–1946, chemist. *DNB.*

Franzelin, Joannes Baptista, 1816–1886, Cardinal, theologian. *Cath. Ency.*

Fraser, Alexander, 1824–1898, army officer.
Boase.

Fraser, Sir Andrew Henderson Leith, 1848–
1919, Indian civil servant. *DNB.*

Fraser, Augusta Zelia (Webb): see *Index*, I,
900.

Fraser, James Keith, 1832–1895, army officer.
Burke.

Frazer, Sir James George: see *Index*, I, 901.

Frederic, Harold, 1856–1898, London correspondent of the *New York Times. DAB.*

Fredrik, Oscar: see Oscar Fredrik.

Freeman, Edward Augustus: see *Index*, I,
901, and II, App. A.

Freeman, Edward Augustus (*continued*)
Shall we give up Greek? 1554
Loyalty, 1651
On the study of history, 1782
Jowett's *Thucydides,* 1888
Impressions of the United States, 1932, 1944
The House of Lords, 1999
Prospects of Home Rule, 2506
House of Lords and the county councils, 2703
House of Habsburg in South-Eastern Europe, 2834
Parallels to Irish Home Rule, 2862
Notice: 488

The Austrian power, **FM** 6302

The sacrifice of education, **NC** 1616

Freeman, Frank; prob. a pseudonym.

Letter: **FM** 526

Fremantle, Sir Arthur James Lyon: see *Index,* I, 902.

Note: **NatR-II** 1608

Fremantle, Sir Edmund Robert: see *Index,* I, 902.

The loss of H.M.S. *Captain,* **FM** 5161
Torpedoes, 5303
Discipline and seamanship in the navy, 5902

Ironclads and torpedo flotillas, **NC** 1199

Fremantle, William Henry: see *Index,* I, 902.

Theology under changed conditions, **FortR** 2575
Letter: 2647

Individualists and socialists, **NC** 3074

French, Alfred J.; possibly the Alfred J. French in Allibone and *BMCat.*

Russia and England, **FortR** 3649

Frere, Sir Henry Bartle Edward: see *Index,* I, 902.

Future of Zululand and South Africa, **FortR** 1962
Abolition of slavery in India and Egypt, 2008

Have we a colonial policy? **NatR-II** 69

The Basutos and the constitution of the Cape, **NC** 545
The Transvaal, 547

The Scotch land question, 651

Freshfield, Douglas William: see *Index,* I, 902.

Val Maggia, **FM** 5543

Frewen, Moreton: see *Index,* I, 902.

Progress to poverty, **FortR** 2250
National policy of the United States, 3009
The Transatlantic cattle trade, 3079
Silver up to date, 3315
Currency crisis in the United States, 3370
Letter: 3527
See: 3517

Silver and the fall of prices, **NatR-II** 854
Silver in the Congress [of the U.S.], 1515
American "sound money" problem, 1806
American politics, 1820
The American elections of 1896, 1944
Our relations to westward, 2446
Letter: 2004

Gold scarcity, **NC** 1195
Europe revisited, 1435, 1461 collab.
The Craig Brook salmon hatchery, 3527

Friedländer, Eberhard David, b.1799, professor, political economist. *Biograficheskiĭ slovar professorov (Dorpat: Kaiserliche Universität),* ed. G. V. Livitsky, (Iurev, 1902), pp. 605–606.

Prussian government, administration, **FQR** 339

Frisby, Alfred: see *Index,* I, 903.

Has conservatism increased in England? **FortR** 1864
The next reform bill, 1939

Frost, Percival; perhaps Percival Frost, 1817–1898, mathematician, fellow of King's Coll. Camb., in *DNB.*

Certain clerical obliquities of mind, **FortR** 1185

Froude, James Anthony: see *Index,* I, 903.

South Africa once more, **FortR** 1626
A lesson on democracy, 1973

The Swedenborgians, **FM** 2542
Materialism: Miss Martineau and Mr. Atkinson, 2839
The Homeric life, 2873
King Alfred, 2928
Doubts concerning Reineke Fuchs, 3008
Kircaldy of Grange, 3094
Burton's *History of Scotland,* 3121

Fuller, Morris Joseph (*continued*)
The poor-law system in relation to the Church, 670
The Lambeth Pan-Anglican Conference, 737
The Archbishop's jurisdiction [Canterbury], 937
Bishop-elect's oath of canonical obedience, 1012

Fuller-Maitland, J. A.: see Maitland, J. A. Fuller.

Fullerton, William Morton, b.1865, political scientist. *LCCat.*

English and Americans, **FortR** 2920, 2952
At Arcachon, 4015

To the brink of Pirene, **NatR-II** 1626

Bion of Smyrna, **NC** 1928

Fung Yee, late sec. of Chinese Legation, London. See *NC* no. 1827.

A Chinese view of railways in China, **NC** 1827

Furley, John, 1836–1919, Red Cross director. *WWW.*

The Red Cross, **NC** 1216

Furrell, James Wyburd: see *Index,* I, 904, and II, App. A.

The colour question, **NC** 1095

Fyfe, Henry Hamilton, 1869–1951, drama critic. *WWW.*

A permanent Shakespearean theatre, **FortR** 4451

Fyffe, Charles Alan: see *Index,* I, 904.

The coming land bill, **FortR** 2282
The arguments of a peer, 2304

The punishment of infanticide, **NC** 42

Fysh, Philip Oakley, 1835–1919, Australian politician. *WWW.*

Letter: **NatR-II** 2459

Fytche, Albert, 1820–1892, army officer in Burma. Buckland.

Burma, **FortR** 1575

G

Gabbett, Henry Singer, Irish physician. *Irish Gentry.*

Beneficent germs, **NC** 3481

Gaffney, Fannie (Smith), feminist. *Amer. WW/1915.*

A woman's criticism of Women's Congress, **NC** 3531

Gagarin, Ivan Sergeevich, or Jean Xavier, 1814–1882, statesman, polemicist. *Cath. Ency.*

See: **Ram** 1040

Gage, Moreton Foley, 1873–1953, army officer. *WWW.*

A trip from Uganda to Khartoum, **NatR-II** 2473

Gainsford, Robert John, 1807/08–1870, attorney of Sheffield. Newman, *L&D,* XIV, 393.

Foundation schools in Ireland, **DR** 121
Statistics of Irish and English crime, 126
Lord J. Russell's Education Bill, 758

Who were the persecutors? [on Bancroft, *History of U.S.*], 761
Catholic reformatory schools, 782
English and Irish crime, 830
Hillard's *Six Months in Italy,* 876
Sunday on Protestant principles, 886
Joseph Wolff, 969
Austria and Hungary, 996
Established Church in Ireland, 1013
The Roman state, 1033
?Reformatory schools, 1092
The early Irish Church, 1275
See: 1100

Gainsford, William Dunn, b.1843, barrister. *M at B.*

International trade, **NatR-II** 412
Bimetallism and currency, 853
Letter: 378

Gairdner, James: see *Index,* I, 904.

Bible study in the fifteenth century, **FortR** 56, 67
Authenticity of *Paston Letters,* 110
Jack Cade's Rebellion, 723
Historical element in Shakespeare's Falstaff, 933

Notice: 306

Sundays, ancient and modern, **FM** 4629
State papers, reign of Henry VIII, 4857
Katharine of Arragon, 4933

Galdemar, Ange. *BMCat.*

Victorien Sardou and *Thermidor*, **FortR** 3220
The Comédie-Française in London, 3378
The dynasty of the Brohans, 3387

Gale, Frederick: see *Index*, I, 904.

Cricket old and new, **FortR** 4005
Forty years in the lobby of the House of Commons, 4075

Galiano, Antonio: see Alcalá Galiano, Antonio.

Gallaher, George R. S., bank manager. *BMCat.*

Luck, merit, and success, **NatR-II** 1146

Gallatly, William, 1850–1914, tutor, mathematical writer. Venn.

The girl graduate, **NatR-II** 1061

Gallenga, Antonio Carlo Napoleone: see *Index*, I, 904.

Catherine de Medici, **FQR** 598
Copyright in Italy, 605
Italian drama, 614
Education in Italy, 629
The women of Italy, 641
The aristocracy of Italy, 652

Massimo d'Azeglio, **FortR** 507
Italy; her home and foreign policy, 1818
Finland, 1910

The age we live in, **FM** 1581
[John] Bull and Nongtongpaw, 1988
Foscolo and English hospitality, 2050
England and Yankee-land, 2119

Italian social life, **NatR-II** 224
A dark page in Italian history, 350
Italy in England, 713
Mr. Gladstone and Italy, 867

Galletti, di Cadilhac, Countess Margaret Isabella: see *Index*, I, 904.

The Vergaro: a tale, **NQM** 73

Galloway, Countess M. A. A.: see Stewart, M. A. A.

Galloway, Thomas: see *Index*, I, 904.

Laplace's *Celestial Mechanics*, **FQR** 59
Pontécoulant: physical astronomy, 114
Herschel and Fresnel: theories of light, 170
Fourier, *Theory of Heat, Interior of Earth,* 197
Poisson, *Capillary Action*, 212
Geology and climatology of Asia, 232
Arago on lunar influence, 277
French, English biographies, Newton, 279

Galt, Sir Alexander Tilloch, 1817–1893, finance minister of Canada. *DNB.*

Galt, fils, to a friend of Galt, père, **FM** 1522

Galt, John: see *Index*, I, 904.

The Hurons—a Canadian tale, **FM** 10
Canadian sketches: bell of St. Regis, 29
American traditions, 123, 268, 368
Letters on West Indian slavery, 135, 149, 161
Guelph in Upper Canada, 137
Pot versus kettle, 146
Lessening the West Indian distress, 204
Ancient commerce of England, 299
Nathan Butt to Dr. Bowring, 423
The free-trade question, 480, 507
The whole West Indian question, 580
The joke, 599
My father's house: a tale, 618
The gude wife, 635
The Mem, or schoolmistress, 721
An autumn in the north, 749, 757, 765, 776, 787
Anonymous publications, 817
The metropolitan emigrant, 859
Sea-fed engine, for propelling vessels, 936
The statesman, 1020
Letter: 1024
See: 346

Galt, William, 1808–1892, pioneer in railway reform. Boase.

Purchase of the railways by the state, **FortR** 997

Galt-Gamble, Thomas E.

The Royal Dublin Society, **NatR-II** 1114

Galton, Arthur Howard: see *Index*, I, 905.

Why I entered, and left, the Roman Catholic Church, **NatR-II** 2447, 2454
Final impressions of the Roman Catholic Church, 2475
Government House [on colonial governors], 2533

Galton, Sir Douglas Strutt: see *Index*, I, 905.

Army hospital services, **FortR** 2059

Demography, **NC** 2083
Feeble-minded children, 2529

Galton, Sir Francis: see *Index*, I, 905.

The efficacy of prayer, **FortR** 880
Causes which operate to create scientific
men, 934
Mental imagery, 1729
The visions of sane persons, 1810
Photographic chronicles, 1872
The anthropometric laboratory, 1891
Medical family registers, 2069
Measurement of character, 2200
Temper in English families, 2606
Signals between neighbouring stars, 3876

Hereditary improvement, **FM** 5391
The history of twins, 5737

Religion in human evolution, **NatR-II** 1611

Psychometric facts, **NC** 282
Generic images, 334
The sacrifice of education, 1668
Identification by finger-tips, 2090
Identification offices in India and Egypt,
3685

Gambetta, Léon, 1838–1882, French statesman. *Grand Larousse.*

The French Republic and M. Gambetta,
FortR 1960

Gambier, James William, b.1841, naval officer. *LCCat., Navy List*/92, p. 394.

An exchange for Gibraltar, **FortR** 3366
The true discovery of America, 3454
The Papacy: its position and aims, 3662
Foreign policy of England, 3707
Turkish question: its religious aspect, 3864
Russia on the Bosphorus, 3960
England and the European concert, 3980
Our military prestige abroad, 4517
A plea for an Anglo-Russian alliance, 4550

The life of Midhat Pasha, **NC** 125

Gambier-Parry, Ernest: see *Index*, I, 905.

Compulsory games at public schools, **NatR-
II** 927
Servants and domestic service, 970

Games, Stephen H. W. Hughes-: see Hughes-
Games.

Gandini, Luigi Alberto, Italian writer at end
of 19th century. *EUI, BMCat.*

Court of Ferrara in the fifteenth century,
ScotR 467

Ganem, Halil, politician, ed. *La France internationale. BMCat., Bib.Nat.Cat.*

Europe's stake in the Soudan, **FortR** 2170

Garden, Francis: see *Index*, I, 905.

?Religious, philosophical guides: Mansel,
Maurice, **FM** 3909

Gardiner, Samuel Rawson: see *Index*, I, 905.

Spanish and Venetian diplomacy [under
James I], **FortR** 148
The case against Sir Walter Raleigh, 402

James I. and Lord Digby, **FM** 5197
John Inglesant [by J. H. Shorthouse], 6510

Gardner, Fitzroy, 1856–1936, journalist.
WWW.

Tory press and Tory party, **NatR-II** 1427

Gardner, Herbert Colstoun, 1st Baron Burghclere, 1846–1921. *Venn.*

Specimen of a translation of the *Georgics*,
NC 3258

Gardner, Sir James Tynte Agg, 1846–1928,
barrister, M.P. *WWW.*

Compulsory temperance, **FortR** 2203

Gardner, Percy: see *Index*, I, 905.

The Hellenic after-world, **FortR** 2326

Impressions of American universities, **NC**
3408

Gargan, Denis, 1819–1903, president Maynooth College. *DNB.*

Letter: **DR** 1978

Garner, Charles, thought reader. *BMCat.,
Athenaeum,* Dec. 29, 1888, pp. 880–881.

A thought-reader's experiences, **NC** 1353

Garnett, Lucy Mary Jane, d.1934, traveller in
the East. *WWW, Yearbook*/1904, p. 336.

The Philippine Islanders, **FortR** 4146

Women under Islam, **NC** 2686

Famous sultanas, **ScotR** 646

Garnett, Richard, 1835–1906: see *Index*, I,
906.

Shelley's last days, **FortR** 1476

Hananda, the miracle worker, **FM** 5341
The purple head, 5958

Note: **NatR-II** 623

Public libraries and their catalogues, **NQM** 172

Garrett, Elizabeth: see Anderson, Elizabeth (Garrett).

Garrett, Fydell Edmund: see *Index*, I, 906.

Paul Kruger, **FortR** 4470

How we lost Africa, **NatR-II** 1526

Gartlan, Peter M'Evoy, lawyer, cousin of C. W. Russell. Russell, "Memorial Notes," vol. 20, p. 3.

The Irish State prosecution, **DR** 332, 349
Jesse's *Life of [George] Brummell*, 345

Garvin, James Louis, 1868–1947, journalist. *DNB.*

The future of Irish politics, **FortR** 3634
A party with a future, 3690
Coventry Patmore: praise of the odes, 3915
Lord Rosebery's apostasy, 4043
The end of the new unionism, 4088
Parnell and his power, 4207
Disraeli of Liberalism [Lord Rosebery], 4229
Why is Unionism unpopular? 4323
A cabinet of commonplace, 4541

The German danger in the Far East, **NatR-II** 2505

Gascoigne, Frederick Richard Thomas Trench, 1851–1937, army officer. *WWW.*

To within a mile of Khartoum, **NC** 1160

Gaskell, Lady Catherine Henrietta (Wallop), 1856/57–1935, wife of Rt. Hon. Charles George Milnes Gaskell, q.v. Burke, *Times*, Aug. 22, 1935, p. 14b.

A farm that pays, **NC** 1046
Women of to-day, 1787
Some talk about clergymen, 2288
"My stay in the highlands," 2438
Old Wenlock and its folklore, 2527

Gaskell, Rt. Hon. Charles George Milnes: see *Index*, I, 906.

The position of the Whigs, **NC** 657
The country gentleman, 765
The Yorkshire Association, 1009
William Cobbett, 1243
The memorials of the dead, 1440

Gaskell, Elizabeth Cleghorn: see *Index*, I, 904.

Shams, **FM** 4303
French life, 4427, 4436, 4448

Gasquet, Francis Aidan, born Francis Neil Gasquet, 1846–1929, cardinal, historian. *DNB.*

Adrian IV. and Ireland, **DR** 1878
The Venerable Richard Whiting, 2074 collab.
Religious instruction in England [in 14th, 15th centuries], 2408
English monasteries on eve of suppression, 2426
Pre-Reformation English Bible, 2444
How our fathers were taught in Catholic days, 2571
Biblical criticism, thirteenth century, 2607
Scholarship in thirteenth century, 2647
Notices: 2570, 2674

Gasquet, Joseph Raymond, 1838–1902, physician. *Surgeon Index*/3rd s.

Alcohol: its action and uses, **DR** 1683
Recent research on nerves and brain, 1728
The brain and the mind, 1758
Physiological psychology of St. Thomas, 1816
Arguments for the existence of God, 1970
Lightfoot's [conception of] St. Ignatius, 2065
Teaching of the Twelve Apostles, 2099
Apostles' Creed and rule of faith, 2135, 2164
Early history of the Mass, 2193, 2215, 2231
Celebration of Mass in ante-Nicene times, 2244
Hypnotism, 2268
The canon of the New Testament, 2382
Translation "Full of Grace" in Luke, 2446
The cures at Lourdes, 2453
History of Baptism and Confirmation, 2470
Notices of Catholic continental periodicals: 2119, ?2226
Notices: ?1826, 2006, 2019, 2029, 2144, 2158, 2211, 2307, 2358, 2485

Lunacy law reform, **NC** 1136

Gathorne-Hardy, Alfred Erskine, 1845–1918, barrister. Burke.

Fallow deer at home, **NatR-II** 119
The examination of prisoners: Emile Gaboriau, 186
Western waters, 492
Out of the depths, 966

Gathorne-Hardy, Gathorne, 1st Earl of Cranbrook, 1814–1906, statesman. *DNB.*

Hereditary pauperism and boarding-out, **NatR-II** 104
Christopher North, 154
Dismemberment disguised, 433
Lord Iddesleigh, 532

Gatti, Vincenzo Maria, 1811–1882, Dominican apologist. *DEI.*

Pronouncement on Rosmini's works, **DR** 1562

Gattie, George Byng, of the civil service. *BMCat.*

Letter: **NatR-II** 1139

Gattie, Walter Montagu, b.1853/54. Foster, *WW*/1932 under his son, V. R. Montagu Gattie.

History of a monopoly [lighthouses and pilots], **FortR** 2809
What English people read, 2864
The physique of European armies, 2941

Gatty, Charles Tindal, 1850/51–1928, antiquary, museum curator. *Tablet,* June 16, 1928.

A criticism of Dr. Julian's *Dictionary,* **DR** 2563

Note: **FortR** 2509

Gaussen, Perceval David Campbell, 1862–1928, barrister. *WWW.*

The spirit of the age, **NatR-II** 425

Gautier, Countess F., prob. Florence Gautier, author of *How to see Tivoli and Hadrian's Villa,* Rome, 1902. *RG*/1904.

The story of Tusculum, **ScotR** 648

Gaye, Arthur: see *Index,* I, 906.

Ekenames and nicknames, **NatR-II** 926
The centenary of White's *Selborne,* 977
"Snake Jim Hollunder?" [on Heligoland], 1040
Modern school-bills, 1098
German or Greek? 1163
Seven and three [as numbers], 1415

Geddes, Sir Patrick: see *Index,* I, 906.

University systems, **FortR** 3422

Scottish university reform, **ScotR** 199

Geffcken, Friedrich Heinrich: see *Index,* I, 906, and II, App. A.

North American fisheries disputes, **FortR** 2953
Change of government in Germany, 2984

Church and state in Germany, **NC** 1704
The French in Germany, 1748
Compulsory insurance in Germany, 2096
The war-chests of Europe, 2620
Turkish reforms and Armenia, 2852

Geikie, Sir Archibald: see *Index,* I, 907.

Scenery and the imagination, **FortR** 3356

Geikie-Cobb, William Frederick, 1857–1941, divine. *WWW.*

Church crisis and disestablishment, **NC** 3552
The prospects of Anglicanism, 3666

Gell, Edith Mary Lyttelton, 1860–1944, writer of inspirational books. *WWW.*

Squandered girlhood, **NC** 2322

Gell, Philip Lyttelton, 1852–1926, president British South Africa Co. *WWW.*

John Richard Green, **FortR** 2035

Reform in the Public Service, **NC** 3679

Gennadius, Joannes: see *Index,* I, 907.

The proper pronunciation of Greek, **NC** 2826
Erasmus and the pronunciation of Greek, 2868

George II, 1683–1760, king of Great Britain and Ireland. *DNB.*

Secret instructions to General Wolfe, **FM** 430

George, Henry, 1839–1897, economist. *DAB.*

England and Ireland: an American view, **FortR** 1922

The "reduction to iniquity," **NC** 1018
Socialism and rent-appropriation, 1099 collab.

Gerard, Jane Emily: see *Index,* I, 907.

Transylvanian superstitions, **NC** 1164

Gerard, John, S.J., 1840–1912. Sutcliffe.

Notice: **DR** 2347

Gergerès, Jean-Baptiste. *Bib.Nat.Cat.*

The Conversion of Hermann the Pianist [by Gergerès], **Ram** 687

Gheyn, Joseph Van den, S.J., 1854–1913, Asiatic scholar. *LCCat.*

Notice: **DR** 1965

Ghosh, A. Sarathkumar: see *Index*, I, 907, and II, App. A.

Great Britain's duty: India, **NatR-II** 2089

Ghosh, Nanda Lal, b.1861, barrister in India. Venn.

Social reforms in India, **NatR-II** 500

Ghulam-us-Saqlain, Khwaji

The Mussalmans of India, **NC** 2760

Gibb, John: see *Index*, I, 907.

A religious poem of the ninth century [Heliand], **FM** 6348

Gibbins, Henry de Beltgens, 1865–1907, economist, historian. *DNB.*

"Made in Germany" and how to stop it, **FortR** 4292

Gibbon, Edward, 1737–1794, historian. *DNB.*

An inedited letter, **FM** 2828

Gibbs, Edward J., writer on political subjects. *BMCat.*

Future Irish policy, **NatR-II** 463
Ancient Rome and modern London, 1299

Gibbs, Henry. *RG.*

Letter: **NatR-II** 2368

Gibbs, Henry Hucks: see *Index*, I, 908.

Bi-metallism, **FortR** 2521

The gold question, **NatR-II** 47
The Empire and the gold standard, 1919
Bimetallism in Europe: Great Britain, 1978
Reply of Bimetallic League to Gold Standard Defence Association, 2006
Letter: 853

Gibbs, Herbert Cokayne: see *Index*, I, 908.

The currency question—for laymen, **NatR-II** 1707
The Indian crisis and a remedy, 2134

Gibson, Edward, 1837–1913, 1st Baron Ash-

bourne, Lord Chancellor of Ireland. *DNB.*

The Home Rule Bill and the army, **NatR-II** 1410
The crowning mercy [defeat of Home Rule Bill], 1482
W. H. Smith as a colleague, 1518

Gibson, Frederick Edward, Madras civil service. *Army List/76,* p. 754.

Letter: **FM** 5852

Gibson, James Arthur, b.1866/67, chemist. See *NC* no. 3407, pp. 92, 93.

The open-air cure of consumption, **NC** 3407
The Nordrach cure [for consumption], 3433
The cry of the consumptives, 3550

Gibson, William, 1868–1942, 2nd Baron Ashbourne. Burke, *WWW* under Ashbourne.

Abbé Grégoire and the French Revolution, **NC** 2441
Activity in the Roman congregations, 3466

Gibson, William Sidney: see *Index*, I, 908.

Londiniana, **DR** 799
Celebrated judges of England, 925

Gielgud, Adam: see *Index*, I, 908, and II, App. A.

The Danubian principalities, **FortR** 304
European Turkey and its subject races, 341
Notice: 369

Giffen, Sir Robert: see *Index*, I, 908.

Financial questions for reformed parliament, **FortR** 463
Russian railways, 478
The question of Central Asia, 514
Mr. Gladstone's work in finance, 559
Taxes on land, 789
The liquidations of 1873–76, 1401
The case against bimetallism, 1615
Bagehot as an economist, 1685
Notices: 406, 425, 435, 443, 456, 488, 513, 526, 547, 568, 626

Value of Ireland to Great Britain, **NC** 1250
A problem in money, 1794
The American silver bubble, 1921
The monetary chaos, 3193

Gigot, Albert, 1835–1913, French administrator. *Larousse XXᵉ Siècle.*

The government of Paris, **FortR** 2005

Gilbert, Sir John Thomas, 1829–1898, Irish historian, antiquary. *DNB.*

O'Curry's *Ancient Irish Historical Literature,* **DR** 1000
Life of John O'Donovan, 1014
The public records of Ireland, 1029

Gilbert, Josiah, 1814–1892, portrait painter. Boase.

Titian, **FM** 5925

Gilbert, William: see *Index,* I, 908.

The London medical schools, **FortR** 1541

Gildea, William, 1833–1925, divine. *WWW.*

The case for the tithe-owner, **NatR-II** 1044

Gildea, William L., 1855–1914, R.C. canon. *Tablet,* Nov. 14, 1914, p. 681.

One of Canon Gore's *Dissertations,* **DR** 2526
Ottley's *Doctrine of Incarnation,* 2566
Notices: 2651, 2738

Giles, Herbert Allen: see *Index,* I, 908.

Present state of affairs in China, **FortR** 1621

Mesmerism and spiritualism in China, **FM** 6147
On Chinese fans, 6172

The book language of China, **NC** 376
Chinese poetry in English verse, 2511

Gilkes, Arthur Herman, 1849/50–1922, headmaster of Dulwich. *WWW,* Foster.

The worship of athletics, **NatR-II** 2061

Gilliatt-Smith, Ernest: see Smith, Frederick Ernest Gilliatt.

Gillie, Laurence, 1825–1854, prof. at Irish Coll. Paris. Boase.

Summary of French Catholic publications, **DR** 619, 640

Gillies, Robert Pearse: see *Index,* I, 908.

Schubert's *Travels in Sweden,* **FQR** 8
Modern German tragedy, 24
The German pocket-books for 1828, 27
Works of Henry Kleist, 51
Notices: 39, 66
Trans: 92

Recollections of Sir Walter Scott, **FM** 855, 878, 891, 899
Goethe's *Tasso,* 941
O'Hanlon and his wife, 981
Humours of the North, in 7 installments from 1031 to 1503
German philosophy, 1082
Respectability, 1122
John Bull's castle, 1348
Recollections of James Hogg, 1371
Recollections of Germany, 1400

Gillow, John, 1814–1877, prof. at Ushaw College. Boase.

Catholic higher education, **DR** 1273

Suppression of the English college at Douay, **Ram** 608

Gilzean-Reid, Hugh: see Reid, Hugh Gilzean.

Girdlestone, Edward: see *Index,* I, 908.

"Landowners, land, and those who till it," **FM** 4924

Gissing, George Robert: see *Index,* I, 909.

By the Ionian Sea, **FortR** 4457, 4486, 4501, 4514, 4529

The day of silence, **NatR-II** 1516
A capitalist, 1574
A lodger in Maze Pond, 1691

Giunchi, D. Antonius, Italian theologian. *BMCat.*

Letter: **Ram** 1003

Gladstone, Florence M. *BMCat.*

The Gledstanes of olden time, **ScotR** 523

Gladstone, Herbert John, Viscount Gladstone, 1854–1930, statesman. *DNB.*

See: **FortR** 2176

A first visit to India, **NC** 1433
Ireland blocks the way, 2223

Gladstone, Mary: see Drew, Mary Gladstone.

Gladstone, William Ewart: see *Index,* I, 909.

The Conservative collapse, **FortR** 1689
Stray letters [to Henry Raikes], 4141

On the Influence of Authority [by George C. Lewis], **NC** 1, 61
Montenegro, 27
Aggression on Egypt, 71
The colour-sense, 87
The county franchise, 100
Last words on the county franchise, 132

Glover, Sir John: see *Index*, I, 911.

Why I shall vote for the Unionist candidate, **NC** 2251

Goadby, Edwin N.: see *Index*, I, 911, and II, App. A.

The Gothenburg licensing system, **FortR** 3596

Gobie, Miss E. C. W. van, afterwards Walrée, Dutch novelist; used "Christine Müller" as pseud. *BMCat., FM* no. 5281, p. 169n.

The burgomaster's family, in 9 installments from **FM** 5281 to 5355

Goddard, George Frederick: see *Index*, I, 911, and *CCD*/76.

Letters of Bernardo Tasso, **FM** 5503

The Dolomites of the Tyrol, **NQM** 64

Godfernaux, André, 1864–1906, dramatist, philosopher. *EUI.*

Philosophy of the Dreyfus case, **FortR** 4328

Godkin, Edwin Lawrence: see *Index*, I, 911.

An American view of Ireland, **NC** 747
American view of popular government, 1238
American Home Rule, 1281
American opinion on the Irish question, 1445

Godkin, Georgina Sarah: see *Index*, I, 911.

Notice: **FortR** 142

Godkin, James, 1806–1879, writer on Ireland. *DNB.* (For *Index* I art., see App. A, below.)

The Irish land question, **FortR** 30
Ireland without church establishment, 85
The Irish Presbyterians, 130
The old Church of Ireland, 184
The case of Ireland, 205
Fenianism and the Irish Church, 477
Ireland and Scotland, 486
Notice: 472

Godley, Hon. Eveline Charlotte, d.1951, fellow Royal Hist. Soc. *WWW.*

A playgoer's protest, **NatR-II** 2370
General Wolfe's letters, 2509

Godley, John Arthur, 1st Baron Kilbracken,

1847–1932, under-sec. of state for India. *DNB.*

See: **FortR** 2176

Godsall, B. M.; perhaps Byam Martin Godsal, 1856–1935, in *Landed Gentry.*

"Round pegs in square holes" [English immigrants in America], **NC** 2945

Godwin, Edward, R.C. canon, prof. of philosophy at Oscott. *BMCat.*

See: **DR** 2714

Godwin, Edward William, 1833–1886, architect. *DNB.*

Decoration of St. Paul's Cathedral, **FM** 5583

The Greek home according to Homer, **NC** 1289

Goethe, Johann Wolfgang von: see *Index*, I, 911.

The Italian merchant, a tale, **FM** 246
The tale, 448
Fragment, 464
Maxims and reflections, 5787

Goff, William, b.1841/42, of Dublin. Foster.

The sun's radiation of heat, **NatR-II** 1135

Goh, or **Go,** Daigoro, b.1862, Japanese businessman. *BMCat., WW in Japan*/1915.

A Japanese view of new Japan. **NC** 2000

Gohier, Urbain Degoulet, 1862–1951, French journalist. *Grand Larousse.*

Anglophobia—a French warning, **NatR-II** 2344
Roman Catholic Church in France, 2368

Goldie, Francis, S.J. 1836–1912, Sutcliffe.

Art books of 1895, **DR** 2546

Goldie, Sir George Dashwood Taubman, 1846–1925, founder of Nigeria. *DNB.*

"Spheres of influence" [occupation of Uganda], **NC** 2328

Goldsmid, Sir Frederic John: see *Index*, I, 911.

Egypt: non-political control, **FortR** 2052

Portugal and the Congo, **NatR-II** 167
Sir Bartle Frere in Sind, 208

Goldsmid, Sir Julian, 1838–1896, M.P. Boase.

England and the Conference, **FortR** 2187
Ismail: a vindication, 2320
See: 2176

Questions of the day in India, **NC** 849

Goldsmid, Nathaniel, 1806/07–1860, barrister.
Foster.

Notices: **Ram** 560, 569 collab.

Goldsmith, Henry C., naval officer. *Navy List*/90

Newfoundland and the fishery question, **NatR-II** 1004

Goldsmith, or **Goldsmit,** Isidor Albertovich, c.1845–1890, revolutionary and journalist, left Russia in 1884. See art. cited below and *Deyateli revolyutsionnogo dvizheniyz*, II, i (Moscow, 1929), 290–291.

Why I left Russia, **NC** 1139

Gonner, Edward Carter Kersey, 1862–1922, prof. of economics, Liverpool. *WWW.*

The foreigner in England, **FortR** 2833

Gonzalez Llana, Manuel, d.1902 or earlier, statesman and historian. *EUI.*

Political parties in Spain, **FortR** 2415

Goodenough, James Graham, 1830–1875, naval officer. *DNB.*

Education in the navy, **FM** 5200

Goodrich, Lawrence Charles, b.1853/54. Foster, *F.O. List.*

France and the slave trade in Madagascar, **NC** 889

Goodrich-Freer, Ada (or Adela) M.: see *Index,* I, 912.

Psychical research and a "haunted" house, **NC** 3151
Horticulture as a profession, 3560

Alleged haunting of B— — — House, **ScotR** 661 collab.

Goodwin, Charles Wycliffe, 1817–1878, Egyptologist. *DNB.*

The story of Saneha, **FM** 4515

Goodwin, Harvey: see *Index,* I, 912.

The unity of nature: a speculation, **NC** 377

God and nature, 421
The philosophy of crayfishes [on Huxley's *The Crayfish*], 506
Man's place in nature, 609
The fallacy of materialism, 793
The uniformity of nature, 1191
Comte's famous fallacy, 1325
Comte's atheism, 1420
Belief and doubt, 1497
The sacrifice of education, 1670
Wallace on "Darwinism," 1839
Bees and Darwinism, 1942

Gordon, Alexander, author of *The Folks o'Carglen, or, Life in the North,* 1891. *BMCat.* (See *Index,* I, 912, for Mac art.)

The Scotch farm-labourer, **ScotR** 255

Gordon, Alice Mary (Brandreth), d.1929, wife of James Edward Henry Gordon (d.1893), and later of John George Butcher, 1st Baron Danesforth. *Times,* June 17, 1929, p. 19.

Development of decorative electricity, **FortR** 3046
Women as students in design, 3489

The careers of university-educated women, **NC** 2762

Gordon, Arthur Charles Hamilton: see *Index,* I, 912.

Mr. Gladstone, **FortR** 4140

An Irish compromise? **NatR-II** 1677

Gordon, Charles, 11th Marquess of Huntly, 1847–1937. Burke.

Eastern notes, **FortR** 2251

Gordon, Charles George, "Chinese Gordon," 1833–1885, general. *DNB.*

Gordon's campaign in China, **FortR** 4503, 4521

'Memo' on classes in the Soudan, **NC** 1793
Letter: 3030

Gordon, Ishbel Maria (Majoribanks), Marchioness of Aberdeen, 1857–1939, philanthropist. *DNB.*

Household clubs, **NC** 2176
The International Council of Women, 3493

Gordon, James Edward Henry: see *Index,* I, 912.

The latest electrical discovery, **NC** 2177

Gordon, John, R.C. priest of Inverness.

Power of the Pope in the Middle Ages, **DR** 414

Gordon, John Campbell, 7th Earl of Aberdeen, 1847–1934, statesman. *DNB.*

The Affirmation Bill, **FortR** 2016
Union of Presbyterian churches, 2318

Gordon, Sir Thomas Edward, 1832–1914, army officer. *DNB.*

The problem of the Middle East, **NC** 3619

Gordon-Cumming, Constance Frederica: see *Index,* I, 912.

Wild tribes of the Sierras, **NatR-II** 100
The lowlands of Moray, fourteenth, nineteenth centuries, 255
Sunny days in Malta, 479
Police work in Ceylon, 1169

Oiling the waves, **NC** 704
The locust war in Cyprus, 893
Locusts and farmers of America, 1083
Strange medicines, 1422

A legend of vanished waters [Loch Spynie], **ScotR** 64

Gore, George, 1826–1908, electro-chemist. *DNB.*

Promotion of scientific research, **FortR** 994

Gore, John Ellard, 1845–1910, writer on astronomy. *DNB.*

The mystery of gravitation, **NatR-II** 1238

Gore, Spencer W., writer on sports. *BMCat.*

Harrow cricket, **NatR-II** 1603

Gore-Browne, Wilfrid, 1858–1928, bishop of Kimberley. Venn.

The private soldier's wrongs, **NC** 1962

Gorst, Sir John Eldon, 1835–1916: see *Index,* I, 913.

The state of the opposition, **FortR** 1968 collab.
Elections of the future, 2103
The Kingdom of the Nizam, 2160

Conservative programme of social reform, **NC** 2774
The voluntary schools, 3013
School children as wage-earners, 3492

Goschen, George Joachim: see *Index,* I, 913.

Since 1880, **NC** 1126

Goss, Charles Frederick, 1855–1893, barrister. Venn.

Morocco—the world's last market, **NC** 2062
Muley Hassan, 2274

Gosse, Sir Edmund William: see *Index,* I, 913.

Ibsen, the Norwegian satirist, **FortR** 917
The Royal Academy in 1881, 1808
The Salon of 1882, 1919
Equestrian sculpture for London, 2161
Samuel Johnson, 2248
Mademoiselle Aïssé, 2659
A nun's love letters, 2697
Ibsen's social dramas, 2785
Edward FitzGerald, 2843
The protection of American literature, 2968
Ibsen's new drama [*The Lady from the Sea*], 3029
An election at the English Academy, 3091
Letter: 2638

The Lofoden Islands, **FM** 5253
Norwegian poetry since 1814, 5354
Present condition of Norway, 5514
John Webster, 5550

The tyranny of the novel, **NatR-II** 1270

A Dutch poetess [Tesselschade Visscher], **NQM** 144

The French Society of Authors, **NC** 1495

Gosse, Philip Henry, 1810–1888, zoologist. *DNB.*

Wanderings at Kew, **FM** 2616

Gossip, George Hatfeild Dingley, 1841–1907, writer on chess and international politics. *BMCat., Landed Gentry.*

Protection versus free trade in Australia, **FortR** 2960
England in Nicaragua and Venezuela, 3730
Venezuela: from an American point of view, 3774
The mournful case of Cuba, 4124

Gough, Henry, 1821–1906, heraldist. *LCCat.,* Allibone.

Heraldry, British and foreign, **ScotR** 353
Book-plates, 397

Gour, Sir Hari Singh, 1866–1949, barrister. *WWW.*

The Hindu theory of marriage, **NatR-II** 1226

Gourlay, Henry

Current sophisms about labour, **NatR-II** 1390

Gradwell, Robert, 1825–1906, chaplain to the Pope. *Landed Gentry.*

Christianity in Lancashire in Roman and Celtic times, **DR** 1933

Graeme-Sutherland, Alexander Malcolm, 1845–1908, Lord of the Barony of Graemeshall. *WWW.*

The Crofters Bill in Orkney, **NatR-II** 438

Graham, Sir Cyril Clerke, 1834–1895, sec. of state for colonies. Boase.

The Dominion of Canada, **FM** 5392

Graham, Sir Gerald, 1831–1899, army officer. *DNB.*

Last words with General Gordon, **FortR** 2547

Graham, Henry Grey, 1842–1906, writer on Scottish history. *DNB.*

Russel of *The Scotsman,* **FM** 6322

Rural Scotland in the last century, **ScotR** 469

Graham, Herbert

Public and private prosecutors, **FortR** 53

Graham, James Edward, 1850–1929, Scottish advocate. *Landed Gentry.*

Religious education in England, **ScotR** 233
Lord Tennyson, 585
Taxation of land values, 667
Negotiations which preceded the war in South Africa, 677

Graham, Peter Anderson: see *Index,* I, 914, and II, App. A.

Ruin of English agriculture, **NatR-II** 1340

Graham, Robert Bontine Cunninghame: see *Index,* I, 914.

Idealism and masses, **NC** 1971
Father Archangel of Scotland, 2451
In the Tarumensian woods, 2621
Hulderico Schmidel, 2835
Alvar Nuñez, 2961

Graham, William, 1839–1911, economist. *DNB.*

Side-lights on the Second Empire, **FortR** 3538, 3554

Chats with Jane Clermont, **NC** 2479, 2508
Collectivist prospect in England, 2683

Graham-Campbell, Sir Rollo Frederick, 1868–1946, police magistrate. *WWW.*

The Judicature Acts at work, **NatR-II** 2486

Grange, Mrs. Amy Mary, novelist. *BMCat.*

The Archduchess Isabel, **DR** 2009
A passage in the history of Charles I, 2379
Fall of the Knights of the Temple, 2502

Grant, Sir Alexander: see *Index,* I, 914.

Tukárám—a study of Hinduism, **FortR** 363
Nature and origin of moral ideas, 764

Grant, Alexander Ronald, 1820–1903, divine. Venn.

Evils of competitive examinations, **NC** 513

Grant, Allan Ewen, 1862–1903, army physician in Madras. Crawford, *Indian Medical Services,* p. 373.

Letter: **NatR-II** 1189

Grant, Arthur: see *Index,* I, 914, and II, App. A.

Scottish origin of the Merlin myth, **ScotR** 377

Grant, Sir Charles: see *Index,* I, 914.

The poor of India, **NC** 119

Grant, Charles, 1841–1889: see *Index,* I, 914, and II, App. A.

Gottfried Keller: modern novel in Germany, **NatR-II** 82

Grant, Colin C., 1832–1889, R.C. bishop of Aberdeen. *Catholic Directory for Scotland/*1890, pp. 197–200.

Where St. Patrick was born, **DR** 2063, 2100

The land question in the Highlands, **NatR-II** 410

The Culdees [earliest Christians in Scotland], **ScotR** 202
Notice: 179

Grant, Daniel, b.1826, M.P. for Marlybone, 1880. LCCat., *House of Commons Registers.*

The tenure of land in Europe, **FM** 5206

Grant, George Munro: see *Index*, I, 914.

Canada and the Empire, **NatR-II** 1889

Grant, Thomas, 1816–1870, R.C. bishop of Southwark. *DNB.*

The sacred congregations of Rome, **DR** 547
The Inquisition, 587 collab.
Are heroes always heroic? 654
The Concordat with Austria, 785
St. Thomas Becket, 953
Notice: 824

Catholicity in India, **Ram** 886 collab.

Grant, W. A.; possibly William Grant, 1821–1849, the only W. Grant in registers of Ushaw Coll., where Richardson, publisher of the *Dublin*, says he was educated (Richardson to H. R. Bagshawe, May 15, 1848, Bagshawe Papers) and whose death is recorded in the *Rambler*, Mar. 1849, p. 548.

See **Ram** 10

Grant Duff, Sir Mountstuart Elphinstone: see *Index*, I, 914.

Must we then believe Cassandra? **FortR** 1096
England and Russia in the East, 1204
Balthasar Gracian, 1339
A plea for a rational education, 1384
Emilio Castelar, 1474, 1485
Sir Stafford Northcote, 1546
Chesterfield's *Letters to his Son*, 1588
South Africa, 1838

Theology in Holland, **FM** 4309
Belgium, 4662

The Life of Arthur Stanley, **NatR-II** 1534
Walter Bagehot, 2380

Russia, **NC** 5, 17
The five nights' debate [on Eastern question], 58
The situation [on Eastern question], 153
Is the popular judgment in politics more just than that of the higher orders? 167
Senior's *Conversations*, 206
The late debate [on Eastern question], 219
British interests in the East, 432
After six years [away from England], 1424
A bird's-eye view of India, 1715
Notice: 2401

Granville, Augustus Bozzi, 1783–1872, physician, Italian patriot. *DNB.*

Diet, **LR (1829)** 6

Granville, Joseph Mortimer, 1833–1900, physician. Boase.

"Drink," **NatR-II** 1200
A new theory of gout, 1815
Is insanity increasing? **NC** 288
Worry, 628

Grattan, Thomas Colley, 1792–1864, journalist. *DNB.* (See below, App. A.)

Industrial and moral state of Belgium, **FQR** 549

Graves, Charles Larcom, 1856–1944, Irish music critic. Grove.

Boycotting no remedy in music, **NatR-II** 568

Gray, Sir Albert, 1850–1928, civil servant in Ceylon. *WWW.*

The backwoods of Ceylon, **FortR** 1700

Gray, John Miller: see *Index*, I, 915.

Scottish arms and tartans, **ScotR** 437

Green, Alice Sophia Amelia (Stopford), 1848–1929, historian. *WWW, LCCat.*

Woman's place in world of letters, **NC** 3128
English and Dutch in the past, 3571
Growing bureaucracy and parliamentary decline, 3656
A visit to the Boer prisoners, 3764

Green, Emma Martha, b.1858, novelist; daughter of the Rev. George Clark Green in Venn and *CCD/76*. *LCCat., RG*; in *BMCat.* she appears as "Edith M. Green," but her mother's name (see Venn) was Emma.

Agricultural education of natives [in So. Africa], **FortR** 4395

Native unrest in South Africa, **NC** 3555

Green, Everard, 1844–1926, writer on heraldry, *WWW.*

Plea for the resurrection of heraldry, **NC** 2950

Green, Joseph Henry, 1791–1863, surgeon, philosopher. *DNB.*

?British Association: Bristol meeting, **FM** 1013

Green, Thomas Louis, 1799–1883, R.C. priest and controversialist. *Cath.Ency.*

The Oaths [required of an M.P.], **Ram** 1119

Green, Sir William Henry Rhodes, 1823–1912, army officer. *WWW*.

The "great wall" of India, **NC** 1140

Greene, Richard, d.1888/89, F.A.S.; grandson of Richard Greene, Lichfield antiquary in *DNB*. See *FM* no. 2013, pp. 731, 734; *Antiquaries*, 2nd s. vol. 12, p. 381.

Shakspeare's monument at Stratford, **FM** 2013

Greenwood, Frederick: see *Index*, I, 915.

A conversation in a balcony, **FortR** 2830
Extension of trade, 2888
The coming session: breakers ahead, 3007
Gladstone-Hartington controversy, 3206
The political outlook, 3255

Suggested by Cobbett's ghost, **NatR-II** 1305
Free trade a variable expedient, 1351
The Farreresqueries of free trade, 1380
The personal gratification bill, 1457
Young genius, 1479
Rosemary, 1631
The squeeze, 1829
Reflections [on foreign affairs], 1880

The recent change in European affairs, **NC** 1628
Distractions of German statesmanship, 1663
Misery in great cities, 1709
Wool-gatherings [on love and kindness], 1749
The newspaper press, 1876
The press and government, 1900
The law of the beasts, 3181
England at war, 3233
The Anglo-American future, 3311
The cry for new markets, 3444
The Chinese revolt, 3710
The working man and the War charges, 3730

Greg, Louis

The agnostic at church, **NC** 666

Greg, Percy: see *Index*, I, 916.

The Lords as a senate, **FortR** 2225
The future of the peerage, 2245

The future value of gold, **FM** 3863
The Rochdale pioneers, 3994

The working classes, **NatR-II** 50
Representation of the people: redistribution, 133
American poetry, 162
Stimulants and narcotics, 266
The new Radicals, 287

Some uses of a parliamentary seat, 352
Why should we break up the marriage code? 514
The gates of Hades [belief in ghosts], 763

Greg, William Rathbone: see Index, I, 916, and II, App. A.

Grant Duff's lecture on *Rocks Ahead*, **FortR** 1110
Employment of our Asiatic forces in European wars, 1475
Rectifications, 1495

England's future attitude towards Europe and the world, **FM** 4552
The Jamaica problem, 4630
Failure of "natural selection" in man, 4900
The cost of a Napoleon [III], 5071
The condition of French politics, 5194
Suum Cuique: moral of Paris catastrophe, 5223
Strikes, short hours, poor-law and *laissez-faire*, 5343

Harriet Martineau [her *Autobiography*], **NC** 68
The soul and future life, 96
Is the popular judgment in politics more just than that of the higher orders? 200
Foreign policy of Great Britain, 214
Verify your compass [on conscientiousness], 262
The grave perplexity before us [problem of labor], 283
Rocks ahead and harbours of refuge, 308

Gregory XVI, Pope, 1765–1846. *Cath.Ency.*

Allocution [on Tonquin martyrs], **DR** 179

Gregory, Francis Ambrose, 1848–1927, missionary to Madagascar. *WWW*.

The French in Madagascar, **NC** 3052

Gregory, Lady Isabella Augusta: see *Index*, I, 917

Through Portugal, **FortR** 2094
Glimpses of the Soudan, 2148

Ireland, real and ideal, **NC** 3374

Gregory, John Walter, 1864–1932, geologist, explorer. *DNB*.

An expedition to Mount Kenya, **FortR** 3475

Proposed German barrier across Africa, **NC** 2881

Gregory, Sir Richard Arman, 1864–1952, scientist. *WWW*.

The spectroscope in recent chemistry, **FortR** 3684

Mars as a world, **NatR-II** 2408

Gregory, Robert: see *Index*, I, 917.

Church [of England] during present century, **NatR-II** 4, 42, 90
Is crime increasing with spread of education? 405
The laity in the Church of England, 564
Extension of the episcopate, 681

Influence upon morality of a decline in religious belief, **NC** 24
Religion and the rates, 823
Why I shall vote for the Unionist candidate, 2247

Gregory, Sir William Henry, 1817–1892, statesman. *DNB*.

The Arundel Society, **NC** 982
Egypt and the Soudan, 1103
Loyalty of the Indian Mohammedans, 1354
More words on Daniel O'Connell, 1692

Greig, David, d.1903, Scottish divine. *CCD/* 1903; *Clergy Directory*/1904.

Speculative basis of modern unbelief, **FortR** 2171

Grenfell, Henry Riversdale: see *Index*, I, 917.

Banking and commercial legislation, **NC** 289
What is a pound? 593
What is a standard [on bimetallism]? 718
The enclosure of commons, 1185

Grenfell, William Henry, Baron Desborough, 1855–1945, public servant, sportsman. *DNB*.

Gladstone and the currency, **FortR** 3404
Oxford *v.* Yale, 3545

Tarpon-fishing, **NatR-II** 2360

Lost in the Rockies, **NC** 2217

Grenville, Richard Plantagenet, 2nd Duke of Buckingham and Chandos, 1797–1861. *Complete Peerage, DNB*.

See: **Ram** 674

Greswell, William Henry Parr: see *Index*, I, 917.

The Germans in So. Africa, **FortR** 2217, 3757

Emigration and "Friendly Societies," 2453
The crisis in Newfoundland, 3619
So. Africa: the high commissionership, 3799
Federalism in So. Africa, 3949
England and France in West Africa, 4050
King Alfred's country, 4334
The Dutch Church and the Boers, 4402
Some aspects of the Boer War, 4417

The late Sir Bartle Frere, **NatR-II** 193
Colonial governors, 397
The Colonial Conference and imperial defence, 526
Our first amphictyonic council, 635
Colonization and the Friendly Societies, 742
A poet's corner, 826
Wordsworth and the Quantock hills, 903
The Imperial Federation League, 911
A Somersetshire valley, 1218
South African policy, 1502

Greville, Lady Beatrice Violet (Graham), 1842–1932, wife of Algernon William Fulke Greville, 2nd Baron Greville. Burke, *Complete Peerage*.

Social reforms for the London poor, **FortR** 2121

Our ideals, **FM** 6369

Men-servants in England, **NatR-II** 1250
The new wedlock, 1285
Victims of vanity, 1406

Women and worship in Burmah, **NC** 2232

Grey, Albert Henry George, 4th Earl Grey, 1851–1917, statesman. *DNB*.

Proportional v. majority representation, **NC** 1070
Proportional representation, 1094 collab.

Grey, Sir George, 1812–1898, colonial governor. *DNB*.

The death-laments of savages, **FortR** 651

Grey, Gordon

Competitive examinations, **FortR** 2494

Grey, Sir Henry George: see *Index*, I, 917.

The referendum, **NatR-II** 1552

Past and future policy in South Africa, **NC** 292
How shall we retain the colonies? 313
South Africa, 527
Ireland, 733
Ireland and the Empire, 898, 919
The House of Commons, 978

The prospect in South Africa, 1384
The government and the tithes, 1823
The Irish Land Purchase Bill, 1904
In peril from parliament, 1951, 1981
Protection—free trade—fair trade, 2148

Grey, Henry M., explorer. *BMCat.*

The future of Morocco, **NatR-II** 2248

Grey, Maria Georgina (Shirreff), 1816–1906, writer on education. *DNB.*

Men and women, **FortR** 1639, 1814

Idols of society, **FM** 5530

Grey-Egerton, Lady Henrietta Elizabeth Sophia (Denison), d.1924, wife of Sir Philip le Belward Grey-Egerton. Burke under Egerton and Denison.

Camp life in Morocco, **NC** 2195
Alaska and its glaciers, 2329

Gribble, Norah (Royds): see *Index,* I, 918.

Conduct and Greek religion, **FortR** 3058

Griffin, Sir Lepel Henry, 1838–1908, Anglo-Indian administrator. *DNB.*

House of Commons and Indian finance, **FortR** 993
The Eastern question, 1014
The Indian civil service examinations, 1145
Indian princes at home, 2089
A visit to Philistia [America], 2124
The harvest of democracy, 2149
England's place in India [attack on W. S. Blunt], 2289
Peace or war, 2307
The Burman and his creed, 3008
The Bengáli in politics, 3223
The Amir of Afghanistan, 3309

England and France in Asia, **NC** 2473
The lotos eaters [the opium trade], 2552
Chitral and the frontier policy, 2765
Kashmir, 2846
Russia, Persia, and England, 2952
Breakdown of the "forward" frontier policy, 3178

Griffith, T. B.

The temperance question, **DR** 2330

Griffith-Boscawen, Sir Arthur Sackville Trevor, 1865–1946, M.P., civil servant. *WWW.*

The Church in Wales, **NatR-II** 1385
A warning from Wales, 1477
The attack on the Church, 1587 collab.
A recent visit to Japan, 1870

Church reform, 1949
Raiding the clergy, 2124
Some personal impressions of the army, 2529

Griffiths, Arthur George Frederick: see *Index,* I, 918.

Newgate, **FortR** 1923
Why have a hangman? 2095
?Armed strength of England, 2295 collab.
The pictures at the Garrick Club, 2435
An Algerian winter-resort: Biskra, 3618
Advancement in the army, 3710
Our second line of defence [the army], 3767
Egypt and its frontier, 3783
To Akasheh [in the Soudan], 3806
The conquest of the Soudan, 3878
After Khartoum, 3940
Khartoum in sight, 4014
Kitchener and Khartoum, 4175
Butler's *Life of Colley,* 4242
Hotels at home and abroad, 4320
The conduct of the war, 4387
The War Office, 4405
Our military needs, 4431
Heroes of the war, and others, 4522

French penal colonies, **NC** 1417

Grimes, Thomas, 1798–1850, schoolmaster, journalist. Information from the librarian at Friends' House, London.

Affghanistan, **DR** 252
Algeria, 260

Mexican antiquities, **FQR** 209

Groom-Napier, Charles Ottley, 1839–c.1895, miscellaneous writer. Boase.

Autobiography of a vegetarian, **FM** 5836

Groome, Francis Hindes: see *Index,* I, 918.

Gipsy folk-tales, **NatR-II** 740

Grose, Thomas Hodge, 1845–1906, registrar of Oxford University. *DNB.*

Letter: **FortR** 3668

Grote, Harriet: see *Index,* I, 918.

Letters of Sir George Cornewall Lewis, **FM** 5118

Groves, Edward C., Irish parson of Dublin. Russell, "Early Reviewers," pp. 82, 83

Maynooth College, **DR** 28
The fisheries of Ireland, 56
Bishop of Exeter and the Catholic Oath, 94

Guest, Lady Cornelia Henrietta Maria (Spencer-Churchill), 1846/47–1927, wife of Ivor Bertie Guest, 1st Baron Wimborne. Burke; *Times*, Jan. 24, 1927, p. 7c.

The ritualist conspiracy, **NC** 3353
Ritualism and the general election, 3726

Gull, Sir William Withey: see *Index*, I, 919.

The nursing crisis at Guy's Hospital, **NC** 447
The ethics of vivisection, 693

Gumley, N. W.

The oratory of the recess [of parliament], **NatR-II** 126

Gundry, Richard Simpson: see *Index*, I, 919.

Progress in China, **FortR** 2875
Judicial torture in China, 2932
Russia and China, 3274
Missionaries in China, 3399
Corea, China, and Japan, 3563
Ancestor worship in China, 3600
Hong Kong and the Straits Settlements, 3656
English industry, Eastern competition, 3712
China, England, and Russia, 3863
China: spheres of interest, open door, 4300
The Yangtze region, 4333
The last palace intrigue at Peking, 4462

China and her tributaries, **NatR-II** 187
India and Thibet, 551
The position in Thibet, 755
The Chinese atrocities, 1212
Notre-Dame de Boulogne, 1330
France, England, and Siam, 1446
Our Lady of Pootoo [Buddhist goddess], 1511

Gurney, Archer Thompson: see *Index*, I, 919.

France as it is, **FortR** 57

Political economy, **NatR-II** 402
British House of Peers, 442

Gurney, Edmund: see *Index*, I, 919.

Critics and class-lists, **DR** 2061

On some disputed points in music, **FortR** 1277
The ethics of pain, 1868
A musical crisis, 1951
Transferred impressions and telepathy, 2013 collab.
Phantasms of the living, 2022 collab.

On the controversy of life, **FM** 6081
On song, 6145
The human ideal, 6486

Evidence in matters extraordinary [psychical research], **NatR-II** 242
Aspects of mesmerism, 330 collab.
Letter: 524

On music and musical criticism, **NC** 193, 320
Thought-reading, 727 collab.
Wagner and Wagnerism, 829
Mesmerism, 917 collab.
Apparitions, 994, 1015, both collab.
Letters on phantasms, 1463

Guthrie, Walter Murray, 1869–1911, M.P. *Landed Gentry.*

The South African war hospitals, **NC** 3724

Guy, Robert Ephrem, 1833–1899, English Benedictine. *Benedictine Bibliog.*

Calderwood and Mill upon Hamilton, **DR** 1133
M'Cosh's *Intuitions of the mind* and *Examination of Mill's Philosophy*, 1181

Guy, William Augustus, 1810–1885, medical statistician, sanitary reformer. *DNB.*

The sanitary question, **FM** 2368
The Sanitary Commission and the health of the metropolis, 2380
1774 and 1844; or, The prisoner and the labourer, 2408
Church Lane, St. Giles', 2427
The plague of beggars, 2440
The Public Health Bill, 2510
Work and wages, 2656
Cholera gossip, 2674
Thomas Carlyle and John Howard, 2713
Neglected health, 3257
Military hospitals a century ago, 3335
Mortality in the army, 3716
Consumption in the Guards, 3750
See: 2440

Guyot, Yves: see *Index*, I, 919.

The new French chamber, **NC** 1222
Où allons-nous? 2344
Socialism in France, 2487
The Dreyfus drama and its significance, 3413

Gwyn, Francis, 1648–1734, privy councillor. DNB.

Mr. Francis Gwyn's journal, **FortR** 2509

Gwynn, Stephen Lucius: see *Index*, I, 919.

Mr. Robert Louis Stevenson, **FortR** 3575
Posthumous works of R. L. Stevenson, 4101
The autumn's books, 4553

H

Habershon, Samuel Osborne, 1825–1889, physician. *DNB*.

The nursing crisis at Guy's Hospital, **NC** 448

Hadden, James Cuthbert: see *Index*, I, 920.

Multiplication of musicians, **NatR-II** 2043

The change of our musical pitch, **NC** 2837
The regulation of street music, 2943
The authorship of "Rule Britannia," 3039
The teaching of music in schools, 3144
The Wagner mania, 3322
The tinkering of hymns, 3596

Music in early Scotland, **ScotR** 220
The national music of Scotland, 239
Ecclesiastical music in Scotland, 265
Literary materials of first Scottish psalter, 302
Scottish paraphrases, 417
Songs of Scotland before Burns, 474
Plagiarism and coincidence, 524
Music in Old England, 538
George Thomson, 569
Mendelssohn, Moscheles, and Chopin in Scotland, 624

Hadden, Robert Henry, 1854–1909, divine. *WWW*.

The city parochial charities, **NC** 554

Haddow, Robert

The miners of Scotland, **NC** 1594

Haden, Sir Francis Seymour: see *Index*, I, 920.

The art of the painter-etcher, **NC** 1868
The Royal Society of Painter Etchers, 2045

Hadfield, Matthew Ellison, 1812–1885, architect of Sheffield. Boase.

Town churches, **Ram** 195 collab.

Hæber, Dr. F.

Homburg, **FortR** 2493

Haeckel, Ernst Heinrich Philipp August, 1834–1919, German scientist. *NDB*.

Huxley and Karl Vogt, **FortR** 3701

Haffkine, Waldemar Mordecai Wolff, 1860–1930, bacteriologist. *WWW*.

Vaccination against Asiatic cholera, **FortR** 3336

Haggard, Sir Henry Rider: see *Index*, I, 920.

An olive branch from America, **NC** 1473

Haines, Herbert, d.1892, barrister. Venn.

Open coast towns, international law, **NatR-II** 844
Food supplies and international law, 865
A plea for scholarships, 943
The evil May-Day [1517], 1013
France and Heligoland, 1046
Letters: 735, 808, 957, 996, 1146, 1234, 1299

Hake, Alfred Egmont: see *Index*, I, 921, and II, App. A.

The American tariff war, **FortR** 3001 collab.

Goschen's mission [bank reform], **NatR-II** 1240
Letter: 948

Haldane, Elizabeth Sanderson, 1862–1937, humanitarian. *DNB*.

Friendly Societies for women, **NatR-II** 1956

Haldane, John Scott, 1860–1936, scientist. *DNB*.

Vitalism, **NC** 3343

Haldane, Louisa Kathleen (Trotter), wife of John Scott Haldane, q.v. *DNB* under her husband.

Training in patriotism, **NatR-II** 1165

Haldane, Richard Burdon: see *Index*, I, 921.

Is a National party possible? **FortR** 2628

Lord Salisbury and the House of Lords, **NatR-II** 1675

Haldane-Duncan, Robert Adam Philips, 3rd Earl of Camperdown, 1841–1918, lord of admiralty. *WWW* under Camperdown.

Floods, **NC** 950
Who is to pay for the [Boer] War? 3633

Hale, Sir Lonsdale Augustus: see *Index*, I, 921.

Autumn manoeuvres, for civilians, **NatR-II** 1685
Unreadiness of the volunteers, 2180

Hale, Sir Lonsdale Augustus (*continued*)
Professional ignorance in the army, **NC** 1448
Das I. Garde-Dragoner-Regiment, 1761
The war-game, 2003
An army without leaders, 2892
Our peace training for war, 3602
The home generals, 3678
The staff work in the [Boer] War, 3713

Hales, John Wesley: see *Index*, I, 921.

King Lear, **FortR** 1117

Old English metrical romances, **FM** 5716
At Stratford-on-Avon, 6039

Milton's Macbeth, **NC** 2134

Halévy, Ludovic, 1834–1908, French dramatist. *Grand Larousse.*

See: **FortR** 3736

Halhed, William B., Liverpool merchant. *Blackwood Papers Cat.*

On commercial "corners," **NC** 635

Haliburton, Thomas Chandler, 1796–1865, humorist, lawyer. *DNB.*

The old judge, in 11 installments from **FM** 2190 to 2398

Halil-Ganem: see Ganem, Halil.

Hall, Agnes (Crombie), 1777–1846, misc. writer. *DNB, Blackwood Papers Cat.*

Autobiography of a Scottish borderer, **FM** 609
Lochead's daughter, 863

Hall, Basil: see *Index*, I, 921.

On the law of storms, **FQR** 526

Basil Hall on mechanics' institutes, **FM** 5

Hall, Christopher Newman, 1816–1902, Congregational divine. *DNB.*

Nonconformists and Unionism, **FortR** 3049

Hall, Fitzedward, 1825–1901, philologist. *DNB.*

English rational and irrational, **NC** 493

Hall, George Rome, 1835–1896, divine. Boase.

Present feeling of the working classes, **NatR-II** 881
The British workman, 915
Public health and politics, 946

Hall, Sir Hugh, 1848–1940. barrister, journalist. *WWW.*

The law of theft, **NatR-II** 572
Irish traits of thought and speech, 973

Hall, Joseph, assoc. member Institute of Civil Engineers.

Letter: **NatR-II** 348

Hall, Theodore Hall, b.1854, barrister. Allibone, *M at B.*

The rural boroughs, **NatR-II** 170

Hall, William Edward: see *Index*, I, 922.

Monte Cassino, **FortR** 271, 278

Hallam, Arthur Henry, 1811–1833, subject of Tennyson's *In Memoriam. DNB.*

Sorelli's Italian translation of Milton, **FQR** 251

Hallam, Henry: see *Index*, I, 922.

Sismondi's *History of France,* **FQR** 81

Hallett, Frederick F. *BMCat.*

Our new wheat-fields at home, **NC** 516

Hallett, Holt Samuel: see *Index*, I, 922, and II, App. A.

British trade and China, **FortR** 4111
Western nations and Eastern markets, **NC** 2539
New British markets: western China, 2793
France and Russia in China, 3089
The partition of China, 3232
Lord Salisbury's score in China, 3296
The war-cloud in the farthest East, 3579

Hallett, Wyndham Hughes: see Hughes-Hallett, James Wyndham.

Halpin, James, R.C. canon. *Irish CD/1926.*

Temperance legislation, **DR** 2216
Temperance and the social question, 2403
Notice: 2583

Hambleton, Godfrey William, b.1852, medical writer. Venn, *Medical WW/1915.*

Letter: **FortR** 3121

Hamerton, Philip Gilbert: see *Index*, I, 922.

The artistic spirit, **FortR** 26
Housing of national art treasures, 70
The place of landscape painting, 138
Leslie, 167
Proudhon as a writer on art, 194

Gustave Doré's Bible, 235
Two art philosophers [H. Taine, C. Lévêque], 270
A canoe voyage, 373
The philosophy of etching, 590
Claude Tillier, unknown satirist, 604
Letter: 3237

Hamilton, Adam, O.S.B., 1841–1908. *Benedictine Bibliog.*

Ancient Benedictine customs, **DR** 2049
The nuns of Syon, 2110
Benedictine government, 2299
Bishops of Exeter in thirteenth, fourteenth centuries, 2487
Notice: 2212

Hamilton, Alexander Henry Abercromby, 1829–1911, J.P. *Landed Gentry.*

Quarter sessions, in 11 installments from **FM** 5820 to 5998
The new education bill [Agricultural Children's Act], 5828
Trial of two Quakers in time of Cromwell, 6086
Strafford, 6113

Hamilton, C.; possibly Mrs. Catherine Jane Hamilton of Dublin in *Index*, I, 923, and II, App. A.

Ireland's only chance, **NatR-II** 519

Hamilton, C. J.; possibly Mrs. Catherine Jane Hamilton of Dublin, in previous entry.

Land League ballads, **NatR-II** 889

Hamilton, Lord George Francis: see *Index*, I, 923.

Is our sea-power to be maintained? **NatR-II** 1508
Ocean highways, 1590

Hamilton, Sir Ian Standish Monteith, 1853–1947, army officer. *DNB.*

Our true policy in India, **FortR** 2796

Hamilton, James, 2nd duke of Abercorn, 1838–1913, M.P. *DNB.*

Spoliation of Irish landlords, **NatR-II** 2012

Hamilton, Lady Margaret Frances (Hely-Hutchinson), 1856/57–1937, wife of Douglas James Proby Hamilton, later Proby. Burke under Abercorn; *Times*, Mar. 4, 1937, p. 16b under Proby.

Household clubs, **NC** 2214

Hamilton, Mary A. Baillie: see under Baillie-Hamilton, Mary A.

Hamilton, Lady Maud Caroline (Lascelles), 1846/47–1938, wife of Lord George Francis Hamilton, q.v. Burke under Abercorn; *Times*, Apr. 6, 1938, p. 14e.

Mission women, **NC** 1072

Hamilton, Sir Richard Vesey: see *Index*, I, 923.

Our invasion scares and panics, **NC** 2896

Hamilton, Sir Robert George Crookshank, 1836–1895, gov. of Tasmania. *DNB.*

Ruin of the civil service, **NC** 1931
Lending money to Australia, 2265

Hamilton-Hoare, Henry William: see *Index*, I, 923.

Book of Job and Plato's dialogue on justice, **FortR** 1206
Thomas Hobbes, 2204

Pensées of Pascal, **NatR-II** 56
Club sketches of old London, 490

The English Bible: Wyclif to Coverdale, **NC** 3288
The English Bible from Henry VIII to James I, 3454

Hamley, Sir Edward Bruce: see *Index*, I, 924.

Snow pictures [travels in Canada], **FM** 2540
Peace campaigns of Ensign Faunce, in 12 installments from 2572 to 2718

Our geographical position and future trade, **NatR-II** 143

The armies of Russia and Austria, **NC** 170
The Channel tunnel, 713
The second division at Tel-El-Kebir, 791
The volunteers in time of need, 1102
The defencelessness of London, 1545
The question of imperial safety, 1556

Hammill, Fred

Labour representation, **FortR** 3492

Hammond, Walter John. *BMCat.*

Liberating the slaves in Brazil, **NC** 1574

Hampson, John Nicoll, 1866–1940, army officer. Burke.

Britain v. France and Russia, **NatR-II** 2168

Hanbury, Robert William, 1845–1903, politician. *DNB.*

Our army, **FortR** 3227

Hanbury, Robert William (*continued*)
An Irish compromise? **NatR-II** 1680

The spoilt child of Europe [Greece], **NC** 378

Hancock, Charles

Visit to the familistère at Guise, **FortR** 3344
Working-class settlements in Mulhouse and Milan, 3525

Hancock, William Neilson, 1820–1888, economist. Boase.

Ireland, **FortR** 1655

Handley, Hubert, b.1853/54, divine, biblical critic. Foster, *CCD/1902*.

Why men will not be clergymen, **NC** 1184

Hankin, Ernest Hanbury, 1865–1939, Indian government service. *WWW.*

Bhowáni, the cholera-goddess, **NC** 2997

Hankin, St. John Emile Clavering, 1869–1909, playwright. *DNB.*

Old friends with a new face [revised spelling of Indian names], **FortR** 3997

The sins of St. Lubbock [bank holiday], **NC** 3087

Hannay, David: see *Index*, I, 926.

The paintings of Mr. [Dante Gabriel] Rossetti, **NatR-II** 9

Hannigan, Denis F., Irish misc. writer. *BMCat.*

Letter: **NatR-II** 842

Hardie, James Keir, 1856–1915, socialist, labor leader. *DNB.*

Fair and bad trade: the views of labour, **NatR-II** 1365

Chamberlain's programme, **NC** 2318
The Independent Labour Party, 2682
Independent Labour Party's programme, 3401 collab.

Hardinge, William Money, b.1854/55, novelist. Foster, *BMCat.*

Chrysanthema, **NC** 241
French verse in English, 586

Hardman, Frederick: see *Index*, I, 927.

?State and prospects of Mexico, **FQR** 852
The writings of Charles Sealsfield, 897

Hardy, Alfred E. Gathorne: see Gathorne-Hardy, Alfred E.

Hardy, Ernest George, 1852–1925, Roman historian. *WWW.*

Provinces of the Roman Empire [by Mommsen], **ScotR** 223

Hardy, Harold, b.1863/64, writer. Foster, *BMCat.*

Letter: **NatR-II** 1310

Hardy, Horatio Nelson: see *Index*, I, 929.

Our great London hospitals, **FM** 5580, 5617
The first London dispensaries, 5677

Hardy, John Frederic, 1826–1886, proctor of Cambridge University; Alpinist. Venn.

Idle days in the High Alps, **FM** 5520
Things we have eaten, 5563

Hardy, Reginald, late a West India planter; perhaps a pseudonym.

A ride through the sugar-canes, **FM** 2702

Hardy, Thomas: see *Index*, I, 929.

For conscience sake, **FortR** 3052
The midnight baptism, 3077
Letter: 2627

An indiscretion in the life of an heiress, **NQM** 147
The distracted young preacher, 173
Fellow-townsmen, 215
Notice: 198

Hare, Thomas: see *Index*, I, 929.

An electoral reform, **FortR** 98
Keystone of parliamentary reform, 164
Responsibility in representative government, 209
Charitable endowments, 426
Public and private property, 571, 601
Estates of endowments as instruments, 665
Representative government, 1175
The Reform Bill of the future, 1428
Representation and misrepresentation, 2275

Representation in practice and theory, **FM** 3939
Representation of locality and intelligence, 3964

Harkness, Margaret Elise, writer on labor problems. *BMCat.*

A week on a labour settlement [in Australia], **FortR** 3533

The municipality of London, **NatR-II** 28, 76

Women as civil servants, **NC** 625
Railway labour, 782

Harlez, Charles Joseph de, 1832–1889, Orientalist, prof. Univ. of Louvain. *Cath. Ency.*

The primitive religion of the Chinese, **DR** 1924
So-called "Sacred Books" of China, 1986
The system of Lao-tze, 2026
History of Chinese philosophy, 2072
The Buddhistic schools, 2177
Buddhist propaganda in Christian countries, 2230
A new system of Biblical history, 2286
Infanticide in China, 2341
The propagation of Islam, 2401
Buddhist sects in Japan, 2464
Notices: 1779, 1941

Harlin, T.; possibly the Thomas Harlin, B.A. of Cambridge, 1856, in Venn, who went to Australia.

Ceylon, **FM** 3973

Harmsworth, Alfred Charles William, Viscount Northcliffe, 1865–1922, newspaper proprietor. *DNB.*

"Ordinary business principles," **NC** 3695

Harnack, Adolf: see *Index*, I, 929.

The Apostles' Creed, **NC** 2433

Harness, Arthur, 1838–1927, army officer, R.A. *WWW.*

The Zulu campaign, **FM** 6274

Harness, Nathaniel A.; perhaps a pseudonym.

A spiritualistic seance, **NQM** 5
Spiritualism in England, 33

Harper, Charles George, 1863–1943, illustrator. *WWW, LCCat.*

The Great Central Railway, **FortR** 4262
The government and London architecture, 4340

Harper, Samuel Browne A., b.1814/1815, R.C. priest. Venn, Gorman.

The philosophy of religion [on W. H. Smith's *Thorndale*], **DR** 877
Notice: 874

Harper, Thomas Norton, 1821–1893, S.J., philosopher. Boase.

From logic to God, **DR** 1909

Dublin palace "fiction," **Ram** 627 collab.
?A visit to the coast of Albania, 816

Harries, Henry: see *Index*, I, 929.

The progress of weather study, **NatR-II** 1049

Harris, Alfred: see *Index*, I, 929.

Untried remedy for Irish grievances, **NatR-II** 121
Letter: 335

Harris, Annie M.; perhaps used pseudonym "Annie Armitt" (see Part C below). *BMCat.*

Mystic novels, **ScotR** 73
The story of Mary Shelley, 374

Harris, Sir Augustus Henry Glossop, 1852–1896, actor. *DNB.*

The national theatre, **FortR** 2384

Harris, Elizabeth Furlong Shipton, 1822–1852, author of *From Oxford to Rome.* Boase under Harris, Furlong Elizabeth Shipton, but see *BMCat.* and H&L.

Letter: **DR** 454

Harris, Frank, 1856–1931, born James Thomas Harris, man of letters; ed. *Fortnightly Rev. DNB.*

The Radical programme: housing of poor, **FortR** 2096
Natural laws and the Home Rule problem, 2488
Randolph Churchill's resignation, 2555
Our true foreign policy, 2723
What our navy should be, 2760
A modern idyll, 3099
Montes, the matador, 3110
A triptych, 3130
Elder Conklin, 3228
A straight flush, 3257
Profit and loss, 3267
Notes: 2503, 2627, 2871, 3040

Harris, George Robert Canning: see *Index*, I, 929.

The development of cricket, **NatR-II** 74

Harris, George Robert Canning (*continued*)
A fortnight in French Cochin China and Cambodgia, 151

Harris, Sir Henry Percy, 1856–1941, barrister. *WWW*.

London County Council, **NatR-II** 1690 collab.
The London housing problem, 2409

Harris, Susan (Hamilton), Countess of Malmesbury, 1854–1935, wife of 3rd Earl of Malmesbury. Burke, *Complete Peerage*.

The future of marriage, **FortR** 3182

The Primrose League, **NatR-II** 441

Harris, W.

India's expectations, **FM** 5795

Harris, Walter Burton: see *Index*, I, 930.

Tiflis, **NatR-II** 1837
Morocco question and [Spanish-American] War, 2200

Harris, William, 1826–1911, of Birmingham. *LCCat.*; *Biograph*, 2 (1879), 399–404.

A year of the Birmingham school-board, **FortR** 1139

Harris, William James, 1835–1911, M.P. *WWW*.

Protection: workman's point of view, **NatR-II** 211
Economic condition of Ireland, 431
Decay of British agriculture, 639
Reply to Randolph Churchill [on free trade], 651

Harrison, Alfred Allen, writer on history of Berkshire, *Cath.WW*/1927.

Sir Francis Englefield, **DR** 2535

Harrison, Charles: see *Index*, I, 930.

The City Unification Commission, **FortR** 3375

Harrison, Ethel B. (Harrison), 1851/52–1916, wife of Frederic Harrison, q.v. *Times*, June 7, 1916, p. 7e.

An educational interlude, **FortR** 3771

Mothers and daughters, **NC** 2532
Smoke [smoking by women], 2634

Harrison, F. Bayford: see *Index*, I, 930.

Home Rule in the eighteenth century, **FortR** 2485

The censuses of the century, **NatR-II** 1132

Harrison, Frederic: see *Index*, I, 930.

Iron-masters' trade-union, **FortR** 9
The limits of political economy, 28
Good and evil of trade-unionism, 127
Industrial co-operation, 158
Our Venetian constitution, 380
Culture: a dialogue [on Matthew Arnold], 455
The transit of power, 490
The Trades-union Bill, 605
The positivist problem, 633
The romance of the peerage, 687
Cairnes on Comte and political economy, 696
The subjective synthesis, 707
Bismarckism, 736
The effacement of England, 752
The Revolution of the Commune, 779
The fall of the Commune, 799
The monarchy, 866
Mr. Brassey on work and wages, 888
Certain metaphysical problems, 901
The revival of authority, 914
The religion of inhumanity, 955
Public affairs, 996, 1004, 1012, 1021, 1029, 1045, 1053
The Conservative reaction, 1030
France, 1062
Mr. Lewes's *Problems of Life and Mind*, 1068
Past and present, 1276
Cross and crescent, 1311
Church and state, 1357
The Republic and the Marshal [MacMahon], 1416
The French Workmen's Congress, 1464
The English school of jurisprudence, 1512, 1524, 1545
Austin and Maine on sovereignty, 1512
Bentham's and Austin's analysis of law, 1524
The historical method, 1545
First impressions of the new [French] Republic, 1558
On the choice of books, 1567
Historical side of the conflict of laws, 1632
Conflict of laws analytically considered, 1642
Martial law in Kabul, 1645, 1679
Empire and humanity, 1671
A few words about the nineteenth century, 1897
Curiosities of the law of treason, 1909, 1917
Review of the year [on Positivism], 2272

The Life of George Eliot, 2284
Apologia pro fide nostra [positivism], 2769
The future of agnosticism, 2787
What the Revolution of 1789 did, 2828
The Irish leadership, 3037
Editorial horseplay [the Elgin Marbles], 3074
A survey of the thirteenth century, 3123
The emancipation of women, 3131
Bard of the Dimbovitza [Roumanian songs], 3150
How to drive Home Rule home, 3258
Mr. Huxley's controversies, 3268
Mr. Huxley's ironicon [sic], 3295
Situation abroad and at home, 3323
Rome revisited, 3365
The evolution of our race [on Pearson's *National Life and Character*], 3384
The royal road to history, 3418
Constantinople as an historic city, 3484
The problem of Constantinople, 3497
The municipal museums of Paris, 3552
An antiquarian ramble in Paris, 3556
The reaction and its lessons, 3703
Letter: 2647

Influence upon morality of a decline in religious belief, **NC** 23
The soul and future life, 45, 56, 99
Is the popular judgment in politics more just than that of the higher orders? 168
Creeds, old and new [impact of science and philosophy on religion], 500, 518
The creed of a layman, 563
Pantheism, and cosmic emotion, 619
The deadlock in the House of Commons, 622
The crisis of parliamentary government, 662
A few words about the eighteenth century, 826
The ghost of religion, 977
Agnostic metaphysics, 1033
A pedantic nuisance [original spelling of ancient names], 1232
More words about names, 1271
The Bishop of Carlisle on Comte, 1342
The two paths [on contemporary culture], 1501
Picture exhibitions, 1569
The sacrifice of education, 1617
Bryce's *American Commonwealth*, 1649
Are we making way [with the party system]? 1710
A breakfast-party in Paris, 1739
The new trades-unionism, 1783
Lord Rosebery and the London County Council, 1888
A Pompeii for the twenty-ninth century, 1926

Give back the Elgin Marbles, 1975
The centenary of Edward Gibbon, 2613
Theological pessimism, 2791
Ruskin as master of prose, 2816
Unto This Last [by Ruskin], 2848
Matthew Arnold, 2898
John Addington Symonds, 2946
John Stuart Mill, 2993
The modern Machiavelli [on Frederick Greenwood], 3174
On style in English prose, 3299
The historical method of Froude, 3341
Historical method of Freeman, 3376
Notices: 1654, 1655, 1699, 2592, 2709, 2710

Harrison, Henry, of Newcastle-on-Tyne. P.O. *Directory* /87

Letter: **NatR-II** 679

Harrison, Sir Henry Leland, 1837–1892, Indian civil servant. Boase, Buckland.

The religious tendencies of India, **DR** 1288
Indian theism, 1308

Harrison, Mary, writer of cook books. *BMCat.*

Cookery as a business, **NC** 2428

Harrison, Mary St. Leger (Kingsley), 1852–1931, novelist. *DNB.*

Youngest of the saints [General Gordon], **FortR** 2366
The other side of the moon [on Amiel], 2459

Harrod, Henry Dawes, b.1858, barrister. Gorman, *Cath.WW* /1927.

The Society of St. Vincent de Paul, **DR** 1864
The dwellings of the poor, 1915
Catholic boys' clubs, 1947
Royal Commission and homes of poor, 1972
Notice: 1930

Hart, Edward Styche

The Catholic vote, **NatR-II** 351

Hart, Ernest Abraham, 1835–1898, medical journalist and reformer. *DNB,* 1st suppl.

Condition of our state hospitals, **FortR** 139
Infirmaries for pauper sick, 217
Forty years in the desert [wastelands in Ireland], 2082

The British Jews, **FM** 3197

Hypnotism and humbug, **NC** 2147

Hart, Ernest Abraham (*continued*)
Cholera and our protection against it, 2300
The revival of witchcraft, 2357
Cholera and the Sultan, 2644

Hart, R. E. S.: see *Index*, I, 930, and II, App. A.

Zola's philosophy of life, **FortR** 3841

Hart, Sir Robert, 1835–1911, inspector-general of customs in China. *DNB.*

The Peking legations, **FortR** 4530

Hartley, May (Laffan): see *Index*, I, 931.

Convent boarding-schools, **FM** 5562

Hartshorne, Bertram Fulke, 1844–1921, barrister. *LCCat.*, Burke under Torrington.

The Weddas [in Ceylon], **FortR** 1240
The Rodiyas [in Ceylon], 1308
A chapter of Buddhist folk-lore, 1496

Harvey, Augustus A., 1839–1903, merchant, statesman in Newfoundland. *Ency. Canada*, Newfoundland suppl.

The Newfoundland fisheries dispute, **FortR** 2986 collab.

Harvey, Robert, de Genève; possibly Robert Harvey, surgeon general, 1842–1901, in *WWW*, but no evidence that he was ever in Switzerland; or Robert Harvey, Bachelier ès Lettres, in *BMCat.*

Edited: **NC** 177

Hastie, Andrew H., misc. writer. *BMCat.*

The telephone tangle, **FortR** 4209

The estate duty and the road round it, **NC** 2672

Hastings, Warren, 1732–1818, governor-general of India. *DNB.*

Origin and destination of the soul, **FM** 1861, 1873
Effects of moral causes on prosperity of nations, 1881

Hatchard, Marian L.

Portraiture in England, **NatR-II** 378 collab.
Miscalled cases of thought transference, 524 collab.

Hatherly, Stephen Georgeson, 1827–1905, organist. Pratt, *Music.* (See *Index*, I, 932.)

Byzantine ecclesiastical music, **ScotR** 256

Coptic ecclesiastical music, 277
Translated Greek office-books, 347

Hattersley

The Arabian Nights' Entertainments, **DR** 164
Fraser's *Travels in Koordistan and Mesopotamia*, 175
See: 153

Hatton, Harold Finch: see Finch-Hatton.

Haughton, George Dunbar, 1807–c.1888, divine. Boase.

New Clerical Subscription Act, **FortR** 42
Bishops and clerical subscription, 100
Notices: 82, 151, 253, 298, 326

Atheism, poetry, and music, **FM** 5568

Haulleville, Baron Prosper de, 1830–1898, Belgian historian. Seyn, *LCCat.*

On a letter of Montalembert's, **DR** 1538

Haussonville, Comte d': see Cléron, Gabriel Paul Othenin de.

Havelock-Allan, Sir Henry Marshman, 1830–1897, army officer. *DNB.*

A national training to arms, **FortR** 1242
Constantinople and our road to India, 1325
A general voluntary training versus conscription? 3904
England's military position, 3978

Haweis, Hugh Reginald: see *Index*, I, 932.

The coming crisis in Morocco, **FortR** 3198
Ghosts and their photos, 3317
The King, the Pope, and Crispi, 3524
Rubinstein, 3587
Morocco up to date, 4322

Haweis, Mary Eliza (Joy): see *Index*, I, 932.

The revolt of the daughters, **NC** 2543

Hawkins, Charles, 1812–1892, surgeon. *BMCat.*, *Surgeon Index*/2nd s.

Ether and chloroform, **DR** 599

Hawkins, J. M.

"Junius" and his time, **FM** 5592

Hawthorne, Julian: see *Index*, I, 932, and *Amer. WWW.*

Theeda: an allegory, **FM** 6310

Calladon, 6328
Rumpty-dudget, 6333

Mrs. Gainsborough's diamonds, **NQM** 137

Hawthorne, Nathaniel, 1804–1864, Amer. novelist. *DAB.*

The ghost of Doctor Harris, **NC** 3590

Hawtrey, Sir Ralph George, b.1879, economist. *WW/1969.*

The speed of warships, **FortR** 4009

The schoolboy's view of schoolmasters, **NatR-II** 2496

Hay, Beatrice J.

Letter: **NatR-II** 1086

Hay, Hon. Claude George Drummond, 1862–1920, businessman, M.P. *WWW*, Burke under Kinnoull.

Toryism and toil, **FortR** 3987 collab.

Hay, William Delisle, F.R.G.S., misc. writer. Allibone.

New Guinea question; a colonial point of view, **NatR-II** 73

Hayden, Mary Teresa, 1861/62–1942, prof. Univ. Coll. Dub. *Studies: an Irish Quarterly Review of Letters*, Sept. 1942, pp. 369–371; *WWW.*

The chansons de geste, **DR** 2229, 2431

Hayllar, Thomas Child, b.1835, barrister. Venn.

The Chinese view of missionaries, **NC** 2832

Hayman, Henry: see *Index*, I, 933.

Popular preaching, **BentQR** 15

Recent editions, Aristophanes and Sophocles, **DR** 1921
On the *Teaching of the Twelve Apostles*, 1946
Explorations of ancient sites in Rome, 1959
Jowett's *Politics of Aristotle*, 2010
John Henry Cardinal Newman, 2250
"Constitution of Athenians" ascribed to Aristotle, 2274
Gardiner's *Civil War*, 2338
Notice: 2335

The statistics of morality, **FortR** 2524

The rights of laymen in the Church, **NatR-II** 214
Voluntary schools, 367

The Byron ladies, 582
The voluntary schools crisis, 1510

Martin Luther, **NQM** 154

Hayman, John Marshall, b.1825, barrister. Venn.

English field sports, **BentQR** 29
Earl of Dundonald, 38

Hayter, Arthur Divett, 1st Baron Haversham, 1835–1917, army officer. *WWW* under Haversham.

Army promotion and retirement, **FortR** 1344
[Western] Ireland beyond the pale, 2549

Have we an army reserve? **NC** 1245

Haythornthwaite, Peter, 1846–1914, R.C. priest, chaplain to W. G. Ward. *Tablet*, Feb. 14, 1914. *Ward as Catholic*, p. 382.

Mrs. Inchbald, **DR** 1955

Hayward, Abraham: see *Index*, I, 933, and II, App. A.

Goethe's *Posthumous Works*, **FQR** 282, 326

Lady Herbert's *Impressions of Spain*, **FortR** 372

The drama in Paris, **FM** 4495
Spiritualism, 4505
Writings of Edmund About, 4560
Charles de Bernard, 4591
Lord Palmerston, 4602
Politics and prospects of Spain, 4603
Policy and prospects of the government, 4612
Clubs, 4633
Reform Bill and the government, 4642
Salons, 4651
Parliamentary reform, 4655
The ministry, 4679
The Reform League and the parks, 4689
Field-Marshal Viscount Combermere, 4700
Ministerial prospects, 4725
Ministerial prospects and reform, 4744
The Mexican drama [on politics], 4794
The Conservative transformation, 4819
More about Junius, 4828
Caucasian administration and Irish difficulty [on Disraeli], 4861
Caucasian administration in trouble [on Disraeli], 4870
Kinglake's *Invasion of the Crimea*, 4886
Religious creed of the Caucasian champion [Disraeli], 4901
Spain, 4920

Hayward, Abraham (*continued*)
The ministry and the Irish Church, 4937
Whist and whist-players, 4964
The Irish Church Bill, 5004
The Irish land question, 5046
Imperialism in 1870, 5145
John Stuart Mill [the *Autobiography*], 5490

Hayward, John Williams, b.1828, physician. *LCCat., Surgeon Index*/1st s.

A climate for the consumptive, **NatR-II** 1375

Hayward, Robert Baldwin, 1829–1903, mathematician. *DNB.*

Proportional representation, **NC** 964

Hazeltine, Mayo Williamson, 1841–1909, literary ed. of *N.Y. Sun. Amer.WWW.*

Studies of New York society, **NC** 2210

Hazlitt, William: see *Index*, I, 934.

On the punishment of death, **FM** 157

Head, Sir Edmund Walker: see *Index*, I, 934.

Translation from the Edda, **FM** 4582
Ballads from the Spanish, 4636a
The death of old King Gorm, 4651a
Visit of Thorfinn to King Magnus, 4833a

Spanish painters, **FQR** 310

Headley, Tanfield George, 1835–1905, solicitor, deacon. *Venn.*

Unity of Christians, **NatR-II** 791

Healy, John, 1841–1918, Irish R.C. bishop. *WWW.*

University education in Ireland, **DR** 2201

Healy, Timothy Michael: see *Index*, I, 935.

The Irish Parliamentary party, **FortR** 1965
Ireland and the Tory party, 2106
The Irish and the government, 2239

Heath, James Pulling. *Kelly's Directory for Devonshire*/83.

Irish land legislation, **NatR-II** 261
The lion's share of world's trading, 578

Heathcote, John Moyer, 1834–1912, tennis player. *DNB.*

Some developments of tennis, **NatR-II** 1591

Heather-Bigg, Ada, feminist. *RG.*

Female labour in the nail trade, **FortR** 2474

Portraiture in England, **NatR-II** 378 collab.
Miscalled cases of thought transference, 524 collab.

Women and the glove trade, **NC** 2136
What is "fashion"? 2349
A cry against home work, 2680

Heaton, Sir John Henniker: see *Index*, I, 937, and II, App. A, under Henniker-Heaton.

Universal penny postage, **FortR** 2525
Imperial five-farthing postage, 3476
Postal and telegraphic progress under Victoria, 3966
Imperial penny postage: revolt of the [colonies], 4169

The centenary of Australia, **NatR-II** 686

A penny post for the Empire, **NC** 1880
Post office "plundering and blundering," 2412
A postal Utopia, 3287
An imperial telegraph system, 3478
Sixpenny telegrams, 3684

Hedley, John Cuthbert, 1837–1915, O.S.B., bishop; ed. *Dublin Rev.*, 1879–1884. *Cath. Ency.*

Christian schools of Alexandria, **DR** 1086, 1118, 1149
Origen at Caesarea, 1168
St. Cyril and the tumults of Alexandria, 1187
Tizzani on St. Cyprian, 1219
St. Jerome, 1227
The case of St. Liberius, 1248
St. John Damascene, 1266
Fra Paolo Sarpi, 1309
Lacordaire and conferences of Notre Dame, 1334
St. Thomas of Aquin [by R. B. Vaughan], 1344, 1449
Evolution and faith, 1359
Father Baker's *Sancta Sophia*, 1565
The Douai Diaries, 1630
Address on school-work, 1634
To our readers, 1662
Catholicism and culture, 1663
Catholicism and Mr. W. H. Mallock, 1677
Cardinal Newman, 1698
Pope Leo XIII and modern studies, 1720
Text-books of philosophy, 1731
?Dr. Ward's *Doctrinal Essays*, 1741
Everlasting punishment, 1762
?The revision of the New Testament, 1784
Canonization of the Eighth of December, 1810
The Pope [and his political independence], 1822

The Holy See, and the Clergy of Ireland, 1881
Beginnings [of belief], 1892
?New Testament Vaticanism, 1904
?Christendom in ideal and in fact, 1913
Pope Leo XIII and the Freemasons, 1926
Mr. Henry George and the land, 1985
Catholic union and Catholic parties, 2001
The letters of the Popes, 2013
Dr. Mivart on faith and science, 2089
Can the Scriptures err? 2127
Physical science and faith, 2639
Notices: 1193, 1561
See: 1250

Heeley, Wilfred Lucas, 1833–1876, Indian civil servant. Venn, *Journal Rutgers Univ. Lib.*, 29 (June 1966), 43.

Sir Philip Sidney, **OxCam** 1, 15
Kingsley's *Sermons for the Times*, 8
Mr. Macaulay, 20
Froude's *History of England*, 37

Heeren, Arnold Hermann Ludwig, 1760–1842, historian, editor. *ADB.*

Notice: **FQR** 353

Helm, Elijah, 1837–1904, economic writer. *LCCat.*, *Times*, Dec. 13, 1904, p. 10d.

The Wolcott Commission: bimetallist view, **NatR-II** 2037

Helps, Sir Arthur: see *Index*, I, 936.

Uncle Tom's Cabin, **FM** 3001
Friends in council abroad, 3416, 3428, 3437
The India Bill, 3707
The Thames and its difficulties, 3759
War, 3828

Hemming, George Wirgman: see *Index*, I, 936.

The Ordnance Survey [of Great Britain and Ireland], **BentQR** 31

Past and future of Cambridge University, **NC** 855

Hemsterhuys, Francis, 1721–1790, Dutch philosopher. *EUI.*

Hemsterhuys on atheism, **FM** 5685

Henderson, James Scot: see *Index*, I, 936.

Hegel as a politician, **FortR** 712
Schelling's life and letters, 727
Reasoned realism [G. H. Lewes and positivism], 1200

Heneage, Everard Henry Fieschi, b.1860. Venn.

Foxhunters and farmers, **NatR-II** 1683

Henley, William Ernest: see *Index*, I, 936.

[Tommaso] Salvini, **NatR-II** 158
Tory press and Tory party, 1430

Hennell, Thomas: see *Index*, I, 937, and II, App. A.

"Standing Orders" of parliament and private bill legislation, **FortR** 256

Hennessy, John Pope: see Pope-Hennessy, John.

Hennessy, William Maunsell, 1829–1889, Irish scholar. *DNB.*

Trans: **FM** 5465

Henniker-Heaton, John: see Heaton, John Henniker.

Hennin, G. de

The coming crisis in Turkey, **FortR** 2528
A partition of Turkey, 2662

Henriques, Alfred Gutteres, barrister. Allibone.

The nursing crisis at Guy's Hospital, **NC** 449

Henslow, John Stevens: see *Index*, I, 937.

Dutrochet's *New Researches on Vegetable Physiology*, **FQR** 136
De Candolle's *Vegetable Physiology*, 269

Henson, Herbert Hensley: see *Index*, I, 937.

Foreign missions, **NatR-II** 2106
Mr. Kensit [controversy among Protestants], 2181
The confessional in the national Church, 2225
The British Sunday, 2326
The Archbishops' judgment, 2363
The Mivart episode, 2460

Hepburn, Arnold, asst. sec. of Bimetallic League.

Bimetallic side of the American crisis, **NatR-II** 1930

Heraud, John Abraham: see *Index*, I, 937.

Poetical genius as a creative power, **FM** 7
?On human perfectibility, 18

Heraud, John Abraham (*continued*)

Poetry of the Magyars [by Bowring], 20 collab.

Odes from the German of Klopstock, 30

?*The Dominie's Legacy* [by Picken; and Bulwer's *Pelham*], 37 collab.

?Mr. Edward Lytton Bulwer's novels, 57 collab.

?Place-men and parliamentary reporters, 120 collab.

Galt's *Life of Byron*, 127 collab.?

Mr. Godwin's novels, 129 collab.?

Southey's *Life of Bunyan*, 175 collab.?

Grant's notes on Byron's *Cain*, 200

Shelley: "The Wandering Jew," 229 collab. at least

Godwin's *Thoughts on Man*, 232 collab. at least

Landor's poems, 250 collab.

Rationalism, 262

Oliver Yorke at home, 270, 296, 341

Colloquy with Robert Southey, 270

German poetry, 275, 315, 369

Taylor's *Historic Survey of German Poetry*, 275

A conversation with Landor, 296

French, German, English philosophy, 300

Beowulf, the Niebelungen Lied, Klopstock, Stolberg, 315

Historical romance: Sir Walter Scott and his imitators, 340, 359

A dialogue with Goethe, 341

Burger, Gotter, Voss, and Holty, 369

Coleridge's philosophy [*Aids to Reflection*], 400

Cunningham's *Maid of Elvar*, 408

Letter on the doctrine of St. Simon, 409 collab.?

Historical drama [Pennie and Collier], 410

Lord Byron's juvenile poems, 439 collab.?

Sacred History of the World [by Sharon Turner], 456, 811

Landscape of the *Waverley Novels*, 481

Wordsworth's *Poetical Works*, 482

Asinarii scenici, 506 collab.?

Œuvres de Platon, 509

Illustrations of Byron's poetry, 528 collab.?

Taylor's *Life of Cowper*, 547

Hayward's translation of Goethe's *Faust*, 551

The Bridgewater treatises, 579, 598, 869, 1147, all collab.?

Dr. Chalmers and Sir Charles Bell, 598 collab.?

The Book of Enoch, 620 collab.?

Fanaticism and the natural historian of enthusiasm [Isaac Taylor], 657

Blackie's and Syme's translations of *Faust*, 716

Reminiscences of Coleridge, 740

Lord Byron's dramas, 767 collab.?

Coleridgeiana, 774

Odd thoughts on strange subjects, 799

A chapter of accidents, 826

Wordsworth's new volume of poetry, 830

Coleridge's *Table-Talk*, 844

Rev. Wm. Kirby and Doctor Roget, 869 collab.?

Asinarii scenici [Browning's *Paracelsus* and Taylor's *Philip van Artevelde*], 925 collab. at least

J. Sheridan Knowles' plays, 932

Southey's *Life of Cowper*, 972

Ion [by T. N. Talford] and *The Provost of Bruges*, 984

Isaac Taylor's *Physical Theory of Another Life*, 1000

Words on books [by Landor and Bulwer-Lytton], 1067 collab. at least

Carlyle's *French Revolution*, 1095

Rev. W. J. Irons on final causes, 1107

Dr. Buckland and Dr. Prout, 1147 collab.?

The poetry of Shelley, 1208

Notes: 876, 885, 1082

See: 25

Herbert, Alfred; perhaps the Alfred Herbert, B.A. 1868, Anglican divine, educator in Venn.

Edmund of Abingdon and the universities, **DR** 2633

Edward Thring of Uppingham, 2665

Notices: 2475?, 2709

Herbert, Arthur Robert Kenney: see Kenney-Herbert, A. R.

Herbert, Auberon Edward William Molyneux: see *Index*, I, 937.

The Canadian confederation, **FortR** 393

State education: a help or hindrance? 1711

A politician in trouble about his soul, 2006, 2031, 2080, 2113, 2147

"The Rake's Progress" in Irish politics, 3038

Slow destruction of the New Forest, 3059

Under the yoke of the butterflies [the idle rich], 3134, 3166

Sacrifice of education to examination, **NC** 1665

The last bit of natural woodland, 2094

A cabinet minister's vade-mecum, 2460

Herbert, Edward Henry Charles, 1837–1870, diplomat. Boase.

[Introduction to] "Thanasi Vaya," **FortR** 682

Herbert, George Robert Charles: see *Index,* I, 937.

Liberty and socialism, **NatR-II** 24
Liberty and Property Defence League, 338
Cripps versus free trade, 708

Reform of the House of Lords, **NC** 1089

Herbert, Henry Howard Molyneux: see *Index,* I, 937.

Imperial administration, **FortR** 1528
Lucius Carey, Lord Falkland, 1959
The Cape in 1888, 2722
Australia in 1888, 2806
Letter: 2627

The first of March, 1711 [on *Spectator* and *National Rev.*], **NatR-II** 3
The art of preaching, 70
Letters by Ruricola, 129, 160, 166, 221, 256, 286
Hadrian's "Address to His Soul," 267
A word to country gentlemen, 310
A vigil in Stonehenge, 317

National insurance, **NC** 490

Herbert, Mary Elizabeth (A'Court), Baroness of Lea, 1822–1911. *WWW, LCCat.*

The Russian Church, **DR** 2359
The Eucharistic Congress at Jerusalem, 2407
Six weeks in Russia, 2467
Catholic Episcopate in Russian Poland, 2499
Notice: 2520

Herbert, St. Leger Algernon, 1850–1885, war correspondent. *DNB.*

Our colonial policy, **FortR** 2139

Herford, Charles Harold: see *Index,* I, 938.

Ibsen's *Love's Comedy,* **FortR** 4403

Herford, Ivan S. Andrew: see *Index,* I, 938.

The Wise and Foolish Virgins, **NatR-II** 809

Herkless, William Robertson, 1849–1900, prof. of law, Glasgow Univ. *LCCat.,* Boase.

Legal position of a chairman, **ScotR** 500

Herkomer, Sir Hubert von, 1849–1914, painter. *WWW.*

Painting in enamels, **FortR** 4113

Heron, Denis Caulfield, 1826–1881, Dublin barrister. Boase.

Audin's *Henry VIII,* **DR** 510

Hérou, maintop-man of the frigate *Belle Poule* (see FM no. 1607); perhaps P. N. M. Hérou in *Bib.Nat.Cat.*

Budget of a blue jacket of the *Belle Poule* frigate, **FM** 1607, 1617, 1626

Herries, Edward, 1821–1911, diplomatic service. *WWW.*

Letter: **NatR-II** 213

Herring, George, 1832–1906, philanthropist. *DNB.*

Hydrophobia: treatment by Pasteur, **NatR-II** 940
Letter: 1028

Herschel, Sir John Frederick William: see *Index,* I, 938.

On atoms, **FortR** 7
On the origin of force, 33

Hervey, Felton: see Hervey-Bathurst, Sir Felton Elwell.

Hervey, Thomas Kibble, 1799–1859, poet, critic. *DNB.*

Life and writings of Mrs. Hemans, **DR** 34

Hervey-Bathurst, Sir Felton Elwell, 1782–1819, aide-de-camp to Duke of Wellington. Burke under Bathurst.

Letter on the battle of Waterloo, **NC** 2363

Heseltine, J. P., economist.

Great Britain's duty [re bimetallism], **NatR-II** 2088

The scramble for gold, **NC** 2507
The gold question, 2637

Hester, Jane: see Reilly, Jane Hester.

Heward, Edward Vincent: see *Index,* I, 938.

The menacing comet, **FortR** 4361

A glance at the comets, **NQM** 111

Tobacco in relation to health, **NC** 3116
Elizabethan rejoicings, 3153

Hewitt, James, 4th Viscount Lifford, 1811–1887. *Complete Peerage* under Lifford

The Irish land question, **NC** 524
The "Canker-Worm"—outdoor relief, 830

Hewlett, Henry Gay: see *Index*, I, 938.

Heinrich Heine's life and work, **FM** 5871
The nemesis of the Renaissance, 6062

The devil in English poetry, **NQM** 133

Barry Cornwall, **NC** 229
The works of Sir Henry Taylor, 519
County characteristics—Kent, 620
County characteristics—Sussex, 1031
County characteristics—Surrey, 1173
Charles the First as picture collector, 1909
Forged literature, 2004
Why I voted for Mr. Gladstone, 2261
Notices: 487, 1754, 1861

Hewlett, Maurice Henry: see *Index*, I, 938.

The Judgment of Borso, **FortR** 4283, 4296
Anima semplicetta, or The Duchess of Nona, 4313, 4327
St. Gervase of Plessy: a mystery, 4555

A materialist's paradise, **NatR-II** 1184

A mediaeval preacher [Nicholas Bozon], **NC** 1932
Notice: 2042

Heygate, Charles B. Kelly/92.

Dissatisfaction in the West Indian Colonies, **NatR-II** 1268

Heygate, Frederick William, 2nd Bart., 1822–1894. Burke.

An elected peerage, **NatR-II** 320

A suggestion as to Home Rule, **NC** 330

Heywood, C., translator.

Trans: **FortR** 3986

Hicks, Edward Lee: see *Index*, I, 939.

On the names of the Greeks, **NC** 689

Higgin, George, 1833–1892, civil engineer. I.C.E. *Minutes*, 112 (1893), 349–353.

Industrial and commercial Spain, **FortR** 2363

Higgins, Anthony, 1840–1912, U.S. senator. *Amer. WWW.*

American "sound money" problem, **NatR-II** 1806

Higgins, Gilbert, C.R.L., 1849–1940, R.C. priest. *Cath.WW*/1941, *Irish CD*/1941.

Notices: **DR** 2347, 2387, 2497, 2509, 2531, 2543, 2686, 2709, 2720, 2729, 2738

Higgins, William Mullinger, writer on geology, lecturer at Guy's Hospital. *BMCat.*, Allibone.

The water we should not drink, **FM** 5100

Hildyard, Sir Henry John Thoroton, 1846–1916, army officer. *WWW*/1928.

A regiment of infantry, **NC** 1430

Hill, Mrs.; prob. Annie (Scott) Hill, wife of George Birkbeck Hill, under her husband in *DNB*/2nd suppl.

Timon of Athens, **OxCam** 40 collab.
Twelfth Night; or, What You Will, 54 collab.

Hill, Alexander Staveley, 1825–1905, barrister, politician. *DNB.*

Cattle-ranche country of Canada, **NatR-II** 64
Behring Sea arbitration award, 1470

Hill, Alfred: see *Index*, I, 939.

Procedure of the High Court of Justice, **NC** 808

Hill, Arthur: see *Index*, I, 939.

Familiar Photographs in Verse, **FM** 6206

Hill, Caroline Southwood (Smith), wife of James Hill. *DNB*/1921 under her daughter Octavia Hill.

Joan of Arc, **NC** 2754

Hill, Charles, sec. Working-Men's Lord's Day Rest Association. Allibone.

A plea for Sunday observance, **NatR-II** 1014

The day of rest, **NC** 987

Hill, Frank Harrison: see *Index*, I, 939.

The Duc de Broglie, **FortR** 1377
Antithetic fallacies, 1395
Political adventure of Lord Beaconsfield, 1452, 1466, 1477, 1498

The Queen in politics, **NatR-II** 1269
French lessons for English politicians, 1388
Gaps in agnostic evolution, 1773

Home Rule: the English answer, **NC** 1259
The Government of Ireland Bill, 1280

Hoare, Henry William: see Hamilton-Hoare, Henry William.

Hoare, Hugh Edward, 1854–1929, businessman. *WWW.*

Homes of the criminal classes, **NatR-II** 16, 60

Hoare, John Newenham, b.1836/37, divine. *BMCat., Alum. Dub.*

Religion of the ancient Egyptians, **NC** 254

Hobart, Vere Henry: see *Index,* I, 941.

The budget and the national debt, **FortR** 403
The International and the Manchester School, 841

A trip to Scotland, **FM** 3556
A chapter on the sea, 3620
Autumn travels, 3742
Modern English literature, 3873
Points of view, 3942

Hobart-Hampden, Lady Albinia: see Donaldson, Lady Albinia Frederica (Hobart-Hampden).

Hobart-Hampden, Augustus Charles: see *Index,* I, 941.

Turkey and England, **NC** 1111
An Anglo-Turkish alliance, 1114
A strategical view of Turkey, 1224

Hobhouse, Arthur: see *Index,* I, 941.

Forfeiture of property by married women, **FortR** 657
Reflections on the Afghan imbroglio, 1733

Hobhouse, Emily, 1860–1926, humanitarian. *LCCat.; Times,* June 10, 1926, p. 9e.

Women workers, **NC** 3623

Hobson, John Atkinson: see *Index,* I, 941.

Influence of Henry George in England, **FortR** 4042

Cost of a shorter working day, **NatR-II** 985
Can England keep her trade? 1120

Hobson, William Francis, d.1892, chaplain to the forces. Venn.

Of the general depression, **NatR-II** 390
Letters: 145, 184, 267, 334, 402

Hodge, Harold, 1862–1937, barrister, ed. *Saturday Review. WWW.*

Toryism and toil, **FortR** 3987 collab.

The teacher problem, 4280

Hodges, Joseph Sydney Willes, 1829–1900, painter. Boase.

After-images, **NC** 913

Hodges, W. J.

Increase of revenue, **NatR-II** 1006
State-owned railways, 1059
State granaries, 1072
To allay Irish discontent, 1131

Hodgkin, Thomas, 1798–1866, physician. *DNB.*

Classification of languages: Balbi's *Ethnographical Atlas,* **FQR** 16
Notices: 39, 53, 155

Hodgson, Charles E., naval chaplain. *Navy List/76.*

Our arctic voyage, **FM** 5882

Hodgson, Hon. Edward Jarvis, judge superior court, Prince Edward Island. *WW/1903.*

An American view of the Boer War, **NC** 3706

Hodgson, William Ballantyne, 1815–1880, educational reformer. *DNB.*

Trans: **NC** 759

Hodgson, William Earl: see *Index,* I, 942, and II, App. A.

Our weekly reviews, **FortR** 3275

Why conservatism fails in Scotland, **NatR-II** 87
A review of fashionable thought, 237
The cuckoo, 428
Party politics and national life, 562
Conservatism in Scotland, 796
Conservative plea for rights of man, 904
An economic cure for socialism, 948
The fair Ophelia of a highland glen, 1126
The degradation of British sports, 1181
The Mahatma period, 1202
Men of letters and the state, 1235
"Trout-fishing begins," 1258
A prig in the Elysian Fields, 1272
The candidate for West Drum, 1312
The revival of ethics, and of laughter, 1329
"The controverted question" [what is agnosticism?], 1352
Disabilities of democracy, 1379
A modern conversation, 1447
Evolutionary ethics [Spencer's *Ethics*], 1473
Heresies in salmon-fishing, 1548
Letter: 492

Hodson, George Hewitt, 1817–1904, divine. Venn.

Letter: **NatR-II** 201

Hoey, Frances Sarah (Johnston), 1830–1908, novelist, translator, wife of John Cashel Hoey. *DNB.*

Recent Irish poetry, **DR** 1109 collab.
Trollope's [*Phineas Finn*], 1292 collab.?
Mr. Aubrey de Vere's *Irish Odes*, 1301 collab.
?*Lothair* [by Disraeli], 1324 collab.?
Jane Austen and her novels, 1336
The Erckmann-Chatrian novels, 1345
Dickens and Thackeray, 1351
The fall of Paris, 1362 collab.?
The works of Charles Lever, 1395
?The novels of Anthony Trollope, 1413
?Paris, 1531

Only an episode, **NQM** 49
Dark cybel, 55
No sign, 62
Kate Cronin's dowry, 105
Esau's choice, 129

Hoey, John Baptist Cashel, 1828–1892, barrister; sub-ed. of *Dublin Review* under W. G. Ward. Boase.

Recent Irish poetry, **DR** 1109 collab.
Wanted a policy for Ireland, 1113
Irish land question, 1132
The new Parliament, 1142
Signs of an Irish policy, 1152
The state of affairs [in Italy], 1182
The state of Ireland, 1192
Irish questions, 1202
An Irish session, 1212
Rome and the revolution, 1221
The Duke of Wellington's *Despatches*, 1224
The case of Ireland before parliament, 1231
Ireland and the new ministry, 1262
Mr. Gladstone's Irish policy, 1271
Catholic home politics, 1284
Trollope's [*Phineas Finn*], 1292 collab?
Landlord and tenant question in Ireland, 1296, 1304
Mr. Aubrey de Vere's *Irish Odes*, 1301 collab.
Is Ireland irreconcilable? 1314
?*Lothair* [by Disraeli], 1324 collab.?
The Land Bill and the Lords, 1325
The fall of the French Empire, 1338
Pius IX and the revolution, 1340
Paris and France, 1356
The fall of Paris, 1362 collab.?
The International Society, 1378
The Pope and Europe in 1872, 1387
The Queen's colleges in Ireland, 1421

Irish University Bill, 1433
Marshal MacMahon's government of France, 1450
The situation in France, 1460
Fall of Mr. Gladstone's government, 1469
Duc de Broglie and crisis in France, 1477
Protestation of 1789 and Irish Catholic Oath, 1504
The European situation, 1517
Ireland and O'Connell, 1526
?French Catholic universities, 1536
?Republican victory in France, 1558
?The impending war [the Russo-Turkish War], 1570
The cloud in the East, 1580
The War [Russo-Turkish], 1591
General Ignatieff, 1596
Marshal MacMahon's appeal to France, 1602
?Turkey and Russia, 1609
?French President and new Chamber of Deputies, 1613
?The winter campaign [Russo-Turkish War], 1620
?England and Russia, 1632
?The Peace of Berlin, 1660
Notice: 1193

Hoffer, Leopold, writer on chess. *BMCat.*

The chess masters of to-day, **FortR** 2542

Höfler, Konstantin von, 1811–1897, German historian. *Grosse Brockhaus.*

Political system of the Popes, **Ram** 1016, 1035, 1072

Hofmeyr, Adrian, an Afrikander. *BMCat.*

The future of South Africa, **NatR-II** 2502

Hogan, John F., 1858–1918, R.C. priest, president St. Patrick's Coll. Maynooth. *WWW.*

Popes as promoters of university education, **DR** 2427

Hogarth, David George: see *Index,* I, 942.

Cycling in the desert, **NatR-II** 1891

Hogarth, George: see *Index,* I, 942.

Ecclesiastical music, **DR** 5 collab.
Italian music, 138

Hogarth, Janet Elizabeth, 1865–1954, editor and essayist, wife of William Leonard Courtney. *WWW.* (See *Index,* I, 942.)

Literary degenerates, **FortR** 3628

Hogarth, Janet Elizabeth (*continued*)
Sudermann's novels, 3794
Madame Geoffrin and her daughter, 4019
The monstrous regiment of women, 4051
Trans: 3573, 3574, 3932, 3969, 3979, 4003, 4032, 4066, 4096, 4148

Hogarth, W. D.

The present discontent in Cyprus, **FortR** 2857

Hogben, John, b.1853, misc. writer, of Edinburgh. *BMCat.*, *Yearbook*/1922.

The mystical side of Wordsworth, **NatR-II** 612

Hogg, Mrs. Edith F.: see *Index*, I, 942.

School children as wage earners, **NC** 3152
The fur-pullers of south London, 3197

Hogg, James: see *Index*, I, 942.

The unearthly witness, **FM** 105
?Strange letter of a lunatic, 145
The barber of Duncow, a ghost story, 185
Aunt Susan, 248
The separate existence of the soul, 314
The mountain-den men, 437
Ewan M'Gabhar, 472
A remarkable Egyptian story, 513
The Shepherd's *Noctes*, 576 collab.
History of a border beauty, 651
The Frasers in the Correi [in Scotland], 665
Anecdotes of ghosts and apparitions, 780
A very ridiculous sermon, 790
The Turners, 950
Helen Crocket, 1001
See: 467, 497

Unpublished letters of James Hogg, **ScotR** 212

Hogg, Thomas Jefferson, see *Index*, I, 942.

The history of the fine arts, **FQR** 115
History of Gnosticism, 127
The fine arts of the middle ages, 161

Hoggan, George, 1837–1891, surgeon. *Surgeon Index*/2nd s.

Vivisection, **FM** 5670

Holberg, Ludvig, Baron Holberg, 1684–1754, Danish playwright. *Ency. Brit.*/11th ed.

Erasmus Montanus: Danish comedy, **FM** 5220

Hole, Hugh Marshall, 1865–1941, Rhodesian civil service. *WWW*.

Native Rhodesia, **NatR-II** 2083

Hole, Samuel Reynolds: see *Index*, I, 943.

A Surrey Garden, **NC** 3274

Holland, Bernard Henry: see *Index*, I, 943.

Charitable endowments, **NatR-II** 1027
A view of Roman Catholicism, 1766
The conversion of Manning, 1848
The Christian motive, 1906
Some Irish history and a moral, 1962
The Irish claim and some replies, 1990
Present position of Anglican Church, 2039
An Eton master [William Johnson], 2123
Present popularity of Omar Khayyam, 2316
A prebendary [Warre-Cornish's *Sunningwell*], 2432
Legal disabilities of trade unions, **NC** 2717

Holland, Sir Henry: see *Index*, I, 943.

Connexion of physical sciences [von Humboldt and Mary Somerville], **BentQR** 24

Holland, Lionel Raleigh, 1865–1936, M.P., barrister. *WWW*.

Mr. Goldwin Smith and Canada, **NatR-II**, 726
Poverty in old age, 1839
Metropolitan water question, 1945
The report on old-age pensions, 2194

Holland, Sir Thomas Erskine: see *Index*, I, 943.

The reform of the statute book, **FortR** 321
Egypt, the Suez Canal, 2053
International law between Japan and China, 3652
Pacific blockade, 3983
Lessons of the Peace Conference, 4376

Proposed removal of the courts of law, **FM** 4163

Hollingshead, John: see *Index*, I, 943.
Note: **FortR** 2067

Hollis, William Ainslie, 1839–1922, Brighton physician. Venn.

Abattoirs, **NatR-II** 1421

Holloway, George, 1825–1892, businessman. Boase.

Solution of Irish land question, **NatR-II** 654
How to revive industries without taxing food, 679
Old-age pensions, 1254

Holme, Frederick: see *Index*, I, 944.
The Scilly Islands, **FM** 2094

Holmes, Edward, 1797–1859, music critic.
DNB.

Derode's *New Theory of Harmony,* **FQR**
72
Mozart, 93
Fétis—music made easy, 142
Beethoven, 202
Notice: 168

Prospects of the opera, **FM** 2435
Lyric drama in 1848, 2490
Hector Berlioz, 2507
The two operas, 2590
?The late opera season, 2637
?Operatic and musical matters, 2712
?The late musical season, 2770
Mozart's pianoforte, 2842
Our musical spring, 2855
?The opera and concert season, 2879
?The English choir, 2916
?Opening of the musical season, 2965
New compositions for the harp, 3082
?The music of the season, 3097
See: 2803

Holmes, Oliver Wendell, 1809–1894, American author. *DAB.*

Letter: **FortR** 2655

Holmes, Thomas Rice Edward: see *Index,* I, 944.

Hodson of Hodson's horse, **NatR-II** 201
Sir William Napier, 324
Sir Herbert Edwardes, 773
Lieutenant Mackenzie's ride, 1404

Holmes, Timothy, 1825–1907, surgeon. *DNB.*

Letter: **NatR-II** 2396

Holms, James Douglas, writer on politics.

Alternative for shorter parliaments? **ScotR**
318

Holms, John, 1830–1891, Glasgow businessman. Boase.

Our army and the people, **NC** 126, 141
Shorter parliaments, 260

Holyoake, George Jacob: see *Index,* I, 944.

Growth of co-operation in England, **FortR**
2616

Impatience in politics, **NC** 64
The new principle of industry, 220
State socialism, 323
A stranger in America, 469

Theory of political epithets, 741
American and Canadian notes, 892
Emigrant education, 3345

Hook, Theodore Edward, 1788–1841, novelist, wit. *DNB.*

?April fools, **FM** 803 collab.

Hooper, George: see *Index,* I, 944.

Unexpected results of Crimean War, **FortR**
87

Hooper, James, of Norwich. *BMCat.*; C. K. Shorter, *George Borrow and his Circle* (Boston, 1913), p. 355n.

George Borrow, **NatR-II** 1827

Hope, A. J. Beresford: see Beresford-Hope, A. J.

Hope, Anne (Fulton), 1809–1887, critic of historians. *DNB.*

Jervis on the Church of France, **DR** 1456
Jervis on Jansenistic and Gallican movement, 1466
Ranke's and Green's histories of England, 1521
Ranke's *History of England,* 1543
Simon de Montfort, Earl of Leicester, 1611
Froude and St. Thomas of Canterbury, 1626
Notice: 1635

Hope, William, 1834–1909, army officer. Burke under Linlithgow.

Ordnance department and Colonel Hope, **FortR** 2503

Hopkins, Jane Ellice: see *Index,* I, 945.

The moral treatment of insanity, **FM** 5915

Hopkins, John Satchell, 1825–1898, businessman. Boase.

Drink as a trade, **NatR-II** 1697
Letter: 405

Hopkins, Manley: see *Index,* I, 945.

Letter: **NatR-II** 92

Hopkins, Martin, of Natal.

Trans: **FM** 6492

Hopkins, Tighe: see *Index,* I, 945.

Some famous pirates, **NatR-II** 1182

Hopkins, William: see *Index*, I, 945.

Physical theories of life, **FM** 3983, 4001
The Glaciers of the Alps [by Tyndall], 4052

Hopkinson, Sir Alfred: see *Index*, I, 945.

Garden allotments, **FM** 6068

Hopper, William Robinson, 1836–1904, divine. Venn.

Iron master's view of strikes, **FortR** 59

Hopwood, John, 1859–1913, prof. at Oscott. *Oscotian*, 13 (1913), 140–145.

Sir Kenelm Digby, **DR** 2595
Maitland's *Roman Canon Law in the Church of England*, 2703
Notices: 2543, 2558, 2570, 2606, 2628, 2651, 2674, 2686, 2709, 2729

Hordern, Peter: see *Index*, I, 945.

Budhist schools in Burmah, **FM** 5990
Educational missions in India, 6020
Among the Burmese, 6076, 6088, 6092, 6104, 6114, 6126

Hornby, Sir Edmund John Phipps, 1857–1947, army officer. *WWW*.

Letter: **NC** 1015

Hornby, Sir Geoffrey Thomas Phipps, 1825–1895, admiral. *DNB*.

What our navy should be, **FortR** 2762
The loss of the *Victoria*, 3403

Hornby, James John, 1826–1909, provost of Eton. *DNB*.

Letter: **FortR** 2647

Horne, Herbert Percy, 1864–1916, architect, connoisseur. *WWW*, *LCCat*.

The Strand improvements, **FortR** 3261
Michelangelo, 3312
Venetian missals, 3570

Horne, Richard Henry or Hengist: see *Index*, I, 945.

"Damned" tragedies, **FM** 1713
The fine and froggy art of swimming, 1746
The character of the ghost in *Hamlet*, 2106
Confessions of a nervous soldier, 2477
On the drowning of Shelley, 5142
Eyes and eye-glasses, 5878
The Wonder-Working Magician [by Calderon], 6143

The Countess von Labanoff, **NQM** 115

Horne, Thomas Hartwell, 1780–1862, biblical scholar. *DNB*.

Notices: **FQR** 39, 66, 90, 103, 132, 144, 204, 254

Horsfall, Thomas Coglan, 1841–1932, public citizen of Manchester. *WWW*.

Painting and popular culture, **FM** 6299

Horsfield, Herbert Knight, b.1856, misc. writer. *Yearbook/1904*.

From a simian point of view, **NatR-II** 1205
Outside the chamber of mirrors, 1292
In the club smoking room, 1361

Horsley, John William: see *Index*, I, 946.

Suicide, **FortR** 1793

Horsley, Sir Victor Alexander Haden, 1857–1916, physiologist. *DNB*.

On the analysis of voluntary movement, **NC** 2052
The morality of "vivisection," 2312

Horton, Robert Forman: see *Index*, I, 946.

The doomed board schools, **FortR** 3831
The Free Church in England, 3947

The Roman danger [Catholicism], **NatR-II** 2410

Horton, Samuel Dana, 1844–1895, economist. *Amer.WWW*.

Arguments for the outlawry of silver, **FortR** 3425

Hosken, William: see *Index*, I, 946.

The future of South Africa, **FortR** 4433

Hoskins, James Thornton, b.1844/45. Foster, *BMCat*.

A Liberal on the House of Lords, **NatR-II** 261

Hoskyns, Chandos Wren, 1812–1876, writer on agriculture, barrister. *DNB*.

Present state of the land question, **FortR** 772

Hoste, James William, b.1861/62, divine. Foster.

Disraeli on national education, **FortR** 3808

Houldsworth, Sir William Henry, 1834–1917, M.P. *WWW*.

Closing of the Indian mints, **NatR-II** 1462
The currency question—for laymen, 1708

Houssaye, Arsène, 1815–1896, French author. *Grand Larousse.*

Alfred de Musset, **FortR** 2811, 2818

Hovey, Richard, 1864–1900, American poet. *DAB.*

Maurice Maeterlinck, **NC** 2725

Howard, Rev. A. J. Dominican preacher.

The principle of individualisation, **DR** 2643

Howard, E. G.: see *Index*, I, 947.

Ancient and modern painted glass, **NatR-II** 609

Howard, Henry, 1757–1842, of Corby Castle, soldier, proponent of Catholic emancipation. Gillow.

Letter: **DR** 47

Howard, Henry Charles, 1833–1898, 18th Earl of Suffolk. Burke.

Foxhunters and farmers, **NatR-II** 1663

Howard, James, 1821–1889, agriculturalist. *DNB.*

The railway commissioners, **FM** 6067

Landowning as a business, **NC** 702
The farmers and the Tory party, 869

Howard, Lady Mabel Harriet (Macdonnell), d.1942, wife of Henry C. Howard. *WWW*, and *WWW/*1916 under her husband.

Nursing the poor in their homes, **NC** 3379

Howard, Philip Henry, 1801–1883, M.P., Roman Catholic antiquary. Boase.

?Arundel Castle: the Fitzalans and Howards, **DR** 1619
?The household books of Lord William Howard, 1818
?Catholic memories of [Durham], 1846

Howe, Samuel, b.1854. *LCCat.*

The spoiling of St. Paul's, **FortR** 4266

Howe, W. H.

Methods of voting, **FortR** 4089

Howell, George: see *Index*, I, 947.

The state of our trade, **FortR** 2558

Fluctuations in trade and wages, 2581

Trade-unions, **FM** 6131
Strikes: their cost and results, 6238

The caucus system and the Liberal party, **NQM** 157

International Association, **NC** 191
Financial condition of trades unions, 767
The dwellings of the poor, 867
The House of Lords, 1023

Howie, James Muir, physician. *Med.Reg/*84

The nerve-rest cure, **NC** 1483

Howitt, William, 1792–1879, misc. writer. *DNB.*

Literature of aristocracy, and of genius, **DR** 27

The disasters of Jan Nadeltreiber, **FM** 110

Howlett, James Aidan, O.S.B., 1856–1909, R.C. canon. Snow.

Mosaic authorship of the Pentateuch, **DR** 2324
Some recent views on inspiration, 2390
The higher criticism and archaeology, 2442
The Book of Daniel, 2488
Biblical science and the Bible, 2523
Textual criticism of the New Testament, 2622
Textual criticism of the Hebrew text, 2681
Wellhausen and the chronicler, 2717
Notices: 2347, 2373, 2387, 2400, 2425, 2448, 2475, 2485, 2497, 2520, 2531, 2583, 2594, 2628, 2651, 2663, 2674, 2686, 2699, 2709, 2720, 2729, 2738

Howorth, Sir Henry Hoyle: see *Index*, I, 947.

The Tsar's new gospel of peace, **NC** 3416
Our Indian troops, 3586

Hozier, Sir Henry Montague: see *Index*, I, 947.

Bulwarks of Empire, **FortR** 2294
Lloyd's, 2451

The German and British armies, **NC** 886
Our actual military strength, 1557

Hsiu-ch'u, Wang, 17th-century Chinese writer from Yangchow.

The sack of Yangchow in 1644, **NC** 3440

Huband, William George, 1845–1912, Irish barrister. Venn.

Intermediate education in Ireland, **FM** 6035

Hubbard, Hon. Evelyn, 1852–1934, banker. *WWW.*

The rupee difficulty, **NatR-II** 1475

Hubbard, Henry William, 1856–1906, physician. *Surgeon Index*/3rd s. (See *Index*, I, 948.)

Homicide as a misadventure [patent medicines], **NatR-II** 1063

Hubbard, John Gellibrand, 1st Baron Addington, 1805–1889, banker, M.P. *DNB.*

Forty years of income tax, **NatR-II** 130
Threatened conflict [Church disestablishment], 533

A census of religions, **NC** 542
The Church and parliament, 1331

Huddleston, Tristram Frederick Croft, 1848–1936, administrator at Cambridge. *WWW.*

The universities and national defence, **NatR-II** 2518

Hudson, John, 1860–1923, divine. Venn.

Thoughts on church hymns, **NatR-II** 750

Hudson, William Henry, 1841–1922: see *Index*, I, 948, and II, App. A.

The serpent's tongue, **FortR** 3396
The serpent's strangeness, 3490
The common crow, 3642

The naturalist on the Pampas, **NC** 1830

Hueffer, Ford Madox: see Ford, Ford Madox

Hueffer, Francis, born Franz Hüffer: see *Index*, I, 948.

Richard Wagner, **FortR** 846
Robert Schumann, 956
Popular and artistic song in Germany, 992
Arthur Schopenhauer, 1314
Chopin, 1394
Modern Italian poets, 1792
Liszt's life and works, 2508
English music during the Queen's reign, 2601

The Wagner Festival of 1876, **FM** 5748

Richard Wagner, *Ring of the Niblung*, **NQM** 48
Provençal poetry during the middle ages, 76
The reformation, thirteenth century, 100
Literary aspects of Schopenhauer's work, 116
The story of Dr. Faustus, 127

Current literature and criticism, 143, 151, 161, all collab.

Hügel, Baron Carl Alexander Anselm von, 1796–1870, naturalist, traveller. *ADB.*

Escape of Prince Metternich, **NatR-II** 41

Hügel, Baron Friedrich von, 1852–1925, theologian. *DNB.*

The Church and the Bible, **DR** 2452, 2479, 2500

Note: **NatR-II** 41

Huggins, Sir William, 1824–1910, astronomer. *DNB.*

The new star in Auriga, **FortR** 3224

Comets, **NC** 753
The sun's corona, 1122
Violins, 1170
The new astronomy, 3124

Hughes, Hugh Price: see *Index*, I, 948.

Irresponsible wealth, **NC** 1967
John Wesley, 2017

Hughes, Margaret Watts, also called Mrs. Watts Hughes. *BMCat., LCCat.*

The art of singing, **NC** 857

Hughes, Reginald, 1843–1924, barrister. *Alpine Journal*, 36 (1924), 379–381.

The Alps in 1898, **NC** 3412

Hughes, Thomas: see *Index*, I, 948, and App. A.

Richard Ford, **FM** 3781
Hodson of Hodson's Horse, 3819
See: 5853

Hughes-Games, Stephen Herbert Wynne, b.1861/62, divine. *CCD*/1902, Foster under Games.

The Reverend Thomas Edward Brown: poet, **FortR** 4533

Hughes-Hallett, James Wyndham, 1852–1927, army officer. *WWW.*

The staging of Shakespeare, **FortR** 4512

Hugo, Victor, 1802–1885, French poet, novelist. *Grand Larousse.*

See: **FQR** 586

Huish, Marcus Bourne, 1843–1921, ed. *Art Journal*, barrister. Venn.

Is Japanese art extinct? **NC** 1523
Ten years of British art, 1819
Whence comes this great multitude of painters? 2305

Hull, Edward, 1829–1917, Irish geologist. *WWW.*

Letter: **NatR-II** 770

Hullah, John Pyke: see *Index*, I, 949.

Meyerbeer's *L'Africaine*, **FortR** 65
Gluck's *Iphigenia in Tauris*, 260

Henry Lawes, **FM** 3347
The Organ, 3455
Handel, 3638
Mendelssohn's *Letters*, 4386, 4466

Hulme-Beaman, A: see Beaman, Ardern George Hulme.

Hume, Martin Andrew Sharp, 1843–1910, historian of Spain. *DNB.*

A palace in the Strand, **FortR** 3411
Philip II. in his domestic relations, 3865
The defeat of the Armada, 3996

More light on Antonio Perez, **NC** 2660
How the sceptre of the sea passed to England, 3170

Hume, W. H.

The industrial crisis in France, **NatR-II** 218

Humphery, George R.

The reading of the working classes, **NC** 2385

Humphreys, Edward Rupert, 1820–1893, classicist, misc. writer. *BMCat., LCCat.*

See: **FM** 3594

Humphreys, G. E.

The "Juliet" of Miss Mary Anderson, **NatR-II** 269
Les Ecréhous [Channel islets], 491 collab.

Humphreys, Henry Temple, 1839–1891, civil engineer. I.C.E. *Minutes*, 108 (1892), 403.

The protest against over-examination, **NC** 1639

Humphreys, J. T. C.

Is England going to keep Ireland? **NatR-II** 120

Humphreys, Jennett: see *Index*, I, 949.

English: its ancestors, its progeny, **FM** 6545

Humphry, Hugh McNab, b.1855, barrister. Allibone, *M at B.*

Settlements of land in England, **NatR-II** 223

Hunnybun, William Martin, 1837–1932, sec. Catholic School Committee. Venn.

Evening schools, **DR** 2367

Hunt, Alfred William, 1830–1896, landscape painter. *DNB.*

Modern English landscape-painting, **NC** 439
Turnerian landscape—an arrested art, 1996

Hunt, James Henry Leigh: see *Index*, I, 949.

The tapiser's tale, **FM** 3689
The shewe of faire seeming, 3727
English poetry vs. Cardinal Wiseman, 3924

Hunt, Leigh: see Hunt, James Henry Leigh.

Hunt, R. R., of Aukland, New Zealand.

Letter: **NatR-II** 1142

Hunt, William Holman: see *Index*, I, 949.

Artistic copyright, **NC** 281

Hunter, Henry, Poor Law official of Scotland. *BMCat.*

Scottish Poor Law reform, **ScotR** 293

Hunter, Isabel Wilson

Trans: **FortR** 4118

Hunter, Kate Marion, plague officer, Poona. *Med. Reg./99, Surgeon Index/2nd s.*

Fighting the bubonic plague in India, **NC** 3307

Hunter, Sir Robert: see *Index*, I, 950.

The future of the city charities, **NC** 1817
A fair taxation of ground-rents, 2068
Places and things of interest and beauty, 3268

Hunter, William Alexander: see *Index,* I, 950.

Cross's labour bills, **FortR** 1182
Poor relief in foreign countries, 1198
Parties and the distribution of seats, 1712
Notice: 626

Hunter, Sir William Wilson: see *Index,* I, 950.

A forgotten Oxford movement—1681, **FortR** 3797

Some aspects of Indian finance, **FM** 6246

Sun-spots and famines, **NC** 102 collab.
The ruin of Aurangzeb, 1407
A river of ruined capitals [the Hugli], 1503
Our missionaries, 1568

Hunting, J. D. *BMCat.*

Women and tobacco, **NatR-II** 914

Huntington, George, 1825–1905, divine. *DNB.*

Authorized systematic lay agency, **NatR-II** 798

Hurd, Sir Archibald Spicer, 1869–1959, naval writer. *LCCat., WWW.*

The navy and the engineering dispute, **NC** 3251
British ships in foreign navies, 3266
Coal, trade, and the Empire, 3368
An all-British cable system, 3418
Retardation of navy by engineers' strike, 3439
Lessons of the [Boer] War, 3743

Hurlbert, William Henry: see *Index,* I, 950, and II, App. A.

Catholic Italy and temporal power, **FortR** 2359
A republic *in extremis* [France], 2885
The outlook in France, 3022, 3051

What are the United States coming to? **FM** 3541

The Democratic victory in America, **NC** 1074
State Christianity and the French elections, 1204

Hurley, Patrick, d.1907, R.C. priest. *Irish CD/1909.*

The Irish at Nantes [Robert Barry and Cornelius O'Keefe], **DR** 2310, 2329

Hussey, Thomas John, 1797–1866/67(?), divine, astronomer. *BMCat., Alum. Dub.,* disappears from *CCD* after 1867.

De Lambre's *Astronomy of the Eighteenth Century,* **FQR** 26
Caillié's *Travels in Africa,* 137
Salverte, *The Occult Sciences of the Ancients,* 150
Notices: 66, 79, 90, 132, 144, 155, 204, 229

Hutchinson, Horatio, or Horace, Gordon: see *Index,* I, 950.

The decrease of the salmon, **FortR** 4496

The parlous condition of cricket, **NatR-II** 2470
Letter: 1484

Hutchinson, James G.

Progress and wages: a workman's view, **NC** 1052

Hutchinson, Sir Jonathan, 1828–1913, surgeon. *DNB.*

On cruelty to animals, **FortR** 1287

Hutchinson, Thomas; possibly Thomas Hutchinson, 1815/16–1903, nephew of William Wordsworth, in Venn.

Wordsworth's *"Castle of Indolence* Stanzas," **FortR** 3568

Hutchison, John, 1842–1924, rector of Glasgow High School. James Acland and Thomas Muir, *History of the High School of Glasgow,* 1878.

Melanchthon: history of education, **FM** 5879

Hutchison, T.

The kingdom of Fife, **FM** 6011

Hutton, George Clark, 1825–1908, Presbyterian divine. *DNB.*

Scotch disestablishment vote, **ScotR** 114

Hutton, Henry Dix, 1825–1907, scholar. Crone.

The Irish Land Bill of 1870, **FortR** 670
The Irish University question, 828

Hutton, James: see *Index,* I, 950.

Notice: **FortR** 335

Hutton, John, 1847–1921, M.P., county alderman. *WWW.*

The aged poor, **NatR-II** 2275

Cottage homes for the aged poor, **NC** 3273

Hutton, Richard Holt: see *Index*, I, 950.

Walter Bagehot, **FortR** 1399
The poetry of Arthur Hugh Clough, 2040

The atheistic view of life, **FM** 6286

M. Renan and Christianity, **NatR-II** 1350

Influence upon morality of a decline in religious belief, **NC** 38
The soul and future life, 82
Is the popular judgment in politics more just than that of the higher orders? 166
The biologists on vivisection, 663
The Metaphysical Society, 1167
Notices: 1979, 2520

Huvétys, Peter, president of Blackrock College, Dublin. *IrishCD* /89.

Catholic education in England and Ireland, **DR** 1950

Huxley, Henrietta Anne (Heathorn), b.1825/26, wife of Thomas Henry Huxley. Huxley, *Life*, I, 39.

The gold diggings at Bathurst, **NC** 3484

Huxley, Thomas Henry: see *Index*, I, 951.

Methods and results of ethnology, **FortR** 21
Improving natural knowledge, 170
Physical basis of life, 561
Scientific aspects of positivism, 596
Administrative nihilism, 818
Hypothesis that animals are automata, 1095
Technical education, 1426
William Harvey, 1434
Science and morals, 2545
An apologetic irenicon, 3280

Influence upon morality of a decline in religious belief, **NC** 37
The soul and future life, 83
Sensation and unity of structure of sensiferous organs, 293
On the method of Zadig, 452
The State and the medical profession, 959

Interpreters of Genesis and of nature, 1213
Mr. Gladstone and Genesis, 1239
The evolution of theology: an anthropological study, 1251, 1260
Scientific and pseudo-scientific realism, 1368
Science and pseudo-science, 1387
An olive branch from America, 1479
Science and the bishops, 1481
The struggle for existence, 1511
Agnosticism, 1651, 1684
Value of witness to the miraculous, 1682
Agnosticism and Christianity, 1724
Natural inequality of men, 1812
Natural rights and political rights, 1824
Capital—the mother of labour, 1847
Government: anarchy or regimentation, 1877
Lights of the Church and of science, 1893
Aryan question and pre-historic man, 1955
Keepers of the herd of swine [Gladstone's biblical criticism], 1974
Mr. Gladstone's controversial method, 2015
Hasisadra's adventure, 2055
Professor Tyndall, 2501
Mr. Balfour's attack on agnosticism, 2728
See: 10, 81, 120, 151, 188, 236, 266, 311, 366, 423, 521

Hyde, Henry Baring

Letter: **NatR-II** 121

Hyndman, Henry Mayers: see *Index*, I, 954.

Cavour, **FortR** 1386
Irish needs and Irish remedies, 1666
Lights and shades of American politics, 1783
Wealth and ability, 2649

Australian colonies and confederation, **FM** 5873

The bankruptcy of India, **NC** 226, 284
Bleeding to death [on Indian empire], 475
The dawn of a revolutionary epoch, 534
Something better than emigration, 1073
Socialism and rent appropriation, 1099 collab.
The Radicals and socialism, 1211

I

Ibrahim-Hilmy: see Hilmy, Ibrahim.

Ignatius of St. Paul, Father: see Spencer, George.

Ilbert, Sir Courtenay Peregrine: see *Index*, I, 951.

The Society of Comparative Legislation, **NC** 2785

Iles, Daniel, 1855–1912, professor at Oscott. *Oscotian*, 12 (1912), 87–94.

Notice: **DR** 2358

Im Thurn, Everard Ferdinand, 1852–1932, colonial administrator. *WWW*.

Our public schools: Marlborough, **NQM** 212

Inge, William Ralph, 1860–1954, divine. *WWW*.

Disestablishment, **NatR-II** 1260

Ingleby, Clement Mansfield, 1823–1886, Shakespearean critic. *DNB*.

From fable to fact, **FortR** 58
The ideality of the rainbow, 109
Notice: 726

Inglefield, Sir Edward Augustus, 1820–1894, admiral. *DNB*.

Letter: **FortR** 3235

Ingram, John H., 1849–1916, literary scholar. *Biograph*, I (1879), 111–114; *LCCat*.

Note: **NQM** 135

Ingram, Thomas Dunbar, 1826–1901, Irish historical writer, lawyer. *DNB*.

Two Centuries of Irish History, **FortR** 2793

Gladstone and the Irish union, **NC** 1490

Innes, Alexander Taylor: see *Index*, I, 951.

Church crisis, **FortR** 1362

Where are the letters? [extra-sensory pre-science], **NC** 1436
The Psychical Society's ghosts, 2123

Innes, Allan; possibly Allan Rose Innes, a son of James Rose Innes, 1799–1873, of Muiryfold in *Landed Gentry*.

Financial relations of England and Ireland, **FortR** 3913

Innes, James John Mc'Leod, 1830–1907, army officer. *DNB*.

Roberts and Indian Frontier policy, **FortR** 4036

Irby, Adelina Paulina, 1831–1911, humanitarian. *Times*, Sept. 18, 1911, p. 8b. (See *Index*, I, 952.)

A Russian lady's book [by Olga de Novikoff], **FM** 6283

Don Miraglia, **NatR-II** 2350

Irvine, George, translator of Schiller's *Bride of Messina*, 1837. *BMCat*.

Jean Paul F. Richter, **DR** 188
German prose writers, 226
Johann Gottfried von Herder, 292
Oehlenschläger's *Autobiography*, 343
Notice: 180

Irvine, John William, b.1835/36, divine. Foster, *CCD*/76.

A study for Colonel Newcome [on Thackeray], **NC** 2467

Irving, David: see *Index*, I, 952.

Greek texts of the Roman law, **FQR** 178
Theodosian Code, 221
Pronunciation of the Greek language, 304
Civil law, 388

Irving, Edward, 1792–1834, divine. *DNB*.

Recollections of a Scottish clergyman, **FM** 49
Recent manifestations of spiritual gifts, 338, 357, 371

Irving, George

The military and the magistrates, **FortR** 3408

Irving, Sir Henry, born John Henry Brodribb, 1838–1905, actor. *DNB*.

The American audience, **FortR** 2273
Acting: an art, 3611
The theatre in relation to the state, 4147

An actor's notes on Shakespeare, **NC** 19, 35, 271, 1415
The third murderer in *Macbeth*, 19
Hamlet and Ophelia, 35
"Look here, upon this picture, and on this," 271
Coquelin on actors and acting, 1415
Actor-managers, 1890
Some misconceptions about the stage, 2302

Irving, Henry Brodribb, 1870–1919, actor-manager. *WWW*.

The art and status of the actor, **FortR** 4447

The true story of Eugene Aram, **NC** 3156

Irwin, Margaret Hardinge, d.1940, Scottish champion of women's industrial rights. *WWW*.

The Shop Seats Bill movement, **FortR** 4307

Isemonger, Edwin Empson, colonial official. *Colonial List*/96.

Debased silver and British trade, **NatR-II** 1614

Ives, Levi Silliman, 1797–1867, American

Episcopal bishop, Catholic convert. *DAB.*

Mediaeval Manichaeism and the Inquisition, **DR** 1176
The Holy See and Spanish Inquisition, 1201

J

Jack, William: see *Index*, I, 952.

The proposed Manchester University, **FortR** 1461

Jackson, Clement Nugent, b.1845/46, of Oxford University Athletic Club. See *FortR* 62 o.s. (1894), 373, Foster.

Sport and travel in Norway, **FortR** 2211

Jackson, Edmund, R.C. priest, convert in 1899. Gorman.

Oxford Movement: twelve years' converts, **DR** 2689
Notice: 2720

Jackson, Henry, 1831–1879, novelist. *DNB.*

A first friendship, in 9 installments from **FM** 4231 to 4305
Gilbert Rugge, in 21 installments from 4434 to 4614

Jackson, Henry, 1839–1921, prof. of Greek, Camb. *DNB.*

Notices: **FortR** 396, 415

Jackson, John Edward, 1805–1891, antiquary. *DNB.*

Amye Robsart, **NC** 691

Jackson, Lowis (or Louis) d'Aguilar, b.1840, civil engineer, writer on card games. *BMCat.*, Burke under Jackson of Arsley.

Card-playing and free whist, **NatR-II** 1077

Jackson, Nicholas Lane, 1849–1937, writer on sports. *BMCat.*, *WWW* under Lane-Jackson.

Professionalism and sport, **FortR** 4399

Jackson, Robert Raynsford: see *Index*, I, 953.

India and Lancashire, **FortR** 1268

Jackson, Sir Thomas Graham, 1835–1924, architect. *DNB.*

Architecture—a profession or an art, **NC** 2361

Jacobs, Joseph: see *Index*, I, 953.

The mean [typical] Englishman, **FortR** 4301
The dying of death, 4321
A romance in scholarship, 4355
The paths of glory [*Who's Who*], 4391

The God of Israel, **NC** 354
Recollections of Sir Edward Burne-Jones, 3410

Jacobus, Russell P. *LCCat.*

Bourget's *André Cornélis*, **FortR** 3675
Maurice Barrès and Walter Pater, 3743, 3773

James, Mrs. A. G. F. Eliot, writer on India. *BMCat.*, Allibone.

Tobacco culture in England, **NatR-II** 470

James, Ernest Edward, b.1861/62. Foster.

Letter: **NatR-II** 511

James, Henry, 1843–1916: see *Index*, I, 953.

Guy de Maupassant, **FortR** 2688
Pierre Loti, 2706
The *Journal* of the Brothers de Goncourt, 2756
Story-teller at large: Henry Harland, 4109

James, Sir Henry Evan Murchison, 1846–1923, colonial official. *WWW.*

On the way home [from India], **NatR-II** 1496
Some further reflections on India, 1536

James, Montague Rhodes: see *Index*, I, 953.

The scrap-book of Canon Alberic, **NatR-II** 1702

Jameson, Andrew, Lord Ardwall, 1845–1911, Scottish judge. *DNB.*

Jurisdiction of English courts over Scotsmen, **ScotR** 156

Jane, Frederick Thomas: see *Index*, I, 954.

The *Maine* disaster and after, **FortR** 4108

Janet, Paul: see *Index*, I, 954.

La philosophie de Diderot, **NC** 579

Japp, Alexander Hay: see *Index*, I, 954.

The electric telegraphs, **FM** 6448

The Scottish border, **ScotR** 430

Jarves, James Jackson: see *Index*, I, 954.

?The London Art Exhibitions of 1870, **FM** 5093

Notes on modern Italian art, 5143

Jastrow, Henriette

Workers' insurance in Germany, **FortR** 3929

Jay, Arthur Osborne Montgomery, 1858–1945, divine. Venn.

Letter: **FortR** 3902

Jeaffreson, John Cordy, 1831–1901, barrister, author. *WWW*.

Hinchbrock, in 9 installments from **FM** 3321 to 3401

Jeans, James Stephen, 1846–1913, sec. British Iron Trade Assn. *WWW, BMCat*.

The American tariff, **FortR** 3298
The new railway rates, 3325
Railway development at home and abroad, 3479

The Panama Canal and its prospects, **NC** 1513
American railways and British farmers, 1927
The coal crisis, 2482
The labour war in the United States, 2623

Jebb, Eglantyne Louisa (Jebb): see *Index*, I, 954.

Handwork for children, **NC** 775

Jebb, Heneage Horsley, 1849/50–1913, divine. Foster, *Landed Gentry*.

The coming revolt of the clergy, **NC** 3180

Jebb, Sir Richard Claverhouse: see *Index*, I, 954.

A tour of the Troad [Asia Minor], **FortR** 2019
Plea for a British institute at Athens, 2033

Old comedy on a new stage [Aristophanes' *Birds*], 2127
Homeric Troy [on Schliemann], 2153
Ancient organs of public opinion, 2233

Jefferies, Richard, 1848–1887, naturalist. *DNB*.

The power of the farmers, **FortR** 1059
Nature and books, 2588

The future of farming, **FM** 5492
John Smith's shanty, 5511
A railway-accidents bill, 5553
The farmer at home, 5577
The labourer's daily life, 5616
The Shipton accident, 5647
The story of Swindon, 5674
Field-faring women, 5723
High-pressure agriculture, 5842
An English homestead, 5874
Unequal agriculture, 5929
A great agricultural problem, 6034

The defense of sport, **NatR-II** 67

The size of farms, **NQM** 35
On allotment gardens, 44
Village organization, 59
The spirit of modern agriculture, 83
The future of country society, 117

Jefferson, Thomas, 1743–1826, president of U.S. *DAB*.

See: **FortR** 4167

Jeffery, Walter, 1861–1922, journalist in New South Wales. *WWW*.

Builder of Empire: George Grey, **FortR** 4189 collab.
The sea story of Australia, 4349 collab.

Jeffray, R. J., businessman with large interests in Queensland. *FortR* no. 1942, p. 295.

Queensland planters, **FortR** 1942

Jeffrée, F.

The Jews in France, **DR** 2085, 2095

Jekyll, Gertrude: see *Index*, I, 957, and *WWW*/1940.

House decoration, **NatR-II** 1659

Jellett, Henry, 1821–1901, archdeacon of Cloyne, dean of St. Patrick's, Dublin. *WWW, Times*, Jan. 2, 1902, p. 4e.

Churchman's view of rights of laity, **NatR-II** 426

Jenkin, Henry Charles Fleeming: see *Index*, I, 957.

Technical education, **FortR** 525

Mrs. Siddons as Lady Macbeth, **NC** 138 collab.

Jenkins, John Edward: see *Index*, I, 957.

Liberalism and disestablishment, **FortR** 1478

Two solutions [to the Malthusian problem], **FM** 5187

Jenkins, Robert Charles: see *Index*, I, 957.

The new patronage bill, **FortR** 3355

Jenner, George Francis Birt: see *Index*, I, 957

Women at the Swiss universities, **FortR** 1190

Jennings, George Henry, 1833–1894, journalist, *LCCat., Times*, Nov. 21, 1894, p. 10d.

Letter: **FortR** 3538

Jennings, Mrs. Kate Vaughan. *BMCat.*, Allibone.

Rahel and Varnhagen von Ense, **FM** 5331
Louis Börne, 6055

Jennings, Louis John: see *Index*, I, 957.

The Calcutta cyclone of 1864, **Fort R** 96
Unsettled problems of American politics, 1281
Jobbery in our public offices, 2733

A model government office, **NC** 1948
The trade league against England, 1968

Jennings, William, 1825–1862, prof. of philosophy at Maynooth. Boase.

Tendencies of modern logic, **DR** 732
Authority in philosophy, 757
Faber on the Blessed Sacrament, 769
Christian theism, 788
Parisis on philosophical tradition, 917
The Roman Campagna, 952
Notice: 760
See: 737, 905

Jephson, Arthur Jermy Mounteney, 1858–1908, African traveller. *DNB*.

Stanley and Emin Pasha, **FortR** 3030

Jephson, Lady Harriet Julia (Campbell), d.1930, artist. *WWW*.

The French Canadian *habitant*, **NatR-II** 1403

Jephson, Henry L.: see *Index*, I, 957.

Royalty and viceroyalty in Ireland, **FortR** 2299

Irish absenteeism, **NC** 446
The Irish Parliament of 1782, 1144
"Passing the wit of man!" [Gladstone's views on Ireland], 2346
The Irish fiasco, 2775

Jephson, John Mounteney, 1819–1865, divine, journalist, antiquary. Boase.

Palgrave's *History of Normandy and England*, **FM** 3616

Jerdan, William: see *Index*, I, 958.

The grand force [advertising], **FM** 4955
The greatest wonder [lack of common sense in legislation], 4962

Jerningham, Frederick William, 1813–1870, army officer, author of a pamphlet on emigration. Burke under Stafford, *BMCat*.

Emigration, **Ram** 6

Jerningham, Sir Hubert Edward Henry: see *Index*, I, 958.

The French people, **NC** 3355

Jerram, Charles Stanger, 1838–1914, classical scholar. *LCCat.*, Foster.

Newman from Newman's view, **NatR-II** 1076

Jerrold, William Blanchard, 1826–1884, journalist. Boase.

The manufacture of public opinion, **NC** 873

Jervois, Sir William Francis Drummond: see *Index*, I, 958.

Home rule for the navy, **NC** 1983

Jesse, Edward, 1780–1868, naturalist. *DNB*.

Thames fishing, **FM** 650

Jessop, Gilbert Laird, 1874–1955, cricket player. *WWW*.

Run-getting, **NatR-II** 2071
Hints to young bowlers, 2286
Some hints on captaincy in cricket, 2441.

Jessopp, Augustus: see *Index*, I, 958.

My return to Arcady, **NC** 617
The Arcady of our grandfathers, 717
Superstition in Arcady, 783
Village life in Norfolk 600 years ago, 818
The coming of the friars, 879
Clouds over Arcady [on agricultural labor], 911
Daily life in a mediaeval monastery, 951
Peasants' homes in Arcady, 970
The prophet of walnut-tree yard, 1029
The black death in East Anglia, 1069, 1117
A swain of Arcady, 1156
The little ones and the land, 1231
The Church and the villages: what hope? 1261
Letters and letter-writers, 1308
The building up of a university, 1343
Hill-digging and magic, 1358
Trials of a country parson, 1380, 1443
A warning to the S.P.R. [Society for Psychical Research], 1398
Doris, 1494
Snowed up in Arcady, 1535
Who owns the churches? 1578
Cathedral-room for neglected records, 1645
Mr. Dandelow, 1737
Are they grievances? [splits within the Church], 1790
The land and its owners in past times, 1831
Village almshouses, 1884
Random roaming, 1990
Pity the poor birds! 2001
1799: a rustic retrospect, 2073
Our worn-out parsons, 2101
A suggestion for my betters [study of history], 2140
Castle Acre, 2166
A fourteenth-century parson, 2230
Swanton mill, 2283
St. William of Norwich, 2388
"Robbing God," 2423
The career of the Rev. Luke Tremain, 2446
A word for our cathedral system, 2509
Simon Ryan the Peterite, 2559, 2572
The parish priest in England before the Reformation, 2639
St. Martin of Tours, 2691
The celestial empire of the West [Rome and the Anglican Church], 2763
Church defence or Church reform? 2872
The baptism of Clovis, 2983
Hints on Church reform, 3085
Moles, 3155
Parish life in England, 3225, 3257
The clergy and the laity, 3371
The cry of the villages, 3475
The elders of Arcady, 3650
The lake-dwellers, 3745
Notices: 1660, 1696, 1912, 1980, 2201

Jeune, Lady Susan Mary Elizabeth: see *Index*, I, 958, and II, App. A.

Saving the innocents, **FortR** 2362
Helping the fallen, 2387
The homes of the poor, 2907
The servant question, 3234
The poor children's holiday, 3376
The revolt of the daughters, 3471
Where to spend a holiday, 3539
The ethics of shopping, 3594
The decay of the chaperon, 4523

The creed of the poor, **NatR-II** 732
Recollections of [William E.] Forster, 756
Technical education for women in England and abroad, 820
Women of today, yesterday, and to-morrow, 941
"General" Booth's scheme, 1106
Extravagance in dress, 1394
Amusements of the poor, 1423

Jevons, William Alfred, *BMCat.*

The land laws, **FortR** 1786

Jevons, William Stanley: see *Index*, I, 958.

Philosophy of inductive inference, **FortR** 991
The use of hypothesis, 1009
The post-office telegraphs, 1215
Cruelty to animals, 1255
The future of political economy, 1305

Jewsbury, Geraldine Endsor, 1812–1880, novelist. *DNB.*

Trans: **FQR** 773

The Greville memoirs, **FM** 5627
Prince Albert [by Theodore Martin], 5645

Jex-Blake, Sophia, 1840–1912, physician. *DNB.*

The practice of medicine by women, **FortR** 1137

Medical women, **NC** 1486
Medical women in fiction, 2351

Jex-Blake, Thomas William: see *Index*, I, 958. See: **OxCam** 38

Jeyes, Samuel Henry, 1857–1911, journalist. *WWW.*

Foreign pauper immigration, **FortR** 3101
Our gentlemanly failures, 3930

Joel, Jonathan Edmondson, b.1844, barrister. Allibone.

The law relating to the married, **NatR-II** 1143

Johns, Bennett George: see *Index*, I, 958.

Literature [of street ballads], **NatR-II** 106
How the blind dream, 299

The traffic in sermons, **NC** 2160
Protective colour in animals, 2286

Johnson, Dr.

Records of olden outlaws, **DR** 88

Johnson, Christopher, 1816–1894, surgeon living in Lancaster, *Surgeon Index*/2nd s.

English agriculture, **DR** 296

Johnson, Frederick C. O.: see Ormsby-Johnson, F. C.

Johnson, Lionel Pigot, 1867–1902, Catholic poet. *DNB.* For an art. in *Index*, I, see below, App. A.

The work of Mr. Pater, **FortR** 3544

Johnson, Robert Arthur, 1874–1938, barrister, comptroller Royal Mint. *WWW.*

Oxford Liberalism, **NatR-II** 2052 collab.

Johnson, William Knox, b.1868, barrister. *Yearbook*/1904, Foster.

The Empress Catharine II, **FortR** 3877
Giacomo Leopardi: poet, philosopher, 4142

Johnston, Alfred Wintle, writer on Orkney Islands. *BMCat.*

Letter: **NatR-II** 438

Johnston, Charles: see *Index*, I, 959, and *Amer.WWW.*

The world's baby-talk, **FortR** 3862

Johnston, Sir Harry Hamilton, 1858–1927, explorer, administrator in Africa. *DNB.*

British East Africa, **FortR** 2753
Where is Stanley? 2765
The ethics of cannibalism, 2780
Are our foreign missions a success? 2808
England and Germany in Africa, 2972
Development of tropical Africa, 3010
The Boer question, 3529

British missions in Africa, **NC** 1487
The value of Africa, 1905

Johnston, Robert Mackenzie, 1844–1918, statistician to gov't of Tasmania. *WWW*, *LCCat.*

Attack on the credit of Australasia, **NC** 2194.

Johnstone, Sir James, 1841–1895, army officer. Boase.

A description of Manipur, **NC** 2053

Johnstone, William A.

From Canton to Mandalay, **FortR** 4077

Johnstone, William Henry, 1819/20–1901, divine. Venn.

Letter: **NatR-II** 1341

Jolly, William, inspector of schools. Allibone, *Imperial Calendar*, 1869–1896.

Professional training of teachers, **FortR** 1085

Jones, Alfred Stowell, 1832–1920, specialist on sewage disposal. *WWW.*

Pollution of the Thames, **FortR** 2486

Jones, Arthur Coppen, 1866–1901, physician. *BMCat., Surgeon Index*/2nd s.

The benefits of vivisection, **FortR** 3316

Jones, C. Rachel (Gurney): see *Index*, I, 960.

Historic memorials of the Norfolk coast, **FM** 6434, 6439

Jones, Charles Sheridan, b.1876, misc. writer. *LCCat., BMCat.*

The housing question and the L.C.C. [London County Council], **FortR** 4547

Jones, Harry, 1823–1900: see *Index*, I, 960.

The parish priest, **FM** 4423, 4473, 4539
The priest in the congregation, 4583
The priest in the world, 4616
The priest in the school, 4649

Our farmers in chains, **NatR-II** 986, 1022
The reform of public dinners, 1064
Christian colonies: brotherhoods, 1091

Town and country parsons, **NC** 2037
Some day dreams [unity among Christian churches], 2426
Total abstinence and temperance movement, 3033

Jones, Harry Longueville: see *Index*, I, 960.

The fine arts in the middle ages in France, **FQR** 502, 519
Versailles, 538

Jones, Henry Arthur, 1851–1928, dramatist. *DNB.*

The actor-manager, **FortR** 2965

Letter: **NatR-II** 1426

The theatre and the mob, **NC** 903
Religion and the stage, 1084
The first-night judgment of plays, 1728
Dr. Pearson on the modern drama, 2463

Jones, William Basil, 1827–1897, bishop of St. Davids. *DNB.*

Homer and the Homeric Age [by Gladstone], **BentQR** 2
Müller and Donaldson on Greek literature, 37

Jones, William Bence: see *Index,* I, 961.

The Irish Land question, **FM** 5847

Landowning as a business, **NC** 686

Jònsonn, Jòn, 1829–c.1868, Icelandic farmer.

Autobiography of a modern Icelander, **FM** 5883

Jordan, Denham: see *Index,* I, 961.

Old guns and their owners, **FortR** 3909 collab.
In the twilight, 4302 collab.

When life stirs, **NatR-II** 1571 collab.
Leafless woods and grey moorlands, 1648 collab.

Jordan, Sir John Newell, 1852–1925, diplomatist. *DNB.*

Modern China, **NC** 1295
Trans: 937

Jörgensen, Adolf Ditlev, 1840–1897, Danish historian. *EUI.*

View of the Schlesvig-Holstein question, **NC** 3210

Joyce, James Augustine, 1882–1941, novelist. *DNB.*

Ibsen's [*When We Dead Awaken*], **FortR** 4435

Joyce, Patrick Weston, 1827–1914, Irish antiquary. Crone, Hyamson.

Spenser's Irish rivers, **FM** 6030

Judd, John Wesley, 1840–1916, geologist. *WWW.*

Chemical action of marine organisms, **FortR** 3455

Postscript: **NC** 1481

Jung, Sir Salar, 1863–1889, Indian statesman. Boase.

Europe revisited, **NC** 1435, 1461 both collab.

Jusserand, Jean Adrien Antoine Jules, 1855–1932, French diplomat and litterateur. *WWW.*

Wayfaring life in the middle ages, **NQM** 199, 211

A French ambassador at the court of Charles II, **NC** 2102
Journey to England in 1663, 2239
Journey to Scotland in 1435, 2771
Did Chaucer meet Petrarch? 2947
Ronsard and his Vendômois, 3097
French ignorance of English literature in Tudor times, 3269

K

Kater, Edward, 1816/17–1866, F.R.S., member Royal Irish Academy. Boase, death certicate at Somerset House.

Printing and publishing at home and abroad, **FQR** 596
Engraving, ancient and modern, 606, 617

Katscher, Leopold, b.1853, Hungarian writer. *EUI, BMCat.*

The Salvation Army, **NatR-II** 280
Rural Tuscany, 481

Taine, **NC** 1296

German life in London, 1409
Alfred de Musset, 2371

Kaufmann, Moritz: see *Index,* I, 962.

German socialism, **FortR** 2247

French socialism, **NatR-II** 644
Socialism and the Papacy, 934

Adam Smith and his foreign critics, **ScotR** 187
Goethe's *Faust* and modern thought, 327
Ruskin as a practical teacher, 446

Kay, David, 1823/24–1898, misc. writer, F.R.G.S. *Times*, Dec. 22, 1898, p. 1a.

Home rule in Austria-Hungary, **NC** 1229

Kay, James Taylor: see *Index*, I, 962.

The classification of literature, **NC** 1051
How to catalogue books, 2427
The parliaments of the world, 2656

Kay-Shuttleworth, Sir James Phillips, 1804–1877, educator, M.P. *DNB.*

The Education Act and Code of 1870, **FortR** 1256

Kaye, Sir John William: see *Index*, I, 962, and II, App. A.

Notice: **FortR** 479

See: **FM** 2595

Keane, David Deady, 1810–1870, barrister. Venn.

Illustrations of discount, **FM** 1800

Kearley, Hudson Ewbanke, first Viscount Devonport, 1856–1934, businessman. *DNB.*

The Royal Patriotic Fund, **FortR** 3498

Keary, Charles Francis: see *Index*, I, 963.

Modern experiential philosophy, **FM** 5696
The "Song of Roland," 6469

The younger Pitt as an orator, **NatR-II** 213

Phases of early religious development, **NC** 212
Roumanian peasants and their songs, 772

Keary, Sir Henry D'Urban, 1857–1937, army officer. *WWW.*

Dacoity in upper Burma, **NatR-II** 1023

Keate, John, 1773–1852, headmaster of Eton. *DNB.*

Letter: **FM** 569

Keating, Francis Amboor, b. 1852/53, silk merchant in Melbourne. Foster.

The economic problem: an Australian appeal, **NatR-II** 2101

Keats, John, 1795–1821, poet. *DNB.*

Some unedited letters of John Keats, **FortR** 3439

Keay, John Seymour: see *Index*, I, 963.

The spoliation of India, **NC** 874, 980, 990

Kebbel, Thomas Edward: see *Index*, I, 963.

English love of Latin poetry, **FortR** 47
Pope's *Essay on Man*, 642
Jane Austen, 658
The reign of Queen Anne, 681
The first Lord Malmesbury, 695
Political reputations, 715
The House of Lords, 1912
Mr. Lecky and George III, 1927
Shooting, 1977
The county system, 2012
Lord Lyndhurst, 2129
Tory party under Wyndham and Bolingbroke, 2158
John Wilson Croker, 2242
Jane Austen at home, 2280
English love of sport, 2452

Lord Macaulay of Rothley, **FM** 3659
Bolingbroke as a statesman, 4331
Party, 4355
Writings of Bolingbroke, 4589
Partridges and politics, 6220
An English rural walk, 6350
Village life of George Eliot, 6379
Mr. Thrale, 6406

Coalitions: a centenary anniversary, **NatR-II** 19
The middle classes, 49
Miss Austen and George Eliot, 89
Tory prime ministers, in 8 installments from 220 to 377
Mr. Pitt, 220
Lord Liverpool, the Duke of Portland, Mr. Perceval, 241
Mr. Canning, 268
Duke of Wellington, 300
Sir Robert Peel, 339, 349
Lord Derby, 364
Lord Beaconsfield, 377
Old "Young England" and new, 539
The House of Brocas [by Montagu Burrows], 563
Old and new Oxford, 580
Canning, Castlereagh, and Wellington, 641
Partridge-shooting, 757
The early pheasants, 933
Lord Iddesleigh, 1082
September, 1191
The greatness of Pitt, 1234
The plough and the platform, 1271
Yeomen and sportsmen, 1301
Gamekeepers, 1345
The Radical rush, 1412
Autumn thoughts, 1629
The retrospect of the reign, 2028

Personal rule, **NC** 256
Political novels of Lord Beaconsfield, 355
A Conservative view of the elections, 450
Conservative party and late election, 459

Kebbel, Thomas Edward (*continued*)
The state of parties, 565
The spirit of party, 688
Party obligations to-day, 828
The House of Lords: its abolition, 958
Democracy and party, 1583
Party prospects [for the Unionists], 1833
Is free education a bribe? 2063
The good sense of the English people, 2716
European coalitions against England, 2932
"England at War," 3249
Is the party system breaking up? 3441
Notice: 1976

Keddie, Henrietta: see *Index*, I, 964.

Meg of Elibank, **FM** 3535
The Laird's seam, 3586
A wooing and wedding of 17——, 3607
Lady Strathmore's daughter, 3680, 3690
Squire Bolton's transgression, 3714, 3724, 3738
Hector Garret of Otter, 3794, 3804
Rae Gifford, 4481
Abigail, 4581
The minister's Sandy and Jess, 4632
Em's first and last lodger, 4693
A lost man, 4702
Two salutations, 4782
Adam and Mally; Scottish farm-life, 5090
Prince Paul's betrothal, 5113
The dominie's sons, 5122

Keen, Benjamin, 1794/95–1839, barrister. Death certificate at Somerset House, which gives 40 as age at death; birthdate given (from Venn) seems more likely since he took his B.A. in 1816.

De Bausset, *Memoirs of Napoleon,* **FQR** 17

Keene, Henry George: see *Index*, I, 964.

Lord Ripon's policy [on India], **FortR** 2048
Belgian socialism, 3602
Socialism at home and abroad, 3752

The Indian Civil Service, **NatR-II** 483
Women of Indian history, 485
The poverty of India, 627
The disorder of the age, 749
The marriage question, 799
Age of Reason: literary aspects of the French Revolution, 906
Home rule for India, 991
Letters: 786, 911, 1007

Keer, William Brown, b.1826/27, divine. Foster, *CCD*/76.

From India by the Euphrates route, **FM** 5600

Kegan Paul, Trench, & Co., London, publishers.

An olive branch from America, **NC** 1480

Keightley, Thomas, 1789–1872, historian. *DNB.*

Von Hammer's *History of the Assassins,* **FQR** 20
Magnusen, *The Edda Doctrine, Its Origin,* 35
Niebuhr's *Roman History,* 44, 187, 272
Illyrian poetry, 50
Scandinavian mythology, 84
History of the Knights Templars, 101
Early Roman history, 112
Wilken and Michaud: history of the Crusades, 129
The Northern runes, 225
Geijer's *History of Sweden,* 284
History of the Phoenicians, Carthaginians, 329
Bojardo's and Ariosto's *Orlando,* 343
Notice: 53

Life and writings of Henry Fielding, **FM** 3679, 3693
On the life of Edmund Spenser, 3896

Keith, H. C. A., translator. *BMCat.* under Philip Kent, pseud.

?Balzac's view of the artistic temperament, **NatR-II** 860 collab.

Keith, James

Our great competitor [U.S.A.], **NC** 1414

Kélékian, Diran, or Dikran: see *Index*, I, 964, and II, App. A.

La Turquie et son souverain, **NC** 3012

Kelly, Matthew, 1814–1858, Irish antiquary, professor at Maynooth. *DNB.*

St. Etienne-du-Mont, Paris, **DR** 253
The Irish Church, 281
Life of Bishop Bedell, 311
Irish Archaeological Society, 324
French religious liberty: the Jesuits, 334
Cauchy's *Religious Orders,* 358
The Works of Edmund Spenser, 360
Bokhara, 378
Round towers of Ireland, 382
Catholic Ireland, A.D. 600, 420
The aristocracies of Ireland, 449
Irish Evangelicals, 460
Miscellany of the Celtic Society, 632
Eloquence in theological seminaries, 786

History of the Reformation in Ireland, **Ram** 460, 467
Life of Richard Creagh, 489

Retrospective proselytism in Ireland, 508
Historical notices of patron saints, 528

Kelly, Walter Keating, 1806–1873, journalist; ed. *FQR*, 1844–1846. *Alum. Dub.*, death certificate at Somerset House, R.L.F.

?*Letters of the Queen of Navarre*, **FQR** 688
Freiligrath's *Poems*, 815
Men and manners in Auvergne in 1665, 831
Adalbert von Chamisso, 872
Notice: 771
See: 678, 763

Kelly, William, musicologist. *BMCat.*

Letter: **Ram** 75

Kelsall, Thomas Forbes, d.1872, friend of Thomas L. Beddoes. Beddoes, *Complete Works*, ed. E. Gosse, (2 vols. [1928]), I, ix.

Thomas Lovell Beddoes, **FortR** 876

Keltie, Sir John Scott: see *Index*, I, 964.

Stanley's expedition, **FortR** 2969
South African problems, 3087

Kemball, Sir Arnold Burrowes: see *Index*, I, 965.

The Imperial British East Africa Company, **FortR** 3437

Kemble, Frances Anne: see *Index*, I, 965.

See: **FM** 862

Kemble, John Mitchell, 1807–1857, philologist, historian. *DNB.*

German origin of the Latin language, **FQR** 246
Rask's *Anglo-Saxon Grammar*, 265
?*Factory Hanseatic merchants in London*, **FM** 3107
?*History of the Prussian Court*, 3115
?*Courts of the House of Brunswick in Germany and England*, 3144
Queens of England of the House of Hanover, 3374
Macaulay's *History of England*, 3438
Pauli's *History of England*, 3546

Kemp, Dixon, 1839–1899, yachtsman. *LCCat.*, *BMCat.*

Yachting: racing, **FortR** 2077

Kemp, George, 1807/1808–1885, physician, chemist. Venn.

See: **FM** 4220

Kemp, Thomas Lindley, d.1858, Scottish physician in Essex. *Surgeon Index*/1st s.; Edinburgh P.O. Directories, 1858, 1859.

Liebig's philosophy, **DR** 521
State of chemical science, 753
Food and its adulterations, 772

Kempe, John Edward: see *Index*, I, 965.

An Athenian archbishop of the dark ages, **FM** 6451

Kendall, Henry, divine, author of *The Kinship of Man*, Boston, 1888. *LCCat.*

Natural heirship, **NC** 1196

Kenealy, Arabella, 1864–1938, novelist, physician. *WW*/1900, *WWW.*

The talent of motherhood, **NatR-II** 1086
The physical conscience, 1158

Woman as an athlete, **NC** 3453, 3479

Kenealy, Edward Vaughan Hyde, 1819–1880, barrister, man of letters. *DNB.*

Life of [Henry] Flood, **DR** 263
Arundines Cami, 279
Life of Grattan, 303
Dunlop's *Travels in Central America*, 469
Prescott's *Conquest of Peru*, 482

Table-talk of the late John Boyle, **FM** 1564, 1580
Letther from Brallaghan: account of the late Richard Milliken, 1650
Sickund letther from Brallaghan, 1657
[Note to] epistles of Aristaenetus, 1711
The late William Maginn, 1738
Oliver Yorke at home, 1768
Titmarsh's travels in Ireland [*Irish Sketch Book*], 1824
A continental tour, 1883, 1928
Note: 1743
See: 1246, 1392

Kennard, Nina H.: see *Index*, I, 965.

Why women write, **NatR-II** 194
Rachel-Crémieux correspondence, 527
Voltaire and England, 1320

Rachel, **NC** 939
Faust, "ein Fragment" [by Goethe], 1059
Gustave Flaubert and George Sand, 1340
Ferdinand Lassalle, 2095

Kennedy, Benjamin Hall, 1804–1889, classicist, prof. at Cambridge. *DNB.*

The lost tales of Miletus, **FortR** 355

Kennedy, C. W.; perhaps Charles William Kennedy, b.1850, barrister in *M at B,* and Foster.

The present House of Commons and the roll of the Long Parliament, **FM** 6499

Kennedy, Hugh Arthur: see *Index,* I, 965.

Velasquez and his king [Philip IV], **NC** 1985
The drama of the moment, 2086
The paintings at Pompeii, 2688
A dialogue on the drama, 2799
Shakespeare, Falstaff, and Queen Elizabeth, 2888

Kennedy, Samuel, doctor. *Med.Reg./*1903.

Mattei v. the knife: cancer, **NatR-II** 1047
Letter: 1069

Kennett-Barrington, Sir Vincent Hunter Barrington, 1844–1903, Red Cross commissioner. *WWW.*

Letter: **NatR-II** 865

Kenney-Herbert, Arthur Robert: see *Index,* I, 965, and *Army List/*87.

The literature of cookery, **NatR-II** 1672, 1757
Aesthetics of the dinner table, 1923

The art of dining, **NC** 3266
The art of cooking, 2309
The art of household management, 2445

Kent, Armine Thomas, 1856–1903, journalist. *Otia: Poems, Essays and Reviews* (1905), pp. 1, 9.

Leigh Hunt as a poet, **FortR** 1832

Della Crusca and Anna Matilda [Hannah Cowley], **NatR-II** 252

Kent, Clement Boulton Roylance: see Roylance-Kent, C. B.

Kent, William Charles Mark: see *Index,* I, 965.

Notice: **DR** 1019

Kent, William Henry, 1857–1935, R.C. priest, linguist. *Tablet,* Apr. 27, 1935.

The unity of theology, **DR** 2147
Catholic theology in England, 2287
Primitive church and the See of Peter, 2456
Eastern devotion to St. Joseph, 2476
The Life of Cardinal Manning [by E. S. Purcell], 2528

Froude and the Council of Trent, 2550
Dr. Lea's *History of Indulgences,* 2584
Philosophy of the Renaissance, 2624
William Ewart Gladstone, 2629
Liturgical books of the Russian Church, 2656
Dr. Fairbairn on Catholicism, 2671
Pastor's *Popes of the Renaissance,* 2675
The making of French literature, 2695
The eve of the English Reformation, 2706
The Syriac *Testament of Our Lord,* 2710
A [nameless] Russian champion of the Church, 2724
Theology and modern thought, 2733
Notices: 2485, 2570, 2606, 2651, 2686, 2699, 2709, 2720, 2729, 2738

Kenyon, Sir Frederic George: see *Index,* I, 965.

Great palace of Byzantium, **ScotR** 249

Keogh, Edward Stephen, 1833–1887, Catholic priest of the London Oratory. Gillow.

Replies to Lord Acton, **DR** 1494 collab.
Notices: 1193, 1222

Keppel, Lady Susan Mary, 1868–1953, wife of Sir Walter Beaupré Townley. Burke under Albermarle.

Byeways in Sicily, **NatR-II** 1384

Keppel, William Coutts: see *Index,* I, 966.

Notes on Canadian matters, **FM** 3580, 3600, 3622
British Columbia and Vancouver's Island, 3788
Volunteer course at Hythe School of Musketry, 3998

The Channel tunnel, **NC** 712
Electric light and force, 742
House-lighting by electricity, 876
Cycling and cyclists, 1081
The unity of the Empire, 1100
Electrical transmission of power, 2150

Ker, Charles Henry Bellenden: see *Index,* I, 966.

The north of Italy and the Tyrol, **FQR** 285

Ker, David, 1842–1914, novelist. *LCCat.,* Foster.

?Story of the Woodhouslee ghost, **FM** 5470 collab.

Ker, Robert, b.1843, Canadian divine. *LCCat.*

Prospects of Canadian confederation, **ScotR** 133

Kernahan, John Coulson, 1858–1943, novelist. *WWW, BMCat.*

Rosetti and the moralists, **FortR** 3055
Philip Marston, the blind poet, 3168
The poems of Louise Chandler Moulton, 3351

Is Emerson a poet? **NatR-II** 2532

Frederick Locker-Lampson, **NC** 2821

Kershaw, John, 1816–1890, canon of Salford. Boase.

Catholic education question in England and Ireland, **DR** 1949

Kershaw, John Baker Cannington, b.1862, chemist, writer on fuels and trade. *LCCat.*

The future of British trade, **FortR** 4035
Joint stock enterprise, 4452

Key, Sir Astley Cooper, 1821–1888, naval officer. *DNB.*

Naval defence of the colonies, **NC** 1312

Keyser, Alfred

The Malay Peninsula, **NC** 2454

Khusrau, or Khusro, Amir Dihlávi, 1253–1325, Hindustan poet. Beale.

The story of the dog-worshipper, **FM** 5101
See: 5237

Kidd, Benjamin: see *Index,* I, 966.

Balfour's *Foundations of Belief,* **NatR-II** 1694
Note: 1611

The civil service as a profession, **NC** 1326
Social Evolution, 2700

Kidd, Joseph, 1824–1918, M.D. *Surgeon Index*/3rd s. (See *Index,* I, 966.)

The Engandine: summer and winter, **NC** 1571
Last illness of Lord Beaconsfield, 1730

Kilian, Dr. E. H.

The Bukowina, **FM** 5753
Austria and Turkey, 5826
The Bulgarians, 5867

King, E. Augusta: see *Index,* I, 966.

Mediaeval medicine, **NC** 2431
Deaths under chloroform, 3263
Death and torture under chloroform, 3304

King, Edward, S. J., 1874–1936. Sutcliffe.

Dramatic art and church liturgy, **DR** 2677

King, Richard John: see *Index,* I, 967.

The forest of Dartmoor, **FortR** 319

[Note to] Thrieve Castle, **FM** 2817
Robert Herrick and his vicarage, 3055
Sketches from Belgium, 3398, 3420, 3562
The châteaux of Rubens and Teniers, 3681
A pilgrimage to St. David's, 5185
Plymouth, 5399
Bodley and the Bodleian, 5431
The folk-lore of Devonshire, 5499
Some old-fashioned parsons, 5539
A day at Fotheringhay, 5588
Charles Kingsley, 5660
Cleveland [northeast Yorkshire], 5666
Runes and rune-stones, 5821

King, William, 1809–1886, geologist. *DNB.*

On certain phenomena of the Atlantic [on the cable], **FM** 4374

Kingdon, George Renorden, S.J., 1821–1893. Sutcliffe.

Letter: **DR** 1550

Kinglake, Alexander William: see **Index,** I, 967.

Mr. Hayward, **FortR** 2163
Bernal Osborne, 2230 collab.

Kinglake, Robert Arthur. *BMCat., DNB* under his brother Alexander William, q.v.

Letter: **NatR-II** 970

Kingsbury, George Chadwick, M.D. *Med. Reg./99.*

Hypnotism, crime and the doctors, **NC** 1991

Kingscote, Adeline Georgiana Isabella (Wolff), d.1908, traveller, linguist. *BMCat., LCCat., Landed Gentry.*

A Brahmin school-girl, **NC** 1648
The decline of Indian taste, 2002

Kingsford, Anna (Bonus): see *Index,* I, 967.

The uselessness of vivisection, **NC** 673

Kingsley, Charles: see *Index*, I, 967.

Should we fear the Romish priests? **FM** 2448
Yeast, 2479, 2487, 2495, 2511, 2518, 2533
The Bothie of Toper-na-Fuosich [by A. H. Clough], 2546
Poetry of sacred art, 2563
Recent novels, 2576
Recent poetry and verse, 2591
North Devon, 2605, 2669, 2690
Lytton and Mrs. Grundy, 2685
Readables and unreadables, 2734
Tennyson, 2763
Mr. and Mrs. Browning, 2819
The prevailing epidemic, 2848
Little books with large aims, 2869
This year's song-crop [Browning, Beddoes, Meredith], 2917
Hypatia, in 16 installments from 2923 to 3084
Alexander Smith and Alexander Pope, 3145
Thoughts on Shelley and Byron, 3155
Palmerston and the presbytery of Edinburgh, 3171
Poems by Matthew Arnold, 3181
Frederick Tennyson's poems, 3234
Sydney Smith, 3368
Tennyson's *Maud*, 3387
Hours with the Mystics, 3514
Paraguay, Brazil, and the Plate, 3539
"A mad world, my masters," 3687
My winter-garden, 3711
Chalk-stream studies, 3773
The irrationale of speech, 3866
Superstition, 4656
Science, 4664
"A charm of birds," 4773
Journal of Our Life in the Highlands [by Queen Victoria], 4838
Note: 3560
See: 4816

Kingsley, George Henry: see *Index*, I, 967.

Chamois hunting, **FM** 2877
A German first of September, 3131
Last salmon before close time, 3560

Kingsley, Henry: see *Index*, I, 967.

The discovery of the Albert N'Yanza, **FortR** 291
The last two Abyssinian books, 452

Wild sports of the Far South [Australia], **FM** 3850

Sir Philip Sidney, **NQM** 42

Kingsley, Mary Henrietta: see *Index*, I, 967.

Liquor traffic with West Africa, **FortR** 4100

Dodos [West African Negroes], **NatR-II** 1844
The throne of thunder, 1864
Fishing in West Africa, 1999
African religion and law, 2065

Kingston, John, retired naval chaplain. *CCD/* 1902.

Church defence, **NatR-II** 956
Letter: 862

Kinloch-Cooke, Sir Clement, 1854–1944, editor, lawyer. *WWW*.

Samoa, **NC** 1248
France and the New Hebrides, 1300
Europe in the Pacific, 1344

Kinnear, John Boyd: see *Index*, I, 968, and II, App. A.

Representation of minorities, **FortR** 186
The question of the House of Lords, 622
The coming land question, 1617

Kipling, Joseph Rudyard: see *Index*, I, 968.

One view [an Indian looks at the English], **FortR** 2914
The lamentable comedy of Willow Wood, 2948

The white seal, **NatR-II** 1466

Kirchhammer, Alexander, 1847–1909, Austrian army officer. *Österreich. Biograph.*

Military impotence of Great Britain, **NC** 572

Kirkus, William, 1830–1907, divine. *LCCat.*

Romanism, Anglicanism, Evangelicalism, **FortR** 267
Elizabeth and her England, 344
Notices: 513, 577, 611

Kirkwood, Townsend Molloy, 1842–1919, of Bengal civil service. *Landed Gentry.*

The impending famine, **FortR** 3893

Kirwan, Andrew Valentine: see *Index*, I, 968.

Charles Gutzkow's *Paris*, **FQR** 699
The Congress of Vienna, 762
Maret, Duke of Bassano, 768
Culinary literature and cookery, 780
The French and English bar, 787
Navy of France, 795

Thiers's *History of the Consulate and Empire*, 830

Ports of France, and admiralty of England, **FM** 1546 collab.
Right of search, 1680 collab.
The classics of the table, in 8 installments from 1942 to 2046
Histoire du Consulat et de L'Empire [by Thiers], 2059, 2973
The Fall of Napoleon [by J. Mitchell], 2087
The late Sir William Follett, 2092
French newspapers and newspaper writers, 2202
?Memoranda of Madrid in 1845, 2227
?*Gatherings from Spain* [by Richard Ford], 2277
Chronique de Paris, 2307, 2422, 2799, 2864, 2913
Life of Henry IV [by G. P. R. James], 2321
Louis XIV, and the Court of France [by Julia Pardoe], 2328
Girondists, Jacobins, and Lamartine, 2357
Chapter on the art of eating, 2389
Reveries of a gastronome, 2439
France: her revolutions, 2461
?Spanish affairs, 2470
?Republican literature [in France], 2482
Lamartine's *Raphael*, 2557
Of the English bar, 2728
Ledru Rollin's *Decline of England*, 2748
History of French Journals, 2834
History of the Restoration in France [by Lamartine], 2895
The coup d'état in France, 2932
State and prospects of France, 2952
Advocates and juries, 3030
?The Empire in France, 3042
Napoleon III—invasion: French pamphlets, 3059
?Law reform, 3079
Modern French memoirs, 3083, 3142
?*The Restoration in 1822–23*, 3091
Bonaparte, Hudson Lowe, and Dr. O'Meara, 3122
?Dr. Véron's *Memoirs*, 3169
?Paris gossip, 3186
Villemain's *Memoirs*, 3192
Recent French literature, 3356
Montalembert and John Wilson Croker, 3472
French romantic literature, 3483
?France and French affairs, 3629
Memoirs of St. Simon, 3664
Lord Normanby and *A Year of Revolution*, 3677
French memoirs [Guizot, Louis Blanc], 3735
Montalembert and the emperor of the French, 3808
Alexis de Tocqueville, 3852

?The Roman question: the Pope, 3864
The peace of Villafranca, 3884
Naples, France, and Austria, 3894
Piedmont and Italy in 1849 and 1859, 3904
Madame Récamier, 3954
Life five-and-thirty years ago, 4004
France and Paris forty, thirty, and twenty years ago, 4023, 4036, 4068
Editors and newspaper writers of last generation, 4185, 4217, 4233
Physicians of a bygone generation, 4270
The late Sir Benjamin Brodie, 4293
A fortnight in Ireland in 1863, 4329
A fortnight in Paris in 1863, 4339
A fortnight in Belgium in 1863, 4364
See: 2567

Kitchener, Horatio Herbert: see *Index*, I, 968.

The future of the fellah, **FortR** 2392

Kitchin, Frederick Harcourt: see *Index*, I, 968.

The casualties of war and industry, **NC** 3753

Kitchin, George William: see *Index*, I, 968.

Why I voted for Gladstone, **NC** 2264

Klausen, Rudolf Heinrich, 1807–1840, German classical scholar. *ADB*.

Religious system of the ancients, **DR** 75

Klausner-Dawoc, Ludwig, 1848–1912(?), German writer. *Wer Ist's/1911/1912*.

The German Emperor, **FortR** 4545

Klein, Louis Léopold Martial Baynard de Beaumont, 1849–1934, French R.C. converted to Unitarianism. Anne Holt, *Walking Together* (1938), pp. 229, 233; *BMCat*.

Mental evolution in man, **DR** 2183
Deep-sea explorations and their results, 2234
Evolution and ethics, 2393
Notice: 2358

Knatchbull-Hugessen, Edward Hugessen: see *Index*, I, 968.

Public schools and schoolmasters, **FM** 5778

The duty of moderate Liberals, **NC** 722
What will the peers do? 1058
Gladstone on "The Irish Demand," 1382
Gladstone's "plain speaking," 1745

Knatchbull-Hugessen, Eva Mary: see *Index*, I, 969.

The higher education of women, **NatR-II,** 833

Newnham College from within, **NC** 1418

Knight, Joseph, 1829–1907, journalist. *DNB.*

The real Cyrano de Bergerac, **FortR** 4156
Letter: 4330
Notices: 387, 415, 520, 547

Dixon's *History of Two Queens*, **FM** 5458

Knight, William Angus: see *Index*, I, 969.

The doctrine of metempsychosis, **FortR** 1508
Note: 3952

Correlation of moral forces, **NatR-II** 1378

Ethical philosophy and evolution, **NC** 217
The protest against over-examination, 1637
Criticism as a trade, 1760
Criticism as theft, 2884

Scottish university reform, **ScotR** 195
Scottish universities commission: curricula and degrees, 271

Knight-Horsfield, H.: see Horsfield, Herbert Knight.

Knighton, William: see *Index*, I, 969.

Hindu households, **FortR** 1813

Village life in Oudh, **FM** 4410, 4418

Demoniacal possession in India, **NC** 508
Religious fairs in India, 587

Knoblauch, Hendrick B., an Afrikander.

A Cape farmer in Kent, **NatR-II** 1204

Knödel, Dr. Karl

Woman and socialism, **FortR** 3604

Knollys, William Wallingford: see *Index*, I, 969.

Mobs and revolutions, **FortR** 2538
A hundred years ago, 2748
Lord Napier of Magdala, 2931
War in the future, 2983

Our disasters in Affghanistan [in 1841], **NQM** 84

Boy soldiers, **NC** 325

Knowles, Sir James Thomas: see *Index*, I, 970.

Recent science: **NC** 10, 34, 81, 120, 151, 188, 236, 266, 311, 366, 423, 521

The proposed Channel tunnel, 697, 710
Thought-reading, 727, collab.
A society for enforcement of sanitary laws, 968a
Westminster Abbey: the cloisters, 1679
Disfigurement of Westminster Abbey, 1896
The joke about the Elgin Marbles, 2018
Aspects of Tennyson, 2345
Canon MacColl on Islam, 2859 collab.
Gladstone as a contributor to the *Nineteenth Century*, 3310
Wireless telegraphy and "brain-waves," 3474
Edited: 710
Notes: 32, 1468, 1653, 1665, 1712, 1838, 2145, 2185, 2247, 3583, 3599, 3690, 3691, 3754, 3757
Notice: 2593

Knowles, Sir Lees, 1857–1928, M.P. *WWW.*

Horseflesh, **NC** 1853

Knox, Alexander Andrew: see *Index*, I, 970.

Sicily of Thucydides and Theocritus, **NC** 665
About Voltaire, 776

Knox, Edmund Francis Vesey: see *Index*, I, 970.

Ireland and bimetallism, **NatR-II** 2030

Knox, Thomas Francis, 1822–1882, superior of the London Oratory. *DNB.*

Father Ryder, **DR** 1242

Knox-Little, William John: see *Index*, I, 970.

"Protestant science" and Christian belief, **NC** 2449

Koe, Arthur Baring

An African adventure, **NC** 3347

Kogălniceanŭ, Mihail, 1817–1891, Roumanian scholar. *BMCat., LCCat.,* suppl.

?Moldo-Wallachia, **FM** 3446

Kopsch, H.

The British bounty to Asia, **NatR-II,** 2128

Korn, Friedrich, 1803–1850, German scholar. *ADB* under Nork.

See: **FM** 2504

Koźmian, Stanislaus, 1811–1885, Polish poet, journalist. *Cath.Ency.*

The Slavonians, **DR** 129

Krausse, Alexis Sidney, 1859–1904, journalist. *WWW*.

The British record in China, **FortR** 4166

Kravchinsky, Sergius Mikhailovitch: see *Index*, I, 970.

The moujiks and the Russian democracy, **FortR** 2530
The Mir and the police, 2561
The Russian famine and the Revolution, 3188

Kropotkin, Prince Peter, or Petr, Aleksyeevich, 1842–1921, Russian anarchist. *Ency.Brit.*, 14th ed.

The Russian Revolutionary Party, **FortR** 1914

Russian prisoners, **NC** 803
The fortress prison of St. Petersburg, 863
Outcast Russia: journey to Siberia, 935
The exile in Siberia, 976
Finland: a rising nationality, 1110
The coming war [on Afghan frontier], 1128
What geography ought to be, 1220
In French prisons, 1255
The scientific bases of anarchy, 1371
The coming anarchy, 1434
Breakdown of our industrial system, 1534
The coming reign of plenty, 1559

The industrial village of the future, 1606
The French Revolution and its lesson, 1717
Brain work and manual work, 1843
Mutual aid among animals, 1923, 1952
Mutual aid among savages, 2021
Mutual aid among barbarians, 2152
Recent science: 2209, 2268, 2330, 2384, 2439, 2514, 2567, 2681, 2780, 2897, 2974, 3070, 3135, 3203, 3333, 3434, 3574, 3761
Mutual aid in the mediaeval city, 2616, 2635
The present condition of Russia, 2813
Mutual aid amongst modern men, 2867
Mutual aid amongst ourselves, 2941
Some of the resources of Canada, 3262
The small industries of Britain, 3705

Kropotkin, Princess Sophia (Ananieu), 1856–1938, wife of Prince Peter Kropotkin. George Woodcock and Ivan Avakumovic, *The Anarchist Prince* (1950), pp. 170–171, 437.

Higher education of women in Russia, **NC** **3230**

Kyan, William E., 1814–1852?, priest, accompanied Wiseman to English Coll. at Rome. Newman, *L&D*, XI, 344.

Ecclesiastical seminaries, **DR** 124

L

Labilliere, Francis Peter, 1840–1895, barrister. *Australian Ency.*

England and its advocates, **NatR-II** 176

Labouchere, Henry Du Pré, 1831–1912, journalist, M.P. *DNB*.

A democrat on the coming democracy, **FortR** 2009
Radicals and Whigs, 2137
People and peers, 2212
The promised land, 2372

Lach-Szyrma, Wladyslaw Somerville, 1841–1915, divine. *LCCat.*, Allibone.

Letter: **NatR-II** 956

Lacordaire, Jean Théodore, 1801–1870, French entomologist. *Grand Larousse*.

Notice: **FQR** 266

Lafargue, Paul, 1842–1911, French socialist. *Grand Larousse*.

Socialism in France from 1876–1896, **FortR** 4010

Lagden, Godfrey Yeatman, 1851–1934, civil servant. *WWW*.

A walk to Coomassie, **NC** 960

Laing, Francis Henry, 1816–1889, R.C. priest. Venn.

Catholic tradition and Scripture, **DR** 463

Laing, Samuel, 1812–1897: see *Index*, I, 971.

A plain view of British interests, **FortR** 1443
The Convention with Turkey, 1492
A month in Connemara, 2102
Rational radicalism, 2126
Peace with Russia, 2332
Ireland and the general election, 2382
Gladstone as a theologian, 2412
Our railway system, 2444

The crisis in Indian finance, **NC** 460

Laing-Meason, Adam B., S.J., 1821–1854, Sutcliffe.

Celebrated visions of the Blessed Virgin, **Ram** 547
Rites and ceremonies: Holy Water, 563

Laister, J., superintendent Postal Telegraph School, London. Blackwood Corres.

Letter: **NatR-II** 420

Lakeman, James B., factory inspector in London. *BMCat.*

Table of wages, **NC** 1451

Lamartine, Alphonse de: see *Index*, I, 971.

See: **FQR** 243

Lamb, Charles: see *Index*, I, 971.

See: **FM** 6075

Lamb, Robert, 1812–1872, divine. Boase.

The manufacturing poor, **FM** 2405, 2549
Manchester, 3101
The Church among the tall chimneys, 3261
An essay on humbug, 3363
A Whit-week in Manchester, 3477
An essay on popularity, 3542
An essay on crotchets, 3646
Manchester Exhibitions of 1857, 3648
A threnode to the east wind, 3719
Our failures, 3789
Hymns for congregational worship, 4017
The philosophy of marriage, 4035
Meeting of Association for Advancement of Science, 4161
Manufacturing districts and classes, 4256
Our manfacturing districts, 4362

Lambert, Agnes, d.1917, misc. writer. *WWW.*

Recent contribution to English history [Bridgett's *History of the Holy Eucharist*], **DR** 1786

The ceremonial use of flowers, **NC** 218, 441
Oldest epic [the *Song of Roland*], 667
False coin [on natural religion], 1005
Leprosy: present and past, 1025, 1040
Thrift among the children, 1263, 1438
The private life of Sir Thomas More, 2107
Aspects of Tennyson: the real Thomas Becket, 2352
Neglecting our customers [on British trade], 3388, 3428

Lambert, Sir John, 1815–1892, civil servant. *DNB.*

Parliamentary franchises, **NC** 1799

Lampakes, Georgios, professor of Christian archaeology, Athens. *ScotR*, 28 (1896), 409.

Recent archaeology in Euboia, **ScotR** 169

Lamy, Thomas Joseph, 1827–1907, prof. of theology at Louvain. *Louvain Bibliog., LCCat.*

The Christians of the East, **DR** 1681
The education question in Belgium, 1697
The Greek Church, 1738
The Russian Church, 1776
Oriental patrology: St. Ephrem, 1968

Lancaster, Henry Hill: see *Index*, I, 971.

Professorial elections [on Ferrier's *Scottish Philosophy*], **FM** 3543

Lancaster-Woodburne, George Burgess: see under Woodburne, George Burgess Lancaster.

Landis, Charles Kline, 1835–1900, founder of Vineland, New Jersey settlement. *LCCat.*

Settlement of Vineland in New Jersey, **FM** 5639

Landolt, or **Landott,** F., mathematician.

Notices: **DR** 2079, 2144, 2199

Landor, Arnold Henry Savage, 1865–1924, anthropologist, traveller. *WWW, BMCat.*

A visit to Corea, **FortR** 3531
Sacred mountain, Siao-Outai-Shan, China, 3547
Burning questions of Japan, 3564

Landor, Edward Wilson, 1811–1878, Australian solicitor. *Austral.Dic.Biog.*, II.

The maelstrom, **FM** 732

Landor, Walter Savage: see *Index*, I, 972.

Latin poetry: *The Writings of Catullus*, **FQR** 672
The Idyls of Theocritus, 691
Francesco Petrarca, 734

Harold, and *Amymone*, **FM** 2508
To C. Cuthbert Southey on Robert Southey, 2797
Imaginary conversations, 3412, 3462
On orthography, 3445
See: 2940

Lane, Laura M. (perhaps later Laura Bogue Luffmann in *BMCat.* since Laura Lane collab. with Charles Bogue Luffman, q.v., in *Temple Bar*, 106 [Oct. 1895], 207–219), misc. writer.

Revival of spiritual ideal, France, **NatR-II** 1435

Lane-Fox, Florence

Can a national school of opera exist? **NatR-II** 759

Lane-Poole, Stanley Edward: see *Index*, I, 972

The beginning of art, **FortR** 2000

Swift and Ireland, **FM** 6442
Dr. Sheridan [friend of Swift's], 6482

Lord Stratford de Redcliffe, **NatR-II** 1644
Sir Charles Newton, 1668

Notice: **NC** 2206

Lang, Andrew: see *Index*, I, 972.

Mythology and fairy tales, **FortR** 951
Homer and his recent critics, 1149
Three new novels [by W. Black, G. Macdonald, R. Broughton], 1323
Titian, 1329
Emile Zola, 1899
In the wrong paradise, 2116
Lady book lovers, 2533
M. Renan's later works, 2548
Byways of Greek song, 2641
Lucian, 2727
Charles Dickens, 4213
Mr. Frazer's theory of totemism, 4293
Papers of the Scottish Reformation, 4491
Letters: 2627, 4197

Rabelais and the Renaissance, **FM** 5063
Kalevala, Finnish national epic, 5317
Gerard de Nerval, 5424
The *Gripis-Spa*, 5518
Egypt and the pre-Homeric Greeks, 6202
The romance of the first radical, 6321
Mr. Carlyle's Reminiscences, 6396
Max Müller's philosophy of mythology, 6428
Primitive belief and savage metaphysics, 6519
See: 5276

Homer and the higher criticism, **NatR-II** 1245
A critical taboo, 1306
The *Song of Roland* and the *Iliad*, 1342

Théodore de Banville, **NQM** 156

Comparative study of ghost stories, **NC** 1118
Myths and mythologists, 1230
Egyptian divine myths, 1322

Demeter and the pig, 1393
Ghost-stories and beast-stories, 2702
The false Pucelle, 2755
Are savage gods borrowed from missionaries? 3411

Lang, John, c.1817–1864, Australian novelist. Serle.

The Wetherbys, **FM** 3062, 3072, 3081, 3093, 3103

Lang, Leonora Blanche: see *Index*, I, 972.

Paul de St. Victor, **NatR-II** 496
Morals and manners in Richardson, 922
Records of Scotch family [*Caldwell Papers*], 1026
Rousseau's ideal household, 1179
A poseuse of the 18th century [Mme. de Genlis], 1297

Lang, Sir Robert Hamilton: see *Index*, I, 973.

The Austrians in Bosnia, **FortR** 1638

Lang, (William) Cosmo Gordon, Baron Lang of Lambeth, 1864–1945, archbishop of Canterbury. *DNB.*

The war relief funds, **NC** 3594

Langtoft, Geoffrey, political writer. *RG/* 1900–1904.

Socialism and anarchism, **FortR** 4516

Langton, Edward, member Executive Council of Victoria.

Colonial custom-houses, **FM** 6105

Lankester, Sir Edwin Ray: see *Index*, I, 973.

The Present Evolution of Man, **FortR** 3853
Letter: 3884

Recent progress in biology, **NC** 1161
Pasteur and hydrophobia, 1303

Lansbury, George, 1859–1940, labour leader, politician. *DNB.*

A Socialist view of the government, **NatR-II** 1738

Larner, George J., bird fancier.

Homing pigeons in war-time, **NC** 3469

Lart, Charles Edmund, 1867–1947, naval officer. Venn.

The dearth of naval engineers, **NC** 3644

Lascelles, Hon. Gerald William, 1849–1928, sportsman, forester. *WWW.*

The chase of the wild fallow deer, **NC** 1327

Lascelles-Scott, Wentworth

Modern explosives, **NC** 2596

Laslett-Browne, H.

Common sense and crime, **FortR** 3678

Latham, Robert Gordon, 1812–1888, ethnologist, philologist. *DNB.*

Plot and personae of *Titus Andronicus*, **FM** 5124

Latham, William; perhaps the barrister, 1836–1915, in *WWW* and Venn.

Modern reforms in paper money, **FortR** 198

Lathbury, Bertha (Price), wife of Daniel C. Lathbury, q.v. *WWW*/1928 under her husband.

Agnosticism and women, **NC** 429

Lathbury, Daniel Conner: see *Index*, I, 973.

Constitutional question in the United States, **FortR** 551
The European concert [the Eastern question], 1722
Radicals and Irish ideas, 1836
Atheists in parliament, 1861

Notice: **Ram** 1120 collab.

Latimer, Lewis. *RG.*

A French abbé of the seventeenth century, **NatR-II** 1356

Lattimer, William; perhaps writer on trade depression in *BMCat.*

The evils of "piece work," **NC** 290

Laughton, Sir John Knox: see *Index*, I, 973.

The sovereignty of the sea, **FortR** 295

Du Quesne and the French navy, **FM** 5615
Venetian navy in sixteenth century, 5730
Thurot, 6009
Paul Jones, "the pirate," 6045
Vice-Admiral Baron von Tegetthoff, 6060
Weather forecasting, 6207
Henry John Codrington, 6366
Our winter storms, 6412
Privateering in the eighteenth century, 6447, 6455
The French privateers, 6493, 6504

Laurie, Arthur Pillans, 1861–1949, chemist, educator. *WWW.*

Is it to be civil war? [Scottish rail strike], **NC** 2027

Laurie, Simon Somerville, 1829–1909, educational reformer. *DNB.*

Montaigne as an educationalist, **FM** 6304
The House of Lords and education, 6318
Secondary education in Scotland, **ScotR** 349

Laurie, Thomas Werner, publisher. *BMCat.*

Author, agent, and publisher, **NC** 2839

Laveleye, Emile Louis Victor de: see *Index*, I, 974.

The future of France, **FortR** 735
The clerical party in Belgium, 900
Causes of war in existing European situation, 922
Alienation of public lands in colonies, 1056
The European situation, 1169
British interests in the present crisis, 1375
England and the [Franco-Turkish] War, 1433
Belgian politics, 1494
Two foreign opinions on Treaty of Berlin, 1520
Prince Bismark, 1529
Italian politics, 1569
The Austro-German alliance, 1646
Bimetallism and free trade, 1824
Egypt for the Egyptians, 1974
The European terror, 2021
Scotch and other townships, 2328

The future of gold, **NC** 631
Laws of war: maritime capture, 754
Laws of war: warfare on land, 762
Democracy in Switzerland, 1189

Law, Alice. *BMCat.*

A new Caroline commonplace book, **FortR** 4330
William Cowper, 4448

Law, Sir Edward Fitzgerald: see *Index*, I, 974.

The present condition of Russia, **FortR** 1900
International rivalries in Central Africa, 2185
The presidential election campaign, 2252

The awakening of Persia, **NC** 1806

Law, Thomas Graves: see *Index*, I, 974.

Dr. Smith on the Pentateuch, **DR** 1233

Archangel Leslie of Scotland: a sequel, **NC** 2481
Devil-hunting in Elizabethan England, 2540

Legend of the Archangel Leslie, **ScotR** 324
John Major, Scottish scholastic, 357
Biblical studies, middle ages, 384
The Spanish blanks and Catholic earls, 405

Lawless, Emily: see *Index*, I, 974, and *WWW/* 1916.

Notes in the Morbihan [Brittany], **NatR-II** 243

A dredging ground, **NC** 608
How Art Kavanagh fought Richard the King, 1924
Irish chronicles: Gerald the Great, 1954, 2013
A bardic chronicle, 2115
The builder of the round towers, 2719
The ethics of literary forgery, 3053
Florentine gardens in March, 3427
North Clare, 3457

Lawley, Francis Charles: see *Index*, I, 974.

Last six days of Secessia [of the Confederacy], **FortR** 62

Lawrance, Hannah: see *Index*, I, 974.

?The modern troubadours, **FM** 1961
?Carlovingien romances of the middle ages, 2371

Lawrence, Edmund, of Armagh, political writer. *BMCat.*

Coalitions, **NatR-II** 473
Letters: 403, 420, 779

Lawrence, George Alfred, 1827–1876, novelist. *DNB.*

Sword and gown, in 8 installments from **FM** 3836 to 3911
Barren honour, in 10 installments from 4134 to 4227

Lawrence, William Frederic, 1844–1935, M.P. *WWW.*

The English in Egypt, **NatR-II** 716

Lawson, Harry Lawson Webster Levy, 2nd Baron Burnham, 1862–1933, M.P., newspaper proprietor. *DNB.*

South Africa: Rhodesian affairs, **FortR** 3798
The county council election, 4072
Cape politics and Colonial policy, 4199

Lawson, J. H.

Co-operative stores, **NC** 277

Lawson, Sir Wilfrid, 1829–1906, M.P. *DNB.*

The drink difficulty, **NC** 280
Classes, masses, glasses, 1347

Lawson, William Ramage, writer on British and American economy, ed. *Edinburgh Courant. BMCat., Blackwoods Papers Cat.* (See *Index*, I, 974.)

The Argentine crisis [finances], **FortR** 2995
An averted crash in the City, 3026

Poetry and prose of crofter question, **NatR-II** 251
Kaffir finance, 1869
Russia's sinews of war, 2147
Company promoting *à la mode*, 2206
The financial strain on France, 2229
The coming Russian loan, 2311
German finance, 2372
The war chest of the Boers, 2403
The investor's opportunity, 2512

Layard, Amy

Scraps from the chronicles of Venice, **NatR-II** 125

Layard, Florence, daughter of Lt. Gen. Frederick Peter Layard. *Blackwood Papers Cat.*

Burma and the Burmese, **FortR** 2615

What women write and read, **NatR-II** 645

Oriental myths and Christian parallels, **ScotR** 287

Layard, George Somes: see *Index*, I, 975.

How to live on £700 a year, **NC** 1516
The doom of the domestic cook, 2354
The gentle art of book lending, 2773

Lazeu, Dr. *Boyle's Court Guide/*1843, p. 505.

The Spanish theatre, **DR** 265

Leach, Arthur Francis: see *Index*, I, 975.

The House of Lords, **FortR** 1946
Our oldest school [St. Peter's, York], 3287
The schoolboys' feast, 3751

The origin of Oxford, **NatR-II** 1913

Leadam, Isaac Saunders: see *Index*, I, 975.

Substitutes for trial by jury in Ireland, **FortR** 1907

Tenant-right, **FM** 6496

Leahy, David, barrister. *BMCat.*

"Romanism in Ireland," **DR** 208, 221, 228
"Unity" and "Catholicity" of "English Protestant Church," 234

Leahy, John Pius, 1802–1890, Bishop of Dromore. *Irish Monthly,* 18 (1890), 561 ff., 646 ff.

Switzerland—convents of Argau, **DR** 254

Leahy, Patrick, 1806–1875, archbishop of Cashel. *DNB.*

State provision for Irish clergy, **DR** 325

Leake, Désirée Mary (Image), d.1937, wife of Percy Dewe Leake. *BMCat., WWW/* 1950 under her husband.

A girls' lodging-house, **NC** 3394

Lean, Francis, army officer. *Army List.*

The progress of heavy artillery, **FortR** 1601

Leary, Thomas Humphrys Lindsay, b.1826/ 27, divine. Foster, *CCD/*1902.

The religious element in Chaucer, **NQM** 45
Mr. Tennyson's *Queen Mary,* 66
The popular preaching of the past, 131

Le Bas, Charles Theodore, 1835–1858, judge in Delhi. *Haileybury Memorials.*

How we escaped from Delhi, **FM** 3691.

Lebon, André, b.1859, French politician. *Larousse XXᵉ Siècle.*

French feeling towards England, **NatR-II** 1547

Lecky, Elisabeth: see *Index,* I, 975, and II, App. A.

A visit to the Grande Chartreuse, **NC** 2010
A warning to imperialists, 2953
The House in the Wood [1899 peace conference], 3467

Lecky, William Edward Hartpole: see *Index,* I, 975.

The political outlook, **FortR** 3251

History of the Evangelical Movement, **NC** 342
A "nationalist" parliament, 1269
Gladstone and the income tax, 1426
Notice: 1911

Ledger, Edmund, 1841–1913, divine, astronomer. Venn.

Stars and molecules, **NC** 2797
The new planet, "Eros," 3451
Some unseen stars, 3707

Lee, Arthur Bolles: see *Index,* I, 976.

Spinozism, **FM** 6007

Lee, Fitzhugh, 1835–1905, American army officer. *WWW, LCCat.*

Cuba and her struggle for freedom, **FortR** 4126

Lee, Frederick George: see *Index,* I, 976.

French clergy exiles in England, **NatR-II** 785

The Order of Corporate Reunion, **NC** 648
The O.C.R. and its work, 3370

Lee, Sir Sidney: see *Index,* I, 976.

Shakespeare and Pembroke, **FortR** 4073

Shakespeare in France, **NC** 3480
Shakespeare and the modern stage, 3597

Leeds, William Henry: see *Index,* I, 976, and II, App. A.

Modern architecture and architectural study, **FQR** 177
Russian novels and novelists: Bulgarin, 188
Russian poetry: Pushkin and Rilaeev, 222
Zagoskin's historical romances, 270
Present architecture in Germany, 324
Principles of Grecian architecture, 348
Landscape and ornamental gardening, 372
Lichtenberg and Hogarth, 378
Russian Annuals, 385
Athenian architecture and polychrome embellishment, 417
Influence of construction on style in architecture, 435
Grecian and Italian architecture contrasted, 448
Present state of art in Russia, 470
Russian novel writing, 481
Lomonosov and his contemporaries, 539
Architecture at home and abroad, 560
Notice: 215

Architectural design and decoration, **FM** 8
The Athenaeum club-house, 17
The fine arts in Russia, 31
Buckingham Palace, 43
Strictures on art and exhibitions, 99
The Suffolk Street exhibition, 243

Pie-crust; or, Architectural madness [on Peter Legh], 285
Our Royal-Academical lounge, 414
Somerset House annual [exhibition], 838
The last of the lairds, 1012
A batch of architects, 1052
Russian fabulists, 1291, 1664
Ramble in St. James's Bazar; on the Nelson monument, 1359
Boutiques and gin-palaces, 1392, 1542
Wightwickism [on Wight's *Palace of Architecture*], 1479
The last sitting [for a portrait], 1834
Architectural revivalism and Puginism, 1875
Public structures [Houses of Parliament and British Museum], 2756

Lees, George Frederic Williams, 1858/59–1938, critic, translator. *LCCat., Times,* Apr. 30, 1938, p. 1.

Some writers on war, **FortR** 4509

Lefevre, George John Shaw: see Shaw-Lefevre, George John.

Lefroy, William, 1836–1909, dean of Norwich. *DNB.*

National Church Sustentation Fund, **NatR-II** 1828

Le Gallienne, Richard Thomas, 1866–1947, poet. *DNB.*

Grant Allen, **FortR** 4381

Death and two friends, **NC** 2622
Notices: 2404, 2591

Legge, Arthur Edward John, 1863–1934, poet, army officer. *LCCat.,* Burke under Dartmouth.

On temperaments, **NatR-II** 1242

Legge, George Francis: see *Index,* I, 976.

Divination in the seventeenth century, **NatR-II** 837
The origin of modern occultism, 899
Colonel Olcott's theosophy, 924
Triumphant democracy in seventeenth century, 1038
The Spanish Inquisition, **ScotR** 316
Witchcraft in Scotland, 332
Mediaeval belief in witchcraft, 388
Some heretic gospels, 410
The origin of our civilisation, 460
Serapis—a study in religions, 528
Primitive religion and magic, 556

Legge, Heneage, 1845–1911, army officer, M.P. *WWW.*

Letter: **NatR-II** 1035

The religion of the undergraduate, **NC** 2841

Leggo, William, 1822–1888, Canadian lawyer. Wallace.

Imperial federation: a Canadian view, **ScotR** 99, 134
The fishery question: a Canadian view, 151, 160
The Hudson's Bay route, 176

Legh, Thomas Wodehouse: see *Index,* I, 976.

Personal experiences of Bulgaria, **NatR-II** 665
A case of paternal desertion, 2485

Leigh, Hon. Francis Dudley, 3rd Baron Leigh, 1855–1938, army officer. *WWW.*

Horse ambulances, **NC** 3002

Leigh, James Wentworth, 1838–1921, divine. Venn.

Labour organization, **FortR** 2664

Leigh, John George

The powers and Samoa, **FortR** 4223
The Samoan crisis and its causes, 4271
Gains and losses in the Pacific, 4390

Leighton, Frederic: see *Index,* I, 977.

Letter: **NC** 380

Leighton, Stanley, 1837–1901, politician, antiquary. *DNB.*

Gordon or Gladstone? **NatR-II** 333
Establishment and endowment of nonconformity, 436
The municipalities on their trial, 576
Nonconformity in Wales, 739
Colonial Office and colonies, 1060
History of a small estate in Wales, 2520

Leland, Charles Godfrey: see *Index,* I, 977.

Yokohama pidgin, **NQM** 183
Shelta, the tinkers' talk, 204

Lemoinne, John Marguerite Emile, 1815–1892, French journalist and politician. *Larousse XXᵉ Siècle.*

The situation [the Eastern question], **NC** 152

Leng, John, 1828–1906, newspaper proprietor. *DNB.*

An Irish compromise? **NatR-II** 1681

Leo XIII, Pope (Gioacchino Vincenzo Raffaele Luigi Pecci), 1810–1903. *Cath. Ency.*

Encyclical [on the Apostolic See], **DR** 1647
Encyclical [on man's obedience to God], 1687
Encyclical [on Thomas Aquinas], 1711
Letters on St. Thomas Aquin, St. Alfonso, and to Société Scientifique of Brussels, 1722
Encyclical on Christian marriage, 1733
Papal brief on Belgium, 1754
On S. Thomas of Aquin, 1765
On the Society for the Propagation of the Faith: letter to Cardinal Guibert, 1777
Bishops and missionaries in England and Scotland, 1799
Encyclical on political power, 1800
Two letters to the bishops of Italy, 1823
Letters to the bishops of Sicily, 1835
Letter to the bishops of Ireland, 1847
Encyclical on St. Francis of Assisi, 1859
Letters on studies and on the Rosary, 1893
Encyclical to the bishops of France, 1916
Encyclical on freemasonry, 1927
Encyclical on ordering Rosary during October, 1938
Encyclical on the constitution of Christian states, 2002
Letter to the bishops of England, 2003
Brief in favour of the Society of Jesus, 2039
Letters: To the bishops of Hungary; Constituting an episcopal hierarchy in India, 2040
Letter to the bishops of Brazil, 2141
Encyclical on liberty, 2155
On conclusion of jubilee year, 2170
Encyclical on duties of Christian citizens, 2222
Encyclical to clergy and people of Italy, 2263
Apostolic letter on the Anglo-Benedictine congregation, 2276
Encyclical on abolition of slavery, 2277
Encyclical on condition of labour, 2291
Apostolic letter on Anglican ordinations, 2554

Leopardi, Giacomo, 1798–1837, poet. *Enci. Ital.*

A dialogue with a mummy, **NatR-II** 960

Lepper, Charles H. *RG*/1900–1904.

Thibet, **NC** 1183

Leppington, C. H. d'Eyncourt: see *Index*, I, 977.

The stage-work and wages, **NatR-II** 1140
Lessons in socialism, 1209
A striking electoral anomaly, 1336
Mental and moral character of mobs, 1375

Leproust, Louis-Pierre, b.1768/69, canon of Tours. *Bib.Nat.Cat., Ram* no. 522, p. 192.

Leaves from the journal of a confessor, **Ram** 522, 530

Le Roux, Henri, called Hugues, 1860–1925, French misc. writer. *Larousse XXᵉ Siècle.*

Phases of crime in Paris, **FortR** 3160
Table-talk of Renan, 3291
The Rajahs of Saràwak, 3548

Leroux, Louis Pierre; prob. the son of Pierre Leroux, 1797–1871 in *Larousse XXᵉ Siècle.*

Pierre Leroux's doctrine of humanity, **FortR** 850

Leroy, Amélie Claire: see *Index*, I, 977.

Leconte de Lisle, **FortR** 3671

Charles Baudelaire and Edgar Poe, **NC** 2424

Victor Hugo, the poet, **ScotR** 536

Leroy-Beaulieu, Pierre-Paul, 1843–1916, French economist. *Larousse XXᵉ Siècle.*

The foreign policy of France, **FortR** 2087

Leslie, Charles, 1785–1870, army officer. *Landed Gentry.*

Scotland and the Scotch, **DR** 210

Leslie, Thomas Edward Cliffe: see *Index*, I, 977.

Political economy and tenure of land, **FortR** 261
Emigration from Ireland, 419
Ireland in 1868, 474
Nations and international law, 518
Westphalia and the Ruhr basin, 569
Political economy of Adam Smith, 730
The gold question and prices in Germany, 903
The gold mines and prices in England, 960
Taxation on the working classes, 1027
Agricultural wages in Europe, 1054
Auvergne, 1105
Maine's *Early History of Institutions,* 1131

Lewes, George Henry (*continued*)
Mr. Darwin's hypotheses, 489, 506, 517, 542
Dickens in relation to criticism, 838
Imaginary geometry and truth of axioms, 1075
Spiritualism and materialism, 1244, 1257
The course of modern thought, 1338
Dread and dislike of science, 1473
Notices: 11, 20, 39, 50, 61, 73, 93, 105, 114, 124, 132, 142, 151, 161, 173, 182, 212, 243, 315, 353

On the London Library, **FM** 1462
The state murder [adapted from George Sand], 1986, 2000
The history of pantomimes, 2147
Morrell's *History of Modern Philosophy*, 2244
Grumble about Christmas books, 2282 collab.
The condition of authors, 2295
Death-in-life, 2344
Recent novels [including *Jane Eyre*], 2397
A Frenchwoman [Mme. de Staël], 2451
Life and works of Leopardi, 2529
A great discovery [circulation of blood], 3395
Owen and the science of life, 3433
Dwarfs and giants, 3499, 3512
Life in its simpler forms, 3570
A precursor of the *Vestiges*, 3660
The physician's art: Dr. Watson, 3684
The murders at Deutz, 3780
Carlyle's *Frederick the Great*, 3799

Lewin, Walter, misc. writer. *BMCat.*

Letters in America, **ScotR** 2

Lewis, Sir Charles Edward, 1825–1893, M.P. Boase.

Prospects of the Conservatives, **NC** 819

Lewis, David, 1814–1895, Roman Catholic convert in 1846, writer on canon law. Newman, *L&D*, XI, 344.

Wordsworth's *Letters to M. Gondon*, **DR** 462
Protestant learning, 496
Protestant honesty, 503
Ffoulkes on Christendom's divisions, 1189
Chronicle of Evesham Abbey, 1319
Canon Estcourt on Anglican ordination, 1441
Secular education, 1897
The Church after the Conquest, 2062
Stubbs on English ecclesiastical law, 2087
Vicars capitular, 2191
Notices: 1203, 1222, 1263, collab.

A "loyal" bishop in the middle ages [Gilbert Folliot], **Ram** 314

Lewis, Mrs. Elizabeth Alicia Maria. *LCCat.*

A reformation of domestic service, **NC** 2342

Lewis, George Cornewall: see *Index*, I, 979, and II, App. A.

Spix and Martius's *Travels in Brazil*, **FQR** 122
History of the Amphictyonic confederacy, 139
Codification, and the laws of England, 147
French Revolution of 1830, 152
Mythology, religion of ancient Greece, 158
The Brunswick revolution, 165
Ancient municipal institutions of France, 189
Thierry's *History of the Gauls*, 236
Notices: 144, 168

Roman book-trade under the Empire, **FM** 4204

Lewis, Sir George Henry, 1st bart., 1833–1911, solicitor. *DNB.*

Marriage and divorce, **FortR** 2312

Lewis, George Pitt: see Pitt-Lewis, G.

Lewis, Henry Harrison, 1863–1965, war correspondent. *Amer. WWW.*

General Wood at Santiago, **FortR** 4249

Lewis, John Delaware: see *Index*, I, 980.

Clergy and laity, **FortR** 1108
A visible church, 1731

Lewis, Mary A.: see *Index*, I, 980.

Our future masters, **FortR** 2377

Lewis, Sarah, feminist. *BMCat.*

Social position of governesses, **FM** 2442

Lewis, William Bevan: see Bevan-Lewis, William.

Ley, James Peard, b.1807, barrister. Venn, *M at B.*

Note: **NC** 948

Leys, John Kirkwood: see *Index*, I, 980.

?Life at Scottish universities, **NatR-II** 515

Lhotsky, Johann, b.1795, alive in 1865, botan-

Linton, Eliza (Lynn): see *Index*, I, 981.

Pasteur's life and labours, **FortR** 2349
A retrospect, 2383
The higher education of woman, 2522
Womanhood in old Greece, 2552, 2592
The Roman matron and the Roman lady, 2623
The women of chivalry, 2646
Italian women in the middle ages, 2681
French political women, 2720
An eighteenth-century abbé [Ferdinando Galiani], 2746
The irresponsibilities of genius, 2757
Characteristics of English women, 2794, 2802
Literature: then and now, 2938
Our illusions, 3069
Henry Drummond's discovery [law of altruism], 3551
Viewy folk, 3789
Letter: 2627

Alfred de Musset, **FM** 3623
Daniele Manin, 3666
Lone-house Dale, 3703
Reminiscences of Walter Savage Landor, 5104

The stage as a profession for women, **NatR-II** 275
The future supremacy of women, 474
Threatened abdication of man [women's suffrage], 875
The Philistine's coming triumph, 1767
The tyrannies of private life, 1779
Class sympathies, 1803

Meliora latent, **NQM** 24
The mad Willoughbys, 39
By the law, 58
Misericordia, 122
Our professor, 155

The judicial shock to marriage, **NC** 2034
The wild women, 2071, 2111
The partisans of the wild women, 2182
A picture of the past, 2311

L'Isle Adam, Auguste Villiers de: see Villiers de L'Isle Adam, Auguste.

Lister, Hon. Martin, 1857–1897, British resident, Negri Sembilan. Burke/1914 under Ribblesdale.

Trade in the Malay Peninsula, **NC** 2141

Lister, Hon. Sir Reginald, 1865–1912, diplomat. *WWW.*

Archaic statues of the Acropolis museum, **NC** 2465
Delphi, 2701

Lister, Samuel Cunliffe: see *Index*, I, 981.

Who profits by free trade? **NatR-II** 1363

Lister, Thomas, 4th Baron Ribblesdale, 1854–1925, sportsman. *WWW* under Ribblesdale.

Lord Peterborough, **FortR** 2351

Queen's plates [prize money], **NatR-II** 581

The art of conversation, **NC** 1746
Hunting at Gibraltar, 1856
A railway journey with Parnell, 2138
The House of Lords, 2790

Lister, Thomas Henry: see *Index*, I, 981.

American poetry [on Bryant], **FQR** 235
Chateaubriand's *Works*, 244
Rush's *Residence in England*, 288
D'Haussez, *Great Britain in 1833*, 293
Madame de Staël, 321

Lister, Sir Thomas Villiers: see *Index*, I, 981.

The exhibiting of pictures, **NC** 541

Little, A. Clarke. *BMCat.*

Iceland and the Faröe Islands, **DR** 2694

Little, Alicia Helen Neva (Bewicke): see *Index*, I, 981.

In the wild west of China, **NC** 2866

Little, Archibald John: see *Index*, I, 981.

Two cities: London and Peking, **FortR** 4288

Little, James Stanley, 1856–1940, critic. *WWW.*

The future of landscape art, **NC** 2082

Little, Sydney Hamilton, 1849/50–1895, divine; consul at Cadiz. Foster, Gorman, who gives 1843 as birthdate.

The conversion of England, **DR** 1936
Church music and church choirs, 2097

Little, W. J. Knox: see Knox-Little, W. J.

Littlejohn, Abram Newkirk, 1824–1901, bishop of Long Island. *DAB.*

An American churchman's view of laity in the Episcopal Church, **NatR-II** 488

Liu, Ta-Jên.

Liu Ta-Jên's mission to England, **NC** 505

Livesey, Sir George Thomas, 1834–1908, director So. Metropolitan Gas Co. *DNB.*

The eight-hours system in gas-works, **FortR** 3241
Letter: 2934

Workmen directors, **NatR-II** 1847

Llana, M. G.: see Gonzalez Llana, Manuel

Lloyd, Clifford Bartholomew, 1845–1915, under sec. of state in Egypt, 1885. *Landed Gentry.*

Note: **NC** 1793

Lloyd, Hannibal Evans, 1771–1847, philologist, translator. *DNB.*

Förster's *Life of Frederick-William I*, **FQR** 368
Notices: 79, 103
See: 317, 464

Lloyd, Howel William, 1816–1893, educator; at Cath. Univ. Coll. Boase.

Letter: **DR** 1614

Lloyd, Thomas, ed. of the *Statist. BMCat.*

The American crisis, **NatR-II** 1908
British interests and the Wolcott Commission [bimetallism], 2036
Shall the Indian government ruin India? 2222

Lloyd, William Watkiss, 1813–1893, classical and Shakespearean scholar. *DNB.*

General Cesnola's *Cyprus*, **NQM** 145

Loch, Sir Charles Stewart: see *Index*, I, 982.

Confusion in medical charities, **NC** 2273
Manufacturing a new pauperism, 2743
Fallacies about old age pensions, 3377

Lockett, Jeannie (Beattie), Australian writer. E. M. Miller, *Australian Literature*, Melbourne, 1940.

Female labour in Australia, **NC** 1198

Lockhart, John Gibson: see *Index*, I, 982, and II, App. A.

The Doctor [William Maginn], **FM** 163
?Ars ridendi; or Hook and Hood, 183 collab.
[Attack on Bulwer], 522
See: 427, 435

Lockhart, Mary Elizabeth, 1812–1870, Fran-

ciscan nun, staff writer for *DR.* Gillow, Gorman.

St. Jane Frances de Chantal, **DR** 1199
Female life in prison, 1237
Madame de Lafayette and Madame de Montagu, 1321
Notice: 1193

Lockhart, William, 1820–1892, R.C. divine. *DNB.*

John Henry Cardinal Newman, **DR** 2249
Reminiscences of Cardinal Manning, 2331
Letters: 1141, 1173, 1519
Notice: 2043

Lockwood, Amelius Richard Mark, 1st Baron Lambourne, 1857–1928, politician. *DNB.*

Thomas Day, **NC** 3139

Lockyer, Sir Joseph Norman: see *Index*, I. 984.

Sun-spots and famines, **NC** 102 collab.
What the sun is made of, 194
The chemical elements, 273
The history of a star, 1788
New stars, 2171
Astronomy and mythology of ancient Egyptians, 2238

Lodge, Henry Cabot, 1850–1924, Amer. senator. *DAB.*

Parliamentary obstruction in the United States, **NC** 2012
The home of the Cabots, 3111

Lodge, Sir Oliver Joseph, 1851–1940, scientist. *DNB.*

The interstellar ether, **FortR** 337

Lord Rayleigh, **NatR-II** 2205

Lo Feng-luh, Sur Chih Chen, 1850–1903, Chinese diplomat. *WWW.*

Symbols as written language, **NatR-II** 2381

Loftus, Lord Augustus William Frederick Spencer, 1817–1904, diplomat. *DNB.*

Commercial unity with the colonies, **NC** 2356

Logan, Mary Simmerson: see *Index*, I, 984, and *Amer. WWW.*

A night in India, **NC** 2606
Night travelling in India, 2690

Lomax, John Acton, b.1860/61. Foster.

American and English girls, **NatR-II** 823
Free law? a scheme, 1196

Lombroso, Cesare: see *Index,* I, 984.

Physical insensibility of woman, **FortR** 3187

Long, George, 1800–1879, classical scholar. *DNB.*

Heeren, *On the Polity and Commerce of the Great Nations of Antiquity,* **FQR** 109

Long, James, "Merlin" of the *Field* newspaper, writer on agriculture. *BMCat.*

British farmer and foreign produce, **FortR** 3395
The agricultural programme, 3793

Can the Empire feed its people? **NC** 2862
Consumption in cattle conveyable to man, 3184

Long, Robert Edward Crozier, 1872–1938, journalist. *WWW.*

The Russian railway policy in Asia, **FortR** 4373

Longe, Francis Davy, 1831–1905, barrister. Foster, *Landed Gentry.*

Law of trade combinations in France, **FortR** 432, 439

Longfield, Mountifort, 1802–1884, Irish judge. *DNB.*

Land tenure in Ireland, **FortR** 1717

Longley, James Wilberforce, 1849–1922, judge and historian of Nova Scotia. Wallace.

Canada and imperial federation, **FortR** 3060

Sir Wilfrid Laurier at Washington, **NatR-II** 2120

Longman, Charles James, 1852-1934, publisher, ed. *Fraser's Mag.,* 1881–1882. *WWW.*

International copyright, **FM** 6386

Longman, Frederick William, b.1846, historian. Foster, *LCCat.*

Recollections of a winter in Brazil, **FM** 5313

Longman, William, 1813–1877, publisher, Alpinist. *DNB.*

Six weeks in Tyrol, **FM** 5374
Impressions of Madeira, 5707

Longridge, C. C.; perhaps Cecil C. Longridge: see *Month,* 58 (Nov. 1886), 378, and Gorman, where he is called "Capt."

Novelists and novels, **DR** 2021

Lonsdale, Margaret, biographer. *BMCat.*

The present crisis at Guy's Hospital, **NC** 433
Doctors and nurses, 464
Platform women, 971

Lorac, Luis de

The situation in Belgium, **NatR-II** 1645

Lord, Millicent; wife of Walter Frewen Lord, q.v. *BMCat.*

Notice: **NC** 1915

Lord, Percival Barton, 1808–1840, diplomat, surgeon. *DNB.*

Animal magnetism, **FQR** 297

Lord, Thomas, shopkeeper.

Co-operative stores, **NC** 301

Lord, Walter Frewen, 1861–1927, barrister, prof. of history. Venn.

Our reign in the Ionian Islands, **NC** 1690
The works of Henrik Ibsen, 1744
The English conquest of Java, 1855
Pasquale de Paoli, 2069
Italia non farà da se [claim of not needing foreign assistance], 2174
Protection and the Empire, 2418
Gift to England in 1662 [Tangier], 2499
Goree: a lost possession of England, 3113
The story of Murat and Bentinck, 3361
Lord Beaconsfield's novels, 3420
Notice: 1805

Lorimer, Louise: see *Index,* I, 985, and II, App. A.

Drummond of Hawthornden, **ScotR** 695

Loring, Nele; possibly son of Henry Nele Loring, b.1811/12, divine, in Foster.

Five thousand miles with range-cattle, **NC** 2031

Loti, Louis-Marie-Julien Viaud, called Pierre, 1850–1923, French novelist. *Grand Larousse.*

Rêve, **FortR** 2738

Lottner, Carl

The Edda, **FM** 4128

Louis-Philippe, King of France: see *Index*, I, 985.

See: **FortR** 240

Lovat-Fraser, James Alexander, 1868–1938, barrister, M.P. *WWW.*

Ancient Scottish parliament, **NatR-II** 1421

Low, Sir Alfred Maurice: see *Index*, I, 985, and *WWW/*1940.

Episodes of the month, **NatR-II** 1946 collab.
The month in America, in 46 installments from 1971 to 2521
President McKinley, 2000
American affairs, 2534

Low, Frances H., misc. writer. *Blackwood Papers Cat.*

A remedy for baby-farming, **FortR** 4078
Mrs. Gaskell's short tales, 4350

How poor ladies live, **NC** 3081, 3146
A woman's criticism of the Women's Congress, 3509

Low, Robert Cunliffe, 1838–1911, general. *DNB.*

Risings on Indian frontier, **NatR-II** 2068

Low, Sir Sidney James Mark: see *Index*, I, 985.

Lowell in his poetry, **FortR** 3122
Fall of the Rosebery government, 3677
The darkest hour for England [May 1797], 4377

A word for the reviewers, **NatR-II** 1248
The consolations of M. Renan, 1286
Newspaper copyright, 1310
Ireland's decay and Ulster's defiance, 1422
The Tory press and the Tory party, 1431
Kossuth and Hungarian war of liberation, 1579
The armed peace—new style, 1821
Journalism as a career, 2214
The case for dissolution, 2309
Ought we to have a coalition? 2389

If the House of Commons were abolished? **NC** 2668
The decline of the House of Commons, 2731

A foreign affairs committee, 2812
The decline of Cobdenism, 2967
The Olney doctrine and America's foreign policy, 3031
Should Europe disarm? 3352
The Liberal collapse: a case for coalition, 3400
Hypocrisies of the Peace Conference, 3458
The future of the great armies, 3526
South African problems and lessons, 3569
The military weakness of England, 3584
The breakdown of voluntary enlistment, 3613
Enigmas of Empire, 3664

Lowe, Charles, 1848–1931, journalist. *WWW, LCCat.*

New emperor [Wilhelm II] and new chancellor [Bismarck], **NatR-II** 1190

The German newspaper press, **NC** 2130

Lowe, Richard Norton

Letter: **NatR-II** 1060

Lowe, Robert, 1st viscount Sherbrooke: see *Index*, I, 985.

Birmingham plan of public-house reform, **FortR** 1318
Shall we create a new university? 1328
Have we abolished imprisonment for debt? 1337
The New Reform Bill, 1398
Foreign dominions of the Crown, 1407
Mr. Gladstone on manhood suffrage, 1415
Imperialism, 1510
A simple way out of the Indian difficulty, 1599

Is the popular judgment in politics more just than that of the higher orders? **NC** 201
Recent attacks on political economy, 240
Reciprocity and free trade, 316
Docility of an "imperial" parliament, 425
Obstruction or "clôture," 499
Legislation for Ireland, 511
Business in the House of Commons, 581
What shall we do with our bankrupts? 621
The clôture and the Tories, 671
What is money? 698
Parliamentary oaths, 756

Lowell, Francis Cabot, III, 1855–1911, American judge. *Amer. WWW; Massachusetts Historical Society: Proceedings*, 44 (Apr. 1911), 580–581.

?English and American federalism, **FortR** 2676

Lowndes, Marie Adelaide (Belloc), 1868–1947, novelist. *WWW*/1950 under Belloc, *LCCat.*

Barthélmy Saint-Hilaire, **FortR** 3764

Lowry, James Corry Jones, 1835–1897, of County Tyrone, colonel, high sheriff. *Irish Gentry.*

Spoliation of Irish landlords, **NatR-II** 2013

Lowry-Corry, Somerset Richard, 4th Earl Belmore, 1835–1913, governor of New South Wales. Burke, Venn under Corry (Lowry Corry).

Letter: **NatR-II** 1604

Lowther, Henry Cecil, 1869–1940, army officer. *WWW.*

Lion hunting beyond the Haud, **NC** 2810
Among the liars [in Crete], 3107

Lowther, James William, 1st Viscount Ullswater, 1855–1949, speaker of the House of Commons. *DNB.*

Some Anglo-French problems, **NatR-II** 1716

Löwy, Albert, or Abraham, 1816–1908, Biblical archaeologist. *DNB.*

The apocryphal character of the Moabite stone, **ScotR** 164

Loyd-Lindsay: see Lindsay, R. J.

Loyson, Charles, called Père Hyacinthe: see *Index*, I, 986.

Paganism in Paris, **NC** 405

Luard, Henry Richards, 1825–1891, registrar of Camb. Univ. *DNB.*

Edited: **FM** 4638

Lubbock, Sir John: see *Index*, I, 986.

Habits of ants, **FortR** 1336
Relations between plants and insects, 1348
Fruits and seeds, 1789
Liberal versus Conservative finance, 2132
Manual instruction, 2519
The government of London, 3173
Letter: 2638
Notice: 298

London government, **NatR-II** 1660

On the imperial policy of Great Britain, **NC** 3

Preservation of ancient national monuments, 15

The history of money, 369
Our national balance-sheet, 838
Proportional representation, 988, 1094 collab.
The London water supply, 2162
London and the water companies, 2739
Bank holidays, a plea for one more, 3109
Financial relations of Great Britain and Ireland, 3202

Lubbock, Montagu, 1842–1925, M.D. in Paris and London. *WWW.*

On the development of the colour-sense, **FortR** 1904

The plague, **NC** 3063

Lubbock, Nevile, 1839–1914, banker, president West India Comm. *WWW.*

Loyalty in the West Indies, **NatR-II** 2110

The revival of the West Indies, **NC** 941

Lucas, Edward, 1822–1899, brother of Frederick Lucas, q.v. Gorman.

Mill, *On Liberty*, **DR** 1278

Lucas, Edward Verrall: see *Index*, I, 986.

Poetry for children, **FortR** 3852

Lucas, Frederick, 1812–1855, journalist, founded the *Tablet. DNB.*

Henry of Monmouth, **DR** 154
Halsted's *Life of Margaret Beaufort*, 165
Duke of Marlborough—usages of war, 537

Lucas, Herbert, S.J. 1852–1933, Sutcliffe.

The "Missa Catechumenorum" in the Greek liturgies, **DR** 2375
The early Gallican liturgy, 2392, 2419
Textual criticism and the Acts of the Apostles, 2440

Lucas, Joseph. *BMCat.*

Petty Romany [clans of gipsies], **NC** 503

Lucas, Locksley, of British Columbia.

Confederation, **NatR-II** 1209
Loyal British Columbia, 1253
Immorality of Chinamen [immigrants in America], 1325
Boom cities [in western U.S.], 1455

Lucy, Sir Henry William: see *Index*, I, 986.

In young parliamentary days, **FortR** 3238
From Cape Town to Cairo, 3482

A new house for the Commons, **FM** 6383

Parliamentary forms and reforms, **NQM** 139

Parliamentary manners, **NC** 1157
New rules and the old complaint [in parliament], 1675

Ludlow, John Malcolm Forbes: see *Index*, I, 986.

Ferdinand Lassalle, **FortR** 581
Old guilds and new trade societies, 628

The French Insurrection of June, **FM** 2512
Froude's *Nemesis of Faith*, 2588
Benzole, 2649
"Labour and the poor," 2675
Queen's College and the *Quarterly*, 2722
Hervey's *Ten Years in India*, 2784
Italian patois books, 3265, 3282
Literature from the two Sicilies, 3504
What Every Christian Must Know, 3550
See: 3903

Luffmann, Charles Bogue, misc. writer. *BMCat.*

A winter's camp in Gippsland [Australia], **NatR-II** 2384

Lugard, Lady Flora Louisa: see Shaw, Flora Louisa.

Lugard, Frederick John Dealtry: see *Index*, I, 986.

British officials and French accusations, **FortR** 3292

England and France in Nile Valley, **NatR-II** 1742
Routes in Africa, 1756
Slatin Pasha and the Sudan, 1853

England and France on the Niger, **NC** 2757
New British markets [in tropical Africa], 2807
Slavery under the British flag, 2891
Liquor traffic in Africa, 3200

Lupton, James Irvine, b.1830/31, veterinary surgeon. *BMCat.*, Foster.

British and American horses, **NC** 2586

Lushington, Godfrey, 1832–1907, barrister, sec. in Home Office. *WWW.*

Trade-union triumph: Allen v. Flood, **NatR-II** 2111
Dreyfus case: scope of enquiry, 2257
Dreyfus affair: de Beaurepaire and Dupuy, 2278

The conspiracy against Dreyfus, 2319
The court-martial at Rennes [Dreyfus case], 2345
The verdict at Rennes [Dreyfus case], 2354

Oxford, **OxCam** 26
See: 45

Lushington, Vernon, 1832–1912, barrister. *WWW.*

Courts martial, **NatR-II** 1468

Carlyle, **OxCam** 23, 31, 35, 62, 65
Two pictures [by Rossetti and Madox Brown], 45

Lusk, Hugh Hart, 1837–1926, barrister in New Zealand. *New Zealand Biog.*

Maori Mahommedanism, **FortR** 120

Lützow, Francis Count, 1849–1916. *WWW/* 1928.

The Bohemian question, **NC** 3389
Austria at the end of the century, 3581

Luys, Jules Bernard, 1828–1895, physician. *Larousse XXᵉ Siècle.*

Latest discoveries in hypnotism, **FortR** 2963, 2975

Lyall, Sir Alfred Comyn: see *Index*, I, 987.

Religion of an Indian province, **FortR** 837
Our religious policy in India, 853
Religious situation in India, 882
Relation of witchcraft to non-Christian religions, 939
Missionary religions, 1065
Divine myths in India, 1188
Formation of clans and castes in India, 1324
Influence upon religious beliefs of a rise in morality, 1457
Relations of religion to Asiatic states, 1879
Progress in India, 2398
Brahmanism and *The Foundations of Belief*, 3717
Theological situation in India, 4194

Official polytheism in China, **NC** 1899
Frontiers and protectorates, 2091
Permanent dominion in Asia, 2803
India under Queen Victoria, 3121
Europe on brink of Seven Years' War, 3276
Notices: 2402, 2589

Lyell, Charles, 1767–1849, botanist, student of Dante. *DNB.*

Rossetti's *Dante*, **FQR** 121 collab.

Lyell, Sir Charles, 1797–1875: see *Index*, I, 987.

Rossetti's *Dante*, **FQR** 121 collab.

Lynch, Hannah: see *Index*, I, 987; also II, App. A.

M. Paul Hervieu, **FortR** 3860
The love-letters of Guy de Maupassant, 4021
Alphonse Daudet, 4133
Zola versus Tolstoi, 4392

Lynch, Henry J., 1824–1870, inspector of schools. Newman, *L&D*, XV, index.

Cloister Life of Charles V., **DR** 749

Lynch, Patrick, 1851/52–1921, provost of Salford. *Tablet*, Jan. 15, 1921.

Maynooth College: its centenary history, **DR** 2516
Notices: 2253, 2335, 2347, 2358

Lyne, Hamilton P.

"As sheep led to slaughter" [dock strike], **NatR-II** 1107
Letter: 655

Lys, Francis de.

See: **Ram** 522, 530

Lys, Francis John, 1863–1947, Oxford educator. *WWW*.

India Civil Service and the universities, **FortR** 3353

Lysaght, Mrs. Elizabeth J., novelist. Allibone, *Blackwood Papers Cat.*

Barbie Vaughan: a novel, **NQM** 17

Lyttelton, Alfred, 1857–1913, lawyer, statesman. *DNB*.

Is golf a first-class game? **NatR-II** 1484
Prisoners in the witness-box, 2099
Cricket reform, 2357
Letter: 1675

Lyttelton, Arthur Temple, 1852–1903, suffragen bishop of Southampton. *DNB*.

A guess at the origin of *Hamlet*, **NatR-II** 1953

Lyttelton, Dame Edith Sophy (Balfour), 1865–1948. *WWW*, *LCCat*.

Some recent fiction, **NatR-II** 1528
Sequel to Gibbon's love-story, 2054
Red Pottage, 2416

Lyttelton, Edward: see *Index*, I, 987.

Athletics in public schools, **NC** 393

Lyttelton, Sir Neville Gerald, 1845–1931, general. *DNB*.

Some Eton and Harrow matches, **NatR-II** 1749

Lyttelton, Hon. Robert Henry, 1854–1939, solicitor, cricketer. Venn.

Eton cricket, **NatR-II** 1585

Lytton, Lady Constance Georgiana, 1869–1923, suffragette. *WWW*.

Some recent fiction, **NatR-II** 1530

Lytton, Edward George Earle Lytton Bulwer: see Bulwer-Lytton.

Lytton, Edward Robert Bulwer: see *Index*, I, 988.

Heinrich Heine's *Last Poems and Thoughts*, **FortR** 663
Old plays and old players: Garrick as Hamlet, 755, 763
Germany: past, present, and future, 785
Beethoven, 874
A novelty in French fiction, 1081
Stage in relation to literature, 2051, 2067
Le style c'est l'homme, 2177
Notice: 1194

An essayist [Montaigne], **NatR-II** 13

A new love poet [Wilfrid Scawen Blunt], **NC** 649
Miss Anderson's Juliet, 1067

Lytton, Lady Rosina: see Bulwer-Lytton, Rosina.

Lytton, Victor Alexander George Robert Bulwer, 2nd earl of Lytton: see Bulwer-Lytton, Victor Alexander George Robert.

M

MacColl, Malcolm (*continued*)
Lambeth decision, 4351
Lambeth decision and the law, 4406
See: 4056

Supernatural religion, **FM** 5594
Tractarianism and ritualism, 6429
Labédoyère's doom, 6476

Fallacies about Turks, Bulgarians, and Russians, **NC** 116
Canon MacColl on Islam, 2859 collab.

McCrea, Frederick Bradford, 1833–1914, army officer, *WWW*.

?"Ordinary Business Principles," **NC** 3696

McCulloch, David, b.1832. *LCCat*.

Canadian protection vindicated, **FortR** 1582

McCulloch, John Ramsay: see *Index*, I, 990, and II, App. A.

Wine trade of France, **FQR** 78
Letting of land: metayer system, 96
Present state of Spain, 107 collab.
History of the Hanseatic League, 162
Whale fishery, 173
Prussian commercial policy, 227, 271

MacCunn, Florence Anne: see *Index*, I, 990.

Scotch divines and English bishops, **ScotR** 337
Chronicle of de Joinville [*Life of St. Louis*], 625

MacDonagh, Michael: see *Index*, I, 990, and II, App. A.

Can we rely on our war news? **FortR** 4106
Royal visit to Ireland, 4440

Night in the reporters' gallery, **NC** 2727
In the sub-editor's room, 3216
Quaint side of Parliament, 3236
Unparliamentary expressions, 3349
Evolution of the parliamentary oath, 3521
The bye-ways of rural Ireland, 3681, 3708

MacDonald, Arthur, 1856–1936, anthropologist. *Amer. WWW*.

Criminal contagion, **NatR-II** 1361

MacDonald, Colin, 1845–1918, divine. *Fasti*, VII, 99.

Transition in the Highlands, **ScotR** 214

Macdonald, Frederika (Richardson), translator; prob. wife of John F. Macdonald. *BMCat*. under her name and his.

Buddhism and mock Buddhism, **FortR** 2317

Antoine Wiertz, **FM** 5308
Penitence of Rajah Yayati, 6360

Macdonald, Georgiana: see Burne-Jones, Lady Georgiana (Macdonald).

Macdonald, Henry James, known as Harry, b.1835/36, English-born American journalist, brother of Lady Georgiana (Macdonald) Burne-Jones. Burne-Jones, *Memorials*, index, Foster.

The Song of Hiawatha, by Longfellow, **OxCam** 6

MacDonald, J. L.; possibly James Leonard Macdonald, b.1832/33, in *Alum.Dub*. and Foster.

The fruit-farming fiasco in California, **NatR-II** 1759

MacDonald, James Ramsay, 1866–1937, writer on socialism. *DNB*.

Independent Labour Party's programme, **NC** 3401 collab.

Modern socialism, **ScotR** 311
Andrew Fletcher, 407

Macdonald, John, journalist, war correspondent. See both *NC* arts.

With Baker and Graham in the Soudan, **NC** 1007
Fellah soldiers, old and new, 3357

Macdonald, John; perhaps of Birmingham.

Birmingham, **NC** 1309

Macdonald, John, b.1851, barrister. *M at B*.

Monks of La Trappe, **FM** 5302

Macdonald, John Archibald Murray: see *Index*, I, 991.

Labour movement, **NC** 1849

Macdonald, John Hay Athole: see *Index*, I, 991.

Volunteers, **NatR-II** 1845

Macdonell, James: see *Index*, I, 991.

Paris under the monarchy of the Restoration, **FortR** 1594

Modern spirit, **FM** 4760
Politics of young England, 4833, 4850
Trades unionism in the City, 4888, 4906
Irish politics and priests, 5072

Proposed Roman Catholic University for Ireland, 5248
Plea for Black Bartholomew, 5405
Protestant restoration in France, 5471
New army of France, 5675
Our future army, 5693
Competitive system [in civil service], 5917

Macdonell, Sir John: see *Index,* I, 991.

New aspects of the land question, **FortR** 862
Karl Marx and German socialism, 1136
German railways, 1222
Blasphemy and the common law, 2039
Is the caucus a necessity? 2397

Legal position of the Dardanelles and the Suez Canal, **FM** 6058

Fetich of publicity, **NC** 2917
England's duties as a neutral, 3280
Future of Egypt, 3385
Neutrals and the [Boer] War, 3611
Imperial federation, 3658
Usages of war in South Africa, 3771

MacDonnell, John, 1795/96–1892, commissioner of local government board. Burke's *Ireland, Alum. Dub.*

?Rise and fall of Chartism, **DR** 170

McDonnell, Sir Richard Graves, 1814–1881, colonial governor. *DNB.*

Poland, England, and Russia, **FM** 1410
Russian alliance, 1497
Past year and present prospects, 1511
What does our Russian ally mean to do? 1512
Foreign policy and home prospects, 1535

MacDougall, Sir Patrick Leonard: see *Index,* I, 991.

Have we an army? **NC** 906
Our system of infantry tactics, 1134

McEwen, Alexander; possibly Alexander MacEwen, political writer in *BMCat.*

Note: **NC** 118

MacFadyen, Alfred N.; possibly Alfred Newth Macfadyen in *BMCat.*

Trans. and intro. note, **NC** 3093

McFall, Frances Elizabeth (Clarke): see *Index,* I, 992, and II App. A.

"Marriage Questions in Fiction," **FortR** 4085

Macfarren, Sir George Alexander: see *Index,* I, 992.

Royal Academy of Music, **NC** 752

MacFie, Matthew: see *Index,* I, 992.

Life in San Francisco, **FortR** 36
True north-west passage, 140

MacGauley or **M'Gauley,** James William, c.1800–1867, prof. of natural philosophy in Ireland. *DNB,* Crone.

Chemistry, **DR** 270

McGrath, John, Irish nationalist.

Ireland's difficulty—England's opportunity, **FortR** 3871

McGrath, Sir Patrick Thomas, 1868–1929, statesman, journalist. *DNB.*

"French Shore" [of Newfoundland], **FortR** 4396

French rights in Newfoundland, **NatR-II** 2208

France in Newfoundland, **NC** 3403

MacGregor, John, 1850–1936, of the Legislative Council of New Zealand. *New Zealand Biog.*

Compulsory arbitration at work, **NatR-II** 2362

McHardy, Alexander Burness, 1842–1917, army officer. *WWW.*

Soldier's barrack-room, **NC** 1917

McHardy, Coghlan McLean, writer on naval affairs. *BMCat.*

Electors and the navy, **NatR-II** 2506

McIlquham, Mrs. Harriett, feminist. *BMCat.*

"Of women in assemblies," **NC** 2023

McIlwraith, Sir Malcolm, 1865–1941, barrister. *WWW.*

Delagoa Bay arbitration, **FortR** 4505

McIntosh, William Carmichael, 1838–1931, zoologist, prof. at St. Andrews. *DNB.*

Sir William Henry Flower, **ScotR** 675

Macintyre, James; possibly James Macintyre, publisher, in Boase.

Theophraste Renaudot; old journalism and new, **NC** 2468

McIntyre, John, 1855–1934, R.C. archbishop of Birmingham. *WWW.*

Modern faith and the Bible, **DR** 2561
Notices: 2583, 2628, 2674, 2738

Mackarness, Frederic Michael Coleridge: see *Index*, I, 992.

What England has done for the Zulus, **FortR** 2218
Future of South Africa, 2343

Mackarness, John Fielder, 1820–1889, bishop of Oxford. *DNB.*

Sisters-in-law, **NC** 1338

Mackay, Charles: see *Index*, I, 992.

President Johnson and reconstruction of the Union, **FortR** 219
A week in Prince Edward Island, 255

Burns and Béranger, **NC** 418
Boileau and Pope, 653
Mystery of Shakespeare's sonnets, 1027
English songs, ancient and modern, 1071
Ascertainment of English, 1821

Mackay, John, 1826/27–1896, Scotsman who lived twenty years in Canada. Adam Gunn and John Mackay, *Sutherland and the Reay Country,* Glasgow, 1897. (See *Index,* I, 993.)

An old Scots society [in Boston, Mass.], **ScotR** 279
Death of Gustavus Adolphus, 359

Mackay, Thomas: see *Index,* I, 993, and *Times,* Feb. 26, 1912, p. 11d.

Politics and the Poor Law, **FortR** 3614

Old-age pensions: economic objections, **NatR-II** 1255
Unpopularity of the Poor Law, 1318
Golf, 1500
People's banks, 1522
Enthusiasm or hysteria [in politics]? 1589
Empiricism in politics, 1758
Unpopularity of the House of Commons, 1899
Letter: 1498

McKendrick, John Gray, 1841–1926, prof. of physiology at Glasgow. *WWW.*

Human electricity, **FortR** 3209
Electric fishes, 3423

Scottish university reform, **ScotR** 197

McKenna, Ethel M. M.

From an eighteenth-century escritoire, **FortR** 4552

Mckenzie, Charles Kenneth, 1788–1862, foreign service officer. Boase, *Gent.Mag.,* Oct. 1862, p. 504.

Humboldt's *Account of Cuba,* **FQR** 69
Mexico, 86

McKenzie, Frederick Arthur, 1869–1931, Canadian journalist. *LCCat., WWW.*

Tammany, **NC** 3209

Mackenzie, Sir George Sutherland, 1844–1910, explorer, colonial administrator. *DNB.*

British East Africa and Mombasa railway, **FortR** 3205
Troubles in Uganda, 3231
Uganda and East African protectorates, 3582

Mackenzie, Gordon Thomson, judge in India. *BMCat.,* Gorman, which gives middle name as Thomas.

Royal patronage in India, **DR** 2361
Marlborough, 2457
Experiment in education [in Madras], 2549
Notice: 2558

Mckenzie, John, 1835–1899: see *Index,* I, 993.

England and South Africa, **NC** 847

Mackenzie, Sir Morell: see *Index,* I, 993.

Specialism in medicine, **FortR** 2323, 2356
Is medicine a progressive science? 2476
Reform of the College of Surgeons, 2944
Influenza, 3090
New yachting, 3115

Health-seeking in Tenerife and Madeira, **NC** 1736
Dreadful revival of leprosy, 1798

McKerlie, Helen G.: see *Index,* I, 993.

Elizabeth, Queen of Roumania, **NatR-II** 727

Mackey, E., M.D.; possibly Edward Mackey of Brighton in *Med.Reg./89.*

Miracles and medical science, **DR** 1752

Mackey, Henry Benedict, O.S.B., 1846–1906, canon in R.C. Church; *Benedictine Bibliog.*

St. Francis de Sales, **DR** 1806, 1830, 1856, 1876
Land and works of St. Francis de Sales, 2175

St. Francis de Sales as a preacher, 2591, 2603, 2612

Mackinlay, James Boniface, O.S.B., 1853–1922. *Benedicti Familiae.*

City of our martyrs [Douai], **DR** 1903

Mackintosh, Sir James: see *Index,* I, 993.

Notice of M. Dumont, **FQR** 117

Macknight, Thomas, 1829–1899, political writer, journalist. *DNB.*

Edmund Burke, **FM** 2912, 2920

Mackonochie, Alexander Heriot, 1825–1887, divine. *DNB.*

Disestablishment and disendowment, **NC** 49
Separation of Church and State, 228

MacLachlan, Paul, priest of Falkirk in Scotland. *CD/41.*

Scottish monks, **DR** 404

Maclagan, Robert, 1820–1894, army officer. Boase.

India: the English and the natives, **NatR-II** 171

Maclagan, Thomas John, 1838–1903, M.D. *Surgeon Index/3rd s.*

Is typhoid fever contagious? **NC** 370
Influenza and salicin, 2170

Maclaren, Charles, 1782–1866, ed. the *Scotsman. DNB.*

Dupin, *Commercial Powers of France,* **FQR** 21
Duke Bernard's *Travels in North America,* 77

M'Laren, Walter Stowe Bright, 1853–1912, industrialist, M.P. *WWW.*

Dairy schools, **FortR** 2692

McLaughlin, Frances; possibly Frances MacLaughlin in *BMCat.*

Problem of domestic service, **NatR-II** 1137

Macleane, Douglas, 1856–1925, canon of Salisbury. *WWW.*

The Church as a profession, **NatR-II** 2337

McLennan, Donald, 1833–1891, editor, barrister. Boase.

Notice: **FortR** 173

MacLennan, John Ferguson: see *Index,* I, 994.

Kinship in ancient Greece, **FortR** 227, 236
Worship of animals and plants, 629, 637, 659
Levirate and polyandry, 1359
Exogamy and endogamy, 1371

McLeod, D. F., R.C. priest.

Coptic Church, **DR** 583

MacLeod, Henry Dunning: see *Index,* I, 994.

Monometallist creed, **NC** 2661
Bimetallism, 2766

Maclure, Alexander Logan, 1860–1932, Scottish barrister, gov't. official. *WWW.*

America as a power, **NC** 2940

McMahon, Alexander Ruxbon, 1828/29–1899, F.R.G.S. Death certificate, Somerset House. (See *Index,* I, 994.)

Situation in Burmah, **NatR-II** 365
Burma and the Burmese, 498

McMahon, Patrick, 1813–1875, Irish M.P. Boase.

Trinity College, Dublin, **DR** 86
Irish election committees, 101
The Commons on controverted elections, 141
Power: Popery—Protestantism, 162, 196, 204
Crown grants of fisheries in Ireland, 236
Lingard's *History of England,* 250
Depopulation: fixity of tenure, 275
Laing's *Travels,* 286
Irish fisheries, 494
[Mrs.] Sinnett's *Byways of History,* 495
Death of Dr. [John Shaw] Campbell, 501
Sanatory [sic] reform, 518 collab.
Measures for Ireland, 525
Ireland: spirit of recent legislation, 565
Impediments to Prosperity of Ireland, 586
Ireland: review of the session, 594
Ireland: a peasant proprietary, 608
Our resources: land, labour, and trade, 724
Irish sea-fisheries, 744
Lord Cloncurry, 765
Irish waste lands, 781
Catholic University and legal education, 815
Appeal in criminal cases, 893

Macmillan, George Augustin: see *Index,* I, 995.

Letter: **FortR** 2033

Macmillan, Hugh: see *Index,* I, 995.

An early Celtic college, **FM** 6343

Macnaghten, Francis, 1798–1869, Bengal civil
servant. Burke; *Bengal Civil Servants,* pp.
304–305.

Deville's *Letters on Bengal,* **FQR** 4

Macnaghten, Russell Elliot: see *Index,* I, 995.

Temperance and the public-houses, **NatR-II**
962
Letter: 1029

MacNamara, James F., of Royal Irish Constabulary.

Immorality of hypnotism, **NatR-II** 1131
Aggressive teetotaller, 1142

Macnamara, Thomas James: see *Index,* I,
995.

Secondary Education Commission, **FortR**
3735
Joints in our educational armour, 4286
Progressivism at London School Board,
4535

New Education Bill, **NC** 2929
Local support of education, 3037
Higher education and the state, 3455

McNaughton, John Hugh, 1829–1891, American author, composer. *Amer. WWW.*

The Red Man, **NC** 1132

McNeill, George Powell, 1860–1931, Scottish
advocate. Grant.

Huchown of the Awle Ryale [medieval
chronicles], **ScotR** 204

MacNeill, John Gordon Swift, 1849–1926,
Irish politician, jurist. *DNB.*

House of Lords, **FortR** 3585
Mr. Lecky and Irish affairs, 3741
Irish lord-lieutenancy, 4016

McNeill, Ronald John: see *Index,* I, 995, and
II, App. A.

Ibsenism: *Little Eyolf,* **NatR-II** 1964

Macnish, Robert: see *Index,* I, 995.

Punch and Judy, **FM** 205
Singular passage in my own life, 215
Who murdered Begbie? 291
Philosophy of Burking, 344
Victims of susceptibility, 443
Books of aphorisms, 491
Philosophy of sneering, 602
Journey from Paris to Ostend, 773

MacPherson, William Charteris, b.1861/62,

student of the Middle Temple. *Foster,
LCCat.*

Representative peers of Scotland, *ScotR*
481

Macquoid, Katharine Sarah: see *Index,* I,
996.

On the Rue Froide, **NQM** 36
Mill of St. Herbot: a Breton story, 69

Macrae, Charles Colin, 1843–1922, barrister,
practised in Calcutta. *WWW.*

Jurisdiction over Englishmen in India,
FortR 2066

Macray, John, 1796–1878, bookseller, librarian. Boase.

Notices: 30 in **FQR** from 12 to 341

McSkimmin, Samuel, of Carrickfergus, Ireland.

Irish Insurrection of 1803, **FM** 1011, collab. at least

McTaggart, John McTaggart Ellis, 1866–
1925, philosopher. *DNB.*

University for Wales, **NatR-II** 1541

M'Vail, Sir David Caldwell, 1845–1917,
physician. *WWW.*

?Medical reform, **ScotR** 14
Scottish university reform, 198

Madden, Sir John, 1844–1918, Australian
chief justice. *WWW.*

Cyclones and hurricanes, **NatR-II** 2276

Madden, Richard Robert, 1798–1886, misc.
writer. *DNB.*

Calumnies against the "Society of Jesus,"
DR 994

Portugal and its rulers, **FQR** 898

Madison, James, 1751–1836, president of the
U.S. *DAB.*

See: **FortR** 4167

Maeterlinck, Maurice: see *Index,* I, 996, and
Grand Larousse.

Evolution of mystery, **FortR** 4458
Kingdom of matter, 4518

Magee, William Connor: see *Index,* I, 996.

Betting, gambling, and my critics, **FortR**
2894

Magnus, Lady Katie (Emanuel) (*continued*)
Higher education of women, 812
Letter: 833

Magnus, Laurie: see *Index*, I, 997.

German poet of revolt [A. Holz], **FortR**
3938

Progress in German universities, **NC** 3378

Magnus, Sir Philip: see *Index*, I, 997.

Trade and training in Germany, **NatR-II**
1996

Magnússon, Eiríkr, 1833–1913, Danish
scholar. *LCCat.*

Saga of Gunnlavg and Rafn, **FortR** 555
collab.

Maguire, James Rochfort, 1855–1925, South
African entrepreneur, friend of Cecil
Rhodes. *DNB.*

See: **FortR** 3811, 3900, 4122

Maguire, John, 1801–1865, D.D., vicar-
general under Wiseman. Newman, *L&D*,
XIII, index.

Chateaubriand's *English Literature*, **DR** 30
Perceval's *Peace Offering* and *Roman
Schism*, 71
Wiseman and Turton, 147
A. P. Perceval, and the *Dublin Review*, 177

Translations of the Scriptures, **Ram** 889
German Jews and French reviewers, 943
Letter: 1050
Notice: 923

Maguire, Thomas Miller, 1849–1920, military
historian. *LCCat.*

Surprise in war, **NatR-II** 2158
Military education of officers, 2530

Mahaffy, Sir John Pentland: see *Index*, I,
997.

Trinity College, Dublin, **FortR** 740

Tercentenary of Trinity College, Dublin,
NC 2241
Sham education, 2333
The future of education, 2437
Recent archaeology, 2580
The proposed Nile reservoir, 2598
Present position of Egyptology, 2624
Provincial patriotism [Home Rule], 2770
International jealousy, 2907
The modern Babel, 3024
About Alexandria, 3084
Modern education, 3195

How to circumvent "cramming," 3382
Recent fuss about the Irish language, 3511

Mahon, J. L., socialist, pres. of Independent
Labour Party. *BMCat.* and *NatR-II* 21
(Mar. 1893), cover.

Liberals and Labour party, **NatR-II** 1409
Labour party and general election, 1600

The crisis in the post office, **NC** 1901

Mahony, Francis Sylvester, S.J., 1804–1866,
Irish humorist. *DNB.*

[Letitia Elizabeth] Landon, **FM** 611
Father Prout's apology for Lent, 685
Father Prout's plea for pilgrimages, 690
Father Prout's carousal, 702
Dean Swift's madness, 710
The rogueries of Tom Moore, 726
Literature and the Jesuits, 736
The songs of France, 747, 758, 764, 777
The songs of Italy, 782, 793
Pierre-Jean de Béranger, 795
Notte romane nel palazzo Vaticano, 807
The days of Erasmus, 819
Hugo's *Hunchback of Notre Dame*, 841
Henry O'Brien, 847
Modern Latin poets, 851, 861, 873
Parliamentary report of *Fraser's Magazine*,
895 collab.
The Reliques of Father Prout, 922
The songs of Horace, 973, 983, 996, 1007,
1019
Crichton [by W. H. Ainsworth], 1027

Mahony, Martin Francis, 1831–1882, novelist.
BMCat., Irish Gentry.

Misadventures of Mr. Catlyne, Q.C., **FM**
5322, 5332, 5337, 5350, 5359

News from Irish emigrants, **NC** 1681 collab.

Mahony, Richard John, 1827–1892, Irish agriculturist. Boase.

Is there hope for Ireland? **FortR** 2496

Maier, Julius, writer on electricity. *BMCat.*

Recent progress in electricity, **FortR** 2313

Maillard, Mrs. Annette Marie, novelist.
BMCat., Eng.Cat.

Madeleine, the Rosière, **Ram** 477, 483, 490,
497, 506

Main, John Frederic, 1854/55–1892, prof. at
Royal College of Science. Boase.

The Upper Engadine in winter, **FortR** 2271

Main, Robert: see *Index*, I, 997.

The future of our navy, **FortR** 121

Maine, Charles Sumner: see *Index*, I, 997.

The international tribunals of Egypt, **FortR** 2348

Maine, Sir Henry James Sumner: see *Index*, I, 997.

"Introduction" to the *Indian Evidence Act*, **FortR** 916
Feudal property in France and England, 1347
Ancient ideas respecting codes, 1583
The king, in relation to early civil justice, 1857
The king and his successor, 1882
South Slavonians and Rajpoots, **NC** 114
Godkin on popular government, 1252

Maitland, Edward; perhaps the Edward Maitland, 1824–1879, journalist in *DNB*. (See below, App. A.)

Misrepresentation of majorities, **FortR** 700

Maitland, Frederic William, 1850–1906, prof. of law, Cambridge. *DNB*.

Canon MacColl's new convocation, **FortR** 4374

Maitland, John Alexander Fuller, 1856–1936, music critic. *DNB*.

Over production in musical world, **NatR-II** 1664
The new *Orfeo*, **NC** 1987
Falstaff and the new Italian opera, 2392
The influence of Bayreuth, 2982
Wanted—an opera, 3303

Maitland, Margaret Mary; possibly Margaret Maitland, trans., in *BMCat*.

Vittoria Accoramboni, **NC** 3406

Maitland, William, of Santa Cruz, California.

A mountain vineyard in California, **NC** 1585
The ruin of the American farmer, 2306

Majendie, Sir Vivian Dering: see *Index*, I, 998.

Nitro-glycerine and dynamite, **FortR** 2029

Malan, Charles Hamilton, 1837–1881, army officer. *BMCat.*, *Times*, May 26, 1881, p. 12e.

The recruiting difficulty, **FortR** 275

Malato, Charles, 1857–1938, French anarchist. *LCCat.*, *N.Y. Times*, Nov. 10, 1938, p. 27i.

Some anarchist portraits, **FortR** 3542

Malcolm, George, of Invergarry. *BMCat.*

Deer forests, **NC** 1406

Malcolm, James Aratoon, b.1868 in Persia, journalist, contractor. *Balliol Coll. Register*, 2nd ed. Oxford, 1934.

An Armenian's cry for Armenia, **NC** 1947

Malkin, Arthur Thomas, 1803–1888, Alpinist. Venn, *Alpine Journal*, 14 (Feb. 1889), 235, 275.

My Highland home, **FM** 4210
Mountaineering in 1861, 4307

Malleson, George Bruce: see *Index*, I, 999.

The modern Mark Antony [Boulanger], **FortR** 3152
Advance of Russia towards India, **NatR-II** 298
Rivalry of England and Russia, 535

Mallock, Mary Margaret: see *Index*, I, 999.

Charles Kingsley, **DR** 2227
Metaphysical basis of Protestantism, 2573
Restaurants for labouring classes, **NatR-II** 1405

Mallock, William Hurrell: see *Index*, I, 999.

General Gordon's message [on religion], **FortR** 2191
Wealth and the working classes, 2568, 2589, 2618, 2463
The scientific bases of optimism, 2784
"Cowardly Agnosticism," 2812
Science and the revolution, 2883
Labouchere: the democrat, 2916
A Catholic theologian [Sebastian Bowden], 2989
Reason alone [insufficient for belief in God], 3013
Public life and private morals, 3041
Marriage and free thought, 3119
A human document, in 7 installments from 3141 to 3207
Amateur Christianity, 3213
Poetry and Lord Lytton, 3222
Social remedies of Labour party, 3352
Fabian economics, 3463, 3481
A socialist in a corner [Bernard Shaw], 3504
The heart of life, in 9 installments from 3572 to 3672

Mallock, William Hurrell (*continued*)
Bi-metallism and nature of money, 3839
The unrecognised essence of democracy, 4000
A study of natural religion [Crozier], 4034
The individualist, in 9 installments from 4165 to 4270
The logic of non-dogmatic Christianity, 4410
Letters: 2638, 2649

The *Golden Ass* of Apuleius, **FM** 5856

Radicalism and the people, **NatR-II** 7
Radicalism of the market-place, 36
A Greek ballad of tenth century, 61a
Radicalism and working classes, 79
Conservatism and socialism, 123
Landlords and national income, 140
How to popularize unpopular political truths, 363
The old order changes, in 9 installments from 379 to 465
"Go ye and teach!" hint to political organizations, 653
Conservatism and diffusion of property, 719
A rival of Marco Polo [Ibn Batoutah], 736
Radicals and the unearned increment, 836
Wanted—a new Corrupt Practices Act, 1328
A common ground of agreement for all parties, 1400
Causes of the national income, 1411, 1426, 1439, 1449, 1461
Comedy of Christian Science, 2273
The rights of the weak, 2468

Is life worth living? **NC** 77, 129
A colloquy [on fine arts], 208
Faith and verification, 231
Dogma, reason, and morality, 249
The logic of toleration, 261
Dialogue on human happiness, 351
Atheistic Methodism, 400
Atheism and the rights of man, 438
Atheism and repentance, 466
The philosophy of Conservatism, 514
Radicalism, 560
The religion of humanity, 2824
The buck-jumping of labour, 3161
Herbert Spencer in self-defence, 3337
Does the Church of England teach anything? 3387
Intellectual future of Catholicism, 3359

Malone, Sylvester, 1822–1906, Irish ecclesiastical historian. *DNB.*

"Corpus Missal" and its probable date, **DR** 1772
Nomenclature of the days of the week, 1829

Church discipline and Protestant historians, 1890
Adrian IV. and Ireland, 1911
The vicissitudes of "vigil," 1935
Where was St. Patrick born? 2034, 2088
Notice: 1941

Malortie, Baron Carl de: *Index,* I, 999, and *EUI.*

Egypt for the Egyptians, **FortR** 2078
Road to the East and its protection, **NatR-II** 111
Our work in Egypt, 329

Manby, Cordy

Letter: **NatR-II** 962

Manby, Edward

Note on affairs in Chili, **FortR** 3107

Mann, Sir John, 1863–1955, misc. writer. *WWW.*

Regulation of the drink traffic, **ScotR** 402

Mann, Tom: see *Index,* I, 1000.

Letter: **FortR** 2934

Development of the labour movement, **NC** 1864

Manners, Fitzalan George John, 1866–1901, of the Scots Guard. *BMCat.,* Burke under Rutland.

The Irish guards, **NC** 3673

Manners, Sir George Espec John: see *Index,* I, 1000.

Glimpses at a game-book, **NatR-II** 1274

Manners, Lady Janetta: see *Index,* I, 1000, and II, App. A.

A sequel to "Rich man's dwellings," **NatR-II** 142
Letters from an idle woman's post-bag, 177
Emancipation of English bondmen and bondwomen, 197
The East Leicestershire election, 400
Bürger and Bauer life in Homberg and the Taunus region, 454
Are rich landowners idle? 684

Massage, **NC** 1350

Manners, Lord John James Robert: see *Index,* I, 1000.

Trip across the Spanish frontier, **FM** 1438, 1459

Manning, Henry Edward: see *Index*, I, 1000.

Catholic Church in England, **DR** 1039
Father Faber, 1059
Cardinal Wiseman's sermons, 1104
Memorial of Cardinal Wiseman, 1107
?Russia [and Catholicism], 1584
Frederic Ozanam, 1585
Dr. Ward's retirement, 1650 collab.
Works and wants of the Church in England, 1665
William George Ward, 1839
How shall Catholics vote at the parliamentary election? 1989
Henry VIII and English monasteries, 2106
Henry VIII and suppression of monasteries, 2160
Leo XIII on "The Condition of Labour," 2290
Note: 1551
Notices: ?1083, 1930, 2068
See: 745

Our national vice [intemperance], **FR** 2513
Distress in London: outdoor relief, 2674
Local Governments Bill: the drink trade, 2717
Education Commission and school rate, 2827

True story of the Vatican Council, **NC** 8, 11, 33, 43, 54
An Englishman's protest [on Church and State unity], 476
An Englishman's protest [against the parliamentary oath], 696
Parliamentary oaths, 766
Is Education Act of 1870 just? 799
Religion and the rates, 822
Is Christianity of England worth preserving? 842
A pleading for the worthless, 1521
Irresponsible wealth, 1965

Letter: **Ram** 712

Manohar, Rajah Murli. *BMCat.*, under Muralīmanohara.

Industries of ancient India, **NC** 2070

Mansel, Henry Longueville: see *Index*, I, 1000.

Modern German philosophy, **BentQR** 13

Mansfield, Charles Blackford, 1819–1855, chemist, Christian Socialist. *DNB.*

Hints from Hygea, **FM** 2703

Mansfield, Robert Blachford, 1824–1908, misc. writer, oarsman. *DNB.*

Shooting in Albania, **FM** 3652

March-Phillipps, Evelyn: see Phillipps, Evelyn March

March-Phillipps, Lisle: see Phillipps, Lisle March

Marindin, Charles Randal, 1851–1929, magistrate in the Indian civil service. "Bengal Civil Fund Family Register," at India Office, II, 672.

Episode of the Bakrid, **NatR-II** 2397

Marindin, George Eden: see *Index*, I, 1001.

Eton in eighty-five, **FortR** 2321

Mario, Jessie Meriton White: see *Index*, I, 1001.

Experience of ambulances, **FM** 5940, 5947, 5961
Garibaldi in France, **FM** 5977, 5988, 5996
Italy and the United States, **NC** 2035

Marjoribanks, Edward, 2nd Baron Tweedmouth, 1849–1909, politician. *DNB.*

Our sea fishermen, **FortR** 2389

Mark,   , Esq.

Murat's *Sketch of the United States*, **FQR** 256

Markby, Sir William: see *Index*, I, 1001.

Why I voted for Gladstone, **NC** 2259

Markham, Sir Clements Robert: see *Index*, I, 1001.

Lord Fairfax at Colchester, **FortR** 1291

Need for an Antarctic expedition, **NC** 2828
Notice: 487

Markoff, or **Markov,** Anatolius V., 1866/67–1916, F.R.G.S., LL.D. Death certificate, Somerset House; *BMCat.*

Policy of Russia, **NatR-II** 2146

Marks, Alfred; possibly Alfred David Thomas Marks, 1869–1946, in Venn.

Letter: **NatR-II** 2403

Marras, Americo, or Americ, William Palfrey de Lamiliere (later Burrell), b.1840/41, barrister. Foster, *M at B* under Burrell, William Palfrey.

Notices: **FortR** 488, 577

Marriott, Edward Frere. *BMCat.*

Indian currency policy, **FortR** 4187

Marriott, John Arthur Ransome, 1859–1945, historian, educator. *DNB.*

A great Anglo-Indian: Sir William Hunter, **FortR** 4468
Lord Rosebery's chance, 4544

Imperial note in Victorian poetry, **NC** 3703
Cabinet government or departmentalism? 3740

Marriott, Sir William Thackeray, 1834–1903, judge-advocate-general. *DNB.*

Egypt, 1882–1892, **FortR** 3221
The political outlook, 3256
Situation in Egypt, 3622
Zebehr Pasha, 3669
Notices: 415, 553

Devastation of the Soudan, **NatR-II** 1371
Primrose League, 1684

Birmingham caucus, **NC** 731

Marryat, Charles, brother of Frederick Marryat, the novelist. *BMCat.*

Letter: **FQR** 149

Marryat, Rosalind. *BMCat.*

"Sanitary Aid" [Committee], **NC** 997

Marsh, Frederick Thomas, divine. *CCD/82, BMCat.*

Letter: **NatR-II** 959

Marshall, Alfred: see *Index*, I, 1001.

Mill's theory of value, **FortR** 1250

Marshall, Beatrice, translator from the German, daughter of Emma (Martin) Marshall. *BMCat., DNB* 1st suppl., under her mother.

Nietzsche and Richard Wagner, **FortR** 4128

Marshall, Charles, traveller. *BMCat.*

The new dominion [Canada], **FM** 5139
The free-grant lands of Canada, 5159
Characteristics of Mormonism, 5207
Salt Lake City, 5221
The original prophet [Joseph Smith], 5400

Marshall, Florence A. (Thomas): see *Index*, 1001, and II, App. A.

Music and the people, **NC** 526
Music for the masses, 2240

Marshall, Frederic, or Frederick: see *Index*, I, 1001, and II, App. A.

Justice abroad, **FortR** 1071
Paris as an English residence, 2327

The reign of the "nouvelles couches," [new generation] in France, **NC** 1602
Society and democracy in France, 1708

Marshall, Pembroke, captain. See *FortR no.* 3018.

Child-life insurance, **FortR** 3018, 3095

Marshall, Thomas William M., 1818–1877, Catholic controversialist. *DNB.*

Developments of Protestantism, **DR** 409
The Russo-Greek and Oriental churches, 486
The American Church, 1333
Authority and the Anglican Church—Garbett and Liddon, 1437
Anglicans of the day, 1522

Rood-screens, **Ram** 27
?Sketches ecclesiastical and secular, 45, 81, 99, 112
Nuns as teachers of schools, 507

Marston, John Westland, 1819–1890, dramatist. *DNB.*

Realism in dramatic art [Zola], **NQM** 194

Marston, Philip Bourke, 1850–1887, poet. *DNB.*

His word of honour, **NQM** 81

Marston, Robert Bright, 1853–1927, publisher, writer on fishing. *WWW.*

Letter: **NatR-II** 1850

Corn stores for war-time, **NC** 2880
Our urgent need of a reserve of wheat, 3295
The Thames as a salmon river, 3448

Martin, Arthur Patchett: see *Index*, I, 1002.

The great Australian strike, **NatR-II** 1081
Robert Lowe as a journalist, 1497
Lord Sherbrooke and Sir Alfred Stephen, 1604
James Anthony Froude, 1657
An Australian's reflections on the [Boer] War, 2421

Martin, Bradley, Jun., 1873–1963, American businessman. *Amer.WWW.*

Is the lavish expenditure of wealth justifiable? **NC** 3395
American imperialism, 3716

Martin, Jean Pierre Paulin: see *Index*, I, 1002.

A Roman Catholic view of ritualism, **NC** 135
The education question in France, 327
The present state of the French church, 389
French clergy and the present republic, 473
The French educational system, 770

Martin, Marion E. (Blackney), d.1855, wife of Robert Martin of Ross. Burke's *Ireland* under her husband; see *FM* no. 2158.

?The legend of Gelnhausen, **FM** 2158
?Kingdom of Sardinia, 3386
See: 2276

Martin, Mary Emma (LeBreton), novelist, wife of Herbert Martin. *BMCat.*, *R.G.*

John Aikin, M.D., **FM** 6175
Beauchamp and Co., 6423
"Lord of all," 6484

Martin, Sir Theodore: see *Index*, I, 1002.

Who are you? or, The Modern Salathiel, **FM** 1432
The dead alive, 1712 collab.
My namesake, 1759 collab.
A night at Peleg Longfellow's, 1843 collab.
[Introduction to] Madonna Pia, 3130a
The Gladiator of Ravenna, 3581
A word about our theatres, 3696
Shakspeare, and his stage interpreters, 4172
Plays, players, and critics, 4393
The drama in London, 4511

An eye-witness of John Kemble, **NC** 406

Martineau, James: see *Index*, I, 1003.

Influence upon morality of a decline in religious belief, **NC** 22
The Creed of Christendom [by W. R. Greg], 815
The Gospel of Peter, 2405, 2471
The Foundations of Belief [by A. J. Balfour], 2730

Martineau, John: see *Index*, I, 1003.

Purchase in the Church, **NC** 395

Martinengo-Cesaresco, Countess Evelyn Lilian Hazeldine (Carrington): see *Index*, I, 1003.

Armenian folk songs, **FM** 5782
Folk lullabies, 6367

Nature in folk-songs, **NatR-II** 283
The agricultural crisis in north Italy, 611

Historical Rimini, 1307

Through the Graubanden to the Engadin, **NQM** 28
Nino Bixio, 61
In the Italian highlands, 132

The peasant in north Italy, **ScotR** 193

Marvin, Charles Thomas: see *Index*, I, 1003.

The oil wells of Burma, **NatR-II** 923
Letter: 535

Marwick, Sir James David, 1826–1908, legal, historical writer. *DNB.*

Early Scottish burghs, **ScotR** 21

Marx, Francis, writer on Russia and the East. *BMCat.*

Russia under Alexander II, **FortR** 713

The River Amoor, **FM** 3301, 4078
Ladak and Tibet, 3439
Last naval campaign in the Pacific, 3507

Marzials, Sir Frank Thomas: see *Index*, I, 1003.

Edmond Scherer, **NatR-II** 247

Maskell, William, ?1814–1890, divine, Catholic convert, 1850. *DNB.*

Letter: **DR** 1347
Notices: 600, ?641

Mason, Miss; possibly the Emily Virginia Mason, 1815–1909, niece of Senator Mason of Virginia in Gorman and *LCCat.*

Kate Gearey; or, Irish life in London, **Ram** in 9 installments from 377 to 440

Mason, Alfred Bishop, 1851–1933, American lawyer. *Amer.WWW.*

American view of emigration, **FortR** 1080

Mason, Arthur James, 1851–1928, prof. of divinity at Cambridge. *DNB.*

An ancient City church [Barking], London, **NC** 3292

Mason, Charles Welsh, the elder, b.1830/31, writer on Spanish literature. Venn, *BMCat.*

Spanish poetry before A.D. 1500, **FM** 4982

Mason, James, M.D. in Blyth, Northumberland. *Med.Reg./99.*

Quack medicines, **NatR-II** 1131

Massey, Gerald: see *Index*, I, 1003.

Charles Lamb, **FM** 4762

Myth and totemism, **NatR-II** 776

Massingham, Henry William: see *Index*, I, 1004.

The trend of trade unionism, **FortR** 3270
What Gladstone ought to do, 3331

The ethics of editing, **NatR-II** 2429
The decline of liberalism, 2452

The future of Lord Rosebery, **NC** 3557

Masson, David: see *Index*, I, 1004, and II, App. A.

On emotional culture, **FM** 1935
The pulpit in the nineteenth century, 1976
The three devils: Luther's, Milton's, Goethe's, 2008
Administration reform "movement," 3351
Bain, *The Senses and the Intellect*, 3443
Sylvester's *Du Bartas*, 3787

The story of Gifford and Keats, **NC** 2193

Masson, George Joseph Gustave: see *Index*, I, 1004.

Notices: **DR** 1767, 1779, 1790

Massue de Ruvigny, Melville Amadeus Henry Douglas Heddle de la Caillmotte de, 9th Marquis de Ruvigny and Raineval, 1868–1921, genealogist. *WWW*, under Ruvigny.

The Carlist cause, **FortR** 4046 collab.
The Carlist policy in Spain, 4173 collab.

"Legitimism" in England, **NC** 3164 collab.

Matheson, Frederick J., an American.

The U.S. and Cuban independence, **FortR** 4123

Matheson, George: see *Index*, I, 1005.

Agnosticism, **ScotR** 23

Mathew, Theobald F., 1834–1872, prof. at Thurlow. M. Russell, "Early Reviewers," pp. 209–210.

The origin of Greek philosophy, **DR** 945
Mystery of the blessed Eucharist, 1071

Mathews, Anne (Jackson), 1782/83–1869, actress. Boase.

Anecdotes of actors, **FM** 1597, 1620, 1638, 1679

Matthews, John Hobson, 1858–1914, R.C. antiquary. *Tablet*, Jan. 31, 1914.

Welsh church history by non-Catholic writers, **DR** 2481
Notice: 2387

Maude, Francis, 1798–1886, naval officer. Boase.

Letter: **NatR-II** 104

Maude, Francis Cornwallis, 1828–1900 army officer. *WWW*.

Slavery and Fanampóana in Madagascar, **FortR** 3149
The military situation in Madagascar, 3194
The deadlock in Madagascar, 3382
Madagascar, 3560, 3591

Maude, Frederic Natusch: see *Index*, I, 1005.

Imperial insurance, **NatR-II** 1519
The Influence of Sea Power [by Mahan], 1557

Maudsley, Henry, 1835–1918, psychologist. *WWW*.

Sex in mind and in education, **FortR** 1040
Hallucinations of the senses, 1505
Materialism and its lessons, 1613
Heredity in health and disease, 2461

Maughan, William Charles, d.1914, chartered accountant. *LCCat., County Direct. of Scotland/75* and */86.*

Argyllshire, **ScotR** 450

Maunder, Edward Walter, 1851–1928, writer on astronomy. *WWW*.

The oldest picture-book of all [the sky], **NC** 3720

Maurice, Frederick Denison: see Maurice, John Frederick Denison.

Maurice, Sir John Frederick: see *Index*, I, 1005.

Can we hold our own [against military attack]? **FortR** 2713
Critics and campaigns, 2730
The naval manoeuvres, 2749
Our true policy in India, 2797

The Zeit-Geist under drill, 2825

Omdurman, **NC** 3398
Terms used in modern gunnery, 3572

Maurice, John Frederick Denison: see *Index*, I, 1005.

Thoughts on Jewish disabilities, **FM** 2391
The Denison case, 3551

Mavor, James, 1854–1925, prof. of political economy at Univ. of Toronto. *WWW*.

The "malaise": Mr. Giffen's address, **NatR-II** 666

"Setting the poor on work," **NC** 2461

Mawdsley, James, 1848–1902, trade union leader. *DNB*.

Great Britain's opportunity, **NatR-II** 2075

Maxim, Sir Hiram Stevens, 1840–1916, engineer. *DNB*.

Progress in aerial navigation, **FortR** 3269

The prospects of flying, **NatR-II** 1624

Max Müller, Friedrich: see *Index*, I, 1006.

A note on "Missionary Religions," **FortR** 1066
On spelling, 1248
Metaphor as a mode of abstraction, 2532
The simplicity of language, 2591
Some lessons of antiquity, 2800
Coincidences, 3826, 4153
How to work, 3914
Dean Liddell, 4220
A prime minister [Gaurîshankar] and a child-wife, 4235

Popol Vuh [sacred writings], **FM** 4197
The science of religion, 5069, 5078, 5087, 5103
Darwin's philosophy of language, 5422, 5432, 5442

Mythology among the Hottentots, **NC** 669
Forgotten bibles, 1008
The savage, 1082
The lesson of "Jupiter," 1197
Solar myths, 1218
The sacrifice of education, 1615
Can we think without words? 1677
Lady Toad, 1779
The "enormous antiquity" of the East, 2047
Esoteric Buddhism, 2389, 2444
Mohammedanism and Christianity, 2531
The alleged sojourn of Christ in India, 2642
Why I am not an agnostic, 2671

The Kutho-Daw, 2811
A real Mahâtman, 2978
The Schleswig-Holstein question, 3108
Literature before letters, 3563
Confucianism, 3714
Taoism, 3729
Buddhism and Christianity, 3744
Note: 2919
Notice: 2588

Maxse, Frederick Augustus, 1833–1900, admiral, political writer. *DNB*.

Our uncultivated lands, **FortR** 708

"Judas" [defence of Joseph Chamberlain], **NatR-II** 1478
The European outlook, 1494
The referendum, 1551
The position of Liberal Unionists, 1570
"Fraternal France," 1763
Anglophobia, 1920
Europe and Greece, 2009
Face to face in West Africa, 2132
Admiral Lord Lyons, 2247
My chiefs in Crimea [Admirals Dundas and Lyons], 2262
Lord Raglan's traducers, 2272
The war correspondent at bay, 2287
The civil war in France, 2324
A glimpse of South Africa, 2453
See: 1932

Maxse, Frederick Ivor, 1862–1958, army officer. *WWW*.

Problems of the Far East [by Curzon], **NatR-II** 1640
Our military problem, 1816, 1826, 1836
The last of the Dervishes, 2391
Inaccurate history [W. S. Churchill, *River War*], 2430

Maxse, Leopold James, 1864–1932, journalist, ed. of *NatR-II*, 1893–1932. *DNB*.

Episodes of the month, **NatR-II** in 89 installments from 1456 to 2527; 1932, 1946 collab.
The British case against Venezuela, 1860
Mr. Rhodes' raid, 1893
A colonial chronicle, in 17 installments from 2023 to 2209
Great Britain's duty: "the bimetallic intrigue," 2091
Economic problem: an apology to Lord Farrer, 2103
The military terror in France, 2186
Cavaignac's vindication of Dreyfus, 2190
Key to the mystery [of the Dreyfus case], 2219

Maxse, Leopold James (*continued*)
Greater Britain, in 26 installments from 2220 to 2538
Russia and Dreyfus, 2224
International aspects of the Dreyfus scandal, 2254
The Dreyfus case, 2259
The Dreyfus affair: sins of the syndicate, 2280
Notes: 1818, 2062, 2128, 2139, 2141, 2161

Maxwell, Sir Herbert Eustace: see *Index*, I, 1006.

The rural voter, **NatR-II** 1232
Country gentlemen, 1327
Heresies in salmon fishing, 1578
Lord Randolph Churchill, 1701
Birds, **NC** 1969
The Scottish railway strike, 1998
Woodlands, 2067
Gardens, 2133
The last great Roman [Stilicho], 2281
Walling the cuckoo [on Mrs. Linton and women's rights], 2321
The craving for fiction, 2417
The conduct of friendship, 2452
Bores, 2530
Love, 2597
A Scottish vendetta, 2647
Intellectual detachment, 2777
Tuberculosis in man and beast, 3364
The militia, 3600
Our allies at Waterloo, 3717
Are we really a nation of amateurs? 3772
Archaeology in the south-west of Scotland, **ScotR** 22
Saved [the Constitution], 153
See: 130

Maxwell, Sir John Maxwell Stirling-, 1866–1956, patron of the arts. *WWW.*

St. Paul's, **NatR-II** 2300

Maxwell, Hon. Marcia Constable, b.1839. Lodge under Herries.

Madame Necker, **NC** 3520

Maxwell, Mary Elizabeth (Braddon): see Braddon, Mary Elizabeth.

Maxwell, Patrick, 1826–1906, army officer. *Times,* July 17, 1906, p. 8b.

Trans: **NatR-II** 960

Maxwell, Sir Peter Benson, 1817–1893, barrister. Boase.

Cunningham's *London,* **DR** 613

State bishops, 646
Byle's *Sophisms of Free Trade and Popular Political Economy,* 662

Maxwell, William Stirling: see Stirling-Maxwell, William.

Maxwell-Scott, Mary Monica (Hope-Scott): see *Index,* I, 1007.

Barbour's *Legends of the Saints,* **DR** 2059

The Scots Guards in France, **ScotR** 12
The Scots brigade, 50
Life of St. Margaret [Queen of Scotland], 54
The Lennox [family], 84
Winifred, Countess of Nithsdaill, 101
Scottish Catholics under Mary and James, 110
St. Magnus of the Orkneys, 159 collab.
The Chevalier de Feuquerolles, 215

May, Henry

The Bank of England, **FortR** 2292
The London stock exchange, 2379

May, Henry John: see *Index,* I, 1007.

Naval warfare, **NatR-II** 2080

Mayers, William Frederick: see *Index,* I, 1007.

Journey across China in twelfth century, **FM** 4801
The Panthays of Yün-nan, 5363

Mayne, Charles Blair, 1855–1914, army officer. *LCCat., Times,* Nov. 28, 1914, p. 11d.

Church parade in the army, **NatR-II** 2531

Mayo, Thomas, 1790–1871, physician, authority on mental diseases. *DNB.*

Buckle's *History of Civilization,* **FM** 3888
Relations of the public to practice of medicine, 4008
Insanity and its moral preventive, **LR(1829)** 9

Mazzini, Giuseppe: see *Index,* I, 1007.

Dante Allighieri, **FQR** 773

Letter to members of Oecumenical Council, **FortR** 692
Italy and the republic, 760
Renan and France, 1022
The Eastern question, 1352

Mead, Frederick, 1847–1945, barrister. *WWW.*

The accused as a witness, **NC** 2159

Meakin, James Edward Budgett, 1866–1906, historian of the Moors. *DNB.*

The Morocco pirates, **ScotR** 622

Meason, Malcolm Ronald Laing: see *Index,* I, 1007, and *MWT,* 15th ed.

The reorganization of our army, **DR** 1782

Our Indian army, **FM** 5810

Detective police, **NC** 851

Mecredy, Richard James, 1861–1924, cycling enthusiast. *WWW.*

Cycling, **FortR** 3105
Winter cycling, 3157
Cycles and tyres for 1893, 3326

Medhurst, Sir Walter Henry: see *Index,* I, 1007.

The Chinese as colonists, **NC** 222

Medley, George Webb, 1826–1898, trade expert. *Boase.*

The lion's share of the world's trade, **NC** 1282
Fair-trade fog and fallacy, 1374

Medwin, Thomas, 1788–1869, biographer of Shelley, army officer. *DNB.*

The sacrifice, **FM** 1132, 1145
Hazlitt in Switzerland, 1301
Canova, 1366

Meinhold, Johannes Wilhelm, 1797–1851, German poet. *ADB.*

The Convent Witch, **FM** 2502

Meldrum, David Storrar: see *Index,* I, 1008.

The Row'tilly girl, **NatR-II** 1323
The comedy of courtship, 1358

Melegari, Dora: see *Index,* I, 1008, and *EUI.*

A love episode in Mazzini's life, **NC** 2748

Melia, Raphael, naturalized in England, 1849; religious author. *Boase.*

See: **DR** 1241

Melvin, James

Italy as it is, **FortR** 1889

Mendíbil, Pablo, 1788–1832, Spanish émigré, prof. of Spanish literature, King's Coll. London. *Athenaeum,* Jan. 7, 1832, p. 19.

?Castilian poetry, **FM** 206
?*A Year in Spain,* 218
Life of Count Campomanes, 237

Menpes, Mortimer, 1860–1938, artist. *WWW,* Mallet.

Shilito Jessop, artist, **NatR-II** 1594

Menzies, Allan: see *Index,* I ,1008.

The legend of Orendel, **ScotR** 368
The romance of *King Rother,* 406
Spielmann romances—Salman and Morolf, 438

Meredith, George: see *Index,* I, 1008.

Vittoria, in 21 installments from **FortR** 163 to 359
Robert Lytton's poems, 510
Beauchamp's career, in 17 installments from 1079 to 1218
The tragic comedians, 1741, 1750, 1759, 1768, 1777
Diana of the Crossways, 2181, 2194, 2214, 2226, 2240, 2246
Concession to the Celt, 2517
One of our conquerors, in 8 installments from 3006 to 3088
Letter: 2627
Notices: 369, 387, 472, 479, 594

Austrian poets, **FM** 2999
South Germany in the autumn of 1866, 4793

Mrs. Meynell's essays [*Rhythm of Life* and *Colour of Life*], **NatR-II** 1895

The house on the beach, **NQM** 101
Comedy, and the uses of the comic spirit, 106
Case of General Ople and Lady Camper, 119
The tale of Chloe, 182

Meredith, Marie (Vulliamy), 1838/39–1885; 2nd wife of George Meredith. Jack Lindsay, *George Meredith,* 1956, pp. 135, 260–261.

Notice: **FortR** 435

Meredith, Mary Ellen (Peacock) Nicolls, 1821–1861, whose 2nd husband was George Meredith. Peacock, *Works,* I, cix.

Soyer's *Modern Housewife,* **FM** 2883
Gastronomy and civilization, 2915 collab.

Merivale, Herman: see *Index*, I, 1008.

Daru's *History of Brittany*, **FQR** 13
French histories of English revolution [Guizot], 57
Béranger, 280
German military history, sixteenth century, 322
Frederic the Great, 332
?Guizot's *Course of Modern History*, 383

Are the *Paston Letters* authentic? **FortR** 74
The architecture of London, 214
Junius, Francis, and Lord Mansfield in December, 1770, 481
American scenery, 541
The colonial question in 1870, 656
The wanderings of Ulysses, 788

Westward: a grandfather's dream, **FM** 5039, 5051

Merivale, John Herman: see *Index*, I, 1009.

Rey, *Judicial Institutions of England Compared with France*, **FQR** 32
Meyer, *Judicial Institutions of Europe*, 70

Merivale, John Herman, colliery manager. *BMCat.*

Explosions in collieries, **NC** 548

Merivale, Louisa Anne: see *Index*, I, 1009, and II, App. A.

Italian poetry and patriotism, **FM** 4311, 4382

Merle, Gibbons, d.1855, journalist, author. Boase, *BMCat.*

A newspaper editor's reminiscences, **FM** 1383, 1477, 1484, 1577

Merriman, John Xavier, 1841–1926, South African statesman. *DNB.*

Some South African questions, **FortR** 2925

The closer union of the Empire, **NC** 1389

Mervyn, Henry

Lord Malmesbury's *Memoirs*, **NatR-II** 232

Metcalfe, Sir Charles Hubert Theophilus, 1853–1928, civil engineer. *DNB.*

British influence in South Africa, **FortR** 2801 collab.

Metcalfe, Hope Cranstoun, born c.1866, misc. writer. Venn, *BMCat., Yearbook*/1904.

The Carlist cause, **FortR** 4046 collab.

The Carlist policy in Spain, 4173 collab.

"Legitimism" in England, **NC** 3164 collab.

Metcalfe, John Henry, b.1830, of Wensleydale, Yorkshire. *LCCat.*

Rabbit pest in Australia, **NatR-II** 1020

Metcalfe, William, 1870–1950, divine. *Fasti, VII,* 451, and IX, 650.

Modern Greek folk-lore, **ScotR** 558
Greek hymns and hymn-writers, 614
South African crisis, 664
The future in South Africa, 690
Letter: 571
Trans: 513

Metcalfe, William Musham, 1840–1916, ed. *Scot Rev. WWW, LCCat.*

Commentators and the Book of Genesis, **ScotR** 6
Mrs. Carlyle's *Letters* [ed. J. A. Froude], 26
Walt Whitman, 33
Theology of St. Paul, 44
The Eddic poems, 53
Frederick Denison Maurice, 55
The Scottish language, 60
Froude's *Carlyle's Life in London*, 77
Archbishop Hamilton's *Catechism*, 82
Hampole's *Psalter*, 90
Natural Law in the Spiritual World [by Henry Drummond], 97
Laing's *Popular and Romance Poetry of Scotland*, 98
Founding of the Congo Free State, 103
York mystery plays, 108
Records of Argyll, 111
Greville Memoirs, 119
Barbour's *Legends of the Saints*, 128
The Caldwell papers, 130
Burton's *Anatomy of Melancholy*, 140
Spencer's "Unknowable," 157
Thomas of Erceldoune, 168
Charles Darwin, 208
Jamieson's *Dictionary* [*of the Scottish Language*], 222
The romance Robert Bruce related, 225
Principal Tulloch, 231
The romance of Sir Tristrem, 252
The Vikings, 267
Mr. Lecky on Ireland, 308
Lux Mundi [by Charles Gore], 317
A publisher [John Murray], 322
Laurence Oliphant, 328
Norse discovery of America, 335
Corea, 461
?Purcell and Cardinal Manning, 522
Lord Roberts in India, 557

Farthest North [on arctic exploration], 560
Korea and the Koreans, 593
Mr. Gross on Scottish guilds, 604
?Glasgow and its records, 612
Travels in Tibet, 626
Mr. Fielding on Buddhism, 633
?Early struggles for the Indian trade, 640
Mrs. Oliphant's *Autobiography*, 647
Rudyard Kipling's prose, 655
Hudson Bay Company, 672
Yiddish literature, 686
Notices: 188, 320, 404
See: 21

Mew, James: see *Index*, I, 1010.

Macchiavelli's *Mandragola*, **FortR** 3202
The modern Persian stage, 3816

Ausonius, **FM** 6188

The *Persiles* of Cervantes, **NatR-II** 1452

The Hebrew hell, **NC** 1918
The Christian hell, 2119
The Muslim hell, 2181
Gongora, 3117

Meyer, Ludwig von, of Austria.

The Austrian Empire, **Ram** 1067
Present state of Austria, 1073 collab.

Meynell, Alice Christiana Gertrude (Thompson), 1847–1922, poet, essayist. *DNB*.

Symmetry and incident, **FortR** 3569

Meynell, Charles, 1828–1882, philosopher. *DNB*.

Prospects of Catholic philosophy, **Ram** 833
Ideology of St. Thomas, 895
Modern poets, 910
The philosophy of the absolute, 948
Rosmini and Gioberti, 1003
The limits of our thought, 1038
Letter: 991
Notices: 927, 940

Meynell, Wilfrid: see *Index*, I, 1010.

The Life of Cardinal Manning, **NC** 2883
Gladstone and the Roman Catholic Church, 3313

Meyrick, Frederick: see *Index*, I, 1010.

Letter: **Ram** 712

Meysey-Thompson, Henry Meysey, 1st Baron Knaresborough, 1845–1929, M.P. Burke.

Letter: **NatR-II** 2366

Real grievances of the Uitlanders, **NC** 3247

Meysey-Thompson, Richard Frederick, 1847–1926, army officer. *WWW*.

Ethics of horse-racing, **NatR-II** 2312

Michel, Francisque, 1809–1887, French scholar. *Grand Larousse*.

Letter: **FQR** 398

Michalowitz, later **Michelsen,** Edward Henry, 1795–1870, prof. of literature. R.L.F., Boase, and *BMCat.* under Michelsen.

Pozzo di Borgo, **DR** 74
Mehemet Ali, 92

Philosophy of Kant, **FQR** 550

Michie, Alexander: see *Index*, I, 1010.

Our future policy in China, **NatR-II** 2178
Persons and politics in Peking, 2230

Li Hung Chang, **NC** 2973

Michie, Sir Archibald, 1810–1899, barrister. *WWW*.

Colonial and Indian custom-houses, **FM** 6056

Middleton, George Alexander Thomas, architect. *BMCat.*

Deception in ancient buildings, **NC** 3086

Midhat Pasha, 1822–1884, Turkish statesman. *Ency. Brit.*, 11th ed.

Past, present, and future of Turkey, **NC** 179

Mijatovics, Countess Elodie (Lawton), d.1908, writer on Serbian folk songs. *BMCat.*, *Times*, Dec. 14, 1908, p. 13d, under Mijatovich.

Panslavism: its rise and decline, **FortR** 970

Milbank, Harry Vane

Letter: **NatR-II** 1131

Milbanke, Ralph Gordon Noel, 13th Baron Wentworth, 1839–1906. Burke.

The Settled Land Bill, **FortR** 1694

Milburn, James Booth, 1860–1923, ed. the *Tablet*. *WWW*.

The Ecclesiastical Titles Bill, **DR** 2503

Milburn, James Booth (*continued*)
The Church and the universities, 2631, 2667
Mediaeval grammar schools, 2683
Notices: 2347, 2358, 2373, 2400, 2425, 2438, 2475, 2497

Mildmay, Henry; perhaps Sir Henry Carew St. John Mildmay, 1787/88–1848, in Foster; possibly a pseudonym.

Some passages in the life of an idler, **FM** 151, 201, 273, 489
A glance at Russia in 1835, 903

Miley, John, 1805?–1861, R.C. priest, ecclesiastical historian. *DNB.*

Gibbon: his Protestant editors, **DR** 167

Milford

Notice: **FQR** 353

Mill, John Stuart: see *Index*, I, 1011.

Endowments, **FortR** 578
Thornton on labour and its claims, 586, 598
Leslie on the land question, 686
Treaty obligations, 741
Maine, on *Village Communities,* 778
Berkeley's life and writings, 817
Grote's *Aristotle,* 915
Chapters on socialism, 1550, 1559, 1568
Letters to Professor Nichol, 3952
Notices: 702, 937

The Negro question, **FM** 2677
Recent writers on reform, 3845
A few words on non-intervention, 3925
Utilitarianism, 4146, 4155, 4165
The contest in America, 4192

Millar, Alexander Hastie: see *Index*, I, 1011.

Wedding-tour of James VI in Norway, **ScotR** 389
A Scottish merchant of the sixteenth century, 419
Sir Walter Scott, 435
John Stuart Blackie, 506
The Annandale Family Book, 535
Pickle the Spy [by Andrew Lang], 555
Hanoverian letters before Culloden, 590
The *Wedderburn Book,* 656
Recent Scottish historians, 683

Miller, Edward, 1825–1901, divine. Foster, *LCCat.*

Confessions of a village tyrant, **NC** 2494

Miller, Mrs. Florence Fenwick, 1854–1935, physiologist; wife of Frederick A. Ford but retained her maiden name. *WWW.*

William Ellis as an educationist, **FM** 6487

Insect communists, **NatR-II** 1003

Miller, William, 1795–1861, general in Peruvian army. *DNB.*

Peruvian empire previous to Spaniards, **FM** 1955

Miller, William Galbraith, 1848–1904, advocate. H. C. Miller, *William Galbraith Miller* (Glasgow, 1904), pp. 5, 19, 38.

Anglicizing of the Scottish universities, **ScotR** 209

Millet, Francis Davis, 1846–1912, painter, traveller. *WWW.*

The new Bulgaria, **NQM** 153

Millican, Kenneth William, 1853–1915, surgeon. *Surgeon Index*/3rd s.

The medical schism, **NC** 1518

Milligan, William: see *Index*, I, 1012.

Wyclif and the Bible, **FortR** 2324

Millin, George Francis: see *Index*, I, 1012.

Recreant leaders, **FortR** 4219
Old age pensions made easy, 4252

Millington, F. A.

Conservative papers among poor, **NatR-II** 661
Arnold Forster's scheme for Ireland, 674
Danger of a protectionist agitation, 734
Midnight drinking in London, 830
A tax on Christian names, 874

Mills, Alexius J. Felix, R.C. priest of London. *Irish Monthly,* 21 (1893), 216.

The Gordon Riots, **DR** 1430, 1436
Letter: 1263

Mills, Arthur: see *Index*, I, 1012.

Imperial Federation League, **FortR** 2287
Is the House of Lords worth preserving? 2487

Blues and buffs [Whigs and Tories], **FM** 6279, 6288, 6298, 6301

The Suez Canal, **NatR-II** 53

The London School Board, 388
The labour question, 1268

Representative government in the colonies, NC 481

Mills, Lawrence Heyworth, 1837–1918, prof. of Zend Philology at Oxford. *LCCat., WWW.*

Zoroaster and the Bible, NC 2505

Milman, Angelina Frances, called Lena, d.1914, translator, daughter of Gen. Sir George Bryan Milman and wife of Edward A. W. Clarke. Burke.

Trans: **FortR** 3528, 3532

Milman, Henry Hart: see *Index*, I, 1012.

Clerical Subscription Commission, **FM** 4521

Milne, Arthur Dawson, 1867–1932, surgeon, served in Africa. *WWW.*

Life on the Nile south of Fashoda, NC 3517

Milne, James: see *Index*, I, 1013.

Consult Sir George Grey! **FortR** 4460

Milner, Lady Violet Georgina (Maxse), Viscountess Milner, 1871/72–1958. *WWW, Times*, Oct. 11, 1958, p. 8.

An English master [Hubert Parry], **NatR-II** 1535

Milnes, Richard Monckton: see *Index*, I, 1013.

Swinburne's *Chastelard*, **FortR** 224
The House of Lords, 829
Swinburne's "Bothwell," 1067
Lord Melbourne, 1436
Phenomena of the imagination, 1542
Samuel Wilberforce, Bishop of Oxford, 1674
Notes on *Endymion* [by Disraeli], 1765
Alexander von Humboldt at Berlin, **FM** 4037
See: 25

Minardi, Tommaso, 1787–1871, Italian painter, writer on art. *DEI.*

The Christmas of Christian art, **Ram** 974

Minto, William: see *Index*, I, 1014.

Mrs. Gaskell's novels, **FortR** 1504
The Letters of Charles Dickens, 1650

Edgar Allan Poe, 1713
Foes in council, 1925

Contesting the counties, **FM** 6276

"Saddling the Right Horse" [on the Eastern question], **NC** 265
John Donne, 444
Wordsworth's great failure, 1762
Why I voted for Gladstone, 2263
Notice: 487

Mitchell, Edmund, 1861–1917, novelist. *WWW.*

The Chinaman abroad, **NC** 2650

Mitchell, John, 1785–1859, army officer. *DNB.*

On military promotion, **FM** 603
On manners, fashion, and things in general, 717, 729, 846, 1176, 1285, 1351, 1428, 1516, 1656, 1841, 1940
Bombardinio in Italy, 864
Bombardinio at Rome, 875
On manners, war, and Prince Pückler Muskau, 893
Affectation—male and female, 1002
Tableaux of the most eminent soldiers of the eighteenth century, 1464, 1529, 1538, 1557, 1563
Schulenberg, Max Emmanuel, and Charles XII, 1464
Prince Eugene, 1529
The Duke of Marlborough, 1538
Marshal Saxe, 1557
Frederick II, 1563
Military tableaux; or, Scenes from the wars of Napoleon, 1884, 1896, 1914, 1931, 1967, 1999
Principal campaigns of Napoleon, in 11 installments from 2146 to 2256
See: 1852

Mitchell, William, treasurer of Scottish Home Rule Assoc. *Westminster Rev.*, 133 (1890), 57.

Scotland and home rule, **ScotR** 207
Letter: 280

Mitford, Algernon Bertram Freeman: see *Index*, I, 1014.

A ride through Yedo, **FortR** 677
Tales of old Japan, 688, 704

The Tower of London, **NC** 728

Mitford, John Thomas Freeman: see *Index*, I, 1014.

Reasons for doubt in the Church of Rome, **NC** 386, 422

Mivart, St. George Jackson: see *Index*, I, 1014.

Church architecture, **DR** 1461
Spencer's *Psychology*, in 9 installments from 1487 to 1715
Liberty of conscience, 1572
Catholic politics, 1875
The conversion of England, 1923
Weismann's hypotheses [about heredity], 2189
Darwinism, 2202
Herbert Spencer on justice, 2296
Science in fetters, 2472, 2486
Letters: 1551, 1573, 1936, 2089
Notice: 2199

The assumptions of agnostics, **FortR** 957
Organic nature's riddle, 2285, 2301
The rights of reason, 2410
An explanation, 2450
Hermann Lotze, 2653
Denominational science, 3698
Life from the lost Atlantis, 3807
Recent Catholic apologists, 4389
Letter: 3716

National education, **NatR-II** 62

Force, energy and will, **NC** 175
The meaning of life, 286
The government of life, 299
A limit to evolution, 1028
Modern Catholics and scientific freedom, 1155
A visit to some Austrian monasteries, 1318
Catholic Church and biblical criticism, 1425
Catholicity and reason, 1496
Sins of belief and unbelief, 1608
Happiness in hell, 2320, 2355, 2382
Evolution in Huxley, 2436
Christianity and Roman paganism, 2485
The *Index* and my articles on hell, 2496
Spencer versus Balfour, 2795
The burial service, 3050
Reminiscences of Thomas Henry Huxley, 3215
Catholic's view of *Helbeck of Bannisdale*, 3362
The new psychology, 3421
What church has "continuity?" 3510
The continuity of Catholicism, 3588
Scripture and Roman Catholicism, 3620

Mockler-Ferryman, Augustus Ferryman: see *Index*, I, 1015.

See: **FortR** 3734

Moeller, Jean, 1806–1862, prof. at the Catho-

lic Univ. of Louvain. *Louvain Bibliog.*, pp. 161–163.

The Archbishop of Cologne, **DR** 82
Wallenstein, 102

Moffat, John Smith: see *Index*, I, 1015.

The future of South Africa, **NC** 3661

Moffat, Robert Scott, 1843–1895, economist. *LCCat.*

On national unity, **NatR-II** 39
Competition and industrial organization, 342
Realism *v.* Idealism, 512
Our food supply, 866
Criminal members of Parliament, 931
Procedure in parliament, 1221
Reference library of the British Museum, 1397
Letter: 332

Mohnike, Gottlieb Christian Friedrich, 1781–1841, theologian, literary historian. *ADB.*

The Gutenberg jubilee in Germany, **FQR** 589
Notice: 600

Mohsin-ul-Mulk, Nawab (Syed Maulvi Mehdi Ali), 1837–1907, reform leader of Indian Muslims. *WWW.*

Attack on Native States of India, **NC** 1770

Moir, David Macbeth: see *Index*, I, 1015.

The wounded spirit, **FM** 46, 74, 130
?The Asiatic cholera, 323
Letters to the learned professions, 362
?The contagious character of cholera, 433
Horae sinicae, 701 collab., 728?, 816 collab., 1173 collab.
Occult science, 1453
See: 380

Moir, George: see *Index*, I, 1015, and II, App. A.

Italian tragedy [on Manzoni], **FQR** 5
Ernest Schultze, 14
Manzoni, *The Betrothed*, 22
Wieland, 41
Wallenstein [by Schiller], 106
Daemonology and witchcraft, 134
Modern French tragedy: Hugo's *Hernani*, 151
Correspondence of Schiller and Goethe, 164
German pocket books for 1831, 167

German manners in the 16th century, 172
Danish drama: Oehlenschläger, 184
German criminal trials, 196
French drama [de Vigny, Hugo], 208
French literature [Hugo Balzac], 220
Minor French theatre: Scribe and his co-adjutors, 226
The German ultra-liberal press: Börne and Heine, 237
Present state of French literature, 263
Pellico's memoirs of his captivity, 276
Menzel's *Tour in Austria*, 289
Pellico's *Tragedies*, 296
Notices: 103, 194, 215, 229, 241, 254

Molden, Berthold. *BMCat.*

Papacy: Hungary and the Vatican, **FortR** 3663

Molesworth, Sir Guilford Lindsey, 1828–1925, engineer. *WWW.*

Political economy: strikes, **NatR-II** 957

Molesworth, William Nassau, 1816–1890, historian. *DNB.*

The reform question, 1832 to 1848, **FortR** 388
The reform question, 1848–1866, 412

Momerie, Alfred Williams: see *Index*, I, 1016.

Religion: its future, **FortR** 3306

Monckton, Miss; niece of William Monckton, 2nd Viscount Galway. See *FM* no. 419.

Recollections of Madame du Barri, **FM** 419
Recollections of Monsieur de Calonne, 460

Moncreiff, Henry James: see *Index*, I, 1016.

The "Affair Simpson," **FM** 6354

Moncreiff, James, 1811–1895: see *Index*, I, 1016, and II, App. A.

A visit to my discontented cousin, **FM** 4968, 4978, 4987, 4997, 5006

Money-Coutts, Francis Burdett Thomas, 5th Baron Latymer, 1852–1942, poet, barrister. Venn, Burke.

Letter: **NatR-II** 212

Monier-Williams, Sir Monier: see *Index*, I, 1016.

The religion of Zoroaster, **NC** 544
The Pārsīs, 566
Muhammad and his teaching, 740

Monk, John, capt. in Royal Marines. *BMCat.* and *Army List*/27.

Paixhans' *New Maritime Force, Artillery,* **FQR** 46

Monkhouse, William Cosmo, 1840–1901, poet, critic. *DNB.*

The worship of the ugly, **NatR-II** 1849

Monroe, James, 1758–1831, president of the United States. *DAB.*

See: **FortR** 4167

Monsell, William: see *Index*, I, 1016.

Catholic intermediate education, **DR** 1542

Catholic policy, **Ram** 1084

Montagu, John Scott: see Douglas-Scott-Montagu, J. W. E.

Montagu, Samuel, 1st Baron Swaything, 1832–1911, banker, M.P. *DNB.*

Dangers of modern finance, **FortR** 3185
Silver and Indian finance, 3279

Montagu, Walter, 1603?–1677, abbot, almoner to Henrietta Maria. *DNB.*

See: **Ram** 911

Montagu, William Drogo, 7th Duke of Manchester, 1823–1890. Burke.

Letters: **NatR-II** 107, 853

Isolated free trade, **NC** 611

Montague, William Edward: see *Index*, I, 1016.

Bourbon [island near Mauritius], **FM** 6140
Mauritius, 6151, 6165

Montalembert, Charles Forbes René, Comte de: see *Index*, I, 1017.

Letter: **DR** 351

Montefiore, Leonard Abraham, 1853/54–1879. Foster, *BMCat.*

Heine in relation to religion and politics, **FortR** 1391

Liberty in Germany, **NC** 205, 234, 272
Alsace-Lorraine since 1871, 371

Monteith, Robert Joseph Ignatius, 1812–1884, of Carstairs, businessman. Venn.

Our martyrs of the 16th century, **Ram** 991

Montgomery, George, 1818–1871, R.C. priest.
Newman, *L&D*, XI, index.

The *Dublin Review* and the converts, **Ram**
835

Montgomery, Hugh de Fellenberg: see *Index*,
I, 1017.

Organization of real credit, **NatR-II** 1346
A Unionist policy for Ireland, 1796
Spoliation of Irish landlords, 2018
Letter: 1678

Montgomery, J. T., university extension official.

"Classes, masses" at Oxford, **NatR-II** 775

Montgomery, Jessie Douglas, misc. writer.
BMCat.

Macbeth, considered as a Celt, **NatR-II** 845

Montrésor, C. A., misc. writer. *BMCat.*

Madame de Maintenon of Wurtemberg,
NatR-II 855

Moon, Sir Ernest Robert: see *Index*, I, 1017.

Railway traffic and charges, **NC** 1279

Moore, Edward: see *Index*, I, 1017.

Dante as a religious teacher, **FortR** 3991,
4048

Moore, George Augustus, 1852–1933, Irish
novelist. *DNB.*

Turgueneff, **FortR** 2680
Some of Balzac's minor pieces, 2876
Our dramatists and their literature, 2884
Meissonier and the Salon Julian, 2967
New pictures in the National Gallery, 3004
The Royal Academy, 3225
La Débâcle [by Zola], 3247
Preface to *The Bending of the Bough*, 4413

Moore, Harold Edward: see *Index*, I, 1017,
and *BMCat.*

How to multiply small holdings, **NC** 2678

Moore, Henry Charles, 1862–1933, journalist.
WWW.

Burmese traits, **FortR** 3284

Moore, John Bassett, 1860–1947, American
lawyer and undersec. of state. *Amer.
WWW.*

The United States and Great Britain, **NatR-
II** 1873

Moore, Julian. *BMCat.*

Book collecting as a fine art. **FortR** 3718
Lost principle of beauty in architecture,
4375

Moore, Niven, 1794/95–1889, diplomat in
the Near East, in Boase; *Times*, Feb. 19,
1889, p. 9.

Turkey and Russia, **FQR** 65

Moore, Sir William Harrison: see *Index*, I,
1017.

Constitution making, Australia, **NatR-II**
2152

Moorhouse, James, 1826–1915, Anglican
bishop of Melbourne. *DNB.*

The morality of vivisection, **NC** 2327

Moran, Patrick Francis, 1830–1911, R.C.
churchman. *DNB.*

Evidences of St. Peter from the catacombs,
DR 868
The letters of St. Ignatius, 881
Monuments of the catacombs, 898
Syriac letters of St. Clement, 912
The birthplace of St. Patrick, 1725
Catholics of Ireland one hundred years ago,
1808

Morant, Lilian Caroline, wife of Percy S.
Ricketts. *Landed Gentry*, under Morant.

The vulgarising of Oberammergau, **NC**
3754

Moreing, Charles Algernon, *BMCat., WWW/
1940*, under his son Adrian Charles
Moreing.

Great Britain's opportunity in China, **NC**
3248
A recent business tour in China, 3342
An all-British railway to China, 3534

Moreton, Henry John, 3rd Earl Ducie, 1827–
1921, M.P. Burke.

Expedition of Philip II to England, **FortR**
1580

An episode of the Armada, **NC** 1180

Morgan, Conwy Lloyd, 1852–1936, psychologist, philosopher. *DNB.*

Limits of animal intelligence, **FortR** 3398

The morality of animals, **NatR-II** 1213

Morgan, Edward Strachan, writer on Italy. *BMCat.*

Secret societies in the Two Sicilies, **FortR** 2650

Rome and malaria, **NatR-II** 669
Monti di Pietà, 801
The Roman family, 871
Italy as a field for emigration, 1161

Morgan, Frank Alton, writer on fruit-growing. *RG.*

The fruit-growing revival, **NC** 1634

Morgan, Sir George Osborne: see *Index*, I, 1018.

Land law reform, **FortR** 1647

Disestablishment in Wales, **NC** 1205
Well-meant nonsense about emigration, 1397
"The House was still sitting when we went to press," 1432
The progress of Welsh disestablishment, 2026

Morgan, Henry George, b.1851/52, divine. Foster, *CCD*/1934.

The clergy and politics, **NatR-II** 366
Retiring pensions for the clergy, 699
Thoughts for defenders of the Church, 1445

Morgan-Richardson, C.: see Richardson, Morgan C.

Morison, James Augustus Cotter: see *Index*, I, 1018.

The significance of ritualism, **FortR** 365
Religious utopias in United States, 381
Ireland for the British, 470
St. Bernard of Clairvaux, 834
Abortiveness of French revolutions, 965
The reign of Louis XIV, 1031, 1042
Is a republic possible in France? 1063
Isaac Casaubon [by Mark Pattison], 1146
Madame de Maintenon, 1251, 1260
Carlyle's *Reminiscences,* 1790
Scientific v. bucolic vivisection, 2278
Notices: 151, 379, 464, 504, 540

Morison, Sir Theodore, 1863–1936, educator. *WWW.*

Sir Syed Ahmad Khan Bahadur, **NatR-II** 2174
A Muhamadan university, 2217

Morland, William Courtenay, 1818–1909, barrister. *Landed Gentry, M at B.*

Letter: **NatR-II** 184

Morley, Sir George, 1873–1942, politician. *WWW.*

The revolt of Strephon, **NatR-II** 1150

Morley, Henry: see *Index*, I, 1018.

Fiedler's *Journey through Greece,* **FQR** 607

Three old Yorkshire poems, **FortR** 473
Palingenesis, 535
Spenser's "Hobbinol," 570
Pictures at the Royal Academy, 870
Notices: 472, 553

?Tea table literature [Tupper's works], **FM** 3021
Conrad Gesner, 3049
Anatomy in long clothes, 3153
Cyrano de Bergerac, 3325

Notices: **NC** 70, 108, 143, 223

Morley, John: see *Index*, I, 1018.

England and the annexation of Mysore, **FortR** 316
France in the seventeenth century, 362
Causeries, 367, 378
Public affairs, in 8 installments from 368 to 434 (all ? except no. 405)
Edmund Burke, 370, 382, 390, 420
Young England and the political future, 394
England and the European crisis, 404
Froude on science of history, 433
Anonymous journalism, 438
The Liberal programme, 442
The genesis of morals, 487
Joseph de Maistre, 497, 505, 539
The political prelude, 519
Old parties and new policy, 532
The chamber of mediocrity [Commons], 552
On *The Ring and the Book,* 574
Lecky's first chapter [of *History of European Morals*], 587
Condorcet, 647, 655
Letter to some ladies, 669
Vauvenargues, 672
Carlyle, 694
Fortnightly Review and positivism, 701
The life of Turgot, 706
France and Germany, 718
England and the [Franco-Prussian] War, 725
A note to Colonel Chesney's letter, 733
Byron, 737

Morley, John (*continued*)

Two discourses [by Turgot] at the Sorbonne, 805
Voltaire at Berlin, 814
Irish policy in the eighteenth century, 842
Rousseau's influence on European thought, 860
Rousseau at Les Charmettes, 889
Rousseau and Theresa Le Vasseur, 897
Rousseau in Paris, 904
The *New Heloïsa*, 911
The five gas-stokers, 920
Pater's essays [on the Renaissance], 942
The death of J. S. Mill, 954
The struggle for national education, 973, 982, 989
Mill's doctrine of liberty, 978
Mill's *Autobiography*, 1013
M. Victor Hugo's new romance [*Quatre-vingt-treize*], 1034
On compromise, 1038, 1055, 1069, 1078
Mr. Flint's *Philosophy of History*, 1084
A recent work on supernatural religion [by W. R. Cassels], 1092
Mill's three essays on religion, 1099, 1118
Diderot, 1121, 1143, 1155, 1191, 1208
The Liberal eclipse, 1130
A day at Sedan, 1168
Home and foreign affairs, in 80 installments from 1227 to 1957
Taine's new work [*l'Ancien Régime*], 1238
Macaulay, 1245
Some recent travels, 1259
Robespierre, 1280, 1289
On popular culture, 1306
A new work on Russia, 1334
An address to some miners, 1343
Turgot in Limousin, 1361
Three books of the eighteenth century, 1388, 1413
Memorials of a man of letters [Macvey Napier], 1459
Diderot at Saint Petersburg, 1470
Lancashire, 1483
A political epilogue, 1502
An economic address, 1516
The impoverishment of India not proven, 1535
The plain story of the Zulu War, 1557
Further remarks on Zulu affairs, 1570
French Republic and the Catholic Church, 1577
The House of Commons, 1609
A word with some critics, 1633
England and Ireland, 1788
Cobden's first pamphlets, 1804
The policy of commercial treaties, 1815
Conciliation with Ireland, 1817
The Journals of Caroline Fox, 1877
The Life of James Mill [by Alexander Bain], 1902

Egyptian policy, 1930
Valedictory, 1956
The Radical programme: religious equality, 2165
Maine, *Popular Government*, 2418
Notes: 1029, 1530, 1661, 4083?
Notices: 369, 379, 387, 396, 406, 415, 425, 435, 443, 456, 479, 488, 496, 504, 513, 526, 547, 602, 858, 1536
Trans: 691, 936

Irish revolution and English liberalism, **NC** 778
The government of Ireland, 1357, 1376
French revolutionary models, 1532
A New Calendar of Great Men [by Comte], 2169
Matthew Arnold, 2857
Lecky on democracy, 2923
Arbitration with America, 2979
Guicciardini, 3204
Notices: 1661, 1750

Moroji, Nana

Letter: **NatR-II** 1078

Morris, James, of Catholic Collegiate School, London, brother of bishop William P. Morris. Bagshawe, and Morris to Bagshawe, Apr. 14 [1851], Bagshawe Papers.

The government criminal returns, **DR** 584

Morris, John, S.J., 1826–1893, sec. to Cardinal Wiseman. *DNB.*

Darwin, *On the Origin of Species*, **DR** 947
The English Poor Law and Catholic poor, 955
St. Thomas and Battle Abbey, 965
Popular education in England, 983
Gladstone on the Elizabethan settlement, 2133
Gladstone and Blessed John Fisher, 2207
Jesuits and seculars in reign of Elizabeth, 2213
Probability and faith, 2352
Notices: 964, 971
See: 953, 1046

Proposal for a priest's portfolio, **Ram** 330
Letter: 1019

Morris, John Brande: see *Index*, I, 1019.

Vindication of Tridentine Canon of Scripture, **DR** 426
Forbearance towards some not yet converted, 434
Faith of Catholics: Waterworth, 438
Christian use of Psalms of David, 467
Letter: ?1190

Dr. Dixon's *Introduction to the Bible*, **Ram** 516
Theologia male ferrata, 806
Notices: 560, 1005
See: 541

Morris, Sir Lewis: see *Index*, I, 1019.

An olive branch from America, **NC** 1474

Morris, Sir Malcolm Alexander, 1849–1924, surgeon. *WWW, LCCat.*

The prevention of consumption, **FortR** 4163

The superfluous vaccination commission, **NC** 3042

The progress of medicine, 3112

Morris, Hon. Martin Henry FitzPatrick, 2nd Baron Killanin, 1867–1927. Burke.

At sea, **NC** 2986
The philosophy of poetry, 3536

Morris, Mowbray Walter: see *Index*, I, 1019.

Charles Dickens, **FortR** 1975

Morris, William, 1834–1896, poet. *DNB.*

The saga of Gunnlaug and Rafn, **FortR** 555 collab.
The revival of architecture, 2707
The revival of handicraft, 2766

Westminster Abbey and its monuments, **NC** 1678

The story of the unknown church, **OxCam** 4
The churches of North France, 12
A dream, 17
Men and Women [by Browning], 19
Frank's sealed letter, 25
Ruskin and the *Quarterly*, 36 collab.
Gertha's lovers, 39, 47
"Death the avenger" and "Death the friend," 44
Svend and his brethren, 46
Lindenborg pool, 49
The hollow land, 53, 57
Golden wings, 64
See: 13

Morris, William Bullen, R.C. priest at Brompton Oratory. *CD/69.*

The Apostle of Ireland and his critics, **DR** 1739
St. Martin and St. Patrick, 1851
Edmund Burke and the Revolution, 2723

Morris, William O'Connor: see *Index*, I, 1019.

Lord Cornwallis, **BentQR** 12

The Digest of the Law Commission, **FortR** 512
The Irish Land Bill, 675
The Civil Code of New York, 714
Home Rule, 830
The Irish Domesday Book, 1290
The landed system of Ireland, 3761
Irish Land Bill of Lord Salisbury, 3814
Financial relations: Gt. Britain and Ireland, 3946
Captain Mahan's *Nelson*, 3971
Irish Local Government Bill, 4116
Report of Commission [on Irish land acts], 4201
Wellington [by Herbert Maxwell], 4404
Contemporary Ireland, 4499

The census of Ireland, **FM** 4137
Irish History and Irish Character [by Goldwin Smith], 4164
The marriage law of the Empire, 4176
Irish policy of Disraeli, 4887

Military lessons of the War of 1870, **NQM** 91

Local government in Ireland, **ScotR** 339
Reminiscences of Marshal Macdonald, 366
Marshal Macmahon, 428
Moltke, 448
Wolseley's *Life of Marlborough*, 455
The Commonwealth and Protectorate, 480
Princes of the House of Condé, 518
Land system of Ireland, 546
Financial relations of Great Britain and Ireland, 562
The Life of Nelson [by A. T. Mahan], 567
Gardiner's *Commonwealth and Protectorate*, 595
Local government in Ireland, 607
Prince Bismarck, 619
Sir Robert Peel, 629
Roundell Earl of Selborne, 642

Morrison, Robert, 1782–1834, missionary to China. *DNB.*

Horae Sinicae, **FM** 701 collab.

Morrison, William Douglas, 1852–1943, prison chaplain. *WWW.*

Are our prisons a failure? **FortR** 3485
Prison reform: prisons and prisoners, 4119

The increase of crime, **NC** 2228

Morrow, Forbes St. John, 1860–1949, barrister, politician. *WWW.* (See *Index*, I, 1020.)

Redistribution bill, **FortR** 4329

Irish revolutionary movement, **NatR-II** 2253

Morse, John Torrey, Jr., 1840–1937, lawyer, biographer. *Amer.WWW*.

The ballot in the U.S., **FM** 5064

Morten, Violet Honnor, 1861–1913, wrote on nursing. *Times,* July 15, 1913, p. 11c.

Hospital chaos, **NatR-II** 2396

Mortimer-Granville, Joseph: see Granville, Joseph Mortimer.

Morton, William; perhaps man of this name, b.1834/35, divine, in Foster and *CCD/* 76.

Moral aspects of political economy, **FM** 5981

Morton, William Kinniburgh. Scottish solicitor. *BMCat., Blackwood Papers Cat.*

The Crofters Act in Shetland, **ScotR** 299

Moseley, Henry Nottidge, 1844–1891, naturalist. *DNB*.

Francis Maitland Balfour, **FortR** 1961

Mosenthal, Henry de

The inventor of dynamite [Alfred Nobel], **NC** 3356

Moss, Frederick James, b.1864, schoolmaster in India. Venn.

A South Sea island and its people [the Maoris], **FortR** 3442

Moss, Hezekiah

Illustrations of national customs, **FM** 1941

Motais, Alexandre, 1837–1886, abbé of Rennes, scientist. *EUI*.

Plato's *Atlantis* and the *Periplus* [of Hanno], **DR** 2025

Mott, Albert Julius, misc. writer. *BMCat*.

Alcohol and total abstinence, **NatR-II** 165
The resources of Ireland, 493
English farms and the price of food, 656
English farms and cost of increased production, 802
The fruit-growing folly, 821
[Wallace's] *Darwinism,* 974

Moule, Horace Mosley: see *Index,* I, 1020.

?Henry Taylor's *Plays and Poems, FM* 4956
The story of Alcestis, 5254

Moulton, Sir John Fletcher: see *Index,* I, 1020.

Old-age pensions, **FortR** 3196
The political outlook, 3252
What Gladstone ought to do, 3329

Moulton, Louise (Chandler), 1835–1908, American poet, novelist. *Amer.WWW*.

Letter: **FortR** 2655

Mourey, Gabriel, 1865–1943, French critic. *Grand Larousse*.

Joris Karl Huysmans, **FortR** 3932
On recent poetry in France, 4028

Moxly, Joseph Henry Sutton, died c.1909, divine. *BMCat.,* disappears from *CCD* after 1909; called "the late" in 1911 ed. of his *Theory of Tides*.

Witness of the monuments, **NatR-II** 1445

Moyes, James, 1851–1927, R.C. canon, ed. *Dublin Rev.,* 1892–1903. *New Catholic Dictionary,* N.Y., 1929.

The claim for Home Rule, **DR** 2015
Papal jubilee: early English pilgrimages, 2374
Notes on social science, 2384
Warham, an English primate of the Reformation, 2434
"Bidding the bedes," 2446
Papal jurisdiction in medieval England, 2458
The rosary, 2460
Synodal sermon in days of Queen Mary, 2556
How English Catholics prayed in fourteenth century, 2650
Nova et vetera, 2662
Lord Halifax and neo-Anglicanism, 2664
Note: 2400
Notices: 2079, 2131, 2211, 2280, 2347, 2373, 2412, 2425, 2448, 2638, 2663, 2674

Mozley, Anne: see *Index,* I, 1021.

Novels by Edward Bulwer Lytton, **BentQR** 3
Adam Bede and recent novels, 14
Tennyson, *Idylls of the King,* 25
George Sand, 32

Mozley, James Bowling: see *Index,* I, 1021.

Indian conversion, **BentQR** 6

Mozoomdar, Protap Chunder, 1840–1905, Indian journalist. Buckland under Mozumdar, Pratap Chandra, and Hyamson.

Present day progress in India, **NC** 3766

Mudford, William: see *Index,* I, 1021.

Felix Binocular, a legal sketch, **FM** 221

Mudie, Robert, 1777–1842, misc. writer.
DNB.

?Fishes and fishing, **DR** 32

Muhammad 'Abd al-Halīm Pasha, Prince of
Egypt, 1831–1894, governor general of
Sudan. Hill.

Egypt and the Soudan, **NC** 1127
A reply to my critics, 1188

Muir, Matthew Moncrieff Pattison, 1848–
1931, chemist. *WWW.*

Residual phenomena, **FM** 6163

Muir, Sir William, 1819–1905, Indian administrator, principal of Edin. Univ.
DNB.

The Sources of Islam, **NC** 3767

Muirhead, John Henry: see *Index,* I, 1021.

Professor William Wallace, **FortR** 3954
What imperialism means, 4487

Mulhall, Marion (Murphy): see *Index,* I,
1022.

Celtic sources of the *Divina Commedia,*
DR 2551
Hiberno-Danish predecessors of Columbus,
2608

Müller, Friedrich Maximilian: see Max Müller, Friedrich.

Mulligan, J. J., of Nottingham.

St. Joseph and Mr. Pugin, **Ram** 330

Mullinger, James Bass: see *Index,* I, 1022.

The multiplication of universities, **FM** 6091

Mulock, Dinah Maria: see *Index,* I, 1022.

Hyas the Athenian, **FM** 2471
The self-seer, 2545, 2552, 2565
Alwyn's first wife, 3306, 3317
The double house, 3501
Last House in C—— Street, 3522
On living in perspective, 4695

Merely players [on theatre and morality],
NC 1321

Munby, Arthur Joseph, 1828–1910, poet, barrister. *DNB.*

?Primogeniture, **FM** 5154

Munro, James, 1832–1908, premier of Victoria, Australia. *DNB.*

Red-deer shooting, **NatR-II** 781

Munro, John, 1848/49–1930, prof. of engineering, Bristol Univ. *WWW, Times,*
March 16, 1931, p. 8a.

New sources of electric power [peat], **NC**
2675

Munro, Robert, 1835–1920, physician, anthropologist. *WWW.*

Prehistoric trepanning, **FortR** 3324

Munro, Robert, 1853–1919, divine. *Fasti—
Free Church.*

The founder of modern pessimism [Scho-
penhauer], **ScotR** 203

Murphy, Dominick, 1809–1875, of St. Pat-
rick's, Cork. *Irish CD/*1876, letter to this
Index from the librarian, Univ. Coll.
Cork.

Etruria-Celtica, **DR** 294
Ursuline and Presentation Orders [of nuns],
309
Nestorian Christians of Kurdistan, 323
Scriptural difficulties of geology, 331
Irish language and literature, 336
Scenes in Rome: Becker's *Gallus,* 344
The Christians of Abyssinia, 346
Chateaubriand's *Life of De Rancé,* 355
Maronites and Druses [in Syria], 366
Ripa's *Residence at Peking,* 368
Faber's *Sir Lancelot,* 375
Prichard's *Natural History of Man,* 383
The Reformation in Sweden, 389
Rome, ancient and modern, 408
Irish eloquence: Curran, 412
Benedictines of St. Maur: Mabillon, 430
Temples and tombs of Egypt and Palestine,
437
Order of Mercy and its foundress, 444
Walsh's *Popular Irish Songs,* 456
Fortune's *Wanderings in China,* 468
Early Jesuit missions in North America,
470
Dr. Channing, 529
Curzon's *Visits to the Levant,* 548
Authorship of the *Imitation of Christ,* 572
Life and death of Oliver Plunkett, 596
Essays of an Octogenarian: James Roche,
636
Notices: 373, 391, 422
See: 274

Murphy, James, R.C. priest. Russell, "Early Reviewers," p. 216.

    Legends of St. Patrick [by Aubrey De Vere], **DR** 1411

Murphy, Jeremiah, d.1915, chancellor of diocese of Cloyne. *Irish CD/1916.*

    Mivart on faith and science, **DR** 2115

    The case of Galileo, **NC** 1276

Murphy, Joseph John: see *Index,* I, 1023.

    Letter: **NatR-II** 617

Murray, Alexander Stuart: see *Index,* I, 1023.

    Cyprus and Mycaenae, **NC** 264
    The sculptures of Olympia, 531
    Exploration in Greece, 760

Murray, Arthur Mordaunt, 1852–1920, army officer. *WWW.*

    Armed strength of Germany in 1889, **FortR** 2886

Murray, Sir Charles Augustus: see *Index,* I, 1023.

    Sketches from Egypt: the dahabiah, **FM** 3768

Murray, George Gilbert Aimé, 1866–1957, prof. of Greek, Oxford. *WWW.*

    Letter: **NC** 3211

Murray, the Hon. Henry Anthony, 1810–1865, traveller, naval officer. *LCCat.,* Burke under Dunmore.

    Burton's *Pilgrimage to Meccah,* **FM** 3392
    Dead Sea Route; Pilgrimage to Mecca [by R. Burton], 3452
    Campaigns of Paskiewitch and Omer Pacha in Asia, 3492
    United States through English eyes, 3946

Murray, James, d.1835, an ed. of the *Times. History of the Times* (1935–1952), I, 419–420.

    Portugal, **FQR** 34
    The Greek Revolution and European diplomacy, 116
    Sovereignty and settlement of Greece, 131

Murray, James A.

    Omar Khayyam, **FortR** 3892

Murray, Sir John, 1841–1914: see *Index,* I, 1024.

    See: **FortR** 3688

Murray, Sir John, 1851–1928: see *Index,* I, 1024.

    Letter: **FM** 3472

Murray, John Clark: see *Index,* I, 1024.

    Sir William Hamilton, **ScotR** 138
    Helen Keller, 261
    Summer school of philosophy, 346

Murray, Kenric Bright, sec. to London Chamber of Commerce, 1882, and of various exhibitions. *WW/1905;* disappears after *WW/1923.* (See *Index,* I, 1025, and II, App. A.)

    The Imperial Institute, **FortR** 2570

Murray, Margaret (Polson), 1844–1927, Canadian patriot. *Canadiana.*

    Women's clubs in America, **NC** 3657

Murray, Patrick Aloysius: see *Index,* I, 1025.

    Lamartine's poetry, **DR** 168
    Brothers of the Christian Schools, 194
    Thomas Moore, 217
    Palmer's *Letters to Wiseman,* 268
    Persecution of slander—*Edinburgh Review:* Borrow's *Bible in Spain,* 290
    O'Connell and Brougham, 313
    Publications on the Irish question, 326
    Ireland and its Rulers: O'Connell and the people, 342
    Hood's poems, 416
    Dickens's *Pictures from Italy,* 428
    Theological errors: Bronson's *Review,* 1056
    Spiritism and modern devil-worship, 1204
    O'Brien on justifying faith, 1243
    Ritualistic divinity and law, 1270 collab.
    Molloy on geology and revelation, 1311
    The world turned atheist, 1386
    The Vatican Council, 1425
    Pomponio Leto on the Vatican Council, 1563
    Note: 1089
    Notices: 353, 1052, 1145, 1213, 1222, 1241, 1330
    See: 208, 412

Murray, Robert Fuller, 1863–1894, poet. Boase.

    An impossible correspondence, 1892, **NC** 2409

Mursell, Arthur, divine, apparently a Roman Catholic. *BMCat.*

    Why I shall vote for the Unionist candidate, **NC** 2252

Myers, Ernest James: see *Index*, I, 1025.

A bather's ideal, **FM** 6319
Macaulay, 6374
English satire in the nineteenth century, 6467
Whigs and Liberals, 6522

Myers, Frederic William Henry: see *Index*, I, 1025.

Jebb's translations, **FortR** 1002
Giuseppe Mazzini, 1454, 1467
Virgil, 1548
Marcus Aurelius Antoninus, 1908
A new eirenicon [on J. R. Seeley], 1963
Transferred impressions and telepathy, 2013 collab.
Phantasms of the living, 2022 collab.
Personal recollections of Duke of Albany, 2167
Human personality, 2385
Darwin and agnosticism, 2669
Matthew Arnold, 2711
Letter: 2647

Aspects of mesmerism, **NatR-II** 330 collab.

Psychical research, 1634
Man's survival of death, 2216

George Sand, **NC** 13
Archbishop Trench's poems, 93
Victor Hugo, 304, 314
Ernest Renan, 594
Renan and miracles, 605
Thought-reading, 727 collab.
Mesmerism, 917 collab.
Apparitions, 994, 1015 both collab.
Multiplex personality, 1337
The disenchantment of France, 1547
Tennyson as prophet, 1676
Science and a future life, 2030
Modern poets and the meaning of life, 2339
Notice: 1755

Mylne, Robert Scott, 1853/54–1920, divine. Foster; Royal Soc. Edin., *Proceedings*, 41 (1920–1921), 203.

Needs of the Welsh Church, **NatR-II** 432

Master masons of Scotland, **ScotR** 458
Christina, Queen of Sweden, 532

N

Nadal, Ehrman Syme: see *Index*, I, 1025.

Notes of a Virginian journey, **NC** 2275

Napier, Sir Francis: see *Index*, I, 1025.

The Highland crofters, **NC** 1104

Napier, Robert William: see *Index*, I, 1026.

The North-West frontier policy, **NC** 3252
The Caucasus and Tirah, 3282

Napoleon III, Louis, 1808–1873, emperor of France. *Grand Larousse.*

The Empress Eugénie, **FM** 5599

Nash, Augustus, of Sydney, N.S.W.

Democracy in New South Wales, **FortR** 2566

Nash, Thomas, 1844/45–1885, Manchester barrister. Boase; *Momus*, Feb. 9, 1885.

The Lords and the [3rd] Reform Bill, **FortR** 2174

Nash, Vaughan: see *Index*, I, 1026.

Home Office and deadly trades, **FortR** 3321
The lock-out in the coal trade, 3429
The Employers' Liability Bill, 3469

Nassif, Ahmed or Amin, editor, of Cairo.

W. M. Metcalfe to Bute, March 12, 1888, Bute Papers, refers to A. Nassif, editor, of Cairo; see *ScotR* no. 161.

Egypt on eve of English invasion, **ScotR** 161
Egypt under the English invasion, 171

Naz, Sir Virgile, 1825–1901, barrister. *WWW.*

Letter: **NatR-II** 1357

Neate, Charles: see *Index*, I, 1026.

See: **LR(1829)** 22

Neilson, George, 1858–1923, historian. *DNB.*

The motes in Norman Scotland, **ScotR** 610

Nelson, Horatio, 3rd Earl Nelson: see *Index*, I, 1027.

Unity in the Church of Christ, **NC** 607
Small holdings, 1215
The relief funds, 3616

Nelson, James Henry, 1838/39–1898, barrister in India. Boase.

Administration of justice in Madras, **FortR** 1728

Nettleship, Henry: see *Index*, I, 1027.

Catullus, **FortR** 1469

Neuman, or **Neumann,** Berman Paul, b.1853, English writer. *WW*/1927.

The case against capital punishment, **FortR** 2865
Take care of the boys, 4171

Congregationalism seen from the pews, **NC** 1945

Neville, F.; very possibly Frederick Neville, b.1829/30, in Foster, whose name at birth and as late as 1876 (see *CCD*/76), was Frederick Howson Potter, a divine.

Literature for the blind, **NatR-II** 1142
Letter: 875

Neville, Henry F., 1822–1889, rector of Cath. Univ. of Ireland. Boase.

The demands of Ireland, **DR** 1696
Theology, past and present, at Maynooth, 1710

Nevin, Robert Jenkins, 1839–1906, Amer. divine. *Amer.WWW.*

A notable secession from the Vatican, **NC** 706

Nevins, later Probyn-Nevins, Henry Willis: see *Index*, I, 1027.

Cardinal Newman on eternity of punishment, **NC** 2381 collab.

Nevinson, Henry Woodd: see *Index*, I, 1027.

Scenes in a barrack school, **NC** 2903

Newbigging, Thomas, civil engineer, of Manchester.

Gas industry of the United Kingdom, **ScotR** 167

Newdegate, Sir Edward Newdigate, 1825–1902, army officer. *WWW.*

Our antiquated drill and tactics, **FortR** 4449

Newman, Ernest: see *Index*, I, 1027.

Gustave Flaubert, **FortR** 3729
Wagner's *Ring* and its philosophy, 4127

Newman, Francis William: see *Index*, I, 1027.

The new Christology, **FortR** 1007
Organized priesthood, 1023
Parliamentary government, 1032

English policy in Europe, **FM** 4065

The American quarrel, 4085
Duties of England to India, 4166
?The decypher of ancient inscriptions, 4294
The future of the national Church, 4322
M'Culloch on taxation, 4350
Land tenure question, 4422
Corporal punishments, 4513
Religious toleration, 4570
Cuneiform inscriptions, 4597
Functions of upper house of Parliament, 4772
Marriage laws, 4788
Currency [by Bonamy Price], 4988
Government from above and from below, 5105
The internal relations of Europe, 5130
On the causes of the Crimean War, 5156
Malthusianism, true and false, 5198
Epicureanism, ancient and modern, 5256
Drink traffic and the Permissive Bill, 5278
Regeneration of Sunday, 5429
Literature and Dogma [by Matthew Arnold], 5450
The Life and Teachings of Mohammed, 5452
Authorship of the *Odyssey,* 5483
Strivings of ancient Greece for union, 5537
Moral character of Roman conquest, 5547
Religion at the bar of ethics, 5558
Ancient and modern history, 5596, 5611, 5624, 5638
The dangerous glory of India, 5602
Vegetarianism, 5641
Alexander the Great, 5683
Essay on poetical translation, 5701
What was primitive Christianity? 5710
On national universities, 5715
On a university curriculum, 5735
The Papal Drama, 5745
The capitalist in society [on Holyoake's *History of Cooperation*], 5747
Weakness of Roman Empire, 5768
English capital and foreign loans, 5770
On cruelty, 5802
Etruscan translation, 5834
The future of the Roman Church, 5854
The Crimean War, 5866
Etruscan interpretation, 5905
Local control of the drink traffic, 5919
On modern automatism, 5932
Disestablishment and disendowment, 5960
English orthography, 5985
Free trade in land, 5997
Teaching English, 6004
Jewish proselytism before the War of Titus, 6061
Negro slavery under English rule, 6137
Negro slavery in the American union, 6142
Letters: 5870, 6049
Note: 5922

Newman, John Henry: see *Index*, I, 1028.

["Retraction of anti-Catholic statements"], **DR** 285

Lyra Innocentium [by John Keble], 419

Greek tragedy, **LR(1829)** 7

On the inspiration of scripture, **NC** 956

On eternity of punishment, 2381 collab.

Correspondence with Bishop of La Rochelle [Villecourt], **Ram** 209 collab.

The mission of the Isles of the North, 986, 995

The ancient saints, 990, 1009, 1046, 1056

Temporal prosperity a note of the Church, 991

Questions and answers [on laymen studying theology], 991

Prospect of war [in Crimea], 991

Contemporary events, 993, 1000

Rheims and Douay version of Holy Scripture, 994

On consulting the faithful in matters of doctrine, 997

Lay students in theology, 998

Designs and prospects of Russia, 998

Letters: 52, 363, 966, 996, 1050

Note: 988

Notice: 1005

See: 615

Newmarch, William: see *Index*, I, 1028.

Failure of the Glasgow Bank, **FortR** 1536

Amending our bankruptcy legislation, 1565

Newton, Sir Charles Thomas: see *Index*, I, 1028.

Classical archaeology, **NatR-II** 32, 99

The religion of the Greeks, **NC** 182, 209

Newton-Robinson, Charles Edmund, 1853–1913, gemologist. *WWW*.

The Marlborough gems, **NC** 3515

Nichol, John: see *Index*, I, 1028.

Scotch universities, **FortR** 2100

Recent poems and plays, **OxCam** 63

Nichol, John Pringle, 1804–1859, astronomer. *DNB*.

Mortality of different populations, **FQR** 311

?Rae's *New Principles of Political Economy,* 355

Nicholl, Mrs. Edith Mary, later Mrs. Bowyer:

see *Index*, I, 818 under Bowyer, and II, App. A under Nicholl.

Impressions of a modern Arcadian [in Virginia], **FortR** 2411

Nichols, John Gough, 1806–1873, publisher, antiquary. *DNB*.

The old Countess of Desmond, **DR** 1005

Nicholson, John Gambril F., poet. *BMCat*.

Degeneracy of modern sonnet, **NatR-II** 1072

Nicholson, Joseph Shield: see *Index*, I, 1028.

Letter: **FortR** 3527

Orthodox political economy, **NatR-II** 387

Mr. Giffen's attack on bimetallists, **NC** 1807

Economic principles and university reform, **ScotR** 314

Nickisson, George William, publisher and editor of *Fraser's Mag.,* c.1842–1847. Thackeray, *Letters,* II, 41; Mill, *Earlier Letters,* II, 723, n. 1.

See: **FM** 2120

Nicolson, Sir Arthur: see *Index*, I, 1028.

Men and manners in Constantinople, **FortR** 2373

Nicolson, William, 1827–1907, Congregational minister; studied at Univ. of Finland. *Congregational Year Book/*1908.

The University of Finland, **ScotR** 278

Three Finnish scholars, 307

Nietzsche, Friedrich Wilhelm, 1844–1900, German philosopher. *Grosse Brockhaus*.

The case of Wagner, **FortR** 3693

Nightingale, Florence: see *Index*, I, 1028.

A note on pauperism, **FM** 4948

A "note" of interrogation, 5425

What will be our religion in 1999? 5443

The people of India, **NC** 204

Our Indian stewardship, 895

Ninet, John, prob. the John Ninet in *BMCat*. who wrote books in French on Middle East at this time.

Origin of the National Party in Egypt, **NC** 809

Nisbet, Hume, 1849–c.1921, artist, critic. *Australian Ency., WWW.*

The Papuan and his master, **FortR** 3056

Nisbet, John: see *Index,* I, 1028.

Forest science: its aim and scope, **NatR-II** 814

Niven, Robert, b.1846/47, barrister; in Australia 1872–1876. Foster, *FM no.* 6169, p. 511n.

William Lloyd Garrison, **FortR** 1886

Squatters and proprietors in Victoria, **FM** 6169

Nobili-Vitelleschi, Marchese Francesco, 1829–1906, Italian statesman. Tosi under Vitelleschi.

The political condition of Italy, **FortR** 2034

Italian policy in the East, **NC** 896
The dawn of the new Italy, 1036
The political situation of Europe, 1108
The Italian Senate, 2491
On inductive morality, 2988

Noble, James Ashcroft: see *Index,* I, 1029, and *Academy,* April 11, 1896, p. 304.

A Lancashire poets' corner, **FM** 6401
A pre-Raphaelite magazine [*The Germ*], 6507

Edgar Allan Poe, **NQM** 118

Noel, Geoffrey C. *RG.*

The settling day [with France], **FortR** 4244

Noel, Robert Ralph, army officer, writer on phrenology in German, translator of German books. *BMCat., Army List/75.* (See *Index,* I, 1029.)

Conversations with Prince Metternich, **FM** 3931
Recollections of the stage, 5654

Noel, Roden Berkeley Wriothesley: see *Index,* I, 1029.

Metaphor and "pathetic fallacy" [in poetry], **FortR** 292

Corsica, **FM** 6139

The Earl of Albermarle, **NatR-II** 1300

The soul and future life, **NC** 85

Nolan, John Philip, 1838–1912, army officer, M.P. for Galway. Crone, *WWW.*

A Home Ruler's views, **FortR** 2442

Nolan, Pierce L., Irish barrister. *Cath.WW/* 1917.

Irishmen in the French Revolution, **DR** 2220

Norman, Charles Boswell, army officer. Allibone.

France: finances and freedom, **NatR-II** 435
Re-organization of Indian army, 574

The French army of to-day, **NC** 924
The colonies of France, 1000

Norman, Sir Henry: see *Index,* I, 1029.

A study of Longfellow, **FortR** 1989
Ralph Waldo Emerson, 2084
Theories and practice of modern fiction, 2118

Our vacillation in China, **NC** 3676

Norman, Sir Henry Wylie, 1826–1904, army officer, colonial governor. *DNB.*

The scientific frontier [between India and Afghanistan], **FortR** 1538
Lord Lawrence and the Mutiny, 2020

Letter: **NatR-II** 2459

Norman, Ménie Muriel: see *Index,* I, 1029, and II, App. A.

In Ruthenia, **FortR** 2999

Norris, Edward Samuel, 1832–1908, J.P. *WWW.*

Fresh work for parliament, **NatR-II** 648
Some abuses in public speaking, 667
A Royal foundation [Hospital of St. Katharine], 772

Northcote, Hon. Amyas Stafford, 1864–1923, J.P. Burke under Iddesleigh.

American life through English spectacles, **NC** 2458
Corruption in American politics, 2568

Northcote, Hon. Arthur Francis, 1852–1943, Anglican divine. *WWW.*

Ritualists and Anglicans, **NC** 408

Northcote, Henry Stafford: see *Index,* I, 1029.

The constitutional question, **NatR-II** 1673
Note: 676

Canada's highway to the Pacific, **NC** 668

Northcote, James Spencer, 1821–1907, ed.

Rambler, pres. of Oscott Coll., archeologist. *DNB*.

Notices: **DR** 1736, 1745

?Roman affairs, in 9 installments from **Ram** 9 to 120
The Roman catacombs, 32, 46, 55, 69, 82, 100
The Neapolitan catacombs, 230
Cardinal Pacca's *Memoirs*, 232, 238
Rossi on the Christian inscriptions of Rome, 239
Celebrated sanctuaries of the Madonna, 250, 257, 263, 275, 288, 307
The miracle of St. Januarius, 280
Devotions to the Blessed Sacrament, in 8 installments from 332 to 439
The Roman revolution, 372
Pilgrimages to Jerusalem, 410
Translations and editors, 418
Protestant controversialists, 419
The Roman catacombs, 421
Christian pilgrimages, 426
Dr. Mackay's *Popular Delusions*, 428
Manners and customs of the Sardinians, 442
A pilgrimage to La Salette, 446, 451
Uncle Tom's Cabin [by Harriet Beecher Stowe], 449
Cloister Life of Charles V [by Stirling], 456
Strickland's *Life of Mary Queen of Scots*, 463
Money and morals, 471
The priest and the parson, 475
Medieval games and festivals, 476
The temporal sovereignty of the Pope, 478
American slavery and Protestantism, 481
Inscription on chair of St. Mark, 482
?*Legends of the Madonna*, 485
A few more words on La Salette, 486
Protestantism and Catholicity on slavery, 499
Historical notices of patron saints, 504, 512, ?520 collab.
Memoir of Cardinal Mezzofanti, 509
Morality and religion of England, 523
Tombs of heretics in the Roman catacombs, 525
Secret societies, 531
Memorandums on Ireland, 534
St. Gregory and St. Anselm, 539, 550
Anecdotes of the Roman Revolution, 540
?Table-turning and table-talking, 541
To the readers of the *Rambler*, 545
Translations: good and bad, 552
Anecdotes of the Roman Republic, 564
Catholic hymnology, 578
Recent Protestant tourists in Italy, 587 collab.?

The life of an editor, 592
English nuns during French Revolution, 593, 600
England and English three hundred years ago, 601
?Protestant authors and Catholic readers, 607
?The fish as symbol in early Christian art, 754
The symbolism of the catacombs, 1007
Signs of martyrdom in catacombs, 1047
Edited: 507
Letters: 258, 1019
Notes: 317, 338
Notices: 241, 267, 337, 346, 457, 465, 487, 501, 510, 543, 560, 569, 576, 582, 590, 597, 614, 643
Trans: ?409, 454, ?522, ?530
See: 343

Northcote, Sir Stafford Henry: see *Index*, I, 1030.

Figures, facts and fallacies, **NatR-II** 45
Conservative and Liberal finance, 116
Letters of Wellesley and Iddesleigh, 676, collab.

Northcote, Walter Stafford: see *Index*, I, 1030.

Jane Austen's novels, **NC** 3653

Norton, Charles Eliot, 1827–1908, editor, prof. of art, Harvard Univ. *DAB*.

On emigration, **FortR** 616

Notley, Frances Eliza Millett (Thomas), b.1820, novelist. Allibone.

A sea changeling, **NQM** 32

Novikoff, Olga Alexeena: see *Index*, I, 1030, and II, App. A.

Russia and [reunion] of Europe, **FortR** 3937
Russia and her patients [Turkey, Austria, France], 4069

Russia Before and After the War, **FM** 6266
Emperor Alexander's reforms, 6363
The new departure in Russia, 6464
The tercentenary of Siberia, 6475
Trans: 6548

The temperance movement in Russia, **NC** 764
Religious basis of Russian policy, 2853

Nugent, Sir Charles Butler Peter Hodges, 1827–1899, army officer. *WWW*.

Letter: **NatR-II** 291

O

Oakeley, Frederick: see *Index*, I, 1030.

The recent conversions, **DR** 406
Dr. Pusey's sermon on absolution, 410
Rite of ordination, 421
Church music and choral regulations, 429
Devotional use of the breviary, 433
Formby on Christian psalmody, 450
The Office of Holy Week, 490
Allies's *Journal in France*, 542
Faber's *Hymns*, 560
Ways and means of the Church, 563
Church offices and popular devotions, 611
Dr. Pusey's teaching and practice, 616
Protestant ideas of the Confessional, 634
Meyrick on the Church of Spain, 660
Miss Sellon and her sisterhood, 665
Cardinal Wiseman's *Essays*, 702
The ceremonies of the Church, 714
Modern ascetic divinity—Father Faber, 725
The Newcomes, 798
Phenomena of Anglicanism [on union with Rome], 828
Recreations and their moral influence, 837
"Souperism," [i.e., proselytism], 840
Dodsworth on Protestant delusions, 844
The Creator and the Creature [by F. W. Faber], 854
Anglican propagandism, 861
Crotchets and crotchettiness, 871
The Messiah [Handel's] at Exeter Hall, 880
Religious disabilities of Catholic prisoners, 883
Jubilee of St. Cuthbert's College, 890
The Abbé Massé's *Life of St. Edmund of Canterbury*, 906
Prison and workhouse grievances, 924
Cardinal Wiseman's *Tour in Ireland in 1858*, 927
Tractarian Movement, 1040, 1051, 1060, 1081
Church music, 1242
The *Month* on church choirs, 1254
On a liberal education, 1287
The use and abuse of ritual, 1502
See: 1046

Consecration of Bishop of Bruges, **Ram** 131
Importance of religious ceremonial, 535
Our most noble selves, 1067
Preaching and public speaking, 1074
English public schools and colleges in Catholic times, 1101
Letters: 44, 123, 169, 391, 562, 991, 1050

Oakley, Charles Selby: see *Index*, I, 1030.

Women in assemblies, **NC** 2998

Oakley, John: see *Index*, I, 1030.

Royal Commission on Church Courts, **FM** 6397

Oates, Austin G., private sec. to Herbert Vaughan, q.v. J. G. Snead-Cox, *Life of Cardinal Vaughan* (1910), II, 482.

Catholic poor children, **DR** 2053
Notices: 2373, ?2485, 2686, 2699, 2720, 2729

O'Brien, Charlotte Grace, 1845–1909, Irish social reformer. *DNB.*

The emigration and waste-land clauses, **FortR** 1812

The Irish "poor man," **NC** 523
Eighty years [1800–1880 in Ireland], 559
The emigrant in New York, 1044

O'Brien, Edward William, 1837–1909. *Irish Gentry; Times,* Jan. 26, 1909, p. 11d.

The radical programme for Ireland, **NC** 1179

O'Brien, Murrough: see *Index*, I, 1031.

Irish rents, improvements, and landlords, **FortR** 1735
Experiments in peasant proprietorship, 1745

O'Brien, Richard Barry: see *Index*, I, 1031.

Mr. Goldwin Smith, **FortR** 2136

Irish wrongs and English remedies, **NC** 1202
Federal union with Ireland, 1228
Three attempts to rule Ireland justly, 1268
Playing at "coercion" [with Ireland], 1402

O'Brien, William, 1852–1928: see *Index*, I, 1031.

Mr. Morley's task in Ireland, **FortR** 3282

A Unionist policy for Ireland, **NatR-II** 1795

If Ireland sent her M.P.s to Washington? **NC** 2926

O'Callaghan-Westropp, George, 1864–1944, army officer. *WWW.*

Spoliation of Irish landlords, **NatR-II** 2016

O'Connell, Daniel, 1775–1847, Irish political leader, co-founder of *Dublin Rev. DNB.*

Six Months in a Convent, **DR** 14

See: **FM** 1237

O'Connell, John, 1810–1858, Irish M.P. *DNB.*

"No-Popery" current, **DR** 37
Recent opinions upon America, 39
Ireland, past and present, 52
Miseries and beauties of Ireland, 91
Memoirs of Scott [by J. G. Lockhart], 112
Why is Ireland exempt from income tax? 264
The grievances of Ireland, 308
See: 90

O'Connell, Maurice, 1803–1853, Irish M.P., story teller. Boase.

Sporting in Ireland, **DR** 215
See: 207

O'Connor, D. Moncrieff

Holy Trinity in the *Divina Commedia*, **DR** 2527
The "Alcestis" of Euripides as a type of Redemption, 2658
Renascence of Catholicism in France, 2690
Notices: 2485, 2509, 2570, 2651, 2663, 2709

O'Conor, Charles Owen, 1838–1906, Irish politician. *DNB.*

The unsolved Irish problem, **NatR-II** 1514
The over-taxation of Ireland, 1973

O'Conor-Eccles, Charlotte: see *Index,* I, 1031.

A royal elopement [Princess Clémentine and Prince Sobieski], **DR** 2242

Hospital where the plague broke out, **NC** 3546

Oday Partap Singh, Rajah of Bhinga, C.S.I. *BMCat.*

Decay of landed aristocracy in India, **NC** 2216
"Russud"—an Indian grievance, 2483
The cow agitation in India, 2566

O'Donnell, Sir Charles Routledge, 1794–1870, Irish army officer. Boase.

Notes on the Russian army of 1828, **FM** 55
Journey from Hermanstadt to Bucharest, 88

O'Dwyer, Edward Thomas, 1842–1917, Irish bishop. *WWW.*

University education for Irish Catholics, **NC** 3405

Ogilvy, David William Stanley, 8th Earl of Airlie, 1856–1900. Burke.

Belligerent claims and neutral rights, **FortR** 1353

Agricultural prospects, 1604
The United States as a field for agricultural settlers, **NC** 552
Is our yeomanry worth preserving? 2126
Officers' expenses in the cavalry, 2723

Ogle, Nathaniel. *BMCat.*

Custody of Infants' Bill, **FM** 1295

O'Grady, Standish, 1846–1928, publicist. *WWW.*

The Irish small farmer, **FortR** 1686
Carlyle as a political teacher, 2375
The new Irish movement, 3912

O'Hagan, John: see *Index,* I, 1032.

Reform of the Dublin University, **DR** 477
M'Carthy's poems, 577
Carlyle's works, 597
The case of Mr. O'Keeffe, 1442

The hopes of Ireland, **Ram** 1024

O'Hara, Robert Patrick, 1836–1885, Irish barrister. Boase, Venn.

Royalty and viceroyalty in Ireland, **FortR** 2300

Öhlenschläger, Adam Gottlob, 1779–1850, Danish playwright. *Ency.Brit./* 11th ed.

See: **FM** 5210

Ohlson, J. L., sec. of West India Committee.

Letter: **FM** 5971

O'Keeffe, Deville, officer of the Swiss Guards of Louis XVI; prob. an Irishman.

?Journal of an officer of the Swiss Guards, **FM** 4756

Olcott, Henry Steel, 1832–1907, founder of N.Y. Theosophical Soc. *DAB.*

The genesis of theosophy, **NatR-II** 913
Theosophy, the "divine wisdom," 947

Oldfield, Josiah, 1863–1953, physician. *WWW, LCCat.*

Vegetarian still, **NC** 3331

Oldham, Alice, d.1907, president of Alexandra Coll., Dublin. *BMCat.; Alexandra College, Dublin* (Dublin, 1919), p. 34.

The history of socialism, **NatR-II** 1075, 1087, 1101

The unsocial evil, 3725
The zoologist about town, 3752
Hints for vagabonds, 3758, 3784, 3816, 3833, 3841, 3963
The battle-fields of 1859, 3937
Where fancy is bred, 4112
Notes from Numidia, 4205, 4222, 4235, 4261
A Derby Day among the Arabs, 4345
A rough ride on classic ground, 4373
The lion-hunters of Algeria, 4414
Tunis and Carthage, 4458
Primary education in Ireland, 5684
A recent Irish election, 5712

Ormsby-Johnson, Frederick Colpoys, 1858–1932, army officer. *WWW* under Johnson.

Marine garrisons for naval bases, **FortR** 3905
Maritime expeditions: sea-power, 4365

Ormsby, Robert: see *Index*, I, 1036.

Origen against Celsus, **DR** 1693
The character of Cicero, 1737
Notice: 1756

Inspection of convents, **Ram** 503
?Cardinal Wiseman and the Tractarians, 524

Orpen, Joseph Millerd, 1828–1923, colonial administrator in S. Africa and Rhodesia. *DSAB.*

The God who promised victory to the Matabele, **NC** 2968
Representation of the colonies, 3293

Orr, Alexandra Sutherland (Leighton): See *Index*, I, 1036.

The future of English women, **NC** 181

Orsi, Count Joseph, or Giuseppe, d.1897. *Titled Nobility.*

Escape of Louis Napoleon from Ham, **FM** 6162
Louis Napoleon's expedition to Boulogne, August 1840, 6205
My life in Paris during the Commune, 6239

Osborn, Percy Lancelot, translator from Greek. *BMCat.*

Note: **FortR** 4058

Osborn, Robert Durie: see *Index*, I, 1036.

Another side of a popular story [on India], **FortR** 1935

Letter: **FM** 5872

Osborn, Sherard: see *Index*, I, 1036.

Our admiralty, **FortR** 371

Osborne, Fanny Georgiana (Pitt-Rivers), Duchess of Leeds, 1836–1896, wife of 9th Duke of Leeds. *Complete Peerage.*

Note: **NC** 2363

Oscar Fredrik II, 1829–1907, King of Sweden. *Ency. Brit.*/11th ed.

To a friend, **NC** 1671
Charles the Twelfth, 1878, 1897
The Lion King of Sweden [Charles VII], 2386
Charles the Twelfth and the campaign of 1712–13, 2515

Oss, Steven, or Salomon, Frederik van, b.1868, Dutch financial writer. *BMCat., LCCat.*

The gold-mining madness in the city, **NC** 2814
Consols at 110, 2911
The Westralian mining "boom," 3014
The "limited-company" craze, 3284

O'Sullivan, D. R.

Tierra Del Fuego, **FortR** 3310

O'Sullivan, Samuel: see *Index*, I, 1037.

A fishing excursion into Galway, **FM** 872

Ottley, Henry, 1811–1878, misc. writer. Boase.

?Germany—past and future, **FM** 3329
?German federative reform, 4379
The Royal Academy Commission, 4402
Diplomacy and diplomatic history, 4460, 4472, 4482, 4502
The American case: the *Alabama* claims, 5297
British policy: Persia, Central Asia, 5487
The Brussels Conference, 5643

Otway, Sir Arthur John, 1822–1912, M.P. *WWW.*

Fallacies of the French press, **NC** 1408

Ouida: see de la Ramée, Marie Louise.

Owen, George S.; perhaps Rev. George Owen, prof. of Chinese, Univ. of London, in *Times*, Feb. 9, 1914, p. 1a.

Reform policy of Chinese Emperor, **NatR-II** 2351

Owen, John Fletcher, 1839–1924, army officer. *WWW.*

Military forces of our colonies, **FortR** 4428

Owen, Sir Richard: see *Index*, I, 1037.

Argument of "infirmity" in Lewes' review of *Reign of Law*, **FM** 4811
Milton and Galileo, 4976
The "Jardin d'Acclimatation" [during sieges of Paris], 5269
On longevity, 5284
On petroleum and oil-wells, 5726

Vivisection: its pains and uses, **NC** 660

Oxenham, Henry Nutcombe, 1829–1888, disciple of Döllinger. *DNB.*

Letter: **DR** 1540

Attitude of Christians toward Old Testament, **NatR-II** 179
Moral authority of Frederick the Great, 476
Madame de Maintenon, 557

Catholic education, **Ram** 1050
George Eliot's novels, 1066
The Neo-Protestantism of Oxford, 1078
Religious novels, 1093
Pugin testimonial, 1104
See: 1116

P

Page, Arnold

Assurance investments, **FortR** 1643

Paget, H., of Harrow.

Aspects of rabbit farming, **NatR-II** 1095

Paget, Sir James: see *Index*, I, 1038.

Escape from pain: discovery [of ether], **NC** 390
Vivisection: its pains and uses, 659
Recreation, 936

Paget, John C., writer on naval affairs. *BMCat.*

Recent naval warfare, **FM** 6038

Paget, Stephen, 1855–1926, biographer, essayist. *DNB.*

Letter: **FortR** 4420

Paget, Violet: see *Index*, I, 1038.

The legend of Madame Krasinska, **FortR** 2930
An eighteenth-century singer [Antonio Vivarelli], 3159
Beauty and sanity, 3681
Deterioration of soul, 3818
Modern art: Whistler, Sargent, and Besnard, 4017
An agnostic's notes on Wm. James, 4366
Letter: 2638

Tuscan peasant plays, **FM** 5899
The Academy of the Árcadi, 6069, 6073
Italian musical life in eighteenth century, 6095, 6101, 6112
Hoffmann's *Kreisler*, 6127
Metastasio and the opera, 6159, 6168, 6174
A culture-ghost, 6362
In Umbria, 6415
Apollo the fiddler, 6525

Transformations of chivalric poetry, **NatR-II** 95
The value of the ideal, 346

Musical expression and composers of eighteenth century, **NQM** 110

Tuscan sculpture of the Renaissance, **NC** 2227

Paget, Countess Walburga Ehrengarde Helena (de Hohenthal), 1839–1929. *WWW.*

Peasant proprietors in Germany, **NatR-II** 516
A visit to Count Mattei, 999
Count Mattei's system, 1035
An unscientific view of vivisection, 1189
Letter: 1024

Common sense in dress and fashion, **NC** 831
Vegetable diet, 2192

Paley, Frederick Apthorp: see *Index*, I, 1039.

Pre-Homeric legends of the Argonauts, **DR** 1670
On the origin of the "Solar Myth," 1694
Religious tests and nationalising the universities, **FortR** 573
Origin of written Greek literature, **FM** 6264
Greek dinners, 6375
Mr. Darwin on earth-worms, 6474
Antiquity of our agricultural terms, 6546
Classical studies in English universities, **Ram** 164
See: 202

Paley, W. B.: see *Index*, I, 1039.

The Roman roads of Britain, **NC** 3380

Palgrave, Francis Turner: see *Index*, I, 1039.

English pictures in 1865, **FortR** 52

Papillon, E. C. *BMCat.*

Teplitz, **NatR-II** 928

Pardo Bazan, Countess Emilia, 1852–1921, Spanish novelist, critic. *WWW, EUI.*

The women of Spain, **FortR** 2838

Pardoe, Julia Sophia, 1806–1862, misc. writer. *DNB, R.L.F.*

Rise and progress of Magyar literature, **FQR** 665

Pilgrimages in Paris, **FM** 1789, 1812, 1839, 1864
An adventure in Bythnia, 1891
Glimpses of the gifted, 1924
Il Ghirlandajo, 1968
The poet of Prague, 2026
A night in the Champ de Mars, 2069
Life of Count de Guiche, 2134

Pardon, George Frederick, 1824–1884, misc. writer. *DNB.*

See: **FM** 3513

Pareto, Vilfredo, 1848–1923, Italian economist. *DEI.*

On Italy, **FortR** 4254

Parisis, Pierre Louis, 1795–1866, bishop of Langres, later of Arras. *LCCat., Grand Larousse.*

Christian education, **Ram** 15
On Catholic journalism, 376

Parke, Thomas Heazle, 1857–1893, African traveller; surgeon-major. *DNB.*

How General Gordon was really lost, **NC** 2212

Parker, Charles, 1800–1881, architect. Boase.

Town churches, **Ram** 231

Parker, Charles Stuart, 1829–1910, politician. *DNB.*

Free trade and cheap sugar, **FortR** 4144

Parker, Edward Harper: see *Index*, I, 1041.

Missionaries in China, Corea, Burma, **DR** 2578

The Burmo-Chinese frontier and the Kak-hyen tribes, **FortR** 3982
Corea, 4074

Trans: **NC** 2956

Parker, George Frederick: see *Index*, I, 1041.

Intellectual progress in the United States, **NC** 2571
Cry for fraudulent money in America, 2995

Parker, Gilbert: see next entry.

Parker, Sir Horatio Gilbert George: see *Index*, I, 1041.

International Council of Women, **FortR** 4310

Canadian military life, **NatR-II** 1231
The tall master, 1334
At the sign of the eagle, 1443

Parker, John William, Sr., 1782–1870, publisher; published *Fraser's Mag.*, 1847–1863. *DNB, CBEL.*

Makers, sellers, buyers of books, **FM** 2981 collab.

Parker, John William, Jun., 1820–1860, publisher; ed. *Fraser's Mag.*, 1847–1860. See *FM* no. 4053, *DNB* under his father.

A happy New Year, **FM** 2535
The first half of the nineteenth century, 2805
Makers, sellers, buyers of books, 2981 collab.
England at war, 3203
Charles David Badham: in memoriam, 3630
Robert Stephen Rintoul, 3728
The expensive luxury of waste, 3797
William John Broderip, 3844
Notes: 3472, 3855

Parker, Lewis

Canada: an emigrant's journal, **NQM** 37

Parkes, Sir Henry: see *Index*, I, 1041.

Our growing Australian empire, **NC** 953
Australia and the imperial connection, 999

Parkes, Kineton, 1865–1938, art critic. *WWW.*

English silks, **NatR-II** 1783

Parkin, Sir George Robert, 1846–1922, educationist, imperialist. *DNB.*

British statesmanship, **NatR-II** 1867

Parkinson, Cyril: see *Index*, I, 1041.

Colliery explosions: their prevention, **NatR-II** 983
A western trout-stream [the Monnow in Wales], 1043
Fruit-culture in Worcestershire orchards, 1080
A winter cruise on the Severn Sea, 1102

Parkinson, Henry, 1852–1924, vice-pres. of Oscott College. *WWW.*

Notice: **DR** 2438

Parkinson, Joseph Charles, b.1832, clerk at Somerset House. *BMCat., LCCat.*

The casual poor of London, **FortR** 179
Uniform poor-rate for London, 196

Parr, Cecil Francis, 1847–1928, barrister. *WWW.*

Random recollections of Corsica, **NatR-II** 964

Parry, Sir Charles Hubert Hastings, 1848–1918, composer, musicologist. *DNB.*

Purcell, **NatR-II** 1797

Parry, Sir Edward Abbott: see *Index,* I, 1041.

The insolvent poor, **FortR** 4121
The Workmen's Compensation Act, 4477

Parsloe, Joseph, writer on railroads. *BMCat.*

Railway rates and fares, **FortR** 1173
Our railway system, 2445

See: **FM** 6067

Railway reform, **NQM** 125

Parsons, Daniel: see *Index,* I, 1041.

?The religious census of England, **Ram** 568
Our picture in the census [of 1851], 574, 580
Preston Hall and our new dignitaries, 759, 765, 772, 777, 784, 792
?Dr. John Bird Sumner at Bath, 785
Notice: 576

Parsons, Florence Mary (Wilson), 1864–1934, lecturer. *WWW.*

Anent the Whitefoords, **ScotR** 644

Parsons, Gertrude (Hext), 1812–1891, misc. writer. Boase.

The new crook in the lot, in 11 installments from **Ram** 5 to 146

Parsons, Harold George: see *Index,* I, 1041.

Australian federation, **FortR** 4348

Parsons, John Langdon, 1837–1903, Australian administrator. Johns, *Australian Biog. Dic.,* 1934.

Northern Territory of South Australia, **NatR-II** 147

Pater, Walter Horatio: see *Index,* I, 1042.

Leonardo Da Vinci, **FortR** 634
Sandro Botticelli, 705
Pico Della Mirandola, 811
The poetry of Michelangelo, 820
Wordsworth, 1039
A fragment on *Measure for Measure,* 1100
Demeter and Persephone, 1223, 1233
A study of Dionysus, 1313
The school of Giorgione, 1402
Character of the humourist: Charles Lamb, 1511
The beginnings of Greek sculpture, 1665, 1678
The marbles of Aegina, 1684
Style, 2773
Giordano Bruno, 2856
Prosper Mérimée, 3019
Raphael, 3271

Notre Dame d'Amiens, **NC** 2549
Vézelay, 2594
Notices: 1697, 1803

Paterson, Arthur Henry: see *Index,* I, 1042.

Canadian immigrants, **NatR-II** 1724

Patmore, Coventry Kersey Dighton: see *Index,* I, 1042.

An English classic: William Barnes, **FortR** 2535
Knowledge, opinion, and inequality, 2624
"Distinction," 2958
Three essayettes, 3236
Mrs. Meynell, poet and essayist, 3299
Mr. F. Thompson, a new poet, 3451

Architects and architecture, **FM** 3037
Emanuel Swedenborg, 3568
Dramatic treasure-trove, 3813

Paton, John Brown: see *Index,* I, 1042.

What are the Falk Laws? **FortR** 1052
Church and State in Germany, 1122

Patterson, Arthur John, 1835–1899, prof. of English, Budapest Univ. Szinnyeí: see *Index,* I, 1042.

Electoral laws of Hungary, **FortR** 244
Country life in Hungary, 294
A Hungarian election, 307
From Agram to Zara, 852, 861
Dualism in Austria-Hungary, 2390

Patterson, James Laird: see *Index,* I, 1043.

Reasons for not despairing of a national return to the faith, **DR** 1787

Patterson, John Letcher, 1861–1936/37, American scholar. *Amer.WW*/1936–1937, 1938–1939.

Pulvis Olympicus, **ScotR** 520
Satyr-drama and Euripides' Cyclops, 598

Patterson, Richard, a Belfast merchant.

Mercantile Ireland v. Home Rule, **NatR-II** 664

Patterson, Robert Hogarth: see *Index*, I, 1043.

The war of the banks, **FortR** 299
The currency and its reforms, 358
The state and the currency, 422
California, 1730

Pattison, Andrew Seth Pringle: see Pringle-Pattison, Andrew Seth.

Pattison, Emilia Frances (Strong): see Dilke, Lady Emilia Frances.

Pattison, Mark: see *Index*, I, 1044.

The age of reason, **FortR** 1340
Books and critics, 1410
Industrial shortcomings, 1756
Etienne Dolet, 1763
Note: 1369

English letter-writers, **FM** 3291
The Birmingham Congress, 3667
Antecedents of the Reformation 3817
Philanthropic societies in reign of Queen Anne, 3969

Middle-class education, **NQM** 206

Patton, Robert, midshipman on *Bellerophon* at Trafalgar.

Note: **NC** 3556

Paul, Charles Kegan: see *Index*, I, 1044.

The production and life of books, **FortR** 2017

Edward Irving [by Margaret Oliphant], **FM** 4290
Mary Wollstonecraft, 6066

?Our public schools: Eton, **NQM** 163
The poets of the Oxford Catholic Movement, 177
Cardinal Newman and his work, 187
Mr. Hardy's novels, 196
Note: 162
Notice: 198

The proper use of the City churches, **NC** 419
Faith and unfaith, 768
Clergymen as head-masters, 901
An experiment [in class understanding], 1050

Stories of old Eton days, 2296
See: 1480

Paul, Francis

[Brunetière] on Victor Hugo, **NatR-II** 575
Wagner's letters to Frau Eliza Wille, 607

Paul, Herbert Woodfield: see *Index*, I, 1044.

Aspects of Tennyson: classical poems, **NC** 2364
The decay of classical quotation, 2916
Sterne, 3045
Gibbon's *Life and Letters*, 3073
The apotheosis of the novel, 3114
The new learning, 3211
The Philosophical Radicals, 3275
The art of letter-writing, 3323
The great tractarian [George Savile], 3437
The father of letters [Cicero], 3529
Prince of journalists [Swift], 3589
The autocrat [John Selden], 3636

Paul, Sir James Balfour, 1846–1931, geneologist. *LCCat., Times*, Sept. 16, 1931, p. 17b.

Lady Warriston, **ScotR** 298
Scottish heraldry, 373
Edinburgh in 1629, 445
Processions, 574
Scottish municipal heraldry, 584

Paul, Margaret Agnes (Colvile), wife of Charles Kegan Paul, q.v. *BMCat., DNB* under her husband.

Old fashioned gardening, **NC** 398

Paul, Nancy

Modern nurses, **NatR-II** 1970

Pauli, Reinhold, 1823–1882, German historian. *ADB.*

Prussia and Germany, **FM** 5171

Paull, Harry Major, 1854–1934, playwright, art critic. *WWW.*

National Gallery and common sense, **FortR** 4103
Dramatic convention: the soliloquy, 4281

Paver, R., of South Africa.

Letter: **NatR-II** 136

Payn, James: see *Index*, I, 1044.

The midway inn [on contemporary life], **NC** 306
The critic on the hearth, 317
The literary calling and its future, 381
Sham admiration in literature, 415

Peel, Hon. Sidney Cornwallis, 1870–1938. *WWW*.

A seventeenth century Chesterfield [Francis Osborne], **NC** 3041
Nicholas Culpeper, 3286

Pelham, Henry Francis: see *Index*, I, 1045.

The younger Pliny, **FortR** 1667

Pell, Albert, 1820–1907, agriculturist, M.P. *DNB*.

Administration of local taxes, **NatR-II** 31

Pellew, Fleetwood Hugh, 1838–1906, commissioner of Dacca. Burke under Exmouth.

Lord Ripon's statesmanship: Indian Rent Bill, **NatR-II** 114

Pelly, Sir Lewis, 1825–1892, army officer, M.P. *DNB*.

British India, **FortR** 64
Glimpses of Carlyle, 3216

Pemberton, Edmund Leigh, 1823–1910, barrister, M.P. *WWW*.

Private bill legislation, **FortR** 2353

Reform in the tenure of land, **NatR-II** 386
Tithes, considered by a tithe-payer, 978

Pennell, Elizabeth (Robins): see *Index*, I, 1045.

A century of women's rights, **FortR** 2992
The two [art] salons [in Paris], 3226, 3371, 3507
The French salons, 3664
John Everett Millais, 3857 collab.
Twenty years of cycling, 3989 collab.
The centenary of lithography, 4215 collab.

Pennell, Joseph: see *Index*, I, 1045.

John Everett Millais, **FortR** 3857 collab.
Twenty years of cycling, 3989 collab.
Cycles and cycling, 4060, 4227
The centenary of lithography, 4215 collab.

Wood-engraving, **NatR-II** 1720

Art and the daily paper, **NC** 3190

Penrose-Fitzgerald, C. C.: see Fitzgerald, C. C. Penrose.

Percival, Henry Robert, 1854–1903, American divine. *Amer.WWW, LCCat*.

The future of the Christian religion, **NC** 3537

Percival, John, 1834–1918, schoolmaster and bishop of Hereford. *DNB*.

Slow growth of moral influence in politics, **NC** 3702

Percy, Henry George, Earl Percy and 7th Duke of Northumberland, 1846–1918, M.P. Burke.

What is a Whig? **NatR-II** 37
The Franchise Bill and the House of Lords, 174
Considerations for small [land] holders, 1746
Letter: 545

Perdicaris, Ion H., b.1840, foreign resident in Tangier. His *The Hand of Fate* (1921), pp. 11, 277 ff.

Consular protection in Morocco, **FortR** 2712

England and North Africa, **NatR-II** 1231

Pérez, Antonio Gonzalo: see *Index*, I, 1046.

The Spaniards in Cuba, **NC** 3327

Perrin, Mark, b.1791/92, B.A. from Trinity Coll. Dublin, 1815. *Alum. Dub*.

A Poor Law for Ireland, **DR** 25

Perry, Charles Copland, b.1853/54, writer on education. Foster, *BMCat*.

Germany as an object-lesson, **NC** 3443

Perry, George Gresley: see *Index*, I, 1046.

The grievances of High Churchmen, **NC** 1767

Perry, Harold Arthur: see *Index*, I, 1046.

France and judicial reform in Egypt, **NatR-II** 8
England and France in the East, 58
The friendship of France, 159
The fate of Marocco, 311
French interests in Egypt, 416
England in the Mediterranean, 587

The protest against over-examination, **NC** 1638

Perry, Sir Thomas Erskine: see Index, I, 1046.

A morning with Auguste Comte, **NC** 104
The future of India, 253

Perry, Walter Copland: see *Index*, I, 1046.

The recent excavations in Pergamon, **FortR** 1840

Benndorf's travels in Lycia and Caria, 2472

An apology for jingoism, **NatR-II** 306
Needlework as Art, 471

The sirens, in ancient literature and art, **NC** 881

Peterson, William, 1856–1921, classical scholar, educationist. *DNB.*

The Universities Bill, **ScotR** 226

Petre, Ralph William, 1856–1884, diplomat; sec. to English legation at Brussels. Gillow.

Belgium and the Holy See, **DR** 1753
Prospects in Belgium, 1797
Projects of the liberals in Belgium, 1888

Petre, William Joseph Petre, 13th Baron Petre, 1847–1893, R.C. prelate. Boase.

Large or small schools, **DR** 1641

Petrie, Sir William Matthew Flinders: see *Index*, I, 1046.

The study of man, **NatR-II** 1915

Pettersson, Sven Otto, b.1848, prof., writer on oceanography. *LCCat., BMCat.*

International fishery legislation, **NC** 3424

Pettifer, H. J., sec. Workingmen's Assoc. for Defence of British Industry. *BMCat.*

Technical education, **NatR-II** 531

Pettigrew, James Bell, 1834–1908, anatomist. *DNB.*

Flight natural and artificial, **FM** 6377

Petty-Fitzmaurice, Edmond George: see *Index*, I, 1047.

Home Rule: in Austria, **NC** 1257
Rural enclosures and allotments, 1352 collab.

Pfoundes, C. S. W.

Australia and annexation, **NatR-II** 463

Phelps, Arthur, 1837–1920, Lt. Gen. of Bombay Army. *WWW.*

What ails trade? **NatR-II** 238

Phelps, Edward John: see *Index*, I, 1047.

The Constitution of the U.S., **NC** 1520, 1529

Phillimore, Catherine Mary: see *Index*, I, 1047.

The Memoirs of Madame de Tourzel, **NatR-II** 228
Donatello, and façade of Duomo, 620

Phillimore, Richard Fortescue, 1864–1940, admiral. *DNB.*

A ride to Tokar, **NatR-11** 1187

Phillimore, Walter George Frank, 1st Baron Phillimore, 1845–1929, judge. *DNB.*

Mr. Gladstone, **FortR** 4138

Phillipps, Ambrose Lisle: See DeLisle, Ambrose L. M. Phillipps.

Phillipps, Evelyn March, d.1915, writer on labour and Italian art. *LCCat., Landed Gentry.*

A dock lodging-house, **FortR** 3212
The working lady in London, 3246
Small farms, 3314
Women's trade-unions, 3389
New factory bill: as it affects women, 3508
Women's newspapers, 3566
Factory legislation for women, 3637
Peasants of Romagna, 4006

Phillipps, Lisle March, 1863–1917, writer on art. *LCCat.*

Chartered Company [South Africa], **NatR-II** 2159

Phillips, Sir Claude: see *Index*, I, 1048.

Venetian art at the New Gallery, **FortR** 3615
Pictures of the year, 3653
The salons, 3832
Munich and Bayreuth, 3866

"Fair women," Grafton Gallery, **NatR-II** 1598
Notes on the National Gallery, 1656

Millais's works at Burlington House, **NC** 3253
The salons, 3316
The Van Dyck exhibition at Antwerp, 3558
The "Perseus and Andromeda" of Titian, 3651

Phillips, Edwin, ed. of the *Railway Service Gazette. BMCat.*

The internal working of railways, **FortR** 1035

Phillips, Henry Arthur Deuteros, writer on Indian law, ed. the *Calcutta Review*. *BMCat.*

The Indian revenue and intoxicants, **DR** 1974

Phillips, Janet, novelist, wife of Alfred Phillips. *RG, BMCat.*

Mr. Harris and Mr. Oliphant, **NatR-II** 1173

Phillips, John Roland, or Rowland: see *Index,* I, 1048.

?Justices of the Peace, **FM** 5394
Coroners, 6032
City companies and technical education, 6393

Phillips, Sir Lionel: see *Index,* I, 1048.

From inside Johannesburg [on the Jameson raid], **NC** 3150

Phillips, Walter Alison, 1864–1950, journalist, professor. *WWW.*

Walter von der Vogelweide, **NC** 2958
Influence of Machiavelli on the Reformation in England, 3036

Phillips, William: see *Index,* I, 1048.

Parliamentary eloquence, **FM** 212, 251, 274, 290, 304

Phillips, William Hallett, 1853–1897, American author. *LCCat.*

The United States and Cuba, **NatR-II** 1959

Phipps, Constantine Henry, 1st Marquis of Normanby, 2nd Earl of Mulgrave, 1797–1863, statesman. *DNB.*

Letter: **Ram** 151

Picken, Andrew, 1788–1833, Scottish author. *DNB.*

A legend of MacAlister More, **FM** 6
?Mrs. M'Crie, 40
?The only daughter: a Scottish tale, 174
The Cliffords of Craven, 794
The Jordans of Grange and the old maids of Balmogy, 835
Confessions of a metempsychosis, 877
The Baron of Courtstown, 886
Letter: 313
See: 284

Pickering, Charles J., student of Persian poetry. *BMCat.*

The Persian poetry of Avicenna, **NatR-II** 952
Firdausî's lyrical poetry, 963
A Persian Chaucer [Rûdagî], 997
The beginnings of Persian literature, 1030
The last singers of Bukhârâ, 1042
'Umar of Nîshâpûr, 1090
The Rubâ'iyât of Abû Sa'îd, 1129
Nasir of Balkh, 1164

Pickering, William Alexander, 1840–1907, civil servant in Straits Settlements. *WWW.*

The Chinese in the Straits of Malacca, **FM** 5860

Pictet, Raoul Pierre, 1846–1929, Swiss physician. *Grand Larousse.*

The liquefaction of oxygen, **NC** 177

Picton, James Allanson: see *Index,* I, 1048.

Moral aspects of religious difficulty, **FortR** 1082

Piggot, John, Jr., d.1877/78, F.S.A., historian. *BMCat., Antiquaries/2nd s., vol. 7, p. 378.*

The Historical Manuscripts Commission, **FM** 5319, 5494, 5656, 6028
Arctic expeditions, 5692
Character of Mary Tudor, 5728
Cistercian abbeys of Yorkshire, 5855

Piggott, Sir Francis Taylor: see *Index,* I, 1048.

Japanese customs, **FortR** 3200
New Japan, 3263
Artistic Japan, 3322

Pigott, Richard: see *Index,* I, 1049.

The Parnellite programme, **FortR** 2330

Pike, Laurence W.

Cruel case of the wounded war-horse, **NC** 3663

Pike, Luke Owen, 1835–1915, barrister. *LCCat.,* Foster.

The pleasures of difficulty, **FM** 4440

Piling,   ; or possibly Pi Ling.

Letter: **NatR-II** 187

Pincott, Frederic, translator of Hindi, writer on India. *BMCat.*

Primary education in India, **NatR-II** 138

The Indian National Congress, 870
Home Rule not wanted for India, 996
What is education? 1041
The eight-hours movement, 1089
The Hindû marriage agitation, 1134
Discontent in India, 1209
Letters: 483, 699, 1002, 1078

Pinsent, Robert John, 1834–1893, Newfoundland judge. Boase.

French fishery claims in Newfoundland, **NC**
1850

Pitman, Frederick Islay, 1863–1942, stockbroker, rowing "blue" at Cambridge. Venn.

Well rowed, Cambridge! **FortR** 2621

Pitra, Louis-Guillaume, of Lyons, president of the Committee of Police, 1789.

A contemporary narrative of the fall of the Bastille, **FortR** 1732

Pitt-Lewis, George: see *Index*, I, 1049.

The protection of innocent prisoners, **NC**
2933
New great reform in the criminal law, 3358
The law as to "contructive murder," 3472

Pius II, Pope (Enea Silvio de' Piccolomini), 1405–1464. *Cath. Ency.*

How I became Pope: by Pius the Second, **NC** 3093

Pius IX, Pope: see *Index*, I, 1049.

Encyclical and Syllabus [of principal errors censored], **DR** 1115
Brief in favour of *La Civiltà Cattolica,* 1164
Apostolic letters related to the Council, 1252
Brief addressed to Dr. Ward, 1328
Urbis et orbis, 1347
Brief addressed to Charles Perin, 1508
Briefs on liberal Catholicism, 1548
Brief [on assent to Papal infallibility], 1583

Encyclicals on Immaculate Conception and on Holy See, **Ram** 108
Allocution in secret consistory, April 20, 1849, 141, 151
Encyclical on present state of affairs in Italy, 209
Allocution at secret consistory of May 20, 1850, 242

Place, Francis, 1771–1854, Utilitarian, philanthropist. *DNB.*

See: **FM** 364

Platzer, Simon, Tyrolese priest. See *Ram,* 9 (Jan. 1852), 33.

The fugitive, an historical sketch, **Ram** 371, 378

Playfair, Sir Lyon: see *Index*, I, 1050.

Organisation of a teaching profession, **FortR** 1331
Selecting and training civil servants for India, 1380
Effects of western competition on the eastern states of America, **FM** 6292
On patents and the new patent bill, **NC** 18
Lord Armstrong and technical education, 1591
The presidential election in the United States, 1627
A great university for London, 2827

Plimsoll, Samuel, 1824–1898, M.P., writer on mercantile shipping. *DNB.*

Parliamentary procedure, **FortR** 2539

Explosions in collieries, **NC** 525
Cheap fish for London, 883
Twelve millions wasted in the sea, 1672, 1720
"Trusts": an alarm, 2049

Plowden, Trevor John Chichele, 1843–1887, army officer, diplomatist. Boase.

Turkish Arabia, **FortR** 2135

Plumptre, Edward Hays: see *Index*, I, 1050.

Letter: **FortR** 2655

Plunkett, Edward: see *Index*, I, 1050.

The "silver streak" [the Channel], **NC** 582
Proposed Channel tunnel, 681
The Channel tunnel, 683
England and the Suez Canal, 790

Plunkett, Sir Horace Curzon, 1854–1932, Irish statesman. *DNB.*

Woman suffrage in Wyoming, **FortR** 2947
Ireland to-day and to-morrow, 3472

Co-operative stores for Ireland, **NC** 1598
"Balfourian amelioration" in Ireland, 3759

Podmore, Frank, 1855–1910, writer on psychical research. *DNB.*

In defence of phantasms, **NatR-II** 1278

Poe, Edgar Allan, 1809–1849, poet. *DAB.*

Unknown correspondence, **NQM** 135

Poel, William, 1852–1934, actor, stage-director. *DNB.*

Letter: **FortR** 4476

The stage in Shakspeare's day, **NatR-II** 1039

Poer, John Henry de la, 5th Marquess of Waterford, 1844–1895. Burke.

On the latest land programme, **NC** 1809

Pole, William: see *Index*, I, 1050.

Conventions at whist, **FortR** 1572
Aërial navigation, 1766
The Bergsturz at Elm, 1865
Letter: 3269

Polignac, Prince Camille Armand Jules Marie de, 1832–1913. *Titled Nobility*; *Times*, Nov. 17, 1913, p.11d.

Ulster and the Confederate states, **NC** 2406

Pollard, William, 1828–1893, Quaker. *DNB.*

The peace-at-any-price party, **FM** 6336

Pollock, Alexander Matthew, d.1865, priest in Dublin. *BMCat.*, Allibone.

The Irish and English universities, **DR** 4 collab.

Pollock, Sir Charles Edward, 1823–1897, judge. *DNB.*

Reminiscences of Judah Philip Benjamin, **FortR** 4083

Pollock, Sir Frederick: see *Index*, I, 1050.

Spinoza's philosophy, **FortR** 948
On cosmic philosophy, 1158
Fitzjames Stephen's *Law of Evidence,* 1292
William Kingdon Clifford, 1578
History of English law as a branch of politics, 1850
History of the science of politics, 1936, 1947, 1952, 1988
John Milton, 2998

See: **FM** 5127, 5448

A fresh puzzle of Home Rule, **NatR-II** 1465
Hobbes, 1623
Sir James Fitzjames Stephen, 1760
"Hidden dangers," 1991
King Alfred, 2289

Benedict de Spinoza, **NC** 140
The sacrifice of education, 1666
Recollections of Ernest Renan, 2304

Pollock, Lady Juliet (Creed): see *Index*, I, 1051.

Vie de Shakespeare [by Victor Hugo], **FM** 4497
See: 3744, 3760, 3769, 3783, 3792, 3802, 5037

For and against the play, **NC** 44
The *Hamlet* of the Seine, 1348

Pollock, Walter Herries: see *Index*, I, 1051.

Eton worthies, **FortR** 2475

Sir Francis Drake, **NatR-II** 29
A glance at the stage, 326
Faust at the Lyceum, 409
A note on plagiarism, 1262
Should Shakespeare's plays be acted? 1277
Episode tiré des mémoires inédits du Marquis de _____ (1780), 1369a, 1412a
The Tory press and the Tory party, 1429

Alexandre Dumas, **NC** 509
Shakespearian criticism, 729

Pollock, Sir William Frederick: see *Index*, I, 1051.

Some recent biographies, **FortR** 2092

Russian dinners, **FM** 3842
Richardson, Miss Austen, Scott, 3927
The Antiquity of Man, [by Lyell], 4316
The portraits at South Kensington, 4668, 4781, 4880
Milman's *Annals of St. Paul's Cathedral*, 4943
Lord Vernon's *Inferno di Dante*, 4974
Faraday, 5061
The Royal Academy Exhibition [1872], 5326
Royal Academy Exhibtion [1873], 5447
An artist's dream, 5504
See: 4851, 5037

Smoke prevention, **NC** 564

Pollon, C. C. de, d.1832, editor in Copenhagen. Erslew (1847 ed.) II, 576.

Notice: **FQR** 215

Poncins, Vicomte Edmond de, b.1866. *Titled Nobility.*

The Menelik myth, **NC** 3435

Ponsonby, Arthur Augustus William Harry, Baron Ponsonby of Shulbrede, 1871–1946. Burke.

Tycho Brahe, **NC** 3670

Ponsonby, Charles Frederick Ashley Cooper: see *Index,* I, 1051.

A court of lunacy, **NC** 1244

Ponsonby, Lady Mary Elizabeth (Bulteel), 1832–1916, lady-in-waiting to Queen Victoria. *LCCat.; Times,* Oct. 17, 1916, p. 11c, and Dec. 26, p.9e.

An attempt at optimism, **NC** 2991
The rôle of women in society, 3762

Pontifex, Dudley David, b.1855, barrister. Venn.

Billiards, **NC** 3213

Poole, Maria Spencer Ruscombe, 1815–1881, Catholic nun known as Sister Mary Imelda. Newman, *L&D,* XI, 352–353.

The modern pilgrim's progress [Puseyism], **Ram** 468

Poole, Reginald Stuart: see *Index,* I, 1051.

Palgrave's *Journey through Arabia,* **FortR** 35
Pagan and Muslim Arabs, 108
Reforms in Persia, 976

Poole, Stanley Edward Lane-: see Lane-Poole, Stanley Edward.

Pope, L. J., of Edgbaston.

Letter: **NatR-II** 887

Pope-Hennessy, Sir John: see *Index,* I, 1052.

Sir Walter Raleigh in Ireland, **NC** 643
What do the Irish read? 1003
Lord Beaconsfield's Irish policy, 1054
The Chinese in Australia, 1543
The African bubble, 1892
Is Central Africa worth having? 1933

Porritt, Edward, 1860–1921, journalist. *WWW.*

American utopia [reform of municipal governments], **NatR-II** 1638
The disappointment of New York [political corruption], 1785

Portal, George Raymond, 1826/27–1889, divine, of Burghclere, Newbury. *Times,* Apr. 6, 1889, p.12b.

The two million [newly enfranchised electors], **NatR-II** 309
Letter: 145

Postgate, John Percival, 1853–1926, classicist. *WWW.*

The science of meaning, **FortR** 4007

Shall women graduate at Cambridge? **NatR-II** 631

Pote, Benjamin Edward, 1795/96–1862, journalist; ed. *FQR.* Obit. in *Norwich Mercury,* May 14, 1862, p.3. (See *Index,* I, 1052.)

Pazos, *Historical and Political Memoirs,* **FQR** 340
Ancient Persian poetry, 416
Davids' *Turkish Grammar,* 420
South America, 429
Tamil historical manuscripts, 441
History of Ottoman poetry, 449
?Fresnel's *History of the Arabs,* 462
Causes of war between Buenos Ayres and Bolivia, 463
Lassen, *Ancient Persian Inscriptions,* 464
The Hanoverian Constitution, and Royal Patent of November, 473 collab.
European and Asiatic poetry, 488
American literature [on] Chinese and Egyptian writing, 493
Dutch literature, 496 collab. at least
Phoenician inscriptions, 499
?Sillig's *Dictionary of the Artists of Antiquity,* 505
Polish poetry, 507
Schlegel's *Essay on Egypt,* 509
Chile, Peru, and American blockades, 520
?Arabs in Italy, Sicily, &c., 521
Progress of chemistry, 527 collab.
Creuzer and Knight: ancient figurative language, 528
Proceedings in India: usurpation of Oude, 530 collab.
Russia, Persia, Turkey, and France, 543 collab.
Arabian Nights, 552
English, classical, and Oriental literature, 561
Whist, par Deschappelles, 562
Ethiopians: apocryphal books of Isaiah and Enoch, 563
Turkey, Egypt, France, Russia, Asia, and the British Ministry, 564
The Druzes: their creed and its sources, 664
Note: 486

Potter, Beatrice: see Webb, Beatrice (Potter).

Potter, George: see *Index,* I, 1052.

The Church of England and the people, **FortR** 840

Imperial emigration, **Nat-R-II** 14

The labourers and the vote, **NC** 124
The workman's view of "fair trade," 629

Potter, John Phillips, 1793–1861, divine. Boase, *LCCat.* (See *Index,* I, 1052, under Rev. Potter.)

Bishop Heber, **LR(1829)** 24

Pottinger, Sir Henry, 1834–1909, barrister, novelist. *WWW.*

Elk-hunting, **FortR** 2668
Trout-fishing, 2705
Wild shooting, 2775
Nordanskär [a Swedish islet], 2846
A visit to a great estate [in Norway], 2957
An island deer-forest, 3042
A handful of lead [hunting in Norway], 3165

Powell, Baden: see *Index* I, 1052.

See: **FM** 3867

Progress of mathematics, **LR(1829)** 19

Powell, George Herbert: see *Index,* I, 1052.

Revival of Jacobinism, **NatR-II** 1281

Powell, Sir George Smyth Baden: see Baden-Powell, Sir G. S.

Powell, Hew David Steuart, b.1850/51. Foster.

Letter: **NatR-II**, 517

Powell, Joseph Louis

Theories of the beautiful and sublime, **DR** 2548
The Berkshire White Horse; and moraines in the Thames valley, 2572

Powell, T. E., vice-president Bimetallic League. See *NatR-II* cover for July 1896.

Mr. Henry D. Macleod, *Bimetallism,* **NatR-II** 1686
The American silver rebellion, 1890
Bimetallic side of the American crisis, 1929

Powell, Thomas, 1809–1887, journalist, *DAB,* Allibone.

Literary characters, **FM,** 33, 62, 231
James Hogg, 33
The bard of hope [Thomas Campbell], 62
The Wellington administration, 83
Wordsworth, 231
Men and manners, in 10 installments from 652 to 766

Power, John O'Connor, Irish M.P. *BMCat.,* Thom/80, p. 417.

Fallacies about Home Rule, **FortR** 1612

The Irish in England, 1677

The Irish land agitation, **NC** 379
The new reform [Redistribution Bill], 1077
Ireland: plan for congested districts, 1872

Power, Lawrence Geoffrey, 1841–1921, Canadian statesman. Wallace.

Canadian opinion on Home Rule, **DR** 2027

Power, Matthew A., S.J., 1857–1926, Sutcliffe.

[Book of] John IV. 35, **DR** 2219

Powys, Thomas Littleton, 4th Baron Lilford, 1833–1896. Burke.

Destruction of British birds, **NatR-II** 1563

Poynder, John P. Dickson: see Dickson-Poynder, J. P.

Poynter, Sir Edward John, 1836–1919, painter, president of Royal Academy, *DNB.*

Beauty and realism, **FortR** 786

Pozzoni, Cesare, Italian writer on politics and economics. *BMCat.*

Old and new economists in Italy, **FortR** 1156

Prandi, Fortunato, d.1868, Italian revolutionary, deputy. Tosi.

Rosini's *Nun of Monza,* **FQR** 102
Rossetti's *Dante,* 121 collab.
Bianca Cappello: the Medici family, 123
Notice: 144

Pressensé, Francis Dehault de: see *Index,* I, I, 1053.

The relations of France and England, **NC** 2877
England and the continental alliances, 3011
The Cretan question, 3076
The powers and the East, 3105
France, Russia, and the England of the Jubilee, 3148
The Dual and the Triple Alliance, 3206
France and England, 3264

Prestage, Edgar, 1869–1951, prof. Portuguese literature, London Univ. *WWW,* Gorman.

Brother Luiz de Sousa, **DR** 2513

Preston, Harriet Waters, 1836–1911, essayist. *DAB.*

An American on America, **NatR-II** 78

Preston, Thomas Scott, 1824–1891, R.C. priest in N.Y. *LCCat., Amer. WWW.*

Letter: **DR** 1407

Preston-Thomas, Herbert: see *Index,* I, 1053 and II, App. A.

Vaccination and the *Britannica,* **NatR-II** 863

Prestwich, Sir Joseph, 1812–1896, geologist. *DNB.*

The position of geology, **NC** 2464
The greater antiquity of man, 2735

Price, Bonamy: see *Index,* I, 1053, and II, App. A.

Austria and Hungary, **FM** 4201
The principles of currency, 4324
England and her colonies, 4372
The political temper of the nation, 4407
Bank Charter Act of 1844, 4550
Banks and banking, 4728
The controversy on free banking, 4835, 4856
Oxford, 4913
Credit and crises, 5000
Reply to the article on currency, 5018
D. Wilder of Boston on gold and currency, 5259
Lombard Street [by Walter Bagehot], 5479
What is money? 6259
What is a bank? 6287

Price, Cormell, 1835/36–1910, schoolmaster. *Times,* May 6, 1910, p.1a.

Shakespeare's minor poems, **OxCam** 14
Unhealthy employments, 28 collab.
Lancashire and *Mary Barton* [by Mrs. Gaskell], 41
?Work of young men in present age, 52

Price, Edward, 1804–1858, R.C. journalist. Newman, *L&D,* XII, index.

Notice: **DR** 719

Price, Eleanor Catherine: see *Index,* I, 1053, and *Yearbook/*1922.

Henri Beyle and his critics, **ScotR** 479

Price, Sir Richard Dansey Green [born Green, became Price in 1861], 1803–1887, solicitor. *BMCat.,* Boase.

Rebeccaism, **NC** 578

Prichard, J. V.

See: **FM** 5579

Priestley, Lady Eliza L. G. St. J. (Chambers), 1836–1909. *Landed Gentry, Times,* July 17, 1909 p. 13c.

Pasteur, **NC** 1560
The mysteries of malaria, 1718
The realm of the microbe, 2048
Housekeeping schools, 2301
Penalties of ignorance, 2732
Nurses à la mode, 3049
French and English research, 3142
Winged carriers of disease, 3456

Priestley, Sir William Overend, 1829–1900, physician. *DNB.*

The sacrifice of education, **NC** 1669

Primrose, Archibald Henry, 5th Earl of Rosebery, 1847–1929, statesman. *DNB.*

Letter: **ScotR** 280

Pringle, Edward J., a Carolinian. *LCCat.*

Slavery in the southern states, **FM** 3022

Pringle-Pattison, Andrew Seth: see *Index,* I, 1054.

Three years under the new ordinances, **ScotR** 492

Prior, Edward Schroder, 1852–1932, architect. *WWW.*

Ruskin's museum at Sheffield, **NatR-II** 307

Probyn, John Webb, 1828–1915, writer on history and economics. Venn, *BMCat.*

Italy and Rome, **FortR** 781
Church and state in Italy, 824
Sicily, 859
Religious liberty and atheism, 1707

Probyn-Nevins, Henry Willis: see Nevins, Henry Willis Probyn.

Procter, Anne Benson (Skepper), wife of Bryan Waller Procter, q.v. *DNB* under her husband, *BMCat.*

Mr. Hayward, **FortR** 2163

Procter, Bryan Waller: see *Index,* I, 1054.

The man-hunter, **FM** 103
Judgment of the annuals, 759
Death of the Rev. Edward Irving, 778

See: **NC** 229

Procter, L. J. *BMCat.*

Native tribes on the Zambési River, **FM**
4645

Dr. Livingstone, 5367

Proctor, Richard Anthony: see *Index,* I, 1054.

Total solar eclipses, **FortR** 2515
The everlasting hills, 2701
Capital and culture in America, 2739

Coloured suns, **FM** 4834
The great nebula in Orion, 4843
Lands and seas of another world, 4893
News from Sirius, 4907
The great nebula in Argo, 4926
The two comets of the year 1868, 4939,
4980
The ever-widening world of stars, 4991
The sun's journey through space, 5008
Professor Tyndall's theory of comets, 5019
The Rosse telescope, 5033
Discoveries respecting the aurora, 5053
Greatest sea wave ever known, 5102
The planet Saturn, 5119
A novel way of studying stars, 5134
The eclipse of the present month, 5150
Meteors and meteor systems, 5166
The sun's corona, 5178
What, then, *is* the corona? 5192
The study of astronomy, 5234
A new survey of the northern heavens, 5274
Movements in the star-depths, 5365
The coming transit of Venus, British pre-
parations, 5408
The coming transit of Venus, foreign pre-
parations, 5439
The rings of Saturn, 5868
The religion of the great pyramid, 5907

The certainties of chance, **NatR-II** 707

The sun's corona, **NC** 928
The new star in the Andromeda nebula,
1200
Whence came the comets? 1273

Prosser, Francis Richard Wegg: see Wegg-
Prosser, Francis Richard.

Prothero, George Walter: see *Index,* I, 1055.

Why should we learn history? **NatR-II** 1655
Resolutions of the House of Commons, 1713

A liberal education: the function of a university, **ScotR** 542

Prothero, Rowland Edmund: see *Index,* I,
1055.

Irish novelists on Irish peasants, **NatR-II**
807

Tithe rent-charges and peasant tenancies,
953
The clergy and the land, **NC** 1550
Frederick the Third and the new Germany,
1619
Is an "Agricultural Department" desirable?
1691
French boycotting and its cure, 1956
Théodore de Banville, 2087
The London County Council, 2187
New letters of Edward Gibbon, 2965
A day in provincial France, 3125
Childhood and school days of Byron, 3226
Notices: 1656, 1752, 1913, 1978, 2202,
2403, 2525

Provand, Andrew Dryburgh: see *Index,* I,
1056.

The coal problem, **NatR-II** 2498

Employers' liability, **NC** 2475

Prowett, Charles Gipps: see *Index,* I, 1056.

The Emperor Julian, **FM** 5186
Lucian, 5460
Apuleius, 5476
Philo the Jew, 5581

Pryde, Thomas

Heine's visit to London, **NatR-II** 657

Pugin, Augustus Welby Northmore, 1812–
1852, architect, ecclesiologist. *DNB.*

Ecclesiastical architecture in England, **DR**
213, 245

Pullar, Adeline. *BMCat.*

A Swedish system of handwork, **FortR** 2566

Pulsford, Edward, 1844–1919, English-Aus-
tralian publicist and politician. *Australian
Biographical Dictionary,* ed. F. Johns,
1934.

An Australian lesson [in trade], **NC** 1597

Purbrick, Edward Ignatius, S.J., 1830–1914.
Sutcliffe.

Christian art, **DR** 1090

Purcell, Edmund Sheridan, 1823–1899, journalist, biographer. Gillow.

Father de Ravignan, **DR** 891
*Anne Sherwood, or Social Institutions of
England,* 914
The Church of Portugal, 931
The Italian Revolution, 950

Bonapartism [in Italy], 967
Living English poets, 980
Döllinger and temporal power of the Popes, 987
The Law of Divorce, 988
Papal allocutions, 1009
Pugin and Turner, 1011
Sicily: the Italian revolution and the Papacy, 1018
Modern intellectualism and the Catholic Church, 1030
Catholic Congress of Malines, 1050
Belgian constitution and Church, 1103
Cardinal Manning in his Anglican days, 2332
Notices: 944, 971, 1002, 1019, 1027

Poisoning the wells of Catholic criticism, **NC** 2906
Ethics of suppression in biography, 2996

Purnell, Charles W.

Politics in Australasia, **FortR** 1453

Purves, James, 1853–1922, solicitor before

Supreme Court, Scotland. *BMCat.*, Records of Soc. of Solicitors to Supreme Court. (See *Index*, I, 1056, where art. is wrongly attrib. to James Liddell Purves.)

Overbury's characters, **FM** 6327
Tyningtown, 6388
Aethelston: a northern sketch, 6528
Lost love: a Lothian tale, 6533
Old Scotch judges, 6549

Salmon leistering [spearing], **NatR-II** 1123

Pyne, Evelyn, poet. *BMCat.*

A Surrey home, **NatR-II** 987
The garden of death, 1133
A temple of silence, 1215

Pyne, William Henry, 1769–1843, painter, *DNB.*

The greater and lesser stars of old Pall Mall, **FM** 1493, 1517, 1540, 1548, 1575, 1588, 1635
Sir David Wilkie and his friends, 1618

Q

Quick, James, clerk at board of trade. Boase and Courtney, III, 1321; in *Imperial Calendar* from 1874 to 1914.

The Cornish pilchard fisheries, **FM** 5898

Quilter, Harry: see *Index*, I, 1057.

Courage [on equality of women], **FortR** 3657

An artist on art [E. J. Poynter], **FM** 6314

Relation of criticism to production in art, **NatR-II** 1730

"In the days of her youth" [women's education], **NC** 2761

Quilter, Sir William Cuthbert, 1841–1911, art collector, politician. *DNB.*

Pure beer, **NC** 1364

Quin, Michael Joseph: see *Index*, I, 1057.

Economy of the earth, **DR** 1
Rienzi, 3
Ecclesiastical music [on G. Hogarth], 5 collab.
Raumer's *England in 1835*, 6
Maria Monk's "Black Nunnery," 7
The Edom of the prophecies, 8
Wraxall's *Memoirs*, 15

Recent poetry, 17
The Protestant Association, 21
The Danube and Black Sea, 59
The French in Africa, 80
Lynch's *Measures for Ireland*, 135
Temperance movement in Ireland, 176
Hungary and Transylvania, 186
The [contemporary] stage, 190
Parties in church and state, 191
?Economy of the atmosphere, 192
The Circassians, 197
Foreign affairs, 199
The wants of Ireland, 209
Recent poetry, 211
Navigable Polar Sea, 212
Mental epidemics, 214
Agricultural improvement in Ireland, 219
Propagation of the Faith, 241
Peel's government, 248
Spain and her resources, 269
See: 14, 69

Quin, Windham Thomas Wyndham, 4th Earl of Dunraven, 1841–1926, Irish politician. *DNB.*

Democracy and the House of Lords, **NatR-II** 206
The real truth about Tory democracy, 567
A word with the physicians, 1257

Quin, W. T. W. (*continued*)
Moose-hunting in Canada, **NC** 328
Days in the woods, 431
A Colorado sketch, 494
Wapiti-running on the plains [of America], 504
A glimpse at Newfoundland, 539
"The Revolutionary Party" [in English politics], 612

Sheep-hunting in the mountains, 644
The future "Constitutional Party," 846
The House of Lords, 957
Opening national institutions on Sunday, 972
The future of Toryism, 1652
Commercial union within the Empire, 2019
The invasion of destitute aliens, 2231

R

Raby, Richard, 1816–1881, teacher in Munich. Boase.

Mystery of the passion at Ober Ammergau, **Ram** 317, 736
Döllinger's *Heathenism and Judaism,* 884
The Archbishop of Cologne and Prussian diplomacy, 963
Letter: 909

Radcliffe, Francis Reynolds Yonge, 1851–1924, barrister. *WWW.*

The volunteers as a military force, **NatR-II** 66
A few Stuart papers, 746
The future of the Tory Party, 1337
Toryism and progression, 1383
Letter: 128

Rae, John: see *Index,* I, 1057.

The Scotch village community, **FortR** 2386

An empire of crofters, **NatR-II** 894

Rae, William Fraser: see *Index,* I, 1058.

Richard Brinsley Sheridan, **FortR** 440
John Wilkes, 529
Notices: 496, 553

Political clubs and party organization, **NC** 174
International copyright, 646
Karlsbad, 1061
The centenary of *The Times,* 1079
The jubilee of the Reform Club, 1272
Play and players on the Riviera, 1828
The Egyptian newspaper press, 2267
More about Sheridan, 3241

Rafiüddin Ahmad: see Ahmad, Rafiüddin.

Raikes, Henry Cecil, 1838–1891, politician. *DNB.*

Job and his comforters, **FortR** 2144
Joseph and his brethren, 2184
Redistribution by different lights, 2259
Conservatives on themselves, 2311

Redistribution of political power, **NatR-II** 17
New law of elections, 83
Women's suffrage, 254
The Radical programme, 382
The radical at home, 1124

Public business in the House of Commons, **NC** 368
Parliamentary obstruction, 533
The functions of an opposition, 811

Raikes, Henry St. John Digby, 1863–1943, barrister. *WWW.*

Edited: **FortR** 4141

Rait, Sir Robert Sangster, 1874–1936, Scottish historian. *DNB.*

A Scot abroad [James Keith], **ScotR** 671

Raleigh, Sir Walter Alexander, 1861–1922, literary critic. *DNB.*

Tudor Translations [ed. W. E. Henley], **FortR** 3697

Ralston, William Ralston Shedden: see *Index,* I, 1058.

Polish Insurrection of 1863, **FortR** 144
A Russian poet, 317
The Roman Molière [Plautus], 408
Russian popular legends, 579

New Tales from the Norse, **FM** 5368
Sicilian fairy tales, 5793

Turkish story-books, **NC** 2
Russian revolutionary literature, 29
Henri Gréville's [i.e., Alice Durand's] sketches of Russian life, 215
Beauty and the Beast, 248
Count Leo Tolstoy's novels, 297
Cinderella, 372
"Puss in Boots," 807

Ramée, Marie Louise de la: see de la Ramée, Marie Louise.

Ramière, Henri, 1821–1884, French Jesuit, journalist. *Grand Larousse.*

Catholic liberalism, **DR** 1518, 1537
The Church's social conflict, 1549
On religious unity and toleration, 1560

Rampini, Charles Joseph Galliari, 1840–1907, sheriff of Dumfries. Grant.

Battle of Otterburn, **ScotR** 70
The burning of Frendraught, 178
Florence Wilson, 257
Correspondence of an old Scotch factor, 306

Ramsay, Agnata Frances: see Butler, Agnata Frances (Ramsay).

Ramsay, Lady Florence Mary (Hilton), 1855/ 56–1936. *Times,* Mar. 23, 1936, p. 1b.

Letter: **NatR-II** 645

Ramsay, George Gilbert: see *Index,* I, 1058.

Secondary education in Scotland, **FM** 5792, 5809

Ramsay, J.

Mr. Irving and Diderot's *Paradox,* **NatR-II** 149

Ramsay, Walter Marlow, d.1910, divine. *CCD*/1910, obit. in *Guardian,* Mar. 24, 1910.

University of London, its influence in Scotland, **FM** 5844

Ramsay, Sir William, 1852–1916, chemist, prof. at Univ. of Glasgow. *DNB.*

Deaths under chloroform, **NC** 3278

Ramsden, Frederick Wollaston, 1839–1898, of the British consular service. *FortR* no. 4179, pp. 507n., 526.

A diary at Santiago, **FortR** 4179, 4196

Ramsden, Lady Helen Guendolen (Seymour), 1846–1910, artist. *WWW,* Burke under Somerset.

Extravagance in dress, **NC** 3746

Ramsden, Hermione Charlotte, 1867–1951, misc. writer. Burke.

The new mysticism in Scandinavia, **NC** 3605

Ramsden, Richard; prob. the Richard Ramsden, 1841–1921, barrister in Venn.

A good word for territorialism, **FortR** 1698

Randell, James S.; possibly the James Randell, 1848/49–1884, divine in Foster.

Friendly Societies, **FortR** 1721

Randolph, Edmund, Jun., 1850–1889, architect, novelist. Gillow.

Catholic political associations, **DR** 1866

Rankin, Daniel J.: see *Index,* I, 1059, and II, App. A.

The Portuguese in East Africa, **FortR** 2913
The Chinde entrance to the Zambesi River, 3304

Rankin, James H., 1831–1902, minister of Muthill. *BMCat., LCCat.*

The Church of Scotland, **NatR-II** 25

Ransom, Edwin: see *Index,* I, 1059, and II, App. A.

A visit to Shamyl's country, **FM** 5383

Rasch, Sir Frederic Carne, 1847–1914, army officer. *WWW.*

Long speeches and bores, **FortR** 4054

The War Office, **NC** 3219

Rathbone, William: see *Index,* I, 1059.

Reform in parliamentary business, **FortR** 1772
The House of Lords, 1845
Great Britain and the Suez Canal, 1938
Irish disaffection: causes and cure, 2403
Failure of government by groups, 3731

Local government in England and Wales, **NC** 821, 835

Rau, R. Vasudeva: see Vāsudeva Rāu, R.

Raupert, John Godfrey Ferdinand, 1858–1929, R.C. priest. *LCCat.,* Gorman.

What will be the creed of the future? **DR** 2576

Rawlings, Benjamin Burford, writer on hospitals. *Yearbook*/1916, *Blackwood Papers Cat.*

Hospital administration, **FM** 6421
The finance of unendowed hospitals, 6431
Among the tors [on Dartmoor], 6503
The case of the special hospitals, 6518

Rawlinson, Sir Henry Creswicke: see *Index,* I, 1059.

The Afghan crisis, **NC** 247

Rawlinson, Sir Henry Creswicke (*continued*)
The results of the Afghan War, 349
The situation in Afghanistan, 402
The Russian advance in Central Asia, 1113

Rawlinson, Sir Robert, 1810–1898, civil engineer. *DNB.*

Domestic sanitary arrangements, **FM** 5379

Rawlinson, William George, 1840–1928, art collector. *DNB.*

Turner's drawings at the Royal Academy, **NC** 1254

Read, Carveth, 1848–1931, prof. of philosophy and psychology, Univ. of London. *WWW.*

De Maillet, **FortR** 966

Read, Clare Sewell, 1826–1905, authority on farming. *WWW.*

English tenant right, **NatR-II** 43

Reade, Amos, novelist. *BMCat.*

Visit to a Kerry nationalist, **NatR** 680
What to do about land, 853
Primrose League *v.* National League in Ireland, 931

Reade, Compton: see *Index,* I, 1060.

The agricultural problem, **NatR-II** 1149
Tithe redemption, 1917

Reaney, George Sale, Broad Church divine, once a Congregationalist. *BMCat., CCD/96.*

Outcast London, **FortR** 2537

Civil and moral benefits of drill, **NC** 3617

Redding, Cyrus, 1785–1870, journalist. *DNB.*

Tegoborski's *Austrian Finance,* **FQR** 767

Retrospective gleanings, **FM** 2021, 2249
Wilkie and Haydon, 2338
Hints upon history, 2384
London from the crow's nest, 2541
A scene in Franconia, 2633
Words about Oxford, 2709
Joseph Mallord William Turner, 2936
Wine, its Use and Taxation, 3353

Redford, George, 1817–1895, physician, art critic. *Athenaeum,* Nov. 2, 1895, p. 615.

Art sales and Christie's, **NC** 1428

Redmayne, R. T.

Currency, **NatR-II** 897
Currency and the case of Ireland, 1020
Letters: 853, 1079

Redmond, Edward, d.1885, prof. of theology at St. Edmund's, Ware. *Tablet,* April 18, 1885, p. 622.

Assumption of the Blessed Virgin Mary, **DR** 1335
Notices: ?1927, ?1306

Redmond, John Edward: see *Index,* I, 1060.

Irish Local Government Bill, **FortR** 3208
A plea for amnesty, 3296
The lesson of South Meath, 3307

Readjustment of the Union, **NC** 2290
Second thoughts on the Home Rule Bill, 2374
What next? [after rejection of Home Rule], 2474
What has become of Home Rule? 2653
"Killing Home Rule by kindness," 2844
Ireland and the next session, 3055
Promised Irish Local Government Bill, 3189
The Centenary of '98 [the Irish Insurrection], 3271

Reed, Sir Edward James: see *Index,* I, 1060.

Dr. Herz and the French Republic, **FortR** 3898

Reed, Henry Byron, 1855–1896, journalist. *Boase.*

Letter: **NatR-II** 325

Reed, Thomas Brackett, 1839–1902, American statesman. *DAB.*

Silver and the tariff at Washington, **FortR** 3517

Rees, Sir John David: see Index, I, 1060.

A fortnight in Finland, **NatR-II** 1487
The outskirts of Europe, 1612

Our day's sport in India, **NC** 1540
The Persia of the Shah, 1738
Meddling with Hindu marriages, 1949
An Indian funeral sacrifice, 2229
Life in a Russian village, 2577
The Bab and Babism, 2957
Fighting the famine in India, 3078
Among the elephants, 3308
A Hindu home, 3580

Rees, William Lee, 1836–1907, in consular service. *LCCat., F.O. List/1901*

German conduct in Samoa, **NC** 1624

Reeve, Christina Georgina Jane (Gollop), wife of Henry Reeve, q.v. *Blackwood Papers Cat.*

Historical cookery, **FM** 6541

Reeve, Henry, 1813–1895: see *Index*, I, 1060.

George Villiers, Earl of Clarendon, **FM** 5108
William Longman, 5974

Reeves, Hon. William Pember, 1857–1932, New Zealand barrister, journalist. *WWW.*

Five years' reform in New Zealand, **NatR-II** 1901
The functions of a governor-general, 1955
Compulsory arbitration in labour disputes, 2084
Criticisms of Australasian democracy, 2175
The New Zealand Old-Age Pensions Act, 2260
Colonial governments as money-lenders, 2537
Letter: 2459

Regnard, Albert Adrien, 1836–1903, physician. *EUI.*

Chaumette and first Commune of Paris, **FortR** 831

Reich, Emil, 1854–1910, historian. *DNB.*

Hungary at the close of her first millennium, **NC** 2935
The Jew-baiting on the Continent, 2987
Zionism, 3154
Austria-Hungary and the Ausgleich, 3260

Reichardt, Annie: see *Index*, I, 1062, and II, App. A.

Mohammedan women, **NC** 2057

Reichensperger, August, 1808–1895, German Catholic statesman. *Cath. Ency.*

The theory of party, **Ram** 1021

Reid, Andrew, b. 1848, political writer. *Yearbook/*1904.

The new party, **FortR** 3648
History in advertisements, 4345

Reid, Arnot. *BMCat.*

How a provincial paper is managed, **NC** 1310
Twenty-four hours in a newspaper office, 1385
The English and the American press, 1439

Reid, Donald, Jun., 1833–1919, of Dunedin, New Zealand. *Ency. of New Zealand,* 1966.

Great Britain's duty, **NatR-II** 2090

Reid, Donald N. *Blackwood Papers Cat.*

The disaffection in Behar, **FortR** 3513

Reid, Sir George Archdall O'Brien, 1860–1929, physiological writer. *WWW.*

Reflex action, instinct, and reason, **FortR** 3763
The Present Evolution of Man, 3884

Reid, Sir George Houstoun, 1845–1918, colonial politician. *DNB.*

The "Commonwealth of Australia," **NC** 2077

Reid, Gilbert, 1857–1927, divine, wrote on China. *LCCat.*

Shall the Open Door be closed? **NatR-II** 2234

Reid, Sir Hugh Gilzean, 1836–1911, journalist. *WWW.*

Religious life in Scotland, **FortR** 250

Reid, Robert Threshie: see *Index*, I, 1062.

Our obligations in Egypt, **FortR** 2202

Reid, Sir Thomas Wemyss: see *Index*, I, 1062.

Rural Roumania, **FortR** 1543
Public opinion and its leaders, 1724
Mr. [William Edward] Forster, 2457

Modern newspaper enterprise, **FM** 5817
?Gossip and gossip [the "society journals"], 6198

[W. E.] Forster and his colleagues, **NC** 1613
The Liberal outlook, 2208
The House of Lords: abolish its veto, 2556
The political situation, 2692
The burden of Egypt, 2909
A northern pilgrimage, 2990
Why Russia distrusts England, 2994
"The integrity of the Ottoman Empire," 3103
Reminiscences of English journalism, 3137
Impressions [of Eastern Europe and Russia], 3198
Gladstone and his party, 3325
The newspapers, in 14 installments from 3568 to 3770
"Ordinary business principles," 3692
Notice: 3022

Reilly, Jane Hester, 1774–1813, daughter of John Reilly of County Down.

A lady's journey from Dublin to London, **NC** 3289

Reinach, Joseph, 1856–1921, French journalist. *WWW.*

Scrutin de liste [on universal suffrage], **NC** 624
Revision of the French constitution, 672
The Channel tunnel, 714
Parisian newspapers, 758
Egyptian question and the French alliance, 789
The unmounted Bucephalus [France], 824
Republican prospects in France, 908
Sympathy between France and England, 1120
Gladstone and the Irish Bill, 1291
The true position of French politics, 1378

Renan, Ernest: see *Index,* I, 1062.

Marc-Aurèle, **NC** 437

Renouf, Sir Peter le Page: see *Index,* I, 1062.

Carlyle's *Past and Present,* **DR** 302
Veneration of saints in early Church, 330, 340
The Papal supremacy, 361
Difficulties of ante-Nicene Fathers, 376
"Saint Worship," and monotheistic religions, 991
See: 362

Repington, Charles à Court, 1858–1925, army officer, military expert. *DNB.*

French naval policy in peace and war, **NC** 3060
Lessons of the [Boer] War, 3742

Reuter, Julio Nathanael, prof. of Sanscrit and comparative literature at Helsingfors. *BMCat.,* Edward Westermarck, *Memories of My Life,* (1929) p. 149.

Russia in Finland, **NC** 3459

Réville, Albert, 1826–1906, French protestant theologian. *Grand Larousse.*

"Dawn of creation," **NC** 1237

Rew, Sir Robert Henry, 1858–1929, agriculturist. *WWW,* Debrett/1921.

Technical agricultural education, **NatR-II** 1093

Reynolds, Henry Revell, Jun., 1827–1896, divine. Venn, Boase under his father.

Road repair, **NatR-II** 348

Rhodes, Cecil John, 1853–1902, imperialist. *DNB.*

See: **FortR** 3936

Letter: **NC** 3418

Rhodes, Matthew John, 1817–1891, barrister. Venn, Gorman.

Modern principles of government, **DR** 948
The Minister's Wooing, 951
P[ère] Félix on progress, 959

Letter: **Ram** 991

Rhys, Ernest Percival: see *Index,* I, 1063.

The new mysticism [on Fiona Macleod], **FortR** 4469
Letters: 2627, 2638

Rhŷs, Sir John, 1840–1915, Celtic scholar. *DNB.*

Welsh fairies, **NC** 2108

Early ethnology of British Isles, **ScotR** 274
A non-Aryan element in the Celtic family, 284
Mythographical treatment of Celtic ethnology, 295
The peoples of ancient Scotland, 304
The spread of Gaelic in Scotland, 315
National names of the aborigines of British Isles, 326

Ricarde-Seaver, Francis Ignatius, 1836–1906, army officer. Rosenthal.

British influence in South Africa, **FortR** 2801 collab.
Boer, Africander, and Briton in the Transvaal, 2676, 3749

Rice, Thomas Spring: see Spring-Rice, Thomas.

Richards, Herbert, 1848–1916, fellow of Wadham College, Oxford. *WWW.*

Church of England and universities, **FortR** 1195

Richards, John Morgan, 1841–1918, businessman, proprietor of the *Academy. WWW.*

Letter: **NatR-II** 1063

Richards, Owen William, 1873–1949, physician. *Landed Gentry, WWW.*

Oxford Liberalism, **NatR-II** 2052 collab.

Richards, R. C.; possibly the Roger Charnock Richards, Sr., barrister, in Venn under his son.

The landord's preferential position, **FortR** 2962

Richards, Thomas; possibly Thomas Richards, surgeon, in *BMCat.*

The philosophy of apparitions, **FM** 89
Fatal presentiments, 173

Richards, Walter John Bruce, 1835/36–1904, R.C. editor. Gorman, Foster.

Character of the Covenant sacrifice, **DR** 2218

Richardson, Sir Benjamin Ward: see *Index,* I, 1063.

The Thames, **FortR** 2658
Letter: 2647

Woman as a sanitary reformer, **FM** 6349
The seed-time of health, 6473
National education, 6520
Race and life on English soil, 6538

Richardson, C. Morgan. *BMCat.*

A manufactured land question, **NatR-II** 1965
Plunder by death duties, 2164

Richardson, Frederick Austin, R.C. abbé, prof. at the Institute St. Louis, Brussels. *BMCat.*

"The Sacrifices of Masses," **DR** 2205

Richardson, Frederika: see Macdonald, Frederika (Richardson).

Richardson, G.; prob. the George Richardson, 1813–1901, of Dudley Grammar School, R.C. canon of Manchester. Gorman, under Mrs. Elizabeth Richardson.

Notices: **DR** 2347, 2373, 2412

Richey, Alexander George, 1830–1883, Irish historian. *DNB.*

Impressions of the Irish Land Bill, **FortR** 1797

The Teutonic and the Celtic epic, **FM** 5527

Richmond, Sir William Blake, 1842–1921, artist. *DNB.*

Lord Leighton and his art, **NC** 2901

Richter, Emil: see *Index,* I, 1063.

?Parliamentary difficulties in Austria, **FortR** 4053

Richter, Jean Paul, 1847–1937: see *Index,* I, 1063, and II, App. A.

Recent criticism on Raphael, **NC** 1450
Guilds of the early Italian painters, 1957
Art studentship of early Italian painters, 2271

Richter, Jean Paul Friedrich, 1763–1825: see *Index,* I, 1063, 1194, and II, App. A.

Mme. de Staël's *Allemagne,* **FM** 4, 45
Chrestomathy; or, Analects and apologues, 744, collab.
Recollections of the fairest hours, 1652
Detached thoughts, 1676

Rickaby, Joseph John, S.J., 1845–1932. *LCCat., Sutcliffe.*

What has the Church to do with science? **DR** 1980
Notice: ?2186

Rickards, Sir George Kettilby: see *Index,* I, 1064.

The commercial crisis of 1857 and currency, **BentQR** 4

Rickett, Arthur: see Compton-Rickett, Arthur.

Ridge, John James, 1847–1908, physician. *LCCat., Surgeon Index*/2s.

Letter: **NatR-II** 1200

Ridge, William Pett, c.1860–1930, novelist; of the Birkbeck Institution. *WWW, Times,* Sept. 30, 1930, p. 14d.

Club life in East London, **NatR-II** 1198

Ridgeway, Sir Joseph West, 1844–1930, soldier, administrator. *DNB.*

The new Afghan frontier, **NC** 1459

Ridsdale, E. S.; perhaps the Sir Edward Aurelian Ridsdale, 1864–1923, sheriff and scientist, in *WWW.*

Letter: **NatR-II** 1135

Riess, Dr. H., S.J., Gymnasial Director. *BMCat.*

Trans: **DR** 1649

Riley, Athelstan: see *Index,* I, 1064.

Conspiracy [religion in education], **NatR-II** 1592
Education and the Conservative party, 2117

The education settlement of 1870, **NC** 2865

Rinder, Frank, 1863–1937, writer on art. *WWW.*

Fragments of Caithness folk-lore, **ScotR** 487
Legendary lore of inner Hebrides, 508
Sutherland folk-lore, 537
The Kelmscott Press, 684

Ritchie, David George: see *Index,* I, 1065.

Note: **ScotR** 449

Ritchie, Leitch, 1797–1865, novelist. *DNB:* Ritchie to Brougham, Dec. 3, 1836, Univ. Coll. London, says he will be 40 in June.

Lebrun, *The Voyage to Greece,* **FQR** 47
French criminal trials, 85
Méry and Barthélemy, *The Son of the Man,* 100
Greek romances, 108
Notices: 39, 53, 103, 118

Ritter, Ludwig

Rare pottery and porcelain, **NQM** 11

Rivett-Carnac, John Henry, 1838–1923, Indian civil service. *WWW.*

Swiss rifle clubs, **NC** 3665

Rivington, Luke, 1838–1899, R.C. priest. *Cath. Ency.*

Allies' *Per Crucem ad Lucem,* **DR** 2240
The Lincoln Judgment, 2262
Anglican claim to historical Christianity, 2275
Independent national churches, 2289
Anglican writers and Council of Ephesus, 2326, 2342
Primitive saints and See of Rome, 2395
The Acacian troubles, 2432
Papal supremacy: Council of Ephesus, 2482
[William Bright] on the Roman See, 2534
The situation, 1897 [Holy See and Church of England], 2567
Dr. Pusey's *Eirenicon,* 2625
Notices: 2520, 2686

Robb, James Hampden, 1846–1911, American banker. *Amer. WWW, N.Y. Times,* Jan. 22, 1911, sec. III, p. ii.

Buying Niagara, **NC** 1349

Roberts, A. W.; perhaps the Arthur William Roberts, b.1851, barrister, in *M at B.*

Low prices and hostile tariffs, **NatR-II** 374

Roberts, Alexander, 1826–1901, classical and biblical scholar. *DNB.*

Revised version of English New Testament, **FM** 6410

Progress of theology in Scotland, **ScotR** 1

Roberts, C. T., of Ipswich.

Letter: **NatR-II** 494

Roberts, Charles, 1836–1901: see *Index,* I, 1065, and *Surgeon Index/2s.*

Physical condition of the masses, **FortR** 2640

Roberts, Frederick Sleigh, 1st Earl Roberts, 1832–1914, field-marshal. *DNB.*

Letter: **FortR** 3133

The present state of the army, **NC** 777
Free trade in the army, 1011

Roberts, John William, O.S.F. *BMCat.,* see *DR* 10 n.s. (1868), 231.

Dr. Ward on intellect, **Ram** 1133

Roberts, L. M.

The Burns and Dunlop correspondence, **FortR** 3715

Pierre Loti and the sea, **ScotR** 501

Roberts, Margaret, b.1833, novelist. *LCCat.*

A story of 1848–1849, **FM** 4018

Roberts, Morley: see *Index,* I, 1065.

The war game in South Africa, **FortR** 4237

Roberts, W.

Life on a guinea a week, **NC** 1531

Roberts, William; perhaps early work by contributor who follows.

Administration of justice in America, **FortR** 3169
Fruit-growing in California, 3285
Wine-growing in California, 3342

Robertson, James Burton (*continued*)
Writings of Augustus William von Schlegel, 154, 165
Trans: 218

Robertson, James Craigie: see *Index*, I, 1065.

An inedited fragment, **FM** 3305
Noctes Ambrosianae [by John Wilson], 3397
Boswell's *Letters*, 3578
Barthomley, 3731

Robertson, John George: see *Index*, I, 1065.

A German court theatre, **NatR-II** 1712

Gustav Freytag, **ScotR** 509

Robertson, John Mackinnon, 1856–1933, critic. *DNB.*

Mr. Lang on the origin of religion, **FortR** 4197

Robertson, Thomas Campbell: see *Index*, I, 1066.

The English in India, **FQR** 140

Robinson, Agnes Mary Frances: see Darmesteter, Agnes Mary Frances (Robinson).

Robinson, Charles Henry: see *Index*, I, 1066.

Civilisation in the Western Soudan, **NC** 3318

Robinson, Charles John, 1833–1898, divine. Boase.

Annals of a border county, **FM** 5162

Robinson, Edward Kay, 1857–1928, naturalist; ed. *Civil and Military Gazette*, Lahore. *WWW.*

India and the viceroyalty, **FortR** 3699
The Afghan alliance, 3719

The era of the torpedo, **NatR-II** 84

The man of the future, **NC** 850

Robinson, Frances Mabel, misc. writer. *BMCat., MWT* 15th ed. under her sister, Madame Darmesteter, q.v.

Our working women and their earnings, **FortR** 2608
Pawnbroking in England and abroad, 2728
The Paris salons of 1891, 3094

Robinson, Frederick, 1826–1901, army surgeon. Munk, IV, *Surgeon Index*/2s.

Recruits and recruiting, **NatR-II** 282

Robinson, Henry Crabb: see *Index*, I, 1067.
See: **FM** 303

Robinson, Sir Hercules George Robert, 1st Baron Rosmead, 1824–1897, colonial governor. *DNB.*

The Swaziland question, **FortR** 2923

Robinson, John, servant. *BMCat.*

A butler's view of men-service, **NC** 2225

Robinson, Sir John: see *Index*, I, 1067.

A voice on the colonial question, **FM** 4942

South Africa as it is, **NC** 1421
Sir George Grey, 3372

Robinson, Sir John Charles, 1824–1913, art connoisseur. *DNB.*

Art collections and provincial museums, **NC** 455, 482
Light and water-colours, 1284
On spurious works of art, 2117
Our national art museums and galleries, 2331
English art connoisseurship, 2643
Rembrandt and Sir Joshua Reynolds, 2722
Art connoisseurship in England, 2838
Picture conservation, 2914
Our public art museums, 3212
Reorganisation of national art museums, 3390

Robinson, Kendall, of Blyth. *BMCat.*

Our junior conservatives, **NatR-II** 355

Robinson, Louis: see *Index*, I, 1067, and *Medical Who's Who*/1915.

Every-day cruelty, **FortR** 3526

The science of change of air, **NatR-II** 1888

Darwinism in the nursery, **NC** 2128
The meaning of a baby's footprint, 2213
Darwinism and swimming: a theory, 2476

Robinson, Mabel: see Robinson, Frances Mabel.

Robinson, Margaret, translator of Frederik Van Eeden. *BMCat.*

A Dutch fairy tale [by Van Eeden], **NC** 3638

Robinson, Sir Robert Spencer: see *Index*, I, 1067.

Dangers and warnings of the *Inflexible*, **NC** 137

England as a naval power, 413
The navy and the admiralty, 1086
Letter: 582

Robinson, Thomas, d.1916, physician. *WWW/*
1928.

Modern life and sedatives, **NatR-II** 1314

Robinson, Wilfrid Cuthbert, 1848–1922, R.C.
historian. *Cath. WW/*1919, information
from librarian at Bayswater.

Father Augustine de Backer, **DR** 1590
Penal times in Holland, 2433
An electoral experiment in Belgium, 2468

Roby, John: see *Index*, I, 1067.

The Jew of York, **FM** 992
Staithes: the smuggler's daughter, 1044

Roche, James, 1770–1853, Irish banker. *DNB.*

The Bible and the Reformation, **DR** 69
Men of Letters and Science [by Brougham],
379
O'Conor's *Military History of Ireland*, 392
D'Aubigné's *Reformation*, 405
Brougham's *Men of Letters and Science—*
D'Alembert, 452
Johnson, his contemporaries and biog-
raphers, 476
Gibbon and his biographers, 508

Rochefort, Henri, 1831–1913, French journalist, politician. *Grand Larousse.*

The Revolution of September, 1870, **FortR**
1077
The Boulangist movement, 2724

Rock, Daniel, 1799–1871, R.C. ecclesiologist.
DNB.

Discovery [of Ebn Batoota's travels], **DR** 50
Fallacious evidence of the senses, 72

Rock, Joseph

The new era at Hyderabad, **FortR** 3972

Rod, Edouard, 1857–1910, Swiss author.
Grand Larousse.

Private life of an eminent politician [fiction],
NatR-II 1373, 1386, 1395, 1407

Rodd, James Rennell: see *Index*, I, 1067.

The poet of the Klephts, **NC** 2076

Roe, Sir Charles Arthur, 1841–1927, Bengal
civil service. *LCCat., WWW.*

Is there really a "crisis" in the Church? **NC**
3502
The return of the exile [from India], 3769

Roebuck, John Arthur: see *Index*, I, 1068.

Châteaubriand's *Historical Discourses*, **FQR**
198

Whig professions and performance, **FM**
2459, 2468

Rogers, Frederic: see *Index*, I, 1068.

South Africa, **NQM** 170

The soul and future life, **NC** 84
The integrity of the British Empire, 86
The causes of the Zulu War, 291
Mozley's *Essays*, 318
South African policy, 341

Rogers, Henry: see *Index*, I, 1068.

Les Apôtres [by Renan], **FortR** 282

Rogers, James Edwin Thorold: see *Index*, I,
1068.

England and the Black Death, **FortR** 137
The Peasants' War of 1381, 189
The House of Lords, 2206

Bribery and its remedies, **FM** 4710
Exclusion of clergy from House of Com-
mons, 4770
Capital, labour, profit, 5073
Parliament and higher education, 6422

Rogers, James Guinness: see *Index*, I, 1068.

Political dissent, **FortR** 1419

Social aspects of disestablishment, **NC** 31
The Church Congress on Nonconformity,
105
Mr. Forster's defence of the Church, 149
The union of the Liberal party, 348
A Nonconformist's view of the election, 430
Results of the Burials Bill, 532
Town and country politics, 723
The ministry and the clôture, 787
Chatter v. work in parliament, 1035
Gladstone as a foreign minister, 1141
Gladstone and the Irish Bill, 1290
A suspended conflict [Church and State],
1351
The middle class and new Liberalism, 1782
The Congregationalist Council, 2075
Shall Uganda be retained? 2348
The position of the Liberal party, 2517
Nonconformist forebodings [on gov't policy],
2663
The general election, 2788
A septuagenarian's retrospect, 2874

Rogers, James Guinness (*continued*)
The new Education Bill, 2930
The massacres in Turkey, 3006
The Liberal leadership, 3048
"The integrity of the Ottoman Empire,"
3104
Is the Liberal party in collapse? 3231
Gladstone and the Nonconformists, 3314
The Tsar's proposed conference, 3367
The Liberal collapse, 3399
The nation and the ritualists, 3429
Liberalism and its cross-currents, 3539
Wanted a leader, 3688

Rolleston, Charles: see *Index*, I, 1068.

To-day in Morocco, **NatR-II** 1171

Rolph, John F.

Letter: **NatR-II** 267

Romanes, George John: see *Index*, I, 1069.

Beginning of nerves in animal kingdom,
FortR 1514
A reply to "Fallacies of Evolution" [*ER* no.
3203], 1628
Scientific evidence of organic evolution,
1866
Mivart on instinct, 2341
Mivart on rights of reason, 2433

Animal intelligence, **NC** 230
Recreation, 350
Hypnotism, 496
Intelligence of ants, 596, 616
The fallacy of materialism, 792
The Darwinian theory of instinct, 1037
Physiological selection, 1359
Mental differences between men and women,
1403
Darwin's latest critics, 1875
Primitive natural history, 1920
Why I shall vote for the Unionist candi-
date, 2254
Notices: 487, 2043, 2400

Romilly, Frederick, 1810–1887, commissioner
of customs. Boase.

Free trade principles and taxation, **FM** 6263

Rooper, George: see *Index*, I, 1069.

Bolsover Forest, **FM** 4881, 4910, 4932

Roose, Edward Charles Robson, 1848–1905,
physician. *DNB.*

Health-resorts and their uses, **FortR** 2365
Wear and tear of London life, 2421
Rest and repair in London life, 2448

Infection and disinfection, 2562
The London water supply, 2799
The art of prolonging life, 2836
Lepers and leprosy in Norway, 2901
Clothing as a protection against cold, 3447
The spread of diphtheria, 3581
Climate of South Africa, its curative influ-
ence, 3748

Roose, Pauline W.: see *Index*, I, 1069.

Carlyle and old women, **NatR-II** 1053

Roosevelt, Theodore, 1858–1919, president of
U.S. *WWW.*

Books on big game, **FortR** 4105

Roscoe, Edward Stanley: see *Index*, I, 1069.

The Judicature Acts in English law, **FM**
5769
The education of barristers, 5785
Some legal customs, 5812
The extradition of criminals, 5839
Marine insurance in England, 5995

Roscoe, Henry, 1800–1836, biographer, barrister. *DNB.*

French histories of English revolution, **FQR**
58

Rose, Edward: see *Index*, I, 1069.

Shakespeare and history, **FM** 5804
Fairy plays, 5850
A northern *Hamlet* [by Ohlenschläger],
5928
Italian masks, 5941
Wagner as a dramatist, 6170

Rose, Henry John: see *Index*, I, 1069.

Neapolitan superstitions, **FQR** 45

See: **FM** 4673

Rose, Hugh James, 1795–1838: see *Index*, I,
1070.

Catholicism in Silesia, **FQR** 23
Simond's *Travels in Italy and Sicily*, 37
Foreign views of the Catholic question, 89
Wessenberg, Catholic Church in Germany,
98

Rose, W. Kinnaird

Macedonia, **FortR** 1624
The Russian Bayard [General Scobeleff],
1949

Rosenberg, Adolphus, of London. *BMCat.*

The condition of Palestine, **FM** 5704

Rosmini-Serbati, Antonio, 1797–1855, philosopher. Newman, *L&D,* XI, index.

See: **Ram** 829

Ross, Adelaide (Sandars): see *Index,* I, 1070.

Reminiscences of Lady Byron, **NC** 3470

Ross, Edward Charles Russell, 1841–1896, expert marksman, barrister. Boase.

Deer-stalking in the past, **FortR** 2495

Ross, Janet Ann (Duff-Gordon): see *Index,* I, 1070.

A Burmese "ilpon" [tale], **FM** 5840
Popular songs of Tuscany, 5912

Lewis Devrient, **NatR-II** 1065
A stroll in Boccaccio's country, 1580

Byron at Pisa, **NC** 2122
Ovid metamorphosed, 2226
Michelangelo, 2314

Rossetti, Dante Gabriel, 1828–1882, poet, painter. *DNB.*

Hand and soul [on Chiaro], **FortR** 739
Notice: 946

Rossetti, William Michael: see *Index,* I, 1070.

Shelley in 1812–13, **FortR** 747

British sculpture, **FM** 4092
The London exhibitions of 1861, 4159
Royal Academy Exhibitions, 4236, 4337, 4455, 4553
The fine art of the International Exhibition, 4244
Mr. Madox Brown's exhibition, 4544

Rossiter, Mrs. Elizabeth, social worker.

Unnatural children [bad health of the poor], **FortR** 1911

Child life for children, **NC** 638

Rossiter, William, d.1897, writer and lecturer for workers. Boase.

The continental Sunday, **NC** 1004
Artisan atheism, 1373, 1431

Rothschild, Constance Flower de, 1843–1931, later wife of first Baron Battersea. Burke, *LCCat.*

The Hebrew woman, **NQM** 71

Rothschild, Ferdinand James de, known as Baron, 1839–1898, art collector. *DNB.*

The expansion of art, **FortR** 2260

Century for century [Augustin Filon on England], **NC** 1541
The Memoirs of the Comte de Brienne, 1620
The Comte de Clermont, 1874
French eighteenth-century art, 2175
Financial causes of the French Revolution, 2359, 2383

Rothschild, Sir Lionel Walter, 2nd Baron Rothschild, 1868–1937, banker, zoologist. *DNB.*

The birds of the Bass Rock, **NC** 3360

Rothschild, Sir Nathan Meyer, 1st Baron Rothschild, 1840–1915, banker, philanthropist. *DNB.*

India's currency problem, **NatR-II** 2212

Round, John Horace: see *Index,* I, 1070.

The protectionist revival, **NatR-II** 1732
Battle of Hastings, 1968

The English libro d'oro [of real nobility], **NC** 2575
A visit to Queen Elizabeth, 3003
The Elizabethan religion, 3064
The sacrifice of the Mass, 3118
Historical research, 3393
Cromwell and the electorate, 3575

Roundell, Charles Savile, 1827-1906, barrister. *WWW,* Foster.

Agrarianism, **FortR** 780

Rous, John Edward Cornwallis, 2nd Earl of Stradbroke, 1794–1886. Burke.

The Peninsular War, **NatR-II** 1608

Rouse, Dr. E.

On the authority of S. Alphonsus, **DR** 1451

Routh, William, 1845–1912, divine. Venn.

Cry of the superannuated, **NatR-II** 1435

Routledge, Florence. *BMCat.*

Trades unionism among women, **FortR** 3081 collab.

Routledge, Robert Warne, 1837/38–1899, literary agent. Boase.

A volunteer battalion, **NC** 1410

Rowbotham, John Frederick: see *Index,* I, 1071.

The place of music in culture, **NatR-II** 758
Dancing as a fine art, 1000

Rowbotham, John Frederick (*continued*)
English and German music, 1139
Letter: 1162

The Wagner bubble, **NC** 1605
How to obtain a school of English opera, 2781

Rowe, James Boone, 1825–1888, R.C. priest, of the London Oratory. Newman, *L&D*, XIII, index.

English Catholic poor-schools, **DR** 1185

Rowe, Sir Reginald Percy Pfeiffer, 1868–1945, civil administrator. *WWW, LCCat.*

Proposed Pan-Anglican festival, **FortR** 3232

Rowett, Ellen

A visit to the Queen of Burmah, **FM** 6513

Rowlatt, Sir Sidney Arthur Taylor, 1862–1945, judge. *DNB.*

State of the bar, **NatR-II** 1928

Rowley, James, 1834–1906, schoolmaster, historian. *BMCat.*, memoir in Rowley, *Wordsworth and Other Essays*, Bristol, 1927.

Green's *History of the English People*, **FM** 5724, 5749
Career and character of Francis Bacon, 6093
The writing of history, and Stuart rule in England, 6133

Burke and the French Revolution, **NatR-II** 595

Rowsell, Francis Wallace: see *Index*, I, 1071.

Malta, **NC** 207
The Domesday Book of Bengal, 384
Administrative machinery of Egypt, 642
The English in Egypt, 872

Roy, Charles Smart, 1854–1897, physician. Venn.

Waist-belts and stays, **NatR-II** 784 collab.

Roylance-Kent, Clement Boulton: see *Index*, I, 1071, and *Yearbook*/1904, under Kent.

Russian intrigues in South-Eastern Europe, **FortR** 3390
House of Lords since the Reform Act, 3586
The new French naval programme, 3845

The persecuted Russian Jews, **NatR-II** 1185
The decay of originality, 1228

Rubinstein, Joseph Samuel, writer on law. *BMCat.*

The law's delay, **FortR** 3750

Rücker, Sir Arthur William, 1848–1915, physicist. *Times*, Nov. 2, 1915, p. 15c.

Hermann von Helmholtz, **FortR** 3565

Rudd, G. Edward; possibly the George Edward Rudd, b.1865/66, in Foster.

Dignity of parliament, **NatR-II** 767

Rudler, Frederick William, 1840–1915, librarian Museum of Practical Geology. *WWW.*

Notice: **NC** 487

Ruffer, Sir Marc Armand, 1859–1917, physician in Egypt. *WWW.*

The new science: preventive medicine, **NC** 2139
The morality of "vivisection," 2313

Rule, Martin Luther, 1834–1926, R.C. priest. Venn.

Archbishop Lanfranc and his modern critics, **DR** 1795
Freeman's *William Rufus*, 1833
Notice: 1812

Rumy, Károly György, 1780–1847, scholar. Maria Kepp, *Rumy Károly György Göttingában* (Budapest, 1938), p. 98.

Language and literature of the Magyars, **FQR** 56

Runciman, James: see *Index*, I, 1071.

King Plagiarism and his court [attack on Rider Haggard], **FortR** 2933

A common-place man [John Leighton], **NatR-II** 191

Runciman, John F., 1866–1916, musicologist. Pratt, *Music.*

Musical criticism and critics, **FortR** 3530

Ruskin, John: see *Index*, I, 1071.

Essays on political economy, **FM** 4229, 4250, 4281, 4315
Modern warfare, 5835

Lecture [on science and religion], **NC** 128
The three colours of Pre-Raphaelitism, 244, 252

Russell, Charles William (continued)
Mignet's Mary Stuart, 655
Anglican views of church history, 667
The lamas of Tibet, 670
Historians of the Council of Trent, 675
Japan, 678
Treatise "Against all Heresies," 683
Novel morality—the novels of 1853, 693
Catholic and Protestant hermeneutics, 700
De Saulcy's Dead Sea and Bible Lands, 707
Whately and the Board of Irish National Education, 710
The Emigrant Milesian, 716
Callistus and his accuser, 717
Formularies of the Anglican Church, 726
Guizot's Cromwell, 734
Recent historians of the Papacy: Riddle and Robertson, 741
Milman's Latin Christianity, 746, 797
The Church of the Catacombs [by Wiseman], 748
Huc's Chinese Empire, 756
Marsden's Puritan's, 759
De Vere's poems, 762
The Maynooth endowment, 768
Burton's Pilgrimage to El Medinah, 773
Pope Callistus on the Trinity, 784
Fabiola [by Wiseman] and Callista [by Newman], 803
Peel's Memoirs, 806
The religious war of words, 807 collab.
Burton's Meccah and East Africa, 810
Recent antiquarian discoveries in Italy, 831
The St. Barnabas judgment, 833
Huc's Christianity in China, 843, 884
Prince de Broglie's Reign of Constantine, 845
Lord Campbell's Chief Justices of England, 850
Döllinger's Relation of Heathenism and Judaism to Christianity, 862
The Confessional controversy, 894
Abbé Domenech's Missionary Life in Texas and Mexico, 908
Cornwallis correspondence, 915
Gilbert's History of Dublin, 929
Newland's Life of Antonio De Dominis, 933
Carlyle's Frederick the Great, 935
Ancient Egyptian history, 943
Roger Bacon, 956
Oliphant's Japan, 958
Froude's Edward VI and Mary [Tudor], 972
Recent discoveries at Carthage, 976
Essays and Reviews, 979, 989
Antiquities of the Irish Academy, 985
Moran's Life of Oliver Plunket, 998
De Vere's Inisfail, 999
D'Abbadie's Ethiopic literature, 1007
Porson, 1008
Marshall's Christian Missions, 1010
Stanhope's Life of Pitt, 1022

Döllinger's Protestantism and the Papacy, 1032
The Jewish catacomb at Rome, 1047
?The laureate [Tennyson], 1067
Froude's Mary Stuart, 1078
?The Viceroys of Ireland, 1137
Canon Oakeley's Lyra Liturgica, 1156
?Master of the Rolls' Irish publications, 1244
Subterranean Rome, 1294
Mary Queen of Scots—the casket papers, 1303
Mary Queen of Scots, 1330a
The Carte Papers, 1401
?Saint Caecilia and Roman society, 1482
The Babington Conspiracy—Mary Stuart, 1483
Aubrey de Vere's Alexander the Great, 1485
Fair play in literature [toward Catholicism], 1500
?Mary Tudor [by De Vere and Tennyson], 1525
Critical history of the sonnet, 1567, 1579
?The Earl of Strafford, 1569
Note: 940
Notices: 353, 373, 381, 391, 403, 411, 422, 432, 443, 465, 470, 479, 502, 513, 534, 562, ?581, 629, 641, 770, 796, 816, 836, 846, 855, 864, 909, 920, 928, ?1213, 1286, 1426, 1480
See: 388, 454, 577, 578, 588, 592, 752, 774, 778, 817, 819, 868, 872, 883, 906, 912, 1015, 1026, 1127, 1166, 1376

Russell, Sir Edward Richard: see Index, I, 1072.

Irving's interpretations of Shakesepeare, FortR 2088
Irving's work [as an actor], 2219
Irving's King Lear, NC 2335

Russell, Francis Albert Rollo: see Index, I, 1072.

A department of health, NC 2028

Russell, Frank Shirley: see Index, I, 1072.

War horses, NC 1181
The War Office, 3220

Russell, Geoffrey; perhaps a pseudonym.

Alfred Waters, FM 1727

Russell, George William Erskine: see Index, I, 1072.

The coming session, FortR 1981

Protest against Whiggery, NC 862
The new Liberalism, 1766
Reformation and reunion [with Rome], 2955

The mass: primitive and Protestant, 3082
Land and lodging-houses, 3166
Ritualism and disestablishment, 3415
Lambeth and "liberation," 3553

Russell, Harold John Hastings: see *Index*, I, 1072.

Protection of wild birds, **NC** 3186

Russell, Jesse Watts, 1786–1875, antiquary. Boase.

Ancient history of Sunbury, **FM** 3593
Origin of the name England, 3624
Antiquities of the Jumnah, 3672
Ancient name of Island of Mersey, 3730
Early history of Isle of Thanet, 3858

Russell, John, Viscount Amberley: see *Index*, I, 1073.

Liberals, Conservatives, and the Church, **FortR** 76
The Church of England, 354, 374
Latter-Day Saints, 635, 644
Can war be avoided? 782
Experiences of spiritualism, 1017

Russell, John Cecil: see *Index*, I, 1073.

Annals of a Publishing House [Blackwoods], **FortR** 4044
Our game books, 4421

Russell, John Francis Stanley, 2nd Earl Russell, 1865–1931, barrister. Burke.

Electricity in country houses, **NatR-II** 1391 collab.

Russell, John Scott: see *Index*, I, 1073.

Steam-carriages, **FQR** 250

Russell, Katharine Louisa (Stanley): see *Index*, I, 1073.

The claims of women, **FortR** 748

Russell, Mary Annette (Beauchamp), Countess Russell, 1866–1941, writer known as "Elizabeth." *DNB.*

Present feeling in Germany [toward England], **NatR-II** 2404
The pious pilgrimage, 2483

Russell, Matthew, S.J., 1834–1912, ed. of *Irish Monthly. WWW.*

Notice: **DR** 1072

Russell, Rollo: see Russell, Francis Albert Rollo.

Russell, Sir Thomas Wallace: see *Index*, I, 1073.

The land purchase question, **FortR** 2915
The Irish Land Bill, 2946, 3609
Irish local government, 3144
The Irish education question, 3180
The political outlook, 3253
American side-lights on Home Rule, 3338
Government and evicted tenants, 3483
Experiment [of the Irish Congested Districts Board], 3522

Position of Liberal Unionists, **NatR-II** 1567
An Irish landlord's budget, 1613

Résumé of Irish land problem, **NC** 1774
The actual and political Ireland, 1818
Ireland then and now, 1862
Compensation or confiscation [on temperance], 1894
The lessons of a decade, 2295
The money-lending inquiry, 3330

Russell, William Clark: see *Index*, I, 1073.

The Lady Maud, in 8 instalments from **FM** 6489 to 6544

Russell, Sir William Howard: see *Index*, I, 1073.

De profundis [the Atlantic cable], **FortR** 89

Arundines Nili [on Egypt], **FM** 5079

Memories of Ischia, **NC** 905
A part of a ghost, 2619

Rutson, Albert Osliff, 1836–1890, barrister. Boase.

Turkey in Europe, **FortR** 1286

Ruvigny: see under Massue de Ruvigny.

Ruxton, George William, 1837–1899. *Irish Gentry.*

Crimes Bill for Ireland, **NatR-II** 603
Union versus separation, 688
The way to change a law is to break it, 754
Gladstone's inconsistencies, 779
Salisbury-Balfour success [reducing crime in Ireland], 862
Let Gladstone speak [on Irish Home Rule], 874
Gladstonians should fight fairly, 908
Irish mountebanks and mendicants, 968
Notes about Ireland, 1020
Sunday in Ireland under Parnellites, 1033
Baiting a bishop, 1072
Mr. Parnell, 1131

Ryan, William Burke, 1810–1874, obstetrician. Plarr.

Child-murder—obstetric morality, **DR** 888
King James II's *Irish Army List,* 970
Notice: 909

Ryder, E. A. *BMCat.*

Crisis in trade, **FM** 6167

Ryder, George Dudley, 1810–1880, convert to Rome, 1846. Newman, *L&D,* XI, index.

On the Study of Words [by R. C. Trench], **Ram** 573

Ryder, Henry Ignatius Dudley: see *Index,* I, 1074.

Miracles: their possibility and probability, **DR** 1499

Catholic miracles, 1529
M. Emery, Superior of St. Sulpice, 2081
Harnack on the "De Aleatoribus," 2179
Letter: 1532

A Jesuit reformer and poet, **NC** 1172
Revelations of after-world, 1375
On certain ecclesiastical miracles, 2084
Pope and Anglican archbishops, 3141
The ethics of war, 3460

Ryley, Edward: see *Index,* I, 1074.

M. Libri and the libraries of France, **DR** 704
Notice: 1222
See: 1046, 1100

The Prison Discipline Act, **Ram** 1054
The Poor-Law Amendment Act, 1063

Ryley, John Horton. *LCCat.*

Letter: **NatR-II** 1355

S

Sablukov, Nikolay Alexandrovich, 1776–1848, Russian general. *Bol'shaía sovetskaía entsiklopediía,* vol. 37, p. 561.

Reminiscences of Paul I of Russia, **FM** 4571, 4578

Sackville-West, Reginald Windsor, 7th Earl De La Warr, 1817–1896. Burke.

Some educational errors, **FortR** 2169

France and North Africa, **NC** 630

Sadler, Michael Ernest: see *Index,* I, 1074.

The facts about university extension, **NC** 2632

Saffi, Aurelio: see *Index,* I, 1074.

Italy and the Pope, **FortR** 356, 391

St. Cheron, Alexandre de, French statesman, ed. *L'université catholique. Bib. Nat. Cat.*

Life of Frederic Hurter, **Ram** 218, 225

St. Helier, Lady Mary: see Jeune, Lady Susan Mary

St. John, Bayle, 1822–1859, journalist. *DNB.*

Russegger's *Travels in Egypt,* **FQR** 686 collab.
Pallme's *Travels in Kordofan,* 765 collab.
Ethnological Societies of London and Paris, 766

English and French rivalry in eastern Africa, 776 collab.
French aggressions in the Pacific. 805
Ship canal across the American isthmus, 817 collab.?

De re vehiculari [history of coaches], **FM** 1691, 1706
Michel de Montaigne, 2232

St. John, Horace Stebbing Roscoe, 1832–1888, journalist. *DNB.*

Erman's *Travels in Siberia,* **DR** 519

St. John, James Augustus: see *Index,* I, 1074.

Christianity in China, **FQR** 124
Russegger's *Tavels in Egypt,* 686 collab.?
Pallme's *Travels in Kordofan,* 765 collab.?
English and French rivalry in eastern Africa, 776 collab.
Fontanier's Eastern mission, 785
Guizot and the right of search, 835
The surveys of the Indian navy, 845
Capefigue's *Europe since the Accession of Louis Philippe,* 873
The English in Borneo, 882
?The diffusion of Christianity, 901

St. John, M. Georgina S., born c.1833, daughter of George St. John. Newman, *L&D,* XIV, index.

Tyborne, **DR** 963

Book hawking, 968
Notices: 954, 964

St. John, Percy Bolingbroke, 1821–1889, newspaper correspondent. *DNB.*

?Ship canal across the American isthmus, **FQR** 817 collab.

Sainte-Beuve, Charles Augustin, 1804–1869, French writer and critic. *Grand Larousse.*

?Victor Hugo's poems and novels, **FQR** 87 collab.

Sainteville, de: see De Sainteville or de Sainteville

Saintsbury, George Edward Bateman: see *Index,* I, 1075.

Charles Baudelaire, **FortR** 1199
Modern English prose, 1232
Jules Sandeau, 1427
Victor Cherbuliez, 1438
Théophile Gautier, 1449
Gustave Flaubert, 1458
An anniversary [Voltaire and Rousseau], 1465
Charles de Bernard, 1479
Octave Feuillet, 1488
Henry Murger, 1497
Alexandre Dumas, 1515
Chamfort and Rivarol, 1544
Saint-Evremond, 1600
Two men of letters [Charles Lever and Théophile Gautier], 1622
Ernest Renan, 1690
The Four Winds of the Spirit [by Victor Hugo], 1819
A new life of Voltaire [by J. Parton], 1827
Miss Ferrier's novels, 1890
A study of sensibility, 1941
The present state of the novel, 2636, 2671
Anthony Hamilton, 3005
The novels of Hall Caine, 3597

French tragedy before Corneille, **FM** 6219

A paradox on Quinet, **NatR-II** 40
John Gibson Lockhart, 198
Guy de Maupassant, 1463

Sala, George Augustus Henry: see *Index,* I, 1075.

Marie Antoinette's milliners' bills, **FortR** 2626
Letter: 2627

Salmon, Edward [G.], 1865–1955, ed., misc. writer. *WWW,* see *NC* no. 1299.

What boys read, **FortR** 2425
Domestic service and democracy, 2691

Socialism experiments by colonisation, 3603
Australian federation, 3666
From Cobden to Chamberlain, 3821
1497–1897: East and West, 3944
The colonial empire of 1837, 3968
Imperial federation, 4551

The working classes and religion, **NatR-II** 715
The democracy and the drama, 788
The crown and the colonies, 912
Beaconsfield—after ten years, 1141

What the working classes read, **NC** 1299
What girls read, 1328
Literature for the little ones, 1466

Salmon, George: see *Index,* I, 1075.

Spirit rapping, **FortR** 177

Salmoné, Habib Anthony, 1860–1904, prof. of Arabic, King's Coll. London. Buckland, *WWW.*

The press in Turkey, **NC** 2657
The real rulers of Turkey, 2745
Is the Sultan of Turkey the true Khaliph of Islam? 2875
The massacres in Turkey, 3009

Salt, Henry Stephens: see *Index,* I, 1075.

The humanities of diet, **FortR** 3855

Confessions of an Eton master, **NC** 1085

Sampson, Donat: see *Index,* I, 1075.

The potato, **DR** 2204
French expedition to Ireland in 1798, 2587

Samuel, Sir Saul, 1820–1900, agent-general for New South Wales. *WWW.*

Letter: **FortR** 2934

Samuels, Emma Margaret (Irwin), d.1904, social reform. *Times,* June 25, 1904, p. 10e.

Adoption of street Arabs by state, **FortR** 4065

Samuelson, Bernard: see *Index,* I, 1075.

Technical education in Saxony, **FortR** 1822

Sanctis, Dr. Bartolomeo de, mathematician and physician. R.L.F.

Notices: **FQR** 39, 53

Sand, George, 1804–1876, French novelist, pseudonym of Aurore (Dupin) Dudevant. *Grand Larousse.*

See: **FM** 1986, 2000

Sandars, Thomas Collett, 1825–1894, barrister, classical scholar. *DNB.*

Stanley's *Sinai and Palestine,* **FM** 3516
Kemble's *State Papers,* 3583
Buckle's *History of Civilization in England,* 3650
Livingstone's *Travels in South Africa,* 3686
Chronicle of current history, in 14 installments from 4005 to 4133

Sanday, William: see *Index,* I, 1075.

Marcion's gospel, **FortR** 1166

Sandberg, Samuel Louis Graham: see *Index,* I, 1075.

The city of Lhása, **NC** 1780
A Tibetan poet and mystic [Milaraspa], 3548

Sanders, Alfred J.

An Italian nun [Galileo's daughter], **NatR-II** 864

Sanderson, John

The Transvaal and the Zulu countries, **FortR** 1481

Sandford, Charles Waldegrave, 1828–1903, bishop of Gibraltar. *WWW.*

The English Church on the Continent, **FortR** 2189

Sandford, Francis Richard John, Baron Sandford, 1824–1893, served in Education and Colonial offices. *DNB.*

Elementary education a municipal charge, **FortR** 3083

Sandwith, Humphry: see *Index,* I, 1076, and II, App. A.

Michael Obrenovitch, Prince of Servia, **FortR** 671
Heterodox view of the Eastern question, 756
Earl Russell, the Commune, and Christianity, 794
Servia, and its new prince, 931
Public health, 1128
From Belgrade to Samakov, 1652
A trip into Bosnia, **FM** 5493
From Belgrade to Constantinople, 5846
How the Turks rule Armenia, **NC** 139

San Giuliano, Antonino Paternò-Castello, Marchese de, 1852–1914, Italian politician. *Enci. Ital.*

The Italian colony on the Red Sea, **NC** 2285

Sannomiya, Alethea Yayeno (Raynor), b.1846. *Peerage of Japan* under her son, Baron S. Sannomiya

A Shinto funeral, **NC** 3043

Sarcey, Francisque, 1827–1899, French journalist, drama critic. *Grand Larousse.*

The Comédie Française, **NC** 337
The Palais-Royal Theatre, 474

Sarel, E. A.

Letter: **NatR-II** 254

Sargant, George Herbert. *BMCat.*

Free dinners at national schools, **FortR** 2633

Sargent, John Young, b.1828/29, dean of Hertford Coll. Oxford in 1885. Foster, *BMCat.*

Mexico and her railways, **FortR** 2002
A journey across the Fjeld [in Norway], **FM** 3879

Sars, Johan Ernst Welhaven, 1835–1917, prof. of history at Univ. of Christiania. *LCCat., EUI.*

Case for Norwegian liberalism, **FortR** 3682

Sasī Chandra Datt: see Dutt, Shoshee Chunder

Sassoon, Sir Edward Albert, 1856–1912, M.P. Burke.

Great Britain's opportunity, **NatR-II** 2072
The crusade against silver, **NC** 1286
The taxation of ground values, 3336

Saunders, Thomas Bailey: see *Index,* I, 1076.

Noiré on the origin of reason, **ScotR** 170
The Faust legend, 216
Development of the Faust legend, 230
Darwinism and the origin of reason, 259
Notice: 188

Saunders, William H., army private.

Letters from a soldier in Egypt, **NC** 1149

Savage, Sir George Henry, 1842–1921, physician. *WWW.*

Homicidal mania, **FortR** 2752

Savage, Marmion W.: see *Index,* I, 1076.

Religion and philosophy reconciled, **FortR** 157
Irish judicial establishment, 193

The woman of business, in 15 installments from 562 to 674

The three Racans, **FM** 3215

Savage-Landor, Arnold Henry: see Landor, Arnold Henry Savage.

Saville, Miss S. E.

Weaver birds, **ScotR** 611
A garden of palms, 630
Concerning birds, 702

Say, Léon, 1826–1896, French politician, economist. *Grand Larousse.*

France and England in Egypt, **FortR** 2062

Sayce, Archibald Henry: see *Index,* I, 1076.

Examination-system at the universities, **FortR** 1164
A ramble in Syracuse, 1197
Discovery of an Etruscan book, 3320

Assyrian discoveries, **FM** 5556
Forgotten empire in Asia Minor [Hittite], 6316

Story-telling in the East, **NatR-II** 762

Sayer, Frederick, 1832–1868, military historian. Boase.

The dangers of Madeira, **FortR** 48

Scanlon, Thomas

Committee on Old Age Pensions, **FortR** 4184

Scannell, Thomas Bartholomew, 1854–1917, theologian, historian. *WWW.*

The English Constitution, **DR** 2047
Pius VII at Savona, 2075
Talleyrand's diplomatic letters, 2271
The internuncio at Paris, 2288
Pastor's *History of the Popes,* 2337, 2501
Alexander VI, 2524
Notes on foreign periodicals, 2322
Notices of Catholic continental periodicals, 2187, 2267, 2295
Notices: 2019, 2029, 2043, 2056, 2068, 2079, 2131, 2144, 2173, 2186, 2199, 2211, 2225, 2238, 2280, 2307, 2321, 2347, 2358, 2373, 2387, 2400, 2412, 2425, 2438, 2448, 2475, 2663

Schäfer, Sir Edward Albert Sharpey, 1850–1935, physiologist. *DNB.*

Mr. Coleridge's attack, **NatR-II** 2291
Letter: 2236

Scherer, Edmond: see *Index,* I, 1076.

Note: **FortR** 1659

Schiff, A. G.

The rehabilitation of silver, **FortR** 3426

Schiller, Johann Christoph Friedrich, von, 1759-1805, German poet. *ADB.*

See: **FM** 156

Schlesinger, Dr. Max, 1822–1881. *LCCat.*

Count Bismarck, **FortR** 274, 287

Schletter, Pauline, novelist. *BMCat.*

A Magyar musician [Lizst], **NatR-II** 668
The modern Spanish novel, 760
The peasant women of Galicia, 774
First special correspondent [Melchior Grimm], 849
On Tuscan rhymes, 900
Trans: 815, 816

Schloss, David Frederick: see *Index,* I, 1076, also Foster and *UJE.*

The sweating system, **FortR** 2260, 2939
Healthy homes for the working classes, 2699
The labour problem, 2872
The road to social peace, 3043
The dearness of "cheap" labour, 3311

The Jew as a workman, **NC** 1988

Schmidt, Hermann, political economist, bimetallist. *BMCat.*

Bimetallic side of American crisis, **NatR-II** 1931

Schmitz, Leonora

Robert Schumann, **FortR** 122
On the study of music, 199

Schnadhorst, Francis, 1840–1900, Liberal party organizer. *WWW.*

The caucus and its critics, **NC** 735

Schnitzer, Eduard Carl Oscar Theodor, known as Emin Pasha, 1840–1892, physician and governor of Equatoria. Hill.

Letters from Central Africa, **FortR** 2605

Schobel, Victor Januarius, 1848–1915, prof. at Oscott. *Tablet,* Aug. 7, 1915.

Notice: **DR** 2373

Schomberg, George Augustus, 1821–1907, general in Royal Marines. *WWW.*

Shall we retain the marines? **NC** 853

Schooling, John Holt, 1859–1927, actuary, statistician. *WWW.*

Naval strength of the seven sea-powers, **FortR** 4481
The armaments of seven navies, 4492

Written gesture [handwriting], **NC** 2724

Schooling, William, F.R.A.S.

Colour-music, **NC** 2783

Schreiner, Olive Emilie Albertina, 1855-1920, novelist. *DNB.*

Three dreams in a desert, **FortR** 2619
Stray thoughts on South Africa, 3104, 3784, 3824, 3840
Letter: 2638

Schultz, Robert Weir, later Robert S. Weir, 1860/61–1951, architect, of London. *BMCat.*; later name in Kelly/1917–1940 and *The Builder*, 180 (Apr.–June 1951), p. 663.

Sancta Sophia, Constantinople, **ScotR** 491

Schuster, Ernest Joseph, 1850–1924, barrister, educated in Germany. *WWW.*

The anti-Jewish agitation in Germany, **FortR** 1785

Schwartz, Alexander Joseph: see *Index*, I, 1077 and *CCD*/1904.

Wittenberg and Cologne, **FM** 5393
The ethics of St. Paul, 5440
The new birth, according to St. Paul, 5488

Schwert, Rudolph von, capt. in 17th Pomeranian Uhlans.

A German view of the British Army, **FortR** 1636

Sclater, Philip Lutley: see *Index*, I, 1077.

Difficulties in zoological distribution, **NC** 250
Animals of New Guinea, 1297
Fur-seal question, 2416

Sclater-Booth, George, 1st Baron Basing, 1826–1894, barrister, M.P. *DNB.*

Local government in rural districts, **NC** 1372

Scofield, Joseph Alan, novelist. *BMCat.*

Land owners and labourers, **NatR-II** 494
"Local option" in the new Local Government Bill, 710

Scoones, William Baptiste: see *Index*, I, 1077.

Civil service examinations, **NC** 739
Is examination a failure? 1662
Selection of army officers, 2484

Scott, Catherine, sec. Metropolitan Assoc. for Befriending Young Servants.

Note: **NC** 2903

Scott, Francis, 1806–1884, barrister, M.P. Boase.

English county asylums, **FortR** 1605

Scott, George Alexander, 1862–1933, barrister, sportsman. Venn.

Rype-shooting in Norway without dogs, **FortR** 3509

Scott, Hon. Mary Monica Maxwell: see Maxwell-Scott, Mary Monica.

Scott, Robert Henry: see *Index*, I, 1078.

Recent progress in weather knowledge, **FortR** 950

Scott, Robert Pickett, 1856–1931, educator. Venn, *WWW.*

The new Education Office, **FortR** 4412

Scott, T. J.; perhaps the Thomas James Scott, b.1828/29, divine, in Foster and *CCD*/1902.

Gladstone's five parliaments, **NatR-II** 650

Scott, Walter: see *Index*, I, 1078.

On the supernatural: works of Hoffmann, **FQR** 2
Molière, 38
Revolutions of Naples in 1647 and 1648, 92
"Farewell to his Readers," 243

Letter: **NC** 2689

Scott, William Bell: see *Index*, I, 1078.

Ornamental art in England, **FortR** 720

Art season of 1871, **FM** 5227
A Scottish kirk sessions-book, 5831
Portfolio of ancient engravings, 6149, 6152

Scott-Moncrieff, Colin Campbell, 1836–1916, army officer, engineer. *WWW*.

Irrigation in Egypt, **NC** 1097

Scott-Moncrieff, William George, 1846–1927, advocate. *WWW*.

Sir John Clerk of Penicuik, **ScotR** 415
See: 13

Scrutton, Sir Thomas Edward, 1856–1934, judge. *DNB*.

Are twelve millions wasted in the sea? **NC** 1688

Seaton, Robert Cooper, 1853–1915, barrister, schoolmaster. Venn, *LCCat*.

Attitude of Carlyle and Emerson towards Christianity, **NatR-II** 200

Seccombe, John Thomas, physician, magistrate, created "Laurence or [Lawrence] Bishop of Caerleon." H. R. T. Brandreth, *Dr. Lee of Lambeth* (1951), pp. 120, 129, *BMCat*.

Note: **NC** 648

Second, Albéric, 1817–1887, French dramatist. *Grande Encyclopédie*.

Monsieur Lecocq and his lodgers, **FM** 2086, 2091

Seebohm, Frederic: see *Index*, I, 1079.

The Black Death in English history, **FortR** 75, 84
Population of England before Black Death, 188
The Oxford Reformers of 1498, in 7 installments from 245 to 333
On the Christian hypothesis, 476
Sir Thomas Moore and Henry VIII's book against Luther, 499
The land question, 641, 652, 660
National compulsory education, 699
Westminster Review on the land question, 750

Interference with domestic handicrafts, **NC** 142
Imperialism and socialism, 436
The historical claims of tenant right, 535

Seeley, Sir John Robert: see *Index*, I, 1079.

Georgian and Victorian expansion, **FortR** 2613
A Midland university [at Birmingham], 2654

Ethics and religion, 2810

Our insular ignorance, **NC** 1214

Seeley, Robert Benton, 1798–1866, author, publisher. *DNB*.

?Political conduct of the clergy, **FM** 327
?The Whig executive, 352
?Shipping interest, silk manufacture, and glove trade, 373
?On [political] parties, 383, 402, 440
?Hints to electors, 455
?Whig foreign policy, 484
?Remonstrance to the Whig aristocracy, 511

Séguin, Leo or Léon, student at Ecole Normale in Paris; served at Ministry of War under Commune. See *FortR* no. 963, p. 17.

The ministry of war under the Commune, **FortR** 881

Selby-Bigge, Lewis Amherst: see *Index*, I, 1079.

College discipline, **NC** 2611

Sellar, Alexander Craig: see *Index*, I, 1079.

School and university system in Scotland, **FM** 4899
Governor of Madras [William Adam], 6425

Private bill legislation, **NC** 1098

Sellar, William Young: see *Index*, I, 1080.

Scotch university reform, **FM** 3436
Froude's *Caesar*, 6211

Seller, William, 1798–1869, ed. of medical journals. *Prods. of Royal Soc. of Edin.*, VII (1872), 26

Kemp's *Indications of Instinct*, **DR** 754

Sellers, Edith: see *Index*, I, 1080.

Liebknecht, German socialist, **FortR** 3823
Dr. Carl Peters, 3908

Guyot of Provins, **NatR-II** 1735
Old-Age Relief Law in Copenhagen, 1943
Story of a philanthropic pawn-shop, 2002
An open-air reformatory, 2340

The people's kitchens in Vienna, **NC** 2659
A people's kitchen in London, 2718
The old-age homes in Austria, 2800
Dr. Von Miquel, "the Kaiser's own man," 3175

Selous, Frederick Courteney, 1851–1917, hunter, explorer. *DNB.*

Mashunaland and the Mashunas, **FortR** 2821

The Matabele War, **NatR-II** 1573

Sendall, Sir Walter Joseph, 1832–1904, colonial governor. *DNB.*

Charles Stuart Calverley, **FortR** 2179

Senior, Nassau William: see *Index*, I, 1080.

A leaf of Eastern history, **FortR** 1370
Conversations with Thiers, 1403, 1409
Guizot at Val Richer, 1431
Conversations with Prince Napoleon, 1608
Conversations with Adolphe de Circourt, 1659

Sir Walter Scott's novels, **LR (1829)** 2
Internal corn trade, 10
See: 18

Behind the scenes in English politics [Crimean crisis], **NC** 1925

Service, James, 1823–1899, politician, pioneer colonist of Melbourne. *DNB.*

Note: **NC** 1087

Seton-Karr, Sir Henry, 1853–1914, M.P., sportsman. *WWW.*

The finest deer in the world, **NatR-II** 851

Seton-Karr, Heywood Walter, 1859–1938, hunter, archaeologist. *WWW.*

A fresh field for the sportsman [Alaska], **FortR** 2571

Seton-Karr, Walter Scott: see *Index*, I, 1080.

Six months in India, **FM** 3434, 3442

Lord Ripon's new Indian policy, **NatR-II** 15
Our game laws, 135
Bengal Tenancy Bill, 297
Ecclesiastical grants in India, 786
Two Hampshire farms, 1242
Consule Planco, 1784

Sewall, May (Wright), 1844–1920, feminist. *WWW, LCCat.*

International Council of Women, **FortR** 4311

Sewell, Elizabeth Missing: see *Index*, I, 1081.

Reign of pedantry in girls' schools, **NC** 1515

Seymour, Edward Adolphus Seymour: see *Index*, I, 1081.

Spanish Church and exchequer, **FortR** 13

Seymour, Sir Edward Hobart, 1840–1929, admiral. *DNB.*

Present state of the Panama Canal, **NC** 2168

Seymour, Francis George Hugh, 5th Marquess of Hertford, 1812–1884. *Complete Peerage.*

Army reform: long service v. short, **NatR-II** 107

Seymour, Frederick Beauchamp Paget, 1st Baron Alcester, 1821–1895, admiral. *DNB.*

What our navy should be, **FortR** 2763

Seymour, Henry Danby, 1820–1877, M.P. for Poole. Boase.

Public affairs, **FortR** 351 collab. at least
Prospects of the session, 376

Seymour, Michael Culme-: see Culme-Seymour, Michael.

Shadwell, Arthur: see *Index*, I, 1081.

Rabies and muzzling, **NatR-II** 988
The English public-house, 1722
A model public-house and its lessons, 1744
Intemperance past and present, 1781
The decline of drunkenness, 1817
The German colony in London, 1835
The forces of temperance, 1859
The economic aspects of the bicycle, 1938
The hidden dangers of cycling, 1975
The Canadian enigma, 2069
Suicide by typhoid fever, 2112
Should inebriates be imprisoned? 2153
Journalism as a profession, 2192
The transports and the troops, 2385
Proprietors and editors, 2455

The London water supply, **NC** 3423
The plague in Oporto, 3567

Shairp, John Campbell: see *Index*, I, 1081.

Shelley as a lyric poet, **FM** 6195
Canon [J. B.] Mozley, 6254
The prophetic power of poetry, 6364
The earliest Scottish university [St. Andrews], 6517, 6524

Shakespear, John Davenport, army officer. *Army List.*

Fire-damp, **NC** 549

Shand, Alexander Innes: see *Index,* I, 1081.

Novelists and their patrons, **FortR** 2482

The centenary of the *Times,* **NatR-II** 685

Sharkey, Sir Seymour John, 1847–1929, neurologist. *WWW.*

Doctors and nurses, **NC** 463
Morphinomania, 1449

Sharp, James, 1613–1679, archbishop of St. Andrews. *DNB.*

Letter to Earl of Middleton, **ScotR** 81 collab.

Sharp, William: see *Index,* I, 1083.

The Rossettis, **FortR** 2441
Edward Burne-Jones, 4162
A group of Celtic writers [including W. B. Yeats], 4222
The divine adventure, 4370, 4386
Iona, 4430, 4444
The dramas of D'Annunzio, 4504
Letter: 2655

[Dante] Rossetti in prose and verse, **NatR-II** 552
The Royal Academy and the Salon, 584
The sonnet in America, 846
American literature, 1125
The art of the year, 1438
The house of Usna, 2469

"La jeune Belgique" [young Belgian writers], **NC** 2453
The new winter-land [French North Africa], 2510
The art treasures of America, 3340, 3359
The Gael and his heritage, 3755

Sharp, William Joseph Curran, 1839–1891, mathematician. Venn.

Selection of public servants, **NatR-II** 956

Sharpe, Sutton, b.1843, nephew of Samuel Sharpe, 1799–1881, in *DNB.* Doris Gunnell, *Sutton Sharpe et ses Amis Français* (Paris, 1925), pp. 24–25.

Moderation and total abstinence, **FortR** 2241

Shaw, Albert: see *Index,* I, 1083.

Local government in America, **FortR** 1954

Shaw, Charles G.

Landed estate and farming in Scotland, **ScotR** 147
Local government in Scotland, 229

Shaw, Edith Mary: see *Index,* I, 1083.

How poor ladies might live, **NC** 3099

Shaw, Flora Louisa: see *Index,* I, 1083.

Dry-nursing the Colonies, **FortR** 2868
British South Africa Company, 2887

Shaw, Frederick George, civil engineer. *BMCat.,* I.C.E. *List of Members* (1904), p. 148.

Matabililand, **NatR-II** 1834

Shaw, George Bernard: see *Index,* I, 1083.

What Gladstone ought to do, **FortR** 3332
To your tents, Oh Israel! 3427 collab.
The religion of the pianoforte, 3470
Mallock's proposed trumpet performance, 3486

Shaw, Thomas, Baron Shaw, later Baron Craigmyle, 1850–1937, M.P. *DNB.*

The educational peace of Scotland, **NC** 3056

Shaw-Lefevre, George John: see *Index,* I, 1083.

The conscience clause, **FortR** 135
Economic law and English land-ownership, 1320
Greece at the Congress of Berlin, 1499
The Channel Islands, 1627
Representation and misrepresentation, 2274
Trawlers and undersized fish, 4466

Trans: **FM** 5281 to 5355, in 9 installments.

Duke of Argyll and Irish Land Bill, **NC** 599
Public works in London, 779
The Agricultural Holdings Act, 916
Statues and monuments of London, 946
The question of the land, 1190
Home rule: precedents, 1256
The Liberal split, 1333
Public buildings in London, 1621
Constantinople revisited, 1970
The naval policy of France, 2112
The London water supply, 3391

Shaylor, Joseph, 1844–1923, bookseller, publisher. *WWW.*

On the selling of books, **NC** 3040
Booksellers and bookselling, 3465

Shea, Charles E.; perhaps the Charles Edward Shea in *BMCat*.

The tithe-payer and tithe-owner, **NatR-II** 1066

Shebbeare, Charles John, 1865–1945, divine. *WWW*.

Antiquarianism in modern art, **NatR-II** 1325

Shee, William Archer, b.1810, critic, brother of Martin Archer Shee. *Landed Gentry*, *BMCat*.

Painters and their patrons, **NC** 888

Sheehan, Patrick Augustus, 1852–1913, priest, novelist. Crone.

Recent works on St. Augustine, **DR** 2125

Shelford, Sir William, 1834–1905, civil engineer. *DNB*.

Development of North-West Canada, **NatR-II** 449

Shelley, Henry Charles. *BMCat*.

Thomas Hood's first centenary, **FortR** 4291

Shelley, Percy Bysshe, 1792–1822, poet. *DNB*.

See: **FortR** 2527

Letters from Italy, **FM** 3948
See: 229

Shepherd, Lady Mary (Primrose), 1777–1847, philosopher; second wife of Sir Samuel Shepherd. See *DNB* under husband.

Lady Shepherd's metaphysics, **FM** 413

Sheppard, John George, 1816–1869, historian. Boase.

La Chanson d'Antioche, **FortR** 238

Sheppard, Nathan, 1834–1888, American prof. *LCCat., Athenaeum,* Sept. 7, 1872, p. 305.

Premier and president, **FM** 5351
Friction between the U.S. and England, 5406

Sherer, John Walker: see *Index,* I, 1084.

Frau Rath, **FM** 5597

Shettle, George Thomas, divine. *BMCat.,* *CCD*/1902; last appearance/1952.

Coming and going, **NatR-II** 1343

Shield, Alice: see *Index,* I, 1084, and Gorman.

The Cardinal of York, **DR** 2537
The Orange conspiracy of 1688, 2552
Queen Clementina [wife of Old Pretender], 2621
Last Stuart princess [Louisa Mary, daughter of James II], 2678

Shindler, Robert: see *Index,* I, 1084.

President Garfield, **NC** 615

Shipley, Sir Arthur Everett: see *Index,* I, 1084.

Death, **NC** 1133

Shipley, Orby: see *Index,* I, 1084.

Fifty versions of "Dies Irae," **DR** 1853, 1868 collab.
Dryden as a hymnodist, 1931
Notices: 2118, 2358

Authority in the Church of England, **FortR** 1746

Doubt in the Church of England, **NC** 329

Shippard, Sir Sidney Godolphin Alexander, 1837–1902, colonial official. *DNB*.

Are we to lose South Africa? **NC** 3491. 3523
South African problems and lessons, 3570

Shirreff, Emily Anne Eliza: see *Index,* I, 1084.

Girton College, **FortR** 969

Shishkoff, Nicholas, Russian member of Relief Committee of Red Cross in Samara.

The horrors of hunger, **NC** 2145
Famine relief in Samara, 2185
A Russian comment on "England at war," 3312

Shore, Henry Noel, 5th Baron Teignmouth, 1847–1926, naval officer. Burke.

Recent literature in China, **NatR-II** 624
Doctoring in China, 858

Shore, Thomas Teignmouth, 1841–1911, divine. *WWW*.

Auricular confession, **NC** 2687
What is church authority? 2720

Shorthouse, Joseph Henry: see *Index,* I, 1084.

The agnostic at church, **NC** 708

An apologue, 738
Frederick Denison Maurice, 998

Shrewsbury, Countess Anna Theresa (Cockerell), 1836–1912, wife of Charles John Chetwynd, 19th Earl of Shrewsbury. *Complete Peerage.*

Prevention [of vice], **NC** 1221

Shuckburgh, Evelyn Shirley: see *Index,* I, 1084.

Modern miracles, **NC** 810

Shuttleworth, James Kay: see under Kay-Shuttleworth, James.

Sibbald, Andrew T.

The brain and the mind, **DR** 1961
The nerves and over-pressure, 1996
Blue water, 2163
Aëropaedia, 2206

Original institution of the Turkish army, **NatR-II** 398
Islam as a political system, 808

Standing armies and conscription, **ScotR** 224
Cession of Heligoland, 290
The Euxine and the Caspian, 333

Sibley, Walter Knowsley, 1862–1944, dermatologist. *WWW.*

Left-leggedness, **NC** 1870

Sichel, Edith: see *Index,* I, 1084.

The Letters of Mary Sibylla Holland, **FortR** 4362

Sichel, Walter Sidney: see *Index,* I, 1084.

The spirit of Toryism, **FortR** 4029
The two Byrons, 4158
Romanism in fiction, 4264

The constitutional aspect of the House of Lords, **NatR-II** 226
The stage *Faust,* 362

The letters of Heinrich Heine, **NC** 1017

Sickert, Walter Richard, 1860–1942, painter. *WWW.*

Whistler to-day, **FortR** 3203

Sidebotham, Henry, b.1837/38, divine; held livings in Gibraltar and Mentone. Foster, *CCD/96.*

Monte Carlo, **NC** 1689

Sidgwick, Arthur, 1839/40–1920, schoolmaster. Venn, *WWW.*

Our public schools: Rugby, **NQM** 190

Sidgwick, Henry: see *Index,* I, 1084.

Benthamism in politics and ethics, **FortR** 1356
Economic method, 1555
What is money? 1571
The wages-fund theory, 1623
Bi-metallism, 2520

Political prophecy and sociology, **NatR-II** 1665

On historical psychology, **NC** 410

Sidney, Algernon, 1622–1683, republican. *DNB.*

A treatise on love, **NC** 948

Sidney, Samuel: see *Index,* I, 1085.

Four-in-hand driving as a fine art, **NQM** 96

Siemens, Sir Charles William [born Karl Wilhelm], 1823–1883, German-born inventor, engineer. *ADB.*

New theory of the sun, **NC** 699

Sieveking, Albert Forbes: see *Index,* I, 1085.

Edited: **FortR** 3439

Siewers, Carl, translator of Hans Christian Andersen. *BMCat.*

Scheme of Scandinavian unification, **FortR** 3683
Trans: 3781

Will Norway become a republic? **NatR-II** 98

Trans: **NC** 1306

Sim, Charles Alexander, army officer. *Army List/96.*

Some reasons for the school board rate, **FortR** 3809

Simcox, Edith Jemima: see *Index,* I, 1085.

Custom and sex, **FortR** 849
Cause and design, 910
New books, 1019
Ideals of feminine usefulness, 1692
Morris's *Hopes and Fears for Art,* 1921
Notices: 937, 946, 953, 962, 972, 980, 988

Unremunerative industry, **FM** 6115

Simcox, Edith Jemima (*continued*)
The industrial employment of women, 6148
Consolations, 6413
A diptych, 6420
Midsummer noon, 6430
Love and friendship, 6446
At anchor, 6457
A turning point in the history of co-opera-
tion, 6534

George Eliot, **NC** 584
Co-operative shirtmaking, 1010
The capacity of women, 1453
The native Australian family, 3496

Simcox, George Augustus: see *Index*, I, 1085,
and *CBEL*.

Charles Kingsley, **FortR** 1319
Miss Martineau, 1350
Barry Cornwall, 1360
Maxims of wisdom, 1620
Henry Thomas Buckle, 1669
A new poet [James Thomson], 1710
Swinburne's trilogy [*Chastelard, Bothwell,
Mary Stuart*], 1881

Old and young—cities and men, **FM** 5920

Evolution and a priori ethics, **NatR-II** 88

Natural religion, **NC** 761

Simeon, Sir John, 1815–1870, M.P. Newman,
L&D, XIV, 257n.

Persecution of nuns during the French Revolution, **Ram** 584

Simmons, Alfred. *BMCat.*

The ideas of the new voters, **FortR** 2270

Simmons, Sir John Lintorn Arabin, 1821–
1903, army officer, R.E. *DNB.*

The Channel tunnel, **NC** 711
The weakness of the army, 836
The critical condition of the army, 884
The inefficiency of the army, 2222
The French Empress and the German War,
2284
The transformation of the army, 2843
The excessive armies of Russia, 3507

Simon, Sir John, 1816–1904, sanitary reformer, pathologist. *DNB.*

Early social self-government, **NC** 2562

Simon, John Allsebrook, 1st Viscount Simon,
1873–1954, statesman. *WWW.*

Bicycles as railway luggage, **FortR** 4317

Simon, Jules François Simon Suisse: see *Index*, I, 1085.

A patriarch about French women, **FortR**
2771

Simon, Oswald John, 1855–1932, leader of
British Jewry. *UJE.*

The mission of Judaism, **FortR** 3868
The unity of the religious idea, 4268

The return of the Jews to Palestine, **NC**
3346

Simonds, William Barrow, 1820–1911, M.P.
WWW.

Tithes, **NatR-II** 603
Letter: 130

Simpson, Albert, Lancashire businessman.

Great Britain's opportunity: silver v. cotton, **NatR-II** 2074

Simpson, Elizabeth Mary, wife of Richard
Simpson, q.v. Gorman.

Trans: **Ram** 901

Simpson, John Palgrave: see *Index*, I, 1086.

?The King of Bavaria and Lola Montez, **FM**
2413
?The witches' stone, 2417

Simpson, Mary Charlotte Mair: see *Index*, I,
1086.

Notes: **FortR** 1370, 1403, 1608, 1659

Simpson, Richard: see *Index*, I, 1086.

Religion and modern philosophy, **Ram** 249,
256, 262, 270
Galileo and his condemnation, 369
Newman's style and method of argument,
498
?Wiseman and the Tractarians, 524
Interesting discoveries in the Holy Land,
549
Science and religion, 551
Recent Protestant tourists in Italy, 587
collab.?
Travels in Transcaucasia, 603
Waterworth's *England and Rome*, 604
Beethoven's Missa Solemnis, 605
The plurality of worlds, 610
Magic, 624, 640
Huc's *Chinese Empire*, 625, 630
Sporting and morals in Norway and Sweden,
631
Gleanings from the "Broad Church," 655

Simpson, Richard (*continued*)
   Lingard's alleged cardinalate, 1011
   The Roman question, 1015 collab., 1062
   A few words on philology, 1018
   A plea for bores, 1020
   Darwin, *On the Origin of Species,* 1028
   Reform, 1034
   The House of Lords, 1043
   The philosopher's stone, 1048
   The spirit-rappers, 1057
   The Grand Remonstrance, 1071
   Present state of Austria, 1073 collab.
   Edward Campion, in 8 parts from 1075 to
      1135
   Dr. Ward's philosophy, 1086
   Reason and faith, 1090, 1100
   ?Religion and civilisation, 1092
   Recollections of Pugin, 1104
   Manning on the papal sovereignty, 1110
   Tocqueville's *Remains,* 1114
   Moral law and political legislation, 1123
   Marshall on Christian missions, 1125
   Enlargement of the *Rambler,* 1130 collab.
   Individual, corporation, and state, 1131
   Dante's philosophy of love, 1132
   Galileo and Mendelssohn, 1134
   Current and/or Contemporary Events, 1006
      collab., 1014, 1023 collab., 1032 collab.,
      1042 collab., 1061 collab., 1088 collab.,
      1097 collab., 1112, 1129
   Edited: 845 collab., 855, 911, 1049, 1058,
      1072
   Letters: 920, 991, 997, ?1019, 1050 collab.,
      1087, 1098
   Notes: ?806, 966
   Notices: 560, 569, 606, 614, 628, 635, 650,
      658, 664, 705, ?718, 774, 781, 789, 797,
      805, 813, 821, 828, 834, 841, 849, 857,
      866, 872, 885, 891, 897, 905, 912, 919,
      927, 934, 945, 952, 958, 965, 973, 979,
      1013, 1022, ?1031, 1041, 1068 collab.,
      1111, 1113 collab., 1120 collab., 1136
   Trans: 974, 988, 1001, 1059
   See: 402, 441, 724, 731, 747, 972, 1037,
      1067

Simpson, William, brother of Richard Simpson, q.v. Gorman.

   Catholicity and nationality, **Ram** 778 collab.
   Antecedents of the French Revolution, 786,
      794 both collab.
   Protestantism in the East, 787 collab.
   Father Southwell and his capture, 815 col-
      lab.
   Life and martyrdom of Thomas Alfield, 843
      collab.
   Lord Montague's troubles, 933
   Edited: 845 collab.
   Notice: 658
   See: 773

Simpson, William: see *Index,* I, 1086.

   Imperial Delhi and the English Raj, **FM**
      5903
   The Schliemannic Ilium, 5943
   Mycenae, 5993
   Buddhist remains in Afghanistan, 6255
   The Prince of Wales' feathers, 6404
   "The Lord of the World" [Hindu diety], 6526

Sinclair, William Macdonald: see *Index,* I,
   1087.

   Protest of the Church of England, **NatR-II**
      1884

Singh, Oday Pertap: see Oday Pertap Singh.

Singleton, Mary Montgomerie: see Currie,
   Mary Montgomerie

Sinnett, Alfred Percy, 1840–1921, journalist,
   editor. *WWW.*

   Anglo-Indian complications, **FortR** 2083

   Esoteric Buddhism, **NC** 2414
   Behind the scenes of nature, 2618

Sinnett, Edward William Percy, 1799/1800–
   1844, journalist. Allibone; death certificate at Somerset House.

   Russian survey of north eastern coast of
      Siberia, **FQR** 571
   Pückler Muskau, *The South-Eastern Picture
      Gallery,* 608

Sinnett, Jane (Fry), 1805/06–1870, wife of
   Edward W. Percy Sinnett, q.v. Death certificate at Somerset House, *BMCat.*

   Schiller, **DR** 239
   Colonization and emigration, 546

   Zschokke's *Autobiography,* **FQR** 774
   The heroic ages of the North, 828
   Johann Gottlieb Fichte, 855
   The Countess Hahn-Hahn's novels, 865
   Johann Gottlieb v. Herder, 892

Sinnott, N.

   ?Nature and the poets, **DR** 1382

Sittenfeld, Konrad, 1862–1918, German editor, writer. *Grosse Brockhaus* under
   pseud. Konrad Alberti.

   Gustav Freytag, **NatR-II** 622

Skelton, Sir John: see *Index,* I, 1087.

   ?Ninian Holdfast, **FM** 3334
   Italy, and art in Italy, 3389, 3402
   Sketches on the north coast, 3464, 3471,

3494, 3515, 3538, 3545
Ruskin on Homer and Tennyson, 3478
A midsummer day with the poets, 3506
Charlotte Brontë [by Mrs. Gaskell], 3601
What are the functions of the artist? 3606
Northern lights: city poems and sermons, 3685
Charles James Napier, 3698
Poems from Eversley [by Charles Kingsley], 3741
Catarina in Venice, 3751, 3762, 3772
People who are not respectable, 3805
Professional sectarianism, 3840
Chambers and Macaulay, 3853
The barons of Buchan, 3876
Pitt and Canning, 3905
Long vacation readings, 3918
William the Silent, 3959
On toleration, 3976
A raid among the rhymers, 3990
A "last word" on Macaulay, 4026
Ruskin at the sea-side, 4047
Abolishing the writing of books, 4060
The inquisition in England, 4083
The sphynx, 4119
Thalatta! Thalatta! a study at sea, 4173, 4184, 4193, 4203, 4213, 4223
Early Scottish poetry, 4174
The ordeal by oath [enfranchisement], 4239
What is truth? 4262
Autumn days, 4279
Robert Browning, 4301
Robertson of Ellon, 4354
A campaigner at home, in 11 installments from 4412 to 4498
Nooks and byways, 4536, 4555, 4599
John Dryden, 4567
The passion of Martin Holdfast, 4639
Church politics in Scotland, 4660
Swinburne and his critics, 4703
Dallas, *The Gay Science*: criticism, 4712
Politics in our parish, 4738
Poetry and George Eliot, 4908
Prussia and Mr. Carlyle, 4919
William Morris and Matthew Arnold, 4944
The poetry of the year, 5028
Dr. Robert Lee of Edinburgh, 5044
Poems of Dante Gabriel Rossetti, 5080
Mr. Disraeli's *Lothair*, 5094
Temptation of Stephen Holdfast, 5153, 5163
The trial of Mary Stuart, 5255, 5263
Ornithological reminiscences, 5557
A cruise in the Baltic, 5732
Bibliomania in 1879, 6197
The *Crookit Meg*: a story of the year one, 6261, 6270, 6275, 6285, 6291
Pauper children in Scotland, 6315
Note: 4396
See: 4465

Skelton, Reginald Albert, misc. writer. *BMCat.*

Statistics of suicide, **NC** 3721

Skene, Felicia Mary Frances: see *Index*, I, 1087.

Prison visiting, **FM** 6355

Skinner, Charles Lancelot Andrewes, 1853–1934, army officer. Venn.

Secondary education, **FortR** 3810

Skottowe, Britiffe Constable, 4th Baron Skottowe in the peerage of France, 1857–1925. *WWW.*

Mr. Chamberlain, **NatR-II** 1896

Slagg, John: see *Index*, I, 1088.

The commercial treaty with France, **FortR** 1342

True "scientific frontier" of India, **NC** 1165
The National Indian Congress, 1275

Slater, John William. *BMCat., Kelly's Suburban Directory* (1892), p. 298.

Laws and government of "brutes," **NatR-II** 1016
Letter: 871

Smalley, George Washburn, 1833–1916, American correspondent of the *Times*. *DAB.*

A visit to Prince Bismarck, **FortR** 3383

Notes on New York, **NC** 1369
Checks on democracy in America, 2582

Smart, Henry Hawley, 1833–1893, army officer, novelist. *DNB.*

Present state of the turf, **FortR** 2376

Smart, William: see *Index*, I, 1088.

The old economy and the new, **FortR** 3120
Is money a mere commodity? 3432

Smeaton, William Henry Oliphant, 1856–1914, novelist, journalist. *WWW, LCCat.*

A lost art [table talk], **ScotR** 699

Smiles, Samuel: see *Index*, I, 1088.

Robert Stephenson, **FM** 3917

Smirnove, John, d.1844/45, sec. to Russian embassy, London. Letters to W. J. Hooker, 1830–1836, Kew Gardens Lib., *Proc. Linnaean Society*, I, 245.

?Russian literature, **FQR** 25 collab.

Smirnove, W.

See: **FQR** 25

Smith, Alfred, d.1949/50, missionary. *CCD/*
1949/50.

The French v. the London Missionary Society in Madagascar, **NatR-II** 204

Smith, Alys W. Pearsall: see Russell, Alys
W. P. S.

Smith, Arthur

The brain-power of plants, **NatR-II** 843
The tithe question and Church reform, 956
Evolution v. specific creations, 1229
Letter: 654

Smith, Bernard, 1815–1903, R.C. priest. Gorman.

Rawlinson's *Herodotus,* **DR** 974
Notice: 981

Smith, Charles, army officer. *Army List/*69.

Notice: **FortR** 602

Smith, Emily Tennyson (Bradley): see *Index,*
I, 1089; also *BMCat.* under maiden name,
and *DNB* 2nd suppl. under G. G. Bradley.

A stone book, **NC** 2025

Smith, Francis Montagu, army officer, asst.
supt., Royal Gunpowder Factory. *Army*
*List/*69.

Gunpowder and modern artillery, **FM** 5112

Smith, Frederick Ernest Gilliat, 1857/58–
1935, man of letters. *Tablet,* Mar. 2, 1935,
p. 275.

Cultus of the Blessed Virgin in Sarum Bre-
viary, **DR** 2303
England's ancient saints, 2414
Two mediaeval Christmas offices, 2465

Smith, George, 1831–1895, philanthropist, social reformer. *DNB.*

Our canal population, **FortR** 1126

Smith, George Barnett: see *Index,* I, 1089.

Thomas Love Peacock, **FortR** 975
Brockden Brown, 1507
An Irish novelist [William Carleton], 3906
The English Terence [Richard Cumberland],
4407

A singer from Killarney [A. P. Graves], **FM**
5456
Mr. [Spencer] Walpole on England, 6123
Walter Bagehot, 6153

Drummond of Hawthornden, **NQM** 20
Nathaniel Hawthorne, 38
Philip Massinger, 60

James Russell Lowell, **NC** 1145
Memorable dissolutions, 2207
Napoleon on himself, 3059

Smith, George Gregory, 1865–1932, writer on
English and Scottish literature. Foster,
LCCat.

Two chancellors: Betoun and Wolsey, **ScotR**
185

Smith, George Vance: see *Index,* I, 1089.

The Second Advent and the church ques-
tion, **NC** 197
A reviser on the new revision [of the New
Testament], 592
Revision of the Bible, 1298
Heresy and schism, 2629

Smith, Gilbert Leslie, Indian civil servant. A.
C. Tupp, *The Indian Civil Service List of*
1885 (Allahabad, 1885), pp. 74-75.

The [National] Congress and modern India,
NatR-II 847

Smith, Goldwin: see *Index,* I, 1089.

Mommsen's *History of Rome,* **BentQR** 26

The aim of reform, **FortR** 845
Political destiny of Canada, 1346
The defeat of the Liberal party, 1374
The policy of aggrandizement, 1390
University extension, 1429
Whigs and Liberals, 1447
The Eastern crisis, 1463
A word for indignation meetings, 1487
The fallacy of Irish history, 2123
Oxford revisited, 3462

The colleges of Oxford, **FM** 2953
Imperialism, 3596
Why not the Lords too? 3947
Conservatism and female suffrage, **NatR-II**
675
Invitation to celebrate the French Revolu-
tion, 745

Can Jews be patriots? **NC** 172
The Jewish question, 633
The machinery of elective government, 670
The Channel tunnel 684
Peel and Cobden, 726
The "Home Rule" fallacy, 734
The Jews, 780
Why send more Irish to America? 861
The political history of Canada, 1293

The moral of the late crisis, [Irish separatism], 1314
American statesmen, 1506, 1562, 1586
The question of disestablishment, 2106
The contest for the presidency, 2277
The situation at Washington, 2430
The impending revolution [on the Irish question], 2537
The House of Lords [its reorganization], 2554
Failure of party government, 3461
Notice: 2519

Smith, Sir Henry Babington, 1863–1923, civil servant and financier. *DNB*.

Ladysmith after the siege, **NatR-II** 2440

Smith, Henry Herbert: see *Index*, I, 1090.

Rural enclosures and allotments, **NC** 1352 collab.
English and Dutch dairy farming, 3025 collab.

Smith, Isaac Gregory: see *Index*, I, 1090.

Slipshod English, **NatR-II** 655

Smith, James, 1790?–1866, R.C. journalist. *Dict. of Catholic Biog.*, N.Y., 1961.

Notice: **DR** 62

Smith, James Parker: see *Index*, I, 1090.

Liberal Unionists, **NatR-II** 1569

Smith, John, R.C. priest, of Formly, near Liverpool. *CD/41*.

Waterton and natural history, **DR** 146

Smith, John Campbell, 1828–1914, Scottish advocate. Grant.

The marriage law of Scotland, **FortR** 460

Smith, Laura Alexandrine, *BMCat*.

Workers' songs, **NC** 1584
On some war-songs of Europe, 1776
The music of Japan, 2673

Smith, Lucy Toulmin, 1838–1911, scholar, librarian. *DNB*.

New edition of *The Paston Letters,* **FM** 5382

Smith, Nowell Charles, 1871–1961, literary critic. *WW/1960*, and obit./1962.

Coleridge and his critics, **FortR** 3691
The poetry of William Morris, 4052

Smith, Philip Vernon, 1845–1929, divine. *WWW*.

Mahmal and British troops in Egypt, **NatR-II** 63
Church action as to vestments and ritual, 184
Reform and the representation of minorities, 249
Women's suffrage, 279
Church question and the coming election, 371
Letter: 893

Smith, Reginald Bosworth: see *Index*, I, 1091.

The Liberal party and Home Rule, **NatR-II** 413
Mohammedanism in Africa, **NC** 1491
The crisis in the Church, 3430

Smith, Richard John, 1786–1855, actor. *Gent. Mag.*, 197 (Mar. 1855), 322–325.

Boat ahoy! **FM** 1818

Smith, Robert Pearsall, of Philadelphia; brother of Lloyd Pearsall Smith, ed., in *DAB*, and father of Logan Pearsall Smith in *DNB/1950*. LCCat., BMCat. [especially the entry under Smith for George H. Putnam's analysis of Smith's work in international copyright], and L. P. Smith, *Unforgotten Years* (1938), pp. 60–61, 138.

An olive branch from America [on Anglo-American copyright], **NC** 1468

Smith, Samuel: see *Index*, I, 1091.

Social reform, **NC** 860

Smith, Sydney: see *Index*, I, 1091.

"Letters on the subject of the Catholics," **FM** 1192

Smith, Sydney Fenn: see *Index*, I, 1092.

Gladstone and Cardinal Manning, **NC** 2922

Smith, T. T. Vernon, civil engineer, prob. a Canadian. *No. American Rev.* 99, (Oct. 1864), 483.

Our new wheat-fields in the North-West, **NC** 326

Smith, Thomas Parker, 1836–1917, physician. *Surgeon Index/3s*.

Vegetarianism, **FortR** 3724

Smith, W. Allen.

State emigration, **NatR-II** 650

Smith, W. Jardine, Australian colonist.

The imperial connection, **FM** 5242
Empire or no empire? 5371
Australian federation, 5983

Blue-blooded boys, **NC** 925

Smith, William Anderson, 1842–1906, writer on Scotland. *Glasgow Herald,* July 25, 1906, p. 9viii.

The state of the Highlands, **ScotR** 5
The future of the Highlands, 24
Scottish fisheries under the Fishery Board, 394
Fish-hatching, 499

Smith, William Garnet: see *Index,* I, 1092.

The women of George Meredith, **FortR** 3805

Smith, William Henry, 1825–1891, statesman. *DNB.*

The navy; its duties and capacity, **NatR-II** 227

Smith, William Wilberforce, d.1896, physician. *Med. Direct./97.*

Letter: **NatR-II** 784

Smyth, Mrs. A. Gillespie: see *Index,* I, 1093, and II, App. A.

Rencontres on the road, in 7 installments from **FM** 319 to 542

The dead alive, 679

Smyth, Patrick James, 1826–1885, Irish politician. *DNB.*

Young Ireland, **FortR** 1753

Smyth, Sir Warington Wilkinson, 1817–1890, mineralogist. *DNB.*

Edward Forbes, **FM** 3304
Sir Henry T. de la Beche, 3357

Smythe, Lady Emily Anne (Beaufort): see *Index,* I, 1093.

East Roumelia, **NC** 307

Snagge, Sir Thomas William, 1837–1914, judge. *WWW.*

Fifty years of English county courts, **NC** 3183

Snead-Cox, John George: see Cox, John George Snead.

Snell, Merwin-Marie. *LCCat.*

The triumph of St. Thomas, **DR** 2676

Sneyd, Henry, 1838–1920. *Landed Gentry.* (See *Index,* I, 1094.)

Koran v. Turkish reform, **FM** 5832

Snow, Herbert, 1847–1930, physician. *WWW.*

Count Mattei, his treatment of cancer, **NatR-II** 1024
The knife v. Mattei, 1069

Increase of cancer, **NC** 1898

Snow, Terence Benedict, 1838–1905, Benedictine abbot. *BMCat., Benedictine Bibliog.*

Hallucinations, **DR** 2498
The Lollards, 2511
Craft guilds in the fifteenth century, 2620

Soissons, Guy Jean Raoul Eugène Charles Emmanuel de Savoie-Carignan: see *Index,* I, 1094.

Maeterlinck's latest drama, **FortR** 4549

Solly, Henry, 1812/13–1903, divine, ed. *Workingman's Magazine. BMCat., Times,* Mar. 5, 1903, p. 8b.

Working men's clubs, **FM** 4529
Trade schools of north Germany, 5897

Technical education, **NC** 1030

Somerset, George Fitzroy Henry, 3rd Baron Raglan, 1857–1921, governor of Isle of Man. *Burke.*

The militia, **NatR-II** 1857

Somerset, Henry Charles Somers Augustus, 1874–1945, army officer. *WWW.*

Great Britain, Venezuela, and the United States, **NC** 2831
Army manoeuvres in France, 3752

Sommerville, W. A.

Rowton houses—from a resident, **NC** 3530

Sorabji, Cornelia, 1866–1954. (See *Index,* I, 1094.)

Stray thoughts of an Indian girl, **NC** 2114
Urmi—a poisoned queen, 2340
The Parsees, 2469

Achthar—a queen, 2948
Legal status of women in India, 3381
An Indian plague story, 3528

Sosnosky, Theodor von, b.1866, Viennese political and military author. *Grosse Brockhaus, Wer Ist's/* 1935.

The future of the British army, **FortR** 4450

Sotheby, Hans William, 1826/27–1874, barrister. Foster. (For *Index,* I, art., see below, App. A.)

Belli's *Sonnets in the Roman Dialect,* **FortR** 1025

Life and writing of Thomas de Quincey, **FM** 4051, 4058

Southern, Henry, 1799–1853, editor, diplomat. *DNB.*

The Pyrenees, **FQR** 63
Memoirs of Vidocq, 73
Louis Bonaparte's *Answer to Scott's "History of Napoleon,"* 75
Victor Hugo's poems and novels, 87 collab.?
Bourrienne's *Memoirs of Napoleon,* 105
French novels: Paul de Koch, 125
Jacotot's system of education, 130
Fontanier's *Travels in Asiatic Turkey,* 143
The Belgian Revolution, 154
Spirit of the twelfth and thirteenth centuries, 157
Victor Hugo's *Notre Dame,* 192
Saint-Simon's *Memoirs:* the court of Louis the Fourteenth, 206
Penal colonies, 224
Memoirs of Louis XVIII, 228
Gouverneur Morris, 247
French novels, 249
The Revolution of 1830, 252
The young Napoleon, 264
Victor Hugo, *Le Roi s'Amuse,* 265
American systems of prison discipline, 281
Notices: 66, 90, 118

Belgium: by an eye-witness, **FM** 153

Southey, Robert: see *Index,* I, 1094.

History of Arabs and Moors in Spain, **FQR** 1

Life of Sir Philip Sydney, **FM** 4865, 4873, 4885
See: 6075

Jacobinism [a manuscript letter], **NatR-II** 1314

Letter: **NC** 921

Spaeth, Charles A.

Proposed address of British army to Queen, **NatR-II** 343

Spalding, Henry, 1840–1907, army officer, translator of Russian literature. *Army Lists, BMCat.*

The Mazeppa legend, **NatR-II** 1152

Spalding, John Lancaster, 1840–1916, Catholic prelate and educator. *DAB.*

Postion of Catholics in the United States, **DR** 1761

Sparrow, Walter Shaw, 1862–1940, writer on art and architecture. *WWW, LCCat.* (See below, App. A.)

Goethe as stage manager, **NC** 3100

Spaur, Thérèse (Giraud), Countess de, formerly wife of Edward Dodwell, 1776/77–1832, later wife of Bavarian minister to Rome. Ward, *Wiseman,* I, 495; Venn under Edward Dodwell.

The flight of the Pope, **Ram** 454

Spear, Mrs. F.

An Italian goldsmith [Salvatore Farina], **FortR** 4182

Spearman, Edmund Robert: see *Index,* I, 1095.

Mistaken identity and police anthropometry, **FortR** 2929
Prisoners on the move, 3720
Juvenile reformatories in France, 4107

"Known to the police," **NC** 2631
Women in French prisons, 2750

Spedding, James: see *Index,* I, 1095.

Improvement of reading department in British Museum, **FM** 3986
Arnold on translating Homer, 4108
Negotiations with Spain, 4326
Miss Kate Terry in Viola, 4575
Gardiner's *Prince Charles and the Spanish Marriage,* 5086
The *Merchant of Venice,* 5699
Note: 4228

Teaching to read, **NC** 46
Charles Tennyson Turner, 353
Dr. Abbott and Queen Elizabeth, 397

Speight, H. perhaps Harry Speight, b.1855, Yorkshire antiquary who published in Bradford: see *BMCat., LCCat.*

Letter: **NatR-II** 1020

Spence, Catherine Helen: see *Index,* I, 1096.

Principles of representation, **FortR** 215, collab.

Spence, Magnus, school teacher of Kirkwall, Shetland. Metcalfe addresses.

Standing Stones and Maeshowe of Stennes, **ScotR** 422

Spence, Thomas William Leisk, 1845–1923, sec. to Board of Lunacy. *WWW.*

Pauper lunacy and ordinary pauperism, **ScotR** 470

Spencer, Lady Charlotte Frances Frederica (Seymour) Countess Spencer of Althorp, 1835–1903. *Complete Peerage.*

Note: **FM** 5123
See: 5129

Spencer, Hon. George, or in Passionist Order, Father Ignatius of St. Paul, 1799–1864. Boase.

Letters: **Ram** 183, 287

Spencer, Herbert: see *Index,* I, 1096.

Mill *versus* Hamilton, **FortR** 41
The origin of animal-worship, 678
Morals and moral sentiments, 769
Specialized administration, 823
Replies to criticisms, 998, 1006
A note on the preceding article, 1124
Rejoinder [to arts. by J. F. McLennan], 1372
Ceremonial government, 1424, 1439, 1450, 1460, 1471, 1490
Political institutions, in 8 installments from 1743 to 1820
The ethics of Kant, 2732
The late Professor Tyndall, 3461
Balfour's dialectics, 3647
[James] Ward's *Naturalism and Agnosticism,* 4371
Letters: 3853, 4427

Origin and function of music, **FM** 3649

Religion: a retrospect and prospect, **NC** 944
Retrogressive religion, 1012
Agnosticism and the religion of humanity, 1063
The factors of organic evolution, 1265, 1278
A counter criticism, 1514
Absolute political ethics, 1820
On justice, 1841, 1854
Lord Salisbury on evolution, 2830
The Duke of Argyll's criticisms, 3119
What is social evolution? 3339
Letter: 2795

Spender, A. F.; perhaps the A. F. Spender in *WWW/1950.*

Little Eyolf [by Ibsen], **DR** 2565
Impressions of the Holy Land, 2611
The catacombs of Syracuse, 2716, 2725
Notices: 2583, 2594, 2606, 2618, 2628, 2651, 2720, 2729

Spender, Edward Harold, 1864–1926, journalist. *WWW,* Foster.

A visit to Andorra, **FortR** 3901
Tennyson, 4038

Spielmann, Marion Harry Alexander: see *Index,* I, 1096.

Wood-engraving in England and America, **NatR-II** 1695
The rivals of *Punch,* 1747

G. F. Watts, **NC** 3061
The National Gallery in 1900, 3680

Spilsbury, Albert Gybbon, b.1849, army officer. *BMCat., LCCat.* under Gybbon-Spilsbury.

The *Tourmaline* expedition, **FortR** 4247

Spink, Charles Anselm, c.1816–1885, schoolmaster. *Acton-Simpson Corres.,* I, 73n.

Trans: **Ram** 953

Spink, William, Scottish solicitor. *BMCat., Edinburgh Directories,* 1866–1922.

Shakespeare as a dramatic model, **NatR-II** 375

Spottiswoode, George Andrew, 1827–1899, printer, ed. of industrial newspaper. Boase.

Religion in elementary schools, **NC** 2784

Spring-Rice, Thomas, 2nd Baron Monteagle: see *Index,* I, 1097.

A Unionist policy for Ireland, **NatR-II** 1792
Railway monopoly in Ireland, 2315

Abolition of landlords, **NC** 557
The Crimes Act, 1152
The Evicted Tenants Bill, 2600
The latest Irish land bill, 2736
The Irish land question to-day, 2927
The new Irish policy, 3132

Squire, William Barclay, 1855–1927, musicologist, critic. *DNB.*

A great singer [Elizabeth Billington], **NatR-II** 1813

Stack, John Herbert: see *Index*, I, 1097, and II, App. A.

Proposed remedies for Irish wrongs, **FortR** 457
Anthony Trollope's novels, 564
Some recent English novels, 787
Life of Charles Dickens [by Forster], 836
Notice: 496

The duties of the State, **FM** 5321

Stähele, Andreas, Swiss-born London bookseller. See printed prospectus of his business enclosed in letter to Rowland Hill, Nov. 16, 1826, Univ. Coll. London.

Rizo, *Modern Greek Literature*, **FQR** 10 collab.

Stairs, William Grant, 1863–1892, captain, traveller. *DNB*.

Shut up in the African forest, **NC** 1984
From the Albert Nyanza to the Indian Ocean, 2058

Standing, Percy Cross: see *Index*, I, 1097.

Significance of the Siamese visit, **NC** 3127

Stanford, Sir Charles Villiers: see *Index*, I, 1097.

Hubert Parry's *Judith*, **FortR** 2758
Verdi's *Falstaff*, 3346
Musical criticism in England, 3515

Sullivan's *Golden Legend*, **NatR-II** 504

The Wagner bubble, **NC** 1623

Stanford, Vere Fane-Benett, 1839–1894, army officer, M.P. *Landed Gentry*.

Madeira as a health resort. **FortR** 3062

Stanhope, Edward: see *Index*, I, 1097.

Lessar's triumph on the [Afghanistan] border, **NatR-II** 319

Stanhope, Philip Henry: see *Index*, I, 1097.

Legends of Charlemagne, **FM** 4667
Arabic philosophy in mediaeval Europe, 4723

Staniforth, Captain

Retzsch's *Outlines to Shakespeare*: **Hamlet,** **FQR** 52

Stanley, Sir Arthur, 1869–1947, philanthropist, M.P. *DNB*.

The sick and wounded in South Africa, **NatR-II** 2480

Stanley, Arthur Penrhyn: see *Index*, I, 1097.

Letter: **DR** 1263

Aids to Faith, and *Replies to "Essays and Reviews,"* **FM** 4245
Theology of the nineteenth century, 4520
The gains of the Church of England in 1865, 4608
Variations of the Roman Church, 6282
Inverawe and Ticonderoga, 6337

Absolution, **NC** 131
The Eucharist, 169
Baptism, 364
The creed of the early Christians, 479

Stanley, Edward: see *Index*, I, 1098.

Brand's *Peru*, **LR (1829)** 15

Stanley, Edward Henry, 15th Earl of Derby, 1826–1893, statesman. *DNB*.

Letter: **FortR** 2638

Ireland and the Land Act, **NC** 632

Stanley, Edward Lyulph: see *Index*, I, 1098.

The Greville Journals, **FortR** 1109
Indian immigrants in Mauritius, 1162
The new Domesday Book, 1263
National education and the London School Board, 1631
Notice: 289

Industrial schools and the Home Office, **NC** 658
Farming and taxation, 797
French elementary education, 832
The House of Lords, 1022
The House of Commons and the Church, 2124
Religion at London School Board, 2478
The education settlement of 1870, 2845
Mr. Diggle and Mr. Riley, 2889

Stanley, Henrietta Maria, Lady Stanley of Alderley, 1807–1895, wife of Edward John Stanley. *Complete Peerage*.

Recollections of women's education, **NC** 344

Stanley, Henry Edward John: see *Index*, I, 1098.

Radical theorists on land, **FortR** 2283
Two days in the Brixworth Union, 2337

Preservation of the colonies, **NatR-II** 1153
Gunners and gunsmiths, 1325
Jesse Collings, [on land allotments], 1353
State regulation of the price of bread, 1381
The Royal Welsh Land Commission, 1464, 1555

Stanley, Sir Henry Morton, 1841–1904, explorer, journalist. *DNB.*

African legends, **FortR** 3373

Issue between Great Britain and America, **NC** 2860
Boer indictments of British policy, 3090
"Splendid isolation" or what? 3294

Stanley, Hon. Maude Alethea, 1833–1915, organizer of clubs for working girls. *WWW.*

West-End improvements, **NC** 588
Clubs for working girls, 1644

Stannard, Arthur; prob. the civil engineer, husband of Mrs. Henrietta E. V. Stannard in *DNB,* 2nd suppl.

Gordon at Gravesend, **NC** 1125

Stansfeld, Sir James: see *Index,* I, 1098.

Note: **FortR** 1352

Medical women, **NC** 60

Stanton, Richard Mary, 1820–1901, priest of the Oratory, London. Newman *L&D, XI,* index.

John Henry Cardinal Newman, **DR** 2248

Stanton, Vincent Henry: see *Index,* I, 1098.

A contribution to political economy, **FortR** 1101

Staples, Robert, Jr., 1847–1895, high sheriff, Queen's County. Venn, *BMCat.*

Local government in Ireland, **FortR** 2489

Representation of Ireland, **NatR-II** 86
Cultivation of tobacco in Ireland, 336

Stapleton, Augustus Granville: see *Index,* I, 1098.

Jewish disabilities, **FM** 2403

Stapleton, Miles Thomas, 8th Baron Beaumont, 1805–1854, writer on European politics. Burke. *BMCat.*

Turkey and its foreign diplomacy, **DR** 45
Montémont's *London,* 55
France: equality and centralization, 109

Staratsky, G. V.

Ivan Tourguénief, **DR** 1922

Statham, Francis Reginald, 1844–1908, misc. writer. *DSAB.*

A story of annexation in South Africa, **FortR** 1748

How to get out of South African difficulty, 1780
Paul Kruger, 4094

The Chartered Company [in Africa], **NatR-II** 1842
The real Robert Elsmere, 1927
Arthur Hugh Clough, 1998
The Transvaal, 2008

Statham, Henry Heathcote: see *Index,* I, 1098.

At the Royal Academy, **FortR** 1274, 1378, 4467
Modern English architecture, 1298
The musical cultus of the day, 1592
Handel, 1657
Beethoven, 1676
How public improvements are carried out, 1978
Mozart, 2138
The Bach festival, 3643
Mendelssohn, 3738
Academy and New Gallery exhibitions, 3820
Proposed new government offices, 3895
Leighton and Watts: two ideals in art, 3924
The Paris salons, 3975, 4136
Handel and the Handel festivals, 3993
Academy, New Gallery, and Guildhall, 4305
The truth about Ruskin, 4423
The Paris Exhibition, 4483

Place of Sterndale Bennett in music, **FM** 5652

London as a Jubilee city, **NatR-II** 2032
Treatment of ancient buildings, 2063
The street music question, 2185

The genius of Handel, **NC** 3672

Staunton, Andrew Aylmer, army surgeon, R.A. *Army List/*40.

Scenes in the desert, **FM** 1422, 1431, 1491, 1510

Staunton, Michael, 1788–1870, journalist of Dublin. Crone.

State and prospects of Ireland, **DR** 13
Irish absenteeism, 31
Retribution due to Ireland, 116

Stead, James Lister, 1864–1915, journalist. *WWW.*

Friendly Societies and pensions, **NatR-II** 1696

Stead, William Thomas: see *Index,* I, 1099.

The policy of coercion [on the Ottoman Empire], **FortR** 1725

Stephen, Leslie (*continued*)
The scepticism of believers, 1393
Newman's theory of belief, 1411, 1418
Dreams and realities, 1503
An attempted philosophy of history, 1693
Bradlaugh and his opponents, 1720
Spinoza [by Frederick Pollock], 1757
Thomas Paine, 3401
Pascal, 3977

University organisation, FM 4837
The Comtist utopia, 4986
?Lecky's *History of European Morals*, 5005
Baths of Santa Catarina, 5026
Dr. Pusey and Dr. Temple, 5031
The Broad Church, 5060
The religious difficulty, 5081
The Alps in the last century, 5109
Matthew Arnold and Church of England, 5128
Sports and university studies, 5148
Elwin's edition of Pope, 5176
Voysey and Purchas, 5188
Future of university reform, 5233
Religion as a fine art, 5280
Darwinism and divinity, 5299
Voltaire [by John Morley], 5318
Social macadamisation, 5335
A bad five minutes in the Alps, 5362
Shaftesbury's *Characteristics*, 5387
The Fable of the Bees [by Mandeville], 5436
Jonathan Edwards, 5480
University endowments, 5526
Ruskin's recent writings, 5555
Sidgwick's *Methods of Ethics*, 5653

Biography, NatR-II 1483
Matthew Arnold, 1509
Luxury, 1546
Duties of authors, 1577
A substitute for the Alps, 1588
The choice of books, 1705
Coleridge's *Letters*, 1717
Evolution of editors, 1833
National biography, 1843
John Byrom, 1855
Arthur Young, 1875
Oliver Wendell Holmes, 1885
Wordsworth's youth, 1974
Gibbon's autobiography, 1987
Jowett's Life, 2022
Johnsoniana, 2060
Life of Tennyson, 2085
The importation of German, 2107
The Browning letters, 2298
Southey's letters, 2325
Cosmopolitan spirit in literature, 2369
John Donne, 2386
John Ruskin, 2428
Lord Herbert of Cherbury, 2461
Walter Bagehot, 2482

Suppression of poisonous opinions, NC 834, 844
Belief and conduct, 1595
Cardinal Newman's scepticism, 1994
Bishop Butler's apologist [W. E. Gladstone], 2870
Thomas Henry Huxley, 3760

Stephen, William, 1834–1901, Scottish Anglican divine. *Aberdeen Graduates.*

?Walter Scott and the Blair Adam Antiquarian Club, ScotR 685

Stephen, William, 1840–1912, Scottish Free Church divine. *Fasti-Free Church*, pp. 350–351.

?Walter Scott and the Blair Adam Antiquarian Club, ScotR 685

Stephens, Frederic George: see *Index*, I, 1101.

William Henry Hunt, FM 4593
Costume in sculpture, 4741

Stephens, George, 1813–1895, runic archaeologist. *DNB.*

Old popular ballads and songs of Sweden, FQR 569, 593
Bernadotte and Charles XIV John, 581
Punishments and prisons in Sweden, 628
Sweden as it is, 643, 654
Foreign correspondence, 680, 695
Notices: 578, 600

Sterling, John: see *Index*, I, 1102.

Characteristics of German genius, FQR 671

Stern, Charlotte Elizabeth, writer on the Bible. *BMCat.*

The Mahdi and Mohammedan predictions, NC 995

Steuart, John Alexander, 1861–1932, novelist. *LCCat., WWW.*

Ireland as a field for tourists, FortR 3854
Authors, publishers, and booksellers, 4076

Steveni, James William Barnes: see *Index*, I, 1102, and *Yearbook*/1922.

Queen Elizabeth and Ivan the Terrible, NC 2493

Stevenson, Francis Joseph

Australasia or Australia? NatR-II 273

Stevenson, Francis Seymour: see *Index*, I, 1102.

What the labourers want, **FortR** 2458

Stevenson, Joseph S.: see *Index*, I, 1102.

Ancient Teutonic rhythmic gospel harmony, **FQR** 174

Stevenson, Robert Louis: see *Index*, I, 1102.

Lord Lytton's *Fables in Song*, **FortR** 1060
Morality of the profession of letters, 1794

The old Pacific capital [Monterey], **FM** 6347

The gospel according to Walt Whitman, **NQM** 152
Story of a lie, 192

Steward, M.

Letter: **NatR-11** 104

Steward, Sarah, of Norfolk.

Women and women's suffrage, **NatR-II** 332

Stewart, Charles; perhaps the novelist in *BMCat*.

Notice: **FortR** 61

Stewart, David: see *Index*, I, 1103.

Wheel overboard, **FM** 121
Bartholomew Fair, 134

Stewart, George, Jun., 1848–1906, journalist. Wallace.

Life and times of Longfellow, **ScotR** 143
Emerson, the thinker, 205

Stewart, Countess Mary Arabella Arthur (Cecil), 1850–1903, wife of Alan Plantagenet Stewart, 10th Earl of Galloway. *Complete Peerage*.

Women and politics, **NC** 1287
A glimpse of Russia, 1395
Free Greece, 1563
Globe-trotting in New Zealand, 2282
Wagner at Bayreuth, 2641

Stigand, William: see *Index*, I, 1103.

The war of the Comunidades, **FortR** 885

Stillman, William James: see *Index*, I, 1103.

Italy, **FortR** 1649
Austro-Hungary, 1701
Greece and the Greeks, 1744

The Cretan insurrection of 1866–1868, **FM** 4949

The belligerent Papacy, **NatR-II** 2297

The *Decameron* and its villas, **NC** 3519

Stirling, Archibald William, 1856/57–1923, solicitor, journalist. *WWW*, Foster.

The political outlook in Queensland, **FortR** 2772

Stirling, James Hutchison: see *Index*, I, 1104.

Was Sir William Hamilton a Berkeleian? **FortR** 312
De Quincey and Coleridge upon Kant, 444
Kant refuted by dint of muscle, 896
Stirling, Hegel, and the mathematicians, 944

Stirling-Maxwell, William: see *Index*, I, 1104.

Lavengro [by George Borrow], **FM** 2826
Cloister-life of Charles V, 2835, 2851
The Bridgewater Gallery, 2884
Tauromachia; or Spanish Bullfights, 2966
Disraeli's *New Curiosities of Literature*, 3035
Sir Robert Strange, 3352
The law of marriage and divorce, 3375
Pius IX and Lord Palmerston [by Montalembert], 3517
High and low latitudes, 3627
William Hickling Prescott, 3835

Stobart, later Greenhalgh, Mabel Annie (Boulton), 1862–1954, in military hospital service. *WWW*, *LCCat*.

New lights on Ibsen's *Brand*, **FortR** 4318

Stobart, W. L.

Rosebery and the Liberal party, **FortR** 3679
Leaderless Liberals and Rosebery, 4131

Stobie, W.: see *Index*, I, 1104.

An incident of real life in Bengal, **FortR** 2629

Stock, Eugene, 1836–1928, sec. of Church Missionary Society. *WWW*.

The Church Missionary Society, **FortR** 2776

Stock, St. George William Joseph, b.1850, writer on philosophy. *LCCat.*, *BMCat*.

Diary of Bishop of Killalla, **FortR** 4216

Erasmus, **FM** 5761, 5774

Origins of political economy, **ScotR** 636

Stockton, Frank Richard, 1834–1902, novelist. *DAB*.

The watchmaker's wife, **NatR-II** 1419

Stoffel, Eugène Georges Henri Céleste, Baron, 1823–1907, French military writer. *Grand Larousse, LCCat.*

Military forces of Prussia, **FM** 5252, 5260

Stoker, Abraham, commonly called Bram, 1847–1912, barrister, journalist. *WWW,* Crone.

Actor-managers, **NC** 1889

Stokes, Alfred W., chemist.

Letter: **NatR-II** 1069

Stokes, Margaret M'Nair: see *Index,* I, 1104.

Petrie's *Ancient Music of Ireland,* **FM** 3753

Stokes, Scott Nasmyth, 1821–1891, barrister, inspector of schools. Boase.

Ecclesiastical Titles Bill, **Ram** 391
Controversy on the poor-school grant, 837
Industrial education, 851
The Royal Commission on Education, 975
The Royal Commission and the *Tablet,* 982
Elementary school books, 1064
Administration of charitable trusts, 1079
The Education Commission, 1108
The Commission on Education, 1115
The revised educational code, 1122

Stokes, Whitley, 1830–1909, Irish editor, scholar. *DNB.*

Danish ballads, **FM** 2976, 3309
Servian proverbs, 3344
Tuscan proverbs, 3554
Mythology of Finnland, 3598
Adamnán's vision, 5169

Stone, Mrs. Elizabeth, novelist. *BMCat.*

A chat about good cheer, **FM** 6468

Stone, Jean Mary: see *Index,* I, 1104.

Missing page from *Idylls of the King,* **DR** 2134
Henrietta Maria [wife of Charles I], 2165
The youth of Mary Tudor, 2194
Mary, Queen of England, 2217
Philip and Mary, 2233
Persecution under Elizabeth, 2300
Queen Elizabeth and the revolution, 2394, 2454
Pictures of the Reformation period, 2623, 2654

Corporate re-union in reign of Charles I, **ScotR** 238

Tudor intrigues in Scotland, 454
Runic Crosses of Northumbria, 521
The Royal Library, 652

Stopford, James George Henry, 5th Earl of Courtown, 1823–1914. Burke.

Celts and Teutons in Ireland, **NatR-II** 550

Stopford, John George Beresford, army officer. *Army List/*1900.

The volunteers, **NC** 3585
Volunteers and insecurity of England, 3646
Soldier settlers in South Africa, 3677

Storr, John Stephens, 1829–1895, philanthropist, social reformer. Boase, *Times,* Jan. 8, 1895, p. 10.

The anarchy of London, **FortR** 959

Story, Alfred Thomas, 1842–1934, misc. writer. *WWW.*

Sluys, 1340, **NatR-II** 1967
A French naval hero [Jean Bart], 2064

Story, Robert Herbert: see *Index,* I, 1104.

Dax, **FM** 6340

The Kirk, and Presbyterian union, **NatR-II** 1512

Story, William Wetmore: see *Index,* I, 1104.

A conversation with Marcus Aurelius, **FortR** 923

Story-Maskelyne, Mervyn Herbert Nevil: see *Index,* I, 1105.

The science of colour, **FM** 3408
New metals, 3419
Teneriffe, 3746
Admiral Smyth, 4636

Stothert, James Augustine, 1816/17–1882, advocate and then R.C. priest in Scotland. P. F. Anson, *The Catholic Church in Modern Scotland,* 1937; Grant gives birth as May 5, 1816.

?Responsibilities of writers of fiction, **Ram** 411
Catholic novelists, 479
?Patron saints of Scotland, 520 collab.?
Living novelists, 556
Note: 577
Notices: 473, 569
See: 500

Stott, David. *BMCat.*

Decay of bookselling, **NC** 2676

Stuart-Glennie, John Stuart: see *Index,* I, 1106, and II, App. A.

The Women's Suffrage Bill, **FortR** 2814
Unionist policy, 3732

Buckle in the East, **FM** 4352
Buckle's contribution to new philosophy of history, 5419
At a Highland hut, 5607
MacPherson, Burns, and Scott, 6277

Modern Greek, **ScotR** 571
Greek folk, revealed in their poesy, 606
Strath of Achéron; its Homeric ghosts, 700

Stuart-Wortley, Charles Beilby, Baron Stuart of Wortley, 1851–1917, barrister, M.P. Burke under Wharncliff.

Merchandise marks legislation, **NatR-II** 1369
The election of 1895, 1771

Stuart-Wortley, Jane (Wenlock), d.1900, wife of James Archibald Stuart-Wortley. Burke under Wharncliff.

The East End represented by Mr. Besant, **NC** 1451

Studd, Arthur Haythorne, 1863–1919, artist. Venn.

A Spanish experience, **NatR-II** 1531

Sturges, Octavius, 1833–1894, physician. *DNB.*

Doctors and nurses, **NC** 462

Sturgis, Julian Russell: see *Index,* I, 1107.

Michael and I, **NQM** 203

Wanted: a leader, **NC** 1305

Stutfield, George Herbert, b.1855/56, barrister. Foster, *M at B.*

Handicaps [in horse racing], **NatR-II** 2160

Modern gambling and gambling laws, **NC** 1792
Racing in 1890, 1881

Stutfield, Hugh Edward Millington: see *Index,* I, 1107.

Position of affairs in Eastern Soudan, **FortR** 3053

Investors and their money, **NatR-II** 1812

Company-monger's elysium, 1838
Higher rascality [finance], 2136
The company scandal: a City view, 2242

Stutzer, Albert; perhaps the German agricultural chemist, 1849–1916, in *EUI.*

Purchase of books in Germany, **FM** 5806

Sullivan, Mr.; possibly John Sullivan, q.v.

Shakespeare's autobiographical poems, **DR** 110

Sullivan, in Rome for Centenary of 1867, possibly priest. See *DR* 1210, p. 472n.

Centenary [of SS. Peter and Paul] of 1867, **DR** 1210

Sullivan, Alexander Martin: see *Index,* I, 1107.

Why send more Irish out of Ireland? **NC** 882

Sullivan, Edward: see *Index,* I, 1107.

Isolated free trade, **NC** 610

Sullivan, John, teacher, of Cork. *Cork P.O. Directory,* 1842–43; see *DR* no. 320.

Prescott's *Conquest of Mexico,* **DR** 320
China, 335
?Kendal's Texan expedition, 356

Sully, James: see *Index,* I, 1107.

Aesthetics of human character, **FortR** 776
Basis of musical sensation, 855
Perception of musical form, 986
Hartmann's philosophy of the unconscious, 1284
Civilisation and noise, 1525
Herder, 1953
Dream as a revelation, 3339
New study of children, 3721
The child in recent English literature, 3916
Philosophy and modern culture, 4397
Notices: 767, 906

Humorous aspect of childhood, **NatR-II** 1856
Uses of humour, 2050

George Henry Lewes, **NQM** 193
Illusions of perception, 214

Scientific optimism, **NC** 639
Genius and insanity, 1143

Swinton, Alan Archibald Campbell: see *Index,* I, 1108.

Electrical engineering, **NC** 3606

Sybel, Heinrich Carl Ludolf von: see *Index,* I, 1109.

The German Empire, **FortR** 743
First partition of Poland, 1073

Sykes, Thomas Percy, 1855–1919, headmaster Great Horton Boys' School, Bradford. *Yorkshire Observer,* June 16, 1919.

The factory half-timer, **FortR** 2899

Sylvester, Walter, d.1925, R.C. priest, F.S.A. of Scotland. Gorman, *CD for Scot./1925.*

Communions of the knights-errant, **DR** 2588
Divided hosts at treaty Communions, 2668

Syme, David: see *Index,* I, 1109.

Restrictions on trade, **FortR** 940

Symington, Alexander Macleod, 1833–1891, Scottish divine. Blackwood Corres., *Glasgow Graduates.* (See *Index,* I, 1109.)

East Africa and the slave trade, **ScotR** 235

Symonds, John Addington: see *Index,* I, 1109.

Arthur Hugh Clough, **FortR** 548
Poliziano's Italian poetry, 974
Popular songs of Tuscany, 999
The *Orlando Innamorato* of Boiardo, 1008
Blank verse of Milton, 1107
Lucretius, 1115
Debt of English to Italian literature, 1135
Hesiod, 1153
Eleatic fragments, 1183
Sophocles, 1189
Florence and the Medici, 1420, 1440
Davos in winter, 1486
Arnold's *Selections from Wordsworth,* 1640
Folgore da San Gemignano, 1784
Fletcher's *Valentinian,* 2507
Benvenuto Cellini's character, 2550
Shelley's separation from his first wife, 2586
Progress of thought in our time, 2600
Realism and idealism, 2637
The model, 2661
Beauty, composition, expression, characterization, 2678
Caricature, fantastic, grotesque, 2698
The *Memoirs of Count Carlo Gozzi,* 2754
Comparison of Elizabethan with Victorian poetry, 2783

A page of my life, 2895
Lyrism of English romantic drama, 2927
Among the Euganean Hills, 2971
Second idyl of Theocritus, 3066
Painter's *Palace of Pleasure* and English romantic drama, 3117
Swiss athletic sports, 3129
La Bête Humaine [by Emile Zola], 3132
Venetian melancholy, 3328
The new spirit [of the Renaissance], 3345
A Jesuit doctrine of obedience, 3368
Journey in South Italy, 3424
Letters: 2617, 2638

Montepulciano, **FM** 6490
A Venetian medley, 6542

Symonds, Sir Thomas Matthew Charles, 1813–1894, admiral. *DNB.*

What our navy should be, **FortR** 2761
The needs of the Navy, 3402

Symons, Arthur: see *Index,* I, 1110.

J. K. Huysmans, **FortR** 3191
A Spanish music-hall, 3215
Henley's poetry, 3245
Where to spend a holiday, 3540
George Meredith, 4030
Gérard de Nerval, 4062
Aubrey Beardsley, 4117
Stéphane Mallarmé, 4193
Balzac, 4273
Villiers de L'Isle Adam, 4315
John Donne, 4358
Ernest Dowson, 4461
The art of Watts, 4488

Frederic Mistral, **NatR-II** 396
Paul Verlaine, 1298

Symons, Jelinger Cookson, 1809–1860, misc. writer, barrister. *DNB.*

Education of the working classes, **DR** 280

Synnott, Nicholas Joseph, 1856–1920, Irish barrister. *WWW, Tablet,* Aug. 21, 1920.

?County administration, **DR** 1815
Liberty, laisser-faire, and legislation, 1899
Influence of fatalism on public opinion, 2051

Dangers to British sea-power, **FortR** 3945

Szabad, Imre, b.1822, Hungarian exile, lieut. col. in U.S. army in Civil War. *LCCat.,* see *FM* no. 4853, p. 385.

Libby Prison [Richmond, Virginia], **FM** 4853

T

Ta-Jên Liu: see Liu, Ta-Jên

Talbot, Edward Stuart: see *Index,* **I,** 1110.

Pusey and the High-Church movement, **FortR** 2007

Talbot, John, 1791–1852, 16th Earl of Shrewsbury, philanthropist. *Complete Peerage.*

Recent charges, **DR** 276
The Reformation and its consequences, 288

Talbot, Hon. Sir Reginald Arthur James, 1841–1929, army officer. *WWW.*

Battle of Abu-Klea, **NC** 1236

Tanner, Joseph Robson, 1860–1931, Fellow of St. John's Coll. Cambridge. *WWW.*

Degrees for women at Cambridge, **FortR** 3957

Taran, Nathaniel

An international money question, **FortR** 576

Tarver, John Charles: see *Index,* **I,** 1110.

Head masters and their schools, **FortR** 4332
Public schools and public services, 4520

Tatham, Hon. Frederick Spence, 1865–1934, Natal barrister. *WWW.*

The future of South Africa, **NC** 3660

Tattersall, William, 1847–1914, expert on cotton trade. *WWW, LCCat.*

Lancashire and the cotton duties, **FortR** 3766

Taubman-Goldie, George: see Goldie, George Dashwood Taubman.

Taylor, Annie R., b.1855, alive in 1903, missionary to Tibet. Isabel S. Robson, *Two Lady Missionaries in Tibet* (1909), pp. 11–112.

An Englishwoman in Tibet, **NatR-II** 1471
Notes on Tibet, 1554

Taylor, Arnold Dawes, 1852–1922, divine. Venn.

Hodge and his parson [the rural laborer], **NC** 2173

Taylor, Aucher Cornwall, 1849–1897, in the civil service. *F.O. List/84* and /1901.

The civil service, **FM** 5687

Taylor, Benjamin, 1846–1913, Scottish journalist. *Glasgow Herald,* Jan. 10, 1913, p. 8vii.

Commercial sovereignty of the seas, **FortR** 4240
The struggle for industrial supremacy, 4524

A study in trade unionism, **NC** 3279
Coal supplies of the world, 3324
The coming struggle in the Pacific, 3363
Sea-power and sea-carriage, 3487
The Bulwer-Clayton Treaty, 3625
The burden of coal, 3722

Disposal of the dead, **ScotR** 296
Mineral leases and royalties, 325
The Darien expedition, 344
Local taxation in Scotland, 482
Spain and the Jacobites, 519

Taylor, Sir Charles, 1817–1876, ed. *Court Journal.* Boase.

Fishing in Norway, **FortR** 99

Taylor, Charles Bell, 1829–1909, opthalmic surgeon. *DNB.*

Pasteur's prophylactic, **NatR-II** 1028
Letter: 988

Taylor, Cooke: see Cooke-Taylor, Richard Whately

Taylor, Frances Magdalen, sometimes called Fanny or Fauny Margaret Taylor, 1832–1900, nurse in Crimean War. Boase.

Works of charity, **DR** 829
Miss Sewell and Miss Yonge, 899
Adam Bede [by George Eliot], 930
Notices: 874, 909

Taylor, George, 1772–1851: see *Index,* **I,** 1111, and **II,** App. A.

French finance, **FQR** 175
Foreign poor: home colonies in Belgium and France, 307
Pauperism in France, 349

Taylor, Helen: see *Index*, I, 1111, and II, App. A.

Trollope's defence of fox-hunting, **FortR** 649
Sir Thomas More on politics of today, 703
Paris and France, 771
A new attack on toleration, 827
Note: 1550

Edited: **FM** 4727, 4786, 4796

Taylor, Sir Henry: see *Index*, I, 1111.

Infant Bridal, and other Poems [by Aubrey De Vere], **FM** 4439
The Habitual Criminals Bill, 4975
Mr. Mill on the subjection of women, 5047

Carlyle's *Reminiscences*, **NC** 597
Four Centuries of English Letters, 627
An academy of literature, 921

Taylor, Henry Yates Jones, misc. writer, of Gloucester. See *NatR-II* no. 908.

Revival of famous fruit trees, **NatR-II** 908
Where were women's rights in the last century? 1176
How poison was detected a hundred years ago, 1292
The cuckoo in the west of England, 1421
Letter: 715

Taylor, Ida Ashworth: see *Index*, I, 1111.

The art of dying, **NC** 2610
Lord Edward Fitzgerald, 3237
Powder and paint, 3549

Taylor, Isaac, 1829–1901: see *Index*, I, 1111.

The great missionary failure, **FortR** 2755
Missionary finance, 2764
Note: 2776

Certain Etruscan interpretations, **FM** 5922

Taylor, John Francis: see *Index*, I, 1111.

Bismarck and Richelieu, **FortR** 4180
Sipodo and Bernard [two assassins], 4510

Taylor, Peter Alfred, 1819–1891, radical politician. *DNB.*

Anti-vaccination, **NC** 721

Taylor, Sedley: see *Index*, I, 1112.

A real "saviour of society" [profit-sharing], **NC** 489
Profit-sharing, 585
Profit-sharing in agriculture, 773

Taylor, Whately Cooke: see Cooke-Taylor, Richard Whately.

Taylor, William, 1765–1836, writer on German literature and French Revolution. *DNB.*

Southern Germany, **FQR** 19
Notice: 39

Taylor, William Cooke, 1800–1849, misc. writer. *DNB.*

The Byzantine historians, **FQR** 234
Schlegel and the Oriental Translation Fund, 268
Jewish emancipation, 274
Meditations of Marcus Antonius, translated into Persian, 277
Mohammed and Mohammedanism, 287
Dumas's *Gaul and France*, 300
Jacquemont's *Letters from India*, 306
Cousinéry's *Travels in Macedonia*, 319
Central Asia, 323
Dumas's *Travelling Impressions*, 325
New Arabian tales, 336
Depping's *Jews in the Middle Ages*, 340
Objects and advantages of statistical science, 375

Tchertkoff, Vladimir Grigorevich: see Chertkóv, Vladimir Grigorevich.

Teague, John Jessop, 1856–1929, divine. *WWW.*

A seventeenth-century prelate [Bishop Ken], **NC** 1840

Telesforo de Trueba y Cossio: see Trueba y Cossio, Telesforo.

Telford, John, 1851–1936, Wesleyan minister, writer on hymnology. *WWW.*

Hymnology of the Christian church, **ScotR** 358

Temple, Sir Richard: see *Index*, I, 1112.

Political effect of religious thought in India, **FortR** 1991
Growth of population in India, 3193
A parliamentary view of the Victoria Nyanza railway, 3214
Superannuation of elemenary teachers, 3349
French movements in Eastern Siam, 3392

Social science at Birmingham, **NatR-II** 199
Our Indo-Chinese frontier, 579
Polynesian labour traffic, 1309

Thackeray, William Makepeace (*continued*)
About a Christmas book, 2143
A literary man, Laman Blanchard, 2174
Some illustrated children's books, 2189
For a continuation of *Ivanhoe*, 2229, 2240
Grumble about Christmas-books, 2282 collab.
?Mr. Thackeray in the United States, 3054
Letter: 1266
See: 427, 435, 485, 501, 522, 538, 548, 560,
562, 574, 585, 606, 607, 619, 622, 631,
636, 662, 663, 666, 684, 694, 705,
738, 739, 745, 775, 809, 821, 831, 868,
909, 959, 1024, 1069, 1079, 1179, 1257,
1331, 1353, 1364, 1414, 1462, 1528

Thicknesse, Ralph Thicknesse: see *Index*, I,
1113, and II, App. A.

Letter: **NC** 491

Thijm, Petrus Paul Maria Alberdingk, 1827–
1904, Dutch Catholic theologian; professor at Louvain. *Cath. Ency.*

Recent works on the state of Germany, **DR**
1783, 1807
Notice: 2019

Thin, George, d.1903, physician. *BMCat., Surgeon Index*/2nd s.

The Leprosy Commission in India, **FortR**
3458

Thomas, Bertha: see *Index*, I, 1113.

Intellectual wild oats, **FM** 5548
A professor extraordinary, 5575
Latest intelligence from Venus [on woman's
suffrage], 5625
Critics in wonderland, 5759
Wagner's Niebelungen trilogy, 5827
Bassano, 5944
Technical training for girls, 6156
Autobiography of an agnostic, 6405

How I became a Conservative, **NatR-II** 1147

The fortunes of the Sundew family, **NQM**
134

Thomas, David Alfred, first Viscount Rhondda, 1856–1918, statesman, colliery proprietor. *DNB.*

The Mines (Eight Hours) Bill, **FortR** 3495

Thomas, Edward A., 1838–1890, U.S. assoc.
judge in Wyoming Territory. *Amer.
WWW.* and *FortR* no. 1846, p. 414.

The Latter Day Saints as they are, **FortR**
1846

Thomas, Herbert Preston: see Preston-
Thomas, Herbert.

Thomas, William Jenkyn, b.1870, divine,
schoolmaster. Venn.

The Church in Wales, **NatR-II** 1160

Thompson, Charles Halford, writer on economics. *BMCat.*

Free trade or reciprocity, **FM** 6010
Reciprocity, 6144

Thompson, Edward Healy, c.1813–1891, translator; sub. ed. *Dublin Rev.*, 1863–1865.
Newman, *L&D*, XI, 358; Gillow.

Foreign periodical literature, **DR** 1043,
1053, 1063, 1074, 1082, 1093, 1105,
?1125, ?1134, all collab.
Letter: 1603
Notices: ?1106, 1116

Allies' *Journal in France*, **Ram** 117, 128
Christian Rome, 168, 178
Religious toleration, 561
English and foreign historians: massacre of
St. Bartholomew, 565
Notices: 560

Thompson, Francis, 1859–1907, poet. *DNB.*

Irish minstrelsy, **DR** 2161
The *Macbeth* controversy, 2182

Thompson, Harriet Diana, 1811–1896, wife of
Edmund Healy Thompson, q.v. Gillow.

Foreign periodical literature, **DR** 1043,
1053, 1063, 1074, 1082, 1093, 1105, 1125,
1134, all collab.
The principles of '89, 1085, 1108
Notice: 1106?

M. Guizot's appeal to our common Christianity, **Ram** 484, 491

Thompson, Sir Henry: see *Index*, I, 1113.

Food and feeding, **NC** 315, 331
Diet in relation to age and activity, 1130
The progress of cremation, 1500
Why "vegetarian"? 3267, 3302

Thompson, Richard Frederick Meysey: see
Meysey-Thompson, Richard Frederick.

Thompson, Stephen: see *Index*, I, 1113.

The lessons of emigration, **NatR-II** 859

Thoms, Peter Perring, writer on China. *BMCat.*

Horae Sinicae, **FM** 701, 816, 1173, all collab.

Threlfall, T. R. (*continued*)
The Trades Union Congress, 2298
Political future of "Labour," 2518
Senussi and his threatened holy war, 3618

Thring, George Herbert, 1859–1941, secretary
of Incorp. Soc. of Authors. *WWW.*

Attempts at copyright legislation, **FortR**
4093
Lord Monkswell's Copyright Bill, 4426

Thring, Sir Henry: see *Index*, I, 1115.

The fallacy of "imperial federation," **NC**
1227
Local government, 1528
The Local Government Bill, 1546
The rural voter: law, land and labour, 2155
The copyright bills, 3671
Lessons of the [Boer] War, 3741

Thruston, Edmund Heathcote, 1863–1948,
army officer. Venn.

Anarchy in Uganda, **NatR-II** 2290

Thurber, Francis Beatty, 1842–1907, merchant. *Amer. WWW.*

Breakers ahead: land, trade, and labour
questions, **NC** 674

Thurston, Herbert Henry Charles, S.J., 1856–
1939, Sutcliffe.

Jubilee indulgence *a poena et a culpa*, **DR**
2700

The mediaeval Sunday, **NC** 3495

Thwaite, Benjamin Howarth, civil engineer.
BMCat.

The Venezuelan dispute, **FortR** 3759

London fog: a scheme to abolish it, **NatR-
II** 1355
Electricity in country houses, 1391 collab.

New sources of electric power, **NC** 2674
The commercial war between Germany and
England, 3038

Tieck, Johann Ludwig: see *Index*, I, 1115.

The superfluities of life, **FM** 1684, 1687

Tierney, Mark Aloysius, 1795–1862, R.C.
priest. *DNB.*

Letters: **Ram** 560, 917

Tille, Alexander, 1866–1912, German political
scientist. *Grosse Brockhaus.*

Trans: **FortR** 3701

Tillett, Benjamin, 1860–1943, labor leader.
DNB.

Our naval weakness, **NatR-II** 1903

Tilley, Arthur Augustus: see *Index*, I, 1115.

New school of fiction [Henry James and W.
D. Howells], **NatR-II** 18
Development of classical learning, 217
Ivan Turgénieff, 258, 341
Eclipse of *esprit* in France, 538
Gogol, father of Russian realism, 1601

Tilley, Henry Arthur: see *Index*, I, 1115.

Three days at Wilna [in Poland], **FM** 4384
Polish women and the Insurrection, 4395
Russia and the Caucasus, 4424

Tillman, Benjamin Ryan, 1848–1918, U.S.
senator. *DAB.*

Political outlook in the United States, **NatR-
II** 1921

Tipping, Edward

Compensation for Irish landlords, **NatR-II**
182

Tirard, Sir Nestor Isidore Charles, 1853–1928,
physician. *WWW.*

Hospital problems: children of the poor,
NatR-II 150

Disease in fiction, **NC** 1332

Tobias, D. E. *BMCat.*

A Negro on the position of the Negro in
America, **NC** 3576

Tod, John, misc. writer. *BMCat.*

Edited: **ScotR** 139

Todd, William Gowan: see *Index*, I, 1116.

Mozley's *Augustinianism*, **DR** 791
Passaglia on the prerogatives of Mary, 813
The Irish in England, 823
Christ, the Church, and the Bible, 839
Formalism, a charge against the Church,
860
Notices: 846, 864

The mission of the laity, **Ram** 921

Toft, Peter: see *Index*, I, 1116.

Volundur, a Scandinavian legend, **FM** 5210
Sketch of [Ludwig] Holberg's life, 5220

Tollemache, Lionel Arthur, see *Index*, I, 1116.

Historical prediction, **FortR** 484

Sir G. C. Lewis and longevity, 582
Literary egotism, 595
Do military inventions promote peace? 765
The new cure for incurables [euthanasia], 926
Tennyson's social philosophy, 1026
Charles Austin, 1132
Courage and death, 1225
The Upper Engadine, 1237
Hell and the divine veracity, 1421
Lord Tollemache and his anecdotes, 3235

Sir Richard Owen and memories, **NatR-II** 1448

Tolstoi, Count Leo Nikolayevich: see *Index,* I, 1116.

Work while ye have the light, **FortR** 3000, 3011
The relations of Church and State, 3065

What makes people to live, **FM** 6548

Toole, John Lawrence, 1830–1906, actor, theatre manager. *DNB.*

New humour and the non-humourists, **NatR-II** 1437

Torrens, Sir Robert, 1814–1884, first premier of South Australia. *DNB.*

The Land Laws, **FortR** 1823

Torrens, William Torrens McCullagh: see *Index,* I, 1116.

The East African slave-trade, **FortR** 2709

Malpractices at elections, **FM** 6414
Registry of title, 6440

The government of London, **NC** 517
Transplanting to the colonies, 568

Towle, Eleanor Ashworth: see *Index,* I, 1116.

Literary courtships, **FortR** 4335

Towle, George Makepeace, 1841–1893, American journalist. *DAB.*

Harvard and Yale Universities, **FortR** 445

Townsend, Charles Collingwood, army officer. *BMCat., Army List/93.*

Electricity in India, **NC** 3542

Townsend, Horace, 1859–1922, London correspondent of *New York Herald. Amer. WWW.*

The Alaskan Boundary question, **FortR** 4336

Townsend, or **Townshend,** Horatio: see *Index,* I, 1116.

The present state of Ireland, **FM** 906

Townsend, Meredith White: see *Index,* I, 1117.

Christianity in India, **FM** 5965
?Can India be Christianised, 5999

Townshend, Richard Baxter, 1846–1923, teacher. Venn.

A trial by lynch law, **NC** 2269
My maverick [western U.S.], 2390
The common mule, 3595
Stray shots and a moral [on western U.S.], 3609

Toynbee, Harry Valpy. *Boyle's Court Guide* (Jan. 1900), p. 853. (See *Index,* I, 1117.)

Position of the Friendly Societies, **NC** 3477

Tozer, Henry Fanshawe, 1829–1916, traveller, geographer. *WWW.*

?Pilgrimage to Compostella [in Spain], **FM** 4467

Traill, Anthony: see *Index,* I, 1117.

Conservative view of the Irish Land Bill, **FortR** 1811

Landowners' convention in Dublin, **NatR-II** 677
Spoliation of Irish landlords, 2014
The Irish Land Acts at work, 2141

"Hands off Trinity" [Trinity Coll. Dublin], **NC** 3442

Traill, Henry Duff: see *Index,* I, 1117.

The Provincial Letters [by Pascal], **FortR** 1217
Paul Louis Courier, 1330
The England of to-day, 1661
Analysis of humour, 1945
Below the opposition gangway, 1979
Lord Westbury and Bishop Wilberforce, 1996
South Kensington Hellenism, 2058
A pious legend examined [Coleridge], 2276
J. R. Lowell, 2340
Parnell and Butt: a dialogue, 3171
The awakened candidates, 3244
Two modern poets [William Watson, John Davidson], 3613
Peel and his predecessors, 3641
The revolution in Grub Street, 3667
Lord Salisbury's triumph, 3692

Traill, Henry Duff (*continued*)
  Our neglected Tories, 3817
  The analytical humorist, 3833
  Sir George Tressady [by Mrs. Humphry Ward], 3880
  The new realism, 3902
  Our learned philhellenes, 3939
  The literature of the Victorian era, 3965
  Letter: 2647

  What is public opinion? **NatR-II** 327
  The plague of tongues [campaign oratory], 392
  Hobbes and the modern radical, 439
  The other side of the medal, 610
  The evolution of humour, 682
  Pope, 936
  Robert Browning, 945
  The abdication of Mrs. Grundy, 1121
  The county councillor, 1194
  Mr. Tree's Hamlet, 1276
  Stage-struck, 1294
  Irving's Becket [performance in Tennyson's play], 1399
  Two proper prides, 1433
  For weary citizens [on Home Rule Bill], 1472
  In Cabinet council, 1503
  Our Cleopatra [Egypt], 1558
  Lords and Commons, 1610
  The autumn holiday, 1755
  The Unionist leaders: Lord Salisbury, 1868
  Gladstone's return, 1905
  Ibsenism: the craze, 1963

  The democracy and foreign policy, **NC** 243
  Political optimism, 485
  Political fatalism, 507
  The allies, 732
  The politics of literature, 912
  Brutes on their master, 973
  The novel of manners, 1193
  Act for the suspension of parliament, 1391
  Our minor poets, 2149, 2179
  Aspects of Tennyson, 2324, 2573
  The anonymous critic, 2492
  About that skeleton [modern drama], 2669
  The burden of Egypt, 2908
  Notices: 2521, 2711

Trant, William. *BMCat.*

  Trade unionism in India, **FortR** 1614

Tree, Sir Herbert Beerbohm, 1852–1917, actor. *DNB.*

  The London stage, **FortR** 2964
  Hamlet—from an actor's prompt book, 3733
  The staging of Shakespeare, 4476

Tregarthen, Hugh Philipps, b.1860/61. Foster.

Pauperism, distress, and the coming winter, **NatR-II** 646
  The Elberfeld poor-law system, 794
  Competitive examination, 804
  Letter: 525

Tregellas, Walter Hawken, 1831–1894, misc. writer. *DNB.*

  County characteristics—Cornwall, **NC** 1485

Tremenheere, Hugh Seymour: see *Index*, I, 1117.

  Thriftless thrift, **FortR** 1863

  State aid and control in industrial insurance, **NC** 484

Tremenheere, John Henry: see *Index*, I, 1117.

  Revolutions and Russian conquests in Central Asia, **NQM** 102

Trench, John Townsend, 1834–1909. Burke under Ashtown.

  Irish interests, **FortR** 2478

Trench, Maria, b.1828, daughter of Thomas Trench, 1st cousin of Francis Chenevix Trench. Debrett/1908, p. 67; *BMCat.;* Trench, *Letters,* II, 80n. (See *Index*, I, 1118, where her art. in *Mac* is wrongly placed under Maria Marcia Fanny Trench.)

  Girl-children of the state, **NC** 806
  English sisterhoods, 1032

Trench, Richard Chenevix, 1807–1886, poet, Archbishop of Dublin. *DNB.*

  Three days of the famine at Schull, **FM** 2333

Trepplin, Ernest Charles, b.1856/57. Foster.

  English and Dutch dairy farming, **NC** 3025 collab.

Trevelyan, George Macaulay: see *Index*, I, 1118.

  Carlyle as an historian, **NC** 3535

Trevelyan, George Otto: see *Index*, I, 1118.

  The dawk bungalow [satire on administration in India], **FM** 4626, 4635
  ?America in its religious aspect, 4761

Trevor, George: see *Index*, I, 1118.

  Ritual litigation, **NatR-II** 455

Trevor, Philip Christian William: see *Index*, I, 1118.

The Catholicism of the British army, **NC** 3301

Tripp, Clavell

German versus British trade in the East, **NC** 3235

Tritton, Joseph Herbert, 1844–1923, banker. *WWW*.

The American crisis, **NatR-II** 1910

Trollope, Anthony: see *Index*, I, 1118.

The Belton estate, in 16 installments from **FortR** 2 to 153
Henry Taylor's poems, 12
On anonymous literature, 37
The Irish Church, 69
Public schools, 102
The civil service, 112
The fourth commandment, 162
The gentle Euphemia, 237
Mr. Freeman on morality of hunting, 640
The Eustace diamonds, in 20 installments from 792 to 928
Lady Anna, in 13 installments from 945 to 1044
Cicero as a politician, 1349
Cicero as a man of letters, 1396
Kafir Land, 1435
Iceland, 1493
George Henry Lewes, 1539
Notices: 50, 82, 93, 173, 182, 222, 253, 264, 273, 343, 379, 602

Novel-reading [Dickens, Thackeray], **NC** 259

Trollope, Frances Eleanor: see *Index*, I, 1119.

Anne Furness, in 14 installments from **FortR** 698 to 804
Italian realistic fiction, 1849

Mrs. Jack, **NQM** 108
The curé's housekeeper, 126

Trollope, Henry Merivale: see *Index*, I, 1119, and II, App. A.

Molière, **FM** 5938

Schoolboys and their ways, **NatR-II** 332

Trollope, Theodosia (Garrow), 1825–1865, first wife of T. A. Trollope, q.v. *DNB*. (See below, App. A.)

Trans: **FQR** 858

Trollope, Thomas Adolphus: see *Index*, I, 1119, and II, App. A.

Celebrated Crimes [by Alexander Dumas], **FQR** 684
?Jean Jacques Rousseau, 745
The plague of Milan in 1630, 800
Vico and the Princess Belgiojoso, 812
Foreign correspondence: 824, 837, 862, 877, 890
Recent Italian political poems [by Giusti], 858
Episode in the history of Lucca, 893
Leonora Casaloni, in 10 installments from **FortR** 483 to 550

A heroine and a mock-hero in the days of the Fronde, **FM** 1867, 1870
?The Mancinis: an Italian episode in French history, 4916

Caucus and camorra [Italian political caucus], **NatR-II** 271
Was I also hypnotized? 995

History of Italian folk-song, **NQM** 160

Trotter, Coutts: see *Index*, I, 1119.

The story of Tonga, **FortR** 2642

New Guinea, **NC** 880

A new religion [Shiah branch of Islam], **ScotR** 356

Trotter, Louisa Kathleen: see Haldane, Louisa Kathleen (Trotter).

Troubetzkoy, Princess Amélie (Rives), 1863–1945, American novelist. *Amer. WWW*.

Was it a crime? **FortR** 2917

Troup, John Rose, 1847/48–1919, member of Stanley's expedition for relief of Emin Pasha. *Times*, Dec. 1, 1919, p. 16e.

Stanley's rear-guard, **FortR** 3017

Troutbeck, Henry, 1866–1923, surgeon. *Venn*.

Letter: **NC** 3140

Trueba y Cossio, Telesforo de, 1798–1835, novelist, historian. *EUI*.

The Spanish novelists, **FQR** 43

Trumbull, Matthew Mark, 1789–1894, American army officer. *Heitman*.

Aristocracy in America, **NC** 1169

Tsêng, Marquis Chitsê, 1837–1890, envoy to France and England. H. A. Giles, *A Chinese Biographical Dictionary*, 1898.

The diary of the Marquis Tsêng, **NC** 937

Tuck, Edward, 1842–1938, American banker. *Amer. WWW.*

Is bimetallism a delusion? **NC** 2703

Tuckett, Coldstream, of The Croft, Bristol. J. Wright & Co., *Bristol and Clifton Directory,* 1884.

Letter: **NatR-II** 150

Tuckey, Charles Lloyd, 1855–1925, physician. *Surgeon Index*/3rd s. (See *Index*, I, 1119.)

Faith-healing as a medical treatment, **NC** 1631

Tuckwell, Gertrude Mary, 1861–1951, sec. Women's Trade Union League. *WWW.*

A seventeen hours' working day, **FortR** 4276
The Government Factory Bill of 1900, 4463

Commercial manslaughter [lead-poisoning], **NC** 3332

Tufnell, Edward Carleton: see *Index*, I, 1119.

Letters on Croatia and Italy, **FQR** 176
Toulotte's *History of the Roman Emperors,* 191

Tufnell, Henry, 1805–1854, politician. *DNB.*

The United States, **FQR** 166

Tugwell, George. 1830–1910, divine, writer on Devonshire natural history. *CCD*/76; Eliot, *Letters*, II, 243n.

Science by the seaside, **FM** 3509
Wanderings on Exmoor, 3656

Tuke, James Hack: see *Index*, I, 1120.

Peasant proprietors at home, **NC** 477
Irish emigration, 556
With the emigrants, 745
State aid to emigrants, 1092
News from some Irish emigrants, 1681

Tuke, John Batty, 1835–1913, physician. *WWW.*

Lunatics as patients, not prisoners, **NC** 1693
Habitual drunkards, 2413

Tulloch, Alexander Bruce, 1838–1920, army officer. *WWW.*

Lesson in "payment of members," **NC** 2776

Tulloch, John: see *Index*, I, 1120.

Coleridge as spiritual thinker, **FortR** 2256

?Port Royal and the Port Royalists, **FM** 3903
The life of Schleiermacher, 4056
Our past and our future, 6193
Gladstone as a man of letters, 6232
Burton's *Reign of Queen Anne*, 6265
Last years of the Prince Consort, 6293

Dean Stanley as a spiritual teacher, **NC** 655
Luther and recent criticism, 985

The Church of Scotland and the coming election, **ScotR** 107

Tupper, Sir Charles: see *Index,* I, 1120

The question of preferential tariffs, **FortR** 3242

Federating the Empire: a colonial plan, **NC** 2105
How to federate the Empire, 2188

Tupper, Sir Charles Hibbert, 1855–1927, Canadian lawyer, statesman. Wallace.

The Manitoba school question, **NatR-II** 1865
Crocodile tears and fur seals, 1912
Functions of a governor-general, 1942

Turgenev or Turgenieff, Ivan Sergilevitch: see *Index*, I, 1120, and *Ency. Brit.*, 11th ed.

Faust: a story in nine letters, **FortR** 3528
Hamlet and Don Quixote, 3532

See: **FM** 3255

A study from Turgenieff ["Live Relics"], **ScotR** 42
The mesmerist, 141
The white lady, 232
The old brigadier, 613
The dog, 631

Turnbull, William Barclay David Donald, 1811–1863, barrister, antiquary. *DNB.*

The Kirk of Scotland, **DR** 277
The Scottish schism, 307
History of St. Andrews, 312

Turner, Sir Alfred Edward, 1842–1918, army officer. *WWW.*

The epistles of the Mahdi, **NatR-II** 1392
Irish official life, 1409

Turner, Charles Edward: see *Index*, I, 1120.

Nicholas Alexeivitch Nekrasoff, **FortR** 1851

Studies in Russian literature, in 8 installments from **FM** 5931 to 6000

Turner, Freedrick Storrs, misc. writer. *BMCat.* (See *Index*, I, 1121.)

Dr. Priestley, **FM** 5598

Opium and England's duty, **NC** 678

Turner, Godfrey Woodsworth: see *Index*, I, 1121.

Amusements of the English people, **NC** 115

Turner, S., miner, of Barnsley, Yorkshire. Robinson's *Barnsley Directory*, 1902.

Will the miners strike? **NatR-II** 1095

Tuttiett, Mary Gleed: see *Index*, I, 1121, and II, App. A.

Under false colours, **FM** 6449

The advantage of fiction, **NC** 2871

Tuttle, Herbert, 1846–1894, American historian. *DAB.*

Parties and politics in Germany, **FortR** 1358 German politics, 1619

Tweedie, Ethel Brilliana (Harley), d.1940, philanthropist. *WWW* under Mrs. Alec Tweedie; *LCCat.*

Danish butter-making, **FortR** 3645

Twigge, Robert William, 1851/52–1915, privy chamberlain to the Pope, F.S.A. *Tablet*, Sept. 4, 1915, p. 308.

Albi and the Albigensians, **DR** 2429 The mediaeval service books of Aquitaine, 2450, 2490, 2547, 2602 A Gascon city [Auch] and its church, 2466 Notices: 2475, 2497

Twining, Louisa, 1820–1911, writer on art and social subjects, especially on the poor. *WWW.*

Fifty years of women's work, **NatR-II** 596 The working of the Poor Law, 729 Poor Law infirmaries and their needs, 879

Workhouse visiting and management, **NQM** 191

Workhouse cruelties, **NC** 1341 Women as public servants, 1972 Women as official inspectors, 2550

Twist, A. C., an Englishman who emigrated to California in 1893.

Fruit ranching, **NC** 2664

Tyler, Sir Henry Whately: see *Index*, I, 1121.

The Cape, **NC** 255

Tylor, Sir Edward Burnett: see *Index*, I, 1121.

Origin of language, **FortR** 225 The religion of savages, 303 History of games, 1581 Huxley as anthropologist, 3687 Notices: 233, 353, 479, 513

The matriarchal family system, **NC** 2959

Tyndall, John: see *Index*, I, 1121.

Constitution of the universe, **FortR** 133 Relations of radiant heat to chemical constitution, 183 Miracles and special providences, 407 Chemical rays, and light of the sky, 567 Climbing in search of the sky, 646 From Portsmouth to Oran to see the eclipse, 762 "Materialism" and opponents, 1203 Fermentation and disease, 1302 Science and man, 1406 The electric light, 1549 Goethe's *Farbenlehre*, 1681 A story of the lighthouses, 2778, 2791 Recollections of Thomas Carlyle, 2904 Phthisis [tuberculosis], 3121

Dust and disease, **FM** 5059

Spontaneous generation, **NC** 122, 148 Virchow and evolution, 238 The sabbath, 512 On rainbows, 968 A story of our lighthouses, 1572

Tyrrell, Robert Yelverton: see *Index*, I, 1121.

The old school of classics and the new, **FortR** 2666 *Robert Elsmere* as a symptom, 2826 Mr. Browning in a passion, 2860 *Jude the Obscure* [by Thomas Hardy], 3812 Letter: 2638

Tyrwhitt, Richard St. John: see *Index*, I, 1122.

Limits of modern art-criticism, **NC** 221

Tytler, John, 1790–1837, physician, Oriental scholar. Crawford, *Indian Medical Service*, p. 64.

Wilson's *Sanscrit Dictionary*, **FQR** 369

Tytler, Patrick Fraser: see *Index*, I, 1122.

Norman conquest of England, **FQR** 146

U

Ullathorne, William Bernard, 1806–1889, R.C. Bishop of Birmingham. *DNB.*

Bishop [Robert William] Willson, **DR** 2070 Letter: 1497

Bishop of Birmingham and Lord J. Russell, **Ram** 296
Pilgrimage to Subiaco and Grotto of St. Benedict, 764, 771, 776, 783, 791
Letters: 52, 296

Underhill, George Frederick, misc. writer. *BMCat.*

Fox-hunting and agriculture, **NC** 3285

Ungern-Sternberg, Peter Alexander von, Baron, 1806–1868, German novelist. *ADB.*

See: **FM** 2539

Upcott, Sir Frederick Robert, 1847–1918, civil engineer. *WWW.*

See: **FM** 6111

Upton, Roger Dawson, 1827–1881, army officer; wrote *Newmarket and Arabia.* Boase.

Arabian horses, **FM** 5857
The Bedaween of the Arabian desert, 5914

Urlichs, Karl Ludwig, 1813–1889, German philologist, archaeologist. *EUI, ADB.*

Christian antiquities, **DR** 77
Roman history [by Arnold, Michelet, Niebuhr], 142

Urquhart, David: see *Index,* I, 1122.

Designs of Russia against Turkey, **FQR** 350 collab. at least
?Character of Turkish travellers, 364 collab.
Russian policy in Greece, 381
Travellers in Turkey, 395 collab. at least

V

Valentine, E. S., army officer, of Capetown. *BMCat.*

American parallel to present campaign [in Boer War], **FortR** 4441

Vambéry, Arminius, 1832–1913, prof. Oriental languages, Univ. of Budapest. *WWW.*

Slave trade and life in Central Asia, **FortR** 398
Russia and England; Batoum and Cyprus, 2512
The Transcaspian railway, 2565
Letter: 2567

Russo-Afghan Boundary Commission, **NatR-II** 229
My lecturing tour in England, 345
Russian propaganda, 1402
Great Britain and her rivals in Asia, 2145

England and Russia in Asia, **NC** 451
Will Russia conquer India? 1078, 1093
The future of Russia in Asia, 1825
The situation in central Asia, 2243
The Shah of Persia in England, 2546

Vandam, Albert Dresden: see *Index,* I, 1122.

A chat about Renan, **FortR** 3290
1793–1893, 3410

A pretender [Duc d'Aumale], 3561
Beginnings of the [Third French] Republic, 3726, 3736
Jules Simon, 3834
"King of Journalists" [E. de Girardin], 3994
Side-lights of the revanche idea, 4091
The spy-mania and the revanche idea, 4170
The Paris market-women, 4354
Poets as legislators, 4482

Van de Velde, Madame M.S.: see Velde, Madame M. S. van de

Vane, Lady Margaret (Gladstone), d.1916, wife of Sir Henry Ralph Fletcher Vane. *WWW/*1916 under her husband, *Landed Gentry* under Gladstone.

The autocrat of the sick-room, **NatR-II** 2162
Boarding-out under ladies' committees, 2250

Vane-Tempest-Stewart, Theresa (Chetwynd-Talbot), Marchioness of Londonderry, 1856–1919. *Complete Peerage,* VIII, 117.

"Conservative" Compensation (Workmen's) Bill, **NC** 3162

Van Even, Edward, 1821–1905, Belgian historian. Seyn.

Quentin Metsys, **ScotR** 696

Vardy, Albert Richard, 1841–1900, divine, schoolmaster. *WWW.*

Notices: **FortR** 93, 161, 173

Varley, Richard, b.1850/51. Foster.

Emigration of English paupers to Western Australia, **NatR-II** 699

Vāsaudeva Rāu, R.

Did Omar destroy the Alexandrian library? **NC** 2645

Vaughan, Herbert Alfred, 1832–1903, Cardinal Archbishop of Westminster, ed. of *Dublin Rev. DNB.*

Popular devotion in Spain, **DR** 1035
California and the Church, 1136
English Catholic university education, 1208
Popular education in England, 1218
National tendencies and duties of Catholics, 1239
The revolution in Spain, 1283
?The pilgrimage to Pontigny, 1484
The evangelisation of Africa, 1671
Sad experience of Catholics in non-Catholic universities, 1871
Government and education in Ireland, 2169
Baltimore centenary, 2208
Cremation and Christianity, 2221
Catholics and technical education, 2245
How to save the voluntary schools, 2304
England's devotion to St. Peter, 2308, 2323
Saving our schools and their Catholic teaching, 2317
Triangular battle for education, 2559
Note: 2115

Leo the thirteenth and civil power, **NC** 1509
The Life of Cardinal Manning [by E. S. Purcell], 2882

Vaughan, John Stephen, 1853–1925, Bishop of Sebastopolis. *WWW.*

Bishop Clifford's theory of days of creation, **DR** 1852
Olier and Dupanloup, 1995
Social disturbances—cause and cure, 2035
Ethics of animal suffering, 2101
Faith and folly [anti-religious science], 2151
Faith and reason, 2178
Final destiny of the earth, 2228
Theism as a scientific hypothesis, 2311
Notes on foreign periodicals, 2346, 2386, 2424
Blessed Trinity in material creation, 2360
The social difficulty, 2415
Notices, 1874, 2347, 2373, 2412, 2475, 2520

Vaughan, Robert, 1795–1868, Congregational divine; ed. *Brit. Quart. Rev.,* 1845–1865. *DNB.*

Sir James Stephen, **FM** 3908

Vaughan, Robert Alfred, 1823–1857, Congregational divine. *DNB.*

Art and history, **FM** 3657

Vaughan, Roger William Beade, 1834–1883, Catholic priest. *DNB.*

Gaume controversy on classical studies, **DR** 1163
The Ladder of Perfection, 1290
See: 1208

Vecchia, Giovanni Dalla: see *Index,* I, 1123.

The situation in Italy, **NC** 3715

Veer, Léon

French politics, **FM** 5251

Veitch, John, 1829–1894, man of letters; prof. of logic at St. Andrew's. *DNB.*

Mr. Gladstone's ancestors, **FM** 6296

Veitch, John Leith, b.1855, journalist. *BMCat.,* Allibone.

Ireland under her own parliament, **NatR-II** 418

Veitch, Sophie Frances Fane, misc. writer. *BMCat.*

Religious novels, **ScotR** 15
?Echoes of the eighteenth century, 80
George Eliot, 89
Victoria: a monograph, 121
Current fiction, 123
Fallacies of reading lists, 131
?Ethics and art in recent novels, 132
Historical novels of James Grant, 194

Velde, Madame M. S. van de, misc. writer. *BMCat.*

Dumas fils and his plays, **FortR** 3747

Venables, Edmund: see *Index,* I, 1123.

Reminiscences of E. A. Freeman, **FortR** 3218

The future cathedral of Liverpool, **NC** 647

Venables, George Stovin: see *Index,* I, 1123.

The French police, **FQR** 662
Schiller's *Minor Poems,* 793

Venables, George Stovin (*continued*)
?German political squibs, 844
Niebuhr and Dahlmann on the French Revolution, 870

Carlyle in society and at home, **FortR** 2028
Byron and his biographers, 2065
Carlyle's Life in London [by J. A. Froude], 2235

Venables, Gilbert, 1844/45–1888, journalist. Foster.

Civil and religious marriage, **NatR-II** 102
Ophelia's madness, 270

Venturi, Emilie: see *Index*, I, 1123.

Answer to [John] Morley's letter, **FortR** 684
Trans: 1352

Vere, Aubrey de: see De Vere, Aubrey

Verlaine, Paul, 1844–1896, French poet. *Grand Larousse.*

Notes on England, **FortR** 3523
Shakespeare and Racine, 3550

Verner, William Willoughby Cole: see *Index*, I, 1123.

Machine guns and coast defence, **NatR-II** 806
A reminiscence of Prince Rudolf of Austria, 832
Bird life in Romney Marsh, 951
A diligence journey in Spain, 1159

Dungeness or Dover [as a harbor]? **NC** 2270

Verney, Sir Edmund Hope: see *Index*, I, 1123.

Rural education, **NC** 3319

Verney, Frances Parthenope: see *Index*, I, 1123.

Sentimental religion, **FM** 4891
Dean Milman, 4929
Female education in France, 5011
The objects of art, 5085
Evidence historical, religious, and scientific, 5250
How Gilbert Sherard fared in the flood, 6491

Peasant properties in France, **NatR-II** 658

Foreign opinions on peasant properties, **NC** 1208
Rural Italy and peasant properties, 1242
Allotments, 1288
Rural life in Russia, 1365
Six generations of czars, 1716

Verney, Frederick William, 1846–1913, barrister. *WWW.*

The Women's Protective League, **FortR** 2615
Trades-unions among women, 2741

Our armies in India, **NC** 1146
The Anglo-French convention in Siam, 2890

Verney, Sir Harry, 1801–1894, army officer. *DNB.*

A route from the Atlantic to Pacific through British territory, **FM** 4973

Vernon, George William Henry Venables, 7th Baron Vernon, 1854–1898, army officer. *WWW.*

Over-mortgaging the land, **NC** 2011
The settlement of landed property, 2172
How to attract capital to the land, 2415
Dairy farming, 2885

Vernon-Harcourt, Leveson Francis, 1839–1907, civil engineer. *DNB.*

Civil engineering as a profession, **NatR-II** 2523

Verres, Joseph, 1849–1904, R.C. priest. *Tablet,* Mar. 5, 1904.

Outcome of Lutheranism in Prussia, **DR** 1988

Verschoyle, John Stuart, 1853–1915, divine, sub.-ed. *Fort. Rev.* under Frank Harris. Venn; H. H. Johnston, *The Story of My Life* (Indianapolis, 1923), p. 218.

The condition of Kerry, **FortR** 2516
The character of Shelley, 2543
In the forests of Navarre and Aragon, 2878
Balfour's work in west of Ireland, 3250
Where to spend a holiday, 3541
Rhodes and Jameson, 3782
See: 3811, 3900, 4122

Vetch, Robert Hamilton, 1841–1916, army officer. *WWW.*

Account of the Taiping rebellion, **FortR** 4503

Vickers, John, author of *The New Koran. BMCat.*

The future of Turkey, **FM** 5075

Victor, Horace: see *Index*, I, 1124.

Eastern women, **FortR** 2877

Vieusseux, André, or Andrea, 1789/90–1858, soldier, writer. Boase.

Botta's *History of Italy,* **FQR** 11
Italian literature, eighteenth century, 49
Oginski's *Memoirs on Poland,* 71
Dialects and literature of Southern Italy, 110
Ferrario, *On Chivalry and Romance, and Italian Romantic Poetry,* 148
Present state of Egypt, 171
Poland in 1830, 181
Political state of Switzerland, 213
Foscolo and his times, 219
Modern Rome, and the Papal government, 257
Count Pecchio's works on England, 262
Arrivabene, *Charitable Institutions of England,* 265
Manno's *History of Sardinia,* 289
History of modern Italian freedom, 292
The French in Algiers, 305
Austrian government and Italian liberals, 314
The Italian Insurrection of 1831, 319 collab.
Italy and Europe, 334
Litta's *Celebrated Italian Families,* 340
?Colletta's *History of Naples,* 370
?Italy and the Italians, 377
Notices: 39, 53, 66, 79, 90, 118, 132, 144, 155, 182, 215, 229

Vignoles, Charles Blacker, 1793–1875, prof. of civil engineering, Univ. Coll. London. *DNB.*

The railway system in Ireland, **DR** 10, 125

Vignoles, Henry, civil engineer, prob. a son of Charles Blacker Vignoles, q.v.

A ride through Bosnia, **FM** 5736 collab.

Vignoles, Olinthus John, b.1829, alive in 1886. *CCD/76,* Foster, *LCCat.*

A ride through Bosnia, **FM** 5736 collab.

Vijaya-Raghavan, T. *BMCat.* under Vijayaraghaven, T.

Hindu marriage customs and British law, **NatR-II** 1127

Villalobos, Angel de, prof. King's Coll. London. *BMCat.*; Registers of Admissions to BM Reading Room, July 1842.

Trans: **DR** 265

Villari, Linda: see *Index,* I, 1124.

Barga, **FM** 6031
Leopardi and his father, 6454

Italians and English, **NatR-II** 97
Roman life in the last century, 188
A Venetian playwright [Carlo Gozzi], 417
Impressions of new Rome, 1224
At the edge of Italy [Bosco Chiesanuova], 1417

Villecourt, Clément, 1787–1865, Bishop of La Rochelle. Newman, *L&D,* XII, index.

Correspondence with J. H. Newman, **Ram** 209 collab.

Villiers, Edward Ernest: see *Index,* I, 1124, and II, App. A.

Turkey, Egypt, and Russia: the crisis in the East, **FQR** 309

Villiers, Melius de: see De Villiers, Melius

Villiers de l'Isle Adam, Jean Marie Mathias Philippe Auguste, comte de, 1838–1889, French novelist. *Grand Larousse.*

La Révolte, **FortR** 4045

Vincent, Mr.; possibly the Sir Francis Vincent, 1803–1880, in *Tablet,* July 10, 1880, p. 58.

Pedro of Castile, **DR** 90

Vincent, Sir Charles Edward Howard: see *Index,* I, 1124.

?Recent publications on the [Franco-Prussian] War, **FM** 5293, 5309
Trans: 5252, 5260

Common sense [on tariffs], **NatR-II** 1311
The colonies and the Empire, 1622

Vincent, Charles W. *BMCat.*

The dangers of electric lighting, **NC** 1822

Vincent, James Edmund, 1857–1909, journalist. *DNB.*

The vernacular press of Wales, **NatR** 782

Vinogradoff, Sir Paul Gavrilovitch: see *Index,* I, 1124.

Oxford and Cambridge, **FortR** 2331

Visger, Jean Allan (Pinder): see *Index,* I, 1124.

Old guns and their owners, **FortR** 3909 collab.
In the twilight, 4302 collab.

Visger, Jean Allan (*continued*)
When life stirs, **NatR-II** 1571 collab.
Leafless woods and grey moorlands, 1648 collab.

Viti de Marco, Antonio: see De Vitti de Marco, Antonio

Vogel, Sir Julius: see *Index*, I, 1125.

New Guinea and annexation, **FortR** 2070
Social politics in New Zealand, 3318
The bank panic in Australia, 3369
Government life insurance, 3535
Letter: 3196

The finances of New Zealand, **FM** 5649
The resources of New Zealand, 5952

Greater or lesser Britain, **NC** 55
Cheap telegrams, 113

The British Empire: Mr. Lowe and Lord Blachford, 156
Is it open to the colonies to secede? 1796
A Zollverein of the British dominions, 2289
The scramble for gold, 2506
Greater Britain and the Queen's long reign, 3077

Volkhovsky, Felix Vadimovich, 1846–1914, Russian émigré and journalist. *Dayateli revolyutsionnogo dvizheniya v Rossii* (Moscow, 1929), II, cols. 220–223. (See *Index*, I, 1125.)

My life in Russian prisons, **FortR** 3015

Voysey, Charles, 1828–1912, theistic preacher. *DNB.*

The new reformation, **FortR** 2553

W

Wace, Henry: see *Index*, I, 1125.

Agnosticism, **NC** 1673
Christianity and agnosticism, 1706

Wackerbarth, Francis Diederich, 1813–1884, scientist. Venn.

Swedish poetry. **DR** 848

Waddington, George, 1793–1869, traveller, church historian. *DNB.*

Cailliaud's *Travels*, **FQR** 42

Waddington, Samuel, 1844–1923, poet. *WWW.*

The cradle of the human race, **NC** 3751

Waddington, William Henry, 1826–1894, French statesman. Venn.

Local government in France, **NC** 1566, 1577

Wade, Mark Sweeten, 1858–1929, Canadian physician. Wallace.

The Clondyke gold fields, **FortR** 4012

Wagstaff, E. Wynter

A theory of brain waves, **NatR-II** 1336

Wakefield, Augusta Mary, 1853–1910, student of folk music and crafts. Grove.

Home arts in the [Lake Country], **FortR** 3870

May carols, **NC** 3110

Wakefield, Edward: see *Index*, I, 1126, and II, App. A.

New Zealand and Froude, **NC** 1304
The wisdom of Gombo, 2109

Wakefield, Henry Russell, 1854–1933, Bishop of Birmingham. *WWW.*

Why I voted for Mr. Gladstone, **NC** 2262

Waldo, Frederick Joseph, 1852–1933, physician, barrister. *WWW.*

Murder by measles, **NC** 2944 collab.

Waldstein, later **Walston,** Sir Charles, 1856–1927, prof. of fine art. *WWW* under Walston.

Nihilism and pessimism in Germany, **NC** 187
The eastern pediment of the Parthenon, 1121
Is it Aristotle's tomb? 2050

Walford, Edward, 1823–1897, journalist, editor. *DNB.*

Antagonist systems in Anglican Church, **DR** 630
The synod of Exeter, 631
The Catholic Florist, 637
The Leeds experiment in Anglicanism, 652
Scudamore on secession to Rome, 661
Patterson's *Tour in Egypt,* 664
The Mormons in America, 672
Ireland and Sir Francis Head, 688

The life and writings of St. Paul, 699
Domestic architecture in England, 721
The Doctrine of the Holy Eucharist, 722
Oxford—its past and present, 730, 738
Courts of William IV and Victoria, 975
Cockerell's *Aegina*, 992
Genealogy, 995
Notices: 641, 669, 677, 760

Walhouse, Moreton John, Madras civil servant. Venn under his son, Moreton Edward Walhouse.

Sissipāra; an Indian mountain sketch, **FM** 5484
A Christmas in India, 5512
Southern India: great elephant forest, 5572
Western coast of India, 5679
Scenery of an Indian stream, 5755
Field sports in Madras, 5885
The great fourfold waterfall, 6006

Walker, Annie Louisa: see Coghill, Annie Louisa (Walker).

Walker, Campbell, army officer, Madras Staff Corps. *Army List*/71, BMCat.

Our rule in India, FM 5055, 5131

Walker, Charles

Veto Bill from the trade point of view, **FortR** 3367

Walker, Francis Amasa, 1840–1897, American educator, economist. *DAB*.

Monetary situation and the United States, **NatR-II** 1897

Walker, George, 1803–1879, writer on chess. *DNB*.

Deschapelles, the chess-king, **FM** 1303
Anatomy of the chess automaton, 1332
Chess without the chess-board, 1419
The Café de la Régence, 1505
Ruy Lopez, the chess-bishop, 1595
Mated and checkmated, 1698
A game of chess with Napoleon, 2029

Walker, George Blake. *BMCat*.

Mine inspection, **NC** 1163

Walker, Henry Martyn, 1821–1886, prof. of classics at Oscott. Boase.

Notice: **Ram** 834

Walker, John, 1800–1873, R.C. priest at Scarborough. Newman, *L&D*, XI, index.

Editors and biographers of the Venerable Bede, **DR** 729
See: 435

Walker, John, 1817–1878, R.C. priest. Newman, *L&D*, XI, index, and XII, 11n.

Vigilantius and his times, **DR** 435

Walker, William, Scottish banker, of Edinburgh. See *NatR-II* no. 853.

Letters: **NatR-II** 804, 853, 943

Walkley, Arthur Bingham, 1855–1926, dramatic and literary critic. *DNB*.

Some plays of the day, **FortR** 3348

Wall, Charles Horace, 1784–1851, schoolmaster at Oxford. See evidence for *FM* no. 393. R.L.F.

Schoolmaster's experience in Newgate, **FM** 393, 417, 421, 450, 473
Masters and servants, 515
Hells in London, 593
Household servants, 640
Condition of the people, 649, 691
Imprisonment for debt, 698
Metropolis water supply, 756
Condemned cells, in 9 installments from 1474 to 1636

Wallace, Alfred Russell: see *Index*, I, 1126.

A defence of modern spiritualism, **FortR** 1050, 1058
Humming-birds, 1417
Epping Forest, 1521
Romanes versus Darwin, 2505
American museums, 2631, 2651
Human selection, 2987
English and American flowers, 3137, 3155
Our molten globe, 3281
Are individually acquired characters inherited? 3350, 3362
The ice age and its work, 3430, 3441
The method of organic evolution, 3599, 3616
Expressiveness of speech, 3706
Gorge of the Aar, 3836

Psychological curiosities of scepticism, **FM** 5994

Note: **NQM** 5

Animals and their native countries, **NC** 270
Reciprocity the true free trade, 296
A few words in reply to Mr. Lowe, 336
The origin of species and genera, 396
Antiquity of man in North America, 1484
Why I voted for Gladstone, 2260
Inaccessible valleys, 2360
A suggestion to Sabbath-keepers, 2649

Walpole, F. G.

The wine duties, **FortR** 2336

Walpole, Sir Spencer, 1839–1907: see *Index,* I, 1127.

The Queen's prime ministers, **FortR** 3694

Old age pensions, **NC** 3457
Lord Ellenborough, 3503

Walsh, David, writer on medical subjects. *BMCat.*

Murder by measles, **NC** 2944 collab.

Walsh, Walter, 1847–1912, divine, editor. *WWW.* (See App. A. below.)

Secret societies in Church of England, **NatR-II** 2271

Walsh, William John: see *Index,* I, 1127.

Alleged Gallicanism of Maynooth, **DR** 1721

T. W. Russell and the "Catholic Hierarchy" of Ireland, **FortR** 3192

Walston, Sir Charles: see Waldstein, Charles.

Walters, John Cuming, 1863/64–1933, newspaper editor. *WWW*, death certificate at Somerset House.

Letter: **NatR-II** 1262

Ward, Arnold Sandwith, 1876–1950, correspondent of the *Times. WWW.*

Missionaries in Egypt, **NC** 3700

Ward, Frances Mary (Wingfield), 1816–1898, wife of W. G. Ward. *Tablet,* Aug. 13, 1898, pp. 265–266.

St. Thomas of Canterbury, **DR** 1216, 1229

Ward, Frederick Oldfield: see *Index,* I, 1128.

Signs of the times, **FM** 2447
Vestigia veri, 2570
An episode of 1848, 2664

Ward, H. C., a captain; possibly Capt. Henderson Ward, retired, in *Army List*/91. *BMCat., RG.*

Winter in country of passion play, **NatR-II** 1105

Ward, Henry Constantine Evelyn: see *Index,* I, 1128.

My residence in Bhopal, **NatR-II** 1769

Ward, James, 1843–1925, philosopher, psychologist. *DNB.*

A reply to Mr. Herbert Spencer, **FortR** 4427

Ward, John: see *Index,* I, 1128.

See: **DR** 417

Arts and manufactures in France, **FQR** 68
Present state of the Netherlands, 120
Commercial histories: financial reform, 153
Diffusion of knowledge in France, 201
Duties on foreign books, 214
The City of Refuge, 265
State of religious feeling in France, 273
Notices: 79, 168, 204, 229, 241

Ward, Mary Augusta (Arnold): see *Index,* I, 1128.

A mediaeval Spanish writer [Juan Ruiz], **FortR** 1316
Democracy: An American Novel [by Henry Adams], 1929

The new Reformation, **NC** 1683, 3551
The Apostles' Creed, 2432
Notices: 1858, 2044

Ward, Wilfrid Philip: see *Index,* I, 1129.

The healing art in philosophy, **DR** 1943
R. H. Hutton as a religious thinker, 2120
Scholastic movement and Catholic philosophy, 2269
Sir M. E. Grant Duff's *Notes from a Diary,* 2653

Vatican and Quirinal, **FortR** 4253
Unchanging dogma and changeful man, 4439
Two mottoes of Cardinal Newman, 4475

The clothes of religion, **NatR-II** 183
A Pickwickian positivist [Frederic Harrison], 222

The wish to believe, **NC** 675, 904
Positivism in Christianity, 1454
New wine in old bottles, 1883
Some aspects of Newman's influence, 1940
Witnesses to the unseen, 2060
The rigidity of Rome, 2834
Thomas Henry Huxley: a reminiscence, 2976
Catholic apologetics, 3483
Liberalism and intransigeance, 3667

Ward, William George: see *Index,* I, 1129.

Plea of conscience for seceding from the

Father Coleridge on the Gospels, 1516
Father Newman on ecclesiastical prudence, 1520
Dr. Brownson's philosophy, 1530
Father O'Reilly on society and the Church, 1532
Tradition and Papal Infallibility, 1540
?Mivart's *Lessons from Nature*, 1541
Church and state, 1544
Mivart on rights of conscience, 1551
Mill on causation, 1553
A few more words on Fessler, 1557
Letter to the *Saturday Review*, 1559
Gospel narrative of the Resurrection, 1564
Civil intolerance of religious error: Mivart on liberty of conscience, 1573
Coleridge's *Life of Our Life*, 1586
Hergenröther on church and state, 1606
Two philosophical papers by Dr. Ward, 1623
Catholic college education in England, 1627
Catholic college discipline, 1640
Dr. Ward's retirement, 1650 collab.
Catholic colleges and Protestant schools, 1651
The reasonable basis of certitude, 1655
Free will, 1678
Supplementary remarks on free will, 1704
Ethics in its bearing on theism, 1717
Mr. Shadworth Hodgson on free will, 1747
The extent of free will, 1781
Philosophy of the theistic controversy, 1805
Letter: 1273
Notes: 1040, 1117, 1126, 1133, 1223, 1512, 1532, 1537, 1572, 1576, 1641, 1649
Notices: 479, 1042, 1052, 1072, 1083, 1106, ?1116, 1126, 1135, 1145, 1154, 1165, 1173, 1183, 1193, 1203, 1213, 1222, 1232, 1241, 1253, 1263, 1272, 1286, 1297, 1306, 1317, 1330, 1347, 1358, 1368, 1380, 1388, 1407, 1426, 1462, 1470, 1489, 1497, 1507, 1519, 1528, 1539, 1550, 1561, 1571, 1582, 1614, 1624, 1661, 1701, 1724
Trans: 1514, 1518, 1549, 1560, 1622
See: 417, 1146, 1188, 1189, 1246

Morality of decline in religious belief, **NC** 36
The soul and future life, 98
The reasonable basis of certitude, 150

Rood screens, **Ram** 41
The necessities of Catholic education, 77, 1076
The study of classical Greek and Latin, 107
Letters: 27, 44, 1050
See: 199

Wardell, William Wilkinson, 1823–1899, architect. Boase.

Gothic ecclesiastical building, **Ram** 198
Town churches, 205

Ware, Henry Ryder, 1836–1905, divine. Venn.

Letter: **NatR-II** 672

Waring, Charles, d.1887, civil engineer, I.C.E. *Minutes*, 92 (1888), 410.

Brazil and her railways, **FortR** 2011
The trusteeship of the Suez Canal, 2107
The future of industry, 2236
State purchase of railways, 2468
State purchase of Irish railways, 2536

Waring, Charles Henry, 1818–1887, civil engineer. I.C.E. *Minutes*, 91 (1888), 447.

The bubble-girl [satire on Carlyle], **FM** 2655

Warlow, John Picton, Madras staff corps. *Army List*/85, *F.O. List*/1901.

An Anglo-Turkish alliance, **NC** 1115

Warre-Cornish, Blanche: see *Index*, I, 1129.

A woman poet [Marceline Valmore], **FortR** 3981

Warre-Cornish, Francis Warre: see *Index*, I, 1129.

Greek beauty and modern art, **FortR** 983

Eton reform, **NC** 1194

Warren, Charles Frere Stopford, 1844–1898, divine. Venn.

Fifty versions of "Dies Irae," **DR** 1868 collab.

Warren, Edward Prioleau, 1856–1937, architect. *WWW*.

Westminster "improvement" scheme, **FortR** 4095

Warren, Frederick Pelham, d.1891, naval officer. Boase; *Times*, May 20, 1891, p. 7.

Morocco, **FortR** 2201

Warren, John Byrne Leicester, 3rd Baron de Tabley, 1835–1895, poet. *DNB.*

Atalanta in Calydon [by Swinburne], **FortR** 6
Bibliography of Tennyson, 94
Notice: 264

Warren, Sir Thomas Herbert: see *Index*, I, 1130.

Letter: **FortR** 2647

Warrender, Hugh Valdave, 1868–1926, army officer. *WWW.*

Pass fishing for tarpon, **NC** 3159

Wassilieff or **Vasil'ev,** Iosif, chaplain to Russian embassy at Paris. *BMCat.; Ram* no. 1059, p. 389.

See: **Ram** 1040

Waterfield, Ottiwell Charles, [1830]–1898, educator, businessman. Venn.

The negotiations with M. de Lesseps, **FortR** 2063

Waters, Cyril Aubrey, b.1860/61, misc. writer. *BMCat.,* Foster.

William Gifford, **NatR-II** 882

Waterton, Charles, 1782–1865, naturalist. *DNB.*

"Quarrels of" zoologists, **FM** 798

Waterworth, William B., S.J., 1811–1882, historian. *DNB.*

Absorption of Anglicanism by the Popedom, **Ram** 596

Watkins, Morgan George: see *Index,* I, 1130, and II, App. A.

Sunshine at the Land's End, **FM** 4733
With a trout rod, 5360
Birds of the Humber, 5466
Into ballad-land [Scotland], 5489
Salmon fishing, 5523
On Ottery East Hill, 5582
Angling worthies, 5689
The royal Bengal tiger, 5771
Izaak Walton, 5811
Amongst the sea-birds, 5861
Capture and shooting of wild-fowl, 6017
British quadrupeds, 6052
White of Selborne, 6155
The capercaillie, 6438

Watson, Emma L.

Modern nurses, **NatR-II** 1957

Watson, George Lennox, 1851–1904, naval architect. *DNB.*

Letter: **NatR-II** 563

Watson, John, 1844–1921, Scottish divine. *Fasti,* VII, 305.

The Stewarts in Orkney, **ScotR** 276

Watson, John, d.1928: see *Index,* I, 1130.

Wild ducks and duck decoying, **NatR-II** 916
Workers in woodcraft, 1128

Water poachers, **NC** 1781

Watson, John Selby: see *Index,* I, 1131.

Notices: **FortR** 161, 192, 203

Watson, Sir John William: see *Index,* I, 1131.

The fall of fiction [on Rider Haggard], **FortR** 2744
Tragedy and Stephen Phillips, 4090

Some literary idolatries, **NatR-II** 769
Dr. Johnson on modern poetry, 876
Fiction—plethoric and anaemic, 910
Poetry by men of the world, 938
The siege of Helicon, 965
Lancashire laureate [Edwin Waugh], 1015
Punishment of genius [on Keats], 1037
Critics and their craft, 1113

Watson, Margaret, translator. Allibone.

Frithjof's Saga by Esaias Tegner, **DR** 2585
Minnesinger Walther von der Vogelweide, 2642
The Nibelungenlied, 2712

Watson, Thomas, 1513–1584, Bishop of Lincoln. *DNB.*

Sermon at the prorogation of the synod, **DR** 2556

Watson, Sir Thomas, 1792–1882: see *Index,* I, 1131.

The abolition of zymotic disease, **NC** 28
Hydrophobia and rabies, 109
Small-pox and compulsory vaccination, 180

Watson, William: see Watson, Sir John William.

Watson, William Davy, 1811–1888, misc. writer, barrister. Venn.

English synonyms, **FM** 2887
The use and beauty of words, 2921
Little books with large aims, 3088
The rule of good nuns [*The Ancren Riwle*], 3327
English, Past and Present [by R. C. Trench], 3394
The Verney papers, 3425
Use of proverbs in grave composition, 3675
Bürger and his translators, 3722
Essays and Reviews, 4012

Watt, Thomas M.

Letter: **NatR-II** 603

Watteville, Armand de, 1846–1925, physician. *Surgeon Index*/3rd s.

Sleep and its counterfeits, **FortR** 2593

Watts, George Frederic, 1817–1904, painter, sculptor. *DNB*.

The present conditions of art, **NC** 404
Art needlework, 562
On taste in dress, 804

Watts, Henry Edward, 1826–1904, journalist, translator of *Don Quixote*. *DNB*.

The West India question, **FM** 5992

Watts, Walter Theodore, later (in 1896) Watts-Dunton, 1832–1914, critic. *DNB*.

The future of American literature, **FortR** 3093
Letter: 2638

Alfred de Musset, and physiognomic poetry, **NQM** 140

The truth about Rossetti, **NC** 827
Aspects of Tennyson, 2395, 2472
Reminiscences of Christina Rossetti, 2714
Notice: 2523

Watts, William Lord, b.1850, traveller, geologist. *LCCat*.

On the Vatna Jökull [in Iceland], **FM** 5619

Watts-Dunton, Theodore: see Watts, Walter Theodore.

Waugh, Arthur, 1866–1943, editor, publisher. *WWW*.

Tyranny of the paragraph, **NatR-II** 1389
The new era in letters, 1442

Waugh, Benjamin: see *Index*, I, 1131.

Prevention of cruelty to children, **DR** 2315

Weale, Robert Morey, 1825–1910, divine. Venn.

Letter: **FM** 2892

Weale, William Henry James, 1832–1917, keeper of National Art Library. *BMCat.*, *WWW*.

The Van Eycks, **NC** 3749

Weatherly, Lionel Alexander, b.1852, physician. *Medical WW*/1915.

Letter: **NatR-II** 1278

Webb, Beatrice (Potter), 1858–1943, economist, wife of Sidney Webb. *WWW*.

Dock life of East London, **NC** 1460
East London labour, 1579
Pages from a work-girl's diary, 1589
The lords and the sweating system, 1879
Failure of the Labour Commission, 2602
Arbitration in labour disputes, 3017 collab.
Law and the laundries, 3067 collab.

Webb, Benjamin, 1819–1885, ecclesiologist. *DNB*.

Prospects of art in England, **BentQR** 5
Art exhibitions of 1859, 18
Domestic architecture, 35

Webb, Sidney James: see *Index*, I, 1132.

What Gladstone ought to do, **FortR** 3333
To your tents, oh Israel! 3427 collab.

Arbitration in labour disputes, **NC** 3017 collab.

Webb, Thomas Ebenezer: see *Index*, I, 1132.

The metaphysician [from Hume to Hamilton], **FM** 3962

Webster, Richard Everard, Viscount Alverstone, 1842–1915, judge, M.P. *DNB*.

The attack on the Church, **NatR-II** 1587 collab.

Webster, Robert Grant, 1845–1925, barrister, M.P. Venn.

Metropolitan coal and wine dues, **NatR-II** 553
The Sugar Convention, 872

Webster, Wentworth: see *Index*, I, 1132.

Peasant proprietors and small farmers in France, **FortR** 1774
Home rule in the western Pyrenees, 2690

Wedderburn, Sir David: see *Index*, I, 1132.

English liberalism and Australasian democracy, **FortR** 1273
Mormonism from a Mormon point of view, 1297
Maoris and Kanakas [of New Zealand], 1365
The Dutch in Java, 1430
Modern Japan, 1448, 1455

Wedderburn, Sir David (*continued*)
Two fair cousins, a Chinese romance, 1513
The *Loyal League*: a Japanese romance, 1553
The Deccan, 1723
Denmark, 1821
Notices: 203, 335, 435

Protected princes in India, **NC** 199
Iceland, 480
Second chambers [on House of Lords], 602

Wedgwood, Frances Julia: see *Index*, I, 1132.

Morals and politics, **NatR-II** 1110

Wedmore, Sir T. Frederick: see *Index*, I, 1132.

The impressionists, **FortR** 1987
Genre in the summer exhibitions, 2045
Hablot Browne and book-illustration, 2125
Modern etching, 2595
A chemist in the suburbs, 3084
Poet on the wolds [Frederick Wedmore], 3802

Méryon and Méryon's Paris, **NC** 171
Whistler's theories and art, 346
Jules Jacquemart, 577
The theatrical revival, 816
Orgeas and Miradou, 2792
Music-halls, 2963
The short story, 3255
The theatrical position, 3329
Players and old plays, 3704
The poet's end, 3765

Wegg-Prosser, Francis Richard, 1824–1911, M.P. Newman, *L&D*, XIV, index.

Rome on the Day of Pentecost, 1862, **DR** 1021
Gunpowder and modern warfare, 1707
The Church and liberalism, 1997
Facilities of modern pilgrimage, 2033
Evolution and determinism, 2302
Modern stellar astronomy, 2349
Scientific evidence of the deluge, 2505
Notices: 2054, 2090, 2358, 2459

Letter: **NatR-II** 323

Weightman, Richard Coxe, 1845–1914, American journalist. *Amer. WWW.*

Notes from Washington, **NC** 3488

Weissenborn, Wilhelm W., 1803–1878, classical philologist, director of Weimar Gymnasium. *ADB.*

Letter: **FortR** 2988

Weisser, Friedrich Christoph W., 1761–1836, German man of letters. *ADB.*

Il Bondocani, from *Mährchen der Scherezade,* **FM** 1454

Welby-Gregory, Lady Victoria Alexandrina Maria Louisa (Stuart-Wortley), 1837–1912. *Times,* Apr. 1, 1912, p. 11c.

A royal slave [man to language], **FortR** 4008

Welby-Gregory, Sir William Earle, 1829–1898, M.P. Burke.

Out-door poor relief, **NatR-II** 1397

Welch, Francis Henry, 1840–1910, military surgeon. *BMCat., Surgeon Index*/2nd s.

Care of the sick and wounded in war, **FortR** 4511

Weld, Charles, 1812–1885, J.P., barrister. *Landed Gentry.*

Waterton's *Autobiography,* **DR** 172

Dr. Oliver's *Collections,* **Ram** 848
Rough notes on Ruskin, 881
Note: 974
Letter: 991

Weld, Charles Richard: see *Index*, I, 1133.

The Arctic expeditions, **FM** 2524
Visit to the Grande Chartreuse, 2666
The Leviathan telescope, 2792
The search for Sir John Franklin, 2821, 2907
?The North-West Passage [M'Clure's voyage in search of Franklin], 3152
Forlorn Hope, 3228
Excursions in Eastern Pyrenees, 3843
Earthquakes, 3921
Franklin's fate, and the *Fox,* 3941
Humming-birds, 4207
The Ardennes and Moselle land, 4376
The sketcher in the Eifel, 4621
Notes on Florence, 4690
The Paris Exhibition, 4804
Volcanos, 4858
See: 2450

Weld, Sir Frederick Aloysius, 1823–1891, colonial governor. *DNB.*

Christianity in the Pacific, **Ram** 825
Letter: ?886

Welldon, James Edward Cowell: see *Index*, I, 1133.

The art of reading books, **NatR-II** 1566

Wellesley, Richard Colley: see *Index*, I, 1133.

[Letters of] Wellesley and Iddesleigh, **NatR-II** 676 collab.

Wells, Charles Jeremiah, c. 1799–1879, poet. *DNB.*

A boar-hunt in Brittany, **FM** 2245
Love-passages in life of Perron the Breton, 2326

Wells, Henry Tanworth, 1828–1903, portrait painter. *DNB.*

Government and artists, **NC** 380

Wells, Herbert George: see *Index*, I, 1133.

Rediscovery of the unique, **FortR** 3108
Human evolution, an artificial process, 3869
Morals and civilisation, 3920
The cyclist soldier, 4542

Wells, Joseph: see *Index*, I, 1133.

Universities of Europe in the middle ages, **ScotR** 529

Welsh, John

Last days of the Ottoman Empire, **FortR** 2879

Welsh-Mason, C.: see Mason, Charles Welsh

Wemyss, Millicent Ann Mary: see *Index*, I, 1133, and II, App. A.

The story of an unhappy queen, **NC** 2233

Wenckstern, Otto von: see *Index*, I, 1133.

History of the Hungarian War, in 8 install-ments from **FM** 2905 to 2979
A Campaign with the Russian Army, 3411
Sutlers in the camp [Crimean War], 3423

Wenham, John George, 1820–1895, inspector of R.C. schools in Southwark. Boase.

The Church in Ceylon, **DR** 517
The Portuguese schism in India, 540
Tennent's *Christianity in Ceylon*, 624
Sermons and preachers, 720
?Our elementary schools and their work, 1709
On the formation of knowledge, 1975
See: 1682

Our poor-schools, **Ram** 790
Instruction v. education, 800
Principles of education, 809
What books shall we use in our schools? 874
Letter: 562

Wenley, Robert Mark: see *Index*, I, 1133.

Scotland's new departure in philosophy, **ScotR** 109
Philosophy in Scotland, 269
Interpretation of *The Critical Philosophy* [by Kant], 286
Philosophy of religion, 323
British thought and modern speculation, 348
Religions, metaphysic and religion, 432
The logic of history, 457
Persistence of rationality, 475
See: 72, 122

Werner, Edward Theodore Chalmers, 1864–1954, foreign officer in China. *WWW.*

The China problem and its solution, **FortR** 3627

Wertheimer, Julius, 1859/60–1924, prof. of chemistry, Univ. of Bristol. *WWW, Times,* Aug. 11, 1924, p. 12e.

Homiculture, **NC** 1596

Wesslau, O. E. *BMCat.*

The American tariff war, **FortR** 3001 collab.

West, Sir Algernon Edward, 1832–1921, chair-man of Board of Inland Revenue. *DNB.*

English prisons, **NC** 2873
Lord Randolph Churchill as an official, 2999
Changes in social life, 3101
Our custom house regulations, 3188
A walk through deserted London, 3224
While waiting in a friend's room, 3498
The great unpaid [public servants], 3540
Two reports of the Licensing Commission, 3604
Reform in the Public Service, 3734

West, Sir Leonard Henry, 1864–1950, solicitor. *WWW.*

Separatist attack on fundamental principles [on the Home Rule issue], **NatR-II** 601
A year under county councils, 998

Westgarth, William, 1815–1889, Australian politician. *DNB.*

The unity of the Empire: federation, **NatR-II** 244

Westlake, John: see *Index,* I, 1134.

The Kafir Revolt of 1873, **FortR** 1103

The case of Finland, **NatR-II** 2420

Proportional representation, **NC** 1094 col-lab.

Westmacott, Charles Malloy, 1787/88–1868, journalist. Boase.

?Gossip about arts and artists, **FM** 58

Weston, Jessie. *BMCat.*

Hints for single women, **NatR-II** 1142

Wetherell, Thomas Frederick: see *Index*, I, 1134.

Catholic unity and English parties, **DR** 852
Notice: ?770

The causes of the present war, **Ram** 996
Volunteers and recruits, 1021
Enlargement of the *Rambler*, 1130 collab.
Current events, ?1023, 1069, 1077
Letter: 991
Notice: 1113 collab.

Whall, W. B., master mariner. *BMCat.*

The British merchant service, **NatR-II** 510

Whalley, Percy Charles, army officer. *Army List*/91.

The Royal Artillery, **NatR-II** 1253

Whately, Richard: see *Index*, I, 1134, and II, App. A.

Concerning Scylla and Charybdis, **FM** 4025 collab.

Transportation, **LR (1829)** 5
Juvenile library, 17
See: 18

Whates, Harry Richard: see *Index*, I, 1134.

The Venezuelan dipute [between England and the U.S.], **FortR** 3760
The Venezuelan award, 4363
The out-going government, 4502
Chamberlain, 4531

Wheatley, Henry Benjamin, 1838–1917, Pepys's scholar, bibliographer. *WWW, LCCat.*

Unpublished pages of Pepys's diary, **NC** 2118

Wheatley, Leonard Abercromby, 1835–1895, publisher, translator. Boase, *LCCat.*

Thomas à Kempis and *The Imitation of Christ*, **ScotR** 100

Wheaton, Henry, 1785–1848, American jurist, historian. *DAB.*

Ancient history and constitution of Denmark, **FQR** 260

Modern painting in Germany [on Raczynsky's *History*], 415, 587, 655
Discovery of America by the Northmen, 483

Wheeler, Alfred A.

The Russians in Armenia, **FortR** 1534

Wheeler, Stephen: see *Index*, I, 1135.

The Black Mountain campaign, **FortR** 2774

Whelpley, James Davenport, b.1863, American economist. *Amer. WW*/1935, *BMCat.*

An international wheat corner, **FortR** 4490

Whetstone, Frederick J., past chairman of the Amalgamated Soc. of Engineers.

Fair trade: the views of labour, **NatR-II** 1366

Whewell, William: see *Index*, I, 1135.

Dialogue on English hexameters, **FM** 2394, 2568
Evangeline [by H. W. Longfellow], 2431
Sacred Latin Poetry, 2586
On Macaulay's praise of knowledge, 2620
Göthe's *Herman and Dorothea*, 2678
The Lamps of Architecture [by Ruskin], 2688
?About the Christmas books, 2808
Grote's *Plato*, 4638

Whibley, Charles: see *Index*, I, 1135.

The hates of Napoleon, **FortR** 4020
Language and style, 4226

The *Mimes* of Herodas, **NC** 2121
Italian art at the new gallery, 2534
Art at the salons, 2584
The farce of "university extension," 2617, 2648
The encroachment of women, 2904, 3092
The limits of biography, 3083

Whitaker, Edgar, 1831–1903, prop. and ed. of *Levant Herald* and *Eastern Express. WWW, Times*, Aug. 25, 1903, p. 4d.

The coup d'état in Eastern Roumelia, **NC** 1210

Whitaker, W.

Notice: **FortR** 335

White, Archer Moresby, legal writer. *BMCat.*

Letter: **NatR-II** 1397

White, Arnold: see *Index*, I, 1135.

The truth about the Salvation Army, **FortR** 3239
The unemployed, 3416
Letter: 3588

The Russian bogey, **NatR-II** 2189
The Tsar's manifesto, 2213
Coming crisis in the Transvaal, 2296
The cult of infirmity, 2358
Cankers of a long peace, 2390
Britannia and the colonist, 2459

Invasion of pauper foreigners, **NC** 1527

White, Arthur M.

The War [in South Africa], **ScotR** 668, 680, 692

White, Arthur Silva: see *Index*, I, 1136.

Chartered government in Africa, **NC** 2512
The partition of Africa, 2603
Africanists in council, 2808
Australia as a strategic base, 2900

White, Blanco: see White, Joseph Blanco.

White, H. Anstruther

Moral and merry England, **FortR** 2396

White, Horace, 1834–1916, American journalist, economist. *DAB.*

An American's impressions of England, **FortR** 1187
The financial crisis in America, 1264
The American centenary, 1299
Parliamentary government in America, 1629

White, Ina Mary, afterwards Harrower, daughter of John Forbes White, for whom see *Index*, I, 1137. *BMCat.* under Harrower.

The diary of Jane Porter, **ScotR** 561
Trans: 696

White, James Dundas, 1866–1951, barrister, politician. *WWW.*

Our educational finance, **FortR** 3746

White, John

Laws on compulsory education, **FortR** 1269

White, Joseph Blanco: see *Index*, I, 1137.

Journals and reviews, **LR (1829)** 1
The Course of Time [by Robert Pollok], 11
Spanish poetry and language, 16

White, Robert

Wanted: a Rowton house for clerks, **NC** 3185

White, Hon. Robert, 1861–1936, army officer. Venn.

Prison treatment of juvenile offenders, **NC** 3160

White, Thomas Pilkington: see *Index*, I, 1137, and II, App. A.

Aspects of the modern Scot, **ScotR** 447
The malcontent woman, 477
The Inches of the Forth, 495
The Orkney Isles, 517
Hjaltland, 527
The cycling epidemic, 548
The new woman on the Bible, 578
A corner of Bretonland, 587
The vaunts of modern progress, 605
Dorset and Devon dales, 634
Coercion of custom, 665
Redundancy of spinster gentlewomen, 689

White, Sir William Henry, 1845–1913, naval architect. *DNB.*

The speed of warships, **FortR** 4024

The latest reconstruction of the navy, **NC** 3265
Note: 3266

Whitehead, Henry: see *Index*, I, 1137.

Bells of Carlisle Cathedral, **NatR-II** 304

Working of school banks, **NC** 1455

Whitehead, Samuel Durham. *BMCat.*, which erroneously gives "Dunham"; cf. Nat. Lib. Scot. MS 935, fols. 218–219.

Wace, *Rollo and the Dukes of Normandy*, **FQR** 31
Modern Spanish comedy, 48
Karamsin's *History of Russia*, 60
Ancient national poetry of Spain, 83
Poland under Sobieski, 180
Memoirs of Duplessis Mornay, 312
Notice: 66

Whitehouse, Frederic Cope: see *Index*, I, 1137, and *Amer. WWW*/1942.

England's right to Suez shares, **FortR** 3412
How to save Egypt, 3433

Whiteside, Thomas, 1857–1921, R.C. archbishop of Liverpool. *WWW.*

?Notice: **DR** 2347

Whiteway, Augustine Robert, 1847–1902, barrister. *Landed Gentry.*

Colonial problems of Newfoundland, **NatR-II** 1689

Whiteway, Sir William Vallance, 1828–1908, premier of Newfoundland. *DNB.*

The Newfoundland fisheries dispute, **FortR** 2986 collab.

Whitley, D. Gath

Ice-age and post-glacial flood, **ScotR** 421

Whitman, James

French fishery claims [off Newfoundland], **FM** 5760

Whitman, Sidney: see *Index,* I, 1137.

Count Moltke, field-marshal, **FortR** 3589

Whitmore, Charles Algernon: see *Index,* I, 1137.

Has the session been unfruitful? **NatR-II** 628
Elections for London County Council, 824
The work of the session, 898
Victory [in London County Council elections], 1279
The general election, 1316
Conservatives and London County Council, 1413
The London programme, 1432
London government, 1662
The Progressive check [of the Radicals], 1711
Beautifying London, 1846
English weather, 2020
Our defeat and some morals, 2151
Is Unionist party committed to old-age pensions? 2321
Redistribution, 2374
Where is the incapacity [of the army]? 2438

Whitney, Caspar W., 1864–1929, sportsman, traveller. *WWW.*

Athletics in the United States, **FortR** 3413

Whittaker, Sir Thomas Palmer: see *Index,* I, 1138.

The liquor traffic, **DR** 1691

Proposals of Fair Trade League, **NC** 641
"Temperance" reply to Algernon West, 3626

Whittle, James Lowry: see *Index,* I, 1138.

McKinley's opportunity, **FortR** 3910
Gibraltar as a winter resort, 4004

Egypt after Omdurman, 4287
Bryan and McKinley, 4534

How to save Ireland from an ultramontane university, **FM** 4855
Irish elections and influence of priests, 5041
The future of labour, 5125
Last instalment of Irish policy, 5175

Whyte, John Charles, barrister of Dublin. Thom/60, p. 1563.

See: **Ram** 708

Whyte-Melville, George John, 1821–1878. novelist. *DNB.*

The White Rose, in 14 installments from **FortR** 364 to 475

Captain Digby Grand, in 14 installments from **FM** 2904 to 3038
General Bounce, in 12 installments from 3170 to 3293
The old world and the new, 3326
Huc's *China,* 3336
Westward Ho! [by Kingsley], 3343
Kate Coventry: an autobiography, 3432, 3440, 3451, 3460, 3470, 3480
A peep into the principalities [Wallachia and Moldavia], 3498
The Interpreter, in 12 installments from 3553 to 3673
The yellow gown; a ghost story, 3778
The taming of horses, and Mr. Rarey, 3793
Holmby House, in 15 installments from 3809 to 3950
Compromise, 3971
A ride for the ring, 4028
Good for Nothing, in 12 installments from 4055 to 4167
Strong-minded women, 4387
A week in bed, 4419
Irish Orangeism, 5472

Wickham, Edward Charles, 1834–1910, dean of Lincoln. *DNB.*

Archbishop Benson, **NatR-II** 2033

Wicks, Frederick: see *Index,* I, 1138.

Confederation of the Empire, **NatR-II** 478
Authors, publishers, and reviewers, 1382
Letters: 796, 1262, 1359, 1426

Insignificance of trades union vote, **NC** 2560

Widor, Charles Marie Jean Albert, 1845–1937, musicologist. Grove, 1954 ed.

Gounod, **FortR** 3446

Wightman, James W., army officer in 17th Lancers at Balaclava. *Army List*/66.

The Balaclava charge, **NC** 2218

Wightwick, George, 1802–1872, architect. *DNB*.

The late Charles Mathews, **FM** 923
Blue Friar pleasantries, in 13 installments from 1046 to 1465
On beggars, 2201
Letter: 1479

Wikoff, Henry, 1813–1884, American diplomat, adventurer. *DAB*.

Fanny Elssler, **FM** 1886, 1893, 1900, 1912, all collab.

Wilberforce, Anna Maria (Denman), d.1938, wife of Reginald G. Wilberforce, q.v. *Landed Gentry*.

Note: **NC** 3590

Wilberforce, Henry William, 1807–1873, Catholic journalist. *DNB*.

Slavery and the war in America, **DR** 1066
The war in America, 1110
The Formation of Christendom, [by T. W. Allies], 1131
Champagny on the Roman Empire, 1151
?*Julius Caesar*, by Napoleon III, 1155
The negro in Africa and West Indies, 1161
Jamaica, 1169
New America [mainly on the Mormons], 1186
Manning on England and Christendom, 1198
Montalembert's *Monks of the West*, 1214
The ritualists, 1228
Souvenirs de Famille [de la Ferronnays], 1234
The Church and Napoleon I, 1259
Newman's Oxford *Parochial Sermons*, 1265
Ritualistic divinity and law, 1270 collab.
Life of Father Faber, 1281
Gallican Assembly of 1682, 1291
?Protestant London, 1318
The Convent Committee, 1331
Unity of the Church, 1337
Champagny's *Caesars of the Third Century*, 1343
Pius VII and Napoleon I, 1349
Hampden and Anglicanism, 1361
Pius VII at Savona and Fontainebleau, 1372
Notices: 1286, ?1317

Wilberforce, Reginald Garton, 1838–1914, army officer. *Landed Gentry*.

Remarks of my reviewers [on his *Life of Samuel Wilberforce*], **FortR** 2056

Cardinal Manning, **NC** 2167
Pusey and Bishop Wilberforce, 2778
Cardinal Manning's memory, 2939
Letter: 3140

Wilberforce, Wilfrid Ignatius, 1850–1910, of the British Museum. *Landed Gentry*.

William George Ward, **DR** 2439
Notice: 2438

Wilcox, Arthur Marwood, c.1841–1901, divine and schoolmaster. Venn.

The second-class clergy, **NatR-II** 959

Wilde, James Plaisted, 1st Baron Penzance, 1816–1899, judge. *DNB*.

Protection of national industry, **NatR-II** 630

The free-trade idolatry, **NC** 1253, 1266
Collapse of the free trade argument, 1315

Wilde, Oscar Fingal: see *Index*, I, 1138.

Pen, pencil, and poison, **FortR** 2782
The soul of man under socialism, 3048
A preface to *Dorian Gray*, 3061
Poems in prose, 3519

Shakespeare and stage costume, **NC** 1131
The decay of lying, 1642
Function and value of criticism, 1902, 1930

Wilkins, John William: see *Index*, I, 1138.

?Austrian nationalities and policy, **FM** 3377
?*Richard Cromwell* [by Guizot], 3526

Wilkins, W. Walker: see *Index*, I, 1139, and II, App. A.

Were the ancient Britons savages? **FortR** 197, 218

Wilkins, William Henry, 1860–1905, biographer. *DNB*.

Immigration of destitute foreigners, **NatR-II** 1057
Potato blight in Ireland, 1070
London hospital and its nurses, 1130

Immigration troubles of the United States, **NC** 2110
Hansoms and their drivers, 2367
"How long, O Lord, how long?" [women's working conditions], 2447

Wilkinson, Colonel

Armed strength of England, **FortR** 2295 collab. at least

Wilkinson, E. T., Liberal agent at York.

The new Bribery Act and York election, **NC** 952

Wilkinson, Henry Spenser: see *Index*, I, 1139.

Cartridges, **NatR-II** 1762
Chitral, 1786
Command of the sea and British policy, 1832
Russia's strength, 1924
The value of Constantinople, 1935
Trifling with national defence, 1960
Lord Roberts in Afghanistan, 1982
The defence of London, 1986
Helpless Europe, 1997
The new *Nelson* [by A. T. Mahan], 2040
Moral factors in the [Boer] War, 2367
War and government, 2402

Through the Khyber Pass, **NC** 2462
The general management of the army, 3599

Wilkinson, John Frome: see *Index*, I, 1139, and *CCD*/1902.

Friendly societies for women, **FortR** 4110

Denominational schools, **NatR-II** 1950
Letter: 1254

Wilkinson, Kosmo. *BMCat.*

A plague on both your parties! **FortR** 3639
Timely truths for the outs and ins, 3674

Wilkinson, Thomas William, 1825–1909, president of Ushaw Coll. Newman, *L&D*, XII, index.

Letter: **Ram** 624

Wilks, John, d.1846, swindler, Paris correspondent of *Standard*, son of John Wilks, 1764/65–1854. *DNB.* (See *Index*, I, 1138, under Wilkes.)

Our club at Paris, **FM** 1187, 1202, 1211, 1229, 1255
Talleyrand, 1290, 1302
Reminiscences of men and things, in 16 installments from 1736 to 1917
Reminiscences of Queen Victoria, 1888

Wilks, Sir Samuel: see *Index*, I, 1139.

Vivisection: its pains and uses, **NC** 661

Willdey, C. J. *BMCat.*

The constable Nun'Alvares, **ScotR** 603
Sons of Dom John, 679

Wilbert, Paul Ferdinand, 1844–1912, writer on French history. *WWW.*

Machiavelli, **FortR** 2145

Théodore Agrippa d'Aubigné, **NatR-II** 446
The Service of Man [by Cotter Morison], 619

Willes, Sir James Shaw, 1814–1872, judge. *DNB.*

See: **FM** 3572

Williams, Arthur John, 1833–1911, barrister, M.P. *Landed Gentry.*

A model land law, **FortR** 2583

Williams, Charles: see *Index*, I, 1139.

How we lost Gordon, **FortR** 2316
Thessalian war of 1897, 3976

The advance in the Soudan, **NatR-II** 2157

Williams, Edmund Sydney, 1817–1891, writer on German literature. *Academy*, Sept. 5, 1891, pp. 196–197.

?Ideler's *System of Psychology*, **FQR** 419
Chronicle of Dithmarsch, 420
?German literature, 461
?German influence upon uncultivated nations, 548
See: 397

Williams, Ernest Edwin, 1866–1935, barrister. *WWW.*

Klondike—a study in booms, **NatR-II** 2336
Mr. Chaplin's kite, 2356
Economic revolution in Germany, 2481
The sacrifice of Canada, 2525

Williams, Frederic Condé, 1844–1917, journalist and judge. Venn.

The colonial judge, **NatR-II** 1263
Madagascar and Mauritius, 1357

Williams, Hwfa, chairman of Sandown Park.

Sport under National Hunt Rules, **NatR-II** 1118

Williams, Joseph Powell, 1840–1904, M.P. *WWW.*

Taxation of ground-rents, **NC** 2353

Williams, Leonard: see *Index*, I, 1140.

Can Sagasta save Spain? **FortR** 4047

Williams, Sir Monier: see Monier-Williams.

Williams, Robert, 1843–1886, journalist. Boase, *M at B.*

A few words on Utilitarianism, **FM** 5003
Laissez-faire, 5043

Williams, Rowland: see *Index*, I, 1140.

Theory of clerical obligation, **FortR** 482
Notice: 533

Williams, Thomas Lloyd, Welsh divine. *CCD/* 1902.

The Church and dissent in Wales, **NatR-II** 1138

Williams, W. M. J. *LCCat.*

A poor man's budget, **FortR** 3474
Local taxation: its amount and burden, 3510

Williams, Walter

The [Royal] Academy and the Salon, **NatR-II** 448

Williamson, Robert, 1819–1902, Free Church divine. Ewing, I, 357, and *Fasti-Free Church*, p. 279.

St. Andrews, **ScotR** 510

Williamson, Stephen: see *Index*, I, 1140.

Agricultural and commercial depression, **FortR** 2261

Williamson, William, d.1873, London business-man, learned in Scottish history. See *FM* no. 5470, pp. 381–382.

Story of the Woodhouselee ghost, **FM** 5470 collab.

Willis, C., of Oxford. See *NatR-II* no. 729.

The volunteer movement, **NatR-II** 817
Letter: 729

Willis-Nevins, Henry: see Probyn-Nevins, Henry Willis.

Willmott, Robert Eldridge Aris, 1809–1863, divine, essayist. *DNB*, Venn.

Minor Greek poets: Meleager, **FM** 69
Minor Greek poets: Simonides, 92
Life of Bishop Heber, 102 collab.?
?Lady poets of France: Madame Tastu, 334
The Greek pastoral poets, 853, 867, 881, 898
Familiar letters of Cowley, 927, 985
Musings with favourite old poets, 929
The Greek Pastoral Poets, 949
Letter from Cambridge, 959, 975, 980
Letter from Athens to Oliver Yorke, 995

Chateaubriand upon English literature, 1021
?A soliloquy about the annuals, 1032
Greek comedy: Aristophanes, 1050, 1227, 1243, 1325, 1368
An April voyage [review of poetry], 1075
Alphonso de Lamartine, 1091
The fabulists: Aesop, Phaedrus, Gay, and Fontaine, 1166
The fabulists: Phaedrus, Fontaine, Fenelon, Vanbrugh, Boursault, 1190
A day among the mountains, 1252
Guesses at one or two truths, 1320
Mrs. Hemans and the picturesque school, 1407
Eloquence, 1416, 1445
Hints for biographers, 1418
?Sketches of national literature [of Greece], 1468
?Old china: Aeschylus, Waller, and Byron, 1504
?Sketches of national literature [of Latins], 1508
Pascal and his friends, 1509
Latest biographer of our poets [Robert Bell], 1549
Rural scenes of Pope and Milton, 1560
Shakspeare [De Quincey's art in *Ency. Brit.*], 1584
R. A. Willmott to Oliver Yorke, 1596
A summer holiday, 1598, 1634, 1647
Journal of an autumn in the country, 1605, 1619, 1625
History of a wet afternoon, 1660
Literary parallels: Dante, Virgil, Chaucer, Milton, 1665
?New edition of Campbell's *Poets,* 1672
?Ben Jonson and William Drummond, 1674
Notes in the margins of books, 1678
Characters of celebrated authors, 1688, 1717
May-day in country and town, 1690
A May-noon in a parlour window, 1695
Picture-galleries of England, 1735, 1745
[Thomas] Arnold and [William] Smyth on modern history, 1758
Objects and advantages of literature, 1769, 1776, 1795
Addison, 1842, 1854
Cloudy hours in summer days, 1865
History of a week, 1879
In Pope's garden: Bolingbroke, Arbuthnot, Swift, 1910
Copleston and Keble, 1944
Southey's sale and Southey's poems, 1959
Lectures of Professor Keble, 1963
A poet's friend [Norton Nicholls], 1987
Courses of English reading, 1994
Autumn leaves gathered up, 2006
Writings of the late John Foster, 2010
The pageant of literature, 2018
?Bishops, clergy, and people, 2028

Willmott, Robert Eldridge Aris (*continued*)
?The great [W. G.] Ward business, 2045
?Oakeley's *Letter to the Bishop of London,*
   2056
Poets, painters, and other shadows, 2080
Something between the showers, 2088
Greek and Roman domestic interiors, 2099
Drops from the leaves, 2109
Private life of the Romans, 2116
The Zoology of the English Poets, 2132
Cambridge studies, 2135
Our chimes for the New Year, 2144
Illustrative chapter on straws, 2156
Latin pamphleteers: Sallust, 2161
Newman, 2166
Civilisation, 2209
Life and Correspondence of John Foster,
   2219
Postscript about John Foster, 2254
Wit and Humour [by Leigh Hunt], 2272
Past, present, and coming, 2273
Homes and Haunts of the British Poets, 2290
Minutiae literariae, 2301
Cary, the translator of Dante, 2315
Book-love, 2352
Recent poetry [R. C. Trench, Aubrey De
   Vere], 2381
Life and remains of Sterling, 2421
Southey's *Life and Correspondence,* 2693
Letter: 2419
See: 287, 2042, 2275

Willoughby, Digby, 1845–1901, soldier adventurer. *DNB.*

French aggression in Madagascar, **FortR**
   2574

Willoughby, Edward Francis: see *Index,* I,
   1140.

Notes on the Slavonian races, **FM** 5969

The cholera-inoculation fallacy, **NC** 1182

Willoughby, Howard, 1839–1908, Australian
   journalist. Serle.

"The seamy side of Australia," **NC** 2089

Willoughby, Sir John Christopher, 1859–1918,
   army officer in So. Africa. *WWW.*

How we occupied Mashonaland, **FortR**
   3064

The Jameson expedition, **NC** 3134
Letter: 3150

Wills, Sir Alfred, 1828–1912, judge, Alpinist. *WWW, M at B.*

An Alpine storm, **FM** 4628

Should prisoners be examined **NC** 130

Wills, Charles James: see *Index,* I, 1140.

On things Persian, **FortR** 3815

Wills, Freeman Crofts: see *Index,* I, 1140.

Recreative evenings schools, **NC** 1301

Wills, J. T.; perhaps the John Taylor Wills,
   b.1857/58, barrister, in Foster and
   BMCat. (See *Index,* I, 1140.)

Emin Bey: Gordon's lieutenant, **FortR** 2544
New light on the Bahr-Gazal frontier, 4205

Willson, Henry Beckles: see *Index,* I, 1140.

Newfoundland's opportunity, **FortR** 4234
An overworked minister [Sec. of State for
   the Colonies], 4473

Wilmot, Sir Sydney Eardley: see Eardley-Wilmot, Sir Sydney.

Wilson, Miss A. M.; possibly the Miss Wilson,
   Dominican nun, in Gorman; possibly the
   A. M. Wilson in *Index,* I, 1140.

Catholic antiquities of Kent, **DR** 2522

Wilson, Alexander Johnstone: see *Index,* I,
   1140.

Position of English joint-stock banks, **FortR**
   1500
The eleventh plague of Egypt [European in-
   trigue], 1967
The budget: what Childers should do, 2025
A world in pawn, 2150, 2178
English bankers and the Bank of England
   reserve, 3027

Spanish struggles for liberty, **FM** 5496
Friendly Society legislation, 5587
Trading benefit, burial societies, post-office
   insurance, 5609
Sir Samuel Baker's expedition, 5655
The financial position of Egypt, 5825
British trade, in 13 installments from 5849
   to 5971
The game of Egyptian finance, 6171
Protectionism and free trade, 6456
And Indian romance [finance and public
   works], 6536

Wilson, Andrew, 1852–1912: see *Index,* I,
   1141.

Biology in schools, **FM** 5881

Wilson, Charles, 1817–1896, sheep farmer in
   Australia and later Alderman of Cheltenham. *Times,* Apr. 19, 1896, p. 6c.

Currency and prices, **NatR-II** 699
Currency, prices and finance, 734

Royal Commission on gold and silver, 804
Irish and other difficulties, 841
History and geography of our colonies, 853
The Australian aborigines, 885
West Australian constitution, 908
Proposed aggression on the Soudan, 908
A deficient currency and the natural result, 943
Remedial legislation for Ireland and India, 1033
Scramble for African territory, 1059
Currency and banking, 1059
Cyprus under British rule, 1131
Egyptian canals, 1142
Obelisks, round towers and sun-worship, 1154
The geology of the Channel, 1187
An honest and sufficient currency, 1361
How agriculture is affected by currency, 1409
Letters: 856, 862, 1029

Wilson, Charles Usher, divine in Cape Colony. BMCat., CCD/1902.

The situation in So. Africa, **NC** 3538

Wilson, Edward, of New So. Wales.

Australian federation, **NatR-II** 1727

Wilson, Edward, 1814–1878, Australian politician, journalist. DNB, Australian Ency.

Principles of representation, **FortR** 215, collab.

Wilson, Edward Daniel Joseph, 1814–1913, journalist. Crone, Annual Register/1913, p. 102.

Political crisis in the United States, **NC** 12
England and South Africa, 76
The Marshalate, 106
The "Friends of the Foreigner," 210
The caucus and its consequences, 232
What is a colonial governor? 251
The government and its critics, 278
An Irish ignis fatuus [Gladstone's Irish Church Act], 345
Irish politics and English parties, 387
The common-sense of Home Rule, 426
The clôture in parliament, 467
Unstable equilibrium of parties, 502
The present anarchy, 536
Confiscation and compensation, 606
Notice: 487

Wilson, F. Mary: see Parsons, Florence Mary.

Wilson, Sir Frederick William, 1844–1924,

journalist, M.P. *WWW*.

The agricultural position, **NC** 2902

Wilson, H.

Early Russian fiction, **DR** 2314

Wilson, Helen K.

The Rev. Jeremiah's thorn, **FM** 6461

Wilson, Henry Schütz: see *Index*, I, 1141.

A volume of French souvenirs, **FortR** 1841
Tasso, 2291
Switzerland as a holiday resort, 2498

The Pompeii of the Tannenwald, **NQM** 104

Lucrezia Borgia, **NC** 363
Wallenstein, 871
Vittoria Colonna, 1186
The story of Bianca Cappello, 2023
Frau Aja [Goethe's mother], 2564
Paris prisons during the Terror, 3344

Wilson, Herbert Wrigley: see *Index*, I, 1141.

The human animal in battle, **FortR** 3842
The struggle before us [for naval superiority], 3882
The working of arbitration, 3886
Naval and colonial policy of Germany, 3973
The Bering Sea dispute, 4031
England and Japan, 4097
Our navy against a coalition, 4129

Trafalgar and to-day, **NatR-II** 1939
The downfall of Greece, 2026
Front bench invertebrates, 2154
The truth about the *Maine* disaster, 2179
An Anglo-Russian understanding? 2201
The policy of jingoism, 2245
The invasion of England, 2317
Rapprochement between France and Germany, 2333
Coming storm in the Far East, 2377
Democracy and the [Boer] War, 2378
Causes of reverse [in South Africa], 2401
The man in the cabinet, 2415
First lessons of the [Boer] War, 2425
Great Britain's debt to Japan, 2437
The story of the Boer War, 2477
"They see not" [on military preparedness], 2479
Japan and the new Far East, 2492
Reconstruction or catastrophe? 2516

Protection of our commerce in war, **NC** 2879
Forthcoming naval review, 3122
Growth of the world's armaments, 3281
The naval situation, 3452
Are we misled about the fleet? 3630

Wilson, James, 1832–1907, High Sheriff of Currygrave. Burke's *Ireland*.

Spoliation of Irish landlords, **NatR-II** 2017

Wilson, Sir James, 1853–1926, Indian civil servant in Punjab. *WWW*.

History of an Indian district [Punjab], **NatR-II** 370

Wilson, John, author of *Studies*: see *Index*, I, 1141.

M. Guizot's *Own Time*, **FortR** 436

Wilson, John, 1785–1854: see *Index*, I, 1142.

See: **FM** 364

Wilson, Robert, writer on the medical education of woman. *BMCat*.

Aesculapia victrix, **FortR** 2407

Wilson, Robert William Rankine, b.1845, barrister. *M at B*.

Letter: **NatR-II** 1238

Wilson, Sir Samuel, 1832–1895, Australian politcian. Boase.

Imperial federation, **NatR-II** 234

A scheme for imperial federation, **NC** 1116

Windsor, Arthur Lloyd, c.1833–1913, Australian journalist, once lived at Clifton. Serle.

Goldsmith, **DR** 849

de Windt, Harry: see De Windt, Harry.

Wingfield, Lewis Strange, 1842–1891, traveller, actor, painter. *DNB*.

Realism behind the footlights, **FortR** 2156

Wingfield, Sir Mervyn Edward, 7th Viscount Powerscourt, 1836–1904, a Lord Justice of Ireland in 1902. Burke, *WWW*.

Irish education, **NC** 1234, 2886
Casual notes about Ireland, 1687

Wingfield, William, 1813–1874, Catholic convert in 1845. Newman, *L&D*, XI, index.

Turks and Christians in Albania, **Ram** 571

Wintle, Robert Wintle, b.1825, named Robert Wintle Gilbert, substituted surname of Wintle in 1851, barrister. Foster, *M at B*.

Letters: **NatR-II** 267, 497

Wirgman, Venerable Augustus Theodore,

1846–1917, archdeacon of Port Elizabeth. *WWW*.

The South African conspiracy, **NC** 3587
The Boers and the native question, 3632

Wise, Bernhard Ringrose: see *Index*, I, 1144.

Reminiscences of the Oxford Union, **NatR-II** 1988
Commonwealth of Australia, 2330

Wise, John Richard de Capel: see *Index*, I, 1145.

The clouds and the poor, **FortR** 45

Wiseman, Nicholas Patrick Stephen, 1802–1865, Cardinal Archbishop of England, owner-ed. of *Dub. Rev. DNB*.

The Oxford controversy, **DR** 11
Philosophy of art, 18 collab.
Religion in Italy, 19
Fourth of October [1835: anti-Catholic demonstration], 24
Persecution of Catholics in Prussia, 29
Catholic versions of Scripture, 43
French Catholic literature, 49, 73, 161
De Jorio on Italian gesticulation, 51
High Church theory of authority, 53
Early Italian scientific academies, 57
The Vaudois, 65 collab.
Pugin on ecclesiastical architecture, 66
Montalembert's *St. Elizabeth*, 67
Tracts for the Times, 87, 108, 145
Catholic missions, 89
The Roman Forum, 97
The Holy See in So. America, 105
Italian guides and tourists, 119
Froude's *Remains*, 132
Geraldine: religious institutions, 136
Church architecture of middle ages, 149
Catholicity in England, 169
Persecution in the East, 178
So. American, Spanish and Portuguese ecclesiastical literature, 181
Christian inscription at Autun, 200
Catholic and Anglican churches, 230
Pope Boniface VIII, 240
The Anglican system, 247
Protestanism of the Anglican Church, 258
Ecclesiastical organization, 266
Prayer and prayer-books, 273
The Catholic Church in Russia, 282
Superficial travelling: Dickens, Mrs. Trollope, 283
National holydays, 291
Russia in 1842, 293
Minor rites and offices, 304, 337
Ancient and modern Catholicity, 314
Newman's *Sermons*, 317

Wolf, Lucien (*continued*)

Count Lamsdorff's first failure [in China], 4528

The anti-Jewish agitation, **NC** 555

Wolfe-Barry, Sir John Wolfe: see *Index*, I, 1145.

"Ordinary business principles," **NC** 3694

Wolff, Sir Henry Drummond Charles: see *Index*, I, 1145.

The state of the opposition, **FortR** 1968 collab.
See: 2163

Wolff, Henry William: see *Index*, I, 1145.

Château Malbrouk, **NatR-II** 1092
Hagenau and Trifels, 1116
The early ancestors of our Queen, 1244
Voltaire and King Stanislas, 1289
Suggestion to the coming parish councils, 1639

Wolffsohn, Mrs. Lily: see *Index*, I, 1145, and II, App. A.

The Strozzi, a family history, **NatR-II** 976

The making of a shrine, **NC** 2707

Salvatore Farina, **ScotR** 182
Songs from South Italy, 206
Julius Wolff, 244
More popular songs of Italy, 270
Poetry of Rudolph Baumbach, 305

Wolseley, Sir Garnet Joseph: see *Index*, I, 1145.

Courage, **FortR** 2740
Military genius, 2742
The negro as a soldier, 2770
War, 2779
Is a soldier's life worth living? 2816
The French Revolution and war, 2829
See: 2434, 2569, 2665

France as a military power in 1870 and 1878, **NC** 121
England as a military power in 1854 and 1878, 145
Long and short service. 570

Woltmann, Alfred Friedrich Gottfried Albert, 1841–1880, writer on painting. *ADB.*

Holbein at the National Portrait Exhibition, **FortR** 308

Wood, Alexander, b.1844/45, F.S.A., antiquary. Foster, *BMCat.*

Western Sussex, **DR** 1748, 1768

Wood, Arthur F.; prob. the Arthur Francis Wood in *BMCat.*

Old-age pensions in France, **NC** 3504

Wood, Sir Charles Lindley: see *Index*, I, 1146.

Christian reunion, **NatR-II** 1805

The reunion of Christendom, **NC** 2936
Present crisis in the Church of England, 3414

Wood, Evelyn: see Wood, Sir Henry Evelyn.

Wood, Granville Francis, S.J., 1818–1858, naval officer. *Records of Eng. Province of Soc. of Jesus,* ed. Henry Foley (London, 1883), p. 857.

A visit to Loyola, **Ram** 521

Wood, Sir Henry Evelyn, 1838–1919, field-marshal. *DNB.*

The Crimea in 1854, and 1894, **FortR** 3553, 3562, 3580, 3593, 3606

Wood, Sir Henry Trueman, 1845–1929, historian. *WWW.*

Exhibitions, **NC** 1336
Chicago and its Exhibition, 2190

Wood, John George: see *Index*, I, 1146.

The dulness of museums, **NC** 1381

Wood, Lady Mary Susan Félicie (Lindsay): see *Index*, I, 1146, and II, App. A.

Cavour on the repeal of the union [of England and Ireland], **NC** 2398

Wood, William: see *Index*, I, 1146.

The just punishments of heretics, **NC** 3315

Woodberry, George Edward, 1855–1930, American critic. *DAB.*

Fortunes of literature under the American Republic, **FortR** 1802

Woodburne, George Burgess Lancaster, b.1855, d.1910 or before, barrister. Gorman, *M at B.*

The Quarterly Review and our clergy, **DR** 2139
The friars in Oxford, 2364

Imperial federation and home rule, **NatR-II** 323

Politics, A.D. 1705–1707, 811

Woods, Pasha, Sir Henry Felix, 1843–1929, Admiral in Ottoman Navy. *WWW.*

The armed strength of Turkey, **NC** 1162

Woods, Margaret Louisa (Bradley): see *Index,* I, 1146.

Girlhood of [Lady Stanley of Alderley], **FortR** 3921

French views of an English university, **NC** 3392

Woods, Samuel, 1846–1915, M.P., organizer of miners' unions. *WW/*1916 and 1917 (obit.).

Labour leaders, **NC** 2319

Woolner, Thomas, 1825–1892, sculptor, poet. *DNB.*

A beggar-poet [James Chambers], **NC** 1419

Wootton, A. C., d.1910. *LCCat., Surgeon Index/*2nd s.

Crickets in 1899, **NC** 3562

Wordsworth, Charles, 1806–1892, Bishop of St. Andrews, New Testament reviser. *DNB.*

A chapter of autobiography, **FortR** 2054

Pindar and athletics, **NatR-II** 706

Scotch disestablishment and "papal aggression," **NC** 147

Law of unity in Christian church, 173

Worsfold, William Basil, 1858–1939, barrister, editor. *WWW.*

The Barren Ground of Northern Canada, **FortR** 3278

Social traits of the Dutch in Java, 3337

The gold era in South Africa, 3762

Charlotte Brontë, 4224

Beaconsfield and Imperial unity, **NatR-II** 1176

The poetry of D. G. Rossetti, **NC** 2442

Worsley, Henry, 1829–1893, divine, historian. Boase.

Methods of historical inquiry, **DR** 1769, 2014

Trans: 614

See: 610 collab.

Worth, John

Lives and loves of North American birds, **NC** 2376

Worthington, James William, 1799/1800– 1879, ed. *For. Quart. Rev.* Boase.

?South Australia, **FQR** 585

Ranke's *History of the Popes of Rome,* 592

Christian Doctrines and Modern Science, 632

Wortley, Jane Stuart: see Stuart-Wortley, Jane.

Wratislaw, Albert Henry: see *Index,* I, 1147.

How history is sometimes written, **FM** 5733

The Bloody Parliament of Wilemow, 5851

Wraxall, Sir Frederic Charles Lascelles, 1828– 1865, misc. writer. *DNB.*

Six months at Kertch, **FM** 3588

Wren, Walter: see *Index,* I, 1147, and II, App. A.

Military education, **FortR** 3116

Public schools and private "coaches," **NC** 2056

Wrench, Frederick Stringer, 1849–1926, agriculturist. *WWW.*

Austrian stud farms, **NC** 2198

Improvement of Irish hunters, 2548

Wright, Almroth Edward, 1861–1947, prof. of pathology. *WWW.*

Colour-blindness, **NC** 2197

Colour-shadows, 2752

Wright, Charles Henry Hamilton, 1836–1909, Hebraist, theologian. *DNB.*

Babylonian account of the Deluge, **NC** 677

The site of paradise, 771

The Jews and human sacrifice, 920

Stamping out Protestantism in Russia, 1797

Some great Jewish rabbis, 2224

Wright, Sir Charles Theodore Hagberg, 1862– 1940, librarian. *DNB.*

Russian sects, **NatR-II** 1055

Russian universities, **ScotR** 367

Wright, Thomas, the "Journeyman Engineer": see *Index,* I, 1147.

English republicanism, **FM** 5211

Wright, Thomas (*continued*)
English working classes and Paris Commune,
5219
Condition of the working classes, 5245
Mis-education, 5369
Education and boots, 6346

Concerning the unknown public, **NC** 820
Our craftsmen, 1329

Wright, Thomas, 1810–1877: see *Index,* I, 1147.

French and English "Chansons de Geste,"
FQR 371
Anglo-Latin poets, twelfth century, 382
Michel: French metrical romances, 390
Guizot's Commission Historique and the
English Record Commission, 403
Friar Rush and the frolicsome elves, 418
Diez and Raynouard on the neo-Latin lan-
guages, 452
Grimm's *German Mythology,* 494
Medieval stories, 843
Comic and satirical literature in the middle
ages, 856
On Monkish legends and miracles, 867
Satirical literature of the Reformation, 884
Ancient Scottish life, 895
See: 763

Old English political songs, **FM** 641
Sir Harris Nicolas and Joseph Ritson, 693
National fairy mythology of England, 713
Europe during the middle ages, 772
Popular superstition of modern Greece, 789
On Anglo-Saxon poetry, 840
Ker's *Nursery Rhymes and Proverbs,* 858
Conquest of Ireland by Anglo-Normans, 916
On Anglo-Norman poetry, 970
The Story of Eustace the Monk, 1035

Wright, William Aldis, 1831–1914, Shakespearean and Biblical scholar. *DNB.*

?Robert Herrick, **OxCam** 48

Wrixon, Sir Henry John, 1839–1913, Australian statesman. *Australian Ency.*

The employment of women, **DR** 1020

Wurm, Christian Friedrich, 1803–1859, German historian, journalist. *ADB.*

Dr. Wurm on *The Portfolio,* **FQR** 397

Wyatt, Harold Frazer, 1858/59–1925, writer
on naval and imperial matters. *WWW,*
Foster.

The ethics of Empire, **NC** 3091
War as the test of national value, 3417

Wyatt, Sydney

The proposed miners' federation, **NatR-II,**
949
The mining federations, 1001

Wyllie, John William Shaw: see *Index,* I, 1148.

Masterly inactivity, **FortR** 639
Mischievous activity, 664

Wyndham, Sir Charles, 1837–1919, actor-manager. *DNB.*

Actor-managers, **NC** 1891

Wyndham, Francis Merrik, 1838–1919, R.C.
priest. *Tablet,* Nov. 22, 1919, p. 686;
Foster.

The Maid of Orleans, **DR** 2258

Wyndham, George: see *Index,* I, 1148.

Adventure in Elizabethan literature, **FortR**
4202

Wyndham, Percy Scawen, 1835–1911, M.P.
WWW.

Town and country labourers, **NC** 3545

Wyndham-Quin, Countess Eva Constance Aline
(Bourke), d.1940, wife of 5th Earl of
Dunraven, Burke.

Sport in Nepal, **NC** 1729
A trip to Travancore, 2165

Wyndham-Quin, Windham Thomas: see Quin,
Windham Thomas Wyndham-.

Wynn-Carrington, Charles Robert, 1st Earl
Carrington, 1843–1928, governor of New
So. Wales. Burke.

The land and the labourers, **NC** 3431
Note: 2678

Wynne, Frederick Richards: see *Index,* I, 1148.

Must it be "all or nothing" [in matters of
faith]? **NC** 795

Wynne, George Robert, 1838–1912, divine.
WWW.

The clergy in modern dogmatism and
thought, **FortR** 223
The theory of missionary effort, 349

Wynter, Andrew: see *Index,* I, 1148.

The massacre of the innocents [murder of
infants in London], **FortR** 229

Night and morning on the Thames, **FM** 2339
The post-office, 2695
A gossip about the Lakes, 2760
Preserved meats, 2956
Training schools of Price's Patent Candle Company, 2990
A fortnight in North Wales, 2995

Wenham Lake ice, 3056
New Crystal Palace at Sydenham, 3159
London stout, 3281

Wyse, Sir Thomas, 1791–1862, politician, diplomat. *DNB.*

Education in England, **DR** 23

Y

Yate, Arthur Campbell: see *Index*, I, 1148.

Persia as an ally, **NatR-II** 393

Yates, Edmund Hodgson, 1831–1894, novelist, editor. *DNB.*

About Kensington Gore, **FortR** 2438
Bygone shows, 2460
Letter: 2655

Yeatman-Biggs, Huyshe Wolcott, 1845–1922, divine. *WWW.*

Reconstruction of diocese of Rochester, **NC** 3259

Yeats, William Butler: see *Index*, I, 1149.

The broken gates of death, **FortR** 4099
Irish witch doctors, 4507

The prisoners of the [ancient] gods [many who die, according to Irish peasant beliefs], **NC** 3228

Yeo, Gerald Francis: see *Index*, I, 1149, and II, App. A.

Vivisection in England, **FortR** 1893

Yeo, Isaac Burney: see *Index*, I, 1149, and II, App. A.

On stimulants, **FortR** 1351
Sea or mountain? 1385
Winter quarters, 1637
Health resorts in the Pyrenees, 1719
Health resorts of the western Riviera, 1883
Wintering in the snow, 1913

Food accessories, **NC** 1246
English and foreign spas, 1307
Long life and how to attain it, 1524
The new cure for "growing too fat," 1581
On change of air, 1741
Medicine and society, 2856

Yerburgh, Robert Armstrong, 1853–1916, M.P. *WWW.*

National granaries, **NatR-II** 1854
Our duty towards China, 2334
Count Mouravieff's triumph ["open door" policy in China], 2462

Yorke, Alexander Campbell, 1852–1925, divine. Burke under Hardwicke.

The jackeroo [immigrant to Australia], **NC** 3471

Yorke, Reginald Somers, 1854–1916, customs official. Venn.

Recollections of Wei Hai Wei, with suggestions for a policy in the Far East, **FortR** 4143

Young, Sir Charles Lawrence, Bart., 1839–1887, barrister. Burke.

Allan Glayne: told at Gerard's Chase, **NQM** 85

Young, D., writer on agriculture. *BMCat.*

The Dalmeny experiments, **NC** 3561

Young, Sir Fredrick, 1817–1913, K.C.M.G., vice-president Royal Colonial Institute. *WWW.*

Commercial union of the Empire, **NC** 2954

Young, John, 1835–1902: see *Index*, I, 1149.

Scottish university reform, **ScotR** 196

Young, Norwood: see *Index*, I, 1149.

Gambling at Monte Carlo, **NatR-II** 1088
Systems of gambling, 1222
What the Labour Party may achieve, 1314

Young, Robert b.1858, ed. *Kobe Chronicle*, Japan. *LCCat.*, see *NC* no. 3015.

Commercial morality in Japan, **NC** 3015
The foreign residents in Japan, 3158

Young, Stanley, translator. *BMCat.*

Cyrano de Bergerac, **NC** 3320

Young, Thomas, 1773–1829, physician, Egyptologist. *DNB.*

Notice: **FQR** 53

Younghusband, Sir Francis Edward: see *Index,* I, 1149.

A plea for the control of China, **NatR–II** 2507

The future of Manchuria, **NC** 3261

Younghusband, George John, 1859–1944, army officer. *WWW.*

The invasion of India by Russia, **NC** 2387
Permanent pacification of the Indian frontier, 3240

Yoxall, Sir James Henry, 1857–1925, educationist. *DNB.*

British seamen for British ships, **NC** 3402 collab.

Yriarte, Charles: see *Index,* I, 1150.

Eugène Piot, **FortR** 4347

Le journal d'Eugène Delacroix, **NC** 2847
E. Meissonier, 3291

Z

Zeller, Eduard: see *Index,* I, 1150.

A heathen apocalypse [sources of apocalyptic literature], **NC** 701

Zimmern, Alice: see *Index,* I, 1150.

Plato and theosophy, **NatR-II** 549

Zimmern, Helen, see *Index,* I, 1150.

Eleonora Duse, **FortR** 4464

A Gallician novelist [Leopold von Sacher-Masoch], **FM** 6204
A Swiss novelist [Gottfried Keller], 6273
Jewish home life, 6394
Three trips to Tartarus, 6531

A popular German author [J. V. Scheffel], **NatR-II** 168
Berthold Auerbach, 717
A Styrian novelist [Peter Rosegger], 1211

Count Giacomo Leopardi, **NQM** 120
Trans: 128

Trans: **ScotR** 467

Zincke, Foster Barham: see *Index,* I, 1150.

Channel Islands and land tenure, **FortR** 1219
The peasants of the Limagne, 1522, 1532
Pauperism and territorialism, 1587
The fruits of territorialism, 1683
Gimel on the division of land in France, 1708

Mr. Caird and land-owning cultivators, 1870
Letter: 1698

The United States of America [by Sir Charles Lyell], **FM** 2727
Homer and the Homeric Age [by Gladstone], 3812, 3823
Sexagenarian mountaineering, 5954

Zissler, Louis

Letter: **NatR-II** 1139

Zola, Émile, 1840–1902, French novelist. *Grand Larousse.*

Parisian middle classes [from *History of a Family*], **ScotR** 34

Zucchi, Maria; possibly Mary Percy (Falkiner) Zucchi, in *Index,* I, 891, under Falkiner, Miss M.P., and II, App. A.

The Misericordia of Florence, **DR** 2430

Zuylen van Nyevelt, Baroness Susette Ida van, 1851–1932. *Titled Nobility*; *Nederland's Adelsboek* (Gravenhage), 1904 ed., p. 616; 1935 ed., p. 528.

Austria, **NatR-II** 1201
Elizabeth Stuart and her family in Holland, 1259
The Dutch peasantry, 1295
Exile of the Marquise de Falaiseau, 1441

PART C

INDEX OF PSEUDONYMS, INCLUDING INITIALS

Index of Pseudonyms, Including Initials

All pseudonyms that appear in the text of the periodical, whether solved or not, are in the following index, but not those in publishers' lists even though they may be mentioned in the entries for Part A. Furthermore, because we subscribe to the notion that to some degree a pseudonym conceals the real name, an author's initials at the end of an article or a story, or of an introductory note or postscript, are not treated as pseudonyms if his real name is printed at the start of the item or on the cover of the issue. But if it is printed only in the table of contents, drawn up later at the conclusion of the half year, the temporary concealment is sufficient to warrant placing the initials in the following list. It may be added that fictitious names are not considered pseudonyms: therefore Tom Jenkins ap Jones ap Barnacle in *Fraser's* no. 1607 is not indexed. This is also true of *purely* descriptive names: "an eye-witness" in an article entitled "An account, by an eye-witness, of the wreck of the *Amphitrite*" (*Fraser's* no. 623) is not included below. But where an article entitled "The annexation of the Transvaal" (*Fraser's* no. 5955) is signed at the end "An Eye-Witness," we take this to be partly descriptive but partly secretive, and enter it as a pseudonym. The distinction, however, is imprecise.

In the case of initials, the entry may be under either the last or the first letter. F.R.S., for example, will appear under S. (S.,F.R.) if the initials are those of a name, or are thought to be, but under F. (F.R.S.) if they stand for a title like Fellow of the Royal Society, or seem to. In the latter case the initials are placed after the initials for names. Likewise, pseudonymous initials like A.B.C.D. or X.Y.Z., or the initials of a pseudonym, like T.W.H. for The Whig Hater, are placed under the first letter after the initials for names. Greek or Hebrew initials and names, together with sigla, will be found at the end of Part C.

The numbers are the code numbers in the periodicals indicated by the letter abbreviations in bold type. No distinction is here made, as it is in Part B, between full-fledged articles or stories and short notices, translations, etc. That information is in the entry for Part A. Parentheses surrounding a code number indicate that that particular item is not signed with the pseudonym, but that there is good evidence to show that it could have been. For example, the pseudonymous signature of a three-part article may appear only at the end of Part III, but all three code numbers are placed after the pseudonym, the first two in parentheses. A list of numbers following an unsolved pseudonym does not necessarily imply a common authorship. "Conservative M.P." below, with six entries in the *National Review* from March 1894 to July 1900, may well be two or more men; but "A Conservative Journalist," writing in the same periodical in August 1885 and July 1886, suggests one writer.

In the case of solved pseudonyms, the evidence is given in Part A under the item or items cited. For information about the authors, including the full name of many whose first initials only are given, see Part B above.

Abbreviations:

DR:	*The Dublin Review*		**NC:**	*The Nineteenth Century*
FortR:	*The Fortnightly Review*		**OxCam:**	*The Oxford and Cambridge*
FM:	*Fraser's Magazine*			*Magazine*
NatR-II:	*The National Review*, 1883–		**Ram:**	*The Rambler*
	1900		**ScotR:**	*The Scottish Review*, 1882–
NQM:	*The New Quarterly Magazine*			1900

A

A.—**FM** 1987—**R. A. Willmott**

A.—**FM** 6100

A.—**Ram** 1010, 1029—**Thomas Arnold**, 1823–1900

A.—**Ram** 1073—**J. D. Acton, L. v. Meyer,** and **Richard Simpson**

A.—**Ram** 1101—**J. D. Acton**

A.,A.—**DR** 2425, 2438—**Antony Allaria**

A.,A.—**FM** 3631—**Augustus Andrews?**

A.,A.—**FM** 5395—**Alexander Allardyce**

A.,C.—**DR** 2606, 2618

A.,F.—**DR** 2594, 2628, 2651

A.,F.—**FM** 5636—**Frederick Arnold**

A.,H.—**FM** 5468

A.,H.—**Ram** 1093—**H. N. Oxenham**

A.,J.—**DR** 2606

A.,J.E.—**FM** 3916—**J. E. Addison**

A.,P.—**DR** 2699

A.,R.A.—**FM** 5608, 5626—**R. A. Arnold**

A.,S.—**FM** 2558, 2629, 3740, 4618—**Sarah Austin**

A.,T.J.—**FM** 3929, 3938, 3982, 4007—**Thomas James Arnold**

A.,W.—**FM** 4669, 4697, 4752—**William Allingham**

A.,W.D.—**FM** 3373, 3453, 3496, 3519, 3547, 3654, 3818—**William Delafield Arnold**

A.,W.S.—**FM** 4039

A.B.C.—**FortR** 4055

A.-M.,G.R.—**FM** 5508—**G. R. Aberigh-Mackay**

A.M.D.G.[Ad majorem Dei gloriam]—**Ram** 1101—**Frederick Oakeley?**

Absentee, Homeward-Bound, An—**FM** 1448, 1467

Academicus—**FortR** 4132

Active Politician, An—**NatR-II** 81

Adalet—**NC** 1907, 1973, 2245

Administrator—**FortR** 4416

Afrikander—**FortR** 3334

Afrikander, An—**NatR-II** 2155—**Melius de Villiers**

Alabama Man, An—**FM** 3025

Alberti, Conrad—**NatR-II** 622—**Konrad Sittenfeld**

Alchemist, An—**FM** 1314

American, An— **FM** 4657—**M. D. Conway**

American, An—**FM** 5093—**James Jackson Jarves?**

American, An—**FM** 5351—**Nathan Sheppard**

American Abolitionist, An—**FM** 4504, 4557 —**Moncure D. Conway**

Anglo-African—**NatR-II** 969, 993, 1108

Anglo-Batavian, An—**FM** 4093, 4145

Anglomane—**FM** 1988, 2050, 2119—**Antonio Gallenga**

Anglo-New Zealander—**NatR-II** 473

Anglo-Parisian Journalist, An—**FortR** 4203,

4269, 4309

Annotator of "An Irish Landlord's Budget," The—**NatR-II** 1630

Apprentice of the Law, An—**FM** 1378, 1413, 1456, 1499, 1539, 1615, 1651, 1697, 1707, 1786, 1998, 2038, 2063, 2077, 2090, 2141, 2153, 2281—**P. W. Banks**

Aquarius—**NatR-II** 1077—**Lowis d'Aquilar Jackson**

Architect, An—**FM** 5212, 5244

Ardersier-Macdonald, Charles Oliver, Esq., of Craig-Houlakim, near Whistle-Binkie, N.B.—**FM** 3549—**A. K. H. Boyd**

Armitt, Annie [may be a maiden name]—**ScotR** 73, 374—**Annie M. Harris**

Artisan, An—**FM** 5427

Atkins, T[ommy]—**NatR-II** 2148

Atticus, Herodes—**NatR-II** 105

Audax—**NatR-II** 353

Ausonius—**FortR** 3779

Author of *A Dead Man's Diary*, The—**FortR** 3055—**Coulson Kernahan**

Author of *A First Friendship*, The—**FM** 4434 to 4614 in 21 installments—**Henry Jackson**

Author of *Agnes Tremorne*, The—**FM** 4238—**Isa Blagden**

Author of *A Study in Colour*, The—**NatR-II**, 1619, 1652—**Augusta Zelia Fraser**

Author of "Catarina in Venice," The—**FM** 4173, 4184, 4193, 4203, 4213, 4223—**John Skelton**

Author of "Consolations," The—**FM** 6420, 6430, 6446, 6457—**Edith Simcox**

Author of *Digby Grand*, The—**FM** 3170 to 3293 in 12 installments; 3432 to 3480 in 6 installments—**G. J. Whyte-Melville**

Author of *Digby Grand, The Interpreter*, etc. —**FM** 4055 to 4167 in 12 installments— **G. J. Whyte-Melville**

Author of *Elizabeth and her German Garden* —**NatR-II** 2483—**Mary Annette Russell**

Author of "First and Last," &c., The—**FM** 221—**William Mudford**

Author of *Flemish Interiors*, The—**FM** 5349, 5364, 5459, 5739, 6215—**Julia C. B. Byrne**

Author of "German Home Life"—**FM** 5632 —**Marie von Bothmer**

Author of *Gheel, the City of the Simple*, The—**FM** 5783—**Julia C. B. Byrne**

Author of *Ginx's Baby*, The—**FM** 5187— **John E. Jenkins**

Author of *Gleanings in Natural History*—**FM** 650—**Edward Jesse**

Author of *Greater Britain*—**FortR** 2648, 2656, 2665, 2675, 2685, 2694, 2704, 2798— **Charles Wentworth Dilke**

Author of *Guy Livingstone*, The—**FM** 3836 to 3911 in 8 installments—**George Alfred Lawrence**

Author of *Guy Livingstone, Sword and Gown*, etc., The—**FM** 4134 to 4227 in 10 installments—**George Alfred Lawrence**

Author of *Headlong Hall*, The—**FM** 3655, 3717, 3795, 3958 to 4046 in 9 installments— **Thomas Love Peacock**

Author of "Humours of the North," The— **FM** 1371—**R. P. Gillies**

Author of "India in Mourning," The—**FM** 3699, 3715, 3806—**W. D. Arnold**

Author of *John Halifax, Gentleman*—**FM** 3501, 4695—**Dinah M. Mulock**

Author of *Life in Our Villages*, The—**FortR** 4219, 4252—**George F. Millin**

Author of "Literary Legislators," The—**FM** 2343, 2354, 2362—**G. H. Francis**

Author of *Mademoiselle Mori*, The—**FM** 4018 —**Margaret Roberts**

Author of "Meg of Elibank," The—**FM** 3586, 3607, 3680, 3690, 3714, 3724, 3738, 3794, 3804—**Henrietta Keddie**

Author of "O'Hanlon and his Wife," The— **FM** 1122, 1348—**R. P. Gillies**

Author of *Old Bailey Experience*, The—**FM** 640, 649, 691, 698, 756—**Charles Wall**

Author of *Patty*, The—**NQM** 36, 69—**Katharine S. Macquoid**

Author of *Paul Ferroll*, The—**FM** 4574— **Caroline Clive**

Author of "Premier and President," The—**FM** 5406—**Nathan Sheppard**

Author of *St. Augustine: an Historical Study*, The—**DR** 2232, 2285, 2381—**Philip Burton**

Author of *Sam Slick the Clockmaker, The Attaché*, etc., The—**FM** 2190 to 2398 in 12 installments—**T. C. Haliburton**

Author of *Sir Andrew Wylie*, The—**FM** 10, 29—**John Galt**

Author of *Stumpingford*, The—**Ram** 759, 765, 772, 777, 784, 792—**Daniel Parsons**

Author of *The Annals of the Parish*, The—**FM** 599, 635—**John Galt**

Author of "The Autobiography of Salmo Salar," The—**FM** 4881, 4910, 4932—**George Rooper**

Author of *The Bachelor of the Albany*, The— **FM** 3215—**M. W. Savage**

Author of *The Broken Tryst*, The—**FM** 6449 **Mary Gleed Tuttiett**

Author of "The Constitution of Sweden," The —**FM** 6074

Author of *The Life of Goethe*, The—**FM** 3799 —**George Henry Lewes**

Author of *The Log of the Water-Lily*, The— **FM** 3625—**R. B. Mansfield**

Author of "The Schoolmaster's Experience in Newgate," The—**FM** 515, 593—**Charles Wall**

Author of *The Upper Ten Thousand*, The—

FM 3308, 3348, 3364, 3388, 3409—**Charles Astor Bristed**

Author of *The Wreck of the "Grosvenor,"* The —**FM** 6489 to 6544 in 8 installments—**William Clark Russell**

Author of *Vera*, The—**NatR-II** 468—**Charlotte Dempster**

Author of *Woman's Mission*, The—**FM** 2442 —**Sarah Lewis**

Author of *Yeast* and *The Saint's Tragedy*, The —**FM** 2923 to 3084 in 16 installments— **Charles Kingsley**

Average Liberal Unionist, An—**NatR-II** 1046

B

B.—**DR** 1724, 1745, 1756, 1767, 1802, 2266, 2335, 2358, 2373, 2400, 2425, 2438, 2475, 2720—**Alfons Bellesheim**

B.—**FortR** 3154

B.—**FM** 3413, 4996, 5414, 5678, 5794

B.—**FM** 4852, 4914, 5438, 5822—**Robert Edward Bartlett**

B.—**FM** 5948—**J. G. Bertram**

B.—**NatR-II** 325—**Algernon Borthwick?**

B.—**Ram** 1095

(b.)—**FM** 530, 553, 613

B.,A.—**NatR-II** 1273

B.,A.—**DR** 2497—**Alfons Bellesheim**

B.,A.—**FM** 3028—**Adolphus Bernays**

B.,A.—**FM** 4538

B.,A.K.H.—**FM** 3671, 3688, 3701, 3720, 3747, 3763, 3767, 3790, 3803, 3810, 3820, 3837, 3856, 3877, 3892, 3926, 3936, 3949, 3975, 3988, 4006, 4025, 4045, 4070, 4088, 4098, 4129, 4136, 4148, 4158, 4175, 4195, 4225, 4243, 4265, 4282, 4299, 4321, 4368, 4385, 4405, 4441, 4463, 4499, 4519, 4592, 4606, 4624, 4631, 4685, 4724, 4736, 4771, 4963, 4999, 5012, 5141, 5271, 5329, 5378, 5386, 5401, 5462, 5495, 5559, 5590, 5799, 5901, 5906, 5962, 5970, 5982, 5989, 6016, 6036, 6065, 6082, 6203, 6231, 6378, 6384, 6459, 6466, 6540—**Andrew Kennedy Hutchinson Boyd**

B.,A.R.—**FM** 3523, 3712, 3775

B.,A.S.—**DR** 2663, 2709

B.,A.S.—**FM** 6158

B.,C.—**DR** 2438, 2720

B.,C.—**FM** 5370—**Camille Barrère**

B.,C.A.—**FM** 3355, 3364, 3388, 3409, 3422, 3564—**Charles Astor Bristed**

B.,C.D.—**FM** 3324, 3345, 3465, 3488, 3525, 3536—**Charles David Badham**

B.,C.V.—**DR** 2412—**Christian van den Biesen**

B.,C.v.d.—**DR** 2475, 2531, 2594, 2638, 2651, 2663—**Christian van den Biesen**

B.,E.—**DR** 2019, 2029, 2520, 2543, 2606, 2628, 2651, 2674, 2720—**Edmund Bishop**

B.,E.—**DR** 2459

B.,E.C.—**DR** 2606, 2618, 2651, 2699, 2709, —**E. C. Butler**

B.,E.H.—**DR** 2663

B.,E.V.—**NatR-II** 2292—**Eleanor Vere Gordon Boyle**

B.,F.—**DR** 2663, 2699, 2729—**Francis Bacchus**

B.,G.—**FM** 4694—**Gustave A. Bergenroth**

B.,G.F. [George Fitz-Boodle]—**FM** 1772— **W. M. Thackeray**

B.,G.G.—**FM** 3785

B.,G.S.F. [George Savage Fitz-Boodle]—**FM** 1785, 1796, 1885, 2128—**W. M. Thackeray**

B.,G.—**T.C.C.** [Trinity College Cambridge]— **FM** 3435—**George Brimley**

B.,H.—**DR** 2728—**Henry Bellingham**

B.,H.W.—**DR** 1397—**H. W. Brewer**

B.,I.—**FM** 4238—**Isa Blagden**

B.,J.—**DR** 2211—**James Britten?**

B.,J.—**NatR-II** 836

B.,J.G.—**FM** 5613—**James Glass Bertram**

B.,J.H. [error for B.,T.H.]—**FM** 4286—**Thomas Henry Bullock**

B.,J.W.—**FM** 3574

B.,J.Z.—**FM** 3640, 3665, 3723—**John Zephaniah Bell**

B.,L.M.—**NatR-II** 1137—**Mrs. L. M. Battine**

B.,P.C.—**FM** 4308, 4317, 4327, 4343, 4353, 4366, 4391, 4477, 4490, 4586, 4648, 4776— **Patrick C. Beaton**

B.,R.—**DR** 2638, 2686

B.,R.—**FM** 3913—possibly **Richard Beamish**

B.,R.E.—**FM** 5808, 5939, 5976, 6005, 6023, 6033, 6053, 6107, 6176, 6183—**Robert Edward Bartlett**

B.,S.—**FM** 4878—**Stephen Buckland**

B.,T.A.—**DR** 2006, 2651

B.,T.E.—**DR** 1756—**Thomas Edward Bridgett**

B.,T.H.—**FM** 4218, 4286, 4320, 4453, 4561, 4739—**T. H. Bullock**

B.,W.—**DR** 2485, 2497—**William Barry**

B.,W.—**FM** 4759, 5665

B.,W.R.—**DR** 1756, ?2729—**William Robert Brownlow**

B.,W.R.—**NatR-II** 430—**W. R. Browne**

B.-E.,M.—**FM** 5673, 5734, 5744, 5762, 5777, 5788, 5801, 5926, 5975, 6063, 6075, 6085, 6096, 6108, 6117, 6125, 6190—**Matilda Betham-Edwards**

Bachelor, A—**FM** 4826

Balance of Power—**NatR-II** 1841

Banks, Archibald—**NQM** 25, 40, 47—**Oswald John F. Crawfurd**

Barbara—**NatR-II** 2237

Barbarian Eye, A—**FM** 1781

Baronet, The—**FM** 241—**William Maginn**

Belfast Merchant, A.—**NatR-II** 664—**Richard Patterson**

Berkeleian, A—**FM** 755

Berkshire Clergyman, A—**FM** 2419—**R. A. Willmott**

Bethel, J.—**FM** 103—**Bryan Waller Procter**

Bibo—**FM** 1109

Birmingham Tory, A—**NatR-II** 373

Blackgown, Eli, D.D.—**FM** 2716

Blunt, Benjamin, formerly a Bencherman and Trencherman in the Inner Temple, now a Rentier of the Rue Rivoli in Paris—**FM** 2202—**A. V. Kirwan**

Bombardinio—**FM** 603, 717, 729, 846, 864, 875, 893, 1002—**John Mitchell**

Bon Gaultier—**FM** 1432, 1712, 1759, 1843—**Theodore Martin** and/or **W. E. Aytoun**

Botherall, Sir Charles—**FM** 549, 564, 815—**W. P. Banks**

Bow-wow-wow, Larry—**FM** 1979

Bradley, Moreton C.—**NatR-II** 2406, 2418—**A. Maurice Low**

Brallaghan, Barney—**FM** 1650, 1657—**E. V. H. Kenealy**

Brett, Robert—**NatR-II** 1281

British Citizen, A—**NatR-II** 1445

British Merchant, A—**NatR-II** 1424

British Resident in Cairo, A—**FortR** 2207

Broad, John—**FM** 1386

Broad Churchman, A—**FM** 6351

Brother Peregrine—**FM** 1403, 1420, 1444, 1457, 1494, 1506—**Octavian Blewitt**

Broughshane—**NatR-II** 294

Butt, Nathan—**FM** 423—**John Galt**

C

C.—**DR** 2583

C.—**FM** 2589—**Thomas Carlyle**

C.—**FM** 3147, 3366, 3393, 4742, 5015, 5376, 5813, 6087, 6187

C.—**Ram** 44, 984—**J. M. Capes**

C.—**Ram** 1019, 1027, 1039—**George Conroy,** prob.

C.,A.—**FM** 5307

C.,A.H.—**FM** 3861—**A. H. Clough**

C.,B.—**DR** 2558

C.,C.—**FM** 1580—**E. V. H. Kenealy**

C.,C.—**Ram** 1021, 1127—**J. D. Acton**

C.,C.C.—**FM** 4447, 4532, 4938—**C. C. Chesney**

C.,D.B.—**DR** 2520, 2543, 2570, 2594, 2606, 2618, 2686, 2699—**Dom Bede Camm**

C.,D.J.—**DR** 2520

C.,E.—**DR** 2738

C.,E.—**FM** 5763—**Edward Caird?**

C.,E.—**FM** 5782—**Evelyn Carrington Martinengo-Cesaresco**

C.,E.B.—**FM** 3540—**E. B. Cowell**

C.,E.M.—**DR** 2345, 2356, 2371, 2709—**Ellen Mary Clerke**

C.,F.—**DR** 2606

C.,F.—**Ram** 834, 1012—**Frederick Capes**

C.,F.P.—**FM** 4189, 4840, 4877, 4959—**Frances Power Cobbe**

C.,F.R.—**FM** 5623, 5637, 5646, 5658, 5680, 5698, 5720, 5789, 5800, 5823, 5829, 5884, 5904, 5913—**F. R. Conder**

C.,F.T.—**FM** 4031

C.,G.—**DR** 1965, 2079, 2144, 2158

C.,G.—**FM** 5570, 5571, 5766, 6185

C.,G.—**FM** 6330—**George W. Cox**

C.,G.A.—**NatR-II** 750

C.,G.J.—**FM** 3770, 4149—**G. J. Cayley**

C.,H.C.—**DR** 2709, 2738—**H. C. Corrance**

C.,I.R.—**FM** 3429, 3811, 3824, 3832

C.,J.—**DR** 2558, 2594, 2606, 2618, 2628

C.,J.—**FM** 3737—**John Conington?**

C.,J.—**FM** 5599, 5621, 5676, 5742

C.,J.E.—**FM** 4123

C.,J.E.—**FM** 6178—**Jessie E. Cadell**

C.,J.F.—**NatR-II** 390—**James Frazer Cornish**

C.,J.I.—**DR** 2438, 2448, 2462, 2475, 2558, 2583, 2618

C.,J.J.—**DR** 2387, 2638

C.,J.M.—**FM** 4016 to 4130 in 12 installments—**John Moore Capes?**

C.,L.C.—**DR** 2092, 2119, 2173, 2174, 2212, 2425—**L. C. Casartelli**

C.,M.—**DR** 2543, 2583, 2686

C.,M.D.—**FM** 5257, 5356—**Moncure Daniel Conway**

C. of S. [Chandos of Sudeley]—**FM** 1042—**Egerton Brydges**

C.,P.S.—**FM** 5816—**Percy S. Cunningham**

C.,R.—**DR** 2686

C.,R.—**FM** 5967

C.,R.B.—**NatR-II** 690—**Robert B. Carter,** prob.

C.,T.—**FM** 5357, 5845—**Thomas Croskery**

C.,T.—**Ram** 502, 1102

C.,W.—**FM** 3695

C.,W.G.—**FM** 3359—**William George Clark**

C.S. [Colorado Settler?]—**FM** 6179

Calchas—**FortR** 4541—**J. L. Garvin**

Calpe—**FortR** 4408

Cambridge Man in the West, A—**FM** 3011—
H. Arthur Bright

Candid Conservative, A—**FortR** 2259—**Henry
C. Raikes**

Candid Conservative, A—**NatR-II** 472

Candid Man, A—**FM** 3882

Candidus—**FM** 1012, 1392, 1479, 1542, 1834
—**W. H. Leeds**

Captain, R.N.—**NatR-II** 2251

Captain in Her Majesty's Service, A—**FM**
5449

Captain of an Ocean Steamer, The—**FM** 5657

Carltonensis—**NatR-II** 2309, 2389—**Sidney J.
Low**

Carolinian, A—**FM** 3022—**Edward J. Pringle**

Carroll, Lewis—**FortR** 1165; **NC** 1466—**C. L.
Dodgson**

Catholica—**DR** 2083

Catholic Architect, A—**Ram** 41

Catholic Priest, A—**Ram** 423, 430

Catholicus—**FM** 184

Centurion—**NatR-II** 380

Chaplain of the *Discovery*, The—**FM** 5882—
Charles E. Hodgson

Chess-Player, A.—**FM** 1419, 1505—**George
Walker**

Chinese, A—**FM** 5909

Chorister, A.—**Ram** 429

Churchman, A—**NatR-II** 943, 1084

Church of England Clergyman, A—**FM** 5534

Circumspecte Agatis—**NatR-II** 2126

Clericus—**NatR-II** 615

Coloniensis—**NatR-II** 2427

Colonist, A—**FM** 5371, 5983—**W. Jardine
Smith**

Colonist [in Australia], A—**FM** 5485

Colorado Settler, A—**FM** 6179

Commander, R.N., A—**FM** 4732, 4940, 5013
—**William Dawson**

Commander [in Royal Navy], A—**FM** 5678

Conceptualist, A—**NatR-II** 278

Conservative, A—**FortR** 2569

Conservative, A—**FM** 6141

Conservative, A—**ScotR** 118—**James Ferguson, 1857–1917**

Conservative Journalist, A—**NatR-II** 340, 459

Conservative M.P. [sometimes with an introductory "A"]—**NatR-II** 1545, 1628, 1754,
1934, 2285, 2465

Constitutionalist—**NatR-II** 1266

Consul, A—**NatR-II** 2444

Contributor [to the *National Review*, 1896] A
—**NatR-II** 1876

Cornwall, Barry—**FM** 759—**Bryan Waller
Procter**

Country Doctor, A—**NatR-II** 249

Country Gentleman, A—**FM** 391

Country Gentleman, A—**NatR-II** 310—**H. H.
M. Herbert**

Country Tory, A—**FM** 4738—**John Skelton**

Country Woman, A—**NatR-II** 1423

County Voter, A—**NatR-II** 153

Couplet, Mordaunt, Esq.—**FM** 799, 826—**J. A.
Heraud**

Cowitch, Gabriel—**FM** 362—**D. M. Moir**

Creston—**FortR** 3452, 3502

Crispus—**FM** 1504—**R. A. Willmott?**

Culpepper, Ned—**FM** 120—**William Maginn,**
perhaps with **J. A. Heraud**

Culpepper, Ned, the Tomahawk—**FM** 57—
William Maginn, perhaps with **J. A. Heraud**

Cumberland, Stuart C.—**NC** 1353—**Charles
Garner**

Cutwater, Sir Julius, Bart., K.C.B.—**FM** 1746
—**R. H. Horne**

D

D.—**DR** 2699

D.—**FM** 2677—**J. S. Mill**

D.—**FM** 5348, ?5722—**Francis Dwyer**

D.—**FM** 6019, 6128

D.—**Ram** 731—possibly Richard Simpson

D.,B—**DR** 1119

D.,C—**DR** 2583

D.,C.S.—**DR** 2594, 2606, 2628, 2638, 2674—
C. S. Devas

D.,D.—[but may be D.D.]—**NatR-II** 892

D.,E.M.—**DR** 2720

D.,F.—**DR** 2475, 2485

D.,G.—**DR** 2594, 2606, 2628, ?2638—**Gilbert
Dolan**

D.,H.—**FM** 604

D.,J.J.—**NatR-II** 1242—**Joseph J. Davies**

D.,J.M.—**FM** 3399

D.,J.W.—**DR** 2006

D.,M.E.—**DR** 2651

D.,R.M.—**FM** 6050

D.,W.B.—**FM** 3592, 3745, 3849, 3996, 4168,
4347—**William Badham Donne**

D.N.—**Ram** 989, 1098—**Richard Simpson**

Dangerfield, John, Author of *Grace Tolmer*—
NQM 3, 10, 21, 43, 46, 77, 97, 112—**Oswald
J. F. Crawfurd**

David, Fr.—**DR** 2492, 2544—**David Fleming**

Decem [Dowden, Edward, C.E.M.?]—**FM**
4609—**Edward Dowden**

Defeated Candidate, A—**FortR** 2413

Democratic Tory—**NatR-II** 259

De Paris, Jehan—**FortR** 1985—**Hector Depasse**

Derlax—**Ram** 1050—**Richard Simpson**

Derwent, J. L.—**NatR-11** 418—**John Leith Veitch**

Desultory Reader, A—**NatR-II** 736—**W. H. Mallock**

Devonia—**FM** 3410, 3548, 3582, 3635, 3899

Diamond, Dionysius, M.D.—**FM** 5153, 5163, 5255—**John Skelton**

Diogenes Quis—**FM** 1124, 1136

Diplomate, A—**NatR-II** 2419

Diplomaticus—**FortR** 2378, 2439, 3859, 3872, 3935, 3962, 3999, 4026, 4039, 4081, 4098, 4125, 4154, 4177, 4190, 4217, 4256, 4258, 4282, 4312, 4326, 4342, 4356, 4384, 4429, 4454, 4484, 4500, 4513, 4528—**Lucien Wolf**

Discipulus—**NatR-II** 1011, 1054—**Sir Walter Peace**

Dixi—**FM** 77—**William Maginn**

Dominie, The—**FM** 877, 886—**Andrew Picken**

Don, A—**FM** 4837—**Leslie Stephen**

Doolittle, Dudley Digges—**FM** 2799—**A. V. Kirwan**

Dorset, Sackville—**NatR-II** 638

Drillem, Sergeant—**FM** 1485

Duncannon, Viscount, M.P.—**FM** 390

E

E.—**DR** 1684, 1708, 1813, 2126

E.—**FM** 5697—**T. H. S. Escott**

E.—**NatR-II** 2536—**Ernest Bowen-Rowlands**

E.,A—**FM** 5426

E.,C.—**FM** 6184

E.,C.J.—**FM** 3530—**Charles John Evans**

E.E.—**FM** 3869

E.,E.—**FM** 6437

E.,G.—**FM** 5346

E.,M.B.—**FM** 5671—**Matilda Betham-Edwards**

E.,R.H.—**FM** 5229, 5249, 5262, 5282, 5295— **Robert H. Elliot**

E.,R.P.—**FM** 233

E.,S.—**FM** 5738, 5818

Eastern Hermit—**FM** 6013, 6025, 6037, 6047, 6059, 6070, 6079, 6089, 6098, 6109, 6119, 6129—**William Allingham**

Editor, An—**NatR-II** 1825, 1898

Editor of the Volume [*Alice Sherwin*], The— **Ram** 857

Educator, An, Not a Teaching Machine— **NatR-II** 205

Emeritus—**FortR** 3894

Emin Pasha—**FortR** 2605—**Edward Schnitzer**

English Catholic, An—**NatR-II** 2513

English Elector, An—**FM** 865

English Farmer Now Settled Three Years in the State [Colorado], An—**FM** 6116

English Lady, An—**FM** 5434, 5718

Englishman, An—**FortR** 3313

Englishman, An—**FM** 806

Englishman, An—**NatR-II** 693, 1729

Englishman, An—**NatR-II** 2401, 2479, 2516, —**Herbert Wrigley Wilson**

English Officer, An— **FortR** 4343

English Officer in South Africa, An—**FM** 6024

English resident [in the Lebanon], An—**FortR** 2075—**Laurence Oliphant**

English Resident in Russia, An—**FM** 5750

English Roman Catholic, An—**FM** 5258

English Sea-Captain, An—**FM** 5545

English Tory, An—**FortR** 2144, 2184, 2311 —**Henry C. Raikes**

Ernulphus Eyes-and-Limbs—**FM** 1462

Esmé Stuart—**ScotR** 536—**Amélie Claire Leroy**

Ettrick Shepherd—**FM** 105, 185, 248, 314, 437, 472, 513, 651, 665, 780, 790, 950, 1001— **James Hogg**

Ex-(Colonial) Attorney-General—**NatR-II** 1112

Ex-Governor—**NatR-II** 1025—perhaps **George Ferguson Bowen**

Ex-Liberal M.P., An—**NatR-II** 395

Experienced Junior [at the Bar], An—**FM** 3260

Expertus—**FortR** 4056

Ex-Private Secretary, An—**NatR-II** 1745

Ex-Secretary—**FM** 5370—**Camille Barrère**

Eye-Witness [to post-revolutionary Rome], An —**FM** 2983, 2998, 3009, 3018, 3029

Eye-Witness [to the Annexation of the Transvaal], An—**FM** 5955

Eyewitness [to Tirah Campaign]—**FortR** 4086

F

F.—**FM** 3383—**F. T. Palgrave**

F.—**FM** 5023, 5534, 5668

F.—**FM** 5270—**J. F. Stephen**

F.—**FM** 5308—**Frederika Richardson**

F.—**FM** 5390—**J. G. Fitch**

F.—**FM** 5519—possibly Percy Fitzgerald

F.—**Ram** 991, 1050, 1074—**Frederick Oakeley**

F.—**Ram** 1065—**Florence Bastard**

F.,A.—**FM** 5164—**Alexander Falconer**

F.,C.G.—**FM** 3361—**Charles Granwood Floyd**

F.,D.—**FM** 5340—**Danby Fry?**

F.,E.R.—**FM** 5161, 5303, 5902—**Edmund Robert Freemantle**

F.,F.G.—**FM** 4572—**Frederick Gard Fleay**

F.,G.E.—**FM** 3533

F.,H.—**FM** 4827

F.,H.S.—**FM** 5230, 5610, 5633, 5772—**H. S. Fagan**

F.,I.A.—**FM** 4177—**James Anthony Froude**

F.,J.—**DR** 2729

F.,J.A.—**FM** 3338, 3466, 5038, 5052, 5058, 5074, 5089, 5099, 5117, 5147, 5158, 5672, 5815, 5838, 5859, 6229—**J. A. Froude**

F.,J.E.—**FM** 5776—**John Edward Field**

F.,J.H.—**FM** 4977, 5205

F.,J.S.—**Ram** 688—**John Stanislas Flanagan**

F.,M.F.A.: see M.F.,A.F.

F.,M.G.—**FM** 5285—**Millicent Garrett Fawcett**

F.,M.J.—**DR** 1461—**St. George Mivart**

F.,T.—**FM** 3417, 3431—**Thomas Fisher**

F.,T.—**FM** 3756

F.,T. ["Terence Flynn"]—**FM** 2650, 2659, 2665, 2769, 2994, 3074, 3430

F.,T.G.—**FM** 3786, 4032, 4057, 4081, 4186, 4266—**Thomas Godfrey Faussett**

F.,W.—**FM** 981, 1041—**R. P. Gillies**

F.,W.F.—**Ram** 311, 447, 452—**W. F. Finlason**

F.,W.J.—**FM** 5397, 5418—**W. J. Fitzpatrick**

F.,X.—**DR** 1070

F.R.G.S. [Fellow Royal Geographical Society] —**DR** 1674, 1688

F.R.G.S. [Fellow Royal Geographical Society] —**FM** 4295, 4304, 4313—**Richard F. Burton**

FRIP—**FM** (4), 45—**Jean Paul Friederick Richter**

Fabian Society, The—**FortR** 3427—**G. B. Shaw** and **Sidney Webb**

Fair-Play—**FM** 409—**J. A. Heraud**, collab.?

Family Man, A—**NatR-II** 1556

Fane, Violet—**FortR** 2151—**Mary Montgomerie Singleton**

Felicitas—**NatR-II** 1583

Fidens—**NatR-II** 137

Field Officer, A—**FortR** 2295—**Colonel Wilkinson** and perhaps **Arthur Griffiths**

Finnicus—**NatR-II** 2449

Finsbury Constituent, A—**FM** 1856

Fitz-Boodle—**FM** 1890 to 2009 in 11 installments—**W. M. Thackeray**

Fitz-Boodle, George—**FM** 1805, 1816, 1828, 1845, 1855, 1868, 1874—**W. M. Thackeray**

Fitz-Boodle, George Savage—**FM** 1702, 1708 —**W. M. Thackeray**

Fitz-Pleydell, E.—**FM** 2989

Foreign [i.e., Continental] Liberal, A—**FM** 6529

Foreigner, A—**NatR-II** 195

Former Resident in Russia, A—**FortR** 2861— **E. J. Dillon?**

Free Church Layman, A—**NatR-II** 547; **ScotR** 350—**James Ferguson**, 1857–1917

?Freeman, Frank—**FM** 526

Frenchwoman, A—**FortR** 3286

Fretensis—**NatR-II** 332

Friend to Free Inquiry, A—**FM** 578

G

G.—**DR** 2699

G.—**FortR** 2176—**T. H. S. Escott?**

G.—**FortR** 3266—**Alfred E. W. Gleichen**

G.—**FM** 3914

G.—**FM** 5111, 5120—**W. G. Palgrave**

G.—**FM** 5503—**George Frederick Goddard**

G.—**Ram** 1003—**Antonius Giunchi**

G.,A.—**Ram** 1003—**Antonius Giunchi**

G.,A.G.—**DR** 2400

G.,C.—**FM** 5564, 5663

G.,C.E.S.—**FM** 3342—**Charles E. S. Gleig**

G.,D.—**FM** 3696—**Theodore Martin**

G.,E.—**DR** 2628, 2720

G.,E.C.—**FM** 4303—**Elizabeth Cleghorn Gaskell**

G.,F.—**FortR** 1729—**Francis Galton**

G.,F.—**FM** 3909—**Francis Garden?**

G.,F.—**FM** 3955

G.,F.A.—**DR** 2570, 2674—**F. A. Gasquet**

G.,G.—**FM** 3276

G.,G.A.—**DR** 2400

G.,J.—**FM** 4629—**James Gairdner**

G.,J.G.—**FM** 5200—**James G. Goodenough**

G.,J.R.—**DR** 2006, 2029, 2065, 2119, 2158, 2211, 2358, 2485—**J. R. Gasquet**

G.,J.S.S.—**FM** 4352—**J. S. Stuart-Glennie**

G.,K.—**NatR-II** 110

G.,P.—**FM** 3994—**Percy Greg**

G.,R.—**FM** 5341; **NatR-II** 623—**Richard Garnett**, 1835–1906

G.,R.E.—**DR** 1133, 1181—**Robert Ephrem Guy**

G.,T. [Trinity Graduate?]—**FM** 959, 975, 980, 995, 1032—**Robert Avis Willmott**

G.,T.L.—**Ram** 1119—**Thomas L. Green**

G.,T.R.—**DR** 2226—**Joseph Raymond Gasquet?**

G.,W.—**DR** 2485, 2709, 2720, 2729

G.,W.—**FM** 5595

G.,W.—**NatR-II** 1397

G.,W.L.—**DR** 2651, 2738—**W. L. Gildea**

G.,W.R.—**FM** 4552, 5071, 5194, 5223, 5343 —**William Rathbone Greg**

G.R.—[George Rex]—**FM** 430—**King George II of Great Britain**

General, A—**FM** 5791, 5923
Genosse, Aegir—**FortR** 3755
German, A—**FM** 5632, 6054
Germanicus—**FortR** 4053—**Emil Richter?**
German Lady, A—**NatR-II** 2404—**Mary Annette Russell**
Gladstonian M.P., A—**FortR** 2604
?Glenelg, Phinlay—**NatR-II** 1220
Government Official, A—**FM** 5719
Gower, Erskine—**NatR-II** 1492—**Millicent Fanny Sutherland**

Grabstein, Professor, Phil. D. of Göttingen——**FM** 2106—**R. H. Horne**
Grand, Sarah—**FortR** 4085—**Frances Elizabeth McFall**
Grant, J.—**ScotR** 311—**James Ramsay MacDonald**
Grille—**NatR-II** 2207, 2346, 2501
Grumbler, A—**FM** 2935, 3061, 3118, 3369, 3390, 3676, 3694, 3729, 3757, 3902
Grundy, Jemima—**FM** 1393—**W. M. Thackeray**

H

H.—**DR** 2347
H.—**DR** 2686—**John Hopwood**
H.—**FM** 609, 863—**Agnes (Crombie) Hall**
H.—**FM** 3556, 3620, 3742, 3873, 3942—**V. H. Hobart**
H.—**FM** 5979, 6233
H.—**NatR-II** 473
H.—**Ram** 27—**W. G. Ward**
H.—**Ram** 998—**J. H. Newman**
H.,A.—**DR** ?2475, 2709—**Alfred Herbert**
H.,A.—**FM** 3001, 3707, 3759—**Arthur Helps**
H.,E.A.—**FM** 3197—**Ernest Abraham Hart**
H.,E.R.—**FM** 3594—possibly Edward Rupert Humphreys
H.,F.—**Ram** 1081, 1117—**Florence Bastard**
H.,F.C.—**NQM** 49—**Frances Cashel Hoey**
H.,F.v.—**NatR-II** 41—**Friedrich von Hügel**
H.,G.—**DR** 2387, 2497, 2509, 2531, 2543, 2686, 2709, 2720, 2729, 2738—**Gilbert Higgins**
H.,G.D.—**FM** 3895
H.,H.—**DR** 1921—**Henry Hayman**
H.,H.—**Ram** 998—**J. H. Newman**
H.,H.N.—**FM** 5580, 5617, 5677—**Horatio Nelson Hardy**
H.,I.—**FM** 4386—**John Hullah**
H.,J.—**DR** 2543, 2558, 2570, 2606, 2628, 2651, 2674, 2709, 2729—**John Hopwood**
H.,J.—**DR** 2583—**James Halpin**
H.,J.—**DR** 2583, 2686
H.,J.—**FM** 3347, 3455, 3638, 4466—**John Hullah**
H.,J.—**FM** 4423, 4473, 4539—**Harry Jones, 1823–1900**
H.,J.—**FM** 5786
H.,J.A.—**DR** 2400, 2425, 2448, 2475, 2485, 2497, 2520, 2531, 2583, 2594, 2628, 2651, 2663, 2674, 2686, 2699, 2709, 2720, 2729, 2738—**J. A. Howlett**
H.,J.C.—**DR** 1985, 2089—**John Cuthbert Hedley**
H.,J.E.—**FortR** 3932—**Janet E. Hogarth**
H.,L.C.—**FM** 280
H.,M.N.—**Ram** 258—**J. S. Northcote**

H.,O.—**Ram** 991—**J. H. Newman**
H.,R.—**DR** 2475
H.,R.—**FortR** 4530—**Robert Hart, 1835–1911**
H.,R.—**FM** 3838
H.,T.—**FM** 3781—**Thomas Hughes**
H.,T.—**FM** 5853—perhaps Thomas Hughes
H.,T.E.—**FM** 4163—**Thomas Erskine Holland**
H.,T.W.—**FM** 5048—**Thomas W. Hinchliff**
H.,W.—**FM** 823—**William Maginn?**
H.,W.—**NatR-II** 1292
H.,W.E.—**NatR-II** 492
H.,W.I.—**FM** 389
H.,W.L.—**OxCam** 8—**Wilfred L. Heeley**
HY.,Q.—**FM** 433—**William Dunlop**
Hardbargain, Captain—**FM** 2868, 3123
Hardy, Francis H.—**FortR** 3584, 3830, 3846, 3867, 3896—**Edward James Cattell**
Harrovian, The—**FM** 69, 92—**Robert Aris Willmott**
Hawes, Pyx—**NatR-II** 1421—**William Ainslie Hollis**
Herder—**Ram** 212—**J. M. Capes**
Hermes—**FM** 633—**Isaac Cullimore**
Hermogenes—**FM** 667, 695, 947, 1005, 1120, 1138, 1148, 1336, 1352, 1362—**Isaac Cullimore**
Herodotus, Jun.—**FM** 2866—**G. W. Dasent**
Hibernicus—**FortR** 3742
Hickory, Colonel Richard H., of Cedar Swamp—**FM** 401, 411, 429, 446, 461
Highlander, A.—**NatR-II** 483
His [i.e. Buckle's] Fellow Traveller—**FM** 4352—**J. S. Stuart-Glennie**
His Own Precentor—**FM** 1261
Holmes, W., Esq., M.P. for Haslemere—**FM** 196—**William Maginn**
Holmes, William—**FM** 378—**William Maginn**
Home-Rule M.P., A—**NQM** 195—**Justin McCarthy**
Howlett, Rev. M., of Devonshire—**FM** 3055—**R. J. King**
Huguenot—**NatR-II** 2171, 2202—**Frederick C. Conybeare**

I

I.—**FM** 286
I.,C J.—**NatR-II** 368
I.,H.—**Ram** 991—**J. H. Newman**
I.,J.M.—**DR** 2543, 2594, 2651
I.,K.P.—**FM** 3611, 3633, 3658—**A. K. H. Boyd**
I.,P.—**FM** 752
Ignatius of S. Paul, Passionist, Fr.—**Ram** 183, 287—**George Spencer**
Ignotus—**NatR-II** 1257
Ignotus—**NatR-II** 2333, 2377, 2437, 2492—**H. W. Wilson**
Imperialist—**FortR** 3811, 3900, 4122—**John Verschoyle?** OR **J. R. Maguire?**
Imperialist, An—**NatR-II** 288
Independent Pittite, An—**FM** 352, 373, 383, 402, 440, 455, 484, 511—**Robert Benton Seeley?**
Index—**FortR** 1689—**W. E. Gladstone**
Indian Editor, An—**NQM** 159
Indian Magistrate, An—**NatR-II** 2397
Indian Officer, An—**FortR** 2796—**Ian S. M. Hamilton**
Indian Official, An—**FM** 5398
Indicus—**NatR-II** 908
Indigo, John—**NatR-II** 71

Ingen dá cerda [daughter of the craft]—**FM** 3753—**Margaret McNair Stokes**
Inquirer—**NatR-II** 346
Irish Catholic, An—**FM** 5065
Irish Catholic Barrister, An—**DR** 2016
Irish Conservative, An—**NatR-II** 262
Irish Girl, An—**NatR-II** 1506
Irish Graduate, An—**FM** 5272—**Keningale Cook?**
Irish J.P., An—**NatR-II** 1348
Irish Justice of the Peace, An—**NatR-II** 1314
Irish Landlord—**NatR-II** 909
Irish Liberal, An—**FM** 5215
Irishman, An—**FortR** 2490, 3240
Irishman, An—**FM** 2741—**Aubrey De Vere**
Irishman, An—**NatR-II** 482
Irishman Belonging to No Party, An—**NatR-II** 531
Irishman who is not a Federalist, An—**FM** 5152
Irish Nationalist, An—**FortR** 3705
Irish Unionist, An—**FortR** 4241
It—**NatR-II** 332
Ithi Kefalende—**FM** 2703—**C. B. Mansfield**

J

J.—**DR** 2686, 2699
J.—**FM** 6055—**Kate Vaughan Jennings**
J.,A.—**NatR-II** 1582
J.,A.D.—**Ram** 988—**J. D. Acton**
J.,B.G.—**FM** 3754
J.,E.—**DR** 2720—**Edmund Jackson**
J.,F.W.—**Ram** 6—**Frederick William Jerningham**
J.,G.—**FM** 5627—**Geraldine Jewsbury**
J.,G.E.—**FM** 5645—**Geraldine Endsor Jewsbury**
J.,H.—**FM** 4423, 4473, 4539, 4583, 4616, 4649—**Harry Jones, 1823–1900**

J.,J.—**NatR-II** 261
J.,J.D.—**NatR-II** 1160
J.,J.M.—**DR** 2558
J.,J.M.—**FM** 3616—**John Mounteney Jephson**
J.,W.—**FM** 4955, 4962—**William Jerdan**
J.J.—**Ram** 966—**J. H. Newman**
J.P. [Justice of the Peace]—**NatR-II** 489
Jenkinson, Philemon—**FM** 3176
Johannesburg Resident, A—**FortR** 3790
Jonathan—**FM** 4713—**Moncure D. Conway**
Journeyman Engineer, The—**FM** 5219, 5245, 5369—**Thomas Wright**
Justitia—**Ram** 1104—**H. N. Oxenham**

K

K.—**FortR** 4298
K.—**FM** 4411
K.,A.V.—**FM** 3884—**A. V. Kirwan**
K.,B.—**DR** 2400, 2425, 2448
K.,B.—**FM** 4099
K.,C.—**FM** 3368, 3514, 3560, 3687, 3711, 3773, 3866—**Charles Kingsley**
K.,D.—**FM** 5470—**David Ker?**
K.,E.S.—**DR** 1494—**E. S. Keogh**
K.,G.—**FM** 4220—possibly George Kemp

K.,G.H.—**FM** 3560—**George H. Kingsley**
K.,H.—**FM** 3850—**Henry Kingsley**
K.,H.G.—**NatR-II** 1007—**Henry George Keene**
K.,J.M.—**FM** 1018—**William Maginn**
K.,J.M.—**FM** 3438, 3546—**J. M. Kemble**
K.,L.—**DR** 1448
K.,M.G.—**NatR-II** 750
K.,O.—**FM** 6266, 6363, 6464, 6475, 6548—**Olga (Kiréeff) Novikoff**
K.,R.—**DR** 2531

K.,R.I.—**FM** 2817—**Richard John King**

K.,R.J.—**FM** 3398, 3420, 3562, 5539—**Richard John King**

K.,R.L.—**DR** 2497

K.,T.E.—**FM** 3659—**T. E. Kebbel**

K.,T.M. [assumed misprint for J.M.K.]—**FM** 3374—**J. M. Kemble**

K.,W.H.—**DR** 2485, 2570, 2606, 2651, 2686, 2699, 2709, 2720, 2729, 2738—**William Henry Kent**

Kent, Philip—**NatR-II** 860 collab., 1341—**Darcy Lever**

Kent, Philip—**NatR-II** 860 collab.—**H. C. A. Keith**

Knarf—**FM** 1257, 1266

Knowall, Timothy, Esq.—**FM** 1639

L

L.—**FortR** 3835

L.—**FM** 4169, 5291

L*.—**FM** 732—**E. Wilson Landor**

L.,A.—**FM** 5063, 5518—**Andrew Lang**

L.,A.M.—**FM** 5167

L.,D.—**DR** 1897, 2062, 2087, 2191—**David Lewis**

L.,E.—**FM** 3623, 3666, 3703—**Eliza Lynn Linton**

L.,F.T.—**DR** 2558, 2583, 2594, 2618, 2628, 2651, 2663, 2674, 2709, 2720, 2738

L.,G.H.—**FM** 3395, 3433, 3499, 3512, 3570, 3660, 3684, 3799—**George Henry Lewes**

L.,H.—**FM** 3376

L.,H.—**NatR-II** 1605

L.,H.W.—**NatR-II** 714—**H. W. Linford**

L.,J.M.—**FM** 3550—**J. M. Ludlow**

L.,M.P.—**FM** 3294, 3314, 3449, 3800—**Mark Praeger Lindo**

L.,M.v.—**Ram** 1067—**Ludwig von Meyer**

L.,P.—**DR** 2253, 2335, 2358—**Patrick Lynch**

L.,R.—**FM** 3363, 3477, 3542, 3646, 3648, 3719, 3789, 4017, 4035, 4161, 4256, 4362—**Robert Lamb**

L.,R.O.B. [but may be R.O.B.L.]—**FM** 5067

L.,T.—**DR** 2485

L.,T.E.C.—**FM** 4100—**T. E. C. Leslie**

L.,W.S.—**DR** 1779, 1813—**W. S. Lilly**

L.-A.—**FM** 5848

Lady, A—**FM** 1393—**W. M. Thackeray**

Lady, A—**FM** 5632, 5642, 5651, 5682, 5691, 5709, 5741, 5754, 5767—**Marie von Bothmer**

Lady A—**Ram** 647, 653—**Mary Anne Arundell**

Laicus—**DR** 1479—**James Burns?**

Lanin, E. B.—**FortR** 2871, 2881, 2892, 2902, 2921, 2966, 2982, 2990, 2997, 3032, 3040, 3086, 3133, 3143, 3260, 3460—**Emile Joseph Dillon**

(Late) Common Soldier, A—**FortR** 330—**James F. Fuller**

Late Member of the University of Oxford, A —**Ram** 133, 143, 153—**J. M. Capes**

Late Resident [of the West Indies], A—**FM** 125, 181

Late Resident in the Island [Jamaica], A—**FM** 4623

Latouche, John—**NQM** 8, 15, 22, 30, 41, 70, 86, 107, 113, 146—**Oswald J. F. Crawfurd**

Latouche, Vivian—**FM** 2147—**George Henry Lewes**

Law, John—**FortR** 3533—**Margaret Elise Harkness**

Lawrenny, H.—**FortR** 849, 910—**Edith J. Simcox**

Layman, A—**NatR-II** 1455, 1933

Layman of the Church of England, A—**FM** 327—**Robert Benton Seeley?**

Lector—**Ram** 906

Lee, H. Vernon—**NQM** 110—**Violet Paget**

Lee, Vernon—**FortR** 2638, 2930, 3159, 3681, 3818, 4017, 4366; **FM** 6069, 6073, 6095, 6101, 6112, 6127, 6159, 6168, 6174, 6362, 6415, 6525; **NatR-II** 346—**Violet Paget**

Lex—**FortR** 3730

Libanus—**FM** 4143

Liberal, A—**FortR** 2038

Liberal Unionist—**FortR** 3357

Liberal Unionist—**NatR-II** 672

Liberal Unionist M.P., A—**NatR-II** 1678

Liberal without Adjectives, A—**FortR** 4543

Local Secretary [of the Society for University Extension at Oxford], A—**NatR-II** 775—**J. T. Montgomery**

Locke—**FM** 1046, 1100, 1116—**George Wightwick**

Locke, B.F. [Blue Friar?]—**FM** 1057, 1139, 1163, 1209, 1289, 1304, 1363, 1465, 2201—**George Wightwick**

Locke, Brother—**FM** 1057—**George Wightwick**

London Artisan, A—**FortR** 2122—**T. W. Brockett**

London Editor, A—**NatR-II** 1296, 1308

London M.A.—**NatR-II** 1061—**William Gallatly**

Looker-on, A—**FM** 188

Looker-On, A—**NatR-II** 331

Lover of Christian Art, A—**Ram** 27

Lover of Consistency, A—**Ram** 52

Lover of Ireland, A—**NatR-II** 661

Lover of the Classics, A—**NatR-II** 499

Loyalist—**NatR-II** 1303

M

M.—**DR** 1487, 1515, 1581, 1592, 1621, 1657, 1669—**St. George Mivart**

M.—**DR** 2686, 2699, 2709, 2729

M.—**FortR** 3041, 3119—**W. H. Mallock**

M.—**FM** 451, 1451—**William Maginn**

M.—**FM** 4421

M.—**FM** 4833, 4850, 4888, 4906, 5072, 5248, 5471, 5675, 5693, 5917—**James MacDonnell**

M.—**NatR-II** 2122

M.—**Ram** 166, 176, 186

M.—**Ram** 1003, 1038—**Charles Meynell**

M.,A. [could be M.A.]—**FM** 4062

M.,A.J.—**FM** 5154—**A. J. Munby?**

M.,C.—**FM** 5139, 5400—**Charles Marshall**

M.,C.—**Ram** 991—**Charles Meynell**

M.,C.A.—**FM** 3768—**Charles Augustus Murray**

M.,C.J.—**Ram** 857

M.,C.O.A. [Charles Oliver Ardersier Macdonald]—**FM** 3549—**A. K. H. Boyd**

M.,D.—**DR** 2628

M.,D.—**FM** 3351, 3443, 3787—**David Masson**

M.,D.S.—**NatR-II** 1168, 1314—**D. S. MacColl**

M.,E.—**FM** 5721

M.,E.B.—**FM** 5193, 5214

M.,E.E.—**FM** 5246 (and possibly 5721)

M.,E.H.—**FM** 3910, 3993

M.,F.—**FM** 3507, 4078—**Francis Marx**

M.,F.B. [the "F" may be "Fr."]—**DR** 1640

M.,G.—**FM** 4793—**George Meredith**

M.,G.J.W.—**FM** 3793—**George John Whyte-Melville**

M.,G.T.—**DR** 2558—**G. T. Mackenzie**

M.,G.W.—**FM** 3326, 3336, 3343, 3498, 4387, 4419—**George Whyte-Melville**

M.,H.—**FM** 3325—**Henry Morley**

M.,H.A.—**FM** 3392, 3452, 3492, 3946—**Henry A. Murray**

M.,H.J.—**FM** 6354—**Henry James Moncrieff**

M.,H.M.—**FM** 4956—**Horace Mosley Moule?**

M.,J.—**DR** 2079, 2131, 2211, 2347, 2373, 2384, 2412, 2425, 2448, 2638, 2663, 2674—**James Moyes**

M.,J.—**FortR** 405, ?4083—**John Morley**

M.,J.—**Ram** 1019—**John Morris, 1826–1893**

M.,J.B.—**DR** 1190; **Ram** 806—**John Brande Morris**

M.,J.B.—**DR** 2400, 2425, 2438, 2475, 2497—**James Booth Milburn**

M.,J.C.—**NatR-II** 707

M.,J.H.—**DR** 2387—**John Hobson Matthews**

M.,J.J.—**FM** 416

M.,Jn.—**DR** 2674, 2686, 2699, 2709, 2720, 2729

M.,Jno.—**DR** 2686

M.,J.S.—**FM** 3845—**J. S. Mill**

M.,K.D.—**FM** 6258

M.,L.A.—**FM** 4311, 4382—**Louisa Merivale**

M.,M.—**DR** 2380, 2729

M.,M.—**FM** 2915—**Mary Meredith** and **T. L. Peacock**

M.,M.E.—**FM** 2158, 3386—**Marion E. Martin?**

M.,M.S.—**Ram** 429

M.,N.S.—**FM** 3408, 3419, 3746, 4636—**Nevil Story-Maskelyne**

M.,O.—**Ram** 1066—**Henry N. Oxenham**

M.,R.—**FM** 3774

M.,R.—**Ram** 991—**Robert Monteith**

M.,R.B.—**FM** 3652—**Robert B. Mansfield**

M.,S.—**DR** 1790

M.,T.E.—**FM** 3782

M.,T.F.—**DR** 1071—**T. F. Mathew**

M.,T.W.—**Ram** 27—**Thomas W. Marshall**

M.,W.—**FM** 5729

M.,W.C.—**FM** 5314, 5358, 5567

M.,W.F.—**FM** 5363—**William Frederick Mayers**

M.,W.O'C.—**FM** 4137, 4164, 4176, 4887—**William O'Connor Morris**

M.A. [Master of Arts]—**FM** 1660, 2088, 2109, 2254, 2301—**R. A. Willmott**

M.D. (London)—**NatR-II** 1257

MEM—**FM** 2276—perhaps Marion E. Martin

M.F.,A.F.—**FortR** 3734—perhaps **Augustus Ferryman Mockler-Ferryman**

M'I.,J.—**DR** 2583, 2628, 2674, 2738—**John McIntyre**

M.-M.—**FM** 4010

M. or N.—**FM** 5472—**George Whyte-Melville**

M.P. [Member of Parliament]—**NatR-II** 822, 1488, 1524, 1562

M.P., An—**FortR** 2229

M.P., An—**FM** 6249

Macc dá cherda, or Mac dá cherda [son of the craft]—**FM** 3598, 5169—**Whitley Stokes**

Macdonald, C. A.—**FM** 3615—**A. K. H. Boyd**

McLeod, Fiona—**FortR** 4222, 4370, 4386, 4430, 4444; **NatR-II** 2469; **NC** 3755—**William Sharp**

Malagrowther, Malachi—**NatR-II** 1268

Malet, Lucas—**FortR** 2366, 2459—**Mary St. Leger Harrison**

Maltese, A—**NatR-II** 479

Man, A—**NatR-II** 272

Manchester Conservative, A—**FortR** 2174—**Thomas Nash**

Manchester Man, A—**FM** 3101, 3363, 3477, 3542, 3646, 3648, 3719, 3789, 4017, 4035, 4161, 4256, 4362—**Robert Lamb**

Manhattan, Frank—**FM** 2889, 2931—**Charles Astor Bristed**

Man in the Street, The—**NatR-II** 2415—**H. W. Wilson**

Man of Genius, The—**FM** 760—**John Churchill**

Man-of-War's Man, The—**FM** 121, 134—**David Stewart**

Man on the Shady Side of Fifty, A—**FM** 4004, 4023, 4036, 4068, 4270—**A. V. Kirwan**

Marget, Edith—**NatR-II** 976; **ScotR** 206, 244, 270, 305—**Mrs. Lily Wolffsohn**

Maryland—**NatR-II** 2196

Meliorist— **NatR-II** 546

Member of Convocation, A [at Oxford]—**FortR** 2342

Member of Parliament, A—**FortR** 2229

Member of Parliament, A—**NatR-II** 598

Member of the Bechuanaland Border Police, A—**NatR-II** 1602

Member of the Cambrian Archeological Association, A—**DR** 2203

Member of the Circuit, A—**FM** 1473

Member of the Jacobin Club, A—**FM** 376

Member of the Manx Church, A—**FM** 1437

Menenius—**FM** 1119

Menzies, Sutherland—**FM** 6468—**Mrs. Elizabeth Stone**

Merriton, Mervyn, author of *The Ringwoods of Ringwood*—**NQM** 29—**Henry Coe Coape**

Mikron, Beta—**FM** 3580, 3600, 3788—**William Coutts Keppel**

Milesius—**FortR** 4275

Military Critic of *Westminster Gazette*, The——**NatR-II** 2489

Military Officer, A—**FM** 5816—**Percy Scudamore Cunningham**

Military Officer, A—**FM** 5780

Minute Philosopher, A—**FM** 3711, 3773, 3866—**Charles Kingsley**

Moderate Liberal, A—**NatR-II** 132

Modern Pythagorean, A—**FM** 205, 215, 291, 344, 443, 602, 773—**Robert Macnish**

Monachus—**DR** 1488

Moore, Wentworth—**FortR** 4165 to 4270 in 9 installments—**W. H. Mallock**

Most Loyal Supporter [of Balfour's], A—**FortR** 3926

Mother of a Girton Student, A—**NatR-II** 812

Müller, Christine—**FM** 5281 to 5355 in 9 installments—**Miss E. C. W. van Gobie**

Musical Critic, A—**FortR** 2508—**Francis Hüffer**

N

N.—**DR** 2686, 2699, 2709, 2720, 2738

N.—**NatR-II** 45—**Stafford Henry Northcote**

N.—**Ram** 32, 46, 55, 69, 82, 100, 230, 250, 257, 263, 275, 280, 288, 307, 317, 338—**James Spencer Northcote**

N.,B.—**FM** 1028

N.,D.—**Ram** 989, 1098—**Richard Simpson**

N.,E.—**DR** 2618, 2663, 2674, 2686, 2709

N.,F.—**FM** 5542

N.,J.S.—**DR** 1736, 1745; **Ram** 1019, 1047—**James Spencer Northcote**

N.L.—**DR** 2531, 2558, 2618, 2651, 2686

N.,W.R.—**NatR-II** 1336

N.N.—**Ram** 1098—**J. D. Acton**

Native Literate [of China], A—**FM** 5183

Naturalist, A—**FM** 3399

Naturalist, A—**FM** 3464, 3471, 3494, 3515, 3538, 3545—**John Skelton**

Nauticus—**FortR** 3448, 3520, 3546—**William Laird Clowes**

Naval Officer, A—**FM** 5705, 5892

Nemo—**NatR-II** 252

Nerke—**FM** 2541—**Cyrus Redding**

Nervous Man, A—**NatR-II** 1314

New Yorker, A—**FM** 2699 to 2889 in 10 installments, 3564—**Charles Astor Bristed**

Nimrod—**FM** 879, 911, 962, 990, 1056, 1062, 1089, 1117, 1149, 1174, 1198, 1513, and 1645 to 1760 in 10 installments—**Charles James Apperley**

Nina—**FM** 2475, 2484

Nork, F.—**FM** 2504—**Friedrich Korn**

North-West Civilian, A—**FM** 5766

O

O.—**DR** 1699, 2686, 2699

O.—**FM** 3725, 3752, 3758, 3784, 3816, 3833, 3841, 3937, 3963, 4112—**John Ormsby**

O.—**FM** 5750

O.—**Ram** 271, 277, 282, 290, 300, 309, 316—**George Oliver**

O. [Oratory?]—**Ram** 990, 997, 1009, 1046, 1056—**J. H. Newman**

O.,A.—**DR** 2373, 2485—Austin Oates

O.,A.G.—**DR** 2686, 2699, 2720, 2729—**Austin G. Oates**

O.,F.—**Ram** 131—**Frederick Oakeley**

O.,G.—**Ram** 236, 244, 251—**George Oliver**

O.,H. [Henry of the Oratory?]—**Ram** 991, 1050—**J. H. Newman**

O.,H.—**FM** 3329, 4379, 4402, 5297—**Henry Ottley**

O.,J.—**FM** 3557, 5684, 5712—**John Ormsby**

O.,J.—**NatR-II** 236

O.,J. [John of the Oratory?]—**Ram** 991, 996—**J. H. Newman**

O.,M.O.W.—**FM** 6289—**Margaret O. W. Oli-phant**

O.,M.S.—**FM** 2947, 2959—**Thomas Love Pea-cock**

O.,R.—**DR** 1756—**Robert Ornsby**

O.,W.—**FM** 3702—**William O'Malley**

O'C.,D.M.—**DR** 2485, 2509, 2570, 2651, 2663, 2709—**D. M. O'Connor**

O'D.,C. [Cornelius O'Donoghue]—**FM** 457—**T. C. Croker**

O'D.,M. [Morgan O'Doherty]—**FM** 136, 155, 241, 434, 559, 584, 712, 1367—**William Maginn**

O'L.,J.—**DR** 2618

O.O.O.—**FM** 6116

O.S.F. [Ordo Saint Francis]—**Ram** 1133—**J. W. Roberts**

Object, An—**FM** 1848

Observer—**NatR-II** 1565, 1714, 1726, 1739, 1751, 1788

Observer, An—**FortR** 3467—**Marie Louise de la Ramée**

Observer of the Relations between the Moral and the Material World, An—**FM** 2212

O'Doherty, Morgan (sometimes with title "Sir")—**FM** 76, 404, 434, 491, 603, 717, 729, 1333, 1406—**William Maginn**

O'Donoghue, C.—**FM** 588, 704, 825, 1189—**T. C. Croker**

O'Donoghue, Cornelius—**FM** 645, 656, 676, 741, 942, 1006, 2818, 2872—**T. C. Croker**

O'Donoghue, Ensign—**FM** 265, 784, 954, 979, 1053, 1224, 1228—**T. C. Croker**

Officer in a Marching Regiment, An—**FM** 788, 800—**William Maginn**

Officer of the Royal Artillery, An—**FM** 2776

Official, An—**NatR-II** 2048

Official [in the Indian Civil Service], An—**FM** 6392

Old Apprentice of the Law, An—**FM** 4185, 4217, 4233, 4293—**Andrew Valentine Kirwan**

Old Banker, The (or An)—**NatR-II** 804, 853—**William Walker**

Old Boy [of Greenwich School], An—**FM** 5585

Oldbuck, Jonathan—**NatR-II** 1292

Old Campaigner, An—**FM** 4536, 4555, 4599, 5732—**John Skelton**

Old Colonist [in Australia], An—**FM 5199**

Old Convent-Girl, An—**FM** 5604

Old Diplomatist, An—**NatR-II** 96

Old Educationalist, An—**FM** 6318—**S. S. Laurie**

Old Fogey, An—**NatR-II** 154

Old German Resident [in Alsace-Lorraine], An—**NatR-II** 591

Old Hand, An—**FM** 1210, 1726—**P. W. Banks**

Old Hand, The—**FM** 2108—**P. W. Banks**

Old Harrow Captain, An—**NatR-II** 2086

Old Journalist, An—**FM** 1395

Old Journalist, An—**NatR-II** 1348

Old Man, An—**FM** 1820, 1831, 1919, 1925

Old Matteist, An—**NatR-II** 1035

Old Personal Friend [of Mrs. Oliphant], An—**ScotR** 577—**William Wallace, 1843–1921**

Old Physician, An—**FM** 1219

Old Sailor, An—**FM** 5746

Old-School Tory, An—**NatR-II** 1338

Old Templar, An—**FM** 6539

?O'Lynn, Brian, Jun.—**FM** 1553

One in Earnest—**NatR-II** 385

One Long Resident in India—**FM** 5965—**Meredith Townsend?**

One of the Electors—**FM** 5712—**John Ormsby**

One of Themselves [Vagabonds]—**FM** 3758, 3784, 3816, 3833, 3841, 3963—**John Ormsby**

One of Themselves [Dalesfolk of Cumberland and Westmoreland]—**FM** 5695

One of the Old Staff—**DR** 2086—**Thomas Arnold, 1823–1900**

One of the People Called Christians—**FM** 1440

One of the Reviewed—**FM** 1411

One of the Upper Ten—**NatR-II** 142

One Who Has a Good Memory—**FM** 1736 to 1917 in 16 installments—**John Wilks, d.1846**

One who has great respect for your [Earl Grey's] order and office, etc.—**FM** 582

One Who Has Lived There [Turkey]—**FM** 6177

One Who Has Paid Taxes for over Half a Century—**NatR-II** 874

One Who Has Suffered—**Ram** 1067—**Frederick Oakeley**

One Who Has Taught Boys—**NatR-II** 887

One Who Knows [the Post Office]—**NatR-II** 1451

One Who Loves and Honours English Poetry—**FM** 6180—**William Allingham**

One Who Overheard—**NatR-II** 149a

Ordinary Man, The—**NatR-II** 1625

Oriental Author, An—**FM** 491—**Robert Macnish**

Ouida—**FortR** 2638, 3167, 3204, 3248, 3301, 3354, 3374, 3500, 3558, 3785, 3828, 3849, 3928, 3953, 4001, 4104, 4134, 4185, 4254, 4364; **NatR-II** 1074; **NC** 2685, 2749, 2863, 2977, 3019, 3196—**Marie Louise de la Ramée**

Our Own Correspondent [in Rome]—**Ram** 9, 21, 35, 51, 64, 77, 93, 107, 120—**James Spencer Northcote?**

Our Special Commissioner [in Belfast]—**FortR** 2504

Outisky, Prince—**FortR** 2314—**George Bunsen**

Oxford B.A., An—**FortR** 3650—**Hugh Chisholm**

Oxford Tutor, An—**FortR** 4352

Oxford Tutor, An—**FM** 6341, 6370, 6403

Oxoniensis—**FM** 6400

P

P.—FM 3630, 3728, 3797—**John W. Parker, 1820–1860**

P.—FM 5447, 5504—**W. F. Pollock**

P.—FM 5775, 5824, 6157

P.—FM 6028—**John Piggot**

P.—Ram 167, 248, 1095

P.—Ram 1110—**Richard Simpson**

P.,A.L.—Ram 33—**Ambrose Lisle Phillipps**

P.,B.—FM 3867—perhaps Baden Powell

P.,C.—FM 3568—**Coventry Patmore**

P.,C.—Ram 231—**Charles Parker**

P.,E.—FM 5372

P.,E.S.—**NatR-II**   307—**Edward   Schroeder Prior**

P.,F.—FM 5127, 5448—perhaps Frederick Pollock

P.,F.—**NatR-II** 1200

P.,F.R.W.—**DR** 1707, 2358, 2459; **NatR-II** 323—**F. R. Wegg-Prosser**

P.,F.T.—FM 3602, 3974, 4212—**Francis Turner Palgrave**

P.,G.—Ram 1134—**Richard Simpson**

P.,G.F.—FM 3513—perhaps George Frederick Pardon

P.,G.T.—FM 6224

P.,H.—DR 2497, 2558, 2570, 2583, 2594, 2628, 2651, 2674, 2686, 2699, 2720, 2738

P.,J.—Ram 1019—**Victor de Buck?**

P.,J.C.—FM 6141

P.,J.R.—FM 5394—**John Rowland Phillips?**

P.,J.V.—FM 5579—possibly J. V. Prichard

P.,L.J.—FM 4645—**L. J. Procter**

P.,M.—DR 2686, 2699

P.,M.—FM 3667, 3817, 3969—**Mark Pattison**

P.,M.D.—DR 2709, 2720, 2729

P.,S.C.—**NatR-II** 754

P.,S.M.—FM 4021

P.,V.—Ram 1127—**Victor de Buck?**

P.,W.—**DR** 1481

P.,W.—FM 6160

P.,W.F.—FM 3927, 4974—**W. F. Pollock**

P.Q.R.—Ram 1050—**John Maguire**

Palmoni—FM 1574

"Parent," A [of an Eton and Oxford Son]— FM 6243

Parisian, A.—**NatR-II** 509

Parochus [a parish priest]—**Ram** 437

Peeress, A—**NatR-II** 474

Pember, Austen—**NatR-II** 384, 878, 887, 935, 1097—**Walter Lionel Bicknell**

Perthshire Landlord, A—**NatR-II** 796

Peter Pepper and Co.—FM 79

Philo-Teuton—**NatR-II** 484

Philo-Turk—**FortR** 2373—**Arthur Nicolson**

Pilpay Junior—FM 106—**Thomas Carlyle**

Piper—FM 209—**William Maginn?**

Plymley, Peter [as a persona]—**FM** 1192— **Sydney Smith**

Poor Devil, A—FM 347—**John Churchill** and **William Maginn?**

Potts Ginger—FM 443

Precentor and Schoolmaster of the Parish, The —**FM** 1180

Precentor of the Parish, The—FM 1114, 1261

Professional Painter, A—FM 3640, 3665, 3723 —**John Zephaniah Bell**

Prout, Father [as a persona]—FM 685, 690, 702, 710, 726, 736, 747, 758, 764, 777, 782, 793, 807, 819, 841, 851, 861, 873, 922, 973, 983, 996, 1007, 1019—**Francis S. Mahoney**

Prussian, A—**NatR-II** 1214, 1225

Pundit, A—**FM** 1430

Pungent, Pierce—FM 33, 62, 83, 231, and 652 to 766 in 10 installments—**Thomas Powell**

Q

Q.—**NatR-II** 662, 1021

Qualiscumque—**NatR-II** 267

Quarterly Reviewer, A—**NatR-II** 1882—**William Francis Barry**

Quarterly Reviewer, The—**FortR** 3713—**Malcolm MacColl**

Quis?—**NatR-II** 1094

R

R.—**DR** 1850

R.—**FortR**—3073

R.—FM 5662

R.—Ram 521—**G. F. Wood**

R.,C.—**DR** 2347, 2358

R.,C.—FM 3353—**Cyrus Redding**

R.,C.J.—FM 5162—**Charles John Robinson?**

R.,C.W. [probably an error for C.R.W., q.v.] —FM 4376

R.,E.—**DR** 1451—**E. Rouse**

R.,E.S.—**FM** 5785, 5812—**E. S. Roscoe**
R.,F.—**DR** 2373
R.,F.—**FM** 4966
R.,G.—**DR** 2373, 2412—**George Richardson**
R.,H.—**FM** 5108, 5974—**Henry Reeve**
R.,H.C.—**NatR-II** 1124—**Henry Cecil Raikes**
R.,H.I.D.—**DR** 1532—**H. I. D. Ryder**
R.,J.—**DR** 2186—**Joseph Rickaby?**
R.,J.—**DR** 2335
R.,J.—**FortR** 2837
R.,J.—**FM** 4942—**James Robinson,** 1839–1903
R.,J.—**Ram** 1095
R.,J.C.—**FM** 3397, 3578, 3731—**James Craigie Robertson**
R.,J.W.—**FM** 3593, 3624, 3672, 3730, 3858—**Jesse Watts Russell**
R.,L.—**DR** 2520, 2686—**Luke Rivington**
R.,M.—**DR** 1812—**Martin Rule**
R.,R.—[or R.R.]—**FM** 4280
R.,T.W.—**NatR-II** 120
R.A. [Royal Artillery], though possibly a man's initials, i.e., A.,R.—**FM** 2544
R.A. [Royal Artillery]—**NatR-II** 2495
R.A.J.A. [perhaps Raja]—**FM** 4799
R. ap W. [Richard son of William]—**Ram** 730—**Richard Simpson**
R.S.S. [Royal Society of Scotland?]—**FM** 1947, 2078
Radical, A—**FortR** 2428—**Joseph Chamberlain**
Radical M.P., A—**NatR-II** 1647, 2246, 2270—**Robert Wallace,** 1831–1899
Radical Teetotaler, A—**NatR-II** 1029
Rambler—**NatR-II** 437, 570
Ratepayer—**NatR-II** 2299
Rattlebrain, Rory—**FM** 1225
Rattler, Morgan—**FM** 178, 549, 564, 569, 605, 692, 699, 718, 751, 815, 836, 882, 905, 967, 1476, 1683, 1716, 1719, 1932, 1946, 1990, 2020, 2038, 2063, 2077, 2103, 2141, 2153, 2178, 2215, 2281, 2286, 2311, 2331, 2619, 2634, 2657, 2697, 2754, 2775—**Percival Weldon Banks**
Reader Both of the *National* and the *Quarterly*, A—**NatR-II** 153

Reader of History, A—**FM** 1752
Recent Resident [of Fiji], A—**FM** 5567
Recent Visitor [to Canada], A—**FM** 5139
Reform—**NatR-II** 1131
Regulus—**NatR-II** 1326
Relative of Lady A[rundell], A—**Ram** 674
Resident in Crete, A—**FM** 4949—**W. J. Stillman**
Resident in Paris, A—**NatR-II** 1770
Resident [of China], A—**FM** 5137
Resident [of Brittany], A—**FM** 2245—**Charles J. Wells**
Resident [of South Africa], A—**ScotR** 664—**William Metcalfe**
Resident [of the Continent in 1855], A—**FM** 3393
Retired—**NatR-II** 546
Retired Politician, A—**NatR-II** 81, 196
Retired Practitioner of the Science [of Garroting], A—**FM** 4302
Returned South African, A—**FortR** 3104—**Olive Schreiner**
Reviewer [of *FM* no. 4442], The—**FM** 4450
Reviewer of Dr. Ward's philosophy, The—**Ram** 1086—**Richard Simpson**
Reynolds, John—**NatR-II** 148, 518
Reynolds, John, Citizen and Goldsmith—**NatR-II** 385
Richard ap William [Richard son of William]—**Ram** 726, 737, 752, 760—**Richard Simpson**
Riverside Visitor, The—**FM** 6346—**Thomas Wright,** the "Journeyman Engineer"
Roger B.F. [Blue Friar?]—**FM** 1046, 1071—**George Wightwick**
Romanus—**Ram** 351
Roughhead, Robin—**FM** 313—**William Maginn**
Rude Boreas—**Ram** 1020—**Richard Simpson**
Ruricola—**NatR-II** 129, 160, 166, 221, 256, 286—**H. H. M. Herbert**
?Russell, Geoffrey—**FM** 1727
Rusticus—**NatR-II** 1128—**John Watson**
Ryder, Miles, Esq.—**FM** 1470

S

S.—**DR** 2373
S.—**FortR** 4284, 4316—**George Strachey?**
S.—**FM** 121, 134—**David Stewart**
S.—**FM** 3906, 5098, 5172, 5388, 5457, 5664, 6177
S.—**FM** (5761), 5774—**St. George Stock**
S.—**FM** 5983—**W. Jardine Smith**
S.—**Ram** 27

S.—**Ram** 249, 1104—**Richard Simpson**
S.,A.—**FM** 5393, 5440, 5488—**Alexander Schwartz**
S.,A.C.—**FM** 4224
S.,A.C.—**FM** 4899—**A. C. Sellar**
S.,A.F.—**DR** 2583, 2594, 2606, 2618, 2628, 2651, 2720, 2729—**A. F. Spender**
S.,A.M.—**ScotR** 235—**A. M. Symington**

S.,C. [may be C.S. (Colorado Settler)]—**FM** 6179

S.,C.S.—**FM** 4454

S.,E.—**DR** 2738

S.,E.—**FM** 4431, 6057

S.,E.H.—**FM** 2462

S.,F.-I.T.—**FM** 3474, 3500—**Fitzjames Stephen**, Inner Temple

S.,F.G.—**FM** 4593— **F. G. Stephens**

S.,F.M.—**FM** 5112—**Francis Montagu Smith**

S.,G.—**FM** ?3596, 3947—**Goldwin Smith**

S.,G.—**FM** 6132, 6186

S.,H.—**FM** 3649—**Herbert Spencer**

S.,H.—**FM** 5727, 6024

S.,H.H.—**FM** 5652—**Henry Heathcote Statham**

S.,H.W.—**FM** 4051—**H. W. Sotheby**

S.,I.G.—**NatR-II** 655—**Isaac Gregory Smith**

S.,J.—**DR** 2211

S.,J.—**FM** 516

S.,J.—**FM** 4108, 4228, 5699—**James Spedding**

S.,J.F.—**FortR** 908; **FM** 4449—**James Fitzjames Stephen**

S.,J.J.—**FM** 5412

S.,J.O.—**FM** 3478—**John Skelton**

S.,J.Y.—**FM** 3879—**John Young Sargent**

S.,L.—**FM** 5176, 5280, 5299, 5318, 5335, 5387, 5436—**Leslie Stephen**

S.,L.D.—**DR** 2462

S.,L.M.—**NatR-II** 1119

S.,M.—**Ram** 991—**Matthew John Rhodes**

S.,M.C.M.—**FortR** 1403, 1608, 1659—**Mary Charlotte Mair (Senior) Simpson**

S.,P.—**Ram** 997—**Richard Simpson**

S.,R.—see Y.,A.—R.S.

S.,R.—**Ram** 966, 991, 1004, 1028, 1032, 1075, 1082, 1087, 1094, 1103, 1118, 1135—**Richard Simpson**

S.,R.C.—**DR** 2485, 2638

S.,R.H.—**NatR-II** 1512—**Robert Herbert Story**

S.,R.P.—**Ram** 688, 751, 766—**Richard Simpson**

S.,R.S.—[but perhaps R.S.S. for Royal Society of Scotland]—**FM** 1947, 2078

S.,S.—**FM** 6018

S.,S.N.—**Ram** 837—**Scott Nasmyth Stokes**

S.,T.B.—**DR** 2079, 2144, 2186, 2187, 2199, 2211, 2225, 2238, 2267, 2280, 2307, 2321, 2322, 2358, 2373, 2387, 2400, 2412, 2425, 2438, 2448, 2475, 2663—**T. B. Scannell**

S.,T.C.—**FM** 3516, 3583, 3650, 3686—**Thomas Collett Sandars**

S.,T.M.—**DR** 2475

S.,W.—**FM** 3352, 3627, 3835—**William Stirling-Maxwell**

S.,W.—**FM** 5427

S.,W.B.—**FM** 5227—**William Bell Scott**

S.,W.J.—**FM** 5371—**W. Jardine Smith**

S.,W.W.—**FM** 3357—**W. W. Smyth**

S.,W.Y.—**FM** 3436—**W. Y. Sellar**

S.A.B.S. [Simpson, Acton both signed?]—**Ram** 1050—**Richard Simpson** and **J. D. Acton**

S-K.,W.S.—**FM** 3434, 3442—**Walter Scott Seton-Karr**

Sabertash, Captain Orlando—**FM** 1176, 1285, 1351, 1428, 1516, 1656, 1841, 1884, 1896, 1914, 1931, 1940, 1967, 1999—**John Mitchell**

Sacerdos—**DR** 1479

Sacerdos—**Ram** 353, 437

Sacerdos—**Ram** 806—**W. H. Eyre**

Sacerdos Alter—**DR** 1479

Sailor and a Seldonite, A—**FM** 1680—**A. V. Kirwan** and an older collab.

Sangfroid [Lord Sangfroid]—**NatR-II** 46, 115, 219—**Alfred Austin**

Sanitary Reformer, A—**FM** 3687—**Charles Kingsley**

Scotchman, A—**NatR-II** 483

Scoto-Celt, A—**FM** 4961

Scottish Conservative, A—**NatR-II** 408, 831, 1251, 1333; **ScotR** 441, 502—**James Ferguson**, 1857–1917

Scupper, Nelson Tattersall Lee, Esq., Late Ensign in her Majesty's Horse-Marines—**FM** 1421—**W. M. Thackeray**

Scythicus—**NatR-II** 2433

Selina—**FM** 2100, 2162, 2562

Selwyn—**FM** 342—**Mrs. A. Gillespie Smyth**

Senex—**FM** 906—**Horatio Townsend**, or **Townshend**

Shabrach, Ebenezer—**FM** 617

Shareholder—**NatR-II** 2264

Shastin, Vamadeva—**FortR** 2398—**Alfred C. Lyall**

Shastri, Vamadeo—**FortR** 3717, 4194—**Alfred C. Lyall**

Shirley—**FM** 3389, 3402, 3464, 3471, 3494, 3506, 3515, 3538, 3545, 3601, 3606, 3685, 3698, 3741, 3805, 3840, 3853, 3876, 3905, 3918, 3959, 3976, 3990, 4026, 4047, 4060, 4083, 4119, 4174, 4239, 4262, 4279, 4301, 4354, 4567, 4660, 4712, 4738, 4908, 4919, 4944, 5028, 5044, 5080, 5094, 5255, 5263, 5557, 6197, 6261, 6291—**John Skelton**

Sirion—**NatR-II** 156

Sixteen Years' Resident [in the U.S.A.], A—**FM** 1133, 1144—**John B. Brown**

Sly, Jacob, Mariner—**FM** 422

Small John—**FM** 3054—**W. M. Thackeray**

Smatterling, Vicessimus, B.L.—**FM** 3265, 3282, 3504—**J. M. Ludlow**

Sociologist, A—**NatR-II** 451

Solomons, Ikey, Esq., Junior—**FM** 1323, 1330, 1344, 1354, 1379, 1404, 1412—**W. M. Thackeray**

Somno, B.F. [Blue Friar?]—**FM** 1071—**George Wightwick**

Son of Adam, A—**FortR** 3140

Son of the Marshes—**FortR** 3909, 4302; **NatR-II** 1571, 1648—**Denham Jordan** and **Mrs. Jean A. Visger**

South, Lt. Michael—**FM** 2540, and 2572 to 2718 in 12 installments—**E. B. Hamley**

South, Peregrine—**FM** 1315

South African, A—**FortR** 2996

Spaniard, A—**FortR** 4155

Spinner, Alice—**NatR-II** 1737—**Mrs. Augusta Zelia Fraser**

Staff Officer, A—**FM** 2544

Stein, C.—**FortR** 4044, 4421—**John Cecil Russell**

Stepniak [Son of the Steppe]—**FortR** 2530, 2561, 3188—**Sergius Mikhailovitch Kravchinsky**

Stradling, Matthew, Author of *Cheap John's Action*, etc.—**FM** 5322, 5332, 5337, 5350, 5359—**Martin Francis Mahoney**

Strathbogie Churchman, A—**FM** 1559, 1590

Strathest, John—**ScotR** 139—**John Tod**

Stuart, Esmé—**FortR** 3671; **NC** 2424; **ScotR** 536—**Amélie C. Leroy**

Stubbs, Alfred, C.B.M.I.—**FM** 1737

Student in Vedânta, A—**FortR** 4210

Student of Science, A—**FortR** 3688—perhaps John Murray, 1841–1914

Surgeon, A—**FM** 5677—**H. N. Hardy**

Swing!—**FM** 162

Sylvester, Paul—**NatR-II** 688, 760, 774, 815, 816, 849, 900—**Pauline Schletter**

T

T.—**FM** 3509, 3656—**George Tugwell**

T.—**FM** 5265 (see, T.,W.D.)

T.,A.C.—**FM** 5687—**Aucher Cornwall Taylor**

T.,B.—**FM** 5548, 5575, 5625, 5759, 5827, 5944, 6156—**Bertha Thomas**

T.,D.—**FM** 448, 555—**Thomas Carlyle**

T.,E.F.I.—**FM** 6040

T.,E.P.—**NatR-II** 690

T.,F.S.—**FM** 5598—**F. S. Turner**

T.,G.—**DR** 2699

T.,H.—**FM** 3617

T.,H.—**FM** 4727—**Helen Taylor**

T.,H.A.—**FM** 4424—**H. A. Tilley**

T.,H.F.—**FM** 4467—**Henry Fanshawe Tozer?**

T.,H.P.—**NatR-II** 804—**Hugh P. Tregarthen**

T.,H.Y.J.—**NatR-II** 1421—**H. Y. J. Taylor**

T.,I.—**DR** 2674

T.,J.—**DR** 2475

T.,J. [John Townsend]—**FM** 2675, 2722—**J. M. Ludlow**

T.,J.—**FM** ?3903, 4056, 6265, 6293—**John Tulloch**

T.,M.—**FM** 5407, 6064

T.,M.—**FM** 5965, 5999—perhaps Meredith Townsend

T.,M.A. [Michael Angelo Titmarsh]—**FM** 1334, 1390, 2174—**W. M. Thackeray**

T.,M.D.—**DR** 1061

T.,R.—**DR** 2475, 2497

T.,R.—**FM** 5966

T.,S.—**NatR-II** 1036

T.,W.—**FM** 5752—**Walter Thornbury**

T.,W.D.—**FM** 5265, 5784, 5798, 6074

T.,W.M.—**FM** 1463—**W. M. Thackeray**

Tackletoo, Ephraim—**FM** 1551

Tantivy, Thomas ["Tantivy" was a 17th-century nickname for Tories, used as an adj. as late as 1884]—**NatR-II** 1, 12, 26, 59, 109, 169, 263—**Alfred Austin**

Templar, A—**FM** 1711, 1743—**E. V. H. Kenealy**

?Templeton, A.—**FM** 38

Theatralis—**FM** 72

Theophilus—**FM** 97—**William Maginn?**; 144 perhaps William Maginn

Tithe-owner, A—**NatR-II** 978, 1018

Titmarsh—**FM** 1934, 1992, 2024—**W. M. Thackeray**

Titmarsh, M. A.—**FM** 1449, 1578, 1857, 1862, 1901, 1948—**W. M. Thackeray**

Titmarsh, Michael Angelo—**FM** 1215, 1273, 1460, 1609, 1614, 1631, 1642, 2075, 2143, 2174, 2189, 2229, 2240, 2282 collab.—**W. M. Thackeray**

Topaze—**FM** (3881), (3912), 3943, 4043, 4141

Tory from Principle, not Prejudice, A—**FM** 98

Tourist, A—**NatR-II** 1789

Trade Unionist—**FortR** 2635

Trades Union Official, A—**FortR** 2269—**William J. Davis**

Trim—**FM** 1572

Trinity Bachelor, A—**FM** 1389, 1398, 1417

True Blue—**NatR-II** 128

Truepenny, Pioneer, M.D.—**FM** 492

True Tory, A—**FM** 267

Tuck, B. F. [Blue Friar?]—**FM** 1071—**George Wightwick**

Turkish Patriot, A—**FortR** 3927, 3951

Turner, Matthew Freke—**NQM** 19, 80—**Oswald J. F. Crawfurd**

Two Conservatives—**FortR** 1968—**John Eldon Gorst** and **Henry Wolff**

Two Other Conservatives—**FortR** 1970

Tyger—**FM** 433—**William Dunlop**

U

U.—**FM** 6111—possibly Frederick Robert Up-
cott
U.U.—**ScotR** 692—**Arthur M. White**
U.U., Colonel—**ScotR** 668, 680, 692—**Arthur
M. White**
Uitlander—**FortR** 4295
Ulster Protestant, An—**FM** 5173

Unionist—**NatR-II** 1096, 1188
Unionist, An—**FortR** 3382
Unite, Pleasaunce—**FortR** 4539
Unus de Multis—**FM** 5963—**William Alling-
ham**
Utopian, A—**FM** 4696—**Dorothea Beale**
Utrinque—**FM** 3057

V

V.—**FM** 4433
V.—**FM** 5736—**Henry Vignoles** and **O. J.
Vignoles**
V.—**NatR-II** 1535—**Violet (Maxse) Milner**
V.,E.A.—**FortR** 1352—**Emile Ashurst Ven-
turi**
V.,H.F.—**FM** 3524, 3534
V.,J.—**FM** 5725
V.,J.S.—**DR** 1874, 2373, 2412, 2475, 2520—
J. S. Vaughan
V.,R.—**FM** 3908—**Robert Vaughan**
V.,R.A.—**FM** 3657—**Robert Alfred Vaughan**
V.,R.B.—**DR** 1163—**Robert Bede Vaughan**
V.P.—**Ram** 1127—possibly Victor de Buck
Varon—**FM** 2021, 2249—**Cyrus Redding**
Vazaha—**FortR** 3149, 3194, 3382, 3560, 3591
—**F. C. Maude**
Vera—**NatR-II** 332

Verax—**FM** 4003
Very Particular Man, A—**FM** 3790—**A. K. H.
Boyd**
Veteran—**FortR** 3925
Veteran Journalist, A—**NatR-II** 2214—**Sidney
J. Low**
Viator—**DR** 2576—**J. G. F. Raupert**
Vicar—**NatR-II** 202
Vicar of the Church of England, A—**FM** 5230
Victorian, A—**FM** 5781
Vieux Moustache—**FortR** 2807
Vindex—**DR** 1223
Vindex—**FortR** 3964—**Malcolm McColl**
Visitor to Salt Lake City, A—**FM** 5400—
Charles Marshall
Vox—**Ram** 382
Vox Clamantis—**NatR-II** 92

W

W.—**DR** 2709
W.—**FortR** 3756, 3772, 3813, 3858, 3897
W.—**FM** 221—**William Mudford**
W.—**FM** 287, 3415, 3674, 5773, 5833, (5875),
6048, 6120, 6164
W.—**Ram** 624—**T. W. Wilkinson**
W.—**Ram** 661
W.—**Ram** 886—**Frederick Weld?**
W.—**Ram** 1018, 1125—**Richard Simpson**
W.—**Ram** 1040—**Joseph Wassilieff?**
W*—**FM** 724—**William Harrison Ainsworth**
W.,A.—**FM** 3661, 5353
W.,A.A.M.—**DR** 2543
W.,A.J.—**FM** 5496, 5587, 5609, 5655, and
5849 to 5971 in 13 installments—**Alexander
Johnstone Wilson**
W.,C.—**NatR-II** 853, 856, 862, 1033, 1059,
1187—**Charles Wilson,** of Cheltenham
W.,C.—**Ram** 991 collab.—**Charles Weld**
W.,C.F.S.—**DR** 1868 collab.—**Charles Frere
Stopford Warren**

W.,C.R.—**FM** 3941, 4207, 4376?, 4621—**C. R.
Weld**
W.,F.—**DR** 2520, 2531, 2558
W.,G.—**FM** 1332, 1419, 1505, 1698—**George
Walker**
W.,G.C.H.—**NatR-II** 650
W.,H.—**DR** 1978
W.,J.—**FM** 3527
W.,J.L.—**FM** 5041—**J. Lowry Whittle**
W.,J.W.—**FM** 3377, 3526—**John W. Wilkins?**
W.,L.—**FM** 3588—**Lascelles Wraxall**
W.,M.—**Ram** 521
W.,M.J.—**FM** 5484, 5512, 5572, 5679, 5755,
5885—**M. J. Walhouse**
W.,O.—**FM** 3411, 3423—**Otto von Wenck-
stern**
W.,P. [Patricius Walker]—**FM** 5540, 5552,
5681, 5714, 6150—**William Allingham**
W.,R.—**FM** 5003, 5043—**Robert Williams**
W.,S.—**FM** 4049
W.,T.P.—**ScotR** 548, 578, 605, 665 689—
Thomas Pilkington White

W.,W.—**FM** 3885 3915, 3952, 3960, 4000, 4050

W.,W.D.—**FM** 3327, 3394, 3425, 3722, 4012 —**William Davy Watson**

W.,W.G.—**Ram** 1050, 1076—**William George Ward**

W.,W.S.—**FM** 2577

W-P.,F.R.—**DR** 2054, 2090—**F. R. Wegg-Prosser**

Walker Patricius—**FM** 4807 to 6002 in 20 installments—**William Allingham**

Walkinworm, Ernest—**FM** 2203

Wanderer on a Raft, A—**FM** 5183

Warmont, C. de—**NC** 269—**Charlotte Blennerhassett**

White Republican, A—**FM** 4232, 4252, 4260, 4275, 4298—**Hiram Fuller**

Wiggins, Napoleon Putnam, of Passimaquoddy —**FM** 1611, 1616—**W. M. Thackeray**

Woman, A—**NatR-II** 257, 272, 546

Woman of Holland, A—**NatR-II** 914

Working Man, A—**FM** 5211—**Thomas Wright, the "Journeyman Engineer"**

Writer of "Kleutgen versus Vindex," The— **DR** 1223

Writer of the Article in *Fraser* on the Stock Exchange, The—**FM** 5875

Writer of the article in the *Dublin* on F. Faber, The—**DR** 1281—**H. W. Wilberforce**

Writer of the articles on magic, The—**Ram** 624 —**Richard Simpson**

Writer of "The Fall of Fiction," The—**FortR** 2744—**William Watson**

Writer of the First "X" Article, The—**FortR** 3436

Writer of *The Life of Edmund Campion*, The —**Ram** 1087—**Richard Simpson**

Writer of the notice on Dr. Melia, The— **DR** 1241

Writer of the Paper on Tithes, The—**Ram** 188 —**Frederick Betham**

Writer of "The Present Position of European Politics," The—**FortR** 2567—**C. W. Dilke**

Wykehamist, A—**FM** 5423, 5433, 5446— **George Jennings Davies**

X

X.—**DR** 2025, 2699, 2709, 2720, 2738

X.—**FortR** 2819

X.—**FortR** 3025

X.—**FortR** 3436, 3438, 3450—**Harold Frederic**

X.—**FM** 4485, 6138

X.—**FM** 5817—**T. Wemyss Reid**

X.—**NatR-II** 477, 1635, 1791

X.—**NatR-II** 2505—**James L. Garvin**

X.—**Ram** 991—**Richard Simpson**

X.—**Ram** 1021—**T. F. Wetherell**

X-M.P., An—**FM** 128

X.X.—**DR** 2699

X.X.—**FM** 631

X.Y.—**FortR** 3661

X.Y.—**FM** 4131

X.Y.—**NatR-II** 1572

X.Y.X.—**DR** 2609, 2730

X.Y.Z.—**FortR** 4338

X.Y.Z.—**NatR-II** 1262

X.Y.Z.—**Ram** 1050—**Henry N. Oxenham**

Y

Y.—**DR** 2699

Y.—**FortR** 3742, 4532

Y.—**FM** (5474), 5481, 5497, 5524

Y.—**Ram** 27, 162, 332

Y.,A.—**FM** 3362

Y.,A.–R.S.—**FM** 3481

Y.,C. [Charles Yellowplush]—**FM** 1156, 1186, 1204, 1213, 1221, 1232—**W. M. Thackeray**

Y.,O. [Oliver Yorke]—**FM** 149, 159, 161, 309, 382, 393, 433, 434, 483, 555, 563, 672, 675, 759, 770, 1082, 1120, 1140, 1189, 1237, 1611, 1739, 1861, 1881, 2040

Y.,O. [Oliver Yorke]—**FM** 171, 448—**Thomas Carlyle**

Y.,O. [Oliver Yorke]—**FM** 195, 313, 447, 712, 907, 1024, 1397, 1433—**William Maginn**

Y.,O. [Oliver Yorke]—**FM** 255, 496, 653, 771 —**William Maginn?**

Y.,O. [Oliver Yorke]—**FM** 663, 676, 694, 739—**William Maginn**, prob. with **John Churchill**

Y.,O [Oliver Yorke]—**FM** 1082—**J. A. Heraud**

Y.,R.—**Ram** 909—**Richard Raby**

Y. *Miss. Ap.* [Missionary Apostolic]—**Ram** 424

Y.Z.—**Ram** 991, 1012, 1030, 1040, 1059— **Victor de Buck**

Yellowplush, Charles—**FM** 1140, 1170, 1181, (1401)—**W. M. Thackeray**

Yellowplush, Fitzroy—**FM** 1266—**W. M. Thackeray**

Yorke, Oliver—**FM** 98, 109, 128, 363, 634, 793, 819, 873, 953, 1001, 1029, 1103, 1114, 1474, 1637

Yorke, Oliver—**FM** 212, 251, 274, 290, 304—**William Phillips**

Yorke, Oliver—**FM** 270, 296—**John A. Heraud**

Yorke, Oliver—**FM** 496, 750—**William Maginn?**

Yorke, Oliver—**FM** 576—**William Maginn** and **James Hogg**

Yorke, Oliver—**FM** 652 to 766 in 10 installments—**Thomas Powell**

Yorke, Oliver—**FM** 690, 710, 747, 758, 764, 777, 782, 807, 851, 861, 973, 983, 996, 1007, 1019—**Francis Sylvester Mahoney**

Yorke, Oliver—**FM** 845—**William Maginn**

Yorke, Oliver—**FM** 1462—**G. H. Lewes**

You Know Who—**FM** 1331, 1353, 1364

Young England—**NatR-II** 2528

Young England Peer, A—**FortR** 2249—**A. D. R. W. Cochrane-Baillie**

Your Contributor—**Ram** 558—**Myles O'Reilly**

Z

Z.—**DR** 2471

Z.—**FM** 346—possibly John Galt

Z.—**NatR-II** 1559

Z.—**Ram** 1011—**Richard Simpson**

Z.—**ScotR** 616—**William Wallace, 1843–1921**

Zoologus—**FM** 5269—**Richard Owen**

Zyx—**FortR** 4540

*—**FM** 3183—**W. J. Broderip**

***—**Ram** 974—**Frederick Capes**

***—**Ram** 1095—**Father Caccia**

₊—**FortR** 4070

β [Beta]—**FM** 3591, 3597, 3612, 3621, 3634, 3639, 3653, 3663, 3683, 3704, 3726, 3739, 3749, 3771, 3791, 3801, 3814, 3829—**W. J. Broderip**

Δ [Delta]—**DR** 1041

Δ [Delta]—**FortR** 4164

Δ [Delta]—**FM** 816—**D. M. Moir**

Zeta—**FM** 2709—**Cyrus Redding**

Θ [Theta]—**FM** 288—**Edward Marlborough Fitzgerald?**

Θ [Theta]—**FM** 1536

Θ [Theta]—**FM** 3558

Sigma—**Ram** 991, 996—**Thomas F. Wetherell**

Φ [Phi]—**FM** 3198, 3239, 3263

ΓΝΩΜΩΝ [GNOMON]—**ScotR** 442

προαιρεσις [person of set purpose]—**NatR-II** 432, 506, 589, 615, 704

אנכי בן ירה ['Anoki ben Ierah = I am the son of the moon]—**FM** 4902

Abbreviations and Short Titles

Abbreviations and Short Titles

A

ADB: *Allgemeine Deutsche Biographie*: for details see *Index*, I, 1171.

Aberdeen Graduates, I, II, III: *Roll of the Graduates of the University of Aberdeen*, in 3 vols., 1860–1900, ed. William Johnston; 1901–1925, with supplement 1860–1900, ed. Theodore Watt; and 1926–1955, with supplement 1860–1925, ed. John Mackintosh; Aberdeen, 1906, 1935, and 1960 respectively.

Abraham, *Essays*: George Whitley Abraham, *Essays, Historical, Critical, and Political, Contributed Principally to the "Dublin Review,"* London, 1868.

Acadamy: *a Weekly Review*, 1869–1916; for details see *Index*, I, 1171.

Acton, *Correspondence*: J. Dalberg Acton, *Selections from the Correspondence of the First Lord Acton*, ed. J. N. Figgis and R. V. Laurence, Vol. I, London, 1917.

Acton, *Essays on Church and State*: J. Dalberg Acton, *Essays on Church and State*, ed. Douglas Woodruff, London, 1952.

Acton, *Historical Essays*: J. Dalberg Acton, *Historical Essays and Studies*, ed. J. N. Figgis and R. V. Laurence, London, 1907.

Acton, *History of Freedom*: J. Dalberg Acton, *The History of Freedom and Other Essays*, ed. J. N. Figgis and R. V. Laurence, London, 1907.

Acton-Simpson Corres.: *The Correspondence of Lord Acton and Richard Simpson*, 3 vols., Cambridge, 1971–. All of our quotations, however, were sent to us by the editors before Vols. I and II were published or from the MS. of Vol. III now in preparation.

Allibone: S. A. Allibone, *A Critical Dictionary of English Literature*; for details see *Index*, I, 1171.

Allies, *Per crucem*: T. W. Allies, *Per crucem ad lucem*, 2 vols., London, 1879.

Allingham Corres.: about 800 letters to and from William Allingham at the Library of the University of Illinois.

Allingham, *Diary*: *William Allingham, A Diary*, ed. Helen Allingham and D. Radford, London, 1908.

Allingham, *Varieties*: William Allingham, *Varieties in Prose*, 3 vols., London, 1893.

Allon, *Letters*: *Letters to a Victorian Editor, Henry Allon*, ed. Albert Peel, London, 1929.

Alum. Dub: *Alumni Dublinenses; a register of the Students, Graduates, Professors and Provosts of Trinity College* (1593–1860, with appendix 1860–1868), ed. G. D. Burtchell and T. U. Sadleir, London, 1924.

Amer. WW: *Who's Who in America*; for details see *Index*, I, 1172.

Amer. WWW: *Who Was Who in America*; for details see *Index*, I, 1172.

Annual Register: see *Index*, I, 1172 for details.

Antiquaries: *Proceedings of the Society of Antiquaries of London*, 1843–1859, 1859–1920, London, 1843, etc.

Army List: *The New Annual Army List*, ed. H. G. Hart, London, 1840–1916.

Arnold, *Essays*, I, II, III: Matthew Arnold, *Essays in Criticism*, first, second, and third series: see *Index*, I, 1172, for details.

Arnold, *Essays*, ed. Neiman: *Essays, Letters, and Reviews by Matthew Arnold*, ed. Fraser Neiman, Cambridge, Mass., 1960.

Arnold, *Life*: Thomas Arnold, Jr., *Passages in a Wandering Life*, London, 1900.

Athenaeum: *The Athenaeum; A Journal of Literature, Science, and the Arts*, 151 vols., London, 1828–1921.

Australian Ency.: *The Australian Encyclopaedia*; 10 vols., East Lansing, Michigan, 1958.

B

BMCat.: *British Museum General Catalogue of Printed Books*, London, 1931–1965.

BNB: *Biographie Nationale de Belgique*, Brussels, 1866–1966.

Baden-Powell, *State Aid*: George Baden-Powell, *State Aid and State Interference, Illustrated by Results in Commerce and Industry*, London, 1882.

Badham, *Prose*: Charles David Badham, *Prose Halieutics: or Ancient and Modern Fish Tattle*, London, 1854.

Bagehot, *Studies*: Walter Bagehot, *Literary Studies*, ed. R. H. Hutton, 3 vols., London, 1898.

Bagehot, *Works*: Walter Bagehot, *Collected Works*, ed. St. John-Stevas, 8 vols., Cambridge, Mass., in progress.

Bagshawe: Notebook in the hand of H. R. Bagshawe, executive editor of the *Dublin Review*, 1837–1863, containing an incomplete list of contributors, vols. 1–52 (May 1836–April 1863), drawn up from notes, letters, and memory about 1863. Now in the "*Dublin Review* Papers" in the Westminster Diocesan Archives, London. The Notebook was transcribed with some corrections and some biographical comment by Matthew Russell, "Early Reviewers," q.v.

Bagshawe Papers: Letters, with associated papers, written to H. R. Bagshawe, editor of the *Dublin Review*, 1837–1863, from Cardinal Wiseman, C. W. Russell, various representatives of the printers and publishers, and a number of contributors. These letters are in the Westminster Diocesan Archives, London, where they are called "*Dublin Review* Papers."

Barnett, *Practicable Socialism*: Samuel and Henrietta Barnett, *Practicable Socialism: Essays on Social Reform*, 2nd ed., London, 1894.

Barry, *Memories*: William [Francis] Barry, *Memories and Opinions*, London and N.Y., [1926].

Batho, *Shepherd*: Edith C. Batho, The Ettrick Shepherd, Cambridge, 1927. With a bibliography, pp. 183–221.

Battersby: William Joseph Battersby, *A Complete Catholic Directory, Almanack, and Registry*, 1836, etc.

Bayswater: A set of the *Dublin Review* in Cardinal Manning's Library at the Oblates of St. Charles, Bayswater, London, with extensive markings in the period 1836–1878. The markings are not, according to M. l'Abbé Chapeau, in Manning's hand, but probably in that of Canon Wyndham.

Beale: T. W. Beale, *An Oriental Biographical Dictionary*, revised edition ed. H. G. Keene, London, 1894.

Beesly, *Catiline*: Edward Spencer Beesly, *Catiline, Clodius, and Tiberius*, London, 1878.

Bell, *Novelists*: Mackenzie Bell, *Representative Novelists of the Nineteenth Century*, 3 vols., N.Y., 1927.

Benedicti Familiae: *S. S. Patriarchae Benedicti Familiae Confederatae*, Beatty, Penna. and Rome, 1869.

Benedictine Bibliog.: *A Benedictine Bibliography*, ed. O. L. Kapsner, 2 vols., Collegeville, Minn., 1962.

Bengal Civil Servants: Edward Dodwell and J. S. Miles, *Alphabetical List of the Honourable East India Company's Bengal Civil Servants, 1780–1839*, London, 1839.

Bentley: R. Bentley & Son, Publishers, *A List of the Principal Publications Issued from New Burlington Street 1829–1898*, 8 vols., London, 1893–1920. According to Gettmann, *Bentley*, p. xi, the book was edited by Richard Bentley II. Since there is no pagination, references to "Bentley" are references to the year, printed at the top of the pages, in which materials in, or on, *Bentley's Miscellany, Bentley's Quarterly Review*, or *Temple Bar* appear.

Bentley list: see Bentley.

Bevington, *Saturday Review*: Merle M. Bevington, *The Saturday Review, 1855–1868*, N.Y., 1941.

Bib. Nat. Cat.: *Catalogue Général des Livres Imprimés de la Bibliothèque Nationale*, Paris, 1924–1964.

Bikelas, *Seven Essays*: Demetrios Bikelas, *Seven Essays on Christian Greece*, translated by the Marquess of Bute, London, 1890.

Bishop, *Life*: Nigel Abercombie, *The Life and Work of Edmund Bishop*, London, 1959, with a "Bibliography," pp. 492–508.

Blackie, *Letters to His Wife*: John Stuart Blackie, *Letters to his Wife, with a few Earlier Ones to his Parents*, ed. A. S. Walker, Edin. and London, 1909.

Blackie, *Testimonials*: *Testimonials in Favour of John Stuart Blackie* [as candidate for the Chair in Greek at the University of Edinburgh], Edin., 1852. On pp. 11–12 Blackie submits a partial list of his writings.

Blackwood: "Blackwood's Contributors' Book," a MS. in the National Library of Scotland which lists most of the authors of articles and stories from 1821–1900.

Blackwood Corres.: Correspondence of Blackwood & Sons relating to *Blackwood's Magazine* now in the National Library of Scotland.

Blackwood Papers Cat.: *National Library of Scotland. Catalogue of Manuscripts Acquired Since 1925, Vol. III . . . Blackwood Papers, 1805–1900*, Edinburgh 1968. A catalogue of the "Blackwood Corres." just above.

Blackwood and Sons: Margaret O. Oliphant, *Annals of a Publishing House, William Blackwood and His Sons*, 2 vols., N.Y., 1897; vol. III, 1898, by Mrs. Gerald Porter.

Boase: Frederic Boase, *Modern English Biography*; for details see *Index*, I, 1173.

Boase and Courtney: George C. Boase and William P. Courtney, *Bibliotheca Cornubiensis. A Catalogue of the Writings . . . of Cornishmen*, 2 vols., London, 1874 and 1878. With a Supplement called vol. III, London, 1882.

Borrow, *Life*: W. I. Knapp, *Life, Writings, and Correspondence of George Borrow*, 2 vols., N.Y. and London, 1899.

Boulger, *Central Asian Questions*: Demetrius C. Boulger, *Central Asian Questions. Essays on Afghanistan, China, and Central Asia*, London, 1885.

Bourchier, *Life*: Lady Grogan, *The Life of J. D. Bourchier*, London, 1926.

Bowring, *Korrespondence*: Robert Beer, ed. *Korrespondence Johna Bowringa do Čech*, Prague, 1904.

Boyd, *Autumn Holidays*: [A. K. H. Boyd], *The Autumn Holidays of a Country Parson*, by the Author of *The Recreations of a Country Parson*, London, 1864.

Boyd, *Critical Essays*: [A. K. H. Boyd], *The Critical Essays of a Country Parson*, by the Author of *The Recreations of a Country Parson*, London, 1867.

Boyd, *Everyday philosopher*: [A. K. H. Boyd], *The Every-day Philosopher in Town and Country*, by the Author of *The Recreations of a Country Parson*, London, 1863.

Boyd, *Landscapes*: [A. K. H. Boyd], *Landscapes, Churches, and Moralities*, by the Author of *The Recreations of a Country Parson*, London, 1874.

Boyd, *Leisure Hours*: [A. K. H. Boyd], *Leisure Hours in Town*, by the Author of *The Recreations of a Country Parson*, London, 1862.

Boyd, *Lessons*: [A. K. H. Boyd], *Lessons of Middle Age*, by the Author of *The Recreations of a Country Parson*, London, 1868.

Boyd, *Recreations*, 1st series, or 2nd series, or 3rd series: Andrew Kennedy Hutchison Boyd, *The Recreations of a Country Parson, First Series*, London, 1860; *Second Series*, 1861; *Third Series*, 1886.

Boyle's Court Guide: *Boyle's New Fashionable Court and Country Guide*, London, 1824–1903.

Brabazon, *Thoughts*: Reginald and Mary Jane Brabazon [Earl and Countess of Meath], *Thoughts on Imperial and Social Subjects*, London, 1906.

Brady, *Essays*: W. Maziere Brady, *Essays on the English State Church in Ireland*, London, 1869.

Brassey, *Voyages*: Thomas Brassey, *Voyages and Travels of Lord Thomas Brassey from 1862 to 1894*, ed. Capt. S. Eardley-Wilmot, 2 vols., London, 1895.

Brimley, *Essays*: George Brimley, *Essays*, ed. William George Clark, 3rd edn. London, [1858], 1882.

Bristed, *Pieces*: Charles A. Bristed, *Pieces of a Broken-Down Critic*, 4 vols. in one, Baden Baden, 1858–59.

Brit. Mus. Biog.: James Duff Brown and Stephen S. Stratton, *British Musical Biography*, Birmingham, 1897.

Britten and Boulger: James Britten and G. S. Boulger, *A Biographical Index of Deceased British and Irish Botanists*, London, 1931.

Broderip, *Leaves*: William John Broderip, *Leaves from the Note Book of a Naturalist*, London, 1852.

Buckland: C[harles] E. Buckland, *Dictionary of Indian Biography*, London, 1906.

Buckle, *Life*: A. H. Huth, *The Life and Writings of Henry Thomas Buckle*, N.Y., 1880.

Bunsen, *Memoir*: Frances, Baroness Bunsen, *A Memoir of Baron Bunsen*, 2 vols., London, 1868.

Burke: *John B. Burke's Genealogical and Heraldic History of the Peerage, Baronetage and Knightage*, 99th and 100th eds., London, 1949, 1953; and various earlier editions.

Burke's *Ireland*: *John B. Burke's Genealogical and Heraldic History of the Landed Gentry of Ireland*, London, 1899, 1904.

Burne-Jones, *Memorials*: Georgiana Burne-Jones, *Memorials of Edward Burne-Jones*, 2 vols., London, 1904.

Burtis list: A list of articles by Moncure D. Conway drawn up by Mary Elizabeth

Burtis, author of *Moncure Conway, 1832–1907*, New Brunswick, N.J., 1952, on the basis of a bound volume of *Fraser* articles in the Conway Collection, Columbia Univ. Lib. Miss Burtis considers these articles "without doubt Conway's, on basis of internal evidence alone."

Busk, "Letters": "The Letters of Mrs. Mary Margaret Blair Busk to *Blackwood's Magazine* in the National Library of Scotland, 1825–1850," ed. George Taylor Prig-

more. Unpubl. diss., Texas Tech. College, 1952.

Bute, *Memoir*: David Oswald Hunter Blair, *John Patrick [Crichton-Stuart], Third Marquess of Bute, K.T., 1847–1900*, London, 1921.

Bute Papers: Correspondence relating to the *Scottish Review*, mainly addressed to the Third Marquess of Bute, now in the possession of the present Lord Bute, Isle of Bute, Scotland.

C

CBEL: *Cambridge Bibliography of English Literature*; for details see *Index*, I, 1174.

CCD: *Crockford's Clerical Directory*; for details see *Index*, I, 1174.

CD: *The Catholic Directory and Annual Register*, starting in 1838.

Cairnes, *Economy*: John Elliott Cairnes, *Essays in Political Economy, Theoretical and Applied*, London, 1873.

Canadiana: *Encyclopedia Canadiana*, ed. J. E. Robbins, 10 vols., Ottawa, 1957–1958.

Canadian WWW: *Standard Dictionary of Canadian Biography; the Canadian Who Was Who*. Eds. C. G. D. Roberts and A. L. Tunnell, 2 vols., Toronto, 1934–38.

Carlyle, *Bibliography*: Isaac Watson Dyer, *A Bibliography of Thomas Carlyle's Writings and Annotations*, Portland, Maine, 1928.

Carlyle, *Essays*: Thomas Carlyle, *Critical and Miscellaneous Essays*, in *Works*, Centenary Edition, vols. 26–30, London, 1896–99.

Carlyle, *Letters*: *Letters of Thomas Carlyle, 1826–1836*, ed. C. E. Norton, 2 vols., London and N.Y., 1888.

Carlyle, *Letters to Mill*: *Letters of Thomas Carlyle to John Stuart Mill, John Sterling, and Robert Browning*, ed. Alexander Carlyle, London, 1923.

Carlyle, *Memoirs*: *Memoirs of the Life and Writings of Thomas Carlyle*, ed. R. H. Shepherd, London, 1881.

Casartelli, "Jubilee": L. C. Casartelli, "Our Diamond Jubilee," *Dublin Review*, 118 (Apr. 1896), 245–271.

Casartelli, *Sketches*: L. C. Casartelli, Bishop of Salford, *Sketches in History, Chiefly Ecclesiastical*, N.Y., 1906.

Cath. Ency.: *The Catholic Encyclopedia*, 15 vols., N.Y., 1907–1914. Also see *New Cath. Ency.*, below.

Cath. WW: *The Catholic Who's Who*, London, 1908–.

Chadwick, *Life*: S. E. Finer, *The Life and Times of Sir Edwin Chadwick*, London, 1952. With a bibliography of his writings, pp. 530–540.

Chamberlain, *Memoir*: Joseph Chamberlain, *A Political Memoir, 1880–92*, ed. C. H. D. Howard, London, 1953.

Chambers: *Chambers' Biographical Dictionary*: for details see *Index*, I, 1174.

Champneys, *Patmore*: Basil Champneys, *Memoirs and Correspondence of Coventry Patmore*, 2 vols., London, 1900–1901.

Clarke, *Chips*: Charles Clarke, *Chips from an Old Block*, London, 1871.

Clarkson, *Suez Canal*: Edward Clarkson, *The Suez Navigable Canal, for Accelerated Communication with India*, 2nd ed., London, 1843.

Clifford, *Lectures*: William Kingdon Clifford, *Lectures and Essays*, ed. Leslie Stephen and Frederick Pollock, 2 vols., London, 1879.

Clough, *Correspondence*: *The Correspondence of Arthur Hugh Clough*, ed. Frederick L. Mulhauser, 2 vols., Oxford, 1957.

Cobbe, *Cities*: Frances Power Cobbe, *The Cities of the Past*, London, 1864.

Cobbe, *Darwinism*: Frances Power Cobbe, *Darwinism in Morals, and Other Essays*, London, 1872.

Cobbe, *Hours*: Frances Power Cobbe, *Hours of Work and Play*, London, 1867.

Cobbe, *Pursuits of Women*: Frances Power Cobbe, *Essays on the Pursuits of Women*, 1863.

Cobbe, *Scientific Spirit*: Frances Power Cobbe, *The Scientific Spirit of the Age*, London, 1888.

Cobbe, *Studies*: Frances Power Cobbe, *Studies New and Old of Ethical and Social Subjects*, London, 1865.

Cole, Diary: The manuscript diary of Henry Cole, 1839–1840, at Victoria and Albert Museum, London.

Coleridge, *Life*: *Life and Correspondence of John Duke Coleridge*, ed. E. H. Coleridge, 2 vols., N.Y., 1904.

Complete Baronetage: *Complete Baronetage, 1611–1800*, ed. G[eorge] E[dward] C[okayne], 5 vols. and an index, Exeter, 1900–1909.

Complete Peerage: *The Complete Peerage of England, Scotland, Ireland, Great Britain and the United Kingdom*, by G. E. C[okayne], ed. Vicary Gibbs, 13 vols., London, 1910–1940.

Conway, *Autobiography*: Moncure D. Conway, *Autobiography*, 2 vols., London, 1904.

Conway, "Working with Froude," I and II: Moncure D. Conway, "Working with Froude on 'Fraser's Magazine,' " being 2 arts. in *The Nation*, vol. 59 (Nov. 22 and 29, 1894), 378–379, and 401–402.

Conybeare, *Roman Catholicism*: Frederick C. Conybeare, *Roman Catholicism as a Factor in European Politics*, London, 1901.

Conzemius: Ignaz von Döllinger, *Briefwechsel, 1850–1890*. Vol. I: *Briefwechsel mit Lord Acton, 1850–1869*, ed. Victor Conzemius, Munich, 1963.

Cornwallis, *Letters*: *Selection from the Letters of Caroline Frances Cornwallis*, ed. M. C. Power, London, 1864, with a list of her articles on p. 443.

Courtney, *Making of an Editor*: Janet Elizabeth Courtney, *The Making of an Editor, W. L. Courtney, 1850–1928*, London, 1930.

Courtney, *Studies*: W. L. Courtney, *Studies New and Old*, London, 1888.

Cowell, *Life*: George Cowell, *Life & Letters of Edward Byles Cowell*, London, 1904. With a list of his writings, pp. 464–470.

Crawford, *Indian Medical Service*: D. G. Crawford, *Roll of the Indian Medical Service, 1615–1930*, London, 1930.

Crawfurd, *The Fool*: Oswald J. F. Crawfurd, *The Fool of the Family and Other Tales*, 2 vols., London, 1876.

Crawfurd, *Portugal*: Oswald J. F. Crawfurd, *Portugal Old and New*, London, 1880.

Crichton-Stuart, *Foreign Essays*: John Patrick Crichton-Stuart, 3rd Marquess of Bute, *Essays on Foreign Subjects*, Paisley, 1901.

Crichton-Stuart, *Home Essays*: John Patrick Crichton-Stuart, *Essays on Home Subjects*, Paisley, 1904.

Crone: John S. Crone, *A Concise Dictionary of Irish Biography*, London, 1928.

Cross, *Impressions*: John W. Cross, *Impressions of Dante and the New World, with a Few Words on Bimetallism*, Edin. and London, 1893.

Current Discussion: *Current Discussion. A Collection from the Chief English Essays on Questions of the Time*, edited by Edward L. Burlingame, 2 vols., N.Y., 1878.

Cushing, *Anonyms*: William Cushing, *Anonyms: a Dictionary of Revealed Authorship*, Cambridge, Mass., 1889.

Cushing: *Initials*: William Cushing, *Initials and Pseudonyms*; for details see *Index*, I, 1175.

D

DAB: *Dictionary of American Biography*, 22 vols., N.Y., 1928–1958.

DBF: *Dictionnaire de Biographie Française*, Paris, 1933–.

DCB: *Dictionary of Catholic Biography*, ed. J. J. Delaney and J. E. Tobin, N.Y., 1961.

DEI: *Dizionario Enciclopedica Italiano*, 12 vols., Rome, 1955–1961.

DNB: *Dictionary of National Biography*, London, 1885–1960. For details see *Index*, I, 1175.

DR list: "The Dublin Review. General List of Articles. Vols. I–CXVIII (1836–1896)," *Dublin Review*, 118 (Apr. 1896), 467–520. This list is a combination of the Bagshawe list (see above under Bagshawe) and a marked file at Oscott. Where there was any conflict, the question was submitted to Matthew Russell, author of various articles in the *Irish Monthly* on the *Dublin Review*, and resolved as therein given unless the conflict is still listed: see p. 467n.

DSAB: *Dictionary of South African Biography*, Vol. I, ed. W. J. de Kock, Cape Town, 1968.

Debrett: *Debrett's Baronetage, Knightage and Companionage*, London, various editions.

de la Ramée, *Views*: Marie Louise de la Ramée, *Views and Opinions*, London, 1895.

Delille, *French Writers*: Edward Delille, *Some French Writers*, London, 1893.

De Morgan, *Memoir*: Sophia Elizabeth De Morgan, *Memoir of Augustus De Morgan*, London, 1882. With a list of his writings on pp. 401–415.

Dennis, *Studies*: John Dennis, *Studies in English Literature*, London, 1876.

De Vere, *Essays*: Aubrey De Vere, *Essays, Chiefly Literary and Ethical*, London, 1889.

De Vere, *Essays on Poetry*: Aubrey De Vere, *Essays, Chiefly on Poetry*, 2 vols., London, 1887.

De Vere, *Religious Problems*: Aubrey De Vere, *Religious Problems of the Nineteenth Century*. Essays, ed. J. G. Wenham, London, 1883.

De Vere's list: A list of his own articles that had not been reprinted, drawn up by Aubrey De Vere in Oct. 1889, and published by Matthew Russell, "Unpublished Letters of Aubrey De Vere," *Irish Monthly*, 39 (1911), 427.

Dickens, *Letters*: *The Letters of Charles Dickens*, ed. Madeline House and Graham Storey, Vols. I and II, Oxford, 1965–.

Dickins, *Kemble*: Bruce Dickins, "John Mitchell Kemble and Old English Scholarship, with a bibliography of his writings," *Proc. of the Brit. Academy*, XXV (1939), 51–84. (See the cautious note on his attributions, p. 79n.)

Dilke, *European Politics*: Sir Charles W.

Dilke, *The Present Position of European Politics*, London, 1887.

Dobson, *Vignettes*: Henry Austin Dobson, *Eighteenth Century Vignettes*, 3 vols., London, 1892–1896.

Dolman list: Any list of articles, together with authors, either drawn up for a given issue or described as being on hand by any member of the publishing firm of Charles Dolman, 1836–1858. These are part of the Bagshawe Papers, q.v.

Donne, *Essays*: William Bodham Donne, *Essays on the Drama and on Popular Amusements*, 2nd ed., London, 1863.

Donne list: see Johnson, *Donne*.

Dowden, *Essays*: Edward Dowden, *Essays Modern and Elizabethan*, London, 1910.

Dowden, *New Studies*: Edward Dowden, *New Studies in Literature*, London, 1895.

Dowden, *Studies*: Edward Dowden, *Studies in Literature, 1789–1877*, London, 1882.

Dowden, *Transcripts*: Edward Dowden, *Transcripts and Studies*, London, 1896.

Dramatic Portraits: *Catalogue of Dramatic Portraits* [of actors], ed. Lillian A. Hall, 4 vols., Cambridge, Mass., 1930–1934.

Dugdale, *Barnes*: Giles Dugdale, *William Barnes of Dorset*, London, 1953. With a bibliography, pp. 237–244.

E

EUI: *Enciclopedia Universal Ilustrada*, Barcelona and Madrid, 1907?–1964.

Eastlake, *Correspondence*: Elizabeth Eastlake, *Journals and Correspondence of Lady Eastlake*, ed. Charles E. Smith, 2 vols., London, 1895.

Edwards, *Russians at Home*: H. Sutherland Edwards, *The Russians at Home and the Russians Abroad: Sketches of Russian Life under Alexander II*, 2 vols., London, 1879.

Eliot, *Essays*: *Essays of George Eliot*, ed. Thomas Pinney, N.Y., 1963.

Eliot, *Letters*: *The George Eliot Letters*, ed. Gordon S. Haight, 7 vols., New Haven, 1954–1955.

Ellis, *Ainsworth*: S. M. Ellis, *William Harrison Ainsworth and his Friends*, 2 vols., N.Y. and London, 1911.

Enci. Ital.: *Enciclopedia Italiana*, 36 vols., 3 appendices, Rome, 1929–1961.

Ency. Brit.: *Encyclopaedia Britannica*, various editions.

Ency. Canada: *The Encyclopedia of Canada*, ed. W. S. Wallace, 6 vols., Toronto, 1940; Newfoundland suppl. 1949.

Ency. So. A.: *Encyclopedia of Southern*

Africa, ed. Eric Rosenthal, London and N.Y., 1961.

Eng. Cat.: *The English Catalogue of Books*, London, 1801–1962.

Erslew, Supplement: Thomas Hansen Erslew, ed., *Almindeligt Forfatter – Lexicon for Kongeriget Danmark* (Supplement), 3 vols., Copenhagen, 1858–1868.

Escott Papers: A large collection of letters written for the most part to T. H. S. Escott by various correspondents, the most important for our purposes being those from Joseph Chamberlain. The letters are the property of Mrs. W. E. Denton and are now being catalogued by the National Register of Archives.

Escott, *Politics*: T. H. S. Escott, *Politics and Letters*, London, 1886.

Essays on Research: *Essays on the Endowment of Research*, by Various Writers, [ed. C. E. Appleton], London, 1876.

Everyman's: *Everyman's Dictionary of Literary Biography English and American*, London and N.Y., 1958.

Ewing: William Ewing, ed., *Annals of the Free Church of Scotland, 1843–1900*, 2 vols., Edin., 1914.

F

F. O. List: *The Foreign Office List*, an annual, starting in 1806. The vol. for 1901 gives deaths from 1852–1900; that for 1907, deaths from 1870–1906.

F.R.G.S.: Fellow of the Royal Geographical Society.

Falconer, *Writings of Lang*: C. M. Falconer, *The Writings of Andrew Lang*, Dundee, [privately printed], 1894.

Fasti: *Fasti Ecclesiae Scoticanae*, ed. W. S. Crockett and Francis Grant, 7 vols., Edin., 1915–1928. This book was originally ed. Hew Scott, in 3 vols., London, 1866–1871, and some of our references may be to this first edition.

Fasti – Free Church: John Alexander Lamb, ed., *The Fasti of the United Free Church of Scotland, 1900–1929*, Edin. and London, 1956.

Fawcett, *Essays*: Henry Fawcett and Millicent Garrett Fawcett, *Essays and Lectures on Social and Political Subjects*, London, 1872.

FitzGerald, *Letters*: Edward FitzGerald, *Letters and Literary Remains*, ed. William Aldis Wright, 3 vols., London, 1889.

Forbes, *Camps*: Archibald Forbes, *Camps, Quarters and Casual Places*, 1896.

Forbes, *Memories*: Archibald Forbes, *Memories and Studies of War and Peace*, N.Y., 1895.

Foreign Office List: see above under *F. O. List*.

Forman: H. Buxton Forman, *The Books of William Morris*, London, 1897, with list of some contributors to the *Oxford and Cambridge Magazine*.

Forster Collection: Catalogue of the John Forster Collection of pamphlets and offprints, Victoria and Albert Museum, London.

Foster: *Alumni Oxonienses: The Members of the University of Oxford, 1715–1886*, ed. Joseph Foster, 4 vols., London, 1886–1887.

Francis, *Orators*: George Henry Francis, *The Orators of the Age*, London, 1847.

Freeman, *Essays*: Edward A. Freeman, *Historical Essays*, 4 series, London, 1871–1892.

Froude, *Armada*: James Anthony Froude, *The Spanish Story of the Armada, and Other Essays*, London, 1892.

Froude, *Life*: W. H. Dunn, *James Anthony Froude. A Biography*, 2 vols., Oxford, 1961–1963.

Froude list: A list of articles by J. A. Froude drawn up by his first wife and owned (in March 1962) by Professor Waldo H. Dunn.

Froude, *Studies*: James Anthony Froude, *Short Studies on Great Subjects*, 4 series, London, 1867, 1871, 1877, 1890.

Furnivall: F. J. Furnivall, "Trial-list of Criticism and Notices of Browning's Works, &c," [London], *Browning Society Papers*, I (1881–1884), 89–108, 125–150, 168.

G

Gairdner, *Studies*: James Gairdner and James Spedding, *Studies in English History*, Edin., 1881.

Gallenga, *Episodes*: Antonio Gallenga, *Episodes of my Second Life*, 2 vols., London, 1884. With a list of his articles in II, 90–91.

Gallenga, *Italy*: Antonio Gallenga, *Italy, Past and Present*, 2 vols., London, 1848.

Galloway, *Testimonials*: *Testimonials in favour of T. G. [Thomas Galloway] . . . , as Candidate for the Chair of Natural Philosophy in the University of Edinburgh*, Edin., 1881.

Galt, *The Howdie*: John Galt, *The Howdie, and Other Tales*, ed. W. Roughead, London, 1923.

Gardner, *Greek History*: Percy Gardner, *New Chapters in Greek History*, London, 1892.

Garnett, *Essays*: Richard Garnett (1835–1906), *Essays in Librarianship and Bibliography*, London, 1899.

Garnett, *Twilight of Gods*: Richard Garnett, *The Twilight of the Gods, and Other Tales*, London, 1924.

Gaskell, "Bibliography": Clark S. Northup, "Bibliography," appended to Gerald DeWitt Sanders, *Elizabeth Gaskell*, London, 1929.

Gaskell, *Letters*: Elizabeth Gaskell, *The Letters of Mrs. Gaskell*, ed. J. A. V. Chapple and Arthur Pollard, Cambridge. Mass., 1967.

Gasquet: Francis Aidan Gasquet, *Lord Acton and His Circle*, London, 1906.

Gent. Mag.: *The Gentleman's Magazine*, London, 1731–1880.

Gettmann, *Bentley*: Royal A. Gettmann, *A Victorian Publisher: A Study of the Bentley Papers*, Cambridge, 1960.

Gilbert, *Life*: Rose Mulholland Gilbert, *Life of Sir John T. Gilbert*, London, 1905.

Gillies, *Memoirs*: Robert Pearse Gillies, *Memoirs of a Literary Veteran*, 3 vols., London, 1851.

Gillies, *Recollections*: Robert Pearse Gillies, *Recollections of Sir Walter Scott*, London, 1837.

Gillow: Joseph Gillow, *Dictionary of English Catholics*; for details see *Index*, I, 1178.

Gladstone, *Gleanings*: William Ewart Gladstone, *Gleanings of Past Years, 1843–1879*, 7 vols., London, 1879.

Gladstone, *Irish Question*: W. E. Gladstone, *Special Aspects of the Irish Question, 1886–1890*, London, 1892.

Gladstone, *Life*: John Morley, *The Life of William Ewart Gladstone*, 3 vols., London and N.Y., 1903.

Glasgow Graduates: W. I. Addison, *Roll of Graduates, Glasgow University*, 1727–1897.

Gleason, *Russophobia*: John Howes Gleason, *The Genesis of Russophobia in Great Britain*, Cambridge, Mass., 1950.

Gleig, *Essays*: George Robert Gleig, *Essays Biographical, Historical, and Miscellaneous, Contributed Chiefly to the "Edinburgh" and "Quarterly Reviews,"* 2 vols., London, 1858.

Gohdes: Clarence Gohdes, *American Literature in Nineteenth-Century England*, N.Y., 1944. With an appendix of articles in British periodicals from 1833–1901, pp. 151–180.

Goodwin, *Science and Faith*: Harvey Goodwin, *Walks in the Regions of Science and Faith*, London, 1883.

Gorman, *Converts*: W. S. Gordon Gorman, *Converts to Rome*; for details see *Index*, I, 1178.

Gosse, *Studies*: Edmund W. Gosse, *Studies in the Literature of Northern Europe*, London, 1879.

Grande Encyclopédie: *La Grande Encyclopédie*, 31 vols., Paris, 1886–1902.

Grand Larousse: *Grand Larousse Encyclopédique*, 10 vols., Paris, 1960–1964.

Grant: *The Faculty of Advocates in Scotland, 1532–1943*, ed. Francis J. Grant, Edin., 1944.

Grant, *Metropolis*: [James Grant], *The Great Metropolis*, 2 vols., London, 1836; also 2nd edition, 1837, where so cited.

Grant Duff, *Miscellanies*: Mountstuart E. Grant Duff, *Miscellanies, Political and Literary*, London, 1878.

Grant Duff, *Studies*: Mountstuart E. Grant Duff, *Studies in European Politics*, Edin., 1866.

Greg, *Misc. Essays*: William Rathbone Greg, *Miscellaneous Essays, [First and] Second Series*, London, 1882, 1884.

Grosse Brockhaus: *Der Grosse Brockhaus*, 15th and 16th eds., Leipsig, 1928–1937; Wiesbaden, 1952–1958.

Grove: George Grove, *Dictionary of Music and Musicians*, 5th ed., 10 vols., London, 1954.

Gundry, *China*: R. S. Gundry, *China Present and Past*, London, 1895.

H

H&L: Halkett and Laing, *Dictionary of Anonymous and Pseudonymous English Literature*; for details see *Index*, I, 1179.

Hales, *Folia*: John W. Hales, *Folia Literaria. Essays and Notes on English Literature*, London, 1893.

Hales, *Notes*: John W. Hales, *Notes and Essays on Shakespeare*, London, 1884.

Hamerton, *Thoughts*: Philip Gilbert Hamerton, *Thoughts about Art*, Boston, 1871.

Hansard: Thomas Curson Hansard, *The Parliamentary Debates*, vol. 1–F41, London, 1803 to present.

Harrison, *Choice of Books*: Frederic Harrison, *The Choice of Books and Other Literary Pieces*, London, 1886.

Harrison, *Common Sense*: Frederic Harrison, *The Philosophy of Common Sense*, N.Y., 1907.

Harrison, *Order and Progress*: Frederic Harrison, *Order and Progress*, London, 1875.

Harrison, *Problems*: Frederic Harrison, *National and Social Problems*, London, 1908.

Harrison, *Tennyson, Ruskin, Mill*: Frederic Harrison, *Tennyson, Ruskin, Mill; and Other Literary Estimates*, London, 1900.

Harrison, *The Meaning of History*: Frederic Harrison, *The Meaning of History, and other Historical Pieces*, London, 1894.

Harrowby MSS.: Manuscripts in the possession of Lord Harrowby, Sandon Hall, Staffordshire.

Hayward, *Correspondence*: Abraham Hayward, *A Selection from the Correspondence, from 1834 to 1884*, ed. H. E. Carlisle, 2 vols., London, 1886.

Hayward, *Essays*: Abraham Hayward, *Biographical and Critical Essays. A New Series*, 2 vols., London, 1873.

Hazlitt, *Memoirs*: W. Carew Hazlitt, *Memoirs of William Hazlitt*, 2 vols., London, 1867. With a chronological catalogue of his writings, pp. xxii–xxxii.

Hazlitt, *Works*, ed. Howe: William Hazlitt, *Complete Works*, ed. P. P. Howe, 21 vols., London and Toronto, 1930–1934.

Hazlitt, *Works*, ed. Waller and Glover: William Hazlitt, *Collected Works*, ed. A. R. Waller and Arnold Glover, 13 vols., London, 1902–1906.

Healy, *Maynooth*: John Healy, *Maynooth College: Its Centenary History*, N.Y., 1895.

Healy Thompson Papers: Letters written to Edward Healy Thompson, 1859–1890. Chief correspondents: J. H. Newman, W. G. Ward, H. J. Coleridge, H. E. Manning, and Herbert Vaughan. The letters are the property of the Catholic Record Society and are on loan to the Westminster Diocesan Archives, Archbishop's House, London.

Hedley, *Evolution*: Bishop John Cuthbert Hedley, *Evolution and Faith, with Other Essays*, London, 1931.

Hedley, *Life*: Joseph Anselm Wilson, *The Life of Bishop [John Cuthbert] Hedley*, London, 1930.

Heitman: Francis B. Heitman, *Historical Register and Dictionary of the U.S. Army, 1789 to 1903*, 2 vols., Washington, D.C., 1903.

Helps, *Correspondence*: *Correspondence of Sir Arthur Helps*, ed. E. A. Helps, London and N.Y., 1917.

Heraud, *Memoirs*: Edith Heraud, *Memoirs of John A[braham] Heraud*, London, 1898.

Herbert, *Essays*: Henry Howard Molyneux Herbert, 4th Earl of Carnarvon, *Essays,*

Addresses, and Translations, ed. Sir Robert Herbert, 3 vols., London, 1896.

Herbert, *Life*: Arthur H. Hardinge, *The Life of Henry Howard Molyneux Herbert, fourth Earl of Carnarvon, 1831–1890*, ed. Elisabeth, Countess of Carnarvon, 3 vols., London and Edin., 1925.

Herschel, *Familiar Lectures*: John F. W. Herschel, *Familiar Lectures on Scientific Subjects*, London and N.Y., 1866.

Hill: Richard Hill, *A Biographical Dictionary of the Anglo-Egyptian Sudan*, Oxford, 1951.

Hill, *London Poor*: Octavia Hill, *Homes of the London Poor*, London, 1875.

Hill, *Memoir*: Rosamond and Florence Davenport-Hill, *The Recorder of Birmingham: A Memoir of Matthew Davenport Hill*, London, 1878.

Hobart, *Writings*: *Essays and Miscellaneous Writings*, ed. Mary, Lady Hobart, 2 vols., London, 1885.

Hoey notebooks: J. Cashel Hoey's notebooks, kept when he was sub-editor of the *Dublin Review* under W. G. Ward, from Apr. 1865–Nov. 1878, partly reprinted and cited by Matthew Russell, "Early Reviewers," q.v. Original notebooks cannot now be found.

Hope, *Memoir*: "Memoir" of Mrs. Anne Hope prefixed to her *Life of S. Thomas Becket*, 3rd ed., London, 1891.

Horne, *Bibliography*: Eri J. Shumaker, *A Concise Bibliography of the Complete Works of Richard H. Horne*, Granville, Ohio, 1943.

Hort, *Life and Letters*: A. F. Hort, *Life and Letters of Fenton John Anthony Hort*, 2 vols., London, 1896.

Huxley, *Collected Essays*: Thomas Henry Huxley, *Collected Essays*, 9 vols., London, 1894–1908.

Huxley, *Controverted Questions*: Thomas Henry Huxley, *Essays Upon Some Controverted Questions*, N.Y., 1892.

Hyamson: A. M. Hyamson, *A Dictionary of Universal Biography*, 2nd ed., London, 1951.

I

I.C.E., *List of Members*: Charter, Bye-Laws and List of Members of the Institution of Civil Engineers, a serial from 1867.

I.C.E. *Minutes*: *Institution of Civil Engineers: Minutes of Proceedings*, a serial from 1843.

Index, I: *The Wellesley Index to Victorian Periodicals, 1824–1900*, ed. Walter E.

Houghton, Vol. I, Toronto, 1966.

Index-Catalogue: see *Surgeon Index*, below.

Irish CD: *Irish Catholic Directory, Almanac and Registry*, Dublin, 1881–.

Irish Gentry: see Burke's *Ireland*, above.

Irving, *Civil Law*: David Irving, *An Introduction to the Study of the Civil Law*, 4th ed., London, 1837.

J

Jenkin, *Papers*: [Henry Charles] Fleeming Jenkin, *Papers, Literary, Scientific, etc.*, ed. S. Colvin and J. A. Ewing, 2 vols., London, 1887.

Jessopp, *Arcady*: Augustus Jessopp, *Arcady for Better for Worse*, London, 1887.

Jessopp, *Coming of the Friars*: Augustus Jessopp, *The Coming of the Friars, and Other Historical Essays*, London, 1888.

Jessopp, *Country Parson*: Augustus Jessopp, *The Trials of a Country Parson*, N.Y., 1890.

Jessopp, *Great Pillage*: Augustus Jessopp, *Before the Great Pillage*, London, 1901.

Jessopp, *Peasantry*: Augustus Jessopp, *England's Peasantry, and Other Essays*, London, 1914.

Jessopp, *Random Roaming*: Augustus Jessopp, *Random Roaming, and Other Papers*, London, 1894.

Jessopp, *Studies*: Augustus Jessopp, *Studies by a Recluse in Cloister, Town, and Country*, London, 1893.

Jevons, *Methods*: William Stanley Jevons, *Methods of Social Reform and Other Papers*, London, 1883.

Johnson, *Donne*: Catherine B. Johnson, *William Bodham Donne and his Friends*, N.Y., 1905. With an appendix of his periodical writings, pp. 340–343.

Johnson Papers: Correspondence of J. M. Kemble, W. B. Donne, Edward Fitzgerald, R. C. Trench, Charles Merivale, and others, owned in 1965 by Miss Mary Barham Johnson of Norwich.

Jones, *Essays*: H. Longueville Jones, *Essays and Papers on Literary and Historical Subjects*, London, 1870.

Jones, *Renascence*: Henry A. Jones, *The Renascence of the English Drama*, London, 1895.

K

Kebbel, *Essays*: Thomas E. Kebbel, *Essays upon History and Politics*, London, 1864.

Kelly: Kelly's *London Post Office Directory*; for details see *Index*, I, 1180.

Kelly, *Dissertations*: Matthew Kelly, *Dissertations, Chiefly on Irish Church History*, ed. D. M'Carthy, Dublin, 1864.

Kelly's *London Suburban Directory*: for details see *Index*, I, 1180.

Kenealy, *Brallaghan*: Edward [Vaughan Hyde] Kenealy, *Brallaghan, or The Deipnosophists*, London, 1845.

Kenealy, "Maginn": [E. V. H. Kenealy], "Our portrait gallery (No. XXXIV): William Maginn, LL.D.," *Dub.Univ.Mag.*, 23 (1844), 72–101. Attr. to Kenealy "with the assistance of D. M. Moir" in *DNB* under Maginn.

King, *Sketches*: Richard J. King, *Sketches and Studies: Descriptive and Historical*, London, 1874.

Kingsley, *Letters*: Charles Kingsley, *Letters and Memories of His Life*, ed. his wife, 2 vols., London, 1877.

Kingsley, *Miscellanies*: Charles Kingsley, *Miscellanies . . . Reprinted Chiefly from "Fraser's Magazine" and the "North British Review,"* 2nd ed., 2 vols., London, 1860.

Kingsley, *Sport and Travel*: George H. Kingsley, *Notes on Sport and Travel*, with a Memoir by Mary H. Kingsley, London, 1900.

Kingsley, *Works*: Charles Kingsley, *Works*, 28 vols., London, 1880–1885.

Kipling, *Writings*: Rudyard Kipling, *The Writings in Prose and Verse*, "Outward Bound" ed., 36 vols., N.Y., 1897–1937.

Kirwan, "Essays": Table of Contents of a projected work by Andrew Valentine Kirwan to have been called *Essays Political, Historical, and Miscellaneous*, printed on page facing the title page of his *Modern France*, London, 1863.

Kirwan, *Host and Guest*: Andrew Valentine Kirwan, *Host and Guest. A Book about Dinners, Wines, and Desserts*, London, 1864.

Kirwan, *Modern France*: Andrew Valentine Kirwan, *Modern France; its Journalism, Literature, and Society*, London, 1863.

Kropotkin, *In Prisons*: Petr A. Kropotkin, *In Russian and French Prisons*, London, 1887.

Kropotkin, *Mutual Aid*: Petr A. Kropotkin, *Mutual Aid, a Factor of Evolution*, N.Y., 1902.

L

M

poems in *The Oxford and Cambridge Magazine* of 1856. Now in the William Morris Gallery, Walthamstow.

Macnish, *Pythagorean*: Robert Macnish, *The Modern Pythagorean: a Series of Tales, Essays and Sketches by the Late Robert Macnish*. With the author's life by D. M. Moir, 2 vols., Edin., 1838.

Macnish, *Tales*: Robert Macnish, *Tales, Essays, and Sketches, by the late Robert Macnish, LL.D., with the author's Life by his friend, D. M. Moir*, 2 vols., London, 1844.

Macray: John Macray, "List of Writers in *Foreign Quarterly Review*, Vols. I–XIV., a Contribution to Literary History," *Notes and Queries*, 2nd ser., VIII (Aug. 13, 1859), 124–127.

Macready, *Diaries*: William Charles Macready, *Reminiscences and Selections from his Diaries and Letters*, ed. Sir Frederick Pollock, 2 vols., N.Y., 1875.

Maginn, *Gallery*: William Maginn, *A Gallery of Illustrious Literary Characters, 1830–1838, Drawn by the Late Daniel Maclise, and Accompanied by Notices, Chiefly by Maginn*, ed. William Bates, London, 1873.

Maginn, "Memoir": Robert Shelton Mackenzie, "Memoir of William Maginn," being a preface to Vol. V ("Fraserian Papers") of William Maginn's *Miscellaneous Writings*, 5 vols., N.Y., 1855–1857.

Maginn, *Writings*: William Maginn, *Miscellaneous Writings of the Late Dr. Maginn*, ed. R. Shelton Mackenzie, 5 vols., N.Y., 1855–1857.

Mahony, *Reliques*: Francis Sylvester Mahony, *Reliques of Father Prout*, ed. with introduction, by himself, 2nd enlarged ed., London, 1862.

Mahony, *Works*: Francis S. Mahony, *The Works of Father Prout*, ed. Charles Kent, London and N.Y., 1881.

Mallett: D. T. Mallett, *Index of Artists*, N.Y., 1935; *Supplement*, 1940.

Mallock, *Studies*: W. H. Mallock, *Studies of Contemporary Superstition*, London, 1895.

Manners, *Writings*: *The Collected Writings of Janetta, Duchess of Rutland*, 2 vols., Edin. and London, 1901.

Manning, *Life*: E. S. Purcell, *Life of Cardinal Manning, Archbishop of Westminster*, 2 vols., N.Y., 1898.

Manning, *Miscellanies*: H. E. Manning, *Miscellanies*, 3 vols., London, 1877–1888.

Manning's list: Cardinal Manning's list of the writings of W. G. Ward, including his articles, in *DR*, 8 3rd s. (Oct. 1882), 268–270. Not entirely reliable.

Mansel, *Reviews*: Henry Longueville Mansel, *Letters, Lectures, and Reviews*, ed. H. W. Chandler, London 1873.

Martin, *Essays*: Theodore Martin, *Essays on the Drama*, 1st and 2nd series, 2 vols., London, 1874, 1889.

Martinengo-Cesaresco, *Folk-Songs*: Evelyn Martinengo-Cesaresco, *Essays in the Study of Folk-Songs*, London and Edin., 1886.

Matthews, "Hedley": J. E. Matthews, "Bishop Hedley as Editor [of the *Dublin Review*]," *Dublin Review*, 198 (Apr. 1936), 253–266.

Maude, *Madagascar*: Col. Francis Cornwallis Maude, *Five Years in Madagascar*, London, 1895.

Maurice, *Work and Opinions*: Frederick Barton Maurice, *Sir [John] Frederick Maurice: A Record of his Work and Opinions*, London, 1913.

Max Müller, *Chips*: Friedrich Max Müller, *Chips from a German Workshop*, 5 vols., N.Y., 1874–1881.

Max Müller, *Last Essays*: Friedrich Max Müller, *Last Essays, First Series*, London, 1901.

Maxse Papers: The papers of Frederick Augustus Maxse and some of his descendants, including the papers of Leopold James Maxse, editor of the *National Review*, 1893–1932, now in the West Sussex County Record Office, Chichester.

Maxwell, *Post Meridiana*: Herbert E. Maxwell, *Post Meridiana: Afternoon Essays*, Edin. and London, 1895.

Maxwell-Scott, *Incidents*: Mary M. Maxwell-Scott, *Making of Abbotsford, and Incidents in Scottish History Drawn from Various Sources*, London, 1897.

Mazzini, *Scritti*: Giuseppe Mazzini, *Scritti, Editi ed Inediti, edizione nazionale*, 94 vols., Imola, 1906–1943.

Med. Direc.: *Medical Directory*, 1845–1914, an annual, divided into sections called London, Provincial, Scotland, Ireland, Army, and Dentists.

Med. Reg.: *Medical Register*, 1859–, annual listing of physicians, giving dates of certification.

Melville, *Thackeray*: Lewis Melville [i.e., Lewis Saul Benjamin], *William Makepeace Thackeray. A Biography*, 2 vols., London, 1910.

Meredith, *Works*: *Works of George Meredith*, memorial edition, 29 vols., N.Y., 1909–1912.

Merivale, *Autobiography*: Charles Merivale, *Autobiography with Selections from his Correspondence*, ed. J. A. Merivale, London, 1899.

Merivale, "Memoir": "Herman Merivale, C.B.," by Charles Merivale, *Report and*

Transactions of the Devonshire Society for the Advancement of Science, Literature, and Art, XVI (1884), 570–580. With a list of his articles, pp. 579–580.

Metcalfe Addresses: A MS. list of the addresses of *Scottish Review* contributors, dated 1891, probably in the hand of the editor, William M. Metcalfe, in the Nat. Lib. Scot., MS 3655.

Metcalfe copy: The file of the *Scottish Review*, presented by William Metcalfe, son of the editor, William M. Metcalfe, to the Nat. Lib. Scot. The names or the initials of the authors are marked in pencil at the end of many of the anonymous articles, and, although it is not certain, the hand appears to be that of the son, William Metcalfe.

Miles, *Poets*: *The Poets and Poetry of the Nineteenth Century*, ed. Alfred H. Miles, London, 12 vols. 1905–1907.

Mill, *Bibliography*: John Stuart Mill, *Bibliography of the Published Writings of John Stuart Mill*, ed. from his MS. by Ney MacMinn, J. R. Hainds, James McNab McCrimmon, in *Northwestern University Studies in the Humanities*, No. 12, Evanston, Illinois, 1945.

Mill, *Dissertations*: John Stuart Mill, *Dissertations and Discussions: Political, Philosophical, and Historical*, 3rd ed., 4 vols., London, 1875.

Mill, *Earlier Letters*: John Stuart Mill, *The Earlier Letters, 1812–1848*, ed. Francis E. Mineka, 2 vols., Toronto, 1963; being vols. XII and XIII of the *Collected Works of John Stuart Mill*, ed. F. E. L. Priestley, J. M. Robson, and others, now in progress.

Milman, *Life*: Arthur Milman, *Henry Hart Milman, a Biographical Sketch*, London, 1900.

Minnesota file: A file of the *Rambler* at University of Minnesota with marginal notations of authorships, of questionable authority.

Mivart, *Essays*: St. George Mivart, *Essays and Criticisms*, 2 vols., London, 1892.

Montefiore, *Essays*: Leonard Abraham Montefiore, *Essays and Letters*, London, 1881.

Moore, *Impressions*: George Moore, *Impressions and Opinions*, London, 1891.

Moore, *Studies*: Edward Moore, *Studies in Dante*, 1st, 2nd, and 3rd series, Oxford 1896, 1899, and 1903.

Morley, *Early Life*: F. W. Hirst, *Early Life & Letters of John Morley*, 2 vols., London, 1927.

Morley, *Life*: Henry S. Solly, *The Life of Henry Morley*, London, 1898.

Morley, *Miscellanies*: John Morley, *Critical Miscellanies*, 4 vols., London and N.Y., 1886–1908.

Morley, *Studies*: John Morley, *Studies in Literature*, London, 1891.

Morris, *Works*: *The Collected Works of William Morris*, ed. Mae Morris, 24 vols., London, 1910–1915.

Munk: William Munk, *The Roll of the Royal College of Physicians of London*, 4 vols., 1878, 1955.

Murray Copy: A marked copy of *The Oxford and Cambridge Magazine* of 1856, once owned by Charles Fairfax Murray, now in the Powell Library, University of California at Los Angeles.

Murray diary: MS. diary of Patrick A. Murray, now at Maynooth.

Myers, *Essays*: Frederic W. H. Myers, *Essays Classical & Modern*, London, 1921.

Myers, *Future Life*: Frederic W. H. Myers, *Science and a Future Life, with Other Essays*, London, 1901.

N

NBG: *Nouvelle Biographie Générale*, Paris 1857–1870.

NDB: *Neue Deutsche Biographie*, Berlin, 1953–.

N&Q: *Notes and Queries*; for details see *Index*, I, 1183.

Napier MSS: Correspondence of Macvey Napier with contributors to *Encyclopedia Britannica* and *Edinburgh Review*, June 1829 to Mar. 1847, and MS. copies of certain articles by Brougham, Macaulay, Jeffrey, Cockburn, John Russell, and Adam Sedgwick: BM Add. MSS. 34,614–34,629.

Nat. Lib. Scot.: National Library of Scotland, at Edinburgh.

Navy List: *The Navy List*. An annual published since 1814; lists only officers; includes the staff on each ship.

New Cath. Ency.: *The New Catholic Encyclopedia*, 15 vols., N.Y., 1967.

Newman, *Correspondence*: *Correspondence of John Henry Newman with John Keble and Others, 1839–1845*, ed. The Birmingham Oratory, London, 1917.

Newman, *Essays*: John Henry Newman, *Essays Critical and Historical*, 2 vols., London, 1871.

Newman, *Historical Sketches*: John Henry Newman, *Historical Sketches*, 3 vols., London, 1878–1881.

Newman, *L&D*: John Henry Newman, *The Letters and Diaries*, ed. C. S. Dessain, London, 1961–.

Newman, *Memoir*: Isabel Giberne Sieveking, *Memoir and Letters of Francis W. Newman*, London, 1909.

Newman, *Miscellanies*: Francis W. Newman, *Miscellanies: Chiefly Addresses, Academical and Historical*, 5 vols., London, 1869–1891.

Newman MSS.: Papers of Cardinal Newman, at the Oratory, Birmingham.

Newton, *Essays*: Charles Thomas Newton, *Essays on Art and Archeology*, London, 1880.

New Zealand Biog.: G. H. Scholefield, ed., *Dictionary of New Zealand Biography*, Wellington, N.Z., 1940.

Nicoll, *Macdonell*: W. Robertson Nicoll, *James Macdonell, Journalist*, London, 1890.

Northcote file: Marked file of the *Rambler* from the library of J. Spencer Northcote at Hawksyard Priory, vols. 1–10 (Jan. 1848–Dec. 1858), presumably marked by Northcote.

Northcote list: Copy of a "list of authors of articles in the Rambler" drawn up by Dr. Northcote for Miss Capes. It runs from 1850–1856, and is drawn up volume by volume by author with only the opening page numbers to indicate the articles. It is in the Simpson notebook, q.v. Appended is a fragment, prob. in Northcote's own hand, drawn up in the same manner, but mainly concerned with 1857–1862; from 1858 on it lists contributions by Simpson only.

O

O'Brien, *Irish Wrongs*: Richard Barry O'Brien, *Irish Wrongs and English Remedies, with Other Essays*, London, 1887.

Oliver, *Collections*: George Oliver, *Collections, Illustrating the History of the Catholic Religion*, London, 1857.

Ormsby, *Autumn Rambles*: John Ormsby, *Autumn Rambles in North Africa*, London, 1864.

Orsi, *Recollections*: Count Joseph Orsi, *Recollections of the Last Half-Century*, London, 1881.

Oscott II: MS. attributions of authorship written into the *DR* list, q.v., in the copy of the *Dublin Review* for Apr. 1896 at

Oscott College.

Owen, *Life*: Richard S. Owen, *The Life of Richard Owen*, 2 vols., London, 1894. With a bibliography, II, [333]–382.

OxCam list: "List of articles [and their authors] in *The Oxford and Cambridge Magazine*, 1856, from a list supplied by Mr. Vernon Lushington and Mr. W. Bell Scott" pasted onto the front fly leaf of the Wellesley College copy, Wellesley, Mass. Another copy of this list, with some slight variations, is in the library of Nottingham University and is covered by the same short title. Any significant differences between the two are noted in the text.

P

PMLA: *Publications of the Modern Language Association*.

Palgrave, *Palgrave's Dictionary of Political Economy*, ed. Henry Higgs, 3 vols., London, 1925–1926.

Palgrave, *Eastern Questions*: William G. Palgrave, *Essays on Eastern Questions*, London, 1872.

Palgrave, Opuscula: Francis T. Palgrave, [*Miscellaneous Essays and Reviews, Extracted from Periodicals . . .*], 4 vols., 1847–1897. Presented to the British Mu-

seum by his family in 1941.

Palgrave, *Ulysses*: William Gifford Palgrave, *Ulysses; or, Scenes and Studies in Many Lands*, London, 1887.

Pardoe, Letters: Lola L. Szladits, "A Victorian Literary Correspondence. Letters from Julia Pardoe to Sir John Philippart, 1841–1860," *Bulletin of the N.Y. Public Lib.*, 59 (1955), 367–378.

Pater, *Studies*: Walter H. Pater, *Miscellaneous Studies*, N.Y., 1895.

Pattison, *Essays*: Mark Pattison, *Essays*, ed.

Henry Nettleship, 2 vols., Oxford, 1889. With a list of articles not reprinted here, I, vii.

Payn, *Private Views*: James Payn, *Some Private Views*, London, 1881.

Peacock, *Works*: Thomas Love Peacock, *Works*, ed. H. F. B. Brett-Smith and C. E. Jones, 10 vols., London, 1924–1934. With an "Index Bibliography" of his periodical articles, I, 179–181.

Pearson, *Chances of Death*: Karl Pearson, *The Chances of Death and other Studies in Evolution*, 2 vols., London, 1897.

Plarr: Victor G. Plarr, *Lives of Fellows of Royal College of Surgeons*, 2 vols., London, 1930.

Pollock, *Remembrances*: [William] Frederick Pollock, *Personal Remembrances*, 2 vols., London and N.Y., 1887.

Poole: William F. Poole, *Poole's Index to Periodical Literature*, N.Y., 1848–1938.

Powell, *Notices*: *Notices of the Life of the Late Rev. Baden Powell, M.A.*, n.p., n.d.,

[Bodleian Lib. Cat. gives 1861]. With a list of his publications.

Pratt: Alfred T. C. Pratt, *People of the Period; Being a Collection of the Biographies of . . . Living Celebrities*, 2 vols., London, 1897.

Pratt, *Music*: Waldo S. Pratt, *New Encyclopedia of Music and Musicians*, N.Y., 1924.

Pratt list: Forty-six anonymous articles by David Masson listed in Pratt, q.v., II, 148.

Price list: List of the authorship of articles, stories, and poems in the *Oxford and Cambridge Magazine*, 1856, enclosed in a letter from Cormell Price to Falconer Madan, Nov. 19, 1909, pasted into a copy, once Madan's, now owned by Mr. J. R. Dunlop, Associate Librarian, The City College of New York.

Proctor, *Light Science*: Richard Anthony Proctor, *Light Science for Leisure Hours*, 3 series, London, 1871–1883.

Q

Quin, *Canadian Nights*: W. T. W. Quin (Earl of Dunraven), *Canadian Nights; Sketches of Life and Sport in the Rockies, etc. . . .* , N.Y., 1914.

R

RG: *Nineteenth Century Readers' Guide to Periodical Literature, 1890–1899*; for details see *Index*, I, 1185.

R.G.S.: Royal Geographical Society.

R.L.F.: Royal Literary Fund.

Radical Programme: *The Radical Programme*, with a Preface by the Right Hon. Joseph Chamberlain, M.P., London, 1885.

Raikes, *Life and Letters*: Henry St. John Raikes, *The Life and Letters of Henry Cecil Raikes, Late Her Majesty's Postmaster-General*, London, 1898.

Rambler accounts: Accounts of the *Rambler*, Sept. 1856–Feb. 1859, kept apparently by Richard Simpson while he was acting editor; included in Simpson notebook, q.v.

Ray, *Thackeray*, I, and II: Gordon N. Ray, *Thackeray: The Uses of Adversity, 1811–1846*, N.Y., 1955, and *Thackeray: The Age of Wisdom, 1847–1863*, N.Y., 1958.

Records of the R.G.S.: Letter to this *Index* from the Director's Assistant of the Royal Geographical Society, London.

Reid, *Patmore*: J. C. Reid, *The Mind and Art of Coventry Patmore*, N.Y., 1957. With a bibliography of his contributions to periodicals, pp. 332–338.

Renouf, *Life-Work*: *The Life-Work of Sir Peter le Page Renouf*, ed. W. H. Rylands, G. Maspero, and E. Naville, 1st series, 4 vols., Paris, 1902–1907.

Richardson list: Any list of articles, together with authors, either drawn up for a given issue or described as being on hand by any member of the publishing firm of Thomas Richardson and Son, 1844–1863. These are part of the Bagshawe Papers, q.v.

Robinson, *Diary*: Henry Crabb Robinson, *Diary, Reminiscences and Correspondence*, ed. T. Sadler, 2 vols., Boston, 1869.

Robinson, *Middle Ages*: A. Mary F. Robinson, *The End of the Middle Ages: Essays and Questions in History*, London, 1889.

Robinson, *Transcripts*: Transcripts of the diary of Henry Crabb Robinson at Dr. Williams's Library, London.

Roche, *Essays*: James Roche, *Critical and*

Miscellaneous Essays. By an Octogenarian, 2 vols., Cork, 1850.

Roebuck, *Life*: *Life and Letters of J. A. Roebuck*, ed. R. E. Leader, London, and N.Y., 1897.

Rogers Papers: The papers of James Edwin Thorold Rogers, now owned by Dr. M. A. T. Rogers, Burnham, Bucks.

Roose, *Waste*: E. C. Robson Roose, *Waste and Repair in Modern Life*, London, 1897.

Rosenthal: Eric Rosenthal, ed., *Southern African Dictionary of National Biography*, London, 1966.

Ross, *Old Florence*: Janet A. Ross, *Old Florence and Modern Tuscany*, London, 1904.

Ross, *Three Generations*: Janet A. Ross, *Three Generations of Englishwomen. Memoirs and Correspondence of Mrs. John Taylor, Mrs. Sarah Austin, and Lady Duff Gordon*, 2 vols., London, 1888.

Rossetti, *Fine Art*: William Michael Rossetti, *Fine Art, Chiefly Contemporary: Notices Re-printed, with Revisions*, London and Cambridge, 1867.

Rowley, *Wordsworth*: James Rowley, *Wordsworth and Other Essays*, Bristol, 1927.

Ruskin, *Works*: *The Works of John Ruskin*, ed. E. T. Cook and A. D. O. Wedderburn, 39 vols., London, 1902–1912. With a bibliography of works by Ruskin, XXXVIII, 3–22, and on Ruskin, pp. 130–190.

Russell, "Early Reviewers": Matthew Russell, "The Early *Dublin* Reviewers," *Irish Monthly*, 21 (1893), 78–90, 137–146, and 206–218. The articles make extensive use of the Bagshawe and Hoey notebooks, q.v.

Russell, "Literary work": Matthew Russell, "Dr. [C. W.] Russell's Literary Work," *Irish Monthly*, 22 (1894), 632–642.

Russell, "Memorial Notes": Matthew Russell, "Dr. [C. W.] Russell of Maynooth: Memorial Notes," *Irish Monthly*, 20 (1892), 1–3, 147–156, 264–276, 303–318, 383–388, 415–428, 485–496, 533–546, 594–598, 599–601, 652–658; 21 (1893), 44–50, 263–269, 317–330, 376–389, 410–422, 494–503; 22 (1894), 68–78, 162–168, 193–202, 270–280, 289–301.

S

Sadleir's *Bulwer*: Michael Sadleir, *Bulwer and his Wife: a Panorama, 1803–36*, London, 1933.

Saintsbury, *Essays*: George Saintsbury, *Collected Essays and Papers, 1875–1923*, 4 vols., London, 1924.

Saintsbury, *French Novelists*: George Saintsbury, *Essays on French Novelists*, 2nd ed., London, 1891.

Sambrook, *Dixon*: James Sambrook, *A Poet Hidden: The Life of Richard Watson Dixon, 1833–1900*, London, 1962.

Schmitz, *Mitchell*: John Mitchell, *Biographies of Eminent Soldiers of the Last Four Centuries*, ed. with a memoir of the author by Leonhard Schmitz, Edin. and London, 1865.

ScotR list: A MS. list of the authors of articles in the *Scottish Review*, 1882–1900, in the Nat. Lib. Scot. Probably in the hand of William Metcalfe, the son of the editor, William M. Metcalfe.

Scott, *Criticism*: Walter Scott, *Periodical Criticism*, 5 vols., Edin., 1851, as reprinted in *The Miscellaneous Prose Works of Sir Walter Scott*, 30 vols., Edin., 1834–1871.

Serle: Percival Serle, *Dictionary of Australian Biography*, 2 vols., Sydney, 1949.

Seyn: *Dictionnaire Biographique des Sciences, des Lettres et des Arts en Belgique*, ed. Eugène de Seyn, 2 vols., Brussels, 1935–1936.

Shadwell, *Drink*: Arthur Shadwell, *Drink, Temperance and Legislation*, London, 1902.

Shand, *Hamley*: Alexander I. Shand, *The Life of General Sir Edward Bruce Hamley*, 2 vols., Edin. and London, 1895.

Sharp, *Writings*: *Selected Writings of William Sharp*, ed. Mrs. William Sharp, 7 vols., N.Y., 1912.

Sidgwick, *Essays*: Henry Sidgwick, *Miscellaneous Essays and Addresses*, London, 1904.

Simcox, *Episodes*: Edith Simcox, *Episodes in the Lives of Men, Women, and Lovers*, Boston, 1882.

Simpson notebook: A notebook belonging to Richard Simpson, now at Downside Abbey, containing lists of authorships in the *Home and Foreign Review*, the *Chronicle*, and the *Rambler*, some accounts for the last, and letters to Simpson from J. M. Capes, C. R. Weld, and T. F. Wetherell.

Skelton, *Essays*: John Skelton, *Essays in History and Biography, including the Defence of Mary Stuart*, Edin., 1883.

Skelton, *Essays in Romance*: John Skelton,

Essays in Romance and Studies from Life, Edin. and London, 1878.

Skelton, *Nugae Criticae*: John Skelton, *Nugae Criticae. Occasional Papers Written at the Seaside,* Edin. 1862.

Snow: Terence Benedict Snow, *Obit Book of the English Benedictines from 1600 to 1912. Being the "Necrology of the English Congregation of the Order of St. Benedict from 1600 to 1883"* compiled by Abbot Snow, revised, enlarged and continued by Dom Henry Norbert, Birt, Edin., 1913.

Southey, *Letters*: *Selections from the Letters of Robert Southey,* ed. J. W. Warter, 4 vols., London, 1856.

Spedding, *Reviews*: James Spedding, *Reviews and Discussions, Literary, Political, and Historical, Not Relating to Bacon,* London, 1879.

Spencer, *Essays*: Herbert Spencer, *Essays: Scientific, Political, and Speculative,* 3 vols., London, 1868–1875.

Stanhope, *Retreat from Moscow*: Philip Henry Stanhope, Lord Mahon, *The French Retreat from Moscow and Other Historical Essays. Collected from the "Quarterly Review" and "Fraser's Magazine,"* London, 1876.

Stanley, *Life*: R. E. Prothero and G. G. Bradley, *The Life and Correspondence of Arthur Penrhyn Stanley,* 2 vols., N.Y., 1894. With an Appendix that lists his articles, II, 579–582.

Statham, *Thoughts on Music*: Henry Heathcote Statham, *My Thoughts on Music and Musicians,* London, 1892.

Stebbing, *Verdicts*: William Stebbing, *Some Verdicts of History Reviewed,* London, 1887.

Stephen, *Agnostic's Apology*: Leslie Stephen, *An Agnostic's Apology, and other Essays,* London, 1893.

Stephen, *Fawcett*: Leslie Stephen, *Life of Henry Fawcett,* London, 1885. With an appendix listing his writings, pp. 469–472.

Stephen, *Freethinking*: Leslie Stephen, *Essays on Freethinking and Plainspeaking,* London, 1873.

Stephen, *Hours*: Leslie Stephen, *Hours in a Library,* new ed., 3 vols., London, 1909.

Stephen list: List of articles by James Fitzjames Stephen in his *Life* by Leslie Stephen, London, 1895, pp. 483–486.

Stephen, *Men and Mountains*: *Men, Books, and Mountains: Essays by Leslie Stephen,* ed. S. O. A. Ullmann, Minneapolis, 1956.

Stephen, *Playground*: Leslie Stephen, *The Playground of Europe,* London, 1894.

Stephen, *Studies*: Leslie Stephen, *Studies of a Biographer,* 4 vols., London, 1898–1902.

Sterling, *Essays*: John Sterling, *Essays and Tales,* ed. J. C. Hare, 2 vols., London, 1848.

Stirling-Maxwell, *Essays*: Sir William Stirling-Maxwell, *Miscellaneous Essays and Addresses,* London, 1891.

Stoddart, *Blackie*: Anna M. Stoddart, *John Stuart Blackie: A Biography,* 2 vols., London, 1895.

Stokes, *Bibliography*: *Bibliography of the Publications of Whitley Stokes,* ed. R. I. Best, Halle, 1911.

Stone, *Studies*: Jean M. Stone, *Studies from Court and Cloister,* London, 1905.

Sully, *Sensation and Intuition*: James Sully, *Sensation and Intuition: Studies in Psychology and Aesthetics,* London, 1874.

Surgeon Index: *Index-Catalogue of the Library of the Surgeon-General's Office, United States Army,* 4 series, Washington, 1880–1955.

Sutcliffe: Edmund F. Sutcliffe, *Bibliography of the English Province of the Society of Jesus, 1773–1953,* London, 1957.

Swinburne, *Essays*: Algernon Charles Swinburne, *Essays and Studies,* London, 1875.

Swinburne, *Miscellanies*: Algernon Charles Swinburne, *Miscellanies,* 2nd ed., London, 1895.

Swinburne, *Studies*: A. C. Swinburne, *Studies in Prose and Poetry,* London, 1897.

Symonds, *Byways*: John Addington Symonds, *Italian Byways,* London, 1883.

Symonds, *Essays*: John Addington Symonds, *Essays Speculative and Suggestive,* London, 1890.

Symonds, *Greek Poets*: John Addington Symonds, *Studies of the Greek Poets,* 1st and 2nd series, London, 1873–1876.

Symonds, *Key of Blue*: John Addington Symonds, *In the Key of Blue,* New York, 1893.

Symonds, *Sketches*: John Addington Symonds, *Sketches and Studies in Italy and Greece,* ed. Horatio Brown, 3 vols., London, 1905–1907.

Symonds, *Swiss Highlands*: J. A. Symonds, *Our Life in the Swiss Highlands,* London and Edin. 1892.

Symons, *Studies*: Arthur Symons, *Studies in Prose and Verse,* London, 1904.

Symons, *Symbolist Movement*: Arthur Symons, *The Symbolist Movement in Literature,* London, 1899.

Szinnyei: József Szinnyei, *Magyar írok élete és munkái,* 14 vols., Budapest, 1891–1914.

T

Taylor, *Memoir*: J. W. Robberds, ed., *Memoir of the Life and Writings of the late William Taylor, of Norwich. . . . Correspondence with Robert Southey*, 2 vols. London, 1843.

Taylor, *Profit-Sharing*: Sedley Taylor, *Profit-Sharing between Capital and Labour: Six Essays*, London, 1884.

Taylor, *Surtees*: George Taylor, *A Memoir of Robert Surtees*, ed. James Raine, Durham, 1852. With an account of Taylor by Raine, pp. x–xvi, and his contributions to periodicals, p. xiv.

TBar list: A complete list of names for each article and story, with their addresses and the payments they received, in *Temple Bar*, 1899–1900, now among the Bentley Papers at the University of Illinois, Urbana. In nearly all cases the names are those of the authors. The handwriting has not been identified.

Thackeray "Bibliography": Malcolm Elwin, *Thackeray*, London, 1932. "Bibliography," pp. 372–393.

Thackeray, *Letters*: *The Letters and Private Papers of William Makepeace Thackeray*, ed. Gordon N. Ray, 4 vols., Camb., Mass., 1945–1946.

Thackeray, *New Sketch Book*: W. M. Thackeray, *The New Sketch Book*, ed. Robert S. Garnett, London, 1906.

Thackeray, *Works*: *The Works of William Makepeace Thackeray*, ed. Lady [Anne Thackeray] Ritchie, 26 vols., London, 1910–1911.

Thackeray, *Works*, Furniss ed.: *The Works of William Makepeace Thackeray*, ed. Harry Furniss, 20 vols., London, 1911.

Thième: Hugo P. Thième, *Bibliographie de la littérature Française de 1800 à 1930*, 3 vols., Paris, 1933.

Thom: *Thom's Irish Almanac and Official Directory*, an annual beginning in 1844.

Thomson, *Popular Lectures*: William Thomson, First Baron Kelvin, *Popular Lectures and Addresses*, 3 vols., London, 1889– 1891.

Thomson, *Recollections*: Mrs. Katherine Thomson [Mrs. A. T. Thomson], *Recollections of Literary Characters and Celebrated Places*, 2 vols., London, 1854.

Thornton, *Ethics*: W. T. Thornton, *Old-fashioned Ethics and Common-sense Metaphysics*, London, 1873.

Thorp, *Kingsley*: Margaret Farrand Thorp, *Charles Kingsley, 1819–1875*, Princeton, 1937.

Thrall: Miriam Mulford H. Thrall, *Rebellious Fraser's; Nol Yorke's Magazine in the Days of Maginn, Thackeray, and Carlyle*, N.Y., 1934.

Thursfield, *Navy and the Nation*: George S. Clarke and James R. Thursfield, *The Navy and the Nation; or, Naval Warfare and Imperial Defence*, London, 1897.

Titled Nobility: *The Titled Nobility of Europe. An International Peerage*, ed. Marquis of Ruvigny, London, 1914.

Todhunter, *Whewell*: Isaac Todhunter, *William Whewell. An Account of his Writings*, 2 vols., London, 1876.

Topics of the Time: *Topics of the Time, No. 3. Studies in Literature*, ed. Titus M. Coan, N.Y., 1883.

Tosi: *Dizionari Biografici e Bibliografici Tosi*, ed. A. Ribero, Milan, 1936–.

Traill, *New Fiction*: H. D. Traill, *The New Fiction and Other Essays on Literary Subjects*, London, 1897.

Trench, *Letters*: Richard Chenevix Trench, *Letters and Memorials*, ed. Mary Trench, 2 vols., London, 1888.

Trollope, *What I Remember*: Thomas Adolphus Trollope, *What I Remember*, 3 vols., London, 1887–1889.

Turner, *Studies*: Charles Edward Turner, *Studies in Russian Literature*, London, 1882.

Tyndall, *Fragments*: John Tyndall, *Fragments of Science*, 2 vols., N.Y., 1899.

Tyndall, *New Fragments*: John Tyndall, *New Fragments*, N.Y., 1899.

U

UJE: *Universal Jewish Encyclopedia*, 10 vols., N.Y., 1939–1943.

Ullmann, list: see Stephen, *Men and Mountains*.

Urquhart, *Reminiscences*: David Urquhart, *Reminiscences of William IV. Correspondence between Lord Ponsonby and Mr. Urquhart, 1833 to 1836*, London, [1891].

V

Vandam, *Third Republic*: Albert D. Vandam, *Men and Manners of the Third Republic*, London, 1904.

Vaughan, *Letters*: Herbert, Cardinal Vaughan, *Letters to Lady Herbert of Lea, 1867 to 1903*, ed. Shane Leslie, London, 1942.

Venn: *Alumni Cantabrigienses. Part II, from 1752 to 1900*, ed. J. A. Venn, 6 vols., Cambridge, 1940–1954.

Verney, *Peasant Owners*: Frances P. Verney, *How the Peasant Owner Lives in Parts of France, Germany, Italy, and Russia*, London, 1888.

Verney, *Peasant Properties*: Frances P. Verney, *Peasant Properties and Other Selected Essays*, 2 vols., London, 1885.

W

WW: *Who's Who. An Annual Biographical Dictionary*, London, 1849 to date.

WWW: *Who Was Who*; for details see *Index*, I, 1189.

Wallace: W. S. Wallace, *The Dictionary of Canadian Biography*, 3rd ed., Toronto, 1963.

Wallace, *Life*: J. Campbell Smith and William Wallace, *Robert Wallace. Life and Last Leaves*, London, 1903.

Wallace, *Studies*: Alfred Russell Wallace, *Studies Scientific and Social*, 2 vols., London and N.Y., 1900.

Ward as Catholic: Wilfrid Ward, *William George Ward and the Catholic Revival*, London, 1912.

Ward, *Devotional Essays*: William George Ward, *Essays on Devotional and Scriptural Subjects*, London, 1879.

Ward, *Doctrinal Authority*: William George Ward, *Essays on the Church's Doctrinal Authority*, London, 1880.

Ward, *Doctrinal Decisions*: William George Ward, *The Authority of Doctrinal Decisions which are not Definitions of Faith*, London, 1866.

Ward, *Essays on Theism*: William George Ward, *Essays on the Philosophy of Theism*, ed. Wilfrid Ward, 2 vols., London, 1884.

Ward, *Experiences*: John Ward, C.B., *Experiences of a Diplomatist*, London, 1872.

Ward letters: Collection of letters to and from W. G. Ward, belonging to Father Damian McElrath, Holy Name College, Washington, D.C.

Ward, *Wiseman*: Wilfrid Ward, *The Life and Times of Cardinal Wiseman*, 2 vols., London, 1898.

Ward, *Witnesses*: Wilfrid Ward, *Witnesses to the Unseen and other Essays*, London, 1893.

Warren, "Horne": Alba Houghton Warren, Jr., "Richard Hengist Horne: A Literary Biography," unpublished typescript, n.d., in Princeton Univ. Lib. With a "List of Horne's Contributions to Periodicals."

Watkins, *In the Country*: Morgan G. Watkins, *In the Country: Essays*, London, 1883.

Watson, *Excursions*: William Watson, *Excursions in Criticism: Being Some Prose Recreations of a Rhymer*, London, 1893.

Wedmore, *Studies*: Frederick Wedmore, *Studies in English Art*, 1st and 2nd series, London, 1876, 1880.

Wenckstern, *History*: Otto Wenckstern, *History of the War in Hungary in 1848 and 1849*, London, 1859.

Wer ist's: *Wer ist's? unsere Zeitgenossen*, Leipzig, 1906, etc.

West, *One City*: Algernon E. West, *One City and Many Men*, London, 1908.

Wheaton: Elizabeth Feaster Baker, *Henry Wheaton, 1785–1848*, Philadelphia, 1937. With a list of his writings, p. 320.

Whitaker: *Whitaker's Naval and Military Directory*, London. An annual starting in 1898.

White, "Thackeray": Edward M. White, "Thackeray's Contributions to *Fraser's Magazine*," *Studies in Bibliography*, 19 (1966), 67–84.

Wilberforce, *The Church*: Henry William Wilberforce, *The Church and the Empires*, London, 1874.

Williams, *Life*: *The Life and Letters of Rowland Williams*, ed. Ellen Williams, 2 vols., London, 1874.

Willmott, *Summer Time*: Robert Aris Willmott, *A Journal of Summer Time in the Country*, N.Y., 1852.

Willson list: A list of articles written by Bishop John Cuthbert Hedley, drawn up by R. W. Willson, O.S.B., now at Ampleforth Abbey in Yorkshire.

Wiseman, *Essays*: Nicholas Patrick Stephen, Cardinal Wiseman, *Essays on Various Subjects*, 3 vols., London, 1853.

Wiseman Papers: Letters to and from Cardinal Wiseman in the Westminster Diocesan Archives, London. Includes a ledger sheet for *DR* nos. 33, 37–45.

Wright, *Archæological Subjects*: Thomas Wright, *Essays on Archaeological Subjects*, 2 vols., London, 1861.

Wright, *Literature*: Thomas Wright, *Essays on Subjects connected with the Literature, Popular Superstitions, and History of England in the Middle Ages*, 2 vols., London, 1846.

Wright, *Masters*: Thomas Wright, the "Journeyman Engineer," *Our New Masters*, London, 1873.

Wynter, *Social Bees*: Andrew Wynter, *Our Social Bees . . . and Other Papers*, 10th ed., London, 1869.

Y

Yearbook: *The Literary Yearbook*; for details see *Index*, I, 1190.

APPENDIX

CORRECTIONS AND ADDITIONS TO VOLUME I

Corrections and Additions to Volume I

It would be a marvel, indeed, if the first voyager in unknown seas should lay down the soundings with such accuracy that the very first chart should require no revision.

Hannah Lawrence
British Quarterly Review, May 1847

EXPLANATORY NOTE

This appendix and its index are intended to answer the three general questions which a careful user of Volume I will find himself asking:

(1) Has there been any correction of whatever kind—title, pagination, authorship, evidence—in a given item? Or in any of the introductions? Has any item been added which had been accidentally omitted?

(2) Has there been any alteration in the work or the biography of any contributor?

(3) Have any writings been found by "new" authors who did not appear in Volume I?

To answer (1) the reader should glance at the several entries (by page or code number) in the revisions of each periodical in Part A below. If he does not find the item he is concerned with, he can assume that it remains unchanged. Any items omitted from Volume I are here entered with an "a" (e.g., *Mac* 3a).

For answers to (2) and (3), he should consult the following index. All names that are involved in Part A changes—whether "old" or "new," whether requiring deletion or insertion—are here entered and the particular items cited. Such changes, with only a few exceptions, automatically involve a change in Part B and, if the name has turned out to be a pseudonym, in Part C too. There is no need, therefore, for the index to include these references. For example, the Part A revision of *ER* 2194 shows that the article should have been assigned to George Coode and not Sir John Coode. The index gives both names, each with an *ER* 2194. The Part B entry for Coode, Sir John, must, of course, be corrected in the Part B revisions. The correction links the two names as follows: "**Coode,** Sir John, should be replaced by **Coode,** George, 1807–1869, barrister, in Boase." There is no need to add "to whom the art. belongs"; that goes without saying. Nor any need to provide the evidence for the shift since that has already been given in the Part A revision. It should be noted that in searching for the Part B entry, one looks for the original name, now found wrong, under which he finds the new name. This follows the pattern of "Corrections and Additions."

Those names on which only new biographical information has been found—the solution of initials, a new life date, a vocation, a better source (information that is not covered in the Part A entry)—are marked "Part B" in the index. If such names have already appeared with new biographical facts in Volume II, Part B, or simply with new sources, the index will read "Part B above," and no entry will appear in the Part B revisions, *unless* there was a specific error in Volume I. But the original entry should also be consulted since its information, if any, is still valid. New contributors are preceded by an asterisk (*). Corrected names (like Francis John Foley for S. J. Foley) are not considered new contributors.

The length of the index is explained by its coverage of every change, however minute, including the spelling of a middle name, and even new biographical sources which change nothing in the Part B entry, though they provide new information. As a matter of fact, considering only articles and stories, the wrong attributions so far discovered—outright, prob., or ?—are 84 out of 27,903, which is three-tenths of one per cent (0.301 per cent). The new attributions, including those now found definite in cases of conflict, are 172.

The abbreviations of the eight periodicals indexed here are as follows:

Bk:	*Blackwood's Edinburgh Magazine*	**H&FR:**	*The Home and Foreign Review*
CR:	*The Contemporary Review*	**Mac:**	*Macmillan's Magazine*
CM:	*The Cornhill Magazine*	**NBR:**	*The North British Review*
ER:	*The Edinburgh Review*	**QR:**	*The Quarterly Review*

INDEX

REVISIONS FOR PREFACE

P. vii, l. 22   For Mrs. Paul Glatzer, read Mrs. Paula Glatzer.
P. ix, l. 16   For Mrs. Rose Van Arsdal, read Mrs. Rosemary VanArsdel.
 l. 30   For Hergenham, read Hergenhan.
P. x, l. 23   Miss Lois J. Carrier was the Reference Librarian, and Miss Dorothy E. Ryder, Librarian: see p. 666, n. 12.

REVISIONS FOR INTRODUCTION

P. xxi   The total entries and total articles and stories in *Blackwood's* was 7916, not 7616. Thus, the grand total of entries should have been 28,017, and the total articles and stories 27,903.

REVISIONS FOR PART A

BLACKWOOD'S MAGAZINE

P. 7, l. 9   For James Pringle and Thomas Cleghorn, read Thomas Pringle and James Cleghorn: see *DNB* under both.
P. 8, l. 18   For 1830, read 1835.
P. 8, l. 34   For John Blackwood, read William Blackwood.
P. 9, l. 1, under Editors   Same correction as for p. 7 above.

P. 9, l. 4, under Editors   Add: Alexander Allardyce (in Part B, p. 791) became
Assistant Editor in 1877: see *DNB*, 1st suppl.

344   For Isobel Douglas read **Isabel Douglas:**
Blackwood Papers Cat.

1463, 1476, 1492, 1498, 1528   For Brockendon, read **Brockedon:** *Blackwood Papers
Cat.*

**1630, 1673, 1696, 1729, 1735, 1781, 1805,
1809, 1841**   For John Wilkes, read **John
Wilks:** cf. entries in I, Part B and II, Part
B, respectively.

1716   For "roses" in title, read "noses."

2388   Add to **Aytoun** "collab." He wrote only
the account of the festival, pp. 370–376,
396–398 (*Memoir*, p. 103), and one of
the speeches, pp. 392–393. The remainder
of the article prints the speeches by Prof.
**John Wilson, Sir John McNeill, Henry
Glassford Bell, Archibald Alison,** 1792–
1867, and Colonel **William Mure,** with
some replies and toasts by others.

2429   After See, l. 4, insert "his"; at end of l.
6, substitute 419 for 433.

2808   Delete the last sentence about Story
assigning it to Smith; and substitute: confirmed in Blackwood Corres.

3994   For Kilkenon, read Kilkerran.

4623   For Miss Walker, read **Annie Louisa
Walker:** *Blackwood Papers Cat.*, Blackwood Corres., letter of 1868.

5766   For James Fergusson, 1832–1907, read
James Ferguson, 1857–1917: claimed in
Ferguson to Blackwood, June 17, 1882,
Blackwood Corres.

5932, 6027, 6103   For George C. Macaulay,
read **George Macaulay:** Ewing, Blackwood Corres., and the Blackwood ascription in text of no. 5932.

5945   The full identification of "Mary Wood"
which is made in Part B, p. 1146, is supported by *Blackwood Papers Cat.*

5979   By **George Macaulay:** cf. no. 5932,
etc., above.

6356   For S. J. Foley, read **Francis John
Foley:** *Blackwood Papers Cat.*, Blackwood Corres.

6629   For Constance Eaglestone, which is a

pseudonym, read **R. Constance Sutcliffe:**
Blackwood Papers Cat. under both names.

6764   For Jennette Pryce, read **Jennet Pryce:**
see Part B revision.

6929   For W. J. Hardy, read **William J. M.
Hardy:** Blackwood Corres.

7002   For James Fergusson, 1832–1907, read
James Ferguson, 1857–1917: claimed in
Ferguson to Blackwood, Jan. 18, 1894,
Blackwod Corres.

7169   By **William J. M. Hardy:** cf. no. 6929
above.

7174   For Mrs. Andrews, read **Marian (Hare)
Andrews:** *Blackwood Papers Cat.*

7185   For George G. Stokes, read **George
Joseph Stokes:** cf. text of evidence with
Part B revision.

7204   For Editha E. Bailey—Signature, read
Edith A. Bailey—Signed.

7304   Meldrum had some assistance from
George Douglas Brown: *TLS*, Sept. 3,
1971, p. 1057.

7323   The article was mainly written by
Brown: see *TLS*, Sept. 3, 1971, p. 1057.

7342   By **William J. M. Hardy:** cf. no. 6929
above.

7358   For Duncan M. McVarish, read **Duncan Charles McVarish:** *Blackwood Papers
Cat.*

7412   For H. Garton Sargent, read **Henrietta
Garton Sargent:** *Blackwood Papers Cat.*

7834   For D. M. McVarish, read **D. C. Mc-
Varish:** cf. no. 7358 above; intro. note to
art. calls man who submitted the MS. an
army chaplain: see *CCD/1902* under the
latter name.

7838, 7855   For W. W. Sparroy, who is prob.
W. Wilfrid Sparroy, a pseudonym (see no.
7867 below), read **H. Wilfrid Sparrow;**
these articles, like no. 7867, are on Persia.

7862   By **William J. M. Hardy:** cf. no. 6929
above.

7867   For Wilfrid Sparroy, which is a pseudonym, read **H. Wilfrid Sparrow:** *Blackwood Papers Cat.* under both names.

CONTEMPORARY REVIEW

P. 211, l. 3   In a letter to Strahan of Apr. 20, 1873, Knowles called himself the
"consulting editor," whose "light" duties were to induce new and able writers
to contribute to the Review (see the *Times*, Jan. 17, 1877, p. 9f). It follows

that he was *the* editor at best only from some time after Apr. 1873 to Jan. 1877; indeed, though he was referred to on Jan. 15, 1877 as "the late editor" (*Times*, p. 6d), this was categorically denied by Strahan in the next day's *Times* (p. 6d), who implied, but did not state, that he himself had been editor all along. Certainly he was the editor from Apr. 1870 until at least some time after Apr. 1873.

P. 212, under Editors   For the period Apr. 1870–Jan. 1877, see the previous comment. It appears that in Mar. 1868, and no doubt before and after, Edward Hayes Plumptre was acting in the same capacity of "consulting editor" seeking new contributors: see Hort, *Life and Letters*, II, 92. William Canton was the sub-editor, 1891–1900: see *DNB* and *WWW*/1928.

P. 213, under Bibliographical Note   Add: There are three items in the *Times*, Jan. 15, 16, and 17, 1877, cited above in the revision to p. 211. Alexander Strahan, "Twenty Years of a Publisher's Life," *Day of Rest*, 1 (Apr. 1881), 256–261, is an essay on Alford which mainly centers on the founding of the Review, with a quotation from the Prospectus on p. 259. C. P. Gooch wrote "The Centenary of the Contemporary Review," *CR*, 208 (Jan. 1966), 4–7, but its identification of nineteenth-century editors is inaccurate and most of it deals with the post-1900 period.

5   For Henry Alford, read **John Mitchinson:** claimed in George R. Parkin, *Edward Thring* (1898), II, 307.

12   Delete the attrib. to Alford made on the authority of Miss Maddox. (See end of this entry for a substitution.) The Alford List, drawn up by his wife, and Alexander Strahan the publisher of *CR* (on p. 260 of the paper cited above in the revision of *Index*, I, 213), both assign 6 arts. to Alford in the *CR* for 1866. They should have assigned him 7: Part II of "Recent Poetry" (no. 91) was erroneously placed by Mrs. Alford in 1867 (it came out in Dec. 1866), and her totals were followed by Strahan (see his p. 259). Those 7 were nos. 21, 47, 52, 62, 70, 79, 91. Our total attributions, however, were 10, for we also included nos. 5, 12, and 32, all made on Miss Maddox's general impression without any specific evidence. No. 5 is certainly wrong (see its correction just above); and since 7 other attributions of hers turn out also to be wrong or highly dubious (no. 80 was corrected in time; for nos. 98, 106, 196, 205, 221, and 307, see below), one becomes rather skeptical about nos. 12 and 32 in the face of the Alford List accepted by Strahan. If these are dropped, along with no. 5, our total too would become 7.

But is the List complete? Lists like this, however accurate—as this one seems

to be—are rarely complete; and in this case no. 147, certainly by Alford, was overlooked. We must recognize, therefore, that nos. 12 and/or 32 *might* be his. The safest conclusion is to follow the pagination in both cases with: Unidentified. By Henry Alford, according to Miss Maddox.

26   Add: Pages 513–516 by **W. B. Rands**—in a collection of cuttings from the *CR* owned by his grandson, Allan J. Rands, of Farnham, Surrey; some are known to be by man cited, some are signed with his initials in ink.

32   Delete the attrib. to Alford and substitute: Unidentified. By Henry Alford, according to Miss Maddox: see revision of no. 12.

98 and 106   Delete the attrib. of this two-part art. on Browning to Alford. In the *Life of Alford* by his wife, Browning is never mentioned, which would be curious indeed had this long essay been his; nor is it on the Alford List. It appears in the *Browning Bibliography* (see *Index*, I, 1173) but anonymously. Our only guide was Miss Maddox, of whose sole authority we have seen reason to be skeptical (see revisions of nos. 5 and 12).

173   Pages 262–264 by **Edward Dowden**—Alford to Dowden, Sept. 9, 1867, Hales Autograph Collec. (Lib. of Congress), I, 28, asks for his two small pages on Taine by next Thursday.

196, 205, 221   For Henry Alford, read **W. B.**

Rands—cf. revision of no. 26 above. The series was wrongly attrib. to Alford, though with a ?, by Miss Maddox and corrected in the Appendix to *Index*, I, 1194.

307   Delete the attrib. to Henry Alford. Beginning in 1868 Alford signed his arts. and there is no reason why he shouldn't have signed this had it been his. The only authority is a dubious one, Miss Maddox (see revision of no. 12).

430   Add at end: pages 479–480, 480–481 by **W. B. Rands**—cf. no. 26 above.

431   By **Jakob Frohschammer**. Add to evidence in *Index*, I, 1193, the remark in the *Theological Rev.*, 9 (Jan. 1872), 72n., that the recent arts. in the *CR* signed "A Bavarian Catholic" are "understood in Germany to be written by Professor Froschammer [sic]"; man cited was prof. of theology at Munich (see *ADB*).

527   By **Jakob Frohschammer**: cf. no. 431 above.

590   By **Jakob Frohschammer**: cf. no. 431.

1114   Add: The higher controversy and periodical literature, 516–517, and Editing, 517–520, by **W. B. Rands**—cf. no. 26 above.

1123   Add: Professor Clifford and his critics on *The Ethics of Belief*, 742–748, by **W. B. Rands**—cf. no. 26 above.

1140   The "?" after Rands should be deleted; so should the evidence block. The correct evidence is that for no. 26 above; and Henry S. Richardson is a pseudonym.

1143   Add: The rationale of reviewing, 1144–1147, and Intellectual detachment, 1151–1152, by **W. B. Rands**—cf. no. 26 above.

1153   Add: Parliamentary reporting, 165–167, Muir's *Mahomet*, 173–174, and Glan-Alarch, 180, by **W. B. Rands**—cf. no. 26 above.

1171   Add: Rus in urbe, 511–514, Mr. John Morley's *Essays*, 515–517, and *Social Life in Greece*, 527–528, by **W. B. Rands**—cf. no. 26 above.

1181   Add: Novelists and philosophers, 704–708, by **W. B. Rands**—cf. no. 26 above.

1201   Add: A self-refutation [Newman's *Via Media*], 1093–1098, and Principal Tulloch and Mr. Stopford Brooke, 1100–1102, by **W. B. Rands**—cf. no. 26 above.

1213   Add: Pictures for children, 205–206, and Charlotte Williams Wynn, 209–211, by **W. B. Rands**—cf. no. 26 above.

1216   Add at end: (Comment, pp. 657–659, by **W. B. Rands**—cf. no. 26 above; the reply by Frances Cobbe is cited in no. 1249.)

1225   Add: The cultur-kampf, 422–428, by **W. B. Rands**—cf. no. 26 above.

1226   Add: Pages 447–448 by **W. B. Rands**—cf. no. 26 above.

1237   Add: Toilet artifices, 657–659, and Government officials and literature, 660–661, by **W. B. Rands**—cf. no. 26 above.

1249   After the pagination insert: "The theory of belief—Dr. Newman and Mr. Leslie Stephen," 869–873, and Obiter dicta in public discussion, 874–876, by **W. B. Rands**—cf. no. 26 above.

1280   Add: A hopeful experiment, 392–394, by **W. B. Rands**—cf. no. 26 above.

1328   Add: Difficulties of the pulpit, 402–406, and Mr. Trelawny and his friends, 406–411, by **W. B. Rands**—cf. no. 26 above.

1329   Add Pages 419–420, by **W. B. Rands**—cf. no. 26 above.

1474   In title: for Bushness, read Bushnell.

1655   After author, dates should be 1849–1926, as in I, 1097.

1976   By **James Purves,** not James Liddell Purves, to whom the art. was assigned in I, 1056. The Scottish dialect on p. 350 and the special emphasis on poachers of the "Northern lowlands," pp. 352–353, clearly point to a Scottish author: see Part B above. J. L. Purves in *WWW/1916* lived in Australia and had no connection with Scotland.

2501   By **Kenric Bright Murray,** not Kenric Benjamin Murray to whom the art. was assigned in I, 1025: see Part B above and cf. subject of art. there with subject here.

3495   For Walter Walsh [1847–1912, as identified in Vol I, Part B], read **Walter Walsh,** 1857–1931. After "Signed" add: Walsh's *My Spiritual Pilgrimage from Sectarianism to Free Religion*, 1925, deals with some of the same ideas in a similar style; on this Walsh, see *WWW/1940*.

3649   By **Walter Walsh,** 1857–1931: cf. no. 3495 above.

4156   By **John Frederick Maurice,** prob. Another art. signed Miles and one which begins by referring to the Militia Ballot Act here under discussion—"Where to get men," *CR*, 81 (Jan. 1902), 78–86—was claimed by Maurice in *Work and Opinions*, p. 259; the idea, pp. 495–496, that different nations require different forms of defence is one of Maurice's basic convictions.

4205   By **J. F. Maurice,** prob. This too is signed Miles like the 1902 art. cited in previous entry; Maurice wrote *ER* no. 3986 in Jan. 1899 on Stonewall Jackson, who is a central figure here.

CORNHILL MAGAZINE

P. 324, under Note on Attributions, l. 6 For "Account Books," read "Smith Accounts."

l. 10: For North Hampshire, read Northamptonshire.

P. 324, under Bibliographical Note Add: Spencer L. Eddy, Jr., *The Founding of "The Cornhill Magazine,"* Ball State University, Muncie, Indiana, 1970.

P. 341 For February 1865, read February 1866.

408, 419 For Frances Eleanor Trollope, read **Theodosia Trollope.** Smith Accounts gave "Mrs. T. A. Trollope," who in 1863 and 1864 was Theodosia: see *DNB*.

433 Delete the reprint.

536 For Frances Eleanor Trollope, read **Theodosia Trollope.** Cf. nos. 408, 419 above.

908 For B. Carlill, read **James Briggs Carlill,** on whom see Part B above. This art. and *Mac* 3179, on which see revision below, as well as the *NC* articles in Part B above, deal with the psychology of man and animals.

1079 A **Howard Ninnis,** d.1886, has now been found in Debrett/1908, p. 60, and in Burke under Arran; since the name is very uncommon, this may well be the man to whom Smith, Elder ascribed the art. But the remainder of the entry had best be left standing, and a ? placed after Ninnis.

2186 For H. S. Edwards, read **H. Edwards:** Smith, Elder and *Blackwood Papers Cat.,* where the two have separate entries; in the latter H. Edwards is called a contributor to *CM* on basis of an 1884 letter.

2579 For J. O'Neill, read **John O'Neill,** c.1837–1895: the address in Page is the same as that for this John O'Neill in Boase.

2589 Delete "prob." after **Arthur Grant.** For evidence block, substitute: repr. *Rambles in Arcadia,* 1903.

2650 Smith, Elder calls author Mrs. H. C. Reichardt.

3028 The London address of **Frederick Dixon** in Page matches that in *Kelly's Suburban Directory* (1898), p. 18, and the name is identical.

3390 For B. E. B. F.-P. Castletown, read **B. E. B. Fitz-Patrick,** who was 2nd baron Castletown: see *WWW*/1940.

3494 For Henry Martley, read **Henry Martley Giveen:** like this art., *Temple Bar,* 121 (Nov. 1900), 406–419, is signed Henry Martley, but Bentley attribs. that to Henry Martley Giveen, who is in the *BMCat.*

3582 Mrs. Charles Trigance Franklin was **Lucy (Haywood) Franklin:** in addition to evidence given, see Pollock, *Remembrances,* II, 115.

EDINBURGH REVIEW

4 Here and elsewhere in the early volumes, references to "Cockburn" are to the "Cockburn Record" in the Short Title list, I, 1175.

127 After the pagination, substitute: **James Macdonald,** 1771/72–1810. Claimed by him in Alexander Gillies, *A Hebridean in Goethe's Weimar: the Rev. James Macdonald* (Oxford, 1969), p. 96.

315 Add to evidence: attr. in *DNB* under John Millar; Jeffrey had reviewed Millar in no. 114.

362 By **Sir Robert Grant,** prob. His *The Expediency Maintained of Continuing the System by which the Trade and Government of India Are Now Regulated,* 1813, is largely an expansion of this art., particularly in its attack on Adam Smith; and see the preface, p. xiv, where Grant explains that the book here reviewed is one with which he chiefly intends to deal.

471 By **Alexander Hamilton.** Author says, p. 324, that in the *Asiatic Annual Register* he had published a trans. from the Persian of a memoir of Hyder, who was Tippoo's father; such a memoir was prefixed to book here being reviewed; Tippoo was the Sultan of Mysor—cf. titles of no. 431 and no. 568, which are attr. to Hamilton, the latter just below; in general see *DNB*.

511 For Francis Jeffrey, read **Horace Twiss.** For present evidence, substitute: Jeffrey to [Horace Twiss], Mar. 30, 1810, Nat. Lib. Scot., thanks him for critique of pamphlet from America ["*A Letter on the Genius . . . of the French Government . . . By an American*" stands at head of books on p. 1], and offers, subject to some modifications, to make it the leading art. in the next issue; Jeffrey to Twiss, July 10, sends payment for his former art. The evidence given in support of Jeffrey in Vol. I shows he had planned to review this pamphlet and no doubt would have done so had not Twiss's critique appeared, as it did, out of the blue (see Jeffrey's 1st letter); he probably revised the *MS.* liberally.

517   **R. Payne Knight** wrote pp. 169–177, according to *The English Cyclopedia: Biography*, ed. Charles Knight (6 vols., 1868), III, 736.

568   By **Alexander Hamilton**. Cf. no. 431; on p. 358 here author says "we cited" two Persian authorities (names given) in no. 342, which is by Hamilton, and here quotes passages from that art., pp. 38, 39, almost verbatim—all of which implies that the "we" is personal, not editorial; on pp. 356–357 author reports he published trans. of Shahrukh's observations in *Asiatic Annual Register*—Hamilton published anonymous trans. in this *Register* (see revision of no. 471 above).

591   By **Alexander Hamilton**. In addition to evidence given, see title of no. 471 and its attribution to Hamilton just above here.

663   The Langman MSS. were owned by the late Lady Eleanor Katherine Langman, great-grandniece of Francis Horner.

726   By **James Mill**, prob. Francis Place to Mill, Aug. 29–31, 1815, BM Add MS. 35,152, discussing 2 of Mill's arts., says he has looked at "Continental press" in *ER*; Mill had written on the press in no. 559.

753   By **Douglas Kinnaird**. Attr. by Francis Place in his commonplace book, BM Add MS. 36,623, f.33; Kinnaird was an associate of Place and a close friend of J. C. Hobhouse. Introduction by **Francis Jeffrey**—ibid.

777   Remove "?" after Brougham. Add to the evidence: Hunter Gordon to Brougham, Apr. 25, 1849, Univ. Coll. London, refers to "your" art. in 1816 on Quarantotti; the document at the head of the art. is *"Letter to Roman Catholic Priests of Ireland, in which is discussed Quarantotti's Rescript."*

823   By **James Mill**. Attr. by Francis Place in his commonplace book, BM Add MS. 36,623, f. 74; the two authors relied on in this art. had been frequently cited in Mill's *History of British India*, 1817.

826   Delete P. M. Roget as a collab. The

authors are **Ugo Foscolo**, with "very considerable additions" by **James Mackintosh**, and the tailpiece on Cary's *Dante*, 469–474, by **Samuel Rogers**. In addition to the evidence given (where Foscolo's pages, line 2, should be 453–469, and "Roget's," line 10, was a misreading of "Rogers"), see *Recollections of the Table-Talk of Samuel Rogers*, ed. A. Dyce (N.Y., 1856), pp. 282–283, from which the statement on Mackintosh's additions is taken. No Part II was published.

861   By **Henry Parnell**. Undated list of Parnell's writings in the possession of the present Lord Congleton.

897   Delete what follows the pagination and substitute By **Henry Parnell**. Evidence for no. 861.

900   Delete what follows pagination and insert By **Henry Parnell**. Evidence for no. 861.

1004   The author entry should read: **Richard Chenevix**, 407–419, and **T. C. Grattan**, 420–432. The note cited attribs. [the first] part of art. to a "learned writer" who was the author of "comparative views of the skill, industry, literature, &c. of England and France": see Chenevix bibliog. in Part B. Constable to Jeffrey, Sept. 18, 1822, Nat. Lib. Scot., sends paper on French poetry by Colley Grattan, and Grattan, *Beaten Paths* (1865), pp. 330–331, really claims the second part of the art. Grattan, therefore, is the other "hand," and the art. does *not* appear in Jeffrey's list. It is, however, assigned to the latter by Copinger and the Cockburn Record, suggesting that he revised Grattan's section rather heavily. The note in vol. 38 was by **Jeffrey**—signed The Editor.

1034   Insert "?" after **McCulloch**. After Napier reference insert OR **Henry Parnell?** Evidence for no. 861.

1096   Delete "?" after Macaulay, and the "OR Henry Brougham": the evidence Add as further evidence Margaret Macaulay, "Recollections by a Sister of T. B. Macaulay," in Joseph Macaulay, *Memoirs of the Clan "Aulay"* (1881), p. 239.

1098   Delete "?" after Macaulay, and the "OR Henry Brougham": the evidence given for no. 1096 dictates this change.

1203   By **William Rhind**. Claimed in Rhind to Thomas Coates, Mar. 23, 1830, S.D.U.K. MSS., Univ. Coll. London. Thomson goes out.

1209   Change pagination to 184–196. After the Procter reprint, entry should continue: AND **Francis Jeffrey?**, 196–204. Allan Cunningham to Robert Southey, Apr. 26, 1833, Nat. Lib. Scot., speaks of the attack

made on him in the *ER* by Jeffrey, which
may mean the man or just the editor;
hence the "?"

1210   Delete attr. to McCulloch. Substitute
By **William Empson.** Empson to Thomas
Spring-Rice, 1790–1866, Feb. 15 [1828],
Nat. Lib. of Ireland, says Jeffrey is printing the emigration and postponing the
review of S. M. Phillipps to early in the
next issue—i.e., no. 1213.

1389   Passed on and perhaps revised by Lord
Palmerston; Gleason, *Russophobia*, p. 124;
cf. no. 1973.

1695   The best guess is George Farquhar Graham, a Scottish musician who assisted
Dauney in editing the *Melodies* and who,
according to *DNB*, contributed to *ER*;
nothing else by Graham has been found.
The case for Moir is overstated and Hogarth's art. came out 16 years earlier.

1757   Passed on and perhaps revised by Lord
Palmerston: Gleason, *Russophobia*, p.
271.

1764   Remove "?" after Moir. The letter is
endorsed on covering sheet, "Life of
Schiller, art. VII, April 1841."

1852   Remove "prob." after Jerdan. Add:
Thomas Wright to J. O. Halliwell, Sept.
1843, Edin. Univ. Lib., says proofs of
Jerdan's "Royal Society of Literature"
have been corrected.

1925   Add to evidence: claimed by Milnes in
Reid, *Milnes*, I, 368–369.

2169   **W. H. Hurlbert,** prob. Marked anonymous in Longmans. Comparison with no.
2324 by Hurlbert shows same anti-slavery,
anti-South convictions; it reveals that
Hurlbert had had detailed knowledge of
Story's *Life and Letters* (he quotes the
book four times in the later art.) and in
particular repeats the circumstances of
Story's strong opposition to the Missouri
Compromise; in both arts. the Virginia
policy is characterized as insolent (p. 337
in no. 2169 and pp. 577, 593 in no. 2324);
Hurlbert was at the Harvard Law School,
1852–1853, where the influence of Story
was still both felt and admired. Two reasons why Hurlbert could have withheld
his name or asked for complete anonymity
were his youth and untried abilities, and
the fact that he was a Southerner attacking

the South, a circumstance which was to
lead to his arrest in Richmond in 1861
(see *DAB*).

2193   Repr. *France*, II, not 11.

2194   For John Coode, read **George Coode.**
Attr. in *Register and Magazine of Biography* (1869), II, 220; nothing in *DNB*
account of John Coode suggests any interest in finance.

2324   This *is* by **William Henry Hurlbert** as
suggested, since Longmans adds "N.
York": see *DAB*.

2450   **G. C. Lewis** wrote the tailpiece, 268–
272: *Letters*, p. 373 and n. Greg should
therefore have a collab., even though
Longmans assigns him the whole art.,
since he wrote only 236–268.

2676, etc.   Here and for later arts. of Croskerry (see I, 864), read **Croskery,** as in
Allibone and *DNB*.

2848   By **Edward Maitland,** but *not* Edward
Francis Maitland, Lord Barcaple, to
whom it was assigned on I, 998; had that
been true, Longmans would have called
the author Lord Barcaple. Consequently,
the reference to the *DNB* should be deleted. This may well be Edward Maitland,
1824–1897, who was writing for periodicals in and after 1870 (see *DNB*, 1st
suppl.). *FortR* no. 700, on a similar subject and published in the same year, was
signed Edward Maitland, as was *Westm.
Rev.*, 102 (July 1874), 200–213, which
is certainly by man suggested.

2925   By **W. H. Hurlbert,** prob. Hurlbert
wrote a good deal on the American Civil
War in British journals, and often as if he
were an Englishman (see this appendix
and Part B in *Index*, I and II); on pp.
574–575 Justice Story, on whom Hurlbert
prob. wrote *ER* no. 2169 (see above), is
quoted with approval, as he is elsewhere
in Hurlbert's arts. (*ER* no. 2324, *FM* no.
3541); the explanation of the unusual
secrecy (the art. is specifically marked
"anonymous" in Longmans) supports the
attrib. since, being an American, he would
be anxious to conceal his attack on the
U.S. claims.

3873   Or perhaps Sir Henry Stewart Cunningham (I, 866) who was also a barrister
and writing in the 90s.

HOME AND FOREIGN REVIEW

28   By **William Bernard MacCabe.** Acton to
Simpson, [Oct. 21, 1862], Acton-Simpson
Corres., lists "MacCabe—Christmas" in

plan for Jan. issue. For MacCabe and
H&FR, see *Index*, I, 1194.

44   After pagination, delete remainder of

entry. Art. by **Julius Fröbel.** Claimed in *Vorwert,* dated Mar. 1, 1864, to *Theorie der Politik,* Vol. II, 1864.

51 Item iii is by **John O'Hagan,** prob.: cf. nos. 11, 22, 32, where he did the Irish current events; O'Hagan to Acton, Dec. 7 and Dec. 21, 1863, Woodruff Collection, show that this section was still in his hands, and in letter of Mar. 11, 1864, he offers to overlook the MS. of a "new man" who is to take his place.

74 The date of Acton's letter is Dec. 1863, in reply to Simpson's of Dec. 16, 1863, so that his reference to only two current events in the next number, both of which he will do, applies to the Jan. 1864 issue, as suggested.

76 Add to evidence for Fröbel that he had written no. 44: see above here.

81 Lottner? Very possibly **Friedrich Löttner,** on whom see Part B below.

MACMILLAN'S MAGAZINE

P. 556, under Note on Attributions   Of the four MS. sources mentioned, the first three are now in the British Museum: (1) is Add. MSS. 55997 and 55999; (2) and (3) are bound together in Add. MS. 55998. The correspondence (4) is mainly in the British Museum (Add. MSS. 55281–55845), but much of it is at the University of Reading and some in the Berg Collection, New York Public Library. At the present time (Jan. 1971) the correspondence in the British Museum is not available to readers and that at Reading has no index.

P. 556, under Bibliographical Note   A. J. Gurr, *"Macmillan's Magazine," Review of English Literature,* 6 (Jan. 1965), 39–55, is an able essay which complements and extends the sketch above. For the history of the break-up of the Macmillan collection, see William E. Fredeman's eloquent article, "The Bibliographical Significance of a Publisher's Archive: The Macmillan Papers," *Studies in Bibliography,* 23 (1970), 183–191.

P. 617   March 1883 is Vol. 47, not 48.

3a [Headnote to] Cobbett; or, A rural ride, 40–41. **George Stovin Venables.** Signed.

76a [Headnote to] The boot [poem on Italian unity]; from the Italian of Giuseppe Giusti, 244–245.

125 R. Macdonnell is **John Randal MacDonnell,** whose address in Kelly in 1861 is that on letter of R. MacDonnell to Macmillan, Jan. 2, 1861, Macmillan Papers, Berg Collec., N.Y. Public Lib., acknowledging check for this art.

153a [Headnote to] Sant' Ambrogio; from the Italian of Giusti, 39.

176 For Swinton Boult, read **Swinton Henry Boult,** son of the former, who calls himself "once a competition-wallah" in *NatR-II,* no. 483, above.

190 By **John Malcolm Ludlow.** On Ludlow's list.

224a [Headnote to] Britain's earnest-money for the provinces which saved her Indian Empire in the Mutiny: a story of Mooltan, 230–231. **R. H. W. Dunlop.** Signed R.H.W.D.; Robertson markings; Dunlop is listed as contrib. to this vol., p. vii; he wrote *Service & Adventure . . . during the Mutinies, 1857–1858,* 1858.

267a [Headnote to] Lines written in the Bay of Lerici, by Percy Bysshe Shelley, 122. **Richard Garnett,** 1835–1906. Signed R.G.; Garnett wrote *Relics of Shelley* in this year, 1862, and he contributed no. 62.

279 By **Alexander Smith Kinnear,** prob.: the K.R. signature was derived, apparently, from *Kinnear;* Masson to Mr. Fraser, accountant at Macmillan's, July 2, 1862, Berg Collec., N.Y. Public Lib., tells him to send cheque to "R. S. Kinnear, 41 Heriot Row, Edinburgh (writer of the article 'Leigh Hunt's Poetry')," but no trace of such a Kinnear; author cited above was living at that address in 1862 (*Edinburgh Directory*), and two years earlier had written a paper on Hunt's life and character (*NBR* no. 618), ending with the hope of finding "some future opportunity of expressing our opinions of the poems," which is the subject of this *Mac.* art.; the memorandum and private letter by Carlyle which are briefly quoted in *NBR* no. 618, pp. 371, 372, appear here at length, pp. 239, 239–240.

293a Michael Angelo: a dramatic anecdote —adapted from Friedrich Hebbel by Richard Garnett, 381–385. **C. Friedrich Hebbel.** Title. Adaptation by **Richard Garnett,** 1835–1906, in *DNB.*

378 By **Fitzjames Stephen.** Cf. no. 441 on *Essays and Reviews* (next entry), which is also signed A Lay Churchman; this art., p. 254, deals with the same book; the sharp tone and liberal viewpoint appear in both essays.

441 By **Fitzjames Stephen.** Masson to Alexander Macmillan, Feb. 12, 1864, BM Add. MS 54792, reports: "Fitzjames Stephen wants to write another article on the Essays and Reviews judgment or the *Times* article thereon [see p. 440 here] . . . . I have said 'yes,' and must try somehow to make room for it."

466a [Translator's introduction to] "Resurrecturis: a poem from the Polish of Sigismund Krasinski," 198–200. Trans. by **William Henry Bullock**—signed W.H.B.; Bullock wrote *Polish Experiences . . . of 1863–4,* 1864, published by Macmillan's; he later added Hall to his name.

513 For V. H. Hobart, read **Henry Kingsley:** the essay is repr. in Kingsley's *Hornby Mills,* as stated. The letter to Hobart applies to no. 517.

660 Delete the attrib. to Hughes. The style of no. 795 is clearly different, as are some of the opinions; and since Hughes signed that art., why not this if he had done it?

671 By **Helen Taylor,** as suggested. Emily Davies to Helen Taylor, Aug. 4, 1866, Mill-Taylor Papers, London School of Economics, is glad to hear that her art. has been accepted for *Macmillan;* same to same, Oct. 15, 1866, asks if she is planning to reprint it.

720 For George Grote, read **John Grote.** Signed "The late Professor Grote"; this art. is attr. to John Grote in *DNB;* also see Mayor's intro. note.

859 By **T. E. Kebbel?** Grove to his assistant Craik, [c. Aug. 1, 1868], BM Add. MS. 54793, thanks him for cheque [prob. for his editorial work] and then adds the addresses of what appear to be two new contributors to *Mac* which Craik needs in order to send them cheques—viz. those of Joseph Bennett (for no. 857) and T. E. Kebbel, who would have written the only unassigned art., namely no. 859. To our knowledge neither had contributed before.

861 By **Elizabeth Garrett.** Grove to Alexander Macmillan, July 23, 1868, BM Add. MS. 54793, reports he has "promised Miss Garrett for Sept." Author cited wrote no. 732 and championed the role of women in medicine.

925 Prob. by **Marie Blaze de Bury.** According to Prof. Jacques Voisine of the Sorbonne, who wrote his dissertation on Mme. Blaze de Bury, in a letter to the *Index,* Oct. 4, 1968, the references to *Bérénice* as the first psychological drama in France and to Shakespeare, Calderon, and Goethe as the three greatest dramatic poets (pp. 70, 71) are opinions often expressed by this author; also, the play, *The Rightful Heir,* so staunchly defended against adverse criticism, pp. 73–75, was by her friend Edward Lytton Bulwer.

1021a Hymn[s] on the Transfiguration [by various hands], 543–546. Edited by **A. P. Stanley**—signed The Dean of Westminster.

1101 By **George Parker Bidder,** 1836–1896: attr. in I.C.E. *Minutes,* 125 (1896), 427.

1152 For Noule, read **Moule,** as in Part B.

1169 For Mrs. Creagh read **Matilda E. V. Creagh:** Grove to Macmillan [1871], BM Add. MS. 54793, fols. 64–65, mentions "Khismet" by "Wolseley's sister" as a story ready to be used; see Part B revision.

1227a Frere here printed, with explanatory comment, an 8-line stanza which Scott composed as an appropriate opening to Burns' "Address of Bruce to His Men before Bannockburn."

1253 Delete the "(Part I)" in the title. The author is **Margaret E. Poole,** who had written no. 753: Grove to Macmillan [1871], BM Add. MS. 54793, lists with "Miss Poole" as author among stories they have on hand; soon afterwards she became Mrs. Margaret E. Sandford, under which name she wrote nos. 1397, 3095.

1344 The "prob." should be deleted. The art. was repr. in Simpson's *Meeting the Sun* (1874), pp. 273–280.

1527 By **R. C. Jebb.** Confidently attr. by Charles Tennyson and Christine Fall, *Alfred Tennyson: an Annotated Bibliography* (Athens, Georgia, 1967), p. 99, but without evidence; Jebb wrote no. 836 on another Tennyson poem.

1630 **Maria Trench** is the author but not the Maria Marcia Fanny Trench to whom the art. was given in Part B. The art. is signed M. Trench; Contents gives "Maria Trench," on whom see Part B above.

1725 By **Sarah Austin.** See opening sentence; attr. by Janet Ross, *Three Generations* (1893 ed.), p. 167. The art. is signed Janet Ross, but she simply edited it.

1840 By **H. Sutherland Edwards:** repr. *The Lyrical Drama* (1881), I.

1955   On p. 408 Mackay refers to his "long residence in Canada"; see Part B revision.

1961   By **Laurence Oliphant.** Claimed in letter to Grove, from Constantinople, Feb. 19, 1880, BM Add. MS. 55256, asking that author remain secret.

2072   This story of boyhood bird-nesting is laid in Scotland. Neither Venn nor *CCD/76* mentions any Scottish background of the David Bruce suggested in Part B. However, another **David Bruce,** d.1911, New Zealand minister in *WWW*, was born and bred in Scotland, and is therefore the more likely author.

2172   After the date of the letter, insert: Letter Books.

2422   For J. Thackray Bruce, read **J. Thackray Bunce:** the publisher's list was misread.

2440   The author's name is FitzGerald. The recipient of Macmillan's letter was Mowbray Morris, not Grove; the high praise is sufficient to warrant the substitution of a prob. for the "?".

2459   The author is **Walter Lionel Bicknell** who used Austen or Austin Pember as a pseudonym: see Macmillan index of books (BM Add. MS. 56001) where the entry for Bicknell has "alias Austin Pember" written below it in the same hand and ink; also both have same address in Macmillan Papers, Add. MS. 55997; *BMCat.* has entries under both names, using "Aust*in*" for the second.

2697   Hudson's life dates, 1862–1918, should have been added, since this is not by the naturalist of the same name, 1841–1922, to whom it is now assigned in Part B: see Part B revision.

2886   By **Lionel Johnson,** with some revision by **Hugh William Orange.** Johnson to Campbell Dodgson, Jan. 1890, BM Add. MS. 46363, writes, "You remember that Nero essay which I wrote, and which Orange slightly altered and read [presumably to some Oxford literary society]? He has got it accepted by Macmillan." Macmillan assigns to H. W. Orange, whose full name is in *WWW/1960*; Johnson and Orange were contemporaries at Winchester and New Coll. Attr. to both in Arthur W. Patrick, *Lionel Johnson, Poète et Critique* (Paris, 1939), p. 238.

3018   For Mrs. H. Musgrave, read **Mrs. Beadon:** see revision for no. 3045.

3045   For Mrs. H. Musgrave, read **Mrs. Beadon.** Attr. to latter in *Macmillan*, and the suggestion in text that Mrs. Musgrave was a pseudonym has proved to be so: *Temple Bar*, 93 (Dec. 1891), 555–572, signed H. Musgrave, is assigned to Mrs. Beadon ("Mrs. Musgrave") by the *Temple Bar* ledger, BM Add. MS. 46564, vol. 5.

3153   The "?" may be removed. *Temple Bar*, 103 (Dec. 1894), 507–520, also a story placed in Montana, is assigned to Miss Nellie Mackulin in *Temple Bar* ledger (BM Add. MS. 46564, vol. 5), which explains the pseudonymous initials; *LCCat.* uses a lower case "k" for Ellen Makubin; the Macmillan reading is the same except that the "k" may be a capital.

3179   By **James Briggs Carlill.** Addresses in Kelly's *Suburban Directory* is the same as that for man cited in Venn, under his son Harold F. Carlill.

3192   For Mrs. H. Musgrave, read **Mrs. Beadon:** cf. revision of no. 3045.

3436   For E. Enticknappe, which is a pseudonym, read **Hannah Lynch,** repr. *Dr. Vermont's Fantasy*, 1896.

3461   By **Hannah Lynch:** signed E. Enticknappe—see previous entry.

3628   By **Hannah Lynch:** signed E. Enticknappe—see revision of 3436 above.

3782   For Esther Hallam, which is a pseudonym, read **Esther Hallam Moorhouse:** see *WWW/1960* under Esther Hallam Meynell, and note that Macmillan calls author "Miss."

3943   For Wilfrid Sparroy, which is a pseudonym, read **H. Wilfrid Sparrow:** *Blackwood Papers Cat.*, p. 287.

3963   For Wilfrid Sparroy, a pseudonym, read **H. Wilfrid Sparrow** and **Walter Shaw Sparrow.** See previous entry; but since the art. is signed Two Brothers and the second man was both a writer on art and the brother of Wilfrid Sparrow (see his *Memories of Life and Art* [1925], pp. 60, 191), it seems reasonable to suppose he was co-author; his brother, "Wilfrid Sparroy," prob. sent in the MS. and received the cheque.

NORTH BRITISH REVIEW

Contributed by Mrs. Joanne Shattock

AMONG THE FRASER PAPERS in possession of Mr. A. C. Fraser of Hawick, Roxburghshire, is a small notebook containing memoranda for the *North British Re-*

view, which Fraser kept from March 1850 until the end of 1851. In it he listed prospective reviewers and articles, noted financial details, and planned the numbers from May 1850 to November 1851. One of the entries proves to be of considerable value in identifying the contributors in the period immediately prior to Fraser's editorship. It is headed "Contributors in 1848–9–50 to Feb.*y*" and consists of a list of the names of the forty contributors to the nine issues between February 1848 and February 1850 (Code nos. 140–224), with the number of articles written by each reviewer marked beside his name. (It is cited in the revisions below as "Fraser notebook.") This reads as follows:

CONTRIBUTORS	NUMBER OF ARTICLES
1. Sir David Brewster	10
2. Dr. Anster of Dublin	7
3. David Masson, Esq., London	4
4. J. W. Kaye, Esq., Editor of Atlas	4
5. Cov*y* Patmore, British Museum, London	4
6. James Lorimer, Esq., Edin.	4
7. Dr. Candlish	4
8. Dr. John Brown	3
9. Principal Cunningham	3
10. Mr. DeQuincey	3
11. James Wilson, Esq.	3
12. Dr. Samuel Brown	2
13. Rev. John Cairns	2
14. Rev. J. Godkin, Ireland	2
15. Dr. Kitto, London	2
16. Augustus Trollope, Esq.[1]	2
17. Dr. Gunn of Edin.[2]	2
18. Dr. James Buchanan, Edin.	1
19. Professor Fleming	1
20. Professor Fraser	1
21. Isaac Taylor, Ongar	1
22. Dr. James Hamilton, London	1
23. Dr. MacCrie, Edin.	1
24. Dr. Hetherington[3]	1
25. Dr. George Bell	1
26. Sheriff Gordon[4]	1
27. Alexander Dunlop, Esq.	1
28. James Moncrieff, Esq.	1
29. Patrick Fraser, Esq.	1
30. J. H. Burton, Esq.	1
31. W. Ivory, Esq.	1
32. Samuel Raleigh, Esq.	1

---

[1]"A. Trollope, Esq.," is listed as a possible writer on historical subjects in a later entry in the notebook, "Proposed Staff of writers." This is most likely Thomas Adolphus Trollope, 1810–1892, "a constant contributor to periodical literature": see *Men of the Time*, 7th ed., 1868, and *DNB*.

[2]William Maxwell Gunn, LL.D.: see revisions for Part B.

[3]William Maxwell Hetherington: see revisions for Part B.

[4]John Thomson Gordon: see Part B of Vol. I.

CONTRIBUTORS	NUMBER OF ARTICLES
33. David Dundas Scott, Esq.	1
34. Lord Lovelace	1
35. John Forster, Esq., London[5]	1
36. William Weir, Esq.	1
37. John Robertson, Esq.[6]	1
38. William Paul, Esq.	1
39. M. Von Gremback	1
40. J. M. Duncan, Esq., Edinb.	1

The *Wellesley Index* Vol. I for this period makes forty-five positive identifications and suggests probable or possible authors for fifteen additional articles, leaving twenty-five articles unidentified. Fraser's notebook confirms the forty-five positive identifications in so far as each of the contributors appears on the list and the number of articles attributed to him falls within the total number he supposedly wrote. For the same reason eleven of the fifteen suggested authors could be, and probably are, correct, while four are definitely incorrect. In addition the list introduces twelve new contributors who, in these nine numbers, are responsible for a total of fifteen articles, and attributes thirteen articles to ten reviewers who are known to have written for the Review in earlier or later periods.

One discrepancy which immediately presents itself fortunately has a solution. Fraser's forty contributors wrote, according to the notebook, a total of eighty-four articles. The number of articles in the nine numbers is eighty-five. However, two letters among the Chalmers Papers in New College, Edinburgh, give fairly conclusive evidence as to the author of the additional article and the reason for its omission from the notebook. Mrs. Anne Hanna, wife of the editor, writes to her friend Mrs. Edward Cardwell, wife of the Peelite M.P., on March 7, 1848, that she is "so pleased to hear that Mr. C. was so kind as to write something for the N.B. No one else is to know, but me, not even Mr. Constable, as Mr. H. thinks it is better that he should not be told." On May 16, 1848, she writes to Mrs. Cardwell again, commenting that she is "looking forward with much pleasure to reading the last article in the Review." This is no. 158, "The Budget of 1848—Financial Reform." Cardwell was Secretary to the Treasury in 1845 and an expert on financial questions (see *DNB*), a likely author for such a specialized article. Fraser would most probably have got his information for the notebook from Constable rather than Hanna, since the former conducted the negotiations when he took over the Review, which would account for the omission of Cardwell from the list.

Unfortunately, even when all possibilities have been considered, and "probable" or "possible" contributors have been given the benefit of the doubt, three articles remain completely unidentified during the period—viz., nos. 169, 190, and 200; and three contributors lack a corresponding article—viz., J. M. Duncan, James Buchanan, and David Masson (his 4th art.).

---

[5]"John Forster, Esq., 58 Lincolns Inn Field" appears later in the notebook under "List of persons with whom I have corresponded concerning the N.B. Review . . ." which positively identifies this John Forster as the essayist and biographer: see Part B of Vol. I.

[6]John Robertson: see revisions for Part B.

NOTE ON VOLUME 33, AUGUST 1860

The exact time at which Blaikie took over the Review from Duns and the question of the editorship of the August 1860 number pose something of a problem. Fraser's journal for June 1, 1860, Fraser Papers, records that the "N.B. Review . . . is now in the hands of Blaikie . . . Clark in George Street being publisher." Duns, in a letter to Douglas, December 27, 1884, bound with the "Douglas File" of the Review at the University of Calgary, states that his editorship lasted until the Review "passed into Mr. Clark's hands," which was in or before August 1860, the first number published by Clark. Douglas in a note on a letter from Dr. John Brown, dated January 30, [1861], states that Blaikie's first number was August 1860 (Douglas Papers, Scrapbook I), although Douglas's annotations at this time are not always reliable. Clearly by the summer of 1860 Blaikie was well engrossed in *North British* affairs, as his letter to Fraser of June 15, 1860 (in the Fraser Papers), asking Fraser for advice on contributors and on promoting the Review's interests, indicates.

However, Blaikie's editorship of the August number is still not firmly established. A letter from Brewster to Lord Brougham, June 21, 1860, in the Brougham Papers at University College London, MS. 26,794, referred to in the *Index*, I, 665, suggests another possibility. Brewster writes:

I presume your Lordship has learned from Mr. Forster that he was unable from the shortness of the time, to find a suitable person to review your address. I trust however, that he will succeed for the Novr number which will contain some excellent articles under the new editor.

The Mr. Forster in question is clearly John Forster as further correspondence indicates, and the Brewster letter raises two important issues—Forster's part, if any, in the editing of the number, and Blaikie's not actually taking over the Review until the November number.

On the first point, it seems highly dubious that a man of Forster's eminence should edit, or help to edit, an Edinburgh-based quarterly at the nadir of its influence and prestige, and that, if he had, none of the other editors ever referred to it. On the other hand, Brewster's remark could be interpreted to mean that he had asked Forster, a friend of Brougham's whose additional correspondence in the Brougham Papers indicates that he was particularly interested in Brougham's addresses at this time, to find someone to review Brougham's address of May 18, 1860, on his inauguration as Chancellor of Edinburgh University, as part of a general attempt to help with the August issue. Was Blaikie, then, its editor? On the end-paper at the beginning of vol. 33 in the "Douglas File" at Calgary, Douglas has written: "No. 66 the first No. edited by Dr. Blaikie" (cited in *Index*, I, 665, n. 9)—i.e., the November issue. Moreover, the *Athenaeum*, November 10, 1860, p. 632, states, "The new number of the *North British Review*, the first under its present management, may be almost considered as a new serial"; and the *Spectator* for November 3, 1860, p. 1060, thought the *North British* appeared "to have passed into more vigorous hands."

Clearly, the documents are somewhat contradictory or ambiguous. For the time being, rather than imputing the editorship of the August issue to either Forster or

Blaikie, it would seem wiser to regard the number as a transitional one, similar to the issues of March and May 1850 and August 1857, relying heavily on articles already accepted or submitted and on the support of old contributors. Blaikie must have had some share in the editorial work, but the main organizer, most probably, was Brewster. His correspondence in the Fraser and Brougham Papers shows that he was keenly involved as ever in *NBR* affairs; and he himself contributed two articles to the August number.

NOTE ON "MR. WEBB"

A further reading of BM Add. MS. 37,193, fols. 182, 186, referred to in *Index*, I, 665, n. 11, to support the claim that a "Mr. Webb" was sub-editor under Welsh, indicates that Webb is a misreading of Brewster's difficult hand for Welsh, the editor.

46 The "?" after the author should be deleted. See the revision of no. 144 below for the link of this article to no. 5.

50 The "?" may be deleted since, in addition to evidence given, there is a reference, p. 262, to "our" former art. on capital and drainage, which is no. 43.

71 By **Thomas Cleghorn**. Attr. by D. M. [preface so signed], *Memorial Sketch of Thomas Cleghorn* (1881), p. 54.

85 By **J. W. Kaye**, as suggested: see text of no. 205 and its revision below.

94 By **John Winter Jones**. Anthony Panizzi to Fraser, Oct. 17, 1850, Fraser Papers, says he suggested to Hanna that "Mr. Jones who wrote . . . on Ballads for your review sometime ago" should write on "Public Libraries"—viz., no. 268, where Mr. Jones is identified.

99 The "prob." may be removed. In addition to evidence given, the only two arts. referred to in the text and notes—nos. 18 and 45—are both by Panizzi. The Espinasse reference is to the *Critic*, Sept. 15, 1851, p. 427.

109 For James Maclagan, read **James Buchanan:** attr. in Mrs. Anne Hanna to Dr. Chalmers, Feb. 15, 1847, Chalmers Papers, New College, Edinburgh.

111 By **Patrick Fraser?** Fraser to A. C. Fraser, Mar. 25, 1852, Fraser Papers, says he once wrote in the Review a general art. dealing with the "social and economic existence of the low and the very low orders . . . in the great towns."

118 Pages 291–294 on Cary and 294–299 on Jeremy Taylor are by **William Hanna:** Mrs. Anne Hanna to Grace Chalmers, n.d., Chalmers Papers, says Hanna has made notes for a critical notice of Taylor and will do the same for Cary.

134 By **John Kitto,** prob. Biblical geography was a favorite topic of his: see *DNB* and

BMCat. Preface to work cited in no. 202 says he benefited from researches of travellers, including Wilson, here reviewed. The style is characteristic: cf. no. 191 (see revision below) and no. 202.

136 By **Thomas Adolphus Trollope.** The literary style and the informal manner disassociate the art. from Panizzi (contrast no. 99); in no. 218 (see revision below) Trollope deals with medieval Italian history in a similar way; in Fraser notebook he is listed as possible writer on historical subjects; see footnote 1 in *NBR* Introduction above.

142 For William Cunningham, read **James Godkin.** Fraser notebook gives former only 3 arts. (which must be nos. 182, 193, 211) and latter 2, neither of which is attr. in *Index*, I. Godkin was a missionary to Roman Catholics from the Irish Evangelical Society and author of anti-Catholic works: see *DNB* and *BMCat.* On p. 341 author states he bought all books being reviewed in Dublin.

143 By **William King,** later King-Noel, 1st Earl of Lovelace, prob. Fraser notebook assigns him one art. Pamphlet in Edin. U. Lib. known to be by King, "Review of Rubichon—De l'action de la Noblesse et des Classes Supérieures dans les Sociétés Modernes and of Benoiton de Chateauneuf on the Extinction of Noble Families in France" (1848), shows knowledge of problems of English poor law, some of which are dealt with in this art.

144 By **John Thomson Gordon.** Fraser notebook assigns him one art.; this paper is written in the same *literary* style which is conspicuous in nos. 5 and 46—the abundant use of metaphor, the lofty rhetorical periods, the literary allusions, and the verbosity; the sentiments are often eloquent or exaggerated; the length of all three arts. is relatively short for the *NBR*; cf. pp. 378–380, especially the first paragraph, with no. 5, notably pp. 99 and 107, and no. 46, pp. 154, 161, 161–162.

146 The "prob" may be deleted. To evidence given, citing no. 127, add the fact that Fraser notebook assigns 7 arts. to Anster —which are probably the 7 now in Part B between the notebook limits of no. 140 to no. 224; but for nos. 168, 175, and 207 see revisions below.

147 Delete the "?". Fraser notebook gives Moncreiff one art.

149 Delete the "?". Besides evidence given, Fraser notebook assigns Candlish 4 arts., the other 3 seem to be nos. 185, 195, 224; on no. 224 see revision below.

153 Delete the attrib. to Hugh Miller, since he does not appear in Fraser notebook. By **James Hamilton**, the second suggestion, since he does, and his "The Adaptation of the Sabbath to Man's Intellectual and Moral Nature" in *The Christian Sabbath*, ed. B. W. Noel (1850), pp. 125–141, is in a similar vein.

156 By **David Masson**. Fraser notebook assigns him 4 arts. Besides this, see revisions below of nos. 177 and 197. Masson's concern with social questions is found in nos. 226, 256, 272, and in an art. on Louis Blanc in *Chambers' Edinburgh Journal* for May 1848; in "Proposed Staff" in Fraser notebook he is listed under "Questions of Society."

157 By **John Robertson**. Attr. in Mrs. Anne Hanna to Mrs. Edward Cardwell, Nov. 23, 1848, Chalmers Papers.

158 By **Edward Cardwell**. Attr. in Mrs. Anne Hanna to Mrs. Edward Cardwell, Mar. 7 and May 16, 1848, Chalmers Papers.

162 By **James Godkin**? See revision of no. 142 above. Writer is obviously of evangelical sympathies (pp. 371, 375–376); he approves of Buxton's connection with the Bible Society, pp. 375–377, and other evangelical causes, pp. 377, 379, 381–390; he is concerned with the role of the Irish Church in converting Roman Catholics without tyrannizing, pp. 390–391.

164 By **T. A. Trollope**. Fraser notebook assigns him 2 arts., which seem to be this and no. 218, on which see revision below. Some of the same material was used in his *Impressions of a Wanderer in Italy, Switzerland, France and Spain* (1850), letters III and IV, from Rome in 1847–1848: in particular, the phrasing about Rome as a museum is almost identical (here p. 417, there pp. 33–34); and here, p. 428, the author says he was at Rome when the Pope established the "Consulta" and de-

fended Papal power (cf. p. 42 of the book).

166 By **Isaac Taylor**, 1787–1865. Fraser notebook gives him one art. Section on "Methodism and the Future" in his *Wesley and Methodism* (1851), pp. 297–332, deals with similar points: cf., for example, p. 298 with the art., pp. 494–496.

167 By **J. W. Kaye**. Kaye to Fraser, Sept. 7, 1854, Fraser Papers, says he wrote an art. on the British soldier "5 or 6 years ago" and another on the British officer. This art. concentrates on the role of the soldier, no. 223 on that of the officer.

168 Delete the "prob." See above, no. 146, on Anster.

169 Not William Ivory, whose one art. in this period (Fraser notebook) is established as no. 187.

170 By **M. von Gremback**. Mrs. Anne Hanna to Mrs. Cardwell, Nov. 23, 1848, Chalmers Papers, notes that there is a theological art. in the present number by man cited and adds that he is "a Dutchman." Listed in Fraser's notebook.

175 Delete the "?". Cf. no. 146 above.

176 By **William Weir**? Fraser notebook assigns him one art. Weir was educated in Germany and was concerned with continental affairs in connection with his work on the *Daily News*: see *DNB*.

177 By **David Masson**. Cf. no. 156 above.

179 By **David Dundas Scott**? Fraser notebook assigns him one art. In this essay pp. 347–349 are devoted to points of translation (also note p. 330n.) and Scott was a professional translator of Italian, French, and German works: see *BMCat*.

180 By **Thomas M'Crie**, 1797–1875. Marked as his in file of *NBR* at New College, Edinburgh. Assigned one art. in Fraser notebook.

184 By **Alexander Dunlop**. Mrs. Anne Hanna to Mrs. Cardwell, Feb. 17, 1849, Chalmers Papers, notes that there is an art. by Dunlop in present number; marked as his in New College file; p. 503 of this art. refers back to no. 10, known to be his; Fraser notebook assigns him one art. See Part B revisions below for full name.

191 By **John Kitto**. Fraser notebook assigns him 2 arts., the other being no. 202. Book cited in evidence for no. 202 contains a map of the "Voyages and Travels of St. Paul."

194 Delete the "?". Fraser notebook credits Dr. George Bell with one art. After title and before comma, insert [of births, deaths, and marriages].

197 By **David Masson**. Cf. revision of no. 156. For Masson's interest in Italian politics, see his *Memories of London in the Forties* (1908), chap. III, and *DNB*, 2nd suppl.; in 1851–1852 he was Sec. of the London Soc. of the Friends of Italy.

198 Not by Dr. Hanna since he does not appear in the Fraser notebook. By **John Forster.** Forster contributed one art. between Feb. 1848 and Feb. 1850 (Fraser notebook); Francis Espinasse, the *Critic*, Sept. 1, 1852, pp. 441–442, assigns Forster "a very amusing article . . . on 'Foreign Socialism' " in the *NBR*; of the three possibilities, nos. 156 and 177 have been assigned on good grounds to Masson (see revisions above), but the writer of this art., who deals with France and Belgium as well as Germany, is sharper, more critical of Socialism, and much more hostile to Louis Blanc (on p. 415 he calls him a "flashy journalist") than Masson; he is also amusing, as Masson is not; moreover, in no. 256 Masson mentions many French socialist writers but not a single German; though Espinasse is not always reliable, there seems to be no reason in this case to reject his attrib.

199 By **William Maxwell Hetherington.** This art. is virtually a summary of the material in his *History of the Church of Scotland from the Introduction of Christianity to the Period of the Disruption*, Edin., 1843. One art. listed in Fraser notebook.

203 By **John Fleming,** prob. This learned art. is largely on ethnology, a subject which had been recognized in 1847 by the British Association for the Advancement of Science as an independent discipline; Fleming wrote on many "departments of natural science" (*DNB*); Fraser notebook assigns him one art., and no other scientific essay is unaccounted for from Feb. 1848 through Feb. 1850.

205 By **J. W. Kaye,** as suggested. Fraser notebook assigns Kaye 4 arts.—clearly this one and nos. 167, 213, and 223: see revisions.

206 Delete the "?". Add to evidence given the fact that Fraser notebook assigns Raleigh one art.

207 Delete the "prob." Cf. revision of no. 146.

212 By **Patrick Fraser?** Fraser notebook assigns him one art. His bibliography in *Index*, I, 901, shows that most of his writing was on Scottish history and biography; the present art. combines both.

213 By **J. W. Kaye,** as suggested: the evidence given here and the revision of no. 205 confirm the attribution.

215 By **William Maxwell Gunn.** Fraser notebook assigns him 2 arts. Gunn was concerned with educational questions, especially those connected with religion: see *BMCat.*

218 By **T. A. Trollope.** See first sentence of no. 164 above. In *What I remember*, II, 119, he speaks of sometimes writing "tidbits from the byways of Italian history." Trollope lived in Italy from 1843–1886.

222 By **W. M. Gunn.** Cf. revision of no. 215. The plea for a national system of education with undenominational religious instruction also appears in *National Education—The Gunn Dinner Analysed and the Gunn Rejection Vindicated*, Edin., 1851.

223 By **J. W. Kaye,** as stated. The telescoped evidence is corrected above in revision of no. 167.

224 Delete the "?". See revision of no. 149. Candlish wrote on much the same subject in *Heads of Objection to the Marriage Affinity Bill*, Edin., 1869.

284 Delete "Bonamy Price on Newman . . . Richard Whately on Greg . . . ." By two unidentified writers, under the supervision of Richard Whately. Whately to Fraser, June 19, 1851, Fraser Papers, suggests that a notice of Greg's book, which "the writer" is transcribing, be added to the article on Newman. Whately to Fraser, Oct. 7, 1851, offers to correct the proofs of the notice as the writer is not at hand. Further letters of Dec. 24, 1851 and Jan. 16, 1852 refer to "the reviewers" and "the writers," indicating that the article on Newman was by a different hand, and that both writers were advised and supervised by Whately, a common practice of the Archbishop—see arts. cited in revision of no. 297. Fraser to Whately, June 16, 1851, states that the paper on Newman was placed in his hands by Mr. Price and that the Archbishop had agreed to supervise its passing through the press. There is no further correspondence, however, to suggest that Price was the author of the paper, and not merely an intermediary. (Note, p. 601. Delete "by Whately . . . ."; by **A. C. Fraser.** Fraser to F. W. Newman, Jan. 8, 1852, Fraser Papers, encloses a draft of the note in his own hand, which is reprinted almost verbatim.)

297 Delete Richard Whately. By an unnamed writer, under the supervision of Richard Whately: Whately to Fraser, Oct. 13, 1851, Fraser Papers, offers an art. on the *Memoir* by "an acquaintance of mine." Cf. nos. 324, 340, 350, and revision of no. 284 for Whately's method of "reviewing."

418 By **E. A. Freeman,** and not J. W. Kaye. Claimed in Preface to Freeman's *The History and Conquests of the Saracens* (Oxford, 1856), p. vii.

420 The "prob." may be deleted since the date of the letter is June 23, 1855.

443 By **Abraham Hayward.** Hayward to Fraser, Jan. 11, [1856], Fraser Papers, says he is writing a biographical and critical notice of a contemporary, who is a legal figure; on Mar. 8 he asks for proofs of his art., and in a letter of Apr. 23 encloses a list of names to whom copies of the current number containing his art. should be sent.

448 By **John Muir.** Muir to Fraser, Mar. 31, 1857, Fraser Papers, refers to his art. on Indian literature in the *NBR*. This is the only art. in the Review on this subject.

466 The Note, p. 592, is by **A. C. Fraser,** not Patrick Fraser. P. Fraser to A. C. Fraser, Dec. 25, 1856, Fraser Papers, cannot agree to proposal that a note of apology be printed; A. C. Fraser to P. Fraser, Dec. 26, encloses a draft of the note which was printed virtually verbatim.

476 By **W. H. Hurlbert.** Kingsley to Fraser, Feb. 6, 1856, Fraser Papers, suggests Hurlbert review Mrs. Stowe's *Dred* and consider the whole surrounding question. Hurlbert to Fraser, n.d., promises to send art. on *Dred* for spring number. This art., a year later, does not review *Dred* (Hurlbert had done that in *ER* no. 2324 in Oct. 1856), but the general point of view and various topics here discussed—Brooks' attack on Sumner and Dana's speech upon it, the hostility to Buchanan and support of Fremont, the need to use cannon in Boston to enforce the Fugitive Slave Law—are all found in *ER* no. 2324; furthermore, J. M. Ludlow to Fraser, Apr. 15, 1857, says he is glad to hear that Hurlbert is writing for *NBR*.

486 By **J. W. Kaye.** He wrote on the Mutiny in *ER* no. 2362 (in *Index*, I) two months later with equal authority: there the lack of touch between Sepoy soldiers and English officers appears, p. 554 (cf. here, pp. 268–269) and the same passage from Metcalfe is quoted, p. 562 (as here, p. 257); attr. to Kaye in Douglas file.

514 In last line of evidence the author is Champneys.

560 By **Marie Blaze de Bury.** David Brewster to Mme. Blaze de Bury, May 26, 1859, Columbia Univ., says he has arranged with Mr. Kennedy [publisher of *NBR* at this time] for her "Guizot's Memoirs."

575 By **James Buchanan.** Identified in his *The "Essays and Reviews" Examined* (Edin., 1861), Appendix Note B., p. 246, where he states, "We have elsewhere observed . . ." and quotes p. 360 of this art.

613 By **James Bannerman.** Attr. by James Buchanan, *Analogy, Considered as a Guide to Truth* (Edin., 1864), p. 478n.

618 The last line should read: for Forster see revision of no. 198. The entry should end: The revision of *Mac* no. 279 strongly supports Kinnear.

626 By **J. W. Kaye.** Attr. in Douglas file; in no. 694, pp. 239 and 245 refer back to this art., which, like no. 694, vigorously supports policy of Canning; the art. links nos. 459 and 694.

655 For J. F. MacLennan, read **J. Boyd Kinnear.** Attr. in W. G. Blaikie to Douglas, July 21, 1863, Douglas Scrapbook I, Douglas Papers.

730 By **J. Boyd Kinnear.** Evidence in previous entry.

901 Delete the "prob." Add: Hannah to Douglas, Feb. 19, 1869, Douglas Scrapbook I, returns proofs of his art.

924 In Acton list delete notice 32, which was inserted on the authority of Shaw, *Bibliography* (it was left blank in the Douglas file); every one of the Douglas file attribs. to Acton is confirmed in a letter from Acton to W. G. Ward, Nov. 20, 1869, repr. in Damian McElrath, *Lord Acton: The Decisive Decade, 1864–1874* (Louvain, 1970), p. 77.

QUARTERLY REVIEW

P. 700, l. 9   A longer and more exact description of the Murray "Register" may be found in Hill and Helen Chadwick Shine, *The Quarterly Review under Gifford* (Chapel Hill, 1949), p. 100.

P. 701, ll. 3–6   The compiler of this list was Thomas Poyser: see Boase.

P. 768   In title of Volume 163 for October: for 1866, read 1886.

6   By **John Taylor Coleridge:** see Murray; Robert Southey to Coleridge, Oct. 21, 1823, quoted in *Studia Germanica Gandensia*, 6 (1964), 131, says that since Coleridge is writing on penitentiaries, he will send him material on Millbank (see pp. 432–440). The attr. to George Taylor, 1772–1851, in the source given was apparently an error, but he may have had some hand in it.

15   By **John Philips (or Phillips) Potter.** Repr. *Essays on the Lives of Cowper, Newton, and Heber*, 1830, published anon. but listed under Potter in *BMCat.*; also see evidence in the text, except for the suggestion of John Phillips (sic.) Potter in the *DNB*, who was this man's son.

27   Add: and disposed of in Southey to J. T. Coleridge, May 11, 1825, quoted in *Studia Germanica* (see previous item), 6 (1964), 159, where Southey says he does not know who wrote the paper on Dissenters.

46   For John Miller, read **William Jacob.** Jacob to Macvey Napier, June 24, 1826, Napier MS. 34613, says his last art. in *QR* was on past and present states of England during editorship of J. T. Coleridge [from Mar.–Dec. 1825]. Murray apparently got this one wrong.

47   By **William Stewart Rose.** Attr. by Thomas Keightley, *The Fairy Mythology* (1850), p. 396n.

92   By **William Henry Leeds,** prob. Correspondence with Sharon Turner in mid-1820s, Trin. Coll. Camb., suggests his possible authorship of such an art., and see Part B above; the raffish language (our "square-toed, velvet-capped, penny-wise forefathers," p. 195), and especially the use of *"con amore,"* p. 188, which must appear in half of his papers, point strongly to Leeds; cf. *FQR* no. 177 above.

190   Add to evidence: claimed in Jacob to Napier, Feb. 14, 1829, Napier MS. 34614.

196   Delete the last clause, which suggests Brewster.

209   By **John Fleming,** and not Brewster. In *NBR* no. 58, p. 500n., Brewster himself says that this art. is "from the pen, we believe, of Dr. Fleming."

337   A note in bound volume of Croker's arts. at Camb. Univ. Lib. explains that "this review was written (by F.E.) in the supposition that the book was *genuine.* Mr. Croker was requested to fit it to the true state of the case—namely that the work was a mere forgery—He could do so but imperfectly." F.E., the "unknown new contributor," may have been Francis

Egerton, whose first acknowledged art. was no. 411.

342   Harriet Martineau, *Autobiography* (3 vols., 1877), I, 199–211, supplies some evidence to show that J. W. Croker and J. G. Lockhart provided the satiric ridicule, while Scrope did the political economy. Since the style seems the same throughout, it is more probable that Croker and/or Lockhart rewrote Scrope's article.

386   Remove the "prob.": total evidence is strong.

388   For last clause substitute: only these pages are included in bound volume of Croker's contributions to *QR* at Camb. Univ. Lib.

400   The "prob." should be deleted: the paper is on a list of H. N. Coleridge's *QR* arts. in J. G. Lockhart to John Taylor Coleridge, Aug. 23, 1843, BM Add. MS. 47558. The notice of S. T. Coleridge's death which is requested is on pp. 291–292, presumably by **Lockhart.**

452   Add a "prob." After date in l. 3, insert: Clements Lib.

463   By **J. G. Lockhart.** Lockhart to T. N. Talfourd, Oct. 29, 1835, Huntington Lib., speaks of not receiving Talfourd's authorization to do notice of *Ion* until the Sept. *QR* was already advertised, leaving him only a few hours for the review; otherwise he might have done more justice to the poem.

485   Delete the possibility of W. H. Smith: the evidence given is only that he wrote an art. on modern science for the *QR* at this time; also, the religious position in the first paragraph is far from Smith's agnosticism (see *Story*, pp. 62–76). The Scrope entry should remain as it is; besides the attrib. by Murray, the author remarks, p. 38 (and cf. p. 39) that "on former occasions we have avowed a preference for the theory of [the earth's] central heat," which may refer to nos. 246 and 438, both by Scrope. OR, **W. J. Broderip?** Attr. while Broderip was alive by Louis Berger, *William John Broderip* (Paris, 1856), p. 8, where the art. is described as "the treatise on bridge-building of Dr. Buckland," published in the *QR* under Lockhart; this is supported by the high praise of Buckland, especially on p. 43: only "those who have listened spell-bound to that conversational eloquence with which the Professor is so peculiarly gifted" can imagine the vivid manner of his writing, etc.; this might well be Broderip speaking, since he was a close friend of Buckland's at Oxford (see *Fraser's Mag.*, no. 3825); on p. 54 is a reference to no. 479 by Broderip.

539 By **J. G. Lockhart,** prob., and **H. N. Coleridge:** Coleridge to John Taylor Coleridge, Aug. 19, 1837, BM Add. MS. 47557, referring to this art., remarks: "As to Cottle, no one but myself could have done the thing properly; and besides I did not wish to let Lockhart write anything upon the subject; and he would have done so, if I had declined." Coleridge, then, reviewed Cottle's *Recollections of S. T. Coleridge,* on pp. 25–32. But pp. 1–25 on the *Literary Remains* were apparently written by someone else because H. N. Coleridge, who was its editor, is severely criticized on pp. 1–2, and because a line is drawn across p. 25 above the Cottle review. The letter suggests Lockhart, who might otherwise have gone on to a second book on S. T. Coleridge, and the whole art. is attr. to him in Poole, I, 274. Murray assigns it to H. N. Coleridge, but Coleridge certainly did not write pp. 1–2.

641 After Croker insert a "prob."

643 Since the source which begins the evidence provides conclusive proof, everything that follows "p. 184" should be deleted.

698 William Wordsworth supplied some arguments and information: G. L. Little, "Wordsworth, Lockhart, Barron Field, and the Copyright Act," *N&Q,* 210 (Nov. 1965,), 411–413.

721 After *Essays* in l. 2, add: Egerton, *Personal Reminiscences of the Duke of Wellington* (1903), pp. 81–83, states that **John Gurwood** collaborated with him here and in no. 817; on ibid., pp. 211–235, he prints the memorandum "which the Duke supplied me with" to aid in writing the *Life of Blücher* in *QR* for Sept. 1842 (viz., no. 721).

781 By **John Holmes?** Holmes was on the staff of the British Museum, 1830–1850, serving mainly in dept. of MSS. (see *DNB*) and had written no. 742; author is well acquainted with books, MSS., and libraries; Robert Cowtan, *Memoirs of the British Museum* (1872), p. 37, calls Holmes a frequent contributor to *QR,* but no. 742 was the only paper assigned to him in *Index,* I.

817 Remove the "prob." after Gurwood: see Egerton's statement for no. 721 above in these revisions. In Egerton's book, cited there, he prints, pp. 192–194, another memorandum supplied by the Duke of

Wellington which Egerton was "able to incorporate into his article"—but not as a unit.

825 Delete the suggestion of Elizabeth Eastlake: the evidence is questionable and the art. seems too technical to be hers. This decision then dictates removing the "?" after Brougham.

857 By **J. S. Howson,** prob. The *DNB* names 4 arts. in *QR* as by man cited, three of which are confirmed by Murray, one being repr. under his name; the 4th is described as "Greece"; this is only unattributed art. corresponding to that title; Howson travelled much (see *DNB*) and this paper is not unlike no. 1204 on Algeria.

872 Letter cited in "Lockhart-Croker" shows that Croker revised the MS., which explains Murray's error.

940 By **Johann Philipp von Wessenberg-Ambringen:** see into. note. Edited and trans. by **J. G. Lockhart:** cf. no. 984, where the same method of giving copious extracts joined by a few passing remarks is used, and Lockhart there says, p. 449, that "we" are doing just what "we" did in no. 940. Delete P. H. Stanhope and François Guizot, as well as Lockhart, as possible authors.

946 At end, in place of "as in no. 940," substitute: Oct. 4, 1848, *N&Q* 190 (Mar. 23, 1946), 117, says he expects an art. for Christmas issue from Guizot.

984 By **Thomas George Fonnereau,** author of book being "reviewed" (see *DNB*). **Lockhart** was the editor. Cf. revision of no. 940 above.

1099 In *Fraser* date: for 1839, read 1859.

1136 Since the art. is not in the list of Layard's *QR* arts. in his *Autobiography and Letters,* ed. Bruce (1903), II, 295, Murray's attrib. to Bulwer-Lytton seems very probable. Delete Layard.

1241 After Bidder add his dates, 1806–1878, since there is now a second G. P. Bidder (in Part B revisions).

1695 According to *DNB,* 1st suppl., **Henry Jones** (in *Index,* I, 960) "assisted" Pole in this art.

1864 By **Hans William Sotheby,** who wrote *FortR* no. 1025, *FM* nos. 4051 and 4058, and three arts. on classical novelists in *Temple Bar* (see Edmund Yates, *Recollections,* II, 62). No sign of any arts. by Thomas Hans Sotheby.

1979 The "prob." may be dropped since the attrib. is also made in the *Academy,* Aug. 3, 1878, p. 112.

REVISIONS FOR PART B

NOTE: The evidence for the addition or deletion of an item, or for a correction (like "Remove the '?' before *QR* 000") is found in the Revisions for Part A above. If a change of

Alford, Henry. Delete *CR* 5, 98, 106, 307. Under "See" delete 221 and add

See: 12, 32, 231

Alison, Archibald, 1792–1867. Add

[Speech at Burns' festival], **BK** 2388

Ames, E. F., is **Ames,** Ernest Fitzroy, living in London from 1897 to 1912: *Blackwood Papers Cat.*, Kelly.

Anderson, Elizabeth (Garrett). Add

Women physicians, **Mac** 861

Andrews, Mrs., is **Andrews,** Marion (Hare), in *Blackwood Papers Cat.*

Anster, John. Delete "?" before *NBR* 175.

Antrobus, Clara Louise (Rogers). For Louise, read Louisa. Life dates are 1846–1919: see Bell, *Novelists* (in *Index*, II, Abbreviations and Short Titles).

Austin, Sarah (Taylor). Add

German society forty years since, **Mac** 1725

Aytoun, W. E. Add a "collab." after *Bk* 2388.

Bacon, John MacKenzie. Middle name is Mackenzie.

Bailey, Edith Elma (Sergison) should be replaced by **Bailey,** Edith Anne (Tarratt), d.1919, wife of Henry J. Bailey, brother of 1st baron Glanusk, in Burke, Blackwood Corres.

Bannerman, James. Add

Rationalism in the Church of England, **NBR** 613

Barrow, Sir John, 1764–1848. *QR* 521 should have been preceded by a "?": cf. *Index*, I, Part A.

Beadon, Mrs. Since "Mrs. H. Musgrave" was her pseudonym, the 3 *Mac* articles under that name (p. 1025) belong here.

name or a new biographical fact is not supported by proof, the evidence is in the source or sources cited in Volume I of the *Index*, Part B.

Bear, William Edwin. See Part B above.

Beckett, Sir Edmund. Between 1816 and 1872 his name was Denison, Edmund Beckett: see *DNB*.

Bedford, Miss Jessie. Known as Elizabeth Godfrey, her pseudonym: *Yearbooks* through 1920, *BMCat.* under both names.

Begbie, Agnes H. Middle name was Helen; of Edinburgh; disappeared from the *Directory* in 1943/44.

Bell, George. Delete "?" before *NBR* 194, and "possibly George Hamilton Bell in *BMCat.*"; George Bell, M.D., is in *BMCat.*

Bell, Henry Glassford, 1803–1874, Scottish advocate. *DNB*.

[Speech at Burns' festival], **Bk** 2388

Bicknell, Walter Lionel. Add

The king's daughter [Church of England] in danger, 2459

Bidder, George Parker, 1836–1896. See Part B above. Add

Cipher and cipher-writing, **Mac** 1101

Blackett, J. B., is very probably **Blackett,** John Fenwick Burgoyne, 1821–1856, M.P. for Newcastle, in Foster and *Landed Gentry*.

Blaze de Bury, Baronne Marie Pauline Rose (Stuart). Add

The drama in England and France, **Mac** 925

Guizot's *Memoirs of His Time*, **NBR** 560

Blowitz, Henri George Adolphe Opper de. After Georges insert Stephane. He was born in 1832, not 1825. Source is *WWW*.

Blundell, Mary E. (Sweetman). Born 1858/59: *Times*, Mar. 11, 1930, p. 18b. Also in *WWW*.

Borring, Frances Mary de. The source given provides only her Christian name and implies she was English, at least by birth.

Boult, Swinfon, should be replaced by his son, **Boult,** Swinton Henry, on whom see Part B above.

Bowyer, Edith Mary (Nicholl). This entry is in *RG*, and with "M." instead of Mary in *LCCat.*, but Nicholl was not her maiden name but that of her first husband: see below under Nicholl.

Brewster, Sir David. Delete *QR* 209; also no. 196 under *QR* "See."

Brockendon, William. Should be **Brockedon.**

Broderip, William John. Add

?Buckland's *Bridgewater Treatise*, **QR** 485

Brotherton, Mary Isabella (Rees) Irwin, 1819/20–1910, novelist; married (1) apparently to ——— Irwin, and (2) to Augustus Henry Brotherton, landcape painter. *BM-Cat.* and *Times*, 3 Feb., 1910, p. 11e.

Brougham, Henry Peter. Remove "?" before *ER* 777 and *QR* 825; delete *ER* 897, 1096, 1098.

Brown, George Douglas. Add at start of his list

Novels of John Galt, **Bk** 7304 collab.

Bruce, David. Add at end: or more likely the New Zealand minister, d.1911, in *WWW*.

Bruce, J. Thackray. Delete the entire entry: see Bunce below.

Bryce, Mary R. L. Bryce is her married name: *Blackwood Papers Cat.*

Buchanan, David. Delete *ER* 900.

Buchanan, James. Add

Irons, *Doctrine of Final Causes*, **NBR** 109
The Order of Nature—Baden Powell, 575

Bullock, William Henry: see Hall, William Henry Bullock, below.

Bulwer, Sir Henry Ernest Gascoyone. The third name should be Gascoyne.

Bulwer-Lytton, Edward G. E. L., Baron Lytton. Delete "?" before *QR* 1136.

Bunce, John Thackray. See Part B above.

A chapter of political history, **Mac** 2422

Burton, Mina Elizabeth. Insert Mrs. before Mina: see *Bk.* no. 5959 entry in Vol. I. Letter to Blackwood, Aug. 15, 1884, Nat. Lib. Scot., shows that her husband was an artist; perhaps he was William Shakespeare Burton, 1825–1916, in Mallet.

Calderon, George L. For "L." read Leslie: *BMCat.*

Candlish, Robert Smith. Delete the "?" before *NBR* 149 and 224.

Cardwell, Edward, viscount Cardwell, 1813–1886, statesman. *DNB.*

The budget of 1848, **NBR** 158

Carlill, B., and **Carlill,** James B. should be replaced by **Carlill,** James Briggs. See Part B above. Both articles belong to him: see Part A revisions.

Carr, Joseph Williams Comyms. The third name is Comyns.

Castletown, B. E. B. F-P. Delete this entire entry: see Fitz-Patrick below.

Chadwick, Sir Edwin. The *Mac* "See" should be 198, not 146.

Cheney, Edward. Born 1803: *Journal of Henry Edward Fox, 1818–1830* (1923), p. 231.

Chermside, Richard Seymour Conway. Obit. in *Gent. Mag.*, 223 (Sept. 1867), 402, where life dates are 1823–1867.

Child, Theodore E. Born 1855, not 1846: Boase and *Times*, Nov. 17, 1892, p. 10f.

Church, Mrs. E. M., is **Church,** Elizabeth Mary (Bennett) wife of Charles Marcus Church, dean of Wells: *Prods. Somerset Archaeological . . . Society*, 1915, in obit. of husband.

Cleghorn, Thomas. Add

Whewell's *Indications of the Creator*, **NBR** 17

Clifford, Lucy (Lane). Obit. in *Times*, Apr. 22, 1929, p. 16c, gives first name as Sophia, and W. K. Clifford, (q.v., p. 848) as her husband.

Clutton-Brock, Mrs. E. G. In line 2 the parish is Marden, not Malvern: see the *Mac* entry.

Code, H. B., is **Code,** Henry Brereton, as suggested: *Blackwood Papers Cat.*

Coleridge, Henry Nelson. Delete entry for *QR* 539 and add

Cottle's *Recollections* [of S. T. Coleridge], part of **QR 539**

Coleridge, Sir John Taylor. Remove "?" before *QR* 6.

Collett, Sophia Dobson. Died 1894: *Life and Letters of Raja Rammohun Roy* (3rd ed., Calcutta, 1962), Appendix XI, pp. 508–524, gives biographical sketch.

Colville, James, is the man suggested, who was an educator in Glasgow: Metcalfe Addresses (in Short Title sec. above) and title-pages of his books.

Coode, Sir John, should be replaced by **Coode,** George, 1807–1869, barrister, in Boase.

Cooley, William Desborough, was born in 1794/95: death certificate at Somerset house.

Corrance, Henry Clemence. Born 1857/58: Foster.

Crawford, Emily (Johnstone). Died 1915: *Times,* Jan. 3, 1916, p. 8d, where 84 is given as age of death, which means b. 1831/32, in contradistinction from *MWT*'s 1841. Also in *WW*/1916.

Creagh, Mrs. is **Creagh,** Matilda Emily Victoria (Wolseley) d.1914, sister of General Garnet Wolseley, wife of John Bagwell Creagh of County Cork. Burke under Wolseley of Mount Wolseley.

Croker, John Wilson. Remove "?" before *QR* 641: see original text. Add under *QR*

See: 342

Croskerry, Thomas, should be **Croskery,** Thomas, as Allibone has it; also see *DNB.*

Crosse, Cornelia, A. H., is **Crosse,** Cornelia Augusta Hewitt (Berkeley): *Blackwood Papers Cat.*

Crosse, Landor Richard. Born 1854, son of Andrew and Cornelia A. H. Crosse (see previous entry): *Landed Gentry*/98 under Hamilton of Fyne Court.

Cunningham, Sir Henry Stewart. Add

See: **ER** 3873 [see Part A revision]

Cunningham, William 1805–1861. Delete *NBR* 142.

Daniell, Clarmont John. Life dates are 1835–1898: "Bengal Civil Fund Family Register," I, at India Office.

Darmesteter, Agnes Mary Frances (Robinson). Born in 1856 or 1857 (sources differ); second husband was Emile Duclaux. *Larousse XXᵉ Siècle, MWT*/15th ed., *Times,* Apr. 14, 1944, p. 8b.

Dease, E.; perhaps Edmund Gerald Dease, 1829–1904, high sheriff of Queen's County and M.P., in *Irish Landed Gentry*/1912.

Dease, James A. For "A," read Arthur; life dates are 1826–1874; vice-lieut. of Cavan: *Irish Landed Gentry*/1912.

DeLeon, Edwin. According to *LCCat.,* born in 1828.

Devereux, Humphry Bohun. First name should be Humphrey.

Domvile, Lady Margaret F. (St. Lawrence). For "F." read Frances; died 1929, not 1884; wife of Sir Charles Domvile, bart., who died 1884: Burke, Blackwood Corres.

Douglas, Isobel. First name should be Isabel.

Dowd, James. An Irish divine, ordained 1876: *CCD*/1909, after which he disappears.

Dowden, Edward. Add under *CR*

Notices: 173

Drayson, Alfred Wilkes. *BMCat.* and *LCCat.* give Wilks as middle name; latter adds 1901 as death date.

Drummond, Robert Charles. Captain, Seaforth Highlanders: *Blackwood Papers Cat.*

Dunlop, Alexander, later (in 1849) Alexander Colquhoun-Stirling-Murray. Add

Prospects of the session, **NBR** 184

Dunlop, Robert Henry Wallace, 1823–1887, civil servant in India. Boase, *BMCat.*

Note: **Mac** 224a

Dunlop, William. Born 1792: *LCCat.*

Dwyer, Francis. This Irish soldier of fortune was apparently **Dwyer,** Francis Doyne: called F. D. Dwyer in Harrowby MSS. (see Short Title section above); full name under Philip Anthony Dwyer, prob. his son, in Foster.

Eaglestone, Constance. A pseudonym used by Constance Sutcliffe, under whom this art belongs.

Eastlake, Lady Elizabeth (Rigby). Delete *QR* 825.

Edgcombe, Frederick Joseph Sydney, is the correct name: *Blackwood Papers Cat.* and *Fraser's Mag.* no. 5027 above. In Kelly until 1909.

Edgcumbe, Richard is **Edgcumbe,** Richard John Frederick: *BMCat.*

Edwards, H., Scotsman, contributor to *CM. Blackwood Papers Cat.,* Blackwood Corres.

The Mystery of Edwin Drood, **CM** 2186

Edwards, Henry Sutherland. Delete *CM* 2186; add

Covent Garden and Italian opera, **Mac** 1840

Egerton, Francis. After *QR* 721 insert a "collab."; under *QR* add

See: 337

Ely, George Herbert, is correct: see *RG* for reprint of *Mac* 3638.

Empson, William. Add

Emigration, **ER** 1210

Enticknappe, E. Delete the entire entry. See Hannah Lynch below, who used this pseudonym.

Erroll, Henry, is in *BMCat., LCCat.*

Evershed, Henry. Perhaps man described was of Weston House, Albury, with life dates 1831–1894: *Landed Gentry.*

Falkiner, Miss M. P., is **Falkiner,** afterwards (in 1892 or 1893) Zucchi, Mary Percy: *Blackwood Papers Cat.*

Farrer, James Anson. See *Times,* June 23, 1925, p. 18e.

Ferguson, James 1857–1917. Add

Lt-Col. Patrick Ferguson, **Bk** 5766
Government and Scottish affairs, 7002

Ferguson, Sir Samuel. In title of *Bk* 1716: for "roses," read "noses."

Fergusson, Sir James, 1832–1907. Delete *Bk* nos. 5766, 7002.

Field, Rev. J. E., is **Field,** John Edward, as suggested: *Blackwood Papers Cat., CCD/* 1902.

Findlater, Jane Helen. Died 1946: *WWW.*

Fisher, Roswell Corse. Died 1910; a Canadian lawyer: *Canadian WWW.*

FitzGerald, Charles Lionel. Remove the "?" before *Mac* no. 2440.

Fitzgerald, J. R. For "J.," read James: *Blackwood Papers Cat.*

Fitzgerald, Percy Hetherington. Also see *Times,* Nov. 26, 1925, p. 19f, where the birthdate, however, is apparently wrong; *WW* /1920 confirms the 1834 in *CBEL.*

Fitz-Patrick, B. E. B., Lord Castletown. See Part B above.

Henry Grattan, **CM** 3390

Fleming, John. Remove "?" before *QR* 209. Add

The Slavonians and eastern Europe, **NBR** 203

Fletcher, Henry Charles. Life dates are 1832/ 33–1879: *Times,* Sept. 4, 1879, p. 7f.

Fletcher, Walter John. Life dates are 1842– 1913: *Landed Gentry.*

Foley, S. J., should be **Foley,** Francis John, vice-admiral, in *Blackwood Papers Cat. Navy List/* 87.

Fonnereau, Thomas George, 1789–1850, artist. *DNB.*

Diary of a Dutiful Son, **QR** 984

Forster, John. Add

German Socialism, **NBR** 198

Franklin, L., is **Franklin,** Lucy (Haywood): see Part A revision for *CM* 3582.

Frantz, G. A. Constantin. Delete the *H&FR* article.

Fraser, Alexander Campbell. Add

Notes: **NBR** 284, 466

Fraser, Frederick Alexander MacK. The third name is Mackenzie: Blackwood Corres.

Fraser, Patrick, Lord Fraser. Delete the Note to *NBR* 466. Add

?State of Scottish towns, **NBR** 111
?*Memoirs of Sir R. M. Keith,* 212

Fröbel, Carl Ferdinand Julius. Add

Austria and Germany, **H&FR** 44

Frohschammer, Jakob. Delete the "See" line at end. Add

Catholicism in Bavaria, **CR** 431
Döllinger and the Catholic Church in Bavaria, 527
Crisis in the Catholic Church in Bavaria, 590

Furrell, James Wyburd. Matriculated at Cambridge 1854: Venn.

Fyvie, John. Appears in *Yearbook*/1920.

Garnett, Richard, 1835–1906. Add

Michael Angelo adapted from Friedrich Hebbel, **Mac** 293a
Note: 267a

Ghosh, A. Sarathkumar. Cover of *NatR-II* for Nov. 1897 calls him prof. of economics, Calcutta Univ.

Gielgud, Adam. Full name is Adam Jerzy Konstanty Gielgud. Life dates are 1834–1920. *Polski Slownik Biograficzny,* 1935–.

Giveen, Henry Martley. *BMCat.*

The diplomacy of Ellis minor, **CM** 3494

Gleig, Charles Edward Stuart. Life dates are 1825–c.1906: *Army List*/April 1906, where he appears for the last time.

Goadby, Edwin N. Born 1836: *Biograph,* 1 (1879), 18.

Godkin, James. See Part B above.

Mariolatry, **NBR** 142
?*Memoirs of Sir T. F. Buxton,* 162

Graham, George Farquhar, 1789–1867, Scottish musician. *DNB.*

See: **ER** 1695

Graham, Peter Anderson. Born 1853/54: *Times,* Oct. 27, 1925, p. 19b.

Grant, Arthur. In title of art., "border" should be "Border."

Grant, Charles, 1841–1889. Prof. of English at Univ. of Jena: Boase.

Grant, James Augustus. Delete italics in title to *Bk* 5146.

Grant, Sir Robert. Under "See," remove 335. Add

Orme's Historical Fragments, **ER** 335
Considerations on Trade with India, 362

Grattan, Thomas Colley. See Part B above.

French poetry, **ER** 1004 collab.

Greg, William Rathbone. Add a collab. after *ER* 2450.

Gremback, M. von, a Dutch writer.

Foundations of the Church of Rome, **NBR** 170

Grote, George. Delete *Mac* 720.

Grote, John. Add

What is materialism? **Mac** 720

Guizot, François Pierre Guillaume. Delete *QR* 940.

Gunn, William Maxwell, d.1851, schoolmaster in Edinburgh. *BMCat.* (also under Thomas Guthrie), *Cat. Adv. Lib.*
Scottish university tests, **NBR** 215
Scottish national education, 222

Gurwood, John. Add

Life of Blücher, **QR** 721 collab.

Hake, Alfred Egmont. Son of Thomas Gordon Hake the poet: see *WW*/1916.

Hall, William Henry Bullock. Add
Note: **Mac** 466a

Hallam, Esther. Delete the entire entry: see Moorhouse, Esther Hallam below.

Hallett, Holt Samuel. Born 1841: *MWT*, 15th ed.

Hamilton, Alexander. Add

Catalogue of Tippoo's Library, **ER** 471
Wilk's *History of Mysor*, 568
Letters of Tippoo Sultan, 591

Hamilton, Catherine Jane. Life dates are 1839 /40–1935; Irish novelist: *Irish Book Lover*, 23 (1935), 83.

Hamilton, James. Delete the "?" before *NBR* 153.

Hanna, William. Under *NBR* "See," delete 198. Add
Notices: 118

Hardy, William John, should be replaced by **Hardy,** William J. M., district inspector, Royal Irish Constabulary, Ballymena. Blackwood Corres.

Hart, R. E. S. For his signed art. in *Temple Bar*, 110 (Apr. 1897), 526–536, the *TBar* ledger, BM Add. MS. 46564, vol. 5, adds "Rev." Since not apparently in *CCD*, prob. a Non-conformist.

Harwood, John Berwick. Born 1828: see preface to his *Poems* (1849), p. v. Last letter at Nat. Lib. Scot. is 1889: *Blackwood Papers Cat.*

Hatherly, Stephen George. See Part B above for correct middle name, etc.

Hayward, Abraham. Add
Life and writings of Talfourd, **NBR** 443

Hebbel, Christian Friedrich, 1813–1863, German poet and dramatist. *ADB*.

Michael Angelo: dramatic anecdote, **Mac** 293a

Hendriks, Frederick. See under William Newmarsh, 1820–1882, in *DNB*.

Hennell, Thomas. Perhaps the man of this name, 1838–1920, in *Landed Gentry*, who in turn may have written the book on water supply in the *BMCat.*; in any event, *QR* 1560 and the *FortR* art. cited in text of that entry seem to be by the same author.

Hetherington, William Maxwell, 1803–1865, Scottish divine. *DNB*.

The Ten Years' Conflict, **NBR** 199

Hewitt, W. G., is **Hewitt,** William Graily, since the art. cited, *Mac* 3267, is repr. in the latter's *Knights of Cockayne*, 1894.

Hodgson, William Earl. The *Times*, Jan. 1, 1910, p. 11b, corrects the *WWW* death date to 1909, and says he was "not yet fifty," which implies a birth in or about 1860; he was an angler as well as a journalist.

Holmes, John. Add
?Illustrated books, **QR** 781

Hoole, Elijah. Life dates are 1798–1872; an orientalist and Wesleyan missionary: *DNB*.

Horne, Richard Henry. Add: or Hengist.

Horner, Ann Susan. Born 1815/16; daughter of Leonard Horner, in I, 946: Boase.

Howden, Mrs. F. A. In *Blackwood Papers Cat.*; her Blackwood Corres. suggests she was the wife of John M. Howden, chartered accountant, in *Edinburgh Directories*/ 1885–1940.

Howson, John Saul. Add as his first art.
Lord Nugent's travels—Greece, **QR** 857

Hudson, William Henry, 1841–1922. Delete *Mac* 2697.

Hudson, William Henry, 1862–1918, literary historian; wrote on France and on the Renaissance. *WWW*.

Jacques Tahureau, **Mac** 2697

Hughes, Thomas. Delete *Mac* 660.

Hurlbert, William Henry. Add
Life and Letters of Justice Story, **ER** 2169
The American claims, 2925

United States policy, **NBR** 476

Ivory, William. Under *NBR* "See" delete 169.

Jacob, William. Add
Past and present state of the country, **QR** 46

Jebb, Sir Richard Claverhouse. Add

Tennyson's *Queen Mary,* **Mac** 1527

Jeffrey, Francis. Delete *ER* nos. 511, 1004, "See" 753; add "?" before no. 355, as in text of Part A; add

?Poetry—Cunningham's songs, **ER** 1209 collab.
Notes: 753, 1004

Jeune, Lady Susan Mary Elizabeth (Stewart-Mackenzie). Her second husband, Sir F. H. Jeune, was created Lord St. Helier in 1905, at which time Lady Jeune became the baroness St. Helier: *WWW/1948.* Her dates are c.1849–1931: *Times,* Jan. 26, 1931, p. 12d.

Johnson, Lionel Pigot. See Part B above.

On the character of Nero, **Mac** 2886 collab.

Jones, Henry. Add

See: **QR** 1695 [Part A revision]

Jones, John Winter, Add

The Roxburghe ballads, **NBR** 94

Kaye, Sir John William. Delete *NBR* 418 and the "See" line at the end. Add

The war on the Sutlej, **NBR** 85
Army reform— limited enlistment, 167
Fall of the Sikh Empire, 205
The romance of Indian warfare, 213
?The crisis in India [the Mutiny], 486
India convalescent, 626

Kebbel, Thomas Edward. Add

?The quarrels of friends, **Mac** 859

Keeton, A. E. Bentley adds "Miss" to this signature used for *Temple Bar,* 113 (Feb. 1898), 275–278; possibly daughter of the musician Haydn Keeton in *WWW/1928.*

Kélékian, Diran, or Dikran. Dikran Khan Kelekian is name given on title-page of his *Potteries of Persia,* Paris, 1909, where he is described as "Consul for Persia at New York."

King, afterwards King-Noel, William, 1st earl Lovelace, 1805–1893, writer on agriculture and engineering. Boase under Lovelace, *BMCat.*

?Settlement and poor removal, **NBR** 143

Kinnaird, Douglas James William, 1788–1830, banker, M.P. *DNB.*

Letters from France, **ER** 753

Kinnear, Alexander Smith. Add

Leigh Hunt's poetry, **Mac** 279

Kinnear, John Boyd. Add

Marriage and divorce, **NBR** 655
The national defences, 730

Kitto, John. Add

Lands of the Bible, **NBR** 134
Smith's *Voyage of St. Paul,* 191

Laurence, Sir Percelval Maitland. First name is Perceval.

Lawson, William Ramage. See Part B above.

Layard, Sir Austen Henry. Delete *QR* 1136.

Lecky, Elizabeth (van Dedem). Her full name was Catharina Elisabeth Boldewina Lecky: born 1842: *Times,* May 25, 1912, p. 11c; *Nederland's Adelsboek.* Gravenhage, 1919.

Lee, William. Life dates are 1817–1886, prof. of ecclesiastical history, Glasgow. Boase; *Fasti,* VII, 408.

Leeds, William Henry. Add

Architectural improvements in London, **QR** 92

Lester, Cecil M. The second name is Morris: *Blackwood Papers Cat.*

Lewis, Sir George Cornewall. Add

British taxation, **ER** 2450 collab.

Lockhart, John Gibson. Delete from *QR* list 940 and 984. Add

[Note on Coleridge's death], **QR** 400
Ion; a Tragedy [by T. N. Talfourd], 463
Coleridge's *Literary Remains,* part of 539
Edited: 940, 984
See: 342

Lorimer, Louise. Of Edinburgh, daughter of James Lorimer in *Index,* I, 984: Blackwood Corres.

Lottner, should be replaced by **Löttner,** Friedrich, d.1873, prof. of Sanskrit at T.C.D.; Boase.

Ludlow, John Malcolm Forbes, Add

The restoration, **Mac** 190

Lynch, Mrs. E. M. (Johnson), is very prob. Mrs. Edward Melville Lynch. Page gives her address as "Dunsany, Co. Meath, Ireland"; her suggested husband was a novelist who wrote one book in the New Irish Library, 1894, and another with an Irish setting, 1896: see *BMCat.*

Lynch, Hannah. Add

A page of philosophy, **Mac** 3436
My friend Arcanieva, 3461
A village sovereign, 3628

Macaulay, George Campbell. The four *Bk* arts. are by **Macaulay,** George, 1826–1895, Free Church minister, in Ewing. The *Mac* arts. are correctly assigned.

Macaulay, Thomas Babington. Delete question marks for *ER* 1096, 1098.

MacCabe, William Bernard, now entered in Appendix, I, 1194. Add

Christmas customs and superstitions, **H&FR** 28

M'Crie, Thomas, the younger, 1797–1875, Scottish divine. *DNB.*

Noel on union of Church and State, **NBR** 180

McCulloch, J. R. Insert a "?" before *ER* 1034, and delete *ER* 1210.

MacDonagh, Michael, is in the *Times*, Mar. 1, 1946, p. 7d, and *BMCat.*; *WWW* gives Macdonagh.

Macdonald, James. Add 1771/72–1810, Scottish minister, author of a MS. translated into German and published with a German title (see *BMCat.*)—viz., the book here cited in English, Alexander Gillies, *A Hebridean in Goethe's Weimar: The Rev. James Macdonald* (Oxford, 1969), pp. 142. For the "See" entry, substitute

Lichtenberg's *Miscellaneous Works*, **ER** 127

Macdonald, Leila. Before Leila add Mrs.: *Blackwood Papers Cat.*

Macdonnell, R., should be **MacDonnell,** John Randal, b.1828, in Venn.

McFall, Frances Elizabeth (Clarke), known as Sarah Grand. Life dates are 1855–1943 (*CBEL*'s "b.1862" is incorrect): *WWW* and *Annual Register*/1943, p. 418, under Grand. But latter gives wrong maiden name; *WWW* and *Times*, May 24, 1943, p. 6d, confirm "Clarke."

Mackay, John, on whom see Part B above and cf. Part A revision of *Mac* no. 1955.

Mackintosh, James. Add

Dante, **ER** 826 collab.

MacKubin, Miss, is **Mackubin,** Ellen, or Nellie, Remove "?" before the *Mac* article.

Maclagan, James. Delete *NBR* 109.

MacLennan, or **McLennan,** John Ferguson. Delete *NBR* 655.

McNeill, Sir John. Add

[Speech at Burns' festival], **Bk** 2388

McNeill, Ronald John. The second *Mac* code number should be 3847 not 2847. New sources are Foster, *WWW*/1927.

McVarish, Duncan M., should be **McVarish,** Duncan Charles: *Blackwood Papers Cat.*, *CCD*/1902. Add under *Bk* article

See: 7834

Maitland, Edward. See Part B above.

?Ballot not secret voting, **ER** 2848

Maitland, Edward Francis. Delete *ER* 2848.

Majendie, Lady Margaret Elizabeth (Lindsay). Died 1912: Burke under Crawford.

Mann, Mary E. (Rackham). Born 1848: *Times*, July 15, 1929, p. 19b.

Manners, Lady Janetta (Hughan), Duchess of Rutland. Born 1836, not 1805/06: *Complete Peerage.*

Mansergh, Jessie (Bell). Wife, first, of Henry Mansergh; second, of George De Horne Vaizey.

Marshall, Charles. Since man suggested wrote dialect stories, he would seem to be the author of the art. cited. His life dates, 1795–1882, are in Ewing.

Marshall, Florence A. (Thomas). For "A," read Ashton; a composer and conductor, wife of Julian Marshall: *DNB*/2nd suppl. under his name.

Marshall, Frederic, or Frederick. Prob. not the barrister suggested, who lived at Dulwich; the letters to Blackwood at the Nat. Lib. Scot. are from Brighton. This writer on France is in the *BMCat.*

Martin, John B. Middle name is Biddulph: *Blackwood Papers Cat.*

Martineau, Harriet. First word in title of *ER* 2441 is "Secret," not "Secretary."

Martley, Henry. Delete the entire entry. See revision of *CM* no. 3494.

Masson, David. Add

Recent French social philosophy, **NBR** 156
The Socialist party in France, 177
Vincent Gioberti, 197

Maurice, Sir John Frederick. Add

Militia, volunteers, and regulars, **CR** 4156
Lessons of the [Boer] War, 4205

Mazzini, Guiseppi. First name is Giuseppe.

Meetkerke, Cecilia Elizabeth. Before Cecilia, insert "Mrs."; a misc. writer who was a distant relative of Anthony Trollope: his *Letters,* p. 197.

Meissner, Albert Ludwig. Life dates should be 1832–1909: T. W. Moody and J. C. Beckett, *Queen's Belfast, 1845–1949* (Belfast, 1959), p. 611.

Meldrum, David Storar. Add a collab. to *Bk* 7304.

Merivale, Louisa A. For "A.," read Anne: A. W. Merivale, *Family Memorials,* Exeter, 1884.

Meynell, Esther Hallam (Moorhouse): see **Moorhouse,** Esther Hallam, below.

Mill, James Delete See 726. Then add to list of his arts. in *ER*

Liberty of Continental press, 726
Religion and character of the Hindus, 823

Miller, Hugh, 1802–1856. Delete *NBR* 153.

Miller, John, Q.C. Delete *QR* 46.

Milne, W. C., is **Milne,** William Charles as suggested: the *ER* art. is attr. to him in *DNB.*

Mitchinson, John. Add

Education and school, **CR** 5

Moir, George. Remove "?" before *ER* 1764.

Moncreiff, James. Remove "?" before *NBR* 147.

Moorhouse, Esther Hallam, afterwards Mrs. Gerard Tuke Meynell, d.1955, in *WWW* under Meynell; used Esther Hallam as pseudonym.

The college at Khartoum, **Mac** 3782

Morris, Maurice C. O'Connor. The "C" should be deleted; the life dates are 1827–1901; he was deputy postmaster-general of Jamaica: *Irish Landed Gentry*/1904.

Muir, John, 1810–1882, orientalist. *DNB.*

Indian literature, **NBR** 448

Mure, William. Add

[Speech at Burns' festival], **Bk** 2388

Murray, Kenric (or Kenvic) Benjamin, should be replaced by **Murray,** Kenric Bright, on whom see Part B above.

Musgrave, Mrs. H. Delete the entire entry. See Mrs. Beadon above.

Nicholl, Mrs. Edith Mary, later Mrs. Bowyer (perhaps wife of James T. Bowyer in *BMCat.* who also wrote on Virginia). For Mrs. Bowyer, see *LCCat.* and *CM* no. 3713 in Vol. I. For Mrs. Nicholl, see *BMCat.* and *FortR* no. 2411 above; also Bentley assigns two arts. in *Temple Bar* to Mrs. Edith M. Nicholl, 88 (Feb. 1890), 202–214, and 95 (May 1892), 58–74.

Ninnis, Howard, is very possibly the Howard Ninnis, d.1886, in Debrett/1908, p. 60, and Burke under Arran. Delete the "See" and add

?Our iron-clad navy, **CM** 1079

Norman, Ménie Muriel (Dowie). Died 1945: Burke/1951.

Novikoff, Olga (Kireeff). The middle name is Alexeena; the birthdate in *LCCat.* is 1840.

Oakley-Williams, P. Henry, is Philip Henry Oakley Williams in *BMCat.,* and he signed translations O. Williams and Oakeley Williams. Apparently original surname was Williams.

O'Hagan, John. Add no. 51 to his Current events in *H&FR.*

Olding, W. Herbert. First name is William: *Blackwood Papers Cat.*

Oliphant, Laurence: see *Index,* I, 1032. Add

Backsheesh [in Turkey], **Mac** 1961

O'Meagher, J. B. Prob. the Paris correspondent of the *Times* who had served in the civil war in Spain: *Dublin Rev.,* 13 n.s. (1869), 175n.

O'Neill, J., is **O'Neill,** John, c.1837–1895, scholar; specially learned in oriental and Provençal life, languages, literatures; wrote study of mythology in 1893. Boase.

Orange, H. W., is Orange, Sir Hugh William, 1866–1956, educationist, in *WWW.* Add a "collab." after the *Mac* art.

Owen, Mrs. M. E. First name is Marianne; married to John Owen, a divine (in *CCD*/65): Blackwood Corres.

Palmerston, Lord H. J. T. Add under *ER*

Edited: ?1389, ?1757

Parnell, Henry B. Add to his arts.

Catholics of Ireland, **ER** 861
Turnpike roads, 897
Finance, 900
?Funding system, 1034

Pember, Austen. Delete the entire entry.

Potter, Rev., is **Potter,** John Philips, or Phillips, as suggested; and see Part B above.

Preston-Thomas, Herbert. Born in 1840/41, prob. 1841: obit. in *Times,* Dec. 23, 1909, p. 9c.

Price, Bonamy. Delete *H&FR* 44 and *NBR* 284.

Probert, W. G., is **Probert,** William Geoffrey, as suggested: *Blackwood Papers Cat.*

Procter, Bryan Waller. After *ER* 1209 add: collab. at least, for which see Part A revision above.

Pryce, Jennette. First name is Jennet; wife of Hugh Lewis Pryce, formely Price, divine (d.1895) in Venn under Price: Blackwood Corres.

Purves, James Liddell, should be replaced by **Purves,** James, on whom see Part B above.

Quekett, Mrs. Arthur Edwin. Her own name was **Quekett,** Marion (Adams).

Raleigh, Samuel. Delete "?" before *NBR* 206.

Rands, William Brighty. Add to his *CR* list

The London press, 196, 205, 221
The Higher Criticism and periodical literature, 1114
Editing, 1114
Professor Clifford and his critics, 1123
The rationale of reviewing, 1143
Intellectual detachment. 1143
Parliamentary reporting, 1153
Muir's *Mahomet,* 1153
Glan-Alarch, 1153
Rus in urbe, 1171
Mr. John Morley's *Essays,* 1171
Social life in Greece, 1171
Novelists and philosophers, 1181
A self-refutation, 1201
Principal Tulloch and Stopford Brooke, 1201
Pictures for children, 1213
Charlotte Williams Wynn, 1213
The cultur-kampf, 1225
Toilet artifices, 1237
Government officials and literature, 1237
Theory of belief—Newman and Leslie Stephen, 1249
Obiter dicta in public discussion, 1249
A hopeful experiment, 1280
Difficulties of the pulpit, 1328
Mr. Trelawny and his friends, 1328
Note: 1216
Notices: 26, 430, 1226, 1329

Rankin, Daniel J. Vice-consul at Mozambique, 1885–1886. *F.O. List*/1901.

Ransom, Edwin. Life dates 1841/42–1927. Death certificate at Somerset House.

Ready, Arthur, is **Ready,** Arthur William, as suggested: he edited part of Macaulay's *History*, which is twice quoted and highly praised in the *Mac* art.

Reichardt, Annie. Her husband (see revision of *CM* no. 2650) was a missionary in Damascus: see *CCD/76* under his name, given in I, 1062.

Rhind, William. Surgeon in Edinburgh, 1828–1868: *P.O. Directories.* Add

Dietetics, **ER** 1203

Richter, Jean Paul, 1763–1825, now entered on I, 1194. After "Paul" add Friedrich.

Richter, Jean Paul Friedric, 1847–1937. Delete the "Friedric."

Robertson, A. Fraser. To an art. so signed in *Temple Bar*, 114 (Aug. 1898), 582–588, Bentley adds "Miss"; according to Page, she lived in Edinburgh at the address (in the *Directory*) of John James Robertson.

Robertson, John, d.1875, journalist; sub-ed. *London and Westminster Rev.* Boase.

Life and labours of Mrs. Fry, **NBR** 157

Rogers, Samuel, 1763–1855, poet. *DNB.*

Dante, **ER** 826 collab.

Roget, Peter Mark. Delete *ER* 826.

Rose, William Stewart. Add

Irish Fairy Tales, **QR** 47

Ross, Janet Ann (Duff-Gordon). Middle name was Anne. Delete *Mac* 1725; add at end

Edited: 1725

Sanders, H. M., is **Sanders,** Herbert M.: many arts. in *Temple Bar* in the 90s are so signed.

Sandford, Margaret E. (Poole). Add to *Mac* list:

An hour with some old people, 1253

Sandwith, Humphrey. First name is Humphry.

Sargent, Harry Garton, or Gaston, should be replaced by **Sargent,** Henrietta Garton.

Scott, David Dundas, translator. *BMCat.*

?Niebuhr, **NBR** 179

Sealsfield, Charles. Born Carl Postel or Postl: see *BMCat.* under latter name and A. B. Faust, *Charles Sealsfield*, Baltimore, 1892.

Serrell, George. Born 1849; London barrister and LL.D.: *M at B.*

Shaw, H. S., is **Shaw,** Henry Scott, 1823–c. 1908: *Blackwood Papers Cat.*; *Fasti*, II, 237.

Shearer, C. J., is **Shearer,** Charles James: *Blackwood Papers Cat.*

Simeon, Cornwall. Life dates are 1819/20–1880, barrister and angler. Foster, *BMCat.*

Skene, James Henry. Life dates are 1812–1886; in the foreign service: see p. 141 of book ed. by W. F. Skene, cited in Part B entry, p. 1087.

Smith, Alexander, c.1794–1851, schoolteacher and postmaster of Banff: *LCCat.*; M. H. Abrams, *The Mirror and the Lamp* (N.Y., 1953), p. 149.

Smith, William Henry. Delete *QR* 485.

Smyth, Mrs. A. Gillespie, is **Smyth,** Amelia Gillespie (Keith): *Blackwood Papers Cat.* In her letter of 1869, Blackwood Corres., she calls herself an octogenarian.

Sneyd, Henry. Life dates are 1838–1920: *Landed Gentry.*

Sotheby is **Sotheby,** Hans William, on whom see Part B above. Delete suggestion of Thomas Hans Sotheby.

Southey, Robert. Under *QR* "See," delete no. 27.

Sparrow, H. Wilfrid, writer on Persia, English tutor, etc. (as in I, 1095, under his pseudonym, Wilfrid Sparroy): *BMCat.* under latter name, *Blackwood Papers Cat.* All arts. now under Sparroy belong to Sparrow, but a "collab." should be added to *Mac* 3963.

Sparrow, Walter Shaw. See Part B above.

Art and the women, **Mac** 3963 collab.

Sparroy, Wilfrid, is a pseudonym: see previous entry.

Speedy, Thomas. An estate agent in Edinburgh: *Blackwood Papers Cat.*

Stack, John Herbert. Delete the "?" after the death rate: Boase.

Stanhope, Philip Henry. Delete *QR* 940.

Stanley, Arthur Penrhyn. Add

Edited: **Mac** 1021a [Part A revision]

Stark, John. A printer in Edinburgh (*Blackwood Papers Cat.*) to whom Allibone assigns *Elements of Natural History*, 1828. The information given from Boase may also be true.

Stephen, Sir James Fitzjames. Add

Convocation and Dr. Colenso, **Mac** 378
The law and the Church [on *Essays and Reviews*], 441

Stokes, Sir George Gabriel, should be replaced by **Stokes,** George Joseph, 1859–1935, prof. of philosophy, Univ. Coll. Cork, in *WWW* and *Blackwood Papers Cat.*

Stormonth-Darling, Moir Todd. For Todd, read Tod.

Strachey, George. This "minister" was a diplomat, not a divine.

Strachey, Henrietta Mary Amy (Simpson). Born in 1866 and alive in 1953: *LCCat.,* Burke/1953.

Stuart-Glennie, John Stuart. Life dates are 1829/30–1910: *Scotsman,* July 19, 1910, under Glennie, John Stuart Stuart-.

Sutcliffe, R. Constance. The initial "R" precedes "Constance" in *Blackwood Papers Cat.,* and see Part B above. Add

Memoir of Sir Edward Boehm, **Bk** 6629

Symington, A. M., is **Symington,** Alexander Macleod, as suggested: see Part B above.

Symonds, Emily Morse. Obit. in *Times,* Sept. 12, 1936, p. 14b.

Syrett, Netta. Obit. in *Times,* Dec. 18, 1943, p. 6e.

Taylor, George, 1772–1851. Birthdate in Boase is 1771, but see *Gent. Mag.,* 35 (Mar. 1851), 317, and *DNB* under his son Henry. Delete *QR* 6. Add at end

See: 6

Taylor, Helen. Replace the "See" entry with

Women and criticism, **Mac** 671

Taylor, Isaac, 1787–1865. Add

The future [of Christianity], **NBR** 166

Taylor, Meadows Philip. Should be **Taylor,** Philip Meadows.

Thicknesse, Ralph Thicknesse. Died 1923: *Landed Gentry.*

Thomson, Emily. Her middle name was Newlands: *Blackwood Papers Cat.*

Thomson, John, 1765–1846. Under *ER* "See," delete 1203.

Toynbee, H. V., is **Toynbee,** Harry Valpy: see Part B above.

Trench, Maria Marcia Fanny, should be replaced by **Trench,** Maria, on whom see Part B above.

Trimmer, Joshua. The "?" before *NBR* no. 50 may be removed.

Trollope, Frances Eleanor. Delete *CM* nos. 408, 419, 536.

Trollope, Henry Merivale. Died 1926: genealogical table in L. P. and R. P. Stebbins, *The Trollopes,* 1946.

Trollope, Theodosia (Garrow) on whom see Part B above.

Contemporary Italian poets, **CM** 408, 419
Giovanni Battista Niccolini, 536

Trollope, Thomas Adolphus. Add

Medieval history of Italy, **NBR** 136
Rome: present state and prospects, 164
Pope Joan, 218

Turner, F. S., is **Turner,** Frederick Storrs, as suggested: see Part B above.

Tuttiett, Mary Gleed. She was born in 1846/47: see *Annual Register*/1823 under her pseud., Maxwell Gray.

Twiss, Horace. Add

Letter on the French Government, **ER** 511

Venables, George Stovin. Under his *Mac* article, add

Note: 3a [Part A revision]

Villiers, Edward. His middle name was Ernest: Foster.

Wakefield, Edward. Died 1924; mainly an editor and writer: *New Zealand Biog.*

Walker, Miss, is **Walker,** Annie Louisa, q.v., under whom the *Bk* 4623 art. should be entered.

Walker, Annie Louisa. Add to her list *Bk* 4623. Later married to Henry Coghill, and then signed her work Annie L. Coghill: see see Part B above under Coghill.

Wallace, William, of the Temple. Life dates are 1785/86–1839: Macready, *Diaries,* II, 10–11.

Walsh, Walter, 1847–1912, should have been **Walsh,** Walter, 1857–1931, leader of the Free Religious Movement, in *WWW.*

Watkins, Morgan George. Died 1911: obit. in *Guardian,* Jan. 20, 1911.

Weir, William. Add

?Germany: its state and prospects, **NBR** 176

Wellesley, Arthur, Duke of Wellington. Under *QR* "See," add 721, 817.

Wemyss, Millicent Ann Mary (Kennedy-Erskine). Life dates are 1831–1895: *Landed Gentry*/1937, p. 709; also see p. 2402.

Werner, J. R. This is **Werner,** John Reinhardt, 1861/62–1891, African traveller: *Proceedings Royal Geographical Soc.,* 13 (1891), 616.

Wessenberg-Ambringen, Johann Philipp von, baron, 1773–1858, Austrian statesman, in *Grosse Brockhaus.*

Wessenberg's *Souvenirs,* **QR** 940

Whately, Richard. Delete *NBR* 284 (both the

collab. and the note) and 297. Add at end of *NBR* list

See: 284, 297 [Part A revision for both]

White, John Forbes. Life dates are 1831–1904: Ina Mary White, afterwards Harrower, *John Forbes White,* 1918.

White, Thomas Pilkington. Died 1913: *Army List*/1914, p. 1550.

Wilkes, John. See Part B above, under Wilks, John.

Wilkins, W. Walker. Perhaps first name is William: *BMCat.*

Wilks, John. Born in 1764/65, not 1776, according to *Gent. Mag.,* 196 (Dec. 1854), 629.

Williams, Alexander Malcolm. Disappears from *Glasgow Directory* in 1940.

Wills, Freeman Crofts. Born 1836/37: *Times,* Apr. 28, 1913, p. 10b.

Wilson, John, 1785–1854. Add

[Speech at Burns' festival], **Bk** 2388

de Windt, Harry. Though his arts. are so signed, all the catalogues call him **De Windt,** on whom see Part B above.

Wolff, Cecil D. The middle name is Drummond: *Blackwood Papers Cat.*

Wolffsohn, Lily. Wolffsohn is her married name: see *NC* no. 2707 above and *RG.*

Wood, Lady Mary Susan Félicie (Lindsay). Born 1851/52: see *Times,* Nov. 29, 1937, p. 16b, under Lady Meynell.

Wordsworth, William, 1772–1850, the poet. *DNB.*

See: **QR** 698 [Part A revision]

Wren, Walter. Born 1834: Boase.

Yeo, Isaac Burney. Born 1835: *Surgeon Index.*

Zucchi, Mary Percy (Falkiner): see above under Falkiner, Miss M. P.

REVISIONS FOR PART C

NOTE: The evidence in all cases, unless otherwise indicated (see Oakley, Henry), is given in the Revisions for Part A above. New initials or pseudonyms—used for articles omitted from Volume I (see B.,W.H.) or overlooked because mistaken for genuine names (see Eaglestone, Constance)—are marked with an asterisk.

B.,G.P.,—**Mac** 1101—**George Parker Bidder,** 1836–1896
*B.,W.H.—**Mac** 466a—**William Henry Bullock**
Bavarian Catholic, A.—**CR** 431, 527, 590: delete the "?" after Frohschammer
*D.,R.H.W.—**Mac** 224a—**R. H. W. Dunlop**
*Dean of Westminster, The—**Mac** 1921a— **A. P. Stanley**
*Eaglestone, Constance—**Bk** 6629—**R. Constance Sutcliffe**
*Enticknappe, E.—**Mac** 3436, 3461, 3628— **Hannah Lynch**
F.,L.—**CM** 3582—**Lucy Franklin**
*G.,R.—**Mac** 267a—**Richard Garnett, 1835–ı 1906**
Golden Horn—**Mac** 1961—**Laurence Oliphant**
*Hallam, Esther—**Mac** 3782—**Esther Hallam Moorhouse**
Janus—**Mac** 2886—**H. W. Orange** and **Lionel Johnson**
K.R. [Kinnea*r*?]—**Mac** 279—**A. S. Kinnear**
Lay Churchman, A,—**Mac** 378, 441—**James Fitzjames Stephen**
M.,H., second entry. After initials add: ["Mrs.

H. Musgrave"]. After the 3 *Mac* numbers (3018, 3045, 3192), replace Mrs. H. Musgrave by **Mrs. Beadon**
*Martley, Henry—**CM** 3494—**Henry Martley Giveen**
Miles—**CR** 4156, 4205—**J. F. Maurice**
*Oakley, Henry—**Mac** 3799—**Philip Henry Oakley-Williams** [see entry in Index, I, under *Mac* 3799]
Pember, Austen—*Mac* 2459—**Walter Lionel Bicknell**
R.,K.,—**Mac** 279—is *not* Leigh Hunt, who is the subject of the art. and should be deleted. See K. R. above here
*Richardson, Henry S.—**CR** 1140—**W. B. Rands**
S.T. should be S., T. Misprint
*Sparroy, W. W. [prob. W. Wilfrid Sparroy] —**Bk** 7838, 7855—**H. Wilfrid Sparrow**
*Sparroy, Wilfrid—**Bk** 7867; **Mac** 3943—**H. Wilfrid Sparrow**
Two Brothers—**Mac** 3963—should be **H. Wilfrid Sparrow** and **Walter Shaw Sparrow.** Wilfrid Sparroy was the former's pseudonym

REVISIONS FOR ABBREVIATIONS AND SHORT TITLES

ADB: For *Allegemeine,* read *Allgemeine.*
Bain, *Autobiography*: The date of the edition cited was 1904.
Cockburn: This short title was accidentally omitted. It is a variant form of "Cockburn Record" on p. 1175.
Whewell, *Life*: Also omitted. The reference is to Mrs. Stair Douglas, *Life of William Whewell and Selections from His Correspondence,* London, 1881.

REVISIONS FOR APPENDIX ON PP. 1193–1194

Head, George. For page 702, read 701. Head was not a contributor to Vol. I, so far as we know.

Rands, William Brighty. For *CR* 201, read 221. Delete the "Short Essays" and see above under revisions of Part A.